The Scale of Wisdom

The Scale of Wisdom

A Compendium of Shi'a *Hadith*

M Muhammadi Rayshahri

Translated by

N Virjee, A Kadhim, M Dasht Bozorgi, Z Alsalami, A Virjee

Edited by

N Virjee

British Library Cataloguing-in-Publication Data
A catalogue record for this book is available from the British Library

ISBN 978-1-904063-34-6 (hbk)

This edition first published in 2009

Published by

ICAS Press
133 High Road, Willesden, London NW10 2SW
www.islamic-college.ac.uk

Contents

1. SELF-SACRIFICE 1
1. The virtue of self-sacrifice 1
2. The virtue of altruistic people 1
2. EMPLOYMENT 3
3. Employment and livelihood 3
4. Divine disapproval of offering oneself for hiring 4
5. Employment agents 4
6. Wronging the worker 4
7. Informing [the worker] of wages and the etiquette of payment 4
3. THE PREORDAINED TERM [OF DEATH] 5
8. The preordained term [of death] 5
9. Death is a fortified castle 5
10. Everything has an end 5
11. Every community has a [preordained] end 6
12. Suspended and sealed ends 6
13. What safeguards against the suspended end 6
4. THE HEREAFTER 7
14. The Hereafter 7
15. The greatness of what is in the Hereafter 7
16. The Hereafter is the eternal home 8
17. The superiority of the Hereafter 8
18. Remembrance of the Hereafter 8
19. Working for the Hereafter 9
5. THE BROTHER 9
20. The believers are brothers 9
21. Increasing the number of true brothers 10
22. Brothers' amity 10
23. That which ensures the endurance of amity 11
24. Brotherhood for the sake of Allah 11
25. Brotherhood for the sake of this world 12
26. Informing one's brother of one's love [for him] 12
27. One's amity for another is a proof of reciprocity 13
28. Cutting off relations with brothers 13

29. Maintaining brotherhood 14
30. Types of brothers 14
31. Warning against some forms of brotherhood 14
32. Preserving old brotherhood 15
33. Real brotherhood 15
34. Choosing a brother 16
35. Tolerating the lapse of a brother 16
36. The best of brothers 16
37. The worst of brothers 17
38. Testing brothers 17
39. Advising brothers 18
40. Honouring and glorifying one's brothers 18
41. Fulfilling brothers' needs 19
42. The etiquette of brotherhood 19
6. GOOD MANNERS 20
43. The virtue of good manners 20
44. Good manners and the mind 21
45. Disciplining the self 21
46. That which brings about good manners 21
47. The outcomes of good manners 22
48. Explaining good manners 22
49. The best manners 23
50. Encouraging the teaching of good manners to the family 23
51. How to teach good manners 24
52. Methods of teaching good manners 24
53. Disciplining oneself by the discipline of Allah 25
54. Allah's discipline 25
7. THE CALL FOR PRAYER (*adhān*) 26
55. The virtue of call for prayer 26
56. The caller to prayer 26
57. Reciting the call for prayer in the ears 26
8. HARM 27
58. Avoiding harming people 27
59. Avoiding harming even the ants 27
60. Harming a believer 27

9. THE PRISONER [OF WAR] 28
61. Surrendering oneself to captivity is not allowed 28
62. Kindness to the prisoner of war 29
10. FOOD 29
63. Encouraging little [consumption of] food 29
64. Warning against eating excessively 30
65. Among the vices of gluttony 30
66. Hunger 31
67. Balance of eating 31
68. Table manners 32
11. AMITY 33
69. Encouraging amity 33
70. There is no good in someone who does not like others, nor is he liked by them 34
12. ALLAH 34
71. The meaning of Allah 34
13. GOVERNMENT 35
72. The necessity of government 35
73. The rule of wicked people 37
74. The value of government 37
14. EXPECTATION 38
75. Expectation is a mercy 38
76. Expectations never cease 38
77. Warning against false expectations 39
78. Expectation and death 40
79. The results of high expectations 40
80. Low expectation 41
81. Prohibition of placing one's expectation in other than Allah 41
15. THE [MUSLIM] COMMUNITY 42
82. The status of the Muslim community 42
83. The best of the Muslim community 42
84. The middle nation 43
85. Factors that ensure the goodness of the Muslim nation 43
86. The status of the Muslim community in the Hereafter 44
87. What takes away the splendour of the Muslim community 44
88. The Prophet's (SAWA) fear for his community 45

16. LEADERSHIP (1) 46
89. The importance of divinely appointed leadership 46
90. The superiority of imāma over prophethood 47
91. The essential need for an imām 47
92. The authority is a known imām 48
93. The Imām may be worried and hence, undistinguishable 48
94. Were it not for the Imām, the Earth would have perished 48
95. The summoning of every nation with their imām 49
96. Importance of knowing the Imām 49
97. Conditions of imāma and the qualifications of the imām 50
98. That which is mandatory on just leaders 52
99. The reciprocal duties and rights between the imām and the community 52
100. Your Imāms are your representatives 53
101. One who accepts the leadership of an unrightful leader 53
102. Leaders to the fire 54
103. The false claimants of imāma 54
104. No obedience is due to one who disobeys Allah 54
105. Obligation of revolting against tyrant leaders 55
106. Circumstances where desisting from revolting is allowed 55
107. Electing an Imām 56
108. The tradition of the two weighty things (al-thaqalayn) 56
109. The obligation of clinging on to the Household of the Prophet 56
110. The reason for the oppression against the Household (AS) 58
111. The philosophy of leadership in the viewpoint of the Household (AS) 58
112. Were it not for fear of dissention 58
113. The twelve Imāms 59
114. The knowledge of the Imām 59
17. LEADERSHIP (2) 60
115. Love for Imām ʿAlī and hatred towards him 60
116. ʿAlī is the Imām of the righteous 60
117. ʿAlī is the successor of the holy Prophet (SAWA) 61
118. ʿAlī is the master of every believer 61
119. ʿAlī is with the truth and the Qur'an 62
120. ʿAlī is the gate to the Prophet's knowledge 62
121. ʿAlī and the Prophet (SAWA) are from the same tree 63

122. Miscellaneous 63
123. Imām ʿAlī's knowledge 65
124. Imām ʿAlī's victimization 65
125. What begins with "verily I..." 66
126. What begins with the word "I..." 66
127. Miscellaneous 67
18. FĀṬIMA, THE MOTHER OF THE IMĀMS (AS) 68
128. Fāṭima's (AS) names 68
129. Fāṭima is a part of the Prophet (SAWA) 69
130. Fāṭima is the chief [lady] of the women of the worlds 69
131. Allah's anger for the sake of Fāṭima's anger 70
132. In mourning for Fāṭima (AS) 70
19. IMĀM AL-ḤASAN B. ʿĀLĪ (AS) 71
133. Proofs for his imāma 71
134. Ḥasan is from me and I am from him 71
135. His virtues 71
20. IMĀM ḤUSAYN B. ʿALĪ (AS) 72
136. The birth of Imām Husayn (AS) 72
137. The proof for his imāma 73
138. Ḥusayn is from me and I am from him 73
139. His virtues 74
21. IMĀM ʿALĪ B. AL-ḤUSAYN ZAYN AL-ʿĀBIDĪN (AS) 77
140. Proofs of his imāma 77
141. The status of Imām Zayn al-ʿĀbidīn (AS) 77
22. IMĀM MUḤAMMAD B. ʿALĪ AL-BĀQIR (AS) 79
142. Proofs of his imāma 79
143. He cleaves knowledge open 79
144. His virtues 79
23. IMĀM JAʿFAR B. MUḤAMMAD AL-ṢĀDIQ (AS) 80
145. Proofs of his imāma 80
146. His comportment and his noble character 81
24. IMĀM MŪSĀ B. JAʿFAR AL-KĀẒIM (AS) 83
147. Proofs of his imāma 83
148. The Imām in prison 83
149. His virtues 84

25. IMĀM ʿALĪ B. MŪSĀ AL-RIḌĀ (AS) 85
150. Proofs of his imāma 85
151. Compelling the Imām to be the heir apparent 85
152. His virtues 86
26. IMĀM MUḤAMMAD B. ʿALĪ AL-JAWĀD (AS) 86
153. Proofs of his imāma 86
154. His virtues 87
27. IMĀM ʿALĪ B. MUḤAMMAD AL-HĀDĪ (AS) 89
155. Proofs of his imāma 89
156. His virtues 89
28. IMĀM AL-ḤASAN B. ʿALĪ AL-ʿASKARĪ (AS) 91
157. Proofs of his imāma 91
158. His virtues 91
29. AL-IMĀM AL-QĀʾIM (AS) 93
159. The names of the Imām 93
160. Proofs of his imāma 93
161. Glad tidings of the Mahdī (AS) 94
162. The two occultations of Imām al-Qāʾim 94
163. The difficulty of adhering to the religion during the occultation 95
164. Supplication during the occultation of al-Qāʾim 95
165. [Actively] anticipating relief 96
166. The reappearance of al-Qāʾim after people's despair 96
167. Those who foretell a specific time [for the reappearance of al-Qāʾim] are lying 97
168. The reason for his occultation 97
169. People benefiting from the Imām during his occultation 98
170. The signs of his reappearance 98
171. At the time of the reappearance 99
172. The universe after the reappearance of al-Mahdī 100
30. FAITH 101
173. Faith (Īmān) and Islam 101
174. The reality of faith 101
175. Relation between faith and action 102
176. Faith and sins 103
177. That which completes faith 104
178. Increase of faith 105

179. The levels of faith 105
180. The pillars of faith 106
181. The strongest bonds of faith 106
182. Steadfast and temporary faith 107
183. That which consolidates faith 107
184. The taste of faith 107
185. Inability to taste the sweetness of faith 108
186. That which removes one from faith 108
187. That which repels faith 109
188. The great status of the believer 109
189. The believers are as one body 109
190. Who is the believer? 110
191. The firmness of the believer 113
192. The light of the believer 113
193. The scarcity of the [true] believer 113
194. The signs of the believer 114
195. The best of believers 114
196. The merit of one who believes in the Prophet without having seen him 114
31. TRUSTWORTHINESS 115
197. The necessity of observing the trust 115
198. Universality of trustworthiness 115
199. An untrustworthy man is a man without faith 116
200. The effects of trustworthiness 116
201. People who must not be trusted 116
32. ASSURANCE 117
202. The necessity of observing assurance 117
203. Adhering to sureties 117
204. Respecting covenants of protection 118
33. INTIMACY 118
205. Things that one should get intimate with 118
206. Things that one should not get intimate with 119
207. What brings intimacy with Allah 119
34. MAN 119
208. The dignity of man 119
209. The reason for man's creation 120

210. Man's weakness 121
211. Measuring man's value 121
35. BANES 122
212. There is trial in everything 122
36. MISERLINESS 127
213. Warning against miserliness 127
214. The explanation of miser 128
215. The miser 128
216. The real miser 129
217. The most miserly of people 129
218. The sign of miserliness 130
37. INNOVATION (*al-bid'a*) 130
219. Warning against innovation 130
220. The innovators 131
221. The meaning of innovation 131
222. Rejecting innovators 131
223. The innovator and worship 132
224. Invalidity of the worship of an innovator 132
225. A scholar's duties when faced with the appearance of innovations 132
38. SQUANDERING 132
226. Censure of squandering 132
227. The meaning of squandering 133
39. RIGHTEOUSNESS 133
228. Encouraging the righteousness 133
229. The sign of a righteous person 134
230. Complete righteousness 134
40. THE PURGATORY (*al-Barzakh*) 135
231. The meaning of the purgatory 135
232. The souls of the believers in the purgatory 135
233. The souls of disbelievers in the purgatory 135
41. THE BLESSING 136
234. The meaning of blessing 136
235. That which brings blessing and that which removes it 136
42. CHEERFULNESS 137
236. Encouraging cheerfulness 137

43. INSIGHT 138
237. Insight 138
44. FALSEHOOD 139
238. Warning against following falsehood 139
239. Discerning the truth from falsehood 139
240. The truth disguised as falsehood 140
241. Falsehood cannot be ascertained as the truth 140
45. [ALLAH'S] ANTIPATHY 141
242. Those whom Allah despises 141
243. The people Allah despises most 142
244. Acts despised by Allah 143
245. Malice 144
46. AGGRESSION 144
246. Warning against aggression 144
247. The characteristics of the aggressor 145
248. Fighting against Muslim aggressors 146
249. The blessings of Imām ʿAlī (AS) fighting the aggressors 147
47. WEEPING 147
250. Weeping due to fear of Allah 147
251. Dryness of the eye 149
48. THE LAND 149
252. A fair territory 149
253. You should live in great cities 149
254. The best of lands 150
255. What the people of every land cannot be without 150
49. ELOQUENCE 150
256. The meaning of eloquence 150
257. The most eloquent speech 151
258. Manipulation through speech 151
50. PROPAGATION [OF ISLAM] 151
259. The importance of the propagation of Islam 151
260. What is incumbent upon the propagator of Islam 153
51. THE ORDEAL 155
261. Testing with events, good and bad 155
262. The reason for testing 156

263. The severity of a believer's ordeal 157
264. The role of evil actions in the onset of ordeals 158
265. Whoever is not tried with ordeals is despised by Allah 158
266. The ordeal as a bounty 158
267. Ordeals and admonition 159
268. Sins are offset by ordeals 160
269. The ordeal is the sign of Allah's love, glory be to Him 160
270. Ordeals correspond to the level of one's faith 161
271. The levels that a servant attains as a result of ordeals 161
272. A believer's trial is for his own good 162
273. The most severe trial of servants 162
274. Salvation at the peak of the ordeal 163
275. Remembrance of Allah at the time of an ordeal 163
276. Supplication when seeing a man being tried with an ordeal 163
52. SLANDER 164
277. Warning against slander 164
53. RECIPROCAL INVOCATION OF ALLAH'S CURSE (*Mubāhala*) 165
278. Reciprocal invocation of Allah's curse 165
54. OATH OF ALLEGIANCE 166
279. Swearing allegiance to the Prophet is swearing allegiance to Allah 166
280. Women's allegiance 167
281. Retraction of allegiance 167
282. The Muslims' oath of allegiance to Imām ʿAlī (AS) 168
55. COMMERCE 168
283. The virtue of trading 168
284. Abandoning trading 169
285. The etiquette of trading 169
286. The prohibition of cheating [by giving less than due] in trade 170
287. Enjoinment upon the trader to give charity 170
288. Leniency in selling and buying 171
289. Bargaining 171
290. Equality between one who bargains and one who does not 171
291. The profit of a believer from another 172
292. The iniquity of merchants 172
293. Enjoinment of the merchant's veracity 172

294. The one who promotes his commodity by oaths 173
295. The trade of the Hereafter 173
296. Trading does not divert the believer 174
297. Trade with religion 174
56. REPENTANCE 175
298. Enjoinment of repenting 175
299. The status of one who repents 175
300. The sign of a penitent person 176
301. The acceptance of repentance 176
302. When is repentance accepted? 177
303. Remorse is repentance 177
304. Appropriate confession [of one's sins] 177
305. The pillars of repentance 178
306. Types of repentance 179
307. Sincere repentance 179
308. Postponing repentance 179
309. What is easier than repentance 180
310. Allah conceals the sin of the penitent one 180
311. Changing sins into good deeds 180
312. Speculating on Allah's judgment 181
57. THE REWARD 181
313. The reward for a righteous deed 181
314. The greatest reward 182
315. A man who hears about the reward for a particular action 182
58. REVOLUTION 183
316. The Islamic revolution in the east before the rise of the twelfth Imām 183
317. The role of non-Arabs in the revolution 183
318. The revolution from the city of Qum 184
59. PREDESTINATION 185
319. The fallacy of predestination 185
320. Neither free will nor predestination 186
321. Allah deserves all credit for good deeds 187
322. Actions to be taken against the proponents of determinism 187
60. TYRANT 187
323. Condemnation of tyranny 187

324. The evil end of the tyrants 188
61. COWARDICE 189
325. Censure of cowardice 189
326. The coward and war 189
62. THE DISPUTE 190
327. Reproached dispute 190
328. Positive debating 190
63. EXPERIENCE 191
329. Blessings of experiences 191
330. Harms due to lack of experience 191
64. ANXIETY 192
331. Warning against anxiety 192
65. REQUITAL 193
332. Requital [of deeds] 193
333. The requital of the virtuous 193
334. The requital of criminals 194
66. SPYING 194
335. Prohibition of following up people's flaws 194
336. Consequences of probing other peoples flaws 195
337. Permissibility of spying in war 196
338. What must be given the benefit of the doubt 196
67. THE SITTING AND THE ASSEMBLY 196
339. The most honoured seating 196
340. What must be observed in sittings 197
341. The main seating spot 197
342. Prohibited sitting places 198
343. Assemblies are about trust 198
344. Encouraging the attendance of gatherings where Allah is remembered 199
345. Encouraging the remembrance of Allah upon leaving an assembly 199
68. SITTING COMPANY 200
346. With whom must we sit? 200
347. The right of one's sitting companion 201
348. Whom one should not sit with 201
69. THE CONGREGATION 202
349. Allah's hand is with the congregation 202

350. The interpretation of congregation 203
70. FRIDAY 203
351. Friday 203
352. Bathing on Friday 204
71. BEAUTY 204
353. Allah is beautiful and he loves beauty. 204
354. The beautiful image 205
355. Taking care of one's hair 205
356. Inner beauty 206
72. RITUAL IMPURITY (*al-Janāba*) 206
357. Ritual bathing of *al-janāba* 206
73. THE ARMY 207
358. The army 207
359. The soldiers of Allah 208
74. PARADISE 208
360. Encouraging to aim for paradise 208
361. There is no price for your souls except for paradise 208
362. The price for paradise 209
363. Requirements for entering paradise 209
364. Paradise surrounded by trials 210
365. Those for whom paradise is guaranteed 210
366. Those for whom paradise is forbidden 211
367. The gates of paradise 211
368. The ranks in paradise 212
369. The first to enter paradise 213
370. The masters of the people of paradise 213
371. Inclusiveness of paradise 213
75. MADNESS 214
372. Types of madness 214
373. One who is truly mad 214
76. JIHĀD (1) The Lesser Jihād 215
374. Encouraging of the lesser jihād 215
375. The one who wages jihād 216
376. Aiding those who wage jihād and censure of those who harm them 217
377. The command to struggle with one's hands, tongue, and heart 217

378. Abandoning jihād 218
379. Branches of jihād 218
380. Keeping posts 218
381. The merit of standing guard 218
77. JIHĀD (2): The Greater Jihād 219
382. Forms of jihād 219
383. Enjoinment of combatting the self 220
384. The greater jihād 220
385. What is necessary for combatting the self 221
386. The fruit of struggle 221
78. JIHĀD (3): Striving to Obey Allah 222
387. Encouraging to strive to obey Allah 222
388. The most diligent of people 222
79. IGNORANCE 223
389. Reprehension of ignorance 223
390. The signs of an ignorant 223
391. The most ignorant of people 225
392. What is sufficient to be considered ignorant 225
393. The interpretation of ignorance 226
394. Man is averse to what he is ignorant of 226
80. HELL 227
395. Warning against hell 227
396. The fuel of hell 227
397. The chains and shackles of hell 227
398. The garments of the people of the fire 228
399. The food of the people of the fire 228
400. The drink of the people of the fire 228
401. The first to enter the fire 229
402. The people with the least chastisement 229
403. The people with the greatest chastisement 229
404. The valley of the arrogant 230
405. Those who will be made to remain in hell permanently 230
406. Those who will leave the fire 230
407. The reason for perpetuity in hell 231
81. THE ANSWER 231

408. The answer 231
82. OPEN-HANDEDNESS 232
409. Encouragement of generosity 232
410. The best open-handedness 232
411. The attributes of the open-handed person 233
83. THE NEIGHBOUR 233
412. Neighbourliness 233
413. Annoying one's neighbour 234
414. Visiting the neighbour 234
415. The rights of the neighbour 234
416. The boundary of the neighbourhood 235
84. LOVE 235
417. Love is kinship 235
418. That which brings about love 235
419. Those that must not be endeared 236
420. The blindness of love [from perceiving the truth] 236
421. The sign of love 236
422. The believers' intense love for Allah 237
423. That which brings about the love of Allah 238
424. Those whom Allah loves 238
425. Those that Allah does not like 239
426. The people loved most by Allah 239
427. The signs of God's love towards His servant 240
428. The status of man's position with Allah 240
429. The sign of man's love for Allah 240
430. The highest position 241
431. The incongruity of the love of Allah with the love of the world 241
432. Enjoining the love of Allah 241
433. To love for the sake of Allah 242
434. The love of the Prophet (SAWA) and his Household (AS) 242
435. The conditions for loving the Household (AS) 243
436. Devotion in love 244
437. Man is with whom he loves 244
85. IMPRISONMENT 244
438. Those who may be imprisoned 244

439. Jailing the warrantor until the return of the warranted 245
440. The one imprisoned for life 245
441. Imprisonment after punishment and acknowledgment of the truth 246
442. The rights of the prisoner 246
443. The conduct of the Prophet (SAWA) in imprisoning a suspect 246
86. THE VEIL 247
444. The veil 247
87. THE PILGRIMAGE (ḤAJJ) 248
445. The legislation of Ḥajj and its virtue 248
446. The philosophy of the pilgrimage 248
447. Pilgrimage repels poverty 250
448. That which completes the pilgrimage 250
449. The consequence of abandoning the obligatory pilgrimage 251
450. Deferring [pilgrimage] to the House 251
451. What a lot of clamour and what few pilgrims 251
452. The etiquette of the pilgrim 252
453. The etiquette of iḥrām 252
454. The reward of one who dies on the way to Ḥajj 253
455. The presence of the hidden Imām [al-Mahdī] during Ḥajj 253
88. THE ARGUMENT 254
456. Presenting the argument 254
457. To Allah belongs the conclusive argument 255
458. The surest and most conclusive argument 255
89. THE PROPHETIC TRADITION (ḤADĪTH) 256
459. The value of learning a tradition 256
460. The value of a narrator of traditions 256
461. The reward of those who memorize forty traditions 257
462. Understanding the tradition 257
463. Caution against ascribing lies to the Prophet (SAWA) 257
464. Prohibition of rejecting that tradition whose falsehood is not known 257
465. The soundness of the tradition and its agreement with the Qur'an 258
466. The soundness of a tradition and its agreement with man's nature 258
467. The soundness of a tradition and its agreement with the truth 258
468. The permissibility of transmitting the meaning of the tradition 259
469. What must be observed when transmitting traditions 259

470. The tradition from Ahl al-Bayt is the tradition from the Messenger of Allah 259
471. The all-inclusiveness of the book and the Prophetic practice 260
472. The ambiguous traditions 260
90. LEGAL PUNISHMENTS 260
473. Everything has a bound 260
474. Averting the punishments 261
475. Upholding the penal laws 261
476. No intercession, bail or oath in a legal punishment 261
477. Prohibition of postponement of legal punishments 262
478. Prohibition of transgressing the bounds 262
479. Executing the legal punishment in the land of the enemy 263
480. The role of implementing the penal law in atonement for the sin 263
481. Prohibition of insulting the one being punished 263
482. Those to whom penal law should not be implemented 264
91. WAR 264
483. Reasons of war 264
484. Surprising the enemy 265
485. That which must be observed before the war 265
486. The troops at the forefront of the army 265
487. Military instructions 266
488. War is a trick 267
489. Prohibition of running away from the battle 267
490. Warning against fighting a Muslim 268
491. Supplicating during war 268
492. The fighting of women 268
92. THE WARMONGER 268
493. The punishment of warmonger 268
93. FREEDOM 269
494. The importance of freedom 269
495. All people are free 269
496. The distinguishing trait of the free 270
94. COVETOUSNESS 270
497. Denouncing covetousness 270
498. Denouncing the covetous 271
499. The elements of covetousness 272

95. THE PROFESSION 273
500. The importance of a profession 273
96. THE PROHIBITED (*ḤARĀM*) 274
501. Avoiding the prohibited 274
502. Consuming the prohibited 274
503. The reward of one who has access to the prohibited but abandons it 275
97. THE PARTY 276
504. The party of Allah 276
505. The party of Satan 276
98. PRUDENCE 277
506. The value of prudence 277
507. The danger of not foreseeing the consequences of matters 277
508. Firm resolution and determination 278
509. The interpretation of prudence 278
510. The prudent 278
511. The most prudent of people 279
99. SORROW 279
512. The harms of sorrow 279
513. The causes of sorrow 280
514. Overcoming sorrow 280
515. The reason for sorrow and joy for an unknown cause 282
516. Praiseworthy sorrow 282
100. THE ACCOUNT 283
517. The day of account 283
518. Enjoinment of accounting for one's self 283
519. The fruit of taking account of oneself 284
520. The first thing that man will be asked about 284
521. That which one is not accountable for 285
522. That which one will be held accountable for 285
523. That which will make the account easier on the day of resurrection 286
524. The categories of people during the account 286
525. The adverse account 286
526. Those whose account will be easy 287
527. Those who will enter paradise without accounting 287
528. *Those who will enter the fire without accounting* 288

101. JEALOUSY 289
529. The harms of jealousy 289
530. Every prosperous person is envied 290
531. Jealousy and faith 290
532. The signs of the jealous person 290
102. REGRET 291
533. The person with the greatest regret 291
103. THE GOOD DEEDS 292
534. The blessings of good deeds 292
535. Multiple requital of good deeds 292
104. GOOD-DOING 292
536. The meaning of good-doing 292
537. He who does good benefits his own soul 293
538. The virtue of good-doing 293
539. good-doing to the wrongdoer 294
540. The consequence of the polytheists' acts of good 294
105. MEMORIZING 294
541. The blessing of memorizing 294
542. Memorization in childhood 295
543. That which increases one's capacity to memorize 295
106. RESENTMENT 295
544. Denouncing resentment 295
545. The believer's resentment is short-lived 296
107. SCORN 296
546. Prohibition of scorning people 296
547. Caution against scorning a believer 297
108. THE TRUTH 297
548. The truth 297
549. The weight of the truth 298
550. The necessity of telling the truth even to one's own detriment 298
551. Speaking the truth when pleased or angered 299
552. Accepting the truth 299
553. The criterion of knowing the truth 300
554. The truth can side equally with or against someone 300
109. THE RIGHTS 300

555. The rights of Allah, Most High 300
556. Giving priority to the rights of people 301
557. The greatest of rights 301
558. The rights of the brethren 301
110. HOARDING 302
559. Denouncing hoarding 302
560. Denouncing the hoarder 303
111. WISDOM 304
561. The virtue of wisdom 304
562. Wisdom is the lost property of the believer 305
563. What a wise person must not do 306
564. The interpretation of wisdom 306
565. The fountainhead of wisdom 307
566. What brings about wisdom 307
567. What prevents wisdom 307
568. The effects of wisdom 308
569. Protection of wisdom 308
112. OATH-TAKING 309
570. Prohibition against taking oath by Allah glory be to Him 309
571. Warning against false oaths 309
572. How to commit a tyrant to oath 309
113. THE LAWFUL (*ḤALĀL*) 310
573. Enjoinment to eat the lawful 310
574. The difficulty in seeking the lawful 310
575. The property of the believer is unlawful to use except with his consent 310
114. CLEMENCY 311
576. The virtue of clemency 311
577. What brings about clemency 311
578. The fruits of clemency 312
579. The interpretation of clemency 312
580. Clemency during anger 312
115. FOOLISHNESS 313
581. Reproaching foolishness 313
582. The characteristics of a fool 313
583. Taking the fool as a companion 314

584. The most foolish of people 314
585. Answering the fool 315
116. THE BATHHOUSE 315
586. Encouraging to take bath 315
587. The etiquettes of entering the bathroom 315
117. THE NEED 316
588. Censure of asking for a need 316
589. Granting needs 316
590. The one who refrains from granting the need of his brother 317
591. Undertaking the granting of needs 318
592. The etiquette of seeking a need 318
118. PRECAUTION 319
593. Take precaution with your religion 319
119. LIFE 319
594. The value of life 319
595. Water and life 320
596. That which is better than life 320
597. The real life 320
120. ANIMALS 320
598. The rights of animals 320
121. MODESTY 322
599. The virtue of modesty 322
600. Modesty and faith 323
601. Reprehensible modesty 323
602. The consequences of lack of modesty 323
603. Having modesty with Allah 324
604. The peak of modesty 324
122. THE END 324
605. The danger of a bad end 324
606. What brings about a good final outcome 325
123. SERVICE 325
607. The virtue of serving Muslims 325
124. THE KHARIJITES 326
608. The apostates 326
609. Imām ʿAlī (AS) after the killing of the Kharijites 327

610. The Imām's prohibition of killing the Kharijites after him 328
125. LOSS 328
611. Who is a loser 328
612. To become a loser in the world and the Hereafter 328
613. The biggest losers 329
126. HUMILITY 329
614. The virtue of humility 329
615. The characteristics of the humble 330
127. THE SERMON 330
616. The sermon 330
128. HANDWRITING 331
617. Handwriting 331
129. SINCERITY 332
618. The virtue of sincerity 332
619. The difficulty of sincerity coupled with sincerity 333
620. The sufficiency of few actions 333
621. The dealing of Allah with the sincere ones with His sincere secrecy 333
622. The role of sincerity in the acceptance of actions 334
623. The pure sincerity 334
624. The signs of the sincere 335
625. What brings about sincerity 335
626. The effects of sincerity 336
130. DIFFERENCES 336
627. There is no base for differences in nature 336
628. Encouragement to discard differences 337
629. Explanation of 'the separation of my community is a mercy' 338
630. Explanation of congregation and separation 338
631. The cause of separation 338
131. CREATION 339
632. The origin of creation 339
633. The first thing that Allah – glory be to Him – created 339
634. The creation of the world 340
635. The greatness of what is hidden from us of creation 340
132. THE CREATOR 341
636. *The call of the intellect* to repel probable harm 341

637. Some proofs for the existence of the Creator 341
638. Attributing creation to nature 344
133. CHARACTER 345
639. The importance of good naturedness (character) 345
640. The blessing of good naturedness in this world 345
641. The blessings of good naturedness in the Hereafter 346
642. Explanation of good naturedness 347
643. High moral virtues 347
644. Explanation of noble moral traits 347
645. The best of noble traits 348
646. The fruits of good naturedness 348
647. Denouncing ill naturedness 348
648. The final outcome of the ill-natured person 349
649. The best virtues 349
650. The link between various traits 350
134. ALCOHOL 350
651. Denouncing drinking alcohol 350
652. The reason for the prohibition of alcohol 350
653. The consequence of drinking alcohol 351
654. Interacting [dealing] with an alcohol drinker 351
655. How an alcohol drinker will be resurrected 351
656. Enjoinment of abandoning alcohol even if it be for other than Allah 352
657. The prohibition of that which produces the same effects as alcohol 352
135. FEAR 352
658. The virtue of fearing Allah 352
659. The believer lies between two fears 353
660. The believer lies between hope and fear 353
661. The marks of the fearful one 354
662. Explanation of fearing Allah 354
663. The fruits of fear of Allah 354
664. Caution against fearing other than Allah 355
665. How one should react when in fear of something awesome 356
666. Miscellaneous 356
136. BETRAYAL 357
667. Caution against betrayal 357

668. Explanation of betrayal and the betrayer 358
669. The peak of betrayal 358
137. GOOD 359
670. The virtue of good 359
671. Actions encompassed by goodness 359
672. How the good of this world and the Hereafter is obtained 360
673. Explanation of good 361
674. When Allah wants good for a servant 361
675. When Allah wants good for a community 362
676. Enjoinment of hastening towards good deeds 362
677. The best of matters 363
678. Prohibition of contempt for little good 363
679. The criteria for good and evil 364
680. The characteristics of good people 364
681. What is better than goodness 364
682. The worth of one who guides towards good 365
138. SEEKING a GOOD OUTCOME [FROM ALLAH] 365
683. The virtue of seeking a good outcome [from Allah] 365
139. AMICABLENESS 366
684. The virtue of amicableness 366
140. SUPPLICATION 368
685. The virtue of supplication 368
686. Supplication wards off inescapable fate 369
687. Supplication repels various types of calamity 370
688. Priority with supplication 370
689. Enjoinment of supplication for every need 371
690. Supplication is the key to granting [of a request] 372
691. The conditions for the answering of supplication 372
692. Factors that prevent the answering of supplication 374
693. The etiquettes of supplication 375
694. What the supplicant must not do 379
695. The one whose request is granted without asking 380
696. The role of contentment and despair in answering 380
697. Those whose supplications are answered 381
698. *Supplications that are not answered* 381

699. The reasons for delayed responses 382
700. Supplication is not without effect 382
701. Caution against supplication without knowledge 383
141. THE WORLD 383
702. Naming the 'world' 383
703. The world is the plantation for the Hereafter 383
704. Explanation of the world 384
705. Taking only what is necessary from the world 384
706. The world belongs to one who has abandoned it 385
707. Criticizing the world without knowledge 385
708. Characteristics of the condemned aspect of the world 386
709. Love of the world is the fountainhead of every mistake 386
710. The effects of love of the world 387
711. The world from the viewpoint of Imām ʿAlī (AS) 387
712. Warning against the deceptions of the world 388
713. Verily the world deceives the ignorant 389
714. Warning against being satisfied with the world 389
715. The danger of preferring the world [over the Hereafter] 390
716. The world is the prison of the believer 391
717. The danger of making worldly affairs one's greatest concern 391
718. The lowliness of the world in Allah's eyes 392
719. The difference between the censured world and the Hereafter 392
720. Combining the world and the Hereafter 394
721. The parable of the world 394
722. The world is the house of [trifling] enjoyment 396
723. The world is a place surrounded by trials 397
142. PLIABILITY 397
724. Flattering the transgressors 397
725. The prohibition of compromising the truth 398
143. STATE 398
726. The state [i.e. governance] of senior people 398
727. Sign of the fall of states 398
728. Reasons for the stability of states 398
144. REMEDY 399
729. To treat oneself 399

730. There is a cure for every ailment 399
731. Beware of hastening towards resorting to medicine 400
732. Diet control is the fountainhead of remedies 400
733. The greatest remedy 401
734. Miscellaneous 401
145. RELIGION 401
735. Importance of religion 401
736. The bane of religion 402
737. Encouragement to preserve religion 402
738. Those who have no religion 403
739. The simplicity of religion 403
740. The only religion through which deeds are accepted 404
741. The correct way to understanding religion 404
742. Protecting the religion by means of the world 405
743. Supplication for affirming the heart towards religion 405
744. Characteristics of the preservers of Allah's religion 405
745. The strengthening of religion through a disgraceful people 406
146. DEBT 406
746. Denouncing borrowing 406
747. Permission to incur debt when in need 406
748. Encouragement to write a contract for any loan 407
749. Prohibition of the postponement of repaying debts 407
147. REMEMBRANCE 408
750. The virtue of the remembrance of Allah 408
751. Enjoinment of frequent remembrance [of Allah] 409
752. Enjoinment of engaging in continuous remembrance 409
753. The remembrance of Allah is good at all times 410
754. The ones who remember 410
755. Remember Allah and he will remember you 411
756. The fruits of remembrance 412
757. Enjoinment of remembrance of Allah in certain situations 413
758. The reality of the remembrance [of Allah] 414
759. That which brings about continuous remembrance [of Allah] 415
760. Factors that prevent the remembrance [of Allah] 416
761. The effects of disregarding the remembrance [of Allah] 417

762. Silent remembrance 417
148. DISGRACE 418
763. Disgrace 418
764. A believer must never disgrace himself 418
765. That which brings about disgraces 419
149. SINNING 420
766. Warning against sinning 420
767. Sinning openly 421
768. The worst of sins 421
769. Unforgivable sins 422
770. Warning against committing acts of disobedience in secret 423
771. Taking one's sins lightly and deeming them insignificant 423
772. The grave sins 424
773. Persistent sinning 424
774. Taking pleasure in sinning 425
775. The effects of sins 425
776. The sins that's punishment is hastened [in the life of this world] 427
777. The remedy for sinning 427
778. Things that expiate sins 427
150. LEADERSHIP 431
779. The censure of [the love of] leadership 431
780. The tool required for leadership 431
151. DREAMS 432
781. Glad tidings in dreams 432
782. Categories of dreams 432
783. Interpretation of dreams 433
152. SHOWING OFF 433
784. The censure of showing off 433
785. Showing off and polytheism 435
786. The evil outcome of those who show off 435
787. The distinguishing characteristics of a show off 436
788. Miscellaneous 436
153. OPINION 437
789. That which renders an opinion valid 437
790. The consequences of obstinately holding one's own opinion 437

791. Factors that destroy an opinion 438
792. The government and the validity of its opinion 438
793. Acting on one's opinion in religious matters 438
794. Sincere effort required in formulating one's opinion 438
154. USURY 439
795. Warning against usury 439
796. The wisdom behind the prohibition of usury 440
797. That which leads one to become involved in usury 440
798. The usurer who justifies himself must be fought 440
155. HOPE 441
799. Enjoinment of true hope 441
800. Caution against placing one's hopes in anyone other than Allah 442
156. THE RETURN 442
801. The return of the dead 442
802. The mentioning of specific people to be returned 442
803. The return will not be universal 443
157. COMPASSION 443
804. The enjoinment of compassion towards one another 443
805. Those that are most deserving of compassion 444
158. DIVINE MERCY 444
806. Allah's divine mercy 444
807. Factors that elicit Allah's mercy 445
159. CONSANGUINAL RELATIONS 445
808. Reconciliation with one's kin 445
809. The benefits of maintaining relations with one's kin 446
810. Reconciling with one who cuts you off 447
811. Caution against cutting ties with one's kin 447
812. The least one can do to maintain relations with one's kin 447
160. SUSTENANCE 448
813. The All-Sustainer 448
814. Sustenance is guaranteed 448
815. Greed and increase in sustenance 449
816. Enjoinment of seeking one's livelihood through decent means 450
817. The seeker of his sustenance 451
818. *Worrying about the morrow's sustenance* 451

819. Impatience with regards to one's sustenance 451
820. Factors that elicit the descent of sustenance and increase it 452
821. Things that cut off sustenance 453
822. Encouraging to seek livelihood through lawful (*ḥalāl*) means 453
823. The best livelihood is that which suffices you 454
161. BRIBERY 455
824. Warning against bribery 455
162. SUCKLING 456
825. Suckling 456
826. Types of wet-nurses that should not be employed 456
163. SATISFACTION (1) Satisfaction with Allah's Divine Decree 457
827. The virtue of satisfaction 457
828. Things that incite satisfaction [with Allah's decree] 458
829. The benefits of satisfaction 458
830. The outcomes of dissatisfaction 459
164. SATISFACTION (2) Allah's Pleasure 459
831. Factors that elicit Allah's pleasure 459
832. Signs of Allah's pleasure 460
833. Pleasing people at the expense of Allah's displeasure 461
165. LENIENCY 461
834. The virtue of leniency 461
835. Moderation in worship 462
836. The benefits of leniency 463
166. SCRUTINY 463
837. Man's actions are scrutinized by Allah, the angels and his own limbs 463
838. Enjoinment of self-scrutiny 464
839. Self-scrutiny and self-accountability 465
167. RAMAḌĀN 465
840. The month of Ramaḍān 465
841. Allah's forgiveness in the month of Ramaḍān 467
168. THE SPIRIT 468
842. The spirit 468
843. Spirits are pre-mobilized groups 468
844. The states of the spirit 469
845. The spirit during sleep 469

169. COMFORT 470
846. Factors that bring about comfort 470
847. Seeking comfort in this world 470
170. AGRICULTURE 471
848. The divine recommendation of cultivation and agriculture 471
171. ALMS-TAX (*zakāt*) 472
849. The obligatory alms-tax 472
850. The role of the alms-tax in the increase of wealth 473
851. The one who refuses to pay the alms-tax 473
852. Those who are entitled to receive the alms-tax 474
853. There is a *zakāt* for everything 474
854. Obligatory alms-tax payable on ʿĪd al-Fiṭr 475
172. TIME 476
855. Perception of time 476
856. Denouncing having trust in time 476
857. Denouncing the contending with time 477
858. Criticising time 477
173. FORNICATION 477
859. Prohibition of fornication 477
860. Consequences of fornication 478
861. Every limb has its own share of fornication 479
174. ASCETICISM 480
862. The virtue of asceticism 480
863. The real meaning of asceticism 480
864. Qualities of the one who practices asceticism 481
865. Factors that elicit asceticism 482
866. The benefits of asceticism 483
867. The most abstemious of people 484
175. MARRIAGE 484
868. Enjoinment of marriage 484
869. Denouncing of unmarried people 486
870. The reward for getting fellow Muslims married 486
871. Enjoinment of urgency in the marriage of young women 486
872. The importance of faith when selecting a spouse 487
873. *The censure of demanding an excessive dowry* 488

874. The importance of being careful in selecting a wife 488
875. The rights of the husband 488
876. The rights of the wife 489
877. Serving one's husband 489
878. Serving one's wife 490
879. Mistreating one's husband 490
880. Mistreating one's wife 491
881. Tolerating bad character of a spouse 491
882. The virtuous wife 491
883. The evil wife 492
884. Things to be considered when spending on one's family 492
885. The etiquette of accepting wedding invitations 492
886. Recommendation to announce one's marriage 493
176. VISITING 493
887. Enjoinment of visiting each other for the pleasure of Allah 493
888. The benefits of meeting fellow brothers 494
889. The etiquette of visiting 494
177. VISITATION OF GRAVES 495
890. Visiting the grave of the Prophet (SAWA) 495
891. Visiting the Household of the Prophet (SAWA) 495
892. Visiting the grave of Fāṭima, the daughter of Imām Mūsā a-Kāẓim (AS) 498
893. Visiting the grave of al-Sayyid ʿAbd al-ʿAẓīm al-Ḥasanī 498
894. Visiting the graves of virtuous people 498
895. Visiting the graves of the deceased 499
896. Greeting the people of the graves 499
178. ADORNMENT 499
897. Encouraging adornment 499
898. The best adornment 500
179. RESPONSIBILITY 501
899. Responsibility 501
900. All of you are responsible 501
901. The answerability of the hearing, the sight and the heart 501
180. ASKING (1) [Seeking Knowledge] 502
902. The key to knowledge 502
903. Productive questioning 502

904. That which should not be questioned 503
905. Answering questions that one does not know the answer to 503
181. ASKING (2) [Requesting a Need] 504
906. Prohibition of asking people 504
907. Caution against asking (of people) in spite of being well-off 505
908. Enjoinment of self-sufficiency 506
909. Asking a favour from the right person 506
910. The etiquette of asking 506
911. Warning against turning a beggar away empty-handed 507
182. INSULTING 508
912. Censure of insulting the believer 508
913. Prohibition of insulting even idols and Satan 508
914. Prohibition of insulting people 508
915. The prohibition of insulting parents 509
916. The prohibition of insulting things 509
183. PROSTRATION 510
917. The role of prostration in proximity to Allah 510
918. Prolonging one's prostration 510
919. The effect of prostration 511
920. Prostrating on the earth from Imām Ḥusayn (AS)'s grave 511
184. THE MOSQUE 512
921. The mosque is the house of Allah 512
922. Maintaining the mosques 512
923. The reward for walking to the mosques 513
924. The reward for sitting in the mosque 513
925. Neighbouring the mosque and praying therein 513
926. Etiquettes of the mosque 514
185. GENEROSITY 514
927. The virtue of generosity 514
928. The virtue of the generous person 515
929. The extent of generosity recommended 516
186. SECRECY 516
930. Encouraging keeping a secret 516
931. Those that must not be entrusted with a secret 518
187. HAPPINESS 518

932. What to be happy about 518
933. The basics of happiness 519
934. One who fills others' hearts with happiness 519
935. Whoever makes another believer happy makes Allah happy 520
936. The reward for alleviating a fellow believer of his sorrows 520
188. WASTING 521
937. Denouncing wasting 521
938. Distinguishing characteristics of a wasteful person 521
939. The lowest of wastefulness 522
940. That which is not counted as wastes 522
189. STEALING 523
941. Stealing and its legal punishment 523
942. Those who are not liable to the legal punishment for stealing 523
190. PROSPERITY 524
943. The sign of the prosperous 524
944. That which brings about prosperity 525
945. Things which are considered as prosperity 525
946. The reality of prosperity 526
947. The most prosperous of people 526
191. TRAVEL 527
948. Encouraging to travel and making it short 527
949. Encouraging to travel for recreation 527
950. Etiquettes of travelling 527
951. The prohibited journey 529
192. QUENCHING SOMEONE'S THIRST 529
952. The virtue of quenching someone's thirst 529
953. The duty of one who quenches others 530
193. INTOXICATION 530
954. Every intoxicant is prohibited 530
955. Types of intoxicants 530
194. HOUSING 531
956. Spaciousness and smallness of a house 531
957. Caution against building more housing than necessary for one's living 531
958. Selling a house 532
195. WEAPONRY 532

959. The reward for making weapons 532
960. Weaponry and goodness 533
961. Prohibition of selling weapons to enemies of Islam 533
196. THE RULER (THE SULTAN) 533
962. Beware of associating with a tyrannical ruler 533
963. Denouncing the subservience to a tyrannical ruler 534
964. The virtue of a just ruler 535
197. ISLAM 535
965. Islam the religion of Allah 535
966. The meaning of Islam 536
967. Characteristics of a Muslim 537
968. Fundamentals of Islam 537
198. GREETING OF PEACE (SALĀM) 538
969. The greeting between Muslims 538
970. The virtue of initiating the greeting 539
971. Enjoinment of greeting upon entering one's house 540
972. The obligation of returning a greeting 540
973. The etiquette of greeting 540
199. SUBMISSION 541
974. Submission to the will of Allah 541
200. LISTENING 543
975. The virtue of attentive ears 543
976. Those whose ears have been sealed 543
977. Effective listening 543
978. The obligation incumbent on the hearing 544
201. THE NAME 544
979. Choosing good names 544
980. Changing ugly names 545
202. THE NAMES OF ALLAH 545
981. In the name of Allah, the All-Beneficent, the All-Merciful 545
982. Allah's greatest name sunnah [tradition] 546
203. THE SUNNAH 546
983. Enjoinment of adhering to the Prophet's practices 546
984. The recompense of one who establishes a habitual practice 547
985. *Prohibition of discontinuing a good practice* 547

204. STAYING AWAKE AT NIGHT 548
986. Staying awake at night 548
987. Enjoinment of remaining awake on specific nights 549
205. THE CHIEF 549
988. Characteristics of the chief 549
989. Requirements of chiefdom 549
990. Factors that repel chiefdom 550
206. MANAGEMENT 550
991. Management of the society 550
992. Management of one's self 551
207. PROCRASTINATION 552
993. Prohibition of procrastination 552
208. THE MARKETPLACE 553
994. Place of negligence 553
995. Imām 'Alī (AS)'s exhortation to market traders 554
209. BRUSHING ONE'S TEETH 554
996. Enjoinment of brushing one's teeth 554
997. The benefits of brushing teeth 555
998. Etiquette of brushing teeth 556
210. YOUTH 556
999. Youth 556
1000. Educating youngsters 557
1001. Learning during one's youth 557
1002. The virtue of a worshipping young man 557
1003. The true significance of the word 'fatā' 558
211. THE OBSCURE MATTER 558
1004. Meaning of the obscure matter 558
1005. The danger of obscure matter 559
1006. The necessity of stopping in the face of an obscure matter 559
1007. Obligation to abandon obscure matters 559
212. TREES 560
1008. The importance of planting trees 560
1009. Forbiddance from cutting down trees 560
213. COURAGE 561
1010. The virtue of courage 561

1011. That which engenders courage 561
1012. The most courageous of people 562
1013. The bane of courage 563
214. EVIL 563
1014. The yardstick of good and evil 563
1015. worse than evil 564
1016. The keys to all evils 564
1017. The merging of evils 564
1018. Man's natural tendency for evil 565
215. POLYTHEISM 565
1019. Caution against polytheism 565
1020. Instruction of polytheism 565
1021. The minimum degree of polytheism 566
1022. Hidden polytheism 566
216. SATAN 567
1023. The lesson to be learned from how Allah dealt with Satan 567
1024. Seeking refuge in Allah from Satan 568
1025. Satan's enmity towards man 568
1026. Caution against Satan's temptations 569
1027. Satan worshippers 569
1028. Satan's allurements 569
1029. That which renders one immune from Satan 570
1030. That which brings one under Satan's authority 571
217. POETRY 572
1031. Explanation of the verse of the Qur'an condemning poets 572
1032. Poetry is jihād with the tongue 572
218. THE BATTLE CRY 573
1033. The battle cries 573
1034. The Muslims' victory cry on the day of resurrection 574
219. INTERCESSION 574
1035. Intercession in the life of this world 574
1036. Intercession in the Hereafter 575
1037. Those who will be deprived of intercession 576
1038. The need of all for intercession 577
1039. Types of intercessors 577

1040. The people most deserving of intercession 578
1041. A believer's right to intercession depends on the extent of his deeds 578
1042. The minimum number that a believer can intercede 578
220. WRETCHEDNESS 579
1043. Characteristics of a wretched person 579
1044. The wretched one was wretched as a foetus in his mother's womb 579
1045. That which brings about wretchedness 580
1046. The most wretched of all people 581
1047. The symptoms of wretchedness 581
221. THANKSGIVING 582
1048. Enjoinment of thanksgiving to Allah 582
1049. The virtue of the thankful one 582
1050. The role of thankfulness in the increase (of bounties) 583
1051. The necessity of thanksgiving for the ability to thank 583
1052. True thanksgiving 584
1053. The most thankful of people 585
1054. Enjoinment of thanking one who does good to you 585
1055. One who has not thanked the creature has not thanked the Creator 586
222. DOUBT 586
1056. Doubt in the principles of belief 586
1057. Causes of doubt 587
1058. Effects of doubt 587
1059. Factors that dispel doubt 587
1060. The aspects of doubt 588
223. BEARING WITNESS (IN A COURT OF JUSTICE) 588
1061. Bearing witness with fairness 588
1062. Enjoinment of bearing witness 589
1063. Concealing one's testimony 589
1064. Those whose testimony is deemed valid 590
1065. The etiquette of giving testimony 590
224. MARTYRDOM IN THE WAY OF ALLAH 591
1066. The virtue of martyrdom 591
1067. The reward of seeking martyrdom 592
1068. Honorary martyrdom 592
1069. The reward of one who is wounded in the way of Allah 593

225. FAME 593
1070. Praiseworthy fame 593
1071. Blameworthy fame 594
1072. The censure of clothing or acts of worship that draw attention 594
226. COUNSEL 595
1073. Enjoinment of consultation 595
1074. People whose counsel should not be sought 595
1075. Boundaries of counselling 596
1076. Enjoinment of guiding one who seeks your counsel 596
1077. To consult with the enemy 596
227. OLD AGE 597
1078. Old age 597
1079. Enjoinment of venerating the old 598
228. THE SHĪʿA 599
1080. The virtue of the Shīʿa of the Household of the Prophet 599
1081. The signs of the Shīʿa of Ahl al-Bayt (AS) 599
1082. Those who are not considered to be Shīʿa 600
1083. Types of those who are called Shīʿa 601
1084. Prohibition of extremism for the shīʿa 602
1085. Duties incumbent on the Shīʿa in their interactions with people 602
1086. The station of the Shīʿa on the day of resurrection 603
229. PATIENCE 603
1087. The virtue of patience 603
1088. Patience and great things 604
1089. Perseverance and victory 605
1090. The reward of the patient one 605
1091. The true meaning of patience 606
1092. The patience possessed by the Shīʿa of Ahl al-Bayt (AS) 606
1093. The effects of anxiety 607
1094. Factors that bring about patience 607
230. TRUTHFULNESS 608
1095. The virtue of truthfulness and the truthful 608
1096. Testing people through truthfulness in speech 609
1097. The most truthful of sayings 609
231. *THE FRIEND* 610

1098. The importance of a friend 610
1099. Resemblance of souls 610
1100. People whom one should befriend 611
1101. People whom one must not befriend 611
1102. That which corrupts a friendship 612
1103. The extent of one's friendship 613
1104. The best of companions 614
1105. The right of one's companion 614
232. CHARITY 614
1106. The virtue of charity 614
1107. Allah's firsthand receipt of charities 615
1108. Charity and repelling adversities 615
1109. Charity is the key to (increased) sustenance 616
1110. Every kindly act is considered charity 616
1111. The best form of charity 617
1112. The virtue of giving charity in secret and its good effects 618
1113. The amount of charity to be given 619
1114. The recipients of charity 620
1115. The etiquette of giving 620
233. THE PATH 621
1116. The danger of crossing the path 621
1117. The true meaning of the straight path 621
1118. Crossing the path of the Hereafter (the bridge over hell) 622
234. CHILDHOOD 623
1119. Childhood 623
235. SHAKING HANDS 624
1120. Encouraging the shaking of hands 624
1121. Prohibition of shaking a woman's hand 625
236. PEACEMAKING 625
1122. Peacemaking in war 625
1123. Imām al-Ḥasan (AS)'s peace treaty 626
1124. The importance of making peace between people 626
1125. The permissibility of lying for the sake of reconciliation 627
237. THE PRAYER (1) 628
1126. The virtue of prayer 628

1127. The effects of the prayer 629
1128. The virtue of one who prays 630
1129. Humbleness in prayer 631
1130. Conditions and impediments to the acceptance of the prayer 632
1131. He whose prayer is accepted 634
1132. The role of presence of the heart in the acceptance of the prayer 634
1133. He whose prayer is not counted 635
1134. Prohibition of laziness in prayer 635
1135. Observance of the prescribed timings of the prayer 636
1136. Enjoinment of performing the prayer at the earliest moment of the time prescribed for it 636
1137. Abandonment of the prayer and disbelief 637
1138. Caution against taking the prayer lightly 638
1139. The congregational prayer 638
1140. Duties that the leader of the congregation must observe 639
238. THE PRAYER (2) the Night Prayer 640
1141. The Virtue of the Night Prayer 640
1142. That which causes one to be deprived of the opportunity to perform the night prayer 642
1143. The recompense of one who intends to perform the night prayer, but stays asleep 642
239. THE PRAYER (3) the Friday Prayer 643
1144. The importance of Friday prayer 643
1145. Etiquette of listening to the sermon 644
240. PRAYER (4) INVOKING BLESSINGS ON THE PROPHET AND HIS HOUSEHOLD (SAWA) 644
1146. The virtue of invoking blessings on the Prophet (SAWA) & his Progeny 644
1147. The method of invoking blessings on the Prophet (SAWA) & his Progeny 645
241. SILENCE 645
1148. The virtue of silence 645
1149. The fruits of silence 646
1150. Blameworthy silence 646
242. AFFLICTION 647
1151. The reward for (enduring an) affliction 647
1152. The worst of afflictions 647
1153. To say "indeed we belong to Allah and to Him do we indeed return" 648
1154. The etiquette of dealing with an affliction 648
1155. Factors that ease afflictions 649

1156. Reprehension of gloating at another's affliction 650
243. THE VOICE 650
1157. Praising the lowering of one's voice and denouncing the raising of it 650
244. FASTING 651
1158. The virtue of fasting 651
1159. Enjoinment of fasting out of one's own accord 652
1160. The etiquette of fasting 653
1161. The virtue of fasting in hot and cold weather 653
245. LAUGHTER 654
1162. The praising of smiling 654
1163. The reproaching of laughing too much and too loud 654
246. THE ABASED PEOPLE 655
1164. The abased people 655
1165. The return of power to the abased people 655
1166. Spiritual weakness 656
247. STRAYING FROM THE STRAIGHT PATH 657
1167. Factors that cause one to stray (from the straight path) 657
1168. Those who lead others astray 658
1169. That which destroys the pillars of misguidance 658
248. LIABILITY 659
1170. Liability as a result of squandering the property of others 659
1171. The censure of risking bailing or culpability 659
1172. There is no liability on something borrowed 660
249. HOSPITALITY 660
1173. The virtue of hospitality 660
1174. People whom one should invite as guests 661
1175. Enjoinment of accepting the invitation of a fellow believer 661
1176. Making a special effort for one's guest 661
1177. The etiquette of hospitality 662
250. MEDICINE 663
1178. The real doctor 663
1179. That which makes one needless of medicine 663
1180. Avoiding medicine as much as possible 664
251. FEEDING OTHERS 664
1181. The virtue of feeding a hungry person 664

252. DIVORCE 665
1182. The reprehension of divorce 665
1183. The wisdom in restricting the divorce to three times 666
253. GREED 667
1184. Reprehension of greed 667
1185. Praiseworthy avidity 669
254. PURITY 669
1186. Ritual purification 669
1187. Purifying agents 670
1188. Spiritual purity 670
255. OBEDIENCE 671
1189. Obedience to Allah and its effects 671
1190. He who is entitled to be obeyed 672
1191. He who must not be obeyed 672
256. PERFUME 673
1192. The virtue of using perfume 673
1193. The perfume of women 674
257. THE EVIL OMEN 674
1194. Drawing evil omens 674
258. NAILS 676
1195. Encouraging the clipping of one's nails 676
1196. Encouraging women to leave their nails (long) 676
259. WRONGDOING 676
1197. Caution against wrongdoing 676
1198. Types of wrongdoing 678
1199. The most atrocious type of wrong 678
1200. Granting respite to the wrongdoer 679
1201. The wrongdoer's regret 680
1202. Caution against aiding the wrongdoer 680
1203. Enjoinment of aiding the wronged 681
1204. Being wary of the plea [to Allah] of one who has been wronged 682
260. CONJECTURE 682
1205. Conjecture of the intellectual 682
1206. Enjoinment to entertain good opinion about the deed of a believer 682
1207. The virtue of entertaining good opinions 683

1208. Caution against entertaining low or suspicious opinions 683
1209. The necessity of avoiding that which incites suspicious thoughts 684
1210. instances when suspicion is allowed 685
261. WORSHIP 685
1211. Encouraging worship 685
1212. The role of understanding and conviction in worship 686
1213. Types of worship 687
1214. Types of worshippers 688
1215. The best form of worship 688
1216. Eagerness and vitality in worship 689
262. THE MORAL LESSON 690
1217. Enjoinment of taking lesson from moral advice 690
1218. Things that must be contemplated upon and drawn lessons from 691
1219. The benefits of taking lesson 692
263. SELF-ADMIRATION 692
1220. Reprehension of self-admiration 692
1221. Enjoinment of undervaluing the good that one does 693
1222. Treatment of self-admiration 694
264. THE MIRACLE 694
1223. The miracle is a sign in knowing the Prophets of Allah and the Imams 694
1224. The wisdom behind the diversity of the Prophets' miracles 695
265. HASTE 695
1225. Reproaching hastiness 695
1226. Enjoinment of rushing to do good deeds 696
266. JUSTICE 697
1227. The importance of justice 697
1228. Qualities of a just person 698
1229. Advice to be just and fair with one's friend and enemy 698
1230. The most just of people 699
267. ENMITY 699
1231. Prohibition of showing enmity toward anyone 699
1232. The seed of enmity 700
1233. One who must be considered an enemy 700
1234. Your archenemy 700
1235. Caution against feeling secure from one's enemy 701

1236. Reconciling with one's enemies 701
1237. How to arm oneself against enemies 701
1238. People's hostility towards that which they are ignorant of 701
268. MAKING EXCUSES 702
1239. Caution against doing something one would later have to excuse oneself for 702
1240. Enjoinment of accepting the excuse of one who excuses himself 702
269. GOOD REPUTE 703
1241. Enjoinment of keeping up one's reputation 703
1242. The reward for refraining from tarnishing fellow Muslims' reputations 703
1243. The reward for defending the reputation of a fellow Muslim 704
270. INNER KNOWLEDGE 704
1244. The importance of inner knowledge 704
1245. Impediments to inner knowledge 705
1246. The inner knowledge of the self 705
271. INNER KNOWLEDGE OF ALLAH 706
1247. The virtue of attaining inner knowledge of Allah 706
1248. The fruits of inner knowledge of Allah 707
1249. The description of the one who knows Allah [or the gnostic] 709
1250. The lowest degree of inner knowledge of Allah 709
1251. Attaining inner knowledge of Allah through Allah Himself 709
1252. Prohibition of pondering about Allah's Essence 710
1253. The intellects' incapacity to fathom His Essence 710
1254. The extent to which one is allowed to describe Allah 711
1255. The value of the belief in Allah's divine unity (*tawḥīd*) and its explanation 713
1256. The proof of Allah's divine unity 713
1257. The sights cannot apprehend Him but the hearts behold Him 715
1258. Eternal and Everlasting 716
1259. Living (Omnipresent) 717
1260. All-Knowing (Omniscient) 717
1261. Just 719
1262. The Creator 719
1263. All-Powerful (Omnipotent) 720
1264. The Speaker 721
1265. The One who wills 721
1266. The Manifest and the Hidden 721

1267. The Master 722
1268. The All-Hearing and the All-Seeing 722
1269. The Subtle and the All-Aware 723
1270. The All-Strong and the Almighty 723
1271. The All-Wise 724
1272. The All-Embracing, All-Needless 724
1273. He is everywhere 724
1274. Attributes of His Essence and Attributes of His action 725
1275. Comprehensive attributes 725
272. ACTS OF COMMON COURTESY (1): PERFORMING ACTS OF COMMON COURTESY 726
1276. The Virtue of Common Courtesy 726
1277. Enjoinment of spreading kindness to both good and bad people 727
1278. Circulation of good acts from hand to hand 728
1279. Prohibition of making someone feel obliged for an act of courtesy 728
1280. Completion of a good act 728
1281. Prohibition of holding acts of common courtesy in contempt 729
1282. The mark of acceptance of a good act 729
1283. The reward for good acts 730
273. ACTS OF COMMON COURTESY (2): ENJOINING GOOD AND PROHIBITING WRONG 731
1284. Importance of enjoining good and prohibiting wrong 731
1285. The danger of abandoning the enjoinment of good and the prohibition of wrong 732
1286. He who contents himself with a people's (wrong) action 733
1287. The conditions to be observed by one who enjoins good 733
1288. The lowest level of prohibition of wrong 734
274. HONOUR 735
1289. The explanation of honour 735
1290. Factors that elicit honour 736
1291. That which causes honour to last 737
275. SOLITUDE 737
1292. The virtue of solitude 737
1293. That which drives one to solitude 738
1294. One who must not adopt solitude 738
276. CONDOLENCE 739

1295. Condoling with one who is grief-stricken 739
1296. What to say when giving condolences to a grief-stricken person 739
1297. Congratulating the grief-stricken is more appropriate than condoling him 739
277. SOCIAL INTERACTION 740
1298. The etiquette of social interaction with people 740
1299. The etiquette of social interaction with one's family 740
1300. What is required when interacting with people 741
278. 'ĀSHŪRĀ' 742
1301. 'Āshūrā and weeping for Imām al-Ḥusayn (AS) and his companions 742
279. INFATUATION 743
1302. The reprehensibility of infatuation 743
1303. The reward for one who despite his infatuation restrains himself 744
1304. Infatuation with Allah 744
280. PARTISANSHIP 744
1305. Reprehension of partisanship 744
1306. Praiseworthy partisanship 746
281. INFALLIBILITY 746
1307. The meaning of infallibility 746
1308. Factors that bring about sinlessness 747
1309. The infallibility of the Imām 748
282. VENERATION 748
1310. Veneration of rulers 748
1311. The extent of veneration recommended 749
283. SELF-RESTRAINT 751
1312. Enjoinment of self-restraint 751
1313. Enjoinment of restraining the stomach and the private parts 752
1314. The root of self-restraint 752
1315. The fruit of self-restraint 752
284. PARDON 753
1316. The virtue of pardon 753
1317. Enjoinment of graceful condonance 754
1318. Enjoinment of pardon in spite of one's power (to punish) 755
1319. Pardon and improvement of hearts 755
1320. That which must not be pardoned 756
1321. *Allah's pardon* 756

285. VITALITY 757
1322. The value of vitality 757
1323. That which engenders vitality 758
1324. Enjoinment of seeking vitality from Allah 758
1325. Supplications to ask for vitality 759
1326. Allah's close servants 759
286. THE INTELLECT 760
1327. The value of intellect 760
1328. The role of the intellect in chastisement and reward 762
1329. The authoritativeness of the intellect 763
1330. The explanation of intellect 763
1331. The attributes of an intelligent person 764
1332. That which increases the intellect 766
1333. What is regarded as intellect 766
1334. That which weakens the intellect 767
1335. Evidence of weak intellect 768
1336. The fruit of the intellect 768
1337. The intellect's adversary 769
287. RETREAT IN THE MOSQUE (*I'tikāf*) 769
1338. Retreat in the mosque 769
288. KNOWLEDGE 771
1339. The virtue of knowledge 771
1340. The superiority of knowledge to acts of worship 774
1341. The death of a scholar 775
1342. Looking at the face of a scholar is an act of worship 775
1343. Enjoinment of seeking knowledge 775
1344. The virtue of the seeker of knowledge 776
1345. The blessings of teaching 777
1346. The way the teacher will be resurrected 778
1347. Gaining knowledge for Allah and for other than Allah 779
1348. What is necessary in choosing a teacher 780
1349. The rights of the student to be observed by the teacher 780
1350. The rights of the teacher to be observed by the student 781
1351. Honouring the scholar 782
1352. Duties incumbent on the student 783

1353. The virtue of the scholars 783
1354. The fruit of knowledge 784
1355. The duties incumbent upon a person of knowledge 784
1356. Reprehension of practising without knowledge 785
1357. The necessity of practising upon one's knowledge 785
1358. The severity of the chastisement of the knowledgeable man who abandons his knowledge 787
1359. Reprehension of evil scholars 788
1360. The etiquettes of knowledge 788
1361. The reprehensibility of knowledge that is of no use 789
1362. The various types of knowledge 789
1363. Inspired knowledge 791
1364. The most knowledgeable of people 791
1365. Exclusive confinement of true knowledge to the Household of the Prophet 791
289. LIFESPAN 792
1366. Lifespan 792
1367. Encouraging making the most of one's life 792
1368. He whose life will be a proof against him 793
1369. That which leads to an increase in lifespan 794
1370. The believer and asking for a long life 795
1371. The wisdom behind man's ignorance of the span of his life 795
290. ACTION 796
1372. Enjoinment of righteous action 796
1373. Action and recompense 798
1374. Maintenance of continuous action 798
1375. The best of actions 799
1376. He whose deeds do not benefit him 799
1377. Deeds that one must be cautious of 800
1378. Perfection of a good deed 800
1379. The exposition of deeds to Allah, the Prophet and the Imāms (AS) 801
1380. The book of deeds 802
1381. Embodiment of deeds 802
291. THE COVENANT 803
1382. Enjoinment of fulfilling one's covenant 803
292. RESURRECTION 805

1383. Resurrection 805
1384. The proofs affirming resurrection 805
1385. The drawing near of the Hour 806
1386. Allah's exclusive knowledge of the Hour 807
1387. The portents of the Hour 807
1388. The Day of Rising [from the graves] 808
1389. The description of the [Day of] Congregation 808
1390. The Godwary people on the Day of Resurrection 809
1391. The guilty ones on the Day of Resurrection 809
1392. The Book of Deeds 810
1393. The People of the Right Hand and of the Left Hand 811
293. THE HABIT 812
1394. The role of habit in life 812
1395. Overcoming the habit 813
1396. The difficulty of removing a habit 813
294. 'ĪD – THE FESTIVAL 814
1397. 'Īd – the true festival 814
1398. Nayrūz festival 815
1399. The adornment of the festivals 816
295. THE FAULT 817
1400. Praise for one whose own fault preoccupies him from finding fault in others 817
1401. The reprehension of preoccupying oneself with faults whilst flattering oneself 817
1402. The virtue of concealing faults 818
1403. Encouraging conferring someone's faults to them 819
1404. Reprehensibility of pursuing of people's faults 819
1405. What covers up the faults 820
1406. He who is ignorant of something finds fault with it 821
296. CONDEMNATION 821
1407. The censure of condemnation 821
297. LIFESTYLE 822
1408. The most wholesome lifestyle 822
1409. Factors which spoil one's lifestyle 823
298. DELUSION 823
1410. The danger of delusion and the characteristics of the deluded 823
1411. Deluding oneself about Allah 824

1412. Being deluded by this world 825
1413. Self-delusion 825
299. THE BATTLES (Fought by the Prophet) 826
1414. The battle of Badr 826
1415. The battle of ʿUḥud 827
1416. The battle of Dhāt al-Riqāʿ 828
1417. The battle of Aḥzāb and Banī Qurayẓa 828
1418. The battle of Khaybar 829
1419. The conquest of Makkah 830
1420. The battle of Ḥunayn 831
300. SWINDLING 831
1421. The reproaching of swindling 831
301. USURPATION 832
1422.The prohibition of usurpation 832
302. ANGER 833
1423. Anger is the key to all evils 833
1424. Enjoinment of controlling one's anger 833
1425. Enjoinment of suppressing one's anger 834
1426. The remedy for anger 834
1427. The praiseworthiness of anger for the sake of Allah 835
303. SEEKING FORGIVENESS 835
1428. The virtue of seeking forgiveness 835
1429. Seeking forgiveness and increase in sustenance 836
1430. The seeking of forgiveness by those brought near to Allah 837
1431. Caution against seeking forgiveness alongside persistent sinning 837
304. NEGLIGENCE 838
1432. Caution against negligence 838
1433. That which prevents negligence 839
1434. The distinguishing characteristics of a negligent person 839
1435. The effects of negligence 839
1436. The praise of feigning negligence (or ignorance) 840
305. RANCOUR 840
1437. Warning against rancour 840
1438. That which the heart of a Muslim cannot harbour rancour towards 841
1439. Censure of breaching one's trust 841

306. EXTREMISM (IN RELIGION) 842
1440. Caution against extremism in religion 842
307. RICHES 844
1441. Richness and rebellion 844
1442. Riches and Godwariness 845
1443. The real meaning of being rich 846
1444. The greatest of riches 846
1445. The key to affluence 847
1446. The rich people whose reward will be doubled 848
1447. The rich people's responsibility for the poor people's hunger 848
308. MUSIC 849
1448. Reproaching music 849
1449. The effects engendered by music 849
309. THE UNSEEN 850
1450. The Prophet knows the unseen through Allah's instruction 850
1451. The Imām and the knowledge of the unseen 850
310. BACKBITING 851
1452. Prohibition of backbiting 851
1453. Backbiting and faith 852
1454. The meaning of backbiting 853
1455. People whom one is allowed to backbite 854
1456. Listening to backbiting 855
1457. The reward for deterring backbiting 855
1458. The penance for backbiting 855
311. POSSESSIVENESS 856
1459. The praise of possessiveness 856
1460. Censure of being jealous or over-possessive over one another in the wrong situation 857
312. TRIAL AND TEMPTATION 858
1461. Trial and temptation 858
1462. Kinds of trial 859
1463. Those who are cleared from trials 859
1464. Miscellaneous 860
313. THE VERDICT 860
1465. Those who give verdicts of their own opinion to people 860
1466. The permissibility for a scholar to issue a verdict 861

314. OBSCENE LANGUAGE 862
1467. Caution against the use of obscene language 862
315. PRIDE 863
1468. Reprehension of showing pride 863
1469. That which prevents pride 864
1470. The Prophet's conduct when mentioning a virtue about himself 864
1471. That which one should be proud of 864
316. THE PERSIANS 865
1472. The Persians and faith 865
317. OPPORTUNITY 866
1473. Seize the opportunity 866
318. OBLIGATIONS 867
1474. Enjoinment of fulfilling religious obligations 867
1475. That which Allah has made obligatory for people 868
1476. The sum of all obligations 869
319. IDLENESS 869
1477. Idleness 869
320. CORRUPTION 871
1478. That which corrupts people in general 871
1479. What is corruption and who is the corruptor? 872
1480. That which repels corruption 873
321. MERIT 873
1481. Merits 873
1482. The best of merits 874
1483. The most virtuous of people 875
322. POVERTY 876
1484. The reprehension of poverty 876
1485. Praising poverty 877
1486. Traditions narrated about the virtue of poverty over wealth 878
1487. The interpretation of poverty 879
1488. Praiseworthy and disparaged poverty 881
1489. Humiliating the poor 881
1490. That which banishes poverty 882
1491. That which brings poverty 882
1492. *Allah*'s excuse to the poor 883

1493. The adornment of poverty 883
1494. Blessed are the poor! 884
323. JURISPRUDENCE 885
1495. Encouraging the learning of religion 885
1496. Qualifications of a scholar (faqīh) 886
1497. The power of the jurist over Satan 886
1498. The death of a jurist 887
324. THINKING 887
1499. Encouraging to think 887
1500. There is no worship like thinking 888
1501. That which purifies thought 888
1502. prohibited thinking 889
325. THE GRAVE 889
1503. The grave is the first stage of the Hereafter 889
1504. Questioning in the grave 890
1505. Punishment in the grave 891
326. KILLING 891
1506. The prohibition of killing a soul [I.e. a human being] 891
1507. Killing of a believer 892
1508. The prohibition of suicide 893
327. THE QUR'AN 893
1509. Adhere to the Qur'an 893
1510. The Qur'an is new in every era 895
1511. Learning and teaching the Qur'an 895
1512. Memorizing the Qur'an and the etiquettes of those who memorise it 896
1513. Urging the recitation of the Qur'an 897
1514. Reciting the Qur'an with a good voice 898
1515. The reality of recitation 899
1516. The etiquettes of recitation 899
1517. Those whom the Qur'an curses 901
1518. Listening to the Qur'an 901
1519. Caution against personal interpretation 902
328. THOSE BROUGHT NEAR TO ALLAH 902
1520. The ultimate goal of proximity to Allah 902
1521. The nearest people to Allah 903

1522. What brings one near to Allah 904
329. THE LOAN 905
1523. The virtue of giving loan 905
1524. Enjoinment to give respite to one who is unable to pay 906
330. ECONOMY 907
1525. Encouraging an economical livelihood 907
1526. The role of economising in one's needlessness 908
331. RETRIBUTION (*Qiṣāṣ*) 908
1527. Legislation of retribution and its importance 908
1528. Forgiving the retribution 910
332. DECREE AND DESTINY 910
1529. Decree and destiny 910
1530. The writing of decree and destiny for people in the womb 912
1531. Whatever Allah decrees for a believer is good 912
1532. One who is not content with the decree 913
1533. What is part of fate 913
333. JUDGMENT (in a Court of Justice) 915
1534. The importance of the status of judgment 915
1535. Bringing a case for judgment before a tyrant 916
1536. The danger in the occupation of a judge 917
1537. Seeking judgment 917
1538. The etiquettes of judging 917
1539. The judges whose mistakes Allah remedies 920
1540. Types of judges 920
1541. Just judges 920
1542. Judging with clear evidence 921
1543. The saying of Imām 'Alī: 'this is indeed like a court of justice' 922
334. THE HEART 922
1544. The heart 922
1545. Soundness of the heart 923
1546. The eye of the heart 924
1547. The ear of the heart 924
1548. The drawing near and the turning away of the heart 925
1549. Purity of the heart 925
1550. Expanding of the heart 925

1551. The veil of the heart 926
1552. Hard-heartedness 926
1553. Sickness of the heart 928
1554. What cures the heart 928
1555. What kills the heart 928
1556. What revives the heart 929
1557. What softens the heart 929
1558. What polishes the heart 930
335. EMULATION (*taqlīd*) 931
1559. Disparaged emulation 931
1560. Those who are permitted to be emulated 931
336. GAMBLING 932
1561. Forbidding gambling 932
337. CONTENTMENT 933
1562. The virtue of contentment 933
1563. What brings about contentment 934
1564. The fruit of contentment 934
1565. Those who are not content with the little 935
338. ARROGANCE 935
1566. Warning against arrogance 935
1567. The explanation of arrogance 936
1568. Reprehensibility of an arrogant person 937
1569. Curing arrogance 937
1570. The outcome of arrogance 938
1571. The abode of the arrogant 939
339. WRITING 940
1572. Writing 940
1573. Writing and the personality of the writer 940
1574. Enjoinment of writing knowledge 940
1575. The reward of authorship and writing 941
1576. The etiquette of writing 941
1577. Correspondence 941
340. CONCEALMENT 942
1578. Emphasising the concealing of secrets 942
1579. Praise of the discreet worshipper 943

341. LYING 944
1580. The reprehension of lying 944
1581. Lying and faith 945
1582. Lying is the key to all evil 945
1583. The command to refrain from lying, both seriously and jestingly 946
1584. white lies 946
1585. The consequence of lying 947
1586. The worst of lies 948
1587. Instances where lying is permitted 949
1588. Dissemblance (tawriya) 949
1589. Listening to a lie 949
342. NOBILITY 950
1590. The virtue of nobility 950
1591. The morals of the generous people 950
1592. What is not regarded as the virtues of generous people 951
1593. Encouraging kindness towards the generous 952
1594. The virtue of treating [others] honourably 952
1595. Reprehension of rejecting kindness 953
1596. The most honourable of people 954
1597. Honouring people is honouring oneself 954
343. EARNINGS 954
1598. The best of earnings 954
1599. Encouragement of earning through one's own labour 955
1600. Disparaged earnings 956
344. LAZINESS 957
1601. Laziness 957
345. DISBELIEF 958
1602. Causes of disbelief 958
1603. The lowest level of disbelief 958
346. RECOMPENSE 959
1604. Encouraging the rewarding of goodness with goodness 959
1605. That which should be done and should not be done in recompensing 960
1606. The reprehension of revenge 961
1607. As you give so shall you get 961
347. *DUTY* 962

1608. Description of divine duty 962
1609. Allah does not task any soul beyond its capacity 962
348. SPEAKING 963
1610. The importance of speaking 963
1611. Warning of offensive speech 964
1612. Encouragement of refraining from speech that does not concern oneself 964
1613. The censure of meddlesome speech 965
1614. The prohibition of speaking excessively 965
1615. The merit of speaking over silence 967
1616. The merit of silence over speaking 967
1617. The best of speech 968
1618. The merit of kind speech 968
349. PERFECTION 969
1619. Perfection of man 969
350. SAGACITY 970
1620. The sign of sagacity 970
351. CLOTHING 971
1621. Recommended clothes 971
1622. Economizing in clothes 972
1623. The best clothing in every time period is the clothing of the people of that time 972
1624. The turban 973
1625. Prohibited clothing 974
352. STUBBORNNESS 974
1626. Reproaching stubbornness 974
353. THE TONGUE 976
1627. The value of the tongue 976
1628. The safety of a person lies in guarding his tongue 976
354. VAIN TALK 978
1629. Vain talk 978
355. MEETING ALLAH 979
1630. Yearning to meet Allah 979
356. AMUSEMENT 980
1631. Amusement 980
1632. The effects of amusement 980
1633. Faith and amusement 981

1634. Amusement of believers 981
1635. Associating with the debauched 982
357. SODOMY 982
1636. Caution against sodomy 982
358. TESTING 983
1637. Testing 983
359. PRAISE 984
1638. The censure of praise 984
1639. Praising someone for qualities that he does not have 985
1640. Caution against praising an immoral person 987
1641. Warning of praising oneself 987
360. WOMAN 988
1642. The words of the representative of women with the Prophet 988
1643. The best characteristics of women 989
1644. Righteous women 990
1645. The praise of loving women 990
1646. The censure of the love of women 990
361. GALLANTRY 991
1647. Interpretation of gallantry 991
362. SICKNESS 992
1648. Some reasons behind sickness 992
1649. Concealing one's sickness 993
1650. The reproaching of those who do not fall sick 993
1651. Visiting the sick 994
1652. Etiquettes of visiting the sick 994
363. DISPUTATION 995
1653. The censure of disputation and its effects 995
364. JOKING 996
1654. The praised joking 996
1655. The censured joking 997
365. SOVEREIGNTY 998
1656. The Master of Sovereignty 998
1657. Mixing with kings 998
1658. The best of kings 999
1659. What is appropriate for the kings 999

366. ANGELS 1000
1660. The creation of angels 1000
1661. The description of the angels 1001
1662. The guardian angels 1001
1663. Houses that angels do not enter 1002
367. DEATH 1002
1664. Death 1002
1665. Having certainty in death 1003
1666. Coming close to departing 1004
1667. Interpretation of death 1004
1668. The death of a believer 1005
1669. Remembrance of death 1006
1670. Preparing for death 1007
1671. Wishing for death 1008
1672. The agony of death 1008
1673. The reason for despising death 1009
1674. The appearance of the Prophet and the Imāms to a dying person 1009
1675. Sudden death 1010
1676. Attending funeral processions 1011
1677. Burying the dead 1011
1678. What follows a person after his death 1012
368. WEALTH 1012
1679. Wealth is the substance of desires 1012
1680. The effects of loving wealth 1013
1681. Love for lawful wealth 1013
1682. Reproaching of excessive wealth 1014
1683. He who acquires wealth from illegitimate sources 1015
1684. Wealth is what benefits men 1016
369. PROPHETHOOD (1) General Prophethood 1017
1685. The philosophy of prophethood 1017
1686. Categories of Prophets (AS) 1019
1687. The number of Prophets (AS) 1020
1688. The Arch-Prophets (Ulū al-ʿAzm) 1020
1689. Special characteristics of the Prophets (AS) 1021
370. PROPHETHOOD (2) Specific Prophethood 1022

1690. Adam (AS) 1022
1691. Enoch [Idrīs] (AS) 1024
1692. Noah (AS) [Nūḥ] 1024
1693. Hūd (AS) 1027
1694. Ṣāliḥ (AS) 1028
1695. Abraham (AS) [Ibrāhīm] 1030
1696. Lot (AS) [Lūṭ] 1034
1697. Jacob and Joseph (AS) 1036
1698. Job (AS) [Ayyūb] 1037
1699. Shuʿayb (AS) 1038
1700. Moses and Aaron (AS) (Mūsā and Hārūn) 1040
1701. Moses and Khiār (AS) 1044
1702. Ishmael b. Ḥazqīl (AS) 1047
1703. Elisha (AS) [al-Yasaʿ] 1048
1704. Dhu'l Kifl (AS) 1048
1705. David (AS) [Dāwūd] 1049
1706. Solomon (AS) [Sulaymān] 1050
1707. Zacharias (AS) [Zakariyyā] 1053
1708. John the Baptist (AS) [Yaḥyā] 1054
1709. Jesus (AS) [ʿĪsā] 1055
1710. Irmiyā' (AS) 1059
1711. Jonah (AS) [Yūnus] 1060
371. PROPHETHOOD (3) 1062
1712. Muḥammad, the Messenger of Allah (SAWA) 1062
1713. The Seal of the Prophets 1063
1714. Muḥammad (SAWA) in the words of Muḥammad (SAWA) himself 1063
1715. Muḥammad (SAWA) in the words of ʿAlī (AS) 1064
1716. The universality of the message of Muḥammad (SAWA) 1066
1717. The best family among all people 1066
1718. The characteristics of the Prophet (SAWA) 1066
372. THE STARS 1074
1719. The science of the stars [astronomy] 1074
373. THE VOW 1075
1720. The vow 1075
1721. *The disapproval* of making something obligatory upon oneself 1076

374. ADVISING 1076
1722. Enjoinment of advice 1076
1723. The signs of an adviser 1077
1724. Enjoinment of accepting advice 1078
375. FAIRNESS 1078
1725. Enjoinment of fairness 1078
1726. Enjoinment of fairness towards those who are not fair 1079
1727. Fairness in spite of oneself 1079
1728. Those who are not fair 1080
376. SIGHT 1081
1729. The eye is the scout of the heart 1081
1730. The eyes are the snares of the devil 1081
1731. Those whom looking at is considered worship 1082
1732. Enjoinment of lowering one's gaze 1082
1733. The first glance is a mistake and the second is intentional 1083
1734. He who sees a woman that pleases him 1084
377. DEBATE 1084
1735. Debate 1084
1736. The Imām's answer to one who invited him to debate 1085
378. CLEANLINESS 1085
1737. Enjoinment of cleanliness 1085
1738. Warning against uncleanliness 1086
379. BOUNTIES 1087
1739. The bounties of Allah cannot be enumerated 1087
1740. Negligence of bounties 1088
1741. Embracing bounties 1088
1742. That which causes bounties to remain 1089
1743. Consecutive succession of bounties and gradual baiting [for chastisement] 1090
1744. Proclaiming about the bounties of Allah 1091
1745. The completion of bounties 1092
380. THE SOUL 1092
1746. The carnal soul that prompts to evil 1092
1747. The self-reproaching soul 1093
1748. Teaching the soul, disciplining it and purifying it 1093
1749. The effects of a noble soul 1094

381. HYPOCRISY 1095
1750. Hypocrisy 1095
1751. The description of a hypocrite 1095
1752. The most obvious hypocrites 1097
1753. Caution against the eloquent hypocrite 1098
1754. The description of the resurrection of hypocrites and their end 1098
1755. What eradicates hypocrisy 1099
382. SPENDING (in Charity) 1099
1756. The virtue of spending 1099
1757. The blessing of spending in his way 1100
1758. Spending out of what you love 1101
1759. He who does not spend in obedience of Allah spends in His disobedience 1102
1760. The virtue of the charity given by one who is himself straitened 1102
1761. Those whose spending [in charity] is not accepted 1103
383. TALEBEARING 1103
1762. Caution against talebearing 1103
1763. Reproaching talebearing 1104
384. SUPEREROGATORY PRAYERS 1105
1764. The virtue of supererogatory prayers 1105
1765. Precedence of the obligatory prayers over the supererogatory 1105
385. THE LIGHT 1106
1766. The light of insight 1106
1767. The light of the heart and the light of the face 1106
1768. There is a light for everything good 1107
1769. The light on the day of resurrection 1107
386. PEOPLE 1108
1770. People 1108
1771. The equality of people in rights 1108
1772. Those who are not considered as people [human] 1109
1773. The explanation of the word 'opportunist' 1109
387. SLEEP 1110
1774. Sleep 1110
1775. Caution against excessive sleep 1110
1776. The ascension of spirits to the sky during sleep 1111
1777. The etiquettes of sleeping 1112

388. INTENTION 1114
1778. The role of intention in action 1114
1779. The role of intention in the Hereafter 1115
1780. The reward of an intention to do good 1115
1781. The intention of the believer is better than his action 1116
1782. Enjoinment of having righteous intentions in everything 1117
1783. Good intention 1117
1784. Bad intention 1118
389. MIGRATION 1118
1785. Migration should continue 1118
1786. The best migration 1119
1787. The necessity of migrating from places [populated with] sinners 1119
1788. Prohibition of returning to [a state of] renegation after having migrated [to belief] 1120
390. DESERTION 1121
1789. Warning against desertion 1121
1790. The prohibition of forsaking a brother for more than three days 1122
391. GUIDANCE 1123
1791. General divine guidance 1123
1792. Living with guidance 1123
1793. The reward for guidance 1123
1794. Guidance being exclusively from Allah 1124
1795. Those whom Allah guides 1125
392. THE GIFT 1125
1796. Encouraging giving gifts 1125
1797. The prohibition of gifts to administrators 1126
1798. Prohibition of accepting gifts from polytheist 1126
1799. Enjoinment of accepting a gift 1126
1800. Taking back one's gift 1127
393. OLD AGE 1127
1801. Senility 1127
1802. What breaks out in a human when he becomes senile [in old age] 1128
1803. What brings about senility before its time 1128
394. DESTRUCTION 1128
1804. What brings about destruction 1128
395. AMBITION 1130

1805. The virtue of high ambition 1130
1806. The benefits of high ambition 1130
1807. Low ambition 1131
1808. He whose sole concern is his stomach 1131
396. THE DESIRE 1132
1809. Desire is a worshipped god 1132
1810. Warning against following desire 1132
1811. The effects of yielding to one's desires 1133
1812. Opposing one's desires 1134
1813. Overpowering desire 1135
1814. The most courageous of people is he who overcomes his desires 1136
1815. That which weakens carnal desires 1137
1816. He who overcomes his desires 1137
397. INHERITANCE 1138
1817. Inheritance 1138
1818. Those who are deprived of inheritance 1139
1819. Inheritance of Prophets 1139
398. PIETY 1140
1820. The virtue of piety 1140
1821. The fruit of piety 1141
1822. The role of piety in worship 1141
1823. Interpretation of piety 1142
1824. The most pious of people 1143
399. THE SCALE 1143
1825. Scales of deeds 1143
400. DEVILISH MISGIVINGS 1144
1826. Misgivings in matters of belief 1144
1827. Caution against doubts in ablution and prayers 1144
1828. The treatment of devilish misgivings 1145
401. CONSOLATION 1146
1829. Encouraging consolation 1146
402. THE WILL 1147
1830. Encouraging to make a will 1147
1831. Forbidding causing damages and losses in one's will 1148
403. *ABLUTION* 1148

1832. Ablution 1148
1833. The reason for ablution 1149
1834. The effects of ablution 1150
1835. The virtue of frequent and abundant ablution 1150
1836. Renewal of ablution 1150
404. HUMBLENESS 1151
1837. Encouraging humbleness 1151
1838. Some of the signs of humbleness 1152
1839. The fruit of humbleness 1152
1840. Means to acquire humbleness 1153
1841. Limits of humbleness 1153
405. THE HOMELAND 1154
1842. Patriotism 1154
1843. Defending one's homeland 1155
1844. Separation from one's homeland 1155
406. THE PROMISE 1155
1845. The promise of Allah is true 1155
1846. The promise is a debt 1156
1847. The promise is one of two types of bondage 1156
1848. What should not be promised 1157
1849. Reproaching the breaking of a promise 1157
407. EXHORTATION 1158
1850. The role of exhortation in the revival of the heart 1158
1851. Types of exhorters 1158
1852. There is exhortation in everything 1159
1853. Etiquettes of exhortation 1160
1854. The personal exhorter 1160
1855. Those who do not benefit from exhortation 1161
1856. The exhorter who himself is not exhorted 1161
1857. The silent propagation 1162
408. SUCCESS (Tawfīq) 1162
1858. Success 1162
1859. Success and failure 1164
409. LOYALTY 1165
1860. Encouraging of loyalty 1165

410. SOLEMNITY 1166
1861. Encouraging of solemnity 1166
1862. What brings about solemnity 1166
411. GODWARINESS 1167
1863. The virtue of Godwariness 1167
1864. Godwariness is the key to nobleness 1169
1865. The characteristics of the godwary 1171
1866. What hinders Godwariness 1174
1867. The reality of Godwariness 1174
1868. Explanation of Godwariness 1174
1869. The most Godwary of people 1175
412. DISSIMULATION (Taqiyya) 1176
1870. Legislation of dissimulation and instances it should be observed 1176
1871. Prohibition of surpassing the situations [calling] for dissimulation 1177
413. TRUST (IN ALLAH) 1178
1872. The virtue of trust (in Allah) 1178
1873. The explanation of trust 1179
1874. The fruit of trust [in Allah] 1179
1875. The etiquette of trust 1181
1876. Relying on other than Allah 1182
414. PARENT AND CHILD 1182
1877. The virtue of having children 1182
1878. The trial of having a child 1183
1879. Loving children 1183
1880. Acting childishly for children 1183
1881. The righteous child 1184
1882. Prohibition of hating girls 1184
1883. Enjoinment of being just between children 1185
1884. Enjoinment of being good to one's parents 1185
1885. Enjoinment of being good to one's parents [even] after their death 1186
1886. Heaven is under the feet of mothers 1187
1887. Hurting one's parents 1187
1888. Insolence to one's parents 1188
1889. The right of the parent upon the child 1188
1890. *The right of the child* upon the parent 1189

1891. Upbringing of the child 1189
415. AUTHORITY 1190
1892. The necessity of obeying those vested with authority by Allah 1190
1893. What brings about the reign of evil rulers 1191
1894. Just rulers 1192
1895. Tyrannical rulers 1192
1896. What is obligatory for the ruler with regard to himself 1192
1897. The most important thing a ruler needs in his rule 1193
1898. What is obligatory for the ruler when employing workers 1195
1899. To not seclude oneself [away from one's subjects] 1196
1900. The obligation upon the ruler to give importance to the abased 1196
1901. The characteristics of the friends of Allah 1197
416. SUSPICION 1198
1902. Warning against suspicion 1198
1903. Prohibition of placing oneself in suspect circumstances 1199
417. DESPAIR 1199
1904. The reproaching of despair 1199
1905. The fruits of despair in obtaining what belongs to others 1200
418. THE ORPHAN 1200
1906. Enjoinment of looking after orphans 1200
1907. The consumption of the property of the orphans 1201
419. CONVICTION 1202
1908. The virtue of conviction 1202
1909. Certain knowledge 1203
1910. Interpretation of certainty 1204
1911. The signs of a person of conviction 1204
1912. What corrupts conviction 1205
1913. Weakness of conviction 1205
1914. The fruits of conviction 1206
1915. Increasing conviction 1206
ENDNOTES (ENGLISH) 1209
ENDNOTES (ARABIC) 1303
INDEX 1415
BIBLIOGRAPHY 1424

Preface

Mizan al-Hikmah acts as an encyclopaedia of the most valuable *hadith* of the Prophet of Islam (SAWA) and twelve Imams (AS) which play a key role in understanding the Holy Qur'an and presenting the pure and genuine message of Islam. This book was first published in 1982 in ten volumes and was subsequently re-published several times. The warm and strong reception it received from esteemed researchers and readers all over the Islamic world indicates new generation's spiritual thirst and sincere interest in authentic Islamic sciences and the constructive and positive teachings of Ahl al-Bayt (AS) despite the vast cultural attacks against the sacred religion of Islam.

Without doubt, consciousness of this need has increased the responsibility of the religious scholars who understand these undeniable facts and realise the value and importance of this great task. Based on this necessity of this work and the positive feedback received on the original, a complementary project to *Mizan al-Hikmah* was initiated under the title of *Mawsu'ah Mizan al-Hikmah* in 1987 with the help and cooperation of a group of respected scholars from the Islamic Seminary of Qum.

With Allah's Grace and by the blessing of this work, the Dar al-Hadith Cultural Institute (consisting of the Dar al-Hadith Research Centre and University of Hadith Sciences) was founded. The voluminous nature of *Mizan al-Hikmah* prevented it from fulfilling certain needs, and so it was therefore proposed that a summarised selection of this book be prepared and presented to the dear readers. This summary was to include the most important chapters of the book and the most essential *hadith* so that those interested in understanding and comprehending some of the brilliant concepts and teachings of Islam could benefit from this collection, even while travelling. This selection was compiled and published under the title *Muntakhab Mizan al-Hikmah*, and this condensed edition allowed this work to be presented in other languages.

Allah Almighty has granted the opportunity to prepare this selection to the esteemed scholar Seyyid Hamid Hussaini, along with the supervision and valuable help of Seyyid Muhammad Kazim Tabatabaei. I would also like to thank all the respected brothers in the Dar al-Hadith Cultural Institute who assisted us in the making of this valuable collection. Special thanks go to the translators of The Islamic College in London and their professional editors who managed to translate a huge number of *hadith* while maintaining their subtle points. Finally I have to thank Hujjatul-Islam Muhammad Sharif Mahdavi for his efforts in comparing, reviewing and making the text as consistent as possible, and Mr. Zaid Alsalami who assisted him in this task. I ask Allah Almighty to grant them success and sincerity and to accept this effort with all His grace and generosity, and may everyone, especially the younger generation, benefit from it. May He Almighty make this humble attempt a provision for us in the world hereafter.

Muhammad Muhammadi Rayshahri
24 Rabi' al-Awwal 1423

Introduction

The narrations of the Prophet (SAWA) and twelve Imams (AS) have always been venerated as a primary source in understanding religion and the Qur'an. None other than their very words, these narrations (*hadith*) – together with their conduct and tacit approval of deeds – constitute the triangle of the *sunnah.* The high esteem accorded to the *sunnah* is apparent in the extensive Shi'a and Sunni *hadith* compilations. The study of the *sunnah* underpins all the Islamic sciences, and, without doubt, scholars in all Islamic fiends are indebted to the compilers in every age who arranged and explained these *hadith* to meet the needs of their time.

Today, the need to evaluate the *hadith* has been renewed. No longer is interest in *hadith* limited to academics; the general public too wants access to the foundations of religious knowledge. The original collection of *Mizan al-Hikmah* – which was the outcome of years of painstaking effort by Ayatullah Muhammadi Rayshahri – is one of this era's best responses to this pressing need.

Tracing the development of Shi'a *hadith* works highlights the value of *Mizan al-Hikmah.* Centred on the publication of four canonical works, Shi'a *hadith* study falls into six periods:

1. The initial *hadith* writings.
2. Booklets, or the '400 books'
3. The compilation of the major Shi'a *hadith* collections
4. The completion of the major Shi'a *hadith* collections
5. The exposition of the major Shi'a *hadith* collections
6. The systemization of the major Shi'a *hadith* collections

First period: The initial *hadith* writings. The first Shi'a *hadith* writings materialized during the first century of the Islamic era, from the time of the Prophet (SAWA) to the time of Imam al-Baqir (AS). This time period was characterized by some of the early caliphs' strict prohibition on transcribing *hadith.*

Historical sources mention several books from Companions of the Prophet (SAWA) that no longer exist, such as the book of Salman al-Farsi, the *Kitab al-Khutbah* of Abu Dharr, the treatises of 'Abdullah ibn 'Abbas regarding the verdicts of Imam 'Ali (AS), and the book of Jabir ibn

ʿAbdullah al-Ansari.[1] Other books have survived in part, such as the book of Sulaym ibn Qays.[2] Still others are not accessible but at least are believed to be in the possession of the Imams (AS), such the book of ʿAli (AS),[3] the treatise of Fatima (AS),[4] and the treatise of ʿAli (AS).[5] Extant books from this early period include *Nahj al-Balagha* and *al-Sahifa al-Sajjadiyya*.[6]

Second period: According to a well investigated account, the number of hadith books written in this period was more than 6600. However, gradually a consensus was formed regarding the authenticity of 400 of them.[7] The term '400 books' refers to the corpus of *hadith* works composed from the time of Imam ʿAli (AS) until the time of Imam Hasan al-ʿAskari (AS) (232-260 AH), particularly during the time of the fifth and sixth Imams (AS). After the Minor Occultation, these primary sources allowed for the compilation of the first major collections of *hadith*, such as *al-Kafi* by Thiqatul-Islam al-Kulayni (d. 329), and continued to function as references for later scholars.

These books obviously survived until the time of the authors of the primary Shiʿa collections, or the 'three Muhammads', who relied upon them in their work. A number of them persisted until the time of Muhammad ibn Idris al-Hilli (d. 598 AH), Sayyid ibn Ṭawus (d. 763), al-Shahid al-Thani (d. 966), and al-Kafʿami (d. 905). Some remained until the time of ʿAllama al-Majlisi (d. 1111), Shaykh al-Hurr al-ʿĀmili (d. 1104), and Mirza Husayn Nuri (d. 1320), who used them as references.[8] Historical and biographical sources such as *Rijal al-Najashi*, the *Fihrist* of Shaykh al-Ṭusi (d. 460), and the *Maʿalim al-ʿUlama'* of Ibn Shahrashub reveal the titles of 122 of these 400 works, which Shaykh Agha Buzurg (1293-1389) lists in *al-Dhariʿa*.[9] Today, only sixteen of these initial works still exist, and they have been collected and published by Hasan Mustafawi in *The Sixteen Books*.

How could such valuable keys to the sources of the faith disappear? Shaykh Agha Buzurg attributes their disappearance to both intentional destruction and unintentional neglect. Many of these irreplaceable sources

1. Fuʿad Sezgin mentions Jabir's book as one of the works of the Umayyad era and first century. See *History of Arabic Writings*, p. 123.
2. *Kitab Asrar 'Al Muhammad*, p. 47 (Introduction).
3. *Baṣa'ir al-Darajat*, p. 187.
4. *Baṣa'ir al-Darajat*, p. 173.
5. *al-Fihrist*, p. 30; also see *Bihar al-Anwar*, v. 28, p. 266. Surprisingly, Ibn Nadim adds, "This is the ordering of the chapters in this treatise," but this section of the book is omitted.
6. *al-Dhari'a*, v. 13, p. 345, and v. 15, p. 18; *al-Sahifa al-Sajjadiyya*, edited by Abtahi, v. 657; *Fath al-Abwab*, p. 76.
7. Al-Hurr al-Amili, Muhammad b. al-Hasan, *Wasa'il al-Shi'a*, Qum, Al al-Bayt, 1414, Vol. 30, p. 165.
8. *al-Dhari'a*, vol. 2, p. 134-5.
9. Ibid. pp. 135-167.

went up in flames when extremist Sunnis set afire Shaykh al-Ṭusi's library in 448 AH.[10] However, by that time, many scholars had turned their attention away from these books due to the fact that most of their contents had been indexed in the major *hadith* works, which – unlike the originals – were conveniently arranged in chapters and topics, and so this led to their loss as well.

Third period: The compilation of the major Shi'a *hadith* collections. Until the time of Imam Hasan al-'Askari, a number of the Imams' companions (such as Hamid ibn Ziyad al-Dihqan, Yunus ibn Abd al-Rahman, and Muhammad ibn Yahya) had been able to record the Imams' sayings on topics of their interest to the extent of their presence in the Imams' gatherings. Although some did attempt to organize their collections, no overarching collections appeared during this time, primarily due to the lack of access to the entire corpus of *hadith* work, the continued presence of the Imam among the people, and the authors' personal emphases on particular topics, such as legal commandments.

However, the Minor and Major Occultations provided the impetus for the compilation of Shi'a *hadith*. Despite the Imam's absence, Shi'a society was still growing, and its scholars, jurists, theologians, and exegists needed systematic *hadith* collections to resolve their mounting legal and theological questions.

In response, Thiqatul-Islam al-Kulayni, Shaykh al-Saduq (d. 381), and Shaykh al-Ṭusi devoted their efforts to systemizing the initial books and producing the magnanimous collections *al-Kafi, Man la yahduruhu al-faqih, Madinat al-'Ilm, al-Tahdhib,* and *al-Istibsar* which overshadowed the nonetheless noteworthy books of their predecessors, such as *al-Mahasin* (by Ahmad ibn Muhammad ibn Khalid, d. 274), *Basa'ir al-Darajat* (by Muhammad ibn Saffar, d. 290), and *Qurb al-Isnad* (by al-Himyari al-Qummi, d. 300). Despite the enormity of these works, their efforts were not limited to these; Shaykh al-Saduq wrote *'Uyun Akhbar al-Rida (AS), al-Khisal,* and *al-Amali;* and Shaykh al-Ṭusi wrote *al-Ghayba* and *al-Iqtisad.* But due to their unparalleled comprehensiveness, scholastic rigour, and careful attention to the details of the chains of narration as well as the *hadith* text itself, these first five works gradually came to be known as *the* five *hadith* works of the Shi'a, or the 'five books'. Unfortunately, after the loss of *Madinat al-'Ilm*, they were renamed the 'four books', and these books have survived until the present day.

Some may find it curious that 'four books' have come to prominence in *hadith* science. However, it is worth noting that other religious disciplines also prioritize certain archetypical sources. For example, *al-Āmali* of Abu 'Ali al-Qali, *al-Bayan wa al-Tabyin* of al-Jahiẓ, *Adab al-Katib*

10. Ibid.

of ibn Qutayba, and *al-Āmali* of Sayyid al-Murtaza are known as the 'four books' of literature; *Rijal al-Najashi* and the *Rijal* and *Fihrist* of Shaykh al-Ṭusi are among the 'four books' of Shiʿa biography; *Tamhid al-Qawaʿid* of ibn Turka (d. 835), *Sharh al-Fusus* of Qaysari (d. 748), *Misbah al-'Uns* of ibn Fanari (d.834), and *al-Futuhat al-Makkiyya* of Ibn ʿArabi (d. 638) are known as the 'four books' of theoretical mysticism; and *Miftah al-Falah* of Shaykh Baha'i (d. 1031), *ʿUddat al-Daʿi* of Ibn Fahd al-Hilli (757-841), *Qut al-Qulub* of Makki ibn Abi Ṭalib, and *al-Iqbal* of Sayyid ibn Ṭawus (d. 664) are known as the 'four books' of practical mysticism.

Fourth period: The completion of the major *hadith* compilations. During this time, the need to annotate and offer commentary on these books arose due to their prominence in Shiʿa scholarship and culture. As a result, numerous commentaries proliferated; for instance, a list of commentaries on *al-Kafi* is to be found in *al-Wafi*. The introduction to *Muʿjam Bihar al-Anwar* mentions some twenty-three commentaries on this voluminous book, some only in manuscript form. Similarly, *Man la Yahduruhu al-Faqih, al-Tahdhib,* and *al-Istibsar* acquired their own commentaries as well. Of all these, the most worthy of mention are the commentaries of Mulla Sadra, Mulla Salih al-Mazandarani, and ʿAllama al-Majlisi.

Fifth period: The exposition of the major Shiʿa *hadith* collections. After the compilation of the four foundational *hadith* books in the fifth century Hijri, Shiʿa scholars began to fill in the gaps and catalogue the *hadith* that had not been included in these monumental works. However, none of their works were comprehensive enough to warrant being called a 'completion' of the *hadith* works until the emergence of the three great traditionalists Shaykh al-Hurr al-ʿĀmili (d. 1104), ʿAllama al-Majlisi (d. 1111), and Muhaddith al-Nuri (d. 1320) as well as Ayatullah Burujurdi (d. 1380) who occupied themselves with completing these works through their own encyclopaedic compilations *Wasa'il al-Shiʿa*, *Bihar al-Anwar*, *Mustadrak al-Wasa'il*, and *Jamiʿ Ahadith al-Shiʿa*, respectively. These voluminous collections marked the fourth period of the development of *hadith* literature, which came to a close with the death of Ayatullah Burujurdi (d. 1380).

Sixth period: The systemization of the major *hadith* collections. In this period, *hadith* research developed further, and scholars subjected the *hadith* texts to various inquiries with different aims. Some of them intended to improve ease of access while others sought to refine them and omit redundancies, and still others wrote guides to the *hadith* literature.

In this period – which corresponds to the last century – a new trend in organizing the narrations has emerged, although some scholars have implemented it more than others. Some books, such as *Safinat al-Bihar*, were written *solely* to organize the narrations in *Bihar al-Anwar*, whereas others, such as *Mizan al-Hikmah, Athar al-Sadiqin,* and *al-Hayat* examined a broader range of narrations – including Sunni ones – and then presented them in a new arrangement. While alphabetic arrangement via the focal point of the narrations' words characterizes *Safinat al-Bihar* and *Athar al-Sadiqin*, *al-Hayat* is organized topically. Both methods occur in *Mizan al-Hikmah*; that is, the narrations are separated alphabetically according to key words appearing inside the narrations themselves.

Upon publication, the original compilation of *Mizan al-Hikmah* received a unique reception, and, within a short period, it was translated and reprinted more than twenty times in Persian and Urdu. Religious students, university students, researchers, and preachers celebrated its attention to practical topics (often neglected at the seminary) such as ethics, politics, and the social sciences; its topical organization; its references and cross-references; its inclusion of Qur'anic verses with the *hadith*; its comprehensive treatment of the different topics; and its analysis and commentary lightly sprinkled where necessary. Initially established to complete the work on *Mizan al-Hikmah,* the Dar al-Hadith Research Centre soon became one of the world's largest cultural and academic institutes and added to the blessings of this work.

However, despite its singular features, *Mizan al-Hikmah* had one drawback, and that was its size. Thus, an abridged version was proposed. This present edition is the outcome of years of careful work sifting through the original 15 volumes selecting those *hadith* addressing the most essential contemporary concerns. Like its predecessor, the selections from *Mizan al-Hikmah* – entitled *Muntakhab Mizan al-Hikmah* – met a similar warm reception and, so far, the new collection has been printed in sixteen editions with 34,500 copies in Persian. It is now appearing in English for the first time. The following steps were taken to condense it:

1. The number of headings was reduced from 564 to 419 by removing the less useful or more obscure topics. As a result, the subheadings were reduced from 4,260 to 1,915.
2. Repetitive *hadith* were excluded. While a primary goal was to preserve as much of the original content of *Mizan al-Hikmah* as possible so that all the content available in the original version would be available in the concise version, *Mizan al-Hikmah* did contain many instances of the same narration repeated in different words. After careful selection, the redundant *hadith* were eliminated, leaving the one which appeared to be the most authentic, clear, and comprehensive.
3. In rare instances, it was felt that certain topics did not contain enough narrations to do justice to those topics. In those situations,

with the permission and coordination of the original author, other narrations were added to the collection.

4. The references in the book were modified to account for the omission of many headings, chapters, and narrations. Additionally, an effort was made to increase the utility of the book by making the references complete and adding further links between related topics.
5. In order to preserve as much of the material as possible, efforts were made to maximize the physical capacity of the book, such as reducing the margins and empty space on the pages. Doing so enabled 6,848 narrations of the original 23,030 to be included in the new single volume rather than the original 15 volumes.

We would like to offer our deepest gratitude to the author of *Mizan al-Hikmah* for his kindness, trust, and guidance, as well as to Hujjat al-Islam Sayyid Muhammad Kaẓim Ṭabataba'i for his assistance and efforts in organizing this summary. Finally, as we express our unending gratitude to Allah for granting His humblest servants the opportunity to serve in the propagation of the lustrous teachings of Ahl al-Bayt (AS), we beseech Him to nobly accept this small effort and deepen its influence in spreading Islamic culture, to illuminate the world with the words of Ahl al-Bayt (AS), to prepare the way for the reappearance of the Saviour of humanity, and to increase the eagerness of the world's people to follow the truth.

Sayyid Hamid Husaini
Muhammad Nouri
October, 2008

1

SELF-SACRIFICE

الإيثار

1. The Virtue of Self-Sacrifice

١ ـ فَضلُ الإيثارِ

1. **Imām ʿAlī (AS) said,** 'Self-sacrifice is the highest of virtues.'[1]

١ . الإمامُ عليٌّ عليه‌السلام : الإيثارُ أعلى المَكارِمِ.١

2. **Imām ʿAlī (AS) said,** 'Self-sacrifice is a characteristic of the righteous.'[2]

٢ . عنه عليه‌السلام : الإيثارُ شيمَةُ الأبرارِ.٢

3. **Imām ʿAlī (AS) said,** 'Self-sacrifice is the best kindness and the highest rank of belief.'[3]

٣ . عنه عليه‌السلام : الإيثارُ أحسَنُ الإحسانِ، وأعلى مَراتِبِ الإيمانِ.٣

4. **Imām ʿAlī (AS) said,** 'Self-sacrifice is the best form of worship and the greatest eminence.'[4]

٤ . عنه عليه‌السلام : الإيثارُ أفضَلُ عِبادَةٍ، وأجَلُّ سِيادَةٍ.٤

5. **Imām ʿAlī (AS) said,** 'The best form of generosity is self-sacrifice.'[5]

٥ . عنه عليه‌السلام : أفضَلُ السَّخاءِ الإيثارُ.٥

6. **Imām ʿAlī (AS) said,** 'Treat all people with fairness, but the believers with self-sacrifice.'[6]

٦ . عنه عليه‌السلام : عامِلْ سائرَ النّاسِ بالإنصافِ، وعامِلِ المؤمنينَ بالإيثارِ.٦

7. **Imām ʿAlī (AS) also said,** 'The peak of virtues is self-sacrifice.'[7]

٧ . عنه عليه‌السلام : غايَةُ المَكارِمِ الإيثارُ.٧

8. **Imām ʿAlī (AS) also said,** 'Through self-sacrifice do free people become enslaved.'[8]

٨ . عنه عليه‌السلام : بالإيثارِ يُستَرَقُّ الأحرارُ.٨

(See also: SPENDING (IN CHARITY): section: 1760, 1762)

(أنظر) الإنفاق: باب ١٧٦٠، ١٧٦٢.

2. The Virtue of Altruistic People

٢ ـ فَضلُ المُؤثِرينَ

"[They are as well] for those who were settled in the land and [abided] in faith before them, who love those who migrate toward them, and do not find in their breasts any need for that which is given to them, but

﴿وَالَّذِينَ تَبَوَّءُو الدَّارَ وَالْإِيمَانَ مِن قَبْلِهِمْ يُحِبُّونَ مَنْ هَاجَرَ إِلَيْهِمْ وَلَا يَجِدُونَ فِى صُدُورِهِمْ حَاجَةً مِّمَّا أُوتُوا وَيُؤْثِرُونَ عَلَىٰ

prefer [the Immigrants] to themselves, though poverty be their own lot. And those who are saved from their own greed - it is they who are the felicitous."[9]

أَنفُسِهِمْ وَلَوْ كَانَ بِهِمْ خَصَاصَةٌ وَمَن يُوقَ شُحَّ نَفْسِهِ فَأُولَٰئِكَ هُمُ الْمُفْلِحُونَ﴾ .٩

9. **Abū Hurayra narrated,** 'A man came to the Prophet (SAWA) and complained to him of hunger, so the Prophet (SAWA) sent a messenger to the homes of his wives, but they said that they had nothing but water. The Prophet (SAWA) asked, 'Who can host this man tonight?' 'Alī b. Abī Ṭālib (AS) said, 'I will host him, O Messenger of Allah.' He came to Fāṭima (AS) and asked her, 'What do you have, O daughter of the Prophet?' She said, 'We only have food for tonight, but we would rather give it to our guest.' He (AS) said, 'O Daughter of Muḥammad. Take the children to bed and put off the lamp.' The next morning, 'Alī (AS) came to the Prophet (SAWA) and told him the story. No sooner had he left than Allah, the Exalted, revealed the verse: "*...but prefer [others] to themselves...*"[10]

٩ . الأمالي للطوسي عن أبي هريرة: جاءَ رجُلٌ إلى النّبيِّ ﷺ فَشَكا إليه الجُوعَ، فَبَعثَ رسولُ اللهِ ﷺ إلىٰ بُيوتِ أزواجِه فقُلْنَ: ما عندَنا إلّا الماءُ. فقالَ رسولُ اللهِ ﷺ: مَن لِهٰذا الرَّجُلِ اللّيلةَ؟ فقالَ عليُّ بنُ أبي طالبٍ ﷺ: أنا له يا رسولَ اللهِ. وأتىٰ فاطمةَ ﷺ فقالَ لها: ما عندَكِ يا ابنةَ رسولِ اللهِ؟ فقالتْ: ما عندَنا إلّا قُوتُ الصِّبيةِ، لٰكنّا نُؤثِرُ ضَيفَنا. فقالَ ﷺ: يا ابنةَ محمّدٍ، نَوِّمي الصِّبْيَةَ وأطفئي المِصْباحَ. فلَمّا أصْبَحَ عليٌّ ﷺ غدا على رسولِ اللهِ ﷺ فأخبرَهُ الخبرَ، فلَمْ يَبرَحْ حتّىٰ أنزلَ اللهُ ﷻ: ﴿ويُؤثِرون...﴾ .١٠

10. **'Ā'isha narrated, 'The Prophet** (SAWA) had never spent three consecutive days having eaten to his full until he left this world, although he could have, had he wanted to; but he used to place others before himself.'[11]

١٠ . تنبيه الخواطر عن عائشة: ما شَبِعَ رسولُ اللهِ ﷺ ثلاثةَ أيّامٍ مُتَواليةٍ حتّىٰ فارَقَ الدُّنيا. ولو شاءَ لَشَبِعَ، ولكنَّهُ كانَ يُؤثِرُ علىٰ نَفْسِهِ.١١

11. **Abū al-Ṭufayl narrated,** "Alī (AS) bought a gown, which he liked, but he gave it away in charity. He said, 'I heard the Prophet (SAWA) saying, 'When a person places others before himself, Allah, the Exalted, will place him before others in Paradise on the Day of Resurrection.'[12]

١١ . مجمع البيان عن أبي الطفيل: اشترىٰ عليٌّ ﷺ ثوباً، فأعجَبَهُ فتَصدَّقَ بهِ، وقالَ: سَمِعتُ رسولَ اللهِ ﷺ يقولُ: مَن آثرَ علىٰ نفسِهِ آثرَهُ اللهُ يومَ القيامةِ الجنّةَ.١٢

12. **Imām al-Ṣādiq (AS) said** in regards to the verse, "*They give food, for the love of Him, to the needy, the orphan and the prisoner.*"[13], 'Fāṭima (AS) had some barley which she made into a sweet paste. When they had finished cooking it and placed it on the table, a poor man came and said, 'May Allah have mercy upon you! Feed us from the sustenance Allah has given you.' 'Alī (AS) stood up and gave him a third of it. Soon afterwards, an orphan came and said, 'May Allah have mercy upon you! Feed us from the sustenance Allah has given you.' 'Alī (AS) stood up and gave him a third. Soon afterwards, a

١٢ . الإمامُ الصّادقُ ﷺ ـ في قولِهِ تعالىٰ: ﴿وَيُطْعِمُونَ ٱلطَّعَامَ عَلَىٰ حُبِّهِۦ مِسْكِينًا وَيَتِيمًا وَأَسِيرًا﴾ ـ: كانَ عِندَ فاطمةَ ﷺ شَعيرٌ، فجَعَلوهُ عَصيدةً، فلَمّا أنضجوها ووَضَعوها بَينَ أيديهِم جاءَ مِسكينٌ، فقالَ المِسكينُ: رَحِمَكُمُ اللهُ! أطعِمونا مِمّا رَزَقَكُمُ اللهُ، فقامَ عليٌّ ﷺ فأعطاهُ ثُلثَها. فما لَبِثَ أن جاءَ يَتيمٌ، فقالَ اليَتيمُ: رَحِمَكُمُ اللهُ! أطعِمونا مِمّا رَزَقَكُمُ اللهُ، فقامَ

prisoner came and said, 'May Allah have mercy upon you! Feed us from the sustenance Allah has given you.' So 'Alī (AS) gave him the last third, and they did not even taste it. So in honouring them, Allah, the Exalted, sent down the Qur'anic verses until, *"And your endeavour has been well-appreciated."*[14 15]

عَلِيٌّ ﷺ فَأَعطاهُ ثُلُثَهَا الثّانِيَ. فَما لَبِثَ أن جاءَ أسيرٌ، فَقالَ الأَسيرُ: يَرحَمُكُمُ اللهُ! أطعِمونا مِمّا رَزَقَكُمُ اللهُ، فَقامَ عَلِيٌّ ﷺ فَأَعطاهُ الثُّلُثَ الباقِيَ، وما ذاقوها. فَأَنزَلَ اللهُ فيهِم هٰذِهِ الآيَةَ إلىٰ قَولِهِ: ﴿وَكَانَ سَعْيُكُم مَّشْكُورًا﴾.[١٣]

2

EMPLOYMENT

الإجارة

3. Employment and Livelihood

٣ـ الإجارَةُ وَ المَعيشَةُ

"Is it they who dispense the mercy of your Lord? It is We who have dispensed among them their livelihood in the present life, and raised some of them above others in rank, so that some may take others into service, and your Lord's mercy is better than what they amass."[16]

﴿أَهُمْ يَقْسِمُونَ رَحْمَةَ رَبِّكَ نَحْنُ قَسَمْنَا بَيْنَهُمْ مَعِيشَتَهُمْ فِي الْحَيَاةِ الدُّنْيَا وَرَفَعْنَا بَعْضَهُمْ فَوْقَ بَعْضٍ دَرَجَاتٍ لِيَتَّخِذَ بَعْضُهُمْ بَعْضاً سُخْرِيّاً وَرَحْمَةُ رَبِّكَ خَيْرٌ مِمّا يَجْمَعُونَ﴾.[١٤]

"One of the two women said, 'Father, hire him. Indeed the best you can hire is a powerful and trustworthy man.'"[17]

﴿قالَتْ إِحْدَاهُمَا يَا أَبَتِ اسْتَأْجِرْهُ إِنَّ خَيْرَ مَنِ اسْتَأْجَرْتَ الْقَوِيُّ الْأَمِينُ﴾.[١٥]

13. **Imām 'Alī (AS) said** about the verse: *"It is We who have dispensed among them their livelihood"*, 'Allah, the Exalted, told us that employment is one of the means of people's livelihood. He, in His wisdom, diversified their aspirations, motivations, and other states. Thus, He made man's employment of one another one of the means of people's livelihood … If every one of us was forced to build for himself, make his own furniture, and produce everything himself… the world's conditions would not be bearable and people would not be able to endure them, and would find them impossible. But He ensured its management by diversifying their aspirations so that everyone performs for others that which is

١٣ . الإمامُ عليٌّ ﷺ ـ في قولِهِ تعالىٰ: ﴿نحنُ قَسَمنا بينهم معيشَتهم﴾ ـ: أخبرَنا سبحانَه أنَّ الإجارةَ أحدُ مَعايشِ الخَلْقِ، إذ خالفَ بحكمتِهِ بينَ هِمَمِهم وإرادتِهِم وسائرِ حالاتِهِم، وجعلَ ذلكَ قِواماً لِمَعايِشِ الخَلْقِ، وهُو الرّجُلُ يَستأجِرُ الرّجُلَ ... ولو كانَ الرّجُلُ منّا يُضطَرُّ إلىٰ أن يكونَ بَنّاءً لنفسِهِ أو نَجّاراً أو صانعاً في شيءٍ مِن جميعِ أنواعِ الصَّنائعِ لنفسِهِ ... ما استقامَتْ أحوالُ العالَمِ بتلكَ، ولا اتّسعُوا لَه، ولَعَجِزوا عَنهُ، ولكنّهُ أتْقَنَ تدبيرَهُ لِمخالَفتِهِ بينَ هِمَمِهِم، وكلُّ ما يُطلَبُ مِمّا تَنصَرِفُ إليهِ همّتُهُ ممّا يَقومُ بِهِ بعضُهُم لبعضٍ، ولِيَستَغنيَ بعضُهُم ببعضٍ

compatible with his own capacity, in order for some of them to be served by others and for their conditions to be sound.'[18]

في أبوابِ المَعايِشِ الّتي بها صَلاحُ أحوالِهم.[١٦]

4. Divine Disapproval of Offering Oneself for Hiring

٤ـ كَراهَةُ إجارَةِ النَّفْسِ

14. **'Ammār al-Sābāṭī narrated,** 'I asked Abū Abdillāh (AS) about a man who trades but he can make the same money by working for someone else. He said, 'He should not work for someone else. Rather, he must seek Allah's bounty and engage in trading, for by working for someone else, he restricts Allah's bounty for him.'[19]

١٤ . الكافي عن عمّارٍ السّاباطيّ: قلتُ لأبي عبدِاللهِ ﷺ: الرّجُلُ يَتّجِرُ ، فإنْ هُو آجَرَ نَفسَهُ أُعطِيَ ما يُصيبُ في تجارتِهِ ، فقالَ: لا يُؤاجِرْ نفسَهُ، ولكنْ يَسترزِقُ اللهَ عزّ وجلّ ويَتّجِرُ، فإنّهُ إذا آجَرَ نفسَهُ حَظَرَ على نفسِهِ الرِّزْقَ.[١٧]

5. Employment Agents

٥ـ الدَّلّالُ فِي الإجارَةِ

15. **Muḥammad b. Muslim** narrated from one of the Imāms (AS), that he was asked about a man who accepts a job and before doing any work, he passes it on to another and profits from it himself; to which he replied, 'No, [it is not allowed] unless he does some work on it.'[20]

١٥ . الكافي عن محمّدَ بنِ مسلم عن أحدِهما ﷺ: أنّهُ سُئلَ عنِ الرّجُلِ يَتقبّلُ بالعَمَلِ فلا يَعملُ فيهِ ويَدفَعُهُ إلىٰ آخرَ فيربَحُ فيه ، قالَ: لا ، إلّا أن يَكونَ قد عَمِلَ فيهِ شَيئاً.[١٨]

6. Wronging the Worker

٦ـ ظُلْمُ الأجيرِ

16. **The Prophet (SAWA) said,** 'A man who wrongs a worker in his wage, will have Allah annul his worship and prevent him from smelling the breeze of Paradise, which can be smelled from a distance of five hundred years.'[21]

١٦ . رسولُ اللهِ ﷺ: مَن ظَلَمَ أجيراً أجرَهُ أحبَطَ اللهُ عَمَلَهُ وحَرّمَ علَيهِ ريحَ الجَنّةِ ، وإنّ رِيحَها لَتُوجَدُ مِن مَسيرَةِ خَمسِمائةِ عامٍ.[١٩]

17. **The Prophet (AS) said,** 'Wronging the worker in his wage is a grave sin.'[22]

١٧ . عنه ﷺ: ظُلمُ الأجيرِ أجرَهُ مِن الكبائرِ.[٢٠]

7. Informing [The Worker] of Wages and the Etiquette of Payment

٧ـ إعلامُ الأُجرَةِ وأدَبُ إعطائها

18. **The Prophet (SAWA) said,** 'Give the worker his wage before his sweat dries up, and inform him of his wage while he is still working.'[23]

١٨ . رسولُ اللهِ ﷺ: أعطُوا الأجيرَ أجرَهُ قَبلَ أنْ يَجِفَّ عَرَقُهُ ، وأعْلِمْهُ أجرَهُ وهُو في عملِهِ.[٢١]

19. **Imām ʿAlī (AS) said,** 'The Prophet (SAWA) forbade using the services of a worker before he is informed of his wages.'[24]

١٩ . الإمامُ عليٌّ ﷺ : نَـهىٰ [رسـولُ اللهِ ﷺ] أن يُسْتَعمَلَ أجيرٌ حتّىٰ يُعلمَ ما أُجرتُهُ.[٢٢]

3

THE PREORDAINED TERM [OF DEATH]

الأَجَلُ

8. The Preordained Term [of Death]

٨ـ الأَجَلُ

20. **Imām ʿAlī (AS) said,** 'He [i.e. Allah] created the duration [of every life] and made them short or long; He expedited some and postponed others, and connected their causes with the death.'[25]

٢٠ . الإمامُ عليٌّ ﷺ : خَـلَقَ الآجـالَ فأطـالَها وقَصَّرَها، وقدَّمَها وأخَّـرَها ، ووصَـلَ بـالموتِ أسبابَها.[٢٣]

21. **Imām ʿAlī (AS) said,** 'Nothing is truer than death.'[26]

٢١ . عنه ﷺ : لا شيءَ أصدقُ مِنَ الأجلِ.[٢٤]

22. **Imām ʿAlī (AS) said,** 'What a good remedy death is!'[27]

٢٢ . عنه ﷺ : نِعْمَ الدَّواءُ الأجلُ.[٢٥]

23. **Imām ʿAlī (AS) said,** 'A man's breath is his step towards his death.'[28]

٢٣ . عنه ﷺ : نَفَس المَرءِ خُطاهُ إلىٰ أجَلِهِ.[٢٦]

9. Death is a Fortified Castle

٩ـ الأَجَلُ حِصْنٌ حَصِينٌ

"No soul may die except by Allah's leave, at an appointed time."[29]

﴿وَما كانَ لِنَفْسٍ أنْ تَـمُوتَ إلّا بِـإذْنِ اللهِ كِـتَاباً مُؤَجَّلاً﴾.[٢٧]

24. **Imām ʿAlī (AS) said,** 'Death suffices as a guard.'[30]

٢٤ . الإمامُ عليٌّ ﷺ : كفىٰ بالأجلِ حارِساً.[٢٨]

25. **Imām ʿAlī (AS) said,** 'Death is a fortified castle.'[31]

٢٥ . عنه ﷺ : الأجَلُ حِصْنٌ حَصِينٌ.[٢٩]

10. Everything Has an End

١٠ـ لِكُلِّ شَيءٍ أجَلٌ

26. **Imām ʿAlī (AS) said,** 'Everything has a fixed duration and an end.'[32]

٢٦ . الإمامُ عليٌّ ﷺ : إنّ لكلِّ شيءٍ مُدّةً وأجَلاً.[٣٠]

27. **Imām ʿAlī (AS) said,** 'Allah has made a measure for everything and for every measure an end.'[33]

٢٧ . عنه ﷺ : جَعلَ اللهُ لكلِّ شيءٍ قَدْراً، ولكلِّ قَدْرٍ أجَلاً.[٣١]

11. Every Community has a [Preordained] End

١١ ـ لِكُلِّ أُمَّةٍ أجَلُ

"There is a [preordained] time for every nation: when their time comes, they shall not defer it by a single hour nor shall they advance it."[34]

﴿وَلِكُلِّ أُمَّةٍ أَجَلٌ فَإِذَا جاءَ أَجَلُهُمْ لا يَسْتَأْخِرُونَ ساعَةً وَلا يَسْتَقْدِمُونَ﴾.[٣٢]

"We did not destroy any town but that it had a known term. No nation can advance its time nor can it defer it."[35]

﴿وَما أَهْلَكْنا مِنْ قَرْيَةٍ إلّا وَلَها كِتابٌ مَعْلُومٌ * ما تَسْبِقُ مِنْ أُمَّةٍ أَجَلَها وَما يَسْتَأْخِرُونَ﴾.[٣٣]

(See also: Qur'an 16:61, 20:129, 29:5, 42:14, 23:43)

(أُنظر) النحل : ٦١ و طه : ١٢٩ و العنكبوت : ٥ والشورىٰ : ١٤ و المؤمنون : ٤٣.

12. Suspended and Sealed Ends

١٢ ـ الأجَلُ المُعَلَّقُ وَالأجَلُ المَحتومُ

"It is He who created you from clay, then ordained the term [of your life] - the specified term is with Him - and yet you are in doubt."[36]

﴿هُوَ الَّذِي خَلَقَكُمْ مِنْ طِينٍ ثُمَّ قَضَىٰ أَجَلاً وَأَجَلٌ مُسَمّىً عِنْدَهُ ثُمَّ أَنْتُمْ تَمْتَرُونَ﴾.[٣٤]

28. **Imām al-Ṣādiq (AS) said,** interpreting the above verse: 'The first – undetermined – term is suspended; He can expedite and postpone it as He wishes. As for the specified term, that is what He destines during the Night of Ordainment (*laylat al-qadr*) to occur from that night up to the next year's Night of Ordainment; and that is Allah's statement: *"when their time comes, they shall not defer it by a single hour nor shall they advance it."*'[37]

٢٨ . الإمامُ الصّادقُ ﷺ ـ في تفسيرِ الآيةِ ـ: الأجلُ الّذي غَيرُ مُسمّى مَوقوفٌ ، يُقدِّمُ مِنه ما شاءَ ، ويؤخِّرُ مِنه ما شاءَ ، وأمّا الأجَلُ المُسمّىٰ فهُوَ الّذي يَنزِلُ مِمّا يُريدُ أنْ يكونَ مِن ليلةِ القَدْرِ إلىٰ مِثلِها مِن قابِلٍ ، فذلك قولُ اللهِ: ﴿إذا جَاء أجلُهم لا يستأخِرونَ ساعةً ولا يستقدِمون﴾.[٣٥، ٣٦]

13. What Safeguards Against The Suspended End

١٣ ـ ما يَدفَعُ الأجَلَ المُعَلَّقَ

29. **Imām ʿAlī (AS) said,** 'People's terms are extended by charity.'[38]

٢٩ . الإمامُ عليٌّ ﷺ : بالصَّدَقةِ تُفْسَحُ الآجالُ.[٣٧]

30. **Imām al-Ṣādiq (AS) said,** 'People live by their goodness towards others more than they do according to their [predestined] life terms; they also die due to their sins more than they die due to the end of their terms.'[39]

٣٠. الإمامُ الصّادقُ ﷺ: يَعيشُ النّاسُ بإحسانِهم أكثرَ مِمّا يَعيشُونَ بأعمارِهِم، ويَموتُونَ بذُنوبِهِم أكثرَ مِمّا يَموتُونَ بآجالِهِم.٣٨

(See also: LIFESPAN: section 1371) (أنظر: العُمر: باب ١٣٧١)

4

THE HEREAFTER

الآخرة

14. The Hereafter

١٤ـ الآخِرَة

"Whoever desires the tillage of the Hereafter, We will enhance for him his tillage, and whoever desires the tillage of the world, We will give it to him, but he will have no share in the Hereafter."[40]

﴿مَنْ كَانَ يُرِيدُ حَرْثَ الْآخِرَةِ نَزِدْ لَهُ فِي حَرْثِهِ وَمَنْ كَانَ يُرِيدُ حَرْثَ الدُّنْيَا نُؤْتِهِ مِنْهَا وَمَا لَهُ فِي الْآخِرَةِ مِنْ نَصِيبٍ﴾.٣٩

31. **Imām ʿAlī (AS) said,** 'This life is the aspiration of the wretched, and the Hereafter is the victory of the fortunate.'[41]

٣١. الإمام عليٌّ ﷺ: الدُّنيا مُنيةُ الأشقياءِ، الآخِرةُ فوزُ السُّعداءِ.٤٠

32. **Imām ʿAlī (AS) said,** 'Aim for the Hereafter and this world will submit to you in humility.'[42]

٣٢. عنه ﷺ: عَلَيكَ بالآخِرةِ تأتِكَ الدُّنيا صاغِرةً.٤١

33. **Imām ʿAlī (AS) said,** 'This world is turning away from you and the Hereafter is close to you.'[43]

٣٣. عنه ﷺ: إنّ الدُّنيا مُنقَطِعةٌ عنكَ، والآخِرة قريبةٌ منكَ.٤٢

15. The Greatness of What is in The Hereafter

١٥ـ عَظَمَةُ ما فِي الآخِرَة

"Observe how We have given some of them an advantage over some others; yet the Hereafter is surely greater in respect of ranks and greater in respect of relative merit."[44]

﴿انْظُرْ كَيْفَ فَضَّلْنَا بَعْضَهُمْ عَلَىٰ بَعْضٍ وَلَلْآخِرَةُ أَكْبَرُ دَرَجَاتٍ وَأَكْبَرُ تَفْضِيلًا﴾.٤٣

34. **Imām ʿAlī (AS) said,** 'Every aspect of this world seems greater upon hearing than when it is seen, and every aspect of the Hereafter is greater when it will be seen than when it is heard about. So be satisfied with the hearing in lieu of the seeing and with the tale in lieu of the concealed. [regarding the Hereafter and the unseen you should be content with what you hear and you are informed of by the prophets].'[45]

٣٤. الإمامُ عليٌّ ﷺ : كلُّ شيءٍ مِن الدُّنيا سَماعُهُ أعظمُ مِن عِيانهِ، وكلُّ شيءٍ مِن الآخـرةِ عِـيانُهُ أعظمُ مِن سَماعِهِ، فَلْيَكْفِكُم مِن العِيانِ السَّماعُ، ومِن الغَيبِ الخَبَرُ.٤٤

16. The Hereafter is the Eternal Home

١٦ـالآخِرَةُ دارُ القَرارِ

"O my people! This life of the world is only a [passing] enjoyment, and indeed the Hereafter is the abiding home."[46]

﴿يا قَوْمِ إِنَّمَا هٰذِهِ الْحَيَاةُ الدُّنْيَا مَتَاعٌ وَإِنَّ الْآخِرَةَ هِيَ دَارُ الْقَرَارِ﴾.٤٥

35. **Imām ʿAlī (AS) said,** 'He who builds the home of his lasting residence is sensible.'[47]

٣٥. الإمامُ عليٌّ ﷺ : مَن عَمَّر دارَ إقامتِهِ فـهُوَ العاقلُ.٤٦

36. **Imām ʿAlī (AS) said,** 'This life is an epoch whilst the Hereafter is eternity.'[48]

٣٦. عنه ﷺ : الدُّنيا أمَدٌ، الآخِرَةُ أبَدٌ.٤٧

17. The Superiority of The Hereafter

١٧ـفَضلُ الآخِرَةِ

"Say, 'The enjoyment of this world is little and the Hereafter is better for the Godwary'"[49]

﴿قُلْ مَتَاعُ الدُّنْيَا قَلِيلٌ وَالْآخِرَةُ خَيْرٌ لِمَنِ اتَّقَى﴾.٤٨

37. **Imām ʿAlī (AS) said,** 'There is no compensation for the Hereafter; and this life is not a worthy price for the self.'[50]

٣٧. الامام عليٌّ ﷺ : لَيسَ عنِ الآخرةِ عِوَضٌ، ولَيستِ الدُّنيا للنَّفْسِ بِثَمَنٍ.٤٩

(See also: THE WORLD: section 717)

(أنظر) الدنيا: باب ٧١٧.

18. Remembrance of the Hereafter

١٨ـذِكرُ الآخِرَةِ

38. **Imām ʿAlī (AS) said,** 'Remembrance of the Hereafter is a remedy and a cure, whilst remembrance of worldly life is the worst disease.'[51]

٣٨. الإمامُ عليٌّ ﷺ : ذِكرُ الآخرةِ دَواءٌ وشِفاءٌ، ذِكرُ الدُّنيا أدْوَأُ الأدواءِ.٥٠

39. **Imām ʿAlī (AS) said,** 'He who increases his remembrance of the Hereafter disobeys [Allah] less often.'[52]

٣٩ . عنه ﷺ : مَن أكثَرَ مِن ذِكرِ الآخِرةِ قَلَّتْ مَعصيتُهُ.٥١

19. Working for the Hereafter

١٩ـ العَمَلُ لِلآخِرَةِ

40. **The Prophet (SAWA) said,** 'Work for your life as though you will live forever, and work for the Hereafter as though you will die tomorrow.'[53]

٤٠ . رسولُ اللهِ ﷺ : اعمَلْ لِدُنياكَ كأنّكَ تَعيشُ أبداً ، واعمَلْ لآخرتِكَ كأنّكَ تَموتُ غَداً .٥٢

41. **The Prophet (SAWA) said,** 'He who makes the Hereafter his greatest concern when he wakes up and before he sleeps, Allah instills needlessness in his heart and mends his affairs for him; he will not depart from this life before having collected all his sustenance. But the one who makes this world his greatest concern in his life, Allah instils poverty between his eyes and disbands his affairs; he will not collect from this life more than what was allotted to him.'[54]

٤١ . عنه ﷺ : مَن أصبَحَ وأمسىٰ والآخِرةُ أكبرُ هَمِّهِ جَعلَ اللهُ الغِنىٰ في قلبِهِ، وجَمَع لَه أمرَهُ، ولَم يَخرُج مِن الدُّنيا حتّىٰ يَستكمِلَ رزقَهُ . ومَن أصبحَ وأمسَىٰ والدُّنيا أكبرُ هَمِّهِ جَعَلَ اللهُ الفَقْرَ بينَ عينَيهِ، وشتَّتَ علَيهِ أمْرَه، ولَم يَنَلْ مِن الدُّنيا إلّا ما قُسِمَ لَهُ.٥٣

42. **Imām ʿAlī (AS) said,** 'Working for the Hereafter is of no benefit when it is coupled with the desire for this world.'[55]

٤٢ . الامام عليٌّ ﷺ : لايَنفَعُ العَمَلُ للآخِرَةِ مَعَ الرَّغبَةِ فِي الدُّنيا .٥٤

5

THE BROTHER

الأخُ

20. The Believers are Brothers

٢٠ـ المُؤمِنُ أخُو المُؤمِنِ

"The faithful are indeed brothers. Therefore make peace between your brothers and be wary of Allah, so that you may receive [His] mercy."[56]

﴿إنَّما الْمُؤْمِنُونَ إخْوَةٌ فَأَصْلِحُوا بَيْنَ أَخَوَيْكُمْ وَاتَّقُوا اللهَ لَعَلَّكُمْ تُرْحَمُونَ﴾ .٥٥

43. **The Prophet (SAWA) said,** 'The believers are brothers, their blood is coequal, and they are one hand against others, the most inferior among them is empowered by them to give [to the enemy] protection.'[57]

٤٣ . رسولُ اللهِ ﷺ: المؤمنونَ إخْوَةٌ، تَتَكافىٰ دِماؤهُم، وَهُمْ يَدٌ علىٰ مَن سِواهُم ، يَسْعىٰ بذِمّتِهم أدناهُم.٥٦

44. **Imām ʿAlī (AS) said,** 'Many a brother was not given birth by your own mother.'[58]

٤٤ . الإمامُ عليٌّ ﷺ : رُبَّ أخٍ لَم تَلِدْهُ أُمُّكَ.٥٧

45. **Imām al-Bāqir (AS) said,** 'A believer is the brother of another believer [as if] from his own mother and father.'[59]

٤٥ . الإمامُ الباقرُ ﷺ : المؤمنُ أخو المؤمِن لأبيهِ وأُمِّهِ.٥٨

46. **Imām al-Ṣādiq (AS) said,** 'A believer is the brother of another believer, his eye and his guide; he does not betray him, nor wrong him, nor deceive him, and nor does he rescind a promise he made to him.'[60]

٤٦ . الامام الصادق ﷺ : المُؤمنُ أخو المؤمنِ ، عَينُهُ ودَليلُهُ ، لا يَخونُهُ ، ولا يَظْلِمُهُ ، ولا يَغُشُّهُ ، ولا يَعِدُهُ عِدَةً فيَخْلِفَهُ.٥٩

47. **Imām al-Ṣādiq (AS) said,** 'A believer is the brother of another believer, like a single body. If any part of him suffers, he will feel its pain in his entire body; and their souls are also made of one soul.'[61]

٤٧ . عنه ﷺ: المؤمنُ أخو المؤمنِ كالجَسَدِ الواحدِ، إنِ اشتكَىٰ شيئاً مِنهُ وَجَدَ ألمَ ذلكَ في سائرِ جسدِهِ ، وأرواحُهُما مِن رُوحٍ واحدةٍ.٦٠

(See also: FAITH: section 189)

(انظر) الايمان : باب ١٨٩.

21. Increasing the Number of True Brothers

٢١ ـ الاستِكثارُ مِنَ الإخوانِ

48. **The Prophet (SAWA) said**, 'Seek to increase your brothers [i.e. believing friends], for every believer will make an intercession on the Day of Judgment.'[62]

٤٨ . رسولُ اللهِ ﷺ : استكْثِروا مِن الإخوانِ ؛ فإنَّ لكلِّ مؤمنٍ شَفاعةً يومَ القيامةِ.٦١

49. **Imām ʿAlī (AS) said**, 'Adopt [the friendship of] true brothers and increase in your acquisition of them, for they are an asset in times of prosperity, and a shield during afflictions.'[63]

٤٩ . الإمام عليٌّ ﷺ : عَلَيكَ بإخوانِ الصِّدْقِ فأكْثِرْ مِنِ اكتِسابِهِم؛ فإنَّهُم عُدّةٌ عِندَ الرَّخاءِ ، وجُنّةٌ عِندَ البَلاءِ.٦٢

(See also: THE FRIEND: section 1102)

(أُنظر) الصديق : باب ١١٠٢.

22. Brothers' Amity

٢٢ ـ مَوَدَّةُ الإخوانِ

50. **Imām ʿAlī (AS) said,** 'Do not let your brother be stronger than you are in your amity for him.'[64]

٥٠ . الإمامُ عليٌّ ﷺ : لا يكونُ أخوكَ أقوىٰ مِنكَ علىٰ مَودّتِهِ.٦٣

51. **Imām ʿAlī (AS) said,** 'Love brothers in proportion to [their] piety.'[65]

٥١ . عنه ﷺ : أحْـبِبِ الإخْـوانَ علىٰ قَدْرِ التَّقْوىٰ.٦٤

52. **Imām al-Ṣādiq (AS) said,** 'A man's love for his brother is part of his love for his religion.'[66]

٥٢ . الإمام الصادق ﷺ : مِن حُبِّ الرَّجلِ دِينَه حبُّهُ أخَاهُ.٦٥

23. That Which Ensures the Endurance of Amity

٢٣ ـ ما يوجِبُ بَقاءَ المَوَدَّةِ

53. **Imām al-Ṣādiq (AS) said,** 'O Ibn al-Nuʿmān! If you want your brother's amity for you to be pure, do not make fun of him, do not dispute with him, do not exchange bragging with him, and do not vie with him in evil acts.'[67]

٥٣ . الإمام الصادق ﷺ : يابنَ النُّعمان ، إنْ أردتَ أن يَصْفُوَ لكَ وُدُّ أخيكَ فلا تُمازِحَنَّهُ، ولا تُمارِيَنَّهُ، ولا تُباهِيَنَّهُ ، ولا تُشارَّنَّهُ.٦٦

54. **Imām al-Ṣādiq (AS) said,** 'Brothers need three things among them – they either use them, or else dispute and hate one another – fairness, benevolence, and evasion of jealousy.'[68]

٥٤ . عنه ﷺ : تَحتاجُ الإخْوةُ فيما بَيْنَهُم إلىٰ ثلاثةِ أشياءَ ، فإنِ استَعمَلُوها وإلّا تَبايَنُوا وتَباغَضُوا، وهي : التَّناصُفُ ، والتَّراحُمُ ، ونَفْيُ الحَسَدِ.٦٧

(See also: CHEERFULNESS: 42; LOVE: section 418)

(أنظر) عنوان ٤٢ «البِشر» ؛ المحبّة : باب ٤١٨.

24. Brotherhood for the Sake of Allah

٢٤ ـ الأُخُوَّةُ فِي اللهِ

55. **The Prophet (SAWA) said,** 'Looking at a brother you love for the sake of Allah, the Exalted, is [an act of] worship.'[69]

٥٥ . رسولُ اللهِ ﷺ : النَّظَرُ إلىٰ الأخِ تَوَدُّهُ في اللهِ عزّ وجلّ عِبادَةٌ.٦٨

56. **The Prophet (SAWA) said,** 'A Muslim cannot acquire anything more beneficial as his embracing Islam than a brother he benefits from for the sake of Allah.'[70]

٥٦ . عنه ﷺ : ما استَفادَ امرؤٌ مسلمٌ فائدةً بعدَ فائدةِ الإسلام مثلَ أخٍ يَستَفيدُهُ في اللهِ.٦٩

57. **Imām ʿAlī (AS) said,** 'Love is purified through cultivating friendship for the sake of Allah.'[71]

٥٧ . الإمامُ عليٌّ ﷺ : علىٰ التَّواخِي في اللهِ تَخْلُصُ المَحَبّةُ.٧٠

58. **Imām ʿAlī (AS) said,** 'Brothers, [whose brotherhood is] for the sake of Allah, enjoy an enduring amity, due to the firmness of its foundation.'[72]

٥٨ . عنه ﷺ : الإخْوانُ في اللهِ تعالىٰ تَدُومُ مَودّتُهُم ، لِدَوامِ سَبَبِها.٧١

59. **Imām ʿAlī (AS) said,** 'Brotherhood for the sake of Allah is fruitful.'[73]

٥٩ . الإمامُ عليٌّ ﷺ : بالتَّواخي في اللهِ تُثْمِرُ الأُخُوّة.[٧٢]

(See also: LOVE: section 433)

(أنظر) المحبّة: باب ٤٣٣.

25. Brotherhood for the Sake of this World

٢٥ ـ الإخاءُ لِلدُّنيا

60. **Imām ʿAlī (AS) said**, 'He whose friendship is not for the sake of Allah must be avoided, for his friendship is vile, and his company is doomed.'[74]

٦٠ . الإمامُ عليٌّ ﷺ : مَن لَم تَكُن مَودّتُهُ في اللهِ فاحْذَرْهُ؛ فإنّ مودّتَهُ لَئيمةٌ ، وصُحْبتَه مَشُومةٌ.[٧٣]

61. **Imām ʿAlī (AS) said**, 'He whose brotherhood is for the sake of Allah is bound to gain, while a man who seeks brothers for the sake of this world is bound to lose.'[75]

٦١ . عنه ﷺ : مَن آخَىٰ في اللهِ غَنِمَ ، مَن آخَىٰ في الدُّنيا حُرِمَ.[٧٤]

62. **Imām ʿAlī (AS) said**, 'He who draws close to you for a purpose will abandon you when it is fulfilled.'[76]

٦٢ . عنه ﷺ :مَن وادَّكَ لأمرٍ ولّىٰ عندَانقِضائِهِ.[٧٥]

26. Informing One's Brother of One's Love [for Him]

٢٦ ـ إعلامُ الأخِ بِالحُبِّ

63. **The Prophet (SAWA) said**, 'When one of you likes his companion or brother, he should let him know.'[77]

٦٣ . رسولُ اللهِ ﷺ : إذا أحبَّ أحدُكُم صاحِبَهُ أو أخاهُ فليُعْلِمْهُ.[٧٦]

64. **Biḥār al-Anwār**: A man passed through the mosque, where Abū Jaʿfar and Abū ʿAbdullāh [Imām al-Bāqir and Imām al-Ṣādiq] (AS) were seated, when one of the people present said, 'By Allah, I like this man.' Abū Jaʿfar replied, 'Then let him know, for this will maintain the amity and enhance the affection.'[78]

٦٤ . بحار الأنوار : مَرّ رجلٌ في المسجدِ وأبو جعفرٍ ﷺ جالسٌ وأبو عبدِاللهِ ﷺ، فقالَ له بعضُ جُلَسائهِ: واللهِ، إنّي لَأُحِبُّ هذا الرّجُلَ. قالَ لَه أبو جعفرٍ ﷺ: ألَا فأعْلِمْهُ ؛ فإنَّهُ أبقىٰ لِلمَوَدّة ، وخَيرٌ في الأُلْفةِ.[٧٧]

27. One's Amity for Another is a Proof of Reciprocity

٢٧ ـ مَوَدَّةُ الأخِ دَليلٌ عَلىٰ مَوَدَّتِهِ لِأخيهِ

65. **Imām ʿAlī (AS) said**, 'Ask your hearts about their amities, for they are witnesses that take no bribes.'[79]

٦٥ . الإمامُ عليٌّ ؑ : سَلُوا القُلوبَ عنِ المَوَدّاتِ ؛ فإنّها شَواهِدُ لا تَقْبَلُ الرُّشا .[٧٨]

66. **Imām al-Bāqir (AS) said**, 'Know the amity that your brother has for you in his heart through what you harbour of the same in your own heart.'[80]

٦٦ . الإمامُ الباقرُ ؑ : اعرِفِ المَودّةَ لكَ في قلبِ أخيكَ بما لَهُ في قلبِكَ .[٧٩]

67. **Imām al-Hādī (AS) said**, 'Do not seek sincere amity from a man you have insincere sentiment for, nor honest advice from someone you direct your distrust towards, for another's feelings [*lit.* heart] towards you are similar to your feelings towards him.'[81]

٦٧ . الإمامُ الهاديُّ ؑ : لا تَطلب الصَّفا ممّن كَدّرتَ علَيهِ ، ولا النُّصْحَ ممّن صَرَفْتَ سُوءَ ظَنِّكَ إلَيهِ ، فإنّما قلبُ غيرِكَ لكَ كقلبِكَ لَهُ .[٨٠]

(See also: LOVE: section 428)

(أُنظر) المحبّة : باب ٤٢٨ .

28. Cutting off Relations with Brothers

٢٨ ـ قَطِيعَةُ الإخوانِ

68. **Imām ʿAlī (AS) said**, 'If you want to cut off relations with your brother make sure to leave a place for him in your heart, so he can return to it one day when he so wishes.'[82]

٦٨ . الإمامُ عليٌّ ؑ : إنْ أرَدْتَ قَطِيعةَ أخيكَ فاستَبْقِ لَهُ مِن نفسِكَ بَقيّةً يَرجِعُ إليها إن بَدا لَه ذلكَ يوماً مّا .[٨١]

69. **Imām ʿAlī (AS) said**, 'How awful it is to cut off relations after having maintained them, to turn away after brotherhood, and to have animosity after amity.'[83]

٦٩ . عنه ؑ : ما أقبحَ القَطِيعةَ بعدَ الصِّلَةِ ، والجَفاءَ بعدَ الإخاءِ ، والعَداوةَ بعدَ المَودّةِ![٨٢]

70. **Imām al-Ṣādiq (AS) said**, 'A man who places his amity in the wrong place is bound to suffer abandonment.'[84]

٧٠ . الإمامُ الصادق ؑ : مَن وضَعَ حُبَّهُ في غيرِ موضعِهِ فقد تَعرَّضَ للقَطيعةِ .[٨٣]

(See also: DESERTION: section 390)

(أُنظر) عنوان ٣٩٠ «الهجران» .

29. Maintaining Brotherhood

٢٩ـ وَصلُ الإخوانِ

71. **Imām ʿAlī (AS) said**, 'Do not let your brother be stronger in his avoidance of you than you are in your maintaining relations with him, and do not be stronger in your harm to him than in your kindness towards him.'[85]

٧١. الإمام عليٌّ ﵇: لا يَكُونَنَّ أخوكَ أقوىٰ علىٰ قَطيعتِكَ منكَ علىٰ صِلَتِهِ، ولا تَكُونَنّ علىٰ الإساءَةِ أقوىٰ منكَ علَى الإحسانِ.[٨٤]

72. **Imām al-Ḥusayn (AS) said,** 'The best person is the one who maintains relations with one who cuts him off.'[86]

٧٢. الإمامُ الحسينُ ﵇: إنّ أوْصَلَ النّاسِ مَن وَصَلَ مَن قَطَعَهُ.[٨٥]

30. Types of Brothers

٣٠ـ أقسامُ الإخوانِ

73. **The Prophet (SAWA) said,** 'The most scarce things at the end of time will be a trustworthy brother and a legitimately earned dirham.'[87]

٧٣. رسولُ اللهِ ﷺ: أقلُّ ما يكونُ في آخِرِ الزّمانِ أخٌ يُوثَقُ بِهِ أو دِرْهَمٌ من حَلالٍ.[٨٦]

74. **Imām al-Ṣādiq (AS) said,** 'Brothers are of three [kinds]: one, like food, is needed all the time and he is the wise [friend]. Another is similar to disease, and this is the fool. And the third is like medicine, and this is the tactful [friend].'[88]

٧٤. الإمامُ الصّادقُ ﵇: الإخوانُ ثلاثةٌ: فواحِدٌ كالغِذاءِ الّذي يُحتاجُ إليهِ كلَّ وقتٍ فَهُو العاقلُ، والثّاني في معنَى الدّاءِ وهُو الأحْمَقُ، والثّالثُ في معنَى الدّواءِ فَهُو اللّبِيبُ.[٨٧]

75. **Imām al-Ṣādiq (AS) said**, 'Brothers are three [kinds]: one helps with his own self, and another helps with his wealth, and these two are true in their brotherhood. A third is the one who takes from you what he needs and keeps you for some of his pleasure - do not consider him trustworthy.'[89]

٧٥. عنه ﵇: الإخْوانُ ثلاثةٌ: مُواسٍ بنفسِهِ، وآخَرُ مُواسٍ بمالِهِ؛ وهُما الصّادقانِ في الإخاءِ، وآخَرُ يأخذُ منكَ البُلْغَةَ، ويُريدُكَ لِبَعضِ اللَّذَّةِ، فلا تَعُدَّه مِن أهلِ الثِّقَةِ.[٨٨]

31. Warning Against Some Forms of Brotherhood

٣١ـ النَّهيُ عَن بَعضِ الإخاءِ

76. **Imām ʿAlī (AS) said,** 'The one you need to safeguard yourself against is not your brother.'[90]

٧٦. الإمام عليٌّ ﵇: ليسَ لكَ بأخٍ مَنِ احْتَجْتَ إلىٰ مُداراتِهِ.[٨٩]

77. **Imām ʿAlī (AS) said,** 'Do not take for brother a man who hides your virtues and exposes your lapses.'[91]

٧٧. عنه ﵇: لا تُواخِ مَن يَسْتُرُ مَناقِبَك، ويَنْشُرُ مَثالِبَكَ.[٩٠]

78. **Imām al-Bāqir (AS) said,** 'The worst brother is the one who stays with you in your affluence and abandons you in your poverty.'[92]

٧٨ . الإمامُ الباقرُ عليه السلام : بِئسَ الأَخُ أخٌ يَرعاكَ غَنِيّاً وَيقطعُكَ فَقيراً ⁹¹.

79. **Imām al-Bāqir (AS) said,** 'Do not take for brothers or companions: the fool, the miserly, the coward, and the liar.'[93]

٧٩ . عنه عليه السلام : لا تُقارِنْ ولا تُواخِ أربعةً: الأحْمَقَ، والبَخيلَ، والجَبانَ، والكَذّابَ ⁹².

80. **Imām al-Ṣādiq (AS) said,** 'Be warned against having a brother who wants you for greed, out of fear, or because of food and drink. Instead, seek the brotherhood of the pious even if they are in the darkness of the earth and even if you have to spend your life seeking them.'[94]

٨٠ . الإمامُ الصّادقُ عليه السلام : احذَرْ أن تُواخيَ مَن أرادَكَ لِطَمعٍ أو خَوفٍ أو مَيْلٍ أو للأكلِ والشُّرْبِ، واطلبْ مُواخاةَ الأتقياءِ ولو في ظُلُماتِ الأرضِ، وإنْ أفنيتَ عُمْرَكَ في طلبِهِم ⁹³.

(See also: THE FRIEND: section 1103; LOVE: section 419)

(أُنظر) الصديق: باب ١١٠٣؛ المحبّة: باب ٤١٩.

32. Preserving Old Brotherhood

٣٢ـ المُحافظةُ عَلَى الأُخُوَّةِ القَديمَةِ

81. **The Prophet (SAWA) said,** 'Allah, the Exalted, likes the maintenance of old brotherhood, so maintain it.'[95]

٨١ . رسولُ اللهِ صلى الله عليه وآله : إنَّ اللهَ تعالىٰ يُحِبُّ المُداوَمَةَ علىٰ الإخاءِ القديمِ، فَداوِمُوا علَيهِ ⁹⁴.

82. **Imām ʿAlī (AS) said,** 'Choose the new of everything, but the oldest one from among brothers.'[96]

٨٢ . الإمامُ عليٌّ عليه السلام : اخْتَرْ مِن كلِّ شيءٍ جَدِيدَهُ، ومِن الإخْوانِ أقدَمَهُمْ ⁹⁵.

33. Real Brotherhood

٣٣ـ الأُخُوَّةُ الحَقيقيَّةُ

83. **Imām ʿAlī (AS) said,** 'Your true brother is the one who forgives your lapse, fulfils your need, accepts your excuse, hides your vices, removes your fear, and lives up to your aspiration.'[97]

٨٣ . الإمامُ عليٌّ عليه السلام : إنَّ أخاكَ حَقّاً مَن غَفَرَ زلّتَكَ، وسَدَّ خَلّتَكَ، وقَبِلَ عُذْرَكَ، وسَتَرَ عَوْرَتَكَ، ونَفىٰ وَجلَكَ، وحَقّقَ أملَكَ ⁹⁶.

84. **Imām ʿAlī (AS) said,** 'Your brother is the one who does not abandon you in difficulty, does not forget you at the time of trouble, and does not cheat you when you seek his advice.'[98]

٨٤ . عنه عليه السلام : أخوكَ الّذي لا يَخْذُلُكَ عِندَ الشِّدَّةِ، ولا يَغْفُلُ عنكَ عندَ الجَرِيرةِ، ولا يَخْدَعُكَ حينَ تَسْأَلُهُ ⁹⁷.

34. Choosing a Brother

٣٤ـ اختيارُ الأخِ

85. **Imām ʿAlī (AS) said,** 'He who shuns his brothers for every lapse has few friends.'[99]

٨٥ . الإمامُ عليٌّ ﷺ : مَن جانَبَ الإخْوانَ علىٰ كُلِّ ذَنبٍ قَلَّ أصدِقاؤهُ.[٩٨]

86. **Imām al-Ṣādiq (AS) said,** 'A man who does not befriend [anyone] unless they are flawless will have few friends.'[100]

٨٦ . الإمامُ الصّادقُ ﷺ : مَن لَم يُـؤاخِ إلّا مَـن لا عَيبَ فيهِ قَلَّ صَديقُهُ.[٩٩]

35. Tolerating the Lapse of a Brother

٣٥ـ تَحَمُّلُ زِلَّةِ الأخِ

87. **Imām ʿAlī (AS) said,** 'Tolerate the lapse of your friend for the time of your enemy's attack.'[101]

٨٧ . الإمامُ عليٌّ ﷺ : احتمِـلْ زلّـةَ وَليِّـكَ لوقتِ وَثْبَةِ عَدُوِّكَ.[١٠٠]

88. **Imām ʿAlī (AS) said,** 'Tolerance is the splendour of companions.'[102]

٨٨ . عنه ﷺ : الاحتِمالُ زَيْنُ الرِّفاقِ.[١٠١]

89. **Imām ʿAlī (AS) said,** 'A man who does not endure the lapses of a friend will die in loneliness.'[103]

٨٩ . عنه ﷺ : مَن لم يَحْتَمِلْ زَلَلَ الصَّديقِ ماتَ وحيداً.[١٠٢]

(See also: MANAGEMENT: section 206)

(أُنظر) عنوان ٢٠٦ «السياسة».

36. The Best of Brothers

٣٦ـ خَيرُ الإخوانِ

90. **The Prophet (SAWA) said,** 'The best of your brothers is the one who helps you to obey Allah, prevents you from disobeying Him, and orders you to please Him.'[104]

٩٠ . رسولُ اللهِ ﷺ : خيرُ إخْوانِكَ مَن أعانَكَ علىٰ طاعةِ اللهِ، وصَدَّكَ عن مَعاصِيهِ ، وأمَرَكَ برِضاهُ.[١٠٣]

91. **Imām ʿAlī (AS) said,** 'The best of brothers is the one with the least hesitance in offering [harsh] advice.'[105]

٩١ . الإمامُ عليٌّ ﷺ : خيرُ الإخْوانِ أقلُّهُمْ مُصانَعةً في النَّصيحَةِ.[١٠٤]

92. **Imām ʿAlī (AS) said,** 'The best of your brothers is the one who stands by you, and better than him is he who you don't need anyone else besides, and even when he is in need of you, he spares you.'[106]

٩٢ . عنه ﷺ : خيرُ إخْوانِكَ مَن واساكَ ، وخيرٌ مِنه مَن كَفاكَ ، وإنِ احتاجَ إليكَ أعْفاكَ.[١٠٥]

93. **Imām ʿAlī (AS) said,** 'The best brother is the one whose amity is for the sake of Allah.'[107]

٩٣ . عنه ﷺ : خيرُ الإخْوانِ مَن كانتْ في اللهِ مَودّتُهُ.[١٠٦]

94. **Imām ʿAlī (AS) said,** 'The best of your brothers is the one who rushes to do good and draws you towards it, and orders you to do good and helps you with it.'[108]

٩٤ . عنه عليه السلام : خيرُ إخوانِكَ مَن سارَعَ إلى الخيرِ وجَذَبَكَ إليهِ ، وأمَرَكَ بالبرِّ وأعانَكَ علَيهِ .١٠٧

95. **Imām ʿAlī (AS) said,** 'The best of your brothers is the one who is roused to anger for your sake in [standing up for] what is right.'[109]

٩٥ . عنه عليه السلام : خيرُ إخوانِك مَن كثُرَ إغْضابُهُ لكَ في الحقِّ .١٠٨

96. **Imām ʿAlī (AS) said,** 'The best of brothers is the one who does not let his fellow brothers need anyone other than himself.'[110]

٩٦ . عنه عليه السلام : خيرُ الإخْوانِ مَن لا يُحْوِجُ إخْوانَهُ إلىٰ سِواهُ .١٠٩

97. **Imām al-Ṣādiq (AS) said,** 'The most beloved of my brothers to me is he who confers my faults to me.'[111]

٩٧ . الإمامُ الصّادقُ عليه السلام : أحبُّ إخْواني إليَّ مَن أهْدىٰ عُيُوبي إليَّ .١١٠

(See also: THE FRIEND: section 1106)

(اُنظر الصديق : باب ١١٠٦).

37. The Worst of Brothers

٣٧ ـ شَرُّ الإخوانِ

98. **Imām ʿAlī (AS) said,** 'The worst of brothers is he for whom one [is made] to go out of one's way.'[112]

٩٨ . الإمامُ عليٌّ عليه السلام : شَرُّ الإخوانِ مَن تُكُلِّفَ لَهُ .١١١

99. The Commander of the Faithful (AS) was asked, 'Which is the worst companion?' He replied, 'The one who glamorizes acts of disobedience of Allah to you.'[113]

٩٩ . عنه عليه السلام ـ لَمّا سُئل : أيُّ صاحبٍ شرٌّ ؟ ـ : المُزَيِّنُ لكَ مَعصيةَ اللهِ .١١٢

38. Testing Brothers

٣٨ ـ اختِبارُ الإخوانِ

100. **The Prophet (SAWA) said,** 'When you see three traits in your brother, place your hope in him: bashfulness, trustworthiness, and truthfulness. If you do not see them, do not place your hope in him.'[114]

١٠٠ . رسولُ اللهِ صلى الله عليه وآله : إذا رأيتَ مِن أخيكَ ثلاثَ خِصالٍ فارْجُهُ : الحياءُ ، والأمانةُ ، والصِّدقُ . وإذا لم تَرَها فلا تَرْجُهُ .١١٣

101. **Imām ʿAlī (AS) said,** 'A man who takes a brother after careful selection is bound to have a lasting companionship and a firm amity, whereas a man

١٠١ . الإمامُ عليٌّ عليه السلام : مَن اتَّخَذَ أخاً بعدَ حُسْنِ الاختِبارِ دامَتْ صُحْبَتُهُ وتأكَّدَتْ مَودَّتُهُ . ومَن اتَّخَذَ أخاً مِن غيرِ اختِبارٍ ألجَأهُ الاضطِرارُ إلى

who takes a brother without careful testing is bound to resort to the friendship of evil people.'[115]

مُرافَقَـةِ الأشرارِ.[١١٤]

102. **Imām al-Ṣādiq (AS) said**, 'Test your brothers with two things, which they must possess; otherwise avoid them, avoid them, avoid them: observing the prayers at their prescribed times and helping brothers during hardship as well as ease.'[116]

١٠٢ . الإمامُ الصّادقُ ﷺ : اختبِرُوا إخْـوانَكُـم بخَصلَتَينِ؛ فإنْ كانَتا فيهِم وإلّا فاعْزُبْ ثمّ اعزُبْ ثمّ اعزُبْ: محافظَةٌ علَى الصّلواتِ في مَواقِيتِها، والبِرُّ بالإخْوانِ في العُسْر واليُسرِ.[١١٥]

39. Advising Brothers

٣٩ـ إرشادُ الإخوانِ

103. **The Prophet (SAWA) said**, 'A believer is a mirror for his believing brother; he stays faithful to him in his absence and spares him from what he would hate to see.'[117]

١٠٣ . رسولُ اللهِ ﷺ: المؤمنُ مِرآةٌ لأخيهِ المؤمنِ، يَنْصَحُهُ إذا غابَ عنه، ويُمِيطُ عنه مـا يَكْـرهُ إذا شَهِدَ.[١١٦]

104. **Imām ʿAlī (AS) said**, 'He who advises his brother in private adorns him, and he who advises him publicly degrades him.'[118]

١٠٤ . الإمام عليٌّ ﷺ : مَن وَعَظَ أخاهُ سِرّاً فقَد زانَهُ ، ومَن وعَظَهُ عَلانِيَةً فقَد شانَهُ.[١١٧]

105. **Imām al-Ṣādiq (AS) said**, 'A man who observes bad behaviour in his brother without forbidding him from it – whilst he is able to – has indeed betrayed him.'[119]

١٠٥ . الإمامُ الصّادقُ ﷺ : مَن رأىٰ أخاهُ عَلىٰ أمرٍ يَكرَهُهُ فَلم يَـرُدَّه عَـنهُ وَهُـو يَـقدِرُ عـلَيهَ فـقد خانَهُ.[١١٨]

(See also: GUIDANCE 391; ADVISING 374)

(أنظر) عنوان ٣٩١ «الهداية»، ٣٧٤ «النصح».

40. Honouring and Glorifying One's Brothers

٤٠ـ إكرامُ الإخوانِ وإعظامُهُم

106. **The Prophet (SAWA) said**, 'Any person in my community who acts kindly towards his brother in faith, Allah will grant him the service of the servants of Paradise.'[120]

١٠٦ . رسولُ اللهِ ﷺ: ما في اُمّتي عبدٌ ألْطَفَ أخاهُ في اللهِ بشيءٍ مِن لُطْفٍ إلّا أخْدَمَهُ اللهُ مِن خَـدَمِ الجنّةِ.[١١٩]

107. **Imām al-Ṣādiq (AS) said**, 'A man who honours his believing brother when he comes to [visit] him is, by doing so, honouring Allah, Mighty and Exalted.'[121]

١٠٧ . الإمامُ الصّادقُ ﷺ : مَن أتاهُ أخوهُ المسلمُ فأكرَمَهُ فإنّما أكرَمَ اللهَ عزّ وجلّ.[١٢٠]

(See also: VENERATION 282)

(أنظر) عنوان ٢٨٢ «التعظيم».

41. Fulfilling Brothers' Needs

٤١ ـ قضاءُ حاجَةِ الإخوانِ

108. **Imām ʿAlī (AS) said**, 'Let none of you compel his brother to ask, if you already know about his need.'[122]

١٠٨ . الإمامُ عليٌّ ﷺ : لا يُكلِّفْ أحدُكُم أخـاهُ الطَّلَبَ إذا عَرَفَ حاجتَهُ.[١٢١]

109. **Imām al-Ṣādiq (AS) said**, 'Allah helps the believer as long as the believer helps his brother.'[123]

١٠٩ . الإمامُ الصّادقُ ﷺ : اللهُ في عَونِ المؤمنِ ما كانَ المؤمنُ في عَونِ أخيهِ.[١٢٢]

110. **Imām al-Ṣādiq (AS) said**, 'He who fulfils one need of his believing brother, Allah will fulfil one hundred thousand needs of his on the Day of Resurrection.'[124]

١١٠ . عنه ﷺ : مَن قَضىٰ لأخيهِ المؤمنِ حاجةً قـضىٰ اللهُ عـزّوجلّ له يـومَ القـيامةِ مـائةَ ألفِ حاجةٍ.[١٢٣]

111. **Imām al-Ṣādiq (AS) said**, 'It suffices for a man to depend on his brother to charge him with his need.'[125]

١١١ . عنه ﷺ : كَفىٰ بالمَرْءِ اعتِماداً علىٰ أخيهِ أنْ يُنْزِلَ بِهِ حاجتَهُ.[١٢٤]

(See also: THE NEED: section 585; ASKING (2): section 904; HAPPINESS: section 925, 928)

(أُنظر) الحاجة : باب ٥٨٥ ؛ السؤال(٢) : باب ٩٠٤ ؛ السرور : باب ٩٢٥، ٩٢٨.

42. The Etiquette of Brotherhood

٤٢ ـ أدَبُ الإخاءِ

112. **The Prophet (SAWA) said,** 'When one of you takes a brother, he must ask him his name, his father's name, his tribe and his address. This is part of true brotherhood; otherwise it is a foolish amity.'[126]

١١٢ . رسولُ اللهِ ﷺ : إذا آخىٰ أحَدُكُـم رَجُـلاً فَلْيَسألْهُ عَنِ اسمِهِ وَاسمِ أبيهِ وقَبيلَتِهِ ومَـنزِلِهِ ؛ فَإنّهُ مِن واجِبِ الحَقِّ وصافِي الإخاءِ ، وإلّا فَهِيَ مَوَدَّةٌ حَمْقاءُ.[١٢٥]

113. **The Prophet (SAWA) said**, 'Meet your brother with a joyful face.'[127]

١١٣ . عنه ﷺ : اِلْقَ أخاكَ بوجْهٍ مُنبسِطٍ.[١٢٦]

114. *Biḥār al-Anwār*, narrating from Anas: 'When the Prophet (SAWA) missed the company of any of his brothers for three days, he would ask about him. If he was absent, he would pray for him; and if he was in town, he would visit him; and if he was ill, he would go to see him.'[128]

١١٤ . بحار الأنوار عَن أنَس : كانَ رَسولُ اللهِ ﷺ إذا فَقَدَ الرَّجُلَ مِن إخْوانِهِ ثَلاثَةَ أيّامٍ سَألَ عَنهُ ، فإنْ كانَ غائِباً دَعا لَهُ ، وإنْ كـانَ شـاهِداً زارَهُ ، وإنْ كانَ مَريضاً عادَهُ.[١٢٧]

(See also: FRIEND: 1107)

(أُنظر) الصّديق : باب ١١٠٧.

6

GOOD MANNERS[129] الأدب

43. The Virtue of Good Manners ٤٣ـ فَضلُ الأدَبِ

115. **Imām ʿAlī (AS) said,** 'Good manners are the perfection of man.'[130]

١١٥ . الإمامُ عليٌّ ﷺ : الأدبُ كمالُ الرَّجُلِ .[١٢٨]

116. **Imām ʿAlī (AS) said,** 'O Believer! This knowledge and good manners are the value of your soul so strive to learn them, for however much your knowledge and good manners increase, so will your value and worth accordingly.'[131]

١١٦ . عنه ﷺ : يا مؤمنُ ، إنّ هذا العِلْمَ والأدبَ ثَمَنُ نفسِكَ ، فاجتَهِدْ في تَعلُّمِهِما ، فما يَزيدُ مِن عِلمِكَ وأدبِكَ يَزيدُ في ثَمَنِكَ وقَدْرِكَ .[١٢٩]

117. **Imām ʿAlī (AS) said,** 'Good manners are the best disposition.'[132]

١١٧ . عنه ﷺ : الأدبُ أحْسَنُ سَجِيّةٍ .[١٣٠]

118. **Imām ʿAlī (AS) said,** 'The best inheritance parents bequeath their progeny are good manners.'[133]

١١٨ . عنه ﷺ : خيرُ ما وَرّثَ الآباءُ الأبناءَ الأدبُ .[١٣١]

119. **Imām ʿAlī (AS) said,** 'People need good manners more than gold and silver.'[134]

١١٩ . عنه ﷺ : إنّ النّاسَ إلى صالحِ الأدبِ أحْوَجُ مِنهُم إلى الفِضّةِ والذَّهَبِ .[١٣٢]

120. **Imām ʿAlī (AS) said,** 'Good manners are the best lineage and the noblest means.'[135]

١٢٠ . عنه ﷺ : حُسنُ الأدبِ أفضلُ نَسَبٍ وأشرفُ سَبَبٍ .[١٣٣]

121. **Imām ʿAlī (AS) said,** 'Acquire good manners, for they are the best personal merit.'[136]

١٢١ . عنه ﷺ : عليكَ بالأدبِ فإنَّهُ زَيْنُ الحَسَبِ .[١٣٤]

122. **Imām ʿAlī (AS) said,** 'Good manners may substitute for [noble] lineage.'[137]

١٢٢ . عنه ﷺ : حُسنُ الأدب يَنُوبُ عنِ الحسَبِ .[١٣٥]

123. **Imām ʿAlī (AS) said,** 'There is no personal merit more useful than good manners.'[138]

١٢٣ . عنه ﷺ : لا حسَبَ أنفعُ مِن الأدبِ .[١٣٦]

124. **Imām ʿAlī (AS) said,** 'Spoiled is the noble descent of a man who has no good manners.'[139]

١٢٤ . عنه ﷺ : فَسَدَ حسَبُ مَن ليسَ لَه أدبٌ .[١٣٧]

125. **Imām ʿAlī (AS) said**, 'Good manners are your adornment.'[140]

١٢٥ . عنه ﷺ : زِينتُكُم الأدبُ.[١٣٨]

126. **Imām ʿAlī (AS) said**, 'There is no adornment like good manners.'[141]

١٢٦ . عنه ﷺ : لا زينةَ كالآدابِ.[١٣٩]

44. Good Manners and the Mind

٤٤ ـ الأدَبُ وَ العَقلُ

127. **The Prophet (SAWA) said**, 'Good manners are the beauty of the mind.'[142]

١٢٧ . رسولُ اللهِ ﷺ : حُسنُ الأدبِ زينةُ العقلِ.[١٤٠]

128. **Imām ʿAlī (AS) said**, 'Everything needs the mind, and the mind needs good manners.'[143]

١٢٨ . الإمامُ عليٌّ ﷺ : كلُّ شيءٍ يَحتاجُ إلى العقلِ، والعقلُ يَحتاجُ إلَى الأدبِ.[١٤١]

129. **Imām ʿAlī (AS) said**, 'Good manners in man resemble a tree whose root is the mind.'[144]

١٢٩ . عنه ﷺ : الأدبُ في الإنسانِ كشَجَرةٍ أصلُها العقلُ.[١٤٢]

130. **Imām ʿAlī (AS) said**, 'He whose good manners surpass his reason is like a shepherd among numerous sheep.'[145]

١٣٠ . عنه ﷺ : مَن زادَ أدبُهُ علىٰ عقلِهِ كانَ كالرّاعي بينَ غَنَمٍ كثيرةٍ.[١٤٣]

131. **Imām al-Ḥasan (AS) said**, 'A man devoid of reason cannot have good manners.'[146]

١٣١ . الإمامُ الحسنُ ﷺ : لا أدبَ لِمَن لا عَقلَ لَهُ.[١٤٤]

45. Disciplining The Self

٤٥ ـ تأديبُ النَّفسِ

132. **Imām ʿAlī (AS) said,** 'Take charge of the discipline of your selves and shift them away from their rough habits.'[147]

١٣٢ . الإمامُ عليٌّ ﷺ : تَولَّوْا مِن أنفسِكُم تأديبَها، واعدِلُوا بها عَن ضَراوةِ عاداتِها.[١٤٥]

133. **Imām ʿAlī (AS) said,** 'A man who teaches his own self and disciplines it deserves more reverence than a man who teaches others and disciplines them.'[148]

١٣٣ . عنه ﷺ : مُعلِّمُ نفسِهِ ومُؤدِّبُها أحَقُّ بالإجلالِ مِن معلّمِ النّاسِ ومُؤدِّبِهِم.[١٤٦]

46. That Which Brings About Good Manners

٤٦ ـ مَبادئُ الأدَبِ

134. It is narrated in *Tuḥaf al-'Uqūl*: Allah, most High, told Jesus[149] (AS), 'Refine your heart with piety'.'[150]

١٣٤ . تحف العقول : قالَ اللهُ تعالىٰ لعيسىٰ ﷺ : أدِّبْ قلبَكَ بالخَشيةِ.[١٤٧]

135. *Tanbīh al-Khawāṭir:* Jesus Christ (AS) was asked, 'Who gave you good manners?' He replied, 'No one disciplined me; when I saw the ugliness of ignorance I avoided it.'[151]

١٣٥ . تنبيه الخواطر ـ لَمّا قيلَ لعيسىٰ ﷺ : مَن أدّبَكَ؟ ـ : ما أدّبَـني أحَـدٌ ، رأيتُ قُـبْحَ الجـهلِ فجانَبْتُهُ.١٤٨

136. **Imām ʿAlī (AS) said**, 'Sit with scholars to increase your knowledge, to improve your manners and to purify your soul.'[152]

١٣٦ . الإمامُ عليٌّ ﷺ : جالِسِ العلماءَ يَزْدَدْ علمُكَ ويَحْسُنْ أدبُكَ وتَزكُ نَفْسُكَ.١٤٩

137. **Imām ʿAlī (AS) said**, 'When man's knowledge increases his manners improve and his fear of his Lord increases.'[153]

١٣٧ . عنه ﷺ : إذا زادَ عِلمُ الرَّجُـلِ زادَ أدبُـهُ ، وتضاعَفَتْ خَشيتُه لربِّهِ.١٥٠

47. The Outcomes of Good Manners

٤٧ ـ آثارُ الأدَبِ

138. **Imām ʿAlī (AS) said**, 'The means to purify one's moral virtues is good etiquette.'[154]

١٣٨ . الإمامُ عليٌّ ﷺ : سَبَبُ تـزكيةِ الأخـلاقِ حُسنُ الأدبِ.١٥١

139. **Imām ʿAlī (AS) said**, 'A man who is preoccupied with good manners has fewer vices.'[155]

١٣٩ . عنه ﷺ : مَن كَلِفَ بالأدبِ قَلَّتْ مَساوِيه.١٥٢

140. **Imām ʿAlī (AS) said**, 'The intellect is sharpened by good manners.'[156]

١٤٠ . عنه ﷺ : بالأدبِ تُشْحَذُ الفِطَنُ.١٥٣

(See also: EXPERIENCE: section 329)

(انظر) التجربة : باب ٣٢٩.

48. Explaining Good Manners

٤٨ ـ تفسيرُ الأدَبِ

141. **Imām ʿAlī (AS) said**, 'It suffices you in disciplining yourself to avoid all that you hold in contempt from others.'[157]

١٤١ . الإمامُ عليٌّ ﷺ : كَفاكَ أدباً لنفسِكَ اجتِنابُ ما تَكْرَهُهُ مِن غيرِكَ.١٥٤

142. **Imām ʿAlī (AS) said**, 'It suffices man in disciplining himself to not associate anyone with his Lord in his bounties and desires.'[158]

١٤٢ . عنه ﷺ : كَفىٰ بالعَبدِ أدَباً أن لا يُشرِكَ فى نِعَمِهِ وأرَبِهِ غيرَ ربِّهِ.١٥٥

143. **Imām al-Ṣādiq (AS) said**, 'My father (AS) refined my manners by three [statements].... He said to me: 'O son! A man who befriends a vile person cannot escape blame, and a man who does

١٤٣ . الإمامُ الصّادقُ ﷺ : أدَّبَني أبي ﷺ بثلاثٍ... قالَ لي : يا بُنيَّ مَن يَصْحَبْ صاحبَ السَّوءِ لا

not restrain his words will live in regret, and a man who enters suspicious places will become subject to accusations.'[159]

يَسْلمْ، ومَن لا يُقيّدْ ألفاظَهُ يَنْدَمْ، ومَـن يـدخُلْ مَداخِلَ السُّوءِ يُتَّهمْ.١٥٦

49. The Best Manners

٤٩ ـ أفضلُ الأدَبِ

144. **Imām ʿAlī (AS) said**, 'The best of manners is for man to stop at his limits and to not exceed his status.'[160]

١٤٤ . الإمامُ عليٌّ ﷺ : أفضلُ الأدبِ أن يَـقِفَ الإنسانُ عند حَدِّه ولا يَتعدّىٰ قَدْرَهُ.١٥٧

145. **Imām ʿAlī (AS) said**, 'The best of manners is that which prevents you from committing sins.'[161]

١٤٥ . عنه ﷺ : أحسَنُ الآدابِ مـا كَـفَّكَ عـنِ المَحارمِ.١٥٨

146. **Imām ʿAlī (AS) said**, 'Self-restraint in times of desire and fear is one of the best manners.'[162]

١٤٦ . عنه ﷺ : ضَبْطُ النّفسِ عندَ الرَّغَبِ والرَّهَبِ مِن أفضلِ الأدبِ.١٥٩

50. Encouraging the Teaching of Good Manners to the Family

٥٠ ـ الحَثُّ علىٰ تَأديبِ الأهلِ

147. **The Prophet (SAWA) said**, 'Honour your children and refine their manners and your sins will be forgiven.'[163]

١٤٧ . رسولُ اللهِ ﷺ : أكرِموا أولادَكُم وأحْسِنوا آدابَهُم يُغْفَرْ لكم.١٦٠

148. **Imām ʿAlī (AS)** said to Imām al-Ḥasan (AS), 'The heart of a youth resembles an empty land - it receives all that is thrown into it. This is why I have started to teach you good manners before your heart is hardened and your soul is preoccupied.'[164]

١٤٨ . الإمامُ عليٌّ ﷺ ـ للحسنِ ﷺ ـ: إنّما قَلْبُ الحَدَثِ كالأرضِ الخاليةِ ما أُلقِيَ فيها مِنْ شيءٍ قَبِلَتْهُ، فبادَرْتُكَ بالأدبِ قـبلَ أن يَـقْسُوَ قـلبُكَ ويَشتغِلَ لُبُّكَ.١٦١

149. **Imām al-Ṣādiq (AS) said**, 'When the verse: *"O you who have faith! Protect yourselves and your kin from the Fire…"*[165] was revealed, people asked, 'O Messenger of Allah (SAWA)! How do we protect ourselves and our kin?' He replied, 'Do good deeds and remind your kin about them, and discipline them to obey Allah.'[166]

١٤٩ . الإمامُ الصّادقُ ﷺ : لمّا نَزَلَتْ هذه الآيةُ: ﴿يا أيُّها الّذينَ آمَنوا قُوا أنفسَكُم وأهليكُم ناراً﴾ ١٦٢ قالَ النّاسُ : يا رسولَ اللهِ! كـيفَ نَـقِي أنـفسَنا وَأهلينا؟ قالَ : اعمَلُوا الخيرَ وذَكِّروا بهِ أهْلِيكُم فأدِّبُوهُم على طاعةِ اللهِ.١٦٣

150. **Imām al-Riḍā (AS) said,** 'Instruct the child to give charity with his own hand, be it a piece of bread or a handful of [food] or any other small thing, for everything – no matter how little it is – if done for the sake of Allah and with an honest intention is great.'[167]

١٥٠ . الإمامُ الرِّضا ﷺ : مُرِ الصَّبيَّ فلْيَتَصدَّقْ بيدِهِ بالكِسْرةِ والقَبْضةِ والشَّيءِ وإنْ قَلَّ ، فإنَّ كلَّ شيءٍ يُرادُ بِهِ اللهُ - وإنْ قَلَّ - بعدَ أنْ تَصدُقَ النِّيّةُ فيهِ عظيمٌ . ١٦٤

(See also: PARENT AND CHILD: section 1892; CHILDHOOD 234)

(أُنظر) الوالد والولد: باب ١٨٩٢؛ عنوان ٢٣٤ «الصغر».

51. How to Teach Good Manners

٥١ـ كَيفيَّةُ التَّأديبِ

151. **The Prophet (SAWA) said,** 'Teach your children to pray when they reach the age of seven….and make them sleep in separate beds.'[168]

١٥١ . رسولُ اللهِ ﷺ : علِّموا أولادَكُمُ الصَّلاةَ إذا بَلَغوا سَبْعاً ، ... وفَرِّقوا بينَهُم في المَضاجِعِ . ١٦٥

152. **The Prophet (SAWA) said,** 'A child is a master for seven years, a slave for the next seven years, and a minister for another seven years. By the age of twenty one, you must either approve of his manners or cut him loose, for [by then] you would have fulfilled your obligation toward Allah, most High.'[169]

١٥٢ . عنه ﷺ : الوَلَدُ سَيِّدٌ سبعَ سنينَ ، وعبدٌ سبعَ سنينَ ، ووزيرٌ سبعَ سنينَ ، فإنْ رَضِيتَ أخلاقَهُ لإحدىٰ وعشرينَ ، وإلّا فَاضْرِبْ علىٰ جَنبِهِ ، فقد أعْذَرتَ إلَى اللهِ تعالىٰ . ١٦٦

153. **Imām al-Ṣādiq (AS) said,** 'A boy should be trained to fast between the ages of fifteen and sixteen.'[170]

١٥٣ . الإمامُ الصّادقُ ﷺ : يُؤدَّبُ الصَّبيُّ علَى الصَّومِ ما بينَ خَمْسَ عَشْرةَ سَنةً إلى سِتَّ عَشرةَ سنةً . ١٦٧

(See also: PARENT AND CHILD: section 1893)

(أُنظر) الوالد والولد: باب ١٨٩٣.

52. Methods of Teaching Good Manners

٥٢ـ آدابُ التَّأدِيبِ

154. *Biḥār al-Anwār*: 'The Prophet (SAWA) prohibited disciplining in times of anger.'[171]

١٥٤ . بحار الأنوار : نَهَىٰ رسولُ اللهِ ﷺ عنِ الأدبِ عندَ الغَضَبِ . ١٦٨

155. **Imām 'Alī (AS) said,** 'Punish the wrong-doer by rewarding the good-doer.'[172]

١٥٥ . الإمامُ عليٌّ ﷺ : ازْجُرِ المُسيءَ بِثوابِ المُحسِنِ . ١٦٩

156. **Imām 'Alī (AS) said,** 'You may improve the doers of good by honouring them, and reform the wrongdoers by disciplining them.'[173]

١٥٦ . عنه ﷺ : استِصْلاحُ الأخيارِ بإكْرامِهِمْ ، والأشرارِ بتأديبِهِمْ . ١٧٠

157. **Imām ʿAlī (AS) said**, 'Reprimand your brother by being kind to him, and react to his wrongdoing by being generous to him.'[174]

١٥٧ . عنه عليه السلام : عاتِبْ أخاكَ بالإحسانِ إليـهِ ، وارْدُدْ شرَّهُ بالإنعامِ علَيهِ .[١٧١]

158. **Imām ʿAlī (AS) said**, 'Rehabilitate the wrongdoer by your good deed [towards him], and indicate towards good through your good words.'[175]

١٥٨ . عنه عليه السلام : أَصْلِحِ المُسيءَ بحُسْنِ فِعالِكَ ، ودُلَّ علَى الخيرِ بجَميلِ مَقالِكَ .[١٧٢]

159. A man said, 'I complained to Abū al-Ḥasan [al-Kāẓim] (AS) about a son of mine. He said, 'Do not beat him, but rather ignore him [i.e. depriving him of your company], but not for too long.'[176]

١٥٩ . الإمامُ الكاظمُ عليه السلام ـ عِندَ ما شَكىٰ لَهُ بَعضُهُم إبناً لَهُ ـ : لا تَضرِبْهُ ، واهْجُرْهُ ولا تُطِلْ .[١٧٣]

53. Disciplining Oneself by the Discipline of Allah

٥٣ ـ التَّأدُّبُ بآدابِ الله

160. **Imām ʿAlī (AS) said**, 'He who disciplines himself by following the etiquette of Allah, the Exalted, will have lasting prosperity.'[177]

١٦٠ . الإمامُ عليٌّ عليه السلام : مَنْ تأدَّبَ بآدابِ اللهِ عزّ وجلّ أدّاهُ إلَى الفلاحِ الدائمِ .[١٧٤]

161. **Imām ʿAlī (AS) said**, 'A man who is not reformed through the etiquette of Allah will not be rehabilitated through his self-discipline.'[178]

١٦١ . عنه عليه السلام : مَنْ لم يَصْلُحْ علىٰ أدبِ اللهِ لم يَصْلُحْ علىٰ أدبِ نفسِهِ .[١٧٥]

54. Allah's Discipline

٥٤ ـ تأديبُ الله

162. **Imām ʿAlī (AS) said**, 'Misfortune is a form of discipline for the wrongdoer.'[179]

١٦٢ . الإمامُ عليٌّ عليه السلام : إنّ البلاءَ للظّالمِ أدبٌ .[١٧٦]

163. **Imām Zayn al-ʿĀbidīn (AS) said**, 'O Lord! Discipline me not through Your punishment.'[180]

١٦٣ . الإمامُ زينُ العابدينَ عليه السلام : إلٰهي ، لا تُؤدِّبْني بِعُقوبَتِكَ .[١٧٧]

(See also: THE ORDEAL: section 267) (أنظر) البلاء : باب ٢٦٧

7

THE CALL FOR PRAYER (adhān)

الأذان

55. The Virtue of Call for Prayer

٥٥ـ فَضلُ الأذانِ

164. **The Prophet (SAWA) said,** 'Stand up, Bilāl, and relieve us with the [call for] prayer.'[181]

١٦٤. رسولُ اللهِ ﷺ : قُمْ يا بِلالُ فأرِحْنا بالصَّلاةِ.[١٧٨]

165. **The Prophet (SAWA) said,** 'Satan flees when he hears the call for prayer.'[182]

١٦٥. عنه ﷺ : إنّ الشَّيطانَ إذا سَمِعَ النِّداءَ بالصَّلاةِ هَرَبَ.[١٧٩]

166. **The Prophet (SAWA) said,** 'The inhabitants of Heaven hear nothing from the inhabitants of the earth except for the call for prayer.'[183]

١٦٦. عنه ﷺ : إنّ أهلَ السَّماءِ لا يَسْمَعُونَ مِن أهلِ الأرضِ شَيئاً إلّا الأذانَ.[١٨٠]

56. The Caller to Prayer

٥٦ـ المُؤَذِّنُ

167. **The Prophet (SAWA) said,** 'The caller to prayer is forgiven according to the distance of his voice and his eyes; every wet and dry thing testifies to his credibility; and he receives a reward for everyone that prays in response to his call.'[184]

١٦٧. رسولُ اللهِ ﷺ : يُغْفَرُ للمؤذِّنِ مَدُّ صَوتِهِ وبَصَرِهِ، ويُصدِّقُهُ كلُّ رطْبٍ ويابِسٍ، وله مِن كُلِّ مَن يُصلّي بأذانِه حَسَنةٌ.[١٨١]

168. **Imām ʿAlī (AS) said,** 'Let the most eloquent from among you call for the prayer, and the most knowledgeable from among you lead the prayer.'[185]

١٦٨. الإمامُ عليٌّ ؑ : لِيؤذِّنْ لَكُم أفصَحُكُمْ، وَلْيؤمَّكُمْ أفقهُكُم.[١٨٢]

57. Reciting the Call for Prayer in the Ears

٥٧ـ الأذانُ في الأُذُن

169. **The Prophet (SAWA) said,** 'O ʿAlī! When a son or daughter is born to you, recite the *adhān* in his [or her] right ear and the *iqāma* in the left ear; then Satan will never harm him [or her].'[186]

١٦٩. رسولُ اللهِ ﷺ : يا عليُّ، إذا وُلِدَ لكَ غُلامٌ أو جاريةٌ فأذِّنْ في أُذنِه اليُمنىٰ وأقِمْ في اليُسرىٰ؛ فإنّه لا يَضُرُّهُ الشّيطانُ أبداً.[١٨٣]

170. **Imām al-Ṣādiq (AS) said,** 'He whose manners deviate, recite the *adhān* in his ear.'[187]

١٧٠ . الإمامُ الصّادقُ ﷺ: مَن ساءَ خُلُقُه فأذِّنوا في أُذنِهِ.١٨٤

8

HARM

الإيذاء

58. Avoiding Harming People

٥٨ـ كَفُّ الأذي عَنِ النّاسِ

171. **The Prophet (SAWA) said,** 'Abstain from harming others for this is your charity towards yourself.'[188]

١٧١ . رسولُ اللهِ ﷺ: كُفَّ أذاكَ عنِ النّاسِ ؛ فإنّهُ صَدَقةٌ تَصَدَّقُ بها علىٰ نَفْسِكَ.١٨٥

172. **Imām al-Ṣādiq (AS) said,** 'A man who keeps his hand from harming people is keeping one hand from [harming] them, whilst they would keep many hands from [harming] him [as a result].'[189]

١٧٢ . الإمامُ الصّادقُ ﷺ: مَن كَفَّ يدَهُ عنِ النّاسِ فإنّما يكُفُّ عَنهُم يداً واحدةً ويَكُفّونَ عنه أيادِيَ كثيرةً.١٨٦

(See also: THE NEIGHBOUR: section 413)

(أنظر) الجار: باب ٤١٣.

59. Avoiding Harming Even the Ants

٥٩ـ كَفُّ الأذي حَتّى عَنِ الذَّرِّ

173. **Imām al-Ṣādiq (AS) said,** 'By Allah, the righteous have won indeed! Do you know who they are? They are the ones who do not even harm small ants.'[190]

١٧٣ . الإمامُ الصّادقُ ﷺ: فازَ واللهِ الأبرارُ، أتدري مَن هُم؟ هُمُ الّذينَ لا يُؤذُونَ الذَّرَّ.١٨٧

60. Harming a Believer

٦٠ـ إيذاءُ المُؤمِنِ

"Those who torment faithful men and women undeservedly, certainly bear the guilt of slander and flagrant sin."[191]

﴿وَالّذِينَ يُؤْذُونَ الْمُؤْمِنِينَ وَالْمُؤْمِنَاتِ بِغَيْرِ مَا اكْتَسَبُوا فَقَدِ احْتَمَلُوا بُهْتَاناً وَإِثْماً مُبِيناً﴾.١٨٨

174. **Imām al-Ṣādiq (AS) said,** 'Allah, Mighty and Exalted, said, 'Let a man who harms a

١٧٤ . الإمامُ الصّادقُ ﷺ: قالَ اللهُ عزّ وجلّ: لِيأذَنْ

believing servant of Mine expect a war waged by Me'.'[192]

بِحَربٍ منّي مَن آذىٰ عَبديَ المؤمنَ.١٨٩

175. **The Prophet (SAWA) said,** 'He who harms a believer is as if he has harmed me.'[193]

١٧٥ . رسولُ اللهِ ﷺ: مَن آذىٰ مُؤمناً فَقَدْ آذاني.١٩٠

176. **The Prophet (SAWA) said,** 'He who looks at a believer with a look that scares him, Allah, the most High, will scare him on the Day when no shade will avail except His Shade.'[194]

١٧٦ . عنه ﷺ: مَن نَظَرَ إلىٰ مؤمنٍ نظرةً يُخيفُهُ بها أخافَهُ اللهُ تعالىٰ يومَ لا ظِلَّ إلّا ظِلُّهُ.١٩١

177. **The Prophet (SAWA) said,** 'He who saddens a believer then bestows him the whole world will not have done enough to discharge his sin, and nor will he be rewarded for the gift.'[195]

١٧٧ . عنه ﷺ: مَن أحزَنَ مُؤمناً ثمّ أعطاهُ الدُّنيا لم يَكُنْ ذلكَ كفّارتَه، ولم يُؤجَرْ علَيهِ.١٩٢

9

THE PRISONER [OF WAR]

الأسيرُ

61. Surrendering Oneself to Captivity is Not Allowed

٦١ - لا يَجوزُ الاستِسلامُ لِلأسرِ

178. **Imām ʿAlī (AS) said,** 'He who allows himself to be imprisoned without sustaining severe wounds should not be ransomed by the treasury, rather his family may choose to pay his ransom from his own money.'[196]

١٧٨ . الإمامُ عليٌّ ؈: مَن استُؤسِرَ مِن غيرِ جِراحةٍ مُثقِلةٍ فلا يُفدىٰ مِن بيتِ المالِ، ولكنْ يُفدىٰ مِن مالِهِ إن أحبَّ أهلُهُ.١٩٣

179. **Imām al-Ṣādiq (AS) said,** 'When the Prophet (SAWA) sent ʿAlī (AS) to propagate the Qur'anic chapter al-Barā'a [chapter 9], he sent a few men with him and told them, 'A man who surrenders himself without suffering severe wounds does not belong among us.'[197]

١٧٩ . الإمامُ الصّادقُ ؈: لمّا بَعثَ رسولُ اللهِ ﷺ بِبراءةٍ مَعَ عليٍّ ؈ بَعثَ مَعَهُ أناساً، وقالَ رسولُ اللهِ ﷺ: مَن اسْتُؤسِرَ مِنْ غيرِ جِراحةٍ مُثْقِلةٍ فليسَ مِنّا.١٩٤

62. Kindness to the Prisoner of War

٦٢ـ الإحسانُ إلَى الأسيرِ

"They give food, for the love of Him, to the needy, the orphan and the prisoner"[198]

﴿وَيُطْعِمُونَ الطَّعَامَ عَلىٰ حُبِّهِ مِسْكِيناً وَيَتِيماً وَأَسِيراً﴾ .١٩٥

"O Prophet! Say to the captives who are in your hands, 'If Allah finds any good in your hearts, He will give you [something which is] better than what has been taken away from you, and He will forgive you, and Allah is all-forgiving, all-merciful."[199]

﴿يا أَيُّها النَّبِيُّ قُلْ لِمَنْ فِي أَيْدِيكُمْ مِنَ الْأَسْرىٰ إِنْ يَعْلَمِ اللهُ فِي قُلُوبِكُمْ خَيْراً يُؤْتِكُمْ خَيْراً مِمَّا أُخِذَ مِنْكُمْ وَيَغْفِرْ لَكُمْ وَاللهُ غَفُورٌ رَحِيمٌ﴾ .١٩٦

180. **Imām 'Alī (AS) said,** 'Feeding the prisoner and treating him well is an obligatory duty, even if you are to execute him the next day.'[200]

١٨٠ . الإمامُ عليٌّ (ع) : إطعامُ الأسيرِ والإحسانُ إليهِ حقٌّ واجبٌ ، وإنْ قَتَلْتَه مِن الغدِ .١٩٧

181. **Imām 'Alī (AS)** said to his sons, after Ibn Muljam struck him, 'Imprison this captive and feed him, quench his thirst, and make his captivity endurable.'[201]

١٨١ . عنه (ع) ـ لِابنَيهِ (ع) لمّا ضَرَبه ابنُ مُلْجَم ـ : احبِسُوا هـذا الأسيرَ ، وأطعِمُوهُ ، واسقُوهُ ، وأحْسِنوا إسارَهُ .١٩٨

182. **Imām al-Ṣādiq (AS) said,** 'Feeding the prisoner is the obligatory duty of the person who captured him, even if he intends to execute him the next day; he must be fed, given water, sheltered, and treated well – whether he is a disbeliever or not.'[202]

١٨٢ . الإمامُ الصّادقُ (ع) : إطعامُ الأسيرِ حقٌّ علىٰ مَن أسَرَهُ وإن كان يُرادُ مِن الغدِ قَتْلُهُ ، فإنّه يَنبغي أن يُطعَمَ ويُسْقىٰ ويُظَلَّ ويُرفَقَ بِهِ ، كافراً كان أو غَيْرَهُ .١٩٩

183. **Imām al-Ṣādiq (AS) said,** 'Imām 'Alī (AS) used to feed those who were sentenced to life imprisonment using the money of the Muslim treasury.'[203]

١٨٣ . عنه (ع) : إنّ علياً (ع) كان يُطعِمُ مَن خُلِّدَ في السِّجْنِ مِن بيتِ مالِ المسلمينَ .٢٠٠

10

FOOD

الأكل

63. Encouraging Little [Consumption of] Food

٦٣ـ الحَثُّ علىٰ قِلَّةِ الأكلِ

184. **The Prophet (SAWA) said,** 'A man whose [consumption of] food is little has a healthy stomach

١٨٤ . رسولُ اللهِ (ص) : مَنْ قَلَّ طُعْمُهُ صَحَّ بَطْنُهُ وَصَفَا قَلْبُهُ ، وَمَنْ كَثُرَ طُعْمُهُ سَقُمَ بَطْنُهُ

and a pure heart, and a man whose food is plenty has a sick stomach and a hard heart.'[204]

وقَسا قَلْبُهُ.٢٠١

185. **Imām ʿAlī (AS) said,** 'Eating little is a sign of self-restraint, and eating a lot is a sign of wastefulness.'[205]

١٨٥ . الإمامُ عليٌّ ﷺ : قِلَّةُ الأكْلِ مِنَ العَفافِ ، وكَثْرَتُهُ مِنَ الإسْرافِ.٢٠٢

64. Warning against Eating Excessively

٦٤ـ التَّحذيرُ عَن كَثرَةِ الأكلِ

186. **The Prophet (SAWA) said,** 'Man cannot fill a container worse than his stomach.'[206]

١٨٦ . رسولُ اللهِ ﷺ : ما مَلأ آدَميٌّ وِعاءً شَرّاً مِنْ بَطْنِهِ.٢٠٣

187. **The Prophet (SAWA) said,** 'A man who fills his stomach will not enter the dominion of the heavens and the earth.'[207]

١٨٧ . عنه ﷺ : لا يَدْخُلُ مَلَكُوتَ السَّماواتِ والأرْضِ مَنْ مَلأَ بَطْنَهُ.٢٠٤

188. **The Prophet (SAWA) said,** 'Be warned against excessive food, for it poisons the heart with hardness, slows the limbs in performing acts of obedience, and blocks the souls from hearing counsel.'[208]

١٨٨ . عنه ﷺ : إيّاكُمْ وفُضُولَ المَطْعَمِ ؛ فإنَّهُ يَسِمُ القَلْبَ بالقَسوةِ ، ويُبْطِئُ بالجَوارِحِ عَنِ الطّاعَةِ، ويُصِمُّ الهِمَمَ عَنْ سَماعِ المَوْعِظَةِ.٢٠٥

189. **Imām ʿAlī (AS) said,** 'A man who eats excessively, his health declines and his burden becomes heavier than he can endure.'[209]

١٨٩ . الإمامُ عليٌّ ﷺ : مَنْ كَثُرَ أكْلُهُ قَلَّتْ صِحَّتُهُ، وثَقُلَتْ عَلى نَفْسِهِ مُؤنَتُهُ.٢٠٦

190. **Imām al-Ṣādiq (AS) said,** 'Nothing is more harmful to the heart of a believer than excess food. It leaves him with two traits: hard-heartedness and burning lust.'[210]

١٩٠ . مصباح الشريعة ـ فيما نسبه إلى الإمامِ الصّادقِ ﷺ ـ : لَيسَ شَيْءٌ أضَرَّ على قلب المُؤمِنِ مِنْ كَثْرَةِ الأكْلِ ، وَهِيَ مُورِثَةٌ لِشَيْئَيْنِ: قَسْوَةِ القَلْبِ، وَهَيَجانِ الشَّهْوَةِ.٢٠٧

65. Among the Vices of Gluttony

٦٥ـ مِن مَساوِئِ البِطنَةِ

191. **Imām ʿAlī (AS) said,** 'Astuteness and gluttony cannot coexist.'[211]

١٩١ . الإمامُ عليٌّ ﷺ : لا تَجْتَمِعُ الفِطْنَةُ والبِطْنَةُ.٢٠٨

192. **Imām ʿAlī (AS) said,** 'When the stomach is filled with [even] permissible food, the heart becomes blind to goodness.'[212]

١٩٢ . عنه ﷺ : إذا مُلِئَ البَطْنُ مِنَ المُباحِ عَمِيَ القَلْبُ عَنِ الصَّلاحِ.٢٠٩

193. **Imām ʿAlī (AS) said,** 'Overeating spoils piety.'[213]

١٩٣ . عنه عليه السلام : الشِّبَعُ يُفسِدُ الوَرَعَ .٢١٠

194. **Imām ʿAlī (AS) said,** 'Overeating is the greatest aid to acts of disobedience.'[214]

١٩٤ . عنه عليه السلام : نِعْمَ عَوْنُ المَعاصِي الشِّبَعُ .٢١١

66. Hunger

٦٦ ـ الجُوعِ

195. **The Prophet (SAWA) said,** 'Applaud a man who abstains from food, sleeps hungry, and has patience. These are the ones who will be satiated on the Day of Judgment.'[215]

١٩٥ . رسولُ اللهِ ﷺ : طُوبىٰ لِمَنْ طَوَىٰ وَجَاعَ وَصَبَرَ، أُولٰئكَ الّذِينَ يَشْبَعُونَ يَوْمَ القِيامَةِ .٢١٢

196. In the tradition of al-Miʿrāj (The Prophet's Ascension to the heavens), the Prophet (SAWA) said, 'O Allah! What is the outcome of hunger?' He said, 'Wisdom, protection of the heart, drawing closer to Me, lasting sorrow, less burden on the people, telling the truth, and lack of concern whether one lives in wealth or poverty.'[216]

١٩٦ . في حديثِ المعراج : قال [رسولُ الله ﷺ]: يا رَبِّ، ما مِيراثُ الجُوعِ ؟ قال : الحِكْمَةُ ، وَحِفْظُ القَلْبِ ، والتَّقَرُّبُ إلَيّ ، والحُزْنُ الدّائمُ ، وَخِفَّةُ المَؤونَةِ بَيْنَ النَّاسِ ، وَقَوْلُ الحَقِّ ، وَلا يُبالِي عَاشَ بِيُسْرٍ أَوْ بِعُسْرٍ .٢١٣

197. **Imām ʿAlī (AS) said,** 'How good a helper hunger is at taming the self and breaking its habit.'[217]

١٩٧ . الإمامُ عليٌّ عليه السلام : نِعْمَ العَوْنُ عَلىٰ أَسْرِ النَّفْسِ وَكَسْرِ عادَتِها التَّجَوُّعُ .٢١٤

198. **Imām ʿAlī (AS) said,** 'Hunger and disease cannot coexist.'[218]

١٩٨ . عنه عليه السلام : لَا يَجْتَمِعُ الجُوعُ وَالمَرَضُ .٢١٥

199. **Imām al-Hādī (AS) said,** 'Lack of sleep sweetens sleeping and hunger increases the tastiness of food.'[219]

١٩٩ . الإمامُ الهاديُّ عليه السلام : السَّهَرُ أَلَذُّ لِلمَنَامِ ، والجُوعُ يَزِيدُ فِي طِيبِ الطَّعَامِ .٢١٦

67. Balance of Eating

٦٧ ـ الميزانُ فِي الأكلِ

200. **The Prophet (SAWA) said,** 'Eat when you desire and stop while you still desire.'[220]

٢٠٠ . رسولُ اللهِ ﷺ : كُلْ وَأَنتَ تَشْتَهِي ، وَأَمْسِكْ وَأَنتَ تَشْتَهِي .٢١٧

201. **Imām al-Riḍā (AS) said,** 'A man who wants to be healthy and have a light body must decrease his dinner.'[221]

٢٠١ . الإمامُ الرِّضا عليه السلام : مَنْ أَرادَ أَنْ يَكُونَ صَالِحاً خَفِيفَ الجِسْمِ (وَاللَّحْمِ) فَلْيُقَلِّلْ مِنْ عَشائِه بِاللَّيْلِ .٢١٨

68. Table Manners

٦٨ـ آدابُ الأكلِ

202. **The Prophet (SAWA) said,** 'A man who is eating and is being watched by another, to whom he does not offer to share his food will be afflicted with an incurable disease.'[222]

٢٠٢ . رسولُ اللهِ ﷺ : مَنْ أكَلَ وَذُو عَيْنَيْنِ يَنْظُرُ إلَيْهِ وَلَمْ يُواسِهِ، ابْتُلِيَ بِدَاءٍ لَا دَوَاءَ لَهُ.[٢١٩]

203. **The Prophet (SAWA) said,** 'The believer eats according to the desire of his family, while the hypocrite makes his family eat according to his own desires.'[223]

٢٠٣ . عنه ﷺ : المُؤْمِنُ يَأْكُلُ بشَهْوَةِ أهْلِهِ ، والمُنَافِقُ يَأْكُلُ أهْلُهُ بِشَهْوَتِهِ.[٢٢٠]

204. **Imām ʿAlī (AS) said,** 'Whoever mentions the name of Allah at the beginning of [eating his] food or drink and thanks Allah at the end will never be asked about the favour of this food.'[224]

٢٠٤ . الإمامُ عليٌّ عليه السلام : مَنْ ذَكَرَ اسْمَ اللهِ عِنْدَ طَعَامٍ أوْ شَرَابٍ فِي أوّلِهِ ، وَحَمِدَ اللهَ فِي آخِرِهِ لَمْ يُسْأَلْ عَنْ نَعِيمِ ذٰلِكَ الطَّعَامِ أبَداً.[٢٢١]

205. **Imām ʿAlī (AS) said,** 'Start with salt before you eat. If people knew what [benefits] salt has, they would prefer it to tested medicine.'[225]

٢٠٥ . عنه عليه السلام : ابْدَؤوا بِالمِلْحِ فِي أوَّلِ طَعَامِكُمْ ، فَلَوْ يَعْلَمُ النَّاسُ مَا فِي المِلْحِ لاخْتَارُوهُ عَلَى الدِّرْيَاقِ المُجَرَّبِ.[٢٢٢]

206. **Imām ʿAlī (AS) said,** 'Set hot food aside until it cools down, for when the Prophet (SAWA) was given hot food, he said, 'Set it aside until it cools down, for Allah, Mighty and Exalted, would not feed us fire when blessings lie with that which is cool.'[226]

٢٠٦ . عنه عليه السلام : أقِرُّوا الحَارَّ حَتّىٰ يَبْرَدَ، فإنَّ رَسُولَ اللهِ ﷺ قُرِّبَ إلَيْهِ طَعَامٌ حَارٌّ فَقَالَ : أقِرُّوهُ حَتَّىٰ يَبْرَدَ ، مَا كَانَ اللهُ عزّ وجلّ لِيُطْعِمَنَا النَّارَ ، وَالبَرَكَةُ فِي البَارِدِ.[٢٢٣]

207. **Imām al-Ḥasan (AS) said,** 'There are twelve things that every Muslim should know about the table [manners]; four are mandatory, four are recommended, and four are general manners. The mandatory are: knowledge [of the food], to be content with it, mentioning the name of Allah [before it], and offering thanks to Him [afterwards]. The recommended acts are: ablution before eating, sitting on one's left side, eating with three fingers. And the general manners are: eating from the closest spot to you, taking small bites, chewing well, and looking less at people's faces [while eating].'[227]

٢٠٧ . الإمامُ الحسنُ عليه السلام : فِي المَائدةِ اثْنَتَا عَشرَةَ خَصْلَةً يَجِبُ عَلىٰ كُلِّ مُسْلِمٍ أنْ يَعْرِفَهَا : أرْبَعٌ مِنها فَرْضٌ ، وَ أرْبَعٌ سُنَّةٌ، وأرْبَعٌ تأدِيبٌ.

فَأمَّا الفَرْضُ : فَالمَعْرِفَةُ ، وَالرِّضَا ، وَالتَّسْمِيَةُ ، وَالشُّكْرُ.

وَأمَّا السُّنَّةُ : فَالوُضُوءُ قَبْلَ الطَّعَامِ ، والجُلُوسُ عَلَى الجَانِبِ الأيْسَرِ ، والأكْلُ بِثَلاثِ أصَابِعَ ، وَلَعْقُ الأصَابِعِ.

وَأمَّا التَّأدِيبُ : فَالأكْلُ مِمَّا يَلِيكَ ، وَتَصْغِيرُ اللُّقْمَةِ، وَتَجْوِيدُ المَضْغِ ، وَقِلّةُ النّظَرِ فِي وُجُوهِ النّاسِ.[٢٢٤]

208. **Imām al-Ṣādiq (AS) said,** 'He who washes his hands before and after eating will be blessed at the beginning and at the end of his food. As long as he lives, he will be in comfort, and he will be cured of the ills of his body.'[228]

٢٠٨. الإمامُ الصّادقُ عليه السلام: مَنْ غَسَلَ يَدَهُ قَبْلَ الطَّعامِ وَبَعْدَهُ بُورِكَ لَهُ فِي أَوَّلِهِ وَآخِرِهِ، وَعَاشَ مَاعَاشَ فِي سَعَةٍ، وَعُوفِيَ مِنْ بَلْوىً فِي جَسَدِهِ.[٢٢٥]

209. **Imām al-Ṣādiq (AS) narrated**, on the authority of his fathers about the tradition entailing certain prohibitions of the Prophet (SAWA), 'He prohibited blowing on food or drink.'[229]

٢٠٩. عنه عليه السلام ـ عن آبائِهِ عليهم السلام في حديثِ مَناهي النّبيِّ صلى الله عليه وآله ـ: ونَهَىٰ أنْ يُنْفَخَ فِي طَعَامٍ أو شَرَابٍ.[٢٢٦]

210. **Imām al-Ṣādiq (AS) said,** 'Do not leave your plates uncovered for Satan[230] spits on uncovered plates and takes from them what he wants.'[231]

٢١٠. عنه عليه السلام: لَا تَدَعُوا آنِيَتَكُمْ بِغَيْرِ غِطَاءٍ؛ فإنَّ الشَّيْطَانَ إذَا لَمْ تُغَطَّ الآنِيَةُ بَزَقَ فِيها، وَأَخَذَ مِمَّا فِيهَا مَا شَاءَ.[٢٢٧]

211. **Imām al-Kāẓim (AS),** when he was asked who the contemptible person was, replied, 'The one who eats in the marketplaces.'[232]

٢١١. الإمامُ الكاظمُ عليه السلام ـ لَمّا سُئلَ عنِ السَّفْلَةِ ـ: الّذِي يَأْكُلُ فِي الأَسْوَاقِ.[٢٢٨]

212. It is narrated in *al-Ikhtiṣāṣ*: 'Prolong your seating at the dinner table [observe proper eating manners], for these are times that will not be accounted for as part of your lives.'[233]

٢١٢. الاختصاص: رُويَ: أَطِيلُوا الجُلُوسَ عَلىٰ المَوائِدِ؛ فَإنَّها أوْقَاتٌ لَا تُحْسَبُ مِنْ أعْمارِكُمْ.[٢٢٩]

11

AMITY

الأُلفة

69. Encouraging Amity

٦٩ ـ الحَثُّ عَلى الأُلفَةِ

"It is He who strengthened you with His help and with the means of the faithful. And united their hearts. Had you spent all that is in the earth, you could not have united their hearts, but Allah united them together. Indeed He is all-mighty, all-wise."[234]

﴿هُوَ الَّذِي أَيَّدَكَ بِنَصْرِهِ وَبِالْمُؤْمِنِينَ * وَأَلَّفَ بَيْنَ قُلُوبِهِمْ لَوْ أَنْفَقْتَ ما فِي الْأَرْضِ جَمِيعاً ما أَلَّفْتَ بَيْنَ قُلُوبِهِمْ وَلٰكِنَّ اللهَ أَلَّفَ بَيْنَهُمْ إِنَّهُ عَزِيزٌ حَكِيمٌ﴾.[٢٣٠]

"And remember Allah's blessing upon you when you were enemies, then He brought your hearts together, so you became brothers with His blessing."[235]

﴿وَاذْكُرُوا نِعْمَةَ اللهِ عَلَيْكُمْ إِذْ كُنْتُمْ أَعْداءً فَأَلَّفَ بَيْنَ قُلُوبِكُمْ فَأَصْبَحْتُمْ بِنِعْمَتِهِ إِخْوَاناً﴾.[٢٣١]

213. **Imām ʿAlī (AS) said,** 'Moving mountains is easier than bringing hostile hearts together.'[236]

٢١٣ . الإمامُ عليٌّ ﷺ : إزَالَةُ الرَّوَاسِي أسْهَلُ مِنْ تَأْلِيفِ القُلُوبِ المُتَنَافِرَةِ.٢٣٢

214. **Imām al-Ṣādiq (AS) said,** 'The speed of amity between the hearts of pious people when they meet – even if they do not show their mutual love on their tongues – is like the speed of the rain water when it mixes with the water of rivers. And the distance between the hearts of the wicked when they meet – even if they make a show of love on their tongues – is like the distance between beasts that cannot have mutual affection no matter how long they eat from the same trough.'[237]

٢١٤ . الإمامُ الصّادقُ ﷺ : إنَّ سُرْعةَ ائْتِلَافِ قُلُوبِ الأبْرَارِ إذا الْتَقَوا ـ وَإنْ لَمْ يُظْهِرُوا التَّوَدُّدَ بأَلْسِنَتِهِمْ ـ كَسُرْعَةِ اخْتِلَاطِ ماءِ السَّمَاءِ بِماءِ الأنْهَارِ . وإنَّ بُعْدَ ائْتِلَافِ قُلُوبِ الفُجَّارِ إذَا الْتَقَوا ـ وَإنْ أظْهَرُوا التَّوَدُّدَ بأَلْسِنَتِهِمْ ـ كَبُعْدِ البَهَائِمِ مِنَ التَّعَاطُفِ وَإنْ طَالَ اعْتِلَافُهَا عَلىٰ مِذْوَدٍ واحِدٍ.٢٣٣

70. There is No Good in Someone who Does Not Like Others, Nor is he Liked by Them

٧٠ ـ لا خَيْرَ فِيمَنْ لا يأْلَفُ ولا يُؤْلَفُ

215. **The Prophet (SAWA) said,** 'The best among you are the ones who have the best moral traits, those who like others and are well-liked.'[238]

٢١٥ . رسولُ اللهِ ﷺ : خِيَارُكُمْ أحاسِنُكُمْ أخْلَاقاً، الَّذِينَ يَأْلَفُونَ وَيُؤْلَفُونَ.٢٣٤

216. **The Prophet (SAWA) said,** 'The best of the believers is the one who is loved by the believers, and there is no good to be found in someone who does not like others nor is he liked by them.'[239]

٢١٦ . عنه ﷺ : خَيْرُ المُؤْمِنِينَ مَنْ كَانَ مَأْلَفَةً لِلْمُؤْمِنِينَ ، وَلَا خَيْرَ فِيمَنْ لَا يُؤْلَفُ وَلَا يَأْلَفُ.٢٣٥

12

ALLAH

الله

71. The Meaning of Allah

٧١ ـ معنى «اللهُ»

217. **Imām ʿAlī (AS) said,** 'Allah means the worshipped one, by Whom people are bewildered, and to Whom they are submissive. Allah is the One veiled from the grasp of sights, and the One hidden from imagination and contemplation.'[240]

٢١٧ . الإمامُ عليٌّ ﷺ : اللهُ مَعْناهُ المَعْبُودُ الّذِي يَأْلَهُ فِيهِ الْخَلْقُ وَيُؤْلَهُ إلَيْهِ ، وَاللهُ هُوَ المَسْتُورُ عَنْ دَرْكِ الأبْصَارِ ، المَحْجُوبُ عَنِ الأوْهَامِ وَالخَطَرَاتِ.٢٣٦

218. **Imām ʿAlī (AS),** on the exposition of the word 'Allah, said: 'He is One Whom every creature invokes at the time of need, difficulty, [when] losing hope in everything else and having no means but Him.'[241]

٢١٨ . عنه ﷺ ـ في تفسير قوله: «الله» ـ: هُوَ الّذي يَتَألَّهُ إليهِ عِندَ الحَوائِجِ وَ الشَّدائِدِ كُلُّ مَخلوقٍ عِندَ انقِطاعِ الرَّجاءِ مِن جَميعِ مَن هُوَ دونَهُ، وتَقَطُّعِ الأسبابِ مِن كُلِّ مَن سِواهُ.٢٣٧

219. **Imām al-Bāqir (AS) said,** 'Allah means the One who is worshipped and whom people are too bewildered to comprehend His essence and fathom His identity.'[242]

٢١٩ . الإمامُ الباقرُ ﷺ: اللهُ مَعْنَاهُ المَعْبُودُ الّذِي أَلِهَ الخَلْقُ عَنْ دَرْكِ مَاهِيَّتِهِ والإحَاطَةِ بِكَيْفِيَّتِهِ.٢٣٨

220. **Imām al-Kāẓim (AS)** on the exposition of the word Allah said, 'He who dominates everything, great and small.'[243]

٢٢٠ . الإمامُ الكاظمُ ﷺ ـ في مَعنَى «الله» ـ: اِستَولىٰ عَلىٰ ما دَقَّ وجَلَّ.٢٣٩

221. **Imām al-Riḍā (AS) said,** 'In the name of Allah, Mighty and Exalted, is the attestation to His Lordship and His Oneness.'[244]

٢٢١ . الإمامُ الرِّضا ﷺ: إنَّ في تَسمِيَةِ اللهِ عزّ وجلّ الإقرارُ بِرُبوبِيَّتِهِ وتَوحيدِهِ.٢٤٠

(See also: THE CREATOR 132; THE NAMES OF ALLAH 202)

(أنظر) عنوان ١٣٢ «الخالق»؛ عنوان ٢٠٢ «اسماء الله».

13

GOVERNMENT

الإِمارَةُ

72. The Necessity of Government

٧٢ـضَرورَةُ الإمارَةِ

222. **Imām ʿAlī (AS)** said regarding the arbitration, 'These [people] say, 'There is no need for government!' Indeed there has to be a ruler under whose rule the believer toils and the wicked seeks to make merry.'[245]

٢٢٢ . الإمامُ عليٌّ ﷺ ـ في قَضيّةِ التَّحْكِيم ـ: إنَّ هٰؤلاءِ يَقُولُونَ: لَا إمْرَةَ! وَلَابُدَّ مِنْ أَمِيرٍ يَعْمَلُ فِي إمْرَتِهِ المُؤْمِنُ، وَيَسْتَمْتِعُ الفَاجِرُ.٢٤١

223. **Imām ʿAlī (AS) said,** 'No one can straighten people other than a ruler – be he pious or wicked.'[246]

٢٢٣ . عنه ﷺ: لَايُصْلِحُ النَّاسَ إلَّا أمِيرٌ؛ بَرٌّ أوْ فَاجِرٌ.٢٤٢

224. **Imām ʿAlī (AS) said,** 'Muʿāwiya will prevail over you.' They asked, 'Why do you fight [him] then?' He replied, 'People must have a ruler – be he pious or wicked.'[247]

٢٢٤ . عنه ﷺ: إنَّ مُعاوِيَةَ سَيَظْهَرُ عَلَيْكُمْ، قَالُوا: فَلِمَ نُقَاتِلُ إذاً؟ قَالَ: لَابُدَّ لِلنّاسِ مِنْ أمِيرٍ بَرٍّ أوْ فَاجِرٍ.٢٤٣

225. **Imām ʿAlī (AS)** said regarding the Ḥarūriyya and they say that there is no rule other than Allah's, 'The rule is Allah's, and there are also rulers on earth, but they [retort and] say, 'There is no government' – 'There must be a government for the people under which the believer toils and the wicked and the unbeliever seek to make merry, and in which Allah decrees the final outcome.'[248]

٢٢٥ . عنه ﷺ ـ فِي الحَرُورِيَّةِ وَهُمْ يقولون : لا حُكْمَ إلّا للهِ ـ: الحُكْمُ للهِ ، وَفِي الأرْضِ حُكَّامٌ ، وَلٰكِنَّهُمْ يَقُولُونَ : لَا إمَارَةَ ، وَلَابُدَّ لِلنَّاسِ مِنْ إمَارَةٍ؛ يَعْمَلُ فِيْها المُؤْمِنُ ، ويَسْتَمْتِعُ فِيها الفَاجِرُ وَالكَافِرُ ، وَيُبَلِّغُ اللهُ فِيهَا الأجَلَ .[٢٤٤]

226. **Imām ʿAlī (AS) said,** 'The people have to have a ruler over them, be he pious or wicked, under whose rule the believer toils and the wicked seeks to make merry, and in which Allah decrees the final outcome, and under which the booty is collected, the enemy is fought, the roads are made safe, and the weak is protected from the powerful, until the pious rests and the wicked is cast aside.'[249]

٢٢٦ . عنه ﷺ : لَابُدّ لِلنَّاسِ مِنْ أمِيرٍ بَرٍّ أوْ فاجِرٍ ، يَعْمَلُ فِي إمْرَتِهِ المُؤْمِنُ وَيَسْتَمْتِعُ فِيهَا الكَافِرُ ، وَيُبَلِّغُ اللهُ فِيهَا الأجَلَ ، ويُجْمَعُ بِهِ الفَيْءُ ، وَيُقَاتَلُ بِهِ العَدُوُّ ، وَتَأمَنُ بِهِ السُّبُلُ ، وَيُؤْخَذُ بِهِ لِلضّعِيفِ مِنَ القَوِيِّ ، حَتّى يَسْتَرِيحَ بَرٌّ وَيُسْتَرَاحَ مِنْ فَاجِرٍ .[٢٤٥]

227. **Imām ʿAlī (AS) said,** 'A wild lion is better than an oppressive ruler, while an oppressive ruler is better than lasting schisms.'[250]

٢٢٧ . عنه ﷺ : أسَدٌ حَطُومٌ خَيْرٌ مِنْ سُلْطَانٍ ظَلُومٍ ، وَسُلْطانٌ ظَلُومٌ خَيرٌ مِنْ فِتَنٍ تَدُومُ .[٢٤٦]

228. **Abū al-Bakhtarī said,** 'A man entered the mosque and said, 'There is no rule save Allah's.' Then another man said, 'There is no rule save Allah's.' So [Imām] ʿAlī said, 'There is no rule save Allah's. *"Allah's promise is indeed true. And do not let yourself be upset by those who have no conviction."*[251] You do not know what these [men] are saying; they are saying, 'There [should] be no government'. O People! You are not set straight without a ruler, be he pious or wicked.' They replied, 'We understand about the pious, but what about the wicked?' He said, '[Under whom] the believer toils and the wicked thrives, and Allah decrees the final outcome, your roads become safe, your markets operate, your booty is collected, your enemy is fought, and your weak is protected from the powerful from among you.'[252]

٢٢٨ . كنز العمّال عن أبي البختريّ : دَخَل رَجُلٌ المَسْجِدَ فقَالَ : لَا حُكْمَ إلّا للهِ ، ثُمَّ قَالَ آخَرُ : لَا حُكْمَ إلّا للهِ ، فَقَالَ عَلِيٌّ ﷺ : لَا حُكْمَ إلّا للهِ ﴿إنَّ وَعْدَ اللهِ حَقٌّ وَلَا يَسْتَخِفَنَّكَ الّذِينَ لَا يُوقِنُونَ﴾[٢٤٧] ، فَمَا تَدْرُونَ مَا يَقُولُ هٰؤلَاءِ ، يَقُولُونَ : لَا إمَارَةَ . أيُّهَا النَّاسُ! إنَّهُ لَا يُصْلِحُكُمْ إلَّا أمِيرٌ؛ بَرٌّ أوْ فَاجِرٌ .
قَالُوا : هٰذَا البَرُّ فَقَدْ عَرَفْنَاهُ ، فَمَا بَالُ الفَاجِرِ ؟
فَقَالَ : يَعْمَلُ المُؤْمِنُ ، وَيُمْلَأُ لِلْفَاجِرِ ، ويُبَلِّغُ اللهُ الأجَلَ ، وَتَأمَنُ سُبُلُكُمْ ، وَتَقُومُ أسْوَاقُكُمْ ، وَيُجْبىٰ فَيْئُكُمْ ، وَيُجَاهَدُ عَدُوُّكُمْ ، وَيُؤخَذُ لِلضَّعِيفِ مِنَ الشَّدِيدِ مِنْكُمْ .[٢٤٨]

and that lousy bell. The noise of the bell, I hated with a vengeance. The only time I ever liked it was when it sounded for a free day. On those mornings you'd have this great feeling of anticipation; the word would go out: "They're going up for a free day." The five monitors and the procurator would go up, and then you'd be waiting for the sound of this bell…

…Another thing during Inter week was croquet. Con Heaney used to organise the games; he kept the equipment — the hoops and mallets — and he taught us how to play. Part of the junior field would be marked off with twine. That was the game you played during the exams there was no football played then. Incidentally, croquet was played a lot in Maynooth — again towards the end of the year.

"…grammar and learning by rote."

…Classes were very long, there were five classes a day, but this had increased to seven by the early 1950s. A hard day was when you had maths and the four languages — English, Irish, Latin and Greek. In languages at that time, you spent a lot of time on grammar — grammar and learning by rote. You were liable to be called for declensions, for nouns or verbs. You got plenty of homework, you'd be fully occupied for the four hours of study, if you chose to be. During the last half hour of first study, you'd find that people got a bit restless and during last study, people might even be asleep…

…Some of the books seemed very strange, the maths books in particular. While I'd obviously done arithmetic at school, I hadn't done any geometry or algebra. But a lot of the students from east of the Corrib, from the area around Tuam would have done both of those, in preparation, I suppose, for scholarships of one sort or another. I was completely lost in these mathematical subjects, but I remember being asked to come to the board to prove some theorem or other. I hadn't a clue what it was about and that turned me against maths for the rest of my time in Jarlath's I couldn't understand algebra then, nor do I understand it to this day…

…Classes were streamed but, in five years, you might only be in three classes. When you came into the College, you went to either Junior D or Junior E. Many of those in Junior D went directly to Junior A in second year and did the Inter Cert. In your third year, you stayed on in Junior A and did the Inter Cert again. At that point, you might skip up to Senior One, so you

77. Warning Against False Expectations

٧٧ ـ التَّحذيرُ مِنَ الآمالِ الباطِلَةِ

"Leave them to eat and enjoy and to be diverted by expectations. Soon they will know."[263]

﴿ذَرْهُمْ يَأْكُلُوا وَيَتَمَتَّعُوا وَيُلْهِهِمُ الْأَمَلُ فَسَوْفَ يَعْلَمُونَ﴾.[٢٥٩]

239. **Imām ʿAlī (AS) said,** 'Guard yourselves against false expectation, for many a person who begins the day does not live to see its end, and many a one is envied at the beginning of the night while his mourners have assembled by the end of it.'[264]

٢٣٩ . الإمامُ عليٌّ (ع) : اتَّقوا باطِلَ الأملِ، فَرُبَّ مُسْتَقْبِلِ يوم ليسَ بِمُسْتَدْبِرِه، ومَغْبُوطٍ في أوَّلِ لَيلِهِ[٢٦٠] قامَتْ بَواكِيه في آخرِه.[٢٦١]

240. **Imām ʿAlī (AS) said,** '[False] Expectation is like the mirage - it deceives those who view it and leaves behind those who place their hope on it.'[265]

٢٤٠ . عنه (ع) : الأملُ كالسَّرابِ: يَغُرُّ مَنْ رَآهُ، ويُخْلِفُ مَن رَجاهُ.[٢٦٢]

241. **Imām ʿAlī (AS) said,** 'Wishes blind the eyes of insight.'[266]

٢٤١ . عنه (ع) : الأمانِيُّ تُعْمي عُيُونَ البصائرِ.[٢٦٣]

242. **Imām ʿAlī (AS) said,** 'Expectation is the sultan of the Satans over the hearts of the oblivious.'[267]

٢٤٢ . عنه (ع) : الأملُ سُلطانُ الشَّياطِينِ على قُلُوبِ الغافِلِين.[٢٦٤]

243. **Imām ʿAlī (AS) said,** 'The fruit of expectation is the spoilage of deeds.'[268]

٢٤٣ . عنه (ع) : ثَمَرَةُ الأملِ فَسادُ العَمَلِ.[٢٦٥]

244. **Imām ʿAlī (AS) said,** '[False] Expectation causes the heart to forget, breaks promises, increases oblivion, and brings about grief.'[269]

٢٤٤ . عنه (ع) : إنّ الأملَ يُسْهي القلبَ، ويُكْذِبُ الوَعْدَ، ويُكْثِرُ الغَفْلَةَ، ويُورِثُ الحَسْرَةَ.[٢٦٦]

245. **Imām ʿAlī (AS) said,** 'Expectation drives reason away, breaks promises, encourages oblivion, and brings about grief. So distrust expectation, for it is deceitful and its addict is a sinner.'[270]

٢٤٥ . عنه (ع) : إنَّ الأملَ يُذْهِبُ العقلَ، ويُكْذِبُ الوَعدَ، ويَحُثُّ على الغَفْلَةِ، ويُورِثُ الحَسْرَةَ. فأكْذِبوا الأملَ؛ فإنّه غَرُورٌ، وإنَّ صاحِبَهُ مَأْزُورٌ.[٢٦٧]

246. **Imām al-Ṣādiq (AS) said,** 'How many a favour Allah grants His servant without him having expected them, and how many a hopeful one entertains high hopes when [Allah's] choice favours others.'[271]

٢٤٦ . الإمامُ الصّادقُ (ع) : كَمْ مِنْ نِعمةٍ للهِ على عبدِهِ في غَيْرِ أملِهِ، وكَمْ مِنْ مُؤَمِّلٍ أملاً الخِيارُ في غَيرِه.[٢٦٨]

78. Expectation and Death

٧٨ـ الأمَلُ وَالأجَلُ

247. It has been narrated that the Prophet (SAWA) took three sticks and set one of them in front of him, another one next to it, and the third far away from the two. He then asked, 'Do you know what this is?' to which they replied, 'Allah and His Messenger know better.' He said, 'This one is man, and this is death [next to it], while that one is expectation, which man entertains [about his long life], but death falls upon him prior to his expectation.'[272]

٢٤٧ . تنبيه الخواطر : رُوِيَ أنَّهُ [رسول الله ﷺ] أخَذَ ثلاثةَ أعْوادٍ فَغَرَسَ عُوداً بين يَدَيْهِ والآخَرَ إلىٰ جَنْبِهِ، وأمّا الثّالثُ فأبْعَدَهُ وقالَ : هَل تَدْرُونَ ما هذا ؟ قالوا : اللهُ ورسولُهُ أعْلَمُ . قالَ : هذا الإنسانُ، وهذا الأجلُ، وهذا الأملُ يَتَعاطاهُ ابنُ آدمَ ويَخْتَلِجُهُ الأجلُ دُونَ الأملِ.[٢٦٩]

248. **Imām ʿAlī (AS) said,** 'If man were to see his death [approaching] and the speed at which it draws near to him, he would despise expectation.'[273]

٢٤٨ . الإمامُ عليٌّ ﵇ :لو رأَى العبدُ أجلَهُ وسُرْعَتَهُ إلَيهِ أبْغَضَ الأملَ.[٢٧٠]

249. **Imām ʿAlī (AS) said,** 'Expectation makes one forget death.'[274]

٢٤٩ . عنه ﵇ : الأملُ يُنْسي الأجَلَ.[٢٧١]

250. **Imām ʿAlī (AS) said,** 'The closest thing is death, and the remotest thing is expectation.'[275]

٢٥٠ . عنه ﵇ : أقْرَبُ شَيْءٍ الأجلُ، أبْعَدُ شَيْءٍ الأملُ.[٢٧٢]

251. **Imām ʿAlī (AS) said,** 'A soul does not depart from expectation until it enters the realm of death.'[276]

٢٥١ . عنه ﵇ : لا تَخْلو النَّفْسُ مِنَ الأملِ حتّىٰ تَدْخُلَ في الأجلِ[٢٧٣].

252. **Imām ʿAlī (AS) said,** 'Indeed you are in the days of expectation that is followed by death. So he who works in the days of his expectation before death arrives will benefit from his work and will not be hurt by death.'[277]

٢٥٢ . عنه ﵇ : ألَا وإنّكُمْ في أيّامِ أملٍ مِن وَرائهِ أجلٌ، فَمَنْ عَمِلَ في أيّامِ أملِهِ قَبْلَ حُضُورِ أجلِهِ فَقَدْ نَفَعَهُ عَمَلُهُ ولَم يَضْرُرْهُ أجلُهُ.[٢٧٤]

253. **Imām al-Kāẓim (AS) said,** 'If times of death were revealed, expectations would be debunked.'[278]

٢٥٣ . الإمامُ الكاظمُ ﵇ : لَو ظَهَرتِ الآجالُ افتَضَحَتِ الآمالُ.[٢٧٥]

79. The Results of High Expectations

٧٩ـ ثَمَراتُ طولِ الأملِ

254. It is narrated in *al-Kāfī*: Part of what Allah, the Exalted, told Prophet Moses[279] (AS): 'O Moses! Do not extend your expectation in this world's

٢٥٤ . الكافي : فيما ناجَى اللهُ عزّ وجلّ بهِ موسىٰ ﵇ : يا موسىٰ، لا تُطَوِّلْ في الدُّنْيا أملَكَ

life lest your heart become hard, for the hard-hearted is far from Me.'[280]

فَيَقْسُوَ قَلْبُكَ، والقاسِي القلبِ منّي بَعِيدٌ.[٢٧٦]

255. **Imām ʿAlī (AS) said,** 'A man who has high expectations is deficient in his action.'[281]

٢٥٥. الإمامُ عليٌّ عليه السلام: مَنِ اتَّسَعَ أملُهُ قَصُرَ عَمَلُهُ.[٢٧٧]

256. **Imām ʿAlī (AS) said,** 'As for high expectation, it causes you to forget the Hereafter.'[282]

٢٥٦. عنه عليه السلام: أمّا طُولُ الأملِ فَيُنْسي الآخِرَةَ.[٢٧٨]

80. Low Expectation

٨٠ـ قِصَرُ الأمَلِ

257. **The Prophet (SAWA)** told Ibn Masʿūd, 'Lower your expectation such that when you wake up in the morning, you say, 'I will not see the night' and when you go to sleep at night, you say, 'I will not see the morning.' And be prepared to depart from this life and yearn to meet Allah.'[283]

٢٥٧. رسولُ اللهِ ﷺ ـ لابنِ مسعودٍ ـ: قَصِّرْ أمَلَكَ، فإذا أصْبَحْتَ فَقُلْ: إنّي لا أُمْسِي، وإذا أمْسَيْتَ فَقُلْ: إنّي لا أُصْبِحُ، واعْزِمْ على مُفارَقَةِ الدُّنْيا، وأحِبَّ لِقاءَ اللهِ.[٢٧٩]

258. **Imām ʿAlī (AS) said,** 'A man who is sure about leaving his loved ones, dwelling under the earth, facing the final Account, and that he will be needless of what he leaves behind, and needy of what he has sent forth [for the Hereafter] deserves to shorten his expectation and lengthen his action.'[284]

٢٥٨. الإمامُ عليٌّ عليه السلام: مَنْ أيْقَنَ أنّهُ يُفارِقُ الأحبابَ، ويَسكُنُ التُّرابَ، ويُواجِهُ الحِسابَ، ويَسْتَغْنِي عَمّا خَلَّفَ، ويَفْتَقِرُ إلى ما قَدَّمَ، كانَ حَرِيّاً بِقِصَرِ الأملِ وطُولِ العَملِ.[٢٨٠]

259. **Imām al-Bāqir (AS) said,** 'Equip yourself with low expectation for this world's life.'[285]

٢٥٩. الإمامُ الباقرُ عليه السلام: تَزَوَّدْ مِنَ الدُّنْيا بِقِصَرِ الأملِ.[٢٨١]

81. Prohibition of Placing One's Expectation in Other than Allah

٨١ـ النَّهيُ عَنِ التّأمِيلِ بِغَيرِ اللهِ

260. **The Prophet (SAWA) said,** 'Allah, Mighty and Exalted says, 'I will cut off the expectation of every believer who places it in someone other than Me [and replace it] with despair.'[286]

٢٦٠. رسولُ اللهِ ﷺ: يقولُ اللهُ عزّ وجلّ: لَأقْطَعَنَّ أملَ كُلِّ مُؤمنٍ أمَّلَ دُوني بالإياسِ.[٢٨٢]

261. **Imām ʿAlī (AS) said,** 'He who places his expectation in a human is indeed fearful of him.'[287]

٢٦١. الإمامُ عليٌّ عليه السلام: مَنْ أمَّلَ إنساناً فَقَدْ هابَهُ.[٢٨٣]

(See also: TRUST (IN ALLAH): section 1878)

(انظر) التوكّل: باب ١٨٧٨.

15

THE [MUSLIM] COMMUNITY

الأُمَّة

82. The Status of the Muslim Community

٨٢ـ مَنزِلَةُ الأُمَّةِ الإِسلامِيَّةِ

"You are the best nation [ever] brought forth for mankind: you bid what is right and forbid what is wrong and have faith in Allah. And if the people of the Book had believed, it would have been better for them. Among them some are faithful, but most of them are transgressors."[288]

﴿كُنتُمْ خَيْرَ أُمَّةٍ أُخْرِجَتْ لِلنَّاسِ تَأْمُرُونَ بِالْمَعْرُوفِ وَتَنْهَوْنَ عَنِ الْمُنكَرِ وَتُؤْمِنُونَ بِاللهِ وَلَوْ آمَنَ أَهْلُ الْكِتَابِ لَكَانَ خَيْراً لَهُم مِنْهُمُ الْمُؤْمِنُونَ وَأَكْثَرُهُمُ الْفَاسِقُونَ﴾.٢٨٤

262. **The Prophet (SAWA) said,** 'My nation is a blessed one, whether its first [early Muslims] is the best or its last [at the end of time] is not known.'[289]

٢٦٢. رسولُ اللهِ ﷺ: أُمّتي أُمّةٌ مُبارَكَةٌ، لا يُدرى أوَّلُها خَيْرٌ أو آخِرُها خَيْرٌ.٢٨٥

263. **The Prophet (SAWA) said,** 'This community of mine is a nation compassioned upon by Allah.'[290]

٢٦٣. عنه ﷺ: أُمّتي هذهِ أُمّةٌ مَرحومةٌ.٢٨٦

264. **The Prophet (SAWA) said,** 'Surely you complete seventy communities, of which you are the best and the most honoured before Allah.'[291]

٢٦٤. عنه ﷺ: إنَّكُمْ تُتِمُّونَ سَبعينَ أُمّـةً، أنتُم خَيرُها وأكرَمُها على اللهِ.٢٨٧

265. **The Prophet (SAWA) said,** 'Give good news to this nation of exaltedness, religion, superiority, victory and power in the land.'[292]

٢٦٥. عنه ﷺ: بَشِّرْ هٰذِهِ الأُمَّةَ بالسَّناءِ، والدِّينِ، والرِّفعَةِ، والنَّصرِ، والتَّمكينِ في الأرضِ.٢٨٨

83. The Best of the Muslim Community

٨٣ـ أخيارُ الأُمَّةِ

266. **The Prophet (SAWA) said,** 'The best of my community are the most abstemious in the world and the most desirous of the Hereafter.'[293]

٢٦٦. رسولُ اللهِ ﷺ: خَيْرُ أُمّتي أزْهَدُهُمْ في الدُّنيا، وأرْغَبُهُمْ في الآخِرَةِ.٢٨٩

267. **The Prophet (SAWA) said,** 'The best of my community are those who spend away their youth in Allah's obedience, wean themselves away from the worldly pleasures and are infatuated with the Hereafter. Surely their reward upon Allah is the highest levels of Paradise.'[294]

٢٦٧ . عنه ﷺ: خَيْرُ أُمّتي مَنْ هَدَمَ شَبابَهُ في طاعةِ اللهِ، وفَطَمَ نَفْسَهُ عَنْ لَذّاتِ الدُّنْيا وتَوَلَّهَ بالآخِرَةِ، إنّ جَزاءهُ علَى اللهِ أعلىٰ مَراتِبِ الجنّةِ.[٢٩٠]

268. **The Prophet (SAWA) said,** 'The best of my community are those who when treated foolishly are tolerant, and when wronged they forgive, and when they are hurt are patient.'[295]

٢٦٨ . عنه ﷺ: خَيْرُ أُمّتي مَن إذا سُفِهَ عَلَيْهِمْ احْتَمَلوا، وإذا جُنِيَ عَلَيْهِمْ غَفَروا، وإذا أُوذُوا صَبَروا.[٢٩١]

84. The Middle Nation

٨٤ـ الأُمَّةُ الوَسَطُ

"Thus We have made you a middle nation that you may be witnessed to the people, and that the Apostle may be a witness to you."[296]

﴿وَكَذٰلِكَ جَعَلْناكُمْ أُمَّةً وَسَطاً لِتَكُونوا شُهَداءَ عَلَى النَّاسِ وَيَكُونَ الرَّسُولُ عَلَيْكُمْ شَهِيداً﴾.[٢٩٢]

269. **Imām ʿAlī (AS) said,** 'We are the witnesses of Allah on His creation and His proof on the earth, and we are those regarding whom Allah has said, "*Thus We have made you a middle nation.*"'[297]

٢٦٩ . الإمامُ عليٌّ ﷺ: نَحْنُ شُهَداءُ اللهِ على خَلْقِهِ، وحُجَّتُهُ في أرضِهِ، ونَحْنُ الّذينَ قالَ اللهُ جلّ اسمه: ﴿وَكَذٰلِكَ جَعَلْناكُمْ أُمَّةً وَسَطاً﴾.[٢٩٣]

85. Factors that Ensure the Goodness of the Muslim Nation

٨٥ـ ما يوجِبُ خيرَ الأُمَّةِ

270. **The Prophet (SAWA) said,** 'My nation will continue to thrive as long as they love each other, deliver the trust, refrain from the forbidden, respect the guest, maintain the prayer, and pay the alms-tax (*zakāt*).'[298]

٢٧٠ . رسولُ اللهِ ﷺ: لا تَزالُ أُمّتي بِخَيْرٍ ما تَحابُّوا وأدَّوا الأمانَةَ، واجْتَنَبوا الحَرامَ، وقَرَوُا الضَّيْفَ، وأقامُوا الصَّلاةَ، وآتَوا الزَّكاةَ.[٢٩٤]

271. **The Prophet (SAWA) said,** 'This nation will continue to remain under the supervision and protection of Allah as long as its reciters do not flatter the rulers, its scholars do not declare the vicious ingrates as innocents, and the good people do not approve of the evil ones; if they do that, Allah will take

٢٧١ . عنه ﷺ: لا تَزالُ هٰذِهِ الأُمّةُ تَحْتَ يَدِ اللهِ وفي كَنَفِهِ ما لَم يُداهِنْ قُرّاؤُها أُمَراءَها، ولَم يُزَكِّ عُلَماؤها فُجّارَها، وما لَم يُهِنّ خِيارُها أشرارَها، فإذا فَعَلوا ذٰلكَ رَفَعَ اللهُ عَنْهُمْ يَدَهُ ثُمَّ

away His supervision and give reign to their oppressors over them.'[299]

سَلَّطَ عَلَيْهِمْ جَبابِرَتَهُمْ.٢٩٥

86. The Status of the Muslim Community in the Hereafter

٨٦ـ مَنزِلَةُ الأُمَّةِ الإسلامِيَّةِ فِي الآخِرَةِ

272. **The Prophet (SAWA) said,** 'Among all the prophets, my followers will be the most on the Day of Resurrection.'[300]

٢٧٢ . رسولُ اللهِ ﷺ : أنا أكْثَرُ النَّبِيِّينَ تَبَعاً يومَ القِيامةِ.٢٩٦

273. **The Prophet (SAWA) said,** 'Surely in Paradise there will be one hundred and twenty ranks, of which eighty will be occupied by my community.'[301]

٢٧٣ . عنه ﷺ :إنّ في الجنّةِ عِشْرينَ ومائةَ صَفٍّ، أُمّتي منها ثَمانُونَ صَفّاً.٢٩٧

87. What Takes Away the Splendour of the Muslim Community

٨٧ـ ما يَنزِعُ مَهابَةَ الأُمَّةِ الإسلامِيَّةِ

274. **The Prophet (SAWA) said,** 'Very soon other communities will attack you, like the attack of a hungry man towards a bowl of food.' One present there asked, 'Will we be a minority then?' He said, 'No, you will be the majority, but you will be like the scum of the flood. And in fact Allah will snatch away the awe that your enemy has of you, and He will cast weakness in your hearts!' One present there asked, 'And what is [that] weakness?' He said, 'Love of the world and dislike of death.'[302]

٢٧٤ . الملاحم و الفتن عن ثوبان مَولىٰ رسول اللهِ ﷺ : قال رسول الله ﷺ : يُوشِكُ الأُمم تَداعىٰ عَلَيْكُمْ تَداعِيَ الأكَلَةِ علىٰ قَصْعَتِها.
قالَ قائلٌ مِنْهُمْ: مِنْ قِلّةٍ نَحْنُ يَوْمَئذٍ؟ قالَ: بَلْ أَنْتُمْ كَثِيرٌ، ولٰكنّكُمْ غُثاءٌ كَغُثاءِ السَّيْلِ، وَلَيَنْزِعَنَّ اللهُ مِنْ عَدُوِّكُمُ المَهابةَ منهم، ولَيَقْذِفَنَّ في قُلوبِكُمُ الوَهْنَ!
قالَ قائلٌ: يا رسولَ الله، وما الوَهْنُ؟ قالَ: حُبُّ الدُّنيا وكَراهِيَةُ المَوتِ.٢٩٨

275. **The Prophet (SAWA) said,** 'Whenever my community aggrandizes the world, Allah will remove the splendour of Islam from them.'[303]

٢٧٥ . رسولُ اللهِ ﷺ : إذا عَظَّمَتْ أُمّتي الدُّنيا نَزَعَ اللهُ منها هَيْبَةَ الإسلامِ.٢٩٩

(See also: CONGREGATION 69; DIFFERENCES 130)

(انظر) عنوان ٦٩ «الجماعة»؛ ١٣٠ «الاختلاف».

88. The Prophet's (SAWA) Fear for His Community

٨٨ـ ما يَخافُ النَّبِيُّ عَلىٰ أُمَّتِهِ

276. **The Prophet (SAWA) said,** 'Indeed I fear three things for my community: obeying their greed, following their desires, and an astray leader.'[304]

٢٧٦ . رسولُ اللهِ ﷺ : إنّما أخافُ علىٰ أُمّتي ثَلاثاً : شُحّاً مُطاعاً ، وهَوىً مُتَّبعاً ، وإماماً ضالّاً .[٣٠٠]

277. **The Prophet (SAWA) said,** 'I fear three things for my community: deviation after awareness, the misleading temptations, and the desires of the stomach and the private parts.'[305]

٢٧٧ . عنه ﷺ : ثَلاثةٌ أخافُهُنَّ علىٰ أُمّتي : الضَّلالةُ بَعْدَ المَعْرِفةِ ، ومُضِلّاتُ الفِتَنِ ، وشَهْوَةُ البَطْنِ والفَرْجِ .[٣٠١]

278. **The Prophet (SAWA) said,** 'The worst I fear for my community are three: the downfall of a scholar, the disputation of a hypocrite by means of the Qur'an, and the world which beheads you. So, for your own sakes, be suspicious of this world.'[306]

٢٧٨ . عنه ﷺ : أشَدُّ ما يُتَخَوَّفُ علىٰ أُمّتي ثَلاثةٌ : زَلّةُ عالِمٍ ، أو جِدالُ منافقٍ بِالقرآنِ ، أو دُنيا تَقْطَعُ رِقابَكُمْ فاتَّهِمُوها علىٰ أنفُسِكُمْ .[٣٠٢]

279. **The Prophet (SAWA) said,** 'Verily the most dreadful things that I fear for my community after me are: these unlawful earnings, covert carnal desire [i.e. lust] and usury.'[307]

٢٧٩ . عنه ﷺ : إنّ أخْوَفَ ما أتَخَوَّفُ علىٰ أُمّتي مِن بَعْدي : هٰذهِ المَكاسِبُ المُحَرَّمةُ ، والشَّهْوَةُ الخَفِيّةُ ، والرِّبا .[٣٠٣]

280. **The Prophet (SAWA) said,** 'Certainly the most dreadful things I fear for my community are: [following] desires and entertaining high hopes, for desires obstruct one from the truth and high hopes make one forget the Hereafter.'[308]

٢٨٠ . عنه ﷺ : إنّ أخْوَفَ ما أخافُ عَلى أُمّتِي الهَوىٰ وطُولُ الأملِ ؛ أمّا الهوىٰ فَإنّهُ يَصُدُّ عَنِ الحقِّ ، وأمّا طُولُ الأملِ فَيُنْسي الآخِرَةَ .[٣٠٤]

281. **The Prophet (SAWA) said,** 'Certainly the most dreadful thing I fear for you is the lesser polytheism.' They asked, 'And what is the lesser polytheism, O Messenger of Allah?' He (SAWA) replied, 'It is showing off *(riyā')*.'[309]

٢٨١ . عنه ﷺ : إنّ أخْوَفَ ما أخافُ عَلَيْكُمُ الشِّرْكُ الأصْغَرُ . قالُوا : وما الشِّرْكُ الأصْغَرُ يا رسولَ اللهِ ؟ قال : هُوَ الرِّياءُ .[٣٠٥]

282. **The Prophet (SAWA) said,** 'Verily the most dreadful thing I fear for my community is every well-spoken hypocrite.'[310]

٢٨٢ . عنه ﷺ : إنّ أخْوَفَ ما أخافُ عَلى أُمّتِي كُلُّ مُنافقٍ عَليمِ اللِّسانِ .[٣٠٦]

283. **The Prophet (SAWA) said,** 'The most dreadful thing I fear for my community is the splendour and abundance of worldly possessions.'[311]

٢٨٣ . عنه ﷺ: أخْوَفُ ما أخافُ على أُمّتي زَهْرَةُ الدُّنيا وكَثرَتُها.٣٠٧

16

LEADERSHIP (1)

الإمامة (١)

GENERAL LEADERSHIP (IMĀMA)[312]

الإمامة العامّة

89. The Importance of Divinely Appointed Leadership

٨٩ـ أهمّيّة الإمامة

"Today I have perfected your religion for you, and I have completed My blessing upon you, and I have approved Islam as your religion."[313]

﴿الْيَوْمَ أَكْمَلْتُ لَكُمْ دِينَكُمْ وَأَتْمَمْتُ عَلَيْكُمْ نِعْمَتِي وَرَضِيتُ لَكُمُ الْإِسْلامَ دِيناً﴾.٣٠٨

284. **Imām 'Alī (AS) said,** '*Imāma* is the [structural] system of the [Muslim] community.'[314]

٢٨٤ . الإمامُ عليٌّ ﷺ: الإمامةُ نِظامُ الأُمّةِ.٣٠٩

285. **Imām al-Bāqir (SAWA) said,** 'Islam is based on five: prayer, alms, fasting, the obligatory pilgrimage (*ḥajj*), and the divine guardianship and no other issue has been called for as much as divine guardianship.'[315]

٢٨٥ . الإمامُ الباقرُ ﷺ: بُنِيَ الإسلامُ على خَمْسٍ: علَى الصَّلاةِ، والزَّكاةِ، والصَّومِ، والحَجِّ، والوَلايةِ، ولَمْ يُنادَ بِشَيْءٍ كَما نُودِيَ بالوَلايةِ.٣١٠

286. **Imām al-Kāẓim (AS) said,** '*Imāma* is the light, and that is the purport of His saying [in the Qur'an]: *"So have faith in Allah and His Apostle and the light which We have sent down."*[316] He (AS) said, 'The light is the Imām.'[317]

٢٨٦ . الإمامُ الكاظمُ ﷺ: الإمامةُ هِيَ النُّورُ، وذلكَ قولُهُ عزّوجلّ: ﴿آمِنُوا باللهِ وَرَسُولِهِ والنُّورِ الّذي أنْزَلْنا﴾٣١١، قالَ: النُّورُ هُوَ الإمامُ.٣١٢

287. **Imām al-Riḍā (AS) said,** 'And it was revealed in the Prophet's farewell pilgrimage, during the end of his life: *"Today I have perfected your religion for you..."* and the issue of *imāma* is the completion of the religion.'[318]

٢٨٧ . الإمامُ الرِّضا ﷺ: وأنزَلَ في حِجّةِ الوَداعِ وَهِيَ آخِرُ عُمْرِهِ ﷺ ﴿اليَومَ أكْمَلْتُ لَكُمْ دِينَكُمْ﴾ وأمرُ الإمامةِ مِنْ تَمامِ الدِّينِ.٣١٣

288. **Imām al-Riḍā (AS) said,** 'Verily *imāma* is the basis of the progressive Islam, as well as its lofty branches.'[319]

٢٨٨. عنه ؏: إنّ الإمامةَ أُسُّ الإسلامِ النّامي، وفَرْعُهُ السّامي.٣١٤

289. **Imām al-Riḍā (AS) said,** 'Verily *imāma* is the reins of religion, the ruling system of the Muslims, the prosperity for the world and an honour for the believers.'[320]

٢٨٩. عنه ؏: إنّ الإمامةَ زِمامُ الدِّين، ونظامُ المُسلمينَ، وصَلاحُ الدُّنيا، وعِزُّ المُؤمنينَ.٣١٥

(See also: THE PATH: section 1119)

(أنظر) الصراط: باب ١١١٩.

90. The Superiority of Imāma over Prophethood

٩٠ـ فَضلُ الإمامَةِ عَلى النُّبُوَّةِ

"And when his Lord tested Abraham with certain words, and he fulfilled them, He said, 'I am making you the Imām of mankind.'"[321]

﴿وَإِذِ ابْتَلَى إِبْرَاهِيمَ رَبُّهُ بِكَلِمَاتٍ فَأَتَمَّهُنَّ قَالَ إِنِّي جَاعِلُكَ لِلنَّاسِ إِمَاماً﴾.٣١٦

290. **Imām al-Ṣādiq (AS) said,** 'Verily Allah, Blessed and most High, took Abraham[322] as a slave before He took him as a prophet, and verily Allah took him as a prophet before He took him as an apostle, And verily Allah took him as an apostle before He took him as a friend. And verily Allah took him as a friend before He made him an Imām. And when all these ranks came together in him, He said, *"I am making you the Imām of mankind."*'[323]

٢٩٠. الإمامُ الصّادقُ ؏: إنّ اللهَ تباركَ وتعالىٰ اتَّخَذَ إبراهيمَ عَبداً قَبْلَ أنْ يَتَّخِذَهُ نَبيّاً، وإنَّ اللهَ اتَّخَذَهُ نَبيّاً قَبْلَ أنْ يَتَّخِذَهُ رَسولاً، وإنَّ اللهَ اتَّخَذَهُ رَسولاً قَبْلَ أنْ يَتَّخِذَهُ خَليلاً، وإنَّ اللهَ اتَّخَذَهُ خَليلاً قَبْلَ أنْ يَجْعَلَهُ إماماً، فَلَمّا جَمَعَ لَهُ الأشياءَ قالَ: إنّي جاعِلُكَ لِلنّاسِ إماماً.٣١٧

91. The Essential Need for an Imām

٩١ـ الاضطِرارُ إلَى الإمامِ

291. **Imām al-Bāqir (AS) said,** 'If the Imām was to ever be removed from the earth even for an instant, the whole earth would tremble its inhabitants the way the ocean trembles with those who are on it.'[324]

٢٩١. الإمامُ الباقرُ ؏: لَو أنَّ الإمامَ رُفِعَ مِنَ الأرضِ ساعةً لَماجَتْ بأهْلِها كَما يَموجُ البَحرُ بأهلِه.٣١٨

292. **Imām al-Ṣādiq (AS) said,** 'The earth will never be absent of having an Imām, so that if the believers were to add something [to religion] he

٢٩٢. الإمامُ الصّادقُ ؏: إنّ الأرضَ لا تَخْلُو إلّا وَفيها إمامٌ، كَيما إنْ زادَ المُؤمنونَ شَيئاً

would refute it, and if they were to omit something from it, he would complete it for them [by bringing it back].'[325]

رَدَّهُمْ، وإنْ نَقَصُوا شَيْئاً أتَمَّهُ لَهُم.[٣١٩]

92. The Authority is a Known Imām

٩٢ـ الحُجَّةُ إمامٌ يُعرَفُ

293. **Imām al-Ṣadiq (AS) said,** 'Verily Allah's proof [authority] over His creation will not be established except by an Imām in order that he be known.'[326]

٢٩٣ . الإمامُ الصّادقُ ﵇ :إنَّ الحُجَّةَ لا تَقُومُ للهِ عزّ وجلّ علىٰ خَلْقِهِ إلّا بإمامٍ حتّىٰ يُعْرَفَ.[٣٢٠]

93. The Imām May be Worried and Hence, Undistinguishable

٩٣ـ قَد يَكونُ الإمامُ خائِفاً مَغموراً

294. **Imām 'Alī (AS) said,** 'Yes indeed, the earth will not be devoid of one who upholds the proofs for the sake of Allah - either a manifest and well-known authority, or one who is worried and undistinguishable – so that His proofs and arguments may never be invalid.'[327]

٢٩٤ . الإمامُ عليٌّ ﵇ :اللّٰهُمَّ بَلىٰ، لا تَخْلو الأرضُ مِنْ قائِمٍ للهِ بِحُجَجِهِ، إمّا ظاهِراً مَشْهُوراً، أو خائفاً مَغْموراً لئلّا تَبْطُلَ حُجَجُ اللهِ وبَيِّناتُهُ.[٣٢١]

295. **Imām al-Bāqir (AS) said,** 'The earth will never remain without an Imām, be he apparent or hidden.'[328]

٢٩٥ . الإمامُ الباقرُ ﵇ :لا تَبْقَى الأرضُ بغيرِ إمامٍ ظاهرٍ أو باطنٍ.[٣٢٢]

94. Were it not for the Imām, the Earth Would Have Perished

٩٤ـ لَولَا الإمامُ لَساخَتِ الأرضُ

296. **Imām al-Ṣadiq (AS) said,** 'If the earth were to remain without an Imām, it would perish.'[329]

٢٩٦ . الإمامُ الصّادقُ ﵇ : لَو بَقِيَتِ الأرضُ بِغَيْرِ إمامٍ لَسَاخَتْ.[٣٢٣]

297. **Imām al-Ṣādiq (AS) said,** 'Certainly the earth cannot exist without an authority [of Allah –i.e. a *ḥujja*] therein. In fact, mankind can only prosper

٢٩٧ . عنه ﵇ : إنّ الأرضَ لا تكونُ إلّا وفيها حُجَّةٌ، إنَّهُ لا يُصْلِحُ النّاسَ إلّا ذٰلكَ،

through him, and the earth can only prosper through that.'[330]

ولا يُصْلِحُ الأرضَ إلّا ذاكَ.[٣٢٤]

(See also: THE ARGUMENT, section 88)

(أُنظر) عنوان ٨٨ «الحُجّة».

95. The Summoning of Every Nation With Their Imām

٩٥ـ دَعوَةُ كُلِّ أُمَّةٍ بِإمامِها

"The day We shall summon every group of people with their Imām."[331]

﴿يَوْمَ نَدْعُو كُلَّ أُناسٍ بِإِمامِهِمْ﴾.[٣٢٥]

298. **Imām al-Ṣādiq (AS) said,** 'When the Day of Judgment comes… an address will come from Allah, the Exalted, saying, 'Lo! Whosoever accepts the leadership of an Imām in the worldly abode should follow him wherever he takes him, hence, '*those who were followed will disown the followers...*'[332 333]

٢٩٨ . الإمامُ الصّادقُ عليه السلام : إذا كانَ يومُ القِيامةِ ... يَأتي النِّداءُ مِنْ عِنْدِ اللهِ جلَّ جلالُهُ : ألَا مَنِ ائْتَمَّ بإمامٍ في دارِ الدُّنيا فَلْيَتَّبِعْهُ إلىٰ حَيْثُ يَذْهَبُ بِهِ ، فَحِينَئذٍ ﴿تَبَرَّأَ الَّذينَ اتُّبِعُوا مِنَ الّذينَ اتَّبَعُوا...﴾[٣٢٦ . ٣٢٧]

96. Importance of Knowing the Imām

٩٦ـ أهَمِّيَّةُ مَعرِفَةِ الإمامِ

299. **The Prophet (SAWA) said,** 'Whoever dies without knowing his Imām has died a pagan [pre-Islamic] death.'[334]

٢٩٩ . رسولُ اللهِ صلى الله عليه وآله : مَن ماتَ وَهُوَ لا يَعرفُ إمامَهُ ماتَ مِيتةً جاهليّةً.[٣٢٨]

300. **The Prophet (SAWA) said,** 'Whoever dies without having an Imām has died a pagan [pre-Islamic] death.'[335]

٣٠٠ . عنه صلى الله عليه وآله : مَن ماتَ بغيرِ إمامٍ ماتَ مِيتةً جاهليّةً[٣٢٩ . ٣٣٠]

301. **Imām Ḥusayn (AS),** when asked how to attain knowledge of Allah, replied, 'It is for the people of every time to know their Imām, obedience to whom is mandatory.'[336]

٣٠١ . الإمامُ الحسينُ عليه السلام ـ لَمّا سُئل عَن مَعرفةِ اللهِ ـ : مَعرفةُ أهلِ كُلِّ زمانٍ إمامَهُمُ الّذي يَجِبُ عَلَيهِمْ طاعَتُهُ.[٣٣١]

302. **Imām al-Ṣādiq (AS),** regarding Allah's verse: *"and he who is given wisdom, is certainly given an abundant good."*[337], said, '[It is] obedience to Allah and knowing one's Imām.'[338]

٣٠٢ . الإمامُ الصّادقُ عليه السلام ـ في قولِهِ تعالى : ﴿وَمنْ يُؤْتَ الحِكْمَةَ فَقَدْ أُوتِيَ خَيْرًا كَثِيرًا﴾[٣٣٢] ـ : طاعةُ اللهِ ومعرفةُ الإمامِ.[٣٣٣]

303. **Imām al-Ṣādiq (AS) said,** 'The Imām is a guide between Allah and His creation, therefore whoever acknowledges him is a believer, and whoever rejects him is a disbeliever.'[339]

٣٠٣ . عنه عليه السلام : الإمامُ عَلَمٌ بَيْنَ اللهِ عزّ وجلّ وبَيْنَ خَلْقِهِ ، فَمَنْ عَرَفَهُ كانَ مُؤمناً ، ومَنْ أنْكَرَهُ كانَ كافراً.[٣٣٤]

304. **Imām al-Ṣādiq (AS) said,** 'He who neither knows us nor rejects us is astray, until he returns to the guidance that Allah has made incumbent upon him - that is the obligatory obedience to us. And if he dies in this deviation of his, Allah will do with him as He pleases.'[340]

٣٠٤. عنه ﷺ: مَن لَم يَعْرِفْنا ولَم يُنْكِرْنا كانَ ضالّاً حتّىٰ يَرْجِعَ إلَى الهُدَى الّذي افْتَرَضَ اللهُ عَلَيْهِ مِنْ طاعَتِنا الواجِبَةِ، فإن يَمُتْ علىٰ ضَلالَتِهِ يَفْعَلِ اللهُ بِهِ ما يَشاءُ.[٣٣٥]

97. Conditions of Imāma and the Qualifications of the Imām

٩٧- شَرائِطُ الإمامَةِ وخَصائِصُ الإمامِ

"And amongst them We appointed Imāms who guide [the people] by Our command, when they had been patient and had conviction in Our signs."[341]

﴿وَجَعَلْنا مِنْهُمْ أَئِمَّةً يَهْدُونَ بِأَمْرِنا لَمّا صَبَرُوا وَكانُوا بِآياتِنا يُوقِنُونَ﴾.[٣٣٦]

"Is He who guides to the truth worthier to be followed, or he who guides not unless he is [himself] guided? What is the matter with you?"[342]

﴿أَفَمَنْ يَهْدِي إِلَى الْحَقِّ أَحَقُّ أَنْ يُتَّبَعَ أَمَّنْ لا يَهِدِّي إِلّا أَنْ يُهْدىٰ فَما لَكُمْ كَيْفَ تَحْكُمُونَ﴾.[٣٣٧]

305. **Imām 'Alī (AS) said,** 'None can bear this responsibility [*imāma*] except those who are patient, and have insight and knowledge of the circumstances of this issue.'[343]

٣٠٥. الإمامُ عليٌّ ﷺ: لا يَحمِلُ هٰذا الأمْرَ إلّا أهلُ الصَّبْرِ والبَصَرِ والعِلْمِ بِمَواقِعِ الأمرِ.[٣٣٨]

306. **Imām 'Alī (AS) said,** 'The Imām needs a wise heart, an expressive tongue and a staunch soul [i.e. authority] in establishing the truth.'[344]

٣٠٦. عنه ﷺ: يَحتاجُ الإمامُ إلىٰ قلبٍ عَقُولٍ، ولسانٍ قَؤولٍ، وجَنانٍ علىٰ إقامةِ الحَقِّ صَؤولٍ.[٣٣٩]

307. **Imām 'Alī (AS) said,** 'One who appoints himself as a leader of the people must first begin by educating himself before educating others; he must discipline through his own behaviour, before disciplining with his tongue.'[345]

٣٠٧. عنه ﷺ: مَن نَصَبَ نَفْسَهُ للنّاسِ إماماً فَلْيَبدأ بتعليمِ نَفْسِهِ قَبْلَ تعليمِ غيرِهِ، ولْيَكُنْ تأديبُهُ بسيرَتِهِ، قبلَ تأديبِهِ بِلِسانِهِ.[٣٤٠]

308. **Imām 'Alī said,** 'None can uphold the command of Allah, Glory be to Him, save one who can neither be bribed, nor does he give up, nor follows coveted desires.'[346]

٣٠٨. عنه ﷺ: لا يُقيمُ أمْرَ اللهِ سُبحانَهُ إلّا مَنْ لا يُصانِعُ ولا يُضارِعُ ولا يَتَّبِعُ المَطامِعَ.[٣٤١]

309. **Imām 'Alī (AS) said,** 'Among the definitions of the custodianship of an Imām whose obedience is

٣٠٩. عنه ﷺ: كِبارُ حُدودِ وَلايةِ الإمامِ

obligatory is to know that he is immune from committing mistakes, errors, intentional wrongs, and from all sins, petty and grave. He never makes mistakes or sin, and neither is he ever diverted from the issues that endanger the religion by any sort of diversion. He is the most knowledgeable of all people about what Allah has made lawful and unlawful, His obligations, recommendations and rulings. He stands needless of the entire world whilst they all need him. And he is the most generous and courageous of men.'[347]

المَفْروضِ الطّاعةِ أنْ يُعْلَمَ أنَّهُ مَعْصومٌ مِنَ الخطأِ والزَّلَلِ والعَمْدِ، ومِنَ الذُّنوبِ كُلِّها صغيرِها وكبيرِها، لا يَزِلُّ، ولا يُخْطئُ، ولا يَلْهو بِشَيْءٍ مِنَ الأُمورِ المُوبِقَةِ للدِّينِ، ولا بِشَيْءٍ مِنَ المَلاهي، وأنَّهُ أعْلَمُ النّاسِ بِحَلالِ اللهِ وحَرامِهِ، وفَرائضِهِ وسُنَنِهِ وأحْكامِهِ، مُسْتَغْنٍ عَنْ جَميعِ العالَمِ، وغَيْرُهُ مُحتاجٌ إلَيْهِ، وأنَّهُ أسْخَى النّاسِ وأشْجَعُ النّاسِ.[٣٤٢]

310. **Imām ʿAlī (AS) said,** 'You certainly know that he who is in charge of the honour, the lives, the booty [enforcement of], the commandments and the leadership of the Muslims must not be: a miser, as he would avidly crave their wealth, nor an ignorant man as he would then mislead them with his ignorance, nor crude in his manner for he would estrange them with his crudeness, nor one who deals unjustly with the distributing of wealth thus preferring one group over another, nor one to accept bribes in his ruling lest he forfeit people's rights and pass judgments without them [their rights], nor one to suspend recommended practices whereby he would ruin the community.'[348]

٣١٠. عنه ﷺ: وقَدْ عَلِمْتُمْ أنَّهُ لا يَنبغي أنْ يَكونَ علَى الفُروجِ والدِّماءِ والمَغانِمِ والأحْكامِ وإمامةِ المُسلِمينَ: البَخيلُ فتَكُونَ في أموالِهِمْ نُهْمَتُهُ، ولا الجاهلُ فَيُضِلَّهُمْ بِجَهْلِهِ، ولا الجافي فَيَقْطَعَهُمْ بِجَفائهِ، ولا الحائفُ (الجائف) للدُّولِ فَيَتَّخِذَ قوماً دُونَ قومٍ، ولا المُرْتَشي في الحُكْمِ فَيَذْهَبَ بالحُقوقِ ويَقِفَ بها دُونَ المَقاطِعِ، ولا المُعَطِّلُ للسُّنّةِ فيُهْلِكَ الأُمَّةَ.[٣٤٣]

311. **Imām Ḥusayn (AS),** in his letter to the inhabitants of Kūfa said, 'By my life, an Imām is only one who rules by the Book, a maintainer of justice, bound to the right religion, and controls himself for the sake of Allah.'[349]

٣١١. الإمامُ الحسينُ ﷺ ـ في كتابِهِ إلىٰ أهلِ الكوفةِ ـ: فَلَعَمْري، ما الإمامُ إلّا الحاكمُ بالكِتابِ، القائمُ بالقِسْطِ، الدّائنُ بِدِينِ الحَقِّ، الحابِسُ نَفْسَهُ علىٰ ذاتِ اللهِ.[٣٤٤]

312. **Imām al-Bāqir (AS),** explaining the traits of an Imām, said, '[He must be] of legitimate birth and well-bred, he neither gets distracted nor does he play.'[350]

٣١٢. الإمامُ الباقرُ ﷺ ـ في تَبْيينِ عَلامةِ الإمامِ ـ: طَهارَةُ الوِلادَةِ وحُسْنُ المَنْشأ، ولا يَلْهو ولا يَلْعبُ.[٣٤٥]

313. **Imām al-Riḍā (AS),** describing an Imām, said, 'Thoroughly proficient with leadership and well-versed in politics.'[351]

٣١٣. الإمامُ الرِّضا ﷺ ـ في صِفَةِ الإمامِ ـ: مُضْطَلِعٌ بالإمامةِ، عالِمٌ بالسِّياسَةِ.[٣٤٦]

98. That Which is Mandatory on Just Leaders

٩٨ـ ما فُرِضَ عَلىٰ أئِمَّةِ العَدلِ

314. **Imām ʿAlī (AS) said,** 'Certainly Allah has made me an Imām for His creation, so He has made it mandatory upon me to take into consideration myself, my food, my drink, and my clothing like that of the weak people [of the community], so that the poor may follow me in my poverty and the wealth of the rich does not embolden them to intimidation.'[352]

٣١٤. الإمامُ عليٌّ ﷺ: إنَّ اللهَ جَعَلَني إماماً لِخَلْقِهِ، فَفَرَضَ عَلَيَّ التَّقْديرَ في نَفْسي ومَطْعَمي ومَشْرَبي ومَلْبَسي كَضُعَفاءِ النّاسِ، كَيْ يَقْتَديَ الفقيرُ بِفَقْري، ولا يُطْغِيَ الغَنِيَّ غِناهُ.[٣٤٧]

315. **Imām ʿAlī (AS) said,** 'Verily there is no obligation on the Imām except that which has been devolved on him by Allah, namely to convey exhortations, to strive to give good counsel, to keep the prophetic practice alive, to enforce penalties on those liable to them and to issue shares [of taxes and charity] to those who deserve them.'[353]

٣١٥. عنه ﷺ: إنَّهُ لَيسَ علَى الإمامِ إلّا ما حُمِّلَ مِنْ أمرِ رَبِّهِ: الإبلاغُ في المَوعِظةِ، والاجتهادُ في النَّصيحةِ، والإحْياءُ للسُّنّةِ، وإقامةُ الحُدودِ علىٰ مَسْتَحِقِّيها، وإصدارُ السُّهْمانِ علىٰ أهْلِها.[٣٤٨]

99. The Reciprocal Duties and Rights Between the Imām and the Community

٩٩ـ الحُقوقُ المُتَبادَلَةُ بَينَ الإمامِ وَالأُمَّةِ

316. **Imām ʿAlī (AS) said,** 'It is the duty of an Imām to rule in accordance with what Allah has revealed, and that he delivers what he has been entrusted with. If he does that, then it is the duty of the people to listen to him and to obey him and to hearken [to his call] when they are called.'[354]

٣١٦. الإمامُ عليٌّ ﷺ: حَقٌّ علىٰ الإمامِ أنْ يَحْكُمَ بما أنْزَلَ اللهُ وأنْ يُؤَدّيَ الأمانةَ، فإذا فَعَلَ فَحَقٌّ علَى النّاسِ أنْ يَسْمَعوا لَهُ وأنْ يُطيعوا وأنْ يُجيبوا إذا دُعوا.[٣٤٩]

317. **Imām ʿAlī (AS) said,** 'Now it is obligatory upon a ruler that the distinction he achieves, or the wealth with which he has been exclusively endowed, should not make him change his behaviour towards those under him. Rather the bounties that Allah has bestowed on him should increase him in nearness to his people and in kindness towards his brethren.
Beware then that it is my duty towards you that I should not keep anything secret from you except

٣١٧. عنه ﷺ: أمّا بَعْدُ، فإنَّ حَقّاً عَلَى الوالي ألّا يُغَيِّرَهُ علىٰ رَعِيَّتِهِ فَضْلٌ نالَهُ، ولا طَوْلٌ خُصَّ بِهِ، وأنْ يَزيدَهُ ما قَسَمَ اللهُ لَهُ مِنْ نِعَمِهِ دُنُوّاً مِنْ عِبادِهِ، وعَطْفاً علىٰ إخْوانِهِ.
ألَا وإنَّ لَكُمْ عِندي ألّا أحْتَجِزَ دُونَكُمْ سِرّاً إلّا في حَرْبٍ، ولا أطْويَ دُونَكُمْ أمْراً إلّا في حُكْمٍ، ولا

during war, nor should I decide any matter without consulting you except with regards to the commands of religion, nor should I postpone the fulfilment of any of your rights nor desist until I discharge it fully. And that all of you are equal to me in your rights. When I have done all this, it becomes obligatory upon you to thank Allah for this bounty and to obey me.'[355]

أُوَخِّرَ لَكُمْ حَقّاً عَنْ مَحِلِّهِ، ولا أقِفَ بِهِ دُونَ مَقْطَعِهِ، وأنْ تَكونوا عِندي في الحَقِّ سَواءً، فإذا فَعَلْتُ ذلكَ وَجَبَتْ للهِ عَلَيْكُمُ النِّعْمَةُ ولي عَلَيْكُمُ الطّاعةُ.[٣٥٠]

100. Your Imāms Are Your Representatives

١٠٠ـ أئِمَّتُكُمْ وَفدُكُم

318. **The Prophet (SAWA) said,** 'Verily your Imāms are your representatives before Allah, therefore be careful whom you follow in your religion and your prayers.'[356]

٣١٨ . رسولُ اللهِ ﷺ : إنّ أئمّتَكُمْ وَفْدُكُمْ إلَى اللهِ، فانْظُروا مَنْ تُوفِدونَ في دِينِكُمْ وصَلاتِكُمْ.[٣٥١]

319. **The Prophet (SAWA) said,** 'Your Imāms are your leaders towards Allah, therefore be careful whom you follow in your religion and your prayers.'[357]

٣١٩ . عنه ﷺ : إنّ أئمّتَكُمْ قادَتُكُمْ إلَى اللهِ، فانْظُروا بِمَنْ تَقْتَدونَ في دِينِكُمْ وَصَلاتِكُمْ.[٣٥٢]

101. One Who Accepts the Leadership of an Unrightful Leader

١٠١ـ مَنِ ائتَمَّ بِغَيرِ إمامِ الحَقِّ

320. **Imām al-Bāqir (AS) said,** 'Allah, Blessed and most High said, 'I will certainly punish every Muslim community who accepted the leadership of a tyrant leader who is not chosen by Allah.'[358]

٣٢٠ . الإمامُ الباقرُ ؑ : قالَ اللهُ تبارَكَ وتعالَى: لأُعَذِّبَنَّ كُلَّ رَعِيَّةٍ في الإسلامِ دانَتْ بِوِلايَةِ كُلِّ إمامٍ جائرٍ ليسَ مِنَ اللهِ.[٣٥٣]

321. **Imām al-Ṣādiq (AS) said,** 'Whoever associates with an Imām chosen by Allah, a leader whose leadership is not endorsed by Allah, [is tantamount to having] ascribed a partner to Allah.'[359]

٣٢١ . الإمامُ الصّادقُ ؑ : مَنْ أشْرَكَ مَعَ إمامٍ إمامَتُهُ مِنْ عِنْدِ اللهِ مَنْ لَيسَتْ إمامَتُهُ مِنَ اللهِ كانَ مُشْرِكاً باللهِ.[٣٥٤]

322. **Imām al-Ṣādiq (AS) said,** 'Allah will not accept the good deeds performed by the servants if they accept the custodianship of a tyrant leader who has not been appointed by Allah, most High.'[360]

٣٢٢ . عنه ؑ : لا يَقْبَلُ اللهُ مِنَ العِبادِ الأعمالَ الصّالحةَ الّتي يَعْمَلونَها إذا تَوَلَّوا الإمامَ الجائرَ الّذي ليسَ مِنَ اللهِ تعالى.[٣٥٥]

102. Leaders to the Fire

١٠٢ ـ أئِمَّةُ النّارِ

"We made them leaders who invite to the Fire."[361]

﴿وَجَعَلْناهُمْ أَئِمَّةً يَدْعُونَ إِلَى النَّارِ﴾.[٣٥٦]

323. **Imām ʿAlī (AS) said,** 'Certainly the worst of people before Allah is the oppressive leader who himself has gone astray and misleads others. He destroys the prophetic practice and revives abandoned innovations. I have heard the Messenger of Allah (SAWA) saying, 'On the Day of Resurrection the oppressive leader will be brought without any helper or anyone to advance excuses on his behalf, and then he will be thrown into the Fire of Hell, where he will turn as the hand-mill turns, then he will be confined to its depth.'[362]

٣٢٣ . الإمامُ عليٌّ عليه السلام: إنّ شَرَّ النّاسِ عِنْدَ اللهِ إمامٌ جائرٌ ضَلَّ وضُلَّ بِهِ، فأماتَ سُنَّةً مأخُوذَةً وأحيا بِدْعةً مَتْروكَةً، وإنّي سَمِعْتُ رسولَ اللهِ صلى الله عليه وآله يقولُ: يُؤتىٰ يومَ القِيامَةِ بالإمامِ الجائرِ ولَيسَ مَعَهُ نَصيرٌ ولا عاذِرٌ، فيُلقىٰ في نارِ جَهَنَّمَ، فَيَدُورُ فيها كما تَدورُ الرَّحىٰ، ثُمَّ يُرْتَبَطُ في قَعْرِها.[٣٥٧]

103. The False Claimants of Imāma

١٠٣ ـ مُدَّعِي الإمامَةِ كاذِباً

324. **Imām al-Bāqir (AS),** regarding Allah's verse in the Qur'an: "*On the Day of Resurrection you will see those who attributed lies to Allah with their faces blackened*", said, '[It refers to] whoever says: I am an Imām, whereas he is not an Imām.'[363]

٣٢٤ . الإمامُ الباقرُ عليه السلام ـ في قولِهِ تعالىٰ: ﴿وَيَوْمَ القِيامَةِ تَرَىٰ الَّذِينَ كَذَبُوا عَلَى اللهِ وُجُوهُهُمْ مُسْوَدَّةٌ﴾[٣٥٨] ـ: مَنْ قالَ: إنّي إمامٌ، وليسَ بإمامٍ.[٣٥٩]

325. **Imām al-Ṣādiq (AS) said,** 'One who claims the *Imāma* unrightfully is an infidel.'[364]

٣٢٥ . الإمامُ الصّادقُ عليه السلام: مَنِ ادّعىٰ الإمامةَ ولَيسَ مِنْ أهلِها فَهُوَ كافِرٌ.[٣٦٠]

104. No Obedience is Due to one Who Disobeys Allah

١٠٤ ـ لا طاعَةَ لِمَن لَم يُطِعِ اللهَ

"And they will say, 'Our Lord! We obeyed our leaders and elders, and they led us astray from the way'"[365]

﴿وَقالُوا رَبَّنا إِنّا أَطَعْنا سادَتَنا وَكُبَراءَنا فَأَضَلُّونَا السَّبِيلَا﴾.[٣٦١]

326. **The Prophet (SAWA) said,** 'There is no obedience due to one who disobeys Allah.'[366]

٣٢٦ . رسولُ اللهِ صلى الله عليه وآله: لا طاعةَ لِمَنْ لَمْ يُطِعِ اللهَ.[٣٦٢]

327. **The Prophet (SAWA) said,** 'O ʿAlī, four things are truly back-breaking: a leader who

٣٢٧ . عنه صلى الله عليه وآله: يا عليُّ، أربعةٌ مِنْ قَواصِمِ

disobeys Allah whilst his command is obeyed…'[367]

الظَّهْرِ: إمامٌ يَعصي اللهَ ويُطاعُ أمْرُهُ....٣٦٣

328. **Imām ʿAlī (AS) said,** 'The Prophet (SAWA) dispatched an army, over whom he appointed a commander and ordered them to listen to him and to obey him. He [the commander] set ablaze a fire and ordered them to jump in it. Some people refused to enter it, saying, 'Verily we flee from the fire', whilst others intended to enter it. The Prophet (SAWA) was informed of this, about which he (SAWA) said, 'Had they entered it, they would have remained therein forever [i.e. the Hellfire].' And he said, 'There is no obedience due to [one who calls to] Allah's disobedience. Rather obedience is due [when calling] for the good.'[368]

٣٢٨. الإمامُ عليٌّ ﷺ: بَعَثَ النَّبيُّ ﷺ جَيْشاً وأمَّرَ عَلَيْهِمْ رَجُلاً وأمَرَهُمْ أنْ يَسْتَمِعوا لَهُ ويُطيعوا، فأجَّجَ ناراً وأمَرَهُمْ أنْ يَقْتَحِموا فيها، فأبى قومٌ أنْ يَدْخُلوها وقالوا: إنّا فَرَرْنا مِنَ النّارِ. وأرادَ قومٌ أنْ يَدْخُلوها، فَبَلَغَ ذلكَ النَّبيَّ ﷺ فقالَ: لو دَخَلوها لَم يَزالوا فيها، وقالَ: لا طاعةَ في مَعْصيةِ اللهِ، إنّما الطّاعةُ في المَعْروفِ.٣٦٤

105. Obligation of Revolting Against Tyrant Leaders

١٠٥ـ وُجوبُ الخُروجِ عَلى أئمَّةِ الجَوْرِ

329. **The Prophet (SAWA) said,** 'Verily the grinding stone of Islam will soon turn, so turn alongside the Qur'an wherever it turns. Soon the ruler and the Qur'an will combat each other and separate from each other. In fact there will be kings who will rule over you with one ruling and adhere to a different ruling for themselves. If you obey them, they will lead you astray. And if you disobey them, they will kill you.' They asked, 'O Messenger of Allah, what should we do if we witness such times?' He said, 'You must be like the companions of Jesus, who were cut into pieces with saws and were raised up on crosses. Dying in obedience [of Allah] is better than a life in disobedience.'[369]

٣٢٩. الدرّ المنثور: ـ قال رسولُ اللهِ ﷺ ـ: إنّ رَحَى الإسلامِ سَتَدورُ، فحَيْثُ ما دارَ القرآنُ فدوروا بِهِ، يُوشِكُ السُّلطانُ والقرآنُ أنْ يَقْتَتِلا ويَتَفَرَّقا، إنَّهُ سَيَكونُ عَلَيْكُمْ مُلوكٌ يَحْكُمونَ لَكُمْ بِحُكْمٍ، ولَهُمْ بِغَيْرِهِ، فإنْ أطَعْتُموهُمْ أضَلُّوكُمْ، وإنْ عَصَيْتُموهُمْ قَتَلوكُمْ. قالوا: يا رسولَ اللهِ، فكَيْفَ بنا إن أدرَكْنا ذلكَ؟ قالَ: تَكونونَ كأصْحابِ عيسى: نُشِروا بالمَناشيرِ ورُفِعوا عَلَى الخَشَبِ. مَوتٌ في طاعةٍ خَيْرٌ مِنْ حياةٍ في مَعْصيةٍ.٣٦٥

106. Circumstances Where Desisting from Revolting is Allowed

١٠٦ـ ما يُجَوِّزُ القُعودَ

330. **Imām al-Bāqir (AS) said,** 'If three hundred and thirteen people, the number of fighters at Badr get together in support of an Imām, it is

٣٣٠. الإمامُ الباقرُ ﷺ: إذا اجْتَمَعَ للإمامِ عِدَّةُ أهلِ بَدْرٍ «ثَلاثُمائةٍ وثَلاثةَ عَشَرَ» وَجَبَ عَلَيْهِ

obligatory upon him to rise up [against the unrightful leader] and bring about a change.'[370] [371]

القِيامُ والتَّغْييرُ.٣٦٦

331. **Imām al-Ṣādiq (AS) said,** 'O Sadīr! By Allah, were I to have followers as many as these goats, it would not be permissible for me to desist [from revolt].' Sadīr narrated, 'We disembarked and prayed, and when we finished the prayer, I looked at the goats and counted them, and there were only seventeen!'[372]

٣٣١. الكافي: ـ قالَ الإمامُ الصّادقُ ؑ لسدير ـ: واللهِ يا سَديرُ، لَو كانَ لي شيعةٌ بِعَدَدِ هذهِ الجِداءِ ما وَسِعَني القُعودُ. [قال سدير:] نَزَلْنا وصَلَّينا، فلَمّا فَرَغْنا مِنَ الصَّلاةِ عَطَفْتُ عَلَى الجِداءِ، فعَدَدْتُها فإذا هِيَ سَبعَةَ عَشَرَ.٣٦٧ ٣٦٨

107. Electing An Imām

١٠٧ ـ اختِيارُ الإمام

332. **Imām Mahdī (AS),** when Saʿd b. ʿAbdillāh al-Qummī asked him the reason why people cannot elect an Imām for themselves, replied, 'Would he be a righteous man or a corrupt man?' I said, 'Righteous.' He said, 'Is it possible that the selected individual be actually corrupt, for no one really knows what passes through another's mind, in terms of their righteousness or corruption?' I said, 'Yes'. He said, 'That is the reason why.'[373]

٣٣٢. كمال الدين عَن سَعْدِ بنِ عبدِ اللهِ القُمّيّ ـ لمّا سَألَهُ (الإمام المهدي ؑ) عَنِ العِلّةِ الّتي تَمْنَعُ القومَ من اختيارِ إمامٍ لأنفسِهِم ـ قال: مُصْلِحٌ أو مُفْسِدٌ؟ قلتُ: مُصْلِحٌ، قالَ: فَهَلْ يَجوزُ أنْ تَقَعَ خِيَرَتُهُمْ علَى المُفْسِدِ بَعْدَ أنْ لا يَعلمَ أحدٌ ما يَخْطُرُ بِبالِ غيرِهِ مِن صَلاحٍ أو فسادٍ؟ قلتُ: بلى، قالَ: فَهِيَ العِلَّةُ.٣٦٩

108. The Tradition of The Two Weighty Things (*al-Thaqalayn*)

١٠٨ ـ حَديثُ الثَّقلَين

333. **The Prophet (SAWA) said,** 'Verily I leave behind among you the two weighty things, which as long as you continue to adhere to, you will never go astray after me, and one of which is greater than the other. The Book of Allah is the rope stretched from the heavens to the earth, and my progeny, my household. Behold, verily they will never separate from each other until they meet me at the Heavenly Waters.'[374]

٣٣٣. رسولُ اللهِ ﷺ: إنّي قد تَرَكْتُ فِيكُمُ الثَّقلَيْنِ، ما إنْ تَمَسَّكْتُمْ بِهما لَن تَضِلّوا بَعْدي، وأحَدُهُما أكْبَرُ مِنَ الآخَرِ: كِتابُ اللهِ حَبْلٌ مَمْدودٌ مِنَ السَّماءِ إلَى الأرضِ، وعِتْرَتي أهلُ بَيْتي، ألَا وإنَّهُما لَن يَفْتَرِقا حتّى يَرِدا علَيَّ الحَوضَ.٣٧٠

109. The Obligation of Clinging on to The Household of the Prophet

١٠٩ ـ وُجوبُ مُلازَمةِ أهلِ البَيتِ ؑ

334. **The Prophet (SAWA) said,** 'Indeed the example of my household among you is like that

٣٣٤. رسولُ اللهِ ﷺ: إنّما مَثَلُ أهلِ بيتي فِيكُمْ

of Noah's Ark; whosoever embarked it was saved and whosoever chose to remain behind it was drowned.'[375]

كَمَثَلِ سَفينةِ نُوحٍ ؛ مَنْ رَكِبَها نَجا، ومَنْ تَخَلَّفَ عَنها غَرِقَ.[٣٧١]

335. **Imām ʿAlī (AS) said,** 'Look at the people of the Prophet's household. Adhere to their direction, follow their footsteps, because they will never remove you from guidance, and will never throw you into destruction. If they sit down [i.e. desist from revolting], you sit down, and if they rise up, you rise up.'[376]

٣٣٥. الإمامُ عليٌّ (ع) : انْظُروا أهلَ بيتِ نبيِّكُمْ، فالْزَموا سَمْتَهُمْ، واتَّبِعوا أثَرَهُمْ، فلَنْ يُخرِجوكُمْ مِن هُدىً، ولَنْ يُعيدوكُمْ في رَدىً، فإنْ لَبَدوا فالْبُدوا، وإنْ نَهَضوا فانْهَضوا.[٣٧٢]

336. **Imām ʿAlī (AS) said,** 'Lo! Verily the example of the family of Muḥammad (SAWA) is like that of the stars in the sky. When one star sets, another one rises. So you are in a position that Allah's blessings on you have been perfected and he has shown you what you have wished for.'[377]

٣٣٦. عنه (ع) : ألا إنّ مَثَلَ آلِ محمّدٍ ﷺ كَمَثَلِ نُجومِ السَّماءِ ؛ إذا خَوىٰ نَجْمٌ طَلَعَ نَجْمٌ، فكأنَّكُمْ قد تكامَلَتْ مِنَ اللهِ فيكُمُ الصَّنائعُ، وأراكُمْ ما كُنْتُمْ تأمَلونَ.[٣٧٣]

337. **Imām ʿAlī (AS) said,** 'We are the tree of prophethood, the settling place of the divine message, the place frequented by angels, the mines of knowledge and the springs of wisdom.'[378]

٣٣٧. عنه (ع) : نَحْنُ شَجَرَةُ النُّبوّةِ، ومَحَطُّ الرِّسالةِ، ومُخْتَلَفُ المَلائكةِ، ومَعادِنُ العِلْمِ، ويَنابيعُ الحُكْمِ.[٣٧٤]

338. **Imām ʿAlī (AS) said,** 'Verily the Imāms are the vicegerents of Allah over His creation, and they make the creatures know Allah. None will enter Paradise except he who acknowledges them and who himself is acknowledged by them, and none will enter Hell except he who denies them and is himself denied by them.'[379]

٣٣٨. عنه (ع) : إنّما الأئمّةُ قُوّامُ اللهِ علىٰ خَلْقِهِ، وعُرَفاؤهُ علىٰ عِبادِهِ، ولا يَدْخُلُ الجنّةَ إلّا مَنْ عَرَفَهُمْ وعَرَفوهُ، ولا يَدْخُلُ النّارَ إلّا مَنْ أنْكَرَهُمْ وأنْكَروهُ.[٣٧٥]

339. **Imām ʿAlī (AS) said,** 'We [the Prophet's household] are like the saddle-cushion in the middle. He who slides behind has to come forward to it, while he who has slid too far forward has to return back to it [people should take us as an example].'[380]

٣٣٩. عنه (ع) : نَحْنُ النُّمْرُقَةُ الوُسْطىٰ، بها يَلْحَقُ التّالي وإلَيها يَرْجِعُ الغالي.[٣٧٦]

340. **Imām al-Ṣādiq (AS),** mentioning the status and qualities of the Imāms said, 'Allah has made

٣٤٠. الإمامُ الصّادقُ (ع) ـ في ذِكْرِ حالِ الأئمّةِ

them the [source of] life for mankind, the lamps in the darkness, the keys to expression and the pillars of Islam.'[381]

وصفاتهم ـ : جَعَلَهُمُ اللهُ حياةً للأنامِ، ومَصابيحَ للظَّلامِ، ومَفاتيحَ للكلامِ، ودَعائمَ للإسلامِ.٣٧٧

(See also: KNOWLEDGE: section 1367) (أنظر العلم: باب ١٣٦٧)

110. The Reason For The Oppression Against The Household (AS)

١١٠ـ عِلَّةُ الاستبدادِ علىٰ أهلِ البَيتِ عليهم السلام

341. **Imām ʿAlī (AS) said,** 'As regards to the oppression against us in this matter –in spite of being the foremost in lineage and bearing the strongest relationship to the Messenger of Allah (SAWA)- it [caliphate] was tempting. The hearts of some people coveted it [the leadership] whereas the hearts of others did not care for it. And the Arbiter is Allah.'[382]

٣٤١. الإمامُ عليٌّ عليه السلام : أمّا الاسْتِبدادُ علَينا بهذا المَقامِ ـ ونحنُ الأعْلَونَ نَسَباً والأشَدُّونَ برسولِ اللهِ صلى الله عليه وآله نَوْطاً ـ فإنّها كانتْ أثَرةً، شَحَّتْ علَيها نفوسُ قومٍ وسَخَتْ عنها نفوسُ آخَرينَ، والحَكَمُ اللهُ.٣٧٨

111. The Philosophy of Leadership in the Viewpoint of the Household (AS)

١١١ـ فلسفة الحكم عند أهل البيت عليهم السلام

342. **Imām ʿAlī (AS) said,** 'O Allah! You know that what we did was neither to compete for power nor to acquire anything from the vanities of the world. Rather we only wanted to restore the original characteristics of Your religion and to usher prosperity into Your lands, so that the oppressed from among Your servants may be safe and that Your abolished commands may be re-established.'[383]

٣٤٢. الإمامُ عليٌّ عليه السلام : اللّهُمَّ إنّكَ تَعلَمُ أنّهُ لم يَكُنِ الّذي كانَ مِنّا مُنافسةً في سُلطانٍ، ولا الْتِماسَ شيءٍ مِن فُضولِ الحُطامِ، ولكن لِنَرُدَّ المَعالِمَ مِن دِينِكَ، ونُظهِرَ الإصْلاحَ في بلادِكَ، فيأمَنَ المظلومونَ مِن عِبادِكَ، وتُقامَ المُعَطَّلةُ مِن حُدودِكَ.٣٧٩

(See also: GOVERNMENT: section 74) (أنظر الإمارة: باب ٧٤)

112. Were it Not For Fear of Dissention

١١٢ـ لَولا مَخافَةُ الفُرقَةِ

343. **Imām ʿAlī (AS) said,** 'By Allah, were it not for fear of dissention among the Muslims, that

٣٤٣. الإمامُ عليٌّ عليه السلام : وأيمُ اللهِ، لولا مَخافةُ

they would return to disbelief and that the religion would be damaged, we would indeed have changed the situation [of leadership] as much as possible.'[384]

الفُرقَةِ بَيْنَ المسلمينَ، وأن يَعودوا إلَى الكفرِ ويَعْوَرَّ الدِّينُ، لَكُنّا قد غَيَّرْنا ذلكَ ما استَطَعْنا. ٣٨٠

113. The Twelve Imāms

١١٣ـ الأئِمَّةُ الإثنا عَشَرَ

344. **The Prophet (SAWA) said,** 'The affairs of the people will continue to progress as long as the twelve men govern them ... all of them will be from [the tribe of] Quraysh.'[385]

٣٤٤. رسولُ اللهِ ﷺ: لا يَزالُ أمرُ النّاسِ ماضياً ما وَلِيَهُم اثنا عَشَرَ رجُلاً... كلّهُم مِن قريشٍ. ٣٨١، ٣٨٢

345. **The Prophet (SAWA) said,** 'Verily the number of successors after me is as the number of chiefs of Moses.'[386]

٣٤٥. عنه ﷺ: إنّ عِدّةَ الخُلَفاءِ بَعدي عِدّةُ نُقَباءِ موسىٰ. ٣٨٣

114. The Knowledge of The Imām

١١٤ـ عِلمُ الإمامِ

346. **Imām al-Ṣādiq (AS) said,** 'Verily 'Alī was knowledgeable and knowledge is something that is inherited. In fact, no sooner does a knowledgeable man die than there remains after him one who knows his knowledge or whatever Allah wishes.'[387]

٣٤٦. الإمامُ الصّادقُ ﷺ: إنّ عليّاً كانَ عالِماً والعِلمُ يُتوارَثُ، ولَن يَهْلِكَ عالِمٌ إلّا بَقِيَ مِن بَعدِهِ مَن يَعلَمُ عِلمَهُ أو ما شاءَ اللهُ. ٣٨٤

347. **Imām al-Ṣādiq (AS) said,** 'By Allah, certainly I know the Book of Allah from its beginning to its end, as if it is in my palm. In it is contained the information about the heavens and the earth, about all that existed and all that is to be. Allah, Mighty and Exalted, has said: *"In it is clarification of all things."*'[388] [389]

٣٤٧. عنه ﷺ: واللهِ، إنّي لَأعلَمُ كتابَ اللهِ مِن أوّلِهِ إلىٰ آخِرِهِ كأنّهُ في كَفّي، فيهِ خَبَرُ السّماءِ وخَبَرُ الأرضِ، وخَبَرُ ما كانَ وخَبَرُ ما هو كائنٌ، قالَ اللهُ عزّ وجلّ: فيهِ تِبيانُ كلِّ شيءٍ. ٣٨٥، ٣٨٦

348. **Imām al-Riḍā (AS) said,** 'Whenever Allah selects a person to manage the affairs of His creation, He opens his breast [endows him with tolerance] for that purpose, and he makes springs of wisdom flow in his heart, and bestows knowledge to him by way of inspiration, after which he never again lacks the capacity to answer, nor is confused from finding the right way out.'[390]

٣٤٨. الإمامُ الرِّضا ﷺ: إنّ العبدَ إذا اختارَهُ اللهُ عزّ وجلّ لأُمورِ عِبادِهِ شَرَحَ صَدرَهُ لذلكَ، وأودَعَ قلبَهُ يَنابِيعَ الحِكمَةِ، وألْهَمَهُ العِلمَ إلهاماً، فلَم يَعْيَ بعدَهُ بجوابٍ ولا يَحيرُ فيهِ عنِ الصّوابِ. ٣٨٧

(See also: KNOWLEDGE: section 1365, 1367; THE UNSEEN: section 1453)

(أنظر) العلم: باب ١٣٦٥، ١٣٦٧؛ الغيب: باب ١٤٥٣

17

LEADERSHIP (2) الإمامة (٢)

Particular Imāma

IMĀM ʿALĪ (AS) الإمام علي بن أبي طالب عليه السلام

1 - The Virtues of Imām ʿAlī in the Sayings of the Holy Prophet (SAWA) ١ ـ فضائل الامام على عن لسان النبي ﷺ

115. Love For Imām ʿAlī and Hatred Towards Him ١١٥ ـ حبّ الامام عليٍ وبغضه ﷺ

349. **The Prophet (SAWA) said,** 'Love for ʿAlī consumes sins as fire consumes wood.'[391]

٣٤٩. رسولُ اللهِ ﷺ: حُبُّ عليٍّ يأكُلُ الذُّنوبَ كما تأكُلُ النّارُ الحَطَبَ.[٣٨٨]

350. **The Prophet (SAWA) said,** 'The title of the deeds of a believer is the love for ʿAlī b. Abī Ṭālib.'[392]

٣٥٠. عنه ﷺ: عُنوانُ صحيفةِ المؤمنِ حُبُّ عليِّ بنِ أبي طالبٍ.[٣٨٩]

351. **The Prophet (SAWA) said,** 'When Allah secures the love for ʿAlī in a believer's heart, whenever his foot slips, Allah will secure his foot on the *Ṣirāṭ* [Bridge outstretched over Hell] on the Day of Resurrection.'[393]

٣٥١. عنه ﷺ: ما ثَبَّتَ اللهُ حُبَّ عليٍّ في قلبِ مؤمنٍ فزَلَّتْ به قدمٌ إلّا ثَبَّتَ اللهُ قَدَماً يومَ القيامةِ علَى الصِّراطِ.[٣٩٠]

352. **The Prophet (SAWA)** said to ʿAlī, 'None will love you but a believer and none will hate you but a hypocrite.'[394]

٣٥٢. عنه ﷺ ـ لِعَليٍّ ﷺ ـ: لا يُحِبُّكَ إلّا مؤمنٌ، ولا يُبغِضُكَ إلّا منافقٌ.[٣٩١]

(See also: LOVE: section 434) (انظر) المحبة: باب ٤٣٤

116. ʿAlī is the Imām of the Righteous ١١٦ ـ عليٌّ ﷺ إمامُ البَرَرَةِ

353. **The Prophet (SAWA) said,** "ʿAlī is the Imām of the righteous, and the fighter of the insolent lot. Whoever helps him is helped [by

٣٥٣. رسولُ اللهِ ﷺ: عليٌّ إمامُ البَرَرَةِ، وقاتِلُ الفَجَرَةِ، منصورٌ مَن نَصرَهُ، مَخذولٌ

Allah] and whoever abandons him is abandoned [by Allah].'[395]

مَن خَذَلَهُ.٣٩٢

354. **The Prophet (SAWA) said,** 'It has been revealed to me about ʿAlī that he is the chief of the Muslims, the Imām of the Godwary, and the leader of the bright faced ones.'[396]

٣٥٤. عنه ﷺ: أُوحِيَ إليَّ في عليٍّ بثلاث خصال: أنَّهُ سيِّدُ المسلمينَ، وإمامُ المُتّقينَ، وقائدُ الغُرِّ المُحَجَّلينَ.٣٩٣

355. **The Prophet (SAWA) said,** 'Verily Allah informed me of certain issues regarding ʿAlī b. Abī Ṭālib (AS). I said, 'O Lord, reveal them to me.' He said, 'Listen.' I said, 'I certainly am.' He said, 'Verily ʿAlī is the banner of guidance, the Imām of My friends, the light of those who obey Me. He is the word that I have attached to the Godwary. Whoever loves him loves Me, and whoever obeys him obeys Me.'[397]

٣٥٥. عنه ﷺ: إنّ اللهَ عزّ وجلّ عَهِدَ إليَّ في عليٍّ عَهْداً، قلتُ: يا ربِّ بَيِّنْهُ لي. قالَ: اسْمَعْ. قلتُ: قد سَمِعْتُ، قالَ: إنّ عليّاً رايةُ الهُدىٰ وإمامُ أوليائي ونورُ مَن أطاعَني، وهُوَ الكلمةُ الّتي أَلْزَمْتُها المتّقينَ٣٩٤، مَن أحبَّهُ أحبَّني، ومَن أطاعَهُ أطاعَني.٣٩٥

117. ʿAlī is the Successor of the Holy Prophet (SAWA)

١١٧ـ عليٌّ خَليفَةُ النَّبِيِّ ﷺ

356. **The Prophet (SAWA) said,** 'Certainly my brother, the executor of my will, my minister and my successor from among my family is ʿAlī b. Abī Ṭālib. He will repay my dues and will fulfil my promises, O Banī Hāshim.'[398]

٣٥٦. رسولُ اللهِ ﷺ: إنّ أخي ووصِيّي ووزيري وخليفَتي في أهلي عليُّ بنُ أبي طالبٍ، يَقْضي دَيني، ويُنْجِزُ مَوعِدي يا بني هاشمٍ.٣٩٦

357. **The Prophet (SAWA),** pointing to ʿAlī said, 'Verily this is my brother, the executor of my will, and my successor among you, so listen to him and obey him.'[399]

٣٥٧. عنه ﷺ ـ مُشيراً إلىٰ عليٍّ ﷺ ـ: إنّ هذا أخي ووصيّي وخليفتي فيكُم، فاسْمَعوا لَه وأطيعُوا.٣٩٧

118. ʿAlī is the Master of Every Believer

١١٨ـ عَلِيٌّ ﷺ وَلِيُّ كُلِّ مُؤمِنٍ

358. **The Prophet (SAWA) said,** 'For whosoever I am master, ʿAlī is his master.'[400]

٣٥٨. رسولُ اللهِ ﷺ: مَن كنتُ مَولاهُ فعليٌّ مَولاهُ.٣٩٨

359. **The Prophet (SAWA) said,** 'Certainly ʿAlī is from me and I am from him, and he is the custodian of every believer.'[401]

٣٥٩. عنه ﷺ: إنّ عليّاً منّي وأنا مِنهُ، وهُو وليُّ كلِّ مؤمنٍ بَعدي.٣٩٩

360. **ʿAbd al-Raḥmān b. Abī Laylā said,** 'I witnessed ʿAlī in Ruḥba [Kūfa] summoning out to the people: I summon before Allah whosoever heard the Prophet say on the Day of Ghadīr Khum, 'For whosoever I am master, ʿAlī is his master' to stand and bear witness. [ʿAbd al-Raḥmān said], 'Twelve men from Badr stood up, like as if I am looking at one of them [recollect them one by one], saying, 'We bear witness that we heard the Prophet (SAWA) say on the Day of Ghadīr Khum: 'Do I not have more authority over the believers than their own selves...?' Then we said, 'Yes, O Messenger of Allah.' He then said, 'Then, for whosoever I am master, ʿAlī is his master. O Allah befriend whoever befriends him and fight whoever fights him.'[402]

٣٦٠. تاريخ دمشق عن عبدِ الرّحمٰنِ بنِ أبي ليلىٰ: شَهِدتُ عليّاً في الرُّحبةِ يَنشُدُ النّاسَ: أنْشُدُ اللهَ مَن سَمِعَ رسولَ اللهِ ﷺ يقولُ يومَ غديرِ خُمّ: «مَن كنتُ مولاهُ فعليٌّ مولاهُ» لَمّا قامَ فشَهِدَ، قالَ عبدُ الرّحمٰنِ: فقامَ اثنا عَشَرَ بَدْريّاً، كأنّي أنظُرُ إلىٰ أحدِهِم، فقالوا: نَشهَدُ أنّا سَمِعْنا رسولَ اللهِ ﷺ يقولُ يومَ غديرِ خُمٍّ: ألستُ أولىٰ بالمؤمنينَ ...؟ فقُلنا: بلىٰ يا رسولَ اللهِ، قالَ: مَنْ كنتُ مَولاهُ فعليٌّ مَولاهُ، اللّهمَّ والِ مَن والاهُ وعادِ مَن عاداهُ.[٤٠٠]

119. ʿAlī is with the Truth and the Qur'an

١١٩ـ عَلِيٌّ عليه السلام مَعَ الحَقِّ والقرآن

361. **The Prophet (SAWA) said,** 'Alī is with the truth and the truth is with ʿAlī – it turns wherever he turns [they are inseparable].'[403]

٣٦١. رسولُ اللهِ ﷺ: عليٌّ مَع الحقِّ والحقُّ مَع عليٍّ، يَدورُ حَيثُما دارَ.[٤٠١، ٤٠٢]

362. **The Prophet (SAWA) said,** 'The truth is with ʿAlī wherever he inclines.'[404]

٣٦٢. عنه ﷺ: الحقُّ مع عليٍّ أيْنَما مالَ.[٤٠٣]

363. **The Prophet (SAWA) said,** 'Alī is with the Qur'an and the Qur'an is with ʿAlī. They will never separate until they come to me at the Heavenly Waters.'[405]

٣٦٣. عنه ﷺ: عليٌّ معَ الحقِّ والحقُّ معَ عليٍّ، ولن يَتَفَرّقا حتّىٰ يَرِدا علَيَّ الحوضَ يومَ القيامةِ.[٤٠٤]

364. **The Prophet (SAWA) said,** 'Alī is with the truth and the Qur'an, and the truth and the Qur'an are with ʿAlī, and they will not separate until they come to me at the Heavenly Waters.'[406]

٣٦٤. عنه ﷺ: عليٌّ مَع الحقِّ والقرآنِ، والحقُّ والقرآنُ معَ عليٍّ، ولن يَتَفَرَّقا حتّىٰ يَرِدا علَيّ الحوضَ.[٤٠٥]

120. ʿAlī is the Gate to the Prophet's Knowledge

١٢٠ـ عَلِيٌّ عليه السلام بابُ عِلمِ النَّبِيِّ

365. **The Prophet (SAWA) said,** 'I am the city of knowledge and ʿAlī is its gate,

٣٦٥. رسولُ اللهِ ﷺ: أنا مدينةُ العلمِ وعليٌّ

whosoever wants the knowledge should approach it through its gate.'[407]

بابُها، فمَن أرادَ العلمَ فلْيَأتِ البابَ.[٤٠٦]

366. **The Prophet (SAWA) said,** 'I am the house of wisdom and 'Alī is its door.'[408]

٣٦٦ . عنه ﷺ: أنا دارُ الحِكمةِ وعليٌّ بابُها.[٤٠٧]

367. **The Prophet (SAWA) said,** 'The most superior in judgment from my community and the most learned of my community after me is 'Alī.'[409]

٣٦٧ . عنه ﷺ: أقضىٰ أُمّتي وأعلمُ أُمّتي بَعدي عليٌّ.[٤٠٨]

121. 'Alī and the Prophet (SAWA) are from the Same Tree

١٢١ـ عليّ والنبيّ من شجرةٍ واحدةٍ

368. **The Prophet (SAWA) said,** "Alī and I are from the same tree, and the rest of people are from different trees.'[410]

٣٦٨ . رسولُ اللهِ ﷺ: أنا وعليٌّ مِن شَجَرةٍ واحدةٍ، والنّاسُ مِن أشجارٍ شَتّىٰ.[٤٠٩]

369. **The Prophet (SAWA)** said to 'Alī, 'You are my brother in this world and in the Hereafter.'[411]

٣٦٩ . رسولُ اللهِ ﷺ ـ لِعليٍّ عليه السلام ـ: أنتَ أخي في الدُّنيا والآخِرَةِ.[٤١٠]

370. **The Prophet (SAWA) said,** "Alī is from me and I am from him.'[412]

٣٧٠ . رسولُ اللهِ ﷺ: عليٌّ مِنّي وأنا مِنهُ.[٤١١]

371. **The Prophet (SAWA) said,** "Alī is to me like my head is to my body.'[413]

٣٧١ . عنه ﷺ: عليٌّ مِنّي بمنزلةِ رَأسي مِن بَدَني.[٤١٢]

372. **The Prophet (SAWA) said,** 'Verily 'Alī's flesh is from my flesh and his blood is from my blood.'[414]

٣٧٢ . عنه ﷺ: إنّ عليّاً لَحْمُهُ مِن لَحْمي ودَمُهُ مِن دَمي.[٤١٣]

373. Jābir narrated, 'The Prophet (SAWA) was once in 'Arafa and 'Alī (A.S) was facing him. He then said to him, "Alī, come closer to me and place your five [fingers of your hand] on my five. O 'Alī, you and I have been created from one tree. I am its root and you are its trunk. Ḥasan and Ḥusayn are its branches. Whoever clings onto any of its branches, Allah will make him enter Paradise.'[415]

٣٧٣ . تاريخ دمشق: إنّ النّبيَّ ﷺ كان بعرَفَةَ وعليٌّ تجاهَهُ، فقالَ: يا عليُّ، أُدْنُ مِنّي (و) ضَعْ خَمْسَكَ في خَمْسِي. يا عليُّ، خُلِقْتُ أنا وأنتَ مِن شَجَرةٍ أنا أصلُها وأنتَ فَرعُها، والحَسَنُ والحُسَينُ أغصانُها، مَن تَعَلّقَ بغُصْنٍ مِنها أدخَلَهُ اللهُ الجَنّةَ.[٤١٤]

122. Miscellaneous

١٢٢ـ النَّوادر

374. **The Prophet (SAWA)** said to 'Alī (AS), 'Your position with respect to me is as that of

٣٧٤ . رسولُ اللهِ ﷺ ـ لِعليٍّ عليه السلام ـ: أنتَ مِنّي بمنزلةِ

Aaron[416] to Moses, except that there is no prophet after me.'[417]

هارونَ مِن موسىٰ إلّا أنّه لا نَبيَّ بَعدي.[٤١٥]

375. **The Prophet (SAWA)**, when the issue of the rulership and the successorship [after him] was mentioned, said, 'If you entrust the government to ʿAlī, you will find him a rightly-guided guide, who will take you to the right path.'[418]

٣٧٥. عنه ﷺ ـ عندما ذُكِرَتِ الإمارةُ أو الخلافةُ عندَهُ ـ: إنْ وَلَّيتُموها عَليّاً وجَدْتُموهُ هادِياً مَهْدِيّاً، يَسلُكُ بكُمْ علَى الطَّريقِ المستقيمِ.[٤١٦]

376. **The Prophet (SAWA) said,** 'Whoever wishes to look at Adam for his knowledge, Noah[419] for his understanding, Abraham for his clemency, John [the Baptist][420] son of Zacharias[421] for his abstemiousness, and Moses son of Amran for his might, should look at ʿAlī b. Abī Ṭālib.'[422]

٣٧٦. عنه ﷺ: مَن أرادَ أن يَنظُرَ إلىٰ آدمَ في عِلمِهِ، وإلىٰ نوحٍ في فَهمِهِ، وإلىٰ إبراهيمَ في حِلمِهِ، وإلىٰ يحيىٰ بنِ زكريّا في زُهدِهِ، وإلىٰ موسىٰ بنِ عِمرانَ في بَطْشِهِ، فَلْيَنْظُرْ إلىٰ عليِّ بنِ أبي طالبٍ.[٤١٧]

377. **The Prophet (SAWA) said,** "Alī is the chief of the believers.'[423]

٣٧٧. عنه ﷺ: عليٌّ سيّدُ المؤمنينَ.[٤١٨]

378. **The Prophet (SAWA) said,** "Alī is the pillar of the religion.'[424]

٣٧٨. عنه ﷺ: عليٌّ عَمودُ الدِّينِ.[٤١٩]

379. **The Prophet (SAWA) said,** 'Whoever hurts ʿAlī has in fact hurt me.'[425]

٣٧٩. عنه ﷺ: مَن آذىٰ عليّاً فقدْ آذاني.[٤٢٠]

380. **The Prophet (SAWA) said,** "Alī is the chief of the believers, and wealth is the chief of the hypocrites.'[426]

٣٨٠. عنه ﷺ: عليٌّ يَعْسوبُ المؤمنينَ، والمالُ يَعْسوبُ المنافقينَ.[٤٢١]

381. **The Prophet (SAWA) said,** "Alī's right over this community is like the right of a father over his son.'[427]

٣٨١. عنه ﷺ: حقُّ عليٍّ على هذهِ الأُمّةِ كحَقِّ الوالدِ علَى الوَلَدِ.[٤٢٢]

382. **The Prophet (SAWA) said,** "Alī b. Abī Ṭālib is my confidant.'[428]

٣٨٢. عنه ﷺ: صاحِبُ سِرّي عليُّ بنُ أبي طالبٍ.[٤٢٣]

383. **The Prophet (SAWA) said,** 'Verily ʿAlī and his followers will be the winners on the Day of Resurrection.'[429]

٣٨٣. عنه ﷺ: إنّ عليّاً وشيعتَهُ هُمُ الفائزونَ يومَ القيامةِ.[٤٢٤]

384. **The Prophet (SAWA) said,** 'The remembrance of ʿAlī is worship.'[430]

٣٨٤. عنه ﷺ: ذِكرُ عليٍّ عبادةٌ.٤٢٥

385. **The Prophet (SAWA) said,** 'My hand and that of ʿAlī in administering justice are equal..'[431]

٣٨٥. عنه ﷺ: كَفّي وكَفُّ عليٍّ في العَدلِ سَواءٌ.٤٢٦

2 – The Virtues of Imam Ali in his own Words

٢ ـ فضائل الإمام عليّ عن لسانه

123. Imām ʿAlī's Knowledge

١٢٣ ـ عِلمُ الإمامِ عليٍّ ﷺ

386. **Imām ʿAlī (AS),** in his sermon after having been pledged allegiance to as the Caliph, said, 'O people, ask me before you lose me. Ask me for I have the knowledge of the past and the future. By Allah, if I was set up to judge, I would certainly judge for the people of the Torah with their Torah itself…' He then said, 'Ask me before you lose me. By He who split the seed and originated man, were you to ask me about each and every verse of the Qur'an, I would inform you when the verse was revealed and the reason for its revelation.'[432]

٣٨٦. الإمامُ عليٌّ ﷺ ـ في خُطبتِه لمّا بُويعَ بالخلافة ـ: يامعشرَ النّاسِ، سَلُوني قبلَ أن تَفْقِدوني، سَلُوني فإنّ عندي عِلمَ الأوّلينَ والآخِرينَ. أمَا واللهِ لو ثُنِيَ لي الوِسادُ لَحَكَمْتُ بينَ أهلِ التّوارةِ بتَوراتِهم... ـ ثُمّ قالَ: ـ سَلُوني قبلَ أن تَفْقِدوني، فوالّذي فَلَقَ الحَبّةَ وبَرأَ النَّسَمَةَ لو سَألتُموني عن آيةٍ آيةٍ لأخبَرتُكُم بوقتِ نُزولِها وفي مَن نَزَلَتْ.٤٢٧

387. **Imām ʿAlī (AS) said,** 'I am fused with a hidden knowledge such that were I to disclose it, you would be shaking like ropes hanging from a bucket in a deep well.'[433]

٣٨٧. عنه ﷺ: اندَمَجْتُ على مَكنونِ عِلمٍ لو بُحْتُ بِهِ لاضْطَرَبْتُمُ اضْطِرابَ الأرشيَةِ في الطَّوِيِّ البعيدةِ.٤٢٨

124. Imām ʿAlī's Victimization

١٢٤ ـ مَظلوميّةُ الإمامِ عليٍّ ﷺ

388. **Imām ʿAlī (AS) said,** 'I have been oppressed ever since the Prophet (SAWA) passed away.'[434]

٣٨٨. الإمامُ عليٌّ ﷺ: ما زِلْتُ مُذ قُبِضَ رسولُ اللهِ ﷺ مظلوماً.٤٢٩

389. **Imām ʿAlī (AS) said,** 'No person has faced what I have faced.'[435]

٣٨٩. عنه ﷺ: مالَقِيَ أحدٌ مِن النّاسِ مالَقِيتُ.٤٣٠

390. **Imām ʿAlī (AS) said,** 'I used to think that the ruler oppresses the people, but now the people oppress the ruler!'[436]

٣٩٠. عنه ﷺ: كنتُ أرى أنّ الواليَ يَظلِمُ الرَّعيّةَ، فإذا الرَّعيّةُ تَظلِمُ الواليَ!٤٣١

391. **Imām ʿAlī (AS)** when someone said to him, 'Verily you are greedy for the caliphate', he

٣٩١. عنه ﷺ ـ وقد قيلَ له: إنّكَ على هذا الأمرِ

replied, 'Rather, you are, by Allah, greedier and more remote, while I am more suited as well as more qualified for it. I have only demanded it as a right that is mine, while you are intervening between me and it, and you are keeping me away from it … 'O Allah, I appeal to you for assistance against the Quraysh and all those who have aided them, for verily they have denied me the rights of kinship, lowered my high position, and have grouped together to challenge what is rightfully mine.'[437]

[الخلافة] لَحريصٌ ـ: بَلْ أنـتُم واللهِ لَأحْـرَصُ وأبْعَدُ، وأنا أخصُّ وأقْرَبُ، وإنّما طَلَبتُ حقّاً لي وأنتمُ تَحُولونَ بَيني وبَينَهُ، وتَـضربونَ وَجْـهي دُونَه... اللّهمّ إنّي أستَعديكَ على قُـريشٍ ومَـن أعانَهُم، فإنّهم قَطَعوا رَحِمي، وصَـغَّروا عَـظيمَ مَنزلتي، وأجْـمَعوا عـلى مُـنازَعَتي أمْـراً هُـو لي.٤٣٣

125. What Begins with "Verily I..."

١٢٥ـ ما يبدأ بلفظ «إنّي»

392. **Imām 'Alī (AS) said,** 'Verily I do not encourage you to perform any act of obedience without performing it myself first, nor do I prohibit you from any sin without first refraining from it myself.'[438]

٣٩٢. الإمامُ عليٌّ (ع): إنّي لا أحُثُّكُم على طاعةٍ إلّا وأسْبِقُكُم إلَيها، ولا أنهاكُم عـن مـعصيةٍ إلّا وأتَناهىٰ قَبلَكُم عنها.٤٣٤

393. **Imām 'Alī (AS) said,** 'Verily I am among you, O people, like Aaron was among Pharaoh's clan, like the door of relief [from the burden of sins] for the Children of Israel, like Noah's Ark for Noah's people. And verily I am the Great News, the most veracious person, and very soon you will all know what you have been promised.'[439]

٣٩٣. عنه (ع): إنّي فيكُم أيُّها النّاسُ كـهارونَ في آلِ فِرعونَ، وكبابِ حِطّةٍ في بني إسرائيلَ، وكسفينةِ نوحٍ (ع) فـي قـومِ نـوحٍ، وإنّـي النّبأُ الأعظمُ، والصِّدّيقُ الأكبرُ، وعن قَليلٍ ستَعْلَمونَ ما تُوعَدونَ.٤٣٥

394. **Imām 'Alī (AS) said,** 'Verily I have never fled from the battlefield.'[440]

٣٩٤. عنه (ع): إنّي لَم أفِرَّ مِنَ الزَّحفِ قَطُّ.٤٣٦

126. What Begins with the word "I..."

١٢٦ـ ما يبدأ بلفظ «أنا»

395. **Imām 'Alī (AS) said,** 'I am the one who belittles the world.'[441]

٣٩٥. الإمامُ عليٌّ (ع): أنا الّذي أهَنْتُ الدُّنيا.٤٣٧

396. **Imām 'Alī (AS) said,** 'I am the closest [in resemblance] to the Prophet, the foremost to [enter] Islam, the demolisher of the idols, the combatant of the

٣٩٦. عنه (ع): أنا صِنْوُ رسـولِ اللهِ، والسّـابقُ إلَـى الإسـلامِ، وكـاسِرُ الأصنامِ، ومُـجاهِدُ

faithless, and the suppressor of the antagonists [of Islam]'.[442]

الكفّارِ، وقامعُ الأضدادِ.٤٣٨

397. **Imām ʿAlī (AS) said,** 'I am the flag of guidance, the sanctuary of the Godwary ones, the place of generosity, the ocean of open-handedness, and the mountain of intelligence.'[443]

٣٩٧. عنه ؑ: أنا عَلَمُ الهُدىٰ، وكَهْفُ التُّقىٰ، ومَحَلُّ السَّخاءِ، وبَحرُ النَّدىٰ، وطَودُ النُّهىٰ.٤٣٩

398. **Imām ʿAlī (AS) said,** 'I am Allah's differentiator between Hell and Heaven, and none will enter it but as differentiated by me, I am the greatest distinguisher [between falsehood and truth] and I am the Imām for those after me and the executor of [the will of] those before me.'[444]

٣٩٨. عنه ؑ: أنا قَسيمُ اللهِ بينَ الجَنّةِ والنّارِ، لا يَدخُلُها داخِلٌ إلّا علىٰ حَدِّ قَسْمي، وأنا الفاروقُ الأكبرُ، وأنا الإمامُ لِمَن بَعدي، والمُؤَدّي عَمَّن كانَ قَبلي.٤٤٠

399. **Imām ʿAli (AS) said,** 'I am the leader of the believers and wealth is the leader of the debauched.'[445]

٣٩٩. عنه ؑ: أنا يَعسوبُ المُؤمنينَ، وَالمالُ يَعسوبُ الفُجّارِ.٤٤١

400. **Imām ʿAlī (AS) said,** 'I am the guide and I am the guided. I am the father of the orphans and the destitute, and the guardian of the widows. I am the refuge of every weak person and the haven of every fearful one. I am the leader of the believers to Paradise; I am the strong rope of Allah; I am Allah's firmest handle and the word of Godwariness. I am the eye of Allah, His truthful tongue and His hand.'[446]

٤٠٠. عنه ؑ: أنا الهادي، وأنا المُهتَدي، وأنا أبو اليَتامىٰ والمَساكينِ، وزوجُ الأراملِ، وأنا مَلْجَأُ كلِّ ضعيفٍ، ومأمَنُ كلِّ خائفٍ، وأنا قائدُ المؤمنينَ إلَى الجنّةِ، وأنا حَبلُ اللهِ المتينُ، وأنا عُروَةُ اللهِ الوُثقىٰ، وكلمةُ التّقوىٰ، وأنا عَينُ اللهِ، ولسانُهُ الصّادقُ، ويَدُهُ.٤٤٢

401. **Imām ʿAlī (AS) said,** 'I am the first who will plead for justice before Allah on the Day of Resurrection.'[447]

٤٠١. عنه ؑ: أنا أوّلُ مَن يَجثو لِلخُصومَةِ بينَ يدَيِ اللهِ عزّ وجلّ يومَ القيامةِ.٤٤٣

402. **Imām ʿAlī (AS) said,** 'I was the first to embrace Islam.'[448]

٤٠٢. عنه ؑ: أنا أوّلُ مَن أسلَمَ.٤٤٤

403. **Imām ʿAlī (AS) said,** 'I was the first to pray with the Prophet (SAWA).'[449]

٤٠٣. عنه ؑ: أنا أوّلُ مَن صَلّىٰ مع النّبيِّ ﷺ.٤٤٥

127. Miscellaneous

١٢٧ ـ النّوادرُ

404. **Imām ʿAlī (AS)** narrated that the Prophet (SAWA) said, 'Were it not for you, O ʿAlī, the believers would not have been known after me.'[450]

٤٠٤. عنه ؑ: قالَ رسولُ اللهِ ﷺ: لَوْلاكَ يا عليُّ، ما عُرِفَ المؤمنونَ مِنْ بَعْدي.٤٤٦

405. **Imām ʿAlī (AS) said,** 'By Allah, I would rather pass a night awake on the thorns of prickly bush or be driven in chains as a prisoner than meet Allah and His Messenger on the Day of Resurrection as having wronged anyone ...'
By Allah, even if I am given all the domains of the seven heavens with all that exists under the skies in exchange for disobeying Allah to the extent of snatching away one grain of barley from an ant, I would never do it.'[451]

٤٠٥. عنه (ع): واللهِ، لَأنْ أبيتَ علىٰ حَسَكِ السَّعْدانِ مُسَهَّداً أو أُجَرَّ في الأغْلالِ مُصَفَّداً أحَبُّ إليَّ مِن أنْ ألقى اللهَ ورسولَه يومَ القيامةِ ظالماً ...
واللهِ، لو أُعْطيتُ الأقاليمَ السَّبعةَ بما تحتَ أفلاكِها علىٰ أن أعصِيَ اللهَ في نَمْلةٍ أسْلُبُها جُلْبَ شَعيرةٍ ما فَعَلْتُه.[٤٤٧]

406. **Imām ʿAlī (AS) said,** 'Verily my example among you is as that of a lamp in the darkness, whoever enters its vicinity is enlightened by it.'[452]

٤٠٦. عنه (ع): إنّما مَثَلي بينَكُم كالسِّراجِ في الظُّلْمَةِ، يَستَضيءُ بها مَن وَلَجَها.[٤٤٨]

407. **Imām ʿAlī (AS)** used to say, 'Neither does Allah have a sign bigger than me, nor does Allah have news greater than me [after the holy Prophet (SAWA)].'[453]

٤٠٧. عنه (ع) ـ أنّه كانَ يقولُ ـ: ما للهِ عزّ وجلّ آيةٌ هي أكبرُ مِنّي.[٤٤٩]

408. **Imām ʿAlī (AS) said,** 'I have never doubted the truth ever since it was shown to me.'[454]

٤٠٨. عنه (ع): ما شَكَكْتُ في الحقِّ مُذ أُريتُهُ.[٤٥٠]

18

FĀṬIMA, THE MOTHER OF THE IMĀMS (AS)

أُمُّ الأئمّةِ فاطِمَةُ

128. Fāṭima (AS)'s Names

١٢٨ ـ أسماءُ فاطِمَةَ (ع)

409. **The Prophet (SAWA) said,** 'My daughter was named Fāṭima because Allah, Mighty and Exalted, has weaned her[455] and weaned those who love her from the Fire.'[456]

٤٠٩. رسولُ اللهِ (ص): إنّما سُمِّيَت ابنَتي فاطِمَةُ لأنّ اللهَ عزّ وجلّ فَطَمَها وفَطَمَ مَن أحَبَّها مِنَ النّارِ.[٤٥١]

410. **Imām al-Ṣādiq (AS) said,** 'Fāṭima, salutations of Allah be upon her, has nine names before Allah: Fāṭima, al-Ṣiddīqa (the veracious one), al-Mubārika (the blessed), al-Ṭāhira (the clean), al-Zakiyya (the pure), al-Raḍiyya (the content), al-Marḍiyya (the one

٤١٠. الإمام الصادق (ع): لِفاطِمَةَ سَلامُ اللهِ عَلَيها تِسعَةُ أسماءٍ عِندَ اللهِ عزّ وجلّ: فاطِمَةُ وَالصِّدّيقَةُ والمُبارَكَةُ والطّاهِرَةُ والزَّكِيَّةُ

who pleases Allah), al-Muḥadditha (the one who speaks to angels) and al-Zahrā' (the radiant one).'[457]

والرَّضيَّةُ والمَرضيَّةُ والمُحدَّثَةُ والزَّهراءُ.٤٥٢

411. 'Ammāra narrated, 'I asked Abā 'Abdillāh [al-Ṣādiq] (AS) as to why Fāṭima has been named al-Zahrā', to which he replied, 'Because when she stood for prayers in her prayer niche, her light would radiate for the dwellers of the skies jut as the light of the stars radiates for the dwellers of the earth.'[458]

٤١١. معاني الأخبار عن عمّارة: سألتُ أبا عبدِ اللهِ عن فاطِمَةَ لِمَ سُمِّيت زَهراءَ؟ فقال: لأنّها كانت اذا قامَت في مِحرابِها زَهَر نورُها لأهلِ السَّماءِ كَما يَزهَر نورُ الكواكِبِ لأهلِ الأرضِ.٤٥٣

129. Fāṭima is a Part of the Prophet (SAWA)

١٢٩ - فاطِمَةُ بَضعَةٌ مِنَ النَّبِيِّ

412. **The Prophet (SAWA) said,** 'Fāṭima is a part of me - whoever pleases her pleases me, whoever grieves her grieves me. Fāṭima is the dearest of all people to me.'[459]

٤١٢. رسولُ اللهِ: فاطمةُ بَضعَةٌ منّي، مَن سَرَّها فقد سَرَّني ومَن ساءها فقد ساءني، فاطمةُ أعزُّ النّاس علَيَّ.٤٥٤

413. **The Prophet (SAWA) said,** 'Verily Fāṭima is a part of me, and is the light of my eyes and the fruit of my heart, whatever grieves her grieves me, whatever pleases her pleases me, and indeed she will be the first to join me [after my death] from my household.'[460]

٤١٣. عنه: إنّ فاطمةَ بَضعَةٌ مِنّي، وهي نورُ عَيني، وثَمرَةُ فُؤادي، يَسوؤني ما ساءها، ويَسُرُّني ما سَرَّها، وإنّها أوّلُ مَن يَلحَقُني مِن أهلِ بيتي.٤٥٥

130. Fāṭima is the Chief [Lady] of the Women of the Worlds

١٣٠ - فاطِمَةُ سَيِّدَةُ نِساءِ العالَمينَ

414. **The Prophet (SAWA) said,** 'My daughter Fāṭima is the chief [Lady] of all the women of the worlds.'[461]

٤١٤. رسولُ اللهِ: ابنَتي فاطمةُ سيِّدةُ نساءِ العالَمينَ.٤٥٦

415. **The Prophet (SAWA) said,** 'Fāṭima is the chief [Lady] of the women of Paradise.'[462]

٤١٥. عنه: فاطِمَةُ سَيِّدَةُ نِساءِ أهلِ الجَنَّةِ.٤٥٧

416. **The Prophet (SAWA) said,** 'As for my daughter Fāṭima, she is the Lady of the women of the worlds, from the first to the last.'[463]

٤١٦. عنه: أمّا ابنَتي فاطمةُ فإنّها سيِّدةُ نِساءِ العالَمينَ مِن الأوّلينَ والآخِرينَ.٤٥٨

131. Allah's Anger for the Sake of Fāṭima's Anger

١٣١ ـ غَضَبُ اللهِ لِغَضَبِ فاطِمَةَ عليها السلام

417. **The Prophet (SAWA)** said to Fāṭima (AS), 'Verily Allah is angry at whatever angers you, and is pleased with whatever pleases you.'[464]

٤١٧ . رسولُ اللهِ صلى الله عليه وآله ـ لِفاطمةَ عليها السلام ـ: إنّ اللهَ يَغضَبُ لِغَضَبِكِ، ويَرضىٰ لِرِضاكِ.[٤٥٩]

132. In Mourning for Fāṭima (AS)

١٣٢ ـ في مُصيبَةِ فاطِمَةَ عليها السلام

418. **Imām ʿAlī (AS),** when burying Fāṭima (AS) said, 'O Prophet of Allah, peace be upon you from me and from your daughter, who is joining you and who has hastened to meet you. O Prophet of Allah, my patience with [the demise of] your chosen one [your daughter] has been exhausted, and my power of endurance has weakened, except that I have ground for consolation in having endured the great hardship and heart-rending event of your separation. I laid you down in your grave when your last breath had passed [when your head was] between my neck and chest.
"...Indeed we belong to Allah, and to Him do we intend return."
Now, the trust has been returned and what had been given has been taken back. As to my grief, it knows no bounds, and as to my nights, they will remain sleepless till Allah chooses for me the house in which you are now residing.
Certainly, your daughter would apprise you of the gathering of your community in oppressing her. You ask her in detail and get all the news about the situation. This happened when a long time had not even elapsed [since your demise] and your remembrance had not yet ceased. My salutation be on you both, the salutation of one grief-stricken, not a disgusted or hateful person; for if I go away it is not because I am weary [of you], and if I stay it is not due to lack of belief in what Allah has promised the endurers.'[465]

٤١٨ . الإمامُ عليٌّ عليه السلام ـ عِندَ دَفنِ فاطِمَةَ عليها السلام ـ: السَّلامُ عَلَيكَ يا رسولَ اللهِ عَنّي وَعَن اِبنَتِكَ النّازِلَةِ في جِوارِكَ وَالسَّريعَةِ اللَّحاقِ بِكَ. قَلَّ يا رسولَ اللهِ عَن صَفيَّتِكَ صَبري، وَرَقَّ عَنها تَجَلُّدي؛ إلاّ أنَّ لي في التَّأسّي بِعَظيمِ فُرقَتِكَ وَفادِحِ مُصيبَتِكَ مَوضِعَ تَعَزٍّ ؛ فَلَقَد وَسَّدتُكَ في مَلحودَةِ قَبرِكَ، وَفاضَت بَينَ نَحري وَصَدري نَفسُكَ. فَإنّا للهِ وَإنّا إلَيهِ راجِعونَ. فَلَقَد استُرجِعَتِ الوَديعَةُ، وَأُخِذَتِ الرَّهينَةُ. أمّا حُزني فَسَرمَدٌ، وَأمّا لَيلي فَمُسَهَّدٌ إلى أن يَختارَ اللهُ لي دارَكَ الَّتي أنتَ بِها مُقيمٌ. وَسَتُنَبِّئُكَ ابنَتُكَ بِتَضافُرِ أُمَّتِكَ عَلى هَضمِها فَأحفِها السؤالَ وَاستَخبِرها الحالَ. هٰذا وَلَم يَطُلِ العَهدُ وَلَم يَخلُ مِنكَ الذِّكرُ. وَالسَّلامُ عَلَيكُما سَلامَ مُوَدِّعٍ لا قالٍ وَلا سَئِمٍ. فَإن أنصَرِف فَلا عَن مَلالَةٍ، وَإن أُقِم فَلا عَن سوءِ ظَنٍّ بِما وَعَدَ اللهُ الصّابِرينَ.[٤٦٠]

19

IMĀM AL-ḤASAN B. ʿĀLĪ (AS) الإمام الحسن بن علي

133. Proofs for his Imāma ١٣٣ـ النَّصُّ علىٰ إمامَتِهِ

419. **Imām al-Bāqir (AS) said,** 'When death came to the Commander of the Faithful [Imām ʿAlī] (AS), he said to his son Ḥasan, 'Come closer to me so that I may tell you a secret which the Prophet of Allah (SAWA) told me, and that I may entrust to you what he entrusted to me. And so he did.'[466]

٤١٩. الإمامُ الباقرُ ﷺ: إنّ أميرَ المؤمنينَ صلواتُ اللهِ عليه لمّا حَضرهُ الّذي حَضرهُ قالَ لابنهِ الحسنِ: أُدْنُ منّي حتّىٰ أُسِرَّ إليكَ ما أسرَّ رسولُ اللهِ ﷺ إليَّ، وأئتَمِنَكَ علىٰ ما ائتَمنَني علَيهِ، فَفعَلَ.[٤٦١]

134. Ḥasan is from me and I am from him ١٣٤ـ حَسَنٌ منّي وأنا منهُ

420. **The Prophet said (SAWA),** 'Ḥasan is from me and I am from him. Allah loves the one who loves him. Ḥasan and Ḥusayn are the two most special grandchildren.'[467]

٤٢٠. رسولُ اللهِ ﷺ: حسنٌ منّي وأنا منهُ، أحَبَّ اللهُ مَن أحبَّهُ، الحسنُ والحسينُ سِبْطانِ مِن الأسباطِ.[٤٦٢]

421. **The Prophet (SAWA) said,** 'O Allah, I love him, so You too love him and love whoever loves him.'[468]

٤٢١. عنه ﷺ: اللّهُمَّ إنّي أُحِبُّهُ فأحِبَّهُ، وأحِبَّ مَن يُحِبُّهُ.[٤٦٣]

135. His Virtues ١٣٥ـ فَضائلُهُ ﷺ

422. **Imām Zayn al-ʿĀbidīn (AS) said,** 'Verily Ḥasan b. ʿAlī b. Abī Ṭālib was the best worshipper of his time, the most abstemious and the best of them all. Whenever he went for *ḥajj*, he went on foot, and sometimes even bare-footed. When he remembered death, he cried. When he remembered the grave, he cried. When he was reminded of the Day of Judgment and Resurrection, he cried. When he was reminded of the crossing over the Bridge [outstretched over Hell], he cried. When he was reminded of the great exposure before Allah - exalted be His remembrance - he would gasp in such a way that he would faint. When he stood for his prayers, his limbs

٤٢٢. الإمامُ زينُ العابدينَ ﷺ: إنَّ الحَسَنَ بنَ عَليِّ بنِ أبي طالِبٍ ﷺ كانَ أعبَدَ الناسِ في زَمانِهِ وأزهَدَهُم وأفضَلَهم، وكانَ إذا حَجَّ حجَّ ماشياً وَرُبَّما مَشى حافياً، وكانَ إذا ذُكِرَ المَوتُ بَكى، وإذا ذُكِرَ القَبرُ بَكى، وإذا ذُكِرَ البَعثُ والنُّشورُ بَكى، وإذا ذُكِرَ المَمَرُّ على الصِّراطِ بَكى، وإذا ذُكِرَ العَرضُ على اللهِ تَعالى ذِكرُه شَهِقَ شَهقَةً يُغشى عَلَيهِ مِنها، وكانَ إذا قامَ في صَلاتِهِ ترتَعِدُ فَرائصُهُ بينَ يَدي رَبِّهِ عزّ وجلّ، وكانَ إذا ذُكِرَ

trembled before his Lord. When he was reminded of Paradise and the Fire, he was greatly disturbed as if bitten by a snake, and asked Allah for Paradise and sought refuge in Him from the Fire.'[469]

الجَنَّةُ وَالنارُ اضطَرَبَ اضطِرابَ السَّليمِ وَسأل الله تعالى الجَنَّةَ وَتَعوذَ بِهِ مِنَ النّارِ.[٤٦٤]

423. **al-Manāqib li Ibn Shahr Āshūb** reported: 'Ḥasan b. ʿAlī (AS) passed by some beggars sitting on the ground, eating pieces of bread placed in front of them. They said to him, 'O son of the Prophet's daughter, come and join us for lunch.' [He narrated], 'So he sat down and said, 'Verily Allah does not like the arrogant.' He ate with them until they had all had enough though the amount of food remained the same by virtue of his blessings. Then he invited them to be his guests, and fed them and clothed them.'[470]

٤٢٣. المناقب لابن شهر آشوب: إنَّهُ مَرَّ الحسَنُ بنُ عَليٍّ ؑ عَلى فُقَراءَ وَقَد وَضَعوا كُسَيراتٍ عَلَى الأرضِ وَهُم قُعودٌ يَلتَقِطونَها وَيَأكُلونَها فَقالوا لَهُ: هَلُمَّ يابنَ بِنتِ رَسولِ اللهِ إلى الغَداءِ، قالَ: فَنَزَلَ وَقالَ: إنَّ اللهَ لا يُحِبُّ المُستَكبِرينَ وَجَعَلَ يَأكُلُ مَعَهُم حَتّى اكتَفوا وَالزادُ عَلى حالِهِ بِبَرَكَتِهِ ثُمَّ دَعاهُم إلى ضِيافَتِهِ وَأطعَمَهُم وَكَساهُم.[٤٦٥]

424. A man from Syria narrated, 'I came to Madina and saw a man whose beauty astonished me. So I asked who this man was and was told, 'He is Ḥasan b. ʿAlī.' [The Syrian man said], 'I envied ʿAlī for having such a son. So I went to him and asked, 'Are you the son of Abū Ṭālib?' He replied, 'Indeed I am his [grand] son'. I then said, 'Curses be on you and your father, curses be on you and your father.' He observed silence and did not reply. He then said, 'I see you are a stranger in town. Should you need a ride, we will provide you with one. Should you have any needs, we will fulfil them for you. Should you need any help, we will help you.' He said, 'I left him [in a state] whereby no one on earth was more beloved to me than him.'[471]

٤٢٤. مختصر تاريخ دمشق عن رَجُلٍ مِن أهلِ الشام: قَدِمتُ المَدينَةَ فَرَأَيتُ رَجُلاً بَهَرَني جَمالُهُ، فَقُلتُ: مَن هٰذا؟ قالوا: الحَسَنُ بنُ عَلِيٍّ، قالَ: فَحَسَدتُ عَلِيّاً أن يَكونَ لَهُ ابنٌ مِثلُهُ، قالَ: فَأَتَيتُهُ فَقُلتُ: أنتَ ابنُ أبي طالِبٍ؟ قالَ: إنّي [أبي] ابنُهُ فَقُلتُ: بِكَ وَبِأبيكَ وَبِكَ وَبِأبيكَ، قالَ: وَأَزِمَ لا يَرُدُّ إلَيَّ شَيئاً، ثُمَّ قالَ: أراكَ غَريباً فَلَو استَحمَلتَنا حَمَلناكَ، وَإنِ استَرفَدتَنا رَفَدناكَ، وَإنِ استَعَنتَ بِنا أعَنّاكَ، قالَ: فَانصَرَفتُ عَنهُ وَما فِي الأرضِ أحَدٌ أحَبُّ إلَيَّ مِنهُ.[٤٦٦]

20

IMĀM ḤUSAYN B. ʿALĪ (AS)

الإمامُ الحُسَينُ بنُ عَليٍّ

136. The Birth of Imām Ḥusayn (AS)

١٣٦ - وِلادَةُ الحُسَينِ ؑ

425. **Imām Zayn al-ʿĀbidīn (AS) said,** 'When Ḥusayn (AS) was born, Allah, most High, revealed

٤٢٥. الإمامُ زينُ العابدينَ ؑ: فَلَمّا وُلِدَ

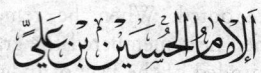

to Gabriel[472] (AS) that a boy had been born to Muḥammad, and to descend to him, to congratulate him, and to tell him that indeed ʿAlī's position with respect to you is as that of Aaron to Moses. So name him with the name of Aaron's son. So Gabriel (AS) descended, congratulated him on behalf of Allah, and then said, 'Verily Allah commands you to name him with the name of Aaron's son'. He [the Prophet] asked, 'And what was his name?' He replied, 'Shubayr.' He said, 'But my language is Arabic.' He said, 'So name him Ḥusayn [i.e. its Arabic equivalent].'[473]

الحُسَينُ ؑ أوحى اللهُ تعالى إلى جَبرَئيلَ ؑ أَنَّهُ قَد وُلِدَ لِمحَمَّدٍ ابن فاهبِط إلَيهِ فَهَنِّئْهُ وَقُل لَهُ إنَّ عَليّاً مِنكَ بِمَنزِلَةِ هارونَ مِن موسى فَسمِّهِ بِاسمِ ابنِ هارونَ فَهَبَطَ جَبرَئيلُ ؑ فَهَنَّاهُ مِنَ اللهِ تعالى ثُمَّ قالَ: إنَّ اللهَ عزّ وجلّ يَأمُرُكَ أن تُسَمّيهِ بِاسمِ ابنِ هارونَ، فَقالَ وَما كانَ اسمُهُ ؟ قالَ: شُبَيراً، قالَ: لِساني عَرَبيٌ، قالَ: سَمِّهِ الحُسَينَ.[٤٦٧]

137. The Proof for his Imāma

١٣٧ ـ النَّصُّ عَلىٰ إمامَتِهِ

426. **Fāṭima (AS) narrated,** 'The Prophet (SAWA) came to me, after I gave birth to Ḥusayn, so I gave him [Ḥusayn] to him [the Prophet] in a yellow cloth, which he cast aside and wrapped him instead in a white cloth. He then said, 'Fāṭima take him, he is indeed an Imām and the son of an Imām. He is the father of nine Imāms; from his loins will come virtuous Imāms, the ninth of whom will be al-Qā'im [the awaited saviour of mankind].'[474]

٤٢٦. فاطمة ؑ: دَخَلَ إليَّ رسولُ اللهِ ﷺ عِندَ وِلادَتي الحُسَينَ ؑ فَناوَلتُهُ إيّاهُ في خِرقَةٍ صَفراءَ، فَرَمى بِها وَأخَذَ خِرقَةً بَيضاءَ وَلَفَّهُ فيها ثُمَّ قالَ: خُذيهِ يا فاطِمَةُ فَإنَّهُ امامُ ابنُ امامٍ أبو الأئِمَّةِ التِسعَةِ، مِن صُلبِهِ ائِمَّةٌ أبرارٌ وَالتّاسِعُ قائِمُهُم.[٤٦٨]

427. **Imām al-Ḥasan (AS) said,** 'Certainly Ḥusayn b. ʿAlī (AS) will be the Imām after my death and after my soul has departed from my body. And with Allah - exalted is His Name – in the Book is the legacy of the Prophet, which Allah has added to him along with the legacy of his father and mother. Indeed Allah knew that you are the best people among His creation, hence he chose from you Muḥammad (SAWA), and Muḥammad chose ʿAlī (AS), and ʿAlī (AS) chose me for the *imāma*, and I have chosen Ḥusayn(AS).'[475]

٤٢٧. الإمامُ الحسنُ ؑ: إنّ الحسينَ بنَ عليٍّ ؑ، بعدَ وفاةِ نَفْسي ومُفارَقَةِ رُوحي جِسْمي، إمامٌ مِن بَعدي، وعندَ اللهِ جلّ اسمُهُ في الكتابِ، وِراثة مِن النّبيِّ ﷺ أضافَها اللهُ عزّ وجلّ لَه في وِراثةِ أبيهِ وأُمّهِ، فعَلِمَ اللهُ أنّكم خِيَرةُ خَلقِهِ، فاصْطَفىٰ مِنكُم مُحمّداً ﷺ، واختارَ محمّدٌ عليّاً ؑ، واختارَني عليٌّ ؑ بالإمامةِ، واخْتَرْتُ أنا الحُسَينَ ؑ.[٤٦٩]

138. Ḥusayn is from me and I am from him

١٣٨ ـ حُسَينٌ مِنّي وأنا مِنهُ

428. **The Prophet (SAWA) said,** 'As for Ḥusayn, he is from me, he is my son, my offspring, and the

٤٢٨. رسولُ اللهِ ﷺ: أمّا الحُسَينُ فَإنَّهُ مِنّي

best of all mankind after his brother. He is the Imām of the Muslims, the Master of the Believers, the vicegerent of the Lord of the Universe, the helper of those who seek assistance, the refuge of those who seek refuge, the proof of Allah on all of His creation. He is the chief of the youth of Paradise, the door to the community's salvation. His command is my command. Obedience to him is obedience to me. Whoever follows him is associated with me and whoever disobeys him cannot be associated with me.'[476]

وَهُوَ ابني وَوَلَدي وَخيرُ الخَلقِ بَعدَ أخيهِ وَهُوَ إمامُ المُسلِمينَ وَمَولى المُؤمِنينَ وَخَليفَةُ رَبِّ العالَمينَ وَغياثُ المُستَغيثينَ وَكَهفُ المُستَجيرينَ وَحُجَّةُ اللهِ عَلى خَلقِهِ أجمَعينَ وَهُوَ سَيِّدُ شَبابِ أهلِ الجَنَّةِ وَبابُ نَجاةِ الأُمَّةِ أمرُهُ أمري وَطاعَتُهُ طاعَتي مَن تَبِعَهُ فَإنَّهُ مِنّي وَمَن عَصاهُ فَلَيسَ مِنّي.[٤٧٠]

429. **al-Barāʾ b. ʿĀzib narrated,** 'I saw the Prophet carrying Ḥusayn and saying, 'O Allah, indeed I love him, so you love him too.'[477]

٤٢٩. بحار الأنوار عن البَراءِ بنِ عازِبٍ: رأيتُ رسولُ اللهِ ﷺ حاملَ الحسينِ عليه السلام وهُو يقولُ: اللّهُمَّ إنّي أُحِبُّهُ فأحِبَّهُ.[٤٧١]

430. **Saʿīd b. Abī Rāshid narrated on the authority of Yaʿlā al-ʿĀmirī,** that he accompanied the Prophet (SAWA) to a meal that he had been invited to. [He narrates], 'The Prophet (SAWA) went ahead towards the people whilst Ḥusayn was playing with the other children. The Prophet (SAWA) wanted to take him, but the child ran from here to there. So the Prophet (SAWA) started to make him laugh until he finally caught him. Then he put one hand behind his neck and the other under his chin, then placed his mouth on Ḥusayn's mouth and kissed him. He then said, 'Ḥusayn is from me and I am from Ḥusayn. May Allah love one who loves Ḥusayn. Ḥusayn is a special grandson from among other grandchildren.'[478]

٤٣٠. المستدرك على الصحيحين عَن يَعلَى العامِريِّ: إنَّهُ خَرَجَ مَعَ رسولُ اللهِ ﷺ إلى طَعامٍ دُعوا لَهُ، قالَ: فاستَقبَلَ رسولُ اللهِ ﷺ أمامَ القَومِ وَحُسَينٌ مَع الغُلمانِ يَلعَبُ فَأرادَ رسولُ اللهِ ﷺ أن يَأخُذَهُ فَطَفِقَ الصَّبيُ يَفِرُّ هاهُنا مَرَّةً وَهاهُنا مَرَّةً فَجَعَلَ رسولُ اللهِ ﷺ يُضاحِكُهُ حَتّى أخَذَهُ، قالَ: فَوَضَعَ إحدى يَديهِ تَحتَ قَفاهُ وَالأُخرى تَحتَ ذِقنِهِ فَوَضَعَ فاهُ عَلى فيهِ يُقَبِّلُهُ، فَقالَ: حُسَينٌ مِنّى وَأنا مِن حُسَينٍ أحَبَّ اللهُ مَن أحَبَّ حُسَيناً، حُسَينٌ سِبطٌ مِنَ الأسباطِ.[٤٧٢]

431. *Sunan al-Tirmidhī*: 'Ibn ʿAbbās narrated, 'The Prophet (SAWA) was carrying Ḥusayn b. ʿAlī on his shoulders, and a man said, 'What a good ride you've mounted on, son!' to which the Prophet (SAWA) said, 'And what a good rider he is!'[479]

٤٣١. سنن الترمذي: كانَ رسولُ اللهِ ﷺ حامِلَ الحُسَينِ ابنِ عَليٍّ عَلى عاتِقِهِ، فَقالَ رَجُلٌ: نِعمَ المَركَبُ رَكِبتَ يا غُلامُ، فقالَ النَبيُّ ﷺ: وَنِعمَ الراكِبُ هُوَ.[٤٧٣]

139. His Virtues

١٣٩ ـ فَضائِلُهُ عليه السلام

432. **The Prophet (SAWA) said,** 'Whoever would like to see the most beloved person to the inhabitants of the

٤٣٢. رسولُ اللهِ ﷺ: مَن أحَبَّ أن يَنظُرَ إلى أحَبِّ أهلِ الأرضِ إلى أهلِ السَّماءِ فَليَنظُر

إلَى الحُسَينِ.[٤٧٤]

heavens from among the inhabitants of the earth should look at Ḥusayn.'[480]

٤٣٣. الإمامُ الحسينُ ﷺ: دَخَلتُ عَلى رسولُ اللهِ ﷺ وَعِندَهُ أبي ابنُ كَعبٍ، فَقالَ لي رسولُ اللهِ ﷺ مَرحَباً بِكَ يا أبا عَبدِاللهِ، يا زَينَ السَمَواتِ وَالأرَضينَ، قالَ لَهُ أبَيٌّ: وَكَيفَ يَكونُ يا رسولَ اللهِ ﷺ زَينُ السَّماواتِ وَالأرَضينَ أحَدٌ غَيرُكَ ؟! قالَ: يا أبَيُّ وَالَّذي بَعَثَني بِالحَقِّ نَبيّاً إنَّ الحُسَينَ بنَ عَليٍّ في السَّماءِ أكبَرُ مِنهُ في الأرضِ، وَإنَّهُ لَمَكتوبٌ عَن يَمينِ عَرشِ اللهِ عزّ وجلّ: مِصباحُ هُدىً وَسَفينَةُ نَجاةٍ وَإمامُ غَيرُ وَهنٍ وَعِزٌّ وَفَخرٌ وَعَلَمٌ وَذُخرٌ.[٤٧٥]

433. **Imām Ḥusayn (AS) said,** 'I visited the Prophet (SAWA) when Ubayy ibn Kaʿb was with him. The Prophet greeted me, saying, 'Welcome O Abā 'Abdillāh, O the beauty of the heavens and the earths.' So Ubayy said, 'How is it possible, O Messenger of Allah, for anyone other than you to be the beauty of the heavens and the earths?' He said, 'O Ubayy I swear by Him who has rightfully sent me down as a messenger, certainly [the worth of] Ḥusayn b. ʿAlī is greater in the heavens than on the earth. And verily it is written [about him] on the right side of Allah's Throne: lamp of guidance, ark of salvation, an Imām, not weak, a [source of] dignity and pride, a landmark and a great treasure.'[481]

٤٣٤. عنه ﷺ ـ مِن كَلامِهِ يَومَ عاشوراءَ ـ: ألا وَإنَّ الدَّعيَّ ابنَ الدَّعيِّ قَد رَكَّزَ بَينَ اثنَتينِ بَينَ السُلَّةِوَالذِلَّةِ وَهَيهاتَ مِنّا الذِلَّةُ يَأبى اللهُ ذٰلك لَنا وَرَسولُهُ وَالمُؤمِنونَ وَحُجورٌ طابَت وَطَهُرَت وَأنوفُ حَميَّةٍ وَنُفوسُ أبيَّةٍ مِن أن تُؤثِرَ طاعَةَ اللِئامِ عَلى مَصارِعِ الكِرامِ.[٤٧٦]

434. **Imām Ḥusayn (AS),** in his speech on the day of 'Āshūrā' said, 'Beware! Now this impostor, son of the impostor [i.e. 'Ubaydullāh b. Ziyād, son of Ziyād b. Abīh][482] has cornered me between two things: between unsheathing the swords, and bearing humiliation. And far be it that we accept humiliation. Verily Allah, His Prophet, the believers, the sacred and pure laps which have nursed us and which abhor disgrace, have all refused that obedience to the ignoble men be chosen over an honourable death.'[483]

٤٣٥. عنه ﷺ ـ مِن كَلامِهِ يَومَ عاشوراءَ ـ: لا وَاللهِ لا أُعطيكُم بِيَدي إعطاءَ الذَّليلِ وَلا أُفِرُّ فِرارَ العَبيدِ.[٤٧٧]

435. **Imām Ḥusayn (AS)** said in his speech on the day of 'Āshūrā', 'By Allah! I shall not give my hand in yours like the giving of one disgraced, and nor shall I flee away like the fleeing of a slave.'[484]

٤٣٦. الإمامُ زينُ العابدينَ ﷺ: سَمِعتُ الحُسَينَ ﷺ يَقولُ: لَو شَتَمَني رَجلٌ في هَذهِ الأُذُنِ ـ وَأومى إلى اليُمنى ـ وَاعتَذَر لي في الأُخرى لَقَبِلتُ ذٰلك مِنهُ، وَذَلِكَ أنَّ أميرَالمُؤمِنينَ عَليَّ بنَ أبي طالبٍ ﷺ حَدَّثَني أنَّهُ سَمِعَ جَدّي رسولُ

436. **Imām Zayn al-ʿĀbidīn (AS) said,** 'I heard Ḥusayn (AS) say, 'If a man were to insult me in this ear – pointing to his right ear – and excuse himself to me in the other, I would accept that [excuse] from him, and that is because the Commander of the Faithful ʿAlī b. Abī Ṭālib (AS) narrated to me that he had heard my grandfather,

the Prophet (SAWA) say, 'The one who does not accept the excuse of someone, be he right or wrong, will not arrive at the Heavenly Waters.'[485]

اللهِ ﷺ يقولُ: لا يَرِدُ الحَوضَ مَن لَم يَقبَلِ العُذرَ مِن مُحقٍّ أو مُبطِلٍ.[٤٧٨]

437. **Ḥudhayfa b. al-Yamān narrated,** 'I saw the Prophet (SAWA) holding the hand of Ḥusayn b. ʿAlī (AS), saying, 'O people! This is Ḥusayn b. ʿAlī, so acknowledge him. By He who holds my life in His Hand, verily he will be in Paradise, those who love him will be in Paradise and those who love his lovers will be in Paradise.'[486]

٤٣٧. حُذَيفَةُ بنِ اليَمانِ: رَأَيتُ النَّبِيَّ ﷺ آخِذاً بِيَدِ الحُسَينِ بنِ عَلِيٍّ ﷺ وهُوَ يَقولُ: يا أيُّها النّاسُ هٰذا الحُسَينُ بنُ عَلِيٍّ فاعرِفوهُ، فَوَالَّذي نَفسي بِيَدِهِ إنَّهُ لَفِي الجَنَّةِ ومُحِبّيهِ فِي الجَنَّةِ ومُحِبّي مُحِبّيهِ فِي الجَنَّةِ.[٤٧٩]

438. **Shuʿayb b. ʿAbd al-Raḥmān al-Khuzāʿī said,** 'A mark was seen on Ḥusayn's back on the day of Ṭaff [ʿĀshūrā'], so they asked Zayn al-ʿĀbidīn [about it], and he replied, 'This is the mark left by the sacks [of food] he carried on his back to the houses of widows, orphans and the destitute.'[487]

٤٣٨. شعيب بن عبد الرحمن الخزاعي: وُجِدَ عَلى ظَهرِ الحُسَينِ بنِ عَلِيٍّ يَومَ الطَّفِّ أثَرٌ، فَسَألوا زَينَ العابِدينَ عَن ذلِكَ فَقالَ: هٰذا مِمّا كانَ يَنقُلُ الجِرابَ عَلى ظَهرِهِ إلى مَنازِلِ الأرامِلِ وَاليَتامى وَالمَساكينِ.[٤٨٠]

439. **al-Sayyid Ibn al-Ṭāwūs** reported in his *al-Luhūf* on the authority of a narrator of traditions: 'Then Ḥusayn (AS) called the enemy to a duel, and he kept on killing whoever stepped up to challenge him, until he had killed a large number of the enemy, upon which he said:

'Death is better than embarking on (a life of) indignity;
And indignity is preferable over plunging into the Fire.'

A reporter has said, 'By Allah, I have never seen a defeated one, whose children, household and companions have all been killed, as calm as him. The men [enemies] were fighting harshly with him and he too was harsh with them with his sword. He attacked an army of thirty thousand, scattered them in front of him as if they were scattered locusts. He then returned to his base, saying, 'There is no power or strength save in Allah, the most High, the Most Supreme.'[488]

٤٣٩. السيد بن طاووس: اللهوف عَن راوي الحَديثِ: ثُمَّ إنَّ الحُسَينَ ﷺ دَعَا النّاسَ إلَى البِرازِ، فَلَم يَزَل يَقتُلُ كُلَّ مَن بَرَزَ إلَيهِ، حَتّى قَتَلَ مَقتَلَةً عَظيمَةً، وهُوَ في ذلِكَ يَقولُ:

القَتلُ أولى مِن رُكوبِ العارِ
وَالعارُ أولى مِن دُخولِ النّارِ

قالَ بَعضُ الرُّواةِ: وَاللهِ ما رَأَيتُ مَكثوراً قَطُّ قَد قُتِلَ وُلدُهُ وأهلُ بَيتِهِ وأصحابُهُ أربَطَ جَأشاً مِنهُ، وإنَّ الرِّجالَ كانَت لَتَشُدُّ عَلَيهِ فَيَشُدُّ عَلَيها بِسَيفِهِ، ولَقَد كانَ يَحمِلُ فيهِم، وقَد تَكَمَّلوا ثَلاثينَ ألفاً، فَيَنهَزِمونَ بَينَ يَدَيهِ كَأَنَّهُمُ الجَرادُ المُنتَشِرُ، ثُمَّ يَرجِعُ إلى مَركَزِهِ وهُوَ يَقولُ: «لا حَولَ ولا قُوَّةَ إلّا بِاللهِ العَلِيِّ العَظيمِ».[٤٨١]

(See also: 'ĀSHŪRĀ' 278)

(أنظر) عنوان ٢٧٨ «عاشوراء».

21

IMĀM ʿALĪ B. AL-ḤUSAYN ZAYN AL-ʿĀBIDĪN (AS)

الإمام علي بن الحسين

140. Proofs of his Imāma

١٤٠ ـ النَّصُّ علىٰ إمامَتِه

440. **Imām al-Bāqir (AS) said,** 'Verily when al-Ḥusayn b. ʿAlī's time of death came near, he called for his eldest daughter Fāṭima bint al-Ḥusayn, and handed over to her a wrapped note. ʿAlī b. al-Ḥusayn was with them, but had a severe stomach ache, the reason for which was unknown. Fāṭima gave the note to ʿAlī b. al- Ḥusayn. Now, by Allah, that note has reached us… By Allah, it contains all that mankind would ever need from the time that Allah created Adam until the end of the world.'[489]

٤٤٠ . الإمامُ الباقرُ ﷺ : إنّ الحسينَ بنَ عليٍّ ﷺ لمّا حَضَرَهُ الّذي حَضَرَهُ ، دَعا ابنَتَهُ الكبرىٰ فاطمةَ بنتَ الحسينِ ﷺ ، فدفعَ إليها كِتاباً مَلفوفاً ، ووَصِيّةً ظاهِرةً . وكانَ عليُّ بنُ الحسينِ ﷺ مَبْطوناً مَعهُم لا يَرَونَ إلّا أنّه لِما بِهِ ، فَدفَعَتْ فاطمةُ الكِتابَ إلىٰ عليِّ بنِ الحسينِ ﷺ ثُمّ صارَ واللهِ ذلكَ الكتابُ إلَينا ... فيهِ واللهِ ما يَحتاجُ إلَيهِ وُلْدُ آدمَ مُنذُ خلقَ اللهُ آدمَ إلى أن تَفْنَى الدُّنيا .٤٨٢

141. The Status of Imām Zayn al-ʿĀbidīn (AS)

١٤١ ـ منزلةُ الإمامِ زينِ العابدينَ ﷺ

441. **The Prophet (SAWA) said,** 'On the Day of Judgment a caller will call, 'Where is the adornment of the worshippers (*zayn al-ʿabidīn*)?' and it is as if I am looking at my son ʿAlī b. al-Ḥusayn b. ʿAlī b. Abī Ṭālib emerging from between the rows.'[490]

٤٤١ . رسولُ اللهِ ﷺ : إذا كانَ يومُ القيامةِ يُنادي مُنادٍ : أينَ زينُ العابدينَ ؟ فكأنّي أنظُرُ إلىٰ وَلَدي عليِّ بنِ الحسينِ بنِ عليِّ بنِ أبي طالبٍ يَخْطِرُ بينَ الصُّفوفِ .٤٨٣

442. **Imām al-Bāqir (AS) said,** 'Verily he used to provide for one hundred households from among the poor of Madina. He liked for the orphans, the needy, the disabled, the poor and the destitute to be present at his food spread. He served them with his own hands. If anyone among them had a family, he used to take the food to their household. He never ate any food but that he first gave charity from it.'[491]

٤٤٢ . الإمامُ الباقرُ ﷺ : إنَّهُ كانَ يَعولُ مائةَ بَيتٍ مِن فُقَراءِ المَدينَةِ وكانَ يُعجِبُهُ أن يَحضُرَ طَعامَهُ اليَتامى وَالأضِرّاءُ وَالزَّمنى وَالمَساكينُ الّذينَ لا حيلَةَ لَهُم وكانَ يُناوِلُهُم بِيَدِهِ وَمَن كانَ مِنهُم لَهُ عِيالٌ حَمَلَهُ إلى عِيالِهِ مِن طَعامِهِ ، وكانَ لا يَأكُلُ طَعاماً حَتّى يَبدَأَ فَيَتَصَدَّقَ بِهِ .٤٨٤

443. **Imām al-Bāqir (AS) said,** 'Verily ʿAlī b. al-Ḥusayn has shared his wealth twice with Allah.'[492]

٤٤٣. عنه عليه السلام: إنَّ عَليَّ بنَ الحُسَينِ عليهما السلام قاسَمَ اللهَ عزّ وجلّ مالَهُ مَرَّتَينِ.[٤٨٥]

444. **Imām al-Ṣādiq (AS) said,** 'My father used to say, ʿAlī b. al-Ḥusayn, when he stood up to pray, was like a tree trunk, with no part of him moving except whatever the wind caused to move.'[493]

٤٤٤. الإمامُ الصّادقُ عليه السلام: كانَ أبي يَقولُ: كانَ عَليُّ بنُ الحُسَينِ عليهما السلام إذا قامَ في الصَّلاةِ كَأَنَّهُ ساقُ شَجَرةٍ لا يَتَحرَّكُ مِنهُ شَيءٌ إلاّ ما حَرَّكَهُ الرّيحُ مِنهُ.[٤٨٦]

445. al-Ṭabarsī narrated in *Iʿlām al-Warā*, 'And ʿAlī b. al-Ḥusayn (AS) had a slave girl, who was once pouring water for him when the jug fell and hurt the Imām's face. He raised his head [looking] at her, and the slave girl said [quoting verses from the Qur'an], 'Verily Allah says: *"And those who suppress their anger."* He said, 'I have suppressed my anger.' She said, *"And excuse the faults of the people."* He said, 'I have excused you.' She said, *"And Allah loves the virtuous."*'[494] He said, 'Go, for you are a free woman for the sake of Allah's pleasure.'[495]

٤٤٥. الطبرسي في إعلام الوَرى: وَكانَت جاريةٌ لِعَليِّ بنِ الحُسَينِ عليهما السلام تَسكُبُ عَلَيهِ الماءَ فَسَقَطَ الابريقُ مِن يَدِها فَشَجَّهُ فَرَفَعَ رَأسَهُ إليها فقالَت الجاريةُ: إنَّ اللهَ يَقولُ: «وَالكاظِمينَ الغَيظَ» فَقالَ: كَظَمتُ غَيظي، قالَت: «وَالعافينَ عَنِ النّاسِ» قالَ: عَفَوتُ عَنكِ قالَت: «وَاللهُ يُحِبُّ المُحسِنينَ»[٤٨٧] قالَ: اذهَبي فَأَنتِ حُرَّةٌ لِوَجهِ اللهِ.[٤٨٨]

446. Muḥammad b. Ṭalḥa al-Shāfiʿī narrated in *Maṭālib al-Saʾūl*, 'A fire set ablaze in the house wherein he was in the state of prostration in his prayers. They [the people of the household] cried, 'O son of the Prophet, O son of the Prophet! Fire! Fire!' But he did not raise his head from prostration until the fire had been extinguished.' He was asked, 'What is it that diverted your attention away from it [the fire]?' He replied, 'The Fire of the Hereafter.'[496]

٤٤٦. محمدُ بنُ طَلحةِ الشافِعيِّ في مَطالِبِ السؤولِ: وَقَعَ الحَريقُ وَالنّارُ في البَيتِ الَّذي هُوَ فيهِ وَكانَ ساجِداً في صَلَوتِهِ فَجَعلوا يَقولونَ لَهُ: يابنَ رَسولِ اللهِ يابنَ رَسولِ اللهِ! النّارَ، النّارَ! فَما رَفَعَ رَأسَهُ مِن سُجودٍ حَتّى أُطفِئَت فَقيلَ لَهُ: ما الَّذي ألهاكَ عَنها؟ فَقالَ: نارُ الآخِرَةِ.[٤٨٩]

447. Abū Naʿīm narrated in *Ḥilyat al-Awliyāʾ*, "ʿAlī b. al-Ḥusayn heard a cry from his house when a group of people was sitting with him. He stood up, went into his house and then returned to his meeting. Someone asked, 'Was the cry due to an accident?' He said, 'Yes.' They extended their condolences and were amazed at his patience. He then said, 'We, the *Ahl al-Bayt* obey Allah in that which we love, and praise Him in that which we dislike.'[497]

٤٤٧. ابو نعيم في حلية الأولياء: سَمِعَ عَليُّ بنُ الحُسَينِ عليهما السلام ناعِيَةً في بَيتِهِ وَعِندَهُ جَماعَةٌ فَنَهَضَ إلى مَنزِلِهِ ثُمَّ رَجَعَ إلى مَجلِسِهِ، فَقيلَ لَهُ: أَمِن حَدَثٍ كانَتِ النّاعِيَةُ؟ قالَ: نَعَم! فَعَزّوهُ وَتَعَجَّبوا مِن صَبرِهِ. فَقالَ: إنّا أهلُ بَيتٍ نُطيعُ اللهَ فيما نُحِبُّ، وَنَحمَدُهُ فيما نَكرَهُ.[٤٩٠]

(See also: PROSTRATION: section 920, 921)

(أنظر) السجود: باب ٩٢٠، ٩٢١.

22

IMĀM MUḤAMMAD B. ʿALĪ AL-BĀQIR (AS)

الإمام محمد بن علي الباقر

142. Proofs of his Imāma

١٤٢ ـ النَّصُّ علىٰ إمامَتِهِ

448. It is narrated in *Kifāyat al-Āthār*. "Alī b. al-Ḥusayn said in his will to his son Muḥammad b. ʿAlī: 'My son! I have chosen you as my successor after me. No one would claim what lies between you and me, and if so Allah would suspend a yoke of fire on his neck on the Day of Resurrection.'[498]

٤٤٨ . كفاية الأثر عن مالك بن أعين الجهني، قال: أوصى عَلِيُّ بنُ الحُسَينِ عليه السلام إبنَهُ مُحَمَّدَ بنَ عَلِيٍّ ـ صلوات الله عليهما ـ فقالَ: يا بُنَيَّ إنّي جَعَلتُكَ خَليفَتي مِن بَعدي، لا يَدّعي فيما بَيني وَ بَينكَ أحَدٌ إلّا قَلَّدَهُ الله يَومَ القِيامَةِ طَوقاً مِن نارٍ.[٤٩١]

143. He Cleaves Knowledge Open

١٤٣ ـ هُوَ يَبقَرُ العِلمَ بَقْراً

449. **The Prophet (SAWA)** said to Jābir b. ʿAbdullāh al-Anṣārī, 'Soon you will be seeing a man from my household, his name will be my name, his feature will resemble mine, and he will cleave the knowledge deeply.'[499]

٤٤٩ . رسولُ الله صلى الله عليه وآله ـ لِجابِرِ بنِ عبدِ الله الأنصاريّ ـ: إنَّكَ سَتُدرِكُ رَجُلاً مِنّي اسمُهُ اسمي وَ شَمائِلُهُ شَمائِلي يَبقَرُ العِلمَ بَقراً.[٤٩٢]

450. **Imām al-Bāqir (AS) said,** 'Verily the truth, harbouring falsehood in its midst, cried out for assistance from me. I cleaved it open from the side and disclosed the truth from its veils until it became manifest and widespread after having being concealed and hidden.'[500]

٤٥٠ . الإمامُ الباقرُ عليه السلام: إنَّ الحَقَّ استَصرَخَني وَقد حَواهُ الباطِلُ في جَوفِهِ، فَبَقَرتُ عَن خاصِرَتِهِ وَاطَّلَعتُ الحَقَّ عَن حُجُبِهِ حَتّى ظَهَرَ وَانتَشَرَ، بَعدَ ما خَفِيَ وَاستَتَرَ.[٤٩٣]

144. His Virtues

١٤٤ ـ فَضائِلُهُ عليه السلام

451. **The Prophet (SAWA) said** to Jābir, 'O Jābir, a boy will be born to my son al-Ḥusayn who shall be called ʿAlī and when Judgment Day comes, a caller will announce, 'Let the master of worshippers rise' and ʿAlī b. al-Ḥusayn will rise, and then from ʿAlī a son will be born by the name of Muḥammad. 'O Jābir, when you see him,

٤٥١ . رسولُ الله صلى الله عليه وآله: يا جابِرُ، يُولَدُ لابني الحسينِ ابنٌ يُقالُ لهُ: عليٌّ، إذا كانَ يومُ القيامةِ نادىٰ مُنادٍ: لِيَقُمْ سيِّدُ العابدينَ، فيقومُ عليُّ بنُ الحسينِ. ويُولَدُ لِعليٍّ ابنٌ يُقالُ لَهُ: محمّدٌ. يا جابِرُ، إنْ رأيتَهُ فأقرِئهُ مِنّي السَّلامَ، واعلَمْ أنَّ

convey my greetings to him and know that your lifespan after seeing him will be short.'[501]

بقاءكَ بعدَ رؤيتِهِ يسيرٌ ٤٩٤.

452. **Imām al-Ṣādiq (AS) said,** 'My father was one who remembered [Allah] a lot. When I walked with him, he would be in constant remembrance of Allah. When I ate food with him, he would be in constant remembrance of Allah. He would be speaking to people but that did not preoccupy him from remembering Allah. I would notice his tongue stick to his palate, uttering, 'There is no god but Allah.' He used to gather us and command us to remember Allah until the sun rose, and he would command whoever could read from among us to read the Qur'an, and whoever could not, to remember Allah.'[502]

٤٥٢ . الإمامُ الصّادقُ عليه السلام: كانَ أبي عليه السلام كَثيرَ الذِّكرِ لَقَد كُنتُ أمشي مَعَهُ وَإنَّهُ لَيَذكُرُ اللهَ، وَآكُلُ مَعَهُ الطَّعامَ وَإنَّهُ لَيَذكُرُ اللهَ، وَلَقد كانَ يُحَدِّثُ القَومَ وَما يَشغَلُهُ ذٰلك عَن ذِكرِ اللهِ وَكُنتُ أرى لِسانَهُ لازِقاً بِحَنَكِهِ يقولُ: لا إلهَ إلّا اللهَ، وَكانَ يَجمَعُنا فَيَأمُرُنا بِالذِّكرِ حَتَّى تَطلُعَ الشَّمسُ وَيَأمُرُ بِالقَراءَةِ مَن كانَ يَقرَأُ مِنّا وَمَن كانَ لا يَقرَأُ مِنّا أمَرَهُ بِالذِّكرِ. ٤٩٥

453. **Imām al-Ṣādiq (AS) said,** 'Abū Jaʿfar had the most beautiful voice.'[503]

٤٥٣ . عنه عليه السلام: وَكانَ أبو جَعفَرٍ عليه السلام أحسَنُ النّاسِ صَوتاً. ٤٩٦

454. **Sulaymān b. Qurm narrated,** 'Abū Jaʿfar Muḥammad b. ʿAlī used to pay us from five hundred to six hundred to one thousand dirhams. He never got tired of granting gifts to his brothers, his visitors, and those who had expectations of his help, and those who entertained hopes of him to assist them.'[504]

٤٥٤ . سُلَيمانَ بنِ قرمٍ: كانَ أبو جَعفَرٍ مُحَمَّدُ بنُ عليٍّ عليهما السلام يُجيزُنا بِالخَمسِمائَةِ دِرهَمٍ إلى السِّتِمائَةِ إلى الألفِ دِرهَمٍ وَكانَ لا يَمُلُّ مِن صِلَةِ الإخوانِ وَقاصِديهِ وَمُؤَمِّليهِ وَراجيهِ. ٤٩٧

23

IMĀM JAʿFAR B. MUḤAMMAD AL-ṢĀDIQ (AS)

الإمامُ جعفرُ بنُ مُحمَّدٍ الصّادقِ

145. Proofs of his Imāma

١٤٥ ـ النَّصُّ عَلىٰ إمامَتِهِ

455. *Biḥār al-Anwār*, 'Hammām b. Nāfiʿ narrated: 'One day Imām al-Bāqir (AS) said to his companions: 'When you lose me, follow this man.

٤٥٥ . بحار الأنوار عن همّام بن نافع، قال: قال أبو جعفر عليه السلام لأصحابه يوماً: إذا افتَقَدتُموني فَاقتَدوا بِهذا، فَهُوَ الإمامُ وَالخَليفَةُ بَعدي،

He is the leader and my successor.' He (AS) then pointed to Abī ʿAbdillah [al-Ṣādiq] (AS).'[505]

وَأشارَ إلىٰ أبي عَبد اللهِ ؑ.٤٩٨

456. **Muḥammad b. Muslim narrated,** 'I was in the presence of Abū Jaʿfar Muḥammad b. ʿAlī al-Bāqir when his son Jaʿfar entered. He had a forelock on his head and had a stick in his hand which he was playing with. Al-Bāqir (AS) took him in his arms and hugged him tightly, then said, 'May my parents be your ransom, you are neither distracted, nor do you play.' He then addressed me and said, 'O Muḥammad! This is your Imām after me, so follow him and benefit from his knowledge. By Allah, verily he is the truthful one [al-Ṣādiq] whom the Prophet (SAWA) described to us. Certainly his followers will be victorious in this world and in the Hereafter.'[506]

٤٥٦ . محمّدَ بنِ مسلم : كنتُ عندَ أبي جعفرٍ محمّدِ بنِ عليٍّ الباقرِ ؑ إذْ دخَلَ جعفرُ ابنُهُ، وعلىٰ رأسِهِ ذُؤابةٌ، وفي يَدِهِ عَصاً يَلْعبُ بها، فأخَذَهُ الباقرُ ؑ وضمَّهُ إليهِ ضمّاً، ثُمّ قالَ: بأبي أنتَ وأُمّي، لا تَلْهو ولا تَلْعبُ. ثُمّ قالَ لي: يا محمّد، هذا إمامُكَ بَعدي، فاقْتَدِ بهِ، واقْتَبِسْ مِن عِلمِهِ، واللهِ إنّهُ لَهُوَ الصّادقُ الّذي وَصَفهُ لنا رسولُ اللهِ ﷺ. إنّ شيعتَهُ مَنصورونَ في الدُّنيا والآخِرَةِ.٤٩٩

146. His Comportment and his Noble Character

١٤٦ - سيرتُهُ وَمكارِمُ أخلاقِهِ

457. **Muḥammad b. Ziyād al-Azdī narrated,** 'I heard Mālik b. Anas, the jurist of Madina say, 'I used to go to visit Jaʿfar b. Muḥammad al-Ṣādiq (AS), and he would place a cushion for me, respect me and say, 'Mālik, indeed I like you.' I would be pleased with this comment and would praise Allah for it.' [Mālik continued], 'He was a man always disposed to one of three states: either he was fasting, or praying, or engaged in Allah's remembrance. He was among the greatest worshippers, the greatest of abstemious people who fear Allah. He narrated many prophetic traditions, was sociable and friendly to sit with, and had much [for us] to benefit from.'[507]

٤٥٧ . محمّدُ بنُ زيادٍ الأزْديّ : سَمِعتُ مالكَ بنَ أنسٍ فقيهَ المدينةِ يقولُ: كنتُ أدخُلُ إلى الصّادقِ جعفرِ بنِ محمّدٍ ؑ فيُقدِّمُ لي مِخَدَّةً، ويَعرفُ لي قَدْراً ويقولُ: يا مالكُ، إنّي أُحِبُّكَ. فكنتُ أسَرُّ بذلكَ وأحمَدُ اللهَ عليه. قالَ: وكانَ ؑ رجُلاً لا يَخْلو مِن إحدىٰ ثلاثِ خِصالٍ: إمّا صائماً، وإمّا قائماً، وإمّا ذاكِراً، وكانَ مِن عُظماءِ العُبّادِ، وأكابِرِ الزُّهّادِ الّذينَ يَخْشَونَ اللهَ عزّ وجلّ، وكانَ كثيرَ الحديثِ، طَيِّبَ المُجالَسةِ، كثيرَ الفوائدِ.٥٠٠

458. **Hishām b. Sālim narrated,** 'When it was dark and part of the night had passed, Abū ʿAbdillāh (AS) would take a sack of bread, meat and money, and carry it on his back to the needy of Madina. He would distribute it among them

٤٥٨ . هشامُ بنُ سالم : كانَ أبو عبدِ اللهِ ؑ إذا اعتَمَّ وَذَهَبَ مِنَ اللّيلِ شَطرُهُ أخَذَ جِراباً فيهِ خُبزٌ وَلَحمٌ وَالدَّراهِمُ فَحَمَلَهُ عَلى عُنُقِهِ ثُمَّ ذَهَبَ بِهِ إلى أهلِ الحاجَةِ مِن أهلِ المَدينَةِ فَقَسَّمَهُ فيهِم

whilst they did not even recognise him. When Abū ʿAbdillāh (AS) passed away, they missed [the aid] and realized that it had in fact been Abū ʿAbdillāh.'[508]

وَلا يَعرِفونَهُ فَلَمّا مَضى أبو عَبدِاللهِ ﵇ فَقَدوا ذٰلك فَعَلِموا أَنَّهُ كانَ أبا عَبدِاللهِ ﵇.[٥٠١]

459. **Muʿallā b. Khunays narrated,** 'Abū ʿAbdillāh (AS) went out on a drizzly night, heading towards the refuge of Banī Sāʿida. So I followed him, when suddenly something fell from him.' He said, 'In the name of Allah, O Allah! Return it back to us.' [He continued], 'I came to him and greeted him, and he asked, 'Are you Muʿallā?' I said, 'Yes, may I be your ransom.' He said, 'Search around with your hands and if you find anything give it to me.' I found pieces of bread, so I extended my hands to give them to him. I was amazed to see a sack of bread on his back. I asked, 'May I be your ransom! Allow me to carry it for you!' He said, 'No! I deserve [the load] more than you but come with me.' He said, 'We came to the refuge of Banī Sāʿida, where we came across a people who were asleep. He placed one or two loafs of bread under the garment of each and every person until he had come to the last person. We then left.' I said, 'May I be your ransom, do these people acknowledge the truth [of leadership]?' He said, 'If they did, we would have given them the flour as well.'[509]

٤٥٩. مُعلّى بن خُنَيسٍ: خَرَجَ أبو عَبدُاللهِ ﵇ في لَيلَةٍ قَد رَشَّتِ السَّماءُ وَهُوَ يُريدُ ظُلَّةَ بَني ساعِدَةٍ فَأتبعتُهُ فَإذا هُوَ قَد سَقَطَ مِنهُ شَيءٌ فَقالَ: بِسمِ اللهِ اللّهمَّ رُدَّ عَلَينا، قالَ: فَأَتَيتُهُ فَسلَّمتُ عَلَيهِ فَقالَ: أنتَ مُعلّىٰ؟ قُلتُ: نَعَم جُعلتُ فِداكَ، فَقالَ لي: التَمِس بِيَدِكَ فَما وَجَدتَ مِن شَيءٍ فَادفَعهُ إلَيَّ قالَ: فَإذا أنا بِخُبزٍ مُنتَثِرٍ، فَجَعلتُ أدفَعُ إلَيهِ ما وَجَدتُ، فَإذا أنا بِجِرابٍ مِن خُبزٍ فَقُلتُ: جُعلتُ فِداكَ أحمِلهُ عَنكَ؟ فَقالَ: لا أنا أولى بِهِ مِنكَ وَلٰكِن امضِ مَعي، قالَ: فَأَتَينا ظُلَّةَ بَني ساعِدَةٍ فَإذا نَحنُ بِقَومٍ نيامٍ فَجَعَلَ يَدُسُّ الرَّغيفَ وَالرَّغيفَينِ تَحتَ ثَوبِ كُلِّ واحِدٍ مِنهُم حَتّى أتى عَلى آخِرَهُم ثُمَّ انصَرَفنا فَقلتُ: جُعلتُ فِداكَ يَعرِفُ هٰؤلاءِ الحقَّ، فَقالَ: لَو عَرَفوا لَواسَيناهُم بِالدَّقَّةِ.[٥٠٢]

460. **Abū ʿAmr al-Shaybānī narrated,** 'I saw Abā ʿAbdillāh (AS) with a spade in his hand and wearing thick clothes, working in his yard with sweat dripping from his back. I stepped forward and said, 'May I be your ransom, allow me to work in your place.' He replied, 'Verily I love for a man [myself] to bear the sun's heat in the quest for a living.'[510]

٤٦٠. أبو عَمرو الشَّيباني: رَأيتُ أبا عَبدِاللهِ ﵇ وَبِيَدِهِ مِسحاةٌ وَعَلَيهِ إزارٌ غَليظٌ يَعمَلُ في حائِطٍ لَهُ وَالعَرَقُ يَتَصابُّ عَن ظَهرِهِ فَقُلتُ: جُعلتُ فِداكَ أعطِني أكفِكَ فَقالَ لي: إنّي أُحِبُّ أن يَتَأذَّى الرَّجُلُ بِحَرِّ الشَّمسِ في طَلَبِ المَعيشَةِ.[٥٠٣]

24

IMĀM MŪSĀ B. JAʿFAR AL-KĀẒIM (AS)

الإمام موسى بن جعفر الكاظم

147. Proofs of his Imāma

١٤٧ ـ النَّصُّ عَلىٰ إمامَتِهِ

461. **Imām al-Ṣādiq (AS)** in reply to Safwān al-Jammāl asking about one who holds this position [of *Imāma*], said, 'One who holds this position does not play and nor is he distracted.' Mūsā b. Jaʿfar, who was then a child entered accompanied by a Makkan she-goat, to whom he was saying, 'Prostrate to your Lord!' So Abū ʿAbdillāh took him and hugged him and said, 'May my parents be your ransom, he never plays and nor is he distracted.'[511]

٤٦١. المناقب لابن شهر آشوب عن صَفوانِ الجَمّالِ: سَألتُ أبا عَبدِاللهِ عليه السلام عَن صاحِبِ هٰذا الأَمرِ، فَقالَ: صاحبُ هذا الأمرِ لا يَلْهو ولا يَلْعبُ. فأقْبَلَ موسىٰ بنُ جعفرٍ وهُو صغيرٌ ومَعَهُ عَناقٌ مكّيّة وهُو يقولُ لها: اسجُدي لربِّكِ، فأخَذَهُ أبو عبدِاللهِ فضَمَّهُ إلَيهِ وقالَ: بأبي وأُمّي، لا يَلْهو ولا يَلْعبُ.[٥٠٤]

148. The Imām in Prison

١٤٨ ـ الإمامُ في السِّجنِ

462. Thawbānī narrated, 'Abū al-Ḥasan Mūsā b. Jaʿfar, for about ten years, performed a single prostration from sunrise until noon. [He continued], 'Hārūn would sometimes climb onto a roof that overlooked the prison cell wherein he had imprisoned Abū al-Ḥasan. He would see Abū al-Ḥasan (AS) in prostration. He asked al-Rabīʿ, 'What is that cloth I see on that spot everyday?' He said, 'O commander of the faithful! That is not a cloth but Mūsā b. Jaʿfar (AS). He performs a prostration every day from sunrise until noon.' Hārūn said, 'He is indeed one of the holy men from the Banī Hāshim.' I asked, 'Then why have you confined him to captivity?' He said, 'Alas! That is how it must be.'[512]

٤٦٢. الثَوباني: كانَت لأَبي الحَسَنِ موسَى بنِ جَعفرٍ عليهما السلام بِضعَ عَشَرةَ سِنَةٍ كُلَّ يَومٍ سَجدَةٌ بَعدَ ابيضاضِ الشَّمسِ إلى وَقتِ الزَّوالِ قالَ: فَكانَ هارونُ رُبَّما صَعَدَ سَطحاً يُشرِفُ مِنهُ عَلى الحَبسِ الَّذي حَبَسَ فيهِ أبا الحَسَنِ عليه السلام فكانَ يَرى أبا الحَسَنِ عليه السلام ساجِداً فَقالَ للرَّبيعِ: ما ذاكَ الثَّوبُ الَّذي أراهُ كُلَّ يَومٍ في ذٰلك المَوضِعِ؟ قالَ: يا أميرَ المُؤمِنينَ ما ذاك بِثَوبٍ وإنّما هُوَ موسَى بنُ جَعفرٍ عليهما السلام لَهُ كُلَّ يَومٍ سَجدَةٌ بَعدَ طُلوعِ الشَّمس إلى وَقتِ الزَّوالِ، قالَ الرَّبيعُ: فَقالَ لي هارونَ: أما إنَّ هٰذا من رُهبانِ بَني هاشِمٍ، قُلتُ: فَما لَكِ فَقَد ضَيَّقتَ عَليهِ في الحَبسِ؟! قالَ: هَيهاتَ لابُدَّ مِن ذٰلك.[٥٠٥]

463. **ʿAlī b. Suwayd narrates,** 'I wrote a letter to Abū al-Ḥasan Mūsā b. Jaʿfar (AS), when he was in captivity, in which I inquired about his health and about many other issues. He held back the

٤٦٣. عليٌّ بن سُوَيدٍ: كَتَبتُ إلىٰ أبي الحسنِ موسىٰ عليه السلام، وهو في الحَبْسِ، كِتاباً أسألُهُ عن حالِه وعن مَسائلَ كثيرةٍ، فاحْتَبسَ الجوابُ علَيَّ

reply from me for months, then he replied in a letter, the text of which is as follows: 'In the name of Allah, the Beneficent, the Merciful ... Certainly you are a man who has been bestowed a special rank by Allah with the household of Muḥammad and has guarded you among those who look after His religion ...'[513]

أشهراً، ثمّ أجابَني بجوابٍ هذِ نُسْخَتُه بسم اللهِ الرَّحمٰنِ الرَّحيمِ ... أمّا بعدُ، فإنّكَ امرؤٌ أنْزَلَكَ اللهُ مِن آلِ محمّدٍ بمَنزلةٍ خاصّةٍ، وحَفِظَ مَوَدّةَ ما اسْتَرعاكَ من دِينِهِ ... الحديث.٥٠٦

149. His Virtues

١٤٩ـ فضائله ﷺ

464. It is narrated in *al-Irshād*: 'It is reported that al-Kāẓim used to supplicate a lot and say, 'O Allah! Indeed I ask You for ease at the time of death and pardon at the time of the account', and he used to repeat this several times. And among his supplications were, 'The sin of Your slave is great, so graceful will be the pardon from You.' He used to weep out of fear of Allah until his beard was soaked with tears. He used to be most diligent with maintaining relations with his family and his kin. He used to visit the poor of Madina at night, for whom he would take a basket of gold, silver, flour and dates. He would deliver all this to them whilst they did not even know where he came from.'[514]

٤٦٤. الإرشاد: رُوِيَ أنّهُ (الكاظم ﷺ) كانَ يَدعو كَثيراً فَيَقولُ: اللّهمَّ إنّي أسألُكَ الرّاحَةَ عِندَ المَوتِ وَالعَفوَ عِندَ الحِسابِ. وَيُكَرِّرُ ذٰلك. وَكانَ مِن دُعائِهِ ﷺ: عَظُمَ الذَّنبُ مِن عَبدِكَ فَلْيَحسُنِ العَفوُ مِن عِندِكَ. وَكانَ يَبكي مِن خَشيَةِ اللهِ حَتّى تَخضَلَّ لِحيَتُهُ بِالدُّموعِ. وَكانَ أوصَلَ النّاسِ لأهلِهِ ورَحِمِهِ وَكانَ يَفتَقِدُ فُقَراءَ المَدينَةِ في اللَّيلِ فَيَحمِلُ إليهِم (الزَّنبيلَ) فيهِ العَينُ وَالوَرِقُ وَالأدِقَّةُ وَالتُّمورِ فَيوصِلُ إلَيهِم ذٰلك وَلا يَعلَمونَ مِن أيِّ جِهَةٍ هُوَ.٥٠٧

465. **Ḥasan b. Muḥammad b. Yaḥyā al-'Alawī said,** 'My grandfather narrated to me that Mūsā b. Ja'far (AS) was called the righteous slave due to his worship and hard work. Our companions narrated that he would enter the mosque of the Prophet (SAWA) and would perform a prostration early in the night. He was heard to say in his prostration, 'My sin from me is great whilst Your pardon from You is graceful. O One who is worthy of being feared and O One who is worthy of granting forgiveness'. He would repeat this until morning. He was generous and noble. He was once informed of someone who spoke ill of him, so he sent for him a tray with one thousand dinars.'[515]

٤٦٥. الحَسَنُ بنُ مُحَمَّدِ بنِ يَحيَى العَلَوِيُّ: حَدَّثَني جَدّي: كانَ موسَى بنُ جَعفَرٍ يُدعىٰ العَبدَ الصّالِحَ مِن عِبادَتِهِ وَاجتِهادِهِ. رَوى أصحابُنا أنَّهُ دَخَلَ مَسجِدَ رسولِ اللهِ ﷺ فَسَجَدَ سَجدَةً في أوَّلِ اللَّيلِ، وَسُمِعَ وَهُوَ يَقولُ في سُجودِهِ: «عَظيمُ الذَّنبِ عِندي فَلْيَحسُنِ العَفوُ عِندَكَ، يا أهلَ التَّقوى وَيا أهلَ المَغفِرَةِ» فَجَعَلَ يُرَدِّدُها حَتّى أصبَحَ وَكانَ سَخِيّاً كَريماً، وَكانَ يَبلُغُهُ عَنِ الرَّجلِ أنَّهُ يُؤذيهِ فَيَبعَثُ إلَيهِ بِصُرَّةٍ فيها ألفُ دينارٍ.٥٠٨

25

IMĀM ʿALĪ B. MŪSĀ AL-RIḌĀ (AS)

الإمامُ عليّ بن موسى الرضا

150. Proofs of his Imāma

١٥٠ ـ النَّصُّ عَلىٰ إمامَتِهِ

466. **ʿAbd al-Raḥmān b. al-Ḥajjāj narrated,** ʿAbū al-Ḥasan Mūsā b. Jaʿfar [al-Kāẓim] (AS) appointed his son ʿAlī (AS) as the executor of his will, and wrote this in a letter to him which sixty of Madina's renowned men bore witness to.ʾ[516]

٤٦٦ . عبدُ الرَّحمٰنُ بنُ الحجّاج : أوصىٰ أبو الحسنِ موسَى بنُ جعفرٍ عليه السلام إلىٰ ابنِه عليٍّ عليه السلام، وكتبَ لهُ كِتاباً أشْهَدَ فيهِ سِتّينَ رجُلاً مِن وُجوهِ أهلِ المدينةِ.[٥٠٩]

151. Compelling the Imām to be the Heir Apparent

١٥١ ـ إجبارُ الإمامِ عَلىٰ وِلايَةِ العَهدِ

467. **Abū al-Ṣalt al-Harawī narrated,** 'Verily Ma'mūn said to al-Riḍā (AS), 'O son of the Prophet ... Verily I see it best for me to relinquish the caliphate and hand it over to you and swear allegiance to you!' So al-Riḍā (AS) said to him, 'If this caliphate indeed belongs to you and Allah has assigned it to you, then it is not permissible for you to remove a garment that Allah has clothed you with and assign it to another instead of yourself. And if the caliphate is not actually yours then it is not permissible for you to assign to me that which is not yours [in the first place].' So Ma'mūn said to him, 'O son of the Prophet! You have to accept this post!' to which the Imām replied, 'I will never do that willingly... for by that [i.e. my acceptance of it] you want the people to say: "'Alī b. Mūsā al-Riḍā did not abstain from worldly pursuits [of leadership] but it is the world that has turned its back on him! Do you not see how he accepted to be the heir apparent in his greed for the caliphate?!" So Ma'mūn became enraged and said, '...I swear to Allah, if you do not accept the position of heir apparent I will force you to it. So you had better accept it or else I will behead you.'[517]

٤٦٧ . ابو الصلت الهروي : إنّ المأمونَ قالَ للرِّضا عليه السلام : يابنَ رسولَ اللهِ... إنّي قد رأيتُ أنْ أعزِلَ نَفْسي عنِ الخِلافةِ، وأجْعَلَها لكَ وأُبايِعَكَ! فقالَ له الرِّضا عليه السلام: إنْ كانتْ هذهِ الخلافةُ لكَ واللهُ جَعلَها لكَ فلا يَجوزُ لكَ أنْ تَخْلَعَ لِباساً ألبَسَكَهُ اللهُ وتَجْعلَهُ لِغَيرِكَ، وإنْ كانتِ الخِلافةُ لَيستْ لكَ فلا يَجوزُ لكَ أن تَجْعلَ لِي ما ليسَ لكَ.
فقالَ له المأمونُ : يابنَ رسولِ اللهِ، فَلابُدَّ لكَ مِن قَبولِ هذا الأمرِ! فقالَ : لَستُ أفْعَلُ ذلك طائعاً أبداً... تُريدُ بذلكَ أن يَقولَ النّاسُ : إنّ عليَّ بنَ موسىٰ الرِّضا لم يَزْهَدْ في الدُّنيا بل زَهِدَتِ الدُّنيا فيهِ ! ألا تَرَونَ كيفَ قَبِلَ وِلايةَ العهدِ طمَعاً في الخِلافة ؟! فغَضِبَ المأمونُ ثُمَّ قالَ : ... فباللهِ أُقسِمُ لَئنْ قَبِلْتَ وِلايةَ العهدِ وإلّا أجْبَرتُكَ علىٰ ذلكَ، فإنْ فَعلتَ وإلّا ضَرِبتُ عُنُقَكَ.[٥١٠]

152. His Virtues

ـ فضائله

468. **al-Harawī narrated,** 'I went to the door of the place in Sarkhas where al-Riḍā was being held captive in chains. I sought permission from the jailor [to visit him] and he said, 'There is no way that you will be able to see him.' I asked, 'Why?' He replied, 'Because he sometimes offers one thousand prayers in the space of one day and night. He stops praying for a while at daybreak, before noon and before sunset. During these times he sits on his prayer mat and converses intimately with his Lord.' I said to him, 'Then request him to grant me permission during these times'. So he asked permission for me [to visit]. I entered and he was sitting on his prayer mat meditating.'[518]

٤٦٨. الهَرَويّ: جِـئتُ إلى بـابِ الدّارِ الّـتي حُبِسَ فـيها الرِّضـا ﷺ بسَـرَخْسَ وقـد قُـيِّدَ، فاستَأذَنتُ علَيهِ السَّجّانَ فقالَ: لا سَبيلَ لَكُم إلَيهِ، فقلتُ: ولِمَ؟ قالَ: لأنّه رُبَّما صلّى في يَومِهِ ولَيلَتِهِ ألفَ رَكعةٍ، وإنّما يَنفَتِلُ مِن صَلاتِهِ ساعةً في صدرِ النّـهارِ وقَـبلَ الزّوالِ وعِـندَ اصْـفِرارِ الشَّمسِ، فهُوَ في هذهِ الأوقاتِ قاعِدٌ في مُصَلّاهُ يُناجي رَبَّهُ. قالَ: فقُلتُ لَه: فاطْلُبْ لِي في هذهِ الأوقاتِ إذْناً علَيهِ، فاستَأذَنَ لِي علَيهِ، فدَخَلتُ علَيهِ وهُو قاعِدٌ في مُصَلّاه مُتفكِّرٌ.٥١١

469. **Ibrāhīm b. al-ʿAbbās narrated,** 'I have never seen Abū al-Ḥasan al-Riḍā (AS) hurt anybody with something he said, nor have I ever seen him interrupt anyone until he had finished, nor refuse to do someone a favour that he was able to do, nor did he ever stretch his legs before anyone sitting with him, nor lean against something while his companion did not, nor did he ever insult any of his servants or workers. And I have never seen him spit or burst into laughter; rather, his laughter was just a smile. When he was ready to eat and the table had been laid, he seated with him at the table all his servants, including the doorman and the stableboy.'[519]

٤٦٩. إبراهيمُ بنُ العبّاسِ: ما رَأيتُ أبا الحَسَنِ الرِّضا ﷺ جَفا أحَداً بِكَلِمَةٍ قَطُّ ولا رَأيـتُهُ قَـطَعَ على أحدٍ كَلامَهُ حَتّى يَفرُغَ مِنهُ، ومـارَدَّ أحَـداً عَن حاجَةٍ يَقدِرُ علَيها ولا مَدَّ رِجلَهُ بَينَ يَـدَي جَليسٍ لَهُ قطُّ ولا اتَّكَى بَينَ يَدَي جَليسٍ لَهُ قَطُّ، ولا رَأيتُهُ شَتَمَ أحَداً مِن مَوالِيهِ ومَمالِيكِهِ قَـطُّ، ولا رَأيتُهُ تَفَلَ ولا رَأيتُهُ يُقَهقِهُ في ضِحكِهِ قَطُّ، بَل كانَ ضِحكُهُ التَّبَسُّمَ، وكانَ إذا خَلا ونَـصَبَ مائِدَتَهُ أجلَسَ مَعَهُ عَلى مائِدَتِهِ مَمالِيكَهُ ومَوالِيهِ حَتَّى البَوّابَ السّائِسَ.٥١٢

26

IMĀM MUḤAMMAD B. ʿALĪ AL-JAWĀD (AS)

الإمام محمّد بن عليّ الجواد

153. Proofs of his Imāma

١٥٣ ـ النَّصُّ عَلىٰ إمامَتِه

470. **The Prophet (SAWA),** in reply to ʿAbdullāh b. Masʿūd regarding the Imāms from Ḥusayn

٤٧٠. رسولُ اللهِ ﷺ ـ لَمّا سَألَهُ عَبدُاللهِ بنُ مَسعودٍ

(AS)'s progeny, said, '... And from the loins of 'Alī [al-Riḍā], his son Muḥammad, the praised and the purest of people in form, and the best of them in character.'[520]

عَنِ الأئِمَّةِ في صُلبِ الحُسَينِ عليه السلام ـ:... وَيَخرُجُ مِن صُلبِ عَليٍّ (الرِّضا) ابنُهُ مُحَمَّدٌ المَحمودُ أطهَرُ النّاسِ خَلقاً وَأحسَنُهُم خُلقاً ٥١٣.

471. **Abdullāh b. Ja'far narrated,** 'Ṣafwān b. Yaḥyā and I visited al-Riḍā (AS), and Abū Ja'far [Imām al-Jawād], who was three years old, was standing there. We asked him [i.e. al-Riḍā], 'May Allah sacrifice us for you. If –God forbid– something happened to you, who will be [the Imām] after you?' He said, 'This son of mine', pointing towards him. We asked, 'While he is still this young?' He replied, 'Of course while he is still this young. Verily Allah, Blessed and most High, made Jesus His divine proof [on earth] when he was just two years old.'[521]

٤٧١ . عبدُ اللهِ بنِ جعفرٍ : دَخَلتُ علىٰ الرِّضا عليه السلام أنا وصَفوانُ بنُ يحيىٰ، وأبو جعفرٍ عليه السلام قائمٌ قد أتىٰ لهُ ثلاثُ سِنينَ ، فقُلْنا له : جَعَلَنا اللهُ فِداكَ ، إنْ ـ وأعوذُ باللهِ ـ حَدَثَ حدَثٌ فَمن يَكونُ بَعدَكَ؟ قالَ : ابْنِي هذا، وأومَأَ إليهِ . قالَ : فقُلْنا لَه: وهُو في هذاالسِّنِّ ؟! قالَ : نَعَمْ ، وهُو في هذا السِّنِّ ، إنَّ اللهَ تبارَكَ وتعالىٰ احْتَجَّ بعيسىٰ عليه السلام وهُو ابنُ سَنَتَينِ . ٥١٤

154. His Virtues

١٥٤ ـ فَضائِلُهُ عليه السلام

472. **Yaḥyā al-Ṣan'ānī narrated,** 'I visited Abū al-Ḥasan al-Riḍā (AS) when he was in Makkah. I saw him peel a banana and feed it to Abū Ja'far. I asked him, 'May I be your ransom, is this the blessed newborn?' He said, 'Yes, O Yaḥyā! This is the newborn the like of whom there is none other born into Islam and upon our *shī'a*, more blessed than him.'[522]

٤٧٢ . يَحيى الصَّنعاني :دَخَلتُ عَلى أبي الحسن الرِّضا عليه السلام وَهُوَ بِمَكَّةَ وَهُوَ يَقشِرُ مَوزاً وَيُطعِمُهُ أبا جَعفَرٍ عليه السلام فَقُلتُ لَهُ : جُعِلتُ فِداكَ هٰذا المَولودُ المُبارَكُ ؟ قالَ : نَعَم يا يَحيى هٰذا المَولودُ الَّذي لَم يولَد في الإسلامِ مِثلُهُ مَولودٌ أعظَمُ بَرَكَةً عَلى شيعَتِنا مِنهُ . ٥١٥

473. **'Abdullāh b. Sa'īd narrated** that Muḥammad b. 'Alī b. 'Umar al-Tannūkhī said to him, 'I saw Muḥammad b. 'Alī [al-Jawād] talking to a bull and the bull shook his head.' Then I said to him, 'No, but [can you not] command the bull to talk to you.' He then recited [the verse]: *"We have been taught the speech of the birds and we have been given out of everything."* He then said [to it], 'Say: there is no god but Allah, the Only One and He has no partner' and stroked its head with his palm. The bull then said, 'There is no god but Allah, the Only One and He has no partner.'[523]

٤٧٣ . عَبدُاللهُ بنُ سَعيدٍ : قالَ لي مُحَمَّدُ بنُ عَليٍّ بنِ عُمَرِ التَّنّوخي : رَأيتُ مُحَمَّدَ بنَ عَليٍّ وَهُوَ يُكَلِّمُ ثَوراً فَحَرَّكَ الثَّورُ رَأسَهُ ، فَقُلتُ لا وَلٰكن تَأمُرُ الثَّورَ أن يُكَلِّمَكَ ، فَقالَ وَعُلِّمنا مَنطِقَ الطَّيرِ وَاوتينا مِن كُلِّ شَيءٍ ثُمَّ قالَ قُل لا إلٰهَ إلّا اللهُ وَحدَهُ لا شَريكَ لَهُ وَمَسَحَ بِكَفِّهِ عَلى رَأسِهِ فَقالَ الثَّورُ لا إله إلّا اللهُ وَحدَهُ لا شَريكَ لَهُ . ٥١٦

474. **ʿAlī b. Ḥassān al-Wāsiṭī,** known as al-ʿAmsh, narrated, 'I brought an item to him from Isfahan made of silver, in order to present it to my master Abū Jaʿfar [al-Jawād]. When the people left his company after he had answered all their questions, he stood up and left. I followed him and met a helper of his from whom I requested to seek permission to see Abū Jaʿfar. I entered and saluted him, and he returned my salutation with signs of dislike on his face. He did not come to sit down, so I approached him and emptied all that was in my sleeve before him. He looked at me in anger, then he looked to the right and left and said, 'Allah has not created me for this, what has play got to do with me?' I asked him to forgive me. He forgave me and then I took the things and left.'[524]

٤٧٤ . عليُّ بنِ حَسّانِ الواسِطيِّ المَعروفِ بِالعَمشِ: حَملتُ مَعي إليهِ ﷺ مِن الآلَـةِ الَّـتي لِـلإصبِهانِ بَعضُها مِن فِضَّةٍ وَقُلتُ أتحُفُ مَولايَ أبا جَـعفرٍ بِها فَلَمّا تَفرَّقَ النّاسُ عنه بَعدَ جَوابِ الجَميعِ قامَ فَمَضى فَاتَّبَعتُهُ فَلقيتُ مُوَفَّقاً فَقُلتُ استَأذِن لي على أبي جَعفرٍ ، فَدَخلتُ وَسَلَّمتُ فَردَّ عَلَيَّ السَّلامَ وَفي وَجهِهِ الكَراهَةُ وَلَم يَأتي بِالجُلوسِ فَدَنوتُ مِنهُ وَأفرَغتُ ما كانَ في كُمّي بَينَ يَدَيهِ فَنَظَرَ إلَيَّ مُغضِباً ثمّ رَنا يَميناً وَشِمالاً وَقالَ ما لِهٰذا خَلَقَني اللهُ ما أنا وَاللَّعبِ؟ فاستَعفَيتُهُ فَعَفا عَنّي فَأخَذتُها فَخَرَجتُ.٥١٧

475. **al-Qāsim b. ʿAbd al-Raḥmān,** who was then a Zaydī, narrated, 'I went to Baghdad. While I was there, I saw the people congratulating each other all of a sudden, exchanging honourable greetings and standing up. I asked, 'What is this?' They replied, 'The son of al-Riḍā [has come].' Then I said, 'Indeed I must see him'. Then he appeared on a male or female donkey. I said, 'May the curse of Allah be upon the supporters of *Imāma* who believe that Allah has made obedience to this [type of person] mandatory.' At that very moment, he turned to me and said, 'O Qāsim b. ʿAbd al-Raḥmān, *"Are we to follow a lone human from ourselves?! Indeed then we would be in error and madness."* [He continued]: 'So I said to myself, 'A sorcerer, by Allah!', and he turned to me again, and said, *"Has the Reminder been cast upon him from among us? Rather he is a self-conceited liar."*[525] [He continued]: 'So I left, believing in *Imāma* and bore witness that verily he is the proof of Allah on His creation and had faith in him.'[526]

٤٧٥ . كشف الغمّة عن القاسِمِ بنِ عَبدِالرَّحمٰنِ ـ وَكانَ زِيديّاً ـ: خَرَجتُ إلى بَغدادَ فَبَينا أنا بِها إذ رَأيتُ النّاسَ يَتَعادونَ وَيَتَشَرَّفونَ وَيَقِفونَ؛ فَقُلتُ: ما هٰذا؟ فَقالوا: ابنُ الرِّضا، فَقُلتُ: وَاللهِ لأنظُرَنَّ إلَيهِ فَطَلَعَ عَلى بَغلٍ أو بَغلَةٍ فَقُلتُ: لَعَنَ اللهُ أصحابُ الإمامَةِ حَيثُ يَقولونَ إنَّ اللهَ افتَرَضَ طاعةَ هٰذا، فَعَدَلَ إليَّ وَقالَ: يا قاسمَ بنَ عبدِالرَّحمٰنِ: «أبَشَراً مِنّا واحِداً نَتَّبِعُهُ إنّا إذاً لَفي ضَلالٍ وَسُعُرٍ»٥١٨ فَقُلتُ في نَفسي ساحِرٌ واللهِ! فَعَدَلَ إلَيَّ فَقالَ: «ءألقِيَ الذِّكرُ عَلَيهِ مِن بَينِنا بَل هُوَ كَذّابٌ أشِرٌ»٥١٩ قالَ: فانصَرَفتُ وَقُلتُ بِالإمامَةِ؛ وَشَهِدتُ أنَّهُ حُجَّةُ اللهِ عَلى خَلقِهِ وَاعتَقَدتُهُ.٥٢٠

27

IMĀM ʿALĪ B. MUḤAMMAD AL-HĀDĪ (AS)

الإمامُ عليُّ بنُ محمّدٍ الهادي

155. Proofs of his Imāma

١٥٥ ـ النَّصُّ عَلىٰ إمامَتِهِ

476. **Imām al-Jawād (AS) said,** ‘Certainly the Imām after me is my son ʿAlī. His command is my command, his word is my word, obedience to him is obedience to me and the *Imāma* after him will rest with his son al-Ḥasan.’[527]

٤٧٦ . الإمامُ الجوادُ عليه السلام : إنّ الإمامَ بَعدي ابْنِي عليٌّ، أمرُهُ أمري، وقَولُهُ قَولي، وطاعَتُهُ طاعَتي، والإمامةُ بعدَهُ في ابنِهِ الحسنِ.[٥٢١]

156. His Virtues

١٥٦ ـ فضائلُه عليه السلام

477. It is narrated in the book *al-Wāḥida*: My brother Ḥusayn b. Muḥammad narrated, saying, ‘I had a friend who used to teach the child of Baghā or Waṣīf.[528] He said to me, ‘The governor, on his return from the Caliph’s palace said to me, ‘Today the commander of the faithful has imprisoned this person known as Ibn al-Riḍā [i.e. the son of al-Riḍā] and has handed him over to ʿAlī b. Karkar, and I heard him say, ‘I am dearer to Allah than the she-camel of Ṣāliḥ[529], so *“Enjoy yourselves in your homes for three days that is a promise not untrue!”*[530] What he meant by that verse or by his speech is not clear. [He said]: I said, ‘May Allah increase your honour, he has made a threat, now see what would happen after three days.
The next day the caliph freed Ibn al-Riḍā and apologised. On the third day Yāghiz, Yaghlūn, Tāmish and a group of people with them assaulted him and killed him, and instated al-Muntaṣir his son as the Caliph.’[531]

٤٧٧ . بحار الأنوار : ذكر الحسن بن محمد جمهور العَمّي فى كتاب الواحدة قال : حدَّثَني أخي الحسينُ بنُ محمّدٍ قالَ : كانَ لي صَديقٌ مُؤَدِّبٌ لِوُلدِ بَغا أو وَصيفٍ ـ الشَّكُّ مِنّي ـ فقالَ لي : قالَ لي الأميرُ ـ مُنْصَرَفَهُ مِن دارِ الخليفةِ ـ : حَبَسَ أميرُ المؤمنينَ هذا الّذي يَقولونَ ابنُ الرِّضا اليومَ، ودفَعَهُ إلىٰ عليِّ بنِ كَرْكَرٍ، فسَمِعتُهُ يقولُ : أنا أكْرَمُ عَلى اللهِ مِن ناقةِ صالحٍ ﴿تَمَتَّعوا في دارِكُمْ ثَلاثةَأيّامٍ ذٰلِكَ وَعدٌ غيرُ مَكذوبٍ﴾[٥٢٢]، وليسَ يُفصِحُ بالآيةِ ولا بالكلامِ، أيُّ شيءٍ هذا؟ قالَ: قلتُ: أعَزّكَ اللهُ تَوَعّدَ، انظُرْ ما يكونُ بعدَ ثلاثةِ أيّامٍ.
فلمّا كانَ مِن الغَدِ أطْلَقَهُ واعْتَذرَ إلَيهِ، فلَمّا كانَ في اليومِ الثّالثِ وَثَبَ علَيهِ ياغزُ ويَغْلونُ وتامِشُ وجَماعةٌ مَعهُم، فقَتَلوهُ وأقْعَدوا المُنْتَصِرَ ولَدَهُ خليفةً.[٥٢٣]

478. A group of people from Isfahan among whom were Abū al-ʿAbbās Aḥmad b. al-Naṣr and

٤٧٨ . كشف الغمّة : حدَّثَ جَماعَةٌ مِن أهلِ إصفِهانَ مِنهُم أبوالعَبّاسِ أحمدُ بنُ النَّصرِ،

Abū Jaʿfar Muḥammad b. ʿAlawiyya, narrated, 'There was a man named ʿAbd al-Raḥmān in Isfahan who was a *shīʿa*. He was asked, 'Why have you accepted the *Imāma* of ʿAlī al-Naqī instead of anyone else from among the people of the time?' So he replied, 'I witnessed that which obligated me to believing such. I was a poor man but outspoken and daring. So the people of Isfahan exiled me and a few others. We came to Mutawakkil to ask for justice. We were at Mutawakkil's gate when the command came to bring ʿAlī b. Muḥammad b. al-Riḍā. I asked those present there who this man was that had been commanded to be brought there. Someone replied, 'He is an ʿAlawī whom the Rāfiḍa believe to be their Imām.' He then said, 'Mutawakkil may have summoned him in order to kill him.' I said, 'I will not move from here until I see who this person is.' [He continued]: 'He came riding on a horse and verily people were standing in a line on the right and left of his path watching him. When I saw him, I stopped and looked at him. Love for him filled my heart. I prayed for him in my heart for Allah to repel from him the evil of Mutawakkil. He moved through the crowd, his sight fixed on the reins of his horse, not looking around. And I was constantly supplicating for him. When he reached me, he turned his face towards me and said, 'May Allah accept your supplication, lengthen your life, and increase your wealth and your children.' After that, we returned to Isfahan. Allah opened phases of wealth upon me, so much so that I have to lock away in my house more than a million dirhams and this is apart from the wealth that is outside my house. I have been blessed with ten sons and I have reached an age in excess of seventy years. This is the reason for my faith in the

وَأبو جَعفرٍ مُحَمَّدُ بنُ عَلويَّةِ، قالوا: كانَ بِإصفِهانَ رَجلٌ يُقالُ لَهُ عَبدُالرَّحمٰنِ وَكانَ شيعيّاً، فَقيلَ لَهُ: ما السَّبَبُ الَّذي أوجَبَ عَلَيكَ القَولُ بِإمامَةِ عَليٍّ النَّقيِّ دونَ غَيرِهِ مِن أهلِ الزَّمانِ؟ فَقالَ: شاهَدتُ ما يوجِبُ عَلَيَّ ذٰلِكَ، وَذٰلك أنّي كُنتُ رَجُلاً فَقيراً وَكانَ لي لِسانٌ وَجُرأةٌ، فَأخرَجَني أهلُ إصفِهانَ سِنةً مِنَ السِّنينَ مَعَ قَومٍ آخَرينَ، (فَجِئنا ـ ظ) إلى بابِ المُتَوَكِّل مُتَظَلِّمينَ، وَكُنّا بِبابِ المُتَوَكِّلِ يَوماً إذ خَرَجَ الأمرُ بِإحضارِ عَليٍّ بنِ مُحَمَّدِ بنِ الرِّضا؛ فَقُلتُ لِبَعضِ مَن حَضَرَ: مَن هٰذا الرَّجُلُ الَّذي قَد أمِرَ بِإحضارِهِ؟ فَقيلَ: هٰذا رَجُلٌ عَلَويٌّ تَقولُ الرافِضَةُ بِإمامَتِهِ، ثُمَّ قالَ: وَنَقدِرُ أنَّ المُتَوَكِّلَ يُحضِرُهُ للقَتلِ، فَقُلتُ: لا أبرَحُ مِن هٰيهُنا حَتّى أنظُرَ إلى هٰذا الرَّجُلِ أيِّ رَجُلٍ هُوَ؟ قالَ: فَأقبَلَ راكِباً عَلى فَرَسٍ وَقَد قامَ النّاسُ صَفَّينِ يُمنَةَ الطَّريقِ وَيُسرَتَها يَنظُرونَ إلَيهِ، فَلَمّا رَأيتُهُ وَقَفتُ فَأبصَرتُهُ فَوَقَعَ حُبُّهُ في قَلبي، فَجَعلتُ أدعو لَهُ في نَفسي بِأن يَدفَعَ اللهُ عنه شَرَّ المُتَوَكِّلِ، فَأقبَلَ يَسيرُ بَينَ النّاسِ وَهُوَ يَنظُرُ إلى عُرفِ دابَّتِهِ لا يَلتَفِتُ، وَأنا دائِمُ الدُّعاءِ لَهُ، فَلَمّا صارَ إلَيَّ أقبَلَ عَلَيَّ بِوَجهِهِ وَقالَ: استَجابَ اللهُ دُعاءَكَ وَطَوَّلَ عُمرَكَ وَكَثَّرَ مالَكَ وَوَلَدَكَ. فانصَرفنا بَعدَ ذٰلك إلى إصفِهانَ، فَفَتَحَ اللهُ عَلَيَّ وُجوهاً مِنَ المالِ حَتّى إنّي أغلِقُ بابي عَلى ما قيمَتُهُ ألفَ ألفَ دِرهَمٍ سِوى مالي خارِجَ داري؛ وَرُزِقتُ عَشَرةً مِنَ الأولادِ وَقَد بَلَغتُ مِن عُمري نَيِّفاً وَسَبعينَ سَنَةً، وَأنا أقولُ بِإمامَةِ هٰذا الَّذي عَلِمَ ما في

Imāma of this man who knew what was in my heart and Allah granted his prayers for me.'[532]

قلبي وَاستَجابَ اللهُ دَعاءَهُ لي.٥٣٢

28

IMĀM AL-ḤASAN B. ʿALĪ AL-ʿASKARĪ (AS)

الإمام الحسن بن علي العسكري

157. Proofs of his Imāma

١٥٧ ـ النَّصُّ علىٰ إمامَتِه

479. **Imām al-Hādī (AS) said,** 'The Imām after me is al-Ḥasan, and after Ḥasan his son al-Qā'im [*lit.* the one who will rise], the one who will fill the land with fairness and justice just as it was filled with tyranny and oppression.'[533]

٤٧٩ . الإمامُ الهاديُّ ؏ : الإمامُ بَعدي الحَسَنُ، وبعدَ الحسنِ ابنُه القائمُ، الّذي يَملأُ الأرضَ قِسْطاً وعدلاً كما مُلِئتْ جوراً وظُلماً.٥٣٣

158. His Virtues

١٥٨ ـ فضائلُه ؏

480. **Muḥammad b. Ismāʿīl narrated,** 'The Abbasids visited Ṣāliḥ b. Waṣīf, and Ṣāliḥ b. ʿAlī and a few other deviated people from this location also visited Ṣāliḥ b. Waṣīf when Abū Muḥammad (AS) [Imām al-ʿAskarī] was in the prison. He said to him, 'Put him in strict confinement and give him no ease.' Ṣāliḥ replied, 'What more can I do with him when I have assigned two of the most evil men I could find to guard him, and surprisingly those two have turned to worship and prayers [as a result of the Imām]!'[534]

٤٨٠ . بحار الأنوار: دخَلَ العبّاسيّونَ على صالحِ ابنِ وَصيفٍ، ودخَلَ صالحُ بنُ عليٍّ وغيرُهُ مِن المُنْحَرِفينَ عن هذهِ النّاحيةِ علىٰ صالحِ بنِ وصيفٍ عندَما حُبِسَ أبو محمّدٍ ؏، فقالَ لَهُ: ضَيِّقْ عليهِ ولا تُوَسِّعْ، فقالَ لَهم صالحٌ: ما أَصْنَعُ بِهِ، وقد وَكَّلْتُ بِهِ رَجلَينِ شَرَّ مَن قَدَرْتُ علَيهِ، فَقد صارا مِنَ العِبادةِ والصّلاةِ إلىٰ أمرٍ عظيمٍ؟!٥٣٤

481. Abū al-Qāsim al-Kūfī narrates in the book *al-Tabdīl*, 'Isḥāq al-Kindī who was the philosopher of his time in Iraq decided to write about contradictions in the Qur'an, and sat alone at home, preoccupied with it. One of his students visited Imām Ḥasan al-ʿAskarī (AS) one day, and Abū Muḥammad (AS) asked him, 'Is there not a

٤٨١ . المناقب لابن شهر آشوب عن أبي القاسمِ الكوفيِّ: إنَّ إسحاقَ الكِنديَّ كانَ فيلسوفَ العِراقِ في زَمانِهِ أخَذَ في تأليفِ تناقضِ القُرآنِ وَشَغَلَ نفسَهُ بِذلك وَتَفَرَّدَ بِهِ في مَنزِلِهِ وَإنَّ بَعضَ تَلامِذَتِه دَخَلَ يَوماً عَلى الإمامِ الحَسَنِ العَسكَريِّ فَقالَ لَهُ أبو مُحَمَّدٍ ؏: أما فيكُم رَجُلٌ

rightly-guided man among you who can stop your teacher al-Kindī from this occupation that he has started with the Qur'an?' The student replied, 'We are his students; how can we object to him on this or on any other issue?' Abū Muḥammad said, 'Will you then convey to him what I am telling him through you?' He said, 'Yes.' He (AS) said, 'Go to him and offer your service to him in his task, as though you want to acquaint yourself with it, and assist him therein. Once the acquaintance has developed, tell him, 'I have a question which I would like to ask you.' Certainly he will allow you. Then ask him, 'If someone who spoke only using [verses of] the Qu'ran was to come to you, would it be possible for his intended speech to be different to what you have understood it to mean?' He will indeed tell you that it is possible, because he is a man who comprehends if he listens. So, if he confirms this, then ask him, 'So that means that that which you have perceived might be different to what he meant, such that you may even be imposing a meaning to a word that is different to its original.'

So the student went to al-Kindī, acquainted himself with him and politely mentioned the issue to him. He asked him to repeat the question, which he did. Then he pondered into it and thought it to be possible in language and acceptable conceptually. He then said, 'I swear by you to tell me from where you have learnt this [argument]?' He [the student] replied, 'It is just something that came to my mind so I presented it to you.' He said, 'No way. Someone like you could not have been guided to this kind of argument nor reached this position [in learning], so tell me from where you have come up with this?' He replied, 'Abū Muḥammad ordered me to [tell you] this.' He then said, 'Now you have told me. Something like this could only have

رَشيدٌ يَردِعُ أستاذَكُم الكِنديِّ عَمّا أخَذَ فيهِ مِن تَشاغُلِهِ بِالقُرآنِ؟ فَقالَ التِّلميذُ: نَحنُ مِن تَلامِذَتِهِ كَيفَ يَجوزُ مِنّا الإعتِراضُ عَلَيهِ في هٰذا أو في غَيرِهِ، فَقالَ لَهُ أبو مُحَمَّدٍ: أتُؤَدّي اللهَ ما ألقيهِ إليكَ؟ قالَ: نَعَم قالَ: فَصِر إلَيهِ وَتَلَطَّف في مُؤانَسَتِهِ وَمَعونَتِهِ عَلى ما هُوَ بِسَبيلِهِ فَإذا وَقَعَتِ الأُنسَةُ في ذٰلك فَقُل قَد حَضَرَتني مَسألَةٌ أسألُكَ عَنها فَإنَّهُ يَستَدعي ذٰلك مِنكَ فَقُل لَهُ إن أتاكَ هٰذا المُتَكَلِّمُ بِهٰذا القُرآنِ هَل يَجوزُ أن يَكونَ مُرادُهُ بِما تَكَلَّمَ مِنهُ غَيرَ المَعاني الَّتي قَد ظَنَنتَها أنَّكَ ذَهَبتَ إليها؟ فَإنَّهُ سَيَقولُ لَكَ إنَّهُ مِنَ الجائِزِ لأنَّهُ رَجُلٌ يَفهَمُ إذا سَمِعَ، فَإذا أوجَبَ ذٰلك فَقُل لَهُ: فَما يُدريكَ لَعَلَّهُ قَد أرادَ غَيرَ الَّذي ذَهَبتَ أنتَ إلَيهِ فَيَكونَ واضِعاً لِغَيرِ مَعانيهِ. فَصارَ الرَّجلُ إلى الكِنديِّ وَتَلَطَّفَ إلى أن ألقى عَلَيهِ هٰذِهِ المَسألَةَ فَقالَ لَهُ: أعِد عَلَيَّ، فَأعادَ عَلَيهِ فَتَفَكَّرَ في نَفسِهِ وَرأى ذٰلك مُحتَمَلاً في اللُّغَةِ وَسائِغاً في النَّظَرِ فَقالَ: أتَيتُ إلَيكَ إلّا أخبَرتَني مِن أينَ لَكَ؟ فَقالَ: إنَّهُ شَيءٌ عَرَضَ بِقَلبي فَأورَدتُهُ عَلَيكَ، فَقالَ: كَلّا ما مِثلُكَ مَن اهتَدى إلى هٰذا وَلا مَن بَلَغَ هٰذِهِ المَنزَلَةَ فَعَرِّفني مِن أينَ لَكَ هٰذا؟ فَقالَ: أمَرَني بِهِ أبو مُحَمَّدٍ فَقالَ: الآنَ جِئتَ بِهِ وَما كانَ لِيَخرُجَ مِثلَ هٰذا إلّا مِن ذٰلك البَيتِ؛ ثُمَّ إنَّهُ دَعا

come from that household.' He then asked for some fire and burnt all that he had written.'[535]

بِالنّارِ وَأحرَقَ جَميعَ ما كانَ أَلَّفَهُ.٥٢٧

29

AL-IMĀM AL-QĀ'IM (AS)

الإمام القائم

159. The Names of the Imām

١٥٩ـ أسماءُ الإمامِ

482. **Imām al-Bāqir (AS),** with reference to the verse of the Almighty: *"And whoever is killed wrongfully, We have certainly given his heir an authority ... for he enjoys the support [of law]*[536], said, 'Allah has named the Mahdī *al-Mansūr* [*lit.* one who enjoys the support of Allah] just as he named the Prophet (SAWA) Aḥmad, Muḥammad and Maḥmūd, and just as he named Jesus the Messiah (AS).'[537]

٤٨٢. الإمامُ الباقرُ ﷺ في قوله تعالى: ﴿وَمَنْ قُتِلَ مظلوماً فقد جَعَلْنا لوليّهِ سُلطاناً ... إنّه كان منصوراً﴾ ٥٢٨ـ: سمَّى اللهُ المهديَّ المنصورَ، كما سمَّى أحمدَ ومحمّد ومحمود، وكما سَمَّى عيسَى المسيحَ ﷺ. ٥٢٩

483. **Imām al-Ṣādiq (AS),** when he was asked the reason for the Qā'im [the twelfth Imām] being named al-Mahdī [*lit.* the guided], said, 'Because verily he is guided to every hidden issue.'[538]

٤٨٣. الإمامُ الصّادقُ ﷺ ـ لمّا سُئلَ عن عِلّةِ تَسميةِ القائمِ بالمَهديِّ ـ: لِأنّه يُهدى إلى كلِّ أمرٍ خَفيٍّ. ٥٣٠

160. Proofs of his Imāma

١٦٠ـ النَّصُّ علىٰ إمامَتِهِ

484. **Imām al-'Askarī (AS),** when asked about the proof [of Allah] and the Imām after him, said, 'My son Muḥammad will be the Imām and the proof after me. Whoever dies without acknowledging him [as the Imām] has died a death of ignorance. Know that certainly he will have an occultation, about which the ignorant will be left confused, the impugners will be ruined and those who predict a specific time [for his reappearance] will lie. Then he will emerge and it is as if I can see the white flags hovering above his head in Najaf [near] Kūfa.'[539]

٤٨٤. الإمامُ العسكريُّ ﷺ ـ وقد سُئلَ عن الحُجّةِ والإمامِ بعدَهُ؟ ـ: ابْني محمّدٌ، وهُو الإمامُ والحُجّةُ بَعدي، مَن ماتَ ولَم يَعرِفْهُ ماتَ مِيتةً جاهليّةً. أمَا إنّ لَه غَيبةً يَحارُ فيها الجاهلونَ، ويَهْلِكُ فيها المُبطِلونَ، ويَكْذِبُ فيها الوَقّاتونَ، ثُمّ يَخرُجُ فكأنّي أنظُرُ إلَى الأعْلامِ البِيضِ تَخفِقُ فوقَ رأسِهِ بِنَجفِ الكوفةِ. ٥٣١

161. Glad Tidings of the Mahdī (AS)

١٦١ ـ البِشارَةُ بِالمَهدِيِّ ؑ

485. **The Prophet (SAWA) said,** 'Glad tidings to you O Fāṭima for verily the Mahdī will be from you [i.e. your descent].'[540]

٤٨٥ . رسولُ اللهِ ﷺ : أبْشِري يا فاطمةُ، فإنّ المهديَّ منكِ.٥٣٢

486. **The Prophet (SAWA) said,** 'The Mahdī will be a man from my offspring, and his face will be like a sparkling star.'[541]

٤٨٦ . عنه ﷺ : المهديُّ رجُلٌ مِن وُلْدي، وجهُهُ كالكَوكبِ الدُّرّيِّ.٥٣٣

487. **The Prophet (SAWA) said,** 'The [Final] Hour will not come until the land has been filled with tyranny and enmity, then a man from my progeny will emerge and will fill it with fairness and justice just as it had been filled with tyranny and enmity.'[542]

٤٨٧ . عنه ﷺ : لا تَقومُ السّاعةُ حتّىٰ تَمْتَلئَ الأرضُ ظُلماً وعُدْواناً، ثُمّ يخرُجُ رجُلٌ مِن عِترتي فيَملَؤُها قِسْطاً وعَدلاً كما مُلِئتْ ظُلماً وعُدْواناً.٥٣٤

488. **The Prophet (SAWA) said,** 'A man from my household will rule, his name will be the same as mine. Even if not more than a day remains of this world, Allah will lengthen that day so that he may rule.'[543]

٤٨٨ . عنه ﷺ : يَلي رجُلٌ مِن أهلِ بيتي يُواطِئُ اسمُه اسمِي، لو لَم يَبْقَ مِن الدُّنيا إلّا يومٌ لَطوَّلَ اللهُ ذلكَ اليومَ حتّىٰ يَليَ.٥٣٥

489. **Imām 'Alī (AS) said,** 'Al-Mahdī will be a man from us, from the progeny of Fāṭima.'[544]

٤٨٩ . الإمامُ عليٌّ ؑ : المهديُّ رجُلٌ مِنّا مِن وُلدِ فاطمةَ.٥٣٦

490. **Imām al-Bāqir (AS) said,** 'When he emerges, he will lean his back against the Ka'ba, and three hundred and thirteen men will assemble with him, and the first thing he will utter will be the verse, "*What remains of Allah's provision is better for you, should you be the faithful.*"[545] He will then say, 'I am the remains of Allah, His proof and His vicegerent upon you. None will salute him except by saying, 'Peace be upon you O remainder of Allah (*baqiyyat Allah*) in His land.'[546]

٤٩٠ . الإمامُ الباقرُ ؑ : فإذا خَرجَ أسْندَ ظَهْرَهُ إلَى الكعبةِ،واجْتَمعَ إليهِ ثلاثُمائةٍ وثلاثةَ عَشَرَ رجُلاً، فأوّلُ ما يَنطِقُ بهِ هذهِ الآيةُ: ﴿بَقِيّةُ اللهِ خيرٌ لكم إنْ كُنتم مؤمنين﴾.٥٣٧ ثُمّ يقولُ: أنا بَقِيّةُ اللهِ وحُجّتُهُ وخليفتُهُ علَيكُم، فلا يُسَلِّمُ إلَيهِ مُسَلِّمٌ إلّا قالَ: السّلامُ عليكَ يا بَقِيّةَ اللهِ في أرضِهِ.٥٣٨

162. The Two Occultations of Imām al-Qā'im

١٦٢ ـ غَيبتا الإمام القائم ؑ

491. **Imām al-Ṣādiq (AS) said,** 'Al-Qā'im will have two occultations, one of which will be long

٤٩١ . الإمامُ الصّادقُ ؑ : للقائمِ غَيبتانِ:

and the other short. During the first, a few elite followers (*shī'a*) will know his location, and during the second one, none will know his location save his selected supporters in faith.'[547]

إحْداهُما طويلةٌ، والأُخرىٰ قصيرةٌ، فالأُولىٰ يَعلَمُ بمكانِهِ فيها خاصّةٌ مِن شيعتِهِ، والأُخرىٰ لا يَعلمُ بمكانِهِ فيها (إلّا) خاصّةُ مواليهِ في دِينِه.[٥٣٩]

(أنظر) الحج: باب ٤٥٥.

(See also: THE OBLIGATORY PILGRIMAGE (*ḤAJJ*): section 455)

163. The Difficulty of Adhering to the Religion during the Occultation of the Imām

١٦٣ ـ صُعوبَةُ التَّمَسُّكِ بِالدِّينِ في غَيبةِ الإمام

492. **The Prophet (SAWA) said,** 'By Him who has sent me down as the bearer of good news, certainly those who are steadfast in their belief in him during his occultation are dearer than red sulphur [elixir].'[548]

٤٩٢ . رسولُ اللهِ ﷺ: والّذي بَعثَني بالحَقِّ بشيراً، إنّ الثّابِتينَ علىٰ القَولِ بهِ في زمانِ غَيبتِهِ لَأعزُّ مِنَ الكِبريتِ الأحْمَرِ.[٥٤٠]

493. **Imām al-Ṣādiq (AS) said** to Ibn Sinān, 'Certainly the rightful owner of this rule will have an occultation, such that the one who adheres to his religion during it will be like one who clutches on to a thorn bush with his hands.' Then he observed silence for a while and then said, 'The rightful owner of this rule will have an occultation, so let the servant be Godwary and adhere to his religion.'[549]

٤٩٣ . الغيبة للنعماني عن الإمامِ الصّادقِ ﷺ: إنّ لِصاحِبِ هذا الأمرِ غَيبةً المُتَمَسِّكُ فيها بدِينِهِ كالخارِطِ لِشَوْكِ القَتادِ بِيَدِهِ.
ـ ثُمّ أطْرَقَ مَليّاً ثُمّ قال: ـ إنّ لِصاحِبِ هذا الأمرِ غَيْبةً فَلْيَتَّقِ اللهَ عَبدٌ ولْيَتَمَسَّكْ بِدِينِهِ.[٥٤١]

(أنظر) الدين: باب ٧٣٩.

(See also: RELIGION: section 739)

164. Supplication during the Occultation of al-Qā'im

١٦٤ ـ الدُّعاءُ عِندَ غَيبةِ القائمِ ﷺ

494. **Imām al-Ṣādiq (AS) said to Ibn Sinān,** 'You will be afflicted with an obscure matter that will leave you with no sign to indicate to the solution, nor a leader to guide the way. None shall be saved from it except the one who recites the '*Supplication of the Drowning Person*'. [The narrator says] I asked the Imām, 'What is the Supplication of the Drowning Person?' The Imām replied, 'You say: *"O Allah, O the Beneficent, O the Merciful, O He who causes the hearts to fluctuate,*

٤٩٤ . بحار الأنوار عن عبد الله بن سنانٍ: قالَ أبو عَبدِ اللهِ ﷺ: سَتُصيبُكُم شُبْهةٌ فَتَبقَونَ بلا عَلَمٍ يُرىٰ ولا إمامِ هُدىً، لا يَنْجو منها إلّا مَن دَعا بدُعاءِ الغَريقِ. قلتُ: وكيفَ دُعاءُ الغَريقِ؟ قالَ: تقولُ: يا اللهُ يا رحمٰنُ يا رحيمُ، يا مُقلِّبَ القلوبِ ثَبِّتْ قلبي علىٰ دِينِكَ. فقلتُ: يا مُقلِّبَ القلوبِ والأبصارِ ثَبِّتْ قلبي علىٰ دِينِكَ! فقالَ: إنّ

affirm my heart upon Your religion." So I said, 'O He who causes the hearts and sights to fluctuate, affirm my heart upon Your religion!' So he said, 'Allah, Mighty and Exalted, is indeed the One who causes the hearts and sights to fluctuate, but you must say exactly as I say: O He who causes the hearts to fluctuate, affirm my heart upon Your religion.'[550]

اللهَ عزّ وجلّ مُقلِّبُ القلوبِ والأبصارِ ولكنْ قُلْ كما أقولُ: يا مُقلِّبَ القلوبِ ثَبِّتْ قلبي على دِينِكَ.٥٤٢

165. [Actively] Anticipating Relief

١٦٥ـ انتِظارُ الفَرَجِ

495. **The Prophet (SAWA) said,** 'The best of the deeds of my community is [actively] anticipating relief from Allah, Mighty and Exalted.'[551]

٤٩٥. رسولُ اللهِ ﷺ: أفضلُ أعمالِ أُمّتي انتظارُ فَرَجِ اللهِ عزّ وجلّ.٥٤٣

496. **Imām Zayn al-ʿĀbidīn (AS) said,** '[Actively] anticipating relief is itself the greatest relief.'[552]

٤٩٦. الإمامُ زينُ العابدينَ ؑ: انتظارُ الفَرَجِ مِن أعظمِ الفَرَجِ.٥٤٤

497. **Imām al-Ṣādiq (AS) said,** 'One who dies anticipating this rule [of the Mahdī] is as one who will be with al-Qā'im in his tent. Not only that, but he possesses the rank of one who fought with the sword in the presence of the Prophet (SAWA).'[553]

٤٩٧. الإمامُ الصّادقُ ؑ: مَن ماتَ مُنتظِراً لهذا الأمرِ كانَ كَمَنْ كانَ مَع القائمِ في فُسْطاطِهِ، لا بَلْ كانَ بمنزلةِ الضّاربِ بينَ يدَي رسولُ اللهِ ﷺ بالسَّيفِ.٥٤٥

498. **Imām al-Kāẓim (AS) said,** 'Anticipating relief is part of the relief itself.'[554]

٤٩٨. الإمامُ الكاظمُ ؑ: انتظارُ الفَرَجِ مِن الفَرَجِ.٥٤٦

166. The Reappearance of al-Qā'im after People's Despair

١٦٦ـ ظُهورُ القائِمِ ؑ بَعدَ يَأسِ النّاسِ

499. **Imām al-Ṣādiq (AS) said,** 'Certainly this rule [of the Mahdī] will not come to you but after having despaired. No by Allah, in order that you may be differentiated from one another.'[555]

٤٩٩. الإمامُ الصّادقُ ؑ: إنّ هذا الأمرَ لا يأتيكُم إلّا بعدَ إياسٍ، لا واللهِ، حتّىٰ تُمَيَّزوا.٥٤٧

500. **Imām al-Riḍā (AS) said,** 'Certainly relief will come after despair.'[556]

٥٠٠. الإمامُ الرِّضا ؑ: إنّما يَجيءُ الفَرَجُ على اليأسِ.٥٤٨

167. Those who Foretell a Specific Time [for the Reappearance of al-Qā'im] are Lying

١٦٧ـكَذَبَ الوَقّاتونَ

501. When Fuḍayl asked, 'Is there a specific time for the reappearance?' al-Imām al-Bāqir (AS) said, 'Those who foretell a specific time [for the reappearance of al-Qā'im] are lying, those who foretell a specific time are lying, those who foretell a specific time are lying.'[557]

٥٠١ . الإمامُ الباقرُ ﷺ ـ وقد سألَه الفُضَيلُ: هَل لهذا الأمرِ وقتٌ ؟ ـ: كَذَبَ الوَقّاتونَ، كَذَبَ الوَقّاتونَ، كَذَبَ الوَقّاتونَ.٥٤٩

168. The Reason for his Occultation

١٦٨ـعِلَّةُ الغَيبَةِ

502. **Imām al-Ṣādiq (AS),** 'The Prophet (SAWA) said, 'Verily occultation will be necessary for the child [i.e. the Mahdī], at which he was asked, 'Why is that, O Messenger of Allah?' He replied, 'He will fear for his life [the time is not safe for his advent].'[558]

٥٠٢ . الإمامُ الصّادقُ ﷺ :قالَ رَسولُ اللهِ ﷺ :لابدّ للغُلامِ من غَيبةٍ، فقيلَ لَهُ: ولِمَ يا رسولُ اللهِ؟ قال: يَخافُ القَتْلَ.٥٥٠

503. When asked about the reason for the occultation, Imām al-Ṣādiq (AS) replied, 'For a reason that we are not allowed to reveal to you. I [i.e. ʿAbdullāh b. al-Faḍl] asked, 'What is the wisdom behind his occultation?' He said, 'The wisdom behind his occultation is the same wisdom behind the occultation of Allah's proofs before him. Certainly the wisdom behind it will not be disclosed until after his reappearance... Verily this command is among the commands of the Almighty Allah, a secret from among the secrets of Allah, a thing of the unseen from among the unseen things of Allah. When we acknowledge that He is All-Wise, we also acknowledge that all His actions are wise, even though the reason behind them may be undisclosed.'[559]

٥٠٣ . كمال الدين عن عبدِ اللهِ بنِ الفَضلِ الهاشِمِيّ: سَمِعتُ الصّادقُ جَعفرَ بنَ مُحمَّدٍ ﷺ يَقولُ: إنّ لِصاحبِ هذَا الأمرِ غَيبةً لابُدَّ مِنها يَرتابُ فيها كلُّ مُبطلٍ. فقُلتُ: وَلِمَ جُعِلتُ فِداكَ؟ قالَ: لِأمرٍ لَم يُؤذنْ لنا في كَشفِهِ لكُم.
قلتُ: فما وجْهُ الحِكمةِ في غَيبتهِ؟ قال: وجْهُ الحِكمةِ في غَيبتهِ وجهُ الحكمةِ في غَيباتِ مَن تقدّمَهُ مِن حُجَجِ اللهِ تعالى ذِكرُهُ، إنّ وجهَ الحكمةِ في ذلكَ لا يَنكشِفُ إلّا بعدَ ظهورِهِ... إنّ هذا الأمرَ أمرٌ مِن أمرِ اللهِ تعالىٰ، وسِرٌّ مِن سرِّ اللهِ، وغيبٌ مِن غَيبِ اللهِ، ومتىٰ عَلِمنا أنّهُ عزّ وجلّ حكيمٌ صدّقْنا بأنّ أفعالَهُ كلَّها حِكمةٌ، وإنْ كانَ وجهُها غيرَ مُنكَشِفٍ.٥٥١

504. **Imām al-Ṣādiq (AS) said,** 'Al-Qā'im (AS) will never reappear until Allah's deposits [i.e. believers born of unbelievers] rise up. When they

٥٠٤ . عنه ﷺ : القائمُ ﷺ لَن يَظهرَ أبداً حتّىٰ تَخرُجَ ودائعُ اللهِ تعالىٰ [يعني بها المؤمنينَ مِن أصلابِ الكافرينَ] فإذا خَرجَتْ ظَهَرَ علىٰ

rise up, he will win over those who revolt from among the enemies of Allah. He will then kill them.'[560]

مَن ظَهرَ مِن أعداءِ اللهِ فقتَلَهُم؟٥٥٢

505. **Imām al-Ṣādiq (AS) said,** 'This rule will not take place until every single type of people will have ruled over people, such that no one will be able to say, 'Indeed were we to rule, we would be just!' And then al-Qā'im will stand with the truth and justice.'[561]

٥٠٥ . عنه ﷺ : ما يكونُ هذا الأمرُ حتّىٰ لا يبقىٰ صِنفٌ مِن النّاسِ إلّا وقد وُلّوا عَلَى النّاسِ، حتّىٰ لا يَقولَ قائلٌ : إنّا لو وُلِّينا لَعَدَلْنا ! ثُمّ يَقومُ القائمُ بالحقِّ والعَدلِ.٥٥٣

506. **Imām al-Kāẓim (AS) said,** 'If there were among you people as many as the numbers [of fighters in the Battle] at Badr, our Qā'im would rise.'[562]

٥٠٦ . الإمامُ الكاظمُ ﷺ : لو كانَ فيكُم عِدّةُ أهلِ بَدرٍ لَقامَ قائمُنا.٥٥٤

169. People Benefiting from the Imām during his Occultation

١٦٩ ـ انتِفاعُ النّاسِ بِالإمامِ في غَيبتِهِ

507. **Imām al-Mahdī (AS) said,** 'The way that people benefit from me during my occultation is as they benefit from the sun when the clouds cover it from the sights. I am indeed a [source of] security for the dwellers of the earth.'[563]

٥٠٧ . الإمامُ المهديُّ ﷺ : أمّا وَجهُ الانْتِفاعِ بي في غَيبَتي فكالانْتِفاعِ بالشَّمسِ إذا غَيَّبها عَنِ الأبصارِ السَّحابُ، وإنّي لَأمانٌ لأهلِ الأرضِ.٥٥٥

170. The Signs of his Reappearance

١٧٠ ـ عَلاماتُ الظُّهورِ

508. **Imām ʿAlī (AS) said,** 'When the preacher perishes and the master of the time deviates, when both thriving hearts and empty hearts fluctuate, when the hopeful ones will perish and those who are destined to fade away will fade away, the believers will remain, and they will be few in number, three hundred or more. The band that fought with the Prophet (SAWA) on the day of Badr will fight alongside them, neither being killed nor dying.'[564]

٥٠٨ . الإمامُ عليٌّ ﷺ : إذا هلَكَ الخاطِبُ٥٥٦ وزاغَ صاحِبُ العَصرِ وبقِيَتْ قلوبٌ تَتَقلّبُ مِن مُخْصِبٍ ومُجْدِبٍ، هلَكَ المُتَمَنّونَ واضْمَحَلَّ المُضْمَحِلّونَ وَبقِيَ المؤمنونَ، وقَليلٌ ما يكونونَ، ثلاثُمائةٍ أو يَزيدونَ، تُجاهِدُ معَهُم عِصابةٌ جاهَدَتْ مَعَ رسولِ اللهِ ﷺ يومَ بَدرٍ، لَم تُقْتَلْ ولَم تَمُتْ.٥٥٧

509. **Imām al-Ṣādiq (AS) said,** 'Certainly there are signs prior to the uprising of al-Qā'im from the Almighty Allah for the believers.' I [i.e. Muḥammad b. Muslim] asked, 'And what are they – may Allah make me your ransom?' He replied,

٥٠٩ . كمال الدين عن محمّدَ بنِ مُسلمٍ : سَمعتُ أبا عبدِاللهِ ﷺ يَقولُ : إنّ قُدّامَ القائمِ عَلاماتٍ تكونُ مِنَ اللهِ عزّ وجلّ للمؤمنينَ، قلتُ : وما هِيَ، جَعَلني اللهُ فِداكَ؟ قالَ : ذلكَ قَولُ اللهِ عزّ وجلّ : ﴿ وَلَنَبْلُوَنَّكُمْ ﴾ يعني المؤمنينَ

'That is His verse: *"We will surely test you*, meaning the believers before the reappearance of al-Qā'im, *with a measure of fear and hunger and a loss of wealth, lives and fruits; and give good news to the patient.*"'[565] [566]

قبلَ خروجِ القائمِ ﷺ ﴿بِشَيْءٍ مِنَ الخَوْفِ والجُوعِ ونَقْصٍ مِنَ الأَمْوالِ والأَنْفُسِ والثَّمَراتِ وبَشِّرِ الصّابِرينَ﴾ ٥٥٨. ٥٥٩

510. **Imām al-Mahdī (AS),** when 'Alī b. Mahzyār asked him, 'O my master, when will this rule be?', replied, 'When the way between you and the Ka'bah will close.'[567]

٥١٠. الإمامُ المهديُّ ﷺ وقد سألَه عليُّ بنُ مهزيارَ: يا سيّدي، متىٰ يكونُ هذا الأمرُ؟ - إذا حِيلَ بينَكم وبينَ سبيلِ الكعبةِ. ٥٦٠

171. At the Time of the Reappearance

١٧١ - عِندَ الظُّهورِ

511. **Imām 'Alī (AS) said,** 'When a caller calls from the sky, 'Certainly the truth is with the progeny of Muḥammad', that is when al-Mahdī will reappear [being circulated] on people's tongues and they will be quenched by his love, and they will not talk about anything but him.'[568]

٥١١. الإمامُ عليٌّ ﷺ: إذا نادىٰ مُنادٍ من السَّماءِ: «إنّ الحَقَّ في آلِ محمّدٍ» فعندَ ذلكَ يَظهرُ المَهديُّ علىٰ أفواهِ النّاسِ، ويُشْرَبونَ حُبَّهُ، فلا يكونُ لَهم ذِكْرٌ غيرُهُ. ٥٦١

512. **Imām al-Bāqir (AS) said,** 'If we were to take rule and our Mahdi [Saviour] would appear, each one of our followers will be more daring than a lion and sharper than the point of a spear. He will trample over our enemies and strike them with his hands, and this will happen with the coming of the mercy of Allah and His relief for His creation.'[569]

٥١٢. الإمامُ الباقرُ ﷺ: إذا وَقَعَ أمرُنا وجاءَ مَهديُّنا كانَ الرَّجُلُ مِن شيعتِنا أجرأَ مِن لَيثٍ وأمضىٰ مِن سِنانٍ يطأُ عَدوَّنا بِرِجليهِ ويَضرِبُهُ بِكَفَّيهِ وذلِكَ عِندَ نُزولِ رَحمَةِ اللهِ وفَرَجِهِ علَى العِبادِ. ٥٦٢

513. **Imām al-Ṣādiq (AS) said,** 'When the Awaited al-Qā'im (may Allah hasten his reappearance) appears, he will rule with justice, all tyranny will be taken away during his ruling, all paths will be safe, the earth will bring out its blessings and all rights will be given to its owner.'[570]

٥١٣. الإمامُ الصّادقُ ﷺ: إذا قامَ القائمُ ﷺ حَكَمَ بالعَدلِ وارتَفَعَ في أيّامِهِ الجَورُ، وأمِنَتْ بِهِ السُّبُلُ، وأخرجَتِ الأرضُ بَرَكاتِها ورَدَّ كُلَّ حَقٍّ إلىٰ أهلِهِ. ٥٦٣

514. **Imām al-Ṣādiq (AS) said,** 'Verily when our Qā'im will rise, Allah will sharpen the sights and the hearing of our followers (*shī'a*) to such an extent that there will be no need for courier between them and al-Qā'im. He will speak to them and they will hear him, and they will see him whilst he is in his own locality.'[571]

٥١٤. عنه ﷺ: إنّ قائمَنا إذا قامَ مَدَّ اللهُ عزّوجلّ لِشيعتِنا في أسماعِهِم وأبصارِهِم، حتّىٰ (لا) يكونَ بينَهُم وبينَ القائمِ بَريدٌ، يُكلِّمُهُم فيَسمَعونَ، ويَنظُرونَ إليهِ وهُوَ في مكانِهِ. ٥٦٤

515. **Imām al-Ṣādiq (AS) said,** 'Very few Arabs will be with al-Qā'im', at which someone said, 'But in fact those who describe this matter from among them are many!' He said, 'People must be purged, distinguished, and sifted, and many people will fall through the sieve.'[572]

٥١٥ . الغيبة للنعماني عن الإمامِ الصّادقِ ﷺ: مَعَ القائمِ ﷺ مِن العربِ شيءٌ يَسيرٌ ، فقيلَ له: إنّ مَن يَصِفُ هذا الأمرَ مِنهُم لَكثيرٌ ! قالَ: لابُدّ للنّاسِ مِن أنْ يُمَحَّصوا ويُمَيَّزوا ويُغَرْبَلوا، وسَيَخرُجُ مِن الغِرْبالِ خَلْقٌ كثيرٌ.٥٦٥

516. **Imām al-Ṣādiq said,** 'When al-Qā'im emerges, many from among those who considered themselves to be with him will leave his command, whereas the likes of those who worship the sun and the moon will enter [his service].'[573]

٥١٦ . عنه ﷺ: إذا خرجَ القائمُ ﷺ خَرَجَ مِن هذا الأمرِ مَن كانَ يرى أنّهُ مِن أهلِهِ، ودخلَ فيهِ شِبْهُ عَبَدَةِ الشَّمسِ والقمرِ.٥٦٦

172. The Universe after the Reappearance of al-Mahdī

١٧٢ ـ العالَمُ بَعدَ ظُهورِ المَهديِّ ﷺ

517. **The Prophet (SAWA) said,** 'Al-Mahdī will reappear among the last ones of my community. Allah will quench him with rain, the land will bring forth its vegetation, wealth will be given in full, livestock will increase and the community will augment.'[574]

٥١٧ . رسولُ اللهِ ﷺ: يَخرُجُ في آخرِ أُمّتي المَهديُّ، يَسْقيهِ اللهُ الغَيْثَ، وتُخرِجُ الأرضُ نَباتَها، ويُعطَى المالُ صِحاحاً، وتَكثُرُ الماشِيَةُ، وتَعْظُمُ الأُمّةُ.٥٦٧

518. **Imām Zayn al-ʿĀbidīn (AS) said,** 'When our Qā'im will rise, Allah will remove all defects from our *shīʿa*. He will make their hearts like pieces of iron, and he will make the strength of a man from among them equal the strength of forty men. They will be the rulers and chiefs of the earth.'[575]

٥١٨ . الإمامُ زينُ العابدينَ ﷺ: إذا قامَ قائمُنا أذْهَبَ اللهُ عن شِيعتِنا العاهَةَ، وجَعلَ قلوبَهُم كزُبَرِ الحديدِ، وجعلَ قُوّةَ الرَّجُلِ مِنهُم قُوّةَ أربعينَ رجُلاً، ويكونونَ حُكّامَ الأرضِ وسَنامَها.٥٦٨

519. **Imām al-Bāqir (AS) said,** 'When al-Qā'im will rise, faith will be presented to every person who declares enmity towards the *Ahl al-Bayt*. If he enters it truly [well and good], but if not, then he will be beheaded lest he pays the poll-tax as do the people of the covenant today. A girdle will be tied onto his waist and he will be exiled from the towns to its outskirts.'[576]

٥١٩ . الإمامُ الباقرُ ﷺ: إذا قامَ القائمُ عَرَضَ الإيمانَ على كلِّ ناصِبٍ، فإنْ دَخلَ فيهِ بِحَقيقةٍ وإلّا ضَرَبَ عُنُقَهُ أو يُؤدّيَ الجِزْيَةَ كما يُؤدّيها اليومَ أهلُ الذِّمّةِ، ويَشُدُّ على وَسَطِهِ الهِمْيانَ، ويُخرِجُهُم مِن الأمْصارِ إلى السَّوادِ.٥٦٩

30

FAITH

الإِيمانُ

173. Faith (*Īmān*) and Islam

١٧٣ـ الإيمانُ وَالإسلامُ

"The Bedouins say, 'We have faith'. Say, 'You do not have faith yet; rather say, 'We have embraced Islam', for faith has not yet entered into your hearts."[577]

﴿قَالَتِ الْأَعْرَابُ آمَنَّا قُلْ لَمْ تُؤْمِنُوا وَلٰكِنْ قُولُوا أَسْلَمْنا وَلَمَّا يَدْخُلِ الْإِيمانُ فِي قُلُوبِكُمْ﴾.[٥٧٠]

520. **Imām al-Bāqir (AS) said,** 'Faith is to attest and to act, whereas Islam is to attest without action.'[578]

٥٢٠. الإمامُ الباقرُ عليه السلام: الإيمانُ إقرارٌ وعملٌ، والإسلامُ إقرارٌ بلا عملٍ.[٥٧١]

521. **Imām al-Ṣādiq (AS) said,** 'Verily faith is that which is embedded in the hearts, whereas Islam is the means by which marriages, inheritances and safeguarding blood take place.'[579]

٥٢١. الإمامِ الصّادقِ عليه السلام: إنّ الإيمانَ ما وَقَرَ في القلوبِ، والإسلامَ ما عليهِ المَناكِحُ والمَوارِيثُ وحَقْنُ الدِّماءِ.[٥٧٢]

174. The Reality of Faith

١٧٤ـ حقيقةُ الإيمانِ

522. **The Prophet (SAWA) said,** 'Faith is not [acquired] through embellishment or wishing. Rather faith is that which is pure in the heart and is certified by actions.'[580]

٥٢٢. رسولُ اللهِ ﷺ: ليسَ الإيمانُ بالتَّحَلّي ولا بالتَّمَنّي، ولكنَّ الإيمانَ ما خَلَصَ في القلبِ وصَدّقَهُ الأعمالُ.[٥٧٣]

523. **The Prophet (SAWA) said,** 'Faith is inner knowledge by means of the heart, attestation with the tongue and action with the limbs.'[581]

٥٢٣. عنه ﷺ: الإيمانُ مَعرِفةٌ بالقلبِ، وقَولٌ باللِّسانِ، وعَملٌ بالأرْكانِ.[٥٧٤]

524. **The Prophet (SAWA) said,** 'Faith is patience and liberality.'[582]

٥٢٤. عنه ﷺ: الإيمانُ، الصَّبرُ والسَّماحةُ.[٥٧٥]

525. **The Prophet (SAWA) said,** 'Every thing has a reality, and a servant will never reach the reality of faith until he acknowledges that whatever afflicts him would never have missed him and whatever has missed him would never have afflicted him.'[583]

٥٢٥. عنه ﷺ: إنّ لكلّ شيءٍ حقيقةً، وما بلَغَ عبدٌ حقيقةَ الإيمانِ حتّى يَعلَمَ أنّ ما أصابَهُ لَم يكُنْ لِيُخْطِئَهُ وما أخْطأهُ لم يَكُن لِيُصيبَهُ.[٥٧٦]

526. **The Prophet (SAWA) said,** 'A servant will never attain the reality of faith until he is angered only for the sake of Allah and is pleased only for Allah. When he does that, he truly becomes deserving of the reality of faith.'[584]

٥٢٦ . عنه ﷺ : لا يَحُقُّ العبدُ حقيقةَ الإيمانِ حتّىٰ يَغْضَبَ للهِ ويَرضىٰ للهِ ، فإذا فَعلَ ذلكَ فَقَدِ استَحَقَّ حقيقةَ الإيمانِ .[٥٧٧]

527. **The Prophet (SAWA) said,** 'A servant will not have faith until he loves for others the good that he loves for himself.'[585]

٥٢٧ . عنه ﷺ : لا يُؤمِنُ عبدٌ حتّىٰ يُحِبَّ للنّاسِ ما يُحبُّ لِنفسهِ مِن الخَيرِ .[٥٧٨]

528. **Imām ʿAlī (AS) said,** 'Faith is sincerity of action.'[586]

٥٢٨ . الإمامُ عليٌّ ؑ : الإيمانُ إخلاصُ العملِ .[٥٧٩]

529. **Imām ʿAlī (AS) said,** 'Faith is patience during calamity, and thankfulness during ease.'[587]

٥٢٩ . عنه ؑ : الإيمانُ صَبرٌ في البَلاءِ ، وشُكْرٌ في الرَّخاءِ .[٥٨٠]

530. **Imām ʿAlī (AS) said,** 'The fountainhead of faith is honesty.'[588]

٥٣٠ . عنه ؑ : رأسُ الإيمانِ الصِّدقُ .[٥٨١]

531. **Imām ʿAlī (AS) said,** 'A servant's faith is not true until his confidence in that which rests in Allah's Hand is more than that which rests in his own hands.'[589]

٥٣١ . عنه ؑ : لا يَصْدُقُ إيمانُ عبدٍ حتّىٰ يَكونَ بما في يَدِ اللهِ سبحانه أوْثَقَ مِنه بما في يَدِهِ .[٥٨٢]

532. **Imām al-Ṣādiq (AS) said,** 'Verily the reality of faith is for you to prefer right, even if it is to your detriment, over wrong, even if it is to your benefit.'[590]

٥٣٢ . الإمامُ الصّادقُ ؑ : إنّ مِن حقيقةِ الإيمانِ أنْ تُؤْثِرَ الحقَّ وإنْ ضَرَّكَ علَى الباطلِ وإنْ نَفَعَكَ .[٥٨٣]

175. Relation between Faith and Action

١٧٥ ـ تآصُرُ الإيمانِ وَالعَمَلِ

533. **The Prophet (SAWA) said,** 'Faith and action are two brothers, bound together with a single rope. Allah will not accept either one without the other.'[591]

٥٣٣ . رسولُ اللهِ ﷺ : الإيمانُ والعملُ أخَوانِ شَريكانِ في قَرَنٍ ، لا يَقْبلُ اللهُ أحدَهُما إلّا بصاحبِهِ .[٥٨٤]

534. **The Prophet (SAWA) said,** 'The *murji'a* have been cursed by seventy prophets. They are

٥٣٤ . عنه ﷺ : لُعِنَتِ المُرجِئةُ علىٰ لِسانِ سَبعينَ نَبيّاً ، الّذينَ يقولونَ : الإيمانُ قَولٌ

those who say that faith is attestation without action.'[592]

بلا عملٍ.[٥٨٥]

535. **Imām ʿAlī (AS) said,** 'If faith was a mere statement, then fasting, prayers, the lawful and the unlawful things would not have been prescribed for it.'[593]

٥٣٥ . الإمامُ عليٌّ ﷺ: لو كانَ الإيمانُ كلاماً لم يَنْزِلْ فيهِ صَومٌ ولا صلاةٌ ولا حلالٌ ولا حرامٌ.[٥٨٦]

536. **Imām al-Kāẓim (AS) said,** 'Faith is all action, and the statement is but part of the action that Allah has made mandatory, which He has explained in His Book.'[594]

٥٣٦ . الإمامُ الكاظمُ ﷺ: الإيمانُ عملٌ كلُّهُ،[٥٨٧] والقَولُ بعضُ ذلكَ العملِ بِفَرضٍ مِن اللهِ بَيَّنَهُ في كِتابهِ.[٥٨٨]

(See also: ACTION 290)

(أُنظر) عنوان ٢٩٠ «العمل».

176. Faith and Sins

١٧٦ ـ الإيمانُ وَالآثامُ

537. **The Prophet (SAWA) said,** 'A sin cannot expel the faithful person from his faith, just as an act of goodness cannot expel an infidel from his faithlessness.'[595]

٥٣٧ . رسولُ اللهِ ﷺ: لا يُخرِجُ المؤمنَ من إيمانِهِ ذَنبٌ، كَما لا يُخرِجُ الكافِرَ مِن كُفرِهِ إحسانٌ.[٥٨٩]

538. **The Prophet (SAWA) said,** 'Whoever sincerely says: 'There is no god but Allah' (*lā ilāha illallāh*) will enter Paradise.' He was asked, 'And where does the sincerity of it [i.e. the statement] lie?' He said, 'In guarding it from what Allah has prohibited.'[596]

٥٣٨ . كنز العمّال عن رسولِ اللهِ ﷺ: مَن قالَ: «لا إلٰه إلّا اللهُ» مُخْلِصاً دَخلَ الجنّةَ. قِيلَ: وما إخلاصُها؟ قالَ: أنْ تَحْجِزَهُ عَن مَحارِمِ اللهِ.[٥٩٠]

539. **The Prophet (SAWA) said,** '[The statement] 'There is no god but Allah' will benefit whoever recites it until he depreciates it. And depreciating its right is when sins are openly committed, and they neither prohibit them, nor do they change them.'[597]

٥٣٩ . عنه ﷺ: لا تَزالُ لا إلٰه إلّا اللهُ تَنْفَعُ مَن قالَها حتّىٰ يُسْتَخَفَّ بها، والاسْتِخْفافُ بِحَقِّها أنْ يَظْهَرَ العملُ بالمَعاصي فلا يُنْكِرُوهُ ولا يُغَيِّرُوهُ.[٥٩١]

540. **Imām al-Kāẓim (AS),** when asked about the grave sins and whether they expel one from faith?', replied, 'Yes.' [And when asked about other than grave sins], said, 'The Prophet (SAWA) said, 'An adulterer would never commit adultery whilst still a believer and a thief would never steal whilst still a believer.'[598]

٥٤٠ . الإمامُ الكاظمُ ﷺ ـ وقد سُئلَ عنِ الكبائرِ: هلْ تُخرِجُ مِن الإيمانِ؟ ـ: نَعَم، وما دُونَ الكبائرِ، قالَ رسولُ اللهِ ﷺ: «لا يَزْني الزّاني وهُو مؤمنٌ ولا يَسْرِقُ السّارقُ وهُو مؤمنٌ».[٥٩٢]

177. That Which Completes Faith

١٧٧ ـ ما يَكمُلُ بِهِ الإيمانُ

541. **The Prophet (SAWA) said,** 'Three qualities, when present in an individual, will complete his faith: a man who does not fear the reproach of an admonisher for the sake of Allah, who never shows off in any of his actions, and who when faced with two matters, one for this world and the other for the Hereafter, he chooses the matter of the Hereafter over the world.'[599]

٥٤١ . رسولُ اللهِ ﷺ : ثلاثةٌ مَن كُنَّ فيهِ يَسْتَكمِلُ إيمانُهُ: رجُلٌ لا يَخافُ في اللهِ لَومةَ لائمٍ، ولا يُرائي بشَيءٍ مِن عَمَلِهِ، وإذا عَرَضَ علَيهِ أمْرانِ أحدُهُما للدُّنيا والآخَرُ للآخِرَةِ، اختارَ أمرَ الآخِرَةِ علَى الدُّنيا.[٥٩٣]

542. **The Prophet (SAWA) said,** 'A servant's faith is incomplete until he loves for his brother what he loves for himself, and until he fears Allah both in times of jesting as well as seriousness.'[600]

٥٤٢ . عنه ﷺ : لا يَسْتَكمِلُ عبدٌ الإيمانَ حتّىٰ يُحِبَّ لأخيهِ ما يُحِبُّ لِنَفْسِهِ، وحتّىٰ يَخافَ اللهَ في مِزاحِهِ وجِدِّهِ.[٥٩٤]

543. **The Prophet (SAWA) said,** 'A servant's faith in Allah is not complete until he has five attributes in him: complete reliance upon Allah, entrusting [his affairs] to Allah, submission to Allah's will, contentment with Allah's decree, and patience in Allah's tribulations. Certainly one who loves for the sake of Allah, hates for the sake of Allah, gives for the sake of Allah, and withholds for the sake of Allah has in fact completed faith.'[601]

٥٤٣ . عنه ﷺ : لا يُكْمِلُ عبدٌ الإيمانَ باللهِ حتّىٰ يكونَ فيه خَمْسُ خِصالٍ: التّوكّلُ علَى اللهِ، والتّفْويضُ إلَى اللهِ، والتَّسْليمُ لأمرِ اللهِ، والرِّضا بِقَضاءِ اللهِ، والصّبرُ علىٰ بَلاءِ اللهِ. إنّه مَن أحَبَّ في اللهِ، وأبْغَضَ في اللهِ، وأعطىٰ للهِ، ومَنعَ للهِ، فَقدِ اسْتَكْمَلَ الإيمانَ.[٥٩٥]

544. **Imām ʿAlī (AS) said,** 'The most perfect in faith from among you is the one with the best character.'[602]

٥٤٤ . الإمامُ عليٌّ ؑ : أكْمَلُكُم إيماناً أحْسَنُكُم خُلقاً.[٥٩٦]

545. **Imām ʿAlī (AS) said,** 'Three attributes, when present in an individual, complete his faith: intellect, clemency and knowledge.'[603]

٥٤٥ . عنه ؑ : ثلاثٌ مَن كُنَّ فيهِ كَمُلَ إيمانُهُ: العقلُ، والحِلْمُ، والعِلمُ.[٥٩٧]

546. **Imām ʿAlī (AS) said,** 'A servant's faith is not complete until he loves one whom Allah, the

٥٤٦ . عنه ؑ : لا يَكْمُلُ إيمانُ عبدٍ حتّىٰ يُحِبَّ مَن أحَبَّهُ اللهُ سبحانه، ويُبغضَ مَن

Glorious, loves and hates one whom Allah, the Glorious, hates.'[604]

أبْغَضَهُ اللهُ سبحانَهُ.٥٩٨

547. **Imām al-Ṣādiq (AS) said,** 'A servant cannot attain the reality of faith until there exist in him three attributes: learning the religion, good [i.e. economical] assessment of his living expenses, and patience in sufferings.'[605]

٥٤٧ . الإمامُ الصّادقُ عليه السلام : لا يَسْتَكمِلُ عبدٌ حقيقةَ الإيمانِ حتّىٰ تكونَ فيه خِصالٌ ثلاثٌ: الفِقهُ في الدِّينِ، وحُسْنُ التَّقديرِ في المَعيشةِ، والصَّبرُ علَى الرَّزايا.٥٩٩

178. Increase of Faith

١٧٨ ـ ازدِيادُ الإيمانِ

"And when His signs are recited to them, they increase their faith."[606]

﴿وَإِذا تُلِيَتْ عَلَيْهِمْ آياتُهُ زَادَتْهُمْ إِيمَاناً﴾.٦٠٠

(See also: Qur'an 2:260, 18:13, 18:14, 33:22, 48:4, 58:22)

(أنظر) البقرة: ٢٦٠ و الكهف: ١٣، ١٤ و الأحزاب: ٢٢ و الفتح: ٤ و المجادلة: ٢٢.

548. **Imām ʿAlī (AS) said,** 'Faith appears as a white spot in the heart. So whenever faith increases in magnitude, the whiteness increases. When faith is completed, the entire heart becomes white.'[607]

٥٤٨ . الإمامُ عليٌّ عليه السلام : إنّ الإيمانَ يَبْدو لُمْظَةً بَيْضَاءَ في القلبِ، فكلَّما ازْدادَ الإيمانُ عِظَماً ازْدادَ البَياضُ، فإذا اسْتُكْمِلَ الإيمانُ ابْيَضَّ القلبُ كُلُّهُ.٦٠١

179. The Levels of Faith

١٧٩ ـ دَرَجاتُ الإيمانِ

549. **The Prophet (SAWA) said,** 'The best of faith is to know that Allah is with you wherever you are.'[608]

٥٤٩ . رسولُ اللهِ صلى الله عليه وآله : أفضلُ الإيمانِ أنْ تَعلمَ أنّ اللهَ معكَ حَيثُ ما كُنتَ.٦٠٢

550. **The Prophet (SAWA) said,** 'The best of faith is patience and liberality.'[609]

٥٥٠ . عنه صلى الله عليه وآله : أفضلُ الإيمانِ الصّبرُ والسَّماحَةُ.٦٠٣

551. **The Prophet (SAWA) said,** 'Faith has more than seventy branches, the best of them is the statement: "There is no god but Allah", and the lowest of them is to remove obstacles from the path. And chastity is a branch of faith.'[610]

٥٥١ . عنه صلى الله عليه وآله : الإيمانُ بِضْعٌ وسَبعونَ شُعْبَةً، فأفْضَلُها قَولُ لا إلٰه إلّا اللهُ، وأدْناها إماطَةُ الأذىٰ عَنِ الطَّريقِ، والحَياءُ شُعْبَةٌ مِن الإيمانِ.٦٠٤

552. **Imām ʿAlī (AS) said,** 'The best of faith is excellent conviction.'[611]

٥٥٢ . الإمامُ عليٌّ عليه السلام : أفضلُ الإيمانِ حُسنُ الإيقانِ.٦٠٥

553. **Imām al-Ṣādiq (AS) said,** 'Certainly faith is ten levels, like the rungs of a ladder, where each rung is climbed one after the other. The one on

٥٥٣ . الإمامُ الصّادقُ عليه السلام : إنّ الإيمانَ عَشْرُ دَرَجاتٍ بِمَنزِلَةِ السُلَّمِ، يُصْعَدُ مِنهُ مِرْقاةً بَعدَ

the second rung cannot say to the one on the first: 'You are nothing' until he completes the ten. Therefore do not knock the one below you down, lest the one above you knocks you down. And when you see one below you in rank, lift him up to your level with gentleness. And do not burden him with that which he cannot bear lest you break him, for verily one who breaks a believer must put him back together again.'[612]

مِرْقاةٍ، فلا يَقُولَنَّ صاحبُ الاثنَين لِصاحِبِ الواحدِ: لَستَ علىٰ شَيءٍ، حتّىٰ يَنْتهيَ إلَى العاشِرِ. فلا تُسْقِطْ مَن هُو دُونَكَ فيُسْقِطَكَ مَن هُو فَوقَكَ، وإذا رأيتَ مَن هُو أسْفَلُ مِنكَ بدرجةٍ فارْفَعْهُ إليكَ برِفْقٍ، ولا تَحْمِلَنَّ علَيهِ ما لا يُطيقُ فَتَكْسِرَهُ، فإنّ مَن كَسَرَ مؤمناً فعلَيهِ جَبْرُهُ.٦٠٦

554. **Imām al-Ṣādiq (AS) said,** 'Certainly Allah has divided faith into seven parts: goodness, honesty, conviction, contentedness, loyalty, knowledge and clemency.'[613]

٥٥٤. عنه ﷺ: إنّ اللهَ عزّ وجلّ وَضعَ الإيمانَ علىٰ سَبْعةِ أسْهُمٍ: علىٰ البِرِّ والصِّدقِ واليقينِ والرِّضا والوَفاءِ والعِلمِ والحِلمِ.٦٠٧

180. The Pillars of Faith

١٨٠ ـ أركانُ الإيمانِ

555. **The Prophet (SAWA) said,** 'Faith is in ten things: inner knowledge, obedience, knowledge, action, piety, striving, patience, conviction, contentedness and submission. And if the individual lacks any one of them, it nullifies the whole structure of his faith.'[614]

٥٥٥. رسولُ اللهِ ﷺ: الإيمانُ في عَشرَةٍ: المعرفةُ، والطّاعةُ، والعِلمُ، والعَملُ، والوَرَعُ، والاجتِهادُ، والصَّبرُ، واليقينُ، والرِّضا، والتَّسليمُ، فأيَّها فقدَ صاحِبُهُ بَطَلَ نِظامُهُ.٦٠٨

556. **Imām ʿAlī (AS) said,** 'Faith rests on four pillars: reliance upon Allah, entrusting one's affairs to Allah, submission to the will of Allah, and contentment with Allah's decree.'[615]

٥٥٦. الإمامُ عليٌّ ﷺ: الإيمانُ علىٰ أربَعةِ أرْكانٍ: التَّوكُّلُ علَى اللهِ، والتَّفْويضُ إلَى اللهِ، والتَّسْليمُ لأمرِ اللهِ، والرِّضا بِقَضاءِ اللهِ.٦٠٩

557. **Imām ʿAlī (AS) said,** 'Excellent chastity, and satisfaction with the bare necessities are among the pillars of faith.'[616]

٥٥٧. عنه ﷺ: حُسْنُ العَفافِ والرِّضا بالكَفافِ مِن دعائمِ الإيمانِ.٦١٠

(See also: ISLAM: section 969)

(اُنظر) الاسلام: باب ٩٦٩.

181. The Strongest Bonds of Faith

١٨١ ـ أوثَقُ عُرَى الإيمانِ

558. **The Prophet (SAWA) said,** 'The strongest bonds of faith are: accepting Allah's guardianship, to love for the sake of Allah and to hate for the sake of Allah.'[617]

٥٥٨. رسولُ اللهِ ﷺ: أوْثَقُ عُرَى الإيمانِ: الوَلايةُ في اللهِ، والحُبُّ في اللهِ، والبُغْضُ في اللهِ.٦١١

559. **The Prophet (SAWA) said,** 'The strongest of bonds is the stance of Godwariness [saying '*lā ilāha illah Allah*'].'[618]

٥٥٩ . عنه ﷺ : أوثَقُ العُرىٰ كَلِمَةُ التَّقوىٰ.٦١٢

182. Steadfast and Temporary Faith

١٨٢ ـ الإيمانُ المُستَقَرُّ وَ المُستَودَعُ

560. **Imām ʿAlī (AS) said,** 'A part of faith is that which is firm and steadfast in the hearts, and another part is that which remains temporarily in the hearts and the breasts up until a certain time.'[619]

٥٦٠ . الإمامُ عليٌّ ﷺ : فمِنَ الإيمانِ ما يكونُ ثابتاً مُستَقِرّاً في القلوبِ ، ومنهُ ما يكونُ عَوارِيَ بَينَ القلوبِ والصُّدورِ ، إلىٰ أجلٍ معلومٍ.٦١٣

183. That Which Consolidates Faith

١٨٣ ـ ما يُثَبِّتُ الإيمانَ

561. **Imām al-Ṣādiq (AS),** when asked what consolidates a servant's faith, replied, 'The thing that consolidates it in him is piety, and that which takes him out of it [i.e. faith] is greed.'[620]

٥٦١ . الإمامُ الصّادقُ ﷺ ـ وقد سُئلَ عمّا يُثَبِّتُ الإيمانَ في العبدِ ـ : الّذي يُثَبِّتُهُ فيهِ الوَرَعُ ، والّذي يُخرِجُهُ مِنهُ الطَّمَعُ.٦١٤

562. **Imām al-Ṣādiq (AS) said,** 'Faith is only consolidated in him through action, and action is a part of it.'[621]

٥٦٢ . عنه ﷺ : لا يَثْبُتُ لَه ٦١٥ الإيمانُ إلّا بالعَمَلِ ، والعَمَلُ مِنهُ.٦١٦

184. The Taste of Faith

١٨٤ ـ طَعمِ الإيمانِ

563. **The Prophet (SAWA) said,** 'Three qualities which, when present in a person, enable him to savour the taste of faith: that nothing is more beloved to him than Allah and His Messenger, that to be burned in the Fire is more beloved to him than to denounce his religion, and that he loves for the sake of Allah and hates for the sake of Allah.'[622]

٥٦٣ . رسولُ اللهِ ﷺ : ثلاثٌ مَن كُنَّ فيه ذاقَ طَعْمَ الإيمانِ : مَن كانَ لا شيءَ أحبُّ إليهِ مِنَ اللهِ ورسولِهِ ، ومن كان لأَنْ يُحرقَ بالنّارِ أحبَّ إليه مِن أنْ يَرْتَدَّ عن دِينِهِ ، ومَن كانَ يُحبُّ للهِ ويُبغضُ للهِ.٦١٧

564. **Imām ʿAlī (AS) said,** 'A servant will never savour the taste of faith until he abandons lying, both in jest and earnestness.'[623]

٥٦٤ . الإمامُ عليٌّ ﷺ : لا يجدُ عبدٌ طعمَ الإيمانِ حتّىٰ يترُكَ الكذبَ هَزْلَهُ وجِدَّهُ.٦١٨

565. **Imām ʿAlī (AS) said,** 'A servant will never savour the taste of faith until he knows that that which afflicts him would never have missed him, and that that which has missed him would never have

٥٦٥ . عنه ﷺ : لا يَجدُ عَبدٌ طعمَ الإيمانِ حتّى يَعلمَ أنَّ ما أصابَهُ لم يكُن لِيُخطِئَهُ ، وأنَّ ما أخطأهُ لم يكُن لِيُصيبَهُ ، وأنَّ الضّارَّ

touched him, and that the only One to induce harm and benefit is Allah, Mighty and Exalted.'[624]

النّافِعَ هوَ اللّهُ عزّ وجلّ.[٦١٩]

566. **Imām ʿAlī (AS) said,** 'Man will never taste the reality of faith until he possesses three qualities: understanding of religion, perseverance in calamities, and a good assessment of his income.'[625]

٥٦٦. عنه ؑ: لا يذوقُ المَرءُ من حَقيقةِ الإيمانِ حتّىٰ يكونَ فيهِ ثلاثُ خصالٍ: الفقهُ في الدِّينِ، والصّبرُ على المَصائبِ، وحُسْنُ التّقديرِ في المَعاشِ.[٦٢٠]

185. Inability to Taste the Sweetness of Faith

١٨٥ ـ عَدَمُ تَذَوُّقِ حَلاوَةِ الإيمانِ

567. **The Prophet (SAWA) said,** 'He whose greatest concern is fulfilling his own desires has the sweetness of faith wrested from his heart.'[626]

٥٦٧. رسولُ اللّهِ ﷺ: مَن كان أكثرُ هـمّهِ نيلَ الشّهَواتِ نُزِعَ مِن قلبهِ حلاوةُ الإيمانِ.[٦٢١]

568. **Imām al-Ṣādiq (AS) said,** 'It is prohibited for your hearts to experience the sweetness of faith until they abstain from this world [i.e. its pleasures].'[627]

٥٦٨. الإمامُ الصّادقُ ؑ: حرامٌ على قلوبِكُم أنْ تعرِفَ حَلاوةَ الإيمانِ حتّىٰ تَزهَدَ في الدّنيا.[٦٢٢]

186. That Which Removes One from Faith

١٨٦ ـ ما يُخرِجُ الإنسانَ مِنَ الإيمانِ

569. **The Prophet (SAWA) said,** 'The most basic level of infidelity is for a man to hear a fellow brother say something and memorize it for future to use against him in order to shame him with it. Those are worthless people indeed.'[628]

٥٦٩. رسولُ اللّهِ ﷺ: أدنَى الكفرِ أنْ يَسمعَ الرّجُلُ مِن أخيهِ الكَلِمَةَ فيَحْفَظَها علَيهِ يُريدُ أنْ يَفْضَحَهُ بها، أُولئكَ لا خَلاقَ لَهُم.[٦٢٣]

570. **Imām al-Ṣādiq (AS) said,** 'The servant can come out of faith through five means, all resembling each other: infidelity, polytheism [i.e. associating anything with Allah], straying from the truth, immorality, and embarking on committing grave sins.'[629]

٥٧٠. الإمامُ الصّادقُ ؑ: قَد يَخْرُجُ [العبدُ] مِن الإيمانِ بخَمْسِ جِهاتٍ مِن الفعلِ كُلُّها مُتَشابِهاتٌ مَعروفاتٌ: الكفرُ، والشِّركُ، والضّلالُ، والفِسقُ، ورُكوبُ الكبائرِ.[٦٢٤]

(See also: POLYTHEISM: section 1023; DISBELIEF: section 1605)

(أنظر) الشرک: باب ١٠٢٣؛ الكفر: باب ١٦٠٥.

187. That Which Repels Faith

١٨٧ ـ ما يُجانِبُ الإيمانَ

571. **The Prophet (SAWA) said,** 'Two traits can never be found in a believer: miserliness and pessimism about one's sustenance.'[630]

٥٧١ . رسولُ اللهِ ﷺ : خَصْلتانِ لا تَجتَمِعانِ في مؤمنٍ : البُخلُ ، وسُوءُ الظَّنِّ بالرِّزقِ.[٦٣٠]

572. **The Prophet (SAWA) said,** 'Two traits can never be found in a believer: avarice and ill-naturedness.'[631]

٥٧٢ . عنه ﷺ : خُلُقانِ لا يَجتَمِعانِ في مؤمنٍ : الشُّحُّ ، وسُوءُ الخُلقِ.[٦٣١]

573. **The Prophet (SAWA) said,** 'The believer can be predisposed to any trait, but he cannot be predisposed to lying or treachery.'[632]

٥٧٣ . عنه ﷺ : يُطبَعُ المؤمنُ على كلِّ خَصلةٍ ولا يُطبَعُ على الكذبِ ولا على الخِيانةِ.[٦٣٢]

574. **Imām al-Ṣādiq (AS) said,** 'Six things cannot be found in a believer: [a feeling of] hardship, anxiety, jealousy, disputatiousness, dishonesty, and aggression.'[633]

٥٧٤ . الإمامُ الصّادقُ ؑ : ستّةٌ لا تكونُ في مؤمنٍ : العُسرُ ، والنَّكَدُ ، والحَسَدُ ، واللَّجاجةُ ، والكِذْبُ ، والبَغْيُ.[٦٣٣]

(See also: LYING: section 1583; TRUSTWORTHINESS: section 199)

(اُنظر) الكذب: باب ١٥٨٣؛ الأمانة: باب ١٩٩.

188. The Great Status of the Believer

١٨٨ ـ عَظَمَةُ المُؤمِنِ

575. **The Prophet (SAWA) said,** 'Verily Allah, exalted be His praise, says: 'By My Might and Exaltedness, I have not created any creature more beloved to Me than My believing servant.'[634]

٥٧٥ . رسولُ اللهِ ﷺ : إنَّ اللهَ جلّ ثَناؤهُ يقولُ: وعِزَّتي وجَلالي ، ما خَلَقتُ مِن خَلْقي خَلْقاً أحَبَّ إلَيَّ مِن عَبديَ المؤمنِ.[٦٣٤]

576. **The Prophet (SAWA) said,** 'The believer is dearer to Allah than His closest angels.'[635]

٥٧٦ . عنه ﷺ : المؤمنُ أكرَمُ على اللهِ مِن ملائكتِهِ المُقَرَّبينَ.[٦٣٥]

577. **Imām al-Ṣādiq (AS) said,** 'The believer is more sanctified than the Kaʿba.'[636]

٥٧٧ . الإمامُ الصّادقُ ؑ : المؤمنُ أعظمُ حُرمَةً مِن الكعبةِ.[٦٣٦]

189. The Believers are as One Body

١٨٩ ـ المُؤمِنونَ كَالجَسَدِ الواحِدِ

578. **The Prophet (SAWA) said,** 'The similitude of the believers in their mutual love, affection and compassion for one another is as one body – if a single limb ails then the rest of the body suffers in insomnia and fever.'[637]

٥٧٨ . رسولُ اللهِ ﷺ : مَثَلُ المُؤمنينَ في توادِّهِمْ وتَعاطُفِهِمْ وتَراحُمِهِمْ مَثَلُ الجَسدِ ؛ إذا اشتكى مِنهُ عُضوٌ تَداعى سائرُ الجَسَدِ بالسَّهَرِ والحُمّى.[٦٣٧]

579. **The Prophet (SAWA) said,** 'The believers' blood is coequal, and they are one hand against others, the most inferior among them is empowered by their protection [of him].'[638]

٥٧٩ . عنه ﷺ : المؤمنونَ تَتَكافَأُ دِماؤهُم ، وهُم يَدٌ علىٰ مَن سِواهُم ، ويَسعىٰ بذِمَّتِهم أدْناهُم .[٦٣٣]

190. Who is the Believer?

١٩٠ ـ مَن هو المُؤمِنُ؟

"The faithful are only those whose hearts tremble [with awe] when Allah is mentioned, and when His signs are recited to them, they increase their faith, and who put their trust in their Lord, maintain the prayer and spend out of what We have provided them. It is they who are truly the faithful. They shall have ranks near their Lord, forgiveness and a noble provision."[639]

﴿إنَّمَا الْـمُؤْمِنُونَ الَّـذِينَ إذَا ذُكِـرَ اللهُ وَجِـلَتْ قُلوبُهُمْ وَإذَا تُلِيَتْ عَلَيْهِمْ آياتُهُ زَادَتْـهُمْ إيـمَاناً وَعَلَى رَبِّهِمْ يَتَوَكَّلُونَ * الَّذِينَ يُقِيمُونَ الصَّلاةَ وَمِمَّا رَزَقْناهُمْ يُنْفِقُونَ * أُولٰئِكَ هُمُ الْـمُؤْمِنُونَ حَقّاً لَـهُمْ دَرَجـاتٌ عِـنْدَ رَبِّـهِمْ وَمَـغْفِرَةٌ وَرِزْقٌ كَرِيمٌ﴾ .[٦٣٤]

(See also: Qur'an 9:71, 12:106, 23:1-11, 28:52-55, 32:15-19, 42:36-39, 48:29, 98:5, 98:7-8)

(أنظر) التوبة : ٧١ و يوسف : ١٠٦ و المؤمنون : ١ ـ ١١ و القصص : ٥٢ ـ ٥٥ و السجدة : ١٥ ـ ١٩ و الشورى : ٣٦ ـ ٣٩ و الفتح : ٢٩ و البيّنة : ٥ . ٧ ـ ٨ .

580. **The Prophet (SAWA) said,** 'The believer is nice and simple, such that he could be mistaken to be stupid because of his simplicity.'[640]

٥٨٠ . رسولُ اللهِ ﷺ : المؤمنُ هَيِّنٌ لَيِّنٌ ، حتّىٰ تَخالَهُ مِن اللِّينِ أحمقَ .[٦٣٥]

581. **The Prophet (SAWA) said,** 'The believer is he whom people trust with their blood and their property.'[641]

٥٨١ . عنه ﷺ : المؤمنُ مَن آمَنَهُ النّاسُ علىٰ دِمائهِم وأموالِهِم .[٦٣٦]

582. **The Prophet (SAWA) said,** 'The believer is he whose soul is inconvenienced because of him but people are at ease.'[642]

٥٨٢ . عنه ﷺ : المؤمنُ الّذي نفسُهُ مِنهُ في عَناءٍ ، والنّاسُ في راحةٍ .[٦٣٧]

583. **The Prophet (SAWA) said,** 'The believer initiates the greeting of peace (*salām*) whereas the hypocrite says, 'Not until it is said to me first!'[643]

٥٨٣ . عنه ﷺ : المؤمن يَبدأ بالسَّلامِ ، والمنافقُ يقولُ : حتّىٰ يُبْدأَ بي ![٦٣٨]

584. **The Prophet (SAWA) said,** 'The believer likes others and is well-liked by them, and there is no good to be found in one who does not get along with others and whom people do not get along with. The best of people is the most useful from among them.'[644]

٥٨٤ . عنه ﷺ : المؤمنُ يألَفُ ويُؤلَفُ ، ولا خيرَ فيمَن لا يألَفُ ولا يُؤلَفُ ، وخيرُ النّاسِ أنفَعهُمْ للنّاسِ .[٦٣٩]

585. **The Prophet (SAWA) said,** 'He whose good deed pleases him and whose sin upsets him is indeed a believer.'[645]

٥٨٥ . عنه ﷺ : مَن سَرَّتْهُ حَسَنتُهُ وساءَتْهُ سَيِّئتُهُ فهُو مؤمنٌ.[٦٤٠]

586. **The Prophet (SAWA) said,** describing the believer, '[He is] subtle in his movements, sweet to look at… he seeks out the loftiest of matters, and has the most outstanding moral ethics… he is not prejudiced against he whom he does not like, nor biased in favour of one he loves… he is hardly a burden, and instead is very helpful… he perfects his actions as if he is being watched, lowers his gaze, is liberal in his giving, and never turns away a beggar… he considers his words carefully and guards his tongue… he neither accepts falsehood from a friend, nor rejects the truth from an enemy… he only learns in order that he might know, and he only seeks to know in order that he may act… When he travels with worldly people, he is the smartest of them, and when he travels with the people of the Hereafter, he is the most pious from among them.'[646]

٥٨٦ . عنه ﷺ ـ يَصِفُ المؤمنَ ـ: لطيفُ الحَرَكاتِ، حُلْوُ المُشاهَدةِ ... يَطلُبُ مِن الأُمورِ أعلاها، ومِن الأخلاقِ أسْناها ... لا يَحيفُ على مَن يُبغِضُ، ولا يأثَمُ فيمَن يُحِبُّ ... قليلُ المؤونةِ، كثير المَعونةِ ... يُحسِنُ في عملِهِ كأنَّهُ ناظِرٌ إلَيهِ، غَضُّ الطَّرْفِ، سَخِيُّ الكَفِّ، لا يَرُدُّ سائلاً ... يَزِنُ كلامَهُ، ويُخْرِسُ لسانَهُ ... لا يَقبَلُ الباطلَ مِن صديقِهِ، ولا يَرُدُّ الحقَّ على عدوِّهِ، ولا يَتعلّمُ إلّا لِيَعْلمَ، ولا يَعلمُ إلّا لِيَعْملَ ... إن سلَكَ مَع أهلِ الدُّنيا كانَ أكيَسَهُم، وإنْ سَلكَ مَع أهلِ الآخرةِ كانَ أورَعَهُم.[٦٤١]

587. **Imām ʿAlī (AS) said,** 'The believer is such that his joy is evident on his face whereas his sorrow is in his heart. His breast is at its widest [i.e. biggest heart] but his ego is at its lowest. He despises high rank and shuns reputation. His grief is long-lasting and his ambition is lofty. His silence is much and his time occupied. He is grateful, extremely patient, and immersed in deep thought. He is thrifty with his needs. He is good-natured and mild-tempered. His soul is firmer than steel whilst he [i.e. his ego] remains lower than a slave.'[647]

٥٨٧ . الإمامُ عليٌّ ؑ : المؤمنُ بِشْرُهُ في وجهِهِ، وحُزنُهُ في قلبِهِ، أوسَعُ شَيءٍ صَدْراً، وأذَلُّ شَيءٍ نَفْساً، يَكْرَهُ الرِّفعةَ، ويَشْنَأُ السُّمْعةَ، طويلٌ غمُّهُ، بَعيدٌ هَمُّهُ، كثيرٌ صَمتُهُ، مَشغولٌ وقتُهُ، شَكورٌ، صَبورٌ، مَغمورٌ بفِكرَتِهِ، ضَنينٌ بخَلّتِهِ، سَهلُ الخَليقةِ، لَيِّنُ العَرِيكةِ، نَفسُهُ أصْلَبُ مِن الصَّلْدِ، وهُو أذَلُّ مِن العبدِ.[٦٤٢]

588. **Imām ʿAlī (AS) said,** 'The believer is grateful in times of prosperity, patient during tribulation, and fearful in times of ease.'[648]

٥٨٨ . عنه ؑ : المؤمنُ شاكرٌ في السَّرّاءِ، صابرٌ في البلاءِ، خائفٌ في الرَّخاءِ.[٦٤٣]

589. **Imām ʿAlī (AS) said,** 'The believer is gullible and kind, secure from his own [lower] self, yet wary and distressed [on account of it].'[649]

٥٨٩ . عنه ؑ : المؤمنُ غِرٌّ كريمٌ، مأمونٌ على نفسِهِ، حَذِرٌ مَحزونٌ.[٦٤٤]

590. **Imām ʿAlī (AS) said,** 'The believer is he who has purified his heart of all that is base.'[650]

٥٩٠ . عنه (ع): المؤمن مَن طَهّرَ قلبَهُ مِن الدَّنِيَّة.٦٤٥

591. **Imām ʿAlī (AS) said,** 'The believer is he who protects his religion by putting his world at stake, whereas the impudent one is he who protects his worldly affairs by putting his religion at stake.'[651]

٥٩١ . عنه (ع): المؤمنُ مَن وَقىٰ دِينَهُ بِـدُنياه، والفاجرُ مَن وقىٰ دُنياهُ بِدِينِه.٦٤٦

592. **Imām Zayn al-ʿĀbidīn (AS) said,** 'The believer is silent in order that he remains safe, and speaks [only] in order to benefit.'[652]

٥٩٢ . الإمامُ زينُ العابدينَ (ع): المؤمنُ يَصمُتُ لِيَسْلَمَ، ويَنْطِقُ لِيَغْنَمَ.٦٤٧

593. **Imām al-Ṣādiq (AS) said,** 'The believer is a great helper, and a very light burden. He is good at economising for his livelihood, and is never stung twice from one hole [i.e. never makes the same mistake again].'[653]

٥٩٣ . الإمامُ الصّادقُ (ع): المؤمنُ حَسَنُ المَعونةِ، خفيفُ المَؤونةِ، جَيِّدُ التَّدبيرِ لِمَعيشتِهِ، لا يُلْسَعُ مِن جُحْرٍ مرّتين.٦٤٨

594. **Imām al-Ṣādiq (AS) said,** 'The believer possesses strength in his religion, prudence in his leniency, faith in conviction, an avid desire for religious understanding, activity in [matters pertaining to] guidance… and prayer during times of preoccupation.'[654]

٥٩٤ . عنه (ع): المؤمنُ لَه قوّةٌ في دِينٍ، وحَزْمٌ في لِينٍ، وإيمانٌ في يَقينٍ، وحِرْصٌ في فِقهٍ، ونَشاطٌ في هُدىً... وصَلاةٌ في شُغلٍ.٦٤٩

595. **Imām al-Ṣādiq (AS) said,** 'The believer is he whose earnings are pure, whose character is beautiful, whose conscience is clean, who gives away whatever is surplus from his wealth, and guards whatever is surplus from his speech.'[655]

٥٩٥ . عنه (ع): المؤمنُ مَن طابَ مَكسَبُهُ، وحَسُنَتْ خَليقَتُه، وصَحَّتْ سَريرَتُهُ، وأنفَقَ الفَضلَ مِن مالِهِ، وأمسَكَ الفَضلَ مِن كلامِهِ.٦٥٠

596. **Imām al-Riḍā (AS) said,** 'The believer is not a believer until he possesses three qualities: a practice [characteristic] of his Lord, a practice of his Prophet (SAWA), and a practice of his guardian (AS). As for the practice of his Lord, it is to conceal secrets; the practice of his Prophet (SAWA) is amicableness towards people; and the practice of his guardian (AS) is patience in both times of ease and difficulty.'[656]

٥٩٦ . الإمامُ الرِّضا (ع): لا يكونُ المؤمنُ مؤمناً حتّىٰ تكونَ فيه ثلاثُ خِصالٍ: سُنّةٌ مِن ربِّهِ، وسُنّةٌ مِن نبيِّهِ ﷺ، وسنّةٌ مِن وليِّهِ (ع)؛ فأمّا السُّنّةُ مِن ربّهِ فكِتْمانُ السِّرِّ، وأمّا السُّنّةُ مِن نبيِّه ﷺ فمُداراةُ النّاسِ، وأمّا السُّنّةُ مِن وليِّهِ (ع) فالصَّبرُ في البَأساءِ والضَّرّاءِ.٦٥١

(See also: ISLAM: section 968) (انظر: الإسلام: باب ٩٦٨)

191. The Firmness of the Believer

١٩١ ـ صَلابَةُ المُؤمِنِ

597. **Imām al-Bāqir (AS) said,** 'The believer is harder than a mountain, for the mountain is dispensable whereas nothing can be taken away from his religion.'[657]

٥٩٧ . الإمامُ الباقرُ ﷺ :المؤمنُ أصْلَبُ مِنَ الجَبلِ، الجَبلُ يُسْتَقَلُّ مِنه، والمؤمنُ لا يُسْتَقَلُّ مِن دِينِهِ شَيءٌ. ٦٥٢

598. **Imām al-Ṣādiq (AS) said,** 'Verily the believer is stronger than pieces of iron, for when a piece of iron enters the fire it changes, whereas the believer, were he to be killed then resurrected and then killed again, his heart would never change.'[658]

٥٩٨ . الإمامُ الصّادقُ ﷺ :إنّ المؤمنَ أشدُّ مِن زُبَرِ الحديدِ، إنّ زُبرَ الحديدِ إذا دَخلَ النّار تغيّرَ، وإنّ المؤمنَ لو قُتِلَ ثُمّ نُشِرَ ثُمّ قُتِلَ لم يَتغيّرْ قلبُهُ. ٦٥٣

192. The Light of the Believer

١٩٢ ـ نورُ المُؤمِنِ

599. **The Prophet (SAWA) said,** 'Hell will say to the believer on Judgment Day: 'Pass through O Believer, because your light has extinguished my flames.'[659]

٥٩٩ . رسولُ اللهِ ﷺ : تَقولُ جَهَنَّمُ لِلمُؤمِنِ يَومَ القِيامَةِ : جُز يا مُؤمِنُ فَقَد أطفَأَ نورُكَ لَهَبي ٦٥٤.

600. **Imām al-Ṣādiq (AS) said,** 'The light of a believer illuminates for the dwellers of the heavens the way the stars of the heavens illuminate for the dwellers of the earth.'[660]

٦٠٠ . الإمامُ الصّادقُ ﷺ : إنَّ المُؤمِنَ لَيَزهَرُ نورُهُ لِأَهلِ السَّماءِ كَما تَزهَرُ نُجومُ السَّماءِ لِأَهلِ الأَرضِ ٦٥٥.

(See also: FEAR: section 663)

(أُنظر) الخوف: باب ٦٦٣.

193. The Scarcity of the [True] Believer

١٩٣ ـ نُدرَةُ المُؤمِنِ

601. **Imām ʿAlī (AS) said,** 'He has not kept His earth free of a knowledgeable man whom all of creation need, who is well-versed with the means of salvation. Such [people] are very few in number, and Allah has expounded this among the communities of the prophets, and made them the example for those to come after them, when He said concerning the people of Noah: *"And none believed with him except a few."*'[661] [662]

٦٠١ . الإمامُ عليٌّ ﷺ : ولَم يُخْلِ أرضَهُ مِن عالمٍ بما يَحتاجُ إليه الخَليقةُ، ومُتَعلِّمٍ على سبيلِ النَّجاةِ، أُولئكَ هُمُ الأقلُّونَ عَدَداً، وقد بَيّنَ اللهُ ذلكَ في أُمَمِ الأنبياءِ، وجَعلَهُم مثَلاً لِمَن تأخّرَ، مثلُ قولِهِ في قومِ نوحٍ: ﴿وما آمَنَ مَعَهُ إلّا قَلِيلٌ﴾. ٦٥٦

602. **Imām al-Ṣādiq (AS) said,** 'The believing woman is scarcer than the believing man, and the believing man is scarcer than red sulphur, and who from among you has ever seen red sulphur [elixir]?!'[663]

٦٠٢. الإمامُ الصّادقُ ﷺ : المؤمنةُ أعَزُّ مِن المؤمنِ، والمؤمنُ أعَزُّ مِن الكبريتِ الأحمرِ، فمَن رأى منكُم الكبريتَ الأحمرَ؟![٦٥٧]

194. The Signs of the Believer

١٩٤ـ عَلاماتُ المُؤمِنِ

603. **Imām Zayn al-ʿĀbidīn (AS) said,** 'The signs of a believer are five: piety [even] when in seclusion, giving charity in spite of lack, patience in the face of calamity, clemency when angered, and truthfulness in spite of fear.'[664]

٦٠٣. الإمامُ زينُ العابدينَ ﷺ : علاماتُ المؤمنِ خمسٌ: الوَرَعُ في الخَلوةِ، والصَّدقةُ في القِلّةِ، والصَّبرُ عند المصيبةِ، والحِلمُ عند الغضبِ، والصِّدقُ عند الخوفِ.[٦٥٨]

604. **Imām al-Ṣādiq (AS),** when he was asked, 'How does a believer know that he is indeed a believer?', replied, 'Through submission to Allah and satisfaction with whatever joy or [source of] annoyance comes his way.'[665]

٦٠٤. الإمامُ الصّادقُ ﷺ ـ وقد سُئلَ: بأيِّ شيءٍ يَعلَمُ المؤمنُ بأنّهُ مؤمنٌ؟ ـ: بالتَّسليمِ للهِ، والرِّضا فيما وَرَدَ علَيهِ مِن سُرورٍ أو سُخطٍ.[٦٥٩]

(See also: THE SHĪʿA: section 1083)

(أنظر) الشيعة: باب ١٠٨٣.

195. The Best of Believers

١٩٥ـ أفضَلُ المُؤمنينَ

605. **Imām ʿAlī (AS) said,** 'The best of believers is the one who is best at dedicating himself, his family and his wealth [for Allah].'[666]

٦٠٥. الإمامُ عليٌّ ﷺ : أفضلُ المؤمنينَ أفضلُهُم تَقْدِمَةً مِن نفسِهِ وأهلِهِ ومالِهِ.[٦٦٠]

606. **Imām ʿAlī (AS) said,** 'The best of believers in terms of faith is he whose giving and withholding, and whose displeasure and pleasure are solely for Allah.'[667]

٦٠٦. عنه ﷺ : أفضلُ المؤمنينَ إيماناً مَن كانَ للهِ أخْذُهُ وعَطاهُ وسَخطُهُ ورِضاهُ.[٦٦١]

(See also: MERIT: section 1485; GODWARINESS: section 1871)

(أنظر) الفضل: باب ١٤٨٥؛ التقوى: باب ١٨٧١

196. The Merit of One Who Believes in the Prophet without Having Seen him

١٩٦ـ فَضلُ مَن يُؤمِنُ بِالرَّسولِ ولَم يَرَهُ

607. **The Prophet (SAWA) said,** 'The faith of one who has seen me is no great wonder, but what

٦٠٧. رسولُ اللهِ ﷺ : ليسَ أيمانُ مَن رآني بعجبٍ

is truly amazing is for the people who have only seen pages with black [ink] on it [i.e. the Qur'an] and have believed in it from beginning to end.'[668]

ولكنّ العَجبَ كلّ العَجبِ لِقومٍ أوا أوْراقاً فـيها سَوادٌ فآمَنوا بهِ أوّلِهِ وآخِرِه.٦٦٢

608. **The Prophet (SAWA) said,** exclaiming, 'When will I see my brothers?!' to which they replied, 'Are we not your brothers?' He said, 'No, you are my companions. My brothers are those who believe in me without having seen me, and I am filled with longing for them.'[669]

٦٠٨. كنز العمّال عنه ﷺ: متىٰ ألْقىٰ إخْواني ؟! قالوا: ألَسْنا إخْوانَكَ ؟ قالَ: بلْ أنـتُم أصْحابي، وإخْواني الّذينَ آمَنوا بِي ولَم يَروني، أنا إلَـيهِم بالأشْواقِ.٦٦٣

31

TRUSTWORTHINESS

الأمانَةُ

197. The Necessity of Observing the Trust

١٩٧ـ وُجوبُ رِعايَةِ الأمانَةِ

"...and those who keep their trusts and covenants"[670]

﴿وَالَّذِينَ هُمْ لِأَمانَاتِهِمْ وَعَهْدِهِمْ رَاعُونَ﴾.٦٦٤

609. **Imām 'Alī (AS) said,** 'The best form of faith is trustworthiness, and the worst vice is betrayal.'[671]

٦٠٩. الإمامُ عليٌّ ﷺ: أفضلُ الإيمانِ الأمانَةُ، أقْبَحُ الأخلاقِ الخِيانَةُ.٦٦٥

610. **Imām al-Bāqir (AS) said,** 'There are three things regarding which Allah, the Exalted, did not allow any flexibility: returning a trust to its owner, be he good or wicked; keeping one's pact with both the good and the wicked; and kindness to one's parents whether they be good or wicked.'[672]

٦١٠. الإمامُ الباقرُ ﷺ: ثلاثٌ لم يَجعلِ اللهُ عزّ وجلّ لأحدٍ فيهنّ رُخصةً: أداءُ الأمانةِ إلى البَـرِّ والفاجرِ، والوفاءُ بـالعَهدِ للـبَرِّ والفـاجرِ، وبِـرُّ الوالِدَينِ برَّينِ كانا أو فاجِرَينِ.٦٦٦

198. Universality of Trustworthiness

١٩٨ـ إطلاقُ وُجوبِ أدائها

611. **Imām 'Alī (AS) said,** 'Do not betray a man who trusts you, even if he betrays you. And do not disclose his secrets even if he discloses yours.'[673]

٦١١. الإمامُ عليٌّ ﷺ: لا تَخُنْ مَنِ ائْتَمَنكَ وإنْ خانَكَ، ولا تُذِعْ سِرَّهُ وإنْ أذاعَ سِرَّكَ.٦٦٧

612. **Imām al-Ṣādiq (AS) said,** 'Fear Allah and return the trust to he who has entrusted it to you, for verily even if the killer of the Commander of the Faithful (AS) left a trust with me, I would return it to him.'[674]

٦١٢ . الإمامُ الصّادقُ ؑ :اتَّقوا اللهَ ،وعلَيكُم بأداءِ الأمانةِ إلىٰ مَنِ ائْـتَمَنكُم ، فـلَو أنّ قـاتِلَ أمـيرِ المؤمنينَ ؑ ائْتَمَنني علىٰ أمانةٍ لَأدَّيْتُها إلَيهِ[٦٦٨].

613. **Imām al-Ṣādiq (AS) said,** 'Return the trust, even to the killer of al-Ḥusayn b. ʿAlī.'[675]

٦١٣ . عنه ؑ :أدُّوا الأمانةَ ولو إلىٰ قاتِلِ الحسينِ بنِ عليٍّ ؑ[٦٦٩].

199. An Untrustworthy Man is a Man Without Faith

١٩٩ ـ لا أيمانَ لِمَن لا أمانَةَ لَهُ

614. **The Prophet (SAWA) said,** 'An untrustworthy man is a man without faith.'[676]

٦١٤ . رسولُ اللهِ ﷺ: لا إيمانَ لِمَن لا أمانةَ لَهُ[٦٧٠].

615. **The Prophet (SAWA) said,** 'He who belittles [the importance of returning] the trust such that he would spoil it when entrusted to him is not one of us.'[677]

٦١٥ . عنه ﷺ : لَيس مِنّا مَن يُحَقِّرُ الأمانةَ حتّىٰ يَسْتَهلِكَها إذا اسْتُودِعَها[٦٧١].

(See also: BETRAYAL 136)

(أنظر) عنوان ١٣٦ «الخيانة».

200. The Effects of Trustworthiness

٢٠٠ ـ آثارُ الأمانَةِ

616. **Luqmān (AS) said,** 'O my son! Return the trust in order to save your life in this world and in the hereafter; and be trustworthy in order to be prosperous.'[678]

٦١٦ . لُقمانُ ؑ : يا بُنيَّ ، أدِّ الأمانةَ تَسلَمْ لكَ دُنياكَ وآخِرتُكَ ، وكُنْ أميناً تَكُنْ غَنيّاً[٦٧٢].

617. **The Prophet (SAWA) said,** 'Trustworthiness begets prosperity and betrayal begets poverty.'[679]

٦١٧ . رسولُ اللهِ ﷺ : الأمانةُ تَجْلِبُ الغَناءَ ، والخِيانةُ تَجْلِبُ الفَقرَ[٦٧٣].

618. **Imām ʿAlī (AS) said,** 'When trustworthiness is fortified, truthfulness increases.'[680]

٦١٨ . الإمامُ عليٌّ ؑ : إذا قَوِيَتِ الأمانةُ كَثُرَ الصِّدقُ[٦٧٤].

619. **Imām al-Ṣādiq (AS) said,** 'Trustworthiness is prosperity.'[681]

٦١٩ . الإمامُ الصّادقُ ؑ : الأمانةُ غِنىً[٦٧٥].

201. People Who Must not be Trusted

٢٠١ ـ مَن نُهِيَ عَنِ ائتِمانِهِم

620. **The Prophet (SAWA) said,** 'A man who trusts an untrustworthy person forfeits Allah's

٦٢٠ . رسولُ اللهِ ﷺ : مَنِ ائْتَمَنَ غيرَ أمينٍ فليسَ

warranty, because He had prohibited him from trusting such a man [in the first place].'[682]

لَهُ على اللهِ ضَمانٌ ، لأنّهُ قد نَهاهُ أنْ يأتَمِنَهُ.٦٧٦

621. **Imām al-Bāqir (AS) said,** 'You were not betrayed by a trustworthy man, rather you trusted a traitor.'[683]

٦٢١ . الإمامُ الباقرُ ﷺ : لَم يَخُنْكَ الأمينُ ، ولكنِ ائتَمَنتَ الخائنَ.٦٧٧

622. **Imām al-Ṣādiq (AS) said,** 'It makes no difference to me to trust a traitor or a careless man.'[684]

٦٢٢ . الإمامُ الصّادقُ ﷺ : ما أُبالي ائتَمَنتُ خائناً أو مُضَيّعاً.٦٧٨

32

ASSURANCE

الأمانُ

202. The Necessity of Observing Assurance

٢٠٢ ـ وُجوبُ رِعايَةِ الأمانِ

623. **The Prophet (SAWA) said,** 'If a man trusts you with his blood [i.e. that you will spare his life] then do not kill him.'[685]

٦٢٣ . رسولُ اللهِ ﷺ : إذا أمِنَكَ الرَّجُلُ على دَمِهِ فلا تَقْتُلْهُ.٦٧٩

624. **The Prophet (SAWA) said,** 'When a man assures another of sparing his life and then kills him, [know that] I renounce the killer, even if the victim is an unbeliever.'[686]

٦٢٤ . عنه ﷺ : مَن أمَّنَ رَجُلاً على دَمِهِ فقتَلَهُ فأنا بَريءٌ مِن القاتلِ ، وإنْ كانَ المَقتولُ كافراً.٦٨٠

203. Adhering to Sureties

٢٠٣ ـ الاعتِصامُ بالذِّمَمِ

625. **Imām ʿAlī (AS) said,** 'Adhere to sureties [that you are liable for] in all firmness.'[687]

٦٢٥ . الإمامُ عليٌّ ﷺ : اعتَصِموا (استَعصِموا) بالذِّمَمِ في أوْتادِها.٦٨١

626. **Imām ʿAlī (AS) said,** in his letter to Mālik al-Ashtar: 'And if you make a covenant between yourself and your enemy or give him a surety [against life or property], then stand by your pact with loyalty and observe your liability with trustworthiness. Make yourself the shield for your word, for there is nothing from Allah's mandates that all people agree upon,

٦٢٦ . عنه ﷺ ـ في عَهدِهِ للأشتَرِ ـ : وإنْ عَقَدتَ بينَكَ وبينَ عَدُوِّكَ عُقْدةً أو ألْبَسْتَهُ مِنكَ ذِمّةً فَحُطْ عَهدَكَ بالوفاءِ وارْعَ ذِمَّتَكَ بالأمانَةِ ، واجعَلْ نفسَكَ جُنّةً دُونَ ما أعطَيتَ ، فإنّهُ ليسَ مِن فرائضِ اللهِ شَيءٌ النّاسُ أشَدُّ علَيهِ اجْتِماعاً مَع تَفرُّقِ أهوائهِم وتَشَتُّتِ آرائهِم مِن

despite their diverse opinions on everything else, as much as they do with regards to respecting the fulfilment of covenants.'[688]

تعظيمِ الوفاءِ بالعُهودِ.٦٨٢

204. Respecting Covenants of Protection

٢٠٤ـ احترامُ الذِّمَمِ

627. **The Prophet (SAWA) said,** 'It is up to my community to protect those who are under them [i.e. non-Muslims living in Muslim lands].'[689] [690]

٦٢٧. رسولُ اللهِ ﷺ: يُجيرُ على أُمَّتي أدناهُم.٦٨٣

628. **The Prophet (SAWA) said,** 'The Muslims are brothers, their blood is co-equal, the weakest among them can grant protection, and they are like one hand [united] against their enemy.'[691]

٦٢٨. عنه ﷺ: المسلِمونَ إخوةٌ، تَتكافأُ دِماؤهُم، يَسْعىٰ بذِمَّتِهِم أدناهُم، وهُم يَدٌ علىٰ مَن سِواهُم.٦٨٤

33

INTIMACY

الأُنسُ

205. Things that One Should get Intimate With

٢٠٥ـ ما يَنبغي منَ الأُنسِ

629. **Imām ʿAlī (AS) said,** 'Do not let anything other than the truth be your comfort, and only falsehood should desert you.'[692]

٦٢٩. الإمامُ عليٌّ ؑ: لا يُؤنِسَنَّكَ إلّا الحقُّ، ولا يُوحِشَنَّكَ إلّا الباطلُ.٦٨٥

630. **Imām al-Ṣādiq (AS) said,** 'Intimacy is found in three: a compatible wife, a kind child, and a loyal friend.'[693]

٦٣٠. الإمامُ الصّادقُ ؑ: الأُنسُ في ثلاثٍ: في الزَّوجةِ المُوافِقَةِ، والوَلَدِ البارِّ، والصَّديقِ المُصافي.٦٨٦

631. **Imām al-Ṣādiq (AS) said,** 'Allah makes the faith of every single believer his own [source of] intimacy, so that he will never feel lonely even if he were to be on the top of a mountain.'[694]

٦٣١. عنه ؑ: ما مِن مؤمنٍ إلّا وقد جَعلَ اللهُ لَه مِن إيمانِهِ أُنساً يَسكُنُ إليه، حتّى لو كانَ علىٰ قُلّةِ جَبلٍ لَم يَستَوحِشْ.٦٨٧

632. **Imām al-ʿAskarī (AS) said,** 'A man who finds intimacy with Allah feels lonely among people.'[695]

٦٣٢. الإمامُ العسكريُّ ؑ: مَن أنِسَ باللهِ استَوحَشَ مِنَ النّاسِ.٦٨٨

206. Things that One Should not get Intimate With

٢٠٦ ـ ما لا يَنبغي من الأُنسِ

633. **Imām ʿAlī (AS) said,** The ignorant fears of what a wise finds intimacy with.'[696]

٦٣٣ . الإمامُ عليٌّ ﷺ : الجاهِلُ يَستوحِشُ مِمّا يَأنسُ بِهِ الحكيمُ .[٦٨٩]

634. **Imām al-Riḍā (AS) said,** 'Being overindulgent in one's intimacy [with people] drives one's dignity away.'[697]

٦٣٤ . الإمامُ الرِّضا ﷺ : الاسْتِرسالُ بالأُنسِ يُذهِبُ المَهابةَ .[٦٩٠]

207. What Brings Intimacy With Allah

٢٠٧ ـ ما يوجِبُ الأُنسَ باللهِ

635. **The Prophet (SAWA) said,** 'He who comes out of the humiliation of disobedience to the dignity of obedience, Allah will grant him intimacy without need for a close friend and elevate him without wealth.'[698]

٦٣٥ . رسولُ اللهِ ﷺ : مَن خَرجَ مِن ذُلِّ المعصيةِ إلى عِزِّ الطّاعةِ آنسَهُ اللهُ عزّ وجلّ بغَيرِ أنيسٍ، وأعانَهُ بغيرِ مالٍ .[٦٩١]

636. **Imām ʿAlī (AS) said,** 'A man who isolates himself away from people[699] will find intimacy with Allah, glory be to Him.'[700]

٦٣٦ . الإمامُ عليٌّ ﷺ : مَنِ انْفَرَدَ عنِ النّاسِ أنِسَ باللهِ سبحانَهُ .[٦٩٢]

34

MAN

الإنسانُ

208. The Dignity of Man

٢٠٨ ـ كَرامةُ بَني آدَمَ

"Certainly We have honoured the Children of Adam, and carried them over land and sea, and provided them with all the good things, and given them an advantage over many of those We have created with a complete preference."[701]

﴿وَلَقَدْ كَرَّمْنا بَنِي آدَمَ وَحَمَلْناهُمْ فِي الْبَرِّ وَالْبَحْرِ وَرَزَقْناهُمْ مِنَ الطَّيِّباتِ وَفَضَّلْناهُمْ عَلى كَثِيرٍ مِمَّنْ خَلَقْنا تَفْضِيلاً﴾ .[٦٩٣]

637. **The Prophet (SAWA) said,** 'Nothing is more honoured by Allah than the son of Adam.' He was asked, 'Not even the angels, O Messenger

٦٣٧ . رسولُ اللهِ ﷺ : ما شَيءٌ أكرمُ على اللهِ مِن ابنِ آدمَ . قيلَ : يا رسولَ اللهِ، ولا الملائكةُ؟! قالَ : الملائكةُ مَجبورونَ،

of Allah?' He said, 'The angels are compelled [by predestination] like the sun and the moon.'[702]

بمنزلةِ الشّمسِ والقمرِ.٦٩٤

638. **The Prophet (SAWA) said,** 'Nothing is better than a thousand of its like, except for man.'[703]

٦٣٨. عنه ﷺ: لَيس شَيءٌ خَيراً مِن ألفٍ مِثلِهِ إلّا الإنسانَ.٦٩٥

639. **Imām al-Ṣādiq (AS),** when 'Abdullāh b. Sinān asked him, 'Is man better or the angels?', replied, 'The Commander of the Faithful (AS) said, 'Allah, the Exalted, gave the angels intellect without desire, He gave the beasts desire without intellect, and He gave both to the sons of Adam. So a man whose intellect prevails over his desire is better than the angels whilst a man whose desire prevails over his intellect is worse that the beasts.'[704]

٦٣٩. الإمامُ الصّادقُ ﷺ ـ وقد سألَهُ عبدُ اللهِ بنُ سِنانٍ: الملائكةُ أفضلُ أمْ بَنو آدمَ؟ ـ: قالَ أميرُ المؤمنينَ عليُّ بنُ أبي طالبٍ ﷺ: إنّ اللهَ عزّ وجلّ ركّبَ في الملائكةِ عقلاً بلا شَهوةٍ، وركّبَ في البهائمِ شَهوةً بلا عقلٍ، وركّبَ في بَني آدمَ كِلْتَيْهِما، فمَنْ غلَبَ عقلُهُ شهوتَهُ فَهُو خيرٌ مِن الملائكةِ، ومَن غلَبتْ شَهوتُهُ عقلَهُ فهُو شَرٌّ مِن البهائمِ.٦٩٦

209. The Reason for Man's Creation

٢٠٩ ـ عِلّةُ خَلقِ الإنسانِ

"I did not create the jinn and the humans except that they may worship Me."[705]

﴿وما خَلقْتُ الجِنَّ والإنسَ إلّا ليَعْبُدُونِ﴾.٦٩٧

"Had your Lord wished, He would have made mankind one community; but they continue to differ, except those on whom your Lord has mercy — and that is why He created them"[706]

﴿ولَوْ شاءَ رَبُّكَ لَجَعَلَ النّاسَ أُمّةً واحِدَةً ولا يَزالُونَ مُخْتَلِفِينَ * إلّا مَنْ رَحِمَ رَبُّكَ ولِذلِكَ خَلَقَهُمْ﴾.٦٩٨

640. **Imām 'Alī (AS) said,** 'You were ordered to fear Allah and you were created for obedience and good deeds.'[707]

٦٤٠. الإمامُ عليٌّ ﷺ: بتقوَى اللهِ أُمِرتُم، وللإحسانِ والطّاعةِ خُلِقتُم.٦٩٩

641. **Imām al-Ḥusayn (AS) said,** 'O People! Allah, exalted be His remembrance, has only created people so that they might know Him; and when they know Him they worship Him; and when they worship Him they become needless of worshipping others by His worship.' A man asked him, 'O son of the Prophet! May my parents be your ransom, what is meant by knowing Allah?' He replied, 'It is that the people of each era must

٦٤١. الإمامُ الحسينُ ﷺ: أيُّها النّاسُ، إنّ اللهَ ـ عزّ وجلّ ذِكْرُهُ ـ ما خَلقَ العِبادَ إلّا ليَعرِفوهُ، فإذا عَرَفُوهُ عَبَدوهُ، فإذا عَبَدوهُ اسْتَغنَوا بعبادتِهِ عن عِبادةِ ما سِواهُ. فقالَ لَه رجلٌ: يابنَ رسولِ اللهِ، بأبي أنتَ وأُمّي فما معرفةُ اللهِ؟ قالَ: معرفةُ أهلِ

know their Imām, to whom obedience is mandatory.'[708]

كلِّ زمانٍ إمامَهُمُ الّذي يَجبُ علَيهِم طاعتُهُ.[٧٠٠]

642. **Imām al-Ṣādiq (AS),** In response to an atheist who asked him, 'For what purpose did He create humanity if He had no need for them and neither was he compelled to create them, and nor would it be proper for Him to create us in vain?', replied, 'He created them to reveal [to them] His wisdom, to execute His knowledge, and to carry out His plan.'[709]

٦٤٢. الإمامُ الصّادقُ عليه السلام ـ في جَوابِ زِنديقٍ سألَهُ: فَلأيِّ عِلّةٍ خَلقَ الخَلقَ وهُو غيرُ مُحتاجٍ إليهِم ولا مُضطَرٍّ إلىٰ خَلْقِهِم، ولا يَليقُ بهِ التَّعَبُّثُ بِنا؟ ـ: خلَقَهُم لإظهارِ حِكمتِهِ، وإنفاذِ علمِهِ، وإمضاءِ تَدبيرِهِ.[٧٠١]

643. **Imām al-Ṣādiq (AS) said,** regarding the verse, *but they continue to differ, except those on whom your Lord has mercy —and that is why He created them"*, 'He created them so that they may perform that which will render them deserving of the mercy of Allah, so that He may confer his mercy upon them.'[710]

٦٤٣. عنه عليه السلام ـ في قولِهِ تعالىٰ: ﴿ولا يَزالونَ مُختلفينَ * إلّا مَن رَحِمَ ربُّكَ ولذلكَ خَلَقهُم﴾ ـ: خَلقَهُم لِيَفعَلوا ما يَستَوجِبونَ بهِ رَحمتَه فيَرحَمَهُم.[٧٠٢]

210. Man's Weakness

٢١٠ ـ ضَعفُ الإنسانِ

"Man was created weak"[711]

﴿خُلِقَ الإنْسانُ ضَعيفاً﴾.[٧٠٣]

644. **Imām 'Alī (AS) said,** 'Pitiable is the son of Adam! His death is hidden [from him], his illnesses are invisible, and his actions are recorded. A mosquito causes him pain, a gasp can kill him, and a little sweat makes him stink.'[712]

٦٤٤. الإمامُ عليٌّ عليه السلام: مِسكينٌ ابنُ آدمَ! مَكتومُ الأجَلِ، مَكنونُ العِلَلِ، مَحفوظُ العَملِ، تُؤلِمُهُ البَقّةُ، وتَقتُلُهُ الشَّرْقةُ، وتُنتِنُهُ العَرْقةُ.[٧٠٤]

211. Measuring Man's Value

٢١١ ـ قيمَةُ الإنسانِ

645. **Imām 'Alī (AS) said,** 'Man ['s worth] is measured according to his two little organs – his heart and his tongue – so that when he fights, he should do so with a firm heart, and when he speaks, he should do so with eloquence.'[713]

٦٤٥. الإمامُ عليٌّ عليه السلام: المرءُ بأصغَرَيهِ: بقلبِهِ ولسانِهِ، إنْ قاتَلَ قاتَلَ بجَنانٍ، وإن نَطقَ نَطقَ بِبَيانٍ.[٧٠٥]

35

BANES[714]

الآفات

212. There is Trial in Every Thing

٢١٢ - لِكُلِّ شَيءٍ آفَةٌ

646. **The Prophet (SAWA) said,** 'The bane of humour is lack of shame; the bane of courage is aggression; the bane of generosity is mentioning one's favours to others; the bane of beauty is arrogance; the bane of worship is abeyance; the bane of speech is lying; the bane of knowledge is forgetfulness; the bane of wisdom is foolishness; the bane of good lineage is pride; and the bane of liberality is wastefulness.'[715]

٦٤٦ . رسولُ اللهِ ﷺ : آفةُ الظَّرْفِ الصَّلَفُ ، وآفةُ الشَّجاعة البغيُ ، وآفةُ السَّماحةِ المَنُّ ، وآفةُ الجَمالِ الخُيَلاءُ ، وآفةُ العِبادةِ الفَتْرةُ ، وآفةُ الحديثِ الكِذبُ ، وآفةُ العلمِ النِّسْيانُ، وآفةُ الحِلمِ السَّفَهُ ، وآفةُ الحَسَبِ الفَخْرُ ، وآفة الجُودِ السَّرَفُ.[٧٠٦]

647. **The Prophet (SAWA) said,** 'The bane of religion is desire.'[716]

٦٤٧ . عنه ﷺ : آفةُ الدِّينِ الهوىٰ.[٧٠٧]

648. **Imām 'Alī (AS) said,** 'For everything there is a bane: the bane of knowledge is forgetfulness; the bane of worship is showing-off; the bane of the conscience is self-admiration; the bane of nobility is pride; the bane of humour is lack of shame; the bane of liberality is wastefulness; the bane of bashfulness is weakness; the bane of clemency is submissiveness; and the bane of stamina is degeneracy.'[717]

٦٤٨ . الإمامُ عليٌّ عليه السلام : لكلِّ شيءٍ آفةٌ، وآفةُ العلمِ النِّسيانُ، وآفةُ العِبادةِ الرِّياءُ ، وآفةُ اللّبِّ العُجْبُ ، وآفةُ النَّجابةِ الكِبْرُ ، وآفةُ الظَّرْفِ الصَّلَفُ ، وآفةُ الجُودِ السَّرَفُ ، وآفةُ الحياءِ الضَّعْفُ ، وآفةُ الحِلمِ الذّلُّ ، وآفةُ الجَلَدِ الفُحْشُ.[٧٠٨]

649. **Imām 'Alī (AS) said,** 'Cowardliness is an affliction.'[718]

٦٤٩ . عنه عليه السلام : الجُبْنُ آفةٌ.[٧٠٩]

650. **Imām 'Alī (AS) said,** 'Desire is the bane of the intellect.'[719]

٦٥٠ . عنه عليه السلام : الهوىٰ آفةُ الألبابِ.[٧١٠]

651. **Imām 'Alī (AS) said,** 'The bane of faith is polytheism idolatry.'[720]

٦٥١ . عنه عليه السلام : آفةُ الإيمانِ الشِّركُ.[٧١١]

652. **Imām 'Alī (AS) said,** 'The bane of certainty is doubt.'[721]

٦٥٢ . عنه عليه السلام : آفةُ اليقينِ الشَّكُّ.[٧١٢]

653. **Imām ʿAlī (AS) said,** 'The bane of bounty is ingratitude.'[722]

٦٥٣. عنه ﷺ: آفةُ النِّعَمِ الكُفْرانُ.٧١٣

654. **Imām ʿAlī (AS) said,** 'The bane of obedience is [the ensuing] disobedience.'[723]

٦٥٤. عنه ﷺ: آفةُ الطّاعةِ العِصْيانُ.٧١٤

655. **Imām ʿAlī (AS) said,** 'The bane of nobility is pride.'[724]

٦٥٥. عنه ﷺ: آفةُ الشَّرَفِ الكِبْرُ.٧١٥

656. **Imām ʿAlī (AS) said,** 'The bane of cleverness is deception.'[725]

٦٥٦. عنه ﷺ: آفةُ الذَّكاءِ المَكْرُ.٧١٦

657. **Imām ʿAlī (AS) said,** 'The bane of worship is showing-off.'[726]

٦٥٧. عنه ﷺ: آفةُ العِبادةِ الرِّياءُ.٧١٧

658. **Imām ʿAlī (AS) said,** 'The bane of generosity is mentioning one's favours to others.'[727]

٦٥٨. عنه ﷺ: آفةُ السَّخاءِ المَنُّ.٧١٨

659. **Imām ʿAlī (AS) said,** 'The bane of religion is suspicion.'[728]

٦٥٩. عنه ﷺ: آفةُ الدِّينِ سوءُ الظَّنِّ.٧١٩

660. **Imām ʿAlī (AS) said,** 'The bane of the intellect is desire.'[729]

٦٦٠. عنه ﷺ: آفةُ العقلِ الهوى.٧٢٠

661. **Imām ʿAlī (AS) said,** 'The obstacles of fate are the bane of glory.'[730]

٦٦١. عنه ﷺ: آفةُ المجدِ عَوائقُ القضاءِ.٧٢١

662. **Imām ʿAlī (AS) said,** 'The bane of the soul is infatuation with this world.'[731]

٦٦٢. عنه ﷺ: آفةُ النّفسِ الوَلَهُ بالدّنيا.٧٢٢

663. **Imām ʿAlī (AS) said,** 'The bane of counsel is the contradiction of opinions.'[732]

٦٦٣. عنه ﷺ: آفةُ المشاوَرةِ انتِقاضُ الآراءِ.٧٢٣

664. **Imām ʿAlī (AS) said,** 'The downfall of kings is bad conduct.'[733]

٦٦٤. عنه ﷺ: آفةُ المُلوكِ سُوءُ السِّيرةِ.٧٢٤

665. **Imām ʿAlī (AS) said,** 'The downfall of ministers is a corrupt heart.'[734]

٦٦٥. عنه ﷺ: آفةُ الوُزَراءِ خُبْثُ السَّريرةِ.٧٢٥

666. **Imām ʿAlī (AS) said,** 'The ruination of scholars is the love for leadership.'[735]

٦٦٦. عنه ﷺ: آفةُ العُلَماءِ حُبُّ الرِّئاسةِ.٧٢٦

667. **Imām ʿAlī (AS) said,** 'The downfall of rulers is weak management.'[736]

٦٦٧. عنه ؑ : آفةُ الزُّعَماءِ ضَعْفُ السِّياسةِ.[٧٢٧]

668. **Imām ʿAlī (AS) said,** 'The ruination of soldiers is disobeying their commanders.'[737]

٦٦٨. عنه ؑ : آفةُ الجُنْدِ مُخالفةُ القادَةِ.[٧٢٨]

669. **Imām ʿAlī (AS) said,** 'The bane of training is the triumph of [one's] habit.'[738]

٦٦٩. عنه ؑ : آفةُ الرِّياضةِ غَلَبةُ العادةِ.[٧٢٩]

670. **Imām ʿAlī (AS) said,** 'The ruination of subjects is abandoning obedience.'[739]

٦٧٠. عنه ؑ : آفةُ الرَّعيّةِ مخالفةُ الطّاعةِ.[٧٣٠]

671. **Imām ʿAlī (AS) said,** 'The bane of piety is lack of contentment.'[740]

٦٧١. عنه ؑ : آفةُ الوَرَعِ قلّةُ القَناعةِ.[٧٣١]

672. **Imām ʿAlī (AS) said,** 'The downfall of judges is greed.'[741]

٦٧٢. عنه ؑ : آفةُ القُضاةِ الطّمعُ.[٧٣٢]

673. **Imām ʿAlī (AS) said,** 'The downfall of the upright is lack of piety.'[742]

٦٧٣. عنه ؑ : آفةُ العُدولِ قلّةُ الوَرَعِ.[٧٣٣]

674. **Imām ʿAlī (AS) said,** 'The ruin of a brave man is the loss of resolve.'[743]

٦٧٤. عنه ؑ : آفةُ الشُّجاعِ إضاعةُ الحَزْمِ.[٧٣٤]

675. **Imām ʿAlī (AS) said,** 'The downfall of the strong man is underestimating the foe.'[744]

٦٧٥. عنه ؑ : آفةُ القويِّ استضعافُ الخَصْمِ.[٧٣٥]

676. **Imām ʿAlī (AS) said,** 'The bane of clemency is submissiveness.'[745]

٦٧٦. عنه ؑ : آفةُ الحِلمِ الذّلُّ.[٧٣٦]

677. **Imām ʿAlī (AS) said,** 'The bane of giving is procrastination.'[746]

٦٧٧. عنه ؑ : آفةُ العَطاءِ المَطْلُ.[٧٣٧]

678. **Imām ʿAlī (AS) said,** 'The bane of economy is miserliness.'[747]

٦٧٨. عنه ؑ : آفةُ الاقتِصادِ البُخلُ.[٧٣٨]

679. **Imām ʿAlī (AS) said,** 'The bane of awe is humour.'[748]

٦٧٩. عنه ؑ : آفةُ الهَيبةِ المِزاحُ.[٧٣٩]

680. **Imām ʿAlī (AS) said,** 'The bane of the quest is failure.'[749]

٦٨٠. عنه ؑ : آفةُ الطَّلَبِ عدمُ النَّجاحِ.[٧٤٠]

681. **Imām ʿAlī (AS) said,** 'The bane of sovereignty is lack of protection.'[750]

٦٨١. عنه ؑ : آفةُ المُلْكِ ضَعْفُ الحِمايةِ.[٧٤١]

682. **Imām ʿAlī (AS) said,** 'The bane of pacts is lack of compliance.'[751]

٦٨٢. عنه ﷺ: آفةُ العُهودِ قلّةُ الرِّعايةِ.٧٤٢

683. **Imām ʿAlī (AS) said,** 'The bane of rule is pride.'[752]

٦٨٣. عنه ﷺ: آفةُ الرِّياسةِ الفَخْرُ.٧٤٣

684. **Imām ʿAlī (AS) said,** 'The bane of narration is lying.'[753]

٦٨٤. عنه ﷺ: آفةُ النَّقْلِ كذبُ الرِّوايةِ.٧٤٤

685. **Imām ʿAlī (AS) said,** 'The bane of knowledge is not putting it into practice.'[754]

٦٨٥. عنه ﷺ: آفةُ العلمِ تركُ العملِ بهِ.٧٤٥

686. **Imām ʿAlī (AS) said,** 'The bane of work is abandoning sincerity.'[755]

٦٨٦. عنه ﷺ: آفةُ العملِ تركُ الإخلاصِ.٧٤٦

687. **Imām ʿAlī (AS) said,** 'The bane of generosity is poverty.'[756]

٦٨٧. عنه ﷺ: آفةُ الجُودِ الفَقرُ.٧٤٧

688. **Imām ʿAlī (AS) said,** 'The ruin of ordinary people is a treacherous scholar.'[757]

٦٨٨. عنه ﷺ: آفةُ العامّةِ العالمُ الفاجرُ.٧٤٨

689. **Imām ʿAlī (AS) said,** 'The bane of justice is a powerful oppressor.'[758]

٦٨٩. عنه ﷺ: آفةُ العَدلِ الظّالمُ القادرُ.٧٤٩

690. **Imām ʿAlī (AS) said,** 'The bane of civilization [and development] is the tyranny of rulers.'[759]

٦٩٠. عنه ﷺ: آفةُ العُمرانِ جَورُ السّلطانِ.٧٥٠

691. **Imām ʿAlī (AS) said,** 'The bane of power is blocking kind deeds.'[760]

٦٩١. عنه ﷺ: آفةُ القُدرةِ منعُ الإحسانِ.٧٥١

692. **Imām ʿAlī (AS) said,** 'The bane of the heart is self-admiration.'[761]

٦٩٢. عنه ﷺ: آفةُ اللبِّ العُجْبُ.٧٥٢

693. **Imām ʿAlī (AS) said,** 'The bane of talking is lying.'[762]

٦٩٣. عنه ﷺ: آفةُ الحديثِ الكذبُ.٧٥٣

694. **Imām ʿAlī (AS) said,** 'The bane of works is the incompetence of workers.'[763]

٦٩٤. عنه ﷺ: آفةُ الأعمالِ عَجزُ العُمّالِ.٧٥٤

695. **Imām ʿAlī (AS) said,** 'The bane of hope is the arrival of death.'[764]

٦٩٥. عنه ﷺ: آفةُ الآمالِ حُضورُ الآجالِ.٧٥٥

696. **Imām ʿAlī (AS) said,** 'The bane of loyalty is betrayal.'[765]

٦٩٦. عنه عليه السلام: آفةُ الوفاءِ الغَدْرُ.[٧٥٦]

697. **Imām ʿAlī (AS) said,** 'The bane of resolve is the passage of an opportunity.'[766]

٦٩٧. عنه عليه السلام: آفةُ الحَزْمِ فَوتُ الأمرِ.[٧٥٧]

698. **Imām ʿAlī (AS) said,** 'The bane of trust is treachery.'[767]

٦٩٨. عنه عليه السلام: آفةُ الأمانةِ الخيانةُ.[٧٥٨]

699. **Imām ʿAlī (AS) said,** 'The ruin of the jurists is lack of piety.'[768]

٦٩٩. عنه عليه السلام: آفةُ الفقهاءِ عدمُ الصِّيانةِ.[٧٥٩]

700. **Imām ʿAlī (AS) said,** 'The bane of liberality is squandering.'[769]

٧٠٠. عنه عليه السلام: آفةُ الجُودِ التّبذيرُ.[٧٦٠]

701. **Imām ʿAlī (AS) said,** 'The ruin of livelihood is lack of prudence [in spending].'[770]

٧٠١. عنه عليه السلام: آفةُ المَعاشِ سُوءُ التّدبيرِ.[٧٦١]

702. **Imām ʿAlī (AS) said,** 'The bane of speech is it being lengthy.'[771]

٧٠٢. عنه عليه السلام: آفةُ الكلامِ الإطالةُ.[٧٦٢]

703. **Imām ʿAlī (AS) said,** 'The bane of wealth is miserliness.'[772]

٧٠٣. عنه عليه السلام: آفةُ الغِنىٰ البُخْلُ.[٧٦٣]

704. **Imām ʿAlī (AS) said,** 'The bane of hope is death.'[773]

٧٠٤. عنه عليه السلام: آفةُ الأمَلِ الأجَلُ.[٧٦٤]

705. **Imām ʿAlī (AS) said,** 'The bane of goodness is a corrupt companion.'[774]

٧٠٥. عنه عليه السلام: آفةُ الخيرِ قَرينُ السُّوءِ.[٧٦٥]

706. **Imām ʿAlī (AS) said,** 'The bane of power is aggression and tyranny.'[775]

٧٠٦. عنه عليه السلام: آفةُ الاقتِدارِ البغيُ والعُتُوُّ.[٧٦٦]

707. **Imām ʿAlī (AS) said,** 'The fountainhead of all afflictions is infatuation with vain pleasures.'[776]

٧٠٧. عنه عليه السلام: رأسُ الآفاتِ الوَلَهُ باللّذّاتِ.[٧٦٧]

708. **Imām ʿAlī (AS) said,** 'The worst affliction of the intellect is arrogance.'[777]

٧٠٨. عنه عليه السلام: شرُّ آفاتِ العقلِ الكِبْرُ.[٧٦٨]

36

MISERLINESS

البُخلُ

213. Warning Against Miserliness

٢١٣ـ التّحذِيرُ عَنِ البُخلِ

"Those who are stingy and bid [other] people to be stingy, and conceal whatever Allah has given them out of His grace; and We have prepared for the faithless a humiliating punishment."[778]

﴿الَّذِينَ يَبْخَلُونَ وَيَأْمُرُونَ النَّاسَ بِالْبُخْلِ وَيَكْتُمُونَ مَا آتَاهُمُ اللهُ مِنْ فَضْلِهِ وَأَعْتَدْنَا لِلْكَافِرِينَ عَذَاباً مُهِيناً﴾.٧٦٩

"Ah! There you are, being invited to spend in the way of Allah; yet among you there are those who are stingy; and whoever is stingy is stingy only to himself. Allah is the All-sufficient, and you are all-needy, and if you turn away He will replace you with another people, and they will not be like you."[779]

﴿ها أَنْتُمْ هٰؤُلاءِ تُدْعَوْنَ لِتُنْفِقُوا فِي سَبِيلِ اللهِ فَمِنْكُمْ مَنْ يَبْخَلُ وَمَنْ يَبْخَلْ فَإِنَّما يَبْخَلُ عَنْ نَفْسِهِ وَاللهُ الْغَنِيُّ وَأَنْتُمُ الْفُقَرَاءُ وَإِنْ تَتَوَلَّوْا يَسْتَبْدِلْ قَوْماً غَيْرَكُمْ ثُمَّ لا يَكُونُوا أَمْثَالَكُمْ﴾.٧٧٠

(See also: Qur'an 4:53; 17:100; 57:24; 68:12)

(أنظر) النساء: ٥٣ و الإسراء: ١٠٠ و الحديد: ٢٤ و القلم: ١٢.

709. **Imām ʿAlī (AS) said,** 'Miserliness encompasses all vices, and it is a rein with which one is led to every defect.'[780]

٧٠٩. الامامُ عليٌّ ؑ : البُخلُ جامعٌ لِمَساوئ العُيوبِ، وهُو زِمامٌ يُقادُ بِهِ إلىٰ كلِّ سُوءٍ.٧٧١

710. **Imām ʿAlī (AS) said,** 'Miserliness is [a source of] shame.'[781]

٧١٠. عنه ؑ : البُخلُ عارٌ.٧٧٢

711. **Imām ʿAlī (AS) said,** 'Miserliness is the garment of wretchedness.'[782]

٧١١. عنه ؑ : البُخلُ جِلْبابُ المَسْكَنَةِ.٧٧٣

712. **Imām ʿAlī (AS) said,** 'Miserliness in giving [to others] what is at hand is a mistrust in God.'[783]

٧١٢. عنه ؑ : البُخلُ بالموجودِ سُوءُ الظَّنِّ بالمَعبودِ.٧٧٤

713. **Imām ʿAlī (AS) said,** 'A man who is miserly with his money will face humiliation, but a man who is miserly with his faith [i.e. he does not readily give it up] will be dignified.'[784]

٧١٣. عنه ؑ : مَن بَخِلَ بمالِهِ ذَلَّ، مَن بَخِلَ بِدِينِهِ جَلَّ.٧٧٥

714. **Imām ʿAlī (AS) said,** 'Miserliness humiliates its companion and honours the one who abandons it.'[785]

٧١٤. عنه ؑ : البُخلُ يُذِلُّ مُصاحِبَهُ، ويُعِزُّ مُجانِبَهُ.٧٧٦

715. **Imām al-Riḍā (AS) said,** 'Miserliness rips one's honour apart.'[786]

٧١٥. الإمامُ الرِّضا ﷺ: البُخلُ يُمَزِّقُ العِرْضَ.٧٧٧

716. **Imām al-Hādī (AS) said,** 'Miserliness is the most blameworthy vice.'[787]

٧١٦. الإمامُ الهاديُّ ﷺ: البُخلُ أذَمُّ الأخلاقِ.٧٧٨

214. The Explanation of Miser

٢١٤ـ تفسيرُ البُخلِ

717. **Imām al-Ḥasan (AS),** when his father asked him about greed, said, '[It is] when you count what is in your hands as a source of honour, while you count what you have given away as a waste.'[788]

٧١٧. الإمامُ الحسنُ ﷺ ـ لَمّا سَألَهُ أبوهُ عنِ الشُّحِّ ـ: أن تَرىٰ ما في يَدَيكَ شَرَفاً وما أنفَقتَ تَلَفاً.٧٧٩

718. **Imām al-Ṣādiq (AS) said,** 'The miser is he who denies what is Allah's right, and spends instead for a purpose other than Allah's sake.'[789]

٧١٨. الإمامُ الصّادقُ ﷺ: إنّما الشَّحيحُ مَن مَنَعَ حَقَّ اللهِ، وأنفَقَ في غَيرِ حَقِّ اللهِ ﷻ.٧٨٠

719. **Imām al-Ṣādiq (AS) said,** 'Greed is worse than miserliness because a miser is parsimonious in spending what he has, whilst a greedy man covets that which others possess in addition to what he himself possesses, such that whatever he sees in the hands of others he wishes to be his – lawfully or unlawfully. He cannot be satiated, and nor does he derive any benefit from what Allah has granted him.'[790]

٧١٩. عنه ﷺ: الشُّحُّ أشَدُّ مِنَ البُخلِ، إنَّ البَخيلَ يَبخَلُ بما في يَدِهِ، والشَّحيحَ يَشُحُّ علىٰ ما في أيدِي النّاسِ وعلىٰ ما في يَدِهِ، حتّىٰ لا يَرىٰ في أيدِي النّاسِ شَيئاً إلّا تَمَنّىٰ أن يكونَ لَهُ بالحِلِّ والحَرامِ، لا يَشبَعُ ولا يَنتَفِعُ بما رَزَقَهُ اللهُ.٧٨١

215. The Miser

٢١٥ـ البَخيلُ

720. **The Prophet (SAWA) said,** 'The least comfortable one among people is the miser.'[791]

٧٢٠. رسولُ اللهِ ﷺ: أقلُّ النّاسِ راحةً البخيلُ.٧٨٢

721. **Imām ʿAlī (AS) said,** 'The miser stores [wealth] for his inheritors.'[792]

٧٢١. الإمامُ عليٌّ ﷺ: البَخيلُ خازِنٌ لِوَرَثَتِهِ.٧٨٣

722. **Imām ʿAlī (AS) said,** 'A miser can have no friend.'[793]

٧٢٢. عنه ﷺ: ليسَ لِبَخيلٍ حبيبٌ.٧٨٤

723. **Imām ʿAlī (AS) said,** 'I wonder at the miser – he expedites the same poverty from which he escapes, and

٧٢٣. عنه ﷺ: عَجِبتُ للبخيلِ يَستعجِلُ الفَقرَ الّذي مِنه هَرَبَ، ويَفوتُهُ الغِنَى الّذي إيّاهُ طَلَبَ،

misses the same richness for which he yearns! So he leads a life of deprivation in this world like the poor, yet he will be judged with the rich in the Hereafter.'[794]

فيعيشُ في الدُّنيا عَيْشَ الفُقراءِ، ويُحاسَبُ في الآخِرةِ حسابَ الأغنياءِ.٧٨٥

724. **Imām ʿAli (AS) said,** 'The greedy is far from Allah, far from the people and close to Hellfire.'[795]

٧٢٤. الإمامُ عليٌّ ﷺ: البَخيلُ بَعيدٌ مِنَ اللهِ، بَعيدٌ مِنَ النّاسِ، قَريبٌ مِنَ النّارِ.٧٨٦

725. **Imām al-Ṣādiq (AS) said,** 'No one should love for others to be rich as much as the misers; for when others become rich, they would subsequently keep away from their wealth.'[796]

٧٢٥. الإمامُ الصّادقُ ﷺ: إنّ أحقَّ النّاسِ بأن يَتمنّىٰ للنّاسِ الغِنىٰ البُخَلاءُ؛ لأنَّ النّاسَ إذا استغْنَوا كَفُّوا عن أموالِهم.٧٨٧

726. **Imām al-Ṣādiq (AS) said,** 'The miser's parsimony suffices as mistrust of his Lord, for a man who is certain of [God's] compensation would give generously.'[797]

٧٢٦. عنه ﷺ: حَسْبُ البخيلِ مِن بُخلِهِ سُوءُ الظَّنِّ بربِّهِ، مَن أيقَنَ بالخَلَفِ جادَ بالعَطيّةِ.٧٨٨

216. The Real Miser

٢١٦ـ البخيلُ حَقُّ البَخيلِ

727. **The Prophet (SAWA) said,** 'The real miser is the one who refuses to pay the mandatory alms-tax from his wealth, and refuses to spend on the necessities of his people, yet he squanders it on other things.'[798]

٧٢٧. رسولُ اللهِ ﷺ: إنّما البَخيلُ حَقُّ البَخيلِ الّذي يَمنعُ الزَّكاةَ المَفروضةَ في مالِهِ، ويَمنعُ البائنَةَ في قومِهِ، وهُو فيما سِوىٰ ذلكَ يُبذِّرُ.٧٨٩

728. **The Prophet (SAWA) said,** 'The real miser is he before whom my name is mentioned and he does not say 'peace be upon him'.'[799]

٧٢٨. عنه ﷺ: البخيلُ حقّاً مَن ذُكِرتُ عِندَهُ فلَم يُصَلِّ علَيَّ.٧٩٠

217. The Most Miserly of People

٢١٧ـ أبخلُ النّاسِ

729. **The Prophet (SAWA) said,** 'The most miserly person is he who refuses to give what Allah has made obligatory [i.e. the alms-tax].'[800]

٧٢٩. رسولُ اللهِ ﷺ: أبْخَلُ النّاسِ مَن بَخِلَ بما افترَضَ اللهُ علَيهِ.٧٩١

730. **The Prophet (SAWA) said,** 'Verily the *most miserly person is he who is miserly with his* greeting [i.e. he does not greet others].'[801]

٧٣٠. عنه ﷺ: إنّ أبخَلَ النّاسِ مَن بَخِلَ بالسَّلامِ.٧٩٢

731. **Imām ʿAlī (AS) said,** 'The most miserly person is he who does not spend his money on himself and stores it away for his inheritors.'[802]

٧٣١. الإمامُ عليٌّ ﷺ: أبخَلُ النّاسِ مَن بَخِلَ علىٰ نفسِهِ بمالِهِ وخلَّفَهُ لِوُرّاثِهِ.٧٩٣

732. **Imām ʿAlī (AS) said,** The worst misery is being miserable by not paying what Allah the Glorious has ordained to pay from one's property.'[803]

٧٣٢. عنه ﷺ : البُخلُ بِإخراجِ مَا افتَرَضَهُ اللهُ سُبحانَهُ مِنَ الأموالِ أقبَحُ البُخلِ.٧٩٤

733. **Imām al-Ṣādiq (AS) said,** 'The Commander of the Faithful (AS) sent someone five camel-loads of dates … at which a man said to him, 'By Allah, he did not even ask you for anything. Indeed, one camel-load would have been enough to recompense him!' The Commander of the Faithful (AS) replied, 'May Allah increase not the people of your type! I am giving and you are the one being miserly?!'[804]

٧٣٣. الإمامُ الصّادقُ ﷺ : إنّ أميرَ المؤمنينَ ﷺ بَعثَ إلىٰ رجُلٍ بخَمسةِ أوْساقٍ مِن تَمرٍ … فقالَ رجُلٌ لأميرِ المؤمنينَ ﷺ : واللهِ ما سألَكَ فُلانٌ، ولقد كانَ يُجْزيهِ مِنَ الخَمسةِ أوْساقٍ وَسَقٌ واحدٌ! فقالَ لَه أميرُ المؤمنينَ ﷺ : لا كَثّرَ اللهُ في المؤمنينَ ضَرْبَكَ! أُعطي أنا وتَبخَلُ أنتَ؟!٧٩٥

218. The Sign of Miserliness

٢١٨ ـ آيةُ البُخلِ

734. **Imām ʿAlī (AS) said,** 'Abundance of excuses [for not giving] is a sign of miserliness.'[805]

٧٣٤. الإمامُ عليٌّ ﷺ : كَثرَةُ العِلَلِ آيةُ البُخلِ.٧٩٦

735. **Imām ʿAlī (AS) said,** 'The miser justifies himself by presenting [many] excuses and justifications.'[806]

٧٣٥. عنه ﷺ : البخيلُ مُتَحَجِّجٌ بالمَعاذِيرِ والتَّعاليلِ.٧٩٧

37

INNOVATION (*al-bidʿa*)[807]

البِدْعَة

219. Warning Against Innovation

٢١٩ ـ التَّحذيرُ مِنَ البِدعةِ٧٩٨

736. **The Prophet (SAWA) said,** 'The worst of matters are the innovations. Certainly, every innovation is a [source of] error and every error is destined for Hell.'[808]

٧٣٦. رسولُ اللهِ ﷺ : شَرُّ الأُمورِ مُحْدَثاتُها ألَا وكُلُّ بدعةٍ ضلالةٌ، ألَا وكلُّ ضَلالةٍ ففي النّارِ.٧٩٩

737. **The Prophet (SAWA) said,** 'Never start a practice based on an innovation; for a man who initiates a bad practice will incur its sin and the sins of the people who act upon it.'[809]

٧٣٧. عنه ﷺ : إيّاكَ أنْ تَسُنَّ سُنّةَ بدعةٍ؛ فإنَّ العبدَ إذا سَنَّ سُنّةً سيّئةً لَحِقَهُ وِزْرُها ووِزْرُ مَن عَمِلَ بها.٨٠٠

738. **Imām ʿAlī (AS) said,** 'No sooner is an innovation initiated than it leaves behind a

٧٣٨. الإمامُ عليٌّ ﷺ : ما أُحْدِثَتْ بِدعةٌ إلّا تُرِكَ

common practice. So eschew innovations and adhere to the clear path. Verily the established traditions are the best, while innovated ones are the worst.'[810]

بها سُنّةٌ، فاتّقوا البِدعَ والْزَموا المَهْيَعَ، إنّ عَوازِمَ الأُمورِ أفضَلُها، وإنَّ مُحْدَثاتِها شِرارُها.[٨٠١]

739. **Imām ʿAlī (AS) said,** 'Nothing destroys religion like innovations.'[811]

٧٣٩. عنه ؑ: ما هَدمَ الدِّينَ مثلُ البِدعِ.[٨٠٢]

220. The Innovators

٢٢٠ـأهلُ البِدَعِ

740. **The Prophet (SAWA) said,** 'The innovators are the worst of all of [God's] creation.'[812]

٧٤٠. رسولُ اللهِ ﷺ: أهلُ البِدَعِ شَرُّ الخَلقِ والخليقةِ.[٨٠٣]

741. **The Prophet (SAWA) said,** 'The innovators are the dogs of the inmates of Hell.'[813]

٧٤١. عنه ﷺ: أهلُ البدعِ كِلابُ أهلِ النّارِ.[٨٠٤]

221. The Meaning of Innovation

٢٢١ـمَعنَى البِدعَةِ

742. **Imām ʿAlī (AS) said,** 'The innovators are those who contradict the command of Allah, His Book and His Messenger; they are those who follow their own opinion and desires, even if they are the majority.'[814]

٧٤٢. الإمامُ عليٌّ ؑ: أمّاأهلُ البِدعةِفالمُخالِفونَ لأمرِ اللهِ ولِكتابهِ ورسولِه، العاملونَ بِرأيِهم وأهوائهِم وإنْ كَثُروا.[٨٠٥]

743. **Imām al-Ṣādiq (AS) said,** 'Anyone who calls people to give him their allegiance, knowing that among them is someone superior to him, is an erroneous innovator.'[815]

٧٤٣. الإمامُ الصّادقُ ؑ: مَن دعا النّاسَ إلىٰ نفسِه وفيهِم مَن هُو أعلمُ مِنه فهُو مُبْتَدِعٌ ضالٌّ.[٨٠٦]

222. Rejecting Innovators

٢٢٢ـالإعراضُ عَن صاحبِ البِدعَةِ

744. **The Prophet (SAWA) said,** 'When a man rejects an innovator, out of dislike for him, Allah will fill his heart with peace and belief.'[816]

٧٤٤. رسولُ اللهِ ﷺ: مَن أعرَضَ عن صاحِبِ بِدعةٍ، بُغْضاً لَهُ، مَلأَ اللهُ قلبَهُ أمْناً وإيماناً.[٨٠٧]

745. **The Prophet (SAWA) said,** 'A man who smiles at an innovator has aided the destruction of his own religion.'[817]

٧٤٥. عنه ﷺ: مَن تَبَسّمَ في وجهِ مُبتَدِعٍ فقد أعانَ علىٰ هَدمِ دِينِه.[٨٠٨]

223. The Innovator and Worship

٢٢٣ ـ المُبتَدِعُ وَ العِبادَةُ

746. **The Prophet (SAWA) said,** 'When a man acts in accordance with an innovation, Satan will leave him to worship and incite humility and tears in him [i.e. that he may continue in its performance].'[818]

٧٤٦ . رسولُ اللهِ ﷺ : مَن عمِلَ في بِدعةٍ خَلّاهُ الشّيطانُ والعِبادةَ، وألْقىٰ عليهِ الخُشوعَ والبُكاءَ.[٨٠٩]

224. Invalidity of the Worship of an Innovator

٢٢٤ ـ بُطلانُ عملِ المُبتَدِعِ

747. **The Prophet (SAWA) said,** 'Little worship following a correct [Prophetic] practice is better than a lot of worship following an innovation.'[819]

٧٤٧ . رسولُ اللهِ ﷺ : عَملٌ قليلٌ في سُنّةٍ خيرٌ مِن عملٍ كثيرٍ في بِدعةٍ.[٨١٠]

748. **The Prophet (SAWA) said,** 'Allah denies the innovator a chance to repent.'[820]

٧٤٨ . عنه ﷺ : أبَى اللهُ لصاحِبِ البدعةِ بالتّوبةِ.[٨١١]

225. A Scholar's Duties when Faced with the Appearance of Innovations

٢٢٥ ـ ما يَجِبُ عَلَى العالِمِ عِندَ ظُهورِ لبِدَعِ

749. **The Prophet (SAWA) said,** 'When innovations arise in my community, the scholar must display his knowledge; and those who do not do this deserve the curse of Allah.'[821]

٧٤٩ . رسولُ اللهِ ﷺ : إذا ظَهَرتِ البِدعُ في اُمّتي فلْيُظهِرِ العالِمُ علمَهُ، فمَن لَم يَفعلْ فعَلَيهِ لَعنةُ اللهِ.[٨١٢]

(See also: DISSIMULATION: section 1873)

(اُنظر) التقيّة : باب ١٨٧٣.

38

SQUANDERING

التَّبذيرُ

226. Censure of Squandering

٢٢٦ ـ ذَمُّ التَّبذِير

"Give the relatives their [due] right, and the needy and the traveller [as well], but do not squander wastefully. Indeed the wasteful are brothers of satans, and Satan is ungrateful to his Lord."[822]

﴿وَآتِ ذَا القُرْبىٰ حَقَّهُ وَالمِسْكِينَ وَابْنَ السَّبِيلِ وَلا تُبَذِّرْ تَبْذِيراً ❊ إِنَّ الْمُبَذِّرِينَ كانُوا إِخْوَانَ الشَّياطِينِ وَكَانَ الشَّيْطَانُ لِرَبِّهِ كَفُوراً﴾.[٨١٣]

750. **Imām ʿAlī (AS) said,** 'Be liberal, but do not squander; and be calculating, but do not be parsimonious.'[823]

٧٥٠. الإمامُ عليٌّ عليه السلام: كُنْ سَمْحاً ولا تكُنْ مُبَذِّراً، وكُنْ مُقَدِّراً ولا تَكُنْ مُقَتِّراً.[٨١٤]

751. **Imām ʿAlī (AS) said,** 'Squandering is the epitome of destitution.'[824]

٧٥١. عنه عليه السلام: التَّبذيرُ عُنوانُ الفاقةِ.[٨١٥]

752. **Imām ʿAlī (AS) said,** 'Squandering is a penniless companion.'[825]

٧٥٢. عنه عليه السلام: التّبذيرُ قَرِينُ مُفْلِسٌ.[٨١٦]

753. **Imām ʿAlī (AS) said,** 'A man who takes pride in squandering will be humiliated by bankruptcy.'[826]

٧٥٣. عنه عليه السلام: مَنِ افْتَخَر بالتَّبذيرِ احتُقِرَ بالإفْلاسِ.[٨١٧]

227. The Meaning of Squandering

٢٢٧ ـ مَعنَى التَّبذِيرِ

754. **Imām al-Ṣādiq (AS) said** about the verse: *"but do not squander wastefully"* – '[It refers to] one who spends for other than the obedience of Allah is a squanderer; and one who spends in the path of good is economical.'[827]

٧٥٤. الإمامُ الصّادقُ عليه السلام ـ في قولِهِ تعالىٰ: ﴿ولا تُبَذِّرْ تَبْذِيراً﴾ ـ: مَن أنْفقَ شيئاً في غيرِ طاعةِ اللهِ فهُو مُبَذِّرٌ، ومَن أنْفقَ في سبيلِ الخيرِ فهُو مُقْتَصِدٌ.[٨١٨]

755. **Imām al-Ṣādiq (AS) said,** in answer to Abū Baṣīr's question about the verse: *"but do not squander wastefully"* – 'When a man spends all his money and remains penniless'. Abū Baṣīr then asked, 'Is spending in such a way for something lawful still called squandering?' He replied, 'Yes.'[828]

٧٥٥. تفسير العيّاشي عن أبي بصيرٍ: سألتُ أبا عبدِ اللهِ عليه السلام في ـ قولِه: ﴿ولا تُبذِّر تبذيراً﴾، قالَ: بَذْلُ الرّجُل مالَهُ ويَقعُدُ ليسَ لَهُ مالٌ، قالَ: فيَكونُ تَبذيرٌ في حلالٍ؟ قالَ: نَعَم.[٨١٩]

39

RIGHTEOUSNESS

البِرُّ

228. Encouraging the Righteousness

٢٢٨ ـ الحَثُّ عَلَى البِرِّ

"Cooperate in righteousness and Godwariness, but do not cooperate in sin and aggression, and be wary of Allah. Indeed Allah is severe in retribution."[829]

﴿وَتَعَاوَنُوا عَلَى البِرِّ وَالتَّقْوَى وَلا تَعَاوَنُوا عَلَى الإِثْمِ وَالْعُدْوَانِ وَاتَّقُوا اللهَ إِنَّ اللهَ شَدِيدُ الْعِقَابِ﴾.[٨٢٠]

756. **The Prophet (SAWA) said,** 'Nothing increases lifespan except righteousness.'[830]

٧٥٦. رسولُ اللهِ ﷺ: لا يَزيدُ في العُمرِ إلّا البِرُّ.[٨٢١]

757. **The Prophet (SAWA) said,** 'The good deed to be rewarded the fastest is righteousness, and the evil deed to be punished the fastest is aggression.'[831]

٧٥٧. عنه ﷺ: إنَّ أسْرَعَ الخيرِ ثواباً البِرُّ، وإنَّ أسْرَعَ الشَّرِّ عِقاباً البَغْيُ.[٨٢٢]

758. **The Prophet (SAWA) said,** 'Three things represent righteousness: liberality from one's self, kind words, and endurance of harm.'[832]

٧٥٨. عنه ﷺ: ثلاثٌ مِن أبوابِ البِرِّ: سَخاءُ النَّفْسِ، وطِيبُ الكلامِ، والصَّبرُ علَى الأذىٰ.[٨٢٣]

759. **Imām al-Bāqir (AS) said,** 'Four things are among the treasures of righteousness: concealing one's need, concealing one's charity, concealing one's pain, and the concealment of catastrophe [befalling oneself].'[833]

٧٥٩. الإمامُ الباقرُ عليه السلام: أربعٌ مِن كُنوزِ البِرِّ: كِتْمانُ الحاجةِ، وكِتْمانُ الصَّدقةِ، وكِتْمانُ الوَجَعِ، وكِتْمانُ المُصيبةِ.[٨٢٤]

229. The Sign of a Righteous Person

٢٢٩ ـ علَامةُ البارِّ

760. **The Prophet (SAWA) said,** 'There are ten signs of a righteous person: he loves for the sake of Allah, hates for the sake of Allah, befriends for the sake of Allah, abandons for the sake of Allah. He becomes angry for the sake of Allah, becomes pleased for the sake of Allah, works for the sake of Allah, beseeches Allah, submits to Allah – fearing Him, awed [by others], pure, sincere, bashful, and watchful – and acts kindly for the sake of Allah.'[834]

٧٦٠. رسولُ اللهِ ﷺ: أمّا علَامةُ البارِّ فعَشَرَةٌ: يُحِبُّ في اللهِ، ويُبْغِضُ في اللهِ، ويُصاحِبُ في اللهِ، ويُفارِقُ في اللهِ، ويَغْضَبُ في اللهِ، ويَرضىٰ في اللهِ، ويَعملُ للهِ، ويَطلُبُ إلَيهِ، ويَخْشَعُ للهِ خائفاً مَخُوفاً طاهِراً مُخْلِصاً مُسْتَحْيِياً مُراقِباً، ويُحْسِنُ في اللهِ.[٨٢٥]

230. Complete Righteousness

٢٣٠ ـ تَمامُ البِرِّ

761. **The Prophet (SAWA) said,** 'Complete righteousness means that you do in secret what is usually done in public.'[835]

٧٦١. رسولُ اللهِ ﷺ: تَمامُ البِرِّ أن تَعملَ في السِّرِّ عَملَ العَلانِيَةِ.[٨٢٦]

40

THE PURGATORY (*al-Barzakh*)

البَرزَخ

231. The Meaning of The Purgatory

۲۳۱ ـ مَعنَى البَرْزَخِ

"And ahead of them is a barrier until the day they will be resurrected"[836]

﴿وَمِنْ وَرَائِهِم بَرْزَخٌ إِلَىٰ يَوْمِ يُبْعَثُونَ﴾ .[٨٣٧]

(See also: Qur'an 3:169-171; 23:99-100; 40:11)

(أنظر) آل عمران: ١٦٩ ـ ١٧١ و المؤمنون: ٩٩ ـ ١٠٠ و غافر: ١١.

762. **Imām al-Ṣādiq (AS) said,** 'By Allah! I fear for you the *barzakh*!' He was asked, 'What is the *barzakh*?' He replied, 'The grave, from the day one dies until the Day of Judgment.'[837]

٧٦٢ . الإمامُ الصّادقُ عليه السلام: واللهِ ، أتَخَوَّفُ عليكُم في البَرزَخِ ! قلتُ: وما البَرْزَخُ ؟ قالَ: القَبرُ ، مُنذُ حينِ مَوتِهِ إلىٰ يومِ القيامةِ .[٨٣٨]

232. The Souls of the Believers in the Purgatory

۲۳۲ ـ أرواحُ المؤمنينَ في البَرزخِ

"Do not suppose those who were slain in the way of Allah to be dead; rather they are living and provided for near their Lord."[838]

﴿وَلَا تَحْسَبَنَّ الَّذِينَ قُتِلُوا فِي سَبِيلِ اللهِ أَمْوَاتاً بَلْ أَحْيَاءٌ عِنْدَ رَبِّهِمْ يُرْزَقُونَ﴾ .[٨٣٩]

763. **Imām al-Ṣādiq (AS) said,** 'The souls of the believers will be in chambers in Paradise, eating of its food and drinking its drinks, and visiting one another, saying, 'Our Lord! Bring the Final Hour, so that You may fulfil what You promised us.'[839]

٧٦٣ . الإمامُ الصادقُ عليه السلام : أرواحُ المؤمنينَ في حُجُراتٍ في الجنّةِ ، يأكُلونَ مِن طَعامِها ، ويَشرَبونَ مِن شَرابِها ، ويَتزاوَرونَ فيها ، ويقولونَ: ربَّنا ، أقِمْ لنا السّاعةَ لِتُنْجِزَ لنا ما وَعَدْتَنا .[٨٣٠]

233. The Souls of Disbelievers in the Purgatory

۲۳۳ ـ أرواحُ الكُفّارِ في البَرزخِ

764. **Imām al-Ṣādiq (AS) said,** 'The souls of disbelievers are in the Fire of Hell, exposed to it, saying, 'Our Lord! Delay the Final Hour, and do not fulfil what You warned us against.'[840]

٧٦٤ . الإمامُ الصّادقُ عليه السلام : إنّ أرواحَ الكُفّارِ في نارِ جَهنّمَ يُعْرَضونَ عليها يقولونَ: ربَّنا ، لا تُقِمْ لنا السّاعةَ ، ولا تُنجِزْ لنا ما وَعَدْتَنا ![٨٣١]

41

THE BLESSING

البَرَكَة

234. The Meaning of Blessing

٢٣٤ـ مَعنَى البَرَكَة

"He has made me blessed, wherever I may be, and He has enjoined me to [maintain] the prayer and to [pay] the zakāt as long as I live."[841]

﴿وَجَعَلَنِي مُبارَكاً أَيْنَ ما كُنْتُ وأَوْصانِي بِالصَّلاةِ وَالزَّكاةِ ما دُمْتُ حَيّاً﴾ .[٨٣٢]

765. **Imām al-Ṣādiq (AS),** with regards to the verse: *"He has made me blessed, wherever I may be"*, said, '[Blessed means] very beneficial [to others].'[842]

٧٦٥ . الإمامُ الصّادقُ عليه السلام ـ في قوله تعالىٰ: ﴿وجَعَلَني مُبارَكاً أيْنَما كُنتُ﴾ ـ: نَفّاعاً .[٨٣٣]

235. That which Brings Blessing and that which Removes it

٢٣٥ـ ما يُوجِبُ البَرَكةَ وما يُزيلُها

"If the people of the towns had been faithful and Godwary, We would have opened to them blessings from the heaven and the earth. But they denied; so We seized them because of what they used to earn."[843]

﴿وَلَوْ أَنَّ أَهْلَ الْقُرَىٰ آمَنُوا وَاتَّقَوْا لَفَتَحْنَا عَلَيْهِمْ بَرَكَاتٍ مِنَ السَّمَاءِ وَالْأَرْضِ وَلٰكِنْ كَذَّبُوا فَأَخَذْنَاهُمْ بِما كانُوا يَكْسِبُونَ﴾ .[٨٣٤]

766. **The Prophet (SAWA) said,** 'Weigh your food, for there is blessing in weighed food.'[844]

٧٦٦ . رَسولُ اللهِ صلى الله عليه وآله : كِيلوا طَعامَكُم، فإنَّ البَرَكةَ في الطَّعامِ المَكِيلِ .[٨٣٥]

767. **The Prophet (SAWA) said,** 'Blessings are in trading and transactions.'[845]

٧٦٧ . عنه صلى الله عليه وآله : إنَّ البَرَكَةَ فِي التِّجارَةِ .[٨٣٦]

768. **The Prophet (SAWA) said,** 'Four things, of which even if only one enters a house, it will destroy it such that it will never again be able to flourish through blessing: betrayal, theft, wine-drinking, and adultery.'[846]

٧٦٨ . عنه صلى الله عليه وآله : أرْبَعٌ لا تَدخُلُ بَيتاً واحدةٌ مِنهُنَّ إلّا خَرِبَ ولَم يَعْمُرْ بالبَرَكةِ: الخِيانةُ، والسَّرِقةُ، وشُربُ الخمرِ، والزِّنا .[٨٣٧]

769. **Imām 'Alī (AS) said,** 'Blessings are multiplied with justice.'[847]

٧٦٩ . الإمامُ عليٌّ عليه السلام : بالعَدلِ تَتَضاعَفُ البَرَكاتُ .[٨٣٨]

770. **Imām ʿAlī (AS) said,** 'When crimes prevail, blessings are lifted away.'[848]

٧٧٠. عنه ﷺ: إذا ظَهَرتِ الجِناياتُ ارْتَفَعتِ البَرَكاتُ.٨٣٩

42

CHEERFULNESS

البِشْر

236. Encouraging Cheerfulness

٢٣٦ ـ الحَثُّ عَلى حُسنِ البِشْرِ

771. **The Prophet (SAWA) said,** 'Cheerfulness removes the grudge [of others].'[849]

٧٧١. رسولُ اللهِ ﷺ: حُسْنُ البِشْرِ يَذهَبُ بالسَّخيمةِ.٨٤٠

772. **The Prophet (SAWA) said,** 'Meet your brother with a cheerful face.'[850]

٧٧٢. عنه ﷺ: اِلْقَ أخاكَ بِوَجْهٍ مُنْبَسِطٍ.٨٤١

773. **The Prophet (SAWA) said,** 'You will not be able to encompass all people with your money, so meet them with cheerful faces and joy.'[851]

٧٧٣. عنه ﷺ: إنَّكُم لَن تَسَعُوا النّاسَ بأموالِكُم، فالْقَوهُم بِطَلاقةِ الوَجهِ وحُسْنِ البِشرِ.٨٤٢

774. **Imām ʿAlī (AS) said,** 'The smile is the trap of amity.'[852]

٧٧٤. الإمامُ عليٌّ ﷺ: البَشاشَةُ حِبالَةُ المَوَدّةِ.٨٤٣

775. **Imām ʿAlī (AS) said,** 'Cheerfulness is the trait of the free.'[853]

٧٧٥. عنه ﷺ: البِشرُ شِيمةُ الحُرِّ.٨٤٤

776. **Imām ʿAlī (AS) said,** 'The cause of love is cheerfulness.'[854]

٧٧٦. عنه ﷺ: سَببُ المَحبّةِ البِشرُ.٨٤٥

777. **Imām ʿAlī (AS) said,** 'The cheerfulness of the believer is on his face, his strength is in his religion, and his sorrow lies in his heart.'[855]

٧٧٧. عنه ﷺ: إنّ بِشرَ المؤمنِ في وَجهِهِ، وقُوّتَهُ في دِينِهِ، وحُزنَهُ في قلبِهِ.٨٤٦

778. **Imām ʿAlī (AS) said,** 'Your cheerfulness shows the generosity of your soul.'[856]

٧٧٨. عنه ﷺ: بِشرُكَ يَدُلُّ على كَرَمِ نفسِكَ.٨٤٧

779. **Imām ʿAlī (AS) said,** 'When you meet your brothers, shake hands with them and show them cheerfulness and joy; thus when you part company all your sins will have gone.'[857]

٧٧٩. عنه ﷺ: إذا لَقِيتُم إخْوانَكُم فَتَصافَحوا، وأظْهِروا لَهمُ البَشاشَةَ والبِشرَ، تَتَفرّقوا وما علَيكُمْ مِن الأوْزارِ قد ذَهَبَ.٨٤٨

780. **Imām ʿAlī (AS) said,** 'The best thing with which people can win the hearts of their loved ones and remove the animosity from the hearts of their enemies is cheerfulness upon meeting, asking about them in their absence, and smiling at them in their presence.'[858]

٧٨٠. عنه عليه السلام: إنَّ أحْسنَ ما يَأْلَفُ بِهِ النّاسُ قلوبَ أوِدّائهِم، ونَفَوا بِهِ الضِّغْنَ عن قُلوبِ أعْدائهِم: حُسنُ البِشرِ عند لِقائهِم، والتَّفَقُّدُ في غَيبتِهِم، والبَشاشةُ بِهِم عند حُضورِهِم.[٨٤٩]

43

INSIGHT

البَصيرَة

237. Insight

٢٣٧ ـ البَصيرَةُ

"Certainly We have created for hell many of the jinn and humans: they have hearts with which they do not understand, they have eyes with which they do not see, they have ears with which they do not hear. They are like cattle; rather they are more astray. It is they who are the heedless."[859]

﴿وَلَقَدْ ذَرَأْنَا لِجَهَنَّمَ كَثِيراً مِنَ الجِنِّ وَالإِنْسِ لَهُمْ قُلُوبٌ لَا يَفْقَهُونَ بِهَا وَلَهُمْ أَعْيُنٌ لا يُبْصِرُونَ بِهَا وَلَهُمْ آذَانٌ لا يَسْمَعُونَ بِهَا أُولٰئِكَ كَالْأَنْعَامِ بَلْ هُمْ أَضَلُّ أُولٰئِكَ هُمُ الْغافِلُونَ﴾.[٨٥٠]

781. **The Prophet (SAWA) said,** 'The blind is not someone who has lost his eyesight, but the one who has lost his insight.'[860]

٧٨١. رسولُ اللهِ ﷺ: ليسَ الأعمىٰ مَن يَعْمىٰ بَصرُهُ، إنَّما الأعمىٰ مَن تَعْمىٰ بَصيرتُهُ.[٨٥١]

782. **Imām ʿAlī (AS) said,** 'Eyesight is useless if the insight goes blind.'[861]

٧٨٢. الإمامُ عليٌّ عليه السلام: نَظَرُ البَصَرِ لا يُجْدي إذا عَمِيَتِ البَصيرةُ.[٨٥٢]

783. **Imām ʿAlī (AS) said,** 'Indeed, the insightful one is he who listens and contemplates, looks and sees, derives benefit from lessons, then he takes a clear path on which he avoids the falls into abysses.'[862]

٧٨٣. عنه عليه السلام: فإنّما البَصيرُ مَن سمِعَ فتَفَكّرَ، ونَظرَ فأبْصرَ، وانْتَفعَ بالعِبَرِ، ثُمّ سَلَكَ جَدَداً واضِحاً يَتَجنّبُ فيهِ الصَّرْعَةَ في المَهاوِي.[٨٥٣]

784. **Imām ʿAlī (AS) said,** 'Vision is not dependent on the eyes, for the eyes may often belie their owners, yet the mind never deceives a man seeking its counsel.'[863]

٧٨٤. عنه عليه السلام: لَيستِ الرَّوِيَّةُ كَالمُعايَنَةِ مَعَ الإبْصارِ؛ فقد تَكذِبُ العُيونُ أهلَها، ولا يَغُشُّ العقلُ مَنِ اسْتَنْصَحَهُ.[٨٥٤]

785. **Imām ʿAlī (AS) said,** 'Losing one's eyesight is easier than losing one's insight.'[864]

٧٨٥. عنه ﷺ : فَقْدُ البَصرِ أهْـوَنُ مِـن فِـقْدانِ البَصيرة.[٨٥٥]

786. **Imām ʿAlī (AS) said,** 'The most insightful person is he who sees his own flaws and refrains from sins as a result.'[865]

٧٨٦. عنه ﷺ : أبْصَرُ النّاسِ مَن أبْـصَرَ عُـيوبَهُ وأقْلَعَ عن ذُنوبِهِ.[٨٥٦]

44

FALSEHOOD

الباطل

238. Warning Against Following Falsehood

٢٣٨ ـ التَّحذيرُ من اتّباع الباطل

"And say, 'The truth has come, and falsehood has vanished. Indeed falsehood is bound to vanish.'"[866]

﴿وَقُلْ جَاءَ الْحَقُّ وَزَهَقَ الْبَاطِلُ إِنَّ الْبَاطِلَ كَانَ زَهُوقاً﴾.[٨٥٧]

"Rather We hurl the truth against falsehood, and it crushes its head, and behold, falsehood vanishes! And woe to you for what you allege [about Allah]."[867]

﴿بَلْ نَقْذِفُ بِالْحَقِّ عَلَى الْبَاطِلِ فَيَدْمَغُهُ فَإِذَا هُوَ زَاهِقٌ وَلَكُمُ الْوَيْلُ مِمَّا تَصِفُونَ﴾.[٨٥٨]

787. **Imām ʿAlī (AS) said,** 'Falsehood is a deceiving deluder.'[868]

٧٨٧. الإمامُ عليٌّ ﷺ : الباطِلُ غَرورٌ خادِعٌ.[٨٥٩]

788. **Imām ʿAlī (AS) said,** 'I will rip falsehood open, until the truth emerges from its belly.'[869]

٧٨٨. عنه ﷺ : فَلأنْقُبَنّ الباطِلَ حتّى يَخرُجَ الحقُّ مِن جَنْبِهِ.[٨٦٠]

789. **Imām ʿAlī (AS) said,** 'Truth is the road to Paradise, and falsehood is the road to Hell; and on each road there is a caller [calling to it].'[870]

٧٨٩. عنه ﷺ : الحقُّ طريقُ الجنّةِ ، والبـاطلُ طريقُ النّارِ، وعلىٰ كُلِّ طريقٍ داعٍ.[٨٦١]

790. **Imām ʿAlī (AS) said,** 'He who supports falsehood oppresses the truth.'[871]

٧٩٠. عنه ﷺ : ظَلَمَ الحقَّ مَنْ نَصرَ الباطلَ.[٨٦٢]

239. Discerning the Truth From Falsehood

٢٣٩ ـ التَّمييزُ بينَ الحقِّ و الباطِلِ

791. **Imām ʿAlī (AS) said,** 'Verily, there is nothing between truth and falsehood but a span

٧٩١. الإمامُ عليٌّ ﷺ : أمَا إنّه ليسَ بينَ الحقِّ

of four fingers ... Falsehood is to say, 'I heard,' while the truth is to say, 'I saw.'[872]

والباطلِ إلّا أربعُ أصابعَ ... الباطلُ أنْ تقولَ: سَمِعتُ ، والحقُّ أنْ تقولَ : رَأيْتُ.[٨٦٣]

240. The Truth Disguised as Falsehood

٢٤٠ ـ التِباسُ الحَقِّ بِالباطِلِ

"And do not mix the truth with falsehood, nor conceal the truth while you know."[873]

﴿وَلا تَلْبِسُوا الْحَقَّ بِالْباطِلِ وَتَكْتُمُوا الْحَقَّ وَأَنْتُمْ تَعْلَمُونَ﴾.[٨٦٤]

792. **Imām ʿAlī (AS) said,** 'If falsehood was isolated from being mixed with the truth, it would not be indefinable by those who aspire it; and if the truth was free from being disguised as falsehood, the tongues of its opponents would still be silenced; but it is often made by taking a little from one and a little from the other.'[874]

٧٩٢. الإمامُ عليٌّ عليه السلام : فلَو أنَّ الباطلَ خَلَصَ مِن مِزاجِ الحقِّ لَم يَخْفَ علَى المُرتادينَ ، ولَو أنَّ الحقَّ خَلَصَ مِن لَبْسِ الباطلِ انْقَطَعتْ عنه ألْسُنُ المُعانِدينَ ، ولكنْ يُؤخَذُ مِن هذا ضِغْثٌ ومِن هذا ضِغْثٌ.[٨٦٥]

793. **Imām ʿAlī (AS) said,** 'Many a wrong was glossed with verses from the Book of Allah, just as the copper dirham is plated with silver coating.'[875]

٧٩٣. عنه عليه السلام : كَم مِن ضَلالةٍ زُخْرِفَتْ بآيةٍ مِن كتابِ اللهِ كما يُزَخْرَفُ الدِّرْهَمُ النُّحاسُ بالفِضّةِ المُمَوَّهَةِ![٨٦٦]

241. Falsehood cannot be Ascertained as the Truth

٢٤١ ـ عدمُ استيقانِ الباطلِ حَقّاً

794. **Imām al-Ṣādiq (AS) said,** 'Allah has refused to present falsehood as a certain truth, and He has refused to present the truth to the heart of a believer as a certain falsehood; He has also refused to present falsehood to the heart of a disbeliever as a certain truth. And had he not done thus, the truth would never be distinguished from falsehood.'[876]

٧٩٤. الإمامُ الصّادقُ عليه السلام : أبَى اللهُ أنْ يُعرِّفَ باطلاً حقّاً، أبَى اللهُ أنْ يجْعَلَ الحقَّ في قلبِ المؤمنِ باطلاً لا شكَّ فيهِ ، وأبَى اللهُ أنْ يَجعَلَ الباطلَ في قلبِ الكافرِ المُخالِفِ حقّاً لا شَكَّ فيهِ ، ولَو لَم يَجْعَلْ هذا هكذا ما عُرِفَ حقٌّ مِن باطلٍ.[٨٦٧]

795. **Imām al-Ṣādiq (AS) said,** 'The heart can never ascertain that the truth is falsehood, nor can it ever ascertain that falsehood is the truth.'[877]

٧٩٥. عنه عليه السلام : لا يَستَيقِنُ القلبُ أنَّ الحقَّ باطلٌ أبداً ، ولا يَستَيقِنُ أنَّ الباطلَ حقٌّ أبداً.[٨٦٨]

45

[ALLAH'S] ANTIPATHY[878]

البُغضُ

242. Those whom Allah Despises

٢٤٢ ـ المَبْغوضونَ إلَى اللهِ

796. **The Prophet (SAWA) said,** 'Allah despises the adulterous old man, the wealthy oppressor, the arrogant pauper, and the persistent beggar; He nullifies the reward of the bragging giver, and he hates the blatantly insolent liar.'[879]

٧٩٦ . رسولُ اللهِ ﷺ : إنَّ اللهَ يُبغِضُ الشّيخَ الزّاني ، والغَنيَّ الظَّلومَ ، والفَقيرَ المُختالَ ، والسّائلَ المُلْحِفَ ، ويُحبِطُ أجرَ المُعطي المَنّانِ ، ويَمقُتُ البَذيخَ الجَريَّ الكَذّابَ.[٨٦٩]

797. **The Prophet (SAWA) said,** 'Allah, the Exalted, despises anyone who is knowledgeable about this world, but ignorant about the Hereafter.'[880]

٧٩٧ . عنه ﷺ : إنَّ اللهَ تباركَ وتعالىٰ يُبغِضُ كلَّ عالِمٍ بالدُّنيا جاهلٍ بالآخِرَةِ.[٨٧٠]

798. **The Prophet (SAWA) said,** 'Allah despises anyone who is ill-mannered, swaggering [in his gait], frequenting the markets, a corpse by night, [sleeping] like a donkey during the day, knowledgeable about this world, but ignorant about the Hereafter.'[881]

٧٩٨ . عنه ﷺ : إنَّ اللهَ تعالىٰ يُبغِضُ كلَّ جَعْظَريٍّ جَوّاظٍ سَخّابٍ في الأسْواقِ ، جِيفةٍ باللّيلِ ، حِمارٍ بالنّهارِ ، عالمٍ بالدُّنيا ، جاهلٍ بالآخِرَةِ.[٨٧١]

799. **The Prophet (SAWA) said,** 'Allah despises a man who does not fight intruders in his home.'[882]

٧٩٩ . عنه ﷺ : إنَّ اللهَ عزّ وجلّ يُبغِضُ رجُلاً يُدخَلُ علَيهِ في بَيتِهِ ولا يُقاتِلُ.[٨٧٢]

800. **Imām ʿAlī (AS) said,** 'Allah, the Exalted, despises the insolent man who is audacious [in committing] acts of disobedience.'[883]

٨٠٠ . الإمامُ عليٌّ ؈ : إنَّ اللهَ سبحانه لَيُبغِضُ الوَقِحَ المُتَجرّي علَى المَعاصي.[٨٧٣]

801. **Imām ʿAlī (AS) said,** 'The Prophet (SAWA) used to say, 'Allah despises the one who frowns at the faces of his brethren.'[884]

٨٠١ . عنه ؈ : كانَ رسولُ اللهِ ﷺ يقولُ : إنَّ اللهَ يُبغِضُ المُعَبِّسَ في وَجهِ إخْوانِهِ.[٨٧٤]

802. **Imām al-Bāqir (AS) said,** 'Allah despises the vile person who displays his vices publicly.'[885]

٨٠٢ . الإمامُ الباقرُ ؈ : إنَّ اللهَ يُبغِضُ الفاحِشَ المُتَفحِّشَ.[٨٧٥]

243. The People Allah Despises Most

٢٤٣ ـ أبغَضُ النّاسِ إلَى اللهِ

803. **The Prophet (SAWA) said,** 'Three people that Allah despises most are: a man who sleeps a lot in the day without having woken up to pray at night, a man who eats a lot without uttering the name of Allah or praising Him upon starting to eat, and a man who laughs a lot without reason.'[886]

٨٠٣. رسولُ اللهِ ﷺ: إنَّ أبغَضَ الخَلقِ إلَى اللهِ ثلاثةٌ: الرَّجُلُ يُكثِرُ النَّومَ بالنّهارِ ولَم يُصَلِّ مِنَ اللّيلِ شَيئاً، والرَّجُلُ يُكثِرُ الأكلَ ولا يُسَمّي اللهَ علىٰ طَعامِهِ ولا يَحمَدُهُ، والرَّجلُ يُكثِرُ الضَّحِكَ مِن غيرِ عَجَبٍ.[٨٧٦]

804. **The Prophet (SAWA) said,** 'Three people that Allah despises most are: an atheist in the Sanctuary [of Makkah], a man who seeks the pre-Islamic pagan practice in the era Islam, and a man who seeks to shed another's blood without any just cause.'[887]

٨٠٤. عنه ﷺ: أبغَضُ النّاسِ إلَى اللهِ ثلاثةٌ: مُلحِدٌ في الحَرَمِ، ومُبتَغٍ في الإسلامِ سُنّةَ الجاهِليّةِ، ومُطَّلِبُ دَمِ امرئٍ بغيرِ حقٍّ لِيُهريقَ دمَهُ.[٨٧٧]

805. **The Prophet (SAWA) said,** 'The most despised, by Allah, from among you are those who roam about gossiping and separating brothers, and seeking out flaws in innocent people.'[888]

٨٠٥. عنه ﷺ: أبغَضُكُم إلَى اللهِ المَشّاؤونَ بالنَّميمةِ، المُفرِّقونَ بينَ الإخوانِ، المُلتَمِسونَ للبُراءِ العَثَراتِ.[٨٧٨]

806. **The Prophet (SAWA) said,** 'The most despised by Allah, the Exalted, from among His creatures is the scholar who frequents the rulers.'[889]

٨٠٦. عنه ﷺ: إنَّ أبغَضَ الخَلقِ إلَى اللهِ تعالى العالِمُ يَزورُ العُمّالَ.[٨٧٩]

807. **The Prophet (SAWA) said,** 'Verily the most despicable from among you to me and the farthest away from me on the Day of Judgment are the prattlers, the pretentious, and the *mutafayhiqūn*.' He was asked, 'O Messenger of Allah! Who are the *mutafayhiqūn*?' He said, 'Those who are arrogant.'[890]

٨٠٧. كنز العمّال عن رسول الله ﷺ: إنّ أبغَضَكُم إلَيَّ وأبعَدَكُم مِنّي يومَ القيامةِ الثَّرثارونَ، والمُتَشَدِّقونَ، والمُتَفَيهِقونَ. قالوا: يا رسولَ اللهِ، ما المُتَفَيهِقونَ؟ قالَ: المُتَكبِّرونَ.[٨٨٠]

808. **Imām ʿAlī (AS) said,** 'The person most despised by Allah from among all His creatures is the backbiter.'[891]

٨٠٨. الإمامُ عليٌّ ﷺ: أبغَضُ الخَلائقِ إلَى اللهِ المُغتابُ.[٨٨١]

809. **Imām ʿAlī (AS) said,** 'The person most despised by Allah, the Exalted, from among His creatures is the one whose greatest concerns are

٨٠٩. عنه ﷺ: أمقَتُ العِبادِ إلَى اللهِ سبحانه مَن

[sating the appetite of] his stomach and his private parts.'[892]

كانَ هِمَّتُهُ (هَمُّهُ) بطنَهُ وفَرْجَهُ.[٨٨٢]

810. **Imām ʿAlī (AS) said,** 'The person most despised by Allah, the Exalted, is the ignorant one.'[893]

٨١٠. عنه ﷺ: أبغَضُ الخَلائقِ إلَى اللهِ تعالىٰ الجاهلُ.[٨٨٣]

811. **Imām ʿAlī (AS) said,** 'The most despised of creatures in the sight of Allah is a man who gathers scattered pieces of knowledge, deceiving [people] in the darkness of chaos, and blinded to what lies hidden in tranquillity. His peers from among the people call him a scholar, but he himself has never benefited one full day from his knowledge.'[894]

٨١١. عنه ﷺ: إنَّ أبغَضَ خَلقِ اللهِ إلَى اللهِ رجُلٌ قَمَشَ عِلْماً، غارّاً في أغْباشِ الفِتْنةِ، عَمِياً بما في غَيبِ الهُدْنةِ، سَمّاهُ أشْباهُهُ مِن النّاسِ عالِماً، ولَم يُغْنَ في العِلمِ يَوماً سالِماً.[٨٨٤]

812. **Imām ʿAlī (AS) said,** 'The person most despised by Allah, the Exalted, is the overbearing scholar.'[895]

٨١٢. عنه ﷺ: أبغَضُ العِبادِ إلَى اللهِ سبحانه العالِمُ المُتَجَبِّرُ.[٨٨٥]

813. **Imām al-Bāqir (AS) narrated,** 'Moses (AS) said, 'O Lord! Who do You despise the most from among Your servants?' He replied, 'The one who [sleeps like] a corpse by night and is idle during the day.'[896]

٨١٣. الإمامُ الباقرُ ﷺ: قالَ موسىٰ ﷺ: يا ربِّ، أيُّ عِبادِكَ أبغَضُ إلَيكَ؟ قالَ: جِيفةٌ باللّيلِ بَطّالٌ بالنّهارِ.[٨٨٦]

814. **Imām al-Ṣādiq (AS) said,** 'The person most despised from among Allah's creatures is a man whose [sharp] tongue people are wary of.'[897]

٨١٤. الإمامُ الصّادقُ ﷺ: إنَّ أبغَضَ خَلقِ اللهِ عبدٌ اتّقَى النّاسُ لِسانَهُ.[٨٨٧]

244. Acts Despised by Allah

٢٤٤ ـ الأعمالُ المَبغوضةُ إلَى اللهِ

815. **The Prophet (SAWA) said,** 'Nothing is more despised by Allah than a full stomach.'[898]

٨١٥. رسولُ اللهِ ﷺ: ليسَ شَيءٌ أبغَضَ إلَى اللهِ مِن بَطنٍ مَلْآنَ.[٨٨٨]

816. **The Prophet (SAWA) said,** 'There is nothing more detested by Allah than greed and bad manners, and indeed they corrupt the deeds the way soil corrupts honey.'[899]

٨١٦. عنه ﷺ: ما شَيءٌ أبغَضُ إلَى اللهِ عزّ وجلّ مِنَ البُخلِ وسوءِ الخُلُقِ، وإنَّهُ لَيُفسِدُ العَمَلَ كَما يُفسِدُ الطِّينُ العَسَلَ.[٨٨٩]

817. **Imām al-Ṣādiq (AS) said,** 'Allah despises excessive sleep and excessive idleness.'[900]

٨١٧. الإمامُ الصّادقُ ﷺ: إنَّ اللهَ يُبْغِضُ كَثْرَةَ النَّومِ وكَثْرَةَ الفراغِ.[٨٩٠]

818. **Imām al-Ṣādiq (AS) said,** ‘Three things deserve the antipathy of Allah, the Exalted: [excessive] sleeping without night-vigil, laughing without a cause, and eating on a full stomach.’[901]

٨١٨. عنه ؑ : ثلاثٌ فيهنَّ المَقْتُ مِن اللهِ عزّ وجلّ: نَومٌ مِن غيرِ سَهَرٍ ، وضِحكٌ مِن غيرِ عجَبٍ ، وأكلٌ على الشِّبَعِ.[٨٩١]

819. **Imām al-Ṣādiq (AS) said,** ‘A man from [the tribe of] Khathʿam came to the Prophet (SAWA), asking, ‘Which deeds are the most despised by Allah, the Exalted?’ The Prophet replied, ‘Associating anyone with Allah.’ The man asked, ‘Then what?’ He said, ‘Cutting off one’s kin.’ The man asked, ‘Then what?’ He said, ‘Enjoining evil and forbidding what is good.’[902]

٨١٩. عنه ؑ : إنَّ رجُلاً مِن خَثْعَم جاءَ إلَى النَّبيِّ ﷺ فقال : أيُّ الأعمالِ أبغَضُ إلَى اللهِ عزّ وجلّ؟ فقالَ : الشِّركُ باللهِ . قالَ: ثُمّ ماذا؟ قالَ : قَطيعةُ الرَّحِمِ . قالَ: ثُمّ ماذا؟ قالَ: الأمرُ بالمُنكرِ والنَّهيُ عن المَعروفِ.[٨٩٢]

820. **Imām al-Riḍā (AS) said,** ‘Allah, the Exalted, despises gossip, wasting money, and persistent begging.’[903]

٨٢٠. الإمامُ الرِّضا ؑ : إنّ اللهَ يُبغِضُ القِيلَ والقالَ ، وإضاعَةَ المالِ ، وكَثرَةَ السُّؤالِ.[٨٩٣]

245. Malice

٢٤٥ ـ البَغْضاءُ

821. **The Prophet (SAWA) said,** ‘You have been sneaked upon by the plague of previous nations: jealousy and malice.’[904]

٨٢١. رسولُ اللهِ ﷺ : دَبَّ إلَيكم داءُ الأُمَمِ قَبلَكُم: البَغْضاءُ والحَسَدُ.[٨٩٤]

822. **Imām al-Ṣādiq (AS) said,** ‘Three things bring about malice: hypocrisy, oppression, and self-admiration.’[905]

٨٢٢. الإمامُ الصّادقُ ؑ : ثلاثةٌ مَكسَبةٌ للبَغْضاءِ: النِّفاقُ ، والظُّلمُ ، والعُجبُ.[٨٩٥]

(See also: ENMITY 267)

(أنظر) عنوان ٢٦٧ «العَداوَة».

46

AGGRESSION

البَغيُ

246. Warning against Aggression

٢٤٦ ـ التَّحذيرُ عَنِ البَغيِ

“But when He delivers them, behold, they commit violations on the earth unduly! O mankind! Your violations are only to your own detriment. [These are]

﴿فَلَمّا أنْجاهُمْ إذا هُمْ يَبْغُونَ فِي الأرْضِ بِغَيْرِ الْحَقِّ يا أيُّها النّاسُ إنَّما بَغْيُكُمْ عَلَى أنْفُسِكُمْ

the wares of the life of this world; then to Us will be your return, whereat We will inform you concerning what you used to do."[906]

مَتاعَ الْحَياةِ الدُّنْيا ثُمَّ إِلَيْنا مَرْجِعُكُمْ فَنُنَبِّئُكُمْ بِما كُنتُمْ تَعْمَلُونَ﴾.[٨٩٦]

"*…and He forbids indecency, wrong, and aggression. He advises you so that you may take admonition.*"[907]

﴿… وَيَنْهىٰ عَنِ الْفَحْشاءِ وَالْمُنْكَرِ وَالْبَغْيِ يَعِظُكُمْ لَعَلَّكُمْ تَذَكَّرُونَ﴾.[٨٩٧]

823. **The Prophet (SAWA) said,** 'The evil deed to be punished the quickest is aggression.'[908]

٨٢٣. رسولُ اللهِ ﷺ: إنَّ أعجَلَ الشَّرِّ عُقوبَةً البَغيُ.[٨٩٨]

824. **Imām ʿAlī (AS) said,** 'Whoever draws the sword of aggression will be killed by it [himself].'[909]

٨٢٤. الإمامُ عليٌّ ﷺ: مَن سَلَّ سَيفَ البَغيِ قُتِلَ بِهِ.[٨٩٩]

825. **Imām ʿAlī (AS) said,** 'Aggression removes [Allah's] favour.'[910]

٨٢٥. عنه ﷺ: البَغيُ يَسلُبُ النِّعمةَ.[٩٠٠]

826. **Imām ʿAlī (AS) said,** 'Aggression brings about destruction.'[911]

٨٢٦. عنه ﷺ: البَغيُ يُوجِبُ الدَّمارَ.[٩٠١]

827. **Imām ʿAlī (AS) said,** 'Avoid aggression, for it expedites death and makes of its doer a lesson to others.'[912]

٨٢٧. عنه ﷺ: إيّاكَ والبَغيَ فإنَّهُ يُعَجِّلُ الصَّرعَةَ، ويُحِلُّ بالعاملِ بهِ العِبَرَ.[٩٠٢]

828. **Imām ʿAlī (AS) said,** 'Aggression leads its perpetrators to the Hellfire.'[913]

٨٢٨. عنه ﷺ: إنَّ البَغيَ يَقودُ أصحابَهُ إلَى النّارِ.[٩٠٣]

829. **Imām al-Ṣādiq (AS) said,** 'Make sure that you never utter one aggressive word, even if you admire [the strength of] yourself and your tribe.'[914]

٨٢٩. الإمامُ الصّادقُ ﷺ: انظُرْ أنْ لا تَكَلَّمَنَّ بِكَلِمَةِ بَغيٍ أبداً، وإنْ أعجَبَتْكَ نَفسُكَ وعَشيرَتُكَ.[٩٠٤]

247. The Characteristics of The Aggressor

٢٤٧ـ صِفَةُ الباغي

830. **Imām al-Ṣādiq (AS),** with regards to the verse: "*But should someone be compelled, without being aggressive or rebellious…*"[915], said, 'The aggressor is whoever rises to fight against the Imām.'[916]

٨٣٠. الإمامُ الصّادقُ ﷺ ـ في قولِهِ تعالى: ﴿فَمَنِ اضْطُرَّ غيرَ باغٍ ولا عادٍ﴾[٩٠٥] ـ: الباغي الّذي يَخرُجُ علَى الإمامِ.[٩٠٦، ٩٠٧]

248. Fighting Against Muslim Aggressors

٢٤٨ ـ قِتالُ أهلِ البَغيِ مِنَ المُسلِمينَ

"If two groups of the faithful fight one another, make peace between them. But if one party of them aggresses against the other, fight the one which aggresses until it returns to Allah's ordinance. Then, if it returns, make peace between them fairly, and do justice. Indeed Allah loves the just."[917]

﴿وَإِنْ طائِفَتَانِ مِنَ الْمُؤْمِنِينَ اقْتَتَلُوا فَأَصْلِحُوا بَيْنَهُمَا فَإِنْ بَغَتْ إِحْدَاهُمَا عَلَىٰ الْأُخْرَىٰ فَقَاتِلُوا الَّتِي تَبْغِي حَتَّىٰ تَفِيءَ إِلىٰ أَمْرِ اللهِ فَإِنْ فاءَتْ فَأَصْلِحُوا بَيْنَهُمَا بِالعَدْلِ وَأَقْسِطُوا إِنَّ اللهَ يُحِبُّ المُقْسِطِينَ﴾.[٩٠٨]

831. **Ḥafs Ibn Ghiyāth said,** 'I asked Abū ʿAbdullah [al-Ṣādiq] (AS) about two groups of believers; one group were rebels and the other group just, and the just group defeated the rebels.' He (AS) said, 'The just group does not have the right to chase the retrieving fugitive or to kill a prisoner or finish off a wounded person, and this is of course when nobody from the rebels are left and no formation from them exists to return so that those who have remained may join them.'[918]

٨٣١. حَفْصُ بْنُ غِيَاثٍ: سَأَلتُ أبا عَبدِ اللهِ عليه السلام عَنِ الطّائِفَتَينِ مِنَ المُؤمِنينَ إحداهُما باغِيَةٌ وَ الأُخرىٰ عادِلَةٌ فَهَزَمَتِ العادِلَةُ الباغِيَةَ؟ فَقالَ: لَيسَ لأَهْلِ العَدلِ أَن يَتبَعوا مُدبِراً و لا يَقتُلوا أسيراً ولا يُجهِزوا عَلَىٰ جَريحٍ، و هٰذا إذا لَمْ يَبقَ مِن أهلِ البَغيِ أَحَدٌ وَ لَم يَكُن لَهُم فِئَةٌ يَرجِعونَ إلَيها.[٩٠٩]

832. **Imām Zayn al-ʿĀbidīn (AS) said,** 'Imām ʿAlī (AS) wrote to Mālik al-Ashtar who was in the frontline in the battle in Baṣra, 'Do not fight those who are not advancing, nor should one who retreats be killed, nor should one finish off a wounded. He who closes the door of his house is safe.'[919]

٨٣٢. الإمام زين العابدين عليه السلام: إنَّ عَلِيّاً عليه السلام كَتَبَ إلىٰ مالِكٍ ـ و هُوَ عَلىٰ مُقَدِّمَتِهِ يَومَ البَصرَةِ ـ بِأَن لا يَطعَنَ في غَيرِ مُقبِلٍ و لا يَقتُلَ مُدبِراً وَ لا يُجيزَ عَلىٰ جَريحٍ و مَن أغلَقَ بابَهُ فَهُوَ آمِنٌ.[٩١٠]

833. **ʿAbdullah Ibn Sharīk,** narrating from his father, 'When the enemy was defeated in the Battle of the Camel, the Commander of the Faithful (AS) said that no one who has fled should be chased, and no one who has been wounded should be finished off, and he who closes the door of his house is safe. On the day of the Battle of Ṣiffīn those who had fought or turned away were killed and the wounded were finished off. Ābān Ibn Taghlib said to ʿAbdullah Ibn Sharīk, 'These two methods are different.' Ibn Sharīk answered, 'Those who are from the Battle of the Camel killed Ṭalḥa and Zubayr, but in this battle

٨٣٣. عَبدُ اللهِ بنُ شَرِيكٍ عَن أبيهِ: لَمّا هُزِمَ النّاسُ يَومَ الجَمَلِ قالَ أميرُ المُؤمِنينَ عليه السلام: لا تَتبَعوا مُوَلِّياً ولا تُجيزوا عَلَىٰ جَريحٍ ومَن أغلَقَ بابَهُ فَهُوَ آمِنٌ، فَلَمّا كانَ يَومُ صِفّينَ قَتَلَ المُقبِلَ وَالمُدبِرَ وأجازَ عَلىٰ جَريحٍ، فَقالَ أبانُ بنُ تَغلِبَ لِعَبدِ اللهِ بنِ شَريكٍ: هٰذِهِ سيرَتانِ مُختَلِفَتانِ، فَقالَ: إنَّ أهلَ الجَمَلِ قَتَلَ طَلحَةَ وَالزُّبَيرَ وإنَّ مُعاوِيَةَ كانَ

Muʿawiya is still present and is himself leading them.'[920]

قائِماً بِعَينِهِ و كانَ قائِدَهُمْ.٩١١

(See also: HUMILITY: 126)

(أُنظر) عنوان ١٢٦ «الخشوع».

249. The Blessings of Imām ʿAlī (AS) Fighting the Aggressors

٢٤٩ ـ بَرَكَةُ قِتالِ الإمامِ عَليٍّ ﷺ البُغاةَ

834. **Imām al-Ṣādiq (AS) said,** 'There was a blessing in the fighting of ʿAlī (AS) against the people of the Qibla, and if ʿAlī (AS) had not fought them no one after him would know how to deal with them.'[921]

٨٣٤. الإمامُ الصّادقُ ﷺ : كانَ في قِتالِ عليٍّ ﷺ أهلَ قِبْلةٍ بَرَكةٌ، ولَو لَم يُقاتِلْهُم عليٌّ ﷺ لَم يَدْرِ أحدٌ بعدَهُ كيفَ يَسيرُ فيهِم.٩١٢

47

WEEPING

البُكاءُ

250. Weeping Due to Fear of Allah

٢٥٠ ـ البُكاءُ مِن خَشيَةِ اللهِ

"When the signs of the All-beneficent were recited to them, they would fall down weeping in prostration."[922]

﴿إذَا تُتْلَىٰ عَلَيْهِمْ آيَاتُ الرَّحْمانِ خَرُّوا سُجَّداً وَبُكِيّاً﴾ .٩١٣

"Weeping, they fall down on their faces, and it increases them in humility."[923]

﴿وَيَخِرُّونَ لِلْأَذْقَانِ يَبْكُونَ وَيَزِيدُهُمْ خُشُوعاً﴾ .٩١٤

835. **The Prophet (SAWA) said,** 'Blessed is a face upon which Allah gazes while it is weeping for a sin out of fear of Allah, the Exalted, and no one else knew about that sin but Him.'[924]

٨٣٥. رسولُ اللهِ ﷺ : طُوبىٰ لِصُورةٍ نَظَرَ اللهُ إلَيها تَبكي علىٰ ذَنبٍ مِن خَشيَةِ اللهِ عزّ وجلّ ، لَم يَطّلِعْ علىٰ ذلكَ الذَّنْبِ غَيْرُهُ.٩١٥

836. **The Prophet (SAWA) said** during the Farewell Sermon, 'And he whose eyes shed tears for the fear of Allah, he will have for every drop of his tears a reward equivalent to the size of Mount Uḥud which will be added to the balance of his [good deeds].'[925]

٨٣٦. عنه ﷺ ـ في خُطبة الوَداعِ ـ: ومَن ذَرَفَتْ عَيناهُ مِن خَشيةِ اللهِ كانَ لَه بكلِّ قَطرةٍ مِن دُموعِهِ مِثلُ جَبَلِ أُحُدٍ يكونُ في ميزانِهِ مِن الأجْرِ.٩١٦

837. **The Prophet (SAWA) said,** 'Seven people will be in the shade of the Throne of Allah, the Exalted, when no shade will avail but His: … and a man who remembered Allah, the Exalted, alone, and his eyes flooded with tears out of fear of Allah.'[926]

٨٣٧. عنه ﷺ : سَبعةٌ في ظِلِّ عَرشِ اللهِ عزّ وجلّ يومَ لا ظِلَّ إلّا ظلُّهُ ... ورجُلٌ ذَكرَ اللهَ عزّ وجلّ خالياً ففاضَتْ عَيناهُ مِن خَشيةِ اللهِ.[٩١٧]

838. **The Prophet (SAWA) said,** 'Whoever sheds a tear as small as the size of a fly out of fear of Allah, Allah will grant him safety on the Day of the Great Terror.'[927]

٨٣٨. عنه ﷺ : مَن خَرَجَ مِن عَينَيهِ مِثلُ الذُّبابِ مِن الدَّمْعِ مِن خَشيَةِ اللهِ آمَنَهُ اللهُ بِهِ يَومَ الفَزَعِ الأكبَرِ.[٩١٨]

839. **Imām ʿAlī (AS) said,** 'The tears in the eyes and the fear in the hearts are part of the mercy of Allah, exalted be His remembrance. When you find them, seize the opportunity for making supplications.'[928]

٨٣٩. الإمامُ عليٌّ عليه السلام : بُكاءُ العُيونِ وخَشْيَةُ القلوبِ مِن رَحْمَةِ اللهِ تعالىٰ ذِكرُهُ، فإذا وَجَدتُموها فاغتَنِموا الدُّعاءَ.[٩١٩]

840. **Imām ʿAlī (AS) said,** 'Weeping out of fear of Allah is the key to [His] mercy.'[929]

٨٤٠. عنه عليه السلام : البُكاءُ مِن خَشيَةِ اللهِ مِفتاحُ الرَّحمةِ.[٩٢٠]

841. **Imām ʿAlī (AS) said,** 'Weeping out of fear of Allah illuminates the heart and shields against returning to the sin.'[930]

٨٤١. عنه عليه السلام : البُكاءُ مِن خَشيةِ اللهِ يُنيرُ القلبَ، ويَعْصِمُ مِن مُعاوَدَةِ الذَّنبِ.[٩٢١]

842. **Imām Zayn al-ʿĀbidīn (AS) said,** 'No drops are more beloved to Allah, the Exalted, than two: a drop of blood [shed] for the sake of Allah, and a teardrop shed by a servant in the darkness of the night solely for Allah's sake.'[931]

٨٤٢. الإمامُ زينُ العابدينَ عليه السلام : ما مِن قَطرةٍ أحَبَّ إلىٰ اللهِ عزّ وجلّ مِن قَطْرَتَينِ : قَطرةُ دَمٍ في سبيلِ اللهِ، وقَطرةُ دَمعَةٍ في سَوادِ اللّيلِ، لا يُريدُ بها عبدٌ إلّا اللهَ عزّ وجلّ.[٩٢٢]

843. **Imām al-Bāqir (AS) said,** 'Every eye will cry on the Day of Judgment except for three: an eye that stayed up [in worship] for the sake of Allah, an eye that filled with tears out of fear of Allah, and an eye that looked away from things prohibited by Allah.'[932]

٨٤٣. الإمامُ الباقرُ عليه السلام : كُلُّ عَينٍ باكيةٌ يومَ القيامةِ غيرَ ثلاثٍ : عينٌ سَهِرَتْ في سبيلِ اللهِ، وعينٌ فاضَتْ مِن خَشيَةِ اللهِ، وعَينٌ غَضّتْ عن مَحارِمِ اللهِ.[٩٢٣]

844. **Imām al-Ṣādiq (AS) said,** 'If weeping does not come naturally to you, force yourself to weep,

٨٤٤. الإمامُ الصّادقُ عليه السلام : إنْ لَم يُجِبْكَ البُكاءُ

for even if a tear as small as a fly's head is shed by you, then congratulations to you.'[933]

فَتَباكَ ، فإنْ خَرجَ مِنكَ مِثلُ رأسِ الذُّبابِ فَبَخٍ بَخٍ.٩٢٤

845. **Imām al-Ṣādiq (AS) said,** 'Every single thing has a measure or a weight, except for tears; for one drop of them can extinguish seas of Fire. If an eye is filled with tears, the face will never be burdened with neediness or humiliation; and if it floods with tears then Allah will make it unlawful for the Fire to touch it. Indeed, if a teary man cries for a community, they all receive mercy.'[934]

٨٤٥. عنه ﷺ : ما مِن شيءٍ إلّا ولَهُ كَيلٌ أو وَزنٌ إلّا الدُّموعَ ، فإنّ القَطرةَ مِنها تُطْفِئُ بِحاراً مِن نارٍ ، وإذا اغْرَوْرَقَتِ العَينُ بمائها لَم يَرْهَقْ وَجهَهُ قَتَرٌ ولا ذِلَّةٌ ، فإذا فاضَتْ حَرَّمَهُ اللهُ على النّارِ ، ولَو أنّ باكياً بكى في أُمَّةٍ لَرُحِموا.٩٢٥

251. Dryness of The Eye

٢٥١ ـ جُمودُ العَينِ

846. **The Prophet (SAWA) said,** 'Dryness of the eye is one of the signs of wretchedness.'[935]

٨٤٦. رسولُ اللهِ ﷺ : مِن عَلاماتِ الشَّقاءِ جُمودُ العَينِ.٩٢٦

847. **Imām ʿAlī (AS) said,** 'Tears only dry up as a result of the hardness of the hearts; and the hearts only harden as a result of an abundance of sins.'[936]

٨٤٧. الإمامُ عليٌّ ﷺ : ما جَفَّتِ الدُّموعُ إلّا لِقَسوةِ القُلوبِ ، وما قَسَتِ القلوبُ إلّا لِكَثرةِ الذُّنوبِ.٩٢٧

48

THE LAND

البَلَد

252. A Fair Territory

٢٥٢ ـ بَلدَةٌ طَيِّبَةٌ

"...a good land and an all-forgiving Lord!"[937]

﴿بَلْدَةٌ طَيِّبَةٌ وَرَبٌّ غَفُورٌ﴾.٩٢٨

"We had placed between them and the towns which We had blessed hamlets prominent [from the main route], and We had ordained the course through them: 'Travel through them in safety, night and day.'"[938]

﴿وَجَعَلْنَا بَيْنَهُمْ وَبَيْنَ الْقُرَى الَّتِي بَارَكْنَا فِيهَا قُرًى ظَاهِرَةً وَقَدَّرْنَا فِيهَا السَّيْرَ سِيرُوا فِيهَا لَيَالِيَ وَأَيَّاماً آمِنِينَ﴾.٩٢٩

(See also: Qur'an 21:71, 21:81, 23:50, 28:29-30, 79:16, 90:1-2, 95:1-3)

(اُنظر: الأنبياء: ٧١، ٨١ و المؤمنون: ٥٠ و القصص: ٢٩، ٣٠ و النازعات: ١٦ و البلد: ١ و ٢، التين: ١ ـ ٣)

253. You Should Live in Great Cities

٢٥٣ ـ عَلَيكُم بِالأمصارِ العِظامِ

848. **Imām ʿAlī (AS) said,** in a letter to al-Ḥārith al-Hamdānī, 'And keep your residence in large

٨٤٨. الإمامُ عليٌّ ﷺ ـ فيما كَتَبَهُ إلى الحارثِ الهَمْدانيِّ ـ : واسكُنِ الأمْصارَ

cities, for they are the gathering places of Muslims; and stay away from places of ignorance and coarseness.'[939]

العِظامَ ، فإنّها جِماعُ المسلمينَ ، واحْذَرْ مَنازِلَ الغَفلَةِ والجَفاءِ.[٩٣٠]

254. The Best of Lands

٢٥٤ ـ خَيرُ البِلادِ

849. **Imām ʿAlī (AS) said,** 'No land claims you more than another; the best land is the one that supports you.'[940]

٨٤٩ . الإمامُ عليٌّ ﷺ : ليسَ بَلَدٌ بأحَقَّ بِكَ مِن بَلَدٍ، خَيرُ البِلادِ ما حَمَلَكَ.[٩٣١]

255. What The People of Every Land Cannot Be Without

٢٥٥ ـ ما لا يَستَغني عَنهُ أهلُ كُلِّ بَلَدٍ

850. **Imām al-Ṣādiq (AS) said,** 'The people of every land cannot be without three [types of people] to whom they rush for the affairs of their life in this world and their Hereafter – and if they lack them, they become savages: a knowledgeable and pious scholar, a good and obeyed ruler, and a trustworthy and experienced physician.'[941]

٨٥٠ . الإمامُ الصّادقُ ﷺ : لا يَستَغْني أهلُ كلِّ بلدٍ عن ثلاثةٍ يُفزَعُ إليهِم في أمرِ دُنياهُم وآخِرَتِهِم ، فإن عَدِموا ذلكَ كانوا هَمَجاً : فَقيهٌ عالِمٌ وَرِعٌ ، وأميرٌ خَيِّرٌ مُطاعٌ ، وطبيبٌ بَصيرٌ ثِقةٌ.[٩٣٢]

49

ELOQUENCE

البَلاغَةُ

256. The Meaning of Eloquence

٢٥٦ ـ تَفسِيرُ البَلاغَةِ

851. **Imām ʿAlī (AS) said,** 'Eloquence is that which is easy [for the speaker] to pronounce and light on the [listener's] intellect.'[942]

٨٥١ . الإمامُ عليٌّ ﷺ : البَلاغةُ ما سَهُلَ على المَنطِقِ وخَفَّ علىٰ الفِطْنَةِ.[٩٣٣]

852. **Imām ʿAlī (AS) said,** 'Eloquence is to answer without delay, and to be correct without mistakes.'[943]

٨٥٢ . عنه ﷺ : البَلاغةُ أنْ تُجِيبَ فلا تُبْطئَ ، وتُصِيبَ فلا تُخْطئَ.[٩٣٤]

853. **Imām ʿAlī (AS) said,** 'Brevity may suffice in accomplishing eloquence.'[944]

٨٥٣ . عنه ﷺ : قد يُكْتَفىٰ مِنَ البَلاغةِ بالإيجازِ.[٩٣٥]

854. **Imām al-Ṣādiq (AS) said,** 'Eloquence is not exemplified by the sharpness of the tongue, nor through excess babbling; rather it is through capturing the intended meaning and aiming at the proof.'[945]

٨٥٤. الإمامُ الصّادقُ ﷺ: لَيسَتِ البَلاغَةُ بِحِدَّةِ اللِّسانِ ولا بِكَثْرَةِ الهَذَيانِ، ولٰكنّها إصابةُ المَعنىٰ وقَصْدُ الحُجّةِ.٩٣٦

855. **Imām al-Ṣādiq (AS) said,** 'Eloquence lies in three things: coming close to the intended meaning, avoiding waffling, and communicating more meaning in fewer words.'[946]

٨٥٥. عنه ﷺ: ثلاثةٌ فيهِنَّ البَلاغةُ: التَّقرُّبُ مِن معنىٰ البُغْيةِ، والتَّبَعُّدُ مِن حَشْوِ الكلامِ، والدَّلالةُ بالقليلِ علىٰ الكثيرِ.٩٣٧

257. The Most Eloquent Speech

٢٥٧ ـ أبلَغُ الكَلامِ

856. **Imām 'Alī (AS) said,** 'The most expressive eloquence lies in that which easily conveys the message, and that which is pleasantly brief.'[947]

٨٥٦. الإمامُ عليٌّ ﷺ: أبلَغُ البَلاغةِ ما سَهُلَ في الصَّوابِ مَجازُهُ وحَسُنَ إيجازُهُ.٩٣٨

857. **Imām 'Alī (AS) said,** 'The best speech is that which is decorated by a pleasant structure and is understood by the elite as well as the laymen.'[948]

٨٥٧. عنه ﷺ: أحسَنُ الكلامِ ما زانَهُ حُسْنُ النِّظامِ، وفَهِمَهُ الخاصُّ والعامُّ.٩٣٩

258. Manipulation Through Speech

٢٥٨ ـ التَّشَدُّقُ فِي الكَلامِ

858. **The Prophet (SAWA) said,** 'The wicked of my nation are the prattlers, the boasters and the haughty, and the best of my nation are the best among them in morals.'[949]

٨٥٨. رسولُ اللهِ ﷺ: شِرارُ أُمَّتي الثَّرثارُونَ، وَالمُتَشَدِّقونَ المُتَفَيهِقونَ، وخِيارُ أُمَّتي أحاسِنُهُم أخلاقاً.٩٤٠

50

PROPAGATION [OF ISLAM]

التَّبليغ

259. The Importance of the Propagation of Islam

٢٥٩ ـ أهَمِّيَّةُ التَّبليغ

"Yet it is not for the faithful to go forth en masse. But why should not there go forth a group from each of their sections to become learned in religion, and to

﴿وَمَا كَانَ ٱلْمُؤْمِنُونَ لِيَنفِرُوا كَآفَّةً فَلَوْلَا نَفَرَ مِن كُلِّ فِرْقَةٍ مِّنْهُمْ طَآئِفَةٌ لِّيَتَفَقَّهُوا فِى ٱلدِّينِ

warn their people when they return to them, so that they may beware?'[950]

وَلِيُنذِرُواْ قَوْمَهُمْ إِذَا رَجَعُوٓاْ إِلَيْهِمْ لَعَلَّهُمْ يَحْذَرُونَ ﴾.٩٤١

859. **The Prophet (SAWA) said,** 'I hereby reiterate what I have said: establish the performance of the prayer, pay the alms-tax, enjoin what is good, and forbid evil. Verily the peak of enjoining what is good and forbidding evil is to heed to my words and propagate them to those who are absent; you must command them to accept [my words] and prohibit them from going against them, for they are the commands from Allah, the Exalted, and from me.'[951]

٨٥٩. رسولُ اللهِ ﷺ : ألا وَإنّي أُجَدِّدُ القَولَ: ألا فَأقيموا الصَّلاةَ، وَآتوا الزَّكاةَ، وَأمُروا بِالمَعروفِ، وَانهَوا عَنِ المُنكَرِ. ألا وَإنَّ رَأسَ الأمرِ بِالمَعروفِ وَالنَّهيِ عَنِ المُنكَرِ أن تَنتَهوا إلى قَولي، وَتُبَلِّغوهُ مَن لَم يَحضُر، وَتَأمُروهُ بِقَبولِهِ، وَتَنهَوهُ عَن مُخالَفَتِهِ؛ فَإنَّهُ أمرٌ مِنَ اللهِ ﷻ وَمِنّي.٩٤٢

860. **The Prophet (SAWA) said,** 'O 'Alī! When Allah guides a man through you, it is better for you than all that the sun shines on.'[952]

٨٦٠. عنه ﷺ : يا عَلِيُّ، لَأن يَهدِيَ اللهُ عَلى يَدَيكَ رَجُلاً خَيرٌ لَكَ مِمّا طَلَعَت عَلَيهِ الشَّمسُ.٩٤٣

861. **The Prophet (SAWA) said,** 'Render Allah beloved to His servants, and He will love you.'[953]

٨٦١. عنه ﷺ : حَبِّبوا اللهَ إلى عِبادِهِ يُحِبَّكُمُ اللهُ.٩٤٤

862. **The Prophet (SAWA) said,** 'Whoever becomes a cause for a man's converting to Islam is guaranteed entry into Paradise.'[954]

٨٦٢. عنه ﷺ : مَن أسلَمَ عَلى يَدَيهِ رَجُلٌ وَجَبَت لَهُ الجَنَّةُ.٩٤٥

863. **The Prophet (SAWA) said,** 'Anyone who calls to what is right will have the same reward as he who follows him, without any decrease in each of their rewards thereof.'[955]

٨٦٣. عنه ﷺ : ما مِن داعٍ يَدعو إلى هُدىً إلّا كانَ لَهُ مِثلُ أجرِ مَنِ اتَّبَعَهُ، لا يَنقُصُ ذلِكَ مِن أُجورِهِم شَيئاً.٩٤٦

864. **The Prophet (SAWA) said,** 'The elect of my community are those who call to [the path] of Allah, the most High, and render Him beloved to His servants.'[956]

٨٦٤. عنه ﷺ : خِيارُ أُمَّتي مَن دَعا إلَى اللهِ تَعالى، وَحَبَّبَ عِبادَهُ إلَيهِ.٩٤٧

865. **Sharīf b. Sābiq al-Taflīsī** narrated on the authority of Ḥammād al-Samdarī: 'I said to Abū 'Abdillāh, Ja'far b. Muḥammad [al-Ṣādiq] (AS), 'I often go to the lands of the idolaters, and people say that if I die there, I will be resurrected with them.' He said to me, 'O Ḥammād! When you are there, do you mention our cause and call people to it?' I said, 'Yes.' He said, 'And when you are in these

٨٦٥. شريفُ بن سابِقِ التفليسي عن حَمّاد السمدري: قُلتُ لِأبي عَبدِاللهِ جَعفَرِ بنِ مُحَمَّدٍ عليه السلام: إنّي أدخُلُ بِلادَ الشِّركِ، وَإنَّ مَن عِندَنا يَقولُ: إن مِتَّ ثَمَّ حُشِرتَ مَعَهُم؟ قالَ: فَقالَ لي: يا حَمّادُ، إذا كُنتَ ثَمَّ، تَذكُرُ أمرَنا وَتَدعو إلَيهِ؟ قالَ: قُلتُ: نَعَم. قالَ: فَإذا كُنتَ في

cities – the cities of Islam – do you mention our cause and call people to it?' I said, 'No.' He said, 'If you die over there, you will be resurrected as a whole community in yourself, and your light will run before you.'[957]

هٰذِهِ المُدُنِ ـ مُدُنِ الإسلامِ ـ تَذكُرُ أمرَنا وَتَدعو إلَيهِ ؟ قالَ: قُلتُ : لا . فَقالَ لي : إنَّكَ إن مِتَّ ثَمَّ حُشِرتَ أُمَّةً وَحدَكَ ، وَسَعى نورُكَ بَينَ يَدَيكَ.٩٤٨

(See also: ENJOINING GOOD AND PROHIBITING WRONG: section 1286)

(أنظر) المعروف (٢): باب ١٢٨٦.

260. What is Incumbent Upon the Propagator of Islam

٢٦٠ ـ ما يَجِبُ عَلَى المُبَلِّغِ

1. Knowledge of the Religion:

١ ـ الفقهُ في الدّينِ

866. **The Prophet (SAWA) said,** 'No one can support [the cause of] the religion of Allah, the Exalted, except for one who is well-versed in all its aspects.'[958]

٨٦٦ . رسولُ اللهِ ﷺ : إنَّ دينَ اللهِ ﷻ لَن يَنصُرَهُ إلّا مَن حاطَهُ مِن جَميعِ جَوانِبِهِ.٩٤٩

2. Referring to the Words of Ahl al-Bayt (AS):

٢ ـ الاستنادُ إلى كَلامِ أهلِ البَيتِ ﷺ

867. **'Abd al-Salām b. Ṣāliḥ al-Harawī said,** 'I heard Abū al-Ḥasan al-Riḍā (AS) saying, 'May Allah have mercy on anyone who revives our cause.' I asked, 'How does he revive your cause?' He replied, 'He learns our sciences and teaches them to the people, for verily if people were to know the goodness in our speech, they would follow us.'[959]

٨٦٧ . عبدُ السلامِ بن صالح الهَرَوي : سَمِعتُ أبا الحسنِ الرِّضا ﷺ يقولُ: رَحِمَ اللهُ عَبداً أحيا أمرَنا. فَقُلتُ لَهُ : فَكَيفَ يُحيي أمرَكُم ؟! قالَ: يَتَعَلَّمُ عُلومَنا وَيُعَلِّمُها النّاسَ ؛ فَإنَّ النّاسَ لَو عَلِموا مَحاسِنَ كَلامِنا لَاتَّبَعونا.٩٥٠

3. Sincerity:

٣ ـ الإخلاص

"I do not ask you any reward for it; my reward lies only with the Lord of all the worlds."[960]

﴿وَمَا أَسْـَٔلُكُمْ عَلَيْهِ مِنْ أَجْرٍ إِنْ أَجْرِىَ إِلَّا عَلَىٰ رَبِّ ٱلْعَـٰلَمِينَ﴾ .٩٥١

868. **The Prophet (SAWA) said,** 'Every single servant who delivers a sermon, Allah, the Exalted, will ask him about it and what he meant by it.'[961]

٨٦٨ . رسولُ اللهِ ﷺ : ما مِن عَبدٍ يَخطِبُ خُطبَةً إلّا اللهُ ﷻ سائِلُه عَنها ما أرادَ بِها.٩٥٢

4. Courage:

٤ ـ الشُّجاعَة

"...such as deliver the messages of Allah and fear Him, and fear no one except Allah, and Allah suffices as reckoner."[962]

﴿ٱلَّذِينَ يُبَلِّغُونَ رِسَـٰلَـٰتِ ٱللَّهِ وَيَخْشَوْنَهُۥ وَلَا يَخْشَوْنَ أَحَدًا إِلَّا ٱللَّهَ وَكَفَىٰ بِٱللَّهِ حَسِيبًا﴾ .٩٥٣

869. **The Prophet (SAWA) said,** 'Speak the truth, and let no one's blame for obeying Allah affect you.'[963]

٨٦٩. رسولُ الله ﷺ: قُل الحقَّ، وَلا تَأخُذكَ في الله لَومَةُ لائِمٍ.٩٥٤

870. **The Prophet (SAWA) said,** 'Let not the fear of people prevent any of you from speaking the truth, when he sees or witnesses it, for telling the truth or reminding [others] of a great event [the Hereafter] will neither hasten death nor delay sustenance.'[964]

٨٧٠. عنه ﷺ: لا يَمنَعَنَّ أحَدَكُم رَهبَةُ النّاسِ أن يَقولَ بِحقٍّ إذا رَآهُ أو شَهِدَهُ؛ فَإنَّهُ لا يُقَرِّبُ مِن أجَلٍ، وَلا يُباعِدُ مِن رِزقٍ أن يَقولَ بِحَقٍّ، أو يُذَكِّرَ بِعَظيمٍ.٩٥٥

5. Honesty:

٥ـ الصِّدقُ

871. **Imām al-Ṣādiq (AS) said,** in what is attributed to him in '*Miṣbāḥ al-Sharīʿa*': 'The best advice is that which does not carry the statement beyond the limits of honesty, nor the act the limits of sincerity.'[965]

٨٧١. الإمامُ الصّادقُ ﷺ ـ فيما يُنسَبُ إلَيهِ في مِصباحِ الشَّريعَةِ ـ: أحسَنُ المَواعِظِ ما لا يُجاوِزُ القَولُ حَدَّ الصِّدقِ، وَالفِعلُ حَدَّ الإخلاصِ.٩٥٦

872. **ʿAmr b. Abī Miqdām said,** 'Abū Jaʿfar (AS) said, when I first went to visit him, 'Learn honesty before speech.'[966]

٨٧٢. عَمرو بن أبي المِقدام: قالَ لي أبو جعفرٍ ﷺ ـ في أوَّلِ دَخلَةٍ دَخَلتُ عَلَيهِ ـ: تَعَلَّموا الصِّدقَ قَبلَ الحَديثِ.٩٥٧

6. Kindness:

٦ـ الرِّفقُ

873. **The Prophet (SAWA) said,** 'Ease and do not cause hardship [when propagating], and comfort and do not nauseate.'[967]

٨٧٣. رسولُ الله ﷺ: يَسِّروا وَلا تُعَسِّروا، وَسَكِّنوا وَلا تُنَفِّروا.٩٥٨

874. **The Prophet (SAWA) said,** 'I have been commanded to be tolerant towards people as much as I have been commanded to deliver the Message.'[968]

٨٧٤. عنه ﷺ: أُمِرتُ بِمُداراةِ النّاسِ كَما أُمِرتُ بِتَبليغِ الرِّسالَةِ.٩٥٩

875. **Imām al-Ṣādiq (AS) said** to 'Umar b. Ḥanẓala, 'O 'Umar! Do not overburden our followers (*shīʿa*), and be kind to them, for people cannot endure what you can.'[969]

٨٧٥. الإمامُ الصّادقُ ﷺ ـ لِعُمرَ بنِ حَنظَلَةَ ـ: يا عُمَرُ، لا تُحَمِّلوا عَلى شيعَتِنا، وَارفُقوا بِهِم؛ فَإنَّ النّاسَ لا يَحتَمِلونَ ما تَحمِلونَ.٩٦٠

7. Good Advice:

٧ـ النُّصحُ

"I communicate to you the messages of my Lord and I am a trustworthy well-wisher for you."[970]

﴿أُبَلِّغُكُمْ رِسَالَاتِ رَبِّي وَأَنَا لَكُمْ نَاصِحٌ أَمِينٌ﴾.٩٦١

876. **Imām ʿAlī (AS) said,** mentioning the virtue of the honourable Prophet (SAWA), 'He [Allah] sent him while the people were straying in perplexity, and engaged in corruption... He (SAWA) advised extensively and kept on the [right] path, and called for wisdom and gentle exhortation.'[971]

٨٧٦. الإمامُ عَليٌّ عليه السلام ـ في ذِكرِ فَضيلَةِ الرَّسولِ الكَريمِ ـ: بَعَثَهُ وَالنّاسُ ضُلّالٌ في حَيرَةٍ، وَحاطِبونَ في فِتنَةٍ... فَبالَغَ صلى الله عليه وآله في النَّصيحَةِ، وَمَضى عَلَى الطَّريقَةِ، وَدَعا إلَى الحِكمَةِ وَالمَوعِظَةِ الحَسَنَةِ.[٩٦٢]

8.Coherence of the Heart and the Tongue:

٨ ـ تَطابُقُ القَلبِ وَاللِسانِ

877. **Imām ʿAlī (AS) said** in the sayings attributed to him, 'When a word comes from the heart, it falls onto the heart; but when it merely comes from the tongue, it will not go farther than the ears.'[972]

٨٧٧. الإمامُ عليٌّ عليه السلام ـ في الحِكَمِ المَنسوبَةِ إلَيهِ ـ: الكَلِمَةُ إذا خَرَجَت مِنَ القَلبِ وَقَعَت فِي القَلبِ، وَإذا خَرَجَت مِنَ اللِسانِ لَم تُجاوِزِ الآذانَ.[٩٦٣]

9. Preaching through Action:

٩ ـ التَبليغُ بِالعَمَلِ

878. **Imām al-Ṣādiq (AS) said,** 'Invite people to what is good with other than your tongues, so that they see tenacity, veracity, and piety in you.'[973]

٨٧٨. الإمامُ الصادقُ عليه السلام: كونوا دُعاةً لِلنّاسِ بِالخَيرِ بِغَيرِ ألسِنَتِكُم؛ لِيَرَوا مِنكُمُ الاجتِهادَ وَالصِّدقَ وَالوَرَعَ.[٩٦٤]

879. **Imām al-Ṣādiq (AS) said,** 'May Allah have mercy on the people who are a lamp and a beacon. They call to our cause with their actions and the best of their efforts.'[974]

٨٧٩. عنه عليه السلام: رَحِمَ اللهُ قَوماً كانوا سِراجاً وَمَناراً؛ كانوا دُعاةً إلَينا بِأعمالِهِم وَمَجهودِ طاقَتِهِم.[٩٦٥]

(See also: ENJOINING GOOD AND PROHIBITING WRONG: section 1289)

(انظر) باب المعروف (٢): ١٢٨٩.

51

THE ORDEAL

البَلاءُ

261. Testing with Events, Good and Bad

٢٦١ ـ الابتِلاءُ بِالشَّرِّ وَالخَيرِ

"We will test you with good and ill by way of test."[975]

﴿وَنَبْلُوكُمْ بِالشَّرِّ وَالْخَيْرِ فِتْنَةً﴾.[٩٦٦]

880. **Imām al-Ṣādiq (AS) said,** 'There is no tension or ease, unless it involves Allah's favour and test.'[976]

٨٨٠ . الإمامُ الصّادقُ عليه‌السلام : ما مِن قَبضٍ ولا بَسطٍ إلّا ولله فيهِ المَنُّ والابْتِلاءُ .[٩٦٧]

881. **Imām al-Ṣādiq (AS) said,** 'There is nothing that has tension or ease from all that Allah has commanded or prohibited except that it involves a test and a judgment from Allah, the Exalted.'[977]

٨٨١ . عنه عليه‌السلام : ليسَ شيءٌ فيهِ قَبضٌ أو بَسطٌ مِمّا أمرَ اللهُ بِهِ أو نهىٰ عنهُ إلّا وفيهِ مِن اللهِ عزّ وجلّ ابْتِلاءٌ وقَضاءٌ .[٩٦٨]

262. The Reason for Testing

٢٦٢ ـ حِكمَةُ الابتِلاءِ

"... so that Allah may test what is in your breasts, and that He may purge what is in your hearts, and Allah knows best what is in the breasts."[978]

﴿وَلِيَبْتَلِيَ اللهُ مَا فِي صُدُورِكُمْ وَلِيُمَحِّصَ مَا فِي قُلُوبِكُمْ وَاللهُ عَلِيمٌ بِذَاتِ الصُّدُورِ﴾ .[٩٦٩]

"We will surely test you until We ascertain those of you who wage jihād and those who are steadfast, and We shall appraise your record."[979]

﴿وَلَنَبْلُوَنَّكُمْ حَتَّىٰ نَعْلَمَ الْمُجَاهِدِينَ مِنْكُمْ وَالصَّابِرِينَ وَنَبْلُوَ أَخْبَارَكُمْ﴾ .[٩٧٠]

"He, who created death and life that He may test you [to see] which of you is best in conduct. And He is the All-mighty, the All-forgiving."[980]

﴿الَّذِي خَلَقَ الْمَوْتَ وَالْحَيَاةَ لِيَبْلُوَكُمْ أَيُّكُمْ أَحْسَنُ عَمَلاً وهُوَ العَزِيزُ الغَفُورُ﴾ .[٩٧١]

882. **Imām ʿAlī (AS) said,** 'Know that Allah, most High, uncovered the people, not because He was ignorant of their well-kept secrets and inner thoughts, but in order to test them [to see] which of them is best in conduct, so that reward becomes the prize and punishment becomes the penalty.'[981]

٨٨٢ . الإمامُ عليٌّ عليه‌السلام : أَلَا إنّ اللهَ تعالىٰ قد كَشفَ الخَلقَ كَشْفةً ، لا أنّه جَهِلَ ما أخْفَوهُ مِن مَصُونِ أسْرارِهِم ومَكْنونِ ضَمائرِهِم ، ولٰكنْ لِيَبلُوَهُم أيُّهُم أحْسَنُ عَملاً ، فيكونَ الثّوابُ جَزاءً والعِقابُ بَواءً .[٩٧٢]

883. **Imām ʿAlī (AS) said,** 'The greater the ordeal and test, the greater the reward and recompense. Do you not see that Allah, the Praiseworthy, tested our precursors from the time of Adam, peace be upon him, to the last generations in this world, with [the creation of] stones that neither harm nor benefit, nor do they see or hear, and He made from them His sacred House, which He made a standing place for people?! But Allah tries His servants with various ordeals, and obligates them with various forms of

٨٨٣ . عنه عليه‌السلام : كُلّما كانتِ البَلوىٰ والاختبارُ أعظمَ كانتِ المَثُوبةُ والجَزاءُ أجْزَلَ ، أَلَا تَرَونَ أنَّ الله سبحانه اختَبرَ الأوَّلِينَ مِن لَدُنْ آدمَ صلواتُ اللهِ عليهِ إلىٰ الآخِرينَ مِن هذاالعالَمِ بأحجارٍ لا تَضُرُّ ولا تَنفَعُ ، ولا تُبصِرُ ولا تَسمَعُ ، فجَعَلَها بَيتَهُ الحَرامَ الّذي جَعَلَهَ اللهُ للنّاسِ قِياماً ...؟! ولكنّ الله يَختبِرُ عِبادَهُ بأنواعِ الشَّدائدِ ، ويَتَعبّدُهُم بأنواعِ المَجاهِدِ ، ويَبْتَليهِم بضُروبِ

struggle, and tests them with various dreads, in order to eradicate vanity from their hearts and instill humility in their souls and that this may open the doors to His favour and the feasible means to His forgiveness.'[982]

المَكارِهِ ؛ إخْراجاً للتَّكَبُّرِ مِن قلوبِهِمْ ، وإسْكاناً للتَّذَلُّلِ في نُفوسِهِم ، وليَجْعلَ ذلكَ أبـواباً فُـتُحاً إلىٰ فضلِهِ ، وأسباباً ذُلُلاً لِعَفوِهِ.[٩٧٣]

884. **Imām 'Alī (AS) said,** 'Verily you will be put in tense perplexity and be finely filtered, until you are turned upside down; then certain people will surpass [others] after having lagged behind, while those who were ahead fall back.'[983]

٨٨٤. عنه ﷺ: لَتُبَلْبَلُنّ بَلْبَلَةً، ولَتُغربَلُنّ غَرْبَلَةً، حتّى يعودَ أسفلُكُم أعلاكم، وأعلاكم أسفلَكُم، وليَسبِقَنّ سَبّاقونَ كانوا قَصَّروا، وليُقَصِّرَنّ سبّاقونَ كانوا سَبَقوا.[٩٧٤]

885. **Imām 'Alī (AS) said,** 'Do not rejoice at wealth and luxury, nor dread poverty and ordeal; for verily gold is tested by the fire and the believer is tested by an ordeal.'[984]

٨٨٥. عنه ﷺ: لا تَفرَحْ بالغَناءِ والرَّخاءِ، ولا تَغتَمَّ بالفقرِ والبلاءِ؛ فإنّ الذَّهبَ يُجَرَّبُ بالنّارِ، والمؤمنُ يُجَرَّبُ بالبلاءِ.[٩٧٥]

263. The Severity of a Believer's Ordeal

٢٦٣ ـ شِدّة ابتِلاءِ المُؤمِنِ

"Do you suppose that you shall enter paradise though there has not yet come to you the like of [what befell] those who went before you? Stress and distress befell them and they were convulsed until the apostle and the faithful who were with him said, 'When will Allah's help [come]?' Look! Allah's help is indeed near!"[985]

﴿أَمْ حَسِبْتُمْ أَنْ تَدْخُلُوا الْجَنَّةَ وَلَمَّا يَأْتِكُمْ مَثَلُ الَّذِينَ خَلَوْا مِنْ قَبْلِكُمْ مَسَّتْهُمُ الْبَأْسَاءُ وَالضَّرَّاءُ وَزُلْزِلُوا حَتَّىٰ يَقُولَ الرَّسُولُ وَالَّذِينَ آمَنُوا مَعَهُ مَتَىٰ نَصْرُ اللهِ أَلَا إِنَّ نَصْرَ اللهِ قَرِيبٌ﴾.[٩٧٦]

886. **Imām 'Alī (AS) said,** 'Verily the ordeal is faster in descending upon a pious believer than rain to the bottom of the earth.'[986]

٨٨٦. الإمامُ عليٌّ ﷺ: إنّ البلاءَ أسرَعُ إلى المؤمنِ التّقيِّ مِن المَطرِ إلىٰ قَرارِ الأرضِ.[٩٧٧]

887. **Imām al-Ṣādiq (AS) said,** 'The prophets have the hardest ordeals from among people, then their successors, then they scale down according to their piety.'[987]

٨٨٧. الإمامُ الصّادقُ ﷺ: إنّ أشدَّ النّاسِ بلاءً الأنبياءُ، ثُمّ الّذين يَلونَهُم، ثُمّ الأمثَلُ فالأمثلُ.[٩٧٨]

888. **Imām al-Bāqir (AS) said,** 'Verily a believer is tested with all calamities and dies in any kind of death, but he does not kill himself.'[988]

٨٨٨. الإمامُ الباقرُ ﷺ: إنّ المؤمنَ يُبتَلىٰ بكُلِّ بَليّةٍ، ويَموتُ بكُلِّ ميتةٍ، إلّا أنّهُ لا يَقتُلُ نفسَهُ.[٩٧٩]

264. The Role of Evil Actions in the Onset of Ordeals

٢٦٤ـ دَورُ الأعمالِ السَّيِّئَةِ في وقوعِ البَلاءِ

"Whatever affliction that may visit you is because of what your hands have earned, and He excuses many [an offense]."[989]

﴿وَما أَصابَكُمْ مِنْ مُصِيبَةٍ فَبِمَا كَسَبَتْ أَيْدِيكُمْ وَيَعْفُو عَنْ كَثِيرٍ﴾.[٩٨٠]

889. **The Prophet (SAWA) said,** 'Allah, most High, revealed to Prophet Job[990], 'Do you know what your sin against Me was that brought ordeals down upon you?' He said, 'No.' He said, 'You entered the court of the pharaoh and uttered two flattering words.'[991]

٨٨٩. رسولُ اللهِ ﷺ: أوْحىٰ اللهُ تعالىٰ إلىٰ أيُّوبَ: هَل تدري ما ذَنبُكَ إليَّ حينَ أصابَكَ البلاءُ؟ قالَ: لا. قالَ: إنّكَ دَخَلتَ علىٰ فِرْعَونَ فَداهَنْتَ في كَلِمتَينِ.[٩٨١]

(See also: SINNING: section 777)

(أُنظر) الذنب: باب ٧٧٧.

265. Whoever is not Tried With Ordeals is Despised by Allah

٢٦٥ـ مَن لَم يُبتَلَ فَهُوَ مَبغوضٌ عِندَ اللهِ

890. **The Prophet (SAWA) said,** 'Allah loathes the withdrawn wicked man, who never sustains any harm to his body or wealth.'[992]

٨٩٠. رسولُ اللهِ ﷺ: إنَّ اللهَ يُبغِضُ العِفْرِيَةَ النِّفْرِيَةَ الّذي لَم يُرْزَأْ في جِسمِهِ ولا مالِهِ.[٩٨٢]

891. **Imām Zayn al-ʿĀbidīn (AS) said,** 'I hate for a man to be immune [to ordeals] in this world's life and not suffer any affliction.'[993]

٨٩١. الإمامُ زينُ العابدينَ عليه السلام: إنّي لَأكرَهُ أنْ يُعافىٰ الرَّجُلُ في الدُّنيا ولا يُصيبَهُ شَيءٌ مِن المَصائبِ.[٩٨٣]

(See also: SICKNESS: section 1652; VITALITY: 1326)

(أُنظر) المرض: باب ١٦٥٢؛ العافية: باب ١٣٢٦.

266. The Ordeal as a Bounty

٢٦٦ـ نِعمَةُ البَلاءِ

892. **The Prophet (SAWA) said,** 'Allah feeds His believing servant with ordeals like a mother feeds her child milk.'[994]

٨٩٢. رسولُ اللهِ ﷺ: إنَّ اللهَ لَيُغذّي عَبدَهُ المؤمنَ بالبلاءِ كما تُغذِّي الوالِدَةُ ولَدَها باللَّبَنِ.[٩٨٤]

893. **The Prophet (SAWA) said,** 'When Allah wants good for a people, he tries them.'[995]

٨٩٣. عنه ﷺ: إذا أرادَ اللهُ بقَومٍ خَيراً ابْتَلاهُم.[٩٨٥]

894. **Imām al-Bāqir (AS) said,** 'Allah, the Exalted, brings trial to the believer like a man brings his family a gift upon his return from a trip; and He

٨٩٤. الإمامُ الباقرُ عليه السلام: إنَّ اللهَ عزّ وجلّ لَيَتعاهَدُ المؤمنَ بالبلاءِ كما يَتعاهَدُ الرَّجُلُ أهلَهُ بالهَدِيّةِ مِن الغَيبةِ، ويَحْميهِ الدُّنيا كما

denies him this world like a doctor puts a patient on diet.’[996]

يَحْمي الطَّبيبُ المريضَ.[٩٨٦]

895. **Imām al-Kāẓim (AS) said,** ‘You will not be believers until you consider the ordeal as a bounty and ease as an affliction, for patience during an ordeal is greater than oblivion during ease.’[997]

٨٩٥. الإمامُ الكاظمُ عليه السلام: لَن تكونوا مؤمنينَ حتّى تَعُدّوا البلاءَ نِعمَةً والرَّخاءَ مُصيبَةً، وذلكَ أنّ الصَّبرَ عِندَ البلاءِ أعظَمُ مِن الغَفلَةِ عندَ الرَّخاءِ.[٩٨٧]

896. **Imām al-‘Askarī (AS) said,** ‘Every single ordeal contains a favour from Allah that encompasses it.’[998]

٨٩٦. الإمامُ العسكريُّ عليه السلام: ما مِن بَلِيَّةٍ إلّا وللهِ فيها نِعمَةٌ تُحيطُ بِها.[٩٨٨]

267. Ordeals and Admonition

٢٦٧ ـ البلاءُ وَ التَّذكيرُ

“Certainly We afflicted Pharaoh’s clan with droughts and loss of produce, so that they may take admonition.”[999]

﴿وَلَقَدْ أَخَذْنَا آلَ فِرْعَوْنَ بِالسِّنِينَ وَنَقْصٍ مِنَ الثَّمَرَاتِ لَعَلَّهُمْ يَذَّكَّرُونَ﴾.[٩٨٩]

897. **Imām ‘Alī (AS) said,** when he set out to pray for rain, ‘Allah tries His servants when they commit evil deeds, with shortage of crops, disallowance of blessings and closing the treasury of bounties, so that a repenting man may repent, a man likely to quit may quit, a man likely to remember may remember, and a man likely to be deterred may be deterred.’[1000]

٨٩٧. الإمامُ عليٌّ عليه السلام ـ وقد خَرَجَ للاستِسقاءِ ـ: إنّ اللهَ يَبتَلي عِبادَهُ عِندَ الأعمالِ السَّيِّئَةِ بنَقصِ الثَّمَراتِ وحَبسِ البَرَكاتِ وإغلاقِ خَزائنِ الخَيراتِ، لِيَتوبَ تائبٌ ويُقلِعَ مُقلِعٌ ويَتَذَكَّرَ مُتَذَكِّرٌ ويَزدَجِرَ مُزدَجِرٌ.[٩٩٠]

898. **Imām al-Ṣādiq (AS) said,** ‘No more than forty nights can pass on a believer without something that saddens him and causes him to remember [Allah’s admonition].’[1001]

٨٩٨. الإمامُ الصّادقُ عليه السلام: المؤمنُ لا يَمْضي علَيهِ أربَعونَ لَيلةً إلّا عَرَضَ لهُ أمرٌ يُحزِنُهُ يُذَكَّرُ بِه.[٩٩١]

899. **Imām al-Ṣādiq (AS) said,** ‘When Allah wants good for a servant who commits a sin, He follows it with a punishment and reminds him to ask for forgiveness. But if Allah, wants bad for a servant who commits a sin, He follows it with a favour that makes him forget to ask for forgiveness and continue sinning. This is the meaning of Allah’s verse, *“We will draw them*

٨٩٩. عنه عليه السلام: إذا أرادَ اللهُ عزّ وجلّ بعبدٍ خيراً فأذْنَبَ ذَنباً تَبِعَهُ بِنَقِمَةٍ ويُذَكِّرُهُ الاستِغفارَ، وإذا أرادَ اللهُ عزّ وجلّ بعبدٍ شَرّاً فأذنَبَ ذَنباً تَبِعَهُ بِنِعمَةٍ لِيُنسِيَهُ الاستِغفارَ ويَتَمادىٰ بِهِ، وهُو قولُ

imperceptibly [into ruin], whence they do not know"[1002]: with favours whenever they sin.'[1003]

الله عـزّ وجـلّ: ﴿سَنَستدرِجُهُم من حيثُ لا يعلمونَ﴾ [٩٩٢] بالنِّعَمِ عند المَعاصي.[٩٩٣]

(See also: GOOD MANNERS: section 54; SICKNESS: section 1652)

(أنظر) الأدب: باب ٥٤؛ المرض: باب ١٦٥٢.

268. Sins are Offset by Ordeals

٢٦٨ ـ تَمحيصُ البَلاءِ لِلذُّنوبِ

900. **Imām ʿAlī (AS) said,** 'Praise be to Allah, Who offset the sins of our followers (*shīʿa*) through their hardships, so that their obedience remains immune through it and they become deserving of reward as a result of it.'[1004]

٩٠٠. الإمامُ عليٌّ (عليه السلام): الحَمدُ للهِ الّذي جَعلَ تَمْحيصَ ذُنوبِ شِيعتِنا في الدُّنيا بمِحْنَتِهِم، لِتَسلَمَ بِها طاعاتُهُم ويَسْتَحِقّوا علَيها ثَوابَها.[٩٩٤]

901. **Imām ʿAlī (AS) said,** 'Whenever Allah punishes a believing servant in this world, [it is only because] He is too Clement, too Glorious, too Generous, and too Kind to requite him with punishment on the Day of Resurrection.'[1005]

٩٠١. عنه (عليه السلام): ما عاقَبَ اللهُ عَبداً مؤمناً في هذهِ الدُّنيا إلّا كانَ اللهُ أحْلَمَ وأمْجَدَ وأجْوَدَ وأكْرَمَ مِن أنْ يَعودَ في عِقابِهِ يومَ القيامةِ.[٩٩٥]

902. **Imām al-Bāqir (AS) said,** 'When Allah, Blessed and most High, wants to honour a servant who has previously committed a sin, He tries him with illness, and if not with that then with need. And if not with that, then He makes his death difficult. But when He wants to humiliate a servant who has done some good previously, He makes his body healthy, or makes his sustenance abundant, or makes his death easy.'[1006]

٩٠٢. الإمامُ الباقرُ (عليه السلام): إنَّ اللهَ تباركَ وتعالىٰ إذا كانَ مِن أمْرِهِ أن يُكرِمَ عَبداً وله عِندَهُ ذَنبٌ ابْتَلاهُ بالسُّقْمِ، فإنْ لَم يَفعَلْ فبالحاجةِ، فإنْ لَم يَفعَلْ شَدَّدَ علَيهِ عندَ المَوتِ. وإذا كانَ مِن أمرِهِ أنْ يُهينَ عَبداً ولَه عندَهُ حَسَنةٌ أصَحَّ بَدنَهُ، فإنْ لم يفعلْ وسَّعَ علَيهِ في مَعيشتِهِ، فإنْ لَم يَفعلْ هَوَّنَ علَيهِ المَوتَ.[٩٩٦]

(See also: SINNING: section 780)

(أنظر) الذنب: باب ٧٨٠.

269. The Ordeal is the Sign of Allah's Love, Glory be to Him

٢٦٩ ـ البَلاءُ عَلامَةُ مَحَبَّةِ اللهِ سُبحانَهُ

903. **Imām al-Ṣādiq (AS) said,** in the presence of Sadīr, 'When Allah loves a servant, He immerses him completely in ordeal. O Sadīr! We and you are in it day and night.'[1007]

٩٠٣. الإمامُ الصّادقُ (عليه السلام) ـ وعندَه سَديرٌ ـ: إنَّ اللهَ إذا أحَبَّ عبداً غَتَّهُ بالبلاءِ غَتّاً، وإنّا وإيّاكُم يا سَديرُ لَنُصبِحُ بهِ ونُمسي.[٩٩٧]

904. **Imām al-Ṣādiq (AS) said,** 'When Allah loves a people, or a certain servant, He pours ordeals down heavily on him, so that whenever he

٩٠٤. عنه (عليه السلام): إذا أحَبَّ اللهُ قَوماً أو أحَبَّ عبداً صَبَّ علَيهِ البلاءَ صَبّاً، فلا يَخرُجُ مِن

exits from a [source of] anguish he falls into another.'[1008]

غَمٍّ إلّا وقعَ في غَمٍّ.٩٩٨

(See also: LOVE: section 436)

(أنظر) المحبّة: باب ٤٣٦.

270. Ordeals Correspond to the Level of One's Faith

٢٧٠ ـ البَلاءُ عَلى قَدرِ الإيمانِ

905. **Imām al-Bāqir (AS) said,** 'The more faith a servant attains, the harder his life becomes.'[1009]

٩٠٥. الإمامُ الباقرُ عليه السلام : كُلَّما ازْدادَ العبدُ إيماناً ازْدادَ ضِيقاً في مَعيشَتِهِ.٩٩٩

906. **Imām al-Bāqir (AS) said,** 'Verily the believer is tested according to the level of his faith.'[1010]

٩٠٦. الكافي عن جابر بن يزيد عن الإمامِ الباقرِ عليه السلام : إنّما يَبتَلِي المُؤمِنُ فِي الدُّنيا عَلى قَدرِ دِينِهِ.١٠٠٠

907. **Imām al-Ṣādiq (AS) said,** 'It is written in the Book of ʿAlī (AS), 'The believer is tested according to the level of his good deeds, so whoever is sound of faith and good deeds, his ordeals are more intense. And that is because Allah, the Exalted, did not make this life a [source of] reward for a believer, nor a [source of] punishment for a disbeliever. However, he whose faith and deeds are weak, his ordeal is also little.'[1011]

٩٠٧. الإمامُ الصّادقُ عليه السلام ـ في كتابِ عليٍّ عليه السلام ـ: إنّما يُبتلىٰ المؤمنُ علىٰ قَدْرِ أعمالِهِ الحَسَنةِ، فمَن صَحَّ دينُهُ وحَسُنَ عملُهُ اشتدَّ بلاؤهُ، وذلكَ أنَّ اللهَ عزّ وجلّ لم يَجعلِ الدُّنيا ثواباً لمؤمنٍ، ولا عُقوبةً لكافرٍ، ومَن سَخُفَ دِينُهُ وضَعُفَ عملُهُ قلَّ بلاؤهُ.١٠٠١

908. **Imām al-Kāẓim (AS) said,** 'A believer is like the two sides of a balance: the more faith he has the more ordeal he sustains, so that he meets Allah, the Exalted, without any sins.'[1012]

٩٠٨. الإمامُ الكاظمُ عليه السلام : مَثَلُ المؤمنِ مَثَلُ كِفَّتَي المِيزانِ: كلّما زِيدَ في إيمانِهِ زِيدَ في بَلائهِ، لِيَلْقَى اللهَ عزّ وجلّ ولا خَطيئةَ لَه.١٠٠٢

271. The Levels that a Servant Attains as a Result of Ordeals

٢٧١ ـ الدَّرَجاتُ الّتي يَبلُغُها العَبدُ بِالبَلاءِ

909. **Imām al-Ṣādiq (AS) said,** 'There is a rank in Paradise which no servant can reach except through suffering harm in his body.'[1013]

٩٠٩. الإمامُ الصّادقُ عليه السلام : إنّ في الجَنّةِ مَنزِلةً لا يَبلُغُها عبدٌ إلّا بالابْتِلاءِ في جَسدِهِ.١٠٠٣

910. **Imām al-Ṣādiq (AS) said,** 'There is a rank that Allah reserves for the servant which he can only attain through one of two things: either the loss of his wealth or through affliction in his body.'[1014]

٩١٠. عنه عليه السلام : إنّه لَيكونُ للعبدِ مَنزِلةٌ عندَ اللهِ فما يَنالُها إلّا بإحدىٰ خَصْلَتَينِ: إمّا بذَهابِ مالِهِ أو بِبَلِيّةٍ في جَسدِهِ.١٠٠٤

(See also: PARADISE: section 368)

(أنظر) الجنّة: باب ٣٦٨.

272. A Believer's Trial is for his Own Good

٢٧٢ ـ ابتِلاءُ المُؤمِنِ خَيرٌ لَهُ

911. **Imām al-Ṣādiq (AS) said,** 'Among what Allah, the Exalted, revealed to Prophet Moses: 'I have not created anything as dear to Me as My believing servant, so when I try him, I do so for his own good, and I make him prosper for his own good, and I shield him for his own good. And I know best what improves My servant, so let him endure My trial and be thankful for My favours, and be content with My decree, and I will record him among the righteous.'[1015]

٩١١ . الإمامُ الصّادقُ عليه السلام ـ فيما أوحىٰ الله تعالىٰ إلىٰ موسىٰ عليه السلام ـ: ما خَلَقتُ خَلْقاً أحَبَّ إليَّ من عَبديَ المؤمنِ ، فإنّي إنّما أبْتَلِيهِ لِمَا هُو خَير لَهُ ، وأُعافِيهِ لِما هُو خيرٌ لَهُ ، وأزْوِي عَنهُ لِما هُوَ خَيرٌ لَهُ ، وأنا أعلَمُ بما يَصلُحُ علَيهِ عبدى ، فلْيَصْبِرْ علىٰ بلائي ، ولْيَشكُرْ نَعْمائي ، ولْيَرْضِ بقَضائي ، أكتُبْهُ في الصِّدِّيقينَ عِندي.[١٠٠٥]

(See also: DECREE: section 1533)

(أُنظر) القضاء: باب ١٥٣٣.

273. The Most Severe Trial of Servants

٢٧٣ ـ أشَدُّ ما ابتُلِيَ بِهِ العِبادُ

912. **Imām ʿAlī (AS) said,** 'Allah does not try anyone with something similar to giving him all the chances [to continue disobeying Him].'[1016]

٩١٢ . الإمامُ عليٌّ عليه السلام : ما ابْتَلىٰ اللهُ أحَداً بمِثلِ الإمْلاءِ لَهُ.[١٠٠٦]

913. **Imām ʿAlī (AS) said,** 'Poverty is part of the trial, and worse than that is the sickness of the body, and worse than that is the sickness of the heart.'[1017]

٩١٣ . عنه عليه السلام : إنّ مِن البلاءِ الفاقةَ ، وأشدُّ مِن ذلكَ مَرضُ البَدنِ ، وأشدُّ مِن ذلكَ مَرضُ القلبِ.[١٠٠٧]

914. **Imām al-Ṣādiq (AS) said,** 'Allah has not tested the servants with anything more severe than having to spend money.'[1018]

٩١٤ . الإمامُ الصّادقُ عليه السلام : ما بَلا اللهُ العِبادَ بشَيءٍ أشَدَّ علَيهِم مِن إخْراجِ الدِّرْهَمِ.[١٠٠٨]

915. **Imām al-Ṣādiq (AS) said,** 'Whoever is plagued by one of three things wishes to die: continuous poverty, a disgraceful wife, and an overpowering enemy.'[1019]

٩١٥ . عنه عليه السلام : ثلاثٌ مَنِ ابتُليَ بواحدةٍ مِنهُنَّ تَمنَّى الموتَ : فَقرٌ مُتَتابعٌ ، وحُرْمَةٌ فاضِحَةٌ ، وعدُوٌّ غالِبٌ.[١٠٠٩]

(See also: TRIAL AND TEMPTATION: section 1464; AFFLICTION: section 1154)

(انظر) الفتنة: باب ١٤٦٤؛ المصيبة: باب ١١٥٤.

274. Salvation at the Peak of the Ordeal

٢٧٤ ـ الفَرَجُ عِندَ تَناهِي البَلاءِ

916. **Imām ʿAlī (AS) said,** 'Salvation comes at the peak of the ordeal.'[1020]

٩١٦ . الإمامُ عليٌّ ﷺ : عندَ تَناهِي البلاءِ يكونُ الفَرَجُ.١٠٢٠

917. **Imām al-Ṣādiq (AS) said,** 'When an ordeal is added to another, relief will result from the ordeal.'[1021]

٩١٧ . الإمامُ الصّادقُ ﷺ : إذا اُضِيفَ البلاءُ إلى البلاءِ كانَ مِنَ البلاءِ عافيةً.١٠٢١

275. Remembrance of Allah at the Time of an Ordeal

٢٧٥ ـ ذِكرُ اللهِ عِندَ البَلاءِ

"Those who, when an affliction visits them, say, 'Indeed we belong to Allah, and to Him do we indeed return."[1022]

﴿الَّذِينَ إِذَا أَصَابَتْهُم مُّصِيبَةٌ قَالُوا إِنَّا لِلَّهِ وَإِنَّا إِلَيْهِ رَاجِعُونَ﴾.١٠٢٢

918. **Imām ʿAlī (AS) said,** 'During every hardship, say, 'There is no power or strength save in Allah, the High and the Great' (*lā ḥawla wa lā quwwata illā billāh al-ʿalīy al-ʿaẓīm*) and you will surmount it.'[1023]

٩١٨ . الإمامُ عليٌّ ﷺ : قُلْ عندَ كلِّ شِدّةٍ: «لا حَولَ ولا قُوّةَ إلّا باللهِ العليِّ العظيمِ» تُكْفَها.١٠٢٣

919. **Imām al-Riḍā (AS) said,** 'I saw my father in a dream, saying, 'Son, whenever you are in hardship, say abundantly, 'O Kind! O Merciful!' (*yā ra'ūf! yā raḥīm!*) Indeed, what you see in a dream is the same as what you see when you are awake.'[1024]

٩١٩ . الإمامُ الرِّضا ﷺ : رأيتُ أبي ﷺ في المَنامِ فقالَ: يا بُنَيَّ ، إذا كُنتَ في شِدّةٍ فأكْثِرْ أنْ تقولَ: «يا رؤوفُ يا رحيمُ»، والّذي تَراهُ في المَنامِ كما تَراهُ في اليَقَظةِ.١٠٢٤

(See also: SUPPLICATION: section 689)

(اُنظر) الدعاء: باب ٦٨٩.

276. Supplication when Seeing a Man being Tried with an Ordeal

٢٧٦ ـ الدُّعاءُ عِندَ رُؤيَةِ المُبتَلى

920. **The Prophet (SAWA) said,** 'When you see people in ordeal, praise Allah without letting them hear you, lest it saddens them.'[1025]

٩٢٠ . رسولُ اللهِ ﷺ : إذا رأيتُمْ أهلَ البلاءِ فاحمَدوا اللهَ ولا تُسمِعوهُم، فإنَّ ذلكَ يَحزُنُهُم.١٠٢٥

921. **Imām al-Bāqir (AS) said,** 'When you see a man in ordeal, say three times, without letting him hear you: 'Praise to Allah Who spared me what He tried you with, though He could have if He willed it so'. He said, 'Whoever says this will never be afflicted with that ordeal.'[1026]

٩٢١ . الإمامُ الباقرُ عليه السلام : تقولُ ثلاثَ مرّاتٍ، إذا نَظَرتَ إلىٰ المُبتلىٰ مِن غيرِ أنْ تُسمِعَهُ : الحمدُ للهِ الّذي عافاني مِمّا ابتلاكَ بهِ ولو شاءَ فعلَ . مَن قالَ ذلكَ لَم يُصِبْهُ ذلكَ البلاءُ أبداً .[١٠١٦]

52

SLANDER

البُهتانُ

277. Warning Against Slander

٢٧٧ ـ التَّحذِيرُ مِنَ البُهتانِ

"Those who torment faithful men and women undeservedly, certainly bear the guilt of slander and flagrant sin."[1027]

﴿وَالَّذِينَ يُؤْذُونَ الْمُؤْمِنِينَ وَالْمُؤْمِناتِ بِغَيْرِ ما اكْتَسَبُوا فَقَدِ احْتَمَلُوا بُهْتاناً وَإِثْماً مُبِيناً﴾ .[١٠١٧]

(See also: Qur'an 17:36, 24:12-15, 49:12)

(أُنظر) الإسراء: ٣٦ والنور: ١٢ ـ ١٥ والحجرات: ١٢.

922. **The Prophet (SAWA) said,** 'Whoever surreptitiously slanders a believing man or a woman, or says about him what is not in him, Allah, the Exalted, will place him on a hill of fire on the Day of Judgment, until he renounces what he said about him.'[1028]

٩٢٢ . رسولُ اللهِ صلى الله عليه وآله : مَن بَهَتَ مؤمناً أو مؤمنةً أو قالَ فيهِ ما ليسَ فيهِ أقامَهُ اللهُ تعالىٰ يومَ القيامةِ علىٰ تَلٍّ مِن نارٍ حتّىٰ يَخرُجَ مِمّا قالَهُ فيهِ .[١٠١٨]

923. **Imām ʿAlī (AS) said,** 'There is no impudence worse than slander.'[1029]

٩٢٣ . الإمامُ عليٌّ عليه السلام : لا قِحَةَ كالبَهْتِ .[١٠١٩]

924. **Imām ʿAlī (AS) said,** 'Slandering an innocent person is more immense than the skies.'[1030]

٩٢٤ . عنه عليه السلام : البُهتانُ علىٰ البَريءِ أعظَمُ مِن السَّماءِ .[١٠٢٠]

925. **Imām Zayn al-ʿĀbidīn (AS) said,** 'Whoever charges others with what is in them provokes them to charge him with what is not in him.'[1031]

٩٢٥ . الإمامُ زينُ العابدينَ عليه السلام : مَن رمىٰ النّاسَ بِما فيهِم رَمَوهُ بِما ليسَ فيهِ .[١٠٢١]

926. **Imām al-Ṣādiq (AS) said,** quoting a wise man, 'Slandering an innocent person is heavier than lofty mountains.'[1032]

٩٢٦ . الإمامُ الصّادقُ عليه السلام ـ ناقِلاً عن حكيمٍ ـ : البُهْتانُ علىٰ البَريءِ أثْقَلُ مِن الجِبالِ الرّاسِياتِ .[١٠٢٢]

53

RECIPROCAL INVOCATION OF ALLAH'S CURSE (*Mubāhala*)

المُبَاهَلَة

278. Reciprocal Invocation of Allah's Curse

٢٧٨ ـ المُباهَلَةُ

"Should anyone argue with you concerning him, after the knowledge that has come to you, say, 'Come! Let us call our sons and your sons, our women and your women, our souls and your souls, then let us pray earnestly and call down Allah's curse upon the liars."[1033]

﴿فَمَنْ حاجَّكَ فِيهِ مِنْ بَعْدِ ما جاءَكَ مِنَ الْعِلْمِ فَقُلْ تَعالَوْا نَدْعُ أَبْناءَنا وَأَبْناءَكُمْ وَنِساءَنا وَنِساءَكُمْ وَأَنْفُسَنا وَأَنْفُسَكُمْ ثُمَّ نَبْتَهِلْ فَنَجْعَلْ لَعْنَةَ اللهِ عَلَى الْكاذِبِينَ﴾.[١٠٣٣]

927. **Imām al-Ṣādiq (AS) said** to Abū al-'Abbās about the reciprocal invocation of Allah's curse, 'You cross your fingers with his fingers and say, 'O Allah! If so-and-so has disputed the truth and attested to a falsehood, then strike him with a bolt from the sky or some torment from You.' Then you exchange curses with him seventy times.'[1034]

٩٢٧ . الإمامُ الصّادقُ ﷺ ـ لأبي العبّاسِ في المُباهَلة ـ: تُشَبِّكُ أصابِعَكَ في أصابِعِهِ ثُمَّ تقولُ: «اللّهُمَّ إنْ كانَ فُلانٌ جَحَدَ حقّاً وأقَرَّ بباطلٍ فأصِبْهُ بِحُسْبانٍ مِن السَّماءِ أو بِعذابٍ مِن عِندِكَ» وتُلاعِنُهُ سَبعينَ مرّةً.[١٠٢٤]

928. **Imām al-Ṣādiq (AS) said,** 'When the Christians of Najrān came to the Prophet (SAWA), their chiefs were al-Ahtam, al-'Āqib and al-Sayyid…they asked, 'To what do you call us?' He said, 'To bear witness that there is no god but Allah and that I am the Messenger of Allah, and that Jesus was a created servant who ate, drank [water] and relieved himself'… the Prophet (SAWA) said, 'Then invoke Allah's curse upon me. If I am telling the truth, the curse will descend upon yourselves and if not, then it will descend upon me.' They said, 'You have spoken fairly.' Then they made an appointment for the challenge. When they returned to their homes, their chiefs told them…'If he comes to invoke curse upon us

٩٢٨ . عنه ﷺ : إنّ نَصارىٰ نَجْرانَ لَمّا وَفَدوا علىٰ رسولِ اللهِ ﷺ وكانَ سيّدُهُم الأهْتَمَ والعاقِبَ والسَّيّدَ ... فقالوا : إلىٰ ما تَدْعون ؟ فقالَ : إلىٰ شَهادَةِ أنْ لا إلهَ إلّا اللهُ وأنّي رسولُ اللهِ وأنّ عيسىٰ عَبدٌ مَخلوقٌ يأكُلُ ويَشْرَبُ ويُحْدِثُ ... فقالَ رسولُ اللهِ ﷺ : فباهِلُوني ، فإنْ كُنتُ صادقاً نزلَتِ اللّعنةُ علَيكُم ، وإنْ كنتُ كاذباً اُنزِلَتْ علَيَّ، فقالوا : أنْصَفْتَ ، فتَواعَدوا للمُباهَلةِ . فلَمّا رجَعوا إلىٰ مَنازِلهم قالَ رؤساؤهُم... : إنْ باهَلَنا بقَومِهِ باهَلْناهُ ، فإنَّهُ ليسَ بِنَبيٍّ ، وإنْ

with his people, we will accept the challenge, because he would not be a prophet, but if he challenges us with his close family, we must not accept, for he would not risk his own family unless he was truthful. When the morning arrived, they came to the Prophet (SAWA), and he was accompanied by the Commander of the Faithful, Fāṭima, al-Ḥasan, and al-Ḥusayn…They got scared and said to the Prophet (SAWA), 'We will give you what you want, so spare us this mutual invocation of curse.' The Prophet (SAWA) made a truce with them that they pay the tax (*jizya*) and they went back.'[1035]

باهَلَنا بأهْلِ بَيتِهِ خاصّةً فلا نُباهِلُهُ ، فإنَّهُ لا يُقْدِمُ علىٰ أهلِ بيتِهِ إلّا وهُو صادقٌ .
فلَمّا أصبَحوا جاؤُوا إلىٰ رسولِ اللهِ ﷺ ومعَهُ أميرُ المؤمنينَ وفاطمةُ والحسنُ والحسينُ صلوات الله عليهم ... فعَرَفوا[١٠٢٥] وقالوا لرسولِ اللهِ ﷺ : نُعْطيكَ الرِّضا فَأعْفِنا من المُباهَلة ، فصالَحَهُم رسولُ اللهِ ﷺ علىٰ الجِزيةِ وانْصَرَفُوا.[١٠٢٦]

54

OATH OF ALLEGIANCE

البَيعَة

279. Swearing Allegiance to the Prophet is Swearing Allegiance to Allah

٢٧٩ ـ بَيعَةُ النَّبِيِ بَيعَةُ اللهِ

"Indeed those who swear allegiance to you, swear allegiance only to Allah: the hand of Allah is above their hands. So whosoever breaks his oath, breaks it only to his own detriment, and whoever fulfills the covenant he has made with Allah, He will give him a great reward."[1036]

﴿إنَّ الَّذِينَ يُبايِعُونَكَ إنَّما يُبايِعُونَ اللهَ يَدُ اللهِ فَوْقَ أَيْدِيهِمْ فَمَن نَكَثَ فَإنَّمَا يَنْكُثُ عَلَىٰ نَفْسِهِ وَمَنْ أَوْفَىٰ بِما عاهَدَ عَلَيْهُ اللهَ فَسَيُؤْتِيهِ أَجْراً عَظِيماً﴾ .[١٠٢٧]

929. **ʿAlī b. Ibrāhīm narrated,** 'In the covenant of al-Riḍwān it was revealed that: *"Allah was certainly pleased with the faithful when they swore allegiance to you under the tree. He knew what was in their hearts…"*[1037] and He put a condition for them that after that they will never dispute with the Prophet (SAWA) about anything he does, or disobey him in anything he might order them to do. Then Allah, the Exalted, said after that verse: *"Indeed those who swear allegiance to you…"*[1038]

٩٢٩ . عليُّ بنُ ابراهيم : ونَزلَتْ في بَيعةِ الرِّضوانِ : ﴿لقد رضِيَ اللهُ عن الْمُؤْمِنِينَ إذْ يُبايِعُونَكَ تَحْتَ الشَّجَرَةِ فَعَلِمَ ما في قُلُوبِهِمْ فَأَنْزَلَ السَّكِينَةَ عَلَيهِمْ وَأَثابَهُمْ فَتْحاً قَرِيباً﴾ واشْتَرطَ علَيهِم أنْ لا يُنكِروا بعدَ ذلكَ علىٰ رسولِ اللهِ ﷺ شيئاً يَفعَلُهُ ، ولا يُخالِفوهُ في شيءٍ يأمُرُهُم بهِ ، فقالَ اللهُ عزّ وجلّ بعدَ نُزولِ آيةِ الرِّضوانِ : ﴿إنّ الّذينَ يُبايِعونَكَ إنَّما يُبايِعُونَ اللهَ﴾ .[١٠٢٨]

930. **Salama b. al-Akwaʿ,** when he was asked, 'Until what term did you give your allegiance to

٩٣٠ . صحيح مسلم عن سَلَمةَ بنِ الأكْوَعِ ـ وقَدسُئل : علىٰ أيِّ شَيءٍ بايَعْتُم رسولَ اللهِ ﷺ يومَ

the Prophet (SAWA) on the day of al-Ḥudaybiyya?', replied, 'Until death.'[1039]

الحُدَيبِيَةِ ؟ ـ: على المَوتِ.١٠٢٩

280. Women's Allegiance

٢٨٠ ـ كيفيّةُ بيعةِ النِّساءِ

"O Prophet! If faithful women come to you, to take the oath of allegiance to you, [pledging] that they shall not ascribe any partners to Allah, that they shall not steal, nor commit adultery, nor kill their children, nor utter any slander that they may have intentionally fabricated, nor disobey you in what is right, then accept their allegiance, and plead for them to Allah for forgiveness. Indeed Allah is all-forgiving, all-merciful."[1040]

﴿يا أَيُّها النَّبِيُّ إِذا جاءَكَ الْمُؤْمِناتُ يُبايِعْنَكَ عَلَى أَنْ لا يُشْرِكْنَ بِاللهِ شَيْئاً وَلا يَسْرِقْنَ وَلا يَزْنِينَ وَلا يَقْتُلْنَ أَوْلادَهُنَّ وَلا يَأْتِينَ بِبُهْتانٍ يَفْتَرِينَهُ بَيْنَ أَيْدِيهِنَّ وَأَرْجُلِهِنَّ وَلا يَعْصِينَكَ فِي مَعْرُوفٍ فَبايِعْهُنَّ وَاسْتَغْفِرْ لَهُنَّ اللهَ إِنَّ اللهَ غَفُورٌ رَحِيمٌ﴾.١٠٣٠

931. **Imām al-Jawād (AS) said,** 'The way in which the women gave allegiance to the Prophet (SAWA) was that he immersed his hand in a bowl filled with water then he took it out. The women then immersed their hands in the bowl as a sign of their acknowledgement and belief in Allah, and belief in his Messenger.'[1041]

٩٣١. الإمامُ الجوادُ عليه السلام: كانَتْ مُبايَعةُ رسولِ اللهِ ﷺ النِّساءَ أنْ يَغْمِسَ يَدَهُ في إناءٍ فيه ماءٌ ثُمّ يُخرِجُها، وتَغمِسَ النِّساءُ بأيدِيهِنَّ في ذلكَ الإناءِ بالإقرارِ والإيمانِ باللهِ والتّصديقِ برسولِهِ.١٠٣١

281. Retraction of Allegiance

٢٨١ ـ نَكثُ البَيعَةِ

"Fulfill Allah's covenant when you pledge, and do not break [your] oaths after pledging them solemnly. And having made Allah a witness over yourselves. Indeed Allah knows what you do."[1042]

﴿وَأَوْفُوا بِعَهْدِ اللهِ إِذا عاهَدْتُمْ وَلا تَنْقُضُوا الْأَيْمانَ بَعْدَ تَوْكِيدِها وَقَدْ جَعَلْتُمُ اللهَ عَلَيْكُمْ كَفِيلاً إِنَّ اللهَ يَعْلَمُ ما تَفْعَلُونَ﴾.١٠٣٢

932. **The Prophet (SAWA) said,** 'Three people Allah will not speak to… and a man who gave his allegiance to an Imām only for the sake of this world, such that if he gives him thereof what he wants he keeps his oath, otherwise he turns away.'[1043]

٩٣٢. رسولُ اللهِ ﷺ: ثلاثةٌ لا يُكلِّمُهُمُ اللهُ... رجُلٌ بايَعَ إماماً لا يُبايِعُهُ إلّا للدُّنيا، إنْ أعطاهُ مِنها ما يُريدُ وَفى لَهُ، وإلّا كَفَّ.١٠٣٣

933. **Imām ʿAlī (AS) said,** 'There is a city in Hell named al-Ḥaṣīna; will you not ask me about it?' He was asked, 'What is in it, O Commander of the Faithful?' He replied, 'In it are the hands of those who violated their covenants.'[1044]

٩٣٣. بحارالأنوار عن الإمام عليّ عليه السلام: إنّ في النّارِ لَمدينةً يُقالُ لها الحَصِينةُ، أفَلا تَسألوني ما فيها؟ فقيلَ لَهُ: وما فِيها يا أميرَ المؤمنينَ؟ قالَ: فيها أيْدي النّاكِثينَ.١٠٣٤

934. **Imām ʿAlī (AS),** when someone asked him, 'For what reason did you fight Ṭalḥa and al-Zubayr?', replied, 'I fought them for violating their oath of allegiance to me and for their killing of my followers (*shīʿa*).'[1045]

٩٣٤ . الإمامُ عليٌّ عليه السلام ـ في جوابِ مَن سأله: على ما قاتلتَ طَلحة والزُّبيرَ ؟ ـ: قاتلْتُهم على نَقْضِهِم بَيْعَتي وقَتْلِهِم شِيعَتي مِن المؤمنينَ.[١٠٣٥]

935. **Imām al-Riḍā (AS) said,** 'A man will not remain immune from a bad fate when he violates his covenant.'[1046]

٩٣٥ . الإمامُ الرِّضا عليه السلام : لا يَعْدَمُ المرءُ دائرةَ السَّوءِ مَعَ نَكْثِ الصَّفْقَةِ.[١٠٣٦]

282. The Muslims' Oath of Allegiance to Imām ʿAlī (AS)

٢٨٢ ـ بَيعَةُ المُسلِمينَ لِلإمامِ عَلِيٍّ عليه السلام

936. **Imām ʿAlī (AS) said,** in his letter to the people of Kufa on his way from Madina to Baṣra, 'People swore allegiance to me being neither forced nor reluctant, but with the sense of obedience and willingly.'[1047]

٩٣٦ . الإمامُ عليٌّ عليه السلام ـ في كتابِهِ إلَى أهلِ الكوفةِ عِندَ مَسيرِهِ مِنَ المَدينَةِ إلى البَصرَةِ ـ: بايَعَني النّاسُ غَيرَ مُستَكرَهينَ، ولا مُجبَرينَ، بَل طائِعينَ مُخَيَّرينَ.[١٠٣٧]

937. **Imām ʿAlī (AS) said,** 'You rushed to me like camels that rush to water, eager to give me your allegiance.'[1048]

٩٣٧ . عنه عليه السلام: تكَأْكَأتُم علَيَّ تكَأْكُؤَ الإبلِ علىٰ حِياضِها؛ حِرْصاً علىٰ بَيْعتي.[١٠٣٨]

55

COMMERCE

التِّجارَةُ

283. The Virtue of Trading

٢٨٣ ـ فَضلُ التِّجارَةِ

"O you who have faith! Do not eat up your wealth among yourselves unrightfully, but it should be trade by mutual consent. And do not kill yourselves. Indeed Allah is most merciful to you."[1049]

﴿يا أَيُّهَا الَّذِينَ آمَنُوا لَا تَأْكُلُوا أَمْوالَكُمْ بَيْنَكُمْ بِالْباطِلِ إِلَّا أَنْ تَكُونَ تِجارَةً عَنْ تَراضٍ مِنْكُمْ وَلَا تَقْتُلُوا أَنْفُسَكُمْ إِنَّ اللهَ كانَ بِكُمْ رَحِيماً﴾.[١٠٣٩]

938. **Imām ʿAlī (AS) said,** 'Practice the various trades, for there is in them independence for you from what is in the hands of others, and indeed Allah loves the one gainfully engaged in a profession.'[1050]

٩٣٨ . الإمامُ عليٌّ عليه السلام: تعرَّضوا للتِّجاراتِ، فإنَّ لَكُم فيها غِنىً عمّا في أيْدي النّاسِ، وإنّ اللهَ عزَّ وجلّ يُحِبُّ المُحترِفَ الأمينَ.[١٠٤٠]

939. **Imām al-Ṣādiq (AS) said,** 'Trading enhances the intellect.'[1051]

٩٣٩ . الإمامُ الصّادقُ عليه السلام : التِّــجارةُ تَـزيدُ فـي العقلِ.[١٠٤١]

284. Abandoning Trading

٢٨٤ ـ تَركُ التِّجارَةِ

940. **Imām al-Ṣādiq (AS) said,** 'Abandoning trading diminishes the intellect.'[1052]

٩٤٠ . الإمامُ الصّادقُ عليه السلام : تَرْكُ التّجارةِ يَـنْقُصُ العقلَ.[١٠٤٢]

941. **Imām al-Ṣādiq (AS),** when the clothes merchant, Muʿādh b. Kathīr told him, 'I intend to leave the market while I have some money in hand', said, 'Then regard for you will fall and you will not be sought for help with anything.'[1053]

٩٤١ . عنه عليه السلام ـ وقد قالَ لَهُ مُعاذُ بنُ كثيرٍ بَـيّاعُ الأكْسِيَةِ : إنّي قد هَمَمْتُ أنْ أدَعَ السُّـوقَ وفـي يَدي شَيءٌ ـ : إذَنْ يَسْقُطَ رأيُكَ ولا يُسْتعانَ بكَ علىٰ شيءٍ.[١٠٤٣]

285. The Etiquette of Trading

٢٨٥ ـ آدابُ التِّجارَةِ

942. **The Prophet (SAWA) said,** 'Whoever sells or buys must avoid five habits, or he should not sell or buy at all: usury, [false] oaths, hiding the defects [of merchandise], praising what he sells, and showing disapproval for what he intends to buy.'[1054]

٩٤٢ . رسولُ اللهِ صلى الله عليه وآله : مَـــن بـــاعَ واشْـــتَرىٰ فلْيَجْتَنِبْ خَمسَ خِـصالٍ، وإلّا فـلا يَـبيعَنَّ ولا يَشْـتَرِيَنَّ: الرِّبـا، والحَـلْفَ، وكِـتْمانَ العَـيبِ، والحمدَ إذا باعَ، والذَّمَّ إذا اشْتَرىٰ.[١٠٤٤]

943. **Imām ʿAlī (AS) said,** 'The timid merchant is often deprived and the bold merchant is often endowed with profit.'[1055]

٩٤٣ . الإمامُ عليٌّ عليه السلام : التّاجرُ الجَبانُ مَحرومٌ، والتّاجرُ الجَسورُ مَرزوقٌ.[١٠٤٥]

944. **Imām ʿAlī (AS) said,** 'O merchants! Knowledge [of trading laws] first, then the trade itself! Knowledge first, then trade! Knowledge first, then trade!'[1056]

٩٤٤ . عنه عليه السلام : يا مَعشَرَ التُّجّارِ، الفِقْهَ ثُمَّ المَتْجَرَ، الفِقْهَ ثُمّ المَتْجَرَ، الفِقْهَ ثُمّ المَتْجَرَ.[١٠٤٦]

945. **Imām ʿAlī (AS) said,** 'O merchants! Start off by seeking a good outcome from Allah, seek the blessing in easy conduct, draw near to customers, beautify yourselves with clemency, refrain from oaths, abandon lies, avoid wronging, be fair to those being wronged, stay away from usury, and *"Observe fully the measure and the balance, with justice, and do not cheat the people of their goods, and do not act wickedly on the earth, causing corruption."*'[1057] [1058]

٩٤٥ . عنه عليه السلام : يــا مَــعشرَ التُّـجّارِ، قَـدِّموا الاسْتِخارةَ، وتَبرَّكوا بـالسُّهولةِ، واقـتَرِبوا مِـن المُبْتاعِينَ، وتَزَيَّنوا بالحِلْمِ، وتَناهَوا عن اليَمينِ، وجانِبوا الكَذِبَ، وتَخافوا (تَجافَوا) عنِ الظُّلْمِ، وأنْصِفوا المظلومِينَ، ولا تَقْرَبوا الرِّبـا، وأوْفُـوا الكَيْلَ والمِيزانَ، ولا تَبْخَسوا النّاسَ أشـياءهُم، ولاتَعْثَوا في الأرضِ مُفسدينَ.[١٠٤٧] [١٠٤٨]

946. **Imām al-Ṣādiq (AS) said,** 'Whoever wants to trade must learn his religion thoroughly in order to know what is allowed and what is forbidden for him; and whoever does not learn about his religion and then practices trading will certainly get entangled into uncertainties and problems.'[1059]

٩٤٦ . الإمامُ الصّادقُ ﷺ : مَن أرادَ التّجارةَ فلْيَتفقَّهْ في دِينِهِ لِيَعلمَ بذلكَ ما يَحِلُّ لَهُ مِمّا يَحْرُمُ علَيهِ ، ومَن لَم يَتَفقّهْ في دِينِهِ ثُمّ اتّجَرَ تَورَّطَ الشُّبُهاتِ.[١٠٤٩]

947. **Imām al-Ṣādiq (AS) said,** 'Any Muslim who excuses another Muslim for a regrettable deal, Allah, the Exalted, will forgive his lapse on the Day of Judgment.'[1060]

٩٤٧ . عنه ﷺ : أيُّما مسلِمٍ أقالَ مسلِماً بَيعَ نَدامَةٍ أقالَهُ اللهُ عزّ وجلّ عَثْرَتَهُ يَومَ القيامةِ.[١٠٥٠]

(See also: WEALTH: section 1671)

(أنظر) التنمية الاقتصادية في الكتاب والسنة / الفصل الرابع: السوق. المال: باب ١٦٧١.

286. The Prohibition of Cheating [by Giving Less than Due] in Trade

٢٨٦ ـ النّهيُ عن التطفيف

"Woe to the defrauders who use short measures, who, when they measure [a commodity bought] from the people, take the full measure, but diminish when they measure or weigh for them."[1061]

﴿وَيْلٌ لِلْمُطَفِّفِينَ * الَّذِينَ إِذَا اكْتَالُوا عَلَى النَّاسِ يَسْتَوْفُونَ * وَإِذَا كَالُوهُمْ أَوْ وَزَنُوهُمْ يُخْسِرُونَ﴾.[١٠٥١]

(See also: Qur'an 6:152, 11:84-85, 26:181-183, 55:7-9)

(أنظر) الأنعام: ١٥٢ و هود: ٨٤، ٨٥ و الشعراء: ١٨١ ـ ١٨٣ و الرحمن: ٧ ـ ٩.

948. **The Prophet (SAWA) said,** 'When you weigh, tip the balance [in favour of the customer].'[1062]

٩٤٨ . رسولُ اللهِ ﷺ : إذا وَزَنْتُم فأرْجِحوا.[١٠٥٢]

949. **Imām al-Ṣādiq (AS) said,** 'The deal is not fulfilled until the balance is tipped [in favour of the customer].'[1063]

٩٤٩ . الإمامُ الصّادقُ ﷺ : لا يكونُ الوفاءُ حتّى يَميلَ المِيزانُ.[١٠٥٣]

287. Enjoinment Upon the Trader to Give Charity

٢٨٧ ـ حَثُّ التّاجِرِ علَى التَّصدُّقِ

950. **The Prophet (SAWA) said,** 'O merchants! Satan and sin are always present during the trade, so mix your trades with charity.'[1064]

٩٥٠ . رسولُ اللهِ ﷺ : يا مَعشرَ التُّجّارِ، إنَّ هذا البَيعَ يَحضُرُهُ اللّغوُ والحَلفُ ، فَشُوبُوهُ بالصَّدَقةِ.[١٠٥٤]

288. Leniency in Selling and Buying

٢٨٨ ـ التَّساهُلُ فِي البَيعِ وَ الشِّراءِ

951. **The Prophet (SAWA) said,** 'May Allah bestow mercy on someone who is liberal when he sells, when he buys, when he judges, and when he is judged.'[1065]

٩٥١ . رسولُ اللهِ ﷺ : رَحِمَ اللهُ عبداً سَمْحاً إذا باعَ، سَمْحاً إذا اشْتَرىٰ، سَمحاً إذا قضىٰ، سَمحاً إذا اقْتَضىٰ.[١٠٥٥]

952. **Imām ʿAlī (AS)** once admonished a man who was selling something, 'I heard the Prophet (SAWA) saying, 'Leniency is one way to profit.'[1066]

٩٥٢ . الإمامُ عليٌّ عليه السلام ـ لِرجُلٍ يُوصيهِ ومَعهُ سِلْعَةٌ يَبيعُها ـ: سَمِعْتُ رسولَ اللهِ ﷺ يقولُ : السَّماحُ وَجهٌ مِن الرِّباحِ.[١٠٥٦]

289. Bargaining

٢٨٩ ـ المُماكَسَةِ

953. **The Prophet (SAWA) said,** 'O ʿAlī! Do not bargain for four things: when selling the sacrificial animal [for the obligatory pilgrimage], the shroud, the servant, and transportation to Makkah.'[1067]

٩٥٣ . رسولُ اللهِ ﷺ : يا عليُّ، لا تُماكِسْ في أربَعةِ أشياءَ : في شِراءِ الأُضْحِيّةِ ، والكفَنِ ، والنَّسَمةِ ، والكَرْيِ إلىٰ مَكّةَ.[١٠٥٧]

954. **Imām ʿAli (AS) said,** 'Bargain even for two dirhams, as he who is wronged is neither praised nor is he rewarded.'[1068]

٩٥٤ . الإمامُ عليٌّ عليه السلام : ماكِسْ عَنْ دِرهَمَيكَ ؛ فَإنَّ المَغبونَ لا مَحمودٌ ولا مَأجورٌ.[١٠٥٨]

290. Equality between One who Bargains and One who does not

٢٩٠ ـ التَّسويَةُ بَينَ المُماكِسِ وغَيرِهِ

955. **Imām al-Ṣādiq (AS) said** regarding a man who has a commodity and marks it for sale at a certain price; he would sell it to any silent buyer for the marked price, but he would make a better offer for the bargainer: 'If he were to make a better offer for two or three men, it would not be a problem; but if he does that for everyone who bargains with him and not for non-bargainers, his deed would not appeal to me, unless he sells it all in one deal.'[1069]

٩٥٥ . الإمامُ الصّادقُ عليه السلام ـ في رجُلٍ عِندَهُ بَيْعٌ، فَسَعّرَهُ سِعْراً مَعلوماً ، فمَنْ سَكَتَ عنهُ مِمّنْ يَشْتري مِنهُ باعَهُ بذلكَ السِّعْرِ ، ومَن ماكَسَهُ وأبى أنْ يَبْتاعَ مِنهُ زادَهُ ـ: لو كانَ يَزيدُ الرَّجُلَين والثَّلاثةَ لم يَكُنْ بذلكَ بَأسٌ ، فأمّا أنْ يَفعَلَهُ بمَنَ أبىٰ علَيهِ وكايَسَهُ ويَمْنَعَهُ مِمَّن لَم يَفْعَلْ ذلك فلا يُعْجِبُني إلّا أنْ يَبيعَهُ بَيْعاً واحِداً.[١٠٥٩]

291. The Profit of a Believer From Another

٢٩١ -رِبحُ المُؤمِنِ عَلَى المُؤمِنِ

956. **Imām al-Ṣādiq (AS) said,** 'The profit of a believer from another is usury, unless he buys with more than one hundred dirhams, whereupon you can profit as much as your day's sustenance; or if he buys it for trading, then you can profit, but be moderate with them.'[1070]

٩٥٦ . الإمامُ الصّادقُ عليه السلام : رِبْحُ المؤمنِ علىٰ المؤمنِ رِبا ، إلّاأنْ يَشْتريَ بأكْثَرَ مِن مائةِ دِرْهَمٍ فاربَحْ علَيهِ قُوتَ يَومِكَ ، أو يَشْتَرِيَهُ للتِّجارةِ فارْبَحُوا علَيهِم وارْفُقوا بهِم.[١٠٦٠]

957. **Imām al-Ṣādiq (AS),** when he was asked about the statement: 'The profit of a believer from another is usury', replied, 'That is when equity prevails, and our Qā'im [i.e. the Mahdī] appears; but for now, it does not matter.'[1071]

٩٥٧ . عنه عليه السلام ـ وقد سُئلَ عنِ الخَبَرِ الّذي رُويَ أنّ رِبْحَ المؤمنِ علىٰ المؤمنِ رِبا ، ما هُو ؟ ـ: ذاكَ إذا ظَهرَ الحقُّ وقامَ قائمُناأهلَ البيتِ ، فأمّا اليومَ فلا بأسَ.[١٠٦١]

292. The Iniquity of Merchants

٢٩٢ -فُجورُ التُّجّارِ

958. **The Prophet (SAWA) said,** 'Verily the merchants are the debauchers.' They asked, 'O Messenger of Allah! But has Allah not made trading lawful?' He said, 'Yes, but they lie when they speak, and they take [false] oaths and incur sins.'[1072]

٩٥٨ . كنز العمّال عن رسول الله صلى الله عليه وآله : إنّ التُّجّارَ هُمُ الفُجّارُ . قالوا : يا رسولَ اللهِ، أليسَ قد أحلَّ اللهُ البَيْعَ ؟ قالَ : بلىٰ، ولكنَّهُم يُحَدِّثونَ فيَكْذِبونَ، ويَحْلِفونَ فيَأثَمونَ.[١٠٦٢]

959. It is narrated in *Kanz al-'Ummāl*: "Alī (AS) used to go to the market and stand in his usual place to say, 'Peace be upon you, O people of the market! Fear Allah in your oaths, for the oath degrades the commodity and drives away the blessing. The merchant is iniquitous except for he who takes and gives only what is right.'[1073]

٩٥٩ . كنز العمّال : كان عليٌّ عليه السلام يَجيءُ إلىٰ السُّوقِ فيقومُ مَقاماً له ، فيقولُ : السّلامُ عليكم أهلَ السُّوقِ ، اتَّقوا اللهَ في الحَلْفِ ، فإنّ الحَلفَ يُزجي السِّلْعَةَ ويَمْحَقُ البَرَكةَ، التّاجرُ فاجرٌ إلّا مَن أخذَ الحقَّ وأعْطاهُ.[١٠٦٣]

293. Enjoinment of the Merchant's Veracity

٢٩٣ -حَثُّ التُّجارِ عَلى الصِّدقِ

960. **The Prophet (SAWA) said,** 'The trustworthy honest Muslim merchant will be with the martyrs on the Day of Judgment.'[1074]

٩٦٠ . رسولُ اللهِ صلى الله عليه وآله : التّاجرُ الأمينُ الصَّدوقُ المسلِمُ معَ الشّهداءِ يَومَ القيامةِ.[١٠٦٤]

961. **The Prophet (SAWA) said,** 'The honest merchant will be in the shade of the Throne on the Day of Judgment.'[1075]

٩٦١ . عنه ﷺ : التّاجرُ الصّدوقُ تحتَ ظِلِّ العرشِ يَومَ القيامةِ.[١٠٦٥]

962. **The Prophet (SAWA),** 'Three types of men at whom Allah will not look [mercifully]: ... and the one who promotes his commodity by lying.'[1076]

٩٦٢ . عنه ﷺ : ثـلاثةٌ لا يَـنْظُرُ اللهُ إلَـيهِم ... والمُزَكّي سِلْعَتَهُ بالكَذِبِ.[١٠٦٦]

294. The One who Promotes his Commodity by Oaths

٢٩٤ ـ التَّحذيرُ مِنَ الحَلفِ فِي التِّجارَةِ

963. **Imām 'Alī (AS) said,** 'O brokers! Curb your use of oaths, for they promote the commodity while obliterating the profit.'[1077]

٩٦٣ . الإمامُ عليٌّ عليه السلام : يـا مَـعاشرَ السَّـماسِرَةِ، أقِلّوا الأيْمانَ ، فإنّها مَـنفقَةٌ للسِّـلْعَـةِ ، مَـمْحَقَةٌ للرِّبْحِ.[١٠٦٧]

964. **Imām al-Ṣādiq (AS) said,** 'Allah, Blessed and most High, loathes the one who promotes his commodity by oaths.'[1078]

٩٦٤ . الإمامُ الصّادقُ عليه السلام : إنّ اللهَ تباركَ وتعالى لَيُبْغِضُ المُنَفِّق سِلْعتَهُ بالأيْمانِ.[١٠٦٨]

295. The Trade of the Hereafter

٢٩٥ ـ تِجارَةُ الآخِرَةِ

"O you who have faith! Shall I show you a deal that will deliver you from a painful punishment? Have faith in Allah and His Apostle, and wage jihād in the way of Allah with your possessions and your persons. That is better for you, should you know."[1079]

﴿يا أَيُّهَاالَّذِينَ آمَنُوا هَـلْ أَدُلُّكُـمْ عَـلَىٰ تِـجارَةٍ تُنْجِيكُمْ مِنْ عَذَابٍ أَلِيم * تُؤْمِنُونَ بِاللهِ وَرَسُولِهِ وَتُجاهِدُونَ فِي سَبِيلِ اللهِ بِأَمْـوَالِكُـمْ وأَنْـفُسِكُمْ ذٰلِكُمْ خَيْرٌ لَكُمْ إِنْ كُنْتُمْ تَعْلَمُونَ﴾ .[١٠٦٩]

965. **The Prophet (SAWA) said,** 'All that you see with your own eye and that your heart finds pleasing, make it for Allah, for this is the trade of the Hereafter. Allah says, *"What is with you depletes, while what is with Allah is eternal"*.'[1080]

٩٦٥ . رسولُ اللهِ ﷺ : كلُّ مـا أبْـصَرْتَهُ بـعَينِكَ واسْتَحْلاهُ قلبُكَ فاجعَلْهُ للهِ، فذلكَ تِجارةُ الآخِرَةِ، لأنَّ اللهَ يـقولُ: ﴿ما عِندَكُم يَنْفَدُ وماعِندَاللهِ باقٍ﴾ .[١٠٧٠][١٠٧١]

966. **The Prophet (SAWA) said,** 'The merchant of this world risks his money and his soul, while the merchant of the Hereafter is a profiting winner: his first profit is his soul and then the sublime Paradise.'[1081]

٩٦٦ . عنه ﷺ : تاجِرُ الدُّنيا مُخاطِرٌ بنفسِهِ ومالِهِ، وتاجِرُ الآخِرَةِ غانِمٌ رابحٌ ، وأوَّلُ رِبْحهِ نَفسُهُ ثُمَّ جَنّةُ المَأوىٰ.[١٠٧٢]

967. **Imām ʿAlī (AS) said,** 'There is no [goods for] trade like good deeds, and no profit like the [divine] reward.'[1082]

٩٦٧. الإمامُ عليٌّ ﷺ: لا تِجارَةَ كالعَمَلِ الصّالحِ، ولا رِبحَ كالثَّوابِ.[١٠٧٣]

968. **Imām ʿAlī (AS) said,** 'The most profiting, among people, is the one who buys the Hereafter at the expense of this world.'[1083]

٩٦٨. عنه ﷺ: أربَحُ النّاسِ منِ اشْتَرىٰ بالدُّنيا الآخِرَةَ.[١٠٧٤]

969. **Imām ʿAlī (AS) said,** 'Whoever sells himself for [a price] less than Paradise, his ordeal is indeed severe.'[1084]

٩٦٩. عنه ﷺ: إنَّ مَن باعَ نَفسَهُ بغيرِ الجَنّةِ فقد عظُمَتْ علَيهِ المِحْنةُ.[١٠٧٥]

970. **Imām ʿAlī (AS) said,** 'Whoever takes the obedience of Allah as a commodity will see profits without even trading.'[1085]

٩٧٠. عنه ﷺ: مَنِ اتَّخَذَ طاعةَ اللهِ بِضاعةً أتَتْهُ الأرْباحُ مِن غيرِ تِجارةٍ.[١٠٧٦]

296. Trading does not Divert the Believer

٢٩٦ ـ عَدَمُ إلهاءِ التِّجارَةِ لِلمُؤمِنِ

"Men whom neither trading nor bargaining distracts from the remembrance of Allah, and the maintenance of prayer and the giving of zakāt. They are fearful of a day wherein the heart and the sight will be transformed."[1086]

﴿رِجالٌ لَا تُلْهِيهِمْ تِجارَةٌ وَلَا بَيْعٌ عَنْ ذِكْرِ اللهِ وَإِقامِ الصَّلَاةِ وَإِيتاءِ الزَّكاةِ يَخافُونَ يَوْماً تَتَقَلَّبُ فِيهِ القُلُوبُ وَالْأَبْصارُ﴾.[١٠٧٧]

971. It is narrated in *Fiqh al-Riḍā* (AS): 'When you are engaged in your trade and prayer time arrives, let not your trading divert you from it; for Allah described a certain people and praised them, saying, *"Men whom neither trade nor sale can divert…"* These people used to trade, but when prayer time arrived they would leave their trade and stand for their prayer. They deserved more reward than non-traders who prayed.'[1087]

٩٧١. بحار الأنوار عن فقه الرضا ﷺ: إذا كُنتَ في تِجارَتِكَ وحَضَرَتِ الصّلاةُ فلا يَشغَلْكَ عنها مَتْجَرُكَ، فإنَّ اللهَ وَصفَ قَوماً ومَدَحَهُم فقالَ: ﴿رِجالٌ لا تُلهيهم تِجارَةٌ وَلَا بَيْعٌ عَنْ ذِكْرِ اللهِ وَإِقامِ الصَّلَاةِ وَإِيتاءِ الزَّكاةِ يَخافُونَ يَوْماً تَتَقَلَّبُ فِيهِ القُلُوبُ وَالْأَبْصارُ﴾. وكانَ هؤلاءِ القَومُ يَتَّجِرونَ، فإذا حَضَرَتِ الصّلاةُ تَرَكوا تِجارَتَهُم وقاموا إلىٰ صَلاتِهِم، وكانوا أعظَمَ أجْراً مِمَّن لا يَتَّجِرُ فيُصَلّي.[١٠٧٨]

297. Trade with Religion

٢٩٧ ـ التِّجارَةُ بالدِّين!

972. **Imām ʿAlī (AS) said,** 'Whoever seeks to eat by sacrificing his religion will only have from his religion as much as he eats.'[1088]

٩٧٢. الإمامُ عليٌّ ﷺ: المُسْتَأكِلُ بدِينِهِ حَظُّهُ مِن دِينِهِ ما يَأكُلُهُ.[١٠٧٩]

973. **Imām ʿAlī (AS) said,** 'Whoever seeks this world through the work of the Hereafter will have his goal set at a greater distance.'[1089]

٩٧٣ . عنه ﷺ : مَن طَلَبَ الدُّنيا بعَمَلِ الآخِرَةِ كانَ أبْعَدَ لَهُ مِمّا طَلَبَ.١٠٨٠

56

REPENTANCE

التَّوبَةُ

298. Enjoinment of Repenting

٢٩٨ ـ الحَثُّ علَى التَّوبَةِ

"It is He who accepts the repentance of His servants, and excuses their misdeeds and knows what you do."[1090]

﴿وَهُوَ الَّذِي يَقْبَلُ التَّوْبَةَ عَنْ عِبادِهِ وَيَعْفُو عَنِ السَّيِّئاتِ وَيَعْلَمُ ما تَفْعَلُونَ﴾.١٠٨١

974. **The Prophet (SAWA) said,** 'Repentance erases whatever precedes it.'[1091]

٩٧٤ . رسولُ اللهِ ﷺ : التَّوبةُ تَجُبُّ ما قَبلَها.١٠٨٢

975. **The Prophet (SAWA) said,** 'He who repents for his sin is like one who has no sin.'[1092]

٩٧٥ . عنه ﷺ : التّائبُ مِن الذَّنبِ كَمَن لا ذَنْبَ لهُ.١٠٨٣

976. **Imām ʿAlī (AS) said,** 'Repentance purifies the hearts and washes away the sins.'[1093]

٩٧٦ . الإمامُ عليٌّ ﷺ : التَّوبَةُ تُطَهِّرُ القُلوبَ وتَغْسِلُ الذُّنوبَ.١٠٨٤

299. The Status of One who Repents

٢٩٩ ـ مَنزِلةُ التّائِبِ

"Indeed Allah loves the penitent and He loves those who keep clean."[1094]

﴿إنَّ اللهَ يُحِبُّ التَّوّابِينَ وَيُحِبُّ المُتَطَهِّرِينَ﴾.١٠٨٥

977. **The Prophet (SAWA) said,** 'There is nothing more beloved to Allah than a penitent believer – man or woman.'[1095]

٩٧٧ . رسولُ اللهِ ﷺ : ليسَ شَيءٌ أحَبَّ إلَى اللهِ مِن مُؤمنٍ تائبٍ أو مُؤمنةٍ تائبةٍ.١٠٨٦

978. **The Prophet (SAWA) said,** 'Every son of Adam is a sinner, but the best of them are the penitent ones.'[1096]

٩٧٨ . عنه ﷺ : كُلُّ بَني آدمَ خَطّاءٌ، وخَيرُ الخَطّائينَ التَّوّابونَ.١٠٨٧

979. **The Prophet (SAWA) said,** 'Allah rejoices for the repentance of His servant more than the barren rejoices for having a child, and more than the lost one who finds his way, and more than the thirsty one who finds water.'[1097]

٩٧٩. عنه ﷺ: لَـلَّهُ أفْـرَحُ بـتَوبةِ عـبدِهِ مِـن العَقيمِ الوالِدِ، ومِن الضّـالِّ الواجِدِ، ومِن الظّمآنِ الوارِدِ.١٠٨٨

300. The Sign of a Penitent Person

٣٠٠ـ عَلامَةُ التّائبِ

980. **The Prophet (SAWA) said,** 'There are four signs to the penitent person: sincerity in his work for the sake of Allah, avoiding misdeeds, adhering to what is right, and eagerness for what is good.'[1098]

٩٨٠. رسولُ اللهِ ﷺ: أمّا عَلامةُ التّائبِ فأربَعةٌ: النَّصيحةُ للهِ في عَمَلِهِ، وتَـرْكُ البـاطِلِ، ولُـزومُ الحَقِّ، والحِرْصُ على الخَيرِ.١٠٨٩

981. **Imām ʿAlī (AS) said,** describing the penitent ones, 'They planted the trees of their sins before their eyes and hearts, and watered them with the water of remorse; thus they produced safety for them and left them with contentment and dignity.'[1099]

٩٨١. الإمامُ عليٌّ ﷺ ـ في وَصفِ التّـائبينَ ـ: غَرَسُوا أشْجارَ ذُنوبِهِم نُصْبَ عُـيونِهِم وقُـلوبِهِم وسَقَوها بمِياهِ النَّدَمِ، فأثْـمَرَتْ لهُـمُ السَّـلامَةَ، وأعْقَبَتْهُمُ الرِّضا والكَرامَةَ.١٠٩٠

982. **Imām Zayn al-ʿĀbidīn (AS)** said in his intimate supplication, 'Place us among those … who extinguish the fire of desires by shedding the water of repentance, and wash the plates of ignorance with the purity of the water of life.'[1100]

٩٨٢. الإمامُ زينُ العابدينَ ﷺ ـ في مُناجاته ـ: واجْعَلْنا مِن الّذينَ ... قَطَعوا أشتارَ نارِ الشَّهَواتِ بنَضْحِ ماءِ التَّوبَةِ، وغَسَلوا أوْعِيَةَ الجَهلِ بِـصَفْوِ ماءِ الحَياةِ.١٠٩١

301. The Acceptance of Repentance

٣٠١ـ قَبولُ التَّوبَةِ

"It is He who accepts the repentance of His servants, and excuses their misdeeds"[1101]

﴿وَهُوَ الَّذِي يَقْبَلُ التَّوْبَةَ عَنْ عِبادِهِ وَيَعْفُو عَـنِ السَّيِّئاتِ﴾.١٠٩٢

983. **Imām ʿAlī (AS) said,** 'A man who is blessed with repentance will not be deprived of its acceptance, and a man who is blessed with seeking forgiveness will not be deprived of forgiveness.'[1102]

٩٨٣. الإمامُ عليٌّ ﷺ: مَن أُعْطِيَ التَّوبَةَ لَم يُحرَمِ القَـبولَ، ومَـن أُعْـطِيَ الاسْـتِغْفارَ لَـم يُـحرَمِ المَغفِرَةَ.١٠٩٣

302. When is Repentance Accepted?

٣٠٢ـ مَتىٰ تُقبَلُ التَّوبَةُ ؟

"But [acceptance of] repentance is not for those who go on committing misdeeds: when death approaches any of them, he says, 'I repent now.' Nor is it for those who die while they are faithless."[1103]

﴿وَلَيْسَتِ التَّوْبَةُ لِلَّذِينَ يَعْمَلُونَ السَّيِّئَاتِ حَتَّى إِذَا حَضَرَ أَحَدَهُمُ الْمَوْتُ قالَ إِنِّي تُبْتُ الْآنَ وَلَا الَّذِينَ يَمُوتُونَ وَهُمْ كُفَّارٌ﴾.[١٠٩٤]

984. **The Prophet (SAWA) said,** 'A man who repents before he sees [the angel of death], Allah will accept his repentance.'[1104]

٩٨٤ . رسولُ اللهِ ﷺ : مَن تابَ قَبْلَ أنْ يُعايِنَ قَبِلَ اللهُ توبَتَهُ.[١٠٩٥]

985. **Imām al-Bāqir (AS) said,** 'When the soul reaches this – and pointed to his throat – there will not remain a chance to repent for the knowledgeable man, but there will remain a chance for the ignorant one.'[1105]

٩٨٥ . الإمامُ الباقرُ عليه السلام : إذا بَلَغَتِ النّفسُ هذهِ ـ وأهْوىٰ بيَدِهِ إلىٰ حَلْقِهِ ـ لَم يَكُن للعالِمِ تَوبَةٌ ، وكانتْ للجاهلِ تَوبَةٌ.[١٠٩٦]

986. **Imām al-Riḍā (AS),** when he was asked about the reason for Allah's drowning the Pharaoh after he believed in Him and attested to His oneness, replied, 'Because he believed after he saw the wrath [of Allah], and belief at such a time is not accepted.'[1106]

٩٨٦ . الإمامُ الرِّضا عليه السلام ـ وقد سُئلَ عن عِلّةِ إغْراقِ اللهِ فِرْعَونَ وقد آمَنَ بهِ وأقَرَّ بتَوحيدِهِ ـ: لأنَّهُ آمنَ عندَ رُؤيةِ البَأْسِ ، والإيمانُ عندَ رُؤيَةِ البَأْسِ غيرُ مَقبولٍ.[١٠٩٧]

303. Remorse is Repentance

٣٠٣ـ النَّدَمُ تَوبَةٌ

987. **The Prophet (SAWA) said,** 'Remorse is repentance.'[1107]

٩٨٧ . رسولُ اللهِ ﷺ : النَّدَمُ تَوبَةٌ.[١٠٩٨]

988. **Imām 'Alī (AS) said,** 'Remorse for a sin counts as seeking forgiveness.'[1108]

٩٨٨ . الإمامُ عليٌّ عليه السلام : النَّدَمُ علىٰ الخَطيئةِ اسْتِغْفارٌ.[١٠٩٩]

989. **Imām 'Alī (AS) said,** 'Remorse of the heart offsets the sin.'[1109]

٩٨٩ . عنه عليه السلام : نَدمُ القلبِ يُكَفِّرُ الذَّنبَ.[١١٠٠]

304. Appropriate Confession [of One's Sins]

٣٠٤ـ حُسنُ الاعتِرافِ

"[There are] others who have confessed to their sins, having mixed up righteous conduct with other that was evil. Maybe Allah will accept their repentance."[1110]

﴿وَآخَرُونَ اعْتَرَفُوا بِذُنُوبِهِمْ خَلَطُوا عَمَلاً صَالِحاً وَآخَرَ سَيِّئاً عَسَىٰ اللهُ أنْ يَتُوبَ عَلَيْهِمْ﴾.[١١٠١]

990. **Imām ʿAlī (AS) said,** 'A sinner who confesses to his sin is better than an obedient man who brags about his deed.'[1111]

٩٩٠ . الإمامُ عليٌّ ﷺ : عاصٍ يُقِرُّ بذَنبِهِ خَيرٌ من مُطيعٍ يَفتَخِرُ بعَمَلِهِ.[١١٠٢]

991. **Imām al-Bāqir (AS) said,** 'By Allah! None will be safe from his sin except the one who admits it.'[1112]

٩٩١ . الإمامُ الباقرُ ﷺ : واللهِ ، ما يَنْجو مِن الذَّنْبِ إلّا مَن أقَرَّ بهِ.[١١٠٣]

992. **Imām al-Bāqir (AS) said,** 'By Allah! Allah wants but two traits to be present in people: to acknowledge His favors so that He may increase them, and to confess their sins so that He may forgive them.'[1113]

٩٩٢ . عنه ﷺ : لا واللهِ ما أرادَ اللهُ تَعالىٰ مِن النّاسِ إلّا خَصْلَتَينِ : أنْ يُقِرّوا لَهُ بالنِّعَمِ فيَزيدَهُم ، وبالذُّنوبِ فَيَغفِرَها لَهُم.[١١٠٤]

305. The Pillars of Repentance

٣٠٥ ـ دَعائِمُ التَّوبَةِ

"But whoever repents after his wrongdoing, and reforms, then Allah shall accept his repentance. Indeed Allah is all-forgiving, all-merciful."[1114]

﴿فَمَنْ تَابَ مِنْ بَعْدِ ظُلْمِهِ وَأَصْلَحَ فَإِنَّ اللهَ يَتُوبُ عَلَيْهِ إِنَّ اللهَ غَفُورٌ رَحِيمٌ﴾.[١١٠٥]

"Indeed I am all-forgiving toward him who repents, becomes faithful and acts righteously, and then follows guidance."[1115]

﴿وَإِنِّي لَغَفَّارٌ لِمَنْ تَابَ وَآمَنَ وَعَمِلَ صَالِحاً ثُمَّ اهْتَدَىٰ﴾.[١١٠٦]

993. **Imām ʿAlī (AS) said,** 'Repentance stands on four pillars: remorse with the heart, asking for forgiveness with the tongue, work with the limbs, and resolve not to repeat [the offense].'[1116]

٩٩٣ . الإمامُ عليٌّ ﷺ : التَّوبَةُ علىٰ أربَعةِ دِعائِمَ : نَدَمٌ بالقَلبِ ، واسْتِغفَارٌ باللِّسانِ ، وعِملٌ بالجَوارِحِ ، وعَزْمٌ أنْ لا يَعودَ.[١١٠٧]

994. **Imām al-Bāqir (AS) said,** in reply to a shaykh from the Nakhaʿ tribe, who said, 'I have been a governor since the time of al-Ḥajjāj until this very day, so is repentance possible for me?' The Imām remained silent, and when I repeated the question, he said, 'No, until you compensate everyone for his lost rights.'[1117]

٩٩٤ . الإمامُ الباقرُ ﷺ ـ وقد سألَهُ شَيخٌ مِن النَّخَعِ: إنّي لَم أزَلْ والِياً مُنذُ زَمنِ الحَجّاجِ إلىٰ يَومي هذا، فهَلْ لي مِن تَوبةٍ ؟ قالَ : فَسَكتَ، ثُمّ أعَدْتُ علَيهِ ،فقالَ ـ : لا ، حتّىٰ تُؤَدّيَ إلىٰ كُلِّ ذي حَقٍّ حَقَّهُ.[١١٠٨]

(See also: SINNING: section 775; SEEKING FORGIVENESS: section 1433)

(أُنظر) الذنب : باب ٧٧٥ ؛ الاستغفار : باب ١٤٣٣.

306. Types of Repentance

٣٠٦ـأنواعُ التَّوبَةِ

995. **The Prophet (SAWA) said,** 'Make a repentance for every sin; public [repentance] for public [sins] and private [repentance] for private [sins].'[1118]

٩٩٥ . رسولُ اللهِ ﷺ : أحْدِثْ لكُ لِّذَنبٍ تَـوبَةً ، السِّرُّ بالسِّرِّ والعَلانِيَةُ بالعَلانِيَةِ.[١١٠٩]

307. Sincere Repentance

٣٠٧ـالتَّوبَةُ النَّصوحُ

"O you who have faith! Repent to Allah with sincere repentance!"[1119]

﴿يـا أَيُّـهَا الَّـذِينَ آمَـنُوا تُـوبُوا إِلَـىٰ اللهِ تَـوْبَةً نَصُوحاً﴾ .[١١١٠]

996. **The Prophet (SAWA) said,** 'Sincere repentance is remorse for the sin as soon as it slips out from you; then you ask Allah for forgiveness, then you never return to it.'[1120]

٩٩٦ . رسولُ اللهِ ﷺ ـوقـد سُـئلَ عـنِ التَّـوبةِ النَّصوحِ ـ: هُو النَّدمُ عـلىٰ الذّنبِ حـينَ يَـفْرُطُ مِنكَ، فتَسْتَغفِرُ اللهَ بِندامَتِكَ عِند الحافِرِ ، ثُـمَّ لا تَعودُ إلَيهِ أبَداً .[١١١١]

997. **Imām al-Hādī (AS)** when he was asked about sincere repentance, said, '[It is] when the inner self becomes identical to the outer behavior, and even better than it.'[1121]

٩٩٧ . الإمامُ الهاديُّ ﷺ ـ وقـد سُـئلَ عـنِ التوبةِالنَّـصُوحِ ـ: أنْ يَكـونَ البـاطِنُ كـالظّاهِرِ وأفْضَلَ مِن ذلكَ .[١١١٢]

308. Postponing Repentance

٣٠٨ـتَأخيرُ التَّوبَةِ

998. **Imām ʿAlī (AS) said,** 'If you commit a misdeed, hasten to erase it with repentance.'[1122]

٩٩٨ . الإمامُ عليٌّ ﷺ : إنْ قارَفْتَ سَيّئةً فعَجِّلْ مَحْوَها بالتَّوبةِ .[١١١٣]

999. **Imām ʿAlī (AS) said,** 'The one who procrastinates in repenting for himself faces the greatest danger from the [sudden] attack of death.'[1123]

٩٩٩ . عنه ﷺ : مُسَوِّفُ نَفسِهِ بالتَّوبةِ ، مِن هُجومِ الأجَلِ علىٰ أعظَمِ الخَطَرِ .[١١١٤]

1000. **Imām al-Jawād (AS) said,** 'Postponing repentance is an illusion, and long procrastination is perplexity.'[1124]

١٠٠٠ . الإمامُ الجوادُ ﷺ : تأخِيرُ التَّوبةِ اغْتِرارٌ، وطُولُ التّسْويفِ حَيْرَةٌ .[١١١٥]

(See also: PROCRASTINATION: 207)

(أنظر) عنوان ٢٠٧ «التسويف».

309. What is Easier Than Repentance

٣٠٩ـ الأهوَنُ مِن التَّوبَةِ

1001. **Prophet Jesus (AS) said,** 'The man who has no debt to people is more comfortable than the one indebted, even if he repayed his debt; and similarly the man who has not committed any sins is more comfortable than he who has committed sins, even if he has sincerely repented and returned [to the right path].'[1125]

١٠٠١. المسيح ؑ: إنَّ مَن لَيس علَيهِ دَيْنٌ مِن النّاسِ أروَحُ وأقَلُّ هَمّاً مِمَّن علَيهِ الدَّينُ وإنْ أحسَنَ القَضاءَ، وكذلكَ مَن لم يَعمَلِ الخَطيئةَ أروَحُ هَمّاً مِمَّن عَمِلَ الخَطيئةَ وإنْ أخلَصَ التَّوبَةَ وأنابَ.١١١٦

1002. **Imām ʿAlī (AS) said,** 'Abandoning sin is easier than asking for forgiveness.'[1126]

١٠٠٢. الإمامُ عليٌّ ؑ: تَرْكُ الذَّنبِ أهْوَنُ مِن طَلَبِ التَّوبةِ.١١١٧

310. Allah Conceals the Sin of the Penitent One

٣١٠ـ سَترُ اللهِ عَلَى التّائِبِ

1003. **Imām ʿAlī (AS) said,** 'Allah turns mercifully to the one who repents, and his limbs are ordered to keep his secret, and all the places on earth to conceal for him [his sin], and the record-keeping angels to forget whatever they wrote about him.'[1127]

١٠٠٣. الإمامُ عليٌّ ؑ: مَن تابَ تابَ اللهُ علَيهِ، وأُمِرَتْ جَوارِحُهُ أنْ تَستُرَ علَيهِ، وبِقاعُ الأرضِ أنْ تَكتُمَ علَيهِ، وأُنسِيَتِ الحَفَظَةُ ما كانتْ تَكتُبُ علَيهِ.١١١٨

311. Changing Sins into Good Deeds

٣١١ـ تَبديلُ السَّيِّئاتِ حَسَناتٍ

"Excepting those who repent, attain faith, and act righteously. For such, Allah will replace their misdeeds with good deeds, and Allah is all-forgiving, all-merciful."[1128]

﴿إلّا مَنْ تابَ وَآمَنَ وَعَمِلَ عَمَلاً صالِحاً فَأُولئكَ يُبَدِّلُ اللهُ سَيِّئاتِهِمْ حَسَناتٍ وَكانَ اللهُ غَفُوراً رَحِيماً﴾.١١١٩

1004. **Imām al-Ṣādiq (AS) narrated,** 'Allah, the Exalted, revealed to Prophet David[1129] – peace be upon him and on our Prophet, 'O David! When My believing servant commits a sin and then returns [to Me] and repents for that sin

١٠٠٤. الإمامُ الصّادقُ ؑ: أوحَى اللهُ عزّوجلّ إلىٰ داودَ النَّبيِّ علىٰ نبيِّنا وآلِهِ وعلَيهِ السّلامُ: يا داودُ، إنّ عَبديَ المؤمنَ إذا أذْنَبَ ذَنباً ثُمّ رَجَعَ

and is ashamed in My presence every time he remembers it, I will forgive him and cause the recording angels to forget it and change it to count as a good deed, and I will not care about it further, for I am the most Merciful.'[1130]

وتابَ مِن ذلكَ الذَّنبِ واسْتَحيىٰ مِنّي عندَ ذِكْرِهِ غَفَرْتُ لَهُ، وأنسَيْتُهُ الحَفَظَةَ وأبْدَلْتُهُ الحسَنَةَ، ولا أُبالي وأنا أرْحَمُ الرّاحِمينَ.[١١٢٠]

(See also: RESURRECTION: section 1395)

(أنظر) المعاد: باب ١٣٩٥.

312. Speculating on Allah's Judgment

٣١٢ـ التَّألّي عَلَى اللهِ

1005. **The Prophet (SAWA) said,** 'Woe to those who foretell [about Allah's actions] from among my community – those who proclaim that *x* will go to Paradise, but *y* will go to the Fire.'[1131]

١٠٠٥. رسولُ اللهِ ﷺ: وَيْلٌ للمُتَألّينَ من أُمَّتي، الَّذينَ يقولونَ: فُلانٌ في الجَنّةِ، وفُلانٌ في النّارِ.[١١٢١]

1006. **The Prophet (SAWA) said,** 'A man said one day, 'I swear by Allah that He will not forgive so and so.' Allah, the Exalted, said, 'Who is he to foretell about what I will do – that I will not forgive this man? I indeed have forgiven him and annulled the work of the foretelling man because of his saying, 'Allah will not forgive him.'[1132]

١٠٠٦. عنه ﷺ: إنَّ رجُلاً قالَ يوماً: واللهِ، لا يَغفِرُ اللهُ لفُلانٍ! فقالَ اللهُ عزّ وجلّ: مَنْ ذا الّذي تَألّىٰ عليَّ أنْ لاأغفِرَ لفُلانٍ؟! فإنّي قد غَفَرتُ لِفُلانٍ، وأحْبَطْتُ عَملَ الثّاني بقولِهِ: لا يَغفِرُ اللهُ لفُلانٍ.[١١٢٢]

57

THE REWARD

الثّوابُ

313. The Reward for A Righteous Deed

٣١٣ـ ثوابُ العَمَلِ الصّالِحِ

1007. **Imām ʿAlī (AS) said,** 'The reward for your work is better than your work itself.'[1133]

١٠٠٧. الإمامُ عليٌّ عليه السلام: ثَوابُ عَمَلِكَ أفضَلُ مِن عَمَلِكَ.[١١٢٣]

1008. **Imām ʿAlī (AS) said,** 'The reward of the Hereafter causes one to forget the toil of this world.'[1134]

١٠٠٨. عنه ﷺ: ثَوابُ الآخِرَةِ يُنْسي مَشَقَّةَ الدُّنيا.١١٣٤

1009. **Imām ʿAlī (AS) said,** 'Allah, the Exalted, decreed reward for obeying Him and chastisement for disobeying Him, in order to protect His servants against His wrath and to herd them to His Paradise.'[1135]

١٠٠٩. عنه ﷺ: إنَّ اللهَ سُبحانَهُ وَضَعَ الثَّوابَ علىٰ طاعَتِهِ والعِقابَ علىٰ مَعصِيَتِهِ ذِيادَةً لِعبادِهِ عَن نِقْمَتِهِ، وحِياشَةً لَهُم إلىٰ جَنَّتِهِ.١١٣٥

1010. **Imām ʿAlī (AS) said,** 'The reward for any work is proportionate to the toil of performing it.'[1136]

١٠١٠. عنه ﷺ: ثَوابُ العَمَلِ علىٰ قَدْرِ المَشَقَّةِ فيهِ.١١٣٦

(See also: REQUITAL: 65)

(أنظر) عنوان ٦٥ «الجزاء».

314. The Greatest Reward

٣١٤ـ أعظمُ المَثوبَةِ

1011. **Imām ʿAlī (AS) said,** 'The greatest reward is the reward [dealt] by fairness.'[1137]

١٠١١. الإمامُ عليٌّ ﷺ: إنَّ أعظَمَ المَثوبَةِ مَثوبَةُ الإنْصافِ.١١٣٧

1012. **Imām ʿAlī (AS) said,** 'The reward for *jihād* is the greatest reward.'[1138]

١٠١٢. عنه ﷺ: ثَوابُ الجهادِ أعظَمُ الثَّوابِ.١١٣٨

1013. **Imām ʿAlī (AS) said,** 'There are two things the reward for which is beyond measure: pardon and justice.'[1139]

١٠١٣. عنه ﷺ: شَيْئانِ لا يُوزَنُ ثَوابُهُما: العَفوُ، والعَدلُ.١١٣٩

315. A Man who Hears About the Reward for a Particular Action

٣١٥ـ مَن بَلَغَهُ ثَوابٌ علىٰ عَمَلٍ

1014. **Imām al-Bāqir (AS) said,** 'If a man hears about Allah's reward for a particular action, and subsequently performs it in order to attain that reward, he will receive it – even if the actual report was contrary to what he had heard.'[1140]

١٠١٤. الإمامُ الباقرُ ﷺ: مَن بَلَغَهُ ثَوابٌ مِن اللهِ علىٰ عَمَلٍ، فعَمِلَ ذلكَ العَمَلَ الْتِماسَ ذلكَ الثَّوابِ أُوتِيَهُ وإنْ لَم يَكُنِ الحَديثُ كَما بَلَغَهُ.١١٤٠

58

REVOLUTION

الثَّوْرَةُ

316. The Islamic Revolution in the East before the Rise of the Twelfth Imām (al-Qā'im)

٣١٦ـ الثَّورَةُ الإسلامِيَّةُ فِي الشَّرقِ قبلَ قيامِ القائمِ عليه السلام

1015. **The Prophet (SAWA) said,** 'There will be a people who will rise from the east to pave the way for al-Mahdī's rule.'[1141]

١٠١٥ . رسولُ اللهِ صلى الله عليه وآله : يَخرُجُ ناسٌ مِن المَشرِقِ فَيُوطِّئونَ للمَهدِيِّ سُلْطانَهُ.[١١٣١]

1016. **'Abdullāh [b. 'Abbās] said,** 'While we were sitting with the Prophet (SAWA), a group of young men passed by us and the face of the Prophet turned pale. We asked, 'O Messenger of Allah! We see a look of dislike on your face.' He said, 'We are members of a household for whom Allah has chosen the Hereafter over this world. And this household of mine will be afflicted by banishment and exile after my demise, until a people will emerge from these parts – and he pointed to the East – with black flags. They will repeatedly demand what is right and will be denied it, so they will fight steadfastly until they are given what they demand. But they will not accept it for themselves, until they give it to a man from my posterity who will fill [the world] with fairness and justice as it was filled with oppression and injustice before. Whoever lives to know them should join them even if he has to crawl on snow.'[1142]

١٠١٦ . الملاحم و الفتن عن عبدِ اللهِ: بينَما نحنُ جُلوسٌ عندَ رسولِ اللهِ صلى الله عليه وآله إذْ مَرَّ فِتْيَةٌ مِن قُرَيشٍ فَتَغيّرَ لونُهُ، فقُلنا : يا رسولَ اللهِ ، إنّا لا نَزالُ نَرىٰ في وَجهِكَ شَيئاً نكرَهُهُ! قالَ: إنّا أهلُ بَيتٍ اخْتارَ اللهُ لَنا الآخِرَةَ علىٰ الدُّنيا، وإنّ أهلَ بَيتي هٰؤلاءِ سَيُصيبُهُم بَعدي بَلاءٌ وتَطْرِيدٌ وتَشْرِيدٌ ، حتّىٰ يَخرُجَ قَومٌ مِن هٰاهُنا ـ وأوْمَأَ بيَدِهِ نحوَ المَشرِقِ ـ مَعَهُم راياتٌ سُودٌ ، يَسْألونَ الحقَّ فلا يُعطَونَهُ ، ويَسْألونَ فلا يُعْطَون فيُقاتِلونَ ويَصْبِرونَ، فيُعْطَونَ ما سَألوا فلا يَقْبَلونَهُ، حتّىٰ يَدْفَعوها إلىٰ رجُلٍ مِن أهلِ بَيتي يَمْلَأُها قِسطاً وعَدْلاً كما مُلِئَتْ ظُلْماً وجَوراً ، فمَنْ أدْرَكَهُم فلْيَأْتِهِم ولَو حَبْواً علىٰ الثَّلْجِ.[١١٣٢]

317. The Role of Non-Arabs in the Revolution

٣١٧ـ دَوْرُ العَجَمِ فِي الثَّورَةِ

1017. **Imām al-Bāqir (AS) said,** 'The companions of al-Qā'im are three hundred and thirteen men from the children of non-Arabs. Some of them are

١٠١٧ . الإمامُ الباقرُ عليه السلام :أصحابُ القائمِ ثلاثُمائَةٍ وثَلاثَةَ عَشَرَ رَجُلاً أولادُ العَجَمِ، بَعضُهُم يُحمَلُ

transported by clouds during the day, and are known by their name, their father's name and their lineage and decorations, and some of them are sleeping in their beds and will meet him [al-Qā'im] in Mecca without a specific time.'[1143]

فِي السَّحابِ نَهاراً يُعرَفُ بِاسمِهِ وَاسمِ أَبِيهِ ونَسَبِهِ وحِليَتِهِ، وبَعضُهُم نائِمٌ عَلىٰ فِراشِهِ فَيُوافيهِ في مَكَّةَ عَلىٰ غَيرِ ميعادٍ.١١٣٣

1018. **Sunan al-Tirmidhi**, narrating from Ṣāliḥ ibn Ṣāliḥ, the servant of ʿAmr ibn Ḥarīth, 'I heard Abū Huraira say: "I mentioned the non-Arabs in front of the Messenger of Allah (SAWA) and he (SAWA) said: "I have trust in them or in some of them more than I have trust in you or in some of you.'[1144]

١٠١٨. سنن الترمذي عن صالح بن أبي صالح مولى عمرو بن حريث: سَمِعتُ أبا هُرَيرَةَ يَقولُ: ذَكَرتُ الأَعاجِمَ عِندَ رَسولِ اللهِ ﷺ فَقالَ النَّبِيُّ ﷺ: لَأَنَا بِهِم أو بِبَعضِهِم أوثَقُ مِنّي بِكُم أو بِبَعضِكُم.١١٣٤

1019. **Imām ʿAlī (AS) said,** 'I can almost see the non-Arabs pitching their tents in the mosque of Kūfa, teaching the Qur'an to the people as it was originally revealed.'[1145]

١٠١٩. الإمامُ عليٌّ ؑ: كأنّي بالعجمِ فَساطِيطُهُم في مسجدِ الكوفةِ، يُعلِّمونَ النّاسَ القرآنَ كما أُنزِلَ.١١٣٥

318. The Revolution from the City of Qum

٣١٨ـ الثَّورَةُ مِن مَدينَةِ قُمّ

1020. **Imām al-Ṣādiq (AS) said,** 'There will come a time when the town of Qum and its people will be an authority (*ḥujja*) over the rest of people. This will be during the time of the occultation of our Qā'im (AS) until his reappearance. And if this was not so, the earth would swallow up its people. Verily, the angels guard Qum and its people from disasters, and no tyrant can aim towards it with evil intentions without being annihilated by Allah, the Annihilator of tyrants.'[1146]

١٠٢٠. الإمامُ الصّادقُ ؑ: سَيأتي زَمانٌ تكونُ بَلدةُ قُمّ وأهلُها حُجَّةً علىٰ الخلائقِ، وذلكَ في زمانِ غَيبَةِ قائمِنا ؑ إلىٰ ظُهورِهِ، ولولا ذلكَ لَساخَتِ الأرضُ بأهلِها. وإنَّ الملائكةَ لَتَدفَعُ البَلايا عَن قُمّ وأهلِهِ، وما قَصدَهُ جَبّارٌ بِسوءٍ إلّا قَصَمَهُ قاصِمُ الجَبّارينَ.١١٣٦

1021. **Imām al-Ṣādiq (AS) said** to ʿAffān al-Baṣrī, 'Do you know the reason for the name Qum?' [ʿAffān] replied, 'Allah, His Messenger, and you know better.' He said, 'It was named Qum because its people will meet with the Qā'im[1147] of the family of Muḥammad, peace be upon him; they will rise with him, stay with him, and support him.'[1148]

١٠٢١. بحار الأنوار عن عَفّانِ البَصريّ: قالَ لي [الإمامُ الصادقُ ؑ]: أتدري لِمَ سُمِّيَ قُمّ؟ قلتُ: اللهُ ورسولُهُ وأنتَ أعلَمُ، قالَ: إنّما سُمِّيَ قُمّ لأنَّ أهلَهُ يَجتَمِعونَ مَعَ قائمِ آلِ محمّدٍ صلواتُ اللهِ عليهِ، ويَقومونَ مَعَهُ ويَستَقيمونَ عليهِ ويَنصُرونَهُ.١١٣٧

1022. **Imām al-Kāẓim (AS) said,** 'A man from Qum will call the people to what is right, and he will be joined by men as firm as iron, who will not be shaken by violent storms. They will not be tired of war, nor will they show cowardice. They will rely solely on Allah, and the good end will be for the pious.'[1149]

١٠٢٢ . الإمامُ الكاظمُ ﷺ : رجُلٌ مِن أهلِ قُمّ يدعو النّاسَ إلىٰ الحقِّ ، يَجْتَمِعُ مَعهُ قَومٌ كَزُبَرِ الحديدِ ، لا تُزِلُّهُمُ الرِّياحُ العَواصِفُ ، ولا يَمَلّونَ مِنَ الحَربِ ، ولا يَجْبُنونَ ، وعلىٰ اللهِ يَتوكّلونَ ، والعاقِبَةُ للمُتّقِينَ.[١١٣٨]

1023. It is narrated in *Biḥār al-Anwār*: 'One of our companions narrated, 'I was sitting with Abū 'Abdillāh (AS) when he recited the verse: *"So when the first occasion of the two [prophecies] came, We aroused against you Our servants possessing great might, and they ransacked [your] habitations, and the promise was bound to be fulfilled."*[1150] We asked, 'Who are those, may we be your ransom?' He said three times, 'By Allah! These are the people of Qum.'[1151]

١٠٢٣ . بحار الأنوار عن بعضِ أصحابِنا : كنتُ عندأبي عبدِ اللهِ ﷺ جالِساً إذْ قَرأَ هذهِ الآيةَ: ﴿فَإذا جاءَ وعدُ أُولاهما بعَثْنا عليكم عِباداً لنا أُولي بأسٍ شديدٍ فجاسُوا خِلالَ الدِّيارِ وكانَ وَعْداً مفعولاً﴾[١١٣٩] فقُلنا : جُعِلْنا فِداكَ ، مَن هٰؤلاءِ ؟ فقالَ ، ثلاثَ مَرّاتٍ : هُمْ واللهِ أهلُ قُمّ.[١١٤٠]

59

PREDESTINATION

الجَبرُ

319. The Fallacy of Predestination

٣١٩ ـ بُطلانُ الجَبرِ

1024. **Imām 'Alī (AS),** exposing the fallacy of predestination, said, 'If it were like this, the concepts of reward, punishment, command, and prohibition would be erroneous. The meaning of promise [of Paradise] and threat [of the Hellfire] would be futile, and there would be no blame for a wrongdoer, nor praise for the good-doer. Furthermore, the good-doer would be more blameworthy than the wrongdoer, and the latter would deserve more praise than the former. This [i.e. predestination] is the claim of the idolators and the foes of the Merciful.'[1152]

١٠٢٤ . الإمامُ عليٌّ ﷺ ـ في بيانِ بُطْلانِ الجَبرِ ـ: لَو كانَ كذلكَ لَبَطلَ الثَّوابُ والعِقابُ ، والأمرُ والنَّهْيُ والزَّجْرُ ، ولَسقَطَ معنىٰ الوَعْدِ والوَعيدِ ، ولَم تَكُنْ علىٰ مُسيءٍ لائمَةٌ، ولا لمُحسنٍ مَحْمَدةٌ ، ولكانَ المُحسنُ أوْلىٰ باللّائمةِ مِن المُذنِبِ ، والمُذنِبُ أولىٰ بالإحسانِ مِن المُحسِنِ، تلكَ مَقالةُ عَبَدَةِ الأوثانِ وخُصَماءِ الرَّحمٰنِ.[١١٤١]

1025. **Imām al-Ṣādiq (AS) said,** 'Anything that you can blame a servant [of Allah] for is his own doing, and whatever you cannot blame him for is

١٠٢٥ . الإمامُ الصّادقُ ﷺ : ما اسْتَطعتَ أنْ تَلومَ العبدَ علَيهِ فهُو مِنهُ، وما لَم تَسْتَطِعْ أنْ تَلومَ

Allah's doing. Allah, the Exalted, will ask the servant, 'Why did you disobey [Me]? Why did you commit sins? Why did you drink wine? Why did you commit adultery?' All of this is the servant's doing. But He will not ask him, 'Why were you sick? Why were you short? Why were you white? Why were you black?' because all of this is Allah's doing.'[1153]

العَبدَ عليهِ فهُو مِن فِعلِ اللهِ ، يقولُ اللهُ تعالىٰ للعبدِ : لِمَ عَصَيْتَ ؟ لِمَ فَسَقْتَ ؟ لِمَ شَرِبْتَ الخَمرَ ؟ لِمَ زَنَيْتَ ؟ فهذا فعلُ العبدِ، ولا يقولُ لَه : لِمَ مَرِضْتَ ؟ لِمَ قَصُرْتَ ؟ لِمَ ابْيَضَضْتَ ؟ لِمَ اسْوَدَدْتَ ؟ لأنَّهُ مِن فِعلِ اللهِ تعالىٰ.[١١٤٢]

1026. **Imām al-Kāẓim (AS) said,** 'Sins cannot be other than one of three cases: either they originate from Allah – which they do not – and in this case it would not be proper for the Lord to punish His servant for what he has not committed; or that they originate from Him and the servant together – which they do not – and in this case it would not be proper for the strong partner to wrong the weak partner; or that they originate from the servant – which they do – and in this case, if Allah forgives, it is due to His kindness and liberality, or if He punishes, it is as a result of the sin and crime of the servant.'[1154]

١٠٢٦ . الإمامُ الكاظمُ عليه السلام : إنّ السَّيّئاتِ لا تَخْلو مِن إحدىٰ ثلاثٍ : إمّا أنْ تكونَ مِن اللهِ ـ ولَيستْ مِنهُ ـ فلا يَنبغي للرَّبِّ أنْ يُعذِّبَ العبدَ علىٰ ما لا يَرْتَكِبُ ، وإمّا أنْ تكونَ مِنهُ ومِن العبدِ ـ ولَيستْ كذلكَ ـ فلا يَنبغي للشَّريكِ القَويِّ أنْ يظلِمَ الشَّريكَ الضَّعيفَ ، وإمّا أنْ تكونَ مِن العبدِ ـ وهِي مِنهُ ـ فإنْ عَفا فبِكَرَمِهِ وجُودِهِ ، وإنْ عاقَبَ فبِذَنبِ العبدِ وجَريرَتِهِ.[١١٤٣]

320. Neither Free Will nor Predestination

٣٢٠ـ لا جَبرَ ولا تَفويضَ

1027. **Imām al-Bāqir and Imām al-Ṣādiq (AS) said,** 'Allah, the Exalted, is too merciful to coerce His servants to sin and then punish them for it. He is also too mighty to want something and it not be accomplished.' Then they were asked whether there is a stance between free will and predestination, to which they replied, 'Yes, [a stance] wider than the space between the earth and the sky.'[1155]

١٠٢٧ . التوحيد عن الإمامِ الباقرِ والإمامِ الصّادقِ عليهما السلام : إنّ اللهَ عزّ وجلّ أرحَمُ بخَلقِهِ مِن أنْ يُجْبِرَ خَلقَهُ علىٰ الذُّنوبِ ثُمّ يُعذِّبَهُم علَيها ، واللهُ أعزُّ مِن أنْ يُريدَ أمراً فلا يكونَ . قالَ : فسُئلا عليهما السلام : هلْ بينَ الجَبرِ والقدَرِ مَنزلةٌ ثالثةٌ ؟ قالا : نَعَمْ ، أوسَعُ مِمّا بينَ السّماءِ والأرضِ.[١١٤٤]

1028. **Imām al-Ṣādiq (AS) said,** according to what Mufaḍḍal b. 'Umar narrated on his authority, 'There is neither predestination nor free will,

١٠٢٨ . بحار الأنوار عن المُفَضَّلِ عن الإمامِ الصّادقِ عليه السلام : لا جَبرَ ولا تَفويضَ ، ولكنْ أمرٌ بينَ

but a stance in between them.' [Mufaḍḍal] asked, 'What is the stance in between?' He replied, 'It is like when you observe a man in sin and you advise him against it but he does not desist from it, so you leave him to his sin. Leaving him to sin after he has rejected your advice does not mean that you commanded him to sin.'[1156]

أمرَينِ . قالَ : قلتُ : ما أمرٌ بينَ أمرَينِ ؟ قالَ : مَثَلُ ذلك مَثَلُ رجُلٍ رأيتَهُ على معصيةٍ فنَهَيْتَهُ فلَم يَنْتَهِ ، فترَكتَهُ ففعلَ تلكَ المعصيةَ، فليسَ حَيثُ لَم يَقْبلْ مِنكَ فتركْتَهُ كُنتَ أنتَ الّذي أمَرتَهُ بالمعصيةِ .[١١٤٥]

321. Allah Deserves All Credit for Good Deeds

٣٢١ـ اللهُ أولىٰ بِالحَسَناتِ

1029. **Imām al-Riḍā (AS) said,** 'Allah, most High, said, 'O son of Adam! By My will you attained free will, and with the help of My favour, you perform your obligations towards Me, and with My power you feel empowered to disobey Me. I created you with sight and hearing, so I deserve more credit for your good deeds than you, while you are to blame for your own misdeeds.'[1157]

١٠٢٩ . الإمامُ الرِّضا عليه السلام : قالَ اللهُ تعالىٰ : يابنَ آدمَ، بِمَشِيَّتي كُنتَ أنتَ الّذي تَشاءُ ، وبِنِعْمَتي أدَّيْتَ إلَيَّ فَرائضي، وبِقُدرَتي قَوِيتَ علىٰ مَعْصيَتي، خَلَقتُكَ سَميعاً بَصيراً ، أنا أوْلىٰ بحَسَناتِكَ مِنكَ ، وأنتَ أوْلىٰ بسَيّئاتِكَ مِنّي .[١١٤٦]

322. Actions to be Taken Against the Proponents of Determinism

٣٢٢ـ ما يَنبغي في مواجهةِ الجَبريَّةِ

1030. **Imām al-Ṣādiq (AS) said,** 'He who claims that Allah coerces His servants to disobey Him or burdens them with that which they cannot endure, you must not eat from an animal that he has slaughtered, nor should you believe his testimony, nor pray behind him, nor give him any part of your alms.'[1158]

١٠٣٠ . الإمامُ الصّادقُ عليه السلام : مَن زعَمَ أنّ اللهَ يَجبُرُ عِبادَه علىٰ المعاصي أو يُكلِّفُهُم ما لا يُطيقونَ فلا تأكُلوا ذَبيحَتَهُ ، ولا تَقْبَلوا شَهادَتَهُ ، ولا تُصَلُّوا وَراءهُ ، ولا تُعطُوهُ مِن الزّكاةِ شيئاً .[١١٤٧]

60

TYRANT

الجَبّارُ

323. Condemnation of Tyranny

٣٢٣ـ ذَمُّ التَّجَبُّرِ وصِفَةُ الجَبابِرَةِ

"But they sought victory and decision (there and then), and frustration was the lot of every powerful obstinate transgressor..."[1159]

﴿وَٱسْتَفْتَحُوا وَخَابَ كُلُّ جَبَّارٍ عَنِيدٍ﴾ .[١١٤٨]

"Such were the "Ād' people: they rejected the Signs of their Lord and Cherisher; disobeyed His Messengers; and followed the command of every powerful, obstinate transgressor."[1160]

﴿وَتِلْكَ عَادٌ جَحَدُوا بِـَٔايَـٰتِ رَبِّهِمْ وَعَصَوْا رُسُلَهُ وَٱتَّبَعُوٓا أَمْرَ كُلِّ جَبَّارٍ عَنِيدٍ﴾.١١٤٩

1031. **The Prophet (SAWA) said,** 'A recalcitrant tyrant is anyone who refuses to say: 'There is no god but Allah.'[1161]

١٠٣١. رسولُ اللهِ ﷺ: كُلُّ جبّارٍ عَنيدٍ مَن أبىٰ أنْ يقولَ: لا إلٰه إلّا اللهُ.١١٥٠

1032. **Imām ʿAlī (AS) said,** 'The work of a tyrant can never be pure.'[1162]

١٠٣٢. الإمامُ عليٌّ ؑ: لايَزْكو عَملُ مُتَجبّرٍ.١١٥١

1033. **Imām ʿAlī (AS) said,** 'Do not address me the way tyrants are addressed, nor should you be reluctant in my presence as it is done in the presence of the oppressors, nor should you associate with me with hypocrisy.'[1163]

١٠٣٣. عنه ؑ: فلا تُكَلِّموني بما تُكَلَّمُ بهِ الجَبابِرَةُ، ولا تَتَحفَّظوا منّي بما يُتَحفَّظُ بهِ عندَ أهلِ البادِرَةِ، ولا تُخالِطوني بالمُصانَعَةِ.١١٥٢

324. The Evil End of the Tyrants

٣٢٤ـ سوءُ عاقِبَةِ الجَبابِرَةِ

1034. **The Prophet (SAWA) said,** 'The tyrants and the arrogant people will be raised on the Day of Judgment in the form of tiny ants, which the rest of the people will trample underfoot – because of their low esteem before Allah.'[1164]

١٠٣٤. رسولُ اللهِ ﷺ: يُحشَرُ الجَبّارونَ والمُتَكبِّرون يومَ القيامةِ في صُورةِ الذَّرِّ، يَطأُهُمُ النّاسُ لِهَوانِهِم علىٰ اللهِ.١١٥٣

1035. **Imām ʿAlī (AS) said,** 'Whoever acts tyrannically will be broken.'[1165]

١٠٣٥. الإمامُ عليٌّ ؑ: مَن تَجَبَّرَ كُسِرَ.١١٥٤

1036. **Imām ʿAlī (AS) said,** 'Allah will humiliate and depose whoever acts tyrannically.'[1166]

١٠٣٦. عنه ؑ: مَن تَجَبَّرَ حَقَّرَهُ اللهُ ووَضَعَهُ.١١٥٥

1037. **Imām ʿAlī (AS) said,** 'Beware of behaving tyrannically with the servants of Allah, for [eventually] Allah annihilates every tyrant.'[1167]

١٠٣٧. عنه ؑ: إيّاكَ والتَّجَبُّرَ علىٰ عبادِ اللهِ؛ فإنَّ كلَّ مُتَجبِّرٍ يَقْصِمُهُ اللهُ.١١٥٦

1038. **Imām al-Ṣādiq (AS) said,** 'The tyrants will be the farthest away from Allah on the Day of Judgment.'[1168]

١٠٣٨. الإمامُ الصّادقُ ؑ: الجَبّارونَ أبْعَدُ النّاسِ مِن اللهِ عزّ وجلّ يومَ القيامةِ.١١٥٧

61

COWARDICE الجُبنُ

325. Censure of Cowardice ٣٢٥ـ ذَمُّ الجُبنِ

1039. **Imām ʿAlī (AS) said,** 'Cowardice is a defect.'[1169]

١٠٣٩ . الإمامُ عليٌّ عليه السلام : الجُبنُ مَنْقَصةٌ.١١٥٨

1040. **Imām ʿAlī (AS) said,** 'Cowardice, greed, and miserliness are vile traits that are the result of distrust in Allah.'[1170]

١٠٤٠ . عنه عليه السلام : الجُبنُ والحِرصُ والبُخلُ غرائزُ سُوءٍ يَجمعُها سُوءُ الظَّنِّ باللهِ سبحانَهُ.١١٥٩

1041. **Imām ʿAlī (AS) said,** 'Beware of cowardice, for it is a [source of] shame and a defect.'[1171]

١٠٤١ . عنه عليه السلام : احْـذَروا الجُـبنَ؛ فـإنَّهُ عـارٌ ومَنْقَصةٌ.١١٦٠

1042. **Imām ʿAlī (AS) said,** 'Sheer cowardice ensues from the impotence of the soul and the weakness of conviction.'[1172]

١٠٤٢ . عنه عليه السلام : شِدّةُ الجُبنِ مِن عَجْزِ النَّـفْسِ وضَعفِ اليقينِ.١١٦١

1043. **Imām al-Ḥasan (AS),** when asked about cowardice, replied, '[It is] aggressiveness with one's friends, and flight from one's enemy.'[1173]

١٠٤٣ . الإمامُ الحسنُ عليه السلام ـ وقد سُئلَ عن الجُبن ـ: الجُرأةُ على الصَّديقِ ، والنُّكُولُ عَن العَدُوِّ.١١٦٢

326. The Coward and War ٣٢٦ـ الجَبانُ وَ الغَزوُ

1044. **The Prophet (SAWA) said,** 'Whoever feels in himself to be a coward should not go to war.'[1174]

١٠٤٤ . رسول الله صلى الله عليه وآله : مَن أحَسَّ مِن نَفسِهِ جُبناً فَلا يَغزُ.١١٦٣

1045. **Imām ʿAlī (AS) said,** 'A coward is not allowed to participate in a campaign, because he would flee fast. However, he must take whatever he was going to use for the conquest [i.e. weaponry] and give it to someone else. Thus, he will have the same reward, without decrease in the reward of the other thereof.'[1175]

١٠٤٥ . الإمامُ عليٌّ عليه السلام : لا يَحِلُّ للجَبانِ أنْ يَغْزوَ لأنَّهُ يَنْهَزِمُ سريعاً ، ولكنْ لِيَنْظُرْ ما كانَ يُريدُ أنْ يَغْزوَ بِهِ فليُجَهِّزْ بِهِ غيرَهُ؛ فإنَّ لَهُ مِثلَ أجـرِهِ ولا يَنْقصُ مِن أجرِهِ شيءٌ.١١٦٤

62

THE DISPUTE

الجِدالُ

327. Reproached Dispute

٣٢٧ ـ الجِدالُ المَذمومُ

"Among the people are those who dispute about Allah without any knowledge, and follow every froward devil"[1176]

﴿وَمِنَ النَّاسِ مَنْ يُجَادِلُ فِي اللهِ بِغَيْرِ عِلْمٍ وَيَتَّبِعُ كُلَّ شَيْطَانٍ مَرِيدٍ﴾.[١١٦٦]

"No one disputes the signs of Allah except the faithless. So do not be misled by their bustle in the towns."[1177]

﴿ما يُجَادِلُ فِي آيَاتِ اللهِ إلَّا الَّذِينَ كَفَرُوا فَلا يَغْرُرْكَ تَقَلُّبُهُمْ فِي البِلادِ﴾.[١١٦٧]

(See also: Qur'an 3:66, 7:71, 8:6, 18:54, 18:56, 19:97, 22:8-9, 22:68, 25:50, 42:35, 43:57)

(أنظر) آل عمران: ٦٦ و الأعراف: ٧١ و الأنفال: ٦ و الكهف: ٥٤، ٥٦ ومريم: ٩٧ و الحج: ٨، ٩، ٦٨ والفرقان: ٥٠ والشورى: ٣٥ والزخرف: ٥٧.

1046. The Prophet (SAWA) said, 'No sooner do a people go astray than they exaggerate in dispute.'[1178]

١٠٤٦. رسولُ اللهِ ﷺ: ما ضَلَّ قَومٌ إلّا أوْثَقوا الجَدَلَ.[١١٦٨]

1047. Imām ʿAlī (AS) said, 'Avoid dispute, for it brings about doubt.'[1179]

١٠٤٧. الإمامُ عليٌّ ؑ: إيّاكُم والجِدالَ؛ فإنّه يُورِثُ الشَّكَّ.[١١٦٩]

(See also: DISPUTATION: 363; Debate: 377)

(أنظر) عنوان ٣٦٣ «المراء»؛ عنوان ٣٧٧ «المناظرة».

328. Positive Debating

٣٢٨ ـ الجِدالُ الحَسَنُ

"Invite to the way of your Lord with wisdom and good advice and dispute with them in a manner that is best. Indeed your Lord knows best those who stray from His way, and He knows best those who are guided."[1180]

﴿ادْعُ إِلَىٰ سَبِيلِ رَبِّكَ بِالْحِكْمَةِ وَالْمَوْعِظَةِ الْحَسَنَةِ وَجَادِلْهُمْ بِالَّتِي هِيَ أَحْسَنُ إِنَّ رَبَّكَ هُوَ أَعْلَمُ بِمَنْ ضَلَّ عَنْ سَبِيلِهِ وَهُوَ أَعْلَمُ بِالْمُهْتَدِينَ﴾.[١١٧٠]

1048. Imām ʿAli (AS) from the wise sayings attributed to him said, 'Command the young with arguing and debating, the adult with thought, and the elder with silence.'[1181]

١٠٤٨. الإمامُ عليٌّ ؑ ـ فِي الحِكَمِ المنسوبَةِ إلَيهِ ـ: مُرُوا الأحداثَ بِالمِراءِ وَالجِدالِ، وَالكُهولَ بِالفِكرِ، وَالشُّيوخَ بِالصَّمتِ.[١١٧١]

1049. Imām al-ʿAskarī (AS) narrated, 'The subject of disputing about religion was mentioned

١٠٤٩. الإمامُ العسكريُّ ؑ: ذُكِرَ عندَ الصّادقِ ؑ الجِدالُ في الدِّينِ، وأنّ رسولَ اللهِ ﷺ والأئمّةَ

in the presence of al-Ṣādiq (AS), and that the Prophet (SAWA) and the infallible Imāms (AS) prohibited it. So al-Ṣādiq (AS) said, 'He never prohibited it absolutely, but only prohibited dispute in ways that are not the best.'[1182]

المعصومينَ عليهم السلام قد نَهَوا عنه، فقالَ الصّادقُ عليه السلام: لَم يُنْهَ عنهُ مطلَقاً، لكنَّهُ نهىٰ عنِ الجِدالِ بغيرِ الّتي هِيَ أحسَنُ.١١٧٢

63

EXPERIENCE

التَّجرِبَةُ

329. Blessings of Experiences

٣٢٩ـ بَرَكاتُ التَّجرِبَةِ

1050. **Imām ʿAlī (AS) said,** 'Experiences are a beneficial knowledge.'[1183]

١٠٥٠. الإمامُ عليٌّ عليه السلام: التّجارِبُ علمٌ مُستفادٌ.١١٧٣

1051. **Imām ʿAlī (AS) said** to his son (AS), 'I started teaching you manners before your heart hardened and your mind became preoccupied in order for you to comprehend with your mind what experienced people have spared you from searching and experiencing. Thus you were spared the hardship of search and the pain of experience.'[1184]

١٠٥١. عنه عليه السلام ـ لابنهِ عليه السلام ـ: فَبادَرْتُك بِالأَدَبِ قَبْلَ أَنْ يَقسوَ قلبُكَ وَيَشتغِلَ لُبُّكَ لتَستَقْبِلَ بجِدِّ رأيِكَ من الأمرِ ما قَد كَفاكَ أهلُ التَّجارِبِ بُغيَتَهُ وتَجرِبَتَهُ، فتكونَ قد كُفِيتَ مَؤونَةَ الطَّلَبِ وعُوفِيتَ مِن عِلاجِ التَّجرِبَةِ.١١٧٤

1052. **Imām ʿAlī (AS) said,** 'Experience suffices as a trainer.'[1185]

١٠٥٢. عنه عليه السلام: كفىٰ بالتَّجارِبِ مُؤدِّباً.١١٧٥

1053. **Imām ʿAlī (AS) said,** 'The worth of a man's opinion is measured by his experience.'[1186]

١٠٥٣. عنه عليه السلام: رأيُ الرّجُلِ علىٰ قَدْرِ تَجرِبَتِهِ.١١٧٦

1054. **Imām ʿAlī (AS) said,** 'Reason is an instinct that is enhanced by knowledge and experience.'[1187]

١٠٥٤. عنه عليه السلام: العَقلُ غَريزةٌ تَزيدُ بالعِلْمِ والتَّجارِبِ.١١٧٧

1055. **Imām ʿAlī (AS) said,** 'Reason is to retain and preserve experiences.'[1188]

١٠٥٥. عنه عليه السلام: العَقلُ حِفْظُ التَّجارِبِ.١١٧٨

330. Harms Due to Lack of Experience

٣٣٠ـ مَضارُّ عَدَمِ التَّجرِبَةِ

1056. **Imām ʿAlī (AS) said,** 'He who does not test things out is bound to be deceived.'[1189]

١٠٥٦. الإمامُ عليٌّ عليه السلام: مَن لَم يُجَرِّبِ الأُمورَ خُدِعَ.١١٧٩

1057. **Imām ʿAlī (AS) said,** 'He who masters his experiences will be safe from harm, while he who feels needless of experiences will be blind to consequences [of actions].'[1190]

١٠٥٧. عنه عليه السلام: مَن أحْكَمَ التَّجارِبَ سَلِمَ مِنَ المَعاطِبِ ، مَن غَنِيَ عَنِ التَّجارِبِ عَمِيَ عنِ العَواقِبِ.[١١٨٠]

1058. **Imām al-Ṣādiq (AS) said,** 'A man with little experience and admiration of his own opinion must not aspire for power.'[1191]

١٠٥٨. الإمامُ الصّادقُ عليه السلام: لا يَطْمَعَنَّ ... القليلُ التَّجربةِ المُعْجَبُ برأيِهِ في رِئاسةٍ.[١١٨١]

64

ANXIETY

الجَزَع

331. Warning Against Anxiety

٣٣١ ـ التّحذيرُ مِنَ الجَزَعِ

"Indeed man has been created covetous: anxious when an ill befalls him and grudging when good comes his way"[1192]

﴿إنَّ الْإِنْسانَ خُلِقَ هَلُوعاً * إذا مَسَّهُ الشَّرُّ جَزُوعاً * وَإذا مَسَّهُ الْخَيْرُ مَنُوعاً﴾.[١١٨٢]

1059. **The Prophet (SAWA) said,** 'Allah detests two sounds: [the sound of] wailing at a catastrophe, and [the sound of] a flute in the time of prosperity.'[1193]

١٠٥٩. رسولُ اللهِ ﷺ: صَوتانِ يُبغِضُهما اللهُ: إعْوالٌ عند مُصيبةٍ، ومِزْمارٌ عند نعمةٍ.[١١٨٣]

1060. **Imām ʿAlī (AS) said,** 'Beware of anxiety, for it cuts off hope, weakens action, and brings sorrow. And know that the way out [of trouble] lies in two things: resourcefulness where a stratagem exists, and perseverance wherever stratagems fail.'[1194]

١٠٦٠. الإمامُ عليٌّ عليه السلام: إيّاكَ والجَزَعَ؛ فإنَّهُ يَقْطَعُ الأملَ، ويُضْعِفُ العملَ، ويُورِثُ الهَمَّ. واعلَمْ أنَّ المَخرَجَ في أمرَينِ: ما كانَتْ فيهِ حِيلةٌ فالاحْتِيالُ، وما لَم تكُنْ فيهِ حِيلةٌ فالاصْطِبارُ.[١١٨٤]

1061. **Imām ʿAlī (AS) said,** 'Overcome anxiety with patience, for anxiety erases [Allah's] reward and augments the catastrophe.'[1195]

١٠٦١. عنه عليه السلام: اغْلِبوا الجَزَعَ بالصَّبرِ، فإنَّ الجَزَعَ يُحبِطُ الأجْرَ ويُعَظِّمُ الفَجيعةَ.[١١٨٥]

1062. **Imām ʿAlī (AS),** upon hearing the weeping of women for the dead killed in the Battle of *Ṣiffīn*, said, 'Do your women prevail over you from what I can hear?! Can you not prohibit them from *making this din?!'*[1196]

١٠٦٢. عنه عليه السلام ـ لمّا سَمِعَ بُكاءَ النِّساءِ على قَتْلى صِفِّينَ ـ: أتَغلِبُكُم نِساؤكُم على ما أسْمَعُ؟! ألا تَنهَونَهُنَّ عن هذا الرَّنينِ؟![١١٨٦]

1063. **Imām al-Bāqir (AS) said,** 'The worst expression of grief is screaming and wailing with loud cries, beating one's face and chest, tearing out one's hair; and a man who takes up wailing is a man who has abandoned patience.'[1197]

١٠٦٣ . الإمامُ الباقرُ ﵇ : أشَدُّ الجَزعِ الصُّـراخُ بالوَيْلِ والعَويلِ ، ولَطْمُ الوَجهِ والصَّـدرِ ، وجَـزُّ الشَّعْرِ . ومَن أقامَ النّواحَةَ فقد تَركَ الصّبرَ . ١١٨٧

1064. **Imām al-Kāẓim (AS) said,** 'The catastrophe is but a single one for the patient man, and two for the wailing one.'[1198]

١٠٦٤ . الإمامُ الكاظمُ ﵇ : المُصيبَةُ للصّابرِ واحدَةٌ، وللجازعِ اثْنَتانِ . ١١٨٨

65

REQUITAL

الجَزاءُ

332. Requital [of Deeds]

٣٣٢ ـ الجَزاءِ

"To Allah belongs whatever is in the heavens and whatever is in the earth, that He may requite those who do evil for what they have done, and reward those who do good with the best [of rewards]."[1199]

﴿وَلِلَّهِ مَا فِي السَّماوَاتِ وَمَا فِي الْأَرْضِ لِيَجْزِيَ الَّذِينَ أَسَاؤُوا بِمَا عَمِلُوا وَيَجْزِيَ الَّذِينَ أَحْسَنُوا بِالْحُسْنَى﴾ . ١١٨٩

1065. **Imām ʿAlī (AS) said,** 'Every single person will face what he has done and will be requited for what he has made.'[1200]

١٠٦٥ . الإمامُ عليٌّ ﵇ : كُلُّ امرئٍ يَلْقَى ما عَمِلَ، ويُجْزىٰ بِما صَنَعَ . ١١٩٠

(See also: THE REWARD 57)

(أنظر) عنوان ٥٧ «الثواب».

333. The Requital of the Virtuous

٣٣٣ ـ جَزاءُ المُحسِنينَ

"When he [Joseph] came of age, We gave him judgment and [sacred] knowledge, and thus do We reward the virtuous."[1201]

﴿وَلَمّا بَلَغَ أَشُدَّهُ آتَيْنَاهُ حُكْماً وَعِلْماً وَكَذٰلِكَ نَجْزِي الْمُحْسِنِينَ﴾ . ١١٩١

"We called out to him, 'O Abraham! You have indeed fulfilled the vision! Thus indeed do We reward the virtuous!'"[1202]

﴿وَنَادَيْنَاهُ أَنْ يَا إِبْرَاهِيمُ ۞ قَدْ صَدَّقْتَ الرُّؤْيَا إِنَّا كَذَٰلِكَ نَجْزِي الْمُحْسِنِينَ﴾ . ١١٩٢

334. The Requital of Criminals

٣٣٤ـ جَزاءُ المُجرِمين

"But whoever disregards My remembrance, his shall be a wretched life ... Thus do We requite him who is a profligate and does not believe in the signs of his Lord. And the punishment of the Hereafter is severer and more lasting."[1203]

﴿وَمَنْ أَعْرَضَ عَنْ ذِكْرِي فَإِنَّ لَهُ مَعِيشَةً ضَنْكاً وَنَحْشُرُهُ يومَ القيامَةِ أعمىٰ ... وَكَذٰلِكَ نَجْزِي مَنْ أَسْرَفَ وَلَمْ يُؤْمِنْ بِآيَاتِ رَبِّهِ وَلَعَذَابُ الْآخِرَةِ أَشَدُّ وَأَبْقَىٰ﴾.[١١٩٣]

"Indeed those who took up the calf [for worship] shall be overtaken by their Lord's wrath and abasement in the life of the world. Thus do We requite the fabricators [of lies]."[1204]

﴿إِنَّ الَّذِينَ اتَّخَذُوا الْعِجْلَ سَيَنَالُهُمْ غَضَبٌ مِنْ رَبِّهِمْ وَذِلَّةٌ فِي الْحَيَاةِ الدُّنْيَا وَكَذٰلِكَ نَجْزِي الْمُفْتَرِينَ﴾.[١١٩٤]

"They shall have hell for their resting place, and over them shall be sheets [of fire], and thus do We requite the wrongdoers."[1205]

﴿لَهُمْ مِنْ جَهَنَّمَ مِهَادٌ وَمِنْ فَوْقِهِمْ غَوَاشٍ وَكَذٰلِكَ نَجْزِي الظَّالِمِينَ﴾.[١١٩٥]

66

SPYING

التَّجَسُّس

335. Prohibition of Following Up People's Flaws

٣٣٥ـ النَّهيُ عَن تَعَقُّبِ عُيوبِ النّاسِ

"Avoid much suspicion. Indeed some suspicions are sins. And do not spy on or backbite one another. Will any of you love to eat the flesh of his dead brother? You would hate it. And be wary of Allah; indeed Allah is all-clement, all-merciful."[1206]

﴿يا أَيُّهَا الَّذِينَ آمَنُوا اجْتَنِبُوا كَثِيراً مِنَ الظَّنِّ إِنَّ بَعْضَ الظَّنِّ إِثْمٌ وَلا تَجَسَّسُوا وَلا يَغْتَبْ بَعْضُكُمْ بَعْضاً أَيُحِبُّ أَحَدُكُمْ أَنْ يَأْكُلَ لَحْمَ أَخِيهِ مَيْتاً فَكَرِهْتُمُوهُ وَاتَّقُوا اللهَ إِنَّ اللهَ تَوَّابٌ رَحِيمٌ﴾.[١١٩٦]

1066. **The Prophet (SAWA) said,** 'Beware of suspicion, for verily suspicion is the greatest lie; and do not probe one another [for information] nor spy on one another.'[1207]

١٠٦٦. رسولُ اللهِ ﷺ: إيّاكُم والظَّنَّ، فإنَّ الظَّنَّ أكْذَبُ الحَديثِ، ولا تَحَسَّسوا، ولا تَجَسَّسوا.[١١٩٧]

1067. **The Prophet (SAWA) said,** 'I have not been ordered to pry open the hearts of people nor to cleave their bellies [for information or flaws].'[1208]

١٠٦٧. عنه ﷺ: إنّي لَم أُومَرْ أنْ أُنَقِّبَ عن قُلوبِ النّاسِ ولا أشُقَّ بطُونَهم.[١١٩٨]

1068. **Thawr al-Kindī narrated** that 'Umar b. al-Khaṭṭāb was making his way through Madina at

١٠٦٨. كنز العمّال: أنّ عمرَ بنَ الخطّابِ كانَ

night when he heard a man singing in his home. He jumped over the fence and said, 'O Enemy of Allah! Did you think that Allah would conceal you while you disobey Him?!' The man retorted, 'What about you, O Commander of the faithful? Do not hasten to punish me, for if I disobeyed Allah once, you did so three times. He has said, '*Do not spy*,' and you did spy [on me]. He also said, '*Enter the homes from their doors*,' but you jumped over my fence and without my permission. And Allah, the Exalted, says, '*Do not enter homes that are not yours until you are invited in and until you greet their owners.*' 'Umar said, 'Is there any good in you, if I decide to pardon you?' The man said, 'Yes.' Then 'Umar pardoned him and departed.'[1209]

يَعُسُّ بالمدينةِ مِن اللّيل، فسمِعَ صَوتَ رجُلٍ في بيتٍ يتَغنّى، فتَسَوّرَ علَيهِ ، فقالَ : يـا عـدوَّ اللهِ، أظنَنْتَ أن اللهَ يَسْـتُرُكَ وأنتَ فـي مَـعصِيَتِهِ ؟ ! فقالَ: وأنتِ يا أميرَ المؤمنينَ، لا تَعْجَلْ علَيَّ ، إن أكُن عَصَيتُ اللهَ واحِـدةً فـقد عَـصَيتَ اللهَ فـي ثلاثٍ:

قالَ: ﴿ولا تَجَسَّسوا﴾ وقد تَـجَسَّسْتَ ، وقـالَ: ﴿وأتُوا البيوتَ مِن أبوابِها﴾ وقد تَسَوَّرْتَ علَيَّ ، وقد دخلْتَ علَيَّ بـغيرِ إذنٍ ، وقـالَ اللهُ تـعالىٰ: ﴿لا تدْخِلُوا بُيوتاً غيرَ بيـوتِكُـم حتّـىٰ تَستـأنِسـوا وتُسلّمـوا علـىٰ أهلِها﴾.[١١٩٩] قـالَ عُمر : فهلْ عندَكَ مِن خيرٍ، إن عَـفَوتُ عـنكَ ؟ قالَ: نَعَم ، فعَفا عنهُ وخَرجَ وتَركَهُ.[١٢٠٠]

336. Consequences of Probing Other Peoples Flaws

٣٣٦ـ آثارُ التَّجسُّسِ عن الناسِ

1069. **The Prophet (SAWA) said,** 'Do not probe for flaws in believers, for a man that probes the flaws of his brother will have Allah probe his own flaws; and when Allah probes the flaws of a man, He will expose him even if he were inside his own home.'[1210]

١٠٦٩ . رسولُ اللهِ ﷺ : لا تَـطلُبوا عَـثَراتِ المؤمنينَ ؛ فإنّ مَـن تَتَبّعَ عَثَراتِ أخيهِ تَـتَبّعَ اللهُ عَثَراتِهِ ، ومَن تَتَبّعَ اللهُ عَثَراتِهِ يَـفْضَحْهُ ولو فـي جَوفِ بَيتِهِ.[١٢٠١]

1070. **The Prophet (SAWA) said,** 'Do not ask the woman who fornicates about her partner in the offense; for just like it was easy for her to commit fornication, so it will be easy for her to accuse an innocent Muslim.'[1211]

١٠٧٠ . عنه ﷺ : لا تَسألوا الفاجِرَةَ: مَن فَجَرَ بكِ ؟ فكما هانَ علَيها الفُجورُ ، يَهونُ علَيها أنْ تَرميَ البَريءَ المسلِمَ.[١٢٠٢]

1071. **Imām al-Ṣādiq (AS) said,** 'Do not probe into the religiosity of people lest you remain without a friend.'[1212]

١٠٧١ . الإمامُ الصّادقُ عليه السلام : لا تُفَتِّشِ النّاسَ عن أديانِهِم فتَبقىٰ بلا صَديقٍ.[١٢٠٣]

1072. **Sunan Abi Dāwūd,** narrating from one of the companions, 'I heard the Messenger of Allah (SAWA) say, 'If you follow the deficiencies

١٠٧٢ . سنن أبي داود عن بعض الأصحاب : سَـمِعتُ رَسُـول اللهِ ﷺ يَـقُولُ: إنَّكَ إنْ اتَـبَعتَ

of people you will corrupt them or be close to corrupting them.'[1213]

عَـــوراتِ النــاس أفسَـدْتَهُم أوكِـدتَ أن تُفسِدَهُم.١٢٠٤

(See also: THE FAULT: section 1406)

(أنظر) العيب: باب ١٤٠٦.

337. Permissibility of Spying in War

٣٣٧-جَوازُ التَّجَسُّسِ فِي الحُروبِ

1073. **Imām al-Riḍā (AS) said,** 'When the Prophet (SAWA) would send an army with a commander that he did not fully trust, he used to send someone whom he trusted to report on the commander's conduct.'[1214]

١٠٧٣. الإمامُ الرِّضا (ع): كانَ رسولُ اللهِ ﷺ إذا بَعثَ جيشاً فاتَّهَم أميراً، بَعثَ مَعهُ مِن ثِقاتِهِ مَن يَتَجَسَّسُ لَه خَبَرَهُ.١٢٠٥

338. What Must be Given the Benefit of the Doubt

٣٣٨-ما يُؤخَذُ فيهِ بِالظّاهِرِ

1074. **Imām al-Ṣādiq (AS) said,** 'Five things must be judged with the benefit of the doubt: allegiance, marriage, inheritance, animal slaughtering, and testimonies. If the person appears to be trustworthy, his testimony must be accepted without investigating his inner thoughts.'[1215]

١٠٧٤. الإمامُ الصّادقُ (ع): خَمسَةُ أشياءَ يَجِبُ علَى النّاسِ أنْ يأخُذوا بِها ظاهِرَ الحُكمِ: الوِلاياتُ، والتَّناكُحُ، والمَواريثُ، والذَّبائحُ، والشّهاداتُ، فإذا كانَ ظاهِرُهُ ظاهِراً مأموناً جازَتْ شهادَتُهُ، ولا يُسألُ عن باطِنِهِ.١٢٠٦

67

THE SITTING AND THE ASSEMBLY

المجلس

339. The Most Honoured Seating

٣٣٩-أشرَفُ المَجالِسِ

1075. **The Prophet (SAWA) said,** 'There is an honour for everything, and the most honoured seating is the one that faces the Qibla (the direction of Makkah).'[1216]

١٠٧٥. رسولُ اللهِ ﷺ: إنّ لكُلِّ شيءٍ شَرَفاً وإنَّ أشرَفَ المَجالِسِ ما استُقْبِلَ بهِ القِبلَةُ.١٢٠٧

1076. **Imām al-Ṣādiq (AS) said,** 'The Prophet (SAWA) used to sit facing the Qibla most of the *time*.'[1217]

١٠٧٦. الإمامُ الصّادقُ (ع): كانَ رسولُ اللهِ ﷺ أكثَرَ ما يَجلِسُ تُجاهَ القِبلَةِ.١٢٠٨

340. What Must Be Observed in Sittings

٣٤٠ـ ما يَنبَغي مُراعاتُهُ فِي المَجالِسِ

"O you who have faith! When you are told, 'Make room,' in sittings, then do make room; Allah will make room for you. And when you are told, 'Rise up!' Do rise up."[1218]

﴿يا أيُّها الَّذِينَ آمَنُوا إذَا قِيلَ لَكُمْ تَفَسَّحُوا فِي الْمَجَالِسِ فَافْسَحُوا يَفْسَحِ اللهُ لَكُمْ وَإذَا قِيلَ انْشُزُوا فَانْشُزُوا﴾.[١٢٠٩]

1077. **The Prophet (SAWA) said,** 'Do not be obscene in your council and meeting lest people avoid you for your bad behaviour; and do not whisper with a man when you are with another.'[1219]

١٠٧٧. رسولُ اللهِ ﷺ: لا تُفحِش في مَجلسكَ لِكَي يَحْذَروكَ بسُوءِ خلقِكَ، ولا تَناجَ مَع رجُلٍ وأنتَ مَعَ آخَرَ.[١٢١٠]

1078. **Imām ʿAlī (AS) said,** describing the Prophet (SAWA), 'He was never seen stretching his leg out in the presence of someone sitting with him.'[1220]

١٠٧٨. الإمامُ عليٌّ ؏ ـ في أوصافِ النَّبيِّ ﷺ ـ: وما رُؤيَ مُقَدِّماً رِجْلَهُ بينَ يَدَيْ جَليسِهِ قَطُّ.[١٢١١]

1079. **Imām al-Bāqir (AS) said,** 'When one of you enters his brother's place, he must sit wherever his host asks him to, because the owner of a house knows its private spots better than a visitor to it.'[1221]

١٠٧٩. الإمامُ الباقرُ ؏: إذا دَخلَ أحدُكُم على أخيهِ في رَحْلِهِ فلْيَقعُدْ حيثُ يأمرهُ صاحبُ الرَّحْلِ، فإنّ صاحبَ الرَّحْلِ أعْرَفُ بِعُورَةِ بَيتِهِ مِن الدّاخلِ عليه.[١٢١٢]

1080. **Imām al-Ṣādiq (AS) said,** 'Whenever the Prophet (SAWA) entered a place, he used to sit in the closest spot from the entrance [lowest place].'[1222]

١٠٨٠. الإمامُ الصّادقُ ؏: كانَ رسولُ اللهِ ﷺ إذا دَخلَ منزلاً قَعَدَ في أدنى المجلسِ حينَ يَدخُلُ.[١٢١٣]

341. The Main Seating Spot

٣٤١ـ صَدرُ المَجالِسِ

1081. **Imām ʿAlī (AS) said,** 'None but a man possessing three virtues is worthy of sitting in the main seat in an assembly: he who answers when asked, speaks when others are not able to, and provides the counsel which is best for his people. He who does not possess any of these and sits there is certainly a fool.'[1223]

١٠٨١. الإمامُ عليٌّ ؏: لا يَجلِسُ في صَدرِ المجلسِ إلّا رجُلٌ فيهِ ثلاثُ خِصالٍ: يُجيبُ إذا سُئلَ، ويَنطِقُ إذا عَجَزَ القومُ عن الكلامِ، ويُشيرُ بالرّأيِ الّذي فيه صَلاحُ أهلِهِ، فمَن لم يَكُنْ فيهِ شَيءٌ مِنهُنَّ فجَلَسَ فهُو أحمَقُ.[١٢١٤]

1082. **Imām ʿAlī (AS) said,** 'Do not hasten to occupy the highest spot in the assembly, for a seat

١٠٨٢. عنه ؏: لا تُسرِعَنَّ إلى أرْفَعِ مَوضِعٍ في المَجلسِ، فإنَّ المَوضِعَ الّذي تُرفَعُ إليهِ

which you are promoted to is better than one you are demoted to.'[1224]

خَيرٌ مِن الموضعِ الّذي تُحَطُّ عنهُ.[١٢١٥]

342. Prohibited Sitting Places

٣٤٢ـ المَجالِسُ الَّتي نُهِيَ عَنها

"Certainly He has sent down to you in the Book that when you hear Allah's signs being disbelieved and derided, do not sit with them until they engage in some other discourse"[1225]

﴿وَقَدْ نَزَّلَ عَلَيْكُمْ فِي الْكِتَابِ أَنْ إِذَا سَمِعْتُمْ آيَاتِ اللهِ يُكْفَرُ بِها وَيُسْتَهْزَأُ بِها فَلا تَقْعُدُوا مَعَهُم حَتّىٰ يَخُوضُوا فِي حَدِيثٍ غَيْرِهِ﴾.[١٢١٦]

1083. **Imām ʿAlī (AS) said,** 'Do not sit at a table on which wine is served, for a man does not know when he is overcome [by death].'[1226]

١٠٨٣ . الإمامُ عليٌّ عليه السلام : لا تَجْلِسوا على مائدةٍ يُشرَبُ علَيها الخمرُ، فإنّ العبدَ لا يَدري متىٰ يؤخَذُ.[١٢١٧]

1084. **Munyat al-Murīd,** 'It is narrated that the Prophet (SAWA) reproached the sitting of a man between two other men unless he has their permission.'[1227]

١٠٨٤ . منية المريد : رُوِيَ أنَّ النَّبيَّ صلى الله عليه وآله نَهىٰ أن يَجلِسَ الرَّجُلُ بَينَ الرَّجُلَينِ إلّا بِإذنِهِما.[١٢١٨]

1085. **Imām ʿAlī (AS) said,** 'He who believes in Allah and the Last Day must not sit in a suspicious place.'[1228]

١٠٨٥ . عنه عليه السلام : مَن كانَ يؤمنُ باللهِ واليومِ الآخِرِ فلا يَقومُ مكانَ رِيبةٍ.[١٢١٩]

1086. **Imām al-Ṣādiq (AS),** with regards to the verse: *"Certainly He has sent down to you in the Book that when you hear Allah's signs being disbelieved and derided, do not sit with them until they engage in some other discourse"*, said, 'It means that [when you hear] someone denying the truth and rejecting it and speaking ill about the Imāms, you should stand up and leave him and never sit with him again no matter who he might be.'[1229]

١٠٨٦ . الإمامُ الصّادقُ عليه السلام ـ في قوله تعالىٰ : ﴿وقد نَزّلَ عليكم في الكتاب أَنْ إذَا سَمِعْتُمْ آيَاتِ اللهِ...﴾ ـ : إنّما عنىٰ بهذا (إذا سمعتم) الرّجُلَ (الّذي) يَجحَدُ الحقَّ ويُكذِّبُ بهِ ويَقَعُ في الأئمّةِ، فقُمْ مِن عندِهِ ولا تُقاعِدْهُ كائناً مَن كانَ.[١٢٢٠]

1087. **Imām al-Ṣādiq (AS) said,** 'A believer must not sit in a place where Allah is disobeyed if he is unable to make a change.'[1230]

١٠٨٧ . عنه عليه السلام : لا يَنبغي للمؤمنِ أنْ يَجلِسَ مَجلساً يُعصىٰ اللهُ فيهِ ولا يَقدِرُ علىٰ تغييرِهِ.[١٢٢١]

(See also: SITTING COMPANY 68)

(انظر) عنوان ٦٨ «المجالسة».

343. Assemblies are about Trust

٣٤٣ـ المَجالِسُ بِالأمانَةِ

1088. **The Prophet (SAWA) said,** 'Observe *trustworthiness in assemblies,* and exposing your

١٠٨٨ . رسولُ اللهِ صلى الله عليه وآله : المَجالسُ بالأمانةِ، وإفْشاءُ

brother's secret [therein] is betrayal, therefore avoid it.'[1231]

سِرِّ أخيكَ خِيانَةٌ ، فاجْتَنِبْ ذلكَ.١٢٣١

344. Encouraging the Attendance of Gatherings where Allah is Remembered

٣٤٤ـ الحَثُّ عَلىٰ حُضورِ مَجالِسِ الذِّكرِ

1089. **The Prophet (SAWA) said,** 'Stay long in the gardens of Heaven.' They asked, 'O Messenger of Allah! What are the gardens of Heaven?' He said, 'Gatherings where Allah is remembered [*dhikr* sessions].'[1232]

١٠٨٩ . رسولُ اللهِ ﷺ : إرْتَعوا في رياضِ الجنّةِ . قالوا : يا رسولَ اللهِ، وما رياضُ الجنّةِ ؟ قالَ : مَجالِسُ الذِّكرِ.١٢٣٢

1090. **The Prophet (SAWA) said,** 'Assemblies are of three kinds: profitable, safe, and blameworthy. The profitable one is that wherein Allah, the Exalted, is remembered; the safe one is that which is silent; and the blameworthy one is the one that engages in vice.'[1233]

١٠٩٠ . عنه ﷺ : المَجالِسُ ثلاثةٌ : غانِمٌ وسالِمٌ وشاحِبٌ١٢٣٤ ، فأمّا الغانمُ فالّذي يَذكُرُ اللهَ تعالى فيهِ، وأمّا السّالمُ فالسّاكِتُ، وأمّا الشّاحِبُ فالّذي يَخوضُ في الباطلِ.١٢٣٥

1091. **Imām ʿAlī (AS) said,** '[You must] attend *dhikr* sessions.'[1234]

١٠٩١ . الإمامُ عليٌّ ﷺ : عليكَ بمَجالِسِ الذِّكرِ.١٢٣٦

1092. **Imām al-Ṣādiq (AS)** asked Fuḍayl, 'Do you sit together and teach the Ḥadīth?' He said, 'Yes, may I be your ransom.' He said, 'These are the assemblies which I love. O Fuḍayl! Keep our cause alive. May Allah bestow mercy on whoever keeps our cause alive. Whoever remembers us – or we are remembered in his presence – and sheds a tear as small as a fly's wing, Allah will forgive his sins, even if they are more than the foam of the sea.'[1235]

١٠٩٢ . قرب الإسناد عن الإمام الصّادق ﷺ ـ لِفُضَيلٍ ـ : تَجلِسونَ وتُحَدِّثونَ ؟ قالَ : نَعَم جُعِلتُ فِداكَ . قالَ : إنَّ تلكَ المَجالِسَ اُحِبُّها ، فأحْيوا أمْرَنا يا فُضيلُ ، فَرَحِمَ اللهُ مَن أحْيا أمْرَنا . يا فُضَيلُ ، مَن ذَكَرَنا أو ذُكِرنا عندَهُ فَخَرجَ مِن عَينِهِ مِثلُ جَناحِ الذُّبابِ غفرَ اللهُ له ذُنوبَهُ ولو كانَ أكثرَ مِن زَبَدِ البحرِ.١٢٣٧

345. Encouraging the Remembrance of Allah Upon Leaving an Assembly

٣٤٥ـ الحَثُّ عَلىٰ ذِكرِ اللهِ تَعالىٰ عِندَ القِيامِ

1093. **The Prophet (SAWA) said,** 'The expiation (*kaffāra*) for sitting in assemblies is to say, 'Glory be to You, O Allah, and Praise be to You; there is no God but You. O Lord! Forgive me and accept my repentance.'[1236]

١٠٩٣ . رسولُ اللهِ ﷺ : إنَّ كَفّارَةَ المَجلِسِ : سُبحانَكَ اللّهمَّ وبِحَمْدِكَ لا إلهَ إلّا أنتَ ، ربِّ تُبْ عَلَيَّ واغفِرْ لي.١٢٣٨

1094. **Imām al-Ṣādiq (AS) said,** 'The Prophet (SAWA) did not leave an assembly, no matter how insignificant, without seeking forgiveness from Allah, the Exalted, twenty-five times.'[1237]

١٠٩٤ . الإمامُ الصّادقُ ؑ : إنّ رسولَ اللهِ ﷺ كانَ لا يَقومُ من مَجلِسٍ ، وإنْ خَفَّ ، حتّىٰ يَستَغْفِرَ اللهَ عزّ وجلّ خَمْساً وعِشرينَ مَرّةً.[١٢٢٩]

68

SITTING COMPANY

المُجالَسَةُ

346. With Whom Must We Sit?

٣٤٦ ـ مَن نُجالِسُ ؟

1095. **Luqmān (AS) said,** 'O my son! Sit with the scholars and impose on them such that you sit knee to knee with them, for Allah, the Exalted, revives the hearts thereby with the light of wisdom like he revives the land with the heavy rain from the sky.'[1238]

١٠٩٥ . لُقمانُ ؑ : يابُنيَّ، جالِسِ العُلَماءَ وزاحِمْهُم برُكْبَتَيْكَ ، فإنّ اللهَ عزّ وجلّ يُحْيي القُلوبَ بنُورِ الحِكمَةِ كما يُحْيي الأرضَ بِوابِلِ السّماءِ.[١٢٣٠]

1096. **The Prophet (SAWA) said,** 'The Disciples said to Prophet Jesus (AS), 'O Spirit of Allah! With whom must we sit?' He said, 'Those who remind you of Allah when you look at them, whose speech increases your knowledge, and whose deeds draw you to the Hereafter.'[1239]

١٠٩٦ . رسولُ اللهِ ﷺ : قالُوا [الحَوارِيّونَ لعيسىٰ ؑ]: يا رُوحَ اللهِ، فمَن نُجالِسُ إذاً ؟ قالَ : مَن يُذَكِّرُكُمُ اللهَ رُؤيَتُهُ ، ويَزيدُ في عِلْمِكُم منطِقُهُ، ويُرَغِّبُكُم في الآخِرَةِ عَمَلُهُ.[١٢٣١]

1097. **The Prophet (SAWA) said,** 'Do not sit but with every scholar who calls you from five states to five states: from doubt to certainty, from hypocrisy to sincerity, from desire to fear [of Allah], from arrogance to humility, and from deceit to advising.'[1240]

١٠٩٧ . عنه ﷺ : لا تَجْلِسوا إلّا عندَ كُلِّ عالِمٍ يَدْعوكُم مِن خَمْسٍ إلىٰ خَمسٍ : مِن الشَّكِّ إلىٰ اليَقينِ ، ومِن الرِّياءِ إلىٰ الإخْلاصِ ، ومِن الرَّغْبَةِ إلىٰ الرَّهبَةِ ، ومِن الكِبْرِ إلىٰ التّواضُعِ ، ومِن الغِشِّ إلىٰ النّصيحَةِ.[١٢٣٢]

1098. **The Prophet (SAWA) said,** 'Feign poverty and love the poor; sit with them and help them, and shun the companionship of the rich and be kind to them and covet not their wealth.'[1241]

١٠٩٨ . عنه ﷺ : تَمَسْكَنوا وأحِبُّوا المَساكِينَ، وجالِسُوهُم وأعِينوهُم ، تَجافَوا صُحْبَةَ الأغْنياءِ وارْحَموهُم وعِفّوا عن أمْوالِهِم.[١٢٣٣]

1099. **Imām 'Alī (AS) said,** 'Sit with the scholars *and your knowledge will increase, your manners will*

١٠٩٩ . الإمامُ عليٌّ ؑ : جالِسِ العُلَماءَ يَزدَدْ

become refined, and your soul will become pure.'[1242]

علمُكَ، ويَحسُنْ أدبُكَ، وتَزكُ نفسُكَ.١٢٣٤

1100. **Imām ʿAlī (AS) said,** 'Sit with the wise and your intellect will be perfected, your soul will be ennobled, and your ignorance will depart from you.'[1243]

١١٠٠. عنه ﷺ: جالِسِ الحُكَماءَ يَكمُلْ عَقلك، وتَشرُفْ نفسُكَ، ويَنْتَفِ عنكَ جَهلُكَ.١٢٣٥

1101. **Imām ʿAlī (AS) said,** 'Sit with the poor and your gratefulness will increase.'[1244]

١١٠١. عنه ﷺ: جالِسِ الفُقَراءَ تَزدَدْ شُكْراً.١٢٣٦

1102. **Imām Zayn al-ʿĀbidīn (AS) said,** 'Sitting with the righteous brings about righteousness.'[1245]

١١٠٢. الإمامُ زينُ العابدينَ ﷺ: مَجالِسُ الصّالِحينَ داعِيَةٌ إلى الصَّلاحِ.١٢٣٧

347. The Right of One's Sitting Companion

٣٤٧ـ حَقُّ الجَليسِ

1103. **Imām Zaynul ʿĀbidīn (AS) said,** 'As for the right of your sitting companion - it is that you lower your wing to him [in humbleness], be fair to him in exchanging words, and do not get up from your seat without his permission, even though the one who sits with you has the right to leave your company without your permission. Forget his shortcomings and remember his virtues, and do not make him listen to anything other than good.'[1246]

١١٠٣. الإمامُ زينُ العابدينَ ﷺ: أمّا حقُّ جَليسِكَ: فأنْ تُلينَ لَهُ جانِبَكَ، وتُنْصِفَهُ في مُجازاةِ اللَّفظِ، ولا تَقومَ مِن مَجلِسِكَ إلّا بإذْنِهِ، ومَن يَجلِسُ إلَيكَ يَجوزُ لَهُ القِيامُ عَنكَ بغَيرِ إذْنِكَ، وتَنسىٰ زَلّاتِهِ، وتَحفَظُ خَيَراتِهِ، ولا تُسْمِعُهُ إلّا خَيراً.١٢٣٨

(See also: THE FRIEND: section 1107)

(أنظر) الصديق: باب ١١٠٧.

348. Whom One Should not Sit with

٣٤٨ـ مَن لا يَنبَغي مُجالَسَتُهُ

1104. **The Prophet (SAWA) said,** 'Beware of sitting with the dead.' He was asked, 'O Messenger of Allah, who are the dead?' He replied, 'Every rich person whose wealth has made a tyrant of him.'[1247]

١١٠٤. رسولُ اللهِ ﷺ: إيّاكُم ومُجالَسَةَ المَوتىٰ! قيلَ: يا رسولَ اللهِ، مَنِ المَوتىٰ؟ قال: كُلُّ غَنيٍّ أطْغاهُ غِناهُ.١٢٣٩

1105. **Imām ʿAli (AS) said,** 'Mixing with the seekers of this world ruins one's religion and weakens certainty.'[1248]

١١٠٥. الإمامُ عليٌّ ﷺ: خُلطَةُ أبناءِ الدُّنيا تَشينُ الدِّينَ، وتُضعِفُ اليَقينَ.١٢٤٠

1106. **Imām ʿAlī (AS) said,** 'Sitting with people of base desires causes heedlessness of one's faith, and invites Satan thereat.'[1249]

١١٠٦. عنه ﷺ: مُجالَسَةُ أهلِ الهَوىٰ مَنْساةٌ للإيمانِ، ومَحْضَرَةٌ للشَّيطانِ.١٢٤١

1107. **Imām al-Ṣādiq (AS) said,** 'Do not take the people of innovation (*bidʿa*) as companions and do not sit with them lest you be considered one of them in people's eyes.'[1250]

١١٠٧. الإمامُ الصّادقُ ﷺ: لا تَصْحَبوا أهلَ البِدَعِ ولا تُجالِسوهُم فتَصيروا عِندَ النّاسِ كواحِدٍ مِنهُم.١٢٤٢

1108. **Imām al-Ṣādiq (AS) said,** 'Beware of sitting with kings and worldly people, for in this there is the erosion of your religion and it will bring about hypocrisy in you, and this is a serious disease from which there is no cure. It will also engender hardheartedness and deprive you of true submission [to Allah]. You must stick to those people who are most like you and the middle classes of people, for it is with them that you find the true jewels [great talents].'[1251]

١١٠٨. عنه ﷺ: إيّاكُم ومُجالَسَةَ المُلوكِ وأبناءِ الدُّنيا، ففي ذلكَ ذَهابُ دِينِكُم ويُعقِبُكُم نِفاقاً، وذلكَ داءٌ دَوِيٌّ لا شِفاءَ لَهُ، ويُورِثُ قَساوَةَ القَلبِ، ويَسْلُبُكُم الخُشوعَ، وعلَيكُم بالأشْكالِ مِنَ النّاسِ والأوْساطِ مِنَ النّاسِ فعِندَهُم تَجِدونَ مَعادِنَ الجَوهرِ.١٢٤٣

69

THE CONGREGATION

الجَماعَة

349. Allah's Hand Is With The Congregation

٣٤٩ـ يَدُ اللهِ مَعَ الجَماعَةِ

1109. **The Prophet (SAWA) said,** 'O people, stay with the congregation and stay away from division.'[1252]

١١٠٩. رسولُ اللهِ ﷺ: أيُّها النّاسُ، علَيكُم بالجَماعَةِ، وإيّاكُم والفُرقَةَ.١٢٤٤

1110. **The Prophet (SAWA) said,** 'Allah's Hand [i.e. divine aid] is with the congregation. Whenever a straying individual deviates, Satan snatches him up like a wolf snatches a sheep straying from the herd.'[1253]

١١١٠. عنه ﷺ: يَدُ اللهِ علَى الجَماعَةِ، فإذا اشْتَذَّ الشّاذُّ مِنهُم اخْتَطَفَهُ الشَّيطانُ كما يَخْتَطِفُ الذِّئبُ الشّاةَ الشّاذَّةَ مِن الغَنَمِ.١٢٤٥

1111. **The Prophet (SAWA) said,** 'Allah's Hand *[i.e. divine aid]* is with the congregation.'[1254]

١١١١. عنه ﷺ: يَدُ اللهِ مَعَ الجَماعةِ.١٢٤٦

1123. **The Prophet (SAWA) said,** 'Each one of you should trim his moustache and the hairs in his nose and he should groom himself for this enhances his beauty.'[1267]

١١٢٣ . عنه ﷺ : لِيَأخُذْ أحدُكُم مِن شارِبِهِ والشَّعْرِ الّذي في أنْفِهِ، ولْيَتَعاهَدْ نَفْسَهُ ، فإنَّ ذلك يَزيدُ في جمَالِهِ.[١٢٥٩]

1124. **Imām al-Ṣādiq (AS) said,** 'Dress up and beautify yourself, for Allah is beautiful and He loves beauty; and make sure it is lawful [beautification].'[1268]

١١٢٤ . الإمامُ الصّادقُ عليه السلام : البَسْ وتَجَمّلْ ، فإنَّ اللهَ جميلٌ يُحِبُّ الجَمالَ ، وليَكُن مِن حَلالٍ.[١٢٦٠]

354. The Beautiful Image

٣٥٤ـ الصُّورَةُ الجَميلَةُ

1125. **The Prophet (SAWA) said,** 'The best thing given to a believer is good character, and the worst thing given to a man is a corrupt heart in a beautiful figure.'[1269]

١١٢٥ . رسولُ اللهِ ﷺ : خَيرُ ما اُعْطِيَ الرّجُلُ المؤمنُ خُلقٌ حَسَنٌ، وشَرُّ ما اُعْطِيَ الرّجُل قلبُ سوءٍ في صُورةٍ حَسَنةٍ.[١٢٦١]

1126. **The Prophet (SAWA) said,** 'Look for goodness in people with beautiful faces for their deeds are more likely to be good.'[1270]

١١٢٦ . عنه ﷺ : اطلُبوا الخيرَ عِندَ حِسانِ الوُجوهِ، فإنَّ فِعالَهُم أحرىٰ أن تكونَ حَسَناً.[١٢٦٢]

1127. **The Prophet (SAWA) said,** 'The bane of beauty is vanity.'[1271]

١١٢٧ عنه ﷺ : آفَةُ الجَمالِ الخُيَلاءُ.[١٢٦٣]

1128. **Imām 'Alī (AS) said,** 'The beauty of a believer's face is a sign of Allah's care for him.'[1272]

١١٢٨ . الإمامُ عليٌّ عليه السلام : حُسْنُ وَجْهِ المؤمنِ مِن حُسنِ عِنايَةِ اللهِ بهِ.[١٢٦٤]

355. Taking Care of One's Hair

٣٥٥ـ إكرامُ الشَّعرِ

1129. **The Prophet (SAWA) said,** 'Beautiful hair is part of Allah's dressing [for you], so make sure to take care of it.'[1273]

١١٢٩ . رسولُ اللهِ ﷺ : الشَّعرُ الحَسَنُ مِن كِسْوَةِ اللهِ فأكْرِموهُ.[١٢٦٥]

1130. **The Prophet (SAWA) said,** 'Whoever keeps his hair long should care for it well, otherwise, he must cut it.'[1274]

١١٣٠ . عنه ﷺ : مَنِ اتَّخذَ شَعراً فليُحْسِنْ وَلايَتَه، أو لِيَجُزَّهُ.[١٢٦٦]

356. Inner Beauty

٣٥٦ـ جَمالُ الباطِنِ

1131. **The Prophet (SAWA) said,** 'Beauty is in the tongue.'[1275]

١١٣١ . رسولُ اللهِ ﷺ : الجَمالُ في اللِّسانِ.[١٢٦٧]

1132. **The Prophet (SAWA) said,** 'There is no beauty better than the intellect.'[1276]

١١٣٢ . عنه ﷺ : لا جَمالَ أحسَنُ مِن العقلِ.[١٢٦٨]

1133. **The Prophet (SAWA) said,** 'There is no clothing more beautiful than good health.'[1277]

١١٣٣ . عنه ﷺ : لا لِباسَ أجمَلُ مِن العافِيَةِ.[١٢٦٩]

1134. **Imām ʿAlī (AS) said,** 'Allah, the Exalted, placed the beauty of woman in her face and of man in his speech.'[1278]

١١٣٤ . الإمامُ عليٌّ ﷺ : إنَّ اللهَ عزّ وجلّ (جَعَلَ) صُورَةَ المَرأةِ في وَجهِها ، وصُورةَ الرّجُلِ في مَنطِقِهِ.[١٢٧٠]

1135. **Imām al-ʿAskarī (AS) said,** 'Physical beauty is the outer beauty, and the beauty of the intellect is inner beauty.'[1279]

١١٣٥ . الإمامُ العسكريُّ ﷺ : حُسنُ الصُّورةِ جَمالٌ ظاهِرٌ ، وحُسنُ العَقلِ جَمالٌ باطِنٌ.[١٢٧١]

72

RITUAL IMPURITY (*al-Janāba*)

الجَنابَةُ

357. Ritual Bathing of *al-Janāba*

٣٥٧ـ غُسلُ الجَنابَةِ

"O you who have faith! When you stand up for prayer, wash your faces and your hands up to the elbows, and wipe a part of your heads and your feet, up to the ankles. If you are junub, purify yourselves."[1280]

(See also: Qur'an 4:43)

﴿يا أيُّها الّذينَ آمَنوا إذا قُمتُمْ إلَى الصَّلاةِ فَاغسِلُوا وُجُوهَكُمْ وَأيْدِيَكُمْ إلَى المَرافِقِ وَامْسَحُوا بِرُؤُوسِكُمْ وَأرْجُلَكُمْ إلَى الكَعْبَيْنِ وَإنْ كُنتُمْ جُنُباً فَاطَّهَّرُوا﴾.[١٢٧٢]

(أنظر النساء : ٤٣).

1136. **Imām ʿAlī (AS) said,** 'A Muslim must not sleep in the state of ritual impurity (*janāba*); he must only sleep in a pure state. If he cannot find water [to perform the major ablution with], he must perform dry ablution (*tayammum*).'[1281]

١١٣٦ . الإمامُ عليٌّ ﷺ : لا يَنامُ المُسلِمُ وهُو جُنُبٌ ، ولا يَنامُ إلّا على طَهورٍ ، فإنْ لَم يَجِدِ الماءَ فلْيَتيَمَّمْ بالصَّعيدِ.[١٢٧٣]

1137. **Imām al-Bāqir (AS) said,** 'A man in a state of ritual impurity, when he wishes to eat or drink,

١١٣٧ . الإمامُ الباقرُ ﷺ : الجُنُبُ إذا أرادَ أنْ

must wash his hands, rinse his mouth and wash his face before he eats or drinks.'[1282]

يَ كُلَ ويَشْرَبَ ، غَسَلَ يَدَهُ وتَمَضْمَضَ وغَسَلَ وَجهَهُ ، وأكَلَ وشَرِبَ.[١٢٧٤]

73

THE ARMY

الجُنْدُ

358. The Army

٣٥٨ـ الجُنـدُ

1138. **Imām ʿAlī (AS),** in his letter to Mālik al-Ashtar when he appointed him governor of Egypt, said, 'Now the army is, by the will of Allah, the fortress of the subjects, the adornment of the rulers, the strength of the religion and the means of peace. The subjects cannot exist without it.'[1283]

١١٣٨ . الإمامُ عليٌّ ﷺ ـ للأشْتَرِ لَمّا وَلّاهُ مِصرَ ـ: فالجُنودُ بإذْنِ اللهِ حُصونُ الرَّعِيَّةِ ، وزَينُ الوُلاةِ ، وعِزُّ الدِّينِ ، وسُبُلُ الأمْنِ ، وليسَ تَقومُ الرَّعِيَّةُ إلّا بِهِم.[١٢٧٥]

1139. **Imām ʿAlī (AS),** in his letter to Mālik al-Ashtar when he appointed him governor of Egypt, said, 'The best commander of the army before you should be he who lends his help to the army equitably and spends from his money on them and on those of their families who remain behind so that all their concerns converge on the one concern for fighting the enemy. Your kindness to them will turn their hearts to you... Therefore, be broad-minded with regard to their desires, continue praising them and recounting the good deeds of those who have shown such deeds, because the mention of good actions shakes the brave and arouses the weak, if Allah so wills.'[1284]

١١٣٩ . عنه ﷺ ـ أيضاً ـ: ولْيَكُنْ آثَرُ رُؤوسِ جُندِكَ عِندَكَ مَن واساهُم في مَعونَتِهِ ، وأفضَلَ علَيهِم مِن جِدَتِهِ ، بما يَسَعُهُم ويَسَعُ مَن وراءَهُم مِن خُلوفِ أهْليهِم ، حتّىٰ يكونَ هَمُّهُم هَمّاً واحِداً في جِهادِ العَدُوِّ ، فإنَّ عَطْفَكَ علَيهِم يَعطِفُ قُلوبَهُم علَيكَ ... فافْسَحْ في آمالِهِم، وواصِلْ في حُسنِ الثَّناءِ علَيهِم، وتَعْديدِ ما أبْلىٰ ذَوو البلاءِ مِنهُم ، فإنَّ كَثرَةَ الذِّكْرِ لِحُسنِ أفْعالِهِم تَهُزُّ الشُّجاعَ ، وتُحرِّضُ النّاكِلَ إنْ شاءَ اللهُ.[١٢٧٦]

1140. **Imām ʿAlī (AS) said,** 'He who forsakes his army aids his enemy.'[1285]

١١٤٠ . عنه ﷺ: مَن خَذَلَ جُندَهُ نَصرَ أضدادَهُ.[١٢٧٧]

1141. **Imām ʿAlī (AS) said,** 'The bane of the army is disobeying their commanders.'[1286]

١١٤١ . عنه ﷺ : آفَةُ الجُندِ مُخالَفَةُ القادَةِ.[١٢٧٨]

359. The Soldiers of Allah

٣٥٩ـ جُنودُ اللهِ

"To Allah belong the hosts of the heavens and the earth, and Allah is all-mighty, all-wise."[1287]

﴿وَلِلّهِ جُنُودُ السَّماواتِ وَالْأَرْضِ وَكَانَ اللهُ عَزِيزاً حَكِيماً﴾.[١٢٧٩]

"No one knows the hosts of your Lord except Him"[1288]

﴿وما يَعْلَمُ جُنودَ رَبِّكَ إلّا هُوَ﴾.[١٢٨٠]

"If you do not help him, then Allah has already helped him....Then Allah sent down His composure upon him, and strengthened him with hosts you did not see"[1289]

﴿إلّا تَنْصُرُوهُ فَقَدْ نَصَرَهُ اللهُ ... فَأَنْزَلَ اللهُ سَكِينَتَهُ عَلَيْهِ وَأَيَّدَهُ بِجُنُودٍ لَمْ تَرَوْهَا﴾.[١٢٨١]

74

PARADISE

الجَنَّة

360. Encouraging to Aim for Paradise

٣٦٠ـ التَّرغيبُ إلَى الجَنَّةِ

"And hasten towards your Lord's forgiveness and a Paradise as vast as the heavens and the earth, prepared for the Godwary."[1290]

﴿وَسارِعُوا إِلَى مَغْفِرَةٍ مِنْ رَبِّكُمْ وَجَنَّةٍ عَرْضُهَا السَّمَاوَاتُ وَالْأَرْضُ أُعِدَّتْ لِلْمُتَّقِينَ﴾.[١٢٨٢]

1142. **Imām ʿAlī (AS) said,** 'Indeed I have not seen anything like Paradise, the seeker whereof is sleeping, nor have I seen anything like the Fire, whose escapee is sleeping.'[1291]

١١٤٢. الإمامُ عليٌّ عليه السلام: ألا وإنّي لَم أرَ كالجَنّةِ نامَ طالِبُها، ولا كالنّارِ نامَ هارِبُها![١٢٨٣]

1143. **Imām ʿAlī (AS) said,** 'Paradise is the best goal.'[1292]

١١٤٣. عنه عليه السلام: الجَنّةُ أفضَلُ غايَةٍ.[١٢٨٤]

1144. **Imām ʿAlī (AS) said,** 'Paradise is the abode of security.'[1293]

١١٤٤. عنه عليه السلام: الجَنّةُ دارُ الأمانِ.[١٢٨٥]

361. There is No Price for Your Souls Except for Paradise

٣٦١ـ لَيسَ لأنفُسِكُم ثَمَنٌ إلّا الجَنّةُ

"Indeed Allah has bought from the faithful their souls and their possessions for Paradise to be theirs."[1294]

﴿إِنَّ اللهَ اشْتَرَى مِنَ الْمُؤْمِنِينَ أَنْفُسَهُمْ وَأَمْوَالَهُمْ بِأَنَّ لَهُمُ الْجَنَّةَ﴾.[١٢٨٦]

1145. **Imām ʿAlī (AS) said,** 'Verily there is no price for your soul except for Paradise, so do not sell it for anything else.'[1295]

١١٤٥. الإمامُ عليٌّ عليه السلام: إنّهُ لَيسَ لأنفُسِكُم ثَمَنٌ إلّا الجَنّةُ، فلا تَبيعوها إلّا بِها.[١٢٨٧]

362. The Price for Paradise

٣٦٢ـ ثَمَنُ الجَنَّةِ

1146. **Imām ʿAlī (AS) said,** 'The price for Paradise is righteous deeds.'[1296]

١١٤٦. الإمامُ عليٌّ عليه السلام: ثَمَنُ الجَنّةِ العَمَلُ الصّالحُ.[١٢٨٨]

1147. **Imām ʿAlī (AS) said,** 'The price for Paradise is abstention from the world.'[1297]

١١٤٧. عنه عليه السلام: ثَمنُ الجَنّةِ الزُّهدُ في الدُّنيا.[١٢٨٩]

1148. **Imām al-Ṣādiq (AS) said,** 'Saying 'There is no god but Allah' is the price for Paradise.'[1298]

١١٤٨. الإمامُ الصّادقُ عليه السلام: قَولُ «لا إلهَ إلّا اللهُ» ثَمَنُ الجَنّةِ.[١٢٩٠]

363. Requirements for Entering Paradise

٣٦٣ـ موجِباتُ دُخولِ الجَنَّةِ

"And whoever does righteous deeds, whether male or female—such shall enter Paradise and they will not be wronged [so much as] the speck on a date-stone."[1299]

﴿وَمَنْ يَعْمَلْ مِنَ الصَّالِحَاتِ مِنْ ذَكَرٍ أَوْ أُنْثَى وَهُوَ مُؤْمِنٌ فَأُولَئِكَ يَدْخُلُونَ الْجَنَّةَ وَلَا يُظْلَمُونَ نَقِيرًا﴾.[١٢٩١]

"This is the Paradise We will give as inheritance to those of Our servants who are Godwary."[1300]

﴿تِلْكَ الْجَنَّةُ الَّتِي نُورِثُ مِنْ عِبَادِنَا مَنْ كَانَ تَقِيًّا﴾.[١٢٩٢]

1149. **The Prophet (SAWA) said,** 'The most effective way my community will enter Paradise is through Godwariness and good character.'[1301]

١١٤٩. رسولُ اللهِ صلى الله عليه وآله: أكثَرُ ما تَلِجُ بهِ اُمَّتي الجَنّةَ: تَقوَى اللهِ وحُسْنُ الخُلقِ.[١٢٩٣]

1150. **The Prophet (SAWA) said,** 'Whoever meets Allah with three things will enter Paradise from any door he likes: good character, fear of Allah in public as well as in solitude, and desisting from disputation even when in the right.'[1302]

١١٥٠. عنه صلى الله عليه وآله: ثلاثٌ مَن لَقِيَ اللهَ عزّ وجلّ بِهِنَّ دَخَلَ الجَنّةَ مِن أيِّ بابٍ شاءَ: مَن حَسُنَ خُلُقُهُ، وخَشِيَ اللهَ في المَغيبِ والمَحْضَرِ، وتَرَكَ المِراءَ وإنْ كانَ مُحِقّاً.[١٢٩٤]

1151. **The Prophet (SAWA)** asked, 'Would you all love to enter Paradise?' They replied, 'Yes, O Prophet of Allah.' He said, 'Shorten your expectations, fix your eyes on death, and feel ashamed in front of Allah to the extent one ought to.'[1303]

١١٥١. تنبيه الخواطر ـ قال رسول الله صلى الله عليه وآله ـ: أكُلُّكُم يُحِبُّ أنْ يَدخُلَ الجَنّةَ؟ قالوا: نَعَم يا رسولَ اللهِ، قالَ: قَصِّروا مِن الأمَلِ، وثَبِّتوا آجالَكُم بينَ أبْصارِكُم، واسْتَحْيوا مِن اللهِ حَقَّ الحَياءِ.[١٢٩٥]

1152. **The Prophet (SAWA) said,** 'Whoever meets his end in *jihād* for the sake of Allah, even for a moment equal to the gasping of a camel, will enter Paradise.'[1304]

١١٥٢. رسولُ اللهِ صلى الله عليه وآله: مَن خُتِمَ لَهُ بِجِهادٍ في سَبيلِ اللهِ ولو قَدْرَ فُواقِ ناقَةٍ دَخَلَ الجَنّةَ.[١٢٩٦]

1153. **Imām al-Ṣādiq (AS) said,** 'There are three things which if a person performs even one, Allah will make Paradise incumbent upon him: to give charity when one is needy oneself, cheerfulness with the whole world, and being just in spite of one's self.'[1305]

١١٥٣ . الإمامُ الصّادقُ ﷺ : ثلاثٌ مَن أتـىٰ اللهَ بواحِدَةٍ مِنْهنَّ أوْجَبَ اللهُ لَهُ الجَنّةَ: الإنْـفاقُ مِـن إقْتارٍ ، والبِشْرُ لِجَميعِ العـالَمِ ، والإنْـصافُ مِـن نَفْسِهِ .[١٢٩٧]

364. Paradise Surrounded by Trials

٣٦٤ ـ الجَنَّةُ مَحفوفَةٌ بِالمَكارِهِ

"Do you suppose that you would enter Paradise, while Allah has not yet ascertained those of you who have waged jihād and not ascertained the steadfast?"[1306]

﴿أَمْ حَسِبْتُمْ أَنْ تَدْخُلُوا الْـجَنَّةَ وَلَـمّا يَـعْلَمِ اللهُ الَّذِينَ جاهَدُوا مِنْكُمْ وَيَعْلَمَ الصّابِرِينَ﴾ .[١٢٩٨]

1154. **Imām ʿAlī (AS) said,** 'Through trials one attains Paradise.'[1307]

١١٥٤ . الإمامُ عليٌّ ﷺ : بالمَكارِهِ تُنالُ الجَنّةُ .[١٢٩٩]

1155. **Imām al-Bāqir (AS) said,** 'Paradise is surrounded by trials and patience. So whoever endures trials in the world will enter Paradise. Hell is surrounded by pleasures and desires. Thus, whoever allows himself its pleasures and desires [of the world] will enter the Fire.'[1308]

١١٥٥ . الإمامُ الباقرُ ﷺ : الجَنّةُ مَحفوفةٌ بالمَكارِهِ والصَّبرِ ، فمَن صَبرَ علىٰ المَكارِهِ في الدُّنيا دَخلَ الجَنّةَ . وجَهنّمُ مَحفوفةٌ بـاللَّذّاتِ والشَّـهَواتِ ، فمَن أعطىٰ نَفْسَهُ لَذَّتَها وشَهْوَتَها دَخلَ النّارَ .[١٣٠٠]

1156. **Imām al-Riḍā (AS) said,** 'Whoever asks Allah for Paradise but does not endure tribulations has in fact ridiculed himself.'[1309]

١١٥٦ . الإمامُ الرِّضا ﷺ : مَن سألَ اللهَ الجَنّةَ ولَم يَصْبِرْ علىٰ الشَّدائدِ فَقدِ اسْتَهْزأ بنَفْسِهِ .[١٣٠١]

365. Those for Whom Paradise is Guaranteed

٣٦٥ ـ مَن ضُمِنَت لَهُ الجَنَّةُ

1157. **The Prophet (SAWA) said,** 'Whoever safeguards, for my sake, what is between his beard [i.e. his tongue] and what is between his legs [i.e. his private parts], I will safeguard Paradise for him.'[1310]

١١٥٧ . رسولُ اللهِ ﷺ : مَن ضَمِنَ لي مـا بـينَ لِحْيَيْهِ وما بينَ رِجْلَيْهِ ضَمِنتُ له الجَنّةَ .[١٣٠٢]

1158. **The Prophet (SAWA) said,** 'Present me with six things and I will present you with Paradise. When you speak, do not lie; when you

١١٥٨ . عنه ﷺ : تَقبّلوا لي بسِتٍّ أتـقبّلْ لَكُم بالجَنّةِ: إذا حَدَّثتُم فلا تَكْذِبوا ، وإذا وَعدْتُم فلا

promise, do not break it; when you are entrusted with something, do not betray; lower your gazes, guard your private parts, restrain your hands and your tongues.'[1311]

تَخلِفوا ، وإذا ائتُمِنتُم فلا تَخونوا ، وغُضّوا أبصارَكُم ، واحفَظوا فُروجَكُم ، وكُفّوا أيديَكُم وألسِنَتَكُم.[١٣٠٣]

366. Those for Whom Paradise is Forbidden

٣٦٦ـ مَن تُحَرَّمُ عَلَيهِ الجَنَّةُ

"Indeed whoever ascribes partners to Allah, Allah shall forbid him [entry into] Paradise. And his refuge shall be the Fire."[1312]

﴿إِنَّهُ مَنْ يُشْرِكْ بِاللهِ فَقَدْ حَرَّمَ اللهُ عَلَيْهِ الْجَنَّةَ وَمَأْوَاهُ النَّارُ﴾.[١٣٠٤]

1159. **The Prophet (SAWA) said,** 'Paradise is forbidden to three types of people: one who is reproachful for his gifts, one who backbites, and one who imbibes alcohol.'[1313]

١١٥٩ . رسولُ اللهِ ﷺ : تَحرُمُ الجنّةُ علىٰ ثلاثةٍ : علىٰ المَنّانِ ، وعلىٰ المُغتابِ ، وعلىٰ مُدمِنِ الخَمرِ.[١٣٠٥]

1160. **The Prophet (SAWA) said,** 'A traitor and a deceiver will not enter Paradise.'[1314]

١١٦٠ . عنه ﷺ : لا يَدخُلُ الجنّةَ خِبٌّ ولا خائنٌ.[١٣٠٦]

1161. **The Prophet (SAWA) said,** 'Whoever assumes responsibility of taking care of a people, then deceives them, Allah forbids him entry into Paradise.'[1315]

١١٦١ . عنه ﷺ : مَنِ استَرعىٰ رَعِيَّةً فغَشَّها حَرَّمَ اللهُ عليهِ الجنّةَ.[١٣٠٧]

367. The Gates of Paradise

٣٦٧ـ أبوابُ الجَنَّةِ

"—Gardens of Eden, whose gates are flung open for them."[1316]

﴿جَنَّاتِ عَدْنٍ مُفَتَّحَةً لَهُمُ الْأَبْوَابُ﴾.[١٣٠٨]

1162. **The Prophet (SAWA),** 'Heaven has eight doors….he who wants to enter any of these eight doors must cling onto four characteristics: Charity, generosity, good manners and refraining from harming any of the servants of Allah Almighty.'[1317]

١١٦٢ . رسولُ اللهِ ﷺ : الجنّةُ لها ثَمانيةُ أبوابٍ... مَن أرادَ الدُّخولَ مِن هٰذهِ الأبوابِ الثّمانيةِ فليَتَمَسَّكْ بأربعِ خِصالٍ : الصَّدَقةِ والسَّخاءِ وحُسنِ الخُلقِ وكَفِّ الأذىٰ عَن عِبادِ اللهِ تعالىٰ.[١٣٠٩]

1163. **Imām 'Alī (AS) said,** 'Paradise has eight doors: a door through which the prophets and the truthful ones will enter, a door through which the martyrs and the righteous will enter, five doors through which our *shī'a* and our lovers will enter

١١٦٣ . الإمامُ عليٌّ ﷺ : إنَّ للجنّةِ ثَمانيةَ أبوابٍ : بابٌ يَدخُلُ مِنهُ النَّبيّونَ والصِّدّيقونَ ، وبابٌ يَدخُلُ مِنهُ الشُّهداءُ والصّالحونَ ، وخَمسةُ أبوابٍ يَدخُلُ مِنها شيعَتُنا ومُحِبّونا ... ، وبابٌ يَدخُلُ مِنهُ

…, a door through which the rest of the Muslims will enter, that is, those that bear witness to 'There is no god but Allah' and who do not bear an atom's weight of enmity towards us, the *Ahl al-Bayt*.'[1318]

سائِرُ المُسلِمينَ مِمَّنْ شَهِدَ أنْ لا إلهَ إلّا اللهُ ، ولَم يَكُنْ في قَلبِهِ مِقْدارُ ذَرَّةٍ مِن بُغْضِنا أهلَ البَيتِ.١٣١٠

(See also: JIHĀD: section 374, 375)

(أنظر) الجهاد: باب ٣٧٤، ٣٧٥

368. The Ranks in Paradise

٣٦٨ ـ دَرَجاتُ الجَنَّةِ

"But whoever comes to Him with faith and he has done righteous deeds, for such shall be the highest ranks."[1319]

﴿ومَنْ يَأْتِهِ مُؤْمِناً قَدْ عَمِلَ الصّالِحاتِ فَأُولئكَ لَهُمُ الدَّرَجاتُ العُلىٰ﴾.١٣١١

1164. **The Prophet (SAWA) said,** 'There is a station in Paradise that none can attain except a just leader, or one who has maintained relations with his kin, or who is forbearing with his family.'[1320]

١١٦٤ . رسولُ اللهِ ﷺ : إنَّ في الجَنّةِ دَرَجةً لا يَنالُها إلّا إمامٌ عادِلٌ ، أو ذو رَحِمٍ وَصُولٌ ، أو ذو عِيالٍ صَبورٌ.١٣١٢

1165. **Imām ʿAlī (AS) said,** describing Paradise, 'There are degrees differing in excellence, and various stations.'[1321]

١١٦٥ . الإمامُ عليٌّ ؑ ـ في صفةِ الجنّةِ ـ : دَرَجاتٌ مُتَفاضِلاتٌ ، ومَنازِلُ مُتَفاوِتاتٌ.١٣١٣

1166. **Imām ʿAlī (AS) said,** 'The people of Paradise will gaze upon the stations of our *shīʿa* just as one of you gazes at the stars on the horizons of the sky.'[1322]

١١٦٦ . عنه ؑ : إنَّ أهْلَ الجَنّةِ لَيَتَراءَوْنَ مَنازِلَ شِيعَتِنا كما يَتَراءىٰ الرّجُلُ مِنكُمُ الكَواكِبَ في أُفُقِ السَّماءِ.١٣١٤

1167. **Imām Zayn al-ʿĀbidīn (AS) said,** 'Adhere to the Qur'an …for Allah has created Paradise, and has made its stations in accordance with the verses of the Qur'an. So whoever reads the Qur'an, it will say to him, 'Read and ascend!' So whoever from among them enters Paradise, there will not be a station higher than theirs except for the prophets and the truthful ones.'[1323]

١١٦٧ . الإمامُ زينُ العابدينَ ؑ : علَيكَ بالقرآنِ ، فإنَّ اللهَ خَلَقَ الجَنّةَ ... وجَعلَ دَرَجاتِها علىٰ قَدْرِ آياتِ القُرآنِ ، فمَن قَرأَ القُرآنَ قالَ لَهُ : إقْرأْ وارْقَ ، ومَن دَخلَ مِنهُمُ الجَنّةَ لَم يَكُنْ في الجَنّةِ أعلىٰ دَرَجةً مِنهُ ما خَلا النَّبيّونَ والصِّدِّيقونَ.١٣١٥

1168. **Imām al-Ṣādiq (AS) said,** 'For the one who occupies the lowest station in Paradise, were the humans and the jinn to appear as guests for him, nothing would diminish from him if he were to provide them all with food and drink.'[1324]

١١٦٨ . الإمامُ الصّادقُ ؑ : إنَّ أدنىٰ أهْلِ الجَنّةِ مَنزِلاً لَو نَزلَ بهِ الثَّقَلانِ ـ الجِنُّ والإنسُ ـ لَوَسِعَهُم طَعاماً وشَراباً ، ولا يَنْقُصُ مِمّا عِندَهُ شَيءٌ.١٣١٦

369. The First to Enter Paradise

٣٦٩ـ أوَّلُ مَن يَدخُلُ الجَنَّةَ

1169. **The Prophet (SAWA) said** to Imām ʿAlī (AS), 'The first four people to enter Paradise will be you, me, Ḥasan and Ḥusayn.'[1325]

١١٦٩ . رسولُ اللهِ ﷺ ـ لعليٍّ ؑ ـ: إنَّ أولَ أربعةٍ يَدْخُلونَ الجَنّةَ: أنا وأنتَ والحَسنُ والحُسينُ.[١٣١٧]

1170. **The Prophet (SAWA) said,** 'The first of people to enter Paradise will be the poor.'[1326]

١١٧٠ . عنه ﷺ : أوَّلُ مَن يَدخُلُ الجَنّةَ من خَلقِ اللهِ الفُقَراءُ.[١٣١٨]

1171. **The Prophet (SAWA) said,** 'The first to enter Paradise will be the martyr and the servant who worshipped his Lord well.'[1327]

١١٧١ . عنه ﷺ : أوَّلُ مَن يَدخُلُ الجَنّةَ شَهيد وعَبدٌ أحسنَ عِبادةَ ربِّهِ.[١٣١٩]

1172. **Imām al-Bāqir (AS) said,** 'Among the people of Paradise, the first to enter therein will be the one who does good to others.'[1328]

١١٧٢ . الإمامُ الباقرُ ؑ : أوَّلُ أهْلِ الجَنّةِ دُخولاً إلىٰ الجَنّةِ أهْلُ المَعروفِ.[١٣٢٠]

370. The Masters of the People of Paradise

٣٧٠ـ سادَةُ أهلِ الجَنَّةِ

1173. **Imām ʿAli (AS) said,** 'The masters of the people of Heaven are the pious and righteous.'[1329]

١١٧٣ . الإمام عليٌّ ؑ : سادَةُ أهلِ الجَنَّةِ الأتقياءِ الأَبرارُ.[١٣٢١]

1174. **Imām ʿAli (AS) said,** 'The masters of the people of Heaven are the sincere.'[1330]

١١٧٤ . عنه ؑ : سادَةُ أهلِ الجَنَّةِ المُخلِصونَ.[١٣٢٢]

1175. **Imām ʿAli (AS) said,** 'The masters of the people of Heaven are the generous and pious.'[1331]

١١٧٥ . عنه ؑ : سادَةُ أهلِ الجَنَّةِ الأَسخِياءُ وَالمُتَّقونَ.[١٣٢٣]

371. Inclusiveness of Paradise

٣٧١ـ شُمولُ الجَنَّةِ

1176. **The Prophet (SAWA) said,** 'All of you shall enter Paradise except for the one who fled from Allah like the fleeing of a camel from its owner.'[1332]

١١٧٦ . رسولُ اللهِ ﷺ : كُلُّكُم يَدخُلونَ الجنّةَ، إلّا مَن شَرَدَ علىٰ اللهِ شِرادَ البَعيرِ علىٰ أهلِهِ.[١٣٢٤]

1177. **Imām Zayn al-ʿĀbidīn (AS) said,** 'O our followers (*shīʿa*)! As for Paradise, it will not escape you sooner or later, but do compete with each other to attain stations therein.'[1333]

١١٧٧ . الإمامُ زينُ العابدينَ ؑ : معاشِرَ شيعتِنا، أمّا الجنّةُ فلَن تَفوتَكُم سَريعاً كانَ أو بَطيئاً، ولكنْ تَنافَسُوا في الدَّرَجاتِ.[١٣٢٥]

75

MADNESS

الجُنونُ

372. Types of Madness

٣٧٢ـ أنواعُ الجُنونِ

1178. **The Prophet (SAWA) said,** 'Youth is a branch of madness.'[1334]

١١٧٨ . رسولُ اللهِ ﷺ : الشَّبابُ شُعْبَةٌ مِن الجُنونِ.١٣٣٦

1179. **Imām ʿAlī (AS) said,** 'Irascibility is a type of madness, since its perpetrator always regrets. If however, he does not regret, his madness is confirmed.'[1335]

١١٧٩ . الإمامُ عليٌّ ﷺ : الحِدَّةُ ضَرْبٌ مِن الجُنونِ ؛لأنَّ صاحِبَها يَنْدَمُ ، فإنْ لَم يَنْدَمْ فجُنونُهُ مُسْتَحكِمٌ.١٣٣٧

1180. **Imām al-Ṣādiq (AS) said,** 'Whoever answers to everything that is asked of him is mad.'[1336]

١١٨٠ . الإمامُ الصّادقُ ﷺ : إنَّ مَن أجابَ في كلِّ ما يُسْأَلُ عَنهُ لَمَجْنونٌ.١٣٣٨

373. One Who is Truly Mad

٣٧٣ـ المَجنونُ الحَقيقيُّ

1181. It is narrated in *Mishkāt al-Anwār*: The Prophet (SAWA) passed by an insane person and asked, 'What is wrong with him?' He was told that he had gone mad. The Prophet (SAWA) then remarked, 'Rather, he is afflicted. The one who has gone mad is the one who prefers this world to the next.'[1337]

١١٨١ . مشكاةالأنوار :مَرَّرسولُاللهِﷺبمَجْنونٍ، فقالَ: ما لَهُ ؟ فقيلَ : إنَّهُ مَجْنونٌ ، فقالَ : بَلْ هُو مُصابٌ ، إنَّما المَجْنونُ مَن آثَرَ الدُّنيا علَى الآخِرَةِ.١٣٣٩

1182. It is narrated in *Mishkāt al-Anwār*: A man passed by the Prophet (SAWA) while he was sitting with his companions. One of them mentioned that he had gone mad. The Prophet (SAWA) replied, 'This man is, in fact, afflicted, since truly one who is mad, be he male or female, is one who has squandered his youth in other than Allah's obedience.'[1338]

١١٨٢ . مشكاةالأنوار : مَرَّ برسولِ اللهِ ﷺ رجُلٌ وهو في أصْحابِهِ ، فقالَ بعضُ القَومِ: مَجْنونٌ! فقالَ النَّبيُّ ﷺ : بَلْ هذا رجُلٌ مُصابٌ، إنَّما المَجْنونُ عَبدٌ أو أمَةٌ أبْلَيا شَبابَهُما في غَيرِ طاعةِ اللهِ.١٣٤٠

1183. It is related from Jābir b. ʿAbdallāh al-Anṣārī that the Prophet (SAWA) passed by one

١١٨٣ . معاني الأخبار : مَرَّ رسولُ اللهِ ﷺ برَجُلٍ مَصْروعٍ ... فقالَ : ما هذا بمَجْنونٍ ، ألَا اُخبِرُكُم

who was affected by madness, and said, 'Shall I inform you of one who is truly mad?' Then he said, 'Indeed one who is mad is one who is haughty in his gait, looking over his shoulders, and swinging his sides from side to side. That is one who is mad and this is one afflicted.'[1339]

بالمَجْنونِ حقَّ المَجْنونِ ؟....قالَ: إنَّ المَجْنونَ حقَّ المَجْنونِ المُتَبَخْتِرُ في مِشيَتِهِ ، النّاظِرُ في عِطْفَيْهِ ، المُحَرِّكُ جَنْبَيهِ بمِنْكَبَيْهِ ، فذاكَ المَجْنونُ وهذا المُبْتلىٰ.١٣٣١

76

JIHĀD (1)

الجِهادُ (١)

The Lesser Jihād[1340]

الجِهادُ الأصغَرُ

374. Encouraging of the Lesser Jihād

٣٧٤ ـ الحَثُّ عَلَى الجِهادِ

"O Prophet! Wage jihād against the faithless and the hypocrites, and be severe with them. Their refuge shall be hell, and it is an evil destination."[1341]

﴿يا أَيُّهَا النَّبِيُّ جاهِدِ الْكُفّارَ وَالْمُنافِقِينَ وَاغْلُظْ عَلَيْهِمْ وَمَأْوَاهُمْ جَهَنَّمُ وَبِئْسَ الْمَصِيرُ﴾.١٣٣٢

"Say, 'If your fathers and your sons, your brethren, your spouses, and your kinsfolk, the possessions that you have acquired, the business you fear may suffer, and the dwellings you are fond of, are dearer to you than Allah, and His Apostle and to waging jihād in His way, then wait until Allah issues His edict, and Allah does not guide the transgressing lot."[1342]

﴿قُلْ إِنْ كَانَ آبَاؤُكُمْ وَأَبْنَاؤُكُمْ... أَحَبَّ إِلَيْكُمْ مِنَ اللهِ وَرَسُولِهِ وَجِهَادٍ فِي سَبِيلِهِ فَتَرَبَّصُوا حَتَّىٰ يَأْتِيَ اللهُ بِأَمْرِهِ وَاللهُ لا يَهْدِي الْقَوْمَ الْفَاسِقِينَ﴾.١٣٣٣

1184. **The Prophet (SAWA) said,** 'Whoever dies, having neither waged a campaign nor having intended to do so, dies on a branch of hypocrisy [in his heart].'[1343]

١١٨٤. رسولُ اللهِ ﷺ: مَن ماتَ ولَم يَغْزُ ، ولَم يُحدِّثْ بِهِ نفسَهُ ، ماتَ علىٰ شُعْبَةٍ مِن نِفاقٍ.١٣٣٤

1185. It is narrated in *Mustadrak al-Wasā'il* that a man went to a mountain to worship Allah and his family had went to the Prophet (SAWA) to complain about him. The Prophet forbade him from it, saying, 'The patience of a Muslim in certain places of *jihād* for one day is better than worshipping for forty years.'[1344]

١١٨٥. مستدرك الوسائل: رُوِيَ أنَّ رجُلاً أتىٰ جَبَلاً لِيَعْبُدَ اللهَ فيهِ ، فجاءَ بِهِ أهلُهُ إلى رَسولِ اللهِ ﷺ فنَهاهُ عَن ذلكَ ، وقالَ له: إنَّ صَبرَ المسلمِ في بعضِ مَواطِنِ الجِهادِ يَوماً واحداً خَيرٌ لَهُ مِن عِبادَةِ أربعينَ سنةً.١٣٣٥

1186. **Imām ʿAlī (AS) said,** 'Indeed *jihād* is one of the gates of Paradise that Allah has opened for his exceptional friends. It is the garment of piety, Allah's fortified defence and a solid shield.'[1345]

١١٨٦ . الإمامُ عليٌّ ﵇ :إنّ الجِهادَ بابٌ مِن أبْوابِ الجَنّةِ فَتَحَهُ اللهُ لِخاصَّةِ أوْلِيائهِ ، وهُو لِباسُ التَّقوىٰ ، ودِرْعُ اللهِ الحَصينَةُ ، وجُنّتُهُ الوَثيقَةُ.[١٣٣٦]

1187. **Imām ʿAlī (AS) said,** '*Jihād* is the pillar of religion and the path of the felicitous.'[1346]

١١٨٧ . عنه ﵇ : الجِهادُ عِمادُ الدِّينِ ، ومِنْهاجُ السُّعَداءِ.[١٣٣٧]

1188. **Imām ʿAlī (AS) said,** 'Verily Allah has made *jihād* obligatory and has magnified it and made it a [source of] triumph and a helper. By Allah, neither one's worldly affairs nor one's religion are set aright except through it.'[1347]

١١٨٨ . عنه ﵇ : إنّ اللهَ فَرضَ الجِهادَ وعَظَّمَهُ وجَعلَهُ نَصْرَهُ وناصِرَهُ. واللهِ ، ما صَلُحتْ دُنيا ولا دِينٌ إلّا بهِ.[١٣٣٨]

1189. **Imām ʿAlī (AS) said,** 'Certainly *jihād* is the noblest of deeds after [acceptance of] Islam, and it is the pillar of religion. The reward for it is great, while at the same time, consistently maintaining one's honour and strength. It is the assault in which there are rewards and good tidings of Paradise after martyrdom.'[1348]

١١٨٩ . عنه ﵇ : إنَّ الجِهادَ أشْرَفُ الأعمالِ بعدَالإسلامِ ، وهُو قِوامُ الدِّينِ ، والأجْرُ فيهِ عَظيمٌ مَع العِزّةِ والمَنَعةِ ، وهُوالكَرّهُ ، فيهِ الحَسَناتُ والبُشْرىٰ بالجنّةِ بَعد الشَّهادَةِ.[١٣٣٩]

1190. **Imām ʿAli (AS) said,** in his letter to his administrator Mikhnaf, 'Indeed it is a duty upon he who has knowledge to struggle against he who turns away from the truth while despising it and he chooses to sleep in blindness and misguidance.'[1349]

١١٩٠ . عنه ﵇ ـفي كتابِه إلىٰ عامِلِه مخْنَفٍ ـ: فإنَّ جِهادَ مَن صَدَفَ عَن الحقِّ رَغْبةً عنهُ ، وعَبَّ في نُعاسِ العَمىٰ والضَّلالِ اخْتِياراً لهُ ، فَريضَةٌ علىٰ العارِفينَ.[١٣٤٠]

(See also: WEAPONRY: section 962)

(اُنظر) السلاح: باب ٩٦٢.

375. The One Who Wages Jihād

٣٧٥ ـ المُجاهِدُ

"Not equal are those of the faithful who sit back—excepting those who suffer from some disability—and those who wage jihād in the way of Allah…"[1350]

﴿لا يَسْتَوِي الْقاعِدُونَ مِنَ الْمُؤْمِنينَ غَيْرُ أُولِى الضَّرَرِ وَالْمُجاهِدُونَ فِي سَبِيلِ اللهِ﴾.[١٣٤١]

1191. **The Prophet (SAWA) said,** 'The deeds of all the worshippers when compared to those who wage *jihād* in the way of Allah is as a gulp of sea-water that a swallow takes into his beak.'[1351]

١١٩١ . رسولُ اللهِ ﷺ : ما أعْمالُ العِبادِ كُلِّهِم عِندالمُجاهِدينَ في سبيلِ اللهِ إلّا كَمِثْلِ خُطّافٍ أخَذَ بمِنْقارِهِ مِن ماءِ البَحرِ.[١٣٤٢]

1192. **The Prophet (SAWA) said,** 'Swords are the keys to Paradise.'[1352]

١١٩٢ . عنه ﷺ : السُّيوفُ مَفاتِيحُ الجَنّةِ.[١٣٤٣]

1193. **Imām ʿAlī (AS) said,** 'The doors of the heavens are opened for those who wage *jihād*.'[1353]

١١٩٣ . الإمامُ عليٌّ ﷺ : المُجاهِدونَ تُفْتَحُ لَهُم أبوابُ السَّماءِ.١٣٤٤

376. Aiding Those Who Wage Jihād and Censure of Those Who Harm Them

٣٧٦ـ إعانَةُ المُجاهِدينَ وذَمُّ إيذائِهِم

1194. **The Prophet (SAWA) said,** 'Whoever equips a warrior, even with a needle or thread, Allah forgives his past and future sins.'[1354]

١١٩٤ . رسولُ اللهِ ﷺ : مَن جَهَّزَ غازياً بسِلْكٍ أو إبْرَةٍ غَفَرَاللهُ لَهُ ما تَقدَّمَ من ذَنبِهِ وما تَأخَّرَ.١٣٤٥

1195. **The Prophet (SAWA) said,** 'Whoever carries a message on behalf of a fighter during war is like one who frees a slave, and he partakes in the reward of the one who actually fought.'[1355]

١١٩٥ . عنه ﷺ : مَن بَلَّغَ رسالةَ غازٍ كانَ كَمَنْ أعْتَقَ رَقَبَةً، وهُو شَريكُهُ في بابِ «ثوابِ» غَزْوَتِهِ.١٣٤٦

1196. **The Prophet (SAWA) said,** 'Be wary of harming those who fight in the way of Allah, for Allah is angered for their sake just as He is for the sake of the Prophet (SAWA), and He answers their prayers just as He answers the prayers of the Prophet (SAWA).'[1356]

١١٩٦ . عنه ﷺ :اتَّقوا أذى المُجاهِدينَ في سبيلِ اللهِ، فإنَّ اللهَ يَغْضَبُ لَهُم كَما يَغْضَبُ للرُّسُلِ، ويَسْتَجيبُ لَهُم كَما يَسْتَجيبُ لَهُم.١٣٤٧

377. The Command to Struggle with One's Hands, Tongue, and Heart

٣٧٧ـ الأمرُ بِالجِهادِ بِالأيدي والألسُنِ والقُلوبِ

1197. **The Prophet (SAWA) said,** 'The prayer of one carrying his sword is seven hundred times better than praying without it.'[1357]

١١٩٧ . رسولُ اللهِ ﷺ :صَلاةُ الرَّجُلِ مُتَقلِّداً بسَيفِهِ تَفْضُلُ على صَلاتِهِ غيرَ مُتَقلِّدٍ بسَبعِمائةِ ضِعْفٍ.١٣٤٨

1198. **Imām ʿAlī (AS) said,** 'Fight in the way of Allah with your hands; and if you are not able to do so then fight with your tongues; and if you are still not able to then fight with your hearts.'[1358]

١١٩٨ . الإمامُ عليٌّ ﷺ : جاهِدوا في سبيلِ اللهِ بأيْديكُم، فإنْ لم تَقْدِروا فجاهِدوا بألْسِنَتِكُم، فإنْ لم تَقْدِروا فجاهِدوا بقُلوبِكُم.١٣٤٩

1199. **Imām ʿAlī (AS) said,** 'By Allah! By Allah! Struggle with your wealth, your selves and your tongues for the sake of Allah.'[1359]

١١٩٩ . عنه ﷺ : اللهَ اللهَ في الجِهادِ بأموالِكُم وأنْفُسِكُم وألْسِنَتِكُم في سبيلِ اللهِ.١٣٥٠

(See also: ENJOINING GOOD AND PROHIBITING WRONG (2): section 1290; POETRY: section 1034)

(اُنظر) المعروف (٢): باب ١٢٩٠؛ الشعر: باب ١٠٣٤

378. Abandoning Jihād

٣٧٨ـ تركُ الجهادِ

1200. **The Prophet (SAWA) said,** 'Allah covers with disgrace the one who abandons *jihād*, and subjects him to poverty, and deprivation in his religion. Verily Allah, blessed and most High, has honoured my community by the solid hooves of its cavalry, and the tips of its lances.'[1360]

١٢٠٠ . رسولُ اللهِ ﷺ : فمَن تَركَ الجِهادَ ألْبسه اللهُ ذُلّاً في نفسِه، وفَقْراً في مَعيشَتِه، ومَحْقاً في دِينهِ. إنّ اللهَ تباركَ وتعالىٰ أعَزَّ اُمّتي بسَنابِكِ خَيْلِها ومَراكِزِ رِماحِها.١٣٦٠

379. Branches of Jihād

٣٧٩ـ شُعَبُ الجهادِ

1201. **Imām 'Alī (AS) said,** '*Jihād* has four branches: enjoining the good, forbidding the wrong, fortitude in the battlefield, and detesting the wicked.'[1361]

١٢٠١ . الإمامُ عليٌّ ﷺ : الجِهادُ علىٰ أرْبَعِ شُعَبٍ: علىٰ الأمرِ بالمَعروفِ والنَّهيِ عنِ المُنكَرِ والصِّدْقِ في المَواطِنِ وشَنَآنِ الفاسِقينَ.١٣٦١

380. Keeping Posts

٣٨٠ـ المُرابطَةُ

"Prepare against them whatever you can of [military] power and war-horses, awing thereby the enemy of Allah, and your enemy, and others besides them, whom you do not know but Allah knows them."[1362]

﴿وَأَعِدُّوا لَهُمْ مَا اسْتَطَعْتُمْ مِنْ قُوَّةٍ وَمِنْ رِبَاطِ الْخَيْلِ تُرْهِبُونَ بِهِ عَدُوَّ اللهِ وَعَدُوَّكُمْ وَآخَرِينَ مِنْ دُونِهِمْ﴾.١٣٦٢

"O you who have faith! Be patient, stand firm, and close [your ranks], and be wary of Allah so that you may be felicitous."[1363]

﴿يَا أَيُّهَا الَّذِينَ آمَنُوا اصْبِرُوا وَصَابِرُوا وَرَابِطُوا وَاتَّقُوا اللهَ لَعَلَّكُمْ تُفْلِحُونَ﴾.١٣٦٣

1202. **The Prophet (SAWA) said,** 'Keeping your posts for a single day is better than the whole world and all that it contains.'[1364]

١٢٠٢ . رسولُ اللهِ ﷺ : رِباطُ يَومٍ في سبيلِ اللهِ خَيرٌ مِن الدُّنيا وما عَلَيها.١٣٦٤

1203. **The Prophet (SAWA) said,** 'Every action will be separated from its owner upon death, except the one who maintained his post for the sake of Allah, since it will be increased and rewarded to him until the Day of Resurrection.'[1365]

١٢٠٣ . عنه ﷺ : كُلُّ عَملٍ مُنْقطِعٌ عَن صاحِبِهِ إذامات إلّا المُرابِطَ في سبيلِ اللهِ ، فإنّهُ يُنْمىٰ لَهُ عَملُهُ ويُجْرىٰ علَيهِ رِزْقُهُ إلىٰ يَومِ القِيامَةِ.١٣٦٥

381. The Merit of Standing Guard

٣٨١ـ فَضلُ الحِراسَةِ

1204. **The Prophet (SAWA) said,** 'Standing guard for a single night for the sake of Allah is

١٢٠٤ . رسولُ اللهِ ﷺ : حَرَسُ لَيلةٍ في سبيلِ اللهِ

better than a thousand nights spent in worship followed by fasting during the day.'[1366]

عزّ وجلّ أفْضَلُ مِن ألفِ لَيلةٍ يُقامُ لَيلُها ويُصامُ نَهارُها.[١٣٥٧]

1205. **The Prophet (SAWA) said,** 'The eyes of two categories of people will never touch the fire: the one who cried out of fear of Allah, and the one who spent the night awake standing guard for the sake of Allah.'[1367]

١٢٠٥. عنه ﷺ: عَيْنانِ لا تَمَسُّهُما النّارُ: عَينٌ بَكَتْ مِن خَشْيَةِ اللهِ، وعَينٌ باتَتْ تَحْرُسُ في سبيلِ اللهِ.[١٣٥٨]

77

JIHĀD (2): The Greater Jihād

الجهاد (٢)
الجِهادُ الأكبَرُ

382. Forms of Jihād

٣٨٢ـ أنواعُ الجِهادِ

1206. **Imām al-Ḥusayn (AS)** was asked about *jihād*, as to whether it was a recommended act or an obligatory one, to which he replied, '*Jihād* comes in four forms, two of which are obligatory, one of which is recommended but can only be undertaken with an obligation, and one which is recommended. The first obligatory *jihād* is that which a man wages against his own self in keeping away from acts of disobedience to Allah. This is one of the greatest forms of *jihād*. Waging *jihād* against those disbelievers who persecute you is also an obligation. As for the *jihād* which is recommended but can only be undertaken with an obligation is to fight the enemy, which is an obligation upon the whole community, and which if they abandon, they are all punishable for it. It is a recommendation upon an Imām, the limit of which is to come and face the enemy and fight them with his community. As for the *jihād* which is recommended, it is [embodied in] every recommended practice which a person performs and strives in its performance, its completion and

١٢٠٦. الإمامُ الحسينُ عليه السلام ـ سُئِلَ عَنِ الجَهادِ: سُنَّةٌ أو فَرِيضةٌ؟ فقالَ عليه السلام ـ: الجِهادُ على أرْبَعَةِ أوْجُهٍ: فجِهادانِ فَرْضٌ وجِهادُ سُنَّةٍ لا يُقامُ إلّا مَعَ فَرْضٍ وجِهادُ سُنَّةٍ، فأمّا أحَدُ الفَرْضَيْنِ فجِهادُ الرَّجُلِ نَفْسَهُ عن مَعاصِي اللهِ وهو مِنْ أعْظَمِ الجِهادِ وَمُجاهَدَةُ الّذين يَلُونَكُمْ مِنَ الكُفّارِ فَرْضٌ. وأمّا الجِهادُ الّذي هو سُنّة لا يُقامُ إلّا مَعَ فَرْض فَإنَّ مجاهَدَةَ العَدُوِّ فرضٌ على جميع الأُمّة لو تركوا الجهاد لَأَتاهم العَذابُ وهذا هو مِنْ عذابِ الأُمَّةِ وهُوَ سُنَّةٌ عَلَى الإمامِ وحَدُّهُ أنْ يَأتِيَ العَدُوَّ مَعَ الأُمَّةِ فيجاهِدَهم. وأمّا الجِهادُ الذي هُوَ سُنّةٌ فكُلُّ سُنّةٍ أقامَها الرَّجُلُ وجاهدَ

its revival. Such an act, and the striving to perform it is one of the best deeds because it is a revival of the Prophetic practice, and the Prophet (SAWA) has said, 'Whoever establishes a good habitual practice, he will get his own reward for it as well as the reward of whoever performs it after him until the Day of Resurrection, without any decrease in their reward thereof.'[1368]

في إقامَتِها وبُلُوغِها وإحيائِها فَالعَمَلُ والسَّعْيُ فيها مِنْ أفضلِ الأَعْمال لِأَنَّها إحياءُ سُنَّةٍ وقَدْ قالَ رسولُ الله ﷺ: «مَنْ سَنَّ سُنَّةً حَسَنَةً فَلَهُ أجْرُها وأجْرُ مَنْ عَمِلَ بِها إلىٰ يَوْمِ القِيامَةِ مِنْ غَيْرِ أن يَنْقُصَ مِنْ أجُورِهِم شَيْئاً».[١٣٥٩]

1207. **Imām ʿAlī (AS) said,** 'The *jihād* of a woman is being a good wife to her husband.'[1369]

١٢٠٧. الإمامُ عليٌّ عليه السلام: جِهادُ المَرأةِ حُسْنُ التَّبَعُّلِ.[١٣٦٠]

383. Enjoinment of Combatting the Self

٣٨٣ ـ الحَثُّ عَلىٰ جِهادِ النَّفسِ

1208. **The Prophet (SAWA) said,** 'The one who truly wages *jihād* is the one who combats his self for the sake of Allah.'[1370]

١٢٠٨. رسولُ اللهِ ﷺ: المُجاهِدُ مَن جاهَدَ نَفْسَهُ في اللهِ.[١٣٦١]

1209. **Imām ʿAlī (AS) said,** '*Jihād* of the self is the dowry for Paradise.'[1371]

١٢٠٩. الإمامُ عليٌّ عليه السلام: جِهادُ النَّفْسِ مَهْرُ الجَنّةِ.[١٣٦٢]

1210. **Imām ʿAlī (AS) said,** 'Prevent your self from fulfilling its desires, and make it hold fast to the Book of Allah during misgivings.'[1372]

١٢١٠. عنه عليه السلام: رُدَّ عَن نَفْسِكَ عِند الشَّهَواتِ، وأقِمْها علىٰ كِتابِ اللهِ عِند الشُّبُهاتِ.[١٣٦٣]

1211. **Imām al-Kāẓim (AS) said,** 'Combat your self to avert it against its desires, for this is incumbent upon you as fighting your enemy.'[1373]

١٢١١. الإمامُ الكاظمُ عليه السلام: جاهِدْ نَفْسَكَ لِتَرُدَّها عَن هَواها، فإنَّهُ واجِبٌ علَيكَ كجِهادِ عَدُوِّكَ.[١٣٦٤]

384. The Greater Jihād

٣٨٤ ـ الجِهادُ الأكبَرُ

1212. **Imām ʿAlī (AS)** relates, 'The Prophet (SAWA) dispatched troops [to a mission]. On seeing the returning armies from the battlefront, he said, 'Blessed are those who have performed the lesser *jihād*, and have yet to perform the greater one.' When asked, 'O Messenger of Allah, what is the greater *jihād*?' the Prophet replied, 'The *jihād* of the self', and added, 'The best *jihād* is that of one who combats his own self that is between his two sides.'[1374]

١٢١٢. معاني الأخبار عن الإمامُ عليٌّ عليه السلام: إنَّ رسولَ اللهِ ﷺ بَعثَ سَرِيّةً، فلَمّا رَجَعوا قالَ: مَرْحَباً بقَومٍ قَضَوُا الجِهادَ الأصْغَرَ وبَقِيَ علَيهِمُ الجِهادُ الأكْبَرُ. قيلَ: يا رسولَ اللهِ، وما الجِهادُ الأكْبَرُ؟ قالَ: جِهادُ النَّفْس. وقالَ عليه السلام: أفْضَلُ الجِهادِ مَن جاهَدَ نَفْسَهُ الّتي بينَ جَنْبَيهِ.[١٣٦٥]

1213. **Imām ʿAlī (AS) said,** 'The best *jihād* is combatting one's self against its desires, and weaning it from the pleasures of this world.'[1375]

١٢١٣ . عنه (عليه السلام) : أفْضَلُ الجِهادِ جِهادُ النَّفْسِ عنِ الهَوىٰ ، وفِطامُها عَن لَذّاتِ الدُّنيا.١٣٦٦

1214. **Imām al-Bāqir (AS) said,** 'There is no greater distinction than *jihād*, and no *jihād* like combatting one's self.'[1376]

١٢١٤ . الإمامُ الباقرُ (عليه السلام) : لا فَضيلةَ كـالجِهادِ ، ولا جِهادَ كمُجاهَدَةِ الهوىٰ.١٣٦٧

385. What is Necessary for Combatting the Self

٣٨٥ ـ ما يَنبَغي في مُجاهَدَةِ النَّفسِ

1215. **Imām ʿAlī (AS) said,** 'Struggle against your self in Allah's worship just as one fights one's enemy, and overcome it just as one overcomes one's opponent, for the strongest of people is he who has triumphed over his self.'[1377]

١٢١٥ . الإمامُ عليٌّ (عليه السلام) : جاهِدْ نَفْسَكَ علىٰ طاعةِ اللهِ مُجاهَدَةَ العَدُوِّ عَدُوَّهُ ، وغالِبْها مُغالَبةَ الضِّدِّ ضِدَّهُ ؛ فإنَّ أقْوىٰ النّاسِ مَن قَوِيَ علىٰ نَفْسِهِ.١٣٦٨

1216. **Imām ʿAlī (AS) said,** 'Gain control of your souls through constant self-struggle.'[1378]

١٢١٦ . عنه (عليه السلام) : امْـلِكُوا أنـفسَكُم بـدوامِ جِهادِها.١٣٦٩

386. The Fruit of Struggle

٣٨٦ ـ ثَمَرَةُ المُجاهَدَةِ

1217. **The Prophet (SAWA) said,** 'Through constant self-struggle are bad habits overcome.'[1379]

١٢١٧ . رسولُ اللهِ ﷺ : بالمُجاهَدَةِ يُغلَبُ سُوءِ العادَةِ.١٣٧٠

1218. **The Prophet (SAWA) said,** 'Struggle against the desires of your self and wisdom will enter your hearts.'[1380]

١٢١٨ . عنه ﷺ : جاهِدوا أنفسَكُم علىٰ شَهَواتِكُم تَحِلَّ قلوبَكُم الحِكمَةُ.١٣٧١

1219. **The Prophet (SAWA) said,** 'Struggle against your selves through reducing food and drink, and the angels will protect you and Satan will flee from you.'[1381]

١٢١٩ . عنه ﷺ : جاهِدوا أنفسَكُم بقِلَّةِ الطَّعامِ والشَّـرابِ ، تُـظِلَّكُمُ المَـلائكةُ ويَـفِرَّ عَـنكُمُ الشَّيطانُ.١٣٧٢

1220. **Imām ʿAlī (AS) said,** 'Struggle against your lower desires, overcome your anger, oppose your bad habits, purify your self, perfect your intellect, and bring to completion the reward that is with your Lord.'[1382]

١٢٢٠ . الإمامُ عليٌّ (عليه السلام) : جاهِدْ شَهْوَتَكَ وغالِبْ غَضَبَكَ وخالِفْ سُوءَ عـادَتِكَ ، تَـزْكُ نَـفْسُكَ ، ويَكْمُلْ عَقلُكَ ، وتَسْتَكمِلْ ثَوابَ ربِّكَ.١٣٧٣

1221. **Imām ʿAlī (AS) said,** 'Controlling the self and combatting with it against its lower desires raises one's stations and multiplies one's rewards.'[1383]

١٢٢١ . عنه (عليه السلام) : رَدْعُ النَّـفْسِ وجِهادُها عـن أهْـوِيَتِها يَـرفَعُ الدَّرَجـاتِ ويُـضاعِفُ الحَسَناتِ.١٣٧٤

1222. **Imām ʿAlī (AS) said,** 'Salvation for the soul is [attained] through self-struggle.'[1384]

١٢٢٢ . عنه ﷺ : بالمُجاهَدَةِ صَلاحُ النَّفْسِ.١٣٧٥

78

JIHĀD (3)
Striving To Obey Allah

الجهاد (٣)
الاجتهاد في طاعة الله

387. Encouraging to Strive to Obey Allah

٣٨٧ ـ الحَثُّ عَلَى الاجتِهادِ في طاعَةِ اللهِ

1223. **Imām ʿAlī (AS) said,** 'You must adopt earnestness, diligence, preparedness and willingness.'[1385]

١٢٢٣ . الإمامُ عليٌّ ﷺ : علَيكُم بالجِدِّ والاجْتهاد، والتّأهُّبِ والاسْتِعدادِ.١٣٧٦

1224. **Imām ʿAlī (AS) said,** 'Obedience to Allah cannot be attained except by one who possesses earnestness and exerts himself to the utmost.'[1386]

١٢٢٤ . عنه ﷺ : طاعَةُ اللهِ سبحانَهُ لا يَحُوزُها إلّا مَن بَذَلَ الجِدَّ ، واسْتَفْرَغَ الجُهْدَ.١٣٧٧

1225. **Imām al-Ṣādiq (AS) said** 'Know that between Allah and His creation there is no proximal angel, nor prophet, nor anything else [to intervene], except for their obedience to Him. So strive to obey Allah!'[1387]

١٢٢٥ . الإمامُ الصّادقُ ﷺ : اعْلَموا أنَّهُ لَيس بينَ اللهِ وبينَ أحَدٍ مِن خَلْقِهِ مَلَكٌ مُقَرَّبٌ ولا نَبِيٌّ مُرْسَلٌ ولا مَن دونَ ذلكَ مِن خَلْقِهِ كُلِّهِم إلّا طاعَتُهُم لَهُ، فاجْتَهِدوا في طاعةِ اللهِ.١٣٧٨

388. The Most Diligent of People

٣٨٨ ـ أشَدُّ النّاسِ اجتِهاداً

1226. **The Prophet (SAWA) said,** 'The most diligent of people is he who abandons sins.'[1388]

١٢٢٦ . رسولُ اللهِ ﷺ : أشَدُّ النّاسِ اجْتِهاداً مَن تَرَكَ الذُّنوبَ.١٣٧٩

1227. **The Prophet (SAWA) said,** 'The best *jihād* is performed by one who awakes in the morning with no intention to wrong anyone.'[1389]

١٢٢٧ . عنه ﷺ : أفْضَلُ الجِهادِ مَن أصْبَحَ لا يَهُمُّ بظُلْمِ أحدٍ.١٣٨٠

1228. When someone addressed Imām al-Bāqir (AS), saying, 'I am weak in my worship, praying and fasting but a little, though I strive to eat only that which is permissible, and be sexually intimate with only those whom it is permissible', the Imām

١٢٢٨ . الإمامُ الباقرُ ﷺ ـ لمّا قالَ لَهُ رجُلٌ : إنّي ضَعيفُ العَملِ قَليلُ الصّلاةِ قليلُ الصَّومِ ، ولكنْ أرْجو أنْ لا آكُلَ إلّا حَلالاً، ولا أنْكِحَ إلّا

replied, 'What *jihād* is there better than restraint of the stomach and the private parts?!'[1390]

حَـلالاً ـ: وأيُّ جِـهادٍ أفْـضَلُ مِـن عِـفَّةِ بَـطْنٍ وفَرْجٍ؟![١٣٨١]

79

IGNORANCE

الجَهل

389. Reprehension of Ignorance

٣٨٩ ـ ذَمُّ الجَهلِ

1229. **Imām ʿAlī (AS) said,** 'Ignorance is the worst affliction.'[1391]

١٢٢٩ . الإمامُ عليٌّ (عليه السلام) : الجَهلُ أدْوَأُ الدّاءِ.[١٣٨٢]

1230. **Imām ʿAlī (AS) said,** 'Ignorance is death for the living and perpetuates wretchedness.'[1392]

١٢٣٠ . عنه (عليه السلام) : الجَهلُ مُميتُ الأحْياءِ ومُخَلِّدُ الشَّقاءِ.[١٣٨٣]

1231. **Imām ʿAlī (AS) said,** 'Ignorance is the ruination of every affair.'[1393]

١٢٣١ . عنه (عليه السلام) : الجَهلُ فَسادُ كُلِّ أمرٍ.[١٣٨٤]

1232. **Imām ʿAlī (AS) said,** 'Ignorance is the root of every evil.'[1394]

١٢٣٢ . عنه (عليه السلام) : الجَهلُ أصْلُ كُلِّ شَرٍّ.[١٣٨٥]

1233. **Imām ʿAlī (AS) said,** 'Greed, voracity, and stinginess are a result of ignorance.'[1395]

١٢٣٣ . عنه (عليه السلام) : الحِرْصُ والشَّرَهُ والبُخْلُ نَتيجَةُ الجَهلِ.[١٣٨٦]

1234. **Imām al-ʿAskarī (AS) said,** 'Ignorance is an enemy.'[1396]

١٢٣٤ . الإمامُ العسكريُّ (عليه السلام) : الجَهلُ خَصْمٌ.[١٣٨٧]

390. The Signs of an Ignorant

٣٩٠ ـ عَلاماتُ الجاهِلِ

1235. **The Prophet (SAWA) said,** 'The ignorant is one who disobeys Allah, even if he is beautiful to look at and of great importance.'[1397]

١٢٣٥ . رسولُ اللهِ ﷺ : إنَّ الجاهِلَ مَن عَصىٰ اللهَ وإنْ كانَ جَميلَ المَنظَرِ عَظيمَ الخَطَرِ.[١٣٨٨]

1236. **The Prophet (SAWA) said,** 'The characteristic of an ignorant person is that he oppresses whoever he associates with, acts unjustly towards his subordinates, flatters his superiors, and his speech is without deliberation.'[1398]

١٢٣٦ . عنه ﷺ : صِفَةُ الجاهِلِ : أنْ يَظلِمَ مَن خالَطَهُ، ويَتَعدّىٰ علىٰ مَن هُو دُونَهُ، ويَتطاوَلَ علىٰ مَن هُو فَوقَهُ، كَلامُهُ بغَيرِ تَدَبُّرٍ....[١٣٨٩]

1237. **Imām ʿAlī (AS) said,** 'An ignorant person does not see his own shortcomings and is not willing to accept any advice given to him.'[1399]

١٢٣٧ . الإمامُ عليٌّ (عليه السلام) : الجاهِلُ لا يَعرِفُ تَقْصيرَهُ ولا يَقبلُ مِنَ النَّصيحِ لَهُ.[١٣٩٠]

1238. **Imām ʿAlī (AS) said,** 'An ignorant person is dead, even though he is living.'[1400]

١٢٣٨ . عنه ﷺ: الجاهِلُ مَيِّتٌ وإنْ كانَ حَيّاً.[١٣٩١]

1239. **Imām ʿAlī (AS) said,** 'The ignorant is one who has allowed himself to be deceived by his desires and whims.'[1401]

١٢٣٩ . عنه ﷺ : الجاهِلُ مَنِ انْخَدَعَ لِهَواهُ وغُرورِهِ.[١٣٩٢]

1240. **Imām ʿAlī (AS) said,** 'You will not see an ignorant person except that he is either committing excess in what he does or falling short of what he ought to do.'[1402]

١٢٤٠ . عنه ﷺ : لا تَرىٰ الجاهِلَ إلّا مُفْرِطاً أومُفَرِّطاً.[١٣٩٣]

1241. **Imām ʿAlī (AS) said,** 'The ignorant is one whose desires have enslaved him.'[1403]

١٢٤١ . عنه ﷺ : إنَّما الجاهِلُ مَنِ اسْتَعْبَدتْهُ المَطالِبُ.[١٣٩٤]

1242. **Imām ʿAlī (AS) said,** 'The ignorant is a slave of his desires.'[1404]

١٢٤٢ . عنه ﷺ : الجاهِلُ عَبدُ شَهْوتِه.[١٣٩٥]

1243. **Imām ʿAlī (AS) said,** 'The deeds of the ignorant are doomed and his knowledge is error.'[1405]

١٢٤٣ . عنه ﷺ : عَملُ الجاهِلِ وبَالٌ ، وعِلمُهُ ضلالٌ.[١٣٩٦]

1244. **Imām ʿAlī (AS) said,** 'The ignorant is one who considers himself knowledgeable about what he is [in actual fact] ignorant of, and he is content with his own opinion. He distances himself from the scholars and he is constantly finding fault with them. He deems invalid the views of those who oppose him, and that which he does not understand he sees as fallacious. If he comes across something that he does not know, he denies it and falsifies it, saying out of ignorance, 'I have never heard of this!' or 'I do not see it as possible! or 'How can it be!' or 'Where is this from?' This is due to his confidence in his own opinion and the paucity of his awareness of his own ignorance.
For this reason he will remain attached to his ignorance, and as a consequence, denies the truth, remains confused in his own ignorance and too proud to seek knowledge.'[1406]

١٢٤٤ . عنه ﷺ : إنَّ الجاهِلَ مَن عَدّ نَفسَهُ ـ بما جَهِلَ مِن مَعرفَةِ العِلمِ ـ عالِماً ، وبِرَأيِهِ مُكْتَفياً ، فمَا يَزالُ للعُلماءِ مُباعِداً وعَلَيهِم زارِياً ، ولِمَن خَالفَهُ مُخَطِّئاً ، ولِمَا لَم يَعْرِفْ مِن الأُمورِ مُضَلِّلاً ، فإذا وَردَ علَيهِ مِن الأُمورِ ما لَم يَعْرِفْهُ أنْكَرَهُ وكَذّبَ بهِ وقالَ بجَهالَتِهِ : ما أعْرِفُ هذا ! وما أراهُ كانَ ! وما أظُنُّ أنْ يَكونَ ! وأنّىٰ كانَ ؟! وذلكَ لِثقَتِهِ برَأْيِه وقِلَّةِ مَعْرِفَتِه بجَهالَتِهِ ! فمَا يَنْفَكُّ بما يَرىٰ مِمّا يَلْتَبِسُ علَيهِ رأيُهُ مِمّا لا يَعْرِفُ للجَهلِ مُسْتَفيداً ، وللحقِّ مُنكِراً ، وفي الجَهالَةِ مُتَحيِّراً ، وعن طَلَبِ العِلمِ مُسْتَكبِراً.[١٣٩٧]

1245. **Imām al-Ṣādiq (AS) said,** 'The attributes of the ignorant are that: he answers before listening,

١٢٤٥ . الإمامُ الصّادقُ ﷺ : مِن أخلاقِ الجاهِلِ

objects before understanding, and passes judgment on that which he does not know.'[1407]

الإجابَةُ قَبلَ أنْ يَسمَعَ ، والمُعارَضَةُ قَبلَ أنْ يَفْهَمَ، والحُكْمُ بما لا يَعْلَمُ.[١٣٩٨]

1246. **Imām al-Hādī (AS) said,** 'The ignorant is a prisoner of his tongue.'[1408]

١٢٤٦ . الإمامُ الهاديُّ عليه السلام : الجاهِلُ أسِيرُ لِسانِهِ.[١٣٩٩]

391. The Most Ignorant of People

٣٩١ـأجهَلُ النّاسِ

1247. **Imām ʿAlī (AS) said,** 'The most ignorant of people is one who is deluded by the praise of a flatterer who beautifies evil to him and renders a sincere advice detestable.'[1409]

١٢٤٧ . الإمامُ عليٌّ عليه السلام : أجْهلُ النّاسِ المُغتَرُّ بقَولِ مادِحٍ مُتَملِّقٍ، يُحسِّنُ لَهُ القَبيحَ ويُبغِّضُ إلَيهِ النَّصيحَ.[١٤٠٠]

1248. **Imām ʿAlī (AS) said,** 'The utter extremity of ignorance is for one to glorify his own ignorance.'[1410]

١٢٤٨ . عنه عليه السلام : غايةُ الجَهلِ تَبَجُّحُ المَرءِ بِجَهْلِهِ.[١٤٠١]

1249. **Imām ʿAlī (AS) said,** 'The greatest form of ignorance is for a person to be ignorant of the condition of his own self.'[1411]

١٢٤٩ . عنه عليه السلام : أعظَمُ الجَهلِ جَهلُ الإنسانِ أمرَ نَفْسِهِ.[١٤٠٢]

392. What is Sufficient to be Considered Ignorant

٣٩٢ـكَفىٰ بِذٰلِكَ جَهلاً

1250. **Imām ʿAlī (AS) said,** 'It suffices for one to be considered ignorant if he commits that which is forbidden.'[1412]

١٢٥٠ . الإمامُ عليٌّ عليه السلام : كَفىٰ بالمرءِ جَهلاً أنْ يَرتَكِبَ مانَهىٰ عَنهُ.[١٤٠٣]

1251. **Imām ʿAlī (AS) said,** 'Self-admiration in one's knowledge is sufficient to be considered ignorance.'[1413]

١٢٥١ . عنه عليه السلام : حَسْبكَ مِن الجَهلِ أنْ تُعجَبَ بعِلْمِكَ.[١٤٠٤]

1252. **Imām ʿAlī (AS) said,** 'It suffices as ignorance to be unaware of one's status.'[1414]

١٢٥٢ . عنه عليه السلام : كفىٰ بالمرءِ جَهلاً أنْ يَجْهَلَ قَدْرَهُ.[١٤٠٥]

1253. **Imām ʿAlī (AS) said,** 'Do not utter all that you know since that is enough to be considered ignorance.'[1415]

١٢٥٣ . عنه عليه السلام : لا تَتَكلّمْ بكُلِّ ما تَعلَمُ فكَفىٰ بذلكَ جَهلاً.[١٤٠٦]

1254. **Imām al-Ṣādiq (AS) said,** '[Possessing] fear of Allah suffices as knowledge, and being conceited towards Him suffices as ignorance.'[1416]

١٢٥٤ . الإمامُ الصّادقُ عليه السلام : كفىٰ بخَشيَةِ اللهِ عِلْماً، وكفىٰ بالاغْتِرارِ باللهِ جَهْلاً.[١٤٠٧]

393. The Interpretation of Ignorance

٣٩٣ـ تَفسيرُ الجَهل

1255. **The Prophet (SAWA) said,** 'Ignorance is to display all that you know.'[1417]

١٢٥٥ . رسولُ اللهِ ﷺ : مِن الجَهل أنْ تُظهِرَ كلَّ ما عَلِمْتَ.[١٤٠٨]

1256. **Imām ʿAlī (AS) said,** 'Relying on this world in spite of all that you face therein is ignorance.'[1418]

١٢٥٦ . الإمامُ عليٌّ عليه السلام : الرُّكونُ إلىٰ الدُّنيا مَع ماتُعايِنُ مِنها جَهلٌ.[١٤٠٩]

1257. **Imām ʿAlī (AS) said,** 'Your desire for the impossible is ignorance.'[1419]

١٢٥٧ . عنه عليه السلام : رَغْبَتُكَ في المُستَحيلِ جَهلٌ.[١٤١٠]

1258. **Imām al-Ḥasan (AS),** when his father asked him the meaning of ignorance, said, 'It is hastening to snatch up an opportunity before having made oneself capable [of fulfilling it], and it is to refuse to answer.'[1420]

١٢٥٨ . الإمامُ الحسنُ عليه السلام ـ لمّا سألَهُ أبوه عن تفسيرِ الجَهلِ ـ: سُرعةُ الوُثوبِ علَى الفُرْصة قبلَ الاسْتِمْكانِ مِنها، والامْتِناعُ عنِ الجَوابِ.[١٤١١]

1259. **Imām al-Ṣādiq (AS) said,** 'Ignorance lies in three things: in constantly changing one's brothers, declaring war without a reason, and spying into affairs that do not concern one.'[1421]

١٢٥٩ . الإمامُ الصّادقُ عليه السلام : الجَهلُ في ثلاثٍ: في تَبدُّلِ الإخْوانِ، والمُنابَذَةِ بغَيرِ بَيانٍ، والتَّجَسُّسِ عمّا لا يَعني.[١٤١٢]

1260. **Imām al-ʿAskarī (AS) said,** 'Ignorance is to laugh without any reason.'[1422]

١٢٦٠ . الإمامُ العسكريُّ عليه السلام : مِن الجَهلِ الضّحكُ من غيرِ عَجَبٍ.[١٤١٣]

394. Man is Averse to What he is Ignorant of

٣٩٤ـ الإنسانُ عَدُوٌّ لِما يَجهَلُ

1261. **Imām ʿAlī (AS) said,** 'People are antagonists of what they are ignorant of.'[1423]

١٢٦١ . الإمامُ عليٌّ عليه السلام : النّاسُ أعْداءُ ما جَهِلوهُ.[١٤١٤]

1262. **Imām ʿAlī (AS) said,** 'He who is ignorant of something tries to find fault with it.'[1424]

١٢٦٢ . عنه عليه السلام : مَن جَهِلَ شيئاً عابَهُ.[١٤١٥]

1263. **Imām ʿAlī (AS) said,** 'I have said four things which Allah has verified with verses He has revealed in His Book… I said: 'He who is ignorant of something will oppose it', and He revealed: *"Rather, they deny that whose knowledge they do not comprehend."*[1425][1426]

١٢٦٣ . عنه عليه السلام : قلتُ أرْبَعاً أنزلَ اللهُ تعالىٰ تَصديقي بها في كِتابِهِ...قُلتُ: مَن جَهِلَ شيئاً عاداهُ، فأنْزلَ اللهُ: ﴿بَلْ كَذَّبوا بِما لَم يُحيطوا بِعلمِهِ﴾[١٤١٦][١٤١٧]

1264. **Imām ʿAlī (AS) said,** 'Do not oppose that which you are ignorant of; for most knowledge lies in that which you cannot fathom.'[1427]

١٢٦٤ . عنه ﷺ : لا تُعادوا ما تَجهَلون ؛ فإنَّ أكثر العِلم فيما لا تعرِفونَ.١٤١٨

(See also: THE FAULT: section 1408)

(أنظر) العيب: باب ١٤٠٨.

80

HELL

جَهَنَّمُ

395. Warning Against Hell

٣٩٥ـ التَّحذِيرُ عَن جَهَنَّم

"Indeed hell is an ambush, a resort for the rebels."[1428]

﴿إنَّ جَهَنَّمَ كانَتْ مِرْصَاداً * لِلطَّاغِينَ مَآباً﴾ .١٤١٩

1265. **Imām ʿAlī (AS) said,** 'Beware of the Fire whose din is ready, whose flames are fierce, and whose pain is ever fresh.'[1429]

١٢٦٥ . الإمامُ عليٌّ ﷺ : احذَروا ناراً لَجَبُها عَتيدٌ، ولَهَبُها شَديدٌ، وعَذابُها أبداً جَديدٌ.١٤٢٠

1266. **Imām ʿAlī (AS) said,** 'The Fire whose rage is fierce, its din is high, its flame is glowing, its blaze is stirring up, its exhalation is furious, its extinction is remote, its fuel is blazing, and its threat is fearful.'[1430]

١٢٦٦ . عنه ﷺ : نارٌ شديدٌ كَلَبُها، عالٍ لَجَبُها، ساطِعٌ لَهَبُها، مُتأجِّجٌ سَعيرُها، مُتَغيِّظٌ زَفيرُها، بَعيدٌ خُمودُها، ذاكٍ وَقودُها، مُتَخوَّفٌ وَعيدُها.١٤٢١

396. The Fuel of Hell

٣٩٦ـ وَقودُ جَهَنَّمَ

"And if you do not—and you will not—then fear the Fire whose fuel will be humans and stones, prepared for the faithless."[1431]

﴿فَإنْ لَمْ تَفْعَلُوا وَلَنْ تَفْعَلُوا فَاتَّقُوا النَّارَ الَّتِي وَقُودُهَا النَّاسُ وَالْحِجَارَةُ أُعِدَّتْ لِلكافِرِينَ﴾ .١٤٢٢

"As for the perverse, they will be firewood for hell."[1432]

﴿وَأَمَّا الْقَاسِطُونَ فَكَانُوا لِجَهَنَّمَ حَطَباً﴾ .١٤٢٣

397. The Chains and Shackles of Hell

٣٩٧ـ سَلاسِلُ جَهَنَّمَ وأغلالُها

"Seize him, and fetter him! Then put him into hell. Then, in a chain whose length is seventy cubits, bind him."[1433]

﴿خُذُوهُ فَغُلُّوهُ * ثُمَّ الْجَحِيمَ صَلُّوهُ * ثُمَّ فِي سِلْسِلَةٍ ذَرْعُهَا سَبْعُونَ ذِرَاعاً فَاسْلُكُوهُ﴾ .١٤٢٤

1267. **Imām al-Ṣādiq (AS) said,** relating what Gabriel (AS) once said to the Prophet (SAWA), 'If

١٢٦٧ . الإمامُ الصّادقُ ﷺ ـ مِن قولِ جبرئيلَ ﷺ لِرسولِ اللهِ ﷺ ـ: لو أنَّ حَلْقةً واحِدةً، مِن

only one link of the chain whose length is seventy cubits was to be tied down on this world, the world would melt by its heat.'[1434]

السّلسلةِ الّتي طولُها سبعونَ ذِراعاً، وُضِعتْ عَلى الدُّنيا لذابَتِ الدُّنيا مِن حَرِّها.١٤٢٥

398. The Garments of the People of the Fire

٣٩٨ـ سَرابيلُ أهلِ النّارِ

1268. **Imām al-Ṣādiq (AS) said,** relating what Gabriel (AS) said to the Prophet (SAWA), 'If only one garment from among the garments of the people of the Fire was to be hung between the sky and the earth, the people of this world would die of its smell.'[1435]

١٢٦٨. الإمامُ الصّادقُ ؏ ـ مِن قَولِ جبرئيلَ ؏ لِرسولِ اللهِ ﷺ ـ: لَو أنّ سِرْبالاً مِن سَرابيلِ أهلِ النّارِ عُلِّقَ بينَ السَّماءِ والأرضِ لَماتَ أهلُ الدُّنيا مِن رِيحِهِ.١٤٢٦

399. The Food of the People of the Fire

٣٩٩ـ طَعامُ أهلِ النّارِ

"They will have no food except cactus, neither nourishing, nor availing against hunger."[1436]

﴿لَيْسَ لَهُمْ طَعامٌ إلّا مِنْ ضَرِيعٍ * لا يُسْمِنُ وَلا يُغْنِي مِنْ جُوعٍ﴾.١٤٢٧

"So he has no friend here today, nor any food except pus."[1437]

﴿فَلَيْسَ لَهُ الْيَوْمَ هٰهُنا حَمِيمٌ * وَلا طَعامٌ إلّا مِنْ غِسْلِينٍ﴾.١٤٢٨

1269. **The Prophet (SAWA) said,** 'If a bucket of the pus [of Hell] was to be poured where the sun rises [over this world], the skulls of the people living where it sets would boil.'[1438]

١٢٦٩. رسولُ اللهِ ﷺ: لَو أنَّ دَلْواً صُبَّ مِن غِسْلينٍ في مَطلَعِ الشّمسِ لَغَلَتْ مِنهُ جَماجِمُ مَن في مَغْرِبِها.١٤٢٩

1270. **Imām al-Ṣādiq (AS) said,** relating what Gabriel said to the Prophet (SAWA), 'If one drop of the cactus [of Hell] was to drop in the drink of the people of this world, they would die of its stench.'[1439]

١٢٧٠. الإمامُ الصّادقُ ؏ ـ مِن قَولِ جبرئيلَ ؏ لِرسولِ اللهِ ﷺ ـ: لَو أنَّ قَطْرَةً مِن الضَّريعِ قَطَرَتْ في شَرابِ أهلِ الدُّنيا لَماتَ أهلُها مِن نَتْنِها.١٤٣٠

400. The Drink of the People of the Fire

٤٠٠ـ شَرابُ أهلِ النّارِ

"And drink boiling water on top of it, drinking like thirsty camels."[1440]

﴿فَشارِبُونَ عَلَيْهِ مِنَ الْحَمِيمِ * فَشارِبُونَ شُرْبَ الْهِيمِ﴾.١٤٣١

1271. **Imām ʿAlī (AS) said,** 'When the *Zaqqūm*[1441] and the cactus will boil in the stomachs of the people of the Fire, like boiling water, they will ask for a drink, and will be given a drink made of pus and festering matter. One will swallow it painfully but will not enjoy it, and death will come to him from all sides though he will not die.'[1442]

١٢٧١ . الإمامُ عليٌّ ﷺ : إنَّ أهلَ النّارِ لَمّا غلىٰ الزَّقُّومُ والضَّريعُ في بُطونِهم كغَلْيِ الحَميمِ سَألوا الشَّرابَ ، فأُتوا بشرابِ غَسّاقٍ وصَديدٍ ، يَتَجرّعُهُ ولا يَكادُ يُسيغُهُ ، ويأتيهِ المَوتُ مِن كلِّ مكانٍ وما هُو بمَيّتٍ .١٤٣٢

401. The First to Enter the Fire

٤٠١ ـ أوّلُ مَن يَدخُلُ النّارَ

1272. **The Prophet (SAWA) said,** 'The first to enter the Fire will be a domineering ruler who did not maintain justice, a rich man possessing wealth who does not give his due from his wealth, and a poor man who is arrogant.'[1443]

١٢٧٢ . رسولُ اللهِ ﷺ : أوّلُ مَن يَدخُلُ النّارَ أميرٌ مُتسلِّطٌ لم يَعْدِلْ ، وذو ثَرْوَةٍ من المالِ لَم يُعْطِ المالَ حقَّهُ ، وفَقيرٌ فَخورٌ .١٤٣٣

402. The People with the Least Chastisement

٤٠٢ ـ أهوَنُ النّاسِ عَذاباً

1273. **The Prophet (SAWA) said,** 'The people of the Fire to experience the least pain will be wearing slippers of fire, whilst their brains will be boiling due to the [intensity of the] heat of their slippers.'[1444]

١٢٧٣ . رسولُ اللهِ ﷺ : أدْنىٰ أهلِ النّارِ عذاباً يَنْتَعِلُ بنَعْلَينِ مِن نارٍ ، يَغْلي دِماغُهُ مِن حَرارَةِ نَعْلَيهِ .١٤٣٤

403. The People with the Greatest Chastisement

٤٠٣ ـ أشَدُّ النّاسِ عَذاباً

1274. **The Prophet (SAWA) said,** 'The person to experience the greatest pain on the Day of Resurrection will be the scholar who did not benefit from his own knowledge.'[1445]

١٢٧٤ . رسولُ اللهِ ﷺ : أشدُّ النّاسِ عَذاباً يَومَ القيامةِ عالِمٌ لم يَنفَعْهُ عِلمُهُ .١٤٣٥

1275. **The Prophet (SAWA) said,** 'The [categories of] people to experience the greatest pain on the Day of Resurrection will be: the man who killed a prophet or was killed by a prophet, the leader of deception.'[1446]

١٢٧٥ . عنه ﷺ : أشدُّ النّاسِ عَذاباً يومَ القيامةِ رجُلٌ قَتلَ نَبيّاً ، أو قَتلَهُ نَبيٌّ ، وإمامُ ضَلالةٍ .١٤٣٦

1276. **Imām ʿAlī (AS) said,** 'The person to experience the greatest punishment will be the man who recompenses good done unto him with evil.'[1447]

١٢٧٦ . الإمامُ عليٌّ ﷺ : أشَدُّ النّاسِ عُقوبةً رجُلٌ كافَأَ الإحْسانَ بالإساءَةِ .١٤٣٧

1277. **Imām ʿAlī (AS) said,** 'The person to experience the greatest pain on the Day of Resurrection will be the one who was dissatisfied with the decree of Allah.'[1448]

١٢٧٧. عنه ﷺ: أشَدُّ النّاسِ عَذاباً يَومَ القيامةِ المُتسخِّطُ لِقضاءِ اللهِ.١٤٣٨

(See also: KNOWLEDGE: section 1360) (أنظر) العلم: باب ١٣٦٠

404. The Valley of the Arrogant

٤٠٤-وادِي المُتَكَبِّرينَ

1278. **Imām al-Ṣādiq (AS) said,** 'Verily there is a valley in Hell reserved for the arrogant, called *Saqar*, which complained to Allah, Mighty and Exalted, about its severe heat and asked His permission to breathe. So it breathed, and thus ignited Hell!'[1449]

١٢٧٨. الإمامُ الصّادقُ ﷺ: إنّ في جهنّمَ لَوادياً للمُتكبِّرينَ يُقالُ لَه: سَقَرُ، شَكا إلىٰ اللهِ عزّ وجلّ شِدّةَ حَرِّهِ، وسَألَهُ أنْ يأذَنَ لَه أنْ يَتنفّسَ، فتَنَفّسَ فأحْرَقَ جَهنّمَ!١٤٣٩

(See also: ARROGANCE: section 1573) (انظر) الكبر: باب ١٥٧٣

405. Those Who Will be Made to Remain in Hell Permanently

٤٠٥-مَن يُخَلَّدُ في جَهَنَّمَ

1279. **Imām al-Kāẓim (AS) said,** 'Allah will not retain anybody in the Fire permanently except the people of disbelief, denial, error and polytheism. And whoever shuns the grave sins from among the believers will not be asked about the minor ones.'[1450]

١٢٧٩. الإمامُ الكاظمُ ﷺ: لا يُخلِّدُ اللهُ فى النّارِ إلّاأهلَ الكُفرِ والجُحودِ وأهلَ الضَّلالِ والشِّركِ، ومَنِ اجْتَنبَ الكبائرَ مِن المؤمنينَ لَم يُسألْ عنِ الصَّغائرِ.١٤٤٠

406. Those Who Will Leave the Fire

٤٠٦-مَن يَخرُجُ مِن النّارِ

1280. **The Prophet (SAWA) said,** 'He who has even an atom's weight of faith in his heart will leave the Fire.'[1451]

١٢٨٠. رسولُ اللهِ ﷺ: يَخرُجُ مِن النّارِ مَن كانَ في قَلبِهِ مِثْقالُ ذَرّةٍ مِن إيمانٍ.١٤٤١

1281. **Imām al-Bāqir (AS) said,** 'Some people will burn in the Fire, until they are burned to ashes [and become pure] – then they will be taken out through intercession.'[1452]

١٢٨١. الإمامُ الباقرُ ﷺ: إنّ قوماً يُحرَقونَ في (بـ)النّـارِ حتّىٰ إذا صاروا حُـمَماً (حَـميماً) أدرَكَتْهُمُ الشَّفاعةُ.١٤٤٢

407. The Reason for Perpetuity in Hell

٤٠٧ـ عِلَّةُ الخُلودِ

1282. **Imām al-Ṣādiq (AS) said,** 'The people of the Fire will be kept permanently in the Fire because their intentions in the world were such that if they were to live forever therein, they would disobey Allah forever. And verily the people of Paradise will also be made to remain in Paradise permanently because their intentions in this world were to obey Allah if only they were to live there forever. So, it is due to their intentions that these and those have their permanent residence.' Then Imām recited the word of Allah, the Exalted: *"Say, 'Everyone acts according to his character"*[1453] and said that it means according to his intention.'[1454]

١٢٨٢ . الإمامُ الصّادقُ عليه السلام : إنّما خُلِّدَ أهلُ النّارِ في النّارِ لأنّ نِيّاتِهِم كانَت في الدُّنيا أنْ لَو خُلِّدوا فيها أنْ يَعْصوا اللهَ أبَداً ، وإنّما خُلِّدَ أهلُ الجَنّةِ في الجنّةِ لأنَّ نِيّاتِهِم كانتْ في الدُّنيا أنْ لو بَقوا فيها أنْ يُطيعوا اللهَ أبداً ، فبِالنِّيّاتِ خُلِّدَ هؤلاءِ وهؤلاءِ ـ ثُمَّ تلا قولَهُ تعالىٰ ـ : ﴿قُلْ كُلٌّ يَعْمَلُ علىٰ شاكِلَتِهِ﴾[١٤٤٣] ، قال : علىٰ نِيَّتِهِ .[١٤٤٤]

81

THE ANSWER

الجَوابُ

408. The Answer

٤٠٨ـ الجَوابُ

1283. **Imām ʿAlī (AS) said,** 'Where there are several answers, the correct one will remain hidden.'[1455]

١٢٨٣ . الإمامُ عليٌّ عليه السلام : إذا ازْدَحَمَ الجَوابُ خَفِيَ الصَّوابُ .[١٤٤٥]

1284. **Imām ʿAlī (AS) said,** 'Sometimes even the eloquent fails to come up with an answer.'[1456]

١٢٨٤ . عنه عليه السلام : رُبَّما أُرتِجَ علىٰ الفَصيحِ الجَوابُ .[١٤٤٦]

1285. **Imām ʿAlī (AS) said,** 'He who rushes to give answers will not perceive the truth.'[1457]

١٢٨٥ . عنه عليه السلام : مَن أسْرَعَ في الجَوابِ لَم يُدرِكِ الصَّوابَ .[١٤٤٧]

1286. **Imām ʿAlī (AS) said,** 'One of the proofs of virtue is giving correct answers.'[1458]

١٢٨٦ . عنه عليه السلام : مِن بُرهانِ الفَضلِ صائبُ الجَوابِ .[١٤٤٨]

1287. **Imām ʿAlī (AS) said,** 'Leave sharpness and reflect instead on the argument, and avoid idle talk in order to be safe from error.'[1459]

١٢٨٧ . عنه عليه السلام : دَعِ الحِدَّةَ وتَفَكَّرْ في الحُجَّةِ وتَحَفَّظْ مِن الخَطَلِ ، تأمَنِ الزَّلَلَ .[١٤٤٩]

1288. **Imām ʿAlī (AS) said,** 'If you remain clement with the ignorant, you give him indeed an adequate answer.'[1460]

١٢٨٨ . عنه ﷺ : إذا حَلُمْتَ عنِ الجاهِلِ فَقَد أوْسَعْتَهُ جَواباً .١٤٥٠

1289. **Imām ʿAlī (AS) said,** 'Many a speech is answered by silence.'[1461]

١٢٨٩ . عنه ﷺ : رُبَّ كلامٍ جَوابُهُ السُّكوتُ .١٤٥١

1290. **Imām al-Ṣādiq (AS) said,** 'He who answers regarding all that is asked is mad.'[1462]

١٢٩٠ . الإمامُ الصّادقُ ﷺ : إنّ مَن أجابَ في كلِّ ما يُسْأَلُ عَنهُ لَمَجنونٌ .١٤٥٢

(See also: ASKING (1): section 907)

(انظر) السؤال (١): باب ٩٠٧.

82

OPEN-HANDEDNESS

الجُودُ

409. Encouragement of Generosity

٤٠٩ ـ التَّرغيبُ بِالجُودِ

1291. **Imām ʿAlī (AS) said,** 'Be openhanded with whatever you find, and you will be commended.'[1463]

١٢٩١ . الإمامُ عليٌّ ﷺ : جُدْ بِما تَجِدُ تُحْمَدْ .١٤٥٣

1292. **Imām ʿAlī (AS) said,** 'Man's open-handedness endears him to his opponents, and his stinginess makes him hated even by his children.'[1464]

١٢٩٢ . عنه ﷺ : جُودُ الرّجُلِ يُحَبِّبُهُ إلىٰ أضْدادِهِ ،وبُخْلُهُ يُبَغِّضُهُ إلىٰ أولادِهِ .١٤٥٤

1293. **Imām ʿAlī (AS) said,** 'Open-handedness is of the nobility of [man's] nature.'[1465]

١٢٩٣ . عنه ﷺ : الجُودُ مِن كَرَمِ الطَّبيعةِ .١٤٥٥

1294. **Imām ʿAlī (AS) said,** 'Open-handedness is a present honour.'[1466]

١٢٩٤ . عنه ﷺ : الجُودُ عِزٌّ مَوجودٌ .١٤٥٦

1295. **Imām al-Ḥusayn (AS) said,** 'He who is open-handed rules.'[1467]

١٢٩٥ . الإمامُ الحسينُ ﷺ : مَن جادَ سادَ .١٤٥٧

410. The Best Open-Handedness

٤١٠ ـ أفضلُ الجودِ

1296. **The Prophet (SAWA) said,** 'The most open-handed of people is he who gives freely of himself and his wealth in the way of Allah.'[1468]

١٢٩٦ . رسولُ اللهِ ﷺ : أجْوَدُ النّاسِ مَن جادَ بنَفسِهِ ومالِهِ في سبيلِ اللهِ .١٤٥٨

1297. **Imām ʿAlī (AS) said,** 'The best form of open-handedness is that expressed in spite of hardship.'[1469]

١٢٩٧ . الإمامُ عليٌّ ؑ : أفضَلُ الجُودِ ما كانَ عن عُسْرَةٍ.[١٤٦٩]

1298. **Imām al-Ḥusayn (AS) said,** 'The most open-handed of people is he who gives without expectation.'[1470]

١٢٩٨ . الإمامُ الحسينُ ؑ : إنّ أجْوَدَ النّاسِ مَن أعطىٰ مَن لا يَرجو.[١٤٧٠]

411. The Attributes of the Open-Handed Person

٤١١ ـ صِفَةُ الجَوادِ

1299. **Imām al-Ṣādiq (AS) said,** 'The open-handed cannot be considered open-handed unless he has three [attributes]: he is generous with his wealth both in times of ease as well as hardship, bestows it on the deserving, and finds the gratitude of the one he gave to greater than what he gave him.'[1471]

١٢٩٩ . الإمامُ الصّادقُ ؑ : لا يكونُ الجَوادُ جَواداً إلّا بثَلاثةٍ: يكونُ سَخيّاً بمالِهِ علىٰ حالِ اليُسْرِ والعُسْرِ، وأنْ يَبْذُلَهُ للمُستحِقِّ، ويَرىٰ أنّ الّذي أخَذَهُ مِن شُكْرِ الّذي أسْدىٰ إلَيهِ أكْثَرُ مِمّا أعْطاهُ.[١٤٧١]

83

THE NEIGHBOUR

الجار

412. Neighbourliness

٤١٢ ـ حُسنُ الجِوارِ

"Worship Allah and do not ascribe any partners to Him, and be good to parents, the relatives, the orphans, the needy, the near neighbour and the distant neighbour, the companion at your side."[1472]

﴿وَاعْبُدُوا اللهَ وَلا تُشْرِكُوا بِهِ شَيْئاً وَبِالْوالِدَيْنِ إِحْساناً وَبِذِي الْقُرْبىٰ وَالْيَتامىٰ وَالْمَساكِينِ وَالْجارِ ذِي الْقُرْبىٰ وَالْجارِ الْجُنُبِ وَالصّاحِبِ بِالْجَنْبِ﴾.[١٤٧٢]

1300. **The Prophet (SAWA) said,** 'One should revere his neighbour as he reveres his mother.'[1473]

١٣٠٠ . رسولُ اللهِ ﷺ : حُرمَةُ الجارِ علَى الإنسانِ كحُرمَةِ اُمِّهِ.[١٤٧٣]

1301. **Imām ʿAlī (AS) said** while on his deathbed, '[Fear] Allah and [keep] Allah in view in the matter of your neighbours, because they were the subject of your Prophet's advice. He continuously advised in their favour such that we thought he would allow them a share in inheritance.'[1474]

١٣٠١ . الإمامُ عليٌّ ؑ ـ عندَ وفاتِهِ ـ : اللهَ اللهَ في جيرانِكُم فإنَّهُم وَصيَّةُ نَبيِّكُم، ما زالَ يُوصي بِهِم حتّىٰ ظَنَنّا أنّهُ سَيُوَرِّثُهُم.[١٤٧٤]

1302. **Imām al-Ṣādiq (AS) said,** 'Neighbourliness causes the lands to thrive and increases life spans.'[1475]

١٣٠٢ . الإمامُ الصّادقُ عليه السلام : حُسنُ الجِوارِ يُعمِّرُ الدِّيارَ، ويَزيدُ في الأعْمارِ.١٤٦٥

1303. **Imām al-Kāẓim (AS) said,** 'Neighbourliness is not only to desist from annoying [one's neighbour], but also to forbear annoyance [from him].'[1476]

١٣٠٣ . الإمامُ الكاظمُ عليه السلام : ليسَ حُسنُ الجِوارِ كَفَّ الأذىٰ، ولكنْ حُسنُ الجِوارِ الصّبرُ علىٰ الأذىٰ.١٤٦٦

413. Annoying One's Neighbour

٤١٣ ـ إيذاءُ الجارِ

1304. **The Prophet (SAWA) said,** 'Whoever believes in Allah and the Day of Resurrection must not annoy his neighbour.'[1477]

١٣٠٤ . رسولُ اللهِ صلى الله عليه وآله : مَن كانَ يُؤمنُ باللهِ واليَومِ الآخِرِ فلا يُؤْذي جارَهُ.١٤٦٧

1305. **Imām al-Riḍā (AS) said,** 'He is not of us whose neighbour is not safe from his troubles.'[1478]

١٣٠٥ . الإمامُ الرِّضا عليه السلام : ليسَ مِنّا مَن لَمْ يأمن جارُهُ بَوائقَهُ.١٤٦٨

(See also: HARM: section 8)

(أنظر) عنوان ٨ «الإيذاء».

414. Visiting the Neighbour

٤١٤ ـ تَفَقُّدُ الجارِ

1306. **Imām 'Alī (AS) said,** 'Among the acts of neighbourliness is visiting one's neighbour.'[1479]

١٣٠٦ . الإمامُ عليٌّ عليه السلام : مِن حُسنِ الجِوارِ تَفَقُّدُ الجـارِ.١٤٦٩

1307. **Imām al-Bāqir (AS) narrated,** 'The Prophet (SAWA) said, 'He has no faith in me who sleeps the night satiated while his neighbour is hungry.' He has also said, 'No sooner do the people in a village sleep at night while there is a hungry man in their midst than Allah will not look at them on the Day of Resurrection.'[1480]

١٣٠٧ . الإمامُ الباقرُ عليه السلام : قالَ رسولُ اللهِ صلى الله عليه وآله : ما آمَنَ بي مَن باتَ شَبْعانَ وجارُهُ جائعٌ. قالَ: وما مِن أهلِ قريةٍ يَبِيتُ و فيهِم جائعٌ، يَنظُرُ اللهُ إليهِم يومَ القِيامَةِ.١٤٧٠

415. The Rights of the Neighbour

٤١٥ ـ حَقُّ الجارِ

1308. **The Prophet (SAWA),** on the rights of the neighbour, said, '[It is] to help him if he asks your help, to lend him if he asks to borrow from you, to satisfy his needs if he becomes poor, to console him if he is visited by an affliction, to congratulate him if he is met with good fortune, to visit him if he becomes ill, to attend his funeral if he dies, not to

١٣٠٨ . رسولُ اللهِ صلى الله عليه وآله ـ في حُقوقِ الجارِ ـ: إنِ اسْتَغاثَكَ أغَثْتَهُ، وإنِ اسْتَقْرَضَكَ أقْـرَضْتَهُ، وإنِ افْتَقَر عُدْتَ علَيهِ، وإنْ أصابَتْهُ مُـصيبَةٌ عَـزَّيْتَهُ، وإنْ أصابَهُ خيرٌ هَنّأتَهُ، وإنْ مَرِضَ عُـدْتَهُ، وإنْ ماتَ اتَّبعتَ جَنازَتَهُ، ولاتَسْتَطِلْ عـلَيهِ بـالبِناءِ

make your house higher than his without his consent lest you deny him the breeze, to offer him fruit when you buy some or to take it to your home secretly if you do not do that, nor send out your children with it so as not to upset his children, nor to bother him by the [tempting] smell of your food unless you send him some.’[1481]

فتحجُبَ عنهُ الرِّيحَ إلّا بإذنِهِ ، وإذا اشْتَرَيتَ فاكِهَةً فأهْدِ لَهُ ، فإنْ لَم تَفعلْ فأدْخِلْها سِرّاً ، ولا تُخرِجْ بها وُلْدَكَ تَغيظُ بها وُلْدَهُ ، ولا تُؤذِهِ بريحِ قِدْرِكَ إلّا أنْ تَغرِفَ لَهُ مِنها .١٤٧١

416. The Boundary of the Neighbourhood

٤١٦ ـ حَدُّ الجارِ

1309. **Imām ʿAlī (AS) said,** ‘The sanctuary of a mosque is forty cubits, and that of a neighbourhood is forty houses on four sides.’[1482]

١٣٠٩ . الإمامُ عليٌّ عليه السلام : حَريمُ المَسجدِ أربعونَ ذِراعاً ، والجِوارُ أربعونَ داراً مِن أربعةِ جَوانِبِها .١٤٧٢

84

LOVE

المَحَبَّةُ

417. Love is Kinship

٤١٧ ـ المَوَدَّةُ قَرابَةٌ

1310. **Imām ʿAlī (AS) said,** ‘Love is acquired kinship.’[1483]

١٣١٠ . الإمامُ عليٌّ عليه السلام : المَوَدَّةُ قَرابَةٌ مُستَفادَةٌ .١٤٧٣

1311. **Imām ʿAlī (AS) said,** ‘Love does not need kinship so much as kinship needs love.’[1484]

١٣١١ . عنه عليه السلام : القَرابَةُ إلى المَوَدَّةِ أحْوَجُ مِن المَوَدَّةِ إلى القَرابَةِ .١٤٧٤

418. That Which Brings About Love

٤١٨ ـ ما يورثُ المَحَبَّةَ

1312. **Imām ʿAlī (AS) said,** ‘Three things bring about love: good temperament, kindness, and humbleness.’[1485]

١٣١٢ . الإمامُ عليٌّ عليه السلام : ثلاثٌ يُوجِبْنَ المَحَبَّةَ : حُسنُ الخُلقِ ، وحُسنُ الرِّفقِ ، والتَّواضُعُ .١٤٧٥

1313. **Imām al-Ṣādiq (AS) said,** ‘Three things bring about love: piety, humbleness, and generosity.’[1486]

١٣١٣ . الإمامُ الصّادقُ عليه السلام : ثلاثةٌ تُورِثُ المَحَبَّةَ : الدِّينُ ، والتَّواضُعُ ، والبَذلُ .١٤٧٦

(See also: CHEERFULNESS: 42; GENEROSITY: section 929)

(أنظر) عنوان ٤٢ «البِشر» ؛ السخاء : باب ٩٢٩.

419. Those Who Must Not Be Endeared

٤١٩ ـ مَن لا يَنبَغي مَوَدَّتُهُ

"You will not find a people believing in Allah and the Last Day endearing those who oppose Allah and His Apostle even though they were their own parents, or children, or brothers, or kinsfolk. [For] such, He has written faith into their hearts."[1487]

﴿لا تَجِدُ قَوْماً يُؤْمِنُونَ بِاللهِ وَالْيَوْمِ الْآخِرِ يُوادُّونَ مَنْ حَادَّ اللهَ وَرَسُولَهُ وَلَوْ كانُوا آبَاءَهُمْ أَوْ أَبْنَاءَهُمْ أَوْ إِخْوَانَهُمْ أَوْ عَشِيرَتَهُمْ أُولٰئِكَ كَتَبَ فِي قُلُوبِهِمُ الْإِيمانَ﴾.١٤٧٧

1314. **Imām ʿAlī (AS) said**, 'Do not offer your friendship to someone who is not loyal.'[1488]

١٣١٤. الإمامُ عليٌّ عليه السلام : لا تَمْنَحَنَّ وُدَّكَ مَن لا وَفاءَ لَهُ.١٤٧٨

1315. **Imām ʿAlī (AS) said,** 'The friendships that are the quickest to break are the friendships made with evildoers.'[1489]

١٣١٥. عنه عليه السلام : أسْرَعُ المَوَدّاتِ انْقِطاعاً مَوَدّاتُ الأشْرارِ.١٤٧٩

1316. **Imām ʿAlī (AS) said,** 'Beware of loving the enemies of Allah, or of harbouring affection for other than the friends of Allah, for verily man will be resurrected with those whom he loves.'[1490]

١٣١٦. عنه عليه السلام : إيّاكَ أنْ تُحِبَّ أعْداءَ اللهِ، أو تُصْفِيَ وُدَّكَ لغَيرِ أولياءِ اللهِ، فإنّ مَن أحَبَّ قَوماً حُشِرَ مَعهُم.١٤٨٠

(See also: THE FRIEND: section 1103; THE BROTHER: section 31; SITTING COMPANY: section 348)

(أُنظر) الصديق: باب ١١٠٣؛ الأخ: باب ٣١؛ المجالسة: باب ٣٤٨.

420. The Blindness of Love [from Perceiving the Truth]

٤٢٠ ـ حُبٌّ يَمنَعُ المَعرِفَةَ

1317. **The Prophet (SAWA) said,** 'Your love for a particular thing makes you blind and deaf.'[1491]

١٣١٧. رسولُ اللهِ صلى الله عليه وآله : حُبُّكَ للشَّيْءِ يُعْمي ويُصِمُّ.١٤٨١

1318. **Imām ʿAlī (AS) said,** 'The lover's eye is blind to the defects of the beloved, and his ear is deaf to the ugliness of his misdeeds.'[1492]

١٣١٨. الإمامُ عليٌّ عليه السلام : عَينُ المُحِبّ عَمِيَةٌ عن مَعايِبِ المَحبوبِ، وأُذُنُه صَمّاءُ عَن قُبْحِ مَساوِيهِ.١٤٨٢

421. The Sign of Love

٤٢١ ـ عَلامَةُ الحُبِّ

1319. **Imām ʿAlī (AS) said,** 'He who loves you forbids you [from committing sin].'[1493]

١٣١٩. الإمامُ عليٌّ عليه السلام : مَن أحَبَّكَ نَهاكَ.١٤٨٣

1320. **Imām ʿAlī (AS) said,** 'He who loves something constantly mentions it.'[1494]

١٣٢٠. عنه عليه السلام : مَن أحَبَّ شيئاً لَهِجَ بذِكْرِهِ.١٤٨٤

422. The Believers' Intense Love for Allah

٤٢٢ ـ شِدَّةُ حُبِّ المُؤمِنينَ لِلّهِ

"Say, 'If your fathers and your sons, your brethren, your spouses, and your kinsfolk, the possessions that you have acquired, the business you fear may suffer, and the dwellings you are fond of, are dearer to you than Allah and His Apostle and to waging jihād in His way, then wait until Allah issues His edict, and Allah does not guide the transgressing lot."[1495]

﴿قُلْ إِنْ كَانَ آبَاؤُكُمْ وَأَبْنَاؤُكُمْ وَإِخْوَانُكُمْ وَأَزْوَاجُكُمْ وَعَشِيرَتُكُمْ وَأَمْوَالٌ اقْتَرَفْتُمُوهَا وَتِجَارَةٌ تَخْشَوْنَ كَسَادَهَا وَمَسَاكِنُ تَرْضَوْنَهَا أَحَبَّ إِلَيْكُمْ مِنَ اللهِ وَرَسُولِهِ وَجِهَادٍ فِي سَبِيلِهِ فَتَرَبَّصُوا حَتَّى يَأْتِيَ اللهُ بِأَمْرِهِ وَاللهُ لا يَهْدِي الْقَوْمَ الْفَاسِقِينَ﴾.[١٤٨٥]

"Among the people are those who set up compeers besides Allah, loving them as if loving Allah—but the faithful have a more ardent love for Allah—though the wrongdoers will see, when they sight the punishment, that power, altogether, belongs to Allah, and that Allah is severe in punishment."[1496]

﴿وَمِنَ النَّاسِ مَنْ يَتَّخِذُ مِنْ دُونِ اللهِ أَنْدَاداً يُحِبُّونَهُمْ كَحُبِّ اللهِ وَالَّذِينَ آمَنُوا أَشَدُّ حُبّاً للهِ وَلَوْ يَرَىٰ الَّذِينَ ظَلَمُوا إِذْ يَرَوْنَ الْعَذَابَ أَنَّ الْقُوَّةَ للهِ جَمِيعاً وَأَنَّ اللهَ شَدِيدُ الْعَذَابِ﴾.[١٤٨٦]

(See also: Qur'an 3:31, 5:51-57, 9:25, 26:77-82, 62:6)

(أُنظر) آل عمران:٣١ والمائدة: ٥١ ـ ٥٧ والتوبة: ٢٥ والشعراء: ٧٧ ـ ٨٢ والجمعة: ٦.

1321. **Imām al-Ḥusayn (AS) said** in one of his supplications attributed to him, 'It is You Who removed the strangers from the hearts of Your lovers so that they never love other than You… What does the one who loses You find?! And what does the one who finds You lose?! He indeed fails who is satisfied with a substitute for You.'[1497]

١٣٢١ . الإمامُ الحسينُ عليه السلام ـ في الدعاء المنسوب إليه ـ: أنتَ الّذي أزَلْتَ الأغْيارَ عن قُلوبِ أحِبّائكَ حتّىٰ لَم يُحِبّوا سِواكَ... ماذا وَجَدَ مَن فَقَدَكَ؟! وما الّذي فَقَدَ مَن وَجَدَكَ؟! لَقد خابَ مَن رَضِيَ دُونَكَ بَدَلاً.[١٤٨٧]

1322. **Imām al-Ṣādiq (AS) said,** 'Man's faith in Allah will not be pure until Allah becomes more beloved to him than his own self, his father, his mother, his children, his wife, his wealth, and all people.'[1498]

١٣٢٢ . الإمامُ الصّادقُ عليه السلام : لا يَمْحَضُ رجُلٌ الإيمانَ باللهِ حتّىٰ يكونَ اللهُ أحَبَّ إلَيهِ مِن نَفْسِهِ وأبيهِ واُمِّهِ ووُلْدِهِ وأهْلِهِ ومالِهِ ومِنَ النّاسِ كُلِّهِم.[١٤٨٨]

1323. **Imām al-Ṣādiq (AS) said,** 'The heart is the sanctuary of Allah, so do not lodge other than Allah in Allah's sanctuary.'[1499]

١٣٢٣ . عنه عليه السلام : القلبُ حَرَمُ اللهِ، فلا تُسْكِنْ حَرَمَ اللهِ غَيرَ اللهِ.[١٤٨٩]

1324. **Imām al-Ṣādiq (AS) said,** 'Love [of Allah] is better than fear [of Him].'[1500]

١٣٢٤ . عنه عليه السلام : الحُبُّ أفْضَلُ مِن الخَوفِ.[١٤٩٠]

423. That which Brings About the Love of Allah

٤٢٣ ـ ما يورِثُ حُبَّ اللهِ

1325. It is narrated in the tradition of the Prophet (SAWA)'s Ascension, 'O Muḥammad, My love is due to those who love each other for My sake, and My love is due to those who are kind to each other for My sake, and My love is due to those who maintain communication with each other for My sake, and My love is due to those who trust Me, and there is no ensign, end or culmination to My love, and whenever I raise an ensign for them I lower another ensign for them.'[1501]

١٣٢٥ . إرشاد القلوب ـ في حديثِ المِعراجِ ـ: يـا محمّدُ، وَجَـبتْ مَـحَبَّتي للـمُتَحابِّينَ فِـيَّ، ووَجَبتْ مَـحَبَّتي للـمُتَعاطِفينَ فِـيَّ، ووَجَـبتْ مَحَبَّتي للـمُتَواصِـلينَ فِـيَّ، ووَجَـبتْ مَـحَبَّتي للمُتَوكِّلينَ عَلَيَّ، ولَيس لمَحَبَّتي عَلَمٌ ولا غايَةٌ ولا نِهايَةٌ، وكُلَّما رَفَعْتُ لَهُم عَلَماً وَضَعْتُ لَـهُم عَلَماً.[١٤٩١]

1326. **Imām al-Ṣādiq (AS) said,** 'Allah, Mighty and Exalted, says, 'The servant endears himself to Me by no better means than what I have made obligatory upon him.'[1502]

١٣٢٦ . الإمامُ الصّادقُ عليه السلام :قالَ اللهُ تباركَ وتعالىٰ: مـا تَـحبَّبَ إليَّ عـبدي بأحَبَّ مِـمّا افْـتَرَضتُ علَيهِ.[١٤٩٢]

1327. **Imām al-Ṣādiq (AS) said,** 'When the believer abandons this world, he is elevated and finds the sweet taste of Allah's love; he appears to the people of this world as if he is confounded in his mind, whereas truly it is they who have confounded the sweetness of Allah's love such that they do not occupy themselves with other than Him.'[1503]

١٣٢٧ . عنه عليه السلام : إذا تَخَلّىٰ المؤمنُ مِـن الدُّنـيا سَما ووَجَدَ حَلاوَةَ حُبِّ اللهِ، وكـانَ عـندَ أهـلِ الدُّنيا كأنَّهُ قد خُولِطَ، وإنَّما خالَطَ القَومَ حَـلاوَةُ حُبِّ اللهِ فلَم يَشْتَغلوا بغَيرِهِ.[١٤٩٣]

424. Those Whom Allah Loves

٤٢٤ ـ الَّذينَ يُحِبُّهُمُ اللهُ

"Indeed Allah loves the virtuous."[1504]

﴿إنَّ اللهَ يُحِبُّ الْمُحْسِنِينَ﴾.[١٤٩٤]

"Indeed Allah loves the penitent and He loves those who keep clean."[1505]

﴿إنَّ اللهَ يُحِبُّ التَّوّابِينَ وَيُحِبُّ الْمُتَطَهِّرِينَ﴾.[١٤٩٥]

"Yes, whoever fulfils his commitments and is wary of Allah—Allah indeed loves the Godwary."[1506]

﴿بَلَىٰ مَنْ أَوْفَىٰ بِـعَهْدِهِ وَاتَّـقَىٰ فَـإنَّ اللهَ يُـحِبُّ الْمُتَّقِينَ﴾.[١٤٩٦]

"And Allah loves the steadfast."[1507]

﴿وَاللهُ يُحِبُّ الصّابِرِينَ﴾.[١٤٩٧]

"Indeed Allah loves those who trust in Him."[1508]

﴿إنَّ اللهَ يُحِبُّ الْمُتَوَكِّلِينَ﴾.[١٤٩٨]

"Indeed Allah loves the just."[1509]

﴿إِنَّ اللهَ يُحِبُّ الْمُقْسِطِينَ﴾.[١٤٩٩]

"Indeed Allah loves those who fight in His way in ranks, as if they were a compact structure."[1510]

﴿إِنَّ اللهَ يُحِبُّ الَّذِينَ يُقاتِلُونَ فِي سَبِيلِهِ صَفّاً كَأَنَّهُمْ بُنْيَانٌ مَرْصُوصٌ﴾.[١٥٠٠]

1328. **The Prophet (SAWA) said,** 'Indeed Allah loves the bashful, clement, chaste and virtuous servant.'[1511]

١٣٢٨. رسولُ اللهِ ﷺ: إنَّ اللهَ يُحِبُّ الحَيِيَّ الحَليمَ العَفيفَ المُتَعفِّفَ.[١٥٠١]

1329. **Imām Zayn al-ʿĀbidīn (AS) said,** 'Indeed Allah loves every sorrowful heart and loves every grateful servant.'[1512]

١٣٢٩. الإمامُ زينُ العابدينَ عليه السلام: إنَّ اللهَ يُحِبُّ كُلَّ قلبٍ حَزينٍ، ويُحِبُّ كُلَّ عبدٍ شَكورٍ.[١٥٠٢]

1330. **Imām al-Bāqir (AS) said,** 'Allah loves the one who is jolly among people without being obscene, is monotheistic in his thought, adorned by patience, and priding himself with the prayer.'[1513]

١٣٣٠. الإمامُ الباقرُ عليه السلام: إنّ اللهَ يُحِبُّ المُداعِبَ في الجَماعةِ بلا رَفَثٍ، المتوحِّدَ بالفِكْرَةِ، المُتَحلّيَ بالصّبرِ، المُتَباهيَ بالصَّلاةِ.[١٥٠٣]

425. Those That Allah does not Like

٤٢٥ـ الَّذينَ لا يُحِبُّهُمُ اللهُ

"Fight in the way of Allah those who fight you, but do not transgress. Indeed Allah does not like transgressors."[1514]

﴿وَقاتِلُوا فِي سَبِيلِ اللهِ الَّذِينَ يُقاتِلُونَكُمْ وَلا تَعْتَدُوا إِنَّ اللهَ لا يُحِبُّ الْمُعْتَدِينَ﴾.[١٥٠٤]

"And Allah does not like the agents of corruption."[1515]

﴿وَاللهُ لا يُحِبُّ الْمُفْسِدِينَ﴾.[١٥٠٥]

"Indeed Allah does not like the wasteful."[1516]

﴿إِنَّهُ لا يُحِبُّ الْمُسْرِفِينَ﴾.[١٥٠٦]

"Indeed He does not like the arrogant."[1517]

﴿إِنَّهُ لا يُحِبُّ الْمُسْتَكْبِرِينَ﴾.[١٥٠٧]

426. The People Loved Most by Allah

٤٢٦ـ أَحَبُّ النّاسِ إلَى اللهِ

1331. **The Prophet (SAWA) said,** 'The most beloved of Allah's servants to Him are those that are the most useful to His servants, and the most persistent of them in establishing His right, those who endear virtue and its practices.'[1518]

١٣٣١. رسولُ اللهِ ﷺ: أحَبُّ عِبادِ اللهِ إلىٰ اللهِ أنْفَعُهُم لِعبادِهِ، وأقْوَمُهُم بحقِّهِ، الّذينَ يُحَبَّبُ إلَيهِمُ المَعروفُ وفِعالُهُ.[١٥٠٨]

1332. **Imām al-Ṣādiq (AS) said,** 'The most beloved of people to Allah, Mighty and Exalted, is a man who is truthful in his speech, careful about his

١٣٣٢. الإمامُ الصّادقُ عليه السلام: أحَبُّ العِبادِ إلىٰ اللهِ عزّ وجلّ رجُلٌ صَدوقٌ في حَديثِهِ، مُحافِظٌ علىٰ صَلَواتِه وما افْتَرَضَ اللهُ علَيهِ،

prayer and all that Allah has made obligatory for him, along with returning whatever he is entrusted with.'[1519]

مَع أداءِ الأمانَةِ.[١٥٠٩]

427. The Signs of God's Love towards His servant

٤٢٧ ـ آثارُ مَحَبَّةِ اللهِ عَبدَهُ

"Say, 'If you love Allah, then follow me; Allah will love you and forgive you your sins, and Allah is all-forgiving, all-merciful.'"[1520]

﴿قُلْ إِنْ كُنْتُمْ تُحِبُّونَ اللهَ فَاتَّبِعُونِي يُحْبِبْكُمُ اللهُ وَيَغْفِرْ لَكُمْ ذُنُوبَكُمْ وَاللهُ غَفُورٌ رَحِيمٌ﴾.[١٥١٠]

1333. **Imām ʿAlī (AS) said,** 'When Allah loves a servant He inspires him with good acts of devotion.'[1521]

١٣٣٣ . الإمامُ عليٌّ عليه السلام : إذا أحَبَّ اللهُ عَبداً ألْهَمَهُ حُسنَ العِبادَةِ.[١٥١١]

1334. **Imām al-Ṣādiq (AS) said,** 'Whoever would like to know that Allah loves him must work in the obedience of Allah and follow us. Has he heard not the speech of Allah, Mighty and Exalted, to His Prophet (SAWA): *"Say, 'If you love Allah…"*?'[1522]

١٣٣٤ . الإمامُ الصّادقُ عليه السلام : مَن سَرَّهُ أن يَعلمَ أنَّ اللهَ يُحِبُّهُ فلْيَعْمَلْ بطاعةِ اللهِ ولْيَتَّبِعْنا، ألَمْ يَسْمَعْ قَولَ اللهِ عزّ وجلّ لنَبيِّهِ صلى الله عليه وآله : ﴿قُلْ إِن كُنتُمْ تُحِبُّونَ ٱللَّهَ فَٱتَّبِعُونِى يُحْبِبْكُمُ ٱللَّهُ وَيَغْفِرْ لَكُمْ ذُنُوبَكُمْ وَٱللَّهُ غَفُورٌ رَّحِيمٌ﴾ ؟![١٥١٢]

428. The Status of Man's Position with Allah

٤٢٨ ـ ميزانُ المَنزِلَةِ عِندَ اللهِ

1335. **Imām al-Ṣādiq (AS) said,** 'Whoever wants to know the status of his position with Allah must first find out what status of position Allah holds with him, for Allah places the servant in the same position whereat the servant places Allah with respect to himself.'[1523]

١٣٣٥ . الإمامُ الصّادقُ عليه السلام : مَن أرادَ أنْ يَعرِفَ كيفَ مَنزِلَتُهُ عِندَ اللهِ فلْيَعْرِفْ كيفَ مَنزِلَةُ اللهِ عِندَهُ، فإنَّ اللهَ يُنزِلُ العَبدَ مِثلَ ما يُنزِلُ العَبدُ اللهَ مِن نَفْسِهِ.[١٥١٣]

429. The Sign of Man's Love for Allah

٤٢٩ ـ عَلامَةُ حُبِّ الإنسانِ للّهِ

1336. **The Prophet (SAWA) said,** 'The sign of [man's] love of Allah is the love of the remembrance of Allah, and the sign of [man's] hatred towards Allah is his hatred towards the remembrance of Allah, Mighty and Exalted.'[1524]

١٣٣٦ . رسولُ اللهِ صلى الله عليه وآله : عَلامَةُ حُبِّ اللهِ تعالىٰ حُبُّ ذِكرِ اللهِ، وعَلامَةُ بُغْضِ اللهِ تعالىٰ بُغْضُ ذِكرِ اللهِ عزّ وجلّ.[١٥١٤]

1337. **Imām al-Ṣādiq (AS) said,** regarding what Allah, most High, revealed to Prophet Moses (AS),

١٣٣٧ . الإمامُ الصّادقُ عليه السلام ـ فيما أوْحىٰ اللهُ تعالىٰ

said, 'He lies who claims that he loves Me, yet when the night covers him up he sleeps away from Me [forgetting Me]. Is it not that every lover loves to be alone with his beloved?!'[1525]

إلىٰ موسىٰ ﷺ ـ: كَذبَ مَن زَعَمَ أنَّهُ يُحِبُّني فإذا جَنَّهُ اللّيلُ نامَ عَنّي، أليسَ كُلُّ مُحِبٍّ يُحِبُّ خَلْوةَ حَبيبِهِ ؟! ١٥١٥

430. The Highest Position

٤٣٠ ـ المَنزِلَةُ الكُبرىٰ

1338. **The Prophet (SAWA) said,** 'Allah, Mighty and Exalted, says, "My servant endears himself to Me with nothing more beloved to Me than what I have made obligatory upon him, and he endears himself to Me through performance of the supererogatory prayers until I love him. Once I love him, I become his hearing with which he hears, his sight with which he sees, his tongue with which he speaks, his hands with which he acts, and his foot with which he walks. When he calls Me I answer him, and when he asks Me I grant him."'[1526]

١٣٣٨ . رسولُ اللهِ ﷺ : قالَ اللهُ: ما تَحبَّبَ إلَيّ عَبدي بشيءٍ أحَبَّ إلَيَّ ممّا افتَرَضْتُهُ علَيهِ ،وإنّهُ لَيَتحبَّبُ إلَيَّ بالنّافِلَةِ حتّىٰ اُحِبَّهُ، فإذا أحْبَبْتُهُ كنتُ سَمْعَهُ الّذي يَسمَعُ بهِ، وبَصرَهُ الّذي يُبصِرُ بهِ، ولِسانَهُ الّذي يَنْطِقُ بهِ، ويَدَهُ الّتي يَبْطِشُ بها، ورِجْلَهُ الّتي يَمشي بها، إذا دَعاني أجَبْتُهُ، وإذا سَألَني أعْطَيتُهُ. ١٥١٦

431. The Incongruity of the Love of Allah Combined with the Love of the World

٤٣١ ـ عَدَمُ اجتِماعِ حُبِّ اللهِ وحُبِّ الدُّنيا

1339. **The Prophet (SAWA) said,** 'The love for Allah and the love for the world cannot ever coexist in one heart.'[1527]

١٣٣٩ . رسولُ اللهِ ﷺ : حُبُّ الدُّنيا وحُبُّ اللهِ لا يَجْتَمِعانِ في قَلبٍ أبداً. ١٥١٧

1340. **Imām al-Ṣādiq (AS) said,** 'By Allah, he who loves this world and befriends other than us does not love Allah.'[1528]

١٣٤٠ . الإمامُ الصّادقُ ﷺ : واللهِ، ما أحَبَّ اللهَ مَن أحَبَّ الدُّنيا ووالَىٰ غيرَنا. ١٥١٨

(See also: THE WORLD: section 721)

(أنظر) الدنيا: باب ٧٢١.

432. Enjoining the Love of Allah

٤٣٢ ـ الحَثُّ عَلىٰ تَحبيبِ اللهِ

1341. **The Prophet (SAWA) said,** 'Allah, Mighty and Exalted, said to Prophet David (AS), "Love Me and encourage My creatures to love Me." He said, 'My Lord, I do love You, but how can I

١٣٤١ . رسولُ اللهِ ﷺ :قالَ اللهُ عزّ وجلّ لداوودَ ﷺ: أحْبِبْني وحَبِّبْني إلىٰ خَلْقي. قالَ: يا رَبِّ، نَعَم أنا اُحِبُّكَ، فكيفَ اُحَبِّبُكَ إلىٰ خَلقِكَ ؟ قالَ: اذْكُرْ

encourage Your creatures to love You?’ Allah said, “Remind them of My blessing and kindness, for if you remind them of that they will love Me.”[1529]

أيـادِيَّ عِـندَهُم، فـإنَّكَ إذا ذَكَـرْتَ لَـهُم ذلكَ أحَبّوني.[١٥١٩]

433. To Love for the Sake of Allah

٤٣٣ ـ الحُبُّ فِي اللهِ

1342. **The Prophet (SAWA) said,** ‘The best of practices is to love for the sake of Allah and to hate for the sake of Allah, most High.’[1530]

١٣٤٢ . رسولُ اللهِ ﷺ : أفْضَلُ الأعْمالِ الحُبُّ في اللهِ والبُغْضُ في اللهِ تعالى.[١٥٢٠]

1343. **The Prophet (SAWA) said** to one of his companions, ‘O servant of Allah! Love for the sake of Allah and hate for the sake of Allah, and befriend for the sake of Allah and contest for the sake of Allah, for Allah’s guardianship is attained only by that, and man will not find the taste of faith — though his prayers and fasting be much — unless he behaves thus. In this present day, the brotherhood and friendship of the people are mainly for the sake of this world; they love each other for its sake and hate each other for its sake.’[1531]

١٣٤٣ . عنه ﷺ ـ لبعضِ أصحابِهِ ـ: يا عبدَ اللهِ، أحْبِبْ في اللهِ، وأبغِضْ في اللهِ، ووالِ في اللهِ، وعادِ في اللهِ، فإنَّهُ لا تُنالُ وَلايةُ اللهِ إلّا بذلكَ، ولا يَجِدُ رَجُلٌ طَعْمَ الإيمانِ ـ وإنْ كَثُرَتْ صَلاتُهُ وصِيامُهُ ـ حتّىٰ يكونَ كذلكَ، وقد صارَتْ مُؤاخاةُ النّاسِ يَومَكُم هذا أكْثَرُها في الدُّنيا، علَيها يَتوادّونَ، وعلَيها يَتَباغَضُونَ.[١٥٢١]

1344. **Imām al-Ṣādiq (AS) said,** ‘No sooner do two believers meet than the better of them is he who loves his brother more.’[1532]

١٣٤٤ . الإمامُ الصّادقُ ؑ : ما الْتَقىٰ مُؤمِنانِ قَطُّ إلّا كانَ أفْضَلُهُما أشَدَّهُما حُبّاً لأخيهِ.[١٥٢٢]

1345. **Imām al-Ṣādiq (AS) said,** ‘Every single person who does not love for religion or hate for religion has no religion.’[1533]

١٣٤٥ . عنه ؑ : كُلُّ مَن لَم يُحِبَّ علَى الدِّينِ ولَم يُبغِضْ علَى الدِّينِ، فلا دِينَ لَهُ.[١٥٢٣]

1346. **Imām al-Jawād (AS) said,** ‘Allah revealed to one of the prophets, “Your asceticism in this world hastens your comfort, and your devotion to Me endears you to Me. But did you oppose an enemy [of Mine] for My sake or did you befriend a friend for Me?”[1534]

١٣٤٦ . الإمامُ الجوادُ ؑ : أوْحَى اللهُ إلىٰ بعضِ الأنبياءِ: أمّا زُهدُكَ في الدُّنيا فَتُعَجِّلُكَ الرّاحَةَ، وأمّا انْقِطاعُكَ إلَيَّ فيُعَزِّزُكَ بِي، ولكنْ هَل عادَيْتَ لي عَدُوّاً ووالَيْتَ لي وَلِيّاً؟[١٥٢٤]

434. The Love of the Prophet (SAWA) and his Household (AS)

٤٣٤ ـ حُبُّ النبيِّ ﷺ وأهلِ بيتِه ؑ

1347. **The Prophet (SAWA) said,** ‘Man is not considered a believer until I am dearer to him

١٣٤٧ . رسولُ اللهِ ﷺ : لا يُؤمنُ عَبدٌ حتّىٰ أكونَ

than his own self, my household dearer to him than his own Household, my family dearer to him than his own family, and my being dearer to him than his own being.'[1535]

أحَبَّ إلَيهِ مِن نَفْسِهِ، وتَكونَ عِتْرَتي إلَيهِ أعَزَّ مِن عِتْرَتِهِ، ويكونَ أهْلي أحَبَّ إلَيهِ مِن أهْلِهِ، وتكونَ ذاتي أحَبَّ إلَيهِ مِن ذاتِهِ.[١٥٢٥]

1348. **The Prophet (SAWA) said,** 'Love Allah for the blessings that He bestows on you every morning; love me because of the love of Allah; and love my household because of love for me.'[1536]

١٣٤٨ . عنه ﷺ : أحِبّوا اللهَ لِما يَغْدوكُم بهِ مِن نِعَمِهِ، وأحِبّوني لِحُبِّ اللهِ، وأحِبّوا أهْلَ بَيْتي لِحُبّي.[١٥٢٦]

1349. **The Prophet (SAWA) said,** 'He who loves us, the holy Household, let him praise Allah for the first blessing.' He was asked, 'What is the first blessing?' to which he replied, 'Legitimate birth, for only he loves us whose birth [i.e. conception] is legitimate.'[1537]

١٣٤٩ . المحاسن عن الإمامِ الصادق عن آبائه عليهم السلام : قالَ رسولُ اللهِ ﷺ : مَن أحَبَّنا أهلَ البيتِ فلْيَحْمَدِ اللهَ علىٰ أوَّلِ النِّعَمِ. قلت: وما أولى النِّعَمِ؟ قالَ: طِيبُ الوِلادَةِ، ولا يُحِبُّنا إلّا مَن طابَتْ وِلادَتُهُ.[١٥٢٧]

1350. It is narrated in *al-Daʿawāt* on the authority of al-Ḥārith al-Hamdānī, 'One day I went to visit the Commander of the Faithful (AS) at noon. He asked, 'What has brought you here?' I answered, 'By Allah, it is love for you.' He said, 'If you are truthful, you will see me at three positions: when your soul comes to this - and then he pointed to his throat –, on the Bridge [outstretched over Hell], and at the Heavenly Waters.'[1538]

١٣٥٠ . الدعوات عن الحارِثِ الهَمْدانيِّ: أتيتُ أميرَ المؤمِنينَ عليه السلام ذاتَ يَومٍ نصفَ النَّهارِ، فقالَ: ما جاءَ بكَ؟ قلتُ: حُبُّكَ واللهِ. قالَ عليه السلام : إنْ كنتَ صادِقاً لَتراني في ثَلاثةِ مَواطِنَ: حَيثُ تَبْلُغُ نَفْسُكَ هذهِ - وأوْمَأ بيدِهِ إلىٰ حَنْجَرَتِهِ - وعِند الصِّراطِ، وعِند الحَوضِ.[١٥٢٨]

1351. **Imām al-Bāqir (AS) said,** regarding the verse of Allah, most High: *"He has held fast to the firmest handle"* [1539], said, 'It is love for us, the Prophet's Household (*Ahl al-Bayt*).'[1540]

١٣٥١ . الإمامُ الباقرُ عليه السلام - في قولِهِ تعالىٰ: ﴿فَقَدِ اسْتَمْسَكَ بِالعُرْوَةِ الوُثْقَىٰ﴾ [١٥٢٩] -: مَودَّتُنا أهلَ البَيتِ.[١٥٣٠]

435. The Conditions for Loving the Household (AS)

٤٣٥ - ما يُشتَرَطُ في حُبِّ أهلِ البَيتِ عليهم السلام

1352. **Imām al-Bāqir (AS) said,** 'By Allah, we have no acquaintance from Allah, nor is there kinship between Allah and us, nor do we possess a [special] argument against Allah, nor do we attain proximity to Allah except through His obedience. So whosoever from among you is obedient to

١٣٥٢ . الإمامُ الباقرُ عليه السلام : واللهِ، ما مَعنا مِن اللهِ بَراءةٌ، ولا بيْنَنا وبَينَ اللهِ قَرابَةٌ، ولا لَنا علىٰ اللهِ حُجَّةٌ، ولا نَتَقَرَّبُ إلىٰ اللهِ إلّا بالطّاعَةِ، فمَن كانَ

Allah, our friendship will benefit him, and whosoever from among you is disobedient to Allah, our friendship will be of no use to him. Woe unto you, do not be deceived! Woe unto you, do not be deceived!'[1541]

مِنكُم مُطيعاً للهِ تَنفَعُهُ ولايَتُنا، ومَن كانَ مِنكُم عاصياً للهِ لَم تَنفَعْهُ وَلايَتُنا. ويْحَكُم لا تَغتَرّوا! ويْحَكُم لاتَغتَرّوا![١٥٣١]

436. Devotion In Love

٤٣٦ ـ إخلاصُ المَحَبَّةِ

1353. **Imām ʿAli (AS) said,** 'Being brothers for the sake of Allah produces sincere love.'[1542]

١٣٥٣. الإمام عليٌّ ؑ: عَلَى التَّواخي فِي اللهِ تَخلُصُ المَحَبَّةُ[١٥٣٢].

1354. **Imām ʿAli (AS) said,** 'He whose friendship is for the sake of Allah is kind in company and his love is genuine.'[1543]

١٣٥٤. الإمام عليٌّ ؑ: مَن كانَت صُحبَتُهُ فِي اللهِ، كانَت صُحبَتُهُ كَريمَةً، ومَوَدَّتُهُ مُستَقيمَةً[١٥٣٣].

437. Man is with Whom he Loves

٤٣٧ ـ المَرءُ مَعَ مَن أحَبَّ

1355. **The Prophet (SAWA) said,** 'Man is with him whom he loves.'[1544]

١٣٥٥. رسولُ اللهِ ﷺ: المَرءُ مَعَ مَن أحَبَّ.[١٥٣٤]

1356. It is narrated in *Kanz al-ʿUmmāl*: A man asked the Prophet (SAWA) about the Final Hour, to whom he asked in turn, 'What have you done to prepare for it?' The man replied, 'I have not prepared much for it [other than the obligatory acts], but I do love Allah and His Messenger.' The Prophet said, 'Then you will be with whom you love.'[1545]

١٣٥٦. كنز العمّال: سأَلَ رجُلٌ رسولَ اللهِ ﷺ عنِ السّاعةِ، فقالَ: ما أعْدَدْتَ لَها؟ قالَ: ما أعْدَدْتُ لَها كبيراً، إلّا أنّي أُحِبُّ اللهَ ورسولَهُ. قالَ: فأنتَ مَعَ مَن أحْبَبْتَ.[١٥٣٥]

85

IMPRISONMENT

الحبس

438. Those Who may be Imprisoned

٤٣٨ ـ مَن يَجوزُ حَبسُهُ

1357. **Imām ʿAlī (AS) said,** 'It is incumbent upon the Imām to imprison the reckless from among

١٣٥٧. الإمامُ عليٌّ ؑ: يَجِبُ علَى الإمامِ أنْ

the scholars, the ignorant from among the physicians, and the bankrupt from among the lease-holders.'[1546]

يَحْبِسَ الفُسّاقَ مِنَ العُلَماءِ، والجُهّالَ مِنَ الأطِبّاءِ، والمَفالِيسَ مِنَ الأكْرِياءِ.١٥٣٦

1358. **Imām ʿAlī (AS) said,** 'If a Muslim woman becomes an apostate, abandoning Islam, she is not killed but is imprisoned for life.'[1547]

١٣٥٨. عنه ؑ: إذا ارْتَدَّتِ المَرأةُ عنِ الإسلامِ لَم تُقْتَلْ، ولكنْ تُحْبَسُ أبداً.١٥٣٧

1359. It is narrated in *al-Kāfī*: Verily the Commander of the Faithful (AS) restricted imprisonment to only three cases: a man consuming the property of an orphan unlawfully, or usurping it, or a man who takes off with what he has been entrusted with.[1548]

١٣٥٩. الكافي: إنّ أميرَ المؤمنينَ ؑ كانَ لا يَرىٰ الحَبْسَ إلّا في ثلاثٍ: رجُلٌ أكلَ مالَ اليَتيمِ، أو غَصَبهُ، أو رجُلٌ اؤتُمِنَ علىٰ أمانةٍ فذَهَبَ بها.١٥٣٨

439. Jailing the Warrantor until the Return of the Warranted

٤٣٩ـ حَبسُ الكَفيلِ إلىٰ حينِ حُضورِ المَكفولِ

1360. **Imām al-Ṣādiq (AS) said,** 'A man was brought to the Commander of the Faithful (AS), who had bailed the life of another man. He imprisoned him, saying, 'Ask for your companion now.'[1549]

١٣٦٠. الإمامُ الصّادقُ ؑ: اُتيَ أميرُ المؤمنينَ ؑ برجُلٍ قد تكفَّلَ بنَفْسِ رجُلٍ، فحَبَسَهُ وقالَ: اطلُبْ صاحِبَكَ.١٥٣٩

440. The One Imprisoned for Life

٤٤٠ـ مَن يُخَلَّدُ في السِّجنِ

1361. **Imām al-Bāqir (AS) said,** about a man who had ordered another man to kill someone, which he had done – 'He who killed him must be killed, and he who ordered the killing must be imprisoned until he dies.'[1550]

١٣٦١. الإمامُ الباقرُ ؑ ـ في رجُلٍ أمَرَ رجُلاً بقتلِ رجُلٍ فقتلَهُ ـ: يُقْتَلُ بهِ الّذي قَتَلَهُ، ويُحْبَسُ الآمِرُ بقَتْلِهِ في السِّجْنِ حتّىٰ يَموتَ.١٥٤٠

1362. **Imām al-Ṣādiq (AS) said,** 'Imām ʿAlī (AS) passed on a judgment between two people whom one was put in jail and the other killed, and he (AS) said, 'The killer is to be killed and the other is to be jailed until he dies with dismay the same way he jailed the prisoner and made him die in dismay.'[1551]

١٣٦٢. الإمامُ الصّادقُ ؑ: قَضىٰ عليٌّ ؑ في رَجُلَينِ أمسَكَ أحَدُهُما وقتَلَ الآخَرُ فقالَ: يُقتَلُ القاتِلُ ويُحبَسُ الآخَرُ حتّىٰ يَموتَ غَمّاً كَما حَبَسَهُ علَيهِ حتّىٰ ماتَ غَمّاً.١٥٤١

441. Imprisonment after Punishment and Acknowledgment of the Truth

٤٤١ـ الحَبسُ بَعدَ إقامَةِ الحَدِّ ومَعرِفَةِ حَقٍّ

1363. **Imām ʿAlī (AS) said,** 'It is unjust for the Imām to imprison the culprit after punishment.'[1552]

١٣٦٣ . الإمامُ عليٌّ عليه السلام : حَبْسُ الإمامِ بعدَ الحَدِّ ظُلْمٌ .١٥٤٢

1364. **Imām ʿAlī (AS) said,** 'Imprisonment after acknowledgment of the truth is injustice.'[1553]

١٣٦٤ . عنه عليه السلام :الحَبسُ بَعدَ مَعرِفَةِ الحقِّ ظُلْمٌ .١٥٤٣

442. The Rights of the Prisoner

٤٤٢ـ حُقوقُ المَحبوسِ

1365. **Imām ʿAlī (AS)** used to inspect the prisons every Friday; he punished the convicts and released those who had no charge against them.'[1554]

١٣٦٥ . الإمامُ عليٌّ عليه السلام : أنَّهُ [عَلِيّاً] كانَ يَعرِضُ السّجونَ في كُلِّ يَومِ جُمُعَةٍ؛ فمَن كانَ علَيهِ حَدٌّ أقامَهُ، ومَن لَم يَكُن علَيهِ حَدٌّ خلّى سَبيلَهُ .١٥٤٤

1366. **Imām al-Ṣādiq (AS) said,** 'It is the duty of the Imām to release the prisoners on financial charges on Fridays and *ʿĪd* [religious festivals] to observe the congregational prayer. He may send them guarded, and when they complete the prayers and the feast, he should return them to the prison.'[1555]

١٣٦٦ . الإمامُ الصّادقُ عليه السلام :علىَ الإمامِ أنْ يُخرِجَ المَحْبوسينَ في الدَّينِ يَومَ الجُمُعَةِ إلَى الجُمُعَةِ، ويَومَ العِيدِ إلَى العِيدِ، فيُرسِلَ مَعهُم، فإذا قَضَوُا الصَّلاةَ والعِيدَ رَدَّهُم إلَى السِّجنِ .١٥٤٥

(See also: THE PRISONER: 9)

(أنظر) عنوان ٩ «الأسير».

443. The Conduct of the Prophet (SAWA) in Imprisoning a Suspect

٤٤٣ـ سيرةُ النبيِّ صلى الله عليه وآله في حَبسِ المتَّهمِ

1367. **Imām al-Ṣādiq (AS) said,** 'The Prophet (SAWA) would imprison for six days he who has been accused of killing, the kin of the killed must come with evidence, and if not, he is freed.'[1556]

١٣٦٧ . الإمام الصادق عليه السلام : إنَّ النَّبِيَّ صلى الله عليه وآله كانَ يَحبِسُ في تُهَمَةِ الدَّمِ سِتَّةَ أيّامٍ، فَإن جاءَ أولياءُ المَقتولِ بِثَبَتٍ وإلّا خَلّىٰ سَبيلَهُ .١٥٤٦

1368. **Sunan Abi Dawūd,** narrating from Ḥakīm narrating from his father said, 'The Prophet (SAWA) jailed a person who was accused of an act [of crime].'[1557]

١٣٦٨ . سنن ابى داود عن حكيم عن ابيه : إنَّ النَّبِيَّ صلى الله عليه وآله حَبَسَ رَجُلاً في تُهمَةٍ .١٥٤٧

86

THE VEIL

الحِجابُ

444. The Veil

٤٤٤ ـ الحِجابُ

"O Prophet! Tell your wives and your daughters and the women of the faithful to draw closely over themselves their chadors [when going out]. That makes it likely for them to be recognized and not be troubled, and Allah is all-forgiving, all-merciful."[1558]

﴿يا أَيُّهَا النَّبِيُّ قُلْ لِأَزْوَاجِكَ وَبَنَاتِكَ وَنِسَاءِ الْمُؤْمِنِينَ يُدْنِينَ عَلَيْهِنَّ مِنْ جَلابِيبِهِنَّ ذٰلِكَ أَدْنَىٰ أَنْ يُعْرَفْنَ فَلا يُؤْذَيْنَ وَكَانَ اللهُ غَفُوراً رَحِيماً﴾.[١٥٤٨]

(See also: Qur'an 24:30-31, 24:58, 33:53, 33:59)

(أُنظر) النور: ٣٠، ٣١، ٥٨ و الأحزاب: ٥٣ و ٥٩.

1369. **Imām ʿAlī (AS) said** to his son al-Ḥasan (AS), 'And curb their eyes by keeping them in veil, for the strict observance of the veil is better for you and for them.'[1559]

١٣٦٩. الإمامُ عليٌّ عليه السلام ـ لابنِهِ الحسنِ عليه السلام ـ: واكْفُفْ علَيهِنَّ مِن أبْصارِهِنَّ بحَجْبِكَ إيّاهُنَّ، فإنَّ شِدَّةَ الحِجابِ خَيرٌ لكَ ولَهُنَّ.[١٥٤٩]

1370. **Imām ʿAlī (AS) said,** 'I was sitting with the Messenger of Allah (SAWA) in Baqīʿ on a cloudy and rainy day, when a woman passed us on a donkey. The foreleg of the donkey slipped into a pit and the woman fell off. The Prophet (SAWA) turned his face away. They [his companions] said, 'O Messenger of Allah, she has trousers on.' He said thrice, 'O Allah! Forgive the women clad in trousers' – 'O people! Wear trousers for they are the most covering of your garments, and safeguard your women by [making them wear] them when they go out.'[1560]

١٣٧٠. عنه عليه السلام: كنتُ قاعداً في البَقيعِ مَع رسولِ اللهِ صلى الله عليه وآله في يَومِ دَجْنٍ ومَطَرٍ، إذ مَرَّتِ امْرَأةٌ علىٰ حِمارٍ، فَهَوتْ يدُ الحِمارِ في وَهْدَةٍ فسَقَطَتِ المَرأةُ، فأعْرَضَ النّبيُّ صلى الله عليه وآله بوجهِهِ، قالوا: يا رسولَ اللهِ، إنّها مُتَسَرْوِلَةٌ. قالَ: اللّهُمَّ اغْفِرْ للمُتَسَرْوِلاتِ ـ ثلاثاً ـ يا أيُّها النّاسُ، اتَّخِذوا السَّراويلاتِ فإنَّها مِن أسْتَرِ ثِيابِكُم، وحَصِّنوا بِها نِساءَكُم إذا خَرَجْنَ.[١٥٥٠]

1371. **Imām ʿAlī (AS) said,** 'Covering the woman is more prosperous to her state and more enduring for her beauty.'[1561]

١٣٧١. عنه عليه السلام: صِيانَةُ المَرأةِ أنعَمُ لِحالِها وأدوَمُ لِجَمالِها.[١٥٥١]

87

THE PILGRIMAGE (ḤAJJ)

الحَجّ

445. The Legislation of Ḥajj and its Virtue

٤٤٥ ـ تَشرِيعُ الحَجِّ وَ فَضلُهُ

"And it is the duty of mankind toward Allah to make pilgrimage to the House—for those who can afford the journey to it."[1562]

﴿وَلِلّٰهِ عَلَىٰ النَّاسِ حِجُّ الْبَيْتِ مَنِ اسْتَطَاعَ إِلَيْهِ سَبِيلاً﴾.[١٥٥٢]

"And proclaim the ḥajj to people: they shall come to you on foot and lean camels from distant places."[1563]

﴿وَأَذِّنْ فِي النَّاسِ بِالْحَجِّ يَأْتُوكَ رِجَالاً وَعَلَىٰ كُلِّ ضَامِرٍ يَأْتِينَ مِنْ كُلِّ فَجٍّ عَمِيقٍ﴾.[١٥٥٣]

"And complete the ḥajj and the ʿumra for Allah's sake."[1564]

﴿وَأَتِمُّوا الْحَجَّ وَالْعُمْرَةَ لِلّٰهِ﴾.[١٥٥٤]

1372. **Imām ʿAlī (AS) said,** in his will at the time of his demise, 'I exhort you, by Allah, by Allah, to take care of the House of your Lord! Do not leave it empty for as long as you live, for if it is deserted you will be given no respite.'[1565]

١٣٧٢. الإمامُ عليٌّ عليه السلام ـ فيما أوصىٰ عِند وفاتِهِ ـ: اللهَ اللهَ في بَيتِ ربِّكمُ، لا تُخْلوهُ ما بَقِيتُم، فإنَّهُ إنْ تُرِكَ لَم تُناظَروا.[١٥٥٥]

1373. **Imām ʿAlī (AS) said,** 'The pilgrimage is the *jihād* of every weak person.'[1566]

١٣٧٣. عنه عليه السلام: الحَجُّ جِهادُ كلِّ ضَعيفٍ.[١٥٥٦]

1374. **Imām ʿAlī (AS) said,** 'Spending one dirham [in charity] during the pilgrimage equals one thousand dirhams.'[1567]

١٣٧٤. عنه عليه السلام: نَفَقةُ دِرْهَمٍ في الحجِّ تَعْدِلُ ألفَ دِرْهَمٍ.[١٥٥٧]

1375. **Imām ʿAlī (AS) said,** 'Those who go to Makkah for obligatory and voluntary pilgrimage (*ḥajj* and *ʿumra*) are the guests of Allah, and His gift to them is forgiveness.'[1568]

١٣٧٥. عنه عليه السلام: الحاجُّ والمُعْتَمِرُ وفْدُاللهِ، ويَحْبوهُ بالمَغفِرَةِ.[١٥٥٨]

446. The Philosophy of the Pilgrimage

٤٤٦ ـ فَلسَفَةُ الحَجِّ

1376. **Imām ʿAlī (AS) said,** 'And He made obligatory for you the pilgrimage to His Sacred House which he made the '*qibla*' for all people.

١٣٧٦. الإمامُ عليٌّ عليه السلام: وفَرَضَ علَيكمُ حَجَّ بَيتِهِ الحَرامِ الّذي جَعَلهُ قِبلَةً للأنامِ، يَرِدُونَهُ

They come to it like the cattle coming to water, and eagerly turn to it like the birds eagerly returning to their nest; He, glory be to Him, made it a sign of their humility before His greatness and their yielding to His Might.'[1569]

وُرودَ الأنْعامِ، ويَألَهونَ إلَيهِ وُلوهَ الحَمامِ، وجَعلَهُ سبحانَهُ عَلامةً لِتَواضُعِهِم لِعظَمَتِهِ وإذْعانِهِم لِعزّتِهِ.[١٥٥٩]

1377. **Imām Zayn al-ʿĀbidīn (AS) said,** 'Perform the *ḥajj* [obligatory pilgrimage] and the *ʿumra* [voluntary pilgrimage] so that your bodies become healthy, your sustenance expanded, and your faith improved; and suffice yourselves with the expenses of people and the expenses of your families.'[1570]

١٣٧٧. الإمامُ زينُ العابدينَ عليه السلام: حِجّوا واعْتَمِروا، تَصِحَّ أجْسامُكُم، وتَتّسِعْ أرْزاقُكُم، ويَصْلُحْ إيمانُكُم، وتُكْفَوا مؤونَةَ النّاسِ ومؤونَةَ عِيالاتِكُم.[١٥٦٠]

1378. **Imām al-Bāqir (AS) said,** 'Pilgrimage calms the hearts.'[1571]

١٣٧٨. الإمامُ الباقرُ عليه السلام: الحَجُّ تَسْكينُ القُلوبِ.[١٥٦١]

1379. **Imām al-Ṣādiq (AS) said,** 'And this is the house by which Allah has demanded the devotion of His creatures to test their obedience in their coming to it, so He prompted them to glorify it and visit it. He made it the station of the prophets and the focal point (*qibla*) for those who pray to Him. It is a branch of His good pleasure and a way that leads to His forgiveness, founded on absolute perfection and ultimate grandeur.'[1572]

١٣٧٩. الإمامُ الصّادقُ عليه السلام: وهذا بَيتٌ اسْتَعبَدَ اللهُ بِهِ خَلقَهُ لِيَخْتَبِرَ طاعَتَهُم في إتْيانِهِ، فحَثَّهُم علىٰ تَعْظيمِهِ وزيارَتِهِ، وقَد جَعلَهُ مَحلَّ الأنبياءِ وقِبْلَةً للمُصَلّينَ لَهُ، وهُو شُعْبَةٌ مِن رِضْوانِهِ، وطَريقٌ يُؤَدّي إلىٰ غُفْرانِهِ، مَنْصوبٌ علىٰ اسْتِواءِ الكَمالِ، ومُجْتَمَعِ العَظَمَةِ.[١٥٦٢]

1380. **Imām al-Ṣādiq (AS) said,** 'There is no place dearer to Allah, most High, than the *masʿā* [place of running between the mounts of al-Ṣafā and al-Marwa in Makkah], for every overbearing person is lowered and debased before Him there.'[1573]

١٣٨٠. عنه عليه السلام: ما مِن بُقْعَةٍ أحَبَّ إلىٰ اللهِ تعالىٰ مِنَ المَسْعىٰ؛ لأنّه يَذِلُّ فيهِ كُلُّ جَبّارٍ.[١٥٦٣]

1381. **Imām al-Riḍā (AS) said,** 'If someone asks why He commanded the pilgrimage, it is answered: in order for people to perform the journey to [i.e. for] Allah, Mighty and Exalted, and ask for increase... in addition to the benefits it has of understanding religion and relating the reports of the Imāms (AS) to every side and region.'[1574]

١٣٨١. الإمامُ الرِّضا عليه السلام: فإنْ قالَ: فَلِمَ أمَرَ بالحَجِّ؟ قيلَ: لِعلَّةِ الوِفادَةِ إلى اللهِ عزّ وجلّ وطَلَبِ الزِّيادَةِ... مَع ما فيهِ مِن التَّفَقُّهِ ونَقْلِ أخْبارِ الأئمّةِ عليهم السلام إلىٰ كُلِّ صُقْعٍ وناحِيَةٍ.[١٥٦٤]

447. Pilgrimage Repels Poverty

٤٤٧ـ نَفيُ الحَجِّ لِلفَقرِ

1382. **The Prophet (SAWA) said,** 'Pilgrimage repels poverty.'[1575]

١٣٨٢ . رسولُ اللهِ ﷺ : الحَجّ يَنفي الفقرَ.[١٥٧٥]

1383. **Imām al-Ṣādiq (AS) said,** 'He who goes to perform the obligatory pilgrimage (*ḥajj*) three times will never be afflicted with poverty.'[1576]

١٣٨٣ . الإمامُ الصّادقُ ﷺ : مَن حَجَّ ثَلاثَ حِجَجٍ لَم يُصِبْهُ فَقرٌ أبداً.[١٥٧٦]

1384. **Imām al-Ṣādiq (AS) said,** 'I have never seen anything faster at attracting wealth and at repelling poverty than habitual pilgrimage (*ḥajj*) to this House.'[1577]

١٣٨٤ . عنه ﷺ : ما رأيتُ شَيئاً أسْرَعَ غِنىً ولا أنْفىٰ للفَقرِ مِن إدْمانِ حَجِّ هذا البَيتِ.[١٥٧٧]

1385. **Imām al-Ṣādiq (AS),** when Isḥāq b. 'Ammār said to him: 'I have made up my mind to go for pilgrimage every year either personally or by sending one man of my household at my cost' – asked, 'Are you determined to do that?' He said, 'Yes'. The Imām said, 'If you do that, then be certain of abundance in your wealth, and take glad tidings of abundance in your wealth.'[1578]

١٣٨٥ . ثواب الأعمال عن إسحاقَ بنِ عمّارٍ : قُلتُ للإمامِ الصادقِ ﷺ : إنّي قد وَطَّنْتُ نَفْسي علىٰ لُزومِ الحَجِّ كلَّ عامٍ بنَفْسي أو بِرَجُلٍ مِن أهلِ بَيْتي بمالي. فقالَ : وقد عَزَمْتَ على ذلكَ ؟ قلتُ : نَعَم، قالَ : فإنْ فَعَلتَ (ذلك) فأيقِنْ بكَثْرَةِ المالِ، و أبْشِرْ بكَثْرَةِ المالِ.[١٥٧٨]

448. That Which Completes the Pilgrimage

٤٤٨ـ ما بِهِ تَمامُ الحَجِّ

1386. **Imām 'Alī (AS) said,** 'Complete your pilgrimage by visiting the Messenger of Allah (SAWA) when you leave to visit the House of Allah, for deserting it is unkind, and that is what you have been commanded to do [i.e. in the Qur'an: *and complete ...*] by observing the rights of the graves that Allah has made incumbent upon you to visit, and ask for [increase in] your sustenance thereat.'[1579]

١٣٨٦ . الإمامُ عليٌّ ﷺ : أتِمّوا برسولِ اللهِ ﷺ حَجَّكُم إذا خَرَجْتُم إلىٰ بَيتِ اللهِ، فإنَّ تَركَهُ جَفاءٌ، وبذلكَ اُمِرْتُم، (وأتِمّوا) بالقُبورِ الّتي ألْزَمَكُمُ اللهُ عزّوجلّ حَقَّها وزِيارَتَها، واطلُبوا الرِّزقَ عِندَها.[١٥٧٩]

1387. **Imām al-Bāqir (AS) said,** 'The pilgrimage is completed by meeting the Imām.'[1580]

١٣٨٧ . الإمامُ الباقرُ ﷺ : تَمامُ الحَجِّ لِقاءُ الإمامِ.[١٥٨٠]

1388. **Imām al-Bāqir (AS) said,** 'Indeed people have been ordered to come to these stones [i.e. the

١٣٨٨ . عنه ﷺ : إنّما اُمِرَ النّاسُ : أنْ يَأتوا هذهِ

edifice of the Ka'ba] to circumambulate them, and then to come to us to inform us of their love and loyalty, and to declare their support for us.'[1581]

الأحْجارَ فيَتطوّفوا بها، ثُمَّ يَأتُونَنا فيُخْبِرونا بوَلايَتِهِم، ويَعْرِضوا علَينا نُصْرَتَهُم.١٥٧١

449. The Consequence of Abandoning the Obligatory Pilgrimage

٤٤٩ـ عاقِبَةُ تَركِ الحَجّ

1389. **The Prophet (SAWA) said,** 'He who postpones the obligatory pilgrimage until he dies, Allah will resurrect him as a Jew or a Christian on the Day of Resurrection.'[1582]

١٣٨٩. رسولُ اللهِ ﷺ: مَن سَوَّفَ الحَجَّ حتّى يَموتَ بَعثَهُ اللهُ يومَ القِيامَةِ يَهودِيّاً أو نَصْرانِيّاً.١٥٧٢

1390. **Imām 'Alī (AS) said,** 'He who abandons the pilgrimage for one of his worldly needs will not be able to satisfy that need until he sees the shaven heads [i.e. after the return of the pilgrims from Makkah].'[1583]

١٣٩٠. الإمامُ عليٌّ ؏: مَن تَرَكَ الحَجَّ لِحاجَةٍ مِن حَوائجِ الدُّنيا لَم يُقْضَ حتّى يَنْظُرَ إلى المُحَلِّقينَ.١٥٧٣

450. Deferring [Pilgrimage] to the House

٤٥٠ـ تَعطيلُ البَيتِ

"Allah has made the Ka'ba, the Sacred House, a [means of] sustentation for mankind."[1584]

﴿جَعَلَ اللهُ الْكَعْبَةَ الْبَيْتَ الْحَرامَ قِياماً لِلنّاسِ﴾.١٥٧٤

1391. **Imām al-Ṣādiq (AS),** when 'Abd al-Raḥmān told him: 'Some of these narrators are saying that it is better for a man to go for pilgrimage once and then to gives alms and maintain his kinship with his relatives [with that money than to go for pilgrimage again]' – said, 'They are wrong. If people were to do that the House would become deserted. Allah has made this House a [means of] sustentation for mankind.'[1585]

١٣٩١. الإمامُ الصّادقُ ؏ ـ لَمّا قالَ لَهُ عبدُ الرّحمٰنِ: إنَّ ناساً مِن هؤلاءِ القُصّاصِ يَقولونَ: إذا حَجَّ رجُلٌ حجّةً ثُمّ تَصَدَّقَ ووَصَلَ كانَ خَيراً لَهُ ـ: كَذَبوا، لَو فَعلَ هذا النّاسُ لَعُطِّلَ هذا البَيتُ، إنَّ اللهَ تعالى جَعلَ هذا البَيتَ قِياماً للنّاسِ.١٥٧٥

451. What a Lot of Clamour and What Few Pilgrims

٤٥١ـ ما أكثَرَ الضَّجيجَ وأقَلَّ الحَجيجَ

1392. **'Abd al-Raḥmān b. Kathīr narrated:** 'I went for pilgrimage with Abū 'Abdillāh [al-Ṣādiq] (AS). When we had gone a certain way, he climbed a

١٣٩٢. بحار الأنوار عن عبدِ الرّحمانِ بنِ كثيرٍ: حَجَجْتُ مَعَ أبي عبدِاللهِ ؏، فلَمّا صِرْنا في بَعضِ الطَّريقِ صَعِدَ على جَبَلٍ فأشْرَفَ فنَظَرَ إلى

hill and looked down at the people and said, 'What a lot of clamour and what few pilgrims!'[1586]

النّاسِ، فقالَ: ما أكْثَرَ الضَّجيجَ وأقَلَّ الحَجيجَ![١٥٧٦]

452. The Etiquette of the Pilgrim

٤٥٢ ـ أدَبُ الحاجِّ

"The hajj [season] is in months well-known; so whoever decides on hajj [pilgrimage] therein, [should know that] there is to be no sexual contact, vicious talk, or disputing during the hajj."[1587]

﴿الْحَجُّ أَشْهُرٌ مَعْلُوماتٌ فَمَنْ فَرَضَ فِيهِنَّ الْحَجَّ فَلا رَفَثَ وَلا فُسُوقَ وَلا جِدالَ فِي الْحَجِّ﴾.[١٥٧٧]

1393. **Imām al-Bāqir (AS) said,** 'The pilgrim to this House is of no worth unless he has three attributes: piety that restrains him from acts of disobedience to Allah, most High; clemency with which he controls his anger; and good companionship with whoever accompanies him.'[1588]

١٣٩٣. الإمامُ الباقرُ عليه السلام: ما يُعْبَأُ بِمَن يَؤُمُّ هذا البَيتَ إذا لَم يَكُن فيهِ ثَلاثُ خِصالٍ: وَرَعٌ يَحْجِزه عن مَعاصي اللهِ تعالى، وحِلْمٌ يَمْلِكُ بِهِ غَضَبَهُ، وحُسْنُ الصَّحابةِ لِمَن صَحِبَهُ.[١٥٧٨]

453. The Etiquette of Iḥrām[1589]

٤٥٣ ـ أدَبُ الإحرامِ

1394. **The Prophet (SAWA) said,** 'When he who makes pilgrimage by means of unlawful money says: "Here I am O Allah! Here I am (*labbayk Allāhumma labbayk*)", Allah will say to him, 'No *labbayka* and no welcome for you. Your pilgrimage is returned to you.'[1590]

١٣٩٤. رسولُ اللهِ صلى الله عليه وآله: مَن حَجَّ بمالٍ حَرامٍ فقالَ: لَبَّيْكَ اللّهُمَّ لَبَّيْكَ، قالَ اللهُ لَهُ: لا لَبَّيْكَ ولا سَعْدَيْكَ، حَجُّكَ مَردودٌ علَيكَ.[١٥٧٩]

1395. **Imām al-Ṣādiq (AS) said,** 'Pilgrimage is of two kinds: the pilgrimage [performed] for Allah and the pilgrimage for the people. So he who goes on pilgrimage for Allah, his reward is upon Allah and will be Paradise, and he who makes pilgrimage for the people, his reward on the Day of Resurrection will be with the people.'[1591]

١٣٩٥. الإمامُ الصّادقُ عليه السلام: الحجُّ حَجّانِ: حَجٌّ للهِ وحَجٌّ للنّاسِ، فمَنْ حَجَّ للهِ كانَ ثَوابُهُ علَى اللهِ الجَنّةَ، ومَن حَجَّ للنّاسِ كانَ ثَوابُهُ علَى النّاسِ يومَ القِيامَةِ.[١٥٨٠]

1396. **Mālik b. Anas narrated:** 'One year I went on pilgrimage with al-Ṣādiq (AS). When his mount came to the place of *iḥrām*, whenever he intended to say *labbayka* [here I am …] his voice would cut off in his throat, and he nearly fell off his mount. So I *said to him*, 'O son of the Prophet, say it, for you must say it', to which he replied, 'O Ibn Abī 'Āmir,

١٣٩٦. الخصال عن مالكِ بنِ أنَس: حَجَجْتُ مع الصّادق عليه السلام سَنةً، فلمّا اسْتَوَتْ بهِ راحِلَتُهُ عِند الإحْرامِ كانَ كُلَّما هَمَّ بالتَّلْبِيَةِ انْقَطعَ الصَّوتُ في حَلْقِهِ، وكادَ يَخِرَّ مِن راحِلَتِهِ، فقلتُ: قُلْ يابنَ رسولِ اللهِ، ولابدَّ لكَ مِن أنْ تَقولَ، فقالَ عليه السلام: يابنَ أبي عامر، كيفَ أجْسُرُ أنْ أقولَ: لَبَّيْكَ اللّهُمَّ

how can I dare say: 'I am here O Allah! I am here' whilst I fear lest He say, 'No *labbayka* and no welcome for you!'[1592]

لَبَّيْكَ ، وأخْشىٰ أنْ يَقولَ عـزّوجلّ لي : لا لَـبَّيْكَ ولا سَعْدَيْكَ! ١٥٨١

1397. **Imām al-Riḍā (AS) said,** 'Indeed they have been ordered to be in the state of *iḥrām* in order that they humble themselves before entering the sanctuary and the safe place of Allah, and so that they do not divert and preoccupy themselves with anything of the affairs of this world and its adornments and pleasures; and so that they be serious in what they are engaged in, journeying to Him and approaching Him with all their being.'[1593]

١٣٩٧ . الإمامُ الرِّضا عليه السلام : إنّما اُمِروا ١٥٨٢ بالإحْرامِ ليَخْشَعوا قَبلَ دُخولِهم حَـرَمَ اللهِ وأمْـنَهُ ، ولِـئلّا يَـلْهوا ويَشْـتَغِلوا بشَـيءٍ مِـن اُمـورِ الدُّنـيا وزِينَتِهـا ولَذّاتِها ، ويكونـوا جادِّيـنَ فـيما هُـم فيهِ ، قاصِدينَ نَحْوَهُ ، مُقْبِلينَ علَيهِ بكُلِّيَّتِهِم. ١٥٨٣

454. The Reward of One Who Dies on the Way to Ḥajj

٤٥٤ ـ ثوابُ مَن ماتَ في طَريقِ الحجّ

1398. **Imām al-Ṣādiq (AS) said,** 'Whoever dies on the road to Makkah, on the way there or back, will be safe from the Great Terror on the Day of Resurrection.'[1594]

١٣٩٨ . الإمامُ الصّادقُ عليه السلام : مَن ماتَ في طَريقِ مَكّةَ ذاهِباً أو جائياً ، أمِنَ مِن الفَزَعِ الأكْبَرِ يومَ القِيامَةِ. ١٥٨٤

1399. **Imām al-Ṣādiq (AS) said,** 'Whoever dies in the state of *iḥrām*, Allah will raise him [obedient to Him] saying, 'Here I am, O Allah' (*labbayka*).[1595]

١٣٩٩ . عنه عليه السلام : مَـن مـاتَ مُـحْرِماً بَـعثَهُ اللهُ مُلَبِّياً. ١٥٨٥

455. The Presence of the Hidden Imām [al-Mahdī] During Ḥajj

٤٥٥ ـ حُضورُ الإمامِ الغائبِ فِي المَوسِمِ

1400. **Imām al-Ṣādiq (AS) said,** 'The people miss their Imām, but he attends the season [of *ḥajj*] and sees them, though they do not see him.'[1596]

١٤٠٠ . الإمامُ الصّادقُ عليه السلام : يَفْقِدُ النّاسُ إمامَهُم فيَشْهَدُ المَوْسِمَ فيَراهُم ولا يَرَوْنَهُ. ١٥٨٦

88

THE ARGUMENT[1597]

الحجة

456. Presenting The Argument

٤٥٦ـ إقامَةُ الحُجَّةِ

"We do not punish [any community] until We have sent [it] an apostle."[1598]

﴿وَما كُنّا مُعَذِّبِينَ حَتَّىٰ نَبْعَثَ رَسُولاً﴾.[١٥٨٧]

"So that he who perishes might perish by a manifest proof, and he who lives may live on by a manifest proof."[1599]

﴿لِيَهْلِكَ مَنْ هَلَكَ عَنْ بَيِّنَةٍ وَيَحْيَىٰ مَنْ حَيَّ عَنْ بَيِّنَةٍ﴾.[١٥٨٨]

(See also: Qur'an 2:256, 2:286, 7:42, 8:42, 9:115, 20:134, 22:71, 26:208-209, 28:46, 28:59, 65:7)

(أنظر) البقرة: ٢٥٦، ٢٨٦ والأعراف: ٤٢ و الأنفال: ٤٢ و التوبة: ١١٥ و طه: ١٣٤ و الحج: ٧١ و العشراء: ٢٠٨ و ٢٠٩ والقصص: ٤٦ و ٥٩ والطلاق: ٧.

1401. **Imām ʿAlī (AS) said,** 'The force of the authority of the argument is greater than the force of the authority of power.'[1600]

١٤٠١ . الإمامُ عليٌّ عليه السلام : قُوّةُ سُلطانِ الحُجّةِ أعظَمُ مِن قُوّةِ سُلطانِ القُدرَةِ.[١٥٨٩]

1402. **Imām ʿAlī (AS) said,** 'He who is true in his speech will be strong in his argument.'[1601]

١٤٠٢ . عنه عليه السلام : مَن صَدَقَتْ لَهجَتُهُ قَوِيَتْ حُجَّتُهُ.[١٥٩٠]

1403. **Imām al-Bāqir (AS),** when he was asked about the argument of Allah with people, replied, 'It is [for them] to say what they know and to stop at what they do not know.'[1602]

١٤٠٣ . الإمامُ الباقرُ عليه السلام ـ وقد سُئلَ عن حُجّةِ اللهِ على العِبادِ ـ: أنْ يَقولوا ما يَعْلَمونَ، ويَقِفوا عِند ما لا يَعْلَمونَ.[١٥٩١]

1404. **Imām al-Ṣādiq (AS) said,** 'Indeed Allah, Mighty and Exalted, will use as an argument against people all that He has given them and all that He has acquainted them with.'[1603]

١٤٠٤ . الإمامُ الصّادقُ عليه السلام : إنّ اللهَ عزّ وجلّ احْتَجَّ على النّاسِ بما آتاهُم وما عَرّفَهُم.[١٥٩٢]

1405. **Imām al-Ṣādiq (AS) said,** 'He who doubts or suspects, and still acts according to either of them [i.e. his doubt or suspicion], Allah will nullify his deed. Indeed the argument of Allah is the clear argument.'[1604]

١٤٠٥ . عنه عليه السلام : مَن شَكَّ أو ظَنَّ فأقامَ على أحَدِهِما أحْبَطَ اللهُ عَمَلَهُ، إنَّ حُجَّةَ اللهِ هِي الحُجَّةُ الواضِحَةُ.[١٥٩٣]

(See also: DIVINE LEADERSHIP (*IMĀMA*): section 91)

(أنظر) الإمامة: باب ٩١.

457. To Allah Belongs the Conclusive Argument

٤٥٧ ـ لِلّٰهِ الحُجَّةُ البالِغَةُ

"Say, 'To Allah belongs the conclusive argument. Had He wished he would have surely guided you all.'"[1605]

﴿قُلْ فَلِلّٰهِ الْحُجَّةُ الْبَالِغَةُ فَلَوْ شَاءَ لَهَدَاكُمْ أَجْمَعِينَ﴾.[١٥٩٤]

1406. **Imām al-Ṣādiq (AS),** with regards to Allah's verse in the Qur'an: *"Say, 'To Allah belongs the conclusive argument"*, said, 'Verily Allah, most High, will ask the servant on the Day of Resurrection, "My servant! Did you know?" If he then answers: "Yes", Allah will tell him, "Then why did you not act upon what you knew?" But if he says, "I was ignorant", He will tell him, "Why did not you learn in order that you may act?!" He will then be disarmed – and that is the conclusive argument.'[1606]

١٤٠٦ . الإمامُ الصّادقُ عليه السلام ـ في قولِهِ تعالىٰ: ﴿قُلْ فلِلّٰهِ الحُجَّةُ البالِغَةُ﴾ ـ: إنَّ اللهَ تعالىٰ يقولُ للعبدِ يومَ القيامَةِ: عَبدي، أكنتَ عالِماً ؟ فإنْ قالَ: نَعَم، قالَ لَهُ: أفلا عَمِلْتَ بما عَلِمْتَ ؟! وإنْ قالَ: كُنتُ جاهِلاً، قالَ لَهُ: أفلا تعلّمْتَ حتّىٰ تَعْمَلَ ؟! فيُخْصَمُ، فتِلكَ الحُجَّةُ البالِغَةُ.[١٥٩٥]

1407. **Imām al-Ṣādiq (AS) said,** 'The Argument existed before the creation of people, it exists alongside creation, and will remain after them.'[1607]

١٤٠٧ . عنه عليه السلام: الحُجَّةُ قَبلَ الخَلقِ، ومَعَ الخَلقِ، وبَعدَ الخَلقِ.[١٥٩٦]

458. The Surest and Most Conclusive Argument

٤٥٨ ـ أوكَدُ الحُجَجِ وأبلَغُها

"Apostles, as bearers of good news and warners, so that mankind may not have any argument against Allah, after the [sending of the] apostles; and Allah is all-mighty, all-wise."[1608]

﴿رُسُلاً مُبَشِّرِينَ وَمُنْذِرِينَ لِئَلَّا يَكُونَ لِلنَّاسِ عَلَىٰ اللهِ حُجَّةٌ بَعْدَ الرُّسُلِ وَكَانَ اللهُ عَزِيزاً حَكِيماً﴾.[١٥٩٧]

1408. **Imām 'Alī (AS) said,** 'O people! Allah, glory be to Him, has no surer argument on His earth than our Prophet Muḥammad (SAWA), and there is no wisdom more conclusive than His Book, the Grand Qur'an.'[1609]

١٤٠٨ . الإمامُ عليٌّ عليه السلام: يا أَيُّها النّاسُ إنَّهُ لَم يَكُنْ للّٰهِ سُبحانَهُ حُجّةٌ في أرضِهِ أوْكَدُ مِن نَبيِّنا محمّدٍ صلى الله عليه وآله، ولا حِكْمَةٌ أبْلَغُ مِن كِتابِهِ القُرآنِ العَظيمِ.[١٥٩٨]

1409. **Imām 'Alī (AS) said,** 'Allah, Blessed and most High, has no more conclusive an argument or wisdom on His earth than His Book.'[1610]

١٤٠٩ . عنه عليه السلام: إنّه لَم يَكُنْ للّٰهِ تباركَ وتعالىٰ في أرْضِهِ حُجَّةٌ ولا حِكْمَةٌ أبْلَغُ مِن كِتابِهِ.[١٥٩٩]

89

THE PROPHETIC TRADITION (ḤADĪTH)

الحَدِيث

459. The Value of Learning a Tradition

٤٥٩ ـ قيمَةُ أخذِ الحَديثِ

1410. **Imām al-Bāqir (AS) said,** 'Truly our tradition enlivens the hearts.'[1611]

١٤١٠ . الإمامُ الباقرُ عليه السلام : إنَّ حَديثَنا يُحْيي القُلوبَ.[١٦٠٠]

1411. **Imām al-Bāqir (AS) said,** 'Indeed one true tradition that you receive from a truthful person is better for you than the whole world and all that it contains.'[1612]

١٤١١ . عنه عليه السلام : لَحَديثٌ واحِدٌ تأخُذُهُ عن صادِقٍ خَيرٌ لَكَ من الدُّنيا وما فِيها.[١٦٠١]

460. The Value of a Narrator of Traditions

٤٦٠ ـ فَضلُ المُحَدِّثِ

1412. **The Prophet (SAWA) said,** 'Whoever transmits to my people one tradition by which a practice is established or a heresy is blocked, will enter Paradise.'[1613]

١٤١٢ . رسولُ اللهِ صلى الله عليه وآله : مَن أدّىٰ إلىٰ اُمَّتي حَديثاً يُقامُ بِهِ سُنّةٌ أو يُثْلَمُ بهِ بِدْعَةٌ فَلهُ الجَنّةُ.[١٦٠٢]

1413. **Imām ʿAlī (AS) said,** 'The Prophet (SAWA) said, 'O Allah! Have mercy on my successors'—thrice. He was asked, 'O Messenger of Allah! Who are your successors?' He said, 'Those who learn my traditions and practices, and then teach them to my community.'[1614]

١٤١٣ . الإمامُ عليٌّ عليه السلام : قال رسول الله صلى الله عليه وآله : اللّهُمَّ ارْحَمْ خُلَفائي ـ ثلاثاً ـ قيلَ : يا رسولَ اللهِ، ومَن خُلَفاؤكَ ؟ قالَ : الّذينَ يَبلّغونَ حَديثي وسُنَّتي، ثُمَّ يُعَلّمونَها اُمَّتي.[١٦٠٣]

1414. **Imām al-Ṣādiq (AS) said,** 'The narrator of traditions who understands religion is better than a thousand worshippers who have neither understanding of religion nor knowledge of traditions.'[1615]

١٤١٤ . الإمامُ الصّادقُ عليه السلام : الرّاويةُ للحَديثِ المُتَفقّهُ في الدِّينِ أفْضَلُ مِن ألفِ عابِدٍ لا فِقْهَ لَهُ ولا رِوايةَ.[١٦٠٤]

1415. **Imām al-Ṣādiq (AS) said,** 'Know the people's positions with respect to us through the amount of their narration of our traditions.'[1616]

١٤١٥ . عنه عليه السلام : اعرِفوا مَنازِلَ النّاسِ مِنّا علىٰ قَدْرِ رِواياتِهم عَنّا.[١٦٠٥]

461. The Reward of Those Who Memorize Forty Traditions

٤٦١ ـ ثَوابُ مَن حَفِظَ أربَعينَ حَديثاً

1416. **The Prophet (SAWA) said,** 'Whoever memorizes forty traditions from which my community benefits in their religious affairs, Allah will raise him on the Day of Resurrection as a learned jurist and a scholar.'[1617]

١٤١٦. رسولُ اللهِ ﷺ: مَن حَفِظَ علىٰ أُمّتي أرْبَعينَ حَديثاً يَنْتَفِعونَ بِها في أمْرِ دينِهِم، بَعثَهُ اللهُ يومَ القِيامَةِ فَقيهاً عالِماً.١٦٠٦

462. Understanding the Tradition

٤٦٢ ـ دِرايَةُ الحَديثِ

1417. **Imām 'Alī (AS) said,** 'Your aim must be to understand [the traditions] rather than just narrating [them].'[1618]

١٤١٧. الإمامُ عليٌّ ﷺ: علَيكُم بالدِّراياتِ لا بالرِّواياتِ.١٦٠٧

1418. **Imām 'Alī (AS) said,** 'The ambition of the foolish is to report [traditions] whereas the ambition of the scholars is to understand the traditions.'[1619]

١٤١٨. عنه ﷺ: هِمَّةُ السُّفَهاءِ الرِّوايَةُ، وهِمَّةُ العُلَماءِ الدِّرايَةُ.١٦٠٨

1419. **Imām al-Ṣādiq (AS) said,** 'One tradition that you understand is better than a thousand traditions that you merely narrate.'[1620]

١٤١٩. الإمامُ الصّادقُ ﷺ: حَديثٌ تَدْرِيهِ خَيرٌ مِن ألفِ حَديثٍ تَرْوِيهِ.١٦٠٩

463. Caution Against Ascribing Lies to the Prophet (SAWA)

٤٦٣ ـ التَّحذيرُ مِنَ الكِذبِ عَلَى الرَّسولِ

1420. **The Prophet (SAWA) said,** 'Whoever deliberately ascribes lies to me, let him take his seat in the Fire.'[1621]

١٤٢٠. رسولُ اللهِ ﷺ: مَن كَذَبَ علَيَّ مُتَعمِّداً فلْيَتَبوّأْ مَقعدَهُ مِن النّارِ.١٦١٠

1421. **The Prophet (SAWA) said,** 'One of the gravest of the grave sins is to attribute to me something that I have not said.'[1622]

١٤٢١. عنه ﷺ: إنّ مِن أكْبرِ الكَبائرِ أنْ يَقولَ الرّجُلُ علَيَّ ما لَم أقُلْ.١٦١١

464. Prohibition of Rejecting that Tradition Whose Falsehood is not Known

٤٦٤ ـ النَّهيُ عَن تَكذيبِ ما لا يُعلَمُ كِذبُهُ

1422. **The Prophet (SAWA) said,** 'Whoever rejects a tradition that is transmitted to him on

١٤٢٢. رسولُ اللهِ ﷺ: مَن رَدَّ حَديثاً بَلغَهُ عنّي

my authority will have me to contend with on the Day of Resurrection. So when you hear a tradition from me that you do not know, say: "Allah knows better."'[1623]

فأنامُخاصِمُهُ يَومَ القِيامَةِ، فإذا بَلَغكُم عنّي حَديثٌ لم تَعرِفوا فقولوا: اللهُ أعْلَمُ.[١٦١٢]

465. The Soundness of the Tradition and its Agreement with the Qur'an

٤٦٥ ـ صِحَّةُ الحَديثِ و مُوافَقَةُ القُرآنِ

1423. **The Prophet (SAWA) said,** 'Compare my tradition with the Book of Allah. If it corresponds with it, then it is from me and I have indeed said it.'[1624]

١٤٢٣. رسولُ اللهِ ﷺ: اعرِضوا حَديثي علىٰ كِتابِ اللهِ، فإنْ وافَقَهُ فهُو مِنّي وأنا قُلتُهُ.[١٦١٣]

1424. **Imām al-Ṣādiq (AS) said,** 'The traditions that do not correspond with the Qur'an are false.'[1625]

١٤٢٤. الإمامُ الصّادقُ ﷺ: ما لَم يُوافِقْ مِنَ الحَديثِ القُرآنَ فهُو زُخْرُفٌ.[١٦١٤]

466. The Soundness of a Tradition and its Agreement with Man's Nature

٤٦٦ ـ صِحَّةُ الحَديثِ و مُوافَقَةُ الفِطرَةِ

1425. **Imām al-Bāqir (AS) said,** 'Whenever a tradition from the household of Muḥammad - peace be upon them all – is transmitted to you, towards which your hearts lean and it seems familiar to you, accept it. And whatever your hearts resent and you reject, then refer it back to Allah and the Prophet and the scholar from the household of Muḥammad (SAWA).'[1626]

١٤٢٥. الإمامُ الباقرُ ﷺ: ماوَرَدَعلَيكُم مِن حَديثِ آلِ محمّدٍ صلواتُ اللهِ علَيهِم فلانَتْ لَهُ قُلوبُكُم وعَرَفْتُموهُ فاقْبَلوهُ، وما اشْمَأزَّتْ مِنهُ قُلوبُكُم وأنكَرْتُموهُ فَرُدّوهُ إلَى اللهِ وإلَى الرّسولِ وإلَى العالِمِ مِن آلِ محمّدٍ ﷺ.[١٦١٥]

467. The Soundness of a Tradition and its Agreement with the Truth

٤٦٧ ـ صِحَّةُ الحَديثِ و مُوافَقَةُ الحَقِّ

1426. **The Prophet (SAWA) said,** 'Whenever a tradition is transmitted to you from me that agrees with the truth, then I have truly said it, and whatever tradition is transmitted to you from me which does not agree with the truth, then I have not said it, for I speak nothing but the truth.'[1627]

١٤٢٦. رسولُ اللهِ ﷺ: ما جاءَكُم عنّي مِن حَديثٍ مُوافِقٍ للحقِّ فأنا قُلتُهُ، وما أتاكُم عنّي مِن حَديثٍ لا يُوافِقُ الحَقَّ فلَم أقُلْهُ، ولَن أقولَ إلّا الحَقَّ.[١٦١٦]

468. The Permissibility of Transmitting the Meaning of the Tradition

٤٦٨ ـ جَوازُ نَقلِ الحَديثِ بِالمَعنى

1427. **The Prophet (SAWA) said,** 'It does not matter if you change the order of the words of a tradition, as long as you render its meaning [exactly].'[1628]

١٤٢٧ . رسولُ اللهِ ﷺ : لا بأسَ في الحَديثِ قَدّمْتَ فيهِ أو أخَّرْتَ ، إذا أصَبْتَ مَعناهُ.[١٦١٧]

1428. **Muḥammad b. Muslim narrated,** 'I asked Abū ʿAbdillāh [al-Ṣādiq] (AS): "I hear a tradition from you and then I add to it or subtract from it." He said, 'If you [do this] intending its meanings, then it does not matter.'[1629]

١٤٢٨ . بحارالأنوار عن محمّدِ بنِ مُسلمٍ : قلتُ لأبي عبدِاللهِ عليه السلام : أسْمَعُ الحَديثَ منكَ فأزيدُ وأنْقُصُ . قالَ : إن كنتَ تُريدُ مَعانِيَهُ فلا بأسَ.[١٦١٨]

469. What Must be Observed when Transmitting Traditions

٤٦٩ ـ ما يَنبَغي مُراعاتُهُ فِي التَّحديثِ

1429. **The Prophet (SAWA) said,** 'Do not narrate to my people from my traditions except those which are perceptible to their intellects.'[1630]

١٤٢٩ . رسولُ اللهِ ﷺ : لا تُحَدِّثوا اُمَّتي مِن أحاديثي إلّا بما تَحْمِلُهُ عُقولُهُم.[١٦١٩]

1430. **Imām ʿAlī (AS) said,** 'Whenever you narrate a tradition, document it to the person from whom you have narrated it. If what he has said is true, its benefit will be yours, but if he has lied, its harm would be against him.'[1631]

١٤٣٠ . الإمامُ عليٌّ عليه السلام : إذا حَدَّثتُم بِحَديثٍ فَاسنِدُوهُ إلَى الّذي حَدَّثَكُم ، فَإن كانَ حَقّاً فَلَكُم وَإن كانَ كَذِباً فعَلَيهِ.[١٦٢٠]

470. The Tradition from Ahl al-Bayt is the Tradition from the Messenger of Allah

٤٧٠ ـ حَديثُ أهلِ البَيتِ حَديثُ رَسولِ اللهِ ﷺ

1431. **Imām al-Ṣādiq (AS) said,** 'My tradition is my father's tradition, and my father's tradition is my grandfather's tradition, and my grandfather's tradition is Ḥusayn's tradition, and Ḥusayn's tradition is Ḥasan's tradition, and Ḥasan's tradition is Imām ʿAlī's tradition, and Imām ʿAlī's tradition is the Messenger of Allah's

١٤٣١ . الإمامُ الصّادقُ عليه السلام : حَديثي حَديثُ أبي ، وحَديثُ أبي حَديثُ جَدّي ، وحَديثُ جَدّي حَديثُ الحُسَينِ ، وحَديثُ الحُسَينِ حَديثُ الحَسَنِ ، وحَديثُ الحَسَنِ حَديثُ أميرِ المُؤمِنينَ عليهم السلام ، وحَديثُ أميرِ المُؤمِنينَ حَديثُ رَسولِ اللهِ ﷺ ، وحَديثُ رَسولِ اللهِ

tradition, and the Messenger of Allah's tradition is the saying of Allah.'[1632]

قولُ اللهِ عزَّ وجلَّ.[١٦٢١]

471. The All-Inclusiveness of the Book and the Prophetic Practice

٤٧١ـ شُموليّةُ الكتاب والسُّنّةِ

1432. **Abū Usāma narrated,** 'I was with Abū 'Abdillāh [al-Ṣādiq] (AS), and there was with him a man from al-Mughīriyyah. The man asked him about some practices. He said, 'There is nothing which the offspring of Adam needs except that it has been expounded in the practices set by Allah and His Messenger. Otherwise He would not have the argument over us that He holds.' The man from al-Mughīriyyah then asked, 'And what is His argument?' Abū 'Abdillāh (AS) said, '[It is] His verse: *"Today I have perfected your religion for you, and I have completed My blessing upon you."*'[1633 1634]

١٤٣٢ . بحار الأنوار عن أبي أُسامةَ: كنتُ عِندَ أبي عبدِ اللهِ عليه السلام وعِندَهُ رجُلٌ من المُغيريَّةِ، فسَأَلَهُ عَن شيءٍ مِن السُّنَنِ، فقالَ: ما مِن شيءٍ يَحتاجُ إليهِ وُلدُ آدمَ إلّا وقد خرَجَتْ فيهِ السُّنَّةُ مِن اللهِ ومِن رسولِهِ، ولولا ذلكَ ما احْتَجَّ علَينا بما احْتَجَّ، فقالَ المُغيريُّ: وبِما احْتَجَّ؟ فقالَ أبو عبدِ اللهِ عليه السلام: قولُهُ: ﴿اليَومَ أَكْمَلْتُ لَكُمْ دِينَكُمْ وأتْمَمْتُ عَلَيكُمْ نِعْمَتِي﴾.[١٦٢٢]

472. The Ambiguous Traditions

٤٧٢ـ مُتَشابِهاتُ الأحاديثِ

1433. **Imām al-Riḍā (AS) said,** 'Some of our traditions are ambiguous like the ambiguous verses of the Qur'an, and some are clear like the clear verses of the Qur'an. Then refer its ambiguous ones to its clear ones, and do not follow its ambiguous ones [blindly] without referring to its clear ones lest you go astray.'[1635]

١٤٣٣ . الإمامُ الرِّضا عليه السلام: إنَّ في أخْبارِنا مُتَشابِهاً كمُتَشابِهِ القُرآنِ، ومُحْكَماً كمُحْكَمِ القُرآنِ، فَرُدّوا مُتَشابِهَها إلىٰ مُحْكَمِها، ولا تَتَّبِعوا مُتَشابِهَها دُونَ مُحْكَمِها فتَضِلّوا.[١٦٢٣]

90

LEGAL PUNISHMENTS[1636]

الحُدُود

473. Everything has a Bound

٤٧٣ـ لِكُلِّ شَيءٍ حَدٌّ

1434. **Imām al-Bāqir (AS) said,** 'Truly Allah, Blessed and most High ... has set a bound for everything, and has made for each one a sign indicating to it, and He has designated a punishment for whoever transgresses that bound.'[1637]

١٤٣٤ . الإمامُ الباقرُ عليه السلام: إنّ اللهَ تباركَ وتعالىٰ...جَعلَ لكُلِّ شيءٍ حَدّاً، و جَعلَ علَيهِ دَليلاً يَدُلُّ علَيهِ، وجَعلَ علىٰ مَن تَعدّىٰ ذلك الحَدَّ حَدّاً.[١٦٢٤]

474. Averting the Punishments

٤٧٤ ـ دَرءُ الحُدودِ

1435. **The Prophet (SAWA) said,** ‘Avert the punishments from the Muslims as much as you can, and if you can find a way out for a Muslim, then make way for him, for it is better for the Imām to err in reprieving than in punishment.’[1638]

١٤٣٥ . رسولُ اللهِ ﷺ : ادْرَؤوا الحُدودَ عنِ المسلِمينَ ما اسْتَطَعْتُم، فإنْ وَجَدتُم للمسلِمِ مَخْرَجاً فَخَلّوا سبيلَهُ؛ فإنَّ الإمامَ لَأَنْ يُخطِئَ في العَفوِ خَيرٌ مِن أنْ يُخْطئَ في العُقوبَةِ.[١٦٢٥]

1436. **The Prophet (SAWA) said,** ‘Avert the punishments through uncertainties.’[1639]

١٤٣٦ . عنه ﷺ : ادْرَؤوا الحُدودَ بالشُّبُهاتِ.[١٦٢٦]

475. Upholding the Penal Laws

٤٧٥ ـ إقامَةُ الحُدودِ

1437. **The Prophet (SAWA) said,** ‘Upholding one of the penal laws of Allah is superior to forty nights of rain on Allah’s land.’[1640]

١٤٣٧ . رسولُ اللهِ ﷺ : إقامَةُ حَدٍّ مِن حُدودِ اللهِ خَيرٌ مِن مَطَرِ أربَعينَ لَيلةً في بِلادِ اللهِ.[١٦٢٧]

1438. **The Prophet (SAWA) said,** ‘A penal law that is exercised on earth is purer than sixty years of worship.’[1641]

١٤٣٨ . عنه ﷺ : حَدٌّ يُقامُ في الأرضِ أزْكىٰ مِن عِبادَةِ سِتّينَ سَنةً.[١٦٢٨]

1439. **Imām al-Ṣādiq (AS) said,** ‘A woman who was honoured amongst her people was once brought to the Prophet (SAWA) charged with theft. He ordered her [hand] to be cut. A group from the tribe of Quraysh came to the Prophet (SAWA) and said, ‘O Messenger of Allah! Must [the hand of] a noble lady such as her be cut like that of *so and so* for such a small mistake?!’ He replied, ‘Yes! Indeed those before you perished because of such a deed. People used to uphold the punishments for the weak ones among them and exempt the strong and the noble ones of them, and therefore they perished.’[1642]

١٤٣٩ . الإمامُ الصّادقُ عن آبائه عليهم السلام : إنّ رسولَ اللهِ ﷺ اُتيَ بامْرأةٍ لَها شَرَفٌ في قَومِها قد سَرَقَتْ، فأمَرَ بقَطْعِها، فاجْتَمعَ إلىٰ رسولِ اللهِ ﷺ ناسٌ مِن قُرَيشٍ وقالوا: يا رسولَ اللهِ، تُقْطَعُ امْرأةٌ شَريفةٌ مثلُ فُلانَةَ في خَطَرٍ يَسيرٍ؟!
قالَ: نَعَم، إنّما هَلكَ مَن كانَ قَبْلَكُم بمِثْلِ هٰذا، كانوا يُقيمونَ الحُدودَ علىٰ ضُعَفائهِم ويَتْرُكونَ أقْوِياءهُم وأشْرافَهُم فهَلَكوا.[١٦٢٩]

476. No Intercession, Bail or Oath in a Legal Punishment

٤٧٦ ـ لا شَفاعَةَ وَلا كَفالَةَ وَلا يَمِينَ في حَدٍّ

1440. **The Prophet (SAWA) said,** ‘Every man who stops the exercise of one of Allah’s penalties

١٤٤٠ . رسولُ اللهِ ﷺ : أيُّما رجُلٍ حالَتْ شَفاعَتُهُ

by his intercession will continue to be exposed to Allah's anger until he ceases.'[1643]

دُونَ حَدٍّ مِن حُدودِ اللهِ، لَم يَزَلْ فـي سَـخَطِ اللهِ حتّىٰ يَنْزِعَ.[١٦٣٠]

1441. **The Prophet (SAWA) said,** 'There is no intercession, bail, or oath in a legal punishment.'[1644]

١٤٤١. عنه ﷺ: لا شَفاعَةَ ولا كفالَةَ ولا يَمينَ في حَدٍّ.[١٦٣١]

1442. **Imām ʿAlī (AS) said,** 'There is no bail for any of Allah's punishments.'[1645]

١٤٤٢. الإمامُ عليٌّ ﷺ: لا كَفالَةَ في حَدٍّ مِن الحُدودِ.[١٦٣٢]

1443. **Imām al-Ṣādiq (AS) said,** narrating on the authority of his father, from his forefathers, from the Prophet (SAWA) - 'He prohibited the use of intercession against the punishments and that he (SAWA) said, 'He who intercedes against one of Allah's punishments in order to annul it, and tries to abolish His punishments will be chastised by Allah, most High, on the Day of Resurrection.'[1646]

١٤٤٣. الإمامُ الصّادقُ ﷺ عن أبيهِ عن آبائهِ ﷺ عن رسولِ اللهِ ﷺ: أنَّهُ نَهىٰ عنِ الشَّفاعَةِ في الحُدودِ، وقالَ: مَن شَفَعَ في حَدٍّ مِن حُدودِ اللهِ لِيُبْطِلَهُ وسَعىٰ في إبْطالِ حُدودهِ عَذَّبَهُ اللهُ تَعالى يَومَ القِيامَةِ.[١٦٣٣]

477. Prohibition of Postponement of Legal Punishments

٤٧٧ ـ النَّهيُ عَنِ النَّظِرَةِ فِي الحُدودِ

1444. **Imām al-Bāqir (AS) narrated,** saying, 'Three people gave witness against a man for committing adultery. Then the Commander of the Faithful (AS) asked, 'Where is the fourth [witness]?' They said, 'He is arriving just now.' The Commander of the Faithful said, 'Punish them, for there is not even one hour of respite to be given in punishments.'[1647]

١٤٤٤. الإمامُ الباقرُ ﷺ: في ثَلاثَةٍ شَهِدوا علىٰ رجُلٍ بالزِّنى، فقالَ أميرُ المؤمنينَ ﷺ: أينَ الرّابِعُ؟ فقالوا: الآنَ يَجيءُ، فقالَ أميرُ المؤمنينَ ﷺ: حُدُّوهُم، فليسَ في الحُدودِ نَظِرَةُ ساعَةٍ.[١٦٣٤]

478. Prohibition of Transgressing the Bounds

٤٧٨ ـ النَّهيُ عَن تَعَدِّي الحُدودِ

"These are Allah's bounds, so do not transgress them, and whoever transgresses the bounds of Allah—it is they who are the wrongdoers."[1648]

﴿تِلْكَ حُدُودُ اللهِ فَلا تَعْتَدُوهَا وَمَنْ يَتَعَدَّ حُدُودَ اللهِ فَأُولٰئِكَ هُمُ الظَّالِمُونَ﴾.[١٦٣٥]

1445. **The Prophet (SAWA) said,** 'On the Day of Resurrection a ruler will be brought forth who had inflicted one lash less than the punishment prescribed. He will plead, 'O my Lord! I did it out

١٤٤٥. رسولُ اللهِ ﷺ: يُؤتىٰ بوالٍ نَقَصَ مِن الحَدِّ سَوطاً فيقولُ: ربِّ رَحمَةً لِعِبادِكَ، فيقالُ لَهُ:

of mercy for Your servants.' He will be told, 'Are you [trying to be] more merciful to them than Me?' Then he will be ordered into the Fire. Another man who had added one lash [to the punishment] will be brought forth, and he will plead, '[O Allah! I did it] to make them stop committing acts of disobedience to You.' Then he too will be ordered into the Fire.'[1649]

أنتَ أرحَمُ بهم مِنّي؟! فيُؤمَرُ بِهِ إلى النّارِ، ويُؤتىٰ بمَن زادَ سَوطاً فيقولُ: لِيَنتَهوا عَن مَعاصيكَ! فيُؤمَرُ بِهِ إلى النّارِ.١٦٣٦

1446. **Imām al-Bāqir (AS) said,** 'The Commander of the Faithful (AS) had ordered Qanbar to execute a man's punishment. Qanbar was rough and beat him three more lashes. So 'Alī (AS) forfeited on his behalf by beating Qanbar three lashes.'[1650]

١٤٤٦. الإمامُ الباقرُ ؑ: إنّ أميرَ المؤمنينَ ؑ أمرَ قَنبراً أن يَضرِبَ رجُلاً حَدّاً، فغَلُظَ قَنبرٌ فَزادَهُ ثلاثةَ أسواطٍ، فأقادَهُ عليٌّ ؑ مِن قَنبرٍ ثلاثةَ أسواطٍ.١٦٣٧

479. Executing the Legal Punishment in the Land of the Enemy

٤٧٩ـ إقامَةُ الحَدِّ بأرضِ العَدُوِّ

1447. **Imām 'Alī (AS) said,** 'I do not execute any legal punishment in the land of the enemy until he leaves it so that he is not overcome and would join the ranks of the enemy.'[1651]

١٤٤٧. الإمامُ عليٌّ ؑ: لا أُقيمُ على أحَدٍ حَدّاً بأرضِ العَدُوِّ حتّىٰ يَخرُجَ مِنها، لِئلّا تَلحَقَهُ الحَمِيَّةُ فيَلحَقَ بالعَدُوِّ.١٦٣٨

480. The Role of Implementing the Penal Law in Atonement for the Sin

٤٨٠ـ دَورُ إقامَةِ الحَدِّ في تَكفيرِ الذَّنبِ

1448. **The Prophet (SAWA) said,** 'Whoever commits a sin and then bears the punishment meted out for that particular sin, then that shall be his atonement.'[1652]

١٤٤٨. رسولُ اللهِ ﷺ: مَن أذنَبَ ذَنباً فأُقيمَ علَيهِ حَدُّ ذلكَ الذَّنبِ فهُو كَفّارَتُهُ.١٦٣٩

1449. **Imām 'Alī (AS) said,** 'When Allah punishes a faithful servant in this world, He is too Bountiful and too Glorious to re-punish him [for the same sin] on the Day of Resurrection.'[1653]

١٤٤٩. الإمامُ عليٌّ ؑ: ما عاقَبَ اللهُ عَبداً مؤمناً في هذهِ الدُّنيا إلّا كانَ أجوَدَ وأمجَدَ مِن أن يَعودَ في عِقابِهِ يَومَ القِيامَةِ.١٦٤٠

481. Prohibition of Insulting the One Being Punished

٤٨١ـ النَّهيُ عَن إهانَةِ المَحدودِ

1450. It is narrated in *Tanbīh al-Khawāṭir*: When the Prophet (SAWA) stoned a man for adultery, a man said to his friend, 'He died on the spot like a

١٤٥٠. تنبيه الخواطر: لمّا رَجَمَ رسولُ اللهِ ﷺ الرَّجُلَ في الزِّنا قالَ رجُلٌ لصاحِبِهِ: هٰذا قَعَصَ

dog.' So when the Prophet (SAWA) was passing with them by the carcass of a dead animal he told them to take a bite out of it. They said, 'O Messenger of Allah! May Allah bless you. How can we bite a carcass?!' He replied, 'What you have bitten from your brother is fouler than that.'[1654]

كَما يَقعصُ الكَلبُ، فمَرَّ النَّبيُّ ﷺ معَهُما بـجِيفَةٍ فقالَ: انْهَشا مِنها، قالا: يا رسولَ اللهِ صلّىٰ اللهُ عليكَ نَـنهَشُ جِـيفَةً؟! قـالَ: مـا أصَـبْتُما مِـن أخيكُما أنْتَنُ مِن هٰذهِ.[١٦٤١]

1451. **'Abd al-Raḥmān b. Abī Laylā narrated:** 'Once 'Alī punished a man who people then began abusing and cursing. So 'Alī said, 'Now this man will not even be questioned with regard to his sin [i.e. your abuse has expiated him of it].'[1655]

١٤٥١. كنز العمّال عن عبد الرحمٰن بن أبي ليلى: إنّ عليّاً أقامَ علىٰ رجُـلٍ حَـدّاً فـجَعلَ النّـاسُ يَسُبّونَهُ ويَلْعَنونَهُ، فقالَ عليٌّ: أمّا عَن ذَنبِهِ هٰـذا فلا يُسْأَلُ.[١٦٤٢]

482. Those to whom Penal Law should not be implemented

٤٨٢ ـ مَن لا حَدَّ عَلَيهِ

1452. **The Prophet (SAWA) said,** 'There is no punishment for he who admits [in committing wrong] after being subdued to a calamity.'[1656]

١٤٥٢. رسولُ اللهِ ﷺ: لا حَدَّ عَلىٰ مُعتَرِفٍ بَعدَ بَلاءٍ.[١٦٤٣]

1453. **Imām 'Ali (AS) said,** 'There is no punishment for he who is compelled [to commit a sin] or for she who is compelled.'[1657]

١٤٥٣. الإمامُ عليٌّ ﷺ: لَيسَ علىٰ مُستكرَهٍ حَدٌّ ولا علىٰ مُستكرَهَةٍ حَدٌّ.[١٦٤٤]

91

WAR

الحَرب

483. Reasons of War

٤٨٣ ـ مَثارُ الحَربِ

1454. **Imām 'Alī (AS) said,** 'Difference is the instigator of wars.'[1658]

١٤٥٤. الإمامُ عليٌّ ﷺ: الخُلفُ مَثارُ الحُروبِ.[١٦٤٥]

1455. **Imām 'Alī (AS) said,** 'Obstinacy is the instigator of wars.'[1659]

١٤٥٥. عنه ﷺ: اللَّجاجُ مَثارُ الحُروبِ.[١٦٤٦]

1456. **Imām 'Alī (AS) said,** 'Abstain from useless, blameable obstinacy, for it will begin wars.'[1660]

١٤٥٦. عنه ﷺ: إيّاكَ ومَذمومَ اللَّجاجِ، فإنَّهُ يُثيرُ الحُروبَ.[١٦٤٧]

484. Surprising the Enemy

٤٨٤ ـ مُباغَتَةُ العَدُوِّ

1457. **Imām ʿAlī (AS) said,** 'Indeed I have called you to fight those people day and night both secretly and openly, and I have told you: 'Attack them before they attack you', for by Allah no sooner are any people attacked in the midst of their abodes than they are disgraced.'[1661]

١٤٥٧ . الإمامُ عليٌّ ﷺ : ألا وإنّي قد دَعَوتُكُم إلىٰ قِتالِ هؤلاءِ القومِ لَيلاً ونَـهاراً ، وسِـرّاً وإعْـلاناً ، وقُلتُ لَكُمْ : اغْزوهُم قَبلَ أنْ يَغْزوكُم ، فواللهِ مـا غُزيَ قَومٌ قَطُّ في عُقْرِ دارِهِم إلّا ذَلّوا.[١٦٤٨]

485. That Which Must be Observed Before the War

٤٨٥ ـ ما يَلزَمُ رِعايَتُهُ قَبلَ الحَربِ

1458. **The Prophet (SAWA) said,** 'Befriend people, give them time, and do not raid them unless you first call them [to Islam]. For you to call all the people of the earth, those who live in houses and those who live in tents, to Islam is dearer to me than for you to bring me their womenfolk and children [as captives], and to kill their men.'[1662]

١٤٥٨ . رسولُ اللهِ ﷺ : تَألَّفوا النّاسَ ، وتَأنَّوهُم ، ولا تُغيروا علَيهِم حتّىٰ تَدْعُوهُم ، فـمَا عـلىٰ الأرضِ مِن أهلِ بَيتِ مَدَرٍ ولا وَبَـرٍ إلّا تَأتـوني بِهِم مسلِمينَ أحَبُّ إلَيَّ مِن أنْ تَأتوني بِـنِسائِهِم وأوْلادِهِم وتَقْتُلوا رِجالَهُم.[١٦٤٩]

1459. **Imām ʿAlī (AS) said** at Ṣiffīn, 'By Allah I did not postpone the war even for one day unless if I hoped a group of people would join me to be guided by me and repose in my light, and I love that more than killing them for their [choosing to remain in] error.'[1663]

١٤٥٩ . الإمامُ عليٌّ ﷺ ـ في صِفّينَ ـ : فواللهِ ما دَفَعْتُ الحَربَ يَوماً إلّا وأنا أطْمَعُ أنْ تَلْحَقَ بي طائفَةٌ فتَهْتَدي بِي ، وتَـعْشو إلىٰ ضَـوْئي ، وذلكَ أحَبُّ إلَيَّ مِن أنْ أقْتُلَها علىٰ ضَلالِها.[١٦٥٠]

1460. **Imām al-Ḥusayn (AS) said,** 'Know that the evil of war is swift, and its taste is bitter. Therefore, he who prepares for it, and sees to its requirements, and does not suffer its wounds before its onset, he is its master; but he who plunges into it before its proper time and before gaining insight into his own effort therein, he is fit not to benefit his people and to ruin himself.'[1664]

١٤٦٠ . الإمامُ الحسينُ ﷺ : ألا إنَّ الحَربَ شَرُّها ذَريعٌ ، وطَعْمُها فَظيعٌ ، فمَن أخَـذَ لَـها اُهْـبَتَها ، واسْتَعَدَّ لَها عُدَّتَها ، ولَم يَألَمْ كُلومَها قَبلَ حُلولِها ، فذاكَ صاحِبُها ، ومَن عاجَلَها قَبلَ أوانِ فُرْصَتِها ، واسْتِبْصارِ سَعيِهِ فيها ، فذاكَ قَمِنٌ ألّا يَنْفَعَ قَومَهُ ، وأنْ يُهْلِكَ نَفْسَهُ.[١٦٥١]

486. The Troops at the Forefront of the Army

٤٨٦ ـ مُقَدَّمَةُ الجَيشِ

1461. **Imām ʿAlī (AS),** in his advice to Ziyād b. al-Naḍr, said, 'Know that the forefront of the

١٤٦١ . الإمامُ عليٌّ ﷺ ـ في وصِيَّتِهِ لزيادِ بـنِ النَّضْرِ ـ : اعْلَمْ أنَّ مُقَدِّمَةَ القومِ عُيونُهُم ، وعُـيونَ

people are their eyes, and that the eyes of the forefront troops are their vanguards; so when you leave your land and approach your enemy do not hesitate to send the vanguards to every side and to some mountain passes, woods, hiding places and every side, lest your enemy attack and lie in ambush for you.'[1665]

المُقَدِّمَةِ طَلائعُهُم، فإذا أنتَ خَرَجْتَ مِن بِلادِكَ ودَنَوْتَ مِن عَدُوِّكَ فلا تَسْأمْ مِن تَوجيهِ الطَّلائعِ في كُلِّ ناحيةٍ وفي بَعضِ الشِّعابِ والشَّجَرِ والخَمَرِ وفي كُلِّ جانبٍ ؛ حتّىٰ لا يُغِيرَكُم عَدُوُّكُم، ويكونَ لَكُم كَمينٌ.١٦٥٢

487. Military Instructions

٤٨٧ ـ إرشاداتٌ عَسكَرِيَّةٌ

1462. **The Prophet (SAWA) said,** 'Messengers and hostages must not be killed.'[1666]

١٤٦٢ . رسولُ اللهِ ﷺ : لا يُقتَلُ الرُّسُلُ ولا الرُّهُنُ.١٦٥٣

1463. **Imām ʿAlī (AS) said,** 'Put the armoured man forward and keep the unarmoured one behind. Grit your teeth because this will make the swords skip off the skull, and dodge on the sides of the spears for it changes the direction of their blades. Close the eyes because it strengthens the spirit and gives peace to the heart. Kill the voices because this will keep off spiritlessness.'[1667]

١٤٦٣ . الإمامُ عليٌّ عليه السلام : فَقَدِّموا الدّارِعَ، وأخِّروا الحاسِرَ، وعَضُّوا علَى الأضْراسِ؛ فإنَّهُ أنبىٰ للسُّيوفِ عنِ الهامِ، والْتَوُوا في أطْرافِ الرِّماحِ؛ فإنَّهُ أمْوَرُ للأسِنَّةِ، وغُضُّوا الأبْصارَ ؛ فإنَّهُ أرْبَطُ للجَأشِ وأسْكَنُ للقُلوبِ، وأمِيتوا الأصْواتَ ؛ فإنَّهُ أطْرَدُ للفَشَلِ.١٦٥٤

1464. **Imām ʿAlī (AS) said,** 'Do not fight them unless they initiate the fighting, because, by the grace of Allah, you are in the right, and to leave them until they begin the fighting will be another proof for your side's right against them. If, by the will of Allah, the enemy is defeated, then do not kill the one who runs away nor strike a helpless person nor finish off the wounded nor inflict harm on women.'[1668]

١٤٦٤ . عنه عليه السلام : لا تُقاتِلوهُم حتّىٰ يَبْدَؤوكُم، فإنَّكُم بِحَمدِ اللهِ علىٰ حُجَّةٍ، وتَرْكُكُم إيّاهُم حتّىٰ يَبْدَؤوكُم حُجَّةٌ اُخْرىٰ لَكُم علَيهِم، فإذا كانَتِ الهَزِيمَةُ بإذْنِ اللهِ فلا تَقْتُلوا مُدْبِراً، ولا تُصيبوا مُعْوِراً، ولا تُجْهِزوا علىٰ جَريحٍ، ولا تَهيجوا النِّساءَ بأذىً.١٦٥٥

1465. **Imām ʿAlī (AS) said,** 'The Prophet (SAWA) prohibited poisoning the land of the polytheists.'[1669]

١٤٦٥ . عنه عليه السلام : نَهىٰ رسولُ اللهِ ﷺ أنْ يُلْقىٰ السَّمُّ في بِلادِ المُشرِكينَ.١٦٥٦

1466. **Imām Zayn al-ʿĀbidīn (AS) said,** 'If you take a captive who then cannot walk further, nor have you a carriage for him, then set him free and do not kill him, for you do not know what would be the Imām's ruling about him.'[1670]

١٤٦٦ . الإمامُ زينُ العابدينَ عليه السلام : إنْ أخَذْتَ الأسيرَ فعَجَزَ عنِ المَشْيِ ولَم يَكُنْ مَعكَ مَحْمِلٌ فأرْسِلْهُ ولا تَقْتُلْهُ ؛ فإنَّكَ لا تَدري ما حُكْمُ الإمامِ فيهِ.١٦٥٧

488. War is a Trick

٤٨٨ ـ الحَربُ خُدعَةٌ

1467. **Imām al-Bāqir (AS) said,** "Alī (AS) used to say: 'I would rather be snatched away by a bird of prey than to attribute a word to the Messenger of Allah (SAWA) that he had not said. I have heard the Messenger of Allah say on the day of the Battle of the Trenches (*khandaq*) that war is trickery, and he used to say: 'Say whatever you wish to say.'[1671]

١٤٦٧ . الإمامُ الباقرُ ﷺ : إنَّ علِيّاً ﷺ كانَ يقولُ : لَأنْ يَخْطَفَني الطَّيرُ أحَبُّ إلَيَّ مِن أنْ أقولَ على رسولِ اللهِ ﷺ ما لَم يَقُلْ ، سَمِعْتُ رسولَ اللهِ ﷺ يقولُ يَومَ الخَندَقِ : الحَربُ خُدْعَةٌ ، ويقولُ : تَكَلَّموا بما أرَدْتُم .[١٦٥٨]

489. Prohibition of Running Away from the Battle

٤٨٩ ـ النَّهيُ عَنِ الفِرارِ مِنَ الحَربِ

"Whoever turns his back [to flee] from them that day—unless [he is] diverting to fight or retiring towards another troop—shall certainly earn Allah's wrath, and his refuge shall be hell, an evil destination."[1672]

﴿وَمَنْ يُوَلِّهِمْ يَوْمَئِذٍ دُبُرَهُ إلّا مُتَحَرِّفاً لِقِتَالٍ أَوْ مُتَحَيِّزاً إلَىٰ فِئَةٍ فَقَدْ بَاءَ بِغَضَبٍ مِنَ اللهِ وَمَأْوَاهُ جَهَنَّمُ وَبِئْسَ الْمَصِيرُ﴾ .[١٦٥٩]

1468. **Imām ʿAlī (AS) said** to his companions in the battle of Ṣiffīn, 'Repeat the attack and be ashamed of running away, for it is a disgrace that remains throughout the generations and a burden on their necks and is a fire on the Day of Reckoning. Therefore, sacrifice your souls for other souls and cheerfully walk to death.'[1673]

١٤٦٨ . الإمامُ عليٌّ ﷺ ـ لأصْحابِهِ في حَربِ صِفّينَ ـ : عاوِدُوا الكَرَّ ، واسْتَحْيوا مِن الفَرِّ ؛ فإنَّهُ عارٌ في الأعْقابِ[١٦٦٠]، ونارُ يَومَ الحِسابِ ، وطِيبوا عَن أنفُسِكُم نَفْساً ، وامْشُوا إلىٰ المَوتِ مَشْياً سُجُحاً .[١٦٦١]

1469. **Imām al-Ṣādiq (AS) said,** 'He who runs away from the battle when faced with two men from the enemy is a deserter indeed, but if he runs away from facing combat with three men, then he is not a deserter.'[1674]

١٤٦٩ . الإمامُ الصّادقُ ﷺ : مَن فَرَّ مِن رجُلَينِ في القِتالِ مِن الزَّحفِ فقَد فَرَّ ، ومَن فَرَّ مِن ثَلاثَةٍ في القِتالِ مِن الزَّحفِ فلَم يَفِرَّ .[١٦٦٢]

1470. **Imām al-Riḍā (AS) said,** 'Allah has prohibited running away from the midst of a battle because of what it does in weakening one's religion and degrading the messengers and the just Imāms (AS).'[1675]

١٤٧٠ . الإمامُ الرِّضا ﷺ : حَرّمَ اللهُ الفِرارَ مِنَ الزَّحْفِ ؛ لِما فيهِ مِنَ الوَهْنِ في الدِّينِ ، والاسْتِخْفافِ بالرُّسُلِ والأئمّةِ العادِلةِ ﷺ .[١٦٦٣]

490. Warning Against Fighting a Muslim

٤٩٠ ـ التَّحذيرُ عَن قِتالِ المُسلِمِ

1471. **The Prophet (SAWA) said,** 'Waging war against a Muslim brother is a sin, and to insult him is a transgression.'[1676]

١٤٧١ . رسولُ اللهِ ﷺ : قِتالُ المسلمِ أخاهُ كُفرٌ، وسِبابُهُ فُسوقٌ.[١٦٦٤]

491. Supplicating During War

٤٩١ ـ الدُّعاءُ عِندَ الحَربِ

1472. **Imām ʿAlī (AS) said,** when confronting an enemy in the battleground, 'O Allah! Hearts have emerged to You and necks have been put forward....O Allah, we complain to You the absence of our Prophet, the great number of our enemies and the dispersion of our desires!'[1677]

١٤٧٢ . الإمامُ عليٌّ ﵇ ـ عِندَ لقاءِ العَدُوِّ مُحارِباً ـ: اللّهُمَّ إليكَ أفْضَتِ القُلوبُ، ومُدَّتِ الأعْناقُ... اللّهُمَّ إنّا نَشكو إلَيكَ غَيْبَةَ نَبِيّنا، وكَثْرَةَ عَدُوِّنا، وتَشَتُّتَ أهْوائنا.[١٦٦٥]

492. The Fighting of Women

٤٩٢ ـ حَربُ النِّساءِ

1473. **Imām al-Bāqir (AS) or Imām al-Ṣādiq (AS) narrated,** 'The Prophet (SAWA) took the women to war in order for them to treat the wounded, but he did not distribute the spoils of war among them but gave them some free gifts instead.'[1678]

١٤٧٣ . الإمامُ الباقرُ أو الإمامُ الصّادقُ ﵉ : إنّ رسولَ اللهِ ﷺ خَرَج بالنِّساءِ في الحَرْبِ حتّىٰ يُداوِينَ الجَرْحىٰ.[١٦٦٦]

(See also: WOMAN: section 1644)

(أنظر) المرأة: باب ١٦٤٤.

92

THE WARMONGER

المُحارِب

493. The Punishment of Warmonger

٤٩٣ ـ جَزاءُ المُحارِبِ

"Indeed the requital of those who wage war against Allah and His Apostles, and try to cause corruption on the earth, is that they shall be slain or crucified, or have their hands and feet cut off from opposite sides or be banished from the land."[1679]

﴿إنَّما جَزَاءُ الَّذِينَ يُحَارِبُونَ اللهَ وَرَسُولَهُ وَيَسْعَوْنَ فِي الْأَرْضِ فَسَاداً أَنْ يُقَتَّلُوا أَوْ يُصَلَّبُوا أَوْ تُقَطَّعَ أَيْدِيهِمْ وَأَرْجُلُهُمْ مِنْ خِلَافٍ أَوْ يُنْفَوْا مِنَ الْأَرْضِ﴾.[١٦٦٧]

1474. **The Prophet (SAWA) said,** 'He who draws his sword [against people] his blood must be shed.'[1680]

١٤٧٤ . رسولُ اللهِ ﷺ : مَن شَهرَ سَيفَهُ فَدَمُهُ هَدْرٌ.[١٦٦٨]

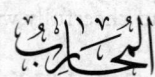

1475. **Imām ʿAlī (AS) said,** 'Kill the armed robber, and as regards to its consequences I am responsible for his blood.'[1681]

١٤٧٥ . الإمامُ عليٌّ ﷺ : اللِّصُّ المُحارِبُ فاقْتُلْهُ ، فَما أصابَكَ فدَمُهُ في عُنُقي .[١٦٦٩]

1476. **Imām al-Bāqir (AS) said,** 'If a man enters your house and intends to assault your family and your wealth, then hit him first if you can, as a thief is a fighter against Allah and His Messenger (SAWA), then kill him, and if something was to happen to you after this, it will be my responsibility.'[1682]

١٤٧٦ . الإمام الباقر ﷺ : إذا دَخَلَ عَلَيكَ رَجُلٌ يُريدُ أهلَكَ وما تَملِكُ فَابدُرهُ بِالضَّربَةِ إنِ ستَطَعتَ ، فَإِنَّ اللِّصَّ مُحارِبٌ للهِ ولِرَسولِهِ فَاقتُلهُ فَما تَبِعَكَ فِيهِ مِن شَيءٍ فَهُوَ عَلَيَّ .[١٦٧٠]

1477. **Imām al-Bāqir (AS) said,** 'Whoever carries weapons by night is a warmonger, unless he is a man about whom there is no misgiving.'[1683]

١٤٧٧ . عنه ﷺ : مَن حمَلَ السِّلاحَ باللَّيلِ فهُو مُحارِبٌ، إلّا أنْ يَكونَ رجُلاً لَيس مِن أهلِ لرِّيبةِ.[١٦٧١]

1478. **Imām al-Bāqir (AS),** when he was asked about banishing the warmonger, said, 'He must be banished from the state. Indeed Imām ʿAlī (AS) banished two men from Kufa to somewhere else.'[1684]

١٤٧٨ . عنه ﷺ ـ وقد سُئلَ عن نَفْيِ المُحارِبِ ـ: يُنْفىٰ مِن مِصرٍ إلىٰ مِصْرٍ، إنّ عَليّاً ﷺ نَفىٰ رجُلَينِ مِن الكُوفةِ إلىٰ غَيرِها .[١٦٧٢]

(See also: USURY: section 800)

(أُنظر) الرباء: باب ٨٠٠.

93

FREEDOM

الحُرِّيَّةُ

494. The Importance of Freedom

٤٩٤ ـ أهَمِّيَّةُ الحُرِّيَّةِ

1479. **Imām al-Ṣādiq (AS) said,** 'There are five attributes such that whoever does not even possess one of them does not have much to admire: loyalty, organisation, modesty, good temper, and the last which brings together all these attribute is freedom.'[1685]

١٤٧٩ . الإمامُ الصّادقُ ﷺ : خَمسُ خِصالٍ مَن لم تَكُنْ فيهِ خَصْلَةٌ مِنها فلَيس فيهِ كَثيرُ مُسْتَمْتَعٍ ، أوَّلُها : الوَفاءُ ، والثّانيةُ : التَّدْبيرُ ، والثّالثةُ : الحَياءُ ، والرّابعةُ : حُسنُ الخُلقِ ، والخامِسةُ ـ وهِي تَجْمَعُ هذهِ الخِصالَ ـ : الحُرِّيّةُ .[١٦٧٣]

495. All People are Free

٤٩٥ ـ النّاسُ كُلُّهُم أحرارٌ

1480. **Imām ʿAlī (AS) said,** 'O people! Indeed Adam did not beget a bondsman or bondswoman, so all people are free.'[1686]

١٤٨٠ . الإمامُ عليٌّ ﷺ : أيُّها النّاسُ ، إنّ آدمَ لَم يَلِدْ عَبداً ولا أمَةً ، وإنّ النّاسَ كلَّهُم أحْرارٌ .[١٦٧٤]

1481. **Imām ʿAlī (AS) said,** 'Do not ever be a slave to others when Allah, glory be to Him, has made you free.'[1687]

١٤٨١ . عنه ﷺ : لا تَكُونَنَّ عَبدَ غَيرِكَ وقَد جَعلَكَ اللهُ سُبْحانَه حُرّاً.[١٦٧٥]

496. The Distinguishing Trait of the Free

٤٩٦ ـ شيمَةُ الحُرِّ

1482. **Imām ʿAlī (AS) said,** 'Cheerfulness is the distinguishing trait of the free.'[1688]

١٤٨٢ . الإمامُ عليٌّ ﷺ : الطَّلاقَةُ شِيمَةُ الحُرِّ.[١٦٧٦]

1483. **Imām ʿAlī (AS) said,** 'Truly modesty and chastity are of the traits of faith, and they are the attributes of the free and the distinguishing marks of the righteous.'[1689]

١٤٨٣ . عنه ﷺ : إنَّ الحَياءَ والعِفَّةَ مِن خَلائقِ الإيمانِ، وإنّهُما لَسَجِيّةُ الأحْرارِ وشِيمَةُ الأبْرارِ.[١٦٧٧]

1484. **Imām ʿAlī (AS) said,** 'The servant of Allah is free so far as he remains content. The free man is a slave as long as he is greedy.'[1690]

١٤٨٤ . عنه ﷺ : العَبدُ حُرٌّ ما قَنِعَ، الحُرُّ عَبدٌ ما طَمِعَ.[١٦٧٨]

1485. **Imām al-Ṣādiq (AS) said,** 'The free is free in all his states: when he is inflicted by a calamity, he shows patience; when afflictions bear down on him, they do not break him, even though he be taken in captivity or defeated and his prosperity turns into poverty, just like the truthful trustworthy Prophet Joseph - blessings of Allah upon him –, whose freedom was not affected even when he was enslaved, defeated and captivated.'[1691]

١٤٨٥ . الإمامُ الصّادقُ ﷺ : إنَّ الحُرَّ حُرٌّ على جميعِ أحْوالِهِ: إنْ نابَتْهُ نائبَةٌ صَبرَ لَها، وإنْ تَداكَّتْ علَيهِ المَصائبُ لَم تَكْسِرْهُ وإنْ اُسِرَ وقُهِرَ واسْتُبْدِلَ بالْيُسرِ عُسراً، كما كانَ يُوسُفُ الصِّدِّيقُ الأمينُ صلواتُ اللهِ علَيهِ: لَم يَضْرُرْ حُرِّيَّتَهُ أنِ اسْتُعبِدَ وقُهِرَ واُسِرَ.[١٦٧٩]

94

COVETOUSNESS

الحِرْص

497. Denouncing Covetousness

٤٩٧ ـ ذَمُّ الحِرص

1486. **Imām ʿAlī (AS),** when asked about covetousness, said, 'It is the desire for something little through the loss of a lot.'[1692]

١٤٨٦ . الإمامُ عليٌّ ﷺ ـ وقد سُئلَ عنِ الحِرصِ: ما هُو؟ ـ: هُو طَلَبُ القَليلِ بإضاعَةِ الكَثيرِ.[١٦٨٠]

1487. **Imām ʿAlī (AS) said,** 'Covetousness is a terminal [source of] distress.'[1693]

١٤٨٧ . عنه ؑ : الحِرْصُ عَناءٌ مُؤبَّدٌ.١٦٨١

1488. **Imām ʿAlī (AS) said,** 'Covetousness stains one's gallantry.'[1694]

١٤٨٨ . عنه ؑ : الحِرصُ يُزْري بالمُرُوَّةِ.١٦٨٢

1489. **Imām ʿAlī (AS) said,** 'Covetousness is the mount of pains.'[1695]

١٤٨٩ . عنه ؑ : الحِرصُ مَطِيَّةُ التَّعَبِ.١٦٨٣

1490. **Imām ʿAlī (AS) said,** 'Covetousness does not increase sustenance, but rather it degrades a person's value.'[1696]

١٤٩٠ . عنه ؑ : الحِرصُ لا يَزيدُ في الرِّزقِ ، ولكنْ يُذِلُّ القَدْرَ.١٦٨٤

(See also: GREED: 253)

(أنظر) عنوان ٢٥٣ «الطمع».

498. Denouncing the Covetous

٤٩٨ ـ ذَمُّ الحَريصِ

1491. **Imām ʿAlī (AS) said,** 'The covetous is a captive of a lowliness whose captivity is never-ending.'[1697]

١٤٩١ . الإمامُ عليٌّ ؑ : الحَريصُ أسِيرُ مَهانَةٍ لا يُفَكُّ أسْرُهُ.١٦٨٥

1492. **Imām ʿAlī (AS),** when asked, 'Which is the worst humility?', said, 'Coveting the world.'[1698]

١٤٩٢ . عنه ؑ ـ وقد سُئلَ : أيُّ ذُلٍّ أذَلُّ ؟ ـ : الحِرصُ على الدُّنيا.١٦٨٦

1493. **Imām ʿAlī (AS) said,** 'Sustenance is allotted, and the covetous is denied.'[1699]

١٤٩٣ . عنه ؑ : الرِّزقُ مَقْسومٌ ، الحَريصُ مَحْرومٌ.١٦٨٧

1494. **Imām ʿAlī (AS) said,** 'The covetous one is poor even if he owns the whole world.'[1700]

١٤٩٤ . عنه ؑ : الحَريصُ فَقيرٌ ولو مَلَكَ الدُّنيا بحَذافيرِها.١٦٨٨

1495. **Imām ʿAlī (AS) said,** 'The one who covets is wretched and miserable.'[1701]

١٤٩٥ . عنه ؑ : مَن حَرَصَ شَقِيَ وتَعَنّى.١٦٨٩

1496. **Imām ʿAlī (AS) said,** 'The covetous one is never satiated.'[1702]

١٤٩٦ . عنه ؑ : الحَريصُ لا يَكْتَفي.١٦٩٠

1497. **Imām al-Ḥusayn (AS) said,** 'Self-restraint does not prevent [the descent of] sustenance, nor does covetousness attract any surplus [sustenance];

١٤٩٧ . الإمامُ الحسينُ ؑ : لَيستِ العِفَّةُ بمانِعَةٍ رِزْقاً ، ولا الحِرصُ بجالِبٍ فَضْلاً ، وإنَّ الرِّزقَ مَقْسومٌ والأجَلَ مَحتومٌ ، وَاسْتِعمالُ

for indeed sustenance is allotted, and death is certain, and covetousness is only asking for sin.'[1703]

الحِرصِ طَالِبُ المَأْثَمِ.١٦٩١

1498. **Imām al-Bāqir (AS) said,** 'The similitude of the one who covets this world is as the caterpillar: the more silk it spins around itself, the harder it makes its exit for itself, until it dies of grief.'[1704]

١٤٩٨ . الإمامُ الباقرُ (ع) : مَثَلُ الحَريصِ علىٰ الدُّنيا مَثَلُ دُودَةِ القَزِّ : كُلَّما ازْدادَتْ مِن القَزِّ علىٰ نَفْسِها لَفّاً كانَ أبْعَدَ لَها مِن الخُروجِ ، حتّىٰ تَموتَ غَمّاً .١٦٩٢

1499. **Imām al-Ṣādiq (AS) said,** 'The Commander of the Faithful, blessings of Allah be upon him, used to say, 'O son of Adam! If only you sought from the world enough to satisfy your needs, indeed the very least from it would be enough to satisfy your needs. But if instead you desire more than your needs, then truly everything that it contains will not suffice you.'[1705]

١٤٩٩ . الإمامُ الصّادقُ (ع) : كانَ أميرُ المؤمنينَ صلواتُ اللهِ علَيهِ يقولُ : ابنَ آدمَ ، إنْ كُنتَ تُريدُ مِن الدُّنيا ما يَكْفيكَ فإنَّ أيْسَرَ ما فيها يَكْفيكَ ، وإنْ كُنتَ إنّما تُريدُ ما لا يَكْفيكَ فإنَّ كُلَّ ما فيها لا يَكْفيكَ .١٦٩٣

(See also: CONTENTMENT: section 1567)

(أنظر) القناعة : باب ١٥٦٧.

499. The Elements of Covetousness

٤٩٩ ـ مادّةُ الحِرصِ

1500. **The Prophet (SAWA) said,** 'Know O 'Alī, that cowardice, miserliness, and covetousness are all a single disposition, brought together through entertaining a low opinion [of Allah].'[1706]

١٥٠٠ . رسولُ اللهِ ﷺ : اعْلَمْ يا عليُّ ، أنّ الجُبْنَ والبُخْلَ والحِرصَ غَريزَةٌ واحِدَةٌ ، يَجْمَعُها سُوءُ الظَّنِّ .١٦٩٤

1501. **The Prophet (SAWA) said,** 'Truly the son of Adam covets what is prohibited.'[1707]

١٥٠١ . عنه ﷺ : إنّ ابنَ آدمَ لَحَريصٌ علىٰ ما مُنِعَ .١٦٩٥

1502. **Imām 'Alī (AS) said,** 'Covetousness and meanness are founded on doubt and lack of trust in Allah.'[1708]

١٥٠٢ . الإمامُ عليٌّ (ع) : علىٰ الشَّكِّ وقِلَّةِ الثِّقَةِ باللهِ ، مَبْنىٰ الحِرصِ والشُّحِّ .١٦٩٦

1503. **Imām 'Alī (AS) said,** 'Intense covetousness arises from ardent gluttony and weakness of faith.'[1709]

١٥٠٣ . عنه (ع) : شِدَّةُ الحِرصِ مِن قُوَّةِ الشَّرَهِ وضَعْفِ الدِّينِ .١٦٩٧

95

THE PROFESSION

الحِرفَةُ

500. The Importance of a Profession

٥٠٠ـ أهَمِّيَّةُ الحِرفَةِ

1504. **The Prophet (SAWA) said,** 'Truly Allah loves the servant who is faithful and engaged in a profession.'[1710]

١٥٠٤ . رسولُ اللهِ ﷺ : إنَّ اللهَ تعالىٰ يُحِبُّ العَبدَ المؤمنَ المُحْتَرِفَ .[١٦٩٨]

1505. It is narrated in *al-Khiṣāl* that whenever the Prophet (SAWA) looked at a man who pleased him, he used to ask, 'Does he have a profession?' If they said, 'No', he would say, 'He has lost his worth in my eye.' They would then ask, 'O Messenger of Allah! Why is that?!' He would reply, 'Because when the believer has no profession, he subsists off his religion.'[1711]

١٥٠٥ . جامع الأخبار عن ابن عبّاس : كانَ رسولُ اللهِ ﷺ إذا نَظَرَ إلىٰ الرّجُلِ فأعْجَبَهُ ، قالَ : هَل لَهُ حِرْفَةٌ ؟ فإنْ قالوا : لا ، قالَ : سَقَطَ مِن عَيْني . قيلَ : وكيفَ ذلكَ يا رسولَ اللهِ ؟! قالَ : لأنَّ المؤمنَ إذا لَم يَكُن لَهُ حِرْفَةٌ يَعيشُ بدِينِهِ .[١٦٩٩]

1506. **Imām ʿAlī (AS) said,** 'Undertake yourselves to trading, for there lies therein your independence from what others possess, and verily Allah, Mighty and Exalted, loves the trustworthy servant who is engaged in a profession.'[1712]

١٥٠٦ . الإمامُ عليٌّ عليه السلام : تَعَرّضوا للتِّجارَةِ ؛ فإنَّ فيها غِنىً لَكُم عَمّا في أيْدي النّاسِ ، وإنَّ اللهَ عزّوجلّ يُحِبُّ العَبدَ المُحْتَرِفَ الأمينَ .[١٧٠٠]

1507. **Imām al-Ṣādiq (AS)** once asked one of his companions about his means of income. He said, 'May I be your ransom. I have given up trading.' Imām asked why, and he answered, 'I am waiting for this rule [i.e. the reign of your government].' Imām said, 'That is strange from you. Your wealth will perish. Do not abandon trading, and seek out the bounty of Allah. Open your door and exhibit your goods, and seek out the sustenance of your Lord.'[1713]

١٥٠٧ . دعائم الإسلام عن جَعفرِ بنِ محمّدٍ عليه السلام أنّه سألَ بعضَ أصْحابِهِ عَمّا يتَصَرَّفُ فيهِ ، فقال : جُعِلتُ فِداكَ ، إنّي كَفَفْتُ يَدي عنِ التِّجارَةِ . قالَ : لِمَ ذلكَ ؟! قالَ : انْتِظاري هذا الأمرَ . قالَ : ذلكَ أعْجَبُ لَكُم ، تَذْهبُ أمْوالُكُم ! لا تَكْفُفْ عنِ التِّجارَةِ والْتمِسْ مِن فَضْلِ اللهِ ، وَافْتَحْ بابَكَ وابْسُطْ بِساطَكَ واسْتَرْزِقْ رَبَّكَ .[١٧٠١]

(See also: COMMERCE: 55; EARNINGS: 343)

(أُنظر) عنوان ٥٥ «التجارة» ؛ عنوان ٣٤٣ «الكسب» .

96

THE PROHIBITED (*ḤARĀM*)

الحَرامُ[١٥]

501. Avoiding the Prohibited

٥٠١ ـ اجتِنابُ المَحارِمِ

1508. **Imām ʿAlī (AS) said,** 'If you wish for noble traits, then avoid the prohibited things.'[1714]

١٥٠٨ . الإمامُ عليٌّ عليه السلام : إذا رَغِبْتَ في المَكارِمِ فاجْتَنِبِ المَحارِمَ.[١٧٠٢]

1509. **Imām ʿAlī (AS) said,** 'One of the best noble traits is the avoidance of prohibited things.'[1715]

١٥٠٩ . عنه عليه السلام : مِن أحْسَنِ المَكارِمِ تَجَنُّبُ المَحارِمِ.[١٧٠٣]

1510. **Imām ʿAlī (AS) said,** 'Even if Allah, glory be to Him, had not forbidden that which He has prohibited, it would have been mandatory for the one possessing intellect to avoid them [at least].'[1716]

١٥١٠ . عنه عليه السلام : لَو لَم يَنْهَ اللهُ سُبحانَهُ عَن مَحارِمِهِ لَوجَبَ أنْ يَجْتَنِبَها العاقِلُ.[١٧٠٤]

502. Consuming the Prohibited

٥٠٢ ـ أكلُ الحَرامِ

1511. **The Prophet (SAWA) said,** 'Worship alongside consumption of the prohibited is like erecting a building on sand—or on water [according to other narrations].'[1717]

١٥١١ . رسولُ اللهِ صلى الله عليه وآله : العِبادَةُ مَع أكْلِ الحَرامِ كالبِناءِ علىٰ الرَّمْلِ ـ وقيلَ : علىٰ الماءِ ـ.[١٧٠٥]

1512. **The Prophet (SAWA) said,** 'Abstaining from eating even one morsel of prohibited food is dearer to Allah than performing two thousand units of voluntary prayers.'[1718]

١٥١٢ . عنه صلى الله عليه وآله : تَرْكُ لُقْمَةِ حَرامٍ أحَبُّ إلىٰ اللهِ من صلاةِ ألفَي رَكْعَةٍ تَطَوُّعاً.[١٧٠٦]

1513. **Imām al-Bāqir (AS) said,** 'When a man accumulates wealth from prohibited sources, neither his obligatory pilgrimage (*ḥajj*) nor his voluntary pilgrimage (*ʿumra*) nor his maintaining kinship will be accepted from him, and it even spoils marriage.'[1719]

١٥١٣ . الإمامُ الباقرُ عليه السلام : إنَّ الرَّجُلَ إذا أصابَ مالاً مِن حَرامٍ لَم يُقْبَلْ مِنهُ حَجٌّ ولا عُمْرَةٌ ولا صِلَةُ رَحِمٍ حتّىٰ أنّه يَفْسُدُ فيهِ الفَرْجُ.[١٧٠٧]

1514. **Imām al-Ṣādiq (AS),** with regards to Allah's verse, *"Then We shall attend to the works they have*

١٥١٤ . الإمامُ الصّادقُ عليه السلام ـ في قولِهِ عزّوجلّ : ﴿وَقَدِمْنَا إِلَىٰ مَا عَمِلُوا مِنْ عَمَلٍ فَجَعَلْنَاهُ

done and then turn them into scattered dust", said, 'By Allah, even though their deeds were whiter than Egyptian cotton, when the prohibited presented itself before them they did not leave it.'[1720]

هَبَاءً مَّنثُورًا﴾ [١٧٠٨] ـ: أمَا واللهِ إنْ كانت أعـمالُهُم أشدَّ بَياضاً مِن القُباطيِّ، ولكنْ كانوا إذا عَرَضَ هُمُ الحرامُ لم يَدَعوهُ. [١٧٠٩]

503. The Reward of One Who has Access to the Prohibited but Abandons it

٥٠٣ـ ثَوابُ مَن قَدَرَ عَلىٰ حَرامٍ فتَرَكَهُ

1515. **The Prophet (SAWA) said,** 'He who has unlawful access to enjoy a woman or a maid but leaves her for fear of Allah, He - Mighty and Exalted - will keep him safe from the Fire, preserve him from the Great Terror, and make him enter Paradise.'[1721]

١٥١٥ . رسولُ اللهِ ﷺ :مَن قَدَرَ علىٰ امرأةٍ أو جاريَةٍ حَراماً فتَرَكَها مَخافَةَ اللهِ حَرَّمَ اللهُ عزّوجلّ علَيهِ النّارَ، وآمَنَهُ اللهُ تَعالىٰ مِن الفَزَعِ الأكبَرِ، وأدْخَلَهُ اللهُ الجَنّةَ. [١٧١٠]

1516. **The Prophet (SAWA) said,** 'No sooner does a man who is able to commit a prohibited act abandon it, only for fear of Allah, than Allah gives him in lieu of it something that is better for him in this present world before the Hereafter.'[1722]

١٥١٦ . عنه ﷺ : لا يَقْدِرُ رَجُلٌ علىٰ حَرامٍ ثُمَّ يَدَعُهُ، لَيس بهِ إلّا مَخافَةُ اللهِ، إلّا أبْدَلَهُ اللهُ في عاجِلِ الدُّنيا قَبْلَ الآخِرَةِ ما هُو خَيرٌ لَهُ مِن ذلكَ. [١٧١١]

1517. **Imām al-Kāẓim (AS) said,** 'The Prophet (SAWA) used to visit the people of the ledge [of the mosque], who were his guests and had migrated to Medina without their families and belongings. The Prophet (SAWA) had lodged them on the ledges of the Mosque. They were four hundred men, and he greeted them every morning and every night. One day he came to them while some of them were mending their sandals, some were patching their garments, and some were cleaning their heads from lice. The Prophet (SAWA) used to provide them with half a bushel of dates every day.

One of the men stood up and said, 'O Messenger of Allah! The dates you provide us with have burned our stomachs!' The Prophet (SAWA) said, 'If I could feed you the whole world surely I would have done it, but [know that] those among you who will live after me will be brought bowls [of food] in the morning and bowls in the evening, and each of you will have a shirt in the morning and another in the

١٥١٧ . الإمامُ الكاظمُ عليه السلام : إنَّ رسولَ اللهِ ﷺ كانَ يأتي أهلَ الصُّفَّةِ وكانوا ضِيفانَ رسولِ اللهِ ﷺ، كانوا هاجَروا مِن أهاليهِم وأموالِهِم إلىٰ المَدينَةِ فأسْكَنَهُم رسولُ اللهِ ﷺ صُفَّةَ المَسجِدِ، وهُم أربَعُمِائةِ رجُلٍ [كان]، يُسَلِّمُ علَيهِم بالغدوةِ والعَشِيِّ، فأتاهُم ذاتَ يومٍ فمِنهُم مَن يَخصِفُ نَعلَهُ، ومِنهُم مَن يَرقَعُ ثَوبَهُ، ومِنهُم مَن يَتَفلّىٰ، وكانَ رسولُ اللهِ ﷺ يَرزُقُهُم مُدّاً مُدّاً مِن تمرٍ في كُلِّ يَومٍ.

فقامَ رجُلٌ مِنهُم فقالَ: يا رسولَ اللهِ، التَّمرُ الّذي تَرْزُقُنا قَد أحْرَقَ بطُونَنا!

فقالَ رسولُ اللهِ ﷺ: أمَا إنّي لَوِ اسْتَطَعْتُ أنْ أُطْعِمَكُمُ الدُّنيا لَأطعَمْتُكُم، ولٰكنْ مَن عاشَ مِنكُم من بَعدي فسَيُغدىٰ علَيهِ بالجِفانِ ويُراحُ علَيهِ بالجِفانِ، ويَغدو أحَدُكُم في قَميصةٍ ويَروحُ في أُخرىٰ، وتُنَجِّدونَ بُيوتَكُم كما تُنَجَّدُ الكَعبَةُ.

evening, and each of you will adorn your houses with curtains and carpets as the Kaʿba is adorned.' A man then rose and exclaimed, 'O Messenger of Allah! We are waiting eagerly for that time. When will it be?!' He (SAWA) said, 'Your time now is better than that time. When you fill your stomachs with the lawful, you might also fill it with the unlawful.'[1723]

فقامَ رجلٌ فقالَ: يا رسولَ اللهِ، إنّا على ذلكَ الزّمانِ بالأشواقِ! فمتىٰ هو؟!
قالَ ﷺ: زمانُكم هٰذا خيرٌ مِن ذلكَ الزّمانِ، إنّكم إنْ مَلأتُم بطونَكم مِن الحَلالِ تُوشِكونَ أنْ تَملؤوها مِن الحَرامِ.١٧١٢

97

THE PARTY

الحِزبُ

504. The Party of Allah

٥٠٤ ـ حِزبُ اللهِ

"Whoever takes for his guardians Allah, His Apostle and the faithful [should know that] the party of Allah is indeed the victorious."[1724]

﴿وَمَنْ يَتَوَلَّ اللهَ وَرَسُولَهُ وَالَّذِينَ آمَنُوا فَإِنَّ حِزْبَ اللهِ هُمُ الْغَالِبُونَ﴾.١٧١٣

1518. **Imām ʿAlī (AS) said,** 'Would you like to be of the victorious party of Allah? Then be Godwary and excel in all your affairs, for Allah is with those who are wary of their duty to Him and those who excel in virtue.'[1725]

١٥١٨. الإمامُ عليٌّ ؑ: أيَسُرُّكَ أنْ تَكونَ مِن حِزبِ اللهِ الغالِبينَ؟ اتّقِ اللهَ سُبحانَهُ وأحْسِنْ في كُلِّ أمورِكَ؛ فإنَّ اللهَ مَعَ الّذينَ اتَّقَوا والّذينَ هُم مُحْسِنونَ.١٧١٤

1519. **Imām al-Ṣādiq (AS) said,** 'We and our followers (*shīʿa*) are the party of Allah, and the party of Allah is the victorious.'[1726]

١٥١٩. الإمامُ الصّادقُ ؑ: نَحنُ وشيعَتُنا حِزبُ اللهِ، وحِزبُ اللهِ هُمُ الغالِبونَ.١٧١٥

505. The Party of Satan

٥٠٥ ـ حِزبُ الشَّيطانِ

"Satan has prevailed upon them, so he has caused them to forget the remembrance of Allah. They are Satan's party. Look! Indeed it is Satan's parties who are the losers!"[1727]

﴿اسْتَحْوَذَ عَلَيْهِمُ الشَّيْطَانُ فَأَنْسَاهُمْ ذِكْرَ اللهِ أُولٰئِكَ حِزْبُ الشَّيْطَانِ أَلَا إِنَّ حِزْبَ الشَّيْطَانِ هُمُ الْخَاسِرُونَ﴾.١٧١٦

1520. **Imām ʿAlī (AS) said,** 'O people! Truly the onset of problems is brought about by following the desires… If the truth were pure there would be no disparity. However, a handful is taken from this [the truth] and a handful from that

١٥٢٠. الإمامُ عليٌّ ؑ: أيُّها النّاسُ، إنّما بَدْءُ وُقوعِ الفِتَنِ أهواءٌ تُتَّبَعُ... ولو أنَّ الحَقَّ خَلَصَ لَم يَكُنِ اختِلافٌ، ولكنْ يُؤخَذُ مِن هٰذا ضِغْثٌ ومِن هٰذا ضِغْثٌ فيُمزَجانِ فيَجيئانِ مَعاً، فهُنالِكَ استَحْوَذَ

[falsehood] and then the two are mixed and appear altogether. And this is where Satan prevails over his followers, and only those who are favoured by Allah are saved.'[1728]

الشّيطانُ علىٰ أوْليائِه، ونَجا الّذينَ سَبَقَتْ لَهُم مِن اللهِ الحُسْنىٰ.[١٧١٧]

1521. **Imām ʿAlī (AS) said** in one of his sermons where he describes the hypocrites, 'They are the companions of Satan, and the incinerating sting of the Fire. They are the party of Satan; indeed it is Satan's parties who are the losers.'[1729]

١٥٢١. عنه عليه السلام ـ مِن خُطبةٍ لَهُ يَصِفُ فيها المُنافِقينَ ـ: فَهُم لُمَةُ الشَّيطانِ، وحُمَةُ النِّيرانِ، أُولٰئكَ حِزبُ الشَّيطانِ، ألَا إنَّ حِزبَ الشَّيطانِ هُمُ الخاسِرونَ.[١٧١٨]

(See also: SATAN: section 1029)

(أُنظر) الشيطان: باب ١٠٢٩.

98

PRUDENCE

الحَزم

506. The Value of Prudence

٥٠٦ـ قِيمَةُ الحَزمِ

1522. **Imām ʿAlī (AS) said,** 'Prudence is sagacity.'[1730]

١٥٢٢. الإمامُ عليٌّ عليه السلام: الحَزْم كِياسَةٌ.[١٧١٩]

1523. **Imām ʿAlī (AS) said,** 'He who adopts prudence is cautious, and he who lacks prudence is reckless.'[1731]

١٥٢٣. عنه عليه السلام: مَن أخَذَ بالحَزمِ اسْتَظْهَرَ، مَن أضاعَ الحَزمَ تَهوَّرَ.[١٧٢٠]

1524. **Imām ʿAlī (AS) said,** 'Planning before action will preserve you from regret.'[1732]

١٥٢٤. عنه عليه السلام: التَّدْبيرُ قَبلَ العَمَلِ يُؤْمِنُكَ مِن النَّدَمِ.[١٧٢١]

1525. **Imām ʿAlī (AS) said,** 'The most intelligent of people is he who looks further into the consequences.'[1733]

١٥٢٥. عنه عليه السلام: أعْقَلُ النّاسِ أنْظَرُهُم في العَواقِبِ.[١٧٢٢]

1526. **Imām al-Ṣādiq (AS) said,** 'Prudence is the lamp-niche of doubt.'[1734]

١٥٢٦. الإمامُ الصّادقُ عليه السلام: الحَزمُ مِشْكاةُ الظَّنِّ.[١٧٢٣]

507. The Danger of Not Foreseeing the Consequences of Matters

٥٠٧ـ خَطَرُ تَركِ النَّظَرِ في عَواقِبِ الأُمورِ

1527. **Imām ʿAlī (AS) said,** 'He who involves himself in matters without considering the consequences exposes himself to troubles.'[1735]

١٥٢٧. الإمامُ عليٌّ عليه السلام: مَن تَورَّطَ في الأُمورِ بغَيرِ نَظَرٍ في العَواقِبِ فَقَد تَعرَّضَ للنَّوائبِ.[١٧٢٤]

508. Firm Resolution and Determination

٥٠٨ـ الحَزمُ وَالعَزمُ

1528. **Imām ʿAlī (AS) said,** 'Victory comes through firm resolution and determination.'[1736]

١٥٢٨ . الإمامُ عليٌّ عليه السلام: الظَّفَرُ بالحَزْمِ والجَزْمِ.[١٧٣٥]

1529. **Imām ʿAlī (AS) said,** 'There is no good in determination without a firm resolution.'[1737]

١٥٢٩ . عنه عليه السلام : لا خَيرَ في عَزمٍ بلا حَزمٍ.[١٧٣٦]

509. The Interpretation of Prudence

٥٠٩ـ تَفسيرُ الحَزمِ

1530. **Imām ʿAlī (AS) said,** 'Prudence is careful consideration of the consequences and consultation of people of reason.'[1738]

١٥٣٠ . الإمامُ عليٌّ عليه السلام : الحَزمُ النَّظَرُ في العَواقِبِ، ومُشاوَرَةُ ذَوي العُقولِ.[١٧٣٧]

1531. **Imām ʿAlī (AS) said,** 'The essence of prudence is stopping in the face of the dubious.'[1739]

١٥٣١ . عنه عليه السلام : أصْلُ الحَزمِ الوُقوفُ عِندَ الشُّبْهَةِ.[١٧٣٨]

1532. **Imām ʿAlī (AS) said,** 'Feeling certainty and quietude before experience is against prudence.'[1740]

١٥٣٢ . عنه عليه السلام : الطُّمَأنينَةُ قَبلَ الخُبْرَةِ خِلافُ الحَزمِ.[١٧٢٩]

510. The Prudent

٥١٠ـ الحازِمُ

1533. **Imām ʿAlī (AS) said,** 'The prudent one is he who is not preoccupied by the delusion of this world from working for his Hereafter.'[1741]

١٥٣٣ . الإمامُ عليٌّ عليه السلام : الحازِمُ مَن لَم يَشْغَلْهُ غُرورُ دُنْياهُ عنِ العَمَلِ لأُخْراهُ.[١٧٣٠]

1534. **Imām ʿAlī (AS) said,** 'The prudent one is he who is selective in his friendships, for man is judged according to his friend.'[1742]

١٥٣٤ . عنه عليه السلام : الحازِمُ مَن تَخيَّرَ لخُلَّتِهِ ؛ فإنَّ المَرْءَ يُوزَنُ بخَليلِهِ.[١٧٣١]

1535. **Imām ʿAlī (AS) said,** 'The prudent one is he whose prosperity does not stop him from working towards the end goal.'[1743]

١٥٣٥ . عنه عليه السلام : الحازِمُ مَن لا يَشْغَلُهُ النِّعْمَةُ عنِ العَملِ للعاقِبَةِ.[١٧٣٢]

1536. **Imām ʿAlī (AS) said,** 'The prudent one is he who puts off punishment when anger prevails, and hastens to reward the good, taking the first possible opportunity to do so.'[1744]

١٥٣٦ . عنه عليه السلام : الحازِمُ مَن يُؤَخِّرُ العُقوبَةَ في سُلطانِ الغَضَبِ، ويُعَجِّلُ مُكافَأةَ الإحْسانِ اغْتِناماً لفُرْصَةِ الإمْكانِ.[١٧٣٣]

511. The Most Prudent of People

٥١١ـ أحزَمُ النّاسِ

1537. **The Prophet (SAWA) said,** 'The most prudent of people is he who is best at controlling his rage.'[1745]

١٥٣٧ . رسولُ اللهِ ﷺ : أحزَمُ النّاسِ أكظَمُهُم للغَيظِ.[١٧٣٤]

1538. **The Prophet (SAWA) said,** 'The most sagacious one from among you is he who remembers death the most, and the most prudent one from among you is he who is the most prepared for it.'[1746]

١٥٣٨ . عنه ﷺ : إنَّ أكيَسَكُم أكثَرُكُم ذِكراً لِلمَوتِ، وإنَّ أحزَمَكُم أحسَنُكُم استِعداداً لَهُ.[١٧٣٥]

1539. **Imām ʿAlī (AS) said,** 'The most prudent one from among you is the one who is most abstemious.'[1747]

١٥٣٩ . الإمامُ عليٌّ (ع) : أحزَمُكُم أزهَدُكُم.[١٧٣٦]

99

SORROW

الحُزنُ

512. The Harms of Sorrow

٥١٢ـ مَضارُّ الحُزنِ

1540. **Prophet Jesus (AS) said,** 'He who has much anxiety, his body starts to ail.'[1748]

١٥٤٠ . عيسى (ع) : مَن كَثُرَ هَمُّهُ سَقُمَ بَدَنُه.[١٧٣٧]

1541. **Imām ʿAlī (AS) said,** 'Worry is half of old age.'[1749]

١٥٤١ . الإمامُ عليٌّ (ع) : الهَمُّ نِصفُ الهَرَمِ.[١٧٣٨]

1542. **Imām ʿAlī (AS) said,** 'Worry wastes away the body.'[1750]

١٥٤٢ . عنه (ع) : الهَمُّ يُذيبُ الجَسَدَ.[١٧٣٩]

1543. **Imām al-Ṣādiq (AS) said,** 'Sorrows are the ailments of the hearts just as illnesses are the ailments of the body.'[1751]

١٥٤٣ . الإمامُ الصّادقُ (ع) : الأحزانُ أسقامُ القُلوبِ، كما أنَّ الأمراضَ أسقامُ الأبدانِ.[١٧٤٠]

(See also: THE WORLD: section 712) (أنظر) الدنيا: باب ٧١٢.

513. The Causes of Sorrow

٥١٣ـ ما يورِثُ الحُزنَ

1544. **The Prophet (SAWA) said,** 'Whoever looks at what other people possess, his sorrow endures and his regret is continuous.'[1752]

١٥٤٤ . رسولُ اللهِ ﷺ : مَن نَظَرَ إلىٰ ما في أيْدي النّاسِ طالَ حُزنُهُ ، ودامَ أسَفُهُ .[١٧٤١]

1545. **The Prophet (SAWA) said,** 'Many a desire lasting but an hour brings about enduring sorrow.'[1753]

١٥٤٥ . عنه ﷺ : رُبَّ شَهْوةِ ساعةٍ تُورِثُ حُزناً طويلاً .[١٧٤٢]

1546. **Imām ʿAlī (AS) said,** 'He who is angry with somebody whom he cannot hurt, his sorrow endures and he inflicts pain on his own soul.'[1754]

١٥٤٦ . الإمامُ عليٌّ ؑ : مَن غَضِبَ علىٰ مَن لا يقدِرُ أنْ يَضُرَّهُ ، طالَ حُزْنُهُ وعَذّبَ نَفْسَهُ .[١٧٤٣]

1547. **Imām ʿAlī (AS) said,** 'I have not seen a wrong-doer resemble a wronged person more than the jealous one: he has an exhausted spirit, a wandering heart, and an inherent sorrow.'[1755]

١٥٤٧ . عنه ؑ : ما رأيتُ ظالِماً أشْبَهَ بمظلومٍ من الحاسِدِ ؟ نَفَسٌ دائمٌ ، وقَلبٌ هائمٌ ، وحُزنٌ لازِمٌ .[١٧٤٤]

1548. **Imām ʿAlī (AS) said,** 'He who is negligent in his work is afflicted with anxiety.'[1756]

١٥٤٨ . عنه ؑ : مَن قَصَّر في العملِ ابْتُلي بالهَمِّ .[١٧٤٥]

1549. **Imām ʿAlī (AS) said,** 'Beware of apprehension, for it kills hope, weakens action, and brings about worry.'[1757]

١٥٤٩ . عنه ؑ : إيّاكَ والجَزَعَ ؛ فإنَّهُ يَقْطَعُ الأملَ ، ويُضعِفُ العَملَ ، ويُورِثُ الهَمَّ .[١٧٤٦]

514. Overcoming Sorrow

٥١٤ـ عِلاجُ الحُزنِ

"Look! The friends of Allah will indeed have no fear nor will they grieve."[1758]

﴿أَلَا إِنَّ أَوْلِيَاءَ اللهِ لا خَوْفٌ عَلَيْهِمْ وَلا هُمْ يحزنون﴾ .[١٧٤٧]

1550. **The Prophet (SAWA) said,** 'Truly Allah, out of His wisdom and grace, placed bliss and happiness in conviction and contentment, and placed worry and sorrow in doubt and discontentment.'[1759]

١٥٥٠ . رسولُ اللهِ ﷺ : إنّ اللهَ ـ بحُكْمِهِ وفَضْلِه ـ جَعلَ الرَّوحَ والفَرحَ في اليقينِ والرِّضا ، وجَعلَ الهَمَّ والحُزنَ في الشَّكِّ والسُّخْطِ .[١٧٤٨]

1551. **The Prophet (SAWA) said,** 'O people! This is the house of pain and not the house of joy, and the house of writhing [in pain] not the house of repose. So he who knows it will neither rejoice for ease and nor will he grieve for misfortune.'[1760]

١٥٥١ . عنه ﷺ : أيُّها النّاسُ ، هٰذهِ دارُ تَرَحٍ لا دارُ فَرَحٍ ، ودارُ الْتِواءٍ لا دارُ اسْتِواءٍ ، فمَن عَرَفها لَم يَفْرَحْ لِرَجاءٍ ، ولَم يَحْزَنْ لِشَقاءٍ .[١٧٤٩]

1552. **The Prophet (SAWA) said,** 'There is remedy in the statement "There is no might or power save in Allah" (*lā ḥawla wa lā quwwata illā billāh*) for ninety-nine ailments, the least of them being anxiety.'[1761]

١٥٥٢ . عنه ﷺ : قَولُ : «لا حَولَ ولا قُوّةَ إلّا باللهِ» فيهِ شِفاءٌ مِن تِسعَةٍ وتِسْعينَ داءً ، أدْناها الهَمُّ .[١٧٥٠]

1553. **Ibn ʿAbbās narrated,** 'I have not profited by any speech after the Messenger of Allah (SAWA) more than by a letter written by ʿAlī b. Abī Ṭālib (AS). He wrote to me, saying, "But now, indeed man grieves for having missed that which he would not have attained anyway, and is overjoyed at attaining that which he would not have missed anyway. So, let your happiness be for what you attain for your Hereafter, and let your regret be for what you miss of it. Do not be happy for what you attain for this world, nor regret sorrowfully what you miss from it, and let your concern be for what comes after death, and peace be with you."'[1762]

١٥٥٣ . مطالب السؤول عن ابنِ عبّاسٍ : ما انْتَفَعْتُ بكلامٍ بَعدَ رسولِ اللهِ ﷺ كانْتِفاعي بكِتابٍ كَتَبَهُ عليُّ بنُ أبي طالبٍ عليه السلام ، فإنَّهُ كَتبَ إلَيَّ : أمّا بَعدُ فإنَّ المَرءَ يَسوؤهُ فَوتُ ما لَم يَكُن لِيُدْرِكَهُ ، ويَسُرُّهُ دَرْكُ ما لَم يَكُن لِيَفوتَهُ ، فلْيَكُنْ سُرورُكَ بما نِلْتَ مِن آخِرَتِكَ ، ولْيَكُن أسَفُكَ علىٰ ما فاتَكَ مِنها ، وما نِلْتَ مِن دُنْياكَ فلا تَكُنْ بِهِ فَرِحاً ، وما فاتَكَ مِنها فلا تَأْسَ علَيهِ حُزْناً ، ولْيَكُنْ هَمُّكَ فيما بَعدَ المَوتِ . والسَّلامُ .[١٧٥١]

1554. **Imām ʿAlī (AS) said,** 'What an excellent repellent of worries conviction is.'[1763]

١٥٥٤ . الإمامُ عليٌّ عليه السلام : نِعْمَ طارِدُ الهُمومِ اليَقينُ .[١٧٥٢]

1555. **Imām ʿAlī (AS) said,** 'Washing clothes takes away worry and sorrow.'[1764]

١٥٥٥ . عنه عليه السلام : غَسْلُ الثِّيابِ يُذهِبُ الهَمَّ والحُزنَ .[١٧٥٣]

1556. **Imām al-Ṣādiq (AS) said,** 'If everything is determined by fate and destiny, then wherefore the sorrow?!'[1765]

١٥٥٦ . الإمامُ الصّادقُ عليه السلام : إنْ كانَ كُلُّ شيءٍ بقَضاءٍ وقَدَرٍ ، فالحُزْنُ لِماذا ؟![١٧٥٤]

1557. **Imām al-Ṣādiq (AS) said,** 'One of the prophets complained of his grief to Allah. So He commanded him to eat grapes.'[1766]

١٥٥٧ . عنه عليه السلام : شَكا نَبيٌّ مِن الأنبياءِ إلىٰ اللهِ الغَمَّ ، فأمَرَهُ بأكْلِ العِنَبِ .[١٧٥٥]

1558. **Imām al-Ṣādiq (AS) said,** 'He who finds himself sorrowful for no reason should wash his head.'[1767]

١٥٥٨ . عنه عليه السلام : مَن وَجَدَ هَمّاً ولا يَدري ما هُو فلْيَغْسِلْ رأسَهُ .[١٧٥٦]

(See also: HAPPINESS: section 935)

(أنظر) السرور : باب ٩٣٥

515. The Reason for Sorrow and Joy for an Unknown Cause

٥١٥ـ عِلَّةُ الحُزنِ والفَرَحِ مِن غَيرِ سَبَبٍ عرَفُ

1559. **Abū Baṣīr narrated,** 'I once went to visit Abū 'Abdillāh [al-Ṣādiq] (AS) along with one of our companions. I said to him, 'O son of the Prophet! Could I but sacrifice myself for you. I grieve and become sorrowful without knowing the cause of that.' So Abū 'Abdillāh (AS) replied, 'Truly that sorrow and joy reaches you from us, for when sorrow or joy comes to us it comes to you too, for indeed we and you are all from the Light of Allah, Mighty and Exalted.'[1768]

١٥٥٩ . علل الشرائع عن أبي بصيرٍ: دَخَلتُ على أبي عبدِ اللهِ ﷺ ومَعي رجُلٌ مِن أصحابِنا، فقُلتُ لَهُ: جُعِلتُ فِداكَ يابنَ رسولِ اللهِ، إنّي لَأغتَمُّ وأحزَنُ مِن غَيرِ أنْ أعرِفَ لِذلكَ سَبباً، فقالَ أبو عبدِ اللهِ ﷺ: إنَّ ذلكَ الحُزنَ والفرحَ يَصِلُ إلَيكُم مِنّا؛ لأنّا إذا دَخلَ علَينا حُزنٌ أو سُرورٌ كانَ ذلكَ داخِلاً علَيكُم، لأنّا وإيّاكُم مِن نُورِ اللهِ عزّوجلّ.[١٧٥٧]

1560. It is narrated in *Biḥār al-Anwār* that the scholar [al-Ṣādiq] (AS) was once asked about why a man may wake up in the morning feeling sad without knowing the reason for his sorrow. He said, 'If that happens to him then he should know that his brother is in sorrow, and similarly if he wakes up happy without a specific reason for that joy. And Allah's help do we seek with regard to the rights of the brothers.'[1769]

١٥٦٠ . بحار الأنوار: رُوِيَ أنّه سُئلَ العالِمُ ﷺ عنِ الرّجُلِ يُصْبحُ مَغْموماً لا يَدْري سَببَ غَمِّهِ، فقالَ: إذا أصابَهُ ذلكَ فلْيَعْلَمْ أنَّ أخاهُ مَغْمومٌ، وكذلكَ إذا أصْبَحَ فَرِحاناً لِغَيرِ سَببٍ يُوجِبُ الفَرَحَ، فباللهِ نَسْتَعينُ على حُقوقِ الإخْوانِ.[١٧٥٨]

516. Praiseworthy Sorrow

٥١٦ـ الحُزنُ المَمدوحُ

1561. **The Prophet (SAWA) said,** 'Allah, Mighty and Exalted, is worshipped through nothing like continuous sorrow.'[1770]

١٥٦١ . رسولُ اللهِ ﷺ: ما عُبِدَ اللهُ عزّوجلّ على مِثلِ طُولِ الحُزنِ.[١٧٥٩]

1562. **Imām Zayn al-Ābidīn (AS) said,** 'Truly Allah loves every sorrowful heart.'[1771]

١٥٦٢ . الإمامُ زينُ العابدينَ ﷺ: إنَّ اللهَ يُحِبُّ كُلَّ قَلبٍ حَزينٍ.[١٧٦٠]

1563. **Imām al-Bāqir (AS) said,** 'I have read in 'Alī's book that the believer spends nights and days in sorrow and only this can benefit him.'[1772]

١٥٦٣ . الإمامُ الباقرُ ﷺ: قَرأتُ في كتابِ عليٍّ ﷺ: إنّ المؤمنَ يُمْسي حَزيناً ويُصبحُ حَزيناً، ولا يَصْلُحُ لَهُ إلّا ذلكَ.[١٧٦١]

1564. **Imām al-Ṣādiq (AS) said,** 'The breath of one who is saddened on our account and is grieved for the oppression done unto us is glorification, and his grief for our cause is worship.'[1773]

١٥٦٤ . الإمامُ الصّادقُ ﷺ: نَفَسُ المَهمومِ لَنا المُغتَمِّ لِظُلْمِنا تَسْبيحٌ، وهَمُّهُ لأمْرِنا عِبادَةٌ.[١٧٦٢]

(See also: WEEPING: 47; THE HEART: section 1554) (أنظر) عنوان ٤٧ «البكاء»؛ القلب: باب ١٥٥٤.

100

THE ACCOUNT

الحِسابُ

517. The Day of Account

٥١٧ـ يَومُ الحِسابِ

1565. **The Prophet (SAWA) said,** 'Truly right now you live the day of action with no accounting therein, and very soon you will live the day of accounting with no action therein.'[1774]

١٥٦٥ . رسولُ اللهِ ﷺ : ألا وإنّكم في يومِ عملٍ وَلا حِسابَ فِيهِ، ويُوشِكُ أنْ تَكونوا في يَومِ حِسابٍ لَيس فيهِ عَملٌ.[١٧٦٣]

1566. **Imām ʿAlī (AS) said,** 'Accountability [for one's actions] will come before the punishment, and the reward will come after the account.'[1775]

١٥٦٦ . الإمامُ عليٌّ ﵇ : الحِسابُ قَبلَ العِقابِ، الثَّوابُ بَعدَ الحِسابِ.[١٧٦٤]

518. Enjoinment of Accounting for One's Self

٥١٨ـ الحَثُّ عَلىٰ مُحاسَبَةِ النَّفسِ

"O you who have faith! Be wary of Allah, and let every soul consider what it sends ahead for tomorrow, and be wary of Allah. Allah is indeed well aware of what you do."[1776]

﴿يا أَيُّهَا الَّذِينَ آمَنُوا اتَّقُوا اللهَ وَلْتَنْظُرْ نَفْسٌ مَا قَدَّمَتْ لِغَدٍ وَاتَّقُوا اللهَ إِنَّ اللهَ خَبِيرٌ بِما تَعْمَلُونَ﴾.[١٧٦٥]

1567. **The Prophet (SAWA) said,** 'Take account of your selves before you are held to account, and evaluate them before you are held for evaluation, and prepare yourselves for the Greatest Exposure.'[1777]

١٥٦٧ . رسولُ اللهِ ﷺ : حاسِبوا أنْفُسَكُم قَبلَ أنْ تُحاسَبوا، وزِنوها قَبلَ أنْ تُوزَنوا، وتَجَهَّزوا للعَرْضِ الأكْبَرِ.[١٧٦٦]

1568. **Imām ʿAlī (AS) said,** 'Restrict your [lower] selves by holding them accountable and control them by opposing them.'[1778]

١٥٦٨ . الإمامُ عليٌّ ﵇ : قَيِّدوا أنْفُسَكُم بالمُحاسَبَةِ، وامْلِكوها بالمُخالَفَةِ.[١٧٦٧]

1569. **Imām Zayn al-Ābidīn (AS) said,** 'O son of Adam! You will continue to thrive as long as you are the admonisher of your self, and as long as accounting for yourself is one of your concerns.'[1779]

١٥٦٩ . الإمامُ زينُ العابدينَ ﵇ : ابنَ آدمَ، إنّكَ لا تَزالُ بخَيرٍ ما كانَ لكَ واعِظٌ مِن نَفْسِكَ، وما كانَتِ المُحاسَبَةُ مِن هَمِّكَ.[١٧٦٨]

1570. **Imām al-Kāẓim (AS) said,** 'The one who does not take account of himself every single day is not one of us. And when he performs a good deed, he should ask Allah to enable him to do more, and when he commits an evil deed, he must seek Allah's forgiveness and repent for it.'[1780]

١٥٧٠ . الإمامُ الكاظمُ ﷺ : لَيس مِنّا مَن لَم يُحاسِبْ نَفْسَهُ في كُلِّ يَومٍ ، فإنْ عَمِلَ خَيراً اسْتَزادَ اللهَ مِنهُ وحَمِدَ اللهَ علَيهِ ، وإنْ عَمِلَ شَيئاً شَرّاً اسْتَغْفَرَ اللهَ وتابَ إلَيهِ .[١٧٦٩]

519. The Fruit of Taking Account of Oneself

٥١٩ـ ثَمَرَةُ المُحاسَبَةِ

1571. **Imām ʿAlī (AS) said,** 'He who takes account of his soul will understand his defects and know his sins. He will repent for the sins and amend the defects.'[1781]

١٥٧١ . الإمامُ عليٌّ ﷺ : مَن حاسَبَ نفسَهُ وقَفَ علىٰ عُيوبِهِ ، وأحاطَ بذُنوبِهِ ، واسْتَقالَ الذُّنوبَ ، وأصْلَحَ العُيوبَ .[١٧٧٠]

1572. **Imām ʿAlī (AS) said,** 'He who takes account of his self profits, he who neglects it is at a loss, and he who fears will be safe.'[1782]

١٥٧٢ . عنه ﷺ : مَن حاسبَ نَفْسَهُ رَبِحَ ، ومَن غَفَلَ عَنها خَسِرَ ، ومَن خافَ أمِنَ .[١٧٧١]

1573. **Imām ʿAlī (AS) said,** 'He who takes account of his self prospers.'[1783]

١٥٧٣ . عنه ﷺ : مَن حاسَبَ نَفسَهُ سَعِدَ .[١٧٧٢]

520. The First Thing that Man Will be Asked About

٥٢٠ـ أوَّلُ ما يُسألُ عَنهُ المَرءُ

1574. **The Prophet (SAWA) said,** 'The first thing that man will be asked about is our love, the people of the Household (*Ahl al-Bayt*).'[1784]

١٥٧٤ . رسولُ اللهِ ﷺ : أوَّلُ ما يُسألُ عَنهُ العَبدُ حُبُّنا أهلَ البيتِ .[١٧٧٣]

1575. **Imām al-Ṣādiq (AS) said,** 'The first thing that man will be asked about when he stands before Allah, Exalted be His Grandeur, is the obligatory prayers, the obligatory alms-tax (*zakāt*), the obligatory fasting, the obligatory pilgrimage (*ḥajj*), and our guardianship (*wilāya*), the people of the Household. If he attests to our guardianship and dies believing that, his prayer, fasting, alms and pilgrimage will all be accepted.'[1785]

١٥٧٥ . الإمامُ الصّادقُ ﷺ : إنَّ أوَّلَ ما يُسألُ عنهُ العَبدُ إذا وَقفَ بينَ يَدَيِ اللهِ جلَّ جلالُهُ الصَّلَواتُ المَفْروضاتُ ، وعنِ الزَّكاةِ المَفْروضَةِ ، وعنِ الصِّيامِ المَفروضِ ، وعنِ الحَجِّ المَفْروضِ ، وعَن وَلايَتِنا أهلَ البيتِ ، فإنْ أقَرَّ بوَلايَتِنا ثُمَّ ماتَ علَيها قُبِلَتْ مِنهُ صَلاتُهُ وصَومُهُ وزَكاتُهُ وحَجُّهُ .[١٧٧٤]

521. That Which One is Not Accountable for

٥٢١ ـ ما لا يُحاسَبُ عَلَيهِ

1576. **The Prophet (SAWA) said,** 'Every bounty will be asked about on the Day of Resurrection except for what was [used] in the way of Allah, most High.'[1786]

١٥٧٦ . رسولُ اللهِ ﷺ : كُلُّ نَعيمٍ مَسؤولٌ عَنهُ يَومَ القِيامَةِ إلّا ما كانَ في سبيلِ اللهِ تعالىٰ . [١٧٧٥]

1577. **Imām ʿAlī (AS) said,** 'Whoever utters the name of Allah on some food that he eats will never be asked [to account for] the bounty of that food.'[1787]

١٥٧٧ . الإمامُ عليٌّ عليه السلام : مَن ذَكَرَ اسمَ اللهِ علىٰ الطَّعامِ لَم يُسألْ عن نَعيمِ ذلكَ الطَّعامِ أبداً . [١٧٧٦]

1578. **Imām al-Bāqir or Imām al-Ṣādiq (AS) said,** 'There are three things which the servant will not be asked about: the cloth he used to cover his private parts, the piece of bread he used to sate his hunger with, and the house that used to protect him from the heat and the cold [the dire necessities of life].'[1788]

١٥٧٨ . الإمامُ الباقرُ أو الإمامُ الصّادقُ عليهما السلام : ثلاثٌ لا يُسألُ عَنها العَبدُ : خِرقَةٌ يُواري بها عَورَتَهُ ، أو كِسْرَةٌ يَسُدُّ بها جَوعَتَهُ ، أو بَيتٌ يَكُنُّهُ مِن الحَـرِّ والبرد . [١٧٧٧]

522. That Which One Will be Held Accountable for

٥٢٢ ـ ما يُحاسَبُ عَلَيهِ

1579. **The Prophet (SAWA) said,** 'On the Day of Resurrection, the feet of the servant will not slip until he is asked about four things: his years and how he spent them, his youth and how he wasted it, his wealth, whence he earned it and how he spent it, and our love, the people of the household (*Ahl al-Bayt*).'[1789]

١٥٧٩ . رسولُ اللهِ ﷺ : لا تَزولُ قَدَما عَبدٍ يَـومَ القِيامَةِ حتّىٰ يُسألَ عَن أربَعٍ : عَن عُـمرِهِ فـيما أفْناهُ ، و(عَن) شَبابِهِ فيما أبْلاهُ ، وعَن مالِهِ مِـن أينَ اكْـتَسَبهُ وفـيما أنْـفَقَهُ ، وعَـن حُـبِّنا أهـلَ البَيتِ . [١٧٧٨]

1580. **Imām al-Ṣādiq (AS),** with regards to Allah's verse: *"You will surely be asked on that day concerning the blessing"*, said, 'This community will be asked about the bounty that Allah bestowed on them in the form of the Messenger of Allah (SAWA), and then in his Household (AS).'[1790]

١٥٨٠ . الإمامُ الصّادقُ عليه السلام ـ في قـولِهِ تـعالىٰ : ﴿لَتُسْألُنَّ يَومَئذٍ عَنِ النَّعيمِ﴾ ـ : تُسألُ هٰذهِ الأُمَّةُ عَمّا أنْعَمَ اللهُ عـلَيهِم بـرسولِ اللهِ ﷺ ثُـمَّ بأهْـلِ بَيتِهِ عليهم السلام . [١٧٧٩]

(See also: THE GRAVE: section 1506)

(أُنظر) القبر : باب ١٥٠٦ .

523. That Which Will Make the Account Easier on the Day of Resurrection

٥٢٣ـ ما يُهَوِّنُ حِسابَ يَومِ القِيامَةِ

1581. **The Prophet (SAWA) said,** 'Be content with what you have been given and your account will be lighter.'[1791]

١٥٨١ . رسولُ اللهِ ﷺ : اقْنَعْ بِما أُوتيتَهُ يَخِفَّ علَيكَ الحِسابُ.[١٧٨٠]

1582. **The Prophet (SAWA) said,** 'Improve your temperament, and Allah will lighten your account.'[1792]

١٥٨٢ . عنه ﷺ : حَسِّنْ خُلقَكَ يُخَفِّفِ اللهُ حِسابَكَ.[١٧٨١]

1583. **Imām al-Ṣādiq (AS) said,** 'Maintaining relations with one's kin makes the account easier on the Day of Resurrection. Then he recited [the verse]: *"And those who join what Allah has commanded to be joined, and fear their Lord, and are afraid of an adverse reckoning."*'[1793]

١٥٨٣ . الإمامُ الصّادقُ ؑ : إنَّ صِلَةَ الرَّحِمِ تُهَوِّنُ الحِسابَ يَومَ القِيامَةِ ، ثُمّ قَرأَ : ﴿(الّذينَ) يَصِلونَ ما أمَرَ اللهُ بِهِ أنْ يُوصَلَ ويَخْشَونَ رَبَّهُم ويَخافُونَ سُوءَ الحِسابِ﴾.[١٧٨٢]

524. The Categories of People During the Account

٥٢٤ـ أصنافُ النّاسِ فِي الحِسابِ

1584. **Imām ʿAlī (AS) said,** 'The people on that day will be of different classes and stations. Some of them will be given an easy account and return to their people happy. Some of them will enter Paradise without giving an account, for they had nothing to do with matters of the worldly life, for indeed the account there is for those who entangle themselves with them [i.e. worldly affairs] here. And some of them will be asked to account for every speck and spot and will be made to suffer the punishment of the Blaze.'[1794]

١٥٨٤ . الإمامُ عليٌّ ؑ : والنّاسُ يَومَئذٍ علىٰ طَبَقاتٍ ومَنازِلَ، فمِنهُم مَن يُحاسَبُ حِساباً يَسيراً ويَنْقَلِبُ إلىٰ أهْلِهِ مَسْروراً ، ومِنهُمُ الّذينَ يَدخُلونَ الجَنّةَ بغَيرِ حِسابٍ ؛ لأنَّهُم لَم يَتَلَبّسوا مِن أمْرِ الدُّنيا بشَيءٍ ، وإنّما الحِسابُ هُناكَ علىٰ مَن تَلَبَّسَ بها هٰاهُنا ، ومِنهُم مَن يُحاسَبُ علىٰ النَّقيرِ والقِطْميرِ ويَصيرُ إلىٰ عَذابِ السَّعيرِ.[١٧٨٣]

525. The Adverse Account

٥٢٥ـ سوءُ الحِسابِ

1585. **Imām al-Ṣādiq (AS),** with regards to Allah's verse: *"and they are afraid of an adverse reckoning"*[1795], said, 'Their bad deeds will be counted against them and their good deeds will be counted for them, and that is the strict reckoning.'[1796]

١٥٨٥ . الإمامُ الصّادقُ ؑ ـ في قولِهِ تعالىٰ: ﴿ويَخافُونَ سُوءَ الحِسابِ﴾ ـ: يُحْسَبُ علَيهِمُ السّيِّئاتُ ويُحْسَبُ لَهُمُ الحَسَناتُ، وهُو الاسْتِقْصاءُ.[١٧٨٤]

526. Those Whose Account Will be Easy

٥٢٦ ـ مَن يُحاسَبُ حِساباً يَسيراً

"Then as for him who is given his record in his right hand, he shall soon receive an easy reckoning."[1797]

﴿فَأَمّا مَنْ أُوتِيَ كِتابَهُ بِيَمِينِهِ * فَسَوْفَ يُحاسَبُ حِساباً يَسِيراً﴾ .١٧٨٥

1586. **Imām al-Bāqir (AS) narrated,** 'The Prophet (SAWA) said, 'Every person who stands to give account will suffer chastisement.' Then someone asked him, 'O Messenger of Allah! What about Allah's verse: *"he shall soon receive an easy reckoning"*?' He replied, 'That is the exposition, meaning the display of the pages [of one's book of deeds].'[1798]

١٥٨٦ . الإمامُ الباقرُ عليه السلام : قالَ رسولُ اللهِ ﷺ : كُلُّ مُحاسَبٍ مُعذَّبٌ ، فقالَ لَهُ قائلٌ يا رسولَ اللهِ ، فأينَ قولُ اللهِ عزّوجلّ : ﴿فَسَوْفَ يُحاسَبُ حِساباً يَسيراً﴾ ؟ قالَ : ذلكَ العَرْضُ ، يَعني التَّصَفُّحَ .١٧٨٦

(See also: RESURRECTION: section 1395)

(أُنظر) المَعاد : باب ١٣٩٥.

527. Those Who Will Enter Paradise Without Accounting

٥٢٧ ـ مَن يَدخُلُ الجَنّةَ بِغَيرِ حِسابٍ

"Say, 'O My servants who have faith! Be wary of your Lord. For those who do good in this world there will be a good [reward], and Allah's earth is vast. Indeed the patient will be paid in full their reward without any reckoning."[1799]

﴿قُلْ يا عِبادِ الَّذِينَ آمَنُوا اتَّقُوا رَبَّكُم لِلَّذِينَ أَحْسَنُوا في هٰذِهِ الدُّنْيا حَسَنَةٌ وَأَرْضُ اللهِ واسِعَةٌ إنَّما يُوَفَّى الصّابِرُونَ أَجْرَهُمْ بِغَيْرِ حِسابٍ﴾ .١٧٨٧

1587. **The Prophet (SAWA) said,** 'Allah, most High, will say: "O My servants who have fought for My sake, were killed and hurt for My sake, and have struggled for My sake! Enter Paradise!" And they will enter it without punishment or account.'[1800]

١٥٨٧ . رسولُ اللهِ ﷺ : يَقولُ اللهُ تعالى : أيْ عِباديَ الّذينَ قاتَلوا في سَبيلي ، وقُتِلوا وأُوذوا في سَبيلي ، وجاهَدوا في سَبيلي ، ادْخُلوا الجَنّةَ ، فيَدخُلونَها بغَيرِ عَذابٍ ولا حِسابٍ .١٧٨٨

1588. **Imām Zayn al-Ābidīn (AS) said,** 'When Allah will bring together the first and the last of people a caller will call out: 'Where are the patient ones that they may all enter Paradise without account?' … The Imām then continued, 'The angels will ask them, 'Who are you?' and they will answer, 'The patient ones.' Again they will ask, 'And what were you patient with?' They will say, 'We were patient with acts of obedience to Allah, and we were patient in keeping away from acts of disobedience to Allah.'[1801]

١٥٨٨ . الإمامُ زينُ العابدينَ عليه السلام : إذا جَمَعَ اللهُ الأوّلينَ والآخِرينَ يُنادي مُنادٍ : أينَ الصّابِرونَ لِيَدْخُلوا الجَنّةَ جَميعاً بغَيرِ حِسابٍ ... : قالَتِ المَلائكةُ لَهُم : ـ مَن أنتُم ؟ قالوا : الصّابرونَ . قالوا : وما كانَ صَبْرُكُم ؟ قالوا : صَبَرْنا على طاعَةِ اللهِ ، وصَبَرْنا عَن مَعصيَةِ اللهِ .١٧٨٩

1589. **Imām Zayn al-Ābidīn (AS) said,** 'When Allah, Mighty and Exalted, will bring together the first and the last of people, a caller will rise and call out so that all people will hear. He will say, 'Where are those who loved each other for Allah' sake?' and a group of people will rise, and they will be told to enter Paradise without accounting.'[1802]

١٥٨٩ . عنه ﷺ : إذا جَمعَ اللهُ عزّوجلّ الأوَّلينَ والآخِرينَ ، قامَ مُنادٍ فنادىٰ يُسمِعُ النّاسَ فيقولُ : أينَ المُتَحابّونَ في اللهِ ؟ قالَ : فيَقومُ عُنُقٌ مِن النّاسِ فيُقالُ لَهُم : اذْهَبوا إلىٰ الجَنّةِ بغَيرِ حِسابٍ .١٧٩٠

1590. **Imām al-Ṣādiq (AS) said,** 'On the Day of Resurrection a group of people will rise; they will come to the gate of Paradise and they will knock at the gate of Paradise. Then they will be asked, 'Who are you?' And they will answer, 'We are the poor.' They will then be asked, '[Have you come] before the Reckoning?!' And they will answer, 'You did not give us anything to hold us accountable for!' Allah, Mighty and Exalted will then say, 'They speak the truth. Enter Paradise!'[1803]

١٥٩٠ . الإمامُ الصّادقُ ﷺ : إذا كانَ يَومُ القِيامَةِ قامَ عُنُقٌ مِن النّاسِ حتّىٰ يَأتوا بابَ الجَنّةِ فيَضْرِبوا بابَ الجَنّةِ ، فيُقالُ لَهُم : مَن أنتُم ؟ فيقولونَ : نحنُ الفُقَراءُ ، فيقالُ لَهُم : أقَبْلَ الحِسابِ؟! فيقولونَ : ما أعْطَيْتُمونا شَيئاً تُحاسِبونا علَيهِ ! فيقولُ اللهُ عزّوجلّ : صَدَقوا ، ادْخُلوا الجَنّةَ .١٧٩١

1591. **Imām al-Ṣādiq (AS) narrated,** 'The Prophet (SAWA) said, 'When the records are spread out and the scales set up, there will be no scales set up for the people of affliction, nor record spread for them.' Then he recited this verse: *"Indeed the patient will be paid in full their reward without any reckoning…"*[1804]

١٥٩١ . عنه ﷺ : قالَ رسولُ اللهِ ﷺ : إذا نُشِرَتِ الدَّواوينُ ونُصِبَتِ المَوازينُ لم يُنْصَبْ لأهلِ البَلاءِ مِيزانٌ ، ولَم يُنْشَرْ لَهُم دِيوانٌ ، وتلا هٰذِه الآيةَ : ﴿... إنَّما يُوَفّىٰ الصّابِرونَ أجْرَهُمْ بِغَيْرِ حِسَابٍ﴾ .١٧٩٢

528. Those Who Will Enter the Fire Without Accounting

٥٢٨ ـ مَن يَدخُلُ النّارَ بِغَيرِ حِسابٍ

1592. **The Prophet (SAWA) said,** 'Truly Allah, Mighty and Exalted, will hold all the creatures to account except those who have associated a partner to Allah, for they will not be given the chance to account on the Day of Resurrection and will be ordered straight to the Fire.'[1805]

١٥٩٢ . رسولُ اللهِ ﷺ : إنّ اللهَ عزّوجلّ يُحاسِبُ كُلَّ خَلقٍ إلّا مَن أشْرَكَ باللهِ ، فإنَّهُ لا يُحاسَبُ يَومَ القِيامَةِ ويُؤْمَرُ بهِ إلىٰ النّارِ .١٧٩٣

1593. **The Prophet (SAWA) said,** 'Six [groups] will enter the Fire before any account because of six [reasons].' He was asked, 'O Messenger of Allah! May Allah's blessings be upon you! Who are they?' He replied, 'The rulers because of their

١٥٩٣ . تنبيه الخواطر عن رسول الله ﷺ : سِتّةٌ يَدخُلونَ النّارَ قَبلَ الحِسابِ بسِتَّةٍ . قيلَ : يا رسولَ اللهِ صلّىٰ اللهُ علَيكَ ، مَن هُم ؟ قالَ : الأُمَراءُ

tyranny, the Arabs because of their prejudice, the landowners because of their arrogance, the merchants because of their treachery, the villagers because of their ignorance, and the scholars because of their jealousy.'[1806]

بالجَورِ ، والعَرَبُ بالعَصَبيَّةِ ، والدَّهاقينُ بالكِبْرِ ، والتُّجّارُ بالخِيانَةِ ، وأهلُ الرُّستاقِ بالجَهالَةِ ، والعُلَماءُ بالحَسدِ.[١٧٩٤]

1594. **Imām al-Ṣādiq (AS) said,** 'Allah will make three [groups] enter the Fire without any account… an unjust leader, a lying merchant, and an adulterous old man.'[1807]

١٥٩٤ . الإمامُ الصّادقُ (ع) : ثَلاثةٌ يُدْخِلُهُمُ اللهُ النّارَ بغَيرِ حِسابٍ ... إمامٌ جائرٌ، وتاجرٌ كَذوبٌ، وشَيخٌ زانٍ.[١٧٩٥]

101

JEALOUSY

الحَسَدُ

529. The Harms of Jealousy

٥٢٩ ـ مَضارُّ الحَسَدِ

"And from the evil of the jealous one when he is jealous."[1808]

﴿وَمِنْ شَرِّ حَاسِدٍ إِذَا حَسَدَ﴾.[١٧٩٦]

1595. **The Prophet (SAWA) said,** 'Allah, Mighty and Exalted, said to Moses son of Amran[1809] (AS), 'Verily the jealous is discontented with My bounties, and wards off the shares I have apportioned to My servants.'[1810]

١٥٩٥ . رسولُ اللهِ (ص) : قالَ اللهُ عزّوجلّ لموسىٰ بنِ عِمرانَ : إنَّ الحاسِدَ ساخِطٌ لِنِعَمي، صادٌّ لِقِسْمي الّذي قَسَمْتُ بينَ عِبادي.[١٧٩٧]

1596. **Imām ʿAlī (AS) said,** 'Jealousy is the spirit's imprisonment.'[1811]

١٥٩٦ . الإمامُ عليٌّ (ع) : الحَسدُ حَبْسُ الرُّوحِ.[١٧٩٨]

1597. **Imām ʿAlī (AS) said,** 'Jealousy is the worst disease.'[1812]

١٥٩٧ . عنه (ع) : الحَسدُ شَرُّ الأمْراضِ.[١٧٩٩]

1598. **Imām ʿAlī (AS) said,** 'The chief of vices is jealousy.'[1813]

١٥٩٨ . عنه (ع) : رأسُ الرَّذائلِ الحَسدُ.[١٨٠٠]

1599. **Imām ʿAlī (AS) said,** 'How capable jealousy is! And how just it is, that it starts off with its perpetrator and ends up killing him!'[1814]

١٥٩٩ . عنه (ع) : للهِ دَرُّ الحَسدِ ما أعْدَلَهُ ! بَدأ بصاحِبِهِ فقتلَهُ.[١٨٠١]

1600. **Imām ʿAlī (AS) said,** 'The fruit of jealousy is the misery of this world and the Hereafter.'[1815]

١٦٠٠ . عنه (ع) : ثَمرَةُ الحَسدِ شَقاءُ الدُّنيا والآخِرَةِ.[١٨٠٢]

1601. **Imām ʿAlī (AS) said,** 'The jealous one sees a loss for the one he is jealous of as a gain for himself.'[1816]

١٦٠١. عنه (ع): الحاسِدُ يَرىٰ أنَّ زَوالَ النِّعمَةِ عَمَّن يَحسُدُهُ نِعمَةٌ علَيهِ.[١٨٠٣]

1602. **Imām ʿAlī (AS) said,** 'I have not seen a wrong-doer resemble a wronged person more than the jealous one: he has an exhausted spirit, a wandering heart, and an inherent sorrow.'[1817]

١٦٠٢. عنه (ع): ما رَأيتُ ظالِماً أشبَهَ بمَظلومٍ مِن الحاسِدِ: نَفَسٌ دائمٌ، وقَلبٌ هائمٌ، وحُزنٌ لازِمٌ.[١٨٠٤]

1603. **Imām ʿAlī (AS) said,** 'That which he suffers is [torment] enough for the jealous one.'[1818]

١٦٠٣. عنه (ع): حَسْبُ الحاسِدِ ما يَلْقىٰ.[١٨٠٥]

1604. **Imām ʿAlī (AS) said,** 'The jealous one has many regrets, and his vices are manifold.'[1819]

١٦٠٤. عنه (ع): الحَسودُ كثيرُ الحَسَراتِ، مُتضاعَفُ السَّيِّئاتِ.[١٨٠٦]

1605. **Imām ʿAlī (AS) said,** 'The jealous one can never rule.'[1820]

١٦٠٥. عنه (ع): الحَسودُ لا يَسودُ.[١٨٠٧]

530. Every Prosperous Person is Envied

٥٣٠ـ كُلُّ ذي نِعمَةٍ مَحسودٌ

1606. **The Prophet (SAWA) said,** 'Seek the assistance of secrecy in fulfilling your needs, for every prosperous person is envied.'[1821]

١٦٠٦. رسولُ اللهِ (ص): استَعينوا علىٰ قَضاءِ حَوائجِكُم بالكِتْمانِ، فإنَّ كُلَّ ذي نِعمَةٍ مَحسودٌ.[١٨٠٨]

531. Jealousy and Faith

٥٣١ـ الحسدُ والإيمانُ

1607. **Imām al-Bāqir (AS) said,** 'Jealousy consumes faith like fire consumes dry wood.'[1822]

١٦٠٧. الإمامُ الباقرُ (ع): إنَّ الحَسَدَ لَيأكُلُ الإيمانَ كما تَأكُلُ النّارُ الحَطَبَ.[١٨٠٩]

1608. **Imām al-Ṣādiq (AS) said,** 'Beware of being jealous of one another, for the origin of disbelief is jealousy.'[1823]

١٦٠٨. الإمامُ الصّادقُ (ع): إيّاكُم أنْ يَحسُدَ بَعضُكُم بَعضاً؛ فإنَّ الكُفرَ أصلُهُ الحَسدُ.[١٨١٠]

532. The Signs of the Jealous Person

٥٣٢ـ عَلامَةُ الحاسِدِ

1609. **Imām al-Ṣādiq (AS) said,** 'Luqmān told his son, 'There are three signs of the jealous person: he backbites someone in his absence, flatters him in his presence, and rejoices at the misery of others.'[1824]

١٦٠٩. الإمامُ الصّادقُ (ع): قالَ لُقمانُ لابنِهِ: للحاسِدِ ثَلاثُ عَلاماتٍ: يَغتابُ إذا غابَ، ويَتَملَّقُ إذا شَهِدَ، ويَشْمَتُ بالمُصيبَةِ.[١٨١١]

102

REGRET

الحَسرَة

533. The Person with the Greatest Regret

٥٣٣ ـ أعظَمُ النّاسِ حَسرَةً

"Warn them of the Day of Regret, when the matter will be decided, while they are [yet] heedless and do not have faith."[1825]

﴿وَأَنْذِرْهُمْ يَوْمَ الْحَسْرَةِ إِذْ قُضِيَ الْأَمْرُ وَهُمْ فِي غَفْلَةٍ وَهُمْ لا يُؤْمِنُونَ﴾.[١٨١٢]

"Lest anyone should say, 'Alas for my negligence in the vicinage of Allah! Indeed I was among those who ridiculed.'"[1826]

﴿أَنْ تَقُولَ نَفْسٌ يَا حَسْرَتَىٰ عَلَىٰ ما فَرَّطْتُ فِي جَنْبِ اللهِ وَإِنْ كُنْتُ لَمِنَ السّاخِرِينَ﴾.[١٨١٣]

"A day when the wrongdoer will bite his hands, saying 'I wish I had followed the Apostle's way.'"[1827]

﴿وَيَوْمَ يَعَضُّ الظّالِمُ عَلَى يَدَيْهِ يَقُولُ يا لَيْتَنِي اتَّخَذْتُ مَعَ الرَّسُولِ سَبِيلاً﴾.[١٨١٤]

1610. **The Prophet (SAWA) said,** 'The person with the most intense remorse on the Day of Resurrection will be the man who sold his Hereafter for the world of others.'[1828]

١٦١٠ . رسولُ اللهِ ﷺ : إنَّ أشَدَّ النّاسِ نَدامَةً يَومَ القِيامَةِ ، رجُلٌ باعَ آخِرَتَهُ بدُنيا غَيرِهِ.[١٨١٥]

1611. **Imām ʿAlī (AS) said,** 'The greatest of regrets on the Day of Resurrection will be the regret of a man who gained wealth through means of disobedience Allah, which was then inherited by a man who spent it in the obedience of Allah, glory be to Him; thus because of it [i.e. the same wealth] the latter entered Paradise whereas the former entered the Fire.'[1829]

١٦١١ . الإمامُ عليٌّ عليه السلام : إنَّ أعْظَمَ الحَسَراتِ يَومَ القِيامَةِ ، حَسْرَةُ رجُلٍ كَسَبَ مالاً في غيرِ طاعَةِ اللهِ ، فوَرِثَهُ رجُلٌ فأنْفَقَهُ في طاعةِ اللهِ سُبحانَهُ ، فدَخَلَ بهِ الجَنّةَ ، ودَخلَ الأوّلُ بهِ النّارَ.[١٨١٦]

1612. **Imām al-Ṣādiq (AS) said,** 'The most regretful person on the Day of Resurrection will be the man who speaks of justice yet acts in opposition to it with others.'[1830]

١٦١٢ . الإمامُ الصّادقُ عليه السلام : إنّ أعظَمَ النّاسِ يَومَ القِيامَةِ (حَسْرَةً) مَن وَصفَ عَدْلاً ثُمَّ خالَفَهُ إلى غَيرِهِ.[١٨١٧]

103

THE GOOD DEEDS

الحَسَنَة

534. The Blessings of Good Deeds

٥٣٤ـ بَرَكاتُ الحَسَنَةِ

1613. **The Prophet (SAWA) said,** 'I have found the good deed to be a light in the heart, an adornment on the face, and strength in action, but I have found the sin to be blackness in the heart, weakness in action, and a blemish on the face.'[1831]

١٦١٣ . رسولُ اللهِ ﷺ : وَجَدْتُ الحَسَنةَ نُوراً في القَلبِ، وزَيْناً في الوَجْهِ، وقُوّةً في العَملِ، ووَجَدتُ الخَطيئةَ سَواداً في القَلبِ، ووَهْناً في العَملِ، وشَيْناً في الوَجْهِ.[١٨١٨]

(See also: THE LIGHT 385)

(اُنظر) عنوان ٣٨٥ «النّور».

535. Multiple Requital of Good Deeds

٥٣٥ـ تَضاعُفُ الحَسَناتِ

"Whoever brings virtue shall receive ten times its likes; but whoever brings vice shall not be requited except with its like, and they will not be wronged."[1832]

﴿مَنْ جَاءَ بِالْحَسَنَةِ فَلَهُ عَشْرُ أَمْثَالِهَا وَمَنْ جَاءَ بِالسَّيِّئَةِ فَلَا يُجْزَىٰ إِلَّا مِثْلَهَا وَهُمْ لَا يُظْلَمُونَ﴾.[١٨١٩]

(See also: Qur'an: 10:26-27, 28:84, 42:23)

1614. **Imām Zayn al-Ābidīn (AS) said,** 'Woe unto him whose ones exceed his tens' - by this he meant that the bad deed is counted one, but the good deeds are counted as ten.[1833]

١٦١٤ . تحف العقول : قالَ الإمامُ زينُ العابدينَ ﷺ: يا سَوْأَتاهْ لِمَن غَلَبَتْ إحْداتُهُ عَشَراتِهِ ـ يُريدُ أنَّ السَّيّئةَ بِواحِدَةٍ والحَسَنةَ بعَشَرَةٍ ـ.[١٨٢٠]

1615. **Imām al-Ṣādiq (AS) said,** 'When the believer excels in his good deed, Allah will enhance each one of his good deeds to equal seven hundred, for Allah, Blessed and most High, says: *"Allah enhances severalfold whomever He wishes."*[1834 1835]

١٦١٥ . الإمامُ الصّادقُ ﷺ : إذا أحْسَنَ المُؤمنُ عمَلَهُ، ضاعَفَ اللهُ عَمَلَهُ لكُلِّ حَسَنةٍ سَبعَمائةٍ، وذلكَ قولُ اللهِ تَبارَكَ وتَعالىٰ: ﴿واللهُ يُضاعِفُ لِمَنْ يَشاءُ﴾.[١٨٢١، ١٨٢٢]

104

GOOD-DOING

الإحْسان

536. The Meaning of Good-Doing

٥٣٦ـ تَفسيرُ الإحسانِ

1616. It is narrated in *Nūr al-Thaqalayn* with regard to Allah's verse: *"Certainly whoever submits*

١٦١٦ . تفسير نور الثقلين : في قولِهِ تعالىٰ: ﴿ومن أحسن ديناً مِمّن أسْلَمَ وَجْهَهُ للهِ وهو

his will to Allah and is a good-doer..."[1836]: It is reported that the Prophet (SAWA) was asked about good-doing, to which he replied, 'It is to worship Allah as if you see Him; for verily even if you do not see Him, indeed He sees you.'[1837]

مُحْسِنٌ﴾١٨٢٣: رُوِيَ أنَّ النَّبيَّ ﷺ سُئلَ عنِ الإحْسانِ، فقالَ: أنْ تَعبُدَ اللهَ كأنَّكَ تَراهُ، فإنْ لَم تَكُن تَراهُ فإنَّهُ يَراكَ.١٨٢٤

537. He Who does Good Benefits his Own Soul

٥٣٧ـ مَن أحسَنَ أحسَنَ لِنَفسِهِ

"If you do good, you will do good to your [own] souls, and if you do evil, it will be [evil] for them."[1838]

﴿إِنْ أَحْسَنْتُمْ أَحْسَنْتُمْ لِأَنْفُسِكُمْ وَإِنْ أَسَأْتُمْ فَلَها﴾١٨٢٥.

1617. **Imām ʿAlī (AS) said,** 'Truly if you do good, then it is your own soul that you honour and do good to, but if you do wrong, it is your own soul that you degrade and wrong.'[1839]

١٦١٧. الإمامُ عليٌّ ﷺ: إنّكَ إنْ أحسَنْتَ فنفسَكَ تُكرِمُ، وإلَيها تُحْسِنُ، إنّكَ إنْ أسأتَ فنفسَكَ تَمْتَهِنُ، وإيّاها تَغْبِنُ.١٨٢٦

(See also: KINDNESS: section 1599)

(انظر) الكرم: باب ١٥٩٩.

538. The Virtue of Good-Doing

٥٣٨ـ فَضلُ الإحسان

"Indeed Allah enjoins justice and kindness and generosity towards relatives, and He forbids indecency, wrong, and aggression. He advices you, so that you may take admonition."[1840]

﴿إِنَّ اللهَ يَأْمُرُ بِالْعَدْلِ وَالْإِحْسانِ وَإِيتاءِ ذِي الْقُرْبىٰ وَيَنْهىٰ عَنِ الْفَحْشاءِ وَالْمُنْكَرِ وَالْبَغْيِ يَعِظُكُمْ لَعَلَّكُمْ تَذَكَّرُونَ﴾١٨٢٧.

1618. **The Prophet (SAWA) said,** 'The hearts have been predisposed to love those who do good to them, and to dislike those who do bad to them.'[1841]

١٦١٨. رسولُ اللهِ ﷺ: جُبِلَتِ القُلوبُ على حُبِّ مَن أحسَنَ إلَيها، وبُغضِ مَن أساءَ إلَيها.١٨٢٨

1619. **Imām ʿAlī (AS) said,** 'Good-doing is incumbent upon you, for it is the best cultivation and the most profitable commodity.'[1842]

١٦١٩. الإمامُ عليٌّ ﷺ: علَيكَ بالإحْسانِ، فإنَّهُ أفْضَلُ زِراعَةٍ، وأرْبَحُ بِضاعَةٍ.١٨٢٩

1620. **Imām ʿAlī (AS) said,** 'What a good provision for the Resurrection good-doing towards people is.'[1843]

١٦٢٠. عنه ﷺ: نِعْمَ زادُ المَعادِ الإحْسانُ إلى العِبادِ.١٨٣٠

1621. **Imām ʿAlī (AS) said,** 'Good-doing is the tithe (*zakāt*) of victory.'[1844]

١٦٢١. عنه ﷺ: زَكاةُ الظَّفَرِ الإحْسانُ.١٨٣١

1622. **Imām ʿAlī (AS) said,** 'He whose good-doing is much his brethren will love him.'[1845]

١٦٢٢ . عنه ﷺ: مَن كَثُرَ إحسانُهُ أحَبَّهُ إخوانُهُ.١٨٣٢

1623. **Imām ʿAlī (AS) said,** 'Hearts are won over through good-doing.'[1846]

١٦٢٣ . عنه ﷺ : بالإحْسانِ تُملَكُ القُلوبُ.١٨٣٣

539. Good-Doing to the Wrongdoer

٥٣٩ـ الإحسانُ إلىٰ مَن أساءَ

1624. **The Prophet (SAWA) said,** 'Do good unto the one who has wronged you.'[1847]

١٦٢٤ . رسولُ اللهِ ﷺ : أحْسِنْ إلىٰ مَن أساءَ إلَيكَ.١٨٣٤

1625. **Imām ʿAlī (AS) said,** 'Indeed your good-doing to the enemies and the jealous ones who scheme against you is more irritating to them than your taking an offensive stance against them, and it is also a motivation for their reform.'[1848]

١٦٢٥ . الإمامُ عليٌّ ﷺ : إنَّ إحْسانَكَ إلىٰ مَن كادَكَ مِن الأضْدادِ والحُسّادِ، لأغْيَظُ علَيهِم مِن مَواقِعِ إساءتِكَ منهُم، وهُو داعٍ إلىٰ صَلاحِهِم.١٨٣٥

(See also: FAIRNESS: section 1728; CONSANGUINAL RELATIONS: section 813)

(أنظر) الإنصاف: باب ١٧٢٨؛ الرحم: باب ٨١٣.

540. The Consequence of the Polytheists' Acts of Good

٥٤٠ـ ما يَتَرتَّبُ علىٰ إحسانِ المُشرِكينَ

1626. **Salmān b. ʿĀmir al-Ḍabbī narrated:** I asked, 'O Messenger of Allah! My father was hospitable to guests, honoured the neighbours, fulfilled his promises, and donated in misfortunes. Of what use will that be to him?' He asked, 'Did your father die a polytheist?' I said, 'Yes!' He said, 'Truly they will be of no use to him, but they will remain for his children, in that they will never be disgraced or humiliated, nor suffer poverty.'[1849]

١٦٢٦ . كنز العمّال عن سلمانِ بنِ عامرٍ الضَّبِّيِّ: قلتُ: يا رسولَ اللهِ، إنَّ أبي كانَ يَقْري الضَّيفَ، ويُكْرِمُ الجارَ، ويَفي بالذِّمَّةِ، ويُعْطي في النّائبَةِ، فما يَنْفَعُهُ ذلكَ؟ قالَ: ماتَ مُشْرِكاً؟ قلتُ: نَعَم. قالَ: أما إنّها لا تَنْفَعُهُ، ولكنّها تَكونُ في عَقِبِهِ أنَّهُم لَن يُخزَوا أبداً، ولَن يُذَلّوا أبداً، ولَن يَفْتَقِروا أبداً.١٨٣٦

105

MEMORIZING

الحِفظ ٢٧٢

541. The Blessing of Memorizing

٥٤١ـ نِعمَةُ الحِفظِ

1627. **Imām al-Ṣādiq (AS),** in a tradition related by al-Mufaḍḍal, said, 'Have you ever thought what

١٦٢٧ . الإمامُ الصّادقُ ﷺ ـ في حديثِ المفضَّلِ ـ:

man's state would have been if from among all of his traits he missed the faculty of memory, and how many problems he would have suffered in his affairs, his livelihood and his experiences if he did not remember what was to his benefit and what was to his detriment, what he had taken and what he had given, and what he had seen and what he had heard? … He would not have learned the way even if he had traversed the same path countless times, or retained a science even if he had kept learning it all his life, or professed a religion, or benefited by an experience, or been able to take a lesson from anything that had happened. Truly he would have lost the very basis of his humanity.'[1850]

أفَرأيتَ لَو نُقِصَ الإنسانُ مِن هذهِ الخِلالِ الحِفْظَ وَحدَهُ كيفَ كانَتْ تكونُ حالُهُ ؟! وكَم مِن خَلَلٍ كانَ يَدخُلُ علَيهِ في أُمورِهِ ومَعاشِهِ وتَجارِبِهِ إذا لَم يَحْفَظْ ما لَهُ وعَلَيهِ، وما أخَذَهُ وما أعطىٰ، وما رأىٰ وما سَمِعَ ...ثُمَّ كانَ لا يَهتدي لطَريقٍ لو سَلَكَهُ ما لا يحصىٰ، ولا يَحفَظُ عِلْماً ولو دَرَسَهُ عُمْرَهُ، ولا يَعْتَقِدُ ديناً، ولا يَنتَفِعُ بتَجرِبَةٍ، ولا يَسْتَطيعُ أن يَعْتَبِرِ شيئاً علىٰ ما مضىٰ، بَل كانَ حَقيقاً أنْ يَنْسَلِخَ مِن الإنسانيّةِ أصْلاً.١٨٣٧

542. Memorization in Childhood

٥٤٢ـ الحِفظُ فِي الصِّغَرِ

1628. **The Prophet (SAWA) said,** 'The similitude of one who learns in his childhood is like carving on stone, whereas the similitude of one who learns in old age is like writing on water.'[1851]

١٦٢٨ . رسولُ اللهِ ﷺ : مَثَلُ الّذي يَتَعلّمُ في صِغَرِهِ كالنَّقشِ في الحَجَرِ ، ومَثَلُ الّذي يَتَعلّمُ في كِبَرِهِ كالّذي يَكتُبُ علَى الماءِ.١٨٣٨

543. That Which Increases One's Capacity to Memorize

٥٤٣ـ ما يَزيدُ فِي الحِفظِ

1629. **The Prophet (SAWA) said,** 'Three things eliminate forgetfulness and incite remembrance: recitation of the Qur'an, brushing the teeth, and fasting.'[1852]

١٦٢٩ . رسولُ اللهِ ﷺ : ثلاثةٌ يُذهِبنَ النِّسيانَ ويُحدِثنَ الذِّكرَ : قِراءةُ القُرآنِ ، والسِّواكُ ، والصِّيامُ.١٨٣٩

106

RESENTMENT

الحِقدُ

544. Denouncing Resentment

٥٤٤ـ ذَمُّ الحِقدِ

1630. **Imām ʿAlī (AS) said,** 'Resentment is the basest of defects.'[1853]

١٦٣٠ . الإمامُ عليٌّ ﷺ : الحِقدُ ألأمُ العُيوبِ.١٨٤٠

1631. **Imām ʿAlī (AS) said,** 'Resentment is the instigator of anger.'[1854]

١٦٣١ . عنه ﷺ : الحِقدُ مَثارُ الغَضَبِ.١٨٤١

1632. **Imām ʿAlī (AS) said,** 'Resentment is the distinguishing characteristic of the jealous.'[1855]

١٦٣٢ . عنه ﷺ : الحِقدُ شِيمَةُ الحَسَدةِ.[١٨٤٢]

1633. **Imām ʿAlī (AS) said,** 'Resentment is a fire that is only extinguished by triumph [over one's opponent].'[1856]

١٦٣٣ . عنه ﷺ :الحِقدُ نارٌ لا تُطْفَأُ إلّا بالظَّفَرِ.[١٨٤٣]

1634. **Imām ʿAlī (AS) said,** 'Resentment is the cause of problems.'[1857]

١٦٣٤ . عنه ﷺ : سَبَبُ الفِتَنِ الحِقْدُ.[١٨٤٤]

1635. **Imām ʿAlī (AS) said,** 'The resentful person has a tormented soul and his anxiety is manifold.'[1858]

١٦٣٥ . عنه ﷺ : الحَقودُ مُعذَّبُ النّفسِ، مُتَضاعَفُ الهَمِّ.[١٨٤٥]

1636. **Imām ʿAlī (AS) said,** 'The resentful person knows no friendship.'[1859]

١٦٣٦ . عنه ﷺ : لا مَودَّةَ لِحَقودٍ.[١٨٤٦]

1637. **Imām al-Hādī (AS) said,** 'Reproof [expressed] is better than resentment [harboured within].'[1860]

١٦٣٧ . الإمامُ الهاديُّ ﷺ : العِتابُ خَيرٌ مِن الحِقْدِ.[١٨٤٧]

1638. **Imām al-ʿAskarī (AS) said,** 'Among people, the person with the least comfort is the resentful one.'[1861]

١٦٣٨ . الإمامُ العسكريُّ ﷺ : أقلُّ النّاسِ راحةً الحَقودُ.[١٨٤٨]

545. The Believer's Resentment Is Short-lived

٥٤٥ـ سُرعةُ ذَهابِ حِقدِ المُؤمِنِ

1639. **Imām al-Ṣādiq (AS) said,** 'The believer's resentment lasts as long as he is seated [in an assembly], but as soon as he rises it vanishes.'[1862]

١٦٣٩ . الإمامُ الصّادقُ ﷺ :المؤمنُ يَحقِدُ مادامَ في مَجلسِهِ، فإذا قامَ ذهبَ عنهُ الحِقدُ.[١٨٤٩]

107

SCORN

التَّحقير

546. Prohibition of Scorning People

٥٤٦ـ النَّهيُ عَن تَحقيرِ النّاس

1640. **Luqmān (AS),** said to his son, 'My son! Do not ever scorn anybody because of his ragged

١٦٤٠ . لقمانُ ﷺ ـ لابنِهِ ـ : يا بُنَيَّ لا تُحَقِّرَنَّ

clothes, for verily your Lord and his Lord is the same One.'[1863]

أحداً بخُلقانِ ثِيابِهِ ؛ فإنَّ ربَّكَ وربَّهُ واحدٌ.١٨٥٠

1641. **The Prophet (SAWA) said,** 'Do not hold any of Allah's creatures in disdain, for you do not know which of them is the friend of Allah.'[1864]

١٦٤١ . رسولُ اللهِ ﷺ : لا يَزرَأنَّ أحدُكُم بأحدٍ من خَلقِ اللهِ فإنَّهُ لا يدري أيُّهُم وليُّ اللهِ.١٨٥١

1642. **Imām al-Ṣādiq (AS) said,** 'He who scorns a poor believer is scorned and detested by Allah until he desists from scorning him.'[1865]

١٦٤٢ . الإمامُ الصّادقُ عليه السلام : مَن حَقَّرَ مؤمناً مِسكيناً لم يَزَلِ اللهُ لَهُ حاقِراً ماقِتاً حتّىٰ يَرجِعَ عن مَحقَرَتِهِ إيّاهُ.١٨٥٢

547. Caution against Scorning a Believer

٥٤٧ ـ التَّحذيرُ مِن تَحقيرِ المُؤمِنِ

1643. **The Prophet (SAWA) said,** 'He who degrades a believing man or woman, or scorns him or her for their poverty or lack of means, Allah, most High, will defame him on the Day of Resurrection, and then will publicly disgrace him.'[1866]

١٦٤٣ . رسولُ اللهِ ﷺ : مَنِ استَذَلَّ مؤمناً أو مؤمنةً ، أو حَقَّرَهُ لفقرِهِ أو قلّةِ ذاتِ يَدِهِ ، شَهَرَهُ اللهُ تعالىٰ يومَ القِيامَةِ ، ثُمّ يَفضَحُهُ.١٨٥٣

1644. **The Prophet (SAWA) said,** 'Do not ever scorn any of the Muslims, for verily the lowest of them is great in the sight of Allah.'[1867]

١٦٤٤ . عنه ﷺ : لا تُحَقِّرَنَّ أحداً مِن المسلمينَ ، فإنَّ صَغيرَهُم عِندَ اللهِ كَبيرٌ.١٨٥٤

1645. **The Prophet (SAWA) said,** 'It is evil enough for the son of Adam to scorn his fellow Muslim brother.'[1868]

١٦٤٥ . عنه ﷺ : حَسْبُ ابنِ آدمَ من الشَّرِّ أن يُحَقِّرَ أخاهُ المسلمَ.١٨٥٥

1646. **Imām al-Ṣādiq (AS) said,** 'Verily Allah, Blessed and most High, says, 'He who insults a friend of Mine has indeed set himself up to fight Me, and I am the fastest to come to the aid of My friends.'[1869]

١٦٤٦ . الإمامُ الصّادقُ عليه السلام : إنَّ اللهَ تَباركَ وتعالىٰ يَقولُ : مَن أهانَ لي وَليّاً فقد أرْصَدَ لمُحارَبَتي ، وأنا أسرَعُ شَيءٍ إلىٰ نُصْرَةِ أوْليائي.١٨٥٦

108

THE TRUTH

الحَقُّ

548. The Truth

٥٤٨ ـ الحَقُّ

"Rather We hurl the truth against falsehood, and it crushes its head, and behold, falsehood vanishes! And woe to you for what you allege [about Allah]."[1870]

﴿بَلْ نَقْذِفُ بِالْحَقِّ عَلَى الْبَاطِلِ فَيَدْمَغُهُ فَإِذَا هُوَ زَاهِقٌ وَلَكُمُ الْوَيْلُ مِمَّا تَصِفُونَ﴾.١٨٥٧

1647. **Imām ʿAlī (AS) said,** 'The truth is the strongest support.'[1871]

١٦٤٧ . الإمامُ عليٌّ ؑ : الحقُّ أقوىٰ ظَهيرٍ .[١٨٥٨]

1648. **Imām ʿAlī (AS) said,** 'Know that the truth is [like] tame mounts, whose owners have mounted them and have been handed their reins. They take them gently until they came to ample shade.'[1872]

١٦٤٨ . عنه ؑ : ألَا وإنَّ الحَقَّ مَطايا ذُلُلٌ ، رَكِبَها أهلُها واُعطُوا أزِمَّتَها ، فسارَتْ بِهِمُ الهُوَيْنا حتّىٰ أتَتْ ظِلّاً ظَليلاً .[١٨٥٩]

1649. **Imām ʿAlī (AS) said,** 'He who seeks might unrightfully will be humiliated, and he who opposes the truth will be afflicted with weakness.'[1873]

١٦٤٩ . عنه ؑ : مَن يَطلُبِ العِزَّ بغَيرِ حقٍّ يَذِلَّ ، ومَن عانَدَ الحقَّ لَزِمَهُ الوَهْنُ .[١٨٦٠]

1650. **Imām al-Ṣādiq (AS) said,** 'No sooner does falsehood stand against the truth than the truth defeats the falsehood, for that is the purport of His verse: *"Rather We hurl the truth against falsehood, and it crushes its head…"*'[1874]

١٦٥٠ . الإمامُ الصّادقُ ؑ : لَيس مِن باطلٍ يَقومُ بإزاءِ الحقِّ إلّا غلَبَ الحقُّ الباطِلَ ، وذلكَ قولُهُ : ﴿بَلْ نَقذِفُ بالحَقِّ علىٰ الباطِلِ فيَدْمَغُهُ ...﴾ .[١٨٦١]

549. The Weight of the Truth

٥٤٩ ـ ثِقَلُ الحَقِّ

"We certainly brought you the truth, but most of you were averse to the truth."[1875]

﴿لَقَدْ جِئْنَاكُمْ بِالْحَقِّ وَلَكِنَّ أَكْثَرَكُمْ لِلْحَقِّ كَارِهُونَ﴾ .[١٨٦٢]

1651. **Imām ʿAlī (AS) said,** 'Truly the truth is heavy but wholesome, whereas falsehood is light but plagued.'[1876]

١٦٥١ . الإمامُ عليٌّ ؑ : إنَّ الحقَّ ثَقيلٌ مَرِيءٌ ، وإنّ الباطِلَ خَفيفٌ وَبِيءٌ .[١٨٦٣]

1652. **Imām al-Bāqir (AS) said,** 'At the time of his death, my father, ʿAlī b. al-Ḥusayn (AS) hugged me close to his chest and said, 'O my son! I advise you as my father advised me at the time of his death, and he proceeded to mention that his father had advised him, saying: 'O my son! Endure the truth even if it be bitter.'[1877]

١٦٥٢ . الإمامُ الباقرُ ؑ : لَمّا حَضَرَتْ أبي عليَّ ابنَ الحسينِ ؑ الوَفاةُ ضَمَّني إلىٰ صَدْرِهِ ثُمَّ قالَ : أيْ بُنَيَّ ، اُوصيكَ بِما أوْصاني أبي حِينَ حَضَرَتْهُ الوَفاةُ ـ وبما ذَكَرَ أنّ أباهُ ؑ أوصاهُ بِهِ ـ : أيْ بُنَيَّ ، اصبِرْ علىٰ الحقِّ وإنْ كانَ مُرّاً .[١٨٦٤]

550. The Necessity of Telling the Truth Even to One's Own Detriment

٥٥٠ ـ وُجوبُ قَولِ الحَقِّ ولَو عَلَى النَّفسِ

1653. **The Prophet (SAWA) said,** 'The most Godwary of people is he who speaks the truth, be it for or against him.'[1878]

١٦٥٣ . رسولُ اللهِ ﷺ : أتْقىٰ النّاسِ مَن قالَ الحقَّ فيما لَهُ وعَلَيهِ .[١٨٦٥]

1654. **Imām ʿAlī (AS) said,** 'It is written on the hilt of one of the Prophet (SAWA)'s swords: 'Speak the truth even if it be against yourself.'[1879]

١٦٥٤. الإمامُ عليٌّ عليه السلام: في قائمةِ سَيفٍ مِن سُيوفِ رسولِ اللهِ ﷺ صَحيفَةٌ فِيها...قُلِ الحقَّ ولو علىٰ نفسِكَ.[١٨٦٦]

1655. **Imām ʿAlī (AS) said,** 'The best of people in the sight of Allah is he who likes to act according to what is right - even if it brings him loss and misery - more than what is wrong, even if it brings him profit and increase of wealth.'[1880]

١٦٥٥. عنه عليه السلام: إنّ أفْضلَ النّاسِ عندَ اللهِ مَن كانَ العَملُ بالحقِّ أحَبَّ إليهِ ـ وإنْ نَقَصَهُ وكَرَثَهُ ـ مِن الباطِلِ وإنْ جَرَّ إلَيهِ فائدةً وزادَهُ.[١٨٦٧]

1656. **Imām al-Kāẓim (AS) said,** 'Speak the truth even if it entails your own ruin, for verily your deliverance is therein... and abandon falsehood even if it entails your deliverance, for truly therein is your ruin.'[1881]

١٦٥٦. الإمامُ الكاظمُ عليه السلام: قُلِ الحقَّ وإنْ كانَ فيهِ هَلاكُكَ، فإنَّ فيهِ نَجاتَكَ... ودَعِ الباطِلَ وإنْ كانَ فيهِ نَجاتُكَ فإنّ فيهِ هَلاكَكَ.[١٨٦٨]

551. Speaking the Truth When Pleased or Angered

٥٥١ ـ قَولُ الحَقِّ فِي الرِّضا وَ الغَضَبِ

1657. **The Prophet (SAWA) said,** 'Lo! Fear of people must never prevent any man from telling the truth when he knows it; truly the best *jihād* is a true word spoken before an unjust ruler.'[1882]

١٦٥٧. رسولُ اللهِ ﷺ: ألَا لا يَمْنَعَنَّ رجُلاً مَهابَةُ النّاسِ أنْ يَتكَلَّم بالحقِّ إذا عَلِمَهُ. ألَا إنّ أفضَلَ الجِهادِ كَلِمَةُ حقٍّ عندَ سُلطانٍ جائرٍ.[١٨٦٩]

1658. **Imām ʿAlī (AS) said** in one of his wills to his son, al-Ḥusayn (AS), 'O my son! I advise you to fear Allah in both affluence and poverty, and to tell the truth both when pleased as well as when angered.'[1883]

١٦٥٨. الإمامُ عليٌّ عليه السلام ـ مِن وصاياهُ لابْنِهِ الحُسينِ عليه السلام ـ: يا بُنيَّ، اُوصيكَ بتَقْوىٰ اللهِ في الغِنىٰ والفَقرِ، وكَلِمَةِ الحقِّ في الرِّضا والغَضَبِ.[١٨٧٠]

552. Accepting the Truth

٥٥٢ ـ قَبولُ الحَقِّ

1659. **The Prophet (SAWA) said,** 'Accept the truth from anyone who comes to you with it – be he lowly or noble, even if he himself is detestable to you. And reject falsehood from anyone who comes to you with it – be he lowly or noble, even if he is beloved to you.'[1884]

١٦٥٩. رسولُ اللهِ ﷺ: اقْبَلِ الحَقَّ مِمَّن أتاكَ بهِ ـ صَغيرٌ أو كَبيرٌ ـ وإن كانَ بَغيضاً، وارْدُدِ الباطِلَ علىٰ مَن جاءَ بهِ مِن صَغيرٍ أو كَبيرٍ وإنْ كانَ حَبيباً.[١٨٧١]

1660. **Imām al-Ṣādiq (AS) said,** 'Honour is that you humble yourself to the truth when you face it.'[1885]

١٦٦٠. الإمامُ الصّادقُ عليه السلام: العِزُّ أنْ تَذِلَّ للحقِّ إذا لَزِمَكَ.[١٨٧٢]

553. The Criterion of Knowing the Truth

٥٥٣ـ ميزانُ مَعرفَةِ الحَقِّ

1661. **Imām ʿAlī (AS) said,** 'Verily the truth is not known through men; know the truth [first] and you will know its people.'[1886]

١٦٦١ . الإمامُ عليٌّ ﷺ : إنّ الحـقَّ لا يُـعرَفُ بالرِّجالِ، اعْرِفِ الحقَّ تَعرِفْ أهلَهُ .[١٨٧٣]

(See also: GOOD: section 679)

(أنظر) الخير: باب ٦٧٩.

554. The Truth Can Side Equally With or Against Someone

٥٥٤ـ لا يَجري الحَقُّ لِأحَدٍ إلّا جَرى عَلَيه

1662. **Imām ʿAlī (AS) said,** 'The truth is the widest thing in description, but the narrowest in practising justice. No sooner does it side with someone than it will side against him [at another time], and no sooner does it side against someone than it will side for him later. And if anyone is to side with it, never going against it, then that would be purely for Allah, glory be to Him.'[1887]

١٦٦٢ . الإمامُ عليٌّ ﷺ : الحقُّ أوْسَعُ الأشياءِ في التَّواصُفِ، وأضْيَقُها فـي التَّـناصُفِ، لا يَـجْري لأحدٍ إلّا جَرى عَلَيهِ، ولا يَجْري عليهِ إلّا جَرى لَهُ، ولَو كانَ لأحَدٍ أنْ يَجْريَ لَهُ ولا يَجْريَ عليهِ لَكانَ ذلكَ خالِصاً للهِ سُبحانَهُ .[١٨٧٤]

1663. **Imām ʿAlī (AS) said,** 'Do not let consideration for a person's right hinder you from upholding the truth when it is against him.'[1888]

١٦٦٣ . عنه ﷺ : لا تَمْنَعَنَّكُم رِعايَةُ الحَقِّ لأحدٍ عن إقامَةِ الحَقِّ علَيهِ .[١٨٧٥]

109

THE RIGHTS

الحُقُوق

555. The Rights of Allah, Most High

٥٥٥ـ حُقوقُ اللهِ تَعالىٰ

1664. **The Prophet (SAWA) said,** 'Truly the rights of Allah, exalted be His praise, are too great to be fulfilled by His servants, and verily the bounties of Allah are too great to be estimated by the servants; but [the least they can do is to] repent to Him morning and night.'[1889]

١٦٦٤ . رسولُ اللهِ ﷺ : إنّ حُقوقَ اللهِ جَلَّ ثَناؤهُ أعْظَمُ مِن أنْ يَقومَ بِها العِبادُ، وإنّ نِعَمَ اللهِ أكثَرُ مِن أنْ يُحْصيَها العِبادُ، ولكنْ أمْسُوا وأصْبِحوا تائبِينَ .[١٨٧٦]

1665. **Imām ʿAlī (AS) said,** 'Allah, glory be to Him, has made it His right upon people to obey

١٦٦٥ . الإمامُ عليٌّ ﷺ : ... لٰكنّهُ سُبحانَهُ جَعَلَ

Him, and has made its requital for them an increase in their reward [for acts of obedience] out of His Grace.'[1890]

حقَّهُ على العِبادِ أنْ يُطيعوهُ، وجَعلَ جَزاءهُم علَيهِ مُضاعَفَةَ الثَّوابِ تَفَضُّلاً مِنهُ.[١٨٧٧]

556. Giving Priority to the Rights of People

٥٥٦ـ تَقديمُ حَقِّ النّاسِ

1666. **Imām ʿAlī (AS) said,** 'Allah, glory be to Him, has made the rights of the people the prelude to His rights; therefore, he who fulfils the rights of Allah's servants ends up fulfilling Allah's rights.'[1891]

١٦٦٦. الإمامُ عليٌّ عليه السلام: جَعلَ اللهُ سبحانَهُ حُقوقَ عِبادِهِ مُقَدِّمَةً لحُقوقِهِ، فمَن قامَ بحُقوقِ عِبادِ اللهِ كانَ ذلكَ مُؤَدّياً إلىٰ القِيامِ بحُقوقِ اللهِ.[١٨٧٨]

557. The Greatest of Rights

٥٥٧ـ أعظَمُ الحُقوقِ

1667. **Imām ʿAlī (AS) said,** 'The greatest of those rights that He, glory be to Him, has made obligatory are the right of the ruler upon the subjects, and the right of the subjects upon the ruler.'[1892]

١٦٦٧. الإمامُ عليٌّ عليه السلام: وأعظَمُ ما افْتَرضَ [اللهُ] سبحانَهُ مِن تلكَ الحُقوقِ: حقُّ الوالي علىٰ الرَّعِيَّةِ، وحقُّ الرَّعِيَّةِ علىٰ الوالي.[١٨٧٩]

558. The Rights of the Brethren

٥٥٨ـ حُقوقُ الإخوانِ

1668. **Imām al-Bāqir (AS) said,** 'Among the rights of the believer upon his fellow believing brother is to satisfy his hunger, cover his body, solve his problems, pay his debt, and when he dies, to substitute him in his family and his children.'[1893]

١٦٦٨. الإمامُ الباقرُ عليه السلام: مِن حقِّ المؤمنِ علىٰ أخيهِ المؤمنِ أن يُشْبِعَ جَوْعَتَهُ، ويُواريَ عَورَتَهُ، ويُفرِّجَ عَنهُ كُرْبَتهُ، ويَقْضيَ دَيْنَهُ، فإذا ماتَ خَلَفَهُ في أهلِهِ ووُلدِهِ.[١٨٨٠]

1669. **Imām al-Ṣādiq (AS) said,** 'He who honours the religion of Allah honours the right of his brethren, and he who takes His religion lightly takes [the right of] his brethren lightly.'[1894]

١٦٦٩. الإمامُ الصّادقُ عليه السلام: مَن عَظّمَ دِينَ اللهِ عظّمَ حقَّ إخْوانِهِ، ومَنِ اسْتَخَفَّ بدِينهِ اسْتَخَفَّ بإخْوانِهِ.[١٨٨١]

1670. **Imām al-Ṣādiq (AS) said,** 'Allah is not worshipped through anything better than fulfilling the right of the fellow believer.'[1895]

١٦٧٠. عنه عليه السلام: ما عُبِدَ اللهُ بشيءٍ أفضَلَ مِن أداءِ حقِّ المؤمنِ.[١٨٨٢]

1671. **Imām al-Ṣādiq (AS) said,** 'The believer has seven rights incumbent upon his fellow believer which are made obligatory by Allah, Mighty and

١٦٧١. عنه عليه السلام: للمؤمنِ علىٰ المؤمنِ سَبْعَةُ حُقوقٍ واجِبَةٍ لَهُ مِن اللهِ عزّوجلّ، واللهُ سائلُهُ

Exalted, and about which Allah will ask him what he did: to esteem him highly in his eyes, to entertain love for him in his heart, to assist him financially from his own wealth, to love for him what he loves for himself, to prohibit [others] from backbiting him, to visit him in his sickness, to attend his funeral procession, and to not say anything but good about him after his death.'[1896]

عَمّا صَنَعَ فيها: الإجْلالُ لَهُ في عَيْنِهِ، والوُدُّ لَـهُ في صَدرِهِ، والمُواساةُ لَهُ في مالِهِ، وأنْ يُحِبَّ لَهُ مـا يُـحِبُّ لنَـفْسِهِ، وأنْ يُـحرِّمَ غِـيبَتَهُ، وأنْ يَعودَهُ في مَرضِهِ، ويُشَيّعَ جَـنازَتَهُ ولا يَـقولَ فيهِ بعدَ مَوتِهِ إلّا خَيراً.[١٨٨٣]

1672. Imām al-Ṣādiq (AS), when he was asked about the right of the believer, said, 'They are seventy rights, of which I will not tell you but of seven of them: … that you should not eat to satiety while he is hungry, or dress yourself while he is naked, and you should be his guide…'[1897]

١٦٧٢. الإمامُ الصّادقُ عليه السلام : وقد سئل عَن حَقِّ المُـؤمِنِ، فَـقالَ: سَـبعونَ حَـقّاً لا اُخـبِرُكَ إلّا بِسَبعَةٍ :... لا تَشبَع ويَجوعُ ولا تَكتَسي ويَعرى؛ وتَكونُ دَليلَهُ.[١٨٨٤]

1673. Imām al-Ṣādiq (AS), expounding on the rights of the believer upon the fellow believer, said, 'The simplest right from among them is to love for him what you love for yourself, and to dislike for him what you dislike for yourself.'[1898]

١٦٧٣. عنه عليه السلام ـ في بيانِ حُقوقِ المؤمنِ على المؤمنِ ـ: أيْسَرُ حقٍّ مِنها أنْ تُحِبَّ لَهُ ما تُحِبُّ لنَفسِكَ، وتَكْرَهَ لَهُ ما تَكْرَهُ لنَفْسِكَ.[١٨٨٥]

1674. Imām al-'Askarī (AS) said, 'The person who best knows the rights of his brethren and is the most diligent of all at fulfilling them is the one who has the greatest esteem in the sight of Allah.'[1899]

١٦٧٤. الإمامُ العسكريُّ عليه السلام : أعْرَفُ النّاسِ بحُقوقِ إخْوانِهِ وأشَدُّهُم قَـضاءً لَـها أعْـظَمُهُم عِـندَ اللهِ شَأناً.[١٨٨٦]

110

HOARDING

الِاحتِكارُ

559. Denouncing Hoarding

٥٥٩ ـ ذَمُّ الاحتِكارِ

1675. The Prophet (SAWA) said, 'Only the perfidious ones hoard.'[1900]

١٦٧٥. رسولُ اللهِ صلى الله عليه وآله : لا يَحْتَكِرُ إلّا الخَوّانونَ.[١٨٨٧]

1676. The Prophet (SAWA) said, 'Only an offender hoards.'[1901]

١٦٧٦. عنه صلى الله عليه وآله : لا يَحْتَكِرُ إلّا خاطئٌ.[١٨٨٨]

1677. Imām 'Alī (AS) said, 'Hoarding is the cause of deprivation.'[1902]

١٦٧٧. الإمامُ عليٌّ عليه السلام : الاحْـتِكارُ داعِـيَةُ الحِرمانِ.[١٨٨٩]

1678. **Imām ʿAlī (AS) said,** 'Hoarding is the habit of the dissolute.'[1903]

١٦٧٨ . عنه ﷺ : الاحْتِكارُ شِيمَةُ الفُجّارِ.١٨٩٠

1679. **Imām ʿAlī (AS) said,** 'Hoarding is a vice.'[1904]

١٦٧٩ . عنه ﷺ : الاحْتِكارُ رَذيلَةٌ.١٨٩١

1680. **Imām ʿAlī (AS) said,** 'Hoarding is the mount of hardship.'[1905]

١٦٨٠ . عنه ﷺ : الاحْتِكارُ مَطِيَّةُ النَّصَبِ.١٨٩٢

1681. **Imām ʿAlī (AS) said,** 'One of the characteristics of the idiots is exhausting themselves by hoarding.'[1906]

١٦٨١ . عنه ﷺ : مِن طَبائعِ الأغْمارِ إتْعابُ النُّفوسِ في الاحْتِكارِ.١٨٩٣

1682. **Imām ʿAlī (AS) said** in a letter he wrote to al-Ashtar when he appointed him governor of Egypt, 'Know - along with this - that most of the merchants and traders are very narrow-minded, and awfully avaricious. They hoard goods for profiteering and fix high prices for goods. This is a source of harm to the people, and a source of shame for the governors in charge. So stop people from hoarding, because verily the Messenger of Allah (SAWA) has prohibited it.'[1907]

١٦٨٢ . عنه ﷺ ـ فيما كَتَبَهُ للأشتَرِ حينَ وَلّاهُ مِصرَ ـ : ... واعْلَمْ ـ مَعَ ذلكَ ـ أنّ في كثيرٍ مِنهُم ضِيقاً فاحِشاً ، وشُحّاً قَبيحاً ، واحْتِكاراً للمَنافِعِ ، وتَحَكُّماً في البِياعاتِ ، وذلكَ بابُ مَضَرَّةٍ للعامَّةِ ، وعَيْبٌ على الوُلاةِ ، فامْنَعْ مِنَ الاحْتِكارِ ؛ فإنَّ رسولَ اللهِ ﷺ مَنعَ مِنهُ.١٨٩٤

1683. **Imām ʿAlī (AS) said,** 'There is no good in any act of hoarding that brings loss to the people and inflates the prices for them.'[1908]

١٦٨٣ . عنه ﷺ : كُلُّ حُكْرَةٍ تَضُرُّ بالنّاسِ وتُغْلي السِّعْرَ علَيهِم فلا خَيرَ فيها.١٨٩٥

1684. **Imām al-Ṣādiq (AS) said,** 'Truly Allah, Mighty and Exalted, showed His bounty to His servants in the seed, but He also plagued them with lice; otherwise the kings would have hoarded it as they hoard gold and silver.'[1909]

١٦٨٤ . الإمامُ الصّادقُ ﷺ : إنَّ اللهَ عزّ وجلّ تَطَوَّلَ على عِبادِهِ بالحَبَّةِ فسَلَّطَ علَيها القُمَّلَةَ ، ولولا ذلكَ لَخَزَنَتْها المُلوكُ كما يَخْزُنونَ الذَّهَبَ والفِضَّةَ.١٨٩٦

560. Denouncing the Hoarder

٥٦٠ ـ ذَمُّ المُحتَكِرِ

1685. **The Prophet (SAWA) said,** 'The hoarder is damned.'[1910]

١٦٨٥ . رسولُ اللهِ ﷺ : المُحْتَكِرُ مَلْعونٌ.١٨٩٧

1686. **The Prophet (SAWA) said,** 'The hoarder in our market is like the apostate in the Book of Allah.'[1911]

١٦٨٦ . عنه ﷺ : المُحتَكِرُ في سُوقِنا كالمُلْحِدِ في كِتابِ اللهِ.١٨٩٨

1687. **The Prophet (SAWA) said,** 'What a wretched servant the hoarder is, for if Allah, most High, lowers the prices he is saddened but if He raises them he rejoices.'[1912]

١٦٨٧ . عنه ﷺ : بِئسَ العَبدُ المُحتَكِرُ ، إنْ أرْخَصَ اللهُ تعالىٰ الأسْعارَ حَزِنَ ، وإنْ أغْلاها اللهُ فَرِحَ .[١٨٩٩]

1688. **The Prophet (SAWA) said,** 'The hoarders and the murderers will be resurrected to occupy the same position in Hell.'[1913]

١٦٨٨ . عنه ﷺ : يُحْشَرُ الحَكّارونَ وقَتَلَةُ الأنْفُسِ إلىٰ جَهَنَّمَ في دَرَجةٍ .[١٩٠٠]

1689. **The Prophet (SAWA) said,** 'He who hoards food for forty days waiting for the rise of its price, he indeed disassociates himself from Allah and Allah disassociates Himself from him.'[1914]

١٦٨٩ . عنه ﷺ : مَن جَمعَ طَعاماً يَتَربّصُ بهِ الغَلاءَ أربَعينَ يَوماً فقد بَرِئَ مِن اللهِ وبَرِئَ اللهُ مِنهُ .[١٩٠١]

1690. **The Prophet (SAWA) said,** 'Any man who buys food and hoards it for forty days waiting for its demand to rise among the Muslims and then sells it, even if he were to donate its value in charity, it would not atone for what he did.'[1915]

١٦٩٠ . عنه ﷺ : أيُّما رجُلٍ اشْتَرىٰ طَعاماً فكَبَسَهُ أربَعينَ صَباحاً يُريدُ بِهِ غَلاءَ المُسلِمينَ ، ثُمَّ باعَهُ فتَصدّقَ بثَمنِهِ لَم يَكُنْ كَفّارَةً لِما صَنَعَ .[١٩٠٢]

1691. **Imām ʿAlī (AS) said,** 'The hoarder is deprived of his bounty.'[1916]

١٦٩١ . الإمامُ عليٌّ ؑ : المُحْتَكِرُ مَحرومُ نِعْمَتَهُ .[١٩٠٣]

1692. **Imām ʿAlī (AS) said,** 'The miserly hoarder gathers for those who will not thank him, and will come to Him who will not excuse him.'[1917]

١٦٩٢ . عنه ؑ : المُحتَكِرُ البَخيلُ جامعٌ لمَن لا يَشْكُرُهُ ، وقادِمٌ على مَنْ لا يَعْذِرُهُ .[١٩٠٤]

111

WISDOM

الحِكْمَةُ

561. The Virtue of Wisdom

٥٦١ ـ فَضلُ الحِكمَةِ

"He gives wisdom to whomever He wishes, and he who is given wisdom is certainly given an abundant good. But none takes admonition except those who possess intellect."[1918]

﴿يُؤْتِي الْحِكْمَةَ مَنْ يَشَاءُ وَمَنْ يُؤْتَ الْحِكْمَةَ فَقَدْ أُوتِيَ خَيْراً كَثِيراً وَما يَذَّكَّرُ إِلّا أُولُوا الْأَلْبابِ﴾ .[١٩٠٥]

1693. **Prophet Jesus (AS) said,** 'Verily wisdom is the light of every heart.'[1919]

١٦٩٣ . عيسى ؑ : إنّ الحِكمَةَ نورُ كُلِّ قَلبٍ .[١٩٠٦]

1694. **Luqmān (AS) said** [advising his son], 'My son, learn wisdom and you will become noble, for verily wisdom directs towards religion, it will elevate the slave over the free person, it raises the poor above the rich and it makes the young precede over the old.'[1920]

١٦٩٤ . لُقمانُ ﷺ ـ مِن وصيَّتِهِ لابنِهِ ـ: يا بُنَيَّ، تَعلَّمِ الحِكمَةَ تَشْرُفْ ؛ فإنَّ الحِكمَةَ تَدُلُّ على الدِّينِ، وتُشرِّفُ العَبْدَ على الحُرِّ، وتَرفَعُ المِسكينَ على الغَنيِّ، وتُقدِّمُ الصَّغيرَ على الكَبيرِ.[١٩٠٧]

1695. **The Prophet (SAWA) said,** 'A word of wisdom that the believer hears is better than the worship of one year.'[1921]

١٦٩٥ . رسولُ اللهِ ﷺ : كَلِمَةُ الحِكمَةِ يَسمَعُها المؤمنُ خَيرٌ مِن عِبادَةِ سَنةٍ.[١٩٠٨]

1696. **The Prophet (SAWA) said,** 'The wise man is almost a prophet.'[1922]

١٦٩٦ . عنه ﷺ: كادَ الحَكيمُ أنْ يَكونَ نَبيّاً.[١٩٠٩]

1697. **Imām ʿAlī (AS) said,** 'Wisdom is the garden of the intelligent ones and the amusement of the noble.'[1923]

١٦٩٧ . الإمامُ عليٌّ ﷺ :الحِكمَةُ رَوضَةُ العُقَلاءِ، ونُزهَةُ النُّبَلاءِ.[١٩١٠]

1698. **Imām ʿAlī (AS) said,** 'Wisdom is a tree that grows in the heart and produces fruit on the tongue.'[1924]

١٦٩٨ . عنه ﷺ : الحِكمَةُ شَجَرَةٌ تَنبُتُ في القَلبِ، وتُثمِرُ على اللِّسانِ.[١٩١١]

1699. **Imām ʿAlī (AS) has said,** 'The one who is known for [his] wisdom is regarded by the eyes with dignity and awe.'[1925]

١٦٩٩ . عنه ﷺ : مَن عُرِفَ بالحِكمَةِ لَحَظَتْهُ العُيونُ بالوَقارِ والهَيبةِ.[١٩١٢]

562. Wisdom is the Lost Property of the Believer

٥٦٢ ـ الحِكمَةُ ضالَّةُ المُؤمِنِ

1700. **Imām ʿAlī (AS) said,** 'Wisdom is the lost property of the believer, so seek it even from the polytheist for you will be more deserving and worthier of it [than him].'[1926]

١٧٠٠ . الإمامُ عليٌّ ﷺ : الحِكمَةُ ضالَّةُ المؤمنِ، فاطلُبوها ولَو عندَ المُشرِكِ تكونوا أحَقَّ بها وأهلَها.[١٩١٣]

1701. **Imām ʿAlī (AS) said,** 'Wisdom is the lost property of the believer, so take wisdom even from the people of hypocrisy.'[1927]

١٧٠١ . عنه ﷺ : الحِكْمَةُ ضالَّةُ المؤمِنِ، فخُذِ الحِكمَةَ ولو مِن أهلِ النِّفاقِ.[١٩١٤]

563. What a Wise Person Must not do

٥٦٣ـ ما لا يَنبَغي لِلحَكيمِ فِعلُهُ

1702. **Imām ʿAlī (AS) said,** 'The one who seeks fulfilment of his need from an unwise person is [himself] not a wise person.'[1928]

١٧٠٢ . الإمامُ عليٌّ ﷺ : لَيس بحَكيمٍ مَن قصَدَ بحاجَتِهِ غَيرَ كَريمٍ.[١٩١٥]

1703. **Imām ʿAlī (AS) said,** 'He who does not deal amicably with someone for whom amicableness is the only option is not a wise person.'[1929]

١٧٠٣ . عنه ﷺ : ليسَ الحَكيمُ مَن لَم يُدارِ مَن لا يَجِدُ بُدّاً مِن مُداراتِهِ.[١٩١٦]

564. The Interpretation of Wisdom

٥٦٤ـ تَفسيرُ الحِكمَةِ

1704. **Imām ʿAlī (AS) said,** 'The opening of wisdom is abandoning the [illicit] pleasures, and the peak of it is to detest the transient things.'[1930]

١٧٠٤ . الإمامُ عليٌّ ﷺ : أوّلُ الحِكمَةِ تَركُ اللَّذّاتِ، وآخِرُها مَقْتُ الفانِياتِ.[١٩١٧]

1705. **Imām ʿAlī (AS) said,** 'From among [the matters of] wisdom is to avoid dispute with one who is above you, to not disesteem anyone below you, to not undertake a task which is outside of your capability, to not have your tongue contradict your heart and neither your word [contradict] your action, to not speak of that which you do not know, and to not abandon a matter as it approaches only to pursue it as it retreats.'[1931]

١٧٠٥ . عنه ﷺ : مِن الحِكمَةِ أنْ لا تُنازِعَ مَن فَوقَكَ، ولا تَسْتَذِلَّ مَن دُونَكَ، ولا تَتَعاطىٰ ما ليسَ في قُدْرَتِكَ، ولا يُخالِفَ لِسانُكَ قَلبَكَ، ولا قَولُكَ فِعلَكَ، ولا تَتَكلّمَ فيما لا تَعلَمُ، ولا تَتْرُكَ الأمرَ عِندَ الإقبالِ وتَطْلُبَهُ عِندَ الإدْبارِ.[١٩١٨]

1706. **Imām al-Bāqir (AS)** when he was asked by Abū Baṣīr regarding the words of Allah's verse, *"and he who is given wisdom..."* said, 'It [wisdom] is obedience to Allah and true knowledge of the Imām.'[1932]

١٧٠٦ . الإمامُ الباقرُ ﷺ ـ وقد سأَلَهُ أبو بصيرٍ عن قولِ اللهِ: ﴿ومَن يُؤْتَ الحِكْمَةَ فَقَد أُوتيَ خَيراً كَثيراً﴾ ـ: هِيَ طاعَةُ اللهِ ومَعرِفَةُ الإمامِ.[١٩١٩]

1707. **Imām al-Ṣādiq (AS) said,** 'Verily wisdom is inner knowledge and deep understanding of religion, for the one who understands among you is truly the wise man.'[1933]

١٧٠٧ . الإمامُ الصّادقُ ﷺ : إنّ الحِكمَةَ المَعرِفَةُ والتَّفَقّهُ في الدِّينِ، فمَن فَقِهَ مِنكُم فهُو حَكيمٌ.[١٩٢٠]

1708. **Imām al-Kāẓim (AS) said,** 'Luqmān was asked, what is the crux of your wisdom?' He said,

١٧٠٨ . الإمامُ الكاظمُ ﷺ : قيلَ لِلُقمانَ: ما يَجْمَعُ

'I do not ask about that which I know already and I do not burden myself with that which does not concern me.'[1934]

مِن حِكْمتِكَ؟ قالَ: لا أسْأَلُ عَمّا كُفِيتُهُ، ولا أتَكلّفُ ما لا يَعْنيني.١٩٢١

565. The Fountainhead of Wisdom

٥٦٥ ـ رأسُ الحِكمَةِ

1709. **The Prophet (SAWA) said,** 'The fountainhead of wisdom is the fear of Allah.'[1935]

١٧٠٩ . رسولُ اللهِ ﷺ : رأسُ الحِكمَةِ مَخافَةُ اللهِ.١٩٢٢

1710. **The Prophet (SAWA) said,** 'Verily the noblest speech is the remembrance of Allah and the fountainhead of wisdom is His obedience.'[1936]

١٧١٠ . عنه ﷺ : إنّ أشْرَفَ الحَديثِ ذِكْرُ اللهِ، ورأسَ الحِكمَةِ طاعَتُهُ.١٩٢٣

1711. **The Prophet (SAWA) said,** 'Verily leniency is the fountainhead of wisdom.'[1937]

١٧١١ . عنه ﷺ : إنّ الرِّفْقَ رأسُ الحِكمَةِ.١٩٢٤

1712. **Imām ʿAlī (AS) said,** 'The fountainhead of wisdom is to be bound to the truth and to obey the one on [the path of] the truth.'[1938]

١٧١٢ . الإمامُ عليٌّ ﷺ : رأسُ الحِكمَةِ لُزومُ الحقِّ وطاعَةُ المُحِقِّ.١٩٢٥

566. What Brings About Wisdom

٥٦٦ ـ ما يورثُ الحِكمَةَ

1713. **Imām ʿAlī (AS) said,** 'Conquer your lustful desire and your wisdom will be perfected.'[1939]

١٧١٣ . الإمامُ عليٌّ ﷺ : اغْلِبِ الشَّهْوَةَ تَكمُلْ لكَ الحِكمَةُ.١٩٢٦

1714. **Imām ʿAlī (AS) said,** 'There is no wisdom except through inerrancy.'[1940]

١٧١٤ . عنه ﷺ : لا حِكمَةَ إلّا بعِصْمَةٍ.١٩٢٧

1715. **Imām al-Ṣādiq (AS) said,** 'Whoever abstains from worldly pleasures, Allah will establish wisdom in his heart and make it flow from his tongue.'[1941]

١٧١٥ . الإمامُ الصّادقُ ﷺ : مَن زَهِدَ في الدُّنيا أثْبَتَ اللهُ الحِكمَةَ في قلبِهِ، وأنْطَقَ بها لِسانَهُ.١٩٢٨

567. What Prevents Wisdom

٥٦٧ ـ ما يَمنَعُ الحِكمَةَ

1716. **The Prophet (SAWA) said,** 'The heart bears wisdom when the stomach is empty, and the heart throws out wisdom when the stomach is full.'[1942]

١٧١٦ . رسولُ اللهِ ﷺ : القَلبُ يَتَحمّلُ الحِكمَةَ عند خُلُوِّ البَطْنِ، القَلبُ يَمُجُّ الحِكمَةَ عند امْتِلاءِ البَطْنِ.١٩٢٩

1717. **Imām ʿAlī (AS) said,** 'Vain desire and wisdom do not come together.'[1943]

١٧١٧ . الإمامُ عليٌّ ﷺ : لا تَجْتَمِعُ الشَّهوَةُ والحِكمَةُ.[١٩٣٠]

1718. **Imām al-Ṣādiq (AS) said,** 'Anger is a destroyer of the wise man's heart, whoever cannot control his anger cannot control his intellect.'[1944]

١٧١٨ . الإمامُ الصّادقُ ﷺ : الغَضَبُ مَمْحَقةٌ لِقَلبِ الحَكيمِ، ومَن لم يَمْلِكْ غَضَبَهُ لَم يَمْلِكْ عَقلَهُ.[١٩٣١]

1719. **Imām al-Kāẓim (AS) said,** 'Verily a seed grows in soft ground and does not grow on stone, in the same way that wisdom thrives in the heart of the humble and does not thrive in the heart of the proud and haughty, because Allah has made humbleness the instrument of the intellect.'[1945]

١٧١٩ . الإمامُ الكاظمُ ﷺ : إنّ الزَّرعَ يَنْبُتُ في السَّهلِ ولا يَنْبُتُ في الصَّفا، فكذلكَ الحِكمَةُ تَعْمُرُ في قَلبِ المُتواضِعِ، ولا تَعْمُرُ في قَلبِ المُتَكبِّرِ الجبّارِ؛ لأنّ اللّهَ جَعلَ التَّواضُعَ آلةَ العَقلِ.[١٩٣٢]

1720. **Imām al-Hādī (AS) said,** 'Wisdom does not avail an immoral character.'[1946]

١٧٢٠ . الإمامُ الهاديُّ ﷺ : الحِكمَةُ لا تَنْجَعُ في الطِّباعِ الفاسِدَةِ.[١٩٣٣]

568. The Effects of Wisdom

٥٦٨ ـ آثارُ الحِكمَةِ

1721. **Imām ʿAlī (AS) said,** 'Whoever has wisdom established [in his heart] for him becomes one who adheres to admonition'[1947]

١٧٢١ . الإمامُ عليٌّ ﷺ : مَن ثَبَتَتْ لَهُ الحِكمَةُ عَرَفَ العِبرَةَ.[١٩٣٤]

1722. **Imām al-Ṣādiq (AS) said,** 'Much contemplation on [matters of] wisdom causes the intellect to flourish.'[1948]

١٧٢٢ . الإمامُ الصّادقُ ﷺ : كَثرةُ النَّظَرِ في الحِكمَةِ تَلْقَحُ العَقلَ.[١٩٣٥]

569. Protection of Wisdom

٥٦٩ ـ المُحافَظَةُ عَلَى الحِكمَةِ

1723. **Imām ʿAlī (AS) said,** 'Verily the wise men ruined and lost wisdom when they deposited it with those who were unworthy of it.'[1949]

١٧٢٣ . الإمامُ عليٌّ ﷺ : إنّ الحُكَماءَ ضَيَّعوا الحِكمَةَ لَمّا وَضَعوها عِندَ غَيرِ أهْلِها.[١٩٣٦]

1724. **Imām al-Kāẓim (AS) said,** 'Do not grant the ignorant ones wisdom for they will not do justice to it, and do not deprive it to those who are worthy of it for you will do injustice to them.'[1950]

١٧٢٤ . الإمامُ الكاظمُ ﷺ : لا تَمْنَحوا الجُهّالَ الحِكمَةَ فتَظْلِموها، ولا تَمْنَعوها أهْلَها فتَظْلِموهُم.[١٩٣٧]

112

OATH-TAKING

الحَلْف

570. Prohibition against Taking Oath by Allah Glory be to Him

٥٧٠ـ النَّهيُ عَنِ الحَلفِ بِاللهِ سُبحانَهُ

"Do not make Allah an obstacle, through your oaths, to being pious and Godwary, and to bringing about concord between people."[1951]

﴿وَلا تَجْعَلُوا اللهَ عُرْضَةً لِأَيْمَانِكُمْ أَنْ تَبَرُّوا وَتَتَّقُوا وَتُصْلِحُوا بَيْنَ النَّاسِ وَاللهُ سَمِيعٌ عَلِيمٌ﴾.[١٩٣٨]

1725. **Imām al-Ṣādiq (AS) said,** 'Do not take oath by Allah whether you are truthful or lying, for verily He says *"Do not make Allah an obstacle, through your oaths."*'[1952]

١٧٢٥ . الإمامُ الصّادقُ عليه السلام : لا تَحْلِفوا باللهِ صادِقينَ ولا كاذِبينَ ؛ فإنّهُ عزّوجلّ يقولُ : ﴿ولا تَجْعَلوا اللهَ عُرْضَةً لأيْمانِكُم﴾.[١٩٣٩]

571. Warning against False Oaths

٥٧١ـ التَّحذيرُ مِنَ الحَلفِ الكاذِبِ

1726. It is narrated in *Thawāb al-A'māl* that Allah Almighty said, 'I will not grant My mercy to he who takes false oaths.'[1953]

١٧٢٦ . ثواب الأعمال : قالَ اللهُ عزّوجلّ : لا اُنيلُ رَحْمَتي مَن تَعرَّضَ للأيمانِ الكاذِبَةِ.[١٩٤٠]

1727. **The Prophet (SAWA) said,** 'Beware of taking false oaths for verily they leave the houses empty of their tenants.'[1954]

١٧٢٧ . رسولُ اللهِ صلى الله عليه وآله : إيّاكُم واليَمينَ الفاجِرَةَ؛ فإنَّها تَدَعُ الدِّيارَ بَلاقِعَ مِن أهلِها.[١٩٤١]

1728. **Imām al-Ṣādiq (AS) said,** 'Whoever takes an oath knowing that he is lying, has surely waged war with Allah.'[1955]

١٧٢٨ . الإمامُ الصّادقُ عليه السلام : مَن حَلفَ على يَمينٍ وهُو يَعلمُ أنّهُ كاذِبٌ فقَد بارَزَ اللهَ عزّوجلّ.[١٩٤٢]

1729. **Imām al-Ṣādiq (AS) said,** 'Lying under a false oath brings about poverty for the heir.'[1956]

١٧٢٩ . عنه عليه السلام : اليَمينُ الصَّبرُ الكاذِبَةُ تُورِثُ العَقِبَ الفَقْرَ.[١٩٤٣]

572. How to Commit a Tyrant to Oath

٥٧٢ـ كَيفيَّةُ تَحليفِ الظّالِمِ

1730. **Imām 'Alī (AS) said,** 'Commit a tyrant to oath whenever you want his oath in a way that it is devoid of the power and strength of Allah, for verily if he falsely takes oath by it, his

١٧٣٠ . الإمامُ عليٌّ عليه السلام : أحْلِفوا الظّالِمَ إذا أرَدْتُم يَمينَهُ بأنّهُ بَريءٌ مِن حَولِ اللهِ وقُوَّتِهِ، فإنَّهُ إذا

chastisement will be hastened, and if he takes oath by Allah whom there is no god but He, it will not be hastened because he has professed the unity of Allah, the all-High.'[1957]

حلفَ بها كاذباً عُوجِلَ العُقوبةَ ، وإذا حلفَ بـالله الّذي لا إلهَ إلّا هو لَم يُعاجَلْ ؛ لأنّهُ قد وَحّدَ اللهَ تعالى.[١٩٤٤]

113

THE LAWFUL (*ḤALĀL*)

الحَلال

573. Enjoinment to Eat the Lawful

٥٧٣ ـ الحَثُّ عَلى أكلِ الحَلالِ

"They ask you as to what is lawful to them. Say, 'All the good things are lawful to you.'"[1958]

﴿يَسْأَلُونَكَ مَاذَا أُحِلَّ لَهُمْ قُلْ أُحِلَّ لَكُمُ الطَّيِّبَاتُ﴾.[١٩٤٥]

"O mankind! Eat of what is lawful and pure in the earth, and do not follow in Satan's steps. Indeed he is your manifest enemy."[1959]

﴿يا أيُّها النّاسُ كُلُوا مِمّا فِي الأَرْضِ حَلالاً طَيِّباً وَلا تَتَّبِعُوا خُطُواتِ الشَّيْطانِ إنَّهُ لَكُمْ عَدُوٌّ مُبِينٌ﴾.[١٩٤٦]

1731. **Imām 'Alī (AS) said,** 'It is incumbent upon you to be bound to the lawful, and excel in goodness to your family, and be in remembrance of Allah at all times.'[1960]

١٧٣١ . الإمامُ عليٌّ ﷺ : عليكَ بلُزومِ الحَلالِ، وحُسنِ البِرِّ بالعِيالِ، وذِكرِ اللهِ في كُلِّ حالٍ.[١٩٤٧]

574. The Difficulty in Seeking the Lawful

٥٧٤ ـ صُعوبَةُ طَلَبِ الحَلالِ

1732. **Imām al-Ṣādiq (AS) said,** 'Sword-combat is easier than seeking the lawful.'[1961]

١٧٣٢ . الإمامُ الصّادقُ ﷺ : مُجادَلَةُ[١٩٤٨] السُّيوفِ أهْوَنُ من طَلَبِ الحَلالِ.[١٩٤٩]

575. The Property of the Believer is Unlawful (*ḥarām*) to Use Except with his Consent

٥٧٥ ـ لا يَحِلُّ مالُ المُؤمِنِ إلّا بِطيبِ نَفسِهِ

1733. **The Prophet (SAWA) said,** 'It is unlawful for anyone to use the property of his brother except by his consent.'[1962]

١٧٣٣ . رسولُ اللهِ ﷺ : لايَحِلُّ لامرِئٍ مِن مالِ أخيهِ شيءٌ إلّا بطِيبِ نَفْسٍ مِنهُ.[١٩٥٠] [١٩٥١]

114

CLEMENCY

الحِلم

576. The Virtue of Clemency

٥٧٦ـفضلُ الحِلم

1734. **The Prophet (SAWA) said,** 'The clement person is almost a prophet.'[1963]

١٧٣٤ . رسولُ اللهِ ﷺ : كـادَ الحَـليمُ أنْ يَكـونَ نَبيّاً .١٩٥٢

1735. **Imām ʿAlī (AS) said,** 'Clemency is the completion of the intellect.'[1964]

١٧٣٥ . الإمامُ عليٌّ ؑ : الحِلمُ تَمامُ العَقلِ .١٩٥٣

1736. **Imām ʿAlī (AS) said,** 'Clemency arranges the affair of the believer.'[1965]

١٧٣٦ . عنه ؑ : الحِلمُ نِظامُ أمْرِ المُؤْمِنِ .١٩٥٤

1737. **Imām ʿAlī (AS) said,** 'The beauty of a man is his clemency.'[1966]

١٧٣٧ . عنه ؑ : جَمالُ الرّجُلِ حِلمُهُ .١٩٥٥

1738. **Imām al-Riḍā (AS),** 'A man cannot be a worshipper until he is clement.'[1967]

١٧٣٨ . الإمامُ الرِّضا ؑ : لا يَكونُ الرّجُلُ عابِداً حتّىٰ يكونَ حَليماً .١٩٥٦

577. What Brings About Clemency

٥٧٧ـما يورثُ الحِلمَ

1739. **Imām ʿAlī (AS) said,** 'With the profusion of the intellect, clemency flourishes.'[1968]

١٧٣٩ . الإمامُ عليٌّ ؑ : بِـوُفورِ العـقلِ يَـتَوفّرُ الحِلمُ .١٩٥٧

1740. **Imām ʿAlī (AS) said,** 'Incumbent upon you is clemency for verily it is the fruit of knowledge.'[1969]

١٧٤٠ . عنه ؑ : علَيكَ بـالحِلمِ ؛ فـإنّهُ ثَـمَرَةُ العِلمِ .١٩٥٨

1741. **Imām ʿAlī (AS) said,** 'Clemency and forbearance are the twins that produce great resolution.'[1970]

١٧٤١ . عنه ؑ : الحِلمُ والأناةُ تَوأمانِ يُنْتِجُهما عُلُوُّ الهِمّةِ .١٩٥٩

1742. **Imām ʿAlī (AS) said,** 'If you are not of the clement ones then feign clemency for verily few people who imitate a group fail to become one of them.'[1971]

١٧٤٢ . عنه ؑ : إنْ لَم تكُن حَليماً فَتَحَلَّمْ ؛ فإنّهُ قَلَّ مَن تَشَبَّهَ بقومٍ إلّا أوْشَكَ أنْ يكونَ مِنهُم .١٩٦٠

578. The Fruits of Clemency

٥٧٨ ـ ثَمَراتُ الحِلمِ

1743. **Imām ʿAlī (AS) said,** 'One who is clement has the upper hand.'[1972]

١٧٤٣ . الإمامُ عليٌّ عليه السلام : مَن حَلُمَ سادَ.[١٩٦١]

1744. **Imām ʿAlī (AS) said,** 'One who is clement with his enemy is victorious.'[1973]

١٧٤٤ . عنه عليه السلام : مَن حَلُمَ عن عَدُوِّهِ ظَفِرَ بِه.[١٩٦٢]

1745. **Imām ʿAlī (AS) said,** 'Verily the first recompense from the qualities of the clement person is that the people will assist him against the ignorant one.'[1974]

١٧٤٥ . عنه عليه السلام : إنّ أوّلَ عِوَضِ الحَليمِ مِن خَصْلَتِهِ، أنّ الناسَ أعْوانُهُ علىٰ الجاهِلِ.[١٩٦٣]

1746. **Imām ʿAlī (AS) said,** 'Clemency in the midst of severe anger will protect one from the anger of the Almighty.'[1975]

١٧٤٦ . عنه عليه السلام : الحِلمُ عِندَ شِدَّةِ الغَضَبِ يُؤمِنُ غَضَبَ الجَبّارِ.[١٩٦٤]

1747. **Imām al-Ṣādiq (AS) said,** 'Clemency suffices as a helper.'[1976]

١٧٤٧ . الإمامُ الصّادقُ عليه السلام : كفىٰ بالحِلمِ ناصِراً.[١٩٦٥]

579. The Interpretation of Clemency

٥٧٩ ـ تَفسيرُ الحِلمِ

1748. **Imām ʿAlī (AS) said,** 'The clement one is he who tolerates his brother.'[1977]

١٧٤٨ . الإمامُ عليٌّ عليه السلام : الحَليمُ مَنِ احْتَمَلَ إخوانَهُ.[١٩٦٦]

1749. **Imām al-Ḥasan (AS),** when asked about clemency, said, '[It is] suppressing one's anger and controlling oneself.'[1978]

١٧٤٩ . الإمامُ الحسنُ عليه السلام ـ وقد سُئلَ عنِ الحِلْمِ ـ: كَظْمُ الغَيظِ ومِلْكُ النَّفْسِ.[١٩٦٧]

580. Clemency During Anger

٥٨٠ ـ الحِلمُ عِندَ الغَضَبِ

1750. **Luqmān (AS) said,** 'The clement person is not known until he is angered.'[1979]

١٧٥٠ . لقمانُ عليه السلام : لا يُعْرَفُ الحَليمُ إلّا عِندَ الغَضَبِ.[١٩٦٨]

1751. **Imām ʿAlī (AS),** when asked about the most clement person, said, 'The one who does not become enraged.'[1980]

١٧٥١ . الإمامُ عليٌّ عليه السلام ـ لمّا سُئلَ عن أحلَمِ الناسِ ـ: الّذي لا يَغْضَبُ.[١٩٦٩]

1752. **Imām Zayn al-ʿĀbidīn (AS) said,** 'The man who finds his clemency in the midst of his anger amazes me.'[1981]

١٧٥٢ . الإمامُ زينُ العابدينَ عليه السلام : إنّهُ لَيُعْجِبُني الرَّجُلُ أنْ يُدرِكَهُ حِلمُهُ عِندَ غَضَبِهِ.[١٩٧٠]

115

FOOLISHNESS

الحُمْقُ

581. Reproaching Foolishness

٥٨١ ـ ذَمُّ الحُمقِ

1753. **Imām ʿAlī (AS) said,** 'Foolishness is the worst disease.'[1982]

١٧٥٣ . الإمامُ عليٌّ ؑ : الحُمْقُ أدْوَأُ الدّاءِ .[١٩٧١]

1754. **Imām ʿAlī (AS) said,** 'The greatest poverty is foolishness.'[1983]

١٧٥٤ . عنه ؑ : أفقَرُ الفقرِ الحُمْقُ .[١٩٧٢]

1755. **Imām ʿAlī (AS) said,** 'A person does not ruin his enemy worse than a fool ruins himself.'[1984]

١٧٥٥ . عنه ؑ : ما العَدُوُّ إلىٰ عَدُوِّهِ أسْوأُ تَضْييعاً مِن الأحمَقِ إلىٰ نَفْسِهِ .[١٩٧٣]

582. The Characteristics of a Fool

٥٨٢ ـ صِفاتُ الأحمَقِ

1756. **Prophet Jesus (AS)** when asked about the traits of the fool said, 'He is one who is proud of himself and his own opinion, who sees all good traits as coming from himself and sees no one better than himself, who has decided that all rights are his and others have no right over him, so this is the fool for whom there is no cure for his disease.'[1985]

١٧٥٦ . عيسى ؑ ـ لَمّا سُئلَ عنِ الأحمَقِ ـ : المُعجَبُ برأيِهِ ونَفْسِهِ ، الّذي يَرىٰ الفَضلَ كُلَّهُ لَه لا علَيهِ ، ويُوجِبُ الحقَّ كُلَّهُ لنَفْسِهِ ولا يُوجِبُ علَيها حقّاً ، فذاكَ الأحمَقُ الّذي لا حِيلةَ في مُداواتِهِ .[١٩٧٤]

1757. **Imām ʿAlī (AS) said,** 'The one who pries into the faults of people, rebukes them and then adopts those faults himself is truly a fool.'[1986]

١٧٥٧ . الإمامُ عليٌّ ؑ : مَن نَظَرَ في عُيوبِ النّاسِ فأنكَرَها ثُمّ رَضِيَها لِنَفْسِهِ فذلكَ الأحمَقُ بعَينِهِ .[١٩٧٥]

1758. **Imām ʿAlī (AS) said,** 'The foolishness of a man is recognised by three things: idle talk, answering something he was not asked, and being careless in matters.'[1987]

١٧٥٨ . عنه ؑ : تُعرفُ حَماقةُ الرّجُلِ بالأشَرِ في النِّعمَةِ ، وكَثرَةِ الذُّلِّ في المِحْنَةِ .[١٩٧٦]

1759. **Imām ʿAlī (AS) said,** 'Among the signs of the fool is his profusely whimsical nature.'[1988]

١٧٥٩ . عنه ؑ : مِن أماراتِ الأحمَقِ كَثرَةُ تَلَوُّنِهِ .[١٩٧٧]

1760. **Imām ʿAlī (AS) said,** 'Do not refute everything that people say to you for that is enough to classify you as foolish.'[1989]

١٧٦٠ . عنه ﷺ : لا تَرُدَّ علىٰ النّاسِ كلَّ ما حَدّثوكَ ؛ فكفىٰ بذلكَ حُمْقاً .[١٩٧٨]

583. Taking the Fool as a Companion

٥٨٣ ـ مُصاحَبَةُ الأحمَقِ

1761. **Imām Zayn al-ʿĀbidīn (AS)** in his counsel to his son al-Bāqir (AS) said, 'My son, beware of taking a fool as a companion or mingling with him; keep away from him and do not converse with him for verily the fool is a lowly person whether he is absent or present. When he talks he exposes his foolishness and when he is silent he displays his inability to express himself. If he acts he spoils and when he is given responsibility he fails it. His own knowledge does not suffice him and others' knowledge is of no benefit to him, he does not follow the one who advises him, his associates do not find rest [from him], his mother wishes to be bereaved of him, his wife wishes to lose him, his neighbour wishes to live far from him and the one who sits with him would rather be absent from his company. If he is the lowest [in status] in the gathering he abases those above him and if he is the highest of them he denigrates the others.'[1990]

١٧٦١ . الإمامُ زينُ العابدينَ ﷺ ـ في وصيّتهِ لابنهِ الباقرِ ﷺ ـ : إيّاكَ يا بُنيَّ أنْ تُصاحِبَ الأحمَقَ أو تُخالِطَهُ ، واهْجُرْهُ ولا تُحادِثْهُ ؛ فإنّ الأحمَقَ هُجْنَةٌ غائباً كانَ أو حاضِراً ، إنْ تَكَلَّم فضَحَهُ حُمقُهُ ، وإنْ سَكَتَ قَصُرَ بهِ عِيُّهُ ، وإنْ عَمِلَ أفسَدَ ، وإنِ اسْتُرعِيَ أضاعَ . لا عِلمُهُ مِن نَفْسِهِ يُغْنيهِ ، ولا عِلمُ غيرهِ يَنْفَعُهُ ، ولا يُطيعُ ناصِحَهُ ، ولا يَستريحُ مقارِنُهُ ، تَوَدُّ أُمُّهُ أنّها ثَكَلَتْهُ ، وامْرَأتُهُ أنّها فَقَدَتْهُ ، وجارُهُ بُعدَ دارِهِ ، وجَليسُهُ الوَحْدةَ مِن مُجالَسَتِهِ . إنْ كانَ أصْغَرَ مَن في المَجلِسِ أعْنىٰ مَن فَوقَهُ ، وإنْ كانَ أكْبَرَهُم أفسَدَ مَن دُونَهُ .[١٩٧٩]

1762. **Imām al-Ṣādiq (AS) said,** 'The one who does not refrain from the friendship of a fool will soon adopt his character.'[1991]

١٧٦٢ . الإمامُ الصّادقُ ﷺ : مَن لَم يَجْتَنِبْ مُصادقَةَ الأحمَقِ أوْشَكَ أنْ يَتَخلّقَ بأخْلاقِهِ .[١٩٨٠]

584. The Most Foolish of People

٥٨٤ ـ أحمَقُ النّاسِ

1763. **Imām ʿAlī (AS) said,** 'The most foolish of people is the one who thinks that he is the most intelligent.'[1992]

١٧٦٣ . الإمامُ عليٌّ ﷺ : أحمَقُ النّاسِ مَن ظَنَّ أنّهُ أعْقَلُ النّاسِ .[١٩٨١]

1764. **Imām ʿAlī (AS) said,** 'The most foolish of people is the one who prevents goodness but expects thanks, and he commits evil and expects the reward of good.'[1993]

١٧٦٤ . عنه ﷺ : أحمَقُ النّاسِ مَن يَمْنَعُ البِرَّ ويَطْلُبُ الشُّكْرَ ، ويَفعَلُ الشَّرَّ ويَتَوقّعُ ثَوابَ الخَيرِ .[١٩٨٢]

1765. **Imām ʿAlī (AS) said,** 'The most foolish of people is he who rebukes others for their vices while he possesses the same.'[1994]

١٧٦٥ . عنه ﷺ : أحمَقُ النّاسِ مَن أنْكَرَ علىٰ غَيرِهِ رَذيلَةً وهُو مُقيمٌ علَيها .[١٩٨٣]

585. Answering the Fool

٥٨٥ـ جَوابُ الأحمَقِ

1766. **Imām ʿAlī (AS) said,** 'Maintaining silence with the fool is the best response.'[1995]

١٧٦٦. الإمامُ عليٌّ ﷺ: السُّكوتُ علىٰ الأحمَقِ أفضَلُ (مِن) جَوابِهِ.[١٩٨٤]

116

THE BATHHOUSE

الحَمّامُ

586. Encouraging to Take Bath

٥٨٦ـ الحَثُّ عَلى الذِّهابِ إلَى الحَمّامِ

1767. **Imām ʿAlī (AS) said,** 'The best of houses is the bathhouse for in it the Fire [of Hell] is remembered and [bodily] dirt is removed.'[1996]

١٧٦٧. الإمامُ عليٌّ ﷺ: نِعمَ البَيتُ الحَمّامُ؛ تُذكَرُ فيهِ النّارُ، ويَذهَبُ بالدَّرَنِ.[١٩٨٥]

1768. **Imām al-Ṣādiq (AS) said,** 'Three things cause weight gain and three others cause weight loss. As for those that cause weight gain – excessive use of the bathhouse, smelling sweet fragrance and wearing soft clothing. And as for those that cause weight loss, they are: eating too many eggs, fish and unripe dates.'[1997]

١٧٦٨. الإمامُ الصادقُ ﷺ: ثَلاثةٌ يُسمِنَّ وثَلاثةٌ يُهزِلْنَ، فأمّا الّتي يُسمِنَّ: فإدْمانُ الحَمّامِ، وشَمُّ الرائحَةِ الطَّيِّبَةِ، ولُبْسُ الثِّيابِ اللَّيِّنَةِ، وأمّا الّتي يُهزِلْنَ: فإدْمانُ أكْلِ البَيضِ، والسَّمَكِ، والطَّلْعِ.[١٩٨٦]

587. The Etiquettes of Entering the Bathroom

٥٨٧ـ آدابُ دُخولِ الحَمّامِ

1769. **Imām al-Ṣādiq (AS) said,** 'Three things destroy the body and may even kill it: eating [cooked] meat that has been left overnight, entering the bathhouse after overeating and having intercourse with the elderly.'[1998]

١٧٦٩. الإمامُ الصّادقُ ﷺ: ثَلاثٌ يَهدِمْنَ البَدَنَ ورُبَّما قَتَلْنَ: أكْلُ القَديدِ الغابِّ، ودُخولُ الحَمّامِ علىٰ البِطْنَةِ، ونِكاحُ العَجائزِ.[١٩٨٧]

1770. **Imām al-Ṣādiq (AS) said,** 'Do not enter the bathhouse except after you have put something in your belly that will cool the heat of the stomach for that strengthens your body. And do not enter the bathhouse with a full stomach.'[1999]

١٧٧٠. عنه ﷺ: لا تَدخُلِ الحَمّامَ إلّا وفي جَوفِكَ شَيءٌ يُطفِئُ عنكَ وهَجَ المَعِدَةِ، وهُو أقْوىٰ للبَدَنِ. ولا تَدخُلْهُ وأنتَ مُمْتَلئٌ مِن الطَّعامِ.[١٩٨٨]

117

THE NEED

الحاجة

588. Censure of Asking for a Need

٥٨٨ ـ ذَمُّ طَلَبِ الحاجَةِ

1771. **Imām ʿAlī (AS) said,** 'Grant to whomsoever you please and you will be his emir; ask your need from whomsoever you please and you will be his prisoner; be free of need from whomsoever you please and you will be his equal.'[2000]

١٧٧١ . الإمامُ عليٌّ عليه السلام : امْنُنْ على مَن شِئْتَ تَكُنْ أميرَهُ، واحْتَجْ إلىٰ مَن شِئْتَ تكُنْ أسيرَهُ، واسْتَغْنِ عَمّن شِئتَ تَكُنْ نَظيرَهُ.[١٩٨٩]

1772. **Imām ʿAlī (AS) said,** 'Whoever you have sought your need from, you have lowered yourself in his eyes.'[2001]

١٧٧٢ . عنه عليه السلام : مَنِ احْتَجْتَ إلَيهِ هُنْتَ علَيهِ.[١٩٩٠]

589. Granting Needs

٥٨٩ ـ قَضاءُ الحَوائِجِ

1773. **Imām al-Ṣādiq (AS) said,** 'Allah said, '[My] Creatures are my dependants, the most beloved ones to Me are those who are the kindest to each other and strive to fulfil others' needs.'[2002]

١٧٧٣ . الإمامُ الصّادقُ عليه السلام : قالَ اللهُ عزّوجلّ : الخَلقُ عِيالي، فأحَبُّهُم إلَيَّ ألْطَفُهُم بهِم، وأسْعاهُم في حَوائجِهِم.[١٩٩١]

1774. **The Prophet (SAWA) said,** 'The one who endeavours to help his brother and benefit him has the reward of the warriors in the way of Allah.'[2003]

١٧٧٤ . رسولُ اللهِ صلى الله عليه وآله : مَن مَشىٰ في عَونِ أخيهِ ومَنْفعتِهِ فلَهُ ثَوابُ المُجاهِدينَ في سبيلِ اللهِ.[١٩٩٢]

1775. **The Prophet (SAWA) said,** 'He who strives to grant the needs of his brother in faith is like he has worshipped Allah for nine thousand years, fasting his days and praying his nights.'[2004]

١٧٧٥ . عنه صلى الله عليه وآله : مَن سَعىٰ في حاجَةِ أخيهِ المؤمنِ فكأنّما عَبدَ اللهَ تِسعَةَ آلافِ سَنةٍ، صائماً نَهارَهُ قائماً لَيلَهُ.[١٩٩٣]

1776. **The Prophet (SAWA) said,** 'The one who grants the need of a fellow believing brother is as one who has worshipped Allah his entire life.'[2005]

١٧٧٦ . عنه صلى الله عليه وآله : مَن قضىٰ لأخيهِ المؤمنِ حاجَةً كانَ كمَنْ عَبدَ اللهَ دَهرَهُ.[١٩٩٤]

1777. **Imām al-Ṣādiq (AS) said,** 'The one who strives for the sake of Allah to fulfil the need of

١٧٧٧ . الإمامُ الصّادقُ عليه السلام : مَن سَعىٰ في حاجَةِ أخيهِ المسلمِ ـ طَلَبَ وَجْهِ اللهِ ـ كَتَبَ اللهُ عزّوجلّ

his Muslim brother, Allah will write for him a million good deeds.'[2006]

لهُ ألفَ ألفِ حَسنةٍ.١٩٩٥

1778. **Imām al-Ṣādiq (AS) said,** 'The one who engages himself in fulfilling the need of his Muslim brother, Allah fulfils his need as long as he remains engaged in fulfilling the need of his brother.'[2007]

١٧٧٨. عنه (ع): مَن كانَ في حاجَةِ أخيهِ المؤمنِ المسلمِ كانَ اللهُ في حاجَتِهِ ما كانَ في حاجَةِ أخيه.١٩٩٦

1779. **Imām al-Ṣādiq (AS) said,** 'The one who strives to fulfil the need of his brother is like the one who runs between *al-Ṣafā* and *al-Marwā*.'[2008 2009]

١٧٧٩. عنه (ع): الماشي في حاجَةِ أخيهِ كالسّاعي بينَ الصَّفا والمَرْوَةِ.١٩٩٧

1780. **Imām al-Ṣādiq (AS) said,** 'The one who grants the need of his believing brother, Allah will grant him one hundred thousand of his needs on the Day of Resurrection, the first of them being Paradise.'[2010]

١٧٨٠. عنه (ع): مَن قَضى لأخيهِ المؤمنِ حاجَةً قَضى اللهُ عزّوجلّ لَهُ يومَ القِيامَةِ مِائةَ ألفِ حاجَةٍ مِن ذلكَ، أوَّلُها الجَنّةُ.١٩٩٨

1781. **Imām al-Ṣādiq (AS) said,** 'Verily granting the need of a fellow believer is more beloved to Allah than twenty obligatory pilgrimages (*ḥajj*) wherein each *ḥajj* the pilgrim donates one hundred thousand (dinars or dirhams).'[2011]

١٧٨١. عنه (ع): لَقَضاءُ حاجَةِ امرِئٍ مؤمنٍ أحَبُّ إلى (اللهِ) مِن عِشرينَ حِجَّةً، كُلُّ حِجَّةٍ يُنفِقُ فيها صاحِبُها مائةَ ألفٍ.١٩٩٩

(See also: ACTS OF COMMON COURTESY (1) 104, section 272; GOOD-DOING: section 41)

(أنظر) عنوان ٢٧٢ «المعروف (١)»: ١٠٤ «الإحسان»: الأخ: باب ٤١.

590. The One who Refrains from Granting the Need of his Brother

٥٩٠ـ مَنِ امتَنَعَ عَن قَضاءِ حاجَةِ أخيهِ

1782. **Imām al-Bāqir (AS) said,** 'Whichever Muslim comes to another Muslim's home to visit or to seek a need, and asks permission to enter but he does not come out [to meet him], the curse of Allah will continuously be upon that Muslim [host] until they both meet again.'[2012]

١٧٨٢. الإمامُ الباقرُ (ع): أيُّما مسلمٍ أتى مسلماً ـ زائراً أو طالِبَ حاجَةٍ وهُو في مَنزِلِهِ ـ فاستَأذَنَ له ولَم يَخرُجْ إلَيهِ، لم يَزَلْ في لَعنَةِ اللهِ عزّوجلّ حتّى يَلتَقِيا.٢٠٠٠

1783. **Imām al-Ṣādiq (AS) said,** 'One who asks his believing brother a need in time of difficulty and he refuses him while being capable of fulfilling that need, either himself or through someone else, Allah will raise him on the Day of

١٧٨٣. الإمامُ الصّادقُ (ع): مَن سألَهُ أخوهُ المؤمنُ حاجَةً مِن ضُرٍّ فمَنَعَهُ مِن سَعةٍ وهُو يَقدِرُ علَيها ـ مِن عِندِهِ أو مِن عندِ غيرِهِ ـ حَشَرهُ اللهُ يومَ

Resurrection in chains from his hands to his neck until Allah completes the account of all of creation.'[2013]

القِيامَةِ مَغْلولَةً يدُهُ إلىٰ عُنُقِهِ حتّىٰ يَفْرُغَ اللهُ مِن حِسابِ الخَلقِ.٢٠٠١

1784. **Imām al-Ṣādiq (AS) said,** 'Whichever one of our brothers comes to one of our followers (*shī'a*) and seeks help from him regarding a need and he does not help him, Allah will afflict him by fulfilling the need of one of our enemies, and for that Allah will punish him on the Day of Resurrection.'[2014]

١٧٨٤ . عنه ﷺ : أيُّما رجُلٍ مِن شِيعَتِنا أتاهُ رجُلٌ مِن إخْوانِنا فاسْتَعانَ بهِ في حاجَةٍ فلَم يُعِنْهُ وهُو يَقْدِرُ، ابْتَلاهُ اللهُ عزّ وجلّ بأنْ يَقْضيَ حوائجَ عَدُوٍّ مِن أعْدائنا يُعذِّبُهُ اللهُ علَيهِ يومَ القِيامَةِ.٢٠٠٢

1785. **Imām al-Ṣādiq (AS) said,** 'Whichever believer withholds his wealth from another believer who is in need, by Allah he will not taste the food of Paradise and he will not drink from the sealed wine [of Paradise].'[2015]

١٧٨٥ . عنه ﷺ : أيُّما مؤمنٍ حَبَسَ مؤمناً عن مالِهِ وهُو مُحتاجٌ إلَيهِ لَم يَذُقْ واللهِ مِن طَعامِ الجَنّةِ، ولا يَشْرَبُ مِن الرَّحيقِ المَخْتومِ.٢٠٠٣

591. Undertaking the Granting of Needs

٥٩١ ـ المُبادَرَةُ إلىٰ قَضاءِ الحَوائجِ

1786. **Imām al-Ṣādiq (AS) said,** 'Verily if a man requests from me a need that he has, I will undertake to grant it fearing that his need gets fulfilled and he will no longer find any use for me [in helping him].'[2016]

١٧٨٦ . الإمامُ الصّادقُ ﷺ : إنَّ الرّجُلَ لَيَسْألُني الحاجَةَ فأُبادِرُ بقَضائها ؛ مَخافَةَ أنْ يَسْتَغْنيَ عنها، فلا يَجِدَ لَها مَوقِعاً إذا جاءَتْهُ.٢٠٠٤

592. The Etiquette of Seeking a Need

٥٩٢ ـ أدَبُ طَلَبِ الحاجَةِ

1787. **Imām 'Alī (AS) said,** 'O Allah please do not make me require a need from bad people from among Your creation, and whatever You make me need, let it be from those with the most beautiful [happiest] faces, who are the most open-handed, have the most eloquent tongues and the least likely to remind me of their favour.'[2017]

١٧٨٧ . الإمامُ عليٌّ ﷺ : اللّهُمَّ لا تَجعَلْ بي حاجَةً إلىٰ أحدٍ مِن شِرارِ خَلْقِكَ، وما جَعَلْتَ بي مِن حاجَةٍ فاجْعَلْها إلىٰ أحْسَنِهِم وَجْهاً، وأسْخاهُم بها نَفْساً، وأطْلَقِهِم بها لِساناً، وأقلِّهِم علَيَّ بها مَنّاً.٢٠٠٥

1788. Someone once said in the presence of Imām Zayn al-'Ābidīn (AS), 'O Allah, free me of need from Your creation.' The Imām immediately responded, 'Not like that! People are in need of

١٧٨٨ . الإمامُ زينُ العابدينَ ﷺ ـ لِمَن قالَ بحَضْرَتِهِ: اللّهُمَّ أغْنِني عَن خَلْقِكَ ـ : لَيسَ هكذا، إنّما النّاسُ بالنّاسِ، ولكنْ قُلْ: اللّهُمَّ

each other, rather say, 'O Allah, free me of need from the bad people from among Your creation.'[2018]

أغْنِني عن شِرارِ خَلْقِكَ.٢٠٠٦

1789. **Imām al-Bāqir (AS) said,** 'Verily the example of one who is in need from someone who has recently attained wealth is that of a dirham [coin] in the mouth of a viper. You are in need of it but at the same time you are in danger of the viper.'[2019]

١٧٨٩ . الإمامُ الباقرُ ﷺ : إنّما مَثَلُ الحاجَةِ إلىٰ مَن أصابَ مالَهُ حَديثاً كمَثَلِ الدِّرْهَمِ في فَمِ الأفعىٰ : أنتَ إلَيهِ مُحْوِجٌ وأنتَ مِنها علىٰ خَطَرٍ.٢٠٠٧

(See also: ASKING (2): section 911)

(أنظر) السؤال (٢): باب ٩١١.

118

PRECAUTION

الاحتياط

593. Take Precaution with your Religion

٥٩٣ ـ احتَط لِدِينِكَ

1790. **Imām 'Alī (AS) said,** 'Your religion is your brother so take precaution with your religion however much you can.'[2020]

١٧٩٠ . الإمامُ عليٌّ ﷺ : أخوكَ دِينُكَ، فاحْتَطْ لدِينِكَ بم شِئتَ.٢٠٠٨

1791. **Imām al-Ṣādiq (AS) said,** 'It is upon you to be resolute and precautious with your religion.'[2021]

١٧٩١ . الإمامُ الصّادقُ ﷺ : لَكَ أنْ تَنْظُرَ الحَزْمَ وتأخُذَ الحائطَةَ لدِينِكَ.٢٠٠٩

1792. **Imām al-Ṣādiq (AS) said,** 'Be precautious with all things that you have the ability to carry out.'[2022]

١٧٩٢ . عنه ﷺ : خُذْ بالاحْتياطِ في جَميعِ ما تَجِدُ إلَيهِ سبيلاً.٢٠١٠

119

LIFE

الحياة

594. The Value of Life

٥٩٤ ـ قيمَةُ الحَياةِ

1793. **Imām 'Alī (AS) said,** 'Know that man gets satiated and wearied with everything except life, because he does not find any comfort in death.'[2023]

١٧٩٣ . الإمامُ عليٌّ ﷺ : اعلَموا أنّهُ لَيس مِن شيءٍ إلّا ويَكادُ صاحِبُهُ يَشبَعُ مِنهُ ويَمَلُّه إلّا الحَياةَ ؛ فإنّهُ لا يَجِدُ في المَوتِ راحةً.٢٠١١

595. Water and Life

٥٩٥ـ الماءُ وَالحَياةُ

"And we made everything living out of water"[2024]

﴿وَجَعَلْنَا مِنَ الْمَاءِ كُلَّ شَيْءٍ حَيٍّ﴾.[٢٠١٢]

1794. **Imām al-Ṣādiq (AS) said,** 'The flavour of water is life.'[2025]

١٧٩٤ . الإمامُ الصادقُ ﷺ : طَعْمُ الماءِ الحياةُ.[٢٠١٣]

596. That Which is Better than Life

٥٩٦ـ ما هُوَ خَيرٌ مِنَ الحَياةِ

1795. **Imām al-ʿAskarī (AS) said,** 'Better than life is that thing which if you lose it you become disgusted with life, and worse than death is that thing which if it comes to you makes you love death.'[2026]

١٧٩٥ . الإمامُ العسكريُّ ﷺ : خَيرٌ مِن الحياةِ ما إذا فَقَدْتَهُ أبْغَضْتَ الحياةَ، وشَرٌّ مِن المَوتِ ما إذا نَزَلَ بِكَ أحْبَبْتَ المَوتَ.[٢٠١٤]

597. The Real Life

٥٩٧ـ الحَياةُ الحَقيقِيَّةُ

1796. **Imām ʿAlī (AS) said,** 'There is no life except through religion, and there is no death except through denial of the certain truth.'[2027]

١٧٩٦ . الإمامُ عليٌّ ﷺ : لا حياةَ إلّا بالدِّين، ولا مَوتَ إلّا بجُحودِ اليَقينِ.[٢٠١٥]

1797. **Imām ʿAlī (AS) said,** 'Monotheism is the life of the soul.'[2028]

١٧٩٧ . عنه ﷺ : التَّوحيدُ حياةُ النَّفسِ.[٢٠١٦]

120

ANIMALS

الحَيَوانُ

598. The Rights of Animals

٥٩٨ـ حُقوقُ الحَيَوانِ

1798. When the Prophet (SAWA) saw a she-camel, whose knees were tied up, carrying her load, he said, 'Where is her owner? Tell him that he should prepare for the lawsuit tomorrow [the Day of Resurrection].'[2029]

١٧٩٨ . رسولُ اللهِ ﷺ ـ لَمّا أبْصَرَ ناقَةً مَعْقولَةً وعلَيها جِهازُها ـ : أينَ صاحِبُها؟ مُروهُ فلْيَسْتَعِدَّ غَداً للخُصومَةِ.[٢٠١٧]

1799. **The Prophet (SAWA) said,** 'Verily Allah loves gentleness and He aids in implementing it,

١٧٩٩ . عنه ﷺ : إنّ اللهَ يُحِبُّ الرِّفْقَ ويُعينُ علَيهِ،

so when you ride a lean animal, dismount it at the right place for if the land is barren and arid then get away from it and if the land is lush and fertile then dismount the animal [and allow it to rest].'[2030]

فإذا رَكِبْتُمُ الدَّوابَّ العُجْفَ فـأَنْزِلوها مَـنازِلَها، فإنْ كانتِ الأرضُ مُـجْدِبَةً فـانْجوا عَـنها، وإنْ كانتْ مُخْصِبةً فأَنْزِلُوها مَنازِلَها.[٢٠١٨]

1800. **The Prophet (SAWA) said,** 'Mount the sound animals and look after them properly and do not treat them as chairs for your conversations in the streets and the markets, for many riding animals are better than their rider and are more remembering of Allah – Blessed and most High.'[2031]

١٨٠٠. عنه ﷺ: ارْكَبوا هـذهِ الدَّوابَّ سـالِمَةً واتَّـدِعُوها سـالِمَةً، ولا تَـتَّخِذوها كَـراسِيَّ لأحاديثِكُم في الطُّرُقِ والأسْواقِ فَرُبَّ مَرْكوبَةٍ خَيرٌ مِن راكِبِها وأكْثَرُ ذِكْراً للهِ تـبارَكَ وتـعالىٰ مِنهُ.[٢٠١٩]

1801. **The Prophet (SAWA) said,** 'The animal has six rights over its owner: once the owner has dismounted the animal he should allow it to graze, he should give it access to water if they pass by it, he should not hit the animal except when it truly deserves it, he should not burden it with a load that it cannot bear, he should not overtask it with a journey that it cannot endure and he should not sit on it for lengthy periods of time.'[2032]

١٨٠١. عنه ﷺ: للدّابّـةِ عـلىٰ صـاحِبِها سِتُّ خِصالٍ: يَعْلِفُها إذا نَزلَ، ويَعْرِضُ علَيها الماءَ إذا مَرَّ بِهِ، ولا يَضْرِبُها إلّا علىٰ حقٍّ، ولا يُحَمّلُها ما لا تُطيقُ[٢٠٢٠]، ولا يُكلّفُها مِن السَّيرِ إلّا طـاقَتَها، ولا يَقِفُ علَيها فُواقاً.[٢٠٢١]

1802. **The Prophet (SAWA) said,** 'Do not hit animals on their faces for verily they praise and glorify Allah.'[2033]

١٨٠٢. عنه ﷺ: لا تَـضْرِبوا الدَّوابَّ عـلىٰ وُجوهِها؛ فإنَّها تُسَبِّحُ بحَمْدِ اللهِ.[٢٠٢٢]

1803. **The Prophet (SAWA) said,** 'A prostitute was forgiven when she passed a panting dog almost dying of thirst at the foot of a well, whereby she took off her shoe and tied it to her headscarf and lowered it into the well to extract water [for the dog], and for that action she was forgiven.'[2034]

١٨٠٣. عنه ﷺ: غُفِرَ لامْرأةٍ مُومِسَةٍ مرَّتْ بكلبٍ علىٰ رأسِ رَكِيٍّ يَـلْهَثُ كـادَ يَـقْتُلُهُ العَـطَشُ، فنَزَعَتْ خُفَّها فأوْثَقَتْهُ بخِمارِها فنَزَعَتْ لَهُ مِـن الماءِ، فغُفِرَ لَها بذلكَ.[٢٠٢٣]

1804. **The Prophet (SAWA) said,** 'No animal, including a bird or any other kind, is killed unjustly except that it will raise a complaint against him [the killer] on the Day of Resurrection.'[2035]

١٨٠٤. عنه ﷺ: ما مِن دابَّةٍ ـ طائرٍ ولا غَيرِهِ ـ يُقتَلُ بغَيرِ الحقِّ إلّا ستُخاصِمُهُ يومَ القِيامَةِ.[٢٠٢٤]

1805. **The Prophet (SAWA) said,** 'Whoever kills a sparrow in vain, it will cry out to Allah against

١٨٠٥. عنه ﷺ: مَن قَتلَ عُصْفوراً عَبَثاً عَجَّ إلىٰ

him on the Day of Resurrection saying, 'O my Lord, so and so killed me in vain and did not kill me for any useful purpose.'[2036]

اللهِ يَومَ القِيامَةِ مِنهُ ، يقولُ: يا رَبِّ، إنّ فُلاناً قَتلَني عَبَثاً ولَم يَقتُلْني لِمَنفَعَةٍ.[٢٠٢٥]

1806. **The Prophet (SAWA) said,** 'If the oppression that you have committed towards animals is forgiven for you, then [realise that] you have been forgiven a lot [of your sins].'[2037]

١٨٠٦ . عنه ﷺ :لَو غُفِرَ لَكُم ما تَأتونَ إلَى البَهائِمِ لَغُفِرَ لَكُم كَثيراً.[٢٠٢٦]

1807. **The Prophet (SAWA) said,** 'Are you not Godwary with respect to this animal that Allah has allowed you to possess?! Because verily it has complained to me that you keep it hungry and tire it out.'[2038]

١٨٠٧ . عنه ﷺ : ألَا تَتَّقي اللهَ في هٰذِهِ البَهيمَةِ الّتي مَلّكَكَ اللهُ تعالىٰ إيّاها ؟! فإنّهُ شَكا إلَيّ أنّكَ تُجيعُهُ وتُدْئبُهُ.[٢٠٢٧]

1808. **The Prophet (SAWA) said,** 'May the curse of Allah be on the one who treats an animal harshly.'[2039]

١٨٠٨ . عنه ﷺ : لَعنَ اللهُ مَن مَثَّلَ بالحَيوانِ.[٢٠٢٨]

1809. It is narrated in *Kanz al-'Ummāl*, from Ibn 'Abbās who said, 'The Prophet (SAWA) forbade the killing of any living thing unless it causes harm.'[2040]

١٨٠٩ . كنز العمّال : نَهىٰ [رسول الله ﷺ] عن قَتلِ كُلِّ ذي رُوحٍ إلّا أنْ يُؤذي.[٢٠٢٩]

1810. **Imām al-Ṣādiq (AS) said,** 'Verily a woman was chastised for the fact that she tied up a cat and left it till it died of thirst.'[2041]

١٨١٠ . الإمامُ الصّادقُ ؑ : إنّ امرأة عُذِّبَتْ في هِرّةٍ رَبَطَتْها حتّىٰ ماتَتْ عَطَشاً.[٢٠٣٠]

121

MODESTY

الحَياءُ

599. The Virtue of Modesty

٥٩٩ ـ فَضلُ الحَياءِ

1811. **Imām 'Alī (AS) said,** 'Modesty is the means to all beauty.'[2042]

١٨١١ . الإمامُ عليٌّ ؑ : الحياءُ سَبَبٌ إلىٰ كُلِّ جَميلٍ.[٢٠٣١]

1812. **Imām 'Alī (AS) said,** 'Modesty is the key to all goodness.'[2043]

١٨١٢ . عنه ؑ : الحياءُ مِفْتاحُ كُلِّ الخَيرِ.[٢٠٣٢]

1813. **Imām 'Alī (AS) said,** 'The most intelligent person is the most modest one.'[2044]

١٨١٣ . عنه ؑ : أعقَلُ النّاسِ أحْياهُم.[٢٠٣٣]

1814. **Imām ʿAlī (AS) said,** 'Modesty prevents ugly actions.'[2045]

١٨١٤ . عنه عليه السلام : الحياءُ يَصُدُّ عنْ فِعْلِ القَبيحِ.[٢٠٣٤]

1815. **Imām ʿAlī (AS) said,** 'The means to chastity is modesty.'[2046]

١٨١٥ . عنه عليه السلام : سَبَبُ العِفَّةِ الحياءُ.[٢٠٣٥]

600. Modesty and Faith

٦٠٠ ـ الحَياءُ وَالإيمانُ

1816. **The Prophet (SAWA) said,** 'Verily every religion has a natural disposition and the natural disposition of Islam is modesty.'[2047]

١٨١٦ . رسولُ اللهِ ﷺ : إنّ لِكُلِّ دِينٍ خُلُقاً ، وإنّ خُلُقَ الإسلامِ الحياءُ.[٢٠٣٦]

1817. **Imām al-Ṣādiq (AS) said,** 'There is no faith for the one who has no modesty.'[2048]

١٨١٧ . الإمامُ الصّادقُ عليه السلام : لا إيمانَ لِمَن لا حياءَ لَهُ.[٢٠٣٧]

601. Reprehensible Modesty

٦٠١ ـ الحَياءُ المَذمومُ

1818. **The Prophet (SAWA) said,** 'There are two types of modesty, modesty springing from the intellect, and a sense of shame arising from foolishness. As for the modesty of the intellect, it is knowledge, and as for the shame from foolishness, it is ignorance.'[2049]

١٨١٨ . رسولُ اللهِ ﷺ : الحياءُ حياءانِ : حياءُ عَقْلٍ وحياءُ حُمْقٍ ، فحَياءُ العَقلِ العِلْمُ ، وحَياءُ الحُمْقِ الجَهْلُ.[٢٠٣٨]

1819. **Imām ʿAlī (AS) said,** 'Shame has been associated with deprivation.'[2050]

١٨١٩ . الإمامُ عليٌّ عليه السلام : قُرِنَ الحياءُ بالحِرْمانِ.[٢٠٣٩]

1820. **Imām ʿAlī (AS) said,** 'Shame prevents sustenance.'[2051]

١٨٢٠ . عنه عليه السلام : الحياءُ يَمْنَعُ الرِّزْقَ.[٢٠٤٠]

1821. **Imām ʿAlī (AS) said,** 'One who is ashamed of speaking the truth is a fool.'[2052]

١٨٢١ . عنه عليه السلام : مَنِ اسْتَحيىٰ مِن قَولِ الحَقِّ فهُو أحمَقُ.[٢٠٤١]

602. The Consequences of Lack of Modesty

٦٠٢ ـ ما يَتَرَتَّبُ عَلىٰ عَدَمِ الحَياءِ

1822. **The Prophet (SAWA) said,** 'From the proverbs of the prophets (AS) only the following saying of the people has remained, "If you do not have modesty then do as you wish".'[2053]

١٨٢٢ . رسولُ اللهِ ﷺ : لم يَبْقَ مِن أمْثالِ الأنْبياءِ عليهم السلام إلّا قَولُ النّاسِ : إذا لَم تَسْتَحيِ فاصْنَعْ ما شِئْتَ.[٢٠٤٢]

1823. **Imām ʿAlī (AS) said,** 'One who is not ashamed in front of people is not ashamed in front of Allah, Glory be to Him.'[2054]

١٨٢٣ . الإمامُ عليٌّ ﷺ :مَن لَم يَسْتَحيِ مِنَ النّاسِ لَم يَسْتَحيِ مِنَ اللهِ سبحانَهُ.٢٠٤٣

603. Having Modesty with Allah

٦٠٣ ـ الاستِحياءُ مِنَ اللهِ

1824. **The Prophet (SAWA) said,** 'Be modest in front of Allah just like your modesty with your righteous neighbours, for verily modesty with Allah increases one's conviction.'[2055]

١٨٢٤ . رسولُ اللهِ ﷺ : اسْتَحْيِ مِنَ اللهِ اسْتِحياءَكَ مِن صالِحي جِيرانِكَ ؛ فإنّ فيها زِيادَةَ اليَقينِ.٢٠٤٤

1825. **The Prophet (SAWA) said,** 'Every one of you should be modest in front of his two angels that are with him, just as you would be modest with two righteous neighbours that are with you day and night.'[2056]

١٨٢٥ . عنه ﷺ لِيَسْتَحيِ أحَدُكُم مِن مَلَكَيهِ اللَّذَينِ معَهُ، كما يَسْتَحْيِي مِن رجُلَينِ صالِحَينِ مِن جِيرانِهِ، وهُما مَعهُ بالليلِ والنّهارِ.٢٠٤٥

1826. **Imām al-Kāẓim (AS) said,** 'Be modest with Allah when in private just as you are modest with people in public.'[2057]

١٨٢٦ . الإمامُ الكاظمُ ﷺ : اسْتَحْيوا مِن اللهِ في سَرائرِكُم كما تَسْتَحْيونَ مِن النّاسِ في عَلانِيَتِكُم.٢٠٤٦

604. The Peak of Modesty

٦٠٤ ـ غايَةُ الحَياءِ

1827. **Imām ʿAlī (AS) said,** 'The peak of modesty is for a man to be modest in the presence of his own self.'[2058]

١٨٢٧ . الإمامُ عليٌّ ﷺ :غايَةُ الحياءِ أنْ يَسْتَحيِيَ المَرءُ مِن نَفْسِهِ.٢٠٤٧

122

THE END

الخاتِمَة

605. The Danger of a Bad End

٦٠٥ ـ خَطَرُ الخاتِمَةِ

1828. **The Prophet (SAWA) said,** 'The believer is continuously fearful of a bad end [to his life] and remains uncertain of attaining the pleasure of Allah until the angel of death appears and takes his soul.'[2059]

١٨٢٨ . رسولُ اللهِ ﷺ : لا يَزالُ المؤمنُ خائفاً من سُوءِ العاقِبَةِ، لا يَتَيقَّنُ الوُصولَ إلىٰ رِضْوانِ اللهِ حتّىٰ يكونَ وَقتُ نَزْعِ رُوحِهِ وظُهورِ مَلَكِ المَوتِ لَهُ.٢٠٤٨

1829. **The Prophet (SAWA) said,** 'Verily a man may carry out the actions of the people of

١٨٢٩ . عنه ﷺ : إنَّ الرّجُلَ لَيعْمَلُ الزَّمَنَ

Paradise for a long period of time, but end his life with the actions of the people of the Hellfire.'[2060]

الطّويلَ بعَمَلِ أهْلِ الجَنّةِ، ثُمّ يُختَمُ لَهُ بعَمَلِ أهْلِ النّارِ.[٢٠٤٩]

1830. **The Prophet (SAWA) said,** 'Do not be amazed by [the good actions of] anyone until you see his end, for verily one may perform good actions for a period of his life that if he were to die during that time he would enter Paradise, but he subsequently changes and then commits evil actions.'[2061]

١٨٣٠. عنه ﷺ: لا علَيكُم أنْ تُعْجَبوا بأحَدٍ حتّىٰ تَنْظُروا بما يُخْتَمُ لَهُ، فإنَّ العامِلَ يَعْمَلُ زَماناً مِن عُمرِهِ أو بُرْهَةً مِن دَهْرِهِ بعَمَلٍ صالحٍ لو ماتَ علَيهِ دَخَلَ الجَنّةَ، ثُمَّ يَتَحَوّلُ فيَعْمَلُ عَمَلاً سَيّئاً.[٢٠٥٠]

(See also: PROSPERITY: section 948)

(أُنظر) السعادة: باب ٩٤٨.

606. What Brings About a Good Final Outcome

٦٠٦ـ موجِباتُ حُسنِ العاقِبَةِ

1831. **Imām ʿAlī (AS) said,** 'If you want Allah to protect you from an evil final outcome [to your life], then know that whatever good that comes is from Allah's grace and divine succour, and whatever bad that comes, know that Allah has delayed it for you and you have already been given respite for it, so be aware of Allah's clemency and pardon for you.'[2062]

١٨٣١. الإمامُ عليٌّ عليه السلام: إنْ أرَدْتَ أنْ يُؤْمِنَكَ اللهُ سُوءَ العاقِبَةِ فاعْلَمْ أنَّ ما تَأْتيهِ مِن خَيرٍ فبفَضْلِ اللهِ وتَوفيقِهِ، وما تَأْتيهِ مِن سُوءٍ فبِإمْهالِ اللهِ وإنْظارِهِ، إيّاكَ وحِلْمَهُ وعَفْوَهُ عَنكَ.[٢٠٥١]

1832. **Imām al-Ṣādiq (AS) said** to some people, 'If you want a good final outcome to your actions and for your soul to be taken while you are in the best of actions then observe the rights of Allah, do not use His bounties to disobey Him, do not allow the fact that Allah is clement with you to delude you [into negligence], and respect and honour everyone who praises us or those who embrace our love.'[2063]

١٨٣٢. الإمامُ الصّادقُ عليه السلام ـ لبعضِ النّاسِ ـ: إنْ أرَدْتَ أنْ يُخْتَمَ بخَيرٍ عَمَلُكَ حتّىٰ تُقْبَضَ وأنتَ في أفْضَلِ الأعْمالِ فعَظِّمْ للهِ حَقَّهُ أن تَبْذُلَ نَعْماءَهُ في مَعاصيهِ، وأنْ تَغْتَرَّ بحِلْمِهِ عَنكَ، وأكْرِمْ كُلَّ مَن وَجَدْتَهُ يُذْكَرُ مِنّا أو يَنْتَحِلُ مَوَدّتَنا.[٢٠٥٢]

123

SERVICE

الخِدمَة

607. The Virtue of Serving Muslims

٦٠٧ـ فَضلُ خِدمَةِ المُسلمينَ

1833. **The Prophet (SAWA) said,** 'No sooner does a Muslim serve a group of Muslims than

١٨٣٣. رسولُ اللهِ ﷺ: أيُّما مُسلمٍ خَدَمَ قوماً

Allah will give him servants equal in number [to the group] in Paradise.'[2064]

مِن المُسلمينَ إلّا أعْطاهُ اللهُ مِثْلَ عَدَدِهِم خُدّاماً في الجَنّةِ.٢٠٥٣

1834. **The Prophet (SAWA) said,** 'The service of a believer to his fellow believing brother is [worthy of] a station of which the reward and grandeur can only be perceived by returning the same service.'[2065]

١٨٣٤. عنه ﷺ: خِدْمَـةُ المؤمنِ لأخيهِ المؤمنِ دَرَجةٌ لا يُدْرَكُ فَضْلُها إلّا بمِثْلِها.٢٠٥٤

1835. **Imām al-Ṣādiq (AS) said,** 'The believers are servants of each other'. (Jamīl narrates), 'I asked, 'How are they servants of each other?' The Imām replied, 'By being of benefit to each other.'[2066]

١٨٣٥. الكافي عن جميل قال الإمام الصّادقُ عليه السلام ـ: المؤمِنونَ خَدَمُ بَعْضُهُم لبَعْضٍ ـ [قالَ جميلٌ:] قلتُ: وكيفَ يَكونونَ خَـدَماً بَـعْضُهم لبَـعْضٍ ؟ قالَ ـ: يُفيدُ بَعْضُهُم بَعْضاً.٢٠٥٥

1836. **Imām al-Ṣādiq (AS) said,** 'Serve your brother, but if he makes you toil then do not serve him.'[2067]

١٨٣٦. الإمامُ الصّادقُ عليه السلام: إخْدِمْ أخاكَ، فـإنِ اسْتَخْدَمَكَ فلا ولا كَرامَةَ.٢٠٥٦

(See also: KNOWLEDGE: SECTION 1353; EMPLOYMENT (2))

(أنظر) العلم: باب ١٣٥٣؛ عنوان ٢ «الإجارة».

124

THE KHARIJITES

الخَوارِج

608. The Apostates[2068]

٦٠٨ ـ المارِقونَ٢٠٥٧

"Say, 'Shall we inform you about the biggest losers in regard to works? Those whose endeavour goes awry in the life of the world, while they suppose they are doing good.'"[2069]

﴿قُلْ هَلْ نُنَبِّئُكُمْ بِالْأَخْسَرِينَ أَعْـمَالاً * الَّـذِينَ ضَلَّ سَعْيُهُمْ فِي الْحَيَاةِ الدُّنْيَا وَهُمْ يَحْسَبُونَ أَنَّهُمْ يُحْسِنُونَ صُنْعاً﴾.٢٠٥٨

1837. It is narrated in *Kanz al-'Ummāl* that while the Prophet (SAWA) was handing out gold bullion on the day of [the battle of] Ḥunayn, a man came to him and said, 'O Muḥammad, act fairly!', The Prophet (SAWA) said, 'Woe to you, if I am not fair then who is fair?' or he said, 'With whom will you find fairness besides me?' after which he said, 'Soon there will come a people like this who will seek the Book of Allah while being its enemy, they will read the Book of Allah but the words will not go higher than their throat. They

١٨٣٧. كنز العمّال عن عبد الله بن عـمرو: إنّ رجُلاً أتىٰ النَّبيَّ ﷺ يَومَ حُنينٍ وهُو يَـقْسِمُ تِـبْراً فقالَ: يا مـحمّدُ، اعْـدِلْ! فـقالَ: وَيْـحَكَ! مَـن يَعْدِلُ إذا لَم أعْدِلْ ؟! ـ أو عِندَ مَن يُلْتَمَسُ العَدلُ بَعدي ؟! ـ ثُمّ قالَ: يُوشِكُ أنْ يأتـيَ قَـومٌ مِـثلُ هٰذا يَسألونَ كِتابَ اللهِ وهُـم أعْـداؤهُ، يَـقْرَؤونَ كِتابَ الله ولا يَحُلُّ حَناجِرَهُم، مُحَلَّقَةً رؤوسُهُم،

will have shaved heads, so when they arise [to revolt] slay their necks.'[2070]

فإذ خَرَجوا فاضْرِبوا رِقابَهُم.٢٠٥٩

1838. Once a man, in the presence of Imām ʿAlī (AS), recited the above-mentioned Qur'anic verse after which the Imām said, 'The *Ḥarūrā'* [i.e. the Kharijites] are from them.'[2071]

١٨٣٨ . الإمامُ عليٌّ عليه السلام ـوقد تَلا رجُلٌ هٰذهِ الآيةَ بحَضْرَتِهِ ـ: أهلُ حَرُوراءَ مِنهُم.٢٠٦٠

1839. **Imām ʿAlī (AS) said,** 'I heard the Prophet (SAWA) saying, 'There will come a people during the last days who will be young and rash-minded, their words will be the best words of the righteous, their prayers will be more than your prayers, their recitation [of the Qur'an] will be more than your recitation, however their faith will not transcend their collarbones - or he said 'throats' -, they will leave the true faith as swiftly as an arrow flies from the bow; therefore kill them.'[2072]

١٨٣٩ . عنه عليه السلام : سَمِعْتُ رسولَ اللهِ صلى الله عليه وآله يقولُ: يَخْرُجُ في آخرِ الزّمانِ قومٌ أحْداثُ الأسْنانِ، سُفَهاءُ الأحْلامِ، قَوْلُهُم مِن خَيرِ أقْوالِ أهْلِ البَرِيَّةِ، صَلاتُهُم أكْثَرُ مِن صَلاتِكُم، وقِراءتُهُم أكْثَرُ مِن قِراءتِكُم، لا يُجاوِزُ إيمانُهُم تَراقِيَهُم - أو قالَ حَناجِرَهُم ـ يَمْرُقونَ مِن الدِّينِ كما يَمْرُقُ السَّهمُ مِن الرَّمِيَّةِ، فاقْتُلوهُم.٢٠٦١

609. Imām ʿAlī (AS) After the Killing of the Kharijites

٦٠٩ ـ الإمام عليّ عليه السلام بَعدَ مَقتَلِ الخَوارجِ

1840. When walking past the slayed bodies of the Kharijites, Imām ʿAlī (AS) said, 'How wretched you are! The one who misled you has brought harm to you', someone then asked, 'Who has misled them O Commander of the Faithful?' he said, 'The deceptive Satan and the carnal soul which commands towards evil have misled them by giving them a false sense of security, giving them a wide opening for disobedience and promising them victory, but through them they have plunged into the Fire.'[2073]

١٨٤٠ . الإمامُ عليٌّ عليه السلام ـ وقَد مَرَّ بقَتْلَى الخَوارجِ ـ: بُؤْساً لَكُم! لَقد ضَرَّكُم مَن غَرَّكُم. فقيلَ لَهُ: مَن غَرَّهُم يا أميرَ المؤمنينَ؟ فقالَ: الشَّيطانُ المُضِلُّ، والأنْفُسُ الأمّارَةُ بالسُّوءِ، غَرَّتْهُم بالأمانيِّ، وفَسَحَتْ لَهُم بِالمَعاصي، ووَعَدَتْهُم الإظْهارَ، فاقْتَحَمَتْ بهِم النّارَ.٢٠٦٢

1841. When the Kharijites had been killed it was said to Imām ʿAlī (AS), 'O Commander of the Faithful, these people have been destroyed in their entirety', to which the Imām (AS) responded, 'Not at all! By Allah they still exist in the loins of men and the wombs of women. Whenever a chief appears from among them he will be cut down till the last of them will be thieves and robbers.'[2074]

١٨٤١ . عنه عليه السلام ـلَمّا قُتلَ الخوارِجُ فقيلَ لَهُ: يا أميرَ المؤمنينَ، هَلكَ القَومُ بأجْمَعِهِم ـ: كَلّا واللهِ، إنَّهُم نُطَفٌ في أصْلابِ الرِّجالِ وقَراراتِ النّساءِ، كُلَّما نَجَمَ مِنهُم قَرْنٌ قُطِعَ، حتّىٰ يكونَ آخِرُهُم لُصوصاً سَلّابِينَ.٢٠٦٣

1842. **Imām ʿAlī (AS) said,** 'O people, I am the one who gouged out the eye of trouble [revolt]. There was

١٨٤٢ . عنه عليه السلام : أيُّها النّاسُ، فإنّي فَقَأْتُ عَينَ

no one except me who dared to advance towards it when its gloom was swelling and its madness was intense [when the uprising was at its peak].'[2075]

الفِتنَةِ ، ولَم يَكُن لِيَجتَرِئَ علَيها أحَدٌ غَيري بَعدَ أنْ ماجَ غَيْهَبُها (ظُلْمَتُها)، واشْتَدَّ كَلَبُها.[٢٠٦٤]

610. The Imām's Prohibition of Killing the Kharijites after Him

٦١٠ـ نهيُ الإمامِ عَن قَتلِ الخَوارجِ بَعدَهُ

1843. **Imām 'Alī (AS) said,** 'Do not fight (or kill) the Kharijites after me, because the one who seeks the truth and mistakes it for something else is not like the one who seeks falsehood and finds it.'[2076],[2077]

١٨٤٣ . الإمامُ عليٌّ ؑ : لا تُـقاتِلوا (تَـقْتُلوا) الخَوارِجَ بَعدي ؛ فلَيس مَن طَلَبَ الحقَّ فأخْطَأهُ، كَمَن طَلَبَ الباطِلَ فأدْرَكَهُ[٢٠٦٥].[٢٠٦٦]

125

LOSS

الخُسْرانُ

611. Who is a Loser

٦١١ـ صِفَةُ الخاسِرِ

1844. **The Prophet (SAWA) said,** 'The loser is the one who is negligent of reforming his Hereafter.'[2078]

١٨٤٤ . رسولُ اللهِ ﷺ : الخاسِرُ مَن غَفَلَ عَن إصْلاحِ المَعَادِ.[٢٠٦٧]

1845. **The Prophet (SAWA) said,** 'The one who spends his life seeking out this world has attained a poor deal and has lost divine succour.'[2079]

١٨٤٥ . عنه ﷺ : المُنْفِقُ عُمرَهُ في طَلَبِ الدُّنيا خاسِرُ الصَّفْقَةِ ، عادِمُ التَّوفيقِ.[٢٠٦٨]

612. To Become a Loser in the World and the Hereafter

٦١٢ـ خَسِرَ الدُّنيا وَالآخِرَةَ

"And among the people are those who worship Allah on the [very] fringe: if good fortune befalls him, he is content with it; but if an ordeal visits him he makes a turnabout, to become a loser in the world and the Hereafter. That is a manifest loss."[2080]

﴿وَمِنَ النَّاسِ مَنْ يَعْبُدُ اللهَ عَلَىٰ حَرْفٍ فَإِنْ أَصَابَهُ خَيْرٌ اطْمَأَنَّ بِهِ وَإِنْ أَصَابَتْهُ فِتْنَةٌ انْقَلَبَ عَلَىٰ وَجْهِهِ خَسِرَ الدُّنْيا وَالْآخِرَةَ ذٰلِكَ هُوَ الْخُسْرَانُ الْمُبِينُ﴾.[٢٠٦٩]

1846. **Imām 'Alī (AS)** when asked about who has the greatest misfortune, said, 'A man who abandons the world for the sake of the world, and therefore he misses out on the world and loses the Hereafter, and a man who worships, struggles and fasts as a display for others, and thus forbids

١٨٤٦ . الإمامُ عليٌّ ؑ ـ وقد سُئلَ : مَنِ العَظيمُ الشَّقاءِ ؟ ـ : رجُلٌ تَرَكَ الدُّنيا للدُّنيا فَفاتَتْهُ الدُّنيا وخَسِرَ الآخِرَةَ ، ورَجُلٌ تَعَبَّدَ واجْتَهَدَ وصامَ رِئاءَ

[himself] the pleasures of this world and also tires himself. And were he to do all that sincerely [for the sake of Allah], he would be deserving of its reward.'[2081]

النّدسِ فذلكَ الّذي حُرِمَ لذّاتَ الدُّنيا ولَحِقَهُ التَّعَبُ الّذي لَو كانَ بهِ مُخْلِصاً لاسْتَحَقَّ ثوابَهُ.[٢٠٧٠]

613. The Biggest Losers

٦١٣ـ أخسَرُ النّاسِ

"Say, 'Shall we inform you about the biggest losers in regard to works? Those whose endeavour goes awry in the life of the world, while they suppose they are doing good.'"[2082]

﴿قُلْ هَلْ نُنَبِّئُكُمْ بِالْأَخْسَرِينَ أَعْمَالاً * الَّذِينَ ضَلَّ سَعْيُهُمْ فِي الْحَيَاةِ الدُّنْيَا وَهُمْ يَحْسَبُونَ أَنَّهُمْ يُحْسِنُونَ صُنْعاً﴾.[٢٠٧١]

1847. **Imām ʿAlī (AS) said,** 'Verily the biggest loser with the worst end of the deal and the most unsuccessful in his striving is the man who exerts himself in the quest for his wealth even though fate does not help him in his aims, and he consequently leaves this world with regret while heading towards the Hereafter, where he will face its ill consequences.'[2083]

١٨٤٧ . الإمامُ عليٌّ ﷺ : إنّ أخْسَرَ النّاسِ صَفْقَةً وأخْيَبَهُم سَعْياً: رجُلٌ أخْلَقَ بَدنَهُ في طَلَبِ مالِهِ ولَم تُساعِدْهُ المَقاديرُ على إرادَتِهِ، فخَرجَ مِن الدُّنيا بحَسْرَتِهِ، وقَدِمَ على الآخِرَةِ بتَبِعَتِهِ.[٢٠٧٢]

126

HUMILITY

الخُشُوعُ

614. The Virtue Of Humility

٦١٤ـ فَضلُ الخُشوعِ[٢٠٧٣]

"Is it not time yet for those who have faith that their hearts should be humbled for Allah's remembrance."[2084]

﴿أَلَمْ يَأْنِ لِلَّذِينَ آمَنُوا أَنْ تَخْشَعَ قُلُوبُهُمْ لِذِكْرِ اللهِ﴾.[٢٠٧٤]

1848. In the tradition recounting the Prophet's Ascension, Allah says, 'No sooner does a servant come to know Me and humble himself before Me than everything is humbled before him.'[2085]

١٨٤٨ . إرشاد القلوب : في حديثِ المِعراجِ : ما عَرَفَني عَبدٌ وخَشَعَ لي إلّا خَشَعَ لَهُ كُلُّ شيءٍ.[٢٠٧٥]

1849. **Imām ʿAlī (AS) said,** 'The best aid for supplication is humility.'[2086]

١٨٤٩ . الإمامُ عليٌّ ﷺ : نِعْمَ عَونُ الدُّعاءِ الخُشوعُ.[٢٠٧٦]

1850. **Imām Zayn al-ʿĀbidīn (AS) said** in his supplication, 'I seek refuge in you from a soul

١٨٥٠ . الإمامُ زينُ العابدينَ ﷺ ـ في الدُّعاءِ ـ:

which is never content, a stomach which is not satisfied and a heart which has no humility.'[2087]

وأعوذُ بكَ مِن نَفْسٍ لا تَـقْنَعُ وبَـطْنٍ لا يَشْبَعُ، وقَلبٍ لا يَخْشَعُ.٢٠٧٧

615. The Characteristics of the Humble

٦١٥ـ صِفاتُ الخاشِعينَ

1851. **The Prophet (SAWA) said,** 'There are four distinguishing marks of the humble ones: they pay constant attention to Allah in private and in public, they carry out good works, they contemplate about the Day of Resurrection, and they engage in intimate supplication with Allah.'[2088]

١٨٥١ . رسولُ اللهِ ﷺ: أمّا علامةُ الخاشِعِ فأربعةٌ: مُراقَبَةُ اللهِ في السِّرِّ والعَلانيَةِ، ورُكوبُ الجَميلِ، والتَّفكُّرُ لِيومِ القِيامَةِ، والمُناجاةُ للهِ.٢٠٧٨

1852. **Imām 'Alī (AS) said,** 'One whose heart is humble, his limbs also humble themselves.'[2089]

١٨٥٢ . الإمامُ عليٌّ ﷺ: مَن خَشَعَ قَلبُهُ خَشَعَت جَوارِحُهُ.٢٠٧٩

(See also: WEEPING 47; THE HEART: section 1554)

(أنظر) عنوان ٤٧ «البكاء»؛ القلب: باب ١٥٥٤.

127

THE SERMON

الخُطبَةُ

616. The Sermon

٦١٦ـ الخُطبَةُ

"We made his kingdom firm and gave him wisdom and conclusive speech."[2090]

﴿وَشَدَدْنَا مُلْكَهُ وَآتَيْنَاهُ الْحِكْمَةَ وَفَصْلَ الْخِطَابِ﴾ ٢٠٨٠.

1853. **Sa'd b. Ibrāhīm narrates** from his father who said, 'The first person to deliver a sermon from the pulpit was Prophet Abraham (AS) when Prophet Lot[2091] (AS) was captured by the Romans and Abraham fought with them till he rescued him from the Romans.'[2092]

١٨٥٣ . سعدُ بنُ إبراهيمَ عن أبيهِ: أوَّلُ مَن خَطَبَ علَى المِنبَرِ إبراهيمُ ﷺ حينَ أُسِرَ لُوطٌ واستَأسَرَتْهُ الرُّومُ، فغَزا إبراهيمُ حتّى استَنقَذَهُ مِن الرُّومِ.٢٠٨١

1854. **Jābir narrates,** 'When he [the Prophet (SAWA)] would deliver a sermon, his eyes would turn red, his voice would be raised, and his fury would intensify as if he was an army watchman warning an army against the danger of imminent enemy attack.'[2093]

١٨٥٤ . جابرٌ: كانَ [النّبيُّ ﷺ] إذا خَطَبَ احْمَرَّتْ عَيناهُ، وعَلا صَوتُهُ، واشتَدَّ غَضَبُهُ، كأنَّهُ مُنذِرُ جَيشٍ يقولُ: صَبَّحَكُم مَسّاكُم!٢٠٨٢

1855. **Abū Umāma narrates,** 'Whenever the Prophet (SAWA) would appoint a commander he would say, 'Keep the sermons short and reduce your speech.'[2094]

١٨٥٥ . المعجم الكبير عن أبي أُمامة : إنَّ رَسولَ اللهِ ﷺ كانَ إذا بَعَثَ أميراً قالَ : أَقصِرِ الخُطبَةَ ، وأقِلِّ الكَلامَ.[٢٠٨٣]

1856. **'Ammār b. Yāsir narrates,** 'The Prophet (SAWA) ordered us to keep our sermons short.'[2095]

١٨٥٦ . سنن أبي داوود عن عمّار بن ياسر : أمَرَنا رَسولُ اللهِ ﷺ بإقصارِ الخُطَبِ.[٢٠٨٤]

1857. **Jābir b. Samura al-Sawā'ī narrates,** 'The Prophet (SAWA) would not prolong his exhortation on Fridays, rather they [his sermons] would be short speeches.'[2096]

١٨٥٧ . سنن أبي داوود عن جابر بن سمرة السّوائيّ : كانَ رَسولُ اللهِ ﷺ لا يُطيلُ المَوعِظَةَ يومَ الجُمُعَةِ ، إنّما هُنَّ كَلِماتٌ يَسيراتٌ.[٢٠٨٥]

(See also: THE FRIDAY PRAYER (3): section 1147; SPEECH: section 1619)

(أنظر) الصلاة (٣): باب ١١٤٧ ؛ الكلام: باب ١٦١٩.

128

HANDWRITING

الخَطُّ

617. Handwriting

٦١٧ ـ الخَطُّ

"You did not use to recite any scripture before it, nor did you write with your right hand, for then the impugners would have been sceptical."[2097]

﴿وَما كُنْتَ تَتْلُوا مِنْ قَبْلِه مِنْ كِتابٍ وَلا تَخُطُّهُ بِيَمِينِكَ إذاً لَارْتابَ الْمُبْطِلُونَ﴾.[٢٠٨٦]

1858. **The Prophet (SAWA) said,** 'Good handwriting increases the clarity of truth.'[2098]

١٨٥٨ . رسولُ اللهِ ﷺ : الخَطُّ الحَسَنُ يَزيدُ الحَقَّ وَضحاً.[٢٠٨٧]

1859. **The Prophet (SAWA),** regarding Allah's verse *"or some vestige of [divine] knowledge"*[2099], said that this means handwriting.'[2100]

١٨٥٩ . عنه ﷺ ـ في قولِهِ تعالىٰ : ﴿أَوْ أَثارَةٍ مِنْ عِلْمٍ﴾[٢٠٨٨] ـ : الخَطُّ.[٢٠٨٩]

1860. **'Atā' b. Yasār narrates,** 'The Prophet (SAWA) was asked about handwriting and he said, 'It was (first) taught by a prophet and those who were with him learned it.'[2101]

١٨٦٠ . الدّر المنثور عن عطاء بن يسار : سُئِلَ رسولُ اللهِ ﷺ عنِ الخَطِّ ، فقالَ : عَلّمَهُ نَبيٌّ ، ومَن كانَ وافَقَهُ عَلِمَ.[٢٠٩٠]

1861. **Imām 'Alī (AS) said,** 'Handwriting is the hand's tongue.'[2102]

١٨٦١ . الإمامُ عليٌّ ﷺ : الخَطُّ لِسانُ اليَدِ.[٢٠٩١]

1862. **Imām 'Alī (AS) said** to his scribe Uubaydullāh b. Abī Rāfi', 'Put cotton flake in the

١٨٦٢ . عنه ﷺ ـ فيما قالَ لِكاتِبِهِ عُبيدِ اللهِ بنِ أبي رافعٍ ـ : ألِقْ دَواتَكَ ، وأطِلْ جِلفَةَ قَلَمِكَ ،

inkpot, keep the nib of your pen long, leave space between lines and join up the letters because this is most suited to creating beautiful handwriting.'[2103]

وَفَرِّجْ بَينَ السُّطورِ، وقَرْمِطْ بَينَ الحُروفِ، فإنَّ ذلكَ أجْدَرُ بصَباحَةِ الخَطِّ.[٢٠٩٢]

1863. **Imām ʿAlī (AS) said,** 'Split the nib of your pen, thicken its blade, slant it to the right and you will beautify your handwriting.'[2104]

١٨٦٣. عنه ؑ: افْتَحْ بَـرْيَةَ قَـلَمِكَ، وأسْـمِكْ شَحْمَتَهُ، وأيْمِنْ قِطَّتَكَ يَجُدْ خَطُّكَ.[٢٠٩٣]

129

SINCERITY

الإخلاص

618. The Virtue of Sincerity

٦١٨ ـ فَضلُ الإخلاصِ

"He said, 'By Your might, I will surely pervert them, except Your exclusive servants amongst them.'"[2105]

﴿قَالَ فَبِعِزَّتِكَ لَأُغْوِيَنَّهُمْ أَجْمَعِينَ * إِلَّا عِبَادَكَ مِنْهُمُ الْمُخْلَصِينَ﴾.[٢٠٩٤]

(See also: Qur'an, 2:112, 2:139, 2:196, 2:207, 2:238, 2:265, 3:20, 6:52, 6:79, 6:162, 12:24, 18:28, 18:110, 22:31, 30:38, 31:22, 37:40, 39:2, 39:3, 39:11, 39:14, 39:29, 40:14,72:18, 72:20, 76:9, 92:20, 97:5)

(أُنظر) البقرة: ١١٢، ١٣٩، ١٩٦، ٢٠٧، ٢٣٨، ٢٦٥ و آل عمران: ٢٠ والأنعام: ٥٢، ٧٩، ١٦٢ و يوسف: ٢٤ والكهف: ٢٨، ١١٠ و الحجّ: ٣١ و الروم: ٣٨ ولقمان: ٢٢ و الصافّات: ٤٠ والزمر: ٢، ٣، ١١، ١٤، ٢٩ و غافر: ١٤ و الجنّ: ١٨، ٢٠ والإنسان: ٩ و الليل: ٢٠ والبيّنة: ٥.

1864. **The Prophet (SAWA) said,** 'The men of knowledge will all be ruined except those who acted [upon their knowledge], and those who act will all be ruined except for the sincere ones from among them, and the sincere ones are indeed in danger.'[2106]

١٨٦٤. رسولُ اللهِ ﷺ: العُلَماءُ كُلُّهُم هَلْكىٰ إلّا العامِلينَ، والعامِلونَ كُلُّهُم هَلْكىٰ إلّا المُخْلِصينَ، والمُخْلِصونَ علىٰ خَطَرٍ.[٢٠٩٥]

1865. **Imām ʿAlī (AS) said,** 'Sincerity is the peak of religion.'[2107]

١٨٦٥. الإمامُ عليٌّ ؑ: الإخْلاصُ غايَةُ الدِّينِ.[٢٠٩٦]

1866. **Imām ʿAlī (AS) said,** 'Sincerity is the worship of those brought near [to Allah].'[2108]

١٨٦٦. عنه ؑ: الإخْلاصُ عِبادَةُ المُقَرَّبينَ.[٢٠٩٧]

1867. **Imām ʿAlī (AS) said,** 'Sincerity is the criterion for worship.'[2109]

١٨٦٧. عنه ؑ: الإخْلاصُ مِلاكُ العِبادَةِ.[٢٠٩٨]

1868. **Imām ʿAlī (AS) said,** 'Sincerity is the summit of faith.'[2110]

١٨٦٨. عنه ؑ: الإخْلاصُ أعْلىٰ الإيمانِ.[٢٠٩٩]

1869. **Imām ʿAlī (AS) said,** 'Salvation is found in sincerity.'[2111]

١٨٦٩ . عنه ﷺ : فـــي الإخْـــلاصِ يَكــونُ الخَلاصُ.٢١٠٠

1870. **Imām ʿAlī (AS) said,** 'Blessed is he whose knowledge and practice, love and hate, acceptance and refusal, speech and silence, and words and actions are sincerely for the sake of Allah.'[2112]

١٨٧٠ . عنه ﷺ : طُوبىٰ لِمَن أخْلَصَ للهِ عَـمَلَهُ وعِلْمَهُ، وحُبَّهُ وبُغْضَهُ، وأخْذَهُ وتَرْكَهُ، وكَلامَهُ وصَمْتَهُ، وفِعْلَهُ وقَولَهُ.٢١٠١

619. The Difficulty of Sincerity

٦١٩ ـ صُعوبَةُ الإخلاصِ

1871. **Imām ʿAlī (AS) said,** 'Perfecting an action is more difficult than [performing] the action itself, and purifying an intention from corruption is tougher for the striving ones than engaging in lengthy *jihād*.'[2113]

١٨٧١ . الإمامُ عليٌّ ﷺ : تَصْفِيَةُ العَمَلِ أشَدُّ مِن العَمَلِ، وتَخْليصُ النِّيّةِ عنِ الفَسادِ أشَدُّ علىٰ العامِلينَ مِن طُولِ الجِهادِ.٢١٠٢

1872. **Imām al-Ṣādiq (AS) said,** 'Persevering with an action until it becomes pure and sincere is harder than [performing] the action itself.'[2114]

١٨٧٢ . الإمامُ الصّادقُ ﷺ : الإبْقاءُ علىٰ العَمَلِ حتّىٰ يَخْلُصَ أشَدُّ مِن العَمَلِ.٢١٠٣

620. The Sufficiency of Few Actions Coupled with Sincerity

٦٢٠ ـ كِفايَةُ القَليلِ مِنَ العَمَلِ مَعَ الإخلاصِ

1873. It is narrated in *al-Kāfī* that Allah – Blessed and most High – addressed Prophet Moses (AS) in intimate conversation saying, 'O Moses, whatever is done for My sake, a little of it is a lot and whatever is done for the sake of others, a lot of it is little.'[2115]

١٨٧٣ . الكافي : فيما ناجىٰ اللهُ تباركَ وتعالىٰ موسىٰ ﷺ : يا موسىٰ، ما اُريدَ بهِ وَجْهي فكَثيرٌ قَليلُهُ، وما اُريدَ بهِ غَيري فقَليلٌ كَثيرُهُ.٢١٠٤

1874. **The Prophet (SAWA) said,** 'Purify your heart and few actions will suffice you.'[2116]

١٨٧٤ . رسولُ اللهِ ﷺ : أخْلِصْ قَلبَكَ يَكْفِكَ القَليلُ مِنَ العَمَلِ.٢١٠٥

621. The Dealing of Allah With the Sincere Ones with His Sincere Secrecy

٦٢١ ـ مُعامَلَةُ اللهِ مَعَ المُخلِصينَ بِخالِصِ سِرِّهِ

1875. **Imām al-Ṣādiq (AS) said** to Mufaḍḍal b. Ṣāliḥ, 'Verily Allah has servants who sincerely engage in transaction with Him in secrecy, so Allah gives them from His pure reward and

١٨٧٥ . عدّة الداعي عن المُفَضّلِ بن صالح : قالُ الإمامُ الصّادقُ ﷺ: إنَّ للهِ عِباداً عامَلوهُ بـخالِصٍ

goodness, for they are the ones who will come on the Day of Resurrection with their book of deeds empty, and when they stand in front of Allah, their books will be filled with the secrets that they had with Him'. [Mufaḍḍal narrates], I asked, 'O my master, why will their books be empty?' The Imām replied, 'Allah holds them in such high regard that He does not even want the guardian angels to be aware of what is between Him and them.'[2117]

مِن سِرِّه، فعامَلَهُم بخالِصٍ مِن بِرِّهِ، فهُمُ الّذينَ تَمُرُّ صُحُفُهُم يومَ القِيامَةِ فُرَّغاً، وإذا وَقَفوا بَينَ يدَيهِ تعالىٰ مَلأَها مِن سِرِّ ما أسَرُّوا إلَيهِ. فقلتُ: يا مَولاي، ولِمَ ذلكَ؟ فقالَ: أجَلَّهُم أنْ تَطَّلِعَ الحَفَظَةُ على ما بَينَهُ وبَينَهُم.٢١٠٦

622. The Role of Sincerity in the Acceptance of Actions

٦٢٢ ـ دَورُ الإخلاصِ في قَبولِ الأعمالِ

1876. **Imām al-Ṣādiq (AS) said,** 'Allah – most High –has said, 'I am the best partner, so whoever associates a partner with Me in his actions I will never accept them, except those actions that have been performed [sincerely for Me].'[2118]

١٨٧٦. الإمامُ الصّادقُ عليه السلام: قالَ اللهُ تبارَكَ وتعالىٰ: أنا خَيرُ شَريكٍ، مَن أشرَكَ بي في عَمَلِهِ لَن أقبَلَهُ، إلّا ما كانَ لي خالِصاً.٢١٠٧

1877. **The Prophet (SAWA) said,** 'If you perform an action, do it sincerely for the sake of Allah because He only accepts from His servants those actions that have been performed sincerely.'[2119]

١٨٧٧. رسولُ اللهِ صلى الله عليه وآله: إذا عَمِلتَ عَمَلاً فاعمَلْ للهِ خالِصاً؛ لأنَّهُ لا يَقبَلُ مِن عِبادِهِ الأعمالَ إلّا ما كانَ خالِصاً.٢١٠٨

623. The Pure Sincerity

٦٢٣ ـ تَمامُ الإخلاصِ

1878. **The Prophet (SAWA) said,** 'Complete sincerity is abstaining from the prohibited things.'[2120]

١٨٧٨. رسولُ اللهِ صلى الله عليه وآله: تَمامُ الإخلاصِ اجتِنابُ المَحارِمِ.٢١٠٩

1879. **Imām al-Ṣādiq (AS) said.** 'Whoever sincerely says "*There is no god but Allah*" will enter Paradise and his sincerity should be such that his testimony of "*There is no god but Allah*" becomes a barrier for him against whatever Allah has forbidden.'[2121]

١٨٧٩. الإمامُ الصّادقُ عليه السلام: مَن قالَ: «لا إلٰهَ إلّا اللهُ» مُخلِصاً دَخَلَ الجَنَّةَ، وإخلاصُهُ أن يَحجِزَهُ «لا إلٰهَ إلّا اللهُ» عَمّا حَرَّمَ اللهُ.٢١١٠

624. The Signs of the Sincere

٦٢٤ـ عَلاماتُ المُخلِصِ

1880. **The Prophet (SAWA) said,** 'Verily for every essential truth is a reality and a servant has not reached the reality of sincerity until he dislikes to be praised [by others] for any act that he does for the sake of Allah.'[2122]

١٨٨٠ . رسولُ اللهِ ﷺ : إنَّ لِكُلِّ حَقٍّ حَقيقةً ، وما بَلغَ عَبدٌ حقيقةَ الإخْلاصِ حتّىٰ لا يُحِبَّ أنْ يُحْمَدَ علىٰ شيءٍ مِن عَمَلٍ للهِ.[٢١١١]

1881. **Imām 'Alī (AS) said,** 'Pure worship is that a man does not hope for anything except his Lord and does not fear anything except [the outcome of] his sin.'[2123]

١٨٨١ . الإمامُ عليٌّ ﷺ : العِبادَةُ الخالِصَةُ أنْ لا يَرجوَ الرّجُلُ إلّا رَبَّهُ ، ولا يَخافَ إلّا ذَنْبَهُ.[٢١١٢]

1882. **Imām al-Ṣādiq (AS) said,** 'The pure action [done out of sincerity], is that which the servant does not wish to be praised for by anyone except Allah – Mighty and Exalted.'[2124]

١٨٨٢ . الإمامُ الصّادقُ ﷺ :العَمَلُ الخالِصُ :الّذي لا تُريدُ أنْ يَحْمَدَكَ عليهِ أحَدٌ إلّا اللهُ عزّوجلّ.[٢١١٣، ٢١١٤]

1883. **The archangel Gabriel (AS),** when he was asked by the Prophet (SAWA) about the meaning of sincerity, replied, 'The sincere one is he who does ask the people anything until he himself finds it, and when he finds it he is pleased. Whenever he has a remainder of a thing, he gives it to others, because if a person does not ask anything from creation, he has established that his servitude is solely for Allah, Mighty and Exalted, and if he finds and he is pleased then he is pleased with Allah and Allah – Blessed and most High – is pleased with him, and if he gives for the sake of Allah then he has reached the station of reliance on his Lord, Mighty and Exalted.' [2125]

١٨٨٣ . معاني الأخبار عَن جَبرئيلَ ﷺ ـ لَمّا سَألَهُ النّبيُّ ﷺ عن تَفسيرِ الإخْلاصِ ـ: المُخْلِصُ الّذي لا يَسألُ النّاسَ شَيئاً حتّىٰ يَجِدَ، وإذا وَجدَ رَضِيَ ، وإذا بَقِيَ عِندَهُ شيء أعْطاهُ فِي اللهِ ، فإنَّ مَن لَم يَسألِ المَخلوقَ فَقَد أقَرَّ للهِ عزّوجلّ بالعُبودِيَّةِ ، وإذا وَجَدَ فرَضِيَ فهُو عنِ اللهِ راضٍ ، واللهُ تباركَ وتعالىٰ عنهُ راضٍ ، وإذا أعطىٰ للهِ عزّوجلّ فهُو علىٰ حَدِّ الثِّقَةِ برَبِّهِ عزّوجلّ.[٢١١٥]

625. What Brings About Sincerity

٦٢٥ـ ما يورِثُ الإخلاصَ

1884. **Imām 'Alī (AS) said,** 'The [root] cause of sincerity is conviction.'[2126]

١٨٨٤ . الإمامُ عليٌّ ﷺ : سَبَبُ الإخلاصِ اليَقينُ.[٢١١٦]

1885. **Imām 'Alī (AS) said,** 'The fruit of knowledge is sincerity of action.'[2127]

١٨٨٥ . عنه ﷺ : ثَمَرةُ العِلمِ إخْلاصُ العَمَلِ.[٢١١٧]

1886. **Imām ʿAlī (AS) said,** 'Reduce your expectations and your actions will become sincere.'[2128]

١٨٨٦ . عنه ﷺ : قَــلِّلِ الآمــالَ تَـخْلُصْ لَك الأعمالُ.[٢١١٨]

1887. **Imām ʿAlī (AS) said,** 'The root of sincerity is despairing of obtaining what is in the hands of men.'[2129]

١٨٨٧ . عنه ﷺ : أصْلُ الإخْلاصِ اليَأسُ مِمّا في أيْدي النّاسِ.[٢١١٩]

626. The Effects of Sincerity

٦٢٦ ـ آثارُ الإخلاصِ

1888. **The Prophet (SAWA) said,** 'Allah said, 'No sooner do I look into a servant's heart and find that he has sincere love for My sole obedience and he seeks My pleasure than I take charge of his plans and affairs.'[2130]

١٨٨٨ . رسولُ اللهِ ﷺ : قالَ اللهُ عزّوجلّ : لا أطَّلِعُ علىٰ قَـلبِ عَـبدٍ فأعْـلَمُ مِـنهُ حُبَّ الإخْـلاصِ لِطاعَتي لِوَجْهي وابْـتِغاءَ مَـرْضاتي إلّا تَـولّيتُ تَقويمَهُ وسياسَتَهُ.[٢١٢٠]

1889. **The Prophet (SAWA) said,** 'No sooner does a servant spend his mornings in a state of sincere devotion for forty days than the springs of wisdom will flow from his heart onto his tongue.'[2131]

١٨٨٩ . عنه ﷺ : ما أخْلَصَ عَـبدٌ للهِ عـزّوجلّ أربَعينَ صباحاً إلّا جَرَتْ يَنابِيعُ الحِكمَةِ مِن قَلبِهِ علىٰ لِسانِه.[٢١٢١]

1890. **Imām ʿAlī (AS) said,** 'The one who purifies his intention distances himself from base qualities.'[2132]

١٨٩٠ . الإمامُ عليٌّ ﷺ : مَن أخْلَصَ النِّيَّةَ تَـنَزّهَ عنِ الدَّنِيَّةِ.[٢١٢٢]

1891. **Imām al-Ṣādiq (AS) said,** 'Verily everything is humbled and awed before the believer', and then he said, 'If he is sincere for Allah, Allah will make everything fear him including the wild and poisonous animals of the land and the birds of the sky.'[2133]

١٨٩١ . الإمامُ الصّادقُ ﷺ : إنَّ المؤمنَ لَيَخشَعُ لَهُ كُلُّ شيءٍ ويَهابُهُ كُلُّ شيءٍ. إذا كانَ مُـخلِصاً للهِ أخافَ اللهُ مِنهُ كُلَّ شـيءٍ، حـتّىٰ هَـوامَّ الأرضِ وسِباعَها وطَيرَ السَّماءِ.[٢١٢٣]

130

DIFFERENCES

الاختِلافُ

627. There is no Base for Differences in Nature

٦٢٧ ـ لا مَبدَأَ لِلإخْتِلافِ فِي الفِطرَةِ

"Mankind were but a single [religious] community; then they differed. And were it not for a prior decree of

﴿وَمَا كَانَ النَّاسُ إلّا أُمَّةً وَاحِدَةً فَاخْتَلَفُوا وَلَوْلا

your Lord, decision would have been made between them concerning about that which they differ."[2134]

كَـمَةٌ سَبَقَتْ مِنْ رَبِّكَ لَـقُضِيَ بَـيْنَهُمْ فِـيما فِـيهِ يَخْتَلِفُونَ﴾. ٢١٢٤

1892. **Imām al-Bāqir (AS) said,** 'Before Prophet Noah (AS), they [mankind] were a single community upon the *fiṭra*[2135] of Allah, neither guided nor in error, thereafter Allah sent the prophets.'[2136]

١٨٩٢. الإمامُ الباقرُ ﷺ: كانوا قَبلَ نُـوحٍ أُمّـةً واحِدَةً على فِـطْرَةِ اللهِ لا مُـهْتَدينَ ولا ضُـلّالاً، فَبعَثَ اللهُ النَّبِيّينَ. ٢١٢٥

628. Encouragement to Discard Differences

٦٢٨ ـ الحَثُّ عَلَىٰ نَبذِ الاختِلافِ

"Hold fast, all together, to Allah's cord, and do not be divided [into sects]. And remember Allah's blessing upon you when you were enemies, then He brought your hearts together, so you became brothers with His blessing."[2137]

﴿وَاعْـتَصِمُوا بِـحَبْلِ اللهِ جَـمِيعاً وَلا تَـفَرَّقُوا وَاذْكُرُوا نِعْمَةَ اللهِ عَلَيْكُمْ إِذْ كُنْتُمْ أَعْدَاءً فَأَلَّفَ بَيْنَ قُلُوبِكُمْ فَأَصْبَحْتُمْ بِنِعْمَتِهِ إِخْوَاناً﴾. ٢١٢٦

1893. **The Prophet (SAWA) said,** 'No sooner does a community differ [between themselves] after their own prophet, than the people of falsehood from amongst them become victorious over the people of truth.'[2138]

١٨٩٣. رسولُ اللهِ ﷺ: ما اخْتَلَفَتْ أُمَّةٌ بَعدَ نَبِيِّها إلّا ظَهرَ أهْلُ باطِلِها علىٰ أهْلِ حقِّها. ٢١٢٧

1894. **Imām ʿAlī (AS) said,** 'Stay with the greater majority, for verily Allah's hand is with the [larger] group. Beware of separation for verily the deviant amongst you is the victim of Satan just as the deviant amongst the cattle is the victim of a wolf.'[2139]

١٨٩٤. الإمامُ عليٌّ ﷺ: والْزَموا السَّوادَ الأعْظَمَ، فإنَّ يَدَ اللهِ مَع الجَماعةِ، وإيّاكُم والفُرْقَةَ، فـإنَّ الشّاذَّ مِن النّاسِ للشَّيطانِ، كما أنّ الشّـاذَّ مِـن الغَنَمِ للذِّئبِ. ٢١٢٨

1895. **Imām ʿAlī (AS) said,** 'By Allah, verily I believe that this group will overcome you, by uniting upon their falsehood and you being divided on your truth.'[2140]

١٨٩٥. عنه ﷺ: واللهِ، لَأظُنُّ أنَّ هٰؤلاءِ القَـومَ سَـيُدالونَ مِـنكُم بـاجْتِماعِهِم عـلىٰ بـاطِلِهِم وتَفَرُّقِكُم عن حقِّكُم. ٢١٢٩

1896. **Imām ʿAlī (AS) said,** 'No sooner do two differing claims arise than one of them is erroneous.[2141]

١٨٩٦. عنه ﷺ: ما اخْتَلَفَتْ دَعْوَتانِ إلّا كانتْ إحْداهُما ضَلالةً. ٢١٣٠

629. Explanation of 'The Separation of My Community is a Mercy'

٦٢٩ ـ تفسيرُ «اختِلافُ أُمَّتي رَحمَةٌ»

1897. **Imām al-Ṣādiq (AS)** was asked by 'Abd al-Mu'min al-Anṣārī, 'Verily some people narrated from the Prophet (SAWA) that he said, "The separation of my community is a mercy" and they were truthful, so I ask that if their separation is a mercy then is their congregation a chastisement?', to which the Imām replied, 'It is not as you understand it nor as they understood it, actually he meant the saying of Allah, *"But why should not there go forth a group from each of their sections…"* so He commanded them to go forth to the Prophet (SAWA) and to frequent him and learn from him then to return to their people and teach them, so what is meant is [physical] separation from their cities, not separation or difference with regards to the religion of Allah, for verily the religion of Allah is one.'[2142]

١٨٩٧ . معاني الأخبار عن عبد المُؤمِن الأنصاريّ : قلت للإمامِ الصّادقِ ﷺ : إنّ قَوماً رَوَوا أنَّ رسولَ اللهِ ﷺ قالَ : إنّ اخْتِلافَ أُمَّتي رَحمَةٌ؟ فقالَ : صَدَقوا . قلتُ : إنْ كانَ اخْتِلافُهُم رَحمَةً فاجْتِماعُهُم عَذابٌ ؟ قالَ : لَيس حيثُ ذَهَبْتَ وذَهَبوا ، إنَّما أرادَ قولَ اللهِ عزّوجلّ : ﴿فَلَولا نَفَرَ مِن كُلِّ فِرْقَةٍ مِنْهُمْ طائِفَةٌ لِيَتَفَقَّهُوا فِي الدِّين﴾ ٢١٣١، فأمَرَهُم أنْ يَنْفِروا إلىٰ رسولِ اللهِ ﷺ ويَخْتَلِفوا إلَيهِ فيَتَعلّموا ثُمَّ يَرْجِعوا إلىٰ قَومِهِم فيُعَلّموهُم ، إنّما أرادَ اخْتِلافَهُم مِن البُلْدانِ ، لا اخْتِلافاً في دِينِ اللهِ ، إنّما الدِّينُ واحِدٌ . ٢١٣٢

630. Explanation of Congregation and Separation

٦٣٠ ـ تَفسيرُ الجَماعةِ وَالفُرقَةِ

1898. **Imām al-Ṣādiq (AS) said,** 'The Prophet (SAWA) was asked about the congregation of his [religious] community, and he said, 'The congregation of my community are those who are the people of truth even if they are few in number.'[2143]

١٨٩٨ . الإمامُ الصّادقُ ﷺ : سُئلَ رسولُ اللهِ ﷺ عَن جَماعَةِ أُمَّتِهِ ، فقالَ : جَماعَةُ أُمَّتي أهلُ الحقِّ وإنْ قَلُّوا . ٢١٣٣

631. The Cause of Separation

٦٣١ ـ علَّةُ الفُرقةِ

1899. **Imām ʿAlī (AS) said,** 'Verily you are brothers in the religion of Allah, nothing has separated you except ill natures and bad consciences, consequently you do not bear the burdens of each other, nor do you advise each other, nor spend on each other, nor love each other.'[2144]

١٨٩٩ . الإمامُ عليٌّ ﷺ : إنَّما أنتُم إخْوانٌ علىٰ دِينِ اللهِ ، ما فَرّقَ بَينَكُم إلّا خُبْثُ السَّرائرِ ، وسُوءُ الضَّمائرِ ، فلا تَوازَرونَ (تأزِرون) ولا تَناصَحونَ ، ولا تَباذَلونَ ولا تَوادّونَ . ٢١٣٤

1900. **Imām ʿAlī (AS) said,** 'If the ignorant ones had kept silent, men would not have differed.'[2145]

١٩٠٠ . عنه ﷺ : لَو سَكَتَ الجاهِلُ ما اخْتَلَفَ النّاسُ . ٢١٣٥

131

CREATION

الخِلقة

632. The Origin of Creation

٦٣٢ـ أصلُ الخِلقةِ

1901. **The Prophet (SAWA) said,** 'Everything has been created from water.'[2146]

١٩٠١. رسولُ اللهِ ﷺ: كلُّ شيءٍ خُلِقَ مِن ماءٍ.[٢١٣٦]

1902. **The Prophet (SAWA) said,** 'The sky of this world was created from a controlled surge.'[2147]

١٩٠٢. عنه ﷺ: خَلقَ اللهُ السَّماءَ الدُّنيا مِن المَوجِ المَكْفوفِ.[٢١٣٧]

1903. **Ḥabbat al-ʿUranī said,** 'One day I heard ʿAlī (AS) take an oath saying, 'By the One who created the sky from smoke and water'.'[2148]

١٩٠٣. بحار الأنوار عن حَبّة العُرَنيِّ: سَمِعْتُ علياً عليه السلام ذاتَ يومٍ يَحْلِفُ: والّذي خَلقَ السَّماءَ مِن دُخَانٍ وماءٍ.[٢١٣٨]

633. The First Thing that Allah – Glory be to Him – Created

٦٣٣ـ أوَّلُ[٢١٣٩] ما خَلَقَ اللهُ عزّ وجلّ

1904. **The Prophet (SAWA) said,** 'Verily the first thing that Allah created was the Pen, and then He commanded it and it wrote everything that is to be.'[2149]

١٩٠٤. رسولُ اللهِ ﷺ: إنَّ أوَّلَ شَيْءٍ خَلقَهُ اللهُ القَلَمُ، فأمَرهُ فكَتَبَ كُلَّ شَيْءٍ يَكونُ.[٢١٤٠]

1905. **The Prophet (SAWA) said,** 'The first thing that Allah created was the intellect.'[2150]

١٩٠٥. عنه ﷺ: أوَّلُ ما خَلَقَ اللهُ العقَلُ.[٢١٤١]

1906. **The Prophet (SAWA) said,** 'The first thing that Allah created was my light.'[2151]

١٩٠٦. عنه ﷺ: أوَّلُ ما خَلقَ اللهُ نُوري.[٢١٤٢]

1907. **The Prophet (SAWA) said,** 'Verily the first thing that Allah – Mighty and Exalted – created was our spirits and then He made them profess His Unity and Majesty, then He created the angels.'[2152]

١٩٠٧. عنه ﷺ: إنَّ أوَّلَ ما خَلقَ اللهُ عزّوجلّ أرْواحُنا، فأنْطَقَها بتَوحيدِهِ وتَمْجيدِهِ، ثُمَّ خَلقَ المَلائكَةَ.[٢١٤٣]

1908. **Imām ʿAlī (AS),** when asked about what Allah first created, said, 'He created light.'[2153]

١٩٠٨. الإمامُ عليٌّ عليه السلام ـ وقد سئلَ عَن أوَّلِ ما خَلقَ اللهُ ـ: خَلقَ النُّورَ.[٢١٤٤]

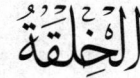

1909. **Imām al-Bāqir (AS) said,** 'The first thing that He created from His creation was the substance that all things come from, and that is water.'[2154]

١٩٠٩ . الإمامُ الباقرُ ﷺ : أوَّلُ شَيءٍ خَلَقَهُ مِن خَلْقِهِ الشّيءُ الّذي جَميعُ الأشياءِ مِنهُ، وهُوَ الماءُ.[٢١٤٥]

634. The Creation of the World

٦٣٤ ـ خَلقُ العالَمِ

"Have the faithless not regarded that the heavens and the earth were interwoven and We disjoined them, and We made every living thing out of water? Will they not then have faith."[2155]

﴿أَوَلَمْ يَرَ الَّذِينَ كَفَرُوا أَنَّ السَّمَاوَاتِ وَالْأَرْضَ كَانَتَا رَتْقًا فَفَتَقْنَاهُمَا وَجَعَلْنَا مِنَ الْمَاءِ كُلَّ شَيْءٍ حَيٍّ أَفَلَا يُؤْمِنُونَ﴾ .[٢١٤٦]

1910. **Imām ʿAlī (AS) said,** 'He did not create things from eternal matter nor after ever-existing models, rather He created whatever He created and fixed limits to them and He shaped whatever He shaped and gave them the best form.'[2156]

١٩١٠ . الإمامُ عليٌّ ﷺ : لَم يَخْلُقِ الأشياءَ مِن أُصولٍ أزَليَّةٍ، ولا مِن أوائلَ أبَديَّةٍ، بَل خَلَقَ ما خَلَقَ فأقامَ حَدَّهُ، وصَوَّرَ ما صَوَّرَ فأحْسَنَ صُورَتَهُ.[٢١٤٧]

1911. **Imām al-Bāqir (AS) said,** 'Verily Allah, Blessed and most High...created things not from a thing and whoever claims that Allah, most High, created things from something has indeed disbelieved.'[2157]

١٩١١ . الإمامُ الباقرُ ﷺ : إنَّ اللهَ تباركَ وتعالىٰ... خَلقَ الأشياءَ لا مِن شَيءٍ، ومَن زَعَمَ أنَّ اللهَ تعالىٰ خَلقَ الأشياءَ مِن شَيءٍ فقد كَفرَ.[٢١٤٨]

635. The Greatness of What is Hidden from Us of Creation

٦٣٥ ـ عَظَمَةُ ما غابَ عَنّا مِنَ الخِلقَةِ

1912. **Imām ʿAlī (AS) said,** 'Glory be to you! How great is Your creation that we see! But how small is every greatness when compared to Your power! How awe-striking is what we see from Your kingdom! But how low this is when compared to what is hidden from us by Your authority.'[2158]

١٩١٢ . الإمامُ عليٌّ ﷺ : سُبحانَكَ ما أعْظَمَ ما نَرىٰ مِن خَلْقِكَ! وما أصْغَرَ كُلَّ عَظيمةٍ في جَنْبِ قُدْرَتِكَ! وما أهْوَلَ ما نَرىٰ مِن مَلَكوتِكَ! وما أحْقَرَ ذلكَ فيما غابَ عَنّا مِن سُلطانِكَ! وما أسْبَغَ نِعَمَكَ في الدُّنيا! وما أصْغَرَها في نِعَمِ الآخِرَةِ![٢١٤٩]

1913. **Imām al-Bāqir (AS) said,** 'Perhaps you think that Allah has only created this single world, and you think that Allah has not created anyone other than yourselves! Nay by Allah, verily Allah has created a million worlds and a million Adams and you are in the last of these worlds and of the last Adams.'[2159]

١٩١٣ . الإمامُ الباقرُ ﷺ : لَعلّكَ تَرىٰ أنَّ اللهَ إنّما خَلقَ هٰذا العالَمَ الواحِدَ، وتَرىٰ أنَّ اللهَ لَم يَخْلُقْ بَشَراً غَيرَكُم! بلىٰ واللهِ، لَقد خَلقَ اللهُ ألفَ ألفِ عالَمٍ، وألفَ ألفِ آدمَ، أنتَ في آخِرِ تلكَ العوالِمِ وأُولئكَ الآدَميّينَ.[٢١٥٠]

132

THE CREATOR

الخالِق

636. The Call of the Intellect to Repel Probable Harm

٦٣٦ ـ دَعوَةُ العَقلِ إلىٰ دَفعِ الضَّرَرِ المُحتَمَلِ

1914. **Imām al-Ṣādiq (AS) said** to ʿAbd al-Karīm b. Abi al-ʿAwjāʾ who was a denier of the origin and the end [resurrection], 'If the matter is as you say [i.e. denial], which of course it is not, then both of us will be saved, however if the matter is as we say, which is of course the truth, then we will be saved and you will be destroyed.' Then ʿAbd al-Karīm turned to his disciples and said, 'I have found anguish and anxiety in my heart, take me from here', so they took him and he died thereafter.'[2160]

١٩١٤ . التوحيد ـ قال الإمامُ الصّادقُ ﷺ لعبدِ الكريمِ بنِ أبي العَوْجاءِ وهُو مُنْكِرٌ للمَبدَأ والمَعادِ ـ: إنْ يَكُنِ الأمُر كما تَقولُ ـ ولَيس كما تَقولُ ـ نَجَوْنا ونَجَوْتَ، وإنْ يَكُنِ الأمرُ كمانَقولُ ـ وهُو كما نَقولُ ـ نَجَوْنا وهَلَكْتَ. فأقْبَلَ عبدُ الكريمِ علىٰ مَن مَعهُ فقالَ: وَجَدتُ في قَلبي حَزازَةً فرُدّوني، فرَدُّوهُ وماتَ.[٢١٥١]

637. Some Proofs for the Existence of the Creator

٦٣٧ ـ مِنْ أدِلَّةِ إثباتِ الصَّانِعِ

1. Innate Nature Regarding Knowing Allah

١ ـ فِطرةُ مَعرفَةِ اللهِ

"So set your heart on the religion as a people of pure faith, the origination of Allah according to which He originated mankind."[2161]

﴿فَأَقِمْ وَجْهَكَ لِلدِّينِ حَنِيفاً فِطْرَةَ اللهِ الَّتِي فَطَرَ النَّاسَ عَلَيْهَا﴾.[٢١٥٢]

1915. **The Prophet (SAWA) said,** 'Every newborn is born upon the origination (*fiṭra*) of Allah, meaning [born] with inner knowledge that affirms that Allah is his Creator and this is the meaning of His words, *"If you ask them, 'Who created the heavens and the earth?' they will surely say, 'Allah'."*[2162],[2163]

١٩١٥ . رسولُ اللهِ ﷺ : كُلُّ مَوْلودٍ يُولَدُ علىٰ الفِطرَةِ، يَعني علىٰ المَعْرِفَةِ بأنّ اللهَ عزّوجلّ خالِقُهُ، فذلكَ قَولُهُ: ﴿ولَئنْ سَأَلْتَهُم مَن خَلَقَ السّماواتِ والأرضَ لَيَقُولُنَّ اللهُ﴾.[٢١٥٣]

1916. **Imām al-ʿAskarī (AS) said** in his explanation of the *basmala*[2164], 'Allah is the one whom all creation deify when they are in need or in

١٩١٦ . الإمامُ العسكريُّ ﷺ ـ في تفسيرِ البَسْمَلَةِ ـ: اللهُ هُو الّذي يَتألَّهُ إلَيهِ عِندَ الحَوائجِ والشَّدائدِ كُلُّ

difficulty or when all their hopes have been severed from all except Him, and when their means of attainment have been cut off from all except Him.'[2165]

مَخْلوقٍ عِندَ انْقِطاعِ الرَّجاءِ مِن كُلِّ مَن هُوَ دُونَهُ، وتَقَطُّعِ الأسْبابِ مِن جَميعِ مَن سِواهُ.[٢١٥٤]

2. The Law of Causality

٢ ـ قانونُ العِلّيّةِ

"Were they created from nothing? Or are they [their own] creators? Did they create the heavens and the earth? Rather they have no certainty."[2166]

﴿أَمْ خُلِقُوا مِنْ غَيْرِ شَيْءٍ أَمْ هُمُ الْخَالِقُونَ * أَمْ خَلَقُوا السَّمَاوَاتِ وَالْأَرْضَ بَلْ لا يُوقِنُونَ﴾.[٢١٥٥]

1917. **Imām al-Bāqir (AS)** was asked by a scholar from Damascus, 'So, the thing, did He create it from something else or from nothing?' The Imām replied, 'He created a thing whereby nothing existed before it. Were He to have created from something then there would be infinite regress and there would always have been something existing alongside Allah when in actual fact Allah existed when nothing else was in existence.'[2167]

١٩١٧ . الإمامُ الباقرُ ﷺ ـ وقد سألَهُ رجُلٌ مِن عُلَماءِ أهلِ الشّامِ: ... فالشَّيْءُ خَلقَهُ مِن شَيْءٍ أو مِن لا شَيءٍ ؟ ـ: خَلقَ الشَّيْءَ لا مِن شَيْءٍ كانَ قَبلَهُ. ولَو خَلقَ الشَّيْءَ مِن شَيْءٍ، إذاً لَم يَكُنْ لَهُ انْقِطاعٌ أبداً، ولَمْ يَزَلِ اللهُ إذاً ومَعهُ شَيْءٌ، ولٰكنْ كانَ اللهُ ولا شَيْءَ مَعهُ.[٢١٥٦]

1918. **Imām al-Ṣādiq (AS)** when asked by Abū Shākir al-Dayṣānī, 'What is the proof that you have a creator?' The Imām (AS) answered, 'I found within myself that there can only be one of two possibilities, that either I was the one who created my own self or that someone other than me created me, so if I created myself, then that can only mean one of two possibilities, either I created myself and I was in existence beforehand or I created myself from non-existence, so if I created myself and I was already in existence beforehand, then I was free of any need to be created by the fact that I already existed. If I was in non-existence then surely you know that non-existence cannot bring about anything into existence. Thus, the third meaning affirms that I have a creator and He is Allah, the Lord of the Worlds.' Then Abū Shakir had no response to the Imām (AS) so he stood up and left.'[2168]

١٩١٨ . الإمامُ الصّادقُ ﷺ ـ لمّا سألَهُ أبو شاكرٍ الدَّيْصانيُّ: ما الدّليلُ علىٰ أنّ لكَ صانِعاً ؟ ـ: وَجَدتُ نَفْسي لا تَخْلو مِن إحْدىٰ جِهَتَينِ: إمّا أنْ أكونَ صَنَعْتُها أنا أو صَنَعَها غَيري ؛ فإن كنتُ صَنَعتُها أنا فلا أخْلو مِن أحدِ مَعْنَيَينِ، إمّا أنْ أكونَ صَنَعتُها وكانتْ مَوجودَةً أو صَنَعْتُها وكانتْ مَعْدومَةً، فإنْ كنتُ صَنَعْتُها وكانتْ مَوجودةً فَقَدِ اسْتَغْنَتْ بوجودِها عن صَنْعَتِها، وإن كانتْ مَعْدومَةً فإنّكَ تَعلمُ أنّ المَعْدومَ لا يُحْدِثُ شَيئاً، فقد ثَبَتَ المَعنىٰ الثّالثُ أنّ لي صانِعاً وهُو اللهُ رَبُّ العالَمِينَ، فقامَ وما أحارَ جَواباً.[٢١٥٧]

3. Order of the Universe

٣ـ نِظامُ العالَم

1919. **Imām ʿAlī (AS) said,** 'O creature that has been equitably created and that has been nurtured and looked after in the darkness of wombs with multiple veils, you were originated from an extract of clay…then you were taken out of your abode to another place you had not seen, and you did not know the means of acquiring its benefits, so who guided you to attain your sustenance from the breast of your mother and who taught you the location of what you required or wanted?'[2169]

١٩١٩ . الإمامُ عليٌّ عليه السلام : أيُّها المَخْلوقُ السَّويُّ، والمُنْشَأُ المَرْعِيُّ، في ظُلُماتِ الأرْحامِ ومُضاعَفاتِ الأستارِ، بُدِئتَ مِن سُلالَةٍ مِن طِينٍ، ووُضِعتَ في قَرارٍ مَكينٍ، إلىٰ قَدَرٍ مَعلومٍ وأجلٍ مَقْسومٍ، تَمُورُ في بَطنِ اُمِّكَ جَنيناً، لا تُحيرُ دُعاءً، ولا تَسمَعُ نِداءً، ثُمّ اُخْرِجْتَ مِن مَقَرِّكَ إلىٰ دارٍ لَم تَشْهَدْها، ولَم تَعرِفْ سُبُلَ مَنافِعِها، فمَنْ هَداكَ لاجْتِرارِ الغِذاءِ مِن ثَدْيِ اُمِّكَ، وعَرّفَكَ عِندَالحاجَةِ مواضِعَ طَلَبِكَ وإرادَتِكَ؟[٢١٥٨]

1920. It is narrated in *Sharḥ Nahj al-Balāgha* that Imām ʿAlī (AS) used to frequently say once he had completed his night prayers, 'I bear witness that the heavens and the earth and what is between them are signs that indicate to You and they bear witness to what You have called us towards. Everything that is a proof for You and demonstrates your Lordship carries the signs of Your bounties and the marks of Your administration and management.'[2170]

١٩٢٠ . شرح نهج البلاغة : كانَ [الإمام عليّ عليه السلام] كثيراً ما يقولُ إذا فَرَغَ مِن صَلاة اللّيلِ ـ: أشهَدُ أنّ السّماواتِ والأرضَ وما بَينَهُما آياتٌ تَدُلُّ علَيكَ، وشَواهِدُ تَشْهدُ بما إلَيهِ دَعوتَ. كلُّ ما يُؤدّي عنكَ الحُجَّةَ ويَشهدُ لكَ بالرُّبوبيّةِ مَوْسومٌ بآثارِ نِعْمَتِكَ، ومَعالِمِ تَدبيرِكَ.[٢١٥٩]

1921. **Imām al-Bāqir (AS) said** with regards to the following verse of Allah – most High– *"But whoever has been blind in this [world], will be blind in the Hereafter"*, said, 'Whoever does not see that there is a great creator behind the creation of the heavens and the earth, the alternating night and day, the orbits of the sun and the moon and all the other wondrous signs *"will be blind in the Hereafter."*' He (AS) then said, 'This means he is blind to what he did not witness and (even) more astray from the (right) way.'[2171]

١٩٢١ . الإمامُ الباقرُ عليه السلام ـ في قولهِ تعالىٰ: ﴿ومَن كانَ في هٰذهِ أعْمىٰ فهُوَ في الآخِرَةِ أعْمىٰ﴾[٢١٦٠] ـ: فمَن لَم يَدُلَّهُ خَلقُ السّماواتِ والأرضِ واخْتِلافُ اللّيلِ والنّهارِ، ودَوَرانُ الفَلَكِ بالشَّمسِ والقَمرِ، والآياتُ العَجيباتُ علىٰ أنّ وَراءَ ذلكَ أمراً هُو أعْظَمُ مِنهُ، ﴿فهُو في الآخِرَةِ أعمىٰ﴾. قالَ: فهُو عمّا لَم يُعايِنْ أعْمىٰ وأضَلُّ سبيلاً.[٢١٦١]

1922. **Imām al-Ṣādiq (AS) said,** 'If you saw a *single door* [on its own], from what normally comprises a pair [of doors], with a protruding attachment, would you ever imagine that this [single door with a protrusion] was created in such a way without purpose? Rather you would certainly know that it was made in such a way to

١٩٢٢ . الإمامُ الصّادقُ عليه السلام : لَو رَأيتَ فَرْداً مِن مِصْراعَيْنِ فيه كَلّوبٌ، أكنتَ تَتَوهّمُ أنَّهُ جُعِلَ كذلكَ بلا مَعنىٰ؟ بَلْ كُنتَ تَعلمُ ضَرورَةً أنّهُ مَصْنوعٌ يَلْقىٰ فَرداً آخَرَ، فتُبْرِزُهُ لِيكونَ في

connect with another part [thus comprising the pair and providing a purpose for the protrusion]. So you would expose the other component in order to unite it [with the first one] and hence reach a useful purpose. In the same way you find a male animal as if he is part of a pair equipped for its female partner, and they unite in order to procreate and preserve [the human race]. So destroyed, defeated and wretched are the claimants of philosophy[2172]. How did their hearts get blinded from this wonderful creation so as to deny the organization and purpose in it?'[2173]

اجْتِماعِهِما ضَرْبٌ مِنَ المَصلَحَةِ، وهٰكذا تَجِدُ الذَّكَرَ مِنَ الحَيوانِ كأنَّهُ فَردٌ مِن زَوْجٍ مُهَيّأٌ مِن فَردٍ أُنثى، فَيلْتَقِيانِ لِما فيهِ مِن دَوامِ النَّسْلِ وبَقائهِ، فَتَبّاً وخَيْبَةً وتَعْساً لِمُنْتَحِلي الفَلسفَةِ، كيفَ عَمِيَتْ قُلوبُهُم عن هٰذهِ الخِلْقَةِ العَجيبَةِ، حتّى أنكَروا التَّدبيرَ والعَمْدَ فيها؟! ٢١٦٢

1923. **Imām al-Ṣādiq (AS) said,** 'Reflect, O Mufaḍḍal, upon the actions that have been designated for mankind such as eating and sleeping… if man were to have to go to sleep while having to think about relaxing his body and reviving his powers, he would probably find it burdensome and turn away [from sleeping], and refuse himself [sleep] till his body would wear out and waste away.'[2174]

١٩٢٣. عنه عليه السلام ـ للمفضل بن عمر ـ : فَكِّرْ يا مُفَضَّلُ في الأفْعالِ الّتي جُعِلَتْ في الإنْسانِ مِن الطُّعْمِ والنَّومِ... لَو كانَ إنّما يَصيرُ إلَى النَّومِ بالتَّفَكُّرِ في حاجَتِهِ إلى راحَةِ البَدَنِ وإجْمامِ قُواهُ كانَ عَسى أنْ يَتَثاقَلَ عَن ذلكَ، فَيَدْمَغُهُ حتّى يَنْهَكَ بَدَنُهُ. ٢١٦٣

4. Cancellation of Firm Intentions and Failure of Ambitions

٤ ـ فَسْخُ العزائمِ ونَقْضُ الهِممِ

1924. **Imām 'Alī (AS),** when asked for a proof to affirm the existence of a creator, said, 'Three things: the changing of states, the weakness of the body's limbs, and the thwarting of ambition.'[2175]

١٩٢٤. الإمامُ عليٌّ عليه السلام ـ وقد سُئلَ عنِ الدَّليلِ علىٰ إثباتِ الصّانِعِ ـ: ثَلاثَةُ أشياءَ: تَحْويلُ الحالِ، وضَعْفُ الأرْكانِ، ونَقْضُ الهِمَّةِ. ٢١٦٤

1925. **Imām al-Ṣādiq (AS),** when asked through what means he knew his Lord, answered, 'By the cancellation of firm intention and the thwarting of ambition, I made a firm intention and it got cancelled, and I had ambition and it was thwarted.'[2176]

١٩٢٥. الإمامُ الصّادقُ عليه السلام ـ وقد سُئلَ: بِما عَرَفْتَ رَبَّكَ؟ ـ: بِفَسْخِ العَزْمِ ونَقْضِ الهَمِّ؛ عَزَمْتُ فَفَسَخَ عَزْمي، وهَمَمْتُ فَنَقَضَ هَمّي. ٢١٦٥

638. Attributing Creation to Nature

٦٣٨ ـ إسنادُ الخَلقِ إلَى الطَّبيعَةِ

1926. **Imām al-Ṣādiq (AS) was** asked by Mufaḍḍal, 'O my master, there is a group of people that

١٩٢٦. الإمامُ الصّادقُ عليه السلام ـ في جوابِ قَولِ

claim that this [creation] is the doing of nature [itself]', the Imām (AS) said, 'Ask them about this nature, does it have knowledge and power to carry out such actions [as creation] or not? For if they answer that it has knowledge and power, then what is preventing them from acknowledging the existence of a creator? – for verily this is His creation. If they claim that nature does these actions without knowledge or without purpose while having witnessed the exactness and wisdom therein, it is [obviously] known that this is the work of a very wise creator, and what they have called 'nature' is the very system running through creation.'[2177]

المُفَضَّلِ: يا مَولايَ، إنّ قَوماً يَزْعُمونَ أنَّ هٰذا مِن فِعلِ الطَّبيعَةِ ـ: سَلْهُمْ عَن هٰذهِ الطَّبيعَةِ: أهِيَ شَيْءٌ لَهُ عِلمٌ وقُدرَةٌ علىٰ مِثْلِ هٰذهِ الأفْعالِ، أمْ لَيست كذلكَ؟ فإنْ أوْجَبوا لَها العِلْمَ والقُدْرَةَ فما يَمْنَعُهُم مِن إثْباتِ الخالِقِ؟ فإنّ هٰذهِ صَنْعَتُهُ، وإنْ زَعَموا أنّها تَفْعَلُ هٰذهِ الأفْعالَ بغَيرِ عِلْمٍ ولا عَمْدٍ وكانَ في أفْعالِها ما قَد تَراهُ مِن الصَّوابِ والحِكمَةِ عُلِمَ أنّ هٰذا الفِعْلَ للخالِقِ الحَكيمِ، وأنّ الّذي سَمَّوهُ طَبيعَةً هُو سُنّةٌ في خَلْقِهِ الجارِيَةُ علىٰ ما أجْراها علَيهِ.[٢١٦٦]

(See also: INNER KNOWLEDGE OF ALLAH (2): 271)

(أُنظر) عنوان ٢٧١ «المعرفة (٢)».

133

CHARACTER

الخُلق

639. The Importance of Good Naturedness (Character)

٦٣٩ـ أهَمّيّةُ حُسنِ الخُلق

1927. **The Prophet (SAWA) said,** 'Islam is to be good-natured.'[2178]

١٩٢٧. رسولُ اللهِ ﷺ: الإسلامُ حُسنُ الخُلق.[٢١٦٧]

1928. **The Prophet (SAWA) said,** 'Good nature is half of religion.'[2179]

١٩٢٨. عنه ﷺ: حُسنُ الخُلقِ نِصفُ الدِّينِ.[٢١٦٨]

1929. **Imām ʿAlī (AS) said,** 'Good naturedness is the fountainhead of every goodness.'[2180]

١٩٢٩. الإمامُ عليٌّ ؑ: حُسنُ الخُلقِ رأسُ كُلِّ بِرٍّ.[٢١٦٩]

640. The Blessing of Good Naturedness in this World

٦٤٠ـ بَرَكاتُ حُسنِ الخُلُقِ في الدُّنيا

1930. **The Prophet (SAWA) said,** 'Good nature establishes love.'[2181]

١٩٣٠. رسولُ اللهِ ﷺ: حُسنُ الخُلقِ يُثبِتُ المَوَدَّةَ.[٢١٧٠]

1931. **Imām al-Ṣādiq (AS) said,** 'Being good-natured brings about an increase in sustenance.'[2182]

١٩٣١ . الإمامُ الصّادقُ عليه السلام : حُسنُ الخُلقِ يَزيدُ في الرِّزقِ.[٢١٧١]

1932. **Imām al-Ṣādiq (AS) said,** 'Verily goodness and good nature cause the homes to flourish and increase in life spans.'[2183]

١٩٣٢ . عنه عليه السلام : إنّ البِرَّ وحُسنَ الخُلقِ يَعْمُرانِ الدِّيارَ، ويَزيدانِ في الأعْمارِ.[٢١٧٢]

1933. **Imām al-Ṣādiq (AS) said,** 'There is no life more wholesome than that lived with a good nature.'[2184]

١٩٣٣ . عنه عليه السلام : لا عَيشَ أهْنَأُ مِن حُسنِ الخُلقِ.[٢١٧٣]

641. The Blessings of Good Naturedness In the Hereafter

٦٤١ ـ بَرَكاتُ حُسنِ الخُلُقِ فِي الآخِرَةِ

1934. **The Prophet (SAWA) said,** 'Verily a servant will definitely reach high ranks and honourable stations in the Hereafter, through his good nature, even if he is weak in his worship.'[2185]

١٩٣٤ . رسولُ اللهِ صلى الله عليه وآله : إنّ العَبدَ لَيَبلُغُ بحُسنِ خُلقِهِ عَظيمَ دَرَجاتِ الآخِرَةِ وشَرَفِ المَنازِل، وإنَّهُ لَضَعيفُ العِبادَةِ.[٢١٧٤]

1935. **The Prophet (SAWA) said,** 'Verily the one with a good nature has the same reward as the one who fasts and prays during the night.'[2186]

١٩٣٥ . عنه صلى الله عليه وآله : إنّ صاحِبَ الخُلقِ الحَسنِ لَهُ مِثلُ أجْرِ الصّائمِ القائمِ.[٢١٧٥]

1936. **The Prophet (SAWA) said,** 'Nothing will be heavier on the scale of deeds than good nature.'[2187]

١٩٣٦ . عنه صلى الله عليه وآله : ما مِن شيءٍ أثقَلُ في الميزانِ مِن حُسنِ الخُلقِ.[٢١٧٦]

1937. **The Prophet (SAWA) said,** 'The most beloved and nearest to me on the Day of Resurrection will be the most good-natured, and the one who is most humble.'[2188]

١٩٣٧ . عنه صلى الله عليه وآله : إنّ أحَبّكُم إلَيَّ وأقرَبَكُم مِنّي يَومَ القِيامَةِ مَجلِساً أحْسَنُكُم خُلقاً، وأشَدُّكُم تَواضُعاً.[٢١٧٧]

1938. **The Prophet (SAWA) said,** 'The believers with the most perfect faith are those who are the most good-natured.'[2189]

١٩٣٨ . عنه صلى الله عليه وآله : أكمَلُ المؤمنينَ إيماناً أحْسَنُهُم خُلقاً.[٢١٧٨]

1939. **Imām 'Alī (AS) said,** 'The distinguishing feature of a believer is his good nature.[2190]

١٩٣٩ . الإمامُ عليٌّ عليه السلام : عُنوانُ صَحيفَةِ المؤمنِ حُسنُ خُلقِهِ.[٢١٧٩]

642. Explanation of Good Naturedness

٦٤٢ ـ تفسيرُ حُسنِ الخُلُق

1940. **Imām ʿAlī (AS) said,** 'Good naturedness is found in three things: abstaining from the forbidden, seeking the lawful and providing peace and comfort for your family.'[2191]

١٩٤٠ . الإمامُ عليٌّ ﷺ : حُسنُ الخُلقِ في ثَلاثٍ : اجْتِنابُ المَحارِمِ ، وطَلَبُ الحَلالِ ، والتَّوسُّعُ على العِيالِ .[٢١٨٠]

1941. **Imām ʿAlī (AS) said,** 'Giving greetings comes from beautiful character.'[2192]

١٩٤١ . عنه ﷺ : إنَّ بَذْلَ التَّحيَّةِ مِن مَحاسِنِ الأخْلاقِ .[٢١٨١]

1942. **Imām al-Ṣādiq (AS),** when he was asked about the meaning and bounds of good naturedness, said, 'Be lenient, make your words pleasant and meet your brother joyfully.'[2193]

١٩٤٢ . الإمامُ الصّادقُ ﷺ ـ لَمّا سُئلَ عَن حَدِّ حُسنِ الخُلقِ ـ : تُلينُ جانِبَكَ ، وتُطيِّبُ كلامَكَ ، وتَلْقى أخاكَ بِبِشْرٍ حَسَنٍ .[٢١٨٢]

643. High Moral Virtues

٦٤٣ ـ معالي الأخلاق

1943. **The Prophet (SAWA) said,** 'Verily Allah loves high moral virtues and detests poor manners.'[2194]

١٩٤٣ . رسولُ اللهِ ﷺ : إنّ اللهَ يُحِبُّ مَعالِيَ الأخْلاقِ ويَكْرَهُ سَفْسافَها .[٢١٨٣]

1944. **Imām ʿAlī (AS) said,** 'I urge you towards the most noble traits for verily they are exalted and possess a high rank, and beware of [adopting] vile traits for verily they derogate noble people and destroy the famous and celebrated.'[2195]

١٩٤٤ . الإمامُ عليٌّ ﷺ : علَيكُم بمَكارِمِ الأخْلاقِ فإنّها رِفعَةٌ ، وإيّاكُم والأخْلاقَ الدَّنِيَّةَ فإنّها تَضَعُ الشَّريفَ وتَهْدِمُ المَجْدَ .[٢١٨٤]

1945. **Imām ʿAlī (AS) said,** 'Persevere in acquiring noble moral traits.'[2196]

١٩٤٥ . عنه ﷺ : ثابِروا على اقْتِناءِ المَكارِمِ .[٢١٨٥]

644. Explanation of Noble Moral Traits

٦٤٤ ـ تفسيرُ مَكارِمِ الأخلاقِ

1946. **The Prophet (SAWA) said,** 'Verily I was deputed to perfect noble moral traits.'[2197]

١٩٤٦ . رسولُ اللهِ ﷺ : إنّما بُعِثْتُ لاُتَمِّمَ مَكارِمَ الأخْلاقِ .[٢١٨٦]

1947. **Imām al-Ṣādiq (AS) said,** 'Verily Allah – Blessed and most High – distinguished the Prophet (SAWA) with noble moral traits, therefore examine yourselves and if you find them within yourselves, then praise Allah and beseech

١٩٤٧ . الإمامُ الصّادقُ ﷺ : إنّ اللهَ تباركَ وتعالى خَصَّ رَسولَهُ ﷺ بمَكارِمِ الأخْلاقِ ، فامْتَحِنوا أنفسَكُم ؛ فإن كانتْ فيكُم فاحْمَدوا اللهَ عزّوجلّ

Him for an increase in them', then the Imām listed ten of them, 'Conviction, contentment, patience, thankfulness, clemency, excellent character, liberality, self-respect, courage and valour.'[2198]

وارغَبوا إلَيهِ في الزّيادَةِ مِنها. فـذكَرَها عَشـرَةً: اليَقينُ، والقَناعَةُ، والصَّبرُ، والشُّكـرُ، والحِـلْمُ، وحُسنُ الخُلقِ، والسَّخاءُ، والغَيرَةُ، والشَّجاعَةُ، والمُروءَةُ.[٢١٨٧]

1948. **Imām al-Ṣādiq (AS)** was asked about noble moral traits, to which he replied, 'Pardoning someone who has oppressed you, repairing broken ties, giving to the one who has deprived you, and speaking the truth even if it is against yourself.'[2199]

١٩٤٨ . عنه (عليه السلام) ـ وقـد سُـئِلَ عـن مَكـارِمِ الأخْلاقِ ـ: العَفْوُ عَـمّنْ ظَـلَمَكَ، وصِـلَةُ مَـن قطَعَكَ، وإعْطاءُ مَن حَرَمَكَ، وقَولُ الحـقِّ ولَـو علىٰ نَفْسِكَ.[٢١٨٨]

645. The Best of Noble Traits

٦٤٥ـ خَيرُ المَكارِمِ

1949. **Imām ʿAlī (AS) said,** 'The best noble moral trait is self-sacrifice.'[2200][2201]

١٩٤٩ . الإمامُ عليٌّ (عليه السلام): خَيرُ المَكارِمِ الإيثارُ.[٢١٨٩]

1950. **Imām ʿAlī (AS) said,** 'The best noble moral traits are the pardoning by one who has the upper hand and the open-handedness of one who is himself in need.'[2202]

١٩٥٠ . عنه (عليه السلام): أحسَنُ المَكارِمِ عَفْوُ المُقْتَدِرِ وجُودُ المُفْتَقِرِ.[٢١٩٠]

1951. **Imām ʿAlī (AS) said,** 'The best moral trait is completing one's favours.'[2203]

١٩٥١ . عنه (عليه السلام): أفضَلُ الكَرَمِ إتْمامُ النِّعَمِ.[٢١٩١]

646. The Fruits of Good Naturedness

٦٤٦ـ ثَمَراتُ حُسنِ الخُلُقِ

1952. **Imām ʿAlī (AS) said,** 'Adorn yourself with good nature and Allah will ease your account.'[2204]

١٩٥٢ . الإمامُ عليٌّ (عليه السلام): حَسِّنْ خُلقَكَ يُخَفِّفِ اللهُ حِسابَكَ.[٢١٩٢]

1953. **Imām al-Ṣādiq (AS) said,** 'Good nature melts away mistakes just as the sun melts away ice.'[2205]

١٩٥٣ . الإمامُ الصّادقُ (عليه السلام): الخُلقُ الحَسنُ يَميثُ الخَطيئَةَ كما تَميثُ الشَّمسُ الجَليدَ.[٢١٩٣]

647. Denouncing Ill Naturedness

٦٤٧ـ ذَمُّ سوءِ الخُلُقِ

1954. **The Prophet (SAWA) said,** 'Being ill-natured is a sin that is not forgiven.'[2206]

١٩٥٤ . رسولُ اللهِ ﷺ: سُـوءُ الخُـلقِ ذَنبٌ لا يُغْفَرُ.[٢١٩٤]

1955. **The Prophet (SAWA) said,** 'Verily the servant with an ill nature will be in the lowest reach of Hell.'[2207]

١٩٥٥ . عنه ﷺ : إنّ العَبدَ لَيَبلُغُ... بِسُوءِ خُلقِهِ أسْفَلَ دَرَجَةٍ في جَهنَّمَ.[٢١٩٥]

1956. **It was said to the Prophet (SAWA)** that, 'Such and such a woman fasts during the days and stands for prayer during the nights, but she is ill-natured and insults her neighbours with her tongue', the Prophet (SAWA) then said, 'There is no good in her, she is of the people of the Hellfire.'[2208]

١٩٥٦ . عنه ﷺ ـ وقد قيلَ لَهُ : إنّ فُلانَةَ تَصومُ النّهرَ وتَقومُ اللّيلَ ، وهِيَ سَيِّئةُ الخُلقِ تُؤْذي جِيرانَها بلِسانِها ـ: لا خَيرَ فيها ، هِيَ مِن أهْلِ النّارِ.[٢١٩٦]

1957. **Imām ʿAlī (AS) said,** 'Ill nature causes life to be miserable and torments the soul.'[2209]

١٩٥٧ . الإمامُ عليٌّ ؑ : سُوءُ الخُلقِ نَكَدُ العَيْشِ وعذابُ النَّفْسِ.[٢١٩٧]

648. The Final Outcome of the Ill-Natured Person

٦٤٨ ـ عاقِبَةُ الخُلُقِ السَّيِّئِ

1958. **Imām ʿAlī (AS) said,** 'Whoever is ill-natured, his family is rendered weary of him.'[2210]

١٩٥٨ . الإمامُ عليٌّ ؑ : مَن ساءَ خُلقُهُ مَلَّهُ أهلُهُ.[٢١٩٨]

1959. **Imām ʿAlī (AS) said,** 'Whoever has low tolerance will see his comfort reduce.'[2211]

١٩٥٩ . عنه ؑ : مَن ضاقَت ساحَتُهُ قَلّتْ راحَتُهُ.[٢١٩٩]

1960. **Imām ʿAlī (AS) said,** 'Whoever is ill-natured, his sustenance will be straitened.'[2212]

١٩٦٠ . عنه ؑ : مَن ساءَ خُلُقُهُ ضاقَ رِزْقُهُ.[٢٢٠٠]

1961. **Imām al-Ṣādiq (AS) said,** 'Eating meat produces flesh [on the body] and the one who avoids meat for forty [consecutive] days will become ill-natured.'[2213]

١٩٦١ . الإمامُ الصّادقُ ؑ : اللَّحْمُ يُنْبِتُ اللَّحْمَ ، ومَن تَرَكَ اللَّحْمَ أربَعينَ يَوماً ساءَ خُلُقُهُ.[٢٢٠١]

1962. **Imām al-Ṣādiq (AS) said,** 'Verily ill nature spoils one's deeds just as vinegar spoils honey.'[2214]

١٩٦٢ . عنه ؑ : إنَّ سُوءَ الخُلقِ لَيُفسِدُ العَملَ كما يُفسِدُ الخَلُّ العسَلَ.[٢٢٠٢]

649. The Best Virtues

٦٤٩ ـ أفضَلُ الأخلاقِ

1963. **Imām ʿAlī (AS) said,** 'The noblest moral virtue is liberality and the most beneficial moral virtue is justice.'[2215]

١٩٦٣ . الإمامُ عليٌّ ؑ : أكْرَمُ الأخْلاقِ السَّخاءُ ، وأعَمُّها نَفْعاً العَدلُ.[٢٢٠٣]

1964. **Imām ʿAlī (AS) said,** 'The most eminent moral traits are humbleness, clemency, and leniency.'[2216]

١٩٦٤ . عنه (ع) : أشرَفُ الخَلائقِ التّواضُعُ والحِلمُ ولينُ الجانبِ.٢٢٠٤

1965. **Imām al-Bāqir (AS),** when asked about the best virtues, said, 'Patience and magnanimity.'[2217]

١٩٦٥ . الإمامُ الباقرُ (ع) ـ وقد سُئلَ عن أفضَلِ الأخلاقِ ـ: الصّبرُ والسّماحَةُ.٢٢٠٥

650. The Link Between Various Traits

٦٥٠ ـ ارتباطُ السَّجايا بَعضِها ببَعضٍ

1966. **Imām ʿAlī (AS) said,** 'When a man has a pure and praiseworthy quality then expect him to have other such qualities.'[2218]

١٩٦٦ . الإمامُ عليٌّ (ع) : إذا كانَ في رَجُلٍ خَلّةٌ رائقَةٌ فانتَظِروا أخَواتِها.٢٢٠٦

1967. **Imām al-Ṣādiq (AS) said,** 'Verily the noble moral traits are all connected and linked to each other.'[2219]

١٩٦٧ . الإمامُ الصّادقُ (ع) : إنّ خِصالَ المَكارِمِ بَعضُها مُقيَّدٌ ببَعضٍ.٢٢٠٧

134

ALCOHOL

الخَمرُ

651. Denouncing Drinking Alcohol

٦٥١ ـ ذَمُّ شُربِ الخَمرِ

1968. **The Prophet (SAWA) said,** 'Alcohol and faith will never be together in the breast or heart of a man.'[2220]

١٩٦٨ . رسولُ اللهِ ﷺ : لا تُجمَعُ الخَمرُ والإيمانُ في جَوفٍ أو قَلبِ رَجُلٍ أبداً.٢٢٠٨

1969. **The Prophet (SAWA) said,** 'Alcohol is the mother of all indecent acts and grave sins.'[2221]

١٩٦٩ . عنه ﷺ : الخَمرُ أُمُّ الفَواحِشِ والكَبائرِ.٢٢٠٩

1970. **The Prophet (SAWA) said,** 'All evil in its entirety has been gathered in one house and drinking alcohol is the key to that house.'[2222]

١٩٧٠ . عنه ﷺ : جُمِعَ الشَّرُّ كُلُّهُ في بَيتٍ، وجُعِلَ مِفتاحُهُ شُربَ الخَمرِ.٢٢١٠

652. The Reason for the Prohibition of Alcohol

٦٥٢ ـ عِلَّةُ تَحريمِ الخَمرِ

1971. **Imām ʿAlī (AS) said,** 'Allah imposed...the abandonment of drinking alcohol in order to safeguard the intellect.'[2223]

١٩٧١ . الإمامُ عليٌّ (ع) : فرَضَ اللهُ... تَركَ شُربِ الخَمرِ تَحصيناً للعَقلِ.٢٢١١

1972. **Imām al-Riḍā (AS) said,** 'Allah forbade alcohol due the corruption that accompanies it, and due to the way in which it alters the drinkers' reason, and how it encourages them to deny Allah, Mighty and Exalted, and to slander Him and His messenger, and for all the other accompaniments of corruption and murder.'[2224]

١٩٧٢ . الإمامُ الرِّضا (ع) : حَرَّمَ اللهُ الخَمرَ لِما فيها مِنَ الفَسادِ، ومِن تَغْيِيرِها عُقولَ شارِبِيها، وحَمْلِها إيّاهُم على إنْكارِ اللهِ عزّوجلّ، والفِرْيَةِ علَيهِ وعلى رُسُلِهِ، وسائرِ ما يكونُ مِنهُم مِنَ الفَسادِ والقَتلِ. ٢٢١٢

653. The Consequence of Drinking Alcohol

٦٥٣ ـ عاقِبَةُ شُربِ الخَمرِ

1973. **Imām ʿAlī (AS) said,** 'When the alcoholic one meets Allah, Mighty and Exalted, he will meet him as an idol worshipper.'[2225]

١٩٧٣ . عنه (ع) : مُدْمِنُ الخَمرِ يَلْقَى اللهَ عزّوجلّ حِينَ يَلْقاهُ كعابِدِ وَثَنٍ. ٢٢١٣

1974. **Imām ʿAlī (AS) said,** 'The one who drinks an intoxicant, his prayers will not be accepted for forty days and nights.'[2226]

١٩٧٤ . الإمامُ عليٌّ (ع) : مَن شَرِبَ المُسْكِرَ لم تُقْبَلْ صَلاتُهُ أربَعينَ يوماً ولَيلَةً. ٢٢١٤

654. Interacting [dealing] with an Alcohol Drinker

٦٥٤ ـ مُعامَلَةُ شارِبِ الخَمرِ

1975. **The Prophet (SAWA) said,** 'When one who drinks alcohol speaks, do not believe him, and if he proposes do not marry him, if he falls sick do not visit him, and if he dies do not attend his funeral, and do not entrust him with anything.'[2227]

١٩٧٥ . رسولُ اللهِ ﷺ : شارِبُ الخَمرِ لا تُصَدِّقوهُ إذا حَدَّثَ، ولا تُزَوِّجوهُ إذا خَطَبَ، ولا تَعودوهُ إذا مَرِضَ، ولا تَحْضَروهُ إذا ماتَ، ولا تأتَمِنوهُ على أمانَةٍ. ٢٢١٥

1976. **The Prophet (SAWA) said,** 'The alcohol drinker is like sulphur, so keep away from him lest he pollute you with his stench for sulphur has a bad stench.'[2228]

١٩٧٦ . عنه ﷺ : مَثَلُ شارِبِ الخَمرِ كَمَثَلِ الكِبْرِيتِ، فاحْذَروهُ لا يُنْتِنْكُم كما يُنْتِنُ الكِبْريتُ. ٢٢١٦

655. How an Alcohol Drinker Will be Resurrected

٦٥٥ ـ صِفَةُ حَشرِ شارِبِ الخَمرِ

1977. **Imām al-Ṣādiq (AS) said,** 'The ones who have quenched themselves in this world with an

١٩٧٧ . الإمامُ الصّادقُ (ع) : إنّ أهلَ الرَّيِّ في

intoxicant [alcohol] will die thirsty, will be resurrected thirsty and will enter the Hellfire thirsty.'[2229]

الدُّنيا مِن المُسْكِرِ يَموتونَ عِطاشاً ، ويُحْشَرونَ عِطاشاً ، ويَدخُلونَ النّار عِطاشاً .[٢٢١٧]

656. Enjoinment of Abandoning Alcohol even if it be for Other than Allah

٦٥٦ ـ الحَثُّ عَلىٰ تَركِ الخَمرِ ولَو لِغَيرِ اللهِ

1978. **The Prophet (SAWA) said,** 'Whoever abandons alcohol for other than the sake of Allah, Allah will quench his thirst [in Paradise] with the sealed wine'. Imām 'Alī (AS) exclaimed, 'For other than Allah?' The Prophet (SAWA) replied, 'Yes, by Allah, for his own protection and well-being.'[2230]

١٩٧٨ . بحار الأنوار قال رسولُ اللهِ ﷺ ـ: مَن تَرَكَ الخَمرَ لغَيرِ اللهِ سَقاهُ اللهُ مِن الرَّحيقِ المَختومِ ، فقالَ عليٌّ ؑ :لغَيرِ اللهِ ؟! قالَ: نَعَم واللهِ ، صِيانَةً لنفسهِ .[٢٢١٨]

657. The Prohibition of that Which Produces the Same Effects as Alcohol

٦٥٧ ـ حُرمَةُ ما فَعَلَ فِعلَ الخَمرِ

1979. **Imām al-Kāẓim (AS) said,** 'Allah did not prohibit alcohol because of its name, rather He prohibited it due to its effects, so whatever produces the same effects as alcohol is [treated as] alcohol.'[2231]

١٩٧٩ . الإمامُ الكاظمُ ؑ :إنّ اللهَ عزّ وجلّ لم يُحَرِّمِ الخَمرَ لاسْمِها، ولٰكنّهُ حَرّمَها لعاقِبَتِها ؛ فما كانَ عاقِبَتُهُ عاقِبَةَ الخَمرِ فهُو خَمرٌ .[٢٢١٩]

135

FEAR

الخَوفُ

658. The Virtue of Fearing Allah

٦٥٨ ـ فَضلُ مَخافَةِ اللهِ

1980. **The Prophet (SAWA) said,** 'The fountainhead of wisdom is the fear of Allah.'[2232]

١٩٨٠ . رسولُ اللهِ ﷺ : رأسُ الحِكمَةِ مَخافَةُ اللهِ .[٢٢٢٠]

1981. **The Prophet (SAWA) said,** 'The person with the highest station in the sight of Allah is the one who fears Him the most.'[2233]

١٩٨١ . عنه ﷺ : أعْلىٰ النّاسِ مَنزِلَةً عِندَ اللهِ أخوَفُهُم مِنهُ .[٢٢٢١]

1982. **The Prophet (SAWA) said,** 'Three things provide salvation…fear of Allah in private, as if you see Him, for verily even though you do not see Him, He surely sees you.'[2234]

١٩٨٢ . عنه ﷺ : ثَلاثٌ مُنْجِياتٌ... خَوفُ اللهِ في السِّرِّ كأنّكَ تَراهُ، فإنْ لَم تَكُن تَراهُ فإنّهُ يرَاكَ.[٢٢٢٢]

1983. **The Prophet (SAWA) said,** 'The one who knows Allah the most is the one who fears Allah the most.'[2235]

١٩٨٣ . عنه ﷺ : مَن كانَ باللهِ أعْرَفَ كانَ مِن اللهِ أخْوَفَ.[٢٢٢٣]

1984. **Imām ʿAlī (AS) said,** 'Fear is the garment of the gnostics.'[2236]

١٩٨٤ . الإمامُ عليٌّ عليه السلام : الخَوفُ جِلْبابُ العارِفينَ.[٢٢٢٤]

1985. **Imām Zayn al-ʿĀbidīn,** (AS) said, 'O son of Adam, you will always be with the good…as long as fear [of Allah] is your motto and grief your cloak.'[2237]

١٩٨٥ . الإمامُ زينُ العابدينَ عليه السلام : ابنَ آدَمَ، لا تَزالُ بخَيرٍ... ما كانَ الخَوفُ لكَ شِعاراً والحُزنُ دِثاراً.[٢٢٢٥]

659. The Believer Lies between Two Fears

٦٥٩ ـ المُؤمِنُ بَينَ مَخافَتَينِ

1986. **Imām al-Ṣādiq (AS) said,** 'The believer lies between two fears, fear of a sin that he has committed in the past and does not know what action Allah has taken [with regards to it], and fear for the remainder of his life in which he does not know what destructive sins he may commit, therefore he always wakes up in the morning fearful and it is only fear that reforms him.'[2238]

١٩٨٦ . الإمامُ الصّادقُ عليه السلام :المؤمنُ بَينَ مَخافَتَينِ: ذَنبٌ قَد مَضىٰ لا يَدْري ما صَنعَ اللهُ فيهِ، وعُمرٌ قَد بَقيَ لا يَدْري ما يَكْتَسِبُ فيهِ مِن المَهالِكِ، فهُو لا يُصْبِحُ إلّا خائفاً ولا يُصْلِحُهُ إلّا الخَوفُ.[٢٢٢٦]

660. The Believer Lies between Hope and Fear

٦٦٠ ـ المُؤمِنُ بَينَ الخَوفِ وَالرَّجاءِ

1987. **The Prophet (SAWA) said,** 'If you knew the extent of Allah's mercy, you would have depended on it and performed only a few deeds, and if you knew the extent of Allah's anger, you would believe that you will not be saved.'[2239]

١٩٨٧ . رسولُ اللهِ ﷺ :لَو تَعْلَمونَ قَدْرَ رَحمَةِ اللهِ لاتَّكَلْتُم علَيها وما عَمِلْتُم إلّا قليلاً، ولَو تَعْلَمونَ قَدْرَ غَضَبِ اللهِ لَظَنَنْتُم بأنْ لا تَنْجوا.[٢٢٢٧]

1988. **Imām al-Ṣādiq (AS) said,** 'Hope in Allah with such hope that it will not embolden you to disobey Him, and fear Allah with such fear that it will not cause you to despair of His mercy.'[2240]

١٩٨٨ . الإمامُ الصّادقُ عليه السلام : ارْجُ اللهَ رَجاءً لا يُجَرّئُكَ علىٰ مَعاصيهِ، وخَفِ اللهَ خَوفاً لا يُؤيِسُكَ مِن رَحمَتِهِ.[٢٢٢٨]

1989. **Imām al-Ṣādiq (AS) said,** 'My father (AS) used to say, 'There is no believing servant except that in his heart are two lights, a light of fear and a light of hope, if they were each to be measured neither would exceed the other.'[2241]

١٩٨٩ . عنه ﷺ : كانَ أبي ﷺ يقولُ: إنّهُ لَيس مِن عَبدٍ مؤمنٍ إلّا و في قَلْبِهِ نُورانِ: نورُ خِيفَةٍ ونورُ رَجاءٍ، لَو وُزِنَ هٰذا لَم يَزِدْ علىٰ هذا، ولَـو وُزِنَ هٰذا لَم يَزِدْ علىٰ هٰذا.[٢٢٢٩]

661. The Marks of the Fearful One

٦٦١ـ عَلاماتُ الخائِفِ

1990. **Imām ʿAlī (AS) said,** 'The one who fears his Lord refrains from wrongdoing.'[2242]

١٩٩٠ . الإمامُ عليٌّ ﷺ : مَن خـافَ رَبَّـهُ كَـفَّ ظُلْمَهُ.[٢٢٣٠]

1991. **Imām al-Ṣādiq (AS) said,** 'A servant is not a believer until he is both fearful and hopeful, and he is not fearful and hopeful until he acts in accordance with what he fears and what he hopes for.'[2243]

١٩٩١ . الإمامُ الصّادقُ ﷺ : لا يكونُ العَبدُ مؤمناً حتّىٰ يكونَ خـائفاً راجِـياً، ولا يكـونُ خـائفاً راجِياً حتّىٰ يكونَ عامِلاً لِما يَخافُ ويَرْجو.[٢٢٣١]

1992. **Imām al-Ṣādiq (AS) said,** 'The fearful one is he whose dread has not left him with a tongue with which to speak.'[2244]

١٩٩٢ . عنه ﷺ : الخائفُ مَن لَم تَدَعْ لَهُ الرَّهْبةُ لِساناً يَنْطِقُ بهِ.[٢٢٣٢]

662. Explanation of Fearing Allah

٦٦٢ـ مَعنىٰ مَخافَةِ اللهِ

1993. **Imām ʿAlī (AS) said,** 'Do not fear oppression from your Lord, rather fear oppression from your own selves.'[2245]

١٩٩٣ . الإمامُ عليٌّ ﷺ : لا تَخافوا ظُلْمَ رَبِّكُـم، ولٰكنْ خافوا ظُلْمَ أنْفُسِكُم.[٢٢٣٣]

1994. **Imām ʿAlī (AS) said,** 'Do not fear anything except your sin, and do not place your hope in anyone except your Lord.'[2246]

١٩٩٤ . عنه ﷺ : لا تَخَفْ إلّا ذَنْبَكَ، لا تَرْجُ إلّا رَبَّكَ.[٢٢٣٤]

1995. **Imām ʿAlī (AS) said,** 'When you fear the Creator you will escape to Him, and when you fear a creature, you will escape from it.'[2247]

١٩٩٥ . عنه ﷺ : إذا خِفْتَ الخالِقَ فَرَرْتَ إلَيهِ، إذا خِفْتَ المَخْلوقَ فَرَرْتَ مِنهُ.[٢٢٣٥]

663. The Fruits of Fear of Allah

٦٦٣ـ ثَمَراتُ مَخافَةِ اللهِ

1996. **The Prophet (SAWA) said,** 'Whoever fears is active during the night, and whoever is active during the night reaches the [desired] station. Verily Allah's commodity is valuable, verily Allah's commodity is *Paradise*.'[2248]

١٩٩٦ . رسولُ اللهِ ﷺ : مَن خافَ أدْلَجَ، ومَـن أدْلَجَ بَلغَ المَنزِلَ. ألَا إنَّ سِلْعَةَ اللهِ غـالِيَةٌ، ألَا إنَّ سِلْعَةَ اللهِ الجَنّةُ.[٢٢٣٦]

1997. **The Prophet (SAWA) said,** 'Allah, Blessed and most High, says, 'By My Honour and Majesty, I do not combine two types of fear for My servant, neither do I combine two types of security for him. If he feels secure from Me [and My punishment] in this world, I will frighten him on the Day of Resurrection, and if he fears Me in this world, I will provide security for him on the Day of Resurrection.'[2249]

١٩٩٧ . عنه ﷺ :قالَ اللهُ تبارَكَ وتعالىٰ: وعِزَّتي وجَلالي، لا أجْمَعُ علىٰ عَبْدي خَوفَينِ، ولا أجْمَعُ لَه أمْنَينِ، فإذا أمِنَني في الدُّنيا أخَفْتُهُ يومَ القِيامَةِ، وإذا خافَني في الدُّنيا أمِنْتُهُ يَومَ القِيامَةِ.[٢٢٣٧]

1998. **Imām ʿAlī (AS) said,** 'Fear is the soul's prison [preventing it] from sinning and is its deterrent from disobedience.'[2250]

١٩٩٨ . الإمامُ عليٌّ عليه السلام: الخَوفُ سِجْنُ النّفْسِ عَنِ الذُّنوبِ، ورادِعُها عنِ المَعاصي.[٢٢٣٨]

1999. **Imām ʿAlī (AS) said,** 'He whose fear increases, his affliction reduces.'[2251]

١٩٩٩ . عنه عليه السلام: مَن كَثُرَتْ مَخافَتُهُ قَلّتْ آفَتُهُ.[٢٢٣٩]

2000. **Imām ʿAlī (AS) said,** 'The fruit of fear is security.'[2252]

٢٠٠٠ . عنه عليه السلام : ثَمرَةُ الخَوفِ الأمنُ.[٢٢٤٠]

2001. **Imām al-Ḥasan (AS) said,** 'The one who is subservient to Allah, Allah will make everything else subservient to him.'[2253]

٢٠٠١ . الإمامُ الحسنُ عليه السلام : مَن عَبدَ اللهَ عَبّدَ اللهُ لَهُ كُلَّ شَيءٍ.[٢٢٤١]

2002. **Imām al-Ṣādiq (AS) said,** 'The one who fears Allah, Allah will make everything fear him, and the one who does not fear Allah, Allah will make him fear everything else.'[2254]

٢٠٠٢ . الإمامُ الصّادقُ عليه السلام : مَن خافَ اللهَ أخافَ اللهُ مِنهُ كُلَّ شَيءٍ، ومَن لَم يَخَفِ اللهَ أخافَهُ اللهُ مِن كُلِّ شَيءٍ.[٢٢٤٢]

2003. **Imām al-Hādī (AS) said,** 'The one who is wary of Allah, Allah will make everyone wary of him.'[2255]

٢٠٠٣ . الإمامُ الهاديُّ عليه السلام : مَنِ اتّقىٰ اللهَ يُتّقىٰ.[٢٢٤٣]

664. Caution Against Fearing Other than Allah

٦٦٤ـ التَّحذيرُ مِن مَخافَةِ غَيرِ اللهِ

2004. **The Prophet (SAWA) said,** 'Allah does not empower anyone over man except one whom he fears. If man was to fear none but Allah, Allah would not allow anyone else to dominate him other than Himself. Man is not assigned to anyone except him in whom he places his hope

٢٠٠٤ . رسولُ اللهِ ﷺ : ما سَلّطَ اللهُ علىٰ ابنِ آدَمَ إلّا مَن خافَهُ ابنُ آدَمَ، ولَو أنّ ابنَ آدَمَ لَم يَخَفْ إلّا اللهَ ما سَلّطَ اللهُ علَيهِ غَيرَهُ ولا وُكِلَ ابنُ آدَمَ إلّا إلىٰ مَن رَجاهُ، ولَو أنّ ابنَ آدَمَ لَم

and if he hopes in none but Allah, he will not be assigned to anyone other than Him.'[2256]

يَرْجُ إلّا اللهَ ما وُكِلَ إلىٰ غَيرِهِ.[٢٢٤٤]

2005. **The Prophet (SAWA) said,** 'Blessed is the one whose fear of Allah preoccupies him from fearing people.'[2257]

٢٠٠٥. عنه ﷺ: طُوبىٰ لِمَن شَغَلَهُ خَوفُ اللهِ عَن خَوفِ النّاسِ.[٢٢٤٥]

2006. **The Prophet (SAWA) said,** 'Do not fear the reproach of blame on the path of Allah.'[2258]

٢٠٠٦. عنه ﷺ: لا تَخَفْ في اللهِ لَوْمَةَ لائمٍ.[٢٢٤٦]

665. How One Should React When in Fear of Something Awesome

٦٦٥ـ ما يَنبَغي عِندَ الخَوفِ مِمّا يُهابُ

2007. **Imām ʿAlī (AS) said,** 'When you fear a matter, dive straight into it for verily the intensity of your wariness of it is greater than what you actually fear.'[2259]

٢٠٠٧. الإمامُ عليٌّ عليه السلام: إذا هِبْتَ أمْراً فقَعْ فيهِ، فإنّ شِدَّةَ تَوقّيهِ أعْظَمُ مِمّا تَخافُ مِنهُ.[٢٢٤٧]

2008. **Imām ʿAlī (AS) said,** 'If you fear the difficulty of a situation, be hard and firm in front of it and it will lower [in difficulty] for you, and wittingly deceive the problems of the age and they will become easy for you.'[2260]

٢٠٠٨. عنه عليه السلام: إذا خِفْتَ صُعوبَةَ أمْرٍ فاصْعُبْ لَهُ يَذِلَّ لكَ، وخادِعِ الزَّمانَ عَن أحْداثِهِ تَهُنْ علَيكَ.[٢٢٤٨]

666. Miscellaneous

٦٦٦ـ النَّوادِرُ

2009. **Imām ʿAlī (AS) said,** 'The one who does not frighten anyone will never fear.'[2261]

٢٠٠٩. الإمامُ عليٌّ عليه السلام: مَن لَم يُخِفْ أحَداً لَم يَخَفْ أبداً.[٢٢٤٩]

2010. **Imām al-Ṣādiq (AS) said,** 'If you enter a place which you fear, then recite this verse, *"My Lord! Admit me with a worthy entrance, and bring me out with a worthy departure, and render me a favourable authority from yourself"*[2262], and if you see someone whom you fear, then recite *'Āyat al-Kursī.*'[2263] [2264]

٢٠١٠. الإمامُ الصّادقُ عليه السلام: إذا دَخَلتَ مَدْخَلاً تَخافُهُ فاقْرَأ هٰذهِ الآيةَ: ﴿رَبِّ أدْخِلْني مُدْخَلَ صِدْقٍ وأخْرِجْني مُخْرَجَ صِدْقٍ واجْعَلْ لي مِن لَدُنْكَ سُلْطاناً نَصيراً﴾[٢٢٥٠]، فإذا عايَنْتَ الّذي تَخافُهُ فاقْرَأ آيةَ الكُرْسِيِّ.[٢٢٥١]

2011. **Imām al-Riḍā (AS) said,** 'Whoever does not fear Allah with regards to small matters will not fear Allah with regards to large matters.'[2265]

٢٠١١. الإمامُ الرِّضا عليه السلام: مَن لَم يَخَفِ اللهَ في القَليلِ لَم يَخَفْهُ في الكَثيرِ.[٢٢٥٢]

136

BETRAYAL
الخِيانَةُ

667. Caution Against Betrayal
٦٦٧ ـ التَّحذيرُ مِنَ الخِيانَةِ

2012. **The Prophet (SAWA) said,** 'Do not betray the one who betrays you lest you be like him.'[2266]

٢٠١٢ . رسولُ اللهِ ﷺ : لا تَخُنْ مَن خانَكَ فتكونَ مِثلَهُ . ٢٢٥٣

2013. **The Prophet (SAWA) said,** 'The one who betrays his trust is not from us.'[2267]

٢٠١٣ . عنه ﷺ : لَيسَ مِنّا مَن خانَ بالأمانَةِ . ٢٢٥٤

2014. **Imām ʿAlī (AS) said,** 'Betrayal is the fountainhead of hypocrisy.'[2268]

٢٠١٤ . الإمامُ عليٌّ ﷺ : الخِيانَةُ رأسُ النِّفاقِ . ٢٢٥٥

2015. **Imām al-Ṣādiq (AS) said,** 'The believer is naturally disposed to all the traits except betrayal and lying.'[2269]

٢٠١٥ . الإمامُ الصّادقُ ﷺ : يُجبَلُ المؤمنُ على كُلِّ طَبيعةٍ إلّا الخِيانَةَ والكَذِبَ . ٢٢٥٦

2016. **Muʿāwiyah b. ʿAmmār narrated,** 'I asked Imām al-Ṣādiq (AS), 'If I entrust some money with a man and he denies that I entrusted him with anything, and then he [in the future] entrusts me with money, can I keep that money [to make up for the money that he took from me]? Imām al-Ṣādiq (AS) replied, 'No, that is betrayal.'[2270]

٢٠١٦ . الكافي عن مُعاويةَ بنِ عمّارٍ : قلت لأبي عبدِالله ﷺ : الرّجُلُ يكونُ لِي علَيهِ الحقُّ فيَجْحَدُنِيهِ ثُمَّ يَسْتَودِعُني مالاً ، ألِيَ أنْ آخُذَ مالي عِندهُ ؟ قال : لا ، هذهِ خِيانَةٌ . ٢٢٥٧

2017. **Abū Thumāma narrated:** 'I came to Abū Jaʿfar [al-Bāqir] (AS) and said to him, 'May I be your ransom! I am a man who wishes to go to Makkah but I have an overdue debt to a Murjiʾite,[2271] so can you please advise me?' The Imām (AS) replied, 'Pay your debt and focus on meeting your Lord without any debt on your shoulders, for verily a believer does not betray [his trust].'[2272]

٢٠١٧ . علل الشرائع عن أبي ثُمامَةَ : دخَلْتُ علىٰ أبي جعفر ﷺ وقلتُ لَه : جُعِلتُ فِداكَ ، إنّي رجُلٌ أُريدُ أنْ اُلازِمَ مكّةَ وعلَيَّ دَينٌ للمُرجِئةِ ، فمَا تقولُ ؟ قالَ : ارجِعْ إلىٰ مُؤدّىٰ دَينِكَ وانظُرْ أنْ تَلقَى اللهَ تعالىٰ ولَيسَ علَيكَ دَينٌ ، فإنّ المؤمنَ لا يَخونُ . ٢٢٥٨

(انظر) عنوان ٣١ «الأمانة».

(See also: THE TRUST: section 31)

668. Explanation of Betrayal and the Betrayer

٦٦٨ـ تَفسيرُ الخِيانَةِ وَالخائِنِ

2018. **The Prophet (SAWA) said,** 'Disclosing the secret of your brother is betrayal, so keep away from that.'[2273]

٢٠١٨. رسولُ اللهِ ﷺ: إفْشاءُ سِرِّ أخيكَ خِيانَةٌ، فاجتَنِبْ ذلكَ.٢٢٥٩

2019. **The Prophet (SAWA) said,** 'As for the signs of the betrayer, there are four: disobedience to the All-Beneficent, disturbance to neighbours, loathing his associates, and being close to tyranny and oppression.'[2274]

٢٠١٩. عنه ﷺ: أمّا عَلامَةُ الخائِنِ فأربَعةٌ: عِصْيانُ الرّحمانِ، وأذَى الجِيرانِ، وبُغْضُ الأقْرانِ، والقُرْبُ إلى الطُّغْيانِ.٢٢٦٠

2020. **Imām ʿAlī (AS) said,** 'The betrayer is the one who busies himself with [the affairs of] others and his today is worse than his yesterday.'[2275]

٢٠٢٠. الإمامُ عليٌّ ؑ: الخائنُ مَن شَغَلَ نفسَهُ بغَيرِ نَفْسِهِ، وكانَ يَومُهُ شَرّاً مِن أمْسِهِ.٢٢٦١

2021. **Imām al-Ṣādiq (AS) said,** 'Whoever from among our companions seeks assistance from one of his brothers, who does not exercise his full efforts [in trying to help him], then he has betrayed Allah and His messenger and the believers.'[2276]

٢٠٢١. الإمامُ الصّادقُ ؑ: أيُّما رجُلٍ مِن أصْحابِنا اسْتَعانَ بهِ رجُلٌ من إخْوانِهِ في حاجَةٍ، فلَم يُبالِغْ فيها بكُلِّ جُهْدِه، فقد خانَ اللهَ ورسولَهُ والمؤمنينَ.٢٢٦٢

2022. **Imām al-Jawād (AS) said,** 'It is sufficient for someone to be classified as a betrayer if he is the trustee of a disloyal person.'[2277]

٢٠٢٢. الإمامُ الجوادُ ؑ: كَفَى بالمَرءِ خِيانَةً أنْ يكونَ أميناً للخَوَنَةِ.٢٢٦٣

669. The Peak of Betrayal

٦٦٩ـ غايَةُ الخِيانَةِ

2023. **Imām ʿAlī (AS) said,** 'The peak of betrayal is disloyalty to a beloved friend and the breaking of vows.'[2278]

٢٠٢٣. الإمامُ عليٌّ ؑ: غايَةُ الخِيانَةِ خِيانَةُ الخِلِّ الوَدودِ، ونَقْضُ العُهودِ.٢٢٦٤

2024. **Imām ʿAlī (AS) said,** 'One of the worst forms of betrayal is being disloyal with things entrusted in one's possession.'[2279]

٢٠٢٤. عنه ؑ: مِن أفْحَشِ الخِيانَةِ خِيانَةُ الوَدائعِ.٢٢٦٥

2025. **Imām ʿAlī (AS) said,** 'Verily the worst betrayal is the betrayal of the [religious] comm-

٢٠٢٥. عنه ؑ: إنّ أعْظَمَ الخِيانَةِ خيانَةُ الاُمّةِ

unity, and the most repulsive deceit is that of the leaders.'[2280]

الأمَنةِ)، وأفْظَعَ الغِشِّ غِشُّ الأئمّةِ.[٢٢٦٦]

137

GOOD

الخَيرُ

670. The Virtue of Good

٦٧٠ ـ فَضلُ الخَيرِ

2026. **The Prophet (SAWA) said,** 'The one who sows good is bound to reap good.'[2281]

٢٠٢٦ . رسولُ اللهِ ﷺ : مَنْ يَزرَعْ خَيراً يُوشِكْ أنْ يَحْصِدَ خَيراً.[٢٢٦٧]

2027. **Imām ʿAlī (AS) said,** 'A good action is an ever-remaining store and a pure yield.'[2282]

٢٠٢٧ . الإمامُ عليٌّ عليه السلام : فِعلُ الخَيرِ ذَخيرَةٌ باقِيَةٌ، وثَمَرةٌ زاكِيَةٌ.[٢٢٦٨]

2028. **Imām ʿAlī (AS) said,** 'The one who plants the tree of goodness will reap the sweetest fruit.'[2283]

٢٠٢٨ . عنه عليه السلام : غارِسُ شَجَرةِ الخَيرِ يَجْتَنيها أحْلى ثَمَرةٍ.[٢٢٦٩]

2029. **Imām ʿAlī (AS) said,** 'The one who does good will be the first to reap its result.'[2284]

٢٠٢٩ . عنه عليه السلام : مَن فَعلَ الخَيرَ فبِنَفْسِه بَدَأ.[٢٢٧٠]

2030. **Imām ʿAlī (AS) said,** 'A good action is easier [to do] than a bad one.'[2285]

٢٠٣٠ . عنه عليه السلام : الخَيرُ أسهَلُ مِن فِعلِ الشَّرِّ.[٢٢٧١]

671. Actions Encompassed by Goodness

٦٧١ ـ جَوامِعُ الخَيرِ

2031. **The Prophet (SAWA) said,** 'All of goodness lies in the awe of Allah.'[2286]

٢٠٣١ . رسولُ اللهِ ﷺ : جِماعُ الخَيرِ خَشيَةُ اللهِ.[٢٢٧٢]

2032. **Imām ʿAlī (AS) said,** 'Three things sum up all of goodness: bestowing of favours, maintaining *covenants* and pacts, and strengthening blood-kinship.'[2287]

٢٠٣٢ . الإمامُ عليٌّ عليه السلام : ثَلاثٌ هُنَّ جِماعُ الخَيرِ: إسْداءُ النِّعَمِ، ورِعايَةُ الذِّمَمِ، وصِلَةُ الرَّحِمِ.[٢٢٧٣]

2033. **Imām ʿAlī (AS) said,** 'All of goodness is contained in those actions which remain, and in contempt for all that is transient.'[2288]

٢٠٣٣ . عنه عليه السلام : جِماعُ الخَيرِ في العَملِ بما يَبقىٰ، والاسْتِهانَةِ بما يَفنىٰ.[٢٢٧٤]

2034. **Imām ʿAlī (AS) said,** 'All of goodness is in friendship for the sake of Allah, enmity for the sake of Allah, love for the sake of Allah and hate for the sake of Allah.'[2289]

٢٠٣٤. عنه ﷺ : جِماعُ الخَيرِ في المُوالاةِ في اللهِ، والمُعاداةِ في اللهِ، والمَحبَّةِ في اللهِ، والبُغْضِ في اللهِ.٢٢٧٥

2035. **Imām Zayn al-ʿĀbidīn (AS) said,** 'I saw goodness in its entirety was summed up in cutting off one's greed for other people's possessions.'[2290]

٢٠٣٥. الإمامُ زينُ العابدينَ ﷺ : رأيتُ الخَيرَ كُلَّهُ قدِ اجْتَمَعَ في قَطْعِ الطَّمَعِ عَمّا في أيْدي النّاسِ.٢٢٧٦

2036. **Imām Zayn al-ʿĀbidīn (AS) said,** 'Goodness in its entirety is man's guarding over himself.'[2291]

٢٠٣٦. عنه ﷺ : الخَيرُ كُلُّهُ صِيانَةُ الإنْسانِ نَفْسَهُ.٢٢٧٧

672. How the Good of this World and the Hereafter is Obtained

٦٧٢ ـ ما يُنالُ بِهِ خَيرُ الدُّنيا وَالآخِرَةِ

2037. **The Prophet (SAWA) said,** 'There are four things which when given to someone, they have indeed been given the good of this world and the Hereafter: a persevering body, a remembering tongue, a thankful heart and a righteous wife.'[2292]

٢٠٣٧. رسولُ اللهِ ﷺ : أربَعٌ مَن أُعْطِيَهُنَّ فَقَد أُعْطِيَ خَيرَ الدُّنيا والآخِرَةِ: بَدناً صابِراً، ولِساناً ذاكِراً، وقَلْباً شاكِراً، وزَوْجَةً صالِحَةً.٢٢٧٨

2038. **Imām ʿAlī (AS) said,** 'The good of this world and the Hereafter has been brought together in the concealing of secrets and the befriending of good people.'[2293]

٢٠٣٨. الإمامُ عليٌّ ﷺ : جُمِعَ خَيرُ الدُّنيا والآخِرَةِ في كِتْمانِ السِّرِّ ومُصادَقَةِ الأخْيارِ.٢٢٧٩

2039. **Imām ʿAlī (AS) said,** 'There are three things which if one possesses, they have been endowed with the good of this world and the Hereafter. They are: contentment with [Allah's] decree, patience in the face of tribulation, and thankfulness in times of ease.'[2294]

٢٠٣٩. عنه ﷺ : ثلاثٌ مَن كُنَّ فيهِ فَقَد رُزِقَ خَيرَ الدُّنيا والآخِرَةِ، هُنَّ: الرِّضا بالقَضاءِ، والصَّبرُ على البَلاءِ، والشُّكْرُ في الرَّخاءِ.٢٢٨٠

2040. **Imām ʿAlī (AS) said,** 'Allah – glory be to Him - does not give His servant any good of this world or the Hereafter except as a result of his good nature and good intention.'[2295]

٢٠٤٠. عنه ﷺ : ما أعطى اللهُ سُبحانَهُ العَبدَ شيئاً مِن خَيرِ الدُّنيا والآخِرَةِ إلّا بحُسْنِ خُلقِهِ وحُسنِ نِيَّتِهِ.٢٢٨١

2041. **Imām ʿAlī (AS) said,** 'There are four things which when given to someone, they have indeed

٢٠٤١. عنه ﷺ : أربَعٌ مَن أُعْطِيَهُنَّ فقد أُعْطِيَ

been given the good of this world and the Hereafter: truthful speech, fulfilment of trust, restraint in [filling] one's stomach [from the forbidden], and a good nature.'[2296]

خَيرَ الدُّنيا والآخِرَة: صِدقُ حَديثٍ، وأداءُ أمانَةٍ، وعِفَّةُ بَطْنٍ، وحُسنُ خُلقٍ.٢٢٨٢

673. Explanation of Good

٦٧٣ـ تفسيرُ الخَيرِ

2042. **Imām ʿAlī (AS) said,** 'Goodness does not lie in the increase of your wealth and of your progeny, rather goodness lies in the increase of your knowledge, and the heightening of your clemency, and in your vying with other people in the worship of Allah. If you do good then you should praise Allah, but if you commit evil then seek forgiveness from Allah.'[2297]

٢٠٤٢. الإمامُ عليٌّ ؈: لَيسَ الخَيرُ أنْ يَكثُرَ مالُكَ ووَلدُكَ، ولكنَّ الخَيرَ أنْ يَكثُرَ عِلمُكَ، وأنْ يَعظُمَ حِلمُكَ، وأن تُباهِيَ النّاسَ بِعِبادَةِ رَبِّكَ، فإنْ أحسَنتَ حَمِدتَ اللهَ، وإن أسَأتَ استَغفَرتَ اللهَ.٢٢٨٣

2043. **Imām al-Ḥasan (AS) said,** 'Absolute goodness that is untainted with evil is being thankful for bounties and having patience in calamity.'[2298]

٢٠٤٣. الإمامُ الحسنُ ؈: الخَيرُ الّذي لا شَرَّ فيهِ: الشُّكرُ مَعَ النِّعمَةِ، والصَّبرُ علَى النّازِلَةِ.٢٢٨٤

674. When Allah Wants Good for a Servant

٦٧٤ـ إذا أرادَ اللهُ بِعَبدٍ خَيراً

2044. **The Prophet (SAWA) said,** 'When Allah wants good for a servant, He makes him proficient in the knowledge of religion, induces him to abstain from the world and gives him insight into his own faults.'[2299]

٢٠٤٤. رسولُ اللهِ ﷺ: إذا أرادَ اللهُ عزّوجلّ بِعَبدٍ خَيراً فَقَّهَهُ في الدِّينِ، وزَهَّدَهُ في الدُّنيا، وبَصَّرَهُ بِعُيوبِ نَفْسِهِ.٢٢٨٥

2045. **The Prophet (SAWA) said,** 'When Allah wants good for a servant, He censures him in his dreams.'[2300]

٢٠٤٥. عنه ﷺ: إذا أرادَ اللهُ بِعَبدٍ خَيراً عاتَبَهُ في مَنامِهِ.٢٢٨٦

2046. **The Prophet (SAWA) said,** 'When Allah wants good for a servant, He sweetens his affairs', at which he was asked, 'How does He sweeten affairs?' The Prophet (SAWA) replied, 'He opens the way for him to do righteous deeds before his death and causes him to die in the state of doing good.'[2301]

٢٠٤٦. كنز العمّال عن أبي عنبة: ـ قال رسول الله ﷺ ـ: إذا أرادَ اللهُ بِعَبدٍ خَيراً عَسَلَهُ. قيلَ: وما عَسَلُهُ؟ قالَ: يَفتَحُ لَهُ عَمَلاً صالِحاً قَبلَ مَوتِهِ ثُمَّ يَقبِضُهُ علَيهِ.٢٢٨٧

2047. **Imām ʿAlī (AS) said,** 'When Allah wants good for a servant, He inspires him with contentment and gives him a righteous spouse.'[2302]

٢٠٤٧ . الإمامُ عليٌّ ﷺ : إذا أرادَ اللهُ بعَبدٍ خَـيراً أَلهَمَهُ القَناعَةَ ، وأصْلَحَ لَه زَوجَهُ .٢٢٨٨

2048. **Imām al-Ṣādiq (AS) said,** 'Verily when Allah wants good for a servant, He marks his heart with a white spot so that his heart is occupied with seeking the truth, then He is faster at fulfilling your needs than a bird flying to its nest.'[2303]

٢٠٤٨ . الإمامُ الصّادقُ ﷺ : إنَّ اللهَ عزّوجلّ إذا أرادَ بعَبدٍ خَيراً نَكَتَ في قَلبِهِ نُكْتَةً بَيْضاءَ ، فَجالَ القَلبُ بطَلَبِ الحقِّ ، ثُمَّ هُو إلىٰ أمْرِكُم أسْرَعُ مِن الطَّيرِ إلىٰ وَكْرِهِ .٢٢٨٩

675. When Allah Wants Good for a Community

٦٧٥ ـ إذا أرادَ اللهُ بِقَومٍ خَيراً

2049. **The Prophet (SAWA) said,** 'When Allah wants good for a community, He increases their scholars and decreases their ignorant ones, so when the scholar speaks, he finds supporters, but when the ignorant one speaks, he is defeated.'[2304]

٢٠٤٩ . رسولُ اللهِ ﷺ : إذا أرادَ اللهُ بـقَومٍ خَـيراً أكثَرَ فُقَهاءَهُم وأقَلَّ جُهّالَهُم ، فإذا تكَـلّمَ الفـقيهُ وَجدَ أعْوانـاً ، وإذا تَكلَّمَ الجـاهِلُ قُهِـرَ .٢٢٩٠

2050. **The Prophet (SAWA) said,** 'Verily when Allah – Blessed and most High – wants a community to remain and thrive, He endows them with moderation and chastity.'[2305]

٢٠٥٠ . عنه ﷺ : إنَّ اللهَ تباركَ وتعالىٰ إذا أرادَ بقَومٍ بَقاءً أو نَماءً رزَقَهُمُ القَصْدَ والعَفافَ .٢٢٩١

2051. **The Prophet (SAWA) said,** 'When Allah wants good for a household, He makes them proficient in the knowledge of religion, He causes the younger ones from among them to revere the elders, He bestows them with moderation in their livelihood and with economy in their spending, He gives them insight into their faults, thus causing them to repent, and when He wants other than that [i.e. good for them] then He leaves them unattended.'[2306]

٢٠٥١ . عنه ﷺ : إذا أرادَ اللهُ بأهلِ بَـيْتٍ خَـيراً فَقّهَهُم فـي الدِّيـنِ ، ووقَّـرَ صَـغيرُهُم كـبيرَهُم ، ورزَقَهُمُ الرِّفـقَ فـي مَـعيشَتِهِم ، والقَـصْدَ فـي نَفَقاتِهِم ، وبَصّرَهُم عُيوبَهُم فـيَتُوبوا مِـنها ، وإذا أرادَ بِهِم غيرَ ذلكَ تَرَكَهُم هَمَلاً .٢٢٩٢

676. Enjoinment of Hastening towards Good Deeds

٦٧٦ ـ الحَثُّ عَلَى المُبادَرَةِ إلَى الخَيراتِ

2052. **The Prophet (SAWA) said,** 'He for whom a door of goodness is opened must seize the

٢٠٥٢ . رسولُ اللهِ ﷺ : مَن فُتِحَ لَهُ بـابُ خَـيرٍ

opportunity for verily he does not know when it will close.'[2307]

قَلْيَنْتَهِزْهُ، فإنّهُ لا يَدْري مَتىٰ يُغْلَقُ عَنهُ.٢٢٩٣

2053. **The Prophet (SAWA) said,** 'Verily Allah loves those good actions which are hastened towards.'[2308]

٢٠٥٣. عنه ﷺ: إنَّ اللهَ يُحِبُّ مِنَ الخَيرِ ما يُعجَّلُ.٢٢٩٤

2054. **Imām ʿAlī (AS) said,** 'Rush to undertake good actions before you are preoccupied with other things.'[2309]

٢٠٥٤. الإمامُ عليٌّ ؑ: بادِروا بعَمَلِ الخَيرِ قَبلَ أنْ تُشْغَلوا عَنه بغَيرِهِ.٢٢٩٥

2055. **Imām al-Ṣādiq (AS) said,** 'My father used to say, 'When you intend to do a good thing, then hasten to undertake it for you do not know what will happen.'[2310]

٢٠٥٥. الإمامُ الصّادقُ ؑ: كانَ أبي يَقولُ: إذا هَمَمْتَ بخَيرٍ فبادِرْ، فإنّكَ لا تَدْري ما يَحْدُثُ.٢٢٩٦

(See also: HASTE: section 1228)

(أنظر العجلة: باب ١٢٢٨).

677. The Best of Matters

٦٧٧ـ خَيرُ الأُمورِ

2056. **The Prophet (SAWA) said,** 'The best of matters are the religious obligations and the worst of them are the innovations.'[2311]

٢٠٥٦. رسولُ اللهِ ﷺ: خَيرُ الأُمورِ عَزائمُها، وشَرُّ الأُمورِ مُحْدَثاتُها.٢٢٩٧

2057. **The Prophet (SAWA) said,** 'The best of matters are those with the best outcomes.'[2312]

٢٠٥٧. عنه ﷺ: خَيرُ الأُمورِ خَيرُها عاقِبَةً.٢٢٩٨

2058. **Imām ʿAlī (AS) said,** 'The best of matters are those that are easy to start, pleasant to finish and whose outcome is praiseworthy.'[2313]

٢٠٥٨. الإمامُ عليٌّ ؑ: خَيرُ الأُمورِ ما سَهُلَتْ مَبادِئُهُ، وحَسُنَتْ خَواتِمُهُ، وحُمِدَتْ عَواقِبُهُ.٢٢٩٩

2059. **Imām al-Kāẓim (AS) said,** 'The best matters are those of the middle way.'[2314]

٢٠٥٩. الإمامُ الكاظمُ ؑ: خَيرُ الأُمورِ أوْسَطُها.٢٣٠٠

678. Prohibition of Contempt for Little Good

٦٧٨ـ النَّهيُ عَن تَحقيرِ القَليلِ مِنَ الخَيرِ

2060. **Imām ʿAlī (AS) said,** 'Do good and do not underestimate it at all, for verily a little good is actually a lot and a small amount of it is much.'[2315]

٢٠٦٠. الإمامُ عليٌّ ؑ: افْعَلوا الخَيرَ ولا تَحْقِروا مِنهُ شيئاً؛ فإنَّ صَغيرَهُ كَبيرٌ، وقَليلَهُ كَثيرٌ.٢٣٠١

2061. **Imām al-Ṣādiq (AS) said,** 'Do not belittle anything that is good, for verily you will see it tomorrow and it will make you happy.'[2316]

٢٠٦١. الإمامُ الصّادقُ ﷺ: لا تُصغِّرْ شيئاً مِنَ الخَيرِ، فإنّكَ تَراهُ غداً حَيثُ يَسُرُّكَ.٢٣٠٢

679. The Criteria for Good and Evil

٦٧٩- ميزانُ الخَيرِ وَ الشَّرِّ

2062. **Imām 'Alī (AS) said,** 'Verily good and evil can only be known through people, so if you want to know good then do good and you will know its people, and if you want to know evil then commit evil and you will know its people.'[2317]

٢٠٦٢. الإمامُ عليٌّ ﷺ: إنّ الخَيرَ والشَّرَّ لا يُعرَفانِ إلّا بالنّاسِ، فإذا أرَدتَ أنْ تَعرِفَ الخَيرَ فاعْمَلِ الخَيرَ تَعرِفْ أهلَهُ، وإذا أرَدتَ أنْ تَعرِفَ الشَّرَّ فاعْمَلِ الشَّرَّ تَعرِفْ أهلَهُ.٢٣٠٣

(See also: THE TRUTH: section 553)

(اُنظر) الحق: باب ٥٥٣.

680. The Characteristics of Good People

٦٨٠- صِفاتُ أهلِ الخَيرِ

2063. It is narrated in the tradition recounting the Prophet's Ascension to the Heavens (*al-mi'rāj*) that Allah addresses the Prophet (SAWA) saying, 'O Aḥmad, Verily the good people and the people worthy of a good Hereafter have gentle countenances and much modesty, they possess little foolishness, they are of much benefit and they are seldom deceptive. People are at ease when with them whereas their souls are exhausted on account of them. Their words are balanced, they take account of their souls and exhaust them [through making them perform good]. Their eyes sleep but their hearts do not, their eyes weep and their hearts are remembering. When people are recorded as being neglectful, they are recorded amongst the remembering ones... Nothing preoccupies them from Allah for a split second. They do not desire much food, neither wish to speak much nor have many clothes. According to them, people are dead and Allah is the Living One, the All-Sustainer.'[2318]

٢٠٦٣. بحار الأنوار: في حديثِ المِعراجِ: يا أحمدُ، إنّ أهلَ الخَيرِ وأهلَ الآخِرَةِ رَقيقَةٌ وُجوهُهُم، كثيرٌ حَياؤهُم، قليلٌ حُمْقُهُم، كثيرٌ نَفْعُهُم، قليلٌ مَكْرُهُم، النّاسُ مِنهُم في راحَةٍ، وأنفسُهُم مِنهُم في تَعَبٍ، كلامُهُم مَوزونٌ، مُحاسِبينَ لأنفُسِهِم مُتعِبينَ لَها، تَنامُ أعيُنُهُم ولا تَنامُ قلوبُهُم، أعيُنُهُم باكِيَةٌ، وقُلوبُهُم ذاكِرَةٌ. إذا كُتِبَ النّاسُ مِن الغافلينَ كُتِبوا مِن الذّاكِرينَ... لا يَشْغَلُهُم عَنِ اللهِ شَيءٌ طَرفَةَ عَينٍ، ولا يُريدونَ كَثرَةَ الطَّعامِ، ولا كَثرةَ الكلامِ، ولا كَثرةَ اللِّباسِ. النّاسُ عِندَهُم مَوتى، واللهُ عِندَهُم حيٌّ قَيّومٌ.٢٣٠٤

681. What is Better Than Goodness

٦٨١- ما هُوَ أفضَلُ مِنَ الخَيرِ

2064. **Imām 'Alī (AS) said,** 'There is nothing better than goodness except its own reward.'[2319]

٢٠٦٤. الإمامُ عليٌّ ﷺ: لَيسَ بخَيرٍ مِنَ الخَيرِ إلّا ثَوابُهُ.٢٣٠٥

2065. **Imām al-Ṣādiq (AS) said,** 'Better than truthfulness is the one who practices it, and better than good is its doer.'[2320]

٢٠٦٥ . الإمامُ الصّادقُ ؑ : أحْسَنُ مِن الصِّدقِ قائلُهُ، وخَيرٌ مِن الخَيرِ فاعِلُهُ.[٢٣٠٦]

2066. **Imām al-Hādī (AS) said,** 'Better than good is its doer, more beautiful than beautiful words is the one who says them and weightier than knowledge is the one who carries it.'[2321]

٢٠٦٦ . الإمامُ الهاديُّ ؑ : خَيرٌ مِن الخَيرِ فاعِلُهُ، وأجمَلُ مِن الجَميلِ قائلُهُ، وأرجَحُ مِن العِلمِ حامِلُهُ.[٢٣٠٧]

(See also: EVIL: section 1017)

(أُنظر) الشرّ: باب ١٠١٧.

682. The Worth of One Who Guides Towards Good

٦٨٢ ـ قيمَةُ الدَّلالةِ عَلَى الخَيرِ

2067. **The Prophet (SAWA) said,** 'The one who guides towards good is just as its doer.'[2322]

٢٠٦٧ . رسولُ اللهِ ﷺ : الدّالُّ على الخَيرِ كفاعِلِهِ.[٢٣٠٨]

2068. **The Prophet (SAWA) said,** 'He who guides towards good has the same reward as the one who does it.'[2323]

٢٠٦٨ . عنه ﷺ : مَن دَلَّ علىٰ خَيرٍ فلَهُ مِثْلُ أجْرِ فاعِلِهِ.[٢٣٠٩]

138

SEEKING A GOOD OUTCOME [FROM ALLAH]

الإِستِخارَة

683. The Virtue of Seeking a Good Outcome [From Allah]

٦٨٣ ـ فَضلُ الاستِخارَةِ

2069. **The Prophet (SAWA) said,** 'When you set out to do something then seek a good outcome for it from your Lord seven times, then look to see what comes to your heart first, for verily there is good in that, meaning, act accordingly.'[2324]

٢٠٦٩ . رسولُ اللهِ ﷺ : إذا هَمَمْتَ بأمْرٍ فاسْتَخِرْ ربَّكَ فيهِ سَبْعَ مرّاتٍ، ثُمّ انظُرْ إلى الّذي يَسْبِقُ إلىٰ قَلبِكَ فإنَّ الخِيرَةَ فيهِ، يَعني: افْعَلْ ذلكَ.[٢٣١٠]

2070. **Imām 'Alī (AS) said,** 'The one who seeks a good outcome [from Allah] does not regret.'[2325]

٢٠٧٠ . الإمامُ عليٌّ ؑ : ما نَدِمَ مَنِ اسْتَخارَ.[٢٣١١]

2071. **Imām 'Alī (AS) said,** 'Seek a good outcome [from Allah] and do not choose [your own

٢٠٧١ . عنه ؑ : استَخِرْ ولا تَتَخَيّرْ فكَم مَن

preference] for verily how many have chosen something within which lay their destruction.'[2326]

تَخَيَّرَ أمراً كانَ هَلاكُهُ فيهِ.[٢٣١٢]

2072. **Imām al-Ṣādiq (AS) said,** 'No sooner does a believing servant seek goodness from Allah than the choice is made for him, even if what he detests occurs [but it will be what is good].'[2327]

٢٠٧٢. الإمامُ الصّادقُ عليه السلام: ما اسْتَخارَ اللهَ عزّوجلّ عَبدٌ مؤمنٌ إلّا خارَ لَهُ وإنْ وَقَعَ ما يَكرَهُ.[٢٣١٣]

2073. **Imām al-Ṣādiq (AS) said** to Ibn Abī Ya'fūr about seeking goodness, 'Magnify Allah, glorify Him and praise Him and send blessings on the Prophet (SAWA) and his family (AS), then say, "O Allah I ask you by the fact that you are the Knower of the unseen and the seen, the All-Beneficent, the All-Merciful, indeed you are the Knower of all the unseen things, I seek goodness from Allah by His Mercy".'[2328]

٢٠٧٣. عنه عليه السلام ـ لابنِ أبي يَعْفورٍ في الاسْتِخارَةِ ـ: تُعَظِّمُ اللهَ وتُمَجِّدُهُ وتَحْمَدُهُ وتُصلّي علىٰ النَّبيِّ وآلِهِ، ثُمّ تقولُ: اللّهُمَّ إنّي أسألُكَ بأنَّكَ عالِمُ الغَيبِ والشَّهادَةِ الرّحمٰنُ الرّحيمُ، وأنتَ عَلّامُ الغُيوبِ، أسْتَخيرُ اللهَ برَحْمتِهِ.[٢٣١٤]

2074. A person asked Imām al-Ṣādiq (AS), 'I seek goodness from Allah when I want to do something but I am unable to make up my mind', so the Imām (AS) said to him, 'Open the Qur'an and look at the first verse that you see and act by it, Allah willing.'[2329]

٢٠٧٤. عنه عليه السلام ـ لِمَن قالَ لَهُ: أُريدُ الشَّيءَ وأستخيرُ اللهَ فيهِ فلا يُوَفَّقُ فيهِ الرَّأيُ ـ: افْتَحِ المُصْحَفَ، فانْظُرْ إلىٰ أوّلِ ما تَرىٰ فَخُذْ بهِ، إنْ شاءَ اللهُ.[٢٣١٥]

2075. **Imām al-Ṣādiq (AS) said,** 'Pray two units of prayer and seek goodness from Allah, and by Allah, no sooner does a Muslim seek goodness from Allah than He surely chooses [the good] for him.'[2330]

٢٠٧٥. عنه عليه السلام: صَلِّ رَكْعَتَينِ واسْتَخِرِ اللهَ. فواللهِ، ما اسْتَخارَ اللهَ مسلمٌ إلّا خارَ لَهُ البَتّةَ.[٢٣١٦]

139

AMICABLENESS

المُداراةُ

684. The Virtue of Amicableness

٦٨٤ ـ فَضلُ المُداراةِ

2076. **The Prophet (SAWA) said,** 'Allah has commanded me to treat people amicably just as He has commanded me to fulfil the religious obligations.'[2331]

٢٠٧٦. رسولُ اللهِ صلى الله عليه وآله: أمَرَني رَبّي بِمُداراةِ النّاسِ كَما أمَرَني بِأداءِ الفَرائضِ.[٢٣١٧]

2077. **The Prophet (SAWA) said,** 'Being amicable towards people is half of faith, and being gentle and kind to them is half of life.'[2332]

٢٠٧٧. عنه ﷺ: مُداراةُ النّاسِ نِصفُ الإيمانِ، والرِّفقُ بِهِم نِصفُ العَيشِ.[٢٣١٨]

2078. **The Prophet (SAWA) said,** 'There are three things that if are not present with someone then their actions are incomplete: piety preventing one from disobeying Allah, a character through which one is amicable towards people, and clemency with which to deal with the rashness of the ignorant.'[2333]

٢٠٧٨. عنه ﷺ: ثَلاثٌ مَن لَم يَكُن فِيهِ لَم يَتِمَّ لَهُ عَمَلٌ: وَرَعٌ يَحجُزُهُ عَن مَعاصِي اللهِ، وخُلُقٌ يُداري بِهِ النّاسَ، وحِلْمٌ يَرُدُّ بِهِ جَهلَ الجاهِلِ.[٢٣١٩]

2079. **Imām ʿAlī (AS) said,** 'The fruit of [strong] intellect is amicableness with people.'[2334]

٢٠٧٩. الإمامُ عليٌّ عليه السلام: ثَمَرَةُ العَقلِ مُداراةُ النّاسِ.[٢٣٢٠]

2080. **Imām ʿAlī (AS) said,** 'The security of this world and the Hereafter lies in amicableness with people.'[2335]

٢٠٨٠. عنه عليه السلام: سَلامَةُ الدِّينِ وَالدُّنيا في مُداراةِ النّاسِ.[٢٣٢١]

2081. **Imām ʿAlī (AS) said,** 'Whoever is amicable towards his enemies is secure from war.'[2336]

٢٠٨١. عنه عليه السلام: مَن دَارىٰ أضدادَهُ أمِنَ المَحارِبَ.[٢٣٢٢]

2082. **Imām ʿAlī (AS) said,** 'Whoever is not improved by the goodness of amicableness will be improved by the evil consequences [of the absence of it].'[2337]

٢٠٨٢. عنه عليه السلام: مَن لَم يُصلِحْهُ حُسنُ المُداراةِ أصلَحَهُ سُوءُ المُكافاةِ.[٢٣٢٣]

2083. **Imām ʿAlī (AS)** when reprimanding his companions said, 'How long should I continue to be amicable with you the way one is amicable with camels with a wounded hump, or to worn clothes which when stitched on one side give way on the other… and verily I know what can improve you and how to straighten your crookedness, but I shall not improve your condition by marring myself.'[2338]

٢٠٨٣. عنه عليه السلام ـ مِن كَلامٍ لَهُ يُوَبِّخُ فِيهِ أصحابَهُ ـ: كَم أُداريكُم كَما تُدارَى البِكارُ العَمِدَةُ، وَالثِّيابُ المُتَداعِيَةُ، كُلَّما حِيصَت مِن جانِبٍ تَهَتَّكَتْ مِن آخَرَ... وإنّي لَعالِمٌ بِما يُصلِحُكُم ويُقِيمُ أوَدَكُم، ولٰكِنّي لا أرى إصلاحَكُم بِإفسادِ نَفْسي.[٢٣٢٤]

140

SUPPLICATION

الدُّعاءُ

685. The Virtue of Supplication

٦٨٥ ـ فَضلُ الدُّعاءِ

"Say, 'What store my Lord would set by you were it not for your supplication? But you impugned [me and my advice] so that will continue to haunt you.'"[2339]

﴿قُل ما يَعْبَأُ بِكُم رَبِّي لَولا دُعاؤُكُم فَقَد كَذَّبتُم فَسَوفَ يَكونُ لِزاماً﴾.[٢٣٢٥]

"Your Lord has said, 'Call Me, and I will hear you[r supplications]!' Indeed those who are disdainful of My worship will enter hell in utter humility."[2340]

﴿وَقالَ رَبُّكُمُ ادعُونِي أَستَجِبْ لَكُمْ إنَّ الَّذِينَ يَسْتَكبِرُونَ عَنْ عِبادَتِي سَيَدْخُلُونَ جَهَنَّمَ داخِرِينَ﴾.[٢٣٢٦]

2084. **The Prophet (SAWA) said,** 'Supplication is the essence of worship and no one who supplicates will be destroyed.'[2341]

٢٠٨٤ . رسولُ اللهِ ﷺ : الدُّعاءُ مُخُّ العِبادَةِ، ولا يَهلِكُ مَعَ الدُّعاءِ أحَدٌ.[٢٣٢٧]

2085. **The Prophet (SAWA) said,** 'Supplication is the weapon of the believer, the pillar of religion, and the light of the heavens and the earth.'[2342]

٢٠٨٥ . عنه ﷺ : الدُّعاءُ سِلاحُ المُؤمِنِ وَعَمودُ الدّينِ وَنورُ السَّماواتِ والأرضِ.[٢٣٢٨]

2086. **The Prophet (SAWA) said,** 'Verily the weakest person is the one who is incapable of supplicating.'[2343]

٢٠٨٦ . عنه ﷺ : إنَّ أعجَزَ النّاسِ مَن عَجَزَ عَنِ الدُّعاءِ.[٢٣٢٩]

2087. **The Prophet (SAWA) said,** 'The best worship is supplication, for when Allah gives permission [and divine succour] for His servant to supplicate, He opens for him the door of mercy. Surely the one who supplicates will never be destroyed.'[2344]

٢٠٨٧ . عنه ﷺ : أفضَلُ العِبادَةِ الدُّعاءُ، فإذا أذِنَ اللهُ لِلعَبدِ في الدُّعاءِ فَتَحَ لَهُ بابَ الرَّحمَةِ، إنّهُ لَن يَهلِكَ مَعَ الدُّعاءِ أحَدٌ.[٢٣٣٠]

2088. **Imām ʿAlī (AS) said** in his counsel to his son Ḥasan (AS), 'Know that the one in whose hands are the treasures of the kingdom of this world and the Hereafter has allowed you to supplicate, He has guaranteed to answer you, He has commanded you to ask Him so He can give you, and He is *the All-Merciful,* the Kind. He has

٢٠٨٨ . الإمامُ عليٌّ ؑ ـ في وَصِيَّتِهِ لِابنِهِ الحَسَنِ ؑ ـ: اِعلَمْ أنَّ الَّذي بِيَدِهِ خَزائنُ مَلَكُوتِ الدُّنيا وَالآخِرَةِ قَد أذِنَ لِدُعائكَ، وتَكَفَّلَ لِإجابَتِكَ، وَأمَرَكَ أن تَسألَهُ لِيُعطِيَكَ، وَهُوَ رَحيمٌ

not placed any barrier between Him and you, He has not committed you to whoever intercedes for you... then He has placed in your hands the keys to His treasures by allowing you to ask from Him, so whenever you wish, open the doors of His treasures by supplicating to Him.'[2345]

كَرِيمٌ، لَم يَجعَلْ بَينَكَ وَبَينَهُ مَن يَحجُبُكَ عَنهُ، وَلَم يُلْجِئكَ إلىٰ مَن يَشفَعُ لَكَ إلَيهِ... ثُمَّ جَعَلَ في يَدِكَ مَفاتيحَ خَزائنِهِ بِما أذِنَ فيهِ مِن مَسألَتِهِ، فَمَتىٰ شِئتَ استَفتَحتَ بِالدُّعاءِ أبوابَ خَزائنِهِ.[٢٣٣١]

2089. **Imām ʿAlī (AS) said,** 'Supplication is the key to mercy and a lantern in the darkness.'[2346]

٢٠٨٩. عنه عليه السلام: الدُّعاءُ مِفتاحُ الرَّحمَةِ وَمِصباحُ الظُّلمَةِ.[٢٣٣٢]

2090. **Imām ʿAlī (AS) said,** 'The most beloved action on this earth with Allah – Mighty and Exalted – is supplication.'[2347]

٢٠٩٠. عنه عليه السلام: أحَبُّ الأعمالِ إلى اللهِ عزّوجلّ فِي الأرضِ الدُّعاءُ.[٢٣٣٣]

2091. **Imām ʿAlī (AS) said,** 'Supplication is the shield of the believer.'[2348]

٢٠٩١. عنه عليه السلام: الدُّعاءُ تُرسُ المُؤمِنِ.[٢٣٣٤]

2092. **Imām al-Ṣādiq (AS) said,** 'I urge you to supplicate, for verily in supplication is a cure for every ailment.'[2349]

٢٠٩٢. الإمامُ الصّادقُ عليه السلام: عَلَيكَ بِالدُّعاءِ، فإنَّ فيهِ شِفاءً مِن كُلِّ داءٍ.[٢٣٣٥]

2093. **Imām al-Ṣādiq (AS) said,** 'Supplicate and do not say, "the matter has already been decreed", for verily there is a station with Allah that can only be attained through supplication.'[2350]

٢٠٩٣. الكافي عن ميسّر بن عبد العزيز عن أبي عبد الله عليه السلام: قال لي: يا ميسّر ادعُ ولا تَقُلْ: إنَّ الأمرَ قَد فُرِغَ مِنهُ، إنَّ عِندَ اللهِ عزّوجلّ مَنزِلَةً لا تُنالُ إلّا بِمَسألَةٍ.[٢٣٣٦]

2094. **Imām al-Ṣādiq (AS) said,** 'Supplication is more useful than a sharp iron spearhead.'[2351]

٢٠٩٤. الإمامُ الصّادقُ عليه السلام: الدُّعاءُ أنفَذُ مِنَ السِّنانِ الحَديدِ.[٢٣٣٧]

2095. **Imām al-Riḍā (AS) said,** 'I urge you to use the weapon of the prophets', upon which he was asked, 'What is the weapon of the prophets?', to which he replied, 'Supplication.'[2352]

٢٠٩٥. الكافي عن الإمامِ الرِّضا عليه السلام: عَلَيكُم بِسِلاحِ الأنبياءِ. فَقيلَ: وما سِلاحُ الأنبياءِ؟ قالَ: الدُّعاءُ.[٢٣٣٨]

686. Supplication Wards off Inescapable Fate

٦٨٦ ـ الدُّعاءُ يَرُدُّ القَضاءَ المُبرَمَ

2096. **The Prophet (SAWA) said,** 'Nothing wards off fate except supplication.'[2353]

٢٠٩٦. رسولُ اللهِ ﷺ: لا يَرُدُّ القَضاءَ إلّا الدُّعاءُ.[٢٣٣٩]

2097. Imām Zayn al-ʿĀbidīn (AS) said, 'Supplication repels descended calamities and those which are yet to descend.'[2354]

٢٠٩٧. الإمامُ زينُ العابدينَ ﵇: الدُّعاءُ يدفَعُ البَلاءَ النّازِلَ وما لم يَنزِل. ٢٣٥٤

2098. Imām al-Kāẓim (AS) said, 'I urge you to supplicate, for verily supplication to Allah and seeking from Allah repels calamity which may have been destined and decreed with just the execution remaining, so if Allah is supplicated and is asked to avert a calamity, it is averted.'[2355]

٢٠٩٨. الإمامُ الكاظمُ ﵇: عَلَيكُم بالدُّعاءِ، فإنَّ الدُّعاءَ للهِ، والطَّلَبَ إلى اللهِ يَرُدُّ البَلاءَ وقَد قُدِّرَ وقُضِيَ ولَم يَبقَ إلّا إمضاؤُهُ، فإذا دُعِيَ اللهُ عزَّ وجلَّ وسُئِلَ صَرفَ البَلاءِ صَرَفَهُ. ٢٣٥٥

687. Supplication Repels Various Types of Calamity

٦٨٧ ـ الدُّعاءُ يَدفَعُ أنواعَ البَلاءِ

2099. The Prophet (SAWA) said, 'Repel the doors of calamity with supplication.'[2356]

٢٠٩٩. رسولُ اللهِ ﵅: إدفَعوا أبوابَ البَلاءِ بالدُّعاءِ. ٢٣٥٦

2100. Imām ʿAlī (AS) said, 'Repel the surges of calamity with supplication. The person who is continuously facing calamities is not more in need of supplication than that person who is free and secure from calamity.'[2357]

٢١٠٠. الإمامُ عليٌّ ﵇: إدفَعوا أمواجَ البَلاءِ بالدُّعاءِ، ما المُبتَلى الَّذي استَدَرَّ بهِ البَلاءُ بأحوَجَ إلَى الدُّعاءِ مِنَ المُعافى الَّذي لا يَأمَنُ البَلاءَ. ٢٣٥٧

2101. Imām al-Ṣādiq (AS) said, 'The one who fears the onset of a calamity and precedes it with supplication, Allah will never afflict him with that calamity.'[2358]

٢١٠١. الإمامُ الصّادقُ ﵇: مَن تَخَوَّفَ بَلاءً يُصيبُهُ فَتَقَدَّمَ فيهِ بالدُّعاءِ لَم يُرِهِ اللهُ عزَّ وجلَّ ذلكَ البَلاءَ أبداً. ٢٣٥٨

(See also: THE ORDEAL: section 275)

انظر: البَلاء، باب ٢٧٥

688. Priority with Supplication

٦٨٨ ـ التَّقَدُّمُ في الدُّعاءِ

"When distress befalls man, he supplicates his Lord, turning to Him penitently. Then, when He grants him a blessing from Himself, he forgets that for which he had supplicated Him before, and sets up equals to Allah that he may lead [people] astray from His way. Say, 'Revel in your ingratitude for a while. Indeed you are among the inmates of the fire.'"[2359]

﴿وَإِذَا مَسَّ الْإِنسَانَ ضُرٌّ دَعَا رَبَّهُ مُنِيبًا إِلَيْهِ ثُمَّ إِذَا خَوَّلَهُ نِعْمَةً مِّنْهُ نَسِيَ مَا كَانَ يَدْعُو إِلَيْهِ مِن قَبْلُ وَجَعَلَ لِلَّهِ أَندَادًا لِّيُضِلَّ عَن سَبِيلِهِ قُلْ تَمَتَّعْ بِكُفْرِكَ قَلِيلًا إِنَّكَ مِنْ أَصْحَابِ النَّارِ﴾. ٢٣٥٩

"Is He who answers the call of the distressed [person] when he invokes Him and removes his distress, and

﴿أَمَّن يُجِيبُ الْمُضْطَرَّ إِذَا دَعَاهُ وَيَكْشِفُ السُّوءَ

makes you the earth's successors…? What! Is there a god besides Allah? Little is that admonition that you take."[2360]

وَيَجْعَلُكُم خُلَفَاءَ الْأَرْضِ أءِ لَهٌ مَّعَ اللهِ قَلِيلاً ما تَذَكَّرُونَ﴾.٢٣٤٦

(See also: Qur'an 39:49, 10:22, 29:65, 30:33, 6:40-41, 6:63, and 17:67)

انظر: الزمر: ٤٩ و يونس: ٢٢ و العنكبوت: ٦٥ والروم: ٣٣. والأنعام: ٤٠، ٤١، ٦٣ و الاسراء: ٦٧.

2102. **The Prophet (SAWA) said,** 'Allah revealed to Prophet David (AS), 'Remember me in the good days so that I may answer [and assist] you in the bad [and difficult] days.'[2361]

٢١٠٢. رسولُ اللهِ ﷺ: أوْحَى اللهُ تَبارَكَ وتَعالىٰ إلىٰ داوود عليه السلام: اُذكُرْني في سَرَّائكَ أستَجِبْ لَكَ في ضَرَّائكَ.٢٣٤٧

2103. **The Prophet (SAWA) said,** 'Acquaint yourself with Allah in times of ease and Allah will acknowledge you in times of difficulty.'[2362]

٢١٠٣. عنه ﷺ: تَعَرَّفْ إلَى اللهِ فِي الرَّخاءِ يَعرِفْكَ فِي الشِّدَّةِ.٢٣٤٨

2104. **Imām al-Bāqir (AS) said,** 'A believer must supplicate Allah in times of ease the same way that he supplicates Allah in times of difficulty.'[2363]

٢١٠٤. الإمامُ الباقرُ عليه السلام: يَنبَغي للمُؤمِنِ أن يَكونَ دُعاؤهُ فِي الرَّخاءِ نَحْواً مِن دُعائهِ فِي الشِّدَّةِ.٢٣٤٩

689. Enjoinment of Supplication for Every Need

٦٨٩ ـ الحَثُّ عَلَى الدُّعاءِ في كُلِّ حاجَةٍ

2105. It is narrated in *Biḥār al-Anwār* that Allah revealed to Prophet Moses (AS), 'O Moses, ask Me for every single thing that you need, even the grass for your sheep to graze and the salt for your dough.'[2364]

٢١٠٥. بحار الأنوار: فيما أوحَى اللهُ إلىٰ موسىٰ عليه السلام: يا موسىٰ، سَلْني كلَّ ما تَحتاجُ إلَيهِ، حتّىٰ عَلَفَ شاتِكَ، ومِلحَ عَجينِكَ.٢٣٥٠

2106. **The Prophet (SAWA) said,** 'Ask Allah for whatever occurs to you from your needs even for the laces of your shoes, for verily if He does not facilitate for it, it will not be facilitated.'[2365]

٢١٠٦. رسولُ اللهِ ﷺ: سَلُوا اللهَ عزّوجلّ ما بدا لَكُم مِن حوائجِكُم حتّىٰ شِسعَ النَّعلِ؛ فإنّهُ إنْ لَم يُيَسِّرْهُ لَم يَتَيسَّرْ.٢٣٥٩

2107. **Imām al-Bāqir (AS) said,** 'Do not deem the smallest of your needs as insignificant, for verily the most beloved of the believers with Allah is the one who asks [Him] the most.'[2366]

٢١٠٧. الإمامُ الباقرُ عليه السلام: لا تُحَقِّرُوا صَغيراً مِن حَوائجِكُم؛ فإنّ أحَبَّ المؤمنينَ إلَى اللهِ تَعالىٰ أسألُهُم.٢٣٥٢

690. Supplication is the Key to Granting [of a Request]

٦٩٠ ـ الدُّعاءُ مِفتاحُ الإجابَةِ

"When My servants ask you about Me, [tell them that] I am indeed nearmost. I answer the supplicant's call when he calls Me. So let them respond to Me, and let them have faith in Me, so that they may fare rightly."[2367]

﴿وَإذا سَألَكَ عِبادِي عَنِّي فَإنِّي قَرِيبٌ أُجِيبُ دَعْوَةَ الدّاعِ إذا دَعانِ فَلْيَسْتَجِيبُوا لِي وَلْيُؤْمِنوا بِي لَعَلَّهُم يَرْشُدُونَ﴾.[٢٣٥٣]

2108. **The Prophet (SAWA) said,** 'When Allah wants to answer or respond to His servant, He allows him [through divine succour] to supplicate.'[2368]

٢١٠٨. رسولُ اللهِ ﷺ: إذا أرادَ اللهُ أن يَستَجِيبَ لعبدٍ أذِنَ لَهُ في الدُّعاءِ.[٢٣٥٤]

2109. **Imām ʿAlī (AS) said,** 'He who knocks on Allah's door, it is opened for him.'[2369]

٢١٠٩. الإمامُ عليٌّ ؑ: مَن قَرَعَ بابَ اللهِ سبحانَهُ فُتِحَ لَهُ.[٢٣٥٥]

2110. **Imām al-Ḥasan (AS) said,** 'Allah has never opened the door of request for anyone only to hold back the door of response.'[2370]

٢١١٠. الإمامُ الحسنُ ؑ: ما فَتَحَ اللهُ عزّوجلّ على أحدٍ بابَ مسألةٍ فَخَزَنَ عَنهُ بابَ الإجابَةِ.[٢٣٥٦]

691. The Conditions for the Answering of Supplication

٦٩١ ـ شُروطُ استِجابَةِ الدُّعاءِ

1. Inner Knowledge:

١ ـ المعرفةُ

2111. A group of people asked Imām al-Ṣādiq (AS), 'We supplicate but are not answered?' the Imām said, 'Because you call upon One whom you do not know.'[2371]

٢١١١. الإمامُ الصّادقُ ؑ ـ و قد سَألَهُ قومٌ: نَدعو فلا يُستَجابُ لنا؟! ـ: لأنّكُم تَدعونَ مَن لا تَعرِفونَهُ.[٢٣٥٧]

2112. Regarding the saying of Allah, *"so let them respond to Me, and let them have faith in Me"* [2372] Imām al-Ṣādiq (AS) said, 'It means that: "they should know that I [Allah] am capable of giving them what they ask Me for".'[2373]

٢١١٢. عنه ؑ ـ في قولِهِ: ﴿فَلْيَستَجِيبُوا لِي وَلْيُؤْمِنُوا بِي﴾[٢٣٥٨] ـ: يَعلَمونَ أنّي أقدِرُ عَلى أن أُعطِيَهُم ما يَسألُونّي.[٢٣٥٩]

2. Acting According to What Inner Knowledge Necessitates:

٢ ـ العملُ بما تقتضيهِ المعرفةُ

2113. **Imām ʿAlī (AS)** when he was asked regarding Allah's verse: *"Call Me and I will hear you[r*

٢١١٣. الإمامُ عليٌّ ؑ ـ لَمّا سُئِلَ عن قولِ اللهِ

supplications]"[2374] – 'So why does it happen that we supplicate and are not answered?' - replied, 'Because your hearts have been treacherous in eight areas, the first of them being that you know Allah but you do not fulfil your right towards Him as is obligatory upon you, so your inner knowledge of Him has not benefited you at all.... so then which supplication will be answered for you with this [state of affairs] after you have blocked its doors and paths?!'[2375]

تعالى: ﴿أُدْعُوني أَسْتَجِبْ لَكُم﴾[٢٣٦٠] فما بالُنا نَدعو فلا نُجابُ ؟ ـ: لأنَّ قُلوبَكُم خانَتْ بِثَماني خِصالٍ: أوّلُها أنَّكُم عَرَفتُمُ اللهَ فلَم تُؤَدُّوا حَقَّهُ كما أوجَبَ عليكُم، فما أغنَتْ عنكُم مَعرِفَتُكُم شَيئاً... فأيُّ دُعاءٍ يُستَجابُ لَكُم مَعَ هذا وقد سَدَدْتُم أبوابَهُ وطُرُقَهُ؟![٢٣٦١]

3. Lawful Earning:

٣ ـ طِيبُ المَكسَبِ

2114. **The Prophet (SAWA) said,** 'Verily a servant raises his hands to Allah [in supplication] while his food is unlawful! So how can his supplications be answered while he is in this state?!'[2376]

٢١١٤. رسولُ اللهِ ﷺ: إنَّ العبدَ لَيَرفَعُ يَدَهُ إلى اللهِ ومَطعَمُهُ حَرامٌ، فكيفَ يُستَجابُ لَهُ وهذا حالُهُ ؟![٢٣٦٢]

2115. **The Prophet (SAWA) said,** 'Make your earnings lawful and your supplication will be answered, for verily when a man raises an unlawful morsel of food to his mouth, his supplication is not answered for forty days.'[2377]

٢١١٥. عنه ﷺ: أطِبْ كَسبَكَ تُستَجَبْ دَعوَتُكَ، فإنَّ الرَّجُلَ يَرفَعُ اللُّقمَةَ إلى فِيهِ (حَراماً)[٢٣٦٣] فما تُستَجابُ لَه دَعوَةٌ أربَعينَ يوماً.[٢٣٦٤]

2116. **Imām al-Ṣādiq (AS) said,** 'If any of you wants his supplication to be answered then he should make a lawful earning and repay people their rights, for verily the supplication of a servant who has unlawful food in his stomach or has wronged anyone from Allah's creation will not be raised to Allah.'[2378]

٢١١٦. الإمامُ الصّادقُ عليه‌السلام: إذا أرادَ أحدُكُم أن يُستَجابَ لَهُ فَليُطَيِّبْ كَسبَهُ ولْيَخرُجْ مِن مَظالِمِ النّاسِ، وإنَّ اللهَ لا يُرفَعُ إلَيهِ دُعاءُ عَبدٍ وفي بَطنِهِ حَرامٌ أو عِندَهُ مَظلِمَةٌ لِأحَدٍ مِن خَلقِهِ.[٢٣٦٥]

4. Presence of the Heart and its Tenderness During Supplication:

٤ ـ حُضورُ القَلبِ ورِقَّتُهُ عِندَ الدُّعاءِ

2117. **The Prophet (SAWA) said,** 'Know that Allah does not answer supplication from a heedless and distracted heart.'[2379]

٢١١٧. رسولُ اللهِ ﷺ: إعلَموا أنَّ اللهَ لا يَستَجيبُ دُعاءً مِن قَلبٍ غافِلٍ لاهٍ.[٢٣٦٦]

2118. **The Prophet (SAWA) said,** 'Seize the opportunity to supplicate during tenderness [of your heart] for verily it is a mercy.'[2380]

٢١١٨. عنه ﷺ: اغتَنِموا الدُّعاءَ عِندَ الرِّقَّةِ فإنَّها رَحمَةٌ.[٢٣٦٧]

2119. **Imām al-Ṣādiq (AS) said,** 'Verily Allah does not answer the supplication that comes from a hard heart.'[2381]

٢١١٩. الإمامُ الصّادقُ ﷺ: إنَّ اللهَ لا يَستَجِيبُ دُعاءً بظَهرِ قلبٍ قاسٍ.[٢٣٦٨]

2120. **Imām al-Ṣādiq (AS) said,** 'When any of you feels softness and compassion, then he should supplicate, for no sooner does the heart soften than it becomes pure and sincere.'[2382]

٢١٢٠. عنه ﷺ: إذا رَقَّ أحدُكُم فَليَدعُ، فإنَّ القلبَ لا يَرِقُّ حَتّى يَخلُصَ.[٢٣٦٩، ٢٣٧٠]

692. Factors that Prevent the Answering of Supplication

٦٩٢ - مَوانِعُ الإجابَةِ

1. Sins:

١ - الذنب

2121. **Imām al-Bāqir (AS) said,** 'Verily a servant asks Allah his need and it is Allah's way that He either grants it very soon or after some time. The servant sins and Allah – Blessed and most High – says to the angels, 'Do not grant him, and deprive him of it for verily he has exposed himself to My displeasure and has made himself deserving of My deprivation.'[2383]

٢١٢١. الإمامُ الباقرُ ﷺ: إنَّ العبدَ يسألُ اللهَ الحاجةَ فيكونُ من شَأنِهِ قضاؤها إلىٰ أجلٍ قريبٍ أو إلىٰ وقتٍ بَطيءٍ، فيُذنِبُ العبدُ ذنباً فيقولُ اللهُ تَبارَكَ وَتعالىٰ للمَلَكِ: لا تَقضِ حاجَتَهُ واحرِمْهُ إيّاها، فإنَّهُ تَعَرَّضَ لِسَخَطي واستَوجَبَ الحِرمانَ مِنّي.[٢٣٧١]

2. Oppression:

٢ - الظُّلمُ

2122. **Imām ʿAlī (AS) said,** 'Allah revealed to Prophet Jesus (AS) saying, 'Tell the community of Israelites that… verily I do not answer the supplication of anyone from among you against whom one of My creation holds a claim of wrong or oppression.'[2384]

٢١٢٢. الإمامُ عليٌّ ﷺ: إنَّ اللهَ عزّ وجلّ أوحىٰ إلىٰ عيسَى بنِ مَريَمَ ﷺ: قُلْ لِلمَلأِ مِن بَني إسرائيلَ... إنّي غَيرُ مُستَجِيبٍ لِأحَدٍ مِنكُم دَعوَةً ولِأحَدٍ من خَلْقي قِبَلَهُ مَظلِمَةٌ.[٢٣٧٢]

2123. **Imām al-Ṣādiq (AS) said,** 'Verily Allah says, 'By My Might and Exaltedness, I do not answer the supplication of one who has been wronged when he calls Me regarding the wrong that has been done unto him, while someone else holds a similar claim of wrong against him.'[2385]

٢١٢٣. الإمامُ الصّادقُ ﷺ: إنَّ اللهَ عزّ وجلّ يَقولُ: وَعِزَّتي وَجَلالي، لا أُجِيبُ دَعوَةَ مَظلومٍ دَعاني في مَظلِمَةٍ ظُلِمَها ولأحدٍ عِندَهُ مِثلُ تِلكَ المَظلِمَةِ.[٢٣٧٣]

3. It Opposing Wisdom:

٣ ـ مُناقَضَتُهُ لِلحِكمَة

2124. **Imām ʿAlī (AS) said,** 'Verily the Kindness of Allah, glory be to Him, does not contradict His Wisdom, therefore not all supplications are answered.'[2386]

٢١٢٤ . الإمامُ عليٌّ ﵇ : إنَّ كَرَمَ اللهِ سُبحانَهُ لا يَنقُضُ حِكمَتَهُ ، فَلِذٰلِكَ لا يَقَعُ الإجابَةُ فـي كُـلِّ دَعوَةٍ[٢٣٧٤، ٢٣٧٥].

4. Describing Allah with Attributes Other than His

٤ ـ توصيفُ اللهِ بِغَيرِ صِفاتِهِ

2125. **Imām al-Ṣadiq (AS) said,** 'A man came to the Commander of the Faithful and said, 'Verily I have supplicated to Allah, but I have not received an answer!', the Imām (AS) said, 'You have described Allah in a manner that He is not worthy of being described, for verily supplication has four stages: sincerity of the heart, making the intention, having true knowledge of the means, and being fair regarding the request. So did you supplicate knowing these four conditions?' He said, 'No', then the Imām (AS) said, 'Then know them now'.'[2387]

٢١٢٥ . الإمامُ الصّادقُ ﵇ : جاءَ رجلٌ إلىٰ أميرِ المـؤمنينَ ﵇ فـقال : إنّـي دَعَـوتُ اللهَ فـلَم أرَ الإجابَةَ ! فقالَ : لقد وَصَفتَ اللهَ بغيرِ صِفاتِهِ ، وإنَّ للـدُّعاءِ أربـعَ خـصالٍ : إخـلاصُ السَّـريرةِ ، وإحضارُ النِّيّةِ ، ومَعرفةُ الوسيلةِ ، والإنصافُ في المسألةِ ، فـهل دَعَـوتَ وأنتَ عـارفٌ بـهذهِ الأربعةِ ؟ قالَ : لا ، قالَ : فاعرِفْهُنَّ[٢٣٧٦].

693. The Etiquettes of Supplication

٦٩٣ ـ آدابُ الدُّعاءِ

1. The *Basmala*:

١ ـ البَسمَلَةُ

2126. **The Prophet (SAWA) said,** 'The supplication that is preceded by *"In the Name of Allah, the all-Beneficent, the all-Merciful"* will not be rejected.'[2388]

٢١٢٦ . رسولُ اللهِ ﷺ : لا يُرَدُّ دُعاءٌ أوَّلُهُ بِسمِ اللهِ الرَّحمٰنِ الرَّحيمِ[٢٣٧٧].

2. Praise:

٢ ـ التَّمجيد

2127. **The Prophet (SAWA) said,** 'Verily every supplication that is not preceded by praise [of Allah] is incomplete.'[2389]

٢١٢٧ . رسولُ اللهِ ﷺ : إنَّ كُلَّ دُعاءٍ لا يَكونُ قَبلَهُ تَمجيدٌ فَهُوَ أَبتَرُ[٢٣٧٨].

3. Blessings upon Prophet Muḥammad (SAWA) and his Family:

٣ ـ الصَّلاةُ عَلىٰ مُحَمَّدٍ وآلِه

2128. **Imām al-Ṣādiq (AS) said,** 'A supplication remains veiled until the supplicant sends blessings on Muḥammad and the family of Muḥammad.'[2390]

٢١٢٨ . الإمامُ الصّادقُ عليه السلام : لا يَزالُ الدُّعاءُ مَحجوباً حَتّىٰ يُصَلّىٰ عَلىٰ مُحَمَّدٍ وعَلىٰ آلِ مُحَمَّدٍ .[٢٣٧٩]

2129. **Imām al-Ṣādiq (AS) said,** 'If anyone has a need from Allah, then he should begin by sending blessings upon Muḥammad and his family, then ask his need. Thereafter he should seal it by sending blessings upon Muḥammad and the family of Muḥammad, for verily Allah is too kind than to just accept the two blessings [at the beginning and at the end] and leave the middle, because the request for blessings on Muhammad and his family is never veiled from Him.'[2391]

٢١٢٩ . عنه عليه السلام : مَن كانَت لَهُ حاجَةٌ إلىٰ اللهِ عزّوجلّ فَلْيَبدَأ بِالصَّلاةِ عَلىٰ مُحَمَّدٍ وآلِهِ ، ثُمَّ يَسألْ حاجَتَهُ ، ثُمَّ يَختِمْ بِالصَّلاةِ عَلىٰ مُحَمَّدٍ وآلِ مُحَمَّدٍ ، فإنَّ اللهَ عزّوجلّ أكرَمُ مِن أن يَقبَلَ الطَّرَفَينِ ويَدَعَ الوَسَطَ إذ كانَتِ الصَّلاةُ عَلىٰ مُحَمَّدٍ وآلِ مُحَمَّدٍ لا تُحجَبُ عَنهُ .[٢٣٨٠]

4. Seeking Intercession of the Righteous:

٤ ـ الاِستِشفاعُ بِالصّالِحينَ

2130. **Imām al-Kāẓim (AS) said,** 'If you have a need from Allah, then say, "O Allah, verily I ask you for the sake of Muḥammad and 'Alī, for verily they have a special station with You.'[2392]

٢١٣٠ . الإمامُ الكاظمُ عليه السلام : إذا كانَت لَكَ حاجَةٌ إلىٰ اللهِ فَقُل : اللّٰهُمَّ إنّي أسألُكَ بِحَقِّ مُحَمَّدٍ وعَلِيٍّ ، فَإنّ لَهُما عِندَكَ شَأناً مِنَ الشَّأنِ .[٢٣٨١]

5. Acknowledgement of Sins:

٥ ـ الإقرارُ بِالذَّنب

2131. **Imām al-Ṣādiq (AS) said,** '[In supplication] praise Allah, then acknowledge your sins, then ask your request.'[2393]

٢١٣١ . الإمامُ الصّادقُ عليه السلام : إنّما هِيَ المِدحَةُ ، ثُمَّ الإقرارُ بِالذَّنبِ ، ثُمَّ المَسألَةُ .[٢٣٨٢]

6. Imploring and Begging:

٦ ـ التَّضرُّعُ والاِبتِهالُ

2132. It is narrated in *Biḥār al-Anwār* that among Allah's exhortations to Prophet Jesus (AS) was, 'O Jesus, call upon Me with a supplication of a sorrowful one, as if he is drowning and has no saviour…and only supplicate Me by imploring Me, with the supplication being your prime concern, for verily if you call Me like that, I will answer you.'[2394]

٢١٣٢ . بحارالأنوار: فيما وَعَظَ اللهُ بِهِ عيسىٰ عليه السلام : يا عيسىٰ ، اُدعُني دُعاءَ الحَزينِ الغَريقِ الّذي لَيسَ لَهُ مُغيثٌ ... ولا تَدْعُني إلّا مُتَضَرِّعاً إلَيَّ وهَمُّكَ هَمّاً واحِداً ، فَإنَّكَ مَتىٰ تَدْعُني كَذٰلِكَ أُجِبْكَ .[٢٣٨٣]

2133. **Imām al-Ḥusayn (AS) said,** 'The Prophet (SAWA) used to raise his hands and implore and

٢١٣٣ . الإمامُ الحسينُ عليه السلام : كانَ رَسولُ اللهِ صلى الله عليه وآله

beg [to Allah] just like the poor man begs for food.'[2395]

يَـرفَعُ يَـدَيهِ إذا ابـتَهَلَ ودَعـا كَـما يَستَطعِمُ المِسكينُ.[٢٣٨٤]

7. Performing Two Units of Prayer:

٧ـأن يُصَلِّيَ رَكعَتَين

2134. **Imām al-Ṣādiq (AS) said,** 'Whoever performs the ablution correctly and thereafter prays two units of prayer, completes its genuflexions and prostrations, sends the salutations [at the end of the prayer], praises Allah and the Prophet (SAWA), then asks his need in the right place will not be disappointed, because whoever seeks good from the right place is never disappointed.'[2396]

٢١٣٤. الإمامُ الصّادقُ ؑ: مَن تَوَضّأَ فَأَحسَنَ الوُضوءَ، ثُمَّ صَلّىٰ رَكعَتَينِ، فَأَتَمَّ رُكوعَهُما وَسُجودَهُما، ثُمَّ سَلَّمَ، وأثنىٰ عَلَى اللهِ عزّوجلّ وعَلىٰ رَسولِ اللهِ ﷺ، ثُمَّ سَألَ حاجَتَهُ، فَقَد طَلَبَ في مَظانِّهِ، وَمَن طَلَبَ الخَيرَ في مَظانِّهِ لَم يَخِب.[٢٣٨٥]

8. Not to Regard One's Own Request as too Much:

٨ـأنْ لا يَستَكثِرَ مَطلوبَهُ

2135. **The Prophet (SAWA) said,** 'Allah revealed unto one of His prophets…, 'If the people of the seven heavens and worlds were all to request from Me and I was to give each one their request, it would not decrease in My Sovereignty even the size of the wing of an insect, and how can My Sovereignty decrease and I am its owner.'[2397]

٢١٣٥. رسولُ اللهِ ﷺ: أوحىٰ اللهُ إلىٰ بَعضِ أنبيائِهِ:... لو أنَّ أهلَ سَبعِ سَماواتٍ وأرَضينَ سَألوني جَميعاً فَأَعطَيتُ كُلَّ واحِدٍ مِنهُم مَسألَتَهُ، ما نَقَصَ ذٰلِكَ مِن مُلكي مِثلَ جَناحِ بَعوضَةٍ، وكَيفَ يَنقُصُ مُلكٌ أنا قَيِّمُهُ؟![٢٣٨٦]

2136. **Imām al-Bāqir (AS) said,** 'Do not regard anything that you seek from Allah as too much, for verily what is with Allah is much greater than you could comprehend.'[2398]

٢١٣٦. الإمامُ الباقرُ ؑ: لا تَستَكثِروا شَيئاً مِمّا تَطلُبونَ، فما عِندَ اللهِ أكثَرُ مِمّا تُقَدِّرونَ.[٢٣٨٧]

9. To Have a High Ambition for What You Seek:

٩ـأنْ يكونَ عالِيَ الهِمَّةِ فيما يَطلُبُ

2137. **The Prophet (SAWA) said,** 'If you were to supplicate, amplify the appeal, as there is nothing great that Allah cannot do.'[2399]

٢١٣٧. رسولُ اللهِ ﷺ: إذا دَعا أحَدُكُم فَليُعظِمِ الرَّغبَةَ؛ فإنَّهُ لا يَتَعاظَمُ[٢٣٨٨] عَلَى اللهِ شَيءٌ.[٢٣٨٩]

2138. **Imām ʿAlī (AS)** in his counsel to his son al-Ḥasan (AS) said, 'Your request you make [from Allah] must be such that its beauty and goodness will remain for you and which its evil consequences will not touch you. Wealth will neither remain for you, and nor will you remain for it.'[2400]

٢١٣٨. الإمامُ عليٌّ ؑ ـ في وصيَّتِهِ إلىٰ ابنِهِ الحسنِ ؑ ـ: وَلتَكُن مَسألَتُكَ فيما يَعنيكَ مِمّا يَبقىٰ لَكَ جَمالُهُ ويُنفىٰ عَنكَ وبالُهُ، والمالُ لا يَبقىٰ لكَ ولا تَبقىٰ لَهُ.[٢٣٩٠]

10. To Supplicate for Everyone:

١٠ ـ تعميمُ الدُّعاءِ

2139. **The Prophet (SAWA) said,** 'When someone supplicates, he should pray for everyone, for it renders his supplication more conducive to being answered, and whoever precedes forty from among his brothers in supplication before supplicating for himself, his supplication for them as well as himself will duly be answered.'[2401]

٢١٣٩ . رسولُ اللهِ ﷺ : إذا دَعا أحَدُ فَلْيُعِمَّ فإنّه أوجَبُ للدُّعاءِ، ومَن قَدَّمَ أربعينَ رَجُلاً مِن إخوانِهِ قَبلَ أن يَدعُوَ لِنفسِهِ استُجِيبَ لَهُ فيهِم وفي نفسِهِ. ٢٣٩١

11. Supplicating in Secrecy:

١١ ـ الإسرارُ بالدُّعاءِ

2140. **The Prophet (SAWA) said,** 'A supplication asked in secret equals seventy supplications asked openly.'[2402]

٢١٤٠ . رسولُ اللهِ ﷺ : دَعوةٌ في السِّرِّ تَعدِلُ سبعينَ دَعوةً في العَلَانِيَةِ. ٢٣٩٢

12. Supplication in Congregation:

١٢ ـ الاجتماعُ في الدُّعاءِ

2141. **Imām al-Ṣādiq (AS) said,** 'No sooner do four people congregate to supplicate together for one matter than they depart with an answer.'[2403]

٢١٤١ . الإمامُ الصّادقُ ؑ : ما اجتَمَعَ أربعةُ رَهطٍ قَطُّ على أمرٍ واحدٍ فَدَعَوا اللهَ إلّا تَفَرَّقُوا عن إجابَةٍ. ٢٣٩٣

13. Being Optimistic about the Answer:

١٣ ـ حُسنُ الظَّنِّ بِالإجابَة

2142. **The Prophet (SAWA) said,** 'Supplicate to Allah while being convinced that He will answer you.'[2404]

٢١٤٢ . رسولُ اللهِ ﷺ : أُدْعُوا اللهَ وأنتُم مُوقِنونَ بالإجابَةِ. ٢٣٩٤

2143. **Imām al-Ṣādiq (AS) said,** 'When you supplicate, be optimistic that your request has been met.'[2405]

٢١٤٣ . الإمامُ الصّادقُ ؑ : إذا دَعَوْتَ فَظُنَّ أنَّ حاجَتَكَ بالبابِ. ٢٣٩٥

14. Selecting a Suitable Time:

١٤ ـ اختيارُ الأوقاتِ المناسِبَةِ

2144. **Imām al-Ṣādiq (AS) said,** The Prophet (SAWA) said, 'The best time to supplicate to Allah, Mighty and Exalted, is the time before dawn', then he recited the verse which is the saying of Prophet Jacob[2406] (AS), *"I shall plead with my Lord to forgive you."*'[2407], then he said, 'He postponed

٢١٤٤ . الإمامُ الصّادقُ ؑ :قالَ رسولُ اللهِ ﷺ: خيرُ وقتٍ دَعَوتُم اللهَ عزّوجلّ فيهِ الأسحارُ، وتلا هذه الآيةَ في قولِ يعقوبَ ؑ: ﴿سَوْفَ أَسْتَغْفِرُ

[supplicating for them] till the time before dawn.'[2408]

لَكُمْ رَبِّي﴾[٢٣٩٦] وقال: أخَّرَهُم إلىٰ السَّحَرِ.[٢٣٩٧]

2145. **Imām al-Ṣādiq (AS) said,** 'There are three times when supplication is not veiled from Allah at all: after completion of an obligatory act, during rainfall, and during the manifestation of a miraculous sign from Allah on the earth [like an eclipse].'[2409]

٢١٤٥. الإمامُ الصّادقُ ﷺ: ثلاثةُ أوقاتٍ لا يُحجَبُ فيها الدُّعاءُ عن اللهِ: في أثَرِ المكتوبةِ، وعند نُزُولِ القَطْرِ، وظُهورِ آيةٍ معجزةٍ للهِ في أرضِهِ.[٢٣٩٨]

15. Insistence:

١٥ ـ الإلحاح

2146. **The Prophet (SAWA) said,** 'Allah has mercy on a servant who seeks a need from Him and insists in supplication, whether it is answered or unanswered for him.'[2410]

٢١٤٦. رسولُ اللهِ ﷺ: رَحِمَ اللهُ عبداً طَلَبَ مِن اللهِ عزّوجلّ حاجةً فَألَحَّ في الدُّعاءِ، أُستُجِيبَ لَهُ أو لم يُستَجَبْ لَهُ.[٢٣٩٩]

2147. **Imām al-Bāqir (AS) said,** 'By Allah, no sooner does a believing servant insist to Allah, Mighty and Exalted, regarding a need than He fulfils it for him.'[2411]

٢١٤٧. الإمامُ الباقرُ ﷺ: واللهِ لا يُلِحُّ عبدٌ مُؤمنٌ علَى اللهِ عزّوجلّ في حاجتِهِ إلّا قضاها لَهُ.[٢٤٠٠]

694. What the Supplicant Must not do

٦٩٤ ـ ما يَنبَغي عَلَى الدَّاعي تَركُهُ

1. Supplication for the Impossible and the Impermissible:

١ ـ الدُّعاءُ لِما لا يَكونُ ولا يَحِلُّ

2148. **Imām 'Alī (AS) said,** 'O supplicant, do not ask for the impossible and the impermissible.'[2412]

٢١٤٨. الإمامُ عليٌّ ﷺ: يا صاحِبَ الدُّعاءِ، لا تَسأل عَمّا لا يَكونُ ولا يَحِلُّ.[٢٤٠١]

2. To Seek a Hasty Response:

٢ ـ الاِستِعجالُ

2149. **Imām al-Ṣādiq (AS) said,** 'The believer continues to remain in goodness, comfort, and mercy from Allah as long as he does not seek a hasty response, then despair and abandon supplication as a consequence'. The Imām was asked, 'How does he hasten?', to which he (AS) replied, 'He says, 'I have supplicated since such and such a time and I do not yet see an answer.'[2413]

٢١٤٩. الكافي عن أبي بصير عن الإمام الصّادق ﷺ: لا يَزالُ المُؤمنُ بخيرٍ ورَجاءٍ رَحمَةً مِنَ اللهِ ما لم يَستَعجِلْ فَيَقنَطُ وَيَترُكُ الدُّعاءَ. قُلتُ لَهُ: كَيفَ يَستَعجِلُ؟ قالَ: يَقولُ: قد دَعَوتُ مُنذُ كَذا وكَذا وما أرَى الإجابَةَ![٢٤٠٢]

3. Do Not Instruct Allah about What is Good for You:

٣ـ أنْ لا يُعَلِّمَ اللهَ ما يُصلِحُهُ

2150. **The Prophet (SAWA) said,** 'Allah, Blessed and most High, has said, 'O son of Adam, obey Me in what I have commanded, and do not instruct Me about what is good for you.'[2414]

٢١٥٠. رسولُ اللهِ ﷺ: قالَ اللهُ تَبارَكَ وتَعالىٰ: يابنَ آدَمَ، أطِعْني فيما أمَرتُكَ، ولا تُعَلِّمْني ما يُصلِحُكَ.[٢٤٠٣]

695. The One Whose Request is Granted without Asking

٦٩٥ـ مَن تُقضىٰ حاجَتُهُ بِلا سُؤالٍ

2151. **Abū Ḥamza narrated,** 'Verily Allah revealed to Prophet David (AS), 'O David, verily no sooner does a servant from among My servants obey Me in what I have commanded him than I give him before he asks Me, and I answer him before he supplicates Me.'[2415]

٢١٥١. بحار الأنوار عن أبي حمزة: إنَّ اللهَ أوحَىٰ إلىٰ داوود ﷺ: يا داوود، إنّه لَيسَ عبدٌ مِن عبادي يُطِيعُني فيما آمُرُهُ إلّا أعطَيتُهُ قَبلَ أن يَسألَني، وأستَجِيبُ له قَبلَ أن يَدعُوَني.[٢٤٠٤]

2152. **The Prophet (SAWA) said,** 'Allah, Mighty and Exalted, says, 'The one who is too preoccupied with My remembrance to ask Me, I give him more than what the ones who ask have been given.'[2416]

٢١٥٢. رسولُ اللهِ ﷺ: يقولُ اللهُ: مَن شَغَلَهُ ذِكري عن مَسألَتي أعطَيتُهُ فوقَ ما أُعْطِي السائلينَ.[٢٤٠٥]

2153. **Fāṭima al-Zahrā' (AS) said,** 'The one who sends up to Allah his pure and sincere worship, Allah, Mighty and Exalted, sends down for him that which will be of most benefit to him.'[2417]

٢١٥٣. فاطمةُ الزَّهراءُ ﷺ: مَن أصعَدَ إلىٰ اللهِ خالصَ عبادَتِهِ أهبَطَ اللهُ عزّوجلّ له أفضَلَ مَصلَحَتِهِ.[٢٤٠٦]

696. The Role of Contentment and Despair in Answering

٦٩٦ـ دورُ الرِّضا وَاليَأسِ في الإجابَةِ

2154. **Imām al-Ḥasan (AS) said,** 'I guarantee that the one who does not harbour anything but contentment in his heart will be answered when he supplicates to Allah.'[2418]

٢١٥٤. الإمامُ الحسنُ ﷺ: أنا الضّامِنُ لِمَن لَم يَهجُسْ في قلبِهِ إلّا الرّضا أن يَدعُوَ اللهَ فَيُستجابَ لَهُ.[٢٤٠٧]

2155. **Imām Zayn al-ʿĀbidīn (AS) said,** 'He who does not place his hope in people for anything and refers all his matters instead to Allah, Allah - Mighty and Exalted - will grant his every need.'[2419]

٢١٥٥. الإمامُ زينُ العابدينَ ﷺ: مَن لم يَرجُ النّاسَ في شيءٍ ورَدَّ أمرَهُ إلى اللهِ عزّوجلّ في جميعِ أمورِهِ استَجابَ اللهُ عزّوجلّ لَهُ في كلِّ شيءٍ.[٢٤٠٨]

697. Those whose Supplications are Answered

٦٩٧ ـ مَن تُستَجابُ دَعوَتُهُ

2156. **The Prophet (SAWA) said,** 'Beware of the supplication of the parent, for verily it is sharper than a sword.'[2420]

٢١٥٦ . رسولُ اللهِ ﷺ : إيّاكُم ودَعوَةَ الوالِدِ ، فإنَّها أحَدُّ مِن السَّيفِ .[٢٤٠٩]

2157. **The Prophet (SAWA) said,** 'The supplications of the children of my community are answered as long as they have not fallen into sins.'[2421]

٢١٥٧ . عنه ﷺ : دعاءُ أطفالِ اُمَّتي مُستَجابٌ ما لَم يُقارِفوا الذُّنوبَ .[٢٤١٠]

2158. **Imām al-Ḥasan (AS) said,** 'The one who recites the Qur'an has a supplication of his answered, be it immediately or later.'[2422]

٢١٥٨ . الإمامُ الحسنُ عليه السلام : مَن قَرَأ القرآنَ كانَت لَهُ دعوةٌ مُجابةٌ إمّا مُعَجَّلَةً وإمّا مُؤَجَّلةً .[٢٤١١]

(See also: WRONGDOING: section 1206)

(اُنظر) الظلم : باب ١٢٠٦.

698. Supplications that are not Answered

٦٩٨ ـ الدَّعواتُ غَيرُ المُستَجابَةِ

2159. **The Prophet (SAWA) said,** 'I asked Allah not to answer the supplication of an enamoured one against his beloved.'[2423]

٢١٥٩ . رسولُ اللهِ ﷺ : سألتُ اللهَ أن لا يَستَجيبَ دعاءَ حبيبٍ على حبيبِهِ .[٢٤١٢]

2160. **Imām al-Ṣādiq (AS) said,** 'There are four kinds of people whose supplications do not get answered: the man who sits in his house saying, 'O my Lord, grant me sustenance', to whom He says, 'Did I not command you to seek [for your sustenance]?', then there is the man who has a wife and supplicates against her, to whom He replies, 'Did I not make you responsible for her [put her affairs in your hands]?', and a man who has wealth and wastes it, who says, 'O my Lord, grant me sustenance', to whom He replies, 'Did I not command you to be economical?'...and a man who has wealth and loans it to someone without keeping any proof [of loan], to whom He replies, 'Did I not command you to take a witness?!'[2424]

٢١٦٠ . الإمامُ الصّادقُ عليه السلام : أربعٌ لا يُستَجابُ لَهُم دعاءٌ : الرجلُ جالسٌ في بَيتِهِ يقولُ : يا ربِّ ارزُقْني ، فيقولُ لَهُ : أَلَم آمُرْكَ بالطَّلَبِ ؟! ورجلٌ كانَت لَهُ امرأةٌ فَدَعا علَيها ، فيقولُ : أَلَم أجعَلْ أمرَها بيدِكَ ؟! ورجلٌ كانَ لَهُ مالٌ فأفسَدَهُ فيقولُ : يا ربِّ ارزُقْني ، فيقولُ لَهُ : أَلَم آمُرْكَ بالاقتِصادِ ؟!... ورجلٌ كانَ لَهُ مالٌ فأدانَهُ بغيرِ بَيِّنَةٍ فَيَقولُ : أَلَم آمُرْكَ بِالشَّهادَةِ ؟![٢٤١٣]

699. The Reasons for Delayed Responses

٦٩٩ـأسبابُ بُطءِ الاستِجابَةِ

2161. **Imām al-Ṣādiq (AS) said,** 'Allah said, 'By My Might, Exaltedness, Greatness and Splendour, verily I protect My friend by not giving him something in this world that will preoccupy him from My remembrance, and [that he may continue to call Me] so that I can hear his voice, and verily I grant the disbeliever his wish for him so that he stops calling Me lest I hear his voice.'[2425]

٢١٦١. الإمامُ الصّادقُ عليه السلام: قالَ اللهُ تعالىٰ: وعِزَّتي وجلالي وعَظَمَتي وبَهائي، إنّي لَأَحمِي وَلِيّي أن أُعطِيَهُ في دارِ الدنيا شيئاً يشغَلُهُ عن ذِكري حتّىٰ يَدعُوَني فأسمَعَ صوتَهُ، وإنّي لَأُعطي الكافرَ مُنيَتَهُ حتّىٰ لايَدعُوَني فَأسمَعَ صوتَهُ بُغضاً لَهُ.[٢٤١٤]

2162. **Imām ʿAlī (AS) said,** 'A delay in response should not dishearten you, for verily the grant [from Allah] is proportional to [the sincerity of] your intention, and maybe the response has been delayed in order for it to be a greater reward for the one who asked and a greater bestowal for the hopeful one, or maybe you asked for something and it was not given to you and instead you are to be granted something better sooner or later, or it may have been kept away from you for your own good, for many a matter that you ask for would be detrimental to your religion [and faith] if it were to be given to you.'[2426]

٢١٦٢. الإمامُ عليٌّ عليه السلام: لا يُقَنِّطَنَّكَ إبطاءُ إجابتِهِ، فإنَّ العطيَّةَ علىٰ قَدْرِ النِّيَّةِ، وربّما أُخِّرَتْ عنك الإجابةُ لِيَكونَ ذلكَ أعظَمَ لِأجرِ السائلِ وأجزَلَ لِعَطاءِ الآمِلِ، وربّما سألتَ الشيءَ فلم تُؤْتاه وأُوتيتَ خيراً مِنهُ عاجِلاً أو آجِلاً، أو صُرِفَ عنكَ لِما هُوَ خيرٌ لكَ، فَلَرُبَّ أمرٍ قد طَلَبْتَهُ وفيهِ هلاكُ دينِكَ لو أُوتيتَهُ.[٢٤١٥]

700. Supplication is not Without Effect

٧٠٠ـعَدَمُ خُلُوِّ الدُّعاءِ مِنَ التَّأثيرِ

2163. **The Prophet (SAWA) said,** 'Verily your Lord is bashful and kind. He would be too ashamed for His servant to open his hands to Him [in supplication] and for Him to return them empty.'[2427]

٢١٦٣. رسولُ اللهِ صلى الله عليه وآله: إنَّ رَبَّكم حَيِيٌّ كريمٌ، يَستَحِيي أن يَبسُطَ العبدُ يَدَيهِ إلَيهِ فَيَرُدَّهُما صِفراً.[٢٤١٦]

2164. **Imām Zayn al-ʿĀbidīn (AS) said,** 'There are three types of outcome from a believer's supplication: either it is stored away for him for

٢١٦٤. الإمامُ زينُ العابدينَ عليه السلام: المؤمنُ مِن دُعائهِ علىٰ ثلاثٍ: إمّا أن يُدَّخَرَ لَهُ، وإمّا أن يُعَجَّلَ لَهُ،

later, or it is hastened for him, or it repels a calamity waiting to afflict him.'[2428]

وإمّا أن يُدفَعَ عنهُ بَلاءٌ يُريدُ أن يُصيبَهُ.٢٤١٧

2165. **Imām al-Ṣādiq (AS) said,** 'The believer would wish that none of his supplications were answered in this world when he sees his beautiful and great rewards [in the Hereafter].'[2429]

٢١٦٥ . الإمامُ الصّادقُ (ع): يَتَمَنّىٰ المؤمنُ أنّه لم يُستَجَبْ لَهُ دَعوَةٌ في الدنيا مِمّا يَرىٰ مِن حُسنِ الثوابِ.٢٤١٨

701. Caution Against Supplication Without Knowledge

٧٠١ـ التَّحذيرُ مِنَ الدُّعاءِ بِغَيرِ عِلمٍ

2166. **Imām al-Ṣādiq (AS) said,** 'Know the ways of your salvation and destruction, so that you would not ask Allah for something that you believe your salvation lies in it, while it brings your destruction. Allah [the Glorious, the Exalted] has said: '*Man prays for evil as he prays for good; for man is given to hasty.*'[2430]

٢١٦٦ . الإمامُ الصّادقُ (ع): اِعرِفْ طُرُقَ نجاتِكَ وهلاكِكَ كي لا تدعُوَ اللهَ بشيءٍ منهُ هلاكُكَ وأنتَ تَظُنُّ فيهِ نجاتَكَ، قالَ اللهُ عزّوجلّ: ﴿وَيَدْعُ الإنسانُ بِالشَّرِّ دُعاءَهُ بِالخَيرِ وَكانَ الإنسانُ عَجولاً﴾.٢٤١٩

141

THE WORLD

الدُّنيا

702. Naming The 'World'

٧٠٢ـ تَسمِيَةُ الدُّنيا

2167. **Imām 'Alī (AS) said,** 'The world has been named *dunyā*[2431] because it is lower than every thing, and the Hereafter has been named *ākhira*[2432] because it contains recompense and reward.'[2433]

٢١٦٧ . الإمامُ عليٌّ (ع): إنّما سُمِّيَتِ الدُّنيا دُنيا لأنّها أدنىٰ مِن كلِّ شيءٍ، وسُمِّيَتِ الآخِرَةُ آخِرَةً لأنّ فيها الجزاءَ والثوابَ.٢٤٢٠

703. The World is the Plantation for the Hereafter

٧٠٣ـ الدُّنيا مَزرَعَةُ الآخِرَةِ

2168. **The Prophet (SAWA) said,** 'The world is the plantation for the Hereafter.'[2434]

٢١٦٨ . رسولُ اللهِ ﷺ: الدنيا مَزرَعَةُ الآخِرَةِ.٢٤٢١

2169. **Imām 'Alī (AS) said,** 'The Hereafter is secured through the world.'[2435]

٢١٦٩ . الإمامُ عليٌّ (ع): بالدنيا تُحرَزُ الآخِرَةُ.٢٤٢٢

2170. **Imām ʿAlī (AS) said,** 'Verily Allah – glory be to Him – has made this world for what is after it and has put its inhabitants to trial so that He may know who from among them has the best deeds, and we have not been created for this world, nor have we been commanded to strive for it.'[2436]

٢١٧٠. عنه ﷺ: إنّ اللهَ سبحانَهُ قد جَعَلَ الدنيا لِما بعدَها، وابتَلىٰ فيها أهلَها، لِيُعلَمَ أيُّهُم أحسَنُ عَمَلاً، ولَسنا للدنيا خُـلِقنا، ولا بـالسَّعيِ فـيها أُمِرنا.٢٤٢٣

2171. **Imām al-Bāqir (AS) said,** 'The world is the best aid for the Hereafter.'[2437]

٢١٧١. الإمامُ الباقرُ ﷺ: نِعمَ العَونُ الدنيا علَى الآخِرَةِ.٢٤٢٤

704. Explanation of the World

٧٠٤ـ تَفسيرُ الدُّنيا

2172. **The Prophet (SAWA) said,** 'The world is cursed along with what is in it, except that through which the pleasure of Allah is sought.'[2438]

٢١٧٢. رسولُ اللهِ ﷺ: الدنيا ملعونةٌ وملعونٌ ما فيها، إلّا ما ابتُغِيَ به وَجهُ اللهِ عزّوجلّ.٢٤٢٥

2173. **Imām Zayn al-ʿĀbidīn (AS) said,** 'The world is of two types: that which causes one to attain [success in the Hereafter] and that which is cursed.'[2439]

٢١٧٣. الإمامُ زينُ العابدينَ ﷺ: الدنيا دُنياءانِ: دنيا بلاغٍ ودنيا ملعونةٌ.٢٤٢٦

705. Taking Only What is Necessary from the World

٧٠٥ـ الأخذُ مِنَ الدُّنيا بِقَدرِ الضَّرورَةِ

2174. **Imām ʿAlī (AS) said** to a man who complained regarding his needs, 'Know that everything that you attain in this world that supersedes your required provision, you are considered to be its treasurer for someone else.'[2440]

٢١٧٤. الإمامُ عليٌّ ﷺ لرجلٍ شكا إليه الحاجةَ: اِعلَم أنّ كلَّ شيءٍ تُصيبُهُ مِن الدنيا فوقَ قُـوتِكَ فإنّما أنتَ فيهِ خازنٌ لِغيرِكَ.٢٤٢٧

2175. **Imām ʿAlī (AS) said** [regarding the world], 'Do not ask in it for what is more than a sufficient means of living and do not seek from it more than what you need.'[2441]

٢١٧٥. عنه ﷺ: لا تَسألُوا فيها فوقَ الكَفافِ، ولا تَطلُبُوا منها أكثرَ مِن البلاغِ.٢٤٢٨

2176. **Imām ʿAlī (AS) said,** 'The world is the abode of the hypocrites and it is not the abode of the pious ones, so take from the world enough to keep your body strong, to keep yourself alive and to gain provision for your Resurrection.'[2442]

٢١٧٦. عنه ﷺ: الدنيا دارُ المُنافِقينَ ولَيستْ بدارِ المُتّقينَ، فَليكُنْ حظُّكَ مِن الدنيا قِوامَ صُـلْبِكَ، وإمساكَ نَفْسِكَ، والتَزَوّدَ لمَعادِكَ.٢٤٢٩

2177. **Imām al-Ṣādiq (AS) said,** 'The status of this world according to me is just as a dead body, where I will only eat from it if I am compelled to do so.'[2443]

٢١٧٧ . الإمامُ الصّادقُ ﵇ : ما منزلةُ الدنيا مِن نفسي إلّا بـمنزلةِ المـيتةِ ، إذا اضـطُرِرتُ إليـها أكَلتُ مِنها .[٢٤٣٠]

706. The World Belongs to One Who Has Abandoned it

٧٠٦ـ الدُّنيا لِمَن تَرَكَها

2178. **The Prophet (SAWA) said,** 'Verily Allah revealed to the world, 'Tire and wear out the one who serves you, and serve the one who serves me you.'[2444]

٢١٧٨ . رسولُ اللهِ ﷺ : أوحَى اللهُ تَبارَكَ وَتَعالىٰ إلى الدنيا : اِخْدِمي مَن خَـدَمَنِي ، وأتْـعِبي مَـن خَدَمَكِ .[٢٤٣١]

2179. **Imām ʿAlī (AS) said,** 'The world is for the one who abandons it and the Hereafter is for the one who seeks it.'[2445]

٢١٧٩ . الإمامُ عليٌّ ﵇ :الدنيالِمَن تَرَكَهاوالآخرةُ لِمَن طَلَبَها .[٢٤٣٢]

2180. **Imām ʿAlī (AS) said,** 'The example of this world is like your shadow for if you stand still, it stands still and if you chase it, it distances itself.'[2446]

٢١٨٠ . عنه ﵇ : مَثَلُ الدنيا كَظِلِّكَ؛ إن وَقَـفتَ وَقَفَ ، وإن طَلَبتَهُ بَعُدَ .[٢٤٣٣]

707. Criticizing the World Without Knowledge

٧٠٧ـ ذَمُّ الدُّنيا مِن دونِ عِلمٍ

2181. **The Prophet (SAWA) said,** 'Do not insult the world for it is the best mount for the believer, because by means of it he attains good and through it he is saved from evil. If a servant [of Allah] says: "May Allah curse the world", the world replies: "May Allah curse the most disobedient one towards his Lord from among us!".'[2447]

٢١٨١ . رسولُ اللهِ ﷺ : لا تَسُبُّوا الدنيا فَنِعمَتْ مَطِيَّةُ المؤمنِ ، فعلَيها يَبلُغُ الخيرَ وبها يَنجو مِن الشرِّ ، إنّهُ إذا قالَ العبدُ : لَـعَنَ اللهُ الدنـيا قـالَتِ الدُّنيا : لَعَنَ اللهُ أعصانا لِرَبِّهِ ![٢٤٣٤]

2182. **Imām ʿAlī (AS) said,** 'O you who insult the world, who have been deceived by its deceit and cheated by its falsities, do you covet the world and then insult it? Should you accuse it or should it accuse you? When did it bewilder it or deceive you?!... Verily the world is an abode of truth for he who is truthful to it, an abode of wellbeing for he

٢١٨٢ . الإمامُ عليٌّ ﵇ : أيُّها الذامُّ للدنيا المُغترُّ بِغُرورِها المَخدُوعُ بِأباطيلِها ، أتَغتَرُّ بـالدنيا ثُـمَّ تَذُمُّها ؟! أنتَ المُتجرِّمُ علَيها أم هـي المُـتجرِّمَةُ علَيكَ ؟! متى استَهوَتْكَ أم مـتىٰ غـرَّتكَ ؟!... إنَّ

who understands it, and an abode of riches for he who collects provision from it [for the next world].'[2448]

الدنيا دارُ صِدقٍ لِمَن صَدَقَها، ودارُ عافيةٍ لِمَن فَهِمَ عنها، ودارُ غِنىً لِمَن تَزَوَّدَ مِنها.[٢٤٣٥]

708. Characteristics of the Condemned Aspect of the World

٧٠٨ ـ خَصائِصُ الدُّنيا المَذمومَةِ

2183. **Imām ʿAlī (AS) said,** 'The world is the marketplace of the losers.'[2449]

٢١٨٣ . الإمامُ عليٌّ عليه السلام: الدنيا سُوقُ الخُسرانِ.[٢٤٣٦]

2184. **Imām ʿAlī (AS) said,** 'The world is the ground of ruin for the intellects.'[2450]

٢١٨٤ . عنه عليه السلام: الدنيا مَصرَعُ العقولِ.[٢٤٣٧]

2185. **Imām ʿAlī (AS) said,** 'The world is the origin of evil and the place of deceit.'[2451]

٢١٨٥ . عنه عليه السلام: الدنيا مَعدِنُ الشرِّ ومحلُّ الغُرورِ.[٢٤٣٨]

2186. **Imām ʿAlī (AS) said,** 'The world is a plantation of evil.'[2452]

٢١٨٦ . عنه عليه السلام: الدنيا مَزرعةُ الشَّرِّ.[٢٤٣٩]

2187. **Imām ʿAlī (AS) said,** 'The world lowers and abases [mankind].'[2453]

٢١٨٧ . عنه عليه السلام: الدنيا تُذِلُّ.[٢٤٤٠]

709. Love of the World is the Fountainhead of Every Mistake

٧٠٩ ـ حُبُّ الدُّنيا رَأسُ كُلِّ خَطيئَةٍ

2188. **The Prophet (SAWA) said,** 'The gravest of the grave sins is love of the world.'[2454]

٢١٨٨ . رسولُ اللهِ صلى الله عليه وآله: أكبَرُ الكبائرِ حُبُّ الدنيا.[٢٤٤١]

2189. **The Prophet (SAWA) said,** 'Love of the world is the origin of every act of disobedience and the beginning of every sin.'[2455]

٢١٨٩ . عنه صلى الله عليه وآله: حُبُّ الدنيا أصلُ كلِّ مَعصيَةٍ وأوّلُ كُلِّ ذَنبٍ.[٢٤٤٢]

2190. **The Prophet (SAWA) said,** 'Searching for what will improve you is not considered love of the world.'[2456]

٢١٩٠ . عنه صلى الله عليه وآله: لَيْسَ مِن حُبِّ الدنيا طَلَبُ ما يُصْلِحُكَ.[٢٤٤٣]

2191. **Imām al-Ṣādiq (AS) said,** 'The fountainhead of every mistake is love of the world.'[2457]

٢١٩١ . الإمامُ الصّادقُ عليه السلام: رأسُ كلِّ خطيئةٍ حُبُّ الدنيا.[٢٤٤٤]

710. The Effects of Love of the World

٧١٠ـ ثَمَراتُ حُبِّ الدُّنيا

2192. **Imām ʿAlī (AS) said,** 'Love of the world corrupts the intellect, it deafens the heart from hearing wisdom and it brings about a painful chastisement.'[2458]

٢١٩٢ . الإمامُ عليٌّ عليه السلام : حُبُّ الدنيا يُفسِدُ العقلَ، وَيُصِمُّ[٢٤٤٥] القلبَ عن سَماعِ الحكمةِ، ويوجِبُ أليمَ العِقابِ.[٢٤٤٦]

2193. **Imām ʿAlī (AS) said,** 'Love of the world engenders greed.'[2459]

٢١٩٣ . عنه عليه السلام : حُبُّ الدنيا يُوجِبُ الطَّمَعَ.[٢٤٤٧]

2194. **Imām al-Ṣādiq (AS) said,** 'The one who attaches his heart to the world has attached his heart to three things, endless worry, false expectation and an unattainable hope.'[2460]

٢١٩٤ . الإمامُ الصّادقُ عليه السلام : مَن تَعَلَّقَ قلبُهُ بالدنيا تَعَلَّقَ قلبُهُ بثلاثِ خِصالٍ: هَمٍّ لا يَفنىٰ، وأمَلٍ لا يُدرَكُ، ورجاءٍ لا يُنالُ.[٢٤٤٨]

2195. **Imām al-Ṣādiq (AS) said,** 'Whoever increasingly becomes ensnared by the world, his distress will be greater when separating from it.'[2461]

٢١٩٥ . عنه عليه السلام : مَن كثُرَ اشتِباكُهُ بالدنيا كانَ أشَدَّ لِحَسرَتِهِ عند فِراقِها.[٢٤٤٩]

711. The World from the Viewpoint of Imām ʿAlī (AS)

٧١١ـ الدُّنيا مِن وِجهَةِ نَظَرِ الإمامِ عَليٍّ عليه السلام

2196. **Imām ʿAlī (AS) said,** 'By Allah, this world of yours is worse in my eyes than the sweat of a pig in the palm of a leper.'[2462]

٢١٩٦ . الإمامُ عليٌّ عليه السلام : واللهِ لَدُنياكُم هذهِ أهوَنُ في عَيني مِن عِراقِ خِنزيرٍ في يَدِ مَجذومٍ.[٢٤٥٠]

2197. **Imām ʿAlī (AS) said,** 'This world of yours is more forsaken [worthless] to me than the sneezing of a goat.'[2463]

٢١٩٧ . عنه عليه السلام : دُنياكُم هذهِ أزهَدُ عِندي مِن عَفطَةِ عَنزٍ.[٢٤٥١]

2198. **Imām ʿAlī (AS) said,** 'Verily your world to me is more worthless than a leaf being gnawed at in the mouth of a locust. What has ʿAlī got to do with perishable things?!'[2464]

٢١٩٨ . عنه عليه السلام : لَدُنياكُم أهوَنُ عِندي مِن وَرَقَةٍ (في) فِي جَرادَةٍ تَقضِمُها،... ما لِعَلِيٍّ ونَعيمٍ يَفنىٰ.[٢٤٥٢]

2199. **Imām ʿAlī (AS) said,** 'Get away from me, O World! Your rein is on your own shoulders as I have released myself from your ditches, removed myself from your snares and avoided walking into your slippery places.'[2465]

٢١٩٩ . عنه عليه السلام : إلَيكِ عَنّي يا دنيا، فحَبلُكِ علىٰ غارِبِكِ، قد انسَلَلتُ مِن مَخالِبِكِ، وأفلَتُّ مِن حَبائلِكِ، واجتَنَبتُ الذَّهابَ في مَداحِضِكِ....[٢٤٥٣]

712. Warning against the Deceptions of the World

٧١٢ ـ التَّحذيرُ مِن غُرورِ الدُّنيا

"To mankind has been made to seem decorous the love of [worldly] desires, including women and children, accumulated piles of gold and silver, horses of mark, livestock and farms. Those are the wares of the life of this world; but Allah – with Him is a good destination."[2466]

﴿زُيِّنَ لِلنّاسِ حُبُّ الشَّهَوَاتِ مِنَ النِّساءِ والْبَنِينَ والْقَناطِيرِ الْمُقَنْطَرَةِ مِنَ الذَّهَبِ والْفِضَّةِ والْخَيْلِ الْمُسَوَّمَةِ والْأَنْعامِ والْحَرْثِ ذٰلِكَ مَتاعُ الْحَياةِ الدُّنْيا واللهُ عِنْدَهُ حُسْنُ الْمَآبِ﴾.[٢٤٥٤]

"So do not let the life of the world deceive you, nor let the Deceiver deceive you concerning Allah."[2467]

﴿فَلا تَغُرَّنَّكُمُ الْحَياةُ الدُّنْيا وَلا يَغُرَّنَّكُمْ بِاللهِ الْغَرُورُ﴾.[٢٤٥٥]

2200. **Imām ʿAlī (AS) said,** 'Verily the world is a house of deception and deceit, it takes a spouse everyday, kills a family every night and splits up a group every hour.'[2468]

٢٢٠٠. الإمامُ عليٌّ (عليه السلام): ألا وإنّ الدنيا دارٌ غَرّارةٌ خَدّاعةٌ، تنكِحُ في كلِّ يومٍ بَعْلاً، وتَقتُلُ في كلِّ ليلةٍ أهلاً، وتُفَرِّقُ في كلِّ ساعةٍ شَملاً.[٢٤٥٦]

2201. **Imām ʿAlī (AS) said,** 'Do not allow the abundance of what amazes you in it to deceive you because it will be only a little that you take from it.'[2469]

٢٢٠١. عنه (عليه السلام): فلا يَغُرَّنَّكُم كَثرةُ ما يُعجِبُكُم فيها لِقِلَّةِ ما يَصحَبُكُم مِنها.[٢٤٥٧]

2202. **Imām ʿAlī (AS) said,** 'It is deceitful, and all that is in it is deceptive. It is perishable and all that is on it will perish. There is no good in any of its provisions except in piety and God-wariness.'[2470]

٢٢٠٢. عنه (عليه السلام): غَرّارةٌ غَرورٌ ما فيها، فانيةٌ فانٍ مَن علَيها، لا خَيرَ في شيءٍ مِن أزوادِها إلّا التَّقوى.[٢٤٥٨]

2203. **Imām ʿAlī (AS) said,** 'Beware of the world, for verily it appears sweet and green, surrounded by carnal and base desires.'[2471]

٢٢٠٣. عنه (عليه السلام): أُحذِّرُكُمُ الدنيا، فإنّها حُلوَةٌ خَضِرَةٌ حُفَّتْ بالشَّهَواتِ.[٢٤٥٩]

2204. **Imām ʿAlī (AS) said,** 'Beware of the world, for verily with regards to its lawful things there is accountability and with regards to its unlawful things there is punishment, its beginning is hardship and its end is annihilation.'[2472]

٢٢٠٤. عنه (عليه السلام): إحذَروا الدنيا، فإنَّ في حلالِها حِساب[اً]، وفي حَرامِها عِقاب[اً]، وأوّلُها عَناءٌ، وآخِرُها فَناءٌ.[٢٤٦٠]

2205. **Imām ʿAlī (AS) said,** 'Beware of this deceptive and deceitful world that has been beautified by its ornaments and has seduced through its delusions… such that it has become like

٢٢٠٥. عنه (عليه السلام): إحذَروا هٰذِهِ الدنيا الخَدّاعةَ الغَدّارةَ، التي قد تَزَيَّنَتْ بِحُلِيِّها، وفَتَنَتْ بِغُرورِها... فأصبَحَتْ كالعَروسِ المَجْلُوَّةِ،

an unveiled bride upon whom everyone's eyes are gazing.'[2473]

والعيونُ إليها ناظِرَةٌ.٢٤٦١

2206. **Imām ʿAlī (AS) said,** 'Beware of the world, for verily it is deceptive, delusive and deceitful, it is a giver that deprives, and one who clothes yet leaves you naked.'[2474]

٢٢٠٦ . عنه (ع) : إحذَروا الدنيا، فإنّها غَـدّارةٌ غَرّارةٌ خَدُوعٌ، مُعطِيَةٌ مَنوعٌ، مُلبِسةٌ نَزُوعٌ.٢٤٦٢

2207. **Imām ʿAlī (AS) said,** 'Beware of the world, for verily it is the enemy of the friends of Allah and the enemy of His enemies too. As for the friends of Allah, it fills them with grief and as for Allah's enemies, it deludes them.'[2475]

٢٢٠٧ . عنه (ع) : اِحذَروا الدنيا، فـإنّها عَـدُوّةُ أولياءِ اللهِ، وعَدُوّةُ أعدائهِ، أمّا أولياؤهُ فَغَمَّتهُم، وأمّا أعداؤهُ فَغَرَّتهُم.٢٤٦٣

713. Verily the World Deceives the Ignorant

٧١٣ ـ إنَّما تَغُرُّ الدُّنيا الجاهلَ

2208. **Imām ʿAlī (AS) said,** 'O World, deceive those who are ignorant of your tricks and who are unaware of the snares of your sly deceptions.'[2476]

٢٢٠٨ . الإمامُ عليٌّ (ع) : غُرّي يا دنيا مَن جَهِلَ حِيَلَكِ وخَفِيَ علَيهِ حبائلُ كَيدِكِ.٢٤٦٤

2209. **Imām ʿAlī (AS) said,** 'The transient world is the booty of the foolish.'[2477]

٢٢٠٩ . عنه (ع) : العاجِلَةُ غُرورُ الحَمقى.٢٤٦٥

2210. **Imām ʿAlī (AS) said,** 'Being happy with the world is foolishness.'[2478]

٢٢١٠ . عنه (ع) : الفَرَحُ بالدُّنيا حُمقٌ.٢٤٦٦

(See also: DELUSION: section 1414)

(أنظر) الغرور: باب ١٤١٤)

714. Warning against Being Satisfied with the World

٧١٤ ـ التَّحذيرُ مِنَ الطُّمَأنينَةِ بِالدُّنيا

"Indeed those who do not expect to encounter Us and who are pleased with the life of this world and satisfied with it, and those who are oblivious of Our signs – it is they whose refuge shall be the Fire because of what they used to earn."[2479]

﴿إنَّ الَّذِينَ لا يَرْجُونَ لِقَاءَنا وَرَضُوا بِالْحَيَاةِ الدُّنْيا واطْمَأَنّوا بِها والَّذِينَ هُمْ عَن آياتِنا غافِلُونَ * أُولـئِكَ مَأْوَاهُمُ النّارُ بِما كانُوا يَكْسِبُونَ﴾ ٢٤٦٧

2211. **Imām ʿAlī (AS)** with regards to Allah's verse: *"Under it there was a treasure belonging to them"* [2480], said, 'that (the treasure) was a golden

٢٢١١ . الإمامُ عليٌّ (ع) ـ في قولِهِ تعالىٰ: ﴿وكانَ تَحتَهُ كَنزٌ لَهُما﴾ ٢٤٦٨ ـ: كانَ ذلكَ الكنزُ لَوحاً مِن

tablet upon which was written... : I wonder at those who see the world and the fluctuating states that people experience, how can they be satisfied with it?'[2481]

ذهبٍ فيه مَكتوبٌ : ... عَجِبتُ لِمَن يَرَى الدنيا وتَصَرُّفَ أهلِها حالاً بعدَ حالٍ كيفَ يَطمئنُّ إلَيها؟! ٢٤٦٩

2212. Imām ʿAlī (AS) said, 'Look at the world through the eyes of those who have renounced it, for verily its inhabitants are quick to depart it and its opulence inflicts distress. So do not allow the abundance of what amazes you therein to deceive you, for it is but a little that you will take with you thereof.'[2482]

٢٢١٢ . عنه ﷺ : أُنظُروا إلى الدنيا نَظَرَ الزاهدِينَ فيها، فإنّها عَن قليلٍ تُزيلُ الساكنَ، وتَفجَعُ المُترَفَ فلا تَغُرَّنّكُم كَثرَةُ ما يُعجِبُكُم فيها لِقلَّةِ ما يَصحَبُكُم مِنها . ٢٤٧٠

2213. Imām ʿAlī (AS) said, 'View the world through the eyes of one who has renounced it and separated from it, and do not view it through the eyes of one who loves it passionately and tenderly.'[2483]

٢٢١٣ . عنه ﷺ : أُنظُرْ إلى الدنيا نَظَرَ الزاهدِ المُفارقِ، ولا تَنظُرْ إلَيها نَظَرَ العاشِقِ الوامِقِ . ٢٤٧١

2214. Imām al-Ṣādiq (AS) said, 'If this world is transient, then why be satisfied with it?'[2484]

٢٢١٤ . الإمامُ الصّادقُ ﷺ : إن كانتِ الدنيا فانيَةً فالطُّمأنينَةُ إلَيها لِماذا ؟! ٢٤٧٢

715. The Danger of Preferring the World [over the Hereafter]

٧١٥ ـ خَطَرُ إيثارِ الدُّنيا

"As for him who was rebellious and preferred the life of this world, his refuge will indeed be hell."[2485]

﴿فَأَمّا مَنْ طَغىٰ * وَآثَرَ الْحَياةَ الدُّنْيا * فَإنَّ الْجَحيمَ هِيَ الْمَأوىٰ﴾ . ٢٤٧٣

2215. Luqmān (AS) said in counsel to his son, 'Sell your world for your Hereafter and you will attain both of them, but do not sell your Hereafter for your world for you will lose them both.'[2486]

٢٢١٥ . لقمانُ ﷺ ـ لابنِهِ وهو يَعِظُهُ ـ : بِعْ دُنياكَ بِآخِرَتِكَ تَربَحْهُما جميعاً، ولا تَبِعْ آخِرَتَكَ بِدُنياكَ تَخْسَرهما جميعاً . ٢٤٧٤

2216. Imām ʿAlī (AS) said, 'The one who worships the world and prefers it over the Hereafter seeks an unhealthy outcome.'[2487]

٢٢١٦ . الإمامُ عليٌّ ﷺ : مَن عَبَدَ الدنيا وآثَرَها على الآخرةِ استَوخَمَ العاقِبةَ . ٢٤٧٥

2217. Imām ʿAlī (AS) said, 'No sooner do people abandon an aspect of their religion in order to

٢٢١٧ . عنه ﷺ : لا يَترُكُ الناسُ شيئاً مِن أمرِ

advance their worldly affairs than Allah will inflict them with something that is more detrimental than that.'[2488]

دينِهِم لاستِصلاحِ دُنياهُم إلّا فتَحَ اللهُ علَيهِم ما هو أضَرُّ مِنهُ.[٢٤٧٦]

(See also: THE HEREAFTER: section 17)

(أنظر) الآخرة: باب ١٧.

716. The World is the Prison of the Believer

٧١٦ـ الدُّنيا سِجنُ المُؤمِنِ

2218. **The Prophet (SAWA) said,** 'The world is not trouble-free for the believer, how can it be when it is his prison and his trial?'[2489]

٢٢١٨. رسولُ اللهِ ﷺ: الدنيا لا تَصفو لِمُؤمنٍ، كيفَ وهِي سِجنُهُ وبلاؤهُ؟![٢٤٧٧]

2219. **Imām al-Ṣādiq (AS) said,** 'The world is the prison of the believer, the grave is his fortress and Paradise is his final abode. The world is the Paradise of the disbeliever, the grave is his prison and the Fire is his final abode.'[2490]

٢٢١٩. الإمامُ الصّادقُ عليه السلام: الدنيا سِجنُ المؤمنِ والقَبرُ حِصنُهُ والجنّةُ مَأواهُ، والدنيا جَنَّةُ الكافِرِ والقبرُ سِجنُهُ والنارُ مَأواهُ.[٢٤٧٨]

717. The Danger of Making Worldly Affairs One's Greatest Concern

٧١٧ـ خَطَرُ جَعلِ الدُّنيا أكبَرَ الهُمومِ

2220. **Imām ʿAlī (AS) said,** 'The one who regards the worldly affairs as his greatest concern, his grief and distress are lengthened.'[2491]

٢٢٢٠. الإمامُ عليٌّ عليه السلام مَن كانَتِ الدنيا أكبرَ هَمِّهِ طالَ شَقاؤهُ وغَمُّهُ.[٢٤٧٩]

2221. **Imām al-Ṣādiq (AS) said,** 'The person who wakes up in the morning and retires at night having worldly affairs as his greatest concern, Allah places poverty between his eyes, scatters his affairs, and he will not take from this world except what Allah has apportioned for him. As for the one who wakes up in the morning and retires at night having the Hereafter as his greatest concern, Allah places needlessness in his heart and brings together his affairs for him.'[2492]

٢٢٢١. الإمامُ الصّادقُ عليه السلام: مَن أصبَحَ وأمسىٰ والدنيا أكبَرُ هَمِّهِ جَعَلَ اللهُ تعالى الفَقرَ بينَ عَينَيهِ وشَتَّتَ أمرَهُ ولم يَنَلْ مِن الدنيا إلّا ما قَسَمَ اللهُ له، ومَن أصبَحَ وأمسىٰ والآخرةُ أكبَرُ هَمِّهِ جَعَلَ اللهُ تعالى الغِنىٰ في قلبِهِ وجَمَعَ لَهُ أمرَهُ.[٢٤٨٠]

718. The Lowliness of the World in Allah's Eyes

٧١٨ـ هَوانُ الدُّنيا عَلَى اللهِ

"Were it not [for the danger] that mankind would be one community, We would have surely made for those who defy the All-beneficent, silver roofs for their houses…yet all that would be nothing but the wares of the life of this world, and the Hereafter near your Lord is for the Godwary."[2493]

﴿وَلَوْلا أن يَكونَ النّاسُ أُمَّةً واحِدَةً لَجَعَلْنا لِمَنْ يَكْفُرُ بِالرَّحْمٰنِ لِبُيُوتِهم سُقُفاً مِنْ فِضَّةٍ وَمَعارِجَ عَلَيْها يَظْهَرُونَ وَلِبُيُوتِهِمْ أَبْوَبًا وَسُرُرًا عَلَيْها يَتَّكِئُونَ وَزُخْرُفًا وَإنْ كُلُّ ذٰلِكَ لَمّا مَتاعُ الْحَياةِ الدُّنْيا والْآخِرَةُ عِنْدَ رَبِّكَ لِلْمُتَّقِينَ﴾ .[٢٤٨١]

2222. **The Prophet (SAWA) said,** 'Allah says, 'Were it not for My believing servant, I would have tied a headband of jewels around the head of the disbeliever.'[2494]

٢٢٢٢ . رسولُ اللهِ ﷺ : يقولُ اللهُ: لولا عَبدي المؤمنُ لَعَصَّبْتُ رأسَ الكافِرِ بعِصابةٍ مِن جَوهَرٍ .[٢٤٨٢]

2223. **The Prophet (SAWA) said,** 'If the world was worth the same as the wing of a mosquito in Allah's eyes, the disbeliever and the insolent person would never get to drink a sip of water from it.'[2495]

٢٢٢٣ . عنه ﷺ : لو أنّ الدنيا كانَت تَعدِلُ عند اللهِ عزّوجلّ جَناحَ بَعوضَةٍ ما سَقَى الكافِرَ والفاجرَ مِنها شَربَةً مِن ماءٍ .[٢٤٨٣]

2224. **Imām ʿAlī (AS) said,** 'The lowliness of the world in Allah's eyes can be seen by the fact that He is not disobeyed except in it, and what is with Him cannot be attained except by abandoning the world.'[2496]

٢٢٢٤ . الإمامُ عليٌّ عليه السلام : مِن هَوانِ الدنيا على اللهِ أنّهُ لا يُعصىٰ إلّا فيها ، ولا يُنالُ ما عندَهُ إلّا بتَركِها .[٢٤٨٤]

2225. **Imām al-Ḥusayn (AS) said,** 'Verily the lowliness of this world in Allah's eyes can be seen by the fact that the head of Prophet John, son of Prophet Zacharias was gifted to a whore from the whores of the Israelites.'[2497]

٢٢٢٥ . الإمامُ الحسينُ عليه السلام : إنَّ مِن هَوانِ الدنيا علىٰ الله تعالىٰ أنَّ رَأسَ يحيى بنِ زكريّا أُهدِيَ إلىٰ بَغِيٍّ مِن بَغايا بني إسرائيلَ .[٢٤٨٥]

719. The Difference between the Censured World and the Hereafter

٧١٩ـ تَضادُّ الدُّنيا الذَّمِيمَةِ وَالآخِرَةِ

2226. **The Prophet (SAWA) said,** 'He who loves his world has harmed his Hereafter.'[2498]

٢٢٢٦ . رسولُ اللهِ ﷺ : مَن أحَبَّ دُنياهُ أضَرَّ بآخرَتِهِ .[٢٤٨٦]

2227. **Imām ʿAlī (AS) said,** 'Verily the world and the Hereafter are two opposing enemies and two different paths, so whoever loves and befriends the world has despised the Hereafter and has made it his enemy. They [the world and the Hereafter] are like the east and the west and whoever walks between them, however much he gets closer to one, he distances himself from the other. After all, they are like two wives of the same husband.'[2499]

٢٢٢٧ . الإمامُ عليٌّ عليه السلام :إنَّ الدنيا والآخِرَةَ عَدُوّانِ مُتَفاوِتانِ، وسَبيلانِ مُختَلِفانِ، فَمَن أحَبَّ الدنيا وتَولّاها أبغضَ الآخِرَةَ وعاداها، وهُما بـمَنزِلَةِ المَشرِقِ والمَغرِبِ وماشٍ بَينَهُما، كُلَّما قَرُبَ مِن واحدٍ بَعُدَ مِنَ الآخَرِ، وهُما بَعدُ ضَرَّتانِ.[٢٤٨٧]

2228. **Imām ʿAlī (AS) said,** 'The bitterness of the world is the sweetness of the Hereafter, and the sweetness of the world is the bitterness of the Hereafter.'[2500]

٢٢٢٨ . عنه عليه السلام : مَرارةُ الدنيا حَلاوةُ الآخِـرَةِ، وحَلاوَةُ الدنيا مَرارَةُ الآخِرَةِ.[٢٤٨٨]

2229. **Imām ʿAlī (AS) said,** 'Seeking to bring together this world and the next is from the deception of the soul.'[2501]

٢٢٢٩ . عنه عليه السلام :طَلَبُ الجمعِ بينَ الدنيا والآخِرةِ مِن خِداعِ النَّفْسِ.[٢٤٨٩]

2230. **Imām ʿAlī (AS) said,** 'No one tastes a worldly pleasure except that he will face a torment on the Day of Resurrection.'[2502]

٢٢٣٠ . عنه عليه السلام : ما التَذَّ أحدٌ مِنَ الدنيا لَذَّةً إلّا كانتْ لَهُ يومَ القيامةِ غُصّةً.[٢٤٩٠]

2231. **Imām ʿAlī (AS) said,** 'The wealth of this world is the poverty of the Hereafter.'[2503]

٢٢٣١ . عنه عليه السلام : ثَروَةُ الدنيا فقرُ الآخِرَةِ.[٢٤٩١]

2232. **Imām Zayn al-ʿĀbidīn (AS) said,** 'By Allah, this world and the next are naught but two scales of a balance, so whichever scale is weightier, it will overpower the other.'[2504]

٢٢٣٢ . الإمامُ زينُ العابدينَ عليه السلام : واللهِ ما الدُّنيا والآخِرَةُ إلّا كَكِفَّتَي المِيزانِ، فأيُّهما رَجَحَ ذَهَبَ بالآخَرِ.[٢٤٩٢]

2233. **Imām al-Ṣādiq (AS) said,** 'The last prophet to enter paradise will be Solomon[2505] son of David (AS) due to what he was given in this world.'[2506]

٢٢٣٣ . الإمامُ الصّادقُ عليه السلام : آخِرُ نـبيٍّ يَـدخُلُ الجنّةَ سُليمانُ بنُ داوود عليه السلام ، وذلك لِما أُعطِيَ في الدنيا.[٢٤٩٣]

(See also: LOVE: section 431)

(أنظر) المحبّة : باب ٤٣١.

720. Combining the World and the Hereafter

٧٢٠ـ اجتماع الدُّنيا وَالآخِرَة

"So Allah gave them the reward of this world and the fair reward of the Hereafter; and Allah loves the virtuous."[2507]

﴿فَآتاهُمُ اللهُ ثَوابَ الدُّنْيا وَحُسْنَ ثَوابِ الْآخِرَةِ واللهُ يُحِبُّ الْمُحْسِنِينَ﴾ .٢٤٩٤

2234. **Imām ʿAlī (AS) said,** Cultivation is of two kinds. Wealth and children are the cultivation of the world and righteous deeds are the cultivation of the Hereafter, and sometimes Allah combines the two for some people.'[2508]

٢٢٣٤ . الإمامُ عليٌّ ﷺ: الحَرثُ حَرثانِ: فحَرثُ الدنيا المالُ والبَنونُ، وحَرثُ الآخرةِ الباقياتُ الصالحاتُ، وقد يَجمَعُهُم الله عزّوجلّ لأقوامٍ.٢٤٩٥

2235. **Imām ʿAlī (AS) said,** 'If you make your religion secondary to your worldly affairs, you have destroyed both your religion and your worldly affairs, and thus you will be among the losers in the Hereafter. But if you make your worldly affairs secondary to your religion, you have safeguarded your religion and your worldly affairs and you will be among the victorious ones in the Hereafter.'[2509]

٢٢٣٥ . عنه ﷺ: إن جَعَلتَ دِينَكَ تَبَعاً لدُنياكَ أهلَكتَ دينَكَ ودُنياكَ وكُنتَ في الآخرةِ مِن الخاسِرينَ، إن جَعَلتَ دُنياكَ تَبَعاً لِدينِكَ أحرَزْتَ دِينَكَ ودُنياكَ وكُنتَ في الآخرةِ مِن الفائزينَ.٢٤٩٦

2236. **Imām al-Kāẓim (AS) said,** 'Allocate for yourselves a portion of the world by taking from it that which is lawful of what you desire, and that which does not breach the honourable virtues and that wherein there is no extravagance. And in this way, use it to assist [and improve] the matters of religion, for it has been narrated that, 'The one who abandons their worldly affairs for their religion is not from us, and neither is the one who abandons their religion for their worldly affairs.'[2510]

٢٢٣٦ . الإمامُ الكاظمُ ﷺ: اِجعَلوا لأنفُسِكُم حظّاً مِن الدنيا بإعطائها ما تَشتَهي مِن الحلالِ وما لا يَثلِمُ المُروّةَ وما لا سَرَفَ فيهِ، واستَعينوا بذلكَ على أمورِ الدِّينِ، فإنّهُ رُوِيَ: ليسَ مِنّا مَن تَرَكَ دُنياهُ لدينِهِ، أو تَرَكَ دِينَهُ لدُنياهُ.٢٤٩٧

721. The Parable of the World

٧٢١ـ مَثَلُ الدُّنيا

"Draw for them the parable of the life of this world: [it is] like the water We send down from the sky. Then the earth's vegetation mingles with it. Then it becomes chaff, scattered by the wind. And Allah is omnipotent over all things."[2511]

﴿وَاضْرِبْ لَهُمْ مَثَلَ الْحَياةِ الدُّنْيا كَماءٍ أَنزَلْناهُ مِنَ السَّماءِ فَاخْتَلَطَ بِهِ نَباتُ الْأَرْضِ فَأَصْبَحَ هَشِيماً تَذْرُوهُ الرِّياحُ وَكانَ اللهُ عَلَىٰ كُلِّ شَيْءٍ مُقْتَدِراً﴾ .٢٤٩٨

2237. **The Prophet (SAWA) said,** 'This world when compared to the Hereafter is just as if one of you dips his finger in the sea and sees what he comes out with.'[2512]

٢٢٣٧. رسولُ اللهِ ﷺ: ما الدنيا في الآخِرَةِ إلّا مِثلُ ما يَجعَلُ أحدُكُم إصبَعَهُ في اليَمِّ فليَنظُرْ بِمَ يَرجِعُ.[٢٤٩٩]

2238. **Imām ʿAlī (AS) said,** 'The parable of this world is like your shadow - if you stop, it stands still, and if you chase it, it distances itself from you.'[2513]

٢٢٣٨. الإمامُ عليٌّ عليه السلام: مَثَلُ الدنيا كَظِلِّكَ؛ إن وَقَفتَ وَقَفَ، وإن طَلَبتَهُ بَعُدَ.[٢٥٠٠]

2239. **Imām al-Bāqir (AS) said,** '[Consider] your sojourn in this world just as a house that you stayed in and [soon] departed from, or an object of perfection that you witnessed in a dream then you awoke and not a thing from it remained with you. I have given you this parable because this world, according to the people of intellect and knowledge of Allah, is just as the shadow in the shade.'[2514]

٢٢٣٩. الإمامُ الباقرُ عليه السلام: أنزِلِ الدنيا كمَنزِلٍ نَزَلتَهُ ثُمّ ارتَحَلتَ عَنهُ، أو كمالٍ وَجَدتَهُ في مَنامِكَ فاستَيقَظتَ ولَيس مَعكَ مِنهُ شيءٌ، إنّي (إنّما) ضَرَبتُ لكَ هذا مَثَلاً لأنّها عِندَ أهلِ اللُبِّ والعِلمِ باللهِ كَفَيْءِ الظِّلالِ.[٢٥٠١]

2240. **Imām al-Bāqir (AS) said,** 'The world in the eyes of the learned ones is like a shadow.'[2515]

٢٢٤٠. عنه عليه السلام: إنّ الدنيا عِندَ العُلَماءِ مِثلُ الظِلِّ.[٢٥٠٢]

2241. **Imām al-Kāẓim (AS) said,** 'The parable of this world is like that of a snake, it is soft to touch but it contains a deadly poison. Men of intellect are cautious whereas children extend their arms towards it.'[2516]

٢٢٤١. الإمامُ الكاظمُ عليه السلام: مَثَلُ الدنيا مَثَلُ الحَيّةِ؛ مَسُّها لَيِّنٌ وفي جَوفِها السُّمُّ القاتِلُ، يَحذَرُها الرِّجالُ ذَوُو العُقولِ، ويَهوِي إلَيها الصِّبيانُ بأيديهِم.[٢٥٠٣]

2242. **Imām al-Kāẓim (AS) said,** 'The parable of this world is that of sea water, however much the thirsty man drinks from it, his thirst intensifies until it kills him.'[2517]

٢٢٤٢. عنه عليه السلام: مَثَلُ الدنيا مَثَلُ ماءِ البحرِ؛ كُلَّما شَرِبَ مِنهُ العَطشانُ ازدادَ عَطَشاً حتّىٰ يَقتُلَهُ.[٢٥٠٤]

2243. **Imām al-Kāẓim (AS) said,** 'The world was embodied to Jesus (AS) in the form of a blue-eyed woman, and he said to her, 'How many have you married?' she said, 'Lots', so he asked, 'So all of them divorced you?', she replied, 'No, rather I killed all of them', then Jesus (AS) said, 'Woe upon your current spouses, for how do they not take a lesson from your previous ones?!'[2518]

٢٢٤٣. عنه عليه السلام: تَمَثَّلَتِ الدنيا للمسيحِ عليه السلام في صُورةِ امرأةٍ زَرْقاءَ، فقالَ لَها: كَم تَزَوَّجتِ؟ فقالَت: كثيراً، قالَ: فَكُلٌّ طَلَّقَكِ؟ قالَت: لا، بَل كُلّاً قَتَلتُ، قالَ المسيحُ عليه السلام: فَوَيحٌ لأزواجِكِ الباقينَ، كيفَ لا يَعتَبِرُونَ بالماضينَ؟![٢٥٠٥]

2244. **Imām al-Kāẓim (AS) said,** 'Luqmān said to his son:...the world is a deep ocean in which many worlds have already drowned, so make Godwariness your boat, faith its content, trust in Allah its sail, reason its custodian, knowledge its guide and patience its inhabitants.'[2519]

٢٢٤٤ . عنه ﷺ : إنّ لُقمانَ قالَ لِابنِهِ:... إنّ الدنيا بحرٌ عميقٌ، قد غَرِقَ فيها عالَمٌ كثيرٌ، فلتَكُنْ سَفينتُكَ فيها تَقوَى اللهِ، وحَشوُها الإيمانُ وشِراعُها التوكُّلُ، وقَيِّمُها العقلُ، ودليلُها العِلمُ، وسُكّانُها الصَّبرُ.[٢٥٠٦]

722. The World is the House of [trifling] Enjoyment

٧٢٢ ـ الدُّنيا دارُ مَتاعٍ

"Allah expands the provision for whomever He wishes, and tightens it. They exult in the life of this world, but compared with the Hereafter the life of this world is but a [trifling] enjoyment."[2520]

﴿اللهُ يَبْسُطُ الرِّزْقَ لِمَن يَشَاءُ وَيَقْدِرُ وفَرِحُوا بِالْحَياةِ الدُّنْيا وَما الْحَياةُ الدُّنْيا فِي الْآخِرَةِ إلّا مَتاعٌ﴾.[٢٥٠٧]

2245. It is narrated in *Tanbīh al-Khawāṭir* that the archangel Gabriel (AS) said to Prophet Noah (AS), 'O prophet who has lived for the longest number of years, how did you find this world?' he replied, 'Like a house which has two doors, I entered through one and then left through the other.'[2521]

٢٢٤٥ . تنبيه الخواطر : رُوِيَ أنّ جَبرئيلَ ﷺ قالَ لنوحٍ ﷺ : يا أطوَلَ الأنبياءِ عُمراً، كيفَ وَجَدتَ الدنيا؟ قال: كَدارٍ لَها بابانِ دَخَلتُ مِن أحَدِهِما وخَرَجتُ مِنَ الآخَرِ.[٢٥٠٨]

2246. **Prophet Jesus (AS) said,** 'Verily this world is a bridge, so cross over it but do not build on it.'[2522]

٢٢٤٦ . عيسى ﷺ : إنّما الدنيا قَنطَرةٌ، فاعبُرُوها ولا تعمُروها.[٢٥٠٩]

2247. **The Prophet (SAWA) said,** 'The world is only an hour [long] so use it in obedience.'[2523]

٢٢٤٧ . رسولُ اللهِ ﷺ : الدنيا ساعةٌ فاجعَلوها طاعةً.[٢٥١٠]

2248. **Imām ʿAlī (AS) said,** 'The world is a transitory and mobile thing, even if it remains for you, you will not remain for it.'[2524]

٢٢٤٨ . الإمامُ عليٌّ ﷺ : الدنيا مُنتَقِلَةٌ فانيةٌ، إن بَقِيَتْ لَكَ لَم تَبقَ لَها.[٢٥١١]

2249. **Imām ʿAlī (AS) said,** 'O people, verily the world is a passage while the Hereafter is a permanent abode, so take [as much as you can] from the passage for the permanent abode.'[2525]

٢٢٤٩ . عنه ﷺ : أيّها الناسُ، إنّما الدنيا دارُ مَجازٍ والآخِرةُ دارُ قَرارٍ، فخُذوا مِن مَمَرِّكُم لِمَقَرِّكُم.[٢٥١٢]

2250. **Imām ʿAlī (AS) said,** 'This world is a transitory place and not a permanent one. The people therein are of two types, the man who has sold his self [to his passions] and thus ruined it,

٢٢٥٠ . عنه ﷺ : الدنيا دارُ مَمَرٍّ لا دارُ مَقَرٍّ، والناسُ فيها رجُلانِ: رجلٌ باعَ فيها نفسَهُ

and the man who has purchased his self [by control against his passions] and thus freed it.'[2526]

فأوبقَها، ورَجُلٌ ابتاعَ نفسَهُ فَأعتَقَها.[٢٥١٣]

723. The World is a Place Surrounded by Trials

٧٢٣ـ الدُّنيا دارٌ بِالبَلاءِ مَحفوفَةٌ

2251. **Imām ʿAlī (AS) said,** '[The world] is a house surrounded by trials, well-known for treachery, whose conditions do not last, whose inhabitants do not remain safe, its states are variable, its ways are changing, life in it is shameful and security in it is non-existent.'[2527]

٢٢٥١. الإمامُ عليٌّ عليه السلام: دارٌ بالبلاءِ مَحفوفَةٌ، وبالغَدْرِ مَعروفَةٌ، لا تَدومُ أحوالُها، ولا يَسلَمُ نُزّالُها، أحوالٌ مُختَلِفَةٌ، تاراتٌ مُتَصَرِّفَةٌ، العَيشُ فيها مَذمومٌ، والأمانُ مِنها مَعدومٌ.[٢٥١٤]

(See also: COMFORT: section 849)

(أنظر الراحة: باب ٨٤٩).

142

PLIABILITY[2528]

المُداهَنَة

724. Flattering the Transgressors

٧٢٤ـ مُداهَنَةُ أهلِ المَعاصي

"Who are eager that you should be pliable, so that they may be pliable [towards you]."[2529]

﴿وَدُّوا لَوْ تُدْهِنُ فَيُدهِنُونَ﴾.[٢٥١٥]

2252. **Imām al-Bāqir (AS) said,** 'Allah revealed to Prophet Shuʿayb[2530], 'Verily I am punishing one hundred thousand members of your community: forty thousand from among the evil doers and sixty thousand from among the good doers.' He said, 'My Lord, evil doers fine, but what about the good doers?' Then Allah, Mighty and Exalted, revealed to him, 'They were pliable with the transgressors and did not express any anger at what angers Me'.'[2531]

٢٢٥٢. الإمامُ الباقرُ عليه السلام: أوحَى اللهُ تَعالىٰ إلى شُعَيبٍ النبيِّ: إنّي مُعَذِّبٌ مِن قومِكَ مائَةَ ألفٍ: أربعينَ ألفاً مِن شِرارِهِم وسِتّينَ ألفاً مِن خِيارِهِم، فقالَ: يا ربِّ، هؤلاءِ الأشرارُ فما بالُ الأخيارِ؟! فَأوحَى اللهُ عزّوجلّ إلَيه: داهَنوا أهلَ المعاصي فلَم يَغضَبوا لِغَضَبي.[٢٥١٦]

2253. **Imām ʿAlī (AS) said,** 'The worst of your brothers is he who flatters you and conceals [from you] your faults.'[2532]

٢٢٥٣. الإمامُ عليٌّ عليه السلام: شَرُّ إخوانِكَ مَن داهَنَكَ في نفسِكَ وساتَرَكَ عَيبَكَ.[٢٥١٧]

2254. **Imām ʿAlī (AS) said,** 'Whoever flatters himself trespasses into the forbidden transgressions.'[2533]

٢٢٥٤. عنه عليه السلام: مَن داهَنَ نفسَهُ هَجَمَت بِهِ على المعاصي المُحَرَّمَةِ.[٢٥١٨]

725. The Prohibition of Compromising the Truth

٧٢٥ـ عدمُ جوازِ المُداهَنَةِ فِي الحَقِّ

2255. **Imām ʿAlī (AS) said,** 'Do not compromise the truth when you come across it and you recognize that it is the truth, lest you suffer clear loss.'[2534]

٢٢٥٥ . الإمامُ عليٌّ ﷺ : لا تُداهِنُوا في الحقِّ إذا وَرَدَ عـلَيكُم وعـرَفتُمُوهُ فـتَخسَرُوا خُسـراناً مُبِيناً.[٢٥١٩]

2256. **Imām ʿAlī (AS) said,** 'By my life, never will I compromise with or be slack when fighting anyone who opposes the truth or one who has fallen into transgression.'[2535]

٢٢٥٦ . عنه ﷺ : ولَعَمْرِي ما علَيَّ مِن قِتالِ مَن خالَفَ الحَقَّ، وخـابَطَ الغَـيَّ، مِـن إدهـانٍ ولا إيهانٍ.[٢٥٢٠]

143

STATE

الدَّوْلَةُ

726. The State [i.e. Governance] of Senior People

٧٢٦ـ دَولَةُ الأكابِرِ

2257. **Imām ʿAlī (AS) said,** 'The governance of senior people [of greater expertise] is one of the greatest advantages whereas the governance of wicked people humiliates noble people.'[2536]

٢٢٥٧ . الإمامُ عليٌّ ﷺ : دَولةُ الأكابِرِ مِن أفضَلِ المَغانِمِ ، دَولةُ اللِئامِ مَذَلَّةُ الكِرامِ.[٢٥٢١]

727. Sign of the Fall of States

٧٢٧ـ علامَةُ إدبارِ الدُّوَلِ

2258. **Imām ʿAlī (AS) said,** 'The fall of states can be discerned by four things: neglect of the fundamentals, embracing peripheral matters, bringing CONTEMPTIBLE ones to the forefront and relegating the virtuous ones.'[2537]

٢٢٥٨ . الإمامُ عليٌّ ﷺ : يُستدَلُّ على إدبارِ الدُّوَلِ بأربَعٍ : تَضييعِ الأصُولِ، والتمسُّكِ بالفروعِ[٢٥٢٢]، وتَقديمِ الأراذِلِ، وتأخيرِ الأفاضِلِ.[٢٥٢٣]

728. Reasons for the Stability of States

٧٢٨ـ عَوامِلُ دَوامِ الدُّوَلِ

2259. **Imām ʿAlī (AS) said,** 'The greatest of the rights that the Glorified [Allah] has made obligatory on man is the right of the ruler over the ruled and the

٢٢٥٩ . الإمامُ عليٌّ ﷺ : وأعظَمُ ما افترَضَ سبحانَهُ مِن تلكَ الحُقوقِ حَقُّ الوالِي على الرَّعِيَّةِ ، وحقُّ

right of the ruled over the ruler... so if the ruled fulfil the rights of the ruler and the ruler fulfils their rights, then the truth attains the position of honour among them, the ways of religion become established, the marks of justice affirmed, the traditions and practices gets implemented correctly, current times improve, the continuance of the state is desired and the ambitions of the enemies are thwarted.'[2538]

الرعيّةِ على الوالِي ... فإذا أدَّتِ الرعيّةُ إلى الوالي حقَّهُ وأدَّى الوالِي إلَيها حَقَّها عَزَّ الحَقُّ بينهم، وقامَت مناهِجُ الدِّينِ، واعتَدَلَتْ مَعالِمُ العَدلِ، وجَرَت علىٰ أذلالِها السُّنَنُ، فَصَلَحَ بذلك الزمانُ، وطُمِعَ في بَقاءِ الدَّولةِ، ويَئسَت مطامِعُ الأعداءِ.[٢٥٢٤]

2260. **Imām ʿAlī (AS) said,** 'Nothing fortifies states like justice.'[2539]

٢٢٦٠. عنه عليه السلام: ما حُصِّنَ الدُّوَلُ بمِثلِ العَدلِ.[٢٥٢٥]

2261. **Imām ʿAlī (AS) said,** 'Make religion the fortress of your state, and thankfulness a protection for your bounties, because every state whose fortress is religion is invincible and every bounty encompassed by thankfulness remains.'[2540]

٢٢٦١. عنه عليه السلام: صَيِّرِ الدِّينَ حِصنَ دَولَتِكَ، والشُّكرَ حِرزَ نِعمَتِكَ، فَكُلُّ دَولَةٍ يَحوطُها الدِّينُ لا تُغلَبُ، وكُلُّ نِعمَةٍ يَحرُزُها الشُّكرُ لا تُسلَبُ.[٢٥٢٦]

2262. **Imām ʿAlī (AS) said,** 'One of the signs of a [stable] government is vigilance in safeguarding matters.'[2541]

٢٢٦٢. عنه عليه السلام: مِن أماراتِ الدَّولةِ اليَقَظَةُ لِحراسَةِ الأُمورِ.[٢٥٢٧]

144

REMEDY

الدَّواءُ

729. To Treat Oneself

٧٢٩ ـ التَّداوي

2263. **Imām al-Ṣādiq (AS) said,** 'A prophet from among the prophets fell sick and said, 'I will not treat myself [with medicine] until the One who made me sick heals me'. Then Allah revealed to him saying, 'I will not heal you until you treat yourself [with medicine] for verily the healing is from Me.'[2542]

٢٢٦٣. الإمامُ الصّادقُ عليه السلام: إنَّ نبيّاً مِنَ الأنبياءِ مَرِضَ، فقالَ: لا أتَداوىٰ حتّىٰ يكونَ الذي أمرَضَنِي هُو الذي يَشفينِي، فأوحَى اللهُ تعالىٰ إلَيهِ: لا أشفِيكَ حتّىٰ تَتَداوىٰ، فإنَّ الشِّفاءَ مِنّي.[٢٥٢٨]

730. There is a Cure for Every Ailment

٧٣٠ ـ لِكُلِّ عِلَّةٍ دَواءٌ

2264. **The Prophet (SAWA) said,** 'Treat yourselves with medicine, for verily Allah has not sent down any

٢٢٦٤. رسولُ اللهِ صلى الله عليه وآله: تَداوَوا فإنَّ اللهَ تعالىٰ لَم

ailment except that he has sent down a cure for it with the exception of death and old age.'[2543]

يُنزِلْ داءً إلّا وقد أنزَلَ اللهُ لَـهُ شِـفاءً، إلّا السّـامَ والهَرَمَ.[٢٥٢٩]

2265. **Imām ʿAlī (AS) said,** 'For every ailment, there is a cure.'[2544]

٢٢٦٥. الإمامُ عليٌّ ؑ: لِكُلِّ عِلّةٍ دَواءٌ.[٢٥٣٠]

731. Beware of Hastening towards Resorting to Medicine

٧٣١ـ إيّاكَ والتَّسَرُّعَ في تَناوُلِ الدَّواءِ

2266. **The Prophet (SAWA) said,** 'Avoid medicine as long as your body can bear the ailment, but if it cannot bear the ailment, then resort to medicine.'[2545]

٢٢٦٦. رسولُ اللهِ ﷺ: تَجَنَّبِ الدَّواءَ ما احتَمَلَ بَدَنُكَ الداءَ، فإذا لم يَحتَمِلِ الداءَ فالدواءُ.[٢٥٣١]

2267. **Imām ʿAlī (AS) said,** 'A Muslim does not seek to treat himself [with medicine] until the ailment overcomes his health.'[2546]

٢٢٦٧. الإمامُ عليٌّ ؑ: لا يَتَداوَى المُسلِمُ حتّىٰ يَغلِبَ مَرَضُهُ صِحَّتَهُ.[٢٥٣٢]

2268. **Imām al-Kāẓim (AS) said,** 'There is no medicine except that it exacerbates another ailment, and there is nothing more beneficial to the body than self-restraint from all except that which the body needs.'[2547]

٢٢٦٨. الإمامُ الكاظمُ ؑ: لَيسَ مِن دواءٍ إلّا وهو يُهَيِّجُ داءً، وليسَ شيءٌ في البَدنِ أنفَعَ مِن إمساكِ اليدِ إلّا عمّا يَحتاجُ إلَيهِ.[٢٥٣٣]

732. Diet Control is the Fountainhead of Remedies

٧٣٢ـ الحِميةُ رَأسُ الدَّواءِ

2269. **Imām ʿAlī (AS) said,** 'Starving out is the best of remedies.'[2548]

٢٢٦٩. الإمامُ عليٌّ ؑ: التَّجوُّعُ أنفَعُ الدواءِ.[٢٥٣٤]

2270. **Imām al-Ṣādiq (AS) said,** 'Dieting from food causes no harm to the sick person.'[2549]

٢٢٧٠. الإمامُ الصادقُ ؑ: لا يَضُـرُّ المَـريضَ ما حَمَيتَ عنهُ الطَّعامَ.[٢٥٣٥]

2271. **Imām al-Ṣādiq (AS) said,** '[Starting to] Diet from food is of no benefit to the sick person after seven days.'[2550]

٢٢٧١. عنه ؑ: لا تَنفَعُ الحِميَةُ لمريضٍ بعدَ سبعَةِ أيّامٍ.[٢٥٣٦]

2272. **Imām al-Kāẓim (AS) said,** 'Diet control is the fountainhead of remedies and the stomach is the house of all ailments, so condition your body while it can be conditioned.'[2551]

٢٢٧٢. الإمامُ الكاظمُ ؑ: الحِميةُ رأسُ الدواءِ، والمَعِدةُ بيتُ الداءِ، عَوِّدْ بَدَناً ما تَعَوَّدَ.[٢٥٣٧]

2273. **Imām al-Kāẓim (AS) said,** 'Diet control is not to avoid eating absolutely anything, rather diet control is to eat lightly.'[2552]

٢٢٧٣ . عنه عليه السلام : لَيسَ الحِميةُ أن تَدَعَ الشيءَ أصلاً لا تأكُلَهُ، ولكنَّ الحِميَةَ أن تأكُلَ مِنَ الشيءِ وتُخَفِّفَ.[٢٥٣٨]

733. The Greatest Remedy

٧٣٣ ـ الدَّواءُ الأكبَرُ

2274. **Imām al-Ṣādiq (AS) said,** 'In the soil of the grave of Ḥusayn (AS) is a healing for every disease, for it is the greatest remedy.'[2553]

٢٢٧٤ . الإمامُ الصّادقُ عليه السلام : في طِينِ قبرِ الحسينِ عليه السلام الشِّفاءُ مِن كلِّ داءٍ وهُوَ الدواءُ الأكبَرُ.[٢٥٣٩]

734. Miscellaneous

٧٣٤ ـ النَّوادِرُ

2275. **Imām ʿAlī (AS) said,** 'It is possible for a medicine to be an ailment and an ailment to be a medicine.'[2554]

٢٢٧٥ . الإمامُ عليٌّ عليه السلام : ربّما كانَ الدَّواءُ داءً والدّاءُ دواءً.[٢٥٤٠]

2276. **Imām ʿAlī (AS) said,** 'The pain of one who cannot bear the bitterness of a remedy will continue.'[2555]

٢٢٧٦ . عنه عليه السلام : مَن لم يَحتَمِلْ مَرارَةَ الدواءِ دامَ ألَمُهُ.[٢٥٤١]

2277. **Imām al-Ḥusayn (AS) said,** 'Do not prescribe any remedy for a [arrogant] ruler, for if it benefits him, he will fail to show gratitude to you, and if it harms him he will accuse you.'[2556]

٢٢٧٧ . الإمامُ الحسينُ عليه السلام : لا تَصِفَنَّ لِمَلِكٍ دواءً، فإن نَفَعَهُ لَم يَحمَدْكَ، وإن ضَرَّهُ اتَّهَمَكَ.[٢٥٤٢]

145

RELIGION

الدِّينُ

735. Importance of Religion

٧٣٥ ـ أهَمِّيَّةُ الدِّينِ

2278. **Imām ʿAlī (AS) said,** 'Whoever gives acute attention to their religion will have a lofty station on the Day of Resurrection.'[2557]

٢٢٧٨ . الإمامُ عليٌّ عليه السلام : مَن دَقَّ في الدِّينِ نَظَرُهُ جَلَّ يومَ القِيامَةِ خَطَرُهُ.[٢٥٤٣]

2279. **Imām ʿAlī (AS) said,** 'Religion is light.'[2558]

٢٢٧٩ . عنه عليه السلام : الدِّينُ نورٌ.[٢٥٤٤]

2280. **Imām ʿAlī (AS) said,** 'There is no life but with religion and no death but with denial of sincere belief.'[2559]

٢٢٨٠ . عنه عليه السلام : لا حياةَ إلّا بالدِّينِ، ولا مَوتَ إلّا بجُحُودِ اليقينِ.[٢٥٤٥]

2281. **Imām ʿAlī (AS) said,** 'Religion immunizes.'[2560]

٢٢٨١ . عنه ﷺ : الدِّينُ يَعصِمُ.[٢٥٤٦]

2282. **Imām ʿAlī (AS) said,** 'Religion is the strongest support.'[2561]

٢٢٨٢ . عنه ﷺ : الدِّينُ أقوَى عِمادٍ.[٢٥٤٧]

2283. **Imām al-Ṣādiq (AS) said,** 'The Commander of the Faithful (AS) would frequently say in his sermons, 'O people! Preserve your religion, for the bad deed of a religious person is better than the good deed of a religion-less person, because the bad deed of a religious person can be forgiven but the good deed of a religion-less person is not accepted.'[2562]

٢٢٨٣ . الإمامُ الصّادقُ ﷺ : كانَ أميرُ المؤمنينَ ﷺ كثيراً مّا يقولُ في خُطبتِهِ : يا أيّها النّاسُ ، دِينَكُم دِينَكم !! فإنّ السيّئةَ فيهِ خيرٌ مِن الحَسَنةِ في غَيرِهِ ، والسيّئةَ فيهِ تُغفَرُ ، والحَسَنةَ في غيرِهِ لا تُقبَلُ.[٢٥٤٨]

736. The Bane of Religion

٧٣٦ ـ آفاتُ الدِّينِ

2284. **Imām ʿAlī (AS) said,** 'The bane of religion is suspiciousness.'[2563]

٢٢٨٤ . الإمامُ عليٌّ ﷺ : آفَةُ الدِّينِ سُوءُ الظَّنِّ.[٢٥٤٩]

2285. **Imām ʿAlī (AS) said,** 'The corruption of religion lies in [the vanities of] this world.'[2564]

٢٢٨٥ . عنه ﷺ : فسادُ الدِّينِ الدنيا.[٢٥٥٠]

2286. **Imām al-Ṣādiq (AS) said,** 'The bane of religion is in jealousy, self-conceit and pride.'[2565]

٢٢٨٦ . الإمامُ الصّادقُ ﷺ : آفَةُ الدِّينِ : الحَسَدُ والعُجبُ والفَخرُ.[٢٥٥١]

737. Encouragement to Preserve Religion

٧٣٧ ـ الحَثُّ عَلَى الحِفاظِ عَلَى الدِّينِ

2287. **Imām ʿAlī (AS) said,** 'If you are faced with a tribulation, shield your life with your wealth. If you are faced with a calamity, then shield your religion with your life, and know that the ruined man is he who destroys his religion himself and that the corrupted one is he who spoils his religion himself.'[2566]

٢٢٨٧ . الإمامُ عليٌّ ﷺ : إذا حَضَرَت بَلِيَّةٌ فاجعَلُوا أموالَكُم دونَ أنفسِكُم ، وإذا نَزَلَت نازلةٌ فاجعَلُوا أنفسَكُم دونَ دِينِكُم ، واعلَمُوا أنَّ الهالِكَ مَن هَلَكَ دِينُهُ ، والحَريبَ مَن حُرِبَ دِينُهُ.[٢٥٥٢]

2288. **Imām al-Ṣādiq (AS)** would say when struck with an affliction, 'All praise be to Allah who did not allow my religion to be afflicted.'[2567]

٢٢٨٨ . الإمامُ الصّادقُ ﷺ ـ كانَ يقولُ عندَ المُصيبةِ ـ : الحمدُ للهِ الذي لم يَجعَلْ مُصِيبَتِي في دِينِي.[٢٥٥٣]

738. Those Who have no Religion

٧٣٨ـ لا دين لِهؤلاء

2289. **Imām al-Bāqir (AS) said,** 'One who subjects himself to the obedience of someone who disobeys Allah has no religion, and the one who subjects himself to attributing a lie or falsity to Allah has no religion, and the one who subjects himself to denying any of Allah's signs has no religion.'[2568]

٢٢٨٩ . الإمامُ الباقرُ عليه السلام : لا دِينَ لِمَن دانَ بطاعةِ مَن عَصَى اللهَ ، ولا دِينَ لِمَن دانَ بِفِريَةٍ باطلٍ على اللهِ ، ولا دِينَ لِمَن دانَ بجُحُودِ شَيءٍ مِن آياتِ اللهِ .[٢٥٥٤]

2290. **Imām al-Ṣādiq (AS) said,** 'He who subjects himself to following an oppressive leader unendorsed by Allah has no religion.'[2569]

٢٢٩٠ . الإمامُ الصّادقُ عليه السلام : لادِينَ لِمَن دانَ بولايةِ إمامٍ جائرٍ لَيسَ مِنَ اللهِ .[٢٥٥٥]

2291. **Imām al-Ṣādiq (AS) said,** 'The one who has no covenant has no religion.'[2570]

٢٢٩١ . عنه عليه السلام : لادِينَ لِمَن لاعَهدَ له .[٢٥٥٦]

2292. **Imām al-Ṣādiq (AS) said,** 'Anyone whose love and hate is not based on religion, has no religion.'[2571]

٢٢٩٢ . عنه عليه السلام : كُلُّ مَن لم يُحِبَّ على الدِّينِ ولم يُبغِضْ على الدِّينِ فلا دينَ لَهُ .[٢٥٥٧]

2293. **Imām al-Kāẓim (AS) said,** 'He who has no valorous qualities has no religion.'[2572]

٢٢٩٣ . الإمامُ الكاظمُ عليه السلام : لادِينَ لِمَن لا مُرُوَّةَ لَهُ .[٢٥٥٨]

2294. **Imām al-Riḍā (AS) said,** 'He who has no piety has no religion.'[2573]

٢٢٩٤ . الإمامُ الرِّضا عليه السلام : لادِينَ لِمَن لاوَرَعَ لَهُ .[٢٥٥٩]

739. The Simplicity of Religion

٧٣٩ـ يَسارُ الدِّينِ

2295. **The Prophet (SAWA) said,** 'O people, verily the religion of Allah is easy.'[2574]

٢٢٩٥ . رسولُ اللهِ صلى الله عليه وآله : يا أيّها الناسُ ، إنَّ دِينَ اللهِ يُسرٌ .[٢٥٦٠]

2296. **The Prophet (SAWA) said,** 'I have been sent [to you] with the upright and liberal religion and whoever defies my prophetic practice is not from me.'[2575]

٢٢٩٦ . عنه صلى الله عليه وآله : بُعِثتُ بِالحَنِيفِيَّةِ السَّمْحَةِ ، ومَن خالَفَ سُنَّتِي فلَيسَ مِنّي .[٢٥٦١]

2297. **The Prophet (SAWA) said,** 'Verily Allah has not sent me with monasticism, rather the best religion with Allah is the upright and liberal one.'[2576]

٢٢٩٧ . عنه صلى الله عليه وآله : إنّ اللهَ لم يَبعَثْنِي بالرَّهبانِيَّةِ ، وإنّ خيرَ الدِينِ عندَ اللهِ الحنيفيّةُ السَّمْحَةُ .[٢٥٦٢]

740. The Only Religion Through Which Deeds are Accepted

٧٤٠ـ الدِّينُ الَّذي لا تُقبَلُ الأعمالُ إلّا بِهِ

"Should anyone follow a religion other than Islam, it shall never be accepted from him"[2577]

﴿وَمَن يَبْتَغِ غَيرَ الْإِسْلامِ دِيناً فَلَن يُقْبَلَ مِنْهُ وَهُوَ فِي الآخِرَةِ مِنَ الخاسِرِينَ﴾.[٢٥٦٣]

2298. It is narrated in *al-Kāfī* that ʿAlī b. Abī Ḥamza narrated from Abū Baṣīr who said: 'I heard him asking Abū ʿAbdullah [al-Ṣādiq] (AS): 'May I be sacrificed for you, please inform me about the religion that Allah has obligated upon His servants. The religion that they cannot afford to be ignorant of and the only religion that will be accepted from them. What is it?' The Imām (AS) replied, 'Bearing witness that there is no god except Allah and that Muḥammad (SAWA) is the Messenger of Allah, establishing the prayer, paying the alms-tax, pilgrimage to the House for those who are able to do so, fasting the month of Ramaḍān.' Then the Imām momentarily paused and then repeated twice, 'and divine guardianship [of the divinely appointed Imāms] (*al-wilāya*).'[2578]

٢٢٩٨ . الكافي عن عليِّ بنِ أبي حمزَةَ عن أبي بصيرٍ، قال: سمعتُهُ يسألُ أبا عبدِاللهِ عليه السلام فقالَ له: جُعِلتُ فِداكَ أخبِرْني عنِ الدِّينِ الذي افتَرَضَ اللهُ عزّوجلّ عَلى العبادِ ما لا يَسَعُهُم جَهلُهُ، ولا يُقبَلُ مِنهُم غيرُهُ ماهو؟ فقالَ: شهادةُ أن لا إلٰهَ إلّا اللهُ، وأنّ محمّداً رسولُ اللهِ صلى الله عليه وآله، وإقامُ الصلاةِ، وإيتاءُ الزكاةِ، وحجُّ البيتِ مَنِ استَطاعَ إلَيهِ سبيلاً، وصومُ شَهرِ رمضانَ. ثُمّ سَكَتَ قليلاً ثُمّ قالَ: والوَلايةُ ـ مَرّتَينِ ـ.[٢٥٦٤]

741. The Correct Way to Understanding Religion

٧٤١ـ المَنهَجُ في مَعرِفَةِ الدِّينِ

2299. **Imām al-Ṣādiq (AS) said,** 'The one who understands his religion from the Book of Allah, mountains will move before he does [in his faith], and the one who enters a matter with ignorance [i.e. accepts religion ignorantly] will leave it in ignorance.'[2579]

٢٢٩٩ . الإمامُ الصّادقُ عليه السلام : مَن عَرَفَ دينَهُ مِن كتابِ اللهِ عزّوجلّ زالَتِ الجِبالُ قبلَ أن يَزُولَ، ومَن دَخَلَ في أمرٍ بِجَهلٍ خَرَجَ منهُ بِجَهلٍ.[٢٥٦٥]

2300. **Imām al-Ṣādiq (AS) said,** 'The one who enters this religion through men will exit it through men just as they caused him to enter it. And whoever enters this religion through the Book and the prophetic practice, mountains will move before he does [in his faith].'[2580]

٢٣٠٠ . عنه عليه السلام :مَن دَخَلَ في هذاالدِّينِ بالرِّجالِ أخرَجَهُ مِنهُ الرِّجالُ كما أدخَلُوهُ فيهِ، ومَن دَخَلَ فيهِ بِالكِتابِ والسُّنَّةِ زالَتِ الجبالُ قَبلَ أن يَزولَ.[٢٥٦٦]

742. Protecting the Religion By Means of the World

٧٤٢ـ صِيانَةُ الدِّين بِالدُّنيا

2301. **Imām ʿAlī (AS) said,** 'Protect your religion by means of your worldly affairs and you will profit in both, but do not use your religion to protect your worldly affairs as you will lose them both.'[2581]

٢٣٠١ . الإمامُ عليٌّ عليه السلام : صُن دِينَكَ بدُنياكَ تَربَحْهُما، ولا تَصُنْ دنياكَ بِدِينِكَ فتَخسَرَهُما.[٢٥٦٧]

2302. **Imām ʿAlī (AS) said,** 'No sooner do people omit any aspect of their religion for the sake of improving their worldly affairs than Allah will open for them something that will be more detrimental to them [than the improvement of their worldly affairs].'[2582]

٢٣٠٢ . عنه عليه السلام : لا يَترُكُ الناسُ شيئاً مِن دِينِهِم لِإصلاحِ دُنياهُم إلّا فَتَحَ اللهُ عَليهِم ما هُوَ أضَرُّ مِنهُ.[٢٥٦٨]

743. Supplication for Affirming the Heart towards Religion

٧٤٣ـ الدُّعاءُ لِتَثبيتِ القَلبِ عَلَى الدِّينِ

2303. **Imām al-Ṣādiq (AS) said,** 'You will be afflicted with an obscure matter that will leave you with no sign to indicate to the solution, nor a leader to guide the way. None shall be saved from it except the one who recites the 'Supplication of the Drowning Person'. [The narrator says] I asked the Imām, 'What is the Supplication of the Drowning Person?' The Imām replied, 'O Allah, O the Beneficent, O the Merciful, O He who causes the hearts to fluctuate, affirm my heart upon Your religion.'[2583]

٢٣٠٣ . كمال الدين عن عبدالله بن سنان : قال أبو عبد الله عليه السلام : سَتُصيبُكُم شُبهَةٌ فَتَبقُونَ بِلا عَلَمٍ يُرىٰ ولا إمامٍ هدىً، ولا يَنجُو مِنها إلّا مَن دَعا بدُعاءِ الغَريقِ. قلتُ : كيفَ دعاءُ الغَريقِ ؟ قالَ : يقولُ : «يا اللهُ يا رحمٰنُ يا رحيمُ يا مُقَلِّبَ القُلوبِ ثَبِّتْ قَلبِي علىٰ دِينِكَ».[٢٥٦٩]

744. Characteristics of the Preservers of Allah's Religion

٧٤٤ـ صِفَةُ المُستَحفِظينَ لِدِينِ اللهِ

2304. **Imām ʿAlī (AS) said,** 'Verily the preservers of Allah's religion are the same people who established the religion and helped it, they guarded it from all sides, they preserved it for the servants of Allah and carefully watched over it.'[2584]

٢٣٠٤ . الإمامُ عليٌّ عليه السلام : إنّما المُستَحفِظُونَ لِدِينِ اللهِ هُمُ الذينَ أقامُوا الدِّينَ ونَصَرُوهُ، وحاطُوهُ مِن جميعِ جَوانِبِهِ، وحَفِظُوهُ علىٰ عِبادِ اللهِ ورَعَوهُ.[٢٥٧٠]

745. The Strengthening of Religion through a Disgraceful People

٧٤٥ـ تأييدُ الدِّينِ بأقوامٍ لا خَلاقَ لَهُم

2305. **The Prophet (SAWA) said,** 'Verily Allah strengthens this religion through an oppressive man.'2585

٢٣٠٥ . رسولُ اللهِ ﷺ : إنّ اللهَ لَيُؤَيِّدُ هذا الدِّينَ بالرَّجُلِ الفاجِرِ.٢٥٧١

2306. **The Prophet (SAWA) said,** 'Verily Allah, Blessed and most High, strengthens this religion through a disgraceful people.'2586

٢٣٠٦ . عنه ﷺ : إنّ اللهَ تَبارَكَ وتَعالىٰ يُؤَيِّدُ هذا الدِّينَ بأقوامٍ لا خَلاقَ لَهُم.٢٥٧٢

146

DEBT

الدَّين

746. Denouncing Borrowing

٧٤٦ـ ذَمُّ الاستدانة

2307. **The Prophet (SAWA) said,** 'Beware of debt for verily it is a source of anxiety in the night and a source of disgrace during the day.'2587

٢٣٠٧ . رسولُ اللهِ ﷺ : إيّاكم والدَّينَ، فإنّه هَمٌّ بالليلِ وذُلٌّ بالنهارِ.٢٥٧٣

2308. **Imām 'Alī (AS) said,** 'Copious debts transform the truthful man into a liar and an achiever into one who is unreliable.'2588

٢٣٠٨ . الإمامُ عليٌّ ع : كَثرَةُ الدَّينِ تُصَيِّرُ الصادِقَ كاذِباً والمُنجِزَ مُخْلِفاً.٢٥٧٤

2309. **Imām al-Ṣādiq (AS) said,** 'Lighten your debts, for verily with little debt comes longer life.'2589

٢٣٠٩ . الإمامُ الصّادقُ ع : خَفِّفوا الدَّينَ، فإنّ في خِفَّةِ الدَّينِ زِيادَةَ العُمُرِ.٢٥٧٥

747. Permission to Incur Debt when in Need

٧٤٧ـ جوازُ الاستِدانَةِ مَعَ الحاجَةِ

2310. **Imām al-Kāẓim (AS) said,** 'One who seeks to gain sustenance for himself and his family in a lawful manner is as the one who fights in the way of Allah. But if he is unable to do so he may incur

٢٣١٠ . الإمامُ الكاظمُ ع : مَن طَلَبَ هذا الرِّزقَ مِن حِلِّهِ لِيَعودَ بِهِ عَلىٰ نَفسِهِ وعِيالِهِ كانَ كالمُجاهِدِ في سبيلِ اللهِ عزّ وجلّ، فإن غَلَبَ

debt, trusting in Allah and His Prophet, in order to ensure provisions for his family.'[2590]

علَيهِ فَلْيَستَدِنْ عَـلَى اللهِ وعَـلىٰ رسـولِهِ ﷺ مـا يَقوتُ بِهِ عِيالَهُ.[٢٥٧٦]

748. Encouragement to Write a Contract for Any Loan

٧٤٨ـ الحَثُّ علىٰ كِتابَةِ الدَّينِ

"O you who have faith! When you contract a loan for a specified term, write it down."[2591]

﴿يا أيُّها الَّذِينَ آمَنُوا إذا تَدايَنْتُم بِدَيْنٍ إلَى أجَلٍ مُسَمًّى فَاكْتُبُوهُ﴾.[٢٥٧٧]

2311. **The Prophet (SAWA) said,** 'There are certain types of people whose supplications are not answered. From among them is the man who lends money to someone for a specified time and neither writes it down nor has anyone witness it.'[2592]

٢٣١١. رسولُ اللهِ ﷺ: أصنافٌ لا يُستَجابُ لَهُم، مِنهُم مَن أدانَ رَجُلاً دَيناً إلىٰ أجَلٍ فلَم يَكتُبْ علَيهِ كِتاباً ولَم يُشهِدْ علَيهِ شُهُوداً.[٢٥٧٨]

749. Prohibition of the Postponement of Repaying Debts

٧٤٩ـ النَّهيُ عَنِ المُماطَلَةِ فِي الدَّينِ

2312. **The Prophet (SAWA) said,** 'Whoever postpones repaying someone their right while he is capable of doing has the sin of an extortionist written down for him as every day passes by.'[2593]

٢٣١٢. رسولُ اللهِ ﷺ: مَن يَمطُلْ علىٰ ذِي حَقٍّ حَقَّهُ وهُو يَقدِرُ علىٰ أداءِ حَقِّهِ فعلَيهِ كُلَّ يومٍ خَطيئةُ عَشّارٍ.[٢٥٧٩]

2313. **The Prophet (SAWA) said,** 'A wealthy man's postponement [in repayment of a debt] is oppression.'[2594]

٢٣١٣. عنه ﷺ: مَطْلُ الغَنِيِّ ظُلْمٌ.[٢٥٨٠]

2314. **Imām ʿAlī (AS) said,** 'The most miserly person with regards to his wealth is the most liberal in squandering away his reputation.'[2595]

٢٣١٤. الإمامُ عليٌّ ﷺ: أبخَلُ الناسِ بِعَرَضِهِ أسخاهُم بِعِرضِهِ.[٢٥٨١]

(See also: CHARITY: section 1117)

(أُنظر) الصدقة: باب ١١١٧.

147

REMEMBRANCE

الذِّكر

750. The Virtue of the Remembrance of Allah

٧٥٠ ـ فَضلُ ذِكرِ اللهِ

"O you who have faith! Do not let your possessions and your children distract you from the remembrance of Allah, and whoever does that – it is they who are the losers."[2596]

﴿يَـٰٓأَيُّهَا ٱلَّذِينَ ءَامَنُوا لَا تُلْهِكُمْ أَمْوَٰلُكُمْ وَلَآ أَوْلَـٰدُكُمْ عَن ذِكْرِ ٱللَّهِ وَمَن يَفْعَلْ ذَٰلِكَ فَأُوْلَـٰٓئِكَ هُمُ ٱلْخَـٰسِرُونَ﴾ .[٢٥٨٢]

(See also: Qur'an, 2:152, 3:41, 3:191, 4:142, 7:180, 7:205, 9:67, 18:24, 18:28, 20:34, 20:42, 24:37, 26:227, 29:45, 33:21, 33:35, 33:41, 62:10, 73:8)

(أنظر) البقرة: ١٥٢ وآل عمران: ٤١، ١٩١ والنساء: ١٤٢ والاعراف: ١٨٠، ٢٠٥ والتوبة: ٦٧ والكهف: ٢٤، ٢٨ وطه: ٣٤، ٤٢ والنور: ٣٧ والشعراء: ٢٢٧ والعنكبوت: ٤٥ والأحزاب: ٢١، ٣٥، ٤١ والجمعة: ١٠ والمزمّل: ٨.

2315. **The Prophet (SAWA) said,** 'Never prefer anything above the remembrance of Allah for verily He says, *"and the remembrance of Allah is surely greater."*'[2597]

٢٣١٥ . رسولُ اللهِ ﷺ : لا تَختارَنَّ عَلىٰ ذِكرِ اللهِ شَيئاً فإنّهُ يقولُ : ﴿وَلَذِكْرُ اللهِ أكْبَرُ﴾ .[٢٥٨٣]

2316. **The Prophet (SAWA) said,** 'There is no action more beloved to Allah Almighty, or more successful as a means of salvation for a servant of Allah from all the evil of this world and the next than the remembrance of Allah.' Someone then asked, 'Not even fighting in the way of Allah?' The Prophet (SAWA) replied, 'If it was not for the remembrance of Allah, there would be no command to fight in the way of Allah.'[2598]

٢٣١٦ . كنز العمّال عن معاذ عنه ﷺ : لَيسَ عَمَلٌ أحَبَّ إلى اللهِ تعالىٰ ولا أنجىٰ لِعَبدٍ مِن كُلِّ سيّئةٍ في الدنيا والآخِرَةِ مِن ذِكرِ اللهِ . قيلَ : ولا القتالُ في سبيلِ اللهِ ؟ قالَ : لولا ذِكرُ اللهِ لم يُؤمَرْ بالقِتالِ .[٢٥٨٤]

2317. **Imām ʿAlī (AS) said,** 'Remembrance is a source of great pleasure for the lovers [of Allah].'[2599]

٢٣١٧ . الإمامُ عليٌّ ؑ : الذِّكرُ لَذَّةُ المُحِبّينَ .[٢٥٨٥]

2318. **Imām ʿAlī (AS) said,** 'Remembrance is sitting in the company of the Beloved One.'[2600]

٢٣١٨ . عنه ؑ : الذِّكرُ مُجالَسَةُ المَحبوبِ .[٢٥٨٦]

2319. **Imām ʿAlī (AS) said,** 'Remembrance of Allah is the natural disposition of every good-doer and the distinguishing mark of every believer.'[2601]

٢٣١٩ . عنه ؑ : ذِكرُ اللهِ سَجِيَّةُ كُلِّ مُحسِنٍ وشِيمَةُ كُلِّ مُؤمِنٍ .[٢٥٨٧]

751. Enjoinment of Frequent Remembrance [of Allah]

٧٥١ـ الحَثُّ عَلىٰ كَثرَةِ الذِّكرِ

"O you who have faith! Remember Allah with a frequent remembrance, and glorify Him morning and evening."[2602]

﴿يا أيُّها الَّذينَ آمَنوا اذكُروا اللهَ ذِكراً كَثيراً * وَسَبِّحوهُ بُكرَةً وَأصيلاً﴾ .٢٥٨٨

2320. **The Prophet (SAWA) said,** 'I urge you to recite the Qur'an and remember Allah frequently, for verily it [will result in] a remembrance for you in the heavens and a light for you in the earth.'[2603]

٢٣٢٠ . رسولُ اللهِ ﷺ : عَليكَ بِتِلاوَةِ القرآنِ وذِكرِ اللهِ كثيراً، فإنَّهُ ذِكرٌ لكَ في السماءِ ونورٌ لكَ في الأرضِ. ٢٥٨٩

2321. **Imām 'Alī (AS) said,** 'Whoever remembers Allah in private, has surely remembered Allah much.'[2604]

٢٣٢١ . الإمامُ عليٌّ (ع) : مَن ذَكَرَ اللهَ في السرِّ فقد ذَكَرَ اللهَ كثيراً. ٢٥٩٠

2322. **Imām al-Ṣādiq (AS) said,** 'Remember Allah frequently as much as you can every hour of the day and night, for verily Allah has commanded [us] to remember Him abundantly.'[2605]

٢٣٢٢ . الإمامُ الصّادقُ (ع) : أكثِروا ذِكرَ اللهِ ما استَطَعتُم في كُلِّ ساعةٍ مِن ساعاتِ الليلِ والنهارِ، فإنَّ اللهَ أمَرَ بكَثرَةِ الذِكرِ لَهُ. ٢٥٩١

2323. **Imām al-Ṣādiq (AS) said,** 'The glorification of Fāṭima al-Zahrā'[2606] (AS) is from the frequent remembrance which Allah mentions, *"Remember Allah with a frequent remembrance."*'[2607]

٢٣٢٣ . عنه (ع) : تَسبيحُ فاطمةَ الزهراءِ (ع) مِنَ الذِكرِ الكثيرِ الذي قالَ اللهُ عزّوجلّ: ﴿اُذكُروا اللهَ ذِكراً كثيراً﴾ . ٢٥٩٢

752. Enjoinment of Engaging in Continuous Remembrance

٧٥٢ـ الحَثُّ عَلىٰ دَوامِ الذِّكرِ

2324. **The Prophet (SAWA) said,** 'Every single hour that passes by the son of Adam, that was devoid of the remembrance of Allah will be grieved for on the Day of Resurrection.'[2608]

٢٣٢٤ . رسولُ اللهِ ﷺ : ما مِن ساعةٍ تَمُرُّ بابنِ آدمَ لَم يَذكُرِ اللهَ فيها إلّا حَسِرَ عليها يومَ القيامةِ. ٢٥٩٣

2325. **Imām 'Alī (AS) said** in the intimate supplication of the month of Sha'ban[2609], 'My God! Inspire me with fervour for Your remembrance until I have become inspired with Your remembrance, and a spiritual zeal for the refreshing salvation of Your Names and the place of Your sanctity.'[2610]

٢٣٢٥ . الإمامُ عليٌّ (ع) ـ في المُناجاةِ الشَّعبانيّةِ ـ: إلٰهي، وألْهِمني وَلَهاً بِذِكرِكَ إلىٰ ذِكرِكَ وهِمَّتي إلىٰ روحِ نَجاحِ أسمائكَ ومَحَلِّ قُدسِكَ. ٢٥٩٤

2326. **Imām ʿAlī (AS) said,** 'I ask You to send blessings on Muḥammad and the family of Muḥammad, and to make me of those who are continuous in Your remembrance and who do not breach Your covenant.'[2611]

٢٣٢٦. عنه ﷺ: أسألُكَ أن تُصَلِّيَ على محمّدٍ وآلِ محمّدٍ، وأن تجعَلَني مِمَّن يُدِيمُ ذِكرَكَ، ولا يَنقُضُ عَهدَكَ.[٢٥٩٥]

753. The Remembrance of Allah is Good at All Times

٧٥٣ـ ذِكرُ اللهِ حَسَنٌ عَلىٰ كُلِّ حالٍ

"Indeed in the creation of the heavens and the earth and the alteration of night and day, there are signs for those who possess intellects. Those who remember Allah standing, sitting, and lying on their sides."[2612]

﴿إنَّ في خَلْقِ السَّماوَاتِ والأَرْضِ واخْتِلَافِ اللَّيلِ والنَّهارِ لَآيَاتٍ لِأُولي الأَلْبابِ * الَّذِينَ يَذْكُرُونَ اللهَ قِيَاماً وَقُعُوداً وَعلىٰ جُنُوبِهِمْ﴾.[٢٥٩٦]

2327. **Imām ʿAlī (AS) said** in counsel to his son Ḥasan at the time of his death (AS), 'and be one to remember Allah at all times.'[2613]

٢٣٢٧. الإمامُ عليٌّ ﷺ ـ مِن وَصاياهُ لِابنِهِ الحسنِ ﷺ عِندَ الوَفاةِ ـ: وكُن للهِ ذاكِراً على كلِّ حالٍ.[٢٥٩٧]

2328. **Imām al-Ṣādiq (AS) narrated,** 'Prophet Moses (AS) said, 'My Lord, I am in a [base] state wherein I esteem You too highly to remember You therein', He said, 'O Moses, remember Me at all times.'[2614]

٢٣٢٨. الإمامُ الصّادقُ ﷺ: قالَ موسىٰ ﷺ: يا ربِّ، إنّي أكونُ في حالٍ أُجِلُّكَ أن أذكُرَكَ فيها. قالَ: يا موسى، أُذكُرْني على كُلِّ حالٍ.[٢٥٩٨]

754. The Ones Who Remember

٧٥٤ـ الذّاكرونَ

2329. **The Prophet (SAWA) said,** 'The one who remembers [Allah] in the midst of the neglectful ones is as one who fights [in the way of Allah] in the midst of others who flee [from the battle].'[2615]

٢٣٢٩. رسولُ اللهِ ﷺ: الذاكِرُ في الغافِلينَ كالمُقاتِلِ في الفارِّينَ.[٢٥٩٩]

2330. **The Prophet (SAWA) said,** 'Everyone will die thirsty except the one who remembers Allah.'[2616]

٢٣٣٠. عنه ﷺ: كُلُّ أحَدٍ يَموتُ عَطْشانَ إلّا ذاكِرَ اللهِ.[٢٦٠٠]

2331. **The Prophet (SAWA) narrated,** 'Verily when Moses, son of Amran (AS) would engage in intimate supplication with his Lord, he said, 'My Lord, are you so far from me that I should call

٢٣٣١. عنه ﷺ: إنّ موسى بنَ عِمرانَ ﷺ لَمّا ناجىٰ رَبَّهُ عزّوجلّ قالَ: يا ربِّ، أبَعيدٌ أنتَ مِنّي

You, or are You so near to me that I should whisper?' so Allah then revealed to Moses, 'I sit in close proximity with the one who remembers Me.'[2617]

فَـأُنادِيَكَ أمْ قَـريبٌ فَـأُناجِيَكَ ؟ فـأَوحَى اللهُ جلّ جلالُهُ : أنا جَلِيسُ مَن ذَكَرَني.[٢٦٠١]

2332. **Imām ʿAlī (AS) said,** 'The one who occupies himself with the remembrance of Allah, Allah beautifies his remembrance [among people].'[2618]

٢٣٣٢ . الإمامُ عليٌّ عليه السلام : مَنِ اشتَغَلَ بذِكرِ اللهِ طَيَّبَ اللهُ ذِكرَهُ.[٢٦٠٢]

2333. **Imām ʿAlī (AS) said,** 'The one who remembers Allah, glory be to Him, is sitting closely with Him.'[2619]

٢٣٣٣ . عنه عليه السلام : ذاكِرُ اللهِ سبحانَهُ مُجالِسُهُ.[٢٦٠٣]

2334. **Imām al-Bāqir (AS) said,** 'The believer remains in a state of prayer as long as he is remembering Allah, whether he is standing, sitting or lying down, for verily Allah says, *"Those who remember Allah standing, sitting and lying on their sides"*.'[2620] [2621]

٢٣٣٤ . الإمامُ الباقرُ عليه السلام : لا يَزالُ المُؤمنُ في صلاةٍ ما كانَ في ذِكرِ اللهِ، قائماً كانَ أو جالِساً أو مُضطَجِعاً، إنّ اللهَ تعالىٰ يقولُ ﴿اَلَّذِينَ يَذْكُرُونَ اللهَ قِياماً وقُعُوداً وعَلَى جُنوبِهِم...﴾.[٢٦٠٤] [٢٦٠٥]

2335. **Imām al-Ṣādiq (AS) said,** 'Verily the one who remembers Allah will never be struck by lightning.'[2622]

٢٣٣٥ . الإمامُ الصّادقُ عليه السلام : إنّ الصاعِقَةَ لا تُصِيبُ ذاكِراً للهِ عزّ وجلّ.[٢٦٠٦]

755. Remember Allah and He Will Remember You

٧٥٥ ـ أُذكُرو اللهَ يَذكُرُكُم

"Remember Me and I will remember you, and thank Me, and do not be ungrateful to Me."[2623]

﴿فَاذْكُرُونِي أذْكُرْكُمْ واشْكُرُوا لِي وَلا تَكفُرُونِ﴾.[٢٦٠٧]

2336. **Imām al-Ṣādiq (AS) said,** 'Allah Almighty said, 'O son of Adam, remember Me within yourself and I will remember you within Myself. O son of Adam, remember Me in secret and I will remember you when [you are] in secret. O son of Adam, remember Me when in an assembly and I will remember you in an assembly which is better than your assembly.'[2624]

٢٣٣٦ . الإمامُ الصّادقُ عليه السلام : قالَ اللهُ تعالىٰ : ابنَ آدمَ، اُذكُرْني في نَفسِكَ أذكُركَ في نَفسي. ابنَ آدمَ اُذكُرني في الخَلاءِ أذكُركَ في خَلاءٍ. ابنَ آدمَ اُذكُرني في مَلَأٍ أذكُرْكَ في مَلَأٍ خَيرٍ مِن مَلَئِكَ.[٢٦٠٨]

756. The Fruits of Remembrance

٧٥٦ـ ثَمَراتُ الذِّكرِ

"*– those who have faith, and whose hearts find rest in the remembrance of Allah. Look! The hearts find rest in the remembrance of Allah.*"[2625]

﴿الَّذِينَ آمَنُوا وَتَطْمَئِنُّ قُلُوبُهُم بِذِكْرِ اللهِ أَلَا بِذِكْرِ اللهِ تَطْمَئِنُّ الْقُلُوبُ﴾.[٢٦٠٩]

2337. **The Prophet (SAWA) said,** 'The remembrance of Allah is a healing for the hearts.'[2626]

٢٣٣٧. رسولُ اللهِ ﷺ: ذِكرُ اللهِ شِفاءُ القُلوبِ.[٢٦١٠]

2338. **The Prophet (SAWA) said,** 'The one who remembers Allah abundantly has freed himself from hypocrisy.'[2627]

٢٣٣٨. عنه ﷺ: مَن أكثَرَ مِن ذِكرِ اللهِ فقد بَرِئَ مِنَ النِّفاقِ.[٢٦١١]

2339. **The Prophet (SAWA) said,** 'The one who remembers Allah abundantly loves Him.'[2628]

٢٣٣٩. عنه ﷺ: مَن أكثَرَ ذِكرَ اللهِ أحَبَّهُ.[٢٦١٢]

2340. **Imām ʿAlī (AS) said,** 'The one whose heart thrives with the continuous remembrance of Allah, his actions will always be good whether done in secret or openly.'[2629]

٢٣٤٠. الإمامُ عليٌّ عليه السلام: مَن عَمَرَ قَلبَهُ بدَوامِ الذِكرِ حَسُنَت أفعالُهُ في السِّرِّ والجَهرِ.[٢٦١٣]

2341. **Imām ʿAlī (AS) said,** 'The root of reforming the heart is in occupying it with the remembrance of Allah.'[2630]

٢٣٤١. عنه عليه السلام: أصلُ صلاحِ القلبِ اشتِغالُهُ بذِكرِ اللهِ.[٢٦١٤]

2342. **Imām ʿAlī (AS) said,** 'Whoever remembers Allah, glory be to Him, Allah enlivens his heart and illuminates his intellect and the innermost core of his heart.'[2631]

٢٣٤٢. عنه عليه السلام: مَن ذَكَرَ اللهَ سبحانَهُ أحيا اللهُ قَلبَهُ ونَوَّرَ عَقلَهُ ولُبَّهُ.[٢٦١٥]

2343. **Imām ʿAlī (AS) said,** 'The remembrance of Allah is a provision for the souls and a close sitting in the company of the Beloved.'[2632]

٢٣٤٣. عنه عليه السلام: ذِكرُ اللهِ قُوتُ النُّفوسِ ومُجالَسَةُ المَحبوبِ.[٢٦١٦]

2344. **Imām ʿAlī (AS) said,** 'I urge you to keep up the remembrance of Allah for verily it is the light of the hearts.'[2633]

٢٣٤٤. عنه عليه السلام: عَليكَ بِذِكرِ اللهِ، فإنَّهُ نورُ القلوبِ.[٢٦١٧]

2345. **Imām ʿAlī (AS) said,** 'Continuous remembrance [of Allah] enlightens the heart and the mind.'[2634]

٢٣٤٥. عنه عليه السلام: دَوامُ الذِكرِ يُنيرُ القلبَ والفِكرَ.[٢٦١٨]

2346. **Imām ʿAlī (AS) said,** 'Verily Allah, Glory be to Him, has made [His] remembrance a polish for the hearts through which they hear after deafness, see after blindness and yield after resistance.'[2635]

٢٣٤٦. عنه ﵍: إنَّ اللهَ سبحانَهُ جَعَلَ الذِّكرَ جَلاءً للقُلوبِ، تَسمَعُ بِهِ بَعدَ الوَقْرَةِ، و تُبصِرُ بِهِ بَعدَ العَشْوَةِ، وتَنقادُ بِهِ بَعدَ المُعانَدَةِ.[٢٦١٩]

2347. **Imām ʿAlī (AS) said** in supplication, 'O He whose name is a remedy and whose remembrance is a healing.'[2636]

٢٣٤٧. عنه ﵍ ـ في الدُّعاءِ ـ: يا مَن اسمُهُ دواءٌ وذِكرُهُ شِفاءٌ.[٢٦٢٠]

2348. **Imām ʿAlī (AS) said,** 'Remembrance [of Allah] is the key to intimacy (with Him).'[2637]

٢٣٤٨. عنه ﵍: الذِّكرُ مِفتاحُ الاُنسِ.[٢٦٢١]

2349. **Imām ʿAlī (AS) said,** 'If you see that Allah, Glory be to Him, has made you intimate with His remembrance, then He loves you. If you see that Allah has made you intimate with His creation and banished you from His remembrance, then He has despised you.'[2638]

٢٣٤٩. عنه ﵍: إذا رَأيتَ اللهَ سُبحانَهُ يُؤنِسُكَ بِذِكرِهِ فقد أحَبَّكَ، إذا رَأيتَ اللهَ يُؤنِسُكَ بِخَلقِهِ ويوحِشُكَ مِن ذِكرِهِ فقد أبغَضَكَ.[٢٦٢٢]

2350. **Imām ʿAlī (AS) said,** 'The remembrance of Allah is a repellent of Satan.'[2639]

٢٣٥٠. عنه ﵍: ذِكرُ اللهِ مَطرَدَةُ الشيطانِ.[٢٦٢٣]

2351. **Imām ʿAlī (AS) said,** 'The remembrance of Allah is a polish for the breasts and a soothing for the hearts.'[2640]

٢٣٥١. عنه ﵍: ذِكرُ اللهِ جَلاءُ الصُّدورِ وطُمأنينَةُ القُلوبِ.[٢٦٢٤]

2352. **Imām ʿAlī (AS) said,** 'Remembrance [of Allah] expands the breasts.'[2641]

٢٣٥٢. عنه ﵍: الذِّكرُ يَشرَحُ الصَّدرَ.[٢٦٢٥]

757. Enjoinment of Remembrance of Allah in Certain Situations

٧٥٧ ـ الحَثُّ عَلى ذِكرِ اللهِ في مَواقِفَ

1. When Facing an Enemy:

أ ـ عِندَ لِقاءِ العَدُوِّ

"O you who have faith! When you meet a host [in battle], then stand firm, and remember Allah greatly so that you may be felicitous."[2642]

﴿يا أيُّها الَّذينَ آمَنوا إذا لَقيتُم فِئَةً فاثبُتوا واذكُرُوا اللهَ كَثيراً لَعَلَّكُم تُفلِحونَ﴾.[٢٦٢٦]

2353. **Imām ʿAlī (AS) said,** 'When you face your enemy in battle, then lessen your speech and increase in the remembrance of Allah.'[2643]

٢٣٥٣. الإمامُ عليٌّ ﵍: إذا لَقيتُم عَدُوَّكُم في الحَربِ فأقِلّوا الكلامَ وأكثِروا ذِكرَ اللهِ عزّ وجلّ.[٢٦٢٧]

2. When Entering the Market Place:

ب ـ عِند دُخولِ الأَسواقِ

2354. **Imām ʿAlī (AS) said,** 'Increase in the remembrance of Allah when you enter the market while people are busy, for verily it will be an expiation of your sins and an increase in good deeds, and you will not be recorded down as being amongst the neglectful ones.'[2644]

٢٣٥٤ . الإمامُ عليٌّ ﷺ : أكثِرُوا ذِكرَ اللهِ عزّ وجلّ إذا دَخَلتُمُ الأسواقَ عِندَ اشتِغالِ النـاسِ، فـإنَّهُ كَفّارةٌ لِلذُّنوبِ وزِيادَةٌ في الحَسَناتِ، ولا تُكتَبُوا في الغافِلينَ .٢٦٢٨

3. During Distress, When Giving Judgment and When Distributing:

ج ـ عند الهَمِّ والحُكم والقِسمَة

2355. **The Prophet (SAWA) said,** 'Remember Allah during your distress when you are distressed, with your tongue when you give judgment and with your hand when distributing anything.'[2645]

٢٣٥٥ . رسولُ اللهِ ﷺ : اُذكُرِ اللهَ عِندَ هَـمِّكَ إذا هَمَمتَ، وعِندَ لِسانِكَ إذا حَكَمتَ، وعِندَ يَدِكَ إذا قَسَمتَ .٢٦٢٩

4. When in Anger:

د ـ عند الغَضَبِ

2356. **The Prophet (SAWA) said,** 'Allah revealed to a prophet from among His prophets, 'O son of Adam, remember Me during your anger and I will remember you during My anger, and I will not destroy you as a result with those whom I destroy.'[2646]

٢٣٥٦ . رسولُ اللهِ ﷺ : أوحَى اللهُ إلى نبيٍّ مِـن أنبيائهِ : ابنَ آدَمَ، اذكُرني عِندَ غضبِكَ أذكُرْكَ عِندَ غَضَبِي ، فلا أمحَقُكَ فيمَن أمحَقُ .٢٦٣٠

5. When Alone and During Pleasures:

هـ ـ في الخَلَواتِ وعند اللَّذّاتِ

2357. **Imām al-Bāqir (AS) said,** 'It is written in the Torah: '...O Moses... remember Me in times of loneliness and when enjoying your pleasures and I will remember you in your times of negligence.'[2647]

٢٣٥٧ . الإمامُ الباقرُ ﷺ : في التَّوراةِ مَكتوبٌ : ... يا موسىٰ ... اُذكُرني في خَلَواتِكَ وعِـندَ سُـرورِ لَذّاتِكَ أذكُرْكَ عِندَ غَفَلاتِكَ .٢٦٣١

758. The Reality of the Remembrance [of Allah]

٧٥٨ ـ حَقيقَةُ الذِّكر

2358. **The Prophet (SAWA) said,** 'Whoever obeys Allah has remembered Him, even if his prayers, his fasts and his recitation of the Qur'an are few.'[2648]

٢٣٥٨ . رسولُ اللهِ ﷺ : مَن أطاعَ اللهَ عزّ وجلّ فَقَد ذَكَرَ اللهَ وإن قَـلَّتْ صَـلاتُهُ وصِـيامُهُ وتِـلاوَتُهُ لِلقرآنِ .٢٦٣٢

2359. **Imām al-Ṣādiq (AS) said,** with regard to the verse of Allah: *"and the remembrance of Allah is greater"* [2649], '[It means] Remembering Allah with regards to what He has made lawful and unlawful.'[2650]

٢٣٥٩ . الإمامُ الصّادقُ ﷺ ـ في قـولِهِ تـعالىٰ: ﴿ولَذِكْرُ اللهِ أَكبَرُ﴾ [٢٦٣٣] ـ: ذِكرُ اللهِ تَعالىٰ عِندَ ما أحَلَّ وحَرَّمَ.[٢٦٣٤]

2360. **Imām al-Ṣādiq (AS) said,** 'There are two types of remembrance, a sincere remembrance which is harmonious with the heart, and a mere remembrance which negates the remembrance of anyone other than Allah.'[2651]

٢٣٦٠ . عنه ﷺ :الذِّكرُ ذِكرانِ:ذِكرٌ خالِصٌ يُوافِقُهُ القَلبُ، وذِكرٌ صارِفٌ يَنفِي ذِكرَ غَيرِهِ.[٢٦٣٥]

2361. **Imām al-Ṣādiq (AS) said,** 'Make your remembrance of Allah for the sake of the fact that He remembers you, for verily He remembers you even though He is needless of you, so His remembrance of you is loftier, more desirable and more complete than your remembrance of Him and it supersedes it…so whoever wishes to remember Allah, most High, should know that as long as Allah does not remember His servant in the context of granting him divine succour to remember Him [in the first place], the servant will not be capable of remembering Him.'[2652]

٢٣٦١ . عنه ﷺ : اِجعَلْ ذِكرَ اللهِ مِن أجلِ ذِكرِهِ لكَ، فإنّهُ ذَكَرَكَ وهُو غَنِيٌّ عنكَ فَذِكرُهُ لكَ أجَلُّ وأشهىٰ وأتَمُّ مِن ذِكرِكَ لَهُ وأسبَقُ... فَمَن أرادَ أن يَذكرَ اللهَ تعالىٰ فَلْيَعلَمْ أنَّهُ ما لَم يَذكُرِ اللهُ العَبدَ بالتوفيقِ لِذِكرِهِ لا يَقدِرُ العَبدُ عَلىٰ ذِكرِهِ.[٢٦٣٦]

2362. **Imām al-Riḍā (AS) said,** 'Whoever remembers Allah but does not vie to meet Him has mocked himself.'[2653]

٢٣٦٢ . الإمامُ الرِّضا ﷺ :مَن ذَكَرَ اللهَ ولم يَستَبِقْ إلى لِقائهِ فَقدِ استَهزَأ بنَفسِهِ.[٢٦٣٧]

759. That Which Brings About Continuous Remembrance [of Allah]

٧٥٩ـ ما يوجِبُ دَوامَ الذِّكرِ

2363. In the tradition recounting the Prophet (SAWA)'s Ascension to the Heavens (*al-mi'rāj*): 'O Aḥmad… be continuous in My remembrance.' The Prophet (SAWA) asked, 'O My Lord, how can I be continuous in Your remembrance?' He replied, 'Through seclusion from people, despising the sweet and the sour [of the world], and clearing your stomach and your house of the world.'[2654]

٢٣٦٣ . بحار الأنوار : في حديثِ المعراجِ : يا أحمَدُ... دُمْ علىٰ ذِكرِي، فقالَ: يا ربِّ، وكَيفَ أدُومُ علىٰ ذِكرِكَ ؟ فقالَ: بالخَلوَةِ عنِ النـاسِ، وبُغضِكَ الحُلوَ والحامِضَ، وفَراغِ بَطنِكَ وبَيتِكَ مِنَ الدنيا.[٢٦٣٨]

2364. **Imām ʿAlī (AS) said,** 'Whoever loves something is engaged in remembrance of it.'[2655]

٢٣٦٤ . الإمامُ عليٌّ ﷺ : مَن أحَبَّ شيئاً لَهِجَ بِذِكرِهِ.[٢٦٣٩]

760. Factors that Prevent the Remembrance [of Allah]

٧٦٠ـ مَوانِعُ الذِّكرِ

"O You who have faith! Do not let your possessions and children distract you from the remembrance of Allah, and whoever does that – it is they who are the losers."[2656]

﴿يا أيُّهَا الَّذينَ آمَنُوا لا تُلْهِكُمْ أمْوالُكُمْ وَلا أوْلادُكُمْ عَنْ ذِكْرِ اللهِ وَمَنْ يَفْعَلْ ذٰلِكَ فَأُولٰئِكَ هُمُ الْخاسِرُونَ﴾ .[٢٦٤٠]

"Indeed Satan seeks to cast enmity and hatred among you through wine and gambling, and to hinder you from the remembrance of Allah and from prayer. Will you, then, relinquish?"[2657]

﴿إنَّما يُرِيدُ الشَّيْطانُ أنْ يُوقِعَ بَيْنَكُمُ الْعَداوَةَ والْبَغْضاءَ فِي الْخَمْرِ والْمَيْسِرِ وَيَصُدَّكُمْ عَنْ ذِكرِ اللهِ وَعَنِ الصَّلاةِ فَهَلْ أَنتُم مُّنتَهُونَ﴾ .[٢٦٤١]

2365. **Imām ʿAlī (AS) said,** 'There is nothing worse from amongst the transgressions than submitting to one's base desires, so do not obey them as they will preoccupy you from [remembering] Allah.'[2658]

٢٣٦٥ . الإمامُ عليٌّ ﷺ : لَيسَ في المعاصِي أشَدُّ مِنِ اتِّباعِ الشَّهوَةِ، فلا تُطِيعُوها فَتَشغَلَكُم عَنِ اللهِ.[٢٦٤٢]

2366. **Imām ʿAlī (AS) said,** 'Anything that distracts you from the remembrance of Allah is classified as gambling.'[2659]

٢٣٦٦ . عنه ﷺ : كُلُّ ما ألهىٰ عن ذِكرِ اللهِ فهو مِن المَيسِرِ.[٢٦٤٣]

2367. **Imām ʿAlī (AS) said,** 'Anything that distracts you from the remembrance of Allah is from Iblīs [Satan].'[2660]

٢٣٦٧ . عنه ﷺ : كُلُّ ما ألهىٰ عن ذِكرِ اللهِ فهو مِن إبليسَ.[٢٦٤٤]

2368. **Imām Zayn al-ʿĀbidīn (AS) said,** 'Verily filling the stomach, weakness of will, the intoxication of being fully satiated and the delusion of power, all hinder and delay one from the performance [of good deeds] and cause one to forget Allah.'[2661]

٢٣٦٨ . الإمامُ زينُ العابدينَ ﷺ : إنَّ قَسوَةَ البِطنَةِ وفَترَةَ المَيلَةِ وسُكرَ الشِّبَعِ وغِرَّةَ المُلكِ مِمّا يُثَبِّطُ ويُبطِئُ عَنِ العَمَلِ ويُنسِي الذِّكرَ.[٢٦٤٥]

761. The Effects of Disregarding the Remembrance [of Allah]

٧٦١ـ آثارُ الإعراضِ عَنِ الذِّكرِ

"But whoever disregards My remembrance, his shall be a wretched life, and on the Day of Resurrection We shall raise him blind. He will say, 'My Lord! Why have you raised me blind, though i used to see! He will say: 'So it is. Our signs came to you, but you forgot them, and thus you will be forgotten today.'"[2662]

﴿وَمَنْ أعْرَضَ عَنْ ذِكرِي فَإنَّ لَهُ مَعيشَةً ضَنْكاً[٢٦٤٦] وَنَحْشُرُهُ يَوْمَ القِيامَةِ أعْمىٰ * قالَ رَبِّ لِمَ حَشَرْتَنِي أعْمىٰ وَقَدْ كُنتُ بَصِيراً * قالَ كَذٰلِكَ أتَتْكَ آياتُنا فَنَسِيتَها وَكَذٰلِكَ الْيَوْمَ تُنْسىٰ﴾.[٢٦٤٧]

"Whoever turns a blind eye to the remembrance of the All-beneficent, We assign him a devil who remains his companion."[2663]

﴿وَمَنْ يَعْشُ عَنْ ذِكرِ الرَّحمٰنِ نُقَيِّضْ لَهُ شَيطاناً فَهُوَ لَهُ قَرِينٌ﴾.[٢٦٤٨]

"And do not be like those who forget Allah, so He makes them forget their own souls. It is they who are the transgressors."[2664]

﴿وَلا تَكُونُوا كَالَّذِينَ نَسُوا اللهَ فَأنْسَاهُمْ أنْفُسَهُم أُوْلَـٰئِكَ هُمُ الْفَاسِقُونَ﴾.[٢٦٤٩]

2369. **Imām ʿAlī (AS) said,** 'Whoever forgets Allah, Glory be to Him, Allah makes him forget himself and blinds his heart.'[2665]

٢٣٦٩ . الإمامُ عليٌّ عليه السلام : مَن نَسِيَ اللهَ سبحانَهُ أنساهُ اللهُ نفسَهُ وأعمىٰ قَلبَهُ .[٢٦٥٠]

762. Silent Remembrance

٧٦٢ـ الذِّكرُ الخَفِيُّ

"And remember your Lord within your heart beseechingly and reverentially, without being loud, morning and evening, and do not be among the heedless."[2666]

﴿واذْكُرْ رَبَّكَ فِي نَفْسِكَ تَضَرُّعاً وَخيفَةً وَدُونَ الجَهْرِ مِنَ الْقَوْلِ بِالغُدُوِّ والآصالِ وَلا تَكُنْ مِنَ الْغافِلِينَ﴾.[٢٦٥١]

2370. **The Prophet (SAWA) said,** 'The best remembrance is the silent type.'[2667]

٢٣٧٠ . رسولُ اللهِ صلى الله عليه وآله : خيرُ الذِّكرِ الخَفِيُّ.[٢٦٥٢]

2371. **Imām al-Bāqir or Imām al-Ṣādiq (AS) said,** 'The angel only writes down what he hears, but when Allah, Mighty and Exalted, has said, "*And remember your Lord within your heart...*", no one knows the reward of that remembrance in the heart of the servant except Allah, most High.'[2668]

٢٣٧١ . الإمامُ الباقرُ أو الإمامُ الصّادقُ عليهما السلام : لا يَكتُبُ المَلَكُ إلّا ما يَسمَعُ ، قالَ اللهُ عزّوجلّ : ﴿وَاذْكُرْ رَبَّكَ في نَفسِكَ﴾ : لا يَعلمُ ثوابَ ذلكَ الذِّكرِ في نَفسِ العَبدِ غيرُ اللهِ تعالىٰ.[٢٦٥٣]

148

DISGRACE

الذِّلَّة

763. Disgrace

٧٦٣-الذِّلَّةُ

2372. **Imām ʿAlī (AS) said,** 'Make do with little rather than disgracing yourself [by begging].'[2669]

٢٣٧٢ . الإمامُ عليٌّ ﷺ : التَّقَلُّلُ ولا التَّذَلُّلُ . ٢٦٥٤

2373. **Imām ʿAlī (AS) said,** 'Death is preferable over a life of disgrace. Frugal living is preferable over begging from others.'[2670]

٢٣٧٣ . عنه ﷺ : المَنِيَّةُ ولا الدَّنِيَّةُ ، والتَّقَلُّلُ ولا التَوَسُّلُ . ٢٦٥٥

2374. **Imām ʿAlī (AS) said,** 'A lifetime of honour can never compensate for an hour of disgrace.'[2671]

٢٣٧٤ . عنه ﷺ : ساعَةُ ذُلٍّ لا تَفي بِعِزِّ الدَّهرِ . ٢٦٥٦

2375. **Imām ʿAlī (AS) said** in one of his intimate supplications, 'O Allah! Let my soul be the first of those precious objects that you will wrest from me, and the first thing to be reclaimed out of all Your bounties held in trust with me.'[2672]

٢٣٧٥ . عنه ﷺ ـ في مُناجاتِهِ ـ : اللّهُمَّ اجعَل نَفسي أوَّلَ كَريمَةٍ تَنتَزِعُها مِن كَرائِمي ، وأوَّلَ وَديعَةٍ تَرتَجِعُها مِن وَدائعِ نِعَمِكَ عِندي . ٢٦٥٧

2376. **Imām al-Ḥusayn (AS) said,** 'Death with dignity is better than living with disgrace', and articulated the following couplet on the day he was martyred:
'Death is better than embarking on (a life of) indignity;[2673]
And indignity is preferable over plunging into the Fire;
By Allah, I will not allow myself any of the two.'[2674]

٢٣٧٦ . المناقب لابن شهرآشوب : قالَ الإمامُ الحسينُ ﷺ : مَوتٌ في عِزٍّ خَيرٌ مِن حياةٍ في ذُلٍّ .
وأنشأ ﷺ في يَومِ قَتلِهِ :
الموتُ خيرٌ من رُكُوبِ العارِ
والعارُ أولىٰ من دُخُولِ النـارِ
واللهِ ما هذا وهذا جاري . ٢٦٥٨

764. A Believer Must Never Disgrace Himself

٧٦٤-لا يَنبَغي لِلمُؤمِنِ أن يُذِلَّ نفسَهُ

2377. **The Prophet (SAWA) said,** 'Whoever succumbs to degrading himself is not considered from among us, the *Ahl al-Bayt*.'[2675]

٢٣٧٧ . رسولُ اللهِ ﷺ : مَن أقَرَّ بِالذُّلِّ طائعاً فَلَيسَ مِنّا أهلَ البيتِ . ٢٦٥٩

2378. **Imām al-Ṣādiq (AS) said,** 'Verily Allah, Blessed and most High, has placed everything at the disposal of the believer except that which brings disgrace upon him.'[2676]

٢٣٧٨ . الإمامُ الصّادقُ عليه السلام : إنَّ اللهَ تَبارَكَ وتعالىٰ فَوَّضَ إلى المؤمنِ كُلَّ شيءٍ إلّا إذلالَ نفسِهِ .[٢٦٦٠]

2379. **Imām al-Ṣādiq (AS) said,** 'A believer must never disgrace himself.' When asked by someone how this disgrace comes about, he replied, 'By going out of his way to obtain that which is beyond his control, he ends up disgracing himself.'[2677]

٢٣٧٩ . مشكاة الأنوار عن داوود الرَّقّي : سمعتُ أبا عبدِاللهِ عليه السلام يقولُ : لا يَنبَغي للمؤمنِ أن يُذِلَّ نفسَهُ ، قيلَ لَهُ : وكيفَ يُذِلُّ نَفسَهُ ؟ قالَ : يَتَعَرَّضُ لِما لا يُطيقُ فَيُذِلُّها .[٢٦٦١]

765. That Which Brings About Disgrace

٧٦٥ ـ ما يورِثُ الذُّلَّ

2380. **The Prophet (SAWA) said,** 'When people are miserly with their dinars and their dirhams [i.e. their wealth] and conclude bargains only upon sampling, and are too busy running after their livestock, and abandon fighting in the way of Allah (*jihād*), Allah brings down such disgrace upon them that can never be revoked until they turn back to their religion.'[2678]

٢٣٨٠ . رسولُ اللهِ صلى الله عليه وآله : إذا ضَنَّ الناسُ بالدِّينارِ والدِّرهَمِ وتَبايَعُوا بالعِينَةِ وتَبِعُوا أذنابَ البَقَرِ وتَرَكُوا الجِهادَ في سبيلِ اللهِ ، أدخَلَ اللهُ علَيهِم ذُلّاً لا يَرفَعُهُ عَنهُم حتّىٰ يُراجِعُوا دِينَهُم .[٢٦٦٢]

2381. **The Prophet (SAWA) said,** 'The most disgraceful of people is he who humiliates others.'[2679]

٢٣٨١ . عنه صلى الله عليه وآله : أذَلُّ الناسِ مَن أهانَ الناسَ .[٢٦٦٣]

2382. **Imām ʿAlī (AS) said,** 'People, in their effort to avoid disgrace, rush headlong into it.'[2680]

٢٣٨٢ . الإمامُ عليٌّ عليه السلام : الناسُ مِن خَوفِ الذُّلِّ مُتَعَجِّلُو الذُّلِّ .[٢٦٦٤]

2383. **Imām ʿAlī (AS) said,** 'He who discloses his problems to others resigns himself to disgrace.'[2681]

٢٣٨٣ . عنه عليه السلام : رَضِيَ بِالذُّلِّ مَن كَشَفَ عن ضُرِّهِ .[٢٦٦٥]

2384. **Imām al-Bāqir (AS) said,** 'There is no disgrace worse than that of greed.'[2682]

٢٣٨٤ . الإمامُ الباقرُ عليه السلام : لا ذُلَّ كَذُلِّ الطَّمَعِ .[٢٦٦٦]

2385. **Imām al-Ṣādiq (AS) said,** 'He who loves life is bound to face disgrace.'[2683]

٢٣٨٥ . الإمامُ الصّادقُ عليه السلام : مَن أحَبَّ الحياةَ ذَلَّ .[٢٦٦٧]

2386. Someone once came to one of the Imāms (AS) complaining about a man who was wronging him. The Imām (AS) replied, 'Be patient with

٢٣٨٦ . كشف الغمة : وفي نَقلٍ : شَكا إلىٰ أبي عَبدِ اللهِ عليه السلام رجُلٌ جارَهُ فَقالَ : اِصبِرْ علَيهِ ، فقالَ :

him.' The man retorted, 'But people are taking me for a disgraced fool.' The Imām replied, 'The disgraced one is actually the one who wrongs others.'[2684]

يَنسُبُنِي الناسُ إلى الذُّلِّ، فقالَ: إنّما الذليلُ مَن ظَلَمَ.[٢٦٦٨]

149

SINNING

الذَّنبُ

766. Warning Against Sinning

٧٦٦ ـ التَّحذِيرُ مِنَ الذَّنبِ

"Renounce outward sins as well as inward ones. Indeed those who commit sins shall be requited for what they used to commit."[2685]

﴿وَذَرُوا ظاهِرَ الإِثْمِ وَباطِنَهُ إنَّ الَّذِينَ يَكْسِبُونَ الإِثْمَ سَيُجْزَوْنَ بِمَا كَانُوا يَقْتَرِفُونَ﴾.[٢٦٦٩]

"Certainly whoever commits misdeeds and is besieged by his iniquity – such shall be the inmates of the Fire, and they shall remain in it [forever]."[2686]

﴿بَلَىٰ مَنْ كَسَبَ سَيِّئَةً وَأَحاطَتْ بِهِ خَطِيئَتُهُ فَأُولٰئِكَ أَصْحابُ النّارِ هُمْ فِيها خالِدُونَ﴾.[٢٦٧٠]

2387. **Imām ʿAlī (AS) said,** 'Sins are a disease the medicine of which is to seek forgiveness, and the cure lies in never committing them again.'[2687]

٢٣٨٧. الإمامُ عليٌّ عليه السلام: الذُّنوبُ الدّاءُ، والدَّواءُ الاستغفارُ، والشِّفاءُ أن لا تَعودَ.[٢٦٧١]

2388. **Imām ʿAlī (AS) said,** 'O man, what has emboldened you to commit sins, and what has deceived you about your Lord, and what has rendered you so complacent about the destruction of your soul!?'[2688]

٢٣٨٨. عنه عليه السلام: يا أيّها الإنسانُ، ما جَرَّأكَ على ذَنبِكَ، وما غَرَّكَ بِرَبِّكَ، وما أنَّسَكَ بِهَلَكَةِ نَفسِكَ!؟[٢٦٧٢]

2389. **Imām ʿAlī (AS) said,** 'How I wonder at people who keep away from certain types of food for fear of harm to themselves, and yet do not keep away from sins for fear of the Fire!?'[2689]

٢٣٨٩. عنه عليه السلام: عَجِبتُ لأقوامٍ يَحتَمُونَ الطَّعامَ مَخافَةَ الأذىٰ كيفَ لا يَحتَمُونَ الذُّنوبَ مَخافةَ النّارِ؟![٢٦٧٣]

2390. **Imām ʿAlī (AS) said,** 'Even if Allah had not fixed punishments and threats for acts of disobedience to Him, we would still be obliged not to disobey Him, simply by way of gratitude to Him for His bounties.'[2690]

٢٣٩٠. عنه عليه السلام: لَو لَم يَتَوَعَّدِ اللهُ علىٰ معصِيَتِهِ لَكانَ يَجِبُ ألّا يُعصىٰ شُكراً لِنِعَمِهِ.[٢٦٧٤]

2391. **Imām ʿAlī (AS) said,** 'Refraining from committing evil deeds is better than performing good deeds.'[2691]

٢٣٩١ . عنه عليه السلام : اجتِنابُ السيّئاتِ أولىٰ مِنِ كتِسابِ الحَسَناتِ.[٢٦٧٥]

2392. **Imām al-Kāẓim (AS) said,** 'The people of intellect have abandoned the excesses of this world, but what about sins? Forsaking worldly excesses is [merely] a virtue whereas abandoning sins is an obligation.'[2692]

٢٣٩٢ . الإمامُ الكاظمُ عليه السلام : إنّ العُقَلاءَ تَرَكُوا فُضولَ الدنيا فكيفَ الذُّنوبُ ؟! وتَركُ الدنيا مِنَ الفَضلِ، وتَركُ الذُّنوبِ مِنَ الفَرضِ.[٢٦٧٦]

2393. It is narrated in *Biḥār al-Anwār,* from the Imāms (AS), 'Strive earnestly and work hard, and even if you do not manage to perform good deeds, at least do not sin, for verily the building of one who continuously builds without destroying [at the same time] will rise tall, even if it be plain and unadorned, whilst the building of one who builds but also destroys will almost never rise up.'[2693]

٢٣٩٣ . بحار الأنوار ـ عنهم عليهم السلام ـ: جِدُّوا واجتَهِدُوا، وإن لَم تَعمَلُوا فلا تَعصُوا، فإنّ مَن يَبنِي ولا يَهدِمُ يَرتَفِعُ بِناؤهُ وإن كانَ يَسيراً، وإنّ مَن يَبنِي ويَهدِمُ يوشِكُ أن لا يَرتَفِعَ بِناؤهُ.[٢٦٧٧]

767. Sinning Openly

٧٦٧ ـ المُجاهَرَةُ بِالذَّنبِ

2394. **Imām ʿAlī (AS) said,** 'Openly and candidly disobeying Allah – glory be to Him – hastens His wrath.'[2694]

٢٣٩٤ . الإمامُ عليٌّ عليه السلام : مُجاهَرَةُ اللهِ سبحانَهُ بالمعاصِي تُعَجِّلُ النِّقَمَ.[٢٦٧٨]

2395. **Imām al-Riḍā (AS) said,** 'The one who commits an evil deed openly is disgraced [by Allah], and the one who hides his evil deed [feeling ashamed of it] is forgiven by Allah.'[2695]

٢٣٩٥ . الإمامُ الرِّضا عليه السلام : المُذِيعُ بالسيّئةِ مَخذُولٌ، والمُستَتِرُ بالسيّئةِ مَغفورٌ لَهُ.[٢٦٧٩]

768. The Worst of Sins

٧٦٨ ـ أعظَمُ الذُّنوبِ

2396. **Imām ʿAlī (AS) said,** 'The worst and gravest of sins is that which its perpetrator takes lightly.'[2696]

٢٣٩٦ . الإمامُ عليٌّ عليه السلام : أشَدُّ الذُّنوبِ ما استَخَفَّ بهِ صاحِبُهُ.[٢٦٨٠]

2397. **Imām ʿAlī (AS) said,** 'The worst of sins in the sight of Allah is the sin which its perpetrator commits persistently.'[2697]

٢٣٩٧ . عنه عليه السلام : أعظَمُ الذُّنوبِ عِندَ اللهِ ذنبٌ أصَرَّ عَليهِ عامِلُهُ.[٢٦٨١]

2398. **Imām al-Bāqir (AS) said,** 'All sins are severe [in requital], but the severest of them are those that result in the growth of [polluted] flesh and blood.'[2698]

٢٣٩٨ . الإمامُ الباقرُ عليه السلام : الذُّنوبُ كُلُّها شَديدةٌ وأشَدُّها ما نَبَتَ عَليهِ اللَّحمُ والدمُ.[٢٦٨٢]

769. Unforgivable Sins

٧٦٩ـ الذُّنوبُ الَّتي لا تُغفَرُ

"Indeed Allah does not forgive that any partner should be ascribed to Him, but He forgives anything besides that to whomever He wishes. And whoever ascribes partners to Allah has indeed fabricated [a lie] in great sinfulness."[2699]

﴿إنَّ اللهَ لَا يَغْفِرُ أنْ يُشْرَكَ بِهِ وَيغْفِرُ مَا دُونَ ذٰلِكَ لِمَن يَشاءُ وَمَن يُشْرِك بِاللهِ فَقَدِ افتَرَىٰ إثْماً عَظِيماً﴾.[٢٦٨٣]

2399. **The Prophet (SAWA) said,** 'The repentance of every sin is acceptable, except for ill-nature, for indeed the ill-natured person is such that every time he manages to get out of one sin, he plunges into another.'[2700]

٢٣٩٩. رسولُ اللهِ ﷺ: لِكُلِّ ذَنبٍ تَوبَةٌ إلّا سُوءَ الخُلُقِ، فإنّ صاحِبَهُ كُلَّما خَرَجَ من ذَنبٍ دَخَلَ في ذَنبٍ.[٢٦٨٤]

2400. **The Prophet (SAWA) said,** 'Beware of the sins that cannot be forgiven: Betraying the spoils, and he who betrays the spoils will be brought with it on Judgment Day, and the consuming of usury, as the consumer of usury will be resurrected from his grave like being deranged by the Devil's touch.'[2701]

٢٤٠٠. عنه ﷺ: إيّاكُم والذُّنوبَ التي لا تُغفَرُ: الغُلُولَ فَمَن غَلَّ شيئاً يَأْتِي بِهِ يومَ القيامةِ، وأكْلَ الرِّبا فإنّ آكِلَ الرِّبا لا يَقومُ إلّا كما يَقومُ الذي يَتَخَبَّطُهُ الشيطانُ مِنَ المَسِّ.[٢٦٨٥]

2401. **Imām ʿAlī (AS) said,** 'One of the firm decisions of Allah in the Wise Reminder (the Qur'an) ... is that it will be of no avail to man to strive with his soul and to act sincerely, if upon leaving this world to meet his Lord he is still guilty of any of the following sins for which he has not repented: that he associated anything else with Allah in his obligatory worship, or appeased his own anger by killing someone, or exposed acts committed by others, or sought fulfilment of his needs from people by introducing an innovation in his religion, or was two-faced in his encounters with people, or mingled among them deceitfully.'[2702]

٢٤٠١. الإمامُ عليٌّ عليه السلام: إنّ مِن عَزائمِ اللهِ في الذِّكرِ الحكيمِ... أنّهُ لا يَنفَعُ عَبداً ـ وإن أجهَدَ نفسَهُ وأخلَصَ فِعلَهُ ـ أن يَخرُجَ مِنَ الدنيا لاقياً رَبَّهُ بِخَصلةٍ مِن هذهِ الخِصالِ لَم يَتُبْ مِنها: أن يُشرِكَ بِاللهِ فيما افتَرَضَ علَيهِ مِن عِبادَتِهِ، أو يَشفِيَ غَيظَهُ بهَلاكِ نَفْسٍ، أو يَعُرَّ بأمرٍ فَعَلَهُ غيرُهُ، أو يَستَنجِحَ حاجةً إلى الناسِ بإظهارِ بِدعَةٍ في دِينِهِ، أو يَلقَى النّاسَ بِوَجهَينِ، أو يَمشِيَ فيهِم بِلِسانَينِ.[٢٦٨٦]

2402. **Imām al-Bāqir (AS) said,** 'Among the sins that are unforgivable is when a man says, 'I wish I would only be punished on account of this one sin [deeming the sin so small that he thinks he can bear the punishment].'[2703]

٢٤٠٢. الإمامُ الباقرُ عليه السلام: مِنَ الذُّنوبِ التي لا تُغفَرُ قولُ الرَّجُلِ: يالَيتَنِي لا أُؤاخَذُ إلّا بهذا![٢٦٨٧]

770. Warning Against Committing Acts of Disobedience in Secret

٧٧٠ـ التَّحذيرُ مِنَ المَعصِيَةِ فِي الخَلَواتِ

2403. **Imām ʿAlī (AS) said,** 'Be on your guard against committing acts of disobedience to Allah in secret, for verily the Witness is the Judge Himself.'[2704]

٢٤٠٣ . الإمامُ عليٌّ عليه السلام : اتَّقوا معاصيَ اللهِ فـي الخَلَواتِ ، فإنّ الشاهِدَ هُو الحاكِمُ.[٢٦٨٨]

2404. **Imām al-Bāqir (AS) said,** 'Allah could not care less about the one who goes out of his way to commit a sin in private [thinking he can hide from Allah].'[2705]

٢٤٠٤ . الإمامُ الباقرُ عليه السلام : مَنِ ارتَكَبَ الذنبَ في الخَلاءِ لم يَعبَأِ اللهُ بهِ .[٢٦٨٩]

771. Taking One's Sins Lightly and Deeming them Insignificant

٧٧١ـ الاستِخفافُ بالذَّنبِ وَاستِصغارُهُ

2405. **The Prophet (SAWA) said,** 'The believer sees his sin as a big boulder which he fears may fall on him, while the disbeliever sees his sin as a fly that has brushed past him.'[2706]

٢٤٠٥ . رسولُ اللهِ صلى الله عليه وآله : إنّ المؤمنَ لَيَرىٰ ذَنبَهُ كَأَنَّهُ تحتَ صَخرَةٍ يَخافُ أن تَقَعَ علَيهِ ، والكافِرَ يَرىٰ ذَنبَهُ كأنّهُ ذُبابٌ مَرَّ علىٰ أنفِهِ .[٢٦٩٠]

2406. **The Prophet (SAWA) said,** 'Verily Iblīs [Satan] is well-pleased with you when you commit petty sins.'[2707]

٢٤٠٦ . عنه صلى الله عليه وآله : إنّ إبليسَ رَضِيَ مِنكُم بالمُحَقَّراتِ .[٢٦٩١]

2407. **The Prophet (SAWA) said,** 'Do not look at the pettiness of the sin, rather look at who it is you have dared to defy.'[2708]

٢٤٠٧ . عنه صلى الله عليه وآله : لا تَنظُرُوا إلىٰ صِغَرِ الذَّنبِ ولكنِ انظُرُوا إلىٰ مَنِ اجتَرَأتُم .[٢٦٩٢]

2408. **Imām ʿAlī (AS) said,** 'The worst of sins in the sight of Allah is the sin which its perpetrator deems insignificant.'[2709]

٢٤٠٨ . الإمامُ عليٌّ عليه السلام : أعظَمُ الذُّنوبِ عِندَ اللهِ سبحانَهُ ذَنبٌ صَغُرَ عِندَ صاحِبِهِ .[٢٦٩٣]

2409. **Imām al-Bāqir (AS) said,** 'There is no greater tribulation than your indifference towards your sins and your satisfaction with your current state of affairs.'[2710]

٢٤٠٩ . الإمامُ الباقرُ عليه السلام : لا مُصيبَةَ كاستِهانَتِكَ بالذنبِ ورِضاكَ بالحالةِ التي أنتَ علَيها .[٢٦٩٤]

2410. **Imām al-Kāẓim (AS) said,** 'Do not deem your petty sins as insignificant, for verily petty sins accumulate and become grave sins.'[2711]

٢٤١٠ . الإمامُ الكاظمُ عليه السلام : لا تَستَقِلُّوا قليلَ الذُّنوبِ، فإنّ قليلَ الذُّنوبِ يَجتَمِعُ حتّىٰ يكونَ كثيراً .[٢٦٩٥]

2411. **Imām al-Riḍā (AS) said,** 'Petty sins lead the way for grave sins, and he who does not fear Allah with regard to small things will not fear Him when it comes to grave things.'[2712]

٢٤١١ . الإمامُ الرِّضا ؑ : الصَّغائرُ مِنَ الذنوبِ طُرُقٌ إلى الكبائرِ ، ومَن لَم يَخَفِ اللهَ في القَليلِ لَم يَخَفْهُ في الكثيرِ .٢٦٩٦

772. The Grave Sins

٧٧٢ ـ كَبائرُ الذُّنوبِ

"If you avoid the grave sins that you are forbidden, We will absolve you of your misdeeds, and admit you to a noble abode."[2713]

﴿إنْ تَجْتَنِبُوا كَبائرَ ما تُنْهَوْنَ عَنْهُ نُكَفِّرْ عَنْكُمْ سَيِّئاتِكُمْ ونُدْخِلْكُم مُدْخَلاً كَريماً﴾ .٢٦٩٧

2412. **The Prophet (SAWA) said,** 'The grave sins are: associating anything with Allah, insolence to one's parents, murdering an innocent soul, and taking an immoral or licentious oath.'[2714]

٢٤١٢ . رسولُ اللهِ ﷺ : الكبائرُ : الإشراكُ بِاللهِ ، وعُقُوقُ الوالدَينِ ، وقَتلُ النَّفْسِ ، واليَمينُ الغَمُوسُ .٢٦٩٨

2413. **Imām 'Alī (AS),** when asked about the gravest of the grave sins, said, 'Feeling secure from Allah's plan, giving up all hope of Allah's munificence, and despairing of Allah's mercy.'[2715]

٢٤١٣ . الإمامُ عليٌّ ؑ ـ لَمّا سُئلَ عن أكبَرِ الكبائرِ ـ : الأمنُ مِن مَكرِ اللهِ ، والإياسُ مِن رَوحِ اللهِ ، والقُنوطُ مِن رَحمَةِ اللهِ .٢٦٩٩

2414. **Imām al-Ṣādiq (AS) said,** 'There are seven grave sins: intentionally killing a believer, falsely accusing a chaste woman of fornication, fleeing from the midst of a battle, returning to a state of renegation after belief[2716], unjustly usurping the property of the orphan, devouring usury after knowledge of its prohibition, and everything else that Allah has threatened to requite with obligatory punishment in the Fire.'[2717]

٢٤١٤ . الإمامُ الصّادقُ ؑ : الكبائرُ سَبعٌ : قَتلُ المؤمنِ مُتَعمِّداً ، وقذفُ المُحصَنَةِ ، والفِرارُ مِنَ الزَّحفِ ، والتَّعَرُّبُ بعدَ الهِجرَةِ ، وأكلُ مالِ اليتيمِ ظُلماً ، وأكلُ الرِّبا بعدَ البَيِّنَةِ ، وكُلُّ ما أوجَبَ اللهُ عليه النارَ .٢٧٠٠

773. Persistent Sinning

٧٧٣ ـ الإصرارُ عَلَى الذَّنبِ

"And those who, when they commit an indecent act or wrong themselves, remember Allah, and plead [Allah's] forgiveness for their sins – and who forgives sins except Allah? - and who do not knowingly persist in what they have committed."[2718]

﴿وَالَّذِينَ إذا فَعَلُوا فاحِشَةً أوْ ظَلَمُوا أنفُسَهُم ذَكَرُوا اللهَ فَاسْتَغْفَرُوا لِذُنُوبِهِمْ وَمَن يَغْفِرُ الذُّنُوبَ إلّا اللهُ وَلَمْ يُصِرُّوا عَلَى ما فَعَلُوا وَهُمْ يَعْلَمُونَ﴾ .٢٧٠١

2415. **The Prophet (SAWA) said,** 'No petty sin remains when persisted upon, and no grave sin remains when repented for' [i.e. the petty sin can

٢٤١٥ . رسولُ اللهِ ﷺ : لا كبيرَ مَعَ الاستِغفارِ ،

be cancelled with persistence and furtherance in it, hence becoming a grave sin, and the grave sin can be annulled with repentance].'[2719]

ولا صغيرَ مع الإصرارِ.[٢٧٠٢]

2416. **Imām al-Bāqir (AS)** with reference to Allah's verse in the Qur'an: *"those who do not knowingly persist in what they have committed"*, said, 'Persistence in sinning is when a person commits a sin, and does not seek forgiveness for it, and moreover, it does not even occur to him to repent for it – that is persistent sinning.'[2720]

٢٤١٦ . الإمامُ الباقرُ عليه السلام ـفي قولِهِ تعالىٰ: ﴿...ولَم يُصِرُّوا...﴾ـ: الإصرارُ أن يُذنِبَ العَبدُ ولا يَستَغفِرَ، ولا يُحَدِّثَ نفسَهُ بالتوبةِ فذلكَ الإصرارُ.[٢٧٠٣]

(See also: SEEKING FORGIVENESS: section 1433)

أنظر: الإستغفار: باب ١٤٣٣.

774. Taking Pleasure in Sinning

٧٧٤ـ الاِبتِهاجُ بِالذَّنبِ

2417. **Imām ʿAlī (AS) said,** 'Whoever takes pleasure in committing acts of disobedience to Allah, Allah will bring disgrace down upon him.'[2721]

٢٤١٧ . الإمامُ عليٌّ عليه السلام : مَن تَلَذَّذَ بمعاصِي اللهِ أورَثَهُ اللهُ ذُلّاً.[٢٧٠٤]

2418. **Imām Zayn al-ʿĀbidīn (AS) said,** 'Beware of enjoying the sin, for verily that enjoyment is worse than the actual perpetration of it.'[2722]

٢٤١٨ . الإمامُ زينُ العابدينَ عليه السلام :إيّاكَ والابتِهاجَ بالذنبِ، فإنّ الابتِهاجَ بهِ أعظَمُ مِن رُكوبِهِ.[٢٧٠٥]

775. The Effects of Sins

٧٧٥ـ آثارُ الذُّنوبِ

2419. **The Prophet (SAWA) said,** 'The sin is also a [source of] misfortune for people other than the perpetrator, for if someone was to expose that sin, he too is afflicted, and if he was to talk about him behind his back, he is also committing a sin, and if he is content thereof and does not bother with others' actions, then it is as if he also partook in the sin.'[2723]

٢٤١٩ . رسولُ اللهِ صلى الله عليه وآله : الذَّنبُ شُؤمٌ علىٰ غيرِ فاعِلِهِ، إن عَيَّرَهُ ابتُلِيَ، وإنِ اغتابَهُ أثِمَ، وإن رَضِيَ بِهِ شارَكَهُ.[٢٧٠٦]

2420. **Imām ʿAlī (AS) said,** 'Tears only dry up and fail to flow as a result of hard-heartedness, and the hearts only harden as a result of an abundance of sins.'[2724]

٢٤٢٠ . الإمامُ عليٌّ عليه السلام : ما جَفَّتِ الدُّموعُ إلّا لِقَسوَةِ القُلوبِ، وما قَسَتِ القُلوبُ إلّا لكَثرَةِ الذُّنوبِ.[٢٧٠٧]

2421. **Imām Zayn al-ʿĀbidīn (AS) said,** 'The sins that prevent rain from falling are: the judges' unjust

٢٤٢١ . الإمامُ زينُ العابدينَ عليه السلام : الذُّنوبُ التي

rulings, the giving of false testimony and the concealing of one's testimony.'[2725]

تَحبِسُ غَيثَ السماءِ: جَورُ الحُكّامِ في القَضاءِ، وشَهادَةُ الزُّورِ، وكِتمانُ الشهادَةِ.٢٧٠٨

2422. **Imām al-Bāqir (AS) said,** 'When the rainfall is less from year to year, it is only because Allah sends it down as and when He wishes, such that when a people commit acts of disobedience to Him, Allah - Mighty and Exalted - withholds the rain that He had ordained for them.'[2726]

٢٤٢٢. الإمامُ الباقرُ عليه السلام: إنّه ما مِن سَنَةٍ أقَلَّ مَطَراً مِن سَنَةٍ، ولكنّ اللهَ يَضَعُهُ حيثُ يشاءُ، إنّ اللهَ عزّوجلّ إذا عَمِلَ قَومٌ بالمعاصِي صَرَفَ عَنهُم ما كانَ قَدَّرَ لَهُم مِنَ المَطَرِ.٢٧٠٩

2423. **Imām al-Ṣādiq (AS) said,** 'When a man commits a sin, a black spot appears on his heart. If he repents, it is effaced, but if he continues committing it, the spot increases and grows until it engulfs the whole heart, and he can never again prosper.'[2727]

٢٤٢٣. الإمامُ الصّادقُ عليه السلام: إذا أذنَبَ الرجُلُ خَرَجَ في قَلبِهِ نُكتَةٌ سَوْداءُ، فإن تابَ انمَحَتْ، وإن زادَ زادَتْ حتّىٰ تَغلِبَ علىٰ قَلبِهِ فلا يُفلِحُ بَعدَها أبداً.٢٧١٠

2424. **Imām al-Ṣādiq (AS) said,** 'Allah never bestows bounties on His servant only to take them away again until and unless he commits a sin, whereby he becomes deserving of Allah's deprivation.'[2728]

٢٤٢٤. عنه عليه السلام: ما أنعَمَ اللهُ علىٰ عبدٍ نِعمَةً فَسَلَبَها إيّاهُ حتّىٰ يُذنِبَ ذَنباً يَستَحِقُّ بذلكَ السَّلبَ.٢٧١١

2425. **Imām al-Ṣādiq (AS) said,** 'Indeed the servant commits a sin, and as a result he is deprived of the Night Prayer. And verily the evil deed pierces into and affects the one who committed it faster than a sharp knife can pierce into meat.'[2729]

٢٤٢٥. عنه عليه السلام: إنّ الرَّجُلَ يُذنِبُ الذنبَ فَيُحرَمُ صلاةَ الليلِ، وإنّ العَمَلَ السَّيِّءَ أسرَعُ في صاحِبِهِ مِنَ السِّكّينِ في اللَّحمِ.٢٧١٢

2426. **Imām al-Ṣādiq (AS) said,** 'There are more people who die as a result of their sins than who die because they have reached their appointed time.'[2730]

٢٤٢٦. عنه عليه السلام: مَن يَموتُ بالذُّنوبِ أكثَرُ مِمَّن يَموتُ بِالآجالِ.٢٧١٣

2427. **Imām al-Riḍā (AS) said,** 'When the governors [of a place] are dishonest, rainfall is withheld [from that place], and when the sultan is unjust the whole country is abased, and when the alms-tax is not paid, livestock die as a result.'[2731]

٢٤٢٧. الإمامُ الرِّضا عليه السلام: إذا كَذَبَ الوُلاةُ حُبِسَ المَطَرُ، وإذا جارَ السُّلطانُ هانَتِ الدَّولةُ، وإذا حُبِسَتِ الزكاةُ ماتَتِ المَواشي.٢٧١٤

(See also: AFFLICTION: section 264 and SUPPLICATION: section 694)

انظر: البلاء: باب ٢٦٤؛ الدعاء: باب ٦٩٤.

776. The Sins that's Punishment is Hastened [in the Life of this World]

٧٧٦ ـ الذُّنوبُ الَّتي تُعَجَّلُ عُقوبَتُها

2428. **The Prophet (SAWA) said,** 'There are three sins whose punishment is hastened in the life of this world and is not delayed until the Hereafter: insolence to one's parents, intimidation of others and ingratitude for a favour.'[2732]

٢٤٢٨ . رسولُ اللهِ ﷺ : ثلاثةٌ مِنَ الذُّنوبِ تُعَجَّلُ عُقوبَتُها ولا تُؤَخَّرُ إلى الآخِرَةِ: عُقوقُ الوالِدَينِ، والبَغيُ على الناسِ، وكُفرُ الإحسانِ.[٢٧١٥]

2429. **Imām al-Bāqir (AS) said** that the following was written in the Book of Imām 'Alī (AS), the Commander of the Faithful, 'The perpetrator of any of the following three misdeeds will not die before seeing their evil consequences in this world. They are: intimidation of others, cutting off one's blood relations and taking false oaths.'[2733]

٢٤٢٩ . الإمامُ الباقرُ ؑ : فـي كِـتابِ أميرِ المؤمنينَ ؑ: ثلاثُ خِصالٍ لا يَموتُ صاحِبُهُنّ حتّىٰ يَـرىٰ وَبـالَهُنَّ: البَـغيُ، وقَـطيعَةُ الرَّحِـمِ، واليَمينُ الكاذِبةُ.[٢٧١٦]

777. The Remedy for Sinning

٧٧٧ ـ دَواءُ الذُّنوبِ

2430. **The Prophet (SAWA) said,** 'There is a remedy for every ailment, and the remedy for sins is seeking forgiveness.'[2734]

٢٤٣٠ . رسولُ اللهِ ﷺ : لِكُـلِّ داءٍ دواءٌ، ودواءُ الذُّنوبِ الاستِغفارُ.[٢٧١٧]

2431. **The Prophet (SAWA) said,** 'The believer is given seventy-two veils of which one is torn off every time he sins. When he repents however, Allah returns the veil to its original state and grants him seven more in addition.'[2735]

٢٤٣١ . عنه ﷺ : لِلمؤمنِ اثنانِ وسَبعونَ ستراً، فإذا أذنَبَ ذنباً انهَتَكَ عَنهُ سِترٌ، فإن تابَ رَدَّهُ اللهُ إلَيهِ وسَبعةً مَعهُ.[٢٧١٨]

778. Things that Expiate Sins

٧٧٨ ـ مُكَفِّراتُ الذُّنوبِ

1. Punishment in this World:

١ ـ العُقوبةُ في الدنيا

2432. **The Prophet (SAWA) said,** 'A believing man or woman will continuously be in a state of physical, financial or domestic affliction so that when they die, they will meet Allah with a clean slate.'[2736]

٢٤٣٢ . رسولُ اللهِ ﷺ : لا يَزالُ البَلاءُ في المؤمنِ والمؤمنةِ في جَسَدِهِ ومالِهِ وولدِهِ حَتّى يَلقَى اللهَ وما علَيهِ مِن خطيئةٍ.[٢٧١٩]

2433. **Imām 'Alī (AS) said,** 'No servant from amongst our followers (*shī'a*) who commits an act that we have forbidden dies without first being

٢٤٣٣ . الإمامُ عليٌّ ؑ : ما مِـنَ الشِّـيعةِ عَـبدٌ يُقارِفُ أمراً نَهَينا عَنهُ فيَموتُ حتّى يُبتَلىٰ بـبَلِيّةٍ

afflicted with a severe calamity which expiates his sins, be it with regard to his wealth, his children or his own soul, such that he meets Allah with a clean slate. Moreover, if any of his sins remain even after that, then they are expiated by the pain and difficulty at the time of death.'[2737]

تُمَحَّصُ بها ذنوبُهُ، إمّا في مالٍ، وإمّا في ولدٍ، وإمّا في نفسِهِ، حتّى يَلقَى اللهَ عزّوجلّ وما لَهُ ذنبٌ، وإنّه لَيَبقىٰ علَيهِ الشيءُ مِن ذنوبِهِ فَيُشَدَّدُ بهِ علَيهِ عِندَ مَوتِه.[٢٧٢٠]

2434. **Imām al-Ṣādiq (AS) said,** 'When Allah wishes good for His servant, He hastens his punishment to the life of this world, and when he wishes bad for a servant, He suspends the punishment of his sins to face him on the Day of Resurrection.'[2738]

٢٤٣٤. الإمامُ الصّادقُ ؛ : إذا أرادَ اللهُ بعَبدٍ خيراً عَجَّلَ عُقوبَتَهُ في الدنيا، وإذا أرادَ بعَبدٍ سوءاً أمسَكَ علَيهِ ذُنوبَهُ حتّىٰ يوافِيَ بها يومَ القيامةِ.[٢٧٢١]

(See also: AFFLICTION: section 268)

انظر: البلاء: باب ٢٦٨.

2. Illnesses:

٢ ـ الأمراضُ

2435. **The Prophet (SAWA) said,** 'Illness wipes away sins.'[2739]

٢٤٣٥. رسولُ اللهِ ؛ : السُّقمُ يَمحُو الذُّنوبَ.[٢٧٢٢]

2436. **The Prophet (SAWA) said,** 'The fever of a single night is expiation for a whole year's sins.'[2740]

٢٤٣٦. عنه ؛ : حُمّىٰ ليلةٍ كَفّارةُ سَنَةٍ.[٢٧٢٣]

2437. **Imām ʿAlī (AS) said,** 'When Allah afflicts a servant with illness, sins shed away from him in proportion to the severity of his ailment.'[2741]

٢٤٣٧. الإمامُ عليٌّ ؛ : إذا ابتَلَى اللهُ عَبداً أسقَطَ عنهُ مِن الذُّنوبِ بقَدْرِ عِلَّتِهِ.[٢٧٢٤]

2438. **Imām ʿAlī (AS) said,** 'The illness that afflicts a child is expiation for his parents' sins.'[2742]

٢٤٣٨. عنه ؛ ـ في المَرَضِ يُصيبُ الصَّبِيَّ ـ: كفّارةٌ لوالِدَيه.[٢٧٢٥]

(See also: SICKNESS: section 1650)

انظر: المرض: باب ١٦٥٠.

3. Sorrows:

٣ ـ الأحزانُ

2439. **The Prophet (SAWA) said,** 'Every fatigue, hardship or sorrow that a believer undergoes, as well as worries that distress him, are a means by which Allah deletes his evil deeds.'[2743]

٢٤٣٩. رسولُ اللهِ ؛ : ما أصابَ المؤمنَ مِن نَصَبٍ ولا وَصَبٍ ولا حَزَنٍ حتّى الهَمُّ يُهِمُّهُ إلّا كَفَّرَ اللهُ بِهِ عَنهُ مِن سيّئاتِهِ.[٢٧٢٦]

2440. **Imām al-Ṣādiq (AS) said,** 'Verily distress takes away the sins of the Muslim.'[2744]

٢٤٤٠. الإمامُ الصّادقُ ؛ : إنّ الهَمَّ لَيَذهَبُ بِذُنوبِ المُسلِمِ.[٢٧٢٧]

2441. **Imām al-Riḍā (AS) said,** 'When anyone from among the followers (*shī'a*) of 'Alī commits a sin or perpetrates an evil deed in the morning, it is expiated by any distress he may undergo by nightfall. So how can the Pen ever write down his evil deeds?!'[2745]

٢٤٤١ . الإمامُ الرِّضا عليه السلام : ما أحَدٌ مِن شيعَةِ عَليٍّ أصبَحَ صَبيحةً أتـى بِسيِّئةٍ أو ارتَكَبَ ذنباً إلّا أمسىٰ وقد نالَهُ غَمٌّ حَطَّ عَنهُ سَيِّئَتَهُ ، فكيف يَجري علَيهِ القَلَمُ ؟! ٢٧٢٨

4. Good Deeds:

٤ ـ الحَسَناتُ

"Maintain the prayer at the two ends of the day, and during the early hours of the night. Indeed good deeds efface misdeeds. That is an admonition for the mindful."[2746]

﴿وأَقِمِ الصَّلاةَ طَرَفَيِ النَّهارِ وَزُلَفاً مِنَ اللّيلِ إنَّ الحَسَناتِ يُذْهِبْنَ السَّيِّئاتِ ذلِكَ ذِكْرىٰ لِلذّاكِرينَ﴾ . ٢٧٢٩

2442. **The Prophet (SAWA) said,** 'When you commit an evil deed then follow it with the performance of a good deed to efface it.'[2747]

٢٤٤٢ . رسولُ اللهِ ﷺ : إذا عَمِلتَ سيّئةً فاعمَلْ حَسَنةً تَمْحوها . ٢٧٣٠

5. Good Character:

٥ ـ حُسنُ الخُلقِ

2443. **The Prophet (SAWA) said,** 'Four qualities, when possessed by a person, cause Allah to transform his evil deeds into good deeds, even if he is sinful from head to toe. They are: honesty, modesty, good character and thankfulness.'[2748]

٢٤٤٣ . رسولُ اللهِ ﷺ : أربَعٌ مَن كُنَّ فيهِ وكانَ مِن قَرنِهِ إلىٰ قَدَمِهِ ذُنوباً بَدَّلَها اللهُ حَسَناتٍ : الصِّدقُ ، والحَياءُ ، وحُسنُ الخُلقِ ، والشُّكرُ . ٢٧٣١

2444. **Imām al-Ṣādiq (AS) said,** 'Verily good character melts away evil deeds as the sun melts away ice, and verily bad character corrupts one's actions like vinegar corrupts honey.'[2749]

٢٤٤٤ . الإمامُ الصّادقُ عليه السلام : إنّ حُسنَ الخُلقِ يُذيبُ الخَطيئةَ كما تُذيبُ الشمسُ الجَليدَ ، وإنّ سوءَ الخُلقِ لَيُفسِدُ العَمَلَ كما يُفسِدُ الخَلُّ العَسَلَ . ٢٧٣٢

6. Bringing Solace to a Grief-stricken Person:

٦ ـ إغاثَةُ المَلهوفِ

2445. **Imām 'Alī (AS) said,** 'Among the things that expiate grave sins are: bringing solace to a grief-stricken person, and providing relief to an anguished person.'[2750]

٢٤٤٥ . الإمامُ عليٌّ عليه السلام : مِن كفّاراتِ الذُّنوبِ العِظامِ : إغاثَةُ المَلهوفِ ، والتَّنفيسُ عنِ المَكروبِ . ٢٧٣٣

7. The Angels' Seeking Forgiveness [on the sinner's behalf]:

٧ ـ استِغفارُ المَلائكَةِ

2446. **Imām al-Ṣādiq (AS) said,** 'Verily Allah, Exalted be His Remembrance, has angels who

٢٤٤٦ . الإمامُ الصّادقُ عليه السلام : إنَّ للهِ عزّ ذِكرُهُ

strip off sins from the backs of our followers (*shīʿa*) like the wind strips the leaves off the trees in autumn, and this is in accordance with His words in the Qur'an, *"they glorify the praise of their Lord and seek forgiveness on behalf of those who believe."* [2751] By Allah this verse refers to none other than you [my followers].'[2752]

ملائكةً يُسقِطونَ الذُّنوبَ عن ظُهورِ شِيعَتِنا كما تُسقِطُ الرِّيحُ الوَرَقَ مِنَ الشَّجَرِ في أوانِ سُقُوطِهِ، وذلكَ قولُهُ عزّوجلّ: ﴿يُسَبِّحُونَ بحَمدِ رَبِّهِم ويَسْتَغْفِرُونَ لِلَّذِينَ آمَنوا﴾ [٢٧٣٤] واللهِ ماأرادَ بهذا غيرَكُم. [٢٧٣٥]

8. Frequent Prostration:

٨ ـ كثرةُ السجودِ

2447. **Imām al-Ṣādiq (AS) said,** 'A man once came to the Prophet (SAWA) and said, 'O Prophet of Allah, my sins have increased and my [performance of] good deeds has weakened', to which the Prophet (SAWA) replied, 'Prostrate yourself to Allah frequently for verily this strips off sins as the wind strips off the leaves from the trees.'[2753]

٢٤٤٧ . الإمامُ الصّادقُ عليه السلام : جاءَ رَجُلٌ إلىٰ رسولِ اللهِ صلى الله عليه وآله فقالَ: يارسولَ اللهِ صلى الله عليه وآله، كَثُرَت ذُنُوبي وضَعُفَ عَمَلِي، فقالَ رسولُ اللهِ صلى الله عليه وآله: أكثِرِ السُّجودَ فإنّه يَحُطُّ الذُّنوبَ كما تَحُطُّ الرِّيحُ وَرَقَ الشَّجَرِ. [٢٧٣٦]

9. Performance of the Obligatory and the Voluntary Pilgrimage (*ḥajj* and *ʿumra*):

٩ ـ الحجُّ والعُمرةُ

2448. **The Prophet (SAWA) said,** 'The voluntary pilgrimage (*ʿumra*) expiates all sins committed since the preceding voluntary pilgrimage, and the reward for an accepted obligatory pilgrimage (*ḥajj*) is Paradise. There are certain sins that can only be forgiven on the plains of ʿArafa [an area near Mecca in which part of the obligatory pilgrimage is performed].'[2754]

٢٤٤٨ . رسولُ اللهِ صلى الله عليه وآله : العُمرَةُ إلى العُمرَةِ كَفّارَةُ ما بينَهُما، والحجّةُ المُتَقَبَّلَةُ ثوابُها الجَنَّةُ، ومِنَ الذُّنوبِ ذنوبٌ لا تُغفَرُ إلّا بعَرَفاتَ. [٢٧٣٧]

10. Sending Blessings on Prophet Muḥammad (SAWA) and his Household:

١١ ـ الصلاةُ علىٰ محمّدٍ وآلِهِ

2449. **Imām al-Riḍā (AS) said,** 'Whoever is not capable of performing actions to expiate his sins should abundantly send blessings on Muḥammad and his household for verily this completely eradicates sins.'[2755]

٢٤٤٩ . الإمامُ الرِّضا عليه السلام : مَن لم يَقدِرْ علىٰ ما يُكَفِّرُ بِهِ ذُنوبَهُ فَلْيُكثِرْ مِنَ الصَّلاةِ علىٰ محمّدٍ وآلِهِ فإنّها تَهدِمُ الذُّنوبَ هَدماً. [٢٧٣٨]

(See also: PRAYER (4): section 1148)

انظر : الصلاة (٤): باب ١١٤٨.

11. Death:

١٢ ـ الموت

2450. **The Prophet (SAWA) said,** 'Death acts as a penance for the sins committed by believers.'[2756]

٢٤٥٠ . رسولُ اللهِ ﷺ : المَوتُ كـفّارةٌ لِـذُنوبِ المؤمنينَ . ٢٧٣٩

150

LEADERSHIP

الرِّئاسَةُ

779. The Censure of [the Love of] Leadership

٧٧٩ ـ ذَمُّ الرِّئاسَةِ

2451. **Imām al-Bāqir (AS) said,** 'Do not ever desire to be a leader for in doing so you will only be a follower.'[2757]

٢٤٥١ . الإمامُ الباقرُ عليه السلام : لا تَطلُبَنَّ أن تكـونَ رَأساً فتكونَ ذَنَباً . ٢٧٤٠

2452. **Imām al-Ṣādiq (AS) said,** 'Beware of those leaders who are taking up the reins of leadership, for by Allah, no sooner does the sound of footsteps from behind them [following them] reach their ears than they themselves perish and destroy others along with them.'[2758]

٢٤٥٢ . الإمامُ الصّادقُ عليه السلام : إيّاكُم وهؤلاءِ الرؤساءَ الذينَ يَتَرأَّسُونَ ، فَوَاللهِ ما خَفَقَتِ النِّعالُ خَلفَ رَجُلٍ إلّا هَلَكَ وأهلَكَ . ٢٧٤١

2453. **Imām al-Ṣādiq (AS) said,** 'One who seeks after leadership perishes.'[2759]

٢٤٥٣ . عنه عليه السلام : مَن طَلَبَ الرئاسةَ هَلَكَ . ٢٧٤٢

2454. **Imām al-Riḍā (AS) said** with reference to someone, 'Indeed he loves leadership', and then said, 'Two rapacious wolves hunting a lamb that has been separated from its shepherd and herd is not nearly as hazardous and perilous as seeking after leadership is to the faith of a Muslim.'[2760]

٢٤٥٤ . الإمامُ الرِّضا عليه السلام ـ بعد ما ذَكَرَ الإمامُ عليه السلام رجُلاً وقالَ : إنَّهُ يُحِبُّ الرئاسةَ ـ : ما ذِئبانِ ضارِيانِ في غَنَمٍ قد تَفَرَّقَ رِعاؤها بِأضَرَّ في دِينِ المُسلمِ مِنَ الرئاسةِ . ٢٧٤٣

780. The Tool Required for Leadership

٧٨٠ ـ آلَةُ الرِّئاسَةِ

2455. **Imām ʿAlī (AS) said,** 'The tool required for leadership is magnanimity.'[2761 2762]

٢٤٥٥ . الإمامُ عليٌّ عليه السلام : آلَـةُ الرئاسةِ سَعَةُ الصَّدرِ . ٢٧٤٤

2456. **Imām ʿAlī (AS) said,** 'He who is generous prevails and rules, whilst he who possesses great

٢٤٥٦ . عنه عليه السلام : مَن جادَ سادَ ، ومَن كَثُرَ مالُهُ

wealth assumes the reins of leadership for himself.'[2763]

رَأسَ.٢٧٤٥

2457. **Imām al-Ṣādiq (AS) said,** 'I sought for leadership and found it in giving good counsel to Allah's servants [and being benevolent].'[2764]

٢٤٥٧. الإمامُ الصّادقُ ؑ: طَلَبتُ الرئاسَةَ فَوَجَدتُها في النَّصيحَةِ لِعِبادِ اللهِ.٢٧٤٦

(See also: THE CHIEF: section 991)

(أنظر) السيّد: باب ٩٩١.

151

DREAMS

الرُّؤيا

781. Glad Tidings in Dreams

٧٨١ـ بُشرى الرُّؤيا

2458. **The Prophet (SAWA),** with regard to Allah's verse in the Qur'an *"for them are glad tidings in the life of this world"*[2765], said, 'This is in reference to the good dream which a believer has and which gives him good news in this world.'[2766]

٢٤٥٨. رسولُ اللهِ ﷺ ـ في قولِهِ تعالىٰ: ﴿لَهُمُ ٱلْبُشْرَىٰ فِى ٱلْحَيَوٰةِ ٱلدُّنْيَا...﴾٢٧٤٧ ـ: هي الرُّؤيا الحَسَنَةُ يَرَى المُؤمنُ فَيُبَشَّرُ بها في دُنياهُ.٢٧٤٨

2459. **The Prophet (SAWA) said,** 'No remnants of prophecy remain today [in people's lives] except glad tidings.' When asked what glad tidings were, he replied, 'True dreams.'[2767]

٢٤٥٩. بحار الأنوار عنه ﷺ: لم يَبقَ مِنَ النبوَّةِ إلّا المُبَشِّراتُ، قالوا: وما المُبَشِّراتُ؟ قال: الرؤيا الصالِحَةُ.٢٧٤٩

2460. **Imām al-Riḍā (AS) said,** 'When the Prophet (SAWA) used to wake up in the morning, he used to first ask his companions, 'Are there any good news?' meaning any good dreams.'[2768]

٢٤٦٠. الإمامُ الرِّضا ؑ: إنّ رسولَ اللهِ ﷺ كانَ إذا أصبَحَ قالَ لأصحابِهِ: هل مِن مُبَشِّراتٍ؟ يَعنِي بِهِ الرُّؤيا.٢٧٥٠

782. Categories of Dreams

٧٨٢ـ أقسامُ الرُّؤيا

2461. **Imām al-Bāqir (AS) said,** 'When people sleep, their spirits go out into the heaven. Whatever the spirit sees while in the heaven is true, and whatever it sees in the air [between earth and the heavens] are just muddled dreams.'[2769]

٢٤٦١. الإمامُ الباقرُ ؑ: إنّ العِبادَ إذا نامُوا خَرَجَت أرواحُهُم إلى السماءِ، فما رَأتِ الرُّوحُ في السماءِ فهُوالحقُّ وما رَأت في الهواءِ فهُو الأضغاثُ.٢٧٥١

2462. **Imām al-Ṣādiq (AS) said,** 'There are three types of dreams: glad tidings from Allah for the

٢٤٦٢. الإمامُ الصّادقُ ؑ: الرؤيا علىٰ ثلاثةِ

believer, ominous dreams from Satan, and muddled dreams.'[2770]

وُجوهٍ: بِشارَةٌ مِنَ اللهِ لِلمُؤمنِ، وتَحذيرٌ مِنَ الشيطانِ، وأضغاثُ أحلامٍ.٢٧٥٢

783. Interpretation of Dreams

٧٨٣ـ تَفسيرُ الرُّؤيا

2463. **The Prophet (SAWA) said,** 'When any of you sees a good dream, then go ahead and interpret it and inform others of it, and if you see a bad dream, then neither interpret it, nor inform others of it.'[2771]

٢٤٦٣. رسولُ اللهِ ﷺ: إذا رَأىٰ أحَدُكُم الرؤيا الحَسَنَةَ فَلْيُفَسِّرْها ولْيُخبِرْ بها، وإذا رَأى الرؤيا القَبيحَةَ فلا يُفَسِّرْها ولا يُخبِرْ بها.٢٧٥٣

2464. **The Prophet (SAWA) said,** 'A dream should only ever be related to a believer who does not harbour jealousy or wrongdoing.'[2772]

٢٤٦٤. عنه ﷺ: الرؤيا لا تُقَصُّ إلّا علىٰ مؤمنٍ خلا مِن الحَسَدِ والبَغيِ.٢٧٥٤

152

SHOWING OFF

الرِّياءُ

784. The Censure of Showing Off

٧٨٤ـ ذَمُّ الرِّياءِ

"Do not be like those who left their homes vainly and to show off to the people, and to bar [other people] from the way of Allah, and Allah comprehends what they do."[2773]

﴿وَلَا تَكُونُوا كَالَّذِينَ خَرَجُوا مِنْ دِيارِهِم بَطَرَاً وَرِئَاءَ النَّاسِ وَيَصُدُّونَ عَنْ سَبِيلِ اللهِ وَاللهُ بِمَا يَعْمَلُونَ مُحِيطٌ﴾.٢٧٥٥

2465. **The Prophet (SAWA) said,** 'Woe betide those who trade their religion for the life of this world – in front of people they are soft-spoken and their words are sweeter than honey, but they are wolves in sheep's clothing[2774], and Allah says regarding them, 'Are they too hopeful in me [while doing nothing]?'[2775]

٢٤٦٥. رسولُ اللهِ ﷺ: ويلٌ للذينَ يَجتَلِبُونَ الدنيا بالدِّينِ، يَلبَسُونَ للناسِ جُلودَ الضَّأنِ مِن لِينِ ألسِنَتِهِم، كلامُهُم أحلىٰ مِن العَسَلِ وقُلوبُهُم قُلوبُ الذِئابِ، يقولُ اللهُ تعالىٰ: أبي يَغتَرُّونَ؟!٢٧٥٦

2466. **The Prophet (SAWA) said,** 'Verily the angel [charged with man's deeds] rises up with man's good deeds, delighted on account of them, but as he is lifting up his good deeds, Allah tells him, 'Go and place them in the *Sijjīn*[2776], as he did not perform these deeds for Me.'[2777]

٢٤٦٦. عنه ﷺ: إنّ المَلَكَ لَيَصعَدُ بعَملِ العَبدِ مُبتَهِجاً بهِ، فإذا صَعِدَ بحَسَناتِهِ يقولُ اللهُ عزّوجلّ: اجعَلُوها في سِجِّينٍ إنّهُ لَيسَ إيّايَ أرادَ بِها.٢٧٥٧

2467. **The Prophet (SAWA) said,** 'The show-off will be called on the Day of Resurrection: O shameless liar! O treacherous one! O show-off! Your deeds are lost, and the reward for your deeds is lost. Go and get your reward from those you intended to please by your actions.'[2778]

٢٤٦٧. عنه ﷺ: إنّ المُرائيَ يُنادىٰ يَومَ القِيامَةِ: يا فاجِرُ! يا غادِرُ! يا مُرائي! ضَلَّ عَمَلُكَ، وبَطَلَ أجرُكَ، اذهَبْ فَخُذْ أجرَكَ مِمَّن كُنتَ تَعمَلُ لَهُ.[٢٧٥٨]

2468. **The Prophet (SAWA) said,** 'Allah, glory be to Him, says, 'I am the most self-sufficient and richest of partners, for whoever performs a deed for Me as well as for someone else alongside Me, [know that] I am free from need of his action and I leave it for the one that he associated with Me.'[2779]

٢٤٦٨. عنه ﷺ: يقولُ اللهُ سبحانَهُ: إنّي أغنَى الشُّرَكاءِ، فَمَن عَمِلَ عَمَلاً ثُمّ أشرَكَ فيهِ غَيرِي فأنا مِنهُ بَرِيءٌ، وهو لِلَّذي أشرَكَ بِهِ دُوني.[٢٧٥٩]

2469. **The Prophet (SAWA) said,** 'Verily Allah does not accept a deed that is performed with even an atom's weight of showing off in it.'[2780]

٢٤٦٩. عنه ﷺ: إنّ اللهَ لا يَقبَلُ عَملاً فيهِ مِثقالُ ذَرَّةٍ مِن رياءٍ.[٢٧٦٠]

2470. **The Prophet (SAWA)** was once asked, 'Where does salvation lie?' to which he replied, 'In that the servant must not perform acts of obedience to Allah whilst intending them for other people [to see].'[2781]

٢٤٧٠. عنه ﷺ ـ حِينَ سَأَلَهُ رَجُلٌ: يا رسولَ اللهِ ﷺ، فِيمَ النَّجاةُ؟ ـ: أن لا يَعمَلَ العَبدُ بطاعَةِ اللهِ يُرِيدُ بها الناسَ.[٢٧٦١]

2471. **Imām ʿAlī (AS) said,** 'How ugly the man who is sick inwardly and beautiful outwardly.'[2782]

٢٤٧١. الإمامُ عليٌّ عليه السلام: ما أقبَحَ بِالإنسانِ باطِناً عَليلاً وظاهِراً جَميلاً![٢٧٦٢]

2472. **Imām ʿAlī (AS) said,** 'O Allah I seek refuge in You from looking good in the gleaming mirror of people's eyes whilst my inward self that I conceal [from others] be ugly in front of You, and from guarding myself [against sins] only for show in front of people whilst You know all there is to know about me, such that I may display my good side to people, leaving the bad deeds for You, in seeking nearness to mere servants of Yours and getting further and further away from Your good pleasure.'[2783]

٢٤٧٢. عنه عليه السلام: اللّهُمّ إنّي أعوذُ بكَ مِن أن تَحسُنَ في لامِعَةِ العُيونِ عَلانِيَتي، وتَقبُحَ فيما أُبطِنُ لكَ سَريرَتي، مُحافِظاً على رِئاءِ الناسِ مِن نَفسِي بجَميعِ ما أنتَ مُطَّلِعٌ علَيهِ مِنّي، فَأُبدِيَ لِلناسِ حُسنَ ظاهِري وأُفضِيَ إلَيكَ بِسُوءِ عَمَلي، تَقَرُّباً إلىٰ عِبادِكَ وتَباعُداً مِن مَرضاتِكَ.[٢٧٦٣]

2473. **Imām al-Bāqir (AS) said,** 'He whose outward appearance is superior to his inward self will have a very light scale of good deeds.'[2784]

٢٤٧٣. الإمامُ الباقرُ عليه السلام: مَن كانَ ظاهِرُهُ أرجَحَ مِن باطِنِهِ خَفَّ مِيزانُهُ.[٢٧٦٤]

2474. **Imām al-Ṣādiq (AS) said,** 'Beware of showing off, for whoever performs good deeds for anyone other than Allah, Allah relegates him to the one he acted for.'[2785]

٢٤٧٤ . الإمامُ الصّادقُ عليه السلام :إيّاك والرياءَ؛فإنّهُ مَن عَمِلَ لِغَيرِ اللهِ وَكَلَهُ اللهُ إلىٰ مَن عَمِلَ لَهُ.[٢٧٦٥]

785. Showing off and Polytheism

٧٨٥ـ الرِّياءُ وَالشِّركُ

2475. **The Prophet (SAWA) said,** 'The worst thing I fear for you is minor polytheism.' When asked what he meant by this, he replied, 'Showing off.'[2786]

٢٤٧٥ . عدّة الداعي عن رسول الله صلى الله عليه وآله : إنّ أخوَفَ ما أخافُ علَيكُمُ الشِّركَ الأصغرَ. قالوا: وما الشِّركُ الأصغَرُ يا رسولَ اللهِ؟ قالَ: الرياءُ.[٢٧٦٦]

2476. **Imām ʿAlī (AS) said,** 'Know that even the slightest showing off is tantamount to polytheism.'[2787]

٢٤٧٦ . الإمامُ عليٌّ عليه السلام : اِعلَمُوا أنَّ يَسِيرَ الرياءِ شِركٌ.[٢٧٦٧]

2477. **Imām al-Bāqir (AS) said,** 'The Prophet (SAWA) was once asked about the interpretation of Allah's words in the Qur'an: *"So whoever expects to encounter his Lord, let him act righteously, and not associate anyone with the worship of Allah"*[2788]. He replied, 'He who performs prayer in order to show people is a polytheist … and he who performs any act commanded by Allah to show people is a polytheist.'[2789]

٢٤٧٧ . الإمامُ الباقرُ عليه السلام: سُئلَ رسولُ اللهِ صلى الله عليه وآله عن تفسيرِ قَولِ اللهِ: ﴿فَمَنْ كانَ يَرْجُو لِقاءَ رَبِّهِ فَلْيَعمَلْ عَمَلاً صَالِحاً وَلَا يُشْرِكْ بِعِبادَةِ رَبِّهِ أحَداً﴾ فقال: مَن صَلَّى مُراءاةَ النـاسِ فهُو مُشرِكٌ... ومَن عَمِلَ عَملاً مِمّا أمَرَ اللهُ بِهِ مُراءاةَ الناسِ فهُو مُشرِكٌ.[٢٧٦٨]

(See also: POLYTHEISM: 215)

انظر: عنوان ٢١٥ «الشرك».

786. The Evil Outcome of those who Show off

٧٨٦ـ سوءُ عاقِبَةِ أهلِ الرِّياءِ

2478. **The Prophet (SAWA) said,** 'Verily the Hellfire and its inmates rage on account of those who used to show off.' When asked how the Hellfire rages, he replied, 'It rages on account of the intense heat with which they are being punished.'[2790]

٢٤٧٨ . مستدرك الوسائل : قال رسولُ اللهِ صلى الله عليه وآله : إنّ النارَ وأهلَها يَعِجُّونَ مِن أهلِ الرياءِ، فقيلَ: يا رسولَ اللهِ، وكيفَ تَعِجُّ النارُ؟! قالَ: مِن حَرِّ النارِ التي يُعَذَّبُونَ بها.[٢٧٦٩]

2479. **Imām al-Ṣādiq (AS) said,** 'On the Day of Resurrection, a servant who used to pray regularly will be brought forth, and he will beg, 'O Lord, I

٢٤٧٩ . الإمامُ الصّادقُ عليه السلام :يُجاءُ بعَبدٍ يَومَ القِيامَةِ قد صَلّىٰ فيقولُ: يا ربِّ صَلَّيتُ ابتِغاءَ وَجهِكَ

prayed in seeking Your pleasure', and he will be told, 'No, you prayed so that people would say how beautiful your prayer was. Take him to the Fire.'[2791]

فيُقالُ لَهُ: بل صَلَّيتَ لِيُقالَ ما أحسَنَ صلاةَ (فلانٍ)٢٧٧٠، اِذهَبُوا بِهِ إلى النارِ.٢٧٧١

787. The Distinguishing Characteristics of a Show off

٧٨٧ـ عَلاماتُ المُرائي

2480. **Imām 'Alī (AS) said,** 'Three characteristics distinguish a show off: he is energetic and active whilst in the presence of people, he is lazy when he is by himself, and he loves to be praised for everything.'[2792]

٢٤٨٠. الإمامُ عليٌّ ﷺ: ثلاثُ علاماتٍ لِلمُرائي: يَنشَطُ إذا رَأى الناسَ، ويَكسَلُ إذا كانَ وَحدَهُ، ويُحِبُّ أن يُحمَدَ في جَميعِ اُمُورِهِ.٢٧٧٢

788. Miscellaneous

٧٨٨ـ النَّوادِرُ

2481. **The Prophet (SAWA) said,** 'Performing actions in secret is better than performing them publicly, except for the one who wishes to set an example.'[2793]

٢٤٨١. رسولُ اللهِ ﷺ: السِّرُّ أفضَلُ مِن العَلانِيَةِ، والعلانِيَةُ لِمَن أرادَ الاقتِداءَ.٢٧٧٣

2482. **Imām al-Bāqir (AS)** was once asked by his companion Zurāra, about a man who performs a good deed which people happen to see, and which he feels good about as a result. Imām replied, 'It does not matter as long as he did not [originally] perform the action for that purpose. Everyone naturally wants people to see them as good.'[2794]

٢٤٨٢. الإمامُ الباقرُ ﷺ ـ لمّا سَألَهُ زرارةُ عن الرَّجُلِ يَعمَلُ الشيءَ مِن الخَيرِ فيَراهُ إنسانٌ فيَسُرُّهُ ذلكَ ـ: لا بَأسَ، ما مِن أحدٍ إلّا وهُو يُحِبُّ أن يَظهَرَ لَهُ في الناسِ الخَيرُ، إذا لَم يَكُن صَنَعَ ذلكَ لذلكَ.٢٧٧٤

2483. **Imām al-Ṣādiq (AS) said,** 'The deed of one who performs it in secret is recorded down as a secret action. If he admits to having performed it [when asked], the previous record is erased and it is recorded instead as a public action. If he subsequently avers it himself, however, the previous record is erased and it is recorded instead as showing off.'[2795]

٢٤٨٣. الإمامُ الصّادقُ ﷺ: مَن عَمِلَ حَسَنَةً سِرّاً كُتِبَت لَهُ سِرّاً، فإذا أقَرَّ بها مُحِيَتْ وكُتِبَت جَهراً، فإذا أقَرَّ بها ثانياً مُحِيَت وكُتِبَت رياءً.٢٧٧٥

153

OPINION

الرَّأيُ

789. That Which Renders an Opinion Valid

٧٨٩ـ ما يوجِبُ إصابَةَ الرَّأيِ

2484. **Imām ʿAlī (AS) said,** 'The [valid] opinion comes from balanced judgment, whilst the impetuous and rash opinion is a vile foundation indeed.'[2796]

٢٤٨٤ . الإمامُ عليٌّ ﷺ : الرَّأيُ مع الأناةِ، وبِئسَ الظَّهيرُ الرأيُ الفَطيرُ.[٢٧٧٦][٢٧٧٧]

2485. **Imām ʿAlī (AS) said,** 'Exchange different opinions with one another and the valid one will emerge thereof.'[2797]

٢٤٨٥ . عنه ﷺ : اِضرِبُوا بعضَ الرأيِ ببعضٍ يَتَوَلَّدْ مِنهُ الصَّوابُ.[٢٧٧٨]

2486. **Imām ʿAlī (AS) said,** 'He who tackles all sides of an opinion [different opinions] will know where the pitfalls lie.'[2798]

٢٤٨٦ . عنه ﷺ : مَنِ استَقبَلَ وُجوهَ الآراءِ عَرَفَ مَواقِعَ الخَطَأِ.[٢٧٧٩]

2487. **Imām ʿAlī (AS) said,** 'The man with the best opinion is he who does not write off the need for a second opinion from someone else.'[2799]

٢٤٨٧ . عنه ﷺ : أفضَلُ الناسِ رَأياً مَن لا يَستَغنِي عن رَأيِ مُشِيرٍ.[٢٧٨٠]

790. The Consequences of Obstinately Holding One's own Opinion

٧٩٠ـ آثارُ الاستِبدادِ بِالرَّأيِ

2488. **Imām ʿAlī (AS) said,** 'He who obstinately holds his own opinion is ruined, and he who consults other people shares in their collective understanding.'[2800]

٢٤٨٨ . الإمامُ عليٌّ ﷺ : مَنِ استَبَدَّ برأيِهِ هَلَكَ، ومَن شاوَرَ الرِّجالَ شارَكَها في عُقُولِها.[٢٧٨١]

2489. **Imām ʿAlī (AS) said,** 'Only an ignorant person is proud of his own opinion.'[2801]

٢٤٨٩ . عنه ﷺ : ما أُعجِبَ برأيِهِ إلّا جاهِلٌ.[٢٧٨٢]

2490. **Imām al-Ṣādiq (AS) said,** 'The one who adamantly holds his own opinion has based it on a shaky and erroneous argument.'[2802]

٢٤٩٠ . الإمامُ الصّادقُ ﷺ : المُستَبِدُّ برأيِهِ مَوقوفٌ علىٰ مَداحِضِ الزَّلَلِ.[٢٧٨٣]

791. Factors that Destroy an Opinion

٧٩١ـ ما يَهدِمُ الرَّأيَ

2491. **Imām ʿAlī (AS) said,** 'Stubbornly insisting upon one's opinion destroys it.'[2803]

٢٤٩١. الإمامُ عليٌّ ﷺ: اللَّجاجةُ تَسُلُّ الرأيَ.[٢٧٨٤]

2492. **Imām al-Ṣādiq (AS) said,** 'A recluse does not have any opinions.'[2804]

٢٤٩٢. الإمامُ الصّادقُ ﷺ: لَيسَ لِحاقِنٍ رأيٌ.[٢٧٨٥]

(See also: STUBBORNNESS: section 352)

انظر: عنوان ٣٥٢ «اللجاج».

792. The Government and The Validity of its Opinion

٧٩٢ـ الدَّولَةُ وصَوابُ الرَّأيِ

2493. **Imām ʿAlī (AS) said,** 'The validity of the opinion of the day changes with governments – when a new government arrives on the scene, so does its opinion [and is accepted as being valid], and when it goes, so does that opinion.'[2805]

٢٤٩٣. الإمامُ عليٌّ ﷺ: صَوابُ الرَّأيِ بالدُّوَلِ، يُقبِلُ بإقبالِها ويَذهَبُ بذَهابِها.[٢٧٨٦]

793. Acting on One's Opinion in Religious Matters

٧٩٣ـ استِعمالُ الرَّأيِ فِي الدِّينِ

2494. **The Prophet (SAWA) said,** 'This community acts upon the Book of Allah for a little while, then it acts upon the practice of the Prophet of Allah for a little while, then it acts upon its own opinion. And when they act based on their own opinion, they themselves go astray and lead others astray too.'[2806]

٢٤٩٤. رسولُ اللهِ ﷺ: تَعمَلُ هذهِ الاُمّةُ بُرهَةً مِن كتابِ اللهِ، ثُمّ تَعمَلُ بُرهةً بِسُنَّةِ رسولِ اللهِ، ثُمّ تَعمَلُ بالرأيِ، فإذا عَمِلُوا بالرأيِ فقد ضَلُّوا وأضَلُّوا.[٢٧٨٧]

2495. **Imām ʿAlī (AS) said,** 'Action is unacceptable when based on any of three things: polytheism, infidelity and one's own opinion. When asked what action based on an opinion meant, he replied, 'It is when you leave the Book of Allah and the practice of His Prophet and act upon your own opinion.'[2807]

٢٤٩٥. كنز العمّال: قالَ الإمامُ عليٌّ ﷺ: ثلاثةٌ لا يُقبَلُ مَعهُنَّ عَمَلٌ: الشِّركُ، والكُفرُ، والرأيُ. قالوا: يا أميرَ المؤمنينَ: ما الرَّأيُ؟ قالَ: تَدَعُ كتابَ اللهِ وسُنَّةَ رسولِهِ وتَعمَلُ بالرَّأيِ.[٢٧٨٨]

794. Sincere Effort Required in Formulating One's Opinion

٧٩٤ـ الاجتِهادُ فِي الرَّأيِ

2496. **The Prophet (SAWA) said,** 'If a governor, sincerely exerts himself when formulating his

٢٤٩٦. رسولُ اللهِ ﷺ: إنَّ الواليَ إذا اجتَهَدَ

opinion [on a legal edict], if his ruling is correct, he is rewarded doubly for it, and if in his ruling he is mistaken, he is still rewarded for his effort.'[2808]

فَأصابَ الحَقَّ فلَهُ أجرانِ، وإنِ اجتَهَدَ فَأخطَأَ الحقَّ فلَهُ أجرٌ واحِدٌ.[٢٧٨٩]

2497. **Imām ʿAlī (AS) said,** 'When someone who is in a position to advise people sincerely exerts himself when formulating his opinion, he is rewarded according to his intention, and has done his duty.[2809]

٢٤٩٧. الإمامُ عليٌّ عليه السلام: مَنِ اجتَهَدَ رَأيَهُ في نَصيحَةِ العامَّةِ فلَهُ ما نَوىٰ، وقد قَضىٰ ما علَيهِ.[٢٧٩٠]

154

USURY

الرِّبا ١٥٤

795. Warning Against Usury

٧٩٥ـ التَّحذيرُ مِن الرِّبا

2498. **The Prophet (SAWA) said,** 'Verily Allah, Mighty and Exalted, curses the usurer, his agent, his scribe and his two witnesses.'[2810]

٢٤٩٨. رسولُ اللهِ ﷺ: إنّ اللهَ عزّ وجلّ لَعَنَ آكِلَ الرِّبا ومُوكِلَهُ وكاتِبَهُ وشاهِدَيهِ.[٢٧٩١]

2499. **The Prophet (SAWA) said,** 'During my Night-Journey up to the heavens, I was taken to a people whose bellies were as large as houses and contained serpents that could be seen from outside their bellies. I asked, 'Who are these people, O Gabriel?' He replied, 'They are the usurers.'[2811]

٢٤٩٩. عنه ﷺ: أتَيتُ ليلةَ أُسرِيَ بِي علىٰ قَومٍ بُطونُهُم كالبيوتِ فيها الحَيّاتُ تُرىٰ مِن خارِجِ بُطونِهِم، فقلتُ: مَن هؤلاءِ يا جَبرئيلُ؟ قالَ: هؤلاءِ أكَلَةُ الرِّبا.[٢٧٩٢]

2500. **Imām al-Bāqir (AS) said,** 'The most despicable of professions [or profits] is the earning from usury.'[2812]

٢٥٠٠. الإمامُ الباقرُ عليه السلام: أخبَثُ المَكاسِبِ، كَسبُ الرِّبا.[٢٧٩٣]

2501. **Imām al-Ṣādiq (AS) said,** 'The usurer only leaves this world after Satan makes him insane.'[2813]

٢٥٠١. الإمامُ الصّادقُ عليه السلام: آكِلُ الرِّبا لا يَخرُجُ مِنَ الدنيا حتّىٰ يَتَخَبَّطَهُ الشيطانُ.[٢٧٩٤]

2502. **Imām al-Ṣādiq (AS) said,** 'A dirham earned by usury is worse in the sight of Allah than

٢٥٠٢. عنه عليه السلام: دِرهَمُ رِبا أعظَمُ عِندَ اللهِ

seventy counts of incest in the Holy Sanctuary of Allah.'[2814]

عزّوجلّ مِن سَبعينَ زَنيةً كلّها بِذاتِ مَحرمٍ فـي بيتِ اللهِ الحرامِ. ٢٧٩٥

796. The Wisdom Behind the Prohibition of Usury

٧٩٦ ـ حِكمَةُ تَحريمِ الرِّبا

2503. **Imām al-Ṣādiq (AS),** when asked by Hishām b. al-Ḥakam about the reason behind the prohibition of usury, replied, 'Were usury to be permissible, people would abandon their trading and other necessities, so Allah prohibited usury in order that man may flee from the unlawful [means of earning] to trade, and resort to buying and selling, and this in turn facilitates borrowing from each other.'[2815]

٢٥٠٣ . الإمامُ الصّادقُ عليه السلام ـ لَمّا سَألَهُ هِشامُ بنُ الحَكَمِ عن عِلَّةِ تَحريمِ الرِّبا ـ: إنّهُ لَو كانَ الرِّبـا حلالاً لَتَرَكَ النّاسُ التِّجاراتِ وما يَحتاجونَ إلَيهِ فحَرَّمَ اللهُ الرِّبا لتَنفِرَ ٢٧٩٦ النـاسُ عـنِ الحـرامِ إلى التِّجاراتِ وإلى البَيعِ والشِّراءِ فَيَتَّصِلَ ذلكَ بَينَهُم في القَرضِ. ٢٧٩٧

2504. **When Imām al-Ṣādiq (AS)** was asked the reason behind the prohibition of usury, he replied, 'So that people may not withhold common courtesy from each other.'[2816]

٢٥٠٤ . عنه عليه السلام ـ لَمّا سُئلَ عن عِلّةِ تحريمِ الرِّبا ـ: لئلّا يَتمانَعَ النّاسُ المَعروفَ. ٢٧٩٨

797. That Which Leads One to Become Involved in Usury

٧٩٧ ـ ما يوجِبُ الارتِطامَ فِي الرِّبا

2505. **Imām ʿAlī (AS) said,** 'Engage yourself firstly in communal relations with people, then the law, and subsequently trading, for by Allah, usury creeps into this community more discreetly than an ant creeps onto a rock.'[2817]

٢٥٠٥ . الإمامُ عليٌّ عليه السلام : مَعاشِرَ النّاسِ، الفِقهَ ثُمَّ المَتجَرَ، واللهِ لَلرِّبا في هذهِ الأُمّةِ أخفىٰ من دَبيبِ النَّملِ علَى الصَّفا. ٢٧٩٩

2506. **Imām ʿAlī (AS) said,** 'Whoever trades without knowledge of legal rulings gets involved in usury.'[2818]

٢٥٠٦ . عنه عليه السلام : مَنِ اتَّجَرَ بغَيرِ فِقهٍ فَقَدِ ارتَطَمَ فِي الرِّبا. ٢٨٠٠

(See also: COMMERCE: section 285)

انظر: التجارة: باب ٢٨٥.

798. The Usurer who Justifies Himself Must be Fought

٧٩٨ ـ آكِلُ الرِّبا مُستَحِلّاً مُحارِبٌ

"O you who have faith! Be wary of Allah, and abandon [all claims to] what remains of usury, should

﴿يا أيُّهَا الّذينَ آمَنُوا اتَّقُوا اللهَ وذَرُوا ما بَقِيَ مِنَ

you be faithful. And if you do not, then be informed of a war from Allah and His apostle. And if you repent, then you will have your principal, neither harming others, nor suffering harm."[2819]

الرِّبَا إن كُنتُم مُّؤمِنِينَ * فَإنْ لَم تَفعَلُوا فَأْذَنُوا بِحَرْبٍ مِنَ اللهِ وَرَسُولِه وَإنْ تُبْتُمْ فَلَكُمْ رُؤُوسُ أمْوَالِكُمْ لَا تَظْلِمُونَ وَلَا تُظْلَمُونَ﴾ .٢٨٠١

2507. **Imām al-Ṣādiq (AS)** was once informed of a man who was extorting usury and calling it *libā*[2820] instead of *ribā* (usury) to justify his actions, with regards to whom Imām said, 'If Allah gave me the power to, I would have him beheaded.'[2821]

٢٥٠٧ . الإمامُ الصّادقُ عليه السلام ـ لَمّا بلَغهُ أنّ رَجلاً كانَ يَأكُلُ الرِّبا ويُسَمِّيهِ اللِّباءَ ـ: لئن أمكَنَنِي اللهُ عزّوجلّ (مِنهُ) لَأضرِبَنَّ عُنُقَهُ.٢٨٠٢

155

HOPE

الرَّجاءُ

799. Enjoinment of True Hope

٧٩٩ ـ الحَثُّ عَلَى الرَّجاءِ الصّادِقِ

"Indeed those who have become faithful and those who have migrated and waged jihād in the way of Allah – it is they who hope for Allah's mercy, and Allah is all-forgiving, all-merciful."[2822]

﴿إِنَّ الَّذِينَ آمَنُوا وَالَّذِينَ هاجَرُوا وَجاهَدُوا فِي سَبِيلِ اللهِ أُولئِكَ يَرْجُونَ رَحْمَتَ اللهِ واللهُ غَفُورٌ رَّحِيمٌ﴾ .٢٨٠٣

2508. **Imām ʿAlī (AS) said,** 'Every hopeful person continues seeking, and every fearful one runs away.'[2823]

٢٥٠٨ . الإمامُ عليٌّ عليه السلام : كلُّ راجٍ طالِبٌ وكُلُّ خائفٍ هارِبٌ.٢٨٠٤

2509. **Imām ʿAlī (AS) said** to a man soliciting advice from him, 'Do not be of those who hope for [bliss in] the life of the Hereafter without action, and delay repentance by having high expectations, and who utter words like the ascetics with regard to this world, though in practice they behave like those who covet it.'[2824]

٢٥٠٩ . عنه عليه السلام ـ لِرَجُلٍ سَألَهُ أن يَعِظَهُ ـ: لا تَكُن مِمَّن يَرجُو الآخِرَةَ بغَيرِ العَمَلِ ويُرَجِّي التَّوبَةَ بطُولِ الأمَلِ، يَقولُ في الدنيا بقَولِ الزاهِدِينَ ويَعمَلُ فيها بعَمَلِ الراغِبينَ.٢٨٠٥

2510. Someone came to Imām al-Ṣādiq (AS) and told him that there was a group of people who were disobeying Allah, but at the same time they were saying that they hoped [in His mercy], and remained thus until death overtook them. Imām (AS) said, 'These are people who swing back and

٢٥١٠ . الإمامُ الصّادقُ عليه السلام ـ لَمّا سُئلَ عن قَومٍ يَعمَلُونَ بالمَعاصِي ويَقولونَ: نَرجُو، فلا يَزالُونَ كذلكَ حتّىٰ يَأتِيَهُمُ الموتُ؟ ـ: هؤلاءِ

forth between their desires. They are lying and are not really hopeful, for the one who hopes for something seeks it, and the one who fears something flees from it.'[2825]

قومٌ يَتَرَجَّحُونَ في الأمانِيِّ كَذَبوا لَيسُوا بِراجِينَ، إنّ مَن رَجا شَيئاً طَلَبَهُ ومَن خافَ مِن شيءٍ هَرَبَ مِنهُ.٢٨٠٦

800. Caution Against Placing One's Hopes in Anyone Other than Allah

٨٠٠ـ التَّحذيرُ مِن رَجاءِ غَيرِ اللهِ

2511. **Imām ʿAlī (AS) said,** 'Place all your hope in Allah, glory be to Him, and do not hope from anyone else apart from Him, for no sooner does anyone place his hope in anyone other than Allah than he fails.'[2826]

٢٥١١. الإمامُ عليٌّ ﷺ: اِجعَلُوا كُلَّ رجائكُم للهِ سبحانَهُ ولا تَرجُوا أحَداً سِواهُ، فإنّهُ ما رَجا أحَدٌ غَيرَ اللهِ تعالىٰ إلّا خابَ.٢٨٠٧

(See also: ASKING (2): section 908; DESPAIR: section 1907)

انظر: السؤال (٢) باب ٩٠٨؛ اليأس: باب ١٩٠٧.

156

THE RETURN[2827]

الرَّجعَةُ

801. The Return of the Dead

٨٠١ـ رَجعَةُ المَوتىٰ

2512. **Imām al-Ṣādiq (AS) said,** 'By Allah, the days and the nights will not come to an end before Allah revives the dead and causes the living to die, and returns rights to those they are due to, and establishes the religion that He has selected for Himself.'[2828]

٢٥١٢. الإمامُ الصّادقُ ﷺ: واللهِ لا تَذهَبُ الأيّامُ واللّيالي حتّىٰ يُحيِيَ اللهُ المَوتىٰ ويُمِيتَ الأحياءَ، ويَرُدَّ الحَقَّ إلى أهلِهِ، ويُقِيمَ دينَهُ الذي ارتَضاهُ لِنَفسِهِ.٢٨٠٨

802. The Mentioning of Specific People to be Returned

٨٠٢ـ مَن اُخبِرَ بِرَجعَتِهِ

2513. **Imām al-Ḥusayn (AS) said,** 'I will be the first to appear at the time of the splitting of the earth. I will come out at the same time of the returning of the Commander of the Faithful (AS) and the rising of our Qāʾim.'[2829]

٢٥١٣. الإمامُ الحسينُ ﷺ: أكُونُ أوَّلَ مَن يَنشَقُّ الأرضُ عَنهُ، فَأخرُجُ خَرجَةً يُوافِقُ ذلكَ خَرجَةَ أميرِ المؤمنينَ وقيامَ قائِمِنا.٢٨٠٩

2514. **Imām al-Ṣādiq (AS) said,** 'The first person to return to the life of this world will be Ḥusayn b. ʿAlī (AS), who will be made to rule until his

٢٥١٤. الإمامُ الصّادقُ ﷺ: أوَّلُ مَن يَرجِعُ إلى الدنيا، الحسينُ ابنُ عليٍّ ﷺ فيُمَلَّكُ حتّىٰ يَسقُطَ

eyebrows will protrude over his eyes as a result of his old age.'[2830]

حاجباهُ على عَينَيهِ مِن الكِبَرِ.[٢٨١٠]

803. The Return will not be Universal

٨٠٣-الرَّجعَةُ لَيسَت عامَّةً

2515. **Imām al-Ṣādiq (AS) said,** 'Verily the Return will not be for everyone, but specific. Only those of absolutely pure faith or pure evil [polytheism] will be brought back to life.'[2831]

٢٥١٥. الإمامُ الصّادقُ عليه السلام: إنّ الرَّجعَةَ لَيست بعامَّةٍ، وهِي خاصّةٌ لا يَرجِعُ إلّا مَن مَحَضَ الإيمانَ مَحضاً أو مَحَضَ الشِّركَ مَحضاً.[٢٨١١]

157

COMPASSION[2832]

الرَّحِم

804. The Enjoinment of Compassion Towards One Another

٨٠٤-الحَثُّ عَلَى التَّراحُمِ

"Muḥammad is the apostle of Allah, and those with him are firm of heart against the unbelievers, compassionate among themselves..."[2833]

﴿مُحَمَّدٌ رَسُولُ اللهِ وَالَّذِينَ مَعَهُ أَشِدَّاءُ عَلَى الكُفَّارِ رُحَماءُ بَيْنَهُمْ﴾.[٢٨١٢]

"...while being of those who have faith and who enjoin one another to patience, and enjoin one another to compassion. They are the People of the Right Hand."[2834]

﴿ثُمَّ كَانَ مِنَ الَّذِينَ آمَنُوا وَتَوَاصَوْا بِالصَّبْرِ وَتَوَاصَوْا بِالمَرْحَمَةِ * أُولَئِكَ أَصْحَابُ المَيْمَنَةِ﴾.[٢٨١٣]

2516. **The Prophet (SAWA) said,** 'The All-Merciful, Blessed and most High, has mercy on those who are merciful (towards others). Have mercy on the dwellers of the earth and the [Lord of the] Heavens will have mercy on you.'[2835]

٢٥١٦. رسولُ اللهِ صلى الله عليه وآله: الراحِمونَ يَرحَمُهُم الرّحمٰنُ تباركَ وتعالىٰ، اِرحَمُوا مَن في الأرضِ يَرحَمْكُم مَن في السماءِ.[٢٨١٤]

2517. **The Prophet (SAWA) said,** 'One of the inmates of the Fire will call out: O Affectionate One, O Liberal Giver, save me from the Fire. So Allah will command one of His angels to take him out that he may come and stand before Him, and Allah will ask him, 'Were you ever compassionate towards a sparrow?'[2836]

٢٥١٧. عنه صلى الله عليه وآله: يُنادي مُنادٍ في النارِ: يا حَنّانُ يا مَنّانُ نَجِّني مِنَ النارِ، فَيأمُرُ اللهُ مَلَكاً فَيُخرِجُهُ حتّىٰ يَقِفَ بينَ يَدَيهِ، فيقولُ اللهُ عزّ وجلّ: هل رَحِمتَ عُصفوراً.[٢٨١٥]

2518. **Imām ʿAlī (AS) said,** 'Have mercy and you will be had mercy upon.'[2837]

٢٥١٨ . الإمامُ عليٌّ عليه السلام : إرحَمْ تُرحَمْ.[٢٨١٦]

2519. **Imām ʿAlī (AS) said,** 'How I wonder at the one who hopes for the mercy of the One above him and yet himself does not have mercy on the one below him.'[2838]

٢٥١٩ . عنه عليه السلام : عَجِبتُ لِمَن يَرجُو رَحمَةَ مَن فَوقَهُ كيفَ لا يَرحَمُ مَن دُونَهُ؟![٢٨١٧]

805. Those That are Most Deserving of Compassion

٨٠٥ـ مَن يَستَحِقُّ الرَّحمَ

2520. **The Prophet (SAWA) said,** 'Be compassionate towards a mighty person who has been dishonoured, a rich man who has become poor, and a scholar who has been forgotten amidst a generation of ignorant people.'[2839]

٢٥٢٠ . رسولُ اللهِ صلى الله عليه وآله : اِرحَمُوا عَزيزاً ذَلَّ، وغَنِيّاً افتَقَرَ، وعالِماً ضاعَ في زمانِ جُهّالٍ.[٢٨١٨]

2521. **The Prophet (SAWA) said,** 'Be compassionate towards the destitute.'[2840]

٢٥٢١ . عنه صلى الله عليه وآله : اِرحَمِ المَساكينَ.[٢٨١٩]

2522. **Imām ʿAlī (AS) said,** 'Show compassion to the young in your family and reverence to the old.'[2841]

٢٥٢٢ . الإمامُ عليٌّ عليه السلام : اِرحَمْ مِن أهلِكَ الصَّغيرَ ووَقِّرْ مِنهُمُ الكَبيرَ.[٢٨٢٠]

158

DIVINE MERCY

الرَّحمَةُ

806. Allah's Divine Mercy

٨٠٦ـ رَحمَةُ اللهِ

2523. **The Prophet (SAWA) said,** 'Verily Allah, most High, created one hundred units of mercy on the day He created the heavens and the earth, each unit of which corresponds to all that is between the sky and the earth. Of these He descended one unit of mercy to the earth, and by virtue of that one unit, everything in creation shows understanding for one another, the mother is affectionate towards her child, and by virtue of the same unit, the birds and the beasts are able to

٢٥٢٣ . رسولُ اللهِ صلى الله عليه وآله : إنّ اللهَ تعالىٰ خَلَقَ مِائةَ رَحمَةٍ يَومَ خَلَقَ السماواتِ والأرضَ، كُلُّ رحمةٍ مِنها طِباقُ ما بينَ السماءِ والأرضِ، فَأهبَطَ رَحمَةً مِنها إلى الأرضِ فَبِها تَراحَمَ الخَلقُ، وبِها تَعطِفُ الوالِدَةُ علىٰ وَلَدِها، وبِها تَشرَبُ الطيرُ والوُحوشُ مِن الماءِ، وبِها

drink water, and all creatures are able to subsist.'[2842]

تَعِيشُ الخلائقُ.٢٨٢١

2524. **The Prophet (SAWA) said,** 'No one shall enter Paradise except by intervention of Allah's divine mercy.' His companions asked, 'Not even you?' to which he replied, 'Not even me, unless Allah encompasses me with His mercy.'[2843]

٢٥٢٤. كنز العمّال عن رسولِ اللهِ ﷺ: لَن يَدخُلَ الجَنَّةَ أحَدٌ إلّا بِرحمَةِ اللهِ. قالوا: ولا أنتَ؟ قالَ: ولا أنا إلّا أن يَتَغَمَّدَنِيَ اللهُ.٢٨٢٢

2525. **The Prophet (SAWA) said,** 'If you knew the worth of Allah's mercy, you would rely solely on that.'[2844]

٢٥٢٥. رسولُ اللهِ ﷺ: لَو تَعلَمُونَ قَدْرَ رحمَةِ اللهِ تعالىٰ لَاتَّكَلتُم علَيها.٢٨٢٣

2526. **Imām Zayn al-ʿĀbidīn (AS) said,** 'It is no small wonder if man is given salvation [on the Day of Resurrection], rather what *is* a wonder is how he manages to end up in eternal damnation in spite of Allah's all-encompassing mercy.'[2845]

٢٥٢٦. الإمامُ زينُ العابدينَ ﷺ: لَيسَ العَجَبُ مِمَّن نَجا كيفَ نَجا، وأمّا العَجَبُ مِمَّنْ هَلَكَ كَيفَ هَلَكَ مَع سَعَةِ رحمةِ اللهِ؟!٢٨٢٤

807. Factors that Elicit Allah's Mercy

٨٠٧ـ موجِباتُ الرَّحمَةِ

2527. **The Prophet (SAWA) said,** 'Elicit Allah's mercy through the performance of the acts of obedience that He has commanded you.'[2846]

٢٥٢٧. رسولُ اللهِ ﷺ: تَعَرَّضُوا لِرَحمَةِ اللهِ بما أمَرَكُم بِهِ مِن طاعَتِهِ.٢٨٢٥

2528. **Imām ʿAlī (AS) said,** 'Allah's remembrance elicits the descent of His mercy.'[2847]

٢٥٢٨. الإمامُ عليٌّ ﷺ: بِـذِكرِ اللهِ تُستَنزَلُ الرحمَةُ.٢٨٢٦

2529. **Imām ʿAlī (AS) said,** 'Spreading mercy [to others] elicits the descent of Allah's mercy.'[2848]

٢٥٢٩. عنه ﷺ: بِبَذلِ الرحمَةِ تُستَنزَلُ الرحمَةُ.٢٨٢٧

159

CONSANGUINEAL RELATIONS

الرَّحِمُ

808. Reconciliation With One's Kin

٨٠٨ـ فَضلُ صِلَةِ الرَّحِمِ

2530. **The Prophet (SAWA) said,** 'Verily the good deed to be rewarded the fastest is reconciliation with one's kin.'[2849]

٢٥٣٠. رسولُ اللهِ ﷺ: إنَّ أعجَلَ الخَيرِ ثَواباً صِلَةُ الرَّحِمِ.٢٨٢٨

2531. **The Prophet (SAWA) said,** 'If you want to be happy the whole year, reconcile with your kin.'[2850]

٢٥٣١. عنهﷺ: سِرْ سَنَةً صِلْ رَحِمَكَ.[٢٨٢٩]

809. The Benefits of Maintaining Relations With One's Kin

٨٠٩ـ آثارُ صِلَةِ الرَّحِمِ

2532. **Fāṭima al-Zahrā' (AS) said,** 'Allah made the maintenance of relations with one's kin obligatory in order to maintain growth in population.'[2851]

٢٥٣٢. فاطمةُ الزَّهراءُؑ: فَرَضَ اللهُ صِلَةَ الأرحامِ مَنماةً لِلعدَدِ.[٢٨٣٠]

2533. **Imām al-Ḥusayn (AS) said,** 'Whoever would like an increase in his lifespan and in his sustenance should maintain relations with his kin.'[2852]

٢٥٣٣. الإمامُ الحسينُؑ: مَن سَرَّهُ أن يُنسَأ في أجَلِهِ، ويُزادَ في رِزقِهِ، فَلْيَصِلْ رَحِمَهُ.[٢٨٣١]

2534. **Imām al-Bāqir (AS) said,** 'Maintaining relations with one's kin purifies one's actions, brings about an increase in wealth, repels misfortunes, eases the account [on the Day of Resurrection], and delays one's appointed time of death.'[2853]

٢٥٣٤. الإمامُ الباقرُؑ: صِلَةُ الأرحامِ تُزَكّي الأعمالَ وتُنْمِي الأموالَ، وتَدفَعُ البَلوىٰ، وتُيَسِّرُ الحِسابَ وتُنسِئُ في الأجَلِ.[٢٨٣٢]

2535. **Imām al-Bāqir (AS) said,** 'Maintaining relations with one's kin improves one's character, brings about open-handedness and cheerfulness, increases in one's sustenance, and delays one's appointed time of death.'[2854]

٢٥٣٥. عنهؑ: صلةُ الأرحامِ تُحَسِّنُ الخُلُقَ وتُسَمِّحُ الكَفَّ وتُطَيِّبُ النَّفْسَ، وتَزِيدُ في الرّزقِ وتُنسِئُ في الأجَلِ.[٢٨٣٣]

2536. **Imām al-Hādī (AS) said,** 'When Allah allowed [Prophet] Moses son of Amran (AS) to converse with Him, Moses (AS) asked, 'My God, what is the reward of one who maintains relations with his kin?' He replied, 'O Moses, I delay the appointed time of his death, and ease the pangs and agonies of death for him.'[2855]

٢٥٣٦. الإمامُ الهاديُّؑ: لَمّا كَلَّمَ اللهُ عزّوجلّ موسى ابنَ عِمرانَؑ قالَ موسىٰ: إلهي... ما جَزاءُ مَن وَصَلَ رَحِمَهُ؟ قالَ: يا موسىٰ، أُنسِأُ[٢٨٣٤] لَهُ أجَلَهُ، وأُهَوِّنُ علَيهِ سَكَراتِ المَوتِ.[٢٨٣٥]

810. Reconciling with One who Cuts You off

٨١٠ـ صِلَةُ القاطِعِ

2537. **The Prophet (SAWA) said,** 'Do not cut off your kin even if they cut you off.'[2856]

٢٥٣٧ . رسولُ اللهِ ﷺ : لا تَقطَعْ رَحِمَكَ وإن قَطَعَتكَ . ٢٨٣٦

2538. **Imām al-Ḥusayn (AS) said,** 'The best reconciler is he who reconciles with one who cut him off.'[2857]

٢٥٣٨ . الإمامُ الحسينُ ﷺ : إنّ أوصَلَ الناسِ مَن وَصَلَ مَن قَطَعَهُ . ٢٨٣٧

811. Caution Against Cutting Ties With One's Kin

٨١١ـ التَّحذيرُ عَن قَطيعَةِ الرَّحِمِ

"May it not be that if you were to wield authority you would cause corruption in the land and cut off the ties of kinship? They are the ones whom Allah has cursed, so he made them deaf and blinded their sight."[2858]

﴿فَهَلْ عَسَيْتُمْ إِنْ تَوَلَّيْتُمْ أَنْ تُفْسِدُوا فِي الْأَرْضِ وَتُقَطِّعُوا أَرْحامَكُمْ ۞ أُولٰئِكَ الَّذِينَ لَعَنَهُمُ اللهُ فَأَصَمَّهُمْ وَأَعْمَىٰ أَبْصارَهُمْ﴾ . ٢٨٣٨

2539. **The Prophet (SAWA) said,** 'Verily the angels do not go to [visit] a people if among them lives one who has cut ties with his kin.'[2859]

٢٥٣٩ . رسولُ اللهِ ﷺ : إنّ الملائكةَ لا تَنزِلُ علىٰ قَومٍ فيهم قاطِعُ رَحِمٍ . ٢٨٣٩

2540. **Imām 'Alī (AS) said,** 'If they cut off ties with their kin, their wealth will be placed at the disposal of evil people.'[2860]

٢٥٤٠ . الإمامُ عليٌّ ﷺ : إذا قَطَعُوا الأرحامَ جُعِلَتِ الأموالُ في أيدِي الأشرارِ . ٢٨٤٠

2541. **Imām al-Ṣādiq (AS) said,** 'The sin that hastens one's death is cutting off ties with one's kin.'[2861]

٢٥٤١ . الإمامُ الصّادقُ ﷺ : الذُّنوبُ التي تُعَجِّلُ الفَناءَ قَطيعَةُ الرَّحِمِ . ٢٨٤١

812. The Least One Can do to Maintain Relations With One's Kin

٨١٢ـ أقَلُّ ما يوصَلُ بِهِ الرَّحِمُ

2542. **The Prophet (SAWA) said,** 'Maintain relations with your kin even if it be with a mere greeting (*salām*).'[2862]

٢٥٤٢ . رسولُ اللهِ ﷺ : صِلُوا أرحامَكُم ولو بِالسَّلامِ . ٢٨٤٢

2543. **Imām al-Ṣādiq (AS) said,** 'Maintain relations with your kin even if it be by offering them a drink of water. The best way to maintain

٢٥٤٣ . الإمامُ الصّادقُ ﷺ : صِلْ رَحِمَكَ ولو بِشَربَةٍ مِن ماءٍ، وأفضَلُ ما تُوصَلُ بِهِ الرَّحِمُ

relations is to refrain from hurting them in any way.'[2863]

كَفُّ الأذىٰ عَنها.[٢٨٤٣]

160

SUSTENANCE

الرِّزقُ

813. The All-Sustainer

٨١٣-الرَّزّاقُ

"Indeed it is Allah who is the All-Sustainer, Powerful, All-Strong."[2864]

﴿إنَّ اللهَ هُوَ الرَّزّاقُ ذُو القُوَّةِ المَتِينُ﴾.[٢٨٤٤]

"Surely your Lord makes plentiful the sustenance for whomever He wishes and straitens it. Indeed He is all-aware, all-seeing about His servants."[2865]

﴿إنَّ رَبَّكَ يَبْسُطُ الرِّزْقَ لِمَن يَشاءُ ويَقْدِرُ إنَّهُ كانَ بِعِبادِهِ خَبِيراً بَصِيراً﴾.[٢٨٤٥]

2544. **Imām ʿAlī (AS) said,** 'No one has the power to withhold or bestow sustenance except the All-Sustainer.'[2866]

٢٥٤٤. الإمامُ عليٌّ عليه السلام: لا يَملِكُ إمساكَ الأرزاقِ وإدرارَها إلّا الرَّزّاقُ.[٢٨٤٦]

2545. **Imām ʿAlī (AS) said,** 'He apportions sustenance, abundantly and sparingly, and He distributes them to those in need as well as to those who prosper, and He is Just in His allotment in order that he may test whomever He wishes with prosperity or with hardship, and that He may test therewith the gratefulness and perseverance expressed by both rich and poor.'[2867]

٢٥٤٥. عنه عليه السلام: وقَدَّرَ الأرزاقَ فَكَثَّرَها وقَلَّلَها، وقَسَّمَها على الضِّيقِ والسَّعَةِ، فَعَدَلَ فيها لِيَبتَلِيَ مَن أرادَ، بِمَيسورِها ومَعسورِها، ولِيَختَبِرَ بذلكَ الشُّكرَ والصَّبرَ مِن غَنِيِّها وفَقيرِها.[٢٨٤٧]

814. Sustenance is Guaranteed

٨١٤-ضَمانُ الرِّزقِ

"There is no animal on the earth, but that its sustenance lies with Allah, and He knows its [enduring] abode and its temporary place of lodging. Everything is in a manifest Book."[2868]

﴿وما مِنْ دابَّةٍ فِي الأرْضِ إلّا عَلَى اللهِ رِزْقُها وَيَعْلَمُ مُسْتَقَرَّها وَمُسْتَوْدَعَها كُلٌّ فِي كِتابٍ مُبِينٍ﴾.[٢٨٤٨]

2546. **The Prophet (SAWA) said,** 'Do not preoccupy yourself away from the duties incumbent upon you in your bid to secure that which is guaranteed to you, for indeed neither will you miss out on that which has been apportioned for

٢٥٤٦. رسولُ اللهِ صلى الله عليه وآله: لا تَتَشاغَلْ عمّا فُرِضَ علَيكَ بِما قد ضُمِنَ لَكَ فإنَّهُ لَيسَ بفائتِكَ ما قد

you, nor will you attain that which has been placed beyond your reach.'[2869]

قُسِّمَ لَكَ ، ولَستَ بِلاحِقٍ ما قد زُوِيَ عنكَ . ٢٨٤٩

2547. **Imām ʿAlī (AS) said,** 'Every living thing has been given its own provision.'[2870]

٢٥٤٧ . الإمامُ عليٌّ (عليه السلام) : لِكُلِّ ذِي رَمَقٍ قُوتٌ . ٢٨٥٠

2548. **Imām ʿAlī (AS) said,** 'This is a crow and this is an eagle, this one a dove and this one an ostrich. He has given each bird an individual name and has guaranteed each one its sustenance.'[2871]

٢٥٤٨ . عنه (عليه السلام) : فهذا غُرابٌ وهذا عُقابٌ ، وهذا حَمامٌ وهذا نَعامٌ ، دَعا كُلَّ طائرٍ باسمِهِ ، وكَفَلَ لَهُ برزقِهِ . ٢٨٥١

2549. **Imām ʿAlī (AS) said,** 'His creatures are His dependants, for whom He has guaranteed the means of subsistence, and apportioned provisions.'[2872]

٢٥٤٩ . عنه (عليه السلام) : عِيالُهُ الخَلائقُ ، ضَمِنَ أرزاقَهُم ، وقَدَّرَ أقْواتَهُم . ٢٨٥٢

2550. **Imām ʿAlī (AS) said,** 'Go out and seek your livelihood for it is guaranteed to the one who goes in search of it.'[2873]

٢٥٥٠ . عنه (عليه السلام) : أُطلُبُوا الرِّزقَ فإنّهُ مَضمونٌ لِطالِبِهِ . ٢٨٥٣

2551. **Imām al-ʿAskarī (AS) said,** 'Do not let [preoccupation with] a sustenance that is guaranteed avert you from an act that is incumbent.'[2874]

٢٥٥١ . الإمامُ العسكريُّ (عليه السلام) : لا يَشغَلْكَ رِزقٌ مَضمونٌ عن عَمَلٍ مَفروضٍ . ٢٨٥٤

815. Greed and Increase in Sustenance

٨١٥ـ الحِرصُ وزِيادةُ الرِّزقِ

2552. **The Prophet (SAWA) said,** 'Sustenance cannot be pulled by the greed of an avaricious person nor repelled by the repugnance of a repugnant person.'[2875]

٢٥٥٢ . رسولُ اللهِ (صلى الله عليه وآله) : إنّ الرِّزقَ لا يَجُرُّهُ حِرصُ حَريصٍ ولا يَصرِفُهُ كَراهِيَةُ كارِهٍ . ٢٨٥٥

2553. **Imām ʿAlī (AS) said,** 'Know that even if a servant was devoid of shrewdness and was feeble in his schemes, it would not reduce the amount of sustenance that Allah has apportioned for him, and even if a servant were to be skilfully shrewd and crafty, it would not do anything to increase the sustenance that Allah has apportioned for him.'[2876]

٢٥٥٣ . الإمامُ عليٌّ (عليه السلام) : إعلَمُوا أنَّ عَبداً وإن ضَعُفَتْ حِيلَتُهُ ، ووَهَنَتْ مَكيدَتُهُ أنّهُ لَن يُنقَصَ مِمّا قَدَّرَ اللهُ لَهُ ، وإن قَوِيَ عَبدٌ في شِدَّةِ الحِيلَةِ وقُوَّةِ المَكيدَةِ أنّهُ لن يُزادَ على ما قَدَّرَ اللهُ لَهُ . ٢٨٥٦

2554. **Imām al-Ṣādiq (AS) said,** 'Since sustenance is duly allotted, what is the use of greed?!'[2877]

٢٥٥٤ . الإمامُ الصّادقُ (عليه السلام) : إن كانَ الرِّزقُ مَقسوماً فالحِرصُ لِماذا ؟! ٢٨٥٧

2555. **Imām al-Ṣādiq (AS) said,** 'Verily Allah, most High, has abundantly distributed sustenance even to the fools, so that intelligent men may take a lesson from this and know that the wealth of this world cannot be obtained by work or cunning.'[2878]

٢٥٥٥. عنه ﷺ: إنّ اللهَ تعالىٰ وَسَّعَ أرزاقَ الحَمقىٰ لِيَعتَبِرَ العُقَلاءُ ويَعلَمُوا أنّ الدنيا ليسَ يُنالُ ما فيها بِعَمَلٍ ولا حِيلَةٍ.[٢٨٥٨]

816. Enjoinment of Seeking One's Livelihood Through Decent Means

٨١٦ـ الحَثُّ عَلَى الإجمالِ في طَلَبِ الرِّزقِ

2556. **The Prophet (SAWA) said,** 'Verily the archangel Gabriel blew into my mind that no soul shall pass away before the depletion of his sustenance in this world, so be wary of your duty to Allah and seek your livelihood through decent means, and let not a delay in your provision cause any of you to seek it through unlawful means, for verily what is with Allah is only acquired through His obedience.'[2879]

٢٥٥٦. رسولُ اللهِ ﷺ: ألا وإنّ الرُّوحَ الأمينَ نَفَثَ في رُوعِي أنّهُ لَن تَمُوتَ نفسٌ حتّىٰ تَستَكمِلَ رِزقَها، فاتَّقُوا اللهَ وأجمِلُوا في الطَّلَبِ، ولا يَحمِلْ أحَدَكُم استِبطاءُ شَيءٍ مِنَ الرِّزقِ أن يَطلُبَهُ بِغَيرِ حِلِّهِ، فإنّهُ لا يُدرَكُ ما عِندَ اللهِ إلّا بطاعَتِهِ.[٢٨٥٩، ٢٨٦٠]

2557. **Imām ʿAlī (AS) said,** 'Take from [the wealth of] this world that which comes to you, and avoid that which evades you, and if you cannot do this, then at least seek your livelihood through decent means.'[2880]

٢٥٥٧. الإمامُ عليٌّ ﷺ: خُذْ مِن الدنيا ما أتاكَ وتَوَلَّ عمّا تَوَلّىٰ عنك، فإن أنتَ لَم تَفعَلْ فَأجمِلْ في الطَّلَبِ.[٢٨٦١]

2558. **Imām al-Ṣādiq (AS) said,** 'Your quest to secure your means of subsistence should be such that it is neither like the earning of a wasteful squanderer, and nor like the greedy man who loves and depends on this world. Rather, you must raise yourself from the level of weakness and incapacity, and bring yourself down [from the level of greed] to the level of an equitable and virtuous man, and seek your earning the way a believer should.'[2881]

٢٥٥٨. الإمامُ الصّادقُ ﷺ: لِيَكُن طَلَبُكَ المَعيشَةَ فَوقَ كَسبِ المُضَيِّعِ، دُونَ طَلَبِ الحَريصِ الراضي بالدنيا المُطمَئنِّ إلَيها، ولكنْ أنزِلْ نفسَكَ مِن ذلكَ بمَنزِلَةِ المُنصِفِ المُتَعَفِّفِ تَرفَعُ نفسَكَ عن مَنزِلَةِ الواهِي الضَّعيفِ وتَكتَسِبُ ما لابُدَّ لِلمُؤمنِ مِنهُ.[٢٨٦٢]

817. The Seeker of his Sustenance

٨١٧ـ الرِّزقُ وطالِبُهُ

2559. **The Prophet (SAWA) said,** 'If man was to flee from his sustenance as he flees from death, it would find him just as death finds him.'[2882]

٢٥٥٩ . رسولُ اللهِ ﷺ : لَو أنَّ ابنَ آدَمَ فَرَّ مِن رِزقِهِ كما يَفِرُّ مِنَ المَوتِ لَأَدرَكَهُ كما يُدرِكُهُ المَوتُ . [٢٨٦٣]

2560. **Imām ʿAlī (AS) said,** 'Sustenance runs after the one who does not run after it.'[2883]

٢٥٦٠ . الإمامُ عليٌّ عليه السلام : الرِّزقُ يَطلُبُ مَن لا يَطلُبُهُ . [٢٨٦٤]

2561. **Imām ʿAlī (AS) said,** 'There are two types of sustenance: the sustenance that you seek out, and the sustenance that seeks you out, which even if you do not pursue it, it pursues you.'[2884]

٢٥٦١ . عنه عليه السلام : إنَّ الرِّزقَ رِزقانِ : رِزقٌ تَطلُبُهُ ، ورِزقٌ يَطلُبُكَ ، فإن أنتَ لَم تَأتِهِ أتاكَ . [٢٨٦٥]

2562. **Imām al-Ṣādiq (AS) said,** 'Verily Allah, Mighty and Exalted, has placed the believers' livelihoods whence they do not anticipate it to come, and that is because when the servant does not know the location of his livelihood, his supplication for it increases.[2885]

٢٥٦٢ . الإمامُ الصّادقُ عليه السلام : إنّ اللهَ عزّ وجلّ جَعَلَ أرزاقَ المؤمنينَ مِن حيثُ لا يَحتَسِبُونَ ، وذلكَ أنَّ العَبدَ إذا لَم يَعرِفْ وَجهَ رِزقِهِ كَثُرَ دُعاؤهُ . [٢٨٦٦]

818. Worrying About the Morrow's Sustenance

٨١٨ـ الاهتِمامُ بِرِزقِ الغَدِ

2563. **The Prophet (SAWA) said,** 'Do not worry about tomorrow's sustenance for every morrow brings its own sustenance.'[2886]

٢٥٦٣ . رسولُ اللهِ ﷺ : لا تَهتَمَّ لِرِزقِ غَدٍ فإنّ كُلَّ غَدٍ يَأتِي بِرِزقِهِ . [٢٨٦٧]

2564. **Imām al-Ṣādiq (AS) said,** 'He who worries about his sustenance is recorded as having sinned.'[2887]

٢٥٦٤ . الإمامُ الصّادقُ عليه السلام : مَنِ اهتَمَّ لِرِزقِهِ كُتِبَ علَيهِ خَطِيئَةٌ . [٢٨٦٨]

819. Impatience with Regards to One's Sustenance

٨١٩ـ استِبطاءُ الرِّزقِ

2565. **The Prophet (SAWA) said,** 'Allah, Glorified and most High, says, "Let my servant be warned that if he is impatient with regard to My sustenance, then I will get angry and open to him a door of this world [and its temptations]".'[2888]

٢٥٦٥ . رسولُ اللهِ ﷺ : يقولُ اللهُ سبحانَهُ وتعالىٰ : لِيَحذَرْ عَبدِي الذي يَستَبطِئُ رزقِي أن أغضَبَ فَأفتَحَ علَيهِ باباً مِن الدنيا ! [٢٨٦٩]

2566. **The Prophet (SAWA) said,** 'Whoever Allah bestows His bounties upon must praise Allah, and whoever is impatient with regards to his sustenance must seek Allah's forgiveness.'[2889]

٢٥٦٦ . عنه ﷺ : مَن أنعَمَ اللهُ تعالىٰ علَيهِ نِـعمَةً فلَيَحمَدِ اللهَ تعالىٰ ، ومَنِ استَبطَأَ (عـلَيهِ) الرِّزقَ فَلَيَستَغفِرِ اللهَ .[٢٨٧٠]

2567. **The Prophet (SAWA) said,** 'He who is impatient with regards to his sustenance must increase his proclamation of Allah's greatness[2890], and he who worries and frets much [about his livelihood] must increase his seeking of forgiveness.'[2891]

٢٥٦٧ . عنه ﷺ : مَن استَبطَأَ الرِّزقَ فَليُكثِرْ مِن التَّكـبيرِ ، ومَـن كَـثُرَهَمُّهُ وغَـمُّهُ فَـليُكثِرْ مِـن الاستِغفارِ .[٢٨٧١]

(See also: SEEKING FORGIVENESS: section 1431)

انظر : الإستغفار : باب ١٤٣١ .

820. Factors that Elicit the Descent of Sustenance and Increase it

٨٢٠ ـ ما يَجلِبُ الرِّزقَ ويَزيدُهُ

2568. **The Prophet (SAWA) said,** 'Sustenance comes to those who feed others faster than a knife can cut through flesh.'[2892]

٢٥٦٨ . رسولُ اللهِ ﷺ : الرِّزقُ أسرَعُ إلىٰ مَن يُطعِمُ الطَّعامَ ، مِن السِّكِّينِ في السَّنامِ .[٢٨٧٢]

2569. **The Prophet (SAWA)** was once asked how one could bring about an increase in one's sustenance, to which he replied, 'Always remain in the state of purity (*ṭahāra*) and your sustenance will be plentiful.'[2893]

٢٥٦٩ . عنه ﷺ ـ لمّا قيلَ لَهُ : أُحِبُّ أن يُوَسَّعَ عَلَيَّ في الرِّزقِ ؟ ـ : دُمْ على الطَّهارَةِ يُوَسَّعْ علَيكَ في الرِّزقِ .[٢٨٧٣]

2570. **The Prophet (SAWA) said,** 'Increase your charity and you will be provided more.'[2894]

٢٥٧٠ . عنه ﷺ : أكثِرُوا مِن الصَّدَقَةِ تُرزَقُوا .[٢٨٧٤]

2571. **Imām ʿAlī (AS) said,** 'Helping out one's brother in faith from one's own wealth, for the sake of Allah, increases sustenance.[2895]

٢٥٧١ . الإمامُ عليٌّ عليه السلام : مُواساةُ الأخِ فـي اللهِ عزّوجلّ تَزِيدُ في الرِّزقِ .[٢٨٧٥]

2572. **Imām ʿAlī (AS) said,** 'Acting with integrity increases one's sustenance.'[2896]

٢٥٧٢ . عنه عليه السلام : استِعمالُ الأمـانَةِ يَـزِيدُ فـي الرِّزقِ .[٢٨٧٦]

2573. **Imām ʿAlī (AS) said,** 'Attract sustenance by giving in charity.'[2897]

٢٥٧٣ . عنه عليه السلام : استَنزِلُوا الرِّزقَ بالصَّدَقَةِ .[٢٨٧٧]

2574. **Imām ʿAlī (AS) said,** 'He who is sincere in his intention receives an increase in sustenance.'[2898]

٢٥٧٤ . عنه عليه السلام : مَن حَسُنَتْ نِـيَّتُهُ ، زِيـدَ فـي رِزقِهِ .[٢٨٧٨]

2575. **Imām al-Bāqir (AS) said,** 'You must pray fervently for your brothers [in faith] in secret, and sustenance will pour down on you.'[2899]

٢٥٧٥ . الإمامُ الباقرُ عليه السلام :علَيكَ بالدعاءِ لإخوانِكَ بظَهْرِ الغَيبِ فإنّهُ يَهِيلُ الرِّزقَ.[٢٨٧٩]

2576. **Imām al-Bāqir (AS) said,** 'Paying the alms-tax (*ẓakāt*) leads to an increase in one's sustenance.'[2900]

٢٥٧٦ . عنه عليه السلام : الزَّكاةُ تَزِيدُ في الرِّزقِ.[٢٨٨٠]

2577. **Imām al-Ṣādiq (AS) said,** 'Whoever is especially kind to his family is increased in sustenance.'[2901]

٢٥٧٧ . الإمامُ الصّادقُ عليه السلام :مَن حَسَّنَ بِرَّهُ أهلَ بَيتِهِ زِيدَ في رِزقِهِ.[٢٨٨١]

2578. **Imām al-Ṣādiq (AS) said,** 'Verily kindness leads to an increase in sustenance.'[2902]

٢٥٧٨ . عنه عليه السلام : إنّ البِرَّ يَزِيدُ في الرِّزقِ.[٢٨٨٢]

2579. **Imām al-Ṣādiq (AS) said,** 'Being good-natured increases in one's sustenance.'[2903]

٢٥٧٩ . عنه عليه السلام :حُسنُ الخُلُقِ يَزِيدُ في الرِّزقِ.[٢٨٨٣]

821. Things that Cut off Sustenance

٨٢١ـ ما يَمحَقُ الرِّزقَ

2580. **The Prophet (SAWA) said,** 'Whoever deprives a fellow Muslim brother of his right, Allah forbids him the benediction of sustenance until he repents.'[2904]

٢٥٨٠ . رسولُ اللهِ صلى الله عليه وآله :مَن حَبَسَ عن أخيهِ المسلمِ شيئاً مِن حَقٍّ حَرَّمَ اللهُ علَيهِ بَرَكـةَ الرِّزقِ إلّا أن يَتوبَ.[٢٨٨٤]

2581. **Imām al-Bāqir (AS) said,** 'Verily when the servant commits a sin, his sustenance eludes him.'[2905]

٢٥٨١ . الإمامُ الباقرُ عليه السلام : إنّ العَبدَ لَيُذنِبُ الذَّنبَ فَيُزوىٰ عنهُ الرِّزقُ.[٢٨٨٥]

2582. **Imām al-Ṣādiq (AS) said,** 'Obtaining wealth through illegal means cuts off one's sustenance.'[2906]

٢٥٨٢ . الإمامُ الصّادقُ عليه السلام : كَثرَةُ السُّحتِ يَمحَقُ الرِّزقَ.[٢٨٨٦]

(See also: BENEDICTION: section 235)

انظر : البركة : باب ٢٣٥.

822. Encouraging to Seek Livelihood Through Lawful (*ḥalāl*) Means

٨٢٢ـ الحَثُّ عَلىٰ طَلَبِ الحَلالِ

2583. **The Prophet (SAWA) said,** 'Worship consists of ten parts of which nine are to do with earning a lawful livelihood.'[2907]

٢٥٨٣ . رسولُ اللهِ صلى الله عليه وآله : العِبادَةُ عَشرَةُ أجزاءٍ تِسعَةُ أجزاءٍ في طَلَبِ الحَلالِ.[٢٨٨٧]

2584. **The Prophet (SAWA) said,** 'He who works hard to provide his family with [a lawful] livelihood is as one who fights in the way of Allah (*jihād*).'[2908]

٢٥٨٤. عنه ﷺ: الكادُّ علىٰ عِيالِهِ كـالمُجاهِدِ في سبيلِ اللهِ.[٢٨٨٨]

2585. **The Prophet (SAWA) said,** 'Verily Allah, most High, loves to see his servant weary from striving to earn his livelihood [lawfully].'[2909]

٢٥٨٥. عنه ﷺ: إنَّ اللهَ تعالىٰ يُـحِبُّ أن يَـرىٰ عَبدَهُ تَعِباً في طَلَبِ الحَلالِ.[٢٨٨٩]

2586. **The Prophet (SAWA) said,** 'Seeking a lawful livelihood is incumbent upon every Muslim man and woman.'[2910]

٢٥٨٦. عنه ﷺ: طَلَبُ الحَلالِ فَريضةٌ علىٰ كُلِّ مُسلمٍ ومُسلمةٍ.[٢٨٩٠]

2587. **The Prophet (SAWA) said,** 'He whose daily bread is earned through his own toil and labour will pass across the *Ṣirāṭ*[2911] as fast as a flash of lightning.'[2912]

٢٥٨٧. عنه ﷺ: مَن أكَلَ مِن كَدِّ يَدِهِ، مَرَّ علىٰ الصِّراطِ كالبَرقِ الخاطِفِ.[٢٨٩١]

2588. **The Prophet (SAWA) said,** 'He whose daily bread is earned through his own toil and labour, Allah will look upon him with mercy and will never expose him to chastisement.'[2913]

٢٥٨٨. عنه ﷺ: مَن أكَلَ مِن كَدِّ يَدِهِ، نَظَرَ اللهُ إلَيهِ بالرَّحمَةِ ثُمَّ لا يُعَذِّبُهُ أبداً.[٢٨٩٢]

2589. **The Prophet (SAWA) said,** 'Cursed! Cursed is the one who brings deprivation to his dependents.[2914]

٢٥٨٩. عنه ﷺ: مَلعونٌ مَلعونٌ مَن ضَيَّعَ مَـن يَعُولُ.[٢٨٩٣]

2590. **Mufaḍḍal b. 'Umar said,** 'Make use of some of the [commodities of this] world to help you in the next world, for I have heard Abū 'Abdallāh [i.e. Imām al-Ṣādiq] (AS) say, 'Make use of some of this [abode] for that one, but do not be a burden on other people.'[2915]

٢٥٩٠. بحار الأنوار عن المـفضّلِ بـنِ عـمرَ: استَعِينُوا بِبعضِ الدنيا على الآخِرَةِ، فإنّي سَمِعتُ أبا عبدِ اللهِ ﷺ يقولُ: إستَعِينُوا بِبعضِ هذهِ علىٰ هذهِ، ولا تَكُونوا كَلّاً على الناسِ.[٢٨٩٤]

823. The Best Livelihood is that Which Suffices you

٨٢٣ـ خَيرُ الرِّزقِ ما يَكفي

2591. **The Prophet (SAWA) said,** 'O Allah provide moderation and sufficiency to Muḥa-

٢٥٩١. رسولُ اللهِ ﷺ: اللّهُمّ ارزُقْ محمّداً وآلَ

mmad and the family of Muḥammad, and to those who love Muḥammad and his family, and provide abundance of wealth and progeny to those who harbour hatred for Muḥammad and his family.'[2916]

محمّدٍ ومَن أحَبَّ محمّداً وآلَ محمّدٍ، العَفافَ والكَفافَ، وارزُقْ مَن أبغَضَ محمّداً وآلَ محمّدٍ المالَ والوَلَدَ.[٢٨٩٥]

2592. **The Prophet (SAWA) said,** 'The best livelihood is that which suffices.'[2917]

٢٥٩٢. عنه ﷺ: خَيرُ الرِّزقِ ما يَكْفِي.[٢٨٩٦]

2593. **The Prophet (SAWA) said,** 'That which is little yet sufficient is better than that which is abundant and distracting [as a result].'[2918]

٢٥٩٣. عنه ﷺ: ما قَلَّ وكَفىٰ خَيرٌ مِمّا كَثُرَ وألهىٰ.[٢٨٩٧]

161

BRIBERY

الرِّشْوَةُ

824. Warning Against Bribery

٨٢٤ـ التَّحذيرُ مِنَ الرِّشوَةِ

2594. **The Prophet (SAWA) said,** 'Beware of bribery for verily it is sheer infidelity, and the briber will not even smell the fragrance of Paradise.'[2919]

٢٥٩٤. رسولُ اللهِ ﷺ: إيّاكُم والرِّشوَةَ فإنّها مَحضُ الكُفرِ، ولا يَشَمُّ صاحِبُ الرِّشوَةِ رِيحَ الجَنَّةِ.[٢٨٩٨]

2595. **The Prophet (SAWA) said,** 'Allah's curse is on the briber, the bribed, and the agent between them.'[2920]

٢٥٩٥. عنه ﷺ: لَعَنَ اللهُ الراشيَ والمُرتَشِيَ والرائشَ الذي يَمشِي بَينَهُما.[٢٨٩٩]

2596. **Imām ʿAlī (AS) said,** 'The ruin of your predecessors lay in the fact that they deprived people of their rights and subsequently resorted to buying them back, and they handled people using unethical means, which they followed.'[2921]

٢٥٩٦. الإمامُ عليٌّ (ع): إنّما أهلَكَ مَن كانَ قَبلَكُم أنَّهُم مَنَعُوا الناسَ الحَقَّ فاشتَرَوهُ، وأخَذُوهُم بالباطِلِ فاقتَدَوهُ.[٢٩٠٠]

2597. **Imām ʿAlī (AS) said,** 'You know full well that he who is in charge of honour, people's lives, war booty, legal commandments and the leadership of the Muslims must not be a miser... nor should he accept bribes in his judgment for he would forfeit their rights, and deprives the rightful from his right.'[2922]

٢٥٩٧. عنه (ع): وقد عَلِمتُم أنَّهُ لا يَنبَغِي أن يكونَ الوالِي علَى الفُروجِ والدِّماءِ والمَغانِمِ والأحكامِ وإمامَةِ المسلمينَ البَخيلُ... ولا المُرتَشي في الحُكمِ فَيَذهَبَ بالحُقوقِ، ويَقِفَ بها دُونَ المَقاطِعِ.[٢٩٠١]

2598. **Imām ʿAlī (AS) said** about Allah's verse in the Qur'an: *"eaters of the unlawful"*[2923], 'This refers to the man who fulfils a need for a fellow brother and then accepts a gift from him.'[2924]

٢٥٩٨ . عنه ﷺ ـ في قولِهِ تعالىٰ: ﴿أَكّالُونَ لِلسُّحْتِ﴾ ـ: هُو الرَّجُلُ يَقضِي لأخِيهِ الحاجَةَ ثُمّ يَقبَلُ هَدِيَّتَهُ.[٢٩٠٢]

2599. **Imām al-Ṣādiq (AS) said,** 'Accepting bribes as a judge or ruler is tantamount to disbelief in Allah.'[2925]

٢٥٩٩ . الإمامُ الصّادقُ ﷺ: الرُّشىٰ في الحُكمِ هُو الكُفرُ باللهِ.[٢٩٠٣]

162

SUCKLING

الرَّضاع

825. Suckling

٨٢٥ـ رِضاعُ المَولُودِ

"Mothers shall suckle their children for two full years – that for such as desire to complete the suckling – and on the father shall be their maintenance and clothing, in accordance with honourable norms."[2926]

﴿وَالوالِداتُ يُرْضِعْنَ أَوْلادَهُنَّ حَوْلَيْنِ كامِلَيْنِ لِمَنْ أَرادَ أَنْ يُتِمَّ الرَّضاعَةَ﴾.[٢٩٠٤]

(See also: Qur'an 46:15 and 65:6)

انظر: الأحقاف: ١٥ والطلاق: ٦.

2600. **The Prophet (SAWA) said,** 'There is no better milk for a child than the milk of his mother.'[2927]

٢٦٠٠ . رسولُ اللهِ ﷺ: ليسَ للصَّبيِّ لَبَنٌ خيرٌ مِن لَبَنِ أُمِّهِ.[٢٩٠٥]

2601. **Imām ʿAlī (AS) said,** 'Take into account who it is that suckles your children, for verily this is what a child grows on.'[2928]

٢٦٠١ . الإمامُ عليٌّ ﷺ: أُنظُرُوا مَن تُرضِعُ أولادَكُم؛ فإنّ الوَلَدَ يَشِبُّ علَيهِ.[٢٩٠٦]

2602. **Imām al-Bāqir (AS) said,** 'Get beautiful wet-nurses to suckle your child and keep away from ugly ones, for verily the milk has an effect [on the child].'[2929]

٢٦٠٢ . الإمامُ الباقرُ ﷺ: إستَرضِعْ لِولدِكَ بِلَبَنِ الحِسانِ، وإيّاكَ والقِباحَ؛ فإنّ اللَّبَنَ قد يُعدِي.[٢٩٠٧]

826. Types of Wet-Nurses that Should not be Employed

٨٢٦ـ مَن لا يَنبَغِي استِرضاعُهُ

2603. **The Prophet (SAWA) said,** 'Do not employ wet-nurses that are stupid or bleary-eyed for verily the milk has an effect [on the child].'[2930]

٢٦٠٣ . رسولُ اللهِ ﷺ: لا تَستَرضِعُوا الحَمقاءَ، ولا العَمشاءَ؛ فإنّ اللَّبَنَ يُعدِي.[٢٩٠٨]

2604. **Imām ʿAlī (AS) said,** 'Protect your children from the milk of prostitutes and madwomen, for verily the milk has an effect [on the child].'[2931]

٢٦٠٤ . الإمامُ عليٌّ ﷺ : تَوَقَّوا علىٰ أولادِكُم لَبَنَ البَغِيِّ مِن النِّساءِ، والمَجنونَةِ؛ فإنّ اللَّبَنَ يُعدِي.٢٩٠٩

2605. **Imām al-Ṣādiq (AS) said,** 'Getting a Christian or a Jewish wet-nurse to suckle a child is better than a *Nāṣibīyya.*'[2932 2933]

٢٦٠٥ . الإمامُ الصّادقُ ﷺ : رِضاعُ اليَهوديّةِ والنَّصرانيّةِ خَيرٌ مِن رِضاعِ الناصِبيّةِ.٢٩١٠

163

SATISFACTION (1)

الرِّضا (١)

Satisfaction With Allah's Divine Decree

الرِّضا بالقضاءِ

827. The Virtue of Satisfaction

٨٢٧ـ فَضلُ الرِّضا

2606. **Imām ʿAlī (AS) said,** 'What an excellent companion satisfaction is.'[2934]

٢٦٠٦ . الإمامُ عليٌّ ﷺ : نِعمَ القَرينُ الرِّضا.٢٩١١

2607. **Imām al-Ḥasan (AS) said,** 'He who trusts whatever Allah has chosen for him to be good, will never wish to be in any situation other than what Allah has chosen for him to be in.'[2935]

٢٦٠٧ . الإمامُ الحسنُ ﷺ : مَنِ اتَّكَلَ على حُسنِ الاختِيارِ مِنَ اللهِ، لَم يَتَمَنَّ أنّهُ في غَيرِ الحالِ التي اختارَها اللهُ لَهُ.٢٩١٢

2608. **Imām al-Ḥasan (AS) said,** 'How can a believer call himself a believer if he is dissatisfied with his lot in life and despises his current circumstances when Allah is the authority above him.'[2936]

٢٦٠٨ . عنه ﷺ : كيفَ يكونُ المؤمنُ مؤمناً وهو يَسخَطُ قِسمَهُ ويُحَقِّرُ مَنزِلَتَهُ والحاكِمُ علَيهِ اللهُ؟!٢٩١٣

2609. **Imām Zayn al-ʿĀbidīn (AS) said,** 'The highest degree of asceticism is equivalent to the lowest degree of piety. And the highest degree of piety is equivalent to the lowest degree of certainty. And the highest degrees of certainty are equivalent to the lowest degrees of ultimate satisfaction (with Allah).'[2937]

٢٦٠٩ . الإمامُ زينُ العابدينَ ﷺ : أعلىٰ دَرَجةِ الزُّهدِ أدنىٰ دَرَجةِ الوَرَعِ، وأعلىٰ دَرَجةِ الوَرَعِ أدنىٰ دَرَجةِ اليَقينِ، وأعلىٰ دَرَجةِ اليَقينِ أدنىٰ دَرَجةِ الرِّضا.٢٩١٤

2610. **Imām Zayn al-ʿĀbidīn (AS) said,** 'Satisfaction with adversities is one of the highest stages of certainty.'[2938]

٢٦١٠. عنه عليه السلام: الرِّضا بمَكروهِ القَضاءِ مِن أعلىٰ دَرَجاتِ اليَقينِ.[٢٩١٥]

2611. **Imām al-Ṣādiq (AS) said,** 'The Prophet (SAWA) never used to utter the words 'if only...' with regards to something that had happened in the past.'[2939]

٢٦١١. الإمامُ الصّادقُ عليه السلام: لَم يَكُن رسولُ اللهِ ﷺ يقولُ لِشَيءٍ قد مَضىٰ: لَو كانَ غَيرَهُ![٢٩١٦]

2612. **Imām al-Ṣādiq (AS) said,** 'The basis of obedience to Allah is to be satisfied with everything that Allah has designed whether he himself likes it or not.'[2940]

٢٦١٢. عنه عليه السلام: رَأسُ طاعَةِ اللهِ الرِّضا بما صَنَعَ اللهُ فيما أحَبَّ العَبدُ وفيما كَرِهَ.[٢٩١٧]

828. Things that Incite Satisfaction [With Allah's Decree]

٨٢٨ـ ما يورِثُ الرِّضا

2613. **Imām ʿAlī (AS) said,** 'The origin of satisfaction is trust in Allah.'[2941]

٢٦١٣. الإمامُ عليٌّ عليه السلام: أصلُ الرِّضا حُسنُ الثِّقَةِ بِاللهِ.[٢٩١٨]

2614. **Imām al-Ṣādiq (AS) said,** 'Verily those who have the greatest knowledge of Allah are the most satisfied with His decree.'[2942]

٢٦١٤. الإمامُ الصّادقُ عليه السلام: إنّ أعلَمَ النّاسِ بِاللهِ أرضاهُم بقَضاءِ اللهِ.[٢٩١٩]

829. The Benefits of Satisfaction

٨٢٩ـ ثَمَراتُ الرِّضا

2615. **The Prophet (SAWA) said,** 'When Allah loves a servant He tests him with tribulations, and if he endures these He selects him [for His proximity], and if he bears them with satisfaction, He distinguishes him [a higher status].'[2943]

٢٦١٥. رسولُ اللهِ ﷺ: إذا أحَبَّ اللهُ عَبداً ابتَلاهُ، فإن صَبَرَ اجتَباهُ، وإن رَضِيَ اصطَفاهُ.[٢٩٢٠]

2616. **The Prophet (SAWA) said,** 'Satisfy yourself with Allah's share [for you] and you will be the richest of people.'[2944]

٢٦١٦. عنه ﷺ: اِرْضَ بِقَسْمِ اللهِ تَكُنْ أغنَى النّاسِ.[٢٩٢١]

2617. **Imām ʿAlī (AS) said,** 'Satisfaction expels sorrow.'[2945]

٢٦١٧. الإمامُ عليٌّ عليه السلام: الرِّضا يَنفِي الحُزْنَ.[٢٩٢٢]

2618. **Imām ʿAlī (AS) said,** 'Verily the one who enjoys the best standards of living is he who is

٢٦١٨. عنه عليه السلام: إنّ أهنَأَ النّاسِ عَيشاً مَن كانَ

satisfied with what Allah has apportioned for him.'[2946]

بما قَسَمَ اللهُ لَهُ راضِياً .٢٩٢٣

2619. **Imām al-Ḥasan (AS) said,** 'I guarantee you that the one who entertains nothing save satisfaction with Allah in his heart, has only to ask Allah and He will answer him.'[2947]

٢٦١٩ . الإمامُ الحسنُ ﵇ : أنا الضّامِنُ لِـمَن لا يَـهجِسُ فـي قَـلبِهِ إلّا الرِّضـا أن يَـدعُوَ اللهَ فَيُستَجابَ لَهُ .٢٩٢٤

2620. **Imām al-Ṣādiq (AS) said,** 'Tranquillity and comfort lie in satisfaction and certainty, whereas worry and sorrow lie in doubt and dissatisfaction.'[2948]

٢٦٢٠ . الإمامُ الصّادقُ ﵇ : الرَّوحُ والرّاحَةُ في الرِّضـا واليَـقينِ ، والهَـمُّ والحُـزْنُ فـي الشَّكِّ والسُّخطِ .٢٩٢٥

830. The Outcomes of Dissatisfaction

٨٣٠ـ ثَمَرَةُ عَدَمِ الرِّضا

2621. **Imām al-Ṣādiq (AS) said,** 'He who is dissatisfied with what Allah has apportioned him accuses Allah with regards to His decree.'[2949]

٢٦٢١ . الإمامُ الصّادقُ ﵇ : مَن لم يَرضَ بما قَسَمَ اللهُ عزّوجلّ ، اِتَّهَمَ اللهَ تعالىٰ في قَضائهِ .٢٩٢٦

2622. **Imām al-Ṣādiq (AS) said,** 'The one who is satisfied with Allah's decree will experience His decree and be rewarded [on account of his satisfaction], whereas the one who is displeased with the decree, not only will he continue to experience the same decree, but Allah will do away with his reward too.'[2950]

٢٦٢٢ . عنه ﵇ : مَن رَضِيَ القَضاءَ أتىٰ عـلَيهِ القَضاءُ وهُو مَأجُورٌ ومَن سَخِطَ القَضاءَ أتىٰ علَيهِ القَضاءُ وأحبَطَ اللهُ أجرَهُ .٢٩٢٧

(See also: JUDGMENT (IN A COURT OF JUSTICE): section 1534)

انظر : القضاء والقدر : باب ١٥٣٤.

164

SATISFACTION (2)

Allah's Pleasure

الرِّضا (٢)

رِضوانُ اللهِ

831. Factors that Elicit Allah's Pleasure

٨٣١ـ موجِباتُ رِضوانِ اللهِ

"Is he who follows [the course] of Allah's pleasure like him who earns Allah's displeasure and whose refuge is Hell, an evil destination?"[2951]

﴿أَفَمَنِ اتَّبَعَ رِضْوانَ اللهِ كَمَنْ باءَ بِسَخَطٍ مِنَ اللهِ وَمأْواهُ جَهَنَّمُ وَبِئْسَ المَصيرُ﴾ .٢٩٢٨

(See also: Qur'an 3:15, 9:21, 9:109, 57:20, 57:27, 5:2, 5:16, 48:29, 59:8, 47:28)

انظر : آل عمران : ١٥ والتوبة : ٢١ ، ١٠٩ والحديد ٢٠ ، ٢٧ والمائدة : ٢ ، ١٦ والفتح : ٢٩ والحشر : ٨ ومحمّد : ٢٨.

2623. It has been narrated in *Biḥār al-Anwār* that Prophet Moses (AS) addressed Allah, saying, 'My Lord, guide me to an action the performance of which will earn me Your good pleasure.' So Allah revealed to him, 'O son of Amran, verily My pleasure lies in that which you will be averse to and you will not be able to endure it.' So Moses fell prostrate, weeping and cried out, 'My Lord! You have selected me to speak to when You have not spoken to any before me, and yet You do not guide me to that action by which I may earn Your pleasure!' So Allah revealed to him, 'Verily My pleasure lies in your pleasure with whatever I decree.'[2952]

٢٦٢٣. بحار الأنوار: رُوِيَ أنّ موسىٰ عليه السلام قالَ: يا رَبِّ، دُلَّني على عَمَلٍ إذا أنا عَمِلتُهُ نِلتُ بِهِ رِضاكَ. فَأوحَى اللهُ إلَيهِ: يابنَ عِمرانَ، إنّ رِضايَ في كُرهِكَ ولَن تُطيقَ ذلكَ... فَخَرَّ موسىٰ عليه السلام ساجِداً باكِياً فقالَ: يا رَبِّ، خَصَصتَني بالكَلامِ، ولَم تُكَلِّمْ بَشَراً قَبلِي، ولَم تَدُلَّني على عَمَلٍ أنالُ بِهِ رِضاكَ! فَأوحَى اللهُ إلَيهِ: إنّ رِضايَ في رِضاكَ بِقَضائي.[٢٩٢٩]

2624. **Imām ʿAlī (AS) said,** 'Three things enable a servant to attain Allah's pleasure: persistence in seeking forgiveness, affability towards people, and frequent giving of charity.'[2953]

٢٦٢٤. الإمامُ عليٌّ عليه السلام: ثلاثٌ يُبلِغْنَ بالعَبدِ رِضوانَ اللهِ: كَثرَةُ الاستِغفارِ، وخَفضُ الجانِبِ، وكَثرَةُ الصَّدَقَةِ.[٢٩٣٠]

2625. **Imām ʿAlī (AS) said,** 'He who dissatisfies [troubles] his body earns Allah's pleasure, and he who is not willing to do so defies Allah.'[2954]

٢٦٢٥. عنه عليه السلام: مَن أسخَطَ بَدَنَهُ أرضىٰ رَبَّهُ، ومَن لَم يُسخِطْ بَدَنَهُ عَصىٰ رَبَّهُ.[٢٩٣١]

2626. **Imām ʿAlī (AS) said,** 'He [Allah] has advised you to be Godwary in all things, and has made it the height of His good pleasure and His sole requirement from His creatures.'[2955]

٢٦٢٦. عنه عليه السلام: أوصاكُم بالتَّقوىٰ، وجَعَلَها مُنتَهىٰ رِضاهُ وحاجَتَهُ مِن خَلقِهِ.[٢٩٣٢]

2627. **Imām ʿAlī (AS) said,** 'Allah's pleasure is linked to His obedience.'[2956]

٢٦٢٧. عنه عليه السلام: رِضا اللهِ سُبحانَهُ مَقرونٌ بطاعَتِهِ.[٢٩٣٣]

2628. **Imām Zayn al-ʿĀbidīn (AS) said,** 'Verily the one who Allah is most pleased with from among you is the one who is the most generous towards his own dependents.'[2957]

٢٦٢٨. الإمامُ زينُ العابدينَ عليه السلام: إنَّ أرضاكُم عِندَ اللهِ أسبَغُكُم على عِيالِهِ.[٢٩٣٤]

832. Signs of Allah's Pleasure

٨٣٢ـ عَلاماتُ رِضا اللهِ

2629. It is narrated in *Biḥār al-Anwār* that Prophet Moses (AS) said, 'O My Lord, what is a sign of Your pleasure with a servant of Yours?' So

٢٦٢٩. بحار الأنوار: رُوِيَ أنّ موسىٰ عليه السلام قالَ: يا رَبِّ أخبِرْني عن آيَةِ رِضاكَ عن عَبدِكَ، فَأوحَى

Allah revealed to him, saying, 'When you see Me preparing My servant for My obedience and averting him from My disobedience, [know that] it is a sign of My pleasure.'[2958]

اللهُ تعالىٰ إلَيه: إذا رَأيتَني أُهَيِّئُ عبدِي لطاعَتي وأصرِفُهُ عن مَعصِيَتي، فذلكَ آيَةُ رِضايَ.[٢٩٣٥]

2630. **Imām ʿAlī (AS) said,** 'The sign of Allah's pleasure with His servant is the satisfaction found in the servant himself with all that Allah decrees, be it in his favour or not.'[2959]

٢٦٣٠. الإمامُ عليٌّ عليه السلام: علامَةُ رِضا اللهِ سبحانَهُ عن العَبدِ، رِضاهُ بما قَضىٰ بهِ سبحانَهُ لَهُ وعلَيهِ.[٢٩٣٦]

833. Pleasing People at the Expense of Allah's Displeasure

٨٣٣ـ مَرضاةُ الخَلقِ وسَخَطُ الخالِقِ

2631. **Imām ʿAlī (AS),** in a letter that he wrote to Muḥammad b. Abū Bakr, said, 'Try to the best of your ability not to displease your Lord by pleasing any of His creatures, for verily Allah can easily substitute a servant for another, but the servant has recourse to no other substitute for Allah.'[2960]

٢٦٣١. الإمامُ عليٌّ عليه السلام ـ فيما كَتَبَ إلىٰ محمّدِ بنِ أبي بكرٍ ـ: إنِ استَطَعتَ أن لا تُسخِطَ رَبَّكَ بِرِضا أحَدٍ مِن خَلقِهِ فَافعَلْ؛ فإنَّ في اللهِ عزّوجلّ خَلَفاً مِن غَيرِهِ، ولَيسَ في شيءٍ سِواهُ خَلَفٌ مِنهُ.[٢٩٣٧]

2632. **Imām al-Ḥusayn (AS) said,** 'He who seeks to please Allah at the expense of displeasing people, Allah suffices him in everything including his affairs with people. But the one who seeks to please people at the expense of Allah's displeasure, Allah relegates him to those very people.'[2961]

٢٦٣٢. الإمامُ الحسينُ عليه السلام: مَن طَلَبَ رِضا اللهِ بِسَخَطِ الناسِ كَفاهُ اللهُ اُمورَ الناسِ، ومَن طَلَبَ رِضا الناسِ بِسَخَطِ اللهِ، وَكَلَهُ اللهُ إلى النّاسِ.[٢٩٣٨]

165

LENIENCY[2962]

الرِّفقُ

834. The Virtue of Leniency

٨٣٤ـ فضلُ الرِّفقِ

2633. **The Prophet (SAWA) said,** 'No sooner is leniency added to something than it adorns it, and no sooner is it taken away from something than it spoils it.'[2963]

٢٦٣٣. رسولُ اللهِ صلى الله عليه وآله: إنّ الرِّفقَ لَم يُوضَعْ على شيءٍ إلّا زانَهُ، ولا نُزِعَ مِن شيءٍ إلّا شانَهُ.[٢٩٣٩]

2634. **The Prophet (SAWA) said,** 'When two people become friends or accompany each other, the

٢٦٣٤. عنه صلى الله عليه وآله: ما اصطَحَبَ اثنانِ إلّا كانَ أعظَمُهُما أجراً وأحَبُّهُما إلى اللهِ عزّوجلّ

one with the greater reward and the most beloved in Allah's eyes is the one who is the most gentle towards his companion.'[2964]

أرفقُهما بصاحِبِهِ.٢٩٤٠

2635. **The Prophet (SAWA) said,** 'When Allah wishes to bestow good on a household, he introduces leniency into it.'[2965]

٢٦٣٥. عنه ﷺ: إذا أرادَ اللهُ بأهلِ بيتٍ خَيراً أدخَلَ علَيهِم بابَ رِفقٍ.٢٩٤١

2636. **The Prophet (SAWA) said,** 'The most intelligent person is he who is the most tolerant towards people.'[2966]

٢٦٣٦. عنه ﷺ: أعقَلُ الناسِ أشَدُّهُم مُداراةً للناسِ.٢٩٤٢

2637. **The Prophet (SAWA) said,** 'Verily Allah, Mighty and Exalted, is lenient and loves leniency in all matters.'[2967]

٢٦٣٧. عنه ﷺ: إنّ اللهَ عزّوجلّ رَفيقٌ يُحِبُّ الرِّفقَ في الأمرِ كُلِّهِ.٢٩٤٣

2638. **Imām ʿAlī (AS) said,** 'Leniency is the key to success.'[2968]

٢٦٣٨. الإمامُ عليٌّ ؑ: الرِّفقُ مِفتاحُ النَّجاحِ.٢٩٤٤

2639. **Imām al-Bāqir (AS) said,** 'Everything has a lock, and the lock of faith is leniency.'[2969]

٢٦٣٩. الإمامُ الباقرُ ؑ: إنّ لِكُلِّ شَيءٍ قُفْلاً وقُفلُ الإيمانِ الرِّفقُ.٢٩٤٥

2640. **Imām al-Kāẓim (AS) said,** 'Moderation is half of one's livelihood.'[2970]

٢٦٤٠. الإمامُ الكاظمُ ؑ: الرِّفقُ نِصفُ العَيشِ.٢٩٤٦

835. Moderation in Worship

٨٣٥ ـ الرِّفقُ فِي العِبادَةِ

2641. **The Prophet (SAWA) said,** 'Verily this religion is firm so penetrate into it gently, and do not arouse aversion for Allah's worship in His servants that they may become like shattered riders who have neither gotten further in their travel nor have any drive left to continue.'[2971]

٢٦٤١. رسولُ اللهِ ﷺ: إنّ هذا الدِّينَ مَتِينٌ فَأوغِلُوا فيهِ برِفقٍ، ولا تُكرِهُوا عِبادَةَ اللهِ إلىٰ عِبادِ اللهِ فتكونوا كالراكِبِ المُنْبَتِّ الذي لا سَفَراً قَطَعَ ولا ظَهْراً أبقىٰ.٢٩٤٧

2642. **Imām ʿAlī (AS) said,** 'Cajole your soul tactfully to worship, and be gentle with it and do not force it. Make allowances for both its weariness and its activity, except for the daily obligations that are incumbent upon it, for it must fulfil them and undertake them at their prescribed times.'[2972]

٢٦٤٢. الإمامُ عليٌّ ؑ: خادِعْ نفسَكَ في العِبادَةِ، وارفُقْ بها ولا تَقهَرْها، وخُذْ عَفوَها ونَشاطَها، إلّا ما كانَ مَكتوباً علَيكَ مِن الفَريضَةِ، فإنّهُ لابُدَّ مِن قَضائها وتَعاهُدِها عندَ مَحَلِّها.٢٩٤٨

(See also: WORSHIP: section 1218)

انظر: العبادة: باب ١٢١٨.

836. The Benefits of Leniency

٨٣٦ـ ثَمَراتُ الرِّفقِ

2643. **The Prophet (SAWA) said,** 'Verily in leniency is to be found abundance and benediction, so whoever is divested of leniency is deprived of good.'[2973]

٢٦٤٣ . رسولُ اللهِ ﷺ : إنّ في الرِّفقِ الزِّيادَةَ والبَرَكَةَ ، ومَن يُحرَمِ الرِّفقَ يُحرَمِ الخَيرَ .٢٩٤٩

2644. **Imām ʿAlī (AS) said,** 'Leniency eases hardships and facilitates difficult situations.'[2974]

٢٦٤٤ . الإمامُ عليٌّ ؏ : الرِّفقُ يُيَسِّرُ الصِّعابَ ، ويُسَهِّلُ شَديدَ الأسبابِ .٢٩٥٠

2645. **Imām al-Ḥusayn (AS) said,** 'For him who is rendered helpless in making a decision and who is at a loss of what to do, moderation is the key.'[2975]

٢٦٤٥ . الإمامُ الحسينُ ؏ : مَن أُحجِمَ عنِ الرَّأيِ وعَيِيَتْ بِهِ الحِيَلُ ، كانَ الرِّفقُ مِفتاحَهُ .٢٩٥١

2646. **Imām Zayn al-ʿĀbidīn (AS) said,** 'The last piece of advice that al-Khiḍr[2976] gave to Prophet Moses (AS) was: 'When a person is lenient towards someone in this world, Allah will be lenient with him on the Day of Resurrection.'[2977]

٢٦٤٦ . الإمامُ زينُ العابدينَ ؏ : كانَ آخِرُ ما أوصىٰ بِهِ الخضرُ موسىٰ بنَ عِمرانَ ؏ : ... ما رَفَقَ أحَدٌ بأحَدٍ في الدنيا إلّا رَفَقَ اللهُ عزّوجلّ به يومَ القِيامَةِ .٢٩٥٢

2647. **Imām al-Ṣādiq (AS) said,** 'If you wish to be honoured [by people] be lenient [towards them], and if you wish to be humiliated then be rough.'[2978]

٢٦٤٧ . الإمامُ الصّادقُ ؏ : إن شِئتَ أن تُكرَمَ فَلِنْ ، وإن شِئتَ أن تُهانَ فاخشُنْ .٢٩٥٣

2648. **Imām al-Ṣādiq (AS) said,** 'One who is lenient and moderate in his affairs will obtain whatever he wants from people.'[2979]

٢٦٤٨ . عنه ؏ : مَن كانَ رفيقاً في أمرِهِ نالَ ما يُريدُ مِنَ الناسِ .٢٩٥٤

166

SCRUTINY (of Man's Actions)

المُراقَبَة

837. Man's Actions are Scrutinized by Allah, the Angels and his own Limbs

٨٣٧ـ مُراقَبَةُ اللهِ والمَلائكَةِ والجَوارحِ

"Indeed Allah is watchful over you."[2980]

﴿إنَّ اللهَ كانَ عَلَيْكُمْ رَقِيباً﴾ .٢٩٥٥

"He says no word but that there is a ready observer beside him."[2981]

﴿ما يَلْفِظُ مِنْ قَوْلٍ إلّا لَدَيْهِ رَقِيبٌ عَتِيدٌ﴾ .٢٩٥٦

2649. **Imām ʿAlī (AS) said,** 'Know O servants of Allah that your own selves monitor you, and your limbs are a watchful eye over you. The truthful guardian angels record your deeds as well as the number of your breaths. Neither can the dark gloomy night conceal you from view, nor can you hide behind a bolted door.'[2982]

٢٦٤٩ . الإمامُ عليٌّ عليه‌السلام : اِعلَمُوا عِبادَ اللهِ أَنَّ علَيكُم رَصَداً مِن أنفُسِكُم، وعُيُوناً من جَوارِحِكُم، وحُفّاظَ صِدْقٍ يَحفَظُونَ أعمالَكُم، وعَدَدَ أنفاسِكم، لا تَستُرُكُم مِنهُم ظُلمَةُ لَيلٍ داجٍ، ولا يُكِنُّكُم مِنهُم بابٌ ذو رِتاجٍ.[٢٩٥٧]

(See also: THE ANGELS: section 1664)

انظر : الملائكة : باب ١٦٦٤.

838. Enjoinment of Self-Scrutiny

٨٣٨ ـ الحَثُّ عَلَى مُراقَبَةِ النَّفْسِ

2650. **The Prophet (SAWA) said,** 'The scriptures of Prophet Abraham (AS) contain the following: '...the rational man, as long as he is of sound reason, must put aside several hours during the day – an hour for conversing with his Lord, an hour for [self-scrutiny and] accounting for himself, an hour to ponder over Allah's favours bestowed upon him, and an hour to spend on his own lawful pleasures, for this one hour will be an aid to him in fulfilling his other hours, as well as a time to recuperate and relax.'[2983]

٢٦٥٠ . رسولُ اللهِ ﷺ : كان فيها [أي صُحُفِ إبراهيم عليه‌السلام]...: على العاقِلِ ما لَم يَكُن مَغلوباً علىٰ عَقلِهِ أن يكونَ لَهُ ساعاتٌ: ساعَةٌ يُناجِي فيها رَبَّهُ عزّوجلّ، وساعَةٌ يُحاسِبُ نَفسَهُ، وساعَةٌ يَتَفَكَّرُ فيما صَنَعَ اللهُ عزّوجلّ إلَيهِ، وساعَةٌ يَخلُو فيها بِحَظِّ نفسِهِ مِنَ الحَلالِ؛ فإنّ هذهِ الساعَةَ عَونٌ لِتلكَ الساعاتِ واستِجمامٌ للقُلوبِ وتَوزِيعٌ لها.[٢٩٥٨]

2651. **Imām ʿAlī (AS) said,** 'Appoint your own self as a scrutinizer over yourself, and use this world to reserve your share in the Hereafter.'[2984]

٢٦٥١ . الإمامُ عليٌّ عليه‌السلام : اِجعَلْ مِن نفسِكَ علىٰ نفسِكَ رَقيباً، واجعَلْ لِآخِرَتِكَ مِن دُنياك نَصيباً.[٢٩٥٩]

2652. **Imām ʿAlī (AS) said,** 'Man must control and survey his own self, scrutinize his heart, and guard his tongue.'[2985]

٢٦٥٢ . عنه عليه‌السلام : يَنبَغِي أن يكونَ الرجُلُ مُهَيمِناً عَلىٰ نَفسِهِ، مُراقِباً قَلبَهُ حافِظاً لِسانَهُ.[٢٩٦٠]

2653. **Imām ʿAlī (AS) said,** 'Allah has mercy on the servant who scrutinizes his sins carefully and fears his Lord.'[2986]

٢٦٥٣ . عنه عليه‌السلام : رَحِمَ اللهُ امرَأً (عَبداً) سَمِعَ حُكْماً فوَعىٰ، ودُعِيَ إلىٰ رَشادٍ فَدَنا، وأخَذَ بِحُجْزَةِ هادٍ فَنَجا، راقَبَ رَبَّهُ، وخافَ ذَنبَهُ.[٢٩٦١]

2654. **Imām ʿAlī (AS) said,** 'The rational man must calculate his soul's misdeeds against religion, reason, ethical virtues and good moral conduct. He must gather this information within himself or write it down in a book and work at eradicating them.'[2987]

٢٦٥٤ . عنه عليه‌السلام : على العاقِلِ أن يُحصِيَ علىٰ نفسِهِ مَساوِيَها في الدِّينِ والرَأيِ والأخلاقِ والأدَبِ، فيَجمَعَ ذلكَ في صَدرِهِ أو في كتابٍ ويَعمَلَ في إزالَتِها.[٢٩٦٢]

2655. **Imām al-Ṣādiq (AS) said,** 'Among the advices that Allah, Blessed and most High, gave to

٢٦٥٥ . الإمامُ الصّادقُ عليه‌السلام : كانَ فيما وَعَظَ اللهُ تَبارَكَ و تَعالىٰ بِهِ عيسَى بنَ مَريَمَ عليه‌السلام أن قالَ

Jesus son of Mary (AS) was, 'O Jesus, wherever you may be, scrutinize yourself on My behalf.'[2988]

له :... يا عيسىٰ ، كُنْ حَيثُما كُنتَ مُراقِباً لي .٢٩٦٣

2656. **Imām al-Ṣādiq (AS) said,** 'The man for whom each day passes exactly the same as another [where there is no change in his character or his deeds] is indeed a loser. And the man for whom the next day is always worse than the previous day is indeed cursed. And the man who never sees to improve himself day after day is indeed at a loss, and whoever passes his days in such loss, death is surely better for him.'[2989]

٢٦٥٦ . عنه ﷺ : مَنِ اعتَدَلَ يَوماهُ فهُو مَغبونٌ ، ومَن كانَ في غَدِهِ شَرّاً مِن يَومِهِ فهُو مَفتونٌ ، ومَن لَم يَتَفَقَّدِ النُّقصانَ في نفسِهِ دام نَقصُهُ ، ومَن دامَ نَقصُهُ فالمَوتُ خَيرٌ لَهُ .٢٩٦٤

(See also: NEGLIGENCE: section 1434)

أنظر : الغفلة : باب ١٤٣٤ .

839. Self-Scrutiny and Self-Accountability

٨٣٩ ـ المُراقَبةُ وَالمُحاسَبةُ

2657. **Imām al-Kāẓim (AS) said,** 'The one who does not take account of himself every single day is not one of us. And when he performs a good deed, he should ask Allah to enable him to do more, and when he commits an evil deed, he must seek Allah's forgiveness and repent for it.'[2990]

٢٦٥٧ . الإمامُ الكاظمُ ﷺ : لَيسَ مِنّا مَن لَم يُحاسِبْ نفسَهُ في كُلِّ يَوم ، فَإن عَمِلَ حَسَناً استَزادَ اللهَ ، وإن عَمِلَ سَيِّئاً استَغفَرَ اللهَ مِنهُ وتابَ إلَيهِ .٢٩٦٥

167

RAMAḌĀN

رَمَضان

840. The Month of Ramaḍān

٨٤٠ ـ شَهرُ رَمَضانَ

"The month of Ramaḍān is the one in which the Qur'an was sent down as guidance to mankind, with manifest proofs of guidance and the Distinguisher. So let those of you who witness it fast [in] it, and as for anyone who is sick or on a journey, let it be a [similar] number of other days. Allah desires ease for you, and He does not desire hardship for you, and so that you may complete the number, and magnify Allah for guiding you, and that you may give thanks."[2991]

﴿شَهْرُ رَمَضانَ الَّذِي أُنْزِلَ فِيهِ الْقُرآنُ هُدىً لِلنَّاسِ وَبَيِّناتٍ مِّنَ الْهُدَىٰ والْفُرقانِ فَمَن شَهِدَ مِنكُمُ الشَّهْرَ فَلْيَصُمْهُ وَمَنْ كانَ مَرِيضاً أو عَلَىٰ سَفَرٍ فَعِدَّةٌ مِّنْ أيَّامٍ أُخَرَ يُرِيدُ اللهُ بِكُمُ الْيُسْرَ وَلا يُرِيدُ بِكُمُ الْعُسْرَ وَلِتُكْمِلُوا العِدَّةَ وَلِتُكَبِّرُوا اللهَ عَلَىٰ ما هَداكُمْ وَلَعَلَّكُمْ تَشْكُرُونَ﴾ .٢٩٦٦

2658. **The Prophet (SAWA) said,** 'Verily Ramaḍān has been thus named because it scorches[2992] away sins.'[2993]

٢٦٥٨ . رسولُ اللهِ ﷺ : إنّما سُمّيَ الرَّمَضانُ لأنّهُ يَرمَضُ الذُّنوبَ.[٢٩٦٧]

2659. **The Prophet (SAWA) said,** 'Verily the gates of the heavens are opened on the first night of the month of Ramaḍān, and are not closed again until the very last night.'[2994]

٢٦٥٩ . عنه ﷺ : إنّ أبوابَ السماءِ تُفتَحُ في أوّلِ ليلةٍ مِن شَهرِ رَمَضانَ، ولا تُغلَقُ إلىٰ آخِرِ ليلةٍ مِنهُ.[٢٩٦٨]

2660. **The Prophet (SAWA) said,** 'If the servant was to fathom the worth of Ramaḍān, he would wish that Ramaḍān lasted the whole year.'[2995]

٢٦٦٠ . عنه ﷺ : لَو يَعلَمُ العَبدُ ما في رَمَضانَ لَوَدَّ أن يكونَ رَمَضانُ السَّنَةَ.[٢٩٦٩]

2661. **The Prophet (SAWA) said,** 'As soon as the month of Ramaḍān sets in, the gates of Hell are locked up, the gates of Paradise are opened, and the devils are bound up.'[2996]

٢٦٦١ . عنه ﷺ : إذا استَهَلَّ رَمَضانُ غُلِّقَتْ أبوابُ النارِ، وفُتِحَتْ أبوابُ الجِنانِ، وصُفِّدَتِ الشَّياطينُ.[٢٩٧٠]

2662. **Imām ʿAlī (AS) said,** 'Verily the Prophet of Allah (AS) addressed us one day, saying, "O people, verily the month of Allah has come to you with benediction, mercy and forgiveness - a month that is the best of months in the sight of Allah, whose days are the best of days, whose nights are the best of nights, and whose hours are the best of hours. It is a month wherein you have been invited to the banquet of Allah and have been made worthy of Allah's magnanimity. Your breaths during this month are considered glorification [of Allah], and your sleep worship. Your actions in it are accepted and your supplication answered..." Upon hearing this, I stood up and asked, 'O Prophet of Allah, what is the best of deeds to be performed in this month?' He replied, 'O Abū al-Ḥasan, the best of deeds in this month is to restrain oneself from all that Allah, Mighty and Exalted, has prohibited.'[2997]

٢٦٦٢ . الإمامُ عليٌّ ؑ : إنَّ رسولَ اللهِ ﷺ خَطَبَنا ذاتَ يومٍ، فقالَ : أيُّها الناسُ، إنّهُ قد أقبَلَ إلَيكُم شَهرُ اللهِ بالبَرَكَةِ والرّحمَةِ والمَغفِرةِ، شَهرٌ هُو عِندَ اللهِ أفضَلُ الشُّهورِ، وأيّامُهُ أفضَلُ الأيّامِ، ولَيالِيهِ أفضَلُ اللَّيالِي، وساعاتُهُ أفضَلُ الساعاتِ، هُو شَهرٌ دُعِيتُمْ فيهِ إلىٰ ضِيافَةِ اللهِ وجُعِلتُم فيهِ مِن أهلِ كَرامَةِ اللهِ، أنفاسُكُم فيهِ تَسبيحٌ، ونَومُكُم فيهِ عِبادَةٌ، وعَمَلُكُم فيهِ مَقبولٌ، ودُعاؤكُم فيهِ مُستَجابٌ...

فقُمتُ فقلتُ : يا رسولَ اللهِ، ما أفضَلُ الأعمالِ في هذا الشَّهرِ؟ فقالَ: يا أباالحسنِ، أفضَلُ الأعمالِ في هذا الشَّهرِ الوَرَعُ عن مَحارِمِ اللهِ عزّوجلّ.[٢٩٧١، ٢٩٧٢]

2663. **Imām al-Bāqir (AS) narrated,** 'At the end of Shaʿbān, when there were only three days left till the month of Ramaḍān, the Prophet (SAWA) told Bilāl, 'Call all the people', so the people gathered together. The Prophet (SAWA) mounted the pulpit,

٢٦٦٣ . الإمامُ الباقر ؑ : قالَ رسولُ اللهِ ﷺ لَمّا حَضَرَ شَهرُ رَمَضانَ وذلكَ لثَلاثٍ بَقِينَ مِن شَعبانَ، قالَ لِبِلالٍ : نادِ في الناسِ، فَجَمَعَ الناسُ

praised Allah and glorified Him, then continued, 'O people, this month that is coming upon you is the chief of all months. One particular night in it is better than a thousand months. During this month, the gates of Hell are locked up, and the gates of Paradise are opened. So whoever, in spite of experiencing this month is not forgiven, has indeed been distanced by Allah.'[2998]

ثُمّ صَعِدَ المِنبَرَ، فَحَمِدَ اللهَ وأثنىٰ علَيهِ، ثُمّ قالَ: أيُّها النّاسُ، إنَّ هذا الشَّهرَ قد حَضَرَكُم وهُو سَيِّدُ الشُّهُورِ، فيهِ ليلةٌ خَيرٌ مِن ألفِ شَهرٍ، تُغلَقُ فيهِ أبوابُ النِّيرانِ، وتُفتَحُ فيهِ أبوابُ الجِنانِ، فَمَن أدرَكَهُ فلَم يُغفَرْ لهُ فَأبعَدَهُ اللهُ.[٢٩٧٣]

2664. **Imām al-Ṣādiq (AS),** in his advice to his children heralding the advent of the month of Ramaḍān, said, 'Exert yourselves [in doing good deeds] for verily in this month sustenance is apportioned, life spans are destined, the names of Allah's select servants who wish to strive towards Him are recorded down, and in this month is a night wherein the good deeds performed equal the deeds of a thousand months.'[2999]

٢٦٦٤. الإمامُ الصّادقُ عليه السلام ـ مِن وَصِيَّتِهِ لِولْدِهِ عِندَ دُخُولِ شَهرِ رَمَضانَ ـ: فاجهَدُوا أنفُسَكُم فإنّ فيهِ تُقسَمُ الأرزاقُ، وتُكتَبُ الآجالُ، وفيهِ يُكتَبُ وَفدُ اللهِ الذين يَفِدُونَ إلَيهِ، وفيهِ ليلةٌ العَمَلُ فيها خَيرٌ مِن العَمَلِ في ألفِ شَهرٍ.[٢٩٧٤]

841. Allah's Forgiveness in the Month of Ramaḍān

٨٤١ ـ غُفرانُ اللهِ في شَهرِ رَمَضانَ

2665. **The Prophet (SAWA) said,** 'He who experiences the month of Ramaḍān and remains unforgiven has indeed been distanced by Allah.'[3000]

٢٦٦٥. رسولُ اللهِ صلى الله عليه وآله: مَن أدرَكَ شَهرَ رَمَضانَ فلَم يُغفَرْ لَهُ فَأبعَدَهُ اللهُ.[٢٩٧٥]

2666. **The Prophet (SAWA),** in his sermon heralding the advent of the month of Ramaḍān, said, 'Verily the most unfortunate is he who is deprived of Allah's forgiveness in this great month.'[3001]

٢٦٦٦. عنه صلى الله عليه وآله ـ في خُطبَتِهِ عندَ إقبالِ شهرِ رمضانَ ـ: إنّ الشَّقِيَّ مَن حُرِمَ غُفرانَ اللهِ في هذا الشَّهرِ العَظيمِ.[٢٩٧٦]

2667. **The Prophet (SAWA) said,** 'If a person remains unforgiven in the month of Ramaḍān, then what other month is there left for him to be forgiven in?!'[3002]

٢٦٦٧. عنه صلى الله عليه وآله: مَن لم يُغفَرْ لَهُ في شَهرِ رمضانَ ففي أيِّ شهرٍ يُغفَرُ لَهُ؟![٢٩٧٧]

2668. **Imām al-Ṣādiq (AS) said,** 'If a person remains unforgiven in the month of Ramaḍān, he will not be forgiven in any other month after it unless he is able to attend the plains of 'Arafa [during the obligatory pilgrimage].'[3003]

٢٦٦٨. الإمامُ الصّادقُ عليه السلام: مَن لَم يُغفَرْ لَهُ في شهرِ رمضانَ لَم يُغفَرْ لَهُ إلى مِثلِهِ مِن قابِلٍ إلّا أن يَشهَدَ عَرَفَةَ.[٢٩٧٨]

168

THE SPIRIT

الرُّوح

842. The Spirit

٨٤٢ـ مَعرِفَةُ الرُّوحِ

"They question you concerning the Spirit. Say, 'The Spirit is of the command of my Lord, and you have not been given of the knowledge except a few [of you].'[3004]

﴿وَيَسْأَلُونَكَ عَنِ الرُّوحِ قُلِ الرُّوحُ مِنْ أَمْرِ رَبِّي وَما أُوتِيتُمْ مِنَ العِلْمِ إلّا قَليلاً﴾.[٢٩٧٩]

(See also: Qur'an 39:42)

انظر: الزمر: ٤٢.

2669. **Imām al-Ṣādiq (AS) said,** 'Verily the spirits neither merge with the body nor are they dependent of it. Rather they are like a thin veil surrounding the body.'[3005]

٢٦٦٩. الإمامُ الصّادقُ عليه السلام: إنّ الأرواحَ لا تُمازِجُ البَدَنَ ولا تُواكِلُهُ، وإنّما هِي كِلَلٌ لِلبَدَنِ مُحيطَةٌ بِهِ.[٢٩٨٠]

2670. **Imām al-Ṣādiq (AS) said,** 'The spirit is a subtle form that is enveloped in a dense shell [i.e. the body].'[3006]

٢٦٧٠. عنه عليه السلام: الرُّوحُ جِسمٌ رَقيقٌ قد أُلبِسَ قالَباً كثيفاً.[٢٩٨١]

843. Spirits are Pre-Mobilized Groups

٨٤٣ـ الأرواحُ جُنودٌ مُجَنَّدَةٌ

2671. **The Prophet (SAWA) said,** 'Spirits are pre-mobilized groups; they are mutually attracted to other spirits that they are in harmony with and they mutually repel those that they differ.'[3007]

٢٦٧١. رسولُ اللهِ ﷺ: الأرواحُ جُنودٌ مُجَنَّدَةٌ، فما تَعارَفَ مِنها ائتَلَفَ، وما تَناكَرَ مِنها اختَلَفَ.[٢٩٨٢]

2672. **Imām ʿAlī (AS) said,** 'Love is when hearts harbour mutual affection due to the harmony between their spirits.'[3008]

٢٦٧٢. الإمامُ عليٌّ عليه السلام: المَوَدَّةُ تَعاطُفُ القُلوبِ في ائتِلافِ الأرواحِ.[٢٩٨٣]

2673. **Shaqīq b. Salama narrated** that a man once came to Imām ʿAlī (AS) and was talking to him. In the course of the conversation, he told Imām ʿAlī (AS) that he loved him. Imām replied, 'That is not true.' The man asked, 'Why, O Commander of the Faithful?' He replied, 'Because

٢٦٧٣. كنز العمّال عن شقيق بن سلمة: جاءَ رَجُلٌ إلىٰ عَلِيٍّ وكَلَّمَهُ، فقالَ في عُرضِ الحديثِ: إنّي أُحِبُّكَ، فقالَ لَهُ عَلِيٌّ: كَذَبتَ. قالَ: لِمَ يا أميرَ

I do not find my heart loving you, and the Prophet (SAWA) said, 'Verily spirits meet each other in the air and sense each other, and those that are in harmony with each other are mutually attracted, and those that clash repel each other.'[3009]

المؤمنينَ ؟ قالَ: لأنّي لا أرىٰ قَلبِي يُحِبُّكَ، قالَ النبيُّ ﷺ: إنّ الأرواحَ كانَت تَـلاقىٰ فـي الهَـواءِ فَتَشامُّ، ما تَعارَفَ مِنها ائتَلَفَ، وما تَناكَرَ مِـنها اختَلَفَ.
فلَمّا كانَ من أمرِ عَلِيٍّ ما كانَ، كانَ مِمَّن خَرَجَ علَيهِ.[٢٩٨٤]

(See also: THE FRIEND: section 1101)

(أنظر: الصديق: باب ١١٠١.)

844. The States of the Spirit

٨٤٤ـ أحوالُ الرُّوحِ

2674. **Imām ʿAlī (AS) said,** 'The body experiences six different states: health, sickness, death, life, sleep and wakefulness, and so does the spirit. Its life is its knowledge and its death ignorance; its sickness is doubt whereas its health is certainty; its sleep is its negligence and its wakefulness is its consciousness.'[3010]

٢٦٧٤. الإمامُ عليٌّ عليه السلام: إنّ لِلجِسمِ سِتَّةَ أحوالٍ: الصِّحّةُ، والمَرَضُ، والمَوتُ، والحَياةُ، والنَّومُ، واليَقظَةُ، وكذلكَ الرُّوحُ، فحياتُها عِلمُها، ومَوتُها جَهلُها، ومَرَضُها شَكُّها، وصِحَّتُها يَقينُها، ونَومُها غَفلَتُها، ويَقَظَتُها حِفظُها.[٢٩٨٥]

845. The Spirit During Sleep

٨٤٥ـ الرُّوحُ عِندَ النَّومِ

2675. **Imām al-Ṣādiq (AS),** when asked by his companion Abū Baṣīr whether the spirit remains with the body during sleep or leaves it, replied, 'No, O Abū Baṣīr, verily if the spirit were to leave the body it would never again return to it. It is actually like the sun that is fixed in its place in the centre of the sky, yet its rays extend out to the earth.'[3011]

٢٦٧٥. الإمامُ الصّادقُ عليه السلام ـ عندما سَألَهُ أبو بصيرٍ عنِ الرُّوحِ عِندَ النَّومِ أخارِجٌ مِنَ البَدَنِ ؟ ـ: لا يا أبا بصيرٍ، فإنَّ الرُّوحَ إذا فارَقَتِ البَدَنَ لَم تَعُدْ إلَيهِ، غَيرَ أنَّها بمَنزِلَةِ عَينِ الشَّمسِ مَركُوزَةٌ فـي السَّماءِ في كَبِدِها، وشُعاعُها في الدنيا.[٢٩٨٦]

2676. **Imām al-Kāẓim (AS) said,** 'When man sleeps, the animal spirit within him remains with his body, and that which leaves it is the rational spirit.'[3012]

٢٦٧٦. الإمامُ الكاظمُ عليه السلام: إنّ المَرءَ إذا نامَ فإنّ رُوحَ الحَيَوانِ باقِيَةٌ في البَدَنِ، والذي يَخرُجُ مِنهُ رُوحُ العَقلِ.[٢٩٨٧]

(See also: SLEEPING: section 1778)

أنظر: النوم: باب ١٧٧٨.

169

COMFORT

الرّاحَة

846. Factors that Bring about Comfort

٨٤٦ـ موجِباتُ الرّاحَةِ

2677. **Imām ʿAlī (AS) said,** 'He who has confidence in the fact that whatever sustenance Allah has apportioned for him will definitely reach him has secured comfort for his heart.'[3013]

٢٦٧٧ . الإمامُ عليٌّ عليه السلام : مَن وَثِقَ بأنَّ ما قَدَّرَ اللهُ لَهُ لَن يَفُوتَهُ استَراحَ قَلبُهُ .٢٩٨٨

2678. **Imām ʿAlī (AS) said,** 'A compatible wife is one of the two main comforts.'[3014]

٢٦٧٨ . عنه عليه السلام : الزَّوجَةُ المُوافِقَةُ إحدَى الرّاحَتَينِ .٢٩٨٩

2679. **Imām ʿAlī (AS) said,** 'He who restricts himself to what is just sufficient for maintenance has secured comfort and leads a carefree life.'[3015]

٢٦٧٩ . عنه عليه السلام : مَنِ اقتَصَرَ على بُلغَةِ الكَفافِ فَقَدِ انتَظَمَ الراحَةَ ، وتَبَوَّأَ خَفضَ الدَّعَةِ .٢٩٩٠

2680. **Imām ʿAlī (AS) said,** 'The greatest comfort lies in practicing abstemiousness in this world.'[3016]

٢٦٨٠ . عنه عليه السلام : الزُّهدُ في الدنيا الراحَةُ العُظمىٰ .٢٩٩١

2681. **Imām al-Ṣādiq (AS) said,** 'Tranquillity and comfort lie in satisfaction and certainty, whereas worry and sorrow lie in doubt and dissatisfaction.'[3017]

٢٦٨١ . الإمامُ الصّادقُ عليه السلام : الرَّوحُ والرّاحَةُ فِي الرِّضا واليَقينِ ، والهَمُّ والحَزَنُ فِي الشَّكِّ والسَّخَطِ .٢٩٩٢

2682. **Imām al-Ṣādiq (AS) said,** 'Absolute tranquillity lies in despairing of [any favours from] people.'[3018]

٢٦٨٢ . عنه عليه السلام : أروَحُ الرَّوحِ اليَأسُ عَنِ النّاسِ .٢٩٩٣

847. Seeking Comfort in this World

٨٤٧ـ طَلَبُ الرّاحَةِ فِي الدُّنيا

2683. **Imām al-Ṣādiq (AS) said,** addressing his companions, 'Do not wish for the impossible.' They retorted, 'Who ever wishes for the impossible?' to which he replied, 'You do. Do you not wish for comfort in this world?' They replied, 'Yes', so he (AS) said, 'Comfort is impossible for the believer to secure in this world.'[3019]

٢٦٨٣ . بحار الأنوار عن الإمام الصادق عليه السلام ـ لأصحابِهِ ـ : لا تَتَمَنَّوا المُستَحيلَ ، قالوا : ومَن يَتَمَنَّى المُستَحيلَ ؟! فقالَ : أنتُم ، ألَستُم تَتَمَنَّونَ الراحَةَ في الدنيا ؟! قالوا : بَلىٰ ، فقالَ : الراحَةُ لِلمُؤمِنِ فِي الدنيا مُستَحيلَةٌ .٢٩٩٤

170

AGRICULTURE

الزِّراعَةُ

848. The Divine Recommendation of Cultivation and Agriculture

٨٤٨ ـ استِحبابُ الزَّرعِ وَالغَرسِ

2684. **The Prophet (SAWA) said,** 'Every single Muslim that plants or cultivates anything of which humans, animals or birds may eat from is counted as charity towards them on his behalf.'[3020]

٢٦٨٤ . رسولُ اللهِ ﷺ : ما مِن مسلِمٍ يَغرِسُ غَرساً أو يَزرَعُ زَرعاً ، فَيَأكُلُ مِنهُ طَيرٌ أو إنسانٌ أو بَهيمَةٌ ، إلّا كانَ لَهُ بِه صَدَقةٌ .[٢٩٩٥]

2685. **Imām al-Bāqir (AS)** narrated that his father used to say, 'The best of occupations is tilling the land, the produce of which is eaten by both the good-doer and the wrongdoer. That which the good-doer eats will seek forgiveness on his [i.e. the grower's] behalf, and that which the wrongdoer eats will curse him [i.e. the wrongdoer]. The birds and animals eat thereof too.'[3021]

٢٦٨٥ . الإمامُ الباقرُ عليه السلام : كانَ أبي يقولُ : خَيرُ الأعمالِ الحَرْثُ ، تَزرَعهُ فَيَأكُلُ مِنهُ البَرُّ والفاجِرُ ، أمّا البَرُّ فما أكَلَ مِن شيءٍ استَغفَرَ لكَ ، وأمّا الفاجِرُ فما أكَلَ مِنهُ مِن شَيءٍ لَعَنَهُ ، ويَأكُلُ مِنهُ البهائمُ والطَّيرُ .[٢٩٩٦]

2686. **Imām al-Bāqir (AS)** narrated that Imām 'Alī (AS) used to say, 'He who, in spite of having water and soil at his disposal, is still poor, is dissociated by Allah.'[3022]

٢٦٨٦ . عنه عليه السلام : كانَ أميرُ المؤمنينَ عليه السلام يقولُ : مَن وَجَدَ ماءً وتُراباً ثُمّ افتَقَرَ فَأبعَدَهُ اللهُ .[٢٩٩٧]

2687. **Imām al-Ṣādiq (AS) said,** 'The farmers are the treasures of mankind for they plant and harvest the good things that Allah has made grow. On the Day of Resurrection, they will occupy the best and nearest position [to Allah] and will be called the blessed ones.'[3023]

٢٦٨٧ . الإمامُ الصّادقُ عليه السلام : الزّارِعُونَ كُنُوزُ الأنامِ ، يَزرَعُونَ طَيِّباً أخرَجَهُ اللهُ عزّوجلّ ، وهُم يومَ القِيامَةِ أحسَنُ الناسِ مَقاماً ، وأقرَبُهُم مَنزِلَةً ، يُدعَوْنَ المُبارَكِينَ .[٢٩٩٨]

2688. **Imām al-Ṣādiq (AS) said** that the verse of Allah in the Qur'an: *"And on Allah do the believers rely"* refers to the farmers.'[3024]

٢٦٨٨ . عنه عليه السلام ـ في قولِ اللهِ عزّوجلّ : ﴿وعَلَى اللهِ فَلْيَتَوَكَّلِ المُؤمِنُونَ﴾ [٢٩٩٩] ـ : الزّارِعُونَ .[٣٠٠٠]

2689. **Imām al-Ṣādiq (AS) said,** 'There is no occupation more beloved to Allah than agricu-

٢٦٨٩ . عنه عليه السلام ـ لَمّا سَألَهُ يزيدُ بنُ هارونَ الواسِطيُّ عنِ الفَلّاحِينَ ـ : هُمُ الزّارِعُونَ كُنوزَ اللهِ

lture, and every single prophet that Allah sent down was a farmer except Prophet Enoch[3025] (AS) who was a tailor.'[3026]

في أرضِهِ، وما في الأعمالِ شَيءٌ أحَبَّ إلى اللهِ مِن الزِّراعَـةِ، ومـا بَـعَثَ اللهُ نـبيّاً إلّا زَرّاعاً إلّا إدريسَ عليه السلام فإنّهُ كانَ خَيّاطاً.٣٠٠١

171

ALMS-TAX (*zakāt*)

الزَّكاةُ

849. The Obligatory Alms-Tax

٨٤٩ـ وُجوبُ الزَّكاةِ

"Take charity from their possessions to cleanse them and purify them thereby, and bless them. Indeed your blessing is a comfort to them, and Allah is all-hearing all-knowing."[3027]

﴿خُذْ مِنْ أمْوالِهِمْ صَدَقَةً تُطَهِّرُهُمْ وَتُزَكِّيهِمْ بِها وَصَلِّ عَلَيهِمْ إنَّ صَلاتَكَ سَكَنٌ لَهُمْ واللهُ سَمِيعٌ عَليمٌ﴾.٣٠٠٢

"And establish the prayer and give the zakāt. Any good that you send ahead for your souls, you shall find it with Allah. Indeed Allah sees best what you do."[3028]

﴿وَأقِيمُوا الصَّلاةَ وَآتُوا الزَّكاةَ وَما تُقَدِّمُوا لأنْفُسِكُمْ مِنْ خَيْرٍ تَجِدُوهُ عِنْدَ اللهِ إنَّ اللهَ بِما تَعْمَلُونَ بَصِيرٌ﴾.٣٠٠٣

2690. **Imām al-Ṣādiq (AS) said,** 'Allah – exalted be His remembrance – has not obligated anything more difficult for this community than paying the alms-tax, and the downfall of the majority of people lies in [their failure to pay] it.'[3029]

٢٦٩٠. الإمامُ الصّادقُ عليه السلام: ما فَرَضَ اللهُ عَزَّ ذِكرُهُ على هذهِ الأُمّةِ أشَدَّ علَيهِم مِنَ الزَّكاةِ، وما تَهلِكُ عامَّتُهُم إلّا فيها.٣٠٠٤

2691. **Imām al-Ṣādiq (AS) said,** 'The prayer of one who does not give the alms-tax is void, and the alms-tax of the impious is void.'[3030]

٢٦٩١. عنه عليه السلام: لا صلاةَ لِمَن لا زكاةَ لَهُ، ولا زكاةَ لِمَن لا وَرَعَ لَهُ.٣٠٠٥

2692. **Imām al-Ṣādiq (AS) said,** 'The alms-tax has been prescribed as a test for the rich and an aid to the poor. If people duly paid the alms-tax on their wealth, there would not remain a single poor or needy Muslim, and all would suffice themselves through what Allah has prescribed. Verily people are only impoverished, needy, hungry and naked as a result of the sins of the wealthy.'[3031]

٢٦٩٢. عنه عليه السلام: إنّما وُضِعَتِ الزَّكاةُ اِختِباراً للأغنِياءِ ومَعُونَةً لِلفُقَراءِ، ولَو أنَّ النّاسَ أدَّوا زكاةَ أموالِهِم ما بَقِيَ مسلمٌ فَقيراً مُحتاجاً، ولَاستَغنىٰ بما فَرَضَ اللهُ عزّوجلّ لَهُ، وإنّ النّاسَ ما افتَقَرُوا، ولا احتاجُوا، ولا جاعُوا، ولا عَرُوا إلّا بِذُنوبِ الأغنياءِ.٣٠٠٦

850. The Role of the Alms-Tax in the Increase of Wealth

٨٥٠ـ دورُ الزَّكاةِ في نَماءِ المالِ

2693. **The Prophet (SAWA) said,** ‘If you want Allah to enrich your wealth then give the alms-tax from it.’[3032]

٢٦٩٣ . رسولُ اللهِ ﷺ : إذا أرَدتَ أن يُثرِيَ اللهُ مالَكَ فَزَكِّهِ.[٣٠٠٧]

2694. **Imām ʿAlī (AS) said,** ‘Strengthen your capital by paying the alms-tax.’[3033]

٢٦٩٤ . الإمامُ عليٌّ (ع) : حَصِّنُوا أموالَكُم بالزَّكاةِ.[٣٠٠٨]

2695. **Imām al-Ḥasan (AS) said,** ‘The giving of the alms-tax never diminishes wealth.’[3034]

٢٦٩٥ . الإمامُ الحسنُ (ع) : ما نَقَصَتْ زكاةٌ مِن مالٍ قطُّ.[٣٠٠٩]

2696. **Imām al-Bāqir (AS) narrated,** ‘We found the following written in the book of the Prophet (SAWA): …When the alms-tax is withheld, the earth withholds all its yield of plants, fruits and minerals.’[3035]

٢٦٩٦ . الإمامُ الباقرُ (ع) : وَجَدنا في كتابِ رسولِ اللهِ ﷺ... إذا مَنَعُوا الزَّكاةَ مَنَعَتِ الأرضُ بَرَكَتَها مِنَ الزَّرعِ والثِّمارِ والمَعادِنِ كُلِّها.[٣٠١٠]

2697. **Imām al-Kāẓim (AS) said,** ‘Verily Allah has fixed the alms-tax as a provision for the poor and a proliferation of your wealth.’[3036]

٢٦٩٧ . الإمامُ الكاظمُ (ع) : إنّ اللهَ عزّوجلّ وَضَعَ الزَّكاةَ قُوتاً للفُقَراءِ وتَوفيراً لأموالِكُم.[٣٠١١]

2698. **Imām al-Riḍā (AS) said,** ‘When the alms-tax is not paid, livestock die as a result.’[3037]

٢٦٩٨ . الإمامُ الرِّضا (ع) : إذا حُبِسَتِ الزَّكاةُ ماتَتِ المَواشي.[٣٠١٢]

(See also: SPENDING: section 1759)

(اُنظر: الإنفاق: باب ١٧٥٩)

851. The One Who Refuses to Pay the Alms-Tax

٨٥١ـ مانِعُ الزَّكاةِ

2699. **Imām al-Bāqir (AS) said,** ‘He who refuses to pay the alms-tax, on the Day of Resurrection Allah will transform his wealth into a cobra with two venom glands that will coil itself around him and be told, ‘Tighten your grip on him just as he was tight-fisted with you in the world.’ This is in accordance with Allah’s verse in the Qur’an: *“They will be collared with what they grudge…”*’[3038 3039]

٢٦٩٩ . الإمامُ الباقرُ (ع) : الذي يَمنَعُ الزَّكاةَ يُحَوِّلُ اللهُ مالَهُ يومَ القيامةِ شُجاعاً مِن نارٍ لَهُ رِيمَتانِ[٣٠١٣] فَيُطَوِّقُهُ إيّاهُ ثُمّ يقالُ لَهُ: الزِمْهُ كما لَزِمَكَ في الدنيا، وهُو قولُ اللهِ ﴿سَيُطَوَّقُونَ ما بَخِلُوا بِهِ يوم القيامة﴾[٣٠١٤، ٣٠١٥]

2700. **Imām al-Ṣādiq (AS) said,** 'Those who refuse to pay the alms-tax ask to be returned to the world at the time of death, as per Allah's verse in the Qur'an: *"When death comes to one of them, he says, 'My Lord! Take me back, that I may act righteously in what I have left behind.'"*[3040 3041]

٢٧٠٠ . الإمامُ الصّادقُ عليه‌السلام : مَن مَنَعَ الزَّكاةَ سَأَلَ الرَّجعَةَ عندَ المَوتِ، وهُو قولُ اللهِ عزّوجلّ: ﴿حَتّىٰ إذا جاءَ أحَدَهُمُ المَوْتُ قالَ رَبِّ ارْجِعُونِ * لَعَلّي أعْمَلُ صالِحاً فيما تَرَكْتُ﴾[٣٠١٦،٣٠١٧]

2701. **Imām al-Ṣādiq (AS) said,** 'There are three types of people that are considered thieves: the one who refuses to pay the alms-tax, the one who spends his wife's dowry unlawfully, and the one who takes a loan with no intention to repay it.'[3042]

٢٧٠١ . عنه عليه‌السلام : السُّرّاقُ ثلاثةٌ: مانعُ الزّكاةِ، ومُستَحِلُّ مُهُورِ النِّساءِ، وكذلكَ مَنِ استَدانَ ولَم يَنوِ قَضاءَهُ.[٣٠١٨]

2702. **Imām al-Ṣādiq (AS) said,** 'He who refuses to pay [as meagre an amount as] a sixteen of a dirham in alms-tax may as well die a Jew or a Christian.'[3043]

٢٧٠٢ . عنه عليه‌السلام : مَن مَنَعَ قِيراطاً مِنَ الزَّكاةِ فَلْيَمُتْ إن شاءَ يَهُودياً وإن شاءَ نَصرانيّاً.[٣٠١٩]

852. Those Who are Entitled to Receive the Alms-Tax

٨٥٢ـ المُستَحِقُّونَ للزَّكاةِ

"Charities are only for the poor and the needy, and those employed to collect them, and those whose hearts are to be reconciled, and for [the freedom of] slaves and the debtors, and in the way of Allah, and for the traveller. [This is] an ordinance from Allah, and Allah is all-knowing, all-wise."[3044]

﴿إنّما الصَّدَقاتُ لِلْفُقَراءِ والمَساكِينِ والعامِلِينَ عَلَيْها والمُؤَلَّفَةِ قُلُوبُهُمْ وَفِي الرِّقابِ والغارِمينَ وَفِي سَبِيلِ اللهِ وابْنِ السَّبِيلِ فَرِيضَةً مِنَ اللهِ واللهُ عَلِيمٌ حَكِيمٌ﴾.[٣٠٢٠]

2703. **Imām al-Ṣādiq (AS),** with regards to Allah's verse in the Qur'an: *"Charities are only for the poor..."*, said, 'The poor man is he who does not beg from people [despite his poverty], the destitute lives in even harsher conditions than him, and the wretched one lives in the most straitened circumstances of all.'[3045]

٢٧٠٣ . الإمامُ الصّادقُ عليه‌السلام ـ في قولِهِ تعالى: ﴿إنّما الصَّدَقاتُ للفُقَراءِ...﴾ ـ: الفَقيرُ الذي لا يَسألُ النّاسَ، والمِسكينُ أجهَدُ مِنهُ، والبائسُ أجهَدُهُم.[٣٠٢١]

(See also: CHARITY: section 1116) (اُنظر الصدقة: باب ١١١٦)

853. There is a Zakāt for Everything[3046]

٨٥٣ـ لِكُلِّ شَيءٍ زَكاةٌ

2704. **Imām ʿAlī (AS) said,** 'The *zakāt* of power is equity.'[3047]

٢٧٠٤ . الإمامُ عليٌّ عليه‌السلام : زكاةُ القُدرَةِ، الإنصافُ.[٣٠٢٢]

2705. **Imām ʿAlī (AS) said,** 'The *zakāt* of beauty is chastity.'[3048]

٢٧٠٥ . عنه ﷺ : زكاةُ الجَمالِ ، العَفافُ.٣٠٢٣

2706. **Imām ʿAlī (AS) said,** 'The *zakāt* of prosperity is goodness to one's neighbours and maintaining relations with one's kin.'[3049]

٢٧٠٦ . عنه ﷺ : زكاةُ اليَسارِ ، بِرُّ الجِيرانِ وصِلَةُ الأرحامِ.٣٠٢٤

2707. **Imām ʿAlī (AS) said,** 'The *zakāt* of health is exerting oneself in Allah's obedience.'[3050]

٢٧٠٧ . عنه ﷺ : زكاةُ الصِّحَّةِ ، السَّعيُ في طاعَةِ اللهِ.٣٠٢٥

2708. **Imām ʿAlī (AS) said,** 'The *zakāt* of courage is fighting in the way of Allah.'[3051]

٢٧٠٨ . عنه ﷺ : زكاةُ الشَّجاعةِ ، الجِهادُ في سبيلِ اللهِ.٣٠٢٦

2709. **Imām ʿAlī (AS) said,** 'Fast, for that is the *zakāt* of the body.'[3052]

٢٧٠٩ . عنه ﷺ : علَيكَ بالصَّومِ ؛ فَإنّهُ زكاةُ البَدَنِ.٣٠٢٧

2710. **Imām al-Ṣādiq (AS) said,** 'Verily upon everything is its *zakāt*, and the *zakāt* of knowledge is to teach it to those who are worthy of it.'[3053]

٢٧١٠ . الإمامُ الصّادقُ ﷺ : إنَّ لِكُلِّ شَيءٍ زكاةً ، وزكاةُ العِلمِ أن يُعَلِّمَهُ أهلَهُ.٣٠٢٨

2711. **Imām al-Ṣādiq (AS) said,** 'Good moral conduct is the *zakāt* of bounties, intercession is the *zakāt* of high status, ailments are the *zakāt* of the body, amnesty is the *zakāt* of victory, and all that you give out *zakāt* on is protected from being snatched away from you.'[3054]

٢٧١١ . عنه ﷺ : المَعروفُ زكاةُ النِّعَمِ ، والشَّفاعةُ زكاةُ الجاهِ ، والعِلَلُ زكاةُ الأبدانِ ، والعَفوُ زكاةُ الظَّفَرِ ، وما أدّيتَ زكاتَهُ فهُو مَأمونُ السَّلْبِ.٣٠٢٩

854. Obligatory Alms-Tax Payable on ʿĪd al-Fiṭr[3055]

٨٥٤ـ زكاةُ الفطرَة

2712. **Imām ʿAlī (AS) said,** 'He who pays the obligatory alms-tax at the end of Ramaḍān, Allah uses it to make up for any deficit in the alms-tax paid on his wealth.'[3056]

٢٧١٢ . الإمامُ عليٌّ ﷺ : مَن أدّى زكاةَ الفِطرَةِ تَمَّمَ اللهُ لَهُ بها ما نَقَصَ مِن زكاةِ مالِهِ.٣٠٣٠

2713. **Imām al-Ṣādiq (AS) said,** 'Giving the alms-tax at the end of the month of Ramaḍān completes and constitutes fasting just as sending blessings on the Prophet (SAWA) at the end of the prayer completes and constitutes the prayer. Verily the one who fasts and yet intentionally does not pay the alms-tax due, his fasting is invalid.'[3057]

٢٧١٣ . الإمامُ الصّادقُ ﷺ : إنّ مِن تَمامِ الصَّومِ إعطاءَ الزَّكاةِ ـ يعني الفِطرَةَ ـ كما أنَّ الصَّلاةَ على النَّبيِّ ﷺ مِن تَمامِ الصَّلاةِ ، لأنّه مَن صامَ ولَم يُؤَدِّ الزَّكاةَ فلا صَومَ لَهُ إذا تَرَكَها مُتَعَمِّداً.٣٠٣١

172

TIME

الزَّمانُ

855. Perception of Time

٨٥٥ـ مَعرِفَةُ الزَّمانِ

2714. **Imām ʿAlī (AS) said,** 'The worth of a man with regard to his perception of things is his knowledge of time.'[3058]

٢٧١٤ . الإمامُ عليٌّ ﷺ : حَسْبُ المَرءِ... مِن عِرفانِهِ، عِلمُهُ بِزَمانِهِ.[٣٠٣٢]

2715. **Imām ʿAlī (AS) said,** 'The man who best understands time is he who is not taken aback by its proceedings.'[3059]

٢٧١٥ . عنه ﷺ : أعرَفُ الناسِ بالزّمانِ، مَن لَم يَتَعَجَّبْ مِن أحداثِهِ.[٣٠٣٣]

2716. **Imām al-Ṣādiq (AS) said,** 'He who knows [the workings of] his time is never overwhelmed by its obscurities.'[3060]

٢٧١٦ . الإمامُ الصّادقُ ﷺ : العالِمُ بِزَمانِهِ، لا تَهجُمُ علَيهِ اللَّوابِسُ.[٣٠٣٤]

856. Denouncing Having Trust in Time

٨٥٦ـ ذَمُّ الثِّقَةِ بِالزَّمانِ

2717. **Imām ʿAlī (AS) said,** 'He who places his trust in time has gone mad.'[3061]

٢٧١٧ . الإمامُ عليٌّ ﷺ : مَن وَثِقَ بِالزَّمانِ صُرِعَ.[٣٠٣٥]

2718. **Imām ʿAlī (AS) said,** 'Whoever trusts time is betrayed by it, and whoever holds it in high esteem is abased by it.'[3062]

٢٧١٨ . عنه ﷺ : مَن أمَنَ الزَمانَ خانَهُ، ومَن أعظَمَهُ أهانَهُ.[٣٠٣٦]

2719. **Imām ʿAlī (AS) said,** 'Whoever trusts time is betrayed by it, whoever attaches great importance to it is abased by it, whoever is angry with time, it spites him even more, and whoever takes refuge with time is forsaken by it. Not everyone who throws hits the target. When the sultan changes so does the time.'[3063]

٢٧١٩ . عنه ﷺ : مَن أمَنَ الزَّمانَ خانَهُ، ومَن تَعَظَّمَ علَيهِ أهانَهُ، ومَن تَرَغَّمَ علَيهِ أرغَمَهُ، ومَن لَجَأَ إلَيهِ أسلَمَهُ، ولَيسَ كُلُّ مَن رَمىٰ أصابَ، وإذا تَغَيَّرَ السُّلطانُ تَغَيَّرَ الزَّمانُ.[٣٠٣٧]

2720. **Imām ʿAlī (AS) said,** 'Time betrays the one who believes he possesses time, and it does not seek to please the one who blames it.'[3064]

٢٧٢٠ . عنه ﷺ : الزَّمانُ يَخُونُ صاحِبَهُ، ولا يَستَعتِبُ لِمَن عاتَبَهُ.[٣٠٣٨]

2721. **Imām ʿAlī (AS) said,** ‘Whoever preoccupies himself with time is occupied by it in turn.’[3065]

٢٧٢١ . عنه ﷺ : مَن تَشاغَلَ بالزَّمانِ شَغَلَهُ .٣٠٣٩

857. Denouncing the Contending with Time

٨٥٧ـ ذَمُّ مُكابَرَةِ الزَّمانِ

2722. **Imām ʿAlī (AS) said,** ‘He who blames time will find no end to his frustration.’[3066]

٢٧٢٢ . الإمامُ عليٌّ ﷺ: مَن عَتَبَ عَلى الزمانِ طالَت مَعتَبَتُهُ .٣٠٤٠

2723. **Imām ʿAlī (AS) said,** ‘Whoever resists time is spited by it even more, and whoever surrenders to it is not safe either.’[3067]

٢٧٢٣ . عنه ﷺ : مَن عانَدَ الزَّمانَ أرغَمَهُ، ومَنِ استَسلَمَ إلَيهِ لَم يَسلَمْ .٣٠٤١

2724. **Imām ʿAlī (AS) said,** ‘Whoever contends with time is thwarted, and whoever is resentful towards it ends up getting angry himself.’[3068]

٢٧٢٤ . عنه ﷺ : مَن كابَرَ الزَّمانَ عَطِبَ، ومن يَنقِمْ علَيهِ غَضِبَ .٣٠٤٢

858. Criticising Time

٨٥٨ـ تَعَيُّبُ الزَّمانِ

2725. Al-Rayyān b. al-Ṣalt narrated that Imām al-Riḍā (AS) recited some verses composed by ʿAbd al-Muṭṭalib:
All of people place the blame on time
When the trouble with time is only ourselves;
We reprove time while the fault lies within us
If time could speak, it would surely mock us.
The wolf shuns the meat of a fellow wolf
Whereas we devour each other in broad daylight.
Attired to deceive with our beautiful clothes,
Yet woe betide the stranger when he approaches us.[3069]

٢٧٢٥ . عيون أخبار الرِّضا عن الرَّيّانِ بنِ الصَّلتِ: أنشَدَنِي الرِّضا ﷺ لعبدِ المُطَّلِبِ:
يَـعِيبُ النـاسُ كُـلُّهُمُ زَمـانا
وما لِـزمانِنا عَـيبٌ سِـوانـا
نَـعِيبُ زَمـانَنا والعَـيبُ فِـينا
ولو نَطَقَ الزَّمـانُ بِـنا هَـجانا
وإنَّ الذِئبَ يَـترُكُ لَـحمَ ذِئبٍ
ويَأكُلُ بَـعضُنا بَـعضاً عِـيانا
لَبِسنا لِلخداعِ مسوكَ طِـيبٍ
ووَيلٌ لِـلغَرِيبِ إذا أتـانا .٣٠٤٣

173

FORNICATION

الزِّنا ١٧٣

859. Prohibition of Fornication

٨٥٩ـ النَّهيُ عَنِ الزِّنا

“Do not approach fornication. It is indeed an indecency and an evil way.”[3070]

﴿وَلا تَـقْرَبُوا الزِّنَـى إنَّـهُ كـانَ فـاحِشَةً وَسـاءَ سَبِيلاً﴾ .٣٠٤٤

(See also: Qur’an 24:33, 25:68)

(أُنظر) النور : ٣٣ و الفرقان : ٦٨

2726. **The Prophet (SAWA) said,** 'Allah's wrath is indeed severe on the married woman who fills her eyes with desire for men other than her husband or looks lustfully at anyone other than her unmarriageable kin [i.e. husband], upon which Allah thwarts every single good deed she has ever committed. And if she welcomes anyone other than her husband in his bed, Allah will rightfully burn her in the Fire after He has chastised her in her grave.'[3071]

٢٧٢٦. رسولُ اللهِ ﷺ: اِشتَدَّ غَضَبُ اللهِ عزّوجلّ عَلَى امرأةٍ ذاتِ بَعلٍ مَلَأَتْ عَينَها مِن غَيرِ زَوجِها أو غَيرِ ذِي مَحرَمٍ مِنها، فإنّها إن فَعَلَتْ ذلكَ أحبطَ اللهُ كُلَّ عَمَلٍ عَمِلَتهُ، فإن أوطَأَتْ فِراشَهُ غَيرَهُ كانَ حَقّاً عَلَى اللهِ أن يُحرِقَها بِالنارِ بعدَ أن يُعَذِّبَها في قَبرِها.[٣٠٤٥]

2727. **Imām 'Alī (AS) said,** 'A man who is possessive [over his own wife] will never commit adultery.'[3072]

٢٧٢٧. الإمامُ عليٌّ عليه السلام: ما زَنىٰ غَيُورٌ قَطُّ.[٣٠٤٦]

2728. **Imām al-Ṣādiq (AS) said,** 'The one to face the severest punishment on the Day of Resurrection will be the man who deposited his sperm in a womb that was forbidden to him.'[3073]

٢٧٢٨. الإمامُ الصّادقُ عليه السلام: إنّ أشَدَّ الناسِ عَذاباً يَومَ القِيامَةِ رَجُلٌ أقَرَّ نُطفَتَهُ في رَحِمٍ تَحْرُمُ علَيهِ.[٣٠٤٧]

2729. **Imām al-Riḍā (AS) said,** 'Fornication has been prohibited due to the corruption it engenders, from murder to illegitimacy to ill-breeding of children to broken lineages and all sorts of other social ills.'[3074]

٢٧٢٩. الإمامُ الرِّضا عليه السلام: حُرِّمَ الزِّنا لِما فيهِ مِنَ الفَسادِ مِن قَتلِ الأنفُسِ، وذَهابِ الأنسابِ، وتَركِ التَّربيَةِ للأطفالِ، وفَسادِ المَوارِيثِ، وما أشبَهَ ذلكَ مِن وُجُوهِ الفَسادِ.[٣٠٤٨]

860. Consequences of Fornication

٨٦٠ـ آثارُ الزِّنا

2730. **The Prophet (SAWA) said,** 'O 'Alī, there are six consequences that result from fornication, three of which are in this world and three in the Hereafter. In this world, it takes away one's beauty, hastens one's death and cuts off one's sustenance. In the Hereafter, it results in an evil reckoning, solicits the indignation of the Merciful Himself and makes one deserving of eternity in the Fire.'[3075]

٢٧٣٠. رسولُ اللهِ ﷺ: يا عليُّ في الزِّنا سِتُّ خِصالٍ: ثلاثٌ مِنها في الدنيا وثلاثٌ في الآخِرَةِ، فأمّا التي في الدنيا فَيَذهَبُ بالبَهاءِ، ويُعَجِّلُ الفَناءَ، ويَقطَعُ الرِّزقَ، وأمّا التي في الآخِرَةِ فَسُوءُ الحِسابِ، وسَخَطُ الرحمٰنِ، والخُلُودُ في النارِ.[٣٠٤٩]

2731. **Imām ʿAlī (AS) said,** 'Fornication brings about poverty.'[3076]

٢٧٣١ . الإمامُ عليٌّ ﷺ : الزِّنا يُورِثُ الفَقرَ.[٣٠٥٠]

2732. **Imām al-Bāqir (AS) said,** 'We found written in the book of the Prophet (SAWA), 'If fornication prevails after my death, incidences of sudden death will increase.'[3077]

٢٧٣٢ . الإمامُ الباقرُ ﷺ :وَجَدْنا في كتابِ رسولِ اللهِ ﷺ : إذا ظَهَرَ الزِّنا مِن بَعدِي كَثُرَ مَوتُ الفَجْأةِ.[٣٠٥١]

2733. **Imām al-Ṣādiq (AS) said,** 'When fornication becomes widespread earthquakes occur as an upshot.'[3078]

٢٧٣٣ . الإمامُ الصّادقُ ﷺ : إذا فَشا الزِّنا ظَهَرَتِ الزَّلازِلُ.[٣٠٥٢]

861. Every Limb has its Own Share of Fornication

٨٦١ـ لِكُلِّ عُضوٍ حَظٌّ مِنَ الزِّنا

2734. **Prophet Jesus (AS) said,** 'Every woman that perfumes herself and leaves her house intending for her perfume to be sensed by others is an adulteress, and every eye [that looks lustfully] is fornicating.'[3079]

٢٧٣٤ . المسيحُ ﷺ: أيُّما امرأةٍ استَعطَرَتْ وخَرَجَتْ لِيُوجَدَ رِيحُها فهِي زانِيَةٌ ، وكُلُّ عَينٍ زانِيَةٌ.[٣٠٥٣]

2735. **Prophet Jesus (AS) said,** 'Do not look intently at one who does not belong to you, for verily your genitals will not commit fornication as long as you guard your gaze [from fornicating]. So if you are able to keep yourself from looking at the apparel of a woman who is not permitted to you, then do so.'[3080]

٢٧٣٥ . عنه ﷺ : لا تَكُونَنَّ حَديدَ النَّظَرِ إلىٰ ما لَيسَ لكَ فإنّهُ لَن يَزنِيَ فَرجُكَ ما حَفِظتَ عَينَكَ ، فإن قَدَرتَ أن لا تَنظُرَ إلىٰ ثَوبِ المرأةِ التي لا تَحِلُّ لكَ فافعَل.[٣٠٥٤]

2736. **The Prophet (SAWA) said,** 'Every breath of man has its share in fornication which he is inevitably aware of at the time. The fornication of the eye is to look [at that which is forbidden to it], and the fornication of the foot is to walk [to where it is forbidden for it], and for the ear to listen [to that which is forbidden].[3081]

٢٧٣٦ . رسولُ اللهِ ﷺ : عَلىٰ كُلِّ نَفَسٍ مِن بَني آدَمَ كُتِبَ حَظٌّ مِنَ الزِّنا أدرَكَ ذلكَ لا مَحالَةَ ، فالعَينُ زِناها النَّظَرُ ، والرِّجلُ زِناها المَشيُ ، والأُذُنُ زِناها الاستِماعُ.[٣٠٥٥]

(See also: SIGHT: section 1734)

(انظر) النظر: باب ١٧٣٤.

174

ASCETICISM

الزُّهْدُ

862. The Virtue of Asceticism

٨٦٢ـ فَضلُ الزُّهدِ

2737. **The Prophet (SAWA) said,** 'People cannot worship Allah with anything better than asceticism from worldly pleasures.'[3082]

٢٧٣٧ . رسولُ اللهِ ﷺ : ما تَعَبَّدُوا للهِ بشَيءٍ مِثلِ الزُّهدِ في الدنيا .[٣٠٥٦]

2738. **Imām ʿAlī (AS) said,** 'Asceticism is the distinguishing characteristic of Godwary people and the natural disposition of those who turn to Allah.'[3083]

٢٧٣٨ . الإمامُ عليٌّ ؑ : الزُّهدُ شِيمَةُ المُتَّقِينَ وسَجِيَّةُ الأوّابِينَ .[٣٠٥٧]

2739. **Imām ʿAlī (AS) said,** 'Verily among the qualities that greatly develop one's faith is abstention from worldly pleasures.'[3084]

٢٧٣٩ . عنه ؑ : إنَّ مِن أعوَنِ الأخلاقِ على الدِّينِ الزُّهدَ في الدنيا .[٣٠٥٨]

2740. **Imām al-Bāqir (AS) said,** 'In one of His conversations with Prophet Moses (AS), Allah told him the following, '...those who seek to adorn themselves [for Me] have no better apparel than abstention from the worldly pleasures that they find indispensable.'[3085]

٢٧٤٠ . الإمامُ الباقرُ ؑ : كانَ فيما ناجَى اللهُ به موسىٰ ؑ : ... ما تَزَيَّنَ لي المُتَزَيِّنُونَ بمِثلِ الزُّهدِ في الدنيا عَمّا بِهِمُ الغِنىٰ عنه .[٣٠٥٩]

2741. **Imām al-Ṣādiq (AS) said,** 'All goodness has been placed in one house, and its key is asceticism and restraint from worldly pleasures.'[3086]

٢٧٤١ . الإمامُ الصّادقُ ؑ : جُعِلَ الخَيرُ كُلُّهُ في بَيتٍ، وجُعِلَ مِفتاحُهُ الزُّهدَ في الدنيا .[٣٠٦٠]

863. The Real Meaning of Asceticism

٨٦٣ـ حَقيقَةُ الزُّهدِ

"So that you may not grieve for what escapes you, nor exult for what comes your way, and Allah does not like any swaggering braggart."[3087]

﴿لِكَيْلا تَأْسَوا عَلَىٰ ما فاتَكُمْ وَلا تَفرَحُوا بِما آتاكُمْ واللهُ لَا يُحِبُّ كُلَّ مُخْتالٍ فَخُورٍ﴾ .[٣٠٦١]

2742. **The Prophet (SAWA) said,** 'Asceticism from worldly pleasures means to cut short one's hopes of this world, to be grateful for every single

٢٧٤٢ . رسولُ اللهِ ﷺ : الزُّهدُ في الدنيا قَصرُ الأمَلِ، وشُكرُ كُلِّ نِعمَةٍ، والوَرَعُ عن

bounty, to have piety and to keep away from all that which Allah has prohibited.'[3088]

كُلِّ ما حَرَّمَ اللهُ.[٣٠٦٢]

2743. **The Prophet (SAWA) said,** 'Asceticism is not to prohibit oneself that which is allowed. Rather it is to find that which is with Allah more secure than that which is in one's own possession.'[3089]

٢٧٤٣ . عنه ﷺ : الزُّهدُ لَيسَ بتَحريمِ الحَلالِ، ولكنْ أن يكونَ بما في يَدَيِ اللهِ أوثَقَ مِنهُ بما في يَدَيهِ.[٣٠٦٣]

2744. **Imām ʿAlī (AS) said,** 'Asceticism is summed up between two phrases in the Qur'an, where Allah, most High, says, *"So that you may not grieve for what has escaped you, nor be exultant at what He has given you."* Therefore, one who neither grieves about past losses nor is overjoyed about the possessions he is granted has perfected his asceticism from both sides.'[3090]

٢٧٤٤ . الإمامُ عليٌّ عليه السلام :الزُّهدُ كَلِمَةٌ بينَ كَلِمَتَينِ، قالَ اللهُ تعالىٰ: ﴿لِكَيْلا تَأْسَوا عَلَىٰ ما فاتَكُمْ وَلا تَفْرَحُوا بِما آتاكُمْ واللهُ لَا يُحِبُّ كُلَّ مُخْتالٍ فَخُورٍ﴾ فَمَن لَم يَأسَ على الماضِي، ولَم يَفرَحْ بالآتي فقد أخَذَ الزُّهدَ بِطَرَفَيهِ.[٣٠٦٤]

2745. **Imām al-Ṣādiq (AS) said,** 'Asceticism is the key to the door of the Hereafter and immunity from the Fire, and it is to abandon all those things that preoccupy you from Allah, neither experiencing regret upon their loss, nor self-admiration for having abandoned them, nor awaiting deliverance from them, nor seeking praise on account of them, and nor anything else in exchange for them. Rather you see their loss as a source of comfort and their presence as a source of misfortune, such that you consistently run away from misfortune and seek refuge in comfort.'[3091]

٢٧٤٥ . الإمامُ الصّادقُ عليه السلام : الزُّهدُ مِفتاحُ بابِ الآخِرَةِ، والبَراءةِ مِنَ النارِ، وهُو تَركُكَ كُلَّ شيءٍ يَشغَلُكَ عنِ اللهِ، مِن غَيرِ تَأسُّفٍ على فَوتِها، ولا إعجابٍ في تَركِها، ولا انتِظارِ فَرَجٍ مِنها، ولا طَلَبِ مَحمَدَةٍ علَيها، ولا عِوَضٍ مِنها، بل تَرىٰ فَوتَها راحَةً وكَونَها آفَةً، وتكونُ أبداً هارِباً مِنَ الآفَةِ، مُعتَصِماً بِالرّاحَةِ.[٣٠٦٥]

864. Qualities of the One who Practices Asceticism

٨٦٤ـ صِفاتُ الزّاهِدِ

2746. **Imām ʿAlī (AS) said,** 'The one who practices asceticism from worldly pleasures is such that he neither allows the prohibited things to overcome his perseverance [in the way of Allah], nor the permissible things to distract him from gratefulness to Allah.'[3092]

٢٧٤٦ . الإمامُ عليٌّ عليه السلام : الزاهدُ في الدنيا مَن لَم يَغلِبِ الحَرامُ صَبرَهُ، ولَم يَشغَلِ الحَلالُ شُكرَهُ.[٣٠٦٦]

2747. **Imām ʿAlī (AS) said,** 'Those who restrain themselves from worldly pleasures are such that their hearts are weeping though outwardly they may laugh, they experience great sorrow though they display joy, and they are filled with self-contempt though they rejoice at all that they have been bestowed.'[3093]

٢٧٤٧ . عنه (عليه السلام) : إنّ الزاهِدينَ في الدنيا تَبكي قلُوبُهُم وإن ضَحِكُوا، ويَشتَدُّ حُزنُهُم وإن فَرِحُوا، ويَكثُرُ مَقتُهُم أنفُسَهُم، وإنِ اغتَبَطُوا بما رُزِقُوا.[٣٠٦٧]

2748. **Imām al-Ṣādiq (AS),** when asked to define the ascetic, said, 'The ascetic is the one who renounces the permissible things in this world for fear of having to account for them, and renounces the forbidden things of this world for fear of punishment for them.'[3094]

٢٧٤٨ . الإمامُ الصّادقُ (عليه السلام) ـ لمّا سُئلَ عن الزاهِدِ في الدنيا ـ: الذي يَترُكُ حَلالَها مخافَةَ حِسابِهِ، ويَترُكُ حَرامَها مَخافَةَ عَذابِهِ.[٣٠٦٨]

2749. **Imām al-Riḍā (AS),** when asked about the qualities of the ascetic, replied, 'He manages to still his hunger without pursuit of food, he is well-prepared for his death, and weary of his life in this world.'[3095]

٢٧٤٩ . الإمامُ الرِّضا (عليه السلام) ـ لمّا سُئلَ عن صِفَةِ الزاهِدِ ـ: مُتَبَلِّغٌ بِدُونِ قُوتِهِ، مُستَعِدٌّ لِيَومِ مَوتِهِ، مُتَبَرِّمٌ بحَياتِهِ.[٣٠٦٩]

865. Factors that Elicit Asceticism

٨٦٥ ـ موجِباتُ الزُّهدِ

2750. **Imām ʿAlī (AS) said,** 'The person best able to practice abstemiousness is he who understands the inferiority of this worldly life.'[3096]

٢٧٥٠ . الإمامُ عليٌّ (عليه السلام) : أحَقُّ الناسِ بالزَّهادَةِ مَن عَرَفَ نَقصَ الدنيا.[٣٠٧٠]

2751. **Imām ʿAlī (AS) said,** 'How can one renounce the pleasures of this world when he has not yet fathomed the worth of the Hereafter?!'[3097]

٢٧٥١ . عنه (عليه السلام) : كيفَ يَزهَدُ في الدنيا مَن لا يَعرِفُ قَدرَ الآخِرَةِ ؟![٣٠٧١]

2752. **Imām al-Bāqir (AS) said,** 'Remember death frequently, for no sooner does man increase his remembrance of death than he begins to renounce this world's life.'[3098]

٢٧٥٢ . الإمامُ الباقرُ (عليه السلام) : أكثِرْ ذِكرَ المَوتِ، فإنّهُ لَم يُكثِرْ إنسانٌ ذِكرَ المَوتِ إلّا زَهِدَ في الدنيا.[٣٠٧٢]

2753. **Imām al-Kāẓim (AS)** once said while standing at a graveside, 'Indeed something that ends with this [i.e. death] is worthy of its beginning being spent in abstemiousness. And

٢٧٥٣ . الإمامُ الكاظمُ (عليه السلام) ـ عند قبرٍ حَضَرَهُ ـ: إنّ شيئاً هذا آخِرُهُ لَحَقيقٌ أن يُزهَدَ في أوَّلِهِ، وإنّ

indeed something that begins with this is worthy of its end being feared with apprehension.’[3099]

شيئاً هذا أوَّلُهُ لَحَقِيقٌ أن يُخافَ آخِرُهُ.[٣٠٧٣]

2754. **Imām al-ʿAskarī (AS) said,** ‘If the inhabitants of this world used their intellect, the world would self-destruct [for it would cease to be of any importance].’[3100]

٢٧٥٤ . الإمامُ العسكريُّ ﷷ :لَو عَقَلَ أهلُ الدنيا خَرِبَتْ.[٣٠٧٤]

(See also: DEATH: section 1671)

(أنظر) الموت: باب ١٦٧١.

866. The Benefits of Asceticism

٨٦٦-ثَمَراتُ الزُّهدِ

2755. **The Prophet (SAWA) said,** ‘Abstaining from the vain pleasures of this world puts the heart and the body at rest, whereas longing for them exhausts the heart and the body.’[3101]

٢٧٥٥ . رسولُ اللهِ ﷺ : الزُّهدُ في الدنيا يُريحُ القَلبَ والبَدَنَ، والرَّغبَةُ فيها تُتعِبُ القَلبَ والبَدَنَ.[٣٠٧٥]

2756. **Imām ʿAlī (AS) said,** ‘He who renounces this worldly life, neither concerning himself with its baseness nor vying for its glory, Allah rewards him with a gift that is unobtainable through any of His creatures, grants him knowledge without the need for learning, secures wisdom in his heart and makes it flow upon his tongue.’[3102]

٢٧٥٦ . الإمامُ عليٌّ ﷷ : مَن زَهِدَ في الدنيا، ولم يَجزَعْ مِن ذُلِّها، ولَم يُنافِسْ في عِزِّها، هَداهُ اللهُ بغَيرِ هِدايَةٍ مِن مَخلوقٍ، وعَلَّمَهُ بغَيرِ تَعليمٍ، وأثبَتَ الحِكمَةَ في صَدرِهِ وأجراها علىٰ لِسانِهِ.[٣٠٧٦]

2757. **Imām ʿAlī (AS) said,** ‘Abstain from the vain pleasures of this world and divine mercy will descend upon you.’[3103]

٢٧٥٧ . عنه ﷷ : اِزهَدْ في الدنيا تَنزِلْ علَيكَ الرَّحمَةُ.[٣٠٧٧]

2758. **Imām ʿAlī (AS) said,** ‘Abstaining from the vain pleasures of this world is the greatest source of comfort.’[3104]

٢٧٥٨ . عنه ﷷ : الزهدُ في الدنيا الراحَةُ العُظمىٰ.[٣٠٧٨]

2759. **Imām Zayn al-ʿĀbidīn (AS) said,** ‘He who renounces the world's vain pleasures finds its afflictions trivial and is not bothered by them as a result.’[3105]

٢٧٥٩ . الإمامُ زينُ العابدينَ ﷷ : مَن زَهِدَ في الدنيا هانَتْ علَيهِ مَصائبُها ولم يَكرَهْها.[٣٠٧٩]

2760. **Imām al-Ṣādiq (AS) said,** ‘It is forbidden for your hearts that they should taste the sweetness of faith until and unless they abstain from the pleasures of this world.’[3106]

٢٧٦٠ . الإمامُ الصّادقُ ﷷ : حَرامٌ علىٰ قُلوبِكُم أن تَعرِفَ حَلاوَةَ الإيمانِ حتّىٰ تَزهَدَ في الدنيا.[٣٠٨٠]

867. The Most Abstemious of People

٨٦٧ـأزهَدُ النّاسِ

2761. **The Prophet (SAWA) said,** 'The most abstemious of people is he who renounces the prohibited things.'[3107]

٢٧٦١ . رسولُ اللهِ ﷺ : أزهَدُ الناسِ مَن اجتَنَبَ الحَرامَ.[٣٠٨١]

2762. **Imām ʿAlī (AS) said,** 'Do not be of those who try to secure the Hereafter by means of the worldly life...they disparage this world using ascetic terms, yet act like those who covet it.'[3108]

٢٧٦٢ . الإمامُ عليٌّ ؑ : لا تَكُنْ مِمَّن يُريدُ الآخِرَةَ بِعَمَلِ الدنيا... يقولُ في الدنيا قَولَ الزاهِدينَ ، ويَعمَلُ فيها عَمَلَ الراغِبينَ.[٣٠٨٢]

2763. **Imām ʿAlī (AS) said,** 'The best level of asceticism is to conceal one's asceticism.'[3109]

٢٧٦٣ . عنه ؑ : أفضَلُ الزُّهدِ إخفاءُ الزُّهدِ.[٣٠٨٣]

2764. **Imām ʿAlī (AS) said,** 'When an abstemious person flees from people, seek after him, and when he seeks after people, flee from him.'[3110]

٢٧٦٤ . عنه ؑ : إذا هَرَبَ الزاهِدُ مِنَ الناسِ فاطْلُبْهُ ، إذا طَلَبَ الزاهِدُ الناسَ فاهْرُبْ مِنهُ.[٣٠٨٤]

2765. **Imām Zayn al-ʿĀbidīn (AS) said,** 'Allah says, 'O son of Adam, be satisfied with what I have given you and you will be among the most abstemious of people.'[3111]

٢٧٦٥ . الإمامُ زينُ العابدينَ ؑ : يقولُ اللهُ : يا ابنَ آدَمَ ، ارْضَ بما آتَيتُكَ تَكُن مِن أزهَدِ الناسِ.[٣٠٨٥]

2766. **Imām al-Kāẓim (AS) said,** 'Verily he who is most persevering in the face of adversity is the most abstemious from among you.'[3112]

٢٧٦٦ . الإمامُ الكاظمُ ؑ : إنّ أصبَرَكُم على البَلاءِ لَأزهَدُكُم في الدنيا.[٣٠٨٦]

175

MARRIAGE

الزَّواج ١٧٥

868. Enjoinment of Marriage

٨٦٨ـالحَثُّ عَلَى الزَّواجِ

"Marry off those who are single among you and the upright ones from among your male slaves and your female slaves. If they are poor, Allah will enrich them out of His grace, and Allah is all-bounteous, all-knowing."[3113]

﴿وَأَنْكِحُوا الْأَيَامَى مِنْكُمْ وَالصَّالِحِينَ مِنْ عِبَادِكُمْ وَإِمَائِكُمْ إِن يَكُونُوا فُقَرَاءَ يُغْنِهِمُ اللهُ مِن فَضْلِهِ وَاللهُ وَاسِعٌ عَلِيمٌ﴾.[٣٠٨٧]

"And of His signs is that He created for you mates from your own selves that you may take comfort in them, and He ordained affection and mercy between

﴿وَمِنْ آيَاتِهِ أَنْ خَلَقَ لَكُم مِنْ أَنْفُسِكُمْ أَزْوَاجاً لِتَسْكُنُوا إِلَيها وَجَعَلَ بَيْنَكُم مَوَدَّةً وَرَحْمَةً إِنَّ فِي

you. There are indeed signs in that for a people who reflect.'[3114]

ذٰلِكَ لَآياتٍ لِّقَوْمٍ يَتَفَكَّرُونَ﴾.[٣٠٨٨]

(See also: Qur'an 3:39, 16:72, 30:32, 25:74)

(أنظر) آل عمران: ٣٩ و النحل: ٧٢ والروم: ٣٢ والفرقان: ٧٤.

2767. **The Prophet (SAWA) said,** 'Whoever wants to meet Allah pure and immaculate should meet him accompanied by a wife.'[3115]

٢٧٦٧. رسولُ اللهِ ﷺ: مَن أحَبَّ أن يَلقَى اللهَ طاهِراً مُطَهَّراً فَلْيَلْقَهُ بزَوجَةٍ.[٣٠٨٩]

2768. **The Prophet (SAWA) said,** 'There is no institution in Islam more beloved and dearer to Allah than marriage.'[3116]

٢٧٦٨. عنه ﷺ: ما بُنِيَ في الإسلامِ بِناءٌ أحَبَّ إلى اللهِ عزّ وجلّ، وأعَزَّ مِنَ التَّزويجِ.[٣٠٩٠]

2769. **The Prophet (SAWA) said,** 'Marriage is my practice, so whoever rejects my practice is not from me.'[3117]

٢٧٦٩. عنه ﷺ: النِّكاحُ سُنَّتِي، فَمَن رَغِبَ عَن سُنَّتي فَلَيسَ مِنّي.[٣٠٩١]

2770. **The Prophet (SAWA) said,** 'When any young person gets married at the prime of his youth, his inner Satan cries out in rage, 'Woe unto him! Woe unto him! Two thirds of his faith have now been secured against me, and he has only to be careful of his duty to Allah in the remaining third.'[3118]

٢٧٧٠. عنه ﷺ: ما مِن شابٍّ تَزَوَّجَ في حَداثَةِ سِنِّهِ إلّا عَجَّ شَيطانُهُ: يا وَيْلَهُ، يا وَيْلَهُ! عَصَمَ مِنّي ثُلُثَي دِينِهِ، فَلْيَتَّقِ اللهَ العَبدُ في الثُّلُثِ الباقِي.[٣٠٩٢]

2771. **The Prophet (SAWA) said,** 'When the servant gets married, he has completed half of his faith, so let him be careful of his duty to Allah in the remaining half.'[3119]

٢٧٧١. عنه ﷺ: إذا تَزَوَّجَ العَبدُ فقدِ استَكمَلَ نِصفَ الدينِ، فَلْيَتَّقِ اللهَ في النِّصفِ الباقي.[٣٠٩٣]

2772. **The Prophet (SAWA) said,** 'A married person asleep is better in the sight of Allah than an unmarried person who fasts and spends his night in prayer.'[3120]

٢٧٧٢. عنه ﷺ: المُتَزَوِّجُ النائمُ أفضَلُ عِندَ اللهِ مِنَ الصائمِ القائمِ العَزَبِ.[٣٠٩٤]

2773. **The Prophet (SAWA) said,** 'Take up a wife for verily that will bring about an increase in your sustenance.'[3121]

٢٧٧٣. عنه ﷺ: اِتَّخِذُوا الأهلَ؛ فإنّه أرْزَقُ لَكُم.[٣٠٩٥]

2774. **The Prophet (SAWA) said,** 'Marry those who are single among you for verily Allah will develop their moral traits [through marriage], He

٢٧٧٤. عنه ﷺ: زَوِّجُوا أياماكُم، فَإنَّ اللهَ يُحسِنُ لَهُم في أخلاقِهِم، ويُوَسِّعُ لَهُم في

will increase their sustenance for them, and will enhance their integrity and gallantry.'[3122]

أرزاقِهم، ويَزيدُهُم في مُرُوّاتِهم.٣٠٩٦

2775. **Imām al-Ṣādiq (AS) said,** 'A two-unit prayer performed by a married person is better than seventy units performed by an unmarried person.'[3123]

٢٧٧٥. الإمامُ الصّادقُ عليه السلام: رَكعَتانِ يُصَلّيهِما مُتَزَوِّجٌ أفضَلُ مِن سَبعينَ رَكعَةً يُصَلّيها غَيرُ مُتَزَوِّجٍ.٣٠٩٧

869. Denouncing of Unmarried People

٨٦٩ـ ذَمُّ العُزّابِ

2776. **The Prophet (SAWA) said,** 'The worst ones from among your dead are the single people.'[3124]

٢٧٧٦. رسولُ اللهِ صلى الله عليه وآله: شِرارُ مَوتاكُمُ العُزّابُ.٣٠٩٨

2777. **The Prophet (SAWA) said,** 'The worst ones from among you are the single ones – two units of prayer performed by a married person is better than seventy units performed by an unmarried person.'[3125]

٢٧٧٧. عنه صلى الله عليه وآله: شِرارُكُم عُزّابُكُم، رَكعَتانِ مِن مُتَأهِّلٍ خَيرٌ مِن سَبعِينَ ركعةً مِن غَيرِ مُتأهِّلٍ.٣٠٩٩

870. The Reward for Getting Fellow Muslims Married

٨٧٠ـ ثَوابُ تَزويجِ الإخوانِ

2778. **Imām al-Ṣādiq (AS) said,** 'He who arranges for a single person to get married will be amongst those whom Allah will regard [with mercy] on the Day of Resurrection.'[3126]

٢٧٧٨. الإمامُ الصّادقُ عليه السلام: مَن زَوَّجَ أعزَباً كانَ مِمَّن يَنظُرُ اللهُ عزّوجلّ إلَيهِ يومَ القِيامَةِ.٣١٠٠

2779. **Imām al-Kāẓim (AS) said,** 'There are three types of people who will be shaded by Allah's Throne on the Day when no shade will avail apart from it: the one who arranged the marriage of a fellow Muslim brother, or served him in some way, or concealed his Muslim brother's faults [from others].'[3127]

٢٧٧٩. الإمامُ الكاظمُ عليه السلام: ثلاثةٌ يَستَظِلّونَ بِظِلِّ عَرشِ اللهِ يَومَ لا ظِلَّ إلّا ظِلُّهُ: رَجُلٌ زَوَّجَ أخاهُ المسلمَ، أو أخدَمَهُ، أو كَتَمَ لَهُ سِرّاً.٣١٠١

871. Enjoinment of Urgency in the Marriage of Young Women

٨٧١ـ الحثّ على التعجيل في تَزويجِ البَناتِ

2780. **Imām al-Riḍā (AS) said,** 'The archangel Gabriel descended to the Prophet (SAWA) and

٢٧٨٠. الإمامُ الرِّضا عليه السلام: نَزَلَ جَبرئيلُ عَلى

told him, 'O Muḥammad, verily your Lord extends salutations on you and says, 'Verily the virgins from among your women are as fruits on a tree, which when they ripen must be plucked otherwise the sun rots them and the wind alters them. So when young women reach marriageable age, they have no other recourse apart from husbands, otherwise they will not be safe from corruption.' The Prophet (SAWA) then climbed the pulpit, gathered the people and informed them of what Allah had commanded him.'[3128]

النبيّ ﷺ فقالَ: يا محمّدُ، إنّ رَبَّكَ يُقرِئُكَ السلامَ، ويقولُ: إنّ الأبكارَ مِنَ النساءِ بمَنزِلَةِ الثَّمرِ على الشَّجَرِ، فإذا أينَعَ الثَّمرُ فلا دَواءَ لَهُ إلّا اجتِناؤهُ وإلّا أفسَدَتْهُ الشَّمسُ، وغَيَّرَتْهُ الرِّيحُ، وإنّ الأبكارَ إذا أدرَكنَ ما تُدرِكُ النساءُ فلا دَواءَ لَهُنَّ إلّا البُعُولُ، وإلّا لَم يُؤمَنْ علَيهِنَّ الفِتنَةُ، فَصَعِدَ رسولُ اللهِ ﷺ المِنبَرَ فَجَمَعَ الناسَ ثُمّ أعلَمَهُم ما أمَرَ اللهُ عزّ وجلّ بِهِ.[٣١٠٢]

872. The Importance of Faith when Selecting a Spouse

٨٧٢-الإهتمامُ بالدينِ في الزَّواجِ

2781. **The Prophet (SAWA) said,** 'He who marries a woman solely for her beauty will not find anything he likes in her, he who marries her for her wealth will be deprived of it as soon as he marries her, so look to marry women of faith.'[3129]

٢٧٨١. رسولُ اللهِ ﷺ: مَن تَزَوَّجَ امرَأةً لا يَتَزَوَّجُها إلّا لِجَمالِها لَم يَرَ فيها ما يُحِبُّ، ومَن تَزَوَّجَها لِمالِها لا يَتَزَوَّجُها إلّا وَكَلَهُ اللهُ إلَيهِ، فعلَيكُم بذاتِ الدِّينِ.[٣١٠٣]

2782. **The Prophet (SAWA) said,** 'The beauty of a woman's faith must be given priority over the beauty of her face.'[3130]

٢٧٨٢. عنه ﷺ: لا يُختارُ حُسنُ وَجهِ المَرأةِ على حُسنِ دِينِها.[٣١٠٤]

2783. **The Prophet (SAWA) said,** 'When someone comes to you with a proposal and you are well-pleased with his faith and his integrity then accept him in marriage, for if you do not, discord and corruption will prevail in the land.'[3131]

٢٧٨٣. عنه ﷺ: إذا جاءَكُم مَن تَرضَونَ دِينَهُ وأمانَتَهُ يَخطُبُ (إلَيكُم) فَزَوِّجُوهُ، إن لا تَفعَلُوهُ تَكُن فِتنَةٌ في الأرضِ وفَسادٌ كبيرٌ.[٣١٠٥]

2784. **Imām al-Ḥasan (AS) said** to man who came to ask his advice about getting his daughter married, 'Marry her to a pious man, for if he loves her he will honour her, and if he comes to dislike her, at least he will not be unjust towards her.'[3132]

٢٧٨٤. الإمامُ الحسنُ عليه السلام ـ لرجلٍ جاءَ إلَيهِ يَستَشِيرُهُ في تَزويجِ ابنَتِهِ ـ: زَوِّجْها مِن رَجُلٍ تَقِيٍّ، فإنّهُ إن أحَبَّها أكرَمَها وإن أبغَضَها لَم يَظلِمْها.[٣١٠٦]

873. The Censure of Demanding an Excessive Dowry[3133]

٨٧٣ـ ذَمُّ غَلاءِ المَهرِ

2785. **The Prophet (SAWA) said,** 'The best women of my community are those that have the prettiest faces and the smallest dowries.'[3134]

٢٧٨٥ . رسولُ اللهِ ﷺ : أفضَلُ نِساءِ اُمَّتي أصبَحُهُنَّ وَجهاً وأقَلُّهُنَّ مَهراً.٣١٠٧

2786. **The Prophet (SAWA) said,** 'The best dowry is the simplest one.'[3135]

٢٧٨٦ . عنه ﷺ : خَيرُ الصَّداقِ أيسَرُهُ.٣١٠٨

2787. **Imām al-Ṣādiq (AS) said,** 'The bane of a woman is her excessive dowry and her disrespect of her husband.'[3136]

٢٧٨٧ . الإمامُ الصّادقُ ؑ : أمّا شُؤمُ المَرأةِ فكَثرَةُ مَهرِها وعُقوقُ زَوجِها.٣١٠٩

874. The Importance of Being Careful in Selecting a Wife

٨٧٤ـ الاهتِمامُ في اختِيارِ الزَّوجَةِ

2788. **The Prophet (SAWA) said,** 'Marry into a good tribe for verily blood is effective [traits and characteristics are inherited].'[3137]

٢٧٨٨ . رسولُ اللهِ ﷺ : تَزَوَّجوا في الحِجزِ الصالِحِ، فإنَّ العِرقَ دَسّاسٌ.٣١١٠

2789. **The Prophet (SAWA) said,** 'Choose carefully for your seed, for verily women give birth to children who resemble their own brothers and sisters.'[3138]

٢٧٨٩ . عنه ﷺ : تَخَيَّروا لِنُطَفِكُم، فإنَّ النساءَ يَلِدْنَ أشباهَ إخوانِهِنَّ وأخَواتِهِنَّ.٣١١١

2790. **Imām al-Ṣādiq (AS) said,** 'The Prophet (SAWA) addressing the people, saying, 'Beware of the verdure that grows in manure.' He was asked, 'What is the verdure that grows in manure?' He replied, 'It is a beautiful woman that comes from an evil environment.'[3139]

٢٧٩٠ . الإمامُ الصّادقُ عن آبائهِ ؑ : أنّ رسولَ اللهِ ﷺ قالَ لِلنّاسِ: إيّاكُم وخَضْراءَ الدِّمَنِ، قيلَ: يا رسولَ الله، وما خضراءُ الدِّمَنِ؟ قالَ: المَرأةُ الحَسناءُ في مَنبِتِ السُّوءِ.٣١١٢

2791. **The Prophet (SAWA) said,** 'Beware of marrying a stupid girl for her company is a waste and her offspring are [like] hyenas.'[3140]

٢٧٩١ . رسولُ اللهِ ﷺ : إيّاكُم وتَزَوُّجَ الحَمْقاءِ، فإنَّ صُحبَتَها ضَياعٌ ووُلْدَها ضِباعٌ.٣١١٣

875. The Rights of the Husband

٨٧٥ـ حُقوقُ الزَّوجِ

2792. **The Prophet (SAWA) said,** 'The person with the greatest right over a woman is her

٢٧٩٢ . رسولُ اللهِ ﷺ : أعظَمُ الناسِ حَقّاً على

husband, and the person with the greatest right over a man is his mother.'[3141]

المرأةِ زَوجُها، وأعظَمُ الناسِ حقّاً عَلَى الرَّجُـلِ أُمُّهُ.٣١١٤

2793. **The Prophet (SAWA) said,** 'Woe unto the woman who angers her husband, and blessed is the woman whose husband is pleased with her.'[3142]

٢٧٩٣ . عنه ﷺ: ويلٌ لِامرأةٍ أغضَبَتْ زَوجَها، وطُوبىٰ لِامرأةٍ رَضِيَ عنها زَوجُها.٣١١٥

2794. **Imām al-Bāqir (AS) said,** 'There is no interceder for a woman more efficient with her Lord than the content of her spouse.'[3143]

٢٧٩٤ . الإمامُ الباقرُ ؈: لا شَفيعَ للمرأةِ أنجَحُ عِند رَبِّها مِن رِضا زَوجِها.٣١١٦

876. The Rights of the Wife

٨٧٦ـ حُقوقُ الزَّوجَةِ

2795. **The Prophet (SAWA) said,** 'The archangel Gabriel continues to bring down so much advice with regard to the [treatment of the] woman that I think she must never be divorced unless she has committed adultery.'[3144]

٢٧٩٥ . رسولُ اللهِ ﷺ: ما زالَ جَبرَئيلُ يُوصِينِي بالمرأةِ حتّىٰ ظَنَنتُ أنَّهُ لا يَنبَغِي طَلاقُها إلّا مِن فاحِشَةٍ مُبَيِّنَةٍ.٣١١٧

2796. **The Prophet (SAWA) said,** 'The right of a woman on her husband is that he feeds her, clothes her, and does not frown his face at her.'[3145]

٢٧٩٦ . عنه ﷺ: حَقُّ المرأةِ علىٰ زَوجِها أن يَسُدَّ جَوعَتَها، وأن يَستُرَ عَورَتَها، ولا يُقَبِّحَ لَها وَجهاً.٣١١٨

2797. **The Prophet (SAWA) said,** 'A man's telling his wife 'I love you' never leaves her heart.'[3146]

٢٧٩٧ . عنه ﷺ: قَولُ الرَّجُلِ للمرأةِ: «إنّي أُحِبُّكِ» لا يَذهَبُ مِن قَلبِها أبداً.٣١١٩

877. Serving One's Husband

٨٧٧ـ خِدمَةُ الزَّوجِ

2798. **The Prophet (SAWA) said,** 'Whichever woman serves her husband for seven days, Allah locks seven doors of Hell to her and opens eight doors of Paradise instead whereof she may enter as she pleases.'
He also said, 'A woman's quenching of her husband's thirst with a glass of water is better for her than a whole year spent fasting during the day and praying at night.'[3147]

٢٧٩٨ . إرشاد القلوب: قالَ رسولُ اللهِ ﷺ: أيُّما امرأةٍ خَدَمَتْ زَوجَها سَبعَةَ أيّامٍ، غَلَّقَ اللهُ عَنها سَبعَةَ أبوابِ النارِ وفَتَحَ لَها ثَمانِيَةَ أبوابِ الجَنَّةِ تدخُلُ مِن أينَما شاءَتْ.
وقالَ ﷺ: ما مِن امرأةٍ تَسقِي زَوجَها شَربَةَ ماءٍ إلّا كانَ خَيراً لَها مِن سَنَةٍ صِيامِ نَهارِها وقِيامِ لَيلِها.٣١٢٠

2799. **Imām al-Ṣādiq (AS) narrated** that Umm Salama [the Prophet's wife] asked the Prophet

٢٧٩٩ . الإمامُ الصّادقُ ؈: سَألَتْ أُمُّ سَلَمَةَ

(SAWA) about the status of women when being of service to their husbands, so he (SAWA) replied, 'Any woman who so much as moves something from one place to another in her husband's house with the intention of improving it is regarded with mercy by Allah, and whoever Allah regards [with mercy] He does not punish.'[3148]

رسولَ اللهِ ﷺ عن فَضلِ النساءِ في خِدمَةِ أزواجِهِنَّ، فقال: أيُّما امرأةٍ رَفَعَتْ مِن بَيتِ زَوجِها شيئاً مِن مَوضِعٍ إلىٰ مَوضِعٍ تُريدُ بِهِ صَلاحاً إلّا نَظَرَ اللهُ إلَيها، ومَن نَظَرَ اللهُ إلَيهِ لَم يُعَذِّبْهُ.[٣١٢١]

2800. **Imām al-Kāẓim (AS) said,** 'The sacred war (*jihād*) of a woman is being a good spouse to her husband.'[3149]

٢٨٠٠. الإمامُ الكاظمُ ﷺ: جِهادُ المَرأةِ حُسنُ التَّبَعُّلِ.[٣١٢٢]

878. Serving One's Wife

٨٧٨ـ خِدمَةُ الزَّوجَةِ

2801. **The Prophet (SAWA) said,** 'If a man quenches his wife's thirst he is rewarded for it.'[3150]

٢٨٠١. رسولُ اللهِ ﷺ: إذا سَقَى الرجلُ امرأتَهُ أُجِرَ.[٣١٢٣]

2802. **The Prophet (SAWA) said,** 'A man's sitting beside his family is more beloved in the sight of Allah than his spending the night in worship in this mosque of mine.'[3151]

٢٨٠٢. عنه ﷺ: جُلوسُ المَرءِ عِندَ عِيالِهِ أحَبُّ إلى اللهِ تعالىٰ مِن اعتِكافٍ في مَسجِدِي هذا.[٣١٢٤]

2803. **The Prophet (SAWA) said,** 'Verily the man who lifts a morsel of food to his wife's mouth is well rewarded.'[3152]

٢٨٠٣. عنه ﷺ: إنَّ الرَّجُلَ لَيُؤجَرُ في رَفعِ اللُّقمَةِ إلىٰ فِي امرأتِهِ.[٣١٢٥]

879. Mistreating One's Husband

٨٧٩ـ إيذاءُ الزَّوجِ

2804. **The Prophet (SAWA) said,** 'If a man has a wife who mistreats him, Allah does not accept her daily prayer, nor any other good deed she performs, even if she was to fast all her life, until and unless she relieves him and pleases him…and the husband will bear the same burden and punishment if he mistreats or oppresses his wife.'[3153]

٢٨٠٤. رسولُ اللهِ ﷺ: مَن كانَ لَهُ امرأةٌ تُؤذِيهِ لَم يَقبَلِ اللهُ صلاتَها ولا حَسَنَةً مِن عَمَلِها حتّىٰ تُعِينَهُ وتُرضِيَهُ وإن صامَتِ الدَّهرَ... وعلَى الرَّجُلِ مِثلُ ذلكَ الوِزرِ والعَذابِ إذا كانَ لَها مُؤذِياً ظالِماً.[٣١٢٦]

2805. **Imām al-Ṣādiq (AS) said,** 'Cursed! Cursed indeed is the woman who troubles and distresses her husband; and blessed! Blessed indeed is the woman who honours her husband, does not trouble him and obeys him in all matters.'[3154]

٢٨٠٥. الإمامُ الصّادقُ ﷺ: مَلعونةٌ مَلعونةٌ امرأةٌ تُؤذِي زَوجَها وتُغِمُّهُ، وسَعيدةٌ سَعيدةٌ امرأةٌ تُكرِمُ زَوجَها ولا تُؤذِيهِ وتُطيعُهُ في جَميعِ أحوالِهِ.[٣١٢٧]

880. Mistreating One's Wife

٨٨٠ـ ايذاء الزوجة

2806. **The Prophet (SAWA) said,** 'I am truly astonished at the man who beats his wife when he is more deserving of the beating than her!'[3155]

٢٨٠٦ . رسولُ اللهِ ﷺ : إنّي لَأَتَعَجَّبُ مِمَّن يَضرِبُ امرَأتَهُ وهُو بِالضَّربِ أولىٰ مِنها ! ٣١٢٨

2807. **The Prophet (SAWA) said,** 'Beware that Allah the Glorious and Exalted and His Messenger dislike he who harms his wife to the extent that she asks for divorce without compensation!'[3156]

٢٨٠٧ . عنه ﷺ : ألا وإنَّ اللهَ عَزَّوجلَّ ورَسُولَهُ بَرِيئانِ مِمَّن أضَرَّ بِامرَأةٍ حتّىٰ تَختَلِعَ مِنهُ . ٣١٢٩

2808. **Imām ʿAlī (AS) said,** in his advise to his son al-Ḥasan, 'Your family should not feel like the most miserable people with you.'[3157]

٢٨٠٨ . الإمامُ عليٌّ عليه السلام ـ فِيما أوصَى ابنَهُ الحسنَ عليه السلام ـ : لايَكُنْ أهلُكَ أشقَى الخَلقِ بكَ . ٣١٣٠

881. Tolerating Bad Character of a Spouse

٨٨١ـ الصَّبرُ عَلىٰ سوءِ خُلُقِ الزَّوجِ والزَّوجة

2809. **The Prophet (SAWA) said,** 'Whoever patiently tolerates and puts up with his wife's bad character [for the sake of Allah], for every day and night of his endurance Allah will grant him the same reward as that granted to Prophet Job (AS) for enduring his afflictions, and for every day and night of her evildoing she will bear a burden as heavy as the sandhills.'[3158]

٢٨٠٩ . رسولُ اللهِ ﷺ : مَن صَبَرَ عَلىٰ سُوءِ خُلُقِ امرَأتِهِ واحتَسَبَهُ ، أعطاهُ اللهُ تعالىٰ بكُلِّ يومٍ ولَيلةٍ يَصبِرُ علَيها مِنَ الثَّوابِ ما أعطىٰ أيُّوبَ عليه السلام عَلىٰ بَلائهِ ، وكانَ علَيها مِنَ الوِزْرِ في كُلِّ يَومٍ ولَيلةٍ مِثلُ رَمْلٍ عالِجٍ . ٣١٣١

2810. **The Prophet (SAWA) said,** 'She who patiently tolerates her husband's bad character will be rewarded equivalent to the reward granted to Āsiya bint Muzāḥim [Pharaoh's wife].'[3159]

٢٨١٠ . عنه ﷺ : مَن صَبَرَتْ عَلىٰ سُوءِ خُلُقِ زَوجِها أعطاها مِثلَ (ثَوابِ) آسِيَةَ بنتِ مُزاحِمٍ . ٣١٣٢

882. The Virtuous Wife

٨٨٢ـ الزَّوجَةُ الصّالِحَةُ

2811. **The Prophet (SAWA) said,** 'There is nothing more beneficial to a believer after his piety and devotion to Allah than a virtuous wife.'[3160]

٢٨١١ . رسولُ اللهِ ﷺ : مااستَفادَ المؤمنُ بعدَ تَقوَى اللهِ عزّوجلّ خَيراً لَهُ مِن زَوجَةٍ صالِحَةٍ . ٣١٣٣

2812. **The Prophet (SAWA) said,** 'The best source of enjoyment in this world is a virtuous wife.'[3161]

٢٨١٢ . عنه ﷺ : خَيرُ مَتاعِ الدنيا المرأةُ الصالِحَةُ . ٣١٣٤

2813. **The Prophet (SAWA) said,** 'A virtuous wife is part of a man's prosperity.'[3162]

٢٨١٣ . عنه ﷺ : مِن سَعادَةِ المَرءِ الزوجَةُ الصالِحَةُ.[٣١٣٥]

(See also: GOOD: section 672)

(أنظر) الخير: باب ٦٧٢.

883. The Evil Wife

٨٨٣ـ الزَّوجَةُ السَّيِّئَةُ

2814. **The Prophet (SAWA) said,** 'The most evil of all things is the evil wife.'[3163]

٢٨١٤ . رسولُ اللهِ ﷺ : شَرُّ الأشياءِ المَرأةُ السّوءِ.[٣١٣٦]

2815. **Imām al-Ṣādiq (AS) said,** 'The believer's worst enemy is an evil wife.'[3164]

٢٨١٥ . الإمامُ الصّادقُ ؑ : أغلَبُ الأعداءِ للمؤمِنِ زَوجَةُ السُّوءِ.[٣١٣٧]

2816. **Imām al-Ṣādiq (AS) said,** 'One of the Prophet's supplications was as follows: I seek refuge in You from a wife who causes me to age before my time.'[3165]

٢٨١٦ . عنه ؑ : كانَ مِن دعاءِ رسولِ اللهِ ﷺ : أعوذُ بِكَ مِنِ امرَأةٍ تُشَيِّبُني قَبلَ مَشِيبِي.[٣١٣٨]

884. Things to be Considered when Spending on One's Family

٨٨٤ـ ما يَنبَغي رِعايَتُهُ في نَفَقَةِ العِيالِ

2817. **The Prophet (SAWA) said,** 'He who goes to the market and buys a gift to take back to his family is as one who is taking charity to a group of needy people. He should begin [giving gifts] to the female members of his family before the males.'[3166]

٢٨١٧ . رسولُ اللهِ ﷺ : مَن دَخَلَ السُّوقَ فاشتَرىٰ تُحفَةً فَحَمَلَها إلىٰ عِيالِهِ كانَ كَحامِلِ صَدَقَةٍ إلىٰ قَومٍ مَحاوِيجَ، ولْيَبدَأْ بِالْإناثِ قَبلَ الذُّكُورِ.[٣١٣٩]

2818. **Imām Zayn al-ʿĀbidīn (AS) said,** 'Verily the one whom Allah is most pleased with from among you is the one who is the most generous towards his dependents.'[3167]

٢٨١٨ . الإمامُ زينُ العابدينَ ؑ : إنَّ أرضاكُم عِندَ اللهِ أسبَغُكُم علىٰ عِيالِهِ.[٣١٤٠]

885. The Etiquette of Accepting Wedding Invitations

٨٨٥ـ أدَبُ استِجابَةِ الدَّعوةِ إلَى العُرُسِ

2819. **The Prophet (SAWA) said,** 'When you are invited to weddings, take your time [in attending] for they incite remembrance of this world's pleasures, and when you are invited to funerals, hasten to attend for they incite remembrance of the Hereafter.'[3168]

٢٨١٩ . رسولُ اللهِ ﷺ : إذا دُعِيتُم إلى العُرُساتِ فَأبطِئُوا فإنّها تُذَكِّرُ الدنيا، وإذا دُعِيتُم إلى الجَنائزِ فَأسرِعُوا فإنّها تُذَكِّرُ الآخِرَةَ.[٣١٤١]

2820. **The Prophet (SAWA) said,** 'When you are invited to a wedding banquet, do accept.'[3169]

٢٨٢٠ . عنه ﷺ : إذا دُعِيَ أحَدُكُم إلىٰ وَلِيمَةِ عُرسٍ فَلْيُجِبْ.[٣١٤٢]

886. Recommendation to Announce One's Marriage

٨٨٦ ـ الحَثُّ عَلىٰ إعلانِ النِّكاحِ

2821. **The Prophet (SAWA) said,** 'Announce this marriage and let it take place in the mosque.'[3170]

٢٨٢١ . رسولُ اللهِ ﷺ : أعلِنُوا هذا النِّكاحَ واجعَلُوهُ في المَساجِدِ.[٣١٤٣]

2822. **The Prophet (SAWA) said,** 'Publicize the marriage, but conceal the engagement.'[3171]

٢٨٢٢ . عنه ﷺ: أظهِرُوا النِّكاحَ وأخفُوا الخِطبَةَ.[٣١٤٤]

176

VISITING

الزِّيارَةُ

887. Enjoinment of Visiting Each Other for the Pleasure of Allah

٨٨٧ ـ الحَثُّ عَلَى التَّزاوُرِ فِي اللهِ

2823. **The Prophet (SAWA) said,** 'He who goes to visit his brother in faith at his home, without any motive on his part, is recorded as having visited Allah, and Allah honours His guest by His own right.'[3172]

٢٨٢٣ . رسولُ اللهِ ﷺ : مَن زارَ أخاهُ المؤمنَ إلىٰ مَنزِلِهِ لا حاجَةً مِنهُ إلَيهِ كُتِبَ مِن زُوّارِ اللهِ، وكانَ حَقيقاً على اللهِ أن يُكرِمَ زائرَهُ.[٣١٤٥]

2824. **Imām ʿAlī (AS) said,** 'Visit each other for the sake of Allah, sit in each other's company for the sake of Allah, give for the sake of Allah and deny for the sake of Allah, keep away from the enemies of Allah and maintain relations with the friends of Allah.'[3173]

٢٨٢٤ . الإمامُ عليٌّ عليه السلام : زُورُوا في اللهِ وجالِسُوا في اللهِ، وأعطُوا في اللهِ وامنَعُوا فِي اللهِ، زايِلُوا أعداءَ اللهِ وواصِلُوا أولياءَ اللهِ.[٣١٤٦]

2825. **Imām al-Bāqir (AS) said,** 'Pay visits to each other in your homes for verily that is a reviving of our teachings, and Allah has mercy on a servant who revives our teachings.'[3174]

٢٨٢٥ . الإمامُ الباقرُ عليه السلام : تَزاوَرُوا في بيوتِكُم فإنّ ذلكَ حَياةٌ لِأمرِنا، رَحِمَ اللهُ عَبداً أحيا أمرَنا.[٣١٤٧]

2826. **Imām al-Ṣādiq (AS) said,** 'He who visits his brother for the sake of Allah and for His

٢٨٢٦ . الإمامُ الصّادقُ عليه السلام : مَن زارَ أخاهُ في اللهِ

pleasure will be raised on the Day of Resurrection walking straddled by two cloths of light, and illuminating thereby anything that he passes.'[3175]

وللهِ، جاءَ يَومَ القِيامَةِ يَخطِرُ بَينَ قُباطِيٍّ مِن نُورٍ لا يَمُرُّ بِشيءٍ إلّا أضاءَ لَهُ.[٣١٤٨]

2827. **Imām al-Ṣādiq (AS) said,** 'Visit each other for verily your visits revive your own hearts and act as a reminder of our traditions, and our traditions in turn awaken affection in you towards each other. If you adopt our traditions you shall be rightly guided and shall attain salvation, and if you abandon them you will stray and perish, so do adopt them and I will guarantee your salvation.'[3176]

٢٨٢٧ . عنه ﷺ: تَزاوَرُوا فإنّ في زِيارَتِكُم إحْياءً لِقُلوبِكُم، وذِكراً لأحادِيثِنا، وأحادِيثُنا تُعَطِّفُ بعضَكُم عَلىٰ بعضٍ، فإن أخَذتُم بها رَشَدتُم ونَجَوتُم، وإن تَرَكتُمُوها ضَلَلتُم وهَلَكتُم، فَخُذُوا بها وأنا بِنَجاتِكُم زَعِيمٌ.[٣١٤٩]

2828. **Imām al-Kāẓim (AS) said,** 'Nothing is more hurtful to Iblīs [Satan] and his army than brothers in faith visiting each other for the sake of Allah.'[3177]

٢٨٢٨ . الإمامُ الكاظمُ ﷺ: لَيسَ شيءٌ أنكىٰ لإبليسَ وجُنودِهِ مِن زِيارَةِ الإخوانِ في اللهِ بعضِهِم لِبعضٍ.[٣١٥٠]

888. The Benefits of Meeting Fellow Brothers

٨٨٨ ـ ثَمَراتُ لِقاءِ الإخوانِ

2829. **The Prophet (SAWA) said,** 'Visiting [each other] makes love grow [between you].'[3178]

٢٨٢٩ . رسولُ اللهِ ﷺ: الزِّيارَةُ تُنبِتُ المَوَدَّةَ.[٣١٥١]

2830. 2835. **Imām al-Jawād (AS) said,** 'Meeting fellow brothers, even very briefly, causes the mind to broaden and develop.'[3179]

٢٨٣٠ . الإمامُ الجوادُ ﷺ: مُلاقاةُ الإخوانِ نُشْرَةٌ وتَلقيحُ العَقلِ، وإن كانَ نَزْراً قَليلاً.[٣١٥٢]

889. The Etiquette of Visiting

٨٨٩ ـ أدَبُ الزِّيارَةِ

2831. **The Prophet (SAWA) said,** 'Visit people at regularly-spaced intervals for that will increase love [between you].'[3180]

٢٨٣١ . رسولُ اللهِ ﷺ: زُرْ غِبّاً تَزدَدْ حُبّاً.[٣١٥٣]

2832. **Imām ʿAlī (AS)** in his will to his son Imām al-Ḥusayn (AS), said, 'Visiting too often brings about boredom.'[3181]

٢٨٣٢ . الإمامُ عليٌّ ﷺ ـ مِن وَصِيَّتِهِ لابنِهِ الحسينِ ﷺ ـ: كَثرَةُ الزِّيارةِ تُورِثُ المَلالَةَ.[٣١٥٤]

2833. **Imām ʿAlī (AS) said,** 'When you are assured of your brother's love for you, then do not worry about when you will meet each other.'[3182]

٢٨٣٣ . عنه ﷺ: إذا وَثِقتَ بِمَوَدَّةِ أخِيكَ، فلا تُبالِ مَتىٰ لَقِيتَهُ ولَقِيَكَ.[٣١٥٥]

177

VISITATION OF GRAVES

زيارة القبور

890. Visiting the Grave of the Prophet (SAWA)

٨٩٠-زِيارَةُ النَّبيِّ ﷺ

2834. **The Prophet (SAWA) said,** 'He who comes to visit me will benefit from my intercession on the Day of Resurrection.'[3183]

٢٨٣٤. رسولُ اللهِ ﷺ: مَن أتانِي زائراً كُنتُ شَفِيعَهُ يَومَ القِيامَةِ.[٣١٥٦]

2835. **The Prophet (SAWA) said,** 'I am informed about the one who sends greetings on me from any part of the earth, whereas I personally listen to the one who greets me at my grave.'[3184]

٢٨٣٥. عنه ﷺ: مَن سَلَّمَ عَلَيَّ في شَيءٍ مِنَ الأرضِ اُبلِغْتُهُ، ومَن سَلَّمَ عَلَيَّ عندَ القَبرِ سَمِعتُهُ.[٣١٥٧]

891. Visiting the Household of the Prophet (SAWA)

٨٩١-زِيارَةُ أهلِ البَيتِ عليهم السلام

2836. **The Prophet (SAWA)** was once asked by his grandson Ḥasan b. ʿAlī (AS), 'O father, what is the reward of one who visits you?' to which he replied, 'My son, he who visits me, during my life or after my death, or visits your father, your brother or yourself becomes deserving of my visiting him on the Day of Resurrection when I will rid him of his sins.'[3185]

٢٨٣٦. رسولُ اللهِ ﷺ -لَمّا سَأَلَهُ الحسنُ بنُ عليٍّ عليه السلام: يا أبَتاهُ، ما جَزاءُ مَن زارَكَ؟-: يا بُنَيَّ، مَن زارَني حَيّاً ومَيّتاً أو زارَ أباكَ أو زارَ أخاكَ أو زارَكَ كانَ حَقّاً عَلَيَّ أن أزُورَهُ يَومَ القِيامَةِ فَاُخَلِّصَهُ مِن ذُنوبِهِ.[٣١٥٨]

2837. **The Prophet (SAWA) said,** 'The one who visits Ḥasan at his resting place will cross the *Ṣirāṭ* firm-footedly on the day when feet shall slip.'[3186]

٢٨٣٧. عنه ﷺ: مَن زارَ الحَسَنَ في بَقِيعِهِ، ثَبَتَ قَدَمُهُ على الصِّراطِ يَومَ تَزِلُّ فيهِ الأقدامُ.[٣١٥٩]

2838. **The Prophet (SAWA) said,** 'A part of me will be buried in the land of Khurāsān, and any believer who visits him, Allah will make Paradise obligatory for him and will forbid the Fire from touching his body.'[3187]

٢٨٣٨. عنه ﷺ: سَتُدفَنُ بَضعَةٌ مِنّي بأرضِ خُراسانَ، لا يَزُورُها مُؤمِنٌ إلّا أوجَبَ اللهُ عزّوجلّ لَهُ الجَنَّةَ وحَرَّمَ جَسَدَهُ على النّارِ.[٣١٦٠]

2839. **Imām al-Ṣādiq (AS) said,** 'He who visits us after our death is as one who visited us in our lifetime.'[3188]

٢٨٣٩ . الإمامُ الصّادقُ ؑ : مَن زارَنا في مَماتِنا فكأنّما زارَنا في حَياتِنا.[٣١٦١]

2840. **Imām al-Ṣādiq (AS) said,** 'Verily there is a grave near Kūfa, which whenever a distressed person comes and prays four units of prayer by the graveside, Allah renders him happy by granting his request.'[3189]

٢٨٤٠ . عنه ؑ : إنَّ إلىٰ جانِبِها [أي جانِبِ الكوفَةِ] قَبراً لا يَأتيهِ مَكروبٌ فَيُصَلّي عِندَهُ أربَعَ رَكعاتٍ، إلّا رَجَعَهُ اللهُ مَسروراً بِقَضاءِ حاجَتِهِ.[٣١٦٢]

2841. **Imām al-Ṣādiq (AS) said,** 'The Prophet (SAWA) has said, 'Between my grave and my pulpit lies a garden from among the gardens of Paradise, and my pulpit rests on one of the waterways of Paradise', because the grave of Fāṭima (AS) is between his grave and his pulpit, and her grave is a garden from among the gardens of Paradise, watered by one of the waterways of Paradise.'[3190]

٢٨٤١ . عنه ؑ : قالَ رسولُ اللهِ ﷺ : ما بينَ قَبرِي ومِنبَرِي رَوضَةٌ مِن رِياضِ الجَنَّةِ، ومِنبَرِي علىٰ تُرْعَةٍ مِن تُرَعِ الجَنَّةِ؛ لأنَّ قَبرَ فاطمةَ صلواتُ اللهِ علَيها بينَ قَبرِهِ ومِنبَرِهِ، وقَبرَها رَوضَةٌ مِن رِياضِ الجَنَّةِ، وإلَيهِ تُرْعَةٌ مِن تُرَعِ الجَنَّةِ.[٣١٦٣]

2842. **Imām al-Ṣādiq (AS) said,** 'Whoever visits Imām Ḥusayn (AS) fully comprehending and acknowledging his right, Allah rewards him with the equivalent of a thousand accepted obligatory pilgrimages (*ḥajj*) and a thousand accepted voluntary pilgrimages (*'umra*), and forgives him all his past and present sins.'[3191]

٢٨٤٢ . عنه ؑ : مَن زارَ الحُسينَ ؑ عارِفاً بِحَقِّهِ كَتَبَ اللهُ لَهُ ثوابَ ألفِ حَجَّةٍ مَقبولَةٍ وألفِ عُمرَةٍ مَقبولَةٍ، وغَفَرَ لَهُ ما تَقَدَّمَ مِن ذَنبِهِ وما تَأخَّرَ.[٣١٦٤]

2843. **Imām al-Ṣādiq (AS) said,** 'Ḥusayn b. 'Alī (AS) was looking towards his Lord...., and he was saying, 'If the visitor to my grave knew what Allah has kept in store for him, his joy would surpass his grief [on my account]' - verily the one who visits him leaves his grave completely free of sins.'[3192]

٢٨٤٣ . عنه ؑ : إنّ الحُسينَ بنَ عليٍّ ؑ عندَ ربِّهِ يَنظُرُ ... ويقولُ: لَو يَعلَمُ زائِرِي ما أعَدَّ اللهُ لَهُ لَكانَ فَرَحُهُ أكثَرَ مِن جَزَعِهِ. وإنّ زائرَهُ لَيَنقَلِبُ وما علَيهِ مِن ذَنبٍ.[٣١٦٥]

2844. **Imām al-Ṣādiq (AS) said,** 'When you go to visit Abā 'Abdillāh (AS) [i.e. Imām al-Ḥusayn], be in a state of sadness and distress, dishevelled and dust-covered, hungry and thirsty, and ask all your needs from him, then leave him, and do not set up camp by his graveside.'[3193]

٢٨٤٤ . عنه ؑ : إذا زُرتَ أبا عبدِاللهِ ؑ فَزُرْهُ وأنتَ حَزينٌ مَكروبٌ شَعْثٌ مُغْبَرٌّ جائعٌ عَطشانُ، فإنَّ الحُسينَ ؑ قُتِلَ حَزيناً مَكروباً شَعِثاً مُغْبَرّاً جائعاً عَطشاناً، واسألْهُ الحوائجَ وانصرِفْ عنهُ ولا تَتَّخِذْهُ وَطَناً.[٣١٦٦]

2845. **Imām al-Ṣādiq (AS) said,** 'He who visits me will be forgiven of all his sins and will not die in poverty.'[3194]

٢٨٤٥ . عنه﵇ : مَن زارَني غُفِرَتْ لَهُ ذُنُوبُهُ ولَم يَمُتْ فَقيراً .[٣١٦٧]

2846. **Imām al-Ṣādiq (AS)** when he was asked what the position of one who visited one of the Imāms would be, replied, 'It is as if he has visited the Prophet (SAWA).'[3195]

٢٨٤٦ . عنه﵇ ـ لَمّا سُئلَ : ما لِـمَن زارَ أحَـداً مِنكُم ؟ ـ : كَمَن زارَ رسولَ اللهِ ﷺ .[٣١٦٨]

2847. **Imām al-Riḍā (AS) said,** 'The superior virtue of visiting the grave of the Commander of the Faithful ʿAlī (AS) over visiting the grave of Imām Ḥusayn (AS) is as the superiority of Imām ʿAlī (AS) over Imām Ḥusayn (AS).'[3196]

٢٨٤٧ . الإمامُ الرِّضا﵇ : فَضلُ زيارَةِ قَبرِ أميرِ المؤمنينَ علىٰ زيارَةِ قَبرِ الحُسينِ كَفَضلِ أمـيرِ المؤمنينَ عَلَى الحُسينِ .[٣١٦٩]

2848. **Imām al-Riḍā (AS)** in reply to Ibn Sinān's question, 'What is the reward of one who goes to visit your father?' said, 'His reward is Paradise, so go and visit him.'[3197]

٢٨٤٨ . عنه﵇ ـ لَمّا سَألَهُ ابنُ سِنانٍ : ما لِـمَن زارَ أباكَ ؟ ـ : لَهُ الجَنَّةُ فَزُرْهُ .[٣١٧٠]

2849. **Imām al-Riḍā (AS) said,** 'Anyone who visits me from amongst my friends, acknowledging and comprehending my right and position will benefit from my intercession on the Day of Resurrection.'[3198]

٢٨٤٩ . عنه﵇ : ما زارَني أحَـدٌ مِـن أولِـيائي عارِفاً بِحَقّي إلّا تَشَفَّعتُ لَهُ يَومَ القِيامَةِ .[٣١٧١]

2850. **Imām al-Riḍā (AS) said,** 'Whoever visits me away from my homeland, I will come to him on the Day of Resurrection in three different places to save him from their terrors: when the records of deeds will be handed out to the left and right, at the *Ṣirāṭ* [the bridge stretching over Hell] and at the Balance [when deeds will be weighed up].'[3199]

٢٨٥٠ . عنه﵇ : مَن زارَني عَلَى بُعدِ دارِي ، أتَيتُهُ يَومَ القِيامَةِ في ثلاثِ مَواطِنَ حتّىٰ اُخَلِّصَهُ مِـن أهوالِها : إذا تَـطايَرَتِ الكُـتُبُ يَـميناً وشِـمالاً ، وعِندَ الصِّراطِ وعِندَ المِيزانِ .[٣١٧٢]

2851. **Imām al-Hādī (AS)** was once asked by Ibrāhīm b. ʿAqaba about visiting the graves of Imām Ḥusayn (AS), Imām al-Kāẓim (AS) and Imām al-Jawād (AS), to which he replied, '[Visiting] Imām Ḥusayn (AS) takes precedence, and this [visiting of the two Imāms] has the greatest and most complete of reward.'[3200]

٢٨٥١ . الإمامُ الهاديُّ﵇ ـ عن إبراهيم بنِ عقبةَ لَمّا سَألَهُ عن زيارَةِ أبي عبدِاللهِ الحُسينِ وعَـن زيـارَةِ أبـي الحَسَـنِ الكـاظم وأبـي جـعفرٍ الجوادِ﵈ ـ : أبوعبدِالله﵇ المُقَدَّمُ، وهذا أجـمَعُ وأعظَمُ أجراً .[٣١٧٣]

2852. **Imām al-ʿAskarī (AS) said** to Abū Hāshim al-Jaʿfarī, 'My grave will be in Surra Man Ra'ā [present day Samarra] and will be a place of security for people on both sides of it [Euphrates].'[3201]

٢٨٥٢ . الإمامُ العسكريُّ عليه السلام ـ لأبي هاشمٍ الجَعفريِّ ـ: قَبري بِسُرَّ مَن رَأى أمانٌ لِأهلِ الجانِبَينِ. [٣١٧٤]

892. Visiting the Grave of Fāṭima, the Daughter of Imām Mūsā al-Kāẓim (AS)

٨٩٢ـ زِيارَةُ فاطِمَةَ بِنتِ موسَى الكاظِمِ

2853. **Imām al-Ṣādiq (AS) said,** 'Verily we have a holy sanctuary called Qum where a woman called Fāṭima from my descent will be buried. Entrance into Paradise will become mandatory for whoever visits her.'[3202]

٢٨٥٣ . الإمامُ الصّادقُ عليه السلام : إنّ... لَنا حَرَماً وهُوَ قُمّ، وسَتُدفَنُ فيه امرَأةٌ مِن وُلدِي تُسَمّىٰ فاطِمَةَ، مَن زارَها وَجَبَت لَهُ الجَنَّةُ. [٣١٧٥]

2854. **Imām al-Jawād (AS) said,** 'Whoever visits the grave of my aunt in Qum is guaranteed Paradise.'[3203]

٢٨٥٤ . الإمامُ الجوادُ عليه السلام : مَن زارَ قَبرَ عَمَّتِي بِقُمَّ فَلَهُ الجَنَّةُ. [٣١٧٦]

893. Visiting the Grave of al-Sayyid ʿAbd al-ʿAẓīm al-Ḥasanī

٨٩٣ـ زِيارَةُ السَّيِّدِ عَبدِ العَظيمِ الحَسَنِيِّ عليه السلام

2855. **Imām al-Hādī (AS)** asked someone from Ray who came to see him, 'Where have you been?' to which the man replied, 'To visit Imām al-Ḥusayn (AS).' Imām (AS) replied, 'Verily if you had visited the grave of ʿAbd al-ʿAẓīm in your own town, it would have been as if you visited Ḥusayn b. ʿAlī (AS).'[3204]

٢٨٥٥ . ثواب الأعمال عن مُحمّدَ بنِ يحيىٰ العَطّار [عن رجلٍ] مِن أهلِ الرَّيّ: دَخَلتُ على أبي الحسَنِ العَسكريِّ عليه السلام فقالَ: أينَ كُنتَ؟ فَقُلتُ: زُرْتُ الحُسينَ عليه السلام، قالَ: أما إنّكَ لو زُرْتَ قَبرَ عبدِ العظيمِ عِندَكُم لَكُنتَ كَمَن زارَ الحُسينَ بنَ عَلِيٍّ عليهما السلام. [٣١٧٧]

894. Visiting the Graves of Virtuous People

٨٩٤ـ زيارةُ قُبُورِ الصُّلَحاءِ

2856. **Imām al-Ṣādiq (AS) said,** 'Whoever is unable to come and visit us, let him go and visit the graves of virtuous people from among our friends, and it will be recorded for him as having visited us.'[3205]

٢٨٥٦ . الإمامُ الصّادقُ عليه السلام : مَن لَم يَقدِرْ علىٰ زِيارَتِنا فَلْيَزُرْ صالِحِي مَوالِينا، يُكتَبْ لَهُ ثَوابُ زِيارَتِنا. [٣١٧٨]

895. Visiting the Graves of the Deceased

٨٩٥ـ زِيارَةُ قُبورِ المَوتىٰ

2857. **Imām ʿAlī (AS) said,** 'Visit [the graves of] your deceased ones for indeed they rejoice at your visit. One should ask for one's requests at the graves of one's father and mother after praying for them.'[3206]

٢٨٤٧ . الإمامُ عليٌّ ﷺ : زُورُوا مَوتاكُم ؛ فإنّهُم يَفرَحُونَ بِزِيارَتِكُم ، ولْيَطلُبِ الرَّجُلُ حاجَتَهُ عِندَ قَبرِ أبيهِ واُمِّهِ بعدَما يَدعُو لَهُما .[٣١٧٩]

2858. **Imām al-Ṣādiq (AS)** was once asked by Dāwūd al-Raqqī, 'Is there any benefit in standing at the grave of one's father, relative or even someone unrelated?' Imām (AS) replied, 'Yes, verily they receive it [the visit] as one would receive a gift, and it makes them happy.'[3207]

٢٨٥٨ . الإمامُ الصّادقُ ﷺ ـ لَمّا سَألَهُ داوود الرَّقِّيُّ : يقومُ الرجُلُ علىٰ قَبرِ أبيهِ وقَرِيبِهِ وغَيرِ قَرِيبِهِ ، هَل يَنفَعُهُ ذلكَ ؟ ـ : نَعَم إنّ ذلك يَدخُلُ علَيهِ كما يَدخُلُ علىٰ أحَدِكُم الهَدِيَّةُ ، يَفرَحُ بِها .[٣١٨٠]

896. Greeting the People of the Graves

٨٩٦ـ التَّسليمُ علىٰ أهلِ القُبورِ

2859. **Imām ʿAlī (AS),** when he passed by graves, would say, 'Peace be upon you O people of the graves, you preceded us and we are following behind you, and we will meet you by Allah's will. As for your houses, they have already found new tenants, your spouses have remarried, your wealth has been distributed – these are the news we have. So what news have you for us?' Then he continued, 'If they were to answer, they would say, 'We found Godwariness to be the best provision [for the grave].'[3208]

٢٨٥٩ . بحار الأنوار : قالَ الإمامُ عليٌّ ﷺ ـ لَمّا مَرَّ على المَقابِرِ فقالَ ـ: السَّلامُ علَيكُم يا أهلَ القُبُورِ ، أنتُم لَنا سَلَفٌ ، ونَحنُ لَكُم خَلَفٌ ، وإنّا إن شاءَ اللهُ بِكُم لاحِقُونَ . أمّا المَساكنُ فَسُكِنَتْ ، وأمّا الأزواجُ فَنُكِحَتْ ، وأمّا الأموالُ فَقُسِّمَتْ ، هذا خَبَرُ ما عِندَنا ، فَلَيتَ شِعرِي ما خَبَرُ ما عِندَكُم ؟ ـ ثُمّ قالَ : ـ أما إنَّهُم إن نَطَقُوا لَقالوا : وَجَدنا التَّقوىٰ خَيرَ زادٍ .[٣١٨١]

178

ADORNMENT

الزِّينَةُ

897. Encouraging Adornment

٨٩٧ـ التَّرغِيبُ بِالزِّينَةِ

"O Children of Adam! Put on your adornment for every occasion of prayer, and eat and drink, but do not waste; indeed Allah does not like the wasteful."[3209]

﴿ يا بَنِي آدَمَ خُذُوا زِينَتَكُمْ عِندَ كُلِّ مَسْجِدٍ وَكُلُوا واشْرَبُوا وَلَا تُسْرِفُوا إنَّهُ لَا يُحِبُّ الْمُسْرِفِينَ ﴾ .[٣١٨٢]

"Say, 'Who has forbidden the adornment of Allah which He has brought forth for His servants and all kinds of lawful things of food....'"[3210]

﴿قُلْ مَنْ حَرَّمَ زِينَةَ اللهِ الَّتِي أخْرَجَ لِعِبادِهِ وَالطَّيِّباتِ مِنَ الرِّزقِ ...﴾.[٣١٨٣]

2860. **The Prophet (SAWA) said,** 'Verily Allah likes it for a believing servant of His, when he goes to visit a fellow brother, to get ready and adorn himself.'[3211]

٢٨٦٠ . رسولُ اللهِ ﷺ : إنّ اللهَ يُحِبُّ ـ إذا خَرَجَ عَبدُهُ المؤمنُ إلىٰ أخيهِ ـ أن يَتَهَيَّأَ لَهُ وأن يَتَجَمَّلَ.[٣١٨٤]

2861. **Imām ʿAlī (AS) said,** 'You should adorn yourself for your fellow Muslim brother when you go to visit him just as you adorn yourself for a stranger for whom you want to make a good first impression.'[3212]

٢٨٦١ . الإمامُ عليٌّ عليه السلام : لِيَتَزَيَّنْ أحدُكُم لأخيهِ المُسلمِ إذا أتاهُ كما يَتَزَيَّنُ للغَريبِ الذي يُحِبُّ أن يَراهُ في أحسَنِ الهَيئَةِ.[٣١٨٥]

(See also: BEAUTY: section 353)

(اُنظر) الجمال: باب ٣٥٣.

898. The Best Adornment

٨٩٨ ـ أحسَنُ الزِّينَةِ

2862. **The Prophet (SAWA) said,** 'The best thing a man can adorn himself with is tranquillity coupled with faith.'[3213]

٢٨٦٢ . رسولُ اللهِ ﷺ : أحسَنُ زِينَةِ الرَّجُلِ السَّكِينَةُ معَ إيمانٍ.[٣١٨٦]

2863. **Imām ʿAlī (AS) said,** 'The best attire is that which enables you to blend in with people, which makes you look presentable in front of them, and which does not give tongues an excuse to wag about you.'[3214]

٢٨٦٣ . الإمامُ عليٌّ عليه السلام : إنّ أحسَنَ الزِّيِّ ما خَلَطَكَ بالناسِ وجَمَّلَكَ بينَهُم وكَفَّ ألسِنَتَهُم عنكَ.[٣١٨٧]

2864. **Imām ʿAlī (AS) said,** 'No one can adorn himself with a better adornment than the obedience of Allah.'[3215]

٢٨٦٤ . عنه عليه السلام : ما تَزَيَّنَ مُتَزَيِّنٌ بِمِثلِ طاعَةِ اللهِ.[٣١٨٨]

2865. **Imām ʿAlī (AS) said,** 'The adornment of your inner selves is more beautiful than the adornment of the outer.'[3216]

٢٨٦٥ . عنه عليه السلام : زِينَةُ البَواطِنِ أجمَلُ مِن زِينَةِ الظَّواهِرِ.[٣١٨٩]

2866. **Imām ʿAlī (AS) said,** 'The adornment of faith is purity of one's innermost thoughts coupled with good actions manifested outwardly.'[3217]

٢٨٦٦ . عنه عليه السلام : زَينُ الإيمانِ طَهارَةُ السَّرائرِ وحُسنُ العَمَلِ في الظّاهِرِ.[٣١٩٠]

179

RESPONSIBILITY

المَسْؤولِيَّة

899. Responsibility

٨٩٩ ـ المَسؤوليَّةُ

"By your Lord, we will question them all concerning what they used to do."[3218]

﴿فَوَرَبِّكَ لَنَسْأَلَنَّهُمْ أَجْمَعِينَ * عَمَّا كَانُوا يَعْمَلُونَ﴾.[٣١٩١]

2867. **Imām ʿAlī (AS) said,** 'Be careful of your duty to Allah with respect to His people as well as His places, for verily you will be answerable even for the places [you frequented] and the animals. Obey Allah and do not disobey Him.'[3219]

٢٨٦٧. الإمامُ عليٌّ (ع): اِتَّقُوا اللهَ في عِبادِهِ وبِلادِهِ فإنَّكُم مَسؤولونَ حتّى عنِ البِقاعِ والبَهائمِ، أطيعُوا اللهَ ولا تَعصُوهُ.[٣١٩٢]

900. All of you are Responsible

٩٠٠ ـ كُلُّكُم مَسؤولٌ!

2868. **The Prophet (SAWA) said,** 'Indeed each of you is a shepherd responsible for his own herd. The commander of the people is their shepherd and responsible for his herd, just as a man looks after his household and is responsible for them, and a woman tends to her husband and children and is responsible for them.'[3220]

٢٨٦٨. رسولُ اللهِ ﷺ: ألا كُلُّكُم راعٍ وكُلُّكُم مَسؤولٌ عن رَعيَّتِهِ، فالأميرُ الذي على النّاسِ راعٍ وهُو مَسؤولٌ عن رَعيَّتِهِ، والرَّجُلُ راعٍ على أهلِ بَيتِهِ وهُو مَسؤولٌ عَنهُم، والمَرأةُ راعِيَةٌ على بَيتِ بَعلِها ووُلْدِهِ وهي مَسؤولَةٌ عَنهُم.[٣١٩٣]

2869. **Imām ʿAlī (AS) said,** 'Every single person is answerable for what he possesses, and for all those who depend on him.'[3221]

٢٨٦٩. الإمامُ عليٌّ (ع): كُلُّ امرِئٍ مَسؤولٌ عمّا مَلَكَتْ يَمينُهُ وعِيالِهِ.[٣١٩٤]

901. The Answerability of the Hearing, the Sight and the Heart

٩٠١ ـ مَسؤوليَّةُ السَّمعِ وَالبَصَرِ وَالفُؤادِ

2870. It has been narrated in *Man La Yaḥḍuruhu al-Faqīh* that a man once came to Imām al-Ṣādiq (AS) saying, 'I have a neighbour whose slave girls sing and play the lute, and sometimes when I go to the outhouse I take my time there so I may listen to them…? So Imām al-Ṣādiq (AS) said to

٢٨٧٠. كتاب من لا يحضره الفقيه: قالَ رجلٌ للصّادقِ (ع): إنّ لي جِيراناً ولَهُم جَوارٍ يَتَغَنَّينَ ويَضرِبنَ بالعُودِ، فرُبَّما دَخَلتُ المَخرَجَ فأُطيلُ

him, 'By Allah! Have you not heard the verse of Allah, Mighty and Exalted, [in the Qur'an], *"Verily the hearing and the sight and the heart, each of those shall be answerable for it"*?!'[3222]

الجُـلُوسَ اسـتِماعاً مِـنّي لَـهُنَّ؟... فـقالَ لَـهُ الصّادقُ ﷺ: تاللهِ أنتَ! أما سَمِعتَ اللهَ عـزّوجلّ يقولُ: ﴿إنَّ السَّمْعَ والبَصَرَ والفُؤادَ كُلُّ أُولئكَ كانَ عنه مَسْؤولاً﴾؟![٣١٩٥]

180

ASKING (1) [Seeking Knowledge]

السُّؤالُ (١) طَلَبُ العِلمِ

902. The Key to Knowledge

٩٠٢ ـ مِفتاحُ العِلمِ

"We did not send [any apostles] before you except as men to whom We revealed – ask the People of the Reminder if you do not know."[3223]

﴿وَمَا أَرْسَلْنا مِن قَبْلِكَ إلَّا رِجالاً نُوحِي إلَيْهِمْ فاسْأَلُوا أَهلَ الذِّكْرِ إنْ كُنْتُمْ لا تَعْلَمُونَ﴾.[٣١٩٦]

2871. **The Prophet (SAWA) said,** 'Knowledge is a treasury, the key to which is the question, so ask and Allah will have mercy on you for verily four people are rewarded [for that question]: the questioner, the speaker, the listener, and the one that admires them.'[3224]

٢٨٧١. رسولُ اللهِ ﷺ: العِلمُ خَزائنُ ومَفاتِيحُهُ السُّؤالُ، فَاسألُوا رَحِمَكُمُ اللهُ فإنّهُ يُؤجَرُ أربَعةٌ: السائلُ، والمُتَكلِّمُ، والمُستَمِعُ، والمُحِبُّ لَهُم.[٣١٩٧]

2872. **The Prophet (SAWA) said,** 'The question is half of knowledge.'[3225]

٢٨٧٢. عنه ﷺ: السُّؤالُ نِصفُ العِلمِ.[٣١٩٨]

903. Productive Questioning

٩٠٣ ـ حُسنُ المَسألَةِ

2873. **The Prophet (SAWA) said,** 'Productive questioning is half of knowledge.'[3226]

٢٨٧٣. رسولُ اللهِ ﷺ: حُسنُ السؤالِ نِصفُ العِلمِ.[٣١٩٩]

2874. **Imām 'Alī (AS) said** to a man who asked him regarding a puzzling issue, 'Ask in order to genuinely comprehend [the matter], and do not ask importunately causing further confusion thereby, for verily the ignorant person willing to learn is like a knowledgeable man, whereas the knowledgeable man who acts haphazardly is like an obstinate ignorant man.'[3227]

٢٨٧٤. الإمامُ عليٌّ ﷺ ـ لِسائلٍ سَألَهُ عن مُعضِلَةٍ ـ: سَلْ تَفَقُّهاً، ولا تَسْألْ تَعَنُّتاً؛ فإنّ الجاهِلَ المُتَعَلِّمَ شَبيهٌ بالعالِمِ، وإنَّ العالِمَ المُتَعَسِّفَ (المُتَعَنِّفَ) شَبيهٌ بالجاهِلِ المُتَعَنِّتِ.[٣٢٠٠]

904. That Which Should not be Questioned

٩٠٤ـ ما لا يَنبَغي فِي السُّؤالِ

"O you who believe! Do not ask about things which, if they are disclosed to you, will upset you. Yet if you ask about them while the Qur'an is being sent down, they shall be disclosed to you. Allah has excused it, and Allah is all-forgiving, all-forbearing."[3228]

﴿يا أَيُّها الَّذِينَ آمَنُوا لا تَسْأَلُوا عَنْ أَشْياءَ إِنْ تُبْدَ لَكُمْ تَسُؤْكُمْ وإِنْ تَسْأَلُوا عَنْها حِينَ يُنَزَّلُ القُرآنُ تُبْدَ لَكُمْ عَفَا اللهُ عَنْها واللهُ غَفُورٌ حَلِيمٌ﴾.٣٢٠١

2875. **The Prophet (SAWA) said,** 'Leave me alone when I part your company, for verily people before you were ruined because of their persistent questioning and contradiction of their prophets. So when I command you with something, carry it out as best as possible, and when I prohibit you something, leave it alone.'[3229]

٢٨٧٥. رسولُ اللهِ ﷺ: ذَرُوني ما تَرَكتُكُم، فإنّما هَلَكَ مَن كانَ قَبلَكُم بكَثرَةِ سُؤالِهِم واختِلافِهِم على أنبيائهِم، فإذا أمَرتُكُم بِشَيءٍ فَأتُوا مِنهُ ما استَطَعتُم، وإذا نَهَيتُكُم عن شَيءٍ فَدَعُوهُ.٣٢٠٢

905. Answering Questions that One does not Know the Answer to

٩٠٥ـ جوابُ ما لا تعلَمُ من الأسئلَةِ

2876. **The Prophet (SAWA)** in his advice to his companion Abū Dharr, said, 'O Abū Dharr! When you are asked about something of which you have no knowledge, say, 'I do not know' and you will be saved from its repercussions. And do not give verdicts about that which you do not know and you will be saved from the chastisement of Allah on the Day of Resurrection.'[3230]

٢٨٧٦. رسولُ اللهِ ﷺ في وَصيّتِه لأبي ذَرٍّ ـ: يا أبا ذَرٍّ، إذا سُئلتَ عن عِلمٍ لا تَعلَمُهُ فَقُل: لا أعلَمُهُ تَنجُ مِن تَبِعَتِهِ، ولا تُفتِ بما لا عِلمَ لكَ بِهِ تَنجُ مِن عَذابِ اللهِ يومَ القِيامَةِ.٣٢٠٣

2877. **Imām 'Alī (AS) said,** 'The scholar never feels ashamed to say 'I have no knowledge about this' when he does not know something.'[3231]

٢٨٧٧. الإمامُ عليٌّ ﷺ: لا يَستَحيِي العالِمُ إذا سُئلَ عمّا لا يَعلَمُ أن يقولَ: لا عِلمَ لي بِهِ.٣٢٠٤

2878. **Imām 'Alī (AS) said,** 'He who abandons saying 'I do not know' is bound to be struck at his most vulnerable spots.'[3232]

٢٨٧٨. عنه ﷺ: مَن تَرَكَ قولَ «لا أدري» أُصِيبَتْ مَقاتِلُهُ.٣٢٠٥

2879. **Imām al-Ṣādiq (AS) said,** 'Verily the one who answers every question posed to him is insane.'[3233]

٢٨٧٩. الإمامُ الصادقُ ﷺ: إنَّ مَن أجابَ في كُلِّ ما يُسألُ عَنهُ لَمَجنونٌ.٣٢٠٦،٣٢٠٧

2880. **Imām al-Ṣādiq (AS) said,** 'When a knowledgeable person is asked about something he does not know, he should say, 'Allah knows better', and none but a knowledgeable man will say that.'[3234]

٢٨٨٠ . عنه ﷺ : للعالِمِ إذا سُئلَ عن شيءٍ وهُو لا يَعلَمُهُ أن يقولَ: اَللهُ أعلَمُ، وليسَ لِغَيرِ العالِمِ أن يقولَ ذلكَ. [٣٢٠٨]

(See also: THE ANSWER 81)

(أنظر) عنوان ٨١ «الجواب».

181

ASKING (2) [Requesting a Need]

السُّؤالُ (٢) (طَلَبُ الحاجَةِ)

906. Prohibition of Asking People

٩٠٦ ـ النَّهيُ عَن سُؤالِ النّاسِ

"[The charities are] for the poor who are straitened in the way of Allah, not capable of moving about in the land [for trade]. The unaware suppose them to be well off because of their reserve. You recognize them by their mark; they do not ask the people importunately. And whatever wealth you may spend, Allah indeed knows it."[3235]

﴿لِلْفُقَرَاءِ الَّذِينَ أُحْصِرُوا فِي سَبِيلِ اللهِ لَا يَسْتَطِيعُونَ ضَرْباً فِي الْأَرْضِ يَحْسَبُهُمُ الْجاهِلُ أَغْنِيَاءَ مِنَ التَّعَفُّفِ تَعْرِفُهُمْ بِسِيماهُمْ لَا يَسْأَلُونَ النَّاسَ إِلْحافاً وَما تُنفِقُوا مِنْ خَيْرٍ فَإِنَّ اللهَ بِهِ عَلِيمٌ﴾. [٣٢٠٩]

2881. **The Prophet (SAWA) said,** 'O Abū Dharr, beware of asking [people] for it is ready humiliation and a poverty which you yourself hasten down [in this world], and it entails lengthy accounting on the Day of Resurrection.'[3236]

٢٨٨١ . رسولُ اللهِ ﷺ : يا أبا ذَرٍّ، إيّاكَ والسؤالَ فإنّهُ ذُلٌّ حاضرٌ، وفَقرٌ تَتَعَجَّلُهُ، وفيهِ حِسابٌ طَويلٌ يَومَ القِيامَةِ. [٣٢١٠]

2882. **The Prophet (SAWA) said,** 'Who can give me their word that they never ask anything from people and I will guarantee them Paradise in return?' A man called Thawbān said, 'I do', and indeed Thawbān never used to ask people for anything.'[3237]

٢٨٨٢ . كنز العمّال : قالَ رسولُ اللهِ ﷺ: مَن يَتَكَفَّلُ لِي أن لا يَسألَ الناسَ شيئاً وأتَكَفَّلُ لَهُ بالجَنَّةِ ؟ قالَ ثَوْبانُ: أنا. فَكانَ ثَوْبانُ لا يَسألُ الناسَ شيئاً. [٣٢١١]

2883. **The Prophet (SAWA) said,** 'No sooner does a servant open the door of begging unto

٢٨٨٣ . عنه ﷺ : ما مِن عبدٍ فَتَحَ علىٰ نَفسِهِ باباً

himself than Allah opens seventy doors of poverty unto him.'[3238]

مِن المَسألَةِ إلّا فَتَحَ اللهُ علَيهِ سَبعينَ باباً مِنَ الفَقرِ.٣٢١٢

2884. **Imām ʿAlī (AS) said,** 'He who asks anything of anyone other than Allah becomes deserving of deprivation.'[3239]

٢٨٨٤. الإمامُ عليٌّ عليه السلام: مَن سَألَ غيرَ اللهِ استَحَقَّ الحِرمانَ.٣٢١٣

2885. **Imām al-Ḥasan (AS) said,** 'Verily begging is not allowed, except in three cases: for paying a large sum of blood money, an escalating debt or an abasing poverty.'[3240]

٢٨٨٥. الإمامُ الحسنُ عليه السلام: إنّ المسألَةَ لا تَحِلُّ إلّا في إحدىٰ ثلاثٍ: دَمٍ مُفجِعٍ، أو دَينٍ مُقرِحٍ، أو فَقرٍ مُدقِعٍ.٣٢١٤

2886. **Imām Zayn al-ʿĀbidīn (AS) said,** 'Asking for the fulfilment of one's needs from people degrades one's life, does away with one's modesty, and makes a mockery of one's own dignity and it is a ready poverty in itself. Refraining from seeking fulfilment of one's needs from people is ready wealth in itself.'[3241]

٢٨٨٦. الإمامُ زينُ العابدينَ عليه السلام: طَلَبُ الحَوائجِ إلى النّاسِ مَذَلَّةٌ للحياةِ، ومَذهَبَةٌ للحَياءِ، واستِخفافٌ بالوَقارِ، وهُو الفَقرُ الحاضِرُ، وقِلَّةُ طَلَبِ الحوائجِ مِنَ النّاسِ هُو الغِنىٰ الحاضِرُ.٣٢١٥

2887. **Imām al-Ṣādiq (AS) said,** 'Our followers [*shīʿa*] are those who do not ask anything from people, even if they were to die of hunger.'[3242]

٢٨٨٧. الإمامُ الصّادقُ عليه السلام: شِيعَتُنا مَن لا يَسألُ النّاسَ ولَو ماتَ جُوعاً.٣٢١٦

(See also: DESPAIR: section 1907)

(انظر) اليأس: باب ١٩٠٧

907. Caution Against Asking (of People) in Spite of Being Well-Off

٩٠٧ـ التَّحذيرُ مِنَ السُّؤالِ عَن ظَهرِ غِنىً

2888. **The Prophet (SAWA) said,** 'Whoever begs in spite of being well-off will be afflicted with headache and stomach pains.'[3243]

٢٨٨٨. رسولُ اللهِ صلى الله عليه وآله: مَن سَألَ عن ظَهرِ غِنىً فَصُداعٌ في الرأسِ وداءٌ في البَطنِ.٣٢١٧

2889. **Imām Zayn al-ʿĀbidīn (AS) said,** 'I assure you by My Lord that no one should ask anything from anyone else unnecessarily, until and unless he is one day compelled by his needs to ask someone for fulfilment of that need.'[3244]

٢٨٨٩. الإمامُ زينُ العابدينَ عليه السلام: ضَمِنتُ على رَبّي أن لا يَسألَ أحَدٌ أحَداً مِن غَيرِ حاجَةٍ إلّا اضطَرَّتهُ حاجَةٌ بالمَسألَةِ يَوماً إلىٰ أن يَسألَ مِن حاجَةٍ.٣٢١٨

2890. **Imām al-Bāqir (AS) said,** 'He who asks others in spite of being well-off will meet Allah with a scarred face on the Day of Resurrection.'[3245]

٢٨٩٠. الإمامُ الباقرُ عليه السلام: مَن سَألَ بظَهرِ غِنىً لَقِيَ اللهَ مَخموشاً وَجهُهُ يومَ القِيامَةِ.٣٢١٩

908. Enjoinment of Self-Sufficiency

٩٠٨ـ الحَثُّ عَلَى الاستِغناءِ عَنِ النّاسِ

2891. **The Prophet (SAWA) said,** 'Whoever asks of us, we give him, and whoever tries to be self-sufficient, Allah enriches him.'[3246]

٢٨٩١ . رسولُ اللهِ ﷺ : مَن سَألَنا أعطَيناهُ، ومَنِ استَغنىٰ أغناهُ اللهُ. [٣٢٢٠]

2892. **The Prophet (SAWA) said,** 'If any of you was to take some rope and bring a bundle of firewood on his back to sell or to use as shelter, it would be better for him than to beg.'[3247]

٢٨٩٢ . عنه ﷺ :لو أنّ أحَدَكُم يَأخُذُ حَبلاً فَيَأتِي بِحُزْمَةِ حَطَبٍ على ظَهرِهِ فَيَبِيعُها فَيَكُفُّ بها وَجهَهُ خَيرٌ لَهُ مِن أن يَسألَ. [٣٢٢١]

909. Asking a Favour from the Right Person

٩٠٩ـ طَلَبُ المَعروفِ مِن أهلِهِ

2893. **The Prophet (SAWA) said,** 'Seek favours and kindness from the compassionate people of my community and you will always remain under their wing of protection.'[3248]

٢٨٩٣ . رسولُ اللهِ ﷺ : أُطلُبُوا المَعروفَ والفَضلَ مِن رُحَماءِ أُمَّتي تَعِيشُوا في أكنافِهِم. [٣٢٢٢]

2894. **Imām 'Alī (AS) said,** 'Your self-respect is firm and only begging causes it to yield, so be careful who you allow it to yield in front of.'[3249]

٢٨٩٤ . الإمامُ عليٌّ عليه السلام : ماءُ وَجهِكَ جامِدٌ يُقْطِرُهُ السُّؤالُ، فَانظُرْ عِندَ مَن تُقطِرُهُ. [٣٢٢٣]

2895. **Imām 'Alī (AS) said,** 'Letting a need go unmet is easier than asking the wrong person for it.'[3250]

٢٨٩٥ . عنه عليه السلام : فَوْتُ الحاجَةِ أهوَنُ مِن طَلَبِها إلىٰ غَيرِ أهلِها. [٣٢٢٤]

(See also: THE NEED: section 592) (أنظر) الحاجة : باب ٥٩٢.

910. The Etiquette of Asking

٩١٠ـ أدَبُ السُّؤالِ

2896. **Imām al-Ṣādiq (AS) said,** 'Do not ask the one who you fear will deny you.'[3251]

٢٨٩٦ . الإمامُ الصّادقُ عليه السلام :لا تَسألْ مَن تَخافُ أن يَمنَعَكَ. [٣٢٢٥]

2897. **Imām al-Ṣādiq (AS) said,** 'Three things bring about deprivation: insistence in one's asking, backbiting and mockery.'[3252]

٢٨٩٧ . عنه عليه السلام : ثلاثةٌ تُورِثُ الحِرمانَ: الإلحاحُ في المَسألَةِ، والغِيبةُ، والهُزءُ. [٣٢٢٦]

911. Warning Against Turning a Beggar Away Empty-Handed

٩١١ ـ التَّحذيرُ عَن رَدِّ السائِلِ

"And as for the beggar, do not chide him."[3253]

﴿وَأَمَّا السَّائِلَ فَلَا تَنْهَرْ﴾.[٣٢٢٧]

2898. **The Prophet (SAWA) said,** 'Do not ever snub the beggar's request, for were it not for the fact that some of them do lie, those who turn beggars away would never prosper.'[3254]

٢٨٩٨. رسولُ اللهِ ﷺ: لا تَقطَعُوا على السائلِ مَسأَلَتَهُ فلَولا أنَّ المَساكينَ يَكذِبُونَ ما أفلَحَ مَن رَدَّهُم.[٣٢٢٨]

2899. **The Prophet (SAWA) said,** 'Look at the beggar and if you find your hearts softening towards him then give him for verily he is honest.'[3255]

٢٨٩٩. عنه ﷺ: أُنظُرُوا إلى السائلِ، فإن رَقَّتْ لَهُ قُلوبُكُم فَأعطُوهُ، فإنّهُ صادِقٌ.[٣٢٢٩]

2900. **Imām ʿAlī (AS) said,** 'Do not turn the beggar away empty handed, even if you can give him but half a grape or a piece of a date.'[3256]

٢٩٠٠. الإمامُ عليٌّ عليه السلام: لا تَرُدَّ سائلاً ولَو مِن شَطرِ حَبَّةِ عِنَبٍ أو شِقِّ تَمرَةٍ.[٣٢٣٠]

2901. **Imām ʿAlī (AS) said,** 'Do not be ashamed to give little, for verily refusing to give anything at all is an act of greater shame.'[3257]

٢٩٠١. عنه عليه السلام: لا تَستَحِ مِن إعطاءِ القَليلِ؛ فإنَّ الحِرمانَ أقَلُّ مِنهُ.[٣٢٣١]

2902. **Imām al-Ḥusayn (AS) said,** 'The needy one loses his self-respect by asking you, so do not lose your self-respect by denying him.'[3258]

٢٩٠٢. الإمامُ الحسينُ عليه السلام: صاحِبُ الحاجةِ لَم يُكرِمْ وَجهَهُ عن سُؤالِكَ فَأكرِمْ وَجهَكَ عن رَدِّهِ.[٣٢٣٢]

2903. **Imām al-Bāqir (AS) said,** 'If the beggar was to know the enormity of begging, no one would ever ask anything of another, and if the one asked was to know the enormity of denying someone, no one would ever deny another again.'[3259]

٢٩٠٣. الإمامُ الباقرُ عليه السلام: لو يَعلَمُ السائلُ ما في المَسألَةِ ما سَألَ أحَدٌ أحَداً، ولَو يَعلَمُ المَسؤولُ ما في المَنعِ ما مَنَعَ أحَدٌ أحَداً.[٣٢٣٣]

2904. **Imām al-Ṣādiq (AS) said,** 'When a man asks me to fulfil a need, I rush to fulfil it fearing lest he ceases to need it, and my assistance will no longer benefit him.'[3260]

٢٩٠٤. الإمامُ الصّادقُ عليه السلام: إنّ الرَّجُلَ لَيَسألُني الحاجَةَ فَأُبادِرُ بقَضائها مَخافَةَ أن يَستَغنِيَ عَنها فلا يَجِدَ لَها مَوقِعاً إذا جاءَتْهُ.[٣٢٣٤]

2905. **Imām al-Ṣādiq (AS) said,** 'Feed [at least] three people. If you then wish to feed more then it is up to you, and if not then you will have at least performed your duty for the Day [of Resurrection].'[3261]

٢٩٠٥. عنه عليه السلام: أطعِمُوا ثلاثةً ثُمّ أنتُم بالخِيارِ علَيهِ، إن شِئتُم أن تَزدادُوا فَازدادُوا وإلّا فقد أدَّيتُم حَقَّ يَومِكُم.[٣٢٣٥]

2906. *Biḥār al-Anwār:* 'The Imāms (AS) said, 'Verily we give to the undeserving in order to act as a deterrent from turning away the deserving.'[3262]

٢٩٠٦ . بحار الأنوار عنهم عليهم السلام : إنّا لَنُعطي غَيرَ المُستَحِقِّ حَذَراً مِن رَدِّ المُستَحِقِّ. ٣٢٣٦

(See also: ACTS OF COMMON COURTESY (1): section 1279)

(أُنظر) المعروف (١): ١٢٧٩.

182

INSULTING

السَّبُّ

912. Censure of Insulting the Believer

٩١٢ـ ذمُّ سِبابِ المُؤمنِ

2907. **The Prophet (SAWA) said,** 'The one who insults a believer is as one who is on the verge of ruin.'[3263]

٢٩٠٧ . رسولُ اللهِ صلى الله عليه وآله : سابُّ المُؤمِنِ كالمُشرِفِ على الهَلَكَةِ. ٣٢٣٧

2908. **The Prophet (SAWA) said,** 'To insult a believer is a gross iniquity, to kill him is infidelity, and to backbite him is an act of disobedience of Allah.'[3264]

٢٩٠٨ . عنه صلى الله عليه وآله : سِبابُ المؤمِنِ فُسوقٌ، وقِتالُهُ كُفرٌ، وأكلُ لَحمِهِ مِن مَعصيَةِ اللهِ. ٣٢٣٨

913. Prohibition of Insulting even Idols and Satan

٩١٣ـ النَّهيُ عن سَبِّ الأصنامِ والشّيطانِ

"Do not abuse those whom they invoke besides Allah, lest they should abuse Allah out of hostility, without any knowledge. That is how to every people we have made their conduct decorous. Then their return will be to their Lord and He will inform them concerning what they used to do.'[3265]

﴿وَلَا تَسُبُّوا الَّذِينَ يَدْعُونَ مِن دُونِ اللهِ فَيَسُبُّوا اللهَ عَدْواً بِغَيرِ عِلْمٍ كَذٰلِكَ زَيَّنَّا لِكُلِّ أُمَّةٍ عَمَلَهُمْ ثُمَّ إِلَىٰ رَبِّهِمْ مَّرْجِعُهُمْ فَيُنَبِّئُهُمْ بِمَا كَانُوا يَعْمَلُونَ﴾. ٣٢٣٩

2909. **The Prophet (SAWA) said,** 'Do not insult Satan but instead seek refuge to Allah from his harm.'[3266]

٢٩٠٩ . رسولُ اللهِ صلى الله عليه وآله : لا تَسُبُّوا الشَّيطانَ وتَعَوَّذُوا بِاللهِ مِن شَرِّهِ. ٣٢٤٠

914. Prohibition of Insulting People

٩١٤ـ النَّهيُ عن سَبِّ النّاسِ

2910. **The Prophet (SAWA) said,** 'Do not insult people lest you procure animosity from them.'[3267]

٢٩١٠ . رسولُ اللهِ صلى الله عليه وآله : لا تَسُبُّوا النّاسَ فتَكتَسِبُوا العَداوةَ بَينَهُم. ٣٢٤١

2911. **Imām ʿAlī (AS) said** to Qanbar when he wished to insult a man who had insulted him, 'Careful Qanbar! Leave your insulter to his disdain and you will please the Beneficent Lord, displease Satan and punish thereby your enemy, for by the One who split the grain and created the breeze, there is no stance better than clemency with which a believer can please his Lord, and nothing like silence to offend Satan, and an idiot is best punished by ignoring him.'[3268]

٢٩١١. الإمامُ عليٌّ ﷺ ـ لِقَنْبَرٍ وقد رامَ أن يَشتِمَ شاتِمَهُ ـ: مَهْلاً يا قَنبرُ! دَعْ شاتِمَكَ مُهاناً تُرْضِ الرّحمٰنَ وتُسخِطُ الشَّيطانَ وتُعاقِبُ عَدُوَّكَ، فَوَالذي فَلَقَ الحَبَّةَ وبَرَأَ النَّسَمَةَ ما أرضَى المؤمنُ رَبَّهُ بِمِثلِ الحِلْمِ، ولا أسخَطَ الشَّيطانَ بِمِثلِ الصَّمتِ، ولا عُوقِبَ الأحمَقُ بِمِثلِ السُّكوتِ عَنهُ.[٣٢٤٢]

2912. **Imām al-Kāẓim (AS)** when he saw two people insulting each other, said, 'The initiator is the more unjust and bears his own sin as well as the sin of his opponent as long as the latter does not retort.'[3269]

٢٩١٢. الإمامُ الكاظمُ ﷺ ـ لَمّا رَأى رَجُلَينِ يَتَسابّانِ ـ: البادِي أظلَمُ، ووِزرُهُ ووِزرُ صاحِبِهِ علَيهِ ما لَم يَعتَدِ المَظلومُ.[٣٢٤٣]

2913. **Imām al-Kāẓim (AS) said,** 'Whenever two people insult each other, the more superior of the two sinks to the level of the more inferior one.'[3270]

٢٩١٣. عنه ﷺ: ما تَسابَّ اثنانِ إلّا انحَطَّ الأعلىٰ إلىٰ مَرتَبةِ الأسفَلِ.[٣٢٤٤]

915. The Prohibition of Insulting Parents

٩١٥ ـ النَّهي عَن سَبّ الوالِدَين

2914. **The Prophet (SAWA) said,** 'The most severe of major sins is for a man to use obscene language at his parents.' He was asked, 'And how does he use obscene language at his parents?' He said, 'That a man uses obscene language at another, and he uses obscene language back at his father and mother.'[3271]

٢٩١٤. رسولُ اللهِ ﷺ: مِن أكبَرِ الكبائرِ أن يَسُبَّ الرجُلُ والِدَيهِ، قيلَ: وكيفَ يَسُبُّ والِدَيهِ؟! قالَ: يَسُبُّ الرجُلَ فَيَسُبُّ أباهُ وأُمَّهُ.[٣٢٤٥]

2915. **The Prophet (SAWA) said,** 'The curse of Allah....be upon he who uses obscene language at his parents.'[3272]

٢٩١٥. عنه ﷺ: لَعَنَ اللهُ... مَن يَسُبُّ والِدَيهِ.[٣٢٤٦]

916. The Prohibition of Insulting Things

٩١٦ ـ النَّهي عَن سَبّ الأشياءِ

2916. **The Prophet (SAWA) said,** 'Do not insult the wind, since it is missioned, and do not insult

٢٩١٦. رسولُ اللهِ ﷺ: لا تَسُبُّوا الرِّياحَ فإنّها

the mountains, the hours, the days and the nights, for you will sin and it will return to you.'[3273]

مَأمُورَةٌ، ولا تَسُبُّوا الجِبالَ ولا السّاعاتِ ولا الأيّامَ ولا اللَّيالِيَ فتَأثَمُوا وتَرجِعَ علَيكُم.[٣٢٤٧]

183

PROSTRATION

السُّجُودُ

917. The Role of Prostration in Proximity to Allah

٩١٧ـ دُورُ السُّجودِ فِى التَّقَرّبِ إلَى اللهِ

2917. **Imām ʿAlī (AS) said,** 'Nothing can bring about proximity to Allah, Glory be to Him, except an abundance of prostration (*sujūd*) and bowing (*rukūʿ*).'[3274]

٢٩١٧ . الإمامُ عليٌّ ﷺ : لا يُقَرِّبُ مِنَ اللهِ سبحانَهُ إلّا كَثرَةُ السُّجودِ والرُّكوعِ.[٣٢٤٨]

2918. **Imām al-Ṣādiq (AS) said,** 'Prostration is the highest degree of worship that man can perform.'[3275]

٢٩١٨ . الإمامُ الصّادقُ ﷺ :السُّجودُ مُنتَهىٰ العِبادَةِ مِن بَني آدَمَ.[٣٢٤٩]

2919. **Imām al-Ṣādiq (AS)** was once asked by Saʿīd b. Yasār whether he should supplicate in the state of prostration or in the state of bowing, to which he replied, 'Supplicate while prostrating for verily the nearest the servant can ever be to Allah is in the state of prostration, so supplicate Allah for your worldly needs as well as for your life in the Hereafter.'[3276]

٢٩١٩ . عنه ﷺ ـ لَمّا قالَ لَهُ سعيدُ بنُ يسارٍ: أدعُو وأنا راكِعٌ أو ساجِدٌ؟ ـ: نَعَم اُدْعُ وأنتَ ساجِدٌ، فإنَّ أقرَبَ ما يَكونُ العَبدُ إلى اللهِ وهُو ساجِدٌ، اُدْعُ اللهَ عزّوجلّ لِدُنياكَ وآخِرَتِكَ.[٣٢٥٠]

918. Prolonging One's Prostration

٩١٨ـ إطالَةُ السُّجودِ

2920. **The Prophet (SAWA) said,** 'If you want Allah to raise you [on the Day of Resurrection] with me, then prolong your prostration to Allah the One, the all-Conqueror.'[3277]

٢٩٢٠ . رسولُ اللهِ ﷺ : إذا أرَدتَ أن يَحشُرَكَ اللهُ مَعي فَأطِلِ السُّجودَ بينَ يَدَي اللهِ الواحِدِ القَهّارِ.[٣٢٥١]

2921. **Imām ʿAlī (AS) said,** 'Prolong your prostration, for there is no act more agonizing for Iblīs [Satan] than to see man in the state of

٢٩٢١ . الإمامُ عليٌّ ﷺ :أطِيلُوا السُّجودَ، فما مِن عَمَلٍ أشَدَّ علىٰ إبليسَ مِن أن يَرَى ابنَ آدَمَ

prostration, for he himself was once commanded to prostrate but refused to do so.'[3278]

ساجِداً، لأنّهُ أُمِرَ بالسُّجودِ فَعَصىٰ.٣٢٥٢

2922. **Imām al-Ṣādiq (AS) said,** 'A group of people once came to the Prophet (SAWA) saying, 'O Prophet of Allah, ask your Lord to secure us a place in Paradise', to which he replied, 'As long as you assist me with lengthy prostrations.'[3279]

٢٩٢٢. الإمامُ الصّادقُ ؑ: إنّ قَوماً أتَوا رسولَ اللهِ ﷺ فقالوا: يا رسولَ اللهِ، اضمَن لَنا علىٰ رَبِّكَ الجَنّةَ، فقالَ: علىٰ أن تُعينوني بِطُولِ السُّجودِ.٣٢٥٣

2923. **Imām al-Ṣādiq (AS) narrated,** 'When 'Alī b. al-Ḥusayn [i.e. Imām Zayn al-'Ābidīn] (AS) used to go down in prostration, he would not raise his head up again until he was dripping with sweat.'[3280]

٢٩٢٣. عنه ؑ: كانَ عليُّ بنُ الحسينِ ؑ ... إذا سَجَدَ لَم يَرفَعْ رَأسَهُ حتّىٰ يَرفَضَّ عَرَقاً.٣٢٥٤

919. The Effect of Prostration

٩١٩ـ أثَرُ السُّجودِ

"Their mark is [visible] on their faces, from the effect of prostration."[3281]

﴿سِيماهُمْ فِي وُجُوهِهِمْ مِنْ أَثَرِ السُّجُودِ﴾.٣٢٥٥

2924. **Imām 'Alī (AS) said,** 'I hate it for a man to have a smooth forehead not having any trace of prostration on it.'[3282]

٢٩٢٤. الإمامُ عليٌّ ؑ: إنّي لأكرَهُ للرَّجُلِ أن تُرىٰ جَبهَتُهُ جَلحاءَ لَيسَ فيها شيءٌ مِن أثَرِ السُّجودِ.٣٢٥٦

2925. **Imām al-Bāqir (AS) said,** 'My father (AS) used to have protruding marks from prostration on his forehead, which he used to cut twice a year, and every time he would do so, he would scrape off five calluses, and came to be nicknamed 'the one with calluses.'[3283]

٢٩٢٥. الإمامُ الباقرُ ؑ: كانَ لأبي ؑ في مَوضِعِ سُجودِهِ آثارٌ ناتِيةٌ، وكانَ يَقطَعُها في السَّنَةِ مَرَّتَينِ، في كُلِّ مَرّةٍ خَمسَ ثَفِناتٍ، فَسُمِّيَ ذا الثَّفِناتِ لذلكَ.٣٢٥٧

920. Prostrating on the Earth from Imām Ḥusayn (AS)'s Grave

٩٢٠ـ السُّجودُ علىٰ تُربَةِ الحُسَينِ ؑ

2926. **Imām al-Ṣādiq (AS) said,** 'Prostrating on the soil from al-Ḥusayn (AS)'s grave pierces the seven veils.'[3284]

٢٩٢٦. الإمامُ الصّادقُ ؑ: السُّجودُ علىٰ تُربَةِ الحُسينِ ؑ يَخرِقُ الحُجُبَ السَّبعَ.٣٢٥٨

184

THE MOSQUE

المَسْجِدُ

921. The Mosque is the House of Allah

٩٢١ ـ المَسجِدُ بَيتُ اللهِ

"The places of worship belong to Allah, so do not invoke anyone along with Allah."[3285]

﴿وَأَنَّ المَسَاجِدَ لِلَّهِ فَلَا تَدْعُوا مَعَ اللهِ أَحَداً﴾.[٣٢٥٩]

2927. **Imām al-Ṣādiq (AS) said,** 'It is incumbent upon you to attend the mosques, for verily they are the houses of Allah on earth. And whoever enters them having purified himself, Allah will purify him of his sins and will record him down as one of its frequenters, so perform many prayers and supplications therein.'[3286]

٢٩٢٧ . الإمامُ الصّادقُ عليه السلام : عَلَيكُم بِإتيانِ المَساجِدِ؛ فإنّها بُيوتُ اللهِ في الأرضِ، ومَن أتاها مُتَطَهِّراً طَهَّرَهُ اللهُ مِن ذُنوبِهِ وكُتِبَ مِن زُوّارِهِ فَأكثِرُوا فيها مِن الصَّلاةِ والدُّعاءِ.[٣٢٦٠]

922. Maintaining the Mosques

٩٢٢ ـ عِمارَةُ المَساجِدِ

"Only those shall maintain Allah's mosques who believe in Allah and the Last Day, and establish the prayer and give the zakāt, and fear no one except Allah. They, hopefully, will be among the guided."[3287]

﴿إنَّما يَعْمُرُ مَساجِدَ اللهِ مَنْ آمَنَ بِاللهِ وَاليَومِ الآخِرِ وَأَقامَ الصَّلَاةَ وَآتَى الزَّكاةَ وَلَمْ يَخْشَ إِلَّا اللهَ فَعَسَىٰ أُولَٰئِكَ أَنْ يَكُونُوا مِنَ المُهْتَدِينَ﴾.[٣٢٦١]

2928. **The Prophet (SAWA)** was asked by Abū Dharr how to maintain the mosques, to which he replied, 'Voices should not be raised therein, nor engrossment in wrongdoing. There should be no buying or selling, and all vain talk must be shunned as long as you are inside. If you do not do this, then you will have no one to blame but yourself on the Day of Resurrection.'[3288]

٢٩٢٨ . رسولُ اللهِ صلى الله عليه وآله ـ وقد سَألَهُ أبو ذَرٍّ عن كَيفيّةِ عِمارَةِ المَساجِدِ ـ: لا تُرفَعُ فيها الأصواتُ، ولا يُخاضُ فيها بالباطِلِ، ولا يُشتَرىٰ فيها ولا يُباعُ، واترُكِ اللَّغوَ ما دُمتَ فيها، فإن لَم تَفْعَل فلا تَلُومَنَّ يَومَ القِيامَةِ إلّا نَفسَكَ.[٣٢٦٢]

2929. **Imām al-Ṣādiq (AS) said,** 'He who builds a mosque, Allah will order a house to be built for him in Paradise.'[3289]

٢٩٢٩ . الإمامُ الصّادقُ عليه السلام : مَن بَنىٰ مَسجِداً بَنَى اللهُ لَهُ بَيتاً في الجَنَّةِ.[٣٢٦٣]

923. The Reward for Walking to the Mosques

٩٢٣ ـ ثَوابُ المَشيِ إلَى المَساجِدِ

2930. **The Prophet (SAWA) said,** 'He who walks to a mosque intending to join the congregation gets the equivalent of seventy thousand good deeds for every step he takes, and he is raised as many levels, and if he dies on the way, Allah assigns seventy thousand angels to visit him in his grave to keep him company in his loneliness and to seek forgiveness for him until the day he is raised again.'[3290]

٢٩٣٠ . رسولُ اللهِ ﷺ : مَن مَشىٰ إلىٰ مَسجِدٍ يَطلُبُ فيهِ الجَماعَةَ كانَ لَهُ بكُلِّ خُطوَةٍ سَبعونَ ألفَ حَسَنةٍ ، ويُرفَعُ لَهُ مِن الدَّرَجاتِ مِثلُ ذلكَ ، و ن ماتَ وهُو علىٰ ذلكَ وكَّلَ اللهُ بِهِ سَبعينَ ألفَ مَلَكٍ يَعُودُونَهُ في قَبرِهِ ، ويُؤنِسُونَهُ في وَحدَتِهِ ، ويَستَغفِرُونَ لَهُ حتّىٰ يُبعَثَ.[٣٢٦٤]

924. The Reward for Sitting in the Mosque

٩٢٤ ـ ثَوابُ الجُلوسِ فِي المَسجِدِ

2931. **The Prophet (SAWA) said,** 'O Abū Dharr, verily for as long as you remain seated in the mosque Allah, most High, will grant you an extra level in Paradise for every breath you take, the angels send salutations on you, and ten good deeds are recorded and ten evil deeds wiped away for every breath you take therein.'[3291]

٢٩٣١ . رسولُ اللهِ ﷺ : يا أبا ذَرٍّ ، إنّ اللهَ تعالىٰ يُعطِيكَ مادُمتَ جالِساً في المَسجِدِ بِكُلِّ نَفَسٍ تَنَفَّستَ دَرَجةً في الجَنَّةِ ، وتُصَلِّي علَيكَ الملائكةُ ، وتُكتَبُ لَكَ بِكُلِّ نَفَسٍ تَنَفَّستَ فيهِ عَشرُ حَسَناتٍ ، وتُمحىٰ عنكَ عَشرُ سَيّئاتٍ.[٣٢٦٥]

925. Neighbouring the Mosque and Praying Therein

٩٢٥ ـ جِوارُ المَسجِدِ وَالصَّلاةُ فيهِ

2932. **Imām 'Alī (AS) said,** 'The prayer of one who lives neighbouring the mosque [yet prays at home] is null and void unless he prays inside the mosque, except if he has an excuse or if he is sick.' When asked who was considered as neighbouring the mosque, he replied, 'Anyone who hears the call to prayer.'[3292]

٢٩٣٢ . بحار الأنوار عن الإمامِ عليٍّ ﷺ : لا صَلاةَ لِجارِ المَسجِدِ إلّا في المَسجِدِ ، إلّا أن يكونَ لَهُ عُذرٌ أو بهِ عِلَّةٌ ، فقيلَ : ومَن جارُ المَسجِدِ يا أميرَ المؤمنينَ ؟ قالَ : مَن سَمِعَ النِّداءَ.[٣٢٦٦]

2933. **Imām 'Alī (AS) said,** 'The sanctuary of the mosque extends to forty cubits[3293], and its neighbouring precinct extends to forty houses on all four sides.'[3294]

٢٩٣٣ . الإمامُ عليٌّ ﷺ : حَريمُ المَسجِدِ أربَعونَ ذِراعاً ، والجِوارُ أربَعونَ داراً مِن أربعَةِ جَوانِبِها.[٣٢٦٧]

926. Etiquettes of the Mosque

٩٢٦ـ آدابُ المَساجِدِ

2934. **The Prophet (SAWA) said,** 'Whoever has eaten this pungent herb [i.e. garlic] should not approach our mosque. As for one who has eaten it and does not come to the mosque [as a result], there is no blame on him for it.'[3295]

٢٩٣٤ . رسولُ اللهِ ﷺ : مَن أكَلَ هذهِ البَقلَةَ المُنتِنَةَ [يَعني الثُّومَ] فلا يَقرَبْ مَسجِدَنا، فأمّا مَن أكَلَهُ ولَم يأتِ المَسجِدَ فلا بَأسَ.[٣٢٦٨]

2935. **The Prophet (SAWA) said,** 'Do not use the mosques as mere passageways until you have prayed two units of prayer therein.'[3296]

٢٩٣٥ . عنه ﷺ : لا تَجعَلُوا المَساجِدَ طُرُقاً حتّىٰ تُصَلُّوا فيها رَكعتَينِ.[٣٢٦٩]

185

GENEROSITY

السَّخاءُ

927. The Virtue of Generosity

٩٢٧ـ فَضلُ السَّخاءِ

2936. **The Prophet (SAWA) said,** 'Allah has made generosity the greatest moral virtue.'[3297]

٢٩٣٦ . رسولُ اللهِ ﷺ : السَّخاءُ خُلُقُ اللهِ الأعظَمُ.[٣٢٧٠]

2937. **The Prophet (SAWA) said,** 'Allah has created every single vicegerent of His with generosity as their natural disposition.'[3298]

٢٩٣٧ . عنه ﷺ : ما جَبَلَ اللهُ ولِيّاً لَهُ إلّا عَلى السَّخاءِ.[٣٢٧١]

2938. **Imām ʿAlī (AS) said,** 'Generosity is a means of nearness [to Allah].'[3299]

٢٩٣٨ . الإمامُ عليٌّ عليه السلام : السَّخاءُ قُربَةٌ.[٣٢٧٢]

2939. **Imām ʿAlī (AS) said,** 'The heart can only be made use of [to the best of its capacity] with generosity.'[3300]

٢٩٣٩ . عنه عليه السلام : لا يُستَعانُ عَلَى اللُّبِّ إلّا بالسَّخاءِ.[٣٢٧٣]

2940. **Imām ʿAlī (AS) said,** 'Generosity is the fruit of the intellect, and contentment is the proof of magnanimity.'[3301]

٢٩٤٠ . عنه عليه السلام : السَّخاءُ ثَمَرَةُ العَقلِ، والقَناعَةُ بُرهانُ النُّبلِ.[٣٢٧٤]

2941. **Imām ʿAlī (AS) said,** 'Generosity cultivates love.'[3302]

٢٩٤١ . عنه عليه السلام : السَّخاءُ يَزرَعُ المَحَبَّةَ.[٣٢٧٥]

2942. **Imām ʿAlī (AS) said,** 'Generosity imparts love and adorns one's character.'[3303]

٢٩٤٢ . عنه عليه السلام : السَّخاءُ يُكسِبُ المَحَبَّةَ ويُزَيِّنُ الأخلاقَ.[٣٢٧٦]

2943. **Imām al-Ṣādiq (AS) said,** 'Generosity is one of the noble traits possessed by prophets. It is the pillar of belief, such that only a true believer will be generous, as well as one who possesses great certainty and high aspiration, for generosity is a gleam from the light of certainty, and the one who knows what he wants finds it easy to give away.'[3304]

٢٩٤٣ . الإمامُ الصّادقُ ﷺ : السَّخاءُ مِن أخلاقِ الأنبياءِ ، وهُو عِمادُ الإيمانِ ، ولا يكونُ مؤمنٌ إلّا سَخيّاً ، ولا يكونُ سَخيّاً إلّا ذو يَقينٍ وهِمَّةٍ عالِيَةٍ ؛ لأنَّ السَّخاءَ شُعاعُ نورِ اليَقينِ ، ومَن عَرَفَ ما قَصَدَ ، هانَ علَيهِ ما بَذَلَ.[٣٢٧٧]

2944. **Imām al-Ṣādiq (AS) said,** 'The best ones from among you are those who are liberal and the worst ones from among you are the miserly.'[3305]

٢٩٤٤ . عنه ﷺ : خِيارُكُم سُمَحاؤكُم وشِرارُكُم بُخَلاؤكُم.[٣٢٧٨]

928. The Virtue of the Generous Person

٩٢٨ ـ فَضلُ السَّخِيِّ

2945. *al-Kāfī*, narrating from 'Alī ibn Ibrāhīm, 'Allah, Mighty and Exalted, revealed to Prophet Moses (AS), 'That you kill not the Sāmirī[3306], for verily he is a generous man.'[3307]

٢٩٤٥ . الكافي عن عليّ بن إبراهيم مرفوعاً : وحىٰ اللهُ عزّوجلّ إلىٰ موسىٰ ﷺ : أن لا تَقتُلِ لسّامِرِيَّ ، فإنّهُ سَخِيٌّ.[٣٢٧٩]

2946. **The Prophet (SAWA) said,** 'The generous person is close to Allah, close to people and close to Paradise.'[3308]

٢٩٤٦ . رسولُ اللهِ ﷺ : السَّخِيُّ قَريبٌ مِنَ اللهِ ، قريبٌ مِن الناسِ ، قَريبٌ مِن الجَنَّةِ.[٣٢٨٠]

2947. **The Prophet (SAWA) said,** 'Relinquish the generous person's sin for verily Allah takes him by the hand every time he slips.'[3309]

٢٩٤٧ . عنه ﷺ : تَجافَوا عن ذَنبِ السَّخِيِّ فإنَّ اللهَ آخِذٌ بيدِهِ كُلَّما عَثَرَ.[٣٢٨١]

2948. **Imām al-Ṣādiq (AS) said,** 'A generous youth burdened by sins is more beloved to Allah than a worshipping but miserly old man.'[3310]

٢٩٤٨ . الإمامُ الصّادقُ ﷺ : شابٌّ سَخِيٌّ مُرَهَّقٌ في الذُّنوبِ أحَبُّ إلى اللهِ عزّوجلّ مِن شَيخٍ عابِدٍ بَخيلٍ.[٣٢٨٢]

2949. **Imām al-Riḍā (AS) said,** 'The generous person partakes of other people's food in order that they may [feel comfortable to] partake of his food, whereas the miser does not partake of others' food so that they may not eat from his.'[3311]

٢٩٤٩ . الإمامُ الرِّضا ﷺ : السَّخِيُّ يَأكُلُ مِن طَعامِ النّاسِ لِيَأكُلُوا مِن طَعامِهِ ، والبَخيلُ لا يَأكُلُ مِن طَعامِ النّاسِ لِئَلّا يَأكُلُوا مِن طَعامِهِ.[٣٢٨٣]

929. The Extent of Generosity Recommended

٩٢٩ـحَدُّ السَّخاءِ

"Do not keep your hand chained to your neck, nor open it altogether, or you will sit blameworthy, regretful."[3312]

﴿وَلا تَجْعَلْ يَدَكَ مَغْلُولَةً إِلىٰ عُنُقِكَ وَلا تَبْسُطْها كُلَّ البَسْطِ فَتَقْعُدَ مَلُوماً مَحْسُوراً﴾.[٣٢٨٤]

2950. **The Prophet (SAWA) said,** 'The most generous of people is he who fulfils payment of the alms-tax due upon him.'[3313]

٢٩٥٠ . رسولُ اللهِ ﷺ :أسخَى الناسِ مَن أدّىٰ زَكاةَ مالِهِ.[٣٢٨٥]

2951. **Imām ʿAlī (AS) said,** 'Generosity is that you contribute willingly from your own wealth, and restrain yourself from other people's wealth.'[3314]

٢٩٥١ . الإمامُ عليٌّ ؑ : السَّخاءُ أن تَكونَ بمالِكَ مُتَبَرِّعاً وعن مالِ غَيرِكَ مُتَوَرِّعاً.[٣٢٨٦]

2952. **Imām al-Ṣādiq (AS) said,** 'The kind and generous person is he who spends his wealth for a right cause.'[3315]

٢٩٥٢ . الإمامُ الصّادقُ ؑ : السَّخِيُّ الكريمُ الذي يُنفِقُ مالَهُ في حَقٍّ.[٣٢٨٧]

2953. **Imām al-Ṣādiq (AS) said,** 'Generosity is when the act of giving is initiated. When it is prompted by a request however, it is merely out of a sense of embarrassment or obligation.'[3316]

٢٩٥٣ . عنه ؑ : السَّخاءُ ما كانَ ابتِداءً، فَأمّا ما كانَ مِن مَسألَةٍ فَحَياءٌ وتَذَمُّمٌ.[٣٢٨٨]

2954. **Imām al-ʿAskarī (AS) said,** 'Generosity has a set limit, and if taken to extremes becomes squandering.'[3317]

٢٩٥٤ . الإمامُ العسكريُّ ؑ : إنّ للسَّخاءِ مِقداراً فإنْ زادَ علَيهِ فهُو سَرَفٌ.[٣٢٨٩]

186

SECRECY

السِّرُّ

930. Encouraging Keeping a Secret

٩٣٠ـالحَثُّ عَلىٰ كِتمانِ السِّرِّ

2955. **Imām ʿAlī (AS) said,** 'Whoever keeps his own secrets has control in his own hands.'[3318]

٢٩٥٥ . الإمامُ عليٌّ ؑ : مَن كَتَمَ سِرَّهُ كانَتِ الخِيَرَةُ بيَدِهِ.[٣٢٩٠]

2956. **Imām ʿAlī (AS) said,** 'Victory comes about through determination, and determination comes

٢٩٥٦ . عنه ؑ : الظَّفَرُ بِالحَزمِ، والحَزمُ بِإجالَةِ

about through carefully weighing up one's ideas, and ideas are formed through guarding secrets.'[3319]

الرَّأيِ، والرَّأيُ بِتَحصِينِ الأسرارِ.[٣٢٩١]

2957. **Imām ʿAlī (AS) said,** 'Your secret is your prisoner which, if let loose, will make you its prisoner.'[3320]

٢٩٥٧. عنه ؑ: سِرُّكَ أسيرُكَ فإن أفشَيتَهُ صِرتَ أسيرَهُ.[٣٢٩٢]

2958. **Imām ʿAlī (AS) said,** 'The bosom of the wise man is the strongbox guarding his secret.'[3321]

٢٩٥٨. عنه ؑ: صَدرُ العاقِلِ صُندوقُ سِرِّهِ.[٣٢٩٣]

2959. **Imām ʿAlī (AS) said,** 'The more the keepers of secrets increase, the more the divulgers of secrets increase.'[3322]

٢٩٥٩. عنه ؑ: كُلَّما كَثُرَ خُزّانُ الأسرارِ كَثُرَ ضُيّاعُها.[٣٢٩٤]

2960. **Imām ʿAlī (AS) said,** 'Shower all your love on your friend but do not shower all your trust on him.'[3323]

٢٩٦٠. عنه ؑ: اُبذُلْ لِصَديقِكَ كُلَّ المَوَدَّةِ ولا تَبذُلْ لَهُ كُلَّ الطُّمأنينَةِ.[٣٢٩٥]

2961. **Imām ʿAlī (AS) said,** 'The most successful of matters is the one that is kept confidential.'[3324]

٢٩٦١. عنه ؑ: أنجَحُ الاُمورِ ما أحاطَ بهِ الكِتمانُ.[٣٢٩٦]

2962. **Imām ʿAlī (AS) said,** 'It does not matter if your secret is unknown.'[3325]

٢٩٦٢. عنه ؑ: لا بَأسَ بأن لا يُعلَمَ سِرُّكَ.[٣٢٩٧]

2963. **Imām al-Ṣādiq (AS) said,** 'Divulging a secret is a breakdown [of trust].'[3326]

٢٩٦٣. الإمامُ الصّادقُ ؑ: إفشاءُ السِّرِّ سُقوطٌ.[٣٢٩٨]

2964. **Imām al-Ṣādiq (AS) said,** 'Your secret is of your own blood, so never let it flow from other than your own veins.'[3327]

٢٩٦٤. عنه ؑ: سِرُّكَ مِن دَمِكَ فلا يَجرِيَنَّ مِن غيرِ أوداجِكَ.[٣٢٩٩]

2965. **Imām al-Riḍā (AS) said,** 'A believer is not a believer unless he possesses three qualities within him: one quality characteristic of his Lord, one quality from His Prophet, and one quality from His vicegerent. The quality that is characteristic of his Lord is guarding a secret, for verily Allah has said, *"Knower of the Unseen, He does not disclose His Unseen to anyone, except to an apostle He approves of."*'[3328] [3329]

٢٩٦٥. الإمامُ الرِّضا ؑ: لا يَكونُ المؤمنُ مؤمناً حتّى يَكونَ فيهِ ثلاثُ خِصالٍ: سُنَّةٌ مِن رَبِّهِ، وسُنَّةٌ مِن نَبيِّهِ، وسُنَّةٌ مِن وَلِيِّهِ، فالسُّنَّةُ مِن رَبِّهِ كِتمانُ سِرِّهِ، قالَ اللهُ عزّوجلّ: ﴿عالِمُ الغَيْبِ فلا يُظْهِرُ عَلىٰ غَيْبِهِ أحَداً * إلّا مَنِ ارْتَضىٰ مِن رَسولٍ﴾[٣٣٠٠] [٣٣٠١]

2966. **Imām al-Jawād (AS) said,** 'Exposing something before it has become consolidated will ruin it.'[3330]

٢٩٦٦. الإمامُ الجوادُ ؑ: إظهارُ الشَّيءِ قبلَ أن يَستَحكِمَ مَفسَدَةٌ لَهُ.[٣٣٠٢]

931. Those that Must not be Entrusted With a Secret

٩٣١ ـ مَن لا يَنبَغي إيداعُهُم سِرّاً

2967. **Imām ʿAlī (AS) said,** ‘Do not confide anything in an ignorant person for he will not be able to guard it.’[3331]

٢٩٦٧ . الإمامُ عليٌّ عليه السلام : لا تُسِرَّ إلى الجاهِلِ شيئاً لا يُطِيقُ كِتمانَهُ.[٣٣٠٣]

2968. **Imām ʿAlī (AS) said,** ‘Do not ever entrust your secret to someone who has no integrity.’[3332]

٢٩٦٨ . عنه عليه السلام : لا تُودِعَنَّ سِرَّكَ مَن لا أمانَةَ لَهُ.[٣٣٠٤]

2969. **Imām ʿAlī (AS) said,** ‘Keep your secret to yourself, and do not share it with someone intelligent as he will be deviated or to an ignorant person as he will betray you.’[3333]

٢٩٦٩ . عنه عليه السلام : اِنفَرِد بِسِرِّكَ؛ ولا تودِعهُ حازِماً فَيَزَلَّ، ولا جاهِلاً فَيَخونَ.[٣٣٠٥]

2970. **Imām ʿAlī (AS) said,** ‘Do not entrust your secret, except to someone who has your absolute trust.’[3334]

٢٩٧٠ . عنه عليه السلام : لا تُودِعْ سِرَّكَ إلّا عِندَ كُلِّ ثِقَةٍ.[٣٣٠٦]

2971. **Imām ʿAlī (AS) said,** ‘The one who is unable to keep his own secret will be unable to keep anyone else's.’[3335]

٢٩٧١ . عنه عليه السلام : مَن ضَعُفَ عَن حِفظِ سِرِّهِ لَم يَقْوَ لِسِرِّ غَيرِهِ.[٣٣٠٧]

2972. **Imām al-Ṣādiq (AS) said,** ‘There are four things that go to waste: …and a secret you entrust to an injudicious person.’[3336]

٢٩٧٢ . الإمامُ الصّادقُ عليه السلام : أربَعةٌ يَذهَبنَ ضَياعاً: ... وسِرٌّ تُودِعُهُ عِندَ مَن لا حَصافَةَ لَهُ.[٣٣٠٨]

187

HAPPINESS

السُّرور

932. What to be Happy About

٩٣٢ ـ ما يَنبَغِي السُّرورُ بِهِ

2973. **Imām ʿAlī (AS) said** to ʿAbdallāh b. ʿAbbās, who said, ‘I have not benefited from any saying after the sayings of the Prophet (SAWA), apart from this one [where the Imām said], ‘Verily man feels happy when he manages to grasp something that he was about to miss, and he is

٢٩٧٣ . الإمامُ عليٌّ عليه السلام ـ لِعَبدِ اللهِ بنِ عبّاسٍ رحمةُ اللهِ علَيهِ وكانَ يقولُ: ما انتَفَعتُ بكلامٍ بَعدَ كلامِ رسولِ اللهِ ﷺ كانتِفاعِي بهذا الكلامِ ـ: أمّا بَعدُ، فإنَّ المَرءَ قد يَسُرُّهُ دَرْكُ ما لَم يَكُن لِيَفُوتَهُ،

saddened when he misses something that he would never had received. So let your happiness lie in all that you can seize of the Hereafter, and let your regret lie in all that which passes you by of it.'[3337]

ويَسُوؤهُ فوتُ ما لَم يَكُن لِيُدرِكَهُ، فَليَكُن سُرُورُكَ بما نِلتَ مِن آخِرَتِكَ، وليَكُنْ أسَفُكَ على ما فاتَكَ مِنها.[٣٣٠٩]

933. The Basics of Happiness

٩٣٣ ـ عَوامِلُ السُّرورِ

2974. **Imām ʿAlī (AS) said,** 'The root of the intellect is power, and its fruit is happiness.'[3338]

٢٩٧٤. الإمامُ عليٌّ عليه السلام: أصلُ العَقلِ القُدرَةُ، وثَمَرَتُها السُّرورُ.[٣٣١٠]

2975. **Imām ʿAlī (AS) said,** 'Happiness is useless without tenderness.'[3339]

٢٩٧٥. عنه عليه السلام: لا يُستَعانُ على السُّرورِ إلّا باللِّينِ.[٣٣١١]

934. One Who Fills Others' Hearts With Happiness

٩٣٤ ـ مَن أودَعَ قَلباً سُروراً

2976. **The Prophet (SAWA) said,** 'There is a place in Paradise called the House of Happiness which none shall enter except those who cheered up the orphans from amongst the believers.'[3340]

٢٩٧٦. رسولُ اللهِ ﷺ: إنّ في الجَنَّةِ داراً يُقالُ لَها دارُ الفَرَحِ لا يَدخُلُها إلّا مَن فَرَّحَ يَتامَى المؤمنينَ.[٣٣١٢]

2977. **The Prophet (SAWA) said,** 'There is a place in Paradise called the House of Happiness which none shall enter except those who cheered up children.'[3341]

٢٩٧٧. عنه ﷺ: إنّ في الجَنَّةِ داراً يقالُ لَها دارُ الفَرَحِ، لا يَدخُلُها إلّا مَن فَرَّحَ الصِّبيانَ.[٣٣١٣]

2978. **Imām ʿAlī (AS) said,** 'By the One whose Hearing encompasses all voices, no sooner does one fill somebody else's heart with happiness than Allah creates a special grace for him from that very happiness, such that when he is faced with a calamity, the grace will pass over it like water flows over a slope, until this [grace] chases it away as wild camels are chased away.'[3342]

٢٩٧٨. الإمامُ عليٌّ عليه السلام: فَوالذي وَسِعَ سَمعُهُ الأصواتَ، ما مِن أحَدٍ أودَعَ قَلباً سُروراً إلّا وخَلَقَ اللهُ لَهُ مِن ذلكَ السُّرورِ لُطفاً، فإذا نَزَلَتْ بهِ نائبَةٌ جَرى إلَيها كالماءِ في انحِدارِهِ حتّى يَطرُدَها عَنهُ، كما تُطرَدُ غَريبَةُ الإبلِ.[٣٣١٤]

2979. **Imām al-Ṣādiq (AS) said,** 'When one of you brings joy to another believer, let him not see it as having only made him happy. Rather, by

٢٩٧٩. الإمامُ الصّادقُ عليه السلام: لا يَرى أحَدُكُم إذا أدخَلَ على مُؤمِنٍ سُروراً أنّه علَيهِ أدخَلَهُ فَقَطْ

Allah, he makes us happy, and by Allah, he makes the Prophet (SAWA) happy too.'[3343]

بَل وَاللهِ علَينا ، بل وَاللهِ عَلىٰ رسولِ اللهِ ﷺ.[٣٣١٥]

935. Whoever makes Another Believer Happy makes Allah Happy

٩٣٥ ـ مَن سَرَّ مُؤمِناً سَرَّ اللهَ

2980. **The Prophet (SAWA) said,** 'Whoever makes another believer happy makes me happy, and whoever makes me happy makes Allah happy.'[3344]

٢٩٨٠ . رسولُ اللهِ ﷺ : مَن سَرَّ مُؤمناً فَقد سَرَّني ، ومَن سَرَّني فَقَد سَرَّ اللهَ.[٣٣١٦]

936. The Reward for Alleviating a Fellow Believer of his Sorrows

٩٣٦ ـ ثَوابُ التَّفريجِ عَنِ المُؤمِنِ

2981. **Imām al-Ṣādiq (AS) said,** 'Whoever alleviates a fellow believer's anguish, Allah will alleviate him of the anguish of the Hereafter, and will bring him out of his grave with a light heart.'[3345]

٢٩٨١ . الإمامُ الصّادقُ ﷺ : مَن نَفَّسَ عَن مؤمنٍ كُربَةً نَفَّسَ اللهُ عَنهُ كُرَبَ الآخِرَةِ ، وخَرَجَ مِن قَبرِهِ وهُو ثَلِجُ الفُؤادِ.[٣٣١٧]

2982. **Imām al-Ṣādiq (AS) said,** 'When Allah will raise the believer out of his grave, another presence will also come out with him and walk ahead of him, and whenever the believer will come across one of the terrors of the Day of Resurrection, the presence will console him saying, 'Do not worry or be saddened…' and the believer will ask, 'Who are you?, at which it will reply, 'I am the happiness that you used to bring upon your fellow believer.'[3346]

٢٩٨٢ . عنه ﷺ : إذا بَعَثَ اللهُ المؤمنَ مِن قَبرِهِ خَرَجَ مَعهُ مِثالٌ يَقدُمُ أمامَهُ ، كُلَّما رَأى المؤمنُ هَوْلاً مِن أهوالِ يومِ القِيامَةِ قالَ لَهُ المِثالُ : لا تَفزَعْ ولا تَحزَنْ.... فيقولُ لَهُ المؤمنُ :... مَن أنتَ ؟ فيقولُ : أنا السُّرورُ الذي كُنتَ أدخَلتَ علىٰ أخيكَ المؤمنِ.[٣٣١٨]

2983. **Imām al-Riḍā (AS) said,** 'Whoever alleviates a believer's worries, Allah will alleviate his heart on the Day of Resurrection.'[3347]

٢٩٨٣ . الإمامُ الرِّضا ﷺ : مَن فَرَّجَ عن مُؤمِنٍ فَرَّجَ اللهُ عن قَلبِهِ يومَ القِيامَةِ.[٣٣١٩]

(See also: THE NEED: section 589)

(أنظر) الحاجة : باب ٥٨٩

188

WASTING

الإسراف

937. Denouncing Wasting

٩٣٧ـ ذَمُّ الإسراف

"O Children of Adam! Put on your adornment on every occasion of prayer, and eat and drink, but do not waste; indeed Allah does not like the wasteful."[3348]

﴿يا بَنِي آدَمَ خُذُوا زِينَتَكُم عِندَ كُلِّ مَسْجِدٍ وَكُلُوا واشْرَبُوا وَلا تُسْرِفُوا إنَّهُ لا يُحِبُّ المُسْرِفِينَ﴾.٣٣٢٠

2984. **Imām ʿAlī (AS) said,** 'Woe betides the wasteful person, how far he is from self-improvement and from redressing his situation.'[3349]

٢٩٨٤ . الإمامُ عليٌّ عليه السلام : وَيحَ المُسرِفِ، ما أبعَدَهُ عن صَلاحِ نفسِهِ واستِدراكِ أمرِهِ!٣٣٢١

2985. **Imām ʿAlī (AS) said,** 'Wasting leads to stagnation [of wealth] whereas thriftiness causes it to thrive.'[3350]

٢٩٨٥ . عنه عليه السلام :السَّرَفُ مَثواةٌ، والقصدُ مَثراةٌ.٣٣٢٢

2986. **Imām Zayn al-ʿĀbidīn (AS) said** in one of his supplications, '...hold me back from wastefulness, fortify my provision against ruin, increase my possessions through blessing them, and set me upon the path of guidance towards good causes in what I spend of it.'[3351]

٢٩٨٦ . الإمامُ زينُ العابدينَ عليه السلام ـ في الدعاءِ ـ: وامنَعْني مِنَ السَّرَفِ، وحَصِّنْ رِزقي مِن التَّلَفِ، ووَفِّرْ مَلَكَتِي بالبَرَكَةِ فيهِ، وأصِبْ بِي سَبيلَ الهِدايَةِ لِلبِرِّ فيما أُنفِقُ مِنهُ.٣٣٢٣

938. Distinguishing Characteristics of a Wasteful Person

٩٣٨ـ عَلاماتُ المُسرِفِ

2987. **The Prophet (SAWA) said,** 'There are four characteristics distinguishing a wasteful person: pride in his wrongdoing, eating that which does not belong to him, refraining from acts of courtesy, and refusal to acknowledge anyone who is of no use to him.'[3352]

٢٩٨٧ . رسولُ اللهِ صلى الله عليه وآله :أمّا علامةُ المُسرِفِ فأربَعةٌ: الفَخرُ بالباطِلِ، ويأكُلُ ما لَيسَ عِندَهُ، ويَزهَدُ في اصطِناعِ المَعروفِ، ويُنكِرُ مَن لا يَنتَفِعُ بِشَيءٍ مِنهُ.٣٣٢٤

2988. **The Prophet (SAWA) said,** 'Eating anything and everything that one desires is wasting.'[3353]

٢٩٨٨ . عنه صلى الله عليه وآله : إنَّ مِنَ السَّرَفِ أن تأكُلَ كُلَّ ما اشتَهَيتَ.٣٣٢٥

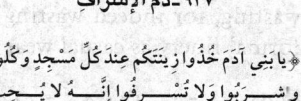

2989. **Imām ʿAlī (AS) said,** 'The giving of wealth to an undeserving cause is squandering and wasting.'[3354]

٢٩٨٩ . الإمامُ عليٌّ عليه السلام :إعطاءُ المالِ في غَيرِ حَقِّهِ تَبذيرٌ وإسرافٌ.[٣٣٢٦]

2990. **Imām al-Ṣādiq (AS)** was once asked by Isḥāq b. 'Ammār, 'Can a believer own ten shirts?' To which he replied, 'Yes.' 'What about twenty?' to which he replied, 'Yes. And no, that would not be wasting, for indeed wasting is when you wear your formal finery as casual wear at home.'[3355]

٢٩٩٠ . الإمامُ الصّادقُ عليه السلام ـوقد سألهُ اسحاقُ بن عمّار ـ: يكونُ للمؤمِنِ عَشـرَةُ أقْـمِصَةٍ؟ قـالَ: نَعَم، قلتُ: وَعِشرينَ ؟ قـالَ: نـعَم، وليسَ ذلكَ مِنَ السَّرَفِ، إنّما السَّرَفُ أن تَجعَلَ ثَوبَ صَونِكَ ثَوبَ بِذْلَتِكَ.[٣٣٢٧]

2991. **Imām al-ʿAskarī (AS) said,** 'Generosity has a set limit, and if taken to extremes becomes squandering.'[3356]

٢٩٩١ . الإمامُ العسكريُّ عليه السلام :إنَّ للسَّخاءِ مِقداراً، فإن زادَ علَيهِ فهُو سَرَفٌ.[٣٣٢٨]

939. The Lowest of Wastefulness

٩٣٩ ـ أدنَى الإسرافِ

2992. **Imām al-Ṣādiq (AS)** when asked about the lowest degree of wastefulness said, 'The lowest degree of wastefulness is to wear one's formal finery as casual wear at home, to spill out the remains of a container [instead of finishing it], and to eat the date and you throw the pits away here and there.'[3357]

٢٩٩٢ . الإمامُ الصّادقُ عليه السلام ـ لَمّا سُئلَ عن أدنَى الإسرافِ ـ: إبـذالُكَ ثَـوبَ صَـونِكَ، وإهـراقُكَ فَضلَ إنائكَ، وأكلُكَ التَّمرَ ورَميُكَ النَّوىٰ هاهُنا وهاهُنا.[٣٣٢٩]

940. That Which is not Counted as Waste

٩٤٠ ـ ما لا يُعَدُّ مِنَ الإسرافِ

2993. **The Prophet (SAWA) said,** 'There is nothing of good to be found in waste, and nothing of waste to be found in good.'[3358]

٢٩٩٣ . رسولُ اللهِ صلى الله عليه وآله : لا خَيرَ في السَّرَفِ، ولا سَرَفَ في الخَيرِ.[٣٣٣٠]

2994. **Imām al-Ṣādiq (AS) said,** 'There is no waste in anything that improves the body...rather waste is found in all that squanders away wealth and harms the body.'[3359]

٢٩٩٤ . الإمامُ الصّادقُ عليه السلام : لَيسَ فـيما أصـلَحَ البَدَنَ إسرافٌ... إنّما الإسرافُ فيما أتلَفَ المـالَ وأضَرَّ بالبَدَنِ.[٣٣٣١]

2995. **Imām al-Kāẓim (AS),** when asked about whether owning ten shirts was considered a waste, replied, 'No, and in fact that is more conducive to longer wear of your clothes. Waste is when you wear your formal finery to unclean places [as casual wear].'[3360]

٢٩٩٥ . الإمامُ الكاظمُ عليه السلام ـوقد سُئلَ عَن عَشَرَةِ أقْمِصَةٍ هَل ذلكَ مِنَ السَّرَفِ ـ: لا، ولكـن ذلكَ أبقىٰ لِـثِيابِهِ، ولكـنَّ السَّـرَفَ أن تَـلبَسَ ثَـوبَ صَونِكَ في المكانِ القَذِرِ.[٣٣٣٢]

189

STEALING

السَّرِقَة

941. Stealing and its Legal Punishment

٩٤١ـ السَّرِقَةِ وَحَدُّها

"As for the thief, man or woman, cut off their hands as requital for what they have earned. [That is] an exemplary punishment from Allah, and Allah is all-mighty, all-wise."[3361]

﴿والسَّارِقُ والسَّارِقَةُ فاقْطَعُوا أيدِيَهُما جَزاءً بِما كَسَبا نَكالاً مِنَ اللهِ واللهُ عَزِيزٌ حَكِيمٌ﴾.[٣٣٣٣]

2996. **Imām al-Riḍā (AS) said,** 'Allah has prohibited stealing because of the financial corruption and murder that would ensue were it to be permissible; and because of all other aggressive crimes that would result such as murder, fighting, and jealous hostilities, and because it would lead to the abandonment of fair trade and industry for earning a living, in exchange for extortion of property where nobody would have rightful ownership of anything [and everything was available for the taking].'
And the reason why the right hand of the thief is to be severed [as punishment] is because he steals things with his right hand, and because it is the best and most useful limb out of all his limbs, so its severing has been prescribed to serve as a deterrent and a lesson to mankind that they must not desire to seize anything that does not belong to them. And because most of the time the theft is committed with the right hand.'[3362]

٢٩٩٦ . الإمامُ الرِّضا عليه السلام : حَرَّمَ اللهُ السَّرِقَةَ لِما فِيها] مِن فَسادِ الأموالِ وقَتلِ النَّفسِ لَو كانَت مُباحَةً، ولِما يَأتي في التَّغاصُبِ مِنَ القَتلِ والتَّنازُعِ والتَّحاسُدِ، وما يَدعُو إلى تَركِ التِّجاراتِ والصِّناعاتِ في المَكاسِبِ، واقتِناءِ الأموالِ إذا كانَ الشَّيءُ المُقتَنىٰ لا يكونُ أحَدٌ أحَقَّ بِهِ مِن أحَدٍ...
وعِلَّةُ قَطعِ اليَمينِ مِنَ السّارِقِ؛ لأنّهُ يُباشِرُ الأشياءَ بِيَمينِهِ، وهِيَ أفضَلُ أعضائهِ وأنفَعُها لَهُ، فَجُعِلَ قَطعُها نَكالاً وعِبرَةً لِلخَلقِ لِئلّا يَبتَغُوا أخذَ الأموالِ مِن غَيرِ حِلِّها، ولأنّهُ أكثَرَ ما يُباشِرُ السَّرِقَةَ بيَمينِهِ.[٣٣٣٤]

942. Those Who are not Liable to the Legal Punishment for Stealing

٩٤٢ـ مَن لا يَجري عَلَيهِ حَدُّ السَّرِقَةِ

2997. **The Prophet (SAWA) said,** 'The thief's hand should only be cut for a theft of a quarter dinar or more.'[3363]

٢٩٩٧ . رسولُ اللهِ صلى الله عليه وآله : لا تُقطَعُ يَدُ السّارِقِ إلّا في رُبعِ دِينارٍ فَصاعِداً.[٣٣٣٥]

2998. **Imām al-Ṣādiq (AS) said,** 'A man who had man who had pilfered a pearl from a girl's earring was brought to the Commander of the Faithful (AS), and he said, 'This is a sneaky theft committed overtly.' He then punished and imprisoned him.'[3364]

٢٩٩٨ . الإمامُ الصّادقُ عليه السلام : إنّ أميرالمؤمنين عليه السلام أُتي برجل اختَلَسَ دُرَّةً مِن أُذُنِ جاريَةٍ قال : هذِهِ الدَّغارَةُ المُعلَنَةُ ، فَضَرَبَهُ وحَبَسَهُ .٣٣٣٦

2999. **Imām 'Alī (AS) said,** 'There are four types of thieves who are not liable to having their hands cut: the pilferer, the fraudster, the one who steals war booty, and the employee who thieves, for these are all acts of deceit.'[3365]

٢٩٩٩ . الإمامُ عليٌّ عليه السلام : أربَعةٌ لا قَطعَ علَيهِم : المُختَلِسُ ، والغُلُولُ ، ومَن سَرَقَ مِنَ الغَنيمَةِ ، وسَرِقَةُ الأجيرِ ؛ فإنّها خِيانَةٌ .٣٣٣٧

3000. **Imām al-Bāqir or Imām al-Ṣādiq (AS) said,** 'Only the thief who breaks into a house or breaks a lock is liable to have his hand cut.'[3366]

٣٠٠٠ . الإمامُ الباقرُ أو الإمامُ الصّادقُ عليهما السلام : لا يُقطَعُ إلّا مَن نَقَبَ بَيتاً أو كَسَرَ قُفلاً .٣٣٣٨

3001. **Imām al-Ṣādiq (AS) said,** 'The employee, or the guest who steals is not liable to have his hand cut because he was in a position of trust.'[3367]

٣٠٠١ . الإمامُ الصّادقُ عليه السلام : لا يُقطَعُ الأجيرُ والضَّيفُ إذا سَرَقَ ؛ لأنّهُما مُؤتَمَنانِ .٣٣٣٩

3002. **Imām al-Ṣādiq (AS) said,** 'The one who steals in a year of famine is not liable to have his hand cut.'[3368]

٣٠٠٢ . عنه عليه السلام : لا يُقطَعُ السّارِقُ في عامِ سَنَةٍ ـ يَعنِي في عامِ مَجاعَةٍ ـ .٣٣٤٠

3003. **Imām al-Ṣādiq (AS) said,** 'The thief who comes and repents of his own accord to Allah, and returns everything that he has stolen back to its owner, is not liable to having his hand cut.'[3369]

٣٠٠٣ . عنه عليه السلام : السّارقُ إذا جاءَ مِن قِبَلِ نَفسِهِ تائباً إلى اللهِ ، ورَدَّ سَرِقَتَهُ عَلىٰ صاحِبِها ، فلا قَطعَ علَيهِ .٣٣٤١

190

PROSPERITY

السَّعادَةُ

943. The Sign of the Prosperous

٩٤٣ ـ عَلامَةُ السَّعيدِ

3004. **The Prophet (SAWA) said** to the Commander of the Faithful, 'Alī (AS), 'Verily the truly prosperous person is the one who loves you and obeys you.'[3370]

٣٠٠٤ . رسولُ اللهِ صلى الله عليه وآله ـ لأميرِ المُؤمنينَ عليه السلام ـ : إنَّ السَّعِيدَ حَقَّ السَّعيدِ مَن أحَبَّكَ وأطاعَكَ .٣٣٤٢

3005. **Imām ʿAlī (AS) said,** 'Prosperous is he who is sincere in his acts of obedience.'[3371]

٣٠٠٥. الإمامُ عليٌّ ﷺ: السَّعيدُ مَن أخلَصَ الطّاعَةَ.[٣٣٤٣]

3006. **Imām al-Ṣādiq (AS) said,** 'One who is not knowledgeable must not be deemed prosperous.'[3372]

٣٠٠٦. الإمامُ الصّادقُ ﷺ: لا يَنبَغي لِمَن لم يَكُن عالِماً أن يُعَدَّ سَعيداً.[٣٣٤٤]

944. That Which brings About Prosperity

٩٤٤ـ ما يوجِبُ السَّعادَةَ

3007. **Imām ʿAlī (AS) said,** 'Act in accordance with knowledge and you will prosper.'[3373]

٣٠٠٧. الإمامُ عليٌّ ﷺ: اِعمَلوا بِالعِلمِ تَسعَدوا.[٣٣٤٥]

3008. **Imām ʿAlī (AS) said,** 'Sit in the company of scholars and you will prosper.'[3374]

٣٠٠٨. عنه ﷺ: جالِسِ العُلماءَ تَسعَدْ.[٣٣٤٦]

3009. **Imām ʿAlī (AS) said,** 'Prosperity lies in adhering to the truth.'[3375]

٣٠٠٩. عنه ﷺ: في لُزومِ الحَقِّ تَكونُ السَّعادَةُ.[٣٣٤٧]

3010. **Imām ʿAlī (AS) said,** 'Whoever takes account of himself prospers.'[3376]

٣٠١٠. عنه ﷺ: مَن حاسَبَ نَفسَهُ سَعِدَ.[٣٣٤٨]

3011. **Imām ʿAlī (AS) said,** 'Whoever exerts his soul in a bid to improve himself prospers, and whoever neglects and abandons his soul to its pleasures attracts misfortune and becomes distant [from Allah].'[3377]

٣٠١١. عنه ﷺ: مَن أجهَدَ نَفسَهُ في إصلاحِها سَعِدَ، مَن أهمَلَ نفسَهُ في لَذّاتِها شَقِيَ وبَعُدَ.[٣٣٤٩]

945. Things which are considered as Prosperity

٩٤٥ـ ما يُعَدُّ مِنَ السَّعادَةِ

3012. **The Prophet (SAWA) said,** 'Four things make up a man's prosperity: virtuous friends, a dutiful child, a compatible wife, and having the source of his livelihood in his own town.'[3378]

٣٠١٢. رسولُ اللهِ ﷺ: أربَعَةٌ مِن سَعادَةِ المَرءِ: الخُلَطاءُ الصّالِحُونَ، والوَلَدُ البارُّ، والمَرأةُ المُؤاتِيَةُ، وأن تَكونَ مَعيشَتُهُ في بَلَدِهِ.[٣٣٥٠]

3013. **Imām ʿAlī (AS) said,** 'Having a heart free from rancour and jealousy is part of a man's prosperity.'[3379]

٣٠١٣. الإمامُ عليٌّ ﷺ: خُلُوُّ الصَّدرِ مِنَ الغِلِّ والحَسَدِ مِن سَعادَةِ العَبدِ.[٣٣٥١]

3014. **Imām ʿAlī (AS) said,** 'Accomplishment of good deeds constitutes prosperity.'[3380]

٣٠١٤. عنه ﷺ: مِنَ السَّعادَةِ، التَّوفيقُ لِصالِحِ الأعمالِ.[٣٣٥٢]

946. The Reality of Prosperity

٩٤٦ـ حَقيقَةُ السَّعادَةِ

3015. **Imām ʿAlī (AS) said,** 'The reality of prosperity is that a man's tasks conclude with success, and the reality of misfortune is that a man's tasks conclude with failure.'[3381]

٣٠١٥. الإمامُ عليٌّ ﷺ : إنّ حَقيقَةَ السَّعادةِ أن يُختَمَ لِلمَرءِ عَمَلُهُ بِالسَّعادَةِ، وإنّ حَقيقَةَ الشَّقاءِ أن يُختَمَ للمَرءِ عَمَلُهُ بِالشَّقاءِ.[٣٣٥٣]

3016. **Imām ʿAlī (AS) said,** 'At the time of the Great Exposure [of our deeds] in front of Allah [on the Day of Resurrection], prosperity and misfortune will materialize in their distinct realities.'[3382]

٣٠١٦. عنه ﷺ : عِندَ العَرضِ عَلَى اللهِ سبحانَهُ تَتَحَقَّقُ السَّعادَةُ مِنَ الشَّقاءِ.[٣٣٥٤]

947. The Most Prosperous of People

٩٤٧ـ أسعَدُ النّاسِ

3017. **The Prophet (SAWA) said,** 'The most prosperous of people is the one who mingles with honourable people.'[3383]

٣٠١٧. رسولُ اللهِ ﷺ :أسعَدُ الناسِ مَن خالَطَ كِرامَ النّاسِ.[٣٣٥٥]

3018. **Imām ʿAlī (AS) said,** 'The most prosperous of people is the one who has abandoned an ephemeral pleasure in exchange for a lasting one.'[3384]

٣٠١٨. الإمامُ عليٌّ ﷺ :أسعَدُ النّاسِ مَن تَرَكَ لَذَّةً فانِيَةً لِلَذَّةٍ باقِيَةٍ.[٣٣٥٦]

3019. **Imām ʿAlī (AS) said,** 'Verily the most prosperous of people in this world is the one who turns away from all that which he knows is detrimental to him, and verily the most unfortunate person is he who follows his whims.'[3385]

٣٠١٩. عنه ﷺ :إنَّ أسعَدَ النّاسِ في الدنيا مَن عَدَلَ عَمّا يَعرِفُ ضُرَّهُ، وإنَّ أشقاهُم مَنِ اتَّبَعَ هَواهُ.[٣٣٥٧]

3020. **Imām ʿAlī (AS) said,** 'The most prosperous person is he who acknowledges our virtue, draws near to Allah through us, is sincere in his love for us, acts upon whatever we have recommended, and refrains from all that we have prohibited. He is indeed of us and will be with us in the place of everlasting abode.'[3386]

٣٠٢٠. عنه ﷺ : أسعَدُ النّاسِ مَن عَرَفَ فَضلَنا، وتَقَرَّبَ إلى اللهِ بِنا، وأخلَصَ حُبَّنا، وعَمِلَ بِما إلَيهِ نَدَبنا، وانتَهىٰ عَمّا عَنهُ نَهَينا، فذاكَ مِنّا وهُو في دارِ المُقامَةِ مَعَنا.[٣٣٥٨]

3021. **Imām ʿAlī (AS) said,** 'The person with the greatest prosperity is the one with the greatest level of abstemiousness.'[3387]

٣٠٢١. عنه ﷺ : أعظَمُ النّاسِ سَعادَةً أكثَرُهُم زَهادَةً.[٣٣٥٩]

191

TRAVEL

السَّفَر

948. Encouraging to Travel and Making it Short

٩٤٨ ـ الحَثُّ عَلَى السَّفَرِ وَقَصرِها

3022. **The Prophet (SAWA) said,** 'Travel and you will be healthy and wealthy.'[3388]

٣٠٢٢ . رسولُ اللهِ ﷺ : سافِروا تَصِحّوا وتَغنَموا.[٣٣٦٠]

3023. **The Prophet (SAWA) said,** 'Travel is a type of chastisement, so when one's travel comes to an end one must hurry back home to one's family.'[3389]

٣٠٢٣ . عنه ﷺ : السَّفَرُ قِطعَةٌ مِنَ العَذابِ، وإذا قَضىٰ أحَدُكُم سَفَرَهُ فَليُسرِعِ الإيابَ إلىٰ أهلِهِ.[٣٣٦١]

949. Encouraging to Travel for Recreation

٩٤٩ ـ الحَثُّ عَلَى التَّنَزُّهِ

3024. **Imām al-Ṣādiq (AS)** was once at his brother 'Abdullāh b. Muḥammad's house when 'Amr b. Ḥurayth entered and asked him, 'What has brought you to this place?' to which he replied, 'Seeking recreation.'[3390]

٣٠٢٤ . الإمامُ الصّادقُ ﷺ ـ لَمّا دَخَلَ عليهِ عمرُو بنُ حُرَيثٍ وهُو في مَنزِلِ أخيهِ عبدِ اللهِ بنِ محمّدٍ فقالَ لَهُ : جُعِلتُ فِداكَ، ما حَوَّلَكَ إلىٰ هذا المَنزِلِ؟ ـ : طَلَبُ النُّزهَةِ.[٣٣٦٢]

3025. **Imām al-Riḍā (AS) said,** 'We had gone out for a picnic when one of the servants forgot to bring the salt. Even though they had slaughtered the plumpest sheep there was for us, it was of no use to us until we left.'[3391]

٣٠٢٥ . الإمامُ الرِّضا ﷺ : لَقَد خَرَجنا إلىٰ نُزهَةٍ لَنا ونَسِيَ بعضُ الغِلمانِ المِلحَ فَذَبَحوا لَنا شاةً مِن أسمَنِ ما يَكونُ فَما انتَفَعنا بِشَيءٍ حتّىٰ انصَرَفنا.[٣٣٦٣]

950. Etiquettes of Travelling

٩٥٠ ـ آدابُ السَّفَرِ

3026. **The Prophet (SAWA) said,** 'If three people are travelling together, they must place one of them in charge.'[3392]

٣٠٢٦ . رسولُ اللهِ ﷺ : إذا كانَ ثلاثةٌ في سَفَرٍ فَليُؤَمِّروا أحَدَهُم.[٣٣٦٤]

3027. **The Prophet (SAWA) said,** 'During a journey, the chief of the people should be their servant.'[3393]

٣٠٢٧ . عنه ﷺ : سَيِّدُ القَومِ خادِمُهُم في السَّفَرِ.[٣٣٦٥]

3028. **The Prophet (SAWA) said,** 'When you go away on a journey, upon your return to your family you should bring them back a gift or a novelty, even if it be a mere stone!'[3394]

٣٠٢٨. عنه ﷺ: إذا خَرَجَ أحَدُكُم إلىٰ سَفَرٍ ثُمّ قَدِمَ علىٰ أهلِهِ فَلْيُهدِهِم ولْيُطرِفهُم ولو حِجارَةً![٣٣٦٦]

3029. **Imām ʿAlī (AS) said,** 'Concern yourself with your companion [on the journey] over the way itself, and with your neighbour before [purchasing] your house.'[3395]

٣٠٢٩. الإمامُ عليٌّ ؑ: سَلْ عَنِ الرَّفيقِ قَبلَ الطَّريقِ، وعنِ الجارِ قَبلَ الدّارِ.[٣٣٦٧]

3030. **Imām ʿAlī (AS) said,** 'Do not accompany on a journey someone who does not consider you worthier than himself the way you consider him worthier than yourself.'[3396]

٣٠٣٠. عنه ؑ: لا تَصحَبَنَّ في سَفَرٍ مَن لا يَرىٰ لكَ الفَضلَ علَيهِ كما تَرىٰ لَهُ الفَضلَ علَيكَ.[٣٣٦٨]

3031. **Imām al-Ṣādiq (AS) said,** 'Commence your journey with the giving of charity, and leave when you wish, for verily you buy the safety of your journey [with charity].'[3397]

٣٠٣١. الإمامُ الصّادقُ ؑ: اِفتَتِحْ سَفَرَكَ بالصَّدقَةِ واخرُجْ إذا بَدا لكَ؛ فإنّكَ تَشتَري سلامَةَ سَفَرِكَ.[٣٣٦٩]

3032. **Imām al-Ṣādiq (AS) narrated** that Luqmān said to his son, 'When you travel in the company of people, consult with them frequently about each of your affairs, make them smile often, and be generous in sharing your provisions with them. When they call you, answer them, and when they ask for your help, assist them. Try to outdo them in three things: long periods of silence, an abundance of prayer, and open-handedness with them with whatever you possess of riding animal, wealth or food.'[3398]

٣٠٣٢. عنه ؑ: قالَ لقمانُ لابنِهِ: إذا سافَرتَ مَع قَومٍ فأكثِرِ استِشارَتَهُم في أمرِكَ وأمرِهِم، وأكثِرِ التَّبَسُّمَ في وُجوهِهِم، وكُن كَريماً علىٰ زادِكَ بَينَهُم، وإذا دَعَوكَ فأجِبهُم، وإذا استَعانُوكَ فَأعِنهُم، واغلِبهُم بثَلاثٍ: طُولِ الصَّمتِ، وكَثرَةِ الصَّلاةِ، وسَخاءِ النَّفسِ بما مَعَكَ مِن دابَّةٍ أو مالٍ أو زادٍ.[٣٣٧٠]

3033. **Imām al-Ṣādiq (AS) said,** 'The ideal courteousness during a journey entails sharing one's provisions freely, joking light-heartedly in matters that do not displease Allah, hardly ever disputing with your travelling companions, and never telling tales about them once you have parted company from them.'[3399]

٣٠٣٣. عنه ؑ: أمّا مُرُوَّةُ السَّفَرِ فَبَذلُ الزادِ، والمِزاحُ في غَيرِ ما يُسخِطُ اللهَ، وقِلّةُ الخِلافِ علىٰ مَن تَصحَبُهُ، وتَركُ الرِّوايَةِ علَيهِم إذا أنتَ فارَقتَهُم.[٣٣٧١]

951. The Prohibited Journey

٩٥١ـ السَّفَرُ المَنهِيُّ عَنهُ

3034. **Imām ʿAlī (AS) said,** 'A man must never go on a journey in which he has cause to fear for his faith or his prayer.'[3400]

٣٠٣٤. الإمامُ عليٌّ ﷺ: لا يَخرُجِ الرَّجُلُ في سَفَرٍ يَخافُ فيهِ على دِينِهِ وصَلاتِهِ.[٣٣٧٢]

3035. **Imām al-Ṣādiq (AS)** was asked by Muḥammad b. Muslim about the situation of a man who becomes ritually impure (*mujnib*) during his journey, and has nothing but snow or ice at his disposal [and therefore cannot perform the obligatory bath to purify himself]. Imām (AS) replied, 'This is a situation of primary necessity, and I do not think that he should ever return to such a place where his religion is at stake.'[3401]

٣٠٣٥. الإمامُ الصّادقُ ﷺ ـ لَمّا سَألَهُ محمّدُ بنُ مسلمٍ عنِ الرَّجُلِ يُجنِبُ في السَّفَرِ، فلا يَجِدُ إلّا الثَّلجَ أو ماءً جامداً ـ: هُو بِمَنزِلَةِ الضَّرُورةِ، ولا أرىٰ أن يَعُودَ إلىٰ هذِهِ الأرضِ التي تُوبِقُ دِينَهُ.[٣٣٧٣]

192

QUENCHING SOMEONE'S THIRST

السَّقيُ

952. The Virtue of Quenching Someone's Thirst

٩٥٢ـ فَضلُ السَّقيِ

3036. **The Prophet (SAWA) said,** 'If a man quenches his wife's thirst he is rewarded for it.'[3402]

٣٠٣٦. رسولُ اللهِ ﷺ: إنّ الرجُلَ إذا سَقى امرَأتَهُ الماءَ أُجِرَ.[٣٣٧٤]

3037. **The Prophet (SAWA) said,** 'If you have committed many sins, then quench people's thirst time after time.'[3403]

٣٠٣٧. عنه ﷺ: إذا كَثُرَت ذُنوبُكَ فاسْقِ الماءَ عَلَى الماءِ.[٣٣٧٥]

3038. **Imām Zayn al-ʿĀbidīn (AS) said,** 'Whoever quenches a believer of his thirst, Allah will quench him from the pure sealed wine [of Paradise].'[3404]

٣٠٣٨. الإمامُ زينُ العابدينَ ﷺ: مَن سَقىٰ مُؤمناً مِن ظَمَأٍ سَقاهُ اللهُ مِنَ الرَّحيقِ المَختومِ.[٣٣٧٦]

3039. **Imām al-Bāqir (AS) said,** ''Whoever gives a drink of water to a thirsty person, Allah will quench him from the pure sealed wine [of Paradise].'[3405]

٣٠٣٩. الإمامُ الباقرُ ﷺ: مَن سَقىٰ ظَمآناً ماءً سَقاهُ اللهُ مِنَ الرَّحيقِ المَختومِ.[٣٣٧٧]

3040. **Imām al-Bāqir (AS) said,** 'Verily the first thing to be rewarded on the Day of Resurrection will be the giving of water.'[3406]

٣٠٤٠. عنه ﷺ: إنّ أوّلَ ما يُبدأُ بِه يَومَ القِيامَةِ صَدَقةُ الماءِ.[٣٣٧٨]

3041. **Imām al-Ṣādiq (AS) said,** 'The best form of charity is to cool down someone's internal heat [by quenching them], and whoever quenches an animal's or any other being's internal heat, Allah will shade him on the Day when no shade will avail except His shade.'[3407]

٣٠٤١. الإمامُ الصّادقُ ﷺ: أفضَلُ الصَّدَقةِ إبرادُ الكَبِدِ الحَرّىٰ، ومَن سَقىٰ كَبِداً حَرّىٰ مِن بَهيمَةٍ أو غَيرِها أظَلَّهُ اللهُ عزّوجلّ يَومَ لا ظِلَّ إلّا ظِلُّهُ.[٣٣٧٩]

953. The Duty of One who Quenches Others

٩٥٣ـ ما يَنبَغي لِلسّاقي

3042. **The Prophet (SAWA) said,** 'The one who gives people to drink should himself drink last of all.'[3408]

٣٠٤٢. رسولُ اللهِ ﷺ: لِيَشرَبْ ساقِي القَومِ آخِرَهُم.[٣٣٨٠]

193

INTOXICATION

السُّكرُ

954. Every Intoxicant is Prohibited

٩٥٤ـ كُلُّ مُسكِرٍ حَرامٌ

3043. **The Prophet (SAWA) said,** 'Keep away from every intoxicant for every intoxicant is prohibited.'[3409]

٣٠٤٣. رسولُ اللهِ ﷺ: احذَرُوا كُلَّ مُسكِرٍ، فإنَّ كُلَّ مُسكِرٍ حَرامٌ.[٣٣٨١]

3044. **Imām al-Bāqir (AS) said,** 'Whatever substance intoxicates when consumed in large amounts is prohibited even in small amounts.'[3410]

٣٠٤٤. الإمامُ الباقرُ ﷺ: ما أسكَرَ كَثيرُهُ فَقَليلُهُ حَرامٌ.[٣٣٨٢]

955. Types of Intoxicants

٩٥٥ـ أنواعُ المُسكِراتِ

3045. **The Prophet (SAWA) said,** 'O Ibn Masʿūd, be wary of the intoxication brought about by sin, for verily the sin intoxicates just as much as alcohol if not more. Allah, most High,

٣٠٤٥. رسولُ اللهِ ﷺ ـ لعبد الله بن مسعود ـ: يابنَ مسعودٍ، إحذَر سُكرَ الخَطيئةِ؛ فإنَّ لِلخَطيئةِ سُكراً كَسُكرِ الشَّرابِ، بل هِي أشَدُّ سُكراً مِنهُ،

says, *"Deaf, dumb, and blind, they will not come back."*[3411][3412]

يــــــقولُ اللهُ تــــعالىٰ: ﴿صُمٌّ بُكْمٌ عُمْيٌ فَهُم لا يَرْجِعُونَ﴾[٣٣٨٣].[٣٣٨٤]

3046. **Imām ʿAlī (AS) said,** 'There are four types of intoxication: the intoxication induced by drink, the intoxication induced by wealth, the intoxication of sleep, and the intoxication induced by power.'[3413]

٣٠٤٦. الإمامُ عليٌّ ؑ: السُّكرُ أربَعُ سَكراتٍ: سُكرُ الشَّرابِ، وسُكرُ المالِ، وسُكرُ النَّومِ، وسُكرُ المُلكِ.[٣٣٨٥]

3047. **Imām ʿAlī (AS) said,** 'The man of reason must be on his guard against the intoxication of wealth, of power, of knowledge, of praise and of youth, for all of these have offensive vapours about them that strip away one's reason and carry away one's dignity.'[3414]

٣٠٤٧. عنه ؑ: يَنبَغي للعاقِلِ أن يَحتَرِسَ مِن سُكرِ المالِ، وسُكرِ القُدرَةِ، وسُكرِ العِلمِ، وسُكرِ المَدحِ، وسُكرِ الشَّبابِ، فإنَّ لِكُلِّ ذلكَ رِياحاً خَبيثَةً تَسلُبُ العَقلَ وتَستَخِفُّ الوَقارَ.[٣٣٨٦]

3048. **Imām ʿAlī (AS) said,** 'The intoxication of heedlessness and arrogance take longer to regain consciousness from than the intoxication of wines.'[3415]

٣٠٤٨. عنه ؑ: سُكرُ الغَفلَةِ والغُرورِ أبعَدُ إفاقَةً مِن سُكرِ الخُمورِ.[٣٣٨٧]

194

HOUSING

المَسكَن

956. Spaciousness and Smallness of a House

٩٥٦ـ سَعَةُ المَسكَنِ وضِيقُهُ

3049. **The Prophet (SAWA) said,** 'Part of a Muslim's prosperity is living in spacious housing.'[3416]

٣٠٤٩. رسولُ اللهِ ﷺ: مِن سَعادَةِ المَرءِ المُسلِمِ المَسكَنُ الواسِعُ.[٣٣٨٨]

3050. **Imām al-Bāqir (AS) said,** 'A misfortunate way of life entails living in a cramped house.'[3417]

٣٠٥٠. الإمامُ الباقرُ ؑ: مِن شَقاءِ العَيشِ ضِيقُ المَنزِلِ.[٣٣٨٩]

957. Caution Against Building more Housing than Necessary for One's Living

٩٥٧ـ التَّحذيرُ مِنَ البِناءِ فَوقَ الكَفافِ

3051. **Imām ʿAlī (AS) said,** 'It is a distressful situation that man amasses what he does not eat and builds wherein he does not live, then he goes

٣٠٥١. الإمامُ عليٌّ ؑ: مِنَ العَناءِ أنَّ المَرءَ يَجمَعُ ما لا يَأكُلُ ويَبني ما لا يَسكُنُ، ثُمَّ يَخرُجُ إلى اللهِ

to Allah, most High, neither carrying the wealth with him, nor shifting the building!'[3418]

تعالىٰ لا مالاً حَمَلَ، ولا بِناءً نَقَلَ!٣٣٩٠

3052. **Imām al-Ṣādiq (AS) said,** 'Every building exceeding the bounds of sufficiency will be a dire curse on its owner on the Day of Resurrection.'[3419]

٣٠٥٢. الإمامُ الصّادقُ ﷺ: كُلُّ بِناءٍ ليسَ بِكَفافٍ فهُو وبالٌ علىٰ صاحِبِهِ يَومَ القِيامَةِ.٣٣٩١

3053. **Imām al-Ṣādiq (AS) said,** 'He who builds in addition to his own house [unnecessarily] will be made to bear its burden on the Day of Resurrection.'[3420]

٣٠٥٣. عنه ﷺ: مَن بَنىٰ فَوقَ مَسكَنِهِ كُلِّفَ حَملَهُ يَومَ القِيامَةِ.٣٣٩٢

958. Selling a House

٩٥٨ـ بَيعُ الدّارِ

3054. **The Prophet (SAWA) said,** 'Whoever sells a house and does not invest the money in something of similar value will not be blessed in it [his money].'[3421]

٣٠٥٤. رسولُ اللهِ ﷺ: مَن باعَ داراً ثُمّ لم يَجعَلْ ثَمَنَها في مِثلِها لَم يُبارَكْ لَهُ فيها.٣٣٩٣

3055. **The Prophet (SAWA) said,** 'Whoever from among you sells a house or some real estate, then let him bear in mind that the money acquired is not worthy of being blessed unless he invests it in something of similar value.'[3422]

٣٠٥٥. عنه ﷺ: مَن باعَ مِنكم داراً أو عَقاراً، فَلْيَعلَمْ أنَّهُ مالٌ قَمَنٌ أن لا يُبارَكَ لَهُ فيهِ إلّا أن يَجعَلَهُ في مِثلِهِ.٣٣٩٤

195

WEAPONRY

السِّلاحُ

959. The Reward for Making Weapons

٩٥٩ـ ثَوابُ صُنعِ الأسلِحَةِ

3056. **The Prophet (SAWA) said,** 'Allah Almighty admits three people into Paradise because of [the casting of] a single arrow [in the path of Allah]: its maker if he intended good in his making of it, its thrower, and he who hands it to him.'[3423]

٣٠٥٦. رسولُ اللهِ ﷺ: إنَّ اللهَ عَزَّوجلَّ يُدخِلُ بِالسَّهمِ الواحِدِ ثلاثَةَ نَفَرٍ الجَنَّةَ: صانِعَهُ يَحتَسِبُ في صَنعَتِهِ الخَيرَ، والرامِيَ بهِ، ومُنبِلَهُ.٣٣٩٥

960. Weaponry and Goodness

٩٦٠ـ السِّلاحُ والخَيرُ

"The faithless are eager that you should be oblivious of your weapons…"[3424]

﴿وَدَّ الَّذِينَ كَفَرُوا لَوْ تَغْفُلُونَ عَنْ أَسْلِحَتِكُم﴾.[٣٣٩٦]

3057. **The Prophet (SAWA) said,** 'All goodness lies in the sword and under the shade of the sword. Only the sword can make people rise up, and the swords are the keys to Paradise and Hell.'[3425]

٣٠٥٧. رسولُ اللهِ ﷺ: الخَيرُ كُلُّهُ في السَّيفِ وتَحتَ ظِلِّ السَّيفِ، ولا يُقِيمُ الناسَ إلّا السَّيفُ، والسُّيُوفُ مَقالِيدُ الجَنَّةِ والنارِ.[٣٣٩٧]

3058. **The Prophet (SAWA) said,** 'Paradise lies under the shade of the swords.'[3426]

٣٠٥٨. عنه ﷺ: الجَنَّةُ تَحتَ ظِلالِ السُّيُوفِ.[٣٣٩٨]

3059. **Imām al-Ṣādiq (AS) said,** 'Verily Allah, Mighty and Exalted, sent His Messenger to preach Islam to the people for ten years, during which they refused to follow him until Allah commanded him to fight them. So goodness lies with the sword and under the sword, and thus will the state of affairs conclude again [in the end].'[3427]

٣٠٥٩. الإمامُ الصّادقُ عليه السلام: إنَّ اللهَ عَزَّ وجلَّ بَعَثَ رسولَهُ بِالإسلامِ إلى الناسِ عَشرَ سِنِينَ، فَأَبَوا أن يَقبَلُوا حتّى أمَرَهُ بالقِتالِ، فالخَيرُ في السَّيفِ وتَحتَ السَّيفِ، والأمرُ يَعُودُ كما بَدَأ.[٣٣٩٩]

961. Prohibition of Selling Weapons to Enemies of Islam

٩٦١ـ النَّهيُ عَن بَيعِ السِّلاحِ لِأعداءِ الدِّينِ

3060. **The Prophet (SAWA),** in his advice to Imām ʿAlī (AS) said, 'O ʿAlī, ten types of people from this community disbelieve in Allah, the Great: … and the one who sells weapons to the enemy.'[3428]

٣٠٦٠. رسولُ اللهِ ﷺ ـ في وَصِيَّتِهِ لعليٍّ عليه السلام ـ: يا عَلِيُّ، كَفَرَ بِاللهِ العَظيمِ مِن هَذِهِ الأُمَّةِ عَشرَةٌ: … وبائعُ السِّلاحِ مِن أهلِ الحَربِ.[٣٤٠٠]

196

THE RULER (THE SULTAN)

السُّلطانُ

962. Beware of Associating with a Tyrannical Ruler

٩٦٢ـ إيّاكم ومُخالَطَةَ السُّلطانِ الجائرِ

3061. **The Prophet (SAWA) said,** 'Beware of associating with the [unjust] ruler for verily it

٣٠٦١. رسولُ اللهِ ﷺ: إيّاكُم ومُخالَطَةَ السُّلطانِ

causes faith to depart. And beware of assisting him for indeed you do not approve of his rule.'[3429]

فإنّهُ ذَهابُ الدِّينِ، وإيّاكُم ومَعُونَتَهُ فإنّكُم لا تَحمَدُونَ أمرَهُ.[٣٤٠١]

3062. **The Prophet (SAWA) said,** 'Whoever adheres to the ruler will be tempted away from the right course, and the closer one gets to the ruler the further away one is from Allah.'[3430]

٣٠٦٢. عنه ﷺ: مَن لَزِمَ السُّلطانَ اُفتُتِنَ، وما يَزدادُ مِنَ السُّلطانِ قُرباً إلّا ازدادَ مِنَ اللهِ بُعداً.[٣٤٠٢]

3063. **The Prophet (SAWA) said,** 'Beware of [going near] the ruler's gates and the retinue guarding them, for verily the nearest of you to the gates and retinue of the ruler is the farthest away from Allah, Mighty and Exalted. And whoever chooses the ruler over Allah, Mighty and Exalted, Allah will strip away his piety and will render him bewildered.'[3431]

٣٠٦٣. عنه ﷺ: إيّاكُم وأبوابَ السُّلطانِ وحَواشِيَها؛ فإنَّ أقرَبَكُم مِن أبوابِ السُّلطانِ وحَواشِيها أبعَدُكم مِنَ اللهِ عَزَّوجلَّ، ومَن آثَرَ السُّلطانَ على اللهِ عَزَّوجلَّ أذهَبَ اللهُ عَنهُ الوَرَعَ وجَعَلَهُ حَيران.[٣٤٠٣]

3064. **Imām ʿAlī (AS) said,** 'The one who associates with the ruler is like one who rides a lion – he is envied for his [high] position, and yet only he best knows his [unstable] situation.'[3432]

٣٠٦٤. الإمامُ عليٌّ ؑ: صاحِبُ السُّلطانِ كَراكِبِ الأسَدِ، يُغبَطُ بمَوقِعِهِ، وهُو أعلَمُ بمَوضِعِهِ.[٣٤٠٤]

3065. **Imām ʿAlī (AS) said,** 'Keep away from the sultan in order to be safe from the deception of Satan.'[3433]

٣٠٦٥. عنه ؑ: باعِدِ السُّلطانَ لِتَأمَنَ خُدَعَ الشَّيطانِ.[٣٤٠٥]

(See also: SOVEREIGNTY: section 1659)

(انظر: الملك: باب ١٦٥٩)

963. Denouncing the Subservience to a Tyrannical Ruler

٩٦٣ ـ ذَمُّ الخُضوعِ لِلسُّلطانِ الجائرِ

3066. **The Prophet (SAWA) said,** 'Whoever yields to a tyrannical ruler in any matter will be his companion in the Fire.'[3434]

٣٠٦٦. رسولُ اللهِ ﷺ: مَن خَفَّ لِسُلطانٍ جائرٍ في حاجَةٍ كانَ قَرِينَهُ في النارِ.[٣٤٠٦]

3067. **The Prophet (SAWA) said,** 'Whoever praises a tyrannical ruler, succumbs to him or humbles himself in front of him in a bid to secure his pleasure, will accompany him to the Fire.'[3435]

٣٠٦٧. عنه ﷺ: مَن مَدَحَ سُلطاناً جائراً وتَخَفَّفَ وتَضَعضَعَ لَهُ طَمَعاً فيهِ، كانَ قَرِينَهُ إلى النارِ.[٣٤٠٧]

3068. **Imām al-Ṣādiq (AS) said,** 'Any believer who is subservient to a ruler, or any other person who is

٣٠٦٨. الإمامُ الصّادقُ ؑ: أيُّما مُؤمِنٍ خَضَعَ

going against his faith in his bid to secure the worldly things that they may have in their grasp, Allah will reduce him to obscurity, will be angry with him and will relegate him to them. And whatever he manages to acquire and possess of the worldly things, Allah will strip them of their benediction.'[3436]

لِصاحِبِ سلطانٍ أو مَن يُخالِفُهُ علىٰ دِينِهِ طَلَباً لِما في يَدَيهِ، أخمَلَهُ اللهُ ومَقَتَهُ علَيهِ ووَكَلَهُ إلَيهِ، فإن هُو غَلَبَ عَلىٰ شَيءٍ مِن دُنياهُ وصارَ في يَدِهِ مِنهُ شَيءٌ، نَزَعَ اللهُ البَرَكَةَ مِنهُ.[٣٤٠٨]

(See also: VENERATION: section 1312)

(أُنظر) التعظيم: باب ١٣١٢.

964. The Virtue of a Just Ruler

٩٦٤ـ فَضلُ السُّلطانِ العادِلِ

3069. **The Prophet (SAWA) said,** 'The just and humble ruler is Allah's Shade and His Lance on this earth.'[3437]

٣٠٦٩. رسولُ اللهِ ﷺ: السُّلطانُ العادِلُ المُتَواضِعُ ظِلُّ اللهِ ورُمحُهُ في الأرضِ.[٣٤٠٩]

3070. **Imām ʿAlī (AS) said,** 'A [just] ruler is the guard of [the laws of] Allah on His earth.'[3438]

٣٠٧٠. الإمامُ عليٌّ عليه السلام: السُّلطانُ وَزَعَةُ اللهِ في أرضِهِ.[٣٤١٠]

3071. **Imām ʿAlī (AS) said,** 'Verily a divine authority safeguards your affairs, so offer him your obedience as is neither late nor reluctant. By Allah, you must do so else Allah will take away the rule of Islam from you, never to return it to you thereafter until it settles with others.'[3439]

٣٠٧١. عنه عليه السلام: إنَّ في سلطانِ اللهِ عِصمَةً لِأمرِكُم، فَأعطُوهُ طاعَتَكُم غَيرَ مُلَوَّمَةٍ (مُتَلَوِّمِينَ) ولا مُستَكرَهٍ بها، واللهِ لَتَفعَلُنَّ أو لَيَنقُلَنَّ اللهُ عَنكُم سلطانَ الإسلامِ، ثُمَّ لا يَنقُلُهُ إلَيكُم أبداً حتّىٰ يَأرِزَ الأمرُ إلىٰ غَيرِكُم.[٣٤١١]

(See also: COMMAND: 13)

(أُنظر) عنوان ١٣ «الإمارة».

197

ISLAM

الإسلامُ

965. Islam the Religion of Allah

٩٦٥ـ الإسلامُ دِينُ اللهِ

"Indeed, with Allah the religion is Islam."[3440]

﴿إنَّ الدِّينَ عِنْدَ اللهِ الْإسْلامُ﴾.[٣٤١٢]

"Should anyone follow a religion other than Islam, it shall never be accepted from him, and he will be among the losers in the Hereafter."[3441]

﴿وَمَنْ يَبْتَغِ غَيرَ الْإسْلامِ دِيْناً فَلَنْ يُقْبَلَ مِنْهُ وَهُوَ فِي الْآخِرَةِ مِنَ الخاسِرِينَ﴾.[٣٤١٣]

3072. **The Prophet (SAWA) said,** 'Islam excels and cannot be surpassed by anything else.'[3442]

٣٠٧٢. رسولُ اللهِ ﷺ: الإسلامُ يَعلُو ولا يُعلىٰ عَلَيهِ.[٣٤١٤]

3073. **The Prophet (SAWA) said,** 'He who performs good acts after having embraced Islam will not be punished for anything that he did in his pre-Islamic state, whilst he who continues to commit bad after having embraced Islam will be taken to account for everything from beginning to end.'[3443]

٣٠٧٣. عنه ﷺ: مَن أحسَنَ في الإسلامِ لَم يُؤاخَذْ بما عَمِلَ في الجاهليّةِ، ومَن أساءَ في الإسلامِ اُخِذَ بِالأوّلِ والآخِرِ.[٣٤١٥]

3074. **Imām ʿAlī (AS) said,** 'There is no distinction higher than Islam.'[3444]

٣٠٧٤. الإمامُ عليٌّ ﷺ: لا شَرَفَ أعلىٰ مِنَ الإسلامِ.[٣٤١٦]

3075. **Imām ʿAlī (AS) said,** 'Verily this Islam is the religion of Allah, which He has chosen for Himself, which He has developed before His eyes, which He has preferred for the best of all His creatures, and whose pillars he has founded upon His love. He has abased other religions by honouring it and humiliated other creeds before its sublimity.'[3445]

٣٠٧٥. عنه ﷺ: إنّ هذا الإسلامَ دِينُ اللهِ الذي اصطَفاهُ لِنفسِهِ، واصطَنَعَهُ على عَينِهِ، وأصفاهُ خِيَرَةَ خَلقِهِ، وأقامَ دَعائمَهُ على مَحَبّتِهِ، أذَلَّ الأديانَ بِعِزَّتِهِ، ووَضَعَ المِلَلَ بِرَفعِهِ.[٣٤١٧]

3076. **Imām ʿAlī (AS),** in his description of Islam, said, 'It is the brightest of all paths, the clearest of all passages, with towering minarets, brightly lit highways and illuminating lamps.'[3446]

٣٠٧٦. عنه ﷺ ـ في وَصفِ الإسلامِ ـ: فهُو أبلَجُ المَناهِجِ، وأوضَحُ (واضِحُ) الوَلائجِ، مُشرِفُ المَنارِ، مُشرِقُ الجَوادِّ، مُضِيءُ المَصابيحِ.[٣٤١٨]

966. The Meaning of Islam

٩٦٦ ـ مَعنَى الإسلامِ

3077. **The Prophet (SAWA) said,** 'Islam is that you submit your heart [to Allah], and that all Muslims feels safe from your tongue and your hand.'[3447]

٣٠٧٧. رسولُ اللهِ ﷺ: الإسلامُ أن تُسلِمَ قَلبَكَ ويَسلَمَ المُسلمونَ مِن لِسانِكَ ويَدِكَ.[٣٤١٩]

3078. **The Prophet (SAWA) said,** 'Islam is good manners.'[3448]

٣٠٧٨. عنه ﷺ: الإسلامُ حُسنُ الخُلقِ.[٣٤٢٠]

3079. **Imām ʿAlī (AS) said,** 'Verily Islam is submission, and submission is conviction, and conviction is certification of something, and certification is attestation, and attestation of

٣٠٧٩. الإمامُ عليٌّ ﷺ: الإسلامُ هُو التسليمُ، والتسليمُ هُو اليَقينُ، واليَقينُ هُو التَّصديقُ، والتصديقُ هُو الإقرارُ، والإقرارُ هُو الأداءُ،

something is fulfilment of it, and fulfilment is the performance of required acts.'[3449]

والأداءُ هُو العَملُ.٣٤٢١

3080. **Imām ʿAlī (AS) said,** 'The ultimate goal of Islam is submission and the ultimate of submission is gaining the blessed abode of Paradise'[3450]

٣٠٨٠. عنه ﷺ: غايَةُ الإسلامِ التسليمُ، غايَةُ التسليمِ الفَوزُ بدارِ النَّعيمِ.٣٤٢٢

(See also: FAITH: section 173)

(أنظر) الإيمان: باب ١٧٣.

967. Characteristics of a Muslim

٩٦٧ـ خَصائِصُ المُسلِمِ

3081. **The Prophet (SAWA) said,** 'A Muslim is the brother of a fellow Muslim - he neither wrongs him nor insults him.'[3451]

٣٠٨١. رسولُ اللهِ ﷺ: المُسلمُ أخُو المُسلِمِ، لا يَظلِمُهُ ولا يَشتُمُهُ.٣٤٢٣

3082. **The Prophet (SAWA) said,** 'A Muslim is the brother of a fellow Muslim - he neither betrays him nor lies to him nor deceives him.'[3452]

٣٠٨٢. عنه ﷺ: المُسلمُ أخُو المُسلمِ، لا يَخُونُهُ ولا يَكذِبُهُ ولا يَخذُلُهُ.٣٤٢٤

3083. **The Prophet (SAWA) said,** 'The Muslim is the mirror of a fellow Muslim.'[3453]

٣٠٨٣. عنه ﷺ: المُسلمُ مِرآةُ المُسلمِ.٣٤٢٥

3084. **The Prophet (SAWA) said,** 'He who wakes up in the morning unconcerned about the situations of fellow Muslims is not a Muslim.'[3454]

٣٠٨٤. عنه ﷺ: مَن أصبَحَ لا يَهتمُّ بِأُمورِ المُسلمينَ فلَيسَ بمُسلمٍ.٣٤٢٦

3085. **Imām ʿAlī (AS) said,** 'Repel treachery, for verily it repels Islam.'[3455]

٣٠٨٥. الإمامُ عليٌّ ﷺ: جانِبُوا الخِيانةَ، فإنّها مُجانِبَةُ الإسلامِ.٣٤٢٧

3086. **Imām ʿAlī (AS) said,** 'Whoever aids and abets wrongdoing towards a fellow Muslim is not a Muslim.'[3456]

٣٠٨٦. عنه ﷺ: مَن أعانَ على مُسلمٍ فقد بَرِئَ مِنَ الإسلامِ.٣٤٢٨

3087. **Imām al-Ṣādiq (AS) said,** 'A Muslim is he whose hand and tongue people feel safe from, whilst a believer (*mu'min*) is he whom people trust with their belongings and their lives.'[3457]

٣٠٨٧. الإمامُ الصّادقُ ﷺ: المُسلمُ مَن سَلِمَ الناسُ مِن يَدِهِ ولِسانِهِ، والمُؤمِنُ مَنِ ائتَمَنَهُ الناسُ على أموالِهِم وأنفُسِهِم.٣٤٢٩

968. Fundamentals of Islam

٩٦٨ـ قَواعِدُ الإسلامِ

3088. **The Prophet (SAWA) said,** 'Islam is naked, and its clothing is modesty, its adornment

٣٠٨٨. رسولُ اللهِ ﷺ: الإسلامُ عُريانٌ؛ فَلِباسُهُ الحَياءُ، وزِينَتُهُ الوَفاءُ، ومُرُوءَتُهُ العَمَلُ الصالِحُ،

loyalty, its valour good deeds, and its pillars piety. Everything has a foundation, and the foundation of Islam is the love for us, the *Ahl al-Bayt* (the household of the Prophet).'[3458]

وعِمادُهُ الوَرَعُ، ولِكُلِّ شَيءٍ أساسٌ وأساسُ الإسلامِ حُبُّنا أهلَ البَيتِ.[٣٤٣٠]

3089. **The Prophet (SAWA) said,** 'The foundation of Islam is love for me and love for my household.'[3459]

٣٠٨٩. عنه ﷺ: أساسُ الإسلامِ حُبّي وحُبُّ أهلِ بَيتِي.[٣٤٣١]

3090. **Imām 'Alī (AS) said,** 'Islam has seven fundamentals: the first is reason, on which perseverance is founded. The second is maintenance of one's honour and honest speech. The third is proper recitation of the Qur'an. The fourth is to love for the sake of Allah and to hate for the sake of Allah. The fifth is the right due to the household of the Prophet (SAWA) and their guardianship. The sixth is the right of one's fellow brothers and their protection. The seventh is close contact with people through fair means.'[3460]

٣٠٩٠. الإمامُ عليٌّ عليه السلام: قَواعِدُ الإسلامِ سَبعٌ: فَأُولَها العَقلُ وعلَيهِ بُنِيَ الصَّبرُ، والثانيّة: صَونُ العِرضِ وصِدقُ اللَّهجَةِ، والثالِثَةُ: تِلاوَةُ القُرآنِ علىٰ جِهَتِهِ، والرابِعَةُ: الحُبُّ في اللهِ والبُغضُ في اللهِ، والخامِسةُ: حَقُّ آلِ محمّدٍ ﷺ ومَعرِفَةُ وَلايَتِهِم، والسادِسَةُ: حَقُّ الإخوانِ والمُحاماةُ علَيهِم، والسّابِعَةُ: مُجاوَرَةُ الناسِ بالحُسنىٰ.[٣٤٣٢]

3091. **Imām al-Bāqir (AS) said,** 'Islam has been founded on five pillars: the establishment of prayer, the giving of the alms-tax, the fast of the month of Ramaḍān, the pilgrimage to the Sanctified House, and [the acknowledgment of] our guardianship, the *Ahl al-Bayt*.'[3461]

٣٠٩١. الإمامُ الباقرُ عليه السلام: بُنِيَ الإسلامُ علىٰ خَمسَ دَعائمَ: إقامِ الصَّلاةِ، وإيتاءِ الزَّكاةِ، وصَومِ شَهرِ رَمَضانَ، وحَجِّ البَيتِ الحَرامِ، والوَلايَةِ لَنا أهلَ البَيتِ.[٣٤٣٣]

3092. **Imām al-Riḍā (AS) said,** 'Verily *Imāma* (divinely appointed leadership of the twelve Imāms) is the ever-growing root of Islam as well as its lofty branch.'[3462]

٣٠٩٢. الإمامُ الرِّضا عليه السلام: إنَّ الإمامَةَ اُسُّ الإسلامِ النامي، وفَرعُهُ السامي.[٣٤٣٤]

198

GREETING OF PEACE (SALĀM)

السَّلامُ

969. The Greeting Between Muslims

٩٦٩ ـ تَحِيَّةُ المُسلِمينَ

"Their call therein will be, 'O Allah! Immaculate are You!' and their greeting therein will be, 'Peace!' and

﴿دَعْواهُم فِيها سُبْحانَكَ اللَّهُمَّ وَتَحِيَّتُهُمْ فِيها

their concluding call, 'All praise belongs to Allah, the Lord of the worlds.'[3463]

سَلَامٌ وَآخِرُ دَعْوَاهُمْ أَنِ الحَمْدُ للهِ رَبِّ العالَمِينَ﴾.[٣٤٣٥]

(See also: Qur'an 4:86, 11:69, 15:52, 16:32, 19:47-62, 24:61, 25:63, 25:75, 33:44, 51:25, 56:26)

(أُنظر) النساء: ٨٦، هود: ٦٩، الحجر: ٥٢، النحل: ٣٢، مريم: ٤٧، ٦٢، النور: ٦١، الفرقان: ٦٣، ٧٥، الأحزاب: ٤٤، الذاريات: ٢٥، الواقعة: ٢٦.

3093. **The Prophet (SAWA) said,** 'The salutation of peace is the greeting towards members of our own creed, and an extension of safety towards people of other creeds living in Muslim lands.'[3464]

٣٠٩٣. رسولُ اللهِ ﷺ: السَّلامُ تَحِيَّةٌ لِمِلَّتِنا، وأمانٌ لِذِمَّتِنا.[٣٤٣٦]

3094. **The Prophet (SAWA) said,** 'The most miserly of all people is he who withholds his greeting.'[3465]

٣٠٩٤. عنه ﷺ: إنَّ أبخَلَ الناسِ مَن بَخِلَ بِالسلامِ.[٣٤٣٧]

3095. **The Prophet (SAWA) said,** 'Spread peace (greetings) around and the good within your own house will increase.'[3466]

٣٠٩٥. عنه ﷺ: أفشِ السلامَ يَكثُر خَيرُ بَيتِكَ.[٣٤٣٨]

3096. **Imām al-Bāqir (AS) said,** 'Verily Allah loves the feeding of food [to others] and the spreading of peace [greetings].'[3467]

٣٠٩٦. الإمامُ الباقرُ ؑ: إنَّ اللهَ يُحِبُّ إطعامَ الطَّعامِ، وإفشاءَ السَّلامِ.[٣٤٣٩]

3097. **Imām al-Ṣādiq (AS) said,** 'The greeting of peace comes before speech.'[3468]

٣٠٩٧. الإمامُ الصّادقُ ؑ: السَّلامُ قَبلَ الكلامِ.[٣٤٤٠]

3098. **Imām al-Ṣādiq (AS) narrated** from his forefathers (AS) that the Prophet (SAWA) said, 'Do not answer the one who begins to talk before having greeted you with peace', and he (AS) said, 'Do not allow anybody to partake of your food until they have greeted with peace.'[3469]

٣٠٩٨. الخصالُ عَن إسماعيلَ بن أبي زيادٍ عَن أبي عبد الله ؑ، عن آبائه ؑ: قالَ رسولُ اللهِ ﷺ: مَن بَدَأ بِالكَلامِ قَبلَ السلامِ فلا تُجيبُوهُ. وقالَ ؑ: لا تَدعُ إلىٰ طَعامِكَ أحَداً حتّى يُسَلِّمَ.[٣٤٤١]

970. The Virtue of Initiating the Greeting

٩٧٠ ـ فَضلُ الابتِداءِ بِالسَّلامِ

3099. **The Prophet (SAWA) said,** 'Verily the nearest people to Allah and His Messenger are those who initiate the greeting of peace.'[3470]

٣٠٩٩. رسولُ اللهِ ﷺ: إنَّ أولَى الناسِ بِاللهِ وبرسولِهِ مَن بَدَأ بِالسلامِ.[٣٤٤٢]

3100. **The Prophet (SAWA) said,** 'The initiator of the greeting is not prone to arrogance.'[3471]

٣١٠٠. عنه ﷺ: البادِئُ بِالسلامِ بَرِيءٌ مِنَ الكِبرِ.[٣٤٤٣]

3101. **Imām ʿAlī (AS) said,** ‘The greeting is rewarded the worth of seventy good deeds, sixty-nine of which are rewarded to the initiator and one to the reciprocator [of the greeting].’[3472]

٣١٠١ . الإمامُ عليٌّ ﷺ : السلامُ سَبعونَ حَسَنةً، تِسعَةٌ وسِتُّونَ لِلمُبتَدي وواحِدَةٌ لِلرّادِّ.[٣٤٤٤]

971. Enjoinment of Greeting Upon Entering One's House

٩٧١ـ الحَثُّ عَلى التَّسليمِ عِندَ دُخولِ البَيتِ

“So when you enter houses, greet yourselves with a salutation from Allah, blessed and good.”[3473]

﴿فَإذَا دَخَلْتُم بُيُوتاً فَسَلِّمُوا عَلَىٰ أنْفُسِكُم تَحِيَّةً مِن عِندِ اللهِ مُبارَكَةً طَيِّبَةً﴾.[٣٤٤٥]

3102. **The Prophet (SAWA) said,** ‘When anyone of you enters his own house, he should greet with peace, for verily it brings down benediction, and angels come to keep him company.’[3474]

٣١٠٢ . رسولُ اللهِ ﷺ : إذا دَخَلَ أحَدُكُم بَيتَهُ فَلْيُسَلِّمْ؛ فإنَّهُ يَنزِلُهُ البَرَكَةُ، وتُؤنِسُهُ المَلائكةُ.[٣٤٤٦]

972. The Obligation of Returning a Greeting

٩٧٢ـ وُجوبُ رَدِّ السَّلامِ

“When you are greeted with a salute, greet with a better one than it, or return it; indeed Allah takes account of all things.”[3475]

﴿وَإذا حُيِّيْتُمْ بِتَحِيَّةٍ فَحَيُّوا بِأحْسَنَ مِنْها أوْ رُدُّوها إنَّ اللهَ كانَ عَلَىٰ كُلِّ شَيءٍ حَسِيباً﴾.[٣٤٤٧]

3103. **The Prophet (SAWA) said,** ‘Greeting with peace is a voluntary act whereas returning it is an obligation.’[3476]

٣١٠٣ . رسولُ اللهِ ﷺ : السلامُ تَطَوُّعٌ، والرَّدُّ فَرِيضَةٌ.[٣٤٤٨]

973. The Etiquette of Greeting

٩٧٣ـ أدَبُ السَّلامِ

3104. **The Prophet (SAWA) said,** ‘The young should greet the old, a single individual should greet two together, the fewer number of people should greet the larger number, the person on horseback should greet the one on foot, the person walking should greet the one standing, and the person standing should greet the one sitting.’[3477]

٣١٠٤ . رسولُ اللهِ ﷺ : يُسَلِّمُ الصغيرُ عَلى الكبيرِ، ويُسَلِّمُ الواحِدُ علىٰ الاثنَينِ، ويُسَلِّمُ القَليلُ علىٰ الكثيرِ، ويُسَلِّمُ الراكِبُ علىٰ الماشي، ويُسَلِّمُ المارُّ علىٰ القائمِ، ويُسَلِّمُ القائمُ علىٰ القاعِدِ.[٣٤٤٩]

3105. **The Prophet (SAWA) said,** ‘There are five things that I will never leave until death: ... and

٣١٠٥ . عنه ﷺ : خَمسٌ لا أدَعُهُنَّ حَتّى المَماتِ:

greeting the young, in order that it may remain a practice after me.'[3478]

...والتَّسليمُ علىٰ الصِّبيانِ لِتكونَ سُنَّةً مِن بَعدي.[٣٤٥٠]

3106. **Imām al-Bāqir (AS) said,** 'Do not extend the greeting of peace ... and to those who drink alcohol, nor to chess and dice players, nor to an effeminate person, nor to a poet who slanders chaste women of fornication, and nor to someone performing his prayer - and that is because the person praying cannot return the greeting, for verily the initiation of the greeting on the part of the greeter is voluntary whereas returning the greeting is obligatory. Nor [greet] the usurer, nor someone who is sitting in the lavatory, nor someone taking a bath, and nor an outrightly corrupt person who openly commits immoral acts.'[3479]

٣١٠٦. الإمامُ الباقرُ عليه السلام: لا تُسَلِّموا علىٰ مَوائِدِ شُرّابِ الخَمرِ، ولا علىٰ صاحِبِ الشِّطرَنجِ والنَّردِ، ولا علىٰ المُخَنَّثِ، ولا علىٰ الشاعِرِ الذي يَقذِفُ المُحصَناتِ، ولا علىٰ المُصَلّي؛ وذلكَ لأنَّ المُصَلّيَ لايَستَطيعُ أن يَرُدَّ السلامَ، لأنَّ التَّسليمَ مِنَ المُسَلِّمِ تَطَوُّعٌ والرَّدَّ علَيهِ فَريضَةٌ، ولا علىٰ آكِلِ الرِّبا، ولا علىٰ رَجُلٍ جالِسٍ علىٰ غائطٍ، ولا علىٰ الذي في الحَمّامِ، ولا علىٰ الفاسِقِ المُعلِنِ بِفِسقِهِ.[٣٤٥١]

3107. **Imām al-Ṣādiq (AS) narrated,** 'The Prophet (SAWA) used to greet women and they used to return his greeting. The Commander of the Faithful (AS) also used to greet women, but he used to dislike greeting young [unmarried] girls and used to say, 'I fear lest their voices may be pleasing to me, whence I would end up with more [consequence] than the reward I anticipated [from the greeting].'[3480]

٣١٠٧. الإمامُ الصّادقُ عليه السلام: كانَ رسولُ اللهِ صلى الله عليه وآله يُسَلِّمُ عَلَى النِّساءِ ويَردُدْنَ علَيهِ، وكانَ أميرُ المؤمنينَ عليه السلام يُسَلِّمُ علىٰ النِّساءِ، وكانَ يَكرَهُ أن يُسَلِّمَ علىٰ الشّابَّةِ مِنهُنَّ، ويقولُ: أتَخَوَّفُ أن يُعجِبَني صَوتُها فَيَدخُلَ عَلَيَّ أكثَرُ مِمّا طَلَبتُ مِنَ الأجرِ.[٣٤٥٢]

199

SUBMISSION

التَّسليمُ

974. Submission to the Will of Allah

٩٧٤ـ التَّسليمُ لإرادَةِ اللهِ

"But no, by your Lord! They will not believe until they make you a judge in their disputes, then do not find in

﴿فَلَا وَرَبِّكَ لَا يُؤْمِنُونَ حَتَّىٰ يُحَكِّمُوكَ فِيمَا شَجَرَ بَيْنَهُمْ ثُمَّ لَا يَجِدُوا فِي أَنفُسِهِمْ حَرَجاً

their hearts any dissent to your verdict and submit in full submission.'[3481]

مِمّا قَضَيتَ ويُسَلِّمُوا تَسْلِيماً﴾.[٣٤٥٣]

3108. It is narrated in *Biḥār al-Anwār* that Allah, most High, revealed to Prophet David (AS) saying, 'I want [something] and you want [something else], and verily only My will is done. Therefore, if you submit to what I want, I will suffice you in what you want. If you do not submit to My will, however, I will exhaust you in your quest for what you want, then only what I want will be.'[3482]

٣١٠٨. بحار الأنوار: أوحَى اللهُ تعالىٰ إلىٰ داوودَ ﷺ: تُرِيدُ وأُرِيدُ، وإنّما يَكونُ ما أُرِيدُ، فإن سَلَّمتَ لِما أُريدُ كَفَيتُكَ ما تُرِيدُ، وإن لَم تُسَلِّم لِما أُرِيدُ أتعَبتُكَ فيما تُرِيدُ، ثُمّ لا يَكونُ إلّا ما أُرِيدُ.[٣٤٥٤]

3109. **Imām al-Bāqir (AS) said,** 'Out of all that Allah has created, the worthiest person of submission to Allah's decree is he who knows Allah.'[3483]

٣١٠٩. الإمامُ الباقرُ ﷺ: أحَقُّ مَن خَلَقَ اللهُ بِالتَّسليمِ لِما قَضَى اللهُ، مَن عَرَفَ اللهَ.[٣٤٥٥]

3110. **Imām al-Bāqir (AS) said,** 'Indeed we desire for ourselves and those we love to be blessed with well-being, but when Allah's command comes, we submit to what He loves.'[3484]

٣١١٠. عنه ﷺ: إنّا لَنُحِبُّ أن نُعافىٰ فِيمَن نُحِبُّ، فإذا جاءَ أمرُ اللهِ سَلَّمنا فيما يُحِبُّ.[٣٤٥٦] [٣٤٥٧]

3111. **Imām al-Ṣādiq (AS)** was once asked how a believer may ascertain that he is indeed a believer, to which he replied, 'Through submission to Allah and satisfaction with whatever source of happiness or discontent that comes his way.'[3485]

٣١١١. الإمامُ الصّادقُ ﷺ ـ لَمّا سُئلَ: بِأيِّ شَيء عَلِمَ المؤمنُ أنّهُ مُؤمِنٌ؟ ـ: بِالتَّسليمِ للهِ، والرِّضا بما وَرَدَ علَيهِ مِن سُرورٍ وسَخَطٍ.[٣٤٥٨]

3112. **Imām al-Ṣādiq (AS) said,** 'The Prophet (SAWA) never used to utter the words 'if only it happened otherwise...' with regards to anything that had already passed.'[3486]

٣١١٢. عنه ﷺ: لَم يَكُن رسولُ اللهِ ﷺ يقولُ لِشيءٍ قد مَضىٰ: لو كانَ غَيرَهُ![٣٤٥٩]

3113. **Imām al-Ṣādiq (AS) said,** 'When a servant says, *'Whatever Allah wills, there is no power and no strength except in Allah'*, Allah says, 'O My angels, My servant has submitted so assist him, hasten to him and grant his request.'[3487]

٣١١٣. عنه ﷺ: إذا قالَ العبدُ: ما شاءَ اللهُ لا حَولَ ولا قُوَّةَ إلّا بِاللهِ، قالَ اللهُ: مَلائكَتي اِستَسلَمَ عَبدي أعِينُوهُ، أدرِكُوهُ، اقضُوا حاجَتَهُ.[٣٤٦٠]

200

LISTENING

الاستماع

975. The Virtue of Attentive Ears

٩٧٥ ـ فَضلُ الأسماعِ الواعِيَةِ

3114. **Imām ʿAlī (AS) said,** 'Even if you are not an articulate scholar, at least be an attentive listener.'[3488]

٣١١٤ . الإمامُ عليٌّ عليه السلام : إذا لَم تَكُن عالِماً ناطِقاً فَكُن مُستَمِعاً واعِياً . [٣٤٦١]

3115. **Imām ʿAlī (AS) said,** 'Indeed the most heedful of all ears is that which is attentive to and accepting of a reminder.'[3489]

٣١١٥ . عنه عليه السلام : ألا إنَّ أسمَعَ الأسماعِ ما وَعىٰ اتَّذكيرَ وقَبِلَهُ . [٣٤٦٢]

976. Those whose Ears have been Sealed

٩٧٦ ـ مَن حُجِبَ سَمعُهُ

"And they will say, 'Had we listened or applied reason, we would not have been among the inmates of the Blaze.'"[3490]

﴿وَقالُوا لَو كُنَّا نَسْمَعُ أوْ نَعْقِلُ ما كُنَّا فِي صْحابِ السَّعِيرِ﴾ . [٣٤٦٣]

3116. **Imām ʿAlī (AS) said,** 'Not every man with a heart is understanding, nor every man with an ear a listener, and nor every man with eyes able to see.'[3491]

٣١١٦ . الإمامُ عليٌّ عليه السلام : ما كُلُّ ذِي قَلبٍ بِلَبِيبٍ ، لا كُلُّ ذِي سَمعٍ بِسَمِيعٍ ، ولا كُلُّ ناظِرٍ بِبَصيرٍ . [٣٤٦٤]

977. Effective Listening

٩٧٧ ـ حُسنُ الاستِماعِ

3117. **Imām ʿAlī (AS) said,** 'Accustom your ear to listen effectively, and do not listen to anything that will not benefit your progress.'[3492]

٣١١٧ . الإمامُ عليٌّ عليه السلام : عَوِّدْ اُذُنَكَ حُسنَ لاستِماعِ، ولا تُصغِ إلىٰ ما لا يَزِيدُ في صَلاحِكَ ستِماعُهُ . [٣٤٦٥]

3118. **Imām ʿAlī (AS) said,** 'The one who listens to the remembrance of Allah in turn remembers [Him].'[3493]

٣١١٨ . عنه عليه السلام : سامِعُ ذِكرِ اللهِ ذاكِرٌ . [٣٤٦٦]

3119. **Imām ʿAlī (AS) said,** 'Whoever listens effectively reaps its benefits immediately.'[3494]

٣١١٩ . عنه عليه السلام : مَن أحسَنَ الاستِماعَ تَعَجَّلَ لانتِفاعَ . [٣٤٦٧]

978. The Obligation Incumbent On the Hearing

٩٧٨ ـ ما فُرِضَ عَلَى السَّمعِ

"Do not follow that of which you have no knowledge. Indeed the hearing, the eyesight, and the heart – all of these are accountable."[3495]

﴿وَلا تَقْفُ ما لَيسَ لَكَ بِهِ عِلْمٌ إنَّ السَّمْعَ والبَصَرَ والفُؤادَ كُلُّ أُولٰئكَ كانَ عَنْهُ مَسؤولا﴾.[٣٤٦٨]

3120. **Imām ʿAlī (AS) said,** 'The obligation incumbent upon the hearing is that it not be used for acts of disobedience, for Allah, Mighty and Exalted, has said, *"Certainly He has sent down to you in the Book that when you hear Allah's signs being disbelieved and derided, do not sit with them until they engage in some other discourse, or else you [too] will be like them"*[3496] [3497].

٣١٢٠ . الإمامُ عليٌّ عليه السلام: فَفَرَضَ على السَّمعِ أن لا تُصغِيَ بِهِ إلى المَعاصِي ، فقالَ عَزَّوجلَّ : ﴿وَقَدْ نَزَّلَ عَلَيْكُم فِي الكِتابِ أنْ إذا سَمِعْتُم آياتِ اللهِ يُكْفَرُ بِها وَيُسْتَهزأُ بِها فَلا تَقْعُدُوا مَعَهُم حَتَّىٰ يَخُوضُوا فِي حَدِيثٍ غَيرِهِ إنَّكُم إذاً مِثْلُهُم إنَّ اللهَ جامِعُ المُنافِقِينَ والكافِرِينَ فِي جَهَنَّمَ جَمِيعاً﴾.[٣٤٦٩]

201

THE NAME

الأسماءُ

979. Choosing Good Names

٩٧٩ ـ اختِيارُ الأسماءِ الحَسَنَةِ

3121. **The Prophet (SAWA) said,** 'Choose good names for yourselves, for verily you will be called by them on the Day of Resurrection: Come O *x son of x* towards your light, or: O *x son of x*, there is no light for you.'[3498]

٣١٢١ . رسولُ اللهِ صلى الله عليه وآله : استَحسِنُوا أسماءَكُم ؛ فإنّكُم تُدعَوْنَ بها يَومَ القِيامَةِ : قُمْ يا فُلانَ ابنَ فُلانٍ إلىٰ نورِكَ ، وقُمْ يا فُلانَ ابنَ فُلانٍ لا نُورَ لَكَ .[٣٤٧٠]

3122. **The Prophet (SAWA) said,** 'Name your children after the prophets.'[3499]

٣١٢٢ . عنه صلى الله عليه وآله : سَمُّوا أولادَكُم أسماءَ الأنبياءِ .[٣٤٧١]

3123. **Imām al-Ṣādiq (AS)** was once asked with regards to naming [one's children] after the Imāms (AS) and whether there was any benefit in doing so, to which he replied, 'Of course, by Allah, and is religion anything but love?! Allah has said, *"Say, 'If you love Allah, then follow me; Allah will love you and forgive you your sins, and Allah is all-forgiving, all-merciful.'"*[3500]

٣١٢٣ . الإمامُ الصّادقُ عليه السلام ـ لَمّا سُئلَ عنِ التَّسميَةِ بِأسماءِ الأئمّةِ ، أفِي ذلك نَفعٌ ؟ ـ : إي واللهِ ، وهَلِ الدِّينُ إلّا الحُبُّ ؟! قالَ اللهُ : ﴿إنْ كُنْتُمْ تُحِبُّونَ اللهَ فاتَّبِعُوني يُحبِبْكُمُ اللهُ ويَغفِرْ لَكُمْ ذُنُوبَكُم﴾ .[٣٤٧٢] [٣٤٧٣]

3124. **Imām al-Kāẓim (AS) said,** 'The very first act of kindness of a man towards his son is to give him a good name, so keep good names for your children.'[3501]

٣١٢٤ . الإمامُ الكاظمُ عليه السلام : أوَّلُ ما يَبَرُّ الرَّجُلُ وَلَدَهُ أن يُسَمِّيَهُ بِاسمٍ حَسَنٍ، فَلْيُحَسِّنْ أحَدُكُمُ اسمَ وَلَدِهِ.[٣٤٧٤]

(See also: PARENT AND CHILD: section 1892)

(أُنظر) الوالد والولد: باب ١٨٩٢.

980. Changing Ugly Names

٩٨٠ ـ استِبدالُ الأسماءِ القَبِيحَةِ

3125. **Imām al-Bāqir (AS) narrated,** 'The Prophet (SAWA) used to change ugly names of people and places [to good names].'[3502]

٣١٢٥ . الإمامُ الباقرُ عليه السلام : كانَ رسولُ اللهِ ﷺ يُغَيِّرُ الأسماءَ القَبيحَةَ في الرِّجالِ والبُلدانِ.[٣٤٧٥]

202

THE NAMES OF ALLAH

أسماءُ اللهِ

981. In the Name of Allah, the All-Beneficent, the All-Merciful

٩٨١ ـ بِسمِ اللهِ الرّحمٰنِ الرَّحيمِ

"It is from Solomon, and it begins in the name of Allah, the All-Beneficent, the All-Merciful."[3503]

﴿إنَّهُ مِنْ سُلَيْمانَ وَإنَّهُ بِسْمِ اللهِ الرَّحْمٰنِ الرَّحِيْمِ﴾.[٣٤٧٦]

3126. **The Prophet (SAWA) said,** 'The phrase 'In the Name of Allah, the All-Beneficent, the All-Merciful' is the key and the opening to every book.'[3504]

٣١٢٦ . رسولُ اللهِ ﷺ : بِسمِ اللهِ الرحمٰنِ الرحيمِ مِفتاحُ كُلِّ كِتابٍ.[٣٤٧٧]

3127. **The Prophet (SAWA) said,** 'Every matter of importance that is not begun with the phrase 'In the Name of Allah, the All-Beneficent, the All-Merciful' is cut short.'[3505]

٣١٢٧ . عنه ﷺ : كُلُّ أمرٍ ذِي بالٍ لا يُبدَأُ فِيهِ بِبِسمِ اللهِ [الرحمٰنِ][٣٤٧٨] الرحيمِ أقطَعُ.[٣٤٧٩]

3128. **Imām al-Ṣādiq (AS) said,** 'Never leave out the phrase 'In the Name of Allah, the All-Beneficent, the All-Merciful', even if it is followed by poetry.'[3506]

٣١٢٨ . الإمامُ الصّادقُ عليه السلام : لا تَدَعْ بِسمِ اللهِ الرحمٰنِ الرحيمِ وإن كانَ بَعدَهُ شِعرٌ.[٣٤٨٠]

3129. **Imām al-Ṣādiq (AS) said,** 'It may sometimes happen that one of our followers (*shī'a)* may leave out the phrase 'In the Name of Allah, the All-Beneficent, the All-Merciful' before a matter, so Allah tests him with a mishap in order to remind him to thank Allah, Blessed and most High, and to praise Him.'[3507]

٣١٢٩ . عنه ﷺ : لَرُبَّما تَرَكَ بَعضُ شِيعَتِنا فـي افتِتاحِ أمرِهِ بِسمِ اللهِ الرحمٰنِ الرحيمِ ، فَـيَمتَحِنُهُ اللهُ بِمَكرُوهٍ لِيُنَبِّهَهُ علىٰ شُكرِ اللهِ تباركَ وتـعالىٰ والثَّناءِ علَيهِ .[٣٤٨١]

982. Allah's Greatest Name

٩٨٢ ـ اسمُ اللهِ الأعظَمُ

3130. **Imām al-Bāqir (AS) said,** 'Verily Allah's greatest Name is composed of seventy-three letters, of which Āsaf [b. Barkhiyya] had but one, with the utterance of which he caused the earth between himself and Bilqīs's throne to sink until he got hold of the throne, and after which [he caused] the earth to return to its former state faster than the blink of an eye. And we [the *Ahl al-Bayt*] have seventy-two letters from the greatest Name, and Allah, Blessed and most High, has exclusive possession of one letter of it with Him in His knowledge of the Unseen.'[3508]

٣١٣٠ . الإمامُ الباقرُ ﷺ : إنَّ اسمَ اللهِ الأعظَمَ علىٰ ثلاثةٍ وسَبعينَ حَرفاً ، وإنّما كانَ عندَ آصَفَ مِنها حَرفٌ واحِدٌ فتَكَلَّمَ بهِ فَخَسَفَ بِالأرضِ ما بَينَهُ وبينَ سَريرِ بِلقِيسَ حتّىٰ تَناوَلَ السَّريرَ بِيَدِهِ ، ثُمّ عادَتِ الأرضُ كما كانَت أسرَعَ مِن طَرفَةِ العَينِ ، ونحنُ عِندَنا مِنَ الاسمِ الأعظَمِ اثنانِ وسَبعونَ حَرفاً ، وحَرفٌ عِندَ اللهِ تَبارَكَ وتعالىٰ استَأثَرَ بهِ في عِلمِ الغَيبِ عِندَهُ ، ولا حَولَ ولا قُوَّةَ إلّا بِاللهِ العَلِيِّ العظيمِ .[٣٤٨٢]

203

Sunnah [Tradition]

السُّنَّة

983. Enjoinment of Adhering to the Prophet's Practices

٩٨٣ ـ الحَثُّ عَلىٰ لُزومِ سُنَّةِ النَّبِيِّ

3131. **The Prophet (SAWA) said,** 'When someone adherent to [the Prophet's] practises does something good it is accepted from him, and even if he makes a mistake, he is forgiven for it.'[3509]

٣١٣١ . رسولُ اللهِ ﷺ : صاحِبُ السُّنَّةِ إن عَمِلَ خَيراً قُبِلَ مِنهُ ، وإن خَلَطَ غُفِرَ لَهُ .[٣٤٨٣]

3132. **Imām Zayn al-ʿĀbidīn (AS) said,** 'The best of deeds in the sight of Allah are those that are performed according to the *Sunnah*, even if they be few in number.'[3510]

٣١٣٢. الإمامُ زينُ العابدينَ ﷺ: إنَّ أفضَلَ الأعمالِ عندَ اللهِ ما عُمِلَ بِالسُّنَّةِ وإن قَلَّ.[٣٤٨٤]

984. The Recompense of One Who Establishes a Habitual Practice

٩٨٤ـ جَزاءُ مَن سَنَّ سُنَّةً

3133. **The Prophet (SAWA) said,** 'Whoever establishes a good habitual practice that people follow even after him, he will get his own reward for it as well as the like of their reward for performing it, without any decrease in their reward thereof. And whoever establishes an evil habitual practice that is followed by people after him, he will be responsible for the burden of his own sin as well as the burden of their sins, without any decrease in their burdens thereof.'[3511]

٣١٣٣. رسولُ اللهِ ﷺ: مَن سَنَّ سُنَّةً حَسَنَةً عُمِلَ بها مِن بَعدِهِ كانَ لَهُ أجرُهُ ومِثلُ أُجورِهِم مِن غَيرِ أن يَنقُصَ مِن أُجورِهِم شيئاً، ومَن سَنَّ سُنَّةً سَيِّئَةً فَعُمِلَ بها بَعدَهُ كانَ علَيهِ وِزرُهُ ومِثلُ أوزارِهِم مِن غَيرِ أن يَنقُصَ مِن أوزارِهِم شيئاً.[٣٤٨٥]

985. Prohibition of Discontinuing a Good Practice

٩٨٥ـ النَّهيُ عَن نَقضِ السُّنَّةِ الصّالِحَةِ

3134. **Imām ʿAlī (AS)** wrote in one of his letters to al-Ashtar, when he appointed him governor of Egypt, 'Do not discontinue a good practice that the pioneers of this community acted upon, by virtue of which there was general unity and through which the subjects prospered. Do not innovate a practice that will infringe on these earlier practices in any way, for then the reward of those who had laid them down will continue, whereas you will be the one to bear the burden of breaching them.'[3512]

٣١٣٤. الإمامُ عليٌّ ﷺ ـ في كتابٍ لَهُ إلى الأشترِ لَمّا وَلّاهُ مِصرَ ـ: لا تَنقُضْ سُنَّةً صالِحَةً عَمِلَ بها صُدورُ هذهِ الأُمَّةِ، واجتَمَعَت بها الأُلفَةُ، وصَلَحَت علَيها الرَّعِيَّةُ، ولا تُحدِثَنَّ سُنَّةً تَضُرُّ بِشَيءٍ مِن ماضي تِلكَ السُّنَنِ، فيَكونَ الأجرُ لِمَن سَنَّها، والوِزرُ علَيكَ بما نَقَضتَ مِنها.[٣٤٨٦]

204

STAYING AWAKE AT NIGHT

السّهر

986. Staying Awake at Night

٩٨٦ ـ السَّهَرُ

3135. **The Prophet (SAWA) said,** 'There is no need to stay awake at night except in three instances: when staying awake to recite the Qur'an, to gain knowledge, and for a bride to be offered to her husband.'[3513]

٣١٣٥. رسولُ اللهِ ﷺ: لا سَهَرَ إلّا في ثلاثٍ: مُتَهَجِّدٍ بالقرآنِ، وفي طَلَبِ العِلمِ، أو عَروسٍ تُهدىٰ إلى زَوجِها.٣٤٨٧

3136. **The Prophet (SAWA) said,** 'There is no need to stay up at night past the last *'ishā'* prayer except in the case of two people: the person performing prayers, and the traveller.'[3514]

٣١٣٦. عنه ﷺ: لا سَهَرَ بعدَ العِشاءِ الآخِرَةِ إلّا لِأحَدِ رَجُلَينِ: مُصَلٍّ أو مُسافِرٍ.٣٤٨٨

3137. **Imām 'Alī (AS) said,** 'Staying awake at night is the garden of those who yearn [for Allah].'[3515]

٣١٣٧. الإمامُ عليٌّ ﷺ: السَّهَرُ رَوضَةُ المُشتاقِينَ.٣٤٨٩

3138. **Imām 'Alī (AS) said,** 'Staying awake at night engaged in acts of obedience to Allah is the springtime of the friends of Allah and the garden of the good-fortuned.'[3516]

٣١٣٨. عنه ﷺ: سَهَرُ الليلِ في طاعَةِ اللهِ رَبيعُ الأولياءِ ورَوضَةُ السُّعَداءِ.٣٤٩٠

3139. **Imām 'Alī (AS) said,** 'The best of worship is for the eyes to remain awake engaged in the remembrance of Allah, Glory be to Him.'[3517]

٣١٣٩. عنه ﷺ: أفضَلُ العِبادَةِ سَهَرُ العُيونِ بذِكرِ اللهِ سبحانَهُ.٣٤٩١

3140. **Imām 'Alī (AS) said,** 'So be conscious of your duty to Allah, O servants of Allah, with the caution of a wise man whose heart is preoccupied with reflection [about the Hereafter], whose body the fear [of Allah] has afflicted with pain, and whose engagement in the night prayer has turned his already short sleep into wakefulness.'[3518]

٣١٤٠. عنه ﷺ: فاتَّقُوا اللهَ عِبادَ اللهِ تَقِيَّةَ ذِي لُبٍّ، شَغَلَ التَّفَكُّرُ قَلبَهُ، وأنصَبَ الخَوفُ بَدَنَهُ، وأسهَرَ التَّهَجُّدُ غِرارَ نَومِهِ.٣٤٩٢

987. Enjoinment of Remaining Awake on Specific Nights

٩٨٧ـ الحَثُّ عَلى إحياءِ هٰذِهِ اللَّيالي

3141. **The Prophet (SAWA) said,** 'He who remains awake on the eve of *ʿīd al-fiṭr*, *ʿīd al-aḍḥā* and on the eve of the 15th of Shaʿbān, his heart will not die on the Day when hearts shall die.'[3519]

٣١٤١. رسولُ اللهِ ﷺ: مَن أحيا لَيلةَ العِيدِ ولَيلةَ النِّصفِ مِن شَعبانَ، لَم يَمُتْ قَلبُهُ يَومَ تَموتُ القُلوبُ.[٣٤٩٣]

3142. **Imām al-Riḍā (AS) narrated,** 'The Commander of the Faithful (AS) did not used to sleep at all on three nights: the 23rd night of the month of Ramaḍān, the eve of *ʿīd al-fiṭr*, and the eve of the 15th of Shaʿbān. And these are the nights when sustenance is allotted, and prescribed times of death and all that is to happen in that year is decreed.'[3520]

٣١٤٢. الإمامُ الرِّضا (عليه السلام): كانَ أميرُ المؤمنينَ (عليه السلام) لا يَنامُ ثلاثَ لَيالٍ: لَيلةَ ثلاثٍ وعِشرينَ مِن شَهرِ رَمَضانَ، ولَيلةَ الفِطرِ، ولَيلةَ النِّصفِ مِن شَعبانَ، وفيها تُقسَمُ الأرزاقُ والآجالُ وما يَكونُ في السَّنَةِ.[٣٤٩٤]

205

THE CHIEF

السَّيِّدُ

988. Characteristics of the Chief

٩٨٨ـ خَصائِصُ السَّيِّدِ

3143. **The Prophet (SAWA) said,** 'The chief of a people should serve them.'[3521]

٣١٤٣. رسولُ اللهِ ﷺ: سَيِّدُ القَومِ خادِمُهُم.[٣٤٩٥]

3144. **Imām al-Ḥusayn (AS)** when asked by his father about what chiefdom involves, replied, '[The ability] To make one's tribe flourish, and [the capacity] to bear the burden of their losses.'[3522]

٣١٤٤. الإمامُ الحسينُ (عليه السلام) ـ لَمّا سَألَهُ أبوهُ عنِ السُّؤدُدِ ـ: إحشاشُ العَشيرَةِ، واحتِمالُ الجَريرَةِ.[٣٤٩٦]

989. Requirements of Chiefdom

٩٨٩ـ ما يوجِبُ السُّؤدَدَ

3145. **Imām ʿAlī (AS) said,** 'Chiefdom is achieved through tolerating hardships.'[3523]

٣١٤٥. الإمامُ عليٌّ (عليه السلام): بِاحتِمالِ المُؤَنِ يَجِبُ السُّؤدُدُ.[٣٤٩٧]

3146. **Imām ʿAlī (AS) said,** 'The truly noble one is he who has been ennobled by his knowledge,

٣١٤٦. عنه (عليه السلام): الشَّريفُ كُلُّ الشَّريفِ مَن شَرَّفَهُ

and true chiefdom belongs to he who is wary of his duty to Allah, his Lord.'[3524]

عِلمُهُ، والسُّؤدُدُ حَقُّ السُّؤدُدِ لِمَنِ اتَّقىٰ اللهَ رَبَّهُ.[٣٤٩٨]

3147. **Imām ʿAlī (AS) said,** 'The virtue characteristic of chiefs is the beauty of their worship.'[3525]

٣١٤٧. عنه ﷺ: فَضيلَةُ السادَةِ حُسنُ العِبادَةِ.[٣٤٩٩]

3148. **Imām ʿAlī (AS) said,** 'There are four virtues that qualify a man for chiefdom: chastity, courtesy, generosity and intelligence.'[3526]

٣١٤٨. عنه ﷺ: أربَعُ خِصالٍ يَسودُ بِها المَرءُ: العِفَّةُ، والأدَبُ، والجُودُ، والعَقلُ.[٣٥٠٠]

3149. **Imām al-Ḥasan (AS) said,** 'The greatest characteristic of chiefdom is giving before one is asked.'[3527]

٣١٤٩. الإمامُ الحسنُ ﷺ: الإعطاءُ قَبلَ السُّؤالِ مِن أكبَرِ السُّؤدُدِ.[٣٥٠١]

990. Factors that Repel Chiefdom

٩٩٠ـ ما يَمنَعُ السُّؤدَدَ

3150. **Imām ʿAlī (AS) said,** 'Engaging in disputes with the lower classes is a source of disgrace for chiefs.'[3528]

٣١٥٠. الإمامُ عليٌّ ﷺ: مُنازَعَةُ السُّفَّلِ تَشينُ السادَةَ.[٣٥٠٢]

3151. **Imām al-Ṣādiq (AS) said,** 'The person who punishes for petty sins should not be coveting chiefdom, and neither should the inexperienced person who proudly holds his own opinion be coveting leadership.'[3529]

٣١٥١. الإمامُ الصّادقُ ﷺ: لا يَطمَعَنَّ... المُعاقِبُ على الذَّنبِ الصغيرِ في السُّؤدُدِ، ولا القَليلُ التَّجرِبَةِ المُعجَبُ بِرَأيِهِ في رئاسَةٍ.[٣٥٠٣]

3152. **Imām al-Ṣādiq (AS) said,** 'A fool can never be chief.'[3530]

٣١٥٢. عنه ﷺ: لا يَسودُ سَفيهٌ.[٣٥٠٤]

206

MANAGEMENT

السِّياسَةُ

991. Management of the Society

٩٩١ـ سِياسَةُ المُجتَمَعِ

3153. **Imām ʿAlī (AS) said,** 'Sovereignty is [efficient] management.'[3531]

٣١٥٣. الإمامُ عليٌّ ﷺ: المُلكُ سِياسَةٌ.[٣٥٠٥]

3154. **Imām ʿAlī (AS) said,** 'The downfall of leading politicians is [due to] their poor management.'[3532]

٣١٥٤ . عنه ﷺ : آفَةُ الزُّعَماءِ ضَعفُ السِّياسَةِ.[٣٥٠٦]

3155. **Imām ʿAlī (AS) said,** 'Good management prolongs one's [term of] leadership.'[3533]

٣١٥٥ . عنه ﷺ : حُسنُ السِّياسَةِ يَستَدِيمُ الرِّياسةَ.[٣٥٠٧]

3156. **Imām ʿAlī (AS) said,** 'Good management acts as a support for one's subjects.'[3534]

٣١٥٦ . عنه ﷺ : حُسنُ السِّياسَةِ قِوامُ الرَّعِيَّةِ.[٣٥٠٨]

3157. **Imām ʿAlī (AS) said,** 'Efficient organisation and avoidance of squandering is part of good management.'[3535]

٣١٥٧ . عنه ﷺ : حسُنُ التَّدبيرِ وتَجَنُّبُ التَّبذيرِ مِن حُسنِ السِّياسَةِ.[٣٥٠٩]

3158. **Imām ʿAlī (AS) said,** 'Disorganisation is the cause of destruction.'[3536]

٣١٥٨ . عنه ﷺ : سُوءُ التَّدبيرِ سَبَبُ التَّدميرِ.[٣٥١٠]

3159. **Imām ʿAlī (AS) said,** 'The yardstick of good management is justice.'[3537]

٣١٥٩ . عنه ﷺ : مِلاكُ السِّياسَةِ العَدلُ.[٣٥١١]

3160. **Imām ʿAlī (AS) said,** 'The peak of good management is the employment of moderation.'[3538]

٣١٦٠ . عنه ﷺ : رَأسُ السِّياسَةِ استِعمالُ الرِّفقِ.[٣٥١٢]

3161. **Imām ʿAlī (AS) said,** 'Tolerance is the adornment of management.'[3539]

٣١٦١ . عنه ﷺ : الاحتِمالُ زَينُ السِّياسَةِ.[٣٥١٣]

992. Management of One's Self

٩٩٢ ـ سِياسَةُ النَّفسِ

3162. **Imām ʿAlī (AS) said,** 'He who is able to manage his own self truly understands management [will be able to manage others].'[3540]

٣١٦٢ . الإمامُ عليٌّ ﷺ : مَن ساسَ نَفسَهُ أدرَكَ السِّياسَةَ.[٣٥١٤]

3163. **Imām ʿAlī (AS) said,** 'Manage your selves with piety, and cure the sick ones from among you with charity.'[3541]

٣١٦٣ . عنه ﷺ : سُوسُوا أنفُسَكُم بالوَرَعِ، وداوُوا مَرضاكُم بالصَّدَقَةِ.[٣٥١٥]

3164. **Imām ʿAlī (AS) said,** 'It is the duty of a king to manage his own self before his army.'[3542]

٣١٦٤ . عنه ﷺ : مِن حَقِّ المَلِكِ أن يَسُوسَ نَفسَهُ قَبلَ جُندِهِ.[٣٥١٦]

(See also: HABIT: section 1398) (انظر: العادة: باب ١٣٩٨)

207

PROCRASTINATION

التَّسويف

993. Prohibition of Procrastination

٩٩٣ ـ النَّهيُ عَنِ التَّسويفِ

3165. **The Prophet (SAWA) said,** 'O Abū Dharr, beware of procrastinating with your [high] hopes, for verily you have today [at your disposal] and have not yet reached tomorrow. When tomorrow comes to you, then be in it as you are in the present; [that way] even if you do not have tomorrow, you will not have regret for all that you neglected today.'[3543]

٣١٦٥ . رسولُ اللهِ ﷺ : يا أبا ذَرٍّ، إيّاكَ والتَّسويفَ بِأمَلِكَ ، فإنَّكَ بِيَومِكَ ولَستَ بما بَعدَهُ، فإن يَكُن غَدٌ لكَ فَكُن في الغَدِ كما كُنتَ في اليَومِ، وان لم يَكُن غَدٌ لكَ لَم تَندَمْ علىٰ ما فَرَّطتَ في اليَومِ.[٣٥١٧]

3166. **Imām ʿAlī (AS) said** in a letter he wrote to one of his companions, 'Seize what you have left of your life, and do not keep [deferring] saying, 'Tomorrow, and the day after tomorrow', for verily those before you were ruined because of their persistent wishful thinking and their procrastination, until suddenly the command of Allah [i.e. death] overtook them while they were heedless.'[3544]

٣١٦٦ . الإمامُ عليٌّ عليه السلام ـ فيما كَتَبَهُ إلىٰ بعضِ أصحابِهِ ـ: فَتَدارَكْ ما بَقِيَ مِن عُمُرِكَ ، ولا تَقُلْ: غَداً وبَعدَ غَدٍ ، فإنّما هَلَكَ مَن كانَ قَبلَكَ بِإقامَتِهِم علَى الأمانِيِّ والتَّسويفِ، حتّىٰ أتاهُم أمرُ اللهِ بَغتَةً وهُم غافِلونَ.[٣٥١٨]

3167. **Imām ʿAlī (AS) said,** 'He whom death overtakes early calls for more time, and he whose death is deferred continues to put forth excuses with further procrastination.'[3545]

٣١٦٧ . عنه عليه السلام : كُلُّ مُعاجَلٍ يَسألُ الإنظارَ ، وكُلُّ مُؤَجَّلٍ يَتَعَلَّلُ بِالتَّسويفِ.[٣٥١٩]

3168. **Imām ʿAlī (AS) said,** 'Do not be like one who hopes for [bliss in] the Hereafter without performance of good deeds, and delays repentance by holding high hopes [of being forgiven] ... when faced with a desire, he is quick to commit a sin but delays the repentance.'[3546]

٣١٦٨ . عنه عليه السلام : لا تَكُن مِمَّن يَرجُو الآخِرَةَ بغَيرِ العَمَلِ، ويُرَجِّي التَّوبَةَ بِطُولِ الأمَلِ ... إن عَرَضَت لَهُ شَهوَةٌ أسلَفَ المَعصِيَةَ وسَوَّفَ التَّوبَةَ.[٣٥٢٠]

3169. **Imām Zayn al-ʿĀbidīn (AS) said** in his *intimate supplication*, 'And help me [by allowing me to] weep on account of my self, for indeed I

٣١٦٩ . الإمامُ زينُ العابدينَ عليه السلام ـ في مُناجاتِهِ ـ: وأعِنّي بِالبُكاءِ عَلىٰ نَفسي ، فقد أفنَيتُ

have wasted my life away with procrastination and high hopes, and I have now stooped to the level of those who despair of any good to come.'[3547]

بِالتَّسويفِ والآمالِ عُمرِي، وقَد نَزَلتُ مَنزِلَةَ الآيِسِينَ مِن خَيرِي.[٣٥٢١]

3170. **Imām al-Bāqir (AS) said,** 'Beware of procrastination for verily it is the sea in which losers drown.'[3548]

٣١٧٠. الإمامُ الباقرُ (عليه السلام): إيّاكَ والتَّسويفَ؛ فإنّهُ بَحرٌ يَغرَقُ فيهِ الهَلْكىٰ.[٣٥٢٢]

3171. **Imām al-Ṣādiq (AS) said,** 'Delaying repentance is an act of self-delusion, and lengthy procrastination is an act of bewilderment.'[3549]

٣١٧١. الإمامُ الصّادقُ (عليه السلام): تَأخِيرُ التَّوبَةِ اغتِرارٌ، وطُولُ التَّسويفِ حَيرَةٌ.[٣٥٢٣]

208

THE MARKETPLACE[3550]

السُّوقُ

994. Place of Negligence

٩٩٤ـ دارُ الغَفْلَةِ

3172. **The Prophet (SAWA) said,** 'The market is a place of distraction and negligence, so whoever occupies himself therein with the glorification of Allah, Allah records for him the worth of a million good deeds.'[3551]

٣١٧٢. رسولُ اللهِ ﷺ: السُّوقُ دارُ سَهْوٍ وغَفلَةٍ، فَمَن سَبَّحَ فيها تَسبِيحَةً كَتَبَ اللهُ لَهُ بها ألفَ ألفِ حَسَنَةٍ.[٣٥٢٤]

3173. **The Prophet (SAWA) said,** 'If you can, do not be the first to enter the market or the last to leave it, as it is the battlefield of Satan and his flag is raised in it.'[3552]

٣١٧٣. رسولُ اللهِ ﷺ: لا تَكونَنَّ ـ إن استَطَعتَ ـ أوَّلَ مَن يَدخُلُ السّوقَ ولا آخِرَ مَن يَخرُجُ مِنها فَإِنَّها مَعرَكَةُ الشَّيطانِ وبِها يَنصِبُ رايَتَهُ.[٣٥٢٥]

3174. **Imām al-Bāqir (AS) said,** 'The most evil of places on earth are the marketplaces, for it is Satan's domain where he unfurls his flag first in the morning, takes up his seat and gives free rein to his offspring, from a vendor niggardly with his measure, to one who is reckless with his scale, to one who thieves off metres [from cloth], or to one who lies about his wares – to all he says, 'Take advantage of this man whose father [Adam (AS)] has died whilst your own father [*Iblīs*] is still

٣١٧٤. الإمامُ الباقرُ (عليه السلام): شَرُّ بِقاعِ الأرضِ الأسواقُ، وهُو مَيدانُ إبليسَ، يَغدُو بِرايَتِهِ، ويَضَعُ كُرسِيَّهُ، ويَبُثُّ ذُرِّيَّتَهُ، فَبَينَ مُطَفِّفٍ في قَفيزٍ، أو طائشٍ في ميزانٍ، أو سارِقٍ في ذِراعٍ، أو كاذِبٍ في سِلعَتِهِ، فيقولُ: علَيكُم بِرَجُلٍ ماتَ أبوهُ وأبُوكُم حَيٌّ، فلا يَزالُ مع

alive.' And he continues to do this from the first one to enter therein to the last one to leave.'[3553]

أوّلِ مَن يَدخُلُ وآخِرِ مَن يَرجِعُ.[٣٥٢٦]

995. Imām ʿAlī (AS)'s Exhortation to Market Traders

٩٩٥ ـ مَوعِظَةُ الإمامِ عَلِيٍّ ؑ لِأهلِ السُّوقِ

3175. **Abū Saʿīd narrated** that Imām ʿAlī (AS) used to come to the market and exhort, 'O market traders, fear Allah and beware of making false oaths, for though it may sell your goods, it eradicates all benediction thereof. The trader [by nature] is corrupt, except those who take only their right, and give back the right due, and upon you be peace.' Then a few days would pass, and he would come there again and exhort them as he did before.'[3554]

٣١٧٥. بحار الأنوار عن أبي سعيد: كانَ عَلِيٌّ ؑ يَأتي السُّوقَ فيقولُ: يا أهلَ السُّوقِ اتَّقوا اللهَ، وإيّاكُم والحَلفَ فإنَّهُ يُنَفِّقُ السِّلعَةَ، ويَمحَقُ البَرَكَةَ، وإنَّ التّاجِرَ فاجِرٌ إلّا مَن أخَذَ الحَقَّ وأعطاهُ، السَّلامُ عَلَيكُم. ثُمَّ يَمكُثُ الأيّامَ ثُمَّ يَأتي فَيقولُ مِثلَ مَقالَتِهِ.[٣٥٢٧]

209

BRUSHING ONE'S TEETH

السِّواكُ

996. Enjoinment of Brushing One's Teeth

٩٩٦ ـ الحَثُّ عَلَى السِّواكِ

3176. **The Prophet (SAWA) said,** 'If it were not for the fact that it would inconvenience my community, I would have commanded them to brush their teeth before every prayer.'[3555]

٣١٧٦. رسولُ اللهِ ﷺ: لَولا أن أشُقَّ عَلىٰ أُمَّتي لَأمَرتُهُم بِالسِّواكِ مَعَ كُلِّ صَلاةٍ.[٣٥٢٨]

3177. **The Prophet (SAWA) said** in his advice to Imām ʿAlī (AS), 'You must brush your teeth at every ablution.'[3556]

٣١٧٧. عنه ﷺ ـ في وَصِيَّتِهِ لِعَلِيٍّ ؑ ـ: عَلَيكَ بِالسِّواكِ عِندَ كُلِّ وُضوءٍ.[٣٥٢٩]

3178. **The Prophet (SAWA)** also said in his advice to Imām ʿAlī (AS), 'O ʿAlī, you must brush your teeth as frequently as possible, for verily a single prayer that you perform after having brushed your teeth is better than forty days worth of prayers performed without doing so.'[3557]

٣١٧٨. عنه ﷺ ـ أيضاً ـ: يا عَلِيُّ، عَلَيكَ بِالسِّواكِ، وإنِ استَطَعتَ أن لا تُقِلَّ مِنهُ فَافعَل، فَإِنَّ كُلَّ صَلاةٍ تُصَلّيها بِالسِّواكِ تَفضُلُ عَلَى الَّتي تُصَلّيها بِغَيرِ سِواكٍ أربَعينَ يَوماً.[٣٥٣٠]

3179. **The Prophet (SAWA) said,** 'Ablution is a main part of faith, and brushing one's teeth is a main part of ablution.'[3558]

٣١٧٩. عنه ﷺ: الوُضوءُ شَطرُ الإيمانِ، والسِّواكُ شَطرُ الوُضوءِ.٣٥٣١

3180. **The Prophet (SAWA) said,** 'Freshen your mouths by brushing, for verily they are the means to the Qur'an.'[3559]

٣١٨٠. عنه ﷺ: طَيِّبوا أفواهَكُم بِالسِّواكِ؛ فإنّها طُرُقُ القرآنِ.٣٥٣٢

3181. **The Prophet (SAWA) said,** 'Gabriel continuously advises me about brushing teeth, that I really thought he would lay it down as an obligation.'[3560]

٣١٨١. عنه ﷺ: مازالَ جَبرئيلُ يُوصيني بالسِّواكِ حتّى ظَنَنتُ أنّهُ سَيَجعَلُهُ فَريضَةً.٣٥٣٣

3182. **Imām al-Ṣādiq (AS)** was once asked, 'Do you consider all of these people as being real human beings?' to which he replied, 'Exclude from them the one who does not brush his teeth,…'[3561 3562]

٣١٨٢. الإمامُ الصّادقُ ﵇ ـ لَمّا سُئلَ: أتَرىٰ هذا الخَلقَ كُلَّهُ مِنَ الناسِ؟ ـ: فقالَ: ألْقِ مِنهُمُ التارِكَ لِلسِّواكِ.٣٥٣٤

997. The Benefits of Brushing Teeth

٩٩٧ ـ مَنافِعُ السِّواكِ

3183. **The Prophet (SAWA) said,** 'Brushing one's teeth increases one's articulacy.'[3563]

٣١٨٣. رسولُ اللهِ ﷺ: السِّواكُ يَزيدُ الرَّجُلَ فَصاحَةً.٣٥٣٥

3184. **Imām al-Ṣādiq (AS) said,** 'There are twelve distinctive features to brushing one's teeth: it is a recommended prophetic practice, it purifies one's mouth, brightens one's eyesight, pleases the Beneficent Lord, whitens the teeth, does away with wretchedness, strengthens one's gums, whets one's appetite for food, takes away phlegm, improves one's memory, multiplies one's rewards for good deeds, and gives pleasure to the angels.'[3564]

٣١٨٤. الإمامُ الصّادقُ ﵇: في السِّواكِ اثنَتا عَشرَةَ خَصلَةً: هُو مِنَ السُّنَّةِ، و مَطهَرَةٌ لِلفَمِ، ومَجلاةٌ لِلبَصَرِ، ويُرضِي الرحمنَ، ويُبَيِّضُ الأسنانَ، ويَذهَبُ بِالحَفرِ، ويَشُدُّ اللِّثَةَ، ويُشَهّي الطَّعامَ، ويَذهَبُ بِالبَلغَمِ، ويَزيدُ فِي الحِفظِ، ويُضاعِفُ بِهِ الحَسَناتُ، وتَفرَحُ بِهِ المَلائكةُ.٣٥٣٦

3185. **Imām al-Ṣādiq (AS) said,** 'You must brush your teeth for it removes temptations of the heart.'[3565]

٣١٨٥. عنه ﵇: علَيكُم بالسِّواكِ؛ فإنّهُ يُذهِبُ وَسوَسَةَ الصَّدرِ.٣٥٣٧

3186. **Imām al-Riḍā (AS) said,** 'Brushing one's teeth brightens the eyesight, increases hair growth, and removes the tendency for frequent weeping.'[3566]

٣١٨٦. الإمامُ الرِّضا ﵇: السِّواكُ يَجلو البَصَرَ، ويُنبِتُ الشَّعرَ، ويَذهَبُ بِالدَّمعَةِ.٣٥٣٨

998. Etiquette of Brushing Teeth

٩٩٨ـ أدَبُ السِّواكِ

3187. **The Prophet (SAWA) said,** 'Brush your teeth in a horizontal manner and not in a vertical manner.'[3567]

٣١٨٧. رسولُ اللهِ ﷺ: إستاكُوا عَرضاً ولا تَستاكُوا طُولاً.[٣٥٣٩]

3188. It is narrated in *Biḥār al-Anwār* that the Prophet (SAWA) used to brush in a horizontal manner whenever he brushed his teeth, and that he would brush his teeth thrice every night: once before going to bed, once when he would wake up for his night worship, and once before going out to perform the dawn prayer. He used to brush with twigs of *Arāk* (a thorny kind of tree) which the archangel Gabriel had told him to do.'[3568]

٣١٨٨. بحار الأنوار: كان النبيُّ ﷺ إذا استاكَ استاكَ عَرضاً، وكانَ يَستاكُ كُلَّ لَيلَةٍ ثلاثَ مَرّاتٍ: مَرَّةً قَبلَ نَومِهِ، ومَرَّةً إذا قامَ مِن نَومِهِ إلىٰ وِردِهِ، ومَرَّةً قَبلَ خُروجِهِ إلىٰ صَلاةِ الصُّبحِ، وكانَ يَستاكُ بالأراكِ أمَرَهُ بذلك جَبرَئيلُ.[٣٥٤٠]

3189. **Imām al-Bāqir (AS) said,** 'Verily brushing one's teeth at dawn before performing the ablution is part of recommended prophetic practice.'[3569]

٣١٨٩. الإمامُ الباقرُ ﷺ: إنّ السِّواكَ في السَّحَرِ قَبلَ الوُضوءِ مِنَ السُّنَّةِ.[٣٥٤١]

210

YOUTH

الشَّبابُ

999. Youth

٩٩٩ـ الشّبابُ

3190. **The Prophet (SAWA) said,** 'Youth is a branch of folly.'[3570]

٣١٩٠. رسولُ اللهِ ﷺ: الشَّبابُ شُعبَةٌ مِنَ الجُنونِ.[٣٥٤٢]

3191. **The Prophet (SAWA) said,** 'The best of your youth are those who act like the old from among you, and the worst of your old ones are those who act like your youth.'[3571]

٣١٩١. عنه ﷺ: خَيرُ شَبابِكُم مَن تَشَبَّهَ بِكُهُولِكُم، وشَرُّ كُهولِكُم مَن تَشَبَّهَ بِشَبابِكُم.[٣٥٤٣]

3192. **Imām 'Alī (AS) said,** 'There are two things whose worth is only known to one who has lost them: youth and health.'[3572]

٣١٩٢. الإمامُ عليٌّ ﷺ: شَيئانِ لا يَعرِفُ فَضلَهُما إلّا مَن فَقَدَهُما: الشَّبابُ، وَالعافِيَةُ.[٣٥٤٤]

1000. Educating Youngsters

١٠٠٠ ـ تَربِيَةُ الأحداثِ

3193. **Imām ʿAlī (AS) said,** 'Verily the heart of a youngster is like an empty plot of land - it accepts whatever is planted therein.'[3573]

٣١٩٣ . الإمامُ عليٌّ عليه السلام : إنّما قَلبُ الحَدَثِ كالأرضِ الخاليَةِ ، ما اُلقِيَ فيها مِن شَيءٍ قَبِلَتهُ.[٣٥٤٥]

3194. **Imām al-Ṣādiq (AS)** asked al-Aḥwal, 'Did you go to Basra?' He replied, 'Yes.' Imām (AS) asked, 'How did you find people's hastening to this matter [of Imāmate] and embracing it?' He replied, 'By Allah, such people were few in number, and even that which they did do was little.' Imām replied, 'You should put it forth to the youngsters, for verily they hasten towards anything good.'[3574]

٣١٩٤ . الكافي عَن إسماعيلَ بنِ عبدِ الخالقِ : سمعت أبا عَبدِالله عليه السلام يقول لأبي جعفر الأحول وأنا أسمع : أتَيتَ البَصرةَ ؟ فَقالَ : نَعَم قالَ : كيفَ رَأيتَ مُسارَعَةَ الناسِ إلى هذا الأمرِ ودُخُولَهُم فيهِ ؟ قالَ : واللهِ إنّهُم لَقليلٌ ، ولَقَد فَعَلُوا وإنّ ذلك لَقليلٌ ، فقالَ : علَيكَ بِالأحداثِ ؛ فإنّهُم أسرَعُ إلىٰ كُلِّ خَيرٍ.[٣٥٤٦]

1001. Learning During One's Youth

١٠٠١ ـ التَّعَلُّمُ فِي الشَّبابِ

3195. **The Prophet (SAWA) said,** 'Learning something during one's youth is like engraving in stone, and learning something when one is old is like writing on the surface of water.'[3575]

٣١٩٥ . رسولُ اللهِ ﷺ : مَن تَعَلَّمَ في شَبابِهِ كانَ بِمَنزِلَةِ الرَّسمِ في الحَجَرِ ، ومَن تَعَلَّمَ وهُو كبيرٌ كانَ بمَنزِلَةِ الكِتابِ علىٰ وَجهِ الماءِ.[٣٥٤٧]

3196. **Imām al-Bāqir (AS) said,** 'If I was brought a young *shīʿa* man undevoted to learning [religious matters], I would discipline him.'[3576]

٣١٩٦ . الإمامُ الباقرُ عليه السلام : لَو اُتيتُ بِشابٍّ مِن شَبابِ الشِّيعَةِ لا يَتَفَقَّهُ (في الدِّينِ) لَأدَّبتُهُ.[٣٥٤٨]

3197. **Imām al-Ṣādiq (AS) said,** 'I only like to see the young man from among you occupied in either of two states: learning or teaching, for if he does not [engage in either of these two], he is wasting his time; and by wasting his time, he will lose out; and by losing out, he will be committing a sin; and by committing a sin, he will dwell in the Fire, by the One who sent Muḥammad with the truth.'[3577]

٣١٩٧ . الإمامُ الصّادقُ عليه السلام : لَستُ اُحِبُّ أن أرىٰ الشّابَّ مِنكُم إلّا غادياً في حالَينِ : إمّا عالِماً أو مُتَعَلِّماً ، فإن لَم يَفعَلْ فَرَّطَ ، فإن فَرَّطَ ضَيَّعَ ، وإنْ ضَيَّعَ أثِمَ ، وإن أثِمَ سَكَنَ النارَ والذي بَعَثَ مُحمّداً بِالحَقِّ.[٣٥٤٩]

1002. The Virtue of a Worshipping Young Man

١٠٠٢ ـ فَضلُ الشّابِّ العابِدِ

3198. **The Prophet (SAWA) said,** 'Verily Allah, most High, boasts about the worshipping young

٣١٩٨ . رسولُ اللهِ ﷺ : إنَّ اللهَ تعالىٰ يُباهِي بالشابِّ العابِدِ المَلائكةَ ، يقولُ : اُنظُرُوا إلىٰ

man to His angels, saying, 'Look at My servant! He has abandoned his desires for My sake.'[3578]

عَبدي ! تَرَكَ شَهوَتَهُ مِن أجلي.٣٥٥٠

3199. **The Prophet (SAWA) said,** 'Verily Allah, most High, loves the penitent young man.'[3579]

٣١٩٩. عنه ﷺ: إنَّ اللهَ تعالىٰ يُحِبُّ الشابَّ التائبَ.٣٥٥١

3200. **The Prophet (SAWA) said,** 'The superiority of a young worshipper who worships Allah in his youth over an old man who worships after he has grown old, is as the superiority of the prophets over the rest of people.'[3580]

٣٢٠٠. عنه ﷺ: فَضلُ الشّابِّ العابِدِ الذي تَعَبَّدَ في صِباهُ على الشيخِ الذي تَعَبَّدَ بعدَ ما كَبِرَت سِنُّهُ كَفَضلِ المُرسَلِينَ علىٰ سائرِ الناسِ.٣٥٥٢

3201. **The Prophet (SAWA) said,** 'Verily Allah loves the young man who spends his entire youth in the obedience of Allah.'[3581]

٣٢٠١. عنه ﷺ: إنَّ اللهَ يُحِبُّ الشابَّ الذي يُفني شَبابَهُ في طاعَةِ اللهِ تعالىٰ.٣٥٥٣

1003. The True Significance of the Word 'Fatā'[3582]

١٠٠٣ ـ تَفسيرُ الفَتىٰ

3202. **Imām al-Ṣādiq (AS)** once asked a man, 'Who do you consider a *fatā*?' to which the man replied, 'A young man.' Imām said, 'No, a *fatā* is a believer, for verily the Companions of the Cave were middle-aged men, yet Allah called them *fitya* [plural of *fatā*] because of their belief.'[3583]

٣٢٠٢. الكافي عَن عليٍّ بنِ إبراهيمَ رَفَعَهُ: قالَ أبو عَبدِاللهِ عليه السلام لرَجُلٍ: ما الفَتىٰ عِندَكُم؟ فقالَ لَهُ: الشابُّ، فقالَ: لا، الفَتىٰ: المُؤمِنُ، إنَّ أصحابَ الكَهفِ كانوا شُيُوخاً فَسَمّاهُمُ اللهُ عَزَّوجلَّ فِتيَةً بِإيمانِهِم.٣٥٥٤

211

THE OBSCURE MATTER

الشُّبهَةُ

1004. Meaning of the Obscure Matter

١٠٠٤ ـ مَعنَى الشُّبهَةِ

3203. **Imām 'Alī (AS) said,** 'The obscure matter has been termed obscure for the very fact that it resembles [and therefore obscures] the truth. The friends of Allah take recourse in conviction as their light therein and the direction of the right path itself as their guide, whereas the enemies of Allah use it to call [others] to deviation and blind following is their guide therein.'[3584]

٣٢٠٣. الإمامُ عليٌّ عليه السلام: إنّما سُمِّيَتِ الشُّبهَةُ شُبهَةً لأنّها تُشبِهُ الحَقَّ، فأمّا أولياءُ اللهِ فَضِياؤهُم فيها اليَقينُ ودَلِيلُهُم سَمتُ الهُدىٰ، وأمّا أعداءُ اللهِ فَدُعاؤهُم فيها الضَّلالُ ودَليلُهُمُ العَمىٰ.٣٥٥٥

1005. The Danger Of Obscure Matter

١٠٠٥ـ خَطَرُ الشُّبهَةِ

3204. **Imām ʿAlī (AS) said,** 'Be on your guard against the obscure matter, for verily it has been set down in order to test people [or lead people astray].'[3585]

٣٢٠٤ . الإمامُ عليٌّ عليه السلام : اِحذَرُوا الشُّبهَةَ ؛ فإنّها وَضِعَت لِلفِتنَةِ .[٣٥٥٦]

1006. The Necessity of Stopping in the Face of an Obscure Matter

١٠٠٦ـ وُجوبُ الوقوفِ عِندَ الشُّبهَةِ

3205. **Imām al-Bāqir (AS) said,** 'Stopping in the face of an obscure matter is better than plunging headlong into disaster.'[3586]

٣٢٠٥ . الإمامُ الباقرُ عليه السلام : الوُقوفُ عِندَ الشُّبهَةِ خَيرٌ مِن الاِقتِحامِ في الهَلَكَةِ وتَركُكَ حديثاً لم تَروِه خيرٌ مِن رِوايَتِكَ حديثاً لَم تُحصِهِ .[٣٥٥٧]

3206. **Imām al-Ṣādiq (AS) said,** 'The most pious of people is he who stops in the face of an obscure matter.'[3587]

٣٢٠٦ . الإمامُ الصّادقُ عليه السلام : أورَعُ النّاسِ مَن وَقَفَ عِندَ الشُّبهَةِ .[٣٥٥٨]

1007. Obligation to Abandon Obscure Matters

١٠٠٧ـ وُجوبُ تَركِ الشُّبُهاتِ

3207. **The Prophet (SAWA) said,** 'Leave that which fills you with doubts for that which does not, for the one who grazes his animals around the protected area risks entering into it.'[3588]

٣٢٠٧ . رسولُ اللهِ صلى الله عليه وآله : دَعْ ما يَرِيبُكَ إلىٰ ما لا يَرِيبُكَ ، فَمَن رَعىٰ حَولَ الحِمىٰ يُوشِكُ أن يَقَعَ فيهِ .[٣٥٥٩]

3208. **The Prophet (SAWA) said,** 'The lawful is evidently clear, and the unlawful is evidently clear, and obscurities fall between these two. He who abandons these obscurities is saved from the prohibited things, whereas one who delves into obscurities also ends up committing prohibited acts and falls into disaster whence he knows not.'[3589]

٣٢٠٨ . عنه صلى الله عليه وآله : حَلالٌ بَيِّنٌ ، وحَرامٌ بَيِّنٌ ، وشُبُهاتٌ بَينَ ذلكَ ، فَمَن تَرَكَ الشُّبُهاتِ نَجا مِنَ المُحَرَّماتِ ، ومَن أخَذَ بِالشُّبُهاتِ ارتَكَبَ المُحَرَّماتِ وهَلَكَ مِن حيثُ لا يَعلَمُ .[٣٥٦٠]

212

TREES

الشَّجَرُ

1008. The Importance of Planting Trees

١٠٠٨ ـ أهَمِّيَّةُ غَرسِ الشَّجَرِ

3209. **The Prophet (SAWA) said,** 'When the Last Hour comes, if any of you happens to be holding a seedling in his hand, then if he is able to, let him not stand until he has planted it.'[3590]

٣٢٠٩. رسولُ اللهِ ﷺ: إن قامَتِ السَّاعةُ وفي يَدِ أحَدِكُم فَسِيلَةٌ، فإنِ استَطاعَ أن لا يَقومَ حتّىٰ يَغرِسَها فَلْيَغرِسْها.[٣٥٦١]

3210. **The Prophet (SAWA) said,** 'Every single Muslim that cultivates or plants anything of which humans, animals or birds may eat from is counted as charity towards them on his behalf.'[3591]

٣٢١٠. عنه ﷺ: ما مِن مُسلِمٍ يَزرَعُ زَرعاً أو يَغرِسُ غَرساً فَيأكُلُ مِنهُ طَيرٌ أو إنسانٌ أو بَهِيمَةٌ إلّا كانَت لَهُ بِهِ صَدَقَةٌ.[٣٥٦٢]

3211. **The Prophet (SAWA) said,** 'Every single person that cultivates something, Allah rewards him as much as the fruit produced by that plant.'[3592]

٣٢١١. عنه ﷺ: ما مِن رَجُلٍ يَغرِسُ غَرساً إلّا كَتَبَ اللهُ لَهُ مِنَ الأجرِ قَدْرَ ما يَخرُجُ مِن ثَمَرِ ذلكَ الغَرسِ.[٣٥٦٣]

3212. **The Prophet (SAWA) said,** 'Whoever plants a tree and patiently maintains it and tends to it until its fruition, every single fruit consumed from that tree is regarded by Allah as charity [on his behalf].'[3593]

٣٢١٢. عنه ﷺ: مَن نَصَبَ شَجرَةً وصَبَرَ علىٰ حِفظِها والقِيامِ علَيها حتّىٰ تُثمِرَ، كانَ لَهُ في كُلِّ شَيءٍ يُصابُ مِن ثَمَرِها صَدَقةٌ عِندَ اللهِ.[٣٥٦٤]

1009. Forbiddance from Cutting Down Trees

١٠٠٩ ـ النَّهْيُ عَنْ قَطعِ الشَّجَرِ

3213. **Imām al-Ṣādiq (AS) said,** 'Do not cut down fruit trees for Allah will pour down punishment unto you.'[3594]

٣٢١٣. الإمامُ الصّادقُ عليه السلام: لا تَقطَعُوا الثِّمارَ فَيَبعَثُ اللهُ عَلَيكُمُ العَذابَ صَبّاً.[٣٥٦٥]

3214. **Imām al-Ṣādiq (AS):** Cutting down a palm tree is [religiously] detested.'[3595]

٣٢١٤. عنه عليه السلام: مَكروهٌ قَطعُ النَّخلِ.[٣٥٦٦]

(See also: AGRICULTURE 170)

(أنظر) عنوان ١٧٠ «الزراعة».

213

COURAGE

الشَّجاعَة

1010. The Virtue of Courage

١٠١٠ـ فَضْلُ الشَّجاعَةِ

3215. **Imām ʿAlī (AS) said,** 'Courage is might at hand.'[3596]

٣٢١٥ . الإمامُ عليٌّ عليه السلام :الشَّجاعَةُ عِزٌّ حاضِرٌ.٣٥٦٧

3216. **Imām ʿAlī (AS) said,** 'Courage is a ready victory and an obvious virtue.'[3597]

٣٢١٦ . عنه عليه السلام :الشَّجاعةُ نُصرةٌ حاضِرةٌ وفضيلةٌ ظاهِرةٌ.٣٥٦٨

3217. **Imām ʿAlī (AS) said,** 'If qualities were to be classified, honesty would be with courage, and cowardice with dishonesty.'[3598]

٣٢١٧ . عنه عليه السلام :لو تَمَيَّزَتِ الأشياءُ لَكانَ الصِّدقُ مَعَ الشَّجاعَةِ، وكانَ الجُبنُ مَعَ الكَذِبِ.٣٥٦٩

3218. **Imām al-Ḥasan (AS)** was once asked about courage, to which he replied, 'It is to know when to stand up to one's opponents, and when to be patient in the face of criticism and slander.'[3599]

٣٢١٨ . الإمامُ الحسنُ عليه السلام ـ وقد سُئلَ عنِ الشَّجاعةِ ـ: مُواقَفَةُ الأقرانِ، والصَّبرُ عِندَ الطِّعانِ.٣٥٧٠

1011. That Which Engenders Courage

١٠١١ـ ما يورِثُ الشَّجاعَةَ

3219. **Imām ʿAlī (AS) said,** 'Courage has been created based on three natural characteristics, each of which has an exclusive merit over the rest. They are: self-esteem, dignity [in the face of humiliation], and seeking a good reputation. If they all attain perfection in the courageous man, he is an invincible hero, distinguished for his boldness in his generation. And if some of them are perfected in him more than others, then his courage will far supersede in those particular qualities over the rest.'[3600]

٣٢١٩ . الإمامُ عليٌّ عليه السلام : جُبِلَتِ الشَّجاعَةُ على ثلاثِ طَبائعَ، لِكُلِّ واحِدةٍ مِنهُنَّ فَضيلَةٌ لَيسَت لِلأُخرى: السَّخاءُ بِالنَّفسِ، والأنَفَةُ مِنَ الذُّلِّ، وطَلَبُ الذِّكرِ، فإنْ تَكامَلَت في الشُّجاعِ كانَ البَطَلَ الذي لا يُقامُ لِسَبيلِهِ، والمَوسومَ بالإقدامِ في عَصرِهِ، وإن تَفاضَلَت فيهِ بَعضُها على بَعضٍ كانَت شَجاعَتُهُ في ذلكَ الذي تَفاضَلَت فيهِ أكثَرَ وأشَدَّ إقداماً.٣٥٧١

3220. **Imām ʿAlī (AS) said,** 'A man's worth is in proportion to the extent of his ambition, his honesty is in proportion to the extent of his gallantry, and his courage is in proportion to the

٣٢٢٠ . عنه عليه السلام : قَدرُ الرَّجُلِ على قَدرِ هِمَّتِهِ، وصِدقُهُ على قَدرِ مُروَّتِهِ، وشَجاعَتُهُ على

extent of his dignity [in the face of humiliation].'[3601]

قَدرِ أنَفَتِهِ.[٣٥٧٢]

3221. **Imām ʿAlī (AS) said,** 'A man's courage is in proportion to the extent of his ambition, and his zeal in proportion to the extent of his ardour.'[3602]

٣٢٢١. عنه ﷺ: شَجاعَةُ الرَّجُلِ عَلىٰ قَدرِ هِمَّتِهِ، وغَيرَتُهُ علىٰ قَدرِ حَمِيَّتِهِ.[٣٥٧٣]

3222. **Imām ʿAlī (AS) said,** '[A man's] courage is in proportion to the extent of [his] ardour [resistance against humiliation].'[3603]

٣٢٢٢. عنه ﷺ: علىٰ قَدرِ الحَمِيَّةِ تكونُ الشَّجاعَةُ.[٣٥٧٤]

1012. The Most Courageous of People

١٠١٢ ـ أشجَعُ النّاسِ

3223. **The Prophet (SAWA) said,** 'Shall I tell you who is the toughest and strongest from among you?' They replied, 'Yes, Messenger of Allah, do tell us', so the Prophet (SAWA) said, 'The strongest and toughest of you is he who, when he is happy, his happiness does not lead him to committing a sin or anything wrong, and when he gets angry, his anger does not prevent him from speaking the truth, and when he is empowered in any way, he does not take hold of that which is not lawfully his.'[3604]

٣٢٢٣. رسولُ اللهِ ﷺ: ألا اُخبِرُكُم بأشَدِّكُم وأقواكُم؟ قالوا: بلىٰ يا رسولَ اللهِ. قالَ: أشَدُّكُم وأقواكُمُ الذي إذا رَضِيَ لَم يُدخِلْهُ رِضاهُ في إثمٍ ولا باطِلٍ، وإذا سَخِطَ لَم يُخرِجْهُ سَخَطُهُ مِن قولِ الحَقِّ، وإذا قَدَرَ لَم يَتَعاطَ ما لَيسَ لَهُ بِحَقٍّ.[٣٥٧٥]

3224. **Imām ʿAlī (AS) said,** 'The most courageous of people is the most generous of them.'[3605]

٣٢٢٤. الإمامُ عليٌّ ﷺ: أشجَعُ النّاسِ أسخاهُم.[٣٥٧٦]

3225. **Imām ʿAlī (AS) said,** 'The most courageous of people is he who conquers his ignorance with clemency.'[3606]

٣٢٢٥. عنه ﷺ: أشجَعُ النّاسِ مَن غَلَبَ الجَهلَ بِالحِلمِ.[٣٥٧٧]

3226. **Imām ʿAlī (AS) said,** 'There is no one more courageous than a man of understanding.'[3607]

٣٢٢٦. عنه ﷺ: لا أشجَعَ مِن لَبيبٍ.[٣٥٧٨]

3227. **Imām ʿAlī (AS) said,** 'The strongest of people is the one with the greatest authority over his own self.'[3608]

٣٢٢٧. عنه ﷺ: أقوَى النّاسِ أعظَمُهُم سُلطاناً علىٰ نَفسِهِ.[٣٥٧٩]

(See also: THE DESIRE: section 1816)

(اُنظر) الهوى: باب ١٨١٦.

1013. The Bane of Courage

١٠١٣ـ آفَةُ الشَّجاعَةِ

3228. **Imām ʿAlī (AS) said,** 'The bane of courage is losing one's judiciousness.'[3609]

٣٢٢٨. الإمامُ عليٌّ عليه السلام: آفَةُ الشَّجاعَةِ إضاعَةُ الحَزمِ.[٣٥٨٠]

3229. **Imām al-ʿAskarī (AS) said,** 'Verily... courage has a limit, which when overstepped becomes foolhardiness.'[3610]

٣٢٢٩. الإمامُ العسكريُّ عليه السلام: إنَّ... للشَّجاعَةِ مِقداراً، فإن زادَ علَيهِ فهُو تَهَوُّرٌ.[٣٥٨١]

214

EVIL

الشَّرُّ

1014. The Yardstick of Good and Evil

١٠١٤ـ مِعيارُ الخَيرِ وَالشَّرِّ

"Warfare has been prescribed for you, though it is repulsive to you. Yet it may be that you dislike something while it is good for you, and it may be that you love something while it is bad for you, and Allah knows and you do not know."[3611]

﴿كُتِبَ عَلَيْكُمُ القِتَالُ وَهُوَ كُرْهٌ لَكُمْ وَعَسَىٰ أَنْ تَكْرَهُوا شَيْئاً وَهُوَ خَيْرٌ لَكُمْ وَعَسَىٰ أَنْ تُحِبُّوا شَيْئاً وَهُوَ شَرٌّ لَكُمْ وَاللهُ يَعْلَمُ وَأَنْتُمْ لا تَعْلَمُونَ﴾.[٣٥٨٢]

"Man prays for evil as [avidly as] he prays for good, and man is overhasty."[3612]

﴿وَيَدْعُ الإنْسانُ بِالشَّرِ دُعاءَهُ بِالخَيْرِ وَكانَ الإنْسانُ عَجُولاً﴾.[٣٥٨٣]

3230. **Imām ʿAlī (AS) said,** 'That good whose end consequence is the Fire is not good, and that hardship whose end consequence is Paradise is not bad. Every bliss other than Paradise is inferior, and every calamity other than the Fire itself is a comfort.'[3613]

٣٢٣٠. الإمامُ عليٌّ عليه السلام: ما خَيرٌ بِخَيرٍ بَعدَهُ النارُ، وما شَرٌّ بِشَرٍّ بَعدَهُ الجَنَّةُ، وكُلُّ نَعيمٍ دُونَ الجَنَّةِ فهُو مَحقورٌ، وكُلُّ بَلاءٍ دُونَ النارِ عافِيَةٌ.[٣٥٨٤]

3231. **Imām ʿAlī (AS) said,** 'Allah, Glorified be He, has sent down a guiding Book wherein He has explained good and evil, so adopt the course of good so that you be rightly guided, and turn away from the direction of evil so that you remain focused on the right way.'[3614]

٣٢٣١. عنه عليه السلام: إنّ اللهَ سبحانَهُ أنزَلَ كِتاباً هادِياً بَيَّنَ فيه الخَيرَ والشَّرَّ، فَخُذُوا نَهجَ الخَيرِ تَهتَدُوا، واصدِفُوا عَن سَمْتِ الشَّرِّ تَقصِدُوا.[٣٥٨٥]

(See also: SUPPLICATION: section 701)

(أنظر) الدعاء: باب ٧٠١.

1015. Worse than Evil

١٠١٥ ـ شَرٌّ مِنَ الشَّرِّ

3232. **The Prophet (SAWA) said,** 'There are two virtues unexcelled by anything better: faith in Allah, and being of benefit to Allah's servants. And there are two iniquities unsurpassed by anything worse: associating something with Allah, and causing harm to Allah's servants.'[3615]

٣٢٣٢. رسولُ اللهِ ﷺ: خَصلَتانِ ليسَ فَوقَهُما مِنَ البِرِّ شَيءٌ: الإيمانُ بِاللهِ والنَّفعُ لِعبادِ اللهِ، وخَصلَتانِ لَيسَ فوقَهُما مِنَ الشَّرِّ شَيءٌ: الشِّركُ بِاللهِ والضُّرُّ لِعِبادِ اللهِ.[٣٥٨٦]

3233. **Imām 'Alī (AS) said,** 'There is nothing worse than an evil deed except for its own punishment, and there is nothing better than a good deed except for its own reward.'[3616]

٣٢٣٣. الإمامُ عليٌّ (ع): إنَّهُ لَيسَ شَيءٌ بِشَرٍّ مِنَ الشَّرِّ إلّا عِقابُهُ، ولَيسَ شَيءٌ بِخَيرٍ مِنَ الخَيرِ إلّا ثَوابُهُ.[٣٥٨٧]

3234. **Imām 'Alī (AS) said,** 'The doer of evil is worse than the evil itself.'[3617]

٣٢٣٤. عنه (ع): فاعِلُ الشَّرِّ شَرٌّ مِنهُ.[٣٥٨٨]

(See also: GOOD: section 681)

(أنظر) الخير: باب ٦٨١

1016. The Keys to All Evils

١٠١٦ ـ مَفاتيحُ الشُّرورِ

3235. **Imām al-Bāqir (AS) said,** 'Verily Allah, Mighty and Exalted, created locks for all evils, and he made the keys to those locks to be alcohol; and lying is worse than alcohol.'[3618]

٣٢٣٥. الإمامُ الباقرُ (ع): إنَّ اللهَ عَزَّوجلَّ جَعَلَ لِلشَّرِّ أقفالاً وجَعَلَ مَفاتيحَ تِلكَ الأقفالِ الشَّرابَ، والكَذِبُ شَرٌّ مِنَ الشَّرابِ.[٣٥٨٩]

3236. **Imām al-Ṣādiq (AS) said,** 'Anger is the key to all evils.'[3619]

٣٢٣٦. الإمامُ الصّادقُ (ع): الغَضَبُ مِفتاحُ كُلِّ شَرٍّ.[٣٥٩٠]

(See also: LYING: section 1584)

(أنظر) الكذب: ١٥٨٤

1017. The Merging of Evils

١٠١٧ ـ جِماعُ الشُّرورِ

3237. **The Prophet (SAWA) said,** 'Verily Satan addresses his devils saying, 'Avail yourselves to meat, intoxicants and women, for verily I do not see the merging together of more evils except through these.'[3620]

٣٢٣٧. رسولُ اللهِ ﷺ: إنَّ إبليسَ يَخطُبُ شَياطينَهُ ويقولُ: عَلَيكُم بِاللَّحمِ والمُسكِرِ والنِّساءِ، فَإنّي لا أجِدُ جِماعَ الشَّرِّ إلّا فيها.[٣٥٩١]

(See also: GOOD: section 671)

(أنظر) الخير: ٦٧١

1018. Man's Natural Tendency for Evil

١٠١٨ـ انطِباعُ الإنسانِ عَلَى الشَّرِّ

3238. **The Prophet (SAWA) said,** 'Force yourselves to do good, and exert yourselves therein, for verily evil is something man naturally tends towards.'[3621]

٣٢٣٨. رسولُ اللهِ ﷺ : تَكَلَّفُوا فِعلَ الخَيرِ وجاهِدُوا نفوسَكُم علَيهِ ؛ فإنَّ الشَّرَّ مَطبوعٌ علَيهِ الإنسانُ.[٣٥٩٢]

3239. **Imām ʿAlī (AS) said,** 'Compel yourself to good virtues, for verily vices are something you have a natural tendency for.'[3622]

٣٢٣٩. الإمامُ عليٌّ عليه السلام : أكرِهْ نفسَكَ على الفَضائلِ، فإنَّ الرذائلَ أنتَ مَطبوعٌ علَيها.[٣٥٩٣]

(See also: SINNING: section 771)

(أُنظر) الذنب: باب ٧٧١.

215

POLYTHEISM[3623]

الشِّرك

1019. Caution Against Polytheism

١٠١٩ـ التَّحذيرُ مِنَ الشِّركِ

"When Luqmān said to his son, as he advised him: 'O my son! Do not ascribe any partners to Allah. Polytheism is indeed a great injustice.'"[3624]

﴿وَإِذْ قالَ لُقْمانُ لِابْنِهِ وَهُوَ يَعِظُهُ يا بُنَيَّ لا تُشْرِكْ بِاللهِ إِنَّ الشِّرْكَ لَظُلْمٌ عَظِيمٌ﴾.[٣٥٩٤]

"Indeed Allah does not forgive that any partner should be ascribed to Him, but He forgives anything besides that to whomever He wishes. And whoever ascribes partners to Allah has certainly strayed into far error."[3625]

﴿إِنَّ اللهَ لا يَغْفِرُ أَن يُشْرَكَ بِهِ وَيَغْفِرُ ما دُونَ ذَٰلِكَ لِمَن يَشاءُ وَمَن يُشْرِكْ بِاللهِ فَقَدْ ضَلَّ ضَلالاً بَعِيداً﴾.[٣٥٩٥]

3240. **The Prophet (SAWA) said,** 'O Ibn Masʿūd, beware of ever associating anything with Allah for even the twinkling of an eye, even if you are to be cut up with a saw, amputated, crucified or burnt with fire.'[3626]

٣٢٤٠. رسولُ اللهِ ﷺ ـ لعبدالله بن مسعود ـ: يابنَ مَسعودٍ، إيّاكَ أن تُشرِكَ بِاللهِ طَرفَةَ عَينٍ وإن نُشِرتَ بِالمِنشارِ، أو قُطِّعتَ، أو صُلِبتَ، أو اُحرِقتَ بِالنارِ.[٣٥٩٦]

1020. Instruction of Polytheism

١٠٢٠ـ تَعليمُ الشِّركِ

3241. **Imām al-Ṣādiq (AS) narrated,** 'Verily the Umayyads used to allow the teaching of faith to

٣٢٤١. الإمامُ الصّادقُ عليه السلام : إنَّ بَني اُمَيَّةَ أطلَقُوا

people but did not permit polytheism to be taught, so that when it came to their converting them [the people] to it, they would not be able to recognise it.'[3627]

لِلنّاسِ تَعليمَ الإيمانِ ولَم يُطلِقْ تَعليمَ الشِّركِ؛ لِكَي إذا حَمَلُوهُم علَيهِ لَم يَعرِفُوهُ.[٣٥٩٧]

1021. The Minimum Degree of Polytheism

١٠٢١ ـ أدنَى الشِّركِ

3242. **Imām al-Bāqir (AS)** was once asked what the absolute minimum of polytheism was, to which he replied, 'It is to call fruit kernels stones and vice versa, and to believe them as such.'[3628]

٣٢٤٢. الإمامُ الباقرُ (ع) ـ لَمّا سُئلَ عن أدنَى الشِّركِ ـ: مَن قالَ لِلنَّواةِ: إنَّها حَصاةٌ، ولِلحَصاةِ: إنّها نَواةٌ، ثُمّ دانَ بهِ.[٣٥٩٨]

3243. **Imām al-Ṣādiq (AS)** was once asked what the absolute minimum of polytheism was, to which he replied, 'It is to contrive a ruling and because of it take side with people or against them.'[3629]

٣٢٤٣. الإمامُ الصّادقُ (ع) ـ لمّا سُئل عَن أدنَى الشرك ـ: مَنِ ابتَدَعَ رَأياً فَأحَبَّ علَيهِ أو أبغَضَ علَيهِ.[٣٥٩٩]

(See also: FAITH: section 186; DISBELIEF: section 1605)

(أُنظر) الإيمان: باب ١٨٦؛ الكفر: باب ١٦٠٥.

1022. Hidden Polytheism

١٠٢٢ ـ الشِّركُ الخَفِيُّ

"And most of them do not believe in Allah without ascribing partners to Him."[3630]

﴿وَما يُؤْمِنُ أَكْثَرُهُمْ بِاللهِ إِلّا وَهُمْ مُشْرِكُونَ﴾.[٣٦٠٠]

3244. **The Prophet (SAWA) said,** 'Beware of committing anything that warrants justification, for verily that is where hidden polytheism is.'[3631]

٣٢٤٤. رسولُ اللهِ (ص): إيّاكَ وما يُعتَذَرُ مِنهُ، فإنَّ فيهِ الشِّركَ الخَفِيَّ.[٣٦٠١]

3245. **Imām al-Ṣādiq (AS) said** when interpreting the Qur'anic verse: *"And most of them do not believe in Allah without ascribing partners to Him"*, 'This is in reference to man's statement: "Were it not for '*x*' I would surely have perished", or "Were it not for '*x*' I would indeed have been afflicted" or "Were it not for '*x*' my family would be at a loss." Do you not see that he has associated a partner to Allah in His Kingdom giving him sustenance and repelling misfortune from him?' He was subsequently asked, 'What if one were to say, "Were it not for Allah granting me *x*'s help, I would have perished…?"

٣٢٤٥. الإمامُ الصّادقُ (ع) ـ في قولِهِ تعالىٰ: ﴿وَما يُؤْمِنُ أَكْثَرُهُمْ...﴾ ـ: هُو الرَّجُلُ يقولُ: لَولا فُلانٌ لَهَلَكتُ، ولَولا فُلانٌ لَأَصَبتُ كذا وكذا، ولَولا فُلانٌ لَضاعَ عِيالي، ألا تَرىٰ أنّهُ قد جَعَلَ للهِ شَريكاً في مُلكِهِ يَرزُقُهُ ويَدفَعُ عَنهُ؟! قالَ [الراوي]: قلتُ: فيقولُ: لَولا أنَّ اللهَ مَنَّ عَلَيَّ

Imām replied, 'There is nothing wrong with saying things like this.'[3632]

بِفلانٍ لَهَلَكتُ ؟ قال: نَعَم، لا بَأسَ بهذا.[٣٦٠٢]

3246. **Imām al-Ṣādiq (AS) said** when interpreting the Qur'anic verse: *"And most of them do not believe in Allah without ascribing partners to Him"*, 'This refers to ascribing partners in Allah's obedience, not [just] in His worship.'[3633]

٣٢٤٦. عنه عليه السلام ـ أيضاً ـ: شِركُ طاعَةٍ ولَيسَ شِركَ عِبادَةٍ.[٣٦٠٣]

3247. **Imām al-Ṣādiq (AS) said,** 'Polytheism is more discreet than the crawling of an ant, and this includes things like turning one's ring to remind oneself, and other such [superstitions].'[3634]

٣٢٤٧. عنه عليه السلام: إنَّ الشِّركَ أخفىٰ مِن دَبِيبِ النَّملِ. وقالَ: مِنهُ تَحويلُ الخاتَمِ لِيَذكُرَ الحاجَةَ وشِبهُ هذا.[٣٦٠٤]

3248. **Imām al-Ṣādiq (AS) said** when interpreting the Qur'anic verse: *"And most of them do not believe in Allah without ascribing partners to Him"*, 'This refers to when people used to say, 'We are being rained on from the storm of *x*, or the storm of *y* [referring to various false gods]. And they used to consult soothsayers and believe whatever they told them.'[3635]

٣٢٤٨. عنه عليه السلام ـ في قولِهِ تعالىٰ: ﴿وما يُؤْمِنُ أَكثَرُهُمْ بِاللهِ إلّا وَهُمْ مُشْرِكُونَ﴾ ـ: كانُوا يَقولونَ: نُمطَرُ بِنَوءِ كذا، وبِنَوءِ كذا، ومِنها أنَّهُم كانوا يَأتُونَ الكُهّانَ فَيُصَدِّقُونَهُم بما يَقولونَ.[٣٦٠٥]

(See also: SHOWING OFF: section 787)

(أنظر) الرياء: باب ٧٨٧.

216

SATAN

الشَّيطانُ

1023. The Lesson to be Learned From how Allah dealt with Satan

١٠٢٣ ـ الاعتِبارُ بِما فَعَلَ اللهُ بِإبليسَ

3249. **Imām ʿAlī (AS) said,** 'So take a lesson from how Allah dealt with Iblīs [Satan], when He thwarted his great works and his extensive efforts, and he had been worshipping Allah for six thousand years, each hour of which was so long that it is not known whether they were years by the reckoning of this world or the next.'[3636]

٣٢٤٩. الإمامُ عليٌّ عليه السلام: فاعتَبِرُوا بما كانَ مِن فِعلِ اللهِ بِإبليسَ؛ إذ أحبَطَ عَمَلَهُ الطَّويلَ وجَهدَهُ الجَهِيدَ (الجميلَ) وكانَ قد عَبَدَ اللهَ سِتَّةَ آلافِ سَنَةٍ، لا يُدرىٰ أمِن سِني الدُّنيا أم مِن سِني الآخِرَةِ عن كِبْرِ ساعَةٍ واحِدَةٍ.[٣٦٠٦]

1024. Seeking Refuge in Allah from Satan

١٠٢٤ـ الاستِعاذَةُ باللهِ مِنَ الشَّيطانِ

"And say, 'My Lord! I seek Your protection from the promptings of the devils; and I seek Your protection, my Lord, from their presence near me.'"[3637]

﴿وَقُلْ رَبِّ أَعُوذُ بِكَ مِنْ هَمَزَاتِ الشَّيَاطِينِ * وَأَعُوذُ بِكَ رَبِّ أَن يَحْضُرُونِ﴾.٣٦٠٧

"When you recite the Qur'an, seek the protection of Allah against the outcast Satan."[3638]

﴿فَإِذَا قَرَأْتَ الْقُرْآنَ فَاسْتَعِذْ بِاللَّهِ مِنَ الشَّيْطَانِ الرَّجِيمِ﴾.٣٦٠٨

3250. **Imām 'Alī (AS) said,** 'I praise Allah and seek His aid against the acts that led to Satan's banishment and his eviction, and [I seek] His protection from his snares and his deceitful ways.'[3639]

٣٢٥٠. الإمامُ عليٌّ (عليه السلام): أحمَدُ اللهَ وأستَعينُهُ على مَداحِرِ الشَّيطانِ ومَزاجِرِهِ (مَزاحِرِهِ)، والاعتِصامِ مِن حَبائلِهِ ومَخاتِلِهِ.٣٦٠٩

1025. Satan's Enmity Towards Man

١٠٢٥ـ عَداوَةُ الشَّيطانِ لِلإنسانِ

"Satan is indeed your enemy, so treat him as an enemy. He only invites his confederates so that they may be among the inmates of the Blaze."[3640]

﴿إِنَّ الشَّيْطَانَ لَكُمْ عَدُوٌّ فَاتَّخِذُوهُ عَدُوًّا إِنَّمَا يَدْعُو حِزْبَهُ لِيَكُونُوا مِنْ أَصْحَابِ السَّعِيرِ﴾.٣٦١٠

3251. **Imām 'Alī (AS) said,** 'Be on your guard against the enemy who covertly penetrates into your hearts and secretly whispers into your ears.'[3641]

٣٢٥١. الإمامُ عليٌّ (عليه السلام): اِحذَروا عَدوّاً نَفَذَ في الصُّدورِ خَفِيّاً، ونَفَثَ في الآذانِ نَجِيّاً.٣٦١١

3252. **Imām al-Ṣādiq (AS) said,** 'Iblīs [Satan] lays out his traps in the Abode of Delusion, intending to ensnare none but our friends [i.e. lovers of the *Ahl al-Bayt*].'[3642]

٣٢٥٢. الإمامُ الصّادقُ (عليه السلام): لقد نَصَبَ إبليسُ حَبائلَهُ في دارِ الغُرورِ، فما يَقصِدُ فيها إلّا أولياءَنا.٣٦١٢

3253. **Imām al-Kāẓim (AS)** was once asked who one's archenemy is that one must fight, to which he replied, 'It is he who is closest to you and yet harbours the most enmity towards you … and he who provokes all your enemies against you, and he is Iblīs [Satan].'[3643]

٣٢٥٣. الإمامُ الكاظمُ (عليه السلام) ـ لَمّا سُئلَ عن أوجَبِ الأعداءِ مُجاهَدَةً ـ: أقرَبُهم إلَيكَ وأعداهُم لَكَ... ومَن يُحَرِّضُ أعداءَكَ علَيكَ، وهُو إبليسُ.٣٦١٣

1026. Caution Against Satan's Temptations

١٠٢٦ ـ التَّحذيرُ مِن فِتَنِ الشَّيطانِ

"O Children of Adam! Do not let Satan tempt you, like he expelled your parents from paradise, stripping them of their garments to expose to them their nakedness. Indeed he sees you – he and his hosts – whence you do not see them. We have indeed made the devils friends of those who have no faith."[3644]

﴿يا بَنِي آدَمَ لا يَفْتِنَنَّكُمُ الشَّيْطانُ كَما أَخْرَجَ أَبَوَيْكُمْ مِنَ الجَنَّةِ يَنْزِعُ عَنْهُما لِباسَهُما لِيُرِيَهُما سَوْآتِهِما إِنَّهُ يَراكُمْ هُوَ وَقَبِيلُهُ مِنْ حَيْثُ لا تَرَوْنَهُمْ إِنَّا جَعَلْنا الشَّياطِينَ أَوْلِياءَ لِلَّذِينَ لا يُؤْمِنُونَ﴾.[٣٦١٤]

3254. **Imām ʿAlī (AS) said,** 'There are three types of temptation: the love of women, which Satan uses as his sword; drinking wine, which Satan uses as his snare; and love of the dinar and dirham [symbols of wealth], which Satan uses as his arrow.'[3645]

٣٢٥٤ . الإمامُ عليٌّ عليه السلام :الفِتَنُ ثلاثٌ :حُبُّ النِّساءِ وهُو سَيفُ الشَّيطانِ، وشُربُ الخَمرِ وهُو فَخُّ الشَّيطانِ، وحُبُّ الدِّينارِ والدِّرهَمِ وهُو سَهمُ الشَّيطانِ.[٣٦١٥]

(See also: TRIAL AND TEMPTATION 312)

(أُنظر) عنوان ٣١٢ «الفتنة».

1027. Satan Worshippers

١٠٢٧ ـ عَبَدَةُ الشَّيطانِ

"Did I not exhort you, O children of Adam, saying, "Do not worship Satan. He is indeed your manifest enemy."[3646]

﴿لَمْ أَعْهَدْ إِلَيْكُمْ يا بَنِي آدَمَ أَنْ لا تَعْبُدُوا الشَّيْطانَ إِنَّهُ لَكُمْ عَدُوٌّ مُبِينٌ﴾.[٣٦١٦]

3255. **Imām ʿAlī (AS) said,** condemning those who follow Satan, 'They have taken Satan as the controller for their affairs, and he has in turn adopted them as his partners [used them as his traps]. He has laid eggs and hatched them in their bosoms, and crawled into their laps, until he saw through their eyes and spoke with their tongues. Thus does he lead them to commit errors and glamorizes their own foolish deeds to them, like the act of one whom Satan has made partner in his domain, speaking lies through his tongue.'[3647]

٣٢٥٥ . الإمامُ عليٌّ عليه السلام ـ في ذَمِّ أتباعِ الشَّيطانِ ـ: اِتَّخَذُوا الشَّيطانَ لِأمرِهِم مِلاكاً، واتَّخَذَهُم لَهُ أشراكاً، فَباضَ وفَرَّخَ في صُدُورِهِم، وَدَبَّ ودَرَجَ في حُجُورِهِم، فَنَظَرَ بِأعيُنِهِم، ونَطَقَ بِألسِنَتِهِم، فَرَكِبَ بِهِمُ الزَّلَلَ، وزَيَّنَ لَهُمُ الخَطَلَ، فِعلَ مَن قد شَرِكَهُ الشَّيطانُ في سُلطانِهِ، ونَطَقَ بالباطِلِ عَلىٰ لِسانِهِ![٣٦١٧]

1028. Satan's Allurements

١٠٢٨ ـ غَواياتُ الشَّيطانِ

"Satan threatens you with poverty and prompts you to [commit] indecent acts. But Allah promises you His forgiveness and grace, and Allah is all-bounteous, all-knowing."[3648]

﴿الشَّيْطانُ يَعِدُكُمُ الفَقْرَ وَيَأْمُرُكُمْ بِالفَحْشاءِ وَاللهُ يَعِدُكُمْ مَغْفِرَةً مِنْهُ وَفَضْلاً وَاللهُ واسِعٌ عَلِيمٌ﴾.[٣٦١٨]

"He makes them promises and gives them false hopes, yet Satan does not promise them anything but delusion."[3649]

﴿يَعِدُهُمْ وَيُمَنِّيهِمْ وَما يَعِدُهُمُ الشَّيْطانُ إلّا غُرُوراً﴾.[٣٦١٩]

"Why did they not entreat when Our might overtook them! But their hearts had hardened and Satan had made to seem decorous to them what they had been doing."[3650]

﴿فَلَوْلا إذْ جاءَهُمْ بَأْسُنا تَضَرَّعُوا وَلٰكِنْ قَسَتْ قُلُوبُهُمْ وَزَيَّنَ لَهُمُ الشَّيْطانُ ما كانُوا يَعْمَلُونَ﴾.[٣٦٢٠]

3256. **Imām ʿAlī (AS) said,** 'O Kumayl! Verily Iblīs [Satan] does not promise them in his own name, rather he promises them in Allah's name in order to cause them to disobey Him, and thus does he entangle them in difficulties.'[3651]

٣٢٥٦. الإمامُ عليٌّ ﷺ ـ لكميل بن زياد ـ: يا كُمَيلُ، إنَّ إبليسَ لا يَعِدُ عن نفسِهِ، وإنّما يَعِدُ عن رَبِّهِ لِيَحمِلَهُم على مَعصِيَتِهِ فَيُوَرِّطَهُم.[٣٦٢١]

3257. **Imām ʿAlī (AS) said,** 'Satan takes charge of him [the servant] and glamorizes the sin to him in order that he commit it, and makes him indulge false hopes of forgiveness in order that he delay it.'[3652]

٣٢٥٧. عنه ﷺ: الشَّيطانُ مُوَكَّلٌ به [أي بالعَبدِ] يُزَيِّنُ لَهُ المَعصيَةَ لِيَركَبَها، ويُمَنِّيهِ التَّوبَةَ لِيُسَوِّفَها.[٣٦٢٢]

3258. **Imām Zayn al-ʿĀbidīn (AS) said** in one of his supplications, 'Were it not for the fact that Satan misleads them from Your obedience, no disobeyer would have ever disobeyed You, and were it not for the fact that he portrays falsehood to them in the likeness of truth, no strayer would have ever strayed from Your path.'[3653]

٣٢٥٨. الإمامُ زينُ العابدينَ ﷺ ـ في دعائهِ ـ: فلولا أنَّ الشَّيطانَ يَختَدِعُهُم عَن طاعَتِكَ ما عَصاكَ عاصٍ، ولَولا أنَّهُ صَوَّرَ لَهُمُ الباطِلَ في مِثالِ الحَقِّ ما ضَلَّ عَن طَريقِكَ ضالٌّ.[٣٦٢٣]

3259. **Imām al-Ṣādiq (AS) said,** 'Iblīs [Satan] addresses his troops saying, 'Sow jealousy and dissention between them, for verily these are tantamount to polytheism in the sight of Allah.'[3654]

٣٢٥٩. الإمامُ الصّادقُ ﷺ: يقولُ إبليسُ لِجُنُودِهِ: أَلقُوا بَينَهُمُ الحَسَدَ والبَغيَ؛ فإنَّهُما يَعدِلانِ عِندَ اللهِ الشِّركَ.[٣٦٢٤]

1029. That which Renders One Immune from Satan

١٠٢٩ ـ ما يَعصِمُ مِنَ الشَّيطانِ

"Indeed he does not have any authority over those who have faith and put their trust in their Lord."[3655]

﴿إنَّهُ لَيْسَ لَهُ سُلْطانٌ عَلَى الَّذِينَ آمَنُوا وَعَلَىٰ رَبِّهِمْ يَتَوَكَّلُونَ﴾.[٣٦٢٥]

"Indeed as for My servants, you do not have any authority over them except the perverse who follow you."[3656]

﴿إنَّ عِبادِي لَيْسَ لَكَ عَلَيْهِمْ سُلْطانٌ إلّا مَنِ اتَّبَعَكَ مِنَ الغاوِينَ﴾.[٣٦٢٦]

3260. **Imām ʻAlī (AS) said,** 'Increase in your supplication and you will be secure from Satan's force.'[3657]

٣٢٦٠. الإمامُ عليٌّ (ع): أكثِرِ الدُّعاءَ تَسلَمْ مِن سَورَةِ الشَّيطانِ.[٣٦٢٧]

3261. **Imām al-Bāqir (AS) said,** 'Guard yourself against Iblīs [Satan] with true dread.'[3658]

٣٢٦١. الإمامُ الباقرُ (ع): تَحَرَّزْ مِن إبليسَ بالخَوفِ الصادِقِ.[٣٦٢٨]

3262. **Imām al-Ṣādiq (AS) said,** 'Iblīs [Satan] said, 'There are five types of people against whom I have no stratagem, whilst I have the rest of people firmly in my grasp: he who clings fast to Allah with a true intention and relies solely on Him in all his affairs, he who is in constant and abundant glorification of Allah day and night, he who pleases for his brother in faith whatever he pleases for himself, he who does not feel anxious about an affliction when it befalls him, and he who is satisfied with whatever Allah has allotted to him and does not worry about his sustenance.'[3659]

٣٢٦٢. الإمامُ الصّادقُ (ع): قالَ إبليسُ: خَمسَةٌ لَيسَ لي فيهِنَّ حِيلَةٌ وسائرُ الناسِ في قَبضَتي: مَنِ اعتَصَمَ باللهِ عن نيّةٍ صادِقةٍ واتَّكَلَ علَيهِ في جَميعِ اُمُورِهِ، ومَن كَثُرَ تَسبيحُهُ في لَيلِهِ ونَهارِهِ، ومَن رَضِيَ لأخِيهِ المؤمنِ بما يَرضاهُ لنفسِهِ، ومَن لَم يَجزَعْ على المُصيبةِ حينَ تُصيبُهُ، ومَن رَضِيَ بما قَسَمَ اللهُ لَهُ ولَم يَهتَمَّ لِرِزقِهِ.[٣٦٢٩]

1030. That Which Brings One Under Satan's Authority

١٠٣٠ـ ما يُسَلِّطُ الشَّيطانَ

"Whoever turns a blind eye to the remembrance of the All-beneficent, We assign him a devil who remains his companion."[3660]

﴿وَمَن يَعْشُ عَنْ ذِكْرِ الرَّحْمٰنِ نُقَيِّضْ لَهُ شَيْطاناً فَهُوَ لَهُ قَرِينٌ﴾.[٣٦٣٠]

(See also: Qur'an 3:155, 7:27, 19:83)

(اُنظر) آل عمران: ١٥٥ والأعراف: ٢٧ و مريم: ٨٣.

3263. **The Prophet (SAWA) narrated,** 'Moses (AS) was once sitting down when Iblīs [Satan] approached him … Moses asked him, 'So inform me about the sin which if the son of Adam were to commit would give you mastery over him.' He replied, 'When he feels proud of himself [for a particular action], and continues to perform that action, deeming his sin insignificant.'[3661]

٣٢٦٣. رسولُ اللهِ (ص): بَينَما موسى (ع) جالِساً إذ أقبَلَ إبليسُ... قالَ موسى: فَأخبِرْني بالذَّنبِ الذي إذا أذنَبَهُ ابنُ آدَمَ استَحوَذتَ علَيهِ. قالَ: إذا أعجَبَتهُ نَفسُهُ، واستَكثَرَ عَمَلَهُ، وصَغُرَ في عَينِهِ ذَنبُهُ.[٣٦٣١]

3264. **Imām ʻAlī (AS) said,** 'Sitting in the company of people who are driven by their base

٣٢٦٤. الإمامُ عليٌّ (ع): مُجالَسَةُ أهلِ الهَوى

desires is the key to obliviousness of one's faith and is the very seat of Satan's presence.'[3662]

مَنساةٌ للإيمانِ ومَحضَرَةٌ للشَّيطانِ.٣٦٦٢

3265. **Imām al-Ṣādiq (AS) said,** 'Satan's strongest forces are [mobilized through] women and anger.'[3663]

٣٢٦٥. الإمامُ الصّادقُ ﷺ : ليسَ لإبليسَ جُندٌ أشَدَّ مِنَ النِّساءِ والغَضَبِ.٣٦٦٣

217

POETRY

الشِّعرُ

1031. Explanation of the Verse of the Qur'an Condemning Poets

١٠٣١ـ تفسيرُ ما وَرَدَ في ذَمِّ الشُّعَراءِ

"As for the poets, [only] the perverse follow them. Have you not regarded that they rove in every valley, and that they say what they do not do? Barring those who have faith and do righteous deeds and remember Allah greatly, and aid each other after they have been wronged. And the wrongdoers will soon know at what goal they will end up."[3664]

﴿وَالشُّعَراءُ يَتَّبِعُهُمُ الغاوُونَ * أَلَمْ تَرَ أَنَّهُمْ فِي كُلِّ وادٍ يَهِيمُونَ * وَأَنَّهُمْ يَقُولُونَ ما لا يَفْعَلُونَ * إِلَّا الَّذِينَ آمَنُوا وَعَمِلُوا الصَّالِحاتِ وَذَكَرُوا اللهَ كَثِيراً وَانْتَصَرُوا مِنْ بَعدِ ما ظُلِمُوا﴾.٣٦٦٤

3266. **Imām al-Bāqir (AS) said** with regards to Allah's verse in the Qur'an: *"As for the poets…"*, 'Have you ever seen a poet being followed by anyone?! They are only people who have devoted themselves to works aside from religion, and hence have strayed and led others astray.'[3665]

٣٢٦٦. الإمامُ الباقرُ ﷺ ـ في قولِهِ تعالى: ﴿والشُّعَراءُ يَتَّبِعُهُمُ الغاوُونَ﴾ ـ: هل رَأيتَ شاعراً يَتَّبِعُهُ أحَدٌ ؟! إنّما هُم قَومٌ تَفَقَّهُوا لِغَيرِ الدِّينِ فَضَلُّوا وأضَلُّوا.٣٦٦٥

1032. Poetry is Jihād With the Tongue

١٠٣٢ـ الشِّعرُ جِهادٌ بِاللِّسانِ

3267. **The Prophet (SAWA)** was once asked about the poets, to which he replied, 'Verily the believer can either fight the enemy with his sword or his tongue, and by the One who has my soul in His Hand, it is as if they [the poets] shower them with arrows [by means of their defamatory poetry].'[3666]

٣٢٦٧. رسولُ اللهِ ﷺ ـ لَمّا سُئلَ عنِ الشِّعرِ ـ: إنّ المُؤمنَ مُجاهِدٌ بِسَيفِهِ ولِسانِهِ، والذي نَفسي بيدِهِ لَكأنّما يَنضِحُونَهم بِالنَّبلِ.٣٦٦٦

3268. **The Prophet (SAWA)** told Ḥassān b. Thābit [who used to write poetry in praise of the Prophet and

٣٢٦٨. عنه ﷺ ـ لِحَسّانَ بنِ ثابتٍ ـ: أُهجُ

in defamation of the polytheists], 'Compose defamatory poetry against the polytheists for verily the archangel Gabriel is with you.'[3667]

المُشركينَ؛ فإنّ جَبرَئيلَ مَعَكَ.[٣٦٣٧]

3269. **The Prophet (SAWA) said,** 'Verily poetry can contain words of wisdom, and verily eloquent rhetoric speech can contain words of enchantment.'[3668]

٣٢٦٩. عنه ﷺ: إنّ مِنَ الشِّعرِ لَحِكَماً، وإنّ مِنَ البَيانِ لَسِحراً.[٣٦٣٨]

3270. **Imām al-Ṣādiq (AS) said,** 'Whoever recites a single verse of poetry praising us [the *Ahl al-Bayt*], Allah, most High, builds a house for him in Paradise.'[3669]

٣٢٧٠. الإمامُ الصّادقُ ؑ: مَن قالَ فينا بَيتَ شِعرٍ بَنَى اللهُ تعالىٰ لَهُ بَيتاً في الجَنَّةِ.[٣٦٣٩]

3271. **Imām al-Ṣādiq (AS) said,** 'No sooner does someone recite a verse of poetry praising us than he is strengthened by the Holy Spirit.'[3670]

٣٢٧١. عنه ؑ: ما قالَ فينا قائلٌ بَيتاً مِنَ الشِّعرِ حتّىٰ يُؤَيَّدَ بِرُوحِ القُدُسِ.[٣٦٤٠]

218

THE BATTLE CRY

الشِّعارُ

1033. The Battle Cry

١٠٣٣ ـ الشِّعارُ فِي الحَرْبِ

3272. **The Prophet (SAWA) said,** commanding his troops to chant a slogan before a battle, 'Make sure your slogan includes one of the Names of Allah, the most High.'[3671]

٣٢٧٢. رسولُ اللهِ ﷺ ـ لَمّا أمَرَ بِالشِّعارِ قَبلَ الحَربِ ـ: لِيَكُنْ في شِعارِكُم اسمٌ مِن أسماءِ اللهِ.[٣٦٤١]

3273. **Imām ʿAlī (AS) said,** 'The battle cry of the Prophet's companions at the Battle of Badr was, *'O victorious one, put them to death!'*[3672]

٣٢٧٣. الإمامُ عليٌّ ؑ: كانَ شِعارُ أصحابِ رسولِ اللهِ ﷺ يومَ بَدرٍ: يا مَنصورُ أمِتْ.[٣٦٤٢]

3274. **Imām ʿAlī (AS)** – One of his battle cries on the day of the Battle of the Camel was, *'It is decreed that they will not be victorious! O Allah, grant us victory over the treacherous people.'*[3673]

٣٢٧٤. عنه ؑ ـ في شِعارٍ لَهُ لِيَومٍ مِن أيّامِ واقِعَةِ الجَمَلِ ـ: حم لا يُنْصَرُونَ، اللّهُمّ انصُرْنا على القَومِ الناكِثِينَ.[٣٦٤٣]

3275. **Imām al-Ṣādiq (AS) said,** 'Our battle cry on the day of the Battle of Badr was, *'Come to us O victory of Allah, come to us!'* … Ḥusayn (AS)'s battle

٣٢٧٥. الإمامُ الصّادقُ ؑ: شِعارُنا يومَ بَدرٍ: يا نَصرَ اللهِ اقتَرِبْ اقتَرِبْ... شِعارُ الحُسَينِ ؑ:

cry was, *'O Muḥammad'*, and our battle cry is also, *'O Muḥammad.'*[3674]

يا محمّدُ، وشِعارُنا: يا محمّدُ.[٣٦٤٤]

1034. The Muslims' Victory Cry on the Day of Resurrection

١٠٣٤ - شِعارُ المُسلِمينَ في القيامَةِ

3276. **The Prophet (SAWA) said,** 'The Muslims' victory cry as they cross the Bridge (*Ṣirāṭ*) on the Day of Resurrection will be, *'There is no god but Allah and on Allah do the trusting ones place their trust.'*[3675]

٣٢٧٦. رسولُ اللهِ ﷺ: شِعارُ المُسلمينَ علىٰ الصِّراطِ يَومَ القِيامَةِ: لا إلٰهَ إلّا اللهُ وعلىٰ اللهِ فَلْيَتَوكَّلِ المُتوكِّلُونَ.[٣٦٤٥]

3277. **The Prophet (SAWA) said,** 'The Muslims' victory cry as they cross the Bridge (*Ṣirāṭ*) on the Day of Resurrection will be, *'Lord! Protect us, protect us.'*[3676]

٣٢٧٧. عنه ﷺ: شِعارُ المؤمنينَ على الصِّراطِ يَومَ القِيامَةِ: رَبِّ، سَلِّمْ سَلِّمْ.[٣٦٤٦]

3278. **The Prophet (SAWA) said,** 'The Muslims' victory cry on the Day of Resurrection, during the darkness of resurrection, will be, *'There is no god but You.'*[3677]

٣٢٧٨. عنه ﷺ: شِعارُ المؤمنينَ يومَ القِيامَةِ في ظُلَمِ القِيامَةِ: لا إلٰهَ إلّا أنتَ.[٣٦٤٧]

219

INTERCESSION

الشّفاعة

1035. Intercession in the Life of this World

١٠٣٥ - الشَّفاعَةُ فِي الدُّنيا

3279. **The Prophet (SAWA) said,** 'Intercede for someone and you will be rewarded.'[3678]

٣٢٧٩. رسولُ اللهِ ﷺ: إشفَعُوا تُؤجَرُوا.[٣٦٤٨]

3280. **The Prophet (SAWA) said,** 'Whoever intercedes for someone settling thereby a financial liability or procuring someone's due profit, Allah will give him a firm footing on the day that feet will stumble.'[3679]

٣٢٨٠. عنه ﷺ: مَن شَفَعَ شَفاعَةً يَدفَعُ بها مَغرَماً أو يُحيِي بها مَغنَماً، ثَبَّتَ اللهُ تعالىٰ قَدَمَيهِ حِينَ تَدحَضُ الأقدامُ.[٣٦٤٩]

3281. **Imām al-Ṣādiq (AS) said,** 'Intercession is the *ẓakāt* of high rank.'[3680]

٣٢٨١ . الإمامُ الصّادقُ عليه السلام : الشَّـفاعةُ زَكـاةُ لجاهِ .[٣٦٥٠]

1036. Intercession in the Hereafter

١٠٣٦ ـ الشَّفاعَةُ فِي الآخِرَةِ

"Say, 'All intercession rests with Allah. To Him belongs the kingdom of the heavens and the earth; then you will be brought back to Him."[3681]

﴿قُلْ للهِ الشَّفاعَةُ جَمِيعاً[٣٦٥١] لَهُ مُلْكُ السَّماواتِ والأرْضِ ثُمَّ إلَيهِ تُرْجَعُونَ﴾ .[٣٦٥٢]

"Who is it that may intercede with Him except with His permission?"[3682]

﴿مَنْ ذا الَّذِي يَشْفَعُ عِنْدَهُ إلّا بِإذْنِهِ﴾ .[٣٦٥٣]

"No one will have the power to intercede [with Allah], except for him who has taken a covenant with the All-beneficent."[3683]

﴿لا يَمْلِكُونَ الشَّفاعَةَ إلّا مَنِ اتَّخَذَ عِندَ الرَّحمٰنِ عَهداً﴾ .[٣٦٥٤]

"Intercession will not avail that day except from him whom the All-beneficent allows and approves of his word."[3684]

﴿يَوْمَئِذٍ لا تَنْفَعُ الشَّفاعَةُ إلّا مَنْ أذِنَ لَهُ الرَّحمٰنُ وَرَضِيَ لَهُ قَوْلاً﴾ .[٣٦٥٥]

(See also: Qur'an 6:51, 70; 32:40; 22:28)

(انظر) الأنعام: ٥١ ، ٧٠ والسجدة: ٤٠ والأنبياء: ٢٨.

3282. **The Prophet (SAWA) said,** 'My intercession will avail those people from my community who love my household.'[3685]

٣٢٨٢ . رسولُ اللهِ صلى الله عليه وآله : شَفاعَتي لِاُمَّتي مَن أحَبَّ أهلَ بَيتي .[٣٦٥٦]

3283. **The Prophet (SAWA) said,** 'On the Day of Resurrection, I will surely intercede for anyone who harbours even a fly's wing's worth of faith in his heart.'[3686]

٣٢٨٣ . عنه صلى الله عليه وآله : لَأَشفَعَنَّ يَومَ القِيامَةِ لِمَن كانَ في قَلبِهِ جَناحُ بَعوضَةٍ إيمانٌ .[٣٦٥٧]

3284. **The Prophet (SAWA) said,** 'When I stand at the Glorious Station, I will intercede on behalf of those of my community who have perpetrated grave sins, and Allah will accept my intercession for them. By Allah, I will not intercede for anyone who hurts my progeny.'[3687]

٣٢٨٤ . عنه صلى الله عليه وآله : إذا قُمتُ المَقامَ المَحمودَ تَشَفَّعتُ في أصحابِ الكَبائرِ مِـن اُمَّـتي ، فَـيُشَفِّعُني اللهُ فِيهِم ، واللهِ لا تَشَفَّعتُ فِيمَن آذىٰ ذُرِّيَّتي .[٣٦٥٨]

3285. **The Prophet (SAWA) said,** 'Every prophet was given the right to a special request which they asked [from Allah], but I suppressed my request in return for the permission to intercede for my community on the Day of Resurrection.'[3688]

٣٢٨٥ . عنه صلى الله عليه وآله : لِكُلِّ نَبِيٍّ دَعوَةٌ قد دَعـا بِـها وقد سَأَلَ سُؤلاً ، وقد خَبَأتُ دَعوَتي لِشَـفاعَتِي لِاُمَّتي يَومَ القِيامَةِ .[٣٦٥٩]

3286. **Imām al-Bāqir (AS) said** with regards to Allah's verse in the Qur'an [addressing the Prophet (SAWA)]: *"Soon your Lord will give you [that with which] you will be pleased"*[3689], '(This is) intercession, by Allah it is intercession, by Allah it is intercession.'[3690]

٣٢٨٦ . الإمامُ الباقرُ ﷺ ـ في قولِهِ تعالىٰ: ﴿ولَسَوْفَ يُعْطِيكَ رَبُّكَ فَتَرْضىٰ﴾ ـ: الشَّفاعَةُ، واللهِ الشَّفاعةُ، واللهِ الشَّفاعَةُ.[٣٦٦٠]

3287. **Imām al-Ṣādiq (AS) said** with regards to Allah's verse in the Qur'an: *"No one will have the power to intercede [with Allah], except for him who has taken a covenant with the All-beneficent"*, '[This means] except for him who has been allowed intercession through his acceptance of the guardianship of the Commander of the Faithful, 'Alī (AS) and the Imāms after him, as this is the covenant with Allah.'[3691]

٣٢٨٧ . الإمامُ الصّادقُ ﷺ ـ في قولِهِ تعالىٰ: ﴿لا يَمْلِكُونَ الشَّفاعَةَ إلّا مَنِ اتَّخَذَ عِندَ الرَّحمٰنِ عَهْداً﴾ ـ: إلّا مَن أُذِنَ لَهُ بِوَلايَةِ أميرِ المؤمنينَ والأئمَّةِ مِن بَعدِهِ فهُو العَهدُ عندَ اللهِ.[٣٦٦١]

1037. Those Who Will Be Deprived of Intercession

١٠٣٧ ـ المَحرومُونَ مِنَ الشَّفاعَةِ

3288. **The Prophet (SAWA) said,** 'Two types of people will not be included in my intercession: the tyrannical and iniquitous ruler and the heretical extremist in matters of religion.'[3692]

٣٢٨٨ . رسولُ اللهِ ﷺ: رَجُلانِ لا تَنالُهُما شَفاعَتي: صاحِبُ سُلطانٍ عَسُوفٌ غَشُومٌ، وغالٍ في الدِّينِ مارِقٌ.[٣٦٦٢]

3289. **The Prophet (SAWA) said,** 'My intercession is intended for those who have committed grave sins [from among the Muslims], except for those guilty of polytheism and injustice to others.'[3693]

٣٢٨٩ . عنه ﷺ: أمّا شَفاعَتِي ففي أصحابِ الكبائرِ ما خَلا أهلَ الشِّركِ والظُّلمِ.[٣٦٦٣]

3290. **The Prophet (SAWA) said,** 'He who does not take his daily prayers seriously will neither benefit from my intercession nor meet me at the Heavenly Pond [of Kawthar], no by Allah.'[3694]

٣٢٩٠ . عنه ﷺ: لا يَنالُ شَفاعَتي مَنِ استَخَفَّ بِصلاتِهِ، ولا يَرِدُ عَلَيَّ الحَوضَ لا واللهِ.[٣٦٦٤]

3291. **The Prophet (SAWA) said,** 'My intercession on behalf of one who does not believe in my intercession will not be accepted by Allah.'[3695]

٣٢٩١ . عنه ﷺ: مَن لم يُؤمِنْ بِشَفاعَتِي فلا أنالَهُ اللهُ شَفاعَتِي.[٣٦٦٥]

3292. **Imām al-Ṣādiq (AS),** when he asked for his relatives to be gathered around him as his death

٣٢٩٢ . الإمامُ الصّادقُ ﷺ ـ لَمّا أمَرَ بِاجتِماعِ قَرابَتِهِ حَولَهُ وقد حَضَرَتهُ الوَفاةُ ـ: إنَّ

approached, said to them, 'Verily our intercession will not avail one who takes his prayer lightly.'[3696]

شَفاعَتَنا لَن تَنالَ مُستَخِفّاً بِالصَّلاةِ.[٣٦٦٦]

3293. **Imām al-Ṣādiq (AS) said,** 'Even if the most favoured angels and all the prophets were to intercede for a Nāṣibī[3697], their intercession would not be accepted.'[3698]

٣٢٩٣. عنه عليه السلام: لَو أنَّ المَلائكَةَ المُقَرَّبينَ والأنبياءَ المُرسَلِينَ شَفَعُوا في ناصِبٍ ما شُفِّعُوا.[٣٦٦٧]

1038. The Need of All for Intercession

١٠٣٨ ـ حاجَةُ الأوَّلينَ وَالآخِرينَ إلَى الشَّفاعَةِ

3294. A man called Abū Ayman once came to Imām al-Bāqir (AS) saying, 'O Abū Ja'far, you delude people by saying, 'Muḥammad's intercession [will help you], Muḥammad's intercession!' At this, the Imām (AS) got so angry that his face was glowering, and said, 'Woe betide you Abū Ayman! If your belly and your private parts keep you away from sin, does that mean they delude you? You would only have to see the atrocities of the Day of Resurrection to need Muḥammad (SAWA)'s intercession. Woe unto you! In any case, do you think that he will only intercede for those whose punishment in the Fire is obligatory?!' Then he continued, saying, 'Every single person, from the first to the last, will need the intercession of Muḥammad (SAWA) on the Day of Resurrection.'[3699]

٣٢٩٤. بحار الأنوار عَن أبي العبّاسِ المكبرِ عَن الإمام الباقرِ عليه السلام ـ وقد قالَ لَهُ أبو أيمنَ: يا أباجعفرٍ، تَغُرُّونَ النّاسَ وتَقولونَ: شَفاعَةُ محمّدٍ، شَفاعَةُ محمّدٍ! فَغَضِبَ عليه السلام حتّىٰ تَرَبَّدَ وَجهُهُ ـ: وَيحَكَ يا أبا أيمَنَ! أغَرَّكَ إن عَفَّ بَطْنُكَ وفَرجُكَ؟! أما لَو قد رَأيتَ أفزاعَ القِيامَةِ لقَدِ احتَجتَ إلىٰ شَفاعَةِ محمّدٍ صلى الله عليه وآله، وَيلَكَ فَهل يَشفَعُ إلّا لِمَن وَجَبَت لَهُ النارُ؟! ثُمَّ قالَ: ما مِن أحَدٍ مِنَ الأوَّلينَ والآخِرِينَ إلّا وهُوَ مُحتاجٌ إلىٰ شَفاعَةِ محمّدٍ صلى الله عليه وآله يومَ القِيامَةِ.[٣٦٦٨]

1039. Types of Intercessors

١٠٣٩ ـ أصْنافُ الشُّفَعاءِ

3295. **The Prophet (SAWA) said,** 'Three types of people have the right to intercede with Allah, and their intercession will be accepted: the prophets, then the scholars, and then the martyrs.'[3700]

٣٢٩٥. رسولُ اللهِ صلى الله عليه وآله: ثلاثةٌ يَشفَعُونَ إلى اللهِ عَزَّوجلَّ فَيُشَفَّعُونَ: الأنبياءُ، ثُمّ العُلَماءُ، ثُمّ الشُّهَداءُ.[٣٦٦٩]

3296. **The Prophet (SAWA) said,** '[The right of] Intercession belongs to the prophets, their vicegerents, the believers and the angels.'[3701]

٣٢٩٦. عنه صلى الله عليه وآله: الشَّفاعَةُ لِلأنْبِياءِ والأوصِياءِ والمُؤمِنينَ والمَلائكةِ.[٣٦٧٠]

3297. **The Prophet (SAWA) said,** 'There are five intercessors: the Qur'an, consanguinity, a trust, your Prophet, and your Prophet's household.'[3702]

٣٢٩٧. عنه صلى الله عليه وآله: الشُّفَعاءُ خَمسَةٌ: القُرآنُ، والرَّحِمُ، والأمانَةُ، ونَبِيُّكُم، وأهلُ بيتِ نَبِيِّكُم.[٣٦٧١]

3298. **The Prophet (SAWA) said,** 'There is no intercessor more effective than repentance.'[3703]

٣٢٩٨. عنه ﷺ: لا شَفيعَ أنجَحُ مِنَ التَّوبَةِ.٣٦٧٢

3299. **Imām ʿAlī (AS) said,** 'The intercessor for all of creation is action according to what is right and adherence to the truth.'[3704]

٣٢٩٩. الإمامُ عليٌّ ﷺ: شافِعُ الخَلقِ العَمَلُ بِالحَقِّ ولُزومُ الصِّدقِ.٣٦٧٣

1040. The People Most Deserving of Intercession

١٠٤٠ ـ أحَقُّ النّاسِ بِالشَّفاعَةِ

3300. **The Prophet (SAWA) said,** 'Verily the closest from among you to me tomorrow [in the Hereafter], and the most eligible of you for my intercession are those who are the most truthful from amongst you, the most conscientious at returning a trust placed in their care, the most good-natured, and the ones who have close ties with people.'[3705]

٣٣٠٠. رسولُ اللهِ ﷺ: إنّ أقرَبَكُم مِنّي غَداً وأوجَبَكُم عَلَيَّ شَفاعَةً: أصدَقُكُم لِساناً، وأدّاكُم لِلأمانَةِ، وأحسَنُكُم خُلقاً، وأقرَبُكُم مِنَ النّاسِ.٣٦٧٤

1041. A Believer's Right to Intercession Depends on the Extent of His Deeds

١٠٤١ ـ شَفاعَةُ المُؤمِنِ عَلىٰ قَدرِ عَمَلِهِ

3301. **The Prophet (SAWA) said,** 'There are people from among the believers who have the right to intercession like Rabīʿa and Muḍar. A believer has the right to intercede on behalf of at least thirty people.'[3706]

٣٣٠١. رسولُ اللهِ ﷺ: في المؤمنينَ مَن يَشفَعُ مِثلَ رَبيعَةَ ومُضَرَ، وأقَلُّ المُؤمنينَ شَفاعَةً مَن يَشفَعُ لِثَلاثينَ إنساناً.٣٦٧٥

3302. **Imām al-Bāqir (AS) said,** 'A man intercedes on behalf of his tribe, or for his family, or even just for two other people, depending on the extent of his deeds, for that is the Glorious Station.'[3707]

٣٣٠٢. الإمامُ الباقرُ ﷺ: يَشفَعُ الرَّجُلُ في القَبيلَةِ، ويَشفَعُ الرَّجُلُ لِأهلِ البَيتِ، ويَشفَعُ الرجُلُ لِلرَّجُلَينِ عَلىٰ قَدرِ عَمَلِهِ، فذلكَ المَقامُ المَحمودُ.٣٦٧٦

1042. The Minimum Number that A Believer Can Intercede

١٠٤٢ ـ أدنَى المُؤمِنينَ شَفاعَةً

3303. **The Prophet (SAWA) said,** 'I intercede and my intercession will be accepted, and ʿAlī will intercede and his intercession will be accepted, and my Ahl al-Bayt will interced and their intercession will be accepted, and the least

٣٣٠٣. قالَ رسولُ اللهِ ﷺ: إنّي أشفَعُ يَومَ القِيامَةِ فَأُشَفَّعُ، ويَشفَعُ عَلِيٌّ فَيُشَفَّعُ، ويَشفَعُ أهلُ بَيتي فَيُشفَعُونَ، وإنَّ أدنَى المُؤمِنينَ شَفاعَةً لَيَشفَعُ في

intercession of a believer is that he will intercede forty of his brothers whom each one of them deserved Hellfire.'[3708]

أربَعينَ مِن إخوانِهِ كُلٌّ قَدِ استَوجَبُوا النّارَ.٣٦٧٧

3304. **Imām al-Bāqir (AS) said,** 'The believer who can intercede the least shall intercede for up to thirty people, and at this time the dweller of Hell will say, '*Now we have no to intercessors, nor do we have any sympathetic friend.*'[3709] [3710]

٣٣٠٤. الإمامُ الباقرُ عليه السلام: إنّ أدنَى المؤمنينَ شَفاعَةً لَيَشفَعُ لِثلاثينَ إنساناً، فعِندَ ذلكَ يقولُ أهلُ النّارِ: ﴿فَما لَنا مِنْ شافِعِينَ * ولا صَدِيقٍ حَمِيمٍ﴾.٣٦٧٨، ٣٦٧٩

220

WRETCHEDNESS

الشَّقاوَة

1043. Characteristics of a Wretched Person

١٠٤٣ـ خَصائصُ الشَّقيِّ

3305. **Imām ʿAlī (AS) said,** 'The wretched one is he who lets himself be deceived by his whims and his delusion.'[3711]

٣٣٠٥. الإمامُ عليٌّ عليه السلام: الشَّقِيُّ مَن انخَدَعَ لِهَواهُ وغُرُورِهِ.٣٦٨٠

3306. **Imām ʿAlī (AS) said,** 'Verily the wretched person is he who is deprived of drawing any benefit from his intellect and the experiences that he has been granted.'[3712]

٣٣٠٦. عنه عليه السلام: إنَّ الشَّقِيَّ مَن حُرِمَ نَفعَ ما أُوتِيَ مِنَ العَقلِ والتَّجرِبَةِ.٣٦٨١

3307. **Imām ʿAlī (AS) said,** 'Be on your guard against sins and restrain yourself from them, for verily the wretched one is he who gives himself free rein to them.'[3713]

٣٣٠٧. عنه عليه السلام: تَوَقَّوُا المَعاصِيَ واحبِسُوا أنفُسَكُم عنها؛ فإنَّ الشَّقِيَّ مَن أطلَقَ فيها عِنانَهُ.٣٦٨٢

1044. The Wretched One was Wretched as a Foetus in His Mother's Womb

١٠٤٤ـ الشَّقِيُّ شَقِيٌّ في بَطنِ أُمِّهِ

3308. **The Prophet (SAWA) said,** 'The prosperous one is he who prospered from when he was in his mother's womb, and the wretched one is he who was wretched from when he was in his mother's womb.'[3714]

٣٣٠٨. رسولُ اللهِ ﷺ: السَّعيدُ مَن سَعِدَ في بَطنِ أُمِّهِ، والشَّقِيُّ مَن شَقِيَ في بَطنِ أُمِّهِ.٣٦٨٣

3309. **Imām al-Ṣādiq (AS) said,** 'Verily Allah, Mighty and Exalted, created prosperity and wretchedness before

٣٣٠٩. الإمامُ الصّادقُ عليه السلام: إنّ اللهَ عزَّ وجلَّ خَلَقَ

He even created His creation. So whoever Allah knows will be prosperous, He will never despise, and even when he commits an evil deed, He will despise the deed but not the person. And if He knows that someone will be wretched, He will never love him, and even when he performs a good deed, He will love the deed but despise the person because of what he is to become.'[3715]

السَّعادَةَ والشَّقاوَةَ قبلَ أن يَخلُقَ خَلقَهُ، فَمَن عَلِمَهُ اللهُ سَعيداً لَم يُبغِضْهُ أبداً، وإن عَمِلَ شَرّاً أبغَضَ عَمَلَهُ ولَم يُبغِضْهُ، وإن كانَ عَلِمَهُ شَقِيّاً لَم يُحِبَّهُ أبداً، وإن عَمِلَ صالحاً أحَبَّ عَمَلَهُ وأبغَضَهُ لِما يَصِيرُ إلَيهِ.[٣٦٨٤]

3310. **Imām al-Ṣādiq (AS) said,** 'Verily Allah, Blessed and most High, may transfer a servant from wretchedness to prosperity, but He never transfers anyone from prosperity to wretchedness.'[3716]

٣٣١٠. عنه عليه السلام: إنّ اللهَ تباركَ وتعالىٰ يَنقُلُ العَبدَ مِنَ الشَّقاءِ إلى السَّعادَةِ، ولا يَنقُلُهُ مِن السَّعادةِ إلى الشَّقاءِ.[٣٦٨٥]

3311. **Imām al-Kāẓim (AS)** was once asked by Ibn Abī 'Umayr about the Prophet (SAWA)'s saying, 'The prosperous one is he who prospered from when he was in his mother's womb, and the wretched one is he who was wretched from when he was in his mother's womb', to which he replied, 'The wretched one is he who, from when he was in his mother's womb, Allah knew would commit acts characteristic of wretched people, and the prosperous one is he who, from when he was in his mother's womb, Allah knew would perform acts characteristic of prosperous people.'[3717]

٣٣١١. التوحيد عن محمّدَ بنِ أبي عُمَيرٍ: سَألتُ أبا الحسنِ موسىٰ بنِ جَعفرٍ عليه السلام عَن معنىٰ قولِ رَسولِ اللهِ صلى الله عليه وآله: «الشَّقِيُّ مَن شَقِيَ في بَطنِ اُمِّهِ، والسَّعيدُ مَن سَعِدَ في بَطنِ اُمِّهِ»، فقالَ: الشَّقِيُّ مَن عَلِمَ اللهُ وهُو في بَطنِ اُمِّهِ أنّهُ سَيَعمَلُ أعمالَ الأشقِياءِ، والسَّعيدُ مَن عَلِمَ اللهُ وهُو في بَطنِ اُمِّهِ أنّهُ سَيَعمَلُ أعمالَ السُّعَداءِ.[٣٦٨٦]

1045. That Which Brings About Wretchedness

١٠٤٥ ـ ما يوجِبُ الشَّقاءَ

3312. **Imām 'Alī (AS) said,** 'The cause of wretchedness is love of this world.'[3718]

٣٣١٢. الإمامُ عليٌّ عليه السلام: سَبَبُ الشَّقاءِ حُبُّ الدُّنيا.[٣٦٨٧]

3313. **Imām al-Ḥusayn (AS) said** in his supplication of 'Arafa, 'O Allah, make me fear you as if I see you, let me prosper through being conscious

٣٣١٣. الإمامُ الحسينُ عليه السلام ـ في دعاءِ يَومِ عَرَفَةَ ـ: اللّهُمّ اجعَلْني أخشاكَ كَأنّي أراكَ، وأسعِدْني

of my duty to You, and keep me from becoming wretched as a consequence of Your disobedience.'[3719]

بِتَقواكَ ، ولا تُشقِني بِمَعصِيَتِكَ .[٣٦٨٨]

1046. The Most Wretched of All People

١٠٤٦ ـ أشقَى النّاسِ

3314. **Prophet Jesus (AS) said,** 'The most wretched of people is he who is reputed amongst people for his knowledge but not known for his action thereof.'[3720]

٣٣١٤ . عيسى عليه السلام : أشقَى النّاسِ مَن هُو مَعروفٌ عندَ الناسِ بِعِلمِهِ مَجهولٌ بِعَمَلِهِ .[٣٦٨٩]

3315. **The Prophet (SAWA) said,** 'The most wretched of all wretched people is he who faces poverty in this world as well as punishment in the Hereafter.'[3721]

٣٣١٥ . رسولُ اللّهِ ﷺ : أشقَى الأشقياءِ مَنِ اجتَمَعَ علَيهِ فَقرُ الدُّنيا وعَذابُ الآخِرَةِ .[٣٦٩٠]

3316. **Imām 'Alī (AS)** when asked who the most wretched of all people was, replied, 'He who sells his Hereafter for someone else's profit in this world.'[3722]

٣٣١٦ . الإمامُ عليٌّ عليه السلام ـ وقد سُئلَ عن أشقَى النّاسِ ـ : مَن باعَ دِينَهُ بِدُنيا غَيرِهِ .[٣٦٩١]

1047. The Symptoms of Wretchedness

١٠٤٧ ـ عَلاماتُ الشَّقاءِ

3317. **The Prophet (SAWA) said,** 'Among the symptoms of wretchedness are: a look of apathy in the eyes, hardness of the heart, intense greed in seeking out one's livelihood, and persistence in committing sins.'[3723]

٣٣١٧ . رسولُ اللّهِ ﷺ : مِن علاماتِ الشَّقاءِ : جُمودُ العَينِ ، وقَسوَةُ القَلبِ ، وشِدَّةُ الحِرصِ في طَلَبِ الرِّزقِ ، والإصرارُ على الذَّنبِ .[٣٦٩٢]

3318. **Imām 'Alī (AS) said,** 'One of the symptoms of wretchedness is swindling one's own friend.'[3724]

٣٣١٨ . الإمامُ عليٌّ عليه السلام : مِن عَلامَةِ الشَّقاءِ غِشُّ الصَّديقِ .[٣٦٩٣]

3319. **Imām 'Alī (AS) said,** 'Among the symptoms of wretchedness is maltreatment of good people.'[3725]

٣٣١٩ . عنه عليه السلام : مِن علاماتِ الشَّقاءِ الإساءَةُ إلى الأخيارِ .[٣٦٩٤]

221

THANKSGIVING
الشُكر

1048. Enjoinment of Thanksgiving to Allah
١٠٤٨ـ الحَثُّ عَلَى الشُكرِ للهِ

"Remember Me, and I will remember you, and thank Me, and do not be ungrateful to Me."[3726]

﴿فاذْكُروني أذْكُرْكُمْ واشْكُروا لي وَلا تَكفُرُونِ﴾.[٣٦٩٥]

3320. **Imām ʿAlī (AS) said,** 'Thankfulness is the adornment of wealth, whereas patience is the adornment of tribulation.'[3727]

٣٣٢٠. الإمامُ عليٌّ عليه السلام: الشُّكرُ زِينَةُ الغِنىٰ، والصَّبرُ زِينَةُ البَلوىٰ.[٣٦٩٦]

3321. **Imām ʿAlī (AS) said,** 'The first duty incumbent upon you towards Allah, Glory be to Him, is thanksgiving for His favours and seeking out His pleasure.'[3728]

٣٣٢١. عنه عليه السلام: أوَّلُ ما يَجِبُ علَيكُم للهِ سبحانَهُ، شُكرُ أيادِيهِ وابتِغاءُ مَراضِيهِ.[٣٦٩٧]

3322. **Imām al-Ṣādiq (AS) said,** 'Every single breath you take necessitates an essential thanks from you, or rather a thousand thanks or more.'[3729]

٣٣٢٢. الإمامُ الصّادقُ عليه السلام: في كُلِّ نَفَسٍ مِن أنفاسِكَ شُكرٌ لازِمٌ لكَ، بَل ألفٌ وأكثَرُ.[٣٦٩٨]

1049. The Virtue of the Thankful One
١٠٤٩ـ فَضلُ الشّاكِرِ

"Rather, worship Allah, and be among the thankful ones."[3730]

﴿بَلِ اللهَ فاعبُدْ وَكُنْ مِنَ الشّاكِرِينَ﴾.[٣٦٩٩]

3323. It is narrated in *Miṣbāḥ al-Sharīʿa*, 'If there was to be an act of worship for Allah's sincere servants to carry out better in the sight of Allah than thanksgiving to Him in every situation, He would have definitely singled out these worshippers for a mention from amongst the rest of creation for their carrying out this special act of worship. And for the very fact that there is no better act of worship than it [i.e. thanksgiving], He has distinguished it from all other acts of worship and has distinguished those who practice

٣٣٢٣. مصباح الشريعة: لَو كانَ عندَ اللهِ عِبادَةٌ تَعَبَّدُ بها عِبادَةُ المُخلِصينَ أفضَلَ مِن الشُّكرِ علىٰ كُلِّ حالٍ لَأطلَقَ لَفظَهُ فيهِم مِن جَميعِ الخَلقِ بها، فَلمّا لَم يَكُن أفضَلُ مِنها خَصَّها

it, saying, *"And very few of My servants are truly thankful."*[3731]

مِن بَينِ العِباداتِ وخَصَّ أربابَها، فقالَ: ﴿وقَليلٌ مِنْ عِبادِيَ الشَّكُورُ﴾.[٣٧٠٠]

3324. **Imām al-Hādī (AS) said,** 'The thankful person prospers more as a result of his thanks than as a result of the bounty which incited the thanks, because bounties are sources of delight [in this world] whereas to thank brings bounties in this world and the hereafter.'[3732]

٣٣٢٤. الإمامُ الهاديُّ عليه السلام: الشاكِرُ أسعَدُ بالشُّكرِ مِنهُ بِالنِّعمَةِ التي أوجَبَتِ الشُّكرَ؛ لأنَّ النِّعَمَ مَتاعٌ، والشُّكرَ نِعَمٌ وعُقبىٰ.[٣٧٠١]

3325. **Imām al-ʿAskarī (AS) said,** 'None but the thankful one knows the true worth of a bounty, and none but the one with inner knowledge [or gnostic] is truly thankful for a bounty.'[3733]

٣٣٢٥. الإمامُ العسكريُّ عليه السلام: لا يَعرِفُ النِّعمَةَ إلّا الشاكِرُ، ولا يَشكُرُ النِّعمَةَ إلّا العارِفُ.[٣٧٠٢]

1050. The Role of Thankfulness in the Increase (of Bounties)

١٠٥٠ - دَورُ الشُّكرِ فِي الزِّيادَةِ

"And when your Lord proclaimed, 'If you are thankful, I will surely increase you [in bounty], but if you are ungrateful, My punishment is indeed severe."[3734]

﴿وَإِذْ تَأَذَّنَ رَبُّكُمْ لَئِنْ شَكَرْتُم لَأَزِيدَنَّكُمْ وَلَئِنْ كَفَرْتُمْ إنَّ عَذابِي لَشَدِيدٌ﴾.[٣٧٠٣]

3326. **The Prophet (SAWA) said,** 'Allah does not open the door of thanks for His servant and keep the door of increase shut.'[3735]

٣٣٢٦. رسولُ اللهِ صلى الله عليه وآله: ما فَتَحَ اللهُ علىٰ عَبدٍ بابَ شُكرٍ فَخَزَنَ عنهُ بابَ الزِّيادَةِ.[٣٧٠٤]

3327. **Imām ʿAlī (AS) said,** 'When Allah bestows a bounty upon a servant, no sooner does the latter feel thankful for it in his heart than he becomes deserving of increase therein before the expression of thanks has even reached his tongue.'[3736]

٣٣٢٧. الإمامُ عليٌّ عليه السلام: ما أنعَمَ اللهُ علىٰ عَبدٍ نِعمَةً فَشَكَرَها بِقَلبِهِ، إلّا استَوجَبَ المَزِيدَ فيها قَبلَ أن يُظهِرَ شُكرَها عَلىٰ لِسانِهِ.[٣٧٠٥]

1051. The Necessity of Thanksgiving for the Ability to Thank

١٠٥١ - وُجوبُ الشُّكرِ عَلَى الشُّكرِ

3328. **Imām Zayn al-ʿĀbidīn (AS) said** in his supplication, 'So how can I ever achieve thanksgiving?! For my thanking You requires thanksgiving in itself. Whenever I say, 'To You belongs

٣٣٢٨. الإمامُ زينُ العابدينَ عليه السلام ـ في المناجاةِ ـ: فكيفَ لي بتَحصيلِ الشُّكرِ، وشُكرِي إيّاكَ يَفتَقِرُ إلىٰ شكرٍ؟! فَكُلَّما قُلتُ: لكَ الحَمدُ، وَجَبَ عَلَيَّ

Praise [Thanks]', it becomes thereby incumbent upon me to say, 'To You belongs Praise [Thanks].'[3737]

لذلكَ أن أقولَ: لكَ الحَمدُ.[٣٧٠٦]

3329. **Imām al-Ṣādiq (AS) said,** 'Allah, most High, revealed to Prophet Moses (AS) saying, 'O Moses, thank Me with the thanks that is due to Me.' Moses asked, 'O Lord, but how can I thank You with the thanks that is due to You, when every single expression of thanks that I may convey has been bestowed upon Me by You?' He replied, 'O Moses, you thank Me with the thanks that is due to Me when you acknowledge that it is indeed from Me.'[3738]

٣٣٢٩. الإمامُ الصّادقُ عليه السلام: أوحَى اللهُ تعالىٰ إلىٰ موسىٰ عليه السلام: يا موسىٰ، اشكُرْني حَقَّ شُكرِي، فقالَ: يا ربِّ كيفَ أشكُرُكَ حَقَّ شُكرِكَ، وليسَ مِن شُكرٍ أشكُرُكَ بِهِ إلّا وأنتَ أنعَمتَ بِهِ عَلَيَّ؟! فقالَ: يا موسىٰ شَكَرتَني حَقَّ شُكري حينَ عَلِمتَ أنَّ ذلكَ مِنّي.[٣٧٠٧]

1052. True Thanksgiving

١٠٥٢ ـ حقيقةُ الشُّكرِ

3330. **Imām ʿAlī (AS) said,** '[True] thanksgiving for every bounty lies in restraining oneself from the things that Allah has prohibited.'[3739]

٣٣٣٠. الإمامُ عليٌّ عليه السلام: شُكرُ كُلِّ نِعمَةٍ الوَرَعُ عن مَحارِمِ اللهِ.[٣٧٠٨]

3331. **Imām ʿAlī (AS) said,** 'When you vanquish your enemy, let your pardon of him serve as thanksgiving for the power [given to you] over him.'[3740]

٣٣٣١. عنه عليه السلام: إذا قَدَرتَ علىٰ عَدُوِّكَ فَاجعَلِ العَفوَ عَنهُ شُكراً لِلقُدرَةِ علَيهِ.[٣٧٠٩]

3332. **Imām al-Bāqir (AS) said,** 'Regard even a little sustenance from Allah as too much for yourself so that you can be thankful.'[3741]

٣٣٣٢. الإمامُ الباقرُ عليه السلام: اِستَكثِرْ لِنفسِكَ مِنَ اللهِ قليلَ الرِّزقِ تَخَلُّصاً إلى الشُّكرِ.[٣٧١٠]

3333. **Imām al-Ṣādiq (AS) said,** 'Thanksgiving for a bounty is accomplished through avoidance of prohibited things, and an expression of complete thanks is when a man says, 'All praise belongs to Allah, the Lord of the worlds.'[3742]

٣٣٣٣. الإمامُ الصّادقُ عليه السلام: شُكرُ النِّعمَةِ اجتِنابُ المَحارِمِ، وتَمامُ الشُّكرِ قولُ الرجُلِ: الحَمدُ للهِ رَبِّ العالَمينَ.[٣٧١١]

3334. **Imām al-Ṣādiq (AS) said,** 'He whom Allah favours with the bestowal of a bounty and who then acknowledges it with his heart has verily conveyed [true] thanks for it.'[3743]

٣٣٣٤. عنه عليه السلام: مَن أنعَمَ اللهُ علَيهِ بنِعمَةٍ فَعَرَفَها بقَلبِهِ، فقد أدّىٰ شُكرَها.[٣٧١٢]

3335. **Imām al-Ṣādiq (AS) narrated,** 'When the Prophet (SAWA) was faced with a situation that

٣٣٣٥. عنه عليه السلام: كانَ رسولُ اللهِ صلى الله عليه وآله إذا وَرَدَ علَيهِ أمرٌ

pleased him, he used to say, 'Praise be to Allah for this bounty', and when he was faced with a situation that made him sorrowful, he used to say, 'Praise be to Allah in every situation.'[3744]

يَسُرُّهُ قالَ: الحَمدُ للهِ علىٰ هذِهِ النِّعمَةِ، وإذا وَرَدَ عليهِ أمرٌ يَغتَمُّ بِهِ قالَ: الحَمدُ للهِ علىٰ كُلِّ حالٍ.[٣٧١٣]

3336. It is narrated in *Miṣbāḥ al-Sharīʿa (The Lantern of the Path)* in what has been attributed to Imām al-Ṣādiq (AS): 'The lowest level of thankfulness is to see the bounty as coming from Allah directly without attaching the heart to any other cause save Allah Mighty and Exalted [does not consider another cause for it]. It consists of being satisfied with what is given, and not disobeying Him by means of His bounty, nor opposing Him in any of His commands and prohibitions as a result of that bounty.'[3745]

٣٣٣٦. مصباح الشريعة ـ فيما نسبه إلى الإمام الصّادق عليه السلام ـ: أدنى الشُّكرِ رُؤيَةُ النِّعمَةِ مِنَ اللهِ مِن غَيرِ عِلَّةٍ يَتَعَلَّقُ القَلبُ بها دُونَ اللهِ والرِّضا بما عطاه، وأن لا تَعصِيَهُ بِنعمَتِهِ و تُخالِفَهُ بِشيءٍ مِن أمرِهِ ونَهيِهِ بِسَبَبِ نِعمَتِهِ.[٣٧١٤]

1053. The Most Thankful of People

١٠٥٣ ـ أشكَرُ النّاسِ

3337. **Imām ʿAlī (AS) said,** 'The most thankful of people is he who is most content whilst the most ungrateful of people is he who is most covetous.'[3746]

٣٣٣٧. الإمامُ عليٌّ عليه السلام: أشكَرُ النّاسِ أقنَعُهُم، وأكفَرُهُم لِلنِّعَمِ أجشَعُهُم.[٣٧١٥]

3338. **Imām Zayn al-ʿĀbidīn (AS) said,** 'The most thankful among you to Allah is he who is most thankful towards people.'[3747]

٣٣٣٨. الإمامُ زينُ العابدينَ عليه السلام: أشكَرُكُم للهِ أشكَرُكُم للناسِ.[٣٧١٦]

1054. Enjoinment of Thanking One Who Does Good To You

١٠٥٤ ـ الحثُّ علىٰ شُكرِ المُحسِنِ

3339. **Imām al-Ḥasan (AS) said,** 'It is blameworthy that you do not thank for a favour done unto you.'[3748]

٣٣٣٩. الإمامُ الحسنُ عليه السلام: اللُّومُ أن لا تَشكُرَ النِّعمَةَ.[٣٧١٧]

3340. **Imām Zayn al-ʿĀbidīn (AS) said,** 'The right of he who does a kindly act towards you is that you thank him and mention his kindness; that you reward him with beautiful words and supplicate for him sincerely in that which is

٣٣٤٠. الإمامُ زينُ العابدينَ عليه السلام: أمّا حَقُّ ذِي المَعروفِ علَيكَ فأن تَشكُرَهُ وتَذكُرَ مَعروفَهُ، وتُكسِبَهُ المَقالَةَ الحَسَنَةَ، وتُخلِصَ لَهُ الدعاءَ فيما بينَكَ وبينَ اللهِ عَزَّوجلَّ، فإذا فَعَلتَ ذلكَ

between you and Allah. If you do that, you have thanked him both secretly and openly. Then if you are able to repay him one day, repay him.'[3749]

كنتَ قد شَكَرتَهُ سِرّاً وعَلانِيَةً، ثُمّ إن قَدَرْتَ علىٰ مُكافَأتِهِ يَوماً كافَيتَهُ.[٣٧١٨]

1055. One Who has not Thanked the Creature has not Thanked the Creator

١٠٥٥ ـ مَن لَم يَشكُرِ المَخلوقَ لَم يَشكُرِ الخالِقَ

3341. **Imām Zayn al-ʿĀbidīn (AS) said,** 'Allah will ask one of His servants on the Day of Resurrection, 'Did you thank *x*?', and the servant will reply, 'No, but I thanked You instead, O Lord.' Allah will reply, 'You have not thanked Me as long as you have not thanked him.'[3750]

٣٣٤١. الإمامُ زينُ العابدينَ عليه السلام: يقولُ اللهُ تباركَ وتعالىٰ لِعبدٍ مِن عَبيدِهِ يَومَ القِيامَةِ: أشَكَرتَ فُلاناً؟ فيقولُ: بَل شَكَرتُكَ يا ربِّ، فيقولُ: لَم تَشكُرْني إذ لَم تَشكُرْهُ.[٣٧١٩]

3342. **Imām al-Ṣādiq (AS) said,** 'Allah curses the one who cuts of the means to kindly acts, who is such that when someone does him a good turn, he is ungrateful and as a result, he deters that person from ever doing the same towards anyone else.'[3751]

٣٣٤٢. الإمامُ الصّادقُ عليه السلام: لَعَنَ اللهُ قاطِعي سَبيلِ المَعروفِ، وهُو الرجُلُ يُصنَعُ إلَيهِ المَعروفُ فَيَكفُرُهُ، فَيَمنَعُ صاحِبَهُ مِن أن يَصنَعَ ذلكَ إلىٰ غَيرِهِ.[٣٧٢٠]

3343. **Imām al-Riḍā (AS) said,** 'Whoever does not thank the one who does him a favour from among Allah's creatures has not thanked Allah either.'[3752]

٣٣٤٣. الإمامُ الرِّضا عليه السلام: مَن لَم يَشكُرِ المُنعِمَ مِنَ المَخلوقينَ لَم يَشكُرِ اللهَ عَزَّوجلَّ.[٣٧٢١]

222

DOUBT

الشَّكُّ

1056. Doubt in the Principles of Belief

١٠٥٦ ـ الشَّكُّ فِي الأُصولِ الإعتِقاديَّةِ

3344. **Imām ʿAlī (AS) said,** 'You must adhere to conviction and keep away from doubt, for there is nothing more detrimental to a man's faith than for doubt to overpower his conviction.'[3753]

٣٣٤٤. الإمامُ عليٌّ عليه السلام: عَلَيكَ بِلُزُومِ اليَقينِ وتَجَنُّبِ الشَّكِّ، فلَيسَ للمَرءِ شَيءٌ أهْلَكَ لِدِينِهِ مِن غَلَبَةِ الشَّكِّ علىٰ يَقينِهِ.[٣٧٢٢]

3345. **Imām ʿAlī (AS) said,** 'I have never doubted the truth since I have been shown it.'[3754]

٣٣٤٥. عنه عليه السلام: ما شَكَكتُ فِي الحَقِّ مُذ أُرِيتُهُ.[٣٧٢٣]

3346. **Imām ʿAlī (AS) said,** 'Verily I am absolutely convinced about my Lord, and do not entertain any obscurity in my religion.'[3755]

٣٣٤٦. عنه عليه السلام: إنّي لَعَلىٰ يَقينٍ مِن رَبِّي، وغَيرِ شُبهَةٍ مِن دِيني.[٣٧٢٤]

3347. **Imām al-Ṣādiq (AS)** with regards to Allah's verse in the Qur'an: *"Indeed Allah desires to repel all impurity from you..."*[3756], said, 'Impurity is doubt, and by Allah, we never doubt in our Lord.'[3757]

٣٣٤٧. الإمامُ الصّادقُ عليه السلام ـ في قولِهِ تعالى: «لِيُذْهِبَ عَنْكُمُ الرِّجْسَ» ـ: الرِّجسُ هُو الشَّكُّ، واللهِ لا نَشُكُّ في رَبِّنا أبداً.[٣٧٢٥]

(See also: CERTAINTY: section 1910) (أنظر اليقين: باب ١٩١٠.)

1057. Causes of Doubt

١٠٥٧ـ أسبابُ الشَّكِّ

3348. **Imām ʿAlī (AS) said,** 'Doubt is the product of ignorance.'[3758]

٣٣٤٨. الإمامُ عليٌّ عليه السلام: الشَّكُّ ثَمَرَةُ الجَهلِ.[٣٧٢٦]

3349. **Imām ʿAlī (AS) said,** 'Whoever is insolent with regards to Allah's command becomes prone to doubting, and whoever doubts, Allah will overcome him, disgraces him with His authority, and belittles him with His Might just as he had shown contempt for His command.'[3759]

٣٣٤٩. عنه عليه السلام: مَن عَتا عن أمرِ اللهِ شَكَّ، ومَن شَكَّ تعالَى اللهُ علَيهِ فَأذَلَّهُ بِسُلطانِهِ، وصَغَّرَهُ بجَلالِهِ كما اغتَرَّ بِرَبِّهِ الكَريمِ وفَرَّطَ في أمرِهِ.[٣٧٢٧]

3350. **Imām ʿAlī (AS) said,** 'Do not give in to misgivings lest you start to doubt, and do not doubt lest you disbelieve, and do not allow yourselves to become negligent [against Allah] lest you fall into self-deception.'[3760]

٣٣٥٠. عنه عليه السلام: لا تَرتابوا فَتَشُكّوا، ولا تَشُكّوا فَتَكفُروا، ولا تُرَخِّصوا لِأنفُسِكُم فَتُدهِنوا.[٣٧٢٨]

1058. Effects of Doubt

١٠٥٨ـ آثارُ الشَّكِّ

3351. **Imām ʿAlī (AS) said,** 'Doubt thwarts faith.'[3761]

٣٣٥١. الإمامُ عليٌّ عليه السلام: الشَّكُّ يُحبِطُ الإيمانَ.[٣٧٢٩]

3352. **Imām ʿAlī (AS) said,** 'Doubt extinguishes the light of the heart.'[3762]

٣٣٥٢. عنه عليه السلام: الشَّكُّ يُطفِئُ نورَ القَلبِ.[٣٧٣٠]

3353. **Imām ʿAlī (AS) said,** 'The consequence of doubt is confusion.'[3763]

٣٣٥٣. عنه عليه السلام: ثَمرَةُ الشَّكِّ الحَيرَةُ.[٣٧٣١]

(See also: CERTAINTY: section 1914) (أنظر اليقين: باب ١٩١٤.)

1059. Factors that Dispel Doubt

١٠٥٩ـ ما يَرفَعُ الشَّكَّ

3354. **Imām ʿAlī (AS) said,** 'Doubts are dispelled through excessive thinking.'[3764]

٣٣٥٤. الإمامُ عليٌّ عليه السلام: بتَكَرُّرِ الفِكرِ يَنجابُ الشَّكُّ.[٣٧٣٢]

3355. **Imām ʿAlī (AS) said,** 'How I wonder at the one who entertains doubts about Allah whilst beholding the very creation of Allah.'[3765]

٣٣٥٥ . عنه عليه السلام : عَجِبتُ لِمَن شَكَّ في اللهِ وهو يَرىٰ خَلقَ اللهِ![٣٧٣٣]

3356. **Imām ʿAlī (AS) said,** 'A sincere person does not entertain misgivings and a person convinced [of his faith] does not doubt.'[3766]

٣٣٥٦ . عنه عليه السلام : مارتـابَ مُـخلِصٌ ولا شَكَّ مُوقِنٌ.[٣٧٣٤]

1060. The Aspects of Doubt

١٠٦٠ ـ شُعَبُ الشَّكِّ

3357. **Imām ʿAlī (AS) said,** 'There are four aspects to doubt: unreasonable debating [born out of a desire to doubt everything], fear, wavering and undue submission. The one who always resorts to unreasonable debating never again sees the light after darkness. The one who is afraid of what befalls him [doubting as a result] is always turning back on his heels. The one who wavers between his misgivings is trampled by Satan underfoot, and the one who succumbs to the perils of this world and the next is destroyed in them both.'[3767]

٣٣٥٧ . الإمامُ عليٌّ عليه السلام : الشَّكُّ علىٰ أربَعِ شُعَبٍ: على التَّمارِي، والهَولِ، والتَّرَدُّدِ، والاستِسلامِ، فَمَن جَعَلَ المِراءَ دَيدَناً لَم يُصبِحْ لَيلُهُ، ومَن هالَهُ ما بَينَ يَدَيهِ نَكَصَ علىٰ عَقِبَيهِ، ومَن تَرَدَّدَ فـي الرَّيبِ وَطِئَتهُ سَنابِكُ الشَّياطينِ، ومَنِ استَسلَمَ لِهَلَكَةِ الدُّنيا والآخِرَةِ هَلَكَ فيهِما.[٣٧٣٥]

223

BEARING WITNESS (IN A COURT OF JUSTICE)

الشَّهادَةُ في القَضاءِ

1061. Bearing Witness with Fairness

١٠٦١ ـ الشَّهادَةُ بِالقِسطِ

"O you who have faith! Be maintainers of justice as witnesses for the sake of Allah, and ill feeling towards a people should never lead you to be unfair. Be fair; that is nearer to Godwariness, and be wary of Allah. Allah is indeed well aware of what you do."[3768]

﴿يا أيُّها الَّذِينَ آمَنُوا كُونُوا قَوّامِينَ للهِ شُـهَداءَ بِالْقِسْطِ وَلا يَجْرِمَنَّكُمْ شَنَآنُ قَوْمٍ عَلَىٰ ألَّا تَعْدِلُوا اعدِلُوا هُوَ أقْرَبُ لِلتَّقوَىٰ وَاتَّقُوا اللهَ إنَّ اللهَ خَبِيرٌ بِما تَعْمَلُونَ﴾.[٣٧٣٦]

3358. **The Prophet (SAWA) said,** 'Verily I am just and only ever bear witness with justice.'[3769]

٣٣٥٨ . رسولُ اللهِ ﷺ : إنّي عَدلٌ لا أشهَدُ إلّا علىٰ عَدلٍ.[٣٧٣٧]

3359. **Imām ʿAlī (AS) said,** 'Fairness is the spirit of bearing witness.'[3770]

٣٣٥٩. الإمامُ عليٌّ عليه السلام: القِسْطُ روحُ الشهادَةِ.[٣٧٣٨]

1062. Enjoinment of Bearing Witness

١٠٦٢ ـ الحَثُّ علىٰ أداءِ الشَّهادَةِ

"And bear witness for the sake of Allah."[3771]

﴿وَأَقِيمُوا الشَّهادَةَ للهِ﴾.[٣٧٣٩]

"The witnesses must not refuse when they are called."[3772]

﴿وَلا يَأْبَ الشُّهَداءُ إذا ما دُعُوا﴾.[٣٧٤٠]

3360. **The Prophet (SAWA) said,** 'He who bears witness in truth for the sake of restoring a fellow Muslim's rights, will come on the Day of Resurrection with a light emanating from his face spreading as far as the eye can see, and all will know him by name and lineage.'[3773]

٣٣٦٠. رسولُ اللهِ ﷺ: مَن شَهِدَ شهادَةَ حَقٍّ لِيُحيِيَ بها حَقَّ امرِئٍ مُسلمٍ أتىٰ يَومَ القِيامَةِ ولِوَجهِهِ نُورٌ مَدَّ البَصَرِ، يَعرِفُهُ الخَلايِقُ باسمِهِ ونَسَبِهِ.[٣٧٤١]

3361. **Imām al-Ṣādiq (AS)** with regards to Allah's verse in the Qur'an: *"The witnesses must not refuse when they are called"*, said, 'When called to bear witness to something that one has indeed witnessed, nobody has the right to say, 'I refuse to bear witness to you.'[3774]

٣٣٦١. الإمامُ الصّادقُ عليه السلام ـ في قوله تعالى: ﴿وَلا يَأْبَ الشُّهَداءُ﴾ ـ: لا يَنبَغي لِأَحَدٍ إذا ما دُعِيَ لشهادَةٍ شَهِدَ علَيها أن يَقولَ: لا أشهَدُ لَكُم.[٣٧٤٢]

3362. **Imām al-Ṣādiq (AS) said,** 'When you are called to bear witness, do respond.'[3775]

٣٣٦٢. عنه عليه السلام: إذا دُعِيتَ إلى الشَّهادَةِ فأجِبْ.[٣٧٤٣]

1063. Concealing One's Testimony

١٠٦٣ ـ كِتمانُ الشَّهادَةِ

"And who is a greater wrongdoer than him who conceals a testimony that is with him from Allah?"[3776]

﴿وَمَنْ أظْلَمُ مِمَّنْ كَتَمَ شَهادَةً عِندَهُ مِنَ اللهِ﴾.[٣٧٤٤]

"And do not conceal testimony; anyone who conceals it, his heart will indeed be sinful. And Allah knows best what you do."[3777]

﴿ولا تَكْتُمُوا الشَّهادَةَ وَمَنْ يَكْتُمْها فَإنَّهُ آثِمٌ قَلْبُهُ وَاللهُ بِما تَعْمَلُونَ عَلِيمٌ﴾.[٣٧٤٥]

3363. **The Prophet (SAWA) said,** 'Whoever conceals his testimony when he is called to give it is as one who bears false testimony.'[3778]

٣٣٦٣. رسولُ اللهِ ﷺ: مَن كَتَمَ شَهادَةً إذا دُعِيَ إلَيها كانَ كَمَن شَهِدَ بالزُّورِ.[٣٧٤٦]

3364. **The Prophet (SAWA) said,** 'Whoever revokes his testimony and conceals it, Allah will

٣٣٦٤. عنه ﷺ: مَن رَجَعَ عن شَهادَتِهِ وكَتَمَها،

make him eat his own flesh in front of all creation and he will enter the Fire chewing his own tongue.'[3779]

أطعَمَهُ اللهُ لَحمَهُ على رُؤوسِ الخَلائقِ، ويَدخُلُ النارَ وهو يَلُوكُ لِسانَهُ.٣٧٤٧

1064. Those whose Testimony is Deemed Valid

١٠٦٤ ـ مَن تَجوزُ شَهادَتُهُ

3365. **Imām ʿAlī (AS) said** to Shurayḥ, 'Know that Muslims are equitable [and admissible as witnesses] towards one another, except for one who has been lashed on account of a crime and has not repented for it [and is therefore, still resentful as a result], one who is known to give false testimony, and one who is a suspect himself.'[3780]

٣٣٦٥. الإمامُ عليٌّ ؑ ـ لِشُرَيحٍ ـ: اِعلَمْ أنّ المسلمينَ عُدولٌ بعضُهُم على بَعضٍ، إلّا مَجلوداً في حَدٍّ لَم يَتُبْ مِنهُ، أو مَعروفاً بشهادَةِ الزُّورِ، أو ظَنِيناً.٣٧٤٨

3366. **Imām al-Ṣādiq (AS) said,** 'I do not accept the testimony of a corrupt person, unless it be against himself.'[3781]

٣٣٦٦. الإمامُ الصادقُ ؑ: لا أقبَلُ شَهادَةَ الفاسِقِ إلّا على نَفسِهِ.٣٧٤٩

3367. **Imām al-Ṣādiq (AS) said,** 'Verily the Commander of the Faithful (AS) never used to accept the testimony of an obscene person, nor one who brought shame on religion through his disgraceful acts.'[3782]

٣٣٦٧. عنه ؑ: إنّ أميرَ المؤمنينَ ؑ كانَ لا يَقبَلُ شَهادَةَ فَحّاشٍ، ولا ذي مُخْزِيَةٍ في الدِّينِ.٣٧٥٠

1065. The Etiquette of Giving Testimony

١٠٦٥ ـ أدَبُ الشَّهادَةِ

3368. **The Prophet (SAWA)** was once asked about bearing witness, to which he replied, 'Do you witness the sun? Thus must you bear witness or else do not.'[3783]

٣٣٦٨. رسولُ اللهِ ﷺ ـ وقد سُئلَ عن الشهادَةِ ـ: هل تَرَى الشمسَ؟ على مِثلِها فَاشهَدْ أو دَعْ.٣٧٥١

3369. **Imām al-Ṣādiq (AS) said,** 'Do not ever bear witness to something unless you know it like the back of your hand.'[3784]

٣٣٦٩. الإمامُ الصّادقُ ؑ: لا تَشهَدَنَّ بشهادَةٍ حتّى تَعرِفَها كما تَعرِفُ كَفَّكَ.٣٧٥٢

224

MARTYRDOM IN THE WAY OF ALLAH

الشَّهادة
القتل في سبيل الله

1066. The Virtue of Martyrdom

١٠٦٦ـ فضلُ الشَّهادةِ

"Do not suppose those who were slain in the way of Allah to be dead; rather they are living and provided for near their Lord."[3785]

﴿ولا تَحْسَبَنَّ الَّذِينَ قُتِلُوا فِي سَبِيلِ اللهِ أَمْواتاً بَلْ أَحْياءٌ عِنْدَ رَبِّهِم يُرْزَقُونَ﴾.٣٧٥٣

3370. **The Prophet (SAWA) said,** 'Above every act of piety is yet a greater act of piety until a man is killed in the way of Allah, and when he is killed in the way of Allah, there is no act of piety greater.'[3786]

٣٣٧٠. رسولُ اللهِ ﷺ: فَوقَ كُلِّ ذي بِرٍّ بِرٌّ حتّى يُقتَلَ الرجُلُ في سبيلِ اللهِ، فإذا قُتِلَ في سبيلِ اللهِ فليسَ فَوقَهُ بِرٌّ.٣٧٥٤

3371. **The Prophet (SAWA) said,** 'The most dignified way to die is to be martyred.'[3787]

٣٣٧١. عنه ﷺ: أشرَفُ المَوتِ قَتلُ الشهادةِ.٣٧٥٥

3372. **The Prophet (SAWA) said,** 'I wish that I may fight in the way of Allah and be killed in the way of Allah, then fight again and be killed again many times over.'[3788]

٣٣٧٢. عنه ﷺ: لَوَدِدتُ أنّي أغزُو في سَبيلِ اللهِ فأُقتَلُ، ثُمّ أغزُو فأُقتَلُ، ثُمّ أغزُو فأُقتَلُ.٣٧٥٦

3373. **The Prophet (SAWA) said,** 'The martyred one is forgiven every sin except his debt [to others].'[3789]

٣٣٧٣. عنه ﷺ: يُغفَرُ للشَّهيدِ كُلُّ ذَنبٍ إلّا الدَّينَ.٣٧٥٧

3374. **The Prophet (SAWA) said,** 'He who faces his enemy and resists until either he is killed or he vanquishes him will not be tormented in the grave.'[3790]

٣٣٧٤. عنه ﷺ: مَن لَقِيَ العَدُوَّ فصَبَرَ حتّى يُقتَلَ أو يَغلِبَ لَم يُفتَنْ في قَبرِهِ.٣٧٥٨

3375. **The Prophet (SAWA) said,** 'Nobody who dies and who has a good position with Allah that pleases him ever wishes to return back to this world, not even to be given the world and all that

٣٣٧٥. عنه ﷺ: ما مِن نفسٍ تَموتُ لها عندَ اللهِ خيرٌ يَسُرُّها أنّها تَرجِعُ إلى الدنيا، ولا أنّ لَـها الدنيا

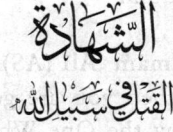

is in it, except the martyr, for he wishes to return to it in order that he may be martyred again because of the virtue that he has seen in martyrdom.'[3791]

وما فيها، إلّا الشهيدَ؛ فإنّهُ يَتَمَنّىٰ أن يَرجِعَ فَيُقتَلَ فِي الدنيا؛ لِما يَرىٰ مِن فَضلِ الشهادَةِ.[٣٧٥٩]

3376. **Imām 'Alī (AS) said,** 'Verily if you are not killed then you are going to die anyway, and I swear by the One Who holds 'Alī's soul in His Hand, a thousand strikes of the sword on one's head is easier to bear than to die in one's bed.'[3792]

٣٣٧٦. الإمامُ عليٌّ عليه السلام: إنّكُم إن لا تُقتَلُوا تَمُوتُوا، والذي نَفسُ عَلِيٍّ بيدِهِ، لَألفُ ضَربَةٍ بالسَّيفِ عَلَى الرَّأسِ أيسَرُ مِن مَوتٍ علىٰ فِراشٍ.[٣٧٦٠]

1067. The Reward Of Seeking Martyrdom

١٠٦٧ ـ ثَوابُ طَلَبِ الشَّهادَةِ

3377. **The Prophet (SAWA) said,** 'Whoever sincerely asks Allah to grant him martyrdom, Allah makes him attain the station of the martyrs, even if he dies in his own bed.'[3793]

٣٣٧٧. رسولُ اللهِ صلى الله عليه وآله: مَن سَأَلَ اللهَ الشهادَةَ بصِدقٍ بَلَّغَهُ اللهُ مَنازِلَ الشُّهَداءِ وإن ماتَ علىٰ فِراشِهِ.[٣٧٦١]

1068. Honorary Martyrdom

١٠٦٨ ـ الشَّهادَةُ الحُكمِيَّةُ

3378. **The Prophet (SAWA) said,** 'Whoever is unjustly killed is a martyr.'[3794]

٣٣٧٨. رسولُ اللهِ صلى الله عليه وآله: مَن قُتِلَ دُونَ مَظلِمَتِهِ فهُو شَهيدٌ.[٣٧٦٢]

3379. **The Prophet (SAWA) said,** 'Whoever loves someone passionately, then suppresses his love in order to remain chaste and dies in the process, is a martyr.'[3795]

٣٣٧٩. عنه صلى الله عليه وآله: مَن عَشِقَ فَكَتَمَ وعَفَّ فَماتَ فهُو شَهيدٌ.[٣٧٦٣]

3380. **The Prophet (SAWA) said,** 'Whoever dies loving the household of Muḥammad dies a martyr.'[3796]

٣٣٨٠. عنه صلى الله عليه وآله: مَن ماتَ علىٰ حُبِّ آلِ محمّدٍ ماتَ شَهيداً.[٣٧٦٤]

3381. **Imām Zayn al-'Ābidīn (AS) said,** 'Whoever dies accepting our guardianship during the occultation of the one who will rise up [the awaited twelfth Imām, al-Mahdī], Allah will grant him the reward of a thousand such martyrs as died in the battles of Badr and 'Uḥud.'[3797]

٣٣٨١. الإمامُ زينُ العابدينَ عليه السلام: مَن ماتَ علىٰ مُوالاتِنا في غَيبةِ قائمِنا أعطاهُ اللهُ أجرَ ألفِ شَهيدٍ مِثلِ شُهَداءِ بَدرٍ واُحُدٍ.[٣٧٦٥]

1069. The Reward of One who is Wounded in the Way of Allah

١٠٦٩ ـ ثَوابُ الجَريحِ في سَبيلِ اللهِ

3382. **The Prophet (SAWA) said,** 'Whoever is wounded in the way of Allah will rise up on the Day of Resurrection, his fragrance as sweet as musk and his colour as vibrant as saffron, and he will have the stamp of a martyr on him. And whoever sincerely asks Allah to grant him martyrdom, Allah grants him the reward of a martyr, even if he dies in his own bed.'[3798]

٣٣٨٢ . رسولُ اللهِ ﷺ : مَن جُرِحَ في سَبيلِ اللهِ جاءَ يَومَ القِيامَةِ رِيحُهُ كَرِيحِ المِسكِ ولَونُهُ لَونُ الزَّعفَرانِ، علَيهِ طابَعُ الشُّهَداءِ، ومَن سَألَ اللهَ الشهادَةَ مُخلِصاً أعطاهُ اللهُ أجرَ شَهيدٍ وإن ماتَ علىٰ فِراشِهِ.[٣٧٦٦]

225

FAME

الشُّهرَةُ

1070. Praiseworthy Fame

١٠٧٠ ـ الشُّهرَةُ المَحمودَةُ

"Did we not exalt your name?"[3799]

﴿وَرَفَعْنا لَكَ ذِكْرَكَ﴾.[٣٧٦٧]

"Confer on me a worthy repute among the posterity."[3800]

﴿واجعَلْ لِي لِسانَ صِدْقٍ فِي الآخِرِينَ﴾.[٣٧٦٨]

(See also: Qur'an 19:50, 20:39, 29:27, 37:78)

(اُنظر) مريم: ٥٠ و طه: ٣٩ والعنكبوت: ٢٧ و الصافات: ٧٨.

3383. **The Prophet (SAWA)** was once asked regarding someone who performs a good deed, and is consequently praised by people on account of it, to which he replied, 'That [praise] is the advance glad tidings for the believer.'[3801]

٣٣٨٣ . رسولُ اللهِ ﷺ ـ لمّا سُئلَ عنِ الرجُلِ الذي يَعمَلُ العَمَلَ مِنَ الخَيرِ، ويَحمَدُهُ الناسُ علَيهِ ـ: تلكَ عاجِلُ بُشرَىٰ المؤمِنِ.[٣٧٦٩]

3384. **The Prophet (SAWA) said,** 'When Allah loves a servant of His from among my community, He radiates love for him into the hearts of His elite servants, the spirits of the angels and the retinue of His throne, in order that they too may love him, and that is one who is truly loved.'[3802]

٣٣٨٤ . عنه ﷺ : إذا أحَبَّ اللهُ عَبداً مِن اُمَّتِي قَذَفَ في قُلوبِ أصفِيائهِ وأرواحِ ملائكَتِهِ وسُكّانِ عَرشِهِ مَحَبَّتَهُ لِيُحِبُّوهُ، فذلكَ المُحَبُّ حقّاً.[٣٧٧٠]

1071. Blameworthy Fame

١٠٧١ـ الشُّهرَةُ المَذمومَةُ

"This is the abode of the Hereafter which We shall grant to those who do not desire to domineer in the earth nor to cause corruption, and the outcome will be in favour of the Godwary."[3803]

﴿تِلْكَ الدَّارُ الْآخِرَةُ نَجْعَلُهَا لِلَّذِينَ لا يُرِيدُونَ عُلُوّاً فِي الْأَرْضِ وَلا فَساداً وَالْعاقِبَةُ لِلْمُتَّقِينَ﴾.٣٧٧١

3385. **The Prophet (SAWA) said,** 'It is bad enough for a man - except for one whom Allah protects from evil - that people should point the finger at him with regard to either his faith or his worldly affairs.'[3804]

٣٣٨٥. رسولُ اللهِ ﷺ: بِحَسْبِ المَرءِ مِنَ الشَّرِّ ـ إلّا مَن عَصَمَهُ اللهُ مِنَ السُّوءِ ـ أن يُشيرَ النّاسُ إلَيهِ بالأصابِعِ في دينِهِ ودُنياهُ.٣٧٧٢

3386. **Imām ʿAlī (AS) said,** 'Every single servant who desires to raise his own status in this world, Allah abases his status in the Hereafter by a greater and longer extent.'[3805]

٣٣٨٦. الإمامُ عليٌّ عليه السلام: ما مِن عَبدٍ يُريدُ أن يَرتَفِعَ فِي الدُّنيا دَرَجَةً، فَارتَفَعَ فِي الدُّنيا دَرَجَةً، إلّا وَضَعَهُ اللهُ فِي الآخِرَةِ دَرَجَةً أكبَرَ مِنها وأطوَلَ.٣٧٧٣

3387. **Imām al-Ṣādiq (AS),** in his description of a believer, said, 'He neither desires repute in this world, nor does he grieve at its disgrace. People have their own matters of significance that they tend to, whilst he occupies himself with his own concerns.'[3806]

٣٣٨٧. الإمامُ الصّادقُ عليه السلام ـ في صِفَةِ المُؤمِنِ ـ: لا يَرغَبُ في عِزِّ الدُّنيا ولا يَجزَعُ مِن ذُلِّها، لِلنّاسِ هَمٌّ قد أقبَلوا عَلَيهِ، ولَهُ هَمٌّ قد شَغَلَهُ.٣٧٧٤

1072. The Censure of Clothing or Acts of Worship that Draw Attention

١٠٧٢ـ ذَمُّ شُهرَةِ اللِّباسِ وشُهرَةِ العِبادَةِ

3388. **Imām al-Ṣādiq (AS) said,** 'It is enough of a disgrace for a man that he should wear such clothes or ride such a beast as draws attention to himself.'[3807]

٣٣٨٨. الإمامُ الصّادقُ عليه السلام: كَفى بِالمَرءِ خِزياً أن يَلبَسَ ثَوباً يَشهَرُهُ، أو يَركَبَ دابَّةً مَشهورَةً.٣٧٧٥

3389. **Imām al-Ṣādiq (AS) said,** 'Verily Allah despises the two forms of attention-seeking: attention-seeking clothes and attention-seeking prayer.'[3808]

٣٣٨٩. عنه عليه السلام: إنَّ اللهَ يُبغِضُ الشُّهرَتَينِ: شُهرَةَ اللِّباسِ وشُهرَةَ الصَّلاةِ.٣٧٧٦

3390. **Imām al-Riḍā (AS) said,** 'If someone makes himself become renown for worshipping, you should doubt his religion, as Allah the Exalted dislikes fame in worshiping and fame in dressing.'[3809]

٣٣٩٠. الإمامُ الرِّضا عليه السلام: مَن شَهَرَ نَفسَهُ بِالعِبادَةِ فَاتَّهِموهُ عَلى دينِهِ؛ فَإِنَّ اللهَ عزّوجلّ يُبغِضُ شُهرَةَ العِبادَةِ وشُهرَةَ اللِّباسِ.٣٧٧٧

3391. **Imām al-Ṣādiq (AS) said,** 'The best and worst of [seeking] fame will land one in the Fire.'[3810]

(See also: CLOTHES: section 1624, 1627)

226

COUNSEL

1073. Enjoinment of Consultation

"Those who answer their Lord, maintain the prayer, and their affairs are (executed) by counsel among themselves, and they spend out of what We have provided them with."[3811]

3392. **Imām ʿAlī (AS) said,** 'Seeking to consult someone [in one's affairs] is guidance in itself, and the one who suffices himself with his own opinion endangers himself.'[3812]

3393. **Imām ʿAlī (AS) said,** 'There is no better support than good counsel.'[3813]

3394. **Imām ʿAlī (AS) said,** 'Seeking counsel has been highly emphasised because the opinion of the counsellor is unadulterated whereas the opinion of the one seeking counsel is polluted with his own whims.'[3814]

1074. People Whose Counsel Should not be Sought

3395. **The Prophet (SAWA) said,** 'O ʿAlī, do not seek counsel from a coward for verily he will confine and narrow the way out for you, nor from the miser for verily he will hold you back from your goal, and nor from the covetous one for verily he will make greediness fair-seeming to you.'[3815]

٣٣٩١ . الإمامُ الصّادقُ ﵇ :الشُّهرَةُ خَيرُها وشَرُّها في النارِ.[٣٧٧٨]

(أنظر) اللّباس: باب ١٦٢٤، ١٦٢٧.

الشُّورىٰ

١٠٧٣ ـ الحَثُّ عَلَى المَشورَةِ

﴿وَالَّذِينَ اسْتَجابُوا لِرَبِّهِم وَأقامُوا الصَّلاةَ وَأمرُهُمْ شُورَىٰ بَيْنَهُمْ وَمِمّا رَزَقناهُم يُنفِقُونَ﴾.[٣٧٧٩]

٣٣٩٢ . الإمامُ عليٌّ ﵇ :الاستِشارَةُ عَينُ الهِدايَةِ، وقد خاطَرَ مَنِ استَغنىٰ بِرأيِهِ.[٣٧٨٠]

٣٣٩٣ . عنه ﵇ : لا ظَهيرَ كالمُشاوَرَةِ.[٣٧٨١]

٣٣٩٤ . عنه ﵇ : إنّما حُضَّ على المُشاوَرَةِ لأنّ رَأيَ المُشيرِ صِرْفٌ، ورَأيَ المُستَشيرِ مَشُوبٌ بالهَوىٰ.[٣٧٨٢]

١٠٧٤ ـ مَن لا يَنبَغي مُشاوَرَتُهُم

٣٣٩٥ . رسولُ اللهِ ﷺ ـ للإمامِ عليٍّ ﵇ ـ: يا عليُّ، لا تُشاوِرْ جَباناً فإنّهُ يُضَيِّقُ علَيكَ المَخرَجَ، ولا تُشاوِرِ البَخيلَ فإنّهُ يَقْصُرُ بكَ عن غايَتِكَ، ولا تُشاوِرْ حَريصاً فإنّهُ يُزَيِّنُ لكَ شَرَهاً.[٣٧٨٣]

3396. **Imām ʿAlī (AS) said,** 'Do not seek counsel from a liar for verily he is like a mirage – he makes that which is far appear near, and he makes that which is near appear far.'[3816]

٣٣٩٦ . الإمامُ عليٌّ ﷺ : لا تَستَشِرِ الكَذّابَ ؛ فإنّهُ كالسَّرابِ : يُقَرِّبُ عـلَيكَ البَـعيدَ ويُـبَعِّدُ عـلَيكَ القَريبَ . ٣٧٨٤

1075. Boundaries of Counselling

١٠٧٥ ـ حُدودُ المَشورَةِ

3397. **Imām al-Ṣādiq (AS) said,** 'Counsel should only be sought whilst fulfilling its four terms. Firstly that the one whose counsel you seek must be a man of intellect. Secondly that he must be a free and religious man. Thirdly, he must be brotherly and friendly, and fourthly that when you disclose your secret to him whereby he knows as much about it as you do, he would keep your secret and guard it well.'[3817]

٣٣٩٧ . الإمامُ الصّادقُ ﷺ : إنّ المَشورَةَ لا تكونُ إلّا بِحُدودِها الأربَعةِ ... فأوَّلُـها أن يكـونَ الذي تُشاوِرُهُ عاقِلاً ، والثانيةُ أن يَكونَ حُرّاً مُـتَدَيِّناً ، والثالثةُ أن يكونَ صَديقاً مُواخِـياً ، والرابـعةُ أن تُطلِعَه علىٰ سِرِّكَ فَيكونَ عِلمُهُ بِهِ كَـعِلمِكَ ثُـمّ يُسِرَّ ذلكَ ويَكتُمَهُ . ٣٧٨٥

1076. Enjoinment of Guiding One who Seeks your Counsel

١٠٧٦ ـ الحَثُّ عَلىٰ إرشادِ المُستَشيرِ

3398. **The Prophet (SAWA) said:**' Be generous to your brother in faith by granting him the knowledge that guides him and the wisdom that shows him the right path.'[3818]

٣٣٩٨ . رسولُ اللهِ ﷺ : تَصَدَّقُوا علىٰ أخِيكُم بِعِلمٍ يُرشِدُهُ ورَأيٍ يُسَدِّدُهُ . ٣٧٨٦

3399. **Imām Zayn al-ʿĀbidīn (AS) said,** 'The right of the one who seeks your counsel is that you point him in the right direction if you know that he is inclined towards a certain opinion, and if you do not know [which way to point out], then you must guide him to someone who does.'[3819]

٣٣٩٩ . الإمامُ زينُ العابدينَ ﷺ : حَقُّ المُستَشيرِ إنْ عَلِمتَ أنَّ لَهُ رَأياً ٣٧٨٧ أشَرتَ علَيهِ ، وإن لَم تَعلَمْ أرشَدتَهُ إلىٰ مَن يَعلَمُ . ٣٧٨٨

3400. **Imām al-Ṣādiq (AS) said,** 'Whoever seeks counsel from a fellow brother and he refuses to advise him with even an opinion either way, Allah wrests him of his opinion.'[3820]

٣٤٠٠ . الإمامُ الصّادقُ ﷺ : مَنِ استَشارَ أخاهُ فَلَم يَنصَحْهُ مَحْضَ الرَّأيِ سَلَبَهُ اللهُ رَأيَهُ . ٣٧٨٩

1077. To Consult with the Enemy

١٠٧٧ ـ إستشارة الأعداء

3401. **Imām ʿAlī (AS) said,** 'Take council with your enemies, so that by knowing their opinions,

٣٤٠١ . الإمامُ عليٌّ ﷺ : اِستَشِرْ أعداءَكَ تَعرِفْ

you be aware of their animosity, goals and intentions.'[3821]

مِن رَأيِهِم مِقدارَ عَداوَتِهِم ومَواضِعَ مَقاصِدِهِم.[٣٧٩٠]

3402. **Imām ʿAlī (AS) said,** 'Take council with your wise enemy, and abstain yourself from the opinion of your ignorant friend.'[3822]

٣٤٠٢. عنه عليه السلام: اِستَشِرْ عَدُوَّكَ العاقِلَ، واحذَرْ رَأيَ صَديقِكَ الجاهِلِ.[٣٧٩١]

227

OLD AGE

الشَّيْبُ

1078. Old Age

١٠٧٨ ـ الشَّيبُ

"It is Allah who created you from [a state of] weakness, then he gave you strength after weakness. Then, after strength, He ordained weakness and old age; He creates whatever He wishes, and He is the All-knowing, the All-powerful."[3823]

﴿اللهُ الَّذي خَلَقَكُمْ مِنْ ضَعْفٍ ثُمَّ جَعَلَ مِنْ بَعْدِ ضَعْفٍ قُوَّةً ثُمَّ جَعَلَ مِنْ بَعْدِ قُوَّةٍ ضَعْفاً وَشَيْبَةً يَخْلُقُ ما يَشاءُ وَهُوَ العَليمُ القَديرُ﴾.[٣٧٩٢]

3403. **The Prophet (SAWA) said,** 'The old man is a youth when it comes to his love for his intimate one, his long life and his abundant wealth.'[3824]

٣٤٠٣. رسولُ اللهِ صلى الله عليه وآله: الشَّيخُ شابٌّ علىٰ حُبِّ أنيسٍ، وطُولِ حَياةٍ، وكَثرَةِ مالٍ.[٣٧٩٣]

3404. **Imām ʿAlī (AS) said,** 'Gray hair is the herald of death.'[3825]

٣٤٠٤. الإمامُ عليٌّ عليه السلام: المَشِيبُ رسولُ المَوتِ.[٣٧٩٤]

3405. **Imām ʿAlī (AS) said,** 'Old age suffices as a warning.'[3826]

٣٤٠٥. عنه عليه السلام: كَفىٰ بالشَّيبِ نَذِيراً.[٣٧٩٥]

3406. **Imām ʿAlī (AS) said,** 'The dignified bearing that comes with old age is more beloved to me than the vigour of youth.'[3827]

٣٤٠٦. عنه عليه السلام: وَقارُ الشَّيبِ أحَبُّ إلَيَّ مِن نَضارَةِ الشَّبابِ.[٣٧٩٦]

3407. **Imām ʿAlī (AS) said,** 'When an intelligent man grows old, his intellect remains young [and sharp], and when the ignorant man grows old, his ignorance too remains young [and more reckless].'[3828]

٣٤٠٧. عنه عليه السلام: إذا شابَ العاقِلُ شَبَّ عَقلُهُ، إذا شابَ الجاهِلُ شَبَّ جَهلُهُ.[٣٧٩٧]

3408. **Imām al-Bāqir (AS) said,** 'Prophet Abraham (AS) woke up one morning to find old age in

٣٤٠٨. الإمامُ الباقرُ عليه السلام: أصبَحَ إبراهيمُ عليه السلام فَرَأىٰ

the form of a white hair in his beard, and said, 'Praise be to Allah, the Lord of the worlds, Who has brought me to this ripe age in which I have never yet disobeyed Him for even the blink of an eye.'[3829]

في لِحيَتِهِ شَيباً شَعرَةً بَيضاءَ، فقالَ: الحَمدُ للهِ رَبِّ العالَمينَ الذي بَلَّغَني هٰذَا المَبلَغَ ولَم أعصِ اللهَ طَرفَةَ عَينٍ.[٣٧٩٨]

3409. **Imām al-Ṣādiq (AS) said,** 'I have never seen anything catch up with something faster than old age catches up with a believer, for verily it is a source of dignity for the believer in this world and a brilliant light for him on the Day of Resurrection. Allah, most High, honoured Abraham (AS) with it [old age], who said, 'What is this, my Lord?' to which Allah replied, 'This is dignity', so Abraham said, 'O my Lord, increase me in dignity then.'[3830]

٣٤٠٩. الإمامُ الصّادقُ عليه السلام: ما رَأيتُ شَيئاً أسرَعَ إلىٰ شيءٍ مِن الشَّيبِ إلَى المؤمنِ، وإنّهُ وَقارٌ للمؤمِنِ في الدنيا، ونورٌ ساطِعٌ يَومَ القِيامَةِ، بهِ وَقَّرَ اللهُ تعالىٰ خَليلَهُ إبراهيمَ عليه السلام، فقالَ: ما هذا يا رَبِّ؟ قالَ لَهُ: هذا وَقارٌ، فقالَ: يا رَبِّ زِدني وَقاراً.[٣٧٩٩]

1079. Enjoinment of Venerating the Old

١٠٧٩ ـ الحَثُّ عَلىٰ إجلالِ الكَبيرِ

3410. **The Prophet (SAWA) said,** 'Venerating Allah includes venerating the old from among the Muslims.'[3831]

٣٤١٠. رسولُ اللهِ ﷺ: مِن إجلالِ اللهِ إجلالُ ذي الشَّيبَةِ المُسلمِ.[٣٨٠٠]

3411. **The Prophet (SAWA) said,** 'Verily venerating me includes honouring the old men of my community.'[3832]

٣٤١١. عنه ﷺ: إنَّ مِن إجلالي تَوقيرَ الشَّيخِ مِن أُمَّتي.[٣٨٠١]

3412. **Imām al-Ṣādiq (AS) said,** 'Exalt the old ones from amongst you and maintain relations between your kin.'[3833]

٣٤١٢. الإمامُ الصّادقُ عليه السلام: عَظِّموا كِبارَكُم وصِلُوا أرحامَكُم.[٣٨٠٢]

3413. **Imām al-Ṣādiq (AS) said,** 'One who neither honours our old nor has mercy on our young is not one of us.'[3834]

٣٤١٣. عنه عليه السلام: ليسَ مِنّا مَن لَم يُوَقِّرْ كَبيرَنا ويَرحَمْ صَغيرَنا.[٣٨٠٣]

228

THE SHĪʿA[3835] — الشِّيعَةُ

1080. The Virtue of the Shīʿa of the Household of the Prophet

١٠٨٠ ـ فَضلُ شيعَةِ أهلِ البَيتِ

3414. **Imām ʿAlī (AS) said,** 'I complained to the Prophet (SAWA) about people's jealousy towards me, so he replied, 'O ʿAlī, the first four people to enter Paradise will be myself, you, Ḥasan and Ḥusayn. The rest of our progeny will be behind us, those who love us will be behind them, and our *shīʿa* will be on either side of us.'[3836]

٣٤١٤ . الإمامُ عليٌّ : شَكَوتُ إلى رسولِ اللهِ حَسَدَ الناسِ إيّايَ ، فقالَ : يا عليُّ ، إنّ أوّلَ أربعةٍ يَدخُلونَ الجَنَّةَ أنا وأنتَ والحَسنُ والحُسينُ ، وذُرِّيَّتُنا خَلفَ ظُهورِنا ، وأحِبّاؤنا خَلفَ ذُرِّيَّتِنا ، وشِياعُنا عَن أيمانِنا وشَمائلِنا .[٣٨٠٤]

3415. **Imām al-Bāqir (AS) said,** 'Umm Salama, the wife of the Prophet (SAWA), was once asked about [the status of] ʿAlī b. Abī Ṭālib (AS), to which she replied, 'I have heard the Prophet (SAWA) say, 'Verily ʿAlī and his *shīʿa* are the victorious ones.'[3837]

٣٤١٥ . الإمامُ الباقرُ : سُئلَت أمُّ سَلَمَةَ زَوجُ النبيِّ عن عليِّ بن أبي طالبٍ ، فقالَت : سَمِعتُ رسولَ اللهِ يقولُ : إنّ عليّاً وشيعَتَهُ هُمُ الفائزونَ .[٣٨٠٥]

1081. The Signs of the Shīʿa of Ahl al-Bayt (AS)

١٠٨١ ـ عَلاماتُ شيعَةِ أهلِ البَيتِ

3416. **Imām ʿAlī (AS)** asked Nawf al-Bakalī, 'Do you know who my *shīʿa* are, Nawf?' to which he replied, 'By Allah, no.' Imām replied, 'My *shīʿa* have parched lips and empty stomachs. They are those whose faces disclose asceticism, for they are ascetics by night, lions by day.'[3838]

٣٤١٦ . الإمامُ عليٌّ ـ لِنَوفٍ البَكاليِّ ـ : أتَدري يا نَوفُ مَن شيعَتي ؟ قالَ : لا وَاللهِ ، قالَ : شيعَتي الذُّبُلُ الشِّفاهِ ، الخُمصُ البُطونِ ، الذينَ تُعرَفُ الرَّهبانيَّةُ في وُجوهِهِم ، رُهبانٌ باللَّيلِ أُسْدٌ بالنَّهارِ .[٣٨٠٦]

3417. **Imām al-Ḥasan (AS) said** in answer to a man who said to him, 'Verily I am one of your *shīʿa*', 'O ʿAbdallāh, if you are truly obedient to us in our commands and prohibitions, then you are telling the truth. But if not, then do not add to your sins by falsely claiming such a dignified position that you are not worthy of. Do not say, 'I

٣٤١٧ . الإمامُ الحسنُ ـ في جوابِ رَجُلٍ قالَ لَهُ : إنّي مِن شِيعَتِكُم ـ : يا عبدَ اللهِ ، إن كُنتَ لَنا في أوامِرِنا وزَواجِرِنا مُطيعاً فقد صَدَقتَ ، وإن كُنتَ بخِلافِ ذلكَ فلا تَزِدْ في ذُنوبِكَ بدَعواكَ مَرتَبَةً شَريفَةً لَستَ مِن أهلِها ، لا تَقُلْ : أنا مِن شِيعَتِكُم ،

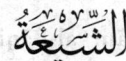

am one of your *shīʿa*', but say rather, 'I am one of your adherents and one of your lovers and an enemy to your enemies.' You are good and aiming towards good.'[3839]

ولكن قُل: أنا مِن مُوالِيكُم ومُحِبِّيكُم ومُعادِي أعدائكُم، وأنتَ في خَيرٍ وإلىٰ خَيرٍ.[٣٨٠٧]

3418. **Imām al-Bāqir (AS) said,** 'Our *shīʿa* are none other than those who are consciously wary of their duty to Allah and obey Him. They are known solely for their humbleness, their humility, their returning promptly whatever is entrusted in their care and their abundant remembrance of Allah.'[3840]

٣٤١٨. الإمامُ الباقرُ ؑ: ما شِيعَتُنا إلّا مَن اتَّقَى اللهَ وأطاعَهُ، وما كانوا يُعرَفُونَ إلّا بالتَّواضُعِ والتَّخَشُّعِ وأداءِ الأمانَةِ وكَثرَةِ ذِكرِ اللهِ.[٣٨٠٨]

3419. **Imām al-Ṣādiq (AS) said,** 'Verily the *shīʿa* of ʿAlī were those who restrained their stomachs and their sexual desires, who struggled and fought intensely, who worked hard for their Creator, who hoped for His reward and feared His punishment. If you have seen such people, then they are the very *shīʿa* of Jaʿfar.'[3841]

٣٤١٩. الإمامُ الصّادقُ ؑ: إنّما شِيعَةُ عليٍّ مَن عَفَّ بَطنُهُ وفَرجُهُ، واشتَدَّ جِهادُهُ، وعَمِلَ لِخالِقِهِ، ورَجا ثَوابَهُ، وخافَ عِقابَهُ، فإذا رأيتَ أُولئكَ فأُولئكَ شِيعَةُ جعفرٍ.[٣٨٠٩]

3420. **Imām al-Ṣādiq (AS) said,** 'Test our *shīʿa* with regard to three things: the prayer times to see how well they observe them, their secrets to see how well they guard them from our enemies, and their wealth to see how they help out their fellow brothers with it.'[3842]

٣٤٢٠. عنه ؑ: اِمتَحِنُوا شِيعَتَنا عِندَ ثَلاثٍ: عِندَ مَواقيتِ الصَّلَواتِ كيفَ مُحافَظَتُهُم علَيها، وعِندَ أسرارِهِم كيفَ حِفظُهُم لَها عَن عَدُوِّنا، وإلىٰ أموالِهِم كيفَ مُواساتُهُم لإخوانِهِم فيها.[٣٨١٠]

3421. **Imām al-Ṣādiq (AS) said,** 'Verily our *shīʿa* are those who possess four eyes: two in their head, as well as two in their heart. Actually, all people are such, except that Allah has opened their [the *shīʿa's*] eyes, and blinded others' [as a result of their rejection of His guidance].'[3843]

٣٤٢١. عنه ؑ: إنّما شِيعَتُنا أصحابُ الأربَعَةِ الأعيُنِ: عَينانِ فِي الرَّأسِ، وعَينانِ فِي القَلبِ، ألا والخَلائقُ كُلُّهُم كذلكَ إلّا أنَّ اللهَ عَزَّ وجلَّ فَتَحَ أبصارَكُم وأعمىٰ أبصارَهُم.[٣٨١١]

1082. Those Who are not Considered to be Shīʿa

١٠٨٢ ـ مَن لَيسَ مِن شيعَةِ أهلِ البَيتِ ؑ

3422. **Imām al-Ṣādiq (AS) said,** 'One who claims to follow us with his tongue, but does the opposite to our actions and deeds is not from among our *shīʿa*.'[3844]

٣٤٢٢. الإمامُ الصّادقُ ؑ: لَيسَ مِن شِيعَتِنا مَن قالَ بِلِسانِهِ وخالَفَنا في أعمالِنا وآثارِنا.[٣٨١٢]

3423. **Imām al-Ṣādiq (AS) said,** 'There is a group of people who claim that I am their Imām, but by

٣٤٢٣. عنه ؑ: قَومٌ يَزعُمُونَ أنّي إمامُهُم، واللهِ ما

Allah, I am no Imām of theirs – may Allah curse them – every time I conceal a secret, they disclose it. Every time I explain a matter, they retort, saying, 'Actually that means such and such.' I am only the Imām of those who obey me.'[3845]

أنا لَهُم بِإمامٍ، لَعَنَهُمُ اللهُ، كُلَّما سَتَرتُ سِتراً هَتَكُوهُ، أقولُ: كذا وكذا، فيقولونَ: إنّما يَعني كذا وكذا، إنّما أنا إمامُ مَن أطاعَني.[٣٨١٣]

3424. **Imām al-Ṣādiq (AS) said,** 'The one who rejects four things is not from among our *shī'a*. They are: the Prophet's Ascension to the heavens, the questioning in the grave, the creation of Heaven and Hell, and intercession.'[3846]

٣٤٢٤. عنه عليه السلام: ليسَ مِن شِيعَتِنا مَن أنكرَ أربَعةَ أشياءَ: المِعراجَ، والمُساءَلَةَ فِي القَبرِ، وخَلقَ الجَنَّةِ وَالنارِ، وَالشَّفاعَةَ.[٣٨١٤]

3425. **Imām al-Ṣādiq (AS)** once asked a man about his tribe and brothers whom he had left back home, which the latter replied by praising them, attesting to their integrity and extolling them. Then Imām (AS) asked, 'Do the rich among them visit the poor when they are ill?' He replied, 'Not much.' 'Do the rich frequent the poor at all?' asked Imām. The man replied, 'Not much.' 'Then, do the rich maintain relations with the poor?' The man replied, 'Verily you are listing virtues that people amongst us rarely possess.' Imām said, 'Then how can these people claim to be *shī'a*?!'[3847]

٣٤٢٥. الكافي عن محمّدِ بنِ عجلان: كنتُ عِند أبي عَبدِ اللهِ عليه السلام فَدخلَ رَجَلٌ فَسَلَّمَ، فَسأَلَهُ: كيفَ مَن خُلّفْتَ مِن إخوانِكَ؟ قالَ: فأحسنَ الثناءَ وزكّىٰ وأطرىٰ. قالَ لهُ: كيفَ عِيادَةُ أغنِيائِهِم علىٰ فُقَرائِهِم؟ فقالَ: قَليلَةٌ، قالَ: وكيفَ مُشاهَدَةُ أغنيائِهِم لِفُقَرائِهِم؟ قالَ: قَليلةٌ، قالَ: فكيفَ صِلَةُ أغنيائِهِم لِفُقَرائِهِم في ذاتِ أيدِيهِم، فقالَ: إنّك لَتَذكُرُ أخلاقاً قَلَّ ما هِيَ فِيمَن عِندَنا. قالَ: فقالَ: فكيفَ تَزعُمُ هؤلاءِ أنَّهُم شِيعَةٌ؟![٣٨١٥]

3426. **Imām al-Kāẓim (AS) said,** 'One who goes into retreat [in order to achieve spiritual upliftment] and who does not attain piety in his heart as a result is not from among our *shī'a*.'[3848]

٣٤٢٦. الإمامُ الكاظمُ عليه السلام: ليسَ مِن شيعَتِنا مَن خَلا ثُمّ لَم يَرُعْ قلبُهُ.[٣٨١٦]

1083. Types of Those who are Called Shī'a

١٠٨٣ ـ أصنافُ مَن يُسَمّىٰ بِالشِّيعَةِ

3427. **Imām al-Bāqir (AS) said,** 'Our *shī'a* are of three types: one type dupe people in our name, one type are like glass which discloses everything that is inside it[3849], and one type are like red gold, which the more it is brandished in the fire, the purer it becomes.'[3850]

٣٤٢٧. الإمامُ الباقرُ عليه السلام: شِيعَتُنا ثلاثةُ أصنافٍ: صِنفٌ يَأكُلونَ النّاسَ بِنا، وصِنفٌ كالزُّجاجِ يَنُمُّ[٣٨١٧]، وصِنفٌ كالذَّهَبِ الأحمَرِ كُلَّما أُدخِلَ النارَ ازدادَ جَودَةً.[٣٨١٨]

3428. **Imām al-Ṣādiq (AS) said,** 'The *shī'a* are of three types: one type who loves us and shows

٣٤٢٨. الإمامُ الصّادقُ عليه السلام: الشِّيعَةُ ثلاثٌ: مُحِبٌّ

affection towards us, and he is one of us. The other type is he who adorns himself through us, and we will serve as an adornment for whoever adorns himself through us. And the third type seeks to cheat people and enrich himself in our name, and whoever does this will be impoverished.'[3851]

وادٌّ فهُو مِنّا، ومُتَزَيِّنٌ بنا ونحنُ زَينٌ لِمَن تَـزَيَّنَ بنا، ومُستَأكِلٌ بِنَا الناسَ، ومَـنِ اسـتَأكَـلَ بِـنَا افتَقَرَ.[٣٨١٩]

1084. Prohibition of Extremism for the Shīʿa

١٠٨٤ ـ نَهيُ الشِّيعَةِ عَنِ الغُلُوِّ

3429. **Imām al-Bāqir (AS) said,** 'O community of *shīʿa* – the *shīʿa* of the household of Muḥammad – be like the middle saddle-cushion, on which the extremist who has slid forward falls back, and with which the follower who is yet to come catches up.' Upon hearing this, a man called Saʿd from among the *anṣār* asked him, 'May I be your ransom, who is an extremist?' He replied, 'They are a group of people who say such things about us that we do not say about ourselves. Neither are these people from among us, nor do we associate ourselves with them.' Then the man asked, 'Who is the follower that is yet to come?' He replied, 'The one who is searching for good and wants it, and who will eventually attain it and be rewarded for it.'[3852]

٣٤٢٩. الكافي عن عَمرو بنِ خالدٍ عَنِ الإمامِ الباقرِ عليه السلام: يا مَعشرَ الشِّيعَةِ ـ شِيعَةَ آلِ مـحمّدٍ ـ كُونُوا النُّمْرُقَةَ الوُسطىٰ، يَرجِـع إليكُـمُ الغـالي، ويَلحَق بِكُمُ التّالي، فقالَ لَهُ رجُلٌ مِن الأنـصارِ يقالُ لَهُ سعدٌ: جُعِلتُ فِداكَ، مَا الغالِي؟ قالَ: قومٌ يَقولُونَ فينا ما لا نَقُولُهُ في أنفُسِنا، فليسَ اُولئكَ مِنّا ولَسنا مِنهُم. قالَ: فَمَا التّالِي، قالَ: المُـرتادُ يُرِيدُ الخَيرَ، يُبَلِّغُهُ الخَيرُ يُوجَرُ علَيهِ.[٣٨٢٠]

1085. Duties Incumbent on the Shīʿa in their Interactions with People

١٠٨٥ ـ ما يَنبَغي لِلشِّيعةِ في مُواجَهَةِ النّاسِ

3430. **Imām al-Ṣādiq (AS) said,** 'O ʿAbd al-Aʿlā, … give my greetings of peace and the mercy of Allah to my *shīʿa*, and tell them: 'Allah has mercy on the servant who incites love in the people towards himself and towards us [when attracting them towards Islam], by displaying to them that which they already like, and keeping from them that which they would reject.'[3853]

٣٤٣٠. الإمامُ الصّادقُ عليه السلام ـ لعبد الأعلى ـ: يا عبدَ الأعلَى... فَـأقرِئهُمُ السـلامَ ورَحـمَةَ اللهِ ـ يَعنِي الشِّيعَةَ ـ وقُل: قالَ لَكُم: رَحِـمَ اللهُ عَـبداً استَجَرَّ مَوَدَّةَ الناسِ إلىٰ نفسِهِ وإلَينا، بأن يُـظهِرَ لَهُم ما يَعرِفُونَ ويَكُفَّ عَنهُم ما يُنكِرُونَ.[٣٨٢١]

3431. **Imām al-Ṣādiq (AS) said,** 'O *shīʿa* community, be an adornment for us [amongst people] and not a disgrace

٣٤٣١. عنه عليه السلام: مَعاشِرَ الشِّيعَةِ، كُونُوا لنا زَيناً،

to us. Say good words to people, guard your tongues and restrain yourselves from mindless chatter and offensive speech.'[3854]

ولا تَكُونُوا علَينا شَيناً ، قُولُوا لِلناسِ حُسناً ، وَاحفَظُوا ألسِنَتَكُم ، وكُفُّوها عنِ الفُضُولِ وقَبيحِ القَولِ .[٣٨٢٢]

1086. The Station of the Shīʿa on the Day of Resurrection

١٠٨٦ ـ مَقامُ الشِّيعَةِ فِي القِيامَةِ

3432. **The Prophet (SAWA) said,** 'On the Day of Resurrection, pulpits will be set up around the Throne for my *shīʿa* and the *shīʿa* of my household, who are sincere in their adherence to our guardianship. Then Allah, Mighty and Exalted, will say, 'Hurry to Me My servants that I may spread My Magnanimity over you, for you have been hurt in the world.'[3855]

٣٤٣٢ . رسولُ اللهِ ﷺ : تُوضَعُ يَومَ القِيامَةِ مَنابِرُ حَولَ العَرشِ لِشِيعَتِي وشِيعَةِ أهلِ بَيتِي المُخلِصِينَ في وَلايَتِنا ، ويقولُ اللهُ عَزَّوجلَّ : هَلُمُّوا يا عبادِي إلَيَّ لَأنشُرَنَّ علَيكُم كَرامَتي ؛ فقد أُوذِيتُم في الدُّنيا .[٣٨٢٣]

3433. **The Prophet (SAWA)** was asked by Ibn ʿAbbās about the verse of Allah in the Qur'an, *"And the Foremost Ones are the foremost ones: they are the ones brought near to Allah"*[3856], to which he replied, 'This refers to ʿAlī and his *shīʿa* – they will be the foremost to enter Paradise, the ones brought near to Allah through His Magnanimity over them.'[3857]

٣٤٣٣ . الأمالي للطوسي : وقد سَأَلَ رسولَ اللهِ ﷺ ابنُ عبّاسٍ عن قولِ اللهِ عَزَّوجلَّ : ﴿والسّابِقُونَ السابِقُونَ ❊ أُولئكَ المُقَرَّبُونَ﴾[٣٨٢٤] ـ فقال : قالَ ي جَبرَئيلُ : ذاكَ عَلِيٌّ وشِيعَتُهُ ، هُمُ السابِقونَ لَى الجَنَّةِ المُقَرَّبُونَ مِنَ اللهِ بكَرامَتِهِ لَهُم .[٣٨٢٥]

229

PATIENCE[3858]

الصَّبرُ

1087. The Virtue of Patience

١٠٨٧ ـ فَضلُ الصَّبرِ

"How many a prophet there has been alongside whom a multitude of godly men fought. They did not falter for what befell them in the way of Allah, neither did they weaken, nor did they abase themselves; and Allah loves the persevering ones."[3859]

﴿وَكَأَيِّنْ مِنْ نَبِيٍّ قاتَلَ مَعَهُ رِبِّيُّون كَثِيْرٌ فَما وَهَنُوا لِما أَصابَهُمْ فِي سَبِيْلِ اللهِ وَما ضَعُفُوا وَما اسْتَكانُوا واللهُ يُحِبُّ الصَّابِرِيْنَ﴾ .[٣٨٢٦]

"And obey Allah and His apostle, and do not dispute, or you will lose heart and your power will be gone. And be patient; indeed Allah is with the patient."[3860]

﴿وَأَطِيْعُوا اللهَ وَرَسُولَهُ وَلا تَنازَعُوا فَتَفْشَلُوا وَتَذْهَبَ رِيْحُكُمْ وَاصْبِرُوا إنَّ اللهَ مَعَ الصَّابِرِينَ﴾ .[٣٨٢٧]

3434. **Prophet Jesus (AS) said,** 'Verily you will never be able to attain that which you love until you are able to endure that which you despise.'[3861]

٣٤٣٤. عيسى (ع): إنّكُم لا تُدرِكُونَ ما تُحِبُّونَ إلّا بِصَبرِكُم على ما تَكرَهُونَ.[٣٨٢٨]

3435. **The Prophet (SAWA)** was once asked what faith was, to which he replied, 'Patience.'[3862]

٣٤٣٥. مسكّن الفؤاد ـ لَمّا سُئلَ عن رسول الله ﷺ ما الإيمان ـ: الصَّبرُ.[٣٨٢٩]

3436. **Imām 'Alī (AS) said,** 'Patience makes light work of calamities.'[3863]

٣٤٣٦. الإمامُ عليٌّ (ع): الصَّبرُ يُهَوِّنُ الفَجيعَةَ.[٣٨٣٠]

3437. **Imām 'Alī (AS) said,** 'Patience in the face of tribulation is better than well-being in times of comfort.'[3864]

٣٤٣٧. عنه (ع): الصَّبرُ على البَلاءِ أفضَلُ مِن العافِيَةِ في الرَّخاءِ.[٣٨٣١]

3438. **Imām al-Ṣādiq (AS) said,** 'The [true] believer is inherently patient against adversities.'[3865]

٣٤٣٨. الإمامُ الصّادقُ (ع): المؤمنُ يُطبَعُ عَلَى الصَّبرِ عَلَى النَّوائبِ.[٣٨٣٢]

3439. **Imām al-Ṣādiq (AS) said,** 'Patience is the peak of faith.'[3866]

٣٤٣٩. عنه (ع): الصَّبرُ رَأسُ الإيمانِ.[٣٨٣٣]

3440. **Imām al-Jawād (AS) said,** 'Patience in the face of a misfortune is itself a misfortune for the one who gloats over your bad luck.'[3867]

٣٤٤٠. الإمامُ الجوادُ (ع): الصَّبرُ عَلَى المُصيبَةِ، مُصيبَةٌ عَلَى الشامِتِ بها.[٣٨٣٤]

1088. Patience and Great Things

١٠٨٨ ـ الصَّبرُ ومَعالِي الأُمورِ

"And your Lord's best word [of promise] was fulfilled for the Children of Israel because of their patience."[3868]

﴿وَتَمَّتْ كَلِمَةُ رَبِّكَ الْحُسْنَىٰ عَلَىٰ بَنِي إِسْرَائِيلَ بِمَا صَبَرُوا﴾.[٣٨٣٥]

"And amongst them We appointed Imāms who guide [the people] by Our command, when they had been patient and had conviction in Our signs."[3869]

﴿وَجَعَلْنَا مِنْهُمْ أَئِمَّةً يَهْدُونَ بِأَمْرِنَا لَمَّا صَبَرُوا وَكَانُوا بِآيَاتِنَا يُوقِنُونَ﴾.[٣٨٣٦]

3441. **Imām 'Alī (AS) said,** 'Through patience are great things accomplished.'[3870]

٣٤٤١. الإمامُ عليٌّ (ع): بالصَّبرِ تُدرَكُ مَعالِي الأُمورِ.[٣٨٣٧]

3442. **Imām 'Alī (AS) said,** 'Whoever patiently endures the path to Allah reaches Him.'[3871]

٣٤٤٢. عنه (ع): مَن صَبَرَ عَلَى اللهِ وَصَلَ إلَيهِ.[٣٨٣٨]

1089. Perseverance and Victory

١٠٨٩ ـ الصَّبرُ وَالنَّصرُ

"How many a small party has overcome a larger party by Allah's will! And Allah is with the patient."[3872]

﴿كَمْ مِنْ فِئَةٍ قَلِيْلَةٍ غَلَبَتْ فِئَةً كَثِيرَةً بِإذْنِ اللهِ واللهُ مَعَ الصَّابِرِيْنَ﴾.[٣٨٣٩]

"Yes, if you persevere and are conscious of your duty to Allah, and should they come upon you suddenly, your Lord will aid you with five thousand marked angels."[3873]

﴿بَلَىٰ إنْ تَصْبِرُوا وَتَتَّقُوا وَيَأْتُوكُم مِنْ فَورِهِمْ هٰذا يُمْدِدْكُمْ رَبُّكُمْ بِخَمْسَةِ آلافٍ مِن المَلائكَةِ مُسَوِّمِينَ﴾.[٣٨٤٠]

3443. **The Prophet (SAWA) said,** 'Verily victory comes with perseverance, and deliverance with hardship, and verily with difficulty comes ease.'[3874]

٣٤٤٣. رسولُ اللهِ ﷺ: إنّ النَّصرَ مَعَ الصَّبرِ، والفَرَجَ مع الكَربِ، وإنّ مَعَ العُسرِ يُسراً.[٣٨٤١]

3444. **The Prophet (SAWA) said,** 'With perseverance, deliverance becomes possible, and whoever knocks at the door persistently will enter it.'[3875]

٣٤٤٤. عنه ﷺ: بِالصَّبرِ يُتَوَقَّعُ الفَرَجُ، ومَن يُدمِنْ قَرعَ البابِ يَلِجْ.[٣٨٤٢]

1090. The Reward of the Patient One

١٠٩٠ ـ ثَوابُ الصّابِرِ

"We will surely test you with a measure of fear and hunger and a loss of wealth, lives and crops; and give good news to the patient – those who when an affliction visits them, say, 'Indeed we belong to Allah, and to Him do we indeed return.' It is they who receive the blessings of their Lord, and [His] mercy, and it is they who are the [rightly] guided."[3876]

﴿وَلَنَبْلُوَنَّكُمْ بِشَيْءٍ مِنَ الخَوْفِ والجُوْعِ وَنَقْصٍ مِنَ الْأَمْوالِ والْأَنْفُسِ والثَّمَراتِ وَبَشِّرِ الصَّابِرِينَ * الَّذِينَ إذا أصابَتْهُمْ مُصِيْبَةٌ قالُوا إنَّا للهِ وَإنَّا إلَيهِ راجِعُونَ * أُولٰئِكَ عَلَيْهِمْ صَلَواتٌ مِنْ رَبِّهِمْ وَرَحمَةٌ وَأُولٰئِكَ هُمُ المُهْتَدُونَ﴾.[٣٨٤٣]

3445. **Imām ʿAlī (AS) said** in his description of the Godwary ones, 'They endured hardship for a short while, and in consequence they secured comfort for a long time.'[3877]

٣٤٤٥. الإمامُ عليٌّ عليه السلام ـ في صفةِ المتّقينَ ـ: صَبَرُوا أيّاماً قَصِيرَةً، أعقَبَتهُم راحَةٌ طَويلَةٌ.[٣٨٤٤]

3446. **Imām al-Ṣādiq (AS) said,** 'Whoever from amongst our *shīʿa* is tried with an affliction and endures it will be granted the reward of a thousand martyrs.'[3878]

٣٤٤٦. الإمامُ الصّادقُ عليه السلام: مَنِ ابتُلِيَ مِن شِيعَتِنا فَصَبَرَ علَيهِ كانَ لَهُ أجرُ ألفِ شَهيدٍ.[٣٨٤٥]

3447. **Imām al-Ṣādiq (AS) said,** 'Whoever, when suffering from an ailment, patiently endures it and considers it a means of proximity to Allah,

٣٤٤٧. عنه عليه السلام: أيُّما رَجُلٍ اشتَكىٰ فَصَبَرَ واحتَسَبَ، كَتَبَ اللهُ لَهُ مِنَ الأجرِ أجرَ

Allah writes down for him the same reward as that of a thousand martyrs.'[3879]

ألفِ شَهيدٍ.[٣٨٤٦]

1091. The True Meaning of Patience

١٠٩١ ـ تَفسيرُ الصَّبرِ

3448. **The Prophet (SAWA) said,** 'Patience is satisfaction [with Allah's decree].'[3880]

٣٤٤٨ . رسولُ اللهِ ﷺ : الصَّبرُ رِضا.[٣٨٤٧]

3449. **Imām 'Alī (AS) said,** 'Patience is that a man bears whatever afflicts him and swallows his anger.'[3881]

٣٤٤٩ . الإمامُ عليٌّ عليه السلام : الصَّبرُ أن يَحتَمِلَ الرجُلُ ما يَنُوبُهُ، ويَكظِمَ ما يُغضِبُهُ.[٣٨٤٨]

3450. **Imām 'Alī (AS) said,** 'Patience is of two types: perseverance in the face of that which you despise, and enduring restraint against that which you love.'[3882]

٣٤٥٠ . عنه عليه السلام : الصَّبرُ صَبرانِ: صَبرٌ على ما تَكرَهُ، وصَبرٌ عمّا تُحِبُّ.[٣٨٤٩]

3451. **Imām 'Alī (AS) said,** 'Patience comes in the form of either persevering in the face of an affliction, or enduring an act of obedience, or restraining oneself against an act of disobedience. And this third type is of a higher calibre than the first two.'[3883]

٣٤٥١ . عنه عليه السلام : الصَّبرُ: إمّا صَبرٌ على المُصيبَةِ، أو على الطاعَةِ، أو عنِ المَعصيَةِ، وهذا القِسمُ الثالثُ أعلىٰ دَرجَةً مِنَ القِسمَينِ الأوَّلَينِ.[٣٨٥٠]

3452. **Imām al-Bāqir (AS)** was once asked about graceful patience[3884], to which he replied, 'That is the patience that is devoid of complaint to other people.'[3885]

٣٤٥٢ . الإمامُ الباقرُ عليه السلام ـ لَمّا سُئلَ عن الصَّبرِ الجميلِ ـ: ذلكَ صَبرٌ ليسَ فيهِ شَكوىٰ إلى الناسِ.[٣٨٥١]

1092. The Patience Possessed by the Shī'a of Ahl al-Bayt (AS)

١٠٩٢ ـ صَبرُ شيعَةِ أهلِ البَيتِ عليهم السلام

3453. *al-Kāfī,* al-Washā' narrates from one of the companions of Imām al-Ṣādiq (AS) that he (AS) said:, 'Verily we are very patient and our *shī'a* are even more patient than us.' His companion asked, 'May I be your ransom, how can your *shī'a* be more patient than yourselves?' He replied, 'Because we are patient in what we already have knowledge of, whereas our *shī'a* are patient in spite of not knowing.'[3886]

٣٤٥٣ . الكافي عن الوَشّاء عن بعضِ أصحابِهِ عن الإمامِ الصّادقِ عليه السلام: إنّا صُبَّرٌ وشِيعَتُنا أصبَرُ مِنّا، قلتُ: جُعِلتُ فِداكَ، كيفَ صارَ شِيعَتُكُم أصبَرَ مِنكُم؟ قالَ: لأنّا نَصبِرُ علىٰ ما نَعلَمُ، وشِيعَتُنا يَصبِرُونَ علىٰ ما لا يَعلَمُونَ.[٣٨٥٢]

1093. The Effects of Anxiety

١٠٩٣ـ آثارُ الجَزَعِ

3454. **Imām ʿAlī (AS) said,** 'Verily if you are patient, the trials of destiny will befall you and you will be rewarded for them, whilst if you are anxious, not only will the trials of destiny still befall you but you will be sinful.'[3887]

٣٤٥٤. الإمامُ عليٌّ عليه السلام : إنّكَ إن صَبَرتَ جَرَت علَيكَ المَقاديرُ وأنتَ مَأجُورٌ، وإن جَزِعتَ جَرَت علَيكَ المَقادِيرُ وأنتَ مَأزُورٌ.[٣٨٥٣]

3455. **Imām ʿAlī (AS) said,** 'You can either have the perseverance of noblemen or else you will taste the suffering, like beasts.'[3888]

٣٤٥٥. عنه عليه السلام : إن صَبَرتَ صَبرَ الأكارِمِ، وإلّا سَلَوتَ سُلُوَّ البَهائمِ.[٣٨٥٤]

3456. **Imām ʿAlī (AS) said,** 'Whoever does not endure his troubles ends up having to endure his ruin [bankruptcy].'[3889]

٣٤٥٦. عنه عليه السلام : مَن لَم يَصبِرْ على كَدِّهِ صَبَرَ على الإفلاسِ.[٣٨٥٥]

3457. **Imām ʿAlī (AS) said,** 'He whose patience gives him no deliverance is destroyed by anxiety.'[3890]

٣٤٥٧. عنه عليه السلام : مَن لَم يُنْجِهِ الصَّبرُ أهلَكَهُ الجَزَعُ.[٣٨٥٦]

1094. Factors that Bring About Patience

١٠٩٤ـ ما يورِثُ الصَّبرَ

3458. **The Prophet (SAWA) said,** 'Whoever tries to be patient, Allah makes him patient, and whoever tries to remain chaste, Allah keeps him chaste, and whoever suffices himself with what he has, Allah enriches him. No servant can ever be granted something better and more sufficient than patience.'[3891]

٣٤٥٨. رسولُ اللهِ ﷺ : مَن يَتَصَبَّرْ يُصَبِّرْهُ اللهُ، ومَن يَستَعفِفْ يُعِفَّهُ اللهُ، ومَن يَستَغنِ يُغنِهِ اللهُ، وما أُعطِيَ عَبدٌ عَطاءً هُو خَيرٌ وأوسَعُ مِن الصَّبرِ.[٣٨٥٧]

3459. **Imām ʿAlī (AS) said,** 'The origin of patience is to have strong conviction in Allah.'[3892]

٣٤٥٩. الإمامُ عليٌّ عليه السلام : أصلُ الصَّبرِ حُسنُ اليَقينِ بِاللهِ.[٣٨٥٨]

3460. **Imām ʿAlī (AS) said,** 'Accustom yourself to persevering in the face of adversity, and what a good trait is the persevering with truth.'[3893]

٣٤٦٠. عنه عليه السلام : عَوِّدْ نَفسَكَ التَّصَبُّرَ (الصَّبرَ) على المَكروهِ، ونِعمَ الخُلقُ التَّصَبُّرُ في الحَقِّ.[٣٨٥٩]

3461. **Imām ʿAlī (AS) said,** 'Perseverance in the face of adversity protects the heart.'[3894]

٣٤٦١. عنه عليه السلام : التَّصَبُّرُ على المَكروهِ يَعصِمُ القَلبَ.[٣٨٦٠]

230

TRUTHFULNESS

الصِّدق

1095. The Virtue of Truthfulness and the Truthful

١٠٩٥ ـ فَضلُ الصِّدقِ وَ الصّادِقِ

"O you who have faith! Be wary of Allah and be with the truthful ones."[3895]

﴿يا أيُّها الَّذِينَ آمَنُوا اتَّقُوا اللهَ وَكُونُوا مَعَ الصَّادِقِينَ﴾.[٣٨٦١]

(See also: Qur'an 5:119, 12:70, 21:63, 33:23, 33:24, 39:33, 59:8)

(أُنظر) المائدة: ١١٩ و يوسف: ٧٠ والأنبياء: ٦٣ و الأحزاب: ٢٣، ص ٢٤ والزمر: ٣٣ والحشر: ٨.

3462. **The Prophet (SAWA) said,** 'Truthfulness is incumbent upon you, for verily it is one of the doors of Paradise.'[3896]

٣٤٦٢. رسولُ اللهِ ﷺ: عليكُم بالصِّدقِ؛ فإنّهُ بابٌ مِن أبوابِ الجَنَّةِ.[٣٨٦٢]

3463. **Imām ʿAlī (AS) said,** 'Truthfulness is the congruity of speech with divine convention, whereas lying removes speech from divine convention.'[3897]

٣٤٦٣. الإمامُ عليٌّ ؑ: الصِّدقُ مُطابَقَةُ المَنطِقِ للوَضعِ الإلهيِّ، الكِذبُ زَوالُ المَنطِقِ عَنِ الوَضعِ الإلهيِّ.[٣٨٦٣]

3464. **Imām ʿAlī (AS) said,** 'Truthfulness is the tongue of the truth.'[3898]

٣٤٦٤. عنه ؑ: الصِّدقُ لِسانُ الحَقِّ.[٣٨٦٤]

3465. **Imām ʿAlī (AS) said,** 'Truthfulness saves you even though you fear it whereas lying ruins you even though you feel safe from it.'[3899]

٣٤٦٥. عنه ؑ: الصِّدقُ يُنجِيكَ وإن خِفتَهُ، الكِذبُ يُردِيكَ وإن أمِنتَهُ.[٣٨٦٥]

3466. **Imām ʿAlī (AS) said,** 'Truthfulness is the goodness of everything whereas lying corrupts everything.'[3900]

٣٤٦٦. عنه ؑ: الصِّدقُ صَلاحُ كُلِّ شيءٍ، الكِذبُ فَسادُ كُلِّ شَيءٍ.[٣٨٦٦]

3467. **Imām ʿAlī (AS) said,** 'Truthfulness is a trust whereas lying is betrayal.'[3901]

٣٤٦٧. عنه ؑ: الصِّدقُ أمانةٌ، الكِذبُ خِيانَةٌ.[٣٨٦٧]

3468. **Imām ʿAlī (AS) said,** 'The worth of a man is measured by the extent of his ambition, and his truthfulness is measured by his integrity.'[3902]

٣٤٦٨. عنه ؑ: قَدرُ الرَّجُلِ علىٰ قَدرِ هِمَّتِهِ، وصِدقُهُ علىٰ قَدرِ مُرُوءَتِهِ.[٣٨٦٨]

3469. **Imām ʿAlī (AS) said,** 'Faith is to prefer to tell the truth, even if it be to your detriment, over lying even though it be to your benefit.'[3903]

٣٤٦٩. عنه ﷺ: الإيمانُ أن تُؤثِر الصِّدقَ حيثُ يَضُرُّكَ، على الكِذبِ حيثُ يَنفَعُكَ.[٣٨٦٩]

3470. **Imām ʿAlī (AS) said,** 'The truthful one is at the height of salvation and dignity, whereas the liar is on the brink of ignominy and degradation.'[3904]

٣٤٧٠. عنه ﷺ: الصادِقُ على شَفا مَنجاةٍ وكَرامَةٍ، والكاذِبُ على شَرَفِ مَهواةٍ ومَهانَةٍ.[٣٨٧٠]

3471. **Imām al-Bāqir (AS) said,** 'Learn to tell the truth before you learn to speak.'[3905]

٣٤٧١. الإمامُ الباقرُ ﷺ: تَعَلَّمُوا الصِّدقَ قَبلَ الحَديثِ.[٣٨٧١]

3472. **Imām al-Ṣādiq (AS) said,** 'Truthfulness is an honour.'[3906]

٣٤٧٢. الإمامُ الصّادقُ ﷺ: الصِّدقُ عِزٌّ.[٣٨٧٢]

3473. **Imām al-Ṣādiq (AS) said,** 'He whose tongue tells the truth is pure of action.'[3907]

٣٤٧٣. عنه ﷺ: مَن صَدَقَ لِسانُهُ زَكا عَمَلُهُ.[٣٨٧٣]

1096. Testing People Through Truthfulness in Speech

١٠٩٦ ـ الإختِبارُ بِصِدقِ الحَديثِ

3474. **Imām al-Ṣādiq (AS) said,** 'Do not be deceived by their [lengthy] prayer or their [abundant] fasting, for verily it may be that a man becomes so attached to his prayer and his fasting that were he to stop doing them, he would be greatly disturbed. Rather test these people through the truth in their speech and their prompt return of goods entrusted in their care.'[3908]

٣٤٧٤. الإمامُ الصّادقُ ﷺ: لا تَغتَرُّوا بِصلاتِهِم ولا بِصِيامِهِم؛ فإنَّ الرجُلَ ربّما لَهِجَ بِالصلاةِ والصومِ حتّى لَو تَرَكَهُ استَوحَشَ، ولكِنِ اختَبِرُوهُم عِندَ صِدقِ الحَديثِ وأداءِ الأمانَةِ.[٣٨٧٤]

3475. **Imām al-Ṣādiq (AS) said,** 'Better than the truth itself is the one who tells it, and better than the good deed itself is the one who performs it.'[3909]

٣٤٧٥. عنه ﷺ: أحسَنُ مِنَ الصِدقِ قائلُهُ، وخَيرٌ مِن الخَيرِ فاعِلُهُ.[٣٨٧٥]

1097. The Most Truthful of Sayings

١٠٩٧ ـ أصدَقُ الأقوالِ

"Allah – there is no god except Him – will surely gather you on the Day of Resurrection, in which there is no doubt; and who is more truthful in speech than Allah?"[3910]

﴿اللهُ لا إلٰهَ إلَّا هُوَ لَيَجْمَعَنَّكُمْ إلَىٰ يَوْمِ القِيامَةِ لا رَيْبَ فِيهِ وَمَنْ أصْدَقُ مِنَ اللهِ حَدِيْثاً﴾.[٣٨٧٦]

3476. **Imām ʿAlī (AS),** when he was asked about the most truthful saying, replied, 'The testimony that there is no god but Allah.'[3911]

٣٤٧٦. الإمامُ عليٌّ ؏ ـ لَمّا سُئلَ عن أصدَقِ الأقوالِ ـ: شَهادَةُ أن لا إلٰهَ إلّا اللهُ.[٣٨٧٧]

3477. **Imām ʿAlī (AS) said,** 'The most truthful of sayings is that which expresses one's feelings.'[3912]

٣٤٧٧. عنه ؏: أصدَقُ المَقالِ ما نَطَقَ بِهِ لِسانُ الحالِ.[٣٨٧٨]

231

THE FRIEND

الصَّدِيق

1098. The Importance of a Friend

١٠٩٨ ـ أهَمِّيَّةُ الصَّدِيقِ

3478. **The Prophet (SAWA) said,** 'Man follows the same creed as his friend, so consider carefully who it is you befriend.'[3913]

٣٤٧٨. رسولُ اللهِ ﷺ: المَرءُ علىٰ دِينِ خَليلِهِ، فَليَنظُر أحَدُكُم مَن يُخالِلُ.[٣٨٧٩]

3479. **Imām ʿAlī (AS) said,** 'One's friend is the closest of one's relations.'[3914]

٣٤٧٩. الإمامُ عليٌّ ؏: الصَّديقُ أقرَبُ الأقارِبِ.[٣٨٨٠]

3480. **Imām ʿAlī (AS) said,** 'He who lacks friends lacks a bare necessity.'[3915]

٣٤٨٠. عنه ؏: مَن لا صَديقَ لَهُ لا ذُخرَ لَهُ.[٣٨٨١]

3481. **Imām ʿAlī (AS) said,** 'Friends are a single soul divided between different bodies.'[3916]

٣٤٨١. عنه ؏: الأصدِقاءُ نَفسٌ واحِدَةٌ في جُسومٍ مُتَفَرِّقَةٍ.[٣٨٨٢]

1099. Resemblance of Souls

١٠٩٩ ـ تَشاكُلُ النُّفوسِ

3482. **Imām ʿAlī (AS) said,** 'Souls are of different kinds. Those that resemble each other are in harmony, and people are more attracted towards those they resemble.'[3917]

٣٤٨٢. الإمامُ عليٌّ ؏: النُّفوسُ أشكالٌ، فما تَشاكَلَ مِنها اتَّفَقَ، والنّاسُ إلىٰ أشكالِهِم أمْيَلُ.[٣٨٨٣]

3483. **Imām ʿAlī (AS) said,** 'Every person is inclined towards one who is like him.'[3918]

٣٤٨٣. عنه ؏: كُلُّ امرِئٍ يَميلُ إلىٰ مِثلِهِ.[٣٨٨٤]

(See also: THE SPIRIT: section 845)

(اُنظر) الروح: باب ٨٤٥.

1100. People whom One Should Befriend

١١٠٠ـ مَن يَنبَغي مُصادَقَتُهُ

3484. **The Prophet (SAWA) said,** 'The most prosperous of people is he who mingles with honourable people.'[3919]

٣٤٨٤ . رسولُ اللهِ ﷺ : أسعَدُ الناسِ مَن خالَطَ كِرامَ الناسِ.[٣٨٨٥]

3485. **Imām ʿAlī (AS) said,** 'The most goodness and righteousness is to be found in the company of people of reason and understanding.'[3920]

٣٤٨٥ . الإمامُ عليٌّ (عليه السلام) : أكثَرُ الصَّلاحِ والصَّوابِ في صُحبَةِ أُولي النُّهىٰ والألبابِ.[٣٨٨٦]

3486. **Imām ʿAlī (AS) said,** 'The one who invites you to the everlasting abode and helps you work towards it is a compassionate friend indeed.'[3921]

٣٤٨٦ . عنه (عليه السلام) : مَن دَعاكَ إلى الدارِ الباقيَةِ وأعانَكَ علَى العَمَلِ لَها، فهُوَ الصَّديقُ الشَّفيقُ.[٣٨٨٧]

3487. **Imām al-Ṣādiq (AS) said,** 'Do not call a man your friend with the true stamp of friendship until you have tested him in three matters: anger him so that you may see whether his anger takes him away from right into wrong; test him with the dinar and the dirham [in money matters]; and travel with him.'[3922]

٣٤٨٧ . الإمامُ الصّادقُ (عليه السلام) : لا تُسَمِّ الرَّجُلَ صَديقاً سِمَةَ مَعرِفَةٍ حتّىٰ تَختَبِرَهُ بثلاثٍ: تُغضِبُهُ فتَنظُرُ غَضَبَهُ يُخرِجُهُ مِنَ الحَقِّ إلى الباطِلِ، وعندَ الدِّينارِ والدِّرهَمِ، وحتّىٰ تُسافِرَ مَعهُ.[٣٨٨٨]

3488. **Imām al-Ṣādiq (AS) said,** 'Befriend one who gives you a good image, and do not befriend one who uses you to boost his own image.'[3923]

٣٤٨٨ . عنه (عليه السلام) : اِصحَبْ مَن تَتَزَيَّنُ بِهِ، ولا تَصحَبْ مَن يَتَزَيَّنُ بكَ.[٣٨٨٩، ٣٨٩٠]

1101. People whom One Must not Befriend

١١٠١ـ مَن لا يَنبَغي مُصادَقَتُهُ

"A day when the wrongdoer will bite his hands, saying, 'I wish I had followed the apostle's way! Woe to me! I wish I had not taken so and so as a friend! Certainly he led me astray from the Reminder after it had come to me, and Satan is a deserter of man."[3924]

﴿وَيَوْمَ يَعَضُّ الظَّالِمُ عَلَىٰ يَدَيْهِ يَقُولُ يَا لَيْتَنِي اتَّخَذْتُ مَعَ الرَّسُولِ سَبِيلاً * يَا وَيْلَتَا لَيْتَنِي لَمْ أَتَّخِذْ فُلاناً خَلِيلاً * لَقَدْ أَضَلَّنِي عَنِ الذِّكْرِ بَعْدَ إِذْ جَاءَنِي وَكَانَ الشَّيْطَانُ لِلْإِنْسَانِ خَذُولاً﴾.[٣٨٩١]

3489. **The Prophet (SAWA) said,** 'It is not good for you to befriend someone who does not have your best interests at heart as he does his own.'[3925]

٣٤٨٩ . رسولُ اللهِ ﷺ : لا خَيرَ لكَ في صُحبَةِ مَن لا يَرىٰ لكَ مِثلَ الذي يَرىٰ لِنَفسِهِ.[٣٨٩٢]

3490. **Imām ʿAlī (AS) said,** 'He who, in his friendship with you, is of no aid to you against your base self, his friendship is a curse on you, if only you knew.'[3926]

٣٤٩٠ . الإمامُ عليٌّ (عليه السلام) : مَن لَم يَصحَبْكَ مُعيناً علىٰ نفسِكَ فَصُحبَتُهُ وَبالٌ علَيكَ إن عَلِمتَ.[٣٨٩٣]

3491. **Imām ʿAlī (AS) said,** 'Beware of befriending corrupt people, immoral people, and those who openly commit acts of disobedience to Allah.'[3927]

٣٤٩١. عنه ؑ: إحذَرْ مُصاحَبَةَ الفُسّاقِ والفُجّارِ والمُجاهِرِينَ بِمَعاصِي اللهِ.٣٨٩٤

3492. **Imām ʿAlī (AS) said,** 'The friend of an ignorant man is always wearied and miserable.'[3928]

٣٤٩٢. عنه ؑ: صَدِيقُ الجاهِلِ مَتعُوبٌ مَنكُوبٌ.٣٨٩٥

3493. **Imām ʿAlī (AS) said,** 'Beware of befriending immoral people, for verily only evil accompanies evil.'[3929]

٣٤٩٣. عنه ؑ: إيّاكَ ومُصاحَبَةَ الفُسّاقِ؛ فإنَّ الشَّرَّ بالشَّرِّ مُلحَقٌ.٣٨٩٦

3494. **Imām ʿAlī (AS),** in his will to his son al-Ḥasan (AS), said, 'O my son, beware of befriending a stupid person, for although he will surely want to be of benefit to you, he will only bring you trouble.'[3930]

٣٤٩٤. عنه ؑ ـ في وصيَّتِهِ لابنِهِ الحَسنِ ؑ ـ: يا بُنَيَّ، إيّاكَ ومُصادَقَةَ الأحمَقِ؛ فإنَّهُ يُرِيدُ أن يَنفَعَكَ فيَضُرُّكَ.٣٨٩٧

3495. **Imām Zayn al-ʿĀbidīn (AS),** in his advice to his son al-Bāqir (AS), said, 'Beware of befriending one who has cut off relations with his kin, for verily I have seen him cursed in the Book of Allah, Mighty and Exalted, on three different occasions.'[3931]

٣٤٩٥. الإمامُ زينُ العابدينَ ؑ ـ في وصيَّتِهِ لابنِهِ الباقِرِ ؑ ـ: إيّاكَ ومصاحَبَةَ القاطِعِ لِرَحِمِهِ؛ فإنّي وَجَدتُهُ مَلعوناً في كتابِ اللهِ عزَّوجلَّ في ثلاثِ مَواضِعَ.٣٨٩٨

3496. **Imām al-Riḍā (AS) said,** 'The ignorant man's friend is always wearied.'[3932]

٣٤٩٦. الإمامُ الرِّضا ؑ: صَديقُ الجاهِلِ في تَعَبٍ.٣٨٩٩

1102. That which Corrupts a Friendship

١١٠٢ ـ ما يُفسِدُ الصَّداقَةَ

3497. **Imām ʿAlī (AS) said,** 'When a man puts his friend to shame, he has indeed parted from him.'[3933]

٣٤٩٧. الإمامُ عليٌّ ؑ: إذا احتَشَمَ الرجُلُ أخاهُ فقد فارَقَهُ.٣٩٠٠

3498. **Imām ʿAlī (AS) said,** 'Jealousy of one's friend stems from weakness in one's love [for him].'[3934]

٣٤٩٨. عنه ؑ: حَسَدُ الصَّديقِ مِن سُقمِ المَوَدَّةِ.٣٩٠١

3499. **Imām ʿAlī (AS) said,** 'Do not let bad opinion of people overcome you, for verily it will not leave any pardon between you and your friend.'[3935]

٣٤٩٩. عنه ؑ: لا يَغْلِبَنَّ علَيكَ سوءُ الظَّنِّ؛ فإنَّهُ لا يَدَعُ بينَكَ وبينَ صَديقٍ صَفْحاً.٣٩٠٢

3500. **Imām ʿAlī (AS) said,** ‘He who penetrates deeply into his friend’s affairs, his love for him comes to an end.’[3936]

٣٥٠٠. عنه (ع): مَنِ استقصىٰ علىٰ صَديقِهِ انقَطَعَت مَوَدَّتُهُ.[٣٩٠٣]

3501. **Imām ʿAlī (AS) said,** ‘He who argues with his brothers has few friends.’[3937]

٣٥٠١. عنه (ع): مَن ناقَشَ الإخوانَ قَلَّ صَديقُهُ.[٣٩٠٤]

3502. **Imām al-Ṣādiq (AS) said,** ‘If you want the exclusive love of your brother, then do not ever make fun of him, nor quarrel with him, nor compete against him, nor be malicious to him.’[3938]

٣٥٠٢. الإمامُ الصّادقُ (ع): إن أرَدتَ أن يَصفُوَ لكَ وُدُّ أخيكَ فلا تُمازِحَنَّهُ، ولا تُمارِيَنَّهُ، ولا تُباهِيَنَّهُ، ولا تُشارَّنَّهُ.[٣٩٠٥]

3503. **Imām al-Hādī (AS) said,** ‘The quarrel corrupts a long friendship and dissolves strong ties, the least of it is that one tries to overcome the other, and strife is the main cause of a break in friendship.’[3939]

٣٥٠٣. الإمامُ الهاديُ (ع): المِراءُ يُفسِدُ الصَّداقةَ القَديمَةَ، ويُحَلِّلُ العُقدَةَ الوَثيقَةَ، وأقَلُّ ما فيهِ أن تَكونَ فيهِ المُغالَبَةُ، والمُغالَبَةُ أُسُّ أسبابِ القَطيعَةِ.[٣٩٠٦]

1103. The Extent of One’s Friendship

١١٠٣ ـ حُدودُ الصَّداقَةِ

3504. **Imām ʿAlī (AS) said,** ‘A sincere friend is he who advises you with regard to your shortcomings, protects you in your absence, and prefers you over himself.’[3940]

٣٥٠٤. الإمامُ عليٌّ (ع): الصَّديقُ الصَّدوقُ: مَن نَصَحَكَ في عَيبِكَ، وحَفِظَكَ في غَيبِكَ، وآثَرَكَ علىٰ نَفسِهِ.[٣٩٠٧]

3505. **Imām ʿAlī (AS) said,** ‘Shower all your love on your friend but do not shower all your trust on him.’[3941]

٣٥٠٥. عنه (ع): اُبذُلْ لِصَديقِكَ كُلَّ المَوَدَّةِ، ولا تَبذُل لَهُ كُلَّ الطُّمأنينَةِ.[٣٩٠٨]

3506. **Imām al-Ṣādiq (AS) said,** ‘Friendship can only succeed when its conditions are fulfilled, and he who fulfils all or some of these conditions may be befriended, and if not, then do not attribute any of your friendship to him. The first of these conditions is that he should treat you in public the same as he treats you in private. Secondly, that your source of pride is a source of pride for him, and your source of shame is a source of shame for him too. Thirdly, that neither position nor wealth should change him towards you. Fourthly, that he

٣٥٠٦. الإمامُ الصّادقُ (ع): لا تَكونُ الصَّداقَةُ إلّا بِحُدودِها، فَمَن كانَت فيهِ هذهِ الحُدودُ أو شَيءٌ مِنهُ، وإلّا فلا تَنسِبْهُ إلىٰ شَيءٍ مِنَ الصَّداقَةِ، فَأَوَّلُها: أن تَكونَ سَريرَتُهُ وعَلانِيَتُهُ لكَ واحِدَةً، والثانيةُ: أن يَرىٰ زَينَكَ زَينَهُ، وشَينَكَ شَينَهُ، والثالثةُ: أن لا تُغَيِّرَهُ عَلَيكَ وِلايَةٌ ولا مالٌ، والرابعةُ: لا يَمنَعُكَ شَيئاً تَنالُهُ مَقدُرَتُهُ،

must not prevent you from obtaining that which you have the capacity for, and fifthly – and this sums up all the other qualities – that he must not give up on you in times of misfortune.’[3942]

والخامسةُ ـ وهي تجمَعُ هذهِ الخِصالَ ـ: أن لا يُسلِمَكَ عِندَ النَّكَباتِ.[٣٩٠٩]

1104. The Best of Companions

١١٠٤ـ أفضلُ الأصحابِ

3507. **The Prophet (SAWA) said,** ‘The best of companions is he who has little discord and much harmony.’[3943]

٣٥٠٧. رسولُ اللهِ ﷺ: خَيرُ الأصحابِ مَن قَلَّ شِقاقُهُ وكَثُرَ وِفاقُهُ.[٣٩١٠]

3508. **Imām ʿAlī (AS) said,** ‘One who aids you in your obedience [to Allah] is the best of companions.’[3944]

٣٥٠٨. الإمامُ عليٌّ ؑ: المُعِينُ على الطاعةِ خَيرُ الأصحابِ.[٣٩١١]

1105. The Right of One’s Companion

١١٠٥ـ حَقُّ الصّاحِبِ

3509. **Imām ʿAlī (AS) said,** ‘Do not cut off a friend, even if he is ungrateful.’[3945]

٣٥٠٩. الإمامُ عليٌّ ؑ: لا تَقطَعْ صَديقاً وإن كَفَرَ.[٣٩١٢]

3510. **Imām Zayn al-ʿĀbidīn (AS) said,** ‘The right of your companion is that you share his company with bounty and fairness. You should honour him as he honours you, and should not let him be the first to extend his generosity. And if he is the first to do so, then repay him. Love him as he loves you, and restrain him from any act of disobedience that he might contemplate. Be a mercy for him, and not a chastisement.’[3946]

٣٥١٠. الإمامُ زينُ العابدينَ ؑ: أمّا حَقُّ الصاحِبِ: فَأن تَصحَبَهُ بالتَّفَضُّلِ والانصافِ، وتُكرِمَهُ كما يُكرِمُكَ، ولا تَدَعَهُ يَسبِقُ إلىٰ مَكرُمَةٍ، فإن سَبَقَ كافَأتَهُ، وتَوَدَّهُ كما يَوَدُّكَ، وتَزجُرَهُ عمّا يَهُمُّ بهِ مِن مَعصيَةٍ، وكُن علَيهِ رَحمَةً، ولا تَكُن علَيهِ عَذاباً.[٣٩١٣]

232

CHARITY

الصَّدَقَة

1106. The Virtue of Charity

١١٠٦ـ فَضلُ الصَّدَقةِ

“Take charity from their possessions to cleanse them and purify them thereby, and bless them. Indeed your blessing is a comfort to them, and Allah is all-hearing, all-knowing.”[3947]

﴿خُذْ مِنْ أَمْوالِهِمْ صَدَقَةً تُطَهِّرُهُمْ وَتُزَكِّيهِمْ بِها وَصَلِّ عَلَيْهِمْ إِنَّ صَلاتَكَ سَكَنٌ لَهُمْ وَاللهُ سَمِيعٌ عَلِيمٌ﴾.[٣٩١٤]

3511. **The Prophet (SAWA) said,** 'The earth on the Day of Resurrection will be scorching, except for the shadow of a believer, for verily his charity will serve him as shade.'[3948]

٣٥١١ . رسولُ اللهِ ﷺ : أرضُ القِيامَةِ نارٌ، ما خَلا ظِلَّ المؤمِنِ فإنَّ صَدَقَتَهُ تُظِلُّهُ . [٣٩١٥]

3512. **The Prophet (SAWA) said,** 'Everyone will only have recourse to the shade provided by charity they had given until their affairs are judged [by Allah].'[3949]

٣٥١٢ . عنه ﷺ : كُلُّ امرِئٍ في ظِلِّ صَدَقَتِهِ حتّىٰ يُقضىٰ بَينَ الناسِ . [٣٩١٦]

3513. **The Prophet (SAWA) said,** 'Verily charity extinguishes the wrath of the Lord.'[3950]

٣٥١٣ . عنه ﷺ: إنَّ الصَّدَقَةَ لَتُطفِئُ غَضَبَ الرَّبِّ . [٣٩١٧]

3514. **Imām 'Alī (AS) said,** 'Charity acts as a shield against the fire.'[3951]

٣٥١٤ . الإمامُ عليٌّ عليه السلام :الصَّدقةُ جُنَّةٌ مِن النارِ. [٣٩١٨]

1107. Allah's Firsthand Receipt of Charities

١١٠٧ ـ تَلَقِّي اللهِ لِلصَّدَقاتِ

"Do they not know that it is Allah who accepts the repentance of His servants and receives the charities, and that it is Allah who is the All-clement, the All-merciful."[3952]

﴿ أَلَمْ يَعْلَمُوا أَنَّ اللهَ هُوَ يَقْبَلُ التَّوبَةَ عَنْ عِبادِهِ وَيَأْخُذُ الصَّدَقاتِ وَأَنَّ اللهَ هُوَ التَّوَّابُ الرَّحِيمُ ﴾ . [٣٩١٩]

3515. **Imām al-Ṣādiq (AS) said,** 'Verily Allah, Blessed and most High, says, 'In My stead, I have entrusted every single thing to the one who grasps it, except for charity, for verily I immediately seize that up in My Hand.'[3953]

٣٥١٥ . الإمامُ الصّادقُ عليه السلام : إنّ اللهَ تبارَكَ وتعالىٰ يقولُ : ما مِن شَيءٍ إلّا وقد وَكَّلتُ مَن يَقبِضُهُ غَيرِي، إلّا الصَّدَقةَ؛ فإنّي أتَلَقَّفُها بِيَدِي تَلَقُّفاً . [٣٩٢٠]

1108. Charity and Repelling Adversities

١١٠٨ ـ الصَّدَقَةُ ودَفعُ البَلاءِ

3516. **The Prophet (SAWA) said,** 'Charity prevents seventy different types of adversities, the simplest of them being elephantiasis and leprosy.'[3954]

٣٥١٦ . رسولُ اللهِ ﷺ : الصَّدَقَةُ تَمنَعُ سَبعينَ نَوعاً مِن أنواعِ البَلاءِ، أهوَنُها الجُذامُ والبَرَصُ . [٣٩٢١]

3517. **The Prophet (SAWA) said,** 'Charity blocks seventy doorways to evil.'[3955]

٣٥١٧ . عنه ﷺ : الصَّدَقةُ تَسُدُّ سَبعِينَ باباً مِن الشَّرِّ . [٣٩٢٢]

3518. **The Prophet (SAWA) said,** 'Charity repels an undignified death.'[3956]

٣٥١٨ . عنه ﷺ : الصَّدَقةُ تَدفَعُ مِيتَةَ السُّوءِ . [٣٩٢٣]

3519. **The Prophet (SAWA) said,** 'Give charity, and cure your sick ones through the giving of charity, for verily charity repels accidents and illnesses, and is a source of increase in your lifespans and your good deeds.'[3957]

٣٥١٩. عنه ﷺ: تَصَدَّقُوا وداوُوا مَرضاكُم بالصَّدَقَةِ؛ فإنَّ الصَّدَقةَ تَدفَعُ عنِ الأعراضِ والأمراضِ، وهِيَ زيادَةٌ في أعمارِكُم وحَسَناتِكُم.[٣٩٢٤]

3520. **Imām ʿAlī (AS) said,** 'Charity is an effective cure.'[3958]

٣٥٢٠. الإمامُ عليٌّ عليه السلام: الصَّدَقةُ دَواءٌ مُنجِحٌ.[٣٩٢٥]

1109. Charity is the Key to (Increased) Sustenance

١١٠٩ ـ الصَّدَقَةُ مِفتاحُ الرِّزقِ

3521. **The Prophet (SAWA) said,** 'Increase your charity and you will be given [increased] sustenance.'[3959]

٣٥٢١. رسولُ اللهِ ﷺ: أكثِرُوا مِنَ الصَّدَقَةِ تُرزَقُوا.[٣٩٢٦]

3522. **Imām ʿAlī (AS) said,** 'Attract sustenance by giving charity.'[3960]

٣٥٢٢. الإمامُ عليٌّ عليه السلام: اِستَنزِلُوا الرِّزقَ بِالصَّدَقةِ.[٣٩٢٧]

3523. **Imām ʿAlī (AS) said,** 'If you are reduced to poverty, then trade with Allah through giving in charity.'[3961]

٣٥٢٣. عنه عليه السلام: إذا أملَقتُم فَتاجِرُوا اللهَ بِالصَّدَقةِ.[٣٩٢٨]

3524. **Imām al-Ṣādiq (AS) said,** 'I am sometimes reduced to poverty, so I trade with Allah through charity.'[3962]

٣٥٢٤. الإمامُ الصّادقُ عليه السلام: إنّي لَأُملِقُ أحياناً، فَأُتاجِرُ اللهَ بِالصَّدَقةِ.[٣٩٢٩]

3525. **Imām al-Ṣādiq (AS) said,** 'Giving in charity helps settle debts and leaves behind blessings.'[3963]

٣٥٢٥. عنه عليه السلام: الصَّدَقةُ تَقضِي الدَّينَ وتُخلِفُ بِالبَرَكَةِ.[٣٩٣٠]

1110. Every Kindly Act is Considered Charity

١١١٠ ـ كُلُّ مَعروفٍ صَدَقَةٌ

3526. **The Prophet (SAWA) said,** 'Verily every single Muslim is to give in charity every single day.' When asked who would be capable of such a thing, he replied, 'Your removal of an obstacle from the road is a charitable act; your guiding someone the way is a charitable act; your visiting the sick is a

٣٥٢٦. بحار الأنوار: رُوِيَ عَنِ النَّبِيِّ ﷺ أنّه قالَ: إنَّ علىٰ كُلِّ مُسلمٍ في كلِّ يومٍ صَدَقةً، قيلَ: مَن يُطِيقُ ذلكَ؟ قالَ ﷺ: إماطَتُكَ الأذىٰ عنِ الطَّريقِ صَدَقةٌ، وإرشادُكَ الرَّجُلَ إلى الطَّريقِ صَدَقةٌ،

charitable act; your enjoinment of good to others is a charitable act; your forbidding others from wrongdoing is a charitable act, and your returning the greeting of peace is a charitable act.'[3964]

وعِيادَتُكَ المَريضَ صَدَقةٌ، وأمرُكَ بالمَعروفِ صَدَقةٌ، ونَهيُكَ عنِ المُنكَرِ صَدَقةٌ، ورَدُّكَ السَّلامَ صَدَقةٌ.٣٩٣١

3527. **The Prophet (SAWA) said,** 'Every kindly act is considered charity.'[3965]

٣٥٢٧. رسولُ اللهِ ﷺ: كُلُّ مَعروفٍ صَدَقةٌ.٣٩٣٢

3528. **The Prophet (SAWA) said,** 'Guard your tongue, for verily this is a charitable act that you perform for your own sake.'[3966]

٣٥٢٨. عنه ﷺ: أمسِكْ لِسانَكَ؛ فإنّها صَدَقةٌ تَصَدَّقُ بها علىٰ نَفسِكَ.٣٩٣٣

3529. **The Prophet (SAWA) said,** 'Abandoning evil [acts] is an act of charity.'[3967]

٣٥٢٩. عنه ﷺ: تَركُ الشَّرِّ صَدَقةٌ.٣٩٣٤

3530. **Imām al-Ṣādiq (AS) said,** 'A charitable act that Allah loves indeed is reconciling people when they have become estranged to one another, and bringing them close together when they have become distanced from each other.'[3968]

٣٥٣٠. الإمامُ الصّادقُ (عليه السلام): صَدَقةٌ يُحِبُّها اللهُ: إصلاحٌ بينَ الناسِ إذا تَفاسَدُوا، وتَقارُبُ بَينَهُم إذا تَباعَدُوا.٣٩٣٥

3531. **Imām al-Ṣādiq (AS) said,** 'Making a deaf person hear without becoming irritated is a wholesome act of charity.'[3969]

٣٥٣١. عنه (عليه السلام): إسماعُ الأصَمِّ مِن غَيرِ تَضَجُّرٍ صَدَقةٌ هَنِيئَةٌ.٣٩٣٦

1111. The Best Form of Charity

١١١١ ـ أفضَلُ الصَّدَقةِ

3532. **The Prophet (SAWA) said,** 'The best form of charity is that you give away when you are healthy and covetous, when you have high hopes of having a lasting life and fear poverty and you do not wait until you are breathing your last, saying: 'this is for *x* and this is for *y*, while that finally will belong to *z*.'[3970]

٣٥٣٢. رسولُ اللهِ ﷺ ـ لَمّا سُئلَ عن أفضَلِ الصَّدَقةِ ـ: أن تَصَدَّقَ وأنتَ صَحيحٌ شَحيحٌ، تَأمُلُ البَقاءَ وتَخافُ الفَقرَ، ولا تُمهِلْ حتّىٰ إذا بَلَغَتِ الحُلقومَ قُلتَ: لِفُلانٍ كذا ولِفُلانٍ كذا، ألا وقَد كانَ لِفُلانٍ.٣٩٣٧

3533. **The Prophet (SAWA) said,** 'The best of people is he who gives away his hard-earned money [in charity].'[3971]

٣٥٣٣. عنه ﷺ: أفضَلُ الناسِ رَجُلٌ يُعطي جُهدَهُ.٣٩٣٨

3534. **The Prophet (SAWA) said,** 'The best form of charity is that which is secretly given to the poor, and from one who himself has little to offer.'[3972]

٣٥٣٤. عنه ﷺ: أفضَلُ الصَّدَقةِ سِرٌّ إلىٰ فَقيرٍ وجُهدٌ مِن مُقِلٍّ.٣٩٣٩

3535. **The Prophet (SAWA) said,** 'The best form of charity is charity with one's tongue through which lives are spared, adversities repelled, and benefits attracted towards one's Muslim brother.'[3973]

٣٥٣٥. عنه ﷺ : إنَّ أفضَلَ الصَّدَقةِ صَدَقةُ اللِّسانِ، تَحقُنُ بِهِ الدِّماءَ، وتَدفَعُ بِهِ الكَريهَةَ، وتَجُرُّ المَنفَعةَ إلى أخيكَ المُسلِمِ.٣٩٤٠

3536. **The Prophet (SAWA) said,** 'The best form of charity is for the Muslim to gain knowledge and then teach it to his fellow Muslim brother.'[3974]

٣٥٣٦. عنه ﷺ : أفضَلُ الصَّدَقةِ أن يَتَعَلَّمَ المَرءُ المُسلِمُ عِلماً ثُمّ يُعَلِّمَهُ أخاهُ المُسلِمَ.٣٩٤١

3537. **The Prophet (SAWA)** when asked about the best act of charity, replied, '[It is the act of charity] towards a kin who harbours secret enmity.'[3975]

٣٥٣٧. عنه ﷺ ـ لَمّا سُئلَ عن أفضَلِ الصَّدَقةِ ـ : علىٰ ذِي الرَّحِمِ الكاشِحِ.٣٩٤٢

3538. **The Prophet (SAWA) said,** 'The best form of charity is to shade someone under one's tent for the sake of Allah.'[3976]

٣٥٣٨. عنه ﷺ : أفضَلُ الصَّدَقةِ ظِلُّ فُسطاطٍ في سَبيلِ اللهِ عزَّ وجلَّ.٣٩٤٣

3539. **The Prophet (SAWA) said,** 'The best act of charity is carried out in the month of Ramaḍān.'[3977]

٣٥٣٩. عنه ﷺ : أفضَلُ الصَّدَقةِ في رَمَضانَ.٣٩٤٤

3540. **Imām al-Ṣādiq (AS) said,** 'The best form of charity is to cool down someone's internal heat [by quenching their thirst].'[3978]

٣٥٤٠. الإمامُ الصّادقُ ﷺ : أفضَلُ الصَّدَقةِ إبرادُ الكَبِدِ الحَرّىٰ.٣٩٤٥

3541. **Imām al-Kāẓim (AS) said,** 'Your assistance of the weak is one of the best forms of charity.'[3979]

٣٥٤١. الإمامُ الكاظمُ ﷺ : عَونُكَ لِلضَّعيفِ مِن أفضَلِ الصَّدَقةِ.٣٩٤٦

1112. The Virtue of Giving Charity in Secret and its Good Effects

١١١٢ـ فَضلُ صَدَقَةِ السِّرِّ وآثارُها

"If you disclose your charities, that is well, but if you hide them and give them to the poor, that is better for you, and it will atone for some of your misdeeds, and Allah is well aware of what you do."[3980]

﴿إنْ تُبْدُوا الصَّدَقاتِ فَنِعِمّا هِيَ وَإنْ تُخْفُوها وَتُؤْتُوها الفُقَراءَ فَهُوَ خَيْرٌ لَكُمْ وَيُكَفِّرُ عَنكُمْ مِنْ سَيِّئاتِكُمْ وَاللهُ بِما تَعْمَلُونَ خَبِيرٌ﴾.٣٩٤٧

3542. **Imām ʿAlī (AS) said,** 'Among the best means by which those who seek nearness to Allah may have recourse to His nearness, Blessed and most High, are: faith in Him and in His messenger ..., giving

٣٥٤٢. الإمامُ عليٌّ ﷺ : إنَّ أفضَلَ ما تَوَسَّلَ بِهِ المُتَوَسِّلُونَ إلى اللهِ سبحانَهُ وتعالىٰ، الإيمانُ بِهِ

charity secretly for verily it atones for one's misdeeds, and giving charity openly for verily it protects against an undignified death.'[3981]

وبرسولِه... وصَدَقةُ السِّرِّ فإنّها تُكَفِّرُ الخَطيئةَ، وصَدَقةُ العَلانيَةِ فإنّها تَدفَعُ مِيتةَ السَّوءِ.[٣٩٤٨]

3543. **Imām al-Bāqir (AS) said,** describing his father Imām Zayn al-ʿĀbidīn (AS), 'He used to go out in the dark night carrying a sack on his back and going from door to door, knocking on each and giving to whoever came out to answer it. He used to cover his face when giving to the poor in order that they may not recognise him.'[3982]

٣٥٤٣. الإمامُ الباقرُ ﷺ ـ في الإمامِ زينِ العابِدينَ ﷺ ـ: إنّهُ كانَ يَخرُجُ في اللَّيلةِ الظَّلماءِ، فَيحمِلُ الجِرابَ على ظَهرِهِ حتّى يَأتيَ باباً باباً، فَيَقرَعَهُ ثمّ يُناوِلَ مَن كانَ يَخرُجُ إلَيهِ، وكانَ يُغَطِّي وَجهَهُ إذا ناوَلَ فَقيراً لِئلّا يَعرِفَهُ.[٣٩٤٩]

3544. **Imām al-Ṣādiq (AS) said,** 'Do not give charity openly for people to see and commend you for it, for verily when you do that, you have already received your reward for it [in their commendation]. However, if you give with your right hand such that your left hand does not come to know it, then the One for whose sake you have secretly given charity will surely reward you for it openly.'[3983]

٣٥٤٤. الإمامُ الصّادقُ ﷺ: لا تَتَصَدَّقْ على أعيُنِ النّاسِ لِيُزَكُّوكَ؛ فإنّكَ إن فَعَلتَ ذلكَ فَقَدِ استَوفَيتَ أجرَكَ، ولكنْ إذا أعطَيتَ بِيَمينِكَ فلا تُطلِعْ علَيها شِمالَكَ؛ فإنّ الذي تَتَصَدَّقُ لَهُ سِرّاً يَجزيكَ عَلانيَةً.[٣٩٥٠]

3545. **Imām al-Ṣādiq (AS) said,** 'By Allah, charity given secretly is better than charity given openly, just as, by Allah, worship performed secretly is better than worship performed openly.'[3984]

٣٥٤٥. عنه ﷺ: الصَّدَقةُ واللهِ في السِّرِّ أفضَلُ مِنَ الصَّدَقةِ في العَلانيَةِ، وكذلكَ واللهِ العِبادةُ في السِّرِّ أفضَلُ مِنها في العَلانيَةِ.[٣٩٥١]

3546. **Imām al-Ṣādiq (AS) said,** 'Verily charity given at night [i.e. secretly in the dark of the night] extinguishes the wrath of the Lord, wipes away grave sins and facilitates one's account [on the Day of Resurrection]. Charity given during the day [in broad daylight] makes one's wealth thrive and increases one's lifespan.'[3985]

٣٥٤٦. عنه ﷺ: إنّ صَدَقةَ الليلِ تُطفِئُ غَضَبَ الرَّبِّ، وتَمحو الذَّنبَ العَظيمَ، وتُهَوِّنُ الحِسابَ، وصَدَقةَ النَّهارِ تُثمِرُ المالَ، وتَزيدُ في العُمرِ.[٣٩٥٢]

1113. The Amount of Charity to be Given

١١١٣ـ حَدُّ الصَّدَقةِ

"Do not keep your hand chained to your neck, nor open it all together, or you will sit blameworthy, regretful."[3986]

﴿وَلا تَجْعَلْ يَدَكَ مَغْلُولَةً إِلَى عُنُقِكَ وَلا تَبْسُطْها كُلَّ البَسْطِ فَتَقْعُدَ مَلُوماً مَحْسُوراً﴾.[٣٩٥٣]

3547. **The Prophet (SAWA) said,** 'The one who gives excessive charity is as the one who withholds it.'[3987]

٣٥٤٧. رسولُ اللهِ ﷺ: المُعتَدي في الصَّدَقةِ كَمانِعِها.[٣٩٥٤]

3548. **Imām al-Kāẓim (AS) said,** 'Do not give away of yourself to your brothers so much that the loss incurred for you supersedes the benefit to them.'[3988]

٣٥٤٨ . الإمامُ الكاظمُ عليه السلام : لا تَبذُلْ لإخوانِكَ مِن نفسِكَ ما ضَرُّهُ علَيكَ أكثَرُ مِن مَنفَعَتِهِ لَهُم.[٣٩٥٥]

1114. The Recipients of Charity

١١١٤ ـ مَواردُ الصَّدَقةِ

"[The charities] are for the poor who are straitened in the way of Allah, not capable of moving about in the land [for trade]. The unaware suppose them to be well-off because of their reserve. You recognise them by their mark; they do not ask people importunately."[3989]

﴿لِلْفُقَراءِ الَّذينَ أُحْصِرُوا فِي سَبيلِ اللهِ لا يَسْتَطِيْعُونَ ضَرْباً فِي الْأَرْضِ يَحْسَبُهُمُ الْجاهِلُ أغْنِياءَ مِنَ التَّعَفُّفِ تَعْرِفُهُمْ بِسِيْماهُمْ لا يَسْأَلُونَ النَّاسَ إلْحافاً وَما تُنفِقُوا مِن خَيرٍ فَإنَّ اللهَ بِهِ عَليمٌ﴾.[٣٩٥٦]

3549. **The Prophet (SAWA) said,** 'The one who is truly poor does not roam around the streets begging, nor can he be turned away with a date or two, or a bite or two. Rather the one who is truly poor is he who restrains himself from asking people and who does not draw attention to himself – that is the one that should be given charity.'[3990]

٣٥٤٩ . رسولُ اللهِ صلى الله عليه وآله : ليسَ المِسكينُ بالطَّوّافِ، ولا بِالذي تَرُدُّهُ التَّمرَةُ والتَّمرَتانِ، واللُّقمَةُ واللُّقمَتانِ، ولكنَّ المِسكينَ المُتَعَفِّفُ الذي لا يَسألُ النّاسَ شيئاً ولا يُفطَنُ لَهُ فَيُتَصَدَّقُ علَيهِ.[٣٩٥٧]

3550. **Imām al-Ṣādiq (AS)** was once asked whether one should give charity to those who beg at people's doors, or whether to withhold it from them and give it to one's poor relatives instead, to which he replied, 'No, rather one should send it to a [poor] relative, for that holds a greater reward.'[3991]

٣٥٥٠ . الإمامُ الصّادقُ عليه السلام ـ لمّا سُئلَ عنِ الصَّدَقةِ علىٰ مَن يَسألُ على الأبوابِ، أو يُمسِكُ ذلكَ عَنهُم ويُعطِيهِ ذَوِي قَرابَتِهِ ؟ ـ : لا، بل يَبعَثُ بها إلىٰ مَن بينَهُ وبينَهُ قَرابَةٌ، فهذا أعظَمُ لِلأجرِ.[٣٩٥٨]

3551. **Imām al-Ṣādiq (AS) said** with regards to Allah's verse in the Qur'an: *"...the beggar and the deprived"*, 'The deprived is the disabled one who is deprived of the use of his hands for working in trade.'[3992]

٣٥٥١ . عنه عليه السلام ـ أيضاً ـ : المَحرومُ المُحارَفُ الذي قد حُرِمَ كَدَّ يَدِهِ في الشِّراءِ والبَيعِ.[٣٩٥٩]

(See also: ALMS-TAX: section 854)

(اُنظر) الزكاة: باب ٨٥٤.

1115. The Etiquette of Giving

١١١٥ ـ أدَبُ العَطاءِ

"O you who have faith! Do not render your charities void by reproaches and affronts, like those who spend their wealth to be seen by people and have no faith in Allah and the Last Day. Their example is that of a

﴿يا أيُّها الَّذِينَ آمَنُوا لا تُبْطِلُوا صَدَقاتِكُمْ بِالْمَنِّ وَالْأذىٰ كَالَّذِي يُنْفِقُ مالَهُ رِئاءَ النَّاسِ وَلا يُؤْمِنُ بِاللهِ وَالْيَوْمِ الْآخِرِ فَمَثَلُهُ كَمَثَلِ صَفْوانٍ عَلَيْهِ

rock covered with soil; a downpour strikes it leaving it bare."[3993]

تُرابٌ فَأصابَهُ وابِلٌ فتَرَكَهُ صَلْداً﴾.[٣٩٦٠]

3552. **The Prophet (SAWA) said,** 'Give in charity without conceitedness, for verily conceitedness does away with your reward [for it].'[3994]

٣٥٥٢. رسولُ اللهِ ﷺ: تَصَدَّقُوا مِن غَيرِ مَخِيلَةٍ؛ فإنَّ المَخِيلَةَ تُبطِلُ الأجرَ.[٣٩٦١]

3553. **Imām ʿAlī (AS) said,** 'Delaying [one's promise of] giving and reproaching someone for a gift embitters the goodness of the favour.'[3995]

٣٥٥٣. الإمامُ عليٌّ عليه السلام: المَطلُ والمَنُّ مُنَكِّدا الإحسانِ.[٣٩٦٢]

(See also: ENJOINING GOOD AND PROHIBITING WRONG (1): section 1281)

(انظر) المعروف (١): باب ١٢٨١.

233

THE PATH

الصِّراطُ[١٥٥]

1116. The Danger of Crossing the Path

١١١٦ ـ خَطَرُ مَعبَرِ الصِّراطِ

3554. **Imām ʿAlī (AS) said,** 'Know that you shall pass the Path [Ṣirāṭ], its slippery way, its fearful slides and its intermittent horrors.'[3996]

٣٥٥٤. الإمامُ عليٌّ عليه السلام: وَاعلَمُوا أنَّ مَجازَكُم على الصِّراطِ ومَزالِقِ دَحضِهِ وأهاوِيلِ زَلَلِهِ وتاراتِ أهوالِهِ.[٣٩٦٣]

1117. The True Meaning of the Straight Path

١١١٧ ـ تَفسيرُ الصِّراطِ المُستَقيمِ

"Guide us on the straight path."[3997]

﴿آهْدِنا الصِّراطَ المُسْتَقِيمَ﴾.[٣٩٦٤]

"Indeed Allah is my Lord and your Lord; so worship Him. This is a straight path."[3998]

﴿إنَّ اللهَ رَبِّي وَرَبُّكُمْ فَاعْبُدُوهُ هٰذا صِراطٌ مُسْتَقِيمٌ﴾.[٣٩٦٥]

"And how could you be faithless while the signs of Allah are recited to you and His apostle is in your midst? And whoever takes recourse in Allah is certainly guided to a straight path."[3999]

﴿وَكَيْفَ تَكْفُرُونَ وَأنْتُمْ تُتْلَىٰ عَلَيكُمْ آياتُ اللهِ وَفِيْكُمْ رَسُولُهُ وَمَنْ يَعْتَصِمْ بِاللهِ فَقَدْ هُدِيَ إلَىٰ صِراطٍ مُسْتَقِيمٍ﴾.[٣٩٦٦]

3555. **Imām al-Ṣādiq (AS) said** regarding the meaning of 'the path', 'It is the way to the inner knowledge of Allah, Mighty and Exalted, and there are actually two paths – one in this world

٣٥٥٥. الإمامُ الصّادقُ عليه السلام ـ في معنى الصِّراطِ ـ: هُوَ الطَّريقُ إلىٰ مَعرِفَةِ اللهِ عَزَّوجلَّ، وهُما صِراطانِ: صِراطٌ في الدُّنيا وصِراطٌ في الآخِرَةِ،

and one in the Hereafter. As for the path in this world's life, it is the *Imām* whom one is obliged to obey. He who acknowledges him in this world and follows his guidance will be able to [successfully] cross the path of the Hereafter, which is a bridge outstretched over the Fire.'[4000]

فأمّا الصِّراطُ الذي في الدُّنيا فهُو الإمامُ المَفروضُ الطاعَةِ، مَن عَرَفَهُ في الدُّنيا واقتَدىٰ بِهُداهُ مَرَّ على الصِّراطِ الذي هو جِسرُ جَهَنَّمَ في الآخرةِ.[٣٩٦٧]

3556. **Imām al-Ṣādiq (AS) said,** 'The straight path is the Commander of the Faithful, ʿAlī (AS).'[4001]

٣٥٥٦. عنه ؑ: الصِّراطُ المُستَقيمُ أميرُ المؤمنينَ عَلِيٌّ ؑ.[٣٩٦٨]

1118. Crossing the Path of the Hereafter (The Bridge over Hell)

١١١٨ـ صِراطُ الآخِرَةِ وَالمُرورُ عَلَيها

3557. **Prophet Moses (AS)** asked Allah, supplicating, 'My God, what is the reward of one who recites Your wisdom [i.e. divine Book] loudly and quietly?' He replied, 'O Moses, he will cross the Bridge like lightning.'[4002]

٣٥٥٧. موسىٰ ؑ ـ في المُناجاةِ ـ: إلٰهي، ما جَزاءُ مَن تلا حِكمَتَكَ سِرّاً وجَهراً؟ قالَ: يا موسىٰ، يَمُرُّ على الصِّراطِ كالبَرقِ.[٣٩٦٩]

3558. **The Prophet (SAWA) said,** 'Those of you who will have the firmest footing on the Bridge are those who have the strongest love for my household.'[4003]

٣٥٥٨. رسولُ اللهِ ﷺ: أثبَتُكُم قَدَماً على الصِّراطِ أشَدُّكُم حُبّاً لِأهلِ بَيتي.[٣٩٧٠]

3559. **The Prophet (SAWA) said,** 'Perform the ritual ablution diligently and you will cross the Bridge like the passing of clouds.'[4004]

٣٥٥٩. عنه ﷺ: أسبِغِ الوُضُوءَ، تَمُرَّ على الصِّراطِ مَرَّ السَّحابِ.[٣٩٧١]

3560. **The Prophet (SAWA) said,** 'The Bridge is thinner than a hair and sharper than a sword.'[4005]

٣٥٦٠. عنه ﷺ: الصِّراطُ أدَقُّ مِنَ الشَّعرَةِ وأحَدُّ مِنَ السَّيفِ.[٣٩٧٢]

3561. **Imām al-Ṣādiq (AS) said** with regard to Allah's verse in the Qur'an: *"Indeed your Lord is in ambush"*[4006], 'There is an arch on the Bridge that no servant having committed an act of injustice can traverse.'[4007]

٣٥٦١. الإمامُ الصّادقُ ؑ ـ في قولِ اللهِ عَزَّ وجلَّ: ﴿إنَّ رَبَّكَ لَبِالْمِرصادِ﴾ ـ: قَنطَرَةٌ على الصِّراطِ لا يَجوزُها عبدٌ بِمَظلِمَةٍ.[٣٩٧٣]

3562. **Imām al-Ṣādiq (AS) said,** 'People will cross the Bridge in classes: some will cross it like lightning, some like a racehorse, some will crawl across it, and some will cross it barely hanging

٣٥٦٢. عنه ؑ: النّاسُ يَمُرُّونَ على الصِّراطِ طَبَقاتٍ: ... فَمِنهُم مَن يَمُرُّ مِثلَ البَرقِ، ومِنهُم مَن يَمُرُّ مِثلَ عَدْوِ الفَرَسِ، ومِنهُم مَن يَمُرُّ حَبْواً،

onto it, with the Fire burning a part of them and leaving a part.'[4008]

ومِنهُم مَن يَمُرُّ مَشْياً ، ومِنهُم مَن يَمُرُّ مُتَعَلِّقاً قد تَأْخُذُ النارُ مِنهُ شيئاً وتَترُكُ شيئاً.٣٩٧٤

234

CHILDHOOD

الصِّغَرُ

1119. Childhood

١١١٩ـ الصِّغَرُ

3563. **The Prophet (SAWA) said,** 'The naughtiness of a boy in his childhood is a sign of an excess of his intellect as an adult.'[4009]

٣٥٦٣. رسولُ اللهِ ﷺ : عَرامَةُ٣٩٧٥ الصَّبيِّ في صِغَرِهِ زِيادَةٌ في عَقلِهِ في كِبَرِهِ.٣٩٧٦

3564. **Imām 'Alī (AS) said,** 'He who does not exert himself in his childhood will not be high-minded when he grows up.'[4010]

٣٥٦٤. الإمامُ عليٌّ ﷺ : مَن لم يُجهِدْ نَفسَهُ في صِغَرِهِ لَم يَنبُلْ في كِبَرِهِ.٣٩٧٧

3565. **Imām 'Alī (AS) said,** 'He who asks questions as a child is able to answer them himself as an adult.'[4011]

٣٥٦٥. عنه ﷺ : مَن سَألَ في صِغَرِهِ أجابَ في كِبَرِهِ.٣٩٧٨

3566. **Imām 'Alī (AS) said,** 'He who does not learn as a child does not progress as an adult.'[4012]

٣٥٦٦. عنه ﷺ : مَن لم يَتَعَلَّمْ في الصِّغَرِ لَم يَتَقَدَّمْ في الكِبَرِ.٣٩٧٩

3567. **Imām 'Alī (AS) said,** 'The ignorant man is a child even though he may be old, while the knowledgeable man is an adult even though he be young.'[4013]

٣٥٦٧. عنه ﷺ : الجاهِلُ صَغيرٌ وإن كانَ شَيخاً، والعالِمُ كَبيرٌ وإن كانَ حَدَثاً.٣٩٨٠

3568. **Imām al-Kāẓim (AS) said,** 'Naughtiness of a boy in his childhood is good, as it will bring clemency to him as an adult.'[4014]

٣٥٦٨. الإمامُ الكاظمُ ﷺ : تُستَحَبُّ عَرامَةُ الغُلامِ في صِغَرِهِ لِيَكونَ حَليماً في كِبَرِهِ.٣٩٨١ ٣٩٨٢

(See also: PARENT AND CHILD: section 1893 and DISCIPLINE: section 50)

(أنظر) الوالد والولد: باب ١٨٩٣؛ الأدب: باب ٥٠.

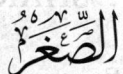

235

SHAKING HANDS

المُصافَحَة

1120. Encouraging the Shaking of Hands

١١٢٠ ـ التَّرغِيبُ بِالمُصافَحَةِ

3569. **The Prophet (SAWA) said,** 'When you meet each other, receive each other with the greeting of peace (*salām*) and a handshake, and when you part company, do so by seeking each other's forgiveness.'[4015]

٣٥٦٩ . رسولُ اللهِ ﷺ: إذا التَقَيتُمْ فَتَلاقَوا بِالتَّسليمِ والتَّصافُحِ، وإذا تَفَرَّقتُم فَتَفَرَّقُوا بِالاستِغفارِ. [٣٩٨٣]

3570. **The Prophet (SAWA) said,** 'Shake hands with each other for verily the handshake takes away resentment.'[4016]

٣٥٧٠ . عنه ﷺ: تَصافَحُوا؛ فإنَّ التَّصافُحَ يُذهِبُ السَّخيمَةَ. [٣٩٨٤]

3571. **The Prophet (SAWA) said,** 'Shake hands with each other for verily it takes away rancour.'[4017]

٣٥٧١ . عنه ﷺ: تَصافَحُوا؛ فإنّهُ يَذهَبُ بِالغِلِّ. [٣٩٨٥]

3572. **Imām al-Bāqir (AS) said,** 'When a man shakes his companion's hand, the one who holds on the longest has the greater reward than the one who lets go. Indeed sins fall off from between them [as a result of it] until finally no sin remains.'[4018]

٣٥٧٢ . الإمامُ الباقرُ عليه السلام: إذا صافَحَ الرجُلُ صاحِبَهُ فَالذي يَلزَمُ التَّصافُحَ أعظَمُ أجراً مِنَ الذي يَدَعُ، ألا وإنَّ الذُّنوبَ لَيَتَحاتُّ فيما بينَهُم حتّىٰ لا يَبقىٰ ذَنبٌ. [٣٩٨٦]

3573. **Imām al-Ṣādiq (AS) narrated,** 'The [early] Muslims were such that when they went on conquests with the Prophet (SAWA) and traversed through dense forests, as they would come back out into the open, they would look at each other and shake each other's hands.'[4019]

٣٥٧٣ . الإمامُ الصّادقُ عليه السلام: كانَ المُسلمونَ إذا غَزَوا مَع رسولِ اللهِ ﷺ ومَرُّوا بمَكانٍ كَثيرِ الشَّجَرِ ثُمّ خَرَجُوا إلى الفَضاءِ نَظَرَ بَعضُهُم إلىٰ بعضٍ فَتَصافَحُوا. [٣٩٨٧]

3574. **Imām al-Ṣādiq (AS) narrated,** 'When the Prophet (SAWA) used to shake someone's hand, he would never be the first to let go, until the other person let go of his hand.'[4020]

٣٥٧٤ . عنه عليه السلام: ما صافَحَ رسولُ اللهِ ﷺ رَجُلاً قَطُّ فَنَزَعَ يَدَهُ حتّىٰ يَكونَ هُو الذي يَنزِعُ يَدَهُ مِنهُ. [٣٩٨٨]

1121. Prohibition of Shaking a Woman's Hand

١١٢١ ـ النَّهيُ عَن مُصافَحَةِ المَرأةِ

3575. **The Prophet (SAWA) said,** 'Verily I do not shake hands with women.'[4021]

٣٥٧٥ . رسولُ اللهِ ﷺ إنّي لَستُ اُصافِحُ النِّساءَ.[٣٩٨٩]

3576. **Imām al-Ṣādiq (AS) said,** 'As for any woman whom one can marry [i.e. not one's immediate relative], one must not shake her hand except from under a cloth, nor clasp her palm.'[4022]

٣٥٧٦ . الإمامُ الصّادقُ عليه السلام : أمّا المرأةُ التي يَحِلُّ لَهُ أن يَتزَوَّجَها فلا يُصافِحْها إلّا مِن وراءِ الثَّوبِ، ولا يَغمِزْ كَفَّها.[٣٩٩٠]

236

PEACEMAKING

الصُّلح

1122. Peacemaking in War

١١٢٢ ـ الصُّلحُ في الحَربِ

"And if they incline toward peace, then you [too] incline toward it, and put your trust in Allah. Indeed He is the All-hearing, the All-knowing."[4023]

﴿وَإنْ جَنَحُوا لِلسَّلْمِ فَاجْنَحْ لَها وَتَوَكَّلْ عَلَى اللهِ إنَّهُ هُوَ السَّمِيْعُ العَلِيْمُ﴾.[٣٩٩١]

3577. **Imām 'Alī (AS) said,** 'I have found conciliation – so long as it is does not enfeeble Islam – to be more beneficial than combat.'[4024]

٣٥٧٧ . الإمامُ عليٌّ عليه السلام : وَجَدتُ المُسالَمَةَ ـ مالَم يَكُن وَهنٌ في الإسلامِ ـ أنجَعَ مِن القِتالِ.[٣٩٩٢]

3578. **Imām 'Alī (AS)** wrote in his letter to al-Ashtar when he appointed him governor of Egypt, 'Do not reject the peace to which your enemy may call you, and wherein the pleasure of Allah lies, for verily peace affords composure to your army, relief to you from your worries, and safety for the country. After the peace entreaty however, be extremely wary of your enemy, because often the enemy draws near in order to take advantage of your negligence. Therefore, act prudently and entertain good opinion about them, though always being on your guard.'[4025]

٣٥٧٨ . عنه عليه السلام ـ مِن كتابِهِ للأشتَرِ لَمّا وَلّاهُ مِصرَ ـ: ولا تَدفَعَنَّ صُلحاً دَعاكَ إلَيهِ عَدُوُّكَ وللهِ فيهِ رِضىً؛ فإنّ في الصُّلحِ دَعَةً لِجُنودِكَ، وراحَةً مِن هُمُومِك، وأمناً لبلادِكَ، ولكِنِ الحذَرَ كُلَّ الحَذَرِ مِن عَدُوِّكَ بَعدَ صُلحِهِ؛ فإنَّ العَدُوَّ رُبّما قارَبَ لِيَتَغَفَّلَ، فَخُذْ بِالحَزمِ، واتَّهِمْ في ذلكَ حُسنَ الظَّنِّ.[٣٩٩٣]

1123. Imām al-Ḥasan (AS)'s Peace Treaty

١١٢٣ ـ صُلحُ الإمامِ الحَسَنِ ﷺ

3579. **Imām ʿAlī (AS) said** in his will to his son after he had been struck by Ibn Muljam, 'Know that Muʿāwiya will oppose you just as he opposed me, and in conciliating and making peace with him, you will be following in the footsteps of your grandfather (AS) when he conciliated with the Banī Ḍamra and the Banī Ashjaʿ tribes … and if instead you wish to fight your enemy, know that you will not find any from among your followers who will be loyal to you anymore than those loyal to your father.'[4026]

٣٥٧٩ . الإمامُ عليٌّ ﷺ ـ في وصيَّتِهِ لابنِهِ الحَسنِ ﷺ لمّا ضَرَبَهُ ابنُ مُلجَمٍ ـ: واعلَمْ أنّ معاويةَ سَيُخالِفُكَ كما خالَفَني، فإن وادَعتَهُ وصالَحتَهُ كُنتَ مُقتَدِياً بِجَدِّكَ ﷺ في مُوادَعَتِهِ بَني ضَمرَةَ وبَني أشجَعَ... فإن أرَدتَ مُجاهَدَةَ عَدُوِّكَ فَلَن يَصلُحَ لكَ مِن شِيعَتِكَ مَن يَصلُحُ لأبيكَ.[٣٩٩٤]

3580. **Imām al-Ṣādiq (AS) said,** 'Verily Ḥasan b. ʿAlī (AS), when he was reproached and opposed by the people for having made peace with Muʿāwiya, people would greet him in the street saying, 'Peace be upon you O degrader of the believers', and he (AS) would reply, 'I am not a degrader of the believers, rather I am elevating the believers. Verily when I saw you having no strength to overpower them [Muʿāwiya's army], I made peace in order that you and I may remain alive in their midst, just like the wise one [al-Khiḍr] damaged the boat in order that it may be spared for its owners. Thus did I act for yours and my benefit in order that we remain alive among them.'[4027]

٣٥٨٠ . الإمامُ الصّادقُ ﷺ: إنّ الحَسنَ بنَ عليٍّ ﷺ لَمّا طُعِنَ واختَلَفَ الناسُ عَليهِ سَلَّمَ الأمرَ لِمعاويةَ، فَسَلَّمَت علَيهِ الشِّيعَةُ «علَيكَ السَّلامُ يا مُذِلَّ المؤمنينَ!» فقالَ ﷺ: ما أنا بِمُذِلِّ المؤمنينَ، ولكِنّي مُعِزُّ المؤمنينَ، إنّي لَمّا رَأيتُكُم لَيسَ بِكُم علَيهِم قُوَّةٌ سَلَّمتُ الأمرَ لِأبقىٰ أنا وأنتُم بينَ أظهُرِهِم، كما عابَ العالِمُ السَّفِينَةَ لِتَبقىٰ لأصحابِها، وكذلكَ نَفسِي وأنتُم لِنَبقىٰ بَينَهُم.[٣٩٩٥]

1124. The Importance of Making Peace Between People

١١٢٤ ـ أهَمِّيَّةُ الإصلاحِ بَينَ النّاسِ

"The faithful are indeed brothers. Therefore make peace between your brothers and be wary of Allah, so that you may receive [His] mercy."[4028]

﴿إنَّما المُؤْمِنُونَ إخْوَةٌ فَأصْلِحُوا بينَ أخَوَيْكُمْ وَاتَّقُوا اللهَ لَعَلَّكُمْ تُرْحَمُونَ﴾.[٣٩٩٦]

"There is no good in much of their secret talks, excepting him who enjoins charity and what is right or reconciliation between people, and whoever does that,

﴿لا خَيْرَ فِي كَثِيرٍ مِنْ نَجْواهُمْ إلَّا مَنْ أمَرَ بِصَدَقَةٍ أوْ مَعْرُوفٍ أوْ إصْلَاحٍ بَيْنَ النَّاسِ وَمَنْ يَفْعَلْ ذٰلِكَ ابْتِغَاءَ مَرْضاةِ اللهِ فَسَوْفَ نُؤتِيهِ

seeking Allah's pleasure, soon We shall give him a great reward.'[4029]

أجْراً عَظِيماً﴾.[٣٩٩٧]

3581. **The Prophet (SAWA) said,** 'Shall I inform you of something that holds a higher status than fasting, praying and giving charity? Making peace between people, for verily sowing dissention between people is indeed calamitous.'[4030]

٣٥٨١. رسولُ اللهِ ﷺ: ألا أُخبِرُكم بِأفضلَ مِن دَرَجَةِ الصِّيامِ والصَّلاةِ والصَّدَقةِ؟ إصلاحُ ذاتِ البَينِ؛ فإنّ فسادَ ذاتِ البَينِ هِي الحالِقةُ.[٣٩٩٨]

3582. **Imām al-Ṣādiq (AS) said,** 'A charitable act most loved by Allah is reconciling between people if they have fallen out, and bringing them together when they have become distanced from one another.'[4031]

٣٥٨٢. الإمامُ الصّادقُ عليه السلام: صَدَقةٌ يُحِبُّها اللهُ: إصلاحُ بَينَ الناسِ إذا تَفاسَدُوا، وتَقارُبُ بَينِهِم إذا تَباعَدُوا.[٣٩٩٩]

3583. **Imām al-Ṣādiq (AS) said** to his companion, Mufaḍḍal, 'If you see two people from amongst our followers (*shī'a*) fighting [over property or the like], use my money to settle the dispute.'[4032]

٣٥٨٣. عنه عليه السلام ـ لِلمفضَّلِ ـ: إذا رَأيتَ بينَ اثنَينِ مِن شِيعَتِنا مُنازَعَةً فافتَدِها مِن مالي.[٤٠٠٠]

1125. The Permissibility of Lying for the sake of Reconciliation

١١٢٥ ـ جَوازُ الكَذِبِ فِي الإصلاحِ

3584. **Imām al-Ṣādiq (AS) said,** 'The reconciler is not a liar.'[4033]

٣٥٨٤. الإمامُ الصّادقُ عليه السلام: المُصلِحُ ليسَ بِكاذِبٍ.[٤٠٠١]

3585. **Imām al-Ṣādiq (AS) said,** 'Utterances fall under three categories: the truth, the lie, and reconciliation between people … you may hear a man saying something about someone, which when they come to hear will lead them to feel malice towards the former. [In such a situation] you may instead tell them, 'I heard *x* speaking such good things about you', contrary to what you had heard.'[4034]

٣٥٨٥. عنه عليه السلام: الكلامُ ثلاثةٌ: صِدقٌ وكِذبٌ وإصلاحٌ بينَ الناسِ... تَسمَعُ مِنَ الرَّجُلِ كلاماً يَبلُغُهُ فَتَخبُثُ نَفسُهُ، فَتَلقاهُ فَتَقُولُ: سَمِعتُ مِن فُلانٍ قالَ فِيكَ مِنَ الخَيرِ كذا وكذا، خِلافَ ما سَمِعتَ مِنهُ.[٤٠٠٢]

237

THE PRAYER (1)

الصَّلاةُ (١)

1126. The Virtue of Prayer

١١٢٦ ـ فَضلُ الصَّلاةِ

"Be mindful of your prayers, and [especially] the middle prayer, and stand in obedience to Allah."[4035]

﴿حافِظُوا عَلَى الصَّلَواتِ وَالصَّلاةِ الوُسْطَىٰ وَقُومُوا لِلّهِ قانِتِينَ﴾.[٤٠٠٣]

"When you have finished the prayers, remember Allah, standing, sitting and lying down, and when you feel secure, perform the [complete] prayers, for the prayer is indeed a timed prescription for the faithful."[4036]

﴿فَإذا قَضَيْتُمُ الصَّلاةَ فَاذْكُرُوا اللهَ قِياماً وَقُعُوداً وَعَلَىٰ جُنُوبِكُمْ فَإذا اطْمَأْنَنْتُمْ فَأَقِيمُوا الصَّلاةَ إنَّ الصَّلاةَ كانَتْ عَلَى المُؤْمِنِينَ كِتاباً مَوْقُوتاً﴾.[٤٠٠٤]

"My Lord! Make me a maintainer of the prayer, and my descendants [too]. Our Lord, accept my supplication."[4037]

﴿رَبِّ اجْعَلْنِي مُقِيمَ الصَّلاةِ وَمِنْ ذُرِّيَّتِي رَبَّنا وَتَقَبَّلْ دُعاءِ﴾.[٤٠٠٥]

3586. **The Prophet (SAWA) said,** 'Everything has a face, and the face of your religion is the prayer.'[4038]

٣٥٨٦. رسولُ اللهِ ﷺ: لِكُلِّ شَيءٍ وَجهٌ، ووَجهُ دِينِكُمُ الصَّلاةُ.[٤٠٠٦]

3587. **The Prophet (SAWA) said,** 'Allah, Exalted be His praise, has made prayer the light of my eyes, and has made prayer as beloved to me as food is to a hungry man, and water to a thirsty man. The hungry man, however, is satiated when he eats, and the thirsty man is quenched when he drinks, but I can never be sated by my prayer.'[4039]

٣٥٨٧. عنه ﷺ: جَعَلَ اللهُ جَلَّ ثناؤهُ قُرَّةَ عَينِي في الصَّلاةِ، وحَبَّبَ إلَيَّ الصَّلاةَ كما حَبَّبَ إلى الجائعِ الطَّعامَ، وإلى الظَّمآنِ الماءَ، وإنَّ الجائعَ إذا أكَلَ شَبِعَ، وإنَّ الظَّمآنَ إذا شَرِبَ رَوِيَ، وأنا لا أشبَعُ مِن الصَّلاةِ.[٤٠٠٧]

3588. **Imām ʿAlī (AS) said,** 'Prayer elicits the descent of divine mercy.'[4040]

٣٥٨٨. الإمامُ عليٌّ عليه السلام: الصَّلاةُ تَستَنزِلُ الرَّحمَةَ.[٤٠٠٨]

3589. **Imām ʿAlī (AS) narrated,** 'The Prophet (SAWA) never put anything before his prayer, neither his dinner nor anything else. When the time for prayer would set in, it was as if he knew neither family nor close friend.'[4041]

٣٥٨٩. عنه عليه السلام: كانَ رسولُ اللهِ ﷺ لا يُؤثِرُ على الصَّلاةِ عَشاءً ولا غَيرَهُ، وكانَ إذا دَخَلَ وَقتُها كأنَّهُ لا يَعرِفُ أهلاً ولا حَمِيماً.[٤٠٠٩]

3590. **Imām ʿAlī (AS) said,** 'Prayer is the pious person's means of proximity [to his Lord].'[4042]

٣٥٩٠. عنه عليه السلام: الصَّلاةُ قُربانُ كُلِّ تَقِيٍّ.[٤٠١٠]

3591. **Imām al-Bāqir (AS) said,** 'Prayer is the pillar of religion and its likeness is as the likeness of the pillar of a tent. If the pillar is stably fixed, the pegs and the ropes remain stable, but if the pillar inclines and breaks, neither peg nor rope remains fixed.'[4043]

٣٥٩١. الإمامُ الباقرُ ؑ: الصَّلاةُ عَمودُ الدِّينِ، مَثَلُها كَمَثَلِ عَمودِ الفُسطاطِ؛ إذا ثَبَتَ العَمودُ يَثبُتُ الأوتادُ والأطنابُ، وإذا مالَ العَمودُ وانكَسَرَ لَم يَثبُتْ وَتِدٌ ولا طُنُبٌ.[٤٠١١]

3592. **Imām al-Ṣādiq (AS) said,** 'The most beloved of all acts to Allah, Mighty and Exalted, is the prayer, and it is the last legacy of the prophets.'[4044]

٣٥٩٢. الإمامُ الصّادقُ ؑ: أحَبُّ الأعمالِ إلى اللهِ عزّوجلَّ الصَّلاةُ، وهي آخِرُ وَصايا الأنبياءِ.[٤٠١٢]

3593. **Imām al-Ṣādiq (AS)** when asked about the best and most beloved deed to Allah, replied, 'I do not know anything after true knowledge [of Allah] to be better than this prayer. Do you not see that the righteous servant Jesus son of Mary even said, *"...and he has enjoined me to [establish] the prayer..."*'[4045] [4046]

٣٥٩٣. عنه ؑ ـ لَمّا سُئلَ عن أفضَلِ الأعمالِ وأحَبِّها إلى اللهِ ـ: ما أعلَمُ شَيئاً بعدَ المَعرِفَةِ أفضَلَ مِن هذهِ الصَّلاةِ، ألا تَرىٰ أنّ العَبدَ الصالِحَ عيسَى بنَ مريمَ قالَ: ﴿وَأوْصانِي بِالصَّلاةِ﴾[٤٠١٣]؟![٤٠١٤]

1127. The Effects of the Prayer

١١٢٧ـ آثارُ الصَّلاةِ

"Recite what has been revealed to you of the Book, and maintain the prayer. Indeed the prayer prevents indecencies and wrongs, and the remembrance of Allah is surely greater. And Allah knows whatever [deeds] you do."[4047]

﴿اتْلُ ما أُوحِيَ إلَيكَ مِنَ الكِتابِ وَأقِمِ الصَّلاةَ إنَّ الصَّلاةَ تَنْهَىٰ عَنِ الْفَحْشاءِ وَالمُنْكَرِ وَلَذِكْرُ اللهِ أكْبَرُ وَاللهُ يَعْلَمُ ما تَصْنَعُونَ﴾.[٤٠١٥]

3594. **The Prophet (SAWA) said,** 'He whose prayer does not prevent him from indecencies and wrong only gets further and further away from Allah.'[4048]

٣٥٩٤. رسولُ اللهِ ﷺ: مَن لم تَنهَهُ صلاتُهُ عنِ الفَحشاءِ والمُنكَرِ لَم يَزدَدْ مِنَ اللهِ إلّا بُعداً.[٤٠١٦]

3595. **The Prophet (SAWA) said** with regards to a man who used to pray with him and yet commits sins, 'Verily his prayer will prevent him [from them] some day or other, and very soon he repented.'[4049]

٣٥٩٥. بحار الأنوار: رُوي عن رسولِ اللهِ ﷺ ـ في رجُلٍ يُصَلّي مَعهُ ويَرتَكِبُ الفَواحِشَ ـ: إنّ صلاتَهُ تَنهاهُ يَوماً ما، فلَم يَلبَث أن تابَ.[٤٠١٧]

3596. **The Prophet (SAWA) said,** 'Verily the pillar of religion is the prayer. It is the first thing to be considered from amongst the deeds of man,

٣٥٩٦. عنه ﷺ: إنّ عَمودَ الدِّينِ الصَّلاةُ، وهِيَ أوّلُ ما يُنظَرُ فيهِ مِن عَمَلِ ابنِ آدَمَ، فإن

so if his prayer is valid, the rest of his deeds will be considered, and if his prayer is void, then the rest of his deeds will not be taken into consideration.'[4050]

صَحَّت نُظِرَ في عَمَلِهِ، وإن لَم تَصِحَّ لَم يُنظَرْ في بَقِيَّةِ عَمَلِهِ.[٤٠١٨]

3597. **Imām ʿAlī (AS) said,** 'Whoever performs his prayer with full knowledge of the right due to it is forgiven.'[4051]

٣٥٩٧. الإمامُ عليٌّ ﵇: مَن أتَى الصَّلاةَ عارِفاً بِحَقِّها غُفِرَ لَهُ.[٤٠١٩]

3598. **Fāṭima al-Zahrā' (AS) said,** 'Allah made the prayer incumbent in order to eliminate one's pride.'[4052]

٣٥٩٨. فاطمةُ الزَّهراءُ ﵍: فَرَضَ اللّهُ الصَّلاةَ تَنزيهاً مِنَ الكِبرِ.[٤٠٢٠]

3599. **Imām al-Bāqir (AS) said,** 'The first thing that the servant will have to account for is his prayer – if accepted, all else will be accepted.'[4053]

٣٥٩٩. الإمامُ الباقرُ ﵇: إنّ أوَّلَ ما يُحاسَبُ بِهِ العَبدُ الصَّلاةُ، فإن قُبِلَت قُبِلَ ما سِواها.[٤٠٢١]

3600. **Imām al-Bāqir (AS) said,** 'Prayer reinforces sincerity and eliminates pride.'[4054]

٣٦٠٠. عنه ﵇: الصَّلاةُ تَثبيتٌ لِلإخلاصِ وتَنزيهٌ عَنِ الكِبرِ.[٤٠٢٢]

3601. **Imām al-Ṣādiq (AS) said,** 'If there was to be a river outside one's house into which he bathed five times a day, would there remain any dirt on his body? Similarly the prayer is the river which purifies [one's soul] – every time one performs a prayer it acts as atonement for one's sins, except for that sin which takes him and keeps away from his faith.'[4055]

٣٦٠١. الإمامُ الصّادقُ ﵇: لَو كانَ عَلى بابِ أحَدِكُم نَهرٌ فاغتَسَلَ مِنهُ كُلَّ يَومٍ خَمسَ مَرّاتٍ هَل كانَ يَبقى عَلى جَسَدِهِ مِنَ الدَّرَنِ شَيءٌ؟ إنَّما مَثَلُ الصَّلاةِ مَثَلُ النَّهرِ الَّذي يُنقي، كُلَّما صَلّى صَلاةً كانَ كَفّارَةً لِذُنوبِهِ إلّا ذَنبٌ أخرَجَهُ مِنَ الإيمانِ مُقيمٌ عَلَيهِ.[٤٠٢٣]

1128. The Virtue of One who Prays

١١٢٨ـ فَضلُ المُصَلّي

3602. **The Prophet (SAWA) said,** 'As long as you are praying, [know that] verily you are knocking at the door of the Almighty King, and the King's door opens for whoever knocks persistently thereat.'[4056]

٣٦٠٢. رسولُ اللّهِ ﷺ: ما دُمتَ فِي الصَّلاةِ فإنَّكَ تَقرَعُ بابَ المَلِكِ الجَبّارِ، ومَن يُكثِرْ قَرعَ بابِ المَلِكِ يُفتَحْ لَهُ.[٤٠٢٤]

3603. **Imām ʿAlī (AS) said,** 'If the praying one knew about the sublimity of Allah covering him, he would never wish to raise his head up from prostration.'[4057]

٣٦٠٣. الإمامُ عليٌّ ﵇: لَو يَعلَمُ المُصَلّي ما يَغشاهُ مِن جَلالِ اللّهِ ما سَرَّهُ أن يَرفَعَ رَأسَهُ مِن سُجودِهِ.[٤٠٢٥]

3604. **Imām ʿAlī (AS) said**, 'When a man stands to pray, Iblīs [Satan] approaches and looks at him jealously because of the mercy of Allah that he can see covering him.'[4058]

٣٦٠٤ . عنه ﷺ: إذا قامَ الرجُلُ إلى الصَّلاةِ أقبَلَ إبليسُ يَنظُرُ إلَيهِ حَسداً ، لِما يَرى مِن رَحمَةِ اللهِ التي تَغشاهُ.[٤٠٣٦]

1129. Humbleness in Prayer

١١٢٩ ـ الخُشوعُ فِي الصَّلاةِ

"Certainly the faithful have attained success – those who are humble in their prayers…"[4059]

﴿قَدْ أَفْلَحَ الْمُؤْمِنُونَ * الَّذِينَ هُمْ فِي صَلاتِهِمْ خاشِعُونَ﴾.[٤٠٣٧]

3605. **The Prophet (SAWA) said,** 'The prayer of one who does not humble himself in his prayer does not count.'[4060]

٣٦٠٥ . رسولُ اللهِ ﷺ: لا صَلاةَ لِمَن لا يَتَخَشَّعُ في صَلاتِهِ.[٤٠٣٨]

3606. **The Prophet (SAWA),** when he was asked about humbleness in prayer, said, 'It is to abase oneself in the prayer, and for the servant to come to his Lord wholeheartedly.'[4061]

٣٦٠٦ . عنه ﷺ ـ لَمّا سُئلَ عنِ الخُشوعِ ـ: اتَّواضُعُ في الصَّلاةِ، وأن يُقبِلَ العَبدُ بِقَلبِهِ كُلِّهِ على رَبِّهِ.[٤٠٣٩]

3607. *Falāḥ al-Sā'il*, narrating from Abū Muḥammad Jaʿfar b. ʿAlī al-Qummī in the book *Zuhd al-Nabī*, 'When the Prophet (SAWA) used to stand for prayer, his face would become pale from fear of Allah, the most High.'[4062]

٣٦٠٧ . فلاح السائل عن أبي محمّد جعفر بن علي القمّي في كتاب زهد النبي ﷺ: كانَ النبيُّ ﷺ إذا قامَ إلى الصَّلاةِ تَرَبَّدَ وَجهُهُ خَوفاً مِنَ اللهِ تعالى.[٤٠٣٠]

3608. **Imām ʿAlī (AS) said,** 'Man should be humble in his prayer, for verily he whose heart is humble before Allah, Mighty and Exalted, his limbs will humble themselves too and will not fidget around.'[4063]

٣٦٠٨ . الإمامُ عليٌّ ﷺ: لِيَخشَعِ الرَّجُلُ في صَلاتِهِ؛ فإنّه مَن خَشَعَ قَلبُهُ للهِ عَزَّوجلَّ خَشَعَت جَوارِحُهُ فلا يَعبَثُ بِشَيءٍ.[٤٠٣١]

3609. It is narrated in *Da'ā'im al-Islām* that any time Imām ʿAlī (AS) would stand for prayer, he would be like a fixed structure or a straight pillar, not moving at all, and sometimes when he would bow or prostrate, [he would be so still that] a bird would perch itself on him. Nobody was ever able to match the prayer of the Prophet (SAWA) apart from ʿAlī b. Abī Ṭālib and ʿAlī b. al-Ḥusayn [i.e. Imām Zayn al-ʿĀbidīn] (AS).'[4064]

٣٦٠٩ . دعائم الإسلام عن عليٍّ صلواتُ اللهِ عليهِ أنَّهُ كانَ إذا دَخَلَ الصَّلاةَ كانَ كَأنَّهُ بِناءٌ ثابِتٌ أو عَمودٌ قائمٌ لا يَتَحَرَّكُ، وكانَ رُبَّما رَكَعَ أو سَجَدَ فَيَقَعُ الطَّيرُ عليهِ، ولَم يُطِقْ أحَدٌ أن يَحكِيَ صَلاةَ رسولِ اللهِ ﷺ إلّا عليُّ بنُ أبي طالبٍ وعليُّ بنُ الحسينِ ﷺ.[٤٠٣٢]

3610. *A'lām al-Dīn*, 'Whenever the Commander of the Faithful ʿAlī (AS) would perform his ablution, the colour of his face would change out of fear of Allah, most High.'[4065]

٣٦١٠ . أعلام الدين: كانَ أميرُ المؤمنينَ ﷺ إذا أخَذَ في الوُضوءِ يَتَغَيَّرُ وَجهُهُ مِن خِيفَةِ اللهِ تعالى.[٤٠٣٣]

3611. *'Uddat al-Dā'ī*: 'Fāṭima al-Zahrā' (AS) used to pant in her prayer due to fear of Allah, most High.'[4066]

٣٦١١ . عدّة الداعي : كانَت فاطِمةُ عليها السلام تَنهَجُ في الصَّلاةِ مِن خِيفَةِ اللهِ تعالىٰ.٤٠٣٤

3612. It is narrated in *Biḥār al-Anwār* that when Imām al-Ḥasan (AS) used to perform his ablution the colour of his face would change and his joints would tremble. When he was asked about this once, he replied, 'It is only fitting for one who stands before the Lord of the Throne that his face should change colour and his joints should tremble.'[4067]

٣٦١٢ . بحار الأنوار من كتاب اللؤلؤيات : كانَ الحَسنُ عليه السلام إذا تَوَضَّأ تَغَيَّرَ لَونُهُ، وارتَعَدَت مَفاصِلُهُ، فقيلَ لَهُ في ذلكَ، فقالَ : حَقٌّ لِمَن وَقَفَ بينَ يَدَي ذِي العَرشِ أن يَصفَرَّ لَونُهُ وتَرتَعِدَ مَفاصِلُهُ.٤٠٣٥

3613. It is narrated in *Da'ā'im al-Islām* that when Imām Zayn al-'Ābidīn (AS) used to perform his ablution and prepare to begin his prayer, his face would become pale and change colour. When asked about this, he replied, 'Verily I am going to stand before the Great King.'[4068]

٣٦١٣ . دعائم الإسلام : كانَ عليّ بن الحسين عليه السلام إذا تَوَضَّأ للصَّلاةِ وأخَذَ في الدُّخولِ فيها اصفَرَّ وَجهُهُ وتَغَيَّرَ لَونُهُ، فقيلَ لَهُ مرّةً في ذلكَ، فقالَ : إنّي اُرِيدُ الوُقُوفَ بينَ يَدَي مَلِكٍ عَظِيمٍ.٤٠٣٦

3614. **Imām al-Bāqir (AS) said:** 'When 'Alī b. al-Ḥusayn (AS) used to stand in his prayer, he was as straight as a tree trunk, and no part of him moved except for that which the wind caused to move.'[4069]

٣٦١٤ . الإمامُ الباقرُ عليه السلام : كانَ عليُّ بنُ الحسينِ صلواتُ اللهِ عليهِما إذا قامَ في الصَّلاةِ كأنّهُ ساقُ شَجرَةٍ لايَتَحَرَّكُ مِنهُ شَيءٌ إلّا ماحَرَّكَهُ الرِّيحُ مِنهُ.٤٠٣٧

3615. **Abū 'Ayyūb narrated,** 'When Abū Ja'far and Abū 'Abdillāh [i.e. Imām al-Bāqir and Imām al-Ṣādiq (AS)] used to stand to pray, their faces would change colour, sometimes reddening and sometimes paling, and it was as if they were intimately conversing with someone they could see.'[4070]

٣٦١٥ . فلاح السائل عن أبي أيوب : كانَ أبو جعفرٍ وأبو عبدِاللهِ عليهما السلام إذا قاما إلى الصَّلاةِ تَغَيَّرَت ألوانُهُما حُمرَةً ومَرَّةً صُفرَةً، وكأنّما يُناجِيانِ شَيئاً يَرَيانِهِ.٤٠٣٨

1130. Conditions and Impediments to the Acceptance of the Prayer

١١٣٠ ـ شَرائطُ وموانعُ قَبولِ الصَّلاةِ

3616. **The Prophet (SAWA) said,** 'If you were to pray so much that you became [as thin as strings], and fasted so much that you [bent over] as arches,

٣٦١٦ . رسولُ اللهِ ﷺ : لَو صَلَّيتُم حتّىٰ تَكونُوا كالأوتارِ، وصُمتُم حتّىٰ تَكُونُوا كالحَنايا، لَم

Allah would not accept any of it unless it was accompanied by piety.'[4071]

يَقبَلِ اللهُ مِنكُم إلّا بِوَرَعٍ.[٤٠٣٩]

3617. **The Prophet (SAWA) said,** 'Allah, most High, revealed to me saying, 'O brother of the prophets and the warners, warn your people not to enter any of My places of worship while having committed a wrong to another servant who holds it against him, for verily I curse him as long as he stands to pray before Me, until he makes amends for that wrong [returns his rights].'[4072]

٣٦١٧. عنه ﷺ: أوحَى اللهُ إلَيَّ أن يا أخا المُرسَلِينَ، يا أخا المُنذِرِينَ، أنذِرْ قَومَكَ لا يَدخُلوا بَيتاً مِن بُيُوتِي ولِأحَدٍ مِن عِبادِي عندَ أحَدِهِم مَظلِمَةٌ؛ فإنّي ألعَنُهُ ما دامَ قائماً يُصَلِّي بينَ يَدَيَّ حتّىٰ يَرُدَّ تلكَ المَظلِمَةَ.[٤٠٤٠]

3618. **The Prophet (SAWA) said,** 'Whoever backbites a Muslim man or woman, Allah, most High, neither accepts his prayer nor his fasting for forty days until its victim has forgiven him.'[4073]

٣٦١٨. عنه ﷺ: مَنِ اغتابَ مُسلماً أو مُسلِمَةً لَم يَقبَلِ اللهُ تعالىٰ صلاتَهُ ولا صِيامَهُ أربَعينَ يَوماً ولَيلةً، إلّا أن يَغفِرَ لهُ صاحِبُهُ.[٤٠٤١]

3619. **The Prophet (SAWA) said,** 'Verily the prayer of one who drinks alcohol is not counted for forty days.'[4074]

٣٦١٩. عنه ﷺ: إنّ مَن شَرِبَ الخَمرَ لَم تُحسَبْ صلاتُهُ أربَعينَ صَباحاً.[٤٠٤٢]

3620. **Imām ʿAlī (AS) said,** 'Look carefully at what [attire] you pray in. If it is not among that which is fitting or permissible for it, then it is not accepted.'[4075]

٣٦٢٠. الإمامُ عليٌّ عليه السلام: أُنظُرْ فِيمَ تُصَلِّي، إن لَم يَكُن مِن وَجهِهِ وحِلِّهِ فلا قَبولَ.[٤٠٤٣]

3621. **Imām Zayn al-ʿĀbidīn (AS),** when he was asked about the condition for the acceptance of the prayer, replied, 'Our guardianship and disassociation from our enemies.'[4076]

٣٦٢١. الإمامُ زينُ العابدينَ عليه السلام ـ وقد سُئلَ عن سَبَبِ قَبولِ الصَّلاةِ ـ: وَلايَتُنا والبَراءةُ مِن أعدائنا.[٤٠٤٤]

3622. **Imām al-Ṣādiq (AS) said,** 'Whoever Allah accepts even one prayer from, He will not chastise, and whoever He accepts even one good deed from He will not chastise.'[4077]

٣٦٢٢. الإمامُ الصّادقُ عليه السلام: مَن قَبِلَ اللهُ مِنهُ صلاةً واحِدَةً لم يُعَذِّبْهُ، ومَن قَبِلَ مِنهُ حَسَنةً لَم يُعَذِّبْهُ.[٤٠٤٥]

3623. **Imām al-Ṣādiq (AS) said,** 'Allah does not accept a single prayer from one who looks at his parents loathingly, even if they oppress him.'[4078]

٣٦٢٣. عنه عليه السلام: مَن نَظَرَ إلىٰ أبَوَيهِ نَظَرَ ماقِتٍ وهُما ظالِمانِ لَهُ، لم يَقبَلِ اللهُ لَهُ صلاةً.[٤٠٤٦]

1131. He Whose Prayer is Accepted

١١٣١ ـ مَن تُقبَلُ صَلاتُهُ

3624. **Imām al-Ṣādiq (AS) said,** 'Allah Almighty said: 'I only accept the prayer of he who has humiliated himself to My Majesty, has refrained himself from carnal desires for My sake, he passes his day with My remembrance, does not act haughty over My creation, feeds the hungry, clothes the undressed, shows compassion to the afflicted and shelters the stranger. The light of such a person will shine like the sun and I shall grant him light in darkness and knowledge in ignorance.
I will preserve him with My honour and guard him with My angels. When he calls me I will answer him, when he asks Me I will grant him. His example is like the story of gardens of Paradise where no fruit will become dry and its state will never change.'[4079]

٣٦٢٤ . الإمام الصادق ؑ : قـالَ اللهُ تَـبارَكَ وتَعالىٰ : إنَّما أقبَلُ الصَّلاةَ مِمَّن تَواضَعَ لِعَظَمَتي ، ويَكُفُّ نَفسَهُ عَنِ الشَّهَواتِ مِن أجـلي ، ويَـقطَعُ نَهارَهُ بِذِكري ، ولا يَتَعاظَمُ عَلىٰ خَلقي ، ويُـطعِمُ الجائِعَ ، ويَكسُو العـارِيَ ، ويَـرحَـمُ المُـصابَ ، ويُـؤوِي الغَـريبَ ، فَـذٰلِكَ يُشـرِقُ نـورُهُ مِـثلَ الشَّمسِ ، وأجعَلُ لَهُ فِي الظُّـلُماتِ نـورًا وفِـي الجَـهالَةِ عِـلمًا ، وأكـلأُهُ بِـعِزَّتي ، وأستَحفِظُهُ بِمَلائِكَتي ، يَدعوني فَأُلَبّيهِ ، ويَسأَلُني فَـأُعطيهِ ، فَـمَثَلُ ذٰلِكَ عِـندي كَـمَثَلِ جَـنّاتِ الفِـردَوسِ ، لا تَيبَسُ ثِمارُها ، ولا تَتَغَيَّرُ عَن حالِها[٤٠٤٧].

1132. The Role of Presence of the Heart in the Acceptance of the Prayer

١١٣٢ ـ دَورُ حُضورِ القَلبِ في قَبولِ الصَّلاةِ

3625. **The Prophet (SAWA) said,** 'Allah does not accept the prayer of the servant whose heart is not present alongside his body.'[4080]

٣٦٢٥ . رسولُ اللهِ ﷺ : لا يَقبَلُ اللهُ صلاةَ عَبدٍ لا يَحضُرُ قَلبُهُ مَع بَدَنِهِ .[٤٠٤٨]

3626. **The Prophet (SAWA) said,** 'Verily the servant performs a prayer where neither a sixth nor a tenth of it may be accepted. Verily only that part of his prayer is accepted from him wherein he was fully conscious.'[4081]

٣٦٢٦ . عنه ﷺ : إنّ العَبدَ لَيُصَلِّي الصَّلاةَ لا يُكتَبُ لَهُ سُـدسُها ولا عُشرُها، وإنّما يُكتَبُ لِلعَبدِ مِـن صَلاتِهِ ما عَقَلَ مِنها .[٤٠٤٩]

3627. **The Prophet (SAWA) said,** 'Two simple units of prayer performed with contemplation are better than standing the whole night in prayer.'[4082]

٣٦٢٧ . عنه ﷺ : رَكعَتانِ خَفيفَتانِ في (ال)ـتَفَكُّرِ خَيرٌ مِن قِيامِ لَيلَةٍ .[٤٠٥٠]

3628. **Imām al-Bāqir and Imām al-Ṣādiq (AS) said,** 'Only that part of your prayer in which you engaged with your full attention is accepted. So if one is inattentive in all of it or careless in his performance of it, that same prayer is crumpled up and thrown back at his face.'[4083]

٣٦٢٨ . الإمامُ الباقرُ والإمامُ الصّادقُ ؑ : ما لَكَ مِن صلاتِكَ الّا ما أقبَلتَ علَيهِ فيها، فإن أوهَمَها كُلَّها أو غَفَلَ عن أدائها لُفَّت فَضُرِبَ بـها وَجـهُ صاحِبِها .[٤٠٥١]

3629. **Imām al-Ṣādiq (AS) said,** 'Whoever performs a two unit prayer fully knowing what he is saying in it, gets up from it with not a single sin left [unforgiven] between him and Allah.'[4084]

٣٦٢٩. الإمامُ الصّادقُ (عليه السلام): مَن صَلّىٰ رَكعتَينِ يَعلَمُ ما يقولُ فيهِما، انصَرَفَ ولَيسَ بَينَهُ وبَينَ اللهِ ذَنبٌ. [٤٠٥٢]

1133. He Whose Prayer is not Counted

١١٣٣ ـ مَن لَيسَ لَهُ صَلاةٌ

3630. **The Prophet (SAWA) said,** 'The prayer of one who does not complete the bowing and prostration is not counted.'[4085]

٣٦٣٠. رسولُ اللهِ (ﷺ): لا صلاةَ لِمَن لا يُتِمُّ رُكوعَها وسُجودَها. [٤٠٥٣]

3631. **The Prophet (SAWA) said,** 'The one who is deliberately aware of who is on his left and who is on his right is not counted as having prayed.'[4086]

٣٦٣١. عنه (ﷺ): مَن عَرَفَ مَن علىٰ يَمينِهِ وشِمالِهِ مُتَعمِّداً في الصَّلاةِ فلا صلاةَ لَهُ. [٤٠٥٤]

3632. **Imām al-Ṣādiq (AS) said,** 'The one who does not pay the alms-tax is not considered as having prayed.'[4087]

٣٦٣٢. الإمامُ الصّادقُ (عليه السلام): لا صلاةَ لِمَن لا زَكاةَ لَهُ. [٤٠٥٥]

3633. **Imām al-Ṣādiq (AS) said,** 'The prayer of a *ḥāqin*, a *ḥāqib* and a *ḥāziq* does not count – a *ḥāqin* is one who suppresses the urge to urinate, a *ḥāqib* is one who suppresses the urge to defecate [before commencing the prayer], and a *ḥāziq* is one whose feet are pinched by wearing narrow shoes.'[4088]

٣٦٣٣. عنه (عليه السلام): لا صلاةَ لِحاقِنٍ ولا لِحاقِبٍ ولا لِحازِقٍ، فالحاقِنُ الذي بِهِ البَولُ، والحاقِبُ الذي بِهِ الغائطُ، والحازِقُ الذي قد ضَغَطَهُ الخُفُّ. [٤٠٥٦]

1134. Prohibition of Laziness in Prayer

١١٣٤ ـ النَّهيُ عَنِ التَّكاسُلِ فِي الصَّلاةِ

"The hypocrites indeed seek to deceive Allah, but it is he who outwits them. When they stand up for prayer, they stand up lazily, showing off to the people and not remembering Allah except a little."[4089]

﴿إنَّ المُنافِقِينَ يُخادِعُونَ اللهَ وَهُوَ خادِعُهُمْ وَإذا قامُوا إلَى الصَّلاةِ قامُوا كُسالىٰ يُراؤُونَ النّاسَ وَلا يَذْكُرُونَ اللهَ إلّا قَلِيلاً﴾. [٤٠٥٧]

3634. It is narrated within the tradition about the Prophet's ascension that [Allah addressed the Prophet (SAWA) saying], 'O Aḥmad, how I wonder at three types of servant: one who starts his prayer knowing full well Who he raises his hands to and in front of Whom he stands, and yet remains drowsy …'[4090]

٣٦٣٤. بحار الأنوار: في حديثِ المِعراجِ: يا أحمدُ، عَجِبتُ من ثَلاثَةِ عَبيدٍ: عَبدٍ دَخَلَ في الصَّلاةِ وهُو يَعلَمُ إلىٰ مَن يَرفَعُ يَدَيهِ وقُدّامَ مَن هُو، وهُو يَنعَسُ... [٤٠٥٨]

3635. **Imām ʿAlī (AS) said,** 'When sleep overcomes you while you are in your prayer, then

٣٦٣٥. الإمامُ عليٌّ (عليه السلام): إذا غَلَبَتكَ عَينُكَ وأنتَ

break your prayer and go to sleep, for verily [in that state] you do not know if you are praying for or against yourself!'[4091]

في الصَّلاةِ فاقطَعِ الصَّلاةَ ونَم؛ فـإنَّكَ لا تَـدري تَدعُو لكَ أو علىٰ نفسِكَ!٤٠٩١

3636. **Imām al-Bāqir (AS) said,** 'Do not stand for prayer lazily, drowsily or sluggishly for verily these are from among the disturbances brought about by hypocrisy, and verily Allah has prohibited the believers from standing for prayer while they are intoxicated, which means when intoxicated by sleep.'[4092]

٣٦٣٦. الإمامُ الباقرُ عليه السلام : لا تَـقُمْ إلى الصَّـلاةِ مُتَكاسِلاً ولا مُتَناعِساً ولا مُتَثاقِلاً؛ فـإنّها مِـن خَلَلِ النِّفاقِ، وإنَّ اللهَ نَهى المؤمنينَ أن يَقومُوا إلى الصَّلاةِ وهُم سُكارىٰ يَعني مِنَ النَّومِ.٤٠٩٢

(See also: LAZINESS: 344)

(أنظر) عنوان ٣٥٤ «الكسل».

1135. Observance of the Prescribed Timings of the Prayer

١١٣٥ ـ المُحافَظَةُ عَلىٰ أوقاتِ الصَّلاةِ

"Woe to them who pray – those who are heedless of their prayers."[4093]

﴿فَوَيْلٌ لِلْمُصَلِّينَ * الَّذِينَ هُمْ عَنْ صَلاتِهِمْ ساهُونَ﴾.٤٠٩٣

"...and who are mindful of their prayers. It is they who will be the inheritors, who will inherit Paradise: they will dwell therein forever."[4094]

﴿وَالَّذِينَ هُمْ عَلَى صَلَواتِهِمْ يُحافِظُونَ * أُولٰئِكَ هُمُ الوارِثُونَ * الَّذِينَ يَرِثُونَ الْفِرْدَوْسَ هُمْ فِيهَا خَـٰلِدُونَ﴾.٤٠٩٤

3637. **The Prophet (SAWA) said,** 'The worth of a man with respect to his religion is measured by his diligence to keeping up his daily prayers [at their specific times].'[4095]

٣٦٣٧. رسولُ اللهِ صلى الله عليه وآله : حَسبُ الرَّجُلِ مِن دِينِهِ، كَثرَةُ مُحافَظَتِهِ علىٰ إقامَةِ الصَّلَواتِ.٤٠٩٥

3638. **Imām 'Alī (AS)** wrote in a letter to Muḥammad b. Abū Bakr, 'Observe the timing of the prayer and perform it at its prescribed time, neither hastening to pray it earlier in order to be free of it, nor delaying it because of some work.'[4096]

٣٦٣٨. الإمامُ عليٌّ عليه السلام ـ مِن كتابِهِ لمحمّدِ بنِ أبي بكرٍ ـ: إرتَقِبْ وَقتَ الصَّلاةِ فَصَلِّها لِـوَقتِها، ولا تَـعَجَّلْ بِـها قَـبلَهُ لِـفَراغٍ، ولا تُـؤخِّرْها عَـنهُ لِشُغلٍ.٤٠٩٦

1136. Enjoinment of Performing the Prayer at the Earliest Moment of the Time Prescribed for it

١١٣٦ ـ الحَثُّ عَلىٰ الصَّلاةِ في أوَّلِ وَقتِها

3639. **Imām al-Bāqir (AS) said,** 'Know that the earliest time is always the best, so hasten to perform

٣٦٣٩. الإمامُ الباقرُ عليه السلام : إعلَمْ أنَّ أوَّلَ الوَقتِ أبداً

good whenever you can. The most beloved acts in the eyes of Allah, Mighty and Exalted, are those that the servant performs regularly, even though they be few in number.'[4097]

أفضَلُ، فَعَجِّلْ بِالخَيرِ ما استَطَعتَ، وأحَبُّ الأعمالِ إلى اللهِ عزَّوجلَّ ما داوَمَ العَبدُ علَيهِ وإن قَلَّ.[٤٠٦٥]

3640. **Imām al-Ṣādiq (AS) said,** 'The virtue of the earliest opportunity over the latest is as the virtue of the Hereafter over this world's life.'[4098]

٣٦٤٠. الإمامُ الصّادقُ ﵇: فَضلُ الوَقتِ الأوَّلِ علَى الآخِرِ كَفَضلِ الآخِرَةِ على الدُّنيا.[٤٠٦٦]

3641. Biḥār al-Anwār, 'al-Qazzāz narrated, 'al-Riḍā (AS) went out to await the arrival of some people who were coming to visit him when the time for prayer set in. He went towards a nearby fort and took shade under a rock, saying, 'Announce the call for prayer.' I replied, 'Why don't we wait for our companions to catch up with us?' He replied, 'May Allah forgive you. Do not ever delay the prayer from the earliest moment of its onset to the latest without a good excuse. You must always pray at the earliest time', so I announced the call for prayer and we prayed.'[4099]

٣٦٤١. بحار الأنوار عن القزّاز: خَرَجَ الرِّضا ﵇ يَستَقبِلُ بعضَ الطّالِبِيِّينَ وجاءَ وقتُ الصَّلاةِ، فَمالَ إلى قَصرٍ هناكَ فَنَزَلَ تحتَ صَخرَةٍ فقالَ: أذِّنْ، فقلتُ: نَنتَظِرُ يَلحَقْ بنا أصحابُنا، فقالَ: غَفَرَ اللهُ لكَ، لا تُؤَخِّرَنَّ صَلاةً عن أوَّلِ وَقتِها إلى آخِرِ وَقتِها مِن غَيرِ عِلَّةٍ، علَيكَ أبَداً بأوَّلِ الوَقتِ، فأذَّنتُ وصَلَّينا.[٤٠٦٧]

1137. Abandonment of the Prayer and Disbelief

١١٣٧ ـ تاركُ الصَّلاةِ وَالكُفرُ

"[They will be] in gardens, questioning concerning the guilty: 'What drew you into Hell?' They will answer, 'We were not among those who prayed.'"[4100]

﴿فِي جَنَّاتٍ يَتَسَاءَلُونَ * عَنِ الْمُجْرِمِينَ * مَا سَلَكَكُمْ فِي سَقَرَ * قَالُوا لَمْ نَكُ مِنَ الْمُصَلِّينَ﴾.[٤٠٦٨]

3642. **The Prophet (SAWA) said,** 'It only takes for a Muslim to deliberately abandon the performance of the daily obligatory prayer or to not perform it out of carelessness, for him to become an infidel (*kāfir*).'[4101]

٣٦٤٢. رسولُ اللهِ ﷺ: مابينَ المسلمِ وبينَ الكافِرِ إلّا أن يَترُكَ الصَّلاةَ الفَريضَةَ مُتَعَمِّداً، أو يَتهاوَنَ بها فلا يُصَلِّيَها.[٤٠٦٩]

3643. **Imām al-Ṣādiq (AS)** was once asked why the one who abandons the prayer is considered an infidel and not the fornicator, to which he replied, 'Because the fornicator and other [such sinners] commits the sin out of a desire that overcomes him, whereas the one who abandons the prayer only does so because he does not take it seriously, deeming it insignificant.'[4102]

٣٦٤٣. الإمامُ الصّادقُ ﵇ ـ لَمّا سُئلَ عن عِلَّةِ تَسميَةِ تارِكِ الصَّلاةِ كافِراً دونَ الزّاني ـ: لِأنَّ الزانيَ وما أشبَهَهُ إنَّما يَعمَلُ ذلكَ لِمَكانِ الشَّهوَةِ لأنَّها تَغلِبُهُ، وتارِكَ الصَّلاةِ لا يَترُكُها إلّا استِخفافاً بها.[٤٠٧٠]

1138. Caution Against Taking the Prayer Lightly

١١٣٨ـ التَّحذيرُ مِنَ الاستِخفافِ بِالصَّلاةِ

3644. **Imām al-Bāqir (AS) said,** 'Do not neglect your prayer, for verily the Prophet (SAWA) said while he was on his death bed, 'The one who takes his prayer lightly is not of me.'[4103]

٣٦٤٤ . الإمامُ الباقرُ ﷺ :لا تَتَهاوَنْ بصلاتِكَ؛ فإنّ النبيَّ ﷺ قالَ عندَ مَوتِهِ: لَيسَ مِنّي مَنِ استَخَفَّ بِصلاتِهِ.[٤٠٧١]

3645. **Abū Baṣīr narrated,** 'I went to Ḥumayda, to condole her for the death of Abū 'Abdillāh (AS) [i.e. Imām al- Ṣādiq], so she cried and said, 'O Abū Muḥammad, if you saw him as death came upon him, he placed his hand over one eye and said, 'Call my relatives and my friends to come to me.' When everyone had gathered around him, he said, 'Verily our intercession will not avail one who takes his prayer lightly.'[4104]

٣٦٤٥ . مستدرك الوسائل عن أبي بصيرٍ :دَخَلتُ علىٰ حُمَيدَةَ أُعَزِّيها بأبي عبدِ اللهِ ﷺ فَبَكَت ثمّ قالَت: يا أبا محمّدٍ، لو شَهِدتَهُ حينَ حَضَرَهُ الموتُ وقد قَبَضَ إحدىٰ عَينَيهِ ثُمّ قالَ: أُدعُوا لي قَرابَتي ومَن يَطُفَ[٤٠٧٢] بي، فلمّا اجتَمَعُوا حَولَهُ قالَ: إنَّ شَفاعَتَنا لَن تَنالَ مُستَخِفّاً بِالصَّلاةِ.[٤٠٧٣]

1139. The Congregational Prayer

١١٣٩ـ صَلاةُ الجَماعَةِ

3646. **Luqmān (AS) said** to his son, exhorting him, 'Pray in congregation, even if you have to stand on an arrowhead [to do so].'[4105]

٣٦٤٦ . لقمانُ ﷺ ـ لابنِهِ وهُو يَعِظُهُ ـ: صَلِّ في جَماعَةٍ ولو عَلَى رَأسِ زُجٍّ![٤٠٧٤]

3647. **The Prophet (SAWA) said** regarding a group of people who used to delay from praying [in congregation] in the mosque [praying instead in their own houses], 'A people who neglect to pray in the mosque almost become deserving of having firewood piled at their doors and set alight so that their houses burn down on them.'[4106]

٣٦٤٧ . رسولُ اللهِ ﷺ ـ في أُناسٍ أبطَؤوا عنِ الصَّلاةِ في المَسجِدِ ـ: لَيُوشِكُ قَومٌ يَدَعُونَ الصَّلاةَ في المَسجِدِ أن نَأمُرَ بحَطَبٍ فَيُوضَعَ علىٰ أبوابِهِم، فَتُوقَدَ علَيهِم نارٌ فتُحرَقَ علَيهِم بُيوتُهُم.[٤٠٧٥]

3648. **The Prophet (SAWA) said,** 'He who prays all five prayers in congregation, you must only believe to be good [keep good opinion about him].'[4107]

٣٦٤٨ . رسولُ اللهِ ﷺ : مَن صَلَّى الخَمسَ في جَماعَةٍ فَظُنُّوا بِهِ خَيراً.[٤٠٧٦]

1140. Duties that the Leader of the Congregation Must Observe

١١٤٠ ـ ما يَلزَمُ مُراعاتُهُ لِلإمامِ

3649. **Imām ʿAlī (AS) said** in his advice to Muḥammad b. Abī Bakr when he appointed him governor of Egypt, 'Look carefully at what your prayer is like, for verily as the leader of the community, you must pray it perfectly and not be careless in its performance. Every leader who leads the prayer for a people is responsible for any defect in their prayer, so perfect it and be mindful with regards to it and you will have the same reward as them without there being any reduction in their reward thereof.'[4108]

٣٦٤٩ . الإمامُ عليٌّ ﷺ ـ في وصيّتِهِ لِمحمّدِ بنِ أبي بكرٍ حينَ وَلّاهُ مِصرَ ـ: وَانظُرْ إلىٰ صلاتِكَ كَيفَ هِيَ فإنّكَ إمامٌ لِقَومِكَ (يَنبَغِي لكَ) أن تُتِمَّها ولا تُخَفِّفَها، فَلَيسَ مِن إمامٍ يُصَلّي بِقَومٍ يَكونُ في صلاتِهِم نُقصانٌ إلّا كانَ علَيهِ، لا يَنقُصُ مِن صلاتِهِم شَيءٌ، وتَمِّمْها وتَحَفَّظْ فيها يَكُن لكَ مِثلَ أُجُورِهِم ولا يَنقُصُ ذلكَ مِن أجرِهِم شَيئاً.[٤٠٧٧]

3650. **Imām ʿAlī (AS)** wrote in a letter to the governors of the cities, saying, 'Lead them in prayer, praying as the weak ones among them do [in consideration towards them], and do not torment them [by performing lengthy prayers].'[4109]

٣٦٥٠ . عنه ﷺ ـ مِن كتابِهِ إلى أُمَراءِ البِلادِ ـ: صَلُّوا بِهِم صلاةَ أضعَفِهِم، ولا تَكُونُوا فَتّانِينَ.[٤٠٧٨]

3651. **Imām al-Ṣādiq (AS)** was asked how to determine the most rightful person to lead the congregation, to which he replied, 'Verily the Prophet (SAWA) said, 'The person who recites the Qur'an the best [i.e. with correct pronunciation] should lead them, and if they all recite similarly, then the one who migrated [from Makkah to Medina] the earliest, and if they all migrated around the same time, then the oldest from among them, and if they are all the same age, then the most knowledgeable from among them with regards to the prophetic practice and the laws of jurisprudence. No one from among you should lead a man in prayer in his own home, nor a man of authority within the sphere of his authority.'[4110]

٣٦٥١ . الإمامُ الصّادقُ ﷺ ـ لَمّا سُئلَ عَمَّن أحَقُّ أن يَؤُمَّ ـ: إنَّ رسولَ اللهِ ﷺ قالَ: يَتَقَدَّمُ القَومَ أقرَؤُهُم لِلقرآنِ، فإن كانُوا في القِراءَةِ سَواءً فَأقدَمُهُم هِجرَةً، فإن كانُوا في الهِجرَةِ سَواءً فَأكبَرُهُم سِنّاً، فإن كانوا في السِّنِّ سَواءً فَلْيَؤُمَّهُم أعلَمُهُم بِالسُّنَّةِ وأفقَهُهُم في الدِّينِ، ولا يَتَقَدَّمَنَّ أحَدُكُمُ الرَّجُلَ في مَنزِلِهِ، ولا صاحِبَ (الـ) سُلطانِ في سُلطانِهِ.[٤٠٧٩]

238

THE PRAYER (2)

الصَّلاةُ (٢)

The Night Prayer

صَلاةُ اللَّيلِ

1141. The Virtue of the Night Prayer

١١٤١ ـ فَضلُ صَلاةِ اللَّيلِ

"And keep vigil for a part of the night, as a superogatory [devotion] for you. It may be that your Lord will raise you to a praiseworthy station."[4111]

﴿ومِنَ اللّيْلِ فَتَهَجَّدْ بِهِ نافِلَةً لَكَ عَسى أَنْ يَبْعَثَكَ رَبُّكَ مَقاماً مَحْمُوداً﴾.[٤٠٨٠]

"Indeed rising in the night is firmer in tread and more upright in respect to speech."[4112]

﴿إنَّ ناشِئَةَ اللّيلِ هِيَ أشَدُّ وَطْأً وَأقوَمُ قِيْلاً﴾.[٤٠٨١]

3652. **The Prophet (SAWA) said,** 'The archangel Gabriel continuously advises me about standing for prayer in the night such that I really thought the good people in my community will never sleep.'[4113]

٣٦٥٢. رسولُ اللهِ ﷺ: ما زالَ جَبرَئيلُ يُوصِيني بقيامِ اللَّيلِ حَتّىٰ ظَنَنتُ أنَّ خِيارَ أُمَّتي لَن يَنامُوا مِنَ اللَّيلِ إلّا قليلاً.[٤٠٨٢]

3653. **The Prophet (SAWA) said,** 'May Allah have mercy on the man who wakes up in the night to pray, and wakes his wife so she too prays, and sprinkles water on her face if she refuses to get up. And Allah has mercy on the woman who wakes up in the night to pray, and wakes her husband to pray too, and sprinkles water on his face if he refuses to get up.'[4114]

٣٦٥٣. عنه ﷺ: رَحِمَ اللهُ رَجلاً قامَ مِنَ الليلِ فَصلّىٰ وأيقَظَ امرَأتَهُ فَصلَّت، فإن أبَت نَضَحَ في وَجهِها الماءَ. رَحِمَ اللهُ امرأةً قامَت مِنَ اللَّيلِ فصَلَّت وأيقَظَت زَوجَها، فإن أبىٰ نَضَحَت في وَجهِهِ الماءَ.[٤٠٨٣]

3654. **The Prophet (SAWA) said,** 'Verily when a servant withdraws to be alone with his Master in the middle of the dark night and intimately

٣٦٥٤. عنه ﷺ: إنَّ العَبدَ إذا تَخَلّىٰ بِسَيِّدِهِ في جَوفِ اللَّيلِ المُظلِمِ وناجاهُ، أثبَتَ اللهُ النورَ في

converses with Him, Allah places divine light into his heart...then He, Exalted be His Splendour, says to His angels, 'O My angels, look at My servant how he seeks solitude to be with Me in the middle of the dark night while the worthless ones remain heedless and the negligent ones sleep. Witness that verily I have forgiven him.'[4115]

قَـبِهِ... ثُـمّ يـقولُ جَـلَّ جـلالُهُ لِـملائكَتِهِ: يـا ملائكَتي، أُنظُرُوا إلىٰ عَبدِي، فقد تَخَلّىٰ بي في جَــوفِ اللَّــيلِ المُــظلِمِ والبـطّالونَ لاهُـونَ، والغافِلونَ نِيامٌ، اشهَدُوا أنّي قد غَفَرتُ لَهُ.[٤٠٨٤]

3655. **The Prophet (SAWA) said,** 'Be mindful for the performing of the night prayer, for verily it was the devoted practice of all righteous people before you, and verily the night vigil is a means of proximity to Allah and a prevention from sin.'[4116]

٣٦٥٥ . عنه ﷺ: علَيكُم بقيامِ اللَّيلِ؛ فإنّهُ دَأْبُ الصالِحينَ قَبلَكُم، وإنَّ قيامَ اللَّيلِ قُـربَةٌ إلى اللهِ، ومَنهاةٌ عنِ الإثمِ.[٤٠٨٥]

3656. **Imām ʿAlī (AS) said,** 'Standing to pray in the night is conducive to the health of the body, is a source of pleasure for the Lord, exposes one to [the descent of] divine mercy, and is adherence to the moral virtues of the prophets.'[4117]

٣٦٥٦ . الإمامُ عليٌّ عليه السلام: قيامُ اللَّيلِ مَصَحَّةٌ لِلبَدَنِ، ومَــــرضاةٌ لِـلـرَّبِّ عَـزَّ وجـلَّ، وتَـعَـرُّضٌ لِلرَّحمَةِ، وتَمَسُّكٌ بأخلاقِ النَّبِيِّينَ.[٤٠٨٦]

3657. **Imām ʿAlī (AS) said,** 'I have never left the night prayer since I heard the Prophet (SAWA) say that the night prayer is a light.' Ibn al-Kawwā' asked, 'Not even on the night of *al-Harīr*[4118]?' to which he replied, 'Not even on the night of *al-Harīr*.'[4119]

٣٦٥٧ . بحارالأنوارعن الإمامِ عليّ عليه السلام: ماتَرَكتُ صلاةَ اللَّيلِ منذُ سَمِعتُ قولَ النـبيِّ ﷺ: صـلاةُ اللَّيلِ نُورٌ. فقالَ ابنُ الكَوّاءِ: ولا ليـلةَ الهَـريرِ؟ قالَ: ولا ليلةَ الهَرِيرِ.[٤٠٨٧]

3658. **Imām al-Ṣādiq (AS) said,** 'A believer's dignity lies in his standing for the night prayer, and his honour lies in abstaining from [tarnishing] other people's good reputations.'[4120]

٣٦٥٨ . الإمامُ الصّادقُ عليه السلام: شَرَفُ المُؤمِنِ صلاتُهُ بالليلِ، وعِزُّ المؤمِنِ كَفُّهُ عن أعراضِ الناسِ.[٤٠٨٨]

3659. **Imām al-Ṣādiq (AS) said,** 'Do not leave the night prayer, for verily the one who is truly in loss is the one who has lost out on the night prayer.'[4121]

٣٦٥٩ . عنه عليه السلام: لا تَدَعْ قِيامَ اللَّيلِ، فإنَّ المَغبونَ مَن غُبِنَ قِيامَ اللَّيلِ.[٤٠٨٩]

3660. **Imām al-Ṣādiq (AS) said,** 'Every single good deed that the servant carries out has a reward mentioned for it in the Qur'an except for the night prayer, for verily Allah has not expressed its reward because of the great significance it holds with Him. Thus, He says, *"Their sides vacate their beds to supplicate their Lord in fear and hope…No one knows what has been kept hidden for them of comfort as a reward for what they used to do.*"'[4122 4123]

٣٦٦٠ . عنه ﷺ :مامِن عَمَلٍ حَسَنٍ يَعمَلُهُ العَبدُ إلّا ولَهُ ثَوابٌ في القرآنِ إلّا صلاةَ اللَّيلِ ؛ فإنَّ اللهَ لَم يُبَيِّنْ ثَوابَها لِعَظيمِ خَطَرِها عِندَهُ، فقالَ: ﴿تَتَجافىٰ جُنُوبُهم عَنِ المَضاجِعِ يَدْعُونَ رَبَّهُمْ خَوْفًا وَطَمَعًا وَمِمَّا رَزَقْنَـٰهُمْ يُنفِقُونَ ❁ فلا تَعْلَمُ نَفسٌ ما أُخْفِيَ لَهُم مِن قُرَّةِ أعْيُنٍ جَزاءً بِما كانوا يَعمَلونَ﴾.[٤٠٩٠، ٤٠٩١]

3661. **Imām al-Ṣādiq (AS) said,** 'The night prayer brightens one's face, the night prayer fragrances one's breath, and the night prayer attracts sustenance.'[4124]

٣٦٦١ . عنه ﷺ :صلاةُ اللَّيلِ تُبَيِّضُ الوَجهَ، وصلاةُ اللَّيلِ تُطَيِّبُ الرِّيحَ، وصلاةُ اللَّيلِ تَجلِبُ الرِّزقَ.[٤٠٩٢]

1142. That Which Causes One to be Deprived of the Opportunity to Perform the Night Prayer

١١٤٢ ـ ما يُوجِبُ الحِرمانَ من صلاةِ الليلِ

3662. **Imām ʿAlī (AS)** was asked by a man, 'I have been deprived of [the opportunity to] pray in the night', to which Imām replied, 'You are one whose sins have imprisoned you.'[4125]

٣٦٦٢ . الإمامُ عليٌّ ﷺ ـ لِرَجُلٍ قالَ لَهُ: إنّي حُرِمتُ الصَّلاةَ باللَّيلِ ـ: أنتَ رَجُلٌ قد قَيَّدَتكَ ذُنوبُكَ.[٤٠٩٣]

3663. **Imām al-Ṣādiq (AS) said,** 'Verily a man tells a lie and he is deprived of the nigh prayer as a result.'[4126]

٣٦٦٣ . الإمامُ الصّادقُ ﷺ : إنّ الرجُلَ لَيَكذِبُ الكِذبَةَ فيُحرَمُ بها صلاةَ اللَّيلِ.[٤٠٩٤]

1143. The Recompense of One Who Intends to Perform the Night Prayer, but Stays Asleep

١١٤٣ ـ أجرُ مَن نَوىٰ صَلاةَ اللَّيلِ فَيَنامُ عنها

3664. **The Prophet (SAWA) said,** 'Every single servant who makes up his mind to wake up at a

٣٦٦٤ . رسولُ اللهِ ﷺ : ما مِن عَبدٍ يُحَدِّثُ نفسَهُ

particular time in the night [to pray] but stays asleep, his sleep is considered charity that Allah accepts on his behalf, and the same reward for that which he intended is written down for him.'[4127]

بقيام ساعةٍ مِنَ اللَّيلِ فَيَنامُ عنها إلّا كـانَ نَـومُهُ صَدَقَةً تَـصَدَّقَ اللهُ بـها عـلَيهِ وكُـتِبَ لَـهُ أجـرُ مانَوىٰ.٤٠٩٥

239

THE PRAYER (3)

الصَّلاةُ (٣)

The Friday Prayer

صَلاةُ الجُمُعَةِ

1144. The Importance of Friday Prayer

١١٤٤ ـ «أهَمِّيَّةُ صَلاةِ الجُمُعَةِ»

"O you who have faith! When the call is made for prayer on Friday, hurry toward the remembrance of Allah, and leave all business. That is better for you, should you know."[4128]

﴿يا أيُّها الَّذِينَ آمَنُوا إذا نُودِيَ لِلصَّلاةِ مِنْ يَوْمِ الجُمُعَةِ فَاسْعَوا إلىٰ ذِكْرِ اللهِ وَذَرُوا البَيْعَ ذٰلِكُم خَيْرٌ لَكُمْ إنْ كُنْتُمْ تَعْلَمُونَ﴾.٤٠٩٦

(See also: Qur'an 63:9)

(أنظر) المنافقون: ٩.

3665. **The Prophet (SAWA) said,** 'Whoever misses three Friday prayers, being indifferent to them, Allah seals his heart.'[4129]

٣٦٦٥. رسولُ اللهِ ﷺ: مَن تَرَكَ ثلاثَ جُمَعٍ تَهاوُناً بها طَبَعَ اللهُ علىٰ قَلبِهِ.٤٠٩٧

3666. **The Prophet (SAWA) said,** 'The Friday prayer is the pilgrimage (*ḥajj*) of the poor.'[4130]

٣٦٦٦. عنه ﷺ: الجُمُعَةُ حَجُّ المَساكِينِ.٤٠٩٨

3667. **The Prophet (SAWA) said,** 'Whoever attends the Friday prayer faithfully and contentedly is able to resume his work [immediately thereafter].'[4131]

٣٦٦٧. عنه ﷺ: مَن أتَى الجُمُعَةَ إيماناً واحتِساباً استَأنَفَ العَمَلَ.٤٠٩٩

3668. **Imām al-Bāqir (AS) said,** 'The Friday prayer is an obligation, and congregating for it in the presence of an *Imām*[4132] is an obligation, so if someone misses three Friday prayers without an excuse, it is as if he has abandoned the performance

٣٦٦٨. الإمامُ الباقرُ ﷺ: صلاةُ الجُمُعَةِ فَرِيضَةٌ، والاجتِماعُ إلَيها فَرِيضَةٌ مع الإمامِ، فـإن تَـرَكَ رَجُلٌ مِـن غَـيرِ عِـلَّةٍ ثـلاثَ جُـمَعٍ فَـقَد تَـرَكَ ثلاثَ فَرائضَ، ولا يَـدَعُ ثـلاثَ فَـرائـضَ مِـن

غَيرِ عِلَّةٍ إلّا مُنافِقٌ.٤١٠٠

of three obligations, and none but a hypocrite abandons three obligations without an excuse.'[4133]

(أنظر) الجمعة: باب ٣٥١.

(See also: FRIDAY: section 351)

١١٤٥ ـ أدبُ سَماعِ الخُطبَةِ

1145. Etiquette of Listening to the Sermon

٣٦٦٩. الإمامُ عليٌّ عليه السلام: لاكلامَ والإمامُ يَخطُبُ ولا التِفاتَ إلّا كما يَحِلُّ في الصَّلاةِ.٤١٠١

3669. **Imām ʿAlī (AS) said,** 'There must be no talking while the leader of the prayer is giving the sermon, nor looking around except to the extent permissible in the prayer.'[4134]

(أنظر) عنوان ١٢٧ «الخطبة».

(See also: THE SERMON 127)

240

الصَّلاة (٤)

PRAYER (4)

الصَّلاةُ عَلَى النَّبِيِّ وآلِهِ

INVOKING BLESSINGS ON THE PROPHET AND HIS HOUSEHOLD (SAWA)

١١٤٦ ـ فَضلُ الصَّلاةِ عَلَى النَّبِيِّ وآله

1146. The Virtue of Invoking Blessings on the Prophet (SAWA) and his Progeny

﴿إنَّ ٱللهَ وَمَلائِكَتَهُ يُصَلُّونَ عَلَى ٱلنَّبِيِّ يا أَيُّهَا ٱلَّذِينَ آمَنُوا صَلُّوا عَلَيهِ وَسَلِّمُوا تَسْلِيماً﴾.٤١٠٢

"Indeed Allah and His angels bless the Prophet; O you who have faith! Invoke blessings on him and invoke Peace upon him in a worthy manner."[4135]

٣٦٧٠. رسولُ اللهِ صلى الله عليه وآله: حَيثُما كُنتُم فَصَلُّوا عَلَيَّ، فإنَّ صلاتَكُم تَبلُغُني.٤١٠٣

3670. **The Prophet (SAWA) said,** 'Wherever you may be, invoke blessings on me for verily your blessing reaches me.'[4136]

٣٦٧١. عنه صلى الله عليه وآله: الصَّلاةُ عَلَيَّ نورٌ على الصِّراطِ.٤١٠٤

3671. **The Prophet (SAWA) said,** 'The invocation of blessings on me is a light on the *Ṣirāṭ*.'[4137]

٣٦٧٢. عنه صلى الله عليه وآله: مَن صَلّى عَلَيَّ في كتابٍ لَم تَزَلِ

3672. **The Prophet (SAWA) said,** 'Whoever invokes blessings on me, writing it on paper, the angels continue to seek forgiveness on his behalf as long as my name remains written on the paper.’[4138]

الملائكةُ تَستَغفِرُ لَهُ مادامَ اسمي في ذلكَ الكتابِ.٤١٠٥

3673. **The Prophet (SAWA) said,** ‘Verily the most miserly of people is he who hears my name mentioned and does not invoke blessings on me.’[4139]

٣٦٧٣. عنه ﷺ: إنَّ أبخَلَ الناسِ مَن ذُكِرتُ عِندَهُ ولَم يُصَلِّ عَلَيَّ.٤١٠٦

3674. **Imām ʿAlī (AS) said,** ‘Every supplication remains veiled [unanswered] until blessings are invoked on the Prophet (SAWA).’[4140]

٣٦٧٤. الإمامُ عليٌّ ؑ: كُلُّ دُعاءٍ مَحجُوبٌ حتّىٰ يُصَلّىٰ على النبيِّ ﷺ.٤١٠٧

3675. **Imām al-Bāqir or Imām al-Ṣādiq (AS) said,** ‘The heaviest thing to be placed on the scales on the Day of Resurrection is the invocation of blessings on Muḥammad and his household (AS).’[4141]

٣٦٧٥. الإمامُ الباقرُ أو الإمامُ الصّادقُ ؑ: أثقَلُ ما يُوضَعُ في المِيزانِ يَومَ القِيامَةِ الصَّلاةُ علىٰ محمّدٍ وعَلىٰ أهلِ بَيتِهِ.٤١٠٨

1147. The Method of Invoking Blessings on the Prophet (SAWA) and his Progeny

١١٤٧ ـ كَيفِيَّةُ الصَّلاةِ عَلَى النَّبِيِّ وآله

3676. **The Prophet (SAWA)** when he was asked how to send blessings on him, replied, ‘Say: O Allah, bless Muḥammad and the family of Muḥammad, just as you blessed Abraham and the family of Abraham, verily you are Praiseworthy and Glorious. And send Your benediction on Muḥammad and on the family of Muḥammad, just as you sent Your benediction on Abraham and on the family of Abraham, verily you are Praiseworthy and Glorious.’[4142]

٣٦٧٦. رسولُ اللهِ ﷺ ـ لَمّا سُئلَ عن كَيفيَّةِ الصَّلاةِ عليهِ ـ: قُولوا: اللّهُمَّ صَلِّ علىٰ محمّدٍ وعلىٰ آلِ محمّدٍ، كما صَلَّيتَ علىٰ إبراهيمَ وعلىٰ آلِ إبراهيمَ إنّكَ حَميدٌ مَجيدٌ، وبارِكْ علىٰ محمدٍ وعلىٰ آلِ محمّدٍ، كَما بارَكتَ علىٰ إبراهيمَ وعلىٰ آلِ إبراهيمَ إنّكَ حَميدٌ مَجيدٌ.٤١٠٩

241

SILENCE

الصَّمتُ

1148. The Virtue of Silence

١١٤٨ ـ فَضْلُ الصَّمتِ

3677. **The Prophet (SAWA) said** to Abū Dharr, exhorting him, ‘There are four things that none

٣٦٧٧. رسولُ اللهِ ﷺ ـ لأبي ذَرٍّ وهو يَعِظُهُ ـ: أربَعٌ لا يُصيبُهُنَّ إلّا مؤمنٌ: الصَّمتُ وهُو أوّلُ

can accomplish apart from the believer: silence, and this is the first stage of worship…’[4143]

العِبادَةِ....٤١١٠

3678. **Imām ʿAlī (AS) said,** ‘Silence is the sign of nobility and the fruit of the intellect.’[4144]

٣٦٧٨. الإمامُ عليٌّ ﵇: الصَّمتُ آيَةُ النُّبلِ وثَمَرَةُ العَقلِ.٤١١١

3679. **Imām ʿAlī (AS) said,** describing the believer, ‘Great is his silence and occupied is his time.’[4145]

٣٦٧٩. عنه ﵇ ـ في صِفةِ المؤمنِ ـ: كثيرٌ صَمتُهُ، مَشغولٌ وَقتُهُ.٤١١٢

1149. The Fruits of Silence

١١٤٩ ـ ثَمَراتُ الصَّمتِ

3680. **The Prophet (SAWA) said,** ‘You must maintain silence for long periods of time for verily it drives Satan away and helps you in matters of your faith.’[4146]

٣٦٨٠. رسولُ اللهِ ﷺ: علَيكَ بطُولِ الصَّمتِ فإنّهُ مَطرَدَةٌ للشَّيطانِ، وعَونٌ لكَ على أمرِ دِينِكَ.٤١١٣

3681. **Imām ʿAlī (AS) said,** ‘Adhere to silence for the very least of its benefits is health.’[4147]

٣٦٨١. الإمامُ عليٌّ ﵇: الزَمِ الصَّمتَ فَأدنى نَفعِهِ السَّلامَةُ.٤١١٤

3682. 3687. **Imām ʿAlī (AS) said,** ‘Silence is the garden of thought.’[4148]

٣٦٨٢. عنه ﵇: الصَّمتُ رَوضَةُ الفِكرِ.٤١١٥

3683. **Imām al-Ḥasan (AS) said,** ‘Indeed the silent one has great earnestness.’[4149]

٣٦٨٣. الإمامُ الحسنُ ﵇: قد أكثَرَ مِن الهَيبَةِ الصّامِتُ.٤١١٦

3684. **Imām al-Ḥasan (AS) said,** ‘How excellent an aid silence is in numerous situations, even if one be an expressive person.’[4150]

٣٦٨٤. عنه ﵇: نِعمَ العَونُ الصَّمتُ في مَواطِنَ كثيرَةٍ وإن كُنتَ فَصيحاً.٤١١٧

3685. **Imām al-Riḍā (AS) said,** ‘Verily silence is one of the doors to wisdom; verily silence secures love; verily it leads one to all good.’[4151]

٣٦٨٥. الإمامُ الرِّضا ﵇: إنَّ الصَّمتَ بابٌ مِن أبوابِ الحِكمَةِ، إنَّ الصَّمتَ يُكسِبُ المَحَبَّةَ إنّهُ دَليلٌ على كُلِّ خَيرٍ.٤١١٨

1150. Blameworthy Silence

١١٥٠ ـ الصَّمتُ المَذمومُ

3686. **Imām ʿAlī (AS) said,** ‘There is no good in keeping silent about a matter of wisdom, just as there is no good in speaking about something one is ignorant of.’[4152]

٣٦٨٦. الإمامُ عليٌّ ﵇: لا خَيرَ في الصَّمتِ عَنِ الحُكمِ، كما أنّهُ لا خَيرَ في القَولِ بالجَهلِ.٤١١٩

3687. **Imām ʿAlī (AS) said** about the distinguishing characteristics of the pious one, 'Verily when he is silent, his own silence does not distress him, and when he laughs he does not do so loudly.'[4153]

٣٦٨٧. عنه عليه السلام ـ في علامةِ المُتَّقي ـ: إن صَمَتَ لَم يَغُمَّهُ، وإن ضَحِكَ لَم يَعلُ صَوتُهُ.[٤١٢٠]

(See also: SPEAKING 348)

(أنظر) عنوان ٣٤٨ «الكلام».

242

AFFLICTION

المُصيبَةُ

1151. The Reward for (Enduring an) Affliction

١١٥١ـ أجرُ المَصائبِ

3688. **Imām al-Ḥasan (AS) said,** 'Afflictions are the keys to reward.'[4154]

٣٦٨٨. الإمامُ الحسنُ عليه السلام: المَصائبُ مَفاتيحُ الأجرِ.[٤١٢١]

1152. The Worst of Afflictions

١١٥٢ـ أشَدُّ المَصائبِ

3689. **Imām ʿAlī (AS)** was once asked what the worst affliction was, to which he replied, 'To be afflicted with a blow to one's faith.'[4155]

٣٦٨٩. الإمامُ عليٌّ عليه السلام ـ لَمّا سُئلَ عن أشَدِّ المَصائبِ ـ: المُصيبَةُ بِالدِّينِ.[٤١٢٢]

3690. **Imām ʿAlī (AS) said,** 'The greatest affliction and source of wretchedness is infatuation with this world.'[4156]

٣٦٩٠. عنه عليه السلام: أعظَمُ المَصائبِ والشَّقاءِ الوَلَهُ بِالدُّنيا.[٤١٢٣]

3691. **Imām ʿAlī (AS) said,** 'The greatest affliction is ignorance.'[4157]

٣٦٩١. عنه عليه السلام: أعظَمُ المَصائبِ الجَهلُ.[٤١٢٤]

3692. **Imām al-Ṣādiq (AS) said** to a man who was experiencing intense grief at the loss of his son, 'You are grieving at the minor affliction and are heedless of the major affliction! If only you prepared yourself for the place that your son has passed away to, your grief would not be so intense, for your affliction at having neglected preparation for it [i.e. the Hereafter] is much greater than the loss of your son.'[4158]

٣٦٩٢. الإمامُ الصّادقُ عليه السلام ـ لِرَجُلٍ قد اشتَدَّ جَزَعُهُ على وَلَدِهِ ـ: يا هذا جَزِعتَ لِلمُصيبَةِ الصُّغرى، وغَفَلتَ عنِ المُصيبَةِ الكُبرى! ولو كنتَ لِما صارَ إليه وَلَدُكَ مُستَعِدّاً لَما اشتَدَّ علَيه جَزَعُكَ، فَمُصابُكَ بتَركِكَ الاستِعدادَ لَهُ أعظَمُ مِن مُصابِكَ بوَلَدِكَ.[٤١٢٥]

1153. To Say "*Indeed we belong to Allah and to Him do we indeed return*" when Struck with an Affliction

١١٥٣ـالاستِرجاعُ[٤١٢٦] عِندَ المُصيبَةِ

"We will surely test you with a measure of fear and hunger and a loss of wealth, lives, and crops; and give good news to the patient – those who, when an affliction visits them, say, 'Indeed we belong to Allah, and to Him do we indeed return.'"[4159]

﴿وَلَنَبْلُوَنَّكُمْ بِشَيْءٍ مِّنَ الخَوْفِ وَالْجُوعِ وَنَقْصٍ مِّنَ الْأَمْوَالِ وَالْأَنْفُسِ وَالثَّمَرَاتِ وَبَشِّرِ الصَّابِرِينَ * الَّذِينَ إِذا أَصابَتْهُمْ مُصِيْبَةٌ قالُوا إِنّا لِلّهِ وَإِنّا إِلَيهِ راجِعُونَ﴾.[٤١٢٧]

3693. **Imām al-Ṣādiq (AS) said:** He who is inspired to utter the words, *'Indeed we belong to Allah, and to Him do we indeed return'* during an affliction, his entrance into Paradise is made obligatory.'[4160]

٣٦٩٣ . الإمامُ الصّادقُ عليه السلام : مَن أُلهِمَ الاستِرجاعَ عندَ المُصيبَةِ وَجَبَت لَهُ الجَنَّةُ.[٤١٢٨]

1154. The Etiquette of Dealing with an Affliction

١١٥٤ـأدَبُ المُصابِ

3694. **The Prophet (SAWA) said,** 'Wailing is an act from the pre-Islamic age of ignorance.'[4161]

٣٦٩٤ . رسولُ اللهِ صلى الله عليه وآله :النِّياحَةُ عملُ الجاهِلِيَّةِ.[٤١٢٩]

3695. **The Prophet (SAWA) said,** 'Among the hidden treasures of goodness are: concealing one's afflictions, one's illnesses and one's charity [from others].'[4162]

٣٦٩٥ . عنه صلى الله عليه وآله :مِن كُنُوزِ البِرِّ: كِتمانُ المَصائبِ والأمراضِ والصَّدَقةِ.[٤١٣٠]

3696. **'Ā'isha narrated,** 'When Ibrāhīm [the Prophet's son] passed away, the Prophet (SAWA) cried such that tears rolled onto his beard, so people said to him, 'O Prophet of Allah, you dissuade people from crying and here you are now crying?!' to which he replied, 'This is not crying, it is compassion, for he who does not have compassion [for others] will not be treated with compassion [by Allah].'[4163]

٣٦٩٦ . الأمالي للطوسي عن عائشة: لَمّا ماتَ إبراهيمُ بَكَى النبيُّ صلى الله عليه وآله حتّى جَرَت دُموعُهُ علىٰ لِحيَتِهِ، فقيلَ لَهُ: يا رسولَ اللهِ، تَنهىٰ عنِ البُكاءِ وأنتَ تَبكي؟! فقالَ: ليسَ هذا بُكاءً، وإنّما هذهِ رَحمَةٌ، ومَن لا يَرحَمْ لا يُرحَمْ.[٤١٣١]

3697. **Abū Hurayra narrated,** 'A man from the family of the Prophet (SAWA) had passed away and the women were gathered around crying for him when 'Umar stood up and prohibited them

٣٦٩٧ . سنن النسائي عن أبي هريرة: ماتَ مَيِّتٌ مِن آلِ رسولِ اللهِ صلى الله عليه وآله فاجتَمَعَ النِّساءُ يَبكِينَ علَيهِ

from doing so, and told them to go away from there. The Prophet (SAWA) then said, 'Leave them O 'Umar, for verily the eye feels teary [at the moment], the heart is afflicted and the pain of the incident is still fresh.'[4164]

قامَ عمرُ يَنهاهُنَّ ويَطرُدُهُنَّ، فقالَ رسولُ اللهِ ﷺ: دَعهُنَّ يا عمرُ، فإنّ العَينَ دامِعةٌ والقَلبَ مُصابٌ والعَهدَ قريبٌ.[٤١٣٢]

3698. **Imām 'Alī (AS) narrated** on the authority of the Prophet (SAWA), 'Two voices are cursed and despised by Allah: howling when struck by an affliction, and singing when blessed with a bounty.'[4165]

٣٦٩٨. الإمامُ عليٌّ ﷺ عن رسولِ اللهِ ﷺ: صَوتانِ مَلعونانِ يُبغِضُهُما اللهُ: إعوالٌ عندَ مُصيبَةٍ، وصَوتٌ عندَ نِعمَةٍ؛ يَعني النَّوحَ والغِناءَ.[٤١٣٣]

(See also: GRIEF 64)

(أنظر) عنوان ٦٤ «الجزع».

1155. Factors that Ease Afflictions

١١٥٥ - ما يُهَوِّنُ المَصائِبَ

3699. **The Prophet (SAWA) said,** 'Afflictions are easy for one who is abstemious in this world.'[4166]

٣٦٩٩. رسولُ اللهِ ﷺ: مَن زَهِدَ في الدنيا هانَت علَيهِ المُصيباتُ.[٤١٣٤]

3700. **The Prophet (SAWA) said,** 'He who finds an affliction too great to bear should think about [the greatness of his affliction resulting from] my passing away from this world, and his own affliction will become easier to bear.'[4167]

٣٧٠٠. عنه ﷺ: مَن عَظُمَت عِندَهُ مُصيبَةٌ فَليَذكُر مُصيبَتَهُ بي؛ فإنّها سَتَهُونُ علَيهِ.[٤١٣٥]

3701. **Imām 'Alī (AS) said,** 'Increase your remembrance of death, the day that you will rise from your graves, and your standing before Allah, Mighty and Exalted, and your afflictions will become easier to bear.'[4168]

٣٧٠١. الإمامُ عليٌّ ﷺ: أكثِروا ذِكرَ المَوتِ، ويومَ خُروجِكُم مِنَ القُبورِ، وقِيامِكُم بَينَ يَدَيِ اللهِ عزّوجلّ، تَهُونُ علَيكُمُ المَصائبُ.[٤١٣٦]

3702. **Imām al-Ṣadiq (AS)** used to say the following when faced with an affliction, 'All praise is due to Allah, Who did not afflict me in my faith, and all praise is due to Allah Who, if He had willed for my affliction to be greater than it is could have made it so, and all praise is due to Allah for the command that He willed to be and it is.'[4169]

٣٧٠٢. الإمامُ الصّادقُ ﷺ - إنّهُ كانَ يقولُ عندَ المُصيبَةِ -: الحَمدُ للهِ الذي لَم يَجعَلْ مُصِيبَتي في دِيني، والحَمدُ للهِ الذي لو شاءَ أن تكونَ مُصيبَتي أعظَمَ مِمّا كانت (كانَت)، والحَمدُ للهِ على الأمرِ الذي شاءَ أن يكونَ وكانَ.[٤١٣٧]

3703. **Imām al-Ṣādiq (AS) said,** 'Verily when someone dies, Allah sends an angel to the most grieved member of his family, who strokes his

٣٧٠٣. عنه ﷺ: إنّ المَيِّتَ إذا ماتَ بَعَثَ اللهُ مَلَكاً

heart and makes him forget the agony of grief, and if it were not for this, the world would never again thrive.'[4170]

إلىٰ أوجَعِ أهلِهِ فَمَسَحَ علىٰ قَلبِهِ فَأنساهُ لَـوعَةَ الحُزنِ، ولولا ذلكَ لَم تَعمُرِ الدنيا.[٤١٣٨]

1156. Reprehension of Gloating at Another's Affliction

١١٥٦ـ ذَمُّ الشَّماتَةِ بِالمُصابِ

3704. **Imām al-Ṣādiq (AS) said,** 'Whoever gloats over an affliction that has befallen his fellow brother does not leave this world until he is tried similarly.'[4171]

٣٧٠٤. الإمامُ الصّادقُ ﷺ: مَن شَمِتَ بمُصيبَةٍ نَزَلَت بأخيهِ لَم يَخرُجْ مِن الدنيا حتّىٰ يُفتَتَنَ.[٤١٣٩]

(See also: CONDOLENCE 276)

(أنظر) عنوان ٢٧٦ «التعزية».

243

THE VOICE

الصَّوت ٢٤٣

1157. Praising the Lowering of one's Voice and Denouncing the Raising of it

١١٥٧ـ مَدحُ خَفضِ الصَّوتِ وَذَمُّ رَفعِه

"Be modest in your bearing, and lower your voice. Indeed the ungainliest of voices is the donkey's voice."[4172]

﴿وَاقْصِدْ فِي مَشْيِكَ وَاغْضُضْ مِنْ صَوْتِكَ إِنَّ أَنْكَرَ الْأَصْوَاتِ لَصَوْتُ الْحَمِيرِ﴾.[٤١٤٠]

3705. **The Prophet (SAWA) said,** 'Verily Allah loves the low voice and despises the raised voice.'[4173]

٣٧٠٥. رسولُ اللهِ ﷺ: إنّ اللهَ يُحِبُّ الصَّوتَ الخَفيضَ، ويُبغِضُ الصَّوتَ الرَّفيعَ.[٤١٤١]

3706. **The Prophet (SAWA) said** in his advice to Abū Dharr, 'O Abū Dharr, lower your voice at funerals, during a battle, and when the Qur'an is being recited.'[4174]

٣٧٠٦. عنه ﷺ ـ في وصيّتِهِ لأبي ذَرٍّ ـ: يا أبا ذَرٍّ، اخفِضْ صَوتَكَ عِندَ الجَنائزِ، وعِندَ القِتالِ، وعِندَ القرآنِ.[٤١٤٢]

3707. **Imām 'Alī (AS) said,** 'Three actions are considered to be gallant: lowering one's gaze, lowering one's voice and walking with deliberation.'[4175]

٣٧٠٧. الإمامُ عليٌّ ﷺ: ثلاثٌ فيهِنَّ المُروءَةُ: غَضُّ الطَّرفِ، وغَضُّ الصَّوتِ، ومَشيُ القَصدِ.[٤١٤٣]

3708. **Imām 'Alī (AS) said,** 'Lowering one's voice, lowering one's gaze, and walking with deliberation

٣٧٠٨. عنه ﷺ: خَفضُ الصَّوتِ، وغَضُّ البَصَرِ،

are among the marks of one's faith and the integrity of one's devoutness.'[4176]

ومَشيُ القَصدِ، مِن أمارَةِ الإيمانِ وحُسنِ التَّدَيُّنِ.[٤١٤٤]

244

FASTING

الصَّوم

1158. The Virtue of Fasting

١١٥٨ ـ فَضلُ الصِّيامِ

"O you who have faith! Prescribed for you is fasting as it was prescribed for those who were before you, so that you may be Godwary."[4177]

﴿يا أيُّها الَّذِينَ آمَنُوا كُتِبَ عَلَيكُمُ الصِّيامُ كَما كُتِبَ عَلَى الَّذِينَ مِنْ قَبْلِكُمْ لَعَلَّكُمْ تَتَّقُونَ﴾.[٤١٤٥]

3709. **The Prophet (SAWA) said,** 'Fasting is incumbent upon you, for verily it severs the roots [of desires] and removes wildness.'[4178]

٣٧٠٩ . رسولُ اللهِ ﷺ : علَيكُم بِالصَّومِ؛ فإنّهُ مَحسَمَةٌ للعُرُوقِ ومَذهَبَةٌ للأشَرِ.[٤١٤٦]

3710. **The Prophet (SAWA) said,** 'Everything has a *zakāt*, and the *zakāt* of the bodies is to fast.'[4179]

٣٧١٠ . عنه ﷺ : لِكُلِّ شَيءٍ زكاةٌ وزكاةُ الأبدانِ الصِّيامُ.[٤١٤٧]

3711. **The Prophet (SAWA) said,** 'Fast and you will be healthy.'[4180]

٣٧١١ . عنه ﷺ : صُومُوا تَصِحُّوا.[٤١٤٨]

3712. **The Prophet (SAWA) said,** 'The fasting person is in constant worship of Allah, even when he is sleeping in his bed, as long as he does not backbite a fellow Muslim.'[4181]

٣٧١٢ . عنه ﷺ : الصائمُ في عِبادَةِ اللهِ وإن كانَ نائماً علىٰ فِراشِهِ، ما لَم يَغتَبْ مُسلِماً.[٤١٤٩]

3713. **The Prophet (SAWA) said,** 'No sooner does a fasting person come upon a group of people eating than his limbs glorify Allah on his behalf, the angels invoke blessings on him, and this invocation of theirs is counted as seeking forgiveness on his behalf.'[4182]

٣٧١٣ . عنه ﷺ : ما مِن صائمٍ يَحضُرُ قَوماً يَطعَمُونَ إلّا سَبَّحَت أعضاؤهُ، وكانَت صَلاةُ الملائكةِ علَيهِ، وكانَت صَلاتُهُم استِغفاراً.[٤١٥٠]

3714. **The Prophet (SAWA) said,** 'Fasting acts as a shield from the Fire.'[4183]

٣٧١٤ . عنه ﷺ : الصَّومُ جُنَّةٌ مِن النارِ.[٤١٥١]

3715. **Fāṭima al-Zahrā' (AS) said,** 'Allah made fasting obligatory in order to reinforce sincere devotion [to Him].'[4184]

٣٧١٥ . فاطمةُ الزَّهراءُ عليها السلام : فَرَضَ اللهُ الصِّيامَ تَثبِيتاً لِلإخلاصِ.[٤١٥٢]

3716. **Imām al-Bāqir (AS) said,** 'The fast and the obligatory pilgrimage (*ḥajj*) pacify the heart.'[4185]

٣٧١٦ . الإمامُ الباقرُ ؑ : الصِّيامُ والحَجُّ تَسكِينُ القُلوبِ.٤١٥٣

3717. **Imām al-Ṣādiq (AS) said,** 'Verily Allah, Blessed and most High, says, 'The fast is solely for Me and I reward for it.'[4186]

٣٧١٧ . الإمامُ الصّادقُ ؑ : إنَّ اللهَ تبارَكَ وتعالىٰ يقولُ: الصَّومُ لِي وأنا أجزِي علَيهِ.٤١٥٤

3718. **Imām al-Ṣādiq (AS) said,** 'A fasting person's sleep is worship, his silence is glorification of Allah, his good deeds are accepted, and his supplication is answered.'[4187]

٣٧١٨ . عنه ؑ : نَومُ الصائمِ عِبادَةٌ، وصَمتُهُ تَسبيحٌ، وعَمَلُهُ مُتَقَبَّلٌ، ودُعاؤهُ مُستَجابٌ.٤١٥٥

3719. **Imām al-Ṣādiq (AS) said,** 'A fasting person has two sources of joy: his joy when he opens his fast and his joy at meeting his Lord.'[4188]

٣٧١٩ . عنه ؑ : لِلصائمِ فَرحَتانِ: فَرحَةٌ عندَ إفطارِهِ، وفَرحَةٌ عندَ لِقاءِ رَبِّهِ.٤١٥٦

3720. **Imām al-Ṣādiq (AS) said,** 'Whoever offers a fasting person something with which to open his fast obtains the same reward as him.'[4189]

٣٧٢٠ . عنه ؑ : مَن فَطَّرَ صائماً فلَهُ مِثلُ أجرِهِ.٤١٥٧

3721. **Imām al-ʿAskarī (AS)** was once asked the reasoning behind the obligation of fasting, to which he replied, 'That the rich may experience the pain of hunger and bestow his generosity thereby upon the poor.'[4190]

٣٧٢١ . الإمامُ العسكريُّ ؑ ـ لمّا سُئلَ عن عِلَّةِ وُجوبِ الصَّومِ ـ: لِيَجِدَ الغَنِيُّ مَسَّ الجُوعِ؛ فَيَمُنَّ على الفَقيرِ.٤١٥٨

1159. Enjoinment of Fasting out of One's Own Accord

١١٥٩ ـ الحَثُّ عَلَى الصِّيامِ تَطَوُّعاً

3722. **The Prophet (SAWA) said,** 'He who fasts a single day of his own accord is rewarded to such an extent that even if he was to be given the whole world's worth of gold for it, the reward he deserves would not be fulfilled until the Day of Resurrection.'[4191]

٣٧٢٢ . رسولُ اللهِ ﷺ : مَن صامَ يَوماً تَطَوُّعاً فلو اُعطِيَ مِلءَ الأرضِ ذَهَباً ماوَفّىٰ أجرَهُ دُونَ يَومِ الحِسابِ.٤١٥٩

3723. **The Prophet (SAWA) said,** 'He who fasts a single day of his own accord, wishing to procure the reward of Allah, [Allah makes] his forgiveness mandatory.'[4192]

٣٧٢٣ . عنه ﷺ : مَن صامَ يَوماً تَطَوُّعاً ابتِغاءَ ثَوابِ اللهِ وَجَبَت لَهُ المَغفِرَةُ.٤١٦٠

3724. **The Prophet (SAWA) said,** 'Whoever [voluntarily] fasts three days every month is considered as having fasted his whole life, for verily Allah, Mighty and Exalted, says, *"Whoever brings virtue shall receive ten times its like."*'[4193 4194]

٣٧٢٤. عنه ﷺ: مَن صامَ ثلاثةَ أيّامٍ مِن كُلِّ شَهرٍ كانَ كَمَن صامَ الدَّهرَ كلّه؛ لأنَّ اللهَ عَزَّ وجلَّ يقولُ: ﴿مَنْ جاءَ بالحَسَنَةِ فلَهُ عَشْرُ أمْثالِها﴾ ٤١٦١. ٤١٦٢

3725. **Imām al-Ṣādiq (AS) said,** 'Verily when a man fasts a single day of his own accord, desiring thereby what is with Allah, Mighty and Exalted, Allah gives him entrance into Paradise because of it.'[4195]

٣٧٢٥. الإمامُ الصّادقُ عليه السلام: إنَّ الرَّجُلَ لَيَصُومُ يَوماً تَطَوُّعاً يُرِيدُ بهِ ما عِندَ اللهِ عَزَّ وجلَّ فَيُدخِلُهُ اللهُ بِهِ الجَنَّةَ. ٤١٦٣

1160. The Etiquette of Fasting

١١٦٠ ـ أدَبُ الصَّومِ

3726. **The Prophet (SAWA) said,** 'Allah, Mighty and Exalted, says, 'He whose limbs do not fast by refraining from what I have prohibited, then there is no need for him to refrain from food and drink for My sake.'[4196]

٣٧٢٦. رسولُ اللهِ ﷺ: يقولُ اللهُ عَزَّ وجلَّ مَن لَم تَصُمْ جَوارِحُهُ عن مَحارِمِي فلا حاجَةَ لي في أن يَدَعَ طَعامَهُ وشَرابَهُ مِن أجلِي. ٤١٦٤

3727. **Imām 'Alī (AS) said,** 'Fasting is just as much keeping away from prohibited things as it is keeping away from food and drink.'[4197]

٣٧٢٧. الإمامُ عليٌّ عليه السلام: الصِّيامُ اجتِنابُ المَحارِمِ كما يَمتَنِعُ الرجُلُ مِن الطَّعامِ والشَّرابِ. ٤١٦٥

3728. **Fāṭima al-Zahrā' (AS) said,** 'What is the fasting person doing with his fast if he is not guarding his tongue, his hearing, his sight and his limbs [from sins]?!'[4198]

٣٧٢٨. فاطمةُ الزَّهراءُ عليها السلام: ما يَصنَعُ الصائمُ بِصِيامِهِ إذا لَم يَصُنْ لِسانَهُ وسَمعَهُ وبَصَرَهُ وجوارِحَهُ؟! ٤١٦٦

3729. **Muḥammad b. Muslim narrated,** 'Abū 'Abdillāh (AS) [i.e. Imām al-Ṣādiq] said, 'When you fast, your hearing must fast, along with your sight, your hair, your skin...' and he listed a number of other things, and said, 'The day that you fast must not be like a day that you do not fast.'[4199]

٣٧٢٩. الكافي عن محمّد بن مسلم: قالَ أبو عبدِ اللهِ عليه السلام: إذا صُمتَ فَلْيَصُمْ سَمعُكَ وبَصَرُكَ وشَعرُكَ وجِلدُكَ وعَدَّدَ أشياءَ غَيرَ هذا، وقالَ: لا يكونُ يومُ صَومِكَ كَيَومِ فِطرِكَ. ٤١٦٧

1161. The Virtue of Fasting in Hot and Cold Weather

١١٦١ ـ فَضلُ الصَّومِ فِي الحَرِّ والشِّتاءِ

3730. **The Prophet (SAWA) said,** 'Fasting in cold weather is an easy thing to do.'[4200]

٣٧٣٠. رسولُ اللهِ ﷺ: الصَّومُ في الشِّتاءِ الغَنيمَةُ البارِدَةُ. ٤١٦٨

3731. **Imām al-Ṣādiq (AS) said,** 'The best *jihād* is fasting in hot weather.'[4201]

٣٧٣١ . الإمامُ الصّادقُ ﷺ : أفضَلُ الجِهادِ الصَّومُ في الحَرِّ.٤١٦٩

3732. **Imām al-Ṣādiq (AS) said,** 'Winter is the springtime of a believer – its nights are long, so he can make use of them to stand in prayer, whereas its days are short and he can make use of them to fast.'[4202]

٣٧٣٢ . عنه ﷺ : الشِّتاءُ رَبيعُ المُؤمِنِ، يَطُولُ فيهِ لَيلُهُ فَيَستَعِينُ بِهِ على قِيامِهِ، ويَقصُرُ فيهِ نَهارُهُ فَيَستَعِينُ بِهِ على صِيامِهِ.٤١٧٠

245

LAUGHTER

الضَّحِكُ

1162. The Praising of Smiling

١١٦٢ ـ مَدحُ التَّبسُّمِ

3733. **Imām ʿAlī (AS) said,** 'The Prophet (SAWA)'s laughter was a smile.'[4203]

٣٧٣٣ . الإمامُ عليٌّ ﷺ : كانَ ضِحكُ النبيِّ ﷺ التبسُّمَ.٤١٧١

3734. **Imām al-Ṣādiq (AS) said,** 'The laughter of a believer is a smile.'[4204]

٣٧٣٤ . الإمامُ الصّادقُ ﷺ : ضِحكُ المؤمِنِ تَبَسُّمٌ.٤١٧٢

3735. **Imām al-Ṣādiq (AS) said,** 'He who smiles at his brother gets the reward of a good deed.'[4205]

٣٧٣٥ . عنه ﷺ : مَن تَبَسَّمَ في وَجهِ أخيهِ كانَت لَهُ حَسَنَةٌ.٤١٧٣

1163. The Reproaching of Laughing too Much and too Loud

١١٦٣ ـ ذَمُّ كَثرَةِ الضِّحكِ وَ القَهقَهَةِ

3736. *Irshād al-Qulūb*, 'In the tradition of the Prophet (SAWA)'s ascension, Allah said, 'How I wonder at the servant who laughs while he does not know whether I am pleased or displeased with him!'[4206]

٣٧٣٦ . إرشاد القلوب : في حديث المِعراج: عَجِبتُ مِن عَبدٍ لايَدري أنّي راضٍ عَنهُ أو ساخِطٌ علَيهِ وهُو يَضحَك!٤١٧٤

3737. **The Prophet (SAWA) said,** 'Beware of laughing too much for verily it kills the heart.'[4207]

٣٧٣٧ . رسولُ اللهِ ﷺ : إيّاكَ وكَثرَةَ الضِّحكِ؛ فإنّهُ يُمِيتُ القَلبَ.٤١٧٥

3738. **The Prophet (SAWA) said,** 'If you knew what I know, you would laugh but a little and you would cry much.'[4208]

٣٧٣٨ . عنه ﷺ : لو تَعلَمُونَ ما أعلَمُ لَضَحِكتُم قليلاً وَلَبَكَيتُم كثيراً.٤١٧٦

3739. **Imām ʿAlī (AS) said,** 'The earnestness of one who laughs too much deteriorates.'[4209]

٣٧٣٩. الإمامُ عليٌّ ﷺ: مَن كَثُرَ ضِحكُه ذَهَبَت هَيبَتُهُ.[٤١٧٧]

3740. **Imām al-Bāqir (AS) said,** 'When you laugh boisterously, say, 'O Allah do not despise me' when you have finished.'[4210]

٣٧٤٠. الإمامُ الباقرُ ﷺ: إذا قَهْقَهتَ فقُلْ حينَ تَفرُغُ: اللّهُمّ لا تَمقُتْني.[٤١٧٨]

3741. **Imām al-Ṣādiq (AS) said,** 'Loud boisterous laughter is from Satan.'[4211]

٣٧٤١. الإمامُ الصّادقُ ﷺ: القَهقَهَةُ مِنَ الشَّيطانِ.[٤١٧٩]

3742. **Imām al-ʿAskarī (AS) said,** 'Laughing without cause stems from ignorance.'[4212]

٣٧٤٢. الإمامُ العسكريُّ ﷺ: مِنَ الجَهلِ الضَّحكُ مِن غَيرِ عَجَبٍ.[٤١٨٠]

246

THE ABASED PEOPLE[4213]

المُستَضعَف

1164. The Abased People

١١٦٤ـ المُستَضعَفون

3743. **The Prophet (SAWA) said,** 'Shall I inform you of the worst of Allah's servants? It is the rude and arrogant person. And shall I inform you of the best of Allah's servants? It is the weak, abased person.'[4214]

٣٧٤٣. رسولُ اللهِ ﷺ: ألا أُخبِرُكُم بِشَرِّ عِبادِ اللهِ؟ الفَظُّ المُتَكبِّرُ، ألا أُخبِرُكم بِخَيرِ عِبادِ اللهِ؟ الضَّعيفُ المُستَضعَفُ.[٤١٨١]

3744. **The Prophet (SAWA) said,** 'Assist me in seeking out the weak people, for verily you are given sustenance and succour only because of the presence of the weak among you.'[4215]

٣٧٤٤. عنه ﷺ: أبغُوني فِي الضُّعَفاءِ، فإنّما تُرزَقُونَ وتُنصَرُونَ بِضُعَفائكُم.[٤١٨٢]

3745. **The Prophet (SAWA) said,** 'Verily Allah gives succour to this community only as a result of [the presence of] the weak among them, their supplication, their prayer and their sincerity.'[4216]

٣٧٤٥. عنه ﷺ: إنّما يَنصُرُ اللهُ هذهِ الأُمَّةَ بِضَعيفِها، بِدَعوَتِهِم وصَلاتِهِم وإخلاصِهِم.[٤١٨٣]

1165. The Return of Power to the Abased People

١١٦٥ـ دَولَةُ المُستَضعَفينَ

"And we desired to show favour to those who were abased in the land, and to make them Imāms, and to

﴿وَنُرِيدُ أَنْ نَمُنَّ عَلَى الَّذِينَ اسْتُضْعِفُوا فِي

make them the heirs, and to establish them in the land.'[4217]

الْأَرْضِ وَنَجْعَلَهُمْ أَئِمَّةً وَنَجْعَلَهُمُ الوارِثِينَ﴾.[٤١٨٤]

3746. **Imām ʿAlī (AS),** with regards to the Qur'anic verse: *"And we desired to show favour to those who were abased..."* said, 'This refers to the progeny of Muḥammad. Allah will send them their rightly guided Saviour [the Mahdī] after their struggle, and he will raise their status and abase their enemy.'[4218]

٣٧٤٦. الإمامُ عليٌّ عليه السلام ـ في قولِهِ تعالىٰ: ﴿ونُرِيدُ أنْ نَمُنَّ على الّذينَ اسْتُضْعِفُوا...﴾ ـ: هُم آلُ محمّدٍ، يَبعَثُ اللهُ مَهدِيَّهُم بَعد جَهدِهِم، فَيُعِزُّهُم ويُذِلُّ عَدُوَّهُم.[٤١٨٥]

1166. Spiritual Weakness

١١٦٦ ـ الإستِضعافُ المَعنَويُّ

"Except the ones who are deemed weak among men, women and children, who have neither access to any means nor are guided to any way. Maybe Allah will excuse them, for Allah is all-excusing, all-forgiving."[4219]

﴿إلّا المُسْتَضعَفِينَ مِنَ الرِّجالِ وَالنِّساءِ وَالوِلْدانِ لا يَسْتَطِيعُونَ حِيْلَةً وَلا يَهْتَدُونَ سَبِيْلاً * فَأُولٰئِكَ عَسَى اللهُ أنْ يَعْفُوَ عَنْهُم وَكانَ اللهُ عَفُوّاً غَفُوراً﴾.[٤١٨٦]

3747. **Imām ʿAlī (AS) said,** 'The term 'weak' cannot be applied to those whom the divine proof has reached, whose ears have heard it and whose hearts have heeded it.'[4220]

٣٧٤٧. الإمامُ عليٌّ عليه السلام: لا يَقَعُ اسمُ الاستِضعافِ علىٰ مَن بَلَغَتهُ الحُجَّةُ فَسَمِعَتها أُذُنُهُ ووَعاها قَلبُهُ.[٤١٨٧]

3748. **Imām al-Bāqir (AS),** with regards to the Qur'anic verse: *"Except the ones who are deemed weak..."*, said, 'This refers to one who is not capable of disbelieving that he may be considered a disbeliever, though neither has he been guided the path of faith that he may have faith. [It also refers to] children, and those people from among men and women who have intellects of children and who are therefore not accountable for their deeds.'[4221]

٣٧٤٨. الإمامُ الباقرُ عليه السلام ـ في قولِهِ تعالىٰ: ﴿إلّا المُستَضعَفِين...﴾ ـ: هُو الذي لا يَستَطيعُ الكُفرَ فَيَكفُرَ ولا يَهتَدِي سَبيلَ الإيمانِ فَيُؤمِنَ، والصِّبيانُ، ومَن كانَ مِن الرِّجالِ والنِّساءِ علىٰ مِثلِ عُقولِ الصِّبيانِ مَرفوعٌ عَنهُمُ القَلَمُ.[٤١٨٨]

3749. **Imām al-Kāẓim (AS) said,** 'The [spiritually] weak person is one whom the divine proof has not reached, and who would not be able to differentiate [even if it did reach him]. If he is able to differentiate [between truth and falsehood] therefore, then he is not considered weak.'[4222]

٣٧٤٩. الإمامُ الكاظمُ عليه السلام: الضَّعيفُ مَن لَم يُرفَعْ إلَيهِ حُجّةٌ، ولَم يَعرِفِ الاختِلافَ، فإذا عَرَفَ الاختِلافَ فليسَ بضَعيفٍ.[٤١٨٩]

247

STRAYING FROM THE STRAIGHT PATH

الضَّلالَة

1167. Factors that Cause One to Stray (from the Straight Path)

١١٦٧ـ موجِباتُ الضَّلالَةِ

"Whoever changes faith for unfaith certainly strays from the right way."[4223]

﴿وَمَنْ يَتَبَدَّلِ الكُفْرَ بِالْإِيْمانِ فَقَدْ ضَلَّ سَواءَ السَّبِيلِ﴾.[٤١٩٠]

"Whoever disbelieves in Allah and His angels, His Books and His apostles and the Last Day, has certainly strayed in far error."[4224]

﴿وَمَنْ يَكْفُرْ بِاللهِ وَمَلائِكَتِهِ وَكُتُبِهِ وَرُسُلِهِ وَاليَوْمِ الآخِرِ فَقَدْ ضَلَّ ضَلالاً بَعِيْداً﴾.[٤١٩١]

"And whoever disobeys Allah and His Apostle has certainly strayed in manifest error."[4225]

﴿وَمَنْ يَعْصِ اللهَ وَرَسُولَهُ فَقَدْ ضَلَّ ضَلالاً مُبِيْناً﴾.[٤١٩٢]

"Have you seen him who has taken his desire to be his god and whom Allah has led astray knowingly, and set a seal upon his hearing and his heart, and drawn a blind on his sight? So who will guide him after Allah? Will you not then take admonition?"[4226]

﴿أفَرَأيْتَ مَنِ اتَّخَذَ إلٰهَهُ هَواهُ وَأضَلَّهُ اللهُ عَلَى عِلمٍ وَخَتَمَ عَلَى سَمْعِهِ وَقَلْبِهِ وَجَعَلَ عَلَى بَصَرِهِ غِشاوَةً فَمَنْ يَهْدِيهِ مِنْ بَعْدِ اللهِ أفَلَا تَذَكَّرُونَ﴾.[٤١٩٣]

3750. **Imām ʿAlī (AS) said,** 'For every misguidance there is a cause, and behind every disloyal act is an obscurity.'[4227]

٣٧٥٠. الإمامُ عليٌّ عليه السلام: لِكُلِّ ضَلَّةٍ عِلَّةٌ، ولِكُلِّ ناكِثٍ شُبهَةٌ.[٤١٩٤]

3751. **Imām ʿAlī (AS) said,** 'Know that indeed the paths to religion are one, and its courses lead straight ahead. Whoever follows them attains the objective, and whoever stops, moving away from them, strays and ends up regretful.'[4228]

٣٧٥١. عنه عليه السلام: ألَا وإنّ شَرائعَ الدِّينِ واحِدَةٌ، وسُبُلَهُ قاصِدَةٌ، مَن أخَذَ بها لَحِقَ وغَنِمَ، ومَن وَقَفَ عَنها ضَلَّ ونَدِمَ.[٤١٩٥]

3752. **Imām ʿAlī (AS) said,** 'Look at the household of your Prophet and adhere to their direction...Do not overtake them, for then you will stray, nor lag behind them lest you fall into ruin.'[4229]

٣٧٥٢. عنه عليه السلام: اُنظُروا أهلَ بَيتِ نَبِيِّكُم فَالْزَمُوا سَمْتَهُم ... لا تَسبِقُوهُم فَتَضِلُّوا، ولا تَتأخَّرُوا عَنهُم فَتَهلِكُوا.[٤١٩٦]

3753. **Imām ʿAlī (AS) said,** 'He who seeks guidance from the wrong source goes astray.'[4230]

٣٧٥٣. عنه ؑ: مَن يَطلُبِ الهِدايَةَ مِن غَيرِ أهلِها يَضِلَّ.٤١٩٧

(See also: GUIDANCE: section 1796)

(أنظر) الهداية: باب ١٧٩٦.

1168. Those who Lead Others Astray

١١٦٨ ـ المُضِلّونَ

3754. **Imām ʿAlī (AS) said,** 'Verily the most evil of people in the sight of Allah is the tyrannical leader who himself has gone astray and through whom others go astray. He abolishes established practices and revives abandoned innovations.'[4231]

٣٧٥٤. الإمامُ عليٌّ ؑ: إنَّ شَرَّ الناسِ عندَ اللهِ إمامٌ جائرٌ ضَلَّ وضُلَّ بِهِ، فَأماتَ سُنَّةً مأخوذَةً (مَعلومَةً)، وأحيا بِدعَةً مَتروكَةً.٤١٩٨

3755. **Imām ʿAlī (AS) said,** 'Verily the most detested of all people in the sight of Allah are two: the man whom Allah has relegated to his own carnal self, so he has deviated from the straight path and is passionately fond of talking about innovations and misguiding others towards the wrong path. He tempts those who are charmed by him. He himself has strayed away from the guidance of his predecessors, and misleads those who follow him during his life as well as after his death. He carries the burden of others' sins and is entangled in his own misdeeds...'[4232]

٣٧٥٥. عنه ؑ: إنّ أبغَضَ الخَلائقِ إلى اللهِ رَجُلانِ: رَجُلٌ وَكَلَهُ اللهُ إلىٰ نَفسِهِ، فهُوَ جائرٌ عَن قَصدِ السَّبيلِ، مَشغوفٌ بكَلامِ بِدعَةٍ ودُعاءِ ضَلالَةٍ، فهُوَ فِتنَةٌ لِمَنِ افتُتِنَ بِهِ، ضالٌّ عن هَديِ مَن كانَ قَبلَهُ، مُضِلٌّ لِمَنِ اقتَدىٰ بِهِ في حَياتِهِ وبعدَ وَفاتِهِ، حَمّالٌ خَطايا غَيرِهِ، رَهنٌ (رَهينٌ) بخَطيئَتِهِ.٤١٩٩

3756. **Imām ʿAlī (AS) said** in his description of the hypocrites, 'I warn you against the hypocrites, for verily they are themselves misguided and they misguide other people. They have slipped and they cause others to slip too.'[4233]

٣٧٥٦. عنه ؑ ـ في صِفَةِ المنافقينَ ـ: أُحَذِّرُكُم أهلَ النِّفاقِ؛ فإنَّهُمُ الضّالّونَ المُضِلّونَ، والزّالّونَ المُزِلّونَ.٤٢٠٠

(See also: GUIDANCE: section 1797)

(أنظر) الهداية: باب ١٧٩٧.

1169. That which Destroys the Pillars of Misguidance

١١٦٩ ـ هادِمُ أركانِ الضَّلالَةِ

3757. **Imām ʿAlī (AS) said,** 'Seek its assistance [i.e. the Qur'an's] in your distress, for verily it contains the cure for the deadliest diseases, namely disbelief and hypocrisy, revolt and misguidance.'[4234]

٣٧٥٧. الإمامُ عليٌّ ؑ: استَعينوا بِهِ [أي بالقرآنِ] علىٰ لَأوائكُم؛ فإنَّ فيهِ شِفاءً مِن أكبَرِ الداءِ، وهُوَ الكُفرُ والنِّفاقُ، والغَيُّ والضَّلالُ.٤٢٠١

3758. **Imām ʿAlī (AS) said,** 'Indeed this Islam is the religion of Allah which he has chosen for

٣٧٥٨. عنه ؑ: إنّ هذا الإسلامَ دِينُ اللهِ الذي

Himself ... and has smashed the pillars of misguidance with its one pillar.'[4235]

اصطَفاهُ لنفسِهِ... وهَدَمَ أركانَ الضَّلالةِ بِرُكنِهِ.[٤٢٠٢]

248

LIABILITY

الضَّمانُ

1170. Liability as a Result of Squandering the Property of Others

١١٧٠ـ ثُبوتُ الضَّمانِ بالإتلافِ

3759. **The Prophet (SAWA) said,** 'The hand is responsible for whatever it takes into its possession until it returns it to its rightful place.'[4236]

٣٧٥٩. رسولُ اللهِ ﷺ: عَلَى اليَدِ ما أخَذَت حتّىٰ تُؤَدِّيَهُ.[٤٢٠٣]

3760. **Imām 'Alī (AS) said,** 'He who practices medicine or veterinary science must first request a cover assurance from the guardian of his client, otherwise he may be held liable.'[4237]

٣٧٦٠. الإمامُ عليٌّ عليه السلام: مَن تَطَبَّبَ أو تَبَيطَرَ فَليَأخُذِ البَراءةَ مِن وَلِيِّهِ، وإلّا فهُوَ لَهُ ضامِنٌ.[٤٢٠٤]

3761. **Imām al-Ṣādiq (AS) said,** 'He who damages anything of the public pathway of the Muslims is liable for it.'[4238]

٣٧٦١. الإمامُ الصّادقُ عليه السلام: مَن أضَرَّ بِشَيءٍ مِن طَرِيقِ المُسلِمينَ فَهُوَ لَهُ ضامِنٌ.[٤٢٠٥]

1171. The Censure of Risking Bailing or Culpability

١١٧١ـ ذَمُّ التَّعَرُّضِ لِلكَفالَةِ وَالضَّمانِ

3762. **Imām 'Alī (AS) said,** 'Do not give a guarantee for something that you are not able to fulfil.'[4239]

٣٧٦٢. الإمامُ عليٌّ عليه السلام: لا تَضمَنْ ما لا تَقدِرُ على الوَفاءِ بِهِ.[٤٢٠٦]

3763. **Imām al-Bāqir (AS) or Imām al-Ṣādiq (AS) said,** 'Do not impose upon yourself any right and be patient against adversities and hardships'[4240]

٣٧٦٣. الإمامُ الباقرُ أوِ الإمامُ الصّادقُ عليهما السلام: لا تُوجِبْ علىٰ نفسِكَ الحُقوقَ واصبِرْ على النَّوائبِ.[٤٢٠٧]

3764. **Imām al-Ṣādiq (AS) said,** 'Bailing is a loss, a penalty and a source of regret.'[4241]

٣٧٦٤. الإمامُ الصّادقُ عليه السلام: الكَفالَةُ خَسارَةٌ، غَرامَةٌ، نَدامَةٌ.[٤٢٠٨]

1172. There is no Liability on Something Borrowed

١١٧٢ـ لا ضَمانَ فِي العارِيَةِ

3765. **Imām al-Ṣādiq (AS) said,** ‘There is no penalty payable by someone who borrows something, which becomes spoilt while in his possession, if he is a trustworthy person.’[4242]

٣٧٦٥. الإمامُ الصّادقُ ؑ: لا غُرمَ علىٰ مُستَعِيرِ عارِيَةٍ إذا هَلَكَت إذا كانَ مَأموناً.٤٢٠٩

249

HOSPITALITY

الضِّيافَةُ

1173. The Virtue of Hospitality

١١٧٣ـ فَضلُ الضِّيافَةِ

3766. **The Prophet (SAWA) said,** ‘He who has faith in Allah and the Last Day must honour his guest.’[4243]

٣٧٦٦. رسولُ اللهِ ﷺ: مَن كانَ يُؤمِنُ بِاللهِ واليَومِ الآخِرِ فَلْيُكرِمْ ضَيفَهُ.٤٢١٠

3767. **The Prophet (SAWA) said,** ‘The guest arrives bringing his own sustenance and leaves taking away the sins of his hosts.’[4244]

٣٧٦٧. عنه ﷺ: الضَّيفُ يَنزِلُ بِرِزقِهِ، ويَرتَحِلُ بِذُنوبِ أهلِ البَيتِ.٤٢١١

3768. **The Prophet (SAWA) said,** 'Sustenance comes to those who feed others faster than a knife can cut though flesh.’[4245]

٣٧٦٨. عنه ﷺ: الرِّزقُ أسرَعُ إلىٰ مَن يُطعِمُ الطَّعامَ مِن السِّكّينِ فِي السَّنامِ.٤٢١٢

3769. **The Prophet (SAWA) said,** ‘Any house which is not visited by guests is not visited by angels either.’[4246]

٣٧٦٩. عنه ﷺ: كُلُّ بَيتٍ لا يَدخُلُ فيهِ الضَّيفُ لا تَدخُلُهُ المَلائكَةُ.٤٢١٣

3770. **Imām ʿAlī (AS) said,** ‘He who has been granted wealth by Allah must use it to maintain relations with his kin and to entertain guests.’[4247]

٣٧٧٠. الإمامُ عليٌّ ؑ: مَن آتاهُ اللهُ مالاً فَلْيَصِلْ بِهِ القَرابَةَ، ولْيُحسِنْ مِنهُ الضِّيافَةَ.٤٢١٤

3771. **Imām ʿAlī (AS)** was once seen sad and asked the reason for it, so he replied, ‘Because it has been seven days since we have had no guests.’[4248]

٣٧٧١. عنه ؑ ـ لَمّا رُئيَ حَزيناً فسُئلَ عن عِلَّتِهِ ـ: لِسَبعٍ أتَتْ لَم يَضِفْ إلَينا ضَيفٌ.٤٢١٥

1174. People Whom One Should Invite as Guests

١١٧٤ ـ مَن يَنبَغي ضِيافَتُهُ

3772. **The Prophet (SAWA) said,** 'Invite one whom you love in the way of Allah to partake of your food as a guest.'[4249]

٣٧٧٢ . رسولُ اللهِ ﷺ : أضِفْ بِطَعامِكَ مَن تُحِبُّ في اللهِ.[٤٢١٦]

3773. **The Prophet (SAWA) said,** 'It is an abominable act to accept the invitation of someone whose banquet is only attended by the rich and not the poor.'[4250]

٣٧٧٣ . عنه ﷺ : يُكرَهُ إجابَةُ مَن يَشهَدُ وَليمَتَهُ الأغنياءُ دُونَ الفُقَراءِ.[٤٢١٧]

1175. Enjoinment of Accepting the Invitation of a Fellow Believer

١١٧٥ ـ الحَثُّ عَلىٰ إجابَةِ دَعوَةِ المُؤمِنِ

3774. **The Prophet (SAWA) said,** 'I advise both the present and the absent ones from my community to accept the invitation of a fellow Muslim, even if it be five miles away, for verily that is a part of religion.'[4251]

٣٧٧٤ . رسولُ اللهِ ﷺ : أُوصِي الشاهِدَ مِن أُمَّتي والغائبَ أن يُجِيبَ دَعوَةَ المُسلِمِ ـ ولَو علىٰ خَمسَةِ أميالٍ ـ ؛ فإنّ ذلكَ مِن الدِّينِ.[٤٢١٨]

3775. **The Prophet (SAWA) said,** 'It is loathsome that a man be invited to a meal and does not accept, or accepts but does not eat.'[4252]

٣٧٧٥ . عنه ﷺ : مِن الجَفاءِ... أن يُدعَى الرَّجُلُ إلىٰ طَعامٍ فلا يُجِيبَ أو يُجِيبَ فلا يَأكُلَ.[٤٢١٩]

3776. **The Prophet (SAWA) said** to Abū Dharr, exhorting him, 'Do not partake of the food of corrupt people.'[4253]

٣٧٧٦ . عنه ﷺ ـ لأبي ذَرٍّ وهُو يَعِظُهُ ـ : لا تَأكُل طَعامَ الفاسِقينَ.[٤٢٢٠]

1176. Making a Special Effort for One's Guest

١١٧٦ ـ التَّكلُّفُ لِلضَّيفِ

3777. **The Prophet (SAWA) said,** 'It is enough of a sin for a [a host] to belittle that which he presents to his fellow brothers, and it is enough of a sin for a people to disparage that which a fellow brother presents to them.'[4254]

٣٧٧٧ . رسولُ اللهِ ﷺ : كَفىٰ بِالمَرءِ إثماً أن يَستَقِلَّ ما يُقَرِّبُ إلىٰ إخوانِهِ، وكَفىٰ بِالقَومِ إثماً أن يَستَقِلُّوا ما يُقَرِّبُهُ إلَيهِم أخُوهُم.[٤٢٢١]

3778. **The Prophet (SAWA) said,** 'No one should go to troubles that they cannot afford for a guest.'[4255]

٣٧٧٨ . عنه ﷺ : لا يَتَكَلَّفَنَّ أحَدٌ لِضَيفِهِ ما لا يَقدِرُ.[٤٢٢٢]

3779. **Imām al-Ṣādiq (AS) said,** 'If your brother comes to your house [uninvited] then offer him whatever you have in the house, and if you invite him, then make a special effort for him.'[4256]

٣٧٧٩ . الإمامُ الصّادقُ ﷺ : إذا أتاكَ أخُوك فَآتِهِ بما عِندَك، وإذا دَعوتَهُ فتَكَلَّفْ لَهُ .[٤٢٢٣]

3780. **Imām al-Riḍā (AS) narrated,** 'A man once invited the Commander of the Faithful, 'Alī (AS) for a meal, so Imām said to him, 'I will accept your invitation provided you fulfil three conditions.' The man asked, 'And what are they, O Commander of the Faithful?' to which he replied, 'Do not bring any special food from outside for me, do not preserve anything in the house especially for me, and do not impose any difficulty on your family.' The man replied, 'You shall have that O Commander of the Faithful' and 'Alī b. Abī Ṭālib accepted his invitation.'[4257]

٣٧٨٠ . الإمامُ الرِّضا ﷺ : دَعا رجُلٌ أميرَ المؤمنينَ ﷺ فقالَ لَهُ : قد أجَبتُكَ على أن تَضمَنَ لي ثلاثَ خِصالٍ . قال: وما هِيَ يا أميرَ المؤمنينَ ؟ قال: لا تُدخِلْ عَلَيَّ شيئاً مِن خارِجٍ، ولا تَدَّخِرْ عَنّي شيئاً في البيتِ، ولا تُجحِفْ بالعِيالِ . قالَ: ذاكَ لكَ يا أميرَ المؤمنينَ، فأجابَهُ عليُّ بنُ أبي طالبٍ ﷺ .[٤٢٢٤]

1177. The Etiquette of Hospitality

١١٧٧ ـ أدَبُ الضِّيافَةِ

3781. **The Prophet (SAWA) said,** 'Whoever wants to be loved by Allah and His Prophet should eat with his guest.'[4258]

٣٧٨١ . رسولُ اللهِ ﷺ : مَن أحَبَّ أن يُحِبَّهُ اللهُ ورسولُهُ فَليَأكُلْ مَعَ ضَيفِهِ .[٤٢٢٥]

3782. **The Prophet (SAWA) said,** 'When one of you is invited for a meal, he must not bring along his son with him too, for verily it is prohibited for him to do so and he enters the house unlawfully.'[4259]

٣٧٨٢ . عنه ﷺ : إذا دُعِيَ أحَدُكُم إلىٰ طَعامٍ فلا يَستَتبِعَنَّ وَلَدَهُ؛ فإنّهُ إن فَعَلَ ذلكَ كانَ حَراماً ودَخَلَ عاصياً .[٤٢٢٦]

3783. **The Prophet (SAWA) said,** 'A guest may expect to be honoured for two nights, then from the third night onwards he is considered to be one of the family and must eat whatever he gets.'[4260]

٣٧٨٣ . عنه ﷺ : الضَّيفُ يُلطَفُ لَيلَتَينِ، فإذا كانتِ اللَّيلةُ الثالثةُ فهُو مِن أهلِ البيتِ يَأكُلُ ما أدرَكَ .[٤٢٢٧]

3784. **The Prophet (SAWA) said,** 'Hospitality towards a guest is incumbent for the first day, the second day and the third day. After that, anything you give him is considered as charity towards him on your behalf.'[4261]

٣٧٨٤ . عنه ﷺ : الضِّيافَةُ أوَّلُ يَومٍ والثاني والثالثُ، وما بعدَ ذلكَ فإنّها صَدَقةٌ تَصَدّق بها علَيهِ .[٤٢٢٨]

3785. **The Prophet (SAWA) said,** 'Hosting a banquet the first day is reasonable, the second day

٣٧٨٥ . عنه ﷺ : الوَليمَةُ أوَّلُ يومٍ حَقٌّ، والثاني

is an act of courtesy, and any more than that is showing-off and seeking repute.'[4262]

مَعروفٌ، وما زادَ رياءٌ وسُمعَةٌ.[٤٢٢٩]

3786. **Imām al-Bāqir (AS) said,** 'When someone enters the house of his fellow brother, he must sit wherever the host tells him to sit for the owner of the house knows the flaws of his own house better than the guest.'[4263]

٣٧٨٦. الإمامُ الباقرُ (عليه السلام): إذا دَخَلَ أحَدُكُم على أخيهِ في رَحلِهِ فَليَقعُدْ حيثُ يَأمُرُ صاحِبُ الرَّحلِ؛ فإنّ صاحِبَ الرَّحلِ أعرَفُ بِعَورَةِ بَيتِهِ مِن الداخِلِ علَيهِ.[٤٢٣٠]

3787. **Ibn Abī Ya'fūr narrated,** 'I saw a guest once at Abī 'Abdillāh's [i.e. Imām al-Ṣādiq] (AS) house, who stood up to get something he needed, so Imām refused for him to do so, and stood up to get it himself, saying, 'The Prophet of Allah (SAWA) prohibited that a guest be allowed to do work.'[4264]

٣٧٨٧. الكافي عن ابن أبي يَعفورٍ: رأيتُ عِندَ أبي عبدِ اللهِ (عليه السلام) ضَيفاً، فقامَ يوماً في بعضِ الحَوائجِ، فَنَهاهُ عن ذلكَ، وقامَ بنفسِهِ إلى تلكَ الحاجَةِ، وقالَ (عليه السلام): نَهى رسولُ اللهِ (صلى الله عليه وآله) عَن أن يُستَخدَمَ الضَّيفُ.[٤٢٣١]

250

MEDICINE

الطِّبُّ

1178. The Real Doctor

١١٧٨ ـ الطَّبيبُ الحَقيقِيُّ

3788. **The Prophet (SAWA) said** to a doctor, 'Verily Allah, Mighty and Exalted, is the (real) doctor, though you are a kind man.'[4265]

٣٧٨٨. رسولُ اللهِ (صلى الله عليه وآله) ـ لِطَبيبٍ ـ: إنّ اللهَ عزّ وجلّ الطَّبيبُ، ولكنّكَ رجُلٌ رَفيقٌ.[٤٢٣٢]

1179. That which Makes One Needless of Medicine

١١٧٩ ـ ما يُستَغنى بِهِ عَنِ الطِّبِّ

3789. **Imām 'Alī (AS) said** in his will to his son, al-Ḥasan (AS), 'O my son, shall I teach you four things which will make you needless of medicine?' He replied, 'Yes, O Commander of the Faithful.' So he said, 'Do not sit to eat unless you are hungry. Stand up from the table while you still desire food. Chew properly. Go to the lavatory before you go to bed. If you put these into practice, you will not need medicine.'[4266]

٣٧٨٩. الخصال عن الأصبغ بن نُباتةَ: قالَ أميرُ المؤمنينَ عليُّ بنُ أبي طالبٍ (عليه السلام) للحَسَن ابنه (عليه السلام): يا بُنيَّ، ألا أُعَلِّمُكَ أربعَ خِصالٍ تَستغني بها عنِ الطِّبِّ؟ فقالَ: بلى يا أميرَ المؤمنينَ، قالَ: لا تَجلِسْ على الطَّعامِ إلّا وأنتَ جائعٌ، ولا تَقُمْ عنِ الطَّعامِ إلّا وأنتَ تَشتَهيهِ، وجَوِّدِ المَضغَ، وإذا نِمتَ فَاعرِضْ نَفسَكَ على الخَلاءِ، فإذا استَعمَلتَ هذا استَغنَيتَ عنِ الطِّبِّ.[٤٢٣٣]

3790. **Imām ʿAlī (AS) said,** 'He who eats food with complete hunger, chews the meal properly and leaves the table while he still desires food and does not retent the faeces at its time will be only ill with the sickness of death '[4267]

٣٧٩٠ . الإمامُ عليٌّ ﷺ : مَن أكَلَ الطَّعامَ عَلَى النَّقاءِ، وأجادَ الطَّعامَ تَمَضُّغاً، وتَرَكَ الطَّعامَ وهُوَ يَشتَهيهِ، ولَم يَحبِسِ الغائِطَ إذا أتىٰ ؛ لَم يَمرَض إلّا مَرَضَ المَوتِ.[٤٢٣٤]

1180. Avoiding Medicine as much as Possible

١١٨٠ ـ تجنب الدواء مَهما أمكَنَ

3791. **The Prophet (SAWA) said,** 'Avoid medicine as long as your body can bear the pain but when it could no longer bear it, only then, the medicine.'[4268]

٣٧٩١ . رسولُ اللهِ ﷺ : تَجَنَّبِ الدَّواءَ مَا احتَمَلَ بَدَنُكَ الدَّاءَ، فَإذا لَم يَحتَمِلِ الدّاءَ فَالدَّواءُ.[٤٢٣٥]

3792. **Imām ʿAlī (AS) said,** 'Get along with your pain as long as it gets along with you[4269]

٣٧٩٢ . الإمامُ عليٌّ ﷺ : اِمشِ بِدائِكَ ما مَشىٰ بِكَ.[٤٢٣٦]

251

FEEDING OTHERS

الإطعامُ

1181. The Virtue of Feeding a Hungry Person

١١٨١ ـ فَضلُ إطعامِ الجائِعِ

"They give food for the love of Him, to the needy, the orphan and the prisoner, [saying], 'We feed you only for the sake of Allah. We do not want any reward from you nor any thanks.'"[4270]

﴿وَيُطعِمُونَ الطَّعامَ عَلَىٰ حُبِّهِ مِسْكِيناً وَيَتِيماً وَأَسِيراً ۞ إنَّما نُطْعِمُكُمْ لِوَجْهِ اللهِ لا نُرِيدُ مِنْكُمْ جَزاءً وَلا شُكُوراً﴾.[٤٢٣٧]

"Or feeding [the needy] on a day of starvation, or an orphan among relatives, or a needy man in desolation."[4271]

﴿أَوْ إِطْعامٌ فِي يَوْمٍ ذِي مَسْغَبَةٍ ۞ يَتِيماً ذا مَقْرَبَةٍ ۞ أَوْ مِسْكِيناً ذا مَتْرَبَةٍ﴾.[٤٢٣٨]

3793. **Imām ʿAlī (AS) said,** 'The nourishment of the body is food whilst the nourishment of the soul is feeding others.'[4272]

٣٧٩٣ . الإمامُ عليٌّ ﷺ : قوتُ الأجسادِ الطَّعامُ، وقوتُ الأرواحِ الإطعامُ.[٤٢٣٩]

3794. **Imām ʿAlī (AS) said,** 'That which you yourself eat gets consumed whereas that which

٣٧٩٤ . عنه ﷺ : ما أكَلتَهُ راحَ، وما أطعَمتَهُ

you feed others diffuses [i.e. the benediction in that sustenance].'[4273]

فاح.[٤٢٤٠]

3795. **Imām al-Bāqir (AS) said,** 'Verily Allah loves the feeding of food to others, and the spilling of blood [offering a sacrifice].'[4274]

٣٧٩٥. الإمامُ الباقرُ عليه السلام: إنّ اللهَ يُحِبُّ إطعامَ الطَّعامِ وهِراقَةَ الدِّماءِ.[٤٢٤١]

3796. **Imām al-Ṣādiq (AS) said,** 'One of the things which gives one obligatory entrance into Paradise and forgiveness is feeding a starving person', then he went on to recite the verse of Allah in the Qur'an: *"or feeding [the needy] on a day of starvation."*[4275]

٣٧٩٦. الإمامُ الصّادقُ عليه السلام: مِن مُوجِباتِ الجَنَّةِ والمَغفِرَةِ إطعامُ الطَّعامِ السَّغبانَ، ثُمَّ تَلا قولَ اللهِ عزّوجلّ: ﴿أوْ إطْعامٌ في يَومٍ ذي مَسْغَبةٍ...﴾.[٤٢٤٢]

3797. **Imām al-Ṣādiq (AS) narrated,** 'Verily the Commander of the Faithful resembled the Prophet (SAWA) the most in the way that he ate. He used to eat bread, vinegar and (olive) oil, and feed others bread and meat.'[4276]

٣٧٩٧. عنه عليه السلام: إنَّ أميرَ المؤمنينَ عليه السلام أشبَهُ النّاسِ طُعمَةً برسولِ اللهِ صلى الله عليه وآله، كانَ يأكُلُ الخُبزَ والخَلَّ والزَّيتَ، ويُطعِمُ النّاسَ الخُبزَ واللَّحمَ.[٤٢٤٣]

(See also: HOSPITALITY 249)

(أُنظر) عنوان ٢٤٩ «الضيافة».

252

DIVORCE

الطَّلاقُ

1182. The Reprehension of Divorce

١١٨٢ ـ ذَمُّ الطَّلاقِ

3798. **The Prophet (SAWA) said,** 'Allah has not made permissible anything more abominable to Him than divorce.'[4277]

٣٧٩٨. رسولُ اللهِ صلى الله عليه وآله: ما أحَلَّ اللهُ شيئاً أبغَضَ إلَيهِ مِن الطَّلاقِ.[٤٢٤٤]

3799. **The Prophet (SAWA) said,** 'Verily Allah, Mighty and Exalted, despises or excludes from His mercy every man who is quick to contract new marriages, and every woman who does so.'[4278]

٣٧٩٩. عنه صلى الله عليه وآله: إنَّ اللهَ عزَّوجلَّ يُبغِضُ أو يَلعَنُ كُلَّ ذَوّاقٍ مِنَ الرِّجالِ، وكُلَّ ذَوّاقَةٍ مِنَ النِّساءِ.[٤٢٤٥]

3800. **Imām al-Bāqir (AS) said,** 'Verily Allah, Mighty and Exalted, despises every man who is quick to contract new divorces and marriages.'[4279]

٣٨٠٠. الإمامُ الباقرُ عليه السلام: إنّ اللهَ عزَّوجلَّ يُبغِضُ كُلَّ مِطلاقٍ ذَوّاقٍ.[٤٢٤٦]

3801. **Imām al-Ṣādiq (AS) said,** 'Nothing is more abominable to Allah from all that He has made permissible than divorce, and verily Allah despises one who is quick to contract new divorces and marriages.'[4280]

٣٨٠١ . الإمامُ الصّادقُ ﷺ : ما مِن شَيءٍ مِمّا أحَلَّهُ اللهُ عَزَّوجلَّ أبغَضَ إلَيهِ مِن الطلاقِ، وإنَّ اللهَ يُبغِضُ المِطلاقَ الذَّوّاقَ.[٤٢٤٧]

3802. **Imām al-Ṣādiq (AS) said,** 'Verily Allah, Mighty and Exalted, loves the house wherein a wedding is taking place, and despises the house wherein a divorce is in process, and nothing is more abominable to Allah than divorce.'[4281]

٣٨٠٢ . عنه ﷺ : إنَّ اللهَ عَزَّوجلَّ يُحِبُّ البيتَ الذي فيهِ العُرسُ، ويُبغِضُ البيتَ الذي فيهِ الطلاقُ، وما مِن شَيءٍ أبغَضَ إلى اللهِ عَزَّوجلَّ مِن الطَّلاقِ.[٤٢٤٨]

1183. The Wisdom in Restricting the Divorce to Three Times

١١٨٣ ـ حِكمَةُ الطَّلاقِ ثَلاثاً

"And if he divorces her, she will not be lawful for him until she marries a husband other than him, and if he divorces her[4282]*, there is no sin upon them to remarry if they think that they can maintain Allah's bounds. These are Allah's bounds, which He clarifies for a people who have knowledge."*[4283]

﴿فَإنْ طَلَّقَها فَلا تَحِلُّ لَهُ مِنْ بَعْدُ حَتَّىٰ تَنْكِحَ زَوْجاً غَيْرَهُ فَإنْ طَلَّقَها فَلا جُناحَ عَلَيْهِما أنْ يَتَراجَعا إنْ ظَنَّا أنْ يُقِيما حُدُودَ اللهِ وَتِلْكَ حُدُودُ اللهِ يُبَيِّنُها لِقَوْمٍ يَعْلَمُونَ﴾.[٤٢٤٩]

3803. **Imām al-Riḍā (AS)** was once asked the reason why a man is not allowed to remarry his divorcée numerous times unless she has married another husband first, to which he replied, 'Verily Allah, Blessed and most High, has permitted revocable divorce twice, and said: *"[Revocable] divorce may be only twice; then [let there be] either an honourable retention, or a kindly release"*[4284], meaning the third time around. Because of his contracting this divorce that Allah despises so, three times over, Allah prohibits him from doing it again, so she [his divorcée] is not lawful for him until she marries another husband [and he divorces her], in order that people do not plunge into divorce, taking it as a light matter, and in order that women may not be caused to suffer in the process.'[4285]

٣٨٠٣ . الإمامُ الرِّضا ﷺ ـ لمّا سُئلَ عن العلّةِ التي من أجلِها لا تَحِلُّ المُطَلَّقَةُ لِلعِدَّةِ لِزَوجِها حتّى تَنكِحَ زَوجاً غيرَهُ ـ: إنَّ اللهَ تبارَكَ و تعالىٰ إنّما أذِنَ في الطلاقِ مَرَّتَينِ، فقالَ عَزَّوجلَّ: ﴿الطَّلاقُ مَرَّتانِ فَإمْساكٌ بِمَعْروفٍ أَوْ تَسْريحٌ بِإحْسانٍ﴾[٤٢٥٠] يَعني في التَّطليقَةِ الثالثةِ، ولِدُخُولِهِ فيما كَرِهَ اللهُ عَزَّوجلَّ لَهُ مِن الطلاقِ الثالثِ حَرَّمَها اللهُ علَيهِ، فلا تَحِلُّ لَهُ مِن بعدُ حتّىٰ تَنكِحَ زَوجاً غَيرَهُ؛ لئلاّ يُوقِعَ الناسُ الاستِخفافَ بِالطلاقِ ولا تُضارَّ النِّساءُ.[٤٢٥١]

3804. **Imām al-Riḍā (AS) said** in a letter that he wrote to Muḥammad Ibn Sinān outlining the reason for restricting the divorce to three times,

٣٨٠٤ . عنه ﷺ ـ مِمّا كَتَبَ إلىٰ محمّدِ بنِ سِنانٍ في عِلَّةِ الطلاقِ ثلاثاً ـ: وعِلَّةُ الطلاقِ ثلاثاً لِما

'The reasoning behind the divorce being permissible three times is to do with the respite it gives [each party to think] between the first to the third time – for in that time, a desire [for one's spouse] may arise or one's rage may subside. Also, [it has been restricted to three] in order to discipline and deter women from disobeying their husbands [time after time] whereby she may have become deserving of separation and distancing for doing something to disobey her husband. The reason why a woman becomes unlawful for a man after nine counts of divorce, where he is absolutely not allowed a woman and is punishable for it, is in order that people do not make a jest of divorce and so that women are not abased, and so that man may consider his situation carefully and vigilantly [before plunging into marriage and divorce], and that he may feel despair at ever coming back together with a woman after having divorced nine times.'[4286]

فيهِ مِن المُهلَةِ فيما بينَ الواحِدَةِ إلى الثلاثِ؛ رَغبَةٍ تَحدُثُ أو سُكونِ غَضَبٍ إن كانَ، ولِيَكُونَ ذلكَ تَخويفاً وتَأديباً للنِّساءِ وزَجراً لهُنَّ عن مَعصيَةِ أزواجِهِنَّ فَاستَحَقَّتِ المرأةُ الفُرقَةَ والمُبايَنَةَ لدُخُولِها فيما لا يَنبَغي مِن مَعصيَةِ زَوجِها، وعِلَّةُ تَحريمِ المرأةِ بعدَ تِسعِ تَطليقاتٍ فلا تَحِلُّ لَهُ أبداً عُقوبَةً؛ لئلّا يُتَلاعَبَ بِالطلاقِ، ولا تُستَضعَفَ المرأةُ، ولِيَكُونَ ناظِراً في اُمورِهِ مُتَيَقِّظاً مُعتَبِراً، ولِيَكونَ يائساً لَها مِن الاجتِماعِ بعدَ تِسعِ تَطلِيقاتٍ.[٤٢٥٢]

253

GREED

الطَّمَعُ

1184. Reprehension of Greed

١١٨٤ ـ ذَمُّ الطَّمَعِ

3805. **The Prophet (SAWA) said,** 'Greed takes away wisdom from the hearts of the knowledgeable men.'[4287]

٣٨٠٥ . رسولُ اللهِ ﷺ : الطَّمَعُ يُذهِبُ الحِكمَةَ مِن قلوبِ العُلَماءِ.[٤٢٥٣]

3806. **The Prophet (SAWA) said,** 'Verily greed is a slippery rock on which the feet of knowledgeable men never become firmly rooted.'[4288]

٣٨٠٦ . عنه ﷺ : إنّ الصَّفاةَ الزُّلالَ الذي لا تَثبُتُ علَيهِ أقدامُ العُلَماءِ الطَّمَعُ.[٤٢٥٤]

3807. **The Prophet (SAWA) said,** 'Beware of greed for it is ready poverty.'[4289]

٣٨٠٧ . عنه ﷺ : إيّاكَ والطَّمَعَ؛ فإنّهُ فَقرٌ حاضِرٌ.[٤٢٥٥]

3808. **Imām 'Alī (AS) said,** 'Greed is an eternal slavery.'[4290]

٣٨٠٨ . الإمامُ عليٌّ عليه السلام : الطَّمَعُ رِقٌّ مُؤَبَّدٌ.[٤٢٥٦]

3809. **Imām ʿAlī (AS) said,** 'Whoever wishes to spend the days of his life as a free man must not allow greed to abide in his heart.'[4291]

٣٨٠٩. عنه عليه السلام: مَن أرادَ أن يَعيشَ حُرّاً أيّامَ حياتِهِ فلا يُسكِنِ الطَّمَعَ قَلبَهُ.[٤٢٥٧]

3810. **Imām ʿAlī (AS) said,** 'The greedy person is shackled in disgrace.'[4292]

٣٨١٠. عنه عليه السلام: الطامِعُ في وَثاقِ الذُّلِّ.[٤٢٥٨]

3811. **Imām ʿAlī (AS) said,** 'The person most neglectful of his own soul is the one who is full of greed.'[4293]

٣٨١١. عنه عليه السلام: أزرى بِنَفسِهِ مَنِ استَشعَرَ الطَّمعَ.[٤٢٥٩]

3812. **Imām ʿAlī (AS) said,** 'No one is more despicable than a greedy person.'[4294]

٣٨١٢. عنه عليه السلام: لا أذَلَّ مِن طامِعٍ.[٤٢٦٠]

3813. **Imām ʿAlī (AS) said,** 'The intellects are most often destroyed as a result of their subservience to bursts of avid desires.'[4295]

٣٨١٣. عنه عليه السلام: أكثَرُ مَصارِعِ العُقولِ تحتَ بُروقِ المَطامِعِ.[٤٢٦١]

3814. **Imām ʿAlī (AS) said,** 'Piety and greed can never come together.'[4296]

٣٨١٤. عنه عليه السلام: لا يَجتَمِعُ الوَرَعُ والطَّمَعُ.[٤٢٦٢]

3815. **Imām al-Bāqir (AS) said,** 'How wretched the servant who is a slave of his own greed, which controls him.'[4297]

٣٨١٥. الإمامُ الباقرُ عليه السلام: بِئسَ العَبدُ عَبدٌ لَهُ طَمَعٌ يَقودُهُ.[٤٢٦٣]

3816. **Imām al-Kāẓim (AS) said** to Hāshim, exhorting him, 'You must beware of greed, and despair of acquiring anything in the possession of others. Suppress the greed in others for verily greed is the key to disgrace, it exploits the intellect, fabricates valorous qualities for itself, tarnishes one's reputation, and does away with one's knowledge.'[4298]

٣٨١٦. الإمامُ الكاظمُ عليه السلام ـ لِهشامٍ وهُو يَعِظُهُ ـ: إيّاكَ والطَّمَعَ، وعلَيكَ باليَأسِ مِمّا في أيدِي النّاسِ، وأمِتِ الطَّمَعَ مِن المَخلوقينَ؛ فإنَّ الطَّمَعَ مِفتاحٌ لِلذُّلِّ، واختِلاسُ العَقلِ، واختِلاقُ المُروّاتِ، وتَدنيسُ العِرضِ، والذَّهابُ بِالعِلمِ.[٤٢٦٤]

3817. **Imām al-Hādī (AS) said,** 'Greed is an evil characteristic.'[4299]

٣٨١٧. الإمامُ الهاديُ عليه السلام: الطَّمَعُ سَجِيَّةٌ سَيِّئَةٌ.[٤٢٦٥]

3818. **Imām al-ʿAskarī (AS) said,** 'How revolting it is for the believer to have an avid desire that disgraces him.'[4300]

٣٨١٨. الإمامُ العسكريُّ عليه السلام: ما أقبَحَ بالمُؤمِنِ أن تكونَ لَهُ رَغبَةٌ تُذِلُّهُ.[٤٢٦٦]

(See also: AVARICE 94)

(أنظر) عنوان ٩٤ «الحرص».

1185. Praiseworthy Avidity[4301]

١١٨٥ ـ الطَّمَعُ المَمدوحُ

"Their sides vacate their beds to supplicate their Lord in fear and hope, and they spend out of what We have provided them."[4302]

﴿تَتَجافَى جُنُوبُهُمْ عَنِ المَضاجِعِ يَدْعُونَ رَبَّـهُمْ خَوْفاً وَطَمَعاً وَمِمَّا رَزَقْناهُمْ يُنْفِقُونَ﴾.[٤٢٦٧]

"Why should we not believe in Allah and the truth that has come to us, avid as we are that our Lord should admit us among the righteous people?"[4303]

﴿وَما لَنا لا نُؤْمِنُ بِاللهِ وَما جاءَنا مِنَ الحَقِّ وَنَطْمَعُ أَن يُدْخِلَنا رَبُّنا مَعَ القَوْمِ الصَّالِحِينَ﴾.[٤٢٦٨]

3819. **Imām Zayn al-ʿĀbidīn (AS) said** in one of his supplications, 'When I consider my sins my Lord, I am horrified [at them], and when I consider Your pardon, I am avidly eager [for it].'[4304]

٣٨١٩. الإمامُ زينُ العابدينَ عليه السلام ـ في الدعاءِ ـ: إذا رَأيتُ مَولايَ ذُنُوبي فَزِعتُ، وإذا رَأيتُ عَـفوَكَ طَمِعتُ.[٤٢٦٩]

3820. **Imām Zayn al-ʿĀbidīn (AS) said** in another one of his supplications, 'For indeed I ask You because of my eternal hope in You and because of the great desire that I entertain about You; which is the graciousness and mercy that You have made obligatory upon Yourself.'[4305]

٣٨٢٠. عنه عليه السلام ـ أيضاً ـ: فإنّما أسألُكَ لِقَديمِ الرَّجاءِ فيكَ، وعَظيمِ الطَّمَعِ منكَ؛ الذي أوجَبتَهُ علىٰ نفسِكَ مِن الرَّأفَةِ والرَّحمَةِ.[٤٢٧٠]

254

PURITY

الطَّهارَةُ

1186. Ritual Purification[4306]

١١٨٦ ـ الطَّهورُ

3821. **The Prophet (SAWA) said,** 'Purification is a portion of faith.'[4307]

٣٨٢١. رسولُ اللهِ صلى الله عليه وآله: الطُّهُورُ شَطرُ الإيمانِ.[٤٢٧١]

3822. **The Prophet (SAWA) said,** 'The first thing that the servant will have to account for is his ritual purification.'[4308]

٣٨٢٢. عنه صلى الله عليه وآله: أوَّلُ مـا يُحاسَبُ بـهِ العَبدُ طَهُورُهُ.[٤٢٧٢]

3823. **The Prophet (SAWA) said,** 'A prayer without ablution is not accepted.'[4309]

٣٨٢٣. عنه صلى الله عليه وآله: لا تُقبَلُ صَلاةٌ بغَيرِ طَهورٍ.[٤٢٧٣]

1187. Purifying Agents

١١٨٧ ـ المُطَهِّراتُ

"And it is He who sends the winds as harbingers of His mercy, and We send down from the sky purifying water."[4310]

﴿وَهُوَ الَّذِي أرسَلَ الرِّياحَ بُشراً بَينَ يَدَي رَحمَتِهِ وَأنزَلنا مِنَ السَّماءِ ماءً طَهُوراً﴾. ٤٢٧٤

(See also: Qur'an 5:6, 9:108)

(أنظر) المائدة: ٦ و التوبة: ١٠٨.

1. Water:

١ ـ الماءُ

3824. **Imām ʿAlī (AS) said,** 'Allah has created water to be a purifier where nothing can make it impure, except for that water whose colour, taste or smell has changed.'[4311]

٣٨٢٤. الإمامُ عليٌّ عليه السلام: خَلَقَ اللهُ الماءَ طَهوراً لا يُنَجِّسُهُ شَيءٌ، إلّا ما غَيَّرَ لَونَهُ أو طَعمَهُ أو رِيحَهُ. ٤٢٧٥

2. The Sun:

٢ ـ الشّمسُ

3825. **Imām al-Bāqir (AS) said,** 'Everything that the sun shines on becomes purified.'[4312]

٣٨٢٥. الإمامُ الباقرُ عليه السلام: كُلُّ ما أشرَقَت عَلَيهِ الشَّمسُ فهُو طاهِرٌ. ٤٢٧٦

3. Earth:

٣ ـ التُّرابُ

3826. **Imām al-Ṣādiq (AS) said,** 'Verily Allah, Mighty and Exalted, made the earth a purifier just as he made water a purifier.'[4313]

٣٨٢٦. الإمامُ الصّادقُ عليه السلام: إنّ اللهَ عَزَّ وجلَّ جَعَلَ التُّرابَ طَهوراً كما جَعَلَ الماءَ طَهوراً. ٤٢٧٧

4. Fire:

٤ ـ النارُ

3827. **Imām al-Kāẓim (AS)** was once asked about gypsum that is burnt along with dried excrement and bone ash, and then used to plaster a mosque, and whether prostration on such plaster is allowed. He replied, 'Verily water and fire [from the kilning process] have purified it.'[4314]

٣٨٢٧. الإمامُ الكاظمُ عليه السلام ـ لمّا سُئلَ عنِ الجِصِّ يُوقَدُ عَلَيهِ بِالعذَرَةِ وعِظامِ المَوتىٰ ثُمَّ يُجَصَّصُ بِهِ المَسجِدُ، أيُسجَدُ عَلَيهِ؟ ـ: إنَّ الماءَ وَالنّارَ قَد طَهَّراهُ. ٤٢٧٨

1188. Spiritual Purity

١١٨٨ ـ الطَّهارَةُ المَعنَويَّةُ

"Indeed Allah desires to repel all impurity from you, O People of the Household, and purify you with a thorough purification."[4315]

﴿إنَّما يُرِيدُ اللهُ لِيُذهِبَ عَنكُمُ الرِّجسَ أهلَ البَيتِ وَيُطَهِّرَكُم تَطهِيراً﴾. ٤٢٧٩

"Take charity from their possessions to cleanse them and purify them thereby, and bless them. Indeed your

﴿خُذْ مِنْ أَمْوالِهِمْ صَدَقَةً تُطَهِّرُهُمْ وَتُزَكِّيهِمْ بِها وَصَلِّ عَلَيْهِمْ إنَّ صَلاتَكَ سَكَنٌ لَهُمْ

blessing is a comfort to them, and Allah is all-hearing, all-knowing.'[4316]

وَاللهُ سَمِيعٌ عَلِيمٌ﴾.[٤٢٨٠]

3828. **Imām ʿAlī (AS) said,** 'Allah has obligated faith in order to purify one from polytheism.'[4317]

٣٨٢٨. الإمامُ عليٌّ عليه السلام: فَرَضَ اللهُ الإيمانَ تطهيراً مِن الشِّركِ.[٤٢٨١]

3829. **Imām ʿAlī (AS) said,** 'Verily being wary of one's duty to Allah is the remedy for the disease of your hearts … and the purifier of the pollution in your souls.'[4318]

٣٨٢٩. عنه عليه السلام: إنَّ تَقوَى اللهِ دَواءُ داءِ قُلوبِكُم... وطَهُورُ دَنَسِ أنفُسِكُم.[٤٢٨٢]

3830. **Imām ʿAlī (AS) said,** 'Since you have no choice but to purify your bodies, then make a point of purifying yourselves of your faults and your sins.'[4319]

٣٨٣٠. عنه عليه السلام: إن كُنتُم لا مَحالَةَ مُتَطَهِّرِينَ فَتَطَهَّرُوا مِن دَنَسِ العُيوبِ والذُّنوبِ.[٤٢٨٣]

(See also: THE HEART: section 1551)

(أنظر) القلب: باب ١٥٥١.

255

OBEDIENCE

الطّاعَة

1189. Obedience to Allah and its Effects

١١٨٩ـ طاعَةُ اللهِ وآثارُها

"O you who have faith! Obey Allah and obey the Apostle and those vested with authority among you."[4320]

﴿يا أَيُّها الَّذِينَ آمَنُوا أَطِيعُوا اللهَ وَأَطِيعُوا الرَّسُولَ وَأُولِي الْأَمْرِ مِنْكُمْ﴾.[٤٢٨٤]

3831. **The Prophet (SAWA) said,** 'Verily what is with Allah can only ever be attained through His obedience.'[4321]

٣٨٣١. رسولُ اللهِ صلى الله عليه وآله: إنَّهُ لا يُدرَكُ ما عِندَ اللهِ إلّا بطاعَتِهِ.[٤٢٨٥]

3832. **Imām ʿAlī (AS) said,** 'Obedience to Allah is the key to every efficient matter and the redressing of every immoral act.'[4322]

٣٨٣٢. الإمامُ عليٌّ عليه السلام: طاعَةُ اللهِ مِفتاحُ كُلِّ سَدادٍ، وصَلاحُ كُلِّ فَسادٍ.[٤٢٨٦]

3833. **Imām ʿAlī (AS) said,** 'The person most worthy of Allah's mercy is the one most diligent in Allah's obedience.'[4323]

٣٨٣٣. عنه عليه السلام: أجدَرُ الناسِ برَحمَةِ اللهِ أقوَمُهُم بالطّاعَةِ.[٤٢٨٧]

3834. **Imām ʿAlī (AS) said,** 'It is incumbent upon you to obey the One whom you hold no excuse to remain ignorant of.'[4324]

٣٨٣٤. عنه عليه السلام: علَيكُم بطاعَةِ مَن لا تُعذَرُونَ بجَهالَتِهِ.[٤٢٨٨]

3835. **Imām al-Hādī (AS) said,** 'He who obeys the Creator is not bothered by the displeasure of the creation [i.e. other people].'[4325]

٣٨٣٥. الإمامُ الهاديُّ ﷺ: مَن أطاعَ الخالِقَ لَم يُبالِ بسَخَطِ المَخلوقِ.[٤٢٨٩]

1190. He who is Entitled to be Obeyed

١١٩٠ـ مَن يَنبَغي طاعَتُهُ

3836. **Imām 'Alī (AS) said,** 'Obey the intelligent man and you will gain, and disobey the ignorant man and you will remain safe.'[4326]

٣٨٣٦. الإمامُ عليٌّ ﷺ: أطِعِ العاقِلَ تَغنَمْ، اِعْصِ الجاهِلَ تَسلَمْ.[٤٢٩٠]

3837. **Imām 'Alī (AS) said,** 'Obey knowledge and disobey ignorance and you will prosper.'[4327]

٣٨٣٧. عنه ﷺ: أطِعِ العِلمَ واعْصِ الجَهلَ تُفلِحْ.[٤٢٩١]

3838. **Imām 'Alī (AS) said,** 'The religion of one who adheres to obeying creatures and disobeying the Creator does not count.'[4328]

٣٨٣٨. عنه ﷺ: لا دِينَ لِمَن دانَ بطاعَةِ المَخلوقِ ومَعصيَةِ الخالِقِ.[٤٢٩٢]

3839. **Imām 'Alī (AS) said,** 'Obey one who is above you [in authority] and the one below you will obey you.'[4329]

٣٨٣٩. عنه ﷺ: أطِعْ مَن فَوقَكَ يُطِعْكَ مَن دُونَكَ.[٤٢٩٣]

3840. **Imām 'Alī (AS) said,** 'He whose heart submits to Allah, his body never tires of Allah's obedience.'[4330]

٣٨٤٠. عنه ﷺ: مَن تَواضَعَ قَلبُهُ للهِ لَم يَسأمْ بَدَنُهُ مِن طاعَةِ اللهِ.[٤٢٩٤]

3841. **Imām al-Hādī (AS) said,** 'He who gives you both his affection and his good opinion is entitled to your giving him your obedience.'[4331]

٣٨٤١. الإمامُ الهاديُّ ﷺ: مَن جَمَعَ لَكَ وُدَّهُ ورَأيَهُ فَاجمَعْ لَهُ طاعَتَكَ.[٤٢٩٥]

1191. He who Must not be Obeyed

١١٩١ـ مَن لا يَنبَغي طاعَتُهُ

"And they will say, 'Our Lord! We obeyed our leaders and elders, and they led us astray from the way. Our Lord! Give them a double punishment and curse them with a mighty curse."[4332]

﴿وَقالُوا رَبَّنا إنّا أطَعْنا سادَتَنا وَكُبَراءَنا فَأضَلُّونا السَّبِيلا * رَبَّنا آتِهِمْ ضِعْفَيْنِ مِنَ العَذابِ وَالْعَنْهُمْ لَعْناً كَبِيراً﴾.[٤٢٩٦]

3842. **The Prophet (SAWA) said,** 'He who pleases a ruler with regard to something that displeases Allah excludes himself from the religion of Allah, Mighty and Exalted.'[4333]

٣٨٤٢. رسولُ اللهِ ﷺ: مَن أرضى سُلطاناً بما يُسخِطُ اللهَ خَرَجَ عن دِينِ اللهِ عزَّ وجلَّ.[٤٢٩٧]

3843. **Imām 'Alī (AS) said,** 'Beware! Beware of obeying your leaders and your elders who felt

٣٨٤٣. الإمامُ عليٌّ ﷺ: ألا فَالحَذَرَ الحَذَرَ مِن

proud of their achievements and boasted about their lineage … and do not obey those who claim to be Muslims [but are hypocrites] whose filth you imbibe alongside your propriety, whose ailments you mix with your healthiness, and whose wrongs you have allowed to infiltrate your rightful matters, while they are the very foundation of vice.'[4334]

طاعَةِ ساداتِكم وكُبَرائكُمُ الَّذينَ تكَبَّرُوا عن حَسَبِهِم، وتَرَفَّعُوا فَوقَ نَسَبِهِم... ولا تُطِيعُوا لأدعِياءَ الذينَ شَرِبتُم بِصَفوِكُم كَدَرَهُم، وخَلَطتُم بِصِحَّتِكُم مَرَضَهُم، وأدخَلتُم في حَقِّكُم باطِلَهُم، وهُم أساسُ الفُسوقِ.[٤٢٩٨]

3844. **Imām ʿAlī (AS) said,** 'He who obeys an negligent person ends up losing his rights, and he who obeys an informant ends up losing his friends.'[4335]

٣٨٤٤. عنه عليه‌السلام: مَن أطاعَ التَّوانِيَ ضَيَّعَ الحُقوقَ، ومَن أطاعَ الواشِيَ ضَيَّعَ الصَّدِيقَ.[٤٢٩٩]

256

PERFUME

الطِّيبُ

1192. The Virtue of Using Perfume

١١٩٢ـ فَضْلُ الطِّيبِ

3845. **The Prophet (SAWA) said,** 'Verily the pleasant fragrance strengthens the heart and acts as an aphrodisiac.'[4336]

٣٨٤٥. رسولُ اللهِ ﷺ: إنّ الرِّيحَ الطَّيِّبَةَ تَشُدُّ القَلبَ وتَزِيدُ في الجِماعِ.[٤٣٠٠]

3846. **The Prophet (SAWA) said,** 'He who perfumes himself for Allah, most High, will be raised on the Day of Resurrection, smelling more fragrant than sweet musk, whereas he who perfumes himself for other than Allah [for an unlawful purpose] will be raised on the Day of Resurrection smelling more putrid than a corpse.'[4337]

٣٨٤٦. عنه ﷺ: مَن تَطَيَّبَ للهِ جاءَ يَومَ القِيامَةِ ورِيحُهُ أطيَبُ مِنَ المِسكِ، ومَن تَطَيَّبَ لِغَيرِ اللهِ جاءَ يَومَ القِيامَةِ ورِيحُهُ أنتَنُ مِن الجِيفَةِ.[٤٣٠١]

3847. **Anas b. Mālik narrated,** 'The Prophet (SAWA) never used to refuse perfume when he was gifted it.'[4338]

٣٨٤٧. سنن النسائي عن أنس بن مالك: كانَ النبيُّ ﷺ إذا أُتِيَ بِطِيبٍ لَم يَرُدَّهُ.[٤٣٠٢]

3848. **Imām ʿAlī (AS) said,** 'Perfume is an amulet [a remedy].'[4339]

٣٨٤٨. الإمامُ عليٌّ عليه‌السلام: الطِّيبُ نُشْرَةٌ.[٤٣٠٣]

3849. **Imām al-Ṣādiq (AS) said,** 'Putting perfume is a practice of the messengers.'[4340]

٣٨٤٩. الإمامُ الصّادقُ عليه السلام : العِطرُ مِن سُنَنِ المُرسَلِينَ.٤٣٠٤

3850. **Imām al-Ṣādiq (AS) narrated,** 'The Prophet (SAWA) used to spend more on perfume than he did on food.'[4341]

٣٨٥٠. عنه عليه السلام : كانَ رسولُ اللهِ صلى الله عليه وآله يُنفِقُ في الطِّيبِ أكثَرَ مِمّا يُنفِقُ في الطَّعامِ.٤٣٠٥

3851. **Imām al-Ṣādiq (AS) said,** 'Whoever perfumes himself first thing in the morning has his intellect [working] with him till nightfall.'[4342]

٣٨٥١. عنه عليه السلام : مَن تَطَيَّبَ أوَّلَ النهارِ لَم يَزَلْ عقلُهُ مَعهُ إلى اللَّيلِ.٤٣٠٦

3852. **Imām al-Kāẓim (AS) said,** 'Man should not leave one day without perfuming himself, and if he is not able to do that, then he should perfume himself every other day, and if he cannot do that, then he should do so every Friday without fail.'[4343]

٣٨٥٢. الإمامُ الكاظمُ عليه السلام : لا يَنبَغِي للرَّجُلِ أن يَدَعَ الطِّيبَ في كُلِّ يَومٍ، فإن لَم يَقدِرْ علَيهِ فَيَومٌ ويَومٌ لا، فإن لَم يَقدِرْ ففي كُلِّ جُمُعَةٍ و لا يَدَعْ.٤٣٠٧

3853. **Imām al-Riḍā (AS) said,** 'Putting perfume is a noble characteristic of the prophets.'[4344]

٣٨٥٣. الإمامُ الرِّضا عليه السلام : الطِّيبُ مِن أخلاقِ الأنبياءِ.٤٣٠٨

1193. The Perfume of Women

١١٩٣ ـ طِيبُ النِّساءِ

3854. **The Prophet (SAWA) said,** 'Perfumes suitable for women are those that have a visible colour and a subtle fragrance and perfumes suitable for men have a distinct fragrance and a transparent colour.'[4345]

٣٨٥٤. رسولُ اللهِ صلى الله عليه وآله : طِيبُ النِّساءِ ما ظَهَرَ لَونُهُ وخَفِيَ رِيحُهُ، وطِيبُ الرِّجالِ ما ظَهَرَ رِيحُهُ وخَفِيَ لَونُهُ.٤٣٠٩

3855. **The Prophet (SAWA) said,** 'Any woman who perfumes herself and goes out among people intending for them to smell her fragrance is an adulteress.'[4346]

٣٨٥٥. عنه صلى الله عليه وآله : أيُّما امرأةٍ استَعطَرَتْ فَمَرَّتْ علىٰ قَومٍ لِيَجِدُوا مِن رِيحِها فهي زانِيَةٌ.٤٣١٠

257

THE EVIL OMEN

الطِّيَرَةُ

1194. Drawing Evil Omens

١١٩٤ ـ التَّطَيُّرُ

3856. **The Prophet (SAWA) said,** 'He who is *driven by an evil omen to abandon fulfilment of*

٣٨٥٦. رسولُ اللهِ صلى الله عليه وآله : مَن رَدَّتهُ الطِّيَرَةُ عَن

his need has indeed associated something with Allah.’[4347]

حاجَتِهِ فَقَد أشرَكَ.[٤٣١١]

3857. **The Prophet (SAWA) said,** ‘He who leaves his home intending to travel, then returns because of an evil omen has indeed disbelieved in what has been revealed to Muhammad.’[4348]

٣٨٥٧ . عنه ﷺ: مَن خَرَجَ يُريدُ سَفَراً فَرَجَعَ مِن طَيرٍ فقد كَفَرَ بما أُنزِلَ على محمّدٍ.[٤٣١٢]

3858. **The Prophet (SAWA) said,** ‘The truest omen is the optimistic auspice.’[4349]

٣٨٥٨ . عنه ﷺ: أصدَقُ الطِّيَرَةِ الفَألُ.[٤٣١٣]

3859. **The Prophet (SAWA) said,** ‘One who draws evil omens or believes evil omens drawn by others, or predicts the future or has his future predicted for him, or practices magic or has magic practiced for him, is not one of us.’[4350]

٣٨٥٩ . عنه ﷺ: ليسَ مِنّا مَن تَطَيَّرَ أو تُطُيِّرَ لَهُ.[٤٣١٤]

3860. **The Prophet (SAWA) said,** ‘The penance for taking an evil omen is complete reliance on Allah.’[4351]

٣٨٦٠ . عنه ﷺ: كَفّارَةُ الطِّيَرَةِ التَّوَكُّلُ.[٤٣١٥]

3861. **The Prophet (SAWA) said,** ‘There is no such thing as an evil omen or bad luck.’[4352]

٣٨٦١ . عنه ﷺ: لا طِيَرَةَ ولا شُؤمَ.[٤٣١٦]

3862. It is narrated in *Makārim al-Akhlāq*: ‘Verily, the Prophet (SAWA) used to like the optimistic auspice and used to dislike the evil omen. He used to tell people who saw something they disliked and took it to mean an evil omen to say: ‘O Allah, none gives good but You, and none repels evil but You, and there is no power and no strength except with You.’[4353]

٣٨٦٢ . مكارم الأخلاق: في الحديث: إنّ النبيَّ ﷺ كانَ يُحِبُّ الفَألَ الحَسَنَ ويَكرَهُ الطِّيَرَةَ، وكانَ يَأمُرُ مَن رَأى شَيئاً يَكرَهُهُ ويَتَطَيَّرُ مِنهُ أن يقولَ: اللّهُمَّ لا يُؤتي الخَيرَ إلّا أنتَ، ولا يَدفَعُ السَّيِّئاتِ إلّا أنتَ، ولا حَولَ ولا قُوَّةَ إلّا بِكَ.[٤٣١٧]

3863. **Imām al-Ṣādiq (AS) said,** ‘The evil omen takes effect according to what you make of it – if you do not take it seriously, it will not be serious, and if you attach great importance to it, it will bear great importance, and if you do not make anything of it, it will not mean anything.’[4354]

٣٨٦٣ . الإمامُ الصّادقُ (ع): الطِّيَرَةُ على ما تَجعَلُها إن هَوَّنتَها تَهَوَّنَت، وإن شَدَّدتَها تَشَدَّدَت، وإن لَم تَجعَلها شَيئاً لَم تَكُن شَيئاً.[٤٣١٨]

258

NAILS

الظُّفُرُ

1195. Encouraging the Clipping of One's Nails

١١٩٥ ـ الحَثُّ على تَقليمِ الأظفارِ

3864. **The Prophet (SAWA) said,** 'Clipping one's nails prevents the worst disease, and yields abundant sustenance.'[4355]

٣٨٦٤. رسولُ اللهِ ﷺ: تقليمُ الأظفارِ يَمنَعُ الداءَ الأعظَمَ، و يُدِرُّ الرِّزقَ. [٤٣١٩]

3865. **Imām al-Bāqir (AS) said,** 'Do cut your nails indeed for verily they are Satan's resting place, and from him ensues forgetfulness.'[4356]

٣٨٦٥. الإمامُ الباقرُ ﷺ: إنَّما قَصُّ الأظفارِ لأنَّها مَقيلُ الشَّيطانِ، ومِنهُ يَكونُ النِّسيانُ. [٤٣٢٠]

3866. **Imām al-Ṣādiq (AS) said,** 'Verily the most hidden and subtle way that Satan has managed to gain control over man is that he has made himself an abode under his nails [i.e. in unclean places].'[4357]

٣٨٦٦. الإمامُ الصّادقُ ﷺ: إنّ أسترَ وأخفىٰ ما يُسَلَّطُ الشَّيطانُ مِن ابنِ آدَمَ أن صارَ أن يَسكُنَ تَحتَ الأظافيرِ. [٤٣٢١]

1196. Encouraging Women to Leave their Nails (Long)[4358]

١١٩٦ ـ الحَثُّ عَلىٰ تَركِ الأظافيرِ لِلنِّساءِ [٤٣٢٢]

3867. It is narrated in *al-Kāfī* on the authority of al-Sakūnī that the Prophet of Allah (AS) said to men, 'Cut your nails', and to women, 'Leave them for verily that is more beautiful for you.'[4359]

٣٨٦٧. الكافي: قالَ رسولُ اللهِ ـ للرِّجالِ ـ: قُصُّوا أظافيرَكُم، وللنِّساءِ: أترُكنَ فإنَّهُ أزيَنُ لَكُنَّ. [٤٣٢٣]

259

WRONGDOING[4360]

الظُّلمُ

1197. Caution Against Wrongdoing

١١٩٧ ـ التَّحذيرُ مِنَ الظُّلمِ

"And Allah does not guide the wrongdoing ones."[4361]

﴿وَاللهُ لا يَهْدِي القَوْمَ الظّالِمِينَ﴾. [٤٣٢٤]

"Indeed the wrongdoers will not be felicitous."[4362]

﴿إنَّهُ لا يُفْلِحُ الظّالِمُونَ﴾. [٤٣٢٥]

3868. **The Prophet (SAWA) said,** 'Beware of wrongdoing for verily it corrupts your hearts.'[4363]

٣٨٦٨. رسولُ اللهِ ﷺ: إيّاكُم والظُّلمَ؛ فإنّهُ يُخرِبُ قُلوبَكُم.[٤٣٢٦]

3869. **The Prophet (SAWA) said,** 'Verily the servant will come on the Day of Resurrection having performed many good deeds which please him, when a man will come, complaining [to Allah], 'O Lord, this man has wronged me', whereupon some of his good deeds will be taken and transferred to the good deeds of the plaintiff. The situation will continue thus until finally he will be left with no good deeds, and then the plaintiff's evil deeds will start being transferred to his own evil deeds, and he will continue to pay for them thus until he will enter the Fire.'[4364]

٣٨٦٩. عنه ﷺ: إنّه لَيأتِي العَبدُ يومَ القِيامَةِ وقد سَرَّتهُ حَسناتُهُ، فَيَجيءُ الرجُلُ فيقولُ: يا ربِّ ظَلَمَني هذا، فَيُؤخَذُ مِن حَسَناتِهِ فَيُجعَلُ في حَسَناتِ الذي سَألَهُ، فما يَزالُ كذلكَ حتّى ما يَبقىٰ لَهُ حَسَنةٌ، فإذا جاءَ مَن يَسألُهُ نَظَرَ إلىٰ سَيِّئاتِهِ فَجُعِلَت مَعَ سيّئاتِ الرَّجُلِ، فلا يَزالُ يُستَوفىٰ مِنهُ حتّىٰ يَدخُلَ النارَ.[٤٣٢٧]

3870. **The Prophet (SAWA) said,** 'Fear wrongdoing, for verily it is a source of darkness on the Day of Resurrection.'[4365]

٣٨٧٠. عنه ﷺ: اتَّقوا الظُّلمَ؛ فإنّهُ ظُلُماتٌ يومَ القِيامَةِ.[٤٣٢٨]

3871. **Imām ʿAlī (AS) said,** 'Wrongdoing is the most painful of all vices.'[4366]

٣٨٧١. الإمامُ عليٌّ ﷺ: الظُّلمُ ألأمُ الرَّذائلِ.[٤٣٢٩]

3872. **Imām ʿAlī (AS) said,** 'Wrongdoing causes feet to slip, snatches away bounties and destroys nations.'[4367]

٣٨٧٢. عنه ﷺ: الظُّلمُ يُزِلُّ القَدَمَ، ويَسلُبُ النِّعَمَ ويُهلِكُ الأُمَمَ.[٤٣٣٠]

3873. **Imām ʿAlī (AS) said,** in denouncing wrongdoing, 'By Allah, I would rather spend a sleepless night on the thorns of the Saʿdān tree [a type of prickly tree], or be driven as a prisoner in shackles, than meet Allah and His Messenger on the Day of Resurrection having wronged any servant or having usurped any kind of worldly wealth. How can I wrong anyone for the sake of this soul that is rapidly hastening towards destruction and is to remain under the earth for a long time?'[4368]

٣٨٧٣. عنه ﷺ ـ في خُطبَةٍ لَهُ يَتبَرّأُ مِن الظُّلمِ ـ: واللهِ لَأن أبيتَ علىٰ حَسَكِ السَّعدانِ مُسَهَّداً، أو أُجَرَّ في الأغلالِ مُصَفَّداً، أحَبُّ إلَيَّ مِن أن ألقَى اللهَ ورسولَهُ يَومَ القِيامَةِ ظالِماً لِبَعضِ العِبادِ، وغاصِباً لِشَيءٍ مِن الحُطامِ، وكيفَ أظلِمُ أحَداً لِنَفسٍ يَسرِعُ إلى البِلىٰ قُفُولُها، ويَطُولُ في الثَّرىٰ حُلُولُها؟![٤٣٣١]

3874. **Imām ʿAlī (AS) said,** 'By Allah, if I was given all the seven domains with all that exists under its celestial spheres in order that I may disobey Allah to the extent of snatching a single grain of barley from an ant, I would not do it.'[4369]

٣٨٧٤. عنه ﷺ ـ أيضاً ـ: واللهِ لو أُعطِيتُ الأقاليمَ السَّبعَةَ بما تَحتَ أفلاكِها، علىٰ أن أعصِيَ اللهَ في نَملَةٍ أسلُبُها جُلبَ شَعيرَةٍ ما فَعَلتُهُ.[٤٣٣٢]

3875. **Imām ʿAlī (AS) said,** 'Beware of wrongdoing, for the living days of one who wrongs others become odious.'[4370]

٣٨٧٥ . عنه عليه السلام : إيّاكَ والظُّلمَ؛ فَمَن ظَلَمَ كَرُهَت أيّامُهُ.[٤٣٣٣]

3876. **Imām ʿAlī (AS) said,** 'Nothing induces the reversal of Allah's bounty or the hastening of His retribution than continuous injustice [to others]; for verily Allah hears the call of the oppressed and lies in wait for the oppressors.'[4371]

٣٨٧٦ . عنه عليه السلام :لَيسَ شَيءٌ أدعىٰ إلىٰ تَغييرِ نِعمَةِ اللهِ وتَعجِيلِ نِقْمَتِهِ مِن إقامَةٍ علىٰ ظُلمٍ؛ فـإنّ اللهَ سَميعُ دَعوَةِ المُـضطَهَدِينَ (المَـظلومِينَ)، وهُـو للظالِمينَ بِالمِرصادِ.[٤٣٣٤]

3877. **Imām ʿAlī (AS) said,** 'The life of one who wrongs others is shattered.'[4372]

٣٨٧٧ . عنه عليه السلام : مَن ظَلَمَ قُصِمَ عُمرُهُ.[٤٣٣٥]

3878. **Imām ʿAlī (AS) said,** 'The one who takes wrongdoing as a mount is thrown off by it.'[4373]

٣٨٧٨ . عنه عليه السلام : راكِبُ الظُّلمِ يَكبُو بِهِ مَركَبُهُ.[٤٣٣٦]

3879. **Imām ʿAlī (AS) said,** 'The one who tyrannises others is ruined by his own tyranny.'[4374]

٣٨٧٩ . عنه عليه السلام : مَن جارَ أهلَكَهُ جَورُهُ.[٤٣٣٧]

3880. **Imām al-Ṣādiq (AS) narrated,** 'The Prophet (SAWA) forbade anyone from eating anything that an ant carries in its mouth or holds in its grip.'[4375]

٣٨٨٠ . الإمامُ الصّادقُ عليه السلام : نهىٰ رسولُ اللهِ صلى الله عليه وآله أن يُؤكَلَ ما تَحمِلُ النَّملَةُ بِفِيها وقَوائمِها.[٤٣٣٨]

1198. Types of Wrongdoing

١١٩٨ ـ أنواعُ الظُّلمِ

3881. **Imām ʿAlī (AS) said,** 'Know that wrongdoing is of three types: the wrongdoing that is unforgivable, the wrongdoing that cannot be left unaccounted, and the wrongdoing that is forgivable and unquestioned. The wrong that is unforgivable is association of anything with Allah …the wrong that is forgivable is when the servant is unjust to himself and wrongs himself with regard to his faults, and the wrong that cannot be left unaccounted is the wrong that people do unto each other.'[4376]

٣٨٨١ . الإمامُ عليٌّ عليه السلام :ألا وإنَّ الظُّلمَ ثلاثةٌ :فَظُلمٌ لا يُغفَرُ، وظُلمٌ لا يُترَكُ، وظُلمٌ مَغفورٌ لا يُطلَبُ، فأمّا الظُّلمُ الذي لا يُغفَرُ فـالشِّركُ بِـاللهِ... وأمّـا الظُّلمُ الذي يُغفَرُ فَظُلمُ العَبدِ نـفسَهُ عـندَ بـعضِ الهَناتِ، وأمّا الظُّلمُ الذي لا يُترَكُ فـظُلمُ العِـبادِ بَعضِهِم بَعضاً.[٤٣٣٩]

(See also: SINNING: section 771)

(اُنظر) الذنب: باب ٧٧١.

1199. The Most Atrocious Type of Wrong

١١٩٩ ـ أفحَشُ الظُّلمِ

3882. **The Prophet (SAWA) said,** 'The wrath of *Allah is indeed severe on one who wrongs*

٣٨٨٢ . رسولُ اللهِ صلى الله عليه وآله : اشتَدَّ غَضَبُ اللهِ عَلىٰ مَن

somebody that has no one to help him apart from Allah.'[4377]

ظَلَمَ مَن لا يَجِدُ ناصِراً غيرَ اللهِ.٤٣٤٠

3883. **Imām ʿAlī (AS) said,** 'Wronging the weak is the most atrocious type of injustice.'[4378]

٣٨٨٣. الإمامُ عليٌّ عليه السلام: ظُلمُ الضَّعيفِ أفحَشُ الظُّلمِ.٤٣٤١

3884. **Imām ʿAlī (AS)** was once asked, 'Which sin hastens punishment down on its perpetrator the fastest?' to which he replied, 'He who wrongs somebody that has no helper save Allah, he who repays bounties with negligence and laxity, and he who displays arrogant and intimidating behaviour towards the poor.'[4379]

٣٨٨٤. عنه عليه السلام ـ لَمّا سُئلَ: أيُّ ذنبٍ أعجَلُ عُقوبَةً لِصاحِبِهِ؟ ـ: مَن ظَلَمَ مَن لا ناصِرَ لَهُ إلّا اللهُ، وجاوَرَ النِّعمَةَ بِالتَّقصيرِ، واستَطالَ بِالبَغيِ على الفَقيرِ.٤٣٤٢

3885. **Imām ʿAlī (AS) said,** 'One of the most atrocious types of injustice is to wrong kind people.'[4380]

٣٨٨٥. عنه عليه السلام: مِن أفحَشِ الظُّلمِ ظُلمُ الكِرامِ.٤٣٤٣

3886. **Imām al-Bāqir (AS)** narrated that when his father, Imām ʿAlī Zayn al-ʿĀbidīn (AS) was approaching death, he hugged him close to his chest and said, 'O my son, I am advising you of the same thing that my father advised me in his will when he was approaching death, and the same thing that he said his father advised him - O my son! Beware of wronging one who has no helper against you but Allah.'[4381]

٣٨٨٦. الإمامُ الباقرُ عليه السلام: لَمّا حَضَرَ عَلِيَّ بنَ الحُسينِ عليه السلام الوَفاةُ ضَمَّني إلىٰ صَدرِهِ، ثُمّ قالَ: يا بُنَيَّ، أوصيكَ بِما أوصاني بِهِ أبي عليه السلام حينَ حَضَرَتهُ الوَفاةُ وبِما ذَكَرَ أنّ أباهُ أوصاهُ بِهِ، قالَ: يا بُنَيَّ، إيّاكَ وظُلمَ مَن لا يَجِدُ علَيكَ ناصِراً إلّا اللهَ.٤٣٤٤

1200. Granting Respite to the Wrongdoer[4382]

١٢٠٠ ـ إمهالُ الظّالِمِ

3887. **The Prophet (SAWA) said,** 'Verily Allah gives such respite to the wrongdoer, until he says [rejoicingly], 'He [Allah] has indeed forgotten about me!' Then Allah seizes him with a terrible seizing. Verily Allah has praised Himself with regard to the way in which He destroys wrongdoers, saying in the Qur'an: *"Thus the wrongdoing ones were rooted out, and all praise belongs to Allah, the Lord of all the worlds."*'[4383] [4384]

٣٨٨٧. رسولُ اللهِ صلى الله عليه وآله: إنَّ اللهَ يُمهِلُ الظّالِمَ حتّىٰ يقولَ: قد أهمَلَني! ثُمّ يَأخُذُهُ أخذَةً رابِيَةً، إنّ اللهَ حَمِدَ نفسَهُ عِندَ هَلاكِ الظّالِمينَ، فقالَ: ﴿فَقُطِعَ دابِرُ القَومِ الّذينَ ظَلَمُوا والحَمدُ للهِ رَبِّ العالَمينَ﴾.٤٣٤٥، ٤٣٤٦

3888. **Imām al-Bāqir (AS) said,** 'Allah gave Pharaoh a long respite of forty years, between His

٣٨٨٨. تفسير نور الثقلين: قالَ الإمامُ الباقرُ عليه السلام:

two addresses to him, then Allah seized him with the punishment of this life and the Hereafter. So forty years passed between the time that Allah said to Prophet Moses (AS) and Prophet Aaron (AS): *"Your supplication has already been granted"* and between the time He actually showed them the answer to their supplication [i.e. through Pharaoh's annihilation].'[4385]

أملَى اللهُ عزّ وجلّ لِفرعَونَ ما بينَ الكَـلِمَتَينِ... أربَعينَ سَنَةً، ثُمّ أخَذَهُ اللهُ نَكالَ الآخِرَةِ والأُولىٰ، وكـانَ بـينَ أن قـالَ اللهُ عـزّوجلّ لمـوسىٰ وهارونَ ﷺ : ﴿قد أُجِيبَتْ دَعوَتُكُما﴾[٤٣٤٧] وبينَ أن عَرَّفَهُ اللهُ تعالىٰ الإجابَةَ أربَعينَ سَنَةً.[٤٣٤٨]

1201. The Wrongdoer's Regret

١٢٠١ ـ نَدامَةُ الظّالِمِ

"A day when the wrongdoer will bite his hands, saying, 'I wish I had followed the Apostle's way!'"[4386]

﴿وَيَوْمَ يَعَضُّ ٱلظَّالِمُ عَلَىٰ يَدَيْهِ يَقُولُ يَا لَـيْتَنِي ٱتَّخَذْتُ مَعَ ٱلرَّسُولِ سَبِيلًا﴾.[٤٣٤٩]

3889. **The Prophet (SAWA) said,** 'Wrongdoing results in regret.'[4387]

٣٨٨٩. رسولُ اللهِ ﷺ : الظُّلمُ نَدامَةٌ.[٤٣٥٠]

3890. **Imām 'Alī (AS) said,** 'The day that justice is brought to the wrongdoer is much more severe than the day oppression is done unto the oppressed.'[4388]

٣٨٩٠. الإمامُ عليٌّ ﷺ : يَومُ العَدلِ على الظّالِمِ أشَدُّ مِن يَومِ الجَورِ على المَظلُومِ.[٤٣٥١]

3891. **Imām al-Bāqir (AS) said,** 'The wronged one profits much more from his oppressor's Hereafter [i.e. his account of deeds] than the oppressor profits from the world [i.e. the wealth or honour] of the one he is wronging.'[4389]

٣٨٩١. الإمامُ الباقرُ ﷺ : ما يَأخُذُ المَظلومُ مِن دِينِ الظّالِمِ أكثَرُ مِمّا يَأخُذُ الظّالِمُ مِن دُنيا المَظلومِ.[٤٣٥٢]

1202. Caution Against Aiding the Wrongdoer

١٢٠٢ ـ التَّحذيرُ مِن إعانَةِ الظّالِمِ

"And do not incline toward the wrongdoers, lest the Fire should touch you, and you will not have any friend besides Allah, then you will not be helped."[4390]

﴿وَلا تَركَنُوا إلَى الَّذِينَ ظَلَمُوا فَتَمَسَّكُمُ النَّارُ وَما لَكُمْ مِنْ دُونِ اللهِ مِنْ أَوْلِياءَ ثُمَّ لا تُنْصَرُونَ﴾.[٤٣٥٣]

3892. **The Prophet (SAWA) said,** 'On the Day of Resurrection, a caller will call out, 'Where are the wrongdoers and their helpers? Whoever prepared the inkwell for them, or tied their purse for them, or supplied them with a pen – gather them all together with them.'[4391]

٣٨٩٢. رسولُ اللهِ ﷺ : إذا كانَ يَومُ القِيامَةِ نادىٰ مُنادٍ: أينَ الظَّلَمَةُ وأعوانُهُم ؟ مَن لاقَ لَهُم دَواةً، أو رَبَطَ لَهُم كِيساً، أو مَدَّ لَهُم مُدَّةَ قَلَمٍ، فاحشُرُوهُم مَعَهُم.[٤٣٥٤]

3893. **Imām al-Ṣādiq (AS) said,** 'The perpetrator of the wrong act, his accomplice and the one who approves of it - all three are equally to blame for the wrong.'[4392]

٣٨٩٣ . الإمامُ الصّادقُ ؑ :العامِلُ بالظُّلمِ والمُعينُ لَهُ والرّاضِي بِهِ شُرَكاءُ ثَلاثَتُهُم. ٤٣٥٥

3894. **Imām al-Ṣādiq (AS) said,** 'If it was not for the fact that the Banī Umayya found people to scribe for them, to shade them, to fight for them, and to attend their gatherings, they would never have been able to snatch away our rights [by themselves].'[4393]

٣٨٩٤ . عنه ؑ : لَولا أنَّ بَني أُمَيَّةَ وَجَدُوا مَن يَكتُبُ لَهُم، ويَجبِي لَهُمُ الفَيءَ، ويُقاتِلُ عَنهُم، ويَشهَدُ جَماعَتَهُم، لَما سَلَبُونا حَقَّنا. ٤٣٥٦

3895. **Imām al-Ṣādiq (AS)** with respect to Allah's verse in the Qur'an: *"And do not incline toward the wrongdoers, lest the Fire should touch you, and you will not have any friend besides Allah, then you will not be helped"*, said, 'This refers to the man who attends to an unjust ruler, wishing his rule to continue in order that he may put his hand in his purse and give him thereof.'[4394]

٣٨٩٥ . عنه ؑ ـ في قولِهِ تعالى: ﴿ولا تَرْكَنُوا إلى الَّذِينَ ظَلَمُوا ...﴾ ـ: هُوَ الرَّجُلُ يَأتِي السُّلطانَ فَيُحِبُّ بَقاءَهُ إلى أن يُدخِلَ يَدَهُ إلى كِيسِهِ فَيُعطِيَهُ. ٤٣٥٧

1203. Enjoinment of Aiding the Wronged

١٢٠٣ ـ الحَثُّ عَلى إعانَةِ المَظلومِ

"Whoever intercedes for a good cause shall receive a share of it, and whoever intercedes for an evil cause shall share its burden, and Allah is proponent over all things."[4395]

﴿مَن يَشْفَعْ شَفاعَةً حَسَنَةً يَكُنْ لَهُ نَصِيبٌ مِنْها وَمَن يَشْفَعْ شَفاعَةً سَيِّئَةً يَكُنْ لَهُ كِفْلٌ مِنْها وَكانَ اللهُ عَلى كُلِّ شَيْءٍ مُقِيتاً﴾. ٤٣٥٨

3896. **The Prophet (SAWA) said,** 'Whoever takes the side of the oppressed over the oppressor will be with me as my companion in Paradise.'[4396]

٣٨٩٦ . رسولُ اللهِ ﷺ : مَن أخَذَ لِلمَظلومِ مِنَ الظّالِمِ كانَ مَعِي فِي الجَنَّةِ مُصاحِباً. ٤٣٥٩

3897. **Imām ʿAlī (AS) said** to Imām Ḥasan and Imām Ḥusayn (AS), 'Speak the truth, and do good deeds to secure a good reward, and be adversaries to the oppressor and aiders of the oppressed.'[4397]

٣٨٩٧ . الإمامُ عليٌّ ؑ ـ للحَسَنَينِ ؑ ـ: قُولا بِالحَقِّ، واعمَلا لِلأجرِ، وكُونا لِلظّالِمِ خَصماً ولِلمَظلومِ عَوناً. ٤٣٦٠

3898. **Imām al-Kāẓim (AS) said** to ʿAlī b. Yaqtīn, 'Verily Allah, most High, has friends just like the friends of the oppressors, with the aid of whom He defends His friends, and you are one of them, O ʿAlī.'[4398]

٣٨٩٨ . الإمامُ الكاظمُ ؑ ـ لِعليِّ بنِ يَقطينٍ ـ: إنّ للهِ تعالى أولياءَ مَعَ أولياءِ الظَّلَمَةِ لِيَدفَعَ بِهِم عَن أوليائِهِ، وأنتَ مِنهُم يا عليُّ. ٤٣٦١

1204. Being Wary of the Plea [to Allah] of One Who Has Been Wronged

١٢٠٤ ـ التَّحذيرُ مِن دَعوةِ المَظلومِ

3899. **The Prophet (SAWA) said,** 'Be on your guard against the plea [to Allah] of one who has been wronged, for verily he asks Allah his right, and verily Allah never denies a right to one whom it is due.'[4399]

٣٨٩٩. رسولُ اللهِ ﷺ: اِتَّقُوا دَعوَةَ المَظلومِ؛ فإنّما يَسألُ اللهُ تعالىٰ حَقَّهُ، وإنَّ اللهَ تعالىٰ لَم يَمنَعْ ذا حَقٍّ حَقَّهُ.[٤٣٦٢]

3900. **The Prophet (SAWA) said,** 'Be on your guard against the plea of one who has been wronged, even if he be a disbeliever, for verily there is no veil preventing his plea from being answered.'[4400]

٣٩٠٠. عنه ﷺ: اِتَّقُوا دَعوَةَ المَظلومِ وإن كانَ كافِراً؛ فإنّهُ لَيسَ دُونَهُ حِجابٌ.[٤٣٦٣]

3901. **Imām 'Alī (AS) said,** 'The most piercing arrow is the plea of the oppressed.'[4401]

٣٩٠١. الإمامُ عليٌّ عليه السلام: أنفَذُ السِّهامِ دَعوَةُ المَظلومِ.[٤٣٦٤]

(See also: SUPPLICATION: section 699)

(أنظر) الدعاء: باب ٦٩٩.

260

CONJECTURE

الظَّنُّ

1205. Conjecture of the Intellectual

١٢٠٥ ـ ظَنُّ العاقِلِ

3902. **Imām 'Alī (AS) said,** 'A man's conjecture is proportionate to the extent of his reason.'[4402]

٣٩٠٢. الإمامُ عليٌّ عليه السلام: ظَنُّ الرَّجُلِ على قَدرِ عَقلِهِ.[٤٣٦٥]

3903. **Imām 'Alī (AS) said,** 'An intellectual man's conjecture is sounder than an ignorant man's certainty.'[4403]

٣٩٠٣. عنه عليه السلام: ظَنُّ العاقِلِ أصَحُّ مِن يَقينِ الجاهِلِ.[٤٣٦٦]

3904. **Imām 'Alī (AS) said,** 'Be wary of the opinions given by believers, for verily Allah has made the truth flow from their tongues.'[4404]

٣٩٠٤. عنه عليه السلام: اتَّقُوا ظُنُونَ المُؤمِنينَ؛ فإنَّ اللهَ تعالىٰ جَعَلَ الحَقَّ علىٰ ألسِنَتِهِم.[٤٣٦٧]

1206. Enjoinment to Entertain Good Opinion about the Deed of a Believer

١٢٠٦ ـ الحَثُّ علىٰ حُسنِ الظَّنِّ بِفِعلِ المُؤمِنِ

3905. **The Prophet (SAWA) said,** 'Make an excuse for your fellow brother, and even if you do

٣٩٠٥. رسولُ اللهِ ﷺ: أُطلُبْ لِأخيكَ عُذراً، فَإنْ

not have an excuse [for his behaviour], then seek out an excuse for him.'[4405]

لم تجِدْ لَهُ عُذراً فَالتَمِسْ لَهُ عُذراً.٤٣٦٨

3906. **Imām ʿAlī (AS) said,** 'See the best in any situation involving a fellow brother, until you experience something from him which proves you wrong, and do not assume the worst about something that your brother may say if you can find the possibility for good therein.'[4406]

٣٩٠٦. الإمامُ عليٌّ عليه السلام: ضَعْ أمرَ أخيكَ علىٰ أحسَنِهِ حتّىٰ يأتِيَكَ مِنهُ ما يَغلِبُكَ، ولا تَظُنَّنَّ بكَلِمَةٍ خَرَجَت مِن أخيكَ سُوءاً وأنتَ تَجِدُ لَها في الخَيرِ مَحمِلاً.٤٣٦٩

1207. The Virtue of Entertaining Good Opinions

١٢٠٧ـ فَضلُ حُسنِ الظَّنِّ

3907. **Imām ʿAlī (AS) said,** 'Entertaining good opinions is a comfort to the heart and [indicates] soundness of faith.'[4407]

٣٩٠٧. الإمامُ عليٌّ عليه السلام: حُسنُ الظَّنِّ راحَةُ القَلبِ وسَلامَةُ الدِّينِ.٤٣٧٠

3908. **Imām ʿAlī (AS) said,** 'Entertaining good opinions reduces anxiety, and saves one from being taken over by sin.'[4408]

٣٩٠٨. عنه عليه السلام: حُسنُ الظَّنِّ يُخَفِّفُ الهَمَّ، ويُنجي من تَقَلُّدِ الإثمِ.٤٣٧١

3909. **Imām ʿAlī (AS) said,** 'The one who thinks the best of people gains their love.'[4409]

٣٩٠٩. عنه عليه السلام: مَن حَسُنَ ظَنُّهُ بِالناسِ حازَ مِنهُمُ المَحَبَّةَ.٤٣٧٢

3910. **Imām ʿAlī (AS) said,** 'The best of piety is to think the best of people.'[4410]

٣٩١٠. عنه عليه السلام: أفضَلُ الوَرَعِ حُسنُ الظَّنِّ.٤٣٧٣

1208. Caution Against Entertaining Low or Suspicious Opinions

١٢٠٨ـ التَّحذيرُ مِن سوءِ الظَّنِّ

"O you who have faith! Avoid much suspicion. Indeed some suspicions are sins."[4411]

﴿يا أيُّها الَّذِينَ آمَنُوا اجْتَنِبُوا كَثِيراً مِنَ الظَّنِّ إنَّ بَعْضَ الظَّنِّ إثْمٌ﴾.٤٣٧٤

3911. **The Prophet (SAWA) said,** 'Beware of suspicion for verily suspicion is the worst of all lies.'[4412]

٣٩١١. رسولُ اللهِ صلى الله عليه وآله: إيّاكُم والظَّنَّ؛ فإنَّ الظَّنَّ أكذَبُ الكَذِبِ.٤٣٧٥

3912. **The Prophet (SAWA) said,** 'If you have assumed the worst [about someone or something], then do not seek to make it true. And if you are jealous [of someone or something] then do not

٣٩١٢. عنه صلى الله عليه وآله: إذا ظَنَنتُم فلا تُحَقِّقوا، وإذا

covet them, and if you draw an evil omen from something, ignore it and walk away.'[4413]

حَسَدتُم فلا تبغُوا، وإذا تطَيَّرتُم فامضُوا.٤٣٧٦

3913. **Imām ʿAlī (AS) said,** 'Verily miserliness, cowardice and greed are all evil impulses caused by entertaining a low opinion of Allah.'[4414]

٣٩١٣. الإمامُ عليٌّ ﷺ: إنّ البُخلَ والجُبنَ والحِرصَ غَرائزُ شَتّى يَجمَعُها سُوءُ الظَّنِّ بِاللهِ.٤٣٧٧

3914. **Imām ʿAlī (AS) said,** 'There is no room for faith with suspicion.'[4415]

٣٩١٤. عنه ﷺ: لا إيمانَ مَعَ سُوءِ الظَّنِّ.٤٣٧٨

3915. **Imām ʿAlī (AS) said,** 'Suspicion corrupts matters and gives rise to evils.'[4416]

٣٩١٥. عنه ﷺ: سُوءُ الظَّنِّ يُفسِدُ الأُمورَ ويَبعَثُ على الشُّرورِ.٤٣٧٩

3916. **Imām ʿAlī (AS) said,** 'Beware of entertaining suspicious thoughts for verily suspicion corrupts worship.'[4417]

٣٩١٦. عنه ﷺ: إيّاكَ أن تُسيءَ الظَّنَّ؛ فإنّ سُوءَ الظَّنِّ يُفسِدُ العِبادَةَ.٤٣٨٠

3917. **Imām ʿAlī (AS) said,** 'The evil person cannot think well of anybody because he can only see people as he himself is predisposed.'[4418]

٣٩١٧. عنه ﷺ: الشِّرّيرُ لا يَظُنُّ بأحَدٍ خَيراً؛ لأنّهُ لا يَراهُ إلّا بِطَبعِ نفسِهِ.٤٣٨١

1209. The Necessity of Avoiding that which Incites Suspicious Thoughts

١٢٠٩ ـ ضَرورَةُ التَّجَنُّبِ عَمّا يُوجِبُ سُوءَ الظَّنِّ

3918. **Imām ʿAlī (AS) said,** 'He who stands in a suspect place cannot blame anyone for thinking suspiciously of him.'[4419]

٣٩١٨. الإمامُ عليٌّ ﷺ: مَن وَقَّفَ نفسَهُ مَوقِفَ التُّهَمَةِ فلا يَلُومَنَّ مَن أساءَ بِهِ الظَّنَّ.٤٣٨٢

3919. **Imām ʿAlī (AS) said,** 'The one who enters bad places naturally stands to be accused, and the one who exposes himself to accusation cannot blame anyone for thinking suspiciously of him.'[4420]

٣٩١٩. عنه ﷺ: مَن دَخَلَ مَداخِلَ السَّوءِ اتُّهِمَ، مَن عَرَّضَ نفسَهُ للتُّهَمَةِ فلا يَلُومَنَّ مَن أساءَ بِهِ الظَّنَّ.٤٣٨٣

3920. **Imām ʿAlī (AS) said,** 'Sitting in the company of bad people engenders suspicious thoughts about good people.'[4421]

٣٩٢٠. عنه ﷺ: مُجالَسَةُ الأشرارِ تُورِثُ سُوءَ الظَّنِّ بِالأخيارِ.٤٣٨٤

3921. **Imām ʿAlī (AS) said,** 'The person in the worst state is the one who does not trust anybody because of his suspiciousness, and who is not *trusted by anybody because of his evil actions.*'[4422]

٣٩٢١. عنه ﷺ: أسوأُ النّاسِ حالاً مَن لَم يَثِقْ بأحَدٍ لِسُوءِ ظَنِّهِ، ولَم يَثِقْ بِهِ أحَدٌ لِسُوءِ فِعلِهِ.٤٣٨٥

3922. **Imām ʿAlī (AS) said,** 'The one who does not think well of people will remain alienated from everybody.'[4423]

٣٩٢٢. عنه ﷺ : مَن لَم يَحسُنْ ظَنُّهُ استَوحَشَ مِن كُلِّ أحَدٍ.٤٣٨٦

1210. Instances when Suspicion is Allowed

١٢١٠ـ مَوارِدُ جَوازِ سوءِ الظَّنِّ

3923. **The Prophet (SAWA) said,** 'Guard yourselves against people with suspicion.'[4424]

٣٩٢٣. رسولُ اللهِ ﷺ : إحتَرِسوا مِنَ النّاسِ بِسوءِ الظَّنِّ.٤٣٨٧

3924. **Imām ʿAlī (AS) said,** 'At a time when good prevails over an era and among its people, if a man suspects another person who has never been seen committing an offence, then he has indeed wronged him. And when corruption prevails over an era and among its people, if a man assumes the best about somebody, then he has indeed deceived himself.'[4425]

٣٩٢٤. الإمامُ عليٌّ ﷺ : إذا استَولَى الصَّلاحُ على الزَّمانِ وأهلِهِ ثُمّ أساءَ رَجُلٌ الظَّنَّ بِرَجُلٍ لَم تَظهَرْ مِنهُ حَوبَةٌ فقد ظَلَمَ، وإذا استَولَى الفَسادُ على الزَّمانِ وأهلِهِ فَأحسَنَ رَجُلٌ الظَّنَّ بِرَجُلٍ فَقد غَرَّرَ.٤٣٨٨

3925. **Imām al-Kāẓim (AS) said,** 'At a time when injustice is more prevalent than good, it is not permitted for anyone to entertain good opinions about another unless he knows him to be such.'[4426]

٣٩٢٥. الإمامُ الكاظمُ ﷺ : إذا كانَ الجَورُ أغلَبَ مِنَ الحَقِّ لَم يَحِلَّ لأحَدٍ أن يَظُنَّ بِأحَدٍ خَيراً حتّى يَعرِفَ ذلكَ مِنهُ.٤٣٨٩

261

WORSHIP

العِبادَةُ

1211. Encouraging Worship

١٢١١ـ الحَثُّ عَلَى العِبادَةِ

"I did not create the jinn and the humans except that they may worship Me."[4427]

﴿وَما خَلَقْتُ الجِنَّ وَالإنْسَ إلّا لِيَعْبُدُونِ﴾.٤٣٩٠

3926. **The Prophet (SAWA) said,** 'The best of people is he who longs for worship and embraces it, loves it with his heart, throws himself into it with his whole body, and devotes himself exclusively to it, such that he is not concerned in what worldly state he wakes up in the morning: in difficulty or in ease.'[4428]

٣٩٢٦. رسولُ اللهِ ﷺ : أفضَلُ النّاسِ مَن عَشِقَ العِبادَةَ فَعانَقَها، وأحَبَّها بِقَلبِهِ، وباشَرَها بِجَسَدِهِ، وتَفَرَّغَ لَها، فَهُوَ لا يُبالي عَلى ما أصبَحَ مِنَ الدُّنيا: عَلى عُسرٍ أم عَلى يُسرٍ.٤٣٩١

3927. **The Prophet (SAWA) said,** 'Worship suffices as an occupation.'[4429]

٣٩٢٧ . عنه ﷺ : كفى بالعِبادَةِ شُغلاً.[٤٣٩٢]

3928. **The Prophet (SAWA) said,** 'Your Lord addresses you, saying, 'O son of Adam! Devote yourself exclusively to My worship and I will fill your heart with wealth and your hands with ready sustenance. O son of Adam! Do not distance yourself from Me or I will fill your heart with poverty and your hands with work [to preoccupy you].'[4430]

٣٩٢٨ . عنه ﷺ : يقولُ رَبُّكُم: يَابنَ آدَمَ، تَفرَّغْ لِعِبادَتي أملأْ قَلبَكَ غِنىً وأملأْ يَدَيكَ رِزقاً. يَابنَ آدمَ، لا تَباعَدْ مِنّي فأملأَ قَلبَكَ فَقراً وأملأَ يَدَيكَ شُغلاً.[٤٣٩٣]

3929. **Imām 'Alī (AS) said,** 'When Allah loves a servant He inspires him to carry out the best forms of worship.'[4431]

٣٩٢٩ . الإمامُ عليٌّ ﷺ : إذا أحَبَّ اللهُ عبداً ألهَمَهُ حُسنَ العِبادَةِ.[٤٣٩٤]

3930. **Imām 'Alī (AS) said,** 'Adoration [of Allah] consists of five things: keeping the stomach empty, reading the Qur'an, performing the night prayer, imploring Allah at dawn, and crying much from fear of Allah.'[4432]

٣٩٣٠ . عنه ﷺ : العُبوديَّةُ خَمسَةُ أشياءَ: خَلاءُ البطنِ، وَقِراءةُ القرآنِ، وقِيامُ اللَّيلِ، والتَّضَرُّعُ عِندَ الصُّبحِ، والبُكاءُ مِن خَشيَةِ اللهِ.[٤٣٩٥]

1212. The Role of Understanding and Conviction in Worship

١٢١٢ـ دورُ التَّفَقُّهِ واليقينِ فِي العِبادَةِ

3931. **The Prophet (SAWA) said,** 'There is no use to worship without conviction.'[4433]

٣٩٣١ . رسولُ اللهِ ﷺ : لا عِبادَةَ إلّا بيَقينٍ.[٤٣٩٦]

3932. **The Prophet (SAWA) said,** 'Worship Allah as if you see Him, for although you may not see Him, indeed He sees you.'[4434]

٣٩٣٢ . عنه ﷺ : أُعبُدِ اللهَ كأنَّكَ تَراهُ، فإن لَم تَكُن تَراهُ، فإنَّهُ يَراكَ.[٤٣٩٧]

3933. **Imām 'Alī (AS) said,** 'Worship without understanding is no good.'[4435]

٣٩٣٣ . الإمامُ عليٌّ ﷺ : لا خَيرَ في عِبادَةٍ لَيسَ فيها تَفَقُّهٌ.[٤٣٩٨]

3934. **Imām Zayn al-'Ābidīn (AS) said,** 'There is no point to worship unless performed with understanding.'[4436]

٣٩٣٤ . الإمامُ زينُ العابدينَ ﷺ : لا عِبادَةَ إلّا بالتَّفَقُّهِ.[٤٣٩٩]

(See also: CONVICTION: 419; JURISPRUDENCE: section 1497)

(أنظر) عنوان ٤١٩ «اليقين»؛ الفقه: باب ١٤٩٧.

1213. Types of Worship

١٢١٣ـ أنواعُ العِبادَةِ

3935. **Prophet Jesus (AS) asked a man,** 'What are you doing?' The man replied, 'I am worshipping.' So he asked, 'Then who is it that supports you [financially]?' He replied, 'My brother', to which Prophet Jesus (AS) said, 'Your brother is a better worshipper than you.'[4437]

٣٩٣٥. عيسى ﷺ ـ لِرجُلٍ ـ: ما تَصنَعُ ؟ قالَ: أتَعَبَّدُ، قالَ: فمَن يَعودُ علَيكَ ؟ قالَ: أخي، قالَ: أخوكَ أعبَدُ مِنكَ.[٤٤٠٠]

3936. **The Prophet (SAWA) said,** 'Worship consists of ten parts, nine of which are to do with earning a lawful living.'[4438]

٣٩٣٦. رسولُ اللهِ ﷺ: العِبادَةُ عَشرَةُ أجزاءٍ، تِسعَةُ أجزاءٍ في طَلَبِ الحَلالِ.[٤٤٠١]

3937. **The Prophet (SAWA) said,** 'A son's looking at his parents with love is a form of worship [of Allah].'[4439]

٣٩٣٧. عنه ﷺ: نَظَرُ الوَلَدِ إلىٰ والِدَيهِ حُبّاً لَهُما عِبادَةٌ.[٤٤٠٢]

3938. **The Prophet (SAWA) said,** 'Looking at [the face of] a scholar is worship, looking at [the face of] a just leader (*imām*) is worship, looking at one's parents with kindness and mercy is worship, and looking at the face of a brother whom you love for the sake of Allah is worship.'[4440]

٣٩٣٨. عنه ﷺ: النَّظَرُ إلَى العالِمِ عِبادَةٌ، والنَّظَرُ إلَى الإمامِ المُقسِطِ عِبادَةٌ، وَالنَّظَرُ إلَى الوالِدَينِ بِرأفَةٍ وَرحمَةٍ عِبادَةٌ، وَالنَّظرُ إلىٰ أخٍ تَوَدُّهُ في اللهِ عَزَّ وجلَّ عِبادَةٌ.[٤٤٠٣]

3939. **The Prophet (SAWA) said,** 'Entertaining the best opinion about Allah is a form of worship of Allah, most High.'[4441]

٣٩٣٩. عنه ﷺ: حُسنُ الظَّنِّ باللهِ مِن عِبادَةِ اللهِ تعالىٰ.[٤٤٠٤]

3940. **Imām ʿAlī (AS) said,** 'Pondering about the dominion of the heavens and the earth is the worship of the sincere ones.'[4442]

٣٩٤٠. الإمامُ عليٌّ ﷺ: التَّفكُّرُ في مَلَكوتِ السَّماواتِ والأرضِ عِبادَةُ المُخلِصينَ.[٤٤٠٥]

3941. **Imām ʿAlī (AS) said,** 'Verily part of worship is to talk to people in a gentle manner and to spread the greeting of peace among them.'[4443]

٣٩٤١. عنه ﷺ: إنّ مِنَ العِبادَةِ لِينَ الكَلامِ وإفشاءَ السَّلامِ.[٤٤٠٦]

3942. **Imām al-Ṣādiq (AS) said,** 'Verily above every act of worship is an even better act of worship, and love for us, the household of the Prophet, is the best act of worship.'[4444]

٣٩٤٢. الإمامُ الصّادقُ ﷺ: إنّ فَوقَ كلِّ عِبادَةٍ عِبادَةً، و حُبُّنا أهلَ البَيتِ أفضَلُ عِبادَةٍ.[٤٤٠٧]

1214. Types of Worshippers

١٢١٤ ـ أنواعُ العُبّادِ

3943. **Imām al-Ṣādiq (AS) said,** 'Worshippers are of three types: people who worship Allah, Mighty and Exalted, out of fear, and that is the worship of a slave; people who worship Allah, Blessed and most High, seeking to be rewarded thereof, and that is the worship of an employee; and people who worship Allah, Mighty and Exalted, out of love for Him, and that is the worship of free men and is the best type of worship.'[4445]

٣٩٤٣. الإمامُ الصّادقُ ﵇ : (إنّ) العُبّادَ ثَـلاثةٌ: قَومٌ عَبَدوا اللهَ عَزَّوجلَّ خَوفاً فتِلكَ عِبادَةُ العَبيدِ، وَقَوم عَبَدوا اللهَ تَبارَكَ وتَـعالىٰ طَـلَبَ الثَّـوابِ فتِلكَ عِبادَةُ الأُجَراءِ، وقَوم عَبَدوا اللهَ عَـزَّوجلَّ حُبّاً لَـهُ فَـتِلكَ عِـبادَةُ الأحـرارِ، وهِـيَ أفـضَلُ العِبادَةِ.[٤٤٠٨]

3944. **Imām al-Ṣādiq (AS) said,** 'He who obeys someone in committing an act of disobedience [to Allah] has indeed worshipped him.'[4446]

٣٩٤٤. عنه ﵇ : مَن أطاعَ رَجُلاً في مَعصِيَةٍ فقَد عَبَدَهُ.[٤٤٠٩]

3945. **Imām al-Jawād (AS) said,** 'Whoever gives a speaker his full attention has indeed expressed a form of worship or adulation to him. If the speaker leads one to Allah through his words, then it is as if one worships Allah [by giving him attention], but if he leads one to Satan through his words, it is as if one worships Satan.'[4447]

٣٩٤٥. الإمامُ الجوادُ ﵇ : مَن أصغىٰ إلىٰ ناطِقٍ فقَد عَبَدَهُ، فإن كانَ النّاطِقُ يُؤَدّي عَنِ اللهِ عَـزَّوجلَّ فقد عَبَدَ اللهَ، وإن كانَ النّاطِقُ يُؤَدّي عنِ الشَّيطانِ فقد عَبَدَ الشَّيطانَ.[٤٤١٠]

1215. The Best Form of Worship

١٢١٥ ـ أفضلُ العِبادَةِ

3946. *Irshād al-Qulūb*: 'In the tradition of the Prophet's Ascension, Allah said: 'O Aḥmad, no worship is dearer to me than silence and fasting.'[4448]

٣٩٤٦. ارشاد القلوب : في حديثِ المِعراجِ : يا أحمدُ، لَيسَ شَيءٌ مِـنَ العِـبادَةِ أحَبَّ إلَـيَّ مِـنَ الصَّمتِ والصَّومِ.[٤٤١١]

3947. **The Prophet (SAWA) said,** 'The best form of worship is to gain an understanding [of religion].'[4449]

٣٩٤٧. رسولُ اللهِ ﷺ : أفضَلُ العِبادَةِ الفِقهُ.[٤٤١٢]

3948. **The Prophet (SAWA) said,** 'The worship deserving of the greatest reward is that which is most discreetly performed.'[4450]

٣٩٤٨. عنه ﷺ : أعظَمُ العِبادَةِ أجراً أخفاها.[٤٤١٣]

3949. **Imām 'Alī (AS) said,** 'The best form of worship is self-restraint.'[4451]

٣٩٤٩. الإمامُ عليٌّ ﵇ : أفضَلُ العِبادَةِ العَفافُ.[٤٤١٤]

3950. **Imām ʿAlī (AS) said,** 'The best form of worship is breaking a habit or an addiction.'[4452]

٣٩٥٠ . عنه ﷺ : أفضَلُ العِبادَةِ غَلَبَةُ العادَةِ.[٤٤١٥]

3951. **Imām ʿAlī (AS) said,** 'The best form of worship is abstinence.'[4453]

٣٩٥١ . عنه ﷺ : أفضَلُ العِبادَةِ الزَّهادَةُ.[٤٤١٦]

3952. **Imām al-Ṣādiq (AS) said,** 'The best form of worship is coming to know Allah and humbling oneself before Him.'[4454]

٣٩٥٢ . الإمامُ الصّادقُ ﷺ : أفضَلُ العِبادَةِ العِلمُ بِاللهِ وَالتَّواضُعُ لَهُ.[٤٤١٧]

3953. **Imām al-Ṣādiq (AS) said,** 'The best form of worship is to be in a state of perpetual reflection about Allah and His power.'[4455]

٣٩٥٣ . عنه ﷺ : أفضَلُ العِبادَةِ إدمانُ التَّفَكُّرِ في اللهِ وفي قُدرَتِهِ.[٤٤١٨]

3954. **Imām al-Ṣādiq (AS) said,** 'By Allah, there is no better way to worship Allah than to fulfil the right of a fellow believer.'[4456]

٣٩٥٤ . عنه ﷺ : واللهِ ما عُبِدَ اللهُ بِشيءٍ أفضَلَ مِن أداءِ حَقِّ المُؤمِنِ.[٤٤١٩]

3955. **Imām al-Ṣādiq (AS) said,** 'The best worshipper among people is he who performs the acts obligatory upon him.'[4457]

٣٩٥٥ . عنه ﷺ : أعبَدُ النّاسِ مَن أقامَ الفَرائضَ.[٤٤٢٠]

3956. **Imām al-Riḍā (AS) said,** 'Worship is not about fasting or praying much, rather worship is to reflect much on the affairs related to Allah.'[4458]

٣٩٥٦ . الإمامُ الرِّضا ﷺ : لَيسَتِ العِبادَةُ كَثرَةَ الصِّيامِ وَالصَّلاةِ، وَإنَّما العِبادَةُ كَثرَةُ التَّفَكُّرِ في أمرِ اللهِ.[٤٤٢١]

3957. **Imām al-Jawād (AS) said,** 'The best form of worship is sincerity.'[4459]

٣٩٥٧ . الإمامُ الجوادُ ﷺ : أفضَلُ العِبادَةِ الإخلاصُ.[٤٤٢٢]

(See also: THINKING: section 1502)

(أنظر) التفكّر: باب ١٥٠٢.

1216. Eagerness and Vitality in Worship

١٢١٦ـ النَّشاطُ فِي العِبادَةِ

3958. **Prophet Jesus (AS) said,** 'With truth I tell you that verily just as the sick man can only look at good food but cannot enjoy it due to the intense pain he suffers, similarly the man engrossed in worldly affairs cannot enjoy worship nor taste its sweetness because of the love that he harbours for worldly possessions.'[4460]

٣٩٥٨ . عيسى ﷺ : بِحقٍّ أقولُ لَكُم: إنَّهُ كَما يَنظُرُ المَريضُ إلَى طَيِّبِ الطَّعامِ فلا يَلتَذُّهُ مَعَ ما يَجِدُهُ مِن شِدَّةِ الوَجَعِ، كذٰلِكَ صاحِبُ الدّنيا لا يَلتَذُّ بِالعِبادَةِ ولا يَجِدُ حَلاوَتَها مَعَ ما يَجِدُ مِن حُبِّ المالِ.[٤٤٢٣]

3959. **The Prophet (SAWA) said,** 'The bane of worship is lassitude.'[4461]

٣٩٥٩ . رسولُ اللهِ ﷺ : آفَةُ العِبادَةِ الفَترَةُ.[٤٤٢٤]

3960. **Imām al-Ṣādiq (AS) said,** 'Do not make worship loathsome to yourselves [by forcing it upon yourselves].'[4462]

٣٩٦٠ . الإمامُ الصّادقُ عليه السلام: لا تُكَرِّهوا إلى أنفُسِكُمُ العِبادَةَ.[٤٤٢٥]

262

THE MORAL LESSON

العِبرَة

1217. Enjoinment of Taking Lesson from Moral Advice

١٢١٧ ـ الحَثُّ عَلَى الاتِّعاظِ بِالعِبَرِ

"So take lesson! O you who have insight."[4463]

﴿فَاعْتَبِرُوا يا أُولِي الأبْصار﴾.[٤٤٢٦]

3961. **The Prophet (SAWA) said,** 'Take lesson, for indeed the moral examples merely passed by your predecessors.'[4464]

٣٩٦١ . رسولُ اللهِ ﷺ: إعتَبِروا؛ فَقَد خَلَتِ المَثُلاتُ فيمَن كانَ قَبلَكُم.[٤٤٢٧]

3962. **Imām 'Alī (AS) said,** 'The believer looks at the world with contemplative consideration, and he only consumes thereof within the bounds of necessity.'[4465]

٣٩٦٢ . الإمامُ عليٌّ عليه السلام: يَنظُرُ المُؤمِنُ إلَى الدّنيا بِعَينِ الاعتِبارِ، ويَقتاتُ مِنها بِبَطنِ الاضطِرارِ.[٤٤٢٨]

3963. **Imām 'Alī (AS) said,** 'The ignorant one rarely takes lesson [from experiences].'[4466]

٣٩٦٣ . عنه عليه السلام: مَن جَهِلَ قَلَّ اعتِبارُهُ.[٤٤٢٩]

3964. **Imām 'Alī (AS) said,** 'The moral lesson is a sincere warner. Whoever contemplates takes lesson, and whoever takes the lesson on board keeps away from making the same mistake twice, and whoever keeps away remains safe.'[4467]

٣٩٦٤ . عنه عليه السلام: الاعتِبارُ مُنذِرٌ ناصِحٌ، مَن تَفَكَّرَ اعتَبَرَ، ومَنِ اعتَبَرَ اعتَزَلَ، ومَنِ اعتَزَلَ سَلِمَ.[٤٤٣٠]

3965. **Imām 'Alī (AS) said,** 'Drawing a lesson [from an experience] leads one to integrity of conduct.'[4468]

٣٩٦٥ . عنه عليه السلام: الاعتِبارُ يَقودُ إلَى الرَّشادِ.[٤٤٣١]

3966. **Imām 'Alī (AS) said,** 'Whoever draws a lesson [from something] gains insight into it, and whoever gains insight into it comprehends it, and whoever comprehends it comes to know it for certain.'[4469]

٣٩٦٦ . عنه عليه السلام: مَنِ اعتَبَرَ أبصَرَ، ومَن أبصَرَ فَهِمَ، ومَن فَهِمَ عَلِمَ.[٤٤٣٢]

1218. Things that Must be Contemplated Upon and Drawn Lessons From

۱۲۱۸ـ ما يَنبَغِي الاعتِبارُ بِهِ

"There is certainly a moral in their accounts for those who possess intellect."[4470]

﴿لَقَدْ كانَ فِي قَصَصِهِمْ عِبْرَةٌ لِأُولِي الْأَلْبابِ﴾.۴۴۳۳

"It is Allah Who alternates the night and the day: verily in that is a moral for those who have insight."[4471]

﴿يُقَلِّبُ اللهُ اللَّيْلَ وَالنَّهارَ إِنَّ فِي ذٰلِكَ لَعِبْرَةً لِأُولِي الْأَبْصارِ﴾.۴۴۳۴

3967. **Imām ʿAlī (AS) said,** 'There is a lesson to be taken from the vicissitudes of this world.'[4472]

۳۹۶۷. الإمامُ عليٌّ ﷺ : في تَصاريفِ الدّنيا اعتِبارٌ.۴۴۳۵

3968. **Imām ʿAlī (AS) said,** 'If only you drew lessons from all that you have lost in what has passed of your life you would look after what is left of it.'[4473]

۳۹۶۸. عنه ﷺ : لَواعتَبَرتَ بِما أضَعتَ مِن ماضي عُمرِكَ لَحَفِظتَ ما بَقِيَ.۴۴۳۶

3969. **Imām ʿAlī (AS) said,** 'So take lesson from how Allah dealt with Satan when he thwarted his long years of good deeds, and all his hard work [because of his outright defiance of Allah].'[4474]

۳۹۶۹. عنه ﷺ : فاعتَبِروا بِما كانَ مِن فِعلِ اللهِ بِإبليسَ؛ إذ أحبَطَ عَمَلَهُ الطَّويلَ، وَجَهدَهُ الجَهيدَ (الجَميلَ).۴۴۳۷

3970. **Imām ʿAlī (AS) said,** 'So take lesson from Allah's intense force, His attacks, His blows and His exemplary punishments that befell the arrogant nations before you.'[4475]

۳۹۷۰. عنه ﷺ : فاعتَبِروا بِما أصابَ الأُمَمَ المُستَكبِرينَ مِن قَبلِكُم؛ مِن بأسِ اللهِ وصَوْلاتِه ووَقائِعِهِ ومَثُلاتِه.۴۴۳۸

3971. **Imām ʿAlī (AS) said,** 'How many the lessons, and how little the contemplation [upon them]!'[4476]

۳۹۷۱. عنه ﷺ : ما أكثَرَ العِبَرَ، وأقَلَّ الاعتِبارَ!۴۴۳۹

3972. **Imām Zayn al-ʿĀbidīn (AS) said,** 'Poor man! Every day he is given three trials whereof he does not even take lesson from a single one. If he contemplated and drew a lesson thereof, these trials and this world would cease to be of importance to him. The first trial is the very day which is deducted from his life – if it was a loss in his wealth that befell him, he would fall into great distress, even though the dirham [i.e. money] can always be substituted but the days of his life will

۳۹۷۲. بحار الأنوار عن الإمام زين العابدين ﷺ : مِسكينٌ ابنُ آدَمَ ! لَهُ في كُلِّ يومٍ ثَلاثُ مَصائبَ لا يَعتَبِرُ بِواحِدَةٍ مِنهُنَّ، ولَو اعتَبَرَ لَهانَت عَلَيهِ المَصائبُ وأمرُ الدّنيا: فأمّا المُصيبَةُ الأُولىٰ: فاليَومُ الّذي يَنقُصُ مِن عُمرِهِ، وإنْ نالَهُ نُقصانٌ في مالِهِ اغتَمَّ بِهِ، والدِّرهَمُ يَخلُفُ عَنهُ وَالعُمرُ لا يَرُدُّهُ شيء.

never again return to him. The second trial is the way in which he goes to great lengths to procure his sustenance, when he will have to account for it all if acquired by lawful means, and he will be punished for it all if acquired by unlawful means. The third trial is the greatest: every day that draws to an end has brought him a step closer to the Hereafter – whether to Paradise or Hellfire, he does not know!'[4477]

والثانِيةُ: أنَّهُ يَستَوفي رِزقَهُ، فإن كانَ حَلالاً حُوسِبَ عَلَيهِ، وإن كانَ حَراماً عُوقِبَ عَلَيهِ. والثّالِثَةُ أعظَمُ مِن ذٰلِكَ ـ قيلَ: وما هِيَ؟ قالَ ـ: ما مِن يَومٍ يُمسي إلّا وقَد دَنا مِنَ الآخِرَةِ مَرحَلَةً، لا يَدري عَلَى الجَنَّةِ أم عَلَى النّارِ؟![٤٤٤٠]

1219. The Benefits of Taking Lesson

١٢١٩ ـ ثَمَرَةُ الاعتِبارِ

3973. **Imām ʿAlī (AS) said,** 'Taking lesson [from past faults] results in immunity [from further faults and sins].'[4478]

٣٩٧٣. الإمامُ عليٌّ عليه السلام: الاعتِبارُ يُثمِرُ العِصمَةَ.[٤٤٤١]

3974. **Imām ʿAlī (AS) said,** 'Continuously taking lessons gives rise to the faculty of insight, and brings about self-restraint.'[4479]

٣٩٧٤. عنه عليه السلام: دَوامُ الاعتِبارِ يُؤَدّي إلَى الاستِبصارِ، ويُثمِرُ الازدِجارَ.[٤٤٤٢]

3975. **Imām ʿAlī (AS) said,** 'He who abundantly and frequently takes lessons [from his experiences] rarely stumbles.'[4480]

٣٩٧٥. عنه عليه السلام: مَن كَثُرَ اعتِبارُهُ قَلَّ عِثارُهُ.[٤٤٤٣]

263

SELF-ADMIRATION

العُجبُ

1220. Reprehension of Self-Admiration

١٢٢٠ ـ ذَمُّ العُجبِ

3976. **Imām ʿAlī (AS) said,** 'There is no loneliness more frightening than self-admiration.'[4481]

٣٩٧٦. الإمامُ عليٌّ عليه السلام: لا وَحدَةَ أوحَشُ مِنَ العُجبِ.[٤٤٤٤]

3977. **Imām ʿAlī (AS) said,** 'Self-admiration shows up your faults.'[4482]

٣٩٧٧. عنه عليه السلام: العُجبُ يُظهِرُ النَّقيصَةَ.[٤٤٤٥]

3978. **Imām ʿAlī (AS) said,** 'Self-admiration is foolishness.'[4483]

٣٩٧٨. عنه عليه السلام: العُجبُ حُمقٌ.[٤٤٤٦]

3979. **Imām ʿAlī (AS) said,** 'An evil deed [of yours] that upsets you is better in the sight of

٣٩٧٩. عنه عليه السلام: سَيِّئَةٌ تَسوؤُكَ خَيرٌ عِندَ اللهِ

Allah than a good deed which you feel proud about.'[4484]

مِن حَسَنَةٍ تُعجِبُكَ.[٤٤٤٧]

3980. **Imām ʿAlī (AS) said,** 'Beware of self-satisfaction lest it increases the number of those against you.'[4485]

٣٩٨٠. عنه ؑ: إيّاكَ أن تَرضىٰ عَن نَفسِكَ فَيَكثُرَ السّاخِطُ عَلَيكَ.[٤٤٤٨]

3981. **Imām ʿAlī (AS) said,** 'The consequence of self-admiration is hatred [of other people towards you].'[4486]

٣٩٨١. عنه ؑ: ثَمَرَةُ العُجبِ البَغضاءُ.[٤٤٤٩]

3982. **Imām ʿAlī (AS) said,** 'Self-admiration is the opposite of proper conduct, and is the bane of the hearts.'[4487]

٣٩٨٢. عنه ؑ: الإعجابُ ضِدُّ الصَّوابِ، وآفَةُ الألبابِ.[٤٤٥٠]

3983. **Imām ʿAlī (AS) said,** 'Self-admiration corrupts reason.'[4488]

٣٩٨٣. عنه ؑ: العُجبُ يُفسِدُ العَقلَ.[٤٤٥١]

3984. **Imām ʿAlī (AS) said,** 'Self-admiration prevents progress.'[4489]

٣٩٨٤. عنه ؑ: الإعجابُ يَمنَعُ الازدِيادَ.[٤٤٥٢]

3985. **Imām al-Bāqir or Imām al-Ṣādiq (AS) said,** 'Verily Allah, Blessed and most High, says, 'Verily from among My servants is he who asks Me to enable him to perform an act of obedience to Me in order that he may procure My love, but I however, withhold that from him in order that he does not come to feel proud of that action of his.'[4490]

٣٩٨٥. الإمامُ الباقرُ أو الإمامُ الصّادقُ ؑ: إنَّ اللهَ تَبارَكَ وتَعالىٰ يَقولُ: إنَّ مِن عِبادي مَن يَسألُني الشَّيءَ مِن طاعَتي لِاُحِبَّهُ، فأصرِفُ ذلكَ عَنهُ لِكَي لا يُعجِبَهُ عَمَلُه.[٤٤٥٣]

3986. **Imām al-Ṣādiq (AS) said,** 'He who is overtaken by self-admiration perishes.'[4491]

٣٩٨٦. الإمامُ الصّادقُ ؑ: مَن دَخَلَهُ العُجبُ هَلَكَ.[٤٤٥٤]

1221. Enjoinment of Undervaluing the Good that One Does

١٢٢١ ـ الحَثُّ عَلَى استِقلالِ الخَيرِ مِنَ النَّفسِ

3987. **The Prophet (SAWA) said,** describing the intelligent person, 'He regards the little good that others do as being much and regards the abundance of good that he himself does as being little.'[4492]

٣٩٨٧. رسولُ اللهِ ﷺ ـ في صِفَةِ العاقِلِ ـ: يَستَكثِرُ قَليلَ الخَيرِ مِن غَيرِه، ويَستَقِلُّ كَثيرَ الخَيرِ مِن نَفسِه.[٤٤٥٥]

3988. **Imām al-Bāqir (AS) said,** 'Undervalue the abundant acts of obedience that you perform for Allah, in contempt of your lower self and in order to expose yourself to Allah's pardon.'[4493]

٣٩٨٨ . الإمامُ الباقرُ عليه السلام : اِستَقلِلْ مِن نَفسِكَ كَثيرَ الطّاعَةِ للهِ؛ إزراءً عَلَى النَّفسِ وتَعَرُّضاً لِلعَفوِ.[٤٤٥٦]

3989. **Imām al-Ṣādiq (AS) said,** 'Iblīs [Satan] – may Allah's curse be on him – says to his troops, 'If I can gain mastery over three things in man, I will no longer care how much good he does for it will not be accepted from him: if he overrates his good deeds, forgets his sins, and is overcome by self-admiration.'[4494]

٣٩٨٩ . الإمامُ الصّادقُ عليه السلام : قالَ إبليسُ ـ لَعنَةُ اللهِ عَلَيهِ ـ لِجُنودِهِ : إذا استَمكَنتُ مِنِ ابنِ آدَمَ في ثَلاثٍ لَم اُبالِ ما عَمِلَ؛ فإنَّهُ غَيرُ مَقبولٍ مِنهُ : إذا استَكثَرَ عَمَلَهُ، ونَسِيَ ذَنبَهُ، ودَخَلَهُ العُجبُ.[٤٤٥٧]

1222. Treatment of Self-Admiration

١٢٢٢ ـ مُعالَجَةُ العُجبِ

3990. **Imām 'Alī (AS) said,** 'What is the matter with man that he is so given to self-admiration when his origin was but a putrid droplet, and his end is as a filthy corpse, and between these states he is but a vessel for excrement?!'[4495]

٣٩٩٠ . الإمامُ عليٌّ عليه السلام : ما لِابنِ آدمَ والعُجبَ ؟! وأوَّلُهُ نُطفَةٌ مَذِرَةٌ، وآخِرُهُ جيفَةٌ قَذِرَةٌ، وَهُوَ بَينَ ذٰلكَ يَحمِلُ العَذِرَةَ؟![٤٤٥٨]

3991. **Imām al-Bāqir (AS) said,** 'Block the path of self-admiration through self-knowledge.'[4496]

٣٩٩١ . الإمامُ الباقرُ عليه السلام : سُدَّ سَبيلَ العُجبِ بِمَعرِفَةِ النَّفسِ.[٤٤٥٩]

3992. **Imām al-Ṣādiq (AS) said,** 'If crossing the *Ṣirāṭ* [Bridge extended over Hell] is a reality, then wherefore the need for self-admiration?!'[4497]

٣٩٩٢ . الإمامُ الصّادقُ عليه السلام : إن كانَ المَمَرُّ عَلَى الصِّراطِ حَقّاً فالعُجبُ لِماذا ؟![٤٤٦٠]

(See also: INNER KNOWLEDGE: section 1248; HAUGHTINESS: section 1571)

(اُنظر) المعرفة (١): باب ١٢٤٨؛ الكبر: باب ١٥٧١.

264

THE MIRACLE

المُعجِزَة

1223. The Miracle is a Sign in Knowing The Prophets of Allah and the Imams

١٢٢٣ ـ المُعجِزَةُ عَلامَةُ مَعرِفَةِ أنبِياءِ اللهِ وحُجَجِهِ

3993. **Imām al-Ṣādiq (AS) said,** 'The miracle is a sign pointing to Allah which none can produce

٣٩٩٣ . الإمامُ الصّادقُ عليه السلام : المُعجِزَةُ عَلامَةٌ للهِ لا

but His prophets, His messengers and His proofs, in order that the truth of the truthful one be distinguished from the lie of the liar.’[4498]

يُعطيها إلّا أنبِياءَهُ ورُسُلَهُ وحُجَجَهُ؛ لِيُعرَفَ بِهِ صِدقُ الصّادِقِ مِن كِذبِ الكاذِبِ.[٤٤٦١]

1224. The Wisdom Behind the Diversity of the Prophets’ Miracles

١٢٢٤ ـ حِكمَةُ اختِلافِ مُعجِزاتِ الأنبِياءِ

3994. **Imām al-Hādī (AS) said** in reply to Ibn Sikkīt’s question about the reason for Allah’s sending Prophet Moses (AS) with the staff [that turned into a snake], his illuminated hand and magic as a resource, and His sending Prophet Jesus (AS) with medicine as a resource, and His sending Prophet Muḥammad (SAWA) with speech and eloquence, ‘Verily when Allah sent Moses (AS), the trend prevalent among the people of the time was magic, so he brought them something from Allah the like of which they were incapable of producing, which thwarted their magic, and with which he demonstrated the proof against them. And verily Allah sent Jesus (AS) at a time when paralytic diseases were widespread and people needed medicine, so he brought them something from Allah the like of which they did not have, and with which he brought life to the dead, cured the blind and the leper with Allah’s permission, and demonstrated the proof against them. And verily Allah sent Muḥammad (SAWA) at an era when the prevalent trend among the people of the time was speech and eloquence – and I think he even said poetry – so he brought to them Allah’s exhortations and wisdoms with which he thwarted their words, and with which he demonstrated the proof against them.’[4499]

٣٩٩٤. الإمامُ الهاديُّ عليه السلام ـ في جَوابِ ابنِ السِّكِّيتِ عَن عِلَّةِ بَعثِ موسىٰ بِالعَصا ويَدِهِ البَيضاءِ وآلَةِ السِّحرِ، وبَعثِ عيسىٰ بِآلَةِ الطِّبِّ، وبَعثِ مُحمَّدٍ ـ صلَّى اللهُ علَيهِ وآلِهِ وعَلىٰ جَميعِ الأنبِياءِ ـ بِالكَلامِ والخُطَبِ ـ: إنَّ اللهَ لَمّا بَعَثَ موسىٰ عليه السلام كانَ الغالِبُ عَلىٰ أهلِ عَصرِهِ السِّحرَ، فأتاهُم مِن عِندِ اللهِ بِما لَم يَكُن في وُسعِهِم مِثلُهُ، وما أبطَلَ بِهِ سِحرَهُم، وأثبَتَ بِهِ الحُجَّةَ عَلَيهِم. وإنَّ اللهَ بَعَثَ عيسىٰ عليه السلام في وَقتٍ قَد ظَهَرَت فيهِ الزَّماناتُ واحتاجَ النّاسُ إلَى الطِّبِّ، فأتاهُم مِن عِندِ اللهِ بِما لَم يَكُن عِندَهُم مِثلُهُ، وبِما أحيا لَهُمُ المَوتىٰ، وأبرَأَ الأكمَهَ والأبرَصَ بِإذنِ اللهِ، وأثبَتَ بِهِ الحُجَّةَ عَلَيهِم. وإنَّ اللهَ بَعَثَ مُحَمَّداً صلى الله عليه وآله في وَقتٍ كانَ الغالِبُ عَلىٰ أهلِ عَصرِهِ الخُطَبَ والكَلامَ ـ وأظُنُّهُ قالَ: الشِّعرَ ـ فأتاهُم مِن عِندِ اللهِ مِن مَواعِظِهِ وحِكَمِهِ ما أبطَلَ بِهِ قَولَهُم، وأثبَتَ بِهِ الحُجَّةَ عَلَيهِم.[٤٤٦٢]

265

HASTE

العَجَلَة

1225. Reproaching Hastiness

١٢٢٥ ـ ذَمُّ العَجَلَةِ

“Man is a creature of hastiness. Soon I will show you My signs. So do not ask Me to hasten.”[4500]

﴿خُلِقَ الإنْسانُ مِنْ عَجَلٍ سَأُرِيكُمْ آياتِي فَلا تَسْتَعْجِلُونَ﴾.[٤٤٦٣]

"Man prays for ill as [avidly as] he prays for good, and man is overhasty."[4501]

﴿وَيَدْعُ الإِنْسانُ بِالشَّرِّ دُعاءَهُ بِالْخَيْرِ وَكانَ الإِنْسانُ عَجُولاً﴾.٤٤٦٤

3995. **The Prophet (SAWA) said,** 'Verily haste has ruined people, and if instead people proceeded with caution no one would be ruined.'[4502]

٣٩٩٥. رسولُ اللهِ ﷺ: إنَّما أهلَكَ النّاسَ العَجَلَةُ، ولو أنَّ النّاسَ تَثَبَّتوا لَم يَهلِكْ أحَدٌ.٤٤٦٥

3996. **The Prophet (SAWA) said,** 'Deliberateness is from Allah whereas haste is from Satan.'[4503]

٣٩٩٦. عنه ﷺ: الأناةُ مِنَ اللهِ، والعَجَلَةُ مِنَ الشَّيطانِ.٤٤٦٦

3997. **Imām ʿAlī (AS) said,** 'Haste causes stumbling.'[4504]

٣٩٩٧. الإمامُ عليٌّ عليه السلام: العَجَلُ يوجِبُ العِثارَ.٤٤٦٧

3998. **Imām ʿAlī (AS) said,** 'Mistakes happen frequently [when work is done] with haste.'[4505]

٣٩٩٨. عنه عليه السلام: مَعَ العَجَلِ يَكثُرُ الزَّلَلُ.٤٤٦٨

3999. **Imām al-Ṣādiq (AS) said,** 'Wholesome results follow cautious procedure whereas regret follows haste.'[4506]

٣٩٩٩. الإمامُ الصّادقُ عليه السلام: مَعَ التَّثَبُّتِ تكونُ السَّلامَةُ، ومَعَ العَجَلَةِ تكونُ النَّدامَةُ.٤٤٦٩

1226. Enjoinment of Rushing to do Good Deeds

١٢٢٦ـ الحَثُّ عَلَى المُبادَرَةِ إلَى الخَيراتِ

4000. **The Prophet (SAWA) said,** 'Verily Allah loves the good that is embarked upon immediately.'[4507]

٤٠٠٠. رسولُ اللهِ ﷺ: إنَّ اللهَ يُحِبُّ مِنَ الخَيرِ ما يُعَجَّلُ.٤٤٧٠

4001. **Imām ʿAlī (AS) said,** 'Deliberateness is recommended in everything except when embarking on opportunities for good-doing.'[4508]

٤٠٠١. الإمامُ عليٌّ عليه السلام: التُّؤَدَةُ مَمدوحَةٌ في كُلِّ شَيءٍ إلّا في فُرَصِ الخَيرِ.٤٤٧١

4002. **Imām al-Bāqir (AS) said,** 'When you think of doing something good, rush to do it immediately for verily you do not know what could happen later [to prevent you from doing it].'[4509]

٤٠٠٢. الإمامُ الباقرُ عليه السلام: إذا هَمَمتَ بِخَيرٍ فبادِرْ؛ فإنَّكَ لا تَدري ما يَحدُثُ.٤٤٧٢

(See also: GOOD: section 676)

(أنظر) الخير: باب ٦٧٦

266

JUSTICE

العَدلُ

1227. The Importance of Justice

١٢٢٧ـ قيمَةُ العَدلِ

4003. **Imām ʿAlī (AS) said,** 'Justice is the base that supports the whole world.'[4510]

٤٠٠٣. الإمامُ عليٌّ عليه السلام: العَدلُ أساسٌ بِه قِوامُ العالَمِ.٤٤٧٣

4004. **Imām ʿAlī (AS) said,** 'Allah, Glory be to Him, made justice a support for mankind, an eliminator of wrongs and sins, and an facilitator for Islam.'[4511]

٤٠٠٤. عنه عليه السلام: جَعَلَ اللهُ سُبحانَهُ العَدلَ قِواماً لِلأنامِ، وتَنزيهاً مِنَ المَظالِمِ والآثامِ، وتَسنِيَةً لِلإسلامِ.٤٤٧٤

4005. **Imām ʿAlī (AS) said,** 'Justice is the support of the masses and the beauty [adornment] of the governors.'[4512]

٤٠٠٥. عنه عليه السلام: العَدلُ قِوامُ الرَّعِيَّةِ وجَمالُ الوُلاةِ.٤٤٧٥

4006. **Imām ʿAlī (AS) said,** 'Justice is the shield of the nations.'[4513]

٤٠٠٦. عنه عليه السلام: العَدلُ جُنَّةُ الدُّوَلِ.٤٤٧٦

4007. **Imām ʿAlī (AS) said,** 'The masses behave righteously through justice.'[4514]

٤٠٠٧. عنه عليه السلام: بِالعَدلِ تَصلُحُ الرَّعِيَّةُ.٤٤٧٧

4008. **Imām ʿAlī (AS) said,** 'Blessings are multiplied through justice.'[4515]

٤٠٠٨. عنه عليه السلام: بِالعَدلِ تَتَضاعَفُ البَرَكاتُ.٤٤٧٨

4009. **Imām ʿAlī (AS) said,** 'Justice brings about order and endurance in authority.'[4516]

٤٠٠٩. عنه عليه السلام: العَدلُ نِظامُ الإمرَةِ.٤٤٧٩

4010. **Imām ʿAlī (AS) said,** 'Nothing can cause nations to flourish like justice.'[4517]

٤٠١٠. عنه عليه السلام: ما عُمِّرَتِ البُلدانُ بِمِثلِ العَدلِ.٤٤٨٠

4011. **Imām ʿAlī (AS)** was once asked which was better, justice or generosity, to which he replied, 'Justice puts things in their rightful place, whereas generosity takes them away from their course. Justice is a general predominant state, whereas generosity is a transient characteristic. Justice is therefore the nobler and better of the two.'[4518]

٤٠١١. عنه عليه السلام ـ لَمّا سُئلَ عَن أفضَلِيّةِ العَدلِ أو الجُودِ ـ: العَدلُ يَضَعُ الاُمورَ مَواضِعَها، والجُودُ يُخرِجُها مِن جِهَتِها، والعَدلُ سائسٌ عامٌّ، والجُودُ عارِضٌ خاصٌّ، فالعَدلُ أشرَفُهُما وأفضَلُهُما.٤٤٨١

4012. **Fāṭima al-Zahrā' (AS) said,** 'Allah has made justice incumbent as a source of tranquillity for the hearts.'[4519]

٤٠١٢. فاطمةُ الزَّهراءُ ؏ : فَــرَضَ ... العَـدلَ تَسكيناً لِلقُلوبِ.[٤٤٨٢]

4013. **Imām al-Ṣādiq (AS) said,** 'Justice is sweeter than water to a thirsty man.'[4520]

٤٠١٣. الإمامُ الصّادقُ ؏ : العَدلُ أحلىٰ مِنَ الماءِ يُصيبُهُ الظَّمآنُ.[٤٤٨٣]

4014. **Imām al-Ṣādiq (AS) said,** 'Justice is sweeter than honey, softer than butter and smells more fragrant than musk.'[4521]

٤٠١٤. عنه ؏ : العَدلُ أحلىٰ مِنَ الشَّهدِ، وألْيَنُ مِنَ الزُّبدِ، وأطيَبُ ريحاً مِنَ المِسكِ.[٤٤٨٤]

1228. Qualities of a Just Person

١٢٢٨ـ صِفاتُ العادِلِ

4015. **The Prophet (SAWA) said,** 'He who treats people in such a way that he never wrongs them, and speaks to them and never lies to them, and when he makes a promise to them he never breaks it, such a person is perfect in his valorous qualities, his justice is manifest, and it becomes obligatory to consider him as one's brother and prohibited to backbite him.'[4522]

٤٠١٥. رسولُ اللهِ ؐ : مَن عامَلَ النّـاسَ فـلَم يَظلِمْهُم، وحَدَّثَهُم فلَم يَكذِبْهُم، ووَعَـدَهُم فـلَم يُخلِفهُم، فهُو مِـمَّن كَـمُلَت مُـروءَتُهُ، وظَـهَرَت عَدالَتُهُ، ووَجَبَت اُخُوَّتُهُ، وحَرُمَت غِيبَتُهُ.[٤٤٨٥]

4016. **The Prophet (SAWA) said,** 'He who associates with people as he himself would like others to associate with him is indeed just.'[4523]

٤٠١٦. عنه ؐ : مَن صاحَبَ النّاسَ بِالَّذي يُحِبُّ أن يُصاحِبوهُ كانَ عَدلاً.[٤٤٨٦]

1229. Advice to be Just and Fair with One's Friend and Enemy

١٢٢٩ـ الوَصِيَّةُ بِالعَدلِ عَلَى الصَّدِيقِ العَدُوِّ

"O you who have faith! Be maintainers of justice, as witnesses for the sake of Allah, and ill feeling for a people should never lead you to be unfair. Be fair; that is nearer to Godwariness, and be wary of Allah.' Allah is indeed well aware of what you do.'[4524]

﴿يا أَيُّها الَّذينَ آمَنُوا كُونُوا قَوّامينَ لِلّهِ شُهَداءَ بِالقِسْطِ وَلا يَجْرِمَنَّكُمْ شَنَآنُ قَوْمٍ عَلَى أَلّا تَعْدِلُوا اعْدِلُوا هُوَ أَقْرَبُ لِلتَّقْوَى وَاتَّقُوا اللهَ إِنَّ اللهَ خَبيرٌ بِما تَعْمَلُونَ﴾.[٤٤٨٧]

4017. **Imām 'Alī (AS) said** in his will to his son al-Ḥusayn (AS), 'I advise you to be wary of your duty to Allah in wealth and poverty ... and [I advise you] of being just towards both friend and foe.'[4525]

٤٠١٧. الإمامُ عليٌّ ؏ ـ فـي وَصِيَّتِهِ لِابنِهِ الحُسَينِ ؏ ـ: اُوصيكَ بِتَقوَى اللهِ في الغِنىٰ والفَقرِ ... وبِالعَدلِ عَلَى الصَّديقِ والعَدُوِّ.[٤٤٨٨]

1230. The Most Just of People ١٢٣٠ـ أعدَلُ النّاسِ

4018. **Imām ʿAlī (AS) said,** 'The most just person is he who uses his strength even-handedly.'[4526]

٤٠١٨. الإمامُ عليٌّ ﷺ: أعدَلُ النّاسِ مَن أنصَفَ عَن قُوَّةٍ.٤٤٨٩

4019. **Imām ʿAlī (AS) said,** 'The most just from all creation is he who judges best according to the truth.'[4527]

٤٠١٩. عنه ﷺ: أعدَلُ الخَلقِ أقضاهُم بالحَقِّ.٤٤٩٠

4020. **Imām ʿAlī (AS) said,** 'The peak of justice is for a person to be just in himself.'[4528]

٤٠٢٠. عنه ﷺ: غايَةُ العَدلِ أن يَعدِلَ المَرءُ في نَفسِهِ.٤٤٩١

267

ENMITY العَداوَةُ

1231. Prohibition of Showing Enmity Toward Anyone ١٢٣١ـ النَّهيُ عَنِ المُعاداةِ

4021. **The Prophet (SAWA) said,** 'Gabriel has not exhorted me against anything like he has exhorted me against showing enmity towards people.'[4529]

٤٠٢١. رسولُ اللهِ ﷺ: ما عَهِدَ إلَيَّ جَبرَئيلُ ﷺ في شَيءٍ ما عَهِدَ إلَيَّ في مُعاداةِ الرِّجالِ.٤٤٩٢

4022. **The Prophet (SAWA) said,** 'After idol-worship, I have not been prohibited with anything as significantly as I have been prohibited hostility towards people.'[4530]

٤٠٢٢. عنه ﷺ: ما نُهيتُ عن شَيءٍ بَعدَ عِبادَةِ الأوثانِ ما نُهيتُ عَن مُلاحاةِ الرِّجالِ.٤٤٩٣

4023. **The Prophet (SAWA) said,** 'Whoever shows hostility towards others, his gallantry wanes and his kindness vanishes.'[4531]

٤٠٢٣. عنه ﷺ: مَن لاحَى الرِّجالَ سَقَطَت مُروءَتُهُ وذَهَبَت كَرامَتُهُ.٤٤٩٤

4024. **Imām ʿAlī (AS) said,** 'The peak of ignorance is showing enmity towards people.'[4532]

٤٠٢٤. الإمامُ عليٌّ ﷺ: رَأسُ الجَهلِ مُعاداةُ النّاسِ.٤٤٩٥

4025. **Imām al-Bāqir (AS) said,** 'Beware of antagonistic dispute for verily it corrupts the heart and engenders hypocrisy.'[4533]

٤٠٢٥. الإمامُ الباقرُ ﷺ: إيّاكُم والخُصومَةَ؛ فإنَّها تُفسِدُ القَلبَ وتُورِثُ النِّفاقَ.٤٤٩٦

1232. The Seed of Enmity

١٢٣٢ـ بَذرُ العَداوَةِ

4026. **Imām ʿAlī (AS) said,** 'The cause of enmity is lack of consideration [for others].'[4534]

٤٠٢٦ . الإمامُ عليٌّ عليه السلام: عِلَّةُ المُعاداةِ قِلَّةُ المُبالاةِ.[٤٤٩٧]

4027. **Imām ʿAlī (AS) said,** 'Everything has a seed, and the seed of enmity is mockery.'[4535]

٤٠٢٧ . عنه عليه السلام: لِكُلِّ شَيءٍ بَذرٌ وبَذرُ العَداوَةِ المِزاحُ.[٤٤٩٨]

1233. One Who Must Be Considered an Enemy

١٢٣٣ـ مَن يَنبَغي أن يُسمّىٰ عَدُوّاً

"O you who have faith! Indeed among your spouses and children you have enemies; so beware of them. And if you excuse, forbear and forgive, then Allah is indeed all-forgiving, all-merciful."[4536]

﴿يا أيُّها الَّذِينَ آمَنُوا إنَّ مِنْ أزْواجِكُمْ وَأوْلادِكُمْ عَدُوّاً لَكُمْ فَاحْذَرُوهُمْ وَإنْ تَعْفُوا وَتَصْفَحُوا وَتَغْفِرُوا فَإنَّ اللهَ غَفُورٌ رَحِيمٌ﴾.[٤٤٩٩]

4028. **Imām ʿAlī (AS) said,** 'Man's stomach is his enemy.'[4537]

٤٠٢٨ . الإمامُ عليٌّ عليه السلام: بَطنُ المَرءِ عَدُوُّهُ.[٤٥٠٠]

4029. **Imām al-Jawād (AS) said,** 'He who conceals [the path] of proper conduct from you in making you follow that which you desire is indeed your enemy.'[4538]

٤٠٢٩ . الإمامُ الجوادُ عليه السلام: قَد عاداكَ مَن سَتَرَ عَنكَ الرُّشدَ اتِّباعاً لِما تَهواهُ.[٤٥٠١]

(See also: SATAN: section 1027)

(اُنظر: الشيطان: باب ١٠٢٧).

1234. Your Archenemy

١٢٣٤ـ أعدىٰ عَدُوِّكَ

4030. **The Prophet (SAWA) said,** 'Your archenemy is your lower self that resides between your two sides.'[4539]

٤٠٣٠ . رسولُ اللهِ صلى الله عليه وآله: أعدىٰ عَدُوِّكَ نَفسُكَ الَّتي بَينَ جَنبَيكَ.[٤٥٠٢]

4031. **Imām ʿAlī (AS) said,** 'The worst enemy of man is his rage and lust, and he who suppresses them will make his status elevate and will reach his goal.'[4540]

٤٠٣١ . الإمامُ عليٌّ عليه السلام: أعدىٰ عَدُوٍّ لِلمَرءِ غَضَبُهُ وشَهوَتُهُ، فَمَن مَلَكَهُما عَلَت دَرَجَتُهُ وبَلَغَ غايَتَهُ.[٤٥٠٣]

1235. Caution Against Feeling Secure from One's Enemy

١٢٣٥ ـ التَّحذيرُ مِن ائتِمانِ العَدُوِّ

4032. **Imām ʿAlī (AS) said,** 'Whoever falls into a sleep of neglect of his enemy is jolted awake by his crafty schemes.'[4541]

٤٠٣٢ . الإمامُ عليٌّ عليه‌السلام : مَن نامَ عَن عَدُوِّهِ أنبَهَتهُ المَكايِدُ .[٤٥٠٤]

4033. **Imām ʿAlī (AS) said,** 'He who overlooks [his enemy] is himself surely not overlooked [by his enemy].'[4542]

٤٠٣٣ . عنه عليه‌السلام : مَن نامَ لَم يُنَمْ عَنهُ .[٤٥٠٥]

4034. **Imām ʿAlī (AS) said,** 'Never underestimate an enemy even if he be weak.'[4543]

٤٠٣٤ . عنه عليه‌السلام : لا تَستَصغِرَنَّ عَدُوّاً وإن ضَعُفَ .[٤٥٠٦]

1236. Reconciling with One's Enemies

١٢٣٦ ـ استِصلاحُ الأعداءِ

4035. **Imām ʿAlī (AS) said,** 'He who reconciles with his enemy increases the numbers [of his friends] on his own side.'[4544]

٤٠٣٥ . الإمامُ عليٌّ عليه‌السلام : مَنِ استَصلَحَ عَدُوَّهُ زادَ في عَدَدِهِ .[٤٥٠٧]

4036. **Imām ʿAlī (AS) said,** 'He who reconciles with the opposition achieves his aim.'[4545]

٤٠٣٦ . عنه عليه‌السلام : مَنِ استَصلَحَ الأضدادَ بَلَغَ المُرادَ .[٤٥٠٨]

1237. How to Arm Oneself Against Enemies

١٢٣٧ ـ ما يَنبَغي التَّسَلُّحُ بِهِ عَلَى الأعداءِ

4037. **Luqmān (AS) said** in his advice to his son, 'O my son, make persuasion and expressing of content from among what you arm yourself with against the enemy to knock him down. Do not try to avoid him so that whatever you have inside be manifested to him, leading him to prepare himself for you [to reciprocate].'[4546]

٤٠٣٧ . لقمانُ عليه‌السلام ـ في وَصِيَّتِهِ لابنِهِ ـ: يا بُنَيَّ، لِيَكُن مِمّا تَتَسَلَّحُ بِهِ عَلىٰ عَدُوِّكَ فَتَصرَعُهُ المُماسَحَةُ وإعلانُ الرِّضا عَنهُ، ولا تُزاوِلْهُ بِالمُجانَبَةِ فيَبدُوَ لَهُ ما في نَفسِكَ فَيَتَأَهَّبَ لَكَ .[٤٥٠٩]

1238. People's Hostility Towards that which they are Ignorant of

١٢٣٨ ـ عَداوَةُ النّاسِ لِما جَهِلوا

4038. **Imām ʿAlī (AS) said,** 'People are hostile towards that which they are ignorant of.'[4547]

٤٠٣٨ . الإمامُ عليٌّ عليه‌السلام : النّاسُ أعداءُ ما جَهِلوا .[٤٥١٠]

(See also: IGNORANCE: section 394)

(أُنظر) الجهل: باب ٣٩٤.

268

MAKING EXCUSES

الاعتِذار

1239. Caution Against doing Something that One would Later have to Excuse Oneself for

١٢٣٩ ـ التَّحذيرُ مِمّا يُعتَذَرُ مِنهُ

4039. **The Prophet (SAWA) said,** 'Keep away from doing that which you must excuse yourself for, for verily that involves hidden polytheism.'[4548]

٤٠٣٩ . رسولُ اللهِ ﷺ: إيّاكَ وما تَعتَذِرُ مِنهُ ؛ فإنَّ فيهِ الشِّركَ الخَفِيَّ.[٤٥١١]

4040. **Imām al-Ḥusayn (AS) said,** 'Keep away from doing that which you must excuse yourself for, for verily the believer neither commits a wrong nor makes excuses for himself, whereas the hypocrite commits wrongs and makes excuses for them everyday.'[4549]

٤٠٤٠ . الإمامُ الحسينُ عليه السلام: إيّاكَ وما تَعتَذِرُ مِنهُ ؛ فإنَّ المُؤمِنَ لا يُسيءُ ولا يَعتَذِرُ، والمُنافِقَ كُلَّ يَومٍ يُسيءُ ويَعتَذِرُ.[٤٥١٢]

4041. *Mishkāt al-Anwār,* narrating from one of the companions of Imām al-Ṣādiq (AS), 'Imām al-Ṣādiq said, 'A believer must never humiliate himself.' When asked how he would humiliate himself, he replied, 'By embarking upon something which he later has to make excuses for.'[4550]

٤٠٤١ . مشكاة الأنوار عن بعضِ أصحابِهِ: قالَ أبو عَبدِ اللهِ عليه السلام: لا يَنبَغي لِلمُؤمِنِ أن يُذِلَّ نفسَهُ، قُلتُ: بِما يُذِلُّ نَفسَهُ؟ قالَ: يَدخُلُ فيما يَعتَذِرُ مِنهُ.[٤٥١٣]

1240. Enjoinment of Accepting the Excuse of One who Excuses himself

١٢٤٠ ـ الحَثُّ عَلىٰ قَبولِ عُذرِ مَنِ اعتَذَرَ

4042. **The Prophet (SAWA) said,** 'He who does not accept an apology from someone, be it from an honest or a liar, will not be with me at the Heavenly Pool [in Paradise].'[4551]

٤٠٤٢ . رسولُ اللهِ ﷺ: مَن لَم يَقبَلِ المَعذِرَةَ مِن مُحِقٍّ أو مُبطِلٍ، لَم يَرِدْ عَلَيَّ الحَوضَ.[٤٥١٤]

4043. **Imām ʿAlī (AS) said,** 'Accept your fellow brother's excuse, and if he has no excuse then find an excuse for him.'[4552]

٤٠٤٣ . الإمامُ عليٌّ عليه السلام: اِقبَلْ عُذرَ أخيكَ، وإن لَم يَكُن لَهُ عُذرٌ فَالتَمِسْ لَهُ عُذراً.[٤٥١٥]

4044. **Imām ʿAlī (AS) said,** 'The most understanding person is he who accepts people's excuses most readily.'[4553]

٤٠٤٤. عنه ﷺ: أعقَلُ النّاسِ أعذَرُهُم لِلنّاسِ.[٤٥١٦]

4045. **Imām Zayn al-ʿĀbidīn (AS) said,** 'If someone insults you on your right hand side, then moves over to your left and apologises to you, accept his apology.'[4554]

٤٠٤٥. الإمام زين العابدين ﷺ: إن شَتَمَكَ رَجُلٌ عَن يَمينِكَ ثُمّ تَحَوَّلَ إلىٰ يَسارِكَ واعتَذَرَ إلَيكَ فَاقبَلْ عُذرَهُ.[٤٥١٧]

269

GOOD REPUTE

العِرضُ

1241. Enjoinment of Keeping Up One's Reputation

١٢٤١ ـ الحَثُّ علىٰ صِيانَةِ العِرضِ

4046. **Imām ʿAlī (AS) said,** 'The most miserly of people with his wares is the most liberal of them with his own reputation [in that he gives it up readily].'[4555]

٤٠٤٦. الإمامُ عليٌّ ﷺ: أبخَلُ النّاسِ بِعَرضِهِ، أسخاهُم بِعِرضِهِ.[٤٥١٨]

4047. **Imām ʿAlī (AS) said,** 'The best form of wealth is that which is used to safeguard one's reputation.'[4556]

٤٠٤٧. عنه ﷺ: أفضَلُ الغِنىٰ ما صِينَ بِهِ العِرضُ.[٤٥١٩]

4048. **Imām ʿAlī (AS) said,** 'He who cares for his reputation must desist from disputation.'[4557]

٤٠٤٨. عنه ﷺ: مَن ضَنَّ بِعِرضِهِ فَلْيَدَعِ المِراءَ.[٤٥٢٠]

4049. **Imām al-Ṣādiq (AS) said,** 'When reputation wanes, it becomes very difficult to restore.'[4558]

٤٠٤٩. الإمامُ الصّادقُ ﷺ: إذا رَقَّ العِرضُ استُصعِبَ جَمعُهُ.[٤٥٢١]

1242. The Reward for Refraining from Tarnishing Fellow Muslims' Reputations

١٢٤٢ ـ ثَوابُ الكَفِّ عَن أعراضِ المُسلِمينَ

4050. **Imām Zayn al-ʿĀbidīn (AS) said,** 'He who refrains from tarnishing fellow Muslims' reputations, Allah, Mighty and Exalted, regards his offence as undone on the Day of Resurrection.'[4559]

٤٠٥٠. الإمامُ زينُ العابدينَ ﷺ: مَن كَفَّ عَن أعراضِ المُسلِمينَ أقالَهُ اللهُ عزَّوجلَّ عَثرَتَهُ يومَ القِيامَةِ.[٤٥٢٢]

1243. The Reward for Defending the Reputation of a Fellow Muslim

١٢٤٣ـ ثَوابُ الدِّفاعِ عَن عِرضِ المُسلِمِ

4051. **The Prophet (SAWA) said,** 'He who guards the reputation of his fellow brother is veiled from the Fire.'[4560]

٤٠٥١ . رسولُ اللهِ ﷺ : مَن رَدَّ عَن عِرضِ أخيهِ كانَ لَهُ حِجاباً مِنَ النّارِ.[٤٥٢٣]

4052. **The Prophet (SAWA) said,** 'He who guards the reputation of his fellow Muslim brother definitely becomes deserving of obligatory entrance into Paradise.'[4561]

٤٠٥٢ . عنه ﷺ : مَن رَدَّ عَن عِرضِ أخيهِ المُسلِمِ وَجَبَت لَهُ الجَنَّةُ البَتَّةَ.[٤٥٢٤]

(See also: BACKBITING: section 1459)

(أنظر) الغيبة: باب ١٤٥٩.

270

INNER KNOWLEDGE[4562]

المَعرِفَةُ

1244. The Importance of Inner Knowledge

١٢٤٤ـ قيمَةُ المَعرِفَةِ

4053. **The Prophet (SAWA) said,** 'The ones from among you with the best faith are the ones with the best inner knowledge.'[4563]

٤٠٥٣ . رسولُ اللهِ ﷺ : أفضَلُكُم إيماناً أفضَلُكُم مَعرِفَةً.[٤٥٢٥]

4054. **Imām ʿAlī (AS) said,** 'Knowledge is the first guide whereas inner knowledge [of Allah] is the ultimate goal.'[4564]

٤٠٥٤ . الإمامُ عليٌّ ﷺ : العِلمُ أوَّلُ دَليلٍ، والمَعرِفَةُ آخِرُ نِهايَةٍ.[٤٥٢٦]

4055. **Imām ʿAlī (AS) said,** 'Inner knowledge is the light of the heart.'[4565]

٤٠٥٥ . عنه ﷺ : المَعرِفَةُ نورُ القَلبِ.[٤٥٢٧]

4056. **Imām al-Ḥusayn (AS) said,** 'The acquisition of knowledge is the seed for [the growth of] inner knowledge.'[4566]

٤٠٥٦ . الإمامُ الحسينُ ﷺ : دِراسَةُ العِلمِ لِقاحُ المَعرِفَةِ.[٤٥٢٨]

4057. **Imām al-Ṣādiq (AS) said,** 'Allah does not accept any act without inner knowledge and inner knowledge only comes through prior action. So, whoever gains knowledge intrinsically, his knowledge will lead him to action, and whoever does not act does not have any inner knowledge.'[4567]

٤٠٥٧ . الإمامُ الصّادقُ ﷺ : لا يَقبَلُ اللهُ عَمَلاً إلّا بِمَعرِفَةٍ، ولا مَعرِفَةَ إلّا بِعَمَلٍ، فمَن عَرَفَ دَلَّتهُ المَعرِفَةُ عَلَى العَمَلِ، ومَن لَم يَعمَلْ فَلا مَعرِفَةَ لَهُ.[٤٥٢٩]

1245. Impediments to Inner Knowledge

١٢٤٥ ـ مَوانِعُ المَعرِفَةِ

"Have you seen him who has taken his desire to be his god and whom Allah has led astray knowingly, and set a seal upon his hearing and his heart, and drawn a blind on his sight? So who will guide him after Allah? Will you not then take admonition?"[4568]

﴿أَفَرَأَيْتَ مَنِ اتَّخَذَ إِلٰهَهُ هَواهُ وَأَضَلَّهُ اللهُ عَلَى عِلْمٍ وَخَتَمَ عَلَىٰ سَمْعِهِ وَقَلْبِهِ وَجَعَلَ عَلَىٰ بَصَرِهِ غِشَاوَةً فَمَنْ يَهْدِيهِ مِنْ بَعْدِ اللهِ أَفَلَا تَذَكَّرُونَ﴾ .[٤٥٣٠]

4058. **The Prophet (SAWA) said,** 'The light of inner knowledge is brought about by hunger whereas distance from Allah is caused by satiety. Proximity to Allah is brought about by loving the poor and drawing near to them, so do not eat to your fill lest the light of inner knowledge be extinguished from your hearts.'[4569]

٤٠٥٨ . رسولُ اللهِ ﷺ : نورُ الحِكمَةِ الجُوعُ، والتَّباعُدُ مِنَ اللهِ الشِّبَعُ، والقُربَةُ إلَى اللهِ حُبُّ المَساكينِ والدُّنُوُّ مِنهُم، لا تَشبَعوا فَيُطفَأَ نورُ المَعرِفةِ مِن قُلوبِكُم.[٤٥٣١]

1246. The Inner Knowledge of the Self

١٢٤٦ ـ مَعرِفَةُ النَّفسِ

4059. **Imām ʿAlī (AS) said,** 'The inner knowledge of the self is the most beneficial of all such knowledge.'[4570]

٤٠٥٩ . الإمامُ عليٌّ عليه السلام : مَعرِفَةُ النَّفسِ أنفَعُ المَعارِفِ.[٤٥٣٢]

4060. **Imām ʿAlī (AS) said,** 'The one who attains knowledge of his own self has obtained the greatest victory indeed.'[4571]

٤٠٦٠ . عنه عليه السلام : نالَ الفَوزَ الأكبَرَ مَن ظَفِرَ بِمَعرِفَةِ النَّفسِ.[٤٥٣٣]

4061. **Imām ʿAlī (AS) said,** 'How can one who is ignorant of his own self expect to know others?!'[4572]

٤٠٦١ . عنه عليه السلام : كَيفَ يَعرِفُ غَيرَهُ مَن يَجهَلُ نَفسَهُ ؟![٤٥٣٤]

4062. **Imām ʿAlī (AS) said,** 'He who gains inner knowledge of his self combats it, and he who remains ignorant of his self, neglects it.'[4573]

٤٠٦٢ . عنه عليه السلام : مَن عَرَفَ نَفسَهُ جاهَدَها، مَن جَهِلَ نَفسَهُ أهمَلَها.[٤٥٣٥]

4063. **Imām ʿAlī (AS) said,** 'He who attains inner knowledge of Allah becomes lonesome; he who attains inner knowledge of his self strips himself [of all that hinders its progress]; he who attains inner knowledge about this world abstains from it; and he who attains inner knowledge about people prefers solitude.'[4574]

٤٠٦٣ . عنه عليه السلام : مَن عَرَفَ اللهَ تَوَحَّدَ، مَن عَرَفَ نَفسَهُ تَجَرَّدَ، مَن عَرَفَ الدّنيا تَزَهَّدَ، مَن عَرَفَ النّاسَ تَفَرَّدَ.[٤٥٣٦]

4064. **Imām ʿAlī (AS) said,** ‘The person who knows his self the best is he who fears his Lord the most.’[4575]

٤٠٦٤. عنه ﷺ: أكثَرُ النّاسِ مَعرِفَةً لِنفسِهِ أخوَفُهُم لِرَبِّهِ.[٤٥٣٧]

4065. **Imām ʿAlī (AS) said,** ‘He who attains inner knowledge of his self attains inner knowledge of his Lord.’[4576]

٤٠٦٥. عنه ﷺ: مَن عَرَفَ نَفسَهُ عَرَفَ رَبَّهُ.[٤٥٣٨]

4066. **Imām ʿAlī (AS) said,** ‘It befits one who knows the dignity of his own self to deem it too great for the vileness of this world.’[4577]

٤٠٦٦. عنه ﷺ: يَنبَغي لِمَن عَلِمَ شَرَفَ نَفسِهِ أن يُنَزِّهَها عَن دَناءَةِ الدّنيا.[٤٥٣٩]

4067. **Imām ʿAlī (AS) said,** ‘It befits one who knows the dignity of his own self to adhere to temperance and self-restraint.’[4578]

٤٠٦٧. عنه ﷺ: يَنبَغي لِمَن عَرَفَ نَفسَهُ أن يَلزَمَ القَناعَةَ والعِفَّةَ.[٤٥٤٠]

4068. **Imām ʿAlī (AS) said,** ‘It befits one who knows the dignity of his own self to never allow a sorrowful and self-cautious state to leave him.’[4579]

٤٠٦٨. عنه ﷺ: يَنبَغي لِمَن عَرَفَ نَفسَهُ أن لا يُفارِقَهُ الحُزنُ والحَذَرُ.[٤٥٤١]

4069. **Imām Zayn al-ʿĀbidīn (AS) said** in one of his supplications, ‘Make us from among those who have attained inner knowledge of their selves and are convinced of their true abode, such that they spend their whole lives in Your obedience.’[4580]

٤٠٦٩. الإمامُ زينَ العابدينُ ﷺ ـ في الدُّعاءِ ـ: واجعَلنا مِنَ الّذين عَرَفوا أنفُسَهُم، وأيقَنوا بِمُستَقَرِّهِم، فكانَت أعمارُهُم في طاعَتِك تَفنىٰ.[٤٥٤٢]

4070. **Imām al-Bāqir (AS) said** in his advice to Jābir al-Juʿfī, ‘There is no inner knowledge like your inner knowledge of your own self.’[4581]

٤٠٧٠. الإمامُ الباقرُ ﷺ ـ في وَصِيَّتِهِ لِجابِرٍ الجُعفيِّ ـ: لا مَعرِفةَ كَمَعرِفَتِكَ بِنَفسِكَ.[٤٥٤٣]

271

INNER KNOWLEDGE OF ALLAH

مَعرِفَةُ اللهِ

1247. The Virtue of Attaining Inner Knowledge of Allah

١٢٤٧ ـ فَضلُ مَعرِفَةِ اللهِ

4071. **Imām ʿAlī (AS) said,** ‘He who attains inner knowledge of Allah has achieved perfection in his knowledge indeed.’[4582]

٤٠٧١. الإمامُ عليٌّ ﷺ: مَن عَرَفَ اللهَ كَمُلَت مَعرِفَتُهُ.[٤٥٤٤]

4072. **Imām ʿAlī (AS) said,** 'The inner knowledge of Allah, Glory be to Him, is the highest of knowable truths.'[4583]

٤٠٧٢. عنه عليه السلام: مَـعرِفةُ اللهِ سُبحانَهُ أعلىٰ المَعارِفِ.[٤٥٤٥]

4073. **Imām ʿAlī (AS) said,** 'I would not be pleased to die as a child and be made to enter Paradise without being able to grow up and get to know my Lord, Mighty and Exalted.'[4584]

٤٠٧٣. عنه عليه السلام: ما يَسُرُّني لو مِتُّ طِفلاً واُدخِلتُ الجَنَّةَ ولم أكبُرْ فأعرِفَ رَبّي عَزَّوجلَّ.[٤٥٤٦]

4074. **Imām ʿAlī (AS) said,** 'The fruit of knowledge is attaining inner knowledge of Allah.'[4585]

٤٠٧٤. عنه عليه السلام: ثَمَرَةُ العِلمِ مَعرِفَةُ اللهِ.[٤٥٤٧]

4075. **Imām ʿAlī (AS) said,** 'He whose heart finds peace in knowing Allah, finds peace in being needless of Allah's creatures.'[4586]

٤٠٧٥. عنه عليه السلام: مَن سَكَنَ قَلبَهُ العِلمُ بِاللهِ سَكَنَهُ الغِنىٰ عَن خَلقِ اللهِ.[٤٥٤٨]

4076. **Imām al-Ṣādiq (AS) said,** 'If people knew the virtue of knowing Allah, Mighty and Exalted, they would never extend their gaze to the splendour and bounties of the life of this world that Allah has granted to the enemies. They would then regard such people's worldly goods to be more insignificant that the dust under their feet, and they would take great pleasure at attaining knowledge of Allah, Mighty and Exalted, and would savour it as if they were tasting the experience of being in the gardens of Paradise with the friends of Allah. Verily the inner knowledge of Allah is an intimate companion in every type of desolation, a friend in every type of loneliness, a light in every darkness, a source of strength from all weakness, and a cure for all ailments.'[4587]

٤٠٧٦. الإمامُ الصّادقُ عليه السلام: لَو يَعلَمُ النّاسُ ما في فَضلِ مَعرِفةِ اللهِ عَزَّوجلَّ ما مَدُّوا أعيُنَهُم إلىٰ ما مَتَّعَ اللهُ بِهِ الأعداءَ مِن زَهرَةِ الحَياةِ الدّنيا ونَعيمِها، وكانَت دُنياهُم أقَلَّ عِندَهُم مِمّا يَطَؤونَهُ بِأرجُلِهِم، ولَنَعِموا بِمَعرِفةِ اللهِ جَلَّ وعَزَّ، وتَلَذَّذوا بِها تَلَذُّذَ مَن لَم يَزَلْ في رَوضاتِ الجِنانِ مَعَ أولِياءِ اللهِ. إنَّ مَعرِفةَ اللهِ عَزَّوجلَّ اُنسٌ مِن كُلِّ وَحشَةٍ، وصاحِبٌ مِن كُلِّ وَحدَةٍ، ونُورٌ مِن كُلِّ ظُلمَةٍ، وقُوَّةٌ مِن كُلِّ ضَعفٍ، وشِفاءٌ مِن كُلِّ سُقمٍ.[٤٥٤٩]

1248. The Fruits of Inner Knowledge of Allah

١٢٤٨ ـ آثارُ مَعرِفَةِ اللهِ

4077. **The Prophet (SAWA) said,** 'He who attains inner knowledge of Allah and aggrandizes Him forbids his mouth from speaking [vain] and

٤٠٧٧. رسولُ اللهِ صلى الله عليه وآله: مَن عَرَفَ اللهَ وعَظَّمَهُ مَنَعَ فاهُ مِنَ الكَلامِ وبَطنَهُ مِنَ الطَّعامِ، وعَنّىٰ

his stomach from eating, and debilitates himself through fasting and praying.'[4588]

نفسَهُ بِالصِّيامِ والقِيامِ.[٤٥٥٠]

4078. **The Prophet (SAWA) said,** 'If you truly knew Allah as He is worthy of being known, you would be able to walk on the seas and the mountains would fall by your command.'[4589]

٤٠٧٨ . عنه ﷺ : لَو عَرَفتُمُ اللّهَ حَقَّ مَعرِفَتِهِ لَمَشَيتُم عَلَى البُحورِ، ولَزالَت بِدُعائكُمُ الجِبالُ.[٤٥٥١]

4079. **The Prophet (SAWA) said,** 'He who is most knowledgeable of Allah is most fearful of Allah.'[4590]

٤٠٧٩ . عنه ﷺ : مَن كانَ بِاللّهِ أعرَفَ كانَ مِنَ اللّهِ أخوَفَ.[٤٥٥٢]

4080. **Imām ʿAlī (AS) said,** 'The least knowledge of Allah leads one to abstain from the vanities of this world.'[4591]

٤٠٨٠ . الإمامُ عليٌّ ؑ : يَسيرُ المَعرِفَةِ يُوجِبُ الزُّهدَ في الدّنيا.[٤٥٥٣]

4081. **Imām ʿAlī (AS) said,** 'Verily it does not befit one who has attained inner knowledge of the grandeur of Allah to behave proudly, for verily the elevation of those who acknowledge His grandeur comes from their abasing themselves in front of Him.'[4592]

٤٠٨١ . عنه ؑ : إنَّهُ لا يَنبَغي لِمَن عَرَفَ عَظَمَةَ اللّهِ أن يَتَعَظَّمَ ؛ فإنَّ رِفعَةَ الّذينَ يَعلَمونَ ما عَظَمَتُهُ أن يَتَواضَعوا لَهُ.[٤٥٥٤]

4082. **Imām ʿAlī (AS) said,** 'The peak of inner knowledge of Allah is fear [of Him].'[4593]

٤٠٨٢ . عنه ؑ : غايَةُ المَعرِفَةِ الخَشيَةُ.[٤٥٥٥]

4083. **Imām ʿAlī (AS) said,** 'The person who best knows Allah asks of Him the most.'[4594]

٤٠٨٣ . عنه ؑ : أعلَمُ النّاسِ بِاللّهِ أكثَرُهُم لَهُ مَسألَةً.[٤٥٥٦]

4084. **Imām al-Bāqir (AS) said,** 'The creature of Allah most eligible for submission to the decree of Allah, Mighty and Exalted, is he who knows Allah, Mighty and Exalted.'[4595]

٤٠٨٤ . الإمامُ الباقرُ ؑ : أحَقُّ خَلقِ اللّهِ أن يُسَلِّمَ لِما قَضَى اللّهُ عَزَّوجلَّ : مَن عَرَفَ اللّهَ عَزَّوجلَّ.[٤٥٥٧]

4085. **Imām al-Ṣādiq (AS) said,** 'He who attains inner knowledge of Allah fears Allah, and he who fears Allah restrains himself from this world.'[4596]

٤٠٨٥ . الإمامُ الصّادقُ ؑ : مَن عَرَفَ اللّهَ خافَ اللّهَ، ومَن خافَ اللّهَ سَخَت نَفسُهُ عَنِ الدّنيا.[٤٥٥٨]

4086. **Imām al-Ṣādiq (AS) said,** 'Verily the person who best knows Allah is the most content with the decree of Allah, Mighty and Exalted.'[4597]

٤٠٨٦ . عنه ؑ : إنَّ أعلَمَ النّاسِ بِاللّهِ أرضاهُم بِقَضاءِ اللّهِ عَزَّوجلَّ.[٤٥٥٩]

(See also: CONVICTION: section 1916; KNOWLEDGE: section 1356)

(انظر) اليقين: باب ١٩١٦؛ العلم: باب ١٣٥٦

1249. The Description of the One who Knows Allah [or the Gnostic]

١٢٤٩ـ صِفَةُ العارِفِ

4087. **Imām ʿAlī (AS) said,** 'The gnostic's face is cheerful and smiley, whereas his heart is apprehensive and sorrowful.'[4598]

٤٠٨٧. الإمامُ عليٌّ ﷺ: العارِفُ وَجهُهُ مُستَبشِرٌ مُتَبَسِّمٌ، وقَلبُهُ وَجِلٌ مَحزونٌ.[٤٥٦٠]

4088. **Imām ʿAlī (AS) said,** 'Longing [for Allah] is the sincerest friend of the gnostics.'[4599]

٤٠٨٨. عنه ﷺ: الشَّوقُ خُلصانُ العارِفينَ.[٤٥٦١]

4089. **Imām ʿAlī (AS) said,** 'Fear is the cloak of the gnostics.'[4600]

٤٠٨٩. عنه ﷺ: الخَوفُ جِلبابُ العارِفينَ.[٤٥٦٢]

4090. **Imām ʿAlī (AS) said,** 'Crying much due to fear of Allah for any possible distance between oneself and Allah is the regular worshipful state of the gnostics.'[4601]

٤٠٩٠. عنه ﷺ: البُكاءُ مِن خِيفَةِ اللهِ لِلبُعدِ عَنِ اللهِ عِبادَةُ العارِفينَ.[٤٥٦٣]

4091. **Imām al-Ṣādiq (AS) said,** 'Trust in Allah and you will attain inner knowledge [of Him].'[4602]

٤٠٩١. الإمامُ الصّادقُ ﷺ: ثِقْ بِاللهِ تَكُن عارِفاً.[٤٥٦٤]

1250. The Lowest Degree of Inner Knowledge of Allah

١٢٥٠ـ أدنَى مَراتِبِ مَعرِفَةِ اللهِ

4092. **Imām al-Kāẓim (AS),** when he was asked about the lowest degree of inner knowledge, replied, 'It is to affirm that there is no god but He, and that He has no likeness or match, and that He is eternal, perpetual and everlasting. He is All-existent and not absent, and that there is nothing like Him.'[4603]

٤٠٩٢. الإمامُ الكاظمُ ﷺ ـ لَمّا سُئلَ عَن أدنَى المَعرِفةِ ـ: الإقرارُ بأنَّهُ لا إلٰهَ غَيرُهُ، ولا شِبهَ لَهُ ولا نَظيرَ وأنَّهُ قَديمٌ، مُثبَتٌ، مَوجودٌ، غَيرُ فَقيدٍ، وأنَّهُ لَيسَ كَمِثلِه شَيءٌ.[٤٥٦٥]

1251. Attaining Inner Knowledge of Allah through Allah Himself

١٢٥١ـ مَعرِفَةُ اللهِ بِاللهِ

4093. **Imām ʿAlī (AS) said,** 'Get to know Allah through Allah, and the Prophet through the message he brought, and those vested with authority through their command to do good, their justice and righteousness.'[4604]

٤٠٩٣. الإمامُ عليٌّ ﷺ: اِعرِفوا اللهَ بِاللهِ، والرَّسولَ بِالرِّسالَةِ، وأُولي الأمرِ بِالأمرِ بِالمَعروفِ والعَدلِ والإحسانِ.[٤٥٦٦]

4094. **Imām al-Ḥusayn (AS) said** in one of his supplications, 'My God! My own concentration on the signs [in nature] prevents me from seeing You, so draw me near to You through Your service that may allow me to reach You. How can something that needs You for its very existence be used to prove Your existence?! Are other things more manifest than You that they be used to point to You?! When were You ever absent that You should need anything to prove Your existence?! Through You alone do I arrive at You, so guide me with Your light to Yourself.'[4605]

٤٠٩٤. الإمامُ الحسينُ ﷺ ـ في الدُّعاءِ ـ: إلٰهي تَرَدُّدي في الآثارِ يُوجِبُ بُعدَ المَزارِ، فاجمَعْني عَلَيكَ بِخِدمَةٍ تُوصِلُني إلَيكَ، كَيفَ يُستَدَلُّ عَلَيكَ بِما هُوَ في وُجودِهِ مُفتَقِرٌ إلَيكَ؟! أيَكونُ لِغَيرِكَ مِنَ الظُّهورِ ما لَيسَ لَكَ حتّىٰ يَكونَ هُوَ المُظهِرَ لَكَ؟! متىٰ غِبتَ حتّىٰ تَحتاجَ إلىٰ دَليلٍ يَدُلُّ عَلَيكَ؟!... بِكَ أستَدِلُّ عَلَيكَ فَاهْدِني بِنورِكَ إلَيكَ.[٤٥٦٧]

4095. **Imām Zayn al-ʿĀbidīn (AS) said** in one of his supplications, 'I have attained knowledge of You through You, and You are the One Who indicated me to Yourself and called me to Yourself, and were it not for You, I would not know who You are.'[4606]

٤٠٩٥. الإقبال عن الإمامِ زينِ العابدينَ ﷺ ـ في الدّعاءِ ـ: بِكَ عَرَفتُكَ وأنتَ دَلَلتَني عَلَيكَ ودَعَوتَني إلَيكَ، ولَولا أنتَ لَم أدرِ ما أنتَ.[٤٥٦٨]

1252. Prohibition of Pondering About Allah's Essence

١٢٥٢ ـ النَّهيُ عَنِ التَّفَكُّرِ في ذاتِ اللهِ

4096. **The Prophet (SAWA) said,** 'Ponder about the creation of Allah, but do not ponder about Allah Himself [His essence] lest you be ruined.'[4607]

٤٠٩٦. رسولُ اللهِ ﷺ: تَفَكَّروا في خَلقِ اللهِ، ولا تَفَكَّروا في اللهِ فتَهلِكوا.[٤٥٦٩]

4097. **Imām al-Ṣādiq (AS) said,** 'Beware of pondering about [the essence of] Allah, for verily pondering about Allah only increases one's bewilderment. Verily Allah, Mighty and Exalted, cannot be perceived by the sights or described by any type of criteria and measurement.'[4608]

٤٠٩٧. الإمامُ الصّادقُ ﷺ: إيّاكُم والتَّفَكُّرَ في اللهِ؛ فإنَّ التَّفَكُّرَ في اللهِ لا يَزيدُ إلّا تِيهاً، إنَّ اللهَ عَزَّوجلَّ لا تُدرِكُهُ الأبصارُ ولا يُوصَفُ بِمِقدارٍ.[٤٥٧٠]

4098. **Imām al-Ṣādiq (AS) said,** 'Ruined is the one who ponders into [the essence of] Allah!'[4609]

٤٠٩٨. عنه ﷺ: مَن نَظَرَ في اللهِ كَيفَ هُوَ هَلَكَ.[٤٥٧١]

(See also: THINKING: section 1504)

(أنظر) التفكّر: باب ١٥٠٤.

1253. The Intellects' Incapacity to Fathom His Essence

١٢٥٣ ـ عَجزُ العُقولِ عَن مَعرِفَةِ كُنهِهِ

4099. **Imām ʿAlī (AS) said,** 'We do not know the essence of Your greatness. All that we do know is

٤٠٩٩. الإمامُ عليٌّ ﷺ: فلَسنا نَعلَمُ كُنهَ عَظَمَتِكَ،

that You are Ever-Living and Self-Subsisting through Whom all things subsist. Drowsiness and sleep do not overtake You, vision does not reach You and sight cannot perceive You.'[4610]

إلّا أنّا نعلَمُ أنّكَ حَيٌّ قَيّومٌ، لا تَأخُذُكَ سِنَةٌ ولا نومٌ، لَم يَنتَهِ إلَيكَ نَظَرٌ، ولَم يُدرِكْكَ بَصَرٌ.٤٥٧٢

4100. **Imām ʿAlī (AS) said** in his description of the angels, 'With all the positions they possess, and with their rank near You and all their love for You, and with their abundant servitude and worship for You, and their lack of attention about You, yet if they were to witness the essence of what is hidden about You from them, they would regard their deeds insignificant, they would reproach themselves and would realize that they have not worshipped You as You deserve to be worshipped, and have not obeyed You as You deserve to be obeyed.'[4611]

٤١٠٠. عنه ﷺ ـ في صِفَةِ المَلائكَةِ ـ: وإنَّهُم عَلىٰ مَكانِهِم مِنكَ، ومَنزِلَتِهِم عِندَكَ، واستِجماعِ أهوائهِم فيكَ، وكَثرَةِ طاعَتِهِم لَكَ، وقِلَّةِ غَفلَتِهِم عَن أمرِكَ، لَو عايَنوا كُنهَ ما خَفِيَ عَلَيهِم مِنكَ لَحَقَّروا أعمالَهُم، ولَزَرَوا عَلىٰ أنفُسِهِم، ولَعَرَفوا أنَّهُم لَم يَعبُدوكَ حَقَّ عِبادَتِكَ، ولَم يُطيعوكَ حَقَّ طاعَتِكَ.٤٥٧٣

4101. **Imām Zayn al-ʿĀbidīn (AS) said** in one of his supplications, 'The intellects are incapable of fathoming the essence of Your Beauty, the sights are restricted to looking at other than the splendour of Your Countenance, and You have not set aside any means for Your creation to get to know You except through their complete incapacity of knowing You.'[4612]

٤١٠١. الإمام زينُ العابدينَ ﷺ ـ في الدّعاءِ ـ: عَجَزَتِ العُقولُ عَن إدراكِ كُنهِ جَمالِكَ، وانحَسَرَتِ الأبصارُ دونَ النَّظَرِ إلىٰ سُبُحاتِ وَجهِكَ، ولَم تَجعَلْ لِلخَلقِ طَريقاً إلىٰ مَعرِفَتِكَ إلّا بِالعَجزِ عَن مَعرِفَتِكَ.٤٥٧٤

4102. **Imām al-Riḍā (AS) said,** 'His essence is a partition [distinction] between Him and His creation.'[4613]

٤١٠٢. الإمامُ الرِّضا ﷺ: كُنهُهُ تَفريقٌ بَينَهُ وبَينَ خَلقِهِ.٤٥٧٥

4103. **Imām al-Riḍā (AS) said** in his description of Allah, Glory be to Him, 'He is too exalted for sight to be able to perceive Him, for imagination to be able to fathom Him, and for the intellect to be able to grasp Him.'[4614]

٤١٠٣. عنه ﷺ ـ في صِفَةِ اللهِ سُبحانَهُ ـ: هُوَ أجَلُّ مِن أن يُدرِكَهُ بَصَرٌ، أو يُحيطَ بِهِ وَهمٌ، أو يَضبِطَهُ عَقلٌ.٤٥٧٦

1254. The Extent to Which One is Allowed to Describe Allah

١٢٥٤ـ نِطاقُ تَوصيفِ الله

4104. **Imām ʿAlī (AS) said,** 'He who [undertakes to] describe Him has defined Him, and he who defines Him has numbered Him, and he who

٤١٠٤. الإمامُ عليٌّ ﷺ: مَن وَصَفَهُ فَقَد حَدَّهُ،

numbers Him has nullified His eternity. He who asks 'How?' [about Allah] has indeed sought to describe Him, and he who asks 'Where?' has indeed confined Him.'[4615]

وَمَن حَدَّهُ فقَد عَدَّهُ، ومَن عَدَّهُ فقد أبطَلَ أزَلَهُ، ومَن قالَ: «كَيفَ؟» فقَدِ استَوصَفَهُ، ومَن قالَ: «أينَ؟» فقَد حَيَّزَهُ.[٤٥٧٧]

4105. **Imām ʿAlī (AS) said,** 'So Exalted be the One Whom the highest ambitions cannot reach and Whom the conjecture of intelligent minds cannot grasp.'[4616]

٤١٠٥. عنه ﷺ: فتَبارَكَ اللهُ الّذي لا يَبلُغُهُ بُعدُ الهِمَمِ، ولا يَنالُهُ حَدسُ الفِطَنِ.[٤٥٧٨]

4106. **Imām ʿAlī (AS) said,** '[He is] One, but not by enumeration. He is everlasting without extremity. He exists without any support.'[4617]

٤١٠٦. عنه ﷺ: واحِدٌ لا بِعَدَدٍ، ودائمٌ لا بِأمَدٍ، وقائمٌ لا بِعَمَدٍ.[٤٥٧٩]

4107. **Imām al-Ṣādiq (AS)** asked a man who said 'Allah is Greater' (*Allāhu Akbar)*, 'Greater than what?' So the man replied, 'Greater than everything', to which Imām (AS) retorted, 'Then you have defined Him.' The man then asked him, 'So what should I say?' Imām replied, 'Say: Allah is too great for description.'[4618]

٤١٠٧. الكافي عن الإمامِ الصّادقِ ﷺ: قالَ رجلٌ عندهُ: اللهُ أكبَرُ، فقالَ: اللهُ أكبَرُ مِن أيِّ شَيءٍ؟ فقالَ: مِن كُلِّ شَيءٍ، فقالَ أبو عَبدِ اللهِ ﷺ: حَدَّدتَهُ، فقالَ الرَّجُلُ: كَيفَ أقولُ؟ قالَ: قُل: اللهُ أكبَرُ مِن أن يُوصَفَ.[٤٥٨٠]

4108. **Imām al-Kāẓim (AS) said,** 'Verily Allah is too High and too Exalted and too Great for the reality of His description to ever be possible, so describe Him as He Himself has described Himself, and desist from anything other than that.'[4619]

٤١٠٨. الإمامُ الكاظمُ ﷺ: إنَّ اللهَ أعلىٰ وأجَلُّ وأعظَمُ مِن أن يُبلَغَ كُنهُ صِفَتِهِ، فَصِفُوهُ بِما وَصَفَ بِهِ نَفسَهُ، وكُفّوا عَمّا سِوىٰ ذٰلكَ.[٤٥٨١]

4109. **Imām al-Hādī (AS) said,** 'Verily the Creator can only be described by that which He Himself has described Himself, and how can the Creator ever be described anyway, Whom the senses are incapable of perceiving and the imaginations unable to grasp and the ideas unable to confine and the sights unable to contain?! He is too exalted for the description of those who undertake to describe, and too high to be attributed by those who seek to attach attributes to Him.'[4620]

٤١٠٩. الإمامُ الهاديُّ ﷺ: إنّ الخالِقَ لا يُوصَفُ إلّا بِما وَصَفَ بِهِ نَفسَهُ، وأنّىٰ يُوصَفُ الخالِقُ الّذي تَعجُزُ الحَواسُّ أن تُدرِكَهُ، والأوهامُ أن تَنالَهُ، والخَطَراتُ أن تَحُدَّهُ، والأبصارُ عَنِ الإحاطَةِ بِهِ؟! جَلَّ عَمّا يَصِفُهُ الواصِفونَ، وتَعالىٰ عَمّا يَنعَتُهُ الناعِتونَ.[٤٥٨٢]

1255. The Value of the Belief in Allah's Divine Unity (*tawḥīd*) and its Explanation

١٢٥٥ـ قيمَةُ التَّوحيدِ وَتَفسيرُهُ

4110. **The Prophet (SAWA) said,** '[Faith in] Allah's divine Unity is half of religion.'[4621]

٤١١٠. رسولُ اللهِ ﷺ: التَّوحيدُ نِصفُ الدِّينِ.[٤٥٨٣]

4111. **Imām ʿAlī (AS) said,** '[Faith in] Allah's divine Unity is the life of the soul.'[4622]

٤١١١. الإمامُ عليٌّ عليه السلام: التَّوحيدُ حَياةُ النَّفسِ.[٤٥٨٤]

4112. **Imām ʿAlī (AS) said,** '[Faith in] Allah's divine Unity is that you do not subject Him to the limitations of your imagination.'[4623]

٤١١٢. عنه عليه السلام: التَّوحيدُ ألّا تَتَوَهَّمَهُ.[٤٥٨٥]

4113. **Imām al-Ṣādiq (AS) said,** '[Faith in] Allah's divine Unity is that you do not deem applicable to your Lord that which applies to you, and [faith in] His divine Justice is that you do not blame Him for that which you are blameworthy.'[4624]

٤١١٣. الإمامُ الصّادقُ عليه السلام ـ لِرَجُلٍ ـ: أمَّا التَّوحيدُ فأن لا تُجوِّزَ عَلىٰ رَبِّكَ ماجازَ عَلَيكَ، وأمَّا العَدلُ فأن لا تَنسِبَ إلىٰ خالِقِكَ ما لامَكَ عَلَيهِ.[٤٥٨٦]

4114. **Imām al-Riḍā (AS) said,** 'The very first step to Allah's worship is to attain inner knowledge of Him, and the origin of attaining inner knowledge of Allah, Exalted be His Praise, is through His divine Unity. The very basis of His divine Unity is to negate any kind of limitation from Him, since the intellects are able to witness that every limited being is created.'[4625]

٤١١٤. الإمامُ الرِّضا عليه السلام: أوَّلُ عِبادَةِ اللهِ مَعرِفَتُهُ، وأصلُ مَعرِفَةِ اللهِ جَلَّ اسمُهُ تَوحيدُهُ، ونِظامُ تَوحيدِهِ نَفيُ التَّحديدِ عَنهُ؛ لِشَهادَةِ العُقولِ أنَّ كُلَّ مَحدودٍ مَخلوقٌ.[٤٥٨٧]

1256. The Proof of Allah's Divine Unity

١٢٥٦ـ دَليلُ التَّوحيدِ

"Whoever invokes besides Allah another god of which he has no proof, his reckoning will indeed rest with His Lord. Indeed the faithless will not be felicitous."[4626]

﴿وَمَنْ يَدْعُ مَعَ اللهِ إلٰهاً آخَرَ لا بُرْهانَ لَهُ بِهِ فَإنَّما حِسابُهُ عِنْدَ رَبِّهِ إنَّهُ لا يُفْلِحُ الْكافِرُونَ﴾.[٤٥٨٨]

4115. **Imām ʿAlī (AS) said** in his will to his son, al-Ḥasan (AS), 'And know my son that if your Lord were to have a partner, his messengers would surely have come to you, and you would have seen the signs of his dominion and his power, and you would know his acts and his attributes. He, however, is One God, just as He as described

٤١١٥. الإمامُ عليٌّ عليه السلام ـ في وَصِيَّتِه لِابنِهِ الحَسَنِ عليه السلام ـ: واعلَمْ يا بُنَيَّ أنَّهُ لَو كانَ لِرَبِّكَ شَريكٌ لَأتَتكَ رُسُلُهُ، ولَرَأيتَ آثارَ مُلكِهِ وسُلطانِهِ، ولَعَرَفتَ أفعالَهُ وصِفاتِهِ، ولٰكِنَّهُ إلٰهٌ واحِدٌ كَما وَصَفَ نَفسَهُ، لا يُضادُّهُ في مُلكِهِ

Himself. He is neither opposed by anyone in His kingdom, nor will He ever cease to be.'[4627]

أحَدٌ ، ولا يَزولُ أبَداً.[٤٥٨٩]

4116. **Imām al-Ṣādiq (AS),** when he was debating with an atheist, said, 'If you say that there are two gods, then they are either in complete agreement on everything or completely separate in all aspects. But when we look at this orderly creation, the continuous orbits, the alternation of night and day, and the sun and the moon, the soundness of the situation and the organisation and sound management of it indicates that the Director [of all creation] is One.'

Then if you still claim that there are two gods, then there must necessarily be some kind of difference between them for them to be two [and therefore distinct from each other], and this distinguishing characteristic between them is itself eternal like them, so you are forced to accept three such beings. And if you hold that there are indeed three, then you have to admit the same thing that we said for two such that they [the three] necessarily have two distinguishing characteristics between them [to differentiate them from each other] so then there are five [such eternal beings] altogether, and thus does the multiplication continue until infinity.'[4628]

٤١١٦ . الإمامُ الصّادقُ ﷺ ـ مِن مُناظَرَتِهِ زِنديقاً ـ: إن قُلتَ : إنَّهُما اثنانِ لَم يَخْلُ مِن أن يَكونا مُتَّفِقَينِ مِن كُلِّ جِهَةٍ ، أو مُفتَرِقَينِ مِن كُلِّ جِهَةٍ ، فلَمّا رَأينا الخَلقَ مُنتَظِماً ، والفَلَكَ جارِياً[٤٥٩٠] ، واختلافَ اللَّيلِ والنَّهارِ والشَّمسِ والقَمَرِ ، دَلَّ صِحَّةُ الأمرِ والتَّدبيرِ وائتِلافُ الأمرِ علىٰ أنَّ المُدَبِّرَ واحِدٌ.

ثُمَّ يَلزَمُكَ إنِ ادَّعَيتَ اثنَينِ فلابُدَّ مِن فُرجَةٍ بَينَهُما حتّىٰ يَكونا اثنَينِ ، فصارَتِ الفُرجَةُ ثالِثاً بَينَهُما قَديماً مَعَهُما فيَلزَمُكَ ثَلاثَةٌ ، فإنِ ادَّعيتَ ثَلاثَةً لَزِمَكَ ما قُلنا في الاثنَينِ حتّىٰ يَكونَ بَينَهُم فُرجَتانِ فيَكونَ خَمساً ، ثُمّ يَتَناهىٰ في العَدَدِ إلىٰ ما لا نِهايَةَ في الكَثرَةِ.[٤٥٩١]

4117. **Imām al-Ṣādiq (AS),** when asked to give proof that Allah is One, said, 'The continuous unity of management [in the cosmos] and the perfection of creation, as Allah, Mighty and Exalted, has said, *"Had there been gods in them (i.e. the heavens and the earth) other than Allah, they would surely have fallen apart."*'[4629] [4630]

٤١١٧ . عنه ﷺ ـ لَمّا سُئلَ عَنِ الدَّليلِ علىٰ أنَّ اللهَ واحِدٌ ـ: اتِّصالُ التَّدبيرِ ، وتَمامُ الصُّنعِ ، كَما قالَ اللهُ عَزَّوجلَّ : ﴿لَو كانَ فيهِما آلِهَةٌ إلّا اللهُ لَفَسَدَتا﴾.[٤٥٩٢]

4118. **al-Tawḥīd,** narrating from Imām al-Riḍā (AS) when a man believing in dualism asked him, 'I believe that the creator of the world are two, so what is the proof that He is One?' The Imām replied, 'Your belief that there are two is proof in itself that He is One, for verily you have only

٤١١٨ . التوحيد عن الإمامِ الرِّضا ﷺ ـ لَمّا سَألَهُ رَجُلٌ مِنَ الثَنَوِيَّةِ : إنّي أقولُ: إنّ صانِعَ العالَمِ اثنانِ ، فما الدَّليلُ علىٰ أنَّهُ واحِدٌ ؟ ـ: قَولُكَ : إنَّهُ اثنانِ دَليلٌ علىٰ أنَّهُ واحِدٌ ؛ لِأنَّكَ لَم تَدَّعِ الثّانِيَ

claimed the second after having affirmed the existence of the One. So, the One is already agreed upon –it is more than one that is controversial [and remains to be proven].'[4631]

إلّا بَعدَ إثباتِكَ الواحِدَ، فالواحِدُ مُجمَعٌ عَـلَيهِ، وأكثَرُ مِن واحِدٍ مُختَلَفٌ فيهِ.[٤٥٩٣]

4119. It is written in *Tafsīr al-Qummī*: 'Then Allah, Mighty and Exalted, answered dualism and those who professed that there were two gods, saying: *"Allah has not taken any offspring, neither is there any god besides Him, for then each god would take away what he created, and some of them would surely rise up against others. Clear is Allah of what they allege!"*[4632] If there were two gods, as you claim, each one of them would seek superiority, and if one of them desired to create a man, the other would desire to oppose him and create an animal, so their joint creation would have to be the product of both their desires, in spite of their differing wills, man and beast at the same time. And this is the most impossible thing that does not even exist. And if this argument is invalid and there is no difference between them, then the whole duality is invalid [with no distinction left between the two] and there is only one. Therefore, this order, unity of arrangement, subsistence of some things through other things, all indicate to One Maker, and this is the purport of Allah's verse in the Qur'an: *"Allah has not taken any offspring neither is there any god besides Him..."* and *"Had there been gods in them (i.e. the heavens and the earth) other than Allah, they would surely have fallen apart."*[4633]

٤١١٩. تفسير القمّي: ثُمّ رَدَّ اللهُ عَلَى الثَّـنَويَّةِ الّذينَ قالوا بِإلٰهَينِ فقالَ اللهُ تَعالىٰ: ﴿ما اتَّخَذَ اللهُ مِنۢ وَلَدٍ وما كانَ مَعَهُ مِن إلٰهٍ...﴾ قالَ: لَـو كـانا إلٰهَينِ كَما زَعَمتُم لَكانا يَختِلفانِ؛ فيَخلُقُ هٰذا ولا يَخلُقُ هٰذا، ويُريدُ هٰذا ولا يُريدُ هٰذا، ويَطلبُ كلُّ واحدٍ مِـنهما الغَـلَبَةَ، وإذا أرادَ أحـدُهُما خَـلْقَ إنسانٍ أرادَ الآخرُ خَلْقَ بَهيمَةٍ، فـيكونُ إنسـاناً بَهيمةً في حالَةٍ واحِدَةٍ، وهٰذا غيرُ مَوجودٍ، فَلَمّا بَطُلَ هٰذا ثَبَتَ التَّدبيرُ والصِنعُ لِواحدٍ، ودَلَّ أيضاً التَّدبيرُ وثـباتُهُ وقِـوامُ بَـعضِهِ بِـبَعضٍ عـلىٰ أنَّ الصّانِعَ واحدٌ وذٰلكَ قَولُهُ: ﴿ما اتَّخَذَ اللهُ مِن وَلَدٍ﴾ إلىٰ قَولِهِ: ﴿لَعَلا بَعْضُهُمْ عَلىٰ بَعْضٍ﴾.[٤٥٩٤]

1257. The Sights Cannot Apprehend Him but the Hearts Behold Him

١٢٥٧ـ لا تُدرِكُهُ الأبصارُ وتراه القلوب

"The sights do not apprehend Him, yet He apprehends the sights, and He is the all-attentive, the All-aware."[4634]

﴿لا تُدْرِكُهُ الْأَبْصارُ وَهُوَ يُدْرِكُ الْأَبْـصارَ وَهُـوَ اللَّطِيفُ الْخَبِيرُ﴾.[٤٥٩٥]

4120. **The Prophet (SAWA) said,** 'When I was taken on my Night Journey to the heavens,

٤١٢٠. رسولُ اللهِ ﷺ: لَمّا أُسرِيَ بي إلى السَّماءِ

Gabriel took me up until a place wherein he himself had never set foot. The veils were pulled away for me and Allah, Mighty and Exalted, showed me whatever He liked from the light of His Greatness.'[4635]

بَلَغَ بي جَبرَئيلُ مَكاناً لَم يَطَأْهُ جَبرَئيلُ قَطُّ، فكُشِفَ لي فأرانِيَ اللهُ عَزَّوجلَّ مِن نورِ عَظَمَتِهِ ما أحَبَّ.[٤٥٩٦]

4121. **Imām ʿAlī (AS) said** in reply to Dhaʿlab's question about his being able to see his Lord, 'Woe to you O Dhaʿlab! I do not worship a Lord Whom I cannot see!' So Dhaʿlab asked, 'But how do you see Him? Describe Him to us.' Imām (AS) replied, 'Woe betide you! Eyes do not see Him by looking with the sights; it is the hearts that behold Him with the realities of faith.'[4636]

٤١٢١. الإمامُ عليٌّ عليه السلام لِذَعلَب لَمّا سَأَلَهُ عَن رُؤيَتِهِ رَبَّهُ: وَيلَكَ يا ذَعلَبُ! لَم أكُن بِالّذي أعبُدُ رَبّاً لَم أرَهُ! قالَ: فكَيفَ رَأيتَهُ؟ صِفْهُ لَنا؟ قالَ: وَيلَكَ! لَم تَرَهُ العُيونُ بِمُشاهَدَةِ الأبصارِ، ولكِنْ رَأتهُ القُلوبُ بِحَقائقِ الإيمانِ.[٤٥٩٧]

4122. **Imām al-Riḍā (AS),** with regards to Allah's verse in the Qur'an: *"The sights do not apprehend Him…"* said, 'The hearts' fancies cannot apprehend Him so how can the eyesights apprehend Him?!'[4637]

٤١٢٢. الإمامُ الرِّضا عليه السلام ـ في قولِهِ تعالى: ﴿لا تُدرِكُهُ الأبصارُ...﴾ ـ: لا تُدرِكُهُ أوهامُ القُلوبِ، فكَيفَ تُدرِكُهُ أبصارُ العُيونِ؟![٤٥٩٨]

4123. **Imām al-ʿAskarī (AS) said,** 'Verily Allah, Blessed and most High, displayed to His Prophet in his heart, whatever He liked from the light of His Greatness.'[4638]

٤١٢٣. الإمامُ العسكريُّ عليه السلام: إنَّ اللهَ تَبارَكَ وتَعالى أرى رَسولَهُ بِقَلبِهِ مِن نورِ عَظَمَتِهِ ما أحَبَّ.[٤٥٩٩]

1258. Eternal and Everlasting

١٢٥٨ـ أزَليٌّ وأبَديٌّ

4124. **Imām ʿAlī (AS) said,** 'Praise be to Allah, the First before every first, and the Last after every last, and His Firstness necessitates that there is no beginning to Him, and His Lastness necessitates that there is no end to Him.'[4639]

٤١٢٤. الإمامُ عليٌّ عليه السلام: الحَمدُ للهِ الأوَّلِ قَبلَ كُلِّ أوَّلٍ، والآخِرِ بَعدَ كُلِّ آخِرٍ، وبِأوَّلِيَّتِهِ وَجَبَ أن لا أوَّلَ لَهُ، وبِآخِرِيَّتِهِ وَجَبَ أن لا آخِرَ لَهُ.[٤٦٠٠]

4125. **Imām ʿAlī (AS) said,** 'He never ceases to exist and will always be, the First before all things without a beginning, and the Last after all things without an end.'[4640]

٤١٢٥. عنه عليه السلام: لا يَزولُ أبَداً ولَم يَزَلْ، أوَّلٌ قَبلَ الأشياءِ بِلا أوَّلِيَّةٍ، وآخِرٌ بَعدَ الأشياءِ بِلا نِهايَةٍ.[٤٦٠١]

4126. **Imām ʿAlī (AS)** was once asked by a Jew, 'When did our Lord, Mighty and Exalted, come to be?', to which he replied, 'O Jew, It is not that our Lord was not and then came to be, for the

٤١٢٦. عنه عليه السلام ـ وقد سَألَهُ رَجُلٌ يَهوديٌّ: مَتى كانَ رَبُّنا عَزَّوجلَّ؟ ـ: يا يَهودِيُّ، (ما كانَ) لَم يَكُنْ

question 'When did x come to be?' is posed regarding something that is not there and then comes to be. He exists without coming into being; He is ever existing having nothing before Him. He is before 'before' itself, before any limit. Limits do not apply to Him for He is the ultimate limit of all limits.'[4641]

رَبُّنا فكانَ، وإنَّما يُقالُ: «مَتىٰ كانَ» لِشَيءٍ لَم يَكُنْ فكانَ، هُوَ كائنٌ بِلا كَينونَةِ كائنٍ لَم يَزَلْ لَيسَ لَهُ قَبلٌ، هُوَ قَبلَ القَبلِ، وقَبلَ الغايَةِ، انقَطَعَتْ عَنهُ الغاياتُ، فهُوَ غايَةُ كُلِّ غايَةٍ.[٤٦٠٢]

4127. **Imām al-Bāqir (AS) said,** 'Verily Allah, Blessed and most High, existed when nothing else did, He is absolute light with no darkness, truthful with no falsehood about Him, all-knowing with no ignorance about Him, ever-living with no death about Him, and He is such today, and thus will He remain forever.'[4642]

٤١٢٧. الإمامُ الباقرُ عليه السلام: إنَّ اللهَ تَبارَكَ وتَعالىٰ كانَ ولا شَيءَ غَيرُهُ، نوراً لا ظَلامَ فيهِ، وصادِقاً لا كِذبَ فيهِ، وعالِماً لا جَهلَ فيهِ، وحَيّاً لا مَوتَ فيهِ، وكذٰلِكَ هُوَ اليَومُ، وكذٰلِكَ لا يَزالُ أبَداً.[٤٦٠٣]

1259. Living (Omnipresent)

١٢٥٩ـ حَيٌّ

"Allah – there is no god except Him – is the Living One, the Self-subsisting."[4643]

﴿اللهُ لا إلٰهَ إلَّا هُوَ الْحَيُّ الْقَيُّومُ﴾.[٤٦٠٤]

4128. **Imām al-Ṣādiq (AS) said,** 'Verily Allah is all knowledge with no ignorance about Him, He is all Life without any death around Him, and all Light with no darkness about Him.'[4644]

٤١٢٨. الإمامُ الصّادقُ عليه السلام: إنَّ اللهَ عِلمٌ لا جَهلَ فيهِ، حَياةٌ لا مَوتَ فيهِ، نورٌ لا ظُلمَةَ فيهِ.[٤٦٠٥]

4129. **Imām al-Kāẓim (AS) said,** 'Allah is Omnipresent without any external source of life … rather He lives through Himself [is Self-existent].'[4645]

٤١٢٩. الإمامُ الكاظمُ عليه السلام: كانَ اللهُ حَيّاً بِلا حَياةٍ حادِثَةٍ... بَل حَيٌّ لِنَفسِهِ.[٤٦٠٦]

1260. All-Knowing (Omniscient)

١٢٦٠ـ عالِمٌ

"With Him are the treasures of the Unseen; no one knows them except Him. He knows whatever there is in land and sea. No leaf falls without His knowing it, nor is there a grain in the darkness of the earth, nor anything fresh or withered but it is in a manifest Book."[4646]

﴿وَعِنْدَهُ مَفاتِحُ الْغَيْبِ لا يَعْلَمُها إلّا هُوَ وَيَعْلَمُ ما فِي الْبَرِّ وَالْبَحْرِ وَما تَسْقُطُ مِنْ وَرَقَةٍ إلَّا يَعْلَمُها وَلا حَبَّةٍ فِي ظُلُماتِ الْأَرْضِ وَلا رَطْبٍ وَلا يابِسٍ إلَّا فِي كِتابٍ مُبِينٍ﴾.[٤٦٠٧]

4130. **Imām ʿAlī (AS) said,** 'The number of droplets of water, or of stars in the sky, or of gusts

٤١٣٠. الإمامُ عليٌّ عليه السلام: ولا يَعزُبُ عَنهُ عَدَدُ قَطرٍ

of wind in the air are not unknown to Him, and neither is the crawling of ants on rocks, nor the settling place of tiny ants in the darkness of the night. He knows the spots where leaves fall and the subtle movement of the pupils of the eyes.'[4647]

الماءِ، ولا نُجومُ السَّماءِ، ولا سَوافِي الرِّيحِ في الهَواءِ، ولا دَبيبُ النَّملِ عَلَى الصَّفا، ولا مَقيلُ الذَّرِّ في اللَّيلَةِ الظَّلماءِ، يَعلَمُ مَساقِطَ الأوراقِ، وخَفِيَّ طَرْفِ الأحداقِ.[٤٦٠٨]

4131. **Imām ʿAlī (AS) said,** 'He knows the howls of beasts in the forests, the sins of the people committed in secret, the fish's frequenting the deep seas and the rising of the waters by tempestuous winds.'[4648]

٤١٣١. عنه ﷺ: يَعلَمُ عَجيجَ الوُحوشِ في الفَلَواتِ، ومَعاصِيَ العِبادِ في الخَلَواتِ، واختِلافَ النِّينانِ في بحارِ الأنوارِ الغامِراتِ، وتلاطُمَ الماءِ بالرِّياحِ العاصِفاتِ.[٤٦٠٩]

4132. **Imām ʿAlī (AS) said,** 'His knowledge pierces through the inside of unknown secrets and encompasses the innermost beliefs of the hearts.'[4649]

٤١٣٢. عنه ﷺ: خَرَقَ عِلمُهُ باطِنَ غَيبِ السُّتُراتِ، وأحاطَ بِغُموضِ عَقائدِ السَّريراتِ.[٤٦١٠]

4133. **Imām al-Bāqir (AS) said,** 'He always knows what is to be, such that His knowledge of it before its coming into being is the same as His knowledge after its coming into being.'[4650]

٤١٣٣. الإمامُ الباقرُ ﷺ: لَم يَزَلْ عالِماً بِما يَكونُ، فعِلمُهُ بِهِ قَبلَ كَونِهِ كعِلمِهِ بِهِ بَعدَ كَونِهِ.[٤٦١١]

4134. **Imām al-Ṣādiq (AS)** was once asked about Allah's knowledge of space [i.e. the concept] and whether He knows it before its coming into existence or during it or after it, to which he replied, 'Most High is Allah! He always knows space before its conception just as He knows it after He has created it, and such is His knowledge of all things like His knowledge of space.'[4651]

٤١٣٤. الإمامُ الصّادقُ ﷺ ـ لَمّا سُئلَ عَن عِلمِهِ بِالمَكانِ: أكانَ قَبلَ تَكوينِهِ أم حِينَهُ وبَعدَهُ؟ ـ: تَعالَى اللهُ! بَل لَم يَزَلْ عالِماً بِالمَكانِ قَبلَ تَكوينِهِ كعِلمِهِ بِهِ بَعدَ ما كَوَّنَهُ، وكَذٰلِكَ عِلمُهُ بِجَميعِ الأشياءِ كعِلمِهِ بِالمَكانِ.[٤٦١٢]

4135. **Imām al-Ṣādiq (AS) said,** 'Knowledge is His very essence and not the object of knowing [or a known], and when He created things and the object of knowledge came into existence, knowledge was projected from Him onto the known things.'[4652]

٤١٣٥. عنه ﷺ: والعِلمُ ذاتُه ولا مَعلومَ... فلَمّا أحدَثَ الأشياءَ وكانَ المَعلومُ وَقَعَ العِلمُ مِنهُ عَلَى المَعلومِ.[٤٦١٣]

4136. **Imām al-Kāẓim (AS) said,** 'The knowledge of Allah cannot be defined by where, nor can Allah's knowledge be described by how. Allah's knowledge cannot be separated from Him, nor can Allah be distinguished from it, and there is no barrier between Allah and His knowledge.'[4653]

٤١٣٦. الإمامُ الكاظمُ ﷺ: عِلمُ اللهِ لا يُوصَفُ مِنهُ بِأينَ، ولا يُوصَفُ العِلمُ مِنَ اللهِ بِكَيفَ، ولا يُفرَدُ العِلمُ مِنَ اللهِ، ولا يُبانُ اللهُ مِنهُ، ولَيسَ بَينَ اللهِ وبَينَ عِلمِهِ حَدٌّ.[٤٦١٤]

1261. Just

١٢٦١ ـ عادِلٌ

"Indeed Allah does not wrong [anyone] [even to the extent of] an atom's weight, and if it be a good deed He doubles its reward, and gives from Himself a great reward."[4654]

﴿ نَّ اللهَ لا يَـظْلِمُ مِـثْقالَ ذَرَّةٍ وَإنْ تَكُ حَسَـنَةً يُضاعِفْها وَيُؤْتِ مِنْ لَدُنْهُ أجْراً عَظِيماً ﴾.[٤٦١٥][٤٦١٦]

4137. **Imām ʿAlī (AS) said,** 'And I bear witness that He is just and acts justly, and is an arbitrator who decides fairly.'[4655]

٤١٣٧ . الإمامُ عليٌّ ﷺ : وأشهَدُ أنَّهُ عَدلٌ عَدَلَ، وحَكَمٌ فَصَلَ.[٤٦١٧]

4138. **Imām ʿAlī (AS)** when asked about faith in Allah's divine justice, replied, '[Faith in] divine justice is that you do not accuse Him of anything.'[4656]

٤١٣٨ . عنه ﷺ ـ لَمّا سُئلَ عنِ العَدلِ ـ: العَدلُ ألّا تَتَّهِمَهُ.[٤٦١٨]

4139. **Imām Zayn al-ʿĀbidīn (AS) said** in his supplication for Friday and for the *ʿĪd al-Aḍḥā*, 'But I know that there is no wrong in Your decree and no hurry in Your vengeance. He alone hurries who fears to miss, and only the weak needs to wrong. But You are exalted, my God, high indeed above all that!'[4657]

٤١٣٩ . الإمامُ زينَ العابدينُ ﷺ ـ في دُعائهِ يَومَ الأضحىٰ والجُمعَةِ ـ: وقَد عَلِمتُ أنَّهُ لَيسَ في حُكمِكَ ظُلمٌ، ولا في نَقمَتِكَ عَجَلَةٌ، وإنّما يَعجَلُ مَن يَخافُ الفَوتَ، وإنَّما يَحتاجُ إلَى الظُّلمِ الضَّعيفُ، وقَد تَعالَيتَ يا إلٰهي عَن ذٰلكَ عُلُوّاً كَبيراً.[٤٦١٩]

4140. **Imām al-Ṣādiq (AS)** was asked about the foundation of religion, to which he replied, '[It is faith in] Allah's divine Unity and divine Justice … [Faith in] Allah's divine Unity is that you do not deem applicable to your Lord that which applies to you, and [faith in] His divine Justice is that you do not attribute to Him that of which you are blameworthy.'[4658]

٤١٤٠ . الإمامُ الصّادقُ ﷺ ـ وقد سُئلَ عَن أساسِ الدِّينِ ـ: التَّوحيدُ والعَدلُ... أمّا التَّوحيدُ فأن لا تُجَوِّزَ عَلىٰ رَبِّكَ ما جازَ عَلَيكَ، وأمّا العَدلُ فأن لا تَنسِبَ إلىٰ خالِقِكَ ما لامَكَ عَلَيهِ.[٤٦٢٠]

1262. The Creator

١٢٦٢ ـ خالِقٌ

"Allah is creator of all things, and He watches over all things."[4659]

﴿ اللهُ خالِقُ كُلِّ شَيْءٍ وَهُوَ عَلَىٰ كُلِّ شَيْءٍ وكَيل ﴾.[٤٦٢١]

4141. *al-Tawḥīd*: 'Marwān b. Muslim narrated, 'Ibn Abī al-ʿAwjāʾ once came to Abū ʿAbdillāh [al-Ṣādiq] (AS) and asked, 'Is it not true that you claim that Allah is the Creator of all things?' to which Abū ʿAbdillāh (AS) replied, 'Yes.' So he retorted, 'I create!'

٤١٤١ . التوحيد عن مروان بن مسلم: دَخَلَ ابنُ أبي العَوجاءِ عَلىٰ أبي عَبدِ اللهِ ﷺ فقالَ: ألَيسَ تَزعَمُ

So the Imām asked him, 'How do you create?!' He replied, 'I defecate in a place, then wait for it, and it becomes a creature, which I have created!' So Abū 'Abdillāh (AS) said, 'Is it not true that the creator of something should know what he has created?' to which he replied yes. Imām continued, 'Well do you know the female from the male [of what you have supposedly created], and do you know its lifespan?' to which he had no answer.'[4660]

أنَّ اللهَ خالِقُ كُلِّ شَيءٍ ؟ فقالَ أبو عَبدِاللهِ ﷺ : بَلىٰ، فقالَ : أنا أخلُقُ ! فقالَ ﷺ لَـهُ : كَـيفَ تَـخلُقُ ؟! فقالَ : أُحدِثُ في المَوضِعِ ثُمَّ ألبَثُ عَنهُ فـيَصيرُ دَوابَّ فأكونُ أنا الّذي خَلَقتُها ! فقالَ أبـو عَـبدِ اللهِ ﷺ : أَلَيسَ خالِقُ الشَّيءِ يَعرِفُ كَـم خَـلقُهُ ؟ قالَ : بَلىٰ، قالَ : فتَعرِفُ الذَّكَرَ مِنها مِنَ الأُنثىٰ، وتَعرِفُ كَم عُمرُها ؟ فسَكَتَ.[٤٦٢٢]

4142. **Imām al-Riḍā (AS) said,** 'The Originator of all things from their conception, and their Inventor from the very beginning with His Power and Wisdom, [He creates] not from anything otherwise the very concept of invention would be nullified, nor for any cause otherwise the very concept of origination would be inapplicable. He creates whatever He pleases however He pleases.'[4661]

٤١٤٢ . الإمامُ الرِّضا ﷺ : الحَمدُ للهِ فاطِرِ الأشياءِ إنشاءً، ومُبتَدِعِها ابتِداءً بِقُدرَتِهِ وحِكمَتِهِ، لا مِن شَيءٍ فَـيَبطُلَ الاختِراعُ، ولا لِـعِلَّةٍ فـلا يَـصِحَّ الابتِداعُ، خَلَقَ ما شاءَ كَيفَ شاءَ.[٤٦٢٣]

1263. All-Powerful (Omnipotent)

١٢٦٣ ـ قادِرٌ

"So I swear by the Lord of the easts and the wests that We are capable…"[4662]

﴿فَلَا أُقْسِمُ بِرَبِّ ٱلْمَشَٰرِقِ وَٱلْمَغَٰرِبِ إِنَّا لَقَٰدِرُونَ﴾.[٤٦٢٤]

4143. **Imām 'Alī (AS)** was once asked, 'Can your Lord fit the world into an egg?' to which he replied, 'Verily Allah, Mighty and Exalted, cannot be attributed with incapacity, but that which you are asking cannot ever be.'[4663]

٤١٤٣ . الإمامُ عليٌّ ﷺ ـ لمّا قيل لَهُ : هل يقدرُ ربُّك على أن يدخل الدنيا في بيضةٍ ـ : إنَّ اللهَ تَبارَكَ وتَعالىٰ لا يُنسَبُ إلَى العَجزِ، والّذي سَألتَني لا يَكونُ.[٤٦٢٥]

4144. **Imām al-Ṣādiq (AS) narrated,** 'Iblīs [Satan] asked Jesus son of Mary (AS), 'Is your Lord capable of fitting the earth inside an egg, without shrinking the earth or enlarging the egg?' So Jesus (AS) replied, 'Woe betide you! Verily Allah can never be ascribed with incapacity, and who is there more powerful than the One who can shrink the earth and enlarge the egg [if He so wills]?!'[4664]

٤١٤٤ . الإمامُ الصّادقُ ﷺ : إنَّ إبليسَ قالَ لِعيسَى ابنِ مَريَمَ ﷺ : أيَقدِرُ رَبُّكَ عَلىٰ أن يُدخِلَ الأرضَ بَيضَةً ؛ لا يُصغِّرُ الأرضَ ولا يُكَبِّرُ البَيضَةَ ؟ فقالَ عيسىٰ ﷺ : وَيلَكَ ! إنَّ اللهَ لا يُوصَفُ بِعَجزٍ، ومَن أقدَرُ مِمَّن يُلَطِّفُ الأرضَ ويُعَظِّمُ البَيضَةَ ؟![٤٦٢٦]

1264. The Speaker

١٢٦٤ ـ مُتَكَلِّمٌ

"And apostles We have recounted to you earlier and apostles we have not recounted to you, and to Moses Allah spoke directly."[4665]

﴿وَرُسُلاً قَدْ قَصَصْناهُمْ عَلَيْكَ مِنْ قَبْلُ وَرُسُلاً لَمْ نَقْصُصْهُمْ عَلَيْكَ وَكَلَّمَ اللهُ مُوسَىٰ تَكْلِيماً﴾ .[٤٦٢٧]

4145. **Imām ʿAlī (AS) said,** 'He expresses information but not through a tongue or voice. He listens but not with the holes and organs of hearing. He speaks but does not utter words; He remembers but does not learn… When He wishes to create something, He says to it 'Be' and it is, but not through a voice that can strike the ears, nor a calling that can be heard. Rather, His speech, Glory be to Him, is an act of His that He creates and incorporates, which did not exist before, for were it an ever-existing thing it would be a second god.'[4666]

٤١٤٥ . الإمامُ عليٌّ (عليه السلام) : يُخبِرُ لا بِلِسانٍ ولَهَواتٍ، ويَسمَعُ لا بِخُروقٍ وأدَواتٍ، يَقولُ ولا يَلفِظُ، ويَحفَظُ ولا يَتَحَفَّظُ ... يَقولُ لِمَن أرادَ كَونَهُ: «كُنْ» فيَكونُ، لا بِصَوتٍ يُقرَعُ، ولا بِنِداءٍ يُسمَعُ، وإنَّما كَلامُه سُبحانَهُ فِعلٌ مِنهُ، أنشَأهُ ومَثَّلَهُ، لَم يَكُنْ مِن قَبلِ ذلكَ كائناً، ولَو كانَ قَديماً لَكانَ إلهاً ثانياً .[٤٦٢٨]

1265. The One who Wills

١٢٦٥ ـ مُريدٌ

"All His command, when He wills something, is to say to it 'Be' and it is."[4667]

﴿إنَّما أمْرُهُ إذا أرادَ شَيْئاً أنْ يَقُولَ لَهُ كُنْ فَيَكُونُ﴾ .[٤٦٢٩]

4146. **Imām al-Kāẓim (AS) said,** 'Verily things come into being solely by His will and His wish; without the need for speech, alternation of breath or utterance with the tongue.'[4668]

٤١٤٦ . الإمامُ الكاظمُ (عليه السلام) : إنَّما تَكونُ الأشياءُ بإرادَتِهِ ومَشيئَتِهِ؛ مِن غَيرِ كلامٍ، ولا تَرَدُّدٍ في نَفَسٍ، ولا نُطقٍ بِلِسانٍ .[٤٦٣٠]

1266. The Manifest and the Hidden

١٢٦٦ ـ ظاهِرٌ وباطِنٌ

"He is the First and the Last, the Manifest and the Hidden, and He has knowledge of all things."[4669]

﴿هُوَ الْأَوَّلُ وَالْآخِرُ وَالظَّاهِرُ وَالْباطِنُ وَهُوَ بِكُلِّ شَيْءٍ عَلِيمٌ﴾ .[٤٦٣١]

4147. **Imām ʿAlī (AS) said,** 'He manifests the wonders of His management for the onlookers, but by virtue of the exaltedness of His Might He is Hidden from the imagination of the thinkers.'[4670]

٤١٤٧ . الإمامُ عليٌّ (عليه السلام) : الظّاهِرُ بِعَجائبِ تَدبيرِهِ لِلنّاظِرينَ، والباطِنُ بِجَلالِ عِزَّتِهِ عَن فِكْرِ المُتَوَهِّمينَ .[٤٦٣٢]

4148. **Imām al-Riḍā (AS) said,** 'He is manifest though indiscernible through direct contact; He is

٤١٤٨ . الإمامُ الرِّضا (عليه السلام) : ظاهِرٌ لا بِتأويلِ

evident though unapprehended by vision; He is hidden though not through withdrawal.'[4671]

المُباشَرَةِ، مُتَجَلٍّ لا بِاستِهلالِ رُؤيَـةٍ، بـاطِنٌ لا بِمُزايَلَةٍ.[٤٦٣٣]

1267. The Master

١٢٦٧ ـ مالِكٌ

"To Allah belongs the kingdom of the heavens and the earth, and Allah has power over all things."[4672]

﴿وَللهِ مُلْكُ السَّماواتِ وَالْأَرْضِ وَاللهُ عَـلَىٰ كُـلِّ شَيْءٍ قَدِيرٌ﴾.[٤٦٣٤]

4149. **Imām ʿAlī (AS) said,** 'Every master other than Him is a slave.'[4673]

٤١٤٩. الإمامُ عليٌّ عليه السلام: كُلُّ مالِكٍ غَيرُهُ مَملوكٌ.[٤٦٣٥]

4150. **Imām ʿAlī (AS),** in his explanation of the phrase *'There is no power or strength save in Allah'*, said, 'Verily we are not masters over anything with Allah, nor are we masters over anything except what He has given us mastery over. So by making us masters over that which He is a superior Master, He has given us responsibility, and by taking away mastership from us He absolves us of our responsibilities.'[4674]

٤١٥٠. عنه عليه السلام ـ في تَفسيرِ لا حَولَ ولا قُوَّةَ إلّا بِاللهِ ـ: إنّا لا نَملِكُ مَعَ اللهِ شَيئاً، ولا نَملِكُ إلّا ما مَلَّكَنا، فمَتىٰ مَلَّكَنا ما هُوَ أملَكُ بِهِ مِنّا كَلَّفَنا، ومَتىٰ أخَذَهُ مِنّا وَضَعَ تَكليفَهُ عَنّا.[٤٦٣٦]

1268. The All-Hearing and the All-Seeing

١٢٦٨ ـ سَميعٌ بصيرٌ

"Allah judges with truth (the sins committed by the eyes) while those whom they invoke besides Him do not judge by anything. Indeed it is Allah who is the All-hearing, the All-seeing."[4675]

﴿وَاللهُ يَقْضِي بِالْحَقِّ وَالَّذِينَ يَدْعُونَ مِنْ دُونِهِ لا يَقْضُونَ بِشَيْءٍ إنَّ اللهَ هُوَ السَّمِيعُ الْبَصِيرُ﴾.[٤٦٣٧]

4151. **Imām ʿAlī (AS) said,** 'He is the All-hearing but not by means of any organ.'[4676]

٤١٥١. الإمامُ عليٌّ عليه السلام: والسَّميعُ لا بِأداةٍ.[٤٦٣٨]

4152. **Imām al-Bāqir (AS) said,** 'Verily He is all-hearing and all-seeing, such that He hears with that by means of which He sees and He sees with that by means of which He hears.'[4677]

٤١٥٢. الإمامُ الباقرُ عليه السلام: إنَّهُ سَميعٌ بَصيرٌ، يَسمَعُ بِما يُبصِرُ، ويُبصِرُ بِما يَسمَعُ.[٤٦٣٩]

4153. **Imām al-Riḍā (AS) said,** 'Because of the fact that the secret trace of a black mustard seed on a massive rock in the darkness of the night, be it in the ground or in the seas, cannot remain hidden from Him, is what compels us to say that He is all-seeing.'[4678]

٤١٥٣. الإمامُ الرِّضا عليه السلام: لَمّا لَم يَخفَ عَلَيهِ خافِيَةٌ مِن أثَرِ الذَّرَّةِ السَّوداءِ، عَلَى الصَّخرَةِ الصَّمّاءِ، في اللَّيلَةِ الظَّلماءِ، تَحتَ الثَّرىٰ وبحار الأنوار، قُلنا: بَصيرٌ.[٤٦٤٠]

1269. The Subtle and the All-Aware

١٢٦٩ ـ لَطيفٌ وخَبيرٌ

"The sights do not apprehend Him, yet He apprehends the sights, and He is the All-attentive, the All-aware."[4679]

﴿ لاتُدْرِكُهُ الْأَبْصارُ وَهُوَ يُدْرِكُ الْأَبْصارَ وَهُوَ اللَّطِيفُ الْخَبِيرُ﴾ .[٤٦٤١]

4154. **Imām al-Riḍā (AS) said,** 'He is subtle not in terms of lack or delicateness or smallness, rather [He is subtle] in His [knowledge and power of] penetration into everything without being perceived. He is all-aware through the fact that nothing escapes His attention or evades Him, independent of experience or consideration of things, for experience and consideration in turn result in two types of knowledge, without which He would not know [if he were to be dependent on them], and would therefore be ignorant.'[4680]

٤١٥٤ . الإمامُ الرِّضا ﷺ: أمّا اللَّطيفُ فلَيسَ علىٰ قِلَّةٍ وقَضافَةٍ وصِغَرٍ ، ولٰكِنَّ ذٰلِكَ عَلَى النَّفاذِ في الأشياءِ ، والامتِناعِ مِن أن يُدرَكَ ، أمّا الخَبيرُ فالّذي لا يَعزُبُ عَنهُ شَيءٌ ولا يَفوتُهُ ، لَيسَ لِلتَّجرِبَةِ ولا لِلاعتِبارِ بِالأشياءِ ، فعِندَ التَّجرِبَةِ والاعتِبارِ عِلمانِ ، ولَولاهُما ما عَلِمَ ؛ لأنَّ مَن كانَ كذٰلِكَ كانَ جاهِلاً .[٤٦٤٢]

1270. The All-Strong and the Almighty

١٢٧٠ ـ قَوِيٌّ عزيزٌ

"So when Our edict came, we delivered Ṣāliḥ and the faithful who were with him by a mercy from Us, and from the [punishment and] disgrace of that day. Your Lord is indeed the All-strong, the All-mighty."[4681]

﴿فَلَمَّا جاءَ أمْرُنا نَجَّيْنا صالِحاً وَالَّذِينَ آمَنُوا مَعَهُ بِرَحْمَةٍ مِنَّا وَمِنْ خِزْيِ يَوْمِئِذٍ إنَّ رَبَّكَ هُوَ الْقَوِيُّ الْعَزِيزُ﴾ .[٤٦٤٣]

"Whoever seeks might [should know that] might belongs entirely to Allah."[4682]

﴿مَن كَانَ يُرِيدُ ٱلْعِزَّةَ فَلِلَّهِ ٱلْعِزَّةُ جَمِيعًا﴾ .[٤٦٤٤]

4155. **Imām ʿAlī (AS) said,** 'And every strong person besides Allah is weak.'[4683]

٤١٥٥ . الإمامُ عليٌّ ﷺ: وكُلُّ قَوِيٍّ غَيرُهُ ضَعيفٌ .[٤٦٤٥]

4156. **Imām ʿAlī (AS) said,** 'Everything humbles before Him, and everything subsists through Him. He is the contentment of every poor, the honour of every disgraced one, and the strength of every weak one.'[4684]

٤١٥٦ . عنه ﷺ : كُلُّ شَيءٍ خاشِعٌ لَهُ ، وكُلُّ شَيءٍ قائمٌ بِهِ ، غِنىٰ كُلِّ فَقيرٍ ، وعِزُّ كُلِّ ذَليلٍ ، وقُوَّةُ كلِّ ضَعيفٍ .[٤٦٤٦]

4157. **Imām ʿAlī (AS) said,** 'Every mighty one besides Him is abased.'[4685]

٤١٥٧ . عنه ﷺ : كُلُّ عَزيزٍ غَيرُهُ ذَليلٌ .[٤٦٤٧]

4158. **Imām ʿAlī (AS) said,** 'Praise be to Allah who wears the cloak of might and majesty, and

٤١٥٨ . عنه ﷺ : الحَمدُ للهِ الّذي لَبِسَ العِزَّ

has chosen them for Himself over the rest of His creation.'[4686]

والكِبرِياء، واختارَهُما لِنَفسِهِ دُونَ خَلقِهِ.[٤٦٤٨]

1271. The All-Wise

١٢٧١ـحَكيمٌ

"This is indeed the true account, for sure. There is no god but Allah, and indeed Allah is the All-mighty, the All-wise."[4687]

﴿إِنَّ هٰذَا لَهُوَ الْقَصَصُ الْحَقُّ وَمَا مِنْ إِلٰهٍ إِلَّا اللهُ وَإِنَّ اللهَ لَهُوَ الْعَزِيزُ الْحَكِيمُ﴾.[٤٦٤٩]

4159. **Imām al-Bāqir (AS)** was once asked why it is that Allah cannot be questioned about what He does, to which he replied, 'Because He only does what is wise and good.'[4688]

٤١٥٩. الإمامُ الباقرُ عليه السلام ـ لَمّا سُئلَ وكَيفَ لا يُسألُ عَمّا يَفعَلُ؟ ـ: لِأنَّهُ لا يَفعَلُ إلّا ما كانَ حِكمَةً وصَواباً.[٤٦٥٠]

1272. The All-Embracing, All-Needless

١٢٧٢ـصَمَدٌ

"Allah is the All-embracing."[4689]

﴿اللهُ الصَّمَدُ﴾.[٤٦٥١]

4160. **Imām al-Ḥusayn (AS) said,** 'The All-embracing is the One Who has no lack within Him; the All-embracing is the One Whose mastership is complete; the All-embracing is the One Who neither eats nor drinks; the All-embracing is the One Who does not sleep; the All-embracing is the Eternal One who is and will always be.'[4690]

٤١٦٠. الإمامُ الحسينُ عليه السلام: الصَّمَدُ: الّذي لا جَوفَ لَهُ، والصَّمَدُ: الّذي قَدِ انتَهىٰ سُؤدَدُهُ، والصَّمَدُ: الّذي لا يَأكُلُ ولا يَشرَبُ، والصَّمَدُ: الّذي لا يَنامُ، والصَّمَدُ: الدّائمُ الّذي لَم يَزَلْ ولا يَزالُ.[٤٦٥٢]

1273. He is Everywhere

١٢٧٣ـهُوَ في كُلِّ مَكانٍ

"And He is with you wherever you may be, and Allah sees best what you do."[4691]

﴿وَهُوَ مَعَكُمْ أَيْنَ مَا كُنتُمْ وَاللهُ بِمَا تَعْمَلُونَ بَصِيرٌ﴾.[٤٦٥٣]

4161. **Imām ʿAlī (AS) said,** describing Allah, Glory be to Him, 'And verily He is everywhere, each and every moment and time, and with every human and Jinn.'[4692]

٤١٦١. الإمامُ عليٌّ عليه السلام ـ في صِفَةِ اللهِ سُبحانَهُ ـ: وإنَّهُ لَبِكُلِّ مَكانٍ، وفي كُلِّ حِينٍ وأوانٍ، ومَعَ كُلِّ إنسٍ وجانٍّ.[٤٦٥٤]

4162. **Imām al-Ṣādiq (AS)** was asked by Abū Jaʿfar regarding Allah's verse in the Qur'an: *"And He is Allah in the heavens and in the earth"*[4693], to which he replied, 'Yes, similarly He is in every place.' I [Abū Jaʿfar] asked, 'In His essence?' Imām

٤١٦٢. الإمامُ الصّادقُ عليه السلام ـ لَمّا سَألَهُ أبو جَعفَرٍ عَن قَولِ اللهِ عَزَّ وجلَّ: ﴿وهُوَ اللهُ في السَّماواتِ وفي الأرضِ﴾[٤٦٥٥] ـ: كَذٰلِكَ هُوَ في كُلِّ مَكانٍ.

replied, 'Woe betide you! Verily places are subject to limits and boundaries, so by your saying that He is in a place in His essence, you are in fact compelled to say that He is contained in objects which are subject to measurement and size. He is, however, distinct from His creation, entirely encompassing what He creates in knowledge, power, control, authority and dominion.'[4694]

قُلتُ: بِذاتِه؟ قالَ: وَيحَكَ! إنَّ الأماكِنَ أقدارٌ، فإذا قُلتَ: في مَكانٍ بِذاتِهِ لَزِمَكَ أن تَقولَ: في أقدارٍ وغَيرِ ذلكَ، ولكِنْ هُوَ بائنٌ مِن خَلقِهِ، مُحيطٌ بِما خَلَقَ عِلماً وقُدرَةً وإحاطَةً وسُلطاناً ومَلكاً. ٤٦٥٦

1274. Attributes of His Essence and Attributes of His Action

١٢٧٤ ـ صِفاتُ الذّاتِ وصِفاتُ الفِعلِ

4163. **Imām al-Ṣādiq (AS) said,** 'Our Lord is luminant in His very essence, Living in His very essence, All-knowing in His very essence, All-embracing in His very essence.'[4695]

٤١٦٣. الإمامُ الصّادقُ عليه السلام: رَبُّنا نوريُّ الذّاتِ، حَيُّ الذّاتِ، عالِمُ الذّاتِ، صَمَديُّ الذّاتِ. ٤٦٥٧

4164. **Imām al-Riḍā (AS) said,** 'Wish and will are among the attributes of action, so whoever claims that Allah, most High, is eternally willing and wishing cannot be considered a monotheist.'[4696]

٤١٦٤. الإمامُ الرِّضا عليه السلام: المَشيئَةُ والإرادَةُ مِن صِفاتِ الأفعالِ، فمَن زَعَمَ أنَّ اللهَ تَعالى لَم يَزَلْ مُريداً شائياً فلَيسَ بِمُوَحِّدٍ. ٤٦٥٨

1275. Comprehensive Attributes

١٢٧٥ ـ جَوامِعُ الصِّفاتِ

4165. **Imām 'Alī (AS) said,** 'The very first step in religion is acknowledging Him, and the perfect way to acknowledge Him is to testify to Him, and the perfect way to testify to Him is to believe in His divine unity, and the perfect way to believe in His divine unity is to regard Him as absolutely pure, and the perfect way to regard Him as absolutely pure is to negate all attributes from Him, for every attribute is a proof of its own distinction from the thing to which it is attributed, and everything that is attached and attributed is distinct from the attribute. Thus, whoever attaches attributes to Allah, Glory be to Him, associates Him with something else, and whoever associates Him regards Him as two, and whoever regards Him as two identifies parts to Him, and whoever identifies parts to Him has indeed misunderstood Him, and whoever misunderstands Him singles

٤١٦٥. الإمامُ عليٌّ عليه السلام: أوَّلُ الدِّينِ مَعرِفَتُهُ، وكَمالُ مَعرِفَتِهِ التَّصديقُ بِهِ، وكَمالُ التَّصديقِ بِهِ تَوحيدُهُ، وكَمالُ تَوحيدِهِ الإخلاصُ لَهُ، وكَمالُ الإخلاصِ لَهُ نَفيُ الصِّفاتِ عَنهُ؛ لِشَهادَةِ كُلِّ صِفَةٍ أنَّها غَيرُ المَوصوفِ، وشَهادَةِ كُلِّ مَوصوفٍ أنَّهُ غَيرُ الصِّفَةِ، فمَن وَصَفَ اللهَ سُبحانَهُ فقَد قَرَنَهُ، ومَن قَرَنَهُ فقَد ثَنّاهُ، ومَن ثَنّاهُ فقَد جَزَّأهُ، ومَن

Him out, and whoever singles Him out has confined Him, and whoever confines Him has enumerated Him. Whoever asks 'In what [is He]?' holds that He is contained, and whoever asks 'On what [is He]?' has excluded Him. He is [a Being] but not through any phenomenon of coming into being, He exists but not from non-existence. He is with everything but not in physical proximity, and is separate from everything but not through physical separation. He acts but without need for movements and instruments. He sees without need for an object of sight from among His creation. He is One such that He has no need for a source of comfort that may keep Him company nor any whom He may miss in his absence.'[4697]

جَزَّأهُ فقد جَهِلَهُ، (ومَن جَهِلَهُ فقد أشارَ إلَيهِ)٤٦٥٩، ومَن أشارَ إلَيهِ فقد حَدَّهُ، ومَن حَدَّهُ فقد عَدَّهُ، ومَن قالَ: «فيمَ؟» فقد ضَمَّنَهُ، ومَن قالَ: «عَلامَ؟» فقد أخلىٰ مِنهُ، كائنٌ لا عَن حَدَثٍ، مَوجودٌ لا عَن عَدَمٍ، مَعَ كُلِّ شَيءٍ لا بِمُقارَنَةٍ، وغَيرُ كُلِّ شَيءٍ لا بِمُزايَلَةٍ، فاعِلٌ لا بِمَعنَى الحَرَكاتِ والآلَةِ، بَصيرٌ إذ لا مَنظورَ إلَيهِ مِن خَلقِهِ، مُتَوحِّدٌ إذ لا سَكَنَ يَستَأنِسُ بِهِ ولا يَستَوحِشُ لِفَقدِهِ.٤٦٦٠

272

ACTS OF COMMON COURTESY (1)[4698]

المَعروف (١)

PERFORMING ACTS OF COMMON COURTESY

فِعلُ المَعروفِ

1276. The Virtue of Common Courtesy

١٢٧٦ ـ فَضلُ المَعروفِ

4166. **Imām ʿAlī (AS) said,** 'Performing common acts of courtesy, bringing solace to a grief-stricken person, and being hospitable to guests is the instrument of leadership.'[4699]

٤١٦٦ . الإمامُ عليٌّ عليه السلام: فِعلُ المَعروفِ، وإغاثَةُ المَلهوفِ، وإقراءُ الضُّيوفِ، آلَةُ السِّيادَةِ.٤٦٦١

4167. **Imām ʿAlī (AS) said,** 'Acts of courtesy are treasures for eternity.'[4700]

٤١٦٧ . عنه عليه السلام: المَعروفُ ذَخيرَةُ الأبَدِ.٤٦٦٢

4168. **Imām al-Ḥusayn (AS) said,** 'Know that acts of courtesy earn praiseworthy results, and end in rewardable gains. If you were to see acts of courtesy personified as a man, you would perceive him to be good and handsome, pleasing for people to behold and transcending all the worlds. And if you were to see acts of vileness personified,

٤١٦٨ . الإمامُ الحسينُ عليه السلام: اعلَموا أنَّ المَعروفَ مُكسِبٌ حَمداً، ومُعقِبٌ أجراً، فلَو رَأيتُمُ المَعروفَ رَجُلاً لَرَأيتُموهُ حَسَناً جَميلاً يَسُرُّ

you would perceive an ugly, revolting, disfigured man, whom the hearts would be averse to and whom the eyes would turn away from in disgust.'[4701]

النّاظِرينَ ويفوقُ العـالَمينَ، ولَـو رَأيـتُمُ اللُّـوْمَ رَجُلاً رَأيتُموهُ سَمِجاً قَبيحاً مَشوماً تَنفِرُ مِنهُ القُلوبُ وتَغُضُّ دُونَهُ الأبصارُ.[٤٦٦٣]

4169. **Imām al-Ṣadiq (AS) said,** 'The first people to enter Paradise will be those who performed acts of common courtesy to others.'[4702]

٤١٦٩. الإمامُ الصّادقُ عليه السلام: أوَّلُ مَن يَدخُلُ الجَنَّةَ أهلُ المَعروفِ.[٤٦٦٤]

4170. **Imām al-Ṣādiq (AS) said,** 'The people who perform acts of courtesy in this world will be the same ones to perform them in the Hereafter, for verily in the Hereafter their scales will be so laden with their good deeds that they will be able to bestow them generously on the sinners [in order to assist them].'[4703]

٤١٧٠. عنه عليه السلام: أهلُ المَعروفِ في الدّنيا هُم أهلُ المَعروفِ في الآخِرَةِ؛ لِأنَّهُم في الآخِرَةِ تَرجَحُ لَـهُمُ الحَسَناتُ، فـيَجودونَ بِـها عَـلىٰ أهـلِ المَعاصي.[٤٦٦٥]

4171. **Imām al-Jawād (AS) said,** 'People who perform acts of courtesy towards others benefit more from them than the receptors of their kindness, for verily they have the reward for them, the [rewarding feeling of] pride for having helped someone as well as a mention. So however much good a man may do for others, it ultimately always starts by benefiting himself, and hence he never seeks thanks for the benefit incurred by himself through helping others.'[4704]

٤١٧١. الإمامُ الجوادُ عليه السلام: أهلُ المَعـروفِ إلَى اصطِناعِهِ أحوَجُ مِن أهلِ الحاجَةِ إلَيهِ؛ لِأنَّ لَهُم أجرَهُ وفَخرَهُ وذِكرَهُ، فمَهما اصطَنَعَ الرَّجُلُ مِن مَعروفٍ فإنَّما يَبدأُ فيهِ بِنَفسِهِ، فلا يَطلُبَنَّ شُكرَ ما صَنَعَ إلىٰ نَفسِهِ مِن غَيرِهِ.[٤٦٦٦]

1277. Enjoinment of Spreading Kindness to Both Good and Bad People

١٢٧٧ ـ الحَثُّ عَلىٰ بَذلِ المَعروفِ إلَى البَرِّ وَالفاجِرِ

4172. **The Prophet (SAWA) said,** 'The peak of good reason after religious devotion is treating people with love, and doing good to both good and bad people.'[4705]

٤١٧٢. رسولُ اللهِ صلى الله عليه وآله: رَأسُ العَقلِ بَـعدَ الدِّيـنِ التَّوَدُّدُ إلَى النّاسِ، واصطِناعُ الخَيرِ إلىٰ كُـلِّ بَـرٍّ وفاجِرٍ.[٤٦٦٧]

4173. **The Prophet (SAWA) said,** 'Perform acts of courtesy to those who are worthy of them as well as those who are not worthy of them, and even if they have no effect on those who deserve them, you are at least worthy of [performing] them.'[4706]

٤١٧٣. عنه صلى الله عليه وآله: اصطَنِعِ الخَيرَ إلىٰ مَن هُوَ أهلُهُ، وإلىٰ مَن هُوَ غَيرُ أهلِهِ، فإن لَم تُصِبْ مَن هُوَ أهلُهُ فأنتَ أهلُهُ.[٤٦٦٨]

(أنظر) السؤال (٢): باب ٩١٣.

(See also: ASKING (2): section 913)

1278. Circulation of Good Acts From Hand to Hand

١٢٧٨ ـ تَداوُلُ الأيدي فِي المَعروفِ

4174. **The Prophet (SAWA) said,** 'He who offers charity to a poor man gets the reward befitting the action, but if forty thousand people pass the same offering from hand to hand until it reaches the poor man, they all receive a complete reward for it.'[4707]

٤١٧٤ . رسولُ اللهِ ﷺ : مَن تَصَدَّقَ بِصَدَقَةٍ عَلىٰ رَجُلٍ مِسكينٍ كانَ لَهُ مِثلُ أجرِهِ، ولَو تَداوَلَها أربَعونَ ألفَ إنسانٍ ثُمّ وَصَلَت إلىٰ مِسكينٍ كانَ لَهُم أجراً كامِلاً .[٤٦٦٩]

4175. **Imām al-Ṣādiq (AS) said,** 'If an act of charity [or courtesy] goes through eighty changes of hands, all of them receive the reward for it, without any decrease in the reward of the initiating good-doer.'[4708]

٤١٧٥ . الإمامُ الصّادقُ ﵇ :لَوجَرَى المَعروفُ عَلى ثَمانينَ كَفّاً لَأُجِروا كُلُّهُم فيهِ ، مِن غَيرِ أن يُنقَصَ صاحِبُهُ مِن أجرِهِ شَيئاً .[٤٦٧٠]

1279. Prohibition of Making Someone Feel Obliged for an Act of Courtesy

١٢٧٩ ـ النَّهيُ عَنِ الامتِنانِ بِالمَعروفِ

4176. **Imām ʿAlī (AS) said,** 'Give life to your act of courtesy by killing it [i.e. by killing your expectation of receiving anything in return].'[4709]

٤١٧٦ . الإمامُ عليٌّ ﵇ : أحْيِ مَعروفَكَ بِإماتَتِهِ .[٤٦٧١]

4177. **Imām ʿAlī (AS) said,** 'If an act of courtesy is done unto you, then be sure to remember it, and if you do an act of courtesy unto someone else, then be sure to forget it.'[4710]

٤١٧٧ . عنه ﵇ : إذا صُنِعَ إلَيكَ مَعروفٌ فَاذكُرْ، إذا صَنَعتَ مَعروفاً فَانْسَهُ .[٤٦٧٢]

4178. **Imām ʿAlī (AS) said,** 'The yardstick [used to measure the goodness] of an act of courtesy is the absence of expectation accompanying it.'[4711]

٤١٧٨ . عنه ﵇ :مِلاكُ المَعروفِ تَركُ المَنِّ بِهِ .[٤٦٧٣]

(See also: CHARITY: section 1117)

(أُنظر) الصدقة: باب ١١١٧.

1280. Completion of a Good Act

١٢٨٠ ـ إتمامُ المَعروفِ

4179. **The Prophet (SAWA) said,** 'Bringing a good act to completion is better than [merely] initiating it.'[4712]

٤١٧٩ . رسولُ اللهِ ﷺ: استِتمامُ المَعروفِ أفضَلُ مِن ابتِدائهِ .[٤٦٧٤]

4180. **Imām ʿAlī (AS) said,** 'One who does not sustain his good action loses it.'[4713]

٤١٨٠ . الإمام عليٌّ ﵇: مَن لَم يُرَبِّ مَعروفَهُ فقَد ضَيَّعَهُ .[٤٦٧٥]

4181. **Imām al-Kāẓim (AS) said,** 'A good favour done to a fellow believer is not considered complete until accompanied by three things: underestimation of the act, concealing it, and hastening its completion. He who underestimates his good turn to a fellow believer has esteemed his brother highly indeed, whereas he who esteems his good turn to be great has deemed his brother to be insignificant. He who conceals the good turn that he has done has honoured his action, and he who hastens to fulfil his promise takes pleasure in the gift too.'[4714]

٤١٨١ . الإمامُ الكاظمُ عليه السلام : الصَّنيعَةُ لا تَتِمُّ صَنيعَةً عِندَ المُؤمِنِ لِصاحِبِها إلّا بِثَلاثَةِ أشياءَ: تَصغيرِها، وسَترِها، وتَعجيلِها، فمَن صَغَّرَ الصَّنيعَةَ عِندَ المُؤمِنِ فقَد عَظَّمَ أخاهُ، ومَن عَظَّمَ الصَّنيعَةَ عِندَهُ فقَد صَغَّرَ أخاهُ، ومَن كَتَمَ ما أولاهُ مِن صَنيعِهِ فقَد كَرَّمَ فِعالَهُ، ومَن عَجَّلَ ما وَعَدَ فقَد هَنِئَ العَطِيَّةَ.[٤٦٧٦]

1281. Prohibition of Holding Acts of Common Courtesy in Contempt

١٢٨١ ـ النَّهيُ عَن تَحقيرِ المَعروفِ

4182. **The Prophet (SAWA) said,** 'Never underestimate any act of common courtesy, even simply meeting a fellow brother with a face displaying pleasure at seeing him.'[4715]

٤١٨٢ . رسولُ اللهِ صلى الله عليه وآله : لا تُحَقِّرَنَّ شَيئاً مِنَ المَعروفِ، ولَو أن تَلقىٰ أخاكَ ووَجهُكَ مَبسوطٌ إلَيهِ.[٤٦٧٧]

4183. **Imām ʿAlī (AS) said,** 'Never deem any act of common courtesy that you are able to carry out as insignificant in comparing it to a greater act, for verily the simple act performed when the need for it arises is more beneficial to its receptor than the great act for which there is no need. Perform for each day good acts that befit it and you will grow on the right course.'[4716]

٤١٨٣ . الإمامُ عليٌّ عليه السلام : لا تَستَصغِرِ شَيئاً مِنَ المَعروفِ قَدَرتَ عَلَى اصطِناعِهِ إيثاراً لِما هُوَ أكثَرُ مِنهُ؛ فإنَّ اليَسيرَ في حالِ الحاجَةِ إلَيهِ أنفَعُ لِأهلِهِ مِن ذٰلكَ الكَثيرِ في حالِ الغَناءِ عَنهُ، واعمَلْ لِكُلِّ يَومٍ بِما فيهِ تَرشُدُ.[٤٦٧٨]

1282. The Mark of Acceptance of a Good Act

١٢٨٢ ـ عَلامَةُ قَبولِ المَعروفِ

4184. **Imām ʿAlī (AS) said,** 'The best act of common courtesy is that which good people are able to benefit from.'[4717]

٤١٨٤ . الإمامُ عليٌّ عليه السلام : خَيرُ المَعروفِ ما اُصيبَ بِهِ الأبرارُ.[٤٦٧٩]

4185. **Imām al-Ṣādiq (AS)** was once asked what the mark of acceptance of a servant with Allah is, to which he replied, 'The mark of acceptance of a

٤١٨٥ . الإمامُ الصّادقُ عليه السلام ـ لَمّا سُئلَ عَن عَلامَةِ قَبولِ العَبدِ عِندَ اللهِ ـ: عَلامَةُ قَبولِ العَبدِ عِندَ

servant with Allah is that his good acts reach the objects of their intention. If not, then that is not the case.'[4718]

اللهِ أن يُصيبَ بِمَعروفِهِ مَواضِعَهُ ، فإن لَم يَكُن كذٰلكَ فلَيسَ كذٰلكَ.[٤٦٨٠]

1283. The Reward for Good Acts

١٢٨٣ـ ثَوابُ المَعروفِ

4186. **The Prophet (SAWA) said,** 'He who leads a blind man forty steps on level ground, even if he was to be rewarded the whole world's worth of gold, it would not be enough to recompense a needle's worth of what that act deserves. And if there is a danger on the path which he averts him from, he will find that act on the Day of Resurrection within his balance of good deeds, larger than one hundred thousand times the expanse of the earth.'[4719]

٤١٨٦ . رسولُ اللهِ ﷺ : مَن قادَ ضَريراً أربَعينَ خُطوَةً عَلىٰ أرضٍ سَهلَةٍ ، لا يَفي بِقَدرِ إبرَةٍ مِن جَميعِهِ طِلاعُ الأرضِ ذَهَباً ، فإن كانَ فيما قادَهُ مَهلَكَةٌ جَوَّزَهُ عَنها وَجَدَ ذٰلكَ في ميزانِ حَسَناتِهِ يَومَ القِيامَةِ أوسَعَ مِنَ الدّنيا مِائةَ ألفِ مَرَّةٍ.[٤٦٨١]

4187. **The Prophet (SAWA) said,** 'A servant [of Allah] entered Paradise because of a thorn branch that he removed from the path of fellow Muslims.'[4720]

٤١٨٧ . عنه ﷺ: دَخَلَ عَبدٌ الجَنَّةَ بِغُصنٍ مِن شَوكٍ كانَ عَلىٰ طَريقِ المُسلِمينَ فأماطَهُ عَنهُ.[٤٦٨٢]

4188. **The Prophet (SAWA) said,** 'He who builds a structure on the road affording shelter to a traveller, Allah will raise him on the Day of Resurrection mounted on a fine-bred camel adorned with pearls, and his face will radiate light for all the dwellers of Paradise.'[4721]

٤١٨٨ . عنه ﷺ: مَن بَنىٰ عَلىٰ ظَهرِ الطَّريقِ ما يَأوي عابِرَ سَبيلٍ بَعَثَهُ اللهُ يَومَ القِيامَةِ عَلىٰ نَجيبٍ مِن دُرٍّ ، ووَجهُهُ يُضيءُ لِأهلِ الجَنَّةِ نوراً.[٤٦٨٣]

4189. **The Prophet (SAWA) said,** 'He who averts an impediment of water or fire from a group of Muslims becomes deserving of obligatory entrance into Paradise.'[4722]

٤١٨٩ . عنه ﷺ : مَن رَدَّ عَن قَومٍ مِنَ المُسلِمينَ عادِيَةَ ماءٍ أو نارٍ وَجَبَت لَهُ الجَنَّةُ.[٤٦٨٤]

4190. **Imām al-Ṣādiq (AS) said,** 'I have witnessed the act of common courtesy to be exactly as its name suggests, and nothing excels the act of common courtesy than its own reward.'[4723]

٤١٩٠ . الإمامُ الصّادقُ ﷺ : رَأيتُ المَعروفَ كَاسمِهِ، ولَيسَ شَيءٌ أفضَلَ مِنَ المَعروفِ إلّا ثَوابُهُ.[٤٦٨٥]

273

ACTS OF COMMON COURTESY (2) المعروف (٢)

ENJOINING GOOD AND PROHIBITING WRONG الأمر بالمعروف والنهي عن المنكر

1284. Importance of Enjoining Good and Prohibiting Wrong ١٢٨٤ ـ أهمّيّةُ الأمرِ بالمعروفِ والنّهيِ عنِ المُنكرِ

"There has to be a nation among you summoning to the good, bidding what is right, and forbidding what is wrong. It is they who are the felicitous."[4724]

﴿وَلْتَكُنْ مِنكُمْ أُمَّةٌ يَدْعُونَ إِلَى الْخَيْرِ وَيَأْمُرُونَ بِالْمَعْرُوفِ وَيَنْهَوْنَ عَنِ الْمُنْكَرِ وَأُولَئِكَ هُمُ الْمُفْلِحُونَ﴾ .٤٦٨٦

"You are the best nation [ever] brought forth for mankind: you bid what is right and forbid what is wrong, and have faith in Allah. And if the People of the Book had believed, it would have been better for them. Among them [some] are faithful, but most of them are transgressors."[4725]

﴿كُنتُمْ خَيْرَ أُمَّةٍ أُخْرِجَتْ لِلنَّاسِ تَأْمُرُونَ بِالْمَعْرُوفِ وَتَنْهَوْنَ عَنِ الْمُنْكَرِ وَتُؤْمِنُونَ بِاللهِ وَلَوْ آمَنَ أَهْلُ الْكِتَابِ لَكَانَ خَيْراً لَهُمْ مِنْهُمُ الْمُؤْمِنُونَ وَأَكْثَرُهُمُ الْفَاسِقُونَ﴾ .٤٦٨٧

"But the faithful, men and women, are comrades of one another: they bid what is right and forbid what is wrong."[4726]

﴿وَالْمُؤْمِنُونَ وَالْمُؤْمِنَاتُ بَعْضُهُمْ أَوْلِيَاءُ بَعْضٍ يَأْمُرُونَ بِالْمَعْرُوفِ وَيَنْهَوْنَ عَنِ الْمُنْكَرِ﴾ .٤٦٨٨

4191. **The Prophet (SAWA) said,** 'Whoever enjoins good and prohibits wrong is the deputy of Allah and the deputy of His Prophet on the earth.'[4727]

٤١٩١ . رسولُ اللهِ ﷺ :مَن أمَرَ بالمعروفِ ونَهى عَنِ المُنكرِ فهُوَ خَليفَةُ اللهِ في الأرضِ، وخَليفَةُ رَسولِهِ. ٤٦٨٩

4192. **The Prophet (SAWA) said,** 'The Prophet (SAWA) said, 'Verily Allah, Mighty and Exalted, despises the weak believer who has no religion [i.e. has no devotion to his religion].' When asked who a believer with no religion is, he replied, 'He who does not prohibit wrong.'[4728]

٤١٩٢ . عنه ﷺ : إنَّ اللهَ تَبارَكَ وتَعالى لَيُبغِضُ المُؤمِنَ الضَّعيفَ الّذي لا زَبْرَ لَهُ، وقالَ: هُوَ الّذي لا يَنهى عَنِ المُنكرِ. ٤٦٩٠

4193. **Imām ʿAlī (AS) said,** 'The basis of Islamic law is the enjoinment of good and the prohibition of wrong.'[4729]

٤١٩٣ . الإمامُ عليٌّ عليه السلام : قِوامُ الشَّريعَةِ الأمرُ بِالمَعروفِ، والنَّهيُ عَنِ المُنكَرِ، وإقامَةُ الحُدودِ.[٤٦٩١]

4194. **Imām ʿAlī (AS) said,** 'All acts of righteousness and striving in the way of Allah are as mere spittle in the deep sea compared to enjoining good and prohibiting wrong.'[4730]

٤١٩٤ . عنه عليه السلام : وماأعمالُ البِرِّ كُلُّها والجِهادُ في سَبيلِ اللهِ عِندَ الأمرِ بِالمَعروفِ والنَّهيِ عَنِ المُنكَرِ، إلّا كَنَفثَةٍ في بَحرٍ لُجِّيٍّ.[٤٦٩٢]

4195. **Imām ʿAlī (AS) said,** 'Enjoinment of good is the best of all acts performed by creation.'[4731]

٤١٩٥ . عنه عليه السلام : الأمرُ بِالمَعروفِ أفضَلُ أعمالِ الخَلقِ.[٤٦٩٣]

4196. **Imām ʿAlī (AS) said,** 'Know that enjoinment of good and prohibition of wrong never reach an end, and never cut off sustenance.'[4732]

٤١٩٦ . عنه عليه السلام : اعلَموا أنَّ الأمرَ بِالمَعروفِ والنَّهيَ عَنِ المُنكَرِ لَم يُقَرِّبا أجَلاً، ولَم يَقطَعا رِزقاً.[٤٦٩٤]

4197. **Imām al-Ḥusayn (AS) said,** 'It is not permissible for a believing eye to watch Allah being disobeyed and close without first changing the situation.'[4733]

٤١٩٧ . الإمامُ الحسينُ عليه السلام : كانَ يُقالُ: لا تَحِلُّ لِعَينٍ مُؤمِنَةٍ تَرَى اللهَ يُعصىٰ فَتَطرِفُ حتّىٰ يُغَيِّرَهُ.[٤٦٩٥]

4198. **Imām al-Bāqir (AS) said,** 'Verily the enjoinment of good and the prohibition of wrong is the path of the prophets, the way of the righteous, a great obligation on which all other obligations are founded and on which ideologies are secured, by which earnings are made lawful, by which iniquities are redressed, through which the earth flourishes, justice is sought from enemies and all affairs are kept upright.'[4734]

٤١٩٨ . الإمامُ الباقرُ عليه السلام : إنَّ الأمرَ بِالمَعروفِ والنَّهيَ عَنِ المُنكَرِ سَبيلُ الأنبياءِ، ومِنهاجُ الصُّلَحاءِ، فَريضَةٌ عَظيمَةٌ بِها تُقامُ الفَرائضُ، وتَأمَنُ المَذاهِبُ، وتَحِلُّ المَكاسِبُ، وتُرَدُّ المَظالِمُ، وتَعمُرُ الأرضُ، ويُنتَصَفُ مِنَ الأعداءِ، ويَستَقيمُ الأمرُ.[٤٦٩٦]

(See also: STRIVING (1): section 379)

(أنظر) الجهاد (١): باب ٣٧٩.

1285. The Danger of Abandoning the Enjoinment of Good and the Prohibition of Wrong

١٢٨٥ ـ خَطَرُ تَركِ الأمرِ بِالمَعروفِ وَالنَّهيِ عَنِ المُنكَرِ

4199. **The Prophet (SAWA) said,** 'You must enjoin good indeed and you shall prohibit wrong otherwise the chastisement of Allah will surely overtake you.'[4735]

٤١٩٩ . رسولُ اللهِ صلى الله عليه وآله : لَتَأمُرُنَّ بِالمَعروفِ ولَتَنهُنَّ عَنِ المُنكَرِ، أو لَيَعُمَّنَّكُم عَذابُ اللهِ.[٤٦٩٧]

4200. **Imām ʿAlī (AS) said** in his last will to Imām Ḥasan and Imām Ḥusayn (AS) after he had

٤٢٠٠ . الإمامُ عليٌّ عليه السلام ـ مِن وَصِيَّتِهِ لِلحَسَنَينِ عليهما السلام

been struck by Ibn Muljam, 'Never abandon the enjoinment of good and the prohibition of wrong lest the evil ones amongst you gain mastery over you whereafter you will supplicate [Allah] but you will not be answered.'[4736]

بعدَ أن ضَرَبَهُ ابنُ مُلجَم: لا تَترُكوا الأمرَ بِالمَعروفِ والنَّهيَ عَنِ المُنكَرِ فَيُوَلّىٰ عَلَيكُم شِرارُكُم ثُمَّ تَدعونَ فلا يُستَجابُ لَكُم.٤٦٩٨

1286. He Who Contents Himself with a People's (Wrong) Action

١٢٨٦ـ مَن رَضِيَ بِفِعلِ قومٍ

4201. **Imām ʿAlī (AS) said,** 'The one who contents himself with the wrong action of a group of people is as one who plunges into it with them, and every person who plunges into wrongdoing is guilty of two sins: the sin of having committed the wrong and the sin of being content with it.'[4737]

٤٢٠١. الإمامُ عليٌّ ﷺ: الرّاضي بِفِعلِ قومٍ كالدّاخِلِ فيهِ مَعَهُم، وعَلىٰ كُلِّ داخِلٍ في باطِلٍ إثمانِ: إثمُ العَمَلِ بِهِ، وإثمُ الرِّضا بِهِ.٤٦٩٩

4202. **Imām al-Jawād (AS) said,** 'He who approves of a wicked deed partakes in it.'[4738]

٤٢٠٢. الإمامُ الجوادُ ﷺ: مَنِ استَحسَنَ قَبيحاً كانَ شَريكاً فيهِ.٤٧٠٠

4203. **Imām al-Jawād (AS) said,** 'He who witnesses a misdeed and abhors it is as one who was absent thereat, whereas he who is absent from a misdeed and yet contents himself with it is as one who witnessed it.'[4739]

٤٢٠٣. عنه ﷺ: مَن شَهِدَ أمراً فكَرِهَهُ كانَ كمَن غابَ عَنهُ، ومَن غابَ عَن أمرٍ فرَضِيَهُ كانَ كمَن شَهِدَهُ.٤٧٠١

1287. The Conditions to be Observed by One Who Enjoins Good

١٢٨٧ـ شَرائطُ الآمِرِ بالمَعروف

4204. **The Prophet (SAWA) said,** 'One who enjoins good should do so using good means.'[4740]

٤٢٠٤. رسولُ اللهِ ﷺ: مَن أمَرَ بِمَعروفٍ فليَكُنْ أمرُهُ ذلكَ بِمَعروفٍ.٤٧٠٢

4205. **The Prophet (SAWA)** was once told, 'We only enjoin that which we ourselves practice absolutely and we only prohibit that which we refrain from absolutely', to which he replied, 'No, rather enjoin good even if you yourself do not practice it absolutely and prohibit wrong even if you yourself do not refrain from it absolutely.'[4741]

٤٢٠٥. عنه ﷺ ـ لَمّا قيلَ لَهُ: لا نَأمُرُ ولا نَنهىٰ إلّا بِما عَمِلنا بِهِ أو انتَهَينا عَنهُ كُلِّهِ ـ: لا، بَل مُروا بِالمَعروفِ وإن لَم تَعمَلوا بِهِ كُلِّهِ، وانهَوا عَنِ المُنكَرِ وإن لَم تَنتَهوا عَنهُ كُلِّهِ.٤٧٠٣

4206. **Imām ʿAlī (AS) said,** 'Verily, it is below my dignity to prohibit people from that which I

٤٢٠٦. الإمامُ عليٌّ ﷺ: إنّي لَأرفَعُ نَفسي أن أنهىٰ

myself do not refrain from, or to enjoin them that which I myself have not performed before them.'[4742]

النّاسَ عَمّا لَستُ أنتَهي عَنهُ، أو آمُرَهُم بِما لا أسبِقُهُم إلَيهِ بعَمَلي.٤٧٠٤

4207. **Imām ʿAlī (AS) said,** 'Allah curses those who enjoin good but abandon its practice, and those who prohibit wrong but commit it themselves.'[4743]

٤٢٠٧. عنه ﷺ: لَعَنَ اللهُ الآمِرينَ بِالمَعروفِ التّارِكينَ لَهُ، والنّاهينَ عَنِ المُنكَرِ العامِلينَ بِهِ.٤٧٠٥

4208. **Imām ʿAlī (AS) said,** 'And prohibit wrong and abstain from it yourselves, for verily you have been commanded to prohibit wrong after abstention from it.'[4744]

٤٢٠٨. عنه ﷺ: وانهَوا عَنِ المُنكَرِ وتَناهَوا عَنهُ؛ فإنَّما اُمِرتُم بِالنَّهيِ بَعدَ التَّناهي.٤٧٠٦

4209. **Imām al-Ṣādiq (AS) said,** 'Verily the one who enjoins good and prohibits wrong should possess three qualities: he should act upon that which he enjoins and abstain from that which he prohibits; he must be just with regards to what he enjoins and just with regards to what he prohibits; and he must be gentle in what he enjoins and gentle in what he prohibits.'[4745]

٤٢٠٩. الإمامُ الصّادقُ ﷺ: إنَّما يَأمُرُ بِالمَعروفِ ويَنهىٰ عَنِ المُنكَرِ مَن كانَت فيهِ ثَلاثُ خِصالٍ: عامِلٌ بِما يَأمُرُ بِهِ وتارِكٌ لِما يَنهىٰ عَنهُ، عادِلٌ فيما يَأمُرُ عادِلٌ فيما يَنهىٰ، رَفيقٌ فيما يَأمُرُ ورَفيقٌ فيما يَنهىٰ.٤٧٠٧

(See also: PROPAGATION (OF ISLAM): section 260; KNOWLEDGE: section 1359; EXHORTATION: section 1858)

(انظر) التبليغ: باب ٢٦٠؛ العلم: باب ١٣٥٩؛ الموعظة: باب ١٨٥٨

1288. The Lowest Level of Prohibition of Wrong

١٢٨٨ ـ أدنىٰ مَراتِبِ النَّهيِ عَنِ المُنكَرِ

4210. **The Prophet (SAWA) said,** 'He who sees wrong being done should redress the situation with his own hand, and if he cannot do so then with his tongue, and if he cannot do so then with his heart [disapproving the act], and that is the weakest level of faith.'[4746]

٤٢١٠. رسولُ اللهِ ﷺ: مَن رَأىٰ مِنكُم مُنكَراً فَلْيُغَيِّرْهُ بِيَدِهِ، فإن لَم يَستَطِعْ فَبِلِسانِهِ، فإن لَم يَستَطِعْ فَبِقَلبِهِ وذٰلكَ أضعَفُ الإيمانِ.٤٧٠٨

4211. **The Prophet (SAWA) said,** 'Indeed fear of people must not prevent any of you from speaking the truth when he sees it fit to remind others of the grandeur of Allah, for neither will it [i.e. speaking the truth] hasten your destined end, nor will it ward off your decreed sustenance.'[4747]

٤٢١١. عنه ﷺ: ألا لا يَمنَعَنَّ أحَدَكُم هَيبَةُ النّاسِ أن يَقولَ الحَقَّ إذا رَآهُ أن يُذَكِّرَ بِعِظَمِ اللهِ، لا يُقَرِّبُ مِن أجَلٍ ولا يُبعِدُ مِن رِزقٍ.٤٧٠٩

4212. **Imām ʿAlī (AS) said,** 'He who abandons the prohibition of wrong with his heart, his hand and his tongue is a dead man walking amongst the living.'[4748]

٤٢١٢ . الإمامُ عليٌّ ﷺ : مَن تَرَكَ إنكارَ المُنكَرِ بقَلبِهِ ويَدِهِ ولِسانِهِ فهُوَ مَيِّتٌ بَينَ الأحياءِ.٤٧١٠

4213. **Imām ʿAlī (AS) said,** 'The Prophet (SAWA) commanded us to meet the sinners with stern faces.'[4749]

٤٢١٣ . عنه ﷺ : أمَرَنا رَسولُ اللهِ ﷺ أن نَلقىٰ أهلَ المَعاصي بِوُجوهٍ مُكفَهِرَّةٍ.٤٧١١

4214. **Imām al-Ṣādiq (AS) said,** 'It is honour indeed for a believer that when he sees wrong being done, Allah, Mighty and Exalted, knows his heart to have rejected it.'[4750]

٤٢١٤ . الإمامُ الصّادقُ ﷺ : حَسبُ المُؤمِنِ عِزّاً إذا رَأىٰ مُنكَراً أن يَعلَمَ اللهُ عَزَّوجلَّ مِن قَلبِهِ إنكارَهُ.٤٧١٢

(See also: STRIVING (1): section 377; ACTS OF COMMON COURTESY (2) section 1288)

(أنظر) الجهاد (١): باب ٣٧٧؛ المعروف (٢): باب ١٢٨٨.

274

HONOUR

العِزَّة

1289. The Explanation of Honour

١٢٨٩ ـ تفسيرُ العِزِّ

"- those who take the faithless for allies instead of the faithful. Do they seek honour with them? [If so,] indeed all honour belongs to Allah."[4751]

﴿الَّذِينَ يَتَّخِذُونَ الْكَافِرِينَ أَوْلِيَاءَ مِن دُونِ الْمُؤْمِنِينَ أَيَبْتَغُونَ عِندَهُمُ الْعِزَّةَ فَإِنَّ الْعِزَّةَ لِلَّهِ جَمِيعًا﴾.٤٧١٣

4215. **Imām ʿAlī (AS) said,** 'Anyone honoured by other than Allah is actually disgraced.'[4752]

٤٢١٥ . الإمامُ عليٌّ ﷺ : العَزيزُ بغَيرِ اللهِ ذَليلٌ.٤٧١٤

4216. **Imām ʿAlī (AS) said,** 'Know that the one who does not abase himself in front of Allah has no honour, and that the one who does not humble himself before Allah has no elevation.'[4753]

٤٢١٦ . عنه ﷺ : إعلَم أنَّهُ لا عِزَّ لِمَن لا يَتَذَلَّلُ للهِ، ولا رِفعَةَ لِمَن لا يَتَواضَعُ للهِ.٤٧١٥

4217. **Imām ʿAlī (AS) said,** 'There is no honour like clemency.'[4754]

٤٢١٧ . عنه ﷺ : ولا عِزَّ كالحِلمِ.٤٧١٦

4218. **Imām Zayn al-ʿĀbidīn (AS) said,** 'Obedience to the [divinely appointed] authorities of command is a completion of one's honour.'[4755]

٤٢١٨ . الإمامُ زينُ العابدينَ ﷺ : طاعَةُ وُلاةِ الأمرِ تَمامُ العِزِّ.٤٧١٧

4219. **Imām al-Ṣādiq (AS) said,** 'Honour is to submit oneself to the truth when it comes to you.'[4756]

٤٢١٩ . الإمامُ الصّادقُ ﷷ : العِزُّ أن تَذِلَّ لِلحَقِّ إذا لَزِمَكَ. ٤٧١٨

1290. Factors that Elicit Honour

١٢٩٠ ـ موجِباتُ العِزِّ

4220. It is narrated in *Biḥār al-Anwār*: Allah, most High, revealed to Prophet David (AS) said, 'O David, verily … I have placed honour in My obedience whilst they seek it in servitude to the ruler and do not find it therefore.'[4757]

٤٢٢٠ . بحار الأنوار : أوحَى اللهُ تَعالىٰ إلىٰ داوودَ ﷷ : يا داوودُ، إنّي ... وَضَعتُ العِزَّ في طاعَتي، وهُم يَطلُبونَهُ في خِدمَةِ السُّلطانِ فلا يَجِدونَهُ. ٤٧١٩

4221. **Luqmān (AS) said** to his son, exhorting him, 'If you want to attract honour in this world, then cut off your greed of drawing advantage from what other people have in their possession; for verily the prophets and the veracious ones achieved what they did by cutting off their greed.'[4758]

٤٢٢١ . لقمانُ ﷷ ـ لِابنِه وهُوَ يَعِظُهُ ـ : إن أردتَ أن تَجمَعَ عِزَّ الدّنيا فَاقطَعْ طَمَعَكَ مِمّا في أيدي النّاسِ ؛ فإنَّما بَلَغَ الأنبِياءُ والصِّدّيقونَ ما بَلَغوا بِقَطعِ طَمَعِهِم. ٤٧٢٠

4222. **Imām ʿAlī (AS) said,** 'There is no honour higher than piety.'[4759]

٤٢٢٢ . الإمامُ عليٌّ ﷷ : لا عِزَّ أعَزُّ مِنَ التَّقوىٰ. ٤٧٢١

4223. **Imām ʿAlī (AS) said** in his intimate supplication, 'My God, it is honour enough for me that I am Your servant, and it is a source of pride for me that You are my Lord.'[4760]

٤٢٢٣ . عنه ﷷ ـ في المُناجاةِ ـ : إلٰهي كَفىٰ لي عِزّاً أن أكونَ لَكَ عَبداً، وكَفىٰ بي فَخراً أن تَكونَ لي رَبّاً. ٤٧٢٢

4224. **Imām ʿAlī (AS) said,** 'Know that verily the one who treats people fairly in spite of himself is only increased by Allah in honour.'[4761]

٤٢٢٤ . عنه ﷷ : ألا إنَّهُ مَن يُنصِفُ النّاسَ مِن نَفسِهِ لَم يَزِدْهُ اللهُ إلّا عِزّاً. ٤٧٢٣

4225. **Imām ʿAlī (AS) said,** 'Be content and you will attain honour.'[4762]

٤٢٢٥ . عنه ﷷ : اِقنَعْ تَعِزَّ. ٤٧٢٤

4226. **Imām al-Bāqir (AS) said,** 'Giving up all hope of benefit from what people possess is an honour for a believer in his religion.'[4763]

٤٢٢٦ . الإمامُ الباقرُ ﷷ : اليَأسُ مِمّا في أيدي النّاسِ عِزٌّ للمُؤمِنِ في دِينِهِ. ٤٧٢٥

4227. **Imām al-Bāqir (AS) said,** 'There are three things through which Allah only increases the Muslim in honour: his pardon of one who has

٤٢٢٧ . عنه ﷷ : ثَلاثٌ لا يَزيدُ اللهُ بِهِنَّ المَرءَ

wronged him, his giving one who has deprived him, and his reconciliation with one who has cut him off.'[4764]

المُسلِمَ إلّا عِزّاً : الصَّفحُ عَمَّن ظَلَمَهُ ، وإعطاءُ مَن حَرَمَهُ ، والصِّلَةُ لِمَن قَطَعَهُ .٤٧٦٤

4228. **Imām al-Ṣādiq (AS) said,** 'He who wishes for honour without noble lineage, wealth without riches and dignity without rulership should remove himself from the disgrace of Allah's disobedience to the honour of His obedience.'[4765]

٤٢٢٨ . الإمامُ الصّادقُ (عليه السلام) : مَن أرادَ عِزّاً بِلا عَشيرَةٍ ، وغِنىً بِلا مالٍ ، وهَيبَةً بِلا سُلطانٍ ، فَليَنقَلْ مِن ذُلِّ مَعصِيَةِ اللهِ إلىٰ عِزِّ طاعَتِهِ .٤٧٦٥

4229. **Imām al-Ṣādiq (AS) said,** 'Every single servant who swallows his anger is increased in honour by Allah, Mighty and Exalted, in this world and in the Hereafter.'[4766]

٤٢٢٩ . عنه (عليه السلام) : ما مِن عَبدٍ كَظَمَ غَيظاً إلّا زادَهُ اللهُ عَزَّوجلَّ عِزّاً في الدّنيا والآخِرَةِ .٤٧٦٦

4230. **Imām al-ʿAskarī (AS) said,** 'No sooner does an honourable man abandon the truth than he is abased, and no sooner does a disgraced man adopt it than he is honoured.'[4767]

٤٢٣٠ . الإمامُ العسكريُّ (عليه السلام) : ما تَرَكَ الحَقَّ عَزيزٌ إلّا ذَلَّ ، ولا أخَذَ بِهِ ذَليلٌ إلّا عَزَّ .٤٧٦٧

(See also: GODWARINESS: section 1866)

(أنظر) التقوى : باب ١٨٦٦ .

1291. That which Causes Honour to Last

١٢٩١ ـ ما يوجِبُ بَقاءَ العِزِّ

4231. **Imām al-Bāqir (AS) said,** 'Seek for everlasting honour through killing greed.'[4768]

٤٢٣١ . الإمامُ الباقرُ (عليه السلام) : اُطلُبْ بَقاءَ العِزِّ بإماتَةِ الطَّمَعِ .٤٧٦٨

4232. **Imām al-Ṣādiq (AS) said,** 'The modesty in one's reservation preserves one's honour longer than the intimacy of encounter [when interacting with people].'[4769]

٤٢٣٢ . الإمامُ الصّادقُ (عليه السلام) : حِشمَةُ الانقِباضِ أبقىٰ لِلعِزِّ من اُنسِ التَّلاقي .٤٧٦٩

275

SOLITUDE

العُزلَة

1292. The Virtue of Solitude

١٢٩٢ ـ فَضلُ العُزلَة

4233. It is narrated in *al-Kāfī*: 'Allah conversed with Prophet Moses saying, 'Be clad in threadbare clothes though having a clean, fresh heart. Be

٤٢٣٣ . الكافي : مِمّا ناجَى اللهُ تَعالىٰ بِهِ موسىٰ : كُن خَلَقَ الثِّيابِ جَديدَ القَلبِ ، تَخفىٰ عَلىٰ

unknown to the people of the earth, though famous among those in the heavens.'[4770]

أهلِ الأرضِ، وتُعرَفُ في أهلِ السَّماءِ.[٤٧٣٢]

4234. **The Prophet (SAWA) said,** 'Solitude is worship.'[4771]

٤٢٣٤. رسولُ اللهِ ﷺ: العُزلَةُ عِبادةٌ.[٤٧٣٣]

4235. **Imām ʿAlī (AS) said,** 'Seclusion is the comfort of the devoted worshippers.'[4772]

٤٢٣٥. الإمامُ عليٌّ ﷺ: الانـفِرادُ راحَـةُ المُتَعَبِّدينَ.[٤٧٣٤]

4236. **Imām ʿAlī (AS) said,** 'He who secludes himself from people seeks company with Allah, Glory be to Him.'[4773]

٤٢٣٦. عنه ﷺ: مَن انفَرَدَ عَنِ النّاسِ أنِسَ بِاللهِ سُبحانَهُ.[٤٧٣٥]

4237. **Imām ʿAlī (AS) said,** 'He who isolates himself from people is safe from their evil.'[4774]

٤٢٣٧. عنه ﷺ: مَنِ اعتَزَلَ النّاسَ سَلِمَ مِن شَرِّهِم.[٤٧٣٦]

1293. That which Drives One to Solitude

١٢٩٣ـ ما يوجِبُ العُزلَةَ

4238. **Imām al-Ṣādiq (AS)** was once asked the reason for his solitude away from people, to which he replied, 'Times have become corrupt and brothers have changed, so I found solitude to be most calming for the heart.'[4775]

٤٢٣٨. الإمامُ الصادقُ ﷺ ـ لَمّا سُئلَ عَن عِلَّةِ اعتِزالِهِ ـ: فَسَدَ الزَّمانُ وتَغَيَّرَ الإخوانُ، فَرَأيتُ الانفِرادَ أسكَنَ لِلفُؤادِ.[٤٧٣٧]

4239. **Imām al-ʿAskarī (AS) said,** 'Estrangement from people comes about as a direct result of knowing them too well.'[4776]

٤٢٣٩. الإمامُ العسكريُّ ﷺ: الوَحشَةُ مِنَ النّاسِ عَلىٰ قَدرِ الفِطنَةِ بِهِم.[٤٧٣٨]

1294. One who Must not Adopt Solitude

١٢٩٤ـ مَن لا يَنبَغي لَهُ العُزلَةُ

4240. **The Prophet (SAWA) said,** 'The believer who mingles with people and tolerates their wrongs is better than the believer who does not mingle with people and does not tolerate their wrongs.'[4777]

٤٢٤٠. رسولُ اللهِ ﷺ: المُؤمِنُ الَّذي يُخالِطُ النّاسَ ويَصبِرُ عَلىٰ أذاهُم أفضَلُ مِنَ المُؤمِنِ الَّـذي لا يُخالِطُ النّاسَ ولا يَصبِرُ عَلىٰ أذاهُم.[٤٧٣٩]

4241. **The Prophet (SAWA) said** to a man who wished to live in the mountains to worship therein, 'Indeed someone's tolerance of what he despises in any part of the Islamic territory for one hour is better than his forty years of worship in isolation.'[4778]

٤٢٤١. عنه ﷺ ـ لِرَجُلٍ أرادَ الجَبَلَ لِيَتَعَبَّدَ فيهِ ـ: لَصَبرُ أحَدِكُم ساعَةً عَلىٰ مـا يَكـرَهُهُ فـي بَـعضِ مَواطِنِ الإسلامِ خَيرٌ مِن عِبادَتِهِ خالِياً أربَـعينَ سَنَةً.[٤٧٤٠]

276

CONDOLENCE التَّعزِيَة

1295. Condoling with One who is Grief-Stricken[4779]

١٢٩٥ ـ تَعزِيَةُ المُصابِ

4242. **The Prophet (SAWA) said,** 'Whoever condoles with a grief-stricken person receives the same reward as him.'[4780]

٤٢٤٢ . رسولُ اللهِ ﷺ : مَن عَزّىٰ مُصاباً كانَ لَهُ مِثلُ أجرِهِ.٤٧٤١

4243. **Imām ʿAlī (AS) said,** 'Whoever condoles with a mother bereaved of her child will be shaded by Allah by the shade of His Throne on the Day when no other shade will avail.'[4781]

٤٢٤٣ . الإمامُ عليٌّ ﷺ : مَن عَزّىٰ الثَّكلىٰ أظَلَّهُ اللهُ في ظِلِّ عَرشِهِ يَومَ لا ظِلَّ إلّا ظِلُّهُ.٤٧٤٢

4244. **Imām al-Ṣādiq (AS) said,** 'The minimum condolence required of you is that the bereaved one sees you present.'[4782]

٤٢٤٤ . الإمامُ الصّادقُ ﷺ : كَفاكَ مِنَ التَّعزِيَةِ بأن يَراكَ صاحِبُ المُصيبَةِ.٤٧٤٣

1296. What to Say when Giving Condolences to a Grief-Stricken Person

١٢٩٦ ـ ما يُقالُ في تَعزِيَةِ المُصابِ

4245. **Imām ʿAlī (AS) narrated** that when the Prophet (SAWA) gave condolences, he would say, 'May Allah recompense you and have mercy on you', and that when he gave congratulations, he would say, 'May Allah bless you and send blessings on you.'[4783]

٤٢٤٥ . الإمامُ عليٌّ ﷺ : كانَ رَسولُ اللهِ ﷺ إذا عَزّىٰ قالَ: آجَرَكُمُ اللهُ ورَحِمَكُم، وإذا هَنّأَ قالَ: بارَكَ اللهُ لَكُم وبارَكَ عَلَيكُم.٤٧٤٤

1297. Congratulating the Grief-Stricken is More Appropriate than Condoling him

١٢٩٧ ـ تَهنِئَةُ المُصابِ أولىٰ مِن تَعزِيَتِه!

4246. **Imām al-Riḍā (AS) said,** when giving condolences to al-Ḥasan b. Sahl, 'Congratulating someone for the reward that is in store for them is more appropriate than condoling them for a transient affliction.'[4784]

٤٢٤٦ . الإمامُ الرِّضا ﷺ ـ في تَعزِيَتِهِ لِلحَسَنِ بن سَهلٍ ـ: التَّهنِئَةُ بِآجِلِ الثَّوابِ أولىٰ مِنَ التَّعزِيَةِ عَلىٰ عاجِلِ المُصيبَةِ.٤٧٤٥

(أنظر) المصيبة: باب ١١٥٣.

(See also: AFFLICTION: section 1153)

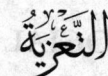

277

SOCIAL INTERACTION

العِشْرَةُ

1298. The Etiquette of Social Interaction with People

١٢٩٨ـأدَبُ العِشرَةِ مَعَ النّاسِ

4247. **Imām ʿAlī (AS) said,** 'Mingle amongst people in such a way that when you die they should weep for you, and when you are alive, they should long for you.'[4785]

٤٢٤٧. الإمامُ عليٌّ ﷺ : خالِطوا النّاسَ مُخالَطَةً إن مِتُّم مَعَها بَكَوا عَلَيكُم، وإن عِشتُم (غِبتُم) حَنُّوا إلَيكُم.[٤٧٤٦]

4248. **Imām ʿAlī (AS)** used to say, 'Let your heart include both need for people as well as needlessness of them – your need for them being in order to speak kindly words to them and to share your joy with them, and your needlessness of them being in order to maintain your integrity and to preserve your self-respect.'[4786]

٤٢٤٨. عنه ﷺ ـ كانَ يَقولُ ـ : لِيَجتَمِعْ في قَلبِكَ الافتِقارُ إلَى النّاسِ، والاستِغناءُ عَنهُم، يَكونُ افتِقارُكَ إلَيهِم في لينِ كَلامِكَ وحُسنِ بِشرِكَ، ويَكونُ استِغناؤكَ عَنهُم في نَزاهَةِ عِرضِكَ وبَقاءِ عِزِّكَ.[٤٧٤٧]

4249. **Imām al-Bāqir (AS) said,** 'The improvement of people's affairs is in coexistence and close cooperation, according to a set measure: two thirds of which are to have awareness and a third of which is to feign ignorance of each other's faults.'[4787]

٤٢٤٩. الإمامُ الباقرُ ﷺ : صَلاحُ شَأنِ النّاسِ التَّعايُشُ والتَّعاشُرُ مِلءَ مِكيالٍ: ثُلثاهُ فِطَنٌ، وثُلثٌ تَغافُلٌ.[٤٧٤٨]

1299. The Etiquette of Social Interaction with One's Family

١٢٩٩ـأدَبُ العِشرَةِ مَعَ الأهلِ

"O you who have faith! It is not lawful for you to inherit women forcibly, and do not press them to take away part of what you have given them, unless they commit a gross indecency. Consort with them in an honourable manner; and should you dislike them, maybe you dislike something while Allah invests it with an abundant good."[4788]

﴿يا أيُّها الَّذِينَ آمَنُوا لا يَحِلُّ لَكُمْ أنْ تَرِثُوا النِّساءَ كَرْهاً وَلا تَعْضُلُوهُنَّ لِتَذْهَبُوا بِبَعْضِ ما آتَيْتُمُوهُنَّ إلّا أنْ يَأْتِينَ بِفاحِشَةٍ مُبَيِّنَةٍ وَعاشِرُوهُنَّ بِالْمَعْرُوفِ فَإنْ كَرِهْتُمُوهُنَّ فَعَسى أنْ تَكْرَهُوا شَيْئاً وَيَجْعَلَ اللهُ فِيهِ خَيْراً كَثِيراً﴾.[٤٧٤٩]

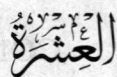

4250. **Imām ʿAlī (AS) said** in his will to his son al-Ḥasan (AS), 'Let your family not become the most miserable of people because of you.'[4789]

٤٢٥٠. الإمامُ عليٌّ ﵇ ـ في وَصِيَّتِهِ لِابنِهِ الحَسَنِ ﵇ ـ: لا يَكُن أهلُكَ أشقى الخَلقِ بِكَ.[٤٧٥٠]

4251. **Imām al-Ṣādiq (AS) said,** 'Verily man needs to adopt three characteristics with respect to his household and his family, even if these are not naturally present within him: pleasant social interaction, calculated generosity, and possessiveness through protectiveness.'[4790]

٤٢٥١. الإمامُ الصّادقُ ﵇: إنَّ المَرءَ يَحتاجُ في مَنزِلِهِ وعِيالِهِ إلىٰ ثَلاثِ خِلالٍ يَتَكَلَّفُها وإن لَم يَكُن في طَبعِهِ ذٰلكَ: مُعاشَرَةٍ جَميلَةٍ، وسَعَةٍ بِتَقديرٍ، وغَيرَةٍ بِتَحَصُّنٍ.[٤٧٥١]

(See also: MARRIAGE: section 175)

(اُنظر) عنوان ١٧٥ «الزواج».

1300. What is Required when Interacting with People

١٣٠٠ ـ ما يَنبَغي في مُخالَطَةِ النّاسِ

4252. **The Prophet (SAWA) said,** 'Associate well with one who associates with you and you will be considered a Muslim.'[4791]

٤٢٥٢. رسولُ اللهِ ﷺ: أحسِنْ مُصاحَبَةَ مَن صاحَبَكَ تَكُن مُسلِماً.[٤٧٥٢]

4253. **Imām ʿAlī (AS) said,** 'Interact with [vile] people with the use of your tongues and your bodies, and part from them with your hearts and your actions.'[4792]

٤٢٥٣. الإمامُ عليٌّ ﵇: خالِطوا النّاسَ بِألسِنَتِكُم وأجسادِكُم، وزايِلوهُم بِقُلوبِكُم وأعمالِكُم.[٤٧٥٣]

4254. **Imām ʿAlī (AS) said,** 'For your brother, offer your blood and your wealth, for your enemy your justice and fairness, and for people in general your joy and your good favour.'[4793]

٤٢٥٤. عنه ﵇: أبذُلْ لِأخيكَ دَمَكَ ومالَكَ، ولِعَدُوِّكَ عَدلَكَ وإنصافَكَ، ولِلعامَّةِ بِشرَكَ وإحسانَكَ.[٤٧٥٤]

4255. **Imām ʿAlī (AS) said,** 'Obligate yourself to adopt affection, and make yourself tolerate the encumbrances of people.'[4794]

٤٢٥٥. عنه ﵇: ألزِم نَفسَكَ التَّوَدُّدَ، وصَبِّر عَلىٰ مُؤوناتِ النّاسِ نَفسَكَ.[٤٧٥٥]

4256. **Imām ʿAlī (AS) said,** 'He who is quick to criticize people in a manner that they dislike, they will talk about him saying that which they do not know.'[4795]

٤٢٥٦. عنه ﵇: مَن أسرَعَ إلَى النّاسِ بِما يَكرَهونَ قالوا فيهِ ما لا يَعلَمونَ.[٤٧٥٦]

4257. **Imām al-Ḥasan (AS) said,** 'Associate with people the way you would like them to associate with you.'[4796]

٤٢٥٧. الإمامُ الحسنُ ﵇: صاحِبِ النّاسَ مِثلَ ما تُحِبُّ أن يُصاحِبوكَ بِهِ.[٤٧٥٧]

4258. **Imām al-Ṣādiq (AS) said,** 'Amicableness towards people is a third of intellect.'[4797]

٤٢٥٨. الإمامُ الصّادقُ عليه السلام: مُجامَلَةُ النّاسِ ثُلثُ العَقلِ.[٤٧٥٨]

4259. **Imām al-Kāẓim (AS) said,** 'Affection towards people is half of intellect.'[4798]

٤٢٥٩. الإمامُ الكاظمُ عليه السلام: التَّوَدُّدُ إلَى النّاسِ نِصفُ العَقلِ.[٤٧٥٩]

(See also: AMICABLENESS 139; LOVE: sections 417-421)

(اُنظر) عنوان ١٣٩ «المداراة»؛ المحبّة: باب ٤١٧ ـ ٤٢١.

278

'ĀSHŪRĀ'[4799]

عاشوراء

1301. 'Āshūrā and weeping for Imām al-Ḥusayn (AS) and his companions

١٣٠١ـ عاشوراءُ والبُكاءُ عَلَى الحُسَينِ عليه السلام وأصحابِهِ

4260. **Imām Zayn al-'Ābidīn (AS) said,** 'Every single believer whose eyes shed tears for the martyrdom of al-Ḥusayn (AS) such that they roll onto his cheeks, Allah prepares chambers for him in Paradise as a result of them wherein he will dwell for ages.'[4800]

٤٢٦٠. الإمامُ زينَ العابدينُ عليه السلام: أيُّما مُؤمِنٍ دَمِعَت عَيناهُ لِقَتلِ الحُسَينِ عليه السلام حَتّىٰ تَسيلَ عَلىٰ خَدِّهِ، بَوَّأَهُ اللهُ بِها فِي الجَنَّةِ غُرَفاً يَسكُنُها أحقاباً.[٤٧٦٠]

4261. **Imām al-Bāqir (AS)** in his discourse about the visitation (*ziyāra*) of al-Ḥusayn (AS) on the day of 'Āshūrā', be it from near or far, said, 'Then let him mourn for al-Ḥusayn (AS) and weep over him, and let him enjoin weeping for him on others in his house who are not in a state of dissimulation, and they should condole with each other for their bereavement of al-Ḥusayn (AS). ... I [i.e. the narrator] asked, 'How should they condole with each other?' to which he replied, 'They should say: 'May Allah make our reward great for our bereavement of al-Ḥusayn, and place us and you among those who avenge his blood with his representative, the Imām Mahdī from the family of Muḥammad, peace be upon them.'[4801]

٤٢٦١. الإمامُ الباقرُ عليه السلام ـ في حَديثِ زِيارَةِ الحُسَينِ عليه السلام يَومَ عاشوراءَ مِن بُعدٍ ـ: ثُمَّ لِيَندُبِ الحسينَ عليه السلام ويَبكيهِ، ويأمُرُ مَن في دارِهِ مِمَّن لا يَتَّقيهِ بِالبُكاءِ عَلَيهِ ... ولِيُعَزِّ بَعضُهُم بَعضاً بِمُصابِهِم بِالحُسَينِ عليه السلام ... قُلتُ: فكَيفَ يُعَزّي بَعضُنا بَعضاً؟ قالَ: تَقولونَ: أعظَمَ اللهُ اُجورَنا بِمُصابِنا بِالحُسَينِ، وجَعَلَنا وإيّاكُم مِنَ الطّالِبينَ بِثارِهِ مَعَ وَلِيِّهِ الإمامِ المَهدِيِّ مِن آلِ مُحَمَّدٍ عليهم السلام.[٤٧٦١]

4262. **Imām al-Ṣādiq (AS) said,** 'Whoever recites a single verse of poetry about al-Ḥusayn (AS),

٤٢٦٢. الإمامُ الصّادقُ عليه السلام: مَن أنشَدَ في

crying as a result and making ten other people cry, becomes deserving of Paradise and so do they.'[4802]

الحُسَينِ عليه السلام بيتاً مِن شِعرٍ فبكىٰ وأبكىٰ عَشرَةً فَلَهُ ولَهُمُ الجَنَّةُ.[٤٧٦٢]

4263. **Imām al-Riḍā (AS) said,** 'He for whom the day of 'Āshūrā' is a day of grief, sorrow and crying, Allah, Mighty and Exalted, will make the Day of Resurrection a day of joy and happiness for him.'[4803]

٤٢٦٣. الإمامُ الرِّضا عليه السلام: مَن كانَ يَومُ عاشوراءَ يَومَ مُصيبَتِهِ وحُزنِهِ وبُكائِهِ، يَجعَلِ اللهُ عزّوجلّ يَومَ القِيامَةِ يَومَ فَرَحِهِ وسُرورِهِ.[٤٧٦٣]

4264. **Imām al-Riḍā (AS) said,** 'Let the weepers weep over someone like Ḥusayn, for verily weeping over him reduces the burden of great sins. Then he continued, saying, 'As soon as the month of Muḥarram would set in, my father (AS) was never seen laughing and he would be overcome by melancholy until after the first ten days had passed. When the tenth day dawned, it was a day of grief and sorrow and crying for him, and he used to say, 'This is the day when al-Ḥusayn (AS) was martyred.'[4804]

٤٢٦٤. عنه عليه السلام: فَعَلىٰ مِثلِ الحُسَينِ فَليَبكِ الباكونَ؛ فإنَّ البُكاءَ عَلَيهِ يَحُطُّ الذُّنوبَ العِظامَ.... كانَ أبي عليه السلام إذا دَخَلَ شَهرُ المُحَرَّمِ لا يُرىٰ ضاحِكاً، وكانَتِ الكَآبَةُ تَغلِبُ عَلَيهِ حَتّىٰ تَمضِيَ عَشرَةُ أيّامٍ، فإذا كانَ يَومُ العاشِرِ كانَ ذٰلكَ اليَومُ يَومَ مُصيبَتِهِ وحُزنِهِ وبُكائِهِ، ويَقولُ: هُوَ اليَومُ الَّذي قُتِلَ فيهِ الحُسَينُ عليه السلام.[٤٧٦٤]

279

INFATUATION

العِشقُ

1302. The Reprehensibility of Infatuation

١٣٠٢ ـ ذَمُّ العِشقِ

4265. **Imām 'Alī (AS) said,** 'Separation from one's beloved is the penalty for infatuation.'[4805]

٤٢٦٥. الإمامُ عليٌّ عليه السلام: الهِجرانُ عُقوبَةُ العِشقِ.[٤٧٦٥]

4266. **Imām 'Alī (AS) said,** 'The one who is infatuated with something, his eyes become blind and his heart becomes sick, such that he sees with unsound eyes and hears with deaf ears, his base desires having torn apart his reason and [love of] *the world having killed* his heart.'[4806]

٤٢٦٦. عنه عليه السلام: ومَن عَشِقَ شَيئاً أعشىٰ (أعمىٰ) بَصَرَهُ وأمرَضَ قَلبَهُ، فَهُوَ يَنظُرُ بِعَينٍ غَيرِ صَحيحَةٍ، ويَسمَعُ بِأُذُنٍ غَيرِ سَميعَةٍ، قَد خَرَقَتِ الشَّهَواتُ عَقلَهُ، وأماتَتِ الدّنيا قَلبَهُ.[٤٧٦٦]

4267. **Imām al-Ṣādiq (AS),** when asked about infatuation, replied, 'Hearts that are empty of the remembrance of Allah are given to taste by Allah the love of other than Him.'[4807]

٤٢٦٧. الإمامُ الصّادقُ عليه السلام ـ لَمّا سُئلَ عَنِ العِشقِ ـ: قُلوبٌ خَلَت مِن ذِكرِ اللهِ فأذاقَها اللهُ حُبَّ غَيرِهِ.[٤٧٦٧]

1303. The Reward for One who Despite his Infatuation Restrains himself

١٣٠٣ـ ثوابُ مَن عَشِقَ وعفَّ

4268. **The Prophet (SAWA) said,** 'Whoever loves someone passionately, then suppresses his love in order to remain chaste and dies in the process, is a martyr.'[4808]

٤٢٦٨. رسولُ اللهِ ﷺ : مَن عَشِقَ فكَتَمَ وعَفَّ فماتَ فَهُوَ شَهيدٌ.٤٧٦٨

4269. **Imām ʿAlī (AS) said,** 'The fighter who is martyred in the way of Allah has no greater reward than the one who is able to sate his lust but restrains himself.'[4809]

٤٢٦٩. الإمامُ عليٌّ ؑ : ما المُجاهِدُ الشَّهيدُ في سَبيلِ اللهِ بِأعظَمَ أجراً مِمَّن قَدَرَ فعَفَّ.٤٧٦٩

1304. Infatuation with Allah

١٣٠٤ـ عِشقُ اللهِ

4270. **The Prophet (SAWA) said,** 'Allah, Mighty and Exalted, says, 'When a servant's predominant state is preoccupation with Me then I make the object of his desire My remembrance and place his pleasure therein. And when I make My remembrance the object of his desire and place his pleasure therein, he becomes infatuated with Me and I with him. And when he becomes infatuated with Me and I with him, I remove all veils between Me and him, and make this state predominate over him where he is never again negligent even when other people are.'[4810]

٤٢٧٠. رسولُ اللهِ ﷺ : يَقولُ اللهُ عزَّ وجلَّ : إذا كانَ الغالِبُ عَلَى العَبدِ الاشتِغالَ بي جَعَلتُ بُغيَتَهُ ولَذَّتَهُ في ذِكري، فإذا جَعَلتُ بُغيَتَهُ ولَذَّتَهُ في ذِكري عَشِقَني وعَشِقتُهُ، فإذا عَشِقَني وعَشِقتُهُ رَفَعتُ الحِجابَ فيما بَيني وبَينَهُ، وصَيَّرتُ ذلكَ تَغالُباً عَلَيهِ، لا يَسهو إذا سَها النّاسُ.٤٧٧٠

(See also: LOVE: section 422)

(أنظر) المحبّة: باب ٤٢٢.

280

PARTISANSHIP

التَّعَصُّبُ

1305. Reprehension of Partisanship

١٣٠٥ـ ذَمُّ التَّعَصُّبِ

"When the faithless nourished bigotry in their hearts, the bigotry of pagan ignorance, Allah sent down His composure upon His Apostle and upon the faithful, and made them abide by the word of Godwariness, for

﴿إذْ جَعَلَ الَّذِينَ كَفَرُوا فِي قُلُوبِهِمُ الْحَمِيَّةَ حَمِيَّةَ الْجاهِلِيَّةِ فَأَنْزَلَ اللهُ سَكِينَتَهُ عَلَى رَسُولِهِ وَعَلَى الْمُؤْمِنِينَ وَأَلْزَمَهُمْ كَلِمَةَ التَّقْوَى وَكَانُوا أَحَقَّ

they were the worthiest of it and deserved it, and Allah has knowledge of all things."[4811]

بِها وَأهْلَها وَكانَ اللهُ بِكُلِّ شَيْءٍ عَلِيماً﴾ .[٤٧٧١]

(See also: Qur'an 19:73, 19:81, 23:33, 23:34, 26:111, 43:52, 43:53, 49:14)

(اُنظر) مريم: ٧٣، ٨١ والمؤمنون: ٣٣، ٣٤ والشعراء: ١١١ والزخرف: ٥٢، ٥٣ والحجرات: ١٤.

4271. **The Prophet (SAWA) said,** 'Whoever is bigoted or partial [to a false cause], or incites partisanship around himself and his own causes [unlawfully], the knot binding him to faith is untied from around his neck.'[4812]

٤٢٧١ . رسولُ اللهِ ﷺ : مَن تَعَصَّبَ أو تُعُصِّبَ لَهُ فقد خَلَعَ رِبْقَ الإيمانِ مِن عُنُقِهِ .[٤٧٧٢]

4272. **The Prophet (SAWA) said,** 'Whoever contains even a mustard seed's weight of partisanship in his heart, Allah will raise him on the Day of Resurrection among the tribes of pagan and clannish Arabia.'[4813]

٤٢٧٢ . عنه ﷺ : مَن كانَ في قَلبِهِ حَبَّةٌ مِن خَردَلٍ مِن عَصَبِيَّةٍ بَعَثَهُ اللهُ يَومَ القِيامَةِ مَعَ أعرابِ الجاهِلِيَّةِ .[٤٧٧٣]

4273. **The Prophet (SAWA) said,** 'One who calls to partisanship is not one of us, nor one who fights for a bigoted cause, nor one who dies a partisan.'[4814]

٤٢٧٣ . عنه ﷺ : لَيسَ مِنّا مَن دَعا إلىٰ عَصَبِيَّةٍ، ولَيسَ مِنّا مَن قاتَلَ (عَلىٰ) عَصَبِيَّةٍ، ولَيسَ مِنّا مَن ماتَ عَلىٰ عَصَبِيَّةٍ .[٤٧٧٤]

4274. **Imām ʿAlī (AS),** condemning Iblīs [Satan], said, 'So he felt proud of his own creation over Adam's, and was racist against him because of his origin. The enemy of Allah, therefore, is the leader of all racist bigots, and the forefather of all those who consider themselves superior, who laid the very foundation of bigotry, and tried to wrest the cloak of might from Allah, and assumed the garb of exultation having shed the veil of self-abasement.'[4815]

٤٢٧٤ . الإمامُ عليٌّ ؑ ـ في ذَمِّ إبليسَ ـ : فافتَخَرَ عَلىٰ آدَمَ بِخَلقِهِ، وتَعَصَّبَ عَلَيهِ لِأصلِهِ، فعَدُوُّ اللهِ إمامُ المُتَعَصِّبينَ، وسَلَفُ المُستَكبِرينَ، الّذي وَضَعَ أساسَ العَصَبِيَّةِ، ونازَعَ اللهَ رِداءَ الجَبرِيَّةِ، وادَّرَعَ لِباسَ التَّعَزُّزِ، وخَلَعَ قِناعَ التَّذَلُّلِ .[٤٧٧٥]

4275. **Imām Zayn al-ʿĀbidīn (AS) said,** 'Blameworthy and punishable partisanship is when a person considers the evil people of his own community to be better and prefers them over the good people of another community. It is not considered partisanship or bigotry to love one's own community, rather it is when a person assists them in spite of their wrongdoing and aids them therein.'[4816]

٤٢٧٥ . الإمامُ زينَ العابدينُ ؑ ـ لَمّا سُئلَ عَنِ العَصَبِيَّةِ ـ : العَصَبِيَّةُ الّتي يَأثَمُ عَلَيها صاحِبُها أن يَرَى الرَّجُلُ شِرارَ قَومِهِ خَيراً مِن خِيارِ قَومٍ آخَرينَ، ولَيسَ مِنَ العَصَبِيَّةِ أن يُحِبَّ الرَّجُلُ قَومَهُ، ولٰكِن مِنَ العَصَبِيَّةِ أن يُعينَ قَومَهُ عَلَى الظُّلمِ .[٤٧٧٦]

1306. Praiseworthy Partisanship

١٣٠٦ـ التَّعَصُّبُ المَمدوحُ

4276. **Imām ʿAlī (AS) said,** ‘And if you cannot avoid partisanship, then let your partisanship be for virtuous qualities, praiseworthy acts, and admirable matters with which the dignified and noble chiefs of the Arab households and the notables of the tribes distinguished themselves, such as attractive manners, great ambitions, momentous positions, and praiseworthy feats. So be partisans of praiseworthy characteristics like protection of one's neighbour, fulfilment of rights, obedience of good people, opposition to the haughty, adoption of virtue, abstention from intimidating others, shunning bloodshed, doing justice to people, suppressing anger, and avoiding corruption in the land.’[4817]

٤٢٧٦. الإمامُ عليٌّ ﷺ : فإن كانَ لابُدَّ مِنَ العَصَبِيَّةِ فلْيَكُن تَعَصُّبُكُم لِمَكارِمِ الخِصالِ، ومَحامِدِ الأفعالِ، ومَحاسِنِ الأُمورِ، الّتي تَفاضَلَت فيها المُجَداءُ والنُّجَداءُ مِن بُيوتاتِ العَرَبِ، ويَعاسيبُ القَبائلِ، بِالأخلاقِ الرَّغيبَةِ، والأحلامِ العَظيمَةِ، والأخطارِ الجَليلَةِ، والآثارِ المَحمودَةِ. فتَعَصَّبوا لِخِلالِ الحَمدِ مِنَ الحِفظِ لِلجِوارِ، والوَفاءِ بِالذِّمامِ، والطّاعَةِ لِلبِرِّ، والمَعصيَةِ لِلكِبرِ، والأخذِ بِالفَضلِ، والكَفِّ عَنِ البَغيِ، والإعظامِ لِلقَتلِ، والإنصافِ لِلخَلقِ، والكَظمِ لِلغَيظِ، واجتِنابِ الفَسادِ في الأرضِ.[٤٧٧٧]

4277. **Imām ʿAlī (AS) said,** ‘If you absolutely must be partisans to a cause, then do so to support the truth and to bring solace to the troubled.’[4818]

٤٢٧٧. عنه ﷺ : إن كُنتُم لا مَحالَةَ مُتَعَصِّبينَ فتَعَصَّبوا لِنُصرَةِ الحَقِّ وإغاثَةِ المَلهوفِ.[٤٧٧٨]

281

INFALLIBILITY

العِصمَة

1307. The Meaning of Infallibility

١٣٠٧ـ مَعنَى العِصمَةِ

4278. **Imām Zayn al-ʿĀbidīn (AS) said,** ‘An Imām from among us can only be infallible. Infallibility is not an outward physical feature that can be noticed which is why it must be documented [in the Qur'an or traditions].’ He was then asked, ‘O son of the Prophet, and what does infallible mean?’ to which he replied, ‘It refers to one who clings fast to the rope of Allah, and the rope of Allah is the Qur'an. They do not separate from each other until the Day of Resurrection, and the Imām guides to the Qur'an and the Qur'an guides to the Imām, which is the purport

٤٢٧٨. معاني الأخبار عن الإمامِ الكاظم عن آبائه عن الإمامِ زينِ العابدينَ ﷺ : الإمامُ مِنّا لا يَكونُ إلّا مَعصوماً، ولَيسَتِ العِصمَةُ في ظاهِرِ الخِلقَةِ فيُعرَفَ بِها، ولِذلكَ لا يَكونُ إلّا مَنصوصاً. فقيلَ لَهُ: يَابنَ رَسولِ اللهِ، فما مَعنَى المَعصومِ؟ فقالَ: هُوَ المُعتَصِمُ بِحَبلِ اللهِ، وحَبلُ اللهِ هُوَ القُرآنُ، لا يَفتَرِقانِ إلَى يَومِ القِيامَةِ، والإمامُ يَهدي إلَى القُرآنِ، والقُرآنُ يَهدي إلَى

of Allah's saying [in the Qur'an]: *"Verily this Qur'an guides to what is most upright."*[4819] [4820]

الإمام، وذٰلكَ قولُ اللهِ عزَّوجلَّ: ﴿إنَّ هٰذا القرآنَ يَهْدي لِلَّتي هِيَ أقْوَمُ﴾.[٤٧٧٩]

4279. **Imām al-Ṣādiq (AS),** in reply to Hishām's question about the meaning of infallible, said, 'The infallible [Imām] is prevented by Allah from all acts which Allah has prohibited, and Allah, Blessed and most High, says: *"And whoever takes recourse in Allah is certainly guided to a straight path."*'[4821] [4822]

٤٢٧٩. الإمامُ الصّادقُ ﷺ ـ لَمّا سَألَهُ هِشامٌ عَن مَعنَى المَعصومِ ـ: المَعصومُ هُوَ المُمتَنِعُ بِاللهِ مِن جَميعِ مَحارِمِ اللهِ، وقالَ اللهُ تَبارَكَ وتَعالىٰ: ﴿ومَن يَعتَصِمْ بِاللهِ فقَد هُدِيَ إلىٰ صِراطٍ مُستَقيمٍ﴾.[٤٧٨٠]

1308. Factors that Bring About Sinlessness

١٣٠٨ ـ موجِباتُ العِصمَةِ

4280. **The Prophet (SAWA) said,** 'Verily Allah, Exalted be His remembrance, protects [from sin] whoever obeys Him, and whoever disobeys Him does not benefit from His protection.'[4823]

٤٢٨٠. رسولُ اللهِ ﷺ: إنَّ اللهَ عزَّ ذِكرُهُ يَعصِمُ مَن أطاعَهُ، ولا يَعتَصِمُ بِهِ مَن عَصاهُ.[٤٧٨١]

4281. **Imām ʿAlī (AS) said,** 'He who is divinely granted infallibility is safe from error.'[4824]

٤٢٨١. الإمامُ عليٌّ ﷺ: من اُلهِمَ العِصمَةَ أمِنَ الزَّلَلَ.[٤٧٨٢]

4282. **Imām ʿAlī (AS) said,** 'Drawing lessons [from past experiences] gives rise to immunity.'[4825]

٤٢٨٢. عنه ﷺ: الاعتِبارُ يُثمِرُ العِصمَةَ.[٤٧٨٣]

4283. **Imām ʿAlī (AS) said,** 'Verily Godwariness is a protection [against sin] for you in your life, and a great profit for you after your death.'[4826]

٤٢٨٣. عنه ﷺ: إنَّ التَّقوىٰ عِصمَةٌ لَكَ في حَياتِكَ، وزُلفىٰ لَكَ بَعدَ مَماتِكَ.[٤٧٨٤]

4284. **Imām ʿAlī (AS) said,** 'Sinlessness is fastened with Godwariness.'[4827]

٤٢٨٤. عنه ﷺ: بِالتَّقوىٰ قُرِنَتِ العِصمَةُ.[٤٧٨٥]

4285. **Imām ʿAlī (AS) said,** 'Wisdom is sinlessness, and sinlessness is a bounty.'[4828]

٤٢٨٥. عنه ﷺ: الحِكمَةُ عِصمَةٌ، العِصمَةُ نِعمَةٌ.[٤٧٨٦]

4286. **Imām ʿAlī (AS) said** in his intimate supplication, 'My God, I have no way to guard myself from sin except through Your protection, and no way to attain good deeds except by Your will. So how can I ever benefit from that which You have preceded with Your will?! And how can I ever guard myself from sins as long as Your protection does not cover me therein?!'[4829]

٤٢٨٦. عنه ﷺ ـ في مُناجاتِهِ ـ: إلٰهي، لا سَبيلَ إلَى الاحتِراسِ مِنَ الذَّنبِ إلّا بِعِصمَتِكَ، ولا وُصولَ إلىٰ عَمَلِ الخَيراتِ إلّا بِمَشيئَتِكَ، فكَيفَ لي بِإفادَةِ ما أسلَفتَني فيهِ مَشيئَتَكَ؟! وكَيفَ لي بِالاحتِراسِ مِنَ الذَّنبِ ما إن لَم تُدرِكني فيهِ عِصمَتُكَ؟![٤٧٨٧]

4287. **Imām al-Bāqir (AS) said,** 'When Allah, most High, knows the good intention of a person, He encompasses him with His protection from all sides.'[4830]

٤٢٨٧. الإمامُ الباقرُ عليه السلام: إذا عَلِمَ اللهُ تَعالىٰ حُسنَ نِيَّةٍ مِن أحَدٍ اكتَنَفَهُ بِالعِصمَةِ.[٤٧٨٨]

(See also: SATAN: section 1031)

(اُنظر) الشيطان: باب ١٠٣١.

1309. The Infallibility of the Imām[4831]

١٣٠٩ ـ عِصمَةُ الإمامِ

4288. **Imām al-Ṣādiq (AS) said,** describing the Imām, 'He is immune from committing all errors, well-protected from all acts of indecency.'[4832]

٤٢٨٨. الإمامُ الصّادقُ عليه السلام ـ في صِفَةِ الإمامِ ـ: مَعصوماً مِنَ الزَّلّاتِ، مَصوناً عَنِ الفَواحِشِ كُلِّها.[٤٧٨٩]

4289. **Imām al-Ṣādiq (AS) said,** 'We are the interpreters of Allah's command, we are the infallible people.'[4833]

٤٢٨٩. عنه عليه السلام: نَحنُ تَراجِمَةُ أمرِ اللهِ، نَحنُ قَومٌ مَعصومونَ.[٤٧٩٠]

4290. **Imām al-Riḍā (AS) said,** 'An Imām is: purified from sins, immune from all flaws.'[4834]

٤٢٩٠. الإمامُ الرِّضا عليه السلام: الإمامُ: المُطَهَّرُ مِنَ الذُّنوبِ، والمُبَرَّأُ عَنِ العُيوبِ.[٤٧٩١]

4291. **Imām al-Riḍā (AS) said,** 'He [i.e. the Imām] is therefore infallible, divinely supported, aided, and shielded; being immune from all mistakes, errors and lapses. Allah has endowed him that in order to make Him His proof on the servants and His witness over creation.'[4835]

٤٢٩١. عنه عليه السلام: ... فَهُوَ مَعصومٌ مُؤَيَّدٌ مُوَفَّقٌ مُسَدَّدٌ، قَد أمِنَ مِنَ الخَطايا والزَّلَلِ والعِثارِ، يَخُصُّهُ اللهُ بِذٰلِكَ لِيَكونَ حُجَّتَهُ عَلىٰ عِبادِهِ وشاهِدَهُ عَلىٰ خَلقِهِ.[٤٧٩٢]

282

VENERATION

التَّعظيمُ

1310. Veneration of Rulers

١٣١٠ ـ تَعظيمُ الاُمَراءِ

4292. **The Prophet (SAWA) said,** 'He who praises a tyrant ruler and is humble and subordinate to him out of greed in him will be his partner in Hellfire.'[4836]

٤٢٩٢. رسول الله صلى الله عليه وآله: مَن مَدَحَ سُلطاناً جائراً وتَخَفَّفَ وتَضَعضَعَ لَهُ طَمَعاً فيهِ كانَ قَرينَهُ إلَى النّارِ.[٤٧٩٣]

4293. **The Prophet (SAWA) said,** 'Whoever likes people to stand up for him should take a seat for himself in the Fire.'[4837]

٤٢٩٣. عنه صلى الله عليه وآله: مَن أحَبَّ أن يَمثُلَ لَهُ الرِّجالُ فَليَتَبَوَّأْ مَقعَدَهُ فِي النّارِ.[٤٧٩٤]

4294. **Bihār al-Anwār,** narrating from Abū Dharr, 'I saw Salmān and Bilāl approaching the Prophet (SAWA) when Salmān threw himself at the Prophet (SAWA)'s feet, kissing them. So the Prophet (SAWA) stopped him from doing that, and said to him, 'O Salmān, do not do unto me as the foreigners do with their kings – I am a servant from among the servants of Allah, eating what a servant eats and sitting how a servant sits.'[4838]

٤٢٩٤ . بحار الأنوار عن أبي ذرٍّ ﵀ : رَأيتُ سَلمانَ وبِلالاً يُقبِلانِ إلَى النَّبِيِّ ﷺ إذ انكَبَّ سَلمانُ عَلىٰ قَدَمِ رَسولِ اللهِ ﷺ يُقَبِّلُها ، فزَجَرَهُ النَّبِيُّ ﷺ عَن ذٰلكَ ، ثُمّ قالَ لَهُ : يا سَلمانُ ، لا تَصنَعْ بي ما تَصنَعُ الأعاجِمُ بِمُلوكِها ، أنا عَبدٌ مِن عَبيدِ اللهِ آكُلُ مِمّا يَأكُلُ العَبدُ ، وأقعُدُ كَما يَقعُدُ العَبدُ .[٤٧٩٥]

4295. **Imām ʿAlī (AS)** was proceeding towards Syria, when the peasants of al-Anbār upon seeing him, dismounted from their mounts and started running towards him. He enquired, 'What is this you are doing?' to which they replied, 'This is the way we respect our leaders.' So he said, 'By Allah, this does not benefit your leaders in any way, whilst you are belabouring yourself in this world and earning misery for yourselves in the Hereafter. How wasteful is the labour in whose wake lies chastisement, and how profitable the composure which brings safety from the Fire!'[4839]

٤٢٩٥ . الإمامُ عليّ ﵇ ـ لدهاقين الأنبار لمّا ترجّلوا لَهُ وَاشتَدُّوا بَينَ يَدَيهِ عند مسيره إلى الشام ـ : ما هٰذا الّذي صَنَعتُموهُ ؟ فَقالوا : خُلقٌ مِنّا نُعَظِّمُ بِهِ اُمَراءَنا ، فقالَ : وَاللهِ ما يَنتَفِعُ بِهٰذا اُمَراؤكُم ! وإنَّكُم لَتَشُقُّونَ عَلى أنفُسِكُم في دُنياكُم ، وتَشقَونَ بِهِ في آخِرَتِكُم ، وما أخسَرَ المَشَقَّةَ وَراءَها العِقابُ ، وأربَحَ الدَّعَةَ مَعَها الأمانُ مِنَ النّارِ ![٤٧٩٦]

1311. The Extent of Veneration Recommended

١٣١١ ـ ما يَنبَغي مِنَ التَّعظيمِ

"That, and whoever venerates the sacraments of Allah – indeed that arises from the godwariness in the hearts."[4840]

﴿ذٰلِكَ وَمَنْ يُعَظِّمْ شَعائِرَ اللهِ فَإنَّها مِنْ تَقْوَى الْقُلُوبِ﴾ .[٤٧٩٧]

"That, and whoever venerates the sacraments of Allah, that is better for him with his Lord. You are permitted [animals of] grazing livestock except for what will be recited to you. So avoid the abomination of idols, and avoid false speech."[4841]

﴿ذٰلِكَ وَمَنْ يُعَظِّمْ حُرُماتِ اللهِ فَهُوَ خَيْرٌ لَهُ عِنْدَ رَبِّهِ وَأُحِلَّتْ لَكُمُ الْأَنْعامُ إلَّا ما يُتْلىٰ عَلَيْكُمْ فَاجْتَنِبُوا الرِّجْسَ مِنَ الْأَوْثانِ وَاجْتَنِبُوا قَوْلَ الزُّورِ﴾ .[٤٧٩٨]

4296. **The Prophet (SAWA) said,** 'Verily venerating Allah's Exaltedness involves honouring the old, the bearer of the Qur'an and the just Imām.'[4842]

٤٢٩٦ . رسولُ اللهِ ﷺ : إنَّ مِن تَعظيمِ جَلالِ اللهِ عَزَّوجلَّ كَرامَةَ ذي الشَّيبَةِ ، وحامِلِ القُرآنِ ، والإمامِ العادِلِ .[٤٧٩٩]

4297. **Imām al-Ṣādiq (AS)** when asked about standing in veneration of someone, replied, 'It is an abominable act, except when standing for a man of religion.'[4843]

٤٢٩٧ . الإمامُ الصّادقُ ﷺ ـ لَمّا سُئلَ عَنِ القِيامِ تَعظيماً لِلرَّجُلِ ـ: مَكروهٌ إلّا لِرَجُلٍ في الدِّينِ.[٤٨٠٠]

4298. **Imām al-Kāẓim (AS) said,** 'Venerate the scholar for his knowledge and abandon argumentation with him. Depreciate the ignorant man for his ignorance but do not drive him away. Rather draw him near and teach him.'[4844]

٤٢٩٨ . الإمامُ الكاظمُ ﷺ : عَظِّمِ العالِمَ لِعِلمِهِ ودَعْ مُنازَعتَهُ، وصَغِّرِ الجاهِلَ لِجَهلِهِ ولا تَطرُدْهُ، ولٰكِن قَرِّبْهُ وعَلِّمْهُ.[٤٨٠١]

Shahīd al-Awwal (may Allah sanctify his soul) wrote in his *al-Qawā'id*, 'The veneration of a believer is allowed according to what is current amongst the norms of the time, even though the practice has not been handed down from our forefathers but because of the general laws indicating to it. Allah, most High, says, *"That, and whoever venerates the sacraments of Allah – indeed that arises from the godwariness in the hearts"*, and He, most High, says, *"That, and whoever venerates the sacraments of Allah, that is better for him with his Lord."*, and the Prophet (SAWA) said, 'Do not display hatred towards each other, nor be jealous of each other, nor oppose each other, nor break off relations with each other, but rather be brothers as servants of Allah.' Based on this, standing and veneration through curtsying and the like is allowed, and may even be obligatory if abandonment of it will lead to mutual hatred and breaking of relations or to the insult of a believer. It is authenticated that the Prophet (SAWA) stood up for Fāṭima (AS) and for Ja'far [may Allah be pleased with him] when he arrived from Abyssinia, and he said to the *Anṣār*, 'Stand up for your leader.' It has been reported that he (SAWA) stood up for 'Ikrima b. Abī Jahl when he arrived from Yemen, gladdened by his arrival.'

بيان :

قالَ الشهيدُ قدّس الله روحه في قواعده: يجوز تعظيم المؤمن بما جرت به عادة الزمان وإن لم يكن منقولاً عن السَّلف؛ لدلالة العُمومات عليه، قال تعالىٰ: ﴿ذٰلكَ ومَنْ يُعَظِّمْ شَعائرَ اللهِ فإنَّها مِن تَقوَى القُلوبِ﴾ وقالَ تعالىٰ: ﴿ ذٰلكَ ومَن يُعَظِّمْ حُرُماتِ اللهِ فهُوَ خَيرٌ لَهُ عِندَ رَبِّه﴾ ولقول النبيّ ﷺ : لاتَباغَضوا ولا تَحاسَدوا ولا تَدابَروا ولا تَقاطَعوا وكونوا عِبادَ اللهِ إخواناً . فعلىٰ هذا يجوز القيام والتعظيم بانحناءٍ وشبهه، وربّما وجب إذا أدّىٰ تركه إلَى التباغض والتقاطع أو إهانة المؤمن. وقد صحّ أنَّ النبيَّ ﷺ قام إلىٰ فاطِمَةَ ﷺ وإلىٰ جَعفرٍ ﷺ لَمّا قَدِمَ مِن الحَبشَةِ، وقال للأنصار: قُوموا إلىٰ سَيِّدِكُم. ونُقِل أنَّهُ ﷺ قامَ لِعِكرِمَةَ بنِ أبي جَهلٍ لَمّا قَدِم مِنَ اليَمنِ فَرَحاً بِقُدومِه.

283

SELF-RESTRAINT

العِفَّة

1312. Enjoinment of Self-Restraint

١٣١٢ـ الحَثُّ عَلَى العَفافِ

"Those who cannot afford marriage should be continent until Allah enriches them out of His grace."[4845]

﴿وَلْيَسْتَعْفِفِ الَّذِينَ لا يَجِدُونَ نِكاحاً حَتَّى يُغْنِيَهُمُ اللهُ مِنْ فَضْلِهِ﴾.٤٨٠٢

"The unaware suppose them to be well-off because of their reserve."[4846]

﴿يَحْسَبُهُمُ الْجاهِلُ أَغْنِياءَ مِنَ التَّعَفُّفِ﴾.٤٨٠٣

4299. **The Prophet (SAWA) said,** 'Verily Allah, Mighty and Exalted, loves the reserved and shy and chaste person, and despises the bawdy and importunate beggar.'[4847]

٤٢٩٩. رسولُ اللهِ ﷺ : إنَّ اللهَ يُحِبُّ الحَيِيَّ المُتَعَفِّفَ ، ويُبغِضُ البَذِيَّ السّائلَ المُلحِفَ.٤٨٠٤

4300. **Imām ʿAlī (AS) said,** 'The fighter who is martyred in the way of Allah has no greater reward than the one who is able to sate himself but remains chaste. The chaste person may well become one of the angels.'[4848]

٤٣٠٠. الإمامُ عليٌّ ؑ : ما المُجاهِدُ الشَّهيدُ في سَبيلِ اللهِ بِأعظَمَ أجراً مِمَّن قَدَرَ فَعَفَّ ، لَكادَ العَفيفُ أن يَكونَ مَلَكاً مِنَ المَلائكَةِ.٤٨٠٥

4301. **Imām ʿAlī (AS) said,** 'Self-restraint is the root of all good.'[4849]

٤٣٠١. عنه ؑ : العِفَّةُ رَأسُ كُلِّ خَيرٍ.٤٨٠٦

4302. **Imām ʿAlī (AS) said,** 'Self-restraint is the best part of spiritual chivalry (*futuwwa*).'[4850]

٤٣٠٢. عنه ؑ : العِفَّةُ أفضَلُ الفُتُوَّةِ.٤٨٠٧

4303. **Imām ʿAlī (AS) said,** 'Self-restraint protects the soul from all sides and keeps it away from base things.'[4851]

٤٣٠٣. عنه ؑ : العَفافُ يَصونُ النَّفسَ ويُنَزِّهُها عَنِ الدَّنايا.٤٨٠٨

4304. **Imām ʿAlī (AS) said,** 'The *zakāt* of beauty is chastity.'[4852]

٤٣٠٤. عنه ؑ : زَكاةُ الجَمالِ العَفافُ.٤٨٠٩

4305. **Imām al-Ṣādiq (AS) said,** 'Restrain yourselves from other people's women and your own women will remain chaste.'[4853]

٤٣٠٥. الإمامُ الصّادقُ ؑ : عِفّوا عَن نِساءِ النّاسِ تَعِفَّ نِساؤكُم.٤٨١٠

1313. Enjoinment of Restraining the Stomach and the Private Parts

١٣١٣ـ الحَثُّ عَلىٰ عِفَّةِ البَطنِ وَالفَرجِ

4306. **The Prophet (SAWA) said,** 'Most of my community who will enter the Fire will be as a result of two cavities: the stomach and the private parts.'[4854]

٤٣٠٦. رسولُ اللهِ ﷺ: أكثَرُ ما تَلِجُ بِهِ اُمَّتيَ النّارَ الأجوَفانِ: البَطنُ والفَرجُ.[٤٨١١]

4307. **The Prophet (SAWA) said,** 'Verily Moses (AS) engaged himself for eight or ten years in restraining his private parts and his stomach.'[4855]

٤٣٠٧. عنه ﷺ: إنَّ موسىٰ ـ صلّى اللهُ عليهِ و سَلَّم ـ آجَرَ نفسَهُ ثَمانِيَ سِنينَ، أو عَشراً، عَلىٰ عِفَّةِ فَرجِهِ وطَعامِ بَطنِهِ.[٤٨١٢]

4308. **Imām al-Bāqir (AS) said,** 'Allah can be worshipped with no act better than restraint of the stomach and the private parts.'[4856]

٤٣٠٨. الإمامُ الباقرُ ؑ: ما عُبِدَ اللهُ بِشَيءٍ أفضَلَ مِن عِفَّةِ بَطنٍ وفَرجٍ.[٤٨١٣]

1314. The Root of Self-Restraint

١٣١٤ـ أصلُ العَفافِ

4309. **Imām ʿAlī (AS) said,** 'The root of self-restraint is contentment, and its fruit is fewer sorrows.'[4857]

٤٣٠٩. الإمامُ عليٌّ ؑ: أصلُ العَفافِ القَناعَةُ، وثَمَرَتُها قِلَّةُ الأحزانِ.[٤٨١٤]

4310. **Imām ʿAlī (AS) said,** 'Satisfaction with one's lot leads to self-restraint.'[4858]

٤٣١٠. عنه ؑ: الرِّضا بِالكَفافِ يُؤَدّي إلَى العَفافِ.[٤٨١٥]

4311. **Imām ʿAlī (AS) said,** 'The worth of a man is proportionate to his ambition ... and his chastity is in proportion with his sense of self-worth.'[4859]

٤٣١١. عنه ؑ: قَدرُ الرَّجُلِ عَلىٰ قَدرِ هِمَّتِهِ... وعِفَّتُهُ عَلىٰ قَدرِ غَيرَتِهِ.[٤٨١٦]

4312. **Imām ʿAlī (AS) said,** 'He who uses his intellect restrains himself.'[4860]

٤٣١٢. عنه ؑ: مَن عَقَلَ عَفَّ.[٤٨١٧]

1315. The Fruit of Self-Restraint

١٣١٥ـ ثَمَرَةُ العِفَّةِ

4313. **The Prophet (SAWA) said,** 'As for self-restraint, from it branches out satisfaction, resignation, good fortune, comfort, a sense of consideration, humbleness, a sense of remembrance, contemplation, magnanimity and generosity. These are the many ramifications for the

٤٣١٣. رسولُ اللهِ ﷺ: أمّا العَفافُ: فَيَتَشَعَّبُ مِنهُ الرِّضا، والاستِكانَةُ، والحَظُّ، والرّاحَةُ، والتَّفَقُّدُ، والخُشوعُ، والتَّذَكُّرُ، والتَّفَكُّرُ، والجُودُ،

intelligent man who practices self-restraint and is satisfied with Allah and with his share.'[4861]

والسَّخاءُ، فهذا ما يَتَشَعَّبُ لِلعاقِلِ بِعَفافِهِ رِضىً بِاللهِ وبِقِسمِهِ.[٤٨١٨]

4314. **Imām ʿAlī (AS) said,** 'Self-restraint weakens carnal desire.'[4862]

٤٣١٤. الإمامُ عليٌّ عليه السلام: العِفَّةُ تُضعِفُ الشَّهوَةَ.[٤٨١٩]

4315. **Imām ʿAlī (AS) said,** 'The fruit of self-restraint is contentment.'[4863]

٤٣١٥. عنه عليه السلام: ثَمَرَةُ العِفَّةِ القَناعَةُ.[٤٨٢٠]

4316. **Imām ʿAlī (AS) said,** 'The fruit of self-restraint is preservation [of oneself].'[4864]

٤٣١٦. عنه عليه السلام: ثَمَرَةُ العِفَّةِ الصِّيانَةُ.[٤٨٢١]

4317. **Imām ʿAlī (AS) said,** 'He who practices self-restraint, his burden decreases and his worth in Allah's eyes increases.'[4865]

٤٣١٧. عنه عليه السلام: مَن عَفَّ خَفَّ وِزرُهُ، وعَظُمَ عِندَ اللهِ قَدرُهُ.[٤٨٢٢]

4318. **Imām ʿAlī (AS) said,** 'Actions are purified through practice of self-restraint.'[4866]

٤٣١٨. عنه عليه السلام: بِالعَفافِ تَزكو الأعمالُ.[٤٨٢٣]

284

PARDON

العَفوُ

1316. The Virtue of Pardon

١٣١٦ـ فَضيلَةُ العَفوِ

"The requital of evil is an evil like it. So whoever pardons and conciliates, his reward lies with Allah. Indeed He does not like the wrongdoers."[4867]

﴿وَجَزاءُ سَيِّئَةٍ سَيِّئَةٌ مِثْلُها فَمَنْ عَفا وَأَصْلَحَ فَأَجْرُهُ عَلَى اللهِ إِنَّهُ لا يُحِبُّ الظّالِمينَ﴾.[٤٨٢٤]

"... those who spend in ease and adversity, and suppress their anger, and pardon [the faults of] the people, and Allah loves the virtuous."[4868]

﴿الَّذينَ يُنفِقُونَ فِي السَّرّاءِ وَالضَّرّاءِ وَالْكاظِمِينَ الْغَيْظَ وَالْعافِينَ عَنِ النّاسِ وَاللهُ يُحِبُّ الْمُحْسِنِينَ﴾.[٤٨٢٥]

4319. **The Prophet (SAWA) said,** 'If you are faced by anger, avert it through pardon, for verily a caller will call out on the Day of Resurrection: 'Whoever has a claim for a reward from Allah should stand up', and none will stand except the pardoners. Have you not heard the verse of Allah, most High, *"So whoever pardons and conciliates, his reward lies with Allah"*?!'[4869]

٤٣١٩. رسولُ اللهِ صلى الله عليه وآله: إذا عَنَّت لَكُم غَضبَةٌ فَادرَؤوها بِالعَفوِ؛ إنَّهُ يُنادي مُنادٍ يَومَ القِيامَةِ: مَن كانَ لَهُ عَلَى اللهِ أجرٌ فَليَقُم، فَلا يَقومُ إلّا العافونَ، ألَم تَسمَعوا قَولَهُ تَعالى: ﴿فَمَن عَفا وأصلَحَ فَأجرُهُ عَلَى اللهِ﴾؟![٤٨٢٦]

4320. **The Prophet (SAWA) said,** 'Verily Allah is all-pardoning and loves pardon.'[4870]

٤٣٢٠ . عنه ﷺ : إنَّ اللهَ عَفُوٌّ يُحِبُّ العَفوَ.[٤٨٢٧]

4321. **The Prophet (SAWA) said,** 'Pardoning is incumbent upon you, for verily pardoning [others] only increases the servant's honour, so pardon each other's faults and Allah will grant you honour.'[4871]

٤٣٢١ . عنه ﷺ : عَلَيكُم بِالعَفوِ ؛ فَإنَّ العَفوَ لا يَزيدُ العَبدَ إلّا عِزّاً فَتَعافَوا يُعِزَّكُمُ اللهُ.[٤٨٢٨]

4322. **The Prophet (SAWA) said,** 'He who pardons much is given an increase in his lifespan.'[4872]

٤٣٢٢ . عنه ﷺ : مَن كَثُرَ عَفوُهُ مُدَّ في عُمرِهِ.[٤٨٢٩]

4323. **The Prophet (SAWA) said,** 'Excuse the lapses of those who make mistakes frequently and Allah will protect you against misfortunes.'[4873]

٤٣٢٣ . عنه ﷺ : تَجاوَزوا عَن عَثَراتِ الخاطِئينَ يَقيكُمُ اللهُ بِذٰلكَ سُوءَ الأقدارِ.[٤٨٣٠]

4324. **Imām al-Bāqir (AS) said,** 'Regret for having pardoned someone is better and easier to bear than regret for having punished them.'[4874]

٤٣٢٤ . الإمامُ الباقرُ عليه السلام : النَّدامَةُ عَلَى العَفوِ أفضَلُ وأيسَرُ مِنَ النَّدامَةِ عَلَى العُقوبَةِ.[٤٨٣١]

4325. **Imām al-Ṣādiq (AS) said,** 'Three of the noble characteristics in this world and in the Hereafter are: to pardon one who has wronged you, to reconcile with one who has cut you off, and to be clement with one who has been rash towards you.'[4875]

٤٣٢٥ . الإمامُ الصّادقُ عليه السلام : ثَلاثٌ مِن مَكارِمِ الدّنيا والآخِرَةِ: تَعفو عَمَّن ظَلَمَكَ، وتَصِلُ مَن قَطَعَكَ، وتَحلِمُ إذا جُهِلَ عَلَيكَ.[٤٨٣٢]

1317. Enjoinment of Graceful Condonance

١٣١٧ ـ الحَثُّ عَلَى الصَّفحِ الجَميلِ

"We did not create the heaven and the earth and whatever is between them except with the Truth, and indeed the hour is bound to come. So condone with a graceful condonance."[4876]

﴿وَما خَلَقْنا السَّماواتِ وَالْأَرْضَ وَما بَيْنَهُما إلَّا بِالْحَقِّ وَإنَّ السَّاعَةَ لَآتِيَةٌ فَاصْفَحِ الصَّفْحَ الْجَمِيلَ﴾.[٤٨٣٣]

4326. **Imām ʿAlī (AS) said,** 'He who rebukes [someone for] a sin has not pardoned it.'[4877]

٤٣٢٦ . الإمامُ عليٌّ عليه السلام : ما عَفا عَنِ الذَّنبِ مَن قَرَّعَ بِهِ.[٤٨٣٤]

4327. **Imām al-Riḍā (AS),** with regards to Allah's verse in the Qur'an: *"So condone with a graceful condonance"*, said, 'It is to pardon without punishing, censuring or scolding.'[4878]

٤٣٢٧ . الإمامُ الرِّضا عليه السلام ـ في قَولِه تَعالىٰ: ﴿فَاصْفَحِ الصَّفْحَ الْجَمِيلَ﴾ ـ: عَفوٌ مِن غَيرِ عُقوبَةٍ، ولا تَعنيفٍ، ولا عَتبٍ.[٤٨٣٥]

1318. Enjoinment of Pardon in Spite of One's Power (to Punish)

١٣١٨ـ الحَثُّ عَلَى العَفوِ عِندَ القُدرَةِ

4328. **The Prophet (SAWA) said,** 'He who pardons when having the power to punish, Allah will pardon him on the Day of great difficulty [i.e. the Day of Resurrection].'[4879]

٤٣٢٨. رسولُ اللهِ ﷺ: مَن عَفا عِندَ القُدرَةِ عَفا اللهُ عَنهُ يومَ العُسرَةِ.[٤٨٣٦]

4329. **Imām ʿAlī (AS) said,** 'When you are empowered to vanquish your enemy, let your pardon of him act as thanks for having been given power over him.'[4880]

٤٣٢٩. الإمامُ عليٌّ ﷺ: إذا قَدَرتَ عَلىٰ عَدُوِّكَ فَاجعَلِ العَفوَ عَنهُ شُكراً لِلقُدرَةِ عَلَيهِ.[٤٨٣٧]

4330. **Imām ʿAlī (AS) said,** 'Pardon is the *zakāt* of triumph.'[4881]

٤٣٣٠. عنه ﷺ: العَفوُ زَكاةُ الظَّفَرِ.[٤٨٣٨]

4331. **Imām al-Ḥusayn (AS) said,** 'Verily the most forgiving of people is he who pardons when having the power to punish.'[4882]

٤٣٣١. الإمامُ الحسينُ ﷺ: إنَّ أعفَى النّاسِ مَن عَفا عِندَ قُدرَتِه.[٤٨٣٩]

(See also: RECOMPENSE: section 1608)

(أنظر: المكافأة: باب ١٦٠٨)

1319. Pardon and Improvement of Hearts

١٣١٩ـ العَفوُ وإستِصلاحُ القُلوبِ

4332. **The Prophet (SAWA) said** to a man who came to him complaining about his servants, 'Pardon their faults and through it their hearts will improve.' So he (SAWA) replied, 'O Prophet of Allah, verily they vary in their bad behaviour', so he replied, 'Pardon them', so he did.'[4883]

٤٣٣٢. رسولُ اللهِ ﷺ ـ لِرَجُلٍ شكا إليه خَدَمَه ـ: أعفُ عَنهُم تَستَصلِحْ بِهِ قُلوبَهُم، فَقالَ: يا رَسولَ اللهِ، إنَّهُم يَتَفاوَتونَ في سُوءِ الأدَبِ، فَقالَ: أعفُ عَنهُم، فَفَعَلَ.[٤٨٤٠]

4333. **Imām ʿAlī (AS)** in his will to his son al-Ḥasan (AS), said, 'If any of them deserves punishment for a sin, then censure gracefully, for verily censure accompanied by pardon is more severe [i.e. more effective] than striking for a person with intellect.'[4884]

٤٣٣٣. الإمامُ عليٌّ ﷺ ـ في وَصِيَّتِهِ لِابنِهِ الحَسَنِ ﷺ ـ: إذا استَحَقَّ أحَدٌ مِنهُم ذَنباً فأحسِنِ العَذلَ؛ فإنَّ العَذلَ مَعَ العَفوِ أشَدُّ مِنَ الضَّربِ لِمَن كانَ لَهُ عَقلٌ.[٤٨٤١]

(See also: ENMITY: section 1238)

(أنظر: العداوة: باب ١٢٣٨)

1320. That which Must not be Pardoned

١٣٢٠ـ ما لا يَنبَغي مِنَ العَفوِ

4334. **Imām ʿAlī (AS) said,** 'Pardon spoils a sinful man just as much as it can reform a decent man.'[4885]

٤٣٣٤. الإمامُ عليٌّ ﷺ: العَفوُ يُفسِدُ مِنَ اللَّئيمِ بِقَدرِ إصلاحِهِ مِنَ الكَريمِ.[٤٨٤٢]

4335. **Imām ʿAlī (AS) said,** 'Reward the good deed and condone the misdeed as long as it is not a breach of religion or does not weaken the authority of Islam.'[4886]

٤٣٣٥. عنه ﷺ: جازِ بِالحَسَنَةِ وتَجاوَزْ عَنِ السَّيِّئَةِ ما لَم يَكُن ثَلماً فِي الدِّينِ أو وَهناً في سُلطانِ الإسلامِ.[٤٨٤٣]

1321. Allah's Pardon

١٣٢١ـ عَفوُ اللهِ

"Indeed Allah is all-excusing, all-forgiving."[4887]

﴿إنَّ اللهَ كانَ عَفُوّاً غَفُوراً﴾.[٤٨٤٤]

4336. **The Prophet (SAWA),** when ʿĀ'isha asked him about what to supplicate on the grand Night of Ordainment (*laylat al-qadr*), replied, 'You should say: O Allah verily you are all-pardoning and You love to pardon, so pardon me.'[4888]

٤٣٣٦. رسولُ اللهِ ﷺ ـ لَمّا سَأَلَتهُ عائشَةُ عَنِ الدُّعاءِ في لَيلَةِ القَدرِ ـ: تَقولينَ: اللّهُمَّ إنَّكَ عَفُوٌّ تُحِبُّ العَفوَ، فَاعفُ عَنّي.[٤٨٤٥]

4337. It is narrated in *Tanbīh al-Khawāṭir* that a Bedouin once asked the Prophet, 'O Prophet of Allah, who will hold creation to account on the Day of Resurrection?' to which he replied, 'Allah, Mighty and Exalted.' He said, 'By the Lord of the Ka'ba, we will be saved indeed!' The Prophet asked, 'And how is that O Bedouin friend?' He replied, 'Because the generous one pardons when he has the power.'[4889]

٤٣٣٧. تنبيه الخواطر: قالَ أعرابيٌّ: يا رَسولَ اللهِ، مَن يُحاسِبُ الخَلقَ يَومَ القِيامَةِ؟ قالَ: اللهُ عزَّ وجلَّ، قالَ: نَجَونا ورَبِّ الكَعبَةِ! قالَ: وكَيفَ ذاكَ يا أعرابِيُّ؟! قالَ: لِأنَّ الكَريمَ إذا قَدَرَ عَفا.[٤٨٤٦]

4338. **Imām ʿAlī (AS) said,** 'Verily Allah, most High, will certainly interrogate you, O community of His servants, about your actions, be they small or big, and be they open or secret. If He punishes you, then it because you have wronged yourselves, and if He pardons, then it is because He is too generous.'[4890]

٤٣٣٨. الإمامُ عليٌّ ﷺ: إنَّ اللهَ تَعالىٰ يُسائلُكُم مَعشَرَ عِبادِهِ عَنِ الصَّغيرَةِ مِن أعمالِكُم وَالكَبيرَةِ، والظّاهِرَةِ والمَستورَةِ، فإن يُعَذِّبْ فأنتُم أظلَمُ، وإن يَعفُ فهُوَ أكرَمُ.[٤٨٤٧]

4339. **Imām ʿAlī (AS) said** in his intimate supplication, 'My Lord I think about Your pardon and my mistakes seem insignificant to me, then I remember the awesomeness of Your

٤٣٣٩. عنه ﷺ ـ في المُناجاةِ ـ: إلٰهي أُفَكِّرُ في عَفوِكَ فتَهونُ عَلَيَّ خَطيئَتي، ثُمَّ أذكُرُ

chastisement and my tribulation seems great indeed.'[4891]

العَظيمَ مِن أخذِكَ فتَعظُمُ عَلَيّ بَلِيَّتي.[٤٨٤٨]

4340. **Imām ʿAlī (AS) said,** 'O Allah expose me to Your pardon but do not expose me to Your justice.'[4892]

٤٣٤٠. عنه ﷺ: اَللّٰهُمَّ احمِلني عَلىٰ عَفوِكَ ولا تَحمِلْني عَلىٰ عَدلِكَ.[٤٨٤٩]

4341. **Imām ʿAlī (AS) said,** 'He who keeps himself aloof from Allah's prohibitions is quickly embraced by Allah's pardon.'[4893]

٤٣٤١. عنه ﷺ: مَن تَنَزَّهَ عَن حُرُماتِ اللهِ سارَعَ إلَيهِ عَفوُ اللهِ.[٤٨٥٠]

4342. **Imām ʿAlī (AS) said,** 'But Allah tries His servants with various tribulations, renders them to worship Him through struggles, tests them with various types of distresses, all in order to extract pride out from their hearts, and to settle humbleness in their souls, and in order to make all these open doors to His grace an easy means to His pardon.'[4894]

٤٣٤٢. عنه ﷺ: ولٰكِنَّ اللهَ يَختَبِرُ عِبادَهُ بِأنواعِ الشَّدائدِ، ويَتَعَبَّدُهُم بِأنواعِ المَجاهِدِ، ويَبتَليهِم بِضُروبِ المَكارِهِ؛ إخراجاً لِلتَّكَبُّرِ مِن قُلوبِهِم، وإسكاناً لِلتَّذَلُّلِ في نُفوسِهِم، ولِيَجعَلَ ذٰلكَ أبواباً فُتُحاً إلىٰ فَضلِهِ، وأسباباً ذُلُلاً لِعَفوِهِ.[٤٨٥١]

4343. **Imām al-Ṣādiq (AS)** used to say, 'O Allah, verily Your worthiness of pardoning is more than my worthiness of punishment.'[4895]

٤٣٤٣. الإمامُ الصّادقُ ﷺ ـ كانَ يَقولُ ـ: اللّٰهُمَّ إنَّكَ بِما أنتَ لَهُ أهلٌ مِنَ العَفوِ، أولىٰ مِنّي بِما أنا لَهُ أهلٌ مِنَ العُقوبَةِ.[٤٨٥٢]

(See also: MERCY: section 808)

(أنظر) الرّحمة: باب ٨٠٨.

285

VITALITY

العافِيَةُ

1322. The Value of Vitality

١٣٢٢ ـ قَيمة العافيَة

4344. **Imām ʿAlī (AS) said,** 'Vitality is the most beneficial of bounties.'[4896]

٤٣٤٤. الإمامُ عليٌّ ﷺ: العافِيَةُ أهنىٰ النِّعَمِ.[٤٨٥٣]

4345. **Imām ʿAlī (AS) said,** 'There is no garment more beautiful than vitality.'[4897]

٤٣٤٥. عنه ﷺ: لا لِباسَ أجمَلُ مِنَ العافِيَةِ.[٤٨٥٤]

4346. **Imām ʿAlī (AS) said,** The pleasure of living is to be found through vitality.'[4898]

٤٣٤٦. عنه ﷺ: بِالعافِيَةِ تُوجَدُ لَذَّةُ الحَياةِ.[٤٨٥٥]

4347. **Imām al-Ṣādiq (AS) said,** 'Vitality is a subtle bounty – when present it is forgotten, and when lost it is remembered.'[4899]

٤٣٤٧. الإمامُ الصّادقُ ؑ: العافِيَةُ نِعمَةٌ خَفِيَّةٌ، إذا وُجِدَت نُسِيَت، وإذا فُقِدَت ذُكِرَت.٤٨٥٦

1323. That which Engenders Vitality

١٣٢٣ ـ ما يورِثُ العافِيَةَ

4348. **The Prophet (SAWA) said,** 'He who sends peace and blessings on me once, Allah opens for him a door of vitality.'[4900]

٤٣٤٨. رسولُ اللهِ ﷺ: مَن صَلّىٰ عَلَيَّ مَرَّةً فَتَحَ اللهُ عَلَيهِ باباً مِنَ العافِيَةِ.٤٨٥٧

4349. **Imām ʿAlī (AS) said,** 'Vitality has ten parts, nine of which lie in silence except for the remembrance of Allah, and one part of which lies in abandoning the company of fools.'[4901]

٤٣٤٩. الإمامُ عليٌّ ؑ: العافِيَةُ عَشرَةُ أجزاءٍ، تِسعَةٌ مِنها في الصَّمتِ إلّا بِذِكرِ اللهِ، وواحِدٌ في تَركِ مُجالَسَةِ السُّفَهاءِ.٤٨٥٨

4350. **Imām al-Ṣādiq (AS) said,** 'He who would like extensive vitality should have piety in Allah.'[4902]

٤٣٥٠. الإمامُ الصّادقُ ؑ: مَن سَرَّهُ طولُ العافِيَةِ فَليَتَّقِ اللهَ.٤٨٥٩

1324. Enjoinment of Seeking Vitality from Allah

١٣٢٤ ـ الحَثُّ عَلىٰ طَلَبِ العافِيَةِ مِنَ اللهِ

4351. **The Prophet (SAWA),** when he heard a man ask Allah for patience, said, 'You have asked Allah to be tried, so now ask Him for the solution.'[4903]

٤٣٥١. رسولُ اللهِ ﷺ ـ لَمّا سَمِعَ رَجُلاً يَسأَلُ اللهَ الصَّبرَ ـ: سَأَلتَ اللهَ البَلاءَ، فَاسأَلهُ المُعافاةَ.٤٨٦٠

4352. **The Prophet (SAWA) said,** 'Allah is not asked anything more beloved to Him than to be asked for vitality.'[4904]

٤٣٥٢. عنه ﷺ: ما سُئِلَ اللهُ شَيئاً أحَبَّ إلَيهِ مِن أن يُسأَلَ العافِيَةَ.٤٨٦١

4353. **The Prophet (SAWA) said,** 'Ask Allah for vitality, for verily after conviction no one is given anything better than vitality.'[4905]

٤٣٥٣. عنه ﷺ: سَلُوا اللهَ المُعافاةَ، فَإِنَّهُ لَم يُؤتَ أحَدٌ بَعدَ اليَقينِ خَيراً مِنَ المُعافاةِ.٤٨٦٢

4354. *al-Daʿawāt*: 'It is narrated that the Prophet (SAWA) visited a sick man and asked him about his health.' The man said 'You led us in the evening prayer and recited the chapter the Catastrophe [Qur'an, 101], and I said, 'O Allah ! If

٤٣٥٤. الدعوات: رُوِيَ أنَّ النَّبِيَّ ﷺ دَخَلَ عَلىٰ مَريضٍ، قالَ: ما شَأنُكَ؟ قالَ: صَلَّيتَ بِنا صَلاةَ

I have committed a sin for which you will want to punish me in the Hereafter, hasten it in this very world, and now I am in such as you see me.' He (SAWA) said: 'Indeed, it was bad what you said. You should have said, 'Our Lord, grant us good in this world and good in the Hereafter and protect us from the punishment of the Fire!' and he prayed for him until he recovered.'[4906]

المَغرِبِ فقرأتَ القارِعَةَ، فقلتُ: اللّهمَّ إن كانَ لي عندكَ ذَنبٌ تريدُ أن تُعذِّبني بِهِ في الآخِرَةِ فَعَجِّلْ ذلكَ في الدُّنيا؛ فَصِرتُ كَما ترى! فقال ﷺ: بِئسَما قُلتَ، ألا قُلتَ: رَبَّنا آتِنا في الدّنيا حَسَنَةً وفي الآخِرَةِ حَسَنَةً وقِنا عَذابَ النّارِ؟! فَدَعا لَهُ حَتّى أفاقَ.[٤٨٦٣]

4355. **Imām Zayn al-ʿĀbidīn (AS)** bumped into the shoulder of a man circumambulating the *Kaʿba* saying, 'O Allah verily I ask You for patience', upon which the Imām said, 'You have asked to be tried! Say instead: O Allah verily I ask You for vitality, and for the ability to thank You for my vitality.'[4907]

٤٣٥٥. الإمامُ زينُ العابدينَ عليه‌السلام ـ لَمّا ضَرَبَ عَلى كَتِفِ رَجُلٍ يَطوفُ بِالكَعبَةِ ويَقولُ: اللّهُمَّ إنّي أسأَلُكَ الصَّبرَ ـ: سَألتَ البَلاءَ! قُلِ: اللّهُمَّ إنّي أسأَلُكَ العافِيَةَ، والشُّكرَ عَلَى العافِيَةِ.[٤٨٦٤]

1325. Supplications to Ask for Vitality

١٣٢٥ ـ دُعاءٌ في طَلَبِ العافِيَةِ

4356. **Imām al-Kāẓim (AS) said,** 'O Allah verily I ask You for vitality, and I ask You for gracious vitality, and I ask You for the ability to thank You for vitality, and I ask You for thankfulness for having granted me the ability to thank You for vitality.'[4908]

٤٣٥٦. الإمامُ الكاظمُ عليه‌السلام: اللّهُمَّ إنّي أسألُكَ العافِيَةَ، وأسألُكَ جَميلَ العافِيَةِ، وأسألُكَ شُكرَ العافِيَةِ، وأسألُكَ شُكرَ شُكرِ العافِيَةِ.[٤٨٦٥]

1326. Allah's Close Servants

١٣٢٦ ـ الضَّنائِنُ

4357. **Imām al-Bāqir (AS) said,** 'Verily Allah, Mighty and Exalted, has certain protégés whom He tenaciously guards against tribulation, such that He gives them *life* through vitality, sustains them with vitality, causes them to die in vitality, resurrects them again in vitality, and makes them dwell in Paradise in vitality.'[4909]

٤٣٥٧. الإمامُ الباقرُ عليه‌السلام: إنَّ للهِ عزَّ وجلَّ ضَنائِنَ يَضُنُّ بِهِم عَنِ البَلاءِ، فَيُحييهِم في عافِيَةٍ، ويَرزُقُهُم في عافِيَةٍ، ويُميتُهُم في عافِيَةٍ، ويَبعَثُهُم في عافِيَةٍ، ويُسكِنُهُمُ الجَنَّةَ في عافِيَةٍ.[٤٨٦٦]

286

THE INTELLECT[4910] العَقلُ

1327. The Value of Intellect ١٣٢٧ ـ قِيمَةُ العَقلِ

"He gives wisdom to whomever He wishes, and He who is given wisdom, is certainly given an abundant good. But none takes admonition except those who possess intellect."[4911]

﴿يُؤْتِي الْحِكْمَةَ مَنْ يَشاءُ وَمَنْ يُؤْتَ الْحِكْمَةَ فَقَدْ أُوتِيَ خَيْراً كَثِيراً وَما يَذَّكَّرُ إِلَّا أُولُوا الْأَلْبابِ﴾.[٤٨٦٧]

"And they will say, 'Had we listened or applied reason, we would not have been among the inmates of the Blaze.'"[4912]

﴿وَقالُوا لَوْ كُنّا نَسْمَعُ أَوْ نَعْقِلُ ما كُنّا فِي أَصْحابِ السَّعِيرِ﴾.[٤٨٦٨]

4358. **The Prophet (SAWA) said,** 'The very basis of man is his intellect, and the man devoid of intellect has no religion.'[4913]

٤٣٥٨. رسولُ اللهِ ﷺ: قِوامُ المَرءِ عَقلُهُ، ولا دِينَ لِمَن لا عَقلَ لَهُ.[٤٨٦٩]

4359. **Imām ʿAlī (AS) said,** 'Allah has only assigned man with an intellect so that it may one day deliver him.'[4914]

٤٣٥٩. الإمامُ عليٌّ ﷺ: ما استَودَعَ اللهُ امرأً عقلاً إلّا استَنقَذَهُ بِهِ يوماً ما.[٤٨٧٠]

4360. **Imām ʿAlī (AS) said,** 'The intellect is the strongest foundation.'[4915]

٤٣٦٠. عنه ﷺ: العَقلُ أقوىٰ أساسٍ.[٤٨٧١]

4361. **Imām ʿAlī (AS) said,** 'The intellect is immune from wrong and commands good-doing.'[4916]

٤٣٦١. عنه ﷺ: العَقلُ مُنَزَّهٌ عَنِ المُنكَرِ آمِرٌ بِالمَعروفِ.[٤٨٧٢]

4362. **Imām ʿAlī (AS) said,** 'The intellect sets right all matters.'[4917]

٤٣٦٢. عنه ﷺ: العَقلُ مُصلِحُ كُلِّ أمرٍ.[٤٨٧٣]

4363. **Imām ʿAlī (AS) said,** 'The intellect is a ladder upwards towards the *'Illiyyūn* [the loftiest heavens].'[4918]

٤٣٦٣. عنه ﷺ: العَقلُ رُقِيٌّ إلى عِلِّيِّينَ.[٤٨٧٤]

4364. **Imām ʿAlī (AS) said,** 'The intellect is the messenger of the truth.'[4919]

٤٣٦٤. عنه ﷺ: العَقلُ رَسولُ الحَقِّ.[٤٨٧٥]

4365. **Imām ʿAlī (AS) said,** 'Verily the most sufficient of riches is the intellect.'[4920]

٤٣٦٥ . عنه عليه السلام : إنَّ أغنَى الغِنَى العَقلُ.[٤٨٧٦]

4366. **Imām ʿAlī (AS) said,** 'The intellect is the friend of the believer.'[4921]

٤٣٦٦ . عنه عليه السلام : العَقلُ خَليلُ المَرءِ.[٤٨٧٧]

4367. **Imām al-Bāqir (AS) said,** 'There is no affliction worse than a lack of intellect.'[4922]

٤٣٦٧ . الإمامُ الباقرُ عليه السلام : لا مُصيبَةَ كَعَدَمِ العَقلِ.[٤٨٧٨]

4368. **Imām al-Ṣādiq (AS) said,** 'Verily Allah, exalted be His praise, created the intellect, and it is the very first thing He created amongst all the spiritual beings from the right hand side of His Throne out of His Light.'[4923]

٤٣٦٨ . الإمامُ الصّادقُ عليه السلام : إنَّ اللهَ جلَّ ثَناؤهُ خَلَقَ العَقلَ، وهُوَ أوَّلُ خَلقٍ خَلَقَهُ مِنَ الرُّوحانيّينَ عَن يَمينِ العَرشِ مِن نورِهِ.[٤٨٧٩]

4369. **Imām al-Ṣādiq (AS) said,** 'Allah created the intellect out of four things: from knowledge, power, light and volition. Then He caused it to subsist through knowledge and be eternal in the divine Dominion.'[4924]

٤٣٦٩ . عنه عليه السلام : خَلَقَ اللهُ تَعالىٰ العَقلَ مِن أربَعَةِ أشياءَ: مِنَ العِلمِ، والقُدرَةِ، والنّورِ، والمَشيئَةِ بِالأمرِ، فجَعَلَهُ قائماً بِالعِلمِ، دائماً في المَلَكوتِ.[٤٨٨٠]

4370. **Imām al-Ṣādiq (AS) said,** 'There is no wealth more productive than the intellect and no poverty lower than stupidity.'[4925]

٤٣٧٠ . عنه عليه السلام : لا غِنىٰ أخصَبُ مِنَ العَقلِ، ولا فَقرَ أحَطُّ مِنَ الحُمقِ.[٤٨٨١]

4371. **Imām al-Ṣādiq (AS) said,** 'There is no wealth more profiting than the intellect.'[4926]

٤٣٧١ . عنه عليه السلام : لا مالَ أعوَدُ مِنَ العَقلِ.[٤٨٨٢]

4372. **Imām al-Ṣādiq (AS) said,** 'The intellect is the guide of the believer.'[4927]

٤٣٧٢ . عنه عليه السلام : العَقلُ دَليلُ المُؤمِنِ.[٤٨٨٣]

4373. **Imām al-Kāẓim (AS),** in his advice to Hishām b. al-Ḥakam, said, 'O Hishām, nothing has been bestowed upon the servants better than the intellect. The sleep of a man of intellect is better than the night vigil of an ignorant man. Every single prophet that Allah has sent down has been a man of intellect, whose intellect supersedes the labour of all diligent workers. The servant is not considered as having fulfilled an obligatory act from among the acts made incumbent by Allah until he understands it.'[4928]

٤٣٧٣ . الإمامُ الكاظمُ عليه السلام ـ في وَصِيَّتِهِ لِهشامِ ابنِ الحَكَمِ ـ: يا هِشامُ، ما قُسِّمَ بَينَ العِبادِ أفضَلُ مِنَ العَقلِ، نَومُ العاقِلِ أفضَلُ مِن سَهَرِ الجاهِلِ، وما بَعَثَ اللهُ نَبِيّاً إلّا عاقِلاً حَتّىٰ يَكونَ عَقلُهُ أفضَلَ مِن جَميعِ جَهدِ المُجتَهِدينَ، وما أدَّى العَبدُ فَريضَةً مِن فَرائضِ اللهِ حَتّىٰ عَقَلَ عَنهُ.[٤٨٨٤]

4374. **Imām al-Riḍā (AS) said,** 'The friend of every man is his intellect and his enemy is his ignorance.'[4929]

٤٣٧٤ . الإمامُ الرِّضا عليه‌السلام : صَديقُ كُلِّ امرِئٍ عَقلُهُ وعَدُوُّهُ جَهلُهُ.[٤٨٨٥]

1328. The Role of the Intellect in Chastisement and Reward

١٣٢٨ - دَورُ العَقلِ فِي العِقابِ وَ الثَّوابِ

4375. **The Prophet (SAWA)** asked a group of people who were praising a man, 'How is the man's intellect?' to which they replied, 'O Prophet of Allah, we are telling you about his endeavours at worship and other good acts, and you are asking us about his intellect?!' So he replied, 'Verily the stupid person suffers as a result of his stupidity worse than the licentiousness of an immoral person. The servants will rise up in rank in the Hereafter and will receive great proximity towards their Lord in proportion to their intellects.'[4930]

٤٣٧٥ . رسولُ اللهِ ﷺ - لِقَومٍ أثنَوا عَلى رَجُلٍ - : كَيفَ عَقلُ الرَّجُلِ ؟ قالوا : يا رَسولَ اللهِ ، نُخبِرُكَ عَنِ اجتِهادِهِ فِي العِبادَةِ وأصنافِ الخَيرِ ، وتَسألُنا عَن عَقلِهِ ؟! فقالَ : إنَّ الأحمَقَ يُصيبُ بِحُمقِهِ أعظَمَ مِن فُجورِ الفاجِرِ ، وإنَّما يَرتَفِعُ العِبادُ غَداً فِي الدَّرَجاتِ ويَنالونَ الزُّلفىٰ مِن رَبِّهِم عَلىٰ قَدرِ عُقولِهِم.[٤٨٨٦]

4376. **The Prophet (SAWA) said,** 'Verily all good is grasped through the intellect, and the man devoid of intellect has no religion.'[4931]

٤٣٧٦ . عنه ﷺ : إنَّما يُدرَكُ الخَيرُ كُلُّهُ بِالعَقلِ ، ولا دينَ لِمَن لا عَقلَ لَهُ.[٤٨٨٧]

4377. **Imām al-Ḥasan (AS) said,** 'Both the abodes [of the world and the Hereafter] are grasped by the intellect, and whoever is deprived of the intellect is deprived of them both.'[4932]

٤٣٧٧ . الإمامُ الحسنُ عليه‌السلام : بِالعَقلِ تُدرَكُ الدّارانِ جَميعاً ، ومَن حُرِمَ مِنَ العَقلِ[٤٨٨٨] حُرِمَهُما جَميعاً.[٤٨٨٩]

4378. **Imām al-Bāqir (AS) said,** 'When Allah created the intellect He said to it, 'Come forward' so it came forward, then commanded it, 'Go back' and it went back. Then He said to it, 'By my Honour and Exaltedness, I have not created anything better than you. It is you that I command, and you that I prohibit from things, and you that I punish and you that I reward.'[4933]

٤٣٧٨ . الإمامُ الباقرُ عليه‌السلام : لَمّا خَلَقَ اللهُ العَقلَ قالَ لَهُ : أقبِل فَأَقبَلَ ، ثُمَّ قالَ لَهُ : أدبِر فَأَدبَرَ ، فَقالَ : وعِزَّتي وجَلالي ما خَلَقتُ خَلقاً أحسَنَ مِنكَ[٤٨٩٠] ، إيّاكَ آمُرُ وإيّاكَ أنهىٰ ، وإيّاكَ اُثيبُ وإيّاكَ اُعاقِبُ.[٤٨٩١]

4379. **Imām al-Bāqir (AS) narrated,** 'Among what was revealed to Moses (AS) was, 'I take My servants to account according to the level of *intellect* that I have given them.'[4934]

٤٣٧٩ . عنه عليه‌السلام - مِمّا اُوحِيَ إلىٰ موسىٰ عليه‌السلام - : أنا اُؤاخِذُ عِبادي عَلىٰ قَدرِ ما أعطَيتُهُم مِنَ العَقلِ.[٤٨٩٢]

4380. **Imām al-Bāqir (AS) said,** 'I found written in the Book [i.e. the Book ascribed to Imām 'Alī (AS)] that the worth and value of every man is his knowledge. Verily Allah, Blessed and most High, will take people to account according to the intellects that He has given them in this world's life.'[4935]

٤٣٨٠. عنه عليه السلام: وَجَدتُ فِي الكِتابِ [يَعني كِتاباً لِعَلِيٍّ عليه السلام] أنَّ قيمَةَ كُلِّ امرِئٍ وقَدرَهُ مَعرِفَتُهُ، إنَّ اللهَ تَبارَكَ وتَعالىٰ يُحاسِبُ النّاسَ عَلىٰ قَدرِ ما آتاهُم مِنَ العُقولِ في دارِ الدّنيا.[٤٨٩٣]

4381. **Imām al-Kāẓim (AS) said,** 'He who wants wealth without the need for riches, and comfort of the heart free from jealousy, and security in his faith should implore Allah, Mighty and Exalted, in his plea for Him to perfect his intellect.'[4936]

٤٣٨١. الإمامُ الكاظمُ عليه السلام: مَن أرادَ الغِنىٰ بِلا مالٍ، وراحَةَ القَلبِ مِنَ الحَسَدِ، والسَّلامَةَ فِي الدِّينِ، فَلْيَتَضَرَّعْ إلَى اللهِ عَزَّ وجلَّ في مَسأَلَتِهِ بِأن يُكمِلَ عَقلَهُ.[٤٨٩٤]

1329. The Authoritativeness of the Intellect

١٣٢٩ ـ حُجِّيَّةُ العَقلِ

4382. **Imām al-Kāẓim (AS) said,** 'Verily Allah has two authoritative proofs over people: a manifest proof and an inward proof. The manifest proof is represented by the prophets and messengers and *Imāms* (AS), and the inward proof is represented by the intellects.'[4937]

٤٣٨٢. الإمامُ الكاظمُ عليه السلام: إنَّ للهِ عَلَى النّاسِ حُجَّتَينِ: حُجَّةً ظاهِرَةً، وحُجَّةً باطِنَةً، فأمّا الظّاهِرَةُ فَالرُّسُلُ والأنبِياءُ والأئمَّةُ عليهم السلام، وأمّا الباطِنَةُ فَالعُقولُ.[٤٨٩٥]

4383. **Imām al-Kāẓim (AS)** in his advice to Hishām b. al-Ḥakam, said, 'Allah has only sent His prophets and messengers to His servants in order that they may come to an understanding of Allah, so the ones who best heed their call are those who have the best inner knowledge, and the ones who know Allah's command the best are those that have the best intellects, and those that have the most perfect intellects will be the ones with the highest status in this world and in the Hereafter.'[4938]

٤٣٨٣. عنه عليه السلام ـ في وَصِيَّتِهِ لِهِشامِ بنِ الحَكَمِ ـ: ما بَعَثَ اللهُ أنبِياءَهُ ورُسُلَهُ إلىٰ عِبادِهِ إلّا لِيَعقِلوا عَنِ اللهِ، فأحسَنُهُم استِجابَةً أحسَنُهُم مَعرِفَةً، وأعلَمُهُم بِأمرِ اللهِ أحسَنُهُم عَقلاً، وأكمَلُهُم عَقلاً أرفَعُهُم دَرَجَةً فِي الدّنيا والآخِرَةِ.[٤٨٩٦]

1330. The Explanation of Intellect

١٣٣٠ ـ تَفسيرُ العَقلِ

4384. **The Prophet (SAWA) said,** 'Verily the intellect is a lasso used to restrain ignorance, and the carnal soul is like the vilest of beasts which if left unrestrained will go wild.'[4939]

٤٣٨٤. رسولُ اللهِ صلى الله عليه وآله: إنَّ العَقلَ عِقالٌ مِنَ الجَهلِ، والنَّفسَ مِثلُ أخبَثِ الدَّوابِّ، فإن لَم تُعقَلْ حارَت.[٤٨٩٧]

4385. **The Prophet (SAWA) said,** 'The intellect is a light that Allah has created for mankind and which He has ordained to illuminate the heart, in order that with it, he may know the difference between the visually manifest things and the unseen things.'[4940]

٤٣٨٥ . عنه ﷺ : العَقلُ نورٌ خَلَقَهُ اللهُ لِلإنسانِ، وجَعَلَهُ يُضيءُ عَلَى القَلبِ ؛ لِيَعرِفَ بِهِ الفَرقَ بَينَ المُشاهَداتِ مِنَ المُغَيَّباتِ.[٤٨٩٨]

4386. **Imām ʿAlī (AS) said,** '[To be a man of] intellect is that you say only that which you know and act upon what you say.'[4941]

٤٣٨٦ . الإمامُ عليٌّ ﵇ : العَقلُ أن تَقولَ ما تَعرِفُ، وتَعمَلَ بِما تَنطِقُ بِهِ.[٤٨٩٩]

4387. **Imām ʿAlī (AS) said,** '[To be a man of] intellect is to preserve your experiences, and the best of all that you have experienced is that which has taught you a lesson.'[4942]

٤٣٨٧ . عنه ﵇ : العَقلُ حِفظُ التَّجارِبِ، وخَيرُ ما جَرَّبتَ ما وَعَظَكَ.[٤٩٠٠]

4388. **Imām ʿAlī (AS) said,** 'There are two divisions of intellect: the natural intellect and the intellect of experience, and both of them produce benefit.'[4943]

٤٣٨٨ . عنه ﵇ : العَقلُ عَقلانِ: عَقلُ الطَّبعِ وعَقلُ التَّجرِبَةِ، وكِلاهُما يُؤَدّي المَنفَعَةَ.[٤٩٠١]

4389. **Imām al-Ḥasan (AS)** when asked about the intellect, said, 'To suppress one's annoyance until the opportunity arises.'[4944]

٤٣٨٩ . الإمامُ الحسنُ ﵇ ـ لَمّا سُئلَ عَنِ العَقلِ ـ: التَّجَرُّعُ لِلغُصَّةِ حَتّىٰ تَنالَ الفُرصَةَ.[٤٩٠٢]

4390. **Imām al-Ḥasan (AS),** when his father asked him regarding the intellect, said, 'It is for the heart to safeguard what you have deposited therein.'[4945]

٤٣٩٠ . عنه ﵇ ـ لَمّا سَأَلَهُ أبوهُ ﵇ عَنِ العَقلِ ـ: حِفظُ قَلبِكَ ما استَودَعتَهُ.[٤٩٠٣]

1331. The Attributes of an Intelligent Person

١٣٣١ ـ صِفاتُ العاقِلِ

4391. **The Prophet (SAWA) said,** 'The attribute of a man of intellect is that he is clement towards one who behaves rashly with him, overlooks the fault of one who wrongs him, is humble even towards one who is lower than him in rank, tries to get ahead of those above him in his quest for good. Whenever he wishes to speak, he contemplates: if what he wants to say is good, he says it and benefits as a result, and if it is bad, then he keeps quiet and remains safe as a result. When a temptation arises before him, he holds fast to Allah and guards his

٤٣٩١ . رسولُ اللهِ ﷺ : صِفَةُ العاقِلِ أن يَحلُمَ عَمَّن جَهِلَ عَلَيهِ، ويَتَجاوَزَ عَمَّن ظَلَمَهُ، ويَتَواضَعَ لِمَن هُوَ دونَهُ، ويُسابِقَ مَن فَوقَهُ في طَلَبِ البِرِّ، وإذا أرادَ أن يَتَكَلَّمَ تَدَبَّرَ؛ فَإِنْ كانَ خَيراً تَكَلَّمَ فَغَنِمَ، وإن كانَ شَرّاً سَكَتَ فَسَلِمَ، وإذا عَرَضَت لَهُ فِتنَةٌ استَعصَمَ بِاللهِ وأمسَكَ يَدَهُ ولِسانَهُ، وإذا رَأىٰ فَضيلَةً انتَهَزَ بِها، لا يُفارِقُه

hand and his tongue: if he sees virtue in it, he seizes it, neither losing his modesty thereat nor displaying any greed. These are ten qualities by which a man of intellect may be known.'[4946]

الحَباءُ، ولا يَبدو مِنهُ الحِرصُ، فتِلكَ عَشرُ خِصالٍ يُعرَفُ بِها العاقِلُ.[٤٩٠٤]

4392. **The Prophet (SAWA) said,** 'The most intelligent of people is he who is best at dealing with people.'[4947]

٤٣٩٢. عنه ﷺ: أعقَلُ النّاسِ أشَدُّهُم مُداراةً لِلنّاسِ.[٤٩٠٥]

4393. **Imām ʿAlī (AS) said,** 'The chest of a man of intellect is the strongbox of his secret.'[4948]

٤٣٩٣. الإمامُ عليٌّ عليه السلام: صَدرُ العاقِلِ صُندوقُ سِرِّهِ.[٤٩٠٦]

4394. **Imām ʿAlī (AS)** was asked to describe a man of intellect, to which he replied, 'He is the one who puts things in their place.' The he was asked, 'So describe to us the ignorant man', to which he replied, 'I have already done so.'[4949]

٤٣٩٤. عنه عليه السلام ـ وَقَد سُئل عَنِ العاقِلِ ـ: هُوَ الّذي يَضَعُ الشَّيءَ مَواضِعَهُ. فقيلَ: فَصِفْ لَنا الجاهِلَ، فقالَ: قَد فَعَلتُ.[٤٩٠٧]

4395. **Imām al-Ṣādiq (AS) said,** 'The man of intellect is never stung twice from the same hole.'[4950]

٤٣٩٥. الإمامُ الصّادقُ عليه السلام: لا يُلسَعُ العاقِلُ مِن جُحرٍ مَرَّتَينِ.[٤٩٠٨]

4396. **Imām al-Ṣādiq (AS)** was asked what the intellect was, to which he replied, 'It is that with which The Beneficent God is worshipped and with which Paradise is attained.' So the man asked, 'So what about that which even Muʿāwiya possessed?' He replied, 'That is a vicious thing, that is devilry, and resembles intellect, though it is not intellect.'[4951]

٤٣٩٦. عنه عليه السلام ـ لمّا سُئل عن العقل ـ: ما عُبِدَ بِهِ الرَّحمٰنُ وَاكتُسِبَ بِهِ الجِنانُ. قالَ: قُلتُ: فَالّذي كانَ في مُعاوِيَةَ؟ فقالَ: تِلكَ النَّكراءُ، تِلكَ الشَّيطَنَةُ، وهِيَ شَبيهَةٌ بِالعَقلِ ولَيسَت بِالعَقلِ.[٤٩٠٩]

4397. **Imām al-Ṣādiq (AS) said,** 'The man of intellect must be well aware of the times he lives in, attentive of his affairs and guarding of his tongue.'[4952]

٤٣٩٧. عنه عليه السلام: عَلَى العاقِلِ أن يَكونَ عارِفاً بِزَمانِهِ، مُقبِلاً عَلىٰ شَأنِهِ، حافِظاً لِلِسانِهِ.[٤٩١٠]

4398. **Imām al-Kāẓim (AS) said,** 'Verily the man of intellect never talks to one whom he fears will belie him, nor asks of one whom he fears will deny him, nor promises that which he is not able to fulfil, nor hopes for that which will dash his hopes, nor attempts to advance towards that which he fears he will be incapable of reaching.'[4953]

٤٣٩٨. الإمامُ الكاظمُ عليه السلام: إنَّ العاقِلَ لا يُحَدِّثُ مَن يَخافُ تَكذيبَهُ، ولا يَسألُ مَن يَخافُ مَنعَهُ، ولا يَعِدُ ما لا يَقدِرُ عَلَيهِ، ولا يَرجو ما يُعَنَّفُ بِرَجائِهِ، ولا يَتَقَدَّمُ عَلىٰ ما يَخافُ العَجزَ عَنهُ.[٤٩١١]

4399. Imām al-Kāẓim (AS) said, 'Verily the man of intellect contents himself with less worldly things when accompanied with wisdom, and does not content himself with less wisdom and more worldly things, and this is why their trade [of the transient for the permanent] profits them.'[4954]

٤٣٩٩. عنه ﷺ: إنَّ العاقِلَ رَضِـيَ بِالدُّونِ مِنَ الدّنيا مَعَ الحِكمَةِ، ولَم يَرضَ بِالدُّونِ مِنَ الحِكمَةِ مَعَ الدّنيا؛ فَلِذٰلكَ رَبِحَت تِجارَتُهُم.[٤٩١٢]

1332. That which Increases the Intellect

١٣٣٢ ـ ما يَزيدُ العَقلَ

4400. Imām ʿAlī (AS) said, 'The intellect is an intrinsic thing that increases with knowledge and experiences.'[4955]

٤٤٠٠. الإمامُ عليٌّ ﷺ: العَقلُ غَريزَةٌ تَزيدُ بِالعِلمِ والتَّجارِبِ.[٤٩١٣]

4401. Imām ʿAlī (AS) said, 'By abandoning that which does not concern you, your intellect will be completed.'[4956]

٤٤٠١. عنه ﷺ: بِتَركِ ما لا يَعنيكَ يَتِمُّ لَكَ العَقلُ.[٤٩١٤]

4402. Imām al-Ḥusayn (AS), when he reminded Muʿāwiya of [the use of] his intellect, said, 'The intellect is only perfected through following the truth', to which Muʿāwiya replied, 'There is only one thing in your chests [i.e. you attribute everything to the truth].'[4957]

٤٤٠٢. الإمامُ الحسينُ ﷺ ـ لَمّا تَذاكَروا العَقلَ عِندَ مُعاوِيَةَ ـ: لا يَكمُلُ العَقلُ إلّا بِاتِّباعِ الحَقِّ، فَقالَ مُعاوِيَةُ: ما في صُدورِكُم إلّا شَيءٌ واحِدٌ.[٤٩١٥]

4403. Imām al-Ṣādiq (AS) said, 'Frequent study of matters of knowledge opens the intellect.'[4958]

٤٤٠٣. الإمامُ الصّادقُ ﷺ: كَثرَةُ النَّظَرِ في العِلمِ يَفتَحُ العَقلَ.[٤٩١٦]

4404. Imām al-Ṣādiq (AS) said, 'Frequent study of matters of wisdom fertilizes the intellect.'[4959]

٤٤٠٤. عنه ﷺ: كَثرَةُ النَّظَرِ في الحِكمَةِ تَلقَحُ العَقلَ.[٤٩١٧]

4405. Imām al-Ṣādiq (AS) said, 'The perfection of the intellect lies in three things: humility before Allah, strong conviction, and silence except when speaking good.'[4960]

٤٤٠٥. عنه ﷺ: كَمالُ العَقلِ في ثَلاثَةٍ: التَّواضُعِ للهِ، وحُسنِ اليَقينِ، والصَّمتِ إلّا مِن خَيرٍ.[٤٩١٨]

1333. What is Regarded as Intellect

١٣٣٣ ـ ما يُعتَبَرُ بِهِ العَقلُ

4406. The Prophet (SAWA) said, 'Indeed among the signs of intellect are withdrawal from the Abode of Delusion [i.e. this worldly life] and frequenting instead the Abode of Eternity, making provisions for the sojourn in the graves and preparation for the Day of Resurrection.'[4961]

٤٤٠٦. رسولُ اللهِ ﷺ: ألا وإنَّ مِن عَلاماتِ العَقلِ التَّجافي عَن دارِ الغُرورِ، والإنابَةَ إلىٰ دارِ الخُلودِ، والتَّزَوُّدَ لِسُكنَى القُبورِ، والتَّأَهُّبَ لِيَومِ النُّشورِ.[٤٩١٩]

4407. **Imām ʿAlī (AS) said,** 'The intellect of every man can be determined by the words that flow on his tongue.'[4962]

٤٤٠٧. الإمامُ عليٌّ ﷺ: يُستَدَلُّ علىٰ عَقلِ كُلِّ امرِئٍ بِما يَجري عَلىٰ لِسانِهِ.[٤٩٢٠]

4408. **Imām ʿAlī (AS) said,** 'Your messenger is the interpreter of your intellect, and your letter is the most eloquent at expressing your true self.'[4963]

٤٤٠٨. عنه ﷺ: رَسولُكَ تَرجُمانُ عَقلِكَ، وكِتابُكَ أبلَغُ ما يَنطِقُ عَنكَ.[٤٩٢١]

4409. **Imām ʿAlī (AS) said,** 'There are six things by which people's intellects may be tested: clemency at the time of anger, patience at the time of fear, calculation when faced with a desire, Godwariness at all times, amicableness, and minimal engagement in disputation.'[4964]

٤٤٠٩. عنه ﷺ: سِتَّةٌ تُختَبَرُ بِها عُقولُ النّاسِ: الحِلمُ عِندَ الغَضَبِ، والصَّبرُ عِندَ الرَّهَبِ، والقَصدُ عِندَ الرَّغَبِ، وتَقوَى اللهِ في كُلِّ حالٍ، وحُسنُ المُداراةِ، وقِلَّةُ المُماراةِ.[٤٩٢٢]

4410. **Imām ʿAlī (AS) said,** 'There are six things by which men's intellects may be tested: the company they keep, their dealings, ruling, their disassociation from power and government, their wealth and their poverty.'[4965]

٤٤١٠. عنه ﷺ: سِتَّةٌ تُختَبَرُ بِها عُقولُ الرِّجالِ: المُصاحَبَةُ، والمُعامَلَةُ، والوِلايَةُ، والعَزلُ، والغِنىٰ، والفَقرُ.[٤٩٢٣]

4411. **Imām ʿAlī (AS) said,** 'People's intellects can be tested when they speak impulsively.'[4966]

٤٤١١. عنه ﷺ: عِندَ بَديهَةِ المَقالِ تُختَبَرُ عُقولُ الرِّجالِ.[٤٩٢٤]

4412. **Imām ʿAlī (AS) said,** 'A man's opinion is the measure of his intellect.'[4967]

٤٤١٢. عنه ﷺ: رَأيُ الرَّجُلِ ميزانُ عَقلِهِ.[٤٩٢٥]

4413. **Imām ʿAlī (AS) said,** 'The abundance of correct acts is an indication of flourishing intellect.'[4968]

٤٤١٣. عنه ﷺ: كَثرَةُ الصَّوابِ تُنبِئُ عَن وُفورِ العَقلِ.[٤٩٢٦]

4414. **Imām ʿAlī (AS) said,** 'When intellect is complete speech decreases.'[4969]

٤٤١٤. عنه ﷺ: إذا تَمَّ العَقلُ نَقَصَ الكَلامُ.[٤٩٢٧]

4415. **Imām ʿAlī (AS) said,** 'He whose intellect is perfected regards carnal desires with disdain.'[4970]

٤٤١٥. عنه ﷺ: مَن كَمُلَ عَقلُهُ استَهانَ بِالشَّهَواتِ.[٤٩٢٨]

1334. That which Weakens the Intellect

١٣٣٤ـ ما يُضعِفُ العَقلَ

4416. **Imām ʿAlī (AS) said,** 'Whims and carnal desires cause the intellect to disappear.'[4971]

٤٤١٦. الإمامُ عليٌّ ﷺ: ذَهابُ العَقلِ بَينَ الهَوىٰ والشَّهوَةِ.[٤٩٢٩]

4417. **Imām ʿAlī (AS) said,** 'The loss of the intellect occurs in the quest for all that is superfluous.'[4972]

٤٤١٧ . عنه عليه السلام: ضَياعُ العُقولِ في طَلَبِ الفُضولِ.[٤٩٣٠]

4418. **Imām ʿAlī (AS) said,** 'Man's admiration and satisfaction with himself is a proof of his weak intellect.'[4973]

٤٤١٨ . عنه عليه السلام : إعجابُ المَرءِ بِنَفسِهِ دَليلٌ عَلىٰ ضَعفِ عَقلِهِ.[٤٩٣١]

4419. **Imām ʿAlī (AS) said,** 'Whoever keeps the company of an ignorant man incurs a loss in his intellect.'[4974]

٤٤١٩ . عنه عليه السلام : مَن صَحِبَ جاهِلاً نَقَصَ مِن عَقلِهِ.[٤٩٣٢]

4420. **Imām ʿAlī (AS) said,** 'Whenever a man makes a joke, a part of his intellect trickles away.'[4975]

٤٤٢٠ . عنه عليه السلام : ما مَزَحَ امرُؤٌ مَزحَةً إلّا مَجَّ مِنَ عَقلِهِ مَجَّةً.[٤٩٣٣]

4421. **Imām ʿAlī (AS) said,** 'He who abandons listening to intellectual people, his own intellect dies.'[4976]

٤٤٢١ . عنه عليه السلام : مَن تَرَكَ الاستِماعَ مِن ذَوي العُقولِ ماتَ عَقلُهُ.[٤٩٣٤]

4422. **Imām al-Bāqir (AS) said,** 'No sooner does an iota of pride enter a man's heart than he incurs a loss in his intellect.'[4977]

٤٤٢٢ . الإمامُ الباقرُ عليه السلام: ما دَخَلَ قَلبَ امرِئٍ شَيءٌ مِنَ الكِبرِ إلّا نَقَصَ مِن عَقلِهِ.[٤٩٣٥]

1335. Evidence of Weak Intellect

١٣٣٥ ـ ما يَدُلُّ عَلىٰ ضَعفِ العَقلِ

4423. **Imām ʿAlī (AS) said,** 'When intellect is little, superfluity thrives.'[4978]

٤٤٢٣ . الإمامُ عليٌّ عليه السلام : إذا قَلَّتِ العُقولُ كَثُرَ الفُضولُ.[٤٩٣٦]

4424. **Imām ʿAlī (AS) said,** 'He whose intellect is weak has bad oratory.'[4979]

٤٤٢٤ . عنه عليه السلام : مَن قَلَّ عَقلُهُ ساءَ خِطابُهُ.[٤٩٣٧]

4425. **Imām ʿAlī (AS) said,** 'Evidence of lack of intellect is keeping company with ignorant people.'[4980]

٤٤٢٥ . عنه عليه السلام : مِن عَدَمِ العَقلِ مُصاحَبَةُ ذَوي الجَهلِ.[٤٩٣٨]

4426. **Imām ʿAlī (AS) said,** 'Overly high aspirations are a result of a corrupt intellect.'[4981]

٤٤٢٦ . عنه عليه السلام: كَثرَةُ الأَماني مِن فَسادِ العَقلِ.[٤٩٣٩]

1336. The Fruit of the Intellect

١٣٣٦ ـ ثَمَرَةُ العَقلِ

4427. **Imām ʿAlī (AS) said,** 'The fruit of the intellect is steadfastness [in the path of Allah].'[4982]

٤٤٢٧ . الإمامُ عليٌّ عليه السلام: ثَمَرَةُ العَقلِ الاستِقامَةُ.[٤٩٤٠]

4428. **Imām ʿAlī (AS) said,** 'The fruit of the intellect is adherence to the truth.'[4983]

٤٤٢٨. عنه ﷺ : ثَمَرَةُ العَقلِ لُزومُ الحَقِّ.[٤٩٤١]

4429. **Imām ʿAlī (AS) said,** 'The fruit of the intellect is contempt for this worldly life and repression of one's whims.'[4984]

٤٤٢٩. عنه ﷺ : ثَمَرَةُ العَقلِ مَقتُ الدّنيا، وقَمعُ الهَوىٰ.[٤٩٤٢]

4430. **Imām ʿAlī (AS) said,** 'The intellect is a tree the fruit of which is generosity and modesty.'[4985]

٤٤٣٠. عنه ﷺ : العَقلُ شَجَرَةٌ، ثَمَرُها السَّخاءُ والحَياءُ.[٤٩٤٣]

1337. The Intellect's Adversary

١٣٣٧ ـ عَدُوُّ العَقلِ

4431. **Imām ʿAlī (AS) said,** 'The caprice is the intellect's adversary.'[4986]

٤٤٣١. الإمامُ عليٌّ ﷺ : الهَوىٰ عَدُوُّ العَقلِ.[٤٩٤٤]

4432. **Imām ʿAlī (AS) said,** 'Many a slavish mind is subservient to an overpowering caprice!'[4987]

٤٤٣٢. عنه ﷺ : كَم مِن عَقلٍ أسيرٍ تَحتَ هَوىً أميرٍ![٤٩٤٥]

4433. **Imām ʿAlī (AS) said,** 'Allah has made obligatory...the abandonment of drinking alcohol in order to safeguard the intellect.'[4988]

٤٤٣٣. عنه ﷺ : فَرَضَ اللهُ... تَركَ شُربِ الخَمرِ تَحصيناً لِلعَقلِ.[٤٩٤٦]

4434. **Imām ʿAlī (AS) said,** 'Know that entertaining high hopes distracts the intellect and causes one to forget their remembrance [of Allah].'[4989]

٤٤٣٤. عنه ﷺ : إعلَموا أنَّ الأمَلَ يُسهي العَقلَ، ويُنسي الذِّكرَ.[٤٩٤٧]

4435. **Imām al-Ṣādiq (AS) said,** 'The caprice is awake while the intellect is asleep.'[4990]

٤٤٣٥. الإمامُ الصّادقُ ﷺ : الهَوىٰ يَقظانُ والعَقلُ نائمٌ.[٤٩٤٨]

(See also: THE DESIRE 396)

(أنظر) عنوان ٣٩٦ «الهوى».

287

RETREAT IN THE MOSQUE
(*Iʿtikāf*)

الاعتكاف

1338. Retreat in the Mosque

١٣٣٨ ـ الاعتكاف

"And [remember] when We made the House a place of spiritual reward for mankind and a sanctuary, [declaring], 'Take the venue of prayer from Abraham's

﴿وَإذْ جَعَلْنا الْبَيْتَ مَثابَةً لِلنّاسِ وَأمْناً وَاتَّخِذُوا مِن مَقامِ إبْراهِيمَ مُصَلًّى وَعَهِدنا إلىٰ إبْراهِيمَ

Station.' We charged Abraham and Ishmael [with its upkeep, saying], 'Purify My House for those who go around it, for those who make it a retreat and for those who bow and prostrate.'[4991]

وَإِسْماعِيلَ أَنْ طَهِّرا بَيْتِيَ لِلطَّائِفِينَ وَالْعاكِفِينَ وَالرُّكَّعِ السُّجُودِ﴾.٤٩٩١

4436. **Anas narrated:** 'The Prophet (SAWA), if he was in town, would retreat in the mosque the last ten nights of the month of Ramaḍān, and if he was travelling, would retreat in the mosque twenty nights the following year.'[4992]

٤٤٣٦. كنز العمّال: كانَ [النَّبِيُّ ﷺ] إذا كانَ مُقيماً اعتكَفَ العَشرَ الأواخِرَ مِن رَمَضانَ، وإذا سافَرَ اعتَكَفَ مِنَ العامِ المُقبِلِ عِشرينَ.٤٩٩٢

4437. *Man La Yaḥḍuruhu al-Faqīh* narrates from Maymūn b. Mihrān, 'I was once sitting in the presence of al-Ḥasan b. 'Alī (AS) when a man came to him, saying, 'O son of the Prophet of Allah, verily *x* is claiming money from me that I owe him and he wants to arrest me.' So he replied, 'By Allah, I do not have money to pay your debt on your behalf.' So he asked, 'Then talk to him.' So he (AS) put on his sandals, whereupon I asked him, 'O son of the Prophet of Allah, have you forgotten the fact that you are in a state of retreat?' So he replied, 'No, I have not forgotten, but I have heard my father (AS) narrating from the authority of [my grandfather], the Prophet of Allah (SAWA) that he had said, 'He who strives to fulfil a fellow Muslim brother's need is as if he has worshipped Allah, Mighty and Exalted, for nine thousand years, fasting during the day and standing in prayer at night.'[4993]

٤٤٣٧. كتاب من لا يحضره الفقيه عن مَيمون بن مِهران: كُنتُ جالِساً عِندَ الحَسَنِ ابنِ عَلِيٍّ ﷺ فأتاهُ رَجُلٌ فقالَ لَهُ: يَابنَ رَسولِ اللهِ، إنَّ فُلاناً لَهُ عَلَيَّ مالٌ ويُريدُ أن يَحبِسَني، فقالَ: وَاللهِ ما عِندي مالٌ فأقضِيَ عَنكَ. قالَ: فَكَلِّمْهُ، قالَ: فلَبِسَ ﷺ نَعلَهُ، فقُلتُ لَهُ: يَابنَ رَسولِ اللهِ، أنَسيتَ اعتِكافَكَ؟ فقالَ لَهُ: لَم أنسَ، ولكِنّي سَمِعتُ أبي ﷺ يُحَدِّثُ عَن (جَدّي) رَسولِ اللهِ ﷺ أنَّهُ قالَ: مَن سَعىٰ في حاجَةِ أخيهِ المُسلِمِ فَكَأنَّما عَبَدَ اللهَ عَزَّوجلَّ تِسعَةَ آلافِ سَنَةٍ، صائماً نَهارَهُ، قائماً لَيلَهُ.٤٩٩٣

4438. **Imām al-Ṣādiq (AS) said,** 'The Prophet (SAWA) used to retreat in the mosque the last ten nights [of Ramaḍān], where a tent of fur would be pitched for him, and he would roll up the skirting and lay out his bedding.'[4994]

٤٤٣٨. الإمامُ الصّادقُ ﷺ: كانَ رَسولُ اللهِ ﷺ إذا كانَ العَشرُ الأواخِرُ [يَعني مِن رَمَضانَ] اعتَكَفَ في المَسجِدِ، وضُرِبَت لَهُ قُبَّةٌ مِن شَعرٍ، وشَمَّرَ الميزَرَ وطَوىٰ فِراشَهُ.٤٩٩٤

4439. **Imām al-Ṣādiq (AS) said,** 'Retreat can only be in a congregational mosque wherein the congregational prayer is led by a just *imām*.'[4995]

٤٤٣٩. عنه ﷺ: لَا اعتِكافَ إلّا في مَسجِدِ جَماعَةٍ قَد صَلّىٰ فيهِ إمامُ عَدلٍ بِصَلاةِ جَماعَةٍ.٤٩٩٥

288

KNOWLEDGE

العِلمُ

1339. The Virtue of Knowledge

١٣٣٩ ـ فَضلُ العِلمِ

"Say, 'Are those who know equal to those who do not know?' Only those who possess intellect take admonition."[4996]

﴿قُلْ هَلْ يَسْتَوِي الَّذِينَ يَعْلَمُونَ وَالَّذِينَ لا يَعْلَمُونَ إِنَّما يَتَذَكَّرُ أُولُوا الأَلْبابِ﴾ .٤٩٥٤

"Allah will raise those of you who have faith and those who have been given knowledge in rank, and Allah is well aware of what you do."[4997]

﴿يَرْفَعِ اللهُ الَّذِينَ آمَنُوا مِنْكُمْ وَالَّذِينَ أُوتُوا العِلْمَ دَرَجاتٍ وَاللهُ بِما تَعْمَلُونَ خَبِيرٌ﴾ .٤٩٥٥

4440. **The Prophet (SAWA) said,** 'When committing a sin, the knowledgeable man is guilty of the one sin whereas the ignorant man is guilty of two [i.e. the sin itself and the sin of ignorance].'[4998]

٤٤٤٠ . رسولُ اللهِ ﷺ : ذَنبُ العالِمِ واحِدٌ، وذَنبُ الجاهِلِ ذَنبانِ.٤٩٥٦

4441. **The Prophet (SAWA) said,** 'Knowledge is the root of all good, whereas ignorance is the root of all evil.'[4999]

٤٤٤١ . عنه ﷺ : العِلمُ رَأسُ الخَيرِ كُلِّهِ، والجَهلُ رَأسُ الشَّرِّ كُلِّهِ.٤٩٥٧

4442. **The Prophet (SAWA) said,** 'The quest for knowledge is incumbent upon every Muslim... by virtue of it the Lord is obeyed and worshipped, consanguinal relations are maintained, and the lawful is distinguished from the prohibited. Knowledge leads to action and action follows it. The fortunate ones are inspired by it whereas the wretched ones are deprived of it.'[5000]

٤٤٤٢ . عنه ﷺ : طَلَبُ العِلمِ فَريضَةٌ عَلىٰ كُلِّ مُسلِمٍ... بِهِ يُطاعُ الرَّبُّ ويُعبَدُ، وبِهِ تُوصَلُ الأرحامُ، ويُعرَفُ الحَلالُ مِنَ الحَرامِ، العِلمُ إمامُ العَمَلِ والعَمَلُ تابِعُهُ، يُلهَمُ بِهِ السُّعَداءُ، ويُحرَمُهُ الأشقِياءُ.٤٩٥٨

4443. **The Prophet (SAWA) said,** 'The worthiest of people are those who have the most knowledge, and the least of them in worth are those with the least knowledge.'[5001]

٤٤٤٣ . عنه ﷺ : أكثَرُ النّاسِ قيمَةً أكثَرُهُم عِلماً، وأقَلُّ النّاسِ قيمَةً أقَلُّهُم عِلماً.٤٩٥٩

4444. **The Prophet (SAWA) said,** 'The people who are closest to the rank of prophethood are the people of knowledge and striving.'[5002]

٤٤٤٤ . عنه ﷺ : أقرَبُ النّاسِ مِن دَرَجَةِ النُّبُوَّةِ أهلُ الجِهادِ وأهلُ العِلمِ.٤٩٦٠

4445. **The Prophet (SAWA) said,** 'On the Day of Resurrection, the ink of the scholars will be weighed up against the blood of the martyrs, and the ink of the scholars will preponderate over the blood of the martyrs.'[5003]

٤٤٤٥. عنه ﷺ: يُوزَنُ يومَ القِيامَةِ مِدادُ العُلَماءِ ودِماءُ الشُّهَداءِ فيَرجَحُ مِدادُ العُلَماءِ عَلىٰ دِماءِ الشُّهَداءِ.٤٩٦١

4446. **Imām ʿAlī (AS) said,** 'The fountainhead of all virtues is knowledge and the peak of all virtues is knowledge.'[5004]

٤٤٤٦. الإمامُ عليٌّ ﷺ: رَأسُ الفَضائلِ العِلمُ، غايَةُ الفَضائلِ العِلمُ.٤٩٦٢

4447. **Imām ʿAlī (AS) said,** 'Knowledge commands, action drives, and the carnal soul is the obstinate mount.'[5005]

٤٤٤٧. عنه ﷺ: العِلمُ قائدٌ، والعَمَلُ سائقٌ، والنَّفسُ حَرونٌ.٤٩٦٣ ٤٩٦٤

4448. **Imām ʿAlī (AS) said,** 'Knowledge is the lamp of the intellect.'[5006]

٤٤٤٨. عنه ﷺ: العِلمُ مِصباحُ العَقلِ.٤٩٦٥

4449. **Imām ʿAlī (AS) said,** 'Knowledge is indeed a good guide.'[5007]

٤٤٤٩. عنه ﷺ: العِلمُ نِعمَ الدَّليلُ.٤٩٦٦

4450. **Imām ʿAlī (AS) said,** 'Knowledge is the noblest source of repute.'[5008]

٤٤٥٠. عنه ﷺ: العِلمُ أشرَفُ الأحسابِ.٤٩٦٧

4451. **Imām ʿAlī (AS) said,** 'Knowledge is the lost property of the believer.'[5009]

٤٤٥١. عنه ﷺ: العِلمُ ضالَّةُ المُؤمِنِ.٤٩٦٨

4452. **Imām ʿAlī (AS) said,** 'Knowledge is such a dignified thing that he who is not proficient at it claims to be so, and one is pleased for it to be attributed to him. And ignorance is such a rebuked thing that even the one who possesses it claims to be free of it.'[5010]

٤٤٥٢. عنه ﷺ: كَفىٰ بِالعِلمِ شَرَفاً أن يَدَّعِيَهُ مَن لا يُحسِنُهُ، ويَفرَحَ بِهِ إذا نُسِبَ إلَيهِ، وكَفىٰ بِالجَهلِ ذَمّاً يَبرَأُ مِنهُ مَن هُوَ فيهِ.٤٩٦٩

4453. **Imām ʿAlī (AS) said,** 'There is no treasure more profitable than knowledge.'[5011]

٤٤٥٣. عنه ﷺ: لا كَنزَ أنفَعُ مِنَ العِلمِ.٤٩٧٠

4454. **Imām ʿAlī (AS) said,** 'There is no source of dignity like knowledge.'[5012]

٤٤٥٤. عنه ﷺ: لا شَرَفَ كَالعِلمِ.٤٩٧١

4455. **Imām ʿAlī (AS) said,** 'Every container becomes cramped by what is placed therein,

٤٤٥٥. عنه ﷺ: كُلُّ وِعاءٍ يَضيقُ بِما جُعِلَ فيهِ

except the container that holds knowledge, for verily it expands because of it.'[5013]

إلّا وِعاءَ العِلمِ ؛ فإنَّهُ يَتَّسِعُ بِهِ.[٤٩٧٢]

4456. **Imām ʿAlī (AS) said,** 'When Allah wishes to repudiate someone, he deprives him of knowledge.'[5014]

٤٤٥٦. عنه عليه السلام : إذا أرذَلَ اللهُ عَبداً حَظَرَ عَلَيهِ العِلمَ.[٤٩٧٣]

4457. **Imām ʿAlī (AS) said,** 'Knowledge is life.'[5015]

٤٤٥٧. عنه عليه السلام : العِلمُ حَياةٌ.[٤٩٧٤]

4458. **Imām ʿAlī (AS) said,** 'Verily knowledge is the life of the hearts, the light of the eyes from blindness and the strength of the bodies against weakness.'[5016]

٤٤٥٨. عنه عليه السلام : إنَّ العِلمَ حَياةُ القُلوبِ، ونورُ الأبصارِ مِنَ العَمىٰ، وقُوَّةُ الأبدانِ مِنَ الضَّعفِ.[٤٩٧٥]

4459. **Imām ʿAlī (AS)** once took Kumayl out to the desert, and when they reached the desert, he let out a deep sigh and said, 'O Kumayl, knowledge is better than wealth, for knowledge guards you while you guard wealth, and wealth is reduced by spending, whereas knowledge increases by spending it, and any good produced by wealth [respect and honour] ceases when it ceases to exist.'[5017]

٤٤٥٩. عنه عليه السلام ـ لِكُمَيلٍ لَمّا أخَذَ بِيَدِهِ وأخرَجَهُ إلَى الجَبّانِ[٤٩٧٦] فلَمّا أصحَرَ تَنَفَّسَ الصُّعَداءَ وقالَ ـ: يا كُمَيلُ، العِلمُ خَيرٌ مِنَ المالِ، العِلمُ يَحرُسُكَ وأنتَ تَحرُسُ المالَ، والمالُ تَنقُصُهُ النَّفَقَةُ، والعِلمُ يَزكو عَلَى الإنفاقِ، وصَنيعُ المالِ يَزولُ بِزَوالِهِ.[٤٩٧٧]

4460. **Imām ʿAlī (AS) said,** 'The treasurers of wealth perish during their own lifetimes, whereas the knowledgeable ones remain alive for all time, their individual selves may pass away, but the likes of them [remembering them] continue to remain in the hearts.'[5018]

٤٤٦٠. عنه عليه السلام : هَلَكَ خُزّانُ الأموالِ وهُم أحياءٌ، والعُلَماءُ باقونَ ما بَقِيَ الدَّهرُ، أعيانُهُم مَفقودَةٌ، وأمثالُهُم فِي القُلوبِ مَوجودَةٌ.[٤٩٧٨]

4461. **Imām ʿAlī (AS) said,** 'The scholar is alive even when he is dead, whereas the ignorant man is dead even though he may be alive.'[5019]

٤٤٦١. عنه عليه السلام : العالِمُ حَيٌّ وإن كانَ مَيِّتاً، الجاهِلُ مَيِّتٌ وإن كانَ حَيّاً.[٤٩٧٩]

4462. **Imām al-Bāqir (AS) said,** Verily a heart that does not have any knowledge is like a ruined house that has no inhabitants.[5020]

٤٤٦٢. الإمامُ الباقرُ عليه السلام : إنَّ قَلباً لَيسَ فيهِ شَيءٌ مِنَ العِلمِ كالبَيتِ الخَرابِ الَّذي لا عامِرَ لَهُ.[٤٩٨٠]

4463. **Imām al-Ṣādiq (AS) said,** 'Verily the scholars are the heirs of the prophets.'[5021]

٤٤٦٣. الإمامُ الصّادقُ عليه السلام : إنَّ العُلَماءَ وَرَثَةُ الأنبِياءِ.[٤٩٨١]

1340. The Superiority of Knowledge to Acts of Worship

١٣٤٠ ـ فَضلُ العِلمِ عَلَى العِبادَةِ

4464. The Prophet (SAWA) said, ‘A little knowledge is better than a lot of worship.’[5022]

٤٤٦٤ . رسولُ اللهِ ﷺ : قَليلُ العِلمِ خَيرٌ مِن كَثيرِ العِبادَةِ.٤٩٨٢

4465. The Prophet (SAWA) said, ‘To sleep having knowledge is better than to pray in ignorance.’[5023]

٤٤٦٥ . عنه ﷺ : نَومٌ مَعَ عِلمٍ خَيرٌ مِن صَلاةٍ عَلىٰ جَهلٍ.٤٩٨٣

4466. The Prophet (SAWA) said, ‘Verily the knowledgeable man is superior to the [mere] worshipper as the sun is to the stars, and the worshipper is superior to the one who does not worship as the superiority of the moon to the stars.’[5024]

٤٤٦٦ . عنه ﷺ : إنَّ فَضلَ العالِمِ عَلَى العابِدِ كفَضلِ الشَّمسِ عَلَى الكَواكِبِ ، وفَضلُ العابِدِ عَلىٰ غَيرِ العابِدِ كفَضلِ القَمَرِ عَلَى الكَواكِبِ.٤٩٨٤

4467. The Prophet (SAWA) said, ‘An hour spent by a knowledgeable man lying on his bed thinking about his deeds is better than seventy years spent by the worshipper performing acts of worship.’[5025]

٤٤٦٧ . عنه ﷺ : ساعَةٌ مِن عالِمٍ يَتَّكِئُ عَلىٰ فِراشِهِ يَنظُرُ في عَمَلِهِ ، خَيرٌ مِن عِبادَةِ العابِدِ سَبعينَ عاماً.٤٩٨٥

4468. The Prophet (SAWA) said, ‘The knowledgeable man is superior to the [mere] worshipper by seventy degrees, the distance between two degrees spanning the gallop of a horse for seventy years; and this is because Satan plants an innovation amongst people which the knowledgeable man notices and prohibits, whilst the worshipper attends to his worship neither taking any notice of it nor recognising it.’[5026]

٤٤٦٨ . عنه ﷺ : فَضلُ العالِمِ عَلَى العابِدِ بِسَبعينَ دَرَجَةً ، بَينَ كُلِّ دَرَجَتَينِ حُضْرُ الفَرَسِ سَبعينَ عاماً ؛ وذلكَ أنَّ الشَّيطانَ يَضَعُ البِدعَةَ لِلنّاسِ فَيُبصِرُها العالِمُ فيَنهىٰ عَنها ، والعابِدُ مُقبِلٌ عَلىٰ عِبادَتِهِ لا يَتَوَجَّهُ لَها ولا يَعرِفُها.٤٩٨٦

4469. The Prophet (SAWA) said, ‘By the One Who holds Muḥammad’s soul in His Grasp! Verily one knowledgeable man is more difficult for Satan to bear than seventy worshippers, for the worshipper serves himself whilst the knowledgeable man serves others.’[5027]

٤٤٦٩ . عنه ﷺ : وَالَّذي نَفسُ مُحَمَّدٍ بِيَدِهِ! لَعالِمٌ واحِدٌ أشَدُّ عَلىٰ إبليسَ مِن ألفِ عابِدٍ ؛ لأنَّ العابِدَ لِنَفسِهِ والعالِمَ لِغَيرِهِ.٤٩٨٧

4470. Imām al-Bāqir (AS) said, ‘Revising knowledge for an hour is better than staying up the whole night in worship.’[5028]

٤٤٧٠ . الإمامُ الباقرُ ﷺ : تَذاكُرُ العِلمِ ساعَةً خَيرٌ مِن قِيامِ لَيلَةٍ.٤٩٨٨

4471. **Imām al-Bāqir (AS) said,** 'The knowledgeable man who is beneficial [to others] as a result of his knowledge is better than seventy thousand worshippers.'[5029]

٤٤٧١. عنه ؑ: عالِمٌ يُنتَفَعُ بِعِلمِهِ، أفضَلُ مِن سَبعينَ ألفِ عابِدٍ.٤٩٨٩

1341. The Death of a Scholar

١٣٤١ ـ مَوتُ العالِمِ

4472. **The Prophet (SAWA) said,** 'The death of a scholar is an affliction that cannot be compensated and a void that cannot be filled, for he is a star that has been obliterated. The death of a whole tribe is easier to bear than the death of a scholar.'[5030]

٤٤٧٢. رسولُ اللهِ ﷺ: مَوتُ العالِمِ مُصيبَةٌ لا تُجبَرُ وثُلمَةٌ لا تُسَدُّ، وهُوَ نَجمٌ طُمِسَ، ومَوتُ قَبيلَةٍ أيسَرُ مِن مَوتِ عالِمٍ.٤٩٩٠

(See also: JURISPRUDENCE: section 1500)

(اُنظر) الفقه: باب ١٥٠٠.

1342. Looking at the Face of a Scholar is an Act of Worship

١٣٤٢ ـ النَّظَرُ إلىٰ وَجهِ العالِمِ عِبادَةٌ

4473. **The Prophet (SAWA) said,** 'Looking at the face of a scholar out of love for him is an act of worship.'[5031]

٤٤٧٣. رسولُ اللهِ ﷺ: النَّظَرُ في وَجهِ العالِمِ حُبّاً لَهُ عِبادَةٌ.٤٩٩١

4474. **Imām al-Ṣādiq (AS)** was once asked regarding the Prophet (SAWA)'s saying, 'Looking at the faces of scholars is an act of worship', to which he replied, 'It refers to the scholar whom looking at reminds you of the Hereafter, and whoever is not thus, then looking at him is a trial.'[5032]

٤٤٧٤. الإمامُ الصّادقُ ؑ ـ لَمّا سُئلَ عَن قَولِ النَّبِيِّ ﷺ: النَّظَرُ في وُجوهِ العُلَماءِ عِبادَةٌ ـ: هُوَ العالِمُ الّذي إذا نَظَرتَ إلَيهِ ذَكَّرَكَ الآخِرَةَ، ومَن كانَ خِلافَ ذلكَ فَالنَّظَرُ إلَيهِ فِتنَةٌ.٤٩٩٢

(See also: SIGHT: section 1733)

(اُنظر) النظر: باب ١٧٣٣.

1343. Enjoinment of Seeking Knowledge

١٣٤٣ ـ الحَثُّ عَلىٰ طَلَبِ العِلمِ

4475. **The Prophet (SAWA) said,** 'Seek knowledge even in China, for verily to seek knowledge is an obligation on every Muslim.'[5033]

٤٤٧٥. رسولُ اللهِ ﷺ: اُطلُبوا العِلمَ ولَو بِالصّينِ، فإنَّ طَلَبَ العِلمِ فَريضَةٌ عَلىٰ كُلِّ مُسلِمٍ.٤٩٩٣

4476. **The Prophet (SAWA) said,** 'Seeking knowledge is an obligation on every Muslim. Indeed Allah loves those who strive in their quest for knowledge.'[5034]

٤٤٧٦. عنه ﷺ: طَلَبُ العِلمِ فَريضَةٌ عَلىٰ كُـلِّ مُسلِمٍ، ألا إنَّ اللهَ يُحِبُّ بُغاةَ العِلمِ.٤٩٩٤

4477. **The Prophet (SAWA) said,** 'He who cannot endure the submissiveness entailed in learning for an hour will remain submissive to ignorance forever.'[5035]

٤٤٧٧. عنه ﷺ: مَن لَم يَصبِر عَلىٰ ذُلِّ التَّـعَلُّمِ ساعَةً بَقِيَ في ذُلِّ الجَهلِ أبداً.٤٩٩٥

4478. **Imām al-Ṣādiq (AS) said,** 'If people knew [the benefits] of seeking knowledge, they would seek it even if they had to shed blood or dive into the deepest seas.'[5036]

٤٤٧٨. الإمامُ الصّادقُ ﷺ: لَو عَلِمَ النّاسُ ما في طَلَبِ العِلمِ لَطَلَبوهُ ولَو بِسَفكِ المُـهَجِ وخَـوضِ اللُّجَجِ.٤٩٩٦

1344. The Virtue of the Seeker of Knowledge

١٣٤٤ـ فَضْلُ طالِبِ العِلم

4479. **The Prophet (SAWA) said,** 'The seeker of knowledge among ignorant people is as the living one among the dead.'[5037]

٤٤٧٩. رسولُ اللهِ ﷺ: طالِبُ العِلمِ بَينَ الجُهّالِ كَالحَيِّ بَينَ الأمواتِ.٤٩٩٧

4480. **The Prophet (SAWA) said,** 'There are two insatiable types of people who are never satisfied by their quest: the seeker of knowledge and the seeker after this world.'[5038]

٤٤٨٠. عنه ﷺ: مَنهومانِ لايَشبَعُ طـالِبُهُما: طالِبُ العِلمِ وطالِبُ الدّنيا.٤٩٩٨

4481. **The Prophet (SAWA) said,** 'When death comes to the seeker of knowledge whilst he is in that state [of seeking knowledge], he dies as a martyr.'[5039]

٤٤٨١. عنه ﷺ: إذا جاءَ المَوتُ لِطالِبِ العِـلمِ وهُوَ عَلىٰ هٰذهِ الحالَةِ ماتَ وهُوَ شَهيدٌ.٤٩٩٩

4482. **The Prophet (SAWA) said,** 'He who goes out to seek knowledge is indeed on the path of Allah until he returns.'[5040]

٤٤٨٢. عنه ﷺ: مَن طَلَبَ العِلمَ فهُوَ في سَبيلِ اللهِ حَتّىٰ يَرجِعَ.٥٠٠٠

4483. **The Prophet (SAWA) said,** 'He who seeks knowledge is as one who spends his day fasting and his night praying. Verily a chapter of knowledge that a man learns is better for him than for him to have as much gold as a mountain and give it all away in the way of Allah.'[5041]

٤٤٨٣. عنه ﷺ: مَن طَلَبَ العِلمَ فهُوَ كالصّائمِ نَهارَهُ، القائمِ لَيلَهُ، وإنَّ باباً مِـنَ العِـلمِ يَـتَعَلَّمُهُ الرَّجُلُ خَيرٌ لَهُ مِن أن يَكونَ أبـو قُـبَيسٍ ذَهَـباً فأنفَقَهُ في سَبيلِ اللهِ.٥٠٠١

4484. **The Prophet (SAWA) said,** 'He who goes out to seek knowledge, Allah guarantees his sustenance for him.'[5042]

٤٤٨٤. عنه ﷺ: مَن طَلَبَ العِلمَ تَكَفَّلَ اللهُ لَـهُ بِرِزقِهِ.[٥٠٠٢]

4485. **The Prophet (SAWA) said,** 'The seeker of knowledge is the seeker of mercy; the seeker of knowledge is the pillar of Islam and is given his recompense with the prophets.'[5043]

٤٤٨٥. عنه ﷺ: طالِبُ العِلمِ طالِبُ الرَّحمَةِ، طالِبُ العِلمِ رُكنُ الإسلامِ، ويُعطىٰ أجرَهُ مَعَ النَّبيّينَ.[٥٠٠٣]

4486. **The Prophet (SAWA) said,** 'Verily the angels spread their wings over the seeker of knowledge and seek forgiveness for him.'[5044]

٤٤٨٦. عنه ﷺ: إنَّ طالِبَ العِلمِ تَبسُطُ لَهُ المَلائكَةُ أجنِحَتَها وتَستَغفِرُ لَهُ.[٥٠٠٤]

4487. **The Prophet (SAWA) said,** 'He who traverses a path in order to gain knowledge thereupon, Allah makes him traverse the path to Paradise.'[5045]

٤٤٨٧. عنه ﷺ: مَن سَلَكَ طَريقاً يَطلُبُ فيهِ عِلماً، سَلَكَ اللهُ بِهِ طَريقاً إلَى الجَنَّةِ.[٥٠٠٥]

4488. **The Prophet (SAWA) said,** 'He who goes out to seek knowledge is himself sought after by Paradise.'[5046]

٤٤٨٨. عنه ﷺ: مَن كانَ في طَلَبِ العِلمِ كانَتِ الجَنَّةُ في طَلَبِهِ.[٥٠٠٦]

4489. **The Prophet (SAWA) said,** 'Verily everything seeks forgiveness for the seeker of knowledge, including the fishes in the sea, the reptiles on the land, and the predators and livestock of the earth.'[5047]

٤٤٨٩. عنه ﷺ: إنَّ طالِبَ العِلمِ لَيَستَغفِرُ لَهُ كُلُّ شَيءٍ؛ حَتّىٰ حِيتانُ البَحرِ، وهَوامُّ الأرضِ، وسِباعُ البَرِّ وأنعامُهُ.[٥٠٠٧]

4490. **Imām ʿAlī (AS) said,** 'He who is overtaken by death whilst he is seeking knowledge, there remains but a difference of one level between him and the Prophets.'[5048]

٤٤٩٠. الإمامُ عليٌّ عليه السلام: مَن جاءَتهُ مَنِيَّتُهُ وهُوَ يَطلُبُ العِلمَ فبَينَهُ وبَينَ الأنبياءِ دَرَجَةٌ.[٥٠٠٨]

1345. The Blessings of Teaching

١٣٤٥ ـ بَرَكاتُ التَّعليمِ

4491. It is narrated in *Tanbīh al-Khawāṭir*: Allah, most High, revealed to Prophet Moses (AS) saying, 'O Moses, learn good and teach it to people, for verily I enlighten the graves of the teachers and the learners of good, so that they never feel afraid in their resting place.'[5049]

٤٤٩١. تنبيه الخواطر: أوحَى اللهُ تَعالىٰ إلىٰ موسى: يا موسىٰ، تَعَلَّمِ الخَيرَ وعَلِّمْهُ النّاسَ؛ فإنّي مُنَوِّرٌ لِمُعَلِّمي الخَيرِ ومُتَعَلِّميهِ قُبورَهُم؛ حَتّىٰ لا يَستَوحِشوا بِمَكانِهِم.[٥٠٠٩]

4492. **Prophet Jesus (AS) said,** 'He who has knowledge, acts upon what he knows and teaches

٤٤٩٢. عيسى عليه السلام: مَن عَلِمَ، وعَمِلَ، وعَلَّمَ، عُدَّ

it to others is regarded as great in the greatest Kingdom [of the heavens].'[5050]

فِي المَلَكوتِ الأعظمِ عَظيماً.[٥٠٥٠]

4493. **The Prophet (SAWA) said,** 'The best form of charity is for a man to gain knowledge and then teach it to his fellow brother.'[5051]

٤٤٩٣. رسولُ اللهِ ﷺ: أفضَلُ الصَّدَقَةِ أن يَعلَمَ المَرءُ عِلماً ثُمَّ يُعَلِّمَهُ أخاهُ.[٥٠٥١]

4494. **The Prophet (SAWA) said,** 'Any man who has been granted knowledge by Allah but who suppresses it, in spite of knowing it, will meet Allah, Mighty and Exalted, on the Day of Resurrection bridled with a rein of fire.'[5052]

٤٤٩٤. عنه ﷺ: أيُّما رَجُلٍ آتاهُ اللهُ عِلماً فكَتَمَهُ وهُوَ يَعلَمُهُ، لَقِيَ اللهَ عزَّوجلَّ يومَ القِيامَةِ مُلجَماً بِلِجامٍ مِن نارٍ.[٥٠٥٢]

4495. **Imām 'Alī (AS) said,** 'Allah does not obligate the ignorant to learn until He has obligated the knowledgeable to teach.'[5053]

٤٤٩٥. الإمامُ عليٌّ ﷺ: ما أخَذَ اللهُ على أهلِ الجَهلِ أن يَتَعَلَّموا حَتّى أخَذَ على أهلِ العِلمِ أن يُعَلِّموا.[٥٠٥٣]

4496. **Imām 'Alī (AS) said,** 'Everything decreases with giving away except knowledge.'[5054]

٤٤٩٦. عنه ﷺ: كلُّ شَيءٍ يَنقُصُ علَى الإنفاقِ إلّا العِلمَ.[٥٠٥٤]

4497. **Imām al-Bāqir (AS) said,** 'He who teaches someone a matter of guidance receives the same reward as he who practices it, without any decrease in the latter's reward thereof.'[5055]

٤٤٩٧. الإمامُ الباقرُ ﷺ: مَن عَلَّمَ بابَ هُدىً فلَهُ مِثلُ أجرِ مَن عَمِلَ بهِ، ولا يُنقَصُ اُولئكَ مِن اُجورِهِم شيئاً.[٥٠٥٥]

4498. **Imām al-Bāqir (AS) said,** 'For the teacher of good, all the animals on the land and the fish in the sea seek forgiveness on his behalf, as do all creatures great and small in Allah's earth and sky.'[5056]

٤٤٩٨. عنه ﷺ: مُعَلِّمُ الخَيرِ يَستَغفِرُ لَهُ دَوابُّ الأرضِ، وحِيتانُ البُحورِ، وكُلُّ صَغيرَةٍ وكَبيرَةٍ في أرضِ اللهِ وسَمائهِ.[٥٠٥٦]

4499. **Imām al-Ṣādiq (AS) said,** 'Verily upon everything is its *zakāt*, and the *zakāt* of knowledge is to teach it to those who are worthy of it.'[5057]

٤٤٩٩. الإمامُ الصّادقُ ﷺ: إنَّ لِكُلِّ شَيءٍ زَكاةً، وزَكاةُ العِلمِ أن يُعَلِّمَهُ أهلَهُ.[٥٠٥٧]

1346. The Way the Teacher Will be Resurrected

١٣٤٦ ـ صِفَةُ حَشْرِ المُعَلِّمِ

4500. **The Prophet (SAWA) said,** 'Shall I inform you who the absolutely most generous one is? Allah is the Absolutely Most Generous One, and I am the most generous of Adam's offspring, and the most generous from amongst you all after me is the man who has been taught knowledge and subsequently spreads his knowledge to others. He

٤٥٠٠. رسولُ اللهِ ﷺ: ألا اُخبِرُكُم عَنِ الأجوَدِ الأجوَدِ؟ اللهُ الأجوَدُ الأجوَدُ، وأنا أجوَدُ وُلدِ آدَمَ، وأجوَدُكُم مِن بَعدي رَجُلٌ عَلَّمَ عِلماً فنَشَرَ

will be raised on the Day of Resurrection as a community in himself, and after him is the man who is generous in giving up his life for Allah, Mighty and Exalted, and is killed for Him.'[5058]

عِلمَهُ، يُبعَثُ يَومَ القِيامَةِ أُمَّةً وَحدَهُ، ورَجُلٌ جادَ بِنَفسِهِ للهِ عَزَّوجلَّ حَتّىٰ يُقتَلَ.[٥٠١٨]

1347. Gaining Knowledge for Allah and for Other than Allah

١٣٤٧ ـ التَعَلُّمُ للهِ ولِغَيرِ اللهِ

4501. **The Prophet (SAWA) said,** 'He who seeks knowledge for Allah, no sooner does he learn even a chapter of it than it increases him in humility within himself, in humbleness in front of people, it increases his fear of Allah and his striving in religion, and that is the one who benefits from the knowledge, so he should acquire. And he who seeks knowledge for this world and for status amongst people and for a favoured position with the ruler, no sooner does he learn even a chapter of it than it only increases his arrogance within himself, his presumptuousness with people, his self-delusion about Allah and his estrangement from religion. That is the one who does not benefit from his knowledge, and must subsequently refrain from it and stop furnishing proof for the case against himself in order not to feel regret and shame on the Day of Resurrection.'[5059]

٤٥٠١. رسولُ اللهِ ﷺ: مَن طَلَبَ العِلمَ للهِ لَم يُصِبْ مِنهُ باباً إلّا ازدادَ بِهِ في نَفسِهِ ذُلّاً، وفِي النّاسِ تَواضُعاً، وللهِ خَوفاً، وفِي الدِّينِ اجتِهاداً، وذٰلكَ الّذي يَنتَفِعُ بِالعِلمِ فَليَتَعَلَّمْهُ، ومَن طَلَبَ العِلمَ لِلدّنيا والمَنزِلَةِ عِندَ النّاسِ والحَظوَةِ عِندَ السُّلطانِ لَم يُصِبْ مِنهُ باباً إلّا ازدادَ في نَفسِهِ عَظَمَةً، وعَلى النّاسِ استِطالَةً، وبِاللهِ اغتِراراً، ومِنَ الدِّينِ جَفاءً، فذٰلكَ الّذي لا يَنتَفِعُ بِالعِلمِ، فَلْيَكُفَّ وَليُمسِكْ عَنِ الحُجَّةِ عَلىٰ نَفسِهِ، والنَّدامَةِ والخِزيِ يَومَ القِيامَةِ.[٥٠١٩]

4502. **The Prophet (SAWA) said,** 'He who desires knowledge in order that he may beguile people will never even smell the fragrance of Paradise.'[5060]

٤٥٠٢. عنه ﷺ: مَنِ ابتَغَى العِلمَ لِيَخدَعَ بِهِ النّاسَ لَم يَجِدْ رِيحَ الجَنَّةِ.[٥٠٢٠]

4503. **The Prophet (SAWA) said,** 'Whoever gains knowledge for the sake of anything other than Allah, most High, should take himself a seat in the Fire.'[5061]

٤٥٠٣. عنه ﷺ: مَن تَعَلَّمَ العِلمَ لِغَيرِ اللهِ تَعالىٰ فَلْيَتَبَوَّأْ مَقعَدَهُ مِن نارٍ.[٥٠٢١]

4504. **Imām 'Alī (AS) said,** 'Take of knowledge whatever seems good to you, but beware of seeking knowledge for four reasons: in order that you may contend with the scholars, or in order to wrangle with foolish people, or that you may show off

٤٥٠٤. الإمامُ عليٌّ ؑ: خُذوا مِنَ العِلمِ ما بَدا لَكُم، وإيّاكُم أن تَطلُبوهُ لِخِصالٍ أربَعٍ: لِتُباهوا بِهِ العُلَماءَ أو تُماروا بِهِ السُّفَهاءَ، أو تُراؤوا بِهِ فِي

with it in gatherings, or in order that people may look up to you to lead them.'[5062]

المَجالِسِ، أوتَصرِفوا وُجوهَ النّاسِ إلَيكُم لِلتَّرَؤُّسِ.[٥٠٢٢]

4505. **Imām al-Ṣādiq (AS) said,** 'He who gains knowledge for the sake of Allah, acts upon it for the sake of Allah and teaches it for the sake of Allah is called great in the kingdom of the heavens, and it is exclaimed about him: 'Indeed he gains knowledge for Allah, acts for Allah and teaches for Allah!'[5063]

٤٥٠٥. الإمامُ الصّادقُ عليه السلام: مَن تَعَلَّمَ للهِ وعَمِلَ للهِ وعَلَّمَ للهِ دُعِيَ في مَلَكوتِ السَّماواتِ عَظيماً، فقيلَ: تَعَلَّمَ للهِ، وعَمِلَ للهِ، وعَلَّمَ للهِ![٥٠٢٣]

1348. What is Necessary in Choosing a Teacher

١٣٤٨ـ ما يَنبَغي في اختِيارِ المُعَلِّم

4506. **Prophet Jesus (AS) said,** 'Take the truth even if it be from wrongdoers, but do not take falsehood even if it be from the righteous – be critics of speech.'[5064]

٤٥٠٦. عيسى عليه السلام: خُذوا الحَقَّ مِن أهلِ الباطِلِ، ولا تأخُذوا الباطِلَ مِن أهلِ الحَقِّ، كونوا نُقّادَ الكَلامِ.[٥٠٢٤]

4507. **The Prophet (SAWA) said,** 'Knowledge is a part of religion [just as] prayer is a part of religion, so be careful who you take this knowledge from.'[5065]

٤٥٠٧. رسولُ اللهِ صلى الله عليه وآله: العِلمُ دِينٌ، الصَّلاةُ دِينٌ، فَانظُروا عَمَّن تَأخُذونَ هٰذا العِلمَ.[٥٠٢٥]

4508. **Imām ʿAlī (AS) said,** 'Take wisdom from whoever brings it to you, and look at that which is being said and do not look at who is saying it.'[5066][5067]

٤٥٠٨. الإمامُ عليٌّ عليه السلام: خُذِ الحِكمَةَ مِمَّن أتاكَ بِها، وَانظُرْ إلىٰ ما قالَ، ولا تَنظُرْ[٥٠٢٦] إلىٰ مَن قالَ.[٥٠٢٧][٥٠٢٨]

4509. **Imām al-Kāẓim (AS) said,** 'Knowledge can only be gained from a divine scholar, and recognition of that scholar is through the intellect.'[5068]

٤٥٠٩. الإمامُ الكاظمُ عليه السلام: لا عِلمَ إلّا مِن عالِمٍ رَبّانِيٍّ، ومَعرِفَةُ العالِمِ بِالعَقلِ.[٥٠٢٩]

(See also: WISDOM: section 562)

(اُنظر) الحكمة: باب ٥٦٢.

1349. The Rights of the Student to be Observed by the Teacher

١٣٤٩ـ حُقوقُ المُتَعَلِّمِ عَلَى المُعَلِّمِ

4510. **The Prophet (SAWA) said,** 'Be gentle towards those whom you teach as well to those whom you learn from.'[5069]

٤٥١٠. رسولُ اللهِ صلى الله عليه وآله: لِينُوا لِمَن تُعلِّمونَ، ولِمَن تَتَعَلَّمونَ مِنهُ.[٥٠٣٠]

4511. **Imām Zayn al-ʿĀbidīn (AS) said,** 'The right of your subjects through the knowledge you possess is to know that Allah has made you a custodian over them on account of the knowledge He has bestowed on you and the storehouses [of wisdom] which He has opened up for you. If you teach people well, and do not mistreat them, and do not get bored of [teaching] them, then Allah will increase His grace upon you. But if you withhold your knowledge from people or treat them harshly when they seek knowledge from you, then it will be Allah's right to deprive you of knowledge and its magnificence, and to make you fall from your place in the people's hearts.'[5070]

٤٥١١ . الإمامُ زينُ العابدينَ :أمّا حَقُّ رَعِيَّتِكَ بِالعِلمِ: فأن تَعلَمَ أنَّ اللهَ عَزَّوجلَّ إنَّما جَعَلَكَ قَيِّماً لَهُم فيما آتاكَ مِنَ العِلمِ، وفَتَحَ لَكَ مِن خَزائنِهِ، فإذا أحسَنتَ في تَعليمِ النّاسِ ولَم تَخرُقْ بِهِم ولَم تَضجَرْ عَلَيهِم زادَكَ اللهُ مِن فَضلِهِ، وإن أنتَ مَنَعتَ النّاسَ عِلمَكَ أو خَرَقتَ بِهِم عِندَ طَلَبِهِمِ العِلمَ كانَ حَقّاً عَلَى اللهِ عَزَّوجلَّ أن يَسلُبَكَ العِلمَ وبَهاءَهُ، ويُسقِطَ مِنَ القُلوبِ مَحَلَّكَ.[٥٠٣١]

4512. **Imām al-Ṣādiq (AS) said,** 'The knowledgeable man must not be harsh when he teaches, and he must not be disdainful when he learns.'[5071]

٤٥١٢ . الإمامُ الصّادقُ :عَلَى العالِمِ إذا عَلَّمَ أن لا يَعنُفَ، وإذا عُلِّمَ أن لا يَأنَفَ.[٥٠٣٢]

4513. **Imām al-Ṣādiq (AS)** with regards to Allah's verse in the Qur'an: *"Do not turn your cheek disdainfully from the people"*[5072], said, 'That people should be equal in your eyes when it comes to [sharing] knowledge.'[5073]

٤٥١٣ . عنه ـ في قولهِ تعالىٰ: (وَلاتُصَعِّرْ خَدَّكَ لِلنّاسِ)[٥٠٣٣] ـ: لِيَكُنِ النّاسُ عِندَكَ فِي العِلمِ سَواءً.[٥٠٣٤]

1350. The Rights of the Teacher to be Observed by the Student

١٣٥٠ ـ حُقوقُ المُعَلِّمِ عَلَى المُتَعَلِّمِ

4514. **The Prophet (SAWA) said,** 'There are three types of people whose right none will deem lightly apart from the hypocrite whose hypocrisy is obvious: the old person in Islam, the just leader, and the teacher of good.'[5074]

٤٥١٤ . رسولُ اللهِ :ثَلاثَةٌ لا يَستَخِفُّ بِحَقِّهِم إلّا مُنافِقٌ: ذو شَيبَةٍ فِي الإسلامِ، وإمامٌ مُقسِطٌ، ومُعَلِّمُ الخَيرِ.[٥٠٣٥]

4515. **Imām ʿAlī (AS) said,** 'It is a scholar's right upon you that you greet people in general as a whole but single him out with your greeting, that you sit in front of him, that you do not point to him with your hand, nor make hints against him with your eyes, nor say, '*but* X *said*' in opposition to his statements, nor backbite anyone in his presence, nor whisper secrets to others in his

٤٥١٥ . الإمامُ عليٌّ :مِن حَقِّ العالِمِ عَلَيكَ أن تُسَلِّمَ عَلَى القَومِ عامَّةً وتَخُصَّهُ دونَهُم بِالتَّحِيَّةِ، وأن تَجلِسَ أمامَهُ، ولا تُشيرَنَّ عِندَهُ بِيَدِكَ، ولا تَغمِزَنَّ بِعَينَيكَ، ولا تَقولَنَّ: «قالَ فُلانٌ» خِلافاً لِقَولِهِ، ولا تَغتابَنَّ عِندَهُ أحَداً، ولا تُسارَّ في

gathering, nor pull on his robe, nor insist for him to continue if he is tired, nor show disinclination at the length of his speech, for verily it [i.e. his speech] is as a palm tree from which you [should] anxiously wait for something to fall from it for you.'[5075]

مَجلِسِهِ، ولا تَأخُذَ بِثَوبِهِ، ولا تَلِجَّ[٥٠٣٦] عَلَيهِ إذا مَلَّ، ولا تُعرِضَ مِن طُولِ صُحبَتِهِ، فَإنَّما هِيَ بِمَنزِلَةِ النَّخلَةِ تَنتَظِرُ مَتىٰ يَسقُطُ عَلَيكَ مِنها شَيءٌ.[٥٠٣٧]

4516. **Imām ʿAlī (AS) said,** 'It is not part of the moral virtues of a believer that he should flatter or be jealous except in the quest for knowledge.'[5076]

٤٥١٦. عنه عليه السلام: لَيسَ مِن أخلاقِ المُؤمِنِ التَّمَلُّقُ ولا الحَسَدُ إلّا في طَلَبِ العِلمِ.[٥٠٣٨]

4517. **Imām Zayn al-ʿĀbidīn (AS) said,** 'The right of the one who trains you in knowledge is to magnify him, to revere his sessions, to listen to him attentively, and to pay attention to him with devotion. You should not raise your voice to him, nor answer a question that someone has asked him about something, so that he will be the one to answer. You should not address anyone else in his session, nor backbite anyone in his presence. You must defend him if anyone ever speaks ill of him in your presence, conceal his faults and publicise his virtues. You should not sit in the company of his enemy, nor be hostile towards his friend. If you fulfil this right, Allah's angels bear witness that you frequented him and learned from his knowledge for the sake of Allah, exalted be His Name, and not for the sake of people.'[5077]

٤٥١٧. الإمامُ زَينُ العابِدينَ عليه السلام: حَقُّ سائِسِكَ بِالعِلمِ: التَّعظيمُ لَهُ، والتَّوقيرُ لِمَجلِسِهِ، وحُسنُ الاستِماعِ إلَيهِ، والإقبالُ عَلَيهِ، وأن لا تَرفَعَ عَلَيهِ صَوتَكَ، وأن لا تُجيبَ أحَداً يَسألُهُ عَن شَيءٍ حَتّىٰ يَكونَ هُوَ الَّذي يُجيبُ، ولا تُحَدِّثَ في مَجلِسِهِ أحَداً، ولا تَغتابَ عِندَهُ أحَداً، وأن تَدفَعَ عَنهُ إذا ذُكِرَ عِندَكَ بِسوءٍ، وأن تَستُرَ عُيوبَهُ، وتُظهِرَ مَناقِبَهُ، ولا تُجالِسَ لَهُ عَدُوّاً، ولا تُعادِيَ لَهُ وَلِيّاً، فإذا فَعَلتَ ذٰلِكَ شَهِدَ لَكَ مَلائِكَةُ اللّٰهِ بِأنَّكَ قَصَدتَهُ وتَعَلَّمتَ عِلمَهُ للّٰهِ جَلَّ اسمُهُ لا لِلنّاسِ.[٥٠٣٩]

1351. Honouring the Scholar

١٣٥١ـ تَكريمُ العالِمِ

4518. **The Prophet (SAWA) said,** 'He who goes forth to meet the scholars has indeed come forth to meet me, and he who visits the scholars has indeed visited me, and he who sits in the company of the scholars has indeed sat in my company, and whoever sits in my company is as if he has sat in the company of my Lord.'[5078]

٤٥١٨. رسولُ اللّٰهِ ﷺ: مَنِ استَقبَلَ العُلَماءَ فَقَدِ استَقبَلَني، ومَن زارَ العُلَماءَ فَقَد زارَني، ومَن جالَسَ العُلَماءَ فَقَد جالَسَني، ومَن جالَسَني فَكَأنَّما جالَسَ رَبّي.[٥٠٤٠]

4519. **Imām ʿAlī (AS) said,** 'When you see a scholar, be a servant to him.'[5079]

٤٥١٩. الإمامُ عليٌّ عليه السلام: إذا رَأيتَ عالِماً فَكُن لَهُ خادِماً.[٥٠٤١]

4520. **Imām ʿAlī (AS) said,** 'He who shows reverence to a scholar has revered his Lord.'[5080]

٤٥٢٠ . عنه عليه السلام : مَن وَقَّرَ عالِماً فقد وَقَّرَ رَبَّهُ .[٥٠٤٢]

1352. Duties Incumbent on the Student

١٣٥٢ ـ ما يَنبَغي عَلَى المُتَعَلِّمِ

4521. **al-Khiḍr (AS) said** to Prophet Moses (AS), 'O Moses, devote yourself exclusively to knowledge if you want it, for verily knowledge is for the one who devotes himself exclusively to it.'[5081]

٤٥٢١ . الخضرُ عليه السلام ـ لِموسىٰ عليه السلام ـ : ياموسىٰ ، تَفَرَّغ لِلعِلمِ إن كُنتَ تُريدُهُ ، فإنَّ العِلمَ لِمَن تفَرَّغَ .[٥٠٤٣]

4522. **The Prophet (SAWA) said,** 'A person's intellect is incomplete until ten qualities come together in him…that he must never tire of seeking knowledge his whole life.'[5082]

٤٥٢٢ . رسولُ اللهِ ﷺ : لا يَتِمُّ عَقلُ المَرءِ حَتّىٰ يَتِمَّ فيهِ عَشرُ خِلالٍ ... لا يَسأمُ مِن طَلَبِ العِلمِ طُولَ عُمرِهِ .[٥٠٤٤]

4523. **Imām ʿAlī (AS) said,** 'The student must discipline himself in his quest for knowledge, and not become bored of learning, nor overestimate what he already knows.'[5083]

٤٥٢٣ . الإمامُ عليٌّ عليه السلام : عَلى المُتَعَلِّمِ أن يُدئبَ نَفسَهُ في طَلَبِ العِلمِ ، ولا يَمَلَّ مِن تَعَلُّمِهِ ، ولا يَستَكثِرَ ما عَلِمَ .[٥٠٤٥]

4524. **Imām ʿAlī (AS) said,** 'Only he who lengthens his study attains knowledge.'[5084]

٤٥٢٤ . عنه عليه السلام : لا يُحرِزُ العِلمَ إلّا مَن يُطيلُ دَرسَهُ .[٥٠٤٦]

4525. **Imām ʿAlī (AS) said,** 'He who gives a great deal of thought to what he learns masters his knowledge, and comes to understand that which he could not understand before.'[5085]

٤٥٢٥ . عنه عليه السلام : مَن أكثَرَ الفِكرَ فيما تَعَلَّمَ أتقَنَ عِلمَهُ ، وفَهِمَ ما لَم يَكُن يَفهَمُ .[٥٠٤٧]

1353. The Virtue of the Scholars

١٣٥٣ ـ فَضلُ العُلَماءِ

4526. **The Prophet (SAWA) said,** 'The scholars are Allah's trustees over His creation.'[5086]

٤٥٢٦ . رسولُ اللهِ ﷺ : العُلَماءُ أُمَناءُ اللهِ عَلىٰ خَلقِهِ .[٥٠٤٨]

4527. **The Prophet (SAWA) said,** 'The superiority of the scholar over others is as the superiority of the prophet over his community.'[5087]

٤٥٢٧ . عنه ﷺ : فَضلُ العالِمِ عَلىٰ غَيرِهِ كَفَضلِ النَّبِيِّ عَلىٰ أُمَّتِهِ .[٥٠٤٩]

4528. **Imām ʿAlī (AS) said,** 'The scholars are the governors over people.'[5088]

٤٥٣٨ . الإمامُ عليٌّ عليه السلام : العُلَماءُ حُكّامٌ عَلَى النّاسِ .[٥٠٥٠]

4529. **Imām al-Ṣādiq (AS) said,** 'The scholars from among our *Shīʿa* are stationed at the forefront next to where Satan and his demons are, preventing them from coming out to the weak *Shīʿa* and from letting Satan and his followers gain mastery over them.'[5089]

٤٥٢٩ . الإمامُ الصّادقُ ﵇: عُلَماءُ شيعَتِنا مُرابِطونَ فِي الثَّغرِ الّذي يَلي إبليسَ وعَفاريتَهُ، يَمنَعونَهُم عَنِ الخُروجِ عَلىٰ ضُعَفاءِ شيعَتِنا، وعَن أن يَتَسَلَّطَ عَلَيهِم إبليسُ وشيعَتُهُ.[٥٠٥١]

1354. The Fruit of Knowledge

١٣٥٤ ـ ثَمَرَةُ العِلمِ

"And of humans and beasts and cattle there are likewise diverse hues. Only those of Allah's servants having knowledge fear Him. Indeed Allah is all-mighty, all-forgiving."[5090]

﴿وَمِنَ النَّاسِ وَالدَّوابِّ وَالْأَنْعامِ مُخْتَلِفٌ أَلْوانُهُ كَذٰلِكَ إِنَّما يَخْشَى اللهَ مِنْ عِبادِهِ الْعُلَماءُ إِنَّ اللهَ عَزِيزٌ غَفُورٌ﴾.[٥٠٥٢]

4530. **Imām ʿAlī (AS) said,** 'The fruit of knowledge is action in accordance with it.'[5091]

٤٥٣٠ . الإمامُ عليٌّ ﵇: ثَمَرَةُ العِلمِ العَمَلُ بِهِ.[٥٠٥٣]

4531. **Imām ʿAlī (AS) said,** 'The fruit of knowledge is worship.'[5092]

٤٥٣١ . عنه ﵇: ثَمَرَةُ العِلمِ العِبادَةُ.[٥٠٥٤]

4532. **Imām ʿAlī (AS) said,** 'The fruit of knowledge is sincerity of action.'[5093]

٤٥٣٢ . عنه ﵇: ثَمَرَةُ العِلمِ إخلاصُ العَمَلِ.[٥٠٥٥]

4533. It is narrated in *Miṣbāḥ al-Sharīʿa* that Imām al-Ṣādiq (AS) said, 'Fear [of Allah] is the legacy of knowledge, and knowledge is the ray of inner understanding and the heart of faith. So he who is devoid of fear cannot be knowledgeable, even if he is precise in obscure sciences.' Allah, most High, has said, *"Only those of Allah's servants having knowledge fear Him."*[5094]

٤٥٣٣ . مصباح الشريعة ـ فيما نسبه إلى الإمامِ الصّادقِ ﵇ ـ: الخَشيَةُ مِيراثُ العِلمِ، والعِلمُ شُعاعُ المَعرِفَةِ وقَلبُ الإيمانِ، ومَن حُرِمَ الخَشيَةَ لا يَكونُ عالِماً وإن شَقَّ الشَّعرَ بِمُتَشابِهاتِ العِلمِ، قالَ اللهُ تَعالىٰ: ﴿إنَّما يَخْشَى اللهَ مِن عِبادِهِ العُلَماءُ﴾.[٥٠٥٦]

1355. The Duties Incumbent Upon a Person of Knowledge

١٣٥٥ ـ ما يَنبَغي عَلَى العالِمِ

4534. **The Prophet (SAWA) said,** 'Whoever says: 'I am a knowledgeable man' is indeed ignorant.'[5095]

٤٥٣٤ . رسولُ اللهِ ﷺ: مَن قالَ: أنا عالِمٌ فَهُوَ جاهِلٌ.[٥٠٥٧]

4535. **Imām ʿAlī (AS) said,** 'The scholar is the one who is never satiated with knowledge, and never becomes full of it.'[5096]

٤٥٣٥ . الإمامُ عليٌّ ﵇: العالِمُ مَن لا يَشبَعُ مِنَ العِلمِ، ولا يَتَشبَّعُ بِهِ.[٥٠٥٨]

4536. **Imām ʿAlī (AS) said,** 'The scholar is the one who never gets bored of gaining knowledge.'[5097]

٤٥٣٦. عنه ﷺ : العالِمُ الّذي لا يَمَلُّ مِن تَعَلُّمِ العِلمِ.[٥٠٥٩]

1356. Reprehension of Practising without Knowledge

١٣٥٦ ـ ذمّ العمل بلا علم

4537. **The Prophet (SAWA) said,** 'He who acts contrary to what he knows, his immoral acts supersede his righteous acts.'[5098]

٤٥٣٧. رسولُ اللهِ ﷺ : مَن عَمِلَ عَلىٰ غَيرِ عِلمٍ كانَ ما يُفسِدُ أكثَرَ مِمّا يُصلِحُ.[٥٠٦٠]

4538. **The Prophet (SAWA) said,** 'The one who worships without any knowledge [of his actions] is as a donkey in a mill.'[5099]

٤٥٣٨. عنه ﷺ : المُتَعَبِّدُ بِغَيرِ فِقهٍ كالحِمارِ في الطّاحونِ.[٥٠٦١]

4539. **Imām al-Ṣādiq (AS) said,** 'He who acts without any insight is as the one who travels off the path, whom walking faster only avails to take him further away from the path.'[5100]

٤٥٣٩. الإمامُ الصادقُ ﷺ: العامِلُ عَلىٰ غيرِ بَصيرَةٍ كَالسّائرِ عَلىٰ غَيرِ الطَّريقِ، ولا يَزيدُهُ سُرعَةُ السَّيرِ مِنَ الطَّريقِ إلّا بُعداً.[٥٠٦٢]

1357. The Necessity of Practising Upon One's Knowledge

١٣٥٧ ـ وجوب العمل بالعلم

4540. **The Prophet (SAWA) said,** 'Advise each other with knowledge, for verily your betrayal of someone in their knowledge is worse than your betraying him in their wealth, and verily Allah will question you on the Day of Resurrection.'[5101]

٤٥٤٠. رسولُ اللهِ ﷺ : تَناصَحوا فِي العِلمِ؛ فإنَّ خِيانَةَ أحَدِكُم في عِلمِهِ أشَدُّ مِن خِيانَتِهِ في مالِهِ، وإنَّ اللهَ سائلُكُم يَومَ القِيامَةِ.[٥٠٦٣]

4541. **The Prophet (SAWA) said,** 'The ambition of knowledgeable people is greater awareness, whereas the ambition of fools is telling stories.'[5102]

٤٥٤١. عنه ﷺ : هِمَّةُ العُلَماءِ الوِعايَةُ، وهِمَّةُ السُّفَهاءِ الرِّوايَةُ.[٥٠٦٤]

4542. **The Prophet (SAWA) said,** 'A group from among the dwellers of Paradise will look down upon a group from among the inmates of Hell, saying, 'What brought you into the Fire when we ourselves entered Paradise by virtue of your education and instruction?!' upon which they will reply, 'Verily we used to enjoin good but did not act upon it.'[5103]

٤٥٤٢. عنه ﷺ : يَطَّلِعُ قَومٌ مِن أهلِ الجَنَّةِ عَلىٰ قَومٍ مِن أهلِ النّارِ فيَقولونَ: ما أدخَلَكُمُ النّارَ وقَد دَخَلنا الجَنَّةَ لِفَضلِ تَأديبِكُم وتَعليمِكُم؟! فيَقولونَ: إنّا كُنّا نَأمُرُ بِالخَيرِ ولا نَفعَلُهُ.[٥٠٦٥]

4543. **Imām ʿAlī (AS) said,** 'Verily people abstain from gaining knowledge because of the numerous instances they witness of the people's lack of action in accordance with what they know.'[5104]

٤٥٤٣. الإمامُ عليٌّ عليه السلام: إنَّما زَهَّدَ النّاسَ في طَلَبِ العِلمِ كَثرَةُ ما يَـرَونَ مِـن قِـلَّةِ مَـن عَـمِلَ بِـما عَلِمَ.[٥٠٦٦]

4544. **Imām ʿAlī (AS) said,** 'The whole world is ignorance apart from the areas of knowledge, and all of knowledge will be held punishable apart from that which is acted upon.'[5105]

٤٥٤٤. عنه عليه السلام: الدّنيا كُلُّها جَهلٌ إلّا مَواضِـعَ العِلمِ، وَالعِلمُ كُلُّه حُجَّةٌ إلّا ما عُمِلَ بِهِ.[٥٠٦٧]

4545. **Imām ʿAlī (AS) said,** 'Knowledge without action is a curse, and action without knowledge is straying in error.'[5106]

٤٥٤٥. عنه عليه السلام: العِلمُ بِلا عَمَلٍ وَبالٌ، العَمَلُ بِلا عِلمٍ ضَلالٌ.[٥٠٦٨]

4546. **Imām ʿAlī (AS) said,** '[To see] An impudent yet knowledgeable man and a religious but ignorant man is a mortal blow to me, for the ignorant man dupes people with his religiosity whilst the knowledgeable man drives them away through his impudence.'[5107]

٤٥٤٦. عنه عليه السلام: قَصَمَ ظَهري عـالِمٌ مُـتَهَتِّكٌ، وجـاهِلٌ مُـتَنَسِّكٌ، فـالجاهِلُ يَـغُشُّ النّـاسَ بِتَنَسُّكِهِ، والعالِمُ يُنَفِّرُهُم بِتَهَتُّكِهِ.[٥٠٦٩]

4547. **Imām ʿAlī (AS) said,** 'When you hear a narration, think of putting it into practice and not with the reasoning of just narrating it, for verily the narrators of knowledge are many but those who attend to it are few.'[5108]

٤٥٤٧. عنه عليه السلام: اعقِلوا الخَبَرَ إذا سَمِعتُموهُ عَقلَ رِعايَةٍ لا عَقلَ رِوايَـةٍ؛ فـإنَّ رُواةَ العِـلمِ كَـثيرٌ ورُعاتَهُ قَليلٌ.[٥٠٧٠]

4548. **Imām ʿAlī (AS) said,** 'He who appoints himself a leader of people must begin by teaching himself before teaching others. And his discipline of them must be through his own example rather than through his words. The one who teaches and disciplines himself is more worthy of esteem than the one who teaches and disciplines people.'[5109]

٤٥٤٨. عنه عليه السلام: مَن نَصَبَ نَفسَهُ لِلنّاسِ إماماً فعَلَيهِ أن يَبدَأ بِتَعليمِ نَفسِهِ قَـبلَ تَـعليمِ غَـيرِهِ، وَليَكُن تَأديبُهُ بِسيرَتِهِ قَبلَ تَأديبِهِ بِلِسانِهِ، ومُعَلِّمُ نَفسِهِ ومُؤَدِّبُها أحَقُّ بِالإجلالِ مِن مُعَلِّمِ النّـاسِ ومُؤَدِّبِهِم.[٥٠٧١]

4549. **Imām ʿAlī (AS) said,** 'It is incumbent upon the knowledgeable man to act upon what he knows, and then to seek to learn that which he does not know.'[5110]

٤٥٤٩. عنه عليه السلام: عَلَى العالِمِ أن يَعمَلَ بِما عَلِمَ، ثُمَّ يَطلُبَ تَعَلُّمَ ما لَم يَعلَمْ.[٥٠٧٢]

4550. **Imām ʿAlī (AS) said,** 'Knowledge is linked to action, so he who knows acts. And knowledge calls for action, so if one answers [the call] it remains, and if not it departs from him.'[5111]

٤٥٥٠ . عنه (عليه السلام) : العِلمُ مَقرونٌ بِالعَمَلِ، فمَن عَلِمَ عَمِلَ والعِلمُ يَهتِفُ بِالعَمَلِ، فإن أجابَهُ وإلّا ارتَحَلَ عَنهُ.٥٠٧٣

1358. The Severity of the Chastisement of the Knowledgeable Man Who Abandons His Knowledge

١٣٥٨ـ تَشديدُ العُقوبَةِ عَلَى العالِمِ التّارِكِ لِعِلمِه

4551. **The Prophet (SAWA) said,** 'Verily the inmates of the Fire will be tormented by the stench of the knowledgeable man who had abandoned his knowledge.'[5112]

٤٥٥١ . رسولُ اللهِ ﷺ : إنَّ أهلَ النّارِ لَيَتَأذَّونَ مِن ريحِ العالِمِ التّارِكِ لِعِلمِهِ.٥٠٧٤

4552. **Imām ʿAlī (AS) said,** 'Those who know and those who do not know are not equal in the sight of Allah with regards to their chastisement. May Allah make us and you benefit from the knowledge we have and make it be reserved solely for His pleasure; verily He is all-hearing, responsive.'[5113]

٤٥٥٢ . الإمامُ عليٌّ (عليه السلام) : لا يَستَوي عِندَ اللهِ في العُقوبَةِ الّذينَ يَعلَمونَ والّذينَ لا يَعلَمونَ، نَفَعَنا اللهُ وإيّاكُم بِما عَلِمنا، وجَعَلَهُ لِوَجهِهِ خالِصاً، إنَّهُ سَميعٌ مُجيبٌ.٥٠٧٥

4553. **Imām ʿAlī (AS) said,** 'A knowledgeable man's blunder is as the destruction of a boat which itself sinks and drowns [those aboard it].'[5114]

٤٥٥٣ . عنه (عليه السلام) : زَلَّةُ العالِمِ كانكِسارِ السَّفينَةِ تَغرَقُ، وتُغرِقُ.٥٠٧٦

4554. **Imām al-Ṣādiq (AS) said,** 'Verily the ignorant man is forgiven seventy sins before the knowledgeable man is forgiven a single one.'[5115]

٤٥٥٤ . الإمامُ الصّادقُ (عليه السلام) : إنَّهُ يُغفَرُ لِلجاهِلِ سَبعونَ ذَنباً قَبلَ أن يُغفَرَ لِلعالِمِ ذَنبٌ واحِدٌ.٥٠٧٧

4555. **Imām al-Ṣādiq (AS) said,** 'The one amongst people to be the most severely punished will be the knowledgeable man who has not benefited from his knowledge one bit.'[5116]

٤٥٥٥ . عنه (عليه السلام) : أشَدُّ النّاسِ عَذاباً عالِمٌ لا يُنتَفَعُ مِن عِلمِهِ بِشَيءٍ.٥٠٧٨

4556. It is narrated in *Biḥār al-Anwār*, 'Allah revealed to Prophet David (AS), saying, 'Verily the least of what I will do to a knowledgeable man who does not act upon his knowledge, which is worse than seventy punishments, is that I remove the sweetness of My remembrance from his heart.'[5117]

٤٥٥٦ . بحارالأنوار : أوحَى اللهُ تبارك وتعالى إلى داوُدَ (عليه السلام) : إنَّ أهوَنَ ما أنا صانِعٌ بِعالِمٍ غَيرِ عامِلٍ بِعِلمِهِ أشَدُّ مِن سَبعينَ عُقوبَةً ؛ أن اُخرِجَ مِن قَلبِهِ حَلاوَةَ ذِكري.٥٠٧٩

(See also: FAITH: section 185; HELL: section 403)

(اُنظر) الإيمان: باب ١٨٥، جهنّم: باب ٤٠٣.

1359. Reprehension of Evil Scholars

١٣٥٩ ـ ذَمُّ عُلَماءِ السُّوءِ

4557. **Prophet Jesus (AS) said,** 'How can one whose worldly life is dearer to him than his Hereafter be considered among the people of knowledge, whilst he pursues his worldly life and considers that which harms him more beloved than that which benefits him?!'[5118]

٤٥٥٧ . عيسى عليه السلام : كَيفَ يَكونُ مِن أهلِ العِلمِ مَن دُنياهُ عِندَهُ آثَرُ مِن آخِرَتِهِ وهُوَ مُقبِلٌ عَلىٰ دُنياهُ، وما يَضُرُّهُ أحَبُّ إلَيهِ مِمّا يَنفَعُهُ؟![٥٠٨٠]

4558. **Prophet Jesus (AS) said,** 'The dinar [i.e. wealth] is religion's affliction, and the knowledgeable man is religion's doctor. So when you see the doctor drawing the affliction upon himself, be suspicious of him and know that he does not advise others well.'[5119]

٤٥٥٨ . عنه عليه السلام : الدِّينارُ داءُ الدِّينِ، والعالِمُ طَبيبُ الدِّينِ، فإذا رَأيتُمُ الطَّبيبَ يَجُرُّ الدّاءَ إلىٰ نَفسِهِ فَاتَّهِموهُ، وَاعلَموا أنَّهُ غَيرُ ناصِحٍ لِغَيرِهِ.[٥٠٨١]

4559. **The Prophet (SAWA) said,** 'Verily the worst of all evil are the evil scholars, and verily the best of all good are the good scholars.'[5120]

٤٥٥٩ . رسولُ اللهِ ﷺ : ألا إنَّ شَرَّ الشَّرِّ شِرارُ العُلَماءِ، وإنَّ خَيرَ الخَيرِ خِيارُ العُلَماءِ.[٥٠٨٢]

4560. **The Prophet (SAWA) said,** 'He who does not increase in guidance in spite of an increase in his knowledge only gets further away from Allah.'[5121]

٤٥٦٠ . عنه ﷺ : مَنِ ازدادَ عِلماً ولَم يَزدَدْ هُدىً، لَم يَزدَدْ مِنَ اللهِ إلّا بُعداً.[٥٠٨٣]

4561. **Imām al-Ṣādiq (AS) said,** 'Cursed, cursed indeed is the knowledgeable man who frequents an unjust ruler, aiding him in his injustice.'[5122]

٤٥٦١ . الإمامُ الصّادقُ عليه السلام : مَلعونٌ مَلعونٌ عالِمٌ يَؤُمُّ سُلطاناً جائراً، مُعيناً لَهُ عَلىٰ جَورِهِ.[٥٠٨٤]

4562. **Imām al-ʿAskarī (AS),** in his description of evil scholars, said, 'They cause more harm to the weak ones from among our *Shīʿa* than the army of Yazīd did to Ḥusayn b. ʿAlī (AS) and his companions, for they snatched away their lives and their property, whereas these evil scholars… enter doubt and obscurity into the weak ones from among our *Shīʿa* and lead them astray.'[5123]

٤٥٦٢ . الإمامُ العسكريُّ عليه السلام ـ في صِفَةِ عُلَماءِ السُّوءِ ـ: وهُم أضَرُّ عَلىٰ ضُعَفاءِ شيعَتِنا مِن جَيشِ يَزيدَ عَلى الحُسَينِ بنِ عَلِيٍّ عليهما السلام وأصحابِهِ، فإنَّهُم يَسلُبونَهُمُ الأرواحَ والأموالَ، وهٰؤلاءِ عُلَماءُ السُّوءِ... يُدخِلونَ الشَّكَّ والشُّبهَةَ عَلىٰ ضُعَفاءِ شيعَتِنا فيُضِلّونَهُم.[٥٠٨٥]

1360. The Etiquettes of Knowledge

١٣٦٠ ـ آدابُ العِلمِ

4563. **Imām al-Ṣādiq (AS) narrated,** 'A man once came to the Prophet (SAWA) asking, 'O Prophet of Allah, what is knowledge?' to which he replied,

٤٥٦٣ . الإمامُ الصّادقُ عليه السلام : جاءَ رَجُلٌ إلىٰ رَسولِ اللهِ ﷺ فقالَ: يا رسولَ اللهِ، ما العِلمُ؟ قالَ:

'Paying attention [being silent].' The man asked, 'Then what?' He replied, 'Listening.' He asked, 'Then what?' The Prophet replied, 'Memorising.' The man asked, 'Then what?' He replied, 'Acting upon it.' He asked, 'Then what O Prophet of Allah', to which he replied, 'Spreading it.'[5124]

الإنصاتُ ، قالَ: ثُمَّ مَه؟ قالَ: الاستِماعُ ، قالَ: ثُمَّ مَه؟ قالَ: الحِفظُ ، قالَ: ثُمَّ مَه؟ قالَ: العَمَلُ بِهِ ، قالَ: ثُمَّ مَه يارَسولَ اللهِ؟ قالَ: نَشرُهُ.[٥٠٨٦]

1361. The Reprehensibility of Knowledge That is of No Use

١٣٦١ ـ ذَمُّ عِلمٍ لا يَنفَعُ

4564. **The Prophet (SAWA)** used to say, 'O Allah, I seek refuge in You from knowledge that does not benefit, from a heart that is not fearful, and from a self that is never sated, from a supplication that is unheard.'[5125]

٤٥٦٤ . رسولُ اللهِ ﷺ ـ كانَ يَقولُ ـ: اللّهُمَّ إنّي أعوذُ بِكَ مِن عِلمٍ لا يَنفَعُ ، ومِن قَلبٍ لا يَخشَعُ ، ومِن نَفسٍ لا تَشبَعُ ، ومِن دَعوَةٍ لا يُستَجاب لَها.[٥٠٨٧]

4565. **Imām ʿAlī (AS) said,** 'And know that there is no good in knowledge that is of no use, and that one cannot benefit from knowledge that is not worthy of being learnt.'[5126]

٤٥٦٥ . الإمامُ عليٌّ عليه السلام: وَاعلَم أنَّهُ لا خَيرَ في عِلمٍ لا يَنفَعَ ، ولا يُنتَفَعُ بِعِلمٍ لا يَحُقُّ تَعَلُّمُهُ.[٥٠٨٨]

4566. **Imām al-Kāẓim (AS) narrated,** 'The Prophet (SAWA) once entered the mosque to find a large group of people gathered around a man, so he asked, 'Who is this?' to which they replied, 'A most learned scholar (*ʿallāma*).' He then asked, 'And what is a most learned scholar?' to which they replied, '[He is] the most knowledgeable of all people about Arab ancestry and events, and pre-Islamic history, and Arab poetry.' So the Prophet said, 'That is knowledge which neither harms one who remains ignorant of it nor avails one who knows it.'[5127]

٤٥٦٦ . الإمامُ الكاظمُ عليه السلام: دَخَلَ رَسولُ اللهِ ﷺ المَسجِدَ فإذا جَماعَةٌ قَد أطافوا بِرَجُلٍ ، فقالَ: ما هٰذا؟ فقيلَ: عَلّامَةٌ ، قالَ: وما العَلّامَةُ؟ قالوا: أعلَمُ لنّاسِ بِأنسابِ العَرَبِ ووَقائعِها ، وأيّامِ الجاهِلِيَّةِ ، وبِالأشعارِ والعَرَبِيَّةِ ، فقالَ النَّبِيُّ ﷺ: ذاكَ عِلمٌ لا يَضُرُّ مَن جَهِلَهُ ، ولا يَنفَعُ مَن عَلِمَهُ.[٥٠٨٩]

1362. The Various Types of Knowledge

١٣٦٢ ـ أنواعُ العُلومِ

4567. **The Prophet (SAWA) said,** 'Verily knowledge is but three things: an unambiguous [a decisive] verse, or an upright obligatory act, or an established recommended act[5128], and anything else apart from these is a virtue.'[5129]

٤٥٦٧ . رسولُ اللهِ ﷺ: إنّما العِلمُ ثَلاثَةٌ: آيَةٌ مُحكَمَةٌ أو فَريضَةٌ عادِلَةٌ ، أو سُنَّةٌ قائمَةٌ[٥٠٩٠] ، وما خَلاهُنَّ فَهُوَ فَضلٌ.[٥٠٩١]

4568. **The Prophet (SAWA) said,** 'There are two types of knowledge: the knowledge of ideologies, and the knowledge of physical bodies.'[5130]

٤٥٦٨ . عنه ﷺ : العِلمُ عِلمانِ: عِلمُ الأديانِ، وعِلمُ الأبدانِ.[٥٠٩٢]

4569. **The Prophet (SAWA) saying,** 'Knowledge is too great to be encompassed, so take the best from each thing.'[5131]

٤٥٦٩ . عنه ﷺ : العِلمُ أكثَرُ مِن أن يُحصىٰ فَخُذْ مِن كُلِّ شَيءٍ أحسَنَهُ.[٥٠٩٣]

4570. **The Prophet (SAWA) said,** 'The best type of knowledge is that which benefits.'[5132]

٤٥٧٠ . عنه ﷺ : خَيرُ العِلمِ ما نَفَعَ.[٥٠٩٤]

4571. **Imām ʿAlī (AS) said,** 'There are four categories of sciences: juristic science for religions, medicine for physical bodies, grammar for language, and astronomy for knowledge of the times.'[5133]

٤٥٧١ . الإمامُ عليٌّ ؑ : العُلومُ أربَعَةٌ : الفِقهُ لِلأديانِ، والطِّبُّ لِلأبدانِ، والنَّحوُ لِلّسانِ، والنُّجومُ لِمَعرِفَةِ الأزمانِ.[٥٠٩٥]

4572. **Imām ʿAlī (AS) said,** 'The best type of knowledge is that which improves you.'[5134]

٤٥٧٢ . عنه ؑ : خَيرُ العُلومِ ما أصلَحَكَ.[٥٠٩٦]

4573. **Imām al-Bāqir (AS) said,** 'Know that there is no knowledge like the quest for integrity, and there is no integrity better than the integrity of the heart [i.e. the soul].'[5135]

٤٥٧٣ . الإمامُ الباقرُ ؑ : اِعلَمْ أنَّهُ لا عِلمَ كطَلَبِ السَّلامَةِ، ولا سَلامَةَ كسَلامَةِ القَلبِ.[٥٠٩٧]

4574. **Imām al-Ṣādiq (AS) said,** 'If only there were whips over my companions' heads that they may gain an understanding of the difference between the lawful and the unlawful.'[5136]

٤٥٧٤ . الإمامُ الصّادقُ ؑ : لَيتَ السِّياطَ عَلىٰ رُؤوسِ أصحابي حَتّىٰ يَتَفَقَّهوا فِي الحَلالِ والحَرامِ.[٥٠٩٨]

4575. **Imām al-Ṣādiq (AS) said,** 'Knowledge is not acquired through learning. Rather it is a light that illuminates in the heart of one who wants Allah, Blessed and most High, to guide him. So if you want knowledge, first seek out within yourself true servitude [to Allah], and seek knowledge according to its use, and ask Allah to make you understand, and He will make you understand.'[5137]

٤٥٧٥ . عنه ؑ : لَيسَ العِلمُ بِالتَّعَلُّمِ، إنَّما هُوَ نورٌ يَقَعُ في قَلبِ مَن يُريدُ اللهُ تَبارَكَ وتَعالىٰ أن يَهدِيَهُ، فإن أرَدتَ العِلمَ فَاطلُب أوَّلاً في نَفسِكَ حَقيقَةَ العُبودِيَّةِ، وَاطلُبِ العِلمَ بِاستِعمالِهِ، وَاستَفهِمِ اللهَ يُفهِمْكَ.[٥٠٩٩]

1363. Inspired Knowledge

١٣٦٣ـ العِلمُ اللّدُنِّيُّ

4576. **The Prophet (SAWA) said,** 'The knowledge of the hidden is one of the secrets of Allah, Mighty and Exalted, and one of Allah's commands which He divulges into the hearts of whom He wills from among His servants.'[5138]

٤٥٧٦. رسولُ اللهِ ﷺ : عِلمُ الباطِنِ سِرٌّ مِن أسرارِ اللهِ عَزَّ وجلَّ، وحُكمٌ مِن حُكمِ اللهِ، يَقذِفُه في قُلوبِ مَن شاءَ مِن عِبادِهِ.[٥١٠٠]

4577. **The Prophet (SAWA) said,** 'If you feared Allah with the fear that He is worthy of, you would be taught the knowledge after which no ignorance ever remains.'[5139]

٤٥٧٧. عنه ﷺ : لَو خِفتُمُ اللهَ حَقَّ خِيفَتِهِ لَعُلِّمتُمُ العِلمَ الّذي لا جَهلَ مَعَهُ.[٥١٠١]

4578. **Imām al-Bāqir (AS) said,** 'He who acts upon what he knows is taught by Allah that which he does not know.'[5140]

٤٥٧٨. الإمامُ الباقرُ عليه السلام : مَن عَمِلَ بِما يَعلَمُ عَلَّمَهُ اللهُ ما لا يَعلَمُ.[٥١٠٢]

(See also: DIVINE LEADERSHIP (*IMĀMA*): section 114) (أُنظر) الإمامة : باب ١١٤.

1364. The Most Knowledgeable of People

١٣٦٤ـ أعلَمُ النّاسِ

4579. **The Prophet (SAWA) said,** 'The most knowledgeable of people is he who adds other people's knowledge to his own.'[5141]

٤٥٧٩. رسولُ اللهِ ﷺ : أعلَمُ النّاسِ مَن جَمَعَ عِلمَ النّاسِ إلىٰ عِلمِهِ.[٥١٠٣]

4580. **The Prophet (SAWA)** was once asked, 'I would love to be the most knowledgeable of all people', to which he replied, 'Be wary of your duty to Allah and you will be the most knowledgeable of people.'[5142]

٤٥٨٠. عنه ﷺ ـ لَمّا قيلَ لَهُ: أُحِبُّ أن أكونَ أعلَمَ النّاسِ ـ: اِتَّقِ اللهَ تَكُن أعلَمَ النّاسِ.[٥١٠٤]

4581. **Imām 'Alī (AS) said,** 'The most knowledgeable of people is he who is infatuated with knowledge.'[5143]

٤٥٨١. الإمامُ عليٌّ عليه السلام : أعلَمُ النّاسِ المُستَهتَرُ بِالعِلمِ.[٥١٠٥]

1365. Exclusive Confinement of True Knowledge to the Household of the Prophet *(Ahl al-Bayt)*

١٣٦٥ـ انحِصارُ العِلمِ الصَّحيحِ بِأهلِ البَيتِ عليهم السلام

4582. **Imām 'Alī (AS) said,** 'If you were to acquire knowledge from its source, and drink water at its freshest, and amass good at its origin, and adopt a

٤٥٨٢. الإمامُ عليٌّ عليه السلام : لَوِ اقتَبَستُمُ العِلمَ مِن مَعدِنِهِ، وشَرِبتُمُ الماءَ بِعُذوبَتِهِ، وَادَّخَرتُمُ الخَيرَ

path at its clearest point, and adopt the path of truth at its most proper, the paths would open themselves to you indeed and the signs would become manifest to you.'[5144]

مِن مَوضِعِهِ، وأخَذتُمُ الطَّريقَ مِن واضِحِهِ، وسَلَكتُم مِنَ الحَقِّ نهجَهُ، لَنَهَجَت بِكُمُ السُّبُلُ، وبَدَت لَكُمُ الأعلامُ.[٥١٠٦]

4583. **Imām al-Bāqir (AS) said** to Salama b. Kuhayl and al-Ḥakam b. ʿUtayba, 'Go to the east and go to the west but you will never find true knowledge except for what comes from us, the household of the Prophet.'[5145]

٤٥٨٣. الإمامُ الباقرُ ﵇ ـ لسَلَمَةَ بنِ كُهَيلٍ والحَكَمِ ابنِ عُتَيبَةَ ـ: شَرِّقا وغَرِّبا لَن تَجِدا عِلماً صَحيحاً إلّا شَيئاً يَخرُجُ مِن عِندِنا أهلَ البَيتِ.[٥١٠٧]

289

LIFESPAN

العُمُرُ

1366. Lifespan

١٣٦٦ ـ العُمُرُ

"Allah created you from dust, then from a drop of [seminal] fluid, then He made you mates. No female conceives or delivers except with His knowledge, and no elderly person advances in years, nor is anything diminished from his life, but it is [recorded] in a Book. That is indeed easy for Allah."[5146]

﴿وَاللهُ خَلَقَكُمْ مِنْ تُرابٍ ثُمَّ مِنْ نُطْفَةٍ ثُمَّ جَعَلَكُمْ أزْوَاجاً وَما تَحْمِلُ مِنْ أُنْثَىٰ وَلا تَضَعُ إلَّا بِعِلْمِهِ وَما يُعَمَّرُ مِنْ مُعَمَّرٍ وَلا يُنْقَصُ مِنْ عُمُرِهِ إلَّا فِي كِتابٍ إنَّ ذٰلِكَ عَلَى اللهِ يَسِيرٌ﴾.[٥١٠٨]

4584. **Imām ʿAlī (AS) said,** 'Verily your lifespan is the total number of your breaths, and there is a watcher over them counting them.'[5147]

٤٥٨٤. الإمامُ عليٌّ ﵇: إنَّ عُمرَكَ عَدَدُ أنفاسِكَ، وعَلَيها رَقيبٌ يُحصيها.[٥١٠٩]

4585. **Imām ʿAlī (AS) said,** 'Verily nobody will receive one day of his lifespan except that another day will be taken from him from his end.'[5148]

٤٥٨٥. عنه ﵇: إنَّهُ لَن يَستَقبِلَ أحَدُكُم يَوماً مِن عُمرِهِ إلّا بِفِراقِ آخَرَ مِن أجَلِهِ.[٥١١٠]

1367. Encouraging Making the Most of One's Life

١٣٦٧ ـ الحَثُّ عَلىٰ اغتِنامِ العُمُرِ

4586. **The Prophet (SAWA) said,** 'Be even more niggardly with your life than with your dirham and your dinar [i.e. your money].'[5149]

٤٥٨٦. رسولُ اللهِ ﷺ: كُنْ عَلىٰ عُمرِكَ أشَحَّ مِنكَ عَلىٰ دِرهَمِكَ ودينارِكَ.[٥١١١]

4587. **The Prophet (SAWA) said,** 'Verily lifespan is fixed and no one will surpass that which has been allotted to him, so rush to make the most of it before time runs out.'[5150]

٤٥٨٧ . عنه ﷺ : إنَّ العُمرَ مَحدودٌ لَن يَتَجاوَزَ أحَدٌ ماقُدِّرَ لَهُ، فبادِروا قَبلَ نَفاذِ الأجَلِ.[٥١١٢]

4588. **Imām 'Alī (AS) said,** 'Your yesterday has passed on, your tomorrow is uncertain, and your today is to be taken advantage of.'[5151]

٤٥٨٨ . الإمامُ عليٌّ ﷺ: ماضي يَومِكَ فائتٌ ، وآتيهِ مُتَّهَمٌ ، ووَقتُكَ مُغتَنَمٌ.[٥١١٣]

4589. **Imām 'Alī (AS) said,** 'How fast the hours in a day go by, and how fast the days in a month, and how fast the months in a year, and how fast the years in a lifetime!'[5152]

٤٥٨٩ . عنه ﷺ : ما أسرَعَ السّاعاتِ فِي اليَومِ، وأسرَعَ الأيّامَ فِي الشَّهرِ، وأسرَعَ الشُّهورَ فِي السَّنَةِ، وأسرَعَ السِّنينَ (السَّنَةَ) فِي العُمرِ![٥١١٤]

4590. **Imām 'Alī (AS) said,** 'O people! [take advantage of] Now! Now before regret sets in, and before *"anyone should say, 'Alas for my negligence in the vicinage of Allah!'"*[5153] [5154]

٤٥٩٠ . عنه ﷺ : أيُّها النّاسُ! الآنَ الآنَ مِن قَبلِ النَّدَمِ، ومِن قَبلِ ﴿أن تَقولَ نَفسٌ يا حَسرَتى عَلى ما فَرَّطتُ في جَنبِ اللهِ﴾[٥١١٥]![٥١١٦]

4591. **Imām 'Alī (AS) said,** 'Allah has mercy on the man who knows that his breaths are but his steps towards his end, so he hastens to perform good deeds and cuts short his high hopes.'[5155]

٤٥٩١ . عنه ﷺ : رَحِمَ اللهُ امرأً عَلِمَ أنَّ نَفَسَهُ خُطاهُ إلى أجَلِهِ، فبادَرَ عَمَلَهُ وقَصَّرَ أمَلَهُ.[٥١١٧]

4592. **Imām 'Alī (AS) said,** 'Be cautious of wasting away your lives in that which will not last for you, for whatever has passed of them never returns.'[5156]

٤٥٩٢ . عنه ﷺ : إحذَروا ضَياعَ الأعمارِ فيما لا يَبقى لَكُم، فَفائتُها لا يَعودُ.[٥١١٨]

4593. **Imām 'Alī (AS) said,** 'Verily your lifetime is the ransom for your eternal prosperity if you spend it in the obedience of your Lord.'[5157]

٤٥٩٣ . عنه ﷺ : إنَّ عُمرَكَ مَهرُ سَعادَتِكَ إن أنفَدتَهُ في طاعَةِ رَبِّكَ.[٥١١٩]

1368. He whose Life will be a Proof Against Him

١٣٦٨ ـ مَن يَكونُ عُمُرُهُ حُجَّةً عَلَيهِ

"They shall cry therein for help: 'Our Lord! Bring us out, so that we may act righteously – different from what we used to do!' 'Did we not give you a life long

﴿وَهُمْ يَصْطَرِخُونَ فِيهَا رَبَّنَا أَخْرِجْنَا نَعْمَلْ صَالِحاً غَيْرَ الَّذِي كُنَّا نَعْمَلُ أَوَلَمْ نُعَمِّرْكُم مَا

enough that one who is heedful might take admonition? And [moreover] the warner had [also] come to you. Now taste [the consequence of your deeds], for the wrongdoers have no helper.''[5158]

يَتَذَكَّرُ فِيهِ مَنْ تَذَكَّرَ وَجاءَكُمُ النَّذِيرُ فَذُوقُوا فَما لِلظَّالِمِينَ مِنْ نَصِيرٍ﴾. ٥١٢٠

4594. **The Prophet (SAWA) said,** 'On the Day of Resurrection, it will be announced, 'Where are the sixty year olds?' for this is the age referring to which Allah, most High, has said, *"Did we not give you a life long enough that one who is heedful might take admonition?"*[5159]

٤٥٩٤ . رسولُ اللهِ ﷺ: إذا كانَ يومُ القِيامَةِ نودِيَ: أينَ أبناءُ السِّتّينَ ؟ وهُوَ العُمرُ الّذي قالَ اللهُ تَعالىٰ: ﴿أوَلَمْ نُعَمِّرْكُم ما يَتَذَكَّرُ فيهِ مَن تَذَكَّرَ﴾. ٥١٢١

4595. **Imām 'Alī (AS) said,** 'The age up to which Allah accepts the excuse of His servants for certain things is sixty years.'[5160]

٤٥٩٥ . الإمامُ عليٌّ عليه السلام: العُمرُ الّذي أعذَرَ اللهُ فيهِ إلى ابنِ آدَمَ سِتّونَ سَنَةً. ٥١٢٢

4596. **Imām 'Alī (AS) said,** 'So alas for every negligent one that his age be a proof against him, and that the days of his life should lead him to perdition!'[5161]

٤٥٩٦ . عنه عليه السلام: فيالَها حَسرَةً علىٰ كُلِّ ذي غَفلَةٍ أن يَكونَ عُمُرُهُ عَلَيهِ حُجَّةً، وأن تُؤَدِّيَهُ أيّامُهُ إلَى الشِّقوَةِ! ٥١٢٣

4597. **Imām al-Bāqir (AS) said,** 'When a man reaches forty years of age, it is said to him, 'Be on your guard, for now you have no excuse', and the forty-year old man is no longer as worthy of being excused as the twenty-year old man.'[5162]

٤٥٩٧ . الإمامُ الباقرُ عليه السلام: إذا أتَت عَلَى العَبدِ أربَعونَ سَنَةً قيلَ لَهُ: خُذْ حِذرَكَ؛ فإنَّكَ غَيرُ مَعذورٍ، ولَيسَ ابنُ أربَعينَ سَنَةً أحَقَّ بِالعُذرِ مِن ابنِ عِشرينَ سَنَةً. ٥١٢٤

1369. That which Leads to an Increase in Lifespan

١٣٦٩ ـ ما يَزيدُ فِي العُمُرِ

4598. **The Prophet (SAWA) said,** 'Remain mostly in the state of purity and Allah will increase your lifespan.'[5163]

٤٥٩٨ . رسولُ اللهِ ﷺ: أكثِرْ مِنَ الطَّهورِ يَزِدِ اللهُ في عُمرِكَ. ٥١٢٥

4599. **The Prophet (SAWA) said,** 'Whoever would like his sustenance to be amplified and his destined end to be postponed should maintain relations with his kin.'[5164]

٤٥٩٩ . عنه ﷺ: مَن سَرَّهُ أن يُبسَطَ لَهُ في رِزقِهِ ويُنسَأَ لَهُ في أجَلِهِ فَلْيَصِلْ رَحِمَهُ. ٥١٢٦

4600. **Imām 'Alī (AS) said,** 'He who wishes to remain alive – though there is no remaining forever – should eat his breakfast early, wear good

٤٦٠٠ . الإمامُ عليٌّ عليه السلام: مَن أرادَ البَقاءَ ـ ولا بَقاءَ ـ فَلْيُباكِرِ الغَداءَ، وَلْيُجَوِّدِ الحِذاءَ، وَلْيُخَفِّفِ الرِّداءَ،

shoes, dress in light clothing, and lessen his sexual intercourse with women.'[5165]

وَليُقِلَّ غُشيانَ النِّساءِ.[٥١٢٧]

4601. **Imām al-Bāqir (AS) said,** 'Command our *Shī'a* to visit the grave of al-Ḥusayn b. 'Alī (AS), for verily going there increases sustenance, extends one's life, and repels evil forces.'[5166]

٤٦٠١ . الإمامُ الباقرُ عليه السلام : مُروا شيعَتَنا بِزيارَةِ قَبرِ الحُسَينِ بنِ عَليٍّ عليه السلام ؛ فإنَّ إتيانَهُ يَزيدُ فِي الرِّزقِ، ويَمُدُّ فِي العُمرِ، ويَدفَعُ مَدافِعَ السُّوءِ.[٥١٢٨]

4602. **Imām al-Ṣādiq (AS) said,** 'He who has good intentions is given an increase in lifespan.'[5167]

٤٦٠٢ . الإمامُ الصّادقُ عليه السلام : مَن حَسُنَت نِيَّتُهُ زيدَ في عُمرِهِ.[٥١٢٩]

4603. **Imām al-Ṣādiq (AS) said,** 'He who excels in his good treatment of his family is given an increase in his lifespan.'[5168]

٤٦٠٣ . عنه عليه السلام : مَن حَسُنَ بِرُّهُ بِأهلِ بَيتِهِ زيدَ في عُمرِهِ.[٥١٣٠]

4604. **Imām al-Ṣādiq (AS) said,** 'If you would like Allah to increase your lifespan then please your parents.'[5169]

٤٦٠٤ . عنه عليه السلام : إن أحبَبتَ أن يَزيدَ اللهُ في عُمرِكَ فَسُرَّ أبَوَيكَ.[٥١٣١]

(See also: CONSANGUINAL RELATIONS: section 811)

(اُنظر: الرَّحِم: باب ٨١١).

1370. The Believer and Asking for a Long Life

١٣٧٠ ـ المُؤمِنُ وطَلَبُ طولِ العُمُرِ

4605. **Fāṭima al-Zahrā' (AS) said** in her intimate supplication, 'O Allah, by Your knowledge of the unseen, and Your power over creation, keep me alive so long as You know that life is good for me, and cause me to die when death is good for me.'[5170]

٤٦٠٥ . فاطمةُ الزَّهراءُ عليها السلام ـ فِي المُناجاةِ ـ : اللّهُمَّ بِعِلمِكَ الغَيبَ، وقُدرَتِكَ عَلَى الخَلقِ، أحيِني ما عَلِمتَ الحَياةَ خَيراً لي، وتَوَفَّني إذا كانَتِ الوَفاةُ خَيراً لي.[٥١٣٢]

4606. **Imām Zayn al-'Ābidīn (AS) said** in his supplication for noble moral traits, 'And let me live so long as my life is spent in Your obedience, but when my life becomes a breeding ground for Satan, then take me to You.'[5171]

٤٦٠٦ . الإمامُ زَينُ العابدينَ عليه السلام ـ مِن دُعائِهِ في مَكارِمِ الأخلاقِ ـ : وعَمِّرني ما كانَ عُمري بِذلَةً في طاعَتِكَ، فإذا كانَ عُمري مَرتَعاً لِلشَّيطانِ فَاقبِضني إلَيكَ.[٥١٣٣]

1371. The Wisdom Behind Man's Ignorance of the Span of His Life

١٣٧١ ـ حِكمَةُ جَهلِ الإنسانِ بِمِقدارِ عُمُرِهِ

4607. **Imām al-Ṣādiq (AS) said,** 'Contemplate now O Mufaḍḍal about the fact that man's lifespan

٤٦٠٧ . الإمامُ الصّادقُ عليه السلام : تَأمَّلِ الآنَ يا مُفَضَّلُ

has been kept concealed from his knowledge; for verily if he was to know the span of his life, and if it were short, he would never take pleasure in living, while being always in anticipation of death and the time that he knows. In fact, he would be like someone whose wealth has perished or is close to perishing, so he feels a sense of poverty and terror at the thought of losing his wealth and a fear of poverty. The feeling which the man who knows that he is going to lose his life is much more intense, for the one whose wealth is diminishing still continues to hope that some of it will be replaced enabling him to live off that, whereas he who is certain of the loss of his life, is taken over by despair. And if instead his lifespan was to be long, and he knew this, he would be certain of staying alive and would therefore become absorbed in vain pleasures and sins, and would act to gratify his desires intending to repent at the end of his life… And if you retort by saying that right now, even though his lifespan is concealed from him and he is anticipating death, he still yields to vile sins and commits forbidden acts, we would reply that the way this matter has been decreed is exactly how it is at the moment, and if man, in spite of that [i.e. his ignorance of his death] does not desist from and shun sins then that is because of his own heedless merriment and the hardness of his heart, and not because of a mistake in divine planning!'[5172]

ما سُتِرَ عَنِ الإنسانِ عِلمُهُ مِن مُدَّةِ حَياتِهِ ؛ فإنَّهُ لَو عَرَفَ مِقدارَ عُمرِهِ وكانَ قَصيرَ العُمرِ لَم يَتَهنَّأْ بِالعَيشِ مَعَ تَرَقُّبِ المَوتِ وتَوَقُّعِهِ لِوَقتٍ قَد عَرَفَهُ ، بَل كانَ يَكونُ بِمَنزِلَةِ مَن قَد فَنِيَ مالُهُ أو قارَبَ الفَناءَ ، فقَدِ استَشعَرَ الفَقرَ والوَجَلَ مِن فَناءِ مالِهِ وخَوفِ الفَقرِ ، عَلىٰ أنَّ الّذي يَدخُلُ عَلَى الإنسانِ مِن فَناءِ العُمرِ أعظَمُ مِمّا يَدخُلُ عَلَيهِ مِن فَناءِ المالِ ، لِأنَّ مَن يَقِلُّ مالُه يَأمَلُ أن يَستَخلِفَ مِنهُ فيَسكُنُ إلىٰ ذٰلكَ ، ومَن أيقَنَ بِفَناءِ العُمرِ استَحكَمَ عَلَيهِ اليَأسُ ، وإن كانَ طَويلَ العُمرِ ثُمَّ عَرَفَ ذٰلكَ وَثِقَ بِالبَقاءِ ، وَانهَمَكَ فِي اللَّذّاتِ والمَعاصي ، وعَمِلَ عَلىٰ أنَّهُ يَبلُغُ مِن ذٰلكَ شَهوَتَهُ ثُمَّ يَتوبُ في آخِرِ عُمرِهِ…

فإن قُلتَ : وها هُوَ الآنَ قَد سُتِرَ عَنهُ مِقدارُ حَياتِه وصارَ يَتَرَقَّبُ المَوتَ ، في كُلِّ ساعَةٍ يُقارِفُ الفَواحِشَ ويَنتَهِكُ المَحارِمَ! قُلنا : إنَّ وَجهَ التَّدبيرِ في هٰذا البابِ هُوَ الّذي جَرىٰ عَلَيهِ الأمرُ فيهِ ، فإن كانَ الإنسانُ مَعَ ذٰلكَ لا يَرعَوي ولا يَنصَرِفُ عَنِ المَساوِئِ فإنَّما ذٰلكَ مِن مَرَحِهِ[٥١٣٤] ومِن قَساوَةِ قَلبِهِ ، لا مِن خَطَأٍ فِي التَّدبيرِ.[٥١٣٥]

290

ACTION

العَمَلُ

1372. Enjoinment of Righteous Action

١٣٧٢ ـ الحَثُّ عَلى العَمَلِ الصّالِحِ

"Whoever acts righteously, [whether] male or female, should he be faithful – We shall revive him with a good life and pay them their reward by the best of what they used to do."[5173]

﴿مَنْ عَمِلَ صالِحاً مِنْ ذَكَرٍ أوْ أُنْثَىٰ وَهُوَ مُؤْمِنٌ فَلَنُحْيِيَنَّهُ حَياةً طَيِّبَةً وَلَنَجْزِيَنَّهُمْ أجْرَهُمْ بِأحْسَنِ ما كانُوا يَعْمَلُونَ﴾ .[٥١٣٦]

4608. **The Prophet (SAWA) said,** 'Three things follow a person when he dies: his family, his wealth and his deeds. Two of those retreat and only one remains: his family and wealth retreat and his deeds remain with him.'[5174]

٤٦٠٨ . رسولُ اللهِ ﷺ : يَتبَعُ المَيِّتَ ثَلاثَةٌ : أهلُه ومالُه وعَمَلُهُ ، فيَرجِعُ اثنانِ ويَبقىٰ واحِدٌ ؛ يَرجِعُ أهلُهُ ومالُه ويَبقىٰ عَمَلُهُ .[٥١٣٧]

4609. **Imām ʿAlī (AS) said,** 'I enjoin you with action indeed, then to take it to its completion, then to maintain it regularly, then to persevere in its performance and then to be pious. Verily you have been destined for a great end, so betake yourselves to your destined end.'[5175]

٤٦٠٩ . الإمامُ عليٌّ ﷺ : العَمَلَ العَمَلَ ، ثُمَّ النِّهايَةَ النِّهايَةَ ، والاستِقامَةَ الاستِقامَةَ ، ثُمَّ الصَّبرَ الصَّبرَ ، والوَرَعَ الوَرَعَ ، إنَّ لَكُم نِهايَةً فَانتَهوا إلىٰ نِهايَتِكُم .[٥١٣٨]

4610. **Imām ʿAlī (AS) said,** 'He who lags behind as a result of his deeds will not be accorded a front position because of his lineage.'[5176]

٤٦١٠ . عنه ﷺ : مَن أبطَأَ بِهِ عَمَلُهُ ، لَم يُسرِعْ بِهِ نَسَبُهُ (حَسَبُه) .[٥١٣٩]

4611. **Imām ʿAlī (AS) said,** 'Do not be among those who hope for the Hereafter without acting ... admiring the righteous people and yet not acting like them, and despising the sinners whilst he is one of them ... he fears for others worse chastisement than what he himself deserves for his sin, and for himself hopes for greater [reward] than his actions deserve ... When he acts he falls short of the action, and when he asks something, he exaggerates ... so he is presumptuous in his speech though performing little action.'[5177]

٤٦١١ . عنه ﷺ : لا تَكُن مِمَّن يَرجو الآخِرَةَ بِغَيرِ العَمَلِ ... يُحِبُّ الصّالِحينَ ولا يَعمَلُ عَمَلَهُم ، ويُبغِضُ المُذنِبينَ وهُوَ أحَدُهُم ... يَخافُ عَلىٰ غَيرِهِ بِأدنىٰ مِن ذَنبِهِ ، ويَرجو لِنَفسِهِ بِأكثَرَ مِن عَمَلِهِ ... يُقَصِّرُ إذا عَمِلَ ، ويُبالِغُ إذا سَألَ ... فَهُوَ بِالقَولِ مُدِلٌّ ، ومِنَ العَمَلِ مُقِلٌّ ![٥١٤٠]

4612. **Imām al-Ṣādiq (AS) said,** 'He from whom Allah accepts a single prayer, He will not punish, nor he from whom He accepts a single good deed.'[5178]

٤٦١٢ . الإمامُ الصّادقُ ﷺ : مَن قَبِلَ اللهُ مِنهُ صَلاةً واحِدَةً لَم يُعَذِّبْهُ ، ومَن قَبِلَ مِنهُ حَسَنَةً ... لَم يُعَذِّبْهُ .[٥١٤]

4613. **Imām al-Ṣādiq (AS) said,** 'If you act but a little, you will enjoy many bounties.'[5179]

٤٦١٣ . عنه ﷺ : إعمَلوا قَليلاً تَتَنَعَّموا كَثيراً .[٥١٤٢]

4614. **Imām al-Hādī (AS) said,** 'People transact through wealth in this world and through deeds in the Hereafter.'[5180]

٤٦١٤ . الإمامُ الهاديُّ ﷺ : النّاسُ فِي الدُّنيا بِالأَموالِ ، وفِي الآخِرَةِ بِالأَعمالِ .[٥١٤٣]

1373. Action and Recompense

١٣٧٣ ـ العَمَلُ وَالجَزاءُ

"It will be neither after your hopes not the hopes of the People of the Book: whoever commits evil shall be requited for it, and he will not find for himself any guardian or helper besides Allah. And whoever does righteous deeds, whether male or female, should he be faithful – such shall enter Paradise and they will not be wronged [so much as] the speck on a date-stone."[5181]

﴿لَيْسَ بِأمانِيِّكُمْ وَلا أمانِيِّ أهْلِ الْكِتابِ مَنْ يَعْمَلْ سُوءً يُجْزَ بِهِ وَلا يَجِدْ لَهُ مِنْ دُونِ اللهِ وَلِيّاً وَلا نَصِيراً * وَمَنْ يَعْمَلْ مِنَ الصَّالِحاتِ مِنْ ذَكَرٍ أوْ أُنْثَى وَهُوَ مُؤْمِنٌ فَأُولَئِكَ يَدْخُلُونَ الجَنَّةَ وَلا يُظْلَمُونَ نَقِيراً﴾.٥١٤٤

4615. **The Prophet (SAWA) said,** 'Just as grapes can never be harvested from thorn bushes, thus can the wrongdoers never come up to the level of the righteous, for they are two distinct paths, whichever one of them you take is where you will arrive.'[5182]

٤٦١٥. رسولُ اللهِ ﷺ: كَما لا يُجتَنىٰ مِنَ الشَّوكِ العِنَبُ كَذٰلكَ لا يَنزِلُ الفُجّارُ مَنازِلَ الأبرارِ، وهُما طَريقانِ، فَأَيَّهُما أخَذتُم أدرَكتُم إلَيهِ.٥١٤٥

(See also: REQUITAL 65)

(أنظر) عنوان ٦٥ «الجزاء».

1374. Maintenance of Continuous Action

١٣٧٤ ـ المُداوَمَةُ عَلَى العَمَلِ

4616. **Imām ʿAlī (AS) said,** 'Act continuously, act continuously! For verily Allah has not decreed any end to the believer's actions except death.'[5183]

٤٦١٦. الإمامُ عليٌّ عليه السلام: المُداوَمَةَ المُداوَمَةَ! فإنَّ اللهَ لَم يَجعَلْ لِعَمَلِ المُؤمِنينَ غايَةً إلّا المَوتَ.٥١٤٦

4617. **Imām ʿAlī (AS) said,** 'The little that you perform continuously is weightier than the great amount that you perform with boredom.'[5184]

٤٦١٧. عنه عليه السلام: قَليلٌ تَدومُ عَلَيهِ، أرجىٰ مِن كَثيرٍ مَملولٍ مِنهُ.٥١٤٧

4618. **Imām al-Bāqir (AS) said,** 'There is nothing more beloved to Allah than the performance of an action that is maintained regularly, even if it be little.'[5185]

٤٦١٨. الإمامُ الباقرُ عليه السلام: ما مِن شَيءٍ أحَبَّ إلَى اللهِ عزّ وجلّ مِن عَمَلٍ يُداوَمُ عَلَيهِ، وإن قَلَّ.٥١٤٨

4619. **Imām al-Ṣādiq (AS) said,** 'If a man performs a certain action, he should maintain it regularly for the duration of a year, then he may move on to another act if he wishes, and that is so that the grand Night of Ordainment (*laylat al-qadr*) is included in his year of performing that particular act, when whatever Allah wills therein happens.'[5186]

٤٦١٩. الإمامُ الصّادق عليه السلام: إذا كانَ الرَّجُلُ عَلىٰ عَمَلٍ فَلْيَدُمْ عَلَيهِ سَنَةً، ثُمَّ يَتَحَوَّلُ عَنهُ إن شاءَ إلىٰ غَيرِهِ؛ وذٰلكَ أنَّ لَيلَةَ القَدرِ يَكونُ فيها في عامِهِ ذٰلكَ ما شاءَ اللهُ أن يَكونَ.٥١٤٩

1375. The Best of Actions

١٣٧٥ ـ أفضَلُ الأعمالِ

4620. **The Prophet (SAWA) said,** 'The best of deeds is the most difficult of them.'[5187]

٤٦٢٠ . رسولُ اللهِ ﷺ: أفضَلُ الأعمالِ أحمَزُها.[٥١٥٠]

4621. **The Prophet (SAWA) said,** 'The best of deeds is that which is most regular, even if be something small.'[5188]

٤٦٢١ . عنه ﷺ: أفضَلُ العَمَلِ أدوَمُهُ وإن قَلَّ.[٥١٥١]

4622. **The Prophet (SAWA) said,** 'The best of deeds in the sight of Allah is the happiness that you bring to a fellow believer, either by driving away his hunger or by relieving him of his distress.'[5189]

٤٦٢٢ . عنه ﷺ: أحَبُّ الأعمالِ إلَى اللهِ سُرورٌ (الذي) تُدخِلُهُ عَلَى المُؤمِنِ، تَطرُدُ عَنهُ جَوعَتَهُ أو تَكشِفُ عَنهُ كُربَتَهُ.[٥١٥٢]

4623. **Imām ʿAlī (AS) said,** 'The best of deeds is that which you force yourself to do.'[5190]

٤٦٢٣ . الإمامُ عليٌّ عليه السلام: أفضَلُ الأعمالِ ما أكرَهتَ عَلَيهِ نَفسَكَ.[٥١٥٣]

4624. **Imām ʿAlī (AS) said,** 'The best of deeds is that whose objective is Allah's pleasure.'[5191]

٤٦٢٤ . عنه عليه السلام: أفضَلُ العَمَلِ ما أُريدَ بِهِ وَجهُ اللهِ.[٥١٥٤]

4625. **Imām ʿAlī (AS) said,** 'The best of deeds is adherence to the truth.'[5192]

٤٦٢٥ . عنه عليه السلام: أفضَلُ الأعمالِ لُزومُ الحَقِّ.[٥١٥٥]

4626. **Imām al-Ṣādiq (AS),** when asked about the best of deeds, replied, 'Performing the prayer at its prescribed time, being kind to one's parents and combat in the way of Allah (*jihād*), Mighty and Exalted.'[5193]

٤٦٢٦ . الإمامُ الصّادقُ عليه السلام ـ لَمّا سُئلَ عَن أفضَلِ الأعمالِ ـ: الصَّلاةُ لِوَقتِها، وبِرُّ الوالِدَينِ، والجِهادُ في سَبيلِ اللهِ عَزَّوجلَّ.[٥١٥٦]

1376. He whose Deeds do not Benefit him

١٣٧٦ ـ مَن لا يَنفَعُهُ عَمَلُهُ

4627. **The Prophet (SAWA) said,** 'There are three qualities which if a person does not possess, his action remains incomplete: piety which safeguards him from acts of disobedience to Allah, a good nature by means of which he maintains amicable relations with people, and clemency by means of which he retorts the rashness of the ignorant.'[5194]

٤٦٢٧ . رسولُ اللهِ ﷺ: ثَلاثٌ مَن لَم تَكُنْ فيهِ لَم يَقُمْ لَهُ عَمَلٌ: وَرَعٌ يَحجُزُهُ عَن مَعاصي اللهِ عَزَّوجلَّ، وخُلُقٌ يُداري بِهِ النّاسَ، وحِلمٌ يَرُدُّ بِهِ جَهلَ الجاهِلِ.[٥١٥٧]

4628. **The Prophet (SAWA) said,** 'There are three sins to which the company of a good deed is to no avail: association of anything with Allah, insolence to one's parents, and fleeing from the midst of a battle.'[5195]

٤٦٢٨ . عنه ﷺ: ثَلاثَةٌ لا يَـنفَعُ مَـعَهُنَّ عَـمَلٌ: الشِّركُ بِـاللهِ، وعُـقوقُ الوالِـدَينِ، والفِـرارُ مِـنَ الزَّحفِ.[٥١٥٨]

4629. **The Prophet (SAWA) said,** 'He who does not guard his tongue has not performed any good deeds.'[5196]

٤٦٢٩ . عنه ﷺ: ما عَمِلَ مَن لَم يَحفَظْ لِسانَهُ.[٥١٥٩]

4630. **Imām al-Bāqir (AS) said,** 'A good deed accompanied by doubt and denial is to no avail.'[5197]

٤٦٣٠ . الإمامُ الباقرُ ؑ: لا يَنفَعُ مَعَ الشَّكِّ والجُحودِ عَمَلٌ.[٥١٦٠]

4631. **Imām al-Ṣādiq (AS) said,** 'Allah does not accept a good deed from a believer as long as he harbours ill will against a fellow believing brother.'[5198]

٤٦٣١ . الإمامُ الصّادقُ ؑ: لا يَقبَلُ اللهُ مِن مُؤمِنٍ عَمَلاً وهُوَ مُضمِرٌ عَلىٰ أخيهِ المُؤمِنِ سُوءاً.[٥١٦١]

(See also: PRAYER (1): section 1132; SPENDING: section 1763)

(اُنظر: الصلاة (١): باب ١١٣٢؛ الإنفاق: باب ١٧٦٣)

1377. Deeds that One Must be Cautious of

١٣٧٧ - الأعمالُ الَّتي يَنبَغي الحَذَرُ مِنها

4632. **Imām ʿAlī (AS) said,** 'Be cautious of every deed which the doer is pleased to perform himself but hates Muslims at large to perform it.'[5199]

٤٦٣٢ . الإمامُ عليٌّ ؑ: احذَرْ كُلَّ عَمَلٍ يَرضاهُ صاحِبُهُ لِنَفسِهِ، ويَكرَهُهُ لِعامَّةِ المُسلِمينَ.[٥١٦٢]

4633. **Imām ʿAlī (AS) said,** 'Be cautious of every deed which is performed in secret but is embarrassing to perform in public.'[5200]

٤٦٣٣ . عنه ؑ: احذَرْ كُلَّ عَمَلٍ يُعمَلُ بِهِ فِـي السِّرِّ، ويُستَحىٰ مِنهُ فِي العَلانِيَةِ.[٥١٦٣]

4634. **Imām ʿAlī (AS) said,** 'Beware of any deed whose performance would be deplored by its doer if mentioned to him.'[5201]

٤٦٣٤ . عنه ؑ: إيّاكَ وكُلَّ عَمَلٍ إذا ذُكِرَ لِصاحِبِهِ أنكَرَهُ.[٥١٦٤]

1378. Perfection of a Good Deed

١٣٧٨ - إتقانُ العَمَلِ

4635. **The Prophet (SAWA) said,** 'Verily Allah, most High, loves for you to perfect a good deed when you perform it.'[5202]

٤٦٣٥ . رسولُ اللهِ ﷺ: إنَّ اللهَ تَعالىٰ يُـحِبُّ إذا عَمِلَ أحَدُكُم عَمَلاً أن يُتقِنَهُ.[٥١٦٥]

4636. **Imām al-Ṣādiq (AS) narrated,** 'When Ibrāhīm, the son of the Prophet (SAWA) passed away, the Prophet (SAWA) saw a gap in his grave, which he filled with his hand, and then said, 'When any of you performs a good deed, he should perfect it.'[5203]

٤٦٣٦. الإمامُ الصّادقُ ﷺ: لَمّا ماتَ إبراهيمُ ابنُ رَسولِ اللهِ ﷺ رَأى النَّبِيُّ ﷺ في قَبرِهِ خَلَلاً فسَوّاهُ بِيَدِهِ، ثُمَّ قالَ: إذا عَمِلَ أحَدُكُم عَمَلاً فَلْيُتقِنْ.[٥١٦٦]

1379. The Exposition of Deeds to Allah, The Prophet and The Imāms (AS)

١٣٧٩ـ عَرضُ الأعمالِ عَلَى اللهِ والنَّبِيِّ ﷺ والأئمَّةِ ﷺ

"And say, 'Go on working, for Allah will see your conduct, and His Apostle and the faithful [as well], and you will be returned to the Knower of the sensible and the Unseen, and He will inform you concerning what you used to do.'"[5204]

﴿وَقُلِ اعْمَلُوا فَسَيَرَى اللهُ عَمَلَكُمْ وَرَسُولُهُ وَالْمُؤْمِنُونَ وَسَتُرَدُّونَ إِلَىٰ عالِمِ الْغَيْبِ وَالشَّهادَةِ فَيُنَبِّئُكُمْ بِما كُنْتُمْ تَعْمَلُونَ﴾.[٥١٦٧]

4637. **The Prophet (SAWA) said,** 'People's deeds are presented every Monday and Thursday. The deeds of one who seeks forgiveness are forgiven to him, and those of the repentant are pardoned, whilst the deeds of those who harbour rancour are returned to them because of their rancour until they repent for them.'[5205]

٤٦٣٧. رسولُ اللهِ ﷺ: تُعرَضُ الأعمالُ يَومَ الاثنَينِ والخَميسِ، فمِن مُستَغفِرٍ فيُغفَرُ لَهُ، ومِن تائبٍ فيُتابُ عَلَيهِ، ويُرَدُّ أهلُ الضَّغائنِ بِضَغائنِهِم حَتّىٰ يَتوبوا.[٥١٦٨]

4638. **The Prophet (SAWA) said,** 'Verily your deeds are exposed to me every day, and whatever good I see I ask Allah to increase them for you, and whatever bad I see, I seek forgiveness from Allah for you.'[5206]

٤٦٣٨. عنه ﷺ: إنَّ أعمالَكُم تُعرَضُ عَلَيَّ كُلَّ يَومٍ، فَما كانَ مِن حَسَنٍ استَزَدتُ اللهَ لَكُم، وما كانَ مِن قَبيحٍ استَغفَرتُ اللهَ لَكُم.[٥١٦٩]

4639. **Imām al-Ḥusayn (AS) said,** 'Verily the deeds of this community are exposed to Allah, most High, every single morning.'[5207]

٤٦٣٩. الإمامُ الحسينُ ﷺ: إنَّ أعمالَ هٰذهِ الأُمَّةِ ما مِن صَباحٍ إلّا وتُعرَضُ عَلَى اللهِ تَعالىٰ.[٥١٧٠]

4640. **Imām al-Ṣādiq (AS)** was asked about Allah's verse: *"And say, 'Go on working, for Allah will see your conduct, and His Apostle and the faithful [as well]"*, replied, 'It is us that He means [by the faithful].'[5208]

٤٦٤٠. الإمامُ الصّادقُ ﷺ ـ لَمّا سُئلَ عَن قَولِهِ تَعالىٰ: ﴿وَقُلِ اعْمَلُوا فَسَيَرَى اللهُ عَمَلَكُمْ وَرَسُولُهُ وَالْمُؤْمِنُونَ﴾ ـ: إيّانا عَنى.[٥١٧١]

4641. **Imām al-Riḍā (AS),** when 'Abdullāh b. Abān said to him, 'Verily a group of your adherents have asked me to request you to supplicate Allah on their behalf', replied, 'By Allah, verily I

٤٦٤١. الإمامُ الرِّضا ﷺ ـ وقد قالَ عَبدُ اللهِ بنُ أبانَ لَهُ: إنَّ قَوماً مِن مَواليكَ سَألوني أن تَدعُوَ اللهَ لَهُم ـ: وَاللهِ إنّي لَأَعرِضُ أعمالَهُم عَلى

am the one who presents their deeds to Allah every day.'[5209]

اللهِ في كُلِّ يومٍ.[٥١٧٢]

1380. The Book of Deeds

١٣٨٠ ـ كِتابُ الأعمالِ

"This is Our book, which speaks truly against you. Indeed We used to record what you used to do."[5210]

﴿هَذَا كِتابُنا يَنْطِقُ عَلَيْكُمْ بِالْحَقِّ إنَّا كُنَّا نَسْتَنْسِخُ ما كُنْتُمْ تَعْمَلُونَ﴾.[٥١٧٣]

(See also: Qur'an 6:61, 10:21, 13:11, 19:79, 23:62, 10:12, 50:17, 50:18, 54:25, 54:53, 82:10-12, 86:4)

(أُنظر) الأنعام: ٦١ ويونس: ٢١ والرعد: ١١ ومريم: ٧٩ والمؤمنون: ٦٢ ويس: ١٢ و ق: ١٧، ١٨ والقمر: ٢٥، ٥٣ والإنفطار: ١٠ ـ ١٢ والطارق: ٤.

4642. **Imām 'Alī (AS) said,** 'The angel on man's right [shoulder] records his good deeds, whilst the angel on the left records his evil deeds. The two angels of the day record the servant's deeds by day, and the two angels of the night record the servant's deeds by night.'[5211]

٤٦٤٢. الإمامُ عليٌّ عليه السلام: صاحِبُ اليَمينِ يَكتُبُ الحَسَناتِ، وصاحِبُ الشِّمالِ يَكتُبُ السَّيِّئاتِ، ومَلَكا النَّهارِ يَكتُبانِ عَمَلَ العَبدِ بِالنَّهارِ، ومَلَكا اللَّيلِ يَكتُبانِ عَمَلَ العَبدِ فِي اللَّيلِ.[٥١٧٤]

(See also: THE ANGELS: section 1664; SCRUTINY (OF MAN'S ACTIONS): 839; RESURRECTION: section 1394)

(أُنظر) الملائكة: باب ١٦٦٤؛ المراقبة: باب ٨٣٩؛ المعاد: باب ١٣٩٤.

1381. Embodiment of Deeds

١٣٨١ ـ تَجَسُّمُ الأعمالِ

"So whoever does an atom's weight of good will see it, and whoever does an atom's weight of evil will see it."[5212]

﴿فَمَنْ يَعْمَلْ مِثْقالَ ذَرَّةٍ خَيْراً يَرَهُ * وَمَنْ يَعْمَلْ مِثْقالَ ذَرَّةٍ شَرّاً يَرَهُ﴾.[٥١٧٥]

"The day when every soul will find present whatever good it has done; and as to whatever evil it has done it will wish there were a far distance between it and itself. Allah warns you to beware of [disobeying] Him, and Allah is most kind to [His] servants."[5213]

﴿يَوْمَ تَجِدُ كُلُّ نَفْسٍ ما عَمِلَتْ مِنْ خَيْرٍ مُحْضَراً وَما عَمِلَتْ مِنْ سُوءٍ تَوَدُّ لَوْ أنَّ بَيْنَها وَبَيْنَهُ أمَداً بَعِيداً وَيُحَذِّرُكُمُ اللهُ نَفْسَهُ وَاللهُ رَؤُوفٌ بِالْعِبادِ﴾.[٥١٧٦]

4643. **The Prophet (SAWA) said,** 'Verily when the believer will come out of his grave, his deeds will come to him personified in a good form, and he will address it asking? 'Who are you, for by Allah I see you to be a veracious man indeed?!' to which it will reply, 'I am your [good] deed', and it will be a source of light for him and lead him into Paradise. And verily when the disbeliever comes out of his grave, his deeds will come to him

٤٦٤٣. رسولُ اللهِ صلى الله عليه وآله: إنَّ المُؤمِنَ إذا خَرَجَ مِن قَبرِهِ صُوِّرَ لَهُ عَمَلُهُ في صورَةٍ حَسَنَةٍ، فيَقولُ لَهُ: ما أنتَ فَوَاللهِ إنّي لَأراكَ امرَأَ الصِّدقِ؟! فيَقولُ لَهُ: أنا عَمَلُكَ، فيَكونُ لَهُ [نوراً أو قائداً[٥١٧٧]] إلَى الجَنَّةِ. وإنَّ الكافِرَ إذا خَرَجَ مِن قَبرِهِ صُوِّرَ لَهُ عَمَلُهُ في صورَةٍ سَيِّئَةٍ، وبِشارَةٍ سَيِّئَةٍ فيَقولُ: مَن

personified in an ugly form with an ugly countenance, to which he will ask, 'Who are you for verily I see you to be an ugly man indeed?!' and it will reply, 'I am your [evil] deeds', and it will rush off with him to plunge into the Fire.'[5214]

أنتَ فَوَاللهِ إنّي لَأراكَ امرَأَ السَّوءِ؟! فيَقولُ: أنا عَمَلُكَ، فيَنطَلِقُ بِهِ حَتّىٰ يَدخُلَ النّارَ.[٥١٧٨]

(See also: DEATH: section 1680)

(أنظر) الموت: باب ١٦٨٠.

291

THE COVENANT[5215]

العَهد

1382. Enjoinment of Fulfilling One's Covenant

١٣٨٣ ـ الحَثُّ عَلَى الوَفاءِ بِالعَهدِ

"And those who fulfil their covenants when they pledge themselves."[5216]

﴿وَالْمُوفُونَ بِعَهْدِهِمْ إذا عاهَدُوا﴾.[٥١٧٩]

(See also: Qur'an 23:8, 19:54, 61:2-3, 70:32, 16:91)

(انظر) المؤمنون: ٨ و مريم: ٥٤ و الصّف: ٢، ٣ والمعارج: ٣٢ والنحل: ٩١.

4644. **The Prophet (SAWA) said,** 'Muslims [make and] fulfil their promises according to what is permissible.'[5217]

٤٦٤٤. رسولُ اللهِ ﷺ: المُسلِمونَ عِندَ شُروطِهِم فيما أُحِلَّ.[٥١٨٠]

4645. **The Prophet (SAWA) said,** 'Verily whoever wrongs any of the people of the covenant (*ahl al-dhimma*), or denies him some of his right, or burdens him beyond that which he is capable of, or takes something from him without his consent, then I will hold it against him on the Day of Resurrection.'[5218]

٤٦٤٥. عنه ﷺ: ألا مَن ظَلَمَ مُعاهَداً، أوِ انتَقَصَهُ، أو كَلَّفَهُ فَوقَ طاقَتِهِ، أو أخَذَ مِنهُ شَيئاً بِغَيرِ طِيبِ نَفسٍ مِنهُ، فَأنا حَجيجُه يَومَ القِيامَةِ.[٥١٨١]

4646. **The Prophet (SAWA) said,** 'When they break a covenant, Allah allows their enemy to gain mastery over them.'[5219]

٤٦٤٦. عنه ﷺ: إذا نَقَضوا العَهدَ سَلَّطَ اللهُ عَلَيهِم عَدُوَّهُم.[٥١٨٢]

4647. **The Prophet (SAWA) said,** 'He who does not keep a promise has no religion.'[5220]

٤٦٤٧. عنه ﷺ: لا دِينَ لِمَن لا عَهدَ لَهُ.[٥١٨٣]

4648. **Imām 'Alī (AS) said,** 'Verily promises are chains on people's necks until the Day of Resur-

٤٦٤٨. الإمامُ عليٌّ عليه السلام: إنَّ العُهودَ قَلائدُ في

rection. So whoever fulfils them is delivered by Allah, and whoever breaks them is forsaken by Allah, and whoever takes them lightly will have to contend with the One Who has placed special emphasis on them and Who has enjoined upon His creation to fulfil them.'[5221]

الأعناقِ إلىٰ يَومِ القِيامَةِ، فمَن وَصَلَها وَصَلَهُ اللهُ، ومَن نَقَضَها خَذَلَهُ اللهُ، ومَنِ استَخَفَّ بِها خاصَمَتهُ إلَى الّذي أكَّدَها وأخَذَ خَلقَهُ بِحِفظِها.[٥١٨٤]

4649. **Imām ʿAlī (AS),** in a letter he wrote to al-Ashtar when he appointed him governor of Egypt, said, 'Among all things made incumbent by Allah, there is nothing on which people are more strongly united, in spite of the difference of their opinions and the diversity of their views, than the respect for fulfilling promises.'[5222]

٤٦٤٩. عنه عليه السلام ـ مِن كِتابِهِ لِلأشتَرِ لَمّا وَلّاهُ مِصرَ ـ: لَيسَ مِن فَرائضِ اللهِ شَيءٌ النّاسُ أشَدُّ عَلَيهِ اجتِماعاً ـ مَعَ تَفَرُّقِ أهوائهِم، وتَشَتُّتِ آرائهِم ـ مِن تَعظيمِ الوَفاءِ بِالعُهودِ.[٥١٨٥]

4650. **Imām ʿAlī (AS) said,** 'Fulfilment of a promise is part of faith.'[5223]

٤٦٥٠. عنه عليه السلام: حُسنُ العَهدِ مِنَ الإيمانِ.[٥١٨٦]

4651. **Imām ʿAlī (AS) said,** 'He who does not observe his promises and his guarantee does not have conviction in Allah.'[5224]

٤٦٥١. عنه عليه السلام: ما أيقَنَ بِاللهِ مَن لَم يَرْعَ عُهودَهُ وذِمَّتَهُ.[٥١٨٧]

4652. **Imām al-Bāqir (AS) said,** 'There are three things wherein Allah, Mighty and Exalted, has not granted anyone a concession ... the fulfilment of one's promise, be it to the good person or the bad.'[5225]

٤٦٥٢. الإمامُ الباقرُ عليه السلام: ثَلاثٌ لَم يَجعَلِ اللهُ عَزَّوجلَّ لِأحَدٍ فيهِنَّ رُخصَةً: ... الوَفاءُ بِالعَهدِ لِلبَرِّ والفاجِرِ.[٥١٨٨]

4653. **Imām al-Bāqir (AS)** with regards to Allah's verse: *"Do not be like her who would undo her yarn, breaking it up after [spinning it to] strength, by making your oaths a means of [mutual] deceit among yourselves ..."*[5226], said, 'The one who undid her yarn was a woman from the tribe of Banī Taym b. Murrah, called Rābiṭa (Rāyṭa), daughter of Kaʿb b. Saʿd b. Taym b. Kaʿb b. Luʿayya b. Ghālib. She was a stupid woman who would spin hair, and after she had spun it, she would undo it then start to spin it all over again. So Allah said, *"Do not be like her who would undo her yarn ..."* Verily Allah, Blessed and most High, has commanded the fulfilment of the oath and has prohibited its breaking, and has made this a parable for them.'[5227]

٤٦٥٣. عنه عليه السلام ـ في قولِهِ تعالىٰ: ﴿وَلا تَكونوا كَالَّتي نَقَضَتْ غَزْلَها مِنْ بَعْدِ قُوة﴾[٥١٨٩] ـ: الّتي نَقَضَت غَزلَها امرَأةٌ مِن بَني تَيمِ بنِ مُرَّةَ يُقالُ لَها: رابِطَةُ (ريطَةُ) بِنتُ كَعبِ بنِ سَعدِ بنِ تَيمِ بنِ كَعبِ بنِ لُؤَيِّ بنِ غالِبٍ، كانَت حَمقاءَ تَغزِلُ الشَّعرَ، فإذا غَزَلَت نَقَضَتهُ ثُمَّ عادَت فَغَزَلَتهُ، فقالَ اللهُ: ﴿وَلا تَكونوا كَالَّتي نَقَضَتْ غَزلَها مِنْ بَعْدِ قُوة﴾ إنَّ اللهَ تَبارَكَ وتَعالىٰ أمَرَ بِالوَفاءِ ونَهىٰ عَن نَقضِ العَهدِ، فضَرَبَ لَهُم مَثَلاً.[٥١٩٠]

4654. **Imām al-Ṣādiq (AS),** when asked about the verse: *"O you who have faith! Keep your agreements"*, replied, '[It refers to] promises.'[5228]

٤٦٥٤ . الإمامُ الصّادقُ ﵇ ـ لَمّا سُئلَ عَن قولِهِ تَعالى: ﴿يا أيُّها الَّذينَ آمَنوا أوْفوا بِالعُقودِ﴾ ـ: العُهودِ.[٥١٩١]

292

RESURRECTION

المَعادُ

1383. Resurrection

١٣٨٣ ـ المَعادُ

4655. **Luqmān (AS) said** to his son, exhorting him, 'O my son, if you are in doubt about death, then try to avert yourself from falling asleep and you will not be able to, and if you are in doubt about the Resurrection, then try to avert yourself from waking up and you will never be able to do that either.'[5229]

٤٦٥٥ . لقمانُ ﵇ ـ لِابنِهِ وهُوَ يَعظُهُ ـ: يا بُنَيَّ، إن تَكُ في شَكٍّ مِنَ المَوتِ فَارفَعْ عَن نَفسِكَ النَّومَ ولَن تَستَطيعَ ذلكَ، وإن كُنتَ في شَكٍّ مِنَ البَعثِ فَارفَعْ عَن نَفسِكَ الانتِباهَ ولَن تَستَطيعَ ذلكَ.[٥١٩٢]

4656. **The Prophet (SAWA) said,** '(The Day of) Resurrection will be a field of activity wherein a successful man will be delighted at what he has bagged for himself, and a regretful man will grieve at what he has missed out on.'[5230]

٤٦٥٦ . رسولُ اللهِ ﷺ: المَعادُ مِضمارُ العَمَلِ، فَمُغتَبِطٌ بِما احتَقَبَ غانِمٌ، ومُبتَئِسٌ بِما فاتَهُ نادِمٌ.[٥١٩٣]

4657. **Imām Zayn al-ʿĀbidīn (AS)** said in one of his exhortations, 'Know O son of Adam that beyond this [life] is something greater, more horrendous and more painful for the hearts – the Day of Resurrection. That is the day when people will be gathered and that will be an eventful day wherein Allah will gather people from the first to the last.'[5231]

٤٦٥٧ . الإمامُ زينُ العابدينَ ﵇ ـ مِن مَواعِظِهِ ـ: اِعلَمْ يابنَ آدَمَ أنَّ مِن وَراءِ هذا أعظَمَ وأفظَعَ وأوجَعَ لِلقُلوبِ يَومَ القِيامَةِ، ذلكَ يَومٌ مَجموعٌ لَهُ النّاسُ وذلكَ يَومٌ مَشهودٌ، يَجمَعُ اللهُ فيهِ الأوَّلينَ والآخِرينَ.[٥١٩٤]

1384. The Proofs Affirming Resurrection

١٣٨٤ ـ دَلائلُ إثباتِ المَعادِ

"Did you suppose that We created you aimlessly, and that you will not be brought back to Us?"[5232]

﴿أفَحَسِبتُم أنَّما خَلَقناكُم عَبَثاً وأنَّكُم إلَينا لا تُرجَعونَ﴾.[٥١٩٥]

"We did not create the sky and the earth and whatever is between them in vain. That is a conjecture of the

﴿أم نَجعَلُ الَّذينَ آمَنوا وعَمِلوا الصّالِحاتِ

faithless. So woe to the faithless for the Fire! Shall We treat those who have faith and do righteous deeds like those who cause corruption on the earth? Shall We treat the Godwary like the vicious?"[5233]

كَـالْمُفْسِدينَ فِـي الْأَرْضِ أمْ نَـجْعَلُ الْـمُتَّقِينَ كَالْفُجَّارِ﴾.[٥١٩٦]

"He draws comparisons for Us, and forgets his own creation. He says, 'Who shall revive the bones when they have decayed? Say, 'He will revive them Who produced them the first time, and He has knowledge of all creation."[5234]

﴿وَضَرَبَ لَنا مَثَلاً وَنَسِيَ خَلْقَهُ قالَ مَـنْ يُـحْيِي الْعِظامَ وَهِيَ رَمِيمٌ * قُلْ يُحْيِيهَا الَّـذِي أنْشَأها أوَّلَ مَرَّةٍ وَهُوَ بِكُلِّ خَلْقٍ عَلِيمٌ﴾.[٥١٩٧]

"Man says, 'Shall I, when I have died, be brought forth alive?' Does not man remember that We created him before when he was nothing?"[5235]

﴿وَيَقُولُ الْإنْسانُ ءَإذَا ما مِتُّ لَسَوْفَ أُخْرَجُ حَيّاً * أوَلا يَذْكُرُ الْإنْسانُ أنَّا خَلَقْناهُ مِنْ قَبْلُ وَلَمْ يَكُ شَيْئاً﴾.[٥١٩٨]

"It is He who originates the creation, and then He will bring it back – and that is more simple for Him. His is the loftiest description in the heavens and the earth. And He is the All-mighty, the All-wise."[5236]

﴿وَهُوَ الَّذِي يَبْدَأُ الْخَلْقَ ثُمَّ يُعِيدُهُ وَهُوَ أهْوَنُ عَلَيْهِ وَلَهُ الْمَثَلُ الْأعْلَىٰ فِي السَّماواتِ وَالْأرْضِ وَهُوَ الْعَزِيزُ الْحَكِيمُ﴾.[٥١٩٩]

"So observe the effects of Allah's mercy: how He revives the earth after its death! Indeed He is the reviver of the dead, and He has power over all things."[5237]

﴿فَانْظُرْ إلَىٰ آثارِ رَحْمَةِ اللهِ كَيْفَ يُحْيِي الْأرْضَ بَعْدَ مَوْتِها إنَّ ذٰلِكَ لَمُحْيِي الْمَوْتَىٰ وَهُوَ عَلىٰ كُلِّ شَيْءٍ قَدِيرٌ﴾.[٥٢٠٠]

"It is Allah who sends the winds and they raise a cloud; then We drive it toward a dead land and with it revive the earth after its death. Likewise will be the resurrection [of the dead]."[5238]

﴿وَاللهُ الَّذِي أرْسَلَ الرِّياحَ فَتُثِيرُ سَحاباً فَسُقْناهُ إلَىٰ بَلَدٍ مَيِّتٍ فَأحْيَيْنا بِهِ الْأرْضَ بَعْدَ مَوْتِها كَذٰلِكَ النُّشُورُ﴾.[٥٢٠١]

1385. The Drawing Near of the Hour[5239]

١٣٨٥ ـ اِقتِرابُ السّاعَةِ

"Mankind's reckoning has drawn near to them, yet they are disregardful in [their] obliviousness."[5240]

﴿اقْـتَرَبَ لِـلنَّاسِ حِسابُهُمْ وَهُمْ فِـي غَـفْلَةٍ مُعْرِضُونَ﴾.[٥٢٠٢]

4658. It is narrated in *al-Ja'fariyyāt* that the Prophet (SAWA) said, 'The time between when I was sent down [as a messenger] and the Hour is as these two', indicating to the space between his index finger and his middle finger. He then continued, 'By the One who has my soul in His Grasp, verily I find the Hour to be upon me already.'[5241]

٤٦٥٨. الجعفريّات عن رسولِ اللهِ ﷺ: بُعِثتُ أنا والسّاعَةُ كَهاتَينِ ـ وأشارَ بِإصبَعِهِ: السَّبّابَةِ والوُسطىٰ ثُمَّ قالَ ـ: وَالّذي نَفسِي بِيَدِه إنّي لَأجِدُ السّاعةَ بَينَ كِتفَيَّ.[٥٢٠٣]

4659. **Imām 'Alī (AS) said,** 'The Hour [Judgment Day] showed its face and its signs have appeared to the clever.'[5242]

٤٦٥٩. الإمامُ عليٌّ ؑ: أسفَرَتِ السّاعَةُ عَن وَجهِها، وظَهَرَتِ العَلامَةُ لِمُتَوَسِّمِها.[٥٢٠٤]

1386. Allah's Exclusive Knowledge of the Hour

١٣٨٦ ـ تَفَرُّدُ اللهِ بِعِلمِ السّاعَةِ

"The people question you concerning the Hour. Say, 'Its knowledge is only with Allah.' What do you know, maybe the Hour is near."[5243]

﴿يَسْأَلُكَ النَّاسُ عَنِ السَّاعَةِ قُلْ إِنَّما عِلْمُها عِنْدَ اللهِ وَما يُدْرِيكَ لَعَلَّ السَّاعَةَ تَكُونُ قَرِيباً﴾.[٥٢٠٥]

4660. **Imām al-Ṣādiq (AS) narrated,** 'Jesus son of Mary (AS) asked Gabriel (AS), 'When will the Hour come?' upon which Gabriel started to tremble so severely that he fainted from it. When he came to his senses, he said, 'O Spirit of Allah, the questioned one does not know that any more than the questioner does. To Him belongs all that is in the heavens and the earth, and it [the Hour] will take you all by surprise.'[5244]

٤٦٦٠ . الإمامُ الصّادقُ عليه السلام : قالَ عيسَى بنُ مَريَمَ عليهما السلام لِجَبرَئيلَ عليه السلام : مَتىٰ قِيامُ السّاعَةِ ؟ فَانتَفَضَ جَبرَئيلُ انتِفاضَةً اُغمِيَ عَلَيهِ مِنها ، فلَمّا أفاقَ قالَ : يا روحَ اللهِ ، ما المَسؤولُ أعلَمُ بِها مِنَ السّائلِ ، ولَهُ مَن في السَّماواتِ والأرضِ ، لا تَأتيكُم إلّا بَغتَةً.[٥٢٠٦]

1387. The Portents of the Hour

١٣٨٧ ـ أشراطُ السّاعَةِ

"Do they await anything except that the Hour should overtake them suddenly? Certainly its portents have come. Of what avail to them will their admonition be when it overtakes them?"[5245]

﴿فَهَلْ يَنْظُرُونَ إِلّا السَّاعَةَ أَنْ تَأْتِيَهُمْ بَغْتَةً فَقَدْ جاءَ أَشْراطُها فَأَنَّىٰ لَهُمْ إِذا جاءَتْهُمْ ذِكْراهُمْ﴾.[٥٢٠٧]

"And the Trumpet will be blown, and whoever is in the heavens will swoon and whoever is on the earth, except whomever Allah wishes. Then it will be blown a second time, behold, they will rise up, looking on!"[5246]

﴿وَنُفِخَ فِي الصُّورِ فَصَعِقَ مَنْ فِي السَّماواتِ وَمَنْ فِي الأَرْضِ إِلَّا مَنْ شاءَ اللهُ ثُمَّ نُفِخَ فِيهِ أُخْرَىٰ فَإِذا هُمْ قِيامٌ يَنْظُرُونَ﴾.[٥٢٠٨]

"When the earth is rocked with a terrible quake,"[5247]

﴿إِذا زُلْزِلَتِ الأَرْضُ زِلْزالَها﴾.[٥٢٠٩]

"No indeed! When the earth is crumbled into fragments,"[5248]

﴿كَلَّا إِذَا دُكَّتِ الأَرْضُ دَكّاً دَكّاً﴾.[٥٢١٠]

"And the mountains move with an awful motion."[5249]

﴿وَتَسِيرُ الْجِبالُ سَيْراً﴾.[٥٢١١]

"And the mountains will be like carded wool."[5250]

﴿وَتَكُونُ الْجِبالُ كَالْعِهْنِ الْمَنْفُوشِ﴾.[٥٢١٢]

"And when the seas are merged."[5251]

﴿وَإِذَا الْبِحارُ فُجِّرَتْ﴾.[٥٢١٣]

"When the sun is wound up, and when the stars fall."[5252]

﴿إِذَا الشَّمْسُ كُوِّرَتْ * وَإِذَا النُّجُومُ انْكَدَرَتْ﴾.[٥٢١٤]

"And when the stars are scattered."[5253]

﴿وَإِذَا الْكَوَاكِبُ انْتَثَرَتْ﴾.[٥٢١٥]

"And the sky will be split open – for it will be frail that day."[5254]

﴿وَانْشَقَّتِ السَّماءُ فَهِيَ يَوْمَئِذٍ واهِيَةٌ﴾.[٥٢١٦]

1388. The Day of Rising [from the Graves]

١٣٨٨ـ يَومُ الخُروجِ

"The day when they hear the Cry in all truth. That is the Day of rising [from the dead]."[5255]

﴿يَوْمَ يَسْمَعُونَ الصَّيْحَةَ بِالْحَقِّ ذَلِكَ يَوْمُ الْخُرُوجِ﴾.[٥٢١٧]

4661. **Imām Zayn al-ʿĀbidīn (AS) said,** 'Man's worst hours are three in number: the hour wherein he will see the angel of death with his own eyes, the hour when he will rise up from his grave, and the hour when he will stand before Allah, Blessed and most High.'[5256]

٤٦٦١. الإمامُ زينُ العابدينَ (ع): أشَدُّ ساعاتِ ابنِ آدَمَ ثَلاثُ ساعاتٍ: السّاعَةُ الّتي يُعايِنُ فيها مَلَكَ المَوتِ، والسّاعَةُ الّتي يَقومُ فيها مِن قَبرِهِ، والسّاعَةُ الّتي يَقِفُ فيها بَينَ يَدَيِ اللهِ تَبارَكَ وتَعالىٰ.[٥٢١٨]

1389. The Description of the [Day of] Congregation

١٣٨٩ـ صِفَةُ المَحشَرِ

4662. **The Prophet (SAWA) said,** 'Man will die in the state that he has lived, and will be raised in the same state that he died.'[5257]

٤٦٦٢. رسولُ اللهِ (ص): يَموتُ الرَّجُلُ علىٰ ما عاشَ عَلَيهِ، ويُحشَرُ عَلىٰ ما ماتَ عَلَيهِ.[٥٢١٩]

4663. **Prophet (SAWA) said,** 'He who dies is resurrected with the clothes he dies in.'[5258 5259]

٤٦٦٣. عنه (ص): المَيِّتُ يُبعَثُ فى ثِيابِهِ الّتى يَموتُ فيها.[٥٢٢٠]

4664. **The Prophet (SAWA) said,** 'Everyone on the Day of Judgment will be thirsty.'[5260]

٤٦٦٤. عنه (ص): كُلُّ مَن وَرَدَ القِيامَةَ عَطشانُ.[٥٢٢١]

4665. **Imām ʿAlī (AS) said,** 'Listen O negligent and fickle one to someone who exhorts and expounds. The Day of Resurrection has been made a day of exposition, questioning, bestowal and exemplary punishment. It is the day when men's deeds will be upturned, and all sins will be computed, when people's pupils will melt with grief and expectant women will deliver what they carry in their wombs.'[5261]

٤٦٦٥. الإمامُ عليٌّ (ع): اِسمَعْ يا ذَا الغَفلَةِ والتَّصريفِ مِن ذي الوَعظِ والتَّعريفِ، جُعِلَ يَومُ الحَشرِ يَومَ العَرضِ والسُّؤالِ والحِباءِ والنَّكالِ، يَومَ تُقلَبُ إلَيهِ أعمالُ الأنامِ، وتُحصىٰ فيهِ جَميعُ الآثامِ، يَومَ تَذوبُ مِنَ النُّفوسِ أحداقُ عُيونِها، وتَضَعُ الحَوامِلُ ما في بُطونِها.[٥٢٢٢]

4666. **Imām ʿAlī (AS) said,** 'And that is the day when Allah will gather all people from the first to the last, standing in subjugation in order to discuss the account [of their deeds] and the recompense for their actions. They will be bridled with their own sweat while the earth trembles under them. Those amongst them in the best state will be those who manage to find a stable place for their feet to stand and an open space for them to breathe!'[5262]

٤٦٦٦ . عنه ﷺ : وذلكَ يَومٌ يَجمَعُ اللهُ فيهِ الأوَّلينَ والآخِرينَ لِنِقاشِ الحِسابِ وجَزاءِ الأعمالِ، خُضوعاً قِياماً، قَد ألجَمَهُمُ العَرَقُ، ورَجَفَت بِهِمُ الأرضُ، فَأحسَنُهُم حالاً مَن وَجَدَ لِقَدَمَيهِ مَوضِعاً، ولِنَفسِهِ مُتَّسَعاً! ٥٢٢٣

1390. The Godwary People on the Day of Resurrection

١٣٩٠ ـ المُتَّقونَ فِي القِيامَةِ

4667. **The Prophet (SAWA),** with regards to Allah's verse: *"The Day We shall gather the Godwary toward the All-beneficent, as incoming guests"*[5263], said, 'Verily these incoming guests will only enter mounted. They are the men who were wary of their duty to Allah, so Allah loved them, distinguished them and is well-pleased with their deeds, and has therefore named them the Godwary.'[5264]

٤٦٦٧ . رسولُ اللهِ ﷺ ـ في قولِهِ تعالى: ﴿يَومَ نَحشُرُ المُتَّقينَ إِلَى الرَّحمٰنِ وَفداً﴾ ـ : إنَّ الوَفدَ لا يَكونونَ إلّا رُكباناً، اُولئكَ رِجالٌ اتَّقَوا اللهَ فأحَبَّهُمُ اللهُ وَاختَصَّهُم ورَضِيَ أعمالَهُم، فسَمّاهُمُ المُتَّقينَ. ٥٢٢٤

1391. The Guilty Ones on the Day of Resurrection

١٣٩١ ـ المُجرِمونَ فِي القِيامَةِ

4668. **Imām al-Ṣādiq (AS) said,** 'He who meets his fellow Muslims two-facedly and hypocritically [lit. having two-tongues] will be raised on the Day of Resurrection with two tongues of Fire.'[5265]

٤٦٦٨ . الإمامُ الصّادقُ ﷺ : مَن لَقِيَ المُسلِمينَ بِوَجهَينِ ولِسانَينِ، جاءَ يَومَ القِيامَةِ ولَهُ لِسانانِ مِن نارٍ. ٥٢٢٥

4669. **Imām al-Ṣādiq (AS) said,** 'Whoever wrongfully consumes his fellow brother's property and does not return it to him will be made to devour a burning log of fire on the Day of Resurrection.'[5266]

٤٦٦٩ . عنه ﷺ : مَن أكَلَ مِن مالِ أخيهِ ظُلماً ولَم يَرُدَّهُ عَلَيهِ، أكَلَ جَذوَةً مِنَ النّارِ يَومَ القِيامَةِ. ٥٢٢٦

4670. **Imām al-Ṣādiq (AS) said,** 'Whoever recites the Qur'an in order to deceive people thereby will be raised on the Day of Resurrection with a bony face without any flesh therein.'[5267]

٤٦٧٠ . عنه ﷺ : مَن قَرَأَ القُرآنَ لِيَأكُلَ بِهِ النّاسَ جاءَ يَومَ القِيامَةِ ووَجهُهُ عَظمٌ لا لَحمَ فيهِ. ٥٢٢٧

4671. **Imām al-Ṣādiq (AS) said,** 'Verily the proud ones will be transformed into tiny ants that people will trample underfoot until Allah finishes the account.'[5268]

٤٦٧١. عنه ﷺ: إنَّ المُتَكَبِّرِينَ يُـجعَلونَ فـي صُوَرِ الذَّرِّ يَتَوَطَّؤُهُمُ النّاسُ حَتّىٰ يَفرُغَ اللهُ مِـنَ الحِسابِ.[٥٢٢٨]

4672. **Imām al-Ṣādiq (AS) said,** 'When the Day of Resurrection comes, a caller will announce [on Allah's behalf], 'Where are those who obstructed My friends?' and a group of people with no flesh on their faces will stand, and it will be said of them, 'These are the people who troubled the believers, who declared enmity towards them, who opposed them and treated them harshly because of their religion.' Then they will be ordered into Hell.'[5269]

٤٦٧٢. عنه ﷺ: إذا كانَ يومَ القِيامَةِ نادىٰ مُنادٍ: أينَ الصَّدودُ لِأَولِيائي؟ فيَقومُ قَومٌ لَـيسَ عَـلىٰ وُجـوهِهِم لَـحمٌ، فـيُقالُ: هٰـؤلاءِ الّـذينَ آذَوُا المُؤمِنينَ ونَصَبوا لَهُم وعانَدوهُم وعَنَّفوهُم فـي دِينِهِم، ثُمَّ يُؤمَرُ بِهِم إلىٰ جَهَنَّمَ.[٥٢٢٩]

1392. The Book of Deeds

١٣٩٢ ـ كِتابُ الأعمالِ

"We have attached every person's omen to his neck, and We shall bring it out for him on the Day of Resurrection as a wide open book that he will encounter. 'Read your book! Today your soul suffices as your own reckoner.'"[5270]

﴿وَكُلَّ إِنْسانٍ أَلْزَمْناهُ طائِرَهُ فِي عُنُقِهِ وَنُخْرِجُ لَهُ يَومَ الْقِيامَةِ كِتاباً يَلْقاهُ مَنْشُوراً * اقْـرَأْ كِـتابَكَ كَفىٰ بِنَفْسِكَ الْيَوْمَ عَلَيْكَ حَسِيباً﴾.[٥٢٣٠]

4673. **Imām al-Bāqir (AS),** with regards to Allah's verse: *"We have attached every person's omen to his neck"*, said, 'The good and the evil he has done is with him wherever he is, and he cannot separate them until he is given his book about his deeds on the Day of Resurrection.'[5271]

٤٦٧٣. الإمامُ الباقرُ ﷺ ـ في قَولِه تَعالىٰ: ﴿وَكُلَّ إنسانٍ أَلْزَمْناهُ طائرَهُ في عُنُقِه﴾ ـ: يَقولُ: خَيرُهُ وشَرُّهُ مَعَهُ حَيثُ كانَ، لا يَستَطيعُ فِراقَـهُ حَـتّىٰ يُعطىٰ كِتابَهُ يَومَ القِيامَةِ بِما عَمِلَ.[٥٢٣١]

4674. **Imām al-Ṣādiq (AS),** with regards to Allah's verse: *'Read your book! Today your soul suffices as your own reckoner'*, said, 'The servant will be reminded of everything that he had done and that was recorded against him, as if he had done it that very hour, and because of that they will say, *"Woe to us! What a book this is! It omits nothing, big or small, without enumerating it?!"*'[5272 5273]

٤٦٧٤. الإمامُ الصّادقُ ﷺ ـ في قولِهِ تَعالىٰ ـ: ﴿اِقْرَأْ كِتابَكَ كَفىٰ بِنَفْسِكَ اليَومَ﴾ ـ: يُذَكَّرُ العَبدُ جَميعَ ما عَمِلَ وما كُتِبَ عَلَيهِ؛ كأنَّهُ فَعَلَهُ تِـلكَ السّاعَةِ، فلِذلكَ قالوا: ﴿يا وَيْلَتَنا ما لِهٰذا الكِتابِ لا يُغادِرُ صَغيرَةً وَلا كَبيرَةً إلّا أحْصاها﴾؟![٥٢٣٢]

4675. **Imām al-Ṣādiq (AS) said,** 'When the Day of Resurrection comes, man will be handed his book and told, 'Read it.' [The reporter of the tradition

٤٦٧٥. عنه ﷺ: إذا كانَ يَومُ القِيامَةِ دُفِعَ إلَـى

then asked him], 'And will he know what is in it?' to which he replied, 'Verily he will remember it. There will not remain a single moment, a single word, a single footstep or anything that he did which he will not remember, as if he had done it that very hour. And this is why they will say, *"Woe to us! What a book this is! It omits nothing, big or small, without enumerating it."*[5274]

الإنسانِ كِتابُه، ثُمَّ قيلَ لَهُ: اقرَأهُ. [قالَ الرّاوي:] قُلتُ: فيَعرِفُ ما فيهِ؟ فقالَ: إنَّهُ يَذكُرُهُ فَما مِن لَحظَةٍ ولا كَلِمَةٍ ولا نَقْلِ قَدَمٍ ولا شَيءٍ فَعَلَهُ إلّا ذَكَرَهُ؛ كأنَّهُ فَعَلَهُ تِلكَ السّاعَةَ، فلِذٰلكَ قالوا: ﴿يا وَيْلَتَنا ما لِهٰذا الكِتابِ لا يُغادِرُ صَغيرَةً وَلا كَبيرَةً إلّا أحْصاها﴾». ٥٢٣٣

1393. The People of the Right Hand and of the Left Hand

١٣٩٣ ـ أصحابُ اليَمينِ والشمال

4676. **Imām al-Ṣādiq (AS) said,** 'Verily when Allah, Blessed and most High, will wish to deal with the believer's account, He will give him his book in his right hand and will then take him to account for all that is between him and Himself, and will say, 'My servant, you have committed such and such and have done such and such!' and he will reply, 'Yes, my Lord, I have done that.' And Allah will say, 'I have forgiven you for them and have transformed them into good deeds', so people will ask, 'Glory be to Allah, did this man not have a single evil deed?!' and this is the purport of Allah's verse: *"Then as for him who is given his record in his right hand, he shall soon receive an easy reckoning, and he will return to his folks joyfully."*[5275 5276]

٤٦٧٦. الإمامُ الصّادقُ عليه السلام: إنَّ اللهَ تَبارَكَ وتَعالىٰ إذا أرادَ أن يُحاسِبَ المُؤمِنَ أعطاهُ كِتابَهُ بِيَمينِهِ وحاسَبَهُ فيما بَينَهُ وبَينَهُ، فيَقولُ: عَبدي، فَعَلتَ كَذا وكَذا وعَمِلتَ كَذا وكَذا! فيَقولُ: نَعَم يا رَبِّ قَد فَعَلتُ ذٰلكَ، فيَقولُ: قَد غَفَرتُها لَكَ وأبدَلتُها حَسَناتٍ، فيَقولُ النّاسُ: سُبحانَ اللهِ أما كانَ لِهٰذا العَبدِ سَيِّئَةٌ واحِدَةٌ؟! وهُوَ قَولُ اللهِ عَزَّوجلَّ: ﴿فَأَمّا مَن اُوتِيَ كِتابَهُ بِيَمينِهِ فَسَوْفَ يُحاسَبُ حِساباً يَسيراً وَيَنْقَلِبُ إلىٰ أهْلِهِ مَسروراً﴾. ٥٢٣٤

4677. **Imām al-Ṣādiq (AS) said,** 'Verily when Allah, Blessed and most High, wishes to requite his servant with evil [as a result of his deeds], He will take him to account for them in front of everyone, and will reduce him to tears [on account of the proofs against him], and will give him his book in his left hand, and this is the purport of Allah's verse: *"But as for him who is given his record from behind his back, he will pray for annihilation, and he will enter the Blaze. Indeed he used to be joyful among his folk."*[5277 5278]

٤٦٧٧. الإمامُ الصّادقُ عليه السلام: إنَّ اللهَ تَبارَكَ وتَعالىٰ ... إذا أرادَ بِعَبدٍ شَرّاً حاسَبَهُ عَلىٰ رُؤوسِ النّاسِ، وبَكَّتَهُ ٥٢٣، وأعطاهُ كِتابَهُ بِشِمالِهِ، وهُوَ قَولُ اللهِ عَزَّوجلَّ: ﴿وَأمّا مَنْ اُوتِيَ كِتابَهُ وَراءَ ظَهْرِهِ فَسَوْفَ يَدْعو ثُبوراً * وَيَصْلىٰ سَعيراً * إنّهُ كانَ في أهْلِهِ مَسروراً﴾. ٥٢٣٦

(See also: THE RECKONING: section 526)

(انظر: الحساب: باب ٥٢٦.)

293

THE HABIT

العادَة

1394. The Role of Habit in Life

١٣٩٤ ـ دورُ العادَةِ فِي الحَياةِ

4678. **Imām ʿAlī (AS) said,** 'Habit is second nature.'[5279]

٤٦٧٨ . الإمامُ عليٌّ ﷺ : العادَةُ طَبعٌ ثانٍ .٥٢٣٧

4679. **Imām ʿAlī (AS) said,** 'A habit holds every man under its authority.'[5280]

٤٦٧٩ . عنه ﷺ : لِلعادَةِ عَلىٰ كُلِّ إنسانٍ سُلطانٌ .٥٢٣٨

4680. **Imām ʿAlī (AS) said,** 'He who obeys habits does not attain high levels.'[5281]

٤٦٨٠ . عنه ﷺ : غَيرُ مُدرِكِ الدَّرَجاتِ مَن أطاعَ العاداتِ .٥٢٣٩

4681. **Imām ʿAlī (AS) said,** 'Your tongue will urge you to whatever you have accustomed it [to say], and your inner self will require you to do whatever you have made it fond of.'[5282]

٤٦٨١ . عنه ﷺ : لِسانُكَ يَستَدعيكَ ما عَوَّدتَهُ ، ونَفسُكَ تَقتَضيكَ ما أَلِفتَهُ .٥٢٤٠

4682. **Imām ʿAlī (AS) said,** 'Do not hasten to resort to anger lest it prevail over you by becoming a habit.'[5283]

٤٦٨٢ . عنه ﷺ : لا تُسرِعَنَّ إلَى الغَضَبِ فيَتَسَلَّطَ عَلَيكَ بِالعادَةِ .٥٢٤١

4683. **Imām ʿAlī (AS) said** in his will to his son, al-Ḥasan (AS), 'Verily the heart of a young person is like the untilled earth, which accepts whatever is placed therein. I, therefore, urge you to hasten to self-discipline before your heart hardens, and your mind becomes preoccupied.'[5284]

٤٦٨٣ . عنه ﷺ ـ في وَصِيَّتِه لِابنِه الحَسَنِ ﷺ ـ : إنَّما قَلبُ الحَدَثِ كالأرضِ الخالِيَةِ ما اُلقِيَ فيها مِن شَيءٍ قَبِلَتهُ ، فبادَرتُكَ بِالأدَبِ قَبلَ أن يَقسُوَ قَلبُكَ ، ويَشتَغِلَ لُبُّكَ .٥٢٤٢

4684. **Imām ʿAlī (AS),** was once offered a sweet called *fālūdhaj*,[5285] so he placed it in front of him, saying, 'Verily you have a fragrant smell, are of a beautiful colour, and taste delicious, but I hate to habituate my soul [to anything] since it has not yet formed any habits.'[5286]

٤٦٨٤ . عنه ﷺ ـ لَمّا اُتِيَ بِفالوذَجٍ فوُضِعَ قُدّامَهُ ـ : إنَّكَ طَيِّبُ الرّيحِ حَسَنُ اللَّونِ طَيِّبُ الطَّعمِ ، ولٰكن أكرَهُ أن اُعَوِّدَ نَفسي ما لَم تَعتَدْ .٥٢٤٣

4685. **Imām ʿAlī (AS) said,** 'Habituate yourself to performing noble actions and to bear the burdensome consequences [of your actions], and your soul will be elevated as a result, your Hereafter will flourish, and your admirers will increase.'[5287]

٤٦٨٥ . عنه (ع) : عَوِّدْ نَفسَكَ فِعلَ المَكارِمِ، وتَحَمُّلَ أعباءِ المَغارِمِ، تَشرُفْ نَفسُكَ، وتَعمُرْ آخِرَتُكَ، ويَكثُرْ حامِدوكَ.[٥٢٤٤]

4686. **Imām al-Ḥasan (AS) said,** 'Habits are overpowering, for he who forms a habit to something in secret and during his free times is plagued by them in public and when occupied.'[5288]

٤٦٨٦ . الإمامُ الحسنُ (ع) : العاداتُ قاهِراتٌ، فَمَنِ اعتادَ شَيئاً في سِرِّهِ وخَلَواتِهِ، فَضَحَهُ في عَلانِيَتِهِ وعِندَ المَلأ.[٥٢٤٥]

1395. Overcoming the Habit

١٣٩٥ ـ غَلَبَةُ العادَةِ

4687. **Imām ʿAlī (AS) said,** 'Virtue is overcoming one's habit.'[5289]

٤٦٨٧ . الإمامُ عليٌّ (ع) : الفَضيلَةُ غَلَبَةُ العادَةِ.[٥٢٤٦]

4688. **Imām ʿAlī (AS) said,** 'The best of worship is to overcome one's habit.'[5290]

٤٦٨٨ . عنه (ع) : أفضَلُ العِبادَةِ غَلَبَةُ العادَةِ.[٥٢٤٧]

4689. **Imām ʿAlī (AS) said,** '[Only] Through overcoming one's habits are the highest of stations attained.'[5291]

٤٦٨٩ . عنه (ع) : بِغَلَبَةِ العاداتِ الوُصولُ إلىٰ أشرَفِ المَقاماتِ.[٥٢٤٨]

4690. **Imām ʿAlī (AS) said,** 'Change your habits and your acts of obedience will become easier for you.'[5292]

٤٦٩٠ . عنه (ع) : غَيِّروا العاداتِ تَسهُلْ عَلَيكُمُ الطّاعاتُ.[٥٢٤٩]

4691. **Imām ʿAlī (AS) said,** 'Subjugate your souls to abandon their habits, drive them to perform acts of obedience, make them bear the burdensome consequences of their actions, adorn them with the performance of noble acts, and protect them against the pollution of sins.'[5293]

٤٦٩١ . عنه (ع) : ذَلِّلوا أنفُسَكُم بِتَركِ العاداتِ، وَقودوها إلىٰ فِعلِ الطّاعاتِ، وحَمِّلوها أعباءَ المَغارِمِ، وحَلّوها بِفِعلِ المَكارِمِ، وصونوها عَن دَنَسِ المَآثِمِ.[٥٢٥٠]

1396. The Difficulty of Removing a Habit

١٣٩٦ ـ صُعوبَةُ نَقلِ العاداتِ

4692. **Imām ʿAlī (AS) said,** 'The most difficult of things to manage is the removal of habits.'[5294]

٤٦٩٢ . الإمامُ عليٌّ (ع) : أصعَبُ السِّياساتِ نَقلُ العاداتِ.[٥٢٥١]

٤٦٩٣. عنه ﷺ: كُلُّ شَيءٍ يُستَطاعُ، إلّا نَقلَ الطِّباعِ.٥٢٥٢

4693. **Imām ʿAlī (AS) said,** 'Everything is achievable, except the removal of an ingrained habit.'[5295]

٤٦٩٤. عنه ﷺ: أيُّها النّاسُ، تَوَلَّوا مِن أنفُسِكُم تَأديبَها، وَاعدِلوا بِها عَن ضَراوَةِ عاداتِها.٥٢٥٣

4694. **Imām ʿAlī (AS) said,** 'O people, take upon yourselves your own training, and turn away from the voracious dictates of your habits.'[5296]

294

ʿĪD – THE FESTIVAL

العيد

1397. ʿĪd – The True Festival

١٣٩٧ ـ العيدُ الحَقيقي

﴿قالَ عيسَى ابنُ مَريَمَ اللّهُمَّ رَبَّنا أنزِل عَلَينا مائِدَةً مِنَ السَّماءِ تَكونُ لَنا عيداً لِأوَّلِنا وَآخِرِنا وَآيَةً مِنكَ وَارزُقنا وَأنتَ خَيرُ الرّازِقينَ﴾.٥٢٥٤

"Jesus son of Mary said, 'O Allah! Our Lord! Send down to us a table from the sky, to be a festival for us, for the first ones and the last ones among us and as a sign from You, and provide for us; for you are the best of providers.'[5297]

٤٦٩٥. الإمامُ عليٌّ ﷺ ـ قالَ في بَعضِ الأعيادِ ـ: إنَّما هُوَ عيدٌ لِمَن قَبِلَ اللهُ صِيامَهُ وشَكَرَ قِيامَهُ، وكُلُّ يَومٍ لا يُعصَى اللهُ فيهِ فَهُوَ عيدٌ.٥٢٥٥

4695. **Imām ʿAlī (AS) said** regarding one of the festivals, 'Verily it is only a festival for he whose fasts Allah has accepted and whose prayers He has acknowledged, and every day in which we do not disobey Allah is a day of celebration.'[5298]

٤٦٩٦. بحار الأنوار عن سُوَيدِ بنِ غَفلَةَ: دَخَلتُ عَلَيهِ [يَعني أميرَ المُؤمِنينَ ﷺ] يَومَ عيدٍ، فَإِذا عِندَهُ فاثورٌ عَلَيهِ خُبزُ السَّمراءِ وصَحفَةٌ فيها خَطيفَةٌ ومِلبَنَةٌ٥٢٥٦، فَقُلتُ: يا أميرَ المُؤمِنينَ، يَومُ عيدٍ وخَطيفَةٌ؟! فَقالَ: إنَّما هٰذا عيدُ مَن غُفِرَ لَهُ.٥٢٥٧

4696. **Suwayd b. Ghafla narrated,** 'I went to visit him [i.e. Imām ʿAlī] (AS) on one of the festivals, and he had a small table in front of him on which was wheat bread, and a plate of *khaṭīfa*[5299] and *milbana*[5300], so I asked, 'O Commander of the Faithful, it is a day of celebration and you are eating *khaṭīfa*?!, to which he replied, 'It is only a day of celebration for whoever has been forgiven.'[5301]

1398. Nayrūz Festival[5302]

١٣٩٨ ـ عيدُ النَّيروزِ

4697. **Imām ʿAlī (AS),** when he was brought a gift for Nayrūz, exclaimed, 'What is this?' to which they replied, 'O Commander of the Faithful, today is Nayrūz.' He replied, 'Make everyday Nayrūz for us [i.e. through your good actions].'[5303]

٤٦٩٧ . الإمامُ عليٌّ عليه السلام ـ لمّا أُتيَ بِهَدِيَّةِ النَّيروزِ ـ: ما هذا؟ قالوا: يا أميرَ المُؤمِنينَ، اليَومُ النَّيروزُ، فقالَ عليه السلام: اِصنَعوا لَنا كُلَّ يَومٍ نَيروزاً! [٥٢٥٨]

4698. **Imām ʿAlī (AS) said,** 'Our Nayrūz is everyday.'[5304]

٤٦٩٨ . عنه عليه السلام: نَيْروزُنا كُلَّ يَومٍ. [٥٢٥٩]

4699. **Imām al-Ṣādiq (AS)** said to Muʿallā b. Khunays when he came to visit him for Nayrūz, 'Do you know what this day is?' to which he replied, 'May I be your ransom, this is a day to which the Persians attach great importance and in which they give each other gifts.' So Imām al-Ṣādiq (AS) said, 'By the Ancient House in Makkah! That is only because of a much older reason which I will explain to you so that you may understand … O Muʿallā, verily the day of Nayrūz is the day when Allah took the servants' covenants from them that they would worship Him and that they would not associate anything with Him, and that they would believe in His prophets and His divine proofs, and that they would believe in the Imāms (AS). This is also the day when the sun rose for the first time … Every day of Nayrūz is a day when we await the Relief [the coming of the Awaited Saviour], for verily it is one of our special days and one of the days of our *shīʿa*. The Persians have kept its significance whereas you have lost it…This is the first day of the Persians' new year, and they have managed to stay alive since having been only thirty thousand in number. The pouring of water on the day of Nayrūz has become a practice…'[5305]

٤٦٩٩ . الإمامُ الصّادقُ عليه السلام ـ لمُعلّى بن خُنيس لمّا دخَلَ عليه يومَ النَّيروزِ ـ: أتعرِفَ هٰذا اليَومَ؟ قُلتُ: جُعِلتُ فِداكَ، هٰذا يَومٌ تُعَظِّمُهُ العَجَمُ وتَتَهادىٰ فيهِ، فقالَ أبوعَبدِاللهِ الصّادِقُ عليه السلام: والبَيتِ العَتيقِ الّذي بِمَكَّةَ! ما هٰذا إلّا لِأمرٍ قَديمٍ أُفَسِّرُهُ لَكَ حَتّىٰ تَفهَمَهُ… يا مُعَلّى، إنَّ يَومَ النَّيروزِ هُوَ اليَومُ الّذي أخَذَ اللهُ فيهِ مَواثيقَ العِبادِ أن يَعبُدوهُ ولا يُشرِكوا بِهِ شَيئاً وأن يُؤمِنوا بِرُسُلِهِ وحُجَجِهِ، وأن يُؤمِنوا بِالأئمَّةِ عليهم السلام، وهُوَ أوَّلُ يَومٍ طَلَعَت فيهِ الشَّمسُ… وما مِن يَومِ نَيروزٍ إلّا ونَحنُ نَتَوَقَّعُ فيهِ الفَرَجَ لِأنَّهُ مِن أيّامِنا وأيّامِ شيعَتِنا، حَفِظَتهُ العَجَمُ وضَيَّعتُموهُ أنتُم… وهُوَ أوَّلُ يَومٍ مِن سَنَةِ الفُرسِ فَعَاشُوا وَهُمْ ثَلاثُونَ أَلْفاً فَصَارَ صَبُّ الْمَاءِ فِي النَّيرُوزِ سُنَّةً…. [٥٢٦٠]

4700. **Imām al-Ṣādiq (AS) said,** 'On the day of Nayrūz, take a bath and wear your cleanest clothes, and perfume yourself with the best of fragrances, and fast on that day.'[5306]

٤٧٠٠. عنه ﷺ: إذا كانَ يَومُ النَّيروزِ فَاغتَسِلْ وَالبَسْ أنظَفَ ثِيابِكَ، وتَطَيَّبْ بِأطيَبِ طِيبِكَ، وتَكونُ ذلكَ اليَومَ صائماً.[٥٢٦١]

4701. It is narrated in *Biḥār al-Anwār*: 'It has been related that Manṣūr [Dawāniqī][5307] ordered Imām Mūsā al-Kāẓim (AS) to sit with him to receive gifts and greetings for the day of Nayrūz, so that he may take the gifts presented to him, so Imām replied, 'Verily I have examined the traditions from my grandfather the Prophet (SAWA) and have not found a single tradition about this festival. Rather it is a practice of the Persians which Islam eradicated, and God forbid that we should revive what Islam has eradicated.' So Manṣūr said, 'We only celebrate it as a matter of policy for our army, so I request you by Allah the Great to sit down', so he sat down ...'[5308 5309]

٤٧٠١. بحار الأنوار: حُكِيَ أنَّ المَنصورَ تَقَدَّمَ إلىٰ موسَى بنِ جَعفَرٍ ﷺ بِالجُلوسِ لِلتَّهنِئَةِ في يَومِ النَّيروزِ وقَبضِ ما يُحمَلُ إلَيهِ، فَقالَ: إنّي قَد فَتَّشتُ الأخبارَ عَن جَدّي رَسولِ اللهِ ﷺ فَلَم أجِدْ لِهٰذا العيدِ خَبَراً، وإنَّهُ سُنَّةُ الفُرسِ ومَحاها الإسلامُ، ومَعاذَ اللهِ أن نُحيِيَ ما مَحاها الإسلامُ. فَقالَ المَنصورُ: إنَّما نَفعَلُ هٰذا سِياسَةً لِلجُندِ، فَسَألتُكَ بِاللهِ العَظيمِ إلّا جَلَستَ. فَجَلَسَ ...[٥٢٦٢، ٥٢٦٣]

1399. The Adornment of the Festivals

١٣٩٩ ـ زينَةُ الأعيادِ

4702. **The Prophet (SAWA) said,** 'Adorn your festivals with frequent chants of *Allāhu Akbar* (Allah is the Greatest).'[5310]

٤٧٠٢. رسولُ اللهِ ﷺ: زَيِّنوا أعيادَكُم بِالتَّكبيرِ.[٥٢٦٤]

4703. **The Prophet (SAWA) said,** 'Adorn the two festivals (*'id al-fiṭr* and *'id al-aḍḥā*) with frequent chants of *lā ilāha illallāh* (There is no god but Allah), *Allāhu Akbar* (Allah is the Greatest), *al-Ḥamdu lillāh* (All praise is due to Allah), and with glorification of Allah.'[5311]

٤٧٠٣. عنه ﷺ: زَيِّنوا العيدَينِ بِالتَّهليلِ والتَّكبيرِ والتَّحميدِ والتَّقديسِ.[٥٢٦٥]

4704. It is narrated in *Kanz al-'Ummāl*: The Prophet (SAWA) used to go out in the streets on the two festivals chanting *lā ilāha illallāh* (There is no god but Allah) and *Allāhu Akbar* (Allah is the Greatest) in a loud voice.'[5312]

٤٧٠٤. كنز العمّال: كانَ ﷺ يَخرُجُ فِي العيدَينِ رافِعاً صَوتَهُ بِالتَّهليلِ والتَّكبيرِ.[٥٢٦٦]

295

THE FAULT

العَيب

1400. Praise for One whose Own Fault Preoccupies him from Finding Fault in Others

١٤٠٠ـ مَدحُ مَن شَغَلَهُ عَيبُهُ عَن عُيوبِ النّاسِ

4705. **Imām ʿAlī (AS) said,** 'Blessed be the one whose own fault preoccupies him from finding faults in others.'[5313]

٤٧٠٥. الإمامُ عليٌّ ﷺ: طوبىٰ لِمَن شَغَلَهُ عَيبُهُ عَن عُيوبِ النّاسِ.٥٢٦٧

4706. **Imām ʿAlī (AS) said,** 'The most intelligent of people is he who is well aware of his own faults and blind to others' faults.'[5314]

٤٧٠٦. عنه ﷺ: أعقَلُ النّاسِ مَن كانَ بِعَيبِهِ بَصيراً، وعَن عَيبِ غَيرِهِ ضَريراً.٥٢٦٨

4707. **Imām ʿAlī (AS) said,** 'He who observes his own faults is preoccupied from others' faults.'[5315]

٤٧٠٧. عنه ﷺ: مَن أبصَرَ عَيبَ نَفسِهِ شُغِلَ عَن عَيبِ غَيرِهِ.٥٢٦٩

4708. **Imām al-Ṣādiq (AS) said,** 'The most beneficial thing for a man is his precedence over others at knowing his own fault.'[5316]

٤٧٠٨. الإمامُ الصّادقُ ﷺ: أنفَعُ الأشياءِ لِلمَرءِ سَبقُهُ النّاسَ إلىٰ عَيبِ نَفسِهِ.٥٢٧٠

4709. **Imām al-Ṣādiq (AS) said,** 'When you see a man inspecting other people's sins and forgetting his own sins, then know that he is deluding himself.'[5317]

٤٧٠٩. عنه ﷺ: إذا رَأيتُمُ العَبدَ مُتَفَقِّداً لِذُنوبِ (النّاسِ) ناسِياً لِذُنوبِهِ، فَاعلَموا أنَّهُ قَد مُكِرَ بِهِ.٥٢٧١

1401. The Reprehension of Preoccupying Oneself with the Faults of Whilst Flattering Oneself

١٤٠١ـ ذَمُّ الاشتِغالِ بِعُيوبِ النّاسِ ومُداهَنَةِ النَّفسِ

4710. **Prophet Jesus (AS) said,** 'O iniquitous servants, you blame others based on what you conjecture about them and do not blame yourselves in that which you know for certain [of your own wrong doings]?!'[5318]

٤٧١٠. عيسى ﷺ: يا عَبيدَ السَّوءِ، تَلومونَ النّاسَ عَلَى الظَّنِّ، ولا تَلومونَ أنفُسَكُم عَلَى اليَقينِ؟!٥٢٧٢

4711. *Kanz al-'Ummāl*: 'The Prophet (SAWA) said, 'How can you notice a speck in your brother's eye but overlook the tree stump in your own?!'[5319]

٤٧١١. كنز العمّال: قالَ رسولُ اللهِ ﷺ: يُبصِرُ أحَدُكُمُ القَذىٰ في عَينِ أخيهِ، ويَنسى الجِذعَ ـ أو قالَ: الجِذْلَ ـ في عَينِه![٥٢٧٣]

4712. **The Prophet (SAWA) said,** 'The fault that lies within a man's own self is more than enough to prevent him from prying into other people's faults, which he himself possesses but to which he is blind; or from blaming others for that which he himself is unable to abandon; or from bothering the one he is sitting next to by prying into matters that are none of his business.'[5320]

٤٧١٢. رسولُ اللهِ ﷺ: كَفىٰ بِالمَرءِ عَيباً أن يَنظُرَ مِنَ النّاسِ إلىٰ ما يَعمىٰ عَنهُ مِن نَفسِهِ، ويُعَيِّرَ النّاسَ بِما لا يَستَطيعُ تَركَهُ، ويُؤذي جَليسَهُ بِما لا يَعنيهِ.[٥٢٧٤]

4713. **Imām 'Alī (AS) said,** 'The one who pries into others' faults, disapproves of them, and then adopts them for himself, is truly a fool.'[5321]

٤٧١٣. الإمامُ عليٌّ ؑ: مَن نَظَرَ في عُيوبِ النّاسِ فأنكَرَها ثُمَّ رَضِيَها لِنَفسِهِ، فذٰلكَ الأحمَقُ بِعَينِهِ.[٥٢٧٥]

4714. **Imām 'Alī (AS) said,** 'The greatest fault is when one criticises others for the same faults present in oneself.'[5322]

٤٧١٤. عنه ؑ: أكبَرُ (أكثَرُ) العَيبِ أن تَعيبَ ما فيكَ مِثلُه.[٥٢٧٦]

1402. The Virtue of Concealing Faults

١٤٠٢ ـ فَضلُ سَترِ العُيوبِ

4715. **The Prophet (SAWA) said,** 'He who conceals a fellow believer's shameful act is as if he has revived a newborn girl buried-alive[5323] from her grave.'[5324]

٤٧١٥. رسولُ اللهِ ﷺ: مَن سَتَرَ عَلىٰ مُؤمِنٍ خِزيَةً فكأنَّما أحيا مَوؤودَةً مِن قَبرِها.[٥٢٧٧]

4716. **The Prophet (SAWA) said,** 'He who knows a fellow brother's evil deed and conceals it [from others], Allah will conceal his faults on the Day of Resurrection.'[5325]

٤٧١٦. عنه ﷺ: مَن عَلِمَ مِن أخيهِ سَيِّئَةً فسَتَرَها، سَتَرَ اللهُ عَلَيهِ يَومَ القِيامَةِ.[٥٢٧٨]

4717. **Imām al-Bāqir (AS) said,** 'It is the duty of a believer towards a fellow believer to conceal seventy of his grave sins!'[5326]

٤٧١٧. الإمامُ الباقرُ ؑ: يَجِبُ لِلمُؤمِنِ عَلَى المُؤمِنِ أن يَستُرَ عَلَيهِ سَبعينَ كَبيرَةً![٥٢٧٩]

4718. It is narrated in *Tanbīh al-Khawāṭir* that Prophet Jesus (AS) was passing with his disciples by the corpse of a dog, when the disciples exclaimed, 'What an awful stench this dog has!' to

٤٧١٨. تنبيه الخواطر: رُوِيَ أنّ عيسىٰ ؑ مَرَّ والحَوارِيّونَ عَلىٰ جيفَةِ كَلبٍ، فقالَ الحَوارِيّونَ: ما أنتَنَ ريحَ هٰذا الكَلبَ! فقالَ

which Prophet Jesus (AS) retorted, 'How white are his teeth!'[5327]

عيسى ﷺ: ما أشَدَّ بَياضَ أسنانِهِ! ٥٣٨٠

1403. Encouraging Conferring Someone's Faults to them

١٤٠٣ ـ الحَثُّ عَلىٰ إهداءِ العُيوبِ

4719. **Imām ʿAlī (AS) said,** 'He who informs you of your faults will guard you in your absence, whereas he who flatters you with respect to your faults will point the finger at you in your absence.'[5328]

٤٧١٩ . الإمامُ عليٌّ ﷺ: مَن كاشَفَكَ في عَيبِكَ حَفِظَكَ في غَيبِكَ ، مَن داهَنَكَ في عَيبِكَ عابَكَ في غَيبِكَ . ٥٣٨١

4720. **Imām ʿAlī (AS) said,** 'Nothing prevents anyone from among you from disclosing to a fellow brother a fault that he fears in him, except for the very fear that he too will disclose the same fault to him. You are all accomplices in your rejection of the next world and loving this world.'[5329]

٤٧٢٠ . عنه ﷺ: ما يَمنَعُ أحَدَكُم أن يَستَقبِلَ أخاهُ بِما يَخافُ مِن عَيبِهِ إلّا مَخافَةَ أن يَستَقبِلَهُ بِمِثلِهِ ، قَد تَصافَيتُم عَلىٰ رَفضِ الآجِلِ وحُبِّ العاجِلِ! ٥٣٨٢

4721. **Imām al-Ṣādiq (AS) said,** 'The most beloved of my brothers to me is he who confers my faults to me.'[5330]

٤٧٢١ . الإمامُ الصّادقُ ﷺ: أحَبُّ إخواني إلَيَّ مَن أهدىٰ إلَيَّ عُيوبي . ٥٣٨٣

1404. Reprehensibility of Pursuing of People's Faults

١٤٠٤ ـ ذَمُّ تَتَبُّعِ العُيوبِ

"Woe to every scandal-monger and slanderer."[5331]

﴿وَيْلٌ لِكُلِّ هُمَزَةٍ ٥٣٨٤ لُمَزَةٍ﴾ . ٥٣٨٥

4722. **The Prophet (SAWA) said,** 'Do not seek to pursue the faults of believers, for verily whoever pursues the faults of believers, Allah will pursue his faults, and whoever's faults Allah pursues, He will expose him, even if he be in the confines of his own home.'[5332]

٤٧٢٢ . رسولُ اللهِ ﷺ: لا تَتَّبِعوا عَوراتِ المُؤمِنينَ ؛ فإنَّهُ مَن تَتَبَّعَ عَوراتِ المُؤمِنينَ تَتَبَّعَ اللهُ عَورَتَهُ ، ومَن تَتَبَّعَ اللهُ عَورَتَهُ فَضَحَهُ ولَو في جَوفِ بَيتِهِ . ٥٣٨٦

4723. **Imām ʿAlī (AS) said,** 'Anticipating attentively for a fault [in someone] is a fault in itself.'[5333]

٤٧٢٣ . الإمامُ عليٌّ ﷺ: تَأمُّلُ العَيبِ عَيبٌ . ٥٣٨٧

4724. **Imām ʿAlī (AS),** in a letter he wrote to al-Ashtar when he appointed him governor of Egypt,

٤٧٢٤ . عنه ﷺ ـ مِن كِتابِهِ لِلأشتَرِ لَمّا وَلّاهُ

said, 'The furthest of your subjects from you, and the worst of them in your view should be the one who is the most eager to pursue people's shortcomings, because people do have faults and the ruler is the most appropriate person to conceal them, so do not ever seek to discover those faults which are hidden from you.'[5334]

مِصرَ ـ: وَلْيَكُنْ أبعَدَ رَعِيَّتِكَ مِنكَ، وأشنَأهُم عِندَكَ، أطلَبُهُم لِمَعايِبِ النّاسِ؛ فإنَّ فِي النّاسِ عُيوباً، الوالي أحَقُّ مَن سَتَرَها، فلا تَكشِفَنَّ عَمّا غابَ عَنكَ مِنها.[٥٢٨٨]

4725. **Imām ʿAlī (AS) said,** 'Do not ever rejoice at someone else's mistake, for verily you yourself will never be immune to committing mistakes.'[5335]

٤٧٢٥. عنه عليه السلام: لا تَبتَهِجَنَّ بِخَطاءِ غَيرِكَ؛ فإنَّكَ لَن تَملِكَ الإصابَةَ أبَداً.[٥٢٨٩]

4726. **Imām ʿAlī (AS) said,** 'He who finds faults will be accused of them himself, and he who insults will be retorted to [with worse].'[5336]

٤٧٢٦. عنه عليه السلام: مَن عابَ عِيبَ، ومَن شَتَمَ أُجيبَ.[٥٢٩٠]

4727. **Imām al-Ṣādiq (AS) said,** 'The furthest a servant can be from Allah is when he associates in a brotherly manner with someone while at the same time making note of all his faults in order to one day reproach him.'[5337]

٤٧٢٧. الإمامُ الصّادقُ عليه السلام: أبعَدُ ما يَكونُ العَبدُ مِنَ اللهِ أن يَكونَ الرَّجُلُ يُواخي الرَّجُلَ وهُوَ يَحفَظُ (عَلَيهِ) زَلّاتِهِ لِيُعَيِّرَهُ بِها يَوماً ما.[٥٢٩١]

(See also: CONDEMNATION 296; SPYING: section 335)

(أُنظر) عنوان ٢٩٦ «التعيير»؛ التجسس: باب ٣٣٥.

1405. What Covers Up the Faults

١٤٠٥ ـ ما يُغَطّي العُيوبَ

4728. **The Prophet (SAWA) said,** 'Knowledge and wealth cover up every fault, whereas ignorance and poverty disclose every fault.'[5338]

٤٧٢٨. رسولُ اللهِ ﷺ: العِلمُ والمالُ يَستُرانِ كُلَّ عَيبٍ، والجَهلُ والفَقرُ يَكشِفانِ كُلَّ عَيبٍ.[٥٢٩٢]

4729. **Imām ʿAlī (AS) said,** 'Tolerance is the grave of faults.'[5339]

٤٧٢٩. الإمامُ عليٌّ عليه السلام: الاحتِمالُ قَبرُ العُيوبِ.[٥٢٩٣]

4730. **Imām ʿAlī (AS) said,** 'The intellect is the coverer of faults.'[5340]

٤٧٣٠. عنه عليه السلام: غِطاءُ العُيوبِ العَقلُ.[٥٢٩٤]

4731. **Imām ʿAlī (AS) said,** 'He who covers himself with the cloak of modesty, people cannot see his flaws.'[5341]

٤٧٣١. عنه عليه السلام: مَن كَساهُ الحَياءُ ثَوبَهُ، لَم يَرَ النّاسُ عَيبَهُ.[٥٢٩٥]

4732. **Imām ʿAlī (AS) said,** 'He who covers himself with the cloak of knowledge, his faults remain hidden from people.'[5342]

٤٧٣٢. عنه عليه السلام: مَن كَساهُ العِلمُ ثَوبَهُ، اختَفىٰ عَنِ النّاسِ عَيبُهُ.[٥٢٩٦]

4733. **Imām ʿAlī (AS) said,** 'Your faults will remain concealed as long as your good fortune assists you.'[5343]

٤٧٣٣ . عنه عليه السلام : عَيبُكَ مَستورٌ ما أسعَدَكَ جَدُّكَ .[٥٢٩٧]

1406. He who is Ignorant of Something Finds Fault with it

١٤٠٦ ـ مَن جَهِلَ شَيئاً عابَهُ

4734. **Imām ʿAlī (AS) said,** 'He who is incapable of getting to know something will find fault with it.'[5344]

٤٧٣٤ . الإمامُ عليٌّ عليه السلام : مَن قَصُرَ عَن مَعرِفَةِ شَيءٍ عابَهُ .[٥٢٩٨]

4735. **Imām ʿAlī (AS) said,** 'He who is ignorant of something finds fault with it.'[5345]

٤٧٣٥ . عنه عليه السلام : مَن جَهِلَ شَيئاً عابَهُ .[٥٢٩٩]

(See also: IGNORANCE: section 296)

(انظر) الجهل : باب ٢٩٦.

296

CONDEMNATION

التَّعيير

1407. The Censure of Condemnation

١٤٠٧ ـ ذَمُّ التَّعيير

4736. **al-Khiḍr (AS),** in his advice to Prophet Moses (AS) said, 'O son of ʿImrān, do not ever condemn somebody for a mistake, and cry over your own mistake [instead].'[5346]

٤٧٣٦ . الخضرُ عليه السلام ـ في وَصِيَّتِهِ لِموسىٰ عليه السلام ـ : يَابنَ عِمرانَ ، لا تُعَيِّرَنَّ أحَداً بِخَطيئَةٍ ، وَابكِ عَلىٰ خَطيئَتِكَ .[٥٣٠٠]

4737. **The Prophet (SAWA) said,** 'The one who condemns a fellow brother for a sin that he has already repented for will not die before committing it himself.'[5347]

٤٧٣٧ . رسولُ اللهِ ﷺ : مَن عَيَّرَ أخاهُ بِذَنبٍ قَد تابَ مِنهُ لَم يَمُتْ حَتّىٰ يَعمَلَهُ .[٥٣٠١]

4738. **The Prophet (SAWA) said,** 'The one who exposes someone's monstrous deed is as the one who initiated it, and the one who condemns a believer for something will not die before becoming guilty of it himself.'[5348]

٤٧٣٨ . عنه ﷺ : مَن أذاعَ فاحِشَةً كانَ كَمُبتَدِئِها ، ومَن عَيَّرَ مُؤمِناً بِشَيءٍ لَم يَمُتْ حَتّىٰ يَركَبَهُ .[٥٣٠٢]

4739. **The Prophet (SAWA) said,** 'If one of your servants commits adultery, lash her with the

٤٧٣٩ . عنه ﷺ : إذا زَنَت خادِمُ أحَدِكُم فَليَجلِدْها

prescribed punishment but do not censure her.'[5349]

الحَدَّ ولا يُعَيِّرْها.[٥٣٠٣]

4740. **The Prophet (SAWA) said,** 'If your Muslim brother condemns you for whatever he knows about you, then do not condemn him back for whatever you know about him. You will have a reward whereas he will carry a sin.'[5350]

٤٧٤٠. عنه ﷺ: إن عَيَّرَكَ أخوكَ المُسلِمُ بِما يَعلَمُ فيكَ فَلا تُعَيِّرْهُ بِما تَعلَمُ فيهِ؛ يَكونُ لَكَ أجراً وعَلَيهِ إثماً.[٥٣٠٤]

4741. **Imām al-Bāqir (AS) said,** 'Anybody who discredits a believer's self-esteem will die an evil death, and he becomes deserving of never again returning to a good end.'[5351]

٤٧٤١. الإمامُ الباقرُ عليه السلام: ما مِن إنسانٍ يَطعَنُ في عَينِ مُؤمِنٍ إلّا ماتَ بِشَرِّ ميتَةٍ، وكانَ قَمِناً أن لا يَرجِعَ إلىٰ خَيرٍ.[٥٣٠٥، ٥٣٠٦]

4742. **Imām al-Ṣādiq (AS) said,** 'He who reviles a believer will be reviled by Allah in both this world and the Hereafter.'[5352]

٤٧٤٢. الإمامُ الصّادقُ عليه السلام: مَن أنَّبَ مُؤمِناً أنَّبَهُ اللهُ فِي الدّنيا والآخِرَةِ.[٥٣٠٧]

4743. **Imām al-Ṣādiq (AS) said,** 'Do not express malicious gloating at your brother [for a sin or misfortune] for Allah will have mercy on him as a result and make it befall you instead.' He also said, 'He who gloats over an affliction that has befallen his brother will not leave this world until he has been tried similarly.'[5353]

٤٧٤٣. عنه عليه السلام: لا تُبدي الشَّماتَةَ لِأخيكَ فَيَرحَمَهُ اللهُ ويُصَيِّرَها بِكَ. مَن شَمَتَ بِمُصيبَةٍ نَزَلَت بِأخيهِ لَم يَخرُجْ مِنَ الدّنيا حَتّىٰ يُفتَتَنَ.[٥٣٠٨]

297

LIFESTYLE

العَيشُ

1408. The Most Wholesome Lifestyle

١٤٠٨ ـ أهنأُ العَيشِ

4744. **Imām 'Alī (AS) said,** 'The most wholesome lifestyle is achieved through letting go of unnecessary formalities.'[5354]

٤٧٤٤. الإمامُ عليٌّ عليه السلام: أهنَى العَيشِ اطّراحُ الكُلَفِ.[٥٣٠٩]

4745. **Imām 'Alī (AS) said,** 'The most pleasant [type] of life is [a life of] contentment.'[5355]

٤٧٤٥. عنه عليه السلام: أطيَبُ العَيشِ القَناعَةُ.[٥٣١٠]

4746. **Imām 'Alī (AS) said,** 'The man with the most comfortable lifestyle is he whom Allah,

٤٧٤٦. عنه عليه السلام: أنعَمُ النّاسِ عَيشاً مَن مَنَحَهُ اللهُ

Glory be to Him, has granted contentment and to whom he has given a virtuous wife.'[5356]

سُبحانَهُ القَناعَةَ، وأصلَحَ لَهُ زَوجَهُ.٥٣١١

4747. **Imām al-Ṣādiq (AS) said,** 'There is no lifestyle more wholesome than [living] good-naturedly.'[5357]

٤٧٤٧. الإمامُ الصّادقُ عليه السلام: لا عَيشَ أهنَأُ مِن حُسنِ الخُلقِ.٥٣١٢

1409. Factors Which Spoil One's Lifestyle

١٤٠٩ - ما يُكَدِّرُ العَيشَ

4748. **Imām al-Ṣādiq (AS) said,** 'Three things spoil one's lifestyle: an oppressive ruler, a bad neighbour, and a loathsome wife.'[5358]

٤٧٤٨. الإمامُ الصّادقُ عليه السلام: ثَلاثَةٌ تُكَدِّرُ العَيشَ: السُّلطانُ الجائرُ، والجارُ السَّوءُ، والمَرأةُ البَذِيَّةُ.٥٣١٣

4749. **Imām al-Ṣādiq (AS) said,** 'There are five things which if one where to lose just one of them it would render his life incomplete, his intellect short-lived, and his heart preoccupied. The first of these is health of the body; the second is security; the third is ample sustenance; the fourth is a compatible companion. [The narrator says], 'I asked, 'What is a compatible companion?' to which he replied, 'The virtuous wife, the virtuous son and the virtuous friend. And the fifth one, which sums up these four things, is tranquillity.'[5359]

٤٧٤٩. عنه عليه السلام: خَمسُ خِصالٍ مَن فَقَدَ واحِدَةً مِنهُنَّ لَم يَزَلْ ناقِصَ العَيشِ زائلَ العَقلِ مَشغولَ القَلبِ، فأوَّلُها: صِحَّةُ البَدَنِ، والثّانِيَةُ: الأمنُ، والثّالِثَةُ: السَّعَةُ في الرِّزقِ، والرّابِعَةُ: الأنيسُ المُوافِقُ - [قال الراوي:] قُلتُ: وما الأنيسُ المُوافِقُ؟ قالَ: الزَّوجَةُ الصّالِحَةُ، والوَلَدُ الصّالِحُ، والخَليطُ الصّالِحُ - والخامِسَةُ: وهِيَ تَجمَعُ هٰذِهِ الخِصالَ: الدَّعَةُ.٥٣١٤

298

DELUSION

الغُرُور

1410. The Danger of Delusion and the Characteristics of the Deluded

١٤١٠ - خَطَرُ الغُرورِ وصِفَةُ المَغرُورِ

4750. **Imām ʿAlī (AS) said,** 'Blessed be the one whom the assassins of delusion have not killed.'[5360]

٤٧٥٠. الإمامُ عليٌّ عليه السلام: طُوبىٰ لِمَن لَم تَقتُلْهُ قاتِلاتُ الغُرورِ.٥٣١٥

4751. **Imām ʿAlī (AS) said,** 'The intoxication of heedlessness and delusion are harder to resume consciousness from than the intoxication of wines.'[5361]

٤٧٥١. عنه عليه السلام: سُكرُ الغَفلَةِ والغُرورِ أبعَدُ إفاقَةً مِن سُكرِ الخُمُورِ.٥٣١٦

4752. **Imām ʿAlī (AS) said,** 'He who is deluded by a mirage [the world] will lose all means [of happiness].'[5362]

٤٧٥٢. عنه ﷺ: مَن غَرَّهُ السَّرابُ تَقَطَّعَت بِهِ الأسبابُ.[٥٣١٧]

4753. **Imām ʿAlī (AS) said,** 'Between you and the moral exhortation is a veil of inadvertency.'[5363]

٤٧٥٣. عنه ﷺ: بَينَكُم وبينَ المَوعِظَةِ حِجابٌ مِن الغِرَّةِ.[٥٣١٨]

4754. **Imām Zayn al-ʿĀbidīn (AS) said,** 'Many a deluded and captivated man [by his own desires] awakes in the morning oblivious and joyful, eating and drinking, unaware that perhaps Allah's wrath has already befallen him for something and as a result of which he will enter the Fire of Hell.'[5364]

٤٧٥٤. الإمامُ زينُ العابدينَ ﷺ: رُبَّ مَغرورٍ مَفتونٍ يُصبحُ لاهِياً ضاحِكاً يَأكُلُ ويَشرَبُ، وهو لا يَدرِي لَعلَّهُ قد سَبَقَت لَهُ مِنَ اللهِ سَخَطَةٌ يَصلىٰ بها نارَ جَهَنَّمَ.[٥٣١٩]

4755. **Imām al-Ṣādiq (AS) said,** 'He who places his trust in three things is indeed deluded: He who believes in the impossible, relies on someone who cannot be trusted, and avidly desires that which he does not possess.'[5365]

٤٧٥٥. الإمامُ الصّادقُ ﷺ: مَن وَثِقَ بثلاثَةٍ كانَ مَغروراً: مَن صَدَّقَ بما لا يكونُ، ورَكَنَ إلىٰ مَن لا يَثِقُ بِهِ، وطَمِعَ فيما لا يَملِكُ.[٥٣٢٠]

1411. Deluding Oneself About Allah

١٤١١ ـ الإغتِرارُ بِاللهِ

"O man! What has deceived you about your generous Lord, Who created you and proportioned you, and gave you an upright nature, and composed you in any form that He wished?"[5366]

﴿يا أَيُّها الْإِنْسانُ ما غَرَّكَ بِرَبِّكَ الْكَرِيمِ * الَّذِي خَلَقَكَ فَسَوَّاكَ فَعَدَلَكَ * فِي أَيِّ صُورَةٍ ما شاءَ رَكَّبَكَ﴾.[٥٣٢١]

4756. **The Prophet (SAWA) said,** 'O Ibn Masʿūd, do not be under any delusion about Allah, and do not be under any delusion with respect to your righteousness, your knowledge, your deeds, your goodness or your worship.'[5367]

٤٧٥٦. رسولُ اللهِ ﷺ: يابنَ مَسعودٍ، لا تَغتَرَّنَّ باللهِ، ولا تَغتَرَّنَّ بِصَلاحِكَ وعِلمِكَ وعَمَلِكَ وبِرِّكَ وعِبادَتِكَ.[٥٣٢٢]

4757. **Imām ʿAlī (AS) said,** 'Verily part of keeping oneself immune from sins is that you do not delude yourself about Allah.'[5368]

٤٧٥٧. الإمامُ عليٌّ ﷺ: إنّ مِن العِصمَةِ ألّا تَغتَرّوا بِاللهِ.٥٣٢٣

4758. **Imām ʿAlī (AS) said,** 'Verily being under a delusion about Allah is when the servant persists in committing acts of disobedience and expects Allah to forgive him.'[5369]

٤٧٥٨. عنه ﷺ: إنَّ مِنَ الغِرَّةِ باللهِ أن يُصِرَّ العَبدُ علَى المَعصيَةِ ويَتَمَنّىٰ علَى اللهِ المَغفِرَةَ.٥٣٢٤

4759. **Imām ʿAlī (AS) said,** 'Many a person approaches Allah's punishment as a result of His good favour towards him while being ungrateful, and many a person is deluded as a result of Allah's concealment of his sins, and many a person is captivated by the good things said about him!'[5370]

٤٧٥٩. عنه ﷺ: كم مِن مُستَدرَجٍ بالإحسانِ إلَيهِ، ومَغرورٍ بِالسَّترِ علَيهِ، ومَفتونٍ بِحُسنِ القَولِ فيهِ!.٥٣٢٥

1412. Being Deluded By This World

١٤١٢ ـ الاِغتِرارُ بِالدُّنيا

4760. **Imām ʿAlī (AS) said,** 'Be wary of this world's delusion, for verily it always reclaims the charms and attractions with which it deceives people, and it troubles the one who adopts it as a place of tranquillity and a permanent dwelling.'[5371]

٤٧٦٠. الإمامُ عليٌّ ﷺ: اِتَّقُوا غُرورَ الدنيا؛ فإنّها تَستَرجِعُ أبداً ما خَدَعَت بهِ مِن المَحاسِنِ، وتُزعِجُ المُطمَئنَّ إلَيها والقاطِنَ.٥٣٢٦

4761. **Imām ʿAlī (AS) said,** 'The soul's trust in this world is one of the greatest delusions.'[5372]

٤٧٦١. عنه ﷺ: سُكونُ النفسِ إلَى الدنيا مِن أعظَمِ الغُرورِ.٥٣٢٧

(See also: THE WORLD: section 714)

(أُنظر) الدنيا: باب ٧١٤.

1413. Self-Delusion

١٤١٣ ـ الاِغتِرارُ بِالنَّفسِ

4762. **Imām ʿAlī (AS) said,** 'Your own sense of honour has deluded you, such that it became the source of disgrace for you. So fear the indecent acts that you commit, for perhaps through that you will be guided.'[5373]

٤٧٦٢. الإمامُ عليٌّ ﷺ: غَرَّكَ عِزُّكَ، فَصارَ قُصارُ ذلكَ ذُلَّكَ، فَاخشَ فاحِشَ فِعلِكَ، فَعَلَّكَ بهذا تُهدىٰ.٥٣٢٨

4763. **Imām ʿAlī (AS) said,** 'He who is ignorant deludes himself, and his present is consequently worse than his past.'[5374]

٤٧٦٣ . عنه عليه السلام : مَن جَهِلَ اغتَرَّ بنفسِهِ، وكانَ يَومُهُ شَرّاً مِن أمسِهِ.[٥٣٢٩]

299

THE BATTLES (Fought by the Prophet)

الغَزوَةُ

1414. The Battle of Badr

١٤١٤ ـ غَزوَةُ بَدرٍ

"Certainly Allah helped you at Badr, when you were abased [in the enemy's eyes]. So be wary of Allah so that you may give thanks. When you were saying to the faithful, 'Is it not enough for you that your Lord should aid you with three thousand angels sent down?'"[5375]

﴿وَلَقَدْ نَصَرَكُمُ اللهُ بِبَدْرٍ وَأَنْتُمْ أَذِلَّةٌ فَاتَّقُوا اللهَ لَعَلَّكُمْ تَشْكُرُونَ * إِذْ تَقُولُ لِلْمُؤْمِنِينَ أَلَنْ يَكْفِيَكُمْ أَنْ يُمِدَّكُمْ رَبُّكُمْ بِثَلاثَةِ آلافٍ مِنَ الْمَلائِكَةِ مُنْزَلِينَ﴾ .[٥٣٣٠]

(See also: Qur'an 3:12-13, 4:77-78, 8:1, 8:19, 8:36, 8:38-41, 8:67, 8:71, 22:19)

(أُنظر) آل عمران: ١٢، ١٣ والنساء: ٧٧، ٧٨ والأنفال: ١، ١٩، ٣٦، ٣٨ـ ٤١، ٦٧، ٧١ و الحجّ: ١٩.

4764. **Imām ʿAlī (AS) said,** 'The feature of the Prophet (SAWA)'s companions on the day of [the battle of] Badr was like white wool.'[5376]

٤٧٦٤ . الإمامُ عليٌّ عليه السلام : سِيماءُ أصحابِ رسولِ اللهِ ﷺ يومَ بَدرٍ الصُّوفُ الأبيضُ.[٥٣٣١]

4765. **Imām ʿAlī (AS) said,** 'I was indeed looking at us all in the battle of Badr while we all sought refuge with the Prophet (SAWA) when he was the closest one from among us to the enemy, and he was the bravest of people on that day.'[5377]

٤٧٦٥ . عنه عليه السلام : لقد رَأيتُنا يومَ بدرٍ ونحنُ نَلُوذُ برسولِ اللهِ ﷺ وهُو أقرَبُنا إلَى العَدُوِّ، وكانَ مِن أشَدِّ الناسِ يَومَئذٍ بَأساً .[٥٣٣٢]

4766. **Imām ʿAlī (AS) said,** 'When we came to Badr, the only horse rider among us was Miqdād b. Aswad. I had been watching us all on the eve of Badr, and all of us slept apart from the Prophet (SAWA). Verily he stood by the roots of a tree, praying and supplicating until morning.'[5378]

٤٧٦٦ . عنه عليه السلام : لقد حَضَرنا بَدراً وما فِينا فارِسُ غيرَ المِقدادِ بنِ الأسوَدِ، ولقد رَأيتُنا ليلةَ بَدرٍ وما فِينا إلّامَن نامَ غيرَ رسولِ اللهِ ﷺ، فإنّهُ كانَ مُنتَصِباً في أصلِ شَجَرةٍ يُصَلّي ويَدعُو حتّى الصَّباحِ.[٥٣٣٣]

1415. The Battle of ʿUḥud

١٤١٥ ـ غَزوَةُ اُحُدٍ

"When you left your family at dawn to settle the faithful in their positions for battle – and Allah is all-hearing, all-knowing."[5379]

﴿وَإِذْ غَدَوْتَ مِنْ أَهْلِكَ تُبَوِّئُ الْمُؤْمِنِينَ مَقاعِدَ لِلْقِتالِ وَاللهُ سَمِيعٌ عَلِيمٌ﴾ .٥٣٣٤

4767. **Ibn Masʿūd narrated:** Verily on the day of the battle of ʿUḥud, your women were behind the Muslims delivering the last strokes to the wounded from among the polytheists ... when Abū Sufyān came and said, 'I esteem Hubal!' So the Prophet (SAWA) told [the Muslims] to say, 'Allah is the Most Sublime and The Most Exalted', so they said, 'Allah is the Most Sublime and the Most Exalted!' Then Abū Sufyān said, 'We have 'Uzza[5380] on our side and you do not!' So the Prophet told them to say, 'Allah is our Guardian and the disbelievers have no guardian.'[5381]

٤٧٦٧ . ابن مسعود : إنَّ النِّساءَ كُنَّ يومَ اُحُدٍ خَلفَ المسلمينَ يُجهِزْنَ عَلى جَرحَى المشركينَ ... فجاءَ أبو سُفيانَ فقالَ : أعلُ هُبَلُ! فقالَ رسولُ اللهِ ﷺ : قولوا : اللهُ أعلىٰ وأجَلُّ ، فقالوا : اللهُ أعلىٰ وأجَلُّ ، فقالَ أبو سفيانَ : لنا ٥٣٣٥ العُزّىٰ ولا عُزّىٰ لَكُم! فقالَ رسولُ اللهِ ﷺ : قُولوا : اللهم مولانا و الكافرون لا مولى لهم ٥٣٣٦ . ٥٣٣٧

4768. **Anas narrated:** 'Verily on the day of the battle of ʿUḥud, the Prophet (SAWA)'s incisors were broken and his head was wounded, so while taking out the blood from it, he said, 'How will a people who wounded their prophet and broke his teeth ever succeed, whilst he only calls them to Allah?!' So Allah revealed the verse: *"You have no hand in the matter."*[5382 5383]

٤٧٦٨ . أنس : إنَّ رسولَ اللهِ ﷺ كُسِرَت رَباعِيَتُهُ يومَ اُحُدٍ ، وشُجَّ في رَأسِهِ ، فَجَعَلَ يَسلُتُ الدَّمَ عَنهُ ويقولُ : كيفَ يُفلِحُ قومٌ شَجُّوا نَبِيَّهُم وكَسَرُوا رَباعِيَتَهُ ، وهُو يَدعُوهم إلَى اللهِ ؟! فَأنزَلَ اللهُ عَزَّوجلَّ : ﴿لَيسَ لَكَ مِنَ الأَمْرِ شَيْءٌ أَوْ يَتُوبَ عَلَيْهِمْ أَوْ يُعَذِّبَهُمْ فَإِنَّهُمْ ظَـٰلِمُونَ﴾ ٥٣٣٨ . ٥٣٣٩

4769. **Imām ʿAlī (AS) said,** 'On the day of ʿUḥud, when the number of people around the Prophet (SAWA) was diminishing, I looked at the dead and could not see the Prophet (SAWA) among them, so I said [to myself], 'By Allah, he would never have run away, and I do not see him among the dead, but I can see Allah being angry with us for what we have done and has therefore taken His prophet away from us. I see nothing better for myself, therefore, than to fight until I am killed, so I broke the sheath of my sword and went to attack the people, and they cleared the way for me, when suddenly I came upon the Prophet (SAWA) right in their midst.'[5384]

٤٧٦٩ . الإمامُ عليٌّ عليه السلام : لَمّا انجَلىٰ الناسُ عَن رسولِ اللهِ ﷺ يومَ اُحُدٍ نَظَرتُ فِي القَتلىٰ فلَم أرَ رسولَ اللهِ ﷺ ، فقلتُ : واللهِ ما كانَ لِيَفِرَّ وما أراهُ فِي القَتلىٰ ، ولكن أرَى اللهَ غَضِبَ علَينا بما صَنَعنا فرَفَعَ نَبِيَّهُ ، فما فِيَّ خيرٌ مِن أن اُقاتِلَ حتّىٰ اُقتَلَ ، فكَسَرتُ جَفنَ سَيفِي ، ثُمّ حَمَلتُ على القومِ فَأفرَجُوا لي ، فإذا أنا برسولِ اللهِ ﷺ بَينَهُم . ٥٣٤٠

1416. The Battle of Dhāt al-Riqāʿ

١٤١٦ ـ غَزوَةُ ذاتِ الرِّقاعِ

4770. **Imām al-Ṣādiq (AS) narrated,** ʻIn the battle of Dhāt al-Riqāʿ, the Prophet (SAWA) descended under a tree on the side of a valley when a flood came and separated him from his companions. A man from among the polytheists saw him whilst the Muslims were standing on the side of the valley waiting for the flood to subside. One of the polytheists said to his people, ʻI will kill Muḥammad! So he came and drew his sword against the Prophet (SAWA), saying, ʻWho will save you now from me O Muḥammad?!' to which he replied, ʻMy Lord and your Lord', upon which the archangel Gabriel (AS) threw him down from his horse and he fell onto his back. The Prophet (SAWA) then stood up, took the sword and sat on his chest, saying, ʻWho will save you now from me, O Ghawrith?' to which he replied, ʻYour magnanimity and generosity O Muḥammad' at which he left him. The man stood up, saying, ʻBy Allah, you are indeed better and nobler than me.'[5385]

٤٧٧٠ . الإمامُ الصّادقُ ؑ : نَزَلَ رسولُ اللهِ ﷺ في غزوةِ ذاتِ الرِّقاعِ تَحتَ شَجرَةٍ علىٰ شَفيرِ وادٍ، فَأقبَلَ سَيلٌ فَحالَ بَينَهُ وبَينَ أصحابِهِ ،فَرآهُ رَجُلٌ مِن المُشركينَ ؛ والمسلمونَ قِيامٌ علَى شَفيرِ الوادِي يَنتَظِرُونَ متَى يَنقَطِعُ السَّيلُ، فقالَ رجُلٌ مِن المُشركينَ لقومِهِ : أنا أقتُلُ محمّداً ! فَجاءَ وشَدَّ علىٰ رسولِ اللهِ ﷺ بالسَّيفِ، ثُمَّ قالَ : مَن يُنجِيكَ مِنّي يا محمّدُ ؟! فقالَ : رَبّي ورَبُّكَ، فَنَسَفَهُ جَبرَئيلُ ؑ عن فَرَسِهِ فَسَقَطَ علىٰ ظَهرِهِ، فقامَ رسولُ اللهِ ﷺ وأخَذَ السَّيفَ وجَلَسَ علىٰ صَدرِهِ، وقالَ : مَن يُنجِيكَ مِنّي يا غَورثُ ؟ فقالَ : جُودُكَ وكَرَمُكَ يا محمّدُ، فَتَرَكَهُ، فقامَ وهُو يَقولُ : واللهِ لَأنتَ خَيرٌ مِنّي وأكرَمُ.[٥٣٤١]

1417. The Battle of Aḥzāb[5386] and Banī Qurayẓa

١٤١٧ ـ غَزوَةُ الأحزابِ وبَني قُرَيظَةَ

4771. **Yazīd b. al-Aṣamm narrated:** ʻWhen Allah, Mighty and Exalted, exposed the factions [to be vanquished by the Muslims], the Prophet (SAWA) returned home to wash his head, when Gabriel came to him, saying, ʻMay Allah pardon you! You put down your weapons whilst the angels of the heavens have not! Come and join us at the fortress of Banī Qurayẓa.' So the Prophet (SAWA) called [his companions] and they joined them at the fortress.'[5387]

٤٧٧١ . يزيد بن الأصم : لَمّا كَشَفَ اللهُ الأحزابَ ورَجَعَ النبيُّ ﷺ إلىٰ بَيتِهِ يَغسِلُ رَأسَهُ، أتاهُ جِبريلُ فقالَ : عَفا اللهُ عنكَ ! وَضَعتَ السلاحَ ولم تَضَعْهُ ملائكةُ السماءِ ! اِئتِنا عندَ حِصنِ بَني قُرَيظَةَ، فَنادَى رسولُ اللهِ ﷺ فَأتاهُم عِندَ الحِصنِ.[٥٣٤٢]

4772. **Imām al-Bāqir (AS),** with regards to the verse: *"He says, I have squandered immense wealth"*[5388], said, ʻThis refers to ʻAmr b. ʻAbd Wudd when ʻAlī b. Abī Ṭālib proposed to him to

٤٧٧٢ . الإمامُ الباقرُ ؑ ـ في قولِهِ تعالىٰ : ﴿يقولُ أهلَكتُ مالاً لُبَداً﴾ [٥٣٤٣] ـ : هو عَمرُو بنُ عبدِ وَدٍّ حينَ عَرَضَ علَيهِ عليُّ بنُ أبي طالبٍ الإسلامَ

submit to Allah [i.e. embrace Islam] on the day of al-Khandaq [the trench], to which he retorted, 'And what about the immense wealth I have spent on you?!' for he had spent great wealth in obstructing the cause of Allah, so 'Alī (AS) killed him.'[5389]

يومَ الخَندَقِ وقالَ: فَأينَ ما أنفقتُ فيكُم مالاً لُبَداً؟! وكانَ أنفَقَ مالاً في الصَّدِّ عن سبيلِ اللهِ، فَقَتَلَهُ عَلِيٌّ (ع).[٥٣٤٤]

4773. **Imām al-Ṣādiq (AS) narrated,** 'When the Prophet (SAWA) was digging the trench [with his companions], they hit upon a large rock, so the Prophet (SAWA) took the pickaxe from the Commander of the Faithful 'Alī (AS)'s hand or Salmān's hand and hit the rock with a blow that shattered it into three pieces. So the Prophet (SAWA) said, 'With this blow of mine, the treasures of the Khosrau and the Caesar have been opened to me', upon which one man said to his companions, 'He gives us promises of the treasures of the Khosrau and the Caesar [with his strength], whilst neither one of us even has the ability to go and relieve himself.'[5390]

٤٧٧٣. الإمامُ الصّادقُ (ع): لَمّا حَفَرَ رسولُ اللهِ ﷺ الخَندَقَ مَرّوا بِكُديَةٍ، فَتَناوَلَ رسولُ اللهِ ﷺ المِعوَلَ مِن يَدِ أميرِ المؤمنينَ (ع) أو مِن يَدِ سلمانَ (رض) فَضَرَبَ بها ضَربَةً فَتَفَرَّقَت بِثلاثِ فِرَقٍ، فقالَ رسولُ اللهِ ﷺ: لَقَد فُتِحَ عَلَيَّ في ضَربَتي هذهِ كُنوزُ كِسرىٰ وقَيصَرَ، فقالَ أحَدُهُما لِصاحِبِهِ: يَعِدُنا بِكُنوزِ كِسرىٰ وقَيصَرَ وما يَقدِرُ أحَدُنا أن يَخرُجَ يَتَخَلّىٰ![٥٣٤٥]

1418. The Battle of Khaybar

١٤١٨ـ غَزوَةُ خَيبَرَ

4774. **Burayda narrated,** 'On the day of Khaybar, Abū Bakr took the flag [in order to attempt the conquest of the fortress of Khaybar] but returned without having conquered it. Then the next day, 'Umar took it and did not conquer it, and instead Ibn Muslima was killed so the people retreated even further. So the Prophet (SAWA) said, 'I will deposit this flag of mine with a man who loves Allah and His Prophet, and whom Allah and His Prophet love, and he will not return without conquering it.' So we rested ourselves assured that the conquest would be tomorrow. So the Prophet (SAWA) performed the morning prayer then called for the flag, and stood up. And every single one of us who held a position with the Prophet (SAWA) hoped that it would be him, until I myself stretched forward and craned my neck due to the

٤٧٧٤. بُرَيدة: لَمّا كانَ يومُ خَيبَرَ أخَذَ اللِّواءَ أبو بكرٍ، فَرَجَعَ ولَم يُفتَحْ لَهُ، فَلَمّا كانَ مِنَ الغَدِ أخَذَ عُمَرُ ولَم يُفتَحْ لَهُ، وقُتِلَ ابنُ مُسلِمَةَ ورَجَعَ النّاسُ، فقالَ رسولُ اللهِ ﷺ: لَأَدفَعَنَّ لِوائي هذا إلىٰ رَجُلٍ يُحِبُّ اللهَ ورسولَهُ ويُحِبُّهُ اللهُ ورسولُهُ، لَن يَرجِعَ حتّىٰ يُفتَحَ علَيهِ. فَبِتنا طَيِّبَةً أنفُسُنا أنَّ الفَتحَ غَداً، فَصَلّىٰ رسولُ اللهِ ﷺ الغَداةَ ثُمَّ دَعا بِاللِّواءِ وقامَ قائماً، فما مِنّا مِن رَجُلٍ لَهُ مَنزِلَةٌ مِن رسولِ اللهِ ﷺ إلّا وهُوَ يَرجو أن يَكونَ ذلكَ

position I had near him. Then he called ʿAlī b. Abī Ṭālib, who was afflicted with pain in his eyes. So the Prophet (SAWA) wiped his hands over them, deposited the flag with him, and he conquered it!'[5391]

الرَّجُلَ؛ حتّىٰ تَطاوَلتُ أنا لهـا ورَفَـعتُ رَأسِـي لِمَنزِلَةٍ كانَت لي مِنهُ فَدَعا عليَّ بنَ أبي طـالبٍ وهو يَشتَكِي عَينَيهِ فَمَسَحَها ثمَّ دَفَعَ إلَيهِ اللِّـواءَ فَفُتِحَ لَهُ!٥٣٤٦

1419. The Conquest of Makkah

١٤١٩ـ غَزوَةُ الفَتحِ

4775. **Kanz al-ʿUmmāl narrated,** 'On the day of the conquest [of Makkah], when the Prophet (SAWA) entered Makkah, he sent for Ṣafwān b. Umayya, Abū Sufyān b. Ḥarb and Ḥārith b. Hishām. [ʿUmar said], 'I said, 'Allah has placed them in our grip, and I will make them taste the consequences of what they have done.' The Prophet (SAWA), however, said, 'My stance with you is as the stance that Joseph[5392] took with his brothers when he said to them, *"There shall be no reproach on you today. Allah will forgive you, and He is the most merciful of the merciful."*[5393] [ʿUmar narrated], 'I turned away from the Prophet (SAWA) in shame and disgust at what had escaped from my mouth. And the Prophet (SAWA) said to them what he had to say.'[5394]

٤٧٧٥. كنز العمّال: لَمّا كانَ يومُ الفَتحِ ورسولُ اللهِ ﷺ بمكَّةَ، أرسَلَ إلىٰ صَفوانَ بـنِ أُمَـيَّةَ وإلىٰ أبي سُفيانَ بنِ حَربٍ وإلَى الحارثِ ابنِ هِشـامٍ، قالَ عمرُ: فَقُلتُ: قَد أمكَنَ اللهُ مِنهُم لَأعـرِفَنَّهُم بما صَنَعُوا، حـتىٰ قـالَ رسـولُ اللهِ ﷺ: مَـثَلِي ومَثَلُكُم كَما قالَ يـوسفُ لِإخـوَتِهِ: ﴿لا تَثْرِيبَ عَلَيكُمُ اليومَ يَغفِرُ اللهُ لَكُم وهُو أَرْحَمُ الرّاحِمِينَ﴾٥٣٤٧، قالَ عمرُ: فَانفَضَحتُ حَياءً مِن رسولِ اللهِ ﷺ؛ كَراهِيَةَ أن يَكونَ بَدَرَ مِـنّي وقـد قالَ لَهُم رسولُ اللهِ ﷺ ما قالَ.٥٣٤٨

4776. **Imām ʿAlī (AS) said,** 'Verily the Prophet (SAWA) marched to Badr in the month of Ramaḍān, and conquered Makkah in the month of Ramaḍān too.'[5395]

٤٧٧٦. الإمامُ عليٌّ ﷺ: إنَّ رسولَ اللهِ ﷺ سارَ إلىٰ بَدرٍ في شهرِ رَمَضانَ، وافتَتَحَ مَكَّـةَ فـي شـهرِ رَمَضانَ.٥٣٤٩

4777. **Imām al-Riḍā (AS) narrated,** 'The Prophet (SAWA) entered Makkah on the day of the conquest of Makkah and there were idols around the Ka'ba, three hundred and sixty of them in total. He started to knock them over with a baton he held in his hand, saying, *"The truth has come and falsehood has vanished. Indeed falsehood is bound to vanish."*[5396] The truth has come and falsehood will not resurface or return.' Then he started to throw them [the idols] down on their faces.'[5397]

٤٧٧٧. الإمامُ الرِّضا ﷺ: دَخَلَ رسولُ اللهِ ﷺ يومَ فتحِ مكَّـةَ والأصـنامُ حَـولَ الكـعبَةِ، وكـانَت ثلاثَمِائةٍ وسِتِّينَ صَنَماً، فَجَعَلَ يَطعَنُها بِمِخصَرَةٍ في يَدِهِ ويـقولُ: ﴿جاءَ الحَقُّ وزَهَقَ الباطلُ إنَّ الباطلَ كانَ زَهُوقاً﴾، جـاءَ الحَـقُّ ومـا يُبدِئُ الباطِلُ وما يُعيدُ. فَجَعَلَت تُكَبُّ لِوَجهِها.٥٣٥٠

1420. The Battle of Ḥunayn — ١٤٢٠ـ غزوةُ حُنَينٍ

4778. **Imām al-Ṣādiq (AS) narrated,** 'The Prophet (SAWA) did not encounter a worse day than the day of the battle of Ḥunayn, and that was because the Arabs revolted against him.'[5398]

٤٧٧٨. الإمامُ الصّادقُ ﷺ : مامَرَّ بالنبيِّ ﷺ يومٌ كانَ أشَدَّ علَيهِ مِن يومِ حُنَينٍ، وذلكَ أنَّ العَـرَبَ تَباغَتْ علَيهِ.٥٣٥١

300

SWINDLING — الغِشُّ

1421. The Reproaching of Swindling — ١٤٢١ـ ذَمُّ الغِشِّ

4779. **The Prophet (SAWA) said,** 'He who swindles a fellow Muslim brother, Allah snatches away the benediction in his sustenance, thwarts his efforts at earning a livelihood, and relegates him to his own base self.'[5399]

٤٧٧٩. رسولُ اللهِ ﷺ : مَن غَشَّ أخاهُ المُسلِمَ نَزَعَ اللهُ عَنهُ بَرَكَةَ رِزقِهِ، وأفسَدَ علَيهِ مَـعيشَتَهُ، ووَكَلَهُ إلىٰ نفسِهِ.٥٣٥٢

4780. **The Prophet (SAWA) said,** 'He who sells a flawed commodity, not stating it, remains despised by Allah, and the angels continuously curse him.'[5400]

٤٧٨٠. عنه ﷺ : مَن باعَ عَيباً لَم يُبَيِّنْهُ لَم يَزَلْ في مَقتِ اللهِ، ولَم تَزَلِ المَلائكةُ تَلعَنُهُ.٥٣٥٣

4781. It is narrated in *al-Targhīb wa al-Tarhīb*: 'Verily the Prophet (SAWA) once passed by a pile of wheat, so he placed his hand in and his fingers hit upon some moisture, at which he asked the vendor, 'What is this O vendor of wheat?' to which he replied, 'The rain fell on it O Prophet of Allah.' The Prophet then asked him, 'Then why did you not place it at the top of the pile that people might see it?! He who swindles us is not of us.'[5401]

٤٧٨١. الترغيب والترهيب : إنَّ رسولَ اللهِ ﷺ مَرَّ علىٰ صُبْرَةِ طَـعامٍ، فَأدخَـلَ يَـدَهُ فـيها فَـنالَت أصابِعُهُ بَلَلاً، فقالَ: ما هذا يا صاحِبَ الطَّعامِ؟ قالَ: أصابَتهُ السماءُ يـارسولَ اللهِ. قـالَ: أفَـلا جَعَلتَهُ فَوقَ الطَّعامِ حتّىٰ يَراهُ الناسُ؟! مَن غَشَّنا فَلَيسَ مِنّا.٥٣٥٤

4782. **Imām ʿAlī (AS) said** in his instruction to one of his representatives, 'Verily the worst act of treachery is the treachery against a Muslim community, and the worst act of swindling is the swindling of the leaders.'[5402]

٤٧٨٢. الإمامُ عليٌّ ﷺ ـ مِن عَهدِهِ إلىٰ بـعضِ عُمّالِهِ ـ: إنَّ أعظَمَ الخِيانَةِ خِيانَةُ الاُمَّةِ، وأفـظَعَ الغِشِّ غِشُّ الأئمَّةِ.٥٣٥٥

4783. **Imām ʿAlī (AS) said,** 'He who swindles people in matters of religion is an antagonist of Allah and His Prophet.'[5403]

٤٧٨٣ . عنه عليه السلام : مَن غَشَّ النّاسَ في دِينِهِم فَهُو مُعانِدٌ للهِ ورسولِهِ.[٥٣٥٦]

4784. **Imām al-Ṣādiq (AS) said,** 'He who swindles us is not of us.'[5404]

٤٧٨٤ . الإمامُ الصّادقُ عليه السلام : لَيسَ مِنّا مَن غَشَّنا.[٥٣٥٧]

4785. **Imām al-Kāẓim (AS)** once passed by Hishām b. al-Ḥakam selling fine cloth in the shade, so he said to him, 'O Hishām, verily the sale of goods in the shade is considered fraud, and verily fraud is not allowed.'[5405]

٤٧٨٥ . الإمامُ الكاظمُ عليه السلام ـ لَمّا مَرَّ بِهِشامِ بنِ الحَكَمِ وهو يَبيعُ السّابِرِيَّ فِي الظِّلالِ ـ: يا هِشامُ، إنَّ البَيعَ فِي الظِّلِّ غِشٌّ، وإنَّ الغِشَّ لا يَحِلُّ.[٥٣٥٨]

301

USURPATION

الغصب

1422. The Prohibition of Usurpation

١٤٢٢ ـ حُرمَةُ الغَصبِ

4786. **The Prophet (SAWA) said,** 'He who usurps the property of a believer without having right to it, Allah continues to abandon him, despising all the good and righteous deeds that he performs, not recording them among his good deeds until and unless he repents and returns the property that he seized to its rightful owner.'[5406]

٤٧٨٦ . رسولُ اللهِ ﷺ : مَنِ اقتَطَعَ مالَ مؤمِنٍ غَصباً بغَيرِ حَقِّهِ لَم يَزَلِ اللهُ مُعرِضاً عَنهُ، ماقِتاً لِأعمالِهِ الَّتي يَعمَلُها مِنَ البِرِّ والخَيرِ، لا يُثبِتُها في حَسَناتِهِ حتّى يَتوبَ ويَرُدَّ المالَ الذي أخَذَهُ إلى صاحِبِهِ.[٥٣٥٩]

4787. **The Prophet (SAWA) said,** 'He who usurps someone's land wrongfully will meet Allah [on the Day of Resurrection] wrathful towards him.'[5407]

٤٧٨٧ . عنه ﷺ : مَن غَصَبَ رَجُلاً أرضاً ظُلماً لَقِيَ اللهَ تعالى وهُو علَيهِ غَضبانُ.[٥٣٦٠]

4788. **The Prophet (SAWA) said,** 'It is not permissible for a Muslim to seize the property of his fellow brother without right to it, and that is because Allah, Mighty and Exalted, has forbidden the property of a Muslim to another Muslim.'[5408]

٤٧٨٨ . عنه ﷺ : لا يَحِلُّ لِامرِئٍ مُسلمٍ أن يَأخُذَ مالَ أخِيهِ بغَيرِ حَقِّهِ؛ وذلكَ لِما حَرَّمَ اللهُ عَزَّوجلَّ مالَ المُسلمِ علَى المُسلمِ.[٥٣٦١]

4789. **Imām ʿAlī (AS) said,** 'One usurped stone in a house is a guarantee for its ruin.'[5409]

٤٧٨٩ . الإمامُ عليٌّ عليه السلام : الحَجَرُ الغَصيبُ[٥٣٦٢] في الدارِ رَهنٌ على خَرابِها.[٥٣٦٣]

4790. **Imām al-Ṣādiq (AS)** was once asked about one who has taken land without right to it and built upon it, to which he replied, 'The building is to be destroyed and the land returned to its rightful owner. The entire lineage of a wrongdoer holds no right.'[5410]

٤٧٩٠ . الإمامُ الصّادقُ ؑ ـ لَمّا سُئلَ عَمَّن أخَذَ أرضاً بِغَيرِ حَقِّها وبَنىٰ فيها ـ: يُرفَعُ بِناؤهُ، وتُسلَّمُ التُّربَةُ إلىٰ صاحِبِها؛ ليسَ لِعِرقِ ظالِمٍ حَقٌّ.٥٣٦٤

4791. **Imām al-Mahdī (AS) said,** 'It is not permissible for anyone to use the property of another without his permission.'[5411]

٤٧٩١ . الإمامُ المهديُّ ؑ : لا يَحِلُّ لأحدٍ أن يَتصرَّفَ في مالِ غَيرِهِ بغَيرِ إذنِهِ.٥٣٦٥

302

ANGER

الغَضَبُ

1423. Anger is the Key to All Evils

١٤٢٣ ـ الغَضَبُ مِفتاحُ كُلِّ شَرٍّ

4792. **The Prophet (SAWA) said,** 'Anger is a smouldering ember [kindled by] Satan.'[5412]

٤٧٩٢ . رسولُ اللهِ ﷺ : الغَضَبُ جَمرَةٌ مِنَ الشيطانِ.٥٣٦٦

4793. **Imām ʿAlī (AS) said,** 'Rage is a type of madness because the one enraged feels regret later on, and if he does not feel regret, then his madness has become ingrained.'[5413]

٤٧٩٣ . الإمامُ عليٌّ ؑ : الحِدَّةُ ضَربٌ مِنَ الجُنونِ؛ لأنَّ صاحِبَها يَندَمُ، فإن لَم يَندَمْ فَجُنونُهُ مُستَحكِمٌ.٥٣٦٧

4794. **Imām al-Ṣādiq (AS) said,** 'Anger is the key to all evils.'[5414]

٤٧٩٤ . الإمامُ الصّادقُ ؑ : الغَضَبُ مِفتاحُ كُلِّ شَرٍّ.٥٣٦٨

4795. **Imām al-Ṣādiq (AS) said,** 'Anger is such that it destroys the heart of even the wise man.'[5415]

٤٧٩٥ . عنه ؑ : الغَضَبُ مَمحَقَةٌ لِقَلبِ الحَكيمِ.٥٣٦٩

1424. Enjoinment of Controlling One's Anger

١٤٢٤ ـ الحَثُّ علىٰ مِلكِ الغَضَبِ

4796. **The Prophet (SAWA) said,** 'The Prophet (SAWA) said, 'Shall I tell you who is the toughest and strongest from among you? The one who controls himself when he is angry.'[5416]

٤٧٩٦ . رسولُ اللهِ ﷺ : ألا اُخبِرُكُم بِأشَدِّكُم؟ مَن مَلَكَ نَفسَهُ عِندَ الغَضَبِ.٥٣٧٠

4797. **Imām al-Bāqir (AS) said,** 'There is no strength like being able to repel one's anger.'[5417]

٤٧٩٧ . الإمامُ الباقرُ (عليه السلام): لا قُوَّةَ كَرَدِّ الغَضَبِ.[٥٣٧١]

4798. **Imām al-Ṣādiq (AS) said,** 'He who has no control over his anger has no control over his reason.'[5418]

٤٧٩٨ . الإمامُ الصّادقُ (عليه السلام): مَن لَم يَملِكْ غَضَبَهُ لَم يَملِكْ عَقلَهُ.[٥٣٧٢]

1425. Enjoinment of Suppressing One's Anger

١٤٢٥ ـ الحَثُّ عَلىٰ كَظمِ الغَيظِ

"...and those who suppress their anger, and excuse [the faults of] the people."[5419]

﴿وَالْكاظِمِينَ الْغَيْظَ وَالْعافِينَ عَنِ النّاسِ﴾.[٥٣٧٣]

"Those who forgive when angered."[5420]

﴿وَإِذا ما غَضِبُوا هُمْ يَغْفِرُونَ﴾.[٥٣٧٤]

4799. **The Prophet (SAWA) said,** 'Verily there is a door to Hell, the entrance into which will be reserved for one who vented his anger through committing an act of disobedience to Allah, most High.'[5421]

٤٧٩٩ . رسولُ اللهِ ﷺ: إنَّ لِجَهَنَّمَ باباً لا يَدخُلُها إلّا مَن شَفىٰ غَيظَهُ بِمَعصيَةِ اللهِ تعالىٰ.[٥٣٧٥]

4800. **The Prophet (SAWA) said,** 'He who curbs his anger, Allah will curb His punishment from him.'[5422]

٤٨٠٠ . عنه ﷺ: مَن كَفَّ غَضَبَهُ كَفَّ اللهُ عَنهُ عَذابَهُ.[٥٣٧٦]

4801. **Imām al-Bāqir (AS) said,** 'He who suppresses his anger despite being able to vent it, Allah will fill his heart with peace and security on the Day of Resurrection.'[5423]

٤٨٠١ . الإمامُ الباقرُ (عليه السلام): مَن كَظَمَ غَيظاً وهو يَقدرُ علىٰ إمضائهِ حَشا اللهُ قَلبَهُ أمناً وإيماناً يومَ القِيامَةِ.[٥٣٧٧]

4802. **Imām al-Ṣādiq (AS) said,** 'What a good dose anger is for he who can swallow it ...'[5424]

٤٨٠٢ . الإمامُ الصّادقُ (عليه السلام): نِعمَ الجُرعَةُ الغَيظُ لِمَن صَبَرَ علَيها ....[٥٣٧٨]

1426. The Remedy for Anger

١٤٢٦ ـ دَواءُ الغَضَبِ

4803. **The Prophet (SAWA) said,** 'O ʿAlī, do not get angry, and if you do get angry, then sit down and reflect upon the power of your Lord over His creation and His clemency towards them. And whenever anyone tells you [condescendingly] to fear Allah, expel your anger and remind yourself of your clemency.'[5425]

٤٨٠٣ . رسولُ اللهِ ﷺ: يا عليُّ، لا تَغضَبْ، فإذا غَضِبتَ فَاقعُدْ وتَفَكَّرْ في قُدرَةِ الرَّبِّ علَى العِبادِ وحِلمِهِ عَنهُم، وإذا قيلَ لكَ: اتَّقِ اللهَ فَانبِذْ غَضَبَكَ، وراجِعْ حِلمَكَ.[٥٣٧٩]

4804. **Imām ʿAlī (AS) said,** 'Remedy your anger with silence, and your carnal desire through your reason.'[5426]

٤٨٠٤ . الإمامُ عليٌّ عليه السلام : داوُوا الغَضَبَ بالصَّمتِ ، والشَّهوَةَ بالعَقلِ .[٥٣٨٠]

1427. The Praiseworthiness of Anger for the Sake of Allah

١٤٢٧ ـ مدحُ الغَضَبِ للهِ

4805. **Imām Zayn al-ʿĀbidīn (AS) said,** 'Prophet Moses (AS) [addressed Allah] saying, 'O Lord, who are your special people whom You will shade with the shade of Your Throne on the day when no shade will avail except Your Shade?' So Allah revealed to him, '... and those who are angered when the things that I have prohibited are deemed lawful [by people], the way a leopard is angered when it is wounded!'[5427]

٤٨٠٥ . الإمامُ زين العابدين عليه السلام : قالَ موسى عليه السلام : يا ربِّ ، مَن أهلُكَ الذينَ تُظِلُّهُم في ظِلِّ عَرشِكَ يومَ لا ظِلَّ إلّا ظِلُّكَ ؟ فَأوحَى اللهُ إلَيهِ : ... والذينَ يَغضَبُونَ لِمَحارِمي إذا استُحِلَّت مِثلَ النَّمِرِ إذا جُرِحَ ![٥٣٨١]

4806. **Imām ʿAlī (AS) said,** 'He [the Prophet] (SAWA) never used to get angry over worldly matters, but when he did get angry for the sake of the truth, he was unrecognisable and nothing could restrain his anger until he had triumphed in his case [for the truth].'[5428]

٤٨٠٦ . الإمامُ عليٌّ عليه السلام : كانَ ﷺ لا يَغضَبُ للدنيا ، فإذا أغضَبَهُ الحقُّ لَم يَعرِفْهُ أحَدٌ ولم يَقُمْ لِغَضَبِهِ شَيءٌ حتّىٰ يَنتَصِرَ لَهُ .[٥٣٨٢]

4807. **Imām ʿAlī (AS) said,** 'He who displays his ill-feeling towards the immoral people and gets angry for the sake of Allah, Allah will get angry for his sake and will render him well-pleased on the Day of Resurrection.'[5429]

٤٨٠٧ . عنه عليه السلام : مَن شَنِئَ الفاسِقينَ وغَضِبَ للهِ ، غَضِبَ اللهُ لَهُ وأرضاهُ يومَ القِيامَةِ .[٥٣٨٣]

303

SEEKING FORGIVENESS

الاستِغفارُ

1428. The Virtue of Seeking Forgiveness

١٤٢٨ ـ فَضْلُ الاستِغفارِ

"And those who, when they commit an indecent act or wrong themselves, remember Allah, and plead [Allah's] forgiveness for their sins – and who forgives sins except Allah? – and who do not knowingly persist in what they have committed."[5430]

﴿وَالَّذِينَ إذا فَعَلُوا فاحِشَةً أَوْ ظَلَمُوا أَنْفُسَهُمْ ذَكَرُوا اللهَ فَاسْتَغْفَرُوا لِذُنُوبِهِمْ﴾ .[٥٣٨٤]

"Whoever commits evil or wrongs himself and then pleads Allah for forgiveness, will find Allah all-forgiving, all-merciful."[5431]

﴿وَمَنْ يَعْمَلْ سُوءًا أَوْ يَظْلِمْ نَفْسَهُ ثُمَّ يَسْتَغْفِرِ اللهَ يَجِدِ اللهَ غَفُوراً رَحِيماً﴾ .[٥٣٨٥]

4808. **Luqmān (AS)** in his advice to his son, said, 'O my son, do not let the rooster be smarter than you – it rises at dawn seeking forgiveness whilst you sleep!'[5432]

٤٨٠٨ . لقمانُ ؑ ـ في وصيَّتِه لابنِه ـ: يا بُنَيَّ، لا يكونُ الدِّيكُ أكيَسَ مِنكَ، يقومُ في وَقتِ السَّحَرِ ويَستغفِرُ، وأنتَ نائمٌ![٥٣٨٦]

4809. **The Prophet (SAWA) said,** 'The best supplication is seeking forgiveness.'[5433]

٤٨٠٩ . رسولُ اللهِ ﷺ: خَيرُ الدعاءِ الاستِغفارُ.[٥٣٨٧]

4810. **The Prophet (SAWA) said,** 'The best act of worship is seeking forgiveness.'[5434]

٤٨١٠ . عنه ﷺ: خَيرُ العِبادَةِ الاستِغفارُ.[٥٣٨٨]

4811. **The Prophet (SAWA) said,** 'Increase your seeking of forgiveness, for verily Allah, Mighty and Exalted, has only taught you to seek forgiveness because He wants to forgive you.'[5435]

٤٨١١ . عنه ﷺ: أكثِروا مِن الاستِغفارِ؛ فإنَّ اللهَ عَزَّوجلَّ لم يُعَلِّمْكُمُ الاستِغفارَ إلّا وهُو يُريدُ أن يَغفِرَ لَكُم.[٥٣٨٩]

4812. **Imām 'Alī (AS) said,** 'I am surprised at the one who despairs whilst he has [the ability to seek] forgiveness!'[5436]

٤٨١٢ . الإمامُ عليٌّ ؑ: عَجِبتُ لِمَن يَقنَطُ ومَعهُ الاستِغفارُ![٥٣٩٠]

4813. **Imām 'Alī (AS) said,** 'Perfume yourselves with seeking forgiveness so that you are not exposed by the stench of sins.'[5437]

٤٨١٣ . عنه ؑ: تَعَطَّروا بالاستِغفارِ لا تَفضَحْكُم رَوائحُ الذُّنوبِ.[٥٣٩١]

4814. **Imām 'Alī (AS) said,** 'He who is given the opportunity to seek forgiveness is not deprived forgiveness.'[5438]

٤٨١٤ . عنه ؑ: مَن أُعطِيَ الاستِغفارَ لم يُحرَمِ المَغفِرَةَ.[٥٣٩٢]

4815. **Imām al-Ṣādiq (AS) said,** 'Verily when a servant commits a sin, it is kept on hold from morning until night, so if he seeks forgiveness for it, it is not recorded against him.'[5439]

٤٨١٥ . الإمامُ الصّادقُ ؑ: إنَّ العَبدَ إذا أذنَبَ ذَنباً أُجِّلَ مِن غُدوَةٍ إلى الليلِ، فإنِ استَغفَرَ اللهَ لم يُكتَبْ علَيهِ.[٥٣٩٣]

1429. Seeking Forgiveness and Increase in Sustenance

١٤٢٩ ـ الاستِغفارُ وزِيادَةُ الرِّزقِ

"Plead with your Lord for forgiveness, then turn to Him penitently. He will provide you with a good

﴿وَأَنِ اسْتَغْفِرُوا رَبَّكُمْ ثُمَّ تُوبُوا إِلَيْهِ يُمَتِّعْكُمْ

provision for a specified term and grant His grace to every meritorious person."[5440]

مَتاعاً حَسَناً إِلَىٰ أَجَلٍ مُسَمًّى وَيُؤْتِ كُلَّ ذِي فَضْلٍ فَضْلَهُ﴾.٥٣٩٤

"O my people! Plead with your Lord for forgiveness, then turn to Him penitently: He will send copious rains for you from the sky, and add power to your [present] power. So do not turn your backs [on Him] as guilty ones."[5441]

﴿وَيا قَوْمِ اسْتَغْفِرُوا رَبَّكُمْ ثُمَّ تُوبُوا إِلَيْهِ يُرْسِلِ السَّماءَ عَلَيْكُمْ مِدْراراً وَيَزِدْكُمْ قُوَّةً إِلَىٰ قُوَّتِكُمْ وَلا تَتَوَلَّوْا مُجْرِمِينَ﴾.٥٣٩٥

4816. **Imām ʿAlī (AS) said,** 'Allah the Glorified has made asking for forgiveness a means for increasing the sustenance of the people and His mercy upon them and He the Glorified has said: "*ask for forgiveness from your Lord, verily He is all-forgiving.*"[5442] Therefore, the mercy of Allah be upon he who repents and asks for abandoning his sin and does good deeds before the arrival of his death.'[5443]

٤٨١٦ . الإمامُ عليٌّ عليه السلام: وقد جَعَلَ اللهُ سبحانَهُ الاستِغفارَ سَبَباً لِدُرورِ الرِّزقِ ورَحمَةِ الخَلقِ، فقالَ سبحانَهُ: ﴿اسْتَغْفِرُوا رَبَّكُمْ إِنَّهُ كانَ غَفّاراً﴾ ٥٣٩٦ فَرَحِمَ اللهُ امرَأً استَقبَلَ تَوبَتَهُ، واستَقالَ خَطيئَتَهُ، وبادَرَ مَنِيَّتَهُ. ٥٣٩٧

4817. **Imām ʿAlī (AS) said,** 'Seeking forgiveness increases sustenance.'[5444]

٤٨١٧ . عنه عليه السلام: الاستِغفارُ يَزِيدُ في الرِّزقِ. ٥٣٩٨

4818. **Imām ʿAlī (AS) said,** 'Seek forgiveness and you will be provided sustenance.'[5445]

٤٨١٨ . عنه عليه السلام: اِستَغفِرْ تُرزَقْ. ٥٣٩٩

(See also: SUSTENANCE: section 821, 822)

(اُنظر) الرزق: باب ٨٢١، ٨٢٢.

1430. The Seeking of Forgiveness by Those Brought Near to Allah

١٤٣٠ ـ استِغفارُ المُقَرَّبينَ

4819. **The Prophet (SAWA) said,** 'Sometimes my heart becomes entangled, so I seek forgiveness from Allah for it seventy times a day.'[5446]

٤٨١٩ . رسولُ اللهِ صلى الله عليه وآله: إنَّهُ لَيُغانُ ٥٤٠٠ عَلىٰ قَلبِي، وإنّي لَأستَغفِرُ اللهَ في كُلِّ يَومٍ سَبعينَ مَرَّةً. ٥٤٠١

1431. Caution Against Seeking Forgiveness Alongside Persistent Sinning

١٤٣١ ـ التَّحذيرُ مِنَ الاستِغفارِ مَعَ الإصرارِ

4820. **Imām ʿAlī (AS) said,** 'Seeking forgiveness alongside persistent sinning is a new sin.'[5447]

٤٨٢٠ . الإمامُ عليٌّ عليه السلام: الاستِغفارُ مَع الإصرارِ ذُنوبٌ مُجَدَّدَةٌ. ٥٤٠٢

4821. **Imām al-Riḍā (AS) said,** 'The one who seeks forgiveness for a sin and then repeats it is as one who mocks his Lord.'[5448]

٤٨٢١ . الإمامُ الرِّضا عليه السلام: المُستَغفِرُ مِن ذَنبٍ ويَفعَلُهُ كَالمُستَهزِئِ بِرَبِّهِ. ٥٤٠٣

4822. **Imām al-Riḍā (AS) said,** 'He who seeks forgiveness with his tongue but does not feel remorse in his heart has fooled himself.'[5449]

٤٨٢٢ . عنه عليه السلام : مَنِ استَغفَرَ بِلِسانِهِ ولم يَـندَمْ بقَلبِهِ فقَدِ استَهزَأَ بنفسِهِ.[٥٤٠٤]

(See also: SINNING: section 775)

(أُنظر) الذنب: باب ٧٧٥.

304

NEGLIGENCE

الغَفلَة

1432. Caution Against Negligence

١٤٣٢ ـ التَّحذيرُ مِنَ الغَفلَةِ

4823. **Imām 'Alī (AS) said,** 'Negligence is deviation [from the straight path].'[5450]

٤٨٢٣ . الإمامُ عليٌّ عليه السلام : الغَفلَةُ ضَلالَةٌ.[٥٤٠٥]

4824. **Imām 'Alī (AS) said,** 'Pitiable indeed is every negligent person that his whole life can be used as evidence against him and that his days lead him to wretchedness!'[5451]

٤٨٢٤ . عنه عليه السلام : فَيالَها حَسرَةً على كُلِّ ذِي غَفلَةٍ أن يكونَ عُمُرُهُ علَيهِ حُجّةً، وأن تُؤَدِّيَهُ أيّامُهُ إلَى الشِّقوَةِ![٥٤٠٦]

4825. **Imām 'Alī (AS) said,** 'So O listener, come to your senses from your intoxication, wake up from your neglect, and reduce your hasty activity.'[5452]

٤٨٢٥ . عنه عليه السلام : فَأَفِقْ أيُّها السامِعُ مِن سَكرَتِكَ، واستَيقِظْ مِن غَفلَتِكَ، واختَصِر مِن عَجَلَتِكَ.[٥٤٠٧]

4826. **Imām 'Alī (AS) said,** 'O people who are not neglected [by Allah] and yet who neglect that which will be taken to account from them - how is it that I see you moving away from Allah and longing for others?!'[5453]

٤٨٢٦ . عنه عليه السلام : أيُّها الناسُ غيرُ المَغفولِ عَنهُم، والتارِكونَ المَأخوذَ مِنهُم، مالي أراكُم عـنِ اللهِ ذاهِبينَ، وإلىٰ غيرِهِ راغِبينَ؟![٥٤٠٨]

4827. **Imām 'Alī (AS) said,** 'How many a negligent person weaves himself a garment in order that he might wear it whilst in reality it is his burial shroud, and who builds himself a house in which he may live but which is in fact his grave.'[5454]

٤٨٢٧ . عنه عليه السلام : كَم مِن غافِلٍ يَنسِجُ ثَوباً لِيَلبَسَهُ وإنّما هُو كَفَنُهُ! ويَبنِي بَيتاً لِـيَسكُنَهُ وإنّـما هـو مَوضِعُ قَبرِهِ![٥٤٠٩]

4828. **Imām al-Ṣādiq (AS) said,** 'If Satan is indeed an enemy, then why the negligence?!'[5455]

٤٨٢٨ . الإمامُ الصّادقُ عليه السلام : إن كانَ الشيطانُ عَدُوّاً فالغَفلَةُ لِماذا؟![٥٤١٠]

(See also: SCRUTINY166)

(أُنظر) عنوان: ١٦٦ «المراقبة».

1433. That which Prevents Negligence

١٤٣٣ ـ ما يَمنَعُ الغَفلَةَ

4829. **The Prophet (SAWA) said,** 'O Abū Dharr, intend to perform good actions even if you do not actually manage to perform them, so that you are not included amongst the negligent.'[5456]

٤٨٢٩ . رسولُ اللهِ ﷺ : يا أباذرٍّ، هُمَّ بـالحَسَنَةِ وإن لم تَعمَلْها ؛ لِكيلا تُكتَبَ مِن الغافِلينَ .[٥٤١١]

4830. **Imām ʿAlī (AS) said,** 'Through constant remembrance of Allah is negligence dispelled.'[5457]

٤٨٣٠ . الإمامُ عليٌّ ﵇ : بِدَوامِ ذِكرِ اللهِ تَنجابُ الغَفـةُ .[٥٤١٢]

4831. **Imām ʿAlī (AS) said,** 'Verily the one who knows the vicissitudes of time will not neglect preparation.'[5458]

٤٨٣١ . عنه ﵇ : إنَّ مَن عَرَفَ الأيّامَ لم يَغفُلْ عنِ الاستِعدادِ .[٥٤١٣]

4832. **Imām al-Bāqir (AS) said,** 'Verily any believer who is mindful of the obligatory prayers and prays them on time is not of the negligent ones.'[5459]

٤٨٣٢ . الإمامُ الباقرُ ﵇ : أيّما مُؤمِنٍ حافَظَ علَى الصَّلواتِ المَفروضَةِ فَصَلّاها لِوَقتِها فَلَيسَ هذا مِن لغافِلينَ .[٥٤١٤]

1434. The Distinguishing Characteristics of a Negligent Person

١٤٣٤ ـ عَلاماتُ الغافِلِ

4833. **Luqmān (AS) said** to his son, exhorting him: 'O my son, everything has a distinguishing characteristic by which it is recognised and witnessed … the negligent person has three distinguishing characteristics: absent-mindedness, amusement, and forgetfulness.'[5460]

٤٨٣٣ . لُقمانُ ﵇ ـ لابنِهِ وهو يَعِظُهُ ـ : يابُنَيَّ ، لِكُلِّ شَيءٍ علامةٌ يُعرَفُ بـها ويُشـهَدُ عـلَيها ... وللـغافِلِ ثـلاثُ عـلاماتٍ : السَّـهوُ ، واللَّـهوُ ، والنِّسيانُ .[٥٤١٥]

4834. **Imām al-Ḥasan (AS) said,** 'Negligence is [manifest] in your abandonment of the mosque and in your obedience of the corrupt.'[5461]

٤٨٣٤ . الإمامُ الحسنُ ﵇ : الغَفلَةُ تَركُكَ المَسجِدَ ، وطاعَتُكَ المُفسِدَ .[٥٤١٦]

1435. The Effects of Negligence

١٤٣٥ ـ آثارُ الغَفلَةِ

4835. **Imām ʿAlī (AS) said,** 'He who prolongs his negligence hastens his own destruction.'[5462]

٤٨٣٥ . الإمامُ عليٌّ ﵇ : مَن طالَت غَفلَتُهُ تَعَجَّلَت هَلَكَتُهُ .[٥٤١٧]

4836. **Imām ʿAlī (AS) said,** 'The one who is overcome by negligence, his heart is dead.'[5463]

٤٨٣٦ . عنه ﵇ : مَن غَلَبَت علَيهِ الغَفلَةُ مـاتَ قَلبُهُ .[٥٤١٨]

4837. **Imām ʿAlī (AS) said,** 'Continued negligence blinds insight.'[5464]

٤٨٣٧ . عنه ﵇ : دَوامُ الغَفلَةِ يُعمِي البَصيرَةَ .[٥٤١٩]

4838. **Imām ʿAlī (AS) said,** 'Beware of negligence and delusion about the respite [that you have been given], for indeed negligence ruins deeds.'[5465]

٤٨٣٨ . عنه عليه السلام : إيّاكَ والغَفلَةَ والاغتِرارَ بالمُهلَةِ ؛ فإنّ الغَفلَةَ تُفسِدُ الأعمالَ .٥٤٢٠

1436. The Praise of Feigning Negligence (or Ignorance)

١٤٣٦ ـ مَدحُ التَّغافُلِ

4839. **Imām ʿAlī (AS) said,** 'Verily half of an intellectual man is tolerating, and the other half is ignoring.'[5466]

٤٨٣٩ . الإمامُ عليٌّ عليه السلام : إنّ العاقِلَ نِصفُهُ احتِمالٌ ، ونِصفُهُ تَغافُلٌ .٥٤٢١

4840. **Imām ʿAlī (AS) said,** 'One of the noblest deeds of a kind person is feigning ignorance of that which he knows already.'[5467]

٤٨٤٠ . عنه عليه السلام : مِن أشرَفِ أعمالِ (أحوالِ) الكَريمِ غَفلَتُهُ عمّا يَعلَمُ .٥٤٢٢

4841. **Imām al-Ṣādiq (AS) said,** 'The proper way to maintain a state of coexistence and mutual intimacy with people is according to a set measure, two thirds of which are alertness and a third of which is to feign ignorance of each other's faults.'[5468]

٤٨٤١ . الإمامُ الصّادقُ عليه السلام : صَلاحُ حالِ التَّعايُشِ والتَّعاشُرِ مِلْءُ مِكيالٍ : ثُلثاهُ فِطنَةٌ وثُلثُهُ تَغافُلٌ .٥٤٢٣

305

RANCOUR

الغِلّ

1437. Warning Against Rancour

١٤٣٧ ـ التَّحذيرُ مِنَ الغِلِّ ٥٤٢٤

"And do not put any rancour in our hearts toward the faithful."[5469]

﴿ولا تَجْعَلْ في قُلُوبِنا غِلّاً لِلَّذِينَ آمَنُوا﴾ .٥٤٢٥

"We will remove whatever rancour there is in their breasts."[5470]

﴿ونَزَعْنا ما فِي صُدُورِهِمْ مِنْ غِلٍّ﴾ .٥٤٢٦

4842. **Prophet Jesus (AS) said,** 'O slaves of this world, you shave your heads [claiming to be ascetics], you shorten your shirts, you bow your heads but do not remove the rancour from your hearts?!'[5471]

٤٨٤٢ . عيسى عليه السلام : يا عَبيدَ الدنيا ، تَحلِقُونَ رُؤوسَكُم وتُقَصِّرُونَ قُمُصَكُم وتُنَكِّسونَ رُؤوسَكُم ولا تَنزِعونَ الغِلَّ مِن قُلوبِكُم ؟!٥٤٢٧

4843. **The Prophet (SAWA) said,** 'If my community does not harbour rancour towards each other, no enemy would ever challenge it.'[5472]

٤٨٤٣ . رسولُ اللهِ ﷺ : إذا لم تَغُلَّ اُمَّتي لم يَقُمْ لَها عَدُوٌّ أبداً .٥٤٢٨

4844. **Imām ʿAlī (AS) said,** 'Rancour is the seed of evil.'[5473]

٤٨٤٤ . الإمامُ عليٌّ ﷷ : الغِلُّ بَذْرُ الشَّرِّ .٥٤٢٩

4845. **Imām ʿAlī (AS) said,** 'Rancour thwarts good deeds.'[5474]

٤٨٤٥ . عنه ﷷ : الغِلُّ يُحبِطُ الحَسَناتِ .٥٤٣٠

4846. **Imām ʿAlī (AS) said,** 'The heart that harbours the most rancour is the heart of the malicious person.'[5475]

٤٨٤٦ . عنه ﷷ : أشَدُّ القُلوبِ غِلّاً قَلبُ الحَقُودِ .٥٤٣١

1438. That Which the Heart of a Muslim Cannot Harbour Rancour Towards

١٤٣٨ ـ مالا يَغُلُّ عَلَيهِ قَلبُ المُسلِمِ

4847. **The Prophet (SAWA) said,** 'There are three things towards which the heart of a Muslim will not harbour rancour: performing acts sincerely to Allah, giving sincere advice to the rulers, and adherence to the community of Muslims; for verily their attraction towards these things encompasses them from all sides [will protect them].'[5476]

٤٨٤٧ . رسولُ اللهِ ﷺ : ثلاثٌ لا يَغُلُّ ٥٤٣٢ عليهِنَّ قلبُ امرئٍ مسلمٍ : إخلاصُ العَمَلِ للهِ ، ومُناصَحَةُ وُلاةِ الأمرِ ، ولزومُ جَماعَةِ المُسلمينَ ؛ فإنَّ دَعوَتَهُم تُحيطُ مِن وَراءِهِم .٥٤٣٣ ٥٤٣٤

1439. Censure of Breaching One's Trust

١٤٣٩ ـ التَّحذيرُ مِنَ الغُلولِ ٥٤٣٥

"A prophet may not breach his trust, and whoever breaches his trust will bring his breaches on the Day of Resurrection…"[5477]

﴿وَما كانَ لِنَبِيٍّ أنْ يَغُلَّ وَمَنْ يَغْلُلْ يَأْتِ بِما غَلَّ يَوْمَ الْقِيامَةِ﴾ .٥٤٣٦

4848. **Ibn ʿAbbās narrated,** 'The verse: *"A prophet may not breach his trust, and whoever breaches his trust will bring his breaches on the Day of Resurrection"* was revealed with regards to a red velvet shawl that got lost on the day of the battle of Badr, so some people started saying that maybe the Prophet (SAWA) had taken it! So Allah revealed the verse: *"A prophet may not breach his trust …"*'[5478]

٤٨٤٨ . ابنُ عبّاسٍ : نَزَلَت هذهِ الآيةُ : ﴿وما كانَ لِنبيٍّ أن يَغُلَّ﴾ في قَطيفَةٍ حَمراءَ افتُقِدَتْ يَومَ بَدرٍ ، فقالَ بعضُ الناسِ : لَعَلَّ رسولَ اللهِ ﷺ أخَذَها ! فَأنزَلَ اللهُ : ﴿وما كانَ لِنبيٍّ أن يَغُلَّ﴾ .٥٤٣٧

4849. It is narrated in *al-Targhīb wa al-Tarhīb*, 'On the day of the battle of Khaybar, some of the Prophet (SAWA)'s companions came to him, [listing who had been martyred], '*x* is a martyr, *y* is a martyr, etc…' until they mentioned a particular man as having been martyred, upon which the Prophet (SAWA) exclaimed, 'No way, verily I have seen him burning in the Fire, clad in a shawl or a cloak that he had taken [as a breach of trust of the war booty].'[5479]

٤٨٤٩. الترغيب والترهيب: لَمّا كانَ يومُ خَيبَرَ أقبَلَ نَفَرٌ مِن أصحابِ النبيِّ ﷺ فقالوا: فلانٌ شَهيدٌ، وفلانٌ شَهيدٌ، وفلانٌ شهيدٌ، حتّىٰ مَرُّوا علىٰ رَجُلٍ فقالوا: فلانٌ شَهيدٌ، فقالَ رسولُ اللهِ ﷺ: كَلّا، إنّي رَأيتُهُ فِي النارِ في بُردَةٍ غَلَّها، أو عَباءَةٍ غَلَّها.[٥٤٣٨]

4850. **Imām al-Ṣādiq (AS) said,** 'Breach of trust includes anything that is taken unlawfully from one's leader [in the form of war booty before it has been justly divided], doubtfully usurping the wealth of an orphan and consuming doubtful gains.'[5480]

٤٨٥٠. الإمامُ الصّادقُ عليه السلام: الغُلولُ[٥٤٣٩] كُلُّ شيءٍ غُلَّ عنِ الإمامِ، وأكلُ مالِ اليَتيمِ شُبهَةً، والسُّحْتُ شُبهَةً.[٥٤٤٠]

306

EXTREMISM (IN RELIGION)[5481]

الغُلُوّ

1440. Caution Against Extremism in Religion

١٤٤٠ ـ التَّحذيرُ مِنَ الغُلوِّ فِي الدِّينِ

"O People of the Book! Do not exceed the bounds in your religion, and do not attribute anything to Allah except the truth. The Messiah, Jesus son of Mary, was only an apostle of Allah, and His Word that He cast toward Mary and a spirit from Him. So have faith in Allah and his apostles, and do not say, '[God is] a trinity."[5482]

﴿يا أهْلَ الْكِتابِ لاتَغْلُوا في دِينِكُمْ وَلا تَقُولُوا عَلَى اللهِ إلَّا الْحَقَّ إنَّما الْمَسِيحُ عِيسَى ابْنُ مَرْيَمَ رَسُولُ اللهِ وَكَلِمَتُهُ﴾.[٥٤٤١]

4851. **The Prophet (SAWA) said,** 'Do not elevate me above my rightful position, for verily Allah has made me a servant before He made me a prophet.'[5483]

٤٨٥١. رسولُ اللهِ ﷺ: لاتَرفَعُوني فَوقَ حَقّي؛ فإنَّ اللهَ تعالىٰ اتَّخَذَني عَبداً قبلَ أن يَتَّخِذَني نَبِيّاً.[٥٤٤٢]

4852. **The Prophet (SAWA) said,** 'Two types of people will not be included in my intercession: the tyrannical and iniquitous ruler, and the heretical extremist in matters of religion, who has digressed

٤٨٥٢. عنه ﷺ: صِنفانِ لا تَنالُهُما شَفاعَتي: سُلطانٌ غَشومٌ عَسُوفٌ، وغالٍ فِي الدِّينِ مارِقٌ

from it and who is neither repentant nor willing to give up [his heresy].'[5484]

مِنهُ غيرُ تائبٍ ولانازعٍ.[٥٤٤٣]

4853. **The Prophet (SAWA) said,** 'O 'Alī, your example in this community is as the example of Jesus son of Mary – one group of people loved him and exceeded the bounds in their love for him, and one group of people hated him and exceeded the bounds in their hatred. The following verse was therefore revealed: *"When the son of Mary was cited as an example, behold, your people raise an outcry."*'[5485 5486]

٤٨٥٣. عنه ﷺ ـ لعليّ عليه السلام ـ: ياعليُّ، مَثَلُكَ في هذهِ الأُمَّةِ كَمَثَلِ عيسَى بنِ مَريمَ؛ أحَبَّهُ قَومٌ فَأفرَطوا فيهِ، وأبغَضَهُ قَومٌ فَأفرَطوا فيهِ، قالَ: فَنَزَلَ الوَحيُ: ﴿ولَمّا ضُرِبَ ابنُ مَريمَ مَثَلاً إذا قَومُكَ مِنهُ يَصِدُّونَ﴾.[٥٤٤٤، ٥٤٤٥]

4854. **Imām 'Alī (AS) said,** 'Two types of people will perish in my name: the one who is an extremist in his love for me, and the one who loathes me with a vengeance.'[5487]

٤٨٥٤. الإمامُ عليٌّ عليه السلام: هَلَكَ فِيَّ رَجُلانِ: مُحِبٌّ غالٍ، ومُبغِضٌ قالٍ.[٥٤٤٦]

4855. **Imām 'Alī (AS) said,** 'O Allah, verily I disclaim association with the extremists as Jesus son of Mary's disassociation with the Christians. O Allah degrade them forever, and do not ever help any of them.'[5488]

٤٨٥٥. عنه عليه السلام: اللّهُمّ إنّي بَريءٌ مِنَ الغُلاةِ كَبَراءَةِ عيسَى بنِ مَريمَ مِنَ النَّصارىٰ، اللّهُمّ اخذُلْهُم أبَداً، ولاتَنصُرْ مِنهُم أحَداً.[٥٤٤٧]

4856. **Imām 'Alī (AS) said,** 'Beware of going to extremes with respect to us. Instead take us as servants that have been endeared [by Allah], and say whatever you wish about our virtues.'[5489]

٤٨٥٦. عنه عليه السلام: إيّاكُم والغُلُوَّ فِينا، قُولُوا إنّا عَبِيدٌ مَربُوبُونَ، وقُولوا في فَضلِنا ما شِئتُم.[٥٤٤٨]

4857. **Imām 'Alī (AS) said,** 'Do not exceed in considering us more than divine and say what you want and you will not be exaggerating, and beware of extremism like the extremism of the Christians, as I have renounced myself from the extremists.'[5490]

٤٨٥٧. عنه عليه السلام: لاتَتَجاوَزوابنا العُبوديَّةَ ثُمّ قُولوا ماشِئتُم ولن تَبلُغُوا، وإيّاكُم والغُلُوَّ كَغُلُوِّ النَّصارىٰ؛ فإنّي بَريءٌ مِن الغالِينَ.[٥٤٤٩]

4858. **Imām al-Ṣādiq (AS) said,** 'Be on your guard that the extremists do not corrupt your youth, for verily the extremists are the most evil of Allah's creation for they belittle the Greatness of Allah, and falsely attribute divinity to the servants of Allah. The extremist may return to us but we do not accept him again, whereas we do accept he who

٤٨٥٨. الإمامُ الصّادقُ عليه السلام: اِحذَرُوا علىٰ شَبابِكُمُ الغُلاةَ لايُفسِدُونَهُم؛ فإنَّ الغُلاةَ شَرُّ خَلقِ اللهِ، يُصَغِّرُونَ عَظَمَةَ اللهِ، ويَدَّعُونَ الرُّبوبِيَّةَ لِعِبادِ اللهِ،

is incapable when he tries to adhere to us. At this, he was asked, 'How can that be O son of the Prophet (SAWA)?' to which he replied, 'Because the extremist has become accustomed to abandoning the prayer, the alms-tax, fasting, the pilgrimage, and cannot give up his habit and return to Allah's obedience ever again, whereas he who is incapable, when he attains inner knowledge, begins to act and carry out acts of obedience.'[5491]

والله إنَّ الغُلاةَ شَرٌّ مِن اليَهودِ والنَّصارىٰ والمَجوسِ والذينَ أشرَكُوا، ثُمّ قالَ: إلَينا يَرجِعُ الغالي فلا نَقبَلُهُ، وبنا يَلحَقُ المُقَصِّرُ فَنَقبَلُهُ، فقيلَ لَهُ: كيفَ ذلكَ يا بنَ رسولِ اللهِ؟ قالَ: لأنَّ الغالِيَ قدِ اعتادَ تَركَ الصَّلاةِ والزكاةِ والصيامِ والحَجِّ فلا يَقدِرُ علىٰ تَركِ عادَتِهِ وعلَى الرُّجوعِ إلىٰ طاعَةِ اللهِ عَزَّوجلَّ أبداً، وإنّ المُقَصِّرَ إذا عَرَفَ عَمِلَ وأطاعَ.٥٤٥٠

4859. **Abū Baṣīr narrated,** 'I told Abū 'Abdillāh [i.e. Imām al-Ṣādiq] (AS): 'Verily they are saying things [about you]!' He asked, 'What are they saying?' to which I replied, '[They are saying], 'He knows the number of drops of rain, the number of stars and the leaves on the trees, and the weight of all that is in the sea, and the number of grains of sand.' So he raised his hands to the sky, saying, 'Glory be to Allah, Glory be to Allah. No, by Allah, no one knows this except Allah.'[5492]

٤٨٥٩. أبو بصيرٍ: قلتُ لأبي عبدِاللهِ علَيهِ الصَّلاةُ والسلامُ: إنّهم يقولونَ! قالَ: وما يَقولونَ؟ قلتُ: يقولونَ: يَعلَمُ قَطْرَ المَطَرِ، وعَدَدَ النُّجومِ ووَرَقَ الشَّجَرِ، ووَزنَ ما في البَحرِ، وعَدَدَ التُّرابِ، فرَفَعَ يَدَهُ إلَى السماءِ وقالَ: سبحانَ اللهِ سبحانَ اللهِ، لا واللهِ ما يَعلمُ هذا إلّا اللهُ.٥٤٥١

4860. **Imām al-Riḍā (AS) said,** 'The extremists are disbelievers and the *mufawwiḍa*[5493] are polytheists…'[5494]

٤٨٦٠. الإمامُ الرِّضا عليه السلام: الغُلاةُ كُفّارٌ، والمُفَوِّضَةُ مُشرِكونَ....٥٤٥٢

4861. **Imām al-Riḍā (AS) said,** 'Whoever exceeds the bounds [of their love] for the Commander of the Faithful 'Alī (AS) into worship [of him] is indeed among those who incur Allah's wrath and are astray.'[5495]

٤٨٦١. عنه عليه السلام: مَن تَجاوَزَ بأميرِ المؤمنينَ عليه السلام العُبوديَّةَ فهُوَ مِنَ المَغضوبِ علَيهِم ومِنَ الضالِّينَ.٥٤٥٣

307

RICHES

الغِنىٰ

1441. Richness and Rebellion

١٤٤١ ـ الغِنىٰ وَالطُّغيانُ

"Indeed man becomes rebellious when he considers himself without need."[5496]

﴿كَلّا إنَّ الْإنْسانَ لَيَطْغَىٰ * أنْ رَءاهُ اسْتَغْنَىٰ﴾.٥٤٥٤

4862. **The Prophet (SAWA) said**, 'Verily Satan says, 'The rich man is not safe from me in either one of three situations: either I embellish his riches in his eyes such that he deprives it to whoever has a right to it, or I facilitate its way so that he squanders it in the wrong place; or I make it so beloved to him that he earns it unlawfully.'[5497]

٤٨٦٢ . رسولُ اللهِ ﷺ: إنَّ الشَّيطانَ قالَ: لن يَنجُوَ مِنّي الغَنِيُّ مِن إحدىٰ ثلاثٍ: إمّا أن أُزَيِّـنَهُ فـي عَينِهِ فَيَمنَعَهُ مِن حَقِّهِ، وإمّا أن أُسَهِّلَ علَيهِ سبيلَهُ فَيُنفِقَهُ في غيرِ حَقِّهِ، وإمّا أن أُحَبِّبَهُ إلَيهِ فَيَكسِبَهُ بغيرِ حَقِّهِ.[٥٤٥٥]

4863. **Imām 'Alī (AS),** in his description of the most wonderful thing in man, which is the heart, said, 'If it comes across riches, freedom from need makes it rebellious. If calamity befalls it, it is humbled by anguish.'[5498]

٤٨٦٣ . الإمامُ عليٌّ ﷷ ـ في صفةِ أعجَبِ ما فِي الإنسانِ وهُـو القَـلبُ ـ: إن أفـادَ مـالاً أطـغاهُ الغِنىٰ، وإن أصابَتهُ مُصيبَةٌ فَضَحَهُ الجَزَعُ.[٥٤٥٦]

4864. **Imām al-Ṣādiq (AS) narrated,** 'A rich man, clad in a clean robe, once came to the Prophet (SAWA) and sat near the Prophet (SAWA). Then a poor man clad in dirty clothes came and sat next to the rich man, at which the rich man grabbed his clothes from under his thighs. So the Prophet (SAWA) asked him, 'Do you fear that some of his poverty will rub off onto you?!' so he replied, 'No.' Then he asked, 'Then perhaps you fear that some of your riches will fall upon him?!' to which he replied, 'No.' So he asked, 'Then do you fear that he will make your clothes dirty?!' to which he again replied no. So the Prophet (SAWA) asked him, 'Then what made you do what you just did?' to which he replied [remorsefully], 'O Prophet of Allah, verily I have an associate [i.e. Satan] who embellishes every ugly act to me, and who makes every good act appear ugly to me. Indeed I will give him [the poor man] half my wealth!' So the Prophet (SAWA) asked the poor man, 'Do you accept it?' and he replied, 'No', so the rich man exclaimed, 'But why not?!' so he replied, 'I fear that the same thing that has affected him will affect me!'[5499]

٤٨٦٤ . الإمامُ الصّادقُ ﷷ: جاءَ رجُلٌ مُوسِرٌ إلىٰ رسولِ اللهِ ﷺ نَقِيُّ الثَّـوبِ فَـجَلَسَ إلىٰ رسـولِ اللهِ ﷺ، فجاءَ رَجُلٌ مُعسِرٌ دَرِنُ الثَّوبِ فَـجَلَسَ إلىٰ جَنبِ المُوسِرِ، فَقَبَضَ المُـوسِرُ ثـيابَهُ مِـن تَحتِ فَخِذَيهِ، فقالَ لَهُ رسولُ اللهِ ﷺ: أخِفتَ أن يَمَسَّكَ مِن فَقرِهِ شَيءٌ؟! قالَ: لا، قالَ: فَـخِفتَ أن يُصيبَهُ مِن غِـناكَ شَـيءٌ؟! قـالَ: لا، قـالَ: فَخِفتَ أن يُوَسِّخَ ثِيابَكَ؟! قالَ: لا، قـالَ: فـما حَمَلَكَ علىٰ ما صَنَعتَ؟ فقالَ: يا رسولَ اللهِ، إنَّ لي قَرِيـاً يُزَيِّنُ لي كُـلَّ قَـبيحٍ، ويُـقَبِّحُ لي كُـلَّ حَسَنٍ، وقد جَعَلتُ لَهُ نِصفَ مالي!
فقالَ رسولُ اللهِ ﷺ للمُعسِرِ: أتَـقبَلُ؟ قـالَ: لا، فقالَ لَهُ الرَّجُلُ: ولِمَ؟! قالَ: أخافُ أن يَدخُلَني ما دَخَلَكَ![٥٤٥٧]

1442. Riches and Godwariness

١٤٤٢ ـ الغِنىٰ وَالتَّقوىٰ

"Did He not find you needy, and enrich you?"[5500]

﴿وَوَجَدَكَ عائِلاً فَأَغْنَىٰ﴾.[٥٤٥٨]

4865. **The Prophet (SAWA) said,** 'What a good aid riches can be to Godwariness.'[5501]

٤٨٦٥. رسولُ اللهِ ﷺ: نِعمَ العَونُ علىٰ تقوَى اللهِ تَعالىٰ الغِنىٰ.[٥٤٥٩]

4866. **Imām al-Ṣādiq (AS) said,** 'Ask Allah for riches and vitality in this world's life, and ask him for forgiveness and Paradise for the life hereafter.'[5502]

٤٨٦٦. الإمامُ الصّادقُ (ع): سَلُوا اللهَ الغِنىٰ فِي الدّنيا والعافِيَةَ، وفي الآخِرَةِ المَغفِرَةَ والجَنَّةَ.[٥٤٦٠]

(See also: WEALTH: section 1683; THE WORLD: section 705)

(أُنظر) المال: باب ١٦٨٣؛ الدنيا: باب ٧٠٥.

1443. The Real Meaning of Being Rich

١٤٤٣ـ تَفسيرُ الغِنىٰ

4867. **Imām ʿAlī (AS) said,** 'There is no treasure more precious than contentment.'[5503]

٤٨٦٧. الإمامُ عليٌّ (ع): لا كَنزَ أغنىٰ مِنَ القَناعَةِ.[٥٤٦١]

4868. **Imām ʿAlī (AS) said,** 'There is no wealth like the intellect.'[5504]

٤٨٦٨. عنه (ع): لا غِنىٰ كالعَقلِ.[٥٤٦٢]

4869. **Imām Zayn al-ʿĀbidīn (AS) said,** 'Show your despair of people [and their possessions], for verily that is true wealth.'[5505]

٤٨٦٩. الإمامُ زينُ العابدينَ (ع): أظهِرِ اليَأسَ مِنَ النّاسِ؛ فإنَّ ذلكَ هُوَ الغِنىٰ.[٥٤٦٣]

4870. **Imām al-Hādī (AS) said,** '[Truly] Being rich is to wish for little and to be content with whatever suffices you, and [true] poverty is the voracity of the soul [for more] and severe despondence.'[5506]

٤٨٧٠. الإمامُ الهاديُّ (ع): الغِنىٰ قِلَّةُ تَمَنِّيكَ والرِّضا بما يَكفِيكَ. الفَقرُ شَرَهُ النَّفسِ وشِدَّةُ القُنوطِ.[٥٤٦٤]

(See also: POVERTY: section 1489)

(أُنظر) الفقر: باب ١٤٨٩.

1444. The Greatest of Riches

١٤٤٤ـ أعظَمُ الغِنىٰ

4871. **The Prophet (SAWA) said,** 'He who wishes to be the richest of people should be more trusting of what is in Allah's Hands than what is in others' hands.'[5507]

٤٨٧١. رسولُ اللهِ ﷺ: مَن أرادَ أن يَكونَ أغنَى النّاسِ فَلْيَكُنْ بما في يَدِ اللهِ أوثَقَ مِنهُ بما في يَدِ غَيرِهِ.[٥٤٦٥]

4872. **The Prophet (SAWA) said,** 'Be free from need of people, even for a toothpick.'[5508]

٤٨٧٢. عنه ﷺ: اِستَغنُوا عَنِ النّاسِ ولو بشَوصِ[٥٤٦٦] السِّواكِ.[٥٤٦٧]

4873. **The Prophet (SAWA) said,** 'The best of richness is richness of the self [i.e. its being needless of everyone but Allah].'[5509]

٤٨٧٣. عنه ﷺ: خَيرُ الغِنىٰ غِنَى النفسِ.[٥٤٦٨]

4874. **Imām ʿAlī (AS) said,** 'He who is needless of all but Allah is himself needed by people.'[5510]

٤٨٧٤. الإمامُ عليٌّ عليه السلام : مَنِ استَغنىٰ باللهِ افتَقَرَ الناسُ إلَيهِ.[٥٤٦٩]

4875. **Imām ʿAlī (AS) said,** 'The greatest richness is to despair of [obtaining] what other people possess.'[5511]

٤٨٧٥. عنه عليه السلام : الغِنَى الأكبَرُ اليَأسُ عَمّا في أيدِي الناسِ.[٥٤٧٠]

4876. **Imām ʿAlī (AS) said,** 'Verily the most affluent of riches is intellect, and the worst poverty is stupidity.'[5512]

٤٨٧٦. عنه عليه السلام : إنَّ أغنَى الغِنَى العَقلُ، وأكبَرَ الفَقرِ الحُمقُ.[٥٤٧١]

4877. **Imām al-Bāqir or Imām al-Ṣādiq (AS) said,** 'He who is content with whatever sustenance Allah has provided him is the richest of people.'[5513]

٤٨٧٧. الإمامُ الباقرُ(أ)والإمامُ الصّادقُ عليهما السلام :مَن قَنِعَ بما رَزَقَهُ اللهُ فهُو مِن أغنَى الناسِ.[٥٤٧٢]

4878. **Imām al-Ṣādiq (AS) said,** 'Whoever has been granted three things, receives three other things in addition, and this is the greatest wealth: contentment with what one has been given, despair of other people's possessions, and abandonment of all that is superfluous.'[5514]

٤٨٧٨. الإمامُ الصّادقُ عليه السلام :مَن رُزِقَ ثلاثاً نالَ ثلاثاً وهُو الغِنَى الأكبَرُ: القَناعَةُ بما اُعطِيَ، واليَأسُ مِمّا في أيدِي الناسِ، وتَركُ الفُضولِ.[٥٤٧٣]

1445. The Key to Affluence

١٤٤٥ـ مِفتاحُ الغِنىٰ

4879. **Imām ʿAlī (AS) said,** 'The key to affluence is conviction.'[5515]

٤٨٧٩. الإمامُ عليٌّ عليه السلام : مِفتاحُ الغِنَى اليَقينُ.[٥٤٧٤]

4880. **Imām ʿAlī (AS) said,** 'One cannot be rich unless one has self-restraint.'[5516]

٤٨٨٠. عنه عليه السلام : لا يكونُ غَنيّاً حتّىٰ يكونَ عَفيفاً.[٥٤٧٥]

4881. **Imām ʿAlī (AS) said,** 'He who lives and his only concern is the Hereafter will achieve richness without wealth, will find solace without family, and is honoured without having a clan.'[5517]

٤٨٨١. عنه عليه السلام :مَن أصبَحَ والآخِرَةُ هَمُّهُ استَغنىٰ بغَيرِ مالٍ، واستَأنَسَ بغَيرِ أهلٍ، وعَزَّ بغَيرِ عَشيرَةٍ.[٥٤٧٦]

4882. **Imām al-Bāqir (AS) said,** 'Verily the Godwary people are the rich, and they have been enriched by their possession of very little of this world, therefore their provisions are very light.'[5518]

٤٨٨٢. الإمامُ الباقرُ عليه السلام : إنَّ أهلَ التَّقوىٰ هُمُ الأغنياءُ، أغناهُمُ القَليلُ مِن الدنيا فَمَؤونَتُهُم يَسِيرَةٌ.[٥٤٧٧]

1446. The Rich People Whose Reward Will Be Doubled

١٤٤٦ ـ مَن يُضاعَفُ لَهُ الأجرُ مِنَ الأغنِياءِ

"It is not your wealth, nor your children, that will bring you close to Us in nearness, except those who have faith and act righteously. It is they for whom there will be a twofold reward for what they did, and they will be secure in lofty abodes."[5519]

﴿وَما أَمْوالُكُمْ وَلا أَوْلادُكُمْ بِالَّتِي تُقَرِّبُكُمْ عِنْدَنا زُلْفَىٰ إِلَّا مَنْ آمَنَ وَعَمِلَ صالِحاً فَأُولٰئِكَ لَهُمْ جَزاءُ الضِّعْفِ بِما عَمِلُوا وَهُمْ فِي الْغُرُفاتِ آمِنُونَ﴾.[٥٤٧٨]

4883. **Imām al-Ṣādiq (AS),** when a man mentioned the rich people in his presence, defaming them, replied, 'Be quiet! For verily if the rich man maintains relations with his kin and does good to his fellow brothers [with the aid of his riches], Allah doubles his reward for him, for Allah has said, *"It is not your wealth, nor your children, that will bring you close to Us in nearness, except those who have faith and act righteously. It is they for whom there will be a twofold reward for what they did, and they will be secure in lofty abodes."*'[5520]

٤٨٨٣ . الإمامُ الصّادقُ عليه السلام ـ لَمّا ذَكَرَ رجُلٌ عندَهُ الأغنياءَ ووَقَعَ فيهِم ـ : أُسكُتْ ! فإنَّ الغَنيَّ إذا كانَ وَصُولاً لِرَحِمِهِ بارّاً بِإخوانِهِ ، أضعَفَ اللهُ لَهُ الأجرَ ضِعفَينِ ؛ لأنَّ اللهَ يقولُ : ﴿وما أموالُكُم ولا أولادُكُم بالّتي تُقَرِّبُكُم عِندَنا زُلفىٰ إلّا مَن آمَنَ وعَمِلَ صالِحاً فأُولئكَ لَهُم جَزاءُ الضِّعْفِ بِما عَمِلُوا وهُمْ في الغُرُفاتِ آمِنونَ﴾ الآية.[٥٤٧٩]

1447. The Rich People's Responsibility for The Poor People's Hunger

١٤٤٧ ـ مَسؤولِيَّةُ الأغنِياءِ عَن جوعِ الفُقَراءِ

4884. **Imām 'Alī (AS) said,** 'Verily Allah, Glory be to Him, allotted the food provisions of the poor within the wealth of the rich, so no poor man goes hungry except as a result of what a rich man has denied him, and Allah, most High, will question him about that.'[5521]

٤٨٨٤ . الإمامُ عليٌّ عليه السلام : إنّ اللهَ سبحانَهُ فَرَضَ في أموالِ الأغنياءِ أقواتَ الفُقَراءِ ، فما جاعَ فَقيرٌ إلّا بما مُتِّعَ بهِ غَنيٌّ ، واللهُ تعالىٰ سائلُهُم عن ذلكَ.[٥٤٨٠]

4885. **Imām 'Alī (AS) said,** 'Verily Allah made it obligatory on the rich in their wealth a proportion to what would also suffice the poor from among them, so if they go hungry or are naked or exhausted, it is only because of the rich people's deprivation of them. And Allah has a right to take them to account for it on the Day of Resurrection and to punish them for it.'[5522]

٤٨٨٥ . عنه عليه السلام : إنَّ اللهَ فَرَضَ علَى الأغنياءِ في أموالِهِم بقَدْرِ ما يَكفِي فُقَراءَهُم ، وإن جاعُوا وعَرُوا وجَهَدُوا فَبِمَنعِ الأغنياءِ ، وحَقٌّ عَلَى اللهِ أن يُحاسِبَهُم يَومَ القِيامَةِ ويُعذِّبَهُم علَيهِ.[٥٤٨١]

4886. **Imām 'Alī (AS) said,** 'There is no burden greater than the burden that a rich person carries for depriving the needy.'[5523]

٤٨٨٦ . عنه عليه السلام : لا وِزرَ أعظَمُ مِن وِزرِ غَنيٍّ مَنَعَ المُحتاجَ.[٥٤٨٢]

308

MUSIC[5524]

الغِناءُ

1448. Reproaching Music

١٤٤٨ـ ذَمُّ الغِناءِ

"So avoid the abomination of idols, and avoid false speech."[5525]

﴿فَاجْتَنِبُوا الرِّجْسَ مِنَ الْأَوْثانِ وَاجْتَنِبُوا قَوْلَ الزُّورِ﴾.٥٤٨٣

4887. **The Prophet (SAWA) said,** 'Verily Allah, Mighty and Exalted, sent me as a mercy to the worlds, and in order to eradicate string instruments, the flute and others pre-Islamic pagan practices.'[5526]

٤٨٨٧. رسولُ اللهِ ﷺ: إنَّ اللهَ بَعَثَني رَحمَةً للعالَمينَ، ولِأمحَقَ المَعازِفَ والمَزاميرَ وأُمورَ الجاهِليّةِ.٥٤٨٤

4888. **The Prophet (SAWA) said,** 'Two sounds are cursed in this world as well as in the Hereafter: the sound of the flute played [in celebration] for a bounty, and the twang [of string instruments played] during a calamity.'[5527]

٤٨٨٨. عنه ﷺ: صَوتانِ مَلعونانِ فِي الدنيا والآخِرَةِ: مِزمارٌ عندَ نِعمَةٍ، ورَنَّةٌ عندَ مُصيبَةٍ.٥٤٨٥

4889. **Imām al-Ṣādiq (AS) said,** 'Singing (or music) is one of the things that Allah, Mighty and Exalted, has threatened to requite with the Fire, and this is the purport of Allah's verse: *"Among the people is he who buys diversionary words that he may lead [people] astray from Allah's way without any knowledge, and he takes it in derision."*'[5528] [5529]

٤٨٨٩. الإمامُ الصّادقُ ؑ: الغِناءُ مِمّا أوعَدَ اللهُ عَزَّوجلَّ علَيهِ النارَ، وهُو قَولُهُ عَزَّوجلَّ: ﴿ومِنَ الناسِ مَن يَشْتَري لَهْوَ الحَديثِ لِيُضِلَّ عن سَبيلِ اللهِ بِغَيْرِ عِلْمٍ ويَتَّخِذَها هُزُواً أُولئكَ لَهُم عَذابٌ مُهينٌ﴾.٥٤٨٦

1449. The Effects Engendered by Music

١٤٤٩ـ ميراثُ الغِناءِ

4890. **The Prophet (SAWA) said,** 'Music is a charm of adultery.'[5530]

٤٨٩٠. رسولُ اللهِ ﷺ: الغِناءُ رُقْيَةُ الزِّنا.٥٤٨٧

4891. **The Prophet (SAWA) said,** 'Three things harden the heart: listening to diversionary words (*lahw*)[5531], hunting, and frequenting the sultan.'[5532]

٤٨٩١. عنه ﷺ: ثلاثٌ يُقسِينَ القَلبَ: استِماعُ اللهوِ، وطَلَبُ الصَّيدِ، وإتيانُ بابِ السُّلطانِ.٥٤٨٨

4892. **Imām al-Ṣādiq (AS) said,** 'Music engenders hypocrisy.'[5533]

٤٨٩٢ . الإمامُ الصّادقُ عليه السلام : الغِناءُ يُورِثُ النِّفاقَ .[٥٤٨٩]

(See also: AMUSEMENT 356)

(أُنظر) عنوان ٣٥٦ «اللهو» .

309

THE UNSEEN

الغَيبُ

1450. The Prophet Knows the Unseen Through Allah's Instruction

١٤٥٠ ـ النَّبِيُّ يَعلَمُ الغَيبَ بِتَعليمِ اللهِ

4893. **Imām al-Ṣādiq (AS) narrated,** 'The Prophet (SAWA)'s she-camel got lost in the battle of Tabūk, so the hypocrites started to say [mockingly], 'He talks to us about the Unseen but does not even know where his own she-camel is!' So the archangel Gabriel (AS) came to him and informed him of what they were saying, and told him that his she-camel was in a particular valley, with its reins attached to a large tree. So the Prophet (SAWA) made the call for congregational prayer, and when the people had gathered, he told them, 'O people, verily my she-camel is in such and such a valley', so they ran to bring it for him.'[5534]

٤٨٩٣ . الإمامُ الصّادقُ عليه السلام : ضَلَّت ناقَةُ رسولِ اللهِ صلى الله عليه وآله في غَزوَةِ تَبُوكَ ، فقالَ المُنافقونَ : يُحَدِّثُنا عَنِ الغَيبِ ولا يَعلَمُ مَكانَ ناقَتِهِ ! فأتاهُ جَبرَئيلُ عليه السلام فَأَخبَرَهُ بما قالوا ، وقالَ : إنَّ ناقَتَكَ في شِعْبِ كذا ، مُتَعَلِّقٌ زِمامُها بشَجَرَةِ بَحرٍ . فَنادىٰ رسولُ اللهِ صلى الله عليه وآله : الصلاةَ جامِعَةً ، قالَ : فاجتَمَعَ الناسُ ، فقالَ : أيُّها الناسُ ، إنّ ناقَتي بِشِعبِ كذا ، فَبادَرُوا إلَيها حتّىٰ أتَوها .[٥٤٩٠]

1451. The Imām and the Knowledge of the Unseen

١٤٥١ ـ الإمامُ وعِلمُ الغَيبِ

4894. **Imām 'Alī (AS) said,** when one of his companions (from the tribe of Kalb) told to him, 'Indeed you have been given knowledge of the Unseen, O Commander of the Faithful', Imām 'Alī (AS) laughed, saying, 'O brother of Kalb, this is not knowledge of the Unseen, but instruction from the Possessor of Knowledge. Verily the knowledge of the Unseen is the knowledge of the Hour, and what Allah, Glory be to Him, has listed in his verse: *"Indeed the knowledge of the Hour is*

٤٨٩٤ . الإمامُ عليٌّ عليه السلام ـ لَمّا قالَ لَهُ بعضُ أصحابِهِ (وكانَ كَلبِيّاً) : لَقَد أُعطِيتَ يا أميرَ المؤمنينَ عِلمَ الغَيبِ ، فَضَحِكَ عليه السلام ـ : يا أخا كَلبٍ ، لَيسَ هُوَ بعِلمِ غَيبٍ ، وإنّما هُو تَعَلُّمٌ مِن ذِي عِلمٍ ، وإنَّما عِلمُ الغَيبِ عِلمُ الساعَةِ ، وما عَدَّدَهُ اللهُ سبحانَهُ بقولِهِ :

with Allah. He sends down the rain, and He knows what is in the wombs."[5535]

«إنّ اللهَ عِندَهُ عِلمُ السّاعَةِ ويُنَزِّلُ الغَيثَ ويَعلَمُ ما في الأرحامِ» ٥٤٩١. ٥٤٩٢

4895. **Imām al-Ṣādiq (AS),** when asked, 'Does the *Imām* know the Unseen?' replied, 'No, but whenever he wishes to know something, Allah makes him know it.'[5536]

٤٨٩٥. الإمامُ الصّادقُ (ع) ـ لَمّا سُئلَ: هل يَعلَمُ الإمامُ بالغَيبِ ـ: لا، ولكن إذا أرادَ أن يَعلَمَ الشيءَ أعلَمَهُ اللهُ ذلكَ. ٥٤٩٣

4896. **Imām al-Kāẓim (AS),** when a man from Persia asked him, 'Do you know the Unseen', replied, 'Abū Jaʿfar (AS) [i.e. Imām al-Bāqir] said, 'Knowledge is expounded for us so we know it, and it can be taken away from us so we do not know.' And he said, 'Allah, Mighty and Exalted, entrusted his secret to Gabriel (AS), and Gabriel entrusted it to Muḥammad (SAWA), and Muḥammad (SAWA) entrusted it to those whom Allah willed.'[5537]

٤٨٩٦. الإمامُ الكاظمُ (ع) ـ لَمّا سَألَهُ رَجُلٌ مِن أهلِ فارِسَ: أتَعلَمونَ الغَيبَ؟ ـ: قالَ أبو جعفرٍ (ع): يُبسَطُ لَنا العِلمُ فنَعلَمُ، ويُقبَضُ عنّا فلا نَعلَمُ. وقالَ: سِرُّ اللهِ عَزَّوجلَّ أسَرَّهُ إلى جَبرَئيلَ (ع)، وأسَرَّهُ جَبرَئيلُ إلى محمّدٍ ﷺ، وأسَرَّهُ محمّدٌ إلى مَن شاءَ اللهُ. ٥٤٩٤

310

BACKBITING

الغِيبَةُ

1452. Prohibition of Backbiting

١٤٥٢ ـ النَّهيُ عنِ الغِيبَةِ

"And do not backbite about one another. Will any of you love to eat the flesh of his dead brother? You would hate it. And be wary of Allah; indeed Allah is all-clement, all-merciful."[5538]

«ولا يَغْتَبْ بَعْضُكُمْ بَعْضاً أيُحِبُّ أحَدُكُمْ أنْ يأكُلَ لَحْمَ أخِيهِ مَيْتاً فَكَرِهْتُمُوهُ واتَّقُوا اللهَ إنَّ اللهَ تَوّابٌ رَحيمٌ». ٥٤٩٥

4897. **The Prophet (SAWA) said,** 'On the night that I was taken on my Night-Journey [to the heavens], I passed by a group of people scratching their own faces with their nails, so I asked, 'O Gabriel, who are these people?' so he replied, 'These are people who backbit about other people and disparaged their reputations.'[5539]

٤٨٩٧. رسولُ اللهِ ﷺ: مَرَرتُ ليلةَ أُسريَ بي على قومٍ يَخمِشونَ وُجوهَهُم بأظفارِهِم، فقلتُ: يا جَبرَئيلُ، مَن هؤلاءِ؟ فقالَ: هؤلاءِ الذينَ يَغتابونَ الناسَ ويَقَعونَ في أعراضِهِم. ٥٤٩٦

4898. **The Prophet (SAWA) said,** 'Backbiting is worse than adultery', at which he was asked, 'How so?' He replied, 'A man commits adultery, then repents, and Allah pardons him for it, whereas the

٤٨٩٨. عنه ﷺ: الغِيبَةُ أشَدُّ مِن الزِّنا، قيلَ: وكيفَ؟ قالَ: الرجلُ يَزني ثُمّ يَتوبُ فيَتوبُ اللهُ عليهِ، وإنّ صاحِبَ الغِيبَةِ لا يُغفَرُ لَهُ حتّى

backbiter is not forgiven until his victim forgives him.'[5540]

يَغفِرَ لَهُ صاحِبُهُ.٥٤٩٧

4899. **Imām ʿAlī (AS) said,** 'Backbiting is the attempt of one who is incapable [of doing better himself].'[5541]

٤٨٩٩ . الإمامُ عليٌّ ﷺ : الغِيبَةُ جُهدُ العاجِزِ.٥٤٩٨

4900. **Imām al-Ḥusayn (AS) said** to a man who was backbiting about a man in his presence, 'Stop backbiting, for verily it is the food of the dogs of Hell.'[5542]

٤٩٠٠ . الإمامُ الحسينُ ﷺ ـ لِرجُلٍ اغتابَ عِندَهُ رجُلاً ـ : يا هذا كُفَّ عنِ الغِيبَةِ؛ فإنّها إدامُ كِلابِ النارِ.٥٤٩٩

4901. **Imām al-Ṣādiq (AS) said,** 'Do not backbite lest you become a victim of backbiting, and do not dig a hole for your brother lest you fall in it yourself, for you will be paid back whatever you put in.'[5543]

٤٩٠١ . الإمامُ الصّادقُ ﷺ : لا تَغتَبْ فتُغتَبُ، ولا تَحفِرْ لِأخِيكَ حُفرَةً فَتَقَعَ فيها ؛ فإنَّكَ كما تَدينُ تُدانُ.٥٥٠٠

4902. **Imām al-Ṣādiq (AS) said,** 'A man once came and told ʿAlī b. al-Ḥusayn (AS) [i.e. Imām Zayn al-ʿĀbidīn], 'Verily *x* has said that you are astray and that you are an innovator!' So ʿAlī b. al-Ḥusayn (AS) said to him, 'Neither have you observed the right of the man you sat with by transmitting to us what he spoke about, nor have you observed my right by informing me of something about my brother which I would not have known! … Beware of backbiting for verily it is the food of the dogs of Hell, and know that whoever frequently talks about people's faults, the frequency of his backbiting is a witness [to the fact] that he only finds faults in others according to the extent present in himself.'[5544]

٤٩٠٢ . عنه ﷺ : قالَ رَجُلٌ لعليِّ بنِ الحسينِ ﷺ : إنَّ فُلاناً يَنسُبُكَ إلىٰ أنّكَ ضالٌّ مُبتدِعٌ! فقالَ لَهُ عليُّ بنُ الحسينِ ﷺ : ما رَعَيتَ حقَّ مُجالَسَةِ الرجُلِ حيثُ نَقَلتَ إلَينا حَديثَهُ، ولا أدَّيتَ حَقّي حيثُ أبلَغتَني عن أخي ما لَستُ أعلَمُهُ!... إيّاكَ والغِيبَةَ فإنّها إدامُ كِلابِ النارِ، وَاعلَمْ أنّ مَن أكثَرَ مِن ذِكرِ عُيوبِ الناسِ شَهِدَ علَيهِ الإكثارُ أنّهُ إنّما يَطلُبُها بقَدرِ ما فيهِ.٥٥٠١

1453. Backbiting and Faith

١٤٥٣ ـ الغيبَةُ وَالدِّينُ

4903. **The Prophet (SAWA) said,** 'Backbiting eats away at a Muslim man's faith faster than a gangrenous sore can eat away to the inside.'[5545]

٤٩٠٣ . رسولُ اللهِ ﷺ : الغِيبَةُ أسرَعُ في دِينِ الرجُلِ المُسلمِ مِن الآكِلَةِ في جَوفِهِ.٥٥٠٢

4904. **The Prophet (SAWA) said,** 'Whoever backbites a fellow Muslim man or woman, Allah neither accepts his prayer *nor his fasting* for forty days and

٤٩٠٤ . عنه ﷺ : مَنِ اغتابَ مُسلِماً أو مُسلمَةً لم يَقبَلِ اللهُ صَلاتَهُ ولا صيامَهُ أربَعينَ يَوماً ولَيلةً،

nights, until and unless the victim of his backbiting forgives him.'[5546]

إلّا أن يَغفِرَ لَهُ صاحِبُهُ.٥٥٠٣

4905. **The Prophet (SAWA) said,** 'On the Day of Resurrection, a man will be brought forth to stand before Allah, and his book of deeds will be presented to him, and he will not see any of his good deeds therein, upon which he will exclaim, 'My God, this is not my book! For verily I do not see any of my acts of obedience therein?!' So he will be told, 'Verily your Lord neither loses nor forgets [deeds], but your deeds have gone because of your backbiting people.' Then another man will be brought forth, and will be presented his book of deeds, and he will see many acts of obedience recorded therein, and will exclaim, 'My God, this is not my book! For verily I did not perform all these acts of obedience!' and he will be told, 'It is because so and so backbit you, so his deeds have been transferred to you.'[5547]

٤٩٠٥. عنه ﷺ: يُؤتىٰ بأحَدٍ يَومَ القِيامَةِ يُوقَفُ بينَ يَدَيِ اللهِ ويُدفَعُ إلَيهِ كتابُهُ فلا يَرىٰ حَسَناتِهِ، فيقولُ: إلٰهي، ليسَ هذا كتابِي! فإنّي لا أرىٰ فيها طاعَتي؟! فيقالُ لَهُ: إنّ رَبَّكَ لا يَضِلُّ ولا يَنسىٰ، ذَهَبَ عَمَلُكَ بِاغتِيابِ الناسِ. ثُمّ يُؤتىٰ بآخَرَ ويُدفَعُ إلَيهِ كتابُهُ فَيَرىٰ فيهِ طاعاتٍ كثيرَةً، فيقولُ: إلٰهي، ما هذا كتابِي! فإنّي ما عَمِلتُ هذهِ الطّاعاتِ! فيقالُ: لأنَّ فلاناً اغتابَكَ فَدُفِعَت حَسَناتُهُ إلَيكَ.٥٥٠٤

1454. The Meaning of Backbiting

١٤٥٤ـ تَفسيرُ الغيبَةِ

4906. **The Prophet (SAWA) said** to Abū Dharr, 'O Abū Dharr, beware of backbiting, for verily backbiting is worse than adultery…' [Abū Dharr narrates], I asked, 'O Prophet of Allah, and what is backbiting?' to which he replied, 'Your mentioning something about your fellow brother that he would not like.' I asked, 'O Prophet of Allah, and what if the thing mentioned about him was actually true about him?' so he replied, 'Know that if you say something about him that is true then you have indeed backbit about him, and if you what you have said is not true, then you have indeed slandered him.'[5548]

٤٩٠٦ـ رسولُ اللهِ ﷺ ـ لأبي ذرّ ـ: ...يا أباذرٍّ، إيّاكَ والغِيبَةَ؛ فإنَّ الغِيبَةَ أشَدُّ مِن الزِّنا... قلتُ: يارسولَ اللهِ، وما الغِيبَةُ؟ قالَ: ذِكرُكَ أخاكَ بما يَكرَهُ، قتُ: يارسولَ اللهِ، فإن كانَ فيهِ ذاكَ الذي يُذكَرُ بهِ؟ قالَ: اِعلَمْ أنَّكَ إذا ذَكَرتَهُ بما هو فيهِ فقدِ اغتَبتَهُ، وإذا ذَكَرتَهُ بما ليسَ فيهِ فَقَد بَهَتَّهُ.٥٥٠٥

4907. **The Prophet (SAWA) said,** 'Backbiting is to say something about your brother that he would not like.'[5549]

٤٩٠٧. عنه ﷺ: الغِيبَةُ ذِكرُكَ أخاكَ بما يَكرَهُ.٥٥٠٦

4908. It is narrated in *al-Targhīb wa al-Tarhīb*: 'Amr b. Shu'ayb narrated, on the authority of his father,

٤٩٠٨. الترغيب والترهيب عن عَمرِو بن شُعَيبٍ ـ

on the authority of his grandfather that some people spoke about a man in the presence of the Prophet (SAWA), saying, 'He does not eat unless he is fed, and does not go out unless a mount is made ready for him.' The Prophet (SAWA) said, 'You have talked about him behind his back' to which they replied, 'O Prophet of Allah, we have only said what is true!' so he exclaimed, 'It is bad enough to talk about your brother regarding what is true [let alone what is false]!'[5550]

عن أبيهِ عن جدِّهِ ـ: أَنَّهم ذَكَـرُوا عـندَ رسـولِ اللهِ ﷺ رجُلاً فقالوا: لا يَأكُلُ حـتّىٰ يُـطعَمَ، ولا يَرحَلُ حتىٰ يُرحَلَ لَهُ، فقالَ النبيُّ ﷺ: اغتَبتُمُوهُ، فقالوا: يا رسولَ اللهِ، إنّما حَدَّثْنا بما فيهِ! قـال: حَسبُكَ إذا ذَكَرتَ أخاكَ بما فيهِ.[٥٥٠٧]

4909. **Imām al-Kāẓim (AS) said,** 'He who talks about someone behind his back, mentioning what is true about him, and what people already know, then he has not backbit about him, whereas he who talks about someone behind his back about something that is true but that people do not know about, then he has backbit about him.'[5551]

٤٩٠٩. الإمامُ الكاظمُ عليه السلام: مَن ذَكَرَ رجُلاً مِن خَلفِهِ بما هُو فيهِ ممّا عَرَفَهُ الناسُ لم يَغتَبْهُ، ومَن ذَكَرَهُ مِن خَلفِهِ بـما هُـو فـيهِ مـمّا لايَـعرِفُهُ النـاسُ اغتابَهُ.[٥٥٠٨]

1455. People whom One is Allowed to Backbite

١٤٥٥ ـ مَن يَجوزُ اغتِيابُهُ

4910. **The Prophet (SAWA) said,** 'Four types of people are such that talking about them behind their backs is not considered backbiting: the immoral person who makes a public display of his immorality; the dishonest leader who, even if you were to be good to would not appreciate you and if you were to be bad to would not forgive you; those who joke about their [and others'] mothers; and one who is a dissenter, who defames my community, and draws his sword against it.'[5552]

٤٩١٠. رسولُ اللهِ ﷺ: أربَعةٌ لَيست غِيبَتُهُم غِيبَةً: الفاسِقُ المُعلِنُ بِفِسقِهِ، والإمامُ الكَذّابُ إن أحسَنتَ لم يَشكُرْ وإن أسَأتَ لم يَغفِرْ، والمُتَفكِّهونَ بالأُمَّهاتِ، والخارِجُ عنِ الجَماعَةِ الطاعِنُ علىٰ أُمَّتِي الشاهِرُ علَيها بسَيفِهِ.[٥٥٠٩]

4911. **The Prophet (SAWA) said,** 'Until when will you sidestep talking about the impudent person?! Disgrace him [through disclosing his insolent acts] so that people may be on their guard against him.'[5553]

٤٩١١. عنه ﷺ: حتّىٰ مَتىٰ تَرعَوُونَ عن ذِكرِ الفاجِرِ؟! اِهتِكُوهُ حتّىٰ يَحذَرَهُ الناسُ.[٥٥١٠]

1456. Listening to Backbiting

١٤٥٦ـسَماعُ الغيبَةِ

4912. **Imām ʿAlī (AS) said,** 'The one who listens to backbiting is as [bad as] the backbiter.'[5554]

٤٩١٢ . الإمامُ عليٌّ عليه السلام : السـامِعُ لِـلغِيبَةِ كالمُغتابِ.[٥٥١١]

4913. **Imām ʿAlī (AS)** saw a man backbiting someone in the presence of his son, al-Ḥasan (AS), to whom he said, 'O my son, steer your hearing clear of such a person, for verily he took the most repulsive thing from his mind and poured it into yours!'[5555]

٤٩١٣ . عنه عليه السلام ـوقد نَظَرَ إلىٰ رجُلٍ يَغتابُ رجُلاً عندَ ابنِهِ الحسنِ عليه السلام ـ: يابُنَيَّ، نَزِّهْ سَمعَكَ عن مِثلِ هذا؛ فإنّهُ نَظَرَ إلىٰ أخبَثِ ما في وِعائهِ فَأفرَغَهُ في وِعائكَ![٥٥١٢]

4914. **Imām Zayn al-ʿĀbidīn (AS) said,** 'The right of the ears is to keep them pure from listening to backbiting, and from that which is unlawful to listen to.'[5556]

٤٩١٤ . الإمامُ زينُ العابدينَ عليه السلام : حقُّ السَّمعِ تَنزيهُهُ عن سَماعِ الغِيبَةِ، وسَماعِ ما لايَحِلُّ سَماعُهُ.[٥٥١٣]

1457. The Reward for Deterring Backbiting

١٤٥٧ـثَوابُ رَدِّ الغيبَةِ

4915. **The Prophet (SAWA) said,** 'Whoever does a good service to his fellow brother by deterring people from talking behind his back in a gathering where he hears them backbiting him, Allah will repel from him a thousand types of evil in this world as well as in the Hereafter.'[5557]

٤٩١٥ . رسولُ اللهِ صلى الله عليه وآله : مَن تَطَوَّلَ علىٰ أخِيهِ في غِيبةٍ سَمِعَها فيهِ في مَجلِسٍ فَرَدَّها عَنهُ، رَدَّ اللهُ عَنهُ ألفَ بابٍ مِن السُّوءِ فِي الدنيا والآخِرَةِ.[٥٥١٤]

4916. **The Prophet (SAWA) said,** 'He in whose presence a fellow Muslim brother is talked about behind his back, and who does not defend him despite having the ability to do so, Allah disgraces him in this world as well as in the Hereafter.'[5558]

٤٩١٦ . عنه صلى الله عليه وآله : مَن اُغتِيبَ عِندَهُ أخوهُ المسلمُ، فاستَطاعَ نَصرَهُ فلم يَنصُرْهُ، خَذَلَهُ اللهُ فِي الدنيا والآخِرَةِ.[٥٥١٥]

(See also: GOOD REPUTE: section 1245)

(اُنظر) العِرض: باب ١٢٤٥.

1458. The Penance for Backbiting

١٤٥٨ـكَفّارَةُ الاغتِيابِ

4917. **The Prophet (SAWA)** was asked about the penance for backbiting, to which he replied, 'You must seek Allah's forgiveness on behalf of the one

٤٩١٧ . رسولُ اللهِ صلى الله عليه وآله ـوقد سُئلَ عن كَفّارَةِ

you have talked about every time you remember him.'[5559]

الاغتياب ـ: تستغفرُ اللهَ لِمَن اغتبتَهُ كُلَّما ذكَرتَهُ.٥٥١٦

4918. **The Prophet (SAWA) said,** 'When one of you backbites about his fellow brother, he must seek forgiveness from Allah for that is penance for it.'[5560]

٤٩١٨ . عنه ﷺ : إذا اغتابَ أحَدُكُم أخاهُ فليَستغفرِ اللهَ ؛ فإنّها كفّارَةٌ لَهُ.٥٥١٧

311

POSSESSIVENESS[5561]

الغَيرَة

1459. The Praise of Possessiveness

١٤٥٩ـ مدحُ الغَيرةِ

4919. **The Prophet (SAWA) said,** 'Verily possessiveness is part of faith.'[5562]

٤٩١٩ . رسولُ اللهِ ﷺ: إنّ الغَيرَةَ مِن الإيمانِ.٥٥١٨

4920. **The Prophet (SAWA) said,** 'My father Abraham [i.e. the prophet] was very possessive and I am even more possessive than him. Allah abases the one who has no sense of possessiveness from among the believers.'[5563]

٤٩٢٠ . عنه ﷺ: كانَ إبراهيمُ أبي غَيوراً وأنا أغيَرُ مِنهُ ، وأرغَمَ اللهُ أنفَ مَن لا يَغارُ مِن المؤمنينَ.٥٥١٩

4921. **The Prophet (SAWA) said,** 'Verily Allah, most High, is possessive, and verily the believer is possessive. Allah's possessiveness over a believer is when he approaches that which Allah has prohibited him from.'[5564]

٤٩٢١ . عنه ﷺ : إنّ اللهَ تعالى يَغارُ وإنّ المؤمنَ يَغارُ ، وغَيرَةُ اللهِ أن يَأتِيَ المؤمنُ ما حَرَّمَ اللهُ علَيهِ.٥٥٢٠

4922. **The Prophet (SAWA) said,** 'Verily the fragrance of Paradise can be smelt from a distance of five hundred years, but neither the one who is insolent towards his parents not the cuckold will ever smell it.' When asked, 'O Prophet of Allah, what is a cuckold?' he replied, 'It is one whose wife commits adultery with his knowledge of it.'[5565]

٤٩٢٢ . عنه ﷺ : إنّ الجَنّةَ لَتوجَدُ ريحُها مِن مَسيرَةِ خَمسِمائةِ عامٍ ، ولا يَجِدُها عاقٌّ ولا دَيُّوثٌ . قيلَ : يا رسولَ اللهِ ، وما الدَّيُّوثُ ؟ قالَ : الذي تَزني امرأتُهُ وهُو يَعلَمُ بها.٥٥٢١

4923. **Imām 'Alī (AS) said,** 'The worth of a man is in proportion to his ambition ... his courage is

٤٩٢٣ . الإمامُ عليٌّ ﷺ : قَدرُ الرجُلِ على قَدرِ

in proportion to his self-esteem, and his chastity is in proportion to his possessiveness [i.e. over his own wife].'[5566]

هِمَّتِهِ... وشَجاعَتُهُ علىٰ قَدرِ أنَفَتِهِ، وعِفَّتُهُ علىٰ قَدرِ غَيرَتِهِ.[٥٥٢٢]

4924. **Imām ʿAlī (AS) said,** 'A man who is possessive [over his own wife] will never commit adultery.'[5567]

٤٩٢٤. عنه عليه السلام: ما زَنىٰ غَيورٌ قطُّ.[٥٥٢٣]

4925. **Imām ʿAlī (AS) said,** 'Verily Allah is possessive over the believer, so let him who is not possessive become possessive [through a sense of self-worth], for verily he has a degenerative heart.'[5568]

٤٩٢٥. عنه عليه السلام: إنَّ اللهَ يَغارُ للمؤمِنِ، فَلْيَغَرْ مَن لايَغارُ؛ فإنّهُ مَنكوسُ القَلبِ.[٥٥٢٤]

4926. **Imām al-Ṣādiq (AS) said,** 'Verily Allah, Blessed and most High, is very possessive and loves every possessive one, and as a result of His possessiveness [over His servants], he has prohibited indecent acts, both those done in public as well as those done in secret.'[5569]

٤٩٢٦. الإمامُ الصّادقُ عليه السلام: إنّ اللهَ تباركَ وتعالىٰ غَيورٌ يُحِبُّ كُلَّ غَيورٍ، ولِغَيرَتِهِ حَرَّمَ الفَواحِشَ ظاهِرَها وباطِنَها.[٥٥٢٥]

1460. Censure of being Jealous or Over-Possessive over One Another in the Wrong Situation

١٤٦٠ـ ذمُّ التَّغايُرِ في غيرِ مَوضِعِ الغَيرةِ

4927. **Prophet Solomon (AS) said** to his son, 'O son, do not exceed your possessiveness over your family and you will accuse them of wrongdoing, even though they are innocent.'[5570]

٤٩٢٧. سليمانُ عليه السلام لِابنِهِ: يا بُنَيّ لا تُكثِرِ الغَيرَةَ عَلىٰ أهلِكَ فَتُرمىٰ بِالسّوءِ مِن أجلِكَ وإن كانَت بَريئَةً.[٥٥٢٦]

4928. **The Prophet (SAWA) said,** 'There is possessiveness that Allah likes, and possessiveness that Allah dislikes. That which He likes is the possessiveness during doubt or misgiving [about one's wife], and the [over]possessiveness He dislikes is in a situation where there is no [reason to] doubt.'[5571]

٤٩٢٨. رسولُ اللهِ صلى الله عليه وآله: مِن الغَيرَةِ ما يُحِبُّ اللهُ، ومِنها ما يَكرَهُ اللهُ، فأمّا ما يُحِبُّ فالغَيرَةُ فِي الرِّيبةِ، وأمّا ما يَكرَهُ فالغَيرَةُ في غيرِ الرِّيبةِ.[٥٥٢٧]

4929. **The Prophet (SAWA) said,** 'There are two kinds of possessiveness in which Allah likes one of them and dislikes the other: Possessiveness over being accused, which Allah likes, and possessiveness

٤٩٢٩. رسولُ اللهِ صلى الله عليه وآله: غَيرَتانِ أحَدُهُما يُحِبُّهَا اللهُ وَالاُخرىٰ يُبغِضُهَا اللهُ: الغَيرَةُ مِنَ الرِّيبَةِ يُحِبُّهَا اللهُ وَالغَيرَةُ مِن غَيرِ الرِّيبَةِ يُبغِضُهَا

without accusation, which Allah the Exalted dislikes.'[5572]

اللهُ عَزَّوجَلَّ.[٥٥٢٨]

4930. **Imām ʿAlī (AS) said** in his will to his son, al-Ḥasan (AS), 'Beware of being over possessive [of your wife] in a situation that does not necessitate it, for verily that will lead a wife of sound character from among them to become weak.'[5573]

٤٩٣٠. الإمامُ عليٌّ ﷺ ـ فـي وصـيَّتِهِ لابـنِهِ الحسنِ ﷺ ـ: إيّاكَ والتَّـغايُرَ فـي غـيرِ مَـوضِعِ الغَيرَةِ، فإنَّ ذلكَ يَـدعُو الصَّـحيحَةَ مِـنهُنَّ إلَـى السَّقَمِ، ولكن أحكِمْ أمـرَهُنَّ فـإن رَأيتَ عَـيباً فَعَجِّلِ النَّكيرَ علَى الكبيرِ والصغيرِ.[٥٥٢٩، ٥٥٣٠]

4931. **Imām al-Ṣādiq (AS) said,** 'There is no jealous possessiveness [warranted] in what is lawful ...'[5574]

٤٩٣١. الإمامُ الصّادقُ ﷺ: لا غَـيرَةَ فـي الحَلالِ....[٥٥٣١]

312

TRIAL AND TEMPTATION

الفِتنَة

1461. Trial and Temptation

١٤٦١ـ الفِتنَةِ

"Do people imagine that they will be left off (on their own) saying: 'We believe!' and they will not be tried? And indeed We did try those before them, so God certainly knows those who are true, and certainly He knows the liars."[5575]

﴿أحَسِبَ النَّاسُ أنْ يُتْرَكُوا أَنْ يَقُولُوا آمَنَّا وَهُمْ لا يُفْتَنُونَ * وَلَقَدْ فَتَنَّا الَّذِينَ مِنْ قَبْلِهِمْ فَلَيَعْلَمَنَّ اللهُ الَّذِينَ صَدَقُوا وَلَيَعْلَمَنَّ الْكاذِبِينَ﴾.[٥٥٣٢]

"See they not that they are tried once or twice in every year yet they do not turn (to God), and nor do they remember."[5576]

﴿أوَلا يَرَوْنَ أَنَّهُمْ يُفْتَنُونَ فِي كُلِّ عامٍ مَرَّةً أَوْ مَرَّتَيْنِ ثُمَّ لا يَتُوبُونَ وَلَا هُمْ يَذَّكَّرُونَ﴾.[٥٥٣٣]

(See also: Qur'an 7:155)

(أنظر) الأعراف: ١٥٥.

4932. **Muʿammar b. Khallād said,** 'I heard Imām al-Riḍā (AS) say: *"Alif, lām, mīm. Do people imagine that they will be left off (on their own) saying: "We believe!" and they will not be tried"*, and he then asked me, 'What is trial?' I said, 'May my soul be sacrificed for you, what I know is that it is to be tested in religion.' He said, 'They [the believers] will be tried the way gold is tried', he then said, 'They will be purified the way gold is purified.'[5577]

٤٩٣٢. مُعمَّر بنِ خَلّادٍ: سَمِعتُ أبا الحَسَنِ ﷺ يـقولُ: ﴿الم * أحَسِبَ الناسُ أنْ يُتْرَكُوا أنْ يَقُولُوا آمَنّا وهُم لا يُفْتَنُونَ﴾[٥٥٣٤] ثُمّ قالَ لي: ما الفِتنَةُ؟ قلتُ: جُعِلتُ فداكَ الذي عِندَنا الفِتنَةُ في الدِّينِ، فقالَ: يُفتَنُونَ كما يُفتَنُ الذَّهبُ، ثُمّ قالَ: يُخلَصُونَ كما يُخلَصُ الذَّهبُ.[٥٥٣٥]

1462. Kinds of Trial

١٤٦٢ ـ أنواعُ الفِتَنِ

"And know that your wealth and your children are a test [temptation], and that, God, with Him is a mighty reward."[5578]

﴿وَاعْلَمُوا أنَّما أمْوالُكُمْ وَأوْلادُكُمْ فِتْنَةٌ وَأنَّ اللهَ عِنْدَهُ أجْرٌ عَظِيمٌ﴾.[٥٥٣٦]

4933. **The Prophet (SAWA) said,** 'There are three tempting trials: beautiful hair, a beautiful face, and a beautiful voice.'[5579]

٤٩٣٣. رسولُ اللهِ ﷺ: ثلاثٌ فاتِناتٌ: الشَّعرُ الحَسَنُ، والوَجهُ الحَسَنُ، والصَّوتُ الحَسَنُ.[٥٥٣٧]

4934. **The Prophet (SAWA) said,** 'I fear for you the trials that are in good times more than in bad times. You have been struck with tests of bad times and you have endured them with patience, while verily the world remains sweet and luxuriant [to you].'[5580]

٤٩٣٤. عنه ﷺ: لَأنا لِفِتنَةِ السَّرّاءِ أخوَفُ علَيكُم مِن فِتنَةِ الضَّرّاءِ، إنّكُمُ ابتُلِيتُم بِفِتنَةِ الضَّرّاءِ فَصَبَرتُم، وإنّ الدنيا حُلوَةٌ خَضِرَةٌ.[٥٥٣٨]

4935. **Imām ʿAlī (AS) said,** 'Trials are of three kinds: love of women [unlawfully], and this is the sword of the devil; drinking of wine, and this is the snare of the devil; and the love of dinars and dirhams, which is the arrow of the devil. So those who love women will not benefit from life, and those who love drinking will be barred from Heaven, and those who love the dinar and dirham are slaves of the world.'[5581]

٤٩٣٥. الإمامُ عليٌّ عليه السلام: الفِتَنُ ثلاثٌ: حُبُّ النِّساءِ وهُو سَيفُ الشَّيطانِ، وشُربُ الخَمرِ وهُو فَخُّ الشَّيطانِ، وحُبُّ الدِّينارِ والدِّرهَمِ وهُو سَهمُ الشَّيطانِ، فَمَن أحَبَّ النِّساءَ لم يَنتَفِعْ بعَيشِهِ، ومَن أحَبَّ الأشرِبَةَ حَرُمَت علَيهِ الجَنّةُ، ومَن أحَبَّ الدِّينارَ والدِّرهَمَ فهُو عَبدُ الدنيا.[٥٥٣٩]

4936. **Imām ʿAlī (AS)** who was riding, said to a person by the name of Ḥarb who was walking with him, 'Go back, for the walking of someone like you with me is a trial for a governor and a [source of] humiliation for the believer.'[5582]

٤٩٣٦. عنه عليه السلام ـ لرجُلٍ يُسَمّىٰ حَرباً يَمشي مَعهُ وهُو راكِبٌ ـ: ارجِعْ، فإنَّ مَشيَ مِثلِكَ مَع مِثلِي فِتنَةٌ للوالي، ومَذَلَّةٌ للمؤمنِ.[٥٥٤٠]

1463. Those who are Cleared from Trials

١٤٦٣ ـ مَن تَنجَلي عَنهُمُ الفِتَنُ

4937. **The Prophet (SAWA) said,** 'Blessed are the sincere. They are the lanterns of guidance, and all dark trials are cleared away from them.'[5583]

٤٩٣٧. رسولُ اللهِ ﷺ: طُوبىٰ لِلمُخلِصينَ، أُولئكَ مَصابيحُ الهُدىٰ تَنجَلي عَنهُم كلُّ فِتنَةٍ ظَلماءَ.[٥٥٤١]

4938. **The Prophet (SAWA) said,** 'There will come a time with troubles and trials where a

٤٩٣٨. عنه ﷺ: سَتَكُونُ فِتَنٌ يُصبِحُ الرجُلُ فيها

person will rise in the morning a believer and turn a disbeliever in the evening, save those whom Allah, most High, revive with knowledge.'[5584]

مؤمِناً ويُمسِي كافِراً، إلّا مَن أحـياهُ اللهُ تـعالىٰ بالعِلمِ.[٥٥٤٢]

4939. **Imām ʿAlī (AS) said,** 'Know that those who are wary of their duty to Allah will find through Him a way out of the troubles of trials, and a light from darkness.'[5585]

٤٩٣٩. الإمامُ عليٌّ ﷺ: اعلَمُوا أنَّهُ مَن يَتَّقِ اللهَ يَجعَلْ لَهُ مَخرجاً مِن الفِتَنِ، ونوراً مِن الظُّلَمِ.[٥٥٤٣]

1464. Miscellaneous

١٤٦٤ـ النَّوادِرُ

4940. **The Prophet (SAWA) said,** 'Know that my community after me will become swathed with trials like parts of a dark night. At that time a person will be a believer in the morning and a disbeliever in the evening; he will sleep a believer and wake up a disbeliever. Groups will sell their religion for a small offer of the world.'[5586]

٤٩٤٠. رسولُ اللهِ ﷺ: لَيَغشَيَنَّ أُمَّتِي مِن بَعدي فِتَنٌ كَقِطَعِ الليلِ المُظلِمِ، يُصبحُ الرجُلُ فيها مؤمِناً ويُمسِي كافِراً، ويُمسِي مؤمِناً ويُصبحُ كافِراً، يَبيعُ أقوامٌ دِينَهُم بعَرَضٍ مِن الدنيا قَليلٍ.[٥٥٤٤]

4941. **Imām ʿAlī (AS) said,** 'He who ignites the fire of trouble will become its firewood.'[5587]

٤٩٤١. الإمامُ عليٌّ ﷺ: مَن شَبَّ نارَ الفِتنَةِ كانَ وَقوداً لها.[٥٥٤٥]

4942. **Imām ʿAlī (AS) said,** 'A brutal oppressing governor is better than a continuous unrest.'[5588]

٤٩٤٢. عنه ﷺ: والٍ ظَلومٌ غَشومٌ خَيرٌ مِن فِتنَةٍ تَدُومُ.[٥٥٤٦]

4943. **Imām ʿAlī (AS) said,** 'You should be at the time of trouble like a baby camel, neither can it be mounted [and overcome as a result], nor can it be milked [and taken advantage of].'[5589]

٤٩٤٣. عنه ﷺ: كُنْ في الفتنَةِ كَابنِ اللَّبونِ؛ لا ظَهرٌ فيُركَبَ، ولاضَرعٌ فيُحلَبَ (فَيُحتَلَبَ).[٥٥٤٧]

313

THE VERDICT[5590]

الفتوىٰ

1465. Those who Give Verdicts of their Own Opinion to People

١٤٦٥ـ مَن أفتَى النّاسَ بِرَأيِهِ

4944. **The Prophet (SAWA) said,** 'The most audacious from among you at giving verdicts will

٤٩٤٤. رسولُ اللهِ ﷺ: أجرَؤكُم علَى الفَتوىٰ

be the most hasty from among you to enter the Hellfire.'[5591]

أجرَؤكُم علَى النارِ.٥٥٤٨

4945. **Imām al-Bāqir (AS) said,** 'If we were to give verdicts to people according to our opinions and whims, we would be among those who perish. But we give them verdicts based on mere reports handed down from the Prophet (SAWA) and the principles of knowledge that we have, which we have inherited from our forefathers…'[5592]

٤٩٤٥. الإمامُ الباقرُ ﵇: لو كنّا نُفتي النّاسَ بِرأينا وهَوانا لَكُنّا مِنَ الهالِكينَ، ولكِنّا نُفتيهِم بآثارٍ مِن رسولِ اللهِ ﷺ وأُصولِ عِلمٍ عِندَنا، نَتَوارَثُها كابِراً عن كابِرٍ....٥٥٤٩

4946. **Imām al-Ṣādiq (AS) said,** 'Whoever gives a verdict to people from their opinion submits to that which they have no knowledge of, and whoever submits to that which he does not have knowledge of is opposing Allah as he permits and prohibits what he does not have knowledge of.'[5593]

٤٩٤٦. الإمامُ الصّادقُ ﵇: مَن أفتَى النّاسَ بِرَأيِهِ فَقَد دانَ بِما لا يَعلَمُ، ومَن دانَ بِما لا يَعلَمُ فَقَد ضادَّ اللهَ حَيثُ أحَلَّ وحَرَّمَ فِيما لا يَعلَمُ.٥٥٥٠

4947. **Imām al-Ṣādiq (AS) said,** 'Flee from a verdict the way you would flee from a lion, and do not let your neck be a bridge for others.'[5594]

٤٩٤٧. الإمامُ الصّادقُ ﵇: اُهرُبْ مِنَ الفُتيا هَرَبَكَ مِنَ الأسَدِ، ولا تَجعَلْ رَقَبَتَكَ لِلنّاسِ جِسراً.٥٥٥١

(See also: OPINION: section 795)

(اُنظُر) الرأي: باب ٧٩٥.

1466. The Permissibility for a Scholar to Issue a Verdict

١٤٦٦ - جَوازُ الإفتاءِ لِلعالِمِ

4948. **Imām ʿAlī (AS),** in what he wrote to Qutham b. ʿAbbās said, 'Sit for them in the afternoon, and give verdicts to the questioner, teach the ignorant, and discuss with the knowledgeable.'[5595]

٤٩٤٨. الإمامُ عليٌّ ﵇ - فيما كَتَبَ إلى قُثَمَ بنِ العبّاسِ -: واجلِسْ لَهُمُ العَصرَينِ، فَأفتِ المُستَفتيَ، وعَلِّمِ الجاهِلَ، وذاكِرِ العالِمَ.٥٥٥٢

4949. **Imām al-Bāqir (AS),** speaking to Abān b. Taghlib said, 'Sit in the mosque of Madina and give verdicts to the people, for I love to see the likes of you among my followers.'[5596]

٤٩٤٩. الإمامُ الباقرُ ﵇ - لأبانِ بنِ تَغلِبَ -: اِجلِسْ في مَجلِسِ٥٥٥٣ المَدينةِ وأفتِ النّاسَ؛ فإنّي أُحِبُّ أن يُرى في شيعَتي مِثلُكَ.٥٥٥٤

314

OBSCENE LANGUAGE

الفُحشُ

1467. Caution Against the Use of Obscene Language

١٤٦٧ ـ التَّحذيرُ مِنَ الفُحشِ

4950. **The Prophet (SAWA) said,** 'No sooner does obscene language accompany something than it disgraces it, and no sooner does modesty accompany something than it adorns it.'[5597]

٤٩٥٠ . رسولُ اللهِ ﷺ : ما كانَ الفُحشُ في شيءٍ قَطُّ إلّا شانَهُ ، ولا كانَ الحَياءُ في شيءٍ قَطُّ إلّا زانَهُ .[٥٥٥٥]

4951. **The Prophet (SAWA) said,** 'Allah has prohibited Heaven to those who use obscenity, vulgarity, lack shame, and are not concerned about what they say and what is said to them.'[5598]

٤٩٥١ . عنه ﷺ : إنّ اللهَ حَرَّمَ الجَنَّةَ على كُلِّ فَحّاشٍ بَذِيءٍ، قَليلِ الحَياءِ، لا يُبالِي ما قالَ ولا ما قيلَ لَهُ .[٥٥٥٦]

4952. **The Prophet (SAWA) said,** 'The most evil of the servants of Allah are those whose company is abhorred [by people] because of their obscenity.'[5599]

٤٩٥٢ . عنه ﷺ : إنّ مِن شَرِّ عِبادِ اللهِ مَن تُكرَهُ مُجالَسَتُهُ لِفُحشِهِ .[٥٥٥٧]

4953. **Imām ʿAlī (AS) said,** 'A person of dignity would never use obscene language.'[5600]

٤٩٥٣ . الإمامُ عليٌّ عليه السلام : ما أفحَشَ كريمٌ قَطُّ .[٥٥٥٨]

4954. **Imām al-Bāqir (AS) said,** 'Allah hates the user of obscene language and the one who is shameless with it.'[5601]

٤٩٥٤ . الإمامُ الباقرُ عليه السلام : إنَّ اللهَ يُبغِضُ الفاحِشَ المُتَفَحِّشَ .[٥٥٥٩]

4955. **Imām al-Bāqir (AS) said,** 'Say unto people the best of what you would like them to say to you, for Allah hates the curser, swearer, and slanderer of believers, the user of obscene language and to do it shamelessly, and the importunate beggar.'[5602]

٤٩٥٥ . عنه عليه السلام : قُولوا للناسِ أحسَنَ ما تُحِبُّونَ أن يُقالَ لَكُم ؛ فإنَّ اللهَ يُبغِضُ اللَّعّانَ السَّبّابَ الطَّعّانَ علَى المؤمنينَ، الفاحِشَ المُتَفَحِّشَ، السائلَ المُلحِفَ .[٥٥٦٠]

4956. **Imām al-Bāqir (AS) said,** 'The weapon of the wicked is foul language.'[5603]

٤٩٥٦ . عنه عليه السلام : سِلاحُ اللِّئامِ قَبيحُ الكلامِ .[٥٥٦١]

4957. **Imām al-Ṣādiq (AS) said,** 'Obscene language, foulness, and impudence are all from hypocrisy.'[5604]

٤٩٥٧. الإمامُ الصّادقُ ﷺ: الفُحشُ والبَذاءُ والسَّلاطَةُ مِن النِّفاقِ.٥٦٠٤

4958. **Imām al-Ṣādiq (AS) said,** 'A person whose [foul] tongue people dread is in the Fire [i.e. his place is the Fire].'[5605]

٤٩٥٨. عنه ﷺ: مَن خافَ النّاسُ لِسانَهُ فهُو في النّارِ.٥٦٠٥

315

PRIDE

الفَخرُ

1468. Reprehension of Showing Pride

١٤٦٨ـ ذَمُّ التَّفاخُرِ

"Know that the life of this world is just play and diversion, and glitter, and mutual vainglory among you."[5606]

﴿اعْلَمُوا أَنَّما الحَياةُ الدُّنْيا لَعِبٌ وَلَهْوٌ وَزِينَةٌ وَتَفاخُرٌ بَيْنَكُمْ﴾.٥٦٠٦

"Indeed Allah does not like any swaggering braggart."[5607]

﴿إنَّ اللهَ لا يُحِبُّ كُلَّ مُخْتالٍ فَخُورٍ﴾.٥٦٠٧

(See also: Qur'an 4:36; 11:10; 57:23)

(أنظر) النساء: ٣٦ و هود: ١٠ والحديد: ٢٣.

4959. **The Prophet (SAWA) said,** 'Allah revealed unto me that we should be humble, so that nobody shows pride over anybody else, and no one intimidates another.'[5608]

٤٩٥٩. رسولُ اللهِ ﷺ: إنّ اللهَ أوحى إلَيَّ أن تواضَعوا، حتّى لا يَفخَرَ أحَدٌ على أحَدٍ، ولا يَبغي أحَدٌ على أحَدٍ.٥٦٠٨

4960. **The Prophet (SAWA) said,** 'The bane of [noble] lineage is pride of it.'[5609]

٤٩٦٠. عنه ﷺ: آفَةُ الحَسَبِ الافتِخارُ والعُجبُ.٥٦٠٩

4961. **Imām ʿAlī (AS) said,** 'There are two things that have ruined people: fear of poverty and going after pride.'[5610]

٤٩٦١. الإمامُ عليٌّ ﷺ: أهلَكَ النّاسَ اثنانِ: خَوفُ الفقرِ، وطَلَبُ الفَخرِ.٥٦١٠

4962. **Imām ʿAlī (AS) said,** 'Let go of your pride, put down your arrogance, and remember your grave.'[5611]

٤٩٦٢. عنه ﷺ: ضَعْ فَخرَكَ، واحطُطْ كِبرَكَ، واذكُرْ قَبرَكَ.٥٦١١

4963. **Imām ʿAlī (AS) said,** 'There is no stupidity greater than vanity.'[5612]

٤٩٦٣. عنه ﷺ: لا حُمقَ أعظَمُ مِن الفَخرِ.٥٦١٢

4964. **Imām ʿAlī (AS) said,** 'The worst state of the rulers in the eyes of righteous people is for them to be assumed to love pride and be regarded as haughty.'[5613]

٤٩٦٤. عنه عليه السلام: إنَّ مِن أسخَفِ حالاتِ الوُلاةِ عندَ صالِحِ النـاسِ، أن يُـظَنَّ بِـهِم حُبُّ الفَـخرِ، ويُوضَعَ أمرُهُم علَى الكِبرِ. ٥٥٧١

4965. **Imām al-Riḍā (AS) said,** 'The Commander of the Faithful [Imām ʿAlī] (AS) visited Ṣaʿṣaʿa b. Ṣūḥān when he was sick, so when he wanted to leave he stood up and said, 'O Ṣaʿṣaʿa, do not display pride in front of your brothers that I visited you, and fear Allah.'[5614]

٤٩٦٥. الإمامُ الرضا عليه السلام: إنَّ أميرَ المؤمنينَ عليه السلام عادَ صَعصَعةَ بنَ صُوحانَ في مَرَضِهِ، فلمّا قـامَ مِـن عندِهِ قالَ: يا صَعصَعةُ، لا تَفتَخِرَنَّ علىٰ إخوانِكَ بعِيادَتي إيّاكَ واتَّقِ اللهَ. ٥٥٧٢

1469. That Which Prevents Pride

١٤٦٩ ـ ما يَمنَعُ مِنَ الفَخرِ

4966. **Imām ʿAlī (AS) said,** 'What is it with the son of Adam [human being] and pride?! His beginning is a sperm and his end is a carcass. He cannot sustain himself, nor can he repel death.'[5615]

٤٩٦٦. الإمامُ عليٌّ عليه السلام: ما لابنِ آدمَ والفَخرِ؟! أوَّلُهُ نُطفَةٌ، وآخِرُهُ جِيفَةٌ، ولا يَرزُقُ نفسَهُ، ولا يَدفَعُ حَتفَهُ. ٥٥٧٣

4967. **Imām Zayn al-ʿĀbidīn (AS) said,** 'It is surprising to see an arrogant and proud person who yesterday was but a sperm and tomorrow will be but a carcass.'[5616]

٤٩٦٧. الإمامُ زينُ العابدينَ عليه السلام: عَجَباً للمُتَكبِّرِ الفَخورِ الذي كانَ بالأمسِ نُـطفَةً ثُـمّ هُـو غَـداً جِيفَةٌ! ٥٥٧٤

1470. The Prophet's Conduct When Mentioning a Virtue About Himself

١٤٧٠ ـ سيرة النَّبيِّ إذا ذكر لِنَفسِهِ فَضِيلَةً

4968. **Imām ʿAlī (AS) said,** 'When the Prophet (SAWA) would mention a merit of himself, he would say, 'And with no pride'.[5617]

٤٩٦٨. الإمامُ عليٌّ عليه السلام: لقد كانَ رسولُ اللهِ ﷺ إذا ذَكَرَ لنفسِهِ فضيلةً قالَ: ولا فَخرَ. ٥٥٧٥

1471. That Which One Should be Proud of

١٤٧١ ـ ما يَنبَغي الفَخرُ بِهِ

4969. **The Prophet (SAWA) said,** 'Poverty is my pride.'[5618]

٤٩٦٩. رسولُ اللهِ ﷺ: الفَقرُ فَخرِي. ٥٥٧٦

4970. **Imām al-Ṣādiq (AS) said,** 'There are three things that are the pride of a believer and his ornament in this world and the Hereafter: prayer at the end of the night [*night vigil*], his despair of

٤٩٧٠. الإمامُ الصّادقُ عليه السلام: ثـلاثٌ هُـنَّ فَـخرُ المؤمنِ وزَينُهُ في الدنيا والآخِرَةِ: الصـلاةُ فـي

[possessing] that which others own, and his allegiance to the Imām from the progeny of Muḥammad (SAWA).'[5619]

آجِرِ اللّيلِ، وَيأسُهُ مِمّا في أيدي الناسِ، ووَلايَتُهُ الإمامَ مِن آلِ محمّدٍ ﷺ.[٥٥٧٧]

316

THE PERSIANS

الفُرسُ

1472. The Persians and Faith

١٤٧٢ ـ الفُرسُ وَالإيمانُ

4971. **The Prophet (SAWA) said,** 'The people who have the greatest portion of Islam are the people of Persia.'[5620]

٤٩٧١. رسولُ اللهِ ﷺ: أعظَمُ الناسِ نَصيباً في الإسلامِ أهلُ فارِسَ.[٥٥٧٨]

4972. **The Prophet (SAWA),** when he recited the verse *"and if you turn away He will replace you with another people, and they will not be like you"*, some people asked him (SAWA), 'Who are those who will replace us?' He replied, putting his hand on the shoulder of Salmān, 'This man and his people.'[5621]

٤٩٧٢. سنن الترمذي: تلا رسولُ اللهِ ﷺ هذه الآية يوماً: ﴿وإنْ تَتَوَلَّوا يَسْتَبْدِلْ قَوْماً غَيْرَكُمْ ثُمَّ لايَكُونوا أمْثالَكُمْ﴾ قالوا: ومَن يستبدِل بِنا؟ قال: فضربَ رسولُ اللهِ ﷺ على مَنكِبِ سلمانَ ثمّ قالَ: هذا وقومُهُ.[٥٥٧٩]

4973. **The Prophet (SAWA),** when asked about the verse, *"O you who have faith! Should any of you desert his religion, Allah will soon bring a people whom He loves and who love Him"*, said, patting the shoulder of Salmān, 'He and his people.' He then said, 'If religion was suspended from the stars, some men of Persia would take it.'[5622]

٤٩٧٣. مجمع البيان: رُوِيَ أنّ النبيّ ﷺ سُئلَ عن هذهِ الآيةِ: ﴿يا أيُّها الّذينَ آمَنوا مَنْ يَرْتَدَّ مِنكُم عَن دِينِهِ فسَوفَ يَأتِي اللهُ بقَومٍ يُحِبُّهُم ويُحِبُّونَهُ...﴾ فضَرَبَ بيَده على عاتِقِ سلمانَ فقالَ ـ: هذا وذَوُوهُ... لو كانَ الدِّينُ مُعَلّقاً بالثُّرَيّا لَتَناوَلَهُ رِجالٌ مِن أبناءِ فارِسَ.[٥٥٨٠]

4974. **The Prophet (SAWA) said,** 'If knowledge was suspended from the skies, the men of Persia would reach it.'[5623]

٤٩٧٤. رسولُ اللهِ ﷺ: لو كانَ العِلمُ بالثُّرَيّا لَتَناوَلَهُ رِجالٌ مِن فارِسَ.[٥٥٨١]

4975. **The Prophet (SAWA) said,** 'If religion was suspended in the heavens some of the men of Persia would obtain it.'[5624]

٤٩٧٥. عنه ﷺ: لَو أنَّ الدّينَ مُعَلَّقٌ بِالثُّرَيّا لَتَناوَلَهُ رِجالٌ مِن أبناءِ فارِسَ.[٥٥٨٢]

4976. **The Prophet (SAWA),** when non-Arabs were mentioned in front of him, said, 'Verily I

٤٩٧٦. عنه ﷺ ـ لمّا ذُكِرَتِ الأعاجِمُ عِندَهُ ـ: لَأنا

have more trust in them, or in some of them, than I have in you, or in some of you.'[5625]

بِهِم أو بِبَعضِهِم أوثَقُ مِنّي بِكُم أو بِبَعضِكُم.[٥٥٨٣]

317

OPPORTUNITY

الفُرصَةُ

1473. Seize the Opportunity

١٤٧٣ـ إغتنم الفُرصَة

4977. **The Prophet (SAWA) said,** 'If a door of benevolence is open for someone, they should utilize it, for they do not know when it will close.'[5626]

٤٩٧٧. رسولُ اللهِ ﷺ: مَن فُتِحَ لَهُ بابٌ مِن الخَيرِ فَلْيَنتَهِزْهُ؛ فإنّهُ لا يَدري مَتى يُغلَقُ عَنهُ.[٥٥٨٤]

4978. **The Prophet (SAWA) said,** 'Leaving opportunities brings regret.'[5627]

٤٩٧٨. عنه ﷺ: تَركُ الفُرَصِ غُصَصٌ.[٥٥٨٥]

4979. **Imām ʿAlī (AS) said,** 'Opportunity passes away quickly the way clouds pass.'[5628]

٤٩٧٩. الإمامُ عليٌّ ﷺ: الفُرصَةُ تَمُرُّ مَرَّ السَّحابِ، فانتَهِزُوا فُرَصَ الخَيرِ.[٥٥٨٦]

4980. **Imām ʿAlī (AS) said,** 'Opportunity is quick to pass on, and slow to come back.'[5629]

٤٩٨٠. عنه ﷺ: الفُرصَةُ سَريعَةُ الفَوتِ، وبَطيئَةُ العَودِ.[٥٥٨٧]

4981. **Imām ʿAlī (AS) said,** 'Opportunity is a treasure.'[5630]

٤٩٨١. عنه ﷺ: الفُرصَةُ غُنمٌ.[٥٥٨٨]

4982. **Imām ʿAlī (AS) said,** 'Losing an opportunity is distressful.'[5631]

٤٩٨٢. عنه ﷺ: إضاعَةُ الفُرصَةِ غُصَّةٌ.[٥٥٨٩]

4983. **Imām ʿAlī (AS) said,** 'Matters are secured [depending] on their own time.'[5632]

٤٩٨٣. عنه ﷺ: الأُمورُ مَرهونَةٌ بأوقاتِها.[٥٥٩٠]

4984. **Imām ʿAlī (AS) said,** 'Hastening to something before its time arrives is clumsiness, as is delaying after an opportunity [arises].'[5633]

٤٩٨٤. عنه ﷺ: مِنَ الخُرقِ المُعاجَلَةُ قَبلَ الإمكانِ، والأناةُ بعدَ الفُرصَةِ.[٥٥٩١]

4985. **Imām al-Ṣadiq (AS) said,** 'Whoever tarries despite the fleeting opportunity, [lengthening] his investigation into the matter, the [passing] days

٤٩٨٥. الإمامُ الصّادقُ ﷺ: مَنِ انتَظَرَ بمُعاجَلَةِ الفُرصَةِ مُؤاجَلَةَ الاستِقصاءِ سَلَبَتهُ الأيّامُ

will snatch away the opportunity, because it is the nature of days to snatch away [opportunities], just as it is the path [nature] of time to pass away.'[5634]

فُرصَتَهُ؛ لأنّ مِن شَأنِ الأيّامِ السَّلبَ، وسَبيلُ الزَّمَنِ الفَوتُ.٥٥٩٢

(See also: LIFESPAN: section 1369) (أنظر) العمر: باب ١٣٦٩.

318

OBLIGATIONS

الفَرائِضُ

1474. Enjoinment of Fulfilling Religious Obligations

١٤٧٤ ـ الحَثُّ عَلى أداءِ الفَرائِضِ

4986. **The Prophet (SAWA) said,** 'Perform the obligations [laid down by] Allah and you will become the most pious of people.'[5635]

٤٩٨٦ رسولُ اللهِ ﷺ: إعمَلْ بِفَرائِضِ اللهِ تَكُن أتقَى النّاسِ.٥٥٩٣

4987. **Imām ʿAlī (AS) said,** 'Obligations! Obligations! Fulfil them for Allah and it will lead you to Heaven.'[5636]

٤٩٨٧. الإمامُ عليٌّ ﷺ: الفَرائِضَ الفَرائِضَ! أدُّوها إلَى اللهِ تُؤَدِّكُم إلَى الجَنَّةِ.٥٥٩٤

4988. **Imām ʿAlī (AS) said,** 'Make your quest that which Allah has made obligatory upon you, and ask Him to [enable you to] fulfil the right of what He has asked of you.'[5637]

٤٩٨٨. عنه ﷺ: اِجعَلوا ما افتَرَضَ اللهُ عَلَيكُم مِن طَلَبِكُم، وَاسألوهُ مِن أداءِ حَقِّهِ ما سَألَكُم.٥٥٩٥

4989. **Imām ʿAlī (AS) said,** 'Lure your soul to worship, and be lenient towards it, and do not force it. Accept its excuse and take advantage of its vitality, except what has been prescribed for you as an obligation; for they must be performed, and carried out at their right time.'[5638]

٤٩٨٩. عنه ﷺ: خادِعْ نفسَكَ في العِبادَةِ، وارفُقْ بها ولا تقهَرْها، وخُذْ عفوَها ونَشاطَها، إلّا ما كانَ مَكتوباً علَيكَ مِن الفَريضَةِ؛ فإنّهُ لا بُدَّ مِن قَضائها وتَعاهُدِها عِندَ مَحَلِّها.٥٥٩٦

4990. **Imām ʿAlī (AS) said,** 'There is no worship like the performance of obligatory acts.'[5639]

٤٩٩٠. عنه ﷺ: لا عِبادَةَ كَأداءِ الفَرائضِ.٥٥٩٧

4991. **Imām ʿAlī (AS) said,** 'If you were to preoccupy yourself with supererogatory acts instead of the obligatory, you will not gain a single merit by losing an obligation.'[5640]

٤٩٩١. عنه ﷺ: إنّكَ إنِ اشتَغَلتَ بِفَضائلِ النَّوافِلِ عَن أداءِ الفَرائضِ، فلَن يَقومَ فَضلُ تَكسِبُهُ بِفَرضٍ تُضَيِّعُهُ.٥٥٩٨

4992. **Imām al-Ḥasan (AS) said,** 'When Allah with His Generosity and Benevolence made the obligations a duty upon you, He did not do so for a need He has for them. Rather, it is as a result of the Benevolence He has over you - there is no god but He – and in order to distinguish between the bad and the good, and to test what is in your chests, and to purify what is in your hearts.'[5641]

٤٩٩٢. الإمامُ الحسنُ ﵇ : إنّ اللهَ عَزَّوجلَّ بِمَنِّهِ ورَحمَتِهِ لَمّا فَرَضَ عَليكُمُ الفَرائضَ لم يَفرِضْ علَيكُم لِحاجَةٍ مِنهُ إلَيهِ، بَل رَحمَةً مِنهُ إلَيكُم (علَيكُم) لا إلٰهَ إلّا هُو، لِيَميزَ الخَبيثَ مِن الطَّيِّبِ، ولِيَبتَلِيَ ما في صُدورِكُم، ولِيُمَحِّصَ ما في قُلوبِكُم.[٥٥٩٩]

4993. **Imām Zayn al-ʿĀbidīn (AS) said,** 'Those who act according to what Allah has made obligatory are the best of people.[5642]

٤٩٩٣. الإمامُ زينُ العابدينَ ﵇ : مَن عَمِلَ بما افتَرَضَ اللهُ علَيهِ فهُو مِن خَيرِ الناسِ.[٥٦٠٠]

4994. **Imām al-Ṣādiq (AS) said,** 'Allah, Blessed and most High, said, 'There is nothing more beloved to Me, through which My servant may endear himself to Me than through the duties I ask him to fulfil.'[5643]

٤٩٩٤. الإمامُ الصّادقُ ﵇ :قالَ اللهُ تبارَكَ وتعالىٰ: ما تَحَبَّبَ إلَيَّ عبدِي بِأحَبَّ مِمّا افتَرَضتُ علَيهِ.[٥٦٠١]

1475. That which Allah has made Obligatory for People

١٤٧٥ ـ ما فَرَضَ اللهُ سُبحانَهُ عَلَى النّاسِ

4995. **Imām ʿAlī (AS) said,** 'Allah, most High, has made obligatory upon the leaders of justice [truth] to equate themselves with the weak ones from among of people, so that the poor cannot be intimidated as a result of his poverty.'[5644]

٤٩٩٥. الإمامُ عليٌّ ﵇ : إنّ اللهَ تعالىٰ فَرَضَ علىٰ أئمّةِ العَدلِ (الحقِّ) أن يُقَدِّرُوا أنفُسَهُم بِضَعَفَةِ الناسِ، كيلا يَتَبيَّغَ بالفَقيرِ فَقرُهُ.[٥٦٠٢]

4996. **Imām ʿAlī (AS) said,** 'Allah, Glory be to Him, made the provisions of the poor incumbent upon the wealth of the rich; so no poor person goes hungry except as a result of what the rich person enjoys.'[5645]

٤٩٩٦. عنه ﵇ : إنّ اللهَ سبحانَهُ فَرَضَ في أموالِ الأغنياءِ أقواتَ الفُقَراءِ، فما جاعَ فَقيرٌ إلّا بما مُتِّعَ بِهِ غَنيٌّ.[٥٦٠٣]

4997. **Imām ʿAlī (AS) said,** 'Allah made faith incumbent in order to purify [people] from polytheism, and prayer to eliminate arrogance, and the alms-tax as a mediator for sustenance [of the needy].'[5646]

٤٩٩٧. عنه ﵇ : فَرَضَ اللهُ الإيمانَ تَطهيراً مِن الشِّركِ، والصلاةَ تَنزيهاً عنِ الكِبرِ، والزكاةَ تَسبيباً للرِّزقِ.[٥٦٠٤]

4998. **Imām ʿAlī (AS) said,** 'Allah has ordained a duty for all of your body parts, *and* they will be

٤٩٩٨. عنه ﵇ :إنّ اللهَ فَرَضَ علىٰ جَوارِحِكَ كُلِّها

used as proofs and witnesses over you on the Day of Resurrection.'[5647]

فَرائِضَ يَحتَجُّ بها علَيكَ يومَ القِيامَةِ.٥٦٠٥

1476. The Sum of All Obligations

١٤٧٦ـ جامِعُ الفَرائِضِ

4999. **Imām ʿAlī (AS) said,** 'As for what Allah has made obligatory in His Book, they are the pillars of Islam, and they are five pillars. It is on these five pillars that Islam was founded, and He Almighty allocated for each of these obligatory duties four boundaries which everyone must know. The first of them is prayer, then alms-tax (*zakāt*), then fasting, then Ḥajj pilgrimage, then guardianship (*wilāya*), which the latter is the seal of them and it encompasses all obligatory and recommended acts.'[5648]

٤٩٩٩. الإمامُ عليٌّ (ع): أمّا ما فَرَضَهُ اللهُ سبحانَهُ في كتابِهِ فدَعائمُ الإسلامِ، وهِي خَمسُ دَعائمَ. وعلى هذهِ الفَرائضِ الخَمسِ بُنِيَ الإسلامُ، فجَعَلَ سبحانَهُ لكُلِّ فَريضَةٍ مِن هذهِ الفَرائضِ أربَعةَ حُدودٍ لا يَسَعُ أحَداً جَهلُها، أوَّلُها: الصلاةُ، ثُمّ الزكاةُ، ثُمّ الصيامُ، ثُمّ الحَجُّ، ثُمّ الوَلايَةُ، وهِي خاتِمَتُها والجامِعَةُ لِجَميعِ الفَرائضِ والسُّنَنِ.٥٦٠٦

319

IDLENESS

الفَراغُ[١]

1477. Idleness

١٤٧٧ـ الفراغ

"So when you are done with, appoint, and turn eagerly to your Lord."[5649]

﴿فَإذا فَرَغْتَ فَانْصَبْ * وَإلى رَبِّكَ فَارْغَبْ﴾.٥٦٠٧

5000. **The Prophet (SAWA) said,** 'The one to be the most harshly judged on the Day of Resurrection will be the capable yet idle [people]. If work is tiring, idleness is corruptive.'[5650]

٥٠٠٠. رسولُ اللهِ ﷺ: أشَدُّ الناسِ حِساباً يومَ القِيامَةِ المَكفِيُّ الفارِغُ، إن كانَ الشُّغلُ مَجهَدَةً فالفَراغُ مَفسَدَةٌ.٥٦٠٨

5001. **The Prophet (SAWA) said,** 'Verily Allah hates the healthy-bodied idle person, who is neither concerned with his worldly life, nor the Hereafter.'[5651]

٥٠٠١. عنه ﷺ: إنَّ اللهَ يُبغِضُ الصَّحيحَ الفارِغَ، لا في شُغلِ الدنيا ولا في شُغلِ الآخِرَةِ.٥٦٠٩

5002. **The Prophet (SAWA) said,** 'There are two things most people are tested with: health and idleness.'[5652]

٥٠٠٢. عنه ﷺ: خَلَّتانِ كثيرٌ مِن الناسِ فيهِما مَفتونٌ: الصِّحَّةُ والفَراغُ.٥٦١٠

5003. **Imām ʿAlī (AS) said,** 'From idleness comes desire.'[5653]

٥٠٠٣ . الإمامُ عليٌّ ﵇: مِـن الفَـراغِ تكـونُ الصَّبوَةُ.[٥٦١١]

5004. **Imām ʿAlī (AS) said,** 'Know that the world is a place of trial wherein there is no time a person can afford to be idle, for that time will be a source of regret for him on the Day of Resurrection.'[5654]

٥٠٠٤ . عنه ﵇ : اِعلَمْ أنَّ الدنيا دارُ بَلِيَّةٍ لم يَفرُغْ صاحِبُها فيها قَطُّ ساعَةً إلّا كانَت فَـرغَتُهُ عـلَيهِ حَسرةً يومَ القِيامَةِ.[٥٦١٢]

5005. **Imām ʿAlī (AS) said,** 'How deserving man is of having an hour where no one disturbs him!'[5655]

٥٠٠٥ . عنه ﵇ : ما أحَقَّ الإنسانَ أن تكونَ لَهُ ساعَةٌ لا يَشغَلُهُ عَنها شاغِلٌ![٥٦١٣]

5006. **Imām ʿAlī (AS) said,** 'If work is tiring, then continuous idleness is corruptive.'[5656]

٥٠٠٦ . عنه ﵇ : إنْ يَكُنِ الشُّغلُ مَجهَدَةً فاتِّصالُ الفَراغِ مَفسَدَةٌ.[٥٦١٤]

5007. **Imām Zayn al-ʿĀbidīn (AS) said** in his supplication, '...and divert our hearts from every other act of remembrance through Your remembrance, our tongues from every other act of thanksgiving through [being preoccupied with] thanking You, our limbs from every other act of obedience through [being preoccupied with] obedience to You! If You have ordained for us idleness in an occupation, make it an idleness of safety, wherein no ill consequence visits us nor weariness overtakes us as a result! Then the writers of evil deeds may depart from us with a page empty of the mention of our evil deeds, and the writers of good deeds may leave us happy with the good deeds of ours which they have written.'[5657]

٥٠٠٧ . الإمامُ زينُ العابدينَ ﵇ ـ في دعائهِ ـ: وَاشغَلْ قُلوبَنا بِذِكرِكَ عن كُلِّ ذِكـرٍ، وألسِـنَتَنا بِشُكرِكَ عن كُلِّ شُكرٍ، وجَوارِحَنا بطاعَتِكَ عن كُلِّ طاعَةٍ، فإنْ قَـدَّرتَ لنـا فَـراغاً مِـن شُـغلٍ فـاجعَلْهُ فَـراغَ سـلامَةٍ، لاتُـدرِكُنا فـيهِ تَـبِعَةٌ، ولاتَلحَقُنا فيهِ سَأمَةٌ، حتّىٰ يَنصَرِفَ عنّا كُـتّابُ السَّيِّئاتِ بـصَحيفَةٍ خـالِيَةٍ مِـن ذِكـرِ سَـيِّئاتِنا، ويَتَوَلّىٰ كُتّابُ الحَسَناتِ عنّا مَسرورِينَ.[٥٦١٥]

5008. **Imām Zayn al-ʿĀbidīn (AS) said** in his supplication, 'O Allah, bless Muḥammad and his Household, and spare me the concerns which distract me [from any act of worship], employ me in that which You will ask me about tomorrow, and let me pass my days [engaged] in that for which You have created me!'[5658]

٥٠٠٨ . عنه ﵇ ـ مِن دعائهِ في مكارمِ الأخلاقِ ـ: اللّهُمَّ صَلِّ علىٰ محمّدٍ وآلِهِ، واكفِنِي ما يَشغَلُنِي الاهتِمامُ بِهِ، واستَعمِلْني بما تَسألُنِي غَداً عَـنهُ، واستَفرِغْ أيّامِي فيما خَلَقتَنِي لَهُ.[٥٦١٦]

5009. **Imām Zayn al-ʿĀbidīn (AS),** in his supplication said, '...and grant me health for the sake of worshipping [You], and free time accompanied with piety.'[5659]

٥٠٠٩ . عنه ﵇ ـ أيضاً ـ: وارزُقْنِي صِحَّةً في عِبادَةٍ، وفَراغاً في زَهادَةٍ.[٥٦١٧]

5010. **Imām Zayn al-ʿĀbidīn (AS) said** in his supplication on the day of ʿArafa, 'Let me taste, through some of Your boundless plenty, the flavour of being free for what You love, and striving in what brings about proximity with You and to You, and give me a gift from among Your gifts! Make my commerce profitable and my return without loss, fill me with fear of Your station, and make me yearn for the meeting with You.'[5660]

٥٠١٠. عنه عليه السلام ـ مِن دعائهِ في يومِ عَرَفَة ـ: وأذِقْني طَعمَ الفَراغِ لِما تُحِبُّ بِسَعَةٍ مِن سَعَتِكَ، والاجتِهادِ فيما يُزلِفُ لَدَيكَ وعِندَك، وأتحِفْني بتُحفَةٍ من تُحَفاتِكَ، واجعَلْ تِجارَتي رابِحَةً، وكَرَّتي غيرَ خاسِرَةٍ، وأخِفنِي مَقامَكَ، وشَوِّقْني لِقاءَكَ.[٥٦١٨]

5011. **Imām al-Kāẓim (AS) said,** 'Verily Allah, most High, hates the servant who sleeps much; verily Allah, most High, hates the idle servant.'[5661]

٥٠١١. الإمامُ الكاظمُ عليه السلام: إنّ اللهَ تعالىٰ لَيُبغِضُ العَبدَ النَّوّامَ، إنّ اللهَ تعالىٰ لَيُبغِضُ العَبدَ الفارِغَ.[٥٦١٩]

320

CORRUPTION

الفَسَاد [١٧٥]

1478. That Which Corrupts People in General

١٤٧٨ ـ مايُفسِدُ العامَّةَ

1. Sin

١ ـ المَعصِيةُ

"Corruption has appeared in land and sea because of the doings of the people's hands, that He may make them taste something of what they have done, so that they may come back."[5662]

﴿ظَهَرَ الْفَسادُ فِي الْبَرِّ وَالْبَحْرِ بِما كَسَبَتْ أَيْدِي النَّاسِ لِيُذِيقَهُمْ بَعْضَ الَّذِي عَمِلُوا لَعَلَّهُمْ يَرْجِعُونَ﴾.[٥٦٢٠]

5012. **The Prophet (SAWA) said,** 'If a servant [of Allah] was to secretly sin, he would only harm himself, and if he was to commit it openly and he is not stopped, people would be harmed by it.'[5663]

٥٠١٢. رسولُ اللهِ صلى الله عليه وآله: إنّ المَعصيَةَ إذا عَمِلَ بها العَبدُ سِرّاً لم تَضُرَّ إلّا عامِلَها، وإذا عَمِلَ بها عَلانِيَةً ولم يُغَيَّرْ عليهِ أضَرَّت بالعامَّةِ.[٥٦٢١]

(See also: SINNING: section 777)

(أنظر) الذنب: باب ٧٧٧.

2. Dissention

٢ ـ الاختِلافُ

5013. **Imām ʿAlī (AS) said,** 'By Allah, no sooner does a community dissent after their prophet than falsehood prevails over the truth, save that which Allah wills…'[5664]

٥٠١٣. الإمامُ عليٌّ عليه السلام: وأيمُ اللهِ، ما اختَلَفَت اُمَّةٌ بَعدَ نَبِيِّها إلّا ظَهَرَ باطِلُها علىٰ حَقِّها إلّا ما شاءَ اللهُ.[٥٦٢٢]

(See also: DIFFERENCES: section 628)

(أنظر) الإختلاف: باب ٦٢٨.

3. Preventing the truth ٤ـ مَنعُ الحقِّ

5014. **The Prophet (SAWA) said,** 'A community who does not let the weak uphold his rights from the strong without obstacle will never be sanctified.'[5665]

٥٠١٤. رسولُ اللهِ ﷺ: لن تُقَدَّسَ أُمّةٌ لايُؤخَذُ للضَّعيفِ فيها حَقُّهُ مِن القَويِّ غيرَ مُتَعتِعٍ.٥٦٢٣

1479. What is Corruption and who is the Corruptor?

١٤٧٩ـ مَعرِفَةُ الفَسادِ والمُفسِدِ

"Indeed the requital of those who wage war against Allah and His Apostle, and try to cause corruption on the earth, is that they shall be slain…"[5666]

﴿إنَّما جَزاءُ الَّذينَ يُحارِبُونَ اللهَ وَرَسُولَهُ وَيَسْعَوْنَ فِي الْأَرْضِ فَساداً أنْ يُقَتَّلُوا﴾.٥٦٢٤

"She said, 'Indeed when kings enter a town, they devastate it, and reduce the mightiest of its people to the most abased. That is how they act.'"[5667]

﴿قالَتْ إنَّ الْمُلُوكَ إذا دَخَلُوا قَرْيَةً أفْسَدُوها وَجَعَلُوا أعِزَّةَ أهْلِها أذِلَّةً وَكَذٰلِكَ يَفْعَلُونَ﴾.٥٦٢٥

"When they are told, 'Do not cause corruption on the earth', they said, 'We are only reformers!'"[5668]

﴿وَإذا قِيلَ لَهُمْ لا تُفْسِدُوا فِي الْأرْضِ قالُوا إنَّما نَحْنُ مُصْلِحُونَ﴾.٥٦٢٦

"And do not obey the dictates of the profligate, who cause corruption in the land and do not bring about reform."[5669]

﴿وَلا تُطِيعُوا أمْرَ الْمُسْرِفِينَ * الَّذِينَ يُفْسِدُونَ فِي الْأرْضِ وَلا يُصْلِحُونَ﴾.٥٦٢٧

5015. **The Prophet (SAWA) said,** 'There are two kinds of people from my community who if they are sound my community will be sound, and if they are corrupt my community will become corrupt.' The Prophet was asked, 'And who are they O messenger of Allah?' He replied, 'The jurists and the rulers.'[5670]

٥٠١٥. رسولُ اللهِ ﷺ: صِنفانِ مِن أُمَّتي إذا صَلُحا صَلُحَت أُمَّتي، وإذا فَسَدا فَسَدَت أُمَّتي، قيلَ: يارسولَ اللهِ، ومَن هُما؟ قالَ: الفُقَهاءُ والأُمَراءُ.٥٦٢٨

5016. **Imām 'Alī (AS) said,** 'Verily, from corruption comes the loss of provisions.'[5671]

٥٠١٦. الإمامُ عليٌّ ﷺ: إنَّ مِن الفَسادِ إضاعَةَ الزّادِ.٥٦٢٩

5017. **Imām al-Riḍā (AS) said,** 'Of the things that are corruptive are blocking dirhams and dinars and disposing of seeds.'[5672]

٥٠١٧. الإمامُ الرِّضا ﷺ: مِن الفَسادِ قَطعُ الدِّرهَمِ والدّينارِ وطَرحُ النَّوى.٥٦٣٠

1480. That Which Repels Corruption

١٤٨٠ ـ ما يَدفَعُ الفَسادَ

5018. **The Prophet (SAWA) said,** 'Were it not for the praying servants of Allah, the young suckling children, and the grazing animals, punishment would pour down on you.'[5673]

٥٠١٨ . رسولُ اللهِ ﷺ : لولا عِبادٌ للهِ[٥٦٣١] رُكَّعٌ، وصِبيانٌ رُضَّعٌ، وبَهائمُ رُتَّعٌ، لَصُبَّ علَيكُمُ العَذابُ صَبّاً.[٥٦٣٢]

5019. **Imām 'Alī (AS) said,** 'If people were to fear and return to their Lord when calamities befall them and blessings are taken away from them, returning with truth in their intentions, and reverence in their hearts, He would return to them every runaway and loss, and correct for them every corrupt.'[5674]

٥٠١٩ . الإمامُ عليٌّ عليه السلام : لو أنَّ النّاسَ حينَ تَنزِلُ بِهِمُ النِّقَمُ، وتَزولُ عَنهُمُ النِّعَمُ، فَزِعُوا إلىٰ رَبِّهِم بِصِدقٍ مِن نِيّاتِهِم، وَوَلَهٍ مِن قُلوبِهِم، لَرَدَّ علَيهِم كُلَّ شارِدٍ، وأصلَحَ لَهُم كُلَّ فاسِدٍ.[٥٦٣٣]

5020. **Imām al-Ṣādiq (AS) said,** 'Allah repels [corruption] from those of our followers who do not pray, with those of our followers who do pray, and if they were to all agree to not pray, they would be destroyed. And verily Allah repels [chastisement] from those of our followers who do not pay the alms-tax with those of our followers who do pay the alms-tax. And this is the purport of Allah's verse in the Qur'an: *"Were it not for Allah's repelling the people by means of one another, the earth would surely have been corrupted."*'[5675] [5676]

٥٠٢٠ . الإمامُ الصّادقُ عليه السلام : إنَّ اللهَ (لَ)يَدفَعُ بِمَن يُصَلِّي مِن شيعَتِنا عَمَّن لا يُصَلِّي مِن شِيعَتِنا ولو أجمَعُوا علىٰ تَركِ الصلاةِ لَهَلَكُوا، وإنَّ اللهَ لَيَدفَعُ بمَن يُزَكِّي مِن شيعَتِنا عَمَّن لا يُزَكِّي ... وهو قولُ اللهِ عزّ وجلَّ : ﴿ولَولا دَفعُ اللهِ النّاسَ بَعضَهُم بِبَعضٍ لَفَسَدَتِ الأَرضُ﴾.[٥٦٣٤]

321

MERIT

الفَضل

1481. Merits

١٤٨١ ـ الفَضائِلُ

5021. **Imām 'Alī (AS) said,** 'Merits come through good perfection [of character] and noble actions, and not through excess money and eminent feats.'[5677]

٥٠٢١ . الإمامُ عليٌّ عليه السلام : الفَضيلَةُ بحُسنِ الكَمالِ ومَكارِمِ الأفعالِ، لا بكَثرَةِ المالِ وجَلالَةِ الأعمالِ.[٥٦٣٥]

5022. **Imām ʿAlī (AS) said,** 'The merit of chiefs lies in the goodness of their worship.'[5678]

٥٠٢٢ . عنه عليه السلام : فَضيلَةُ السادَةِ حُسنُ العِبادَةِ.[٥٦٣٦]

5023. **Imām ʿAlī (AS) said,** 'So the pious among them are the people of merits; their speech is truth and their dress is moderate.'[5679]

٥٠٢٣ . عنه عليه السلام : فالمُتَّقُونَ فيها هُم أهلُ الفَضائلِ: مَنطِقُهُمُ الصَّوابُ ، ومَلبَسُهُمُ الاقتِصادُ.[٥٦٣٧]

5024. **Imām ʿAlī (AS) said,** 'He who lifts his head [i.e. holds himself] from misjudging has acquired the sum of all the merits.'[5680]

٥٠٢٤ . عنه عليه السلام : لَقَد أخَذَ بجَوامِعِ الفَضلِ مَن رَفَعَ نفسَهُ عن سُوءِ المُجازاةِ.[٥٦٣٨]

5025. **Imām ʿAlī (AS) said,** 'He who is good to one who does bad to him has attained all merits.'[5681]

٥٠٢٥ . عنه عليه السلام : مَن أحسَنَ إلىٰ مَن أساءَ إلَيهِ فقد أخَذَ بجَوامِعِ الفَضلِ.[٥٦٣٩]

5026. **Imām ʿAlī (AS) said,** 'Be forgiving with your power, generous in spite of your own hardship and selflessness [preferring others over yourselves] in spite of your own neediness, and your virtue will be perfected.'[5682]

٥٠٢٦ . عنه عليه السلام : كُن عَفُوّاً في قُدرَتِكَ ، جَواداً في عُسرَتِكَ ، مُؤْثِراً مَعَ فاقَتِكَ ؛ يَكمُلْ لكَ الفَضلُ.[٥٦٤٠]

5027. **Imām Zayn al-ʿĀbidīn (AS) said,** 'When the Day of Judgment comes Allah, Blessed and most High, will gather the first and the last of creation in one place. A caller will cry out, 'Where are the people of merit?' The Imām then said, 'Then a group of people will rise, and the angels will receive them asking them, 'What were your merits?' They will say, 'We used to visit those who cut us off, give to those who deprived us, and forgive those who oppressed us.' It will then be said to them, 'You have spoken the truth. Enter Paradise.'[5683]

٥٠٢٧ . الإمامُ زينُ العابدينَ عليه السلام : إذا كانَ يَومُ القِيامَةِ جَمَعَ اللهُ تبارَكَ وتعالَى الأوَّلينَ والآخِرينَ في صَعيدٍ واحِدٍ ، ثُمّ يُنادِي مُنادٍ: أينَ أهلُ الفَضلِ ؟ قالَ: فَيَقومُ عُنُقٌ مِن الناسِ ، فَتَلقّاهُم المَلائكةُ فيَقولونَ: وما كانَ فَضلُكُم ؟ فيَقولونَ: كنّا نَصِلُ مَن قَطَعَنا ، ونُعطِي مَن حَرَمَنا ، ونَعفُو عَمَّن ظَلَمَنا ، فيقالُ لَهُم: صَدَقتُم ، ادخُلُوا الجَنَّةَ.[٥٦٤١]

5028. **Imām al-Jawād (AS) said,** 'There are four types of merits: the first is wisdom, and its basis is thinking. The second is chastity, and its basis is desire. The third is power, and its basis is anger. The fourth is justice, and its basis is moderation in the faculties of the self.'[5684]

٥٠٢٨ . الإمامُ الجوادُ عليه السلام : الفَضائلُ أربَعةُ أجناسٍ: أحَدُها: الحِكمَةُ ، وقِوامُها في الفِكرَةِ ، والثاني: العِفَّةُ ، وقِوامُها في الشَّهوَةِ ، والثالثُ: القُوَّةُ ، وقِوامُها في الغَضَبِ ، والرابِعُ: العَدلُ ، وقِوامُهُ في اعتِدالِ قُوَى النفسِ.[٥٦٤٢]

1482. The Best of Merits

١٤٨٢ ـ أفضَلُ الفَضائلِ

5029. **Imām ʿAlī (AS) said,** 'Fairness is the best of merits.'[5685]

٥٠٢٩ . الإمامُ عليٌّ عليه السلام : الإنصافُ أفضَلُ الفَضائلِ.[٥٦٤٣]

5030. **Imām ʿAlī (AS) said,** 'Safeguarding the tongue and spreading goodness [to others] are among the best merits of the human.'[5686]

٥٠٣٠ . عنه ﷺ : حِفظُ اللِّسانِ وبَذلُ الإحسانِ مِن أفضَلِ فَضائلِ الإنسانِ.[٥٦٤٤]

5031. **Imām ʿAlī (AS) said,** 'There is not merit greater than goodness [to others].'[5687]

٥٠٣١ . عنه ﷺ: لافَضيلَةَ أجَلُّ مِن الإحسانِ.[٥٦٤٥]

5032. **Imām ʿAlī (AS) said,** 'The fountainhead of merits is the overpowering of anger, and the eradication of desire.'[5688]

٥٠٣٢ . عنه ﷺ : رَأسُ الفَضائلِ مِلكُ الغَضَبِ، وإماتَةُ الشَّهوَةِ.[٥٦٤٦]

5033. **Imām ʿAlī (AS) said,** 'The peak of merits is knowledge.'[5689]

٥٠٣٣ . عنه ﷺ : غايَةُ الفَضائلِ العِلمُ.[٥٦٤٧]

(See also: CHARACTER: section 645, 649)

(أنظر) الخلق: باب ٦٤٥، ٦٤٩.

1483. The Most Virtuous of People

١٤٨٣ ـ أفضَلُ النّاسِ

5034. **The Prophet (SAWA) said,** 'Those among you who have the best status with Allah, most High, are those who prolong their hunger and contemplation. Those of you who are most hated by Allah, most High, are those who sleep, eat and drink excessively.'[5690]

٥٠٣٤ . رسولُ اللهِ ﷺ : أفضَلُكُم مَنزِلَةً عندَ اللهِ تعالىٰ أطوَلُكُم جُوعاً وتَفَكُّراً، وأبغَضُكُم إلَى اللهِ تعالىٰ كُلُّ نَؤومٍ وأكُولٍ وشَروبٍ.[٥٦٤٨]

5035. **The Prophet (SAWA) said,** 'O people! The most virtuous of people is he who is humble from loftiness, is ascetic despite richness, is fair in spite of his strength and forgiving in spite of his power. Verily, the most virtuous of people is a servant who takes what suffices him from this world, takes self-restraint as his companion therein, prepares his provisions to leave [this world], and is ready for the journey [to the Hereafter].'[5691]

٥٠٣٥ . عنه ﷺ : أيُّها النّاسُ، إنّ أفضَلَ النّاسِ مَن تَواضَعَ عَن رِفعَةٍ، وزَهِدَ عن غُنيَةٍ، وأنصَفَ عن قُوَّةٍ، وحَلُمَ عن قُدرَةٍ، ألَا وإنَّ أفضَلَ النّاسِ عَبدٌ أخَذَ مِن الدنيا الكَفافَ، وصاحَبَ فيها العَفافَ، وتَزَوَّدَ للرَّحيلِ، وتَأهَّبَ للمَسيرِ.[٥٦٤٩]

5036. **Imām ʿAlī (AS) said,** 'The most virtuous of Allah's servants according to Allah is a just leader, who is guided and guides [others], and who has established the known tradition, and abolished the unknown innovations.'[5692]

٥٠٣٦ . الإمامُ عليٌّ ﷺ : أفضَلُ عِبادِ اللهِ عِندَ اللهِ إمامٌ عادِلٌ، هُدِيَ وهَدَىٰ، فَأقامَ سُنَّةً مَعلومَةً، وأماتَ بِدعَةً مَجهولَةً.[٥٦٥٠]

5037. **Imām ʿAlī (AS) said,** 'The most virtuous of people according to Allah is he to whom action in accordance with what is right is most beloved-

٥٠٣٧ عنه ﷺ : إنّ أفضَلَ النّاسِ عندَ اللهِ مَن كانَ العَمَلُ بالحَقِّ أحَبَّ إلَيهِ ـ وإن نَقَصَهُ وكَرَثَهُ ـ

even if it damages and worries him – rather than what is false, even if it gives him benefit and increases him.'[5693]

مِن الباطِلِ وإن جَرَّ إلَيهِ فائدَةً وزادَهُ.٥٦٥١

(See also: FAITH: section 195) (أنظر) الإيمان: باب ١٩٥.

322

POVERTY

الفَقرُ

1484. The Reprehension of Poverty

١٤٨٤ـ ذمُّ الفقرِ

5038. **The Prophet (SAWA) said,** 'Poverty is almost disbelief.'[5694]

٥٠٣٨. رسولُ اللهِ ﷺ: كـادَ الفَـقرُ أن يَكـونَ كُفراً.٥٦٥٢

5039. **The Prophet (SAWA) said,** 'O Allah I seek refuge in You from disbelief and poverty.' A person asked, 'Are these two equivalent?' He said, 'Yes.'[5695]

٥٠٣٩. عنه ﷺ: اللّهمّ إنّي أعوذُ بكَ مِن الكُفرِ والفقرِ، فقالَ رجُلٌ: أيَعدِلانِ؟ قالَ: نَعَم.٥٦٥٣

5040. **The Prophet (SAWA) said,** 'If it was not for my Lord's mercy on the poor of my community, poverty would just about be disbelief.'[5696]

٥٠٤٠. عنه ﷺ: لَولا رَحمَةُ رَبّي عَلىٰ فُقَراءِ اُمَّتي، كادَ الفَقرُ يَكونُ كُفراً.٥٦٥٤

5041. **The Prophet (SAWA) said,** 'Poverty is worse than killing.'[5697]

٥٠٤١. عنه ﷺ: الفَقرُ أشَدُّ مِنَ القَتلِ.٥٦٥٥

5042. **Imām ʿAlī (AS) said,** 'Poverty is humiliation for the self, bewilderment for the intellect, and it attracts anxieties.'[5698]

٥٠٤٢. الإمامُ عليٌّ ؈: إنّ الفقرَ مَذَلَّةٌ لِلنَّفسِ، مَدهَشَةٌ لِلعَقلِ، جالِبٌ لِلهُمومِ.٥٦٥٦

5043. **Imām ʿAlī (AS) said,** 'Poverty is the greater death.'[5699]

٥٠٤٣. عنه ؈: الفَقرُ المَوتُ الأكبَرُ.٥٦٥٧

5044. **Imām ʿAlī (AS) said,** 'Poverty silences the sagacious from his proof, and a poor person is a foreigner in his own country.'[5700]

٥٠٤٤. عنه ؈: الفَقرُ يُخرِسُ الفَطِنَ عن حُجَّتِهِ، والمُقِلُّ غَريبٌ في بَلدَتِهِ.٥٦٥٨

5045. **Imām ʿAlī (AS),** speaking to his son Imām Ḥasan (AS), said, 'Do not blame a person who

٥٠٤٥. عنه ؈ ـ لابنِهِ الحسنِ ؈ ـ: لا تَلُمْ إنساناً

tries to seek his ration, for he who does not have a ration, his mistakes increase. O son, a poor person is humiliated, his words are not heard, and his status is not recognized. If a poor person speaks the truth, they call him a liar, and if he is an ascetic, they call him ignorant. O son, those who are tried with poverty are tested in four things: weakness in their certainty, deficiency in their intellect, fragility in their devotion, and lack of shame on their face. So, we seek refuge in Allah from poverty.'[5701]

يَطلُبُ قُوتَهُ، فَمَن عَدِمَ قُوتَهُ كَثُرَت خَطاياهُ. يابُنَيَّ، الفقيرُ حَقيرٌ لا يُسمَعُ كلامُهُ، ولا يُعرَفُ مَقامُهُ، لو كانَ الفَقيرُ صادِقاً يُسَمُّونَهُ كاذِباً، ولو كانَ زاهِداً يُسَمُّونَهُ جاهِلاً. يابُنَيَّ، مَن ابتُلِيَ بالفَقرِ فقدِ ابتُلِيَ بأربَعِ خِصالٍ: بالضَّعفِ في يَقينِهِ، والنُّقصانِ في عَقلِهِ، والرِّقَّةِ في دِينِهِ، وقِلَّةِ الحَياءِ في وَجهِهِ، فَنَعُوذُ باللهِ مِن الفَقرِ.[٥٦٥٩]

5046. **Imām ʿAlī (AS),** speaking to his son Muḥammad b. al-Ḥanafiyya, said, 'O son, I fear for you because of poverty, so seek refuge in Allah from it, for poverty brings diminishment in one's faith, confusion to the intellect and a motive for hatred.'[5702]

٥٠٤٦. عنه عليه السلام ـ لابنِهِ محمّدِ بنِ الحَنَفِيَّةِ ـ: يابُنَيَّ، إنّي أخافُ علَيكَ الفَقرَ، فَاستَعِذْ بِاللهِ مِنهُ؛ فإنَّ الفَقرَ مَنقَصَةٌ للدِّينِ، مَدهَشَةٌ للعَقلِ، داعِيَةٌ لِلمَقتِ.[٥٦٦٠]

5047. **Imām ʿAlī (AS) said,** 'Poverty in one's homeland is like being foreign in it.'[5703]

٥٠٤٧. عنه عليه السلام: الفَقرُ في الوَطَنِ غُربَةٌ.[٥٦٦١]

1485. Praising Poverty

١٤٨٥ ـ مَدحُ الفَقرِ

5048. **The Prophet (SAWA) said,** 'Poverty is my honour, and I am proud of it.'[5704]

٥٠٤٨ ـ رسولُ اللهِ صلى الله عليه وآله: الفَقرُ فَخري وبِهِ أفتَخِرُ.[٥٦٦٢]

5049. **The Prophet (SAWA) said,** 'The poor are the friends of Allah.'[5705]

٥٠٤٩ ـ عنه صلى الله عليه وآله: الفُقَراءُ أصدِقاءُ اللهِ.[٥٦٦٣]

5050. **The Prophet (SAWA) said,** 'O Allah, revive me as a destitute, and make me meet death as a destitute, and resurrect me among the destitute.'[5706]

٥٠٥٠ عنه صلى الله عليه وآله: اللّهُمَّ أحيِني مِسكيناً، وتَوَفَّني مِسكيناً، واحشُرْني في زُمرَةِ المَساكينِ.[٥٦٦٤]

5051. **Imām ʿAlī (AS),** 'Poverty is more decorative for a believer than a rein on the cheek of a horse.'[5707]

٥٠٥١ ـ الإمامُ عليٌّ عليه السلام: الفَقرُ أزيَنُ للمُؤمِنِ مِنَ العِذارِ علىٰ خَدِّ الفَرَسِ.[٥٦٦٥]

5052. **Imām al-Ṣādiq (AS) said,** 'Calamities are endowments from Allah, and poverty is stored with Allah.'[5708]

٥٠٥٢ ـ الإمامُ الصّادقُ عليه السلام: المَصائِبُ مِنَحٌ مِنَ اللهِ، وَالفَقرُ مَخزونٌ عِندَ اللهِ.[٥٦٦٦]

1486. Traditions Narrated about the Virtue of Poverty over Wealth

١٤٨٦ـ ما رُوِيَ في تفضيلِ الفقرِ علَى الغِنىٰ

5053. **The Prophet (SAWA) said,** 'Poverty is convenience, and wealth is punishment.'[5709]

٥٠٥٣ . رسولُ اللهِ ﷺ : الفَقرُ راحَةٌ ، وَالغِنىٰ عُقوبَةٌ .[٥٦٦٧]

5054. **The Prophet (SAWA) said,** 'Poverty is better than wealth, save those who relieve others' debts [with their own wealth] and give during tragedies.'[5710]

٥٠٥٤ . عنه ﷺ : الفَقرُ خَيرٌ مِن الغِنىٰ ، إلّا مَن حَمَلَ في مَغرَمٍ وأعطىٰ في نائبَةٍ .[٥٦٦٨]

5055. **Imām 'Alī (AS) said,** 'The harm of poverty is more praiseworthy than the exuberance of wealth.'[5711]

٥٠٥٥ . الإمامُ عليٌّ ﵇ : ضَرَرُ الفَقرِ أحمَدُ مِن أشَرِ الغِنىٰ .[٥٦٦٩]

5056. **Imām al-Ṣādiq (AS) narrated,** 'Allah said in an intimate conversation with Moses (AS), 'O Moses, when you see poverty coming, then say to it, 'Welcome O garment of the righteous', and when you see wealth coming, say, 'A sin whose punishment has been hastened.'[5712]

Al-Majlisī said, 'To combine both types of traditions [praising and disparaging poverty] and in order to portray that poverty and wealth are both bounties of Allah, most High, it must be said, that He gives each of them [poverty and richness] to whomsoever He wishes according to the complete interests He knows for each. So the servant should endure his poverty, and furthermore be grateful for it, and be grateful for wealth when he is given it, and use it as it is necessary. So with both acting in accordance with what their individual situation requires of them, it is generally agreed that the patient poor man is rewarded more than the grateful rich man. However the levels of their respective situations are completely different, and there can never be an absolute judgment about either side. It seems, therefore, that [a state of] sufficiency is safer and less dangerous than either of the two sides. Hence, the request for it [i.e. sufficiency] features in many supplications, and the Prophet (SAWA) would ask for it for himself and his household (AS).

٥٠٥٦ . الإمامُ الصّادقُ ﵇ في مُناجاةِ موسىٰ ﵇ : يـا مـوسىٰ ، إذا رَأيتَ الفَـقرَ مُـقبِلاً فَـقُل : مَرحَباً بشِعارِ الصالِحينَ ، وإذا رأيتَ الغِنىٰ مُقبِلاً فَقُل : ذَنبٌ عُجِّلَت عُقوبَتُهُ .[٥٦٧٠]

قال المجلسي : مقتضى الجمع بين أخـبارنا أنَّ الفقر والغنىٰ كلٌّ منهما نعمة من نعم الله تـعالىٰ ، يعطي كلّاً منهما من شاء من عباده بحسب مـا يعلم من مصالحه الكاملة ، وعلَى العبد أن يصبر علَى الفقر بل يشكره ويشكر الغـنىٰ إن أعـطاه ويعمل بمقتضاه ، فـمع عـمل كـلٍّ مـنهما بـما تقتضيه حاله فالغالب أنَّ الفقير الصابر أكثر ثواباً من الغنيِّ الشاكر ، لكن مراتب أحوالهما مختلفة غاية الاختلاف ، ولا يمكن الحكم الكـلّيُّ مـن أحد الطرفَين ، والظاهر أنَّ الكفاف أسلم وأقـلُّ خطراً من الجانبَين ؛ ولذا ورد في أكثر الأدعية طلبه وسأله النبيُّ ﷺ لآله وعترته .

Some have said that if this is so, then the best is what the Prophet (SAWA) and most of his companions have chosen in possessing less of the world and distancing oneself from its pleasures.[5713]

وقال بعض: وإذا كان الأمر كذلك فالأفضل ما اختاره لنبيُّ ﷺ وجمهور أصحابه من التقلُّل في الدنيا والبعد عن زهرتها.[٥٦٧١]

Al-Rāghib has said in his *al-Mufradāt*: the word poverty is used with four meanings.

قال الراغب في المفردات: الفقر يستعمل على أربعة أوجه:

The first: the need for bare necessities, that applies to all human beings, as long as they dwell in the realm of this world, or rather, it applies for all existing beings, and this is what is meant in His verse in the Qur'an: *"O mankind! You are the ones who stand in need of Allah, and Allah - He is the All-sufficient, the All- laudable."*[5714]

الأوّل: وجود الحاجة الضروريّة، وذلك عامّ للإنسان مادام في دار الدنيا، بل عامّ للموجودات كلّها، وعلىٰ هذا قوله تعالىٰ: ﴿يا أيُّها النامُ أنتُمُ الفُقَراءُ إلَى اللهِ واللهُ هُو الغَنيُّ الحَميدُ﴾.[٥٦٧٢]

The second: lack of acquisitions, which is mentioned in His verse in the Qur'an: *"[The charities are] for the poor who are straitened in the way of Allah* – until His verse: "*...Charities are only for the poor and the needy.*"[5715]

والثاني: عدم المُقتَنيات، وهو المذكور في قوله: ﴿لِلفُقَراءِ الّذينَ اُحْصِروا في سَبيلِ اللهِ - إلىٰ قوله - يَحسَبُهُمُ الجاهِلُ أغنِياءَ مِنَ التَّعَفُّفِ﴾ ﴿إنّما الصَّدَقاتُ لِلفُقَراءِ والمَساكِينِ﴾.[٥٦٧٣]

The third: poverty of the self, which is voracious greed, denoted by the Prophet (SAWA)'s saying, 'Poverty is almost infidelity', and is opposite to his saying, '[True] Wealth is the needlessness of the self.'

الثالث: فقر النفس، وهو الشَّرَه المَعنيُّ بقوله ﷺ: «كادَ الفَقرُ أن يكونَ كُفراً»، وهو المقابِلُ بقوله: «الغِنَى غِنَى النفسِ» والمعنيُّ بقولهم: مَن عَدم القناعة لم يفده المال غنىً.

The fourth: Being in need of Allah, referred to in his (SAWA) saying, 'O Allah, enrich me through making me needy of You, and do not impoverish me through needlessness of You.' This is what is meant in Allah's verse in the Qur'an: *"My Lord! Indeed I am in need of any good You may send down to me."*[5716] [5717]

الرابع: لفقر إلَى الله المشار إليه بقوله ﷺ: «اللّهُمّ أغنِني بالافتِقارِ إليكَ، ولا تُفقِرْني بالاستِغناءِ عنكَ»، وإيّاه عُنى بقوله تعالىٰ: ﴿رَبِّ إنّي لِما أنْزَلْتَ إلَيَّ مِن خَيرٍ فَقيرٌ﴾.[٥٦٧٤] [٥٦٧٥]

1487. The Interpretation of Poverty

١٤٨٧ - تفسيرُ الفقرِ

5057. *Biḥār al-Anwār:* 'It is narrated in the scriptures of Prophet Enoch (AS)[5718]: There is no wealth with those who are not in need of Me, and there is no poverty for those who are in want of Me.[5719]

٥٠٥٧. بحار الأنوار: في صُحفِ إدريسَ: لا غِنىً لِمَنِ استَغنىٰ عَنّي، ولا فَقرَ بمَنِ افتَقَرَ إلَيَّ.[٥٦٧٦]

5058. **The Prophet (SAWA) said,** 'O people! ... Who are the utterly destitute?' They said, 'A person who does not have any wealth.' He said, 'No, rather the real destitute is he who has not offered any of his money regarding it to be for Allah, even though he has a lot more after that.'[5720]

٥٠٥٨. رسولُ اللهِ ﷺ: أيُّها الناسُ... ما الصُّعلوكُ فيكُم؟ قالوا: الرجُلُ الذي لامالَ لَهُ، فقالَ: بل الصُّعلوكُ حَقَّ الصُّعلوكِ مَن لم يُقَدِّمْ مِن مالِهِ شيئاً يَحتَسِبُهُ عِندَاللهِ وإن كانَ كثيراً مِنَ بَعدِهِ.[٥٦٧٧]

5059. **The Prophet (SAWA) said,** '[True] Poverty is the poverty of the heart.'[5721]

٥٠٥٩. عنه ﷺ: الفَقرُ فقرُ القَلبِ.[٥٦٧٨]

5060. **Imām ʿAlī (AS) said,** 'There is no poverty like ignorance.'[5722]

٥٠٦٠. الإمامُ عليٌّ عليه السلام: لا فقرَ كالجَهلِ.[٥٦٧٩]

5061. **Imām ʿAlī (AS) said,** 'The greatest of poverty is stupidity.'[5723]

٥٠٦١. عنه عليه السلام: أكبَرُ الفَقرِ الحُمقُ.[٥٦٨٠]

5062. **Imām ʿAlī (AS),** when asked what kind of poverty is most severe, said, 'Disbelief after faith.'[5724]

٥٠٦٢. عنه عليه السلام ـ وقد سُئلَ: أيُّ فَقرٍ أشَدُّ؟ ـ: الكُفرُ بعدَ الإيمانِ.[٥٦٨١]

5063. **Imām ʿAlī (AS) said,** 'Poverty of the self is the worst of poverty.'[5725]

٥٠٦٣. عنه عليه السلام: فَقرُ النَّفسِ شَرُّ الفَقرِ.[٥٦٨٢]

5064. **Imām ʿAlī (AS) said,** '[Real] Wealth and poverty come after submission [of our deeds] to Allah.'[5726]

٥٠٦٤. عنه عليه السلام: الغِنىٰ والفَقرُ بعدَ العَرضِ علَى اللهِ.[٥٦٨٣]

5065. **Imām ʿAlī (AS) said,** 'There is no poverty after [having] Heaven, and no wealth after the Hellfire.'[5727]

٥٠٦٥. عنه عليه السلام: لا فَقرَ بعدَ الجَنّةِ، ولا غِنىٰ بعدَ النارِ.[٥٦٨٤]

5066. **Imām Ḥasan (AS),** when asked about poverty, said, 'It is the greed of the self for everything.'[5728]

٥٠٦٦. الإمامُ الحسنُ عليه السلام ـ لمّا سُئلَ عنِ الفَقرِ ـ: شَرَهُ النفسِ إلىٰ كُلِّ شيءٍ.[٥٦٨٥]

5067. **Imām al-Hādī (AS) said,** 'Poverty is the greed of the self and the extremity of despair.'[5729]

٥٠٦٧. الإمامُ الهاديُّ عليه السلام: الفَقرُ شَرَهُ النفسِ وشِدَّةُ القُنوطِ.[٥٦٨٦]

(See also: RICHES: section 1445)

(أُنظر) الغنى: باب ١٤٤٥.

1488. Praiseworthy and Disparaged Poverty

١٤٨٨ ـ الفَقرُ المَمدوحُ والمَذمومُ

5068. **Imām al-Ṣādiq (AS),** when asked about the [meaning of the] saying of Abū Dharr: "There are three things that people hate but I love: I love death and I love poverty and I love tribulation", said, 'This is not as they have understood it. What he meant is that death in the obedience of Allah is more beloved to me than a life of disobedience to Allah; poverty in the obedience of Allah is more beloved to me than wealth [accompanied] with disobedience to Allah, and tribulation [accompanied] with obedience to Allah is more beloved to me than good health with disobedience to Allah.'[5730]

٥٠٦٨ ـ الإمامُ الصّادقُ عليه السلام ـ لمّا سُئلَ عمّا يُروىٰ عن أبي ذَرٍّ: ثلاثةٌ يُبغِضُها النـاسُ وأنا اُحِبُّها: اُحِبُّ المَوتَ واُحِبُّ الفَقرَ واُحِبُّ البَلاءَ ـ: إنّ هذا ليس علىٰ ما يَرَونَ[٥٦٨٧]؛ إنّما عَنىٰ: المَـوتُ فـي طاعَةِ اللهِ أحَبُّ إلَـيَّ مِـن الحَـياةِ فـي مَـعصيَةِ اللهِ، والفَقرُ فـي طـاعةِ اللهِ أحَبُّ إليَّ مِـن الغِـنىٰ في مَعصيَةِ اللهِ، والبَلاءُ في طاعَةِ اللهِ أحَبُّ إلَيَّ مِن الصِّحَّةِ في مَعصيَةِ اللهِ.[٥٦٨٨]

5069. **Imām al-Ṣādiq (AS) said,** 'Poverty with us [i.e. our guardianship] is better than wealth with other than us, and death with us is better than life with other than us.'[5731]

٥٠٦٩. عنه عليه السلام: الفَقرُ مَعَنا خَيرٌ من الغِنىٰ مـع غَيرِنا. والقَتلُ مَعَنا خَيرٌ من الحَياةِ مَع غَيرِنا.[٥٦٨٩]

5070. **Imām al-Ṣādiq (AS) said,** 'Wealth that prevents you from oppression is better than poverty that drives you to sin.'[5732]

٥٠٧٠. عنه عليه السلام: غِنىً يَحجُزُكَ عنِ الظُّلمِ خَيرٌ مِن فَقرٍ يَحمِلُكَ علَى الإثمِ.[٥٦٩٠]

5071. **Imām al-Ṣādiq (AS) said,** 'Poverty is red death.' The narrator said, 'I asked Abū ʿAbdullāh [al-Ṣādiq] (AS), 'Poverty of dinars and dirhams?' He said, 'No, rather poverty in one's faith.'[5733]

٥٠٧١. عنه عليه السلام: الفَـقرُ المَـوتُ الأحـمَرُ، [قالَ الراوي:] فـقلـتُ لأبي عبدِاللهِ عليه السلام: الفَـقرُ مِـن الدِّيـنارِ والدِّرهَـمِ؟ فـقالَ: لا، ولكـن مِـن الدِّينِ.[٥٦٩١]

1489. Humiliating the Poor

١٤٨٩ ـ تحقيرُ الفَقيرِ

5072. **The Prophet (SAWA) said,** 'Whoever degrades a believer, male or female, or humiliates him because of his poverty or lack of ability, Allah, most High, will promulgate him on the Day of Resurrection and then disgrace him.'[5734]

٥٠٧٢. رسولُ اللهِ صلى الله عليه وآله: مَنِ استَذَلَّ مؤمِناً أو مؤمِنَةً أو حَقَّرَهُ لِفَقرِهِ أو قِلَّةِ ذاتِ يَدِهِ، شَهَرَهُ اللهُ تعالى يومَ القِيامَةِ ثُمّ يَفضَحُهُ.[٥٦٩٢]

5073. **Imām ʿAlī (AS) said,** 'Do not humiliate the weak ones from among your brethren; for whoever

٥٠٧٣. الإمامُ عليٌّ عليه السلام: لا تُـحَقِّروا ضُـعفاءَ إخوانِكُم؛ فإنّهُ مَنِ احـتَقَرَ مُـؤمِناً لم يَـجمَعِ اللهُ

humiliates a believer, Allah Almighty will not bring them together in Heaven until he repents.'[5735]

عَزَّوجلَّ بينهما في الجنّةِ إلّا أن يتوبَ.[٥٦٩٣]

5074. **Imām al-Riḍā (AS) said,** 'Whoever meets a poor Muslim and greets him differently to the way he would greet a rich person, will meet Allah, Mighty and Exalted, on the Day of Judgment, and He will be angry with him.'[5736]

٥٠٧٤. الإمامُ الرِّضا ﷺ: مَن لَقِيَ فقيراً مُسلِماً فَسَلَّمَ علَيهِ خِلافَ سَلامِهِ علَى الغَنيِّ، لَقِيَ اللهَ عَزَّوجلَّ يَومَ القِيامَةِ وهُو علَيهِ غَضبانُ.[٥٦٩٤]

1490. That which Banishes Poverty

١٤٩٠ـ مايَنفِي الفَقرَ

5075. **The Prophet (SAWA) said,** 'Keeping relationships with one's kin prolongs one's life and repels poverty.'[5737]

٥٠٧٥. رسولُ اللهِ ﷺ: صِلَةُ الرَّحِمِ تَزيدُ في العُمرِ، وتَنفي الفَقرَ.[٥٦٩٥]

5076. **Imām ʿAlī (AS) said,** 'Cure poverty with charity and giving generously.'[5738]

٥٠٧٦. الإمامُ عليٌّ ﷺ: داوُوا الفَقرَ بالصَّدقَةِ والبَذلِ.[٥٦٩٦]

5077. **Imām al-Bāqir (AS) said,** 'Righteousness and almsgiving in secret banishes poverty.'[5739]

٥٠٧٧. الإمامُ الباقرُ ﷺ: البِرُّ وصَدقَةُ السِّرِّ يَنفِيانِ الفَقرَ.[٥٦٩٧]

5078. **Imām al-Ṣādiq (AS) said,** 'I guarantee that those who economize will never fall poor.'[5740]

٥٠٧٨. الإمامُ الصّادقُ ﷺ: ضَمِنتُ لِمَنِ اقتَصَدَ أن لا يَفتَقِرَ.[٥٦٩٨]

(See also: PILGRIMAGE: section 447)

(أنظر) الحج: باب ٤٤٧.

1491. That which Brings Poverty

١٤٩١ـ مايوجِبُ الفَقرَ

5079. **The Prophet (SAWA) said,** 'He who acts poor will become poor.'[5741]

٥٠٧٩. رسولُ اللهِ ﷺ: مَن تَفاقَرَ افتَقَرَ.[٥٦٩٩]

5080. **The Prophet (SAWA) said,** 'Trustworthiness attracts wealth, and treachery attracts poverty.'[5742]

٥٠٨٠. عنه ﷺ: الأمانَةُ تَجلِبُ الغَناءَ، والخِيانَةُ تَجلِبُ الفَقرَ.[٥٧٠٠]

5081. **Imām ʿAlī (AS) said,** 'Poverty is decreed on those who indulge in it - meaning the world (*dunyā*) - and those who turn away from it will be helped with ease.'[5743]

٥٠٨١. الإمامُ عليٌّ ﷺ: حُكِمَ بالفاقَةِ على مُكثِرِها ـ يَعني الدنيا ـ وأُعِينَ بالراحَةِ مَن رَغِبَ عنها.[٥٧٠١]

5082. **Imām ʿAlī (AS) said,** 'Whoever opens the door of begging to themselves Allah will open for them a door of poverty.'[5744]

٥٠٨٢ عنه ﷺ: مَن فَتَحَ علىٰ نفسِهِ باباً مِن المَسألَةِ فَتَحَ اللهُ علَيهِ باباً مِن الفَقرِ.[٥٧٠٢]

5083. **Imām al-Bāqir (AS) said** to Abū Nuʿmān, 'Do not earn a living from people through us [i.e. in our name], for by that Allah will increase you in nothing but poverty.'[5745]

٥٠٨٣ الإمامُ الباقرُ ﷺ ـ لأبي النُّعمانِ ـ: لا تَستَأكِلْ بِنا النـاسَ، فـلا يَـزيدَكَ اللهُ بـذلكَ إلّا فَقراً.[٥٧٠٣]

5084. **Imām al-Ṣādiq (AS)** narrated from his forefathers (AS), saying, 'Whoever does not ask for Allah's grace will be impoverished.'[5746]

٥٠٨٤ الإمامُ الصّادقُ ﷺ ـ عن آبائهِ ﷺ ـ: مَن لم يَسألِ اللهَ مِن فَضلِهِ افتَقَرَ.[٥٧٠٤]

5085. **Imām al-Ṣādiq (AS) said,** 'Any man who invokes Allah against his son will bequeath to him poverty.'[5747]

٥٠٨٥ عنه ﷺ: أيُّما رَجُلٍ دَعا علىٰ ولَدِهِ أورَثَهُ الفَقرَ.[٥٧٠٥]

1492. Allah's Excuse to the Poor

١٤٩٢ ـ اعتِذارُ اللهِ سُبحانَه مِنَ الفُقَراءِ!

5086. **Imām al-Ṣādiq (AS) said,** 'Allah, Exalted be His praise, explains the reasons and excuses for His believing servant who is needy in this world the same way that a brother would do so to his fellow brother, saying, 'By my Honour and Majesty, I did not make you needy in this world because you were low in My view, so raise this veil and look at what I have compensated you with for this world.' He (AS) then said, 'And he will then raise his head and exclaim, 'That which You deprived me of does not harm me when offset against that which you have compensated me with.'[5748]

٥٠٨٦ الإمامُ الصّادقُ ﷺ: إنّ اللهَ جَلَّ ثَناؤهُ لَيَعتَذِرُ إلىٰ عَبدِهِ المؤمنِ المُحْوِجِ في الدنيا كما يَعتَذِرُ الأخُ إلىٰ أخيهِ، فيَقولُ: وعِزَّتي وجَلالي، ما أحوَجتُكَ في الدنيا مِن هَوانٍ كانَ بِكَ عَلَيَّ، فارفَعْ هذا السَّجْفَ فانظُرْ إلىٰ ما عَوَّضتُكَ مِن الدنيا. قالَ: فَيَرفَعُ فيَقولُ: ما ضَرَّني ما مَنَعتَني مع ما عَوَّضتَني؟![٥٧٠٦]

1493. The Adornment of Poverty

١٤٩٣ ـ زينَةُ الفَقرِ

"[The charities are] for the poor who are straitened in the way of Allah, not capable of moving about in the land [for trade]. The unaware suppose them to be well-off because of their reserve. You recognize them by their mark; they do not ask the people importunately. And whatever wealth you may spend, Allah indeed knows it."[5749]

﴿لِلْفُقَراءِ الَّذِينَ أُحْصِرُوا فِي سَبِيلِ اللهِ لا يَسْتَطِيعُونَ ضَرْباً فِي الْأَرْضِ يَحْسَبُهُمُ الْجاهِلُ أَغْنِياءَ مِنَ التَّعَفُّفِ تَعْرِفُهُمْ بِسِيماهُمْ لا يَسْأَلُونَ النَّاسَ إِلْحافاً﴾.[٥٧٠٧]

5087. **The Prophet (SAWA) said,** ‘Allah has made poverty a trust with His creation. So, those who conceal it, Allah will give them the equivalent of the reward of a fasting and praying person.’[5750]

٥٠٨٧. رسولُ اللهِ ﷺ: إنَّ اللهَ جَعَلَ الفقرَ أمانةً عندَ خَلقِهِ، فَمَن سَتَرَهُ أعطاهُ اللهُ مِثلَ أجرِ الصائمِ القائمِ.[٥٧٠٨]

5088. **Imām ʿAlī (AS) said,** ‘Self-restraint is the adornment of poverty.’[5751]

٥٠٨٨. الإمامُ عليٌّ ؑ: العَفافُ زينةُ الفقرِ.[٥٧٠٩]

5089. **Imām al-Ṣādiq (AS) said,** ‘The hardest thing to store is hiding one’s neediness.’[5752]

٥٠٨٩. الإمامُ الصّادقُ ؑ: أشَدُّ شيءٍ مَؤونةً إخفاءُ الفاقةِ.[٥٧١٠]

1494. Blessed are the Poor!

١٤٩٤ ـ طوبىٰ لِلفُقَراءِ!

5090. **The Prophet (SAWA) said,** ‘Blessed are the needy for their patience, and they are the ones who will see the Kingdom of the heavens and the earth.’[5753]

٥٠٩٠. رسولُ اللهِ ﷺ: طُوبىٰ لِلمَساكينِ بالصَّبرِ، وهُمُ الذينَ يَرَونَ مَلَكوتَ السَّماواتِ والأرضِ.[٥٧١١]

5091. **The Prophet (SAWA) said,** ‘The poor will be the kings of the people of Heaven. All people long for Heaven, whereas Heaven itself longs for the poor.’[5754]

٥٠٩١. عنه ﷺ: الفُقَراءُ مُلوكُ أهلِ الجَنّةِ، والناسُ كُلُّهُم مُشتاقونَ إلَى الجَنّةِ والجَنّةُ مُشتاقةٌ إلَى الفُقَراءِ.[٥٧١٢]

5092. **The Prophet (SAWA) said,** ‘I gazed into Heaven, and I saw that most of its people were the poor.’[5755]

٥٠٩٢. عنه ﷺ: اِطَّلَعتُ في الجَنّةِ فَرأيتُ أكثَرَ أهلِها الفُقَراءَ.[٥٧١٣]

5093. **The Prophet (SAWA) said,** ‘Whoever dies and does not leave behind him a dirham or dinar, there is no person that will enter Heaven richer than him.’[5756]

٥٠٩٣. عنه ﷺ: مَن ماتَ ولم يَترُكْ دِرهَماً ولا دِيناراً لم يَدخُلِ الجَنّةَ أغنىٰ مِنهُ.[٥٧١٤]

5094. **Imām al-Ṣādiq (AS) said,** ‘The last of the Prophets to enter Heaven will be Solomon, because of what he was given in this world.’[5757]

٥٠٩٤. الإمامُ الصّادقُ ؑ: إنَّ آخِرَ الأنبياءِ دُخولاً إلَى الجَنّةِ سُليمانُ، وذلكَ لِما اُعطِيَ مِنَ الدنيا.[٥٧١٥]

5095. **Imām al-Ṣādiq (AS),** speaking to Muḥammad al-Khazzāz, said, ‘Do you not go to the market? Do you not see the fruit that is sold, and the things that you desire?’ al-Khazzāz said, ‘Yes.’ He (AS) said, ‘For everything you see but you

٥٠٩٥. عنه ؑ ـ لمحمّد الخزّاز ـ: أما تَدخُلُ السُّوقَ؟ أما تَرَى الفاكِهَةَ تُباعُ والشيءَ مِمّا تَشتَهيهِ؟ فقلتُ: بَلىٰ، فقالَ: أما إنَّ لكَ بكُلِّ

cannot [afford to] buy, you receive the reward of a good deed.'[5758]

ما تَراهُ ملا تقدِرُ علىٰ شِراهُ حَسَنةً.٥٧١٦

(See also: THE ORDEAL: section 269; LOVE: section 436)

(أنظر) البلاء: باب ٢٦٩؛ المحبة: باب ٤٣٦.

323

JURISPRUDENCE

الفِقْهُ

1495. Encouraging the Learning of Religion

١٤٩٥ ـ الحَثُّ عَلَى التَّفَقُّهِ فِي الدِّين

"Yet it is not for the faithful to go forth en masse. But why should not go forth a group from each of their sections to become learned in religion, and to warn their people when they return to them, so that they may beware?"[5759]

﴿وما كانَ الْمُؤْمِنُونَ لِيَنْفِرُوا كافَّةً فَلَوْلا نَفَرَ مِنْ كُلِّ فِرْقَةٍ مِنْهُمْ طائِفَةٌ لِيَتَفَقَّهُوا فِي الدِّينِ وَلِيُنْذِرُوا قَوْمَهُمْ إِذا رَجَعُوا إِلَيْهِمْ لَعَلَّهُمْ يَحْذَرُونَ﴾.٥٧١٧

5096. **The Prophet (SAWA) said,** 'When Allah wants good for a servant, He educates him in religion and inspires him to its complete path.'[5760]

٥٠٩٦ . رسولُ اللهِ ﷺ : إذا أرادَ اللهُ بِعَبدٍ خَيراً فَقَّهَهُ فِي الدِّينِ، وأَلهَمَهُ رُشدَهُ.٥٧١٨

5097. **The Prophet (SAWA) said,** 'The best of worship is the study of religion.'[5761]

٥٠٩٧ . عنه ﷺ : أفضَلُ العِبادَةِ الفِقهُ.٥٧١٩

5098. **The Prophet (SAWA) said,** 'There is a support for everything, and the support for this religion is education.'[5762]

٥٠٩٨ . عنه ﷺ: إنّ لِكُلِّ شيءٍ دِعامَةً، ودِعامَةُ هذا الدِّينِ الفِقهُ.٥٧٢٠

5099. **Imām ʿAlī (AS) said,** 'Learn the Qur'an for it is the best of speeches, and study it for it is the spring of the hearts.'[5763]

٥٠٩٩ . الإمامُ عليٌّ ﷺ : تَعَلَّموا القرآنَ؛ فإنَّهُ أحسَنُ الحَديثِ، وتَفَقَّهُوا فيهِ فإنَّهُ رَبيعُ القُلوبِ.٥٧٢١

5100. **Imām al-Kāẓim (AS) said,** 'The superiority of a learned person over a worshipper is as the superiority of the sun over the planets, and whoever does not educate themselves in their religion, Allah will not accept a single deed from them.'[5764]

٥١٠٠ . الإمامُ الكاظمُ ﷺ : فَضلُ الفَقيهِ علَى العابِدِ كَفَضلِ الشَّمسِ علَى الكَواكِبِ، ومَن لم يَتَفَقَّهْ في دِينِهِ لم يَرضَ اللهُ لَهُ عَمَلاً.٥٧٢٢

1496. Qualifications of a Scholar (*faqīh*)[5765]

١٤٩٦ ـ خَصائِصُ الفَقيهِ

5101. **Imām ʿAlī (AS) said,** 'A real scholar is one who does not make people lose hope in the mercy of Allah, or cause them to have despair from the mercy of Allah, or make them feel safe from the Allah's cunningness.'[5766]

٥١٠١ . الإمامُ عليٌّ عليه السلام : الفَقيهُ كُلُّ الفَقيهِ مَن لَم يُقَنِّطِ النّاسَ مِن رَحمَةِ اللهِ، ولَم يُؤيِسهُم مِن روحِ اللهِ، ولَم يُؤمِنهُم مِن مَكرِ اللهِ.[٥٧٢٣]

5102. **Imām ʿAlī (AS) said,** 'Shall I inform you of a true learned person? He who does not allow people to commit acts of disobedience to Allah, does not let them lose hope in the mercy of Allah, does not assure them against the devices of Allah, and does not leave the Qur'an in his desire for something other than it.'[5767]

٥١٠٢ . عنه عليه السلام : ألا أُخبِرُكُم بالفَقيهِ حَقِّ الفَقيهِ ؟ مَن لم يُرَخِّصِ النّاسَ في مَعاصِي اللهِ، ولم يُقَنِّطْهُم مِن رَحمَةِ اللهِ، ولم يُؤمِنْهُم مِن مَكرِ اللهِ، ولم يَدَعِ القرآنَ رَغبَةً عَنهُ إلىٰ ما سِواهُ.[٥٧٢٤]

5103. **Imām al-Bāqir (AS)** was once asked a question by a man, to which he duly replied, and to which the man then retorted, 'The jurists do not say this!' The Imām said, 'Woe unto you! Have you ever seen a jurist?! A real jurist is a person who is ascetic from this world, who craves for the Hereafter, and strongly holds onto the tradition of the Prophet (SAWA).'[5768]

٥١٠٣ . الإمامُ الباقرُ عليه السلام ـ وقد سَألَهُ رجُلٌ فأجابَهُ، فقالَ الرجُلُ: إنّ الفُقَهاءَ لا يَقولونَ هذا ! ـ : يا وَيحَكَ ! وهَل رَأيتَ فَقيهاً قَطُّ ؟! إنَّ الفَقيهَ حَقَّ الفَقيهِ : الزاهِدُ في الدنيا، الراغِبُ في الآخِرَةِ، المُتَمسِّكُ بسُنَّةِ النبيِّ صلى الله عليه وآله.[٥٧٢٥]

5104. **Imām al-Ṣādiq (AS) said,** 'There is no man from among you who will become a jurist until they understand the intents of our speech.'[5769]

٥١٠٤ . الإمامُ الصّادقُ عليه السلام : لا يكونُ الرجُلُ مِنكُم فَقيهاً حتّىٰ يَعرِفَ مَعاريضَ كلامِنا.[٥٧٢٦]

5105. **Imām al-Riḍā (AS) said,** 'Among the signs of a jurist are clemency, knowledge, and silence.'[5770]

٥١٠٥ . الإمامُ الرِّضا عليه السلام : مِن علاماتِ الفِقهِ الحِلمُ والعِلمُ والصَّمتُ.[٥٧٢٧]

1497. The Power of the Jurist Over Satan

١٤٩٧ ـ شِدَّةُ الفَقيهِ عَلىٰ إبليسَ

5106. **The Prophet (SAWA) said,** 'One jurist is more powerful over Satan than one thousand worshippers.'[5771]

٥١٠٦ . رسولُ اللهِ صلى الله عليه وآله : فَقيهٌ واحِدٌ أشَدُّ علىٰ إبليسَ مِن ألفِ عابِدٍ.[٥٧٢٨]

5107. **The Prophet (SAWA) said,** 'There is nothing more difficult [*lit.* backbreaking] for Satan than a scholar emerging from a tribe.'[5772]

٥١٠٧ . عنه صلى الله عليه وآله : ما مِن شيءٍ أقطَعَ لِظَهرِ إبليسَ مِن عالِمٍ يَخرُجُ في قَبيلَةٍ.[٥٧٢٩]

5108. **Imām Zayn al-ʿĀbidīn (AS) or Imām al-Bāqir (AS) said,** 'A person educated in religion is more difficult for Satan to bear than the worship of one thousand worshippers.'[5773]

٥١٠٨ . الإمامُ زينُ العابدينَ أو الإمامُ الباقرُ عليهما السلام : مُتَفَقِّهٌ في الدِّينِ أشَدُّ على الشيطانِ مِن عِبادَةِ ألفِ عابِدٍ . ٥٧٣٠

(See also: KNOWLEDGE: section 1342)

(أُنظر) العلم : باب ١٣٤٢.

1498. The Death of a Jurist

١٤٩٨ ـ مَوتُ الفَقيهِ

5109. **Imām al-Ṣādiq (AS) said,** 'When a jurist believer dies a void is left in Islam that nothing can ever again fill.'[5774]

٥١٠٩ . الإمامُ الصّادقُ عليه السلام : إذاماتَ المؤمنُ الفَقيهُ ثُلِمَ في الإسلامِ ثُلمَةٌ لا يَسُدُّها شيءٌ . ٥٧٣١

5110. **Imām al-Ṣādiq (AS) said,** 'No believer's death makes Satan happier more than the death of a jurist.'[5775]

٥١١٠ . عنه عليه السلام : مامِن أحَدٍ يَموتُ مِن المؤمنينَ أحَبَّ إلىٰ إبليسَ مِن مَوتِ فَقيهٍ . ٥٧٣٢

324

THINKING

التَّفَكُّر

1499. Encouraging to Think

١٤٩٩ ـ الحَثُّ عَلَى التَّفَكُّرِ

"Thus does Allah clarify His signs for you so that you may reflect."[5776]

﴿ كَذٰلِكَ يُبَيِّنُ اللهُ لَكُمْ ٱلْآيَاتِ لَعَلَّكُمْ تَتَفَكَّرُونَ ﴾ . ٥٧٣٣

(See also: Qur'an 2:266, 2:269, 3:13, 3:137, 3:191, 6:11, 6:36, 6:50, 6:152, 7:3, 7:176, 7:185, 7:201, 10:24, 10:73, 10:101, 12:109, 12:111, 13:3, 15:75, 16:11, 16:36, 23:85, 25: 50, 25:73, 27:62, 27:69, 29:20, 29:24, 29:35, 29:43, 30:8, 30:9, 30:21, 40:13, 40:58, 40:82, 45:3-5, 45:13, 47:10, 54:4, 54:15, 59:2, 69:11, 73:19, 76:29)

(انظر) البقرة : ٢٦٦ ، ٢٦٩ وآل عمران : ١٣ ، ١٣٧ ، ١٩١ والأنعام : ١١ ، ٣٦ ، ٥٠ ، ١٥٢ والأعراف : ٣ ، ١٧٦ ، ١٨٥ ، ٢٠١ ويونس : ٢٤ ، ٧٣ ، ١٠١ ويوسف : ١٠٩ ، ١١١ ، والرعد : ٣ والحِجر : ٧٥ والنحل : ١١ ، ٣٦ والمؤمنون : ٨٥ والفرقان : ٥٠ ، ٧٣ والنمل : ٦٢ ، ٦٩ والعنكبوت : ٢٠ ، ٢٤ ، ٣٥ ، ٤٣ والروم : ٨ ، ٩ ، ٢١ والمؤمن : ١٣ ، ٥٨ ، ٨٢ والجاثية : ٣ ـ ٥ ، ١٣ و محمد : ١٠ والقمر : ٤ ، ١٥ والحشر : ٢ والحاقّة : ١١ والمزّمّل : ١٩ و الإنسان : ٢٩.

5111. **Imām ʿAlī (AS) said,** 'Thinking instigates goodness and action upon it.'[5777]

٥١١١ . الإمامُ عليٌّ عليه السلام : التفكُّرُ يَدعُو إلَى البِرِّ والعَمَلِ بهِ . ٥٧٣٤

5112. **Imām ʿAlī (AS) said,** 'He who thinks perceives.'[5778]

٥١١٢ . عنه عليه السلام : مَن تَفَكَّرَ أبصَرَ . ٥٧٣٥

5113. **Imām ʿAlī (AS) said,** 'Whoever increases his thinking in whatever he learns, his knowledge will become proficient, and he will come to

٥١١٣ . عنه عليه السلام : مَن أكثَرَ الفِكرَ فيما تَعَلَّمَ أتقَنَ

understand whatever he did not understand before.'[5779]

عِلمَهُ، وفَهِمَ ما لم يَكُن يَفهَمُ.[٥٧٣٦]

5114. **Imām ʿAlī (AS) said,** 'There is no knowledge like thinking.'[5780]

٥١١٤. عنه عليه السلام: لا عِلمَ كالتَّفكُّرِ.[٥٧٣٧]

5115. **Imām ʿAlī (AS) said,** 'Thinking is a transparent mirror.'[5781]

٥١١٥. عنه عليه السلام: الفِكرُ مِرآةٌ صافِيَةٌ.[٥٧٣٨]

5116. **Imām Ḥasan (AS) said,** 'Thinking is the life of the heart of the cognizant.'[5782]

٥١١٦. الإمامُ الحسنُ عليه السلام: التفكُّرُ حَياةُ قَلبِ البَصيرِ.[٥٧٣٩]

5117. **Imām Ḥasan (AS) said,** 'I advise you with Godwariness and continuous thinking, for thinking is the father and mother of all good.'[5783]

٥١١٧. عنه عليه السلام: أُوصيكُم بتَقوَى اللهِ وإدامَةِ التَّفكُّرِ؛ فإنَّ التَّفَكُّرَ أبو كُلِّ خَيرٍ وأُمُّهُ.[٥٧٤٠]

5118. **Imām al-Ṣādiq (AS) said,** 'A thought is the mirror of merits and the penance for vices.'[5784]

٥١١٨. الإمامُ الصّادقُ عليه السلام: الفِكرَةُ مِرآةُ الحَسَناتِ وكَفّارَةُ السَّيِّئاتِ.[٥٧٤١]

1500. There is no Worship like Thinking

١٥٠٠ ـ لا عِبادَةَ كَالتَّفَكُّرِ

5119. The mother of Abū Dharr when asked about the worship of Abū Dharr, said, 'He spent his whole day thinking in a place far away from people.'[5785]

٥١١٩. أُمُّ أبي ذَرٍّ ـ وقد سُئلَت عن عِبادَةِ أبي ذَرٍّ ـ: كانَ نَهارَهُ أجمَعَ يَتفكَّرُ في ناحِيَةٍ عنِ الناسِ.[٥٧٤٢]

5120. **Imām al-Ṣādiq (AS) said,** 'The best of worship is perpetually thinking about Allah and His power.'[5786]

٥١٢٠. الإمامُ الصّادقُ عليه السلام: أفضَلُ العِبادَةِ إدمانُ التَّفكُّرِ في اللهِ وفي قُدرَتِهِ.[٥٧٤٣]

5121. **Imām al-Ṣādiq (AS) said,** 'Thinking for an hour is better than worshipping for a year, for *"Only those who possess intellect take admonition."*'[5787 5788]

٥١٢١. عنه عليه السلام: تَفَكُّرُ ساعَةٍ خَيرٌ مِن عِبادَةِ سَنَةٍ ﴿إنَّما يَتَذَكَّرُ أُولُوا الأَلبابِ﴾.[٥٧٤٤]

(See also: WORSHIP: section 1215, 1217)

(أُنظر) العبادة: باب ١٢١٥، ١٢١٧.

1501. That which Purifies Thought

١٥٠١ ـ ما يُصَفِّي الفِكرَ

5122. **Imām ʿAlī (AS) said,** 'Whoever eats less, their thought will be more purified.'[5789]

٥١٢٢. الإمامُ عليٌّ عليه السلام: مَن قَلَّ أكلُهُ صَفا فِكرُهُ.[٥٧٤٥]

5123. **Imām ʿAlī (AS) said,** 'How can one's thought be purified if they are constantly full.'[5790]

٥١٢٣. عنه عليه السلام: كيفَ تَصفُو فِكرَةُ مَن يَستَديمُ الشِّبَعَ؟![٥٧٤٦]

1502. Prohibited Thinking

١٥٠٢ـ التَّفَكُّرُ المَنهِيُّ عَنهُ

5124. **Imām ʿAlī (AS) said,** 'Thinking outside [the bounds] of wisdom is fantasy.'[5791]

٥١٢٤. الإمامُ عليٌّ ﷺ : الفِكرُ في غَيرِ الحِكمَةِ هَوَسٌ.[٥٧٤٧]

5125. **Imām ʿAlī (AS) said,** 'Whoever thinks much about sins, will be prompted to commit them.'[5792]

٥١٢٥. عنه ﷺ : مَن كَثُرَ فِكرُهُ في المَعاصي دَعَتهُ إلَيها.[٥٧٤٨]

5126. **Imām ʿAlī (AS) said,** 'He who contemplates in the essence of Allah becomes a disbeliever.'[5793]

٥١٢٦. عنه ﷺ : مَن تَفَكَّرَ في ذاتِ اللهِ أَلحَدَ.[٥٧٤٩]

(See also: INNER KNOWLEDGE OF ALLAH: section 1254)

(أنظر) المعرفة (٢): باب ١٢٥٤.

325

THE GRAVE

القَبْرُ

1503. The Grave is the First Stage of the Hereafter

١٥٠٣ـ القَبرُ أوَّلُ مَنازِلِ الآخِرَةِ

5127. **The Prophet (SAWA) said,** 'The grave is the first station of the Hereafter. If one is saved from it, whatever comes after it is easier. And if he is not saved from it, whatever comes after it is no less difficult than it.'[5794]

٥١٢٧. رسولُ اللهِ ﷺ : إنّ القَبرَ أوَّلُ مَنازِلِ الآخِرَةِ، فإن نَجا مِنهُ فما بَعدَهُ أيسَرُ مِنهُ، وإن لم يَنجُ مِنهُ فما بَعدَهُ لَيسَ أقلَّ مِنهُ.[٥٧٥٠]

5128. **The Prophet (SAWA),** when he passed by a grave wherein someone had been buried the day before, and the person's family was crying over the grave, said, 'Two simple units of prayer that you deem insignificant are dearer to the person in this grave than the whole of your world.'[5795]

٥١٢٨. عنه ﷺ ـ لَمّا مَرَّ بقَبرٍ دُفِنَ فيهِ بالأمسِ إنسانٌ وأهلُهُ يَبكُونَ ـ: لَرَكعَتانِ خَفيفَتانِ مِمّا تَحتَقِرونَ أحَبُّ إلى صاحِبِ هذا القَبرِ مِن دُنياكُم كُلِّها.[٥٧٥١]

5129. **The Prophet (SAWA) said,** 'The first [experience of the] justice of the Hereafter is the grave, it does not differentiate between the base-born and the noble.'[5796]

٥١٢٩. عنه ﷺ : أوَّلُ عَدلِ الآخِرَةِ القُبورُ، لا يُعرَفُ شَريفٌ مِن وَضيعٍ.[٥٧٥٢]

5130. **The Prophet (SAWA) said,** 'I have never seen a scene more horrid than the grave.'[5797]

٥١٣٠ . عنه ﷺ : ما رَأيتُ مَنظَراً إلّا والقَبرُ أفظَعُ مِنهُ .[٥٧٥٣]

5131. **Imām 'Alī (AS) said,** 'Live near the graves and you will take a lesson.'[5798]

٥١٣١ . الإمامُ عليٌّ عليه السلام : جاوِرِ القُبورَ تَعتَبِرْ .[٥٧٥٤]

5132. **Imām al-Ṣādiq (AS) said,** 'The grave speaks every day. It says: I am the house of loneliness, I am the house of gloom, I am the house of worms, I am the grave, I am a garden of the gardens of Heaven, or a hole from among the holes of Hell.'[5799]

٥١٣٢ . الإمامُ الصّادقُ عليه السلام : إنّ لِلقَبرِ كلاماً في كُلِّ يَوم، يقولُ : أنا بَيتُ الغُربَةِ ، أنا بيتُ الوَحشَةِ ، أنا بَيتُ الدُّودِ ، أنا القَبرُ ، أنا رَوضَةٌ مِن رِياضِ الجَنّةِ أو حُفرَةٌ مِن حُفَرِ النارِ .[٥٧٥٥]

5133. **Imām al-Kāẓim (AS) said** at a graveside, 'Verily the thing [i.e. life] whose end is this [grave] deserves to be spent in asceticism, and verily the thing [i.e. the Hereafter] which begins with this [grave] deserves to be feared.'[5800]

٥١٣٣ . الإمامُ الكاظمُ عليه السلام ـ عندَ قَبرٍ ـ : إنّ شيئاً هذا آخِرُهُ لَحَقيقٌ أن يُزهَدَ في أوَّلِهِ ، وإنّ شيئاً هذا أوَّلُهُ لَحَقيقٌ أن يُخافَ آخِرُهُ .[٥٧٥٦]

1504. Questioning in the Grave

١٥٠٤ ـ سُؤالُ القَبرِ

5134. **The Prophet (SAWA),** with regards to Allah's verse in the Qur'an: *"Allah fortifies those who have faith with an immutable word in the life of this world and in the Hereafter"*[5801], said, 'In the grave when the dead are interrogated'.[5802]

٥١٣٤ . رسولُ اللهِ ﷺ ـ في قولِهِ تعالىٰ : ﴿يُثَبِّتُ اللهُ الّذينَ آمَنوا بالقَولِ الثّابتِ في الحَياةِ الدُّنيا وفي الآخِرَةِ﴾[٥٧٥٧] ـ : في القَبرِ إذا سُئلَ المَوتىٰ .[٥٧٥٨]

5135. **Imām al-Ṣādiq (AS) said,** 'A dead person will be questioned about five things: his prayer, his alms-tax (*zakāt*), his obligatory pilgrimage (*ḥajj*), his fasting, and his acceptance of our divine guardianship (*wilāya*), the *Ahl al-Bayt*. Our guardianship will address the other four from inside the grave, 'Any deficiency that is in you, I will fill.'[5803]

٥١٣٥ . الإمامُ الصّادقُ عليه السلام : يُسألُ المَيِّتُ في قَبرِهِ عن خَمسٍ : عن صَلاتِهِ ، وزَكاتِهِ ، وحَجِّهِ ، وصيامِهِ ، ووَلايَتِهِ إيّانا أهلَ البَيتِ ، فتَقولُ الوَلايةُ مِن جانِبِ القَبرِ للأربَعِ : ما دَخَلَ فِيكُنَّ مِن نَقصٍ فعَلَيَّ تَمامُهُ .[٥٧٥٩]

5136. **Imām al-Ṣādiq (AS) said,** 'A person will not be questioned in their grave unless they have total pureness of faith or total disbelief.'[5804]

٥١٣٦ . عنه عليه السلام : لا يُسألُ في القَبرِ إلّا مَن مَحَضَ الإيمانَ مَحضاً ، أو مَحَضَ الكُفرَ مَحضاً .[٥٧٦٠]

1505. Punishment in the Grave

١٥٠٥ـ عَذابُ القَبرِ

5137. **Imām ʿAlī (AS) said,** 'O servants of Allah! That which comes after death for those who have not been forgiven is worse than death itself and it is the grave. So, be warned of its tightness, its hardship, its darkness and its loneliness ..... And the hard life that Allah has warned His enemies about is the punishment of the grave.'[5805]

٥١٣٧ـ الإمامُ عليٌّ عليه السلام : يا عِبادَ اللهِ، ما بعدَ المَوتِ لِمَن لم يُغفَرْ لَهُ أشدُّ مِن المَوتِ؛ القَبرُ، فاحذَرُوا ضِيقَهُ وضَنكَهُ وظُلمَتَهُ وغُربَتَهُ... وإنّ المَعيشَةَ الضَّنْكَ الّتي حَذَّرَ اللهُ مِنها عَدُوَّهُ عذابُ القَبرِ.[٥٧٦١]

5138. **Imām ʿAlī (AS) said,** 'If you were to see what the dead from among you have seen, you would become grieved, and you would be frightened, and you would listen and obey. However, what they have seen is veiled from you, and the veil will soon be lifted!'[5806]

٥١٣٨ـ عنه عليه السلام : فإنّكُم لو قد عايَنتُم ما قد عايَنَ مَن ماتَ مِنكُم لَجَزِعتُم ووَهِلتُم وسَمِعتُم وأطَعتُم، ولكنْ مَحجوبٌ عَنكُم ما قد عايَنُوا، وقَريبٌ ما يُطرَحُ الحِجابُ[٥٧٦٢]![٥٧٦٣]

5139. **Imām al-Bāqir (AS) said,** 'Whoever's bowings in his prayer [*rukūʿ*] are perfect will not experience fright in their grave.'[5807]

٥١٣٩ـ الإمامُ الباقرُ عليه السلام : مَن أتَمَّ رُكوعَهُ لم تَدخُلْهُ وَحشَةٌ في قَبرِهِ.[٥٧٦٤]

326

KILLING

القَتلُ

1506. The Prohibition of Killing a Soul [i.e. a Human Being]

١٥٠٦ـ حُرمَةُ قَتلِ النَّفسِ

"That is why We decreed for the children of Israel that whoever kills a soul, without [its being guilty of] manslaughter or corruption on the earth, is as though he had killed all mankind, and whoever saves a life is as though he has saved all mankind."[5808]

﴿مِنْ أَجْلِ ذٰلِكَ كَتَبْنا عَلَىٰ بَنِي إِسْرائيلَ أَنَّهُ مَنْ قَتَلَ نَفْساً بِغَيْرِ نَفْسٍ أَوْ فَسادٍ فِي الأَرْضِ فَكَأَنَّما قَتَلَ النَّاسَ جَمِيعاً وَمَنْ أَحْياها فَكَأَنَّما أَحْيا النَّاسَ جَمِيعاً﴾.[٥٧٦٥]

(See also: Qur'an 4:29, 4:92, 4:93, 5:28, 6:140, 6:151, 18:74, 25:68, 81:9)

(انظر) النساء: ٢٩، ٩٢، ٩٣ والمائدة: ٢٨ والأنعام: ١٤٠، ١٥١ والكهف: ٧٤ والفرقان: ٦٨ والتكوير: ٩.

5140. **The Prophet (SAWA) said,** 'The most aggressive of people is he who kills someone other than his killer, or strikes someone other than one who struck him.'[5809]

٥١٤٠ـ رسولُ اللهِ صلى الله عليه وآله : أعتَى الناسِ مَن قَتَلَ غيرَ قاتِلِهِ، أو ضَرَبَ غيرَ ضارِبِهِ.[٥٧٦٦]

5141. **The Prophet (SAWA) said,** 'The first thing that will be judged between people on the Day of Resurrection is the blood shed [between them].'[5810]

٥١٤١ . عنهﷺ : أوَّلُ ما يُقضىٰ بينَ الناسِ يَومَ القِيامَةِ في الدِّماءِ.[٥٧٦٧]

5142. **The Prophet (SAWA) said,** 'The eradication of the whole world is more insignificant for Allah than the blood that has been shed without right.'[5811]

٥١٤٢ . عنهﷺ : لَزَوالُ الدنيا جَميعاً أهوَنُ علَى اللهِ مِن دَمٍ سُفِكَ بغيرِ حَقٍّ.[٥٧٦٨]

5143. **Imām al-Riḍā (AS) said,** 'Allah forbade the killing of human beings for the reason that creation would be corrupted were it to be permissible, and due to their annihilation and the chaos [that would ensue].'[5812]

٥١٤٣ . الإمامُ الرِّضاؑ : حَرَّمَ اللهُ قَتلَ النـفسِ لِعِلَّةِ فَسادِ الخَلقِ في تَحليلِهِ لو أحَلَّ، وفَـنائهِم وفَسادِ التَّدبيرِ.[٥٧٦٩]

1507. Killing of a Believer

١٥٠٧ ـ قَتلُ المُؤمِنِ

"Should anyone kill a believer intentionally, his requital shall be hell, to remain in it [forever]; Allah shall be wrathful at him and curse him and he shall prepare for him a great punishment"[5813]

﴿وَمَنْ يَقْتُلْ مُؤْمِناً مُتَعَمِّداً فَجَزاؤُهُ جَهَنَّمُ خالِداً فِيها وَغَضِبَ اللهُ عَلَيْهِ وَلَـعَنَهُ وَأعَـدَّ لَـهُ عَـذاباً عَظِيماً﴾.[٥٧٧٠]

5144. **The Prophet (SAWA) said,** 'O people! Will a person be killed whilst I am among you, and it is not known whom the killer is?! If all the people of the heavens and the earth were to get together and kill a Muslim [believer], Allah would punish them all without account and judgment.'[5814]

٥١٤٤ . رسولُ اللهِﷺ : يا أيُّها الناسُ، أيُقتَلُ قَتيلٌ وأنا بَينَ أظهُرِكُم لا يُعلَمُ مَن قَتَلَهُ ؟! لو أنّ أهلَ السماءِ والأرضِ اجتَمَعُوا علىٰ قَتلِ رجُلٍ مُسلمٍ لَعَذَّبَهُم اللهُ بلا عَددٍ ولا حِسابٍ.[٥٧٧١]

5145. **The Prophet (SAWA) said,** 'Whoever helps in the killing of a believer even with a part of a word, he will meet Allah on the Day of Judgment with the following words written between his eyes: 'Doomed from the mercy of Allah.'[5815]

٥١٤٥ . عنهﷺ : مَن أعانَ علىٰ قَتلِ مؤمنٍ بشَطرِ كَلِمَةٍ لَقِيَ اللهَ يَومَ القِيامَةِ مَكتوبٌ بـينَ عَـينَيهِ: آيِسٌ مِن رَحمَةِ اللهِ.[٥٧٧٢]

5146. **Imām al-Bāqir (AS) said,** 'Whoever intentionally kills a believer, Allah will affirm for him all the sins, and will acquit sins from the one he has killed. This is according to Allah's verse in the Qur'an: *"I desire that you earn [the burden of] my sin and your sin, to become one of the inmates of the Fire."*'[5816] [5817]

٥١٤٦ . الإمامُ الباقرُؑ : مَن قَتَلَ مُؤمناً مُتَعمِّداً أثبَتَ اللهُ تعالىٰ عـلَيهِ جَـميعَ الذُّنـوبِ، وبَـرِئَ المَقتولُ مِنها، وذلكَ قولُ اللهِ تـعالىٰ: ﴿أُرِيدُ أن تَبُوأَ بِإثْمِي وإثْمِكَ فتَكونَ مِن أصْحابِ النّارِ﴾[٥٧٧٣].[٥٧٧٤]

5147. **Imām al-Ṣādiq (AS)** was once asked, 'A believer intentionally kills a believer, does he have the right to repent?' The Imām replied, 'If his killing him was due to his belief, then he does not have the right to repentance. But if he killed him due to anger or any other worldly reason, then his repentance is that he be killed for it.'[5818]

٥١٤٧ . الإمامُ الصّادقُ عليه السلام ـ لمّا سُئلَ : المؤمنُ يَقتُلُ المؤمنَ مُتَعمِّداً هَل لَهُ تَوبَةٌ ؟ ـ : إن كانَ قَتَلَهُ لإيمانِهِ فلا تَوبةَ لَهُ ، وإن كانَ قَتَلَهُ لِغَضَبٍ أو لِسَبَبِ شيءٍ مِن أمرِ الدنيا فإنَّ تَوبَتَهُ أن يُقادَ مِنهُ .٥٣٧٥

1508. The Prohibition of Suicide

١٥٠٨ ـ تَحريمُ قَتلِ الإنسانِ نَفسَهُ

"O you who have faith! Do not eat up your wealth among yourselves unrightfully, but it should be trade by mutual consent. And do not kill yourselves. Indeed Allah is most merciful to you."[5819]

﴿يا أَيُّها الَّذِينَ آمَنُوا لَا تَأْكُلُوا أَمْوَالَكُم بَيْنَكُم بِالْباطِلِ إِلَّا أَنْ تَكُونَ تِجارَةً عَنْ تَرَاضٍ مِنكُمْ وَلَا تَقْتُلُوا أَنْفُسَكُمْ إِنَّ اللهَ كانَ بِكُمْ رَحِيماً﴾ .٥٧٧٦

5148. **Imām al-Bāqir (AS) said,** 'A believer may be afflicted with all kinds of misfortunes, and may die in all sorts of ways, but he must not kill himself.'[5820]

٥١٤٨ . الإمامُ الباقرُ عليه السلام : إنّ المؤمنَ يُبتَلىٰ بكُلِّ بَليَّةٍ ويَموتُ بكُلِّ مِيتَةٍ إلّا أنّهُ لا يَقتُلُ نفسَهُ .٥٧٧٧

5149. **Imām al-Ṣādiq (AS) said,** 'Whoever intentionally kills himself will dwell in the Hellfire forever.'[5821]

٥١٤٩ . الإمامُ الصّادقُ عليه السلام : مَن قَتَلَ نفسَه مُتَعمِّداً فهُو في نارِ جَهنَّمَ خالِداً فيها .٥٧٧٨

327

THE QUR'AN

القُرآن

1509. Adhere to the Qur'an

١٥٠٩ ـ عَلَيكُم بِالقُرآنِ

"Certainly We have given you [the surah of] the seven oft-repeated verses and the great Qur'an."[5822]

﴿وَلَقَدْ آتَيْنَاكَ سَبْعاً مِنَ الْمَثَانِي وَالْقُرْآنَ الْعَظِيمَ﴾ .٥٧٧٩

"Certainly We have made the Qur'an simple for the sake of admonishment. So is there anyone who will be admonished?"[5823]

﴿وَلَقَدْ يَسَّرْنَا الْقُرْآنَ لِلذِّكْرِ فَهَلْ مِنْ مُدَّكِرٍ﴾ .٥٧٨٠

5150. **The Prophet (SAWA) said,** 'When matters become obscure for you like the darkness of the

٥١٥٠ . رسولُ اللهِ صلى الله عليه وآله : إذا التَبَسَتِ الأُمورُ علَيكُم

night, then turn to the Qur'an, for it is the mediating intercessor and the trustworthy deviser. Whoever puts it in front of them, it will lead them to Heaven, and whoever puts it behind them, it will drag them to Hell'.[5824]

كَقِطَعِ اللَّيلِ المُظلِمِ فعلَيكُم بالقرآنِ؛ فإنَّهُ شافِعٌ مُشَفَّعٌ، وماحِلٌ مُصَدَّقٌ، ومَن جَعَلَهُ أمامَهُ قادَهُ إلَى الجَنَّةِ، ومَن جَعَلَهُ خَلفَهُ قادَهُ إلَى النارِ.[٥٧٨١]

5151. **The Prophet (SAWA),** when it was said to him that his community will be tested, they asked how they may be delivered from it, to which he replied, 'The noble Book of Allah that cannot be overcome with falsehood, neither from in front nor from behind. It is descended from the all-Wise, the Praised One. Allah will lead astray whoever seeks knowledge in other than it.'[5825]

٥١٥١. عنه ﷺ ـ لَمّا قِيلَ لَهُ: أُمَّتُكَ سَتُفتَتَنُ، فَسُئلَ: ما المَخرَجُ مِن ذلكَ؟ ـ: كتابُ اللهِ العَزيزُ، الذي لا يَأتيهِ الباطِلُ مِن بَينِ يَدَيهِ ولا مِن خَلفِهِ، تَنزيلٌ مِن حَكيمٍ حَميدٍ، مَنِ ابتَغَى العِلمَ في غَيرِهِ أضَلَّهُ اللهُ.[٥٧٨٢]

5152. **The Prophet (SAWA) said,** 'You must adhere to the Qur'an, so take it as an *imām* and a leader.'[5826]

٥١٥٢. عنه ﷺ: علَيكُم بالقرآنِ، فاتَّخِذُوهُ إماماً وقائداً.[٥٧٨٣]

5153. **The Prophet (SAWA) said,** 'The superiority of the Qur'an over any other speech is as the superiority of Allah over His creation.'[5827]

٥١٥٣. عنه ﷺ: فَضلُ القرآنِ علىٰ سائرِ الكلامِ كَفَضلِ اللهِ علىٰ خَلقِهِ.[٥٧٨٤]

5154. **The Prophet (SAWA) said,** 'The Qur'an is rich, and there is no richness without it, and no poverty after it.'[5828]

٥١٥٤. عنه ﷺ: القرآنُ غِنىً، لا غِنىً دونَهُ، ولا فَقرَ بعدَهُ.[٥٧٨٥]

5155. **The Prophet (SAWA) said,** 'Whoever is given the Qur'an, and then doubts that someone has been given something more than him, this person has aggrandized something little and belittled something great.'[5829]

٥١٥٥. عنه ﷺ: مَن أُعطِيَ القرآنَ فَظَنَّ أنّ أحَداً أُعطِيَ أكثَرَ ممّا أُعطِيَ فقد عَظَّمَ صَغيراً وصَغَّرَ كبيراً.[٥٧٨٦]

5156. **The Prophet (SAWA) said,** 'Whoever wants the knowledge of the first and the last should explore the Qur'an.'[5830 5831]

٥١٥٦. عنه ﷺ: مَن أرادَ عِلمَ الأوَّلينَ والآخِرينَ فَلْيُثَوِّرِ القرآنَ.[٥٧٨٧، ٥٧٨٨]

5157. **Imām 'Alī (AS) said,** 'He, most High, has manifested Himself for them in His Book, without them seeing Him, by showing them His power.'[5832]

٥١٥٧. الإمامُ عليٌّ ؏: فَتَجَلّىٰ لَهُم سبحانَهُ في كتابِهِ مِن غَيرِ أن يَكونوا رَأَوهُ بِما أراهُم مِن قُدرَتِهِ.[٥٧٨٩]

5158. **Imām ʿAlī (AS) said,** 'Allah Allah [i.e. I advise you] with the Qur'an, nobody other than you should be quicker in acting according to it.'[5833]

٥١٥٨ . عنه ﷺ : اللهَ اللهَ في القرآنِ ، لا يَسبِقُكُم بالعَمَلِ بِهِ غَيرُكُم .٥٧٩٠

5159. **Imām ʿAlī (AS) said,** 'Learn the Book of Allah Almighty; for it is the best of speech and the most eloquent exhortation. Get educated through it, for it is the spring of the hearts. Get cured by its light, for it is the cure for everything in the heart. Excel in its recitation for it is the best of stories.'[5834]

٥١٥٩ . عنه ﷺ : تَعَلَّمُوا كتابَ اللهِ تباركَ وتعالىٰ ؛ فإنّهُ أحسَنُ الحَديثِ وأبلَغُ المَوعِظَةِ ، وتَفَقَّهُوا فيه فإنّهُ رَبيعُ القُلوبِ ، واستَشفُوا بنُورِهِ فإنّه شِفاءٌ لِما في الصُّدورِ ، وأحسِنُوا تِلاوَتَهُ فإنّهُ أحسَنُ القَصصِ .٥٧٩١

5160. **Imām ʿAlī (AS) said,** 'In it there is the cure for the greatest sickness, which is disbelief, hypocrisy, error, and going astray.'[5835]

٥١٦٠ . عنه ﷺ : إنّ فيهِ شِفاءً مِن أكبَرِ الداءِ ، وهُو الكُفرُ والنِّفاقُ ، والغَيُّ والضَّلالُ .٥٧٩٢

5161. **Imām Zayn al-ʿĀbidīn (AS) said,** 'If everyone from the east to the west was to die, I would not feel lonely if I had the Qur'an with me.'[5836]

٥١٦١ . الإمامُ زينُ العابدينَ ﷺ : لو ماتَ مَن بَينَ المَشرِقِ والمَغرِبِ لَما استَوحَشتُ بعدَ أن يكونَ القرآنُ مَعي .٥٧٩٣

1510. The Qur'an is New in Every Era

١٥١٠ ـ القُرآنُ في كُلِّ زَمانٍ جَديدٌ

5162. **Imām ʿAlī (AS) said,** 'The frequency of its recitation and its falling on ears does not render it old.'[5837]

٥١٦٢ . الإمامُ عليٌّ ﷺ : لا تُخلِقُهُ كَثرَةُ الرَّدِّ ووُلوجُ السَّمعِ .٥٧٩٤

5163. **Imām al-Ṣādiq (AS),** when asked, 'Why is it that the Qur'an only increases in freshness the more it is promulgated and taught?' He replied, 'Because Allah, Blessed and most High, did not make the Qur'an for a certain time and not another, or for certain people and not others. It is new in every time and fresh for all people until the Day of Judgment.'[5838]

٥١٦٣ . الإمامُ الصّادقُ ﷺ ـ لَمّا سُئلَ : ما بالُ القرآنِ لا يَزدادُ علَى النَّشرِ والدَّرسِ إلّا غَضاضَةً ؟ ـ : لأنَّ اللهَ تبارَكَ وتعالىٰ لم يَجعَلْهُ لِزمانٍ دونَ زَمانٍ ، ولا لِناسٍ دونَ ناسٍ ، فهُو في كلِّ زَمانٍ جَديدٌ ، وعِندَ كُلِّ قَومٍ غَضٌّ إلىٰ يَومِ القِيامَةِ .٥٧٩٥

1511. Learning and Teaching the Qur'an

١٥١١ ـ تَعَلُّمُ القُرآنِ وَتَعليمُهُ

5164. **The Prophet (SAWA) said,** 'The best of you are those who learn the Qur'an, and teach it.'[5839]

٥١٦٤ . رسولُ اللهِ ﷺ : خِيارُكُم مَن تَعَلَّمَ القرآنَ وعَلَّمَهُ .٥٧٩٦

5165. **The Prophet (SAWA) said,** 'You must learn the Qur'an, and recite it a lot.'[5840]

٥١٦٥ . عنه ﷺ : علَيكُم بتَعَلُّمِ القرآنِ وكَثرَةِ تِلاوَتِهِ .[٥٧٩٧]

5166. **The Prophet (SAWA) said,** 'Whoever teaches a person the Qur'an, he becomes his master. He should not disappoint him or favour anything over him.'[5841]

٥١٦٦ . عنه ﷺ : مَن عَلَّمَ رجُلاً القرآنَ فهُو مَولاهُ ، لا يَخذُلُهُ ولا يَستأثِرُ علَيهِ .[٥٧٩٨]

5167. **Imām ʿAlī (AS) said,** 'The right of a child incumbent upon his father is that he should give him a good name, good manners, and teach him the Qur'an.'[5842]

٥١٦٧ . الإمامُ عليٌّ عليه السلام : حَقُّ الوَلَدِ علَى الوالِدِ أن يُحَسِّنَ اسمَهُ ، ويُحسِّنَ أدَبَهُ ، ويُعَلِّمَهُ القرآنَ .[٥٧٩٩]

5168. **Imām al-Ṣādiq (AS) said,** 'The believer should be such that he does not die without learning the Qur'an, or without being engaged in learning it.'[5843]

٥١٦٨ . الإمامُ الصّادقُ عليه السلام : يَنبَغي للمؤمنِ أن لا يَموتَ حتّىٰ يَتَعَلَّمَ القرآنَ ، أو يكونَ في تَعلُّمِهِ .[٥٨٠٠]

1512. Memorizing the Qur'an and the Etiquettes of those who Memorise it

١٥١٢ ـ حِفظُ القُرآنِ و أدبُ حافِظِه

5169. **The Prophet (SAWA) said,** 'Whoever has been endowed by Allah the memorization of His Book, and doubts that someone has been given something better than what he has, has despised the greatest bounty.'[5844]

٥١٦٩ . رسولُ اللهِ ﷺ : مَن أعطاهُ اللهُ حِفظَ كتابِهِ فظَنَّ أنَّ أحَداً اُعطيَ أفضَلَ مِمّا اُعطيَ فقد غَمَطَ أفضَلَ النِّعمَةِ .[٥٨٠١]

5170. **The Prophet (SAWA) said,** 'Someone who has none of the Qur'an in their self is like a wrecked house.'[5845]

٥١٧٠ . عنه ﷺ : إنّ الذي ليسَ في جَوفِهِ شيءٌ من القرآنِ كالبَيتِ الخَرِبِ .[٥٨٠٢]

5171. **The Prophet (SAWA) said,** 'How wretched is the one who says that he has forgotten such and such verse – rather it is that he has been forgotten. Remember the Qur'an, for by He who owns my soul, it is stronger at detaching itself from the hearts of men than the detachment of an animal from its shackle.'[5846]

٥١٧١ . عنه ﷺ : بِئسَما لِأحدِكُم أن يَقولَ نَسِيتُ آيَةً كَيتَ وكَيتَ ، بَل هو نُسِّيَ . استَذكِرُوا القرآنَ ، فوالذي نَفسي بيَدِهِ لَهُو أشَدُّ تَفَصِّياً مِن صُدورِ الرِّجالِ مِن النَّعَمِ مِن عُقُلِها .[٥٨٠٣]

5172. **The Prophet (SAWA) said,** 'The bearers of the Qur'an [i.e. those who memorize it] are surrounded by the mercy of Allah and are dressed with the light of Allah.'[5847]

٥١٧٢ . عنه ﷺ : حَمَلَةُ القرآنِ هُمُ المَحفوفُونَ برَحمَةِ اللهِ ، المَلبوسونَ بنُورِ اللهِ عَزَّوجلَّ .[٥٨٠٤]

5173. **The Prophet (SAWA) said,** 'The noblemen of my community are the bearers of the Qur'an [i.e. those who memorize it] and the people of night vigil.'[5848]

٥١٧٣ . عنه ﷺ : أشرافُ أُمّتي حَمَلَةُ القرآنِ وأصحابُ الليلِ.٥٨٠٥

5174. **The Prophet (SAWA) said,** 'The worthiest of people in their humbleness, both secretly and openly, are the bearers of the Qur'an, and the worthiest of people in terms of their prayers and fasting, both secretly and openly, are the bearers of the Qur'an.'[5849]

٥١٧٤ . عنه ﷺ : إنّ أحَقَّ الناسِ بالتَّخَشُّعِ في السِّرِّ والعَلانيَةِ لَحامِلُ القرآنِ، وإنّ أحَقَّ النّاسِ في السِّرِّ والعَلانيَةِ بالصلاةِ والصومِ لَحامِلُ القرآنِ.٥٨٠٦

5175. **The Prophet (SAWA) said,** 'The owner of the Qur'an [i.e. he who has memorized it] should not be harsh towards those who are harsh with him, nor behave ignorantly like those who are ignorant, while he has the words of Allah inside him.'[5850]

٥١٧٥ . عنه ﷺ : لا يَنبغي لِصاحِبِ القرآنِ أن يَحِدَّ مَعَ مَن حَدَّ، ولا يَجهَلَ مَعَ مَن يَجهَلُ وفي جَوفِهِ كلامُ اللهِ.٥٨٠٧

5176. **Imām al-Ṣādiq (AS) said,** 'The memorizer of the Qur'an who acts according to it will be with the envoys, noble and pious.'[5851]

٥١٧٦ . الإمامُ الصّادقُ ؑ : الحافِظُ للقرآنِ العامِلُ بِهِ مَعَ السَّفَرَةِ الكِرامِ البَرَرَةِ.٥٨٠٨

5177. **Imām al-Ṣādiq (AS) said,** 'Whoever forgets a chapter (*ṣurah*) from the Qur'an, it will exemplify to him as a form of a reward and a high station. When he sees it, he will ask, 'Who are you? How great you are! If only you were mine!' and it will say to him, 'Don't you know me? I am chapter so and so, and if you did not forget me I would have elevated you to this place.'[5852]

٥١٧٧ . عنه ؑ : مَن نَسِيَ سُورَةً مِنَ القرآنِ مُثِّلَت لَهُ في صُورَةٍ حَسَنَةٍ ودَرَجَةٍ رَفيعَةٍ، فإذا رَآها قالَ: مَن أنتِ؟ ما أحسَنَكِ! لَيتَكِ لي! فتَقولُ: أما تَعرِفُني؟ أنا سُورَةُ كذا وكذا، لو لم تَنسَني لَرَفَعتُكَ إلى هذا المَكانِ.٥٨٠٩

1513. Urging the Recitation of the Qur'an

١٥١٣ ـ الحَثُّ عَلى تِلاوَةِ القُرآنِ

"Indeed those who recite the Book of Allah and maintain the prayer, and spend out of what We have provided them, secretly and openly, expect a commerce that will never go bankrupt."[5853]

﴿إنَّ الَّذينَ يَتلُونَ كِتابَ اللهِ وأقامُوا الصَّلاةَ وأنفَقُوا مِمّا رَزَقناهُم سِرّاً وعَلانيَةً يَرجُونَ تِجارَةً لَن تَبُورَ﴾.٥٨١٠

5178. **The Prophet (SAWA) said,** 'When one of you would like to converse with his Lord, he should read the Qur'an.'[5854]

٥١٧٨ . رسولُ اللهِ ﷺ : إذا أحَبَّ أحدُكُم أن يُحَدِّثَ رَبَّهُ فَلْيَقرأِ القرآنَ.٥٨١١

5179. **The Prophet (SAWA) said,** 'It will be said to the reciter of the Qur'an, 'Read and rise in rank, and recite as you recited in the world, for your station is as per the last verse that you recited.'[5855]

٥١٧٩ . عنه ﷺ : يقالُ لِصاحِبِ القرآنِ : اِقرأ وَارقَ ورَتِّلْ كما كنتَ تُرَتِّلُ في دارِ الدنيا، فإنّ مَنزِلَتَكَ عندَ آخِرِ آيَةٍ كُنتَ تَقرَؤها.[٥٨١٢]

5180. **The Prophet (SAWA) said,** 'These hearts rust the way metal rusts.' He was asked, 'O Messenger of Allah, and what can clean them?' He replied, 'The recitation of the Qur'an.'[5856]

٥١٨٠ . عنه ﷺ : إنّ هذهِ القُلوبَ تَصدأُ كما يَصدأُ الحَديدُ . قيلَ : يا رسولَ الله، فما جَلاؤها؟ قال: تِلاوَةُ القرآنِ.[٥٨١٣]

5181. **The Prophet (SAWA) said,** 'You must read the Qur'an, for verily reading it is a penance for the sins, protection from the Fire, and a safeguard from punishment.'[5857]

٥١٨١ . عنه ﷺ : علَيكَ بقِراءةِ القرآنِ؛ فإنّ قِراءتَه كَفّارةٌ للذُّنوبِ، وسَترٌ في النارِ، وأمانٌ مِن العذابِ.[٥٨١٤]

5182. **The Prophet (SAWA) said,** 'O son, do not neglect reading the Qur'an, for verily the Qur'an revives the heart, and prevents the committing of the erroneous, wrong and corrupt.'[5858]

٥١٨٢ . عنه ﷺ : يا بُنَيَّ، لا تَغفُلْ عَن قِراءةِ القرآنِ؛ فإنّ القرآنَ يُحيي القَلبَ، ويَنهى عَنِ الفحشاءِ والمُنكَرِ والبَغيِ.[٥٨١٥]

1514. Reciting the Qur'an with a Good Voice

١٥١٤ ـ قِراءَةُ القُرآنِ بِالصَّوتِ الحَسَنِ

5183. **The Prophet (SAWA) said,** 'For everything there is an ornament, and the ornament of the Qur'an is a nice voice.'[5859]

٥١٨٣ . رسولُ اللهِ ﷺ : لكلِّ شيءٍ حِليَةٌ وحِليَةُ القرآنِ الصَّوتُ الحَسَنُ.[٥٨١٦]

5184. **The Prophet (SAWA) said,** 'Decorate the Qur'an with your voices.'[5860]

٥١٨٤ . عنه ﷺ : زَيِّنوا القرآنَ بأصواتِكُم.[٥٨١٧]

5185. **The Prophet (SAWA),** when he was asked about the person with the best voice at reciting the Qur'an, he said, 'He who when you hear his recitation you can see that he fears Allah.'[5861]

٥١٨٥ . عنه ﷺ ـ لمّا سُئلَ عن أحسَنِ الناسِ صَوتاً بالقرآنِ ـ : مَن إذا سَمِعتَ قِراءتَهُ رَأيتَ أنّهُ يَخشَى اللهَ.[٥٨١٨]

5186. **The Prophet (SAWA) said,** 'Read the Qur'an sorrowfully, for verily it came down sorrowfully.'[5862]

٥١٨٦ . عنه ﷺ : اقرَؤوا القرآنَ بالحُزنِ؛ فإنّهُ نَزَلَ بالحُزنِ.[٥٨١٩]

1515. The Reality of Recitation

١٥١٥ ـ حَقُّ التِّلاوَةِ

5187. **Imām al-Ṣādiq,** with respect to Allah's verse in the Qur'an: *"Those to whom We have given the Book follow it as it ought to be followed."*[5863] said, 'They recite its verses and understand its meanings and act according to its laws. They hope for its reward, fear its punishment, take examples from its stories, take lesson from its parables, perform its orders, stay away from what it has prohibited. By Allah, it is not just memorizing its verses, citing its words, reciting its chapters, and learning its parts. They have memorized its words and lost its limits. That which is important is contemplating into its verses, Allah Almighty says: *"[It is] a blessed Book that We have sent down to you, so that they may contemplate its signs."*[5864 5865]

٥١٨٧ . الإمامُ الصّادقُ عليه السلام ـ في قولِهِ تعالىٰ: ﴿الَّذِينَ آتَيناهُمُ الكِتابَ يَتْلُونَهُ حَقَّ تِلاوَتِهِ﴾ ـ: يُرَتِّلُونَ آياتِهِ، ويَتَفَهَّمونَ مَعانِيَهُ، ويَعمَلُونَ بأحكامِهِ، ويَرجُونَ وَعدَهُ، ويَخشَونَ عَذابَهُ، ويَتَمَثَّلُونَ قصَصَهُ، ويَعتَبِرُونَ أمثالَهُ، ويَأتُونَ أوامِرَهُ، ويَجتَنِبونَ نَواهِيَهُ. ما هُوَ واللهِ بِحِفظِ آياتِهِ وسَردِ حُروفِهِ، وتِلاوَةِ سُوَرِهِ ودَرسِ أعشارِهِ وأخماسِهِ، حَفِظُوا حُروفَهُ وأضاعُوا حُدودَهُ وإنّما هو تَدَبُّرُ آياتِهِ، يقولُ اللهُ تعالىٰ: ﴿كِتابٌ أنْزَلناهُ إلَيكَ مُبارَكٌ لِيَدَّبَّروا آياتِهِ﴾.[٥٨٢٠، ٥٨٢١]

1516. The Etiquettes of Recitation

١٥١٦ ـ آدابُ القِراءَةِ

1. Cleaning of the mouth

١ ـ تنظيفُ الفَمِ:

5188. **The Prophet (SAWA) said,** 'Clean the path of the Qur'an.' He was asked, 'O Messenger of Allah, and what is the path of the Qur'an?' He replied, 'Your mouths.' They asked, 'How [should we clean them]?' He said, '[By brushing them] With a tooth cleanser (*siwāk*).'[5866]

٥١٨٨ رسولُ اللهِ صلى الله عليه وآله: نَظِّفُوا طَريقَ القرآنِ، قيلَ: يا رسولَ اللهِ، وما طَريقُ القرآنِ؟ قالَ: أفواهُكُم، قيلَ: بماذا؟ قالَ: بالسِّواكِ.[٥٨٢٢]

2. Seeking refuge

٢ ـ الاستِعاذةُ:

"When you recite the Qur'an seek the protection of Allah against the outcast Satan."[5867]

﴿فَإِذَا قَرَأْتَ الْقُرْآنَ فَاسْتَعِذْ بِاللهِ مِنَ الشَّيْطَانِ الرَّجِيمِ﴾.[٥٨٢٣]

5189. **Imām al-Ṣādiq (AS),** when he was asked about seeking refuge at the beginning of every chapter, said, 'Yes, seek refuge in Allah from the outcast Satan. And he mentioned that the outcast (*al-rajīm*) is the most wicked of Satans.'[5868]

٥١٨٩ . الإمامُ الصّادقُ عليه السلام ـ لمّا سُئلَ عنِ التَّعوُّذِ عندَ افتِتاحِ كُلِّ سُورَةٍ ـ: نَعَم، فَتَعَوَّذْ بِاللهِ مِنَ الشَّيطانِ الرَّجيمِ، وذَكَرَ أنَّ الرَّجيمَ أخبَثُ الشَّياطينِ.[٥٨٢٤]

3. Recitation

٣ ـ التَّرتيلُ :

"recite the Qur'an in a measured tone."[5869]

﴿وَرَتِّلِ الْقُرْآنَ تَرْتِيلاً﴾ .٥٨٢٥

5190. **The Prophet (SAWA),** with regard to Allah's verse in the Qur'an: *"and recite the Qur'an in a measured tone"* said, 'Recite it clearly, do not disperse it prosaically, nor rave it like raving poetry. Stop where it mentions wonders, and move the hearts with it, and do not let your only concern be [to finish] the end of the chapter.'[5870]

٥١٩٠ . رسولُ اللهِ ﷺ ـ في قولِهِ تعالىٰ: ﴿وَرَتِّلِ القُرآنَ تَرتيلاً﴾ ـ: بَيِّنْهُ تِبياناً، ولا تَنثُرْهُ نَثرَ البَقْلِ، ولا تَهُذَّهُ هَذَّ الشِّعرِ، قِفُوا عندَ عَجائبِهِ، حَرِّكُوا بهِ القُلوبَ، ولا يَكُن هَمُّ أحَدِكُم آخِرَ السُّورَةِ.٥٨٢٦

4. Contemplation

٤ ـ التَّدبّرُ :

"[It is] a blessed Book that We have sent down to you, so that they may contemplate its signs, and that those who possess intellect may take admonishment."[5871]

﴿كِتابٌ أَنْزَلْناهُ إِلَيْكَ مُبارَكٌ لِيَدَّبَّرُوا آياتِهِ ولِيَتَذَكَّرَ أُوْلُو الأَلْبابِ﴾ .٥٨٢٧

5191. **Imām ʿAlī (AS) said,** 'Verily, there is no good in recitation that does not have contemplation in it. Verily, there is no good in worship that does not have understanding.'[5872]

٥١٩١ . الإمامُ عليٌّ عليه السلام : ألا لا خَيرَ في قِراءةٍ ليسَ فيها تَدَبُّرٌ، ألا لا خَيرَ في عِبادَةٍ ليسَ فيها تَفَقُّهٌ.٥٨٢٨

5192. **Imām al-Ṣādiq (AS),** when asked about completing the Qur'an in one night, said, 'I do not like it for you to complete it all in less than a month.'[5873]

٥١٩٢ . الإمامُ الصّادقُ عليه السلام ـ لمّا سُئلَ عن قِراءةِ القرآنِ في ليلَةٍ ـ: لا يُعجِبُني أن تَقرَأهُ في أقَلَّ مِن شَهرٍ.٥٨٢٩

5. Humbleness

٥ ـ الخُشوعُ :

"Is it not time yet for those who have faith that their hearts should be humbled for Allah's remembrance and to the truth which has come down [to them], and to be not like those who were given the Book before? Time took its toll on them and so their hearts were hardened, and many of them are transgressors"[5874]

﴿أَلَمْ يَأْنِ لِلَّذِينَ آمَنُوا أَنْ تَخْشَعَ قُلُوبُهُم لِذِكْرِ اللهِ وَما نَزَلَ مِنَ الْحَقِّ وَلَا يَكُونُوا كَالَّذِينَ أُوتُوا الْكِتابَ مِن قَبْلُ فَطالَ عَلَيْهِمُ الأَمَدُ فَقَسَتْ قُلُوبُهُمْ وَكَثِيرٌ مِنْهُمْ فاسِقُونَ﴾ .٥٨٣٠

5193. **The Prophet (SAWA),** when asked about the people who recite the best, replied, 'When you hear their recitation, you see that they fear Allah.'[5875]

٥١٩٣ . رسولُ اللهِ ﷺ: لمّا سُئلَ عن أحسَنِ النّاسِ صَوتاً بالقرآنِ ـ: مَن إذا سَمِعتَ قِراءَتَهُ رَأيتَ أنَّهُ يَخشَى اللهَ.٥٨٣١

5194. **Uyūn Akhbār al-Riḍā (AS),** Imām al-Riḍā (AS) constantly recited the Qur'an in his bed at

٥١٩٤ . عيون أخبار الرِّضا عن رجاءَ بنِ أبي الضحّاكِ ـ في ذكرِ سيرة الإمام الرِّضا عليه السلام وقد

night during the path to Khurāsān. When he would read a verse that mentioned Heaven or Hell, he would cry and ask Allah for Heaven or seek refuge from Hell.'[5876]

صَحبَه إلى خراسان ـ: يُكثِرُ باللّيلِ في فِراشِهِ مِن تِلاوَةِ القرآنِ، فإذا مَرَّ بآيَةٍ فيها ذِكرُ جَنّةٍ أو نارٍ بَكى وسَألَ اللهَ الجَنّةَ وتَعَوَّذَ بِهِ مِنَ النارِ.[٥٨٣٢]

1517. Those Whom the Qur'an Curses

١٥١٧ـ مَن يلعنُه القرآنُ

5195. **The Prophet (SAWA) said,** 'Many a reciter of the Qur'an is cursed by the Qur'an itself.'[5877]

٥١٩٥. رسولُ اللهِ ﷺ: رُبَّ تالِ القرآنِ والقرآنُ يَلعَنُهُ.[٥٨٣٣]

5196. **The Prophet (SAWA) said,** 'You read the Qur'an and it prevents you [from sins]. And if it does not prevent you, then you are not reading it [correctly].'[5878]

٥١٩٦. عنه ﷺ: أنتَ تَقرَأُ القرآنَ ما نَهاكَ، فإذا لم يَنهَكَ فَلَستَ تَقرَؤهُ.[٥٨٣٤]

5197. **The Prophet (SAWA) said,** 'In Hell there is a metal millstone that grinds the heads of criminal reciters and scholars'.[5879]

٥١٩٧. عنه ﷺ: إنّ في جَهَنَّمَ رَحاءً مِن حَديدٍ تُطحَنُ بِها رُؤوسُ القُرّاءِ والعُلَماءِ المُجرِمينَ.[٥٨٣٥]

1518. Listening to the Qur'an

١٥١٨ـ استِماعُ القُرآنِ

"When the Qur'an is recited, listen to it and be silent, maybe you will receive [Allah's] mercy."[5880]

﴿وَإِذَا قُرِئَ الْقُرْآنُ فَاسْتَمِعُوا لَهُ وَأَنصِتُوا لَعَلَّكُمْ تُرْحَمُونَ﴾.[٥٨٣٦]

5198. **The Prophet (SAWA) said,** 'Verily, whoever yearns for Allah should listen to the words of Allah.'[5881]

٥١٩٨. رسولُ اللهِ ﷺ: ألا مَنِ اشتاقَ إلَى اللهِ فَليَستَمِعْ كلامَ اللهِ.[٥٨٣٧]

5199. **The Prophet (SAWA) said,** 'Whoever listens to a verse from the Book of Allah, a multiplied reward will be written for him, and whoever recites a verse from the Book of Allah, they will have a light on the Day of Resurrection.'[5882]

٥١٩٩. عنه ﷺ: مَنِ استَمَعَ إلى آيَةٍ مِن كتابِ اللهِ كُتِبَت لَهُ حَسَنَةٌ مُضاعَفَةٌ، ومَن تَلا آيَةً مِن كتابِ اللهِ كانَت لَهُ نوراً يومَ القيامَةِ.[٥٨٣٨]

5200. **Imām al-Ṣādiq (AS),** when Zurāra asked *him* whether paying attention and listening was obligatory upon one who hears the Qur'an being recited, replied, 'Yes, if the Qur'an is recited in your presence, it is obligatory for you to listen and pay attention.'[5883]

٥٢٠٠. الإمامُ الصّادقُ ﷺ ـ لمّا سَألَهُ زُرارَةُ عن وُجوبِ الإنصاتِ والاستماعِ على مَن يَسمَعُ القرآنَ ـ: نَعَم، إذا قُرِئَ القرآنُ عِندَكَ فقد وَجَبَ عليكَ الاستماعُ والإنصاتُ.[٥٨٣٩]

1519. Caution Against Personal Interpretation

١٥١٩ـ التَّحذيرُ مِن التَّفسيرِ بِالرَّأيِ

5201. **The Prophet (SAWA) said**, 'Allah the Exalted has said, 'Those who interpret My words with their own opinion do not believe in Me.'[5884]

٥٢٠١. رسولُ اللهِ ﷺ: قالَ اللهُ جلَّ جلالُه: ما آمَنَ بي مَن فَسَّرَ بِرَأيِهِ كَلامي. ٥٨٤٠

5202. **The Prophet (SAWA) said,** 'The worst thing I fear for my community after me is for someone to interpret the Qur'an wrongfully.'[5885]

٥٢٠٢. عنه ﷺ: أكثَرُ ما أخافُ علىٰ أُمَّتي مِن بَعدي رجُلٌ يَتَأوَّلُ القرآنَ يَضَعُهُ علىٰ غيرِ مَواضِعِهِ. ٥٨٤١

5203. **Imām al-Ṣādiq (AS) said,** 'Whoever interprets the Qur'an with his own opinion and is correct, will not be rewarded, and if he is wrong, he will bear the burden of a sin.'[5886]

٥٢٠٣. الامام الصادق ؑ: من فَسَرَ القرآنَ برأيهِ فَأصابَ لم يُؤجَرْ، وإن أخطَأَ كانَ إثمُهُ علَيهِ. ٥٨٤٢

328

THOSE BROUGHT NEAR TO ALLAH

المُقَرَّبُونَ

1520. The Ultimate Goal of Proximity to Allah

١٥٢٠ـ غايَةُ التَّقَرُّبِ

"And the Foremost Ones are the foremost ones: they are the ones brought near [to Allah]."[5887]

﴿وَالسَّابِقُونَ السَّابِقُونَ * أُولَـٰئِكَ الْمُقَرَّبُونَ﴾. ٥٨٤٣

"Then if he be of those brought near, then ease, abundance, and a garden of bliss."[5888]

﴿فَأَمَّا إِنْ كانَ مِنَ الْمُقَرَّبِينَ * فَرَوْحٌ وَرَيْحانٌ وَجَنَّةُ نَعِيمٍ﴾. ٥٨٤٤

"A spring where those brought near [to Allah] drink."[5889]

﴿عَيْناً يَشْرَبُ بِها الْمُقَرَّبُونَ﴾. ٥٨٤٥

5204. **The Prophet (SAWA) said,** 'Allah, Mighty and Exalted, has said...., 'My servant can never come close to Me with something more beloved to Me than that which I have made obligatory for him, and he can come close to Me with supererogatory prayers such that I love him. And when I love him,

٥٢٠٤. رسولُ اللهِ ﷺ: قالَ الله عزّ وجلّ...: ما تَقَرَّبَ إلَيَّ عَبدٌ بشيءٍ أحَبّ إلَيَّ مـمّا افتَرَضتُ علَيهِ، وإنّهُ لَيَتقرَّبُ إلَيَّ بالنافِلَةِ حتّىٰ أُحِبَّهُ، فإذا أحبَبتُهُ كنتُ سَمعَهُ الذي يَسمَعُ بِهِ، وبَصَرَهُ الذي

I will become his hearing that he hears with, his sight that he sees with, his tongue that he speaks with, his hand that he strikes with. When he prays to Me, I will answer, and when he asks Me, I will give him.'[5890]

يُبصِرُ بِهِ، ولِسانَهُ الذي يَنطِقُ بِهِ، ويَدَهُ التي يَبطِشُ بها، إن دَعاني أجَبتُهُ، وإن سَألَني أعطَيتُهُ.[٥٨٤٦]

5205. **Imām ʿAlī (AS) said,** 'Whoever has patience for the sake of Allah will reach Him.'[5891]

٥٢٠٥. الإمامُ عليٌّ عليه السلام: مَن صَبَرَ علَى اللهِ وَصَلَ إلَيهِ.[٥٨٤٧]

5206. **Imām ʿAlī (AS) said** in his supplication of Shaʿbān, 'O Allah, grant me the perfection of devotion to You, and illuminate the sight of our hearts with the radiance of looking at You until the sight of our hearts pierces through the veils of light, reaching the source of Exaltedness.'[5892]

٥٢٠٦. عنه عليه السلام ـ في المناجاةِ الشَّعبانيّةِ ـ: إلٰهي هَبْ لي كمالَ الانقِطاعِ إلَيكَ، وأنِرْ أبصارَ قُلوبِنا بِضِياءِ نَظَرِها إلَيكَ، حتّىٰ تَخرِقَ أبصارُ القُلوبِ حُجُبَ النورِ، فَتَصِلَ إلىٰ مَعدِنِ العَظَمَةِ.[٥٨٤٨]

5207. **Imām al-ʿAskari (AS) said,** 'Reaching Allah, Mighty and Exalted, is a journey that cannot be accomplished without mounting the night [i.e. night vigil].'[5893]

٥٢٠٧. الإمامُ العسكريُّ عليه السلام: إنَّ الوُصولَ إلَى اللهِ عَزَّوجلَّ سَفَرٌ لا يُدرَكُ إلّا بامتِطاءِ اللَّيلِ.[٥٨٤٩]

1521. The Nearest People to Allah

١٥٢١ ـ أقرَبُ الخَلق إلى اللهِ

5208. **Imām al-Ṣādiq (AS) narrated,** 'Within what Allah revealed unto David (AS): 'O David, just as the closest people to Allah are the humble ones, so the farthest away from Allah are the proud ones.'[5894]

٥٢٠٨. الإمامُ الصّادقُ عليه السلام: فيما أوحَى اللهُ عَزَّوجلَّ إلىٰ داودَ عليه السلام: يا داودُ، كما أنَّ أقرَبَ الناسِ مِن اللهِ المُتَواضِعُونَ كذلكَ أبعَدُ النّاسِ مِن اللهِ المتَكبرونَ.[٥٨٥٠]

5209. **Imām Zayn al-ʿĀbidīn (AS) said,** 'The closest of you to Allah are those who are the most magnanimous of character.'[5895]

٥٢٠٩. الإمامُ زينُ العابدينَ عليه السلام: إنَّ أقرَبَكُم مِن اللهِ أوسَعَكُم خُلقاً.[٥٨٥١]

5210. **Imām al-Ṣādiq (AS) said,** 'There are three kinds of people who will be the closest to Allah on the Day of Resurrection, until all are judged. They are: a person whose power when he is angered does not allow him to wrong those he has power over; a person who walks between two people and is not biased to either one of them, not even by the width of a small hair; and the person who

٥٢١٠. الإمامُ الصّادقُ عليه السلام: ثلاثةٌ هُم أقرَبُ الخَلقِ إلَى اللهِ يَومَ القِيامَةِ حتّىٰ يَفرُغَ (النّاسُ) مِن الحِسابِ: رجُلٌ لم تَدعُهُ قُدرَتُهُ في حالِ غَضَبِهِ إلىٰ أن يَحيفَ علىٰ مَن تَحتَ يَدَيهِ، ورجُلٌ مَشىٰ

speaks the truth, whether it be for or against him.'[5896]

بينَ اثنَينِ فلم يَمِلْ مَعَ أحَـدِهِما عـلَى الآخَـرِ بشَعيرَةٍ، ورجُلٌ قالَ الحَقَّ فيما لَهُ وعلَيهِ.٥٨٥٢

1522. What Brings One Near to Allah

١٥٢٢ ـ ما يُتَقَرَّبُ بِهِ إلَى اللهِ

5211. **Imām al-Bāqir (AS) said,** 'One of the things that Allah confided to Moses (AS) on the mountain is: 'O Moses, inform your people that those who are close to Me can only come nearer to Me by crying to Me out of awe of Me, and the best worship performed by My worshippers is restraint against committing what I have forbidden. Those who adorn themselves for Me have no better adornment than abstinence from worldly affairs in that which they can manage without.' Moses (AS) asked, 'O most Generous of the generous, so what establishes them upon it?' He said, 'O Moses, as for those who come near to Me with crying from My awe, they are in the loftiest level which they will share with no one.'[5897]

٥٢١١. الإمامُ الباقرُ عليه السلام: كانَ فيما ناجىٰ بِهِ اللهُ موسىٰ عليه السلام علىٰ الطُّورِ أن: يا موسىٰ، أبلِغْ قَومَكَ أنّهُ ما يَتَقَرَّبُ إلَيَّ المُتَقرِّبونَ بـمِثلِ البُكـاءِ مِـن خَشيَتي، وما تَعَبَّدَ لي المُتَعبِّدونَ بمِثلِ الوَرَعِ مِن مَحارِمي، ولا تَزَيَّنَ لي المُتَزيِّنونَ بمِثلِ الزُّهـدِ في الدنيا عمّا بِهِمُ الغِنىٰ عَنهُ.
فقالَ موسىٰ عليه السلام: يا أكرَمَ الأكرَمينَ، فماذا أثبَتَهُم علىٰ ذلكَ؟ فقالَ: يا موسىٰ، أمّا المُـتَقرِّبُونَ إلَيَّ بالبُكاءِ مِن خَشيَتي فَهُم في الرَّفيقِ الأعـلىٰ لا يَشرَكُهُم فيهِ أحَدٌ.٥٨٥٣

5212. **The Prophet (SAWA) said,** 'O 'Alī, if worshippers come close to their Creator through righteous deeds, then you should come close to Him with your intellect and you will beat them.'[5898]

٥٢١٢. رسولُ اللهِ صلى الله عليه وآله: يا عليُّ، إذا تَقَرَّبَ العِبادُ إلىٰ خالِقِهِم بالبِرِّ فَتَقَرَّبْ إلَيهِ بالعَقلِ تَسبِقْهُم.٥٨٥٤

5213. **Imām 'Alī (AS) said,** 'The servant can come near to Allah, glory be to Him, by making his intentions sincere.'[5899]

٥٢١٣. الإمامُ عليٌّ عليه السلام: تَقَرُّبُ العَبدِ إلَى اللهِ سبحانَهُ بِإخلاصِ نِيَّتِهِ.٥٨٥٥

5214. **Imām 'Alī (AS) said,** 'Observe true sincerity and excellent certainty, for they are both the best form of worship [carried out] by those brought near [to Allah].'[5900]

٥٢١٤. عنه عليه السلام: علَيكُم بِصِدقِ الإخلاصِ وحُسنِ اليقينِ، فإنّهُما أفضَلُ عِبادَةِ المُقَرَّبينَ.٥٨٥٦

329

THE LOAN

القَرض

1523. The Virtue of Giving Loan

١٥٢٣ ـ فَضلُ القَرضِ

"Who is it that will lend Allah a good loan, that He may multiply it for him and [that] there may be a noble reward for him."[5901]

﴿مَنْ ذَا الَّذِي يُقْرِضُ اللهَ قَرْضاً حَسَناً فَيُضاعِفَهُ لَهُ وَلَهُ أَجْرٌ كَرِيمٌ﴾. ٥٨٥٧

5215. **The Prophet (SAWA) said,** 'Whoever readily lends [money] to a troubled person and is kind in the request after doing so, Allah will give him for every dirham one thousand kantars[5902] in Heaven.'[5903]

٥٢١٥. رسولُ اللهِ ﷺ: مَن أقرَضَ مَلهوفاً فأحسَنَ طِلبَتَهُ استأنَفَ العَمَلَ وأعطاهُ اللهُ بِكُلِّ دِرهَمٍ ألفَ قِنطارٍ مِن الجَنَّةِ. ٥٨٥٨

5216. **The Prophet (SAWA) said,** 'Whoever gives a loan to a believer and waits until he is able, his money will be regarded as alms-tax, and the angels will pray for him until his loan is returned.'[5904]

٥٢١٦. عنه ﷺ: مَن أقرَضَ مُؤمناً قَرضاً يَنتَظِرُ بهِ مَيسورَهُ كانَ مالُهُ في زَكاةٍ، وكانَ هو في صَلاةٍ مِن المَلائكةِ حتّى يُؤَدِّيَهُ إلَيهِ. ٥٨٥٩

5217. **The Prophet (SAWA) said,** 'Whoever wants his prayers to be answered and his grief to be dispelled should relieve a person in difficulty.'[5905]

٥٢١٧. عنه ﷺ: مَن أرادَ أن تُستَجابَ دَعوَتُهُ وأن تُكشَفَ كُربَتُهُ فَلْيُفَرِّجْ عن مُعسِرٍ. ٥٨٦٠

5218. **The Prophet (SAWA) said,** 'If one's Muslim brother needs a loan from him and he is able to lend him but does not do so, Allah will prohibit for this person the smell of Heaven.'[5906]

٥٢١٨. عنه ﷺ: مَنِ احتاجَ إلَيهِ أخوهُ المُسلمُ في قَرضٍ وهُو يَقدِرُ علَيهِ فلَم يَفعَلْ حَرَّمَ اللهُ علَيهِ ريحَ الجَنّةِ. ٥٨٦١

5219. **Imām ʿAlī (AS) said,** 'He who relies on Him will be sufficed, whoever asks Him will be given, whoever lends for Him, He will repay him, and whoever thanks Him will be rewarded.'[5907]

٥٢١٩. الإمامُ عليٌّ عليه السلام: مَن تَوَكَّلَ علَيهِ كَفاهُ، ومَن سَألَهُ أعطاهُ، ومَن أقرَضَهُ قَضاهُ، ومَن شَكَرَهُ جَزاهُ. ٥٨٦٢

5220. **Imām ʿAlī (AS),** in his will to his son Ḥasan (AS) said, 'And if you find a needy person who is deprived who can carry your provision for

٥٢٢٠. عنه عليه السلام ـ في وصيَّتِهِ لابنِهِ الحسنِ عليه السلام ـ:

you until the Day of Judgment and who will pay you back tomorrow when you need it, then seize the opportunity and let him hold this provision for you. Increase in giving provisions to the poor if you are able to, for you might look for them and not find them. Seize the opportunity to lend someone when you yourself are free from need so that he may repay you in your time of difficulty.'[5908]

وإذا وَجَدتَ مِن أهلِ الفاقةِ مَن يَحمِلُ لكَ زادَكَ إلىٰ يومِ القيامَةِ فيُوافِيكَ بهِ غداً حيثُ تحتاجُ إلَيهِ فاغتَنِمْهُ وحَمِّلْهُ إيّاهُ، وأكثِرْ مِن تَزويدِهِ وأنتَ قادِرٌ علَيهِ فلَعلَّكَ تَطلُبُهُ فلا تَجِدُهُ، واغتَنِمْ مَن استَقرَضَكَ في حالِ غِناكَ، لِيَجعَلَ قَضاءَهُ لكَ في يومِ عُسرَتِكَ.٥٨٦٣

5221. **Imām al-Ṣādiq (AS) said,** 'It is written on the door of Heaven: [The reward for] A loan is multiplied by eighteen, and a donation is by ten, and this is because the loan is not given to anyone other than the hand of a needy person, whereas the donation may fall into the hands of someone not needy.'[5909]

٥٢٢١. الإمامُ الصّادقُ عليه السلام: علىٰ بابِ الجَنّةِ مَكتوبٌ: القَرضُ بثَمانيةَ عَشرَ، والصَّدَقةُ بعَشرَةٍ، وذلكَ أنّ القَرضَ لا يكونُ إلّا في يدِ المُحتاجِ، والصَّدقةُ ربّما وَقَعَت في يَدِ غيرِ مُحتاجٍ.٥٨٦٤

5222. **Imām al-Ṣādiq (AS) said,** 'For me to give a loan is far beloved to me than acquiring that same amount.'[5910]

٥٢٢٢. عنه عليه السلام: لأن أُقرِضَ قَرضاً أحَبُّ إلَيَّ مِن أن أصِلَ بمِثلِهِ.٥٨٦٥

1524. Enjoinment to Give Respite to One who is Unable to Pay

١٥٢٤ ـ الحَثُّ علىٰ إنظارِ المُعسِرِ

"And if [the debtor] is in straits, let there be a respite until the time of ease; and if you remit [the debt] as charity, it will be better for you should you know."[5911]

﴿وإنْ كانَ ذو عُسْرَةٍ فَنَظِرَةٌ إلىٰ مَيْسَرَةٍ وأنْ تَصدَّقُوا خَيْرٌ لَكُمْ إنْ كُنتُمْ تَعلَمُونَ﴾.٥٨٦٦

5223. **The Prophet (SAWA) said,** 'Whoever gives respite to a straitened person, Allah will shade him with His Shade on the Day when no shade will avail other than His Shade.'[5912]

٥٢٢٣. رسولُ اللهِ صلى الله عليه وآله: مَن أنظَرَ مُعسِراً أظَلَّهُ اللهُ بظِلِّهِ يومَ لا ظِلَّ إلّا ظِلُّهُ.٥٨٦٧

5224. **The Prophet (SAWA) said,** 'Fear the imprecations of a person in difficulty.'[5913]

٥٢٢٤. عنه صلى الله عليه وآله: اتَّقُوا دَعوَةَ المُعسِرِ.٥٨٦٨

5225. **The Prophet (SAWA) said,** 'Just as it is not permitted for the one indebted to you to delay repaying you when he is well-off, so it is also not permitted for you to put him in difficulty [by

٥٢٢٥. عنه صلى الله عليه وآله: كما لا يَحِلُّ لِغَريمِكَ أن يَمطُلَكَ وهُو مُوسِرٌ، فكذلكَ لا يَحِلُّ لكَ أن

demanding repayment] when you know that he is straitened.'[5914]

تُعسِرَهُ إذا عَلِمتَ أنّهُ مُعسِرٌ.[٥٨٦٩]

(See also: THE DEBT: section 751)

(أنظر) الدين: باب ٧٥١.

330

ECONOMY

الاقتصاد

1525. Encouraging an Economical Livelihood

١٥٢٥ـ الحَثُّ عَلى الاقتِصادِ فِي المَعيشَةِ

5226. **The Prophet (SAWA) said,** 'Economising in one's expenditure is half of livelihood.'[5915]

٥٢٢٦. رسولُ اللهِ ﷺ: الاقتِصادُ فِي النَّفَقَةِ نِصفُ المَعيشَةِ.[٥٨٧٠]

5227. **The Prophet (SAWA) said,** 'There is no spending more loved by Allah than spending with careful deliberation.'[5916]

٥٢٢٧. عنه ﷺ: ما مِن نَفَقَةٍ أحَبَّ إلَى اللهِ مِن نَفَقَةِ قَصدٍ.[٥٨٧١]

5228. **The Prophet (SAWA) said,** 'Economising, maintaining silence and righteous guidance are one part of the twenty-five parts of prophethood.'[5917]

٥٢٢٨. عنه ﷺ: الاقتِصادُ وحُسنُ السَّمتِ والهَديُ الصالِحُ جُزءٌ مِن بِضعٍ وعِشرينَ جُزءاً مِنَ النُّبوَّةِ.[٥٨٧٢]

5229. **Imām 'Alī (AS) said,** 'Whoever adopts moderation his expenditure will decrease.'[5918]

٥٢٢٩. الإمامُ عليٌّ عليه السلام: مَن تَحَرَّى القَصدَ خَفَّت عَلَيهِ المُؤَنُ.[٥٨٧٣]

5230. **Imām 'Alī (AS) said,** 'Whoever adopts moderation needlessness will continuously accompany him and moderation will make up for his poverty and shortages'[5919]

٥٢٣٠. عنه عليه السلام: مَن صَحِبَ الاقتِصادَ دامَت صُحبَةُ الغِنى لَهُ، وجَبَرَ الاقتِصادُ فَقرَهُ وخَلَلَهُ.[٥٨٧٤]

5231. **Imām 'Alī (AS) said,** He who adopts moderation in richness and poverty has prepared himself against the adversities of the world.'[5920]

٥٢٣١. عنه عليه السلام: مَنِ اقتَصَدَ فِي الغِنى والفَقرِ فَقَدِ استَعَدَّ لِنَوائبِ الدَّهرِ.[٥٨٧٥]

5232. **Imām 'Alī (AS) said,** in his will to his son Imām Ḥasan 'O son, adopt moderation in your livelihood.'[5921]

٥٢٣٢. عنه عليه السلام ـ في وَصيَّتِهِ لابنِهِ الحسنِ عليه السلام عِندَ وفاتِهِ ـ: اقتَصِد يا بُنَيَّ في مَعيشَتِكَ.[٥٨٧٦]

5233. **Imām ʿAlī (AS) said,** 'The characteristic of a believer is moderation and his way of life is development.'[5922]

٥٢٣٣ . عنه ﷺ : المؤمنُ سِيرَتُهُ القَصدُ، وسُنَّتُهُ الرُّشدُ.٥٨٧٧

1526. The Role of Economising in One's Needlessness

١٥٢٦ـ دَورُ الاقتِصادِ فِي الغِنىٰ

5234. **The Prophet (SAWA) said,** 'Whoever economizes, Allah will enrich them.'[5923]

٥٢٣٤ . رسولُ اللهِ ﷺ : مَنِ اقتَصَدَ أغناهُ اللهُ.٥٨٧٨

5235. **Imām ʿAlī (AS) said,** 'Economising is subsistence.'[5924]

٥٢٣٥ . الإمامُ عليٌّ ﷺ : الاقتِصادُ بُلغَةٌ.٥٨٧٩

5236. **Imām ʿAlī (AS) said,** 'Economising increases the little, and wasting destroys the abundant.'[5925]

٥٢٣٦ . عنه ﷺ: الاقتِصادُ يُنمي القليلَ، الإسرافُ يُفني الجزيلَ.٥٨٨٠

5237. **Imām al-Ṣādiq (AS) said,** I guarantee that he who adopts moderation would not become poor'[5926]

٥٢٣٧ . الإمامُ الصّادقُ ﷺ : ضَمِنتُ لِمَنِ اقتَصَدَ أن لا يفتقِرَ.٥٨٨١

331

RETRIBUTION (*Qiṣāṣ*)[5927]

القِصَاصُ

1527. Legislation of Retribution and its Importance

١٥٢٧ـ تَشريعُ القِصاصِ وَاهمِّيتهُ

"There is life for you in retribution, O you who possess intellects! Maybe you will be Godwary."[5928]

﴿وَلَكُم فِي القِصاصِ حَياةٌ يا أُولِي الأَلْبابِ لَعَلَّكُمْ تَتَّقُونَ﴾.٥٨٨٢

"A sacred month for a sacred month, and all sanctities require retribution. So should anyone aggress against you, assail him in the manner he assailed you, and be wary of Allah, and know that Allah is with the Godwary."[5929]

﴿الشَّهْرُ ٱلْحَرَامُ بِالشَّهْرِ ٱلْحَرَامِ وَٱلْحُرُماتُ قِصاصٌ فَمَنِ ٱعْتَدَىٰ عَلَيْكُمْ فَاعْتَدُوا عَلَيْهِ بِمِثْلِ ما ٱعْتَدَىٰ عَلَيْكُمْ وَٱتَّقُوا اللهَ وَٱعْلَمُوا أَنَّ اللهَ مَعَ الْمُتَّقِينَ﴾.٥٨٨٣

"And in it We prescribed for them: a life for a life, an eye for an eye, a nose foe a nose, and an ear for an ear, a tooth for a tooth, and retaliation for wounds. Yet whoever remits out of charity, that shall be an atonement for him. Those who do not judge by who Allah has sent down it is they who are the wrongdoers."[5930]

﴿وكَتَبْنا عَلَيْهِمْ فِيها أَنَّ النَّفْسَ بِالنَّفْسِ وَالْعَيْنَ بِالْعَيْنِ والأَنْفَ بِالأَنْفِ وَالأُذُنَ بِالأُذُنِ والسِّنَّ بِالسِّنِّ وَالْجُرُوحَ قِصاصٌ فَمَنْ تَصَدَّقَ بِهِ فَهُوَ كَفّارَةٌ لَهُ وَمَنْ لَمْ يَحْكُمْ بِما أَنْزَلَ اللهُ فَأُولئِكَ هُمُ الظّالِمُونَ﴾.[٥٨٨٤]

5238. **The Prophet (SAWA) said,** 'O people, verily I am a human being like you, and it might be that my departure from among you is close, so whoever I have afflicted whether it be in their honour, one strand of their hair, their skin, their money, here is the honour, hair, skin, and money of Muḥammad, so they should stand up and take their reprisals! And none of you should say: I fear the enmity and grudge of Muḥammad. Verily, these two are not of my nature and not of my morals.'[5931]

٥٢٣٨. رسولُ اللهِ ﷺ: يا أيُّها الناسُ، إنّما أنا بَشَرٌ مِثلُكُم، ولعلّهُ أن يكونَ قد قَرُبَ مِنّي خُفوقٌ مِن بينِ أظهُرِكُم، فَمَن كُنتُ أصَبتُ مِن عِرضِهِ أو مِن شَعرِهِ أو مِن بَشَرِهِ أو مِن مالِهِ شَيئاً، هذا عِرضُ مُحمّدٍ وشَعرُهُ وبَشَرُهُ ومالُهُ فَليَقُمْ فَلْيَقتَصَّ! ولا يَقولَنَّ أحَدٌ مِنكُم: إنّي أتَخوَّفُ مِن مُحمّدٍ العَداوَةَ والشَّحناءَ، ألا وإنّهُما لَيسَتا مِن طَبيعَتي ولَيسَتا مِن خُلُقي.[٥٨٨٥]

5239. **The Prophet (SAWA) said,** 'O people, revive retribution and revive the truth, and do not disperse. Be Muslims and submit and you will be saved.'[5932]

٥٢٣٩. عنه ﷺ: أيُّها الناسُ، أحيُوا القِصاصَ وأحيُوا الحَقَّ ولا تَفَرَّقُوا، وأسلِموا وسَلِّموا تَسلَموا.[٥٨٨٦]

5240. **Imām ʿAlī (AS) said,** 'Allah ordained faith to be purification from polytheism…and retribution to act as prevention of bloodshed.'[5933]

٥٢٤٠. الإمامُ عليٌّ ؑ: فَرَضَ اللهُ الإيمانَ تَطهيراً مِنَ الشِّركِ... والقِصاصَ حَقناً للدِّماءِ.[٥٨٨٧]

5241. **Imām Zayn al-ʿĀbidīn (AS),** with regard to Allah's verse in the Qur'an: *"There is life for you in retribution"* said, 'Because whoever intends to kill and knows that he will be punished as a result, and refrains from doing so, there will be [a new] life for the person who he intended to kill, for the criminal who wanted to kill, and life for people other than these two who know that retribution is obligatory and they do not dare kill for fear of retribution.'[5934]

٥٢٤١. الإمامُ زينُ العابدينَ ؑ ـ في قولِهِ تعالى: ﴿ولَكُم في القِصاصِ حَياةٌ﴾ ـ: لأنَّ مَن هَمَّ بالقتلِ فَعَرَفَ أنّهُ يُقتَصُّ مِنهُ فكَفَّ لِذلكَ عنِ القَتلِ كانَ حَياةً لِلّذي (كانَ) هَمَّ بِقَتلِهِ، وحَياةً لِهذا الجاني الذي أرادَ أن يَقتُلَ، وحَياةً لِغَيرِهِما مِن الناسِ إذا عَلِموا أنَّ القِصاصَ واجِبٌ لا يَجرؤونَ على القَتلِ مَخافَةَ القِصاصِ.[٥٨٨٨]

1528. Forgiving the Retribution

١٥٢٨ ـ العَفوُ عَنِ القِصاصِ

5242. **The Prophet (SAWA) said,** 'Whoever forgives blood money, their reward will be nothing short of Heaven.'[5935]

٥٢٤٢ . رسولُ اللهِ ﷺ : مَن عَفا عَن دَمٍ لم يَكُن لَهُ ثَوابٌ إلّا الجَنّةُ .٥٨٨٩

5243. **The Prophet (SAWA) said,** 'Any person who is afflicted on their body in any way, and they remit this out of charity, Allah will elevate their level and demote their mistakes.'[5936]

٥٢٤٣ . عنه ﷺ : ما مِن رَجُلٍ مُسلمٍ يُصابُ بشَيءٍ في جَسَدِهِ فيَتَصَدَّقُ بهِ إلّا رَفَعَهُ اللهُ بهِ دَرَجَةً وحَطَّ عَنهُ بهِ خَطيئةً .٥٨٩٠

5244. **Imām al-Ṣādiq (AS),** when asked about Allah's verse: *"Yet whoever remits out of charity, that shall be an atonement for him"*, said, 'His sins will be pardoned according to how much he forgave.'[5937]

٥٢٤٤ . الإمامُ الصادقُ ﷺ ـ لَمّا سُئلَ عن قولِ اللهِ عزّوجلّ : ﴿فَمَنْ تَصَدَّقَ بِهِ فَهُوَ كَفّارَةٌ لَهُ﴾ ـ : يُكَفَّرُ عَنهُ مِن ذُنوبِهِ بقَدرِ ما عَفا .٥٨٩١

(See also: PARDON 284)

(انظر) عنوان ٢٨٤ «العفو».

332

DECREE AND DESTINY

القَضاءُ وَالقَدَرُ

1529. Decree and Destiny

١٥٢٩ ـ القَضاءُ وَالقَدَرُ

"Say, 'Nothing will befall us except what Allah has ordained for us. He is our master, and in Allah let all the faithful put their trust.'"[5938]

﴿قُلْ لَنْ يُصِيبَنا إلّا ما كَتَبَ اللهُ لَنا هُوَ مَوْلانا وَعَلَى اللهِ فَلْيَتَوَكَّلِ الْمُؤْمِنُونَ﴾ .٥٨٩٢

"But in order that Allah may carry through a matter that was bound to be fulfilled."[5939]

﴿وَلٰكِنْ لِيَقْضِيَ اللهُ أمْراً كانَ مَفْعُولاً﴾ .٥٨٩٣

"Indeed We have created everything in a measure."[5940]

﴿إنّا كُلَّ شَيءٍ خَلَقْناهُ بِقَدَرٍ﴾ .٥٨٩٤

5245. **The Prophet (SAWA) said,** 'And everything has its decreed measure, even weakness and cleverness.'[5941]

٥٢٤٥ . رسولُ اللهِ ﷺ : وكُلُّ شيءٍ بقَدَرٍ حتّى العَجزُ والكَيسُ .٥٨٩٥

5246. **The Prophet (SAWA) said,** 'Even if the angels Isrāfīl, Gabriel, Mikā'īl, the bearers of the Throne, and I among them were to pray for you,

٥٢٤٦ . عنه ﷺ : لو دَعا لكَ إسرافيلُ وجبريلُ وميكائيلُ وحَمَلَةُ العَرشِ وأنا فيهم ما تَزَوَّجتَ

you would not marry other than the woman that was written for you.'[5942]

إلّا المرأةَ التي كُتِبَت لكَ.٥٨٩٦

5247. **Imām ʿAlī (AS),** in praising Allah, glory be to Him, said, 'I praise Him for Himself as He has requested praise from His creation, and He made a decreed measure for everything, and for every decree a due date, and for every date a record.'[5943]

٥٢٤٧. الإمامُ عليٌّ ﷺ ـ في تحميدِ اللهِ سبحانَهُ ـ: أحمَدُهُ إلىٰ نفسِهِ كما استَحمَدَ إلىٰ خَلقِهِ، وجَعَلَ لكُلِّ شيءٍ قَدراً، ولِكُلِّ قَدرٍ أجَلاً ولِكُلِّ أجَلٍ كتاباً.٥٨٩٧

5248. **Imām ʿAlī (AS) said,** 'Destiny is one of the secrets of Allah, one of the veils of Allah, one of the amulets of Allah. It is upheld in the veil of Allah and concealed from Allah's creation.'[5944]

٥٢٤٨. عنه ﷺ: القَدَرُ سِرٌّ مِن سِرِّ اللهِ، وسِترٌ مِن سِترِ اللهِ وحِرزٌ مِن حِرزِ اللهِ مَرفوعٌ في حِجابِ اللهِ، مَطويٌّ عَن خَلقِ اللهِ.٥٨٩٨

5249. **Imām ʿAlī (AS),** when asked by a man about destiny said, '[It is] a deep sea, so do not delve into it. The man asked, 'O Commander of the Faithful, inform us about destiny.' The Imām said, 'It is the secret of Allah, so do not trouble yourself with it.' The man then asked [again], 'O Commander of the Faithful, inform us about destiny.' The Imām said, 'Seeing as you are refusing [and insisting], it is a matter between two extremes - neither predestination nor absolute free will.'[5945]

٥٢٤٩. عنه ﷺ ـ وقد سَألَهُ رجُلٌ عنِ القَدَرِ ـ: بَحرٌ عَميقٌ فلا تَلِجْهُ. قالَ: يا أميرَ المؤمنينَ، أخبِرنا عنِ القَدَرِ. قالَ: سِرُّ اللهِ فلا تَتَكَلَّفْهُ. قالَ: يا أميرَ المؤمنينَ، أخبِرنا عنِ القَدَرِ. قالَ: أما إذ أبَيتَ فإنّهُ أمرٌ بَينَ أمرَينِ لا جَبرَ ولا تَفويضَ.٥٨٩٩

5250. **Imām ʿAlī (AS) said,** 'Destiny holds sway over [our] calculations until calamity ruins our calculations.'[5946]

٥٢٥٠. عنه ﷺ: يَغلِبُ المِقدارُ علَى التَّقديرِ، حتّىٰ تكونَ الآفَةُ في التَّدبيرِ.٥٩٠٠

5251. **Imām ʿAlī (AS) said,** 'All things surrender to destiny so much so that [sometimes our] calculations will be ruined.'[5947]

٥٢٥١. عنه ﷺ: تَذِلُّ الأُمورُ للمَقاديرِ حتّىٰ يكونَ الحَتفُ في التَّدبيرِ.٥٩٠١

5252. **Imām al-Ṣādiq (AS) said,** 'Decree and destiny are two creations from among the creations of Allah, and Allah increases in His creation how He wills.'[5948]

٥٢٥٢. الإمامُ الصّادقُ ﷺ: إنّ القَضاءَ والقَدَرَ خَلقانِ مِن خَلقِ اللهِ، واللهُ يَزيدُ في الخَلقِ ما يَشاءُ.٥٩٠٢

5253. **Imām al-Ṣādiq (AS) said,** 'When the Day of Resurrection comes and Allah will gather all His creation, He will ask what He entrusted with

٥٢٥٣. عنه ﷺ: إذا كانَ يَومُ القِيامَةِ وجَمَعَ اللهُ الخَلائقَ سَألَهُم عمّا عَهِدَ إلَيهِم ولم

them, and will not ask about what He destined for them.'[5949]

يَسألُهُم عَمّا قَضىٰ علَيهِم.٥٩٠٣

5254. **Imām al-Ṣādiq (AS) said,** 'When Allah wants something, He decrees it, and when He decrees it He issues His command, and when He issues His command He executes it.'[5950]

٥٢٥٤ . عنه ﷺ: إنّ اللهَ إذا أرادَ شيئاً قَدَّرَهُ، فإذا قَدَّرَهُ قَضاهُ، فإذا قَضاهُ أمضاهُ.٥٩٠٤

5255. **Imām al-Hādī (AS) said,** 'Predeterminations show you what would have never crossed your mind.'[5951]

٥٢٥٥ . الإمامُ الهاديُّ ﷺ: المَقاديرُ تُريكَ ما لَم يَخطُرْ بِبالِكَ.٥٩٠٥

1530. The Writing of Decree and Destiny for People in the Womb

١٥٣٠ - كِتابَةُ القَضاءِ وَالقَدَرِ عَلَى الإنسانِ فِي الرَّحِمِ

5256. **Imām al-Bāqir (AS),** with regards to the creation of the human in the womb said, 'When four months are completed, Allah sends two creative angels...., and they ask, 'O Lord, shall it be wretched or prosperous?' Again, they are commanded, and they then ask, 'O Lord, what is its due date of death, its sustenance, and all other matters relating to its state – [and he listed some of them]-?' And they then go about writing a covenant between his eyes.'[5952]

٥٢٥٦ . الإمامُ الباقرُ ﷺ - في خِلقَةِ الإنسانِ في الرَّحِمِ - : إذا كَمُلَ أربعةُ أشهُرٍ بَعَثَ اللهُ مَلَكَينِ خَلّاقَينِ، ... فيَقولانِ: يا ربِّ، شَقيّاً أو سَعيداً؟ فيُؤمَرانِ، فيقولانِ: يا رَبِّ، ما أجَلُهُ وما رِزقُهُ وكلُّ شيءٍ مِن حالِهِ - وعَدَّدَ مِن ذلك أشياءَ - ؟ ويَكتُبانِ المِيثاقَ بينَ عَينَيهِ.٥٩٠٦

5257. **Imām al-Bāqir (AS),** said, 'And then Allah will reveal unto the two angels, 'Write for him My decree and destiny, and the execution of My command, and reserve My condition of changing [of a divine ruling] (*badā'*) among what you write.'[5953]

٥٢٥٧ . عنه ﷺ - أيضاً - : ثُمّ يُوحي اللهُ إلَى المَلَكَينِ: أُكتُبا علَيهِ قَضائي وقَدَري ونافِذَ أمري واشتَرِطا لِيَ البَداءَ فيما تَكتُبانِ.٥٩٠٧

1531. Whatever Allah Decrees for a Believer is Good

١٥٣١ - ما قَضاهُ اللهُ لِلمُؤمِنِ فَهُوَ خَيرٌ

5258. **The Prophet (AS) said,** 'In every decree of Allah's, Mighty and Exalted, there is good for the believer.'[5954]

٥٢٥٨ . رسولُ اللهِ ﷺ: في كلِّ قَضاءِ اللهِ عَزَّوجلَّ خِيَرَةٌ (خَيرٌ) للمؤمنِ.٥٩٠٨

5259. **Imām al-Ṣādiq (AS) said,** 'How wonderful for a Muslim that Allah does not ordain a fate for him unless it is good for him, even if he was to be cut with scissors it would be for his benefit, and even if he was to own the east side of the world and the west, it would be for his good.'[5955]

٥٢٥٩ . الإمامُ الصّادقُ عليه السلام : عَجِبتُ للمَرءِ المُسلمِ لا يَقضي اللهُ عَزَّوجلَّ لَهُ قَضاءً إلّا كانَ خَيراً لَهُ، وإن قُرِضَ بالمَقاريضِ كانَ خَيراً لَهُ، وإن مَلَكَ مَشارِقَ الأرضِ ومَغارِبَها كانَ خَيراً لَهُ.[٥٩٠٩]

5260. **Imām al-Ṣadiq (AS) said,** 'Any fate that Allah decrees for a believer which he is pleased with, Allah will place good in what He decreed.'[5956]

٥٢٦٠ . عنه عليه السلام : ما قَضَى اللهُ لمؤمنٍ قَضاءً فَرَضِيَ بِهِ إلّا جَعَلَ اللهُ لَهُ الخِيَرَةَ فيما يَقضي.[٥٩١٠]

(See also: THE ORDEAL: section 272)

(أُنظر) البلاء: باب ٢٧٢.

1532. One who is not Content with the Decree

١٥٣٢ ـ مَن لَم يَرضَ بِالقَضاءِ

5261. **The Prophet (SAWA) said,** 'Allah Almighty says, 'Whoever is not pleased with My decree and does not believe in My destiny should beseech another god.'[5957]

٥٢٦١ . رسولُ اللهِ صلى الله عليه وآله : قالَ اللهُ جلَّ جلالُهُ : مَن لم يَرضَ بقَضائي ولم يُؤمِنْ بِقَدَري فَلْيَلتَمِسْ إلهاً غَيري![٥٩١١]

5262. **Imām ʿAlī (AS) said,** 'The people with the worst punishment on the Day of Judgment will be those who resented the decree of Allah.'[5958]

٥٢٦٢ . الإمامُ عليٌّ عليه السلام : أشَدُّ الناسِ عَذاباً يَومَ القِيامَةِ المُتَسَخِّطُ لِقَضاءِ اللهِ.[٥٩١٢]

5263. **Imām ʿAlī (AS) said,** 'Whoever wakes up upset with the world has woken up resentful of the decree of Allah.'[5959]

٥٢٦٣ . عنه عليه السلام : مَن أصبَحَ علَى الدنيا حَزيناً فقد أصبَحَ لِقَضاءِ اللهِ ساخِطاً.[٥٩١٣]

5264. **Imām al-ʿAskarī (AS) said,** 'Since decrees are concealed, wherefore the need for begging?!'[5960]

٥٢٦٤ . الإمامُ العسكريُّ عليه السلام : إذا كانَ المَقضيُّ كائِناً فالضَّراعَةُ لماذا؟![٥٩١٤]

(See also: SATISFACTION WITH ALLAH'S DIVINE DECREE: section 832)

(أُنظر) الرضا (١): باب ٨٣٢.

1533. What is Part of Fate

١٥٣٣ ـ ما هو مِن القَدَرِ

5265. **The Prophet (SAWA) said,** 'The remedy is a part of fate, and He helps whom He wills and however He wills.'[5961]

٥٢٦٥ . رسولُ اللهِ صلى الله عليه وآله : الدَّواءُ مِن القَدَرِ، وهُوَ يَنفَعُ مَن يَشاءُ بما شاءَ.[٥٩١٥]

5266. **The Prophet (SAWA),** when asked, 'Have you seen medicine that we can cure ourselves with, amulets we can protect ourselves with, and things we can do to repel the destiny of Allah?' He replied, 'They are all part of the destiny of Allah.'[5962]

٥٢٦٦ . عنه ﷺ ـ لَمّا سُئلَ : أرأيتَ دَواءً نتَداوىٰ بِهِ، وَرُقىً نَستَرقِي بِها، وأشياءَ نَفعَلُها، هَل تَرُدُّ مِن قَدَرِ اللهِ ؟ ـ: بل هِي مِن قَدَرِ اللهِ.[٥٩١٦]

5267. **Imām ʿAlī (AS),** returning from the Battle of Ṣiffīn, in answer to an old man who asked him about their journey to Syria: 'Is this fate or destiny?' said, 'By He who created the seed and made the human being, we have not gone through a valley or ascended a mountain without it being our fate and destiny…. You might think this to be imperative fate and inevitable destiny. If this were so then promise of reward (*waʿd*) and threat of penalty (*waʿīd*), would cease to apply, and reward and punishment would become null. Allah would not blame the sinners, nor would He praise the good-doers. The benevolent would not be more worthy of reward for good deeds than the sinner, which is the belief of the idol worshippers…. and the Magians. However, Allah has commanded good by choice and forbidden evil by warning, and He is not disobeyed helplessly, nor obeyed forcefully or freely, and nor does He give man absolute control.'[5963]

٥٢٦٧ . الإمامُ عليٌّ عليه السلام ـ عندَ انصِرافِهِ مِن صِفِّينَ في جَوابِ شَيخٍ سَألَهُ عن مَسيرِهِم إلَى الشامِ: أبِقَضاءٍ وقَدَرٍ ؟ ـ: والذي خَلَقَ الحَبَّةَ وبَرَأَ النَّسَمَةَ، ما قَطَعنا وادِياً ولا عَلَونا تَلعَةً إلّا بقَضاءٍ وقَدَرٍ... لعلَّكَ ظَنَنتَه قَضاءً لازِماً وقَدَراً حاتِماً، لو كانَ ذلكَ لَسَقَطَ الوَعدُ والوَعيدُ وبَطَلَ الثَّوابُ والعِقابُ، ولا أتَت لائمَةٌ مِن اللهِ لِمُذنِبٍ ولا مَحمَدَةٌ مِن اللهِ لُمحسِنٍ، ولا كانَ الُمحسِنُ أولىٰ بثَوابِ الإحسانِ مِن المُذنِبِ، ذلكَ مَقالُ أحزابِ عَبَدَةِ الأوثانِ... ومَجُوسِها، ولكنَّ اللهَ أمَرَ بالخَيرِ تَخييراً ونَهىٰ عَنِ الشَّرِّ تَحذيراً، ولم يُعصَ مَغلوباً ولم يُطَعْ مُكرَهاً، ولا يُمَلِّكُ تَفويضاً.[٥٩١٧]

5268. **Ibn Nubāta narrated,** 'The Commander of the Faithful (AS) swerved away from a leaning wall away to another wall, so he was asked, 'O Commander of the Faithful, are you fleeing from the decree of Allah?' He said, 'I flee from the decree of Allah to the destiny of Allah, Mighty and Exalted.'[5964]

٥٢٦٨ . ابن نُباتَة : إنّ أميرَ المؤمنينَ عليه السلام عَدَلَ مِن عِندِ حائطٍ مائلٍ إلىٰ حائطٍ آخَرَ، فقيلَ لَهُ: يا أميرَ المؤمنينَ، تَفِرُّ مِن قَضاءِ اللهِ ؟! قالَ: أفِرُّ مِن قَضاءِ اللهِ إلىٰ قَدَرِ اللهِ عَزَّوجلَّ.[٥٩١٨]

333

JUDGMENT (in a Court of Justice)

القَضاء

1534. The Importance of the Status of Judgment

١٥٣٤ ـ أهَمِّيَّةُ موقِعِ القَضاءِ

"O David! Indeed We have made you a vicegerent on the earth. So judge between people with justice, and do not follow desire, or it will lead you astray from the way of Allah. Indeed those who stray from the way of Allah there is a severe punishment for them because of their forgetting the Day of Reckoning."[5965]

﴿يا دَاوُدُ إنَّا جَعَلْناكَ خَلِيفَةً فِي الْأَرْضِ فَاحْكُمْ بَيْنَ النَّاسِ بِالْحَقِّ وَلَا تَتَّبِعِ الْهَوَىٰ فَيُضِلَّكَ عَنْ سَبِيلِ اللهِ إِنَّ الَّذِينَ يَضِلُّونَ عَنْ سَبِيلِ اللهِ لَهُمْ عَذَابٌ شَدِيدٌ بِمَا نَسُوا يَوْمَ الْحِسابِ﴾.[٥٩١٩]

5269. **Imām ʿAlī (AS) said** to Shurayḥ, 'O Shurayḥ, you are sitting on a seat that only the likes of prophets, successors of prophets or wretched people sit on.'[5966]

٥٢٦٩. الإمامُ عليٌّ عليه السلام ـ لِشُرَيح ـ: يا شُرَيحُ، قد جَلَستَ مَجلِساً لا يَجلِسُهُ إلّا نَبيٌّ أو وَصيُّ نَبيٍّ أو شَقيٌّ.[٥٩٢٠]

5270. **Imām ʿAlī (AS),** in a letter he wrote to al-Ashtar when he made him governor of Egypt, said, '...Then choose for judgment between people the best of your subjects, who are of excellent character and high calibre and for whom no issue or case is hard. They must not lose their temper, disputes should not let him fall astray they should not exceed in their mistakes, and when the truth is made clear to them they should not hesitate to accept it [change their verdict]. They should not lean towards greed. They should not satisfy themselves with the lowest of understanding over the highest, they must be more precautious than anyone else in doubtful and ambiguous matters. They must attach the greatest importance to reasoning, arguments and proofs. They must exhibit the least annoyance at seeing the opponent, be the most patient in scanning details, and most serious in the issuing of a verdict when

٥٢٧٠. عنه عليه السلام ـ مِن كتابٍ كَتَبَهُ للأشتَرِ لَمّا وَلّاهُ علىٰ مِصرَ ـ: ثُمّ اختَرْ لِلحُكمِ بينَ الناسِ أفضَلَ رَعِيَّتِكَ في نَفسِكَ، ممَّن لا تَضيقُ بهِ الاُمورُ، ولا تُمَحِّكُهُ الخُصومُ، ولا يَتَمادىٰ في الزَّلَّةِ، ولا يَحصَرُ مِنَ الفَيءِ إلَى الحَقِّ إذا عَرَفَهُ، ولا تُشرِفُ نَفسُهُ علىٰ طَمَعٍ، ولا يَكتَفي بأدنىٰ فَهمٍ دونَ أقصاهُ، وأوقَفَهُم في الشُّبُهاتِ، وآخَذَهُم بالحُجَجِ وأقَلَّهُم تَبَرُّماً بمُراجَعَةِ الخَصمِ، وأصبَرَهُم علىٰ تَكَشُّفِ الاُمورِ، وأصرَمَهُم عِند

the matter is clear. The praisings of people should not deceive them. They should not be misled by flattery, but unfortunately such people are few. After you have selected such men to act as your judges, make it a point to go through some of their judgments and to check their proceedings.'[5967]

اتِّضاحِ الحُكمِ، مِمّن لا يَزدَهيهِ إطراءٌ، ولا يَستَميلُهُ إغراءٌ، وأُولئكَ قليلٌ، ثُمّ أكثِر تَعاهُدَ (تعهُّدَ) قَضائهِ.٥٩٢١

5271. **Imām al-Ṣādiq (AS) said,** 'Beware of governance, for verily governance is for the leader who is knowledgeable about judgment, just among the Muslims, and for a prophet or the successor of a prophet.'[5968]

٥٢٧١ . الإمامُ الصّادقُ عليه السلام : اتَّقُوا الحُكومَةَ؛ فإنَّ الحُكومَةَ إنّما هي لِلإمامِ العالِمِ بالقَضاءِ، العادِلِ في المُسلمينَ، لِنَبيٍّ أو وَصيِّ نبيٍّ.٥٩٢٢

1535. Bringing a Case for Judgment Before a Tyrant

١٥٣٥ ـ التَّحاكُمُ إلَى الطّاغوتِ

"Have you not regarded those who claim that they believe in what has been sent down to you, and what was sent down before you? They desire to seek the judgment of the Rebel, though they were commanded to defy it."[5969]

﴿أَلَمْ تَرَ إِلَى الَّذِينَ يَزْعُمُونَ أَنَّهُمْ آمَنُوا بِما أُنْزِلَ إِلَيْكَ وَما أُنْزِلَ مِنْ قَبْلِكَ يُرِيدُونَ أَنْ يَتَحاكَمُوا إِلَى الطَّاغُوتِ وَقَدْ أُمِرُوا أَنْ يَكْفُرُوا بِهِ﴾.٥٩٢٣

5272. **Imām al-Ṣādiq (AS),** with regard to two of his companions who went to be judged before a tyrant in a dispute they had about a loan or inheritance, said, 'Whoever goes to be judged before a tyrant and he judges in favour of one of them, whatever he is compensated is unlawful, even if it was rightfully his, because he took it by judgment of a tyrant when Allah has ordered him to reject the tyrant.'[5970]

٥٢٧٢ . الإمامُ الصّادقُ عليه السلام ـ في تَحاكُمِ رَجلَينِ مِن أصحابِهِ إلَى الطاغوتِ وبينَهُما مُنازَعَةٌ في دَينٍ أو مِيراثٍ ـ: مَن تَحاكَمَ إلَى الطاغوتِ فَحُكِمَ لَهُ فإنّما يَأخُذُ سُحتاً وإن كانَ حَقُّهُ ثابِتاً لَهُ، لأنّهُ أخَذَ بحُكمِ الطاغوتِ، وقد أمَرَ اللهُ أن يَكفُرَ بهِ.٥٩٢٤

5273. **Imām al-Ṣādiq (AS) said,** 'Beware of seeking judgment amongst yourselves from oppressors. Rather, try to find a person among you who has some knowledge about our legal edicts and make him judge between you, for I have made such a person [with these qualifications] a judge, so seek judgment from him.'[5971]

٥٢٧٣ . عنه عليه السلام : إيّاكُم أن يُحاكِمَ بعضُكُم بَعضاً إلىٰ أهلِ الجَورِ، ولكنِ انظُرُوا إلىٰ رجُلٍ مِنكُم يَعلَمُ شيئاً مِن قَضايانا فاجعَلُوهُ بينَكُم، فإنّي قد جَعَلتُهُ قاضياً فتَحاكَمُوا إلَيهِ.٥٩٢٥

1536. The Danger in the Occupation of a Judge

١٥٣٦ ـ خُطورَةُ عَمَلِ القَضاءِ

5274. **The Prophet (SAWA) said,** 'Whoever has been [wrongfully] appointed judge has been slaughtered without a knife.' He was asked, 'O Messenger of Allah, and what is meant by slaughtering?' He said, 'The Fire of Hell.'[5972]

٥٢٧٤ . رَسولُ اللهِ ﷺ : مَن جُعِلَ قاضياً فَقَد ذُبِحَ بغيرِ سِكِّينٍ . فقيلَ : يارسولَ اللهِ ، وما الذَّبحُ ؟ قالَ : نارُ جهنَّمَ .[٥٩٢٦]

5275. **The Prophet (SAWA) said,** 'The just judge will be brought forward on the Day of Judgment and will be judged so severely that he will wish that he never judged between two people for so much as a date.'[5973]

٥٢٧٥ . عنه ﷺ : إنَّ القاضيَ العَدلَ لَيُجاءُ بهِ يَومَ القِيامَةِ فَيَلقَىٰ مِن شِدَّةِ الحِسابِ ما يَتَمَنّىٰ أن لا يكونَ قَضىٰ بينَ اثنَينِ في تَمرَةٍ قَطُّ .[٥٩٢٧]

5276. **Imām al-Ṣādiq (AS) said,** 'The Nawāwīs [a place in Hell] complained to Allah about the severity of the heat within them, so He said to them, 'Quiet! For the resting place of the judges is more severe in heat than yours!'[5974]

٥٢٧٦ . الإمامُ الصّادقُ عليه السلام : إنَّ النَّواويسَ[٥٩٢٨] شَكَت إلَى اللهِ عَزَّوجلَّ شِدَّةَ حَرِّها ، فقالَ لَها عَزَّوجلَّ : اسكُني ؛ فإنَّ مَواضِعَ القُضاةِ أشَدُّ حَرّاً مِنكِ ![٥٩٢٩]

1537. Seeking Judgment

١٥٣٧ ـ طَلَبُ القَضاءِ

5277. **The Prophet (SAWA) said,** 'Whoever seeks to be a judge and asks the mediators will be left to himself, and whoever is forced in doing so, Allah will bring down to him an angel to protect him.'[5975]

٥٢٧٧ . رسولُ اللهِ ﷺ : مَنِ ابتَغَى القَضاءَ وسَألَ فيهِ الشُّفَعاءَ وُكِلَ إلىٰ نفسِهِ ، ومَن اُكرِهَ علَيهِ أنزَلَ اللهُ علَيهِ مَلَكاً يُسَدِّدُهُ .[٥٩٣٠]

5278. **Imām al-Ṣādiq (AS) said,** 'A person of little legal knowledge should not desire to be a judge.'[5976]

٥٢٧٨ . الإمامُ الصّادقُ عليه السلام : لا يَطمَعَنَّ قَليلُ الفِقهِ في القَضاءِ .[٥٩٣١]

1538. The Etiquettes of Judging

١٥٣٨ ـ آدابُ القَضاءِ

a. Equity Between Opposing Plaintiffs

أ ـ المُواساةُ بينَ الخُصومِ :

5279. **The Prophet (SAWA) said,** 'Whoever is stricken with having to judge between Muslims must

٥٢٧٩ . رسولُ اللهِ ﷺ : مَنِ ابتُلِيَ بالقَضاءِ بينَ

do so with fairness, in his glance, his indications, his sitting, and his gatherings.'[5977]

المُسلمينَ فَلْيَعدِلْ بَينَهُم في لَحظِهِ وإشارَتِهِ ومَقعدِهِ ومَجلِسِهِ.٥٩٣٢

5280. **Imām ʿAlī (AS),** speaking to Shurayḥ said, 'And act with equity between the Muslims with your face, speech, and sitting, in order that those who are close to you will not hope for bias from you, nor will your enemies despair of your justice.'[5978]

٥٢٨٠. الإمامُ عليٌّ ﷺ ـ لِشُرَيح ـ: ثُمّ واسِ بينَ المسلمينَ بوَجهِكَ ومَنطِقِكَ ومَجلِسِكَ، حتّىٰ لا يَطمَعَ قَريبُكَ في حَيفِكَ، ولا يَيأسَ عَدُوُّكَ مِن عَدلِكَ.٥٩٣٣

b. The Judge Should Not Raise His Voice over the Plaintiff's

ب ـ أن لا يَعلُوَ كلامُهُ كلامَ الخصمِ:

5281. **Imām ʿAlī,** speaking to Abū al-Aswad al-Du'alī when he asked the Imām about the reason why he was discharged from being a judge, when he had neither been treacherous nor committed a crime, replied, 'I saw that your voice was raised above the voice of your plaintiff's.'[5979]

٥٢٨١. الإمامُ عليٌّ ﷺ ـ لأبي الأسوَدِ الدُّؤَليِّ لمّا سَألَهُ عن عِلّةِ عَزلِهِ عنِ القَضاءِ وهُو لم يَخُنْ ولم يَجنِ ـ: إنّي رَأيتُ كلامَكَ يَعلو علىٰ كلامِ الخَصمِ.٥٩٣٤

c. Not Becoming Irritated

ج ـ أنْ لا يَتَضَجَّرَ في مجلسِ القضاءِ:

5282. **Imām ʿAlī (AS) said** to Shurayḥ, 'Beware of becoming bored and irritated in the court of justice, wherein Allah has prescribed a reward and for which there will be good provision for he who judges honestly.'[5980]

٥٢٨٢. الإمامُ عليٌّ ﷺ ـ لِشُرَيح ـ: إيّاكَ والتَّضَجُّرَ والتَّأذِّيَ في مَجلِسِ القَضاءِ، الذي أوجَبَ اللهُ فيهِ الأجرَ، ويُحسِنُ فيهِ الذُّخرَ لِمَن قَضىٰ بالحَقِّ.٥٩٣٥

d. Not Passing Judgment before Listening to Both Sides

د ـ أن لا يَقضيَ قبلَ سماعِ كلامِ الخَصمَينِ معاً:

5283. **The Prophet (SAWA) said** to Imām ʿAlī (AS), 'When two people bring a case against each other before you to be judged, do not judge the first before you hear out the second. If you adhere to this, judging will become clear for you.' Imām ʿAlī (AS) said, 'And after that I continued to be a judge.' The Prophet (SAWA) said [supplicating for him], 'O Allah, make him understand judgment.'[5981]

٥٢٨٣. رسولُ اللهِ ﷺ ـ لِعَليٍّ ﷺ ـ: إذا تَقاضىٰ إلَيكَ رَجُلانِ فلا تَقضِ لِلأوّلِ حتّىٰ تَسمَعَ مِن الآخَرِ؛ فإنّكَ إذا فَعلتَ ذلكَ تَبَيَّنَ لكَ القَضاءُ.
قالَ عليٌّ ﷺ: فما زِلتُ بَعدَها قاضياً، وقالَ لَهُ النبيُّ ﷺ: اللّهُمَّ فَهِّمْهُ القَضاءَ.٥٩٣٦

e. Not Passing Judgment While Angry

هـ ـ عَدَمُ القَضاءِ في الغَضَبِ :

5284. **Imām ʿAlī (AS),** said to Shurayḥ, 'Do not whisper to anyone in your court, and if you get angry leave, and do not judge whilst you are angry.'[5982]

٥٢٨٤ . الإمامُ عليٌّ عليه السلام لِشُرَيح ـ: لا تُسارَّ أحَداً في مَجلِسِكَ، وإن غَضِبتَ فقُمْ، فلا تَقضِيَنَّ فأنتَ غَضبانُ.[٥٩٣٧]

f. Not Passing Judgment Whilst Being Overcome by Sleep

و ـ أن لا يَقضيَ وهو مُثقَلٌ بالنَّومِ :

5285. *Daʿāʾim al-Islām*: 'The Prophet (SAWA) forbade for a judge to pass judgment whilst being angry, hungry or tired.'[5983]

٥٢٨٥ . دعائم الإسلام : نَهىٰ رسولُ اللهِ صلى الله عليه وآله أن يَقضيَ القاضي وهُو غَضبانُ أو جائعٌ أو ناعِسٌ.[٥٩٣٨]

g. Not Passing Judgment While Hungry or Thirsty

ز ـ أن لا يَقضيَ وهو جُوعانُ أو عَطشانُ :

5286. **The Prophet (SAWA) said,** The judge should not pass judgment between two people unless he is satiated with food and water.'[5984]

٥٢٨٦ . رسولُ اللهِ صلى الله عليه وآله : لا يَقضِي القاضِي بَينَ إثنَينِ إلّا وهُوَ شَبعان رَيّان.[٥٩٣٩]

5287. **Imām ʿAlī (AS),** said to Shurayḥ, 'Do not sit in a session of justice until you have eaten.'[5985]

٥٢٨٧ . الإمامُ عليٌّ عليه السلام لِشُرَيح ـ: ولا تَقعُدَنَّ في مَجلِسِ القَضاءِ حتّىٰ تَطعَمَ.[٥٩٤٠]

h. Not Hosting Any of the Plaintiffs as a Guest

ح ـ أن لا يُضيفَ أحدَ الخَصمَينِ :

5288. **Imām al-Ṣādiq (AS) narrated,** 'A person was a guest of the Commander of the Faithful (AS) and stayed with him for some days. He then presented him with a prior dispute that he had not mentioned to the Commander of the Faithful (AS). The Imām said to him, 'Are you making a formal complaint?' He said, 'Yes.' The Imām said, 'Transfer from us [from our house], for the Messenger of Allah (SAWA) forbade the hosting of a plaintiff [for whom one is judge] unless the rival plaintiff is also with him.'[5986]

٥٢٨٨ . الإمامُ الصّادقُ عليه السلام : إنَّ رجُلاً نَزَلَ بأميرِ المؤمنينَ عليه السلام فمَكَثَ عِندَهُ أيّاماً، ثُمّ تَقَدَّمَ إلَيهِ في خُصومَةٍ لم يَذكُرْها لأميرِ المؤمنينَ عليه السلام، فقالَ لَهُ: أخَصمٌ أنتَ؟ قالَ: نَعَم، قالَ: تَحَوَّلْ عنّا، إنَّ رسولَ اللهِ صلى الله عليه وآله نَهىٰ أن يُضافَ الخَصمُ إلّا ومَعَهُ خَصمُهُ.[٥٩٤١]

i. Not Suborning the Witnesses
ط ـ أن لا يُلَقِّنَ الشُّهودَ:

5289. It is narrated in *Mustadrak al-Wasā'il*: The Prophet (SAWA) forbade the judge to favour one of the plaintiffs [over the other] by looking at him too much or paying more attention to him, and he also forbade suborning witnesses.'[5987]

٥٢٨٩ . مستدرك الوسائل: إنّ رسولَ اللهِ ﷺ نَهى أن يُحابِيَ القاضي أحَدَ الخَصمَينِ بكَثرَةِ النَّظَرِ وحُضورِ الذِّهنِ، ونَهى عَن تَلقينِ الشُّهودِ.[٥٩٤٢]

1539. The Judges Whose Mistakes Allah Remedies
١٥٣٩ ـ مَن يُسَدِّدُهُ اللهُ مِن القُضاةِ

5290. **The Prophet (SAWA) said,** 'There is no Muslim judge who does not have two angels guiding him to the truth as long as he does not seek other than this [i.e. the truth]. If he does want other than the truth and intentionally gives wrong edicts, the two angels disown him and entrust him to his own [base] self.'[5988]

٥٢٩٠ . رسولُ اللهِ ﷺ: ما مِن قاضٍ مِن قُضاةِ المُسلمينَ إلّا ومَعَهُ مَلَكانِ يُسَدِّدانِهِ إلَى الحَقِّ مالَم يُرِدْ غيرَهُ، فإذا أرادَ غيرَهُ وجارَ مُتَعمِّداً تَبَرّأَ مِنهُ المَلَكانِ ووَكَلاهُ إلى نفسِهِ.[٥٩٤٣]

5291. **Imām 'Alī (AS) said,** 'The Hand of Allah hovers above the head of the judge with mercy. If he gives unjust rulings, Allah entrusts him to his own self.'[5989]

٥٢٩١ . الإمامُ عليٌّ ؈: يَدُ اللهِ فوقَ رَأسِ الحاكِمِ تُرَفرِفُ بالرَّحمَةِ، فإذا حافَ وَكَلَهُ اللهُ إلىٰ نفسِهِ.[٥٩٤٤]

1540. Types of Judges
١٥٤٠ ـ أصنافُ القُضاةِ

5292. **Imām al-Ṣādiq (AS) said,** 'Judges are of four types, three of them are in the Hellfire, and one in Heaven: a person who knowingly judges wrongfully is in the Hellfire; a person who unknowingly judges wrongfully is in the Hellfire; a person who unknowingly judges with truth is in the Hellfire; and a person who knowingly judges with truth is in Heaven.'[5990]

٥٢٩٢ . الإمامُ الصّادقُ ؈: القُضاةُ أربَعةٌ: ثلاثةٌ في النارِ وواحِدٌ في الجَنّةِ: رجُلٌ قَضىٰ بجَورٍ وهُو يَعلَمُ فهُو في النارِ، ورَجُلٌ قَضىٰ بجَورٍ وهُو لا يَعلَمُ فهُو في النارِ، ورجلٌ قَضىٰ بالحَقِّ وهُو لا يَعلَمُ فهُو في النارِ، ورجُلٌ قَضىٰ بالحَقِّ وهو يَعلَمُ فهُو في الجَنّةِ.[٥٩٤٥]

1541. Just Judges
١٥٤١ ـ قُضاةُ الحقّ

5293. **Imām 'Alī (AS) said,** 'The most just of creation is he who is the best in judging according to the truth.'[5991]

٥٢٩٣ . الإمامُ عليٌّ ؈: أعدَلُ الخَلقِ أقضاهُم بِالحَقِّ.[٥٩٤٦]

5294. **Imām ʿAlī (AS) said,** 'The best of people are the truthful judges.'[5992]

٥٢٩٤ . عنه ﷺ : خَيرُ النّاسِ قُضاةُ الحَقِّ.٥٩٤٧

1542. Judging with Clear Evidence

١٥٤٢ ـ القَضاءُ بِالبَيِّنَةِ

5295. **The Prophet (SAWA) said** to two men when they came to him with a dispute about the inheritance and things that had became effaced, 'One of you might be more agile in his evidence than the other. So if I was to judge something in his favour that was [actually] from the right of his brother, then I am giving him a part of Hell.' Each of the two men asked him, 'O Messenger of Allah, does this right of mine belong to my companion?' He replied, '[No], But go and become brothers and have compassion, and each of you should forgive the other.'[5993]

٥٢٩٥ . رسولَ اللهِ ﷺ ـ لمّا اختصم إليه رَجلانِ في مَواريثَ وأشياءَ قد دَرَسَتْ ـ: لعلَّ بعضَكُم أن يكونَ ألحَنَ بحُجَّتِهِ مِن بَعضٍ ، فَمَن قَضَيتُ لَهُ بشيءٍ مِن حَقِّ أخيهِ فإنّما أقطَعُ لَهُ قِطعَةً مِن النارِ ، فقالَ لَهُ كُلُّ واحِدٍ مِن الرَّجُلَينِ : يا رسولَ اللهِ ، حَقّي هذا لِصاحبي ؟ فقالَ : ولكنِ اذهَبا فَتَوَخَّيا ثُمّ اسْتَهِما ثُمّ لِيُحَلِّلْ كلُّ واحِدٍ مِنكُما صاحِبَهُ.٥٩٤٨

5296. **The Prophet (SAWA),** speaking to Imri' al-Qays who was in a dispute with another person about a piece of land, said, 'Do you have evidence?' He said, 'No'. The Prophet said, 'Then make him swear [by Allah].' He said, 'In that case, by Allah he will take my land!' The Prophet said, 'If by falsely swearing this person takes the land, he will be among those whom Allah will not look at on the Day of Judgment and He will not purify him, and he will be severely punished.' He said, 'The person became frightened as a result and returned the land to him.'[5994]

٥٢٩٦ . عنه ﷺ ـ لامرءِ القيس وقد اختصم هو ورجل في أرض ـ: ألكَ بَيِّنَةٌ ؟ قالَ : لا ، قالَ : فَيَمِّنْهُ ، قالَ : إذَن واللهِ يَذهَبُ بأرضي ! قالَ : إن ذَهَبَ بأرضِكَ بيَمينِهِ كانَ ممَّن لا يَنظُرُ اللهُ إلَيهِ يَومَ لقِيامَةِ ولا يُزَكِّيهِ ولَهُ عَذابٌ أليمٌ . قالَ : فَفَزِعَ الرجُلُ وَرَدَّها إلَيهِ.٥٩٤٩

5297. **Imām ʿAlī (AS) said,** 'There are five things a judge must accept at face value: guardianship, marriage, inheritance, slaughtering, and witnessings. If the witness appears trustworthy, their testimony is permitted, and they should not be asked about their inner aspects.'[5995]

٥٢٩٧ . الإمامُ عليٌّ ﷺ : خَمسَةُ أشياءَ يَجِبُ علَى القاضي الأخْذُ فيها بظاهِرِ الحُكمِ : الوِلايَةُ والمَناكِحُ والمَواريثُ والذَّبايحُ والشَّهاداتُ ، إذا كانَ ظاهرُ الشُّهودِ مَأموناً جازَت شَهادَتُهُم ولا يَسألُ عن باطِنِهم.٥٩٥٠

5298. **Imām al-Ṣādiq (AS) said,** 'When al-Qā'im [the one who will rise] from the household of Muḥammad [i.e. the Mahdī] reappears - peace be

٥٢٩٨ . الإمامُ الصّادقُ ﷺ : إذا قامَ قائمُ آلِ محمّدٍ

upon him and them - he will judge among people as the judging of Prophet David (AS). He will not need evidence as Allah, most High, will inspire into him and he will judge with his knowledge.'[5996]

ـ عليه وعليهمُ السلامُ ـ حَكَمَ بينَ الناسِ بحُكمِ داودَ، لا يَحتاجُ إلىٰ بيِّنةٍ، يُلهِمُهُ اللهُ تعالىٰ فَيَحكُمُ بعلمِه.٥٩٩٦

1543. The Saying of Imām ʿAlī: 'This is Indeed like a Court of Justice'

١٥٤٣ ـ قولُ الإمامِ: أما إنَّها حُكومَةٌ!

5299. **Imām al-Ṣādiq (AS) narrated,** 'Verily, the Commander of the Faithful (AS) made the school children put their writing tablets in front of him so as to choose from them, so he exclaimed, 'This is indeed like a court of justice, and injustice here is like injustice in a verdict! Inform your teacher that if he was to hit you more than three hits for discipline, he will be penalized.'[5997]

٥٢٩٩. الإمامُ الصادقُ عليه السلام: إنَّ أميرَ المؤمنينَ عليه السلام ألقى صِبيانُ الكُتّابِ ألواحَهُم بينَ يدَيهِ لِيُخَيِّرَ بينَهُم، فقال: أما إنّها حُكومَةٌ! والجَورُ فيها كالجَورِ في الحُكمِ! أبلِغوا مُعَلِّمَكُم إن ضَرَبَكُم فوقَ ثلاثِ ضَرَباتٍ في الأدبِ اقتُصَّ مِنهُ.٥٩٩٧

334

THE HEART

القَلْب

1544. The Heart

١٥٤٤ ـ القلبُ

5300. **The Prophet (SAWA) said,** 'Allah, most High, has receptacles on the earth, and verily they are the hearts. The most beloved of hearts to Allah are the softest ones, the purest ones, and the firmest ones: those that are the softest to their brothers, those that are the most pure from sins, and those that are the firmest in the path of Allah.'[5998]

٥٣٠٠. رسولُ اللهِ صلى الله عليه وآله: إنَّ للهِ تعالىٰ في الأرضِ أوانِيَ، ألا وهِيَ القُلوبُ، فأحَبُّها إلَى اللهِ، أرَقُّها وأصفاها وأصلَبُها؛ أرَقُّها للإخوانِ، وأصفاها مِنَ الذُّنوبِ، وأصلَبُها في ذاتِ اللهِ.٥٩٩٨

5301. **The Prophet (SAWA) said,** 'Allah Almighty does not look at your appearances, nor at your possessions, rather he looks at your hearts and actions.'[5999]

٥٣٠١. عنه صلى الله عليه وآله: إنَّ اللهَ تباركَ وتعالىٰ لا يَنظُرُ إلىٰ صُوَرِكُم ولا إلىٰ أموالِكُم ولكنْ يَنظُرُ إلىٰ قُلوبِكُم وأعمالِكُم.٥٩٩٩

5302. **Imām ʿAlī (AS) said,** 'The heart is the book of the sight.'[6000]

٥٣٠٢. الإمامُ عليٌّ عليه السلام: القلبُ مُصحَفُ البَصَرِ.٦٠٠٠

5303. **Imām ʿAlī (AS) said,** 'Verily these hearts are receptacles, and the best of them are the most receptive.'[6001]

٥٣٠٣ . عنه عليه السلام : إنَّ هذهِ القُلوبَ أوعِيَةٌ ، فخَيرُها أوعاها .[٥٩٥٦]

5304. **Imām al-Ṣādiq (AS) said,** 'The place of the intellect is the brain, and the place of cruelty and softness is in the heart.'[6002]

٥٣٠٤ . الإمامُ الصّادقُ عليه السلام : مَوضِعُ العَقلِ الدِّماغُ ، والقَسوَةُ والرِّقَّةُ في القلبِ .[٥٩٥٧]

5305. **Imām al-Ṣādiq (AS) said,** 'The status of the heart to the body is the same as that of a leader among people.'[6003]

٥٣٠٥ . عنه عليه السلام : إنَّ مَنزِلَةَ القلبِ مِن الجَسَدِ بمَنزِلَةِ الإمامِ مِن الناسِ .[٥٩٥٨]

5306. **Imām al-Jawād (AS) said,** 'Seeking Allah with the hearts is more effective than tiring the limbs with actions.'[6004]

٥٣٠٦ . الإمامُ الجوادُ عليه السلام : القَصدُ إلَى اللهِ تعالىٰ بالقُلوبِ أبلَغُ مِن إتعابِ الجَوارحِ بالأعمالِ .[٥٩٥٩]

1545. Soundness of the Heart

١٥٤٥ ـ سَلامةُ القَلبِ

"Do not disgrace me on the day that they will be resurrected, the day when neither wealth nor children will avail, except him who comes to Allah with a sound heart."[6005]

﴿وَلَا تُخزِنِي يَوْمَ يُبْعَثُونَ * يَوْمَ لَا يَنْفَعُ مالٌ وَلا بَنُونَ * إلَّا مَنْ أَتَى اللهَ بِقَلْبٍ سَلِيمٍ﴾ .[٥٩٦٠]

5307. **Imām al-Ṣādiq (AS),** with respect to Allah's verse in the Qur'an: *"except him who comes to Allah with a sound heart"* said, 'A sound heart that meets its Lord having nothing other than Him in it. Every heart that has polytheism or doubt is a failed heart.'[6006]

٥٣٠٧ . الإمامُ الصّادقُ عليه السلام ـ في قولِهِ تعالىٰ : ﴿إلّا مَن أتَى اللهَ بِقَلبٍ سَليمٍ﴾ ـ : القَلبُ السَّليمُ الذي يَلقَىٰ رَبَّهُ ، وليسَ فيهِ أحَدٌ سِواهُ ، وكُلُّ قَلبٍ فيهِ شِركٌ أو شَكٌّ فهُو ساقِطٌ .[٥٩٦١]

5308. **Imām al-Ṣādiq (AS),** also said, 'It is a heart that is safe from the love of this world.'[6007]

٥٣٠٨ . عنه عليه السلام ـ أيضاً ـ : هُو القَلبُ الذي سَلِمَ مِن حَبِّ الدنيا .[٥٩٦٢]

5309. **Prophet Jesus (AS) said,** 'As long as the hearts are not punctured with desires and polluted with greed and hardened by bounties, they will be vessels of wisdom.'[6008]

٥٣٠٩ . عيسى عليه السلام : القُلوبُ ما لم تَخرِقْها الشَّهَواتُ ويُدَنِّسْها الطَّمَعُ ويُقْسِها النَّعيمُ فسوفَ تَكونُ أوعيَةً للحِكمَةِ .[٥٩٦٣]

5310. **Imām ʿAlī (AS) said,** 'Your heart will not be sound unless you love for the believers what you love for yourself.'[6009]

٥٣١٠ . الإمامُ عليٌّ عليه السلام : لا يَسلَمُ لكَ قَلبُكَ حتّىٰ تُحِبَّ للمُؤمنينَ ما تُحِبُّ لنفسِكَ .[٥٩٦٤]

5311. Imām Ḥasan (AS) said, 'The soundest of hearts is the heart that is pure of obscure matters.'[6010]

٥٣١١ . الإمامُ الحسنُ عليه السلام : أسلَمُ القُلوبِ ما طَهُرَ مِن الشُّبُهاتِ.[٥٩٦٥]

5312. Imām al-Bāqir (AS) said, 'There is no knowledge like the acquirement of wellbeing [for oneself], and there is no wellbeing like the soundness of the heart.'[6011]

٥٣١٢ . الإمامُ الباقرُ عليه السلام : لا عِلمَ كَطَلَبِ السَّلامَةِ ، ولا سَلامَةَ كسَلامَةِ القَلبِ.[٥٩٦٦]

1546. The Eye of the Heart

١٥٤٦ ـ عَينُ القَلبِ

5313. The Prophet (SAWA) said, 'If it was not for the devils hovering around the hearts of human beings, they would be able to see the Divine Kingdom (*malakūt*).'[6012]

٥٣١٣ . رسولُ اللهِ صلى الله عليه وآله :لولا أنَّ الشَّياطينَ يَحومُونَ علىٰ قُلوبِ بَني آدمَ لَنَظَرُوا إلَى المَلَكوتِ.[٥٩٦٧]

5314. Imām 'Alī (AS), in his intimate supplication said, 'O Allah, grant me the perfection of devotion to You, and illuminate the sight of our hearts with the radiance of being able to behold You until the sight of our hearts pierces through the veils of light, reaching the source of Exaltedness, and our souls become attached to the glory of Your Sacredness.'[6013]

٥٣١٤ . الإمامُ عليٌّ عليه السلام ـ في المُناجاةِ ـ : إلٰهي هَبْ لي كمالَ الانقِطاعِ إلَيكَ ، وأنِرْ أبصارَ قُلوبِنا بِضِياءِ نَظَرِها إلَيكَ ، حتّىٰ تَخرِقَ أبصارُ القُلوبِ حُجُبَ النُّورِ ، فَتَصِلَ إلىٰ مَعدِنِ العَظَمةِ ، وتَصيرَ أرواحُنا مُعَلّقةً بِعِزِّ قُدسِكَ.[٥٩٦٨]

5315. Imām al-Ṣādiq (AS) said, 'Our followers [*shī'a*] are people who have four eyes: two eyes in the head and two eyes in the heart. Verily, all creation have so, but Allah Almighty has opened your sight and blinded their sight.'[6014]

٥٣١٥ . الإمامُ الصّادقُ عليه السلام : إنّما شيعَتُنا أصحابُ الأربَعةِ الأعيُنِ : عَينانِ في الرَّأسِ ، وعَينانِ في القَلبِ ، ألا والخَلائقُ كُلُّهم كذلكَ ، ألا إنّ اللهَ عَزَّوجلَّ فَتَحَ أبصارَكُم وأعمىٰ أبصارَهُم.[٥٩٦٩]

1547. The Ear of the Heart

١٥٤٧ ـ أُذُنُ القَلبِ

5316. The Prophet (SAWA) said, 'If it were not for the dispersion of your hearts and your excess in speaking, you would hear what I hear.'[6015]

٥٣١٦ . رسولُ اللهِ صلى الله عليه وآله : لولا تَمَزُّعُ قلوبِكُم وتَزَيُّدُكُم في الحَديثِ لَسَمِعتُم ما أسمَعُ.[٥٩٧٠]

5317. Imām al-Ṣādiq (AS) said, 'You have a heart and ears to hear, and verily if Allah wants to guide a servant, He will open the ears of his hearts, and if He wills the opposite, He will seal the ears of his heart so it will never again be sound. This is the

٥٣١٧ . الإمامُ الصّادقُ عليه السلام : إنّ لكَ قَلباً ومَسامِعَ ، وإنَّ اللهَ إذا أرادَ أن يَهدِيَ عَبداً فَتَحَ مَسامِعَ قَلبِهِ ، وإذا أرادَ بِهِ غيرَ ذلكَ خَتَمَ مَسامِعَ قَلبِهِ فلا يَصلُحُ أبداً ، وهُو قَولُ اللهِ تعالىٰ

purport of Allah's verse: *"or are there locks on the hearts?"*[6016 6017]

﴿أم علىٰ قُلُوبٍ أقْفالُها﴾ [٥٩٧١، ٥٩٧٢]

1548. The Drawing Near and the Turning Away of the Heart

١٥٤٨ ـ إقبالُ القَلبِ وإدبارُهُ

5318. **Imām al-Riḍā (AS) said,** 'Hearts draw near and turn away, and become active and frigid. When they draw forward they see and understand, and when they fall back they become dim and weary. Therefore, make use of them when they draw near and are active, and leave them when they are feeble and weary.'[6018]

٥٣١٨ . الإمامُ الرِّضا عليه السلام : إنَّ لِلقُلوبِ إقبالاً وإدباراً ، ونَشاطاً وفُتوراً ، فإذا أقبَلَت بَصُرَت وفَهِمَت ، وإذا أدبَرَت كَلَّت ومَلَّت ، فَخُذُوها عِندَ إقبالِها ونَشاطِها ، واترُكُوها عِندَ إدبارِها وفُتورِها . [٥٩٧٣]

5319. **Imām al-ʿAskarī (AS) said,** 'When the hearts are active commit them [to use], and when they are averse, leave them.'[6019]

٥٣١٩ . الإمامُ العسكريُّ عليه السلام : إذا نَشِطَتِ القُلوبُ فَأودِعْها (فَأودِعُوها) ، وإذا نفرَت فَوَدِّعُوها . [٥٩٧٤]

1549. Purity of the Heart

١٥٤٩ ـ طَهارَةُ القَلبِ

5320. **Prophet Moses (AS) said,** 'O Lord, who are those whom You will shade under the Shade of Your Throne on the Day when no shade will avail other than Your Shade?' He said, 'Allah Almighty revealed, 'Those with pure hearts.'[6020]

٥٣٢٠ . موسىٰ عليه السلام : يارَبِّ ، مَن أهلُكَ الذينَ تُظِلُّهُم في ظِلِّ عَرشِكَ يَومَ لا ظِلَّ إلّا ظِلُّكَ ؟ قالَ : فَأوحَى اللهُ إلَيهِ : الطاهِرَةُ قُلوبُهُم . [٥٩٧٥]

5321. **Imām ʿAlī (AS) said,** 'Purify yourselves from the impurity of carnal desires and you will perceive elevated stations.'[6021]

٥٣٢١ . الإمامُ عليٌّ عليه السلام : طَهِّرُوا أنفُسَكُم مِن دَنَسِ الشَّهَواتِ تُدرِكُوا رَفيعَ الدَّرَجاتِ . [٥٩٧٦]

5322. **Imām ʿAlī (AS) said,** 'The hearts of servants that are pure are places that Allah looks at [with mercy]. So whoever purifies his heart, Allah will look at it.'[6022]

٥٣٢٢ . عنه عليه السلام : قُلوبُ العِبادِ الطاهِرَةُ مَواضِعُ نَظَرِ اللهِ سبحانَهُ ، فَمَن طَهَّرَ قَلبَهُ نَظَرَ إلَيهِ . [٥٩٧٧]

(See also: PURITY: section 1188)

1550. Expanding of the Heart

١٥٥٠ ـ انشِراحُ القَلبِ

"Whomever Allah desires to guide, He opens his breast to Islam, and whomever He desires to lead astray, He

﴿فَمَنْ يُرِدِ اللهُ أَنْ يَهْدِيَهُ يَشْرَحْ صَدْرَهُ لِلْإِسْلامِ وَمَنْ يُرِدْ أَنْ يُضِلَّهُ يَجْعَلْ صَدْرَهُ ضَيِّقاً حَرَجاً كَأَنَّما يَصَّعَّدُ فِي السَّماءِ كَذٰلِكَ يَجْعَلُ

makes his breast narrow and straitened as if he were climbing to a height. Thus does Allah lay [spiritual] defilement on those who do not have faith.'[6023]

اللهُ الرِّجْسَ عَلَى الَّذِينَ لَا يُؤْمِنُونَ﴾.[٥٩٧٨]

"Did We not open your breast for you?"[6024]

﴿أَلَمْ نَشْرَحْ لَكَ صَدْرَكَ﴾.[٥٩٧٩]

5323. **Majmaʿ al-Bayān,** It is narrated in an authenticated tradition: 'When this verse was revealed: *"Whomever Allah desires to guide…"*, the Prophet (SAWA) was asked about the expanding of the breast and what it was. He said, 'It is a light that Allah casts into the heart of a believer and it expands the heart and broadens it.' They asked, 'Is there a sign by which this may be known?' He (SAWA) said, 'Yes, to return to the eternal realm, to shun away from the realm of delusion, and to prepare for death before it comes.'[6025]

٥٣٢٣. مجمع البيان: وَردَتِ الرّوايةُ الصَّحيحة أنّه لمّا نَزَلَت هذهِ الآيَةُ: ـ ﴿فَمَنْ يُرِدِ اللهُ أن يَهدِيَهُ﴾ ـ سُئلَ رسولُ اللهِ ﷺ عن شَرحِ الصَّدرِ ما هُو؟ فقالَ: نورٌ يَقذِفُهُ اللهُ في قَلبِ المؤمنِ فَيَنشَرِحُ لَهُ صَدرُهُ ويَنفَسِحُ.
قالوا: فهَل لذلكَ مِن أمارَةٍ يُعرَفُ بها؟ قالَ ﷺ: نَعَم، الإنابَةُ إلىٰ دارِ الخُلودِ، والتَّجافي عن دارِ الغُرورِ، والاستِعدادُ لِلمَوتِ قَبلَ نُزولِ المَوتِ.[٥٩٨٠]

1551. The Veil of the Heart

١٥٥١ ـ حِجابُ القَلبِ

5324. **The Prophet (SAWA) said,** 'When a believer sins a black dot appears on his heart. If he repents, pulls back and seeks forgiveness his heart is cleansed from the black dot, but if he increases his sins the dot grows larger, and this is the rust that Allah has mentioned in His Book: *"No indeed! Rather their hearts have been sullied by what they have been earning."*'[6026 6027]

٥٣٢٤. رسولُ اللهِ ﷺ: إنَّ المؤمنَ إذا أذنَبَ كانَت نُكتَةٌ سَوداءُ في قَلبِهِ، فإن تابَ ونَزَعَ واستَغفَرَ صُقِلَ قَلبُهُ، فإن زادَ زَادَت، فذلكَ الرانُ الذي ذَكَرَهُ اللهُ في كتابِهِ ﴿كَلَّا بَلْ رانَ علىٰ قُلوبِهِم ما كانُوا يَكسِبُونَ﴾.[٥٩٨١، ٥٩٨٢]

5325. **Imām al-Kāẓim (AS) said,** 'Allah Almighty revealed unto David (AS), 'O David, warn and caution your companions against the love of desires, for those whose hearts are attached to worldly desires, their hearts are veiled from Me.'[6028]

٥٣٢٥. الإمامُ الكاظمُ ﷺ: أوحَى اللهُ تعالىٰ إلىٰ داودَ ﷺ: يا داودُ، حَذِّرْ وأنذِرْ (ونَذِّرْ) أصحابَكَ عن حُبِّ الشَّهَواتِ، فإنّ المُعَلَّقةَ قُلوبُهُم بِشَهَواتِ الدنيا قُلوبُهُم مَحجوبَةٌ عَنّي.[٥٩٨٣]

1552. Hard-heartedness

١٥٥٢ ـ قَسوَةُ القَلبِ

"Then your hearts hardened after that; so they are like stones, or even harder. For indeed there are some stones from which streams gush forth, and indeed there are some of them that split, and water issues from them,

﴿ثُمَّ قَسَتْ قُلُوبُكُمْ مِنْ بَعْدِ ذَلِكَ فَهِيَ كَالْحِجارَةِ أَوْ أَشَدُّ قَسْوَةً وَإِنَّ مِنَ الْحِجارَةِ لَما يَتَفَجَّرُ مِنْهُ الأَنْهارُ وَإِنَّ مِنْها لَما يَشَّقَّقُ فَيَخْرُجُ مِنْهُ الْماءُ وَإِنَّ مِنْها لَما يَهْبِطُ مِنْ

and indeed there are some of them that fall for the fear of Allah. And Allah is not oblivious of what you do.'[6029]

خَشْيَةِ اللهِ وَما اللهُ بِغافِلٍ عَمَّا تَعْمَلُونَ﴾.[٥٩٨٤]

5326. It is narrated in *al-Kāfī* that in one of Allah's intimate conversations with Prophet Moses (AS), He said, 'O Moses, do not prolong your hope in this world for your heart will turn hard, and hard hearts are far away from Me.'[6030]

٥٣٢٦. الكافي: فيما ناجَى اللهُ عَزَّوجلَّ بهِ موسىٰ عليه السلام: يا موسىٰ، لا تُطَوِّلْ في الدُّنيا أمَلَكَ فَيَقسُوَ قَلبُكَ، والقاسي القَلبِ مِنّي بَعيدٌ.[٥٩٨٥]

5327. **Prophet Jesus (AS) said,** 'When an animal is not mounted, trained or used it will become hard to use and its character will change. The same goes for the hearts - if they are not made soft with the remembrance of death, followed by diligent worship, they will harden and become harsh.'[6031]

٥٣٢٧. عيسى عليه السلام: إنّ الدابَّةَ إذا لم تُرتَكَبْ ولم تُمتَهَنْ وتُستَعمَلْ لَتَصعُبُ ويَتَغَيَّرُ خُلقُها، وكذلكَ القُلوبُ إذا لم تُرَقَّقْ بذِكرِ المَوتِ ويَتبَعُها دُؤوبُ العِبادَةِ تَقسُو وتَغلُظُ.[٥٩٨٦]

5328. **The Prophet (SAWA) said,** 'Do not speak excessively without the remembrance of Allah, for excessive speech devoid of the remembrance of Allah hardens the heart. The farthest of people from Allah are the hard-hearted.'[6032]

٥٣٢٨. رسولُ اللهِ ﷺ: لا تُكثِرُوا الكلامَ بغَيرِ ذِكرِ اللهِ؛ فإنَّ كَثرَةَ الكلامِ بغَيرِ ذِكرِ اللهِ قَسوَةُ القَلبِ، إنّ أبعَدَ الناسِ مِن اللهِ القَلبُ القاسي.[٥٩٨٧]

5329. **The Prophet (SAWA) said,** 'Three things harden the heart: listening to distracting words of amusement (*lahw*), hunting, and associating with rulers.'[6033]

٥٣٢٩. عنه ﷺ: ثلاثةٌ يُقسِينَ القَلبَ: استِماعُ اللَّهوِ، وطَلَبُ الصَّيدِ، وإتيانُ بابِ السُّلطانِ.[٥٩٨٨]

5330. **Imām ʿAlī (AS) said,** 'Tears only dry up [i.e. fail to flow] as a result of hardness of the heart, and the hearts only harden as a result of frequent sinning.'[6034]

٥٣٣٠. الإمامُ عليٌّ عليه السلام: ما جَفَّتِ الدُّموعُ إلّا لِقَسوةِ القُلوبِ، وما قَسَتِ القُلوبُ إلّا لكَثرَةِ الذُّنوبِ.[٥٩٨٩]

5331. **Imām ʿAlī (AS) said,** 'Verily too much money corrupts religion and hardens the heart.'[6035]

٥٣٣١. عنه عليه السلام: إنّ كَثرَةَ المالِ مَفسَدَةٌ للدِّينِ، مَقساةٌ لِلقلوبِ.[٥٩٩٠]

5332. **Imām ʿAlī (AS) said,** 'Looking at a miserly person hardens the heart.'[6036]

٥٣٣٢. عنه عليه السلام: النَّظَرُ إلَى البَخيلِ يُقسي القَلبَ.[٥٩٩١]

5333. **Imām al-Bāqir (AS) said,** 'Allah has punishments of the hearts and of the bodies: a difficult livelihood,

٥٣٣٣. الإمامُ الباقرُ عليه السلام: إنَّ للهِ عُقوباتٍ في القُلوبِ والأبدانِ: ضَنْكٌ في المَعيشَةِ ووَهنٌ في العِبادَةِ،

weakness in worship, and the harshest punishment a servant is stricken with is hardness of the heart.'[6037]

وما ضُرِبَ عَبدٌ بِعُقوبَةٍ أعظَمَ مِن قَسوَةِ القَلبِ.[٥٩٩٢]

1553. Sickness of the Heart

١٥٥٣ـ مَرَضُ القَلبِ

"There is sickness in their hearts; then Allah increased their sickness, and there is a painful punishment for them because of the lies they used to tell"[6038]

﴿فِي قُلُوبِهِمْ مَرَضٌ فَزَادَهُمُ اللهُ مَرَضاً وَلَهُمْ عَذابٌ أَلِيمٌ بِما كانُوا يَكْذِبُونَ﴾.[٥٩٩٣]

5334. **Imām 'Alī (AS) said,** 'Beware of disputing and quarrelling, for they sicken the heart against one's brethren and give rise to hypocrisy against them.'[6039]

٥٣٣٤. الإمامُ عليٌّ عليه السلام: إيّاكُم والمِراءَ والخُصومَةَ؛ فإنّهُما يُمرِضانِ القُلوبَ علَى الإخوانِ ويَنبُتُ علَيهِما النِّفاقُ.[٥٩٩٤]

5335. **Imām 'Alī (AS) said,** 'Nothing hurts the heart more than sins.'[6040]

٥٣٣٥. عنه عليه السلام: لا وَجَعَ أوجَعُ للقُلوبِ مِنَ الذُّنوبِ.[٥٩٩٥]

1554. What Cures the Heart

١٥٥٤ـ ما يَشفِي القَلبَ

"O mankind! There has certainly come to you an advice from your Lord, and a cure for what is in the breasts, and a guidance and mercy for the faithful."[6041]

﴿يا أَيُّها النّاسُ قَدْ جاءَتْكُمْ مَوْعِظَةٌ مِنْ رَبِّكُمْ وَشِفاءٌ لِما فِي الصُّدُورِ وَهُدىً وَرَحْمَةٌ لِلْمُؤْمِنِينَ﴾.[٥٩٩٦]

5336. **Imām 'Alī (AS) said,** 'Verily Godwariness is the remedy for the sickness of your hearts, and the sight for the blindness of your hearts, and the cure for the sickness of your bodies, and the correction of the corruption of your chests, and the purification for the pollution of your selves, and the unveiling of the blurriness of your eyes.'[6042]

٥٣٣٦. الإمامُ عليٌّ عليه السلام: إنَّ تَقوَى اللهِ دَواءُ داءِ قُلوبِكُم، وبَصَرُ عَمىٰ أفئدَتِكُم، وشِفاءُ مَرَضِ أجسادِكُم (أجسامِكُم)، وصَلاحُ فَسادِ صُدورِكُم، وطَهورُ دَنَسِ أنفُسِكُم، وجَلاءُ عَشا (غِشاءِ) أبصارِكُم.[٥٩٩٧]

1555. What Kills the Heart

١٥٥٥ـ ما يُميتُ القَلبَ

5337. **The Prophet (SAWA),** in his advice to Abū Dharr said, 'Beware of laughing a lot, for it kills the heart.'[6043]

٥٣٣٧. رسولُ اللهِ صلى الله عليه وآله ـ في مَواعِظِهِ لأبي ذَرٍّ ـ: إيّاكَ وكَثرَةَ الضَّحِكِ؛ فإنّهُ يُميتُ القَلبَ.[٥٩٩٨]

5338. **Imām 'Alī (AS) said,** 'He who loves something that makes his eyes blind and his heart sick is looking with false eyes and hearing with

٥٣٣٨. الإمامُ عليٌّ عليه السلام: مَن عَشِقَ شيئاً أعشىٰ (أعمىٰ) بَصَرَهُ، وأمرَضَ قَلبَهُ، فهُو يَنظُرُ بِعَينٍ

impaired hearing. Lusts have pierced his intellect and the world has killed his heart.'[6044]

غيرِ صَحيحَةٍ، ويَسمَعُ بأُذُنٍ غيرِ سَميعَةٍ، قد خَرَقَتِ الشَّهَواتُ عَقلَهُ، وأماتَتِ الدنيا قَلبَهُ.٥٩٩٩

5339. **Imām ʿAlī (AS) said,** 'One whose piety decreases, his heart dies, and whoever's heart dies will enter the Fire.'[6045]

٥٣٣٩. الإمامُ عليٌّ (ع): مَن قَلَّ وَرَعُهُ ماتَ قَلبُهُ، ومَن ماتَ قَلبُهُ دَخَلَ النارَ.٦٠٠٠

1556. What Revives the Heart

١٥٥٦ ـ ما يُحيي القَلبَ

5340. **Luqmān (AS),** giving advice to his son, said, 'O my son, sit in the company of scholars so much that your knees touch theirs, for Allah Almighty revives the hearts with the light of wisdom like the earth is revived with rain from the sky.'[6046]

٥٣٤٠. لقمانُ (ع) ـ لابنِهِ وهُو يَعِظُهُ ـ: يا بُنَيَّ، جالِسِ العُلَماءَ، وزاحِمْهُم برُكبَتَيكَ؛ فإنَّ اللهَ عَزَّوجلَّ يُحيي القُلوبَ بنُورِ الحِكمَةِ كما يُحيي الأرضَ بوابِلِ السَّماءِ.٦٠٠١

5341. **The Prophet (SAWA) said,** 'Allah Almighty says, 'The discussion of knowledge among My servants revives the dead hearts if by it they seek to fulfil My command.'[6047]

٥٣٤١. رسولُ اللهِ (ص): إنّ اللهَ عَزَّ وجلَّ يقولُ: تَذاكُرُ العِلمِ بينَ عِبادي مِمّا تَحيا علَيهِ القُلوبُ المَيْتَةُ إذا هُم انتَهَوا فيهِ إلىٰ أمري.٦٠٠٢

5342. **Imām ʿAlī (AS),** in his will to his son Imām Ḥasan (AS) said, 'Revive your heart with exhortations, and kill it will asceticism.'[6048]

٥٣٤٢. الإمامُ عليٌّ (ع) ـ مِن وصيَّتِهِ لابنِهِ الحَسَنِ (ع) ـ: أحيِ قَلبَكَ بالمَوعِظَةِ، وأمِتْهُ بالزَّهادَةِ.٦٠٠٣

5343. **Imām ʿAlī (AS) said,** 'Meeting righteous people improves the heart.'[6049]

٥٣٤٣. عنه (ع): لِقاءُ أهلِ الخَيرِ عِمارَةُ القَلبِ.٦٠٠٤

5344. **Imām ʿAlī (AS),** in his will to his son Imām al-Ḥasan (AS) said, 'I advise you to be Godwary, O my son, and to abide by His orders, and to keep your heart alive with His remembrance.'[6050]

٥٣٤٤. عنه (ع) ـ من وصيَّتِهِ لابنِهِ الحسنِ (ع) ـ: اُوصِيكَ بتَقوَى اللهِ ـ أي بُنَيَّ ـ ولُزومِ أمرِهِ، وعِمارَةِ قَلبِكَ بذِكرِهِ.٦٠٠٥

1557. What Softens the Heart

١٥٥٧ ـ ما يُلينُ القَلبَ

5345. **The Prophet (SAWA),** when a person complained to him about the hardness of his heart,

٥٣٤٥. رسولُ اللهِ (ص) ـ لَمّا شَكا إلَيهِ رجُلٌ قَساوَةَ قَلبِهِ ـ: إذا أرَدتَ أن يَلينَ قَلبُكَ فأطعِمِ

said, 'If you want your heart to soften, feed the needy and stroke the head of orphans.'[6051]

المِسكينَ وامسَحْ رَأسَ اليَتيمِ.[٦٠٠٦]

5346. **The Prophet (SAWA) said,** 'Accustom your hearts to being soft, and increase your contemplation and cry much due to fear of Allah.'[6052]

٥٣٤٦. عنه ﷺ: عَوِّدُوا قُلوبَكُمُ الرِّقَّةَ، وأكثِرُوا مِنَ التَّفَكُّرِ والبُكاءِ مِن خَشيَةِ اللهِ.[٦٠٠٧]

5347. **Imām 'Alī (AS),** being seen wearing a wraparound cloth that was worn-out and patched, was asked about it, to which he replied, 'With it the heart becomes humble, the self is humiliated, and the believers follow its example.'[6053]

٥٣٤٧. الإمامُ عليٌّ عليه السلام ـ وقد رُئيَ علَيهِ إزارٌ خَلَقٌ مَرقوعٌ فقيلَ لَهُ في ذلكَ ـ: يَخشَعُ لَهُ القَلبُ، وتَذِلُّ بِهِ النفسُ، ويَقتَدي بِهِ المُؤمنونَ.[٦٠٠٨]

5348. **Imām al-Bāqir (AS) said,** 'Embark upon softening the heart through constant remembrance [of Allah] in places of seclusion.'[6054]

٥٣٤٨. الإمامُ الباقرُ عليه السلام: تَعَرَّضْ لِرِقَّةِ القَلبِ بكَثرَةِ الذِّكرِ في الخَلَواتِ.[٦٠٠٩]

(See also: WEEPING 47)

(اُنظر) عنوان ٤٧ «البكاء».

1558. What Polishes the Heart

١٥٥٨ ـ ما يَجلِي القَلبَ

5349. **The Prophet (SAWA) said,** 'Verily these hearts rust like metal rusts when exposed to water.' He was asked, 'And what can polish them?' He said, 'Remembering death much, and reciting the Qur'an.'[6055]

٥٣٤٩. رسولُ اللهِ ﷺ: إنّ هذهِ القُلوبَ تَصدَأُ كما يَصدأُ الحَديدُ إذا أصابَهُ الماءُ. قيلَ: وما جَلاؤها؟ قالَ: كَثرَةُ ذِكرِ المَوتِ، وتِلاوَةِ القرآنِ.[٦٠١٠]

5350. **The Prophet (SAWA) said,** 'The polish of these hearts is the remembrance of Allah and the recitation of the Qur'an.'[6056]

٥٣٥٠. عنه ﷺ: جَلاءُ هذهِ القُلوبِ ذِكرُ اللهِ وتِلاوَةُ القرآنِ.[٦٠١١]

5351. **Imām 'Alī (AS) said,** 'Revive your heart with exhortations…and enlighten it with wisdom.'[6057]

٥٣٥١. الإمامُ عليٌّ عليه السلام: أحْيِ قَلبَكَ بالمَوعِظَةِ... ونَوِّرْهُ بالحِكمَةِ.[٦٠١٢]

5352. **Imām al-Ṣādiq (AS) said,** 'Hearts have rust like the rust of copper so polish them with seeking forgiveness.'[6058]

٥٣٥٢. الإمامُ الصّادقُ عليه السلام: إنَّ للقُلوبِ صَداءً كصَداءِ النُّحاسِ، فاجلُوها بالاستِغفارِ.[٦٠١٣]

335

EMULATION (*taqlīd*) التَّقليدُ

1559. Disparaged Emulation ١٥٥٩ ـ التَّقليدُ المَذمومُ

"And when they are told, "Come to what Allah has sent down and [come] to the Apostle", they say, "Sufficient for us is what we have found our fathers following." What, even if their fathers did not know anything and were not guided?"[6059]

﴿وَإِذَا قِيلَ لَهُمْ تَعالَوْا إِلَىٰ ما أَنْزَلَ اللهُ وَإِلَى الرَّسُولِ قالُوا حَسْبُنا ما وَجَدْنا عَلَيْهِ آبَاءَنا أَوَلَوْ كانَ آبَاؤُهُمْ لَا يَعْلَمُونَ شَيْئاً وَلَا يَهْتَدُونَ﴾ .[٦٠١٤]

5353. **Imām al-Ṣādiq (AS),** with regard to Allah's verse in the Qur'an: *"They have taken their scribes and their monks as lords besides Allah"*[6060], said, 'By Allah, they did not pray to them nor did they fast for them, rather they permitted for them the prohibited and prohibited the permitted and people followed them.'[6061]

٥٣٥٣ . الإمامُ الصّادقُ عليه السلام ـ في قولِهِ تعالىٰ: ﴿اتَّخَذُوا أَحْبارَهُم ورُهْبانَهُم أرباباً مِن دُونِ اللهِ﴾ ـ: واللهِ ما صَلَّوا لَهُم ولا صامُوا، ولكنَّهُم أحَلُّوا لَهُم حَراماً، وحَرَّموا علَيهِم حَلالاً فاتَّبَعُوهُم.[٦٠١٥]

5354. **Imām al-Ṣādiq (AS),** speaking to one of his companions said, 'Do not be toady, saying, 'I am with the people and I am one of the people!'[6062]

٥٣٥٤ . عنه عليه السلام ـ لِرجُلٍ مِن أصحابِهِ ـ: لا تَكونَنَّ إمَّعَةً، تقولُ: أنا مَعَ الناسِ وأنا كَواحِدٍ مِنَ الناسِ![٦٠١٦]

(See also: PEOPLE: section 1775)

(أُنظر) الناس: باب ١٧٧٥.

1560. Those who are Permitted to be Emulated ١٥٦٠ ـ مَن يَجوزُ تَقليدُهُ

5355. **Imām Ḥasan al-ʿAskarī (AS),** 'Whoever from among the jurists safeguards himself, is protective of his religion, opposes his temptations, is obedient to his Master's commands, then the common people must emulate him, and this is only [applicable to] some of the *Shīʿa* jurists, not all of them.'[6063]

٥٣٥٥ . الإمامُ العسكريُّ عليه السلام: فَأَمّا مَن كانَ مِنَ الفُقَهاءِ صائناً لنفسِهِ حافِظاً لِدينِهِ مُخالِفاً علىٰ هَواهُ مُطِيعاً لأمرِ مَولاهُ فلِلعَوامِّ أن يُقَلِّدُوهُ، وذلكَ لا يكونُ إلّا بَعضَ فُقَهاءِ الشِّيعَةِ لا جَميعَهُم.[٦٠١٧]

336

GAMBLING

القِمارُ

1561. Forbidding Gambling

١٥٦١ ـ النَّهيُ عَنِ القِمارِ

"O you who have faith! Indeed wine, gambling, idols and the divining arrows are abominations of Satan's doing, so avoid them, so that you may be felicitous. Indeed Satan seeks to cast enmity and hatred among you through wine and gambling, and to hinder you from the remembrance of Allah and from prayer. Will you, then, relinquish?"[6064]

﴿يا أيُّها الَّذينَ آمَنوا إنَّما الخَمْرُ وَالمَيْسِرُ وَالأنْصابُ وَالأزْلامُ رِجْسٌ مِنْ عَمَلِ الشَّيْطانِ فَاجْتَنِبُوهُ لَعَلَّكُمْ تُفْلِحونَ * إنَّما يُريدُ الشَّيْطانُ أنْ يُوقِعَ بَيْنَكُمُ العَداوَةَ وَالبَغْضاءَ في الخَمْرِ وَالمَيْسِرِ وَيَصُدَّكُمْ عَنْ ذِكْرِ اللهِ وَعَنِ الصَّلاةِ فَهَلْ أنْتُم مُنْتَهونَ﴾.[٦٠١٨]

5356. **The Prophet (SAWA),** in answer to a question about games of chance when the verse: *"indeed wine, gambling..."* was revealed, said, 'It is anything that can be gambled with, even dice or walnuts.' He was asked, 'So what is the dedication to idols (*anṣāb*)?' He said, 'What they sacrificed for their gods.' He was then asked, 'And what is divining with arrows?' He said, 'Their arrow shafts that they swear by.'[6065 6066]

٥٣٥٦. رسولُ اللهِ ﷺ ـ في الجواب عن الميسر لمّا نزل ﴿إنّما الخمرُ والمَيسِرُ﴾ ـ: كُلُّ ما تُقُومِرَ بِهِ حتّى الكِعابُ والجَوزُ.
قيلَ: فما الأنصابُ؟ قالَ: ما ذَبَحُوهُ لِآلِهَتِهِم.
قيلَ: فما الأزلامُ؟ قالَ: قِداحُهُم التي يَستَقسِمُونَ بها.[٦٠١٩]

5357. **Imām ʿAlī (AS) said,** 'Anything that distracts one from the remembrance of Allah is gambling.'[6067]

٥٣٥٧. الإمامُ عليٌّ ﷺ: كُلُّ ما ألهىٰ عن ذِكرِ اللهِ فهُو مِن المَيسِرِ.[٦٠٢٠]

5358. **Imām al-Bāqir (AS),** when asked about playing chess said, 'A believer is too busy to play.'[6068]

٥٣٥٨. الإمامُ الباقرُ ﷺ ـ لمّا سُئلَ عن اللعبِ بالشَّطرَنجِ ـ: إنّ المُؤمِنَ لَمَشغولٌ عنِ اللّعبِ.[٦٠٢١]

5359. **Imām al-Ṣādiq (AS),** with regard to Allah's verse in the Qur'an: *"Do not eat up your wealth among yourselves wrongfully"* said, 'The people of Quraysh would gamble their families and their

٥٣٥٩. الإمامُ الصادقُ ﷺ ـ في قولِهِ تعالى: ﴿ولا تَأكُلُوا أموالَكُم بَينَكُم بالباطِلِ﴾[٦٠٢٢] ـ: كانَت قُرَيشٌ تُقامِرُ الرجُلَ بأهلِهِ ومالِهِ،

money away, and Allah Almighty prohibited them from doing so.’[6069]

فَنَهاهُمُ اللهُ عَزَّ وجلَّ عَن ذلكَ.[٦٠٢٣]

5360. **al-Sakūnī narrated,** ‘He [Imām al-Ṣādiq (AS)] would condemn the eating of walnuts that children had won from gambling, saying, ‘It is illegally earned [and forbidden] (*suḥt*).’[6070]

٥٣٦٠. السكوني: كانَ يَنْهىٰ [الإمامَ الصادق ﷺ] عَنِ الجَوزِ الذي يَجيءُ بِهِ الصِّبيانُ مِن القِمارِ أنْ يُؤكَلَ، وقالَ: هُو السُّحتُ.[٦٠٢٤]

337

CONTENTMENT

القَناعَة

1562. The Virtue of Contentment

١٥٦٢ ـ فَضلُ القَناعَةِ

5361. *‘Uddat al-Dā‘ī*: ‘Allah Almighty revealed unto Prophet David (AS) saying, ‘I put richness in contentment, whilst they seek it [richness] in abundance of wealth but do not find it.’[6071]

٥٣٦١ عدّة الدّاعي: أوحَىٰ اللهُ تعالىٰ إلىٰ داوودَ ﷺ: وَضَعتُ الغِنىٰ في القَناعَةِ وهُم يَطلُبُونَهُ في كَثرَةِ المالِ فلا يَجِدُونَهُ.[٦٠٢٥]

5362. **The Prophet (SAWA) said,** ‘Contentment is wealth that does not deplete.’[6072]

٥٣٦٢. رسولُ اللهِ ﷺ: القَناعَةُ مالٌ لا يَنفَدُ.[٦٠٢٦]

5363. **Imām ‘Alī (AS),** when asked about Allah’s verse in the Qur’an: *“We shall revive him with a good life”*[6073] said, ‘It is contentment.’[6074]

٥٣٦٣. الإمامُ عليٌّ ﷺ ـ لمّا سُئلَ عن قولِهِ تعالىٰ: ﴿فَلَنُحْيِيَنَّهُ حَياةً طَيِّبَةً﴾ ـ: هِيَ القَناعَةُ.[٦٠٢٧]

5364. **Imām ‘Alī (AS) said,** ‘The most thankful of people are the most content, and the most ungrateful for blessings are the greediest.’[6075]

٥٣٦٤. عنه ﷺ: أشكَرُ الناسِ أقنَعُهُم، وأكفَرُهُم لِلنِّعَمِ أجشَعُهُم.[٦٠٢٨]

5365. **Imām ‘Alī (AS) said,** ‘I searched for wealth and I did not find it other than through contentment. Adhere to contentment and you will become rich.’[6076]

٥٣٦٥. عنه ﷺ: طَلَبتُ الغِنىٰ فما وَجَدتُ إلّا بالقَناعَةِ، عليكُم بالقَناعَةِ تَستَغنُوا.[٦٠٢٩]

5366. **Imām ‘Alī (AS) said,** ‘There is no treasure richer than contentment.’[6077]

٥٣٦٦. عنه ﷺ: لا كَنزَ أغنىٰ مِن القَناعَةِ.[٦٠٣٠]

5367. **Imām Ḥasan (AS) said,** ‘Know that the valour in contentment and satisfaction is greater than the valour in giving.’[6078]

٥٣٦٧. الإمامُ الحسنُ ﷺ: اعلمْ أنَّ مُرُوَّةَ القَناعَةِ والرِّضا أكثرُ مِن مُرُوَّةِ الإعطاءِ.[٦٠٣١]

1563. What Brings About Contentment

١٥٦٣ ـ ما يورِثُ القَناعَةَ

5368. **Imām ʿAlī (AS) said,** 'Contentment is proportionate to the degree of self-restraint.'[6079]

٥٣٦٨ . الإمامُ عليٌّ ﷺ : علىٰ قَدرِ العِفَّةِ تكونُ القَناعَةُ .٦٠٣٢

5369. **Imām ʿAlī (AS) said,** 'He who uses his intellect is content.'[6080]

٥٣٦٩ . عنه ﷺ : مَن عَقلَ قَنِعَ .٦٠٣٣

5370. **Imām al-Ṣādiq (AS) said,** 'Look at those who are less capable than you, and do not look at those who are more capable than you, as it makes you more content in what has been allotted for you.'[6081]

٥٣٧٠ . الإمامُ الصّادقُ ﷺ : أُنظُرْ إلىٰ مَن هُو دُونَكَ في المَقدُرَةِ ولا تَنظُرْ إلىٰ مَن هو فَوقَكَ في المَقدُرَةِ ، فإنّ ذلكَ أقنَعُ لكَ بما قُسِمَ لكَ .٦٠٣٤

1564. The Fruit of Contentment

١٥٦٤ ـ ثَمَرَةُ القَناعَةِ

5371. **The Prophet (SAWA) said,** 'Be content with what has been given to you, and the Account [on the Day of Resurrection] will be made easy for you.'[6082]

٥٣٧١ . رسولُ اللهِ ﷺ : اِقنَعْ بما أُوتِيتَهُ يَخِفَّ علَيكَ الحِسابُ .٦٠٣٥

5372. **Imām ʿAlī (AS) said,** 'The most helpful thing in reforming the self is contentment.'[6083]

٥٣٧٢ . الإمامُ عليٌّ ﷺ : أعوَنُ شيءٍ علىٰ صَلاحِ النَّفسِ القَناعَةُ .٦٠٣٦

5373. **Imām ʿAlī (AS) said,** 'Whoever is content will not be depressed.'[6084]

٥٣٧٣ . عنه ﷺ : مَن قَنِعَ لم يَغتَمَّ .٦٠٣٧

5374. **Imām ʿAlī (AS) said,** 'Through contentment comes dignity.'[6085]

٥٣٧٤ . عنه ﷺ : بالقَناعَةِ يكونُ العِزُّ .٦٠٣٨

5375. **Imām ʿAlī (AS) said,** 'The most blessed of people in his livelihood is he who Allah Almighty has granted contentment to, and has given a righteous spouse.'[6086]

٥٣٧٥ . عنه ﷺ : أنعَمُ الناسِ عَيشاً مَن مَنَحَهُ اللهُ سُبحانَهُ القَناعَةَ وأصلَحَ لَهُ زَوجَهُ .٦٠٣٩

5376. **Imām Ḥusayn (AS) said,** 'Contentment is comfort of the body.'[6087]

٥٣٧٦ . الإمامُ الحسينُ ﷺ : القُنوعُ راحَةُ الأبدانِ .٦٠٤٠

5377. **Imām al-Ṣādiq (AS) said,** 'Whoever accepts from Allah the little livelihood, Allah will accept from him the little in actions [worships].'[6088]

٥٣٧٧ . الإمامُ الصّادقُ ﷺ : مَن رَضِيَ مِن اللهِ بِاليَسيرِ مِن المَعاشِ رَضِيَ اللهُ مِنهُ بِاليَسيرِ مِن العَمَلِ .٦٠٤١

1565. Those Who are not Content with the Little

١٥٦٥ ـ مَن لَم يُقنِعْهُ اليَسيرُ

5378. **Imām ʿAlī (AS) said,** 'Those who are not content with a little will not be content with a lot.[6089]

٥٣٧٨ . الإمامُ عليٌّ عليه السلام : مَن لم يُقنِعْهُ اليسيرُ لم يَنفَعْهُ لكَثيرُ .٦٠٤٢

5379. **Imām al-Ṣādiq (AS) said,** 'Be content with what Allah has allotted for you, do not look at what others have, and do not wish for what you cannot acquire, for whoever is content will be full and whoever is not content will never be full, and take your portion of your hereafter.'[6090]

٥٣٧٩ . الإمامُ الصّادقُ عليه السلام : اقنَعْ بما قَسَمَ اللهُ لكَ ولا تَنظُرْ إلىٰ ما عِندَ غيرِكَ ولا تَتَمَنَّ ما لَستَ نائلَهُ ؛ فإنّهُ مَن قَنِعَ شَبِعَ ومَن لم يَقنَعْ لم يَشبَعْ ، وخُذْ حَظَّكَ مِن آخِرَتِكَ .٦٠٤٣

338

ARROGANCE

الكِبرُ

1566. Warning Against Arrogance

١٥٦٦ ـ التَّحذِيرُ مِنَ الكِبرِ

"Thereat the angels prostrated all of them together, except Iblis; he acted arrogantly and he was one of the faithless."[6091]

﴿فَسَجَدَ الْمَلَائِكَةُ كُلُّهُمْ أَجْمَعُونَ * إِلَّا إِبْلِيسَ اسْتَكْبَرَ وَكَانَ مِنَ الْكَافِرِينَ﴾ .٦٠٤٤

""Get down from it" He said. "It is not for you to be arrogant therein. Be gone! You are indeed among the degraded ones."[6092]

﴿قالَ فَاهْبِطْ مِنْها فَما يَكُونُ لَكَ أَنْ تَتَكَبَّرَ فِيها فَاخْرُجْ إِنَّكَ مِنَ الصَّاغِرِينَ﴾ .٦٠٤٥

5380. **Imām ʿAlī (AS) said,** 'Take lesson from what Allah did to Satan. He foiled his many deeds and his hardworking efforts…. for being arrogant for an instant! So, after Satan who will be saved from Allah's wrath with something like his sin?!'[6093]

٥٣٨٠ . الإمامُ عليٌّ عليه السلام : فاعتَبِرُوا بما كانَ مِن فِعلِ اللهِ بإبليسَ ، إذ أحبَطَ عَمَلَهُ الطَّويلَ وجَهدَهُ الجَهيدَ... عن كِبْرِ ساعَةٍ واحِدَةٍ ! فمَن ذا بَعدَ إبليسَ يَسلَمُ علَى اللهِ بمثلِ مَعصيَتِهِ ؟!٦٠٤٦

5381. **Imām al-Bāqir (AS) said,** 'If any amount of arrogance enters the heart of a person, it will only bring deficiency to the intellect with the same amount of what entered it, whether it be a little or a lot.'[6094]

٥٣٨١ . الإمامُ الباقرُ عليه السلام : ما دَخَلَ قَلبَ امرِئٍ شيءٌ مِن الكِبرِ إلّا نَقَصَ مِن عَقلِهِ مِثلُ ما دَخَلَهُ مِن ذلكَ ، قَلَّ ذلكَ أو كَثُرَ .٦٠٤٧

5382. **Imām al-Ṣādiq (AS) said,** 'Whoever is free from arrogance will obtain dignity.'[6095]

٥٣٨٢ . الإمامُ الصّادق ﷺ : مَن بَرِئَ مِن الكِبرِ نالَ الكَرامَةَ .[٦٠٤٨]

5383. **Imām al-Ṣādiq (AS) said,** 'Grandeur is the robe of Allah, and whoever wants to wrest with Allah in any of it, Allah will throw him onto his face into the Hellfire.'[6096]

٥٣٨٣ . عنه ﷺ : الكِبرُ رِداءُ اللهِ ، فَمَن نازَعَ اللهَ شيئاً مِن ذلكَ أكَبَّهُ اللهُ في النّارِ .[٦٠٤٩]

1567. The Explanation of Arrogance

١٥٦٧ ـ تَفسيرُ الكِبرِ

5384. **The Prophet (AS) said,** 'O Abū Dharr, whoever dies having an atom's weight of arrogance in his heart will never smell the scent of Heaven unless he repents beforehand.' Abū Dharr asked, 'O Messenger of Allah, I am fond of beauty so much so that I wished that the handle of my cane and the lace of my sandal be beautiful. So, should I be afraid of this?' He said, 'How do you see your heart?' Abū Dharr said, 'I see it knowing the truth, and certain of it.' He (SAWA) said, 'That is not arrogance. Rather, arrogance is that you leave the truth and exceed beyond it. You look at people and you do not see their honour as being like your honour or their blood like yours.'[6097]

٥٣٨٤ . رسولُ اللهِ ﷺ : يا أباذَرٍّ ، مَن ماتَ وفي قَلبِهِ مِثقالُ ذَرَّةٍ مِن كِبرٍ لم يَجِدْ رائحَةَ الجَنَّةِ إلّا أن يَتوبَ قبلَ ذلكَ ، فقالَ : يا رسولَ اللهِ ، إنّي لَيُعجِبُني الجَمالُ حتّىٰ وَدِدتُ أنَّ عِلاقَةَ سَوطي وقِبالَ نَعلي حَسَنٌ ، فَهل يُرهَبُ علىٰ ذلكَ ؟ قالَ : كيفَ تَجِدُ قَلبَكَ ؟ قالَ : أجِدُهُ عارِفاً للحَقِّ مُطمَئنّاً إلَيهِ ، قالَ : ليسَ ذلكَ بالكِبرِ ، ولكنَّ الكِبرَ أن تَترُكَ الحَقَّ وتَتَجاوَزَهُ إلىٰ غيرِهِ ، وتَنظُرَ إلَى النّاسِ ولا تَرىٰ أنَّ أحَداً عِرضُهُ كَعِرضِكَ ولا دَمُهُ كَدَمِكَ .[٦٠٥٠]

5385. **Imām 'Alī (AS) said,** 'I sought after humility and did not find it other than through accepting the truth. Accept the truth, for accepting the truth distances one from arrogance.'[6098]

٥٣٨٥ . الإمامُ عليٌّ ﷺ : طَلَبتُ الخُضوعَ فما وَجَدْتُ إلّا بقبولِ الحقِّ ، اقبَلُوا الحَقَّ ، فإنَّ قبولَ الحقِّ يُبَعِّدُ مِن الكِبرِ .[٦٠٥١]

5386. *Al-Kāfī*: 'Imām al-Ṣādiq (AS) narrated, 'The Prophet (SAWA) said, 'The worst of arrogance is degrading people and depreciating the truth.' At this, 'Abd al-A'lā Ibn A'yun asked, 'And what is despising people and depreciating the truth?' He said, 'It is when one is ignorant of the truth and slanders its people, and whoever does this has wrested Allah of His robe.'[6099]

٥٣٨٦ . الكافي عن عبد الأعلى بن أعين : قال أبو عبدالله : قالَ رسولُ اللهِ ﷺ : إنَّ أعظَمَ الكِبرِ غَمصُ الخَلقِ وسَفَهُ الحَقِّ ، قلتُ : وما غَمْصُ الخَلقِ وسَفَهُ الحَقِّ ؟ قالَ : يَجهَلُ الحَقَّ ويَطعَنُ علىٰ أهلِهِ ، فَمَن فَعَلَ ذلكَ فقد نازَعَ اللهَ عَزَّوجلَّ رِداءَهُ .[٦٠٥٢]

5387. *Al-Kāfī*: 'Imām al-Ṣādiq (AS) said, 'Whoever thinks that he is superior to someone else is himself of the arrogant.' Abū Ḥafṣ Ibn Ghiyāth

٥٣٨٧ . الكافي عن حفص بن غياث عن الإمام الصادق ﷺ : مَن ذَهَبَ يَرىٰ أنَّ لَهُ علَى الآخَرِ فَضلاً فهُو مِن المُستَكبِرينَ ، فقلتُ لَهُ : إنّما يَرىٰ

said, 'I asked him: [What if] one sees that they are superior in their being good when they see others committing sins?' The Imām said, 'Far from it, far from it! For maybe he has been forgiven for what he has done and whilst you will be stopped and held accountable. Have you not read the story of the magicians of [the time of] Moses (AS) in the Qur'an?'[6100]

أنَّ لَهُ عليهِ فَضلاً بالعافيَةِ إذا رَآهُ مُرتَكِباً لِلمَعاصي ؟ فقالَ : هَيهاتَ هَيهاتَ ! فَلَعَلَّهُ أن يكونَ قد غُفِرَ لَهُ ما أتىٰ وأنتَ مَوقوفٌ مُحاسَبٌ، أما تَلَوتَ قِصَّةَ سَحَرَةِ موسىٰ عليه السلام .[٦٠٥٣]

1568. Reprehensibility of An Arrogant Person

١٥٦٨ ـ ذَمُّ المُتَكَبِّرِ

5388. **The Prophet (SAWA) said,** 'The most hateful of people are the arrogant.'[6101]

٥٣٨٨ . رسولُ اللهِ صلى الله عليه وآله : أمقَتُ النّاسِ المُتَكبِّرُ .[٦٠٥٤]

5389. **The Prophet (SAWA) said,** 'The most distanced of you from me on the Day of Judgment will be the braggers, who are the arrogant.'[6102]

٥٣٨٩ . عنه صلى الله عليه وآله : إنَّ أبعَدَكُم يَومَ القِيامَةِ مِنّي الثَّرثارُونَ، وهُمُ المُستَكبِرُونَ .[٦٠٥٥]

5390. **Imām ʿAlī (AS) said,** 'How man surprises me! His origin is a sperm and his end is a carcass, and between these two he is a vessel for excrement, and he is still arrogant!'[6103]

٥٣٩٠ . الإمامُ عليٌّ عليه السلام : عَجِبتُ لابنِ آدمَ؛ أوَّلُهُ نُطفَةٌ وآخِرُهُ جِيفَةٌ، وهو قائمٌ بينَهُما وِعاءٌ للغائطِ، ثُمّ يَتَكبَّرُ ![٦٠٥٦]

5391. **Imām ʿAlī (AS) said,** 'Only he who is vile is arrogant.'[6104]

٥٣٩١ . عنه عليه السلام : ما تَكَبَّرَ إلّا وَضيعٌ .[٦٠٥٧]

5392. **Imām al-Ṣādiq (AS) said,** 'A person is arrogant or tyrannical only as a result of a [source of] disgrace he has in himself.'[6105]

٥٣٩٢ . الإمامُ الصّادقُ عليه السلام : ما مِن رَجُلٍ تَكَبَّرَ أو تَجَبَّرَ إلا لِذِلَّةٍ وَجَدَها في نفسِهِ .[٦٠٥٨]

1569. Curing Arrogance

١٥٦٩ ـ عِلاجُ الكِبرِ

5393. **The Prophet (SAWA) said,** 'I admire a man who brings something with his hands to please his family, with which repels arrogance from himself.'[6106]

٥٣٩٣ . رسولُ اللهِ صلى الله عليه وآله : إنّهُ لَيُعجِبُني أن يَحمِلَ الرَّجُلُ الشَّيءَ في يَدِهِ يكونُ مُهنِئاً[٦٠٥٩] لأهلِهِ يَدفَعُ بِهِ الكِبرَ عَن نفسِهِ .[٦٠٦٠]

5394. **The Prophet (SAWA) said,** 'Whoever milks his sheep, patches his own clothes, mends his own sandals, trusts his servants, and carries his own

٥٣٩٤ . عنه صلى الله عليه وآله : مَن حَلَبَ شاتَهُ ورَقَعَ قَميصَهُ وخَصَفَ نَعلَهُ وواكَلَ خادِمَهُ وحَمَلَ مِن سُوقِهِ،

goods from the market is free from arrogance.'[6107]

فقد بَرِئَ مِن الكِبرِ.[٦١٠٧]

5395. **Abū Umāma said,** 'The Prophet (SAWA) went to al-Baqīʿ and some of his companions followed him. He stopped and ordered them to proceed and he then walked behind them. He was asked about this, and he said, 'I heard the beat of your sandals [behind me] and feared that some arrogance would fall into my self.'[6108 6109]

٥٣٩٥ . أبو إمامة : إنّ النبيَّ ﷺ خَرَجَ إلَى البَقيعِ فتَبِعَهُ أصحابُهُ فَوَقَفَ وأمَرَهُم أن يَتَقَدَّموا، ثُمّ مَشىٰ خَلفَهُم، فَسُئلَ عن ذلك فقال: إنّي سَمِعتُ خَفقَ نِعالِكُم، فأشفَقتُ أن يَقَعَ في نفسِي شيءٌ مِن الكِبرِ.[٦١٠٨ ٦١٠٩]

5396. **Imām ʿAlī (AS) said,** '…But Allah tests His worshippers with many different hardships, He makes them engage in different struggles, and He makes them undergo different kinds of misfortunes. All this in order to extract arrogance from their hearts, to establish humbleness in their selves, and to make them open the doors to His Grace.'[6110]

٥٣٩٦ . الإمامُ عليٌّ ﷺ : لكنَّ اللهَ يَختَبِرُ عِبادَهُ بأنواعِ الشَّدائدِ، ويَتَعَبَّدُهُم بأنواعِ المَجاهِدِ، ويَبتَليهِم بضُروبِ المَكارِهِ، إخراجاً للتَّكَبُّرِ مِن قُلوبِهِم، وإسكاناً للتَّذَلُّلِ في نُفوسِهِم، ولِيَجعَلَ ذلكَ أبواباً فُتُحاً إلىٰ فَضلِهِ.[٦١١٠]

5397. **Imām ʿAlī (AS) said,** 'Allah obligated faith as purification from polytheism, and prayer as a deterrent from arrogance.'[6111]

٥٣٩٧ . عنه ﷺ : فَرَضَ اللهُ الإيمانَ تَطهيراً مِن الشِّركِ، والصلاةَ تَنزيهاً عنِ الكِبرِ.[٦١١١]

5398. **Imām Ḥasan (AS) said,** 'It is not appropriate for he who knows the magnitude of Allah to be haughty, for the glory of those who know the magnitude of Allah is that they become humble, and the honour of those who know the Majesty of Allah is that they humiliate themselves to Him.'[6112]

٥٣٩٨ . الإمامُ الحسنُ ﷺ : لا يَنبَغي لِمَن عَرَفَ عَظَمَةَ اللهِ أن يَتَعاظَمَ، فإنّ رِفعَةَ الذينَ يَعلَمونَ عَظَمَةَ اللهِ أن يَتَواضَعوا، و(عِزَّ) الذينَ يَعرِفونَ ما جَلالُ اللهِ أن يَتَذَلَّلوا (لَهُ).[٦١١٢]

1570. The Outcome of Arrogance

١٥٧٠ ـ ثَمَرَةُ الكِبرِ

5399. **The Prophet (SAWA) said,** 'Whoever is arrogant, Allah degrades him.'[6113]

٥٣٩٩ . رسولُ اللهِ ﷺ : مَن يَستَكبِرْ يَضَعْهُ اللهُ.[٦١١٣]

5400. **Imām ʿAlī (AS) said,** 'Greed, arrogance, and jealousy are all motives for falling into sins.'[6114]

٥٤٠٠ . الإمامُ عليٌّ ﷺ : الحِرصُ والكِبرُ والحَسَدُ دَواعٍ إلَى التَّقَحُّمِ في الذُّنوبِ.[٦١١٤]

5401. **Imām ʿAlī (AS) said,** 'An arrogant person has no friend.'[6115]

٥٤٠١. عنه ﷺ: لَيسَ لِمُتَكبِّرٍ صَديقٌ.٦٠٦٩

5402. **Imām ʿAlī (AS) said,** 'He who behaves arrogantly will never learn.'[6116]

٥٤٠٢. عنه ﷺ: لا يَتَعَلَّمُ مَن يَتَكبَّرُ.٦٠٧٠

5403. **Imām ʿAlī (AS) said,** 'He who behaves arrogantly with people will be degraded.'[6117]

٥٤٠٣. عنه ﷺ: مَن تَكبَّرَ علَى النّاسِ ذَلَّ.٦٠٧١

5404. **Imām al-Ṣādiq (AS) said,** 'An arrogant person should not avidly expect good praises.'[6118]

٥٤٠٤. الإمامُ الصّادقُ ﷺ: لا يَطمَعَنَّ ذو الكِبرِ في الثَّناءِ الحَسَنِ.٦٠٧٢

5405. **Imām al-Kāẓim (AS) said,** 'A plant grows in a plain-levelled land and does not grow in a hard rocky place. The same goes for wisdom, as it grows in the humble heart and does not grow in the arrogant haughty heart; for Allah has made humbleness the tool for the intellect, and made arrogance the tool for ignorance. Do you not know that he who turns his head up towards the ceiling will break it, and he who lowers his head will be shaded and sheltered underneath it?! Thus, Allah will abase one who is not humble before Him, and Allah will elevate whoever is humble for Him.'[6119]

٥٤٠٥. الإمامُ الكاظمُ ﷺ: إنّ الزَّرعَ يَنبُتُ في السَّهلِ ولا يَنبُتُ في الصَّفا، فكذلكَ الحِكمَةُ تَعمُرُ في قَلبِ المُتَواضِعِ ولا تَعمُرُ في قَلبِ المُتَكبِّرِ الجَبّارِ؛ لِأنَّ اللهَ جَعَلَ التَّواضُعَ آلَةَ العَقلِ، وجَعَلَ التَّكبُّرَ مِن آلَةِ الجَهلِ، أَلَم تَعلَمْ أنَّ مَن شَمَخَ إلَى السَّقفِ برأسِهِ شَجَّهُ، ومَن خَفَضَ رأسَهُ استَظَلَّ تَحتَهُ وأكَنَّهُ؟! وكذلكَ مَن لم يَتَواضَعْ للهِ خَفَضَهُ اللهُ، ومَن تَواضَعَ للهِ رَفَعَهُ.٦٠٧٣

1571. The Abode of the Arrogant

١٥٧١ـ مَثوَى المُتَكبِّرينَ

"Enter the gates of hell to remain in it [forever]. Evil is the [final] abode of the arrogant."[6120]

﴿فَادْخُلُوا أَبْوَابَ جَهَنَّمَ خَالِدِينَ فِيهَا فَلَبِئْسَ مَثْوَى الْمُتَكَبِّرِينَ﴾.٦٠٧٤

5406. **Imām al-Ṣādiq (AS) said,** 'In Hell there is a valley by the name of Ṣaqar reserved for the arrogant, and it complained to Allah about the extremity of its heat and asked Him to be permitted to breathe. So it breathed and ignited Hell.'[6121]

٥٤٠٦. الإمامُ الصّادقُ ﷺ: إنّ في جَهَنَّمَ لَوادِياً لِلمُتَكبِّرينَ يقالُ لَهُ سَقَرُ، شَكا إلَى اللهِ عَزَّوجلَّ شِدَّةَ حَرِّهِ وسَألَهُ أن يَأذَنَ لَهُ أن يَتَنَفَّسَ، فَتَنَفَّسَ فَأحرَقَ جَهَنَّمَ.٦٠٧٥

339

WRITING

الكِتابُ

1572. Writing

١٥٧٢ ـ الكِتابُ

"By the Pen and what they write."[6122]

﴿ن وَالْقَلَمِ وَما يَسْطُرُونَ﴾.٦٠٧٦

5407. **Imām ʿAlī (AS) said,** 'Books are the gardens of scholars.'[6123]

٥٤٠٧. الإمامُ عليٌّ ﷺ: الكُتُبُ بَساتينُ العُلَماءِ.٦٠٧٧

5408. **Imām ʿAlī (AS) said,** 'A book is the best of conversers.'[6124]

٥٤٠٨. عنه ﷺ: نِعمَ المُحَدِّثُ الكتابُ.٦٠٧٨

5409. **Imām ʿAlī (AS) said,** 'Whoever seeks harmony with books will not miss any tranquillity.'[6125]

٥٤٠٩. عنه ﷺ: مَن تَسَلّىٰ بالكُتُبِ لم تَفُتْهُ سَلوَةٌ.٦٠٧٩

1573. Writing and the Personality of the Writer

١٥٧٣ ـ الكتابَةُ وَشخصيَّةُ الكاتِبِ

5410. **Imām ʿAlī (AS) said,** 'Your messenger is the interpreter of your intellect, and your letter is their most eloquent at expressing your true self.'[6126]

٥٤١٠. الإمامُ عليٌّ ﷺ: رَسولُكَ تَرجُمانُ عَقلِكَ، وكِتابُكَ أبلَغُ ما يَنطِقُ عَنكَ.٦٠٨٠

5411. **Imām ʿAlī (AS) said,** 'A man's book is the title of his intellect and the proof of his virtue.'[6127]

٥٤١١. عنه ﷺ: كِتابُ الرَّجُلِ عُنوانُ عَقلِهِ وبُرهانُ فَضلِهِ.٦٠٨١

5412. **Imām ʿAlī (AS) said,** 'The intellects of the meritorious are around their pens.'[6128]

٥٤١٢. عنه ﷺ: عُقولُ الفُضَلاءِ في أطرافِ أقلامِها.٦٠٨٢

1574. Enjoinment of Writing Knowledge

١٥٧٤ ـ الحَثُّ عَلىٰ كِتابَةِ العِلمِ

5413. **The Prophet (SAWA) said,** 'Capture knowledge through writing.'[6129]

٥٤١٣. رسولُ اللهِ ﷺ: قَيِّدُوا العِلمَ بالكِتابِ.٦٠٨٣

5414. **The Prophet (SAWA) said,** 'Write down knowledge before the departure of the scholars,

٥٤١٤. عنه ﷺ: اكتُبُوا العِلمَ قبلَ ذَهابِ العُلَماءِ،

for the departure of knowledge ensues from the death of scholars.'[6130]

وإنّما ذَهابُ العِلمِ بِمَوتِ العُلَماءِ.٦٠٨٤

5415. **Imām al-Ṣādiq (AS) said,** 'Write, for you will not memorize until you write.'[6131]

٥٤١٥. الإمامُ الصّادقُ ؑ: اكتُبوا؛ فإنّكُم لا تَحفَظونَ حتّىٰ تَكتُبوا.٦٠٨٥

5416. **Imām al-Ṣādiq (AS) said,** 'The heart relies on writing.'[6132]

٥٤١٦. عنه ؑ: القَلبُ يَتّكِلُ علَى الكِتابَةِ.٦٠٨٦

1575. The Reward of Authorship and Writing

١٥٧٥ ـ ثَوابُ التَّأليفِ وَالكِتابَةِ

5417. **The Prophet (SAWA) said,** 'If a believer dies and leaves behind one piece of paper that has knowledge on it, that paper will be a guard for him on the Day of Judgment between him and the Hellfire, and Allah Almighty will give him for every word written on that paper a city seven times larger than the world.'[6133]

٥٤١٧. رسولُ اللهِ ﷺ: المؤمنُ إذا ماتَ وتَرَكَ وَرَقَةً واحِدَةً علَيها عِلمٌ تَكونُ تِلكَ الوَرَقَةُ يَومَ القِيامَةِ سِتراً فيما بَينَهُ وبَينَ النّارِ، وأعطاهُ اللهُ تَباركَ وتَعالىٰ بكُلِّ حَرفٍ مَكتوبٍ علَيها مَدينَةً أوسَعَ مِن الدُّنيا سَبعَ مَرّاتٍ.٦٠٨٧

5418. **The Prophet (SAWA) said,** 'Whoever writes knowledge or a narration on my authority, a reward will continuously be written for him as long as that knowledge and narration exists.'[6134]

٥٤١٨. عنه ﷺ: مَن كَتَبَ عَنّي عِلماً أو حَديثاً لَم يَزَلْ يُكتَبُ لَهُ الأجرُ ما بَقِيَ ذلكَ العِلمُ والحَديثُ.٦٠٨٨

1576. The Etiquette of Writing

١٥٧٦ ـ أدَبُ الكِتابَةِ

5419. **The Prophet (SAWA) said,** '[The phrase] In the name of Allah, the Compassionate, the Merciful is the key [opening] for every book.'[6135]

٥٤١٩. رسولُ اللهِ ﷺ: بِسمِ اللهِ الرَّحمٰنِ الرَّحيمِ مِفتاحُ كُلِّ كِتابٍ.٦٠٨٩

5420. **Imām al-Ṣādiq (AS) said,** 'Do not leave out 'In the name of Allah, the Compassionate, the Merciful' even if what follows is poetry.'[6136]

٥٤٢٠. الإمامُ الصّادقُ ؑ: لا تَدَعْ بِسمِ اللهِ الرَّحمٰنِ الرَّحيمِ وإن كانَ بَعدَهُ شِعرٌ.٦٠٩٠

1577. Correspondence

١٥٧٧ ـ المُكاتَبَةُ

5421. **The Prophet (SAWA) said,** 'The reply to a letter is a right [incumbent upon one] just like the reply to a greeting (*salām*).'[6137]

٥٤٢١. رسولُ اللهِ ﷺ: رَدُّ جَوابِ الكِتابِ حَقٌّ كَرَدِّ السَّلامِ.٦٠٩١

5422. **Imām al-Ṣādiq (AS) said,** 'The contact between brothers is maintained by visiting each other when present, and the contact during travel is maintained through correspondence.'[6138]

٥٤٢٢ . الإمامُ الصّادقُ عليه السلام: التَّواصُلُ بينَ الإخوانِ في الحَضَرِ التَّزاوُرُ، والتَّواصُلُ في السَّفَرِ المُكاتَبةُ.[٦٠٩٢]

5423. **Imām al-Ṣādiq (AS) said,** 'The reply to a letter is obligatory just like the obligation of replying the greeting (*salām*).'[6139]

٥٤٢٣ . عنه عليه السلام: رَدُّ جَوابِ الكتابِ واجِبٌ كَوُجوبِ رَدِّ السَّلامِ.[٦٠٩٣]

340

CONCEALMENT

الكِتمانُ

1578. Emphasising the Concealing of Secrets

١٥٧٨ ـ التَّأكيدُ عَلى كِتمانِ الأسرارِ

5424. **Imām 'Alī (AS) said,** 'To keep silent is wisdom, quietness is safety, and concealing [secrets] is a part of prosperity.'[6140]

٥٤٢٤ . الإمامُ عليٌّ عليه السلام: الصَّمتُ حُكمٌ، والسُّكوتُ سَلامَةٌ، والكِتمانُ طَرَفٌ مِن السَّعادَةِ.[٦٠٩٤]

5425. **Imām Zayn al-'Ābīdīn (AS) said,** 'By Allah I would love to sacrifice the meat of my forearm for two vices of our followers: heedlessness and little concealment [of secrets].'[6141]

٥٤٢٥ . الإمامُ زينُ العابدينَ عليه السلام: وَدِدتُ واللهِ أنّي افتَدَيتُ خَصلَتَينِ في الشِّيعَةِ لنا بِبَعْضِ لَحمِ ساعِدي: النَّزَقُ[٦٠٩٥] وقِلَّةُ الكِتمانِ.[٦٠٩٦]

5426. **Imām al-Bāqir (AS) said,** 'By Allah, the most beloved of my companions to me are those who are the most pious, the most knowledgeable, and the most discrete with our speech.'[6142]

٥٤٢٦ . الإمامُ الباقرُ عليه السلام: واللهِ، إنَّ أحَبَّ أصحابِي إلَيَّ أورَعُهُم وأفقَهُهُم وأكتَمُهُم لِحَديثِنا.[٦٠٩٧]

5427. **Imām al-Ṣādiq (AS) said,** 'Our affairs are hidden and veiled with a covenant, so Allah will humiliate whoever discloses us.'[6143]

٥٤٢٧ . الإمامُ الصّادقُ عليه السلام: إنَّ أمرَنا مَستورٌ مُقَنَّعٌ بالمِيثاقِ، فمَن هَتَكَ علَينا أذَلَّهُ اللهُ.[٦٠٩٨]

5428. **Imām al-Ṣādiq (AS) said,** 'Concealing our secrets is struggling on the path of Allah.'[6144]

٥٤٢٨ . عنه عليه السلام: كِتمانُ سِرِّنا جِهادٌ في سبيلِ اللهِ.[٦٠٩٩]

5429. **Imām al-Ṣādiq (AS) said,** 'Whoever announces our [private] speech is like one who denies us our rights.'[6145]

٥٤٢٩ . عنه عليه السلام: مَن أذاعَ علَينا حَديثَنا فهُو بمَنزِلَةِ مَن جَحَدَنا حَقَّنا.[٦١٠٠]

5430. **Imām al-Ṣādiq (AS) said,** 'He who announces our [private] speech does not kill us accidentally, rather, he kills us intentionally.'[6146]

٥٤٣٠. عنه عليه السلام : ما قَتَلَنا مَن أذاعَ حَديثَنا قتلَ خَطَأٍ ولكنْ قتَلَنا قتلَ عَمدٍ.[٦١٠١]

5431. **Imām al-Ṣādiq (AS) said,** 'The announcer of a secret is a doubter, and he who speaks about it to those who are unworthy of it is a disbeliever.'[6147]

٥٤٣١. عنه عليه السلام : مُذيعُ السِّرِّ شاكٌّ، وقائلُهُ عندَ غيرِ أهلِهِ كافِرٌ.[٦١٠٢]

5432. **Imām al-Ṣādiq (AS),** with respect to Allah's verse in the Qur'an: *"That, because they would defy the signs of Allah and kill the prophets unjustly"*[6148] said, 'By Allah, they did not kill them with their hands, nor did they strike them with their swords, but they listened to their [private] speeches and publicized them, so they were punished because of it and killed.'[6149]

٥٤٣٢. عنه عليه السلام ـ في قولِهِ تعالىٰ: ﴿ذلكَ بأنَّهُمْ كانُوا يَكْفُرُونَ بآياتِ اللهِ ويَقْتُلونَ النَبيِّينَ بغَيرِ الحَقِّ﴾ ـ: واللهِ ما قَتَلُوهُم بأيديهِم ولا ضَرَبُوهُم بأسيافِهِم، ولكنَّهُم سَمِعُوا أحاديثَهُم فَأذاعُوها، فَاُخِذُو عليها فقُتِلُوا.[٦١٠٣]

5433. **Abū Baṣīr narrated,** 'I asked Abū Abdillāh [Imām al-Ṣādiq] (AS) about numerous narrations and he asked, 'Have you concealed anything about me?' So, I was trying to remember if I had, and when he saw how I was, he said, 'Anything you speak to your companions is fine, but publicizing it is when you say it to those other than your companions.'[6150]

٥٤٣٣. أبو بَصيرٍ: سَألتُ أباعبدِاللهِ عليه السلام عن حَديثٍ كثيرٍ، قالَ: هَل كَتَمتَ علَيَّ شيئاً قَطُّ؟ فَبَقِيتُ أتَذَكَّرُ، فلَمّا رَأىٰ ما بي قالَ: أمّا ما حَدَّثتَ بهِ أصحابَكَ فلا بأسَ، إنّما الإذاعَةُ أن تُحَدِّثَ بهِ غيرَ أصحابِكَ.[٦١٠٤]

(See also: DISSIMULATION 412)

(اُنظر) عنوان ٤١٢ «التقية».

1579. Praise of the Discreet Worshipper

١٥٧٩ ـ مَدحُ العَبدِ الكَتومِ

5434. **Imām 'Alī (AS) said,** 'Blessed be every unknown worshipper that no one cares for. He knows people but people do not know him. Allah knows him with satisfaction; they are the lanterns of guidance.'[6151]

٥٤٣٤. الإمامُ عليٌّ عليه السلام : طوبىٰ لِكُلِّ عَبدٍ نُومَةٍ، عَرَفَ النّاسَ ولم يَعرِفْهُ النّاسُ، عَرَفَهُ اللهُ برِضوانٍ، اُولئكَ مَصابيحُ الهُدىٰ، يَكشِفُ اللهُ عَنهُم كُلَّ فِتنَةٍ مُظلِمَةٍ، سَيُدخِلُهُم اللهُ في رَحمَةٍ مِنهُ، ليسَ اُولئكَ بالمَذاييعِ البُذُرِ ولا الجُفاةِ المُرائينَ.[٦١٠٥]

5435. **Imām 'Alī (AS) said,** 'After me there will be dark, blind, obscure afflictions. No one will be saved from them other than a person who is not cared about.' He was asked: 'And who is one who

٥٤٣٥. عنه عليه السلام : إنَّ بَعدِي فِتَناً مُظلِمَةً عَمياءَ مُشَكِّكةً، لا يَبقىٰ فيها إلّا النُّومَةُ. قيلَ: وما

is not cared about, O Commander of the Faithful?' He replied, 'He who people do not know what is inside his self.'[6152]

النُّومَةُ يا أميرَ المؤمنينَ ؟ قالَ : الذي لا يَدري النّاسُ ما في نفسِهِ.[٦١٠٦]

341

LYING

الكِذب

1580. The Reprehension of Lying

١٥٨٠ ـ ذَمُّ الكِذبِ

5436. **The Prophet (SAWA) said,** 'The worst form of usury is lying.'[6153]

٥٤٣٦ . رسولُ اللهِ ﷺ : أربَى الرِّبا الكذبُ.[٦١٠٧]

5437. **The Prophet (SAWA) said,** 'When a servant tells one lie, the angels distance themselves a mile away from him because of his foul smell.'[6154]

٥٤٣٧ . عنه ﷺ : إذا كَذَبَ العَبدُ كِذبَةً تَباعَدَ المَلَكُ مِنهُ مَسيرَةَ مِيلٍ مِن نَتْنِ ما جاءَ بهِ.[٦١٠٨]

5438. **The Prophet (SAWA) said,** 'Lying is one door of the doors of hypocrisy.'[6155]

٥٤٣٨ . عنه ﷺ : إنّ الكذبَ بابٌ مِن أبوابِ النِّفاقِ.[٦١٠٩]

5439. **The Prophet (SAWA) said,** 'A liar only lies because of his disgraceful self, and the origin of mockery is sympathising with people who lie.'[6156]

٥٤٣٩ . عنه ﷺ : لا يَكذِبُ الكاذِبُ إلّا مِن مَهانَةِ نفسِهِ، وأصلُ السُّخريَةِ الطُّمأنينَةُ إلىٰ أهلِ الكذبِ.[٦١١٠]

5440. **Imām ʿAlī (AS) said,** 'Lying is treachery.'[6157]

٥٤٤٠ . الإمامُ عليٌّ ؑ : الكذبُ خِيانَةٌ.[٦١١١]

5441. **Imām ʿAlī (AS) said,** 'The most evil of speech is lying.'[6158]

٥٤٤١ . عنه ؑ : شَرُّ القَولِ الكذبُ.[٦١١٢]

5442. **Imām ʿAlī (AS) said,** 'The sign of faith is that you prefer truthfulness where it is to your own detriment over lying where it is to your benefit.'[6159]

٥٤٤٢ . عنه ؑ : (عَلامَةُ) الإيمانِ أن تُؤثِرَ الصِّدقَ حَيثُ يَضُرُّكَ علَى الكذبِ حَيثُ يَنفَعُكَ.[٦١١٣]

5443. **Imām ʿAlī (AS) said,** 'A liar is degraded and humiliated.'[6160]

٥٤٤٣ . عنه ؑ : الكاذِبُ مُهانٌ ذَليلٌ.[٦١١٤]

5444. **Imām ʿAlī (AS) said,** 'There is no bad thing worse than lying.'[6161]

٥٤٤٤ . عنه ؑ : لا سُوءَ أسوأُ مِن الكذبِ.[٦١١٥]

5445. **Imām al-Kāẓim (AS),** advising Hishām, said, 'An intelligent person does not lie even if his interests are involved.'[6162]

٥٤٤٥. الإمامُ الكاظمُ ﷺ ـ لِهشامٍ وهُو يَعِظُهُ ـ: إنّ العاقِلَ لا يَكذِبُ وإن كانَ فيهِ هَواهُ.[٦١١٦]

1581. Lying and Faith

١٥٨١ ـ الكِذبُ وَالإيمانُ

"Only those fabricate lies who do not believe in the signs of Allah, and it is they who are the liars."[6163]

﴿إنَّما يَفْتَرِي الْكَذِبَ الَّذِينَ لا يُؤْمِنُونَ بِآياتِ اللهِ وَأُولٰئِكَ هُمُ الْكاذِبُونَ﴾.[٦١١٧]

5446. **Imām ʿAlī (AS) said,** 'Cast aside lying, for it opposes faith. A truthful person is on the verge of salvation and dignity, whereas a liar is on the point of falling down and humiliation.'[6164]

٥٤٤٦. الإمامُ عليٌّ ﷺ: جانِبوا الكذبَ؛ فإنّهُ مُجانِبٌ للإيمانِ، الصادِقُ على شَفا مَنجاةٍ وكَرامَةٍ، والكاذِبُ على شرفِ مَهواةٍ ومَهانَةٍ.[٦١١٨]

5447. **Imām al-Bāqir (AS) said,** 'Lying is the wrecker of faith.'[6165]

٥٤٤٧. الإمامُ الباقرُ ﷺ: إنّ الكذبَ هُو خَرابُ الإيمانِ.[٦١١٩]

5448. **Imām al-Ṣādiq (AS),** when asked by Ḥasan b. Maḥbūb, 'Can a believer be miserly?', replied, 'Yes.' [He said] I asked, 'And can he be cowardly?' The Imām replied, 'Yes.' I asked, 'Can he be a liar?' The Imām said, 'No, and nor can he be a traitor.' He then said, 'A believer can be predisposed by nature for everything except treachery and lying.' [6166]

٥٤٤٨. الإمامُ الصّادقُ ﷺ ـ وقد سألهُ الحسن بن محبوب ـ: يكونُ المؤمنُ بَخيلاً؟ قالَ: نَعَم، قلتُ: فيكونُ جَباناً؟ قالَ: نَعَم، قلتُ: فيكونُ كَذّاباً؟ قالَ: لا، ولا خائناً، ثُمّ قالَ: يُجبَلُ المؤمنُ على كُلِّ طَبيعَةٍ إلّا الخِيانَةَ والكذبَ.[٦١٢٠]

(See also: FAITH: section 187)

(انظر: الإيمان.)

1582. Lying is the Key to All Evil

١٥٨٢ ـ الكِذبُ مِفتاحُ كُلِّ شَرٍّ

5449. **The Prophet (SAWA) said,** 'Lying leads to immorality, and immorality leads to the Hellfire.'[6167]

٥٤٤٩. رسولُ اللهِ ﷺ: إنّ الكذبَ يَهدي إلَى الفُجورِ، وإنّ الفُجورَ يَهدي إلَى النّارِ.[٦١٢١]

5450. **Imām al-Bāqir (AS) said,** 'Allah, Mighty and Exalted, made locks for evil, and made the keys to those locks drinking [alcohol], and lying is even worse than drinking.'[6168]

٥٤٥٠. الإمامُ الباقرُ ﷺ: إنّ اللهَ عَزَّوجلَّ جَعَلَ لِلشرِّ أقفالاً، وجَعَلَ مَفاتيحَ تِلكَ الأقفالِ الشَّرابَ، والكذبُ شَرٌّ مِن الشَّرابِ.[٦١٢٢]

5451. **Imām al-ʿAskarī (AS) said,** 'The malicious sins have all been put in one house, and the key for it is lying.'[6169]

٥٤٥١. الإمامُ العسكريُّ ﷺ: جُعِلَتِ الخَبائثُ في بَيتٍ وجُعِلَ مِفتاحُهُ الكذبَ.[٦١٢٣]

1583. The Command to Refrain from Lying, Both Seriously and Jestingly

١٥٨٣ ـ الأمرُ بِتَركِ جِدِّ الكِذبِ وهَزلِهِ

5452. **The Prophet (SAWA) said,** 'Lying is not right, whether it be serious or in jest, nor is it right for a man to make a promise to his child and not fulfil it. Truthfulness leads to righteousness, and righteousness leads to Heaven.'[6170]

٥٤٥٢ . رسولُ اللهِ ﷺ : إنّ الكذبَ لا يَصلَحُ مِنهُ جِدٌّ ولا هَزلٌ ، ولا أن يَعِدَ الرجُلُ ابنَهُ ثُمّ لا يُنجِزَ لَهُ، إنّ الصِّدقَ يَهدي إلَى البِرِّ ، وإنَّ البِرَّ يَهدي إلَى الجَنَّةِ ، وإنّ الكـذبَ يَـهدي إلَـى الفُـجورِ ، وإنّ الفُجورَ يَهدي إلَى النّارِ .[٦١٢٤]

5453. **The Prophet (SAWA) said,** 'Woe unto him who speaks and lies in order to get people to laugh. Woe to him! Woe to him!'[6171]

٥٤٥٣ . عنه ﷺ : وَيلٌ للذي يُـحَدِّثُ فَـيكذِبُ لِيُضحِكَ بِهِ القَومَ ! وَيلٌ لَهُ ، وَيلٌ لَهُ ![٦١٢٥]

5454. **Imām ʿAlī (AS) said,** 'A servant will not experience the taste of faith until he leaves lying, both seriously and in jest.'[6172]

٥٤٥٤ . الإمامُ عليٌّ ؑ : لا يَجِدُ عَبدٌ طَعمَ الإيمانِ حتّىٰ يَترُكَ الكذبَ هَزلَهُ وجِدَّهُ .[٦١٢٦]

5455. **Imām Zayn al-ʿĀbidīn (AS)** would say to his children, 'Be cautious of lies, both big and small, both seriously and in jest, for if a man tells a white lie, he will have the audacity to tell a big lie.'[6173]

٥٤٥٥ . الإمامُ زينُ العابدينَ ؑ ـ كـانَ يـقولُ لِوُلدِهِ ـ : اتَّقُوا الكَذِبَ الصَّغيرَ مِنهُ والكبيرَ ، فـي كلِّ جِدٍّ وهَزلٍ ، فإنّ الرجُلَ إذا كذبَ في الصَّغيرِ اجتَرَأَ علَى الكبيرِ .[٦١٢٧]

1584. White Lies

١٥٨٤ ـ الكُذَيبَةُ

5456. **The Prophet (SAWA) said,** 'It suffices as lying for you to repeat everything that you hear.'[6174]

٥٤٥٦ . رسولُ اللهِ ﷺ : حَسبُكَ مِن الكـذبِ أن تُحَدِّثَ بكُلِّ ما سَمِعتَ .[٦١٢٨]

5457. **The Prophet (SAWA),** when Asmā' bint Yazīd asked him, 'If one of us were to say about something we desired: 'I do not desire it', would this be considered lying?' He replied, 'A lie is written as a lie, and a white lie is written as a white lie.'[6175]

٥٤٥٧ . عنه ﷺ ـ لمّا سَألتَهُ أسماءُ بنتُ يَزيدَ ـ : إن قالَت إحدانا لِشيءٍ تَشتَهيهِ : لا أشتَهيهِ ، يُعَدُّ ذلكَ كِذباً ؟ قال : إنّ الكِذبَ يُكتَبُ كِـذباً حـتّىٰ يُكتَبَ الكُذَيبَةُ كُذَيبَةً .[٦١٢٩]

5458. **ʿAbdullāh b. ʿĀmir narrated,** 'My mother called me one day when the Prophet (SAWA) was sitting in our house, and she said, 'Come here so I can give you something.' The Prophet (SAWA) asked her, 'What did you want to give him?' She said, 'I wanted to give him a date.' So the Prophet (SAWA) said to her, 'If you were not to have given

٥٤٥٨ . عبدُ اللهِ بن عامرٍ : دَعَـتني أُمِّـي يَـوماً ورسولُ اللهِ ﷺ قاعِدٌ في بَيتِنا ، فقالت : ها تَـعالَ أُعطِكَ ، فقالَ لها رسـولُ اللهِ ﷺ : مـا أرَدتَ أن تُعطِيَهُ ؟ قـالت : أرَدتُ أن أُعـطِيَهُ تَـمراً ، فـقالَ

him anything, it would have been written against you as a lie.'[6176]	لَها رسولُ اللهِ ﷺ: أما إنّكِ لو لم تُعطِهِ شيئاً كُتِبَت علَيكِ كِذبَةٌ.٦١٣٠

1585. The Consequence of Lying
١٥٨٥ ـ ثَمَرَةُ الكِذبِ

"Indeed Allah does not guide someone who is a profligate, a liar."[6177]	﴿إِنَّ اللهَ لَا يَهْدِي مَنْ هُوَ مُسْرِفٌ كَذَّابٌ﴾.٦١٣١
"He caused hypocrisy to ensue in their hearts until the day they will encounter Him, because of their going back on what they had promised Allah and because of the lies they used to tell."[6178]	﴿فَأَعْقَبَهُمْ نِفاقاً فِي قُلُوبِهِمْ إِلَى يَوْمِ يَلْقَوْنَهُ بِما أَخْلَفُوا اللهَ ما وَعَدُوهُ وَبِما كانُوا يَكْذِبُونَ﴾.٦١٣٢
5459. **The Prophet (SAWA) said,** 'Lying blackens the face.'[6179]	٥٤٥٩. رسولُ اللهِ ﷺ: إنّ الكَذِبَ يُسَوِّدُ الوَجهَ.٦١٣٣
5460. **The Prophet (SAWA) said,** 'Lying decreases sustenance.'[6180]	٥٤٦٠. عنه ﷺ: الكِذبُ يَنقُصُ الرِّزقَ.٦١٣٤
5461. **Imām ʿAlī (AS) said,** 'The consequence of lying is humiliation in this world and punishment in the Hereafter.'[6181]	٥٤٦١. الإمامُ عليٌّ ﷺ: ثَمَرَةُ الكذبِ المَهانَةُ في الدُّنيا والعَذابُ في الآخِرَةِ.٦١٣٥
5462. **Imām ʿAlī (AS) said,** 'Excessive lying corrupts one's religion and increases one's burden [of sins].'[6182]	٥٤٦٢. عنه ﷺ: كَثرَةُ الكذبِ تُفسِدُ الدِّينَ وتُعظِمُ الوِزرَ.٦١٣٦
5463. **Imām ʿAlī (AS) said,** 'Lying leads to hypocrisy.'[6183]	٥٤٦٣. عنه ﷺ: الكذبُ يُؤَدِّي إلَى النِّفاقِ.٦١٣٧
5464. **Imām ʿAlī (AS) said,** 'Whoever lies corrupts his valour.'[6184]	٥٤٦٤. عنه ﷺ: مَن كَذَبَ أفسَدَ مُرُوَّتَهُ.٦١٣٨
5465. **Imām ʿAlī (AS) said,** 'Whoever is known to lie will be less trusted, and whoever refrains from lying will be trusted in what he says.'[6185]	٥٤٦٥. عنه ﷺ: مَن عُرِفَ بالكذبِ قَلَّتِ الثِّقَةُ بهِ، مَن تَجَنَّبَ الكذبَ صُدِّقَت أقوالُهُ.٦١٣٩
5466. **Imām ʿAlī (AS) said,** 'A liar acquires three things with his lies: Allah's discontentment with him, the people's despising him, and the angels' hatred towards him.'[6186]	٥٤٦٦. عنه ﷺ: يَكتَسِبُ الكاذِبُ بِكِذبِهِ ثلاثاً: سَخَطَ اللهِ علَيهِ، واستِهانَةَ النّاسِ بهِ، ومَقتَ المَلائكَةِ لَهُ.٦١٤٠

5467. **Imām ʿAlī (AS) said,** 'Habitually lying brings about poverty.'[6187]

٥٤٦٧ . عنه ﷺ : اعتِيادُ الكِذبِ يُورِثُ الفَقرَ.[٦١٤١]

5468. **Imām al-Ṣādiq (AS) said,** 'Do not lie, lest your splendour fade away.'[6188]

٥٤٦٨ . الإمامُ الصّادقُ ﷺ : لا تَكذِبْ فَيَذهَبَ بَهاؤكَ.[٦١٤٢]

5469. **Imām al-Ṣādiq (AS) said,** 'When a man lies, he is deprived of the Night Prayer as a result.'[6189]

٥٤٦٩ . عنه ﷺ : إنّ الرجُلَ لَيَكذِبُ الكِذبَةَ فيُحرَمُ بها صَلاةَ الليلِ.[٦١٤٣]

5470. **Imām al-Ṣādiq (AS) said,** 'That which Allah helps [to expose] the liars with is forgetfulness.'[6190 6191]

٥٤٧٠ . عنه ﷺ : إنَّ مِمّا أعانَ اللهُ (بِهِ) علَى الكذّابينَ النِّسيانَ[٦١٤٤].[٦١٤٥]

1586. The Worst of Lies

١٥٨٦ ـ أقبَحُ الكِذبِ

"So who is a greater wrongdoer than him who fabricates a lie against Allah to mislead the people without any knowledge."[6192]

﴿فَمَنْ أَظْلَمُ مِمَّنِ افْتَرَىٰ عَلَى اللهِ كَذِباً لِيُضِلَّ النَّاسَ بِغَيْرِ عِلْمٍ﴾.[٦١٤٦]

"On the Day of Resurrection you will see those who attributed lies to Allah with their faces blackened. Is not the [final] abode of the arrogant in hell?"[6193]

﴿وَيَوْمَ الْقِيامَةِ تَرَى الَّذِينَ كَذَبُوا عَلَى اللهِ وُجُوهُهُمْ مُسْوَدَّةٌ أَلَيْسَ فِي جَهَنَّمَ مَثْوىً لِلْمُتَكَبِّرِينَ﴾.[٦١٤٧]

5471. **Imām ʿAlī (AS) said,** 'There will come a time after me when there will be nothing more hidden than the truth and nothing more manifest than falsehood, and nothing worse than lying about Allah and His Messenger.'[6194]

٥٤٧١ . الإمامُ عليٌّ ﷺ : إنّه سَيَأتِي علَيكُم مِن بَعدِي زَمانٌ ليسَ فيهِ شيءٌ أخفىٰ مِن الحَقِّ ولا أظهَرَ مِن الباطِلِ، ولا أكثَرَ مِن الكذبِ علىٰ اللهِ ورسولِهِ.[٦١٤٨]

5472. **Imām ʿAlī (AS) said,** 'By Allah, falling from the sky or being snatched by a bird would be more beloved to me than to lie about the Messenger of Allah (SAWA).'[6195]

٥٤٧٢ . عنه ﷺ : فواللهِ لَأن أخِرَّ مِن السَّماءِ أو تَخطَفَني الطَّيرُ أحَبُّ إلَيَّ مِن أن أكذِبَ علىٰ رسولِ اللهِ ﷺ.[٦١٤٩]

5473. **Imām al-Ṣādiq (AS) said,** 'A lie breaks the fast of a fasting person.' [Abū Baṣīr said] I asked, 'But who from among us does not lie?!' The Imām replied, 'It is not as you are thinking, rather it is lying about Allah, His Messenger, and the Imāms, praises of Allah be upon him and them.'[6196]

٥٤٧٣ . الإمامُ الصّادقُ ﷺ : إنّ الكِذبَةَ لَتُفَطِّرُ الصائمَ، قلتُ: وأيُّنا لا يكونُ ذلكَ مِنهُ؟! قالَ: ليسَ حيثُ ذَهَبتَ، إنّما ذلكَ الكذبُ علَى اللهِ وعلىٰ رسولِهِ وعلَى الأئمَّةِ صلواتُ اللهِ علَيهِ وعلَيهِم.[٦١٥٠]

5474. **Imām al-Ṣādiq (AS) said,** ‘Lying about Allah and His Messenger (SAWA) is a major sin.’[6197]

٥٤٧٤ . الإمامُ الصّادقُ عليه السلام : الكَذِبُ علَى اللهِ وعلى رسولِهِ صلى الله عليه وآله مِن الكبائرِ.[٦١٥١]

1587. Instances where Lying is Permitted

١٥٨٧ ـ مَوارِدُ جَوازِ الكِذبِ

5475. **Imām al-Ṣādiq (AS) said,** ‘Lying is disparaged except in two situations: to repel the evilness of oppressors and to reconcile between people.’[6198]

٥٤٧٥ . الإمامُ الصّادقُ عليه السلام : الكِذبُ مَذمومٌ إلّا في أمرَينِ : دَفعِ شَرِّ الظَّلَمَةِ، وإصلاحِ ذاتِ البَينِ.[٦١٥٢]

5476. **Imām al-Ṣādiq (AS) said,** ‘Speech is of three kinds: the truth, the lie and the [means of] reconciling between people.’[6199]

٥٤٧٦ عنه عليه السلام : الكلامُ ثلاثةٌ : صِدقٌ، وكِذبٌ، وإصلاحٌ بينَ النّاسِ.[٦١٥٣]

5477. **Imām al-Ṣādiq (AS) said,** ‘A reconciler is not a liar.’[6200]

٥٤٧٧ . عنه عليه السلام : المُصلِحُ ليسَ بكاذِبٍ.[٦١٥٤]

1588. Dissemblance (*tawriya*)[6201]

١٥٨٨ ـ التَّورِيَةُ

“He said, ‘Rather it was this biggest of them who did it! Ask them, if they can speak.’”[6202]

﴿قالَ بَلْ فَعَلَهُ كَبِيرُهُمْ هَذَا فَاسْأَلُوهُمْ إنْ كانُوا يَنْطِقُونَ﴾.[٦١٥٥]

5478. **The Prophet (SAWA) said,** ‘The intelligent man can free himself from lying by using vague speech.’[6203]

٥٤٧٨ . رسولُ اللهِ صلى الله عليه وآله : إنَّ في المَعاريضِ ما يُغني الرجُلَ العاقِلَ عنِ الكذبِ.[٦١٥٦]

5479. **Imām al-Ṣādiq (AS),** when ‘Abdullāh b. Bukayr asked him about a person who wants to visit him and he tells his servant to say: ‘He is not here in this very place’ [and whether that is permissible], replied, ‘There is no problem, it is not lying.’[6204]

٥٤٧٩ . الإمامُ الصّادقُ عليه السلام ـ لمّا سَألَهُ عبدُاللهِ بنُ بكيرٍ عنِ الرجُلِ يُستَأذَنُ علَيهِ فيقولُ لِجاريَتِهِ قُولي : ليسَ هُو هاهُنا؟ ـ لا بَأسَ، ليسَ بكذبٍ.[٦١٥٧] [٦١٥٨]

1589. Listening to a Lie

١٥٨٩ ـ استِماعُ الكِذبِ

“And the Jews who eavesdrop with the aim of [telling] lies [against you].”[6205]

﴿وَمِنَ الَّذِينَ هادُوا سَمَّاعُونَ لِلْكَذِبِ﴾.[٦١٥٩]

5480. **Imām ‘Alī (AS) said,** ‘Do not give your hearing [i.e. attention] to those who have gone astray.’[6206]

٥٤٨٠ . الإمامُ عليٌّ عليه السلام : لا تُمَكِّنِ الغُواةَ مِن سَمعِكَ.[٦١٦٠]

5481. It is narrated in *Biḥār al-Anwār*: Imām al-Ṣādiq (AS) was asked about storytellers and whether it is permitted to listen to them?' He said, 'No', and he (AS) said, 'Whoever listens to a speaker worships him. But if he speaks about Allah [and anything associated], then it is as if he is worshipping Allah, and if he speaks from or about Satan [and anything associated with him], then it is as if he is worshipping Satan.'[6207]

٥٤٨١. بحار الأنوار: سُئلَ الصّادقُ ﷺ عنِ القُصّاصِ: أيَحِلُّ الاستِماعُ لَهُم؟ فقالَ: لا، وقالَ ﷺ: مَن أصغىٰ إلىٰ ناطِقٍ فَقَد عَبَدَهُ، فإن كانَ النّاطِقُ عن اللهِ فقد عَبَدَ اللهَ، وإن كانَ النّاطِقُ عن إبليسَ فقد عَبَدَ إبليسَ.٦١٦١

342

NOBILITY[6208]

الكَرَمُ

1590. The Virtue of Nobility

١٥٩٠ـ فَضلُ الكَرَمِ

5482. **The Prophet (SAWA) said,** 'A man's nobility is his religion.'[6209]

٥٤٨٢. رسولُ اللهِ ﷺ: كَرَمُ الرجُلِ دِينُهُ.٦١٦٢

5483. **The Prophet (SAWA) said,** 'Allah, most High is Generous and He loves the generous.'[6210]

٥٤٨٣. عنه ﷺ: إنّ اللهَ تَعالىٰ كريمٌ يُحِبُّ الكَرَمَ.٦١٦٣

5484. **Imām ʿAlī (AS) said,** 'Graciousness is of great manners.'[6211]

٥٤٨٤. الإمامُ عليٌّ ﷺ: نِعمَ الخُلقُ التَّكَرُّمُ.٦١٦٤

1591. The Morals of The Generous People

١٥٩١ـ أخلاقُ الكِرامِ

"Those who do not give false testimony, and when they come upon vain talk, pass by nobly."[6212]

﴿وَالَّذِينَ لا يَشْهَدُونَ الزُّورَ وَإِذَا مَرُّوا بِاللَّغْوِ مَرُّوا كِرَاماً﴾.٦١٦٥

5485. **Imām ʿAlī (AS) said,** 'He who is noble towards his own self, his desires become contemptible.'[6213]

٥٤٨٥. الإمامُ عليٌّ ﷺ: مَن كَرُمَت نفسُهُ صَغُرَتِ الدُّنيا في عَينِهِ.٦١٦٦

5486. **Imām ʿAlī (AS) said,** 'Nobility is to fulfil obligations.'[6214]

٥٤٨٦. عنه ﷺ: مِن الكَرَمِ الوَفاءُ بالذِّمَمِ.٦١٦٧

5487. **Imām ʿAlī (AS) said,** 'A noble person is he who honours his face from the humiliation of the fire.'[6215]

٥٤٨٧. عنه ﷺ: الكريمُ مَن أكرَمَ عَن ذُلِّ النّارِ وَجهَهُ.٦١٦٨

5488. **Imām ʿAlī (AS) said,** 'A generous person becomes inattentive and is thus [seems to be] tricked.'[6216]

٥٤٨٨ . عنه ؑ : الكريمُ يَتَغافَلُ ويَنخَدِعُ.٦١٦٩

5489. **Imām ʿAlī (AS) said,** 'When a noble person makes a promise he fulfils it, and when he threatens [to punish], he forgives [instead].'[6217]

٥٤٨٩ . عنه ؑ : الكريمُ إذا وَعَـدَ وَفـىٰ ، وإذا تَوَعَّدَ عَفا.٦١٧٠

5490. **Imām ʿAlī (AS) said,** 'Giving advice is of the morals of the noble, whereas cheating is of the morals of the vile.'[6218]

٥٤٩٠ . عنه ؑ : النَّصيحَةُ مِن أخلاقِ الكِرام، الغِشُّ مِن أخلاقِ اللِّئامِ.٦١٧١

5491. **Imām ʿAlī (AS) said,** 'Rushing to forgive is of the morals of the generous, and rushing to take revenge is the habit of the vile.'[6219]

٥٤٩١ . عنه ؑ : المُبادَرَةُ إلَى العَفوِ مِن أخلاقِ الكِرامِ ، المُبادَرَةُ إلَى الانتِقامِ مِن شِيَمِ اللِّئامِ.٦١٧٢

5492. **Imām ʿAlī (AS) said,** 'Noble people possess the merit of initiating good deeds and performing generous acts.'[6220]

٥٤٩٢ . عنه ؑ :لِلكِرامِ فَضيلَةُ المُبادَرَةِ إلىٰ فِعلِ المَعروفِ وإسداءِ الصَّنائعِ.٦١٧٣

5493. **Imām ʿAlī (AS) said,** 'The habitual practice of the generous is munificence.'[6221]

٥٤٩٣ . عنه ؑ : سُنَّةُ الكِرامِ الجُودُ.٦١٧٤

5494. **Imām Ḥasan (AS) said,** 'As for generosity, it entails undertaking acts of common courtesy and giving before being asked.'[6222]

٥٤٩٤ . الإمامُ الحسنُ ؑ : أمّا الكَـرَمُ فـالتَّبَرُّعُ بالمَعروفِ والإعطاءُ قَبلَ السُّؤالِ.٦١٧٥

5495. **Imām Zayn al-ʿĀbidīn (AS) said,** 'A noble person is pleased on account of his generosity, whereas a vile person is proud of what he owns.'[6223]

٥٤٩٥ . الإمامُ زينُ العابدينَ ؑ :إنّ الكريمَ يَبتَهِجُ بفَضلِهِ ، واللَّئيمَ يَفتَخِرُ بمُلكِهِ.٦١٧٦

5496. **Imām al-Ṣādiq (AS) said,** 'Three things show the nobility of a person: good manners, suppressing anger, and casting down one's gaze.'[6224]

٥٤٩٦ . الإمامُ الصّادقُ ؑ : ثلاثةٌ تَدُلُّ علىٰ كَرَمِ المَرءِ : حُسنُ الخُـلُقِ ، وكَـظمُ الغَـيظِ ، وغَـضُّ الطَّرْفِ.٦١٧٧

1592. What is not Regarded as the Virtues of Generous People

١٥٩٢ ـ ما لَيسَ مِن أخلاقِ الكِرامِ

5497. **Imām ʿAlī (AS) said,** 'lying and betrayal are not among the characteristics of the generous people.'[6225]

٥٤٩٧ . الإمامُ عليٌّ ؑ : الكَذِبُ والخِيانَةُ لَيسا مِن أخلاقِ الكِرامِ.٦١٧٨

5498. **Imām ʿAlī (AS) said,** 'It is not among the characteristics of generous people to hasten in taking revenge.'[6226]

٥٤٩٨ . عنه ﷺ : ليسَ مِن شِيَمِ الكِرامِ تَـعجيلُ الانتِقامِ.[٦١٧٩]

5499. **Imām ʿAlī (AS) said,** 'He who does not repay bad with good is not of the noble.'[6227]

٥٤٩٩ . عنه ﷺ : مَن لم يُجازِ الإساءَةَ بالإحسانِ فليسَ مِن الكِرامِ.[٦١٨٠]

5500. **Imām Ḥasan (AS) said,** 'He who counts his favours [to others] destroys his own generosity.'[6228]

٥٥٠٠ . الإمامُ الحسنُ ﷺ : مَن عَدَّدَ نِعَمَهُ مَحَقَ كَرَمَهُ.[٦١٨١]

1593. Encouraging Kindness Towards the Generous

١٥٩٣ ـ الحَثُّ عَلىٰ إكرامِ الكَريمِ

5501. **The Prophet (SAWA) said,** 'Honour the generous of every race of people.'[6229]

٥٥٠١ . رسولُ اللهِ ﷺ : أكرِموا كريمَ كُلِّ قَومٍ.[٦١٨٢]

1594. The Virtue of Treating [Others] Honourably

١٥٩٤ ـ فَضلُ الإكرامِ

5502. **The Prophet (SAWA),** when Salmān entered the room and he (SAWA) was leaning on a cushion, he gave it to Salmān saying, 'O Salmān, any Muslim who visits his Muslim brother, and the latter gives him a cushion [to sit on] in honour of him, Allah will forgive him.'[6230]

٥٥٠٢ . رسولُ اللهِ ﷺ ـ لمّا دَخَلَ علَيهِ سلمانُ وهُو مُتَّكئٌ علىٰ وِسادَةٍ فَألقاها إلَيهِ ـ : يا سلمانُ، ما مِن مُسلمٍ دَخَلَ علىٰ أخيهِ المُسلمِ فَيُلقي لَهُ الوِسادَةَ إكراماً لَهُ إلّا غَفَرَ اللهُ لَهُ.[٦١٨٣]

5503. **The Prophet (SAWA) said,** 'Honouring three people is glorifying the Magnitude of Allah: a Muslim of old age, a just leader, and one who has memorised the Qur'an, who is neither an extremist with regard to it, nor has he shunned it [practicing it] aside.'[6231]

٥٥٠٣ . عنه ﷺ : إنّ مِن عِظَمِ جَلالِ اللهِ تعالىٰ إكرامُ ثلاثةٍ: ذِي الشَّيبَةِ في الإسلامِ، والإمامِ العادِلِ، وحامِلِ القرآنِ غيرِ الغالي ولا الجافي عَنهُ.[٦١٨٤]

5504. **The Prophet (SAWA) said,** 'Whoever honours his brother honours Allah indeed.'[6232]

٥٥٠٤ . عنه ﷺ : مَن أكرَمَ أخاهُ فإنّما يُكرِمُ اللهَ.[٦١٨٥]

5505. **The Prophet (SAWA) said,** 'When a visitor comes to you honour him.'[6233]

٥٥٠٥ . عنه ﷺ : إذا أتاكُم الزّائرُ فَأكرِمُوهُ.[٦١٨٦]

5506. **The Prophet (SAWA) said,** 'Whoever believes in Allah and the Hereafter should honour the people he sits with.'[6234]

٥٥٠٦ . عنه ﷺ: مَن كانَ يُؤمِنُ باللهِ واليَومِ الآخِرِ فَليُكرِمْ جَليسَهُ.[٦١٨٧]

5507. **The Prophet (SAWA) said,** 'Anyone who takes the stirrup of a person [in order to assist him], neither from hope of a reward from him thereof, nor from fear of him will be forgiven.'[6235]

٥٥٠٧ . عنه ﷺ: مَن أخَذَ بِرِكابِ رَجُلٍ لا يَرجُوهُ ولا يَخافُهُ غُفِرَ لَهُ.[٦١٨٨]

5508. **The Prophet (SAWA) said,** 'When one enters a place he is taken aback, so receive him with a welcome.'[6236]

٥٥٠٨ . عنه ﷺ: بالدّاخِلِ دَهشَةٌ فَتَلَقَّوهُ بِمَرحَباً.[٦١٨٩]

5509. **The Prophet (SAWA) said,** 'Be kind to orphans and be good to your neighbour.'[6237]

٥٥٠٩ . عنه ﷺ: أكرِمِ اليَتيمَ، وأحسِنْ إلىٰ جارِكَ.[٦١٩٠]

5510. **The Prophet (SAWA) said,** 'Be kind to your children and teach them good manners.'[6238]

٥٥١٠ . عنه ﷺ: أكرِمُوا أولادَكُم وأحسِنُوا أدَبَهُم.[٦١٩١]

1595. Reprehension of Rejecting Kindness

١٥٩٥ ـ ذَمُّ رَدِّ الكَرامَةِ

5511. **The Prophet (SAWA) said,** 'If one of you is treated kindly do not reject it. Indeed, it is the donkey that rejects kindness.'[6239]

٥٥١١ ـ رسولُ اللهِ ﷺ: إذا عُرِضَ علىٰ أحَدِكُمُ الكَرامَةُ فلا يَرُدَّها؛ فإنّما يَرُدُّ الكَرامَةَ الحِمارُ.[٦١٩٢]

5512. **The Prophet (SAWA) said,** 'Accept generosity [in the form of a gift], and the best of generosity is perfume; it is light to carry and has a fragrant scent.'[6240]

٥٥١٢ . عنه ﷺ: اِقبَلُوا الكرامَةَ، وأفضَلُ الكرامَةِ الطِّيبُ، أخَفُّهُ مَحمِلاً وأطيَبُهُ رِيحاً.[٦١٩٣]

5513. **The Prophet (SAWA) said,** 'A man's honouring of his Muslim brother entails accepting his gift, or for him to give him something of what he owns without burden [troubling himself].'[6241]

٥٥١٣ . عنه ﷺ: مِن تَكرِمَةِ الرجُلِ لأخيهِ المُسلمِ أن يَقبَلَ تُحفَتَهُ، أو يُتحِفَهُ مِمّا عِندَهُ ولا يَتَكَلَّفَ شيئاً.[٦١٩٤]

5514. **Imām al-Ḥusayn (AS) said,** 'Whoever accepts what you give to them has aided you in your generosity.'[6242]

٥٥١٤ . الإمامُ الحسينُ ؈: مَن قَبِلَ عَطاءَكَ فقد أعانَكَ علَى الكَرَمِ.[٦١٩٥]

1596. The Most Honourable of People

١٥٩٦ ـ أكرَمُ النّاسِ

5515. **The Prophet (SAWA) said,** 'I am the most honourable of the children of Adam to my Lord, without pride.'[6243]

٥٥١٥ . رسولُ اللهِ ﷺ : أنا أكرَمُ وُلْدِ آدمَ علىٰ رَبّي ، ولا فَخرَ.[٦١٩٦]

5516. **The Prophet (SAWA),** when a person asked him, 'I want to be the most honoured of people, replied, 'Do not complain about Allah to people and you will be the most honoured of people.'[6244]

٥٥١٦ . عنه ﷺ ـ وقد سَألَهُ رجُلٌ : اُحِبُّ أن أكُونَ أكرَمَ النّاسِ ـ : لا تَشكُوَنَّ اللهَ إلَى الخَلقِ تَكُنْ أكرَمَ النّاسِ.[٦١٩٧]

5517. **Imām ʿAlī (AS) said,** 'There is no honour like Godwariness.'[6245]

٥٥١٧ . الإمامُ عليٌّ ؈ : لا كَرَمَ كالتَّقوىٰ.[٦١٩٨]

(See also: GODWARINESS: section 1866)

(اُنظر) التقوى: باب ١٨٦٦.

1597. Honouring People is Honouring Oneself

١٥٩٧ ـ إكرامُ النّاسِ إكرامُ النَّفسِ

5518. **Imām ʿAlī (AS) said,** 'A kind deed you do for a person is kindness done towards yourself, and with which you decorate your own honour. So, do not seek thanks from someone else for what you have done for yourself.'[6246]

٥٥١٨ . الإمامُ عليٌّ ؈ : إنَّ مَكرُمَةً صَنَعتَها إلىٰ أحَدٍ مِن النّاسِ إنّما أكرَمتَ بها نفسَكَ وزَيَّنتَ بها عِرضَكَ ، فلا تَطلُبْ مِن غيرِكَ شُكرَ ما صَنَعتَ إلىٰ نفسِكَ.[٦١٩٩]

5519. **Imām ʿAlī (AS) said,** 'Habituate yourself to performing noble deeds and paying the debts of others, and your self will be noble.'[6247]

٥٥١٩ . عنه ؈ : عَوِّدْ نفسَكَ فِعلَ المَكارِمِ ، وتَحَمُّلَ أعباءِ المَغارِمِ ، تَشرُفْ نفسُكَ.[٦٢٠٠]

(See also: GOOD-DOING: section 539)

(اُنظر) الإحسان: باب ٥٣٩.

343

EARNINGS

الكَسبُ

1598. The Best of Earnings

١٥٩٨ ـ أطيَبُ الكَسبِ

5520. **The Prophet (SAWA) said,** 'The best of earnings is the earning of traders who when they speak they do not lie, when they are entrusted

٥٥٢٠ . رسولُ اللهِ ﷺ : إنَّ أطيَبَ الكَسبِ كَسبُ التُّجّارِ الذينَ إذا حَدَّثُوا لم يَكذِبُوا ، وإذا ائتُمِنُوا

with something they do not betray, when they promise they do not breach, when they buy they do not defame [the goods], when they sell they do not praise [their own goods], when they are in debt they do not delay its repayment, and if they are owed [money] they do not force [their debtor].'[6248]

لم يَخُونوا، وإذا وَعَدُوا لم يُخلِفُوا، وإذا اشتَرَوا لم يَذُمُّوا، وإذا باعُوا لم يُطرُوا، وإذا كانَ علَيهِم لم يَمطُلُوا، وإذا كانَ لَهُم لَم يُعَسِّرُوا.[٦٢٠١]

5521. **The Prophet (SAWA) said,** 'The best [legitimate] earning of a Muslim is through striving on the path of Allah.'[6249]

٥٥٢١ . عنه ﷺ: أطيَبُ كَسبِ المُسلمِ سَهمُهُ في سَبيلِ اللهِ.[٦٢٠٢]

1599. Encouragement of Earning through One's Own Labour

١٥٩٩ ـ الحَثُّ عَلى التَّكَسُّبِ بِاليَدِ

5522. **Prophet David (AS),** when he walked past a shoemaker said, 'O person, work and eat, for Allah loves the one who works and eats, and does not love those who eat and do not work.'[6250]

٥٥٢٢ . داوود ؑ ـ لَمّا مَرَّ بِإسكافٍ ـ: يا هذا اِعمَلْ وكُل، فَإنَّ اللهَ يُحِبُّ مَن يَعمَلُ ويَأكُلُ، ولا يُحِبُّ مَن يَأكُلُ ولا يَعمَلُ.[٦٢٠٣]

5523. **The Prophet (SAWA) said,** 'There is absolutely no food better consumed than consuming from the earnings of one's own hand, and the prophet of Allah, David (AS) would eat from the labour of his hand.'[6251]

٥٥٢٣ . رسولُ اللهِ ﷺ: ما أكَلَ أحَدٌ طَعاماً قَطُّ خَيراً مِن أن يَأكُلَ مِن عَمَلِ يَدِهِ، وإنَّ نَبيَّ اللهِ داوودَ كانَ يَأكُلُ مِن عَمَلِ يَدِهِ.[٦٢٠٤]

5524. **The Prophet (SAWA) said,** 'The best earning is that of the hands of a worker if he is faithful [honest in his work].'[6252]

٥٥٢٤ . عنه ﷺ: خَيرُ الكَسبِ كَسبُ يَدَيِ العامِلِ إذا نَصَحَ.[٦٢٠٥]

5525. It is narrated in *Man Lā Yaḥḍuruhu al-Faqīh*: 'The Commander of the Faithful (AS) would leave in the midday heat to work, wanting Allah, most High to see him tiring himself out in acquiring a lawful earning.'[6253]

٥٥٢٥ . كتاب من لا يحضره الفقيه: كانَ أميرُ المؤمنينَ ؑ يَخرُجُ في الهاجِرَةِ في الحاجَةِ قد كُفِيَها، يُريدُ أن يَراهُ اللهُ تعالى يُتعِبُ نَفسَهُ في طَلَبِ الحَلالِ.[٦٢٠٦]

5526. **Imām al-Ṣādiq (AS) said,** 'The Commander of the Faithful (AS) freed one thousand slaves as a result of what he earned with his own hands' labour.'[6254]

٥٥٢٦ . الإمامُ الصّادقُ ؑ: إنَّ أميرَ المؤمنينَ ؑ أعتَقَ ألفَ مَملوكٍ مِن كَدِّ يَدِهِ.[٦٢٠٧]

5527. It is narrated in *Man La Yaḥḍuruhu al-Faqīh,* from al-Faḍl b. Abī Qurra: 'We walked into the presence of Abū 'Abdillāh [al-Ṣādiq] (AS) and he was working at fixing his wall, so we said, 'May Allah sacrifice us for you, let us work for you, or let the servants do it.' He said, 'No, let me be, for I desire for Allah to see me working with my hands and earning a lawful livelihood through tiring my own self.'[6255]

٥٥٢٧ . كتاب من لا يحضره الفقيه عن الفَضلُ بن أبي قُرَّة: دَخَلنا علىٰ أبي عبدِاللهِ ﷺ وهُو يَعمَلُ فـي حائطٍ لَهُ، فقُلنا: جَعَلَنا اللهُ فِداكَ، دَعْنا نَعمَلْ لكَ أو تَعمَلْهُ الغِلمانُ، قالَ: لا، دَعُوني فإنّي أشتَهي أن يَرانـيَ اللهُ عَـزَّوجلَّ أعـمَلُ بِـيَدي وأطـلُبُ الحلالَ في أذىٰ نفسِي.[٦٢٠٨]

1600. Disparaged Earnings

١٦٠٠ ـ المَكاسِبُ المَذمومَةُ

5528. **The Prophet (SAWA),** when a person asked him, 'I taught my son this book, so what shall I make him work as?' replied, 'May Allah forgive your father, hand him over to any occupation, but [whatever you do] do not hand him over to five people: Do not give him to a *sayyā'*, nor a goldsmith, nor a butcher, nor a wheat-seller, and nor a slave trader.'
So he asked, 'O Messenger of Allah (SAWA), what is a *sayyā'*?' He replied, 'One who sells shrouds for the dead, wishing death for the people of my community, and indeed I love the births of my community more than all that the sun shines on. As for the goldsmith, he deals with the cheating of my community. The butcher is one who slaughters such that mercy is erased from his heart. The wheat-seller monopolizes the food of my community, and it is more liked by me for a servant to meet Allah as a thief than to meet Him having a monopoly of food for forty days. As for the slave trader, Gabriel (AS) came to me and said, 'O Muḥammad, the most evil of your community are those who sell people.'[6256]

٥٥٢٨ . رسولُ اللهِ ﷺ ـ لمّا قال له رجلٌ: قد عَلَّمتُ ابني هذا الكتابَ ففي أيِّ شيءٍ أُسَلِّمُهُ؟ فقالَ ـ: سَلِّمْهُ للهِ أبوكَ، ولا تُسَلِّمْهُ في خَمسٍ: لا تُسَلِّمْهُ سَيّاءً، ولا صايغاً، ولا قَصّاباً، ولا حَنّاطاً، ولا نَخّاساً.

فقالَ: يا رسولَ اللهِ ﷺ، وما السَّيّاءُ؟ قالَ: الذي يَبيعُ الأكفانَ ويَتَمَنّىٰ مَوتَ أُمَّتي، ولَلمَولُودُ مِن أُمَّتي أحَبُّ إلَيَّ ممّا طَلَعَت علَيهِ الشَّمسُ، وأما الصائغُ فإنّهُ يُعالِجُ غَبنَ أُمّتي، فأمّا القَصّابُ فإنّهُ يَذبَحُ حتّىٰ تَذهَبَ الرَّحمَةُ مِن قَلبِهِ، وأمّا الحَنّاطُ فإنّهُ يَحتَكِرُ الطَّعامَ علىٰ أُمَّـتي، ولَأن يَـلقَى اللهُ العَبدَ سارِقاً أحَبُّ إليَّ مِن أن يَلقاهُ قـدِ احـتَكَرَ طَعاماً أربَعينَ يَوماً. وأمّا النَّخّاسُ فـإنّهُ أتـاني جَبرَئيلُ ﷺ فقالَ: يا محمّدُ، إنَّ شِرارَ أُمَّتِكَ الذينَ يَبيعُونَ النّاسَ.[٦٢٠٩]

(See also: TRADE: 55; THE PROFESSION: 95)

(أُنظر) عنوان ٥٥ «التجارة»؛ عنوان ٩٥ «الحرفة».

344

LAZINESS

الكَسَلُ

1601. Laziness

١٦٠١ ـ الكَسَلُ

5529. **Imām ʿAlī (AS) said,** 'The bane of success is laziness.'[6257]

٥٥٢٩ . الإمامُ عليٌّ عليه السلام : آفةُ النُّجحِ الكَسَلُ.[٦٢١٠]

5530. **Imām ʿAlī (AS) said,** 'A believer desires that which stays, and renounces that which perishes….his laziness is far from him and his energy is constant.'[6258]

٥٥٣٠ . عنه عليه السلام : المؤمنُ يرغَبُ فيما يَبقى، ويَزهَدُ فيما يَفنى... بَعيدٌ كَسَلُهُ، دائمٌ نَشاطُهُ.[٦٢١١]

5531. **Imām ʿAlī (AS) said,** 'Laziness corrupts one's Hereafter.'[6259]

٥٥٣١ . عنه عليه السلام : الكَسَلُ يُفسِدُ الآخِرَةَ.[٦٢١٢]

5532. **Imām ʿAlī (AS) said,** 'Whoever obeys slackness will lose rights.'[6260]

٥٥٣٢ . عنه عليه السلام : مَن أطاعَ التَّوانِيَ ضَيَّعَ الحُقوقَ.[٦٢١٣]

5533. **Imām ʿAlī (AS) said,** 'From slackness comes laziness.'[6261]

٥٥٣٣ . عنه عليه السلام : مِن التَّواني يَتولَّدُ الكَسَلُ.[٦٢١٤]

5534. **Imām ʿAlī (AS) said,** 'Combat slackness with firm will.'[6262]

٥٥٣٤ . عنه عليه السلام : ضادُّوا التَّوانِيَ بالعَزمِ.[٦٢١٥]

5535. **Imām ʿAlī (AS) said,** 'Delaying work is the title for laziness.'[6263]

٥٥٣٥ . عنه عليه السلام : تأخيرُ العَمَلِ عُنوانُ الكَسَلِ.[٦٢١٦]

5536. **Imām al-Bāqir (AS) said,** 'Laziness harms both one's religion [i.e. the Hereafter] and this world.'[6264]

٥٥٣٦ . الإمامُ الباقرُ عليه السلام : الكَسَلُ يُضِرُّ بالدِّينِ والدُّنيا.[٦٢١٧]

5537. **Imām al-Bāqir (AS) said,** 'I hate a man – or I hate for a man – to be lazy in his worldly affairs, and whoever is lazy in his worldly affairs will be lazier in his affairs of the Hereafter.'[6265]

٥٥٣٧ . عنه عليه السلام : إنّي لَأُبغِضُ الرجُلَ ـ أو أُبغِضُ للرَّجُلِ ـ أن يَكونَ كَسلانَ عن أمرِ دُنياهُ، ومَن كَسِلَ عَن أمرِ دُنياهُ فهُوَ عن أمرِ آخرتِهِ أكسَلُ.[٦٢١٨]

5538. **Imām al-Ṣādiq (AS) said,** 'The enemy of work is laziness.'[6266]

٥٥٣٨. الإمامُ الصّادقُ ﷺ : عَـدُوُّ العَـمَلِ الكَسَلُ.٦٢١٩

5539. **Imām al-Ṣādiq (AS) said** to some of his children, 'Beware of becoming lazy and bored, for they will both forbid you from your share in this world and the Hereafter.'[6267]

٥٥٣٩. عنه ﷺ ـ لِبَعضِ وُلدِهِ ـ: إيّاكَ والكَسَلَ والضَّجَرَ؛ فإنّهما يَمنَعانِكَ مِن حَظِّكَ مِن الدُّنيا والآخِرَةِ.٦٢٢٠

345

DISBELIEF

الكُفرُ

1602. Causes of Disbelief

١٦٠٢ ـ موجِباتُ الكُفرِ

5540. **The Prophet (SAWA) said,** 'There are four pillars of disbelief: desire, fear, discontentment and anger.'[6268]

٥٥٤٠. رسول الله ﷺ : أركـانُ الكُـفرِ أربَـعةٌ: الرَّغبَةُ، والرَّهبَةُ، والسَّخَطُ، والغَضَبُ.٦٢٢١

5541. **Imām ʿAlī (AS) said,** 'Disbelief was built on four pillars: corruption, extremism, doubt and suspicion.'[6269]

٥٥٤١. الإمامُ عليٌّ ﷺ : بُنِيَ الكفرُ على أربَعِ دَعائمَ: الفِسقُ، والغُلوُّ، والشَّكُّ، والشُّبهَةُ.٦٢٢٢

5542. **Imām al-Bāqir (AS) said,** 'Every act that is drawn by attestation and submission is faith, and anything that is drawn by refusal and denial is disbelief.'[6270]

٥٥٤٢. الإمامُ الباقرُ ﷺ : كُلُّ شَيءٍ يَجُرُّهُ الإقرارُ والتَّسليمُ فهُو الايمانُ، وكُلُّ شَيءٍ يَجُرُّهُ الإنكارُ والجُحودُ فهُو الكُفرُ.٦٢٢٣

5543. **Imām al-Ṣādiq (AS) said,** 'He who doubts in Allah and His Messenger (SAWA) is a disbeliever.'[6271]

٥٥٤٣. الإمامُ الصّادقُ ﷺ : مَن شَكَّ في اللهِ وفي رسولِهِ ﷺ فهُو كافِرٌ.٦٢٢٤

(See also: FAITH: section 186, 187)

(أنظر) الإيمان: باب ١٨٦، ١٨٧.

1603. The Lowest Level of Disbelief

١٦٠٣ ـ أدنَى الكُفرِ

5544. **The Prophet (SAWA) said,** 'The lowest level of disbelief is when a man hears something from his fellow brother, memorizing it and desiring to expose him by it. There is no share of blessings for these people.'[6272]

٥٥٤٤. رسول الله ﷺ : أدنَى الكُـفرِ أن يَسمَعَ الرجلُ عن أخيهِ الكَلِمَةَ فَيَحفَظَها علَيهِ يُريدُ أن يَفضَحَهُ بها، اُولئكَ لا خَلاقَ لَهُم.٦٢٢٥

5545. **Imām al-Ṣādiq (AS),** when asked about the lowest level of atheism, said, 'Arrogance is part of it.'[6273]

٥٥٤٥ . الإمامُ الصّادقُ ـ لمّا سُئلَ عن أدنَى الإلحادِ ـ: الكِبرُ مِنهُ.٦٢٢٦

5546. **Imām al-Ṣādiq (AS),** when asked about the status of a person who lies when he speaks, who breaks promises when he makes them, and who betrays trusts when entrusted with them, replied, 'These are the lowest of the states of disbelief, even though he may not be a disbeliever.'[6274]

٥٥٤٦ . عنه ـ لمّا سُئلَ عن مَنزلَةِ رجُلٍ إن حَدَّثَ كَذَبَ، وإن وَعَدَ أخلَفَ، وإن ائتُمِنَ خانَ ـ: هي أدنَى المَنازِلِ مِن الكُفرِ وليسَ بكافِرٍ.٦٢٢٧

346

RECOMPENSE

المُكافأةُ

1604. Encouraging The Rewarding of Goodness with Goodness

١٦٠٤ ـ الحَثُّ عَلى مُكافأةِ الإحسانِ بِالإحسانِ

"When you are greeted with a salute, greet with a better one than it, or return it; indeed Allah takes account of all things."[6275]

﴿وَإذا حُيِّيتُمْ بِتَحِيَّةٍ فَحَيُّوا بِأحْسَنَ مِنْها أوْ رُدُّوها إنَّ اللهَ كانَ عَلى كُلِّ شَيْءٍ حَسِيباً﴾.٦٢٢٨

"Is the requital of goodness anything but goodness?"[6276]

﴿هَلْ جَزاءُ الإحْسانِ إلّا الإحْسانُ﴾.٦٢٢٩

5547. **Imām al-Kāẓim (AS),** with regards to Allah's verse: *"Is the requital of goodness anything but goodness?"* said, 'It means that among the believers, disbelievers, righteous and sinful, when good is done unto them they must recompense it. Recompense is not that you do what was done until you see you excel him, for if you repay it exactly as he did unto you, he has the merit in being the initiator.'[6277]

٥٥٤٧ . الإمامُ الكاظمُ ـ في قَولِهِ تَعالىٰ: ﴿هَلْ جَزاءُ الإحْسانِ إلّا الإحْسانُ﴾ ـ: جَرَت في المُؤمنِ والكافِرِ والبَرِّ والفاجِرِ، مَن صُنِعَ إلَيهِ مَعروفٌ فعَلَيهِ أن يُكافِئَ بِهِ، ولَيسَتِ المُكافأةُ أن تَصنَعَ كما صَنَعَ حتّىٰ تَرىٰ فَضلَكَ، فإن صَنَعتَ كما صَنَعَ فلَهُ الفَضلُ بالابتِداءِ.٦٢٣٠

5548. **The Prophet (SAWA) said,** 'Whoever does a good turn to you, recompense it, and if you do not find something to recompense it with, then pray to Allah for him until you think you have compensated him.'[6278]

٥٥٤٨ . رسولُ اللهِ : مَن آتاكُم مَعروفاً فكافِئوهُ، وإن لَم تَجِدوا ما تُكافِئونَهُ فادعُوا اللهَ لَهُ حتّىٰ تَظُنّوا أنَّكُم قد كافَيتُموهُ.٦٢٣١

5549. **Imām ʿAlī (AS),** in his exposition of rights, said, '…Then, from His right, He, glory be to Him, created certain rights for certain people over others. He made them so as to equate with one another. Some of these rights produce other rights, and some rights are such that they do not accrue except with others.'[6279]

٥٥٤٩ . الإمامُ عليٌّ ﷺ ـ في بَيان الحُقوقِ ـ: ثُمّ جَعَلَ سُبحانَهُ مِن حُقوقِهِ حُقوقاً افتَرَضَها لِبَعضِ النّاسِ عَلىٰ بَعضٍ ، فَجَعَلَها تَتَكافَأُ في وُجوهِها . ويُوجِبُ بَعضُها بَعضاً ، ولا يُستَوجَبُ بَعضُها إلّا بِبَعضٍ .[٦٢٣٢]

5550. **Imām ʿAlī (AS) said,** 'Extend your hand in recompense to one who has done good to you, and if you cannot do so, then at least thank him.'[6280]

٥٥٥٠ . عنه ﷺ : أطِلْ يَدَكَ في مُكافَأةِ مَن أحسَنَ إلَيكَ، فإن لَم تَقدِرْ فلا أقَلَّ مِن أن تَشكُرَهُ .[٦٢٣٣]

5551. **Imām ʿAlī (AS) said,** 'If you are greeted with a salute then greet back with one better than it, and when a hand is extended towards you, return it with more that what it did; and the merit for this is with the initiator.'[6281]

٥٥٥١ . عنه ﷺ : إذا حُيِّيتَ بِتَحِيَّةٍ فَحَيِّ بأحسَنَ مِنها، وإذا أُسدِيَت إلَيكَ يَدٌ فكافِئْها بِما يُربي عَلَيها، والفَضلُ مَعَ ذلكَ لِلبادِئِ .[٦٢٣٤]

5552. **Imām al-Kāẓim (AS) said,** 'The act of kindness is like shackles that cannot be unlocked except through recompense or thanks.'[6282]

٥٥٥٢ . الإمامُ الكاظمُ ﷺ : المَعروفُ غُلٌّ لا يَفُكُّهُ إلّا مُكافَأةٌ أو شُكرٌ .[٦٢٣٥]

(See also: THANKSGIVING: section 1056)

(أُنظر) الشكر : باب ١٠٥٦.

1605. That which Should be Done and that which Should not be Done in Recompensing

١٦٠٥ ـ ما يَنبَغي فِي المُكافَأةِ وما لا يَنبَغي

5553. **Imām ʿAlī (AS) said,** 'The worst form of recompense is requital with bad.'[6283]

٥٥٥٣ . الإمامُ عليٌّ ﷺ : أقبَحُ المُكافاةِ المُجازاةُ بِالإساءَةِ .[٦٢٣٦]

5554. **Imām ʿAlī (AS) said,** 'From the perfection of faith is to recompense the bad doer with goodness.'[6284]

٥٥٥٤ . عنه ﷺ : مِن كَمالِ الإيمانِ مُكافاةُ المُسيءِ بِالإحسانِ .[٦٢٣٧]

5555. **Imām al-Ṣādiq (AS) said,** 'Whoever recompenses a foolish person with foolishness has accepted what has come unto them, since they imitated that example.'[6285]

٥٥٥٥ . الإمامُ الصّادقُ ﷺ : مَن كافَأَ السَّفيهَ بِالسَّفَهِ فَقَد رَضِيَ بِما أُتيَ إلَيهِ حَيثُ احتَذىٰ مِثالَهُ .[٦٢٣٨]

5556. **Imām al-Ṣādiq (AS) said,** 'Whoever is kind to you, be kind to them, and whoever belittles you be kind to yourself [by ignoring him].'[6286]

٥٥٥٦ . عنه ﷺ : مَن أكرَمَكَ فأكرِمْهُ ، ومَنِ استَخَفَّكَ فأكرِمْ نَفسَكَ عَنهُ .[٦٢٣٩]

1606. The Reprehension of Revenge

١٦٠٦ ـ ذَمُّ الانتِقامِ

5557. **Imām al-Ṣādiq (AS) said,** 'It is written in the Torah: O son of Adam…If you are oppressed with injustice then be content with My help for you, for My help for you is better than your help for yourself.'[6287]

٥٥٥٧ . الإمامُ الصّادقُ ﷺ إنّ في التَّوراةِ مَكتوباً : يابنَ آدمَ... إذا ظُلِمتَ بِمَظلِمَةٍ فارضَ بِانتِصاري لَكَ؛ فإنَّ انتِصاري لَكَ خَيرٌ مِن انتِصارِكَ لِنفَسِكَ .[٦٢٤٠]

5558. **Imām ʿAlī (AS) said,** 'There is no glory with revenge.'[6288]

٥٥٥٨ . الإمامُ عليٌّ ﷺ : لا سُؤدُدَ مَع انتِقامٍ .[٦٢٤١]

5559. **Imām ʿAlī (AS) said,** 'Hastening to revenge is the greatest of sin.'[6289]

٥٥٥٩ ـ عنه ﷺ : التَّسَرُّعُ إلَى الانتِقامِ أعظَمُ الذُّنوبِ [٦٢٤٢]

5560. **Imām ʿAlī (AS) said,** 'The worst action of an empowered person is revenge.'[6290]

٥٥٦٠ ـ عنه ﷺ : أقبَحُ أفعالِ المُقتَدِرِ الانتِقامُ .[٦٢٤٣]

1607. As you Give so Shall you Get

١٦٠٧ ـ كَما تَدينُ تُدانُ

5561. **Imām ʿAlī (AS) said,** 'As you give so shall you get.'[6291]

٥٥٦١ . الإمامُ عليٌّ ﷺ : كَما تَدينُ تُدانُ .[٦٢٤٤]

5562. **Imām ʿAlī (AS) said,** 'He who digs a hole for his brother will fall in it himself, and he who exposes the veils of others, the shames of his own house will be exposed.'[6292]

٥٥٦٢ . عنه ﷺ : مَن حَفَرَ بِئراً لِأخيهِ وَقَعَ فيها ، ومَن هَتَكَ حِجابَ غَيرِهِ انْكَشَفَتْ عَوراتُ بَيتِهِ .[٦٢٤٥]

5563. **Imām ʿAlī (AS) said,** 'He who mocks will be mocked, and whoever insults will be retorted to. He who sows trees of piety will reap fruits of goodness.'[6293]

٥٥٦٣ . عنه ﷺ : مَن عابَ عِيبَ ، ومَن شَتَمَ أُجيبَ ، ومَن غَرَسَ أشجارَ التُّقىٰ اجتَنىٰ ثِمارَ المُنىٰ .[٦٢٤٦]

5564. **Imām al-Ṣādiq (AS) said,** 'Be good to your fathers and your children will be good to you, and restrain yourselves from other people's women and your own women will be chaste.'[6294]

٥٥٦٤ . الإمامُ الصّادقُ ﷺ : بَرُّوا آباءَكُم يَبَرَّكُم أبناؤكُم، وعِفّوا عَن نِساءِ النّاسِ تَعِفَّ نِساؤكُم.٦٢٤٧

347

DUTY

التَّكليفُ

1608. Description of Divine Duty

١٦٠٨ ـ صِفَةُ تَكلِيفِ اللهِ

5565. **Imām ʿAlī (AS) said,** 'Know that what you have been commanded to do is little and its reward is great. Even if there had been no fear of punishment for revolt and disobedience, which Allah has prohibited, the reward in refraining from them would be enough [incentive] to abstain from pursuing them.'[6295]

٥٥٦٥ . الإمامُ عليٌّ ﷺ : اِعلَمُوا أنّ ما كُلِّفتُم بِهِ يَسيرٌ، وأنّ ثَوابَهُ كثيرٌ، ولو لم يَكُن فيما نَهَى اللهُ عنهُ مِن البَغيِ والعُدوانِ عِقابٌ يُخافُ لَكانَ في ثَوابِ اجتِنابِهِ ما لا عُذرَ في تَركِ طَلَبِهِ.٦٢٤٨

5566. **Imām ʿAlī (AS) said,** 'Allah, glory be to Him, ordered His servants by choice and forbade them by warning. He made duties easy and did not order hard duties. For a little He gives plenty, He is not defeatingly disobeyed nor is He obeyed by force. He did not send prophets playfully, nor did He reveal the Book to creation in amusement. He did not create the Heavens and the earth in vain: *"That is a conjecture of the faithless. So woe to the faithless for the Fire!"*'[6296 6297]

٥٥٦٦ . عنه ﷺ : إنّ اللهَ سبحانَهُ أمَرَ عِبادَهُ تَخييراً، ونَهاهُم تَحذيراً، وكَلَّفَ يَسيراً، ولم يُكَلِّفْ عَسيراً، وأعطىٰ علَى القَليلِ كثيراً، ولم يُعصَ مَغلوباً، ولم يُطَعْ مُكرَهاً، ولم يُرسِلِ الأنبياءَ لَعِباً، ولم يُنزِلِ الكتابَ لِلعِبادِ عَبَثاً، ولا خَلَقَ السماواتِ والأرضَ وما بَينَهُما باطِلاً: ﴿ذلكَ ظَنُّ الَّذِينَ كَفَرُوا فَوَيلٌ للّذينَ كَفَرُوا مِنَ النّارِ﴾ ٦٢٤٩. ٦٢٥٠

1609. Allah does not Task any Soul Beyond its Capacity

١٦٠٩ ـ لا يُكَلِّفُ اللهُ نَفساً إلّا وُسعَها

"Allah does not task any soul beyond its capacity..."[6298]

﴿لَا يُكَلِّفُ اللهُ نَفْساً إِلَّا وُسْعَها لَها ما كَسَبَتْ وَعَلَيْها ما اكْتَسَبَتْ﴾ .٦٢٥١

5567. **The Prophet (SAWA) said,** 'Nine things have been forgiven to my community: the mistake, forgetfulness, that which they do not know, that which they cannot bear, that which they are forced

٥٥٦٧ . رسولُ اللهِ ﷺ: وُضِعَ عن أُمّتي تِسعُ خِصالٍ: الخَطاءُ، والنِّسيانُ، وما لا يَعلَمونَ، وما لا

to do, that which they are compelled to do, the evil omen, [Satan's] insinuations in thinking about [the origin of] creation, and jealousy that is not manifest on the tongue or the hand.'[6299]

يُطيقُونَ، وما اضطُرُّوا إلَيهِ، وما استُكرِهُوا علَيهِ، والطِّيَرَةُ، والوَسوَسَةُ في التَّفَكُّرِ في الخَلقِ، والحَسَدُ ما لم يَظهَرْ بلِسانٍ أو يَدٍ.٦٢٥٢

5568. **Imām al-Ṣādiq (AS) said,** 'Creation was never ordered outside of their capability, for whatever people were ordered to do they are capable of doing, and whatever they are not capable of doing does not apply to them.'[6300]

٥٥٦٨. الإمامُ الصّادقُ (ع): ما أُمِرَ العِبادُ إلّا بِدُونِ سَعَتِهِم، فكُلُّ شيءٍ أُمِرَ النّاسُ بأخذِهِ فهُم مُتَّسِعونَ لَهُ، وما لا يَتَّسِعونَ لَهُ فهُو مَوضوعٌ عَنهُم.٦٢٥٣

348

SPEAKING

الكَلامُ

1610. The Importance of Speaking

١٦١٠ ـ أهَمِّيَّةُ الكَلامِ

5569. **The Prophet (SAWA) said,** 'A person speaks something pleasing Allah, not thinking it will reach anywhere, and Allah writes for it His satisfaction until the day he meets Him, and a person speaks something that displeases Allah not thinking it will reach anywhere, and Allah writes for him His discontentment until the day he meets Him.'[6301]

٥٥٦٩. رسولُ اللهِ ﷺ: إنّ الرجُلَ لَيتكلَّمُ بالكَلِمَةِ مِن رِضوانِ اللهِ ما كانَ يَظُنُّ أن تَبلُغَ ما بَلَغَت يَكتُبُ اللهُ تعالىٰ لَهُ بها رِضوانَهُ إلىٰ يومِ يَلقاهُ، وإنّ الرجُلَ لَيتكلَّمُ بالكَلِمَةِ مِن سَخَطِ اللهِ ما كانَ يَظُنُّ أن تَبلُغَ ما بَلَغَت يَكتُبُ اللهُ لَهُ بها سَخَطَهُ إلىٰ يومِ يَلقاهُ.٦٢٥٤

5570. **Imām 'Alī (AS) said,** 'Many a word is more effective than an assault.'[6302]

٥٥٧٠. الإمامُ عليٌّ (ع): رُبَّ قَولٍ أنفَذُ مِن صَولٍ.٦٢٥٥

5571. **Imām 'Alī (AS) said,** 'The attraction of a woman is in her face and the attraction of a man is in his speech.'[6303]

٥٥٧١. عنه (ع): صُورَةُ المرأةِ في وَجهِها، وصُورَةُ الرجُلِ في مَنطِقِهِ.٦٢٥٦

5572. **Imām 'Alī (AS) said,** 'Many a word is more effective than an arrow.'[6304]

٥٥٧٢. عنه (ع): رُبَّ كلامٍ أنفَذُ مِن سِهامٍ.٦٢٥٧

5573. *Tuḥaf al-'Uqūl*: He ['Alī] (AS) was asked, 'What is the best thing that Allah has created?' He (AS) said, 'Speech.' He was then asked, 'What is the worst thing that Allah has created?' He said, 'Speech.' Then he said, 'With speech faces are

٥٥٧٣. تحف العقول: سُئلَ [عليٌّ] (ع) أيُّ شيءٍ مِمّا خَلَقَ اللهُ أحسَنُ؟ فقالَ (ع): الكلامُ، فقيلَ: أيُّ شيءٍ مِمّا خَلَقَ اللهُ أقبَحُ؟ قالَ: الكلامُ، ثُمّ قالَ: بالكلامِ ابيَضَّتِ الوُجوهُ،

whitened [illuminated] and with speech faces are blackened.'[6305] وبالكلامِ اسودَّتِ الوُجوهُ.٦٢٥٨

(See also: THE TONGUE 353) (انظر) عنوان ٣٥٣ «اللسان»

1611. Warning of Offensive Speech ١٦١١ـ التَّحذيرُ مِنَ الكَلامِ المُستَهجَن

5574. **Imām ʿAlī (AS) said,** 'Beware of using offensive speech, for it confines you to vile people and dispels honourable people from you.'[6306]

٥٥٧٤ . الإمامُ عليٌّ ؛ : إيّاكَ وما يُستَهجَنُ مِن الكَلامِ ؛ فإنّهُ يَحبِسُ علَيكَ اللِّئامَ ويُنَفِّرُ عنكَ الكِرامَ.٦٢٥٩

5575. **Imām ʿAlī (AS) said,** 'Beware of offensive speech, for it harbours hatred in the heart.'[6307]

٥٥٧٥ . عنه ؛ : إيّاكَ ومُستَهجَنَ الكلامِ ؛ فإنّهُ يُوغِرُ القلبَ.٦٢٦٠

5576. **Imām ʿAlī (AS) said,** 'He whose speech is bad is blamed more.'[6308]

٥٥٧٦ . عنه ؛ : مَن ساءَ كلامُهُ كَثُرَ مَلامُهُ.٦٢٦١

5577. **Imām ʿAlī (AS) said,** 'The habit of the vile is vulgar speech.'[6309]

٥٥٧٧ . عنه ؛ : سُنَّةُ اللِّئامِ قُبحُ الكلامِ.٦٢٦٢

1612. Encouragement of Refraining from Speech that does not Concern Oneself ١٦١٢ـ الحَثُّ عَلى تَركِ ما لا يَعني مِنَ الكَلام

5578. **The Prophet (SAWA) said,** 'An intelligent man lessens his speech in things that do not concern him.'[6310]

٥٥٧٨ . رسولُ اللهِ ؛ : مِن فِقهِ الرجُلِ قِلَّةُ كَلامِهِ فيما لا يَعنيهِ.٦٢٦٣

5579. **The Prophet (SAWA) said,** 'The people with the most sins are those who speak the most about things that do not concern them.'[6311]

٥٥٧٩ . عنه ؛ : أكثَرُ النّاسِ ذُنوباً أكثَرُهُم كلاماً فيما لا يَعنيهِ.٦٢٦٤

5580. **The Prophet (SAWA) said,** 'A person comes so close to Heaven until there remains only a spear's throw between it and him, and then he says something, thereby distancing him farther away than Sinai.'[6312]

٥٥٨٠ . عنه ؛ : إنّ الرجُلَ لَيَدنو مِنَ الجَنَّةِ حتّى ما يكونُ بينَهُ وبينَها إلّا قِيدُ رُمحٍ ، فيَتَكلَّمُ بالكَلِمَةِ فيَتَباعَدُ منها أبعَدَ مِن صَنعاءَ.٦٢٦٥

5581. **Imām ʿAlī (AS),** walking past a person speaking meddlesomely, said, 'You dictate to your *two angels the book inscribed* for your Lord, so

٥٥٨١ . الإمامُ عليٌّ ؛ ـ لمّا مَرَّ برجُلٍ يَتَكلَّمُ

speak about issues that concern you and leave whatever does not concern you.'[6313]

5582. **Imām ʿAlī (AS) said,** 'It surprises me that someone should speak about things that neither benefit him in this world, nor will any reward be written for him in the Hereafter.'[6314]

5583. **Imām ʿAlī (AS) said,** 'Beware of prattle, for he who speaks a lot will have a lot of sins.'[6315]

5584. **Imām al-Ḥusayn (AS) said** to Ibn ʿAbbās, 'Do not speak about things that do not concern you, for I fear for you the burden [of sin], and do not speak about things that concern you until you find speaking to be appropriate.'[6316]

1613. The Censure of Meddlesome Speech

5585. **Imām ʿAlī (AS) said,** 'Beware of meddlesome speech, for it exposes your faults that were hidden and provokes your enemies who were silent.'[6317]

5586. **Imām ʿAlī (AS) said,** 'Blessed be he who… donates the excess from his money, and retains the excess in his speech.'[6318]

5587. **Imām al-Ṣādiq (AS) said,** 'The knowledgeable one does not speak meddlesomely.'[6319]

1614. The Prohibition of Speaking Excessively

5588. **Prophet Khiḍr (AS),** in his advice to Prophet Moses (AS) said, 'Do not be talkative and a prattler in speaking, for excessive speech disgraces the knowledgeable and shows up the faults of the foolish.'[6320]

5589. **The Prophet (SAWA) said,** 'Do not speak a lot without the remembrance of Allah, for excessive

بِفُضـولِ الكلامِ ـ: إنّكَ تُملِي علىٰ حافِظَيكَ كِتاباً إلىٰ رَبِّكَ، فَتَكَلَّمْ بما يَعنيكَ ودَعْ ما لا يَعنيكَ.[٦٢٦٦]

٥٥٨٢. عنه عليه السلام: عَجِبتُ لِمَن يَتكلَّمُ بما لا يَنفَعُهُ في دُنياهُ ولا يُكتَبُ لَهُ أجرُهُ في اُخراهُ.[٦٢٦٧]

٥٥٨٣. عنه عليه السلام: إيّاكَ والهَذَرَ؛ فَمَن كَثُرَ كلامُهُ كَثُرَت آثامُهُ.[٦٢٦٨]

٥٥٨٤. الإمامُ الحسينُ عليه السلام ـ لابنِ عبّاسٍ ـ: لا تَتَكَلَّمَنَّ فيما لا يَعنيكَ فإنّي أخافُ علَيكَ الوِزرَ، ولا تَتكَلَّمَنَّ فيما يَعنيكَ حتّىٰ تَرىٰ لِلكلامِ مَوضِعاً.[٦٢٦٩]

١٦١٣ ـ ذَمُّ فُضولِ الكَلامِ

٥٥٨٥. الإمامُ عليٌّ عليه السلام: إيّاكَ وفضولَ الكلامِ؛ فإنّهُ يُظهِرُ مِن عُيوبِكَ ما بَطَنَ، ويُحَرِّكُ علَيكَ مِن أعدائكَ ما سَكَنَ.[٦٢٧٠]

٥٥٨٦. عنه عليه السلام: طوبىٰ لِمَن... أنفَقَ الفَضلَ مِن مالِهِ، وأمسَكَ الفَضلَ مِن لِسانِهِ.[٦٢٧١]

٥٥٨٧. الإمامُ الصّادقُ عليه السلام: العالِمُ لا يَتكلَّمُ بالفُضولِ.[٦٢٧٢]

١٦١٤ ـ النَّهيُ عَن كَثرَةِ الكَلامِ

٥٥٨٨. الخضرُ عليه السلام ـ مِن وصاياهُ لِموسىٰ عليه السلام ـ: لا تكونَنَّ مِكثاراً بالنُّطقِ مِهذاراً، فإنّ كَثرَةَ النُّطقِ تَشينُ العُلَماءَ، وتُبدي مَساويَ السُّخَفاءِ.[٦٢٧٣]

٥٥٨٩. رسولُ اللهِ صلى الله عليه وآله: لا تُكثِروا الكلامَ بغيرِ ذِكرِ

speech without the remembrance of Allah hardens the heart. The farthest of people away from Allah are the hard-hearted.’[6321]

اللهِ ؛ فإنَّ كَثرَةَ الكلامِ بغَيرِ ذِكرِ اللهِ قَسوَةُ القَلبِ، إنّ أبعَدَ النّاسِ مِن اللهِ القَلبُ القاسي.[٦٢٧٤]

5590. **Imām ʿAlī (AS) said,** ‘Beware of speaking too much, for it increases mistakes and engenders boredom.’[6322]

٥٥٩٠. الإمامُ عليٌّ عليه السلام: إيّاكَ وكَثرَةَ الكَلامِ ؛ فإنّهُ يُكثِرُ الزَّلَلَ ويُورِثُ المَلَلَ.[٦٢٧٥]

5591. **Imām ʿAlī (AS) said,** ‘When the intellect is perfected speaking decreases.’[6323]

٥٥٩١. عنه عليه السلام: إذا تَمَّ العَقلُ نَقَصَ الكلامُ.[٦٢٧٦]

5592. **Imām ʿAlī (AS) said,** ‘Your speech is in your shackle [power] as long as you do not speak, and when you speak you become shackled by it. So, guard your tongue like you guard your gold and silver, for many a word snatches away a blessing and brings down vengeance.’[6324]

٥٥٩٢. عنه عليه السلام: الكلامُ في وَثاقِكَ ما لم تَتَكلَّمْ بهِ، فإذا تَكَلَّمتَ بهِ صِرتَ في وَثاقِهِ، فَاخزُنْ لِسانَكَ كما تَخزُنُ ذَهَبَكَ ووَرِقَكَ، فَرُبَّ كَلِمَةٍ سَلَبَت نِعمَةً وجَلَبَت نِقمَةً.[٦٢٧٧]

5593. **Imām ʿAlī (AS) said,** ‘If you speak a word it possesses you and if you withhold it you possess it.’[6325]

٥٥٩٣. عنه عليه السلام: إذا تَكَلَّمتَ بالكَلِمَةِ مَلَكَتكَ، وإذا أمسَكتَها مَلَكتَها.[٦٢٧٨]

5594. **Imām ʿAlī (AS) said,** ‘He who knows that his words form part of his actions, his words lessen except in that which concerns him.’[6326]

٥٥٩٤. عنه عليه السلام: مَن عَلِمَ أنّ كلامَهُ مِن عَمَلِهِ قلّ كلامُهُ إلّا فيما يَعنيهِ.[٦٢٧٩]

5595. **Imām ʿAlī (AS) said,** ‘Do not say what you do not know, or rather, do not say everything you know, for Allah prescribed obligations upon your body parts which He will use as proof against you on the Day of Resurrection.’[6327]

٥٥٩٥. عنه عليه السلام: لا تَقُلْ ما لا تَعلَمُ، بَل لا تَقُلْ كُلَّ ما تَعلَمُ، فإنَّ اللهَ فَرَضَ علىٰ جَوارِحِكَ كُلِّها فَرائضَ يَحتَجُّ بها علَيكَ يَومَ القِيامَةِ.[٦٢٨٠]

5596. **Imām ʿAlī (AS) said,** ‘Speech is like medicine; a little bit of it benefits, and a lot of it kills.’[6328]

٥٥٩٦. عنه عليه السلام: الكلامُ كالدَّواءِ؛ قَليلُهُ يَنفَعُ، وكَثيرُهُ قاتِلٌ.[٦٢٨١]

5597. **Imām ʿAlī (AS) said,** ‘[Balanced] Speech is between two attributes of badness, which are: excessive and too little [speech]; too much is prattle and too little is stammering and hesitation.’[6329]

٥٥٩٧. عنه عليه السلام: الكلامُ بَينَ خَلَّتَي سَوءٍ، هُما: الإكثارُ والإقلالُ، فالإكثارُ هَذَرٌ، والإقلالُ عِيٌّ وحَصَرٌ.[٦٢٨٢]

5598. **Imām al-Bāqir (AS) said,** 'I hate for the size of a person's tongue to exceed his knowledge, just as I hate the extent of a person's knowledge to exceed the extent of his intellect.'[6330]

٥٥٩٨ . الإمامُ الباقرُ (عليه السلام): إنّي لَأَكْرَهُ أن يكونَ مِقدارُ لِسانِ الرجُلِ فاضِلاً علىٰ مِقدارِ عِلمِهِ، كما أكرَهُ أن يكونَ مِقدارُ عِلمِهِ فاضِلاً علىٰ مِقدارِ عَقلِهِ.[٦٢٨٣]

5599. **Imām al-Hādī (AS) said,** 'The ignorant person is the prisoner of his own tongue.'[6331]

٥٥٩٩ . الإمامُ الهاديُّ (عليه السلام): الجاهِلُ أسيرُ لِسانِهِ.[٦٢٨٤]

(See also: SILENCE 241)

(أُنظر) عنوان ٢٤١ «الصمت».

1615. The Merit of Speaking over Silence

١٦٠٥ ـ فَضلُ الكَلامِ عَلَى السُّكوتِ

5600. **Imām ʿAlī (AS) said,** Telling the truth is better than being incapable of speaking or being silent.'[6332]

٥٦٠٠ . الإمامُ عليٌّ (عليه السلام): القولُ بالحَقِّ خيرٌ مِن العِيِّ والصَّمتِ.[٦٢٨٥]

5601. **Imām Zayn al-ʿĀbidīn (AS),** when asked about which of speaking or silence was better, said, 'For each of these two there are harms, and when they are both safe from harm, speaking is better than keeping quiet.' They asked him, 'How is this so, O son of the Prophet (SAWA)?' He said, 'Because Allah Almighty did not send prophets and successors to remain quiet, rather He sent them with speech, nor is Heaven earned by silence, nor is quietness obligated for the vicegerency of Allah, and nor is protection from Hell sought through silence. This is all possible through speech.'[6333]

٥٦٠١ . الإمامُ زينُ العابدينَ (عليه السلام) لمّا سُئلَ عنِ الكلامِ والسُّكوتِ أيُّهُما أفضَلُ؟ فقالَ (عليه السلام): لِكُلِّ واحِدٍ مِنهُما آفاتٌ، فإذا سَلِما مِن الآفاتِ فالكلامُ أفضَلُ مِن السُّكوتِ.
قيلَ: كيفَ ذلكَ يا ابنَ رسولِ اللهِ؟ قالَ: لأنَّ اللهَ عَزَّوجلَّ ما بَعَثَ الأنبياءَ والأوصياءَ بالسُّكوتِ، إنّما بَعَثَهُم بالكلامِ، ولا استُحِقَّتِ الجَنّةُ بالسُّكوتِ، ولا استُوجِبَت وَلايَةُ اللهِ بالسُّكوتِ، ولا تُوُقِّيَتِ النّارُ بالسُّكوتِ، إنّما ذلكَ كُلُّهُ بالكلامِ.[٦٢٨٦]

5602. **Imām al-Bāqir (AS),** addressing a man who talked too much, said: 'O man, you underestimate and belittle speech! Know that when Allah the Glorious and Exalted sent His prophets He did not send them with gold and silver but with speech. God, the Exalted, presented Himself to His creatures through speech, proofs and signs referring to Him.'[6334]

٥٦٠٢ . الإمامُ الباقرُ (عليه السلام) ـ لِرجُلٍ وقَد كَلَّمَهُ بكلامٍ كَثيرٍ ـ: أيُّها الرجُلُ، تَحتَقِرُ الكلامَ وتَستَصغِرُهُ؟! اِعلَمْ أنَّ اللهَ عَزَّوجلَّ لم يَبعَثْ رُسُلَهُ حيثُ بَعَثَها ومَعها ذَهَبٌ ولا فِضَّةٌ، ولكنْ بَعَثَها بالكلامِ، وإنّما عَرَّفَ اللهُ جلَّ وعزَّ نفسَهُ إلى خَلقِهِ بالكلامِ والدَّلالاتِ علَيهِ والأعلامِ.[٦٢٨٧]

1616. The Merit of Silence over Speaking

١٦١٦ ـ ما يفضل السُّكوتَ عَلَى الكَلامِ

5603. **The Prophet (SAWA) said,** 'Silence is better than dictating the vice (to the angels

٥٦٠٣ . رسولُ اللهِ ﷺ: السُّكوتُ خَيرٌ مِن إملاءِ

responsible for recording our deeds) and dictating good deeds is better than silence.'[6335]

الشَّرِّ، وإملاءُ الخَيرِ خَيرٌ مِن السُّكوتِ.[٦٢٨٨]

5604. **Imām ʿAlī (AS) said,** 'Silence that brings you dignity is better than speech which causes disdain.'[6336]

٥٦٠٤ . الإمامُ عليٌّ عليه السلام: صَمتٌ يُكسِبُكَ الوَقارَ خَيرٌ مِن كلامٍ يَكسُوكَ العارَ.[٦٢٨٩]

5605. **Imām ʿAlī (AS) said,** 'Silence that brings you good health is better than speech which causes you blame.'[6337]

٥٦٠٥ . عنه عليه السلام: صَمتٌ يُعقِبُكَ السَّلامَةَ خَيرٌ مِن نُطقٍ يُعقِبُكَ المَلامَةَ.[٦٢٩٠]

5606. **Imām ʿAlī (AS) said,** 'Silence that puts the garment of dignity on you is better than words that brings you remorse.'[6338]

٥٦٠٦ . عنه عليه السلام: صَمتٌ يَكسُوكَ الكرامَةَ خَيرٌ مِن قَولٍ يُكسِبُكَ النَّدامَةَ.[٦٢٩١]

5607. **Imām ʿAlī (AS) said,** 'Being dumb is better than telling lies.'[6339]

٥٦٠٧ . عنه عليه السلام: الخَرَسُ خَيرٌ مِن الكَذِبِ.[٦٢٩٢]

5608. **Imām ʿAlī (AS) said,** 'Inability to speak is better than talking nonsense.'[6340]

٥٦٠٨ . عنه عليه السلام: الحَصَرُ خَيرٌ مِن الهَذَرِ.[٦٢٩٣]

1617. The Best of Speech

١٦١٧ـ أحسَنُ الكَلامِ

5609. **The Prophet (SAWA) said,** 'The best of speech is the speech of Allah.'[6341]

٥٦٠٩ . رسولُ اللهِ صلى الله عليه وآله: أحسَنُ الكلامِ كلامُ اللهِ.[٦٢٩٤]

5610. **Imām ʿAlī (AS) said,** 'The best of speech is that which is not thrown out by the ears, nor is its understanding tiring for people.'[6342]

٥٦١٠ . الإمامُ عليٌّ عليه السلام: أحسَنُ الكلامِ ما لا تَمُجُّهُ الآذانُ ولا يُتعِبُ فَهمُهُ الأفهامَ.[٦٢٩٥]

5611. **Imām ʿAlī (AS) said,** 'The best of speech is that which is adorned by a good structure, and is understood by both the elite and the laymen.'[6343]

٥٦١١ . عنه عليه السلام: أحسَنُ الكلامِ ما زانَهُ حُسنُ النِّظامِ، وفَهِمَهُ الخاصُّ والعامُّ.[٦٢٩٦]

5612. **Imām ʿAlī (AS) said,** 'The best of speech is that which neither bores [due to its length] and nor is it too brief.'[6344]

٥٦١٢ . عنه عليه السلام: خَيرُ الكلامِ ما لا يُمِلُّ ولا يَقِلُّ.[٦٢٩٧]

1618. The Merit of Kind Speech

١٦١٨ـ فَضلُ طيبِ الكَلامِ

"And speak kindly to people."[6345]

﴿وَقُولُوا لِلنَّاسِ حُسناً﴾.[٦٢٩٨]

"Tell My servants to speak in a manner which is the best. Indeed Satan incites ill feeling between them, and Satan is indeed man's manifest enemy."[6346]

﴿وَقُلْ لِعِبادِي يَقُولُوا الَّتِي هِيَ أَحْسَنُ إِنَّ الشَّيْطانَ يَنْزَغُ بَيْنَهُمْ إِنَّ الشَّيْطانَ كانَ لِلْإِنسانِ عَدُوّاً مُبِيناً﴾.٦٢٩٩

5613. **Imām al-Bāqir (AS),** with regard to Allah's verse: *"And speak kindly to people"* said, 'Say to people the best of what you like to be said to you.'[6347]

٥٦١٣. الإمامُ الباقرُ ـ في قولِ اللهِ عزّوجلّ: ﴿وقُولُوا للنّاسِ حُسْناً﴾٦٣٠٠ـ: قولوا للناسِ أحسَنَ ما تُحِبُّونَ أن يُقالَ فيكُم.٦٣٠١

5614. **The Prophet (SAWA),** When a man asked him about the best of actions, said, 'The feeding of food and speaking well.'[6348]

٥٦١٤. رسولُ اللهِ ـ لمّا سَألَهُ رجُلٌ عن أفضَلِ الأعمالِ ـ: إطعامُ الطَّعامِ، وإطيابُ الكلامِ.٦٣٠٢

5615. **Imām Zayn al-ʿĀbidīn (AS) said,** 'Beautiful speech makes wealth thrive, increases sustenance, delays death, brings love in the family, and makes one enter Heaven.'[6349]

٥٦١٥. الإمامُ زينُ العابدينَ: القَولُ الحَسَنُ يُثري المالَ، ويُنمي الرِّزقَ، ويُنسِئُ في الأجَلِ، ويُحَبِّبُ إلى الأهلِ، ويُدخِلُ الجَنَّةَ.٦٣٠٣

5616. **Imām al-Ṣādiq (AS) said,** 'O followers (*shīʿa*) of ours, be an adornment for us and do not be a disgrace to us. Speak well to people, protect your tongues, and prevent it from futile and vulgar speech.'[6350]

٥٦١٦. الإمامُ الصّادقُ: مَعاشِرَ الشِّيعَةِ، كونوا لنا زَيناً ولا تكونوا علَينا شَيناً، قولوا للناسِ حُسناً، وحفَظُوا ألسِنَتَكُم، وكُفُّوها عنِ الفُضولِ وقَبيحِ القَولِ.٦٣٠٤

349

PERFECTION

الكَمالُ

1619. Perfection of Man

١٦١٩ ـ كَمالُ الإنسانِ

5617. **Imām ʿAlī (AS) said,** 'The intelligent person seeks perfection and the ignorant person seeks possession.'[6351]

٥٦١٧. الإمامُ عليٌّ: العاقِلُ يَطلُبُ الكَمالَ، الجاهِلُ يطلُبُ المالَ.٦٣٠٥

5618. **Imām ʿAlī (AS) said,** 'In the perfection of the human being, the existence of his merit lies in his own feeling of inadequacy.'[6352]

٥٦١٨. عنه: مِن كمالِ الإنسانِ ووُفورِ فَضلِهِ استِشعارُهُ بنفسِهِ النُّقصانَ.٦٣٠٦

5619. **Imām ʿAlī (AS) said,** 'Perfection in this world does not exist.'[6353]

٥٦١٩. عنه: الكمالُ في الدُّنيا مَفقودٌ.٦٣٠٧

5620. **Imām ʿAlī (AS) said,** 'The perfection of a man lies in six features: in two of his smallest [features], in two of his largest [features], and in two of his apparent [features]. As for two of his smallest [features] - his heart and his tongue - when he fights he fights with his heart and when he speaks he speaks with his tongue. Two of his largest [features] are his intellect and his determination, and his two apparent [features] are his wealth and his beauty.'[6354]

٥٦٢٠ . عنه ﷺ : كمالُ الرجُلِ بستِّ خِصالٍ : بِأصغَرَيهِ، وأكبَرَيهِ، وهيئَتَيهِ ؛ فأمّا أصغراهُ فقلبُهُ ولِسانُهُ، إن قاتَلَ قاتَلَ بجَنانٍ، وإن تكَلَّمَ تكَلَّمَ بلِسانٍ، وأمّا أكبَراهُ فعقلُهُ وهِمَّتُهُ، وأمّا هَيئَتاهُ فمالُهُ وجَمالُهُ.٦٣٠٨

5621. **Imām ʿAlī (AS) said,** 'The perfection of the human being is the intellect.'[6355]

٥٦٢١ . عنه ﷺ : كمالُ الإنسانِ العَقلُ.٦٣٠٩

5622. **Imām ʿAlī (AS) said,** 'Of the perfection of a person is that he leaves what is not appropriate for him.'[6356]

٥٦٢٢ . عنه ﷺ : مِن كمالِ المَرءِ تَركُهُ ما لا يَجمُلُ بِهِ.٦٣١٠

5623. **Imām ʿAlī (AS) said,** 'Clothe yourself with shyness and armour yourself with loyalty; protect brotherhood...., and your eminence will be perfected.'[6357]

٥٦٢٣ . عنه ﷺ : تَسَربَلِ الحَياءَ وادَّرِعِ الوَفاءَ واحفَظِ الإخاءَ... يَكمُلْ لكَ السَّناءُ.٦٣١١

5624. **Imām al-Bāqir (AS) said,** 'Perfection, all of perfection is education in religion, patience over misfortunes, and apportioning one's livelihood.'[6358]

٥٦٢٤ . الإمامُ الباقرُ ﷺ : الكمالُ كُلُّ الكمالِ التَّفقُّهُ في الدِّينِ، والصَّبرُ علَى النّائبَةِ، وتَقديرُ المَعيشَةِ.٦٣١٢

5625. **Imām al-Ṣādiq (AS) said,** 'There are three features that whoever is blessed with is perfect: intellect, beauty and eloquence.'[6359]

٥٦٢٥ . الإمامُ الصّادقُ ﷺ : ثلاثُ خِصالٍ مَن رُزِقَها كانَ كامِلاً: العَقلُ، والجَمالُ، والفَصاحةُ.٦٣١٣

350

SAGACITY

الكِيَاسَةُ

1620. The Sign of Sagacity

١٦٢٠ـ علامةُ الكِياسَةِ

5626. **The Prophet (SAWA) said,** 'The sagacious person is someone who subjugates himself and acts for that which comes after death.'[6360]

٥٦٢٦ . رسولُ اللهِ ﷺ : الكَيِّسُ مَن دانَ نفسَهُ وعَمِلَ لِما بَعدَ المَوتِ، والعاجِزُ مَن أتبَعَ نفسَهُ وهواها وتَمنّىٰ علَى اللهِ عزَّ وجلَّ الأمانيَّ.٦٣١٤

5627. **The Prophet (SAWA),** when asked, 'Who is the most sagacious of believers?' replied, 'Those who remember death the most, and are the most prepared for it.'[6361]

٥٦٢٧ . عنه ﷺ ـ لمّـا سُـئلَ: مـنَ أكـيَسُ المؤمنينَ ـ: أكثَرهُم ذِكراً لِلمَوتِ وأشَدُّهُم لَـهُ استِعداداً.[٦٣١٥]

5628. **The Prophet (SAWA) said,** 'The highest level of sagacity is piety and the lowest level of stupidity is immorality.'[6362]

٥٦٢٨ . عنه ﷺ : أكيَسُ الكَيْسِ التُّقىٰ، وأحمَقُ الحُمقِ الفُجورُ.[٦٣١٦]

5629. **The Prophet (SAWA) said,** 'The most sagacious of the sagacious is he who takes account of himself and works for the Hereafter, and the stupidest of the stupid is he who allows himself to follow his desires and entertains false expectations from Allah.'[6363]

٥٦٢٩ . عنه ﷺ : أكيَسُ الكَيِّسِينَ مَن حـاسَبَ نفسَهُ وعَمِلَ لِما بَعدَ المَوتِ، وأحـمَقُ الحَـمقىٰ مَـن أتـبَعَ نـفسَهُ هَـواهـا وتَـمَنَّى عـلَى اللهِ الأمانِيَّ.[٦٣١٧]

5630. **Imām ʿAlī (AS) said,** 'The sagacious one is he who knows himself and purifies his actions.'[6364]

٥٦٣٠ . الإمامُ عليٌّ ﷷ : الكَيِّسُ مَن عَرَفَ نفسَهُ وأخلَصَ أعمالَهُ.[٦٣١٨]

5631. **Imām ʿAlī (AS) said,** 'The sagacious one is he whose today is better than his yesterday, and locks away blame from himself.'[6365]

٥٦٣١ . عنه ﷷ : الكَيِّسُ مَن كانَ يَومُهُ خَيراً مِن أمسِهِ، وعَقَلَ الذَّمَّ عن نفسِهِ.[٦٣١٩]

5632. **Imām ʿAlī (AS),** when asked about the most sagacious of people, said, '[It is] he who has insight into what is [conducive to] his growth from his erring, and inclines towards his growth.'[6366]

٥٦٣٢ . عنه ﷷ ـ لمّا سُئلَ عن أكيَسِ النّاسِ ـ: مَن أبصَرَ رُشدَهُ مِن غَيِّهِ فَمالَ إلىٰ رُشدِهِ.[٦٣٢٠]

5633. **Imām ʿAlī (AS) said,** 'The most sagacious from among you is the most pious of you.'[6367]

٥٦٣٣ . عنه ﷷ : أكيَسُكُم أورَعُكُم.[٦٣٢١]

351

CLOTHING

اللِّبَاسُ

1621. Recommended Clothes

١٦٢١ ـ الالبسة الممدوحة

5634. **The Prophet (SAWA) said,** 'The best garment in which you will meet Allah the Exalted in your graves and in the mosque is white cloth.'[6368]

٥٦٣٤ . رسولُ اللهِ ﷺ : أحسَنُ ما زُرتُمُ اللهَ عَزَّ وجلَّ بِهِ في قُبورِكُم ومَساجِدِكُمُ البَياضُ.[٦٣٢٢]

5635. **The Prophet (SAWA) said,** 'Wear white, for it is nicer and purer, and shroud your dead with it.'[6369]

٥٦٣٥ . عنهﷺ : اِلبَسوا البَياضَ ؛ فـإنّهُ أطـيَبُ وأطهَرُ ، وكَفِّنوا فيهِ مَوتاكُم.[٦٣٢٣]

5636. **Imām ʿAlī (AS) said,** 'Wear clothes of cotton, for it is the clothing of the Prophet (SAWA) and our clothing.'[6370]

٥٦٣٦ . الإمامُ عليٌّؑ : اِلبَسوا ثِـيابَ القُـطنِ ؛ فإنّها لِباسُ رسولِ اللهِﷺ ، وهُو لِباسُنا.[٦٣٢٤]

5637. **Imām al-Ṣādiq (AS) said,** 'Linen is of the clothes of the Prophets, and makes one's flesh grow.'[6371]

٥٦٣٧ . الإمامُ الصّادقُؑ : الكَتّانُ مِـن لِـباسِ الأنبياءِ ، وهُو يُنبِتُ اللَّحمَ.[٦٣٢٥]

(See also: ADORNMENT: section 899)

(اُنظر) الزنية : باب ٨٩٩.

1622. Economizing in Clothes

١٦٢٢ ـ الاِقتِصادُ في اللِّباسِ

5638. *Kanz al-ʿUmmāl*: 'He [the Prophet (SAWA)] prohibited clothes that express notoriety (*shuhra*), both thin and thick, soft and rough, long and short. It should be something appropriate between these two and economical.'[6372]

٥٦٣٨ . كنز العمّال : نَهىٰ [النبيُّﷺ] عن الشُّهرَتَينِ ، دِقَّةِ الثِّيابِ وغِلظِها ، ولِينِها وخُشونَتِها ، وطُولِها وقِـصَرِها ، ولكـنْ سَـدادٌ فـيما بَـينَ ذلكَ واقتِصادٌ.[٦٣٢٦]

5639. **Imām ʿAlī (AS)** –describing the pious- said, 'Their speech is truthfulness and they dress economically.'[6373]

٥٦٣٩ . الإمامُ عليٌّؑ ـ في صِفَةِ المُـتّقينَ ـ : مَنطِقُهُمُ الصَّوابُ ، ومَلبَسُهُمُ الاقتِصادُ.[٦٣٢٧]

5640. **Imām al-Ṣādiq (AS) said,** 'Wealth belongs to Allah, and He entrusts it to man as a deposit. He permitted them to eat economically and dress economically.'[6374]

٥٦٤٠ . الإمامُ الصّادقُؑ : المالُ مالُ اللهِ يَضَعُهُ عِندَ الرَّجُلِ وَدايِعَ ، وجَوَّزَ لَهُم أن ياُكُلوا قَصداً ويَلبَسوا قَصداً.[٦٣٢٨]

(See also: FAME: section 1074)

(اُنظر) الشهرة : باب ١٠٧٤.

1623. The Best Clothing in Every Time Period is the Clothing of the People of that Time

١٦٢٣ ـ خَيرُ لِباسِ كُلِّ زَمانٍ لِباسُ أهلِهِ

5641. **Ḥammād b. ʿUthmān narrated,** 'I was in the presence of Abū Abdillāh [al-Ṣādiq] (AS), when a man said to him, 'May Allah make you well, you mentioned that ʿAlī b. Abī Ṭālib (AS) would wear rough clothes and would wear a shirt that was worth four dirhams, and things similar to that, but we see you are wearing good clothes!' [He

٥٦٤١ . حَمّادُ بنِ عُثمانَ : كنتُ حاضِراً عندَ أبي عبدِاللهِؑ إذ قالَ لَهُ رجُلٌ: أصلَحَكَ اللهُ ، ذَكَرتَ أنّ عليَّ بنَ أبي طالبٍؑ كانَ يَـلبَسُ الخَشِـنَ ، يَلبَسُ القَميصَ بأربَعةِ دَراهِمَ ومـا أشـبَهَ ذلكَ ،

said], 'The Imām replied to him, ''Alī b. Abī Ṭālib (AS) wore that in a time in which it would not be disapproved, and if he would wear those clothes today he would be defamed for it. Therefore, the best clothing of every time is the clothing of the people [of that time]. However, when our al-Qā'im [the awaited saviour Imām al-Mahdī, may Allah hasten his appearance] reappears he will be wearing the clothes of 'Alī (AS) and will follow his way of life.'[6375]

ونَرىٰ علَيكَ اللِّباسَ الجَيِّدَ! قالَ فقالَ لَهُ: إنّ عليَّ بنَ أبي طالبٍ ؑ كانَ يَلبَسُ ذلكَ في زمانٍ لا يُنكَرُ، ولَو لَبِسَ مِثلَ ذلكَ اليومَ لَشُهِرَ بهِ، فخَيرُ لِباسِ كُلِّ زمانٍ لِباسُ أهلِهِ. غَيرَ أنّ قائمَنا إذا قامَ لَبِسَ لِباسَ عليٍّ ؑ وسارَ بسِيرَتِهِ.[٦٣٢٩]

5642. **Sufyān al-Thawrī narrated,** 'I asked Abū 'Abdillāh [al-Ṣādiq] (AS), 'You narrate that 'Alī b. Abī Ṭālib (AS) wore rough clothes whilst you wear soft and fine clothes!' He (AS) said, 'Woe unto you! 'Alī b. Abī Ṭālib (AS) lived in a time of difficulty, so if it is a time of ampleness the righteous deserve it more.'[6376]

٥٦٤٢. سُفيانُ الثَّوريِّ: قلتُ لأبي عبدِاللهِ ؑ: أنتَ تَروي أنّ عليَّ بنَ أبي طالبٍ ؑ كانَ يَلبَسُ الخَشِنَ، وأنتَ تَلبَسُ القُوهِيَّ والمَرويَّ! قالَ: وَيحَكَ! إنّ عليَّ بنَ أبي طالبٍ ؑ كانَ في زمانٍ ضِيقٍ، فإذا اتّسَعَ الزّمانُ فأبرارُ الزّمانِ أولىٰ بهِ.[٦٣٣٠]

5643. **Imām al-Riḍā (AS) said,** 'The weak from among my followers want me to sit on wool and wear rough clothes, but this era cannot handle that.'[6377]

٥٦٤٣. الإمامُ الرِّضا ؑ: إنّ أهلَ الضَّعفِ مِن مَوالِيَّ يُحِبّونَ أن أجلِسَ علَى اللُّبُودِ وألبَسَ الخَشِنَ، ولَيس يَتَحَمّلُ الزَّمانُ ذٰلكَ.[٦٣٣١]

5644. **Abū 'Abbād narrated,** 'al-Riḍā (AS) would sit on a straw mat in the summer, and on sackcloth in the winter. He wore rough, thick clothes, and when he appeared in front of people he would adorn himself for them.'[6378]

٥٦٤٤. أبو عبّاد: كانَ جُلوسُ الرِّضا ؑ في الصَّيفِ علىٰ حَصيرٍ، وفي الشِّتاءِ علىٰ مِسْحٍ[٦٣٣٢]، ولُبسُهُ الغَليظُ مِن الثِّيابِ؛ حتّىٰ إذا بَرزَ للنّاسِ تَزَيّنَ لَهُم.[٦٣٣٣]

1624. The Turban

١٦٢٤ ـ العِمامَةُ

5645. **The Prophet (SAWA) said,** 'Turbans are the crowns of the Arabs.'[6379]

٥٦٤٥. رسولُ اللهِ ﷺ: العَمائمُ تِيجانُ العَرَبِ.[٦٣٣٤]

5646. **The Prophet (SAWA) said,** 'Go to mosques without armour and with your heads covered, for the turbans are the crowns of the Muslims.'[6380]

٥٦٤٦. عنه ﷺ: ائْتوا المَساجِدَ حُسَّراً ومُعَصَّبينَ، فإنّ العَمائمَ تِيجانُ المُسلِمينَ.[٦٣٣٥]

5647. **Jābir narrated,** 'The Messenger of Allah (SAWA) entered Makkah in the year of the Conquest wearing a black turban.'[6381]

٥٦٤٧. جابر: إنّ رسولَ اللهِ ﷺ دَخَلَ عامَ الفَتحِ مَكّةَ وعلَيهِ عِمامَةٌ سَوداءُ.[٦٣٣٦]

5648. Imām al-Ṣādiq (AS) said, 'The Messenger of Allah (SAWA) attired 'Alī (AS) with a turban with his own hands. The Prophet (SAWA) lowered the turban down from the front and shortened it from the back the breadth of four fingers, then he said, 'Turn around', and he did so, then he said, 'Turn to the front' so he did, then the Prophet (SAWA) said, 'This is how the crowns of the angels are.'[6382]

٥٦٤٨ . الإمامُ الصّادقُ عليه السلام : عَمَّمَ رسولُ اللهِ صلى الله عليه وآله عليّاً عليه السلام بيَدِهِ، فسَدَلَها مِن بَينِ يَدَيهِ وقَصَّرَها مِن خَلفِهِ قَدرَ أربَعِ أصابِعَ، ثُمّ قالَ : أدبِرْ فأدبَرَ، ثُمّ قالَ: أقبِلْ فأقبَلَ، ثُمّ قالَ: هٰكذا تِيجانُ المَلائكَةِ.[٦٣٣٧]

1625. Prohibited Clothing

١٦٢٥ ـ الألبِسَةُ المَمنوعَةُ

5649. The Prophet (SAWA) said, 'Clothings of silk and gold are forbidden for the males of my community and have been permitted for the females.'[6383]

٥٦٤٩ . رسولُ اللهِ صلى الله عليه وآله : حُرِّمَ لِباسُ الحَريرِ والذَّهَبِ على ذُكورِ اُمَّتي واُحِلَّ لإناثِهِم.[٦٣٣٨]

5650. The Prophet (SAWA) said, 'Whoever wears clothes to show off so other people will look at him, Allah will not look at him until he takes it off.'[6384]

٥٦٥٠ . عنه صلى الله عليه وآله : مَن لَبِسَ ثَوباً يُباهي بهِ لِيَراهُ النّاسُ لَم يَنظُرِ اللهُ إلَيهِ حتّىٰ يَنزَعَهُ.[٦٣٣٩]

5651. Imām al-Ṣādiq (AS) said, 'A man must not wear silk and brocade except in war.'[6385]

٥٦٥١ . الإمامُ الصّادقُ عليه السلام : لا يَلبَسُ الرّجُلُ الحَريرَ والدِّيباجَ إلّا في الحَربِ.[٦٣٤٠]

(See also: FAME: section 1073)

(اُنظر) الشهرة: باب ١٠٧٣.

352

STUBBORNNESS

اللَّجاجُ

1626. Reproaching Stubbornness

١٦٢٦ ـ ذَمُّ اللَّجاجَةِ

5652. The Prophet (SAWA) said, 'Beware of obstinacy; it begins with ignorance and ends with regret.[6386]

٥٦٥٢ . رسولُ اللهِ صلى الله عليه وآله : إيّاكَ واللَّجاجَةَ؛ فإنّ أوَّلَها جَهلٌ وآخِرَها نَدامَةٌ.[٦٣٤١]

5653. Imām 'Alī (AS) said, 'Obstinacy unsheathes opinion.'[6387]

٥٦٥٣ . الإمامُ عليٌّ عليه السلام : اللَّجاجَةُ تَسُلُّ الرّأيَ.[٦٣٤٢]

5654. Imām 'Alī (AS) said, 'A stubborn person does not have a [valid] opinion.'[6388]

٥٦٥٤ . عنه عليه السلام : اللَّجوجُ لا رأيَ لَهُ.[٦٣٤٣]

5655. **Imām ʿAlī (AS) said,** 'A stubborn person does not contemplate.'[6389]

٥٦٥٥ . عنه ؏ : لَيسَ لِلَّجوجٍ تَدبيرٌ . ١٣٤٤

5656. **Imām ʿAlī (AS) said,** 'Stubbornness creates wars and brings hatred to the hearts.'[6390]

٥٦٥٦ . عنه ؏ : اللِّجاجُ يُنتِجُ الحُروبَ ويُوغِرُ القُلوبَ . ١٣٤٥

5657. **Imām ʿAlī (AS) said,** 'Beware that you are not overcome by [the mount of] stubbornness.'[6391]

٥٦٥٧ . عنه ؏ : إيّاكَ أن تَـطيحَ بِكَ مَطِيَّةُ اللِّجاجِ . ١٣٤٦

5658. **Imām ʿAlī (AS) said,** 'Beware of being surmounted by stubbornness.'[6392]

٥٦٥٨ . عنه ؏ : إيّاكَ أن تَـجمَحَ بِكَ مَطِيَّةُ اللِّجاجِ . ١٣٤٧

5659. **Imām ʿAlī (AS) said,** 'Be cautious of stubbornness and you will be safe from its mishaps.'[6393]

٥٦٥٩ . عنه ؏ : احذَرِ اللِّجاجَ تَنجُ مِن كَبوَتِهِ . ١٣٤٨

5660. **Imām ʿAlī (AS) said,** 'Excessiveness in blaming [others] ignites the fires of stubbornness.'[6394]

٥٦٦٠ . عنه ؏ : الإفراطُ في المَلامَةِ يَشُبُّ نيرانَ اللَّجاجَةِ . ١٣٤٩

5661. **Imām ʿAlī (AS) said,** 'The best of morals are those that are the farthest away from stubbornness.'[6395]

٥٦٦١ . عنه ؏ : خَيرُ الأخلاقِ أبعَدُها عَنِ اللِّجاجِ . ١٣٥٠

5662. **Imām ʿAlī (AS) said,** 'He who is stubborn and persistent is the degenerate one whose heart Allah has prevailed over with rust, and the axis of evil hangs over his head.'[6396]

٥٦٦٢ . عنه ؏ : مَن لَجَّ وتَمادىٰ فَهُوَ الراكِسُ الّذي رانَ اللهُ علىٰ قَلبِهِ ، وصارَت دائِرَةُ السَّوءِ علىٰ رَأسِهِ . ١٣٥١

5663. **Imām ʿAlī (AS) said,** 'Beware of hastening matters before their time, or of breaking down when their time is right, or of stubbornness when they are estranged, or of weakness from them when they become clear. So, put every matter in its appropriate place.'[6397]

٥٦٦٣ . عنه ؏ : إيّاكَ والعَجَلَةَ بِالأُمورِ قَبلَ أوانِها ، والتَّسَقُّطَ (التَّساقُطَ ـ التَّثَبُّطَ) فيها عِندَ إمكانِها ، أوِ اللَّجاجَةَ فيها إذا تَنَكَّرَت ، أوِ الوَهنَ عَنها إذَا استَوضَحَت ، فضَع كُلَّ أمرٍ مَوضِعَهُ . ١٣٥٢

353

THE TONGUE

اللِّسان

1627. The Value of the Tongue

١٦٢٧ ـ قيمَةُ اللِّسانِ

5664. **The Prophet (SAWA) said,** 'Beauty is in the tongue.'[6398]

٥٦٦٤. رسولُ اللهِ ﷺ: الجَمالُ في اللِّسانِ.[٦٣٥٣]

5665. **The Prophet (SAWA) said,** 'Eloquence of the tongue is a person's capital.'[6399]

٥٦٦٥. عنه ﷺ: ذَلاقَةُ اللِّسانِ رأسُ المالِ.[٦٣٥٤]

5666. **Imām ʿAlī (AS) said,** 'The tongue is a human's scale.'[6400]

٥٦٦٦. الإمامُ عليٌّ ﷺ: اللِّسانُ ميزانُ الإنسانِ.[٦٣٥٥]

5667. **Imām ʿAlī (AS) said,** 'The core of a human is his tongue and his intellect is his religion.'[6401]

٥٦٦٧. عنه ﷺ: الإنسانُ لُبُّهُ لِسانُهُ، وعَقلُهُ دِينُهُ.[٦٣٥٦]

5668. **Imām ʿAlī (AS) said,** 'Speak and you will be known, for a person is hidden under his tongue.'[6402]

٥٦٦٨. عنه ﷺ: تَكَلَّموا تُعرَفوا؛ فإنَّ المَرءَ مَخبوءٌ تَحتَ لِسانِهِ.[٦٣٥٧]

5669. **Imām ʿAlī (AS) said,** 'Your tongue is the interpreter of your intellect.'[6403]

٥٦٦٩. عنه ﷺ: لِسانُكَ تَرجُمانُ عَقلِكَ.[٦٣٥٨]

(See also: SPEAKING: section 1612)

(أنظر) الكلام: باب ١٦١٢.

1628. The Safety of a Person Lies in Guarding his Tongue

١٦٢٨ ـ سَلامَةُ الإنسانِ في حِفظِ اللِّسانِ

5670. **The Prophet (SAWA) said,** 'The safety of a person lies in guarding his tongue.'[6404]

٥٦٧٠. رسولُ اللهِ ﷺ: سَلامَةُ الإنسانِ في حِفظِ اللِّسانِ.[٦٣٥٩]

5671. **The Prophet (SAWA) said,** 'When a person wakes up in the morning his body parts will plead to the tongue, saying, 'Fear Allah for us, as we depend on you; if you are steadfast we are steadfast, and if you are crooked we are crooked.'[6405]

٥٦٧١. عنه ﷺ: إذا أصبَحَ ابنُ آدمَ فإنَّ الأعضاءَ كُلَّها تُكَفِّرُ اللِّسانَ، فتَقولُ: اِتَّقِ اللهَ فِينا فإنَّما نَحنُ بِكَ؛ فإنِ استَقَمتَ استَقَمنا، وإنِ اعوَجَجتَ اعوَجَجنا.[٦٣٦٠]

5672. **The Prophet (SAWA) said,** 'No person will be safe from sins until he guards his tongue.'[6406]

٥٦٧٢ . عنه ﷺ : لا يَسلَمُ أحَدٌ مِن الذُّنوبِ حتّىٰ يَخزُنَ لِسانَهُ .[٦٣٦١]

5673. **The Prophet (SAWA) said,** 'He who does not guard his tongue has not performed any actions.'[6407]

٥٦٧٣ . عنه ﷺ : ما عَمِلَ مَن لَم يَحفَظْ لِسانَهُ .[٦٣٦٢]

5674. **The Prophet (SAWA) said,** 'The calamity of a person is from his own tongue.'[6408]

٥٦٧٤ . عنه ﷺ : بَلاءُ الإنسانِ مِن اللِّسانِ .[٦٣٦٣]

5675. **The Prophet (SAWA) said,** 'Hold your tongue, for it is a charity that you donate to yourself.'[6409]

٥٦٧٥ . عنه ﷺ : أمسِكْ لِسانَكَ ؛ فإنّها صَدَقَةٌ تَصَدَّقُ بها علىٰ نَفسِكَ .[٦٣٦٤]

5676. **Imām ʿAlī (AS) said,** 'Allah will conceal the faults of he who guards his tongue.'[6410]

٥٦٧٦ . الإمامُ عليٌّ عليه السلام : مَن حَفِظَ لِسانَهُ سَتَرَ اللهُ عَورَتَهُ .[٦٣٦٥]

5677. **Imām ʿAlī (AS) said,** 'The strike of a tongue is harsher than the assault of an arrow-head.'[6411]

٥٦٧٧ . عنه عليه السلام : ضَربُ اللِّسانِ أشَدُّ مِن ضَربِ السِّنانِ .[٦٣٦٦]

5678. **Imām ʿAlī (AS) said,** 'The tongue is a wild beast, if it is left alone it will slay.'[6412]

٥٦٧٨ . عنه عليه السلام : اللِّسانُ سَبُعٌ ، إن خُلِّيَ عَنهُ عَقَرَ .[٦٣٦٧]

5679. **Imām ʿAlī (AS) said,** 'There is nothing that deserves long imprisonment more than the tongue.'[6413]

٥٦٧٩ . عنه عليه السلام : ما مِن شيءٍ أحَقَّ بطُولِ السِّجنِ مِن اللِّسانِ .[٦٣٦٨]

5680. **Imām ʿAlī (AS) said,** 'The Prophet (SAWA) has said, 'The faith of a worshipper will not be upright until his heart is upright, and his heart will not be upright until his tongue is upright.' So, whoever from among you is able to meet his Lord being pure at ease from the blood and property of Muslims and their money, and his tongue free from their honour, then they should do so.'[6414]

٥٦٨٠ . عنه عليه السلام : لَقد قالَ رسولُ اللهِ ﷺ : «لا يَستَقيمُ إيمانُ عَبدٍ حتّىٰ يَستَقيمَ قَلبُهُ ، ولا يَستَقيمُ قَلبُهُ حتّىٰ يَستَقيمَ لِسانُهُ» فمَنِ استَطاعَ مِنكُم أن يَلقَى اللهَ تعالىٰ وهُو نَقِيُّ الرّاحَةِ مِن دِماءِ المُسلمينَ وأموالِهِم ، سَليمُ اللِّسانِ مِن أعراضِهِم ، فلْيَفعَلْ .[٦٣٦٩]

5681. **Imām ʿAlī (AS) said,** 'The tongue of an intelligent man is behind his heart and the heart of a fool is behind his tongue.'[6415]

٥٦٨١ . عنه عليه السلام : لِسانُ العاقِلِ وَراءَ قَلبِهِ ، وقَلبُ الأحمَقِ وَراءَ لِسانِهِ .[٦٣٧٠]

5682. **Imām al-Bāqir (AS) said,** 'This tongue is the key to all good and evil, so a believer must seal his tongue like he seals his gold and silver.'[6416]

٥٦٨٢ . الإمامُ الباقرُ عليه السلام : إنّ هٰذا اللِّسانَ مِفتاحُ كلِّ خَيرٍ وشَرٍّ ، فيَنبَغي للمؤمنِ أن يَختِمَ علىٰ لِسانِهِ كَما يَختِمُ علىٰ ذَهَبِهِ وفِضَّتِهِ .[٦٣٧١]

354

VAIN TALK

اللَّغوُ

1629. Vain Talk

١٦٢٩ ـ اللَّغوُ

"Who avoid vain talk."[6417]

﴿وَالَّذِينَ هُمْ عَنِ اللَّغْوِ مُعْرِضُونَ﴾.[٦٣٧٢]

"Those who do not give false testimony, and when they come upon vain talk, pass by nobly."[6418]

﴿وَالَّذِينَ لا يَشْهَدُونَ الزُّورَ وَإِذا مَرُّوا بِاللَّغْوِ مَرُّوا كِرَاماً﴾.[٦٣٧٣]

(See also: Qur'an 19:62, 28:55, 41:6, 74:45, 78:35)

(أنظر) مريم: ٦٢ والقصص: ٥٥ ولقمان: ٦ والمدّثّر: ٤٥ والنبأ: ٣٥.

5683. **The Prophet (SAWA) said,** 'The worthiest person is he who leaves whatever does not concern him.'[6419]

٥٦٨٣. رسولُ اللهِ ﷺ: أعظَمُ النّاسِ قَدراً مَن تَركَ ما لا يَعنيهِ.[٦٣٧٤]

5684. **Imām ʿAlī (AS) said,** 'Any talk that does not have the remembrance of Allah therein is vain.'[6420]

٥٦٨٤. الإمامُ عليٌّ ؑ: كُلُّ قَولٍ لَيسَ للهِ فيهِ ذِكرٌ فلَغوٌ.[٦٣٧٥]

5685. **Imām ʿAlī (AS) said,** 'Do not interfere with things that do not concern you by abandoning things that do concern you.'[6421]

٥٦٨٥. عنه ؑ: لا تَعَرَّضْ لِما لا يَعنيكَ بِتَركِ ما يَعنيكَ.[٦٣٧٦]

5686. **Imām ʿAlī (AS),** in a letter he wrote to ʿAbdullāh b. ʿAbbās, said, 'Seek what concerns you and leave whatever does not concern you, for in leaving that which does not concern you, you will perceive the things that do concern you.'[6422]

٥٦٨٦. عنه ؑ ـ مِن كِتابٍ لَهُ إلىٰ عبدِاللهِ بنِ العبّاسِ ـ: أمّا بَعدُ، فاطلُبْ ما يَعنيكَ واترُكْ ما لا يَعنيكَ؛ فإنّ في تَركِ ما لا يَعنيكَ دَركَ ما يَعنيكَ.[٦٣٧٧]

5687. **Imām al-Ṣādiq (AS),** with regard to Allah's verse in the Qur'an: *"Who avoid vain talk"*, said, 'It means that when someone fabricates falsities about you or says something about you that is not true and you turn away from it for the sake of Allah.' In another narration, he said, 'It is singing and amusements.'[6423]

٥٦٨٧. الإمامُ الصّادقُ ؑ ـ في قولهِ تعالىٰ: ﴿والّذينَ هُمْ عَنِ اللّغوِ مُعْرِضونَ﴾ ـ: هُو أن يَتَقَوّلَ الرّجُلُ علَيكَ بالباطِلِ، أو يأتِيَكَ بما لَيسَ فيكَ، فتُعرِضَ عَنهُ للهِ.

وفي روايةٍ أُخرى: إنّهُ الغِناءُ والمَلاهي.[٦٣٧٨]

355

MEETING ALLAH

لقاء الله سبحانه وتعالى

1630. Yearning to Meet Allah

١٦٣٠ ـ شوق لقاء الله

5688. It is narrated in *al-Maḥajjat al-Bayḍā'*: Among the narrations about Prophet David (AS) that Allah revealed unto him, '...O David, I have created the hearts of those who long for Me from My Satisfaction and I have blessed them with the light of My Face...' So David said, 'O Lord, and how did they acquire this from You?!' He said, 'As a result of their good opinion, their refraining from the world and its followers, seclusion with Me and intimate conversation with Me, and this is a station that no one will achieve until they refuse the world and its people, do not occupy themselves with anything of its remembrance, devote their hearts to Me and chose Me over all My creation.'[6424]

٥٦٨٨ . المحجّة البيضاء : في أخبارِ داوودَ ﷺ أنَّ اللهَ عَزَّوجلَّ أوحىٰ إلَيهِ : ... يا داوودُ، إنّي خَلَقتُ قُلوبَ المُشتاقينَ مِن رِضواني، وَنَعَّمتُها بِنُورِ وَجهي.. فقالَ داوودُ: يا رَبِّ، بِمَ نالُوا مِنكَ هٰذا؟ قالَ: بِحُسنِ الظَّنِّ، والكَفِّ عَنِ الدُّنيا وأهلِها، والخَلَواتِ بي ومُناجاتِهِم لي، وإنَّ هٰذا مَنزِلٌ لا يَنالُهُ إلّا مَن رَفَضَ الدُّنيا وأهلَها، ولَم يَشتَغِلْ بشيءٍ مِن ذِكرِها، وفَرَّغَ قَلبَهُ لي واختارَني علىٰ جَميعِ خَلقي، فعِندَ ذٰلكَ أعطِفُ علَيهِ فأُفَرِّغُ نَفسَهُ لَهُ وأكشِفُ الحِجابَ فيما بَيني وبَينَهُ؛ حتّىٰ يَنظُرَ إلَيَّ نَظَرَ النّاظِرِ بعَينِهِ إلَى الشّيءِ.[٦٣٧٩]

5689. It is narrated in *al-Maḥajjat al-Bayḍā'*: 'O David, if those who turn away from Me were to know the extent of My anticipation for them, My gentleness towards them and My yearning for them to leave their sins, they would die of yearning for Me and their body parts would be cut up because of My love.'[6425]

٥٦٨٩ . المحجّة البيضاء ـ في أخبار داوودَ ﷺ أيضاً ـ يا داوودُ، لَو يَعلَمُ المُدبِرونَ عَنّي كَيفَ انتِظاري لَهُم، ورِفقي بِهِم، وشَوقي إلىٰ تَركِ مَعاصيهِم، لَماتُوا شَوقاً إلَيَّ وتَقَطَّعَت أوصالُهُم مِن مَحَبَّتي.[٦٣٨٠]

5690. **The Prophet (SAWA) said** in a supplication, 'I ask from You satisfaction with Your decree, a calm life after death, the delight of looking at Your Face, and yearning for seeing and meeting You.'[6426]

٥٦٩٠ . رسولُ اللهِ ﷺ ـ في الدُّعاءِ ـ: أسألُكَ الرِّضا بالقَضاءِ، وبَردَ العَيشِ بَعدَ المَوتِ، ولَذَّةَ النَّظَرِ إلىٰ وَجهِكَ، وشَوقاً إلىٰ رُؤيَتِكَ ولِقائكَ.[٦٣٨١]

5691. **The Prophet (SAWA) said,** 'Whoever would love to meet Allah, Allah [in turn] will love to meet him, and whoever would hate to meet Allah, He too will hate to meet them.'[6427]

٥٦٩١ . عنه ﷺ : مَن أحَبَّ لِقاءَ اللهِ أحَبَّ اللهُ لِقاءَهُ، ومَن كَرِهَ لِقاءَ اللهِ كَرِهَ اللهُ لِقاءَهُ.[٦٣٨٢]

5692. **Imām ʿAlī (AS),** in a letter he wrote to the people of Egypt said, 'And indeed I yearn for meeting Allah, and I am waiting for His good rewards with hope.'[6428]

٥٦٩٢ . الإمامُ عليٌّ عليه السلام ـ مِن كِتابِه إلىٰ أهلِ مِصرَ ـ: وإنّي إلىٰ لِقاءِ اللهِ لَمُشتاقٌ، وحُسنِ ثَوابِهِ لَمُنتَظِرٌ راجٍ.[٦٣٨٣]

5693. **Imām ʿAlī (AS) said,** 'He who wants to meet Allah Almighty must think no more of this world.'[6429]

٥٦٩٣ . عنه عليه السلام: مَن أحَبَّ لِقاءَ اللهِ سُبحانَهُ سَلا عَنِ الدُّنيا.[٦٣٨٤]

356

AMUSEMENT

1631. Amusement

١٦٣١ ـ اللَّهوُ

"Know that the life of this world is just play and diversion, and glitter, and mutual vainglory among you."[6430]

﴿اِعْلَمُوا أَنَّمَا الْحَيَاةُ الدُّنْيَا لَعِبٌ وَلَهْوٌ وَزِينَةٌ وَتَفَاخُرٌ بَيْنَكُمْ﴾.[٦٣٨٥]

"When they sight a deal or a diversion, they scatter off towards it and leave you standing! Say, 'What is with Allah is better than diversion and dealing, and Allah is the best of providers.'"[6431]

﴿وَإِذَا رَأَوا تِجَارَةً أَوْ لَهْواً انْفَضُّوا إِلَيْهَا وَتَرَكُوكَ قائماً قُلْ مَا عِنْدَ اللهِ خَيْرٌ مِنَ اللَّهْوِ وَمِنَ التِّجَارَةِ وَاللهُ خَيْرُ الرَّازِقِينَ﴾.[٦٣٨٦]

5694. **Imām ʿAlī (AS) said,** 'O people, revere Allah, for man was not created in vain that he may amuse himself, nor has he been abandoned to futility that he may be in vain!'[6432]

٥٦٩٤ . الإمامُ عليٌّ عليه السلام: أيُّها النّاسُ، اتَّقوا اللهَ؛ فما خُلِقَ امرؤٌ عَبَثاً فيَلهوَ، ولا تُرِكَ سُدىً فيَلغوَ![٦٣٨٧]

5695. **Imām ʿAlī (AS) said,** 'Amusement is the provision of stupidity.'[6433]

٥٦٩٥ . عنه عليه السلام: اللّهوُ قُوتُ الحَماقَةِ.[٦٣٨٨]

5696. **Imām ʿAlī (AS) said,** 'The worst thing that life is wasted on is play.'[6434]

٥٦٩٦ . عنه عليه السلام: شَرُّ ما ضُيِّعَ فيهِ العُمرُ اللَّعِبُ.[٦٣٨٩]

1632. The Effects of Amusement

١٦٣٢ ـ ثَمَراتُ اللَّهوِ

5697. **Imām ʿAlī (AS) said,** 'Amusement brings discontent to the Merciful, pleases Satan, and it makes one forget the Qur'an.'[6435]

٥٦٩٧ . الإمامُ عليٌّ عليه السلام: اللّهوُ يُسخِطُ الرَّحمٰنَ، ويُرضي الشَّيطانَ، ويُنسي القُرآنَ.[٦٣٩٠]

5698. **Imām ʿAlī (AS) said,** 'Amusement corrupts the wills of determination.'[6436]

٥٦٩٨ . عنه ؑ : اللّهوُ يُفسِدُ عَزائمَ الجِدِّ .[٦٣٩١]

5699. **Imām ʿAlī (AS) said,** 'The farthest of people from success is the one infatuated with amusement and jokes.'[6437]

٥٦٩٩ . عنه ؑ : أبعَدُ النّاسِ مِن النّجاحِ المُستَهتَرُ باللَّهوِ والمِزاحِ .[٦٣٩٢]

5700. **Imām ʿAlī (AS) said,** 'He whose amusement increases his intellect decreases.'[6438]

٥٧٠٠ . عنه ؑ : مَن كَثُرَ لَهوُهُ قَلَّ عَقلُهُ .[٦٣٩٣]

(See also: MUSIC: section 1451)

(اُنظر) الغناء : باب ١٤٥١.

1633. Faith and Amusement

١٦٣٣ ـ الإيمانُ وَاللَّهوُ

5701. **Imām ʿAlī (AS),** describing a believer, said, 'His time is always occupied.'[6439]

٥٧٠١ الإمامُ عليٌّ ؑ ـ في صفةِ المؤمنِ ـ : مَشغولٌ وَقتُهُ .[٦٣٩٤]

5702. **Imām Ḥasan (AS) said,** 'A believer does not occupy himself with amusement lest he becomes negligent, and when he thinks he becomes sad.'[6440]

٥٧٠٢ . الإمامُ الحسنُ ؑ : المؤمنُ لا يَلهو حتّىٰ يَغفُلَ ، فإذا تَفَكّرَ حَزِنَ .[٦٣٩٥]

5703. **Imām al-Ṣādiq (AS),** regarding someone who wanted to go hunting for amusement, said, 'A believer is too busy for that; acquiring the Hereafter preoccupies him away from amusements...' until he said, 'A believer is too busy for all this, and what does he have to do with amusement, for amusement engenders hard-heartedness and hypocrisy.'[6441]

٥٧٠٣ . الإمامُ الصّادقُ ؑ ـ فيمَن طَلَبَ الصَّيدَ لاهِياً ـ : وإنّ المؤمنَ لَفي شُغُلٍ عن ذٰلكَ ، شَغَلَهُ طَلَبُ الآخِرَةِ عَنِ المَلاهي ... وإنَّ المؤمنَ عَن جَميعِ ذلكَ لَفي شُغُلٍ ، ما لَهُ ولِلمَلاهي ؟! فإنَّ المَلاهيَ تُورِثُ قَساوَةَ القَلبِ وتُورِثُ النِّفاقَ .[٦٣٩٦]

1634. Amusement of Believers

١٦٣٤ ـ لَهوُ المُؤمِنِ

5704. **The Prophet (SAWA) said,** 'The amusement most loved by Almighty Allah is competing with horses and archery.'[6442]

٥٧٠٤ . رسولُ اللهِ ﷺ : أحَبُّ اللّهوِ إلى اللهِ تعالى إجراءُ الخَيلِ وَالرَّمي .[٦٣٩٧]

5705. **The Prophet (SAWA) said,** 'The best amusement for a believer is swimming and the best amusement for women is the spinning wheel.'[6443]

٥٧٠٥ . عنه ﷺ : خَيرُ لَهوِ المؤمنِ السِّباحَةُ ، وخَيرُ لهوِ المَرأةِ المِغزَلُ .[٦٣٩٨]

1635. Associating with the Debauched

١٦٣٥ ـ مُجالَسَةُ اللّاهي

5706. **Imām ʿAlī (AS) said,** 'Frequenting with the debauched brings about the forgetting of the Qur'an and brings the presence of the devil.'[6444]

٥٧٠٦ . الإمام عليّ ﷺ: مُجالَسَةُ أهلِ اللّهوِ يُنسِي القُرآنَ ويُحضِرُ الشَّيطانَ.[٦٣٩٩]

5707. **Imām ʿAlī (AS) said,** 'Gatherings of amusement corrupt the faith.'[6445]

٥٧٠٧ . عنه ﷺ: مَجالِسُ اللّهوِ تُفسِدُ الإيمانَ.[٦٤٠٠]

357

SODOMY

اللِّواطُ

1636. Caution Against Sodomy

١٦٣٦ ـ التَّحذِيرُ عَنِ اللِّواطِ

"And Lot, when he said to his people, 'What! Do you commit an outrage none in the world ever committed before you?! Indeed you come to men with desire instead of women! Rather you are a profligate lot."[6446]

﴿وَلُوطاً إِذْ قَالَ لِقَوْمِهِ أَتَأْتُونَ الفَاحِشَةَ مَا سَبَقَكُمْ بِهَا مِنْ أَحَدٍ مِنَ العَالَمِينَ * إِنَّكُمْ لَتَأْتُونَ الرِّجَالَ شَهْوَةً مِنْ دُونِ النِّسَاءِ بَلْ أَنْتُمْ قَوْمٌ مُسْرِفُونَ﴾.[٦٤٠١]

(See also: Qur'an 21:74, 26:165-174, 27:54-55, 29:28-35)

(أنظر) الأنبياء: ٧٤ والشعراء: ١٦٥ ـ ١٧٤ والنمل: ٥٤، ٥٥ والعنكبوت: ٢٨ ـ ٣٥.

5708. **The Prophet (SAWA) said,** 'The most dreadful thing I fear for my community is the action of the people of Lot.'[6447]

٥٧٠٨ . رسولُ اللهِ ﷺ: إنّ أخوَفَ ما أخافُ علىٰ أُمّتي مِن عَمَلِ قَومِ لُوطٍ.[٦٤٠٢]

5709. **The Prophet (SAWA) said,** 'Whoever of my community performs the acts of the people of Lot and dies in that state, his punishment is delayed until he is put in his grave, and when he is put in it he does not stay more than three days therein until the earth casts him to the perished people of Lot with whom he will be resurrected!'[6448]

٥٧٠٩ . عنه ﷺ: مَن يَعمَلْ مِن أُمّتي عَملَ قَومِ لُوطٍ ثُمّ يَموتُ علىٰ ذٰلكَ فهُو مُؤَجَّلٌ إلىٰ أن يُوضَعَ في لَحدِهِ، فإذا وُضِعَ فيهِ لَم يَمكُثْ أكثَرَ مِن ثَلاثٍ حتّىٰ تَقذِفَهُ الأرضُ إلىٰ جُملَةِ قَومِ لُوطٍ المُهلَكينَ فيُحشَرَ مَعَهُم.[٦٤٠٣]

5710. **Imām ʿAlī (AS) said,** 'Allah prescribed faith as purification from polytheism…and the abandonment of sodomy to multiply offspring.'[6449]

٥٧١٠ . الإمامُ عليٌّ ﷺ: فَرَضَ اللهُ الإيمانَ تَطهيراً مِنَ الشِّركِ ... وتَرْكَ اللِّواطِ تَكثيراً للنَّسلِ.[٦٤٠٤]

5711. **Imām al-Ṣādiq (AS) said,** 'Allah has forbidden for every rear end that has been sexually penetrated to sit on the brocade of Heaven.'[6450]

٥٧١١ . الإمامُ الصّادقُ ﷺ: حَرّمَ اللهُ علىٰ كُلِّ دُبُرٍ مُستَنكَحٍ الجُلوسَ علىٰ إستَبرَقِ الجَنّةِ.[٦٤٠٥]

5712. **Imām al-Riḍā (AS) said,** 'The reason for the prohibition of males to males and of females to females is because of what females have been endowed with and the nature of males. Moreover, in males being with males and females being with females, lies the continuity of offspring will cease, corruption of [natural] order, and the destruction of the world.'[6451]

٥٧١٢ . الإمامُ الرِّضا ﷷ : عِلّةُ تَحريمِ الذُّكـرانِ للذُّكرانِ والإناثِ للإناثِ ؛ لِما رُكِّبَ في الإناثِ وما طُبِعَ علَيهِ الذُّكرانُ ، ولِما في إتيانِ الذُّكـرانِ الذُّكرانَ والإناثِ الإناثَ مِـنِ انـقِطاعِ النَّسـلِ ، وفَسادِ التَّدبيرِ ، وخَرابِ الدُّنيا .[٦٤٠٦]

358

TESTING

الاِمتِحانُ

1637. Testing

١٦٣٧ ـ الاِمتِحانُ

5713. **Imām 'Alī (AS) said,** 'Our affair is hard, considerably difficult; no one can bear it save the servant whose heart Allah has tested for faith.'[6452]

٥٧١٣ . الإمامُ عليٌّ ﷷ : إنّ أمـــرَنا صَـــعبٌ مُستَصعَبٌ ، لا يَحمِلُهُ إلّا عَبدٌ مؤمنٌ امـتَحَنَ اللهُ قَلبَهُ للإيمانِ .[٦٤٠٧]

5714. **Imām 'Alī (AS),** in the description of prophets (AS) and saints, said, 'Allah has examined them with hunger, and has tried them with struggles, and has tested them with fears.'[6453]

٥٧١٤ . عنه ﷷ ـ في صفةِ الأنبياءِ عليهم السلام والأولياءِ ـ : قَدِ اختَبَرَهُمُ اللهُ بالمَخمَصَةِ ، وابتَلاهُم بالمَجهَدَةِ ، وامتَحَنَهُم بالمَخاوِفِ .[٦٤٠٨]

5715. **Imām 'Alī (AS) said,** 'Try a man and you will [come to] hate him.'[6454]

٥٧١٥ . عنه ﷷ : اُخبُرْ تَقْلِهِ .[٦٤٠٩][٦٤١٠]

5716. **Imām 'Alī (AS) said,** 'During a test is a person elevated or humiliated.'[6455]

٥٧١٦ . عنه ﷷ : عِندَ الامتِحانِ يُكرَمُ الرّجُلُ أو يُهانُ .[٦٤١١]

5717. **Imām 'Alī (AS) said,** 'A man is tested in his actions and not in his sayings.'[6456]

٥٧١٧ . عنه ﷷ : يُمتَحَنُ الرّجُلُ بفِعلِهِ لا بِقولِهِ .[٦٤١٢]

5718. **Imām 'Alī (AS) said,** 'Three things test men's intellects. They are: wealth, guardianship (*wilāya*) and calamity.'[6457]

٥٧١٨ . عنه ﷷ : ثَلاثٌ يُمتَحَنُ بها عُقولُ الرِّجالِ ، هُنَّ : المالُ ، والوِلايَةُ ، والمُصيبَةُ .[٦٤١٣]

5719. **Imām al-Ṣādiq (AS) said,** 'Socialise with people and test them, and when you test them you will [come to] hate them.'[6458]

٥٧١٩ . الإمامُ الصّادقُ ﷷ : خالِطِ النّاسَ تَخبُرْهُم ، ومتى تَخبُرْهُم تَقْلِهِم .[٦٤١٤]

5720. **Imām al-Ṣādiq (AS) said,** 'Test our followers [*shī'a*] with three things: at times of prayer and how well they observe them, secrets and how they guard them from our enemies, and their wealth and how they aid their brothers with it.'[6459]

٥٧٢٠ . عنه ؑ: اِمتَحِنوا شِيعَتَنا عِندَ ثَلاثٍ: عِندَ مَواقيتِ الصَّلاةِ كيفَ مُحافَظَتُهُم علَيها، وعِندَ أسرارِهِم كيفَ حِفظُهُم لَها عِندَ عَدُوِّنا، وإلىٰ أموالِهِم كيفَ مُواساتُهُم لإخوانِهِم فيها. ٦٤١٥

359

PRAISE

المَدح

1638. The Censure of Praise

١٦٣٨ ـ ذَمُّ المَدحِ

5721. **The Prophet (SAWA) said,** 'Beware of praise, for verily it is slaughter.'[6460]

٥٧٢١ . رسولُ اللهِ ﷺ: إيّاكُم والمَدحَ؛ فإنَّهُ الذَّبحُ. ٦٤١٦

5722. **The Prophet (SAWA) said,** 'A man insulting another man with a sharp knife is better for him than if he was to praise him to his face.'[6461]

٥٧٢٢ . عنه ﷺ: لَو مَشىٰ رجُلٌ إلىٰ رجُلٍ بسِكِّينٍ مُرهَفٍ كانَ خَيراً لَهُ مِن أن يُثني علَيهِ في وَجهِهِ. ٦٤١٧

5723. **The Prophet (SAWA) said,** 'The love of commendation and praise blinds and deafens one from religion, and it makes houses desolate.'[6462]

٥٧٢٣ . عنه ﷺ: حُبُّ الإطراءِ والثّناءِ يُعمي ويُصِمُّ عَنِ الدِّينِ، ويَدَعُ الدِّيارَ بَلاقِعَ. ٦٤١٨

5724. **al-Miqdād b. 'Amr narrated,** 'The Prophet (SAWA) ordered us to throw dust into the faces of the praisers.'[6463]

٥٧٢٤ . المقداد بن عمرو: أمَرَنا رسولُ اللهِ ﷺ أن نَحثُوَ في وُجوهِ المَدّاحِينَ التُّرابَ. ٦٤١٩

5725. **Abū Mūsā narrated,** 'A man was about to praise another man in front of the Prophet (SAWA), so he (SAWA) said, 'Do not let him listen for you will ruin him, and if he hears you he will not succeed.'[6464]

٥٧٢٥ . أبو موسى: إنّ رجُلاً مَدَحَ رجُلاً عِندَ النَّبيِّ ﷺ، فقالَ ﷺ: لا تُسمِعْهُ فتُهلِكَهُ، لَو سَمِعَكَ لَم يُفلِحْ. ٦٤٢٠

5726. **Imām 'Alī (AS) said,** 'O people, know that one who is annoyed by a false accusation about him is not intelligent, and nor is one who accepts the praise of an ignorant person wise.'[6465]

٥٧٢٦ . الإمامُ عليٌّ ؑ: أيُّها النّاسُ، اعلَموا أنّهُ ليسَ بعاقِلٍ مَنِ انزَعَجَ مِن قَولِ الزُّورِ فيهِ، ولا بحَكيمٍ مَن رَضِيَ بثَناءِ الجاهِلِ علَيهِ. ٦٤٢١

5727. **Imām 'Alī (AS) said,** 'If you [must] praise then make it brief, and if you disparage make it short.'[6466]

٥٧٢٧ . عنه ؑ: إذا مَدَحتَ فاختَصِرْ، إذا ذَمَمتَ فاقتَصِرْ. ٦٤٢٢

5728. **Imām ʿAlī (AS) said,** 'I hate it for you to think that I like commendation and listening to praises when, praise be to Allah, I am not so. If I did like for such things to be said, I would abandon it as degradation of myself before Allah Almighty in accepting something that He is more worthy of in Grandeur and Glory. People might be pleased with praises after hardships, but do not praise me good praises for what I have done for Allah Almighty, and done for you in what is left of the rights I have not yet fulfilled, and the obligations I must duly accomplish. So do no speak to me the way you speak to tyrants, and do not evade me as the people of passion are [to be] evaded, and do not meet me with flattery.'[6467]

٥٧٢٨ . عنه عليه السلام : وقَد كَرِهتُ أن يكونَ جالَ في ظَنِّكُم أنّي اُحِبُّ الإطراءَ واستِماعَ الثَّناءِ، ولَستُ ـ بحَمدِ اللهِ ـ كذلكَ. ولَو كُنتُ اُحِبُّ أن يقالَ ذلكَ لَتَرَكتُهُ انحِطاطاً للهِ سبحانَهُ عن تَناوُلِ ما هُو أحَقُّ بهِ مِنَ العَظَمَةِ والكِبرياءِ، ورُبَّما استَحلَى النّاسُ الثَّناءَ بَعدَ البَلاءِ، فلا تُثنوا علَيَّ بجَميلِ ثَناءٍ لإخراجي نَفسي إلَى اللهِ سبحانَهُ وإلَيكُم مِنَ التَّقيَّةِ (البَقيَّةِ) في حُقوقٍ لَم أفرُغْ مِن أدائها وفَرائضَ لابُدَّ مِن إمضائها، فلا تُكَلِّموني بما تُكَلَّمُ بهِ الجَبابِرَةُ، ولا تَتَحَفَّظوا مِنّي بما يُتَحَفَّظُ بهِ عِندَ أهلِ البادِرَةِ، ولا تُخالِطوني بالمُصانَعَةِ.[٦٤٢٣]

5729. **Imām ʿAlī (AS),** when a group of people praised him to his face, said, 'O Allah, You know more about me than I myself do, and I know more about myself than they do. O Allah, make us better than what they think and forgive us that which they do not know.'[6468]

٥٧٢٩ . عنه عليه السلام ـ لَمّا مَدَحَهُ قَومٌ في وَجهِهِ ـ: اللّهُمّ إنّكَ أعلَمُ بي مِن نَفسي، وأنا أعلَمُ بنَفسي مِنهُم. اللّهُمّ اجعَلْنا خَيراً مِمّا يَظُنّونَ، واغفِرْ لَنا ما لا يَعلَمونَ.[٦٤٢٤]

5730. **Imām Zayn al-ʿĀbidīn (AS) said,** 'A believer is silent in order to be safe, and speaks in order to benefit.... If he is praised he fears what they say and he seeks forgiveness from Allah for what they do not know. He is not deceived by the sayings of those who do not know him, and he fears being accountable for the things he has done.'[6469]

٥٧٣٠ . الإمامُ زينُ العابدينَ عليه السلام : المؤمنُ يَصمُتُ لِيَسلَمَ، ويَنطِقُ لِيَغنَمَ... إن زُكِّيَ خافَ مِمّا يَقولونَ، ويَستَغفِرُ اللهَ لِما لا يَعلَمونَ، لا يَغِرُّهُ قَولُ مَن جَهِلَهُ، ويَخافُ إحصاءَ ما عَمِلَهُ.[٦٤٢٥]

1639. Praising Someone for Qualities that he does not have

١٦٣٩ ـ مَدحُ الرَّجُلِ بِما لَيسَ فيهِ

5731. **The Prophet (SAWA) said,** 'O Ibn Masʿūd, if people praise you, saying, 'You fast the day and stay awake at night', and you do not actually do so then do not feel happy about it, for Allah Almighty says, *"Do not suppose those who exult in what they have done, and love to be praised for*

٥٧٣١ . رسولُ اللهِ صلى الله عليه وآله : يابنَ مَسعودٍ، إذا مَدَحَكَ النّاسُ فقالوا: إنّك تَصومُ النَّهارَ وتَقومُ اللّيلَ وأنتَ علىٰ غَيرِ ذلكَ فلا تَفرَحْ بذلكَ؛ فإنَّ اللهَ تعالىٰ يقولُ: ﴿لا تَحْسَبَنَّ الّذينَ يَفرَحُونَ بِما أتَوا

what they have not done, do not suppose them saved from punishment, and there is a painful punishment for them." [6470] [6471]

ويُحِبُّونَ أنْ يُحمَدوا بما لَم يَفْعَلوا فَلا تَحْسَبَنَّهُمْ بِمَفازَةٍ مِنَ العَذابِ ولَهُمْ عَذابٌ أليمٌ﴾.٦٤٢٦

5732. **Imām ʿAlī (AS) said,** 'Whoever praises you with something you do not have then it is a disparagement for you, if you are sane [know].'[6472]

٥٧٣٢. الإمامُ عليٌّ (ع): مَن مَدَحَكَ بما لَيسَ فيكَ فَهُو ذَمٌّ لَكَ إن عَقَلتَ.٦٤٢٧

5733. **Imām ʿAlī (AS) said,** 'Beware of he who praises you with what you do not have for you may be disgraced with qualities that are not in you.'[6473]

٥٧٣٣. عنه (ع): اِحذَرْ مَن يُطرِيكَ بما لَيسَ فيكَ فيُوشِكُ أن تنهَتِكَ بما لَيسَ فيكَ.٦٤٢٨

5734. **Imām ʿAlī (AS),** in his letter to al-Ashtar, said, 'Stick to people of piety and truthfulness, then tell them not to praise you and not to slash you with a wrong that you have not done, for too much praise brings pride and decreases dignity.'[6474]

٥٧٣٤. عنه (ع) ـ من كتابهِ للأشترِ ـ: الصَقْ بأهلِ الوَرَعِ والصِّدقِ، ثُمّ رُضهُمْ على ألّا يُطروكَ، ولا يَبْجَحُوكَ بباطِلٍ لَم تَفعَلْهُ؛ فإنّ كَثرَةَ الإطراءِ تُحدِثُ الزَّهوَ، وتُدني مِن العزّةِ (الغِرَّة).٦٤٢٩

5735. **Imām al-Bāqir (AS) said** to Jābir b. Yazīd al-Juʿfī, 'Know that you will not be a friend of ours unless if all of your countrymen were to gather and claim that you are a bad person, it would not worry you, and if they were all to say that you are a good person, it would not make you any happier. Expose yourself to the Book of Allah, and if you follow its path, abstaining from that which it dictates to be abstained from, wanting what it wants, and fearing that which it frightens about, then be steadfast and rejoice, for what is said about you will not harm you. But if you are contrary to the Qurʾan then what do you have to be proud about?'[6475]

٥٧٣٥. الإمامُ الباقرُ (ع) ـ لجابرِ بنِ يزيدَ الجُعفيِّ ـ: واعلَمْ بأنّكَ لا تكونُ لنا وَليّاً حتّى لَو اجتمَعَ علَيكَ أهلُ مِصرِكَ وقالوا: إنّكَ رجُلُ سَوءٍ لَم يَحزُنْكَ ذلكَ، ولَو قالوا: إنّكَ رجُلٌ صالحٌ لَم يَسُرَّكَ ذلكَ، ولكنِ اعرِضْ نَفسَكَ على كِتابِ اللهِ؛ فإن كنتَ سالِكاً سَبيلَهُ، زاهِداً في تَزهيدِهِ، راغِباً في تَرغيبِهِ، خائفاً مِن تَخويفِهِ، فاثبُتْ وأبشِرْ، فإنّهُ لا يَضُرُّكَ ما قيلَ فيكَ، وإن كنتَ مُبائناً للقرآنِ فماذا الّذي يَغُرُّكَ مِن نَفسِكَ؟!٦٤٣٠

5736. **Imām al-ʿAskarī (AS) said,** 'He who praises one who is not worthy of it, stands to be suspected!'[6476]

٥٧٣٦. الإمامُ العسكريُّ (ع): مَن مَدَحَ غَيرَ المُستحِقِّ فَقد قامَ مَقامَ المُتَّهَمِ.٦٤٣١

1640. Caution Against Praising an Immoral Person

١٦٤٠ ـ التَّحذيرُ مِن مَدحِ الفاجِرِ

5737. **The Prophet (SAWA) said,** 'When an immoral person is praised, the Throne trembles and the Lord is angered.'[6477]

٥٧٣٧ . رسولُ اللهِ ﷺ : إذا مُدِحَ الفـاجِرُ اهـتَزَّ العَرشُ وغَضِبَ الرَّبُّ.[٦٤٣٢]

5738. **The Prophet (SAWA) said,** 'Whoever praises a tyrant ruler and is lenient and subservient to him, out of eagerness [for his reward], then he will be his consort in the Hellfire.'[6478]

٥٧٣٨ . عنه ﷺ: مَن مَدَحَ سُلطاناً جائراً وتَخَفَّفَ وتَضَعضَعَ لَهُ طَمَعاً فيهِ كانَ قَرينَهُ إلَى النّارِ.[٦٤٣٣]

1641. Warning of Praising Oneself

١٦٤١ ـ النَّهيُ عَن تَزكِيَةِ النَّفسِ

"Those who avoid major sins and indecencies, excepting [minor and occasional] lapses. Indeed your Lord is expansive in [His] forgiveness. He knows you best since [the time] He produced you from the earth, and since you were fetuses in the bellies of your mothers. So do not flaunt your piety: He knows best those who are Godwary."[6479]

﴿الَّذِينَ يَجْتَنِبُونَ كَبَائِرَ الْإِثْمِ وَالْفَوَاحِشَ إِلَّا اللَّمَمَ إِنَّ رَبَّكَ وَاسِعُ الْمَغْفِرَةِ هُوَ أَعْلَمُ بِكُمْ إِذْ أَنْشَأَكُمْ مِنَ الْأَرْضِ وَإِذْ أَنْتُمْ أَجِنَّةٌ فِي بُطُونِ أُمَّهَاتِكُمْ فَلَا تُزَكُّوا أَنْفُسَكُمْ هُوَ أَعْلَمُ بِمَنِ اتَّقَىٰ﴾.[٦٤٣]

5739. **Imām al-Ṣādiq (AS),** when asked about Allah's verse in the Qur'an: *"So do not flaunt your piety"* said, 'It refers to when someone says, 'I prayed yesterday and fasted yesterday', and its like. The Prophet (SAWA) then said, 'A group of people would wake up and say, 'We prayed and fasted yesterday', and Imām 'Alī (AS) said, 'But I sleep night and day and if I found any time between that I would sleep too [i.e. making light of his worship in front of people].'[6480]

٥٧٣٩ . الإمامُ الصّادقُ عليه السلام ـ لَمّا سُئلَ عن قولِ اللهِ عزَّوجلَّ: ﴿فلا تُزَكُّوا...﴾ ـ: قولُ الإنسانِ: صَلّيتُ البارِحَةَ وصُمتُ أمسِ ونَحو هٰذا. إنّ قَوماً كانوا يُصبِحونَ فيَقولونَ: صَلَّينا البارِحَةَ وصُمنا أمسِ، فقالَ عليٌّ عليه السلام: لٰكنّي أنامُ اللّيلَ والنّهارَ، ولَو أجِدُ بَينَهُما شيئاً لَنُمتُهُ![٦٤٣٥]

5740. **The Prophet (SAWA) said,** 'Whoever says: 'I am the best of people', then he is the worst of people, and whoever says: 'I am [deserving] of Heaven' is [deserving] of Hell.'[6481]

٥٧٤٠ . رسولُ اللهِ ﷺ : مَن قالَ: إنّي خَيرُ النّاسِ فهُوَ مِن شَرِّ النّاسِ، ومَن قالَ: إنّي في الجَنّةِ فهُوَ في النّارِ.[٦٤٣٦]

360

WOMAN

المَرأةُ

1642. The Words of the Representative of Women with the Prophet

١٦٤٢ ـ كَلامُ وافِدَةِ النِّساءِ مَعَ النَّبِيِّ ﷺ

5741. **Majmaʿ al-Bayān,** 'When Asmā' bint 'Umays returned from Ethiopia with her husband Ja'far b. Abī Ṭālib, she visited the wives of the Prophet (SAWA) and asked them, 'Does the Qur'an say anything about us [women]?' They said, 'No.' So, she went to the Prophet (SAWA) and said, 'O Messenger of Allah, the women are indeed at a loss and failure!' He asked, 'Why is that?' She said, 'Because they are not mentioned with goodness like men are.' So Allah sent down this verse: "*Indeed for Muslim men and women, for believing men and women, for devout men and women, for true men and women, for men and women who are patient and constant, for men and women who humble themselves, for men and women who give in charity, for men and women who fast, for men and women who guard their chastity, and for men and women who engage much in Allah's remembrance, for them has Allah prepared forgiveness and great reward*"[6482] [6483]

٥٧٤١ . مجمع البيان : لمّا رَجَعَت أسماءُ بِنتُ عُمَيسٍ مِنَ الحَبَشةِ مَع زَوجِها جعفرِ بنِ أبي طالبٍ ؑ دخَلَت علىٰ نِساءِ رسولِ اللهِ ﷺ فقالَت : هَل نزل فِينا شَيءٌ مِن القرآنِ ؟ قُلنَ : لا ، فأتَت رسولَ اللهِ ﷺ فقالت : يارسولَ اللهِ ، إنّ النِّساءَ لَفي خَيبَةٍ وخَسارٍ ! فقالَ ﷺ : ومِمَّ ذلكَ ؟ قالَت : لأنّهُنَّ لايُذكَرنَ بخَيرٍ كما يُذكَرُ الرِّجالُ . فأنزَلَ اللهُ تعالىٰ هٰذهِ الآيَةَ ﴿إنّ المُسلِمينَ والمُسلِماتِ وَٱلْمُؤْمِنِينَ وَٱلْمُؤْمِنَٰتِ وَٱلْقَٰنِتِينَ وَٱلْقَٰنِتَٰتِ وَٱلصَّٰدِقِينَ وَٱلصَّٰدِقَٰتِ وَٱلصَّٰبِرِينَ وَٱلصَّٰبِرَٰتِ وَٱلْخَٰشِعِينَ وَٱلْخَٰشِعَٰتِ وَٱلْمُتَصَدِّقِينَ وَٱلْمُتَصَدِّقَٰتِ وَٱلصَّٰٓئِمِينَ وَٱلصَّٰٓئِمَٰتِ وَٱلْحَٰفِظِينَ فُرُوجَهُمْ وَٱلْحَٰفِظَٰتِ وَٱلذَّٰكِرِينَ ٱللَّهَ كَثِيرًا وَٱلذَّٰكِرَٰتِ أَعَدَّ ٱللَّهُ لَهُم مَّغْفِرَةً وَأَجْرًا عَظِيمًا﴾[٦٤٣٧] . [٦٤٣٨]

5742. **al-Bayhaqī narrated** from Asmā' bint Yazīd al-Anṣārī that she went to the Prophet (SAWA) whilst he was with his companions, and said, 'May my mother and father be ransomed for you! I come to you representing women, and know – may my soul be sacrificed for you – that there is no woman that exists in the east or the west who does not agree with me if she was to hear of my visit to you. Allah sent you with the truth to men and women, so we believed in you and in your God who sent you. We women are restricted and limited, confined to your

٥٧٤٢ . الدرّ المنثور : أخرَجَ البَيهَقيُّ عن أسماءَ بِنتِ يَزيدَ الأنصاريّةِ أنّها أتَتِ النّبيَّ ﷺ وهُوَ بَينَ أصحابِهِ ، فقالَت : بأبي أنتَ وأُمّي ! إنّي وافِدَةُ النِّساءِ إلَيكَ ، واعلَمْ ـ نَفسي لَكَ الفِداءُ ـ أنّهُ ما مِن امرأةٍ كائنَةٍ في شَرقٍ ولاغَربٍ سَمِعَت بمَخرَجي هٰذا إلّا وهِيَ علىٰ مِثلِ رأيي ، إنّ اللهَ بَعَثَكَ بالحَقِّ إلَى الرِّجالِ والنِّساءِ ، فآمَنّا بكَ

[men's] houses, fulfillers of your desires, bearers of your children, and you men are superior to us because of the Friday and congregational prayers, visiting the sick, participating in burials, pilgrimage after pilgrimage, and better than all that, fighting (*jihād*) in the path of Allah. When a man from among you goes for the obligatory or voluntary pilgrimage, or is stationed away from home, we protect your property for you, sew your clothes, bring up your children, so what do we share with you in reward, O Messenger of Allah?'
The Prophet (SAWA) turned his whole face to his companions and said, 'Have you ever heard a woman speaking better than she has in her asking about her religion?'
They said, 'O Messenger of Allah, we did not think that a woman could be so guided like this!'
The Prophet (SAWA) then turned towards her and said, 'Leave, O woman, and inform the women after you that for one of you to be a good spouse to her husband, her seeking his satisfaction and her following of what he approves is equivalent to all that you mentioned.'
So the woman left, saying: 'There is no god but Allah (*lā ilāha illallāh*) and aggrandizing Allah (*Allāhu Akbar*) with happiness.'[6484]

وبإلٰهِكَ الّذي أرسَلَكَ، وإنّا مَعشَرَ النِّساءِ مَحصوراتٌ مَقصوراتٌ، قَواعِدُ بُيوتِكُم ومَقضىٰ شَهَواتِكُم وحامِلاتُ أولادِكُم، وإنّكُم مَعاشِرَ الرِّجالِ فَضَّلتُم علَينا بالجُمُعَةِ والجَماعاتِ وعِيادَةِ لمَرضىٰ وشُهودِ الجَنائزِ والحَجِّ بَعدَ الحَجِّ، وأفضَلُ مِن ذلكَ الجِهادُ في سبيلِ اللهِ، وإنّ الرَّجلَ مِنكُم إذا خَرَجَ حاجّاً أو مُعتَمِراً أو مُرابِطاً حَفِظنا لَكُم أموالَكُم، وغَزَلنا لَكُم أثوابَكُم، ورَبَّينا لَكُم أموالَكُم ٦٤٣٩ فما نُشارِكُكُم في الأجرِ يا رسولَ اللهِ؟
فالتَفتَ النّبيُّ ﷺ إلىٰ أصحابِهِ بوَجهِهِ كُلِّهِ، ثُمّ قالَ: هَل سَمِعتُم مَقالَةَ امرأةٍ قَطُّ أحسَنَ مِن مُساءلَتِها في أمرِ دِينِها مِن هٰذهِ؟ فقالوا: يا رسولَ اللهِ، ما ظَنَنّا أنّ امرأةً تَهتَدي إلىٰ مِثلِ هٰذا!
فالتَفتَ النّبيُّ ﷺ إلَيها، ثُمّ قالَ لَها: انصَرِفي أيَّتُها المَرأةُ، وأعلِمي مَن خَلفَكِ مِن النِّساءِ أنّ حُسنَ تَبَعُّلِ إحداكُنّ لزَوجِها وطَلَبَها مَرضاتَهُ واتِّباعَها مُوافَقَتَهُ يَعدِلُ ذلكَ كُلَّهُ. فأدبَرَتِ المَرأةُ وهِي تُهَلِّلُ وتُكَبِّرُ استِبشاراً. ٦٤٤٠

5743. **Abū Saʿīd al-Khudrī narrated,** 'A woman came to the Prophet (SAWA) and said, 'O Messenger of Allah, men leave with your sayings, so allocate one day for us that we can have with you so you can teach us from what Allah has taught you.' So he said, 'Gather on such and such a day such and such a place.' So they gathered and the Prophet (SAWA) came to them and taught them what Allah had taught him.'[6485]

٥٧٤٣. أبو سعيد الخدري: جاءتِ امرأةٌ إلىٰ رسولِ اللهِ ﷺ فقالت: يارسولَ اللهِ، ذَهَبَ الرِّجالُ بحَديثِكَ، فاجعَلْ لَنا مِن نَفسِكَ يَوماً نَأتِيكَ فيهِ تُعَلِّمُنا مِمّا عَلَّمَكَ اللهُ. قالَ: اجتَمِعْنَ يَومَ كَذا وكذا في مَوضعِ كذا وكذا، فاجتَمَعنَ، فأتاهُنَّ النّبيُّ ﷺ فعلَّمَهُنَّ مِمّا عَلّمَهُ اللهُ. ٦٤٤١

1643. The Best Characteristics of Women

١٦٤٣ ـ خِيارُ خِصالِ النِّساءِ

5744. **Imām ʿAlī (AS) said,** 'The good characteristics of women are the bad characteristics of men: pride, cowardice and stinginess. If a woman has pride she will not allow herself to be taken advantage of; if she is

٥٧٤٤. الإمامُ عليٌّ ؑ: خِيارُ خِصالِ النِّساءِ شِرارُ خِصالِ الرِّجالِ: الزَّهوُ، والجُبنُ، والبُخلُ؛ فإذا كانتِ المَرأةُ مَزهُوّةً لَم تُمَكِّنْ مِن نَفسِها،

stingy she will guard her wealth and her spouse's wealth; and if she is cowardly she will be cautious of everything that confronts her.'[6486]

وإذا كانت بَخيلَةً حَفِظَت مالَها ومالَ بَعلِها، وإذا كانت جَبانَةً فَرِقَت مِن كُلِّ شَيءٍ يَعرِضُ لَها.٦٤٤٢

1644. Righteous Women

١٦٤٤ ـ المرأةُ الصالحة

5745. **The Prophet (SAWA) said,** 'One righteous woman is better than one thousand unrighteous men.'[6487]

٥٧٤٥. رسولُ اللهِ ﷺ: المَرأةُ الصّالِحَةُ خَيرٌ مِن ألفِ رَجُلٍ غَيرِ صالِحٍ.٦٤٤٣

5746. **The Prophet (SAWA) said,** 'The world is like a commodity, and there is nothing in this world better than a righteous woman.'[6488]

٥٧٤٦. عنه ﷺ: الدُّنيا مَتاعٌ، ولَيسَ مِن مَتاعِ الدُّنيا شَيءٌ أفضلَ مِنَ المَرأةِ الصّالِحَةِ.٦٤٤٤

5747. **The Prophet (SAWA) said,** 'The righteousness of one believing woman is better than seventy virtuous (*ṣidīq*) men and the corruption of one woman is like the corruption of one thousand corrupt people.'[6489]

٥٧٤٧. عنه ﷺ: بِرُّ المَرأةِ المُؤمِنَةِ كَعَمَلِ سَبعينَ صِدّيقاً، وفُجورُ المَرأةِ المُؤمِنَةِ كَفُجورِ ألفِ فاجِرٍ.٦٤٤٥

1645. The Praise of Loving Women

١٦٤٥ ـ مَدحُ حُبِّ النِّساءِ

5748. **The Prophet (SAWA) said,** 'The more the faith of a servant increases the more his love for women increases.'[6490]

٥٧٤٨. رسولُ اللهِ ﷺ: كُلَّما ازدادَ العَبدُ إيماناً ازدادَ حُبّاً لِلنِّساءِ.٦٤٤٦

5749. **Imām al-Ṣādiq (AS) said,** 'Whoever's love for us increases, their love for women and sweets will increase.'[6491]

٥٧٤٩. الإمامُ الصّادقُ عليه السلام: كُلُّ مَنِ اشتَدَّ لَنا حُبّاً اشتَدَّ لِلنِّساءِ حُبّاً ولِلحَلواءِ.٦٤٤٧

5750. **Imām al-Ṣādiq (AS) said,** 'One of the morals of the prophets, peace of Allah be upon them, is the love of women.'[6492]

٥٧٥٠. عنه عليه السلام: مِن أخلاقِ الأنبياءِ صلّى اللهُ عليهم حُبُّ النِّساءِ.٦٤٤٨

1646. The Censure of the Love of Women[6493]

١٦٤٦ ـ ذَمُّ حُبِّ النِّساءِ٦٤٤٩

5751. **The Prophet (SAWA) said,** 'Satan has no greater force than women and anger.'[6494]

٥٧٥١. رسولُ اللهِ ﷺ: ما لإبليسَ جُندٌ أعظَمَ مِنَ النِّساءِ والغَضَبِ.٦٤٥٠

5752. **Imām ʿAlī (AS) said,** 'There are three temptations: the love of women, and it is the sword of Satan…So, whoever loves women they will not derive profit in their livelihood.'[6495]

٥٧٥٢ . الإمامُ عليٌّ عليه السلام: الفِتَنُ ثلاثٌ: حُبُّ النِّساءِ وهُو سَيفُ الشّيطانِ... فمَن أحَبَّ النِّساءَ لَم يَنتَفِعْ بعَيشِهِ. [٦٤٥١]

5753. **Imām ʿAlī (AS) said,** 'Beware of too much passion for women and being seduced by the sweet temptations of this world, for passion for women is trying and being seduced by worldly temptations is humiliating.'[6496]

٥٧٥٣ . عنه عليه السلام: إيّاكَ وكَثرَةَ الوَلَهِ بالنِّساءِ، والإغراءِ بلَذّاتِ الدُّنيا، فإنَّ الوَلَهَ بالنِّساءِ مُمتَحَنٌ، والغَرِيَّ باللَّذّاتِ مُمتَهَنٌ. [٦٤٥٢]

361

GALLANTRY

المُروءة

1647. Interpretation of Gallantry

١٦٤٧ ـ تَفسيرُ المُروءةِ

5754. **The Prophet (SAWA) said** to a man from Thaqīf, 'O brother from Thaqīf, what is gallantry in your opinion?' He said, 'O Messenger of Allah, it is fairness and peacemaking.' So he (SAWA) said, 'That is how it is in us.'[6497]

٥٧٥٤ . رسولُ اللهِ ﷺ ـ لِرجُلٍ مِن ثَقيفٍ ـ: يا أخا ثَقيفٍ، ما المُروءةُ فيكُم؟ قالَ: يا رسولَ اللهِ، الإنصافُ والإصلاحُ. قالَ: وكذلكَ هِي فينا. [٦٤٥٣]

5755. **Imām ʿAlī (AS),** when asked about gallantry, said, '[It is to] Not do something secretly which you would be ashamed to do in public.'[6498]

٥٧٥٥ . الإمامُ عليٌّ عليه السلام ـ لَمّا سُئلَ عَنِ المُروءةِ ـ: لاتَفعَلْ شيئاً في السِّرِّ تَستَحيي مِنهُ في العَلانِيَةِ. [٦٤٥٤]

5756. **Imām ʿAlī (AS) said,** 'The gallantry of a man will not be complete until he is educated [in religion], economizes in his living, is patient in tragedy when it befalls him, and finds the bitterness of his brethren sweet.'[6499]

٥٧٥٦ . عنه عليه السلام: لا تَتِمُّ مُروءةُ الرَّجُلِ حتّى يَتَفَقَّهَ (في دِينِهِ)، ويَقتَصِدَ في مَعيشَتِهِ، ويَصبِرَ علَى النّائبَةِ إذا نَزَلَت بِهِ، ويَستَعذِبَ مَرارَةَ إخوانِهِ. [٦٤٥٥]

5757. **Imām ʿAlī (AS) said,** 'With gentleness is gallantry completed.'[6500]

٥٧٥٧ . عنه عليه السلام: بالرِّفقِ تَتِمُّ المُروءةُ. [٦٤٥٦]

5758. **Imām ʿAlī (AS) said,** 'With truthfulness is gallantry perfected.'[6501]

٥٧٥٨ . عنه عليه السلام: بالصِّدقِ تَكمُلُ المُروءةُ. [٦٤٥٧]

5759. **Imām Ḥasan (AS),** when asked about gallantry, said, '[It is] Protecting the religion,

٥٧٥٩ . الإمامُ الحسنُ عليه السلام ـ لَمّا سُئلَ عَنِ

dignifying the self, lowering one's wing [in humility], dedication in one's actions, fulfilling rights, and showing love to people.'[6502]

المُروءةِ ـ: حِفظُ الدِّينِ، وإعزازُ النّفسِ، ولِينُ الكَنَفِ، وتَعَهُّدُ الصَّنيعةِ، وأداءُ الحُقوقِ، والتَّحَبُّبُ إلَى النّاسِ.٦٤٥٨

5760. **Imām al-Ṣādiq (AS),** when asked about gallantry said, 'That Allah should not see you where He has prohibited you, and that He does not miss you where He has ordered you.'[6503]

٥٧٦٠. الإمامُ الصّادقُ ؑ ـ لَمّا سُئلَ عَنِ المُروءةِ ـ: لا يَراكَ اللّهُ حَيثُ نَهاكَ، ولا يَفقِدُكَ مِن حَيثُ أمَرَكَ.٦٤٥٩

362

SICKNESS

المَرَض

1648. Some Reasons behind Sickness

١٦٤٨ ـ بَعضُ حِكَمِ المَرَضِ

5761. **The Prophet (SAWA) said,** 'The wrong-doings of a sick person shed away from him like the shedding of leaves from a tree.'[6504]

٥٧٦١. رسولُ اللّهِ ﷺ: المَريضُ تَحاتُّ خَطاياهُ كَما يَتَحاتُّ وَرَقُ الشَّجَرِ.٦٤٦٠

5762. **The Prophet (SAWA) said,** 'No believer and Muslim – man or woman - fall sick except that Allah will wipe out their sins.'[6505]

٥٧٦٢. عنه ﷺ: لا يَمرَضُ مؤمنٌ ولا مؤمنةٌ ولا مسلمٌ ولا مسلمةٌ إلّا حَطَّ اللّهُ بِهِ خَطيئتَهُ.٦٤٦١

5763. **Imām al-Bāqir or Imām al-Ṣādiq (AS) said,** 'Staying awake from sickness or pain for one night carries a greater reward than the worship of one year.'[6506]

٥٧٦٣. الإمامُ الباقرُ أو الإمامُ الصّادقُ ؑ: سَهَرُ لَيلَةٍ مِن مَرَضٍ أو وَجَعٍ أفضَلُ وأعظَمُ أجراً مِن عِبادَةِ سَنَةٍ.٦٤٦٢

5764. **Imām al-Kāẓim (AS) said,** 'When a believer becomes sick, Allah reveals unto the angel on his left [shoulder], 'Do not write a sin for my servant as long as he is in My confinement and My grasp, and He reveals unto the angel on his right [shoulder], 'Write for My servant what you were writing for him in merits when he was healthy.'[6507]

٥٧٦٤. الإمامُ الكاظمُ ؑ: إذا مَرِضَ المؤمنُ أوحَى اللّهُ عَزَّوجلَّ إلىٰ صاحِبِ الشِّمالِ: لا تَكتُبْ علىٰ عَبدي مادامَ في حَبسي ووَثاقي ذَنباً. ويُوحي إلىٰ صاحِبِ اليَمينِ أنِ اكتُبْ لِعَبدي ما كُنتَ تَكتُبُهُ في صِحَّتِهِ مِنَ الحَسَناتِ.٦٤٦٣

(See also: SINNING: section 780)

(أنظر) الذنب: باب ٧٨٠.

1649. Concealing One's Sickness

١٦٤٩ ـ كِتمانُ المَرَضِ

5765. **The Prophet (SAWA) said,** 'Allah Almighty has said, 'Whoever becomes sick three times and does not complain to any of his visitors, I change his flesh to flesh better than what he has and blood better than his blood. If I cure him, then I will cure him and he will have no sin, and if I take him [in death], I will take him to My Mercy.'[6508]

٥٧٦٥ . رسولُ اللهِ ﷺ : قالَ اللهُ عَزَّوجلَّ : مَن مَرِضَ ثلاثاً فلَم يَشكُ إلىٰ أحَدٍ مِن عُوّادِهِ أبدَلتُهُ لَحماً خَيراً مِن لَحمِهِ ودَماً خَيراً مِن دَمِهِ، فإن عافَيتُهُ عافَيتُهُ ولا ذَنبَ لَهُ، وإن قَبَضتُهُ قَبَضتُهُ إلىٰ رَحمَتي.[٦٤٦٤]

5766. **The Prophet (SAWA) said,** 'From among the treasures of righteousness are: concealing one's tragedies, sicknesses and charity.'[6509]

٥٧٦٦ . عنه ﷺ :مِن كُنوزِ البِرِّ :كِتمانُ المَصائبِ، والأمراضِ، والصَّدَقَةِ.[٦٤٦٥]

5767. **Imām ʿAlī (AS) said,** 'Whoever suppresses pain that he has been inflicted with for three days from people and complains to Allah instead, Allah will rightfully cure him from it.'[6510]

٥٧٦٧ . الإمامُ عليٌّ ؑ : مَن كَتَمَ وَجَعاً أصابَهُ ثلاثةَ أيّامٍ مِنَ النّاسِ وشَكا إلَى اللهِ، كانَ حَقّاً علَى اللهِ أن يُعافِيَهُ مِنهُ.[٦٤٦٦]

5768. **Imām ʿAlī (AS) said,** 'Whoever conceals his sickness from physicians has betrayed his body.'[6511]

٥٧٦٨ . عنه ؑ : مَن كَتَمَ الأطِبّاءَ مَرَضَهُ خانَ بَدَنَهُ.[٦٤٦٧]

5769. **Imām ʿAlī (AS) said,** 'Whoever conceals his hidden sickness, his physician will not be able to cure it.'[6512]

٥٧٦٩ . عنه ؑ: مَن كَتَمَ مَكنونَ دائهِ عَجَزَ طَبيبُهُ عَن شِفائهِ.[٦٤٦٨]

1650. The Reproaching of those who do not Fall Sick

١٦٥٠ ـ ذَمُّ مَن لا يَمرَضُ

5770. **Prophet David (AS),** would say, 'O Allah, [do not give me] sickness that weakens me nor health that makes me forget [You], rather a state in between them both.'[6513]

٥٧٧٠ . داوودُ ؑ ـ كانَ يقولُ ـ: اللّهُمّ لا مَرَضٌ يُضنيني، ولا صِحَّةٌ تُنسيني، ولكنْ بينَ ذلكَ.[٦٤٦٩]

5771. **The Prophet (SAWA) said,** 'Continuous health suffices as an ailment.'[6514]

٥٧٧١ . رسولُ اللهِ ﷺ : كَفىٰ بالسَّلامَةِ داءً.[٦٤٧٠]

5772. **The Prophet (SAWA) said,** 'Indeed Allah hates a wicked evil person who does not endure any harm in his body or his wealth.'[6515]

٥٧٧٢ . عنه ﷺ :إنّ اللهَ يُبغِضُ العِفرِيَةَ النِّفرِيَةَ الّذي لَم يُرزَأ في جِسمِهِ ولا مالِه.[٦٤٧١]

5773. **Imām al-Bāqir (AS) said,** 'If a body does not become sick it continues to make merry, and there is no good in a body that [only] makes merry.'[6516]

٥٧٧٣ . الإمامُ الباقرُ (ع) : الجَسَدُ إذا لم يَمرَضْ أشِرَ، ولا خَيرَ في جَسَدٍ يَأشَرُ.٦٤٧٢

1651. Visiting the Sick

١٦٥١ ـ عِيادَةُ المَريضِ

5774. **The Prophet (SAWA) said,** 'Allah Almighty will say on the Day of Resurrection, 'O son of Adam, I became sick and you did not visit Me!' and he will ask, 'O Lord, how can I visit You when You are the Lord of the worlds?' He Almighty will say, 'Did you not know that My servant so and so became sick and you did not visit him?! Did you not know that if you had visited him you would have found Me there with him [visiting a sick person is as visiting Allah]?!'[6517]

٥٧٧٤ . رسولُ اللهِ ﷺ : إنَّ اللهَ عَزَّوجلَّ يقولُ يومَ القِيامَةِ : يابنَ آدمَ، مَرِضتُ فلَم تَعُدْني ! قالَ: ياربِّ، كيفَ أعودُكَ وأنتَ رَبُّ العالَمينَ ؟! قالَ: أما عَلِمتَ أنّ عَبدي فُلاناً مَرِضَ فلَم تَعُدْهُ ؟! أما عَلِمتَ أنّكَ لَو عُدتَهُ لَوَجَدتَني عِندَهُ ؟!٦٤٧٣

5775. **The Prophet (SAWA) said,** 'The one who visits the sick dives into [divine] mercy.'[6518]

٥٧٧٥ . عنه ﷺ : عائدُ المَريضِ يَخوضُ في الرَّحمَةِ.٦٤٧٤

5776. **The Prophet (SAWA) said,** 'Visit the sick and attend funerals, they will remind you of the Hereafter.'[6519]

٥٧٧٦ . عنه ﷺ : عودوا المَريضَ واتبَعوا الجَنازَةَ يُذَكِّرْكُم الآخِرَةَ.٦٤٧٥

5777. **Imām al-Ṣādiq (AS) said,** 'Whoever visits a sick person, seventy thousand angels will escort him seeking forgiveness for him until he returns to his house.'[6520]

٥٧٧٧ . الإمامُ الصّادقُ (ع) : مَن عادَ مَريضاً شَيَّعَهُ سَبعونَ ألفَ مَلَكٍ يَستَغفِرونَ لَهُ حتّى يَرجِعَ إلى مَنزِلِهِ.٦٤٧٦

1652. Etiquettes of Visiting the Sick

١٦٥٢ ـ أدَبُ العِيادَةِ

5778. **The Prophet (SAWA) said,** 'The best kind of visit [of the sick] is the briefest one.'[6521]

٥٧٧٨ . رسولُ اللهِ ﷺ : خَيرُ العِيادَةِ أخَفُّها.٦٤٧٧

5779. **Imām ʿAlī (AS) said,** 'The visitor with the greatest reward with Allah is he who when he visits he sits briefly, unless the sick person likes the company and wants and asks [him to sit longer].'[6522]

٥٧٧٩ . الإمامُ عليٌّ (ع) : إنّ مِن أعظَمِ العُوّادِ أجراً عِندَ اللهِ عَزَّوجلَّ لَمَن إذا عادَ أخاهُ خَفَّفَ الجُلوسَ، إلّا أن يَكونَ المَريضُ يُحِبُّ ذلكَ ويُريدُهُ ويَسألُهُ ذلكَ.٦٤٧٨

5780. **Imām al-Ṣādiq (AS) said,** 'Visiting should be the length of time it takes to milk a camel.'[6523]

٥٧٨٠ . الإمامُ الصّادقُ عليه السلام : العِيادَةُ قَدرُ فُواقِ ناقَةٍ أو حَلَبِ ناقَةٍ.[٦٤٧٩]

5781. **Imām al-Ṣādiq (AS) said,** 'The complete visit of the sick should be just long enough for you to put your hand on his arm, and hasten to leave from him, for the visit of the foolish is harder for the sick person to bear than his pain.'[6524]

٥٧٨١ . عنه عليه السلام : تَمامُ العِيادَةِ للمَريضِ أن تَضَعَ يَدَكَ على ذِراعِهِ وتُعَجِّلَ القِيامَ مِن عِندِهِ ؛ فإنَّ عِيادَةَ النَّوكىٰ أشَدُّ علَى المَريضِ مِن وَجَعِهِ.[٦٤٨٠]

5782. **Al-Kāfī**: 'A servant of Imām al-Ṣādiq (AS) narrated, 'One of his servants became sick so we went to visit him as a group of the servants of Jaʿfar. We met Jaʿfar (AS) on the way, and he asked, 'Where are you going?' We replied, 'We are going to so and so to visit him.' He said, 'Stop.', so we stopped, and he asked, 'Does any of you have an apple or a quince, or a citron, or some perfume or a piece of sandalwood?!' We said, 'No, we do no have any of these?' He said, 'Do you not know that the sick man is comforted by anything that is brought for him.'[6525]

٥٧٨٢ . الكافي عن مولىً لجعفرِ بنِ محمّدٍ عليهما السلام : مَرِضَ بعضُ مَواليهِ فخَرَجنا إلَيهِ نَعودُهُ ونَحنُ عِدَّةٌ مِن مَوالي جعفرٍ ، فاستَقبَلَنا جعفرٌ عليه السلام في بعضِ الطَّريقِ ، فقالَ لنا : أينَ تُريدونَ ؟ فقُلنا: نُريدُ فُلاناً نَعودُهُ ، فقالَ لَنا: قِفوا ، فوَقَفنا ، فقالَ : مَع أحَدِكُم تُفّاحَةٌ، أو سَفَرجَلَةٌ ، أو اُترُجَّةٌ ، أو لَعقَةٌ مِن طِيبٍ، أو قِطعَةٌ مِن عُودِ بَخورٍ ؟ فقُلنا : ما مَعنا شيءٌ مِن هذا، فقالَ: أما تَعلَمونَ أنَّ المَريضَ يَستَريحُ إلىٰ كُلِّ ما اُدخِلَ بِهِ علَيهِ ؟![٦٤٨١]

363

DISPUTATION

المِراءُ

1653. The Censure of Disputation and its Effects

١٦٥٣ ـ ذَمُّ المِراءِ وآثارُهُ

5783. **The Prophet (SAWA) said,** 'A servant will not perfect the reality of faith until he abandons disputation, even if he is right.'[6526]

٥٧٨٣ . رسولُ اللهِ صلى الله عليه وآله : لا يَستَكمِلُ عَبدٌ حَقيقَةَ الإيمانِ حتّىٰ يَدَعَ المِراءَ وإن كانَ مُحِقّاً.[٦٤٨٢]

5784. **The Prophet (SAWA) said,** 'The most pious of people is he who abandons disputation, even if he is right.'[6527]

٥٧٨٤ . عنه صلى الله عليه وآله : أورَعُ النّاسِ مَن تَرَكَ المِراءَ وإن كانَ مُحِقّاً.[٦٤٨٣]

5785. **Imām ʿAlī (AS) said,** 'Beware of disputation and argument, for they sicken the hearts against brothers, and hypocrisy grows from them.'[6528]

٥٧٨٥ . الإمامُ عليٌّ عليه السلام : إيّاكُم والمِراءَ والخُصومَةَ ؛ فإنَّهُما يُمرِضانِ القُلوبَ علَى الإخوانِ ، ويَنبُتُ علَيهِما النِّفاقُ.[٦٤٨٤]

5786. **Imām ʿAlī (AS) said,** 'Whoever wants to hold on to his reputation should abandon disputation.'[6529]

٥٧٨٦ . عنه ﷺ : مَـن ضَـنَّ بـعِرضِهِ فَـلْيَدَعِ المِراءَ.[٦٤٨٥]

5787. **Imām ʿAlī (AS) said,** 'One should not dispute with six types of people: the jurist, the leader, the low, the lewd, the woman, and the child.'[6530]

٥٧٨٧ . عنه ﷺ : سِـتَّةٌ لا يُـمارَونَ: الفَـقيهُ، والرّئـيسُ، والدَّنـيُّ، والبَـذيُّ، والمَـرأةُ، والصَّبيُّ.[٦٤٨٦]

5788. **Imām al-Ṣādiq (AS) said,** 'Humbleness is to…abandon disputation, even if one is right.'[6531]

٥٧٨٨ . الإمامُ الصّادقُ ﷺ : إنّ مِنَ التَّواضُعِ... أن يَترُكَ المِراءَ وإن كانَ مُحِقّاً.[٦٤٨٧]

5789. **Imām al-Hādī (AS) said,** 'Disputation corrupts old friendships, undoes strong ties, and the least of it brings about aggression, and aggression is the basic cause of cutting off relations.'[6532]

٥٧٨٩ . الإمامُ الهاديُّ ﷺ : المِراءُ يُفسِدُ الصَّداقَةَ القَديمَةَ، ويَحلُلُ العُقدَةَ الوَثيقَةَ، وأقلُّ ما فيهِ أن تكونَ فيهِ المُغالَبةُ، والمُغالَبةُ اُسُّ أسبابِ القَطيعَةِ.[٦٤٨٨]

5790. **Imām al-ʿAskarī (AS) said,** 'Do not dispute lest your splendour fade, and do not joke lest people feel defiant towards you.'[6533]

٥٧٩٠ . الإمامُ العسكريُّ ﷺ : لا تُمارِ فـيَذهَبَ بَهاؤكَ، ولا تُمازِحْ فيُجتَرأَ علَيكَ.[٦٤٨٩]

364

JOKING

المِزاح

1654. The Praised Joking

١٦٥٤ ـ المِزاحُ المَحمودُ

5791. **The Prophet (SAWA) said,** 'I joke but I do not speak other than the truth.'[6534]

٥٧٩١ . رسولُ اللهِ ﷺ : إنّي أمزَحُ ولا أقولُ إلّا حَقّاً.[٦٤٩٠]

5792. **The Prophet (SAWA) said,** 'A believer is fun and playful, and a hypocrite is grim and angry.'[6535]

٥٧٩٢ . عنه ﷺ : المؤمنُ دَعِبٌ لَعِبٌ، والمُنافقُ قَطِبٌ غَضِبٌ.[٦٤٩١]

5793. **Tanbīh al-Khawāṭir**: 'An old woman came to the Prophet (SAWA) and he said to her, 'Old people will not enter Heaven.' So she started to cry, and he then said, 'At that time you will not be old, Allah Almighty has said, *"We have created*

٥٧٩٣ . تنبيه الخواطر : أتَتِ امرأةٌ عَجوزٌ إلَى النّبيِّ ﷺ فقالَ ﷺ : لا تَدخُلُ الجَنّةَ عَجوزٌ ؛ فبَكتْ، فقالَ: إنّكِ لستِ يَومئذٍ بعَجوزٍ، قالَ اللهُ

them with a special creation, and made them virgins.'[6536 6537]

تعالىٰ: ﴿إنّا أنْشَأناهُنَّ إنشاءً ❁ فجَعَلْناهُنَّ أبْكاراً﴾ [٦٤٩٢، ٦٤٩٣]

5794. **Imām al-Bāqir (AS) said,** 'Indeed Allah loves those who are playful among people without obscenity.'[6538]

٥٧٩٤. الإمامُ الباقرُ عليه السلام: إنّ اللهَ عَزَّوجلَّ يُحِبُّ المُداعِبَ في الجَماعةِ بلا رَفَثٍ. [٦٤٩٤]

5795. **Imām al-Ṣādiq (AS) said,** 'Every single believer should have playfulness in him.' [The narrator said] I asked, 'What is playfulness?' He replied, 'Joking.'[6539]

٥٧٩٥. الإمامُ الصّادقُ عليه السلام: ما مِن مؤمنٍ إلّا وفيهِ دُعابَةٌ، قتُ: وما الدُّعابَةُ؟ قالَ: المِزاحُ. [٦٤٩٥]

5796. **Imām al-Ṣādiq (AS)** asked Yūnus al-Shaybānī, 'How much do you jest around with each other?' I said, 'Little.' He said, 'This is not how it should be, for playing is part of good character, and through that you bring happiness to your brother, and the Messenger of Allah (SAWA) would jest with people wanting to make them happy.'[6540]

٥٧٩٦. عنه عليه السلام ـ ليونس الشيبانيّ ـ: كيفَ مُداعَبَةُ بَعضِكُم بَعضاً؟ قلتُ: قليلٌ، قالَ: فلا تَفعلوا[٦٤٩٦]، فإنّ المُداعَبَةَ مِن حُسنِ الخُلقِ، وإنّكَ لَتُدخِلُ بها السُّرورَ علىٰ أخيكَ، ولقد كانَ رسولُ اللهِ صلى الله عليه وآله يُداعِبُ الرّجُلَ يُريدُ أن يَسُرَّهُ. [٦٤٩٧]

1655. The Censured Joking

١٦٥٥ ـ المِزاحُ المَذمُومُ

5797. **The Prophet (SAWA) said,** 'O 'Alī, do not joke lest your splendour fade, and do not lie lest your light fade.'[6541]

٥٧٩٧. رسولُ اللهِ صلى الله عليه وآله: يا عليُّ، لا تَمزَحْ فيَذهَبَ بَهاؤكَ، ولا تَكذِبْ فيَذهَبَ نورُكَ. [٦٤٩٨]

5798. **The Prophet (SAWA) said,** 'Excessive joking takes away one's honour.'[6542]

٥٧٩٨. عنه صلى الله عليه وآله: كَثرَةُ المِزاحِ يَذهَبُ بماءِ الوجهِ. [٦٤٩٩]

5799. **Imām 'Alī (AS) said,** 'Every time a person makes a joke, a part of his intellect is thrown out.'[6543]

٥٧٩٩. الإمامُ عليٌّ عليه السلام: ما مَزَحَ امرؤٌ (رجُلٌ) مَزحَةً إلّا مَجَّ مِن عَقلِهِ مَجّةً. [٦٥٠٠]

5800. **Imām 'Alī (AS) said,** 'Joking brings about grudges.'[6544]

٥٨٠٠. عنه عليه السلام: المِزاحُ يُورِثُ الضَّغائنَ. [٦٥٠١]

5801. **Imām 'Alī (AS) said,** 'He who jokes will not be taken seriously.'[6545]

٥٨٠١. عنه عليه السلام: مَن مَزَحَ استُخِفَّ بهِ. [٦٥٠٢]

5802. **Imām 'Alī (AS) said,** 'Many a joke can turn out to be serious.'[6546]

٥٨٠٢. عنه عليه السلام: رُبَّ هَزلٍ[٦٥٠٣] عادَ جِدّاً. [٦٥٠٤]

5803. **Imām al-Ṣādiq (AS) said,** 'A joke is minor swearing.'[6547]

٥٨٠٣. الإمامُ الصّادقُ ﷺ: المِـزاحُ السِّبابُ الأصغَرُ.٦٥٠٥

5804. **Imām al-Ṣādiq (AS) said,** 'Do not joke lest your light fade.'[6548]

٥٨٠٤. عنه ﷺ: لاتَمزَحْ فيَذهَبَ نورُكَ.٦٥٠٦

5805. **Imām al-Ṣādiq (AS) said,** 'When you love someone do not joke and argue with him.'[6549]

٥٨٠٥. عنه ﷺ: إذا أحبَبتَ رَجُلاً فلا تُمازِحْهُ ولاتُمارِهِ.٦٥٠٧

365

SOVEREIGNTY

المُلك

1656. The Master of Sovereignty

١٦٥٦ـ مالِكُ المُلكِ

"Say, "O Allah, Master of all sovereignty! You give sovereignty to whomever You wish, and strip of sovereignty whomever you wish; You make mighty whomever You wish, and you abase whomever You wish; all good is in Your hand. Indeed You have power over all things."[6550]

﴿قُلِ اللّهُمَّ مَالِكَ الْمُلْكِ تُؤْتِي الْمُلْكَ مَنْ تَشَاءُ وَتَنْزِعُ الْمُلْكَ مِمَّنْ تَشَاءُ وَتُعِزُّ مَنْ تَشَاءُ وَتُذِلُّ مَنْ تَشَاءُ بِيَدِكَ الْخَيْرُ إِنَّكَ عَلَى كُلِّ شَيْءٍ قَدِيرٌ﴾.٦٥٠٨

"To Allah belongs the kingdom of the Heavens and the earth, and toward Allah is the destination."[6551]

﴿وَلِلّهِ مُلْكُ السَّمَاوَاتِ وَالْأَرْضِ وَإِلَى اللّهِ الْمَصِيرُ﴾.٦٥٠٩

5806. **The Prophet (SAWA) said,** 'The anger of Allah intensifies towards he who claims that he is the king of the kings, as there is no king other than Allah.'[6552]

٥٨٠٦. رسولُ اللهِ ﷺ: إشتَدَّ غضَبُ اللهِ على مَن زَعَمَ أنَّهُ مَلِكُ الأملاكِ، لا مَلِكَ إلّا اللهُ.٦٥١٠

5807. **Imām 'Alī (AS) said,** 'Every sovereign other than Him is himself owned.'[6553]

٥٨٠٧. الإمامُ عليٌّ ﷺ: كلُّ مالِكٍ غيرَهُ مَملوكٌ.٦٥١١

1657. Mixing with Kings

١٦٥٧ـ خُلطَةُ المُلوكِ

5808. **Imām 'Alī (AS) said,** 'Do not visit kings too much, for if you befriend them they will bore you, and if you advise them they will deceive you.'[6554]

٥٨٠٨. الإمامُ عليٌّ ﷺ: لا تُكثِرَنَّ الدُّخولَ على المُلوكِ؛ فإنّهُم إن صَحِبتَهُم مَلّوكَ، وإن نَصَحتَهُم غَشّوكَ.٦٥١٢

5809. **Imām ʿAlī (AS) said,** 'Status with kings is the key to misfortune and a seed for trial.'[6555]

٥٨٠٩ . عنه ﷷ : المَكانَةُ مِـن المُـلوكِ مِـفتاحُ المِحنَةِ وبَذرُ الفِتنَةِ.٦٥١٣

5810. **Imām al-Ṣādiq (AS) said,** 'There is no neighbour for the sea, no friend for a king, and no price for health.'[6556]

٥٨١٠ . الإمامُ الصّادقُ ﷷ : ليسَ للبحرِ جارٌ، ولا للمَلِكِ صَديقٌ، ولا للعافِيَةِ ثَمَنٌ.٦٥١٤

(See also: THE RULER: section 964)

(أنظر: السلطان: باب ٩٦٤).

1658. The Best of Kings

١٦٥٨ ـ خَيرُ المُلوكِ

5811. **Imām ʿAlī (AS) said,** 'The greatest of kings is he who kills oppression and revives justice.'[6557]

٥٨١١ . الإمامُ عليٌّ ﷷ : خَيرُ المُلوكِ مَن أماتَ الجَورَ وأحيا العَدلَ.٦٥١٥

5812. **Imām ʿAlī (AS) said,** 'The noblest of kings is he who rules his own self and spreads justice.'[6558]

٥٨١٢ . عنه ﷷ : أجَلُّ المُلوكِ مَن مَلَكَ نفسَهُ وبَسَطَ العَدلَ.٦٥١٦

5813. **Imām ʿAlī (AS) said,** 'The wisest of kings is he who rules his own self in favour of his subjects to the extent that they would have no argument against him and rules on the people in a manner that his arguments are established for them.'[6559]

٥٨١٣ . عنه ﷷ : أعقَلُ المُلوكِ مَن ساسَ نفسَهُ لِلرَّعيَّةِ بما يُسقِطُ عنهُ حُجَّتَها، وساسَ الرَّعيَّةَ بما تَثبُتُ بِهِ حُجَّتُهُ علَيها.٦٥١٧

5814. **Imām ʿAlī (AS) said,** 'The king who has the best status is he who during his time people have a good life, and he encompasses his subjects with his justice.'[6560]

٥٨١٤ . عنه ﷷ : أحسَنُ المُلوكِ حالاً مَن حَسُنَ عَيشُ النّاسِ في عَيشِهِ، وعَمَّ رعِيَّتَهُ بعَدلِهِ.٦٥١٨

5815. **Imām al-Ṣādiq (AS) said,** 'The best of kings is he who has been given three features: affection, generosity, and justice.'[6561]

٥٨١٥ . الإمامُ الصّادقُ ﷷ : أفضَلُ المُلوكِ مَن أُعطِيَ ثلاثَ خِصالٍ: الرَّأفَةَ، والجُودَ، والعَدلَ.٦٥١٩

1659. What is Appropriate for the Kings

١٦٥٩ ـ ما يَنبغي لِلملوكِ

5816. **Imām ʿAlī (AS) said,** 'A king is worthier of having mastery over himself before [disciplining] his soldiers.'[6562]

٥٨١٦ . الإمامُ عليٌّ ﷷ : حَقٌّ علَى المَلِكِ أن يَسوسَ نفسَهُ قَبلَ جُندِهِ.٦٥٢٠

5817. **Imām ʿAlī (AS) said,** 'Whoever makes his sovereignty subservient to his religion, all rulers will submit to him. And whoever makes his religion subservient to his sovereignty then all

٥٨١٧ . عنه ﷷ : مَن جَعَلَ مُلكَهُ خادِماً لِدينِهِ انقادَ لَهُ كلُّ سُلطانٍ، ومَن جَعَلَ دِينَهُ خادِماً

people will become greedy for it [i.e. his sovereignty].'[6563]

لمُلكِهِ طَمِعَ فيهِ كلُّ إنسانٍ.٦٥٢١

5818. **Imām ʿAlī (AS) said,** 'When a king builds on the foundations of justice and bases [his rule] on the pillars of reason, then Allah will make his followers victorious and will desert his enemies.'[6564]

٥٨١٨ . عنه ؑ : إذا بُنِيَ المُلكُ على قَواعِدِ العَدلِ ودُعِمَ بدعائمِ العَقلِ، نَصَرَ اللهُ مُوالِيَهُ وخَذَلَ مُعادِيَهُ.٦٥٢٢

366

ANGELS

المَلائِكَة

1660. The Creation of Angels

١٦٦٠ ـ خِلقَةُ المَلائكَةِ

"All praise belongs to Allah, originator of the Heavens and the earth, maker of the angels [His] messengers, possessing wings, two, three or four [of them]. He adds to the creation whatever He wishes, Indeed Allah has power over all things."[6565]

﴿الْحَمْدُ للهِ فَاطِرِ السَّمَاوَاتِ وَالْأَرْضِ جَاعِلِ الْمَلَائِكَةِ رُسُلاً أُولِي أَجْنِحَةٍ مَثْنَىٰ وَثُلَاثَ وَرُبَاعَ يَزِيدُ فِي الْخَلْقِ مَا يَشَاءُ إِنَّ اللهَ عَلَىٰ كُلِّ شَيْءٍ قَدِيرٌ﴾.٦٥٢٣

5819. **The Prophet (SAWA) said,** 'Nothing of what Allah created is more [numerous] than the angels'[6566]

٥٨١٩ . رسولُ اللهِ ﷺ : ما مِن شيءٍ مِمّا خَلَقَ اللهُ أكثَرَ مِن الملائكةِ.٦٥٢٤

5820. **Imām ʿAlī (AS) said,** 'He, Glory be to Him, then created for the inhabiting of His skies and populating the higher strata of his realm a great creation from among His angels. With them He filled the openings of its cavities and populated with them the vastness of its circumference.'[6567]

٥٨٢٠ . الإمامُ عليٌّ ؑ : ثُمَّ خَلَقَ سُبحانَهُ لإسكانِ سَماواتِه، وعِمارَةِ الصَّفيحِ الأعلىٰ مِن مَلَكوتِهِ، خَلقاً بَديعاً مِن مَلائكتِه، ومَلأ بِهِم فُروجَ فِجاجِها، وحَشا بِهِم فُتوقَ أجوائها (أجوابِها).٦٥٢٥

5821. **Imām al-Ṣādiq (AS) said,** 'Allah Almighty created the angels from light.'[6568]

٥٨٢١ . الإمامُ الصّادقُ ؑ : إنّ اللهَ عزَّ وجلَّ خَلَقَ المَلائكةَ مِن النُّورِ.٦٥٢٦

5822. **Imām al-Ṣādiq (AS) said,** 'By He who owns my soul, the number of angels in the Heavens is more than the amount of sand on the earth, and there is not even the space of a footstep in Heaven that does not have an angel glorifying and sanctifying Him, nor is there a tree or a ground without having an angel responsible for it.'[6569]

٥٨٢٢ . عنه ؑ : والّذي نَفسي بِيَدِهِ، لَمَلائكةُ اللهِ في السَّماواتِ أكثَرُ مِن عَدَدِ التُّرابِ في الأرضِ، ومافي السَّماءِ مَوضِعُ قَدَمٍ إلّا وفيها مَلَكٌ يُسَبِّحُهُ ويُقَدِّسُهُ، ولا في الأرضِ شَجَرٌ ولا مَدَرٌ إلّا وفيها مَلَكٌ مُوَكَّلٌ بِها.٦٥٢٧

1661. The Description of the Angels

١٦٦١ـ صِفَةُ المَلائِكَةِ

5823. **Imām ʿAlī (AS),** describing angels said, 'They are the most knowledgeable of Your creation about You, the most fearful of You and the closest to You. They did not come from loins nor did they enter wombs; they were not created from worthless liquid; they were not dispersed by vicissitudes of time. They are on their places [distinct] from You and in their positions near You. Their desires are concentrated in You. Their worship for You is very much. Their neglect from Your command is little. If they were to witness what remains hidden about You, they would belittle their actions.'[6570]

٥٨٢٣ . الإمامُ عليٌّ عليه السلام ـ في صفَةِ الملائكةِ ـ: هُم أعلَمُ خَلقِكَ بكَ، وأخوَفُهُم لكَ، وأقرَبُهُم مِنكَ، لَم يَسكُنوا الأصلابَ، ولَم يُضَمَّنوا الأرحامَ، ولَم يُخلَقوا مِن ماءٍ مَهينٍ، ولَم يَتشَعَّبْهُم رَيبُ المَنونِ، وإنّهُم على مَكانِهِم مِنكَ، ومَنزِلَتِهِم عِندَكَ، واستِجماعِ أهوائهِم فيكَ، وكَثرَةِ طاعَتِهِم لكَ، وقِلَّةِ غَفلَتِهِم عن أمرِكَ، لَو عايَنوا كُنهَ ما خَفِيَ علَيهِم مِنكَ لَحَقَّروا أعمالَهُم.[٦٥٢٨]

5824. **Imām al-Ṣādiq (AS) said,** 'Angels do not eat or drink or copulate, rather they subsist through the breeze of the Throne.'[6571]

٥٨٢٤ . الإمامُ الصّادقُ عليه السلام: إنّ الملائكةَ لا يأكُلونَ، ولا يَشرَبونَ، ولا يَنكِحونَ، وإنّما يَعيشونَ بِنَسيمِ العَرشِ.[٦٥٢٩]

1662. The Guardian Angels

١٦٦٢ـ المَلائِكَةُ الحَفَظَةُ

"He is the All-dominant over His servants, and He sends guards to [protect] you. When death approaches anyone of you, Our messengers take him away and they do not neglect [their duty]."[6572]

﴿وَهُوَ القَاهِرُ فَوْقَ عِبَادِهِ وَيُرْسِلُ عَلَيْكُمْ حَفَظَةً حَتَّىٰ إِذَا جَاءَ أَحَدَكُمُ الْمَوْتُ تَوَفَّتْهُ رُسُلُنَا وَهُمْ لَا يُفَرِّطُونَ﴾.[٦٥٣٠]

5825. **Imām al-Bāqir (AS),** with regard to Allah's verse in the Qur'an: *"He has guardian angels, to his front and his rear, who guard him by Allah's command"*[6573], said, 'By the command of Allah he is protected from falling into a well or from a wall falling onto him, or from being struck with something, until the decree of Allah comes. They [i.e. the angels] leave him alone it and pass him onto his decrees. They are two angels that protect him in the night, and two angels following them that protect him in the day.'[6574]

٥٨٢٥ الإمامُ الباقرُ عليه السلام ـ في قولِهِ تعالىٰ: ﴿لَهُ مَعقِّباتٌ مِنْ بَينِ يَدَيهِ ومِنْ خَلْفِهِ يَحْفَظونَهُ مِنْ أمْرِ اللهِ﴾[٦٥٣١] ـ: بأمرِ اللهِ مِن أن يَقعَ في رَكِيٍّ، أو يَقَعَ علَيهِ حائطٌ، أو يُصيبَهُ شيءٌ؛ حتّىٰ إذا جاءَ القَدَرُ خَلّوا بينَهُ وبينَهُ يَدفَعونَهُ إلَى المَقاديرِ، وهُما مَلَكانِ يَحفَظانِهِ باللَّيلِ، ومَلَكانِ يَحفَظانِهِ بالنَّهارِ يَتَعاقَبانِ.[٦٥٣٢]

5826. **Tafsīr al-Qummī**: *"Indeed, there are over you watchers."*[6575], 'The two angels entrusted with man;' *"noble writers."*[6576], 'They write the good deeds and the bad.'[6577]

٥٨٢٦ . تفسيرِ القمّيِّ: ﴿وإنّ علَيكُم لَحافِظينَ﴾[٦٥٣٣] قالَ: المَلَكانِ المُوَكّلانِ بالإنسانِ، ﴿كِراماً كاتِبينَ﴾[٦٥٣٤] يَكتُبونَ الحَسَناتِ والسَّيِّئاتِ.[٦٥٣٥]

1663. Houses that Angels do not Enter

١٦٦٣ ـ البُيوتُ الَّتي لا تدخُلُها المَلائِكَةُ

5827. **The Prophet (SAWA) said,** 'Gabriel (AS) came to me and said, 'O Muḥammad, how can we [angels] descend to your [people's] houses whilst you do not brush your teeth, you do not purify yourselves with water after excretion, and you do not wash your knuckles [of the dirt on them].'[6578]

٥٨٢٧. رسولُ اللهِ ﷺ: أتاني جَبرئيلُ ؑ فقالَ: يا محمّدُ، كيفَ نَنزِلُ علَيكُم وأنتُم لا تَستاكونَ ولا تَستَنجونَ بالماءِ ولا تَغسِلونَ بَراجِمَكُم[٦٥٣٦]؟![٦٥٣٧]

5828. **Imām al-Bāqir (AS) said,** 'Gabriel (AS) said, 'O Messenger of Allah, we do not enter a house that has in it a picture of a human, nor a place that one urinates in, nor a house that has a dog.'[6579]

٥٨٢٨. الإمامُ الباقرُ ؑ: قالَ جَبرئيلُ ؑ: يا رسولَ اللهِ، إنّا لا نَدخُلُ بَيتاً فيهِ صُورَةُ إنسانٍ، ولا بَيتاً يُبالُ فيهِ، ولا بَيتاً فيهِ كلبٌ.[٦٥٣٨]

367

DEATH

المَوتُ

1664. Death

١٦٦٤ ـ الموتُ

"He, who created death and life that He may test you [to see] which of you is best in conduct. And He is the All-mighty, the All-forgiving."[6580]

﴿الَّذِي خَلَقَ الْمَوْتَ وَالْحَيَاةَ لِيَبْلُوَكُمْ أَيُّكُمْ أَحْسَنُ عَمَلاً وَهُوَ الْعَزِيزُ الْغَفُورُ﴾.[٦٥٣٩]

5829. **The Prophet (SAWA) said,** 'When any of you die, his Resurrection has started; and he sees what good and bad he has [accumulated].'[6581]

٥٨٢٩. رسولُ اللهِ ﷺ: إذا ماتَ أحَدُكُم فَقد قامَت قِيامَتُهُ، يَرىٰ ما لَهُ مِن خَيرٍ و شَرٍّ.[٦٥٤٠]

5830. **The Prophet (SAWA) said,** 'Whoever dies in a certain state, Allah will resurrect him as such.'[6582]

٥٨٣٠. عنه ﷺ: مَن ماتَ علىٰ شيءٍ بَعَثَهُ اللهُ علَيهِ.[٦٥٤١]

5831. **Imām ʿAlī (AS) said,** 'With death one's life ends.'[6583]

٥٨٣١. الإمامُ عليٌّ ؑ: بالمَوتِ تُختَمُ الدُّنيا.[٦٥٤٢]

5832. **Imām ʿAlī (AS) said,** 'Death is the door to the Hereafter.'[6584]

٥٨٣٢. عنه ؑ: المَوتُ بابُ الآخِرَةِ.[٦٥٤٣]

5833. **Imām al-Ṣādiq (AS) said,** 'A group of the people of the past said to their prophet, 'Pray to

٥٨٣٣. الإمامُ الصّادقُ ؑ: إنّ قوماً أتَوا نَبيّاً

your Lord to take death away from us. He did so and Allah took death away from them. They became so many that their houses became crowded and their offspring became too many. A man had to feed his father, mother and grandfather, and his great grandfather, and they had to satisfy them and take care of them. They became too occupied to seek a livelihood, so they said, 'Ask your Lord to return us to our previous state. So, their Prophet asked his Lord and He returned them to their original state.'[6585]

فقالُوا: أُدعُ لَنا ربَّكَ يَرفَعْ عنّا المَوتَ فدَعا لَهُم فَرفَعَ اللهُ تبارَكَ وتعالىٰ عنهُمُ المَوتَ، وكَثُروا حتّىٰ ضاقَت بهِمُ المَنازِلُ وكَثُرَ النَّسلُ، وكانَ الرّجُلُ يُصبحُ فيَحتاجُ أن يُطعِمَ أباهُ واُمَّهُ وجَدَّهُ وجَدَّ جدِّهِ ويُرضِيَهُم [٦٥٤٤] ويَتعاهَدَهُم، فشُغِلوا عن طَلَبِ المَعاشِ، فأتَوهُ فقالوا: سَلْ ربَّكَ أن يَرُدَّنا إلى آجالِنا الّتي كُنّا علَيها، فسَألَ ربَّهُ عَزَّوجلَّ فرَدَّهُم إلىٰ آجالِهِم. [٦٥٤٥]

1665. Having Certainty in Death

١٦٦٥ ـ اليَقينُ بِالمَوتِ

"Every soul shall taste death, and you will indeed be paid your full rewards on the Day of Resurrection. Whoever is delivered from the Fire and admitted to paradise has certainly succeeded. The life of this world is nothing but the wares of delusion."[6586]

﴿كُلُّ نَفْسٍ ذَائِقَةُ الْمَوْتِ وَإِنَّمَا تُوَفَّوْنَ أُجُورَكُمْ يَوْمَ الْقِيَامَةِ فَمَنْ زُحْزِحَ عَنِ النَّارِ وَأُدْخِلَ الْجَنَّةَ فَقَدْ فَازَ وَمَا الْحَيَاةُ الدُّنْيَا إِلَّا مَتَاعُ الْغُرُورِ﴾. [٦٥٤٦]

5834. **Imām al-Ṣādiq (AS),** with regard to Allah's verse in the Qur'an: *"Say, 'Indeed the death that you flee will indeed encounter you."* [6587], said, 'Years are counted, then months, then days, then hours, then breaths *"When their time comes, they shall not defer it by a single hour nor shall they advance it.'*[6588] [6589]

٥٨٣٤. الإمامُ الصّادقُ عليه السلام ـ في قولهِ تعالىٰ: ﴿قُلْ إنّ الموتَ الّذي تَفِرّونَ مِنهُ فإنّهُ مُلاقِيكُم...﴾ [٦٥٤٧] ـ: تَعُدُّ السِّنينَ، ثُمّ تَعُدُّ الشُّهورَ، ثُمّ تَعُدُّ الأيّامَ، ثُمّ تَعُدُّ السّاعاتِ، ثُمّ تَعُدُّ النَّفَسَ ﴿فإذا جاءَ أجَلُهُمْ لا يَسْتَأخِرونَ ساعَةً ولا يَسْتَقدِمونَ﴾. [٦٥٤٨] [٦٥٤٩]

5835. **Imām ʿAlī (AS) said,** 'I have never seen a kind of faith that comes with certainty more resembling to doubt in the human being. Every day he entrusts bodies to the graves and goes to funeral processions, but he returns to the delusion of the world, and he does not relinquish desires and sins. If the poor son of Adam did not have a single sin to deviate him and no reckoning to contemplate with than death that scatters his union, disunites his congregation, orphans his children then it would be a must for him to be cautious of what he is in with the greatest of exhaustion and hardship.'[6590]

٥٨٣٥. الإمامُ عليٌّ عليه السلام: ما رَأيتُ إيماناً مَع يَقينٍ أشبَهَ مِنهُ بشَكٍّ علىٰ هذا الإنسانِ؛ إنّهُ كُلَّ يَومٍ يُوَدِّعُ إلَى القُبورِ ويُشَيِّعُ، وإلىٰ غُرورِ الدّنيا يَرجِعُ، وعنِ الشَّهوَةِ والذُّنوبِ لا يُقلِعُ، فلَو لَم يَكُن لابنِ آدمَ المِسكينِ ذَنبٌ يَتوَكَّفُهُ ولا حِسابٌ يَقِفُ علَيهِ إلّا مَوتٌ يُبَدِّدُ شَملَهُ ويُفَرِّقُ جَمعَهُ ويُوتِمُ وُلدَهُ، لَكانَ يَنبَغي لَهُ أن يُحاذِرَ ما هُوَ فيهِ بأشَدِّ النَّصَبِ والتَّعَبِ. [٦٥٥٠]

5836. **Imām ʿAlī (AS),** in his will to Imām al-Hasan (AS) said, 'My son, know that you have been created

٥٨٣٦. عنه عليه السلام ـ مِن وَصاياهُ لابنِهِ الحسنِ عليه السلام ـ:

for the next world and not for this world, and for annihilation and not to stay, for death and not for life; you are in a transient place, a place which is a path to the Hereafter. You are running away from death from which no one can run away from and which none of its seekers can miss. It has to be experienced so beware lest it catches up with you while you are in a bad state, while you were promising yourself to repent for the sin, but it did not allow you to repent and it made you perish.'[6591]

اعلَمْ يا بُنَيَّ أنَّكَ إنّما خُلِقتَ للآخِرَةِ لا للدُّنيا، وللفَناءِ لا للبَقاءِ، وللمَوتِ لا للحَياةِ، وأنَّكَ في قُلعَةٍ ودارِ بُلغَةٍ وطَريقٍ إلَى الآخِرَةِ، وأنَّكَ طَريدُ المَوتِ الّذي لا يَنجو مِنهُ هارِبُهُ، ولا يَفوتُهُ طالِبُهُ، ولابُدَّ أنَّهُ مُدرِكُهُ، فكُن مِنهُ علىٰ حَذَرٍ أن يُدرِكَكَ وأنتَ علىٰ حالٍ سَيِّئَةٍ، قد كنتَ تُحَدِّثُ نفسَكَ مِنها بالتَّوبَةِ فيَحولُ بينَكَ وبينَ ذلكَ، فإذا أنتَ قد أهلَكتَ نفسَكَ.[٦٥٥١]

5837. **Imām ʿAlī (AS) said,** 'You are running away from death. If you resist it, it will take you, and if you run from it, it will catch you. It is more stuck to you than your own shadow. Death is attached to your forelocks.'[6592]

٥٨٣٧. عنه عليه‌السلام: أنتُم طُرَداءُ المَوتِ، إن أقَمتُم لَهُ أخَذَكُم، وإن فَرَرتُم مِنهُ أدرَكَكُم، وهُو ألزَمُ لَكُم مِن ظِلِّكُم، المَوتُ مَعقودٌ بنَواصيكُم.[٦٥٥٢]

5838. **Imām al-Ṣādiq (AS) said,** 'Allah has not created certainty devoid of doubt more similar to a doubt devoid of certainty like death.'[6593]

٥٨٣٨. الإمامُ الصّادقُ عليه‌السلام: ما خَلَقَ اللهُ عزّوجلّ يَقيناً لا شَكَّ فيهِ أشبَهَ بشَكٍّ لا يَقينَ فيهِ مِن المَوتِ.[٦٥٥٣]

1666. Coming Close to Departing

١٦٦٦ ـ اقتِرابُ الرَّحيلِ

5839. **Imām ʿAlī (AS) said,** 'If you are leaving life behind you and death is drawing forwards, then how quickly will you run into each other.'[6594]

٥٨٣٩. الإمامُ عليٌّ عليه‌السلام: إذا كُنتَ في إدبارٍ والمَوتُ في إقبالٍ، فما أسرَعَ المُلتَقىٰ![٦٥٥٤]

5840. **Imām ʿAlī (AS) said,** 'Departure is imminent.'[6595]

٥٨٤٠. عنه عليه‌السلام: الرَّحيلُ وَشيكٌ.[٦٥٥٥]

5841. **Imām ʿAlī (AS) said,** 'There is no absent thing closer [to us] than death.'[6596]

٥٨٤١. عنه عليه‌السلام: لا غائبَ أقرَبُ مِن المَوتِ.[٦٥٥٦]

1667. Interpretation of Death

١٦٦٧ ـ تَفسيرُ المَوتِ

5842. **Imām Zayn al-ʿĀbidīn (AS),** when asked about death said, 'For a believer, it is like taking off dirty clothes, undoing shackles and heavy chains, and changing into the finest and most scented of clothes. It is the smoothest of mountable animals and the most comforting of abodes. As for the infidel, it is like taking off fine clothes, trans-

٥٨٤٢. الإمامُ زينُ العابدينَ عليه‌السلام ـ لمّا سُئلَ عنِ المَوتِ ـ: لِلمؤمنِ كنَزعِ ثِيابٍ وَسِخَةٍ قَمِلَةٍ، وفَكِّ قُيودٍ وأغلالٍ ثَقيلَةٍ، والاستِبدالِ بأفخَرِ الثِّيابِ وأطيَبِها رَوائحَ، وأوطَأِ المَراكِبِ، وآنَسِ المَنازِلِ؛ وللكافِرِ كخَلعِ ثِيابٍ فاخِرَةٍ، والنَّقلِ

ferring from comfortable abodes, and changing into the dirtiest and roughest of clothes, the most terrifying of stations and the greatest of punishments.'[6597]

عن مَنازِلَ أنيسَةٍ، والاستِبدالِ بأوسَخِ الثِّيابِ وأخشَنِها، وأوحَشِ المَنازِلِ، وأعظَمِ العَذابِ.[٦٥٥٧]

5843. **Imām al-Kāẓim (AS),** when he visited a person immersed in the pangs of death said, 'Death is the purifier which purifies the believers from their sins, so it is the last pain that they are struck with as atonement for the last wrongdoing left in them. For the infidels, death strips them of their good deeds, so it is the last pleasure or leisure they will ever experience, and it will be the last reward of a good deed for them …'[6598]

٥٨٤٣. الإمامُ الكاظمُ عليه السلام ـ لَمّا دَخَلَ على رجُلٍ قد غَرِقَ في سَكَراتِ المَوتِ ـ: المَوتُ هُو المَصْفاةُ يُصَفّي المؤمنينَ مِن ذُنوبِهِم فيكونُ آخِرُ ألَمٍ يُصيبُهُم كَفّارَةَ آخِرِ وِزرٍ بَقِيَ علَيهِم، ويُصَفّي الكافِرينَ مِن حَسَناتِهِم فيكونُ آخِرَ لَذّةٍ أو راحَةٍ تَلحَقُهُم، وهُو آخِرُ ثَوابِ حَسَنَةٍ تكونُ لَهُم....[٦٥٥٨]

5844. **Imām al-Jawād (AS),** when asked about death said, 'It is the sleep that comes to you every night, however its period is long and none will wake from it until the Day of Resurrection. So he who sees in his sleep different kinds of happy states whose extent he cannot fathom and different kinds of terrors he cannot fathom, then how does the happy and the dismayed feel in death? This is death so prepare for it.'[6599]

٥٨٤٤. الإمامُ الجوادُ عليه السلام ـ لمّا سُئلَ عن المَوتِ ـ: هُو النَّومُ الّذي يأتيكُم كُلَّ ليلَةٍ إلّا أنّهُ طويلٌ مُدَّتُهُ لا يُنتَبَهُ مِنهُ إلّا يومَ القيامَةِ، فمَن رأىٰ في نَومِهِ من أصنافِ الفَرَحِ ما لا يُقادِرُ قَدرَهُ، ومِن أصنافِ الأهوالِ ما لا يُقادِرُ قَدرَهُ، فكيفَ حالُ فَرِحٍ في النَّومِ ووَجِلٍ فيهِ؟ هذا هُو المَوتُ، فاستَعِدّوا لَهُ.[٦٥٥٩]

1668. The Death of a Believer

١٦٦٨ ـ مَوتُ المُؤمِنِ

"Those whom the angels take away while they are pure. They say [to them], 'Peace be to you! Enter paradise because of what you used to do.'"[6600]

﴿الَّذِينَ تَتَوَفَّاهُمُ الْمَلَائِكَةُ طَيِّبِينَ يَقُولُونَ سَلَامٌ عَلَيْكُمُ ادْخُلُوا الْجَنَّةَ بِمَا كُنْتُمْ تَعْمَلُونَ﴾.[٦٥٦٠]

5845. **The Prophet (SAWA) said,** 'Death is the basil of a believer.'[6601]

٥٨٤٥. رسولُ اللهِ ﷺ: المَوتُ رَيحانَةُ المؤمنِ.[٦٥٦١]

5846. **The Prophet (SAWA) said,** 'Death is a gift for the believer.'[6602]

٥٨٤٦. عنه ﷺ: تُحفَةُ المؤمنِ المَوتُ.[٦٥٦٢]

5847. **Imām al-Ṣādiq (AS),** with regard to Allah's verse in the Qur'an: *"For them is good news in the life of this world"*[6603], said, 'It is that these two give them glad tidings of Heaven during their death, meaning Muḥammad and ʿAlī (AS).'[6604]

٥٨٤٧. الإمامُ الصّادقُ عليه السلام ـ في قولِهِ تعالىٰ: ﴿لَهُمُ البُشْرىٰ في الحَياةِ الدُّنيا﴾[٦٥٦٣] ـ: هُو أن يُبَشِّراهُ بالجَنّةِ عِندَ المَوتِ، يَعني محمّداً وعليّاً عليهما السلام.[٦٥٦٤]

5848. **Imām al-Riḍā (AS),** when visiting one of his sick companions, asked, ‘How are you?’ He replied, ‘I have met death after you!’ referring to the pain he had endured from his intense sickness’, so he said, ‘How did you find it?’ He said, ‘Very painful.’ He (AS) said, ‘You have not met it, you have only met what is warning you of it and it is introducing you to some of its states…’[6605]

٥٨٤٨ . الإمامُ الرِّضا ؈ ـ في عِيادَةِ رجُلٍ مِن أصحابِهِ ـ: كيفَ تَجِدُكَ ؟ قالَ: لَقِيتُ المَوتَ بَعدَكَ ! ـ يُريدُ ما لَقِيَهُ مِن شِدَّةِ مَرَضِهِ ـ فقالَ: كيفَ لَقِيتَهُ ؟ فقالَ: أليماً شَديداً ، فقالَ: ما لَقِيتَهُ ، إنّما لَقِيتَ ما يُنذِرُكَ بِهِ ويُعرِّفُكَ بعضَ حالِهِ ...[٦٥٦٥]

1669. Remembrance of Death

١٦٦٩ ـ ذِكرُ المَوتِ

5849. **The Prophet (SAWA) said,** ‘Increase the remembrance of the demolisher of desires.’ He was asked, ‘O Messenger of Allah, what is the demolisher of desires?’ He said, ‘Death, for the most sagacious of believers are those who remember death the most and are the most prepared for it.’[6606]

٥٨٤٩ . رسولُ اللهِ ﷺ : أكثِروا مِن ذِكرِ هادِمِ اللَّذّاتِ ، فقيلَ: يا رسولَ اللهِ، فما هادِمُ اللَّذّاتِ ؟ قالَ: المَوتُ ، فإنّ أكيَسَ المؤمنينَ أكثَرُهُم ذِكراً للمَوتِ ، وأشَدُّهُم لَهُ استِعداداً .[٦٥٦٦]

5850. **The Prophet (SAWA) said,** ‘Increase your remembrance of death, for any servant who increases its remembrance, Allah will revive his heart and ease death for him.’[6607]

٥٨٥٠ . عنه ﷺ : أكثِروا ذِكرَ المَوتِ ، فما مِن عَبدٍ أكثَرَ ذِكرَهُ إلّا أحيا اللهُ قلبَهُ وهَوَّنَ علَيهِ المَوتَ .[٦٥٦٧]

5851. **Imām ʿAlī (AS) said** to his son al-Ḥasan (AS), ‘O son, increase your remembrance of death, of that which overcomes it, and of that which you will return to after death such that when it comes to you, you will have taken heed of it and strengthened yourself for it, and you will not let it overcome you by surprise so that it overpowers you.’[6608]

٥٨٥١ . الإمامُ عليٌّ ؈ ـ لابنِهِ الحسنِ ؈ ـ : يابُنيَّ ، أكثِرْ مِن ذِكرِ المَوتِ ، وذِكرِ ما تَهجُمُ علَيهِ وتُفضي بعدَ المَوتِ إلَيهِ ، حتّىٰ يأتيَكَ[٦٥٦٨] وقد أخَذتَ مِنهُ حِذرَكَ وشَدَدتَ لَه أزرَكَ ، ولا يَأتيَكَ بَغتَةً فيَبهَرَكَ .[٦٥٦٩]

5852. **Imām al-Ṣādiq (AS) said,** ‘The remembrance of death kills the desires in the self and uproots the sources of inattentiveness. It strengthens the heart about Allah’s promises, softens one's attitude, breaks the pillars of inclinations, extinguishes the fire of greed, and it degrades the world.’[6609]

٥٨٥٢ . الإمامُ الصّادقُ ؈ : ذِكرُ المَوتِ يُميتُ الشَّهَواتِ في النَّفسِ ، ويَقلَعُ مَنابِتَ الغَفلَةِ ، ويُقَوّي القلبَ بمَواعِدِ اللهِ ، ويُرِقُّ الطَّبعَ ، ويَكسِرُ أعلامَ الهَوىٰ ويُطفِئُ نارَ الحِرصِ ، ويُحَقِّرُ الدُّنيا .[٦٥٧٠]

5853. **Imām al-Ṣādiq (AS) said,** ‘Increase in the remembrance of death, for no sooner does a

٥٨٥٣ . عنه ؈ : أكثِروا ذِكرَ المَوتِ ؛ فإنّهُ ما أكثَرَ

person increase his remembrance of death than he abstains from the world.'[6610]

ذِكرَ المَوتِ إنسانٌ إلّا زَهِدَ في الدُّنيا.[٦٥٧١]

5854. **Imām al-Hādī (AS) said,** 'Remember your death in front of your family; when there will be no doctor to prevent it from you and no beloved to help you.'[6611]

٥٨٥٤. الإمامُ الهاديُّ عليه السلام: أُذكُرْ مَصرَعَكَ بينَ يَدَي أهلِكَ؛ ولا طَبيبَ يَمنَعُكَ، ولا حَبيبَ يَنفَعُكَ.[٦٥٧٢]

1670. Preparing for Death

١٦٧٠ ـ الاستِعدادُ لِلمَوتِ

5855. **The Prophet (SAWA) said,** 'Whoever anticipates death will hasten to do good deeds.'[6612]

٥٨٥٥. رسولُ اللهِ صلى الله عليه وآله: مَنِ ارتَقَبَ المَوتَ سارَعَ في الخَيراتِ.[٦٥٧٣]

5856. **Imām ʿAlī (AS) said,** 'Prepare for death for it overshadows you, and be a group who when it screams at them they awaken, and know that the world is not their abode and therefore they have exchanged it [for the Hereafter]...'[6613]

٥٨٥٦. الإمامُ عليٌّ عليه السلام: اِستَعِدّوا للمَوتِ فقد أظَلَّكُم، وكُونوا قَوماً صِيحَ بِهِم فانتَبَهوا، وعَلِموا أنّ الدُّنيا لَيسَت لَهُم بدارٍ فاستَبدَلوا....[٦٥٧٤]

5857. **Imām ʿAlī (AS) said,** 'When there is something that you do not know when it will take you by surprise, then you must prepare yourself for it before it covers you over.'[6614]

٥٨٥٧. عنه عليه السلام: إنّ أمراً لاتَعلَمُ مَتىٰ يَفجَؤُكَ يَنبَغي أنْ تَستَعِدَّ لَهُ قبلَ أن يَغشاكَ.[٦٥٧٥]

5858. **Imām ʿAlī (AS) said,** 'I am surprised at the one who sees that his lifespan and his breaths are decreasing every day but still does not prepare for death.'[6615]

٥٨٥٨. عنه عليه السلام: عَجِبتُ لمَن يَرىٰ أنّهُ يُنقَصُ كلَّ يَومٍ في نفسِهِ وعُمرِهِ وهُو لا يَتَأهَّبُ للمَوتِ![٦٥٧٦]

5859. **Imām ʿAlī (AS) said,** 'Get ready for death and its difficulties, plan for it before it comes, and prepare for it before it descends.'[6616]

٥٨٥٩. عنه عليه السلام: بادِروا المَوتَ وغَمَراتِهِ، وامهَدوا لَهُ قبلَ حُلُولِهِ، وأعِدُّوا لَهُ قبلَ نُزولِهِ.[٦٥٧٧]

5860. **Imām ʿAlī (AS) said,** 'He who counts tomorrow as another of his days has not given death its true recognition.'[6617]

٥٨٦٠. عنه عليه السلام: ما أنزَلَ المَوتَ حَقَّ مَنزِلَتِهِ مَن عَدَّ غَداً مِن أجَلِهِ.[٦٥٧٨]

5861. **Imām ʿAlī (AS),** when asked about preparing for death, said, '[It is to] Fulfil obligations, refrain from the forbidden and adopt good moral traits, and then to not care whether one should fall onto death or death should fall onto him. By Allah, the son of Abū Ṭālib is not

٥٨٦١. عنه عليه السلام ـ لمّا سُئلَ عنِ الاستِعدادِ للمَوتِ ـ: أداءُ الفَرائضِ، واجتِنابُ المَحارِمِ، والاشتِمالُ علَى المَكارِمِ، ثُمّ لايُبالي أوَقَعَ علَى المَوتِ أم وَقَعَ المَوتُ علَيهِ. واللهِ، مايُبالي ابنُ

concerned whether he falls onto death or death falls onto him.'[6618]

أبي طالبٍ أوَقَعَ علَى المَـوتِ أم وَقَـعَ المَـوتُ علَيهِ.[٦٥٧٩]

1671. Wishing for Death

١٦٧١ ـ تَمَنِّي المَوتِ

5862. **The Prophet (SAWA) said,** 'None of you should pray for death if harm afflicts him, rather he should say, 'O Allah, keep me alive as long as life is good for me, and take me away when death is better for me.'[6619]

٥٨٦٢ . رسولُ اللهِ ﷺ: لا يَتَمنّىٰ أحَدُكُمُ المَوتَ لِضُرٍّ نَزَلَ بهِ، فإن كانَ ولابُدَّ فاعِلاً فلْيَقُل: اللّهُمّ أحيِني ما كانَتِ الحَـياةُ خَـيراً لي، وتَـوَفَّني إذا كانَتِ الوَفاةُ خَيراً لي.[٦٥٨٠]

5863. **The Prophet (SAWA) said,** 'None of you should wish for death unless they have trust in [the goodness of] their actions.'[6620]

٥٨٦٣ . عنه ﷺ: لايَتَمنّىٰ أحَدُكُمُ المَوتَ إلّا أن يَثِقَ بِعَملِهِ.[٦٥٨١]

5864. **Imām ʿAlī (AS) said** to Ḥārith al-Hamdānī, 'Increase the remembrance of death and what comes after death, and do not wish for death without [having fulfilled] the strong condition.'[6621]

٥٨٦٤ . الإمامُ عليٌّ عليه السلام ـ لِلحارثِ الهَمْدانيِّ ـ: وأكثِرْ ذِكرَ المَوتِ وما بعدَ المَـوتِ، ولا تَـتَمَنَّ المَوتَ إلّا بشَرطٍ وَثيقٍ.[٦٥٨٢]

5865. **Imām al-Kāẓim (AS),** said to a man who wished to die, 'Is there a kinship between you and Allah as a result of which He will be partial to you in it [i.e. death]?' He said, 'No.' The Imām then asked, 'So, do you have good deeds that you have done that exceed your bad deeds?' He said, 'No.' The Imām said, 'Therefore, you are wishing for the ultimate ruin!'[6622]

٥٨٦٥ . الإمامُ الكاظمُ عليه السلام ـ لِرجُلٍ يَتَمَنّى المَوتَ ـ: هل بينَكَ وبينَ اللهِ قَرابَةٌ يُحابيكَ لَها؟ قـالَ: لا. قـالَ: فـهَل لكَ حَسَـناتٌ قَـدَّمتَها تَـزيدُ عـلىٰ سَيِّئاتِكَ؟ قالَ: لا. قالَ: فأنتَ إذاً تَتمنّىٰ هَـلاكَ الأبَدِ![٦٥٨٣]

1672. The Agony of Death

١٦٧٢ ـ سَكرَةُ المَوتِ

"Then the agony of death brings the truth: 'This is what you used to shun!'"[6623]

﴿وجاءَتْ سَكْرَةُ الْمَوْتِ بِالْحَقِّ ذَلِكَ مَا كُنْتَ مِنْهُ تَحِيدُ﴾.[٦٥٨٤]

(See also: Qur'an 4:97, 47:27, 56:83-94)

(أُنظر) النساء: ٩٧ و محمّد: ٢٧ والواقعة: ٨٣ ـ ٩٤.

5866. **The Prophet (SAWA) said,** 'Attend to the people who are about to die and dictate to them [the phrase]: *Lā ilāha illallāh (There is no god but Allah)*, and give them glad tidings of Heaven, for

٥٨٦٦ . رسولُ اللهِ ﷺ: اِحضَروا مَوتاكُم ولَقِّنوهُم «لا إلهَ إلّا اللهُ» وبَشِّروهُم بالجَنَّةِ، فإنّ الحَليمَ مِن الرِّجالِ والنِّساءِ يَتَحَيّرُ عندَ ذلكَ المَصرَعِ، وإنّ

even the most forbearant of men and women become perplexed at that instant, and Satan comes as close as he can get to the children of Adam in that state. By He who owns my soul! Seeing the angel of death is more severe than being hit one thousand times by a sword. By He who owns my soul! The soul of a servant will not exit from the world until every vein in him feels pain.'[6624]

الشّيطانَ قرَبُ ما يكونُ مِن ابنِ آدمَ عـندَ ذلكَ المَصرَعِ. والّذي نَـفسي بـيَدِهِ! لَـمُعايَنةُ مَـلَكِ المَوتِ أشَدُّ مِن ألفِ ضَـربَةٍ بـالسَّيفِ. والّـذي نَفسي بيَدِهِ! لا تَخرُجُ نَفسُ عَبدٍ مِن الدّنيا حتّىٰ يَتَألَّمَ كُلُّ عِرقٍ مِنهُ علىٰ حِيالهِ.[٦٥٨٥]

5867. **The Prophet (SAWA) said,** 'If the animals knew about death what you know, you would never be able to eat the fat of them [due to their abstinence from the world].'[6625]

٥٨٦٧ . عنه ﷺ : لو أنّ البَهائمَ يَعلَمْنَ مِن المَوتِ ما تَعلَمونَ أنتُم، ما أكَلتُم مِنها سَميناً![٦٥٨٦]

5868. **Imām ʿAlī (AS) said,** 'Death has difficulties that are more terrible than can ever be described or be comprehended by the intellects of the people of the world.'[6626]

٥٨٦٨ . الإمامُ عليٌّ عليه السلام : إنّ للمَوتِ لَغَمَراتٍ هِيَ أفظَعُ مِن أن تُستَغرَقَ بـصِفَةٍ، أو تَـعتَدِلَ عـلىٰ عُقولِ أهلِ الدّنيا.[٦٥٨٧]

1673. The Reason for Despising Death

١٦٧٣ ـ عِلَّةُ كَراهَةِ المَوتِ

5869. **The Prophet (SAWA) said** to a person who asked him about the reason for [man's] despising of death, 'Do you have wealth?' He said, 'Yes.' The Prophet said, 'And have you given it away [before death should overtake you]?' He said, 'No.' The Prophet said, 'This is why you do not like death.'[6627]

٥٨٦٩ . رسولُ اللهِ ﷺ ـ لِرَجلٍ سَأَله مِـن عِـلَّةِ كَرهَةِ المَوتِ ـ: ألكَ مالٌ؟ قـالَ: نَـعَم. قـالَ: فـقَدَّمتَهُ؟ قـالَ: لا، قـالَ: فـمِن ثَـمّ لا تُـحِبُّ المَوتَ.[٦٥٨٨]

5870. **Imām al-Ḥasan (AS),** in answer to a person about the reason for hating death, said, 'Because you have wrecked your Hereafter and built your world, and you hate to move from a constructed place to a demolished place.'[6628]

٥٨٧٠ . الإمامُ الحسنُ عليه السلام ـ أيـضاً ـ: لِأنّكُم أخرَبتُم آخِـرَتَكُم، وعَـمَّرتُم دُنـياكُـم، وأنـتُم تَكرَهونَ النُّقلَةَ مِن العُمرانِ إلَى الخَرابِ.[٦٥٨٩]

1674. The Appearance of the Prophet and the Imāms to a Dying Person

١٦٧٤ ـ تَمثُّلُ النَّبِيِّ ﷺ وَالأئِمَّةِ عليهم السلام لِلمُحتَضَرِ

5871. **Imām ʿAlī (AS) said,** 'Whoever loves me will find me when they die as they loved me, and

٥٨٧١ . الإمامُ عليٌّ عليه السلام : مَن أحَبَّني وجَدَني عندَ

whoever hates me will see me when they die as they hated me.'[6629]

مَماتِهِ بحَيثُ يُحِبُّ، ومَن أبغَضَني وجَدَني عندَ مَماتِهِ بحَيثُ يَكرَهُ.[٦٥٩٠]

5872. **Imām al-Ṣādiq (AS),** when asked, 'Does a believer hate it when his soul is being taken?', said, 'By Allah no, when the angel of death comes to him to take his soul he will be anguished and the angel of death will say, 'O friend of Allah, do not worry, because by He who sent Muḥammad (SAWA) I am more compassionate and caring for you than a merciful father if he was to be with you. Open your eyes and see.' He said, 'And the Messenger of Allah, the Commander of the Faithful, Fāṭima, Ḥasan and Ḥusayn and the Imāms after him will all appear and it will be said to him, 'This is the Messenger of Allah and….your friends…and there will be nothing more beloved to this person than for his soul to leave and meet the caller.'[6630]

٥٨٧٢ . الإمامُ الصّادقُ (عليه السلام) ـ لمّا سُئلَ: هل يُكرَهُ المؤمنُ علىٰ قَبضِ رُوحِهِ ؟ ـ: لا واللهِ، إنّهُ إذا أتاهُ ملَكُ المَوتِ لقَبضِ رُوحِهِ جَزِعَ عِندَ ذلكَ، فيَقولُ لَهُ ملَكُ المَوتِ: يا وَليَّ اللهِ لا تَجزَعْ، فوالّذي بَعَثَ محمّداً ﷺ لَأنا أبَرُّ بِكَ وأشفَقُ علَيكَ من والِدٍ رَحيمٍ لو حَضَرَكَ، افتَحْ عَينَكَ فانظُرْ. قالَ: ويُمَثَّلُ لَهُ رسولُ اللهِ ﷺ وأميرُ المؤمنينَ وفاطمةُ والحسنُ والحسينُ والأئمةُ من ذُرِّيتِهِم (عليهم السلام) فيقالُ لَهُ: هذا رسولُ اللهِ و... رُفَقاؤكَ... فما شيءٌ أحَبَّ إلَيهِ مِن استِلالِ رُوحِهِ واللُّحوقِ بالمُنادي.[٦٥٩١]

5873. **Imām al-Ṣādiq (AS) said,** 'Every person who is dying and is a follower of us and hates our enemies will be visited by the Messenger of Allah (SAWA), the Commander of the Faithful, Ḥasan and Ḥusayn, and they will make him happy, and give him glad tidings. But if he is not a follower of ours, he will see them in a way that will upset him.' The proof of this is the saying of the Commander of the Faithful (AS) to Ḥārith al-Hamdānī:
'O Ḥār Hamdān, whoever dies will see me,
Both believer and hypocrite alike.'[6631]

٥٨٧٣ . عنه (عليه السلام): ما يَموتُ مُوالٍ لَنا مُبغِضٌ لأعدائنا إلّا ويَحضُرُهُ رسولُ اللهِ ﷺ وأميرُ المؤمنينَ والحسنُ والحسينُ (عليهم السلام) فيَسُرُّوهُ ويُبَشِّروهُ، وإن كانَ غيرَ مُوالٍ لَنا يَراهُم بحَيثُ يَسوؤهُ.
والدّليلُ علىٰ ذلكَ قَولُ أميرِ المؤمنينَ (عليه السلام) لحارثِ الهَمْداني:

يا حارَ هَمْدانَ مَن يَمُتْ يَرَني
مِن مؤمنٍ أو مُنافِقٍ قُبُلا.[٦٥٩٢]

1675. Sudden Death

١٦٧٥ـ مَوتُ الفُجأةِ

5874. **The Prophet (SAWA) said,** 'Sudden death is ease for the believer and a regretful overtaking for the disbeliever.[6632]

٥٨٧٤ . رسولُ اللهِ ﷺ: إنّ مَوتَ الفُجأةِ تَخفيفٌ عنِ المؤمنِ، وأخذَةُ أسَفٍ عنِ الكافرِ.[٦٥٩٣]

5875. **The Prophet (SAWA) said,** 'Sudden death is ease for the believers and a source of anger for the disbelievers.'[6633]

٥٨٧٥ . عنه ﷺ: مَوتُ الفُجأةِ تَخفيفٌ علَى المؤمنينَ، ومَسخَطَةٌ علَى الكافِرينَ.[٦٥٩٤]

5876. **The Prophet (SAWA) said,** 'Among the portents of the Hour are the spread of semi-paralysis and sudden death.'[6634]

٥٨٧٦. عنه ﷺ: مِن أشراطِ السّاعَةِ أن يَفشوَ الفالَجُ وموتُ الفُجاءَةِ.[٦٥٩٥]

1676. Attending Funeral Processions

١٦٧٦ـ تَشييعُ الجَنازَةِ

5877. **The Prophet (SAWA) said,** 'Travel [i.e. walk] two years [in distance] to do good to your parents, travel one year to reconcile with your kin, travel a mile [in distance] to visit a sick person, and travel two miles [in distance] to attend a funeral procession.'[6635]

٥٨٧٧. رسولُ اللهِ ﷺ: سِرْ سَنَتَينِ بِرَّ والِدَيكَ، سِرْ سَنَةً صِلْ رَحِمَكَ، سِرْ ميلاً عُدْ مَريضاً، سِرْ ميلَينِ شَيِّعْ جَنازَةً.[٦٥٩٦]

5878. **The Prophet (SAWA) said,** 'You must walk quietly, and in deliberation when walking in your funeral processions.'[6636]

٥٨٧٨. عنه ﷺ: عَلَيكُم بالسَّكينَةِ، عَلَيكُم بالقَصدِ في المَشيِ بجَنائزِكُم.[٦٥٩٧]

5879. It is narrated in *al-Da'āwāt*: When the Prophet (SAWA) followed a funeral procession, grief would overcome him and he would increase in speaking to his own self, and lessen his talking.[6637]

٥٨٧٩. الدعوات: كانَ رسولُ اللهِ ﷺ إذا تَبِعَ جَنازَةً غَلَبَتهُ كآبَةٌ، وأكثَرَ حديثَ النَّفسِ، وأقَلَّ الكلامَ.[٦٥٩٨]

5880. **Imām al-Ṣādiq (AS) said,** 'The first gift that a believer is able to bestow [others after his death] is that those who follow his funeral procession are forgiven.'[6638]

٥٨٨٠. الإمامُ الصّادقُ عليه السلام: أوّلُ ما يُتحَفُ بهِ المؤمنُ يُغفَرُ لِمَن تَبِعَ جَنازَتَهُ.[٦٥٩٩]

5881. **Imām al-Ṣādiq (AS) said,** 'It is a must for the guardians of the corpse to inform the brothers of the deceased person of his death so that they can attend his funeral and perform the prayers for him, so that they may be rewarded on account of him and the deceased person will be forgiven.'[6639]

٥٨٨١. عنه عليه السلام: يَنبَغي لأولياءِ المَيِّتِ أن يُؤذِنوا إخوانَ المَيِّتِ بمَوتِهِ، فيَشهَدونَ جَنازَتَهُ ويُصَلّونَ علَيهِ، فيَكسِبُ لَهُمُ الأجرَ ويُكسِبُ لِمَيِّتِهِ الاستِغفارَ.[٦٦٠٠]

(See also: MARRIAGE: section 887)

(أنظر) الزواج، باب ٨٨٧.

1677. Burying the Dead

١٦٧٧ـ دفنُ المَيِّتِ

5882. **The Prophet (SAWA) said,** 'If a person dies at the beginning of the day then he should not spend that night anywhere other than in his grave.'[6640]

٥٨٨٢. رسولُ اللهِ ﷺ: إذا ماتَ المَيِّتُ أوّلَ النَّهارِ فلا يَقيلُ إلّا في قَبرِهِ.[٦٦٠١]

5883. **The Prophet (SAWA) said,** 'Do not bury your dead in the night unless you are compelled to.'[6641]

٥٨٨٣ . عنه ﷺ : لاتَدفِنوا مَوتاكُم باللّيلِ إلّا أن تَضطَرّوا.[٦٦٠٢]

5884. **The Prophet (SAWA) said,** 'The most merciful Allah is towards His servant is when he is put in the hole of his grave.'[6642]

٥٨٨٤ . عنه ﷺ : إنّ أرحَمَ ما يَكونُ اللهُ بالعَبدِ إذا وُضِعَ في حُفرَتِهِ.[٦٦٠٣]

5885. **Imām ʿAlī (AS) said,** 'The Messenger of Allah (SAWA) ordered us to bury our dead in the midst of righteous people, for the dead are hurt by evil neighbours in the same way that living people are.'[6643]

٥٨٨٥ . الإمامُ عليٌّ عليه السلام :أمَرَنا رسولُ اللهِ ﷺ أن نَدفِنَ مَوتانا وَسطَ قَومٍ صالِحينَ ؛ فإنّ المَوتىٰ يَتأذّونَ بجارِ السَّوءِ كما يَتأذّىٰ بِهِ الأحياءُ.[٦٦٠٤]

1678. What Follows a Person after his Death

١٦٧٨ ـ ما يَتبَعُ الإنسانَ بَعدَ المَوتِ

5886. **The Prophet (SAWA) said,** 'Three things follow a dead person: his family, his wealth and his actions. Two go back and one stays: his family and wealth go back and his actions stay [with him].'[6644]

٥٨٨٦ . رسولُ اللهِ ﷺ : يَتبَعُ المَيّتَ ثلاثةٌ: أهلُهُ ومالُهُ وعمَلُهُ، فيَرجِعُ اثنانِ ويَبقىٰ واحِدٌ ؛ يَرجِعُ أهلُهُ ومالُهُ، ويَبقىٰ عَمَلُهُ.[٦٦٠٥]

5887. **Imām al-Ṣādiq (AS) said,** 'Six things benefit a person after he passes away: a child who seeks forgiveness for him, a copy of the Qur'an which he leaves behind, a plant that he planted, water that he donated in charity, a well that he had dug, and a tradition that others take from him and [practice] after him.'[6645]

٥٨٨٧ . الإمامُ الصّادقُ عليه السلام :سِتّةٌ يَلحَقنَ المؤمنَ بَعدَ وَفاتِهِ: ولدٌ يَستَغفِرُ لَهُ، ومصحَفٌ يُخَلِّفُهُ، وغَرسٌ يَغرِسُهُ، وصَدَقَةُ ماءٍ يُجريهِ، وقَليبٌ يَحفِرُهُ، وسُنّةٌ يُؤخَذُ بها مِن بَعدِهِ.[٦٦٠٦]

(See also: ACTION: section 1383; HABITIUAL PRACTICE: section 986; RESURRECTION: section 1394)

(أنظر) العمل: باب ١٣٨٣؛ السنة: باب ٩٨٦؛ المعاد: باب ١٣٩٤.

368

WEALTH

المَالُ

1679. Wealth is the Substance of Desires

١٦٧٩ ـ المالُ مادّةُ الشَّهَواتِ

"Wealth and children are an adornment of the life of this world, but lasting righteous deeds are better with your Lord in reward and better in hope."[6646]

﴿الْمَالُ وَالْبَنُونَ زِينَةُ الْحَيَاةِ الدُّنْيَا والبَاقِيَاتُ الصَّالِحَاتُ خَيْرٌ عِنْدَ رَبِّكَ ثَوَاباً وَخَيْرٌ أَمَلاً﴾.[٦٦٠٧]

5888. **The Prophet (SAWA) said,** ‘Dinars and dirhams ruined those before you and will ruin you too.’[6647]

٥٨٨٨ . رسولُ اللهِ ﷺ: إنّ الدِّينارَ والدِّرهَمَ أهلَكا مَن كانَ قَبلَكُم، وهُما مُهلِكاكُم.٦٦٠٨

5889. **The Prophet (SAWA) said,** ‘Satan, may Allah curse him, said, ‘The owner of wealth will not be safe from me in three things that I will overcome him with and leave thereafter: his acquisition of it from unlawful places, his spending it in its unrightful place, and I will make him love it so much that he will deprive it to its rightful due.’[6648]

٥٨٨٩ . عنه ﷺ: قالَ الشَّيطانُ لَعَنَهُ اللهُ: لَن يَسلَمَ مِنّي صاحِبُ المالِ من إحدى ثلاثٍ أغدو علَيهِ بهِنَّ وأرُوحُ: أخذُهُ مِن غيرِ حِلِّهِ، وإنفاقُهُ في غيرِ حَقِّهِ، وأُحَبِّبُهُ إلَيهِ فيَمنَعُهُ مِن حَقِّهِ.٦٦٠٩

5890. **Imām ʿAlī (AS) said,** ‘Wealth is the substance of desires.’[6649]

٥٨٩٠ . الإمامُ عليٌّ ﵇: المالُ مادَّةُ الشَّهَواتِ.٦٦١٠

5891. **Imām ʿAlī (AS) said,** ‘Money strengthens expectations.’[6650]

٥٨٩١ . عنه ﵇: المالُ يُقَوّي الآمالَ.٦٦١١

1680. The Effects of Loving Wealth

١٦٨٠ ـ آثارُ حُبِّ المالِ

“And you love wealth with much fondness.”[6651]

﴿وَتُحِبُّونَ الْمَالَ حُبًّا جَمًّا﴾.٦٦١٢

5892. **Prophet Jesus (AS) said,** ‘Do not look at the wealth of the people of this world, for the glitter of their wealth will take away the light of your faith.’[6652]

٥٨٩٢ . عيسى ﵇: لا تَنظُروا إلى أموالِ أهلِ الدُّنيا؛ فإنَّ بَريقَ أموالِهِم يَذهَبُ بنُورِ إيمانِكُم.٦٦١٣

5893. **Imām ʿAlī (AS) said,** ‘Wealth corrupts the ultimate goal and heightens one’s expectations.’[6653]

٥٨٩٣ . الإمامُ عليٌّ ﵇: المالُ يُفسِدُ المآلَ، ويُوَسِّعُ الآمالَ.٦٦١٤

5894. **Imām ʿAlī (AS) said,** ‘The love of wealth weakens one’s religion and corrupts one’s conviction.’[6654]

٥٨٩٤ . عنه ﵇: حُبُّ المالِ يُوهِنُ الدِّينَ، ويُفسِدُ اليَقينَ.٦٦١٥

1681. Love for Lawful Wealth

١٦٨١ ـ حُبُّ المالِ مِنَ الحَلالِ

5895. **The Prophet (SAWA) said,** ‘Blessed is the righteous wealth for a righteous man.’[6655]

٥٨٩٥ . رسولُ اللهِ ﷺ: نِعمَ المالُ الصّالِحُ للرَّجُلِ الصّالِحِ.٦٦١٦

5896. **Imām ʿAlī (AS) said,** 'Richness in a foreign place is like one's homeland, and poverty in one's homeland is like being a foreigner in it...'[6656]

٥٨٩٦ . الإمامُ عليٌّ ﷺ : الغِنىٰ في الغُربَةِ وَطَنٌ ، والفَقرُ في الوَطَنِ غُربَةٌ .٦٦١٧

5897. **Imām Zayn al-ʿĀbidīn (AS) said,** 'Utilising wealth is the perfection of gallantry.'[6657]

٥٨٩٧ . الإمامُ زينُ العابدينَ ﷺ : إستِثمارُ المالِ تَمامُ المُرُوَّةِ .٦٦١٨

5898. **Imām al-Ṣādiq (AS) said,** 'There is no good in he who does not love to earn lawful wealth with which he can protect his honour, repay his debts and maintain relations with his kin.'[6658]

٥٨٩٨ . الإمامُ الصّادقُ ﷺ : لا خَيرَ فيمَن لا يُحِبُّ جَمعَ المالِ مِن حَلالٍ ، يَكُفُّ بِهِ وَجهَهُ ويَقضي بِهِ دَينَهُ ويَصِلُ بِهِ رَحِمَهُ .٦٦١٩

1682. Reproaching of Excessive Wealth

١٦٨٢ ـ ذَمُّ كَثرَةِ المالِ

"Those who treasure up gold and silver, and do not spend it in the way of Allah, inform them of a painful punishment."[6659]

﴿وَالَّذِينَ يَكْنِزُونَ الذَّهَبَ وَالْفِضَّةَ وَلا يُنْفِقُونَهَا فِي سَبِيلِ اللهِ فَبَشِّرْهُمْ بِعَذَابٍ أَلِيمٍ﴾ .٦٦٢٠

(See also: Qur'an 28:76, 28:82, 70:18, 18:34, 77:20, 9:69, 10:88, 34:35)

(أنظر) القصص: ٧٦، ٨٢ والمعارج: ١٨ والكهف: ٣٤ والحديد: ٢٠ والتوبة: ٦٩ويونس: ٨٨ وسبأ: ٣٥.

5899. **Imām al-Ṣādiq (AS) narrated,** 'In an intimate conversation that Allah had with Prophet Moses (AS), He said, 'Do not envy anyone for having excessive wealth, for with excessive wealth sins increase in [trespassing] obligatory rights.'[6660]

٥٨٩٩ . الإمامُ الصّادقُ ﷺ : فيما ناجَى اللهُ عَزَّ وجلَّ بِهِ موسىٰ ﷺ : ... لا تَغبِطْ أحَداً بكَثرَةِ المالِ ؛ فإنَّ مَعَ كَثرَةِ المالِ تَكثُرُ الذُّنوبُ لِواجِبِ الحُقوقِ .٦٦٢١

5900. **The Prophet (SAWA) said,** 'I do not fear poverty for you, but I fear you vying in your excessive wealth.'[6661]

٥٩٠٠ . رسولُ اللهِ ﷺ : ما أخشىٰ علَيكُمُ الفَقرَ ، ولكنّي أخشىٰ علَيكُمُ التَّكاثُرَ .٦٦٢٢

5901. **Imām ʿAlī (AS) said,** 'Too much wealth corrupts the hearts and produces sins.'[6662]

٥٩٠١ . الإمامُ عليٌّ ﷺ : كَثرَةُ المالِ تُفسِدُ القُلوبَ وتُنشِئُ الذُّنوبَ .٦٦٢٣

5902. **Imām Ḥusayn (AS) said,** 'Your wealth is such that if you do not control it, it will control you, so do not save any of it for it will not stay for you. Consume it before it consumes you.'[6663]

٥٩٠٢ . الإمامُ الحسينُ ﷺ : مالُكَ إن لَم يَكُنْ لَكَ كُنتَ لَهُ ، فلا تُبقِ علَيهِ فإنّهُ لا يُبقي علَيكَ ، وكُلْهُ قَبلَ أن يَأكُلَكَ ٦٦٢٤ ! ٦٦٢٥

5903. **Imām al-Ṣādiq (AS) said,** 'Whenever one's wealth increases, Allah's evidence against him increases. So, if you are able to push it away from

٥٩٠٣ . الإمامُ الصّادقُ ﷺ : ما كَثُرَ مالُ رجُلٍ قطُّ إلّا عَظُمَتِ الحُجّةُ للهِ تعالىٰ علَيهِ ، فإن قَدَرتُم أن

yourselves then do so. He was asked, 'How?' He replied, 'By fulfilling the needs of your brothers from your wealth.'[6664]

تَدفَعوه عَن أنفُسِكُم فافعَلوا، فقيلَ: بماذا؟ قالَ: بقَضاءِ حَوائجِ إخوانِكُم مِن أموالِكُم.[٦٦٢٦]

5904. **Imām al-Ṣādiq (AS) said,** 'I sought after comfort of my heart and I found it in having little wealth.'[6665]

٥٩٠٤. عنه ﷺ: طَلَبتُ فَراغَ القلبِ فوَجَدتُهُ في قِلَّةِ المالِ.[٦٦٢٧]

5905. **Imām al-Riḍā (AS) said,** 'Wealth can only be gathered through five means: through intense miserliness, high expectation, overcoming greed, cutting of kinship, and preferring this world over the Hereafter.'[6666]

٥٩٠٥. الإمامُ الرِّضا ﷺ: لا يَجتَمِعُ المالُ إلّا بخِصالٍ خَمسٍ: بِبُخلٍ شَديدٍ، وأمَلٍ طَويلٍ، وحِرصٍ غالِبٍ، وقَطيعَةِ الرَّحِمِ، وإيثارِ الدُّنيا علَى الآخِرَةِ.[٦٦٢٨]

1683. He who Acquires Wealth from Illegitimate Sources

١٦٨٣ ـ مَن كَسَبَ مالاً مِن غَيرِ حِلِّهِ

5906. **The Prophet (SAWA) said,** 'Allah will impoverish whoever acquires wealth from an illegitimate source.'[6667]

٥٩٠٦. رسولُ اللهِ ﷺ: مَن كَسَبَ مالاً مِن غيرِ حِلِّهِ أفقَرَهُ اللهُ.[٦٦٢٩]

5907. **The Prophet (SAWA) said,** 'He who does not care whence he acquires wealth, Allah will not care whence He will make him enter Hell.'[6668]

٥٩٠٧. عنه ﷺ: مَن لم يُبالِ مِن أينَ اكتَسَبَ المالَ لَم يُبالِ اللهُ مِن أينَ أدخَلَهُ النّارَ.[٦٦٣٠]

5908. **Imām ʿAlī (AS) said,** 'He who acquires wealth from an unlawful source will spend it in a place where he will have no recompense thereof.'[6669]

٥٩٠٨. الإمامُ عليٌّ ﷺ: مَن يَكسِبْ مالاً مِن غَيرِ حَقِّهِ يَصرِفْهُ في غَيرِ أجرِهِ.[٦٦٣١]

5909. **Imām al-Ṣādiq (AS) said,** 'He who acquires wealth from illegitimate sources, the building, the soil and the water [of those places] will reign over him.'[6670 6671]

٥٩٠٩. الإمامُ الصّادقُ ﷺ: مَن كَسَبَ مالاً مِن غَيرِ حِلِّهِ سُلِّطَ علَيهِ البِناءُ والطِّينُ والماءُ.[٦٦٣٢]

5910. **Imām al-Ṣādiq (AS) said,** 'He who acquires wealth unrightfully will be rightfully prevented from keeping it.'[6672]

٥٩١٠. عنه ﷺ: مَن طَلَبَ المالَ بغَيرِ حَقٍّ حُرِمَ بَقاءَهُ لَهُ بِحَقٍّ.[٦٦٣٣]

(See also: THE LAWFUL 113)

(أنظر) عنوان ١١٣ «الحلال».

1684. Wealth is what Benefits Men

١٦٨٤ ـ المالُ ما أفادَ الرِّجالَ

5911. **The Prophet (SAWA) said,** 'You are three partners in your wealth: you, your losses, and your heir, so if you can try not to be the weakest of them then do so.'[6673]

٥٩١١ . رسولُ اللهِ ﷺ : إنّ لكَ في مالِكَ ثـلاثاً شُركاءَ: أنتَ، والتّلَفُ، والوارِثُ، فإنِ استَطَعتَ أن لا تكونَ أعجَزَهُم فافعَلْ.[٦٦٣٤]

5912. **The Prophet (SAWA) said,** 'The son of Adam says: 'My property, my property! My wealth, my wealth!' - O poor man! Where were you when there was property but not you, and do you possess anything other than what you eat and emit, or wear and wear out, or did you donate so it stayed?! Either you will be had mercy on as a result of it [i.e. your wealth] or punished on account of it. So, beware lest that wealth which is not yours be more beloved to you than your own wealth.'[6674]

٥٩١٢ . عنه ﷺ : يقولُ ابنُ آدمَ: مُلكي مُلكي! ومالي مالي! يامِسكينُ! أينَ كنتَ حيثُ كانَ المُلكُ ولَم تَكُن، وهَل لكَ إلّا ما أكَلتَ فأفنَيتَ، أو لَبِستَ فأبلَيتَ، أو تَصَدَّقتَ فأبقَيتَ؟! إمّا مَرحومٌ بِهِ وإمّا مُعاقَبٌ علَيهِ، فاعقِلْ أن لا يكونَ مالُ غيرِكَ أحَبَّ إلَيكَ مِن مالِكَ.[٦٦٣٥]

5913. **Imām 'Alī (AS) said,** 'Wealth is what benefits men.'[6675]

٥٩١٣ . الإمامُ عليٌّ عليه السلام :المالُ ما أفادَ الرِّجالَ.[٦٦٣٦]

5914. **Imām 'Alī (AS) said,** 'Wealth honours its owner as long as he spends it and it humiliates him where he is miserly with it.'[6676]

٥٩١٤ . عنه عليه السلام : المالُ يُكرِمُ صاحِبَهُ ما بَذَلَهُ، ويُهينُهُ ما بَخِلَ بهِ.[٦٦٣٧]

5915. **Imām 'Alī (AS) said,** 'Hold onto wealth according to your need of it, and put the rest away for a day you will need it.'[6677]

٥٩١٥ . عنه عليه السلام :أمسِكْ مِن المالِ بقَدرِ ضَرورَتِكَ، وقَدِّمِ الفَضلَ لِيَومِ حاجَتِكَ.[٦٦٣٨]

5916. **Imām 'Alī (AS) said,** 'The best of wealth is that with which one's dignity is guarded and that through which one's rights are fulfilled.'[6678]

٥٩١٦ . عنه عليه السلام :أفضَلُ المالِ ما وُقِيَ بهِ العِرضُ، وقُضِيَت بهِ الحُقوقُ.[٦٦٣٩]

5917. **Imām 'Alī (AS) said,** 'The best of your wealth is that which helps you with your needs.'[6679]

٥٩١٧ . عنه عليه السلام : خَيرُ مالِكَ ما أعانَكَ على حاجَتِكَ.[٦٦٤٠]

5918. **Imām al-Ṣādiq (AS) said,** 'Allah gave you this excess in wealth in order that you may use it according to how Allah Almighty would like, and He did not give it to you in order for you to store it away.'[6680]

٥٩١٨ . الإمامُ الصّادقُ عليه السلام: إنّما أعطاكُمُ اللهُ هذهِ الفُضولَ مِن الأموالِ لتُوَجِّهوها حيثُ وَجَّهَها اللهُ عزّوجلَّ، ولَم يُعطِكُموها لِتَكنِزوها.[٦٦٤١]

5919. **Imām ʿAlī al-Riḍā (AS) said,** 'The best wealth of a person is what he reserves for charity.'[6681]

٥٩١٩ . الإمامُ الرِّضا عليه السلام : خَيرُ مالِ المَرءِ ذَخائِرُ الصَّدَقَةِ. ٦٦٤

369

PROPHETHOOD (1)
General Prophethood

النُّبُوَّةُ (١)
النُّبُوَّةُ العامَّةُ

1685. The Philosophy of Prophethood

١٦٨٥ ـ فَلسَفَةُ النُّبُوَّةِ

1. Perfection

١ ـ التَّكاملُ

5920. **Imām al-Ṣādiq (AS) said** to an atheist who asked him, 'Wherefore did you establish the [need for and existence of] prophets?' 'When we established that we have a Creator and Maker, supreme over us and over all that He created, and that this Maker is so Wise and Supreme that His creation cannot see Him or touch Him, like they can mutually see each other and contend with each other, it hence becomes established that He has ambassadors among His creation who speak on His behalf to His creation and servants. They guide creation to their advantages and benefits, and to that which will secure their survival and the abandonment of which will destroy them.'[6682]

٥٩٢٠ . الإمامُ الصّادقُ عليه السلام ـ للزِّنديقِ الّذي سألَهُ: مِن أينَ أثبَتَّ الأنبياءَ؟ ـ: إنّا لَمّا أثبَتنا أنّ لَنا خالِقاً صانِعاً مُتَعالِياً عنّا وعن جَميعِ ما خَلَقَ، وكانَ ذلكَ الصّانِعُ حَكيماً مُتَعالِياً لَم يَجُزْ أن يُشاهِدَهُ خَلقُهُ، ولا يُلامِسوهُ، فيُباشِرَهُم ويُباشِروهُ، ويُحاجَّهُم ويُحاجُّوهُ، ثَبَتَ أنَّ لَهُ سُفَراءَ في خَلقِهِ يُعَبِّرونَ عَنهُ إلىٰ خَلقِهِ وعِبادِهِ، ويَدُلُّونَهُم علىٰ مَصالِحِهِم ومَنافِعِهِم، وما بِهِ بَقاؤهُم وفي تَركِهِ فَناؤهُم. ٦٦٤٣

2. Saving Mankind from the Rule of Tyrants

٢ ـ إنقاذُ الإنسانِ مِن وَلايةِ الطَّواغيتِ

"Certainly We raised an apostle in every nation [to preach:] 'Worship Allah, and keep away from the Rebel.' Then among them were some whom Allah guided, and among them were some who deserved to be in error. So travel over the land and then observe how was the fate of the deniers."[6683]

﴿وَلَقَدْ بَعَثْنَا فِي كُلِّ أُمَّةٍ رَسُولاً أَنِ اعْبُدُوا اللهَ وَاجْتَنِبُوا الطَّاغُوتَ فَمِنْهُمْ مَنْ هَدَى اللهُ وَمِنْهُمْ مَنْ حَقَّتْ عَلَيْهِ الضَّلَالَةُ فَسِيرُوا فِي الْأَرْضِ فَانْظُرُوا كَيْفَ كَانَ عَاقِبَةُ الْمُكَذِّبِينَ﴾. ٦٦٤٤

5921. **Imām ʿAlī (AS) said,** 'Allah, Blessed and most High, sent Muḥammad (SAWA) with the truth to bring out His servants from worshipping

٥٩٢١ . الإمامُ عليٌّ عليه السلام : إنّ اللهَ تبارَكَ وتَعالىٰ بَعَثَ مُحمّداً صلى الله عليه وآله بالحَقِّ لِيُخرِجَ عِبادَهُ مِن عِبادَةِ

His creatures into worshipping Him, from the covenants made with His creatures to His covenants, from obedience to His creatures to obedience to Him, and from being under the rule of His creatures to His rule.'[6684]

عِبادِهِ إلىٰ عِبادَتِهِ، ومِن عُهودِ عِبادِهِ إلىٰ عُهودِهِ، ومِن طاعَةِ عِبادِهِ إلىٰ طاعَتِهِ، ومِن وَلايَةِ عِبادِهِ إلىٰ وَلايَتِهِ.[٦٦٤٥]

3. Purifying Morals

٣ ـ تزكيةُ الأخلاقِ

"It is He who sent to the unled [people] an apostle from among themselves, to recite to them His signs, to purify them, and to teach them the Book and wisdom, and earlier they had indeed been in manifest error."[6685]

﴿هُوَ الَّذِي بَعَثَ فِي الْأُمِّيِّينَ رَسُولاً مِنْهُمْ يَتْلُو عَلَيْهِمْ آيَاتِهِ وَيُزَكِّيهِمْ وَيُعَلِّمُهُمُ الْكِتَابَ وَالْحِكْمَةَ وإن كانُوا مِنْ قَبلُ لَفِي ضَلالٍ مُبِينٍ﴾.[٦٦٤٦]

5922. **The Prophet (SAWA) said,** 'I was sent to complete the noble morals virtues.'[6686]

٥٩٢٢. رسولُ اللهِ ﷺ: بُعِثتُ لأُتَمِّمَ مَكارِمَ الأخلاقِ.[٦٦٤٧]

5923. **The Prophet (SAWA) said,** 'Verily I was sent to complete good morals.'[6687]

٥٩٢٣. عنه ﷺ: إنّما بُعِثتُ لأُتَمِّمَ حُسنَ الأخلاقِ.[٦٦٤٨]

5924. **Imām 'Alī (AS) said,** 'So He sent His messengers among them and He sent prophets one after another to help lead them to the covenant of their innate nature, and to remind them of His blessings that they have forgotten, to show them proofs through propagation, to extract for them the treasures of their intellects, and to show them the signs of His potential.'[6688]

٥٩٢٤. الإمامُ عليٌّ عليه السلام: فبَعَثَ فيهِم رُسُلَهُ وواتَرَ إلَيهِم أنبياءَهُ؛ لِيَستَأدُوهُم مِيثاقَ فِطرَتِهِ، ويُذَكِّروهُم مَنسِيَّ نِعمَتِهِ، ويَحتَجُّوا علَيهِم بالتَّبليغِ، ويُثيروا لَهُم دَفائنَ العُقولِ، ويُرُوهُم آياتِ المَقدِرَةِ.[٦٦٤٩]

4. Establishing Equity Among People

٤ ـ قيامُ النّاسِ بالقِسطِ

"Certainly We sent Our apostle with manifest proofs, and We sent down with them the Book and the Balance, so that mankind may maintain justice; and We sent down iron in which there is great might and use for mankind, and so that Allah may know those who help Him and His apostle in [their] absence. Indeed Allah is all-strong, all mighty."[6689]

﴿لَقَدْ أَرْسَلْنَا رُسُلَنَا بِالْبَيِّنَاتِ وَأَنْزَلْنَا مَعَهُمُ الْكِتَابَ وَالْمِيزَانَ لِيَقُومَ النَّاسُ بِالْقِسْطِ وَأَنْزَلْنَا الْحَدِيدَ فِيهِ بَأْسٌ شَدِيدٌ وَمَنَافِعُ لِلنَّاسِ وَلِيَعْلَمَ اللهُ مَنْ يَنْصُرُهُ وَرُسُلَهُ بِالْغَيْبِ إِنَّ اللهَ قَوِيٌّ عَزِيزٌ﴾.[٦٦٥٠]

5. Lifting Differences

٥ ـ رفعُ الاختلافِ:

"Mankind were a single community; then Allah sent the prophets as bearers of good news and as warners, and He

﴿كَانَ النَّاسُ أُمَّةً وَاحِدَةً فَبَعَثَ اللهُ النَّبِيِّينَ

sent down with them the Book with the truth, that it may judge between the people concerning that about which they differed, and none differed in it except those who had been given it, after the manifest proofs had come to them, out of envy among themselves. Then Allah guided those who had faith to the truth of what they differed in, by His will, and Allah guides whomever He wishes to a straight path."[6690]

مُبَشِّرِينَ وَمُنْذِرِينَ وَأَنْزَلَ مَعَهُمُ الْكِتابَ بِالْحَقِّ لِيَحْكُمَ بَيْنَ النَّاسِ فِيما اخْتَلَفُوا فِيهِ وَمَا اخْتَلَفَ فِيهِ إِلَّا الَّذِينَ أُوتُوهُ مِنْ بَعْدِ مَا جَاءَتْهُمُ الْبَيِّنَاتُ بَغْياً بَيْنَهُمْ فَهَدَى اللهُ الَّذِينَ آمَنُوا لِمَا اخْتَلَفُوا فِيهِ مِنَ الْحَقِّ بِإِذْنِهِ وَاللهُ يَهْدِي مَنْ يَشَاءُ إِلَىٰ صِرَاطٍ مُسْتَقِيمٍ﴾.[٦٦٥١]

5925. **Imām ʿAlī (AS) said,** 'Look at the various favours of Allah upon them, when He deputed towards them a prophet who got them to pledge their obedience to Him, and made them unite at his call. [Look] how [Allah's] bounty spread the wings of its favours over them and made flow for them streams of its blessing, and the whole community was covered in blissful prosperity. Consequently they were submerged under its bounty.'[6691]

٥٩٢٥. الإمامُ عليٌّ عليه السلام: أُنظُروا إلىٰ مَواقِعِ نِعَمِ اللهِ علَيهِم حِينَ بَعَثَ إلَيهِم رَسولاً فعَقَدَ بِمِلَّتِهِ طاعَتَهُم، وجَمَعَ علىٰ دَعوَتِهِ اُلفَتَهُم: كيفَ نَشَرَتِ النِّعمَةُ علَيهِم جَناحَ كَرامَتِها، وأسالَت لَهُم جَداوِلَ نَعيمِها، والتَفَّتِ المِلَّةُ بِهِم في عَوائدِ بَرَكَتِها، فأصبَحوا في نِعمَتِها غَرِقِينَ![٦٦٥٢]

6. Completing the Proof [against them]

٦ ـ إتمامُ الحُجّةِ

5926. **The Prophet (SAWA) said,** 'He sent messengers to them so that He would have the ultimate proof against His creation, and His messengers to them are witnesses over them. He sent among them prophets who were bearers of glad tidings and warners that those who contradict His evidence will perish, and that those who were revived by His evidence will be revived. And that servants may comprehend about their Lord that which they did not know, and come to know Him through His Lordship after they had denied it, and that they may profess His divine unity through His Godliness after they had advocated [it] [ascribing a partner for Him].'[6692]

٥٩٢٦. رسولُ اللهِ صلى الله عليه وآله: بَعَثَ إلَيهِمُ الرُّسُلَ لِتكونَ لَهُ الحُجّةُ البالِغَةُ علىٰ خَلقِهِ، ويكونَ رُسُلُهُ إلَيهِم شُهَداءَ علَيهِم، وابتَعَثَ فيهِمُ النَّبيّينَ مُبَشِّرينَ ومُنذِرينَ لِيَهلِكَ مَن هَلَكَ عَن بَيِّنَةٍ، ويَحيىٰ مَن حَيَّ عَن بَيِّنَةٍ، ولِيَعقِلَ العِبادُ عن رَبِّهِم ما جَهِلوهُ، فيَعرِفوهُ بِرُبوبيَّتِهِ بَعدَ ما أنكَروا، ويُوحِّدوهُ بالإلٰهِيّةِ بعد ما عَضَدوا.[٦٦٥٣]

1686. Categories of Prophets (AS)

١٦٨٦ ـ أصنافُ الأنبِياءِ عليهم السلام

"It is not [possible] for any human that Allah should speak to him except through revelation or from behind a curtain, or send a messenger who reveals by His

﴿وَمَا كَانَ لِبَشَرٍ أَنْ يُكَلِّمَهُ اللهُ إِلَّا وَحْياً أَوْ مِنْ وَرَاءِ حِجَابٍ أَوْ يُرْسِلَ رَسُولاً فَيُوحِيَ بِإِذْنِهِ

permission whatever He wishes. Indeed He is all-exalted, all-wise."[6693]

مَا يَشَاءُ إِنَّهُ عَلِيٌّ حَكِيمٌ﴾ .٦٦٥٤

5927. **Imām al-Ṣādiq (AS) said,** 'Prophets and Messengers are of four classes: a prophet who imparts the tidings to his own self and doe not extend to anyone else; a prophet who sees [the Unseen] in his sleep and hears sounds but does not see anything when awake, and he is not sent to anyone and he has a leader [Imām] over him, like how Prophet Abraham (AS) was to Prophet Lot (AS); a prophet who sees in his dream, and he hears and sees the angel, and he is sent to a group, be they small or large, like Prophet Jonah[6694] (AS). Allah said about Prophet Jonah (AS): *"We sent him to a [community of] hundred thousand or more,"*[6695] [He continued], '*or more*' by thirty thousand, and he has an Imām over him too; and a prophet who sees in his sleep, hears the voice, sees while awake, and he himself is an Imām [leader] like the arch-prophets, and Prophet Abraham (AS) was a prophet and not an Imām [leader] until Allah said, *"I am making you the Imām of mankind"*[6696 6697]

٥٩٢٧ . الإمامُ الصّادقُ عليه السلام : الأنبياءُ والمُرسَلونَ علىٰ أربَعِ طَبَقاتٍ: فنَبيٌّ مُنَبّأٌ في نَفسِهِ لا يَعدو غيرَها. ونَبيٌّ يَرىٰ في النَّومِ ويَسمَعُ الصَّوتَ ولا يُعايِنُهُ في اليَقَظَةِ، ولَم يُبعَثْ إلىٰ أحَدٍ وعلَيهِ إمامٌ، مِثل ما كانَ إبراهيمُ علىٰ لُوطٍ عليهما السلام. ونَبيٌّ يَرىٰ في مَنامِهِ ويَسمَعُ الصَّوتَ ويُعايِنُ المَلَكَ، وقد أُرسِلَ إلىٰ طائفةٍ قَلُّوا أو كَثُروا، كيُونُسَ، قالَ اللهُ ليونُسَ: ﴿وأرْسَلْناهُ إلىٰ مِائةِ ألْفٍ أو يَزيدونَ﴾ ٦٦٥٥ ـ قالَ: يَزيدونَ: ثلاثينَ ألفاً ـ وعليهِ إمامٌ. والّذي يَرىٰ في نَومِهِ ويَسمَعُ الصَّوتَ ويُعايِنُ في اليَقَظَةِ وهُو إمامٌ مِثلُ أُولي العَزمِ. وقد كانَ إبراهيمُ عليه السلام نَبيّاً وليسَ بإمامٍ حتّىٰ قالَ اللهُ: ﴿إنّي جاعِلُكَ للنّاسِ إماماً ...﴾ ٦٦٥٦، ٦٦٥٧

1687. The Number of Prophets (AS)

١٦٨٧ ـ عِدَّةُ الأنبِياءِ عليهم السلام

5928. **The Prophet (SAWA),** when Abū Dharr asked about the number of prophets, said, 'One hundred and twenty four thousand prophets.' I asked, 'How many of them are Messengers?' The Prophet said, 'Three hundred and thirteen altogether.' I asked, 'Who was the first of prophets?' He said, 'Adam.'[6698]

٥٩٢٨ . رسولُ اللهِ صلى الله عليه وآله ـ لمّا سَأَله أبو ذرّ عن عدّة الأنبياءِ ـ: مِائةُ ألفٍ وأربَعةٌ وعِشرونَ ألفَ نَبيٍّ. قلتُ: كَمِ المُرسَلونَ مِنهُم؟ قالَ: ثلاثُمِائةٍ وثلاثةَ عَشَرَ جَمّاءَ غَفيراءَ. قلتُ: مَن كانَ أوّلَ الأنبياءِ؟ قالَ: آدمُ. ٦٦٥٨

1688. The Arch-Prophets (*Ulū al-'Azm*)

١٦٨٨ ـ أُولو العَزمِ من الأنبياء

"So be patient just as the resolute among the apostles were patient, and do not seek to hasten [the punishment] for them. The day when they see what they are promised, [it will be] as though they had remained only an hour of a day. This is a proclamation. So shall anyone be destroyed except the transgressing lot?"[6699]

﴿فَاصْبِرْ كَمَا صَبَرَ أُولُوا الْعَزْمِ مِنَ الرُّسُلِ وَلَا تَسْتَعْجِلْ لَهُمْ كَأَنَّهُمْ يَوْمَ يَرَوْنَ مَا يُوعَدُونَ لَمْ يَلْبَثُوا إِلَّا سَاعَةً مِنْ نَهَارٍ بَلَاغٌ فَهَلْ يُهْلَكُ إِلَّا الْقَوْمُ الْفَاسِقُونَ﴾ .٦٦٥٩

5929. **Imām Zayn al-ʿĀbidīn (AS) said** to some of his companions, 'From the Messengers there are five arch-prophets.' We asked, 'Who are they?' He said, 'Noah, Abraham, Moses, Jesus, and Muḥammad, peace of Allah be upon them.' We asked, 'What does *Ulū al-ʿAẓm* mean?' He said, 'They were sent to the east of the earth and the west, to its Jinn and its humans.'[6700]

٥٩٢٩ الإمامُ زين العابدينَ ﷺ ـ لِبعضِ أصحابه ـ: مِنهُم خَمسَةٌ أُولو العَزمِ مِن الرُّسُلِ. قُلنا: مَن هُم؟ قالَ: نُوحٌ، وابراهيمُ، وموسىٰ، وعيسىٰ، ومحمّدٌ صلَّى اللهُ علَيهِم، قُلنا لَهُ: ما معنىٰ أُولو العَزمِ؟ قالَ: بُعِثوا إلىٰ شَرقِ الأرضِ وغَربِها، جِنِّها وإنسِها.[٦٦٠٠]

5930. **Imām al-Ṣādiq (AS),** when Sumāʿa b. Mihrān asked him about Allah's verse in the Qur'an: *"So be patient just as the resolute among the apostles were patient"*, said, 'Noah, Abraham, Moses, Jesus, and Muḥammad, peace be upon him, his progeny and them.' [Sumāʿa said,] I asked, 'How did they become the arch-prophets?' He said, 'Because Noah was sent with a divine book and law (*sharīʿa*), and all who came after him adopted Noah's book, law and teachings, until Abraham (AS) came with the Scriptures being commanded to leave Noah's book without disbelieving in it…'[6701]

٥٩٣٠. الإمامُ الصّادقُ ﷺ ـ لمّا سَألَه سماعةِ بن مِهران عن قوله تعالى: ﴿فاصْبِرْ كَما صَبَرَ أُولو العَزْمِ مِنَ الرُّسُلِ﴾ ـ: نُوحٌ، وإبراهيمُ؛ وموسىٰ، وعيسىٰ، ومحمّدٌ صلَّى الله عَليهِ وآلهِ وعلَيهِم. قلتُ: كيفَ صارُوا أُولي العَزمِ؟ قالَ: لأنَّ نُوحاً بُعِثَ بكِتابٍ وشَريعَةٍ، وكلُّ مَن جاءَ بعدَ نُوحٍ أخذَ بكِتابِ نُوحٍ وشَريعَتِهِ ومِنهاجِهِ، حتّىٰ جاءَ إبراهيمُ ﷺ بالصُّحُفِ وبعَزيمَةِ تَركِ كِتابِ نُوحٍ لا كُفراً بِهِ....[٦٦٠١]

1689. Special Characteristics of the Prophets (AS)

١٦٨٩ ـ خَصائِصُ الأنبِياءِ ﷺ

5931. **The Prophet (SAWA) said,** 'We the prophets have been commanded to speak to people according to the capacity of their intellects.'[6702]

٥٩٣١. رسولُ اللهِ ﷺ: إنّا مَعاشِرَ الأنبياءِ أُمِرنا أن نُكلِّمَ النّاسَ علىٰ قَدرِ عُقولِهِم.[٦٦٠٢]

5932. **The Prophet (SAWA) said,** 'We the prophets are such that our eyes sleep but our hearts do not sleep, and we see behind us as we see in front of us.'[6703]

٥٩٣٢. عنه ﷺ: إنّا مَعاشِرَ الأنبياءِ تَنامُ عُيونُنا ولا تَنامُ قُلوبُنا، ونَرىٰ مِن خَلفِنا كما نَرىٰ مِن بَينِ أيدِينا.[٦٦٠٣]

5933. **The Prophet (SAWA) said,** 'From the morals of the prophets and the righteous ones is smiling when they see people, and shaking hands when they meet each other.'[6704]

٥٩٣٣. عنه ﷺ: مِن أخلاقِ النَّبيِّينَ والصِّدِّيقينَ البَشاشَةُ إذا تَراءوا، والمُصافَحَةُ إذا تَلاقوا.[٦٦٠٤]

5934. **Qatāda narrated,** 'Allah has never sent a prophet without sending him with a handsome face and a pleasant voice.'[6705]

٥٩٣٤. قَتادَة: ما بَعَثَ اللهُ نَبيّاً قَطُّ إلّا بَعَثَهُ حَسَنَ الوَجهِ، حَسَنَ الصَّوتِ.[٦٦٠٥]

5935. **Imām ʿAlī (AS),** describing the prophets (AS), said, 'They were people who were subject to oppression, whom Allah had tried with hunger, afflicted with difficulty, tested with fear, and shaken with troubles. If Allah had wished to open for His prophets treasures of gold, mines of pure gold and grounds of gardens wherever He sent them… He would have done so, but if He did, tests would be invalid, and reward would be inapplicable. Rather, Allah the Glorified, made His prophets strong in their determination, and weak in their appearance as seen from the eyes, with contentment that fills the hearts and eyes with richness, and with poverty that pains the eyes and ears.'[6706]

٥٩٣٥ . الإمامُ عليٌّ ﵇ ـ في صِفَةِ الأنبياءِ: ـ: كـانُوا قَوماً مُستَضعَفِينَ، قَدِ اختَبرَهُمُ اللهُ بالمَخمَصَةِ، وابتَلاهُم بالمَجهَدَةِ، وامتَحَنَهُم بالمَخاوِفِ، ومَخَضَهُم بالمَكارِهِ…
ولو أرادَ اللهُ سبحانَهُ لأنبيائهِ حَيثُ بَعَثَهُم أن يَفتَحَ لَهُم كُنوزَ الذِّهْبانِ، ومَعادِنَ العِقْيانِ، ومَغارِسَ الجِنانِ… لَفعَلَ، ولَو فَعَلَ لَسَقَطَ البَلاءُ، وبَطَلَ الجَزاءُ…
ولكنَّ اللهَ سبحانَهُ جَعَلَ رُسُلَهُ أُولي قُوَّةٍ في عَزائمِهِم، وضَعَفةً فيما تَرَى الأعيُنُ مِن حالاتِهِم، مَعَ قَناعَةٍ تَملَأُ القُلوبَ والعُيونَ غِنىً، وخَصاصَةٍ تَملَأُ الأبصارَ والأسماعَ أذىً.[٦٦٦٦]

5936. **Imām al-Ṣādiq (AS) said,** 'Allah never sent a prophet unless He had made him herd sheep [first], through which He taught him how to manage people.'[6707]

٥٩٣٦ . الإمامُ الصّادقُ ﵇ : ما بَعَثَ اللهُ نَبيّاً قَطُّ حتّىٰ يَستَرعِيَهُ الغَنَمَ، يُعَلِّمُهُ بذلكَ رِعْيَةَ النّاسِ.[٦٦٦٧]

5937. **Imām al-Kāẓim (AS) said,** 'Allah, Almighty, did not send a prophet or a successor unless he was generous.'[6708]

٥٩٣٧ . الإمامُ الكاظمُ ﵇ : ما بَعَثَ اللهُ عَزَّوجلَّ نَبيّاً ولا وَصِيّاً إلّا سَخِيّاً.[٦٦٦٨]

5938. **Imām al-Riḍā (AS) said,** 'Cleanliness is of the morals of the prophets.'[6709]

٥٩٣٨ . الإمامُ الرِّضا ﵇ : مِن أخلاقِ الأنبياءِ التَّنَظُّفُ.[٦٦٦٩]

5939. **Imām al-Riḍā (AS) said,** 'Perfume is of the morals of the prophets.'[6710]

٥٩٣٩ . عنه ﵇ : الطِّيبُ مِن أخلاقِ الأنبياءِ.[٦٦٧٠]

(See also: THE ORDEAL: section 263)

(انظر) البلاء: باب ٢٦٣.

370

PROPHETHOOD (2)
Specific Prophethood

النُّبُوَّة (٢)
النُّبُوَّةُ الخاصَّةُ

1690. Adam (AS)

١٦٩٠ ـ آدمُ ﵇

"O mankind! Be wary of your Lord who created you from a single soul, and created its mate from it, and,

﴿يا أَيُّهَا النّاسُ اتَّقوا رَبَّكُمُ الَّذي خَلَقَكُم مِن

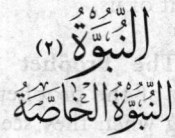

from the two of them, scattered numerous men and women. Be wary of Allah, in whose Name you adjure one another, and the wombs. Indeed Allah is watchful over you.'[6711]

نَفْسٍ وَ حِدَةٍ وَخَلَقَ مِنْها زَوْجَها وَبَثَّ مِنْهُمَا رِجَالاً كَثِيراً وَنِسَاءً وَاتَّقُوا اللهَ الَّذِي تَسَاءَلُونَ بِهِ وَالْأَرْحَامَ إِنَّ اللهَ كَانَ عَلَيْكُمْ رَقِيباً﴾ .[٦٦٧١]

5940. **Imām ʿAlī (AS),** describing the creation of Adam, said, 'Allah collected the hard, soft, sweet and sour of the earth, [making it into] clay by dipping it into water until it became pure, and then kneaded it with moisture till it became gluey. From it He carved an image with curves, joints, limbs and parts. He solidified it until it dried up, for a fixed time and a known duration. Then, He blew into it out of His Spirit whereupon it took the pattern of a human being with a mind that governs him, intelligence which he makes use of…. a mixture of clay of different colours, cohesive materials, divergent contraries and differing properties like heat and cold, softness and hardness.'[6712]

٥٩٤٠ . الإمامُ عليٌّ عليه السلام ـ في صِفَةِ خَلقِ آدمَ عليه السلام ـ: ثُمّ جَمَعَ سبحانَهُ مِن حَزْنِ الأرضِ وسَهْلِها، وعَذْبِها وسَبَخِها، تُربَةً سَنَّها (سَنّاها) بالماءِ حتّىٰ خَلَصَت، ولاطَها بالبَلَّةِ حتّىٰ لَزِبَت، فَجَبَلَ مِنها صُورَةً ذاتَ أحناءٍ ووُصولٍ، وأعضاءٍ وفُصولٍ، أجمَدَها حتّى استَمسَكَت، وأصلَدَها حتّىٰ صَلْصَلَت، لِوَقتٍ مَعدودٍ وأمَدٍ مَعلومٍ. ثُمّ نَفَخَ فيها مِن رُوحِهِ فَمَثُلَت (فتَمثّلَت) إنساناً ذا أذهانٍ يُجيلُها وفِكَرٍ يَتَصَرّفُ بها... مَعجوناً بطِينَةِ الألوانِ المُختَلِفَةِ، والأشباهِ المُؤتَلِفَةِ، والأضدادِ المُتَعادِيَةِ، والأخلاطِ المُتَبايِنَةِ، مِنَ الحَرِّ والبَردِ، والبَلَّةِ والجُمودِ.[٦٦٧٢]

5941. **Imām ʿAlī (AS) said,** 'When He had prepared the earth and enforced His commands, He chose Adam (AS) as the best of His creation and made him the first of human creation.'[6713]

٥٩٤١ . عنه عليه السلام : ...فلَمّا مَهَدَ أرضَهُ، وأنفَذَ أمرَهُ، اختارَ آدَمَ عليه السلام خِيَرَةً مِن خَلقِهِ، وجَعَلَهُ أوّلَ جِبِلَّتِهِ.[٦٦٧٣] [٦٦٧٤]

5942. **Imām al-Ṣādiq (AS) said,** 'Adam was named Adam because he was created from the surface (*adīm*) of the earth.'[6714]

٥٩٤٢ . الإمامُ الصّادقُ عليه السلام : إنّما سُمِّيَ آدَمُ آدَمَ لأنّهُ خُلِقَ مِن أديمِ الأرضِ.[٦٦٧٥]

5943. **Abū al-Miqdām said,** 'I asked Abū al-Jaʿfar [Imām al-Bāqir] (AS), 'What did Allah create Eve from?' He asked, 'What do people say about this?' I said, 'They say that Allah created her from one of the ribs of Adam.' He (AS) said, 'They lie, was He incapable of creating her from something other than his rib.' I said, 'May I be sacrificed for you, O son of the Prophet (SAWA), what did He create her from?' He (AS) said, 'My father told me, informing me from his fathers (AS) that the Prophet (SAWA) said, 'Allah, Blessed and most High, grabbed a handful of clay and mixed it with His right hand – and both His hands are right – and from it He

٥٩٤٣ . أبو المِقدامِ : سألتُ أباجعفرٍ عليه السلام : مِن أيِّ شيءٍ خَلقَ اللهُ حَوّاءَ ـ: أيَّ شيءٍ يقولُ هٰذا الخَلقُ؟
قلتُ: يقولونَ: إنّ اللهَ خَلَقَها من ضِلعٍ مِن أضلاعِ آدَمَ. فقالَ: كَذَبوا، كانَ يُعجِزُهُ أن يَخلُقَها مِن غَيرِ ضِلعِهِ؟! فقلتُ: جُعِلتُ فِداكَ يا ابنَ رسولِ اللهِ مِن أيِّ شيءٍ خَلَقَها؟ فقالَ: أخبَرَني أبي عن آبائهِ: قالَ: قالَ رسولُ اللهِ: إنّ اللهَ تباركَ وتعالىٰ قَبَضَ قَبضَةً مِن طِينٍ فخَلَطَها بيَمينِهِ ـ وكِلتا يَدَيهِ يَمينٌ ـ فخَلَقَ مِنها آدَمَ، وفَضَلَت فَضلَةٌ

created Adam, and with the rest of the clay He created Eve.'[6715]

مِن الطِّينِ فخَلَقَ مِنها حَوّاءَ.[٦٦٧٦]

5944. **Imām al-Riḍā (AS) said** in reply to al-Bazanṭi who asked about the offspring of Adam, 'Eve conceived Hābīl and a sister in one womb, and then Qābīl and a sister in another womb. Hābīl got married with the twin that was with Qābīl, and Qābīl got married to the one that was with Hābīl, then after this it became prohibited.'[6716]

٥٩٤٤. الإمامُ الرِّضا عليه السلام ـ وقد سألَهُ البَزَنطيُّ عن كيفيَّةِ تناسُلِ النّاسِ مِن آدمَ ـ: حَمَلَت حَوّاءُ هابيلَ وأُختاً لَهُ في بَطنٍ، ثُمّ حَمَلَت في البَطنِ الثّاني قابيلَ وأُختاً له في بَطنٍ، فزُوِّجَ هابيلُ الّتي معَ قابيلَ، وتَزوَّجَ قابيلُ الّتي مَعَ هابيلَ، ثُمّ حَدَثَ التَّحريمُ بعدَ ذلكَ.[٦٦٧٧]

1691. Enoch [Idrīs] (AS)

١٦٩١ ـ إدريسُ عليه السلام

"And mention in the Book Idrīs. Indeed he was a truthful one, a prophet, and We raised him to a station exalted."[6717]

﴿وَاذْكُرْ فِي الْكِتَابِ إِدْرِيسَ إِنَّهُ كَانَ صِدِّيقاً نَبِيّاً * وَرَفَعْنَاهُ مَكَاناً عَلِيّاً﴾.[٦٦٧٨]

5945. **The Prophet (SAWA) said,** 'Allah sent down onto Idrīs thirty Books.'[6718] [6719]

٥٩٤٥. رسولُ اللهِ ﷺ: أنزَلَ اللهُ على إدريسَ ثَلاثينَ صَحيفةً.[٦٦٧٩] [٦٦٨٠]

5946. **The Prophet (SAWA) said,** 'The first person who wrote by pen is Enoch (Idrīs) (AS).[6720]

٥٩٤٦. عنه ﷺ: أوّلُ مَن خَطَّ بالقَلمِ إدريسُ.[٦٦٨١]

5947. **Imām al-Ṣādiq (AS) said,** 'Al-Sahla mosque is where the house of Prophet Enoch (AS) was, wherein he would sew.'[6721]

٥٩٤٧. الإمامُ الصّادقُ عليه السلام: مَسجِدُ السَّهلَةِ مَوضِعُ بَيتِ إدريسَ النَّبيِّ عليه السلام الّذي كانَ يَخيطُ فيهِ.[٦٦٨٢]

1692. Noah (AS) [Nūḥ]

١٦٩٢ ـ نوحٌ عليه السلام

"Certainly We sent Noah to his people. He said, 'O my people, worship Allah! You have no other god besides Him. Indeed I fear for you the punishment of a tremendous day."[6722]

﴿لَقَدْ أَرْسَلْنَا نُوحاً إِلَىٰ قَوْمِهِ فَقَالَ يَا قَوْمِ اعْبُدُوا اللهَ مَا لَكُمْ مِنْ إِلَٰهٍ غَيْرُهُ إِنِّي أَخَافُ عَلَيْكُمْ عَذَابَ يَوْمٍ عَظِيمٍ﴾.[٦٦٨٣]

"Relate to them the account of Noah when he said to his people, 'O my people! If my stay [among you] be hard on you and [also] my reminding you of Allah's signs, [for my part] I have put my trust in Allah."[6723]

﴿وَاتْلُ عَلَيْهِمْ نَبَأَ نُوحٍ إِذْ قَالَ لِقَوْمِهِ يَا قَوْمِ إِنْ كَانَ كَبُرَ عَلَيْكُمْ مَقَامِي وَتَذْكِيرِي بِآيَاتِ اللهِ فَعَلَى اللهِ تَوَكَّلْتُ﴾.[٦٦٨٤]

(See also: 11:25-48, 21:76-77, 23:23-30, 26:105-122, 29:14-15, 37:75-82, 51:46, 54:9-17, 66:10, 71:1-28)

(انظر) هود: ٢٥ ـ ٤٨ والأنبياء: ٧٦، ٧٧ والمؤمنون: ٢٣ ـ ٣٠ والشعراء: ١٠٥ ـ ١٢٢ والعنكبوت: ١٤، ١٥ والصافات: ٧٥ ـ ٨٢ والذاريات: ٤٦ والقمر: ٩ ـ ١٧ والتحريم: ١٠ ونوح: ١ ـ ٢٨.

5948. **The Prophet (SAWA) said,** 'The first prophet to be sent down as a messenger was Noah.'[6724]

٥٩٤٨ . رسولُ اللهِ ﷺ : أوّلُ نَبيٍّ أُرسِلَ نُوحٌ.[٦٦٨٥]

5949. **The Prophet (SAWA) said,** 'Allah sent Noah as a prophet for forty years, and he stayed among his people for one thousand years minus fifty, calling them [to the truth]. He stayed alive for sixty years after the flood until the number of people increased and they spread out.'[6725]

٥٩٤٩ . عنه ﷺ : بَعَثَ اللهُ نُوحاً لأربَعينَ سَنةً، ولَبِثَ في قَومِهِ ألفَ سَنةٍ إلّا خَمسينَ عاماً يَدعُوهم، وعاشَ بعدَ الطُّوفانِ سِتّينَ سَنةً حتّىٰ كَثُرَ النّاسُ وفَشَوا.[٦٦٨٦]

5950. **Imām al-Bāqir (AS),** with regard to Allah's verse in the Qur'an: *"And none believed with him except a few"*[6726], said, 'They were eight.'[6727]

٥٩٥٠ . الإمامُ الباقرُ ﵇ ـ في قولِهِ تعالىٰ: ﴿وما آمَنَ مَعَهُ إلّا قَليلٌ﴾[٦٦٨٧] ـ: كانوا ثمانِيَةً.[٦٦٨٨]

5951. **Imām al-Bāqir (AS) said,** 'When Noah (AS) planted a seed a group of people walked by him and started to laugh and mock him, saying, 'He has now become a gardener!' When the palm tree grew and became great and high, he cut it down and worked it, and they said, 'He has become a carpenter!' He then made these into a boat, and a group of people came by, laughing and mocking, saying to him, 'He has now become a sailor in the desert of the earth!', until he finished [building] it.'[6728]

٥٩٥١ . عنه ﵇ : إنّ نُوحاً ﵇ لَمّا غَرَسَ النَّوىٰ مَرَّ علَيهِ قَومُهُ فجَعلوا يَضحَكونَ ويَسخَرونَ ويقولونَ: قد قَعَدَ غَرّاساً! حتّىٰ إذا طالَ النَّخلُ وكانَ جَبّاراً طُوالاً قَطَعَهُ ثُمّ نَحَتَهُ فقالوا: قد قَعَدَ نَجّاراً! ثُمّ ألّفَهُ فجَعَلَهُ سَفينَةً فمَرُّوا علَيهِ فجَعلوا يَضحَكونَ ويسخَرونَ ويقولونَ: قد قَعَدَ مَلّاحاً في فَلاةٍ من الأرضِ! حتّىٰ فَرَغَ مِنها.[٦٦٨٩]

5952. **Imām al-Bāqir (AS) said,** 'There were ten fathers between Adam and Noah (AS), and all of them were prophets.'[6729]

٥٩٥٢ . عنه ﵇ : كانَ بينَ آدَمَ وبينَ نُوحٍ ﵉ عَشرَةُ آباءٍ كلُّهُم أنبياءُ اللهِ.[٦٦٩٠]

His Story in the Qur'an

قِصّتُهُ ﵇ فِي القُرآنِ:

Sending him as a Prophet with a Message

بَعثُهُ وإرسالُهُ:

People after Adam were living as one nation very simply and guilelessly preserving their human nature, until a feeling of haughtiness spread among them and they gradually tried to rise above each other. Corruption spread during the time of Noah (AS) and people turned away from religion and monotheism, and from the tradition of social justice. They began to worship idols, and Allah Almighty mentioned some of them, like Wadd, Suwā', Yaghūth, Ya'ūq, and Nasr (Ṣūrah Nūḥ).

كان الناس بعد آدم ﵇ يعيشون أُمةً واحدةً علىٰ بساطة وسذاجة وهم علَى الفطرة الإنسانيّة؛ حتّىٰ فشا فيهم روح الاستكبار وآل إلَى استعلاء البعض علىٰ البعض تدريجيّاً...

فشاع في زمن نوح ﵇ الفساد في الأرض، وأعرض الناس عن دين التوحيد وعن سنّة العدل الاجتماعيّ، وأقبلوا علىٰ عبادة الأصنام. وقد سمَّى الله سبحانه منها وَدّاً وسُواعاً ويَغوث ويَعوق ونَسراً (سورة نوح).

Classes in society moved farther away from each other. Those who were strong, with wealth and children, bean to neglect the rights of the weak, and the tyrants began to humiliate those below them and rule over them as their desires dictated to them (Ṣūrah al-Aʿrāf, Hūd, Nūḥ).

وتباعدت الطبقات؛ فصار الأقوياء بالأموال والأولاد يضيّعون حقوق الضعفاء، والجبابرة يستضعفون مَن دونهم ويحكمون عليهم بما تهواه أنفسهم (الأعراف ـ هود ـ نوح).

So, Allah sent Noah to them with a divine book and law, calling them to the Oneness of Allah Almighty, and to refute a partner to Him, and to bring equity to the society through giving glad tidings and warnings to them (Qurʾan 2:213).

فبعث الله نوحاً ﵇ وأرسله إليهم بالكتاب والشريعة يدعوهم إلىٰ توحيد الله سبحانه وخلع الأنداد والمساواة فيما بينهم (البقرة: ٢١٣) بالتبشير والإنذار.

His Effort in Propagation

إجتهادُهُ ﵇ في دَعوتِهِ:

...and he (AS) would propagate to his people to believe in Allah and His signs, and he tried his hardest to do so. He called them to the truth day and night, and they did not respond to his call other than with arrogance and haughtiness...

وكان ﵇ يدعو قومه إلَى الإيمان بالله وآياته، ويبذل في ذلك غاية وسعه؛ فيندبهم إلَى الحقّ ليلاً ونهاراً وإعلاناً وإسراراً، فلا يجيبونه إلّا بالعناد والاستكبار...

Staying Among his People

لَبْثُهُ ﵇ في قَومِهِ:

He (AS) stayed among his people for nine hundred and fifty years calling them to Allah Almighty, and they only answered him with mockery and sarcasm. They called him insane and said that he only wanted to rule over them, until he sought help from his Lord (Ṣūrah al-ʿAnkabūt).

لبث ﵇ في قومه ألف سنة إلّا خمسين عاماً يدعوهم إلَى الله سبحانه، فلم يجيبوه إلّا بالهزء والسخرية ورميه بالجنون وأنّه يقصد به أن يتفضّل عليهم، حتّىٰ استنصر ربّه (سورة العنكبوت)...

Making the Ark

صَنْعُهُ ﵇ الفُلْكَ:

Allah Almighty ordered him to make an ark with His guidance and protection.

أمره الله تعالىٰ أن يصنع الفلك بتأييده سبحانه وتسديده فأخذ في صنعها...

The Descent of Punishment and the Starting of the Flood

نُزولُ العَذابِ ومَجيءُ الطوفان:

When the ark was completed, the command of Allah came and water gushed forth from the valley, Allah revealed to him to carry to his boat a pair of every animal and all his family members save those whom Allah had decreed to drown, who were his treacherous wife and his son who

حتّىٰ إذا تمّت صنعة الفلك وجاء أمر الله وفار التنّور أوحَى الله تعالىٰ إليه أن يحمل في السفينة من كلٍّ من الحيوان زوجَين اثنَين، وأن يحمل أهله إلّا من سبق عليه القول الإلٰهيّ بالغرق وهو

refused to board the ark. He was also ordered to take the believers (Ṣurah Hūd, al-Mu'minūn). When they all got onto the boat Allah opened the doors of the sky with pouring water and exploded the springs of water from the earth, meeting each other according to a designated measure (Ṣūrah al-Qamar). The water came up and the boat rose on it, floating above the waves like mountains (Ṣūrah Hūd).

امرأته الخائنة وابنه الذي تخلّف عن ركوب السفينة، وأن يحمل الذين آمنوا (سورتا هود والمؤمنون)، فلمّا حملهم وركبوا جميعاً فتح الله أبواب السماء بماء منهمر وفجّر الأرض عيوناً فالتقى الماء علىٰ أمر قد قُدِر (سورة القمر) وعلا الماءُ وارتفعت السفينة عليه وهي تسير في موج كالجبال (سورة هود)...

Fulfilling of the Command and his Descent onto the Ground with those Accompanying him

قَضاءُ الأمرِ ونُزولُهُ ومَن مَعه ﷺ إلَى الأرضِ :

When the flood encompassed everything and everyone drowned (as is mentioned in Ṣūrah al-Ṣaffāt:77) Allah ordered the earth to swallow its water and the sky to suck up the water, and the boat settled on the mountain of Jūdī…[6730]

فلمّا عمّ الطوفان وأغرق الناس (كما يظهر من سور: الصافّات آية ٧٧) أمر الله الأرض أن تبلع ماءها والسماء أن تقلع وغِيضَ الماء و استوت السفينة علىٰ جبل الجُوديّ...[٦٦٩١]

1693. Hūd (AS)[6731]

١٦٩٣ ـ هـودٌ ﷺ

"And to [the people of] 'Ād, Hūd, their brother. He said, 'O my people, worship Allah! You have no other god besides Him. Will you not then be wary [of Him]?'"[6732]

﴿وَإِلَىٰ عَادٍ أَخَاهُمْ هُوداً قَالَ يَا قَوْمِ اعْبُدُوا اللهَ مَالَكُمْ مِنْ إِلٰهٍ غَيْرُهُ أَفَلَا تَتَّقُونَ﴾ .[٦٦٩٢]

(See also: Qur'an 11:50-60, 23:31-41, 26:123-140, 41:13-16, 46:21-26, 51:41-42, 54:18-22, 69:4-8, 89:6-8)

(أُنظر) هود: ٥٠ ـ ٦٠ والمؤمنون: ١٣ ـ ٤١ والشعراء: ١٢٣ ـ ١٤٠ وفصّلت: ١٣ ـ ١٦ والأحقاف: ٢١ والحاقّة: ٤ ـ ٨ والفجر: ٦ ـ ٨.

5953. **Imām al-Bāqir (AS) said,** 'When Noah's prophethood finished and his time came to an end, Allah Almighty revealed to him: 'O Noah, you have fulfilled your prophethood and your days have come to an end, so put the knowledge you have, the faith, the Great Name, the heritage of knowledge and the legacy of the knowledge of prophethood in the offspring of your progeny…'. Noah informed Sām of the coming of Hūd (AS), and there were prophets between Noah and Hūd. Noah said, 'Allah will send a prophet by the name of Hūd. He will invite his people to Allah and they will refute him. Allah Almighty will destroy them with wind, and so those of you who live to see him must believe in him and follow him, for

٥٩٥٣ . الإمامُ الباقرُ ﷺ : إنّ نُوحاً ﷺ لَمّا انقَضَت نُبُوّتُهُ واستَكمَلَت أيّامُهُ أوحَى اللهُ عَزَّوجلَّ إلَيهِ أن: يا نُوحُ قد قَضَيتَ نُبُوّتَكَ واستَكمَلتَ أيّامَكَ، فاجعَلِ العِلمَ الّذي عِندَكَ والإيمانَ والاسمَ الأكبَرَ ومِيراثَ العِلمِ وآثارَ عِلمِ النُّبُوّةِ في العَقِبِ مِن ذُرّيَّتِكَ...

وبَشَّرَ نُوحٌ ساماً بِهُودٍ ﷺ، وكانَ فيما بينَ نُوحٍ وهُودٍ مِن الأنبياءِ. وقالَ نُوحٌ: إنّ اللهَ باعِثٌ نَبيّاً يُقالُ لَهُ: هُودٌ، وإنّهُ يَدعو قَومَهُ إلَى اللهِ عَزَّوجلَّ فَيُكَذِّبونَهُ واللهُ عَزَّوجلَّ مُهلِكُهُم بالرِّيحِ، فمَن أدرَكَهُ مِنكُم فَليُؤمِنْ بِهِ وليَتَّبِعْهُ فإنّ

Allah will save you from the punishment of the wind.'[6733]

اللهَ عَزَّوجلَّ يُنَجِّيهِ مِن عَذابِ الرِّيحِ.[٦٦٩٣]

5954. **Imām al-Ṣādiq (AS) said,** 'When Allah Almighty sent Hūd (AS), the descendants of Sām believed in him. As for the others, they said, 'Who can be stronger than us?' So they were destroyed with the barren wind. Hūd exhorted them and informed them of Ṣāliḥ (AS).'[6734]

٥٩٥٤. الإمامُ الصّادقُ عليه السلام: لَمّا بَعثَ اللهُ عَزَّوجلَّ هُوداً عليه السلام أسلَمَ لَهُ العَقِبُ مِن وُلدِ سامٍ، وأمّا الآخَرونَ فقالوا: مَن أشَدُّ مِنّا قُوَّةً؟! فاُهلِكوا بالرِّيحِ العَقيمِ، وأوصاهُم هُودٌ وبَشَّرَهُم بصالِحٍ عليه السلام.[٦٦٩٤]

Details of the Story of Hūd and his People 'Ād

إشارة إلى قِصَّةِ هُودٍ وقَومِهِ عادٍ

What the glorious Qur'an mentions about their story is that 'Ād – and they are also called the former 'Ād (Qur'an 53:50), indicating that there was a second 'Ād – was a group of people living in al-Ahqāf[6735] in the Arabian peninsula (Qur'an 46:21) after the people of Noah (Qur'an 7:69).

الذي يذكره القرآن الكريم من قصّتهم هو أنّ عاداً ـ وربّما يسمّيهم عاداً الأولىٰ (النجم: ٥٠) وفيه إشارة إلىٰ أنّ هناك عاداً ثانية ـ كانوا قوماً يسكنون الأحقاف[٦٦٩٥] من شبه جزيرة العرب (الأحقاف: ٢١) بعد قوم نوح (الأعراف: ٦٩)...

...the people were happily enjoying the bounties of Allah until they changed what was in their selves [their behaviour and morals], and paganism became deeply rooted in them and they built a sign on every hill with amusement.

So Allah sent to them their brother Hūd to call them to the Truth guiding them to worship Allah, to refute the idols, and to live with justice and mercy (Qur'an 26:130). He advised them greatly and spread exhortations among them. He enlightened the way, clarified the path, and cut off their excuses from them, and they repaid him with nothing but refusal and denial. So Allah sent punishment down upon them and sent down a barren wind that did not leave anything it came across without rendering it like decayed bones (Qur'an 51:42).[6736]

لم يزل القوم يتنعّمون بنعمة الله حتّىٰ غيّروا ما بأنفسهم، فتعرّقت فيهم الوثنيّة وبنوا بكلّ ريع آيةً يَعبثون...

فبعث الله إليهم أخاهم هوداً يدعوهم إلى الحقّ ويرشدهم إلىٰ أن يعبدوا الله ويرفضوا الأوثان ويعملوا بالعدل والرحمة (الشعراء: ١٣٠) فبالغ في وعظهم وبثّ النصيحة فيهم، وأنار الطريق وأوضح السبيل، وقطع عليهم العذر، فقابلوه بالإباء والامتناع...

فأنزل الله عليهم العذاب، وأرسل إليهم الريح العقيم ما تذر من شيء أتت عليه إلّا جعلته كالرميم (الذاريات: ٤٢)...[٦٦٩٦]

1694. Ṣāliḥ (AS)[6737]

١٦٩٤ ـ صالحٌ عليه السلام

"And to [the people of] Thamūd, Ṣāliḥ, their brother. He said, 'O my people, worship Allah! You have no other god

﴿وَإِلَىٰ ثَمُودَ أَخَاهُمْ صَالِحاً قَالَ يَا قَوْمِ اعْبُدُوا

beside him. There has certainly come to you a manifest proof from your Lord. This she-camel of Allah is a sign for you.'[6738]

اللهَ مَا لَكُمْ مِنْ إِلٰهٍ غَيْرُهُ قَدْ جَاءَتْكُمْ بَيِّنَةٌ مِنْ رَبِّكُمْ هَذِهِ نَاقَةُ اللهِ لَكُمْ آيَةً﴾.[٦٦٩٧]

(See also: Qur'an 11:61-68, 15:80-84, 26:141-159, 27:45-53, 41:17-18, 51:43-45, 54:23-32, 69:4-5, 89:9, 91:11-15)

(انظر) هود ٦١ ـ ٦٨ والحِجْر: ٨٠ ـ ٨٤ والشعراء: ١٤١ ـ ١٥٩ والنمل: ٤٥ ـ ٥٣ وفصّلت: ١٧، ١٨ والذاريات: ٤٣ ـ ٤٥ والقمر: ٢٣ ـ ٣٢ والحاقّة: ٤، ٥ والفجر: ٩ والشمس: ١١ ـ ١٥.

5955. **Imām ʿAlī (AS) said,** 'O people! Satisfaction and discontentment are what gather people [in categories]. And although it was only one man who slaughtered the she-camel of Thamūd, Allah included all of them in the punishment because they all accepted his action, as He Almighty said, '*"But they hamstrung her, whereupon they became regretful."*'[6739] So, it was not long before their land declined by sinking [into the earth] as the spike of a plough pierces weak, unploughed land.'[6740]

٥٩٥٥ـ الإمامُ عليٌّ عليه السلام: أيُّها النّاسُ، إنّما يَجمَعُ النّاسَ الرِّضىٰ والسُّخطُ، وإنّما عَقَرَ ناقَةَ ثَمودَ رجُلٌ واحِدٌ فعَمَّهُمُ اللهُ بالعَذابِ لَمّا عَمُّوهُ بالرِّضا، فقالَ سبحانَهُ: ﴿فعَقَرُوها فأصْبَحُوا نادِمينَ﴾[٦٦٩٨] فما كانَ إلّا أن خارَت أرضُهُم بالخَسفَةِ خُوارَ السِّكَّةِ المُحْماةِ في الأرضِ الخَوّارَةِ.[٦٦٩٩]

5956. **Abū Maṭar said,** 'When the wicked Ibn Muljam, may Allah curse him, struck the Commander of the Faithful (AS), Imām Ḥasan (AS) asked [his father], 'Shall I kill him?' The Imām said, 'No, but detain him and if I die, then kill him. When I die, bury me in this place between the graves of my brothers Hūd and Ṣāliḥ.'[6741]

٥٩٥٦ـ أبو مَطَرٍ: لَمّا ضَرَبَ ابنُ مُلجَمٍ الفاسِقُ لَعَنهُ اللهُ أميرَ المؤمنينَ عليه السلام قالَ لَهُ الحسَنُ: أقتُلُهُ؟ قالَ: لا ولكنِ احبِسْهُ؛ فإذا مُتُّ فاقتُلوهُ، وإذا مُتُّ فادفِنوني في هذا الظَّهرِ في قَبرِ أخَوَيَّ: هُودٍ وصالِحٍ.[٦٧٠٠]

Details of the Story of Ṣaliḥ and his People, Thamūd

إشارة إلى قِصّةِ صالحٍ وقَومِهِ ثَمودَ

Thamūd used to live according to the traditions of past nations and tribes, and their leaders and elders were ruling them. In the city that Ṣāliḥ was sent to there were nine groups of people who were corrupting on the earth and not reforming. (Qur'an 27:48). They rebelled in the earth, worshipped idols and exceeded in their unfairness and oppression. When Thamūd forgot their Lord and went to extremes in their ways, Allah sent the prophet Ṣāliḥ (AS) to them. He was from a dignified and respected house, known for their intellect and contentment (Qur'an 11:62, 27:49). He called them to the Oneness of Allah Almighty, to leave the worshipping of statues, and to live with justice and goodness in their society. He told them not

كانت ثمود تعيش علىٰ سنّة الشعوب والقبائل؛ يحكم فيهم سادتهم وشيوخهم. وقد كانت في المدينة التي بعث فيها صالح تسعة رهط يفسدون في الأرض ولا يصلحون (النمل: ٤٨) فطغوا في الأرض وعبدوا الأصنام وأفرطوا عتوّاً وظلماً.

لمّا نسيت ثمود ربّها وأسرفوا في أمرهم أرسل الله إليهم صالحاً النبيّ عليه السلام، وكان من بيت الشرف

exult on the earth, not to waste, and not to rebel. He warned them of punishment (Qur'an: Ṣūrah Hūd, Ṣūrah Shuʿarā', Ṣūrah Shams and others).

Then they rebelled and plotted, and they sent the most evil of them to kill the she-camel and so he slaughtered it. They said to Ṣāliḥ, 'Bring us what you threatened if you are of the truthful.' Ṣāliḥ (AS) said, 'Make merry in your abodes for three days, this is a threat which is not a lie.' (Qur'an 11:65).

The people of the city plotted and grouped against Ṣāliḥ. They divided the plan among themselves: We will detain him and his family, and then tell his guardian, 'We did not witness the ones who destroyed his family, and we are truthful.' They devised a plot, and Allah devised a plan, but they do not notice (Qur'an 27:50). A thunderbolt seized them as they looked on (Qur'an 51:44). The earthquake seized them, and they lay lifeless prostrate in their homes. So he abandoned them, and said, 'O my people! Certainly I communicated to you the message of my Lord, and I advised you, but you did not like advisers.' (Qur'an 7:78-79, 11:68) And We delivered those who had faith and were Godwary (Qur'an 41:18). A divine caller called after them, 'Verily, Thamūd disbelieved in their Lord. Verily away with Thamūd!'[6742]

والفَخار معروفاً بالعقل والكفاية (هود: ٦٢، النمل: ٤٩) فدعاهم إلىٰ توحيد الله سبحانه، وأن يتركوا عبادة الأصنام، وأن يسيروا في مجتمعهم بالعدل والإحسان، ولا يعلوا في الأرض ولا يسرفوا ولا يطغوا، وأنذرهم بالعذاب (هود، الشعراء، الشمس وغيرها).

ثمّ إنّهم طغوا ومكروا، وبعثوا أشقاهم لقتل الناقة فعقرها، وقالوا لصالح: ائتنا بما تعدنا إن كنت من الصادقين! قال صالح عليه السلام: تمتّعوا في داركم ثلاثة أيّام، ذلك وعد غير مكذوب (هود: ٦٥).

ثمّ مكرت شعوب المدينة وأرهاطها بصالح، وتقاسموا بينهم: لنُبيّتنّه وأهله ثمّ نقولنّ لوليّه: ما شهدنا مَهلِك أهله وإنّا لصادقون، ومكروا مكراً ومكرالله مكراً وهم لايشعرون (النمل: ٥٠) فأخذتهم الصاعقة وهم ينظرون (الذاريات: ٤٤) والرجفة والصيحة فأصبحوا في دارهم جاثمين، فتولّىٰ عنهم وقال: يا قوم لقد أبلغتكم رسالة ربّي ونصحت لكم، ولكن لاتحبّون الناصحين (الأعراف: ٧٩، هود: ٦٧) وأنجَى الله الذين آمنوا وكانوا يتّقون (فصّلت: ١٨) ونادى بعدهم المنادي الإلهيّ: ألا إنّ ثمود كفروا ربَّهم ألا بُعداً لثمود.[٦٧٠١]

1695. Abraham (AS) [Ibrāhīm]

١٦٩٥ ـ إبراهيمُ عليه السلام

"And when his Lord tested Abraham with certain words, and he fulfilled them, He said, 'I am making you the Imām of mankind,' Said he, 'And from among my descendants?' He said, 'My pledge does not extend to the unjust.'"[6743]

﴿وَإِذِ ابْتَلَىٰ إِبْرَاهِيمَ رَبُّهُ بِكَلِمَاتٍ فَأَتَمَّهُنَّ قَالَ إِنِّي جَاعِلُكَ لِلنَّاسِ إِمَاماً قَالَ وَمِنْ ذُرِّيَّتِي قَالَ لا يَنَالُ عَهْدِي الظَّالِمِينَ﴾.[٦٧٠٢]

(See also: Qur'an 3:65-68, 16:120-123, 2:125-132, 2:258, 2:260, 6:74-84, 9:114, 19:41-48, 21:51-73, 26:69-87, 29:16-18, 29:24, 29:27, 37:83-113, 43:26-28, 60:4-5, 53:36-38, 87:18-19, 11:69-76, 14:35-41, 22:26-27)

(أُنظر) آل عمران: ٦٥ ـ ٦٨ والنحل: ١٢٠ ـ ١٢٣ والبقرة: ١٢٥ ـ ١٣٢، ٢٥٨، ٢٦٠ والأنعام: ٧٤ ـ ٨٤ والتوبة: ١١٤ ومريم: ٤١ ـ ٤٨ والأنبياء: ٥١ ـ ٧٣ والشعراء: ٦٩ ـ ٨٧ والعنكبوت: ١٦ ـ ١٨، ٢٤، ٢٧ والصافّات: ٨٣ ـ ١١٣ والزخرف: ٢٦ ـ ٢٨ والممتحنة: ٤، ٥ والنجم: ٣٦ ـ ٣٨ والأعلى: ١٨، ١٩ وهود: ٦٩ ـ ٧٦ وإبراهيم: ٣٥ ـ ٤١ والحجّ: ٢٦، ٢٧.

5957. **The Prophet (SAWA) said,** 'On the 'day of the fire', Abraham was brought to the fire, and when he saw it he said, 'Allah is sufficient for us and He is the best supporter.'[6744]

٥٩٥٧. رسولُ اللهِ ﷺ: أُتِيَ بإبراهيمَ يومَ النّارِ إلَى النّارِ، فلَمّا أبصَرَها قالَ: حَسبُنا اللهُ ونِعمَ الوَكيلُ.٦٧٠٣

5958. **The Prophet (SAWA) said,** 'Allah took Abraham as a friend only because of his feeding of food [to others] and praying of prayers in the night while people were asleep.'[6745]

٥٩٥٨. عنه ﷺ: ما اتَّخَذَ اللهُ إبراهيمَ خَليلاً إلّا لإطعامِهِ الطَّعامَ، وصَلاتِهِ بالليلِ والنّاسُ نِيامٌ.٦٧٠٤

5959. **Ḥassān b. ʿAṭiyya said,** 'The first person to organise an army for war, with a right, left and middle wing was Abraham (AS), when he journeyed to fight those who imprisoned Lot (AS).'[6746]

٥٩٥٩. حَسّانُ بنُ عَطِيّةَ: أوَّلُ مَن رَتَّبَ العَسكَرَ في الحَربِ مَيمَنَةً ومَيسَرَةً وقَلباً إبراهيمُ ﷺ، لَمّا سارَ لِقِتالِ الّذينَ أسَرُوا لُوطاً ﷺ.٦٧٠٥

5960. **Imām al-Bāqir (AS) said,** 'Allah Almighty took Abraham as a friend because he did not refuse anyone, and did not ask anyone other than Allah Almighty.'[6747]

٥٩٦٠. الإمامُ الباقرُ ﷺ: اتَّخَذَ اللهُ عَزَّوجلَّ إبراهيمَ خَليلاً لأنّهُ لَم يَرُدَّ أحَداً، ولَم يَسألْ أحَداً غيرَ اللهِ عَزَّوجلَّ.٦٧٠٦

5961. **Imām al-Ṣādiq (AS) said,** 'Allah Almighty took Abraham as a servant before He took him as a prophet. Allah took him as a prophet before He took him as a messenger. Allah took him as a messenger before He took him as a friend, and Allah took him as a friend before He took him as an Imām. When He gathered all these things in Abraham He said, *"I am making you the Imām of mankind."*'[6748 6749]

٥٩٦١. الإمامُ الصّادقُ ﷺ: إنّ اللهَ تباركَ وتعالى اتَّخَذَ إبراهيمَ عَبداً قَبلَ أن يَتَّخِذَهُ نَبيّاً، وإنّ اللهَ اتَّخَذَهُ نَبيّاً قَبلَ أن يَتَّخِذَهُ رَسولاً، وإنّ اللهَ اتَّخَذَهُ رَسولاً قَبلَ أن يَتَّخِذَهُ خَليلاً، وإنّ اللهَ اتَّخَذَهُ خَليلاً قَبلَ أنْ يَجعَلَهُ إماماً، فلَمّا جَمَعَ لَهُ الأشياءَ قالَ: ﴿إنّي جاعِلُكَ لِلنّاسِ إماماً﴾.٦٧٠٧

The Story of Abraham (AS) in the Holy Qur'an

قِصّةُ إبراهيمَ ﷺ في القرآنِ الكريمِ:

Abraham (AS) from his young childhood till his age of puberty was living in seclusion from the community of his people. He then returned to them and joined his uncle, but saw him and his group worshipping idols and did not accept his or their actions. He started to debate with them about the issue of idol worship (Qur'an 20:51-56, 26:69-77, 37:83-87), and he debated with other people in their beliefs in worshipping the sun, moon, and the stars until he demonstrated the

«كان إبراهيم ﷺ ـ في طفوليّته إلى أوائل تمييزه ـ يعيش في معزل من مجتمع قومه، ثمّ خرج إليهم ولحق بأبيه فوجده وقومه يعبدون الأصنام، فلم يرتض منه ومنهم ذلك... يحاجّ القوم في أمر الأصنام (الأنبياء: ٥١ ـ ٥٦، الشعراء: ٦٩ ـ ٧٧، الصافّات: ٨٣ ـ ٨٧) ويحاجّ أقواماً آخرين منهم يعبدون الشمس والقمر والكوكب في أمرها حتّى ألزمهم الحقّ، وشاع خبره في الانحراف عن الأصنام والآلهة

proof to them. News of him and his deviation from these idols and false gods spread (Qur'an 6:74-82). One day a group went out for congregational worship outside of the city, but he came up with the excuse of being sick. He therefore did not leave with them and he stayed behind. He went to the house where the statues were kept and started demolishing them, reducing them to dust, but he left the big statue for them so that they would refer to it. When they came back and learnt of what had happened to their gods and searched for who the culprit was, they were told: We heard a young person by the name of Abraham mentioning them.

(الأنعام: ٧٤ ـ ٨٢) حتّىٰ خرج القوم ذات يـوم إلىٰ عبادةٍ جامعة خارجَ البلد واعتلّ هو بالسقم فلم يخرج معهم وتخلّف عـنهم، فـدخل بـيت الأصـنام فـراغ عـلىٰ آلهـتهم ضـرباً بـاليمين فجعلهم جُذاذاً إلّا كبيراً لهم لعلّهم إليه يرجعون، فلمّا تراجعوا وعلموا بما حدث بآلهتهم وفتّشوا عمّن ارتكب ذلك قالوا: سمعنا فـتىً يـذكرهم يقال له: إبراهيم.

They brought him to their gathering and put him in front of all the people so that they could witness. They ordered him to speak, saying, 'Are you the one who has done this to our gods, O Abraham?' He said, 'No, rather it was the big one of them who did it, so ask them if they can speak.' He had left the biggest of the statues and had not broken it and had put an axe on its shoulder or something similar to that, so that he could demonstrate that it was the big statue that had broken the other statues.

فأحضروه إلىٰ مجمعهم فأتوا بـه عـلىٰ أعـين الناس لعلّهم يشهدون، فاستنطقوه فقالوا: أأنت فعلت هذا بآلهتنا يا إبراهـيم؟ قـال: بـل فـعله كبيرهم هذا فاسألوهم إن كانوا يـنطقون، وقـد كان أبقىٰ كبيرَ الأصنام ولم يجذّه ووضع الفأس على عاتقه أو ما يقرب من ذلك؛ ليشهد الحـال علىٰ أنّه هو الذي كسر سائر الأصنام.

They said, 'Burn him and help your gods!' So, they built a building and ignited it. All the people participated, and they threw him in the fire, but Allah made it cold and safe for him and nullified their conspiracy (Qur'an 21:57-70, 37:88-98).

قالوا: حَرِّقوه وانصروا آلهتكم، فـبنوا له بـنياناً وأسعروا فيه جحيماً من النار، وقد تشارك فى أمره الناس جميعاً وألقوه في الجحيم، فـجعله الله بَرداً عليه وسلاماً وأبطل كيدهم (الأنـبياء: ٥٧ ـ ٧٠، الصافّات: ٨٨ ـ ٩٨)...

Then when Allah had rescued him from the fire, he began to call people to the upright religion, the religion of monotheism, but only a small group of people believed. Abraham (AS) and some of the believers with him then disclaimed all association with their people, and he disassociated himself from Āzar whom he used to call a father but who was not his real father.[6750] He migrated with his wife and Lot (AS) to the sacred land to call to Allah Almighty without any obstacle impeding them from their oppressive crude people (Qur'an 60:4, 21:71).

ثمّ لمّا أنجاه الله من النار أخذ يدعو إلَى الديـن الحنيف دين التوحيد، فآمن له شرذمة قليلة...

ثمّ تبرّأ هو ﷺ ومـن مـعه مـن المـؤمنين مـن قومهم، وتبرّأ هو من آزر الذي كان يـدعوه أباً ولم يكن بـوالده الحـقيقيّ[٦٧٠٨]، وهـاجر ومـعه زوجته ولوط إلَى الأرض المـقدّسة ليـدعو الله سبحانه من غير معارض يـعارضه مـن قـومه

الجفاة الظالمين (الممتحنة: ٤، الأنبياء: ٧١).

Allah Almighty gave him the glad tidings there of Ishmael and Isaac, and of Jacob after Isaac. Abraham (AS) became very old and he had Ishmael, and then Isaac was born, and Allah blessed him and his two children and their children.

وبشّره الله سبحانه هناك بإسماعيل وبإسحاق ومن وراء إسحاق يعقوب، وقد شاخ وبلغه كبر السنّ فولد له إسماعيل ثمّ ولد له إسحاق، وبارك الله سبحانه فيه وفي ولدَيه وأولادهما.

Then, due to a command from his Lord, Abraham went to the land of Makkah – which was an untilled valley - and he left his son Ishmael to live there who was at that time a young child, and he went back to the sacred land. Ishmael grew up there and a group of Arabs gathered around him who were inhabitants there and the city of Makkah was established from then. Abraham (AS) might have visited Ishmael in the land of Makkah before building Makkah and the House and after it (Qur'an 2:126, 14:35-41). Abraham then built the Kaʿba in it – the Sacred House – with the help of Ishmael. It was the first house made for the people by Allah Almighty as a blessing and a [source of] guidance for all mankind. In it are signs and evidences, the site (*maqām*) of Abraham, and whoever enters it will be safe (Qur'an 2:127-129, 3:96-97). He proclaimed the obligatory pilgrimage to it (*ḥajj*) to people and legislated the rituals of *ḥajj* (Qur'an 22:26-30).

ثمّ إنّه ؑ بأمر من ربّه ذهب إلىٰ أرض مكّة ـ وهي وادٍ غير ذي زرع ـ فأسكن فيه ولده إسماعيل وهو صبيّ ورجع إلى الأرض المقدّسة، فنشأ إسماعيل هناك، واجتمع عليه قوم من العرب القاطنين هناك، وبُنيت بذلك بلدة مكّة.

وكان ؑ ربّما يزور إسماعيل في أرض مكّة، قبل بناء مكّة والبيت وبعد ذلك (البقرة: ١٢٦، إبراهيم: ٣٥ ـ ٤١). ثمّ بنىٰ بها الكعبة البيت الحرام، بمشاركة من إسماعيل. وهي أوّل بيت وُضع للناس من جانب الله مباركاً وهُدىً للعالمين، فيه آيات بيّنات مقام إبراهيم ومن دخله كان آمناً (البقرة: ١٢٧ ـ ١٢٩، آل عمران: ٩٦، ٩٧) وأذّنَ في الناس بالحجّ، وشرّع نسك الحجّ (الحجّ: ٢٦ ـ ٣٠).

Allah then ordered him to slaughter his son Ishmael (AS) [in sacrifice] and so he left with his son to the rituals. When he reached the [place of the] *Saʿī* he said, 'My son! I see in a dream that I am sacrificing you. See what you think.' He said, 'Father! Do whatever you have been commanded. If Allah wills, you will find me to be of the patient.' So when they had both submitted [to Allah's will], and he had laid him down on his forehead, it was called out to him, 'O Abraham! You have indeed

ثمّ أمره الله بذبح ولده إسماعيل ؑ فخرج معه للنُّسك، فلمّا بلغ معه السعي قال: يا بُنيّ إنّي أرىٰ في المنام أنّي أذبحك، قال: يا أبتِ افعل ما تُؤمر ستجدني إن شاء الله من الصابرين، فلمّا أسلما وتلّه للجبين نودي أن: يا إبراهيم، قد

fulfilled the vision!' And so Allah ransomed him with a great sacrifice. (Qur'an 101-107).[6751]

صدّقتَ الرؤيا، وفداه الله سبحانه بـذِبح عـظيم (الصافّات: ١٠١ـ١٠٧).٦٧٠٩

1696. Lot (AS) [*Lūṭ*]

١٦٩٦ ـ لُـوطٌ عليه السلام

"And Lot, when he said to his people, 'What! Do you commit an outrage none in the world ever committed before you?!'"[6752]

﴿وَلُوطاً إِذْ قـالَ لِـقَوْمِهِ أَتَأْتُـونَ الْـفَاحِشَةَ مَـا سَبَقَكُمْ بِهَا مِنْ أَحَدٍ مِنَ الْعَالَمِينَ﴾ .٦٧١٠

(See also: Qur'an 11:77-83, 15:51-77, 21:74-75, 26:160-175, 27:54-58, 29:28-35, 37:133-138, 51:24-37, 54:33-40, 66:10)

(أُنظر) هود: ٧٧ ـ ٨٣ والحِجر: ٥١ ـ ٧٧ والأنبياء: ٧٤، ٧٥ والشعراء: ١٦٠ ـ ١٧٥ والنمل: ٥٤ ـ ٥٨ والعنكبوت: ٢٨ ـ ٣٥ والصافّات: ١٣٣ ـ ١٣٨ والذاريات: ٢٤ ـ ٣٧ والقمر: ٣٣ ـ ٤٠ والتحريم: ١٠.

5962. **Imām al-Bāqir (AS) said,** 'As for the village that was rained upon with rain of punishment, it was the village of Sodom, the village of the people of Lot. Allah rained rocks of baked earth upon them, meaning clay.'[6753]

٥٩٦٢ . الإمامُ الباقرُ عليه السلام : وأمّا القَريَةُ الّتي أُمطِرَت مَطرَ السَّوءِ فهِيَ سَدُومُ قَريَةُ قومِ لُوطٍ ، أمطَرَ اللهُ علَيهِم حِجارَةً مِن سِجِّيلٍ، يقولُ: مِن طِينٍ.٦٧١١

5963. **Imām al-Ṣādiq (AS) said,** 'Allah did not send a prophet after Lot without having dignity among his people.'[6754 6755]

٥٩٦٣ . الإمامُ الصّادقُ عليه السلام : ما بَعَثَ اللهُ نَبيّاً بعدَ لُوطٍ إلّا في عِزٍّ مِن قَومِهِ.٦٧١٢

Details of the Story of Lot and his People

إشارة إلى قِصّةِ لوطٍ عليه السلام وقَومِهِ

Lot (AS) was from Kildān, from the land of Babylon. He was from among the first and foremost of those to believe in Abraham (AS), and he said, *"Indeed I am migrating toward my Lord"*[6756] Allah rescued him with Abraham to the sacred land, the land of Palestine (Qur'an 21:71). Lot resided in one of its cities, which was the city of Sodom as is mentioned in history, the Torah and other narrations.

The people of this city and the other cities surrounding it – as Allah named them 'the towns that were overturned' (Qur'an 9:70) – worshipped idols and committed obscenities, such as sodomy, and they were the first people to practice this among themselves (Qur'an 7: 80). They committed this act in their gatherings without denouncing. This outrageous sin continued to spread until it became a national custom that the general public were practicing.

«كان لوط عليه السلام من كلدان في أرض بـابل ومـن السابقين الأوّلين ممّن آمن بإبراهيم عليه السلام، آمن به وقال: ﴿إنّي مُهاجِرٌ إلىٰ ربِّي﴾ ٦٧١٣، فنجّاه الله مع إبـــراهـــيم إلَـــى الأرض المـــقدّسة أرضِ فلسطين (الأنبياء: ٧١) فنزل في بعض بـلادها وهي مدينة سَدوم علىٰ ما في التواريخ والتوراةَ وبعض الروايات.

وكان أهل المدينة وما والاها من المدائن ـ وقد سمّاها الله في كـلامه بـ «المُـؤتَفِكات»(التـوبة: ٧٠) ـ يعبدون الأصـنام، ويأتـون بـالفاحشة: اللواط، وهم أوّل قوم شاع فيهم ذلك (الأعراف: ٨٠) حتّى كانوا يأتون به في نواديهم مـن غـير إنكار، ولم يَزَل تشيع الفاحشة فيهم حتّىٰ عادت

They neglected women and cut off procreation (Qur'an 29:29).

سُنّة قومية ابتلت به عامّتهم، وتركوا النساء وقطعوا السبيل (العنكبوت: ٢٩).

So Allah sent Lot (AS) to them (Qur'an 26:162) and he called them to have fear in Allah and to relinquish their obscene actions, and to return to the path of nature. He warned them and scared them, but it only increased their rebellion, and their answer was nothing but, 'Bring us the punishment of Allah if you are of the truthful!' They threatened him with expulsion from their city and said to him, *"...if you do not relinquish you will surely be banished"* [6757] and *"They said, 'expel Lot's family from your town! They are indeed a puritanical lot.'"*[6758]

فأرسل الله لوطاً إليهم (الشعراء: ١٦٢) فدعاهم إلىٰ تقوَى الله وترك الفحشاء والرجوع إلىٰ طريق الفطرة، وأنذرهم وخوّفهم، فلم يَزِدهم إلّا عُتوّاً ولم يكن جوابهم إلّا أن قالوا: ائتِنا بعذاب الله إن كنت من الصادقين! وهدّدوه بالإخراج من بلدتهم، وقالوا له: ﴿لَئن لَم تَنْتَهِ يا لُوطُ لَتَكُونَنَّ مِنَ المُخْرَجينَ﴾ [٦٧١٤] و﴿قالوا أخْرِجوا آلَ لُوطٍ مِنْ قَرْيَتِكُم إنّهُمْ أُناسٌ يَتَطَهَّرونَ﴾.[٦٧١٥]

...until rebellion was firmly established in them and they became deserving of the word of punishment, Allah sent to them messengers from among the eminent angels to destroy them. They came to Lot in the form of youths visiting him as guests. This became hard for Lot and a predicament for their sake, because of what he knew about his people and what they would do to them and that they would certainly not leave them. It was not long before the people heard about them and rushed towards him, charging at his house. He went out to them and excessively advised them and reminded them of their youthfulness and maturity, and he even offered them [to marry] his own daughters, saying: 'O my people, these are my daughters: they are purer for you. Be wary of Allah and do not humiliate me with regard to my guests.' He then asked for assistance saying, 'Is there not a single right-minded man among you?' They replied by saying that they had no need for his daughters and would certainly not leave his guests, until Lot lost hope and said, *"If only I had the power to deter you, or could take refuge in a mighty support!"*[6759]

حتّى استقرّ بهم الطغيان وحقّت عليهم كلمة العذاب، فبعث الله رسلاً من الملائكة المكرّمين لإهلاكهم...

فمضوا إلى لوط في صُوَرِ غِلمان مُرد ودخلوا عليه ضيفاً، فشقّ ذلك علىٰ لوط وضاق بهم ذرعاً؛ لِما كان يعلم من قومه أنّهم سيتعرّضون لهم وأنّهم غير تاركيهم البتّة، فلم يلبث دون أن سمع القوم بذلك وأقبلوا يُهرَعون إليه وهم يستبشرون، وهجموا علىٰ داره، فخرج إليهم وبالغ في وعظهم واستثارة فُتوّتهم ورشدهم حتّىٰ عرض عليهم بناته، وقال: يا قوم، إنّ هؤلاء بناتي هنّ أطهر لكم، فاتّقوا الله ولا تخزوني في ضيفي. ثمّ استغاث وقال: أليس منكم رجل رشيد؟! فردّوا عليه أنّه ليس لهم في بناته إربة، وأنّهم غير تاركي أضيافه البتّة، حتّىٰ أيس لوط وقال: ﴿لَوْ أنّ لِي بِكُمْ قُوَّةً أو آوِي إلىٰ رُكْنٍ شَديدٍ﴾.[٦٧١٦]

The angels then said, 'O Lot, we are messengers from your Lord, do not worry, the people will not reach you.' They then blinded the eyes of the

قالت الملائكة عند ذلك: يا لوط إنّا رسل ربّك، طِب نفساً إنّ القوم لن يصلوا إليك. فطمسوا

people and they dispersed them making them insane and they departed (Qur'an 54:37). The Cry then took them over at dawn, and Allah sent down upon them stones of clay, marked by your Lord for the profligate. He upturned their cities on top of them and turned them upside down, and He picked out those therein who were faithful, but did not find other than one house of *muslims* (believers), which was the house of Lot, and He left therein a sign for those who fear a painful punishment (Qur'an 51:37, and other verses).[6760]

أعين القوم فعادوا عـمياناً يـتخبّطون وتـفرّقوا (القمر: ٣٧).
فأخذت الصيحةُ القوم مُشـرِقين، وأرسـل الله عليهم حـجارة مـن طـين مُسـوَّمة عـند ربّك للمسرفين، وقلبَ مدائنهم عليهم فجعل عاليَها سافلَها، وأخرج من كان فيها من المؤمنين فلم يجد فيها غير بيت مـن المسـلمين وهـو بـيت لوط، وترك فيها آية للـذين يـخافون العـذاب الأليم (الذاريات: ٣٧ وغيرها).[٦٧١٧]

1697. Jacob and Joseph (AS) [*Ya'qūb* and *Yūsuf*]

١٦٩٧ ـ يَعقوبُ ويوسُفُ عليهما السلام

"Abraham enjoined this [creed] upon his children, and [so did] Jacob, [saying], 'My children! Allah has indeed chosen this religion for you; so never die except as muslims.' Were you witnesses when death approached Jacob, when he said to his children, 'What will you worship after me?' They said, 'We will worship your God, and the God of your fathers, Abraham, Ishmael, and Isaac, the One God, and to Him do we submit.'"[6761]

﴿وَوَصَّىٰ بِهَا إِبْرَاهِيمُ بَنِيهِ وَيَعْقُوبُ يَا بَنِيَّ إِنَّ اللَّهَ اصْطَفَىٰ لَكُمُ الدِّينَ فَلَا تَمُوتُنَّ إِلَّا وَأَنْتُمْ مُسْلِمُونَ ۞ أَمْ كُنْتُمْ شُهَدَاءَ إِذْ حَضَرَ يَعْقُوبَ الْمَوْتُ إِذْ قَالَ لِبَنِيهِ مَا تَعْبُدُونَ مِنْ بَعْدِي قَالُوا نَعْبُدُ إِلَٰهَكَ وَإِلَٰهَ آبَائِكَ إِبْرَاهِيمَ وَإِسْمَاعِيلَ وَإِسْحَاقَ إِلَٰهاً وَاحِداً وَنَحْنُ لَهُ مُسْلِمُونَ﴾.[٦٧١٨]

5964. *Amālī al-Ṭūsī*, from Mūsā b. Sa'īd al-Rāsibī, who said, 'When Jacob went to Joseph (AS), Joseph came out with a group of people to receive him. He went past the wife of the governor while she was worshipping in one of her rooms. When she saw him she recognised him and called out to him with a sad voice, 'O rider, how long you have rendered me sorrowful - how good piety is indeed in how it frees slaves! And how bad sinning is indeed in how it enslaves the free!'[6762]

٥٩٦٤. الأمالي للطوسي: لَمّا قَدِمَ يَعقوبُ علىٰ يوسفَ عليه السلام خَرَجَ يُوسفُ عليه السلام فاستَقبَلَهُ في مَوكِبِهِ، فَمَرَّ بامرأةِ العَزيزِ وهِيَ تَعبُدُ في غُرفَةٍ لَها، فلَمّا رأتهُ عَرَفَتهُ فنادَتهُ بصَوتٍ حَزينٍ: أيُّـها الرّاكِبُ طالَ ما أحـزَنتَني، مـا أحسَـنَ التَّـقوىٰ كـيفَ حَرَّرَتِ العَبيدَ؟! وما أقبَحَ الخَطيئةَ كيفَ عَبَّدَتِ الأحرارَ؟![٦٧١٩]

5965. **The Prophet (SAWA) said,** 'Joseph was given a good share of beauty.'[6763]

٥٩٦٥. رسولُ اللهِ صلى الله عليه وآله: أُعـطِيَ يُـوسُفُ شَـطرَ الحُسنِ.[٦٧٢٠]

5966. **The Prophet (SAWA) said,** 'The honourable, son of the honourable, son of the honourable, son of the honourable is Joseph, son of Jacob, son of Isaac, son of Abraham.'[6764]

٥٩٦٦. عنه صلى الله عليه وآله: الكريمُ ابنُ الكريمِ ابنِ الكريمِ ابنِ الكريمِ: يُوسفُ بـنُ يَـعقوبَ بـنِ إسـحاقَ بـنِ إبراهيمَ.[٦٧٢١]

5967. **Imām al-Ṣādiq (AS) said,** 'When the sons of Jacob asked him to allow Joseph to go outside with them, he said to them, *'I fear the wolf may eat him while you are oblivious of him'.* [6765] ......, 'Jacob suggested to them an excuse which they later used as a deception for Joseph.'[6766]

٥٩٦٧ـ الإمامُ الصّادقُ ؈ : إنّ بني يَعقوبَ لمّا سَألوا أباهُم يَعقوبَ أن يَأذَنَ ليوسُفَ في الخُروجِ مَعهُم، قالَ لَهم: ﴿إنّي أخافُ أن يأكُلَه الذئبُ وَأنتم غافِلون﴾[٦٧٢٢]... قَرَّبَ يَعقوبُ لَهُم العِلّةَ اعتلّوا بها في يوسُفَ.[٦٧٢٣]

1698. Job (AS) [Ayyūb]

١٦٩٨ـ أيُّوبُ ؈

"And Job, when he called out to his Lord, 'Indeed distress has befallen me, and You are the most merciful of the merciful.' We answered his prayer and removed his distress, and We gave him [back] his family along with others like them, as a mercy from Us, and an admonition for the devout."[6767]

﴿وَأَيُّوبَ إِذْ نَادَىٰ رَبَّهُ أَنِّي مَسَّنِيَ الضُّرُّ وَأَنْتَ أَرْحَمُ الرَّاحِمِينَ * فَاسْتَجَبْنَا لَهُ فَكَشَفْنَا مَا بِهِ مِنْ ضُرٍّ وَآتَيْنَاهُ أَهْلَهُ وَمِثْلَهُمْ مَعَهُمْ رَحْمَةً مِنْ عِنْدِنَا وَذِكْرَىٰ لِلْعَابِدِينَ﴾[٦٧٢٤].

(See also: Qur'an 38:41-44)

(أنظر) ص: ٤١ ـ ٤٤.

5968. **The Prophet (SAWA) said,** 'Allah Almighty revealed unto Job (AS), 'Do you know what your sin to Me was when you were struck with calamities?' He said, 'No.' Allah Almighty said, 'You went to Pharaoh and you flattered him with two words.'[6768]

٥٩٦٨. رسولُ اللهِ ﷺ: قالَ اللهُ عزّوجلَّ لأيُّوبَ: أتدري ما كانَ جُرمُكَ إلَيَّ حتّى ابتَلَيتُكَ؟ قالَ: [لا][٦٧٢٥] يارَبِّ! قالَ: لأنَّكَ دَخَلتَ على فِرعَونَ فادَّهَنتَ بكَلِمَتَينِ.[٦٧٢٦]

5969. **The Prophet (SAWA) said,** 'Job was the most tolerant and patient of people, and the strongest at suppressing his anger.'[6769]

٥٩٦٩. عنه ﷺ: كانَ أيُّوبُ أحلَمَ النّاسِ، وأصبَرَ النّاسِ، وأكظَمَ النّاسِ لِغَيظٍ.[٦٧٢٧]

5970. **Ibn ʿAbbās narrated,** 'The wife of Job (AS) said to him one day, 'If only you supplicated to Allah to cure you!' He said, 'Woe unto you! We enjoyed blessings for seventy years, so lets be patient with calamities in its equivalent!' The narrator says, 'He did not stay after this for long until he was cured.'[6770]

٥٩٧٠. ابن عبّاس: إنّ امرأةَ أيُّوبَ ؈ قالَت لَهُ يوماً: لَو دَعَوتَ اللهَ أن يَشفيَكَ! فقالَ: وَيحَكِ! كُنّا في النَّعماءِ سَبعينَ عاماً فهَلُمَّ نَصبِرْ في الضَّرّاءِ مِثلَها! قالَ: فلَم يَمكُثْ بعدَ ذلكَ إلّا يَسيراً حتّى عوفِيَ.[٦٧٢٨]

5971. **Imām al-Ṣādiq (AS) said,** 'Job was afflicted for seven years without having committed a single sin.'[6771]

٥٩٧١. الإمامُ الصّادقُ ؈ : ابتُلِيَ أيُّوبُ سَبعَ سِنينَ بلا ذَنبٍ.[٦٧٢٩]

5972. **Imām al-Ṣādiq (AS) said,** 'Allah, Blessed and most High, afflicted Job (AS) without him committing a single sin, and he was patient until he was mocked, and prophets do not tolerate being mocked.'[6772]

٥٩٧٢. عنه ؈ : إنّ اللهَ تَبارَكَ وتَعالَى ابتَلَى أيُّوبَ ؈ بلا ذَنبٍ، فصَبَرَ حتّى عُيِّرَ، وإنّ الأنبياءَ لا يَصبِرونَ علَى التَّعييرِ.[٦٧٣٠]

5973. **Imām al-Ṣādiq (AS) said,** 'Job never asked for wellbeing in any of the calamities he was struck with.'[6773]

٥٩٧٣ . عنه ﷺ : ماسَألَ أيُّوبُ ﷺ العافِيَةَ في شَيءٍ مِن بَلائهِ.[٦٧٣١]

1699. Shuʿayb (AS)[6774]

١٦٩٩ ـ شُعَيبٌ ﷺ

"And to [the people of] Midian, Shuʿayb, their brother. He said, 'O my people, worship Allah! You have no other god besides Him. There has certainly come to you a manifest proof from your Lord. Observe fully the measure and the balance, and do not cheat the people of their goods, and do not cause corruption on the earth after its restoration. That is better for you, if you are faithful.'...Those who impugned Shuʿayb became as if they had never lived there. Those who impugned Shuʿayb were themselves the losers."[6775]

﴿وَإِلَىٰ مَدْيَنَ أَخَاهُمْ شُعَيْباً قَالَ يَا قَوْمِ اعْبُدُوا اللهَ مَالَكُمْ مِنْ إِلٰهٍ غَيْرُهُ قَدْ جَاءَتْكُمْ بَيِّنَةٌ مِن رَبِّكُمْ فَأَوْفُوا الْكَيْلَ وَالْمِيزَانَ وَلا تَبْخَسُوا النَّاسَ أَشْيَاءَهُمْ وَلا تُفْسِدُوا فِي الأَرْضِ بَعْدَ إِصْلَاحِهَا ذٰلِكُمْ خَيْرٌ لَكُمْ إِنْ كُنْتُمْ مُؤْمِنِينَ ﴿... الَّذِينَ كَذَّبُوا شُعَيْباً كَأَنْ لَمْ يَغْنَوْا فِيهَا الَّذِينَ كَذَّبُوا شُعَيْباً كَانُوا هُمُ الخَاسِرِينَ﴾.[٦٧٣٢]

(See also: 11:84-95, 15:78-79, 26:176-190, 28:45, 29:36-37, 50:14)

(أُنظر) هود: ٨٤ ـ ٩٥ والحِجر: ٧٨، ٧٩ والعشراء: ١٧٦ ـ ١٩٠ والقصص: ٤٥ والعنكبوت: ٣٦، ٣٧ وق: ١٤.

5974. **Imām al-Ṣādiq (AS) said,** 'Allah Almighty only sent five prophets from the Arabs: Hūd, Ṣāliḥ, Ishmael, Shuʿayb, and Muḥammad, the seal of the prophets, peace of Allah be upon them; and Shuʿayb was one who cried very much.'[6776]

٥٩٧٤ . الإمامُ الصّادقُ ﷺ : لَم يَبعَثِ اللهُ عَزَّوجلَّ مِنَ العَرَبِ إلّا خمسَةَ أنبياءَ: هُوداً وصالِحاً وإسماعيلَ وشُعَيباً ومُحمّداً خاتمَ النَّبيِّينَ صلواتُ اللهِ علَيهِم، وكانَ شُعَيبٌ بَكّاءً.[٦٧٣٣]

Details of the Story of Shuʿayb and his People in the Holy Qur'an*

إشارة إلى قِصّةِ شُعَيبٍ ﷺ وقَومِهِ فِي القُرآنِ الكريمِ:

He (AS) was from Midian – a city on the way to Shām from the Arabian Peninsula – and he was a contemporary of Moses (AS). He married one of his two daughters to Moses on condition that he hire Moses to work for him for eight years, and if he worked for ten years, then it would be his own choice (Qur'an 28:27). Moses served him for ten

كان ﷺ من أهل مدَين ـ مدينة في طريق الشام من الجزيرة ـ وكان معاصراً لموسىٰ ﷺ، وقد زوّجه إحدىٰ ابنتيه علىٰ أن يأجُره ثمانيَ حِجج وإن أتمّ عشراً فمن عنده (القصص: ٢٧)، فخدمه موسىٰ عشر سنين، ثمّ ودّعه وسار بأهله إلىٰ مصر.

* Shuʿayb (AS) was the third Arab prophet whose name was mentioned in the Qur'an, along with Hūd, Ṣāliḥ and Muḥammad (SAWA). Allah Almighty speaks parts of his story in chapters: Aʿrāf [7], Hūd [11], Shuʿarā' [26], Qaṣaṣ [28], and ʿAnkabūt [29].

years, and he then bid farewell to him leaving for Egypt with his family.

His people from Midian worshipped idols and were blessed with security, luxury, fertile land, and cheap prices. Corruption spread among them, and the defrauding of weights and measures became common (Qur'an 11:84, and others). Allah then sent Shuʿayb to them and commanded him to forbid them from worshipping statues, causing corruption on the earth, and defrauding scales and weights. Shuʿayb invited them to what he had been commanded and advised them by warning them [of chastisement] and giving them glad tidings [of Paradise]. He also reminded them of what had happened to the people of Noah, Hūd, Ṣāliḥ, and Lot.

وكان قومه من أهل مَديَن يعبدون الأصنام، وكانوا قوماً مُنعَّمين بالأمن والرفاهية والخصب ورخص الأسعار، فشاع الفساد بينهم والتطفيف بنقص المكيال والميزان (هود: ٨٤ وغيرها)، فأرسل الله إليهم شعيباً وأمره أن ينهاهم عن عبادة الأصنام وعن الفساد في الأرض ونقص المكيال والميزان، فدعاهم إلىٰ ما أُمر به، ووعظهم بالإنذار والتبشير، وذكّرهم ما أصاب قوم نوح وقوم هود وقوم صالح وقوم لوط.

He (AS) excessively debated with them and exhorted them, but it only increased their rebellion, disbelief and corruption (Qur'an: Ṣūrah Aʿrāf, Ṣūrah Hūd, and others). None but a small group of people believed in him, and people started hurting, mocking and threatening the followers of Shuʿayb (AS). They lay in every street corner, threatening and barring from the path of Allah those who believed in Him, seeking to deviate them from the right path (Qur'an 7:86).

وبالغ عليه السلام في الاحتجاج عليهم وعظتهم فلم يزدهم إلّا طغياناً وكفراً وفسوقاً (الأعراف وهود وغيرهما من السور). ولم يؤمنوا به إلّا عدّة قليلة منهم، فأخذوا في إيذائهم والسخرية بهم وتهديدهم عن اتّباع شعيب عليه السلام، وكانوا يقعدون بكلّ صراط يوعدون ويصدّون عن سبيل الله من آمن به ويبغونها عِوَجاً (الأعراف: ٨٦).

They accused him (AS) of being enchanted and that he was a liar (Qur'an 26:185,186). They threatened him and those who believed in him of expulsion from their village unless they reverted back to their creed (Qur'an 7:88). They continued to abuse them until they made him lose hope in them, so he left them to themselves (Qur'an 11:93). Shuʿayb prayed to Allah for victory and said, 'O Lord, give us victory over our people in truth, and You are the best of those who give victory.' Allah *then sent the punishment* that occurred on the cloudy day (Qur'an 26:189), and they were mocking him, saying, 'Throw onto us punishment from the Heavens if you are of the truthful', and the Cry seized them, and the earthquake seized them (Qur'an 11:94, 7:91, 29:37), so they lay lifeless

وأخذوا يرمونه عليه السلام بأنّه مسحور وأنّه كاذب (الشعراء: ١٨٥، ١٨٦) وأخافوه بالرجم، وهدّدوه والذين آمنوا به بالإخراج من قريتهم أو ليعودنّ في ملّتهم (الأعراف: ٨٨). ولم يزالوا به حتّىٰ أيأسوه من إيمانهم، فتركهم وأنفسهم (هود: ٩٣). ودعا الله بالفتح قال: ربّنا افتح بيننا وبين قومنا بالحقّ وأنت خير الفاتحين.
فأرسل الله إليهم عذاب يوم الظُّلّة (الشعراء: ١٨٩)، وقد كانوا يستهزؤون به أن أسقِطْ علينا كسفاً من السماء إن كنت من الصادقين، وأخذتهم الصيحة (هود: ٩٤) والرجفة

prostrate in their homes, and He delivered Shuʿayb and the faithful who were with him (Qurʾan 11:94). So he abandoned them and said, *'O my people! Certainly I communicated to you the messages of my Lord, and I was your well-wisher. So how should I grieve for a faithless lot?'* (Qurʾan 7:93).[6777]

(الأعراف: ٩١، العنكبوت: ٣٧) فأصبحوا في ديارهم جاثمين، ونجّى شعيباً ومن معه من المؤمنين (هود: ٩٤) فتولّىٰ عنهم وقال: يا قوم لقد أبلغتكم رسالات ربّي ونصحت لكم، فكيف آسىٰ علىٰ قوم كافرين ؟! (الأعراف: ٩٣). ٦٧٣٤

1700. Moses and Aaron (AS) (Mūsā and Hārūn)

١٧٠٠ ـ موسىٰ وهارونُ عليهما السلام

"Certainly We gave Moses and Aaron the Distinguisher, as a light and reminder for the Godwary."[6778]

﴿وَلَقَدْ آتَيْنَا مُوسَىٰ وَهَارُونَ الْفُرْقَانَ وَضِيَاءً وَذِكْراً لِلْمُتَّقِينَ﴾. ٦٧٣٥

"and apostles We have recounted to you earlier and apostle We have not recounted to you, and to Moses Allah spoke directly."[6779]

﴿ورُسُلاً قَدْ قَصَصْنَاهُم عَلَيْكَ مِنْ قَبْلُ وَرُسُلاً لَمْ نَقْصُصْهُمْ عَلَيْكَ وَكَلَّمَ اللهُ مُوسَىٰ تَكْلِيماً﴾. ٦٧٣٦

(See also: Qurʾan 2:49-93, 11:17, 11:110, 5:20-26, 14:5-8, 19:51-53, 32:23-24, 33:69, 37:114-122, 40:53-54, 41:45, 46:12, 28:3-46, 8:52-54, 10:75-93, 17:101-104, 20:9-97, 23:45-49, 26:10-68, 38:12, 40:23-46, 43:46-56, 66:11, 8:103-156, 7:159-162, 44:17-33, 51:38-40, 62:5, 73:15-16, 79:15-26)

(اُنظر) البقرة: ٤٩ ـ ٩٣ وهود: ١٧، ١١٠ والمائدة: ٢٠ ـ ٢٦ وإبراهيم: ٥ ـ ٨ ومريم: ٥١ ـ ٥٣ والسجدة: ٢٣، ٢٤ والأحزاب: ٦٩ والصافّات: ١١٤ ـ ١٢٢ والمؤمن: ٥٣، ٥٤ و فصّلت: ٤٥ والأحقاف: ١٢ والقصص: ٣ ـ ٤٦ والأنفال: ٥٢ ـ ٥٤ ويونس: ٧٥ ـ ٩٣ والإسراء: ١٠١ ـ ١٠٤ وطه: ٩ ـ ٩٧ والمؤمنون: ٤٥ ـ ٤٩ والشعراء: ١٠ ـ ٦٨ وص: ١٢ والمؤمن: ٢٣ ـ ٤٦ والزخرف: ٤٦ ـ ٥٦ والتحريم: ١١ والأعراف: ١٠٣ ـ ١٥٦، ١٥٩ ـ ١٦٢ والدخان: ١٧ ـ ٣٣ والذاريات: ٣٨ ـ ٤٠ والصفّ: ٥ والمزّمل: ١٥، ١٦ والنازعات: ١٥ ـ ٢٦.

5975. **Imām al-Ṣādiq (AS) said,** 'Allah revealed unto Moses son of ʿImrān (AS), 'Do you know O Moses why I picked you from My creation and chose you to speak to?' He said, 'No, O Lord.' So Allah revealed to him, 'I looked at the earth and did not find anyone on it more humble before Me than you.'[6780]

٥٩٧٥. الإمامُ الصّادقُ عليه السلام: أوحَى اللهُ إلىٰ موسَى بنِ عِمرانَ عليه السلام: أتَدري يا موسىٰ لِمَ انتَجَبتُكَ مِن خَلقي واصطَفَيتُكَ لِكَلامي؟ فقالَ: لا يا ربِّ، فأوحَى اللهُ إلَيهِ: إنّي اطَّلَعتُ إلَى الأرضِ فلَم أجِدْ علَيها أشَدَّ تَواضُعاً لي مِنكَ. ٦٧٣٧

5976. **The Prophet (SAWA) said,** 'The first prophet from the Children of Israel (*Banī Isrāʾīl*) was Moses and the last of them was Jesus, and [they had] six hundred prophets.'[6781]

٥٩٧٦. رسولُ اللهِ صلى الله عليه وآله: أوّلُ نَبيٍّ من بَني إسرائيلَ موسىٰ، وآخِرُهُم عيسىٰ، وسِتُّمِائةِ نَبيٍّ. ٦٧٣٨

5977. *al-Ṭabaqāt al-Kubrā*: Ibn ʿAbbās narrated, 'The Prophet (SAWA) said, 'I saw Jesus, Moses and Abraham. As for Jesus, he had shrivelled, red skin and broad shoulders. Moses was a well-built person,

٥٩٧٧. الطبقات الكبرىٰ عن ابن عباس: قالَ رسولُ اللهِ صلى الله عليه وآله: إنّي رَأيتُ عيسىٰ وموسىٰ وإبراهيمَ؛ فأمّا عيسىٰ فجَعْدٌ أحمَرُ عَريضُ الصَّدرِ، وأمّا موسىٰ فآدِمٌ جَسِيمٌ سَبْطٌ كأنّهُ مِن

heavy as if he was a gipsy.' He was asked, 'And Abraham?' He said, 'Look at your friend', referring to himself.'[6782]

رِجالِ الزُّطِّ ، فقالوا لَهُ : إبراهيمُ ؟ فقالَ : انـظُروا إلىٰ صـحِبِكُم ؛ يَعني رسولَ اللهِ ﷺ نفسَهُ .[٦٧٣٩]

5978. **Imām ʿAlī (AS) said,** 'Praise be to Allah...who spoke to Moses directly and showed him His great signs without the use of body parts, tools, the organ of speech or the uvula.'[6783]

٥٩٧٨ . الإمامُ عليٌّ ؑ : الحَمدُ للهِ... الّذي كَلَّمَ موسىٰ تَكلِيماً ، وأراهُ مِـن آيـاتِهِ عَـظيماً ، بـلا جَوارِحَ ولا أدَواتٍ ، ولا نُطقٍ ولا لَهَواتٍ .[٦٧٤٠]

5979. **Imām ʿAlī (AS) said** in describing the asceticism of the prophets, 'If you want, I will give a second example of Moses, the interlocutor of Allah (AS), when he said, '*My Lord I am indeed in need of any good You may send down to me!*'[6784] By Allah, he did not ask Him for anything other than bread to eat because he used to eat the herbs of the earth.'[6785]

٥٩٧٩ . عنه ؑ ـ في بيان زهد الأنبياء ـ : وإنْ شئتَ ثَنَّيتُ بموسىٰ كَليمِ اللهِ ؛ حَـيثُ يـقولُ : ﴿رَبِّ إنّي لِما أنْزَلْتَ إلَيَّ مِن خَيرٍ فَقيرٌ﴾[٦٧٤١] واللهِ ، ما سَألَهُ إلّا خُبزاً يأكُلُهُ ، لأنّهُ كانَ يأكُـلُ بَقلَةَ الأرضِ .[٦٧٤٢]

5980. **Imām al-Ṣādiq (AS) said,** 'When the Pharaoh realised that Moses would be the cause of the downfall of his kingdom, he called the divinators and they told him of Moses's lineage and that he was from the Children of Israel. Pharaoh continued to order his men to cut open the stomachs of all the pregnant women from the Children of Israel until he killed in his search more than twenty thousand children, but he was not able to kill Moses because Allah the Almighty protected him.'[6786]

٥٩٨٠ . الإمامُ الصّادقُ ؑ : إنّ فِرعَونَ لَمّا وَقَفَ علىٰ أنّ زَوالَ مُلكِهِ علىٰ يدِ موسىٰ أمرَ بإحضارِ الكَهَنَةِ ، فدَلّوهُ علىٰ نَسَبِهِ وأنّهُ مِن بَني إسرائيلَ ، فلَم يَزَلْ يأمُرُ أصحابَهُ بِشَقِّ بُطونِ الحَوامِلِ مِن بَني إسرائيلَ حتّىٰ قَتَلَ في طَلَبِهِ نَيّفاً و عِشرينَ ألفَ مَولودٍ ، وتَـعَذّرَ عـلَيهِ الوُصـولُ إلىٰ قَـتلِ موسىٰ ؛ لِحفظِ اللهِ تباركَ وتعالىٰ إيّاهُ .[٦٧٤٣]

Details of the Story of Moses and Aaron (AS)

كلامٌ حَولَ قِصَصِ مُوسىٰ وهارونَ ؑ :

He was born in Egypt in an Israeli house at the time when all the male newborns of the Children of Israel were being slaughtered by Pharaoh's order. His mother concealed him in a casket and threw him in the sea. Pharaoh then took him and returned him to his mother [not knowing that she was his mother and thinking her to be a wet-nurse] so that she could nurse him and bring him up, and he grew up in Pharaoh's house.

أنّه تولّد بمصر في بيتٍ إسرائيليّ حـينما كـانوا يذبحون المواليد الذّكور من بني إسرائيل بأمـر فرعون ، وجعلت أُمّه إيّاه في تابوت وألقته في البـحر ، وأخـذ فـرعون إيّـاه ثـمّ ردّه إلىٰ أمّـه للإرضاع والتربية ونشأ في بيت فرعون .

Moses became mature, killed someone from the Pharaoh's tribe [accidentally] and fled from Egypt to Midian in fear that Pharaoh and his men would kill him in retribution [for his action]. He stayed in Midian with Shuʿayb (AS) and married one of his two daughters.

ثمّ بلغ أشدّه وقتل القبطيّ وهرب من مصر إلىٰ مَديَن خوفاً من فرعون وملئه أن يقتلوه قصاصاً.
ثمّ مكث في مَدين عند شعيب النبيّ ﷺ، وتزوّج إحدىٰ بنتيه.

When Moses had fulfilled the stay required of him there, he then left with his family, and saw the fire on the side of Mount Sinai, as they had lost their way in the cold, rainy night. He stopped them there and went to the fire to bring for them a brand from it, or find some guidance at the fire. So when he came to it, Allah called him from the right side of valley in the sacred place of the Tree. He, Almighty, spoke to him and chose him, and gave him the miracles of the staff and the glowing hand among nine other signs. He, Almighty, elected him to give the message to Pharaoh and his people and to save the Children of Israel, and He ordered him to go to him.

ثمّ لمّا قضىٰ موسَى الأجل وسار بأهله آنس من جانب الطور ناراً وقد ضلّوا الطريق في ليلة شاتية، فأوقفهم مكانهم وذهب إلَى النّار ليأتيهم بقبسٍ أو يجد علَى النار هدى، فلمّا أتاها ناداه الله من شاطئ الوادي الأيمن في البقعة المباركة من الشجرة، وكلّمه واجتباه وآتاه معجزة العصا واليد البيضاء في تسع آيات، واختاره للرسالة إلىٰ فرعون وملئه وانجاء بني إسرائيل وأمره بالذهاب إليه.

Moses went to Pharaoh and invited him to the word of Truth and asked to send the Children of Israel with him, and not to punish them. He showed Pharaoh the miracle of the stick and the glowing hand, but he rejected and countered him with the sorcery of the magicians. The magicians came with great magic with pythons and snakes, but Moses threw his stick on the ground and it swallowed what they had faked. The magicians fell down in prostration, saying, 'We believe in the Lord of the worlds, the Lord of Moses and Aaron.' Pharaoh insisted in his disbelief and threatened the magicians and did not believe.

فأتىٰ فرعون ودعاه إلىٰ كلمة الحقّ وأن يرسل معه بني إسرائيل ولا يعذّبهم، وأراه آية العصا واليد البيضاء فأبىٰ، وعارضه بسحر السَّحَرة وقد جاؤوا بسحر عظيم من ثعابين وحيّات، فألقىٰ عصاه فإذا هي تلقف ما يأفكون، فألقي السّحرة ساجدين قالوا: آمنّا بربّ العالمين ربّ موسىٰ وهارون، وأصرّ فرعون علىٰ جحوده وهدّد السَّحَرة ولم يؤمن.

Moses (AS) continuously invited Pharaoh and his followers to belief showing them sign after sign, like the flood, the locusts, the lice, the frogs, the blood, and other manifest signs, but they persisted in their haughtiness. Whenever evil would befall them, they would say, 'O Moses, pray to your Lord for us for what He has bestowed unto you that if you were to take away this evil we will believe in

فلم يزل موسىٰ ﷺ يدعوه وملأه ويريهم الآية بعد الآية كالطوفان والجراد والقمّل والضفادع والدم آياتٍ مفصّلاتٍ وهم يصرّون علَى استكبارهم، وكلّما وقع عليهم الرّجز قالوا: يا موسىٰ، ادع لنا ربّك بما عَهِد عندك لئن كشفت عنّا الرجز لنؤمننّ لك ولنرسلنّ معك بني

you and we will send the Children of Israel with you. But when Allah took away the punishment for an allocated time, they would break their commitment.

إسرائيل، فلمّا كشف الله عنهم الرجز إلىٰ أجـل هم بالغوه إذا هم ينكثون.

Allah then ordered him to leave with the Children of Israel during the night, and they left until they got to the sea shore, with Pharaoh and his soldiers pursuing them. When the two sides sighted each other, Moses' companions said, 'Indeed we have been caught', to which he replied, 'Certainly not! Indeed my Lord is with me. He will guide me.' Then he was commanded to strike the sea with his staff, whereupon it parted. So they crossed the sea, with Pharaoh and his hosts following them. When all of them had reached the shore, Allah closed the water back over them [i.e. Pharaoh and his hosts] and drowned every last one of them.

فأمره الله أن يسري ببني إسرائيل ليلاً، فساروا حتّىٰ بلغوا ساحل البحر، فعقّبهم فرعون بجنوده فلمّا تراءى الفريقان قال أصحاب موسىٰ: إنّا لَمُدرَكون. قال: كلّا إنّ معي ربّي سيهدين. فأُمر بأن يضرب بعصاه البحر فانفلق الماء فجاوزوا البحر، وأتبعهم فرعون وجنوده حتّىٰ إذا ادّاركوا فيها جميعاً أطبق الله عليهم الماء فغرقهم عن آخرهم.

When Allah saved them from Pharaoh and his soldiers extracting them to dry land, and there was no water or plants there, Allah was kind to them and sent down *manna* [a sweet] and quail to them. Moses was ordered to hit a stone with his stick, and from it gushed out twelve springs of water. Every tribe came to know its drinking-place, and they drank and ate from it, and He shaded them with clouds.

ولمّا أنجاهم الله من فرعون وجنوده وأخرجهم إلَى البرّ ولا ماء فيه ولا كلأ أكرمهم الله فأنزل الله عليهم المنّ والسّلوىٰ، وأُمر موسىٰ فضرب بعصاه الحجر فانبجست منه اثنتا عشرة عيناً قد علم كلّ أُناس مشربهم، فشربوا منها وأكلوا منها وظلّلهم الغمام.

Allah then made an appointment with Moses for forty nights for the descent of the Torah on Mount Sinai. Moses chose seventy of his men to let them hear Allah speaking to him. They heard but said, 'We will not believe in you until we see Allah in person, so the thunderbolt seized them as they looked on. Allah then revived them by the request of Moses, and when the tryst was completed Allah sent down the Torah and informed him of al-Sāmirī who was leading his people astray after him, worshipping the calf.

ثمّ واعد الله موسىٰ أربعين ليلةً لنزول التوراة بجبل الطور، فاختار قومه سبعين رجلاً ليسمعوا تكليمه تعالىٰ إيّاه، فسمعوا ثمّ قالوا: لن نؤمن لك حتّىٰ نرى الله جهرةً، فأخذتهم الصاعقة وهم ينظرون، ثمّ أحياهم الله بدعوة موسى، ولمّا تمّ الميقات أنزل الله عليه التوراة وأخبره أنّ السامريّ قد أضلّ قومه بعده فعبدوا العجل.

Moses returned to his people angry and regretful, and he burnt the calf and scattered it into the sea, and expelled al-Sāmirī, saying to him, 'Be gone! It

فرجع موسىٰ إلىٰ قومه غضبان أسفاً، فأحرق العجل ونسفه في اليمّ وطرد السامريّ وقال له:

shall be your lot throughout life to say, 'Do not touch me….' As for the people, they were ordered to repent and kill [those among] themselves [who had worshipped the calf], and they were forgiven after that. But they were haughty in accepting the laws of the Torah until Allah raised the mountain over them.

اذهب فإنّ لك في الحياة أن تقول لا مساس. وأمّا القوم فأُمروا أن يتوبوا ويقتلوا أنفسهم، فتيب عليهم بعد ذلك، ثمّ استكبروا عن قبول شريعة التوراة حتّىٰ رفع الله الطور فوقهم.

They became bored of eating manna and quail and said, 'We will not put up with one kind of food.' So, they asked him to invoke his Lord to bring forth for them of that which the earth grows, of its greens, cucumbers, garlic, lentils, and its onions. They were then ordered to enter the sacred land that Allah had ascribed to them, but they refused so Allah prohibited it to them and struck them with deviation, making them wander on the earth for forty years.'[6787]

ثمّ إنّهم ملّوا المنّ والسّلوىٰ وقالوا: لن نصبر علىٰ طعام واحد، وسألوه أن يدعو ربّه أن يُخرج لهم ممّا تنبت الأرض من بقلها وقثّائها وفومها وعدسها وبصلها، فأُمروا أن يدخلوا الأرض المقدّسة الّتي كتب الله لهم فأبوا، فحرّمها الله عليهم وابتلاهم بالتّيه يتيهون في الأرض أربعين سنة.[٦٧٤٤]

1701. Moses and Khiḍr (AS)

١٧٠١ ـ موسىٰ وَالخِضرُ عليهما السلام

"When Moses said to his lad, 'I will go on [journeying] until I have reached the confluence of the two seas, or have spent a long time [travelling].'…As for the wall, it belonged to two boy orphans in the city. Under it there was a treasure belonging to them. Their father had been a righteous man. So your Lord desired that they should come of age and take out their treasure as a mercy from your Lord. I did not do that of my own accord. This is the interpretation of that over which you could not maintain patience."[6788]

﴿وَإِذْ قَالَ مُوسَىٰ لِفَتَاهُ لَا أَبْرَحُ حَتَّىٰ أَبْلُغَ مَجْمَعَ الْبَحْرَيْنِ أَوْ أَمْضِيَ حُقُباً * ... وَأَمَّا الْجِدَارُ فَكَانَ لِغُلَامَيْنِ يَتِيمَيْنِ فِي الْمَدِينَةِ وَكَانَ تَحْتَهُ كَنْزٌ لَهُمَا وَكَانَ أَبُوهُمَا صَالِحاً فَأَرَادَ رَبُّكَ أَنْ يَبْلُغَا أَشُدَّهُمَا وَيَسْتَخْرِجَا كَنْزَهُمَا رَحْمَةً مِنْ رَبِّكَ وَمَا فَعَلْتُهُ عَنْ أَمْرِي ذٰلِكَ تَأْوِيلُ مَا لَمْ تَسْطِعْ عَلَيْهِ صَبْراً﴾.[٦٧٤٥]

5981. **The Prophet (SAWA) said,** 'May Allah be pleased with my brother Moses, he was shy and said that [which he was not supposed to], and if was to have stayed with his companion [al-Khiḍr] he would have seen the greatest of wonders.'[6789]

٥٩٨١ . رسولُ اللهِ صلى الله عليه وآله : رَحِمَ اللهُ أخي موسىٰ استَحيا فقالَ ذلكَ، لَو لَبِثَ مَع صاحِبِهِ لأبصَرَ أعجَبَ الأعاجِيبِ.[٦٧٤٦]

5982. **Imām al-Ṣādiq (AS) said,** 'Khiḍr was a sent prophet. Allah Almighty sent him to his people, to call them to His Oneness and to acknowledge the prophets, messengers and their scriptures. His miracle was that any time he sat on dry wood or

٥٩٨٢ . الإمامُ الصّادقُ عليه السلام : إنّ الخضرَ كانَ نَبيّاً مُرسَلاً، بَعَثَهُ اللهُ تبارَكَ وتعالىٰ إلىٰ قَومِهِ فدَعاهُم إلىٰ تَوحيدِهِ والإقرارِ بأنبيائهِ ورُسُلِهِ وكُتُبِهِ، وكانَتْ آيَتُهُ أنّهُ كانَ لا يَجلِسُ علىٰ خَشَبَةٍ يابِسَةٍ ولا أرضٍ بَيضاءَ إلّا أزهَرَت

barren land, greenery would sprout from it, and this is why he was called Khiḍr.' [6790] [6791]

خَضِراً، وإنّما سُمِّيَ خضراً لذٰلكَ.[٦٧٤٧]

5983. **Imām al-Ṣādiq (AS) said,** 'The mosque of Sahla has the climate of the rider.' He was asked, 'And who is the rider?' He said, 'Khiḍr (AS).'[6792]

٥٩٨٣. عنه عليه السلام: مَسجِدُ السَّهلَةِ مُناخُ الرَّاكِبِ. قيلَ: ومَنِ الرّاكِبُ؟ قالَ: الخضرُ عليه السلام.[٦٧٤٨]

5984. **Imām al-Riḍā (AS) said,** 'Khiḍr has drunk from the fountain of life, so he is alive and will not die until the horn is blown.'[6793]

٥٩٨٤. الإمامُ الرِّضا عليه السلام: إنّ الخضرَ شَرِبَ مِن ماءِ الحَياةِ فهُو حَيٌّ لا يَموتُ حتّىٰ يُنفَخَ في الصُّورِ، وإنّهُ لَيأتِينا فيُسَلِّمُ فنَسمَعُ صَوتَهُ ولا نَرىٰ شَخصَهُ، وإنّهُ لَيحضُرُ حيثُ ما ذُكِرَ، فمَن ذكَرَهُ مِنكُم فلْيُسَلِّمْ علَيهِ، وإنّهُ لَيحضُرُ المَوسِمَ كُلَّ سَنةٍ فيَقضي جَميعَ المَناسِكِ ويَقِفُ بعَرَفَةَ فيُؤمِّنُ علىٰ دُعاءِ المؤمِنينَ، وسيُؤنِسُ اللهُ بِهِ وَحشَةَ قائمِنا في غَيبَتِهِ، ويَصِلُ بهِ وَحدَتَهُ.[٦٧٤٩]

The Story of Moses and Khiḍr in the Qur'an

قِصّةُ مُوسىٰ والخِضرِ عليهما السلام في القُرآنِ:

The scholar [al-Khiḍr] said, 'Verily you will not be patient with me in things that you see me do, the interpretation of which you do not have knowledge about. How can you be patient about something your knowledge does not comprehend?' Moses promised him that he will be patient and will not disobey him in anything by the will of Allah. The knowledgeable scholar said to him – according to what he requested from Moses and what Moses promised him – 'So if you follow me do not ask me regarding anything until I myself tell you about it.'

قال العالم: إنّك لن تستطيع معي صبراً علىٰ ما تشاهد، من أعمالي التي لا عِلم لك بتأويلها، وكيف تصبر علىٰ ما لم تُحِط به خبراً؟! فوعده موسىٰ أن يصبر ولا يعصيه في أمر إن شاء الله، فقال له العالم ـ بانياً علىٰ ما طلبه منه ووعده به ـ: فإن اتّبعتني فلا تسألني عن شيء حتّىٰ أُحدِث لك منه ذِكراً.

Moses and the scholar started off on their journey until they boarded a ship that had people on it – and Moses did not have any knowledge of what the intention of the scholar was – and the scholar pierced the ship in such a way that it could not be prevented from sinking. This bewildered Moses and made him forget his promise, so he said to the scholar, 'Did you make a hole in it to drown those aboard it? You have certainly done a monstrous thing!' The knowledgeable man said to him, 'Did I not say, indeed you cannot have patience with me?' Moses apologized to him for the promise he had made [and broken] to be patient, saying, 'Do not take me to task for my forgetting, and do not be hard upon me.'

فانطلق موسىٰ والعالم حتّىٰ ركبا سفينة وفيها ناس من الركّاب ـ وموسىٰ خالي الذهن عمّا في قصد العالم ـ فخرق العالمُ السفينة خرقاً لا يؤمَن معه الغرق، فأدهش ذلك موسىٰ وأنساه ما وعده فقال للعالم: أخرقتها لتغرق أهلها؟! لقد جئت شيئاً إمراً! قال له العالم: ألم أقل: إنّك لن تستطيع معي صبراً؟! فاعتذر إليه موسىٰ بأنّه نسي ما وعده من الصبر قائلاً: لا تؤاخذني بما نسيت ولا ترهقني من أمري عسراً.

So they went on until they encountered a boy, and the knowledgeable man killed him. Moses could not control himself from going back on his word, so he reproved the action, saying, 'Did you slay an innocent soul, without [his having slain] anyone? You have certainly done a dire thing!'

The knowledgeable man said again, 'Did I not tell you, indeed you cannot have patience with me?' Moses did not have anything to say to apologize and to prevent him from abandoning him, which he would not be content with. So he requested him that if he was to ask another question, he would [be justified to] break off company with him, saying: 'If I question you about anything after this, do not keep me in your company. You have already got sufficient excuse on my part.' And the knowledgeable man accepted.

فانطلقا فلقيا غلاماً فقتله العالم، فلم يملك موسىٰ نفسه دون أن تغيّر وأنكر عليه ذلك قائلاً: أقتلت نفساً زكيّةً بغير نفس؟! لقد جئت شيئاً نُكراً! قال له العالم ثانياً: ألم أقل لك: إنّك لن تستطيع معي صبراً؟! فلم يكن عند موسىٰ ما يعتذر به ويمتنع به عن مفارقته ونفسه غير راضية بها، فاستدعىٰ منه مصاحبة مؤجّلة بسؤال آخر إن أتى به كان له فراقه، واستمهله قائلاً: إن سألتك عن شيء بعدها فلا تصاحبني قد بلغت من لدنّي عذراً، وقبله العالم.

So they went on, until they came to a town – and they were hungry – so they asked its people for food, but none of them agreed to extend them any hospitality. There was a wall which was about to collapse, so the knowledgeable man erected it. Moses said to him, 'Had you wished, you could have taken a wage for it so we could have satisfied our hunger with it. We are in need of it and the people do not accommodate us!'

فانطلقا حتّىٰ أتيا قرية ـ وقد بلغ بهما الجوع ـ فاستطعما أهلها فلم يضيّفهما أحد منهم، وإذا بجدار فيها يريد أن ينقضّ ويتحذّر منه الناس فأقامه العالم، قال له موسىٰ: لو شئتَ لاتّخذتَ على عملك منهم أجراً فتوسّلنا به إلى سدّ الجوع، فنحن في حاجة إليه والقوم لا يضيّفوننا!

The knowledgeable man said to him, 'This is where you and I shall part. I will inform you about the interpretation of that over which you could not maintain patience.' He then said, 'As for the ship, it belonged to some poor people who work on the sea and earn their living by it. There was a king after them wanting to seize every ship by usurping them, so I damaged it making it faulty so that he would not be interested in it.

فقال له العالم: هذا فراقُ بيني وبينك، سأُنبّئك بتأويل ما لم تستطع عليه صبراً. ثمّ قال: أمّا السفينة فكانت لمساكين يعملون في البحر ويتعيّشون بها، وكان وراءهم ملك يأخذ كلّ سفينة غصباً، فخرقتُها لتكون مَعيبة لا يرغب فيها.

As for the boy, he was a disbeliever and his parents were believers. If he was to live he would be overbearing with them with disbelief and rebellion, but the mercy of Allah encompassed them, so He ordered me to kill the boy so that He can give

وأمّا الغلام فكان كافراً وكان أبواه مؤمنَين، ولو أنّه عاش لأرهقهما بكفره وطغيانه، فشملتهما الرحمة الإلهيّة، فأمرني أن أقتله ليبدلهما ولداً خيراً منه زكاةً وأقرب رُحماً، فقتلته.

them in exchange one better than him in purity and closer to mercy, therefore I killed him.

As for the wall, it belonged to two orphan boys in the city. Under it there was a treasure belonging to them, and their father had been a righteous man. So He ordered me to raise it so that the wall can be erect in order for them to take out their treasure when they come of age. If the wall was to have fallen the treasure would have been exposed and the people would have looted it.'

وأمّا الجدار فكان لغلامَين يتيمَين في المدينة وكان تحته كنز لهما، وكَان أبوهما صالحاً، فشملتهما الرحمة الإلهيّة لصلاح أبيهما، فأمرني أن أُقيمه فيستقيم حتّىٰ يبلغا أشدّهما ويستخرجا كنزهما، ولو انقضّ لظهر أمر الكنز وانتهبه الناس.

He then said, 'I did not do that out of my own accord, rather it is an order from Allah and its interpretation is what I have informed you.' He then left Moses.[6794]

قال: وما فعلت الذي فعلت عن أمري بل عن أمر من الله، وتأويلها ما أنبأتك به، ثمّ فارق موسىٰ [٦٧٥٠]

1702. Ishmael b. Ḥazqīl (AS)

١٧٠٢ـ إسماعِيلُ بن حِزقيلَ

"And mention in the Book Ishmael. Indeed he was true to his promise, and an apostle and a prophet. He used to bid his family to [maintain] the prayer and to [pay] the zakāt and was pleasing to his Lord."[6795]

﴿وَاذْكُرْ فِي الْكِتَابِ إِسْمَاعِيلَ إِنَّهُ كَانَ صَادِقَ الْوَعْدِ وَكَانَ رَسُولاً نَبِيّاً * وَكَانَ يَأْمُرُ أَهْلَهُ بِالصَّلَاةِ وَالزَّكَاةِ وَكَانَ عِنْدَ رَبِّهِ مَرْضِيّاً﴾.[٦٧٥١]

5985. **Imām al-Ṣādiq (AS) said,** 'The Ishmael that Allah mentions in His book *"And mention in the Book Ishmael..."* was not Ishmael son of Abraham, rather he was one of the prophets whom Allah Almighty sent to his people, who took him and skinned his head and face. An angel came to him and said, 'Allah has sent me to you, so command me with whatever you wish.' He said, 'I have an example before me in what will be done to al-Ḥusayn (AS).'[6796]

٥٩٨٥. الإمامُ الصّادقُ ﷷ: إنّ اسماعيلَ الّذي قالَ اللهُ عَزَّ وجلَّ في كِتابِهِ: ﴿واذْكُرْ فِي الكِتابِ إسْماعيلَ...﴾ لَم يَكُن إسماعيلَ بنَ إبراهيمَ، بَل كانَ نَبيّاً مِن الأنبياءِ بَعَثَهُ اللهُ عَزَّ وجلَّ إلىٰ قَومِهِ، فأخَذوهُ فسَلَخوا فَروَةَ[٦٧٥٢] رأسِهِ ووَجهِهِ، فأتاهُ مَلَكٌ فقالَ: إنّ اللهَ بَعَثَني إلَيكَ فَمُرْني بِما شِئتَ، فقالَ: لِي أُسوَةٌ بما يُصنَعُ بالحُسَينِ ﷷ.[٦٧٥٣]

5986. **Imām al-Ṣādiq (AS) said,** 'Ishmael was a messenger and a prophet. A group ruled over him and they peeled the skin off his face and skinned his head. A messenger [angel] came to him from the Lord of the worlds, and said to him, 'Your Lord greets you and says, 'I have seen what has been done to you.' He has ordered me to obey you,

٥٩٨٦. عنه ﷷ: إنّ إسماعيلَ كانَ رَسولاً نَبيّاً، سُلِّطَ علَيهِ قَومُهُ فقَشَروا جِلدَةَ وَجهِهِ وفَروَةَ رأسِهِ، فأتاهُ رَسولٌ مِن رَبِّ العالَمينَ، فقالَ لَهُ: ربُّكَ يُقرِئُكَ السّلامَ ويقولُ: قَد رأيتُ ما صُنِعَ بكَ

so command me with whatever you wish.' So, he said, 'I have an example before me in al-Ḥusayn b. 'Alī (AS).'[6797]

وقد أمَرَني بطاعَتِكَ فمُرْني بما شِئتَ، فقالَ: يكونُ لِي بالحُسَينِ بنِ عليٍّ عليهما السلام أُسوَةٌ. [٦٧٥٤]

5987. It is narrated in *Tafsīr al-Qummī*, with regards to Allah's verse in the Qur'an: *"And mention in the Book Ishmael. Indeed he was true to his promise"*, He made a promise for an appointment and waited for his friend for one year, and his name is Ishmael, son of Hazqīl.'[6798]

٥٩٨٧. تفسيرِ القُمّيِّ: في قولهِ تعالىٰ: ﴿واذْكُرْ في الكِتابِ إسْماعيلَ إنّهُ كانَ صادِقَ الوَعْدِ﴾، قالَ: وَعدَ وَعداً فانتَظَرَ صاحِبَهُ سَنَةً، وهُو إسماعيلُ بنُ حِزقيلَ عليه السلام. [٦٧٥٥] [٦٧٥٦]

1703. Elisha (AS) [al-Yasaʿ]

١٧٠٣ - اليَسَعُ عليه السلام

"and Ishmael, Elisha, Jonah and Lot – each We graced over all the nations."[6799]

﴿وَإِسْمَاعِيلَ وَالْيَسَعَ وَيُونُسَ وَلُوطاً وَكُلّاً فَضَّلْنَا عَلَى الْعَالَمِينَ﴾. [٦٧٥٧]

5988. **Imām al-Riḍā (AS)** – debating with the leader of the Christians, said, 'Elisha (AS) did the same as what Jesus had done (AS) - he walked on water, revived the dead, healed the blind and the leper, but his people did not take him as a god.'[6800]

٥٩٨٨. الإمامُ الرِّضا عليه السلام ـ فيما احتَجَّ بهِ علىٰ جاثِليقِ النَّصارىٰ ـ: إنّ اليَسَعَ قد صَنَعَ مِثلَ ما صَنَعَ عيسىٰ عليه السلام: مَشىٰ علَى الماءِ، وأحيا المَوتىٰ، وأبرَأ الأكمَهَ والأبرَصَ، فلَم تَتَّخِذْهُ اُمّتُهُ رَبّاً. [٦٧٥٨]

1704. Dhu'l Kifl (AS)[6801]

١٧٠٤ - ذُو الكِفلِ عليه السلام

"And Ishmael, Idrīs, and Dhu'l-Kifl each of them was among the patient. We admitted them into Our mercy. Indeed they were among the righteous."[6802]

﴿وَإِسْمَاعِيلَ وَإِدْرِيسَ وَذَا الْكِفْلِ كُلٌّ مِنَ الصَّابِرِينَ * وَأَدْخَلْنَاهُمْ فِي رَحْمَتِنَا إِنَّهُمْ مِنَ الصَّالِحِينَ﴾. [٦٧٥٩]

"And remember Ishmael, Elisha and Dhu'l-Kifl each [of whom was] among the elect."[6803]

﴿وَاذْكُرْ إِسْمَاعِيلَ وَالْيَسَعَ وَذَا الْكِفْلِ وَكُلٌّ مِنَ الأَخْيَارِ﴾. [٦٧٦٠]

5989. **Imām al-Jawād (AS)** – when 'Abd al-'Aẓīm al-Ḥasanī asked him about Dhul Kifl and his name, and whether he was a messenger, said, 'Allah, exalted be His remembrance, sent one hundred and twenty four thousand prophets, of whom three hundred and thirteen were messengers, and Dhul Kifl was one of them, peace of Allah be upon them all. He was after Solomon, son of David (AS), and he used to judge between people like David did before him. He never became angry other than for Allah, and his name was 'Uwaydiyā'.

٥٩٨٩. الإمامُ الجوادُ عليه السلام ـ لَمّا سَألَهُ عبدُ العَظيمِ الحَسَنيُّ عن ذي الكِفلِ ما اسمُهُ؟ وهلَ كانَ مِن المُرسَلينَ؟ ـ: بَعَثَ اللهُ تعالىٰ جَلَّ ذِكرُهُ مِائةَ ألفِ نَبيٍّ وأربَعةً وعِشرينَ ألفَ نَبيٍّ، المُرسَلونَ مِنهُم ثلاثُمِائةٍ وثلاثَةَ عَشَرَ رجُلاً، وإنّ ذا الكِفلِ مِنهُم صلواتُ اللهِ علَيهِم. وكانَ بَعدَ سُليمانَ بنِ داوودَ عليه السلام، وكانَ يَقضي بينَ النّاسِ كما كانَ يَقضي داوودُ، ولَم يَغضَبْ إلّا للهِ عزَّوجلَّ، وكانَ اسمُهُ عُويديا، وهُو الّذي ذَكرَهُ اللهُ تعالىٰ جَلّت

He is the one Allah, Mighty and Exalted, has mentioned in His book, saying *"remember Ishmael, Elisha and Dhu'l-Kifl each [of whom was] among the elect."*[6804]

عظَمتُهُ في كِتابِهِ حيثُ قالَ: ﴿واذْكُرْ إسْماعيلَ واليَسَعَ وذا الكِفْلِ وكُلٌّ مِنَ الأخْيارِ﴾.[٦٧٦١]

1705. David (AS) [Dāwūd]

١٧٠٥ـ داوودُ عليه السلام

"and remember Our servant David, [the man] of strength. Indeed he was a penitent [soul]..."O David! Indeed We have made you a vicegerent on the earth. So judge between people with justice, and do not follow desire, or it will lead you astray from the way of Allah. Indeed those who stray from the way of Allah – there is a severe punishment for them because of their forgetting the Day of Reckoning."[6805]

﴿اصْبِرْ عَلَىٰ مَا يَقُولُونَ وَاذْكُرْ عَبْدَنَا دَاوُدَ ذَا الْأَيْدِ إِنَّهُ أَوَّابٌ * ... يَا دَاوُدُ إِنَّا جَعَلْنَاكَ خَلِيفَةً فِي الْأَرْضِ فَاحْكُمْ بَيْنَ النَّاسِ بِالْحَقِّ وَلَا تَتَّبِعِ الْهَوَىٰ فَيُضِلَّكَ عَنْ سَبِيلِ اللهِ إِنَّ الَّذِينَ يَضِلُّونَ عَنْ سَبِيلِ اللهِ لَهُمْ عَذَابٌ شَدِيدٌ بِمَا نَسُوا يَوْمَ الْحِسَابِ﴾.[٦٧٦٢]

"Certainly We wrote in the Psalms, after the Torah: "Indeed My righteous servants shall inherit the earth."[6806]

﴿وَلَقَدْ كَتَبْنَا فِي الزَّبُورِ مِنْ بَعْدِ الذِّكْرِ أَنَّ الْأَرْضَ يَرِثُهَا عِبَادِيَ الصَّالِحُونَ﴾.[٦٧٦٣]

(See also: Qur'an 4:163, 17:55, 5:78-79, 6:84, 21:78-80, 27:15, 34:10-11)

(أُنظر: النساء: ١٦٣ والإسراء: ٥٥ والمائدة: ٧٨، ٧٩ والأنعام: ٨٤ والأنبياء: ٧٨ ـ ٨٠ والنمل: ١٥ وسبأ: ١٠، ١١.

5990. **Imām ʿAlī (AS) said,** 'Allah Almighty revealed to David (AS), 'You would be a great worshipper, if it was not for the fact that you consume from the treasury and do not labour at all with your own hands.' He said, 'David (AS) then cried, so Allah revealed unto the iron, 'Soften yourself for my worshipper David, and it did.' So, Allah softened the metal for him, and he used to make an armour shield every day, and would sell it for one thousand dirhams. He made three hundred and sixty shields and sold them for three hundred and sixty thousand dirhams, and hence he no longer needed the treasury.'[6807]

٥٩٩٠. الإمامُ عليٌّ عليه السلام: أوحَىٰ اللهُ عَزَّوجلَّ إلىٰ داوودَ عليه السلام: إنّكَ نِعمَ العَبدُ لَولا أنّكَ تأكُلُ مِن بَيتِ المالِ ولا تَعمَلُ بِيَدِكَ شيئاً. قالَ: فبَكىٰ داوودُ عليه السلام، فأوحَى اللهُ عَزَّوجلَّ إلَى الحَديدِ: أنْ لِنْ لِعَبدي داوودَ، فلانَ، فألانَ اللهُ تعالىٰ لَهُ الحَديدَ، فكانَ يَعمَلُ كلَّ يَومٍ دِرعاً فيَبيعُها بألفِ دِرهَمٍ، فعَمِلَ عليه السلام ثلاثَمِائةٍ وسِتّينَ دِرعاً فباعَها بثلاثِمِائةٍ وسِتّينَ ألفاً، واستَغنىٰ عن بَيتِ المالِ.[٦٧٦٤]

5991. **Imām al-Ṣādiq (AS) said,** 'Allah Almighty revealed unto David (AS), 'Why is it that I see you alone?' He said, 'I deserted people and they deserted me because of You.' 'So why is it that I see you quiet?' He said, 'My awe of You has rendered me quiet.' He Almighty asked, 'So why do

٥٩٩١. الإمامُ الصّادقُ عليه السلام: إنّ اللهَ تباركَ وتعالىٰ أوحىٰ إلىٰ داوودَ عليه السلام: ما لِي أراكَ وَحداناً؟ قالَ: هَجَرتُ النّاسَ وهَجَروني فيكَ. قالَ: فَما لِي أراكَ ساكِتاً؟ قالَ: خَشيَتُكَ أسكَتَتني. قالَ: فَما

I see you tired?' He said, 'Your love has tired me.' He Almighty asked, 'So why do I see you poor, whilst I have provided you?' He said, 'Undertaking Your rights has impoverished me.' He Almighty asked, 'So why do I see you humiliated?' He said, 'The greatness of Your indescribable Magnitude has humiliated me, and this is Your right O Master.' Allah Almighty said, 'Then rejoice with grace from Me, for you will have whatever you want when you meet Me. Associate with people to correct their morals, and disassociate from them in their actions, and you will achieve from Me whatever you desire from Me on the Day of Judgment.'[6808]

لِي أراكَ نَصِباً ؟ قالَ : حُبُّكَ أنصَبَني. قالَ : فما لِي أراكَ فقيراً وقَد أفَدتُكَ ؟ قالَ : القِيامُ بِحَقِّكَ أفقَرَني. قالَ : فما لِي أراكَ مُتذَلِّلاً ؟ قالَ : عَظيمُ جَلالِكَ الّذي لا يُوصَفُ ذَلَّلَني ، وحقَّ ذلكَ لكَ يا سيّدي . قالَ اللهُ جَلّ جَلالُهُ: فأبشِرْ بالفَضلِ مِنّي، فلَكَ ما تُحِبُّ يومَ تَلقاني ، خالِطِ النّاسَ وخالِقهُم بأخلاقِهِم وزايِلْهُم في أعمالِهِم تَنَلْ ما تُريدُ مِنّي يومَ القِيامَةِ .٦٧٦٥

5992. It is narrated in *Biḥār al-Anwār*: 'Prophet David (AS) left for the desert by himself, so Allah revealed to him, 'O David, why is it that I see you by yourself?' He said, 'O Allah, my yearning for meeting You has become extreme, and has become an obstruction between me and Your creation.' So, Allah revealed to him, 'Return to them, for if you bring me a runaway servant I will inscribe you in the Tablet as praised.'[6809]

٥٩٩٢ . بحار الأنوار : رُوِيَ أنّ داوودَ ﷺ خَرَجَ مُصحِراً مُنفَرِداً ، فأوحَى اللهُ إليهِ : يا داوودُ ، ما لِي أراكَ وَحدانِيّاً ؟ فقالَ : إلهي اشتَدَّ الشَّوقُ مِنّي إلى لِقائكَ ، وحالَ بَيني وبَينَ خَلقِكَ . فأوحَى اللهُ إليهِ : ارجِعْ إليهِم فإنّكَ إن تأتِني بعَبدٍ آبِقٍ أثبِتْكَ في اللَّوحِ حَميداً .٦٧٦٦

5993. **The Prophet (SAWA) said,** 'David was the greatest worshipper among mankind.'[6810]

٥٩٩٣ . رسولُ اللهِ ﷺ : كانَ داوودُ أعبَدَ البَشَرِ .٦٧٦٧

5994. **The Prophet (SAWA) said,** 'People would visit David thinking that he was sick, whilst there was nothing wrong with him other than his extreme fear of Allah Almighty.'[6811]

٥٩٩٤ . عنه ﷺ : كانَ النّاسُ يَعودُونَ داوودَ ويَظُنّونَ أنّ بِهِ مَرَضاً ، وما بِهِ إلّا شِدَّةُ الخَوفِ مِن اللهِ تعالى .٦٧٦٨

5995. **Imām al-Bāqir (AS) said,** 'As for David, he owned all that was between al-Shāmāt, till the land of Istakhr, and the kingdom of Solomon was the same.'[6812]

٥٩٩٥ . الإمامُ الباقرُ ﷺ : وأمّا داوودُ فمَلَكَ ما بَينَ الشّاماتِ إلى بِلادِ إصطَخرَ ، وكذلكَ كانَ مُلكُ سُلَيمانَ .٦٧٦٩

1706. Solomon (AS) [Sulaymān]

١٧٠٦ ـ سُلَيمانُ ﷺ

"Solomon inherited from David, and he said, 'O people! We have been taught the speech of the birds, and

﴿وَوَرِثَ سُلَيْمَانُ دَاوُدَ وَقَالَ يَا أَيُّهَا النَّاسُ عُلِّمْنَا مَنطِقَ الطَّيْرِ وَأُوتِينَا مِن كُلِّ شَيْءٍ إِنَّ

we have been given out of everything. Indeed this is a manifest advantage.'[6813]

هٰذا لَهُوَ الْفَضْلُ الْمُبِينُ﴾ .٦٧٧٠

(See also: Qur'an 4:163, 6:84, 21:81-82, 34:12-13, 38:30-40, 27:17-44, 2:102)

(أُنظر) النساء: ١٦٣ والأنعام: ٨٤ والأنبياء: ٨١، ٨٢ وسبأ: ١٢، ١٣ وص: ٣٠ ـ ٤٠ والنمل: ١٧ ـ ٤٤ والبقرة: ١٠٢.

5996. **Solomon (AS),** when he saw a male sparrow saying to a female sparrow, 'Why do you deprive me of yourself, for if I wanted I could take Solomon's crown with my beak and throw it in the sea!' Solomon said to him, smiling, 'Are you really able to do so?' The bird said, 'No, O Messenger of Allah, but a man may embellish himself and greaten himself in front of his wife, and a lover cannot be rebuked for what he says.' Solomon then asked the female sparrow, 'Why do you deprive him of yourself when he loves you?' She said, 'O Prophet of Allah, he is not a lover, but a claimant [of love], for he loves someone else besides me!' The words of this sparrow affected Solomon's heart and he cried very much, and secluded himself from people for forty days praying to Allah to empty his heart for his love for Him, and to not mix it with love for anything other than Him.'[6814]

٥٩٩٦ . سُلَيمانُ ﷺ ـ لمّا رأىٰ عُصفوراً يَقولُ لِعُصفورَةٍ: لِمَ تمنَعينَ نَفسَكِ مِنّي، ولو شِئتُ أخَذتُ قُبّةَ سُليمانَ بِمِنقارِي فألقَيتُها في البَحرِ؟! فقال لَهُ وهو يتبسّم ـ: أتُطيقُ أن تَفعَلَ ذلكَ؟! فقالَ: لا يا رسولَ اللهِ، ولكنَّ المَرءَ قد يُزَيِّنُ نفسَهُ ويُعَظِّمُها عِندَ زَوجَتِهِ، والمُحِبُّ لا يُلامُ علىٰ ما يقولُ، فقالَ سُلَيمانُ ﷺ لِلعُصفورَةِ: لِمَ تَمنَعينَهُ مِن نَفسِكَ وهُو يُحِبُّكِ؟ فقالت: يا نَبيَّ اللهِ، إنّهُ لَيس مُحِبّاً ولكنّهُ مُدَّعٍ؛ لأ نّهُ يُحِبُّ مَعي غَيري! فأثَّرَ كلامُ العُصفورَةِ في قَلبِ سُلَيمانَ وبَكىٰ بُكاءً شَديداً واحتَجَبَ عنِ النّاسِ أربَعينَ يَوماً يَدعُو اللهَ أن يُفَرِّغَ قَلبَهُ لمَحَبّتِهِ وأن لا يُخالِطَها بمَحَبَّةِ غَيرِهِ.٦٧٧١

5997. **Solomon (AS) said,** 'We have been given what people [in the past] were given as well as what they were not given, and we know what other people know as well as what they do not know. But we did not find anything better [in all of that] than fearing Allah in secret and in public, and moderation in times of wealth as well as poverty, speaking the truth both in [states of] pleasure and anger, and humility before Allah Almighty in every situation.'[6815]

٥٩٩٧ . عنه ﷺ: أُوتينا ما أُوتِيَ النّاس وما لَم يُؤتَوا، وعَلِمنا ما عَلِمَ الناسُ وما لَم يَعلَموا، فلم نَجِدْ شيئاً فضَلَ مِن خَشيَةِ اللهِ في الغَيبِ والمَشهَدِ، والقَصدِ في الغِنىٰ والفَقرِ، وكَلِمَةِ الحَقِّ في الرِّضا والغَضبِ، والتَّضَرُّعِ إلَى اللهِ عَزَّوجلَّ علىٰ كلِّ حالٍ.٦٧٧٢

5998. **Imām ʿAlī (AS) said,** 'If there was anyone who could secure a ladder to everlasting life or a way to avoid death, it would have been Solomon son of David (AS) who was given control over the domain of the jinn and humans, along with prophethood and a great position [before Allah].

٥٩٩٨ . الإمامُ عليٌّ ﷺ: لَوأ نَّ أحَداً يَجِدُ إلَى البَقاءِ سُلَّماً، أو لِدَفعِ المَوتِ سَبيلاً، لَكانَ ذلكَ سُلَيمانُ بنُ داوودَ ﷺ، الّذي سُخِّرَ لَهُ مُلكُ الجِنِّ والإنسِ،

مَع النُّبُوّةِ وعَظيمِ الزُّلفَةِ ، فلَمّا استَوفىٰ طُعمَتَهُ ، واستَكمَلَ مُدَّتَهُ ، رَمَتهُ قِسِيُّ الفَناءِ بِنِبالِ المَوتِ ، وأصبَحَتِ الدِّيارُ مِنهُ خالِيَةً ، والمَساكِنُ مُعَطَّلَةً ، ووَرِثَها قَومٌ آخَرونَ.[٦٧٧٣]

But when he finished his allotment of sustenance [in this world] and exhausted his [fixed] time, the bow of destruction shot him with the arrow of death, houses became vacant of him and his habitations became empty, and another group of people inherited them.'[6816]

٥٩٩٩. الإمامُ الصّادقُ عليه السلام: كانَ سُلَيمانُ عليه السلام يُطعِمُ أضيافَهُ اللَّحمَ بِالحُوّارىٰ ، وعِيالَهُ الخُشكارَ ، ويأكُلُ هُو الشَّعيرَ (غَيرَ) مَنخولٍ.[٦٧٧٤]

5999. **Imām al-Ṣādiq (AS) said,** 'Solomon (AS) would feed his guests meat in white flour, and his family brown bread with bran, and he himself would eat unsifted barley.'[6817]

٦٠٠٠. عنه عليه السلام: آخِرُ مَن يَدخُلُ الجَنّةَ مِنَ النَّبِيِّينَ سُلَيمانُ بنُ داوودَ عليه السلام ، وذلكَ لِما أُعطِيَ في الدُّنيا.[٦٧٧٥]

6000. **Imām al-Ṣādiq (AS) said,** 'The last person to enter Heaven from among the prophets is Solomon, son of David (AS), because of all that he was given in this world.'[6818]

٦٠٠١. عنه عليه السلام: إنّ سُلَيمانَ بنَ داوودَ عليه السلام قالَ ذاتَ يَومٍ لأصحابِهِ: إنّ اللهَ تَبارَكَ وتَعالىٰ قد وَهَبَ لِي مُلكاً لا يَنبَغي لأحَدٍ مِن بَعدي ، سَخَّرَ لِي الرِّيحَ والإنسَ والجِنَّ والطَّيرَ والوُحوشَ ، وعَلَّمَني مَنطِقَ الطَّيرِ ، وآتاني مِن كُلِّ شيءٍ ، ومَعَ جَميعِ ما أُوتيتُ مِنَ المُلكِ ماتَمَّ لِي سُروري يَوم إلَى اللَّيلِ ، وقد أحبَبتُ أن أدخُلَ قَصري في غَدٍ فأصعَدَ أعلاهُ وأنظُرَ إلىٰ مَمالِكي ، فلا تَأذَنوا لأحَدٍ علَيَّ لِئلّا يَرِدَ علَيَّ ما يُنَغِّصُ علَيَّ يَومي ، فقالوا: نَعَم. فلَمّا كانَ مِنَ الغَدِ أخَذَ عَصاهُ بِيَدِهِ وصَعِدَ إلىٰ أعلىٰ مَوضِعٍ مِن قَصرِهِ ، ووَقَفَ مُتَّكِئاً علىٰ عَصاهُ يَنظُرُ إلىٰ مَمالِكِهِ مَسروراً بِما أُوتِيَ فَرِحاً بِما أُعطِيَ ، إذ نَظَرَ إلىٰ شابٍّ حَسَنِ الوَجهِ واللِّباسِ قَد خَرَجَ علَيهِ مِن بَعضِ زَوايا قَصرِهِ ، فلَمّا أبصَرَهُ سُلَيمانُ قالَ لَهُ: مَن أدخَلَكَ إلىٰ هذا القَصرِ ، وقد أرَدتُ أن أخلُوَ فيهِ اليَومَ ؟!

6001. **Imām al-Ṣādiq (AS) said,** 'Solomon, son of David (AS) one day said to his companions, 'Allah Almighty has endowed upon me a kingdom that no person after me will ever have. He has given me control of the wind, the humans, the jinn, the birds and the animals, and He has taught me the language of the birds. He has given me from everything, and with all that I possess, there has never been a day when my happiness has continued until night. I would like to enter my palace tomorrow and climb atop it and oversee my subjects. So, do not permit anyone to come to me for I do not want anyone to disturb my day.' They said, 'Yes.'
When the next day came, he took his walking staff in his hand and went up to the highest point of his palace. He stood there leaning on his staff looking at his kingdom, happy for where he was and pleased with what had been given to him, when suddenly he saw a young man with a handsome face and neat clothes coming out to him from a corner of the palace.
When Solomon saw him, he asked him, 'Who let you enter the palace when I wanted to be alone here for the day? And with whose per-mission did you enter?' The young man replied, 'The Lord of

this palace let me enter it, and with His permission I entered.' Solomon said, 'Indeed its Lord is more rightful to it than me, so who are you?' He said, 'I am the angel of death.' Solomon asked, 'What has brought you here?' He said, 'I have come to take your soul.' Solomon said, 'Do what you have been commanded to do, for this is the day of my happiness, and Allah Almighty has refused for me to be happy but only in meeting Him.'

So the angel of death took his soul, while he was leaning on his staff. Solomon stayed leaning on his staff while dead until Allah wished so, while the people continued to look at him [from below] thinking him to be alive. People then argued and differed among each other, some saying, 'Solomon has stayed leaning on his staff for all these days, and has neither become tired nor slept nor drunk nor eaten. Surely he must be our lord whom we must worship!' Others said, 'Solomon is a magician, and he is showing us that he can stand there leaning on his staff. He is conjuring our eyes, while it is not actually so!' The believers said, 'Solomon is a servant of Allah and His prophet, and Allah controls his affairs as He wishes.' So when they differed among each other Allah Almighty sent termites who crawled into Solomon's staff. When they had eaten the inside of the staff, it broke and Solomon (AS) fell from his palace onto his face.'[6819]

وبإذنِ مَن دَخَلتَ ؟! فقالَ الشابُّ: أدخَلَني هذا القَصرَ رَبُّهُ وبإذنِهِ دَخَلتُ. فقالَ: ربُّـهُ أحَـقُّ بـهِ مِنّي، فمَن أنتَ ؟ قالَ: أنا مَلَكُ المَـوتِ، قـالَ: وفيما جِئتَ ؟ قالَ: جِئتُ لأقبِضَ رُوحَكَ. قالَ: إمضِ لِما اُمِرتَ بهِ فهٰذا يومُ سُروري، وأبَى اللهُ عَزَّوجلَّ أن يكونَ لِي سُرورٌ دُونَ لِقائهِ. فقَبَضَ مَلَكُ المَوتِ رُوحَهُ وهُو مُـتَّكِئٌ عـلىٰ عَـصاه، فبَقِيَ سُـيمانُ مُتّكِئاً علىٰ عَصاهُ وهُو مَـيِّتٌ مـا شاءَ اللهُ والنّاسُ يَنظُرونَ إلَيهِ وهُم يُقَدِّرونَ أنّـه حَيٌّ، فافتُتِنوا فيهِ واختَلَفوا؛ فمِنهُم مَن قالَ: إنّ سُلَيمانَ قَد بَقِيَ مُتَّكِئاً علىٰ عَصاهُ هـذهِ الأيّـام الكَثيرَةَ ولَم يَتعَبْ ولَم يَنَمْ ولَم يَشرَبْ ولَم يأكُلْ، إنّهُ لَرَبُّنا الّذي يَجِبُ علَينا أن نَعبُدَهُ! وقالَ قَوم: إنّ سُلَيمانَ ساحِرٌ وإنّهُ يُرِينا أنّهُ واقِـفٌ مُـتّكِئٌ علىٰ عَصاهُ، يَسحَرُ أعيُنَنا ولَيس كذلكَ! وقـالَ المؤمنونَ: إنّ سُلَيمانَ، هُو عَبدُ اللهِ ونَبيُّهُ يُدَبِّرُ اللهُ أمرَهُ بما شاءَ؛ فلَمّا اختَلَفوا بَـعَثَ اللهُ عَـزَّوجلَّ الأرَضَةَ فدَبَّت في عَصاةِ سُلَيمانَ، فلَمّا أكَـلَت جَوفَها انكَسَرَتِ العَصا وخَـرَّ سُـلَيمانُ ﷺ مِـن قَصرِهِ علىٰ وَجهِهِ.[٦٧٧٦]

1707. Zacharias (AS) [Zakariyyā]

١٧٠٧ ـ زَكَرِيّا ﷺ

"And Zacharias, when he cried out to his Lord, 'My Lord! Do not leave me without an heir, and You are the best of inheritors.' So We answered his prayer, and gave him John, and remedied his wife ['s infertility] for him. Indeed they were active in [performing] good works, and they would supplicate Us with eagerness and awe and were humble before Us."[6820]

﴿وَزَكَرِيَّا إِذْ نَادَىٰ رَبَّهُ رَبِّ لَا تَذَرْنِي فَرْداً وَأَنْتَ خَيْرُ الْوَارِثِينَ * فَاسْتَجَبْنَا لَهُ وَوَهَبْنَا لَهُ يَحْيَىٰ وَأَصْلَحْنَا لَهُ زَوْجَهُ إِنَّهُمْ كَانُوا يُسَارِعُونَ فِي الْخَيْرَاتِ وَيَدْعُونَنَا رَغَباً وَرَهَباً وَكَانُوا لَنَا خَاشِعِينَ﴾.[٦٧٧٧]

(See also: Qur'an 3:38-41, 19:1-12)

(أنظر) آل عمران: ٣٨ ـ ٤١ ومريم: ١ ـ ١٢.

6002. **The Prophet (SAWA) said,** 'The Children of Israel went to seek out Zacharias in order to kill him, so he left fleeing into the desert. A tree parted open and he entered into it, but the hem of his clothes remained outside, so they came and stood around it, and sawed through him with a saw.'[6821]

٦٠٠٢ . رسولُ اللهِ ﷺ : خَرَجَت بَنو إسرائيلَ في طَلَبِ زَكريّا ليَقتُلوهُ، فخَرَجَ هارِباً في البَـرِّيَّةِ، فانفَرَجَت لَهُ شَجَرَةٌ فدَخَلَ فيها فبَقِيَت هُدبَةٌ مِن ثَـوبِهِ، فـجاؤوا حـتّىٰ قـامُوا عـلَيها فـنَشَروهُ بالمِنشارِ.[٦٧٧٨]

6003. **The Prophet (SAWA) said,** 'Zacharias was a carpenter.'[6822]

٦٠٠٣ . عنه ﷺ : كانَ زَكريّا نَجّاراً.[٦٧٧٩]

1708. John the Baptist (AS) [Yaḥyā]

١٧٠٨ ـ يَحيىٰ ﷺ

"O Zacharias! Indeed we give you the good news of a son, whose name is "John." Never before have We made anyone his namesake… 'O John!' [We said] 'Hold on with power to the Book!' And We gave him judgment while still a child, and a compassion and purity from Us. He was Godwary, and good to his parents, and was not self-willed or disobedient. Peace be to him, the day he was born, and the day he dies, and the day he is raised alive!"[6823]

﴿يا زَكَرِيَّا إِنَّا نُبَشِّرُكَ بِغُلَامٍ اسْمُهُ يَحْيَىٰ لَمْ نَجْعَلْ لَهُ مِنْ قَبْلُ سَمِيّاً * ... يَا يَحْيَىٰ خُذِ الْكِتَابَ بِقُوَّةٍ وَآتَيْنَاهُ الْحُكْمَ صَبِيّاً * وَحَنَاناً مِنْ لَدُنَّا وَزَكَـاةً وَكانَ تَقِيّاً * وَبَرّاً بِوَالِدَيْهِ وَلَمْ يَكُنْ جَبَّاراً عَصِيّاً * وَسَلَامٌ عَلَيْهِ يَوْمَ وُلِدَ وَيَوْمَ يَمُوتُ وَيَوْمَ يُبْعَثُ حَيّاً﴾.[٦٧٨٠]

6004. **The Prophet (SAWA) said,** 'May Allah be pleased with my brother John when he was invited by children to play, and he was small, and he said, 'Was I created to play?!' So, what will there be for those who perceive his statement as a sin?!'[6824]

٦٠٠٤ . رسولُ اللهِ ﷺ : رَحِمَ اللهُ أخي يحيىٰ حِينَ دَعاهُ الصِّبيانُ إلَى اللَّعِبِ وهُو صَغيرٌ فقالَ: أَلِلَّعِبِ خُـلِقتُ ؟! فكـيفَ بـمَن أدرَكَ الحِـنْثَ مِـن مَقالِهِ ؟![٦٧٨١]

6005. **Imām al-Ṣādiq (AS) narrated** from his fathers (AS) the conversation of John with the devil: 'John (AS) asked, 'Have you ever been triumphant over me for any moment?' He [the devil] said, 'No, but you have a feature that pleases me.' John asked, 'And what is that?' He said, 'You are a person who eats too much, so when you break your fast and fill yourself, it prevents you from performing some of your prayers and night vigils.' John (AS) said, 'Therefore I will make a pledge to Allah that I will never fill myself with food until I meet Him.' Satan said to him, 'I will make a pledge to Allah that I will never advise a

٦٠٠٥ . الإمامُ الصّادقُ ﷺ عن آبائهِ : ـ في ذِكرِ حَديثٍ ليحيىٰ ﷺ مَعَ الشَّيطانِ ـ : قالَ يحيىٰ ﷺ: فهَل ظَفِرتَ بِي ساعَةً قَطُّ ؟ قالَ: لا، ولٰكن فيكَ خَصلَةٌ تُعجِبُني. قالَ يحيىٰ: فما هِي ؟ قالَ: أنتَ رَجُلٌ أكُـولٌ، فـإذا أفـطَرتَ أكَـلتَ وبَشِـمتَ فيَمنَعُكَ ذلكَ مِن بَعضِ صَلاتِكَ وقِيامِكَ باللَّيلِ. قالَ يحيىٰ ﷺ: فإنّي أُعطِي اللهَ عَهداً أنّي لا أشبَعُ مِنَ الطَّعامِ حتّىٰ ألقاهُ. قالَ لَهُ إبليسُ: وأنا أُعطي اللهَ عَهداً أنّي لا أنصَحُ مُسلِماً حتّىٰ ألقـاهُ، ثُـمَّ

submitter [*muslim*] again until I meet Him.' So he left and never returned to him after that.'[6825]

خَرَجَ فما عادَ إلَيهِ بعدَ ذٰلكَ.[٦٧٨٢]

6006. **Imām al-Kāẓim (AS) said,** 'John, son of Zacharias (AS), cried and never laughed, and Jesus son of Mary (AS) would laugh and cry, and what Jesus (AS) used to do was better than what John (AS) used to do.'[6826]

٦٠٠٦. الإمامُ الكاظمُ عليه السلام: كانَ يحيَى بنُ زَكريّا عليهما السلام يَبكي ولا يَضحَكُ، وكانَ عيسَى بنُ مَريمَ عليهما السلام يَضحَكُ ويَبكي، وكانَ الّذي يَصنَعُ عيسىٰ عليه السلام أفضَلَ مِن الّذي كانَ يَصنَعُ يحيىٰ عليه السلام.[٦٧٨٣]

1709. Jesus (AS) [ʿĪsā]

١٧٠٩ ـ عيسىٰ عليه السلام

"Indeed the case of Jesus with Allah is like the case of Adam: He created him from dust, then said to him, 'Be' and he was."[6827]

﴿إنَّ مَثَلَ عِيسَىٰ عِنْدَ اللهِ كَمَثَلِ آدَمَ خَلَقَهُ مِنْ تُرَابٍ ثُمَّ قَالَ لَهُ كُنْ فَيَكُونُ﴾.[٦٧٨٤]

"And for their saying, 'We killed the Messiah, Jesus son of Mary, the apostle of Allah' though they did not kill him nor did they crucify him, but so it was made to appear to them. Indeed those who differ concerning him are surely in doubt about him: they do not have any knowledge of that beyond following conjectures, and certainly they did not kill him. Rather Allah raised him up toward Himself, and Allah is all-mighty, all-wise. There is none among the People of the Book but will surely believe in him before his death; and on the Day of Resurrection he will be a witness against them."[6828]

﴿وَقَوْلِهِمْ إنَّا قَتَلْنَا الْمَسِيحَ عِيسَىٰ بْنَ مَرْيَمَ رَسُولَ اللهِ وَمَا قَتَلُوهُ وَمَا صَلَبُوهُ وَلٰكِنْ شُبِّهَ لَهُمْ وَإِنَّ الَّذِينَ اخْتَلَفُوا فِيهِ لَفِي شَكٍّ مِنْهُ مَا لَهُمْ بِهِ مِنْ عِلْمٍ إلَّا اتِّبَاعَ الظَّنِّ وَمَا قَتَلُوهُ يَقِيناً * بَلْ رَفَعَهُ اللهُ إلَيْهِ وَكَانَ اللهُ عَزِيزاً حَكِيماً * وَإِنْ مِنْ أَهْلِ الْكِتَابِ إلَّا لَيُؤْمِنَنَّ بِهِ قَبْلَ مَوْتِهِ وَيَوْمَ الْقِيَامَةِ يَكُونُ عَلَيْهِمْ شَهِيداً﴾.[٦٧٨٥]

(See also: 3:45-58, 19:16-34, 2:87, 2:253, 5:110-118, 23:50, 43:57-65, 62:6, 62:14, 57:27)

(اُنظر) آل عمران: ٤٥ ـ ٥٨ و مريم: ١٦ ـ ٣٤ والبقرة: ٨٧، ٢٥٣ والمائدة: ١١٠ ـ ١١٨ والمؤمنون: ٥٠ والزخرف: ٥٧ ـ ٦٥ والصفّ: ٦، ١٤ والحديد: ٢٧.

6007. **Prophet Jesus (AS) said,** 'My servant is my own two hands; my riding beast is my two feet, my bed is the earth, my pillow is a rock, my warmth in the winter is the east of the earth.... I sleep and I do not possess anything, and I wake up and I do not possess anything, but there is no one on the face of this earth richer than me.'[6829]

٦٠٠٧. عيسى عليه السلام: خادِمي يَدايَ، ودابَّتي رِجلايَ، وفِراشي الأرضُ، ووِسادي الحَجَرُ، ودِفئي في الشِّتاءِ مَشارِقُ الأرضِ... أبِيتُ ولَيسَ لِي شيءٌ، وأُصبِحُ[٦٧٨٦] ولَيسَ لِي شيءٌ، ولَيسَ علىٰ وَجهِ الأرضِ أحَدٌ أغنىٰ مِنّي.[٦٧٨٧]

6008. **The Prophet (SAWA) said,** 'The first prophet from the Children of Israel was Moses (AS) and the last of them was Jesus (AS), and [they had] six hundred prophets.'[6830]

٦٠٠٨. رسولُ اللهِ صلى الله عليه وآله: أوّلُ نَبيٍّ مِن بَني إسرائيلَ موسىٰ، وآخِرُهُم عيسىٰ وستُّمِائةِ نَبيٍّ.[٦٧٨٨]

6009. **The Prophet (SAWA) said,** 'The food of Jesus was broad beans until he was taken up [by Allah], and Jesus never ate anything that had been changed by fire [i.e. cooked] until he was taken up.'[6831]

٦٠٠٩. عنه ﷺ: كانَ طَعامُ عيسَى الباقِلّاءَ حتّىٰ رُفِعَ، ولَم يأكُلْ عيسىٰ شيئاً غَيَّرَتهُ النّارُ حتّىٰ رُفِعَ. ٦٧٨٩

6010. **The Prophet (SAWA) said,** 'O Um Ayman! Did you not know that my brother Jesus never kept dinner for breakfast or breakfast for dinner?! He would eat from the leaves of trees, drink from rainwater, wear hair-cloth, sleep wherever he was, and he would say, 'Every day comes with its own sustenance.'[6832]

٦٠١٠. عنه ﷺ: يا أُمَّ أيمَنَ! أما عَلِمتِ أنّ أخي عيسىٰ كانَ لا يُخبئُ عَشاءً لِغَداءٍ ولا غَداءً لِعَشاءٍ؟! يأكُلُ مِن وَرَقِ الشَّجَرِ، ويَشرَبُ مِن ماءِ المَطَرِ، يَلبَسُ المُسُوحَ، ويَبِيتُ حَيثُ يُمسي، ويَقولُ: يأتي كُلُّ يَومٍ برِزقِهِ. ٦٧٩٠

6011. **The Prophet (SAWA) said,** 'I saw Jesus son of Mary, and lo he was a white-skinned man, and slim like a sword.'[6833]

٦٠١١. عنه ﷺ: رَأيتُ عيسَى بنَ مَريمَ فإذا هُو رجُلٌ أبيَضُ مُبَطَّنٌ ٦٧٩١ مِثلُ السَّيفِ. ٦٧٩٢

6012. **Imām ʿAlī (AS),** describing Jesus (AS) said, 'If you wish I will speak about Jesus son of Mary (AS). He used to use a rock for his pillow, wore rough clothes and ate dry food. His condiment was hunger; his lamp at night was the moon, his shade during the winter was the east of the earth and its west. His fruits and flowers were what the earth grew for the cattle. He had no wife to seduce him, nor any son to grieve him, nor wealth to deviate [his attention], nor greed to disgrace him. His two feet were his riding beast and his two hands his servant.'[6834]

٦٠١٢. الإمامُ عليٌّ ﵇ ـ في صِفَةِ عيسىٰ ﵇ ـ: وإن شِئتَ قُلتُ في عيسَىٰ بنِ مَريمَ ﵇، فلَقد كانَ يَتَوسَّدُ الحَجَرَ، ويَلبَسُ الخَشِنَ، ويأكُلُ الجَشِبَ، وكانَ إدامُهُ الجُوعَ، وسِراجُهُ باللَّيلِ القَمَرَ، وظِلالُهُ في الشِّتاءِ مَشارِقَ الأرضِ ومَغارِبَها، وفاكِهَتُهُ ورَيحانُهُ ما تُنبِتُ الأرضُ لِلبَهائمِ، ولَم تكُن لَهُ زَوجَةٌ تَفتِنُهُ، ولا وَلَدٌ يَحزُنُهُ (يَخزِنُهُ)، ولا مالٌ يَلفِتُهُ، ولا طَمَعٌ يُذِلُّهُ، دابَّتُهُ رِجلاهُ، وخادِمُهُ يَداهُ! ٦٧٩٣

6013. **Imām al-Ṣādiq (AS)** with regard to Allah's verse in the Qur'an: *"He has made me blessed, wherever I may be."*[6835], narrated on the authority of Jesus (AS), that he said, '[It means] One who greatly benefits others.'[6836]

٦٠١٣. الإمامُ الصّادقُ ﵇ ـ في قولِهِ تعالىٰ نَقلاً عن عيسىٰ ﵇: ﴿وجَعَلَنِي مُبارَكاً أيْنَما كُنتُ﴾ ٦٧٩٤ ـ: نَفّاعاً. ٦٧٩٥

The Story of Jesus and his Mother in the Qur'an

قِصّةُ عيسىٰ ﵇ وأُمِّهِ فِي القرآنِ:

The mother of Jesus was Mary daughter of ʿImrān. Her mother was pregnant with her and she vowed

كانت أمّ المسيح مريم بنت عمران حملت بها

to give whatever was in her womb in consecration to serve the mosque, assuming that the child in her belly was a male. But when she gave birth and saw that it was a female, she became unhappy and sorrowful and named her Mary [Maryam], which means servant – and her father 'Imrān had passed away before her birth, so her mother took her to the mosque to hand her over to the priests, among whom was Zacharias (AS). They [the priests] argued about who would have her in his charge, but then agreed on drawing lots in which they all participated. It came out for Zacharias so he took her in his charge, and when she came to the age of maturity, he erected a veil between them and her wherein she used to worship Allah Almighty, and no one would visit her other than Zacharias. Whenever Zacharias entered the prayer niche, he found that she had ready sustenance with her. He asked, 'O Mary, where did you get this from?!' She said, 'It is from Allah; verily Allah provides to whomsoever He likes without measure.' She was truthful, and immaculate, by the protection of Allah [against sins], pure, chosen, and spoken to – the angels spoke to her that Allah had chosen her and purified her. She was one of the obedient ones and one of Allah's signs to the worlds (Qur'an 3:35-44, 19:16, 21:91, 66:12).

أُمّها، فنذرت أن تجعل ما في بطنها إذا وضعته محرّراً يخدم المسجد، وهي تزعم أنّ ما في بطنها ذكر، فلمّا وضعتها وبان لها أنّها أُنثى حزنت وتحسّرت ثمّ سمّتها مريم أي الخادمة ـوقد كان توفّي أبوها عمران قبل ولادتها ـ فأتت بها المسجد تسلّمها للكهنة وفيهم زكريّا، فتشاجروا في كفالتها، ثمّ اصطلحوا علىٰ القرعة وساهموا، فخرج لزكريّا فكفلها، حتّىٰ إذا أدركت ضرب لها من دونهم حجاباً، فكانت تعبد الله سبحانه فيها لا يدخل عليها إلّا زكريّا. وكلّما دخل عليها زكريّا المحراب وجد عندها رزقاً، قال: يامريم أنّىٰ لكِ هذا؟! قالَت: هو من عندالله، والله يرزق من يشاء بغير حساب وقد كانت عليها السلام صدّيقة، وكانت معصومة بعصمة الله، طاهرة، مصطفاة، محدَّثة؛ حدّثها الملائكة بأنّ الله اصطفاها وطهّرها، وكانت من القانتين ومن آيات الله للعالمين (سورة آل عمران آية ٣٥ ـ ٤٤، سورة مريم آية ١٦، سورة الأنبياء آية ٩١، سورة التحريم آية ١٢).

Allah, most High, then sent the Spirit down to her while she was secluded. It manifested to her as a well-proportioned human. He told her that he was a messenger from her Lord that He may gift her, by the will of Allah, a child without a father, and he also informed her of the magnificent miracles that her child would produce. He informed her that Allah would strengthen him with the Holy Spirit, and teach him the Book and the Wisdom, the Torah and the Evangel, and that he would be a messenger to the Children of Israel with miracles and signs. He also informed her of his life and story, and then blew the Spirit into her. She became pregnant from it like a lady bearing a child (Qur'an 3:35-44).

ثمّ إنّ الله تعالىٰ أرسل إليها الرُّوح وهي محتجبة فتمثّل لها بشراً سويّاً، وذكر لها أنّه رسول من ربّها ليهب لها بإذن الله ولداً من غير أب، وبشّرها بما سيظهر من ولدها من المعجزات الباهرة، وأخبرها أنّ الله سيؤيّده بروح القدس، ويعلّمه الكتاب والحكمة والتوراة والإنجيل، ورسولاً إلىٰ بني إسرائيل ذا الآيات البيّنات، وأنبأها بشأنه وقصّته، ثمّ نفخ الروح فيها فحملت بها حمل المرأة بولدها (الآيات من آل عمران: ٣٥ ـ ٤٤).

ثمّ انتبذت مريم به مكاناً قصيّاً، فأجاءها المخاض إلىٰ جذع النخلة، قالت: يا ليتني متُّ قبل هذا وكنت نسياً منسيّاً، فناداها من تحتها أن لا تحزني قد جعل ربّك تحتك سريّاً، وهُزّي إليك بجذع النخلة تساقط عليك رُطباً جنيّاً،

Mary then withdrew with him to a distant place. The birth pangs brought her to the trunk of a date palm. She said, 'I wish I had died before this and become a forgotten thing, beyond recall.' Thereupon he called her from below saying, 'Do not grieve! Your Lord has made a spring to flow at your feet. Shake the trunk of the palm tree; freshly picked dates will drop upon you. Eat, drink, and be comforted. Then if you see any human, say, 'Indeed I have vowed a fast to the All-beneficent, so I will not speak to any human today.' Then carrying him she brought him to her people (Qur'an 19:20-27). His birth, delivery, speech and other aspects of his life were all natural and normal like other humans.

When her people saw her in such a state, they attacked her with accusations, blaming her for what they witnessed as a woman having become pregnant and given birth without a spouse. They said, 'O Mary, you have certainly come up with an odd thing! O sister of Aaron! Your father was not an evil man, nor was your mother unchaste.' Thereat she pointed to him. They said, 'How can we speak to one who is yet a baby in the cradle?!' He said, 'Indeed I am a servant of Allah! He has given me the Book and made me a prophet. He has made me blessed, wherever I may be, and He has enjoined me to [maintain] the prayer and to [pay] the *zakāt* as long as I live, and to be good to my mother, and He has not made me overbearing and rebellious. Peace is to me the day I was born, and the day I die, and the day I am raised alive.' (Qur'an 19:27-33).

Jesus (AS) grew up and became a youth, and lived a normal life as others did: eating, drinking, and they experienced situations that all other creations experience. Jesus (AS) was then given the message to give to the Children of Israel, so he went to invite them to the religion of monotheism, saying, 'I have come to you with a sign from your Lord that I will create for you from clay the form of a bird, and I will breathe into it and it will become a bird by the will of Allah; and I will heal the

فكُلي واشربي وقرّي عيناً فإمّا ترينَّ من البشر أحداً فقولي: إنّي نذرت للرحمٰن صوماً فلن أكلّم اليوم إنسيّاً، فأتت به قومها تحمله (سورة مريم: ٢٠ ـ ٢٧). وكان حمله ووضعه وكلامه وسائر شؤون وجوده من سنخ ما عند سائر الأفراد من الإنسان.

فلمّا رآها قومها ـ والحال هذه ـ ثاروا عليها بالطعنة واللوم بما يشهد به حال امرأة حملت ووضعت من غير بعل، وقالوا: يا مريم، لقد جئت شيئاً فريّاً! يا أُخت هارون ما كان أبوك امرأ سوء وما كانت أُمّك بغيّاً، فأشارت إليه، قالوا: كيف نكلّم من كان في المهد صبيّاً؟! قال: إنّي عبدالله آتاني الكتاب وجعلني نبيّاً، وجعلني مباركاً أينما كنت وأوصاني بالصلاة والزكاة ما دمت حيّاً، وبرّاً بوالدتي ولم يجعلني جبّاراً شقيّاً، والسلام عليَّ يوم ولدت ويوم أموت ويوم أُبعث حيّاً (سورة مريم آية ٢٧ ـ ٣٣)...[٦٧٩٦]

ثمّ نشأ عيسىٰ عليه السلام وشبّ وكان هو وأُمّه علَى العادة الجارية في الحياة البشريّة: يأكلان ويشربان، وفيهما ما في سائر الناس من عوارض الوجود إلىٰ آخر ما عاشا.

ثمّ إنّ عيسىٰ عليه السلام أُوتي الرسالة إلىٰ بني إسرائيل، فانبعث يدعوهم إلىٰ دين التوحيد ويقول: إنّي قد جئتكم بآية من ربّكم أنّي أخلق لكم من الطين كهيئة الطير فأنفُخ فيه فيكون طيراً بإذن الله، وأبرئ الأكمه والأبرص وأُحيي الموتىٰ بإذن الله، وأُنبّئُكُم بما تأكلون وما تدّخرون في بيوتكم، إنّ في ذلك لآية لكم، إنّ الله هو ربّي وربّكم فاعبدوه...
وكان يدعوهم إلى شريعته الجديدة وهو تصديق شريعة موسى عليه السلام، إلّا أنّه نسخ بعض ما حُرّم في التوراة تشديداً على اليهود، وكان يقول: إنّي قد جئتكم بالحكمة ولأُبيِّن لكم بعض الذي

blind and the leper and raise the dead by the will of Allah; and I will inform you of what you eat and what you keep in your houses. Verily in this is a sign for you. Verily Allah is my Lord and your Lord, so worship Him.

تختلفون فيه، وكان يقول: يا بني إسرائيل، إنّي رسول الله إليكم مصدّقاً لما بين يديّ من التوراة مبشّراً برسول يأتي من بعدي اسمه أحمد.

وأنجز ﷺ ما ذكره لهم من المعجزات كخلق الطير، وإحياء الموتى، وإبراء الأكمه والأبرص، والإخبار عن المغيّبات بإذن الله.

He continued to call them to the Oneness of Allah and His new law until he lost hope in them believing, seeing their tyranny and obstinacy, and the haughtiness of the priests and clergies. Therefore, from among the group who believed in him he chose the disciples as his helpers on the path to Allah.

... ولم يزل يدعوهم إلىٰ توحيد الله وشريعته الجديدة حتّىٰ أيس من إيمانهم؛ لِما شاهد من عتوّ القوم وعنادهم واستكبار الكهنة والأحبار عن ذلك، فانتخب من الشرذمة التي آمنت به الحواريّين أنصاراً له إلَى الله.

The Jews revolted against him wanting to kill him, so Allah took him and raised him up to Himself, and the Jews were confused. So, whoever claims that they killed him and whoever claims that they crucified him, [it was not so] rather it was made to appear to them thus.[6837]

ثم إنّ اليهود ثاروا عليه يريدون قتله فتوفّاه الله ورفعه إليه، وشُبِّه لليهود: فمن زاعم أنّهم قتلوه، ومن زاعم أنّهم صلبوه، ولكن شُبّه لهم.

آل عمران: آية ٤٥ ـ ٥٨، الزخرف: آية ٦٣ ـ ٦٥، الصّف: آية ٦ و ١٤، المائدة: آية ١١٠ و ١١١، النساء: آية ١٥٧ و ١٥٨، فهذه جمل ما قصّه لقرآن في عيسى بن مريم وأُمّه.[٦٧٩٧]

1710. Irmiyā' (AS)

١٧١٠ ـ إرمِيا ﷺ

"Or him who came upon a township as it lay fallen on its trellises. He said, 'How will Allah revive this after its death?!'"[6838]

﴿أَوْ كَالَّذِي مَرَّ عَلَىٰ قَرْيَةٍ وَهِيَ خَاوِيَةٌ عَلَىٰ عُرُوشِهَا قَالَ أَنَّىٰ يُحْيِي هَـٰذِهِ اللهُ بَعْدَ مَوْتِهَا ...﴾.[٦٧٩٨]

6014. **Imām al-Bāqir (AS),** when a Christian scholar asked him about a man who copulated with his wife and she became pregnant with two, both in one hour, and she gave birth to both in one hour, and they both died in one hour, and they were both buried in one grave, but one lived for one hundred and fifty years and the other lived for fifty years - who were they? He replied, "Uzair and 'Uzra. Their mother was pregnant with them as you have described, and she gave birth as you described, and 'Uzair and 'Uzra lived for so and so years. Allah then made 'Uzair die for one hundred years, then he was revived and lived with 'Uzra for fifty years. Then they both died together at one time.'[6839]

٦٠١٤. الإمامُ الباقرُ ﷺ ـ لَمّا سَأَلَهُ عالِمٌ نَصرانِيٌّ عن رجُلٍ دَنا مِنِ امرأتِهِ فحَمَلَت باثنَينِ، حَمَلَتهُما جَميعاً في ساعَةٍ واحِدَةٍ، ووَلَدَتهُما في ساعَةٍ واحِدَةٍ، وماتا في ساعَةٍ واحِدَةٍ، ودُفِنا في قَبرٍ واحِدٍ، عاشَ أحَدُهُما خَمسينَ ومِائَةَ سَنَةٍ وعاشَ الآخَرُ خَمسِينَ سَنَةً، مَن هُما؟ ـ: عُزَيرٌ وعُزرَةُ، كانا حَمَلَت أُمُّهُما بِهما علىٰ ما وَصَفتَ ووَضَعَتهُما علىٰ ما وَصَفتَ وعاشَ عُزَيرٌ وعُزرَةُ كذا وكذا سَنَةً، ثُمّ أماتَ اللهُ تباركَ وتعالىٰ عُزَيراً مِائَةَ سَنَةٍ، ثُمّ بُعِثَ وعاشَ مَع عُزرَةَ هذهِ الخَمسينَ سَنَةً، وماتا كِلاهُما في ساعَةٍ واحِدَةٍ.[٦٧٩٩]

6015. **Imām al-Ṣādiq (AS) said,** 'Allah brought death to the prophet Irmiyā' who looked at the ruins of Jerusalem and its surroundings when Nebuchadnezzar invaded it. He said, 'How will Allah revive this after its death?!' So Allah made him die for a hundred years, then He resurrected him. He looked at his organs and how they came together and how they became covered in flesh, and at his limbs and veins and how they were connected together. When he sat upright he said, *'I know that Allah has power over all things'*.'[6840]

٦٠١٥. الإمامُ الصّادقُ عليه السلام : أماتَ اللهُ إرمياءَ النَّبيَّ عليه السلام الّذي نَظَرَ إلىٰ خَرابِ بَيتِ المَقدِسِ وما حَولَهُ حينَ غَزاهُم بُختُ نَصَّرُ، وقالَ: أنّىٰ يُحيي هذهِ اللهُ بَعدَ مَوتِها؟! فأماتَهُ اللهُ مِائَةَ عامٍ ثُمّ أحياهُ، ونَظَرَ إلىٰ أعضائهِ كيفَ تَلتَئمُ وكيفَ تَلبَسُ اللَّحمَ، وإلىٰ مَفاصِلِه وعُروقِهِ كَيفَ تُوصَلُ، فلمّا استَوىٰ قاعداً قالَ: ﴿أعْلَمُ أنّ اللهَ علىٰ كُلِّ شَيْءٍ قَديرٌ﴾ ٦٨٠١،٦٨٠٠.

1711. Jonah (AS) [Yūnus]

١٧١١ـ يونس عليه السلام

"And indeed Jonah was one of the apostles, when he absconded toward the laden ship. Then he drew lots with them and he was the one to be refuted. Then the fish swallowed him while he was blameworthy. And had he not been one of those who celebrate Allah's glory, he would have surely remained in its belly till the day they will be resurrected. Then We cast him on a bare shore, and he was sick. So we made a gourd plant grow above him. We sent him to a [community of] hundred thousand or more, and they believed [in him]. So We provided for them for a while."[6841]

﴿وَإِنَّ يُونُسَ لَمِنَ الْمُرْسَلِينَ * إِذْ أَبَقَ إِلَى الْفُلْكِ الْمَشْحُونِ * فَسَاهَمَ فَكَانَ مِنَ الْمُدْحَضِينَ * فَالْتَقَمَهُ الْحُوتُ وَهُوَ مُلِيمٌ * فَلَوْلَا أَنَّهُ كَانَ مِنَ الْمُسَبِّحِينَ * لَلَبِثَ فِي بَطْنِهِ إِلَىٰ يَوْمِ يُبْعَثُونَ * فَنَبَذْنَاهُ بِالْعَرَاءِ وَهُوَ سَقِيمٌ * وَأَنْبَتْنَا عَلَيْهِ شَجَرَةً مِنْ يَقْطِينٍ * وَأَرْسَلْنَاهُ إِلَىٰ مِائَةِ أَلْفٍ أَوْ يَزِيدُونَ * فَآمَنُوا فَمَتَّعْنَاهُمْ إِلَىٰ حِينٍ﴾ ٦٨٠٢.

(See also: Qur'an: 10:98, 21:87-88, 68:48-50)

(أنظر) يونس: ٩٨ والأنبياء: ٨٧، ٨٨ والقلم: ٤٨ ـ ٥٠.

6016. **The Prophet (SAWA) said,** 'It is not appropriate for a prophet to say: 'I am better in the eyes of Allah than Jonah son of Mattā'.'[6842]

٦٠١٦. رسولُ اللهِ صلى الله عليه وآله : لا يَنبَغي لأحَدٍ أن يَقولَ: أنا عندَ اللهِ خَيرٌ مِن يُونُسَ بنِ مَتّىٰ. ٦٨٠٣

6017. **Imām 'Alī (AS),** when some Jews asked him about a jail which went around the whole world with its prisoner, replied, 'O Jew, as for the jail that circled all parts of the world with its captive, it was the whale that imprisoned Jonah in its stomach.'[6843]

٦٠١٧. الإمامُ عليٌّ عليه السلام ـ لَمّا سَألَهُ بَعضُ اليهودِ عن سِجنٍ طافَ أقطارَ الأرضِ بِصاحِبِهِ ـ: يا يَهوديُّ، أمّا السِّجنُ الّذي طافَ أقطارَ الأرضِ بِصاحِبِهِ فإنّهُ الحُوتُ الّذي حُبِسَ يُونُسُ في بَطنِهِ. ٦٨٠٤

Details of the Story of Jonah (AS)

كلامٌ في قِصّةِ يونس عليه السلام :

Jonah (AS) was a messenger whom Allah Almighty sent to his people, and they were a large group

أنّ يونس عليه السلام كان من الرسل أرسله الله تعالىٰ إلىٰ

exceeding one hundred thousand. He invited them and they did not respond other than to call him a liar and to repudiate him, until the punishment Jonah warned them of came. He then left them.

قومه وهم جمع كثير يزيدون علىٰ مائة ألف فدعاهم فلم يجيبوه إلّا بالتكذيب والردّ، حتّىٰ جاءهم عذاب أوعدهم به يونس، ثمّ خرج من بينهم.

When the punishment came down upon them, and they saw it with their own eyes they all turned to belief and repentance to Allah Almighty. So, Allah lifted the punishment of shame from them in this world. Jonah (AS) then asked about their situation when he saw that the punishment had been raised from them – since he did not know of their [recent] belief and repentance – so he did not return to them. He left angry and upset with them, and his state was like that of one who absconds from his Lord, in a rage, thinking that He would not put him through hardship. He left for the sea in a laden ship, and a large fish came after them. They could not avert it in any way other than to throw one of them overboard so that the fish may swallow him and the boat would be safe from it. They drew lots between themselves and Jonah (AS) was chosen, so they threw him in the sea where the fish swallowed him and the ship was saved.

فلمّا أشرف عليهم العذاب وشاهدوه مشاهدة عيان أجمعوا علَى الإيمان والتوبة إلَى الله سبحانه، فكشف الله عنهم عذاب الخزي في الحياة الدنيا.

ثمّ إنّ يونس ﷺ استخبر عن حالهم فوجد العذاب انكشف عنهم ـ وكأنّه لم يعلم بإيمانهم وتوبتهم ـ فلم يعد إليهم، وذهب لوجهه علىٰ ما به من الغضب والسخط عليهم، فكان ظاهر حاله حال من يأبق من ربّه مغاضباً عليه ظانّاً أنّه لا يقدر عليه، وركب البحر في فُلك مشحون، فعرض لهم حوت عظيم لم يجدوا بدّاً من أن يلقوا إليه واحداً منهم يبتلعه وينجو الفلك بذلك، فساهموا وقارعوا فيما بينهم فأصابت يونس ﷺ، فألقوه في البحر فابتلعه الحوت ونجت السفينة.

Allah, Glory be to Him, kept him alive and well inside the fish's belly for days and nights, and Jonah (AS) knew that this was a trial that Allah was testing him with as a punishment for what he did. He was calling out while inside its belly, *"There is no god except You! You are immaculate! I have indeed been among the wrongdoers!"*

ثمّ إنّ الله سبحانه حفظه حيّاً سويّاً في بطنه أيّاماً وليالي، ويونس ﷺ يعلم أنّها بليّة ابتلاه الله بها مؤاخذة بما فعل، وهو ينادي في بطنه أن ﴿لا إلٰه إلّا أنتَ سُبْحانَكَ إنّي كُنْتُ مِنَ الظّالمينَ﴾.

Allah answered his prayer and ordered the fish to spit him out. It cast him on a bare shore, and he was sick. So Allah Almighty made a gourd plant grow above him so he used its leaves to shadow him. Then when his health was restored, Allah sent him back to his people. They accepted his call and believed in him, so Allah gave them provision until a fixed time.'[6844]

فاستجاب الله له، فأمر الحوت أن يلفظه، فنبذه بالعراء وهو سقيم، فأنبت الله سبحانه عليه شجرة من يقطين يستظلّ بأوراقها، ثمّ لمّا استقامت حاله أرسله إلى قومه، فلبّوا دعوته وآمنوا به فمتّعهم الله إلى حين.[٦٨٠٥]

371

PROPHETHOOD (3)

Muḥammad the Messenger of Allah

النُّبُوَّةُ (٣)

مُحَمَّدٌ رَسُولُ اللهِ

1712. Muḥammad, the Messenger of Allah (SAWA)

١٧١٢ـ مُحَمَّدٌ رَسولُ اللهِ ﷺ

"Muḥammad is the Apostle of Allah."[6845]

﴿مُحَمَّدٌ رَسُولُ اللهِ﴾ ٦٨٠٦.

"There has certainly come to you an apostle from among yourselves. Grievous to him is your distress; he has deep concern for you, and is most kind and merciful to the faithful."[6846]

﴿لَقَدْ جَاءَكُمْ رَسُولٌ مِنْ أَنْفُسِكُمْ عَزِيزٌ عَلَيْهِ مَا عَنِتُّمْ حَرِيصٌ عَلَيْكُمْ بِالْمُؤْمِنِينَ رَؤُوفٌ رَحِيمٌ﴾ ٦٨٠٧.

"O Prophet! Indeed We have sent you as a witness, as a bearer of good news and as a warner and as a summoner to Allah by His permission, and as a radiant lamp."[6847]

﴿يَا أَيُّهَا النَّبِيُّ إِنَّا أَرْسَلْنَاكَ شَاهِداً وَمُبَشِّراً وَنَذِيراً * وَدَاعِياً إِلَى اللهِ بِإِذْنِهِ وَسِرَاجاً مُنِيراً﴾ ٦٨٠٨.

6018. **The Prophet (SAWA),** when a Jew asked him about the reason for him being called Muḥammad, Aḥmad, Abū al-Qāsim, Bashīr, Nadhīr, and Dāʿī – he replied, 'As for Muḥammad, I am praised [*maḥmūd*] in this earth, and Aḥmad is that I am praised in the Heaven. As for Abū al-Qāsim, Allah will divide the Day of Resurrection into two parts; the part (*qisma*) of Hell, and those who disbelieve in me from among the first ones to the last ones will be in the Hellfire; and the part of Heaven, and whoever believes in me from among the first ones to the last ones, and has acknowledged my prophethood will be in Heaven. Al-Dāʿī [the caller] is that I call people to the religion of my Lord Almighty. Al-Nadhīr [the warner] is that I warn people who disobey me about the Hellfire. Al-Bashīr [bringer of good news] is that I bring the good news of Heaven to those who obey me.'[6848]

٦٠١٨. رسولُ اللهِ ﷺ ـ لَمّا سألَهُ يهوديٌّ عَن وَجهِ تَسمِيَتِهِ بمُحمّدٍ وأحمَدَ وأبي القاسِمِ وبَشيرٍ ونَذيرٍ وداعٍ؟ ـ: أمّا مُحمّدٌ فإنّي مَحمودٌ في الأرضِ، وأمّا أحمَدُ فإنّي مَحمودٌ في السَّماءِ، وأمّا أبو القاسِمِ فإنَّ اللهَ عزَّوجلَّ يَقسِمُ يَومَ القِيامَةِ قِسمَةَ النّارِ؛ فمَن كَفَرَ بي مِنَ الأوَّلينَ والآخِرينَ ففي النّارِ، ويَقسِمُ قِسمَةَ الجَنّةِ؛ فمَن آمَنَ بي وأقَرَّ بِنُبُوَّتي ففي الجَنّةِ. وأمّا الدّاعي فإنّي أدعُو النّاسَ إلىٰ دِينِ ربّي عزَّوجلَّ، وأمّا النَّذيرُ فإنّي أُنذِرُ بالنّارِ مَن عَصاني، وأمّا البَشيرُ فإنّي أُبشِّرُ بالجَنّةِ مَن أطاعَني. ٦٨٠٩

1713. The Seal of the Prophets

١٧١٣ ـ خاتَمُ النَّبِيِّينَ ﷺ

"Muhammad is not the father of any man among you, but he is the Apostle of Allah and the seal of the Prophets, and Allah has knowledge of all things."[6849]

﴿ما كانَ مُحَمَّدٌ أبَا أحَدٍ مِنْ رِجالِكُمْ وَلكِنْ رَسُولَ اللهِ وَخاتَمَ النَّبِيِّينَ وَكانَ اللهُ بِكُلِّ شَيْءٍ عَلِيماً﴾.[٦٨١٠]

6019. **The Prophet (SAWA) said,** 'I am the successor after whom there is no prophet.'[6850]

٦٠١٩. رسولُ اللهِ ﷺ: أنا العاقِبُ الّذي لَيسَ بَعدَهُ نَبيٌّ.[٦٨١١]

6020. **Imām al-Ṣādiq (AS) said,** 'Allah, may His remembrance be exalted, sealed the prophets with your prophet, so there will never be a prophet after him, and He sealed the books with your Book, so there will never be a Book after it.'[6851]

٦٠٢٠. الإمامُ الصّادقُ ﷺ: إنّ اللهَ عَزَّ ذِكرُهُ خَتَمَ بِنَبِيِّكُمُ النَّبِيِّينَ فلا نَبيَّ بَعدَهُ أبداً، وخَتَمَ بكتابِكُمُ الكُتُبَ فلا كِتابَ بَعدَهُ أبداً.[٦٨١٢]

6021. **Imām al-Ṣādiq (AS) said,** '.... till Muḥammad came, and he brought the Qur'an and its laws and teachings. So, the permitted (*ḥalāl*) of Muḥammad is permitted until the Day of Resurrection, and his forbidden (*ḥarām*) is forbidden until the Day of Resurrection.'[6852]

٦٠٢١. عنه ﷺ: ...حتّى جاءَ محمّدٌ ﷺ فجاءَ بالقرآنِ وبِشَريعَتِهِ ومِنهاجِهِ، فحَلالُهُ حَلالٌ إلى يَومِ القِيامَةِ، وحَرامُهُ حَرامٌ إلى يَومِ القِيامَةِ.[٦٨١٣]

1714. Muḥammad (SAWA) in the Words of Muḥammad (SAWA) himself

١٧١٤ ـ مُحَمَّدٌ ﷺ عَلى لِسانِ مُحَمَّدٍ ﷺ

6022. **The Prophet (SAWA) said,** 'I have been educated by Allah Himself and 'Alī has been educated by me.'[6853]

٦٠٢٢. رسولُ اللهِ ﷺ: أنا أديبُ اللهِ وعَليٌّ أديبي.[٦٨١٤]

6023. **The Prophet (SAWA) said,** 'O people, verily I am a mercy gifted [to you].'[6854]

٦٠٢٣. عنه ﷺ: أيُّها النّاسُ، إنّما أنا رَحمَةٌ مُهداةٌ.[٦٨١٥]

6024. **The Prophet (SAWA) said,** 'I am the [fulfilment of the] prayer of Abraham which he recited while raising the foundations of the House: *'Our Lord, raise amongst them an apostle from among them, who should recite to them Your signs, and teach them the Book and wisdom and purify them.'*[6855 6856]

٦٠٢٤. عنه ﷺ: أنا دَعوَةُ إبراهيمَ، قالَ وهُو يَرفَعُ القَواعِدَ مِنَ البَيتِ: ﴿رَبَّنا وابعَثْ فِيهِم رَسُولاً مِنْهُم...﴾.[٦٨١٦، ٦٨١٧]

6025. **The Prophet (SAWA) said,** 'I am the chief of the children of Adam, without pride.'[6857]

٦٠٢٥. عنه ﷺ: أنا سَيِّدُ وُلدِ آدَمَ ولا فَخرَ.[٦٨١٨]

6026. **The Prophet (SAWA) said,** 'I am the leader of the messengers, without pride, and I am the seal of the prophets, without pride; and I am the first intercessor and the first mediator, without pride.'[6858]

٦٠٢٦ . عنه ﷺ : أنا قائدُ المُرسَلينَ ولا فَخرَ، وأنا خاتَمُ النَّبيِّينَ ولا فخرَ، وأنا أوّلُ شافِعٍ وأوّلُ مُشَفَّعٍ ولا فَخرَ.[٦٨١٩]

6027. **The Prophet (SAWA) said,** 'I will be the first to enter into the presence of the Noble, all-Conqueror on the Day of Judgment, with His Book and my household, then my community, where I will ask them, 'What did you do with the Book of Allah and with my household?'[6859]

٦٠٢٧ . عنه ﷺ : أنا أوّلُ وافِدٍ علَى العَزيزِ الجَبّارِ يَومَ القِيامَةِ وكِتابُهُ وأهلُ بَيتي ثُمّ أُمَّتي، ثُمّ أسألُهُم: ما فَعَلتُم بكِتابِ اللهِ وبأهلِ بَيتي ؟[٦٨٢٠]

6028. **The Prophet (SAWA) said,** 'Indeed the most pious one from among you and the person most acquainted with Allah is me.'[6860]

٦٠٢٨ . عنه ﷺ : أنا أتقاكُم للهِ، وأعلَمُكُم لِحُدودِ اللهِ.[٦٨٢١]

6029. **The Prophet (SAWA) said,** 'Allah has not created a creation better than me, nor dearer to Him than me.'[6861]

٦٠٢٩ . عنه ﷺ : ما خَلَقَ اللهُ خَلقاً أفضَلَ مِنّي، ولا أكرَمَ علَيهِ مِنّي.[٦٨٢٢]

6030. **The Prophet (SAWA) said,** 'I have been given five things that no prophet before me was given: I was sent to the white, black and red; the earth has been made pure for me and a place for prostration; I have been made victorious with awe; and spoils were permitted for me when they were not permitted to any before me [or to any prophet before me]; and I have been given the collection of wise words [the Qur'an].'[6862]

٦٠٣٠ . عنه ﷺ : أُعطيتُ خَمساً لَم يُعطَهُنَّ نَبيٌّ كانَ قَبلي: أُرسِلتُ إلَى الأبيَضِ والأسوَدِ والأحمَرِ، وجُعِلَت لِيَ الأرضُ طَهوراً ومَسجِداً، ونُصِرتُ بالرُّعبِ، وأُحِلَّت لِيَ الغَنائمُ ولَم تُحَلَّ لأحَدٍ ـ أو قالَ: لنَبيٍّ ـ قَبلي، وأُعطِيتُ جَوامِعَ الكَلِمِ.[٦٨٢٣]

1715. Muḥammad (SAWA) in the Words of ʿAlī (AS)

١٧١٥ ـ مُحَمَّدٌ ﷺ عَلىٰ لِسانِ عليٍّ عليه السلام

6031. **Imām ʿAlī (AS),** when asked about the characteristics of the Prophet (SAWA) while he was sitting with his legs tucked under his sword-belt in the mosque of Kūfa, said, 'The messenger of Allah (SAWA) had white skin tinted with redness, with large black eyes, abundant lank hair, a thick beard, flat hairy cheeks, fine hair on his chest. His neck was [white] like a silver pitcher, he had hair from

٦٠٣١ . الإمامُ عليٌّ عليه السلام ـ لمّا سُئلَ عن صِفَةِ النَّبيِّ ﷺ وهُو مُحْتَبٍ بحَمائلِ سَيفِهِ في مَسجِدِ الكُوفَةِ ـ: كانَ رسولُ اللهِ ﷺ أبيَضَ اللَّونِ مُشرَباً حُمرَةً، أدعَجَ العَينِ، سَبطَ الشَّعرِ، كَثَّ اللِّحيَةِ، سَهلَ الخَدِّ، ذا وَفرَةٍ، دَقيقَ المَسرُبَةِ، كأنّ عُنقَهُ

the top of his chest to his belly flowing like a cane, and he did not have any other hair on his stomach or chest. He had thick hands and feet [big bones], when he walked he walked fast and when he stood up it was like he had been erected from a rock. When he turned he would turn his whole body. The perspiration on in his face was like pearls, and the scent of his perspiration was more fragrant than strong musk. He was neither short nor tall, nor was he frail, nor avaricious. I have never seen someone like him (SAWA) before him or after him.'[6863]

إبريقُ فِضَّةٍ، لَهُ شَعرٌ مِن لَبَّتِهِ إلىٰ سُرَّتِهِ يَجري كالقَضيبِ، لَيسَ في بَطنِهِ ولا صَدرِهِ شَعرٌ غَيرُهُ، شَثْنُ الكَفِّ والقَدَمِ، إذا مَشىٰ كأنّما يَنحَدِرُ مِن صَبَبٍ، وإذا قامَ كأنّما يَنقَلِعُ مِن صَخرٍ، إذا التَفَتَ التَفَتَ جَميعاً، كأنَّ عَرَقَهُ في وَجهِهِ اللُّؤلُؤُ، ولَريحُ عَرَقِهِ أطيَبُ مِن المِسكِ الأذفَرِ، لَيسَ بالقَصيرِ ولا بالطَّويلِ، ولا بالعاجِزِ ولا اللَّئيمِ، لَم أرَ قَبلَهُ ولا بَعدَهُ مِثلَهُ ﷺ.[٦٨٢٤]

6032. **Imām ʿAlī (AS) said,** '...until Allah sent Muḥammad (SAWA) as a witness, a warner and a bringer of glad tidings. He was the best of people as a child, and the most noble of them when old. He was the purest of the pure in character and the most generous of all givers of all time.'[6864]

٦٠٣٢. عنه عليه السلام :... حتّىٰ بَعَثَ اللهُ محمّداً ﷺ شَهيداً وبَشيراً ونَذيراً، خَيرَ البَرِيَّةِ طِفلاً، وأنجَبَها كَهلاً، وأطهَرَ المُطَهَّرينَ شِيمَةً، وأجوَدَ المُستَمطَرينَ دِيمَةً.[٦٨٢٥]

6033. **Imām ʿAlī (AS) said,** 'No sooner was he confronted with two tasks than he took the hardest of them.'[6865]

٦٠٣٣. عنه عليه السلام : لا عَرَضَ لَهُ أمرانِ إلّا أخَذَ بأشَدِّهِما.[٦٨٢٦]

6034. **Imām ʿAlī (AS) said,** 'Allah did not create a human being better than Muḥammad (SAWA).'[6866]

٦٠٣٤. عنه عليه السلام : ما بَرَأ اللهُ نَسمَةً خَيراً مِن محمّدٍ ﷺ.[٦٨٢٧]

6035. **Imām ʿAlī (AS) said,** 'The Prophet (SAWA) was like a roaming physician who has set ready his ointments and heated his instruments. He used them wherever the need arose for curing blind hearts, deaf ears, and dumb tongues. He followed with his medicines the spots of negligence and the places of perplexity. They [the people] did not take the light from the lights of his wisdom nor did they produce flame from the flint of his sparkling knowledge. So in this matter, they are like grazing cattle and hard stones.'[6867]

٦٠٣٥. عنه عليه السلام : طَبيبٌ دَوّارٌ بطِبِّهِ، قد أحكَمَ مَراهِمَهُ، وأحمىٰ (أمضىٰ) مَواسِمَهُ، يَضَعُ ذلكَ حَيثُ الحاجَةُ إلَيهِ، مِن قُلوبٍ عُميٍ، وآذانٍ صُمٍّ، وألسِنَةٍ بُكمٍ، مُتَتَبِّعٌ بدَوائهِ مَواضِعَ الغَفلَةِ ومَواطِنَ الحَيرَةِ، لَم يَستَضيئوا بأضواءِ الحِكمَةِ، ولَم يَقدَحوا بزِنادِ العُلومِ الثّاقِبَةِ، فهُم في ذلكَ كالأنعامِ السّائمَةِ، والصُّخورِ القاسِيَةِ.[٦٨٢٨]

6036. **Imām ʿAlī (AS) said,** 'I am but a servant from among the servants of Muḥammad (SAWA).'[6868]

٦٠٣٦. عنه عليه السلام : إنّما أنا عَبدٌ مِن عَبيدِ محمّدٍ ﷺ.[٦٨٢٩]

1716. The Universality of the Message of Muḥammad (SAWA)

١٧١٦ـ عالَمِيَّةُ رِسالَةِ مُحَمَّدٍ ﷺ

"We did not send you except as a bearer of good news and a warner to all mankind, but most people do not know."[6869]

«وَمَا أَرْسَلْنَاكَ إِلَّا كَافَّةً لِلنَّاسِ بَشِيراً وَنَذِيراً وَلَكِنَّ أَكْثَرَ النَّاسِ لَا يَعْلَمُونَ». ٦٨٣٠

6037. **The Prophet (SAWA) said,** 'I am the messenger of those who live in my time, as well as those who will be born after me.'[6870]

٦٠٣٧. رسول الله ﷺ: أنا رَسولُ مَن أدرَكتُ حَيّاً ومَن يُولَدُ بَعدي. ٦٨٣١

6038. **The Prophet (SAWA) said,** 'Every prophet before me was sent to their people in their own language, but I was sent to all, black and red [skinned], in Arabic.'[6871]

٦٠٣٨. عنه ﷺ: بُعِثَ كلُّ نبيٍّ كانَ قَبلي إلىٰ أُمَّتِهِ بلِسانِ قومِهِ، وبَعَثَني إلىٰ كُلِّ أسوَدَ وأحمَرَ بالعَربيّةِ. ٦٨٣٢

1717. The Best Family Among All People

١٧١٧ـ خَيرُ النّاسِ أُسرَةً

6039. **Imām ʿAlī (AS) said,** 'His family is the best family and his tree is the best tree. Its branches are moderate and its fruits hang down. His birth was in Makkah and his migration was to Ṭayba [Madina]. In it his remembrance was elevated and from it his voice spread.'[6872]

٦٠٣٩. الإمامُ عليٌّ ﷺ: أُسرَتُهُ خَيرُ أُسرةٍ، وشَجَرَتُهُ خَيرُ شَجَرةٍ، أغصانُها مُعتَدِلَةٌ، وثِمارُها مُتَهَدِّلَةٌ، مَولِدُهُ بمَكّةَ، وهِجرَتُهُ بطَيبَةَ، عَلا بِها ذِكرُهُ، وامتَدَّ مِنها صَوتُهُ. ٦٨٣٣

6040. **Imām ʿAlī (AS) said,** 'I testify that Muḥammad is His servant and messenger, and the chief of His creation; whenever Allah divided the line of descent, He put him in the better one.'[6873]

٦٠٤٠. عنه ﷺ: أشهَدُ أنّ محمّداً عَبدُهُ ورَسولُهُ، وسَيِّدُ عِبادِهِ، كُلَّما نَسَخَ اللهُ الخَلقَ فِرقَتَينِ جَعَلَهُ في خَيرِهِما. ٦٨٣٤

1718. The Characteristics of the Prophet (SAWA)

١٧١٨ـ خَصائصُ الرَّسولِ ﷺ

1. A Great Character

١ـ عَلىٰ خُلُقٍ عَظيمٍ

"And indeed you possess a great character."[6874]

«وَإِنَّكَ لَعَلَىٰ خُلُقٍ عَظِيمٍ». ٦٨٣٥

6041. **Imām ʿAlī (AS),** describing the Prophet (SAWA), said, 'He had the most generous of hands, and his chest was the boldest of all. He was the most truthful of people in speech and the

٦٠٤١. الإمامُ عليٌّ ﷺ ـ في صفة النبيّ ﷺ ـ: كان أجوَدَ النّاسِ كَفّاً، وأجرأَ النّاسِ صَدراً، وأصدَقَ

most trustworthy in liability. He was the most lenient of people in disposition, and the kindest of them in social companionship. Those who saw him would spontaneously respect him, and those who associated with him and came to know him loved him. I have never seen anyone like him, before him or after him (SAWA).'[6875]

النّاسِ لَهجَةً وأوفاهمُ ذِمَّةً، وألينَهُم عَريكَةً، وأكرَمَهُم عِشرَةً. مَن رَآهُ بَديهَةً هابَهُ، ومَن خالَطَهُ فعَرَفَهُ أحَبَّهُ، يَقولُ ناعِتُهُ: لَم أرَ قَبلَهُ ولا بَعدَهُ مِثلَهُ.[٦٨٣٦]

6042. **ʿĀ'isha,** when asked about the character of the Prophet (SAWA) in his house, said, 'He was the best of people in character; he neither swore nor was obscene; he did not make a clamour in the markets, and did not return bad with its like, but he would pardon and forgive.'[6876]

٦٠٤٢. عائشةُ ـ لَمّا سُئلَت عن خُلقِ النّبيِّ ﷺ في بَيتِهِ ـ: كانَ أحسَنَ النّاسِ خُلقاً، لَم يَكُن فاحِشاً ولا مُتَفَحِّشاً، ولا صَخّاباً في الأسواقِ، ولا يَجزي بالسَّيِّئَةِ مِثلَها، ولكنْ يَعفو ويَصفَحُ.[٦٨٣٧]

6043. **ʿĀ'isha said,** 'There was no characteristic more hated by the Messenger of Allah (SAWA) than lying, and whenever he found out about any of his companions [as having lied], he would retract from that person until he knew that that person had repented.'[6877]

٦٠٤٣. عائشة: ما كانَ خُلقٌ أبغضَ إلىٰ رَسولِ اللهِ ﷺ مِن الكِذبِ، وما اطَّلَعَ مِنهُ علىٰ شيءٍ عِندَ أحَدٍ مِن أصحابِهِ فيَبخَلُ لَهُ مِن نَفسِهِ حتّىٰ يَعلَمَ أن أحدَثَ تَوبَةً.[٦٨٣٨]

6044. **ʿĀ'isha said,** 'He was the most lenient of people, and the kindest of people. He was as normal as one of your men, except that he laughed and smiled a lot.'[6878]

٦٠٤٤. عائشة: كانَ ﷺ أليَنَ النّاسِ، وأكرَمَ النّاسِ، وكانَ رجُلاً مِن رِجالِكُم إلّا أنّهُ كانَ ضَحّاكاً بَسّاماً.[٦٨٣٩]

6045. **Muḥammad b. al-Ḥanafiyya said,** 'The Messenger of Allah (SAWA) almost never said to something: 'No'. When he was asked to do something that he wanted to do, he would say 'Yes', and if he was asked to do something that he did not want to do he would keep silent, and it [the answer] would be known from his silence.'[6879]

٦٠٤٥. محمّد بنِ الحَنَفيّةِ: كانَ رَسولُ اللهِ ﷺ لا يَكادُ يَقولُ لشيءٍ: لا، فإذا هُو سُئلَ فأرادَ أن يَفعَلَ، قالَ: نَعَم، وإذا لَم يُرِدْ أن يَفعَلَ سَكَتَ، فكانَ قد عُرِفَ ذلكَ مِنهُ.[٦٨٤٠]

6046. **ʿAbdullāh b. al-Ḥārith said,** 'I have never seen someone who smiled more than the Messenger of Allah (SAWA).'[6880]

٦٠٤٦. عبدُاللهِ بن الحارِثِ: ما رَأيتُ أحَداً أكثَرَ تَبَسُّماً مِن رسولِ اللهِ ﷺ.[٦٨٤١]

2. Trustworthy

٢ ـ أمينٌ

6047. **The Prophet (SAWA) said,** 'By Allah, I am trustworthy in the Heavens and trustworthy on the earth.'[6881]

٦٠٤٧ . رسولُ اللهِ ﷺ : أما واللهِ إنّي لَأمينٌ في السَّماءِ وأمينٌ في الأرضِ.[٦٨٤٢]

6048. **Ibn Isḥāq said,** 'The [tribe of] Quraysh used to call the Prophet (SAWA) 'the trustworthy' (*al-amīn*) before revelation had descended onto him.'[6882]

٦٠٤٨ . ابن اسحاق : كانَت قُرَيشُ تُسَمّي رَسولَ اللهِ ﷺ قَبلَ أن يَنزِلَ علَيهِ الوَحيُ : الأمينَ.[٦٨٤٣]

6049. **Ibn Isḥāq said,** 'Khadīja, daughter of Khuwaylid was a female merchant with dignity and wealth. She would employ men with her money and lend them money [to invest], receiving a portion of its profit, and the people of Quraysh were merchants. So when she heard about the Prophet (SAWA) and his being truthful in what he says, his faithfulness in trusts and his great morals, she sent for him and offered for him to take some of her wealth to Syria as a trader.'[6883]

٦٠٤٩ . ابن اسحاق : كانَت خَديجَةُ بِنتُ خُوَيلدٍ امرأةً تاجِرَةً ذاتَ شَرَفٍ ومالٍ، تَستأجِرُ الرِّجالَ في مالِها وتُضارِبُهُم إيّاهُ بشيءٍ تَجعَلُهُ لَهُم، وكانَت قُرَيشُ قَوماً تُجّاراً ، فلَمّا بَلَغَها عن رَسولِ اللهِ ﷺ ما بَلَغَها مِن صِدقِ حَديثِهِ ، وعِظَمِ أمانَتِهِ ، وكَرَمِ أخلاقِهِ ، بَعَثَت إلَيهِ فعَرَضَت علَيهِ أن يَخرُجَ في مالٍ لَها إلَى الشّامِ تاجِراً.[٦٨٤٤]

3. Just

٣ ـ عادِلٌ

6050. **Imām al-Ṣādiq (AS) said,** 'The Prophet (SAWA) would divide his gazes equally among his companions, looking at one and looking at the other all with equality.[6884]

٦٠٥٠ . الإمامُ الصّادقُ ؏ : كانَ رسولُ اللهِ ﷺ يُقَسِّمُ لَحَظاتِهِ بَينَ أصحابِهِ، يَنظُرُ إلىٰ ذا ويَنظُرُ إلىٰ ذا بالسَّوِيَّةِ.[٦٨٤٥]

4. Courageous

٤ ـ شُجاعٌ

6051. **Imām 'Alī (AS) said,** 'When a situation became tense and when two sides came close to each other [in battle], we would seek out the Messenger of Allah (SAWA) for protection, and there was no one closer to the enemy than him.'[6885]

٦٠٥١ . الإمامُ عليٌّ ؏ : كُنّا إذا احمَرَّ البأسُ ولَقِيَ القَومُ القَومَ اتَّقَينا برسولِ اللهِ، فما يَكونُ أحَدٌ أقرَبَ إلَى العَدُوِّ مِنهُ.[٦٨٤٦]

6052. **al-Barā' b. 'Āzib said,** 'When the situation became tense [in battle] we would seek protection

٦٠٥٢ . البَراء بن عازِبٍ : كنّا إذا احمَرَّ البأسُ نَتَّقي

with the Messenger of Allah (SAWA), for verily the courageous was he who was standing close him (SAWA).'[6886]

برسولِ اللهِ ﷺ، وإنّ الشُّجاعَ لَلّذي يُحاذي بِهِ.[٦٨٤٧]

6053. **Anas said,** 'The Prophet (SAWA) was the best of people, the most generous of people, and the most courageous of people. The people of Madina became scared one night, and they ran towards the place that the noise was coming from, and the Prophet (SAWA) met them on his way back from there – as he had preceded them to the noise, mounted on a barebacked horse belonging to Abū Ṭalḥa, and he had his sword hanging from his neck, saying, 'Why are you scared, don't be scared!'[6887]

٦٠٥٣. أنس: كانَ رسولُ اللهِ ﷺ أحسَنَ النّاسِ، وكانَ أجوَدَ النّاسِ، وكانَ أشجَعَ النّاسِ، ولَقد فَزِعَ أهلُ المَدينَةِ ذاتَ لَيلَةٍ، فانطَلَقَ ناسٌ قِبَلَ الصَّوتِ، فتَلَقّاهُم رسولُ اللهِ ﷺ راجِعاً ـ وقَد سَبَقَهم إلَى الصَّوتِ ـ وهُو علىٰ فَرَسٍ لأبي طَلحَةَ عُرْيٍ، في عُنُقِهِ السَّيفُ وهو يقولُ: لم تُراعُوا، لم تُراعُوا.[٦٨٤٨]

5. Compassionate

٥ ـ رَحيمٌ

6054. **Anas said,** 'If the Prophet (SAWA) did not see one of his brothers for three days he would ask about him; if he was away he would pray for him, if he was present he would visit him, and if he was sick he would visit him.'[6888]

٦٠٥٤. أنس: كانَ رسولُ اللهِ ﷺ إذا فَقَدَ الرّجُلَ مِن إخوانِهِ ثَلاثَةَ أيّامٍ سألَ عَنهُ؛ فإن كانَ غائباً دَعا لَهُ، وإن كانَ شاهِداً زارَهُ، وإن كانَ مَريضاً عادَهُ.[٦٨٤٩]

6. Tolerant

٦ ـ حَليمٌ

6055. **Anas said,** 'I was walking with the Prophet (SAWA), and he was wearing a Najrānī robe that had rough sides. A Bedouin came upon him and pulled him by his robe very roughly, so I looked at the side of the Prophet's (SAWA) neck, and the side of the robe had left a mark from the strong pull. He then said, 'O Muḥammad, give me some of Allah's money that you have.' So the Prophet looked at him, laughed and ordered that he be given some.'[6889]

٦٠٥٥. أنس: كُنتُ أمشي مَع رسولِ اللهِ ﷺ وعلَيهِ بُردٌ نَجرانيٌّ غَليظُ الحاشِيَةِ، فأدرَكَهُ أعرابيٌّ فجَذَبَهُ بِردائهِ جَذبَةً شَديدَةً، فنَظَرتُ إلىٰ صَفحَةِ عُنُقِ رسولِ اللهِ ﷺ، وقَد أثّرَ بها حاشِيَةُ الرِّداءِ مِن شِدَّةِ جَذبَتِهِ. ثُمّ قالَ: يا محمّدُ، مُرْ لي من مالِ اللهِ الّذي عِندَكَ. فالتَفَتَ إلَيهِ فضَحِكَ ثُمّ أمَرَ لَهُ بعَطاءٍ.[٦٨٥٠]

7. Shy

٧ ـ حَيِيٌّ

6056. **Musnad Ibn Ḥanbal,** 'The Messenger of Allah (SAWA) was shy and generous.'[6890]

٦٠٥٦. مسند ابن حنبل: كان رسولُ اللهِ ﷺ حَيِيّاً كَريماً.[٦٨٥١]

6057. **Abū Saʿīd al-Khuḍrī said,** 'The Prophet (SAWA) was so shy that no sooner would he be asked for something than he would give it.'[6891]

٦٠٥٧. أبو سعيدٍ الخُدريُ: كانَ رسولُ اللهِ حَيِيّاً لا يُسألُ شيئاً إلّا أعطاهُ.[٦٨٥٢]

8. Humble

٨ـ مُتَواضِعٌ

6058. **The Prophet (SAWA) said,** 'There are five things that I will not leave until I die: Eating low [on the ground] with servants, riding donkeys without saddles, milking the goat with my own hands, wearing wool, and greeting children, so that it becomes a tradition after me.'[6892]

٦٠٥٨. رسولُ اللهِ ﷺ: خَمسٌ لا أدَعُهُنَّ حتّى المَماتِ: الأكلُ علَى الحَضيضِ مَع العَبيدِ، ورُكوبيَ الحِمارَ مُؤْكَفاً، وحَلبيَ العَنزَ بِيَدي، ولُبسُ الصُّوفِ، والتَّسليمُ علَى الصِّبيانِ؛ لِتَكونَ سُنّةً مِن بَعدي.[٦٨٥٣]

6059. **Ibn Masʿūd said,** 'A man came to the Prophet (SAWA) and spoke to him, and his limbs started to tremble, so he said to him, 'Be calm, for I am not a king, I am but the son of a woman who ate jerked meat.'[6893]

٦٠٥٩. ابنُ مسعودٍ: أتىٰ النَّبيَّ ﷺ رجُلٌ فكَلَّمَهُ، فجَعَلَ تَرعُدُ فَرائصُهُ، فقالَ لَهُ: هَوِّن علَيكَ فإنّي لَستُ بمَلِكٍ، إنّما أنا ابنُ امرأةٍ تأكُلُ القَديدَ.[٦٨٥٤]

6060. **Ḥamza b. ʿAbdullāh b. ʿUtba said,** 'The Prophet (SAWA) had characteristics that did not exist in tyrants. There was no red or black person who called him except that he answered. He would also ride a donkey that was barebacked and did not have anything on it [i.e. a saddle].'[6894]

٦٠٦٠. حمزةُ بنُ عبداللهِ بنِ عُتبَةَ: كانَت في النَّبيِّ ﷺ خِصالٌ لَيسَت في الجَبّارينَ، كانَ لا يَدعوهُ أحمَرُ ولا أسوَدُ مِن النّاسِ إلّا أجابَهُ.[٦٨٥٥]

6061. **Imām al-Bāqir (AS) said,** 'Gabriel (AS) came to him three times with the keys of the treasuries of the earth, giving him the choice without Allah Almighty lessening anything of what He had prepared for him on the Day of Judgment. So, he chose humbleness to his Lord, the Exalted and Mighty.'[6895]

٦٠٦١. الإمامُ الباقرُ عليه السلام: ولَقَد أتاهُ جَبرئيلُ عليه السلام بمَفاتيحِ خَزائنِ الأرضِ ثَلاثَ مَرّاتٍ يُخَيِّرُهُ مِن غَيرِ أن يَنقُصَهُ اللهُ تباركَ وتعالىٰ مِمّا أعَدَّ اللهُ لَهُ يَومَ القِيامَةِ شيئاً، فيَختارُ التَّواضُعَ لِربِّهِ جلَّ وعزَّ.[٦٨٥٦]

6062. **Imām al-Bāqir (AS) said,** 'The Prophet (SAWA) ate the food of slaves and would sit in the place of slaves. He would eat low on the ground and sleep on the ground.'[6896]

٦٠٦٢. عنه عليه السلام: كانَ رَسولُ اللهِ ﷺ يأكُلُ أكلَ العَبدِ، ويَجلِسُ جِلسَةَ العَبدِ، وكانَ يأكُلُ علَى الحَضيضِ، ويَنامُ علَى الحَضيضِ.[٦٨٥٧]

9. Relier [on Allah]

٩ـ مُتَوَكِّلٌ

6063. **Imām al-Ṣādiq (AS) narrated,** 'In the battle of Dhāt al-Riqāʿ, the Prophet (SAWA) descended

٦٠٦٣. الإمامُ الصّادقُ عليه السلام: نَزَلَ رسولُ اللهِ ﷺ في

under a tree on the side of a valley when a flood came and separated him from his companions. A man from among the polytheists saw him whilst the Muslims were standing on the side of the valley waiting for the flood to subside. One of the polytheists said to his people, 'I will kill Muḥammad!' So he came and drew his sword against the Prophet (SAWA), saying, 'Who will save you now from me O Muḥammad?!' to which he replied, 'My Lord and your Lord', upon which [the angel] Gabriel (AS) threw him down from his horse and he fell onto his back. The Prophet (SAWA) then stood up, took the sword and sat on his chest, saying, 'Who will save you now from me, O Ghawrith?' to which he replied, 'Your magnanimity and generosity, O Muḥammad' at which he left him. The man stood up, saying, 'By Allah, you are indeed better and nobler than me.'[6897]

غَزوَةِ ذاتِ الرِّقاعِ تَحتَ شَجَرَةٍ علىٰ شَفيرِ وادٍ، فأقبَلَ سَيلٌ فحالَ بَينَهُ وبَينَ أصحابِهِ فرآهُ رجُلٌ مِنَ المُشرِكينَ والمُسلِمونَ قِيامٌ علىٰ شَفيرِ الوادي يَنتَظِرونَ مَتىٰ يَنقَطِعُ السَّيلُ، فقالَ رجُلٌ مَنَ المُشرِكينَ لقَومِهِ: أنا أقتُلُ محمّداً، فجاءَ وشَدَّ علىٰ رسولِ اللهِ ﷺ بالسَّيفِ، ثُمّ قالَ: مَن يُنْجِيكَ مِنّي يا محمّدُ؟! فقالَ: رَبّي ورَبُّكَ، فنَسَفَهُ جَبرئيلُ عليه السلام عن فَرَسِهِ فسَقَطَ علىٰ ظَهرِهِ، فقامَ رسولُ اللهِ ﷺ وأخذَ السَّيفَ وجَلَسَ علىٰ صَدرِهِ وقالَ: مَن يُنْجِيكَ مِنّي يا غورثُ؟! فقالَ: جُودُكَ وكَرمُكَ يا محمّدُ، فتَرَكَهُ فقامَ وهُو يقولُ: واللهِ، لَأنتَ خَيرٌ مِنّي وأكرَمُ.[٦٨٥٨]

10. Patient

١٠ ـ صَبورٌ

6064. **The Prophet (SAWA) said,** 'No one has been hurt the way I have been hurt for the sake of Allah.'[6898]

٦٠٦٤. رسولُ اللهِ ﷺ: ما أُوذِيَ أحَدٌ مِثلَ ما أُوذِيتُ في اللهِ.[٦٨٥٩]

6065. **The Prophet (SAWA) said,** 'I was being hurt for the sake of Allah when no one was being hurt, and I was threatened because of Allah when no one else was being threatened. Thirty days and nights passed once when neither Bilāl nor I had any food that a man may eat save what Bilāl may use to cover his armpits [i.e. leaves].'[6899]

٦٠٦٥. عنه ﷺ: لَقد أُوذِيتُ في اللهِ وما يُؤذىٰ أحَدٌ، وأُخِفْتُ [في] اللهِ وما يُخافُ أحَدٌ، ولَقد أتَت علَيَّ ثَلاثونَ مِن يَومٍ ولَيلَةٍ وما لي ولِبِلالٍ طَعامٌ يأكُلُهُ ذو كَبِدٍ إلّا شيءٌ يُوارِيهِ إبطُ بلالٍ.[٦٨٦٠]

6066. **Ismāʿīl b. ʿAyyāsh said,** 'The Prophet (SAWA) was the most patient of people with regard to people's wrongdoings.'[6900]

٦٠٦٦. إسماعيل بنِ عيّاشٍ: كانَ رسولُ اللهِ ﷺ أصبَرَ النّاسِ علىٰ أوزارِ النّاسِ.[٦٨٦١]

6067. **Ibn Masʿūd said,** 'It is as if I am looking at the Prophet (SAWA) speaking [to us] as one of the past prophets who was hit by his people and made to bleed, wiping the blood from his face, saying, 'O Allah forgive my people for they do not know.'[6901]

٦٠٦٧. ابن مسعودٍ: كأنّي أنظُرُ إلىٰ رسولِ اللهِ ﷺ يَحكي نَبيّاً مِنَ الأنبياءِ ضَرَبَهُ قَومُهُ فأدمَوهُ، وهُو يَمسَحُ الدَّمَ عَن وَجهِهِ ويَقولُ: اللّهُمَّ اغفِرْ لِقَومي فإنّهُم لا يَعلَمونَ.[٦٨٦٢]

11. Ascetic

١١ ـ زاهِدٌ

6068. **The Prophet (SAWA),** when some said to him, 'Why don't you sleep on a bed?' when the straw mat had left a mark on his sides, said, 'What do I have with this world? The example of me and the world is like a rider who rides on a summer's day, and then goes to take shade under a tree for a while during the day, and then rides on leaving it.'[6902]

٦٠٦٨ . رسولُ اللهِ ﷺ ـ وقد قيلَ لَهُ: لوِ اتَّخَذتَ فِراشاً، وهُو علىٰ حَصيرٍ قد أثَّرَ في جَنبَيهِ ـ: ما لِي ولِلدُّنيا؟! ما مَثَلي ومَثَلُ الدُّنيا إلّا كَراكِبٍ سارَ في يَومٍ صائفٍ فاستَظَلَّ تَحتَ شَجَرَةٍ ساعَةً مِن نَهارٍ ثُمّ راحَ وتَرَكَها.[٦٨٦٣]

6069. **Imām al-Bāqir (AS) said,** 'The Prophet (SAWA) did not leave in inheritance a dinar, or a dirham, or a slave, or a slavegirl, or a lamb, or a camel. When he (SAWA) passed away, his shield was pawned to one of the Jews of Madina for twenty measures of barley, as a provision of sustenance for his family.'[6903]

٦٠٦٩ . الإمامُ الباقرُ عليه السلام: إنّ رسولَ اللهِ ﷺ لَم يُورِّثْ دِيناراً ولا دِرهَماً ولا عَبداً ولا وَليدَةً ولا شاةً ولا بَعيراً، ولقد قُبِضَ ﷺ وإنّ دِرعَهُ مَرهونَةٌ عِند يَهوديٍّ مِن يَهودِ المَدينَةِ بعِشرينَ صاعاً مِن شَعيرٍ استَسلَفَها نَفَقَةً لأهلِهِ.[٦٨٦٤]

6070. **'Umar said,** 'I visited the Prophet (SAWA) and he was sitting on a straw mat, so I sat down and saw that he was wearing a loincloth and nothing else, and the mat had made a mark on his side. I saw about a handful of barley there, and a tan hide spread out to one side of the room, and I also saw raw hide hung up, so my eyes gushed with tears. He (SAWA) asked, 'What is making you cry, O son of Khaṭṭāb?' He said, 'O Prophet of Allah, how can I not cry when this mat has made a mark on your side, and I do not see anything in your storage, other than what I see. And there are Kisra and the Caesar with their fruits and rivers, and you are a prophet of Allah and His chosen one, and this is your storage warehouse?!' He said, 'O son of Khaṭṭāb, do you not want us to have the Hereafter and leave the world to them?!'[6904]

٦٠٧٠ . عُمر: دَخَلتُ علىٰ رسولِ اللهِ ﷺ وهُو علىٰ حَصيرٍ، قالَ: فجَلَستُ، فإذا علَيهِ إزارُهُ، ولَيس علَيهِ غَيرُهُ، وإذا الحَصيرُ قد أثَّرَ في جَنبِهِ، وإذا أنا بِقَبضَةٍ مِن شَعيرٍ نَحوِ الصّاعِ، وقَرَظٌ في ناحِيَةٍ في الغُرفَةِ، وإذا إهابٌ مُعَلَّقٌ، فابتَدَرَت عَيناي، فقالَ: ما يُبكيكَ يابنَ الخَطّابِ؟ فقالَ: يا نَبيَّ اللهِ، وما لِيَ لا أبكي وهٰذا الحَصيرُ قد أثَّرَ في جَنبِكَ وهٰذهِ خِزانَتُكَ لا أرىٰ فيها إلّا ما أرىٰ، وذاكَ كِسرىٰ وقَيصرُ في الثِّمارِ والأنهارِ، وأنتَ نَبيُّ اللهِ وصَفوَتُهُ، وهٰذهِ خِزانَتُكَ؟! قالَ: يابنَ الخطّابِ، أما تَرضىٰ أن تَكونَ لَنا الآخِرَةُ ولَهُمُ الدُّنيا؟![٦٨٦٥]

6071. It is narrated in *Makārim al-Akhlāq*: 'Ibn Khūlī came to him (SAWA) with a bowl of honey and milk, and he refused to drink it, saying, 'Two drinks in one meal, and two bowls in one bowl?!' So, he refused to drink it, and he then said, 'I do not prohibit it, but I hate pride, and having to account for the extravagances of this world tomorrow, and I

٦٠٧١ . مكارِمِ الأخلاقِ: جاءَهُ ﷺ ابنُ خولي بإناءٍ فيهِ عَسَلٌ ولَبَنٌ، فأبىٰ أن يَشرَبَهُ، فقالَ: شَربَتانِ في شَربَةٍ، وإناءانِ في إناءٍ واحِدٍ؟! فأبىٰ أن يَشرَبَهُ، ثُمّ قالَ: ما أُحَرِّمُهُ، ولٰكنّي أكرَهُ الفَخرَ والحِسابَ بِفُضولِ الدُّنيا غَداً، وأُحِبُّ

love humbleness, for he who is humble for Allah, Allah will elevate him.'[6905]

التَّواضُعَ، فإنّ مَن تواضَعَ للهِ رَفَعَهُ اللهُ.[٦٨٦٦]

12. Preferring Others Over Himself and his Family

١٢ ـ إيثارُهُ النّاسَ عَلىٰ نَفسِهِ ﷺ وأهلِ بَيتِهِ

6072. **Imām al-Bāqir,** speaking to Muḥammad b. Muslim, said, 'O Muḥammad, you might think that he [meaning the Prophet (SAWA)] filled himself by eating wheat bread for three continuous days from the time Allah sent him until when He took him up?' He answered himself, saying, 'No, by Allah, he never filled himself with wheat bread for three continuous days since the time Allah sent him until He took him [his soul]. I am not saying that he could not find any, for one man would offer him one hundred camels, so if he wanted to eat he could have done so.'[6906]

٦٠٧٢. الإمامُ الباقرُ ﷺ ـ لمحمّدِ بنِ مُسلمٍ ـ: يا محمّدُ، لَعلَّكَ تَرىٰ أنّهُ [يعني رَسولَ اللهِ ﷺ] شَبِعَ مِن خُبزِ البُرِّ ثَلاثةَ أيّامٍ مُتَوالِيَةٍ مِن أن بَعَثَهُ اللهُ إلىٰ أن قَبَضَهُ؟! لا واللهِ، ما شَبِعَ مِن خُبزِ البُرِّ ثَلاثةَ أيّامٍ مُتَوالِيَةٍ مُنذُ بَعَثَهُ اللهُ إلىٰ أن قَبَضَهُ. أما إنّي لا أقولُ: إنّهُ كانَ لا يَجِدُ، لَقد كانَ يُجيزُ الرّجُلَ الواحِدَ بالمِائةِ مِن الإبِلِ، فلو أرادَ أن يأكُلَ لَأكَلَ.[٦٨٦٧]

13. Never Being Angry for Himself

١٣ ـ عَدَمُ غَضَبِهِ ﷺ لِنَفسِهِ

6073. It is narrated in *al-Manāqib*: 'The Prophet (SAWA) would only be angry for the sake of his Lord, and would never be angry for himself.'[6907]

٦٠٧٣. المناقبِ لابنِ شهر آشوبَ: كانَ النَّبيُّ ﷺ ... يَغضَبُ لِرَبِّهِ، ولا يَغضَبُ لِنَفسِهِ.[٦٨٦٨]

6074. **'Ā'isha said,** 'The Prophet (SAWA) never hit anything with his hand, neither a woman nor a slave, only when he fought on the path of Allah (*jihād*), and he never took revenge for anything that was taken from him; only when any of the prohibitions of Allah were violated would he take revenge for the sake of Allah.'[6908]

٦٠٧٤. عائشة: ما ضَرَبَ رَسولُ اللهِ ﷺ شيئاً قَطُّ بِيَدِهِ، ولا امرأةً ولا خادِماً إلّا أن يُجاهِدَ في سَبيلِ اللهِ، وما نِيلَ مِنهُ شيءٌ قَطُّ فيَنتَقِمُ مِن صاحِبِهِ، إلّا أن يُنتَهَكَ شيءٌ مِن مَحارِمِ اللهِ فيَنتَقِمَ للهِ عَزَّ وجلَّ.[٦٨٦٩]

14. Exhausting Himself in Worship

١٤ ـ إجهادُ نَفسِهِ ﷺ في العِبادَةِ

"Ta Ha. We did not send down to you the Qur'an that you should be miserable."[6909]

﴿طٰه * مَا أَنْزَلْنَا عَلَيْكَ القُرْآنَ لِتَشْقَىٰ﴾.[٦٨٧٠]

6075. **Imām 'Alī (AS) said** that when the verse: *"O you wrapped up in your mantle, stand vigil*

٦٠٧٥. الإمامُ عليٌّ ﷺ: لَمّا نَزَلَ علَى النَّبيِّ ﷺ ﴿يا

through the night, except a little" descended onto the Prophet (SAWA), he used to stay up all night until his feet would swell up, so he would pick one foot up, and put the other down, and Gabriel came down to him saying: *"Taha"*, meaning 'the earth is for your feet, O Muḥammad', *"We did not send down to you the Qur'an that you should be miserable"*, and He revealed: *"So recite as much of the Qur'an as is feasible."*[6910]

أيُّها المُزَّمِّلُ* قُمِ اللَّيلَ إلّا قَليلاً﴾[٦٨٧١] قامَ اللَّيلَ كلَّهُ حتّى تَوَرَّمَت قَدَماهُ، فَجَعَلَ يَرفَعُ رِجلاً ويَضَعُ رِجلاً، فهَبَطَ علَيهِ جِبريلُ فقالَ: ﴿طه﴾ يَعني الأرضَ بِقدَمَيكَ يا محمّدُ ﴿ما أنزَلْنا عَلَيكَ القُرآنَ لِتَشقى﴾، وأنزَلَ ﴿فاقرَأوا ما تَيَسَّرَ مِنَ القُرآنِ﴾[٦٨٧٢، ٦٨٧٣]

6076. **Imām al-Bāqir (AS) said,** 'The Prophet (SAWA) was with 'Ā'isha on her night, and she said, 'O Messenger of Allah, why do you exhaust yourself when Allah has forgiven you what is past of your sin and what is to come?' He said, 'O 'Ā'isha, can I not be a thankful servant?!'[6911]

٦٠٧٦. الإمامُ الباقرُ ﷺ: كانَ رَسولُ اللهِ ﷺ عِندَ عائشةَ لَيلَتَها، فقالَت: يا رَسولَ اللهِ، لِمَ تُتعِبُ نَفسَكَ وقد غَفَرَ اللهُ لَكَ ما تَقَدَّمَ مِن ذَنبِكَ وما تأخَّرَ؟ فقالَ: يا عائشةُ، ألا أكونُ عَبداً شَكوراً؟![٦٨٧٤]

372

THE STARS

النُّجُوم

1719. The Science of the Stars [Astronomy][6912]

١٧١٩- عِلمُ النُّجومِ

6077. **Imām 'Alī (AS) said,** 'O people, beware of learning astrology except that which is used for guidance in the land or the sea [astronomy], because it [astrology] leads to divining and an astrologer is like a diviner. And the diviner is like a sorcerer, and a sorcerer is like the disbeliever and the disbeliever will be in Hell.'[6913]

٦٠٧٧. الإمامُ عليٌّ ﷺ: أيُّها النّاسُ، إيّاكُم وتَعَلُّمَ النُّجومِ إلّا ما يُهتَدى بهِ في بَرٍّ أو بَحرٍ، فإنّها تَدعو إلَى الكِهانَةِ، والمُنَجِّمُ كالكاهِنِ، والكاهِنُ كالسّاحِرِ، والسّاحِرُ كالكافِرِ، والكافِرُ في النّارِ.[٦٨٧٥]

6078. **Imām al-Ṣādiq (AS),** when asked about the science of the stars said, 'It [i.e. astronomy] is a science from the sciences of the prophets.'[6914]

٦٠٧٨. الإمامُ الصّادقُ ﷺ ـ لمّا سُئلَ عن عِلمِ النّجومِ ـ: هُو عِلمٌ مِن عِلمِ الأنبياءِ.[٦٨٧٦]

6079. **Imām al-Ṣādiq (AS),** when asked about what was popularly held among people that the studying of the stars [astronomy] was prohibited

٦٠٧٩. عنه ﷺ ـ لَمّا سُئلَ عمّا اشتَهَرَ بينَ النّاسِ مِن حُرمَةِ النَّظَرِ في النُّجومِ وعَن ضَرَرِهِ بالدِّينِ ـ: لَيسَ كما يَقولونَ، لا تَضُرُّ

and harmful to religion, said, 'It is not as they say. It [i.e. astronomy] does not harm your religion.' He then said, 'You are looking into something [a science] where too much of it cannot be achieved and too little of it cannot be benefitted from.'[6915] [6916]

بدِينِكَ. إنّكُم تَنظُرونَ في شَيءٍ مِنها كثيرُهُ لا يُدرَكُ، وقَليلُهُ لا يُنتَفَعُ بِهِ.[٦٨٧٧]

6080. **Imām al-Ṣādiq (AS),** when an atheist asked him about the science of the stars [i.e. astrology] said, 'It is a science whose benefits are few and whose harms are many… an astrologer contradicts Allah in His knowledge, claiming he is refuting Allah in His fate over His creation.'[6917] [6918]

٦٠٨٠. عنه عليه السلام ـ لَمّا سألَهُ زِنديقٌ عن عِلمِ النُّجومِ ـ: هُو عِلمٌ قَلَّت مَنافِعُهُ وكَثُرَت مَضَرّاتُهُ؛ لأنّهُ لا يُدفَعُ بِهِ المَقدورُ ولا يُتَّقىٰ بِهِ المَحذورُ، إن أخبَرَ المُنَجِّمُ بالبَلاءِ لَم يُنجِهِ التَّحَرُّزُ مِن القَضاءِ، وإن أخبَرَ هُو بخَيرٍ لَم يَستَطِعْ تَعجيلَهُ، وإن حَدَثَ بِهِ سُوءٌ لَم يُمكِنْهُ صَرفُهُ، والمُنَجِّمُ يَضادُّ اللهَ في عِلمِهِ بزَعمِهِ أنّهُ يَرُدُّ قَضاءَ اللهِ عَن خَلقِهِ.[٦٨٧٨]

6081. **ʿAbd al-Malik b. Aʿyan said,** 'I asked Abū ʿAbdillāh [al-Ṣādiq] (AS), 'I have been tried by this science [astrology], so when I want something I look at the rising star, and if I see the rising star as evil, I desist from pursuing that thing, and if I see good in the rising star, I pursue the matter.' He asked me, 'Do you predict fate?' I said, 'Yes.' He said, 'Then burn your books.'[6919]

٦٠٨١. عبد الملكِ بنِ أعيَنٍ: قلتُ لأبي عبدِ اللهِ عليه السلام: إنّي قدِ ابتُلِيتُ بهٰذا العِلمِ، فأُريدُ الحاجَةَ؛ فإذا نَظَرتُ إلَى الطّالِعِ ورأيتُ الطّالِعَ الشَّرَّ جَلَستُ ولَم أذهَبْ فيها، وإذا رأيتُ الطّالِعَ الخَيرَ ذَهَبتُ في الحاجَةِ، فقالَ لي: تَقضي؟ قلتُ: نَعَم، قالَ: أحرِقْ كُتُبَكَ.[٦٨٧٩]

373

THE VOW

النَّذر

1720. The Vow

١٧٢٠ـ الوَفاءُ بِالنَّذرِ

"When the wife of Imrān said, 'My Lord, I dedicate to You what is in my belly, in consecration. Accept it from me; indeed You are the All-hearing, the All-knowing.'"[6920]

﴿إِذْ قَالَتِ امْرَأَةُ عِمْرَانَ رَبِّ إِنِّي نَذَرْتُ لَكَ مَا فِي بَطْنِي مُحَرَّراً فَتَقَبَّلْ مِنِّي إِنَّكَ أَنْتَ السَّمِيعُ الْعَلِيمُ﴾.[٦٨٨٠]

"Whatever charity you may give, or vows that you may vow, Allah indeed knows it, and the wrongdoers have no helpers."[6921]

﴿وَمَا أَنْفَقْتُمْ مِنْ نَفَقَةٍ أَوْ نَذَرْتُمْ مِنْ نَذْرٍ فَإِنَّ اللهَ يَعْلَمُهُ وَمَا لِلظَّالِمِينَ مِنْ أَنْصَارٍ﴾.[٦٨٨١]

"They fulfil their vows and fear a day whose ill will be widespread."[6922]

﴿يُوفُونَ بِالنَّذْرِ وَيَخَافُونَ يَوْماً كَانَ شَرُّهُ مُسْتَطِيراً﴾.[٦٨٨٢]

6082. **Imām al-Bāqir (AS),** with regard to Allah's verse in the Qur'an: *"They fulfil their vows"*, said, 'al-Ḥasan and al-Ḥusayn became sick when they were young children, so the Prophet (SAWA) visited them and there were two men with him. One of the two men said [to Imām 'Alī], 'O Abū al-Ḥasan, why don't you make a vow for your two children for Allah to cure them.' He said, 'I will fast for three days in thanks to Allah Almighty. Fāṭima also said the same, and so did their servant Fiḍḍa. Allah Almighty covered them with good health, and so they fasted the next day.'[6923]

٦٠٨٢. الإمامُ الباقرُ عليه السلام ـ في قولهِ تعالىٰ: ﴿يُوفُونَ بالنَّذْرِ﴾ ـ: مَرِضَ الحَسنُ والحُسينُ وهُما صَبيّانِ صَغيرانِ، فعادَهُما رَسولُ اللهِ صلى الله عليه وآله ومَعهُ رجُلانِ، فقالَ أحَدُهُما: يا أبا الحَسَنِ، لو نَذَرتَ في ابنَيكَ نَذراً إن عافاهُما اللهُ، فقالَ: أصومُ ثَلاثَةَ أيّامٍ شُكراً للهِ عَزَّوجلَّ، وكذلكَ قالَت فاطمَةُ، وكذلكَ قالَت جارِيَتُهُم فِضَّةُ، فألبَسَهُما اللهُ عافِيَةً فأصبَحوا صِياماً.[٦٨٨٣]

1721. The [Divine] Disapproval of Making Something Obligatory Upon Oneself

١٧٢١ ـ كَراهَةُ الإيجابِ عَلَى النَّفسِ

6083. *Wasā'il al-Shī'a*, narrating from Isḥāq b. 'Ammār: 'I said to Abu Abdullāh: 'I enforced upon myself [as a vow] two units of prayer to perform while travelling or at home in thanks to Allah: 'Should I pray them while travelling during the daytime?' He said, 'Yes.' He then said, 'I hate the making of things obligatory; which is when a man makes something obligatory upon himself.' I said, 'I did not make them [the two units] obligatory on myself for Allah, but I made it incumbent for myself, to pray in thanks to Allah, and I did not make it obligatory for myself. So can I leave them, if I want?' He said, 'Yes.'[6924]

٦٠٨٣. وسائل الشيعة عن إسحاق بنِ عمّار: قلتُ لأبي عبد اللهِ عليه السلام: إنّي جَعَلتُ على نفسي شُكراً للهِ رَكعتين أُصَلّيهما في السَّفَرِ والحَضَرِ، أفَأُصَلّيهِما في السَّفَرِ بالنَّهارِ؟ فقالَ: نَعَم. ـ ثُمَّ قالَ: إنّي لَأكرَهُ الإيجابَ؛ أن يُوجِبَ الرّجُلُ علىٰ نفسِهِ. قُلتُ: إنّي لَم أجعَلْهُما للهِ علَيَّ، إنّما جَعَلتُ ذلكَ علىٰ نفسي أُصَلّيهما شُكراً للهِ ولَم أُوجِبْهُما علىٰ نَفسي، أفأدَعُهُما إذا شِئتُ؟ قالَ: نَعَم.[٦٨٨٤]

374

ADVISING

النُّصح

1722. Enjoinment of Advice

١٧٢٢ ـ الحَثُّ عَلَى النُّصحِ

"I communicate to you the messages of my Lord and I am a trustworthy well-wisher for you."[6925]

﴿أُبَلِّغُكُمْ رِسَالَاتِ رَبِّي وَأَنْصَحُ لَكُمْ وَأَعْلَمُ مِنَ اللهِ مَا لَا تَعْلَمُونَ﴾.[٦٨٨٥]

(See also: Qur'an 7:79, 7:93, 9:91)

(أُنظر) الأعراف: ٧٩، ٩٣ والتوبة: ٩١.

6084. **The Prophet (SAWA) said,** 'Allah Almighty said, 'The most beloved way that My servant can use to worship Me is through sincerity and advising for My sake.'[6926]

٦٠٨٤. رسولُ اللهِ ﷺ: قالَ اللهُ عَزَّ وجلَّ: أحَبُّ ما تَعَبَّدَ لي بِهِ عَبدي، النُّصحُ لي.[٦٨٨٦]

6085. **The Prophet (SAWA) said** to his companions, 'Religion is advise.' We asked, 'For whom?' He said, 'For the sake of Allah, His Book, His Messenger, the leaders of the Muslims, and the general people.'[6927]

٦٠٨٥. عنه ﷺ ـ لأصحابه ـ: الدِّينُ النَّصيحَةُ، قُلنا: لِمَن؟ قالَ: للهِ، ولكِتابِهِ، ولرَسولِهِ، ولأئمَّةِ المُسلِمينَ، وعامَّتِهِم.[٦٨٨٧]

6086. **The Prophet (SAWA) said,** 'The people who have the greatest status with Allah on the Day of Judgment are those who roamed the earth the most, advising His creatures.'[6928]

٦٠٨٦. عنه ﷺ: إنّ أعظَمَ النّاسِ مَنزِلَةً عِندَ اللهِ يَومَ القِيامَةِ أمشاهُم في أرضِهِ بالنَّصيحَةِ لِخَلقِهِ.[٦٨٨٨]

6087. **The Prophet (SAWA) said,** 'Let the advice a man gives to his brother be the same advice he would give to himself.'[6929]

٦٠٨٧. عنه ﷺ: لِيَنصَحِ الرّجُلُ مِنكُم أخاهُ كنَصيحَتِهِ لنَفسِهِ.[٦٨٨٩]

6088. **Imām ʿAlī (AS) said,** 'Give sincere advice to your brother, whether it be good or bad.'[6930]

٦٠٨٨. الإمامُ عليٌّ عليه السلام: امحَضْ أخاكَ النَّصيحَةَ، حَسَنةً كانَت أو قَبيحَةً.[٦٨٩٠]

6089. **Imām al-Ṣādiq (AS) said,** 'It is obligatory for the believer to advise a fellow believer, present or absent.'[6931]

٦٠٨٩. الإمامُ الصّادقُ عليه السلام: يَجِبُ لِلمؤمنِ على المؤمنِ النَّصيحَةُ لَهُ في المَشهَدِ والمَغيبِ.[٦٨٩١]

6090. **Imām al-Ṣādiq (AS) said,** 'You must advise Allah's creatures for His sake, for you will never meet Him with a deed better than this.'[6932]

٦٠٩٠. عنه عليه السلام: علَيكُم بالنُّصحِ للهِ في خَلقِهِ، فلَن تَلقاهُ بعَمَلٍ أفضَلَ مِنهُ.[٦٨٩٢]

1723. The Signs of an Adviser

١٧٢٣ ـ عَلامَةُ النّاصِحِ

6091. **The Prophet (SAWA) said,** 'As for the signs of the adviser, there are four: he judges with truth, gives the right due from his own self, accepts for people what he accepts for himself, and he does not transgress against anybody.'[6933]

٦٠٩١. رسولُ اللهِ ﷺ: أمّا علامَةُ النّاصِحِ فأربَعةٌ: يَقضي بالحَقِّ، ويُعطي الحَقَّ مِن نَفسِهِ، ويَرضىٰ للنّاسِ ما يَرضاهُ لنَفسِهِ، ولا يَعتدي علىٰ أحَدٍ.[٦٨٩٣]

6092. **Imām ʿAlī (AS) said,** 'It is enough for a person ... when advising, to prohibit what he would not accept for himself.'[6934]

٦٠٩٢. الإمامُ عليٌّ عليه السلام: حَسبُ المَرءِ ...مِن نُصحِهِ نَهيُهُ عَمّا لا يَرضاهُ لنَفسِهِ.[٦٨٩٤]

6093. **Imām ʿAlī (AS) said,** 'He who among people is the best adviser to his own self is the one who is most obedient to his Lord, and the most deceitful of people to his own self is the one who is most disobedient to his Lord.'[6935]

٦٠٩٣. عنه ﷺ: إنّ أنصَحَ النّاسِ لِنَفسِهِ أطوَعُهُم لِرَبِّهِ، وإنّ أغَشَّهُم لِنفسِهِ أعصاهُم لِرَبِّهِ.[٦٨٩٥]

6094. **Imām Zayn al-ʿĀbidīn (AS) said,** 'Excessive advice calls for accusation.'[6936]

٦٠٩٤. الإمامُ زينُ العابدينَ ﷺ: كَثرَةُ النُّصحِ يَدعو إلَى التُّهمَةِ.[٦٨٩٦]

6095. **Imām al-Ṣādiq (AS) said,** '[Good] Advice from a jealous person is impossible.'[6937]

٦٠٩٥. الإمامُ الصّادقُ ﷺ: النَّصيحَةُ مِن الحاسِدِ مُحالٌ.[٦٨٩٧]

6096. **Imām al-Ṣādiq (AS) said,** 'No sooner does a Muslim servant advise his own self for the sake of Allah, and give the rights due from himself, and take the rights due to him than he is given two features: sustenance from Allah which he will be satisfied with, and satisfaction with Allah that will save him.'[6938]

٦٠٩٦. عنه ﷺ: ما ناصَحَ اللهَ عَبدٌ مُسلِمٌ في نَفسِهِ، فأعطَى الحَقَّ مِنها وأخَذَ الحَقَّ لَها، إلّا أُعطِيَ خَصلَتَينِ: رِزقاً مِن اللهِ عَزَّوجلَّ يَقنَعُ بِهِ ورِضىً عنِ اللهِ يُنجيهِ.[٦٨٩٨]

1724. Enjoinment of Accepting Advice

١٧٢٤ ـ الحَثُّ عَلىٰ قَبولِ النَّصيحَةِ

6097. **Imām ʿAlī (AS) said,** 'Blessed be the one who obeys an adviser who guides him, and avoids a deviant person who misleads him.'[6939]

٦٠٩٧. الإمامُ عليٌّ ﷺ: طُوبىٰ لِمَن أطاعَ ناصِحاً يَهديهِ، وتَجَنَّبَ غاوِياً يُرديهِ.[٦٨٩٩]

6098. **Imām ʿAlī (AS) said,** 'He who opposes [good] advice will perish.'[6940]

٦٠٩٨. عنه ﷺ: مَن خالَفَ النُّصحَ هَلَكَ.[٦٩٠٠]

6099. **Imām al-Bāqir (AS) said,** 'Follow he who makes you cry when he advises you, and do not follow he that makes you laugh while he deceives you.'[6941]

٦٠٩٩. الإمامُ الباقرُ ﷺ: اِتَّبِعْ مَن يُبكيكَ وهُوَ لكَ ناصِحٌ، ولا تَتَّبِعْ مَن يُضحِكُكَ وهُوَ لكَ غاشٌّ.[٦٩٠١]

375

FAIRNESS

الإنصاف

1725. Enjoinment of Fairness

١٧٢٥ ـ الحَثُّ عَلَى الإنصافِ

6100. **Imām ʿAlī (AS),** with regard to Allah's verse in the Qur'an: *"Indeed Allah enjoins justice and*

٦١٠٠. الإمامُ عليٌّ ﷺ ـ في قولِه تعالىٰ: ﴿إنّ اللهَ

kindness'[6942], said, 'Justice is fairness, and kindness is courteousness.'[6943]

يَأمُرُ بالعَدْلِ والإحْسانِ﴾ [٦٩٠٢] ـ: العَـــــدلُ: الإنصافُ، والإحسانُ: التَّفَضُّلُ.[٦٩٠٣]

6101. **Imām ʿAlī (AS) said,** 'Fairness is the best of characteristics.'[6944]

٦١٠١. عنه عليه السلام: الإنصافُ أفضَلُ الشِّيَمِ.[٦٩٠٤]

6102. **Imām ʿAlī (AS) said,** 'Fairness brings harmony between hearts.'[6945]

٦١٠٢. عنه عليه السلام: الإنصافُ يُؤلِّفُ القُلوبَ.[٦٩٠٥]

6103. **Imām ʿAlī (AS) said,** 'With fairness relationships last.'[6946]

٦١٠٣. عنه عليه السلام: بالنَّصفَةِ تَدومُ الوُصلَةُ.[٦٩٠٦]

6104. **Imām ʿAlī (AS) said,** 'With fairness relations are increased.'[6947]

٦١٠٤. عنه عليه السلام: بالنَّصفَةِ يَكثُرُ المُواصِلونَ.[٦٩٠٧]

6105. **Imām ʿAlī (AS) said,** 'The *zakāt* of power is fairness.'[6948]

٦١٠٥. عنه عليه السلام: زَكاةُ القُدرَةِ الإنصافُ.[٦٩٠٨]

6106. **Imām al-Bāqir (AS) said,** 'There is no justice like fairness.'[6949]

٦١٠٦. الإمامُ الباقرُ عليه السلام: لا عَدلَ كالإنصافِ.[٦٩٠٩]

1726. Enjoinment of Fairness Towards Those Who are Not Fair

١٧٢٦ ـ الحَثُّ عَلىٰ إنصافِ مَن لا يُنصِفُ

6107. **Imām ʿAlī (AS) said,** 'A believer is fair to one who is not fair to him.'[6950]

٦١٠٧. الإمامُ عليٌّ عليه السلام: المؤمنُ يُنصِفُ مَن لا يُنصِفُهُ.[٦٩١٠]

6108. **Imām ʿAlī (AS) said,** 'The most just of people is he who is fair towards those who do wrong to him.'[6951]

٦١٠٨. عنه عليه السلام: أعدَلُ النّاسِ مَن أنصَفَ مَـن ظَلَمَهُ.[٦٩١١]

6109. **Imām al-Ṣādiq (AS) said,** 'Keep ties to those who cut theirs with you....and be fair to those who dispute with you.'[6952]

٦١٠٩. الإمامُ الصّادقُ عليه السلام: صِلْ مَنْ قَطَعَكَ... وأنصِفْ مَن خاصَمَك.[٦٩١٢]

1727. Fairness in Spite of Oneself

١٧٢٧ ـ الإنتِصافُ مِنَ النَّفسِ

6110. **The Prophet (SAWA) said,** 'Whoever is charitable towards a poor person, and is fair

٦١١٠. رسولُ اللهِ صلى الله عليه وآله: مَن واسَى الفَقيرَ، وأنصَفَ

towards people in spite of himself, then he is the true believer.'[6953]

النّاسَ مِن نَفسِهِ ، فذٰلكَ المؤمِنُ حقّاً.٦٩١٣

6111. **Imām ʿAlī (AS) said,** The fairest of people is he who is fair in spite of himself without someone judging over him.'[6954]

٦١١١. الإمامُ عليٌّ ﷺ: أنصَفُ النّاسِ مَن أنصَفَ مِن نَفسِهِ مِن غَيرِ حاكِمٍ علَيهِ.٦٩١٤

6112. **Imām ʿAlī (AS) said,** 'Indeed he who is fair to people in spite of himself, Allah will only increase him in dignity.'[6955]

٦١١٢. عنه ﷺ: ألا إنّهُ مَن يُنصِفُ النّاسَ مِن نَفسِهِ لَم يَزِدْهُ اللهُ إلّا عِزّاً.٦٩١٥

6113. **Imām ʿAlī (AS) said,** 'It is enough for a person ... endowed with intellect to be fair [to others] in spite of himself ... and [for a person] endowed with fairness to accept the truth when it becomes clear to him.'[6956]

٦١١٣. عنه ﷺ: حَسْبُ المَرءِ... مِن عَقلِهِ إنصافُهُ مِن نَفسِهِ... ومِن إنصافِهِ قَبولُهُ الحَقَّ إذا بانَ لَهُ.٦٩١٦

6114. **Imām ʿAlī (AS),** in his letter to Mālik al-Ashtar said, '...be fair for Allah and be fair to people in spite of yourself, and in spite of your close members of your family, and in spite of those towards whom you have inclinations from among your followers, for if you do not do so you will be oppressing.'[6957]

٦١١٤. عنه ﷺ ـ مِن كتابه للأشتر ـ: أنصِفِ اللهَ وأنصِفِ النّاسَ مِن نَفسِكَ ومِن خاصَّةِ أهلِكَ ومَن لكَ فيهِ هَوىً مِن رَعيّتِكَ، فإنَّكَ إلّا تَفعَلْ تَظلِمْ!...٦٩١٧

6115. **Imām al-Bāqir (AS) said,** 'Allah has a Heaven that no one enters other than three kinds of people: one of them is he who judges himself with truth.'[6958]

٦١١٥. الإمامُ الباقرُ ﷺ: إنّ للهِ جَنّةً لا يَدخُلُها إلّا ثَلاثَةٌ، أحَدُهُم مَن حَكَمَ في نَفسِهِ بالحَقِّ.٦٩١٨

1728. Those Who are Not Fair

١٧٢٨ ـ مَن لا يَنتَصِفُ

6116. **Imām ʿAlī (AS) said,** 'There are three types of people who cannot expect fairness from three other types of people: an intelligent man from a fool, a righteous man from a corrupt man, and a kind man from a vile man.'[6959]

٦١١٦. الإمامُ عليٌّ ﷺ: ثَلاثَةٌ لا يَنتَصِفونَ مِن ثَلاثَةٍ أبداً: العاقِلُ مِنَ الأحمَقِ، والبَرُّ مِنَ الفاجِرِ، والكَريمُ مِنَ اللَّئيمِ.٦٩١٩

6117. **Imām ʿAlī (AS) said,** 'A righteous man cannot expect fairness from a corrupt man, nor can a knowledgeable man expect fairness from an ignorant man.'[6960]

٦١١٧. عنه ﷺ: لا يَنتَصِفُ البَرُّ مِنَ الفاجِرِ، ولا يَنتَصِفُ عالِمٌ مِن جاهِلٍ.٦٩٢٠

376

SIGHT

النَّظَرُ

1729. The Eye is the Scout of the Heart

١٧٢٩ ـ العَينُ رائِدُ القلبِ

6118. **Imām ʿAlī (AS) said,** 'The eye is the messenger of the heart.'[6961]

٦١١٨ . الإمامُ عليٌّ عليه السلام : العَينُ بَريدُ القَلبِ.[٦٩٢١]

6119. **Imām ʿAlī (AS) said,** 'The eye is the spy of the heart, and the messenger of the intellect.'[6962]

٦١١٩ . عنه عليه السلام : العَينُ جاسُوسُ القَلبِ وبَريدُ العَقلِ.[٦٩٢٢]

6120. **Imām ʿAlī (AS) said,** 'The heart is the book of the eye.'[6963]

٦١٢٠ . عنه عليه السلام : القَلبُ مُصحَفُ[٦٩٢٣] البَصَرِ.[٦٩٢٤]

1730. The Eyes are the Snares of the Devil

١٧٣٠ ـ العُيونُ مَصائِدُ الشَّيطانِ

6121. **Prophet Jesus (AS) said,** 'Beware of looking at that which is forbidden, as it is the seed of desires and the plant of corruption.'[6964]

٦١٢١ . عيسى عليه السلام : إيّاكُم والنَّظَرَ إلَى المحذوراتِ ؛ فإنّها بَذرُ الشَّهَواتِ ونَباتُ الفِسقِ.[٦٩٢٥]

6122. **The Prophet (SAWA) said,** 'Beware of futile gazes for they introduce lustful inclinations and produce inattentiveness.'[6965]

٦١٢٢ . رسولُ اللهِ ﷺ : إيّاكُم وفُضولَ النَّظَرِ ؛ فإنَّهُ يَبذُرُ الهوىٰ ، ويُوَلِّدُ الغَفلَةَ.[٦٩٢٦]

6123. **Imām ʿAlī (AS) said,** 'The eyes are the snares of the devil.'[6966]

٦١٢٣ . الإمامُ عليٌّ عليه السلام : العُيونُ مَصائدُ الشَّيطانِ.[٦٩٢٧]

6124. **Imām ʿAlī (AS) said,** 'Blindness is better than looking excessively.'[6967]

٦١٢٤ . عنه عليه السلام : عَمَى البَصَرِ خَيرٌ مِن كَثيرٍ مِن النَّظَرِ.[٦٩٢٨]

6125. **Imām ʿAlī (AS) said,** 'He who lets his sight loose exhausts his present moment, and he whose glances follow each other successively is in constant loss.'[6968]

٦١٢٥ . عنه عليه السلام : مَن أطلَقَ ناظِرَهُ أتعَبَ حاضِرَهُ، مَن تَتابَعَت لَحَظاتُهُ دامَت حَسَراتُهُ.[٦٩٢٩]

6126. **Imām al-Ṣādiq (AS) said,** 'How many a look has brought about long regret!'[6969]

٦١٢٦ . الإمامُ الصّادقُ عليه السلام : كَم مِن نَظرَةٍ أورَثَت حَسرَةً طَويلَةً![٦٩٣٠]

1731. Those Whom Looking at is Considered Worship

١٧٣١ ـ مَن يَكونُ النَّظرُ إلَيهِ عِبادَةً

6127. **The Prophet (SAWA) said,** 'Looking at a scholar is worship, looking at a just leader is worship, looking at one's parents with affection and mercy is worship, and looking at a brother you love for the sake of Allah is worship.'[6970]

٦١٢٧ . رسولُ اللهِ ﷺ : النَّظَرُ إلَى العالِمِ عِبادَةٌ، والنَّظَرُ إلَى الإمامِ المُقسِطِ عِبادَةٌ، والنَّظَرُ إلَى الوالِدَينِ بِرأفَةٍ ورَحمَةٍ عِبادَةٌ، والنَّظَرُ إلَى الأخِ تَوَدُّهُ في اللهِ عَزَّوجلَّ عِبادَةٌ.[٦٩٣١]

6128. **The Prophet (SAWA) said,** 'Looking at three things is worship: looking at the faces of one's parents, at the Book [Qur'an], and at the sea.'[6971]

٦١٢٨ . عنه ﷺ : النَّظَرُ في ثَلاثَةِ أشياءَ عِبادَةٌ: النَّظَرُ في وَجهِ الوالِدَينِ، وفي المُصحَفِ، وفي البَحرِ.[٦٩٣٢]

1732. Enjoinment of Lowering One's Gaze

١٧٣٢ ـ الحَثُّ عَلىٰ غَضِّ البَصَرِ

"Tell the faithful men to cast down their looks and guard their private parts. That is more decent for them. Allah is indeed well aware of what they do. And tell the faithful women to cast down their looks and to guard their private parts, and not to display their charms, except for what is outward."[6972]

﴿قُلْ لِلْمُؤْمِنِينَ يَغُضُّوا مِنْ أَبْصَارِهِمْ وَيَحْفَظُوا فُرُوجَهُمْ ذٰلِكَ أَزْكَىٰ لَهُمْ إِنَّ اللهَ خَبِيرٌ بِمَا يَصْنَعُونَ * وَقُلْ لِلْمُؤْمِنَاتِ يَغْضُضْنَ مِنْ أَبْصَارِهِنَّ وَيَحْفَظْنَ فُرُوجَهُنَّ وَلَا يُبْدِينَ زِينَتَهُنَّ إِلَّا مَا ظَهَرَ مِنْهَا﴾ .[٦٩٣٣]

6129. **The Prophet (SAWA) said,** 'Every limb of man has a part in adultery: the adultery of the eye is looking [unlawfully].'[6973]

٦١٢٩ . رسولُ اللهِ ﷺ : لِكُلِّ عُضوٍ مِن ابنِ آدمَ حَظٌّ مِن الزِّنا: العَينُ زِناها النَّظَرُ.[٦٩٣٤]

6130. **The Prophet (SAWA) said,** 'Lower your gazes [from the forbidden] and you will see wonders.'[6974]

٦١٣٠ . عنه ﷺ : غُضُّوا أبصارَكُم تَرَونَ العَجائبَ.[٦٩٣٥]

6131. **The Prophet (SAWA) said,** 'Whoever fills his gaze with what is prohibited, Allah will fill his eyes with fire on the Day of Judgment, unless he repents and returns.'[6975]

٦١٣١ . عنه ﷺ : مَن مَلأَ عَينَهُ مِن حَرامٍ مَلأَ اللهُ عَينَهُ يَومَ القِيامَةِ مِنَ النّارِ، إلّا أن يَتوبَ ويَرجِعَ.[٦٩٣٦]

6132. **The Prophet (SAWA) said,** 'The anger of Allah is intensified towards a married woman who fills her eyes with [lust for] someone other than her husband and other than those of her blood relatives [*maḥram*].'[6976]

٦١٣٢ . عنه ﷺ : اِشتَدَّ غَضَبُ اللهِ عَزَّوجلَّ علَى امرأةٍ ذاتِ بَعلٍ مَلأت عَينَها مِن غَيرِ زَوجِها أو غَيرِ ذِي مَحرَمٍ مِنها.[٦٩٣٧]

6133. **Imām ʿAlī (AS) said,** 'He who lowers his gaze will rest his heart.'[6977]

٦١٣٣ . الإمامُ عليٌّ ﷺ : مَن غَضَّ طَرفَهُ أراحَ قَلبَهُ. [٦٩٣٨]

6134. **Imām al-Ṣādiq (AS) said,** 'A glance is a poisoned arrow from the arrows of Satan. He who refrains from it [glancing] for the sake of Allah and for nothing other than Him, Allah will grant him a faith, the taste of which he will experience.'[6978]

٦١٣٤ . الإمامُ الصّادقُ ﷺ : النَّظرَةُ سَهمٌ مِن سِهامِ إبليسَ مَسمومٌ، مَن تَرَكَها للهِ عَزَّوجلَّ لا لغَيرِهِ أعقَبَهُ اللهُ إيماناً يَجِدُ طَعمَهُ. [٦٩٣٩]

6135. **Imam al-Riḍā (AS),** in what he wrote in answer to some queries of Muḥammad b. Sinān, said, 'Looking at the hair of veiled women with husbands, and all women besides them is prohibited, for what it arouses in men, and for what that arousal engenders in terms of corruption and embarking upon what is not permitted and not good. And also, what is similar to hair, except those women whom Allah mentions: *"As for women advanced in years"*[6979] ... as there is no problem in looking at the hair of their like.'[6980]

٦١٣٥ . الإمامُ الرِّضا ﷺ ـ مِمّا كَتَبَ في جَوابِ مَسائلِ محمّدِ بنِ سِنانٍ ـ : وحُرِّمَ النَّظَرُ إلىٰ شُعورِ النِّساءِ المَحجوباتِ بالأزواجِ وإلىٰ غَيرِهِنَّ مِن النِّساءِ ؛ لِما فيهِ مِن تَهييجِ الرِّجالِ، وما يَدعو التَّهييجُ إلَيهِ مِن الفَسادِ والدُّخولِ فيما لا يَحِلُّ ولا يَجمُلُ، وكذٰلكَ ما أشبَهَ الشُّعورَ، إلّا الّذي قالَ اللهُ تعالىٰ : ﴿والقَواعِدُ مِن النِّساءِ اللاتي لا يَرجُونَ نِكاحاً ...﴾ [٦٩٤٠] ... فلا بأسَ بالنَّظَرِ إلىٰ شُعورِ مِثلِهِنَّ. [٦٩٤١]

(See also: FORNICATION: section 863)

(أنظر) الزنا : باب ٨٦٣.

1733. The First Glance is a Mistake and the Second is Intentional

١٧٣٣ ـ النَّظرَةُ الأُولىٰ خَطَأٌ وَالثّانِيَةُ عَمدٌ

6136. **The Prophet (SAWA) said to ʿAlī (AS),** 'O ʿAlī, you are allowed the first glance, but the second is against you, not in your favour.'[6981]

٦١٣٦ . رسولُ اللهِ ﷺ ـ لعَليٍّ ﷺ ـ : يا عليُّ، لكَ أوّلُ نَظرَةٍ، والثّانِيَةُ علَيكَ ولا لَكَ. [٦٩٤٢]

6137. **Imām al-Ṣādiq (AS) said,** 'The first glance is allowed to you, but the second is against you and not in your favour. In the third lies your ruin.'[6982]

٦١٣٧ . الإمامُ الصّادقُ ﷺ : أوّلُ النَّظرَةِ لكَ، والثّانِيَةُ علَيكَ ولا لَكَ، والثّالِثَةُ فيها الهَلاكُ. [٦٩٤٣]

6138. **Imām al-Ṣādiq (AS) said,** 'Glance after glance plants desire in the heart, and that is enough of a temptation for the onlooker.'[6983]

٦١٣٨ . عنه ﷺ : النَّظرَةُ بعدَ النَّظرَةِ تَزرَعُ فى القَلبِ الشَّهوَةَ، وكفىٰ بها لِصاحِبِها فِتنَةً. [٦٩٤٤]

1734. He Who Sees a Woman that Pleases Him

١٧٣٤ ـ مَن رَأىٰ امرأةً تُعجِبُهُ

6139. **Imām ʿAlī (AS) said,** 'If one of you sees a woman he is interested in, he should go to his wife, for she possesses whatever he saw. He should not allow the devil a path to his heart, and he should avert his eyes away from her. If he does not have a wife, he should offer two units of prayer and praise Allah a lot, and invoke blessings on the Prophet and his household, then he should ask from the grace of Allah, for He will grant him from His compassion that which will make him free from need.'[6984]

٦١٣٩. الإمامُ عليٌّ ﵇ : إذا رأىٰ أحَدُكُمُ امرأةً تُعجِبُهُ فلْيَأْتِ أهلَهُ ؛ فإنَّ عِندَ أهلِهِ مِثلَ ما رأىٰ ، ولا يَجعَلَنَّ لِلشَّيطانِ إلىٰ قَلبِهِ سَبيلاً ، وليَصرِفْ بَصَرَهُ عَنها ، فإن لَم تَكُنْ لَهُ زَوجَةٌ فَلْيُصَلِّ رَكعَتَينِ ويَحمَدِ اللهَ كثيراً ، ويُصَلّي عَلَى النَّبيِّ وآلِهِ ، ثُمّ ليَسألِ اللهَ مِن فَضلِهِ فإنّهُ يُبيحُ لَهُ برأفتِهِ ما يُغنيهِ .[٦٩٤٥]

377

DEBATE

المُناظَرَةُ

1735. Debate

١٧٣٥ ـ المُناظَرَةُ

6140. **Imām ʿAlī (AS),** in his advice to Kumayl said, 'O Kumayl, in every race there are groups better than groups, so beware of debating with the vile of them, and if they insult you, then tolerate them, and be of those whom Allah has described in His verse: *"and when the ignorant address them, say, 'Peace!'*.[6985] [6986]

٦١٤٠. الإمامُ عليٌّ ﵇ ـ في وَصيَّتِهِ لِكُمَيلٍ ـ : يا كُمَيلُ ، في كُلِّ صِنفٍ قَومٌ أرفَعُ مِن قَومٍ ، فإيّاكَ ومُناظَرَةَ الخَسيسِ مِنهُم ، وإن أسمَعوكَ فاحتَمِلْ وكُن مِنَ الّذينَ وَصَفَهُمُ اللهُ تعالىٰ بقولِهِ : ﴿وإذا خاطَبَهُمُ الجاهِلونَ قالوا سَلاماً﴾ .[٦٩٤٦] [٦٩٤٧]

6141. **Imām al-Ṣādiq (AS)** when al-Ṭayyār asked him about the detesting of debating with people said, 'As for the speech of the likes of you, it is not disliked. He who flies knows how to descend, and if he was to descend he knows how ascend again, so if one is like this, we do not dislike it.'[6987]

٦١٤١. الإمامُ الصّادقُ ﵇ ـ لَمّا سَألَهُ الطَّيّارُ عَن كَراهَةِ مُناظَرَةِ النّاسِ ـ : أمّا كَلامُ مِثلِكَ فَلا يُكرَهُ ، مَن إذا طارَ يُحسِنُ أن يَقَعَ ، وإن وَقَعَ يُحسِنُ أن يَطيرَ ، فمَن كانَ هكذا لا نَكرَهُهُ .[٦٩٤٨]

6142. **Imām al-Ṣādiq (AS) said** to Abū Jaʿfar al-Aḥwal, 'How is Ibn al-Ṭayyār?' al-Aḥwal said, 'He has passed away.' He (AS), 'The mercy of Allah be

٦١٤٢. عنه ﵇ لأبي جعفر الأحول : ما فَعَلَ ابنُ الطَّيّارِ ؟ فقلتُ : تُوُفِّي ، فقالَ : رَحِمَهُ اللهُ ، أدخَلَ

upon him, and may Allah give him mercy and blissfulness, as he would debate for the sake of us Ahl al-Bayt.'[6988]

اللهُ عليهِ الرَّحمَةَ والنَّضرَةَ ؛ فإنَّهُ كانَ يُخاصِمُ عنّا أهلَ البَيتِ.٦٩٤٩

1736. The Imām's Answer to One who Invited him to Debate

١٧٣٦ ـ جَوابُ الإمامِ لِمَن دَعاهُ إلَى المُناظَرَةِ

6143. **Imām Ḥusayn (AS)** replied to a man who said, 'Sit down so we can debate about religion' – 'O you, I am aware of my religion, and my path is clear for me. So, if you are ignorant about your religion then go and seek it. What do I have to do with disputation?! Indeed the devil tempts a person and calls him, saying, 'Debate with people regarding their religion so that they do not think of you as incapable and ignorant.'[6989]

٦١٤٣. الإمامُ الحسينُ ؑ ـ لرجُلٍ قالَ لَهُ: اجلِسْ حتّىٰ نَتَناظَرَ في الدِّينِ ـ: يا هٰذا أنا بَصيرٌ بدِيني مَكشوفٌ علَيَّ هُدايَ، فإن كُنتَ جاهلاً بدِينِكَ فـاذهَبْ واطـلُبْهُ، مـا لي ولـلمُماراةِ؟! وإنَّ الشَّيطانَ لَيُوَسوِسُ لِلرَّجُلِ ويُناجيهِ ويقولُ: ناظِرِ النّاسَ في الدِّينِ كيلا يَظُنّوا بكَ العَجزَ والجَهلَ! ٦٩٥٠

378

CLEANLINESS

النَّظافَةُ

1737. Enjoinment of Cleanliness

١٧٣٧ ـ الحَثُّ علَى النَّظافَةِ

6144. **The Prophet (SAWA) said,** 'Indeed Allah is pleasant and loves all that is pleasant. He is clean and loves cleanliness.'[6990]

٦١٤٤. رسولُ اللهِ ﷺ: إنَّ اللهَ طَيِّبٌ يُحِبُّ الطَّيِّبَ، نَظيفٌ يُحِبُّ النَّظافَةَ.٦٩٥١

6145. **The Prophet (SAWA) said,** 'Purify these bodies and Allah will purify you. For when a servant sleeps in a state of purity, an angel sleeps with him [engaged] in his remembrance. Any time of the night when he turns over, the angel says, 'O Allah forgive Your servant, for he has slept pure.'[6991]

٦١٤٥. عنه ﷺ: طَهِّروا هٰذهِ الأجسادَ طَهَّرَكُمُ اللهُ؛ فإنَّهُ لَيسَ عَبدٌ يَبيتُ طاهِراً إلّا باتَ مَعَهُ مَلَكٌ في شِعارِهِ، ولا يَتَقَلَّبُ ساعَةً مِن اللَّيلِ إلّا قالَ: اللّٰهُمَّ اغفِرْ لعَبدِكَ فإنَّهُ باتَ طاهِراً.٦٩٥٢

6146. **The Prophet (SAWA),** when he saw a man whose hair on his head was dishevelled, whose clothes were dirty, and who had a bad appearance, said, 'It is part of religion to enjoy oneself and to display one's bounties.'[6992]

٦١٤٦. عنه ﷺ ـ لَمّا أبصَرَ رجُلاً شَعِثاً شَعرُ رأسِهِ، وَسِخَةً ثِيابُهُ، سَيِّئَةً حالُهُ ـ: مِن الدِّينِ المُتعَةُ وإظهارُ النِّعمَةِ.٦٩٥٣

6147. **Jābir b. ʿAbdullāh al-Anṣārī said,** 'The Prophet (SAWA) visited us, and he saw an untidy man whose hair was dishevelled, so he said, 'Did this man not find anything with which to tame his hair?!' He then saw another man, who was wearing dirty clothes, so he said, 'Did this man not have any water to wash his clothes with?!'[6993]

٦١٤٧. جابرُ بنُ عبد الله: أتانا رسولُ اللهِ ﷺ فرأىٰ رجُلاً شَعِثاً قد تفَرَّقَ شَعرُهُ، فقالَ: أما كانَ يَجِدُ هٰذا ما يُسَكِّنُ بِه شَعرَهُ؟! ورأىٰ رجُلاً آخَرَ (و) علَيهِ ثيابٌ وسِخَةٌ فقالَ: أما كانَ هذا يَجِدُ ماءً يَغسِلُ بِه ثَوبَهُ؟! ٦٩٥٤

6148. **The Prophet (SAWA) said,** 'Keep yourselves as clean as possible, for Allah Almighty built Islam on cleanliness, and no one will ever enter Heaven unless they are clean.'[6994]

٦١٤٨. رسولُ اللهِ ﷺ: تَنَظَّفوا بكُلِّ ما استَطَعتُم؛ فإنَّ اللهَ تعالىٰ بَنَى الإسلامَ علَى النَّظافَةِ، ولَن يَدخُلَ الجَنَّةَ إلّا كُلُّ نَظيفٍ. ٦٩٥٥

6149. **The Prophet (SAWA) said,** 'Indeed Allah loves the clean worshipper.'[6995]

٦١٤٩. عنه ﷺ: إنّ اللهَ يُحِبُّ النّاسِكَ النَّظيفَ. ٦٩٥٦

6150. **The Prophet (SAWA) said,** 'Whoever wears clothes must clean them.'[6996]

٦١٥٠. عنه ﷺ: مَنِ اتَّخَذَ ثَوباً فلْيُنَظِّفْهُ. ٦٩٥٧

6151. **Imām ʿAlī (AS) said,** 'Clean clothes take away sorrow and grief, and it is [a condition of] purity for prayers.'[6997]

٦١٥١. الإمامُ عليٌّ ﷺ: النَّظيفُ مِنَ الثِّيابِ يُذهِبُ الهَمَّ والحُزنَ، وهُو طَهورٌ للصَّلاةِ. ٦٩٥٨

6152. **Imām al-Bāqir (AS) said,** 'Sweeping of the houses eradicates poverty.'[6998]

٦١٥٢. الإمامُ الباقرُ ﷺ: كَنسُ البُيوتِ يَنفي الفَقرَ. ٦٩٥٩

6153. **Imām al-Ṣādiq (AS) said,** 'Washing dishes and sweeping the courtyard attracts sustenance.'[6999]

٦١٥٣. الإمامُ الصّادقُ ﷺ: غَسلُ الإناءِ وكَسحُ الفِناءِ، مَجلَبَةٌ للرِّزقِ. ٦٩٦٠

6154. **Imām al-Riḍā (AS) said,** 'From the morals of the prophets is cleanliness.'[7000]

٦١٥٤. الإمامُ الرِّضا ﷺ: مِن أخلاقِ الأنبياءِ التَّنَظُّفُ. ٦٩٦١

1738. Warning Against Uncleanliness

١٧٣٨ ـ التَّحذيرُ مِن تَركِ النَّظافَةِ

6155. **The Prophet (SAWA) said,** 'How wretched is the servant who is filthy.'[7001]

٦١٥٥. رسولُ اللهِ ﷺ: بِئسَ العَبدُ القاذُورَةُ. ٦٩٦٢

6156. **The Prophet (SAWA) said,** 'The filthy ones perish.'[7002]

٦١٥٦. عنه ﷺ: هَلَكَ المُتَقذِّرونَ. ٦٩٦٣

6157. **The Prophet (SAWA) said,** 'Do not place dirt behind the door, for it is the shelter of the devil.'[7003]

٦١٥٧. عنه ﷺ: لا تُؤْوُا التُّرابَ خَلفَ البابِ؛ فإنّهُ مَأوَى الشَّيطانِ.٦٩٦٤

6158. **The Prophet (SAWA) said,** 'Do not leave garbage overnight in your houses, and take it out in the daytime, for it is the dwelling place of the devil.'[7004]

٦١٥٨. عنه ﷺ: لا تُبَيِّتوا القُمامَةَ في بُيوتِكُم وأخرِجوها نَهاراً؛ فإنّها مَقعَدُ الشَّيطانِ.٦٩٦٥

6159. **Imām ʿAlī (AS) said,** 'Clean yourselves with water from the bad smells that are offensive, and attend to yourselves; for Allah Almighty hates the dirty from among His servants whose seating companions become disdained as a result of him.'[7005]

٦١٥٩. الإمامُ عليٌّ ﷺ: تَنَظَّفوا بالماءِ مِن النَّتنِ الرِّيحِ الّذي يُتأذّى بِهِ، تَعَهَّدوا أنفُسَكُم؛ فإنّ اللهَ عَزَّوجلَّ يُبغِضُ مِن عِبادِهِ القاذُورَةَ الّذي يَتأنَّفُ بِهِ مَن جَلَسَ إلَيهِ.٦٩٦٦

6160. **Imām ʿAlī (AS) said,** 'Clean your houses of cobwebs, for leaving them in the house brings about poverty.'[7006]

٦١٦٠. عنه ﷺ: نَظِّفوا بُيوتَكُم مِن حَوكِ العَنكَبوتِ؛ فإنّ تَركَهُ في البَيتِ يُورِثُ الفَقرَ.٦٩٦٧

(See also: PURITY 254)

(أنظر) عنوان ٢٥٤ «الطهارة».

379

BOUNTIES

النِّعمَةُ

1739. The Bounties of Allah Cannot be Enumerated

١٧٣٩ ـ نِعَمُ اللهِ لا تُحصى

"And He gave you all that you had asked Him. If you enumerate Allah's blessing, you will not be able to count them. Indeed man is most unfair and ungrateful!"[7007]

﴿وَآتَاكُمْ مِنْ كُلِّ مَا سَأَلْتُمُوهُ وَإِنْ تَعُدُّوا نِعْمَةَ اللهِ لَا تُحْصُوهَا إِنَّ الْإِنْسَانَ لَظَلُومٌ كَفَّارٌ﴾.٦٩٦٨

6161. **The Prophet (SAWA) said,** 'He who does not see the bounties of Allah upon himself other than in his food, drink, and clothes, surely his actions fall short and his punishment is near.'[7008]

٦١٦١. رسولُ اللهِ ﷺ: مَن لَم يَرَ للهِ عَزَّوجلَّ علَيهِ نِعمَةً إلّا في مَطعَمٍ أو مَشرَبٍ أو مَلبَسٍ، فقد قَصُرَ عَمَلُهُ ودَنا عَذابُهُ.٦٩٦٩

6162. **Imām ʿAlī (AS) said,** 'Praise be to Allah whose extolment speakers cannot attain, and whose

٦١٦٢. الإمامُ عليٌّ ﷺ: الحَمدُ للهِ الذي لا يَبلُغُ

bounties cannot be enumerated by those who count.'[7009]

مِـــدحَتَهُ القـائلونَ، ولا يُـحصِي نَـعماءَهُ العادُّونَ.[٦٩٧٠]

6163. **Imām ʿAlī (AS),** in his advice to Kumayl said, 'O Kumayl, you cannot ever be devoid of the bounties of Allah and the good health [given to you by Him], so do not remain without praising Him, exalting Him, glorifying Him, sanctifying Him, thanking Him and remembering Him in every situation.'[7010]

٦١٦٣. عنه ﷺ ـ في وَصيَّتِهِ لِكُميلٍ ـ: يا كُمَيلُ، إنّـهُ لا تَـخلو مِـن نِـعمَةِ اللهِ عَـزَّوجلَّ عِـندَكَ وعـافِيَتِهِ، فـلا تَـخْلُ مِـن تَـحميدِهِ وتَـمجيدِهِ وتَسبيحِهِ وتَقديسِهِ وشُكرِهِ وذِكـرِهِ عـلىٰ كـلِّ حالٍ.[٦٩٧١]

1740. Negligence of Bounties

١٧٤٠ ـ الغَفلَةُ عَنِ النِّعَمِ

6164. **The Prophet (SAWA) said,** 'There are two bounties that most people are tested with: free time and health.'[7011]

٦١٦٤. رسولُ اللهِ ﷺ: نِعمَتانِ مَفتونٌ فيهِما كَثيرٌ مِن النّاسِ: الفَراغُ والصِّحَّةُ.[٦٩٧٢]

6165. **The Prophet (SAWA) said,** 'There are two bounties that people are ungrateful for: safety and good health.'[7012]

٦١٦٥. عنه ﷺ: نِـعمَتانِ مَكـفورَتانِ: الأمـنُ والعافِيَةُ.[٦٩٧٣]

6166. **Imām ʿAlī (AS) said,** 'He who lives in bounties is ignorant of the worth of the calamity.'[7013]

٦١٦٦. الإمامُ عليٌّ ﷺ: مَن كانَ في النِّعمَةِ جَهِلَ قَدرَ البَلِيَّةِ.[٦٩٧٤]

6167. **Imām Ḥasan (AS) said,** 'Bounties are ignored as long as they exist, but when they go they [their worth] are known.'[7014]

٦١٦٧. الإمامُ الحسنُ ﷺ: تُجهَلُ النِّعَمُ ما أقامَت، فإذا وَلَّت عُرِفَت.[٦٩٧٥]

1741. Embracing Bounties

١٧٤١ ـ إحسانُ مُجاوَرَةِ النِّعَمِ

6168. **Imām ʿAlī (AS) said,** 'Appreciate the having of bounties before their departure, for they will leave and testify against their owner with respect to what he has done with them.'[7015]

٦١٦٨. الإمامُ عليٌّ ﷺ: أحسِنوا صُحبَةَ النِّعَمِ قَبلَ فِراقِها؛ فإنّها تَزولُ وتَشهَدُ عـلىٰ صـاحِبِها بـما عَمِلَ فيها.[٦٩٧٦]

6169. **Imām ʿAlī (AS) said,** 'Beware the fleeing of bounties, for not every runaway returns.'[7016]

٦١٦٩. عنه ﷺ: اِحذَروا نِفارَ النِّعَمِ؛ فما كـلُّ شارِدٍ بمَردُودٍ.[٦٩٧٧]

6170. **Imām al-Hādī (AS) said,** 'Meet bounties by treating them well, and plead for an increase in them by giving thanks for them, and know that the self is the most accepting of what it is given

٦١٧٠. الإمامُ الهادي ﷺ: ألقُوا النِّـعَمَ بـحُسنِ مُـجاوَرَتِها؛ والتَـمِسوا الزِّيـادَةَ فـيها بـالشُّكرِ عـلَيها، واعـلَموا أنّ النَّـفسَ أقـبَلُ شـيءٍ لِـما

and the most resistant against that which it has been deprived of.'[7017]

أعطِيَت، وأمنَعُ شَيءٍ لِما مُنِعَت.٦٩٧٨

1742. That which Causes Bounties to Remain

١٧٤٢ـ ما يوجِبُ بَقاءَ النِّعَمِ

"If the people of the towns had been faithful and Godwary, We would have opened to them bounties from the Heaven and the earth. But they denied; so we seized them because of what they used to earn."[7018]

﴿وَلَوْ أَنَّ أَهْلَ الْقُرَىٰ آمَنُوا وَاتَّقَوا لَفَتَحْنَا عَلَيْهِمْ بَرَكَاتٍ مِنَ السَّمَاءِ وَالْأَرْضِ وَلٰكِنْ كَذَّبُوا فَأَخَذْنَاهُمْ بِمَا كَانُوا يَكْسِبُونَ﴾.٦٩٧٩

"That is because Allah never changes a blessing that He has bestowed on a people unless they change what is in their own souls, and Allah is all-hearing, all-knowing."[7019]

﴿ذٰلِكَ بِأَنَّ اللهَ لَمْ يَكُ مُغَيِّرًا نِعْمَةً أَنْعَمَهَا عَلَىٰ قَوْمٍ حَتَّىٰ يُغَيِّرُوا مَا بِأَنْفُسِهِمْ وَأَنَّ اللهَ سَمِيعٌ عَلِيمٌ﴾.٦٩٨٠

6171. **The Prophet (SAWA) said,** 'Allah has servants whom He has chosen for bounties. He establishes these in them as long as they distribute them to people, but if they withhold them [the bounties], He transfers them to other people.'[7020]

٦١٧١. رسولُ اللهِ ﷺ: إنّ للهِ عِباداً اختَصَّهُم بالنِّعَمِ، يُقِرُّها فيهِم ما بَذَلوها للنّاسِ، فإذا مَنَعوها حَوَّلَها مِنهُم إلىٰ غَيرِهِم.٦٩٨١

6172. **Imām ʿAlī (AS) said,** 'He upon whom the bounties of Allah are plenty, people's needs from him increase accordingly. So, if he uses them for Allah in the way he must do so, He causes them to continue and remain. But if he does not use them in the way that he must, He will make them cease and perish.'[7021]

٦١٧٢. الإمامُ عليٌّ (ع): مَن كَثُرَت نِعَمُ اللهِ علَيهِ كَثُرَت حَوائجُ النّاسِ إلَيهِ، فمَن قامَ للهِ فيها بما يَجِبُ فيها عَرَّضَها لِلدَّوامِ والبَقاءِ، ومَن لَم يَقُمْ فيها بما يَجِبُ عَرَّضَها لِلزَّوالِ والفَناءِ.٦٩٨٢

6173. **Imām ʿAlī (AS) said,** 'The least of what you are obliged to do for Allah is to not use His bounties to commit acts of disobedience to Him.'[7022]

٦١٧٣. عنه (ع): أقَلُّ ما يَلزَمُكُم للهِ ألّا تَستَعينوا بِنِعَمِهِ علىٰ مَعاصيهِ.٦٩٨٣

6174. **Imām al-Ṣādiq (AS) said,** 'Bounties will not remain unless after having three things: knowledge of the status of Allah in the blessings [being from Him], fulfilment of thanks for them, and striving with them.'[7023]

٦١٧٤. الإمامُ الصّادقُ (ع): لا تَدومُ النِّعَمُ إلّا بعدَ ثَلاثٍ (إلّا بثَلاثٍ): مَعرِفَةٌ بما يَلزَمُ للهِ سبحانَهُ فيها، وأداءُ شُكرِها، والتَّعَبُ فيها.٦٩٨٤

6175. **Imām al-Ṣādiq (AS) said,** 'He upon whom are great bounties from Allah, people's needs from

٦١٧٥. عنه (ع): مَن عَظُمَت نِعمَةُ اللهِ علَيهِ اشتَدَّت

him increase accordingly. So, seek continuity in your bounties through bearing the expenses [of people], and do not let them cease, for it is seldom that one's bounties cease and return to him again.'[7024]

مَؤونَةُ النّاسِ علَيهِ، فاستَديموا النِّعمَةَ باحتِمالِ المَؤونَةِ ولا تُعَرِّضوها لِلزَّوالِ، فـقَلَّ مَـن زالَتَ عَنهُ النِّعمَةُ فكادَت أن تَعودَ إلَيهِ. [٦٩٨٥]

6176. **Imām al-Kāẓim (AS) said,** 'He who economizes and is content, his bounties will stay, and he who wastes and squanders, his bounties cease to remain with him.'[7025]

٦١٧٦. الإمامُ الكاظمُ ﷷ : مَنِ اقتَصَدَ وقَنَعَ بَقِيَت عـلَيهِ النِّـعمَةُ، ومَـن بَذَّرَ وأسـرَفَ زالَت عنهُ النِّعمَةُ. [٦٩٨٦]

6177. **Imām al-Riḍā (AS) said,** 'Observing justice and benevolence invites the continuation of bounties.'[7026]

٦١٧٧. الإمامُ الرِّضا ﷷ : اِستِعمالُ العَـدلِ والإحسانِ مُؤْذِنٌ بِدَوامِ النِّعمَةِ. [٦٩٨٧]

(See also: SINNING: section 777)

(أُنظر) الذنب: باب ٧٧٧.

1743. Consecutive Succession of Bounties and Gradual Baiting [for Chastisement]

١٧٤٣ ـ تَتابُعُ النِّعَمِ وَالاستِدراجُ

"Let the faithless not suppose that the respite that We grant them is good for their souls: We give them respite only that they may increase in sin, and there is a humiliating punishment for them."[7027]

﴿وَلَا يَحْسَبَنَّ الَّذِينَ كَفَرُوا أَنَّمَا نُمْلِي لَهُمْ خَيْرٌ لِأَنْفُسِهِمْ إِنَّمَا نُمْلِي لَهُمْ لِيَزْدَادُوا إِثْماً وَلَهُمْ عَذَابٌ مُهِينٌ﴾. [٦٩٨٨]

6178. **Imām 'Alī (AS) said,** 'O son of Adam, if you see your Lord, glory be to Him, bestowing bounties upon you in continuous succession while you are disobeying Him, then be cautious of Him.'[7028]

٦١٧٨. الإمامُ عليٌّ ﷷ : يابنَ آدمَ، إذا رَأيتَ ربَّكَ سـبحانَهُ يُـتابِعُ عـلَيكَ نِـعمَهُ وأنتَ تَـعصيهِ فاحذَرْهُ. [٦٩٨٩]

6179. **Imām 'Alī (AS) said,** 'O people, let Allah see you fearing Him at the time of happiness just as you fear Him in time of distress. Certainly he who is given ease [of life] and does not consider it as a means of gradual baiting towards tribulation [wrongdoing], considers himself safe against what is to be feared, while he who is afflicted with straitened circumstances but does not perceive them to be a trial loses the coveted reward.'[7029]

٦١٧٩. عنه ﷷ : أيُّها النّاسُ، لِيَرَكُمُ اللهُ مِن النِّعمَةِ وَجِلِينَ كما يَراكُم مِن النِّقمَةِ فَرِقِينَ ؛ إنَّهُ مَن وُسِّعَ علَيهِ في ذاتِ يَدِهِ فلَم يَرَ ذلكَ استِدراجاً فَقد أمِنَ مَخُوفاً، ومَن ضُيِّقَ علَيهِ في ذاتِ يَدِهِ فلَم يَـرَ ذلكَ اختِباراً فَقد ضَيَّعَ مَأمولاً. [٦٩٩٠]

6180. **Imām 'Alī (AS) said,** 'Very often a favoured person is gradually being driven [towards punishment]

٦١٨٠. عنه ﷷ : رُبَّ مُنعَمٍ عـلَيهِ مُستَدرَجٌ

through these favours; and very often an afflicted person is being done good through his affliction.'[7030]

بالنِّعمىٰ ، ورُبَّ مُبتَلىً مَصنوعٌ لَهُ بالبَلوىٰ.٦٦٩١

6181. **Imām Ḥusayn (AS) said,** 'Allah Almighty's gradual baiting of His servant is that He envelops him with bounties and eradicates thankfulness from him.'[7031]

٦١٨١. الإمامُ الحسينُ ؑ : الاستِدراجُ مِن اللهِ سُبحانَهُ لِعَبدِهِ أن يُسبِغَ عَلَيهِ النِّعَمَ ويَسلُبَهُ الشُّكرَ.٦٦٩٢

1744. Proclaiming about the Bounties of Allah

١٧٤٤ ـ التَّحَدُّثُ بِنعمَةِ اللهِ

"And as for your Lord's blessing, proclaim it!"[7032]

﴿وَأَمَّا بِنِعْمَةِ رَبِّكَ فَحَدِّثْ﴾.٦٦٩٣

6182. **The Prophet (SAWA) said,** 'Allah loves to see the signs of His bounties on His servant.'[7033]

٦١٨٢. رسولُ اللهِ ﷺ : إنَّ اللهَ يُحِبُّ أن يَرىٰ أثَرَ نِعمَتِهِ علىٰ عَبدِهِ.٦٦٩٤

6183. **Abū al-Aḥwaṣ,** narrating from his father said, 'I visited the Prophet (SAWA) and he saw me with a bad appearance, so the Prophet (SAWA) said, 'Do you own anything?' I said, 'Yes, all the wealth that Allah has given me.' He (SAWA) said, 'If you have wealth then it should be seen on you.'[7034]

٦١٨٣. أبو الأحوَصِ عن أبيهِ : دخلتُ على رسول الله ﷺ فرآني سيِّئَ الهيئة، فقال النبيّ ﷺ هل لك من شيء؟ قال: نعم من كلّ المال قد آتاني الله. فقال: إذا كان لك مالٌ فليُرىٰ عليك.٦٦٩٥

6184. **Imām 'Alī (AS) said,** 'Allah is Beautiful and He loves beauty, and He loves to see the sign of His bounties on His servant.'[7035]

٦١٨٤. الإمامُ عليٌّ ؑ : إنّ اللهَ جَميلٌ يُحِبُّ الجَمالَ، ويُحِبُّ أن يَرىٰ أثَرَ النِّعمَةِ علىٰ عَبدِهِ.٦٦٩٦

6185. **Imām al-Ṣādiq (AS) said,** 'When Allah blesses His servant with bounties and it is manifest about him, he is called the beloved of Allah and a proclaimer of Allah's bounties, and when Allah blesses a servant with bounties and he does not show it, he is called the despiser of Allah and a denier of Allah's bounties.'[7036]

٦١٨٥. الإمامُ الصّادقُ ؑ : إذا أنعَمَ اللهُ علىٰ عَبدِهِ بِنعمَةٍ فظَهَرَت علَيهِ سُمِّيَ حَبيبَ اللهِ مُحَدِّثاً بِنِعمَةِ اللهِ، وإذا أنعَمَ اللهُ علىٰ عَبدٍ بِنعمَةٍ فلَم تَظهَرْ علَيهِ سُمِّيَ بَغيضَ اللهِ مُكَذِّباً بنِعمَةِ اللهِ.٦٦٩٧

6186. **Imām al-Ṣādiq (AS) said,** 'Indeed I hate for a man to have been bestowed bounties by Allah and to not show it.'[7037]

٦١٨٦. عنه ؑ : إنّي لَأكرَهُ لِلرّجُلِ أن يَكونَ علَيهِ نِعمَةٌ مِن اللهِ فلا يُظهِرُها.٦٦٩٨

1745. The Completion of Bounties

١٧٤٥ ـ تَمامُ النِّعمَةِ

6187. **The Prophet (SAWA) said,** 'Whoever sleeps and wakes up possessing three things, then bounties for him in this world are complete: he who sleeps and wakes up with a healthy body, safe in his den, with enough sustenance for the day. And if he has a fourth thing then the bounties of this world and the Hereafter are complete in him, and that is faith.'[7038]

٦١٨٧ . رسولُ اللهِ ﷺ : مَن أمسىٰ وأصبحَ وعِندَهُ ثَلاثٌ فقد تَمَّت علَيهِ النِّعمَةُ في الدُّنيا : مَن أصبَحَ وأمسىٰ مُعافىً في بَدَنِهِ ، آمِناً في سَرْبِهِ ، عِندَهُ قُوتُ يَومِهِ ، فإن كانَت عِندَهُ الرّابِعَةُ فَقد تَمَّت علَيهِ النِّعمَةُ في الدُّنيا والآخِرَةِ ؛ وهُو الإيمانُ .[٦٩٩٩]

6188. **Imām ʿAlī (AS) said,** 'Bounties are completed through humbleness.'[7039]

٦١٨٨ . الإمامُ عليٌّ ﷺ : بالتَّواضُعِ تَتِمُّ النِّعمَةُ .[٧٠٠٠]

6189. **Imām ʿAlī (AS) said,** 'Complete the bounties of Allah over you by having patience in obeying Him, and refraining from disobeying Him.'[7040]

٦١٨٩ . عنه ﷺ : استَتِمُّوا نِعمَ اللهِ علَيكُم بالصَّبرِ علىٰ طاعَتِهِ ، والمُجانَبَةِ لِمَعصيَتِهِ .[٧٠٠١]

6190. **Imām al-Ṣādiq (AS) said,** 'Bounties in this world are safety and a healthy body, and the completion of bounties in the Hereafter is entrance into Heaven. And the bounties [of Allah] are not complete until the servant enters Heaven.'[7041]

٦١٩٠ . الإمامُ الصّادقُ ﷺ : النَّعيمُ في الدُّنيا الأمنُ وصِحَّةُ الجِسمِ ، وتَمامُ النِّعمَةِ في الآخِرَةِ دُخولُ الجَنَّةِ ، وما تَمَّتِ النِّعمَةُ علىٰ عَبدٍ قَطُّ لَم يَدخُلِ الجَنَّةَ .[٧٠٠٢]

380

THE SOUL

النَّفسُ

1746. The Carnal Soul that Prompts to Evil

١٧٤٦ ـ النَّفسُ الأمّارَةُ

"Yet I do not absolve my [own carnal] soul, for the [carnal] soul indeed prompts [men] to evil, except inasmuch as my Lord has mercy. Indeed my Lord is all-forgiving, all-merciful."[7042]

﴿وَمَا أُبَرِّئُ نَفْسِي إِنَّ النَّفْسَ لَأَمَّارَةٌ بِالسُّوءِ إِلَّا مَا رَحِمَ رَبِّي إِنَّ رَبِّي غَفُورٌ رَحِيمٌ﴾ .[٧٠٠٣]

6191. **Imām ʿAlī (AS) said,** 'The carnal, seducing soul flatters as a hypocrite flatters, and simulates the characteristics of an agreeing friend, and as soon as it tricks and overcomes him [man], it

٦١٩١ . الإمامُ عليٌّ ﷺ : النَّفسُ الأمّارةُ المُسَوِّلَةُ تَتَملَّقُ تَملُّقَ المُنافِقِ ، وتَتَصَنَّعُ بشِيمَةِ الصَّديقِ المُوافِقِ ، حتّىٰ إذا خَدَعَت وتَمَكَّنَت تَسَلَّطَت

overpowers him as an enemy overpowers and controls him like a controlling tyrant, and hence it [the soul] drives a man towards his ruin.'[7043]

تَسَلُّطَ العَدُوِّ، وتَحَكَّمَت تَحَكُّمَ العُتُوِّ، فأورَدَت مَوارِدَ السُّوءِ.[٧٠٠٤]

6192. **Imām Zayn al-ʿĀbidīn (AS),** in an intimate supplication said, 'O Allah, to You I complain of a soul that prompts to evil, that hastens towards wrongdoing and is fond of disobeying You… it has many faults, yet [entertains] high expectations; when evil strikes it, it worries, and when good comes its way, it withholds it. It inclines to amusement and frivolity, full of inattentiveness and forgetfulness; it hastens me to sin, and stalls me from repentance.'[7044]

٦١٩٢. الإمامُ زينُ العابدينَ عليه السلام ـ في المُناجاةِ ـ: إلٰهي، إليكَ أشكو نَفساً بالسُّوءِ أمّارَةً، وإلَى الخَطيئةِ مُبادِرَةً، وبمَعاصيكَ مُولَعَةً،... كثيرَةَ العِلَلِ، طَويلَةَ الأمَلِ، إن مَسَّها الشَّرُّ تَجزَعْ، وإن مَسَّها الخَيرُ تَمنَعْ، مَيّالَةً إلَى اللَّعِبِ واللَّهوِ، مَملُوّةً بالغَفلَةِ والسَّهوِ، تُسرِعُ بي إلَى الحَوبَةِ، وتُسَوِّفُني بالتَّوبَةِ.[٧٠٠٥]

1747. The Self-Reproaching Soul

١٧٤٧ ـ النَّفسُ اللَّوّامَةُ

"And I swear by the self-blaming soul!"[7045]

﴿وَلَا أُقْسِمُ بِالنَّفْسِ اللَّوَّامَةِ﴾.[٧٠٠٦]

6193. **The Prophet (SAWA),** in his advice to Ibn Masʿūd said, 'O Ibn Masʿūd, increase in the acts of righteousness and good, for both the good [people] and the bad will regret; the good-doer will say, 'If only I had done more good!' And the bad-doer will say, 'I was negligent', and the evidence for this is the verse: *"And I swear by the self-blaming soul!"*'[7046]

٦١٩٣. رسولُ اللهِ صلى الله عليه وآله ـ في وصيَّتِهِ لابنِ مَسعودٍ ـ: يابنَ مَسعودٍ، أكثِرْ مِن الصّالِحاتِ والبِرِّ؛ فإنّ المُحسِنَ والمُسيءَ يَندَمانِ، يَقولُ المُحسِنُ: يا لَيتَني ازدَدتُ مِن الحَسَناتِ! ويقولُ المُسيءُ: قَصَّرتُ، وتَصديقُ ذلكَ قَولُهُ تعالىٰ: ﴿ولا أُقْسِمُ بالنَّفْسِ اللَّوّامَةِ﴾.[٧٠٠٧]

1748. Teaching the Soul, Disciplining it and Purifying it

١٧٤٨ ـ تَعليمُ النَّفسِ وتَأديبُها وتَهذيبُها

"by the soul and Him who fashioned it, and inspired it with [discernment between] its virtues and vices: one who purifies it is certainly felicitous, and one who betrays it certainly fails."[7047]

﴿وَنَفْسٍ وَمَا سَوَّاهَا * فَأَلْهَمَهَا فُجُورَهَا وَتَقْوَاهَا * قَدْ أَفْلَحَ مَنْ زَكَّاهَا * وَقَدْ خَابَ مَنْ دَسَّاهَا﴾.[٧٠٠٨]

6194. **Imām ʿAlī (AS) said,** 'O people, take charge of the disciplining of your selves, and redress them from the wildness of their habits.'[7048]

٦١٩٤. الإمامُ عليٌّ عليه السلام: أيُّها النّاسُ، تَوَلَّوا مِن أنفُسِكُم تأديبَها، واعدِلوا بِها عَن ضَراوَةِ عاداتِها.[٧٠٠٩]

6195. **Imām ʿAlī (AS) said,** 'Rule your souls by continuously struggling with them.'[7049]

٦١٩٥ . عنه عليه السلام : إمـــلِكوا أنــفُسَكُم بــدَوامِ جِهادِها.[٧٠١٠]

6196. **Imām ʿAlī (AS) said,** 'Godwariness is the cure for the sickness of your hearts….and the purification of the pollution of your souls.'[7050]

٦١٩٦ . عنه عليه السلام : إنَّ تَقوَى اللهِ دَواءُ داءِ قُلوبِكُم... وطَهورُ دَنَسِ أنفُسِكُم.[٧٠١١]

6197. **Imām ʿAlī (AS) said,** 'Come closer to your soul by retracting from it [i.e. its carnal desires].'[7051]

٦١٩٧ . عنه عليه السلام : أقبِلْ عـلىٰ نَـفسِكَ بـالإدبارِ عَنها.[٧٠١٢]

6198. **Imām ʿAlī (AS) said,** 'He who censures his soul improves it, and he who praises his soul slaughters it.'[7052]

٦١٩٨ . عنه عليه السلام : مَن ذَمَّ نفسَهُ أصلَحَها ، مَن مَدَحَ نَفسَهُ ذَبَحَها.[٧٠١٣]

6199. **Imām ʿAlī (AS) said,** 'He who does not refine his soul will be disgraced by bad habits.'[7053]

٦١٩٩ . عنه عليه السلام : مَن لَم يُهَذِّبْ نفسَهُ فضَحَهُ سُوءُ العادَةِ.[٧٠١٤]

6200. **Imām ʿAlī (AS) said,** 'He who does not engage himself in remedying the defects in his soul, its whims will overcome him, and he who [lives] in deficiency, then death is surely better for him.'[7054]

٦٢٠٠ . عنه عليه السلام : مَن لَم يَتَعاهَدِ النَّقصَ مِن نفسِهِ غَلَبَ علَيهِ الهَوىٰ ، ومَن كانَ في نَقصٍ فالمَوتُ خَيرٌ لَهُ.[٧٠١٥]

(See also: REMEMBRANCE: section 758; PIETY: section 1823)

(اُنظر) الذكر : باب ٧٥٨ ؛ الورع : باب ١٨٢٣ .

1749. The Effects of a Noble Soul

١٧٤٩ ـ آثارُ كَرامَةِ النَّفسِ

6201. **Imām ʿAlī (AS) said,** 'He who honours his soul will not humiliate it with sins.'[7055]

٦٢٠١ . الإمامُ عليٌّ عليه السلام : مَن كَرُمَت علَيهِ نَفسُهُ لَم يُهِنْها بالمَعصيَةِ.[٧٠١٦]

6202. **Imām ʿAlī (AS) said,** 'He who honours his soul, his desires become insignificant for him.'[7056]

٦٢٠٢ . عنه عليه السلام : مَن كَرُمَت علَيهِ نَفسُهُ هانَت علَيهِ شَهوَتُهُ.[٧٠١٧]

6203. **Imām ʿAlī (AS) said,** 'He who honours his soul, the world becomes small in his eyes.'[7057]

٦٢٠٣ . عنه عليه السلام : مَن كَرُمَت نَفسُهُ صَغُرَتِ الدُّنيا في عَينِهِ.[٧٠١٨]

381

HYPOCRISY

النِّفاقُ

1750. Hypocrisy

١٧٥٠ ـ النِّفاقُ

"So He caused hypocrisy to ensue in their hearts until the day they will encounter Him, because of their going back on what they had promised Allah and because of the lies they used to tell."[7058]

﴿فَأَعْقَبَهُمْ نِفَاقاً فِي قُلُوبِهِمْ إِلَىٰ يَوْمِ يَلْقَوْنَهُ بِمَا أَخْلَفُوا اللهَ مَا وَعَدُوهُ وَبِمَا كَانُوا يَكْذِبُونَ﴾ .[٧٠١٩]

6204. **The Prophet (SAWA) said,** 'Hypocrisy appears as a black dot [on the heart]. Whenever hypocrisy increases in magnitude that black dot increases, and when hypocrisy becomes complete the heart becomes black.'[7059]

٦٢٠٤ . رسولُ اللهِ ﷺ: إنّ النِّفاقَ يَبدو لُمظَةً سوداءَ، فكُلّما ازدادَ النِّفاقُ عِظَماً ازدادَ ذلكَ السَّوادُ، فإذا استَكمَلَ النِّفاقُ اسوَدَّ القَلبُ .[٧٠٢٠]

6205. **Imām ʿAlī (AS) said,** 'Hypocrisy is the brother of polytheism.'[7060]

٦٢٠٥ . الإمامُ عليٌّ عليه السلام: النِّفاقُ أخو الشِّركِ .[٧٠٢١]

6206. **Imām ʿAlī (AS) said,** 'How hideous is the human being whose outer is agreeable while his inner is hypocritical.'[7061]

٦٢٠٦ . عنه عليه السلام: ما أقبَحَ بالإنسانِ ظاهِراً مُوافِقاً، وباطِناً مُنافِقاً ![٧٠٢٢]

6207. **Imām ʿAlī (AS) said,** 'The hypocrisy of a person [stems] from the inferiority he finds within himself.'[7062]

٦٢٠٧ . عنه عليه السلام: نِفاقُ المَرءِ مِن ذُلٍّ يَجِدُهُ في نفسِهِ .[٧٠٢٣]

1751. The Description of a Hypocrite

١٧٥١ ـ صِفَةُ المُنافِقِ

"The hypocrites indeed seek to deceive Allah, but it is He who outwits them. When they stand up for prayer, they stand up lazily, showing off to the people and not remembering Allah except a little, wavering in between: neither with these nor with those. And whoever Allah leads astray, you will never find any way for him."[7063]

﴿إِنَّ الْمُنَافِقِينَ يُخَادِعُونَ اللهَ وَهُوَ خَادِعُهُمْ وَإِذَا قَامُوا إِلَى الصَّلَاةِ قَامُوا كُسَالَىٰ يُرَاؤُونَ النَّاسَ وَلَا يَذْكُرُونَ اللهَ إِلَّا قَلِيلاً ۞ مُذَبْذَبِينَ بَيْنَ ذٰلِكَ لَا إِلَىٰ هٰؤُلَاءِ وَلَا إِلَىٰ هٰؤُلَاءِ وَمَنْ يُضْلِلِ اللهُ فَلَنْ تَجِدَ لَهُ سَبِيلاً﴾ .[٧٠٢٤]

(See also: Qur'an 2:8, 2:20, 3:167-168, 4:61, 4:138, 4:145, 29:10-11, 47:30, 58:14-16)

(أُنظر) البقرة: ٨، ٢٠ وآل عمران: ١٦٧، ١٦٨ والنساء: ٦١، ١٣٨، ١٤٥ والعنكبوت: ١٠، ١١ ومحمد: ٣٠ والمجادلة: ١٤ ـ ١٦.

6208. **The Prophet (SAWA) said,** 'A hypocrite is someone who when he makes a promise he does not fulfil it, when he does something [good], he shows off, when he speaks he lies, when he is entrusted with something he betrays, when he is given sustenance he is heedless, and when he is deprived he resorts to tricks.'[7064]

٦٢٠٨. رسولُ اللهِ ﷺ: المُـنافِقُ مَـن إذا وَعَـدَ أخلَفَ، وإذا فَعَلَ أفشىٰ[٧٠٢٥]، وإذا قـالَ كَـذَبَ، وإذا ائتُمِنَ خـانَ، وإذا رُزِقَ طـاشَ، وإذا مُـنِعَ عاشَ.[٧٠٢٦]

6209. **The Prophet (SAWA) said,** 'A hypocrite has control over his eyes, he cries whenever he wants to.'[7065]

٦٢٠٩. عنه ﷺ: المُنافِقُ يَملِكُ عَـينَيهِ يَـبكي كما يَشاءُ.[٧٠٢٧]

6210. **The Prophet (SAWA) said,** 'Hypocrites have signs through which they are known: their greeting is cursing, their food is greed [gluttony], their earnings are through breaches of trust, they do not come close to the mosques save with contempt, they fulfil their prayers at the very last moment, [they are] haughty people who do not socialize and are not sociable, they are as wood in the night, loud in the day.'[7066]

٦٢١٠. عنه ﷺ: لِلمُنافقينَ عَلاماتٌ يُعرَفونَ بِها: تَحِيَّتُهُم لَعنَةٌ، وطَعامُهُم نُهمَةٌ، وغَنيمَتُهُم غُلولٌ، لا يَقرَبونَ المَساجِدَ إلّا هُجراً، ولا يَأتونَ الصَّلاةَ إلّا دُبُراً، مُستَكبِرينَ لا يَألَفونَ ولا يُؤلَفونَ، خُشُبٌ بِاللَّيلِ سُخُبٌ بِالنَّهارِ.[٧٠٢٨]

6211. **The Prophet (SAWA) said,** 'He whose inner is contrary to his outer is a hypocrite, no matter who he may be.'[7067]

٦٢١١. عنه ﷺ: مَن خالَفَت سَريرَتُهُ عَلانِيَتَهُ فهُو مُنافِقٌ كائناً مَن كانَ.[٧٠٢٩]

6212. **The Prophet (SAWA) said,** 'When humbleness of the body supersedes that which is in the heart then in our view it is hypocrisy.'[7068]

٦٢١٢. عنه ﷺ: ما زادَ خُشوعُ الجَسَدِ على ما في القَلبِ فهُو عِندَنا نِفاقٌ.[٧٠٣٠]

6213. **Imām ʿAlī (AS) said,** 'A hypocrite, when he looks he is frivolous, when he is silent he forgets, when he speaks he prattles, when he becomes wealthy he tyrannizes, when hardship afflicts him he becomes noisy, so he is close to discontentment and far from contentment. The least of things make him discontented with Allah, and he is never content, even with much. He intends to do a lot of evil and commits some of them, and he regrets the evil deeds that pass him by and how he did not manage to commit them.'[7069]

٦٢١٣. الإمامُ عليٌّ عليه السلام: المُنافِقُ إذا نَظَرَ لَـها، وإذا سَكَتَ سَها، وإذا تَكَلَّمَ لَـغا، وإذا استَغنى طَغا، وإذا أصابَتهُ شِدَّةٌ ضَغا، فهُو قَريبُ السُّخطِ بَعيدُ الرِّضا، يُسخِطُهُ علَى اللهِ اليَسيرُ، ولا يُرضيه الكَثيرُ، يَنوي كَثيراً مِن الشَّرِّ ويَعمَلُ بِطائفَةٍ مِنهُ، ويَتَلَهَّفُ على ما فاتَهُ مِن الشَّرِّ كيفَ لَـم يَـعمَلْ بِهِ![٧٠٣١]

6214. **Imām ʿAlī (AS) said,** 'If I was to strike the nose of a believer with my sword to hate me he would never hate me, and if I was to pour down the whole world onto a hypocrite to love me he would never love me, and this is because of what has been destined, as this was passed on through the tongue of the unschooled Prophet (SAWA), saying, "Alī, a believer can never hate you and a hypocrite can never love you."'[7070]

٦٢١٤. عنه ﵇ : لو ضَرَبتُ خَيشومَ المُؤمِنِ بِسَيفي هٰذا علىٰ أن يُبغِضَني ما أبغَضَني، ولو صَبَبتُ الدُّنيا بِجَمّاتِها علَى المُنافِقِ علىٰ أن يُحِبَّني ما أحَبَّني، وذٰلكَ أنّهُ قُضِيَ فانقَضىٰ علىٰ لِسانِ النَّبيِّ الاُمِّيِّ ﷺ، أنّهُ قالَ: يا عليُّ، لا يُبغِضُكَ مُؤمِنٌ، ولا يُحِبُّكَ مُنافِقٌ.[٧٠٣٢]

6215. **Imām Zayn al-ʿĀbidīn (AS) said,** 'A hypocrite prohibits [wrongdoing] but does not refrain from it himself, and he enjoins that which he does not do himself. When he prays he complains, when he bows (*rukūʿ*) he slumps, when he prostrates (*sujūd*) he pecks [prostrating so fast], when he sits he spreads himself out, when he is going to bed his only concern is food even though he is full, and when he wakes up in the morning, his only concern is sleep even though he did not stay up during the night. When he speaks to you he lies, when he makes a promise he does not fulfil it, if you entrust him with anything he betrays it, and if you disagree with him he backbites you.'[7071]

٦٢١٥. الإمامُ زينُ العابدينَ ﵇: المُنافِقُ يَنهىٰ ولا يَنتَهي، ويأمُرُ بما لا يأتي، إذا قامَ في الصَّلاةِ اعترَضَ، وإذا رَكَعَ رَبَضَ، وإذا سَجَدَ نَقَرَ، وإذا جَلَسَ شَغَرَ، يُمسي وهَمُّهُ الطَّعامُ وهُو مُفطِرٌ، ويُصبِحُ وهَمُّهُ النَّومُ ولَم يَسهَرْ، إن حَدَّثَكَ كَذَبَكَ، وإن وَعَدَكَ أخلَفَكَ، وإنِ ائتَمَنتَهُ خانَكَ، وإن خالَفتَهُ اغتابَكَ.[٧٠٣٣]

6216. **Imām al-Ṣādiq (AS) said,** 'There are four signs to a hypocrite: hardheartedness, dryness of the eyes, persistence in sinning, and greed for the world.'[7072]

٦٢١٦. الإمامُ الصّادقُ ﵇ : أربَعٌ مِن عَلاماتِ النِّفاقِ: قَساوَةُ القَلبِ، وجُمودُ العَينِ، والإصرارُ علَى الذَّنبِ، والحِرصُ علَى الدُّنيا.[٧٠٣٤]

1752. The Most Obvious Hypocrites

١٧٥٢ ـ أظهَرُ النّاسِ نِفاقاً

6217. **Imām ʿAlī (AS) said,** 'The most obvious of hypocrites is he who enjoins acts of obedience but does not perform them himself, and prohibits wrongdoing but does not refrain from them himself.'[7073]

٦٢١٧. الإمامُ عليٌّ ﵇: أظهَرُ النّاسِ نِفاقاً مَن أمَرَ بالطّاعَةِ ولَم يَعمَلْ بها، ونَهىٰ عنِ المَعصيَةِ ولَم يَنتَهِ عنها.[٧٠٣٥]

6218. **Imām ʿAlī (AS) said,** 'The most severe of hypocrites is he who enjoins acts of obedience, but does not perform them himself, and prohibits

٦٢١٨. عنه ﵇ : أشَدُّ النّاسِ نِفاقاً مَن أمَرَ بالطّاعَةِ ولَم يَعمَلْ بها، ونَهىٰ عَنِ المَعصيَةِ

wrongdoing but does not refrain from them himself.'[7074]

ولم يَنتَهِ عنها.[٧٠٣٦]

1753. Caution Against the Eloquent Hypocrite

١٧٥٣ ـ التَّحذيرُ مِنَ المُنافِقِ المِنطيقِ

6219. **Imām ʿAlī (AS) said,** 'Verily, the Prophet (SAWA) said to me, 'With respect to my people, I am afraid neither of a believer nor of an unbeliever. As for the believer, Allah will afford him protection because of his belief, and as for the disbeliever, Allah will humiliate him because of his disbelief. But I am afraid about every one from among you who is a hypocrite in his heart and eloquent of speech. He speaks what you hold to be good but does what you dislike.'[7075]

٦٢١٩ . الإمامُ عليٌّ عليه السلام : ولَقد قالَ لي رسولُ اللهِ ﷺ : إنّي لا أخافُ على أُمَّتي مُؤمِناً ولا مُشرِكاً ، أمّا المُؤمنُ فيَمنَعُهُ اللهُ بإيمانِهِ ، وأمّا المُشرِكُ فيَقمَعُهُ اللهُ بشِركِهِ، ولٰكنّي أخافُ علَيكُم كُلَّ مُنافِقِ الجَنانِ ، عالِمِ اللِّسانِ ، يقولُ ما تَعرِفونَ ، ويَفعَلُ ما تُنكِرونَ.[٧٠٣٧]

1754. The Description of the Resurrection of Hypocrites and their End

١٧٥٤ ـ صِفَةُ حَشرِ المُنافِقينَ وعاقِبتُهُم

"Allah has promised the hypocrites, men and women, and the faithless, the Fire of hell, to remain in it [forever]. That suffices them. Allah has cursed them, and there is a lasting punishment for them."[7076]

﴿وَعَدَ اللهُ الْمُنَافِقِينَ وَالْمُنَافِقَاتِ وَالكُفَّارَ نَارَ جَهَنَّمَ خَالِدِينَ فِيهَا هِيَ حَسْبُهُمْ وَلَعَنَهُمُ اللهُ وَلَهُمْ عَذَابٌ مُقِيمٌ﴾ .[٧٠٣٨]

"Indeed the hypocrites will be in the lowest reach of the Fire, and you will never find any helper for them."[7077]

﴿إِنَّ الْمُنَافِقِينَ فِي الدَّرْكِ الأَسْفَلِ مِنَ النَّارِ وَلَنْ تَجِدَ لَهُمْ نَصِيراً﴾ .[٧٠٣٩]

6220. **The Prophet (SAWA) said,** 'He [the hypocrite] will come on the Day of Judgment with two faces and with his tongue hanging out from the back of his head, and with another tongue hanging in front. They will both be ignited with fire until they ignite his body, then it will be said about him: This is the one who was two-faced and two-tongued in the world, and he will be known as such on the Day of Resurrection.'[7078]

٦٢٢٠ . رسولُ اللهِ ﷺ : يَجيءُ يَومَ القِيامَةِ ذو الوَجهَينِ دالِعاً لِسانَهُ في قَفاهُ، وآخَرُ مِن قُدّامِهِ، يَلتَهِبانِ ناراً حتّىٰ يُلهِبا جَسَدَهُ، ثُمّ يُقالُ لَهُ: هٰذا الّذي كانَ في الدُّنيا ذا وَجهَينِ وذا لِسانَينِ، يُعرَفُ بذلكَ يَومَ القِيامَةِ.[٧٠٤٠]

6221. **The Prophet (SAWA) said,** 'A two-faced person in this world will come on the Day of Resurrection with two faces of fire.'[7079]

٦٢٢١ . عنه ﷺ : ذو الوَجهَينِ في الدُّنيا يأتي يَومَ القِيامَةِ ولَهُ وَجهانِ مِن نارٍ.[٧٠٤١]

1755. What Eradicates Hypocrisy

١٧٥٥ ـ ما يَذهَبُ بِالنِّفاقِ

6222. **The Prophet (SAWA) said,** 'Invoking blessings on me and my household takes away hypocrisy.'[7080]

٦٢٢٢. رسولُ اللهِ ﷺ: الصَّلاةُ علَيَّ وعلى أهلِ بَيتي تَذهَبُ بالنِّفاقِ.٧٠٤٢

6223. **The Prophet (SAWA) said,** 'Raise your voices in invocation of blessings on me for it takes away hypocrisy.'[7081]

٦٢٢٣. عنه ﷺ: ارفَعوا أصواتَكُم بالصَّلاةِ علَيَّ؛ فإنّها تَذهَبُ بالنِّفاقِ.٧٠٤٣

382

SPENDING (in Charity)

الإنفاق

1756. The Virtue of Spending

١٧٥٦ ـ فَضلُ الإنفاقِ

"O you who have faith! Spend out of what We have provided you before there comes a day on which there will be no bargaining, neither friendship, nor intercession. And the faithless – they are the wrongdoers."[7082]

﴿يا أيُّها الَّذينَ آمَنُوا أنْفِقُوا مِمّا رَزَقْناكُمْ مِنْ قَبْلِ أنْ يَأتِيَ يَوْمٌ لا بَيْعٌ فِيهِ وَلا خُلَّةٌ وَلا شَفاعَةٌ وَالكافِرُونَ هُمُ الظّالِمُونَ﴾.٧٠٤٤

"Have faith in Allah and His Apostle, and spend out of that wherein He has made you successors. Those of you who have faith and spend [in Allah's way] there is a great reward for them."[7083]

﴿آمِنُوا بِاللهِ وَرَسُولِهِ وَأنْفِقُوا مِمّا جَعَلَكُمْ مُسْتَخْلَفِينَ فِيهِ فَالَّذينَ آمَنُوا مِنْكُمْ وَأنْفَقُوا لَهُمْ أجْرٌ كَبِيرٌ﴾.٧٠٤٥

"And whatever wealth you spend, it is for your own benefit."[7084]

﴿وَما تُنْفِقُوا مِنْ خَيْرٍ فَلِأنْفُسِكُمْ﴾.٧٠٤٦

(See also: Qur'an 2:261-265, 4:8)

(انظر) البقرة: ٢٦١ ـ ٢٦٥ والإنسان: ٨.

6224. **The Prophet (SAWA) said,** 'The ground on the Day of Judgment will be fire except for the shadow of the believer, for his charity will shade him.'[7085]

٦٢٢٤. رسولُ اللهِ ﷺ: أرضُ القِيامَةِ نارٌ ما خَلا ظِلَّ المُؤمنِ؛ فإنَّ صَدَقتَهُ تُظِلُّهُ.٧٠٤٧

6225. **The Prophet (SAWA) said,** 'Whoever gives a dirham in the path of Allah, Allah will write for him five hundred merits.'[7086]

٦٢٢٥. عنه ﷺ: مَن أعطى دِرهَماً في سَبيلِ اللهِ كَتَبَ اللهُ لَهُ سبعَمائةِ حَسَنَةٍ.٧٠٤٨

6226. **The Prophet (SAWA) said** to his companions, 'Which of you loves the money of his heirs more than his own money?' They said, 'O Messenger of Allah, we all love our own money more than the money of our heirs.' He said, 'One's own money is that which is put forward and the money of one's heir [i.e. that which we save and not spend in charity] is that which he leaves behind.'[7087]

٦٢٢٦. الترغيب والترهيب: ـ قال رسولُ اللهِ ﷺ لأصحابِهِ ـ: أيُّكم مالُ وارِثِهِ أحَبُّ إلَيهِ مِن مالِهِ؟ قالوا: يا رسولَ اللهِ، ما مِنّا أحدٌ إلّا مالُهُ أحَبُّ إلَيهِ مِن مالِ وارِثِهِ. قالَ: فإنَّ مالَهُ ما قَدَّمَ، ومالَ وارِثِهِ ما أخَّرَ.[٧٠٤٩]

6227. **Imām ʿAlī (AS) said,** 'Blessings be upon he who spends the excess of his money and guards the excess of his speech.'[7088]

٦٢٢٧. الإمامُ عليٌّ ؑ: طُوبى لِمَن أنفَقَ الفَضلَ مِن مالِهِ وأمسَكَ الفَضلَ مِن كلامِهِ.[٧٠٥٠]

6228. **Imām ʿAlī (AS) said,** 'You will be more overjoyed for what you have given away than the one who asked you for what you have given him.'[7089]

٦٢٢٨. عنه ؑ: إنّكُم أغبَطُ بِما بَذَلتُم مِنَ الرّاغِبِ إلَيكُم فيما وَصَلَهُ مِنكُم.[٧٠٥١]

6229. **Imām ʿAlī (AS),** in his will to his son al-Ḥasan (AS) said, 'You have in your world that with which you can reform your [eternal] abode, so spend rightfully and do not be a storage place for others ['s dues].'[7090]

٦٢٢٩. عنه ؑ ـ في وصيّتِهِ لابنِهِ الحسنِ ؑ ـ: إنّما لكَ مِن دُنياكَ ما أصلَحتَ بِهِ مَثواكَ، فأنفِقْ في حَقٍّ ولا تَكُن خازِناً لِغَيرِكَ.[٧٠٥٢]

6230. **Imām ʿAlī (AS) said,** 'Indeed you are more in need of spending in charity what you have earned than gaining what you accumulate.'[7091]

٦٢٣٠. عنه ؑ: إنّكُم إلى إنفاقِ ما اكتَسَبتُم أحوَجُ مِنكُم إلى اكتِسابِ ما تَجمَعونَ.[٧٠٥٣]

6231. **Imām al-Ṣādiq (AS) said,** 'Cursed! Cursed is he whom Allah has endowed with wealth and he does not donate any of it.'[7092]

٦٢٣١. الإمامُ الصّادقُ ؑ: مَلعونٌ مَلعونٌ مَن وَهَبَ اللهُ لَه مالاً فلَم يَتَصَدَّقْ مِنهُ بشَيءٍ.[٧٠٥٤]

1757. The Blessing of Spending in His Way

١٧٥٧ ـ بَرَكَةُ الإنفاقِ

"Say, 'Indeed my Lord expands the provision for whomever of His servants that He wishes and He tightens it, and He will repay whatever you may spend, and He is the best of providers."[7093]

﴿قُلْ إِنَّ رَبِّي يَبْسُطُ الرِّزْقَ لِمَنْ يَشَاءُ مِنْ عِبَادِهِ وَيَقْدِرُ لَهُ وَمَا أَنْفَقْتُمْ مِنْ شَيْءٍ فَهُوَ يُخْلِفُهُ وَهُوَ خَيْرُ الرَّازِقِينَ﴾.[٧٠٥٥]

6232. *Makārim al-Akhlāq*, narrating from one of the companions of Imām al-Ṣādiq (AS) who said: 'I told Imām al-Ṣādiq (AS), 'based on Allah's saying:

٦٢٣٢. مكارم الأخلاق عن رجلٍ من أصحابِ الإمامِ الصّادقِ ؑ: قلتُ لأبي عبدِ اللهِ ؑ: ... قولُهُ

"whatever you may spend…", I donate but do not see any repayment.' He (AS) asked: 'Have you ever seen Allah not fulfil His promise?' I said, 'No.' He asked, 'Then why do you say this?' I said, 'I do not know.' He said, 'If any of you acquires legitimate wealth and spends it rightfully, then he will not spend a single dirham without Allah repaying it.'[7094]

تــعالىٰ: ﴿وما أنفَقْتُم من شيء فهو يخلفه...﴾ فَأراني أُنفِقُ ولا أرىٰ خَـلَفاً! قـالَ: أفَـتَرَى اللهَ أخلَفَ وَعدَهُ؟! قلتُ: لا، قالَ: فمِمَّ؟ قُـلتُ: لا أدري، قالَ: لَو أنّ أحَدَكُمُ اكتَسَبَ المالَ مِن حِلِّهِ وأنفَقَهُ في حَقِّهِ لَم يُـنفِقْ دِرهَـماً إلّا أخـلَفَ اللهُ علَيهِ.[٧٠٥٦]

6233. **The Prophet (SAWA) said,** 'Absolutely no wealth will ever decrease as a result of charity, so give and do not be afraid.'[7095]

٦٢٣٣. رسولُ اللهِ ﷺ: ما نَقَصَ مالٌ مِن صَدَقَةٍ قَطُّ، فأعطُوا ولا تَجبُنوا.[٧٠٥٧]

6234. **'Ā'isha said,** 'They slaughtered a sheep [to distribute its meat]'. The Prophet (SAWA) asked, 'Is there any of it remaining?' She said, 'Nothing remains other than its shoulder.' He (SAWA) said, 'All of it remains [forever] other than its shoulder.'[7096]

٦٢٣٤. عائشة: أنّهُم ذَبَحوا شاةً، فقالَ النَّبيُّ ﷺ: ما بَقِيَ؟ فقالَت: ما بَقِيَ مِنها إلّا كَتِفُها، قالَ [ﷺ]: بَقِيَ كلُّها غيرَ كَتِفِها.[٧٠٥٨]

6235. **Imām 'Alī (AS) said,** 'He who is certain of the repayment is generous with giving.'[7097]

٦٢٣٥. الإمامُ عليٌّ ؑ: مَن أيقَنَ بالخَلَفِ جادَ بالعَطيَّةِ.[٧٠٥٩]

6236. **Imām al-Ṣādiq (AS) said,** 'Spend and be certain of being repaid.'[7098]

٦٢٣٦. الإمامُ الصّادقُ ؑ: أنفِقْ وأيقِنْ بالخَلَفِ.[٧٠٦٠]

6237. **Imām al-Ṣādiq (AS) said,** 'Charity fulfils the repayment of debts and brings about blessings.'[7099]

٦٢٣٧. عنه ؑ: إنّ الصَّدَقَةَ تَقضي الدَّينَ وتَخلُفُ بالبَرَكَةِ.[٧٠٦١]

(See also: ALMS-TAX: section 852)

(اُنظر) الزكاة: باب ٨٥٢.

1758. Spending Out of What You Love

١٧٥٨ ـ الإنفاقُ بِما تُحبُّ

"You will never attain piety until you spend out of what you hold dear, and whatever you may spend of anything, Allah indeed knows it."[7100]

﴿لَنْ تَنَالُوا الْبِرَّ حَتَّىٰ تُنْفِقُوا مِمَّا تُحِبُّونَ وَمَا تُنْفِقُوا مِنْ شَيْءٍ فَإِنَّ اللهَ بِهِ عَلِيمٌ﴾.[٧٠٦٢]

6238. **Abū al-Ṭufayl said,** "Alī (AS) bought a piece of clothing and liked it, so he gave it away in charity.'[7101]

٦٢٣٨. أبو الطُّفَيلِ: اشتَرىٰ عليٌّ ؑ ثَوباً فأعجَبَهُ فتَصَدَّقَ بهِ.[٧٠٦٣]

6239. **Imām al-Ṣādiq (AS),** when someone saw him donating sugar, and asked him 'Do you give sugar as charity?', replied, 'Yes, there is nothing I love more than it, and I love to donate the thing that I love the most.'[7102]

٦٢٣٩. الإمامُ الصّادقُ ؑ ـ وقد قيل له، وكانَ يَتَصَدَّقُ بالسُّكَّرِ ـ: أتَتَصَدَّقُ بالسُّكَّرِ؟!: نَعَم، إنَّهُ لَيسَ شَيءٌ أحَبَّ إلَيَّ مِنهُ، فأنا اُحِبُّ أن أتَصَدَّقَ بأحَبِّ الأشياءِ إلَيَّ.[٧٠٦٤]

1759. He who does not Spend in Obedience of Allah Spends in His Disobedience

١٧٥٩ ـ مَن لَم يُنفِق في طاعَةِ اللهِ يُنفِق في مَعصِيَتِهِ

6240. **The Prophet (SAWA) said,** 'Whoever withholds his wealth from the righteous discriminatingly, Allah will forcefully distribute his wealth to the evil.'[7103]

٦٢٤٠. رسولُ اللهِ ﷺ: مَن مَنَعَ مالَهُ مِنَ الأخيارِ اختِياراً صَرَفَ اللهُ مالَهُ إلَى الأشرارِ اضطِراراً.[٧٠٦٥]

6241. **Imām al-Ṣādiq (AS) said,** 'No sooner does a servant withhold the spending of a dirham in its rightful place than he will end up spending two dirhams outside of its rightful place.'[7104]

٦٢٤١. الإمامُ الصّادقُ ؑ: ما مِن عَبدٍ يَمنَعُ دِرهَماً في حَقِّهِ إلّا أنفَقَ اثنَينِ في غَيرِ حَقِّهِ.[٧٠٦٦]

6242. **Imām al-Kāẓim (AS) said,** 'Beware of withholding [charity] in the obedience of Allah, for you will spend twice its amount in disobeying Him.'[7105]

٦٢٤٢. الإمامُ الكاظمُ ؑ: إيّاكَ أن تَمنَعَ في طاعَةِ اللهِ، فتُنفِقَ مِثلَيهِ في مَعصيَةِ اللهِ.[٧٠٦٧]

1760. The Virtue of the Charity Given by One who is Himself Straitened

١٧٦٠ ـ فَضلُ إنفاقِ المُقتِرِ

6243. **The Prophet (SAWA) said,** 'There are three things that constitute the realities of faith: the charity given by a person who is himself straitened, your fairness towards people in spite of yourself, and spreading knowledge to those who seek it.'[7106]

٦٢٤٣. رسولُ اللهِ ﷺ: ثَلاثَةٌ مِن حَقائقِ الإيمانِ: الإنفاقُ مِنَ الإقتارِ، وإنصافُكَ النّاسَ مِن نَفسِكَ، وبَذلُ العِلمِ لِلمُتَعلِّمِ.[٧٠٦٨]

6244. **Imām Zayn al-ʿĀbidīn (AS) said,** 'Among the moral virtues of a believer is spending [in charity] according to his financial condition.'[7107]

٦٢٤٤. الإمامُ زينُ العابدينَ ؑ: إنَّ مِن أخلاقِ المُؤمنِ الإنفاقَ علىٰ قَدرِ الإقتارِ.[٧٠٦٩]

1761. Those Whose Spending [in Charity] is Not Accepted

١٧٦١ ـ مَن لا تُقبَلُ نَفَقتُهُ

"Say, 'Spend willingly or unwillingly, it shall never be accepted from you; for you are indeed a transgressing lot.' Nothing stops their charities from being accepted except that they have no faith in Allah and His Apostle and do not perform the prayer but lazily, and do not spend but reluctantly."[7108]

﴿قُلْ أَنْفِقُوا طَوْعاً أَوْ كَرْهاً لَنْ يُتَقَبَّلَ مِنْكُمْ إِنَّكُمْ كُنْتُمْ قَوْماً فَاسِقِينَ * وَمَا مَنَعَهُمْ أَنْ تُقْبَلَ مِنْهُمْ نَفَقَاتُهُمْ إِلَّا أَنَّهُمْ كَفَرُوا بِاللهِ وَبِرَسُولِهِ وَلَا يَأْتُونَ الصَّلَاةَ إِلَّا وَهُمْ كُسَالَىٰ وَلَا يُنْفِقُونَ إِلَّا وَهُمْ كَارِهُونَ﴾ .٧٠٧٠

6245. **Imām al-Bāqir (AS),** when he was asked about Allah's verse in the Qur'an: *"and do not be of the mind to give the bad part of it"*[7109], said, 'When people became Muslims, they had earnings from usury and from unlawful dealings, and a man would mix it in with his money and donate from it. So, Allah prohibited them from doing so, and charity is only correct [when given] out of pure earnings.'[7110]

٦٢٤٥ . الإمامُ الباقرُ عليه السلام ـ لَمّا سُئلَ عن قولِهِ تعالىٰ: ﴿ولا تَيَمَّمُوا الخَبيثَ مِنْهُ تُنْفِقونَ﴾ ٧٠٧١ ـ: كانَ النّاسُ حينَ أسلَموا عِندَهُم مَكاسِبُ مِنَ الرِّبا ومِن أموالٍ خَبيثَةٍ، فكانَ الرّجُلُ يَتعَمَّدُها مِن بَينِ مالِهِ فتَصَدّقَ بها، فنهاهُمُ اللهُ عَن ذٰلكَ، وإنّ الصَّدَقَةَ لا تَصلُحُ إلّا مِن كَسبٍ طَيِّبٍ. ٧٠٧٢

6246. **Imām al-Ṣādiq (AS) said,** 'If people were to earn whence Allah has ordered them to and spend it in that which He has forbidden, then He will not accept it from them. And if they earn what Allah has prohibited them from and spend it in that which He has ordered them to, He will not accept it from them either unless they take it from its rightful place and spend it in its rightful place.'[7111]

٦٢٤٦ . الإمامُ الصّادقُ عليه السلام: لَو أنَّ النّاسَ أخَذوا ما أمَرَهُمُ اللهُ بهِ فأنفَقوهُ فيما نَهاهُم عَنهُ ما قَبِلَهُ مِنهُم، ولو أخَذوا ما نَهاهُمُ اللهُ عَنهُ فأنفَقوهُ فيما أمَرَهُمُ اللهُ بهِ ما قَبِلَهُ مِنهُم؛ حتّىٰ يأخُذوهُ مِن حَقٍّ ويُنفِقوهُ في حَقٍّ. ٧٠٧٣

383

TALEBEARING

النَّمِيمَةُ

1762. Caution Against Talebearing

١٧٦٢ ـ التَّحذيرُ مِنَ النَّميمَةِ

"And do not obey any vile swearer, scandal-monger, and talebearer."[7112]

﴿وَلَا تُطِعْ كُلَّ حَلَّافٍ مَهِينٍ * هَمَّازٍ مَشَّاءٍ بِنَمِيمٍ﴾ .٧٠٧٤

6247. **The Prophet (SAWA) said,** 'Beware of talebearing.'[7113]

٦٢٤٧. رسولُ اللهِ ﷺ : إيّاكُم والنَّميمةَ.٧٠٧٥

6248. **Imām ʿAlī (AS)) said,** 'The Messenger of Allah (SAWA) said to his companions: 'Shall I inform you of the most evil from among you?' They said, 'Yes, O Messenger of Allah.' He continued, 'The talebearers, those who break up loved ones, and those who seek faults in the righteous.'[7114]

٦٢٤٨. الإمامُ عليٌّ ﷺ : قالَ رسولُ اللهِ ﷺ ... لأصحابِهِ: ألا أُخبِرُكُم بشِرارِكُم؟ قالوا: بلىٰ يا رسولَ اللهِ. قالَ: المَشّاؤونَ بالنَّميمَةِ، المُفَرِّقونَ بَينَ الأحِبَّةِ، الباغُونَ لِلبُرَآءِ العَيبَ.٧٠٧٦

6249. **Imām ʿAlī (AS) said,** 'Beware of talebearing, for it plants enmity and distances one from Allah and people.'[7115]

٦٢٤٩. عنه ﷺ : إيّاكَ والنَّميمَةَ؛ فإنّها تَزرَعُ الضَّغينَةَ وتُبَعِّدُ عنِ اللهِ والنّاسِ.٧٠٧٧

6250. **Imām ʿAlī (AS) said,** 'The worst of truthfulness is talebearing.'[7116]

٦٢٥٠. عنه ﷺ : أسوأُ الصِّدقِ النَّميمَةُ.٧٠٧٨

6251. **Imām al-Ṣādiq (AS) said,** 'The greatest of sorcery is slandering, for through it loved ones are broken up, animosity is brought in between sincere friends, blood is shed, houses are demolished, veils are uncovered, and the talebearer is the most evil thing that has laid a step on this earth.'[7117]

٦٢٥١. الإمامُ الصّادقُ ﷺ : إنّ مِن أكبَرِ السِّحرِ النَّميمَةَ؛ يُفَرَّقُ بها بَينَ المُتحابِّينَ، ويُجلَبُ العَداوَةُ علَى المُتَصافِيَينِ، ويُسفَكُ بها الدِّماءُ، ويُهدَمُ بها الدُّورُ، ويُكشَفُ بها السُّتورُ، والنَّمّامُ أشَرُّ مَن وَطِئَ علَى الأرضِ بقَدَمٍ.٧٠٧٩

1763. Reproaching Talebearing

١٧٦٣ـ ذَمُّ السِّعايَةِ

6252. **The Prophet (SAWA) said,** 'He who informs against his brother to a ruler, Allah will destroy all of his deeds, and if the person he informed on is harmed or hurt, Allah Almighty will put the informant with Hāmān [Pharaoh's vizier] on the same level in the Hellfire.'[7118]

٦٢٥٢. رسولُ اللهِ ﷺ: مَن سَعىٰ بأخيهِ إلىٰ سُلطانٍ أحبَطَ اللهُ تعالىٰ عَمَلَهُ كُلَّهُ، وإن وَصَلَ إلَيهِ مَكروهٌ أو أذىً جَعَلَهُ اللهُ تعالىٰ مَعَ هامانَ في دَرَجَةٍ في النّارِ.٧٠٨٠

6253. **Imām al-Ṣādiq (AS) said,** 'An informant is a killer of three: killer of himself, killer of the person who he informed of, and killer of the person he is informing to.'[7119]

٦٢٥٣. الإمامُ الصّادقُ ﷺ: السّاعي قاتِلُ ثَلاثَةٍ: قاتِلُ نَفسِهِ، وقاتِلُ مَن يَسعىٰ بِهِ، وقاتِلُ مَن يَسعىٰ إلَيهِ.٧٠٨١

384

SUPEREROGATORY PRAYERS

النّافِلَة

1764. The Virtue of Supererogatory Prayers

١٧٦٤ ـ فَضلُ النّافِلَةِ

"And keep vigil for a part of the night, as a supererogatory [devotion] for you. It may be that your Lord will raise you to a praiseworthy station."[7120]

﴿وَمِنَ اللَّيْلِ فَتَهَجَّدْ بِهِ نَافِلَةً لَكَ عَسَىٰ أَنْ يَبْعَثَكَ رَبُّكَ مَقَاماً مَحْمُوداً﴾ .٧٠٨٢

6254. **The Prophet (SAWA) said,** 'Hearts have [the capacity to] incline [to worship] and to retract, so when they incline then perform the supererogatory, and when they retract then observe the obligatory.'[7121]

٦٢٥٤ . رسولُ اللهِ ﷺ: إنّ لِلقُلوبِ إقبالاً وإدباراً، فإذا أقبَلَت فتَنَفَّلوا، وإذا أدبَرَت فعلَيكُم بالفَريضَةِ.٧٠٨٣

6255. **Al-Fuḍayl said,** 'I asked Abū Ja'far [al-Bāqir] (AS) about Allah's verse in the Qur'an: *"and those who are watchful of their prayers."*[7122] He said, 'These are the obligatory prayers.' I asked, *"those who are persevering in their prayers."*[7123]? He said, 'They are the supererogatory prayers.'[7124]

٦٢٥٥ . الفُضَيل: سألتُ أبا جعفرٍ عليه السلام عن قَولِ اللهِ عَزَّوجلَّ: ﴿الّذينَ هُمْ علىٰ صَلَواتِهِمْ يُحافِظونَ﴾ ٧٠٨٤ قالَ: هِيَ الفَريضَةُ. قلتُ: ﴿الّذينَ هُمْ علىٰ صَلاتِهِمْ دائِمونَ﴾ ٧٠٨٥ قالَ: هِيَ النّافِلَةُ.٧٠٨٦

1765. Precedence of the Obligatory Prayers over the Supererogatory

١٧٦٥ ـ تَقديمُ الفَرائِضِ عَلَى النَّوافِلِ

6256. **Imām 'Alī (AS) said,** 'There is no leniency with respect to the obligatory, and there is no hardship [imposed] with respect to the supererogatory.'[7125]

٦٢٥٦ . الإمامُ عليٌّ عليه السلام: لا رُخصَةَ في فَرضٍ، ولا شِدَّةَ في نافِلَةٍ.٧٠٨٧

6257. **Imām 'Alī (AS) said,** 'When the supererogatory prayers harm the obligatory ones then leave them.'[7126]

٦٢٥٧ . عنه عليه السلام: إذا أضَرَّتِ النَّوافِلُ بالفَرائضِ فارْفُضوها.٧٠٨٨

6258. **Imām ʿAlī (AS) said,** 'There is no proximity [to Allah] achieved with the supererogatory if they affect the obligatory [prayers] adversely.'[7127]

٦٢٥٨. عنه ﷺ: لا قُربَةَ بالنَّوافِلِ إذا أضَـرَّت بالفَرائضِ.[٧٠٨٩]

385

THE LIGHT

النُّورُ

1766. The Light of Insight

١٧٦٦ـ نُورُ البَصيرَةِ

"Is he who was lifeless, then We gave him life and provided him with a light by which he walks among the people, like one who dwells in a manifold darkness which he cannot leave? To the faithless is thus presented as decorous what they have been doing."[7128]

﴿أَوَمَنْ كَانَ مَيْتاً فَأَحْيَيْنَاهُ وَجَعَلْنَا لَهُ نُوراً يَمْشِي بِهِ فِي النَّاسِ كَمَنْ مَثَلُهُ فِي الظُّلُمَاتِ لَيْسَ بِخَارِجٍ مِنْهَا كَذٰلِكَ زُيِّنَ لِلْكَافِرِينَ مَا كَانُوا يَعْمَلُونَ﴾.[٧٠٩٠]

"O you who have faith! Be wary of Allah and have faith in His Apostle. He will grant you a double share of His mercy and give you a light to walk by, and forgive you, and Allah is all-forgiving, all-merciful."[7129]

﴿يَا أَيُّهَا الَّذِينَ آمَنُوا اتَّقُوا اللهَ وَآمِنُوا بِرَسُولِهِ يُؤْتِكُمْ كِفْلَيْنِ مِنْ رَحْمَتِهِ وَيَجْعَلْ لَكُمْ نُوراً تَمْشُونَ بِهِ وَيَغْفِرْ لَكُمْ وَاللهُ غَفُورٌ رَحِيمٌ﴾.[٧٠٩١]

6259. **Imām Zayn al-ʿĀbidīn (AS),** in a supplication said, 'And grant me a light with which I can walk among people, and through which I can be guided in a manifold darkness, and with which I can enlighten myself from doubts and uncertainties.'[7130]

٦٢٥٩. الإمامُ زينُ العابدينَ ﷺ ـ في الدّعاء ـ: وَهَبْ لي نُوراً أمشي بهِ في النّاسِ، وأهتَدي بهِ في الظُّلُماتِ، وأستَضيءُ بهِ مِن الشَّكِّ والشُّبُهاتِ.[٧٠٩٢]

6260. **Imām al-Ṣādiq (AS) said,** 'Knowledge is not [achieved] through learning; rather it is a light that falls into the heart of one whom Allah Almighty wishes to guide.'[7131]

٦٢٦٠. الإمامُ الصّادقُ ﷺ: لَيسَ العِلمُ بالتَّعلُّمِ، إنّما هُو نُورٌ يَقَعُ في قَلبِ مَن يُريدُ اللهُ تباركَ وتعالىٰ أن يَهدِيَهُ.[٧٠٩٣]

1767. The Light of the Heart and the Light of the Face

١٧٦٧ـ نورُ القَلبِ ونورُ الوَجهِ

6261. **Imām ʿAlī (AS) said,** 'Increase your silence and your thoughts will flourish, your heart will enlighten, and people will be safe from your hands.'[7132]

٦٢٦١. الإمامُ عليٌّ ﷺ: أكثِرْ صَمتَكَ يَتَوفَّرْ فِكرُكَ، ويَستَنِرْ قَلبُكَ، ويَسلَمِ النّاسُ مِن يَدَيكَ.[٧٠٩٤]

6262. **Imām Zayn al-ʿĀbidīn (AS),** when asked about the reason why those who perform the night prayer have the most beautiful faces among people, replied, 'Because they seclude themselves with Allah and so Allah covers them in His light.'[7133]

٦٢٦٢. الامام زين العابدين ﷺ ـلما سُئلَ عن عِلَّةِ كَونِ المُتَهَجِّدينَ باللَّيلِ مِن أحسَنِ النّاسِ وَجهاً ـ: لأنَّهُم خَلَوا باللهِ فكَساهُمُ اللهُ مِن نُورِهِ.[٧٠٩٥]

6263. **Imām al-Ṣādiq (AS) said,** 'I sought for light of the heart and found it in contemplation and crying. I sought for crossing the Bridge [on the Day of Resurrection] and found it in giving charity. I sought for light of the face and found it in the night prayer.'[7134]

٦٢٦٣. الإمامُ الصّادقُ ﷺ : طَلَبتُ نُورَ القَلبِ فوَجَدتُهُ في التَّفَكُّرِ والبُكاءِ، وطَلَبتُ الجَوازَ علَى الصِّراطِ فوَجَدتُهُ في الصَّدَقَةِ، وطَلَبتُ نُورَ الوَجهِ فوَجَدتُهُ في صَلاةِ اللَّيلِ.[٧٠٩٦]

1768. There is a Light for Everything Good

١٧٦٨ ـ عَلىٰ كُلِّ صَوابٍ نُورٌ

6264. **The Prophet (SAWA) said,** 'Prayer is light.'[7135]

٦٢٦٤. رسولُ اللهِ ﷺ : الصَّلاةُ نُورٌ.[٧٠٩٧]

6265. **The Prophet (SAWA) said,** 'Whoever strikes an arrow in the path of Allah will have a light on the Day of Judgment.'[7136]

٦٢٦٥. عنه ﷺ : مَن رَمىٰ بسَهمٍ في سَبيلِ اللهِ كانَ لَهُ نُوراً يَومَ القِيامَةِ.[٧٠٩٨]

6266. **The Prophet (SAWA) said,** 'Do recite the Qur'an, for it is a light for you on the earth and a provision for you in Heaven.'[7137]

٦٢٦٦. عنه ﷺ : علَيكَ بتِلاوَةِ القرآنِ ؛ فإنّهُ نُورٌ لَكَ في الأرضِ، وذُخرٌ لكَ في السّماءِ.[٧٠٩٩]

6267. **The Prophet (SAWA) said,** 'Whoever testifies with a true testimony wanting to uphold the rights of a Muslim person, he will come on the Day of Resurrection and his face will reflect a light as far as the eye can see, and all of creation will know him by name and lineage.'[7138]

٦٢٦٧. عنه ﷺ : مَن شَهِدَ شَهادَةَ حَقٍّ لِيُحيِيَ بِها حَقَّ امرئٍ مُسلِمٍ أتىٰ يَومَ القِيامَةِ ولِوَجهِهِ نُورٌ مَدَّ البَصَرِ، يَعرِفُهُ الخَلايِقُ باسمِهِ ونَسَبِهِ.[٧١٠٠]

6268. **Imām ʿAlī (AS) said,** 'To every truth there is a reality, and for every good thing there is a light.'[7139]

٦٢٦٨. الإمامُ عليٌّ ﷺ : إنّ علىٰ كُلِّ حَقٍّ حَقيقَةً، وعلىٰ كُلِّ صَوابٍ نُوراً.[٧١٠١]

1769. The Light on the Day of Resurrection

١٧٦٩ ـ نورُ المُؤمِنينَ فِي القِيامَةِ

"The day you will see the faithful, men and women, with their light moving swiftly before them and on

﴿يَوْمَ تَرَى الْمُؤْمِنِينَ وَالْمُؤْمِنَاتِ يَسْعَىٰ نُورُهُمْ

their right, [and greeted with the words:] 'There is good news for you today! Gardens with streams running in them, to remain in them [forever]. That is the great success.'[7140]

بَيْنَ أَيْدِيهِمْ وَبِأَيْمَانِهِمْ بُشْرَاكُمُ الْيَوْمَ جَنَّاتٌ تَجْرِي مِنْ تَحْتِهَا الْأَنْهَارُ خَالِدِينَ فِيهَا ذَٰلِكَ هُوَ الْفَوْزُ الْعَظِيمُ﴾.٧١٠٢

6269. **The Prophet (SAWA),** to a man who said, 'I would love to be resurrected on the Day of Resurrection in the light', said, 'Do not oppress anyone and you will be resurrected on the Day of Judgment in [with] light.'[7141]

٦٢٦٩. رسولُ اللهِ ﷺ ـ لِرجُلٍ قالَ: أُحِبُّ أن أُحشَرَ يَومَ القِيامَةِ في النُّورِ ـ: لا تَظلِمْ أحَداً تُحشَرْ يَومَ القِيامَةِ في النُّورِ.٧١٠٣

386

PEOPLE

النّاس

1770. People

١٧٧٠ ـ النّاس

6270. **Imām ʿAlī (AS) said,** 'People are like trees, their drink is one but their fruits are different.'[7142]

٦٢٧٠. الإمامُ عليٌّ ؑ: النّاسُ كالشَّجَرِ؛ شَرابُهُ واحِدٌ وثَمَرُهُ مُختَلِفٌ.٧١٠٤

6271. **Imām al-Ṣādiq (AS) said,** 'There are three things that all people need: security, justice, and comfort.'[7143]

٦٢٧١. الإمامُ الصّادقُ ؑ: ثَلاثَةُ أشياءَ يَحتاجُ النّاسُ طُرّاً إلَيها: الأمنُ، والعَدلُ، والخِصبُ.٧١٠٥

6272. **Imām al-Ṣādiq (AS) said,** 'You should heed those similar to you and those of the middle class, for it is there that you will find the sources of jewels.'[7144]

٦٢٧٢. عنه ؑ: علَيكُم بالأشكالِ مِن النّاسِ والأوساطِ مِن النّاسِ، فعِندَهُم تَجِدونَ مَعادِنَ الجَوهَرِ.٧١٠٦

1771. The Equality of People in Rights

١٧٧١ ـ تَساوِي النّاسِ فِي الحُقوقِ

6273. **The Prophet (SAWA) said,** 'People are as equal as the teeth of a comb.'[7145]

٦٢٧٣. رسولُ اللهِ ﷺ: النّاسُ سَواءٌ كأسنانِ المُشطِ.٧١٠٧

6274. **Imām ʿAlī (AS) said,** 'People are equal to one another in rights.'[7146]

٦٢٧٤. الإمامُ عليٌّ ؑ: النّاسُ في الحَقِّ سَواءٌ.٧١٠٨

6275. **Imām ʿAlī (AS) said,** 'People up to Adam are all equal.'[7147]

٦٢٧٥. عنه ؑ: النّاسُ إلى آدَمَ شَرعٌ سَواءٌ.٧١٠٩

6276. *Sharh Nahj al-Balāgha*: 'Two women came to Imām ʿAlī, one of them was an Arab and the other was a non-Arab. They asked him for assistance. He equally gave money and food to them. One of them protested, saying, 'I am an Arab woman, and she is a non-Arab.' He said, 'By Allah, I do not see in this shade that the children of Ishmael have any merit over the children of Isaac.'[7148]

٦٢٧٦ . شرح نهج البلاغة عن أبي إسحاق الهمْداني : أنّ امرأتَينِ أتَتا عَليّاً (ع) ، إحداهُما مِن العَرَبِ والاُخرىٰ مِن المَوالي فسألَتاه، فَدَفَعَ إلَيهِما دَراهِمَ وطَعاماً بالسَّواء. فقالَت إحداهُما : إنّي امرأةٌ مِن العَرَبِ وهٰذهِ مِن العَجَم! فقالَ : إنّي واللهِ لا أجِدُ لِبَني إسماعيلَ في هذا الفَيءِ فَضلاً علىٰ بَني إسحاقَ .[٧١١٠]

(See also: GODWARINESS: section 1866)

(أنظر) التقوى : باب ١٨٦٦.

1772. Those who are Not Considered as People [Human]

١٧٧٢ ـ مَن لَيس مِنَ النّاسِ

6277. **Imām al-Ṣādiq (AS),** to a man who asked, 'Do you consider all these creatures as people?' said, 'Exclude from among them those who do not brush their teeth, sitting cross-legged in a narrow place, one who interferes in matters that do not concern him, debates about that which he has no knowledge, one who acts sick without an illness, one who falls apart without a calamity, one who opposes his friends in matters of truth that they have agreed upon, a proud person who is proud of his forefathers but he is devoid of their good deeds, so he is like a heath peeling off its bark bit by bit until it reaches its core, and he is like Allah's verse: *"They are like cattle; rather they are more astray"*.[7149 7150]

٦٢٧٧ . الإمامُ الصّادقُ (ع) ـ لِرجُلٍ قالَ لَهُ : أتَرىٰ هذا الخَلقَ كُلَّهُ مِن النّاسِ ؟ : ألقِ مِنهُمُ التّارِكَ للسِّواكِ ، والمُتَربِّعَ في مَوضِعِ الضِّيقِ ، والدّاخِلَ فيما لا يَعنيهِ ، والمُماريَ فيما لا عِلمَ لَهُ ، والمُتَمَرِّضَ مِن غَيرِ عِلَّةٍ ، والمُتَشَعِّثَ مِن غَيرِ مُصيبَةٍ ، والمُخالِفَ علىٰ أصحابِهِ في الحَقِّ وقَدِ اتَّفَقوا علَيهِ ، والمُفتَخِرَ يَفتَخِرُ بآبائهِ وهُو خِلْوٌ مِن صالِحِ أعمالِهِم ، فهُو بمَنزِلَةِ الخَلَنجِ[٧١١١] يُقشَرُ لِحاءً عَن لِحاءٍ حتّىٰ يُوصَلَ إلىٰ جَوهَرِيَّتِهِ ، وهُو كما قالَ اللهُ عزَّ وجلَّ : ﴿إنْ هُمْ إلّا كالأنعامِ بَلْ هُمْ أضَلُّ سَبيلاً﴾[٧١١٢ ٧١١٣].

1773. The Explanation of the Word 'Opportunist'

١٧٧٣ ـ تَفسيرُ كَلِمَةِ «إمَّعَةٍ»

6278. **Imām al-Kāẓim (AS),** to Faḍl b. Yūnus said, 'Do good and speak only good, and do not be an opportunist.' I asked, 'What does it mean to be an opportunist?' He said, 'Do not say: "I am with the people and I am one of the people." The Prophet (SAWA) said, 'O people, there are two paths: the path of good and the path of evil, so the path of evil should not be more loved by you than the path of good.'[7151]

٦٢٧٨ . الإمامُ الكاظمُ (ع) لِفَضلِ ابنِ يُونُسَ : أبلِغْ خَيراً ، وقُلْ خَيراً ولا تَكُن إمَّعَةً . قلتُ : وما الإمَّعَةُ ؟ قالَ : لا تَقُلْ : أنا مَعَ النّاسِ ، وأنا كَواحِدٍ مِن النّاسِ . إنّ رسولَ اللهِ ﷺ قالَ : يا أيُّها النّاسُ ، إنّما هُما نَجدانِ : نَجدُ[٧١١٤] خَيرٍ ونَجدُ شَرٍّ ، فلا يَكُن نَجدُ الشَّرِّ أحَبَّ إلَيكُم مِن نَجدِ الخَيرِ .[٧١١٥]

(See also: EMULATION (*Taqlīd*): section 1561)

(أنظر) تقليد : باب ١٥٦١.

387

SLEEP

النَّوْمُ

1774. Sleep

١٧٧٤ ـ النَّـومُ

"And [did we not] make your sleep for rest?"[7152]

﴿وَجَعَلْنَا نَوْمَكُمْ سُبَاتاً﴾[٧١١٦] .[٧١١٧]

"Allah takes the souls at the time of their death, and those that have not died in their sleep. Then he retains those for whom He has ordained death and releases the others until a specified time. There are indeed signs in that for a people who reflect."[7153]

﴿اللهُ يَتَوَفَّى الْأَنْفُسَ حِينَ مَوْتِهَا وَالَّتِي لَمْ تَمُتْ فِي مَنَامِهَا فَيُمْسِكُ الَّتِي قَضَىٰ عَلَيْهَا الْمَوْتَ وَيُرْسِلُ الْأُخْرَىٰ إِلَىٰ أَجَلٍ مُسَمًّى إِنَّ فِي ذَٰلِكَ لَآيَاتٍ لِقَوْمٍ يَتَفَكَّرُونَ﴾ .[٧١١٨]

6279. **The Prophet (SAWA) said,** 'Sleep is the brother of death, and the people of Heaven do not die.'[7154]

٦٢٧٩ . رسولُ اللهِ ﷺ : النَّومُ أخُو المَوتِ، ولا يَموتُ أهلُ الجَنَّةِ .[٧١١٩]

6280. **Imām al-Riḍā (AS) said,** 'Sleep is the sultan of the brain, and it is the foundation of the body and its [source of] strength.'[7155]

٦٢٨٠ . الإمامُ الرِّضا عليه السلام : إنَّ النَّومَ سُلطانُ الدِّماغِ، وهُو قِوامُ الجَسَدِ وقُوَّتُهُ .[٧١٢٠]

6281. **Imām al-Hādī (AS) said,** 'Staying awake makes sleeping more sweet.'[7156]

٦٢٨١ . الإمامُ الهادي عليه السلام : السَّهَرُ ألَذُّ لِلمَنامِ .[٧١٢١]

1775. Caution Against Excessive Sleep

١٧٧٥ ـ التَّحذيرُ مِن كَثرَةِ النَّومِ

6282. **Imām al-Bāqir (AS) said,** 'Moses (AS) asked [Allah], 'Who from among Your servants is most hated by You?' He Almighty said, '[One who is] a carcass at night and idle [jobless] during the day.'[7157]

٦٢٨٢ . الإمامُ الباقرُ عليه السلام : قالَ موسىٰ عليه السلام : أيُّ عِبادِكَ أبغَضُ إلَيكَ ؟ قالَ : جِيفَةٌ بِاللَّيلِ، بَطّالٌ بِالنَّهارِ .[٧١٢٢]

6283. **The Prophet (SAWA) said,** 'Beware of too much sleep, for excessive sleep will render one poor on the Day of Judgment.'[7158]

٦٢٨٣ . رسولُ اللهِ ﷺ : إيّاكُم وكَثرَةَ النَّومِ ؛ فإنَّ كَثرَةَ النَّومِ يَدَعُ صاحِبَهُ فَقيراً يَومَ القِيامَةِ .[٧١٢٣]

6284. **Imām ʿAlī (AS) said,** 'He who fears a nightly raid will sleep little.'[7159]

٦٢٨٤ . الإمامُ عليٌّ ﷺ : مَن خافَ البَياتَ قَلَّ نَومُهُ.[٧١٢٤]

6285. **Imām ʿAlī (AS) said,** 'How very much does sleep [at night] unravel the firm determinations made during the day!'[7160]

٦٢٨٥ . عنه ﷺ : ما أنقَضَ النَّومَ لعَزائمِ اليَومِ![٧١٢٥]

6286. **Imām al-Ṣādiq (AS) said,** 'Excessive sleeping takes away religion and world.'[7161]

٦٢٨٦ . الإمامُ الصّادقُ ﷺ: كَثرَةُ النَّومِ مَذهَبَةٌ للدِّينِ والدُّنيا.[٧١٢٦]

6287. **Imām al-Kāẓim (AS) said,** 'Do not habituate your eyes to too much sleep, for it is the least thankful in the body.'[7162]

٦٢٨٧ . الإمامُ الكاظمُ ﷺ : لا تُعَوِّدْ عَينَيكَ كَثرَةَ النَّومِ ؛ فإنّها أقَلُّ شَيءٍ في الجَسَدِ شُكراً.[٧١٢٧]

6288. **Imām al-Kāẓim (AS) said,** 'Allah, the Exalted and Noble, hates a servant who excessively sleeps and is idle.'[7163]

٦٢٨٨ . عنه ﷺ : إنّ اللهَ جَلَّ وعَزَّ يُبغِضُ العَبدَ النَّوّامَ الفارِغَ.[٧١٢٨]

6289. **Imām al-ʿAskarī (AS) said,** 'He who sleeps too much sees [disturbing] dreams.'[7164]

٦٢٨٩ . الإمامُ العسكريُّ ﷺ: مَن أكثَرَ المَنامَ رأى الأحلامَ.[٧١٢٩]

1776. The Ascension of Spirits to the Sky During Sleep

١٧٧٦ ـ صُعودُ روحِ المُومِنِ عِندَ النَّومِ إلَى السَّماءِ

6290. **Imām ʿAlī (AS) said,** 'A Muslim will not sleep while in a state of ritual impurity (*janāba*), and he should not sleep without being in a state of purity. If he does not find water then he should perform dry ablution (*tayammum*) with soil, for the spirit of a believer ascends to Allah Almighty and He meets it and blesses it. If his time of death was to have come when in a state [of purity], He places his spirit within the folds of His Mercy, and if his end has not come He sends it back [i.e. his spirit] with His guardian angels and they return it to his body.'[7165]

٦٢٩٠ . الإمامُ عليٌّ ﷺ : لا يَنامُ المُسلمُ وهُو جُنُبٌ، ولا يَنامُ إلّا على طَهورٍ، فإن لَم يَجِدِ الماءِ فلْيَتَيمَّمْ بالصَّعيدِ ؛ فإنَّ رُوحَ المُؤمنِ تَروحُ إلَى اللهِ عَزَّوجلَّ فَيَلقاها ويُبارِكُ علَيها، فإن كانَ أجَلُها قَد حَضَرَ جَعَلَها في مَكنونِ رَحمَتِهِ، وإن لَم يَكُن أجَلُها قَد حَضَرَ بَعَثَ بِها مَعَ اُمَنائهِ مِن مَلائكَتِهِ فيَرُدُّوها في جَسَدِهِ.[٧١٣٠]

(See also: THE SPIRIT: section 837)

(اُنظر) الروح: باب ٨٤٧.

1777. The Etiquettes of Sleeping ١٧٧٧ـ آدابُ النَّومِ

1. Cleanliness ١ ـ النَّظافةُ :

6291. **The Prophet (SAWA) said,** 'None of you should go to sleep with unclean hands, for if he does and is stricken with mental derangement from Satan [as a result] then he has only himself to blame.'[7166]

٦٢٩١ . رسولُ اللهِ ﷺ : لا يَبيتَنَّ أحَدُكُم ويَدُهُ غَمِرَةٌ ، فإن فَعَلَ فأصابَهُ لَمَمٌ لِلشَّيطانِ فلا يَلُومَنَّ إلّا نَفسَهُ .٧١٣١

2. Purity ٢ ـ الطَّهارةُ :

6292. **The Prophet (SAWA) said,** 'Whoever sleeps with ablution [*wuḍū'*] and dies in his sleep is regarded by Allah as a martyr.'[7167]

٦٢٩٢ . رسولُ اللهِ ﷺ : مَن نامَ علَى الوُضوءِ إن أدرَكَهُ المَوتُ في لَيلِهِ فهُو عِندَ اللهِ شَهيدٌ .٧١٣٢

6293. **Imām al-Ṣādiq (AS) said,** 'Whoever purifies himself [ablution] and then goes to his bed, he will sleep and his bed will be like his mosque.'[7168]

٦٢٩٣ . الإمامُ الصّادقُ ﷺ : مَن تَطَهَّرَ ثُمّ أوىٰ إلى فِراشِهِ باتَ وفِراشُهُ كمَسجِدِهِ .٧١٣٣

6294. **Imām al-Ṣādiq (AS) said,** 'Whoever purifies himself [ablution] and then goes to his bed he will sleep and his bed will be like his mosque. So, if he remembers that he is not in a state of ablution, then he should perform dry ablution (*tayammum*) on his clothes, whatever it may be, and if he does so he will be [regarded as] continuously praying and remembering Allah Almighty.'[7169]

٦٢٩٤ . عنه ﷺ : مَن تَطَهَّرَ ثُمّ أوىٰ إلىٰ فِراشِهِ ، باتَ وفِراشُهُ كمَسجِدِهِ ، فإن ذَكَرَ أنّهُ علىٰ غَيرِ وُضوءٍ فلْيَتَيَمَّمْ مِن دِثارِهِ كائناً ما كانَ ، فإن فَعَلَ ذلكَ لَم يَزَلْ في الصَّلاةِ وذِكرِ اللهِ عزّوجلّ .٧١٣٤

3. Relieving Oneself before Sleeping ٣ ـ عَرضُ النَّفسِ علَى الخَلاءِ :

6295. **Imām 'Alī (AS),** to his son al-Ḥasan (AS) said, 'O son, shall I teach you four things that will make you needless of medicine?' He said, 'Yes, O Commander of the Faithful.' He said, 'Do not eat food unless you are hungry and get up from eating whilst you still desire to eat more, chew well, and before you sleep go and relieve yourself. If you do these you will be needless of medicine.'[7170]

٦٢٩٥ . الإمامُ عليٌّ ﷺ لابنهِ الحسنِ ﷺ : يابُنَيَّ ، ألا اُعَلِّمُكَ أربَعَ خِصالٍ تَستَغني بِها عَنِ الطِّبِّ ؟ فقالَ : بلىٰ يا أميرَ المؤمنينَ . قالَ : لا تَجلِسْ علَى الطَّعامِ إلّا وأنتَ جائعٌ ، ولا تَقُمْ عَنِ الطَّعامِ إلّا وأنتَ تَشتَهيهِ ، وجَوِّدِ المَضغَ ، وإذا نِمتَ فاعرِضْ نَفسَكَ علَى الخَلاءِ ، فإذا استَعمَلتَ هٰذا استَغنَيتَ عَنِ الطِّبِّ .٧١٣٥

4. Taking Account of Oneself

٤ ـ المُحاسَبةُ :

6296. **Imām al-Ṣādiq (AS) said,** 'When you head for bed then look at what you have put in your stomach [during the day] and what you have earned in your day, and remember that you are to die and that you will be resurrected.'[7171]

٦٢٩٦ . الإمامُ الصّادقُ عليه السلام : إذا أوَيتَ إلىٰ فِراشِكَ فانظُرْ ما سَلَكتَ في بَطنِكَ وما كَسَبتَ في يَومِكَ ، واذكُرْ أنَّكَ مَيِّتٌ وأنَّ لكَ مَعاداً .[٧١٣٦]

5. Reciting [the Qur'an] and Supplicating at Bedtime

٥ ـ القِراءةُ والدُّعاءُ عِندَ النَّومِ :

6297. **The Prophet (SAWA) said,** 'Whoever recites the chapter of the Qur'an entitled *al-Ikhlāṣ* when he retires to his bed, Allah will forgive fifty years of his sins.'[7172]

٦٢٩٧ . رسولُ اللهِ صلى الله عليه وآله : مَن قَرَأَ ﴿قُلْ هُوَ اللهُ أحَدٌ﴾ حِينَ يأخُذُ مَضجَعَهُ ، غَفَرَ اللهُ عَزَّ وجَلَّ لَهُ ذُنوبَ خَمسينَ سَنَةً .[٧١٣٧]

6298. **The Prophet (SAWA) said,** 'Whoever recites the chapter of the Qur'an entitled *al-Takāthur* when going to sleep will be protected from the trials of the grave.'[7173]

٦٢٩٨ . عنه صلى الله عليه وآله : مَن قَرَأَ ﴿ألْهاكُمُ التَّكاثُرُ﴾ عِندَ مَنامِهِ وُقِيَ فِتنَةَ القَبرِ .[٧١٣٨]

6299. **The Prophet (SAWA) said,** 'When any of you retires to his bed … he should say: O Allah, if You take my soul while I am sleeping then forgive it, and if You send it back to me, then protect it as You protect Your righteous servants.'[7174]

٦٢٩٩ . عنه صلى الله عليه وآله : إذا آوىٰ أحَدُكُم إلىٰ فِراشِهِ … فَلْيَقُلْ : اللّهُمّ إن أمسَكتَ نَفسي في مَنامي فاغفِرْ لَها ، وإن أرسَلتَها فاحفَظْها بما تَحفَظُ بِهِ عِبادَكَ الصّالِحينَ .[٧١٣٩]

6. Sleeping on One's Back or Side

٦ ـ النَّومُ علَى القَفا أو علَى اليَمينِ :

6300. **Imām ʿAlī (AS) said,** 'Sleeping can be in four ways: prophets (AS) sleep straight on their backs and their eyes do not sleep waiting for the revelation of Allah. The believer sleeps on his right side facing the *qibla*. Kings and their children sleep on their left side enjoying what they ate. Satan, his brethren and every insane and deformed person sleeps flat on their front.'[7175]

٦٣٠٠ . الإمامُ عليٌّ عليه السلام : النَّومُ علىٰ أربَعَةِ أوجُهٍ : الأنبياءُ عليهم السلام تَنامُ علىٰ أقفِيَتِهِم مُستَلقِينَ وأعيُنُهُم لا تَنامُ مُتَوَقِّعَةً لِوَحيِ اللهِ عَزَّ وجلَّ ، والمُؤمنُ يَنامُ علىٰ يَمينِهِ مُستَقبِلَ القِبلَةِ ، والمُلوكُ وأبناؤها تَنامُ علىٰ شَمائلِها لِيَستَمرِئوا ما يأكُلونَ ، وإبليسُ وإخوانُهُ وكُلُّ مَجنونٍ وذوعاهَةٍ يَنامُ علىٰ وَجهِهِ مُنبَطِحاً .[٧١٤٠]

7. Supplication When Waking Up

٧ ـ الدُّعاءُ عِندَ الانتِباهِ :

6301. *Biḥār al-Anwār*, 'Ḥudhayfa said, 'When the Prophet (SAWA) retired to his bed he would say, 'In Your name O Allah I die and live', and when

٦٣٠١ . بحار الأنوار : إنَّ النَّبيَّ صلى الله عليه وآله كانَ إذا آوىٰ إلىٰ فِراشِهِ قالَ : «باسمِكَ اللّهُمّ أمُوتُ وأحيا» ، وإذا

he woke up he would say, 'Praise be to Allah who revived us after He caused us to die, and upon Him is the Resurrection.'[7176]

استيقظَ قالَ: «الحمدُ للهِ الّذي أحيانا بَعدَما أماتَنا وإلَيهِ النُّشورُ». ٧١٤١

388

INTENTION

النِّيَّة

1778. The Role of Intention in Action

١٧٧٨ـ دَورُ النِّيَّةِ في العَمَلِ

6302. **The Prophet (SAWA) said,** 'O people, actions are according to intentions, and every person will have what he intended. So, whoever's migration was to Allah and His Messenger then his migration is to Allah and His Messenger, and whoever's migration was to the world to gain from it, or to a woman to marry her, then their migration will be to whatever they migrated to.'[7177]

٦٣٠٢. رسولُ اللهِ ﷺ: يـا أيُّـها النّـاسُ، إنّـما الأعمالُ بالنِّيّاتِ، وإنّما لِكُلِّ امرِئٍ ما نَوىٰ، فمَن كانَت هِجرَتُهُ إلَى اللهِ ورَسولِهِ فـهِجرَتُهُ إلَـى اللهِ ورَسولِهِ، ومَن كانَت هِجرَتُهُ إلىٰ دُنيا يُصيبُها أو امرأةٍ يَتَزَوَّجُها فهِجرَتُهُ إلىٰ ما هاجَرَ إلَيهِ. ٧١٤٢

6303. **The Prophet (SAWA),** when he sent 'Alī on a military expedition with a brigade, and a man said to his brother, 'Lets go on the military expedition with the brigade of 'Alī, we might get a slave or an animal or something of value- said, 'Actions are according to intentions, and every person has what they intend. So whoever goes on a conquest in search of what is with Allah then their reward will be from Allah, and whoever goes on a conquest in search of worldly affairs or intends restraints will not get other than what he intended.'[7178]

٦٣٠٣. عنه ﷺ ـ لَمّا أغزىٰ عَلِيّاً ﷺ في سَرِيَّةٍ، فقالَ رجُلٌ لأخٍ لَهُ: أغزُ بِنا في سَرِيَّةِ عَلِيٍّ لَعلَّنا نُصيبُ خادِماً أو دابَّةً أو شَيئاً نَتَبلَّغُ بِـهِ ـ: إنّـما الأعمالُ بالنِّيّاتِ، ولِكُلِّ امرِئٍ ما نَوىٰ، فمَن غَزا ابتِغاءَ ما عِندَ اللهِ فقد وَقَعَ أجرُهُ علَى اللهِ، ومَـن غَزا يُريدُ عَرَضَ الدُّنيا أو نَوىٰ عِقالاً لَم يَكُن لَـهُ إلّا ما نَوىٰ. ٧١٤٣

6304. **Imām 'Alī (AS) said,** 'Intention is the basis of action.'[7179]

٦٣٠٤. الإمامُ عليٌّ ﷺ: النِّيَّةُ أساسُ العَمَلِ. ٧١٤٤

6305. **Imām Zayn al-'Ābidīn (AS) said,** 'There is no action without intention.'[7180]

٦٣٠٥. الإمامُ زينُ العابدينَ ﷺ: لا عَـمَلَ إلّا بِنيَّةٍ. ٧١٤٥

6306. **Imām al-Ṣādiq (AS) said,** 'A body will not become weak where the intention is strong.'[7181]

٦٣٠٦. الإمامُ الصادقُ ﷺ: ما ضَعُفَ بَدَنٌ عمّا قَوِيَت علَيهِ النِّيَّةُ. ٧١٤٦

1779. The Role of Intention in the Hereafter

١٧٧٩ ـ دَورُ النِّيَّةِ فِي القيامَةِ

6307. **Imām al-Ṣādiq (AS) said,** 'The people of Hell will dwell eternally in Hell because their intentions in the world were such that if they were to remain there forever they would disobey Allah forever, and the people of Heaven will dwell eternally in Heaven because their intentions in the world were such that if they were to remain there forever, they would obey Allah. Therefore, it is according to their intentions that these people and those people will have everlasting abodes. He then recited Allah's verse in the Qur'an: *"Say, 'Everyone acts according to his character'*[7182], and said, [meaning] 'With his intention.'[7183]

٦٣٠٧ . الكافي عن الإمام الصّادق عليه السلام : إنّما خُلِّدَ أهلُ النّارِ في النّارِ لأنّ نِيّاتِهِم كانَت في الدُّنيا أن لو خُلِّدوا فيها أن يَعصُوا اللهَ أبداً ، وإنّما خُلِّدَ أهلُ الجَنّةِ في الجَنّةِ لأنّ نِيّاتِهِم كانَت في الدُّنيا أن لَو بَقُوا فيها أن يُطِيعوا اللهَ أبَداً ، فبِالنِّيّاتِ خُلِّدَ هٰؤلاءِ وهٰؤلاءِ ، ثُمّ تَلا قولَهُ تعالىٰ : ﴿قُلْ كُلٌّ يَعْمَلُ عَلىٰ شاكِلَتِهِ﴾[٧١٤٧] قالَ : علىٰ نِيَّتِهِ.[٧١٤٨]

6308. **Imām al-Ṣādiq (AS) said,** 'Allah will resurrect people according to their intentions on the Day of Judgment.'[7184]

٦٣٠٨ . الإمامُ الصّادقُ عليه السلام : إنّ اللهَ يَحشُرُ النّاسَ علىٰ نِيّاتِهِم يومَ القِيامَةِ.[٧١٤٩]

1780. The Reward of an Intention to do Good

١٧٨٠ ـ ثَوابُ نِيَّةِ الخَيرِ

6309. **The Prophet (SAWA) said,** 'We left groups of people in Madinah, while there was no valley we crossed nor heights we climbed nor hills we descended without them being with us. They said, 'How can they be with us when they did not witness any of this?' He said, '[Because of] their intentions.'[7185]

٦٣٠٩ . رسولُ اللهِ صلى الله عليه وآله : تَرَكنا في المَدينَةِ أقواماً لا نَقطَعُ وادِياً ولا نَصعَدُ صُعوداً ولا نَهبِطُ هُبوطاً إلّا كانُوا مَعَنا . قالُوا : كَيفَ يَكونونَ مَعَنا ولَم يَشهَدوا ؟! قالَ : نِيّاتُهُم.[٧١٥٠]

6310. **The Prophet (SAWA) said,** 'O Abū Dharr, intend to do good, even if you do not [manage to] do it so that you are not written among the inattentive.'[7186]

٦٣١٠ . عنه صلى الله عليه وآله : يا أبا ذرٍّ ، هِمَّ بالحَسَنَةِ وإن لَم تَعمَلْها ، لِكَيلا تُكتَبَ مِن الغافِلينَ.[٧١٥١]

6311. **Imām 'Alī (AS) said,** 'Righteous intention is one of the two actions [it itself is a deed].'[7187]

٦٣١١ . الإمامُ عليٌّ عليه السلام : النِّيَّةُ الصّالِحَةُ أحَدُ العَمَلَينِ.[٧١٥٢]

6312. **Imām ʿAlī (AS) said** to a man who wished his brother was present so that he could see the victory of Allah over His enemies at the Battle of the Camel, 'Did your brother desire to be with us?' He said, 'Yes.' He (AS) said, 'Then he has witnessed us, and groups of people have witnessed us in our army while they are still in the loins of men and the wombs of women. Very soon time will bring them out and faith will become strong through them.'[7188]

٦٣١٢. عنه ؑ ـ لرجلٍ يَوَدُّ حُضورَ أخيهِ ليَشهَدَ نَصرَ اللهِ علىٰ أعدائهِ في الجَمَلِ ـ: أهَوىٰ أخيكَ مَعَنا؟ فقالَ: نَعَم، قالَ: فَقد شَهِدَنا، ولَقد شَهِدَنا في عَسكَرِنا هٰذا أقوامٌ (قَومٌ) في أصلابِ الرِّجالِ وأرحامِ النِّساءِ، سَيَرعَفُ بِهِمُ الزَّمانُ[٧١٥٣]، ويَقوىٰ بِهِمُ الإيمانُ.[٧١٥٤]

6313. **Imām ʿAlī (AS) said,** 'Allah's granting [of rewards] is according to the intention.'[7189]

٦٣١٣. الإمامُ عليٌّ ؑ: علىٰ قدرِ النِّيَّةِ تَكونُ مِنَ اللهِ العَطِيَّةُ.[٧١٥٥]

6314. **Imām al-Bāqir (AS) said,** 'When Allah Almighty knows the good intention of someone He encompasses him with protection [from sins].'[7190]

٦٣١٤. الإمامُ الباقرُ ؑ: إذا عَلِمَ اللهُ تعالىٰ حُسنَ نِيَّةٍ مِن أحَدٍ، اكتَنَفَهُ بالعِصمَةِ.[٧١٥٦]

1781. The Intention of the Believer is Better than his Action

١٧٨١ ـ نِيَّةُ المُؤمِنِ خَيرٌ مِن عَمَلِهِ

6315. **The Prophet (SAWA) said,** 'The intention of the believer is better than his action, and the intention of the disbeliever is worse than his action, and every doer does according to his intention.'[7191]

٦٣١٥. رسولُ اللهِ ﷺ: نِيَّةُ المُؤمِنِ خَيرٌ مِن عَمَلِهِ، ونِيَّةُ الكافِرِ شَرٌّ مِن عَمَلِهِ، وكُلُّ عامِلٍ يَعمَلُ علىٰ نِيَّتِهِ.[٧١٥٧]

6316. **The Prophet (SAWA) said,** 'The intention of a believer is more effective than his action, and same with the evildoer.'[7192]

٦٣١٦. عنه ﷺ: نِيَّةُ المُؤمِنِ أبلَغُ مِن عَمَلِهِ، وكذلكَ الفاجِرُ.[٧١٥٨]

6317. **Imām al-Bāqir (AS) said,** 'The intention of a believer is better than his action, that is because he intends good that he cannot perform, and the intention of the disbeliever is worse than his action because he intends evil and he wishes in evil what he cannot perform.'[7193]

٦٣١٧. الإمامُ الباقرُ ؑ: نِيَّةُ المُؤمِنِ أفضَلُ مِن عَمَلِهِ؛ وذلكَ لأنَّهُ يَنوي مِنَ الخَيرِ ما لا يُدرِكُهُ، ونِيَّةُ الكافِرِ شَرٌّ مِن عَمَلِهِ؛ وذلكَ لأنَّ الكافِرَ يَنوي الشَّرَّ ويأمَلُ مِنَ الشَّرِّ ما لا يُدرِكُهُ.[٧١٥٩]

6318. **Imām al-Ṣādiq (AS),** in answer to the reason behind the superiority of a believer's

٦٣١٨. الإمامُ الصّادقُ ؑ ـ في الجَوابِ عَن عِلَّةِ

intention over his action, 'Because an action could be done as an act of showing-off, but the intention is solely and sincerely for the Lord of the worlds, so He Almighty gives according to the intention what He does not give for the action.'[7194]

فَضلِ نِيَّةِ المُؤمنِ علىٰ عَملِهِ ـ: لأنَّ العَمَلَ رُبَّما كـانَ رِياءً لِـلمَخلوقينَ، والنِّـيَّةُ خـالِصَةٌ لِرَبِّ العالَمينَ، فيُعطي تَعالىٰ علَى النِّيَّةِ مـا لا يُـعطي علَى العَمَلِ.[٧١٦٠]

1782. Enjoinment of Having Righteous Intentions in Everything

١٧٨٢ ـ الحَثُّ عَلَى النِّيَّةِ الصّالحَةِ في كُلِّ شَيءٍ

6319. **The Prophet (SAWA) said,** 'O Abū Dharr, you should have a righteous intention in everything you do, even in sleeping and eating.'[7195]

٦٣١٩. رسولُ اللهِ ﷺ: يا أبا ذرٍّ، لِيَكُن لَكَ في كُلِّ شَيءٍ نِيَّةٌ صالِحَةٌ، حتّىٰ في النَّومِ والأكلِ.[٧١٦١]

6320. **Imām al-Ṣādiq (AS) said,** 'It is important for a servant to have sincere intention in every movement and stillness, for if it was not so he would be regarded as negligent.'[7196]

٦٣٢٠. الإمامُ الصّادقُ ؑ: لابُدَّ لِلعَبدِ مِن خالِصِ النِّيَّةِ في كُلِّ حَرَكَةٍ وسُكونٍ؛ لأنَّهُ إذا لَم يَكُن هذا لمَعنىٰ يَكونُ غافِلاً.[٧١٦٢]

1783. Good Intention

١٧٨٣ ـ حُسنُ النِّيَّةِ

6321. **The Prophet (SAWA) said,** 'The best action is the true intention.'[7197]

٦٣٢١. رسولُ اللهِ ﷺ: أفـضَلُ العَـمَلِ النِّـيَّةُ الصّادِقَةُ.[٧١٦٣]

6322. **Imām ʿAlī (AS) said,** 'Good intention is the beauty of the hearts.'[7198]

٦٣٢٢. الإمامُ عليٌّ ؑ: حُسـنُ النِّـيَّةِ جَـمالُ السَّرائرِ.[٧١٦٤]

6323. **Imām ʿAlī (AS) said,** 'The beautiful intention is the reason for the fulfilment of ambition.'[7199]

٦٣٢٣. عنه ؑ: جَـميلُ النِّـيَّةِ سَـبَبٌ لِـبُلوغِ الاُمنِيَّةِ.[٧١٦٥]

6324. **Imām al-Ṣādiq (AS) said,** 'Allah will increase the sustenance of he whose intention is good.'[7200]

٦٣٢٤. الإمامُ الصّادقُ ؑ: مَن حَسُنَت نِيَّتُهُ زادَ اللهُ في رِزقِهِ.[٧١٦٦]

6325. **Imām al-Ṣādiq (AS),** when asked about the limit of worship required by a person for him to be considered as fulfilling it, said, 'Good intention with obedience.'[7201]

٦٣٢٥. عنه ؑ ـ لَمّا سُئلَ عن حَدِّ العِبادَةِ الّتي إذا فَـعَلَها فـاعِلُها كـانَ مُـؤَدِّياً ـ: حُسـنُ النِّـيَّةِ بالطّاعَةِ.[٧١٦٧]

1784. Bad Intention

١٧٨٤ ـ سوءُ النِّيَّةِ

6326. **Imām ʿAlī (AS) said,** ʻBad intention is a hidden sickness.ʼ[7202]

٦٣٢٦ . الإمامُ عليٌّ عليه السلام : سُوءُ النِّيَّةِ داءٌ دَفينٌ. ٧١٦٨

6327. **Imām ʿAlī (AS) said,** ʻWith corrupt intentions blessings are removed.ʼ[7203]

٦٣٢٧ . عنه عليه السلام : عِندَ فَسادِ النِّيَّةِ تَرتَفِعُ البَرَكَةُ. ٧١٦٩

6328. **Imām ʿAlī (AS) said,** ʻWhen an intention is corrupt calamity befalls.ʼ[7204]

٦٣٢٨ . عنه عليه السلام : إذا فَسَدَتِ النِّيَّةُ وَقَعَتِ البَلِيَّةُ. ٧١٧٠

6329. **Imām al-Ṣādiq (AS) said,** ʻA believer makes an intention to sin, and he is deprived of sustenance [as a result].ʼ[7205]

٦٣٢٩ . الإمامُ الصّادقُ عليه السلام : إنّ المُؤمنَ لَيَنوي الذَّنبَ فيُحرَمُ رِزقَهُ. ٧١٧١

389

MIGRATION

الهِجرَةُ

1785. Migration Should Continue

١٧٨٥ ـ عَدَمُ انقِطاعِ الهِجرَةِ

6330. **The Prophet (SAWA) said,** ʻO people, migrate and hold fast on to Islam, for migration does not stop as long as struggle exists.ʼ[7206]

٦٣٣٠ . رسولُ اللهِ ﷺ : أيُّها النّاس، هاجِروا وتَمَسَّكوا بالإسلامِ ؛ فإنَّ الهِجرَةَ لا تَنقَطِعُ ما دامَ الجِهادُ. ٧١٧٢

6331. **The Prophet (SAWA) said,** ʻThere are two migrations: one of them is that you migrate away from bad deeds, and the other one is your migration to Allah Almighty and His Messenger, and migration does not stop as long as repentance is accepted.ʼ[7207]

٦٣٣١ . عنه ﷺ : الهِجرَةُ هِجرَتانِ : إحداهُما أن تَهجُرَ السَّيِّئاتِ، والاُخرىٰ أن تُهاجِرَ إلَى اللهِ تعالىٰ ورَسولِهِ، ولا تَنقَطِعُ الهِجرَةُ ما تُقُبِّلَتِ التَّوبَةُ. ٧١٧٣

6332. **Imām ʿAlī (AS) said,** ʻMigration stands at its original position. Allah has no need of him who secretly accepts belief or him who openly does so. Migration will not apply to anyone unless

٦٣٣٢ . الإمامُ عليٌّ عليه السلام : الهِجرَةُ قائمَةٌ علىٰ حَدِّها الأوَّلِ، ما كانَ للهِ في أهلِ الأرضِ حاجَةٌ مِن مُستَسَرِّ الاُمَّةِ ومُعلَنِها، لا يَقَعُ اسمُ الهِجرَةِ علىٰ

he recognises the proof [of Allah - an Imām] on the earth. Whoever recognises him and acknowledges him is a migrant. The title 'weak'[7208] does not apply to him whom the proof [of Allah] has reached, and he hears it and his heart comprehends it.'[7209]

أحَدٍ (إلّا) بـمَعرِفَةِ الحُـجَّةِ فـي الأرضِ، فـمَن عَرَفَها وأقَـرَّ بـها فـهُو مُـهاجِرٌ، ولا يَـقَعُ اسـمُ الاستِضعافِ علىٰ مَن بَلَغَتهُ الحُجَّةُ فسَمِعَتها اُذُنُهُ ووَعاها قَلبُهُ.[٧١٧٤]

6333. **Imām al-Bāqir (AS) said,** 'He who willingly enters Islam is a migrant.'[7210]

٦٣٣٣. الإمامُ الباقرُ عليه السلام: مَن دَخَلَ في الإسلامِ طَوعاً فهُو مُهاجِرٌ.[٧١٧٥]

1786. The Best Migration

١٧٨٦ـ أفضَلُ الهِجرَةِ

"and keep away from all impurity!"[7211]

﴿وَالرُّجْزَ فَاهْجُرْ﴾.[٧١٧٦]

6334. **The Prophet (SAWA) said,** 'The best migration is that you abandon all that Allah hates.'[7212]

٦٣٣٤. رسولُ اللهِ صلى الله عليه وآله: أفضَلُ الهِجرَةِ أن تَهجُرَ ما كَرِهَ اللهُ.[٧١٧٧]

6335. **The Prophet (SAWA) said,** 'The best migration is that you abandon all bad.'[7213]

٦٣٣٥. عنه صلى الله عليه وآله: أفـضَلُ الهِـجرَةِ أن تَـهجُرَ السُّوءَ.[٧١٧٨]

6336. **The Prophet (SAWA) said,** 'A migrant is someone who migrates from wrongs and sins.'[7214]

٦٣٣٦. عنه صلى الله عليه وآله: المُهاجِرُ مَن هَـجَرَ الخَـطايا والذُّنوبَ.[٧١٧٩]

1787. The Necessity of Migrating from Places [Populated with] Sinners

١٧٨٧ـ وُجوبُ الهِجرَةِ عَن بِلادِ أهلِ المَعاصي

"Indeed, those whom the angels take away while they are wronging themselves, they ask, "What state were you in?" They reply, 'We were abased in the land.' They say, 'Was not Allah's earth vast enough so that you might migrate in it?' The refuge of such shall be hell, and it is an evil destination."[7215]

﴿إِنَّ الَّذِينَ تَوَفَّاهُمُ الْـمَلَائِكَةُ ظَـالِمِي أَنْـفُسِهِمْ قَالُوا فِيمَ كُنْتُمْ قَالُوا كُنَّا مُسْتَضْعَفِينَ فِي الْأَرْضِ قَالُوا أَلَمْ تَكُنْ أَرْضُ اللهِ وَاسِعَةً فَتُهَاجِرُوا فِـيهَا فَأُولٰئِكَ مَأْوَاهُمْ جَهَنَّمُ وَسَاءَتْ مَصِيراً﴾.[٧١٨٠]

"O My servants who have faith! My earth is indeed vast. So worship [only] Me."[7216]

﴿يَا عِبَادِيَ الَّذِينَ آمَنُوا إِنَّ أَرْضِي وَاسِعَةٌ فَإِيَّايَ فَاعْبُدُونِ﴾.[٧١٨١]

6337. **Imām al-Ṣādiq (AS),** with regard to Allah's verse in the Qur'an: *"O My servants who have faith! My earth is indeed vast. So worship [only] Me"*, said, 'When Allah is disobeyed in a place that you are in, leave it and go somewhere else.'[7217]

٦٣٣٧. الإمامُ الصّادقُ عليه السلام ـ في قولِهِ تعالىٰ: ﴿يا عِبادِيَ الّذِينَ آمَنوا إنَّ أرضي...﴾ ـ: إذا عُصِيَ اللهُ فـي أرضٍ أنتَ فـيها فـاخرُجْ مِـنها إلىٰ غَيرِها.[٧١٨٢]

6338. **The Prophet (SAWA) said,** 'Whoever flees with their religion from one place to another, even if it was the distance of a hand's span of the earth, Heaven becomes obligatory for him and he will be in the company of Abraham and Muḥammad (AS).'[7218]

٦٣٣٨. رسولُ اللهِ ﷺ: مَن فَرَّ بدِينِهِ مِن أرضٍ إلىٰ أرضٍ وإن كانَ شِبراً مِن الأرضِ، استوجَبَ الجَنّةَ وكانَ رَفيقَ إبراهيمَ ومحمّدٍ.٧١٨٣

1788. Prohibition of Returning to [a State of] Renegation after Having Migrated [to Belief] (*al-taʿarrub baʿd al-hijra*)[7219]

١٧٨٨ ـ النَّهيُ عَنِ التَّعرُّبِ بَعدَ الهِجرَةِ

6339. **The Prophet (SAWA),** in his will to 'Alī (AS) said, 'There is no renegation after migration.'[7220]

٦٣٣٩. رسولُ اللهِ ﷺ ـ في وصيَّتِهِ لعليٍّ ﷺ ـ: لا تعَرُّبَ بَعدَ الهِجرَةِ.٧١٨٤

6340. **Imām ʿAlī (AS) said,** 'Among the major sins is the intentional killing of a believer…and regeneration after migration.'[7221]

٦٣٤٠. الإمامُ عليٌّ ﷺ: مِنَ الكَبائرِ قَتلُ المُؤمِنِ عَمداً... وَالتَّعرُّبُ بَعدَ الهِجرَةِ.٧١٨٥

6341. **Imām al-Ṣādiq (AS) said,** 'The one who returns to a state of renegation after migration [to belief] is one who abandons this affair [of Islam] after having acknowledged it.'[7222]

٦٣٤١. الإمامُ الصّادقُ ﷺ: المُتَعرِّبُ بَعدَ الهِجرَةِ التّارِكُ لهٰذا الأمرِ بَعدَ مَعرِفَتِهِ.٧١٨٦

6342. **Imām al-Riḍā (AS) said,** 'Allah has prohibited renegation after migration [to belief] because of [the danger] of denouncing one's religion and leaving the support of the prophets and the divine proofs (AS), and the corruption that would ensue, the nullification of the rights of all those who hold rights [in religion], especially for Bedouins. This is why, if a man were to have acknowledged religion completely, it is not allowed for him to go and live with people who

٦٣٤٢. الإمامُ الرِّضا ﷺ: حَرَّمَ اللهُ التَّعرُّبَ بَعدَ الهِجرَةِ للرُّجوعِ عَنِ الدِّينِ وتَركِ المُوازَرَةِ للأنبياءِ والحُجَجِ ﷺ، وما في ذٰلِكَ مِنَ الفَسادِ وإبطالِ حَقِّ كُلِّ ذي حَقٍّ لِعِلَّةِ سُكنَى البَدوِ؛ ولذلكَ لَو عَرَفَ الرَّجُلُ الدِّينَ كامِلاً لَم يَجُزْ لَهُ

are ignorant [or in disbelief] of it, and as a result of fear for him, for he can never be safe from falling from his position of knowledge and re-entering into ignorance and remaining therein.'[7223]

مُساكَنَةُ أهلِ الجَهلِ، والخَوفِ علَيهِ؛ لأنه لا يُؤمَنُ أن يَقَعَ مِنهُ تَركُ العِلمِ، والدُّخولُ مَع أهلِ الجَهلِ والتَّمادِي في ذلكَ.[٧١٨٧]

390

DESERTION

الهِجرانُ

1789. Warning Against Desertion

١٧٨٩ ـ التَّحذيرُ عَنِ الهِجرانِ

6343. **The Prophet (SAWA) said,** 'A Muslim's desertion of his brother is like shedding his blood.'[7224]

٦٣٤٣ . رسولُ اللهِ ﷺ: هَجرُ المُسلِمِ أخاهُ كَسَفكِ دَمِهِ.[٧١٨٨]

6344. **The Prophet (SAWA) said,** 'O Abū Dharr, beware of deserting your brother, for deeds are not accepted from desertion.'[7225]

٦٣٤٤ . عنه ﷺ: يا أبا ذرٍّ، إيّاكَ وهِجرانَ أخِيكَ؛ فإنَّ العَمَلَ لا يُتَقَبَّلُ مِن الهِجرانِ.[٧١٨٩]

6345. **Imām al-Ṣādiq (AS) said,** 'Satan continues to be happy as long as two Muslims forsake each other, and when they reconcile again his knees tremble and his joints break apart, and he screams out 'Woe unto me, I am perished'.'[7226]

٦٣٤٥ . الإمامُ الصّادقُ عليه السلام: لا يَزالُ إبليسُ فَرِحاً ما اهتَجرَ المُسلِمانِ، فإذا التَقَيا اصطَكَّت رُكبتاه وتَخَلّعَت أوصالُهُ[٧١٩٠]، ونادَىٰ يا وَيلَهُ، ما لَقِىَ مِنَ الثُّبُورِ؟![٧١٩١]

6346. **Imām al-Ṣādiq (AS) said,** 'No sooner do two men who forsake each other part than one of them becomes deserving of disassociation [by Allah] and curse, and both of them may become deserving of it'. Mu'attab said to him, 'May Allah sacrifice me for your sake, this is for the one who wronged, but what about the one who was wronged?' He said, 'Because he does not call his brother to reconciliation and does not forgive him for what he said. I heard my father say, 'When two people dispute with each other and one overcomes the other, the one who has been wronged should return to his friend and says to him 'O brother I am the one at fault', to cut the desertion between them, for Allah Almighty is a

٦٣٤٦ . عنه عليه السلام: لا يَفتَرِقُ رجُلانِ علَى الهِجرانِ إلّا استَوجَبَ أحَدُهُما البَراءةَ واللَّعنَةَ، ورُبَّما استَحقَّ ذلكَ كِلاهُما، فقالَ لَهُ مُعَتّبُ: جَعَلَنِيَ اللهُ فِداكَ، هٰذا الظّالِمُ فما بالُ المَظلومِ؟
قالَ: لأنَّهُ لا يَدعو أخاهُ إلىٰ صِلَتِهِ ولا يَتَغامَسُ[٧١٩٢] لَهُ عَن كَلامِهِ، سَمِعتُ أبي يقولُ: إذا تَنازَعَ اثنانِ فَعازَّ أحَدُهُما الآخَرَ فلْيَرجِع المَظلومُ إلىٰ صاحِبِهِ حتّىٰ يَقولَ لِصاحِبِهِ: أى أخِي أنا الظّالِمُ، حتّىٰ يَقطعَ الهِجرانَ بَينَهُ وبَينَ

Just Judge, and will take the right of the wronged one from the wronger.'[7227]

صاحِبِهِ، فإنّ اللهَ تبارَكَ وتعالىٰ حَكَمٌ عَدلٌ يأخُذُ للمَظلوم مِن الظّالِم.٧١٩٣

1790. The Prohibition of Forsaking a Brother for More than Three Days

١٧٩٠ ـ النَّهيُ عن هِجرَةِ الأخِ فَوقَ ثَلاثٍ

6347. **The Prophet (SAWA) said,** 'Forsaking [one's brother] for more than three days is not allowed.'[7228]

٦٣٤٧. رسولُ اللهِ ﷺ: لا هِجرَةَ فَوقَ ثَلاثٍ.٧١٩٤

6348. **The Prophet (SAWA) said,** 'It is not permitted for a believer to desert his brother for more than three days.'[7229]

٦٣٤٨. عنه ﷺ: لا يَحِلُّ للمُؤمنِ أن يَهجُرَ أخاهُ فَوقَ ثَلاثَةِ أيّامٍ.٧١٩٥

6349. **The Prophet (SAWA) said,** 'Deserting [one's brother] for more than three days is not allowed, and if they meet thereafter and one of them greets the other, and he returns the greeting, they will both share the reward. But if he does not return the greeting, the person who greeted is cleared of sin, and will take the reward alone.'[7230]

٦٣٤٩. عنه ﷺ: لا تَحِلُّ الهِجرَةُ فَوقَ ثَلاثَةِ أيّامٍ، فإنِ التَقَيا فسَلَّمَ أحَدُهُما فَرَدَّ الآخَرُ اشتَرَكا في الأجرِ، وإن لَم يَرُدَّ بَرِئَ هٰذا مِن الإثمِ، وباءَ بِهِ الآخَرُ.٧١٩٦

6350. **The Prophet (SAWA) said,** 'Do not turn your backs to each other and do not cut ties amongst yourselves, and be servants of Allah as brothers. Deserting a believer for [more than] three days [is not allowed] and they must speak [thereafter], but if they do not Allah Almighty turns away from them until they speak.'[7231]

٦٣٥٠. عنه ﷺ: لا تَدابَرُوا، ولا تَقاطَعُوا، وكُونوا عِبادَ اللهِ إخواناً، هَجرُ المُؤمنَينِ ثَلاثاً، فإن تكلَّما وإلّا أعرَضَ اللهُ عَزَّوجلَّ عَنهُما حتّى يَتَكلَّما.٧١٩٧

6351. **The Prophet (SAWA) said,** 'No sooner do two Muslims forsake each other and stay like that for three days without reconciling, then they are regarded as having left Islam and there is no relation between them. Whoever of them precedes in speaking to his brother will precede entrance into Heaven on the Day of Judgment.'[7232]

٦٣٥١. عنه ﷺ: أيُّما مُسلِمَينِ تَهاجَرا فمَكَثا ثَلاثاً لا يَصطَلِحانِ إلّا كانا خارِجَينِ مِن الإسلامِ، ولَم يَكُن بَينَهُما وَلايَةٌ، فأيُّهُما سَبَقَ إلىٰ كلامِ أخيهِ كانَ السّابِقَ إلَى الجَنَّةِ يَومَ الحِسابِ.٧١٩٨

6352. **Imām al-Bāqir (AS) said,** 'Any two believers who forsake each other for more than three days, I disassociate myself from them on the

٦٣٥٢. الإمامُ الباقرُ عليه السلام: ما مِن مُؤمنَينِ اهتَجَرا

third day.' He was asked, 'O son of the Prophet, this is in regard to the one wronging, but what about the wronged?' He (SAWA) said, 'Well why doesn't the wronged one himself go to the wronger and say, 'I am in the wrong, until they reconcile?!'[7233]

فَوقَ ثَلاثٍ إلّا وَبَرِئتُ مِنهُما في الثّالِثَةِ، فقيلَ لَهُ: يابنَ رسولِ اللهِ، هٰذا حالُ الظّالِمِ فما بالُ المَظلومِ؟ فقالَ عليه السلام: ما بالُ المَظلومِ لا يَصيرُ إلَى الظّالِمِ فيَقولُ: أنا الظّالِمُ، حتّىٰ يَصطَلِحا؟![٧١٩٩]

391

GUIDANCE

الهِدايَةُ

1791. General Divine Guidance

١٧٩١ ـ الهِدايَةُ الإلٰهِيَّةُ العامَّةُ

"He said, 'Our Lord is He who gave everything its creation and then guided it."[7234]

﴿قَالَ رَبُّنَا الَّذِي أَعْطَىٰ كُلَّ شَيْءٍ خَلْقَهُ ثُمَّ هَدَىٰ﴾.[٧٢٠٠]

6353. **Imām al-Ṣādiq (AS),** with regard to Allah's verse in the Qur'an: *"Indeed We have guided him to the way, be he grateful or ungrateful"*[7235] said, 'We made them know it [i.e. the right way], they can either take it or leave it.'[7236]

٦٣٥٣. الإمامُ الصّادقُ عليه السلام ـ في قولِهِ عَزَّوجلَّ: ﴿إنّا هَدَيْناهُ السَّبيلَ...﴾[٧٢٠١] ـ: عَرَّفناهُ إمّا آخِذاً وإمّا تارِكاً.[٧٢٠٢]

1792. Living with Guidance

١٧٩٢ ـ الإحياءُ بِالهِدايَةِ

"...and whoever saves a life is as though he had saved all mankind."[7237]

﴿وَمَنْ أَحْيَاهَا فَكَأَنَّمَا أَحْيَا النَّاسَ جَمِيعاً﴾.[٧٢٠٣]

6354. **Imām al-Ṣādiq (AS),** when asked about the above verse, said, 'Whoever takes it [i.e. a person's soul] out of error and into guidance is as if he has revived it. And whoever takes it out from guidance into error is as if he has killed it.'[7238]

٦٣٥٤. الإمامُ الصّادقُ عليه السلام ـ لَمّا سُئل عَنِ الآيَةِ ـ: مَن أخرَجَها مِن ضَلالٍ إلىٰ هُدىٰ فكأنّما أحياها، ومَن أخرَجَها مِن هُدىً إلىٰ ضَلالٍ فَقَد قَتَلَها.[٧٢٠٤]

1793. The Reward for Guidance

١٧٩٣ ـ ثَوابُ الهِدايَةِ

6355. It is narrated in *Biḥār al-Anwār*: 'Prophet David (AS) left for the desert by himself, so Allah revealed to him, 'O David, why is it that I see you by yourself?' He said, 'O Allah, my yearning for meeting You has become extreme, and has become

٦٣٥٥. بحارالأنوار: رُويَ أنّ داوودَ عليه السلام خَرَجَ مُصحِراً مُنفَرِداً، فأوحَى اللهُ إلَيهِ: يا داوودُ، مالِي

an obstruction between me and Your creation.' So, Allah revealed to him, 'Return to them, for if you bring me a runaway servant I will inscribe you in the Tablet as praised.'[7239]

أراكَ وَحدانِيّاً ؟ فقالَ : إلٰهي اشتَدَّ الشَّوقُ مِنّي إلىٰ لِقائكَ ، وحالَ بَيني وبَينَ خَلقِكَ ، فأوحَى اللهُ إلَيهِ : ارجِعْ إلَيهِم ؛ فإنّكَ إن تَأتِني بِعَبدٍ آبِقٍ اُثْبِتْكَ في اللَّوحِ حَميداً .[٧٢٠٥]

6356. **The Prophet (SAWA) said** to Imām 'Alī (AS) when he sent him to Yemen, 'O 'Alī, do not fight anyone without [first] inviting them [to Islam]. By Allah, that Allah should guide a person through your hands is better for you than everything that the sun rises and sets on, and you will have his allegiance, O 'Alī.'[7240]

٦٣٥٦ . رسولُ اللهِ ﷺ ـ لعليٍّ ؑ لَمّا بَعَثَهُ إلَى اليَمَنِ ـ : يا عليُّ ، لا تُقاتِلَنَّ أحَداً حتّىٰ تَدعُوَهُ ، وايمُ اللهِ لَأن يَهدي اللهُ علىٰ يَدَيكَ رجُلاً خَيرٌ لَكَ مِمّا طَلَعَت علَيهِ الشَّمسُ وغَرَبَت ، ولَكَ وَلاؤهُ يا عليُّ .[٧٢٠٦]

6357. **The Prophet (SAWA) said** to a person asking him for advice, 'I advise you not to associate anything with Allah....and call people to Islam, and know that for every person that is guided by you, you will get the reward of having freed a slave from the offspring of Jacob.'[7241]

٦٣٥٧ . عنه ﷺ ـ لرجُلٍ سألَهُ أن يُوصِيَهُ ـ : اُوصِيكَ أن لا تُشرِكَ باللهِ شَيئاً ... وادْعُ النّاسَ إلَى الإسلامِ ، واعلَمْ أنّ لكَ بكُلِّ مَن أجابَكَ عِتقَ رَقَبَةٍ مِن وُلدِ يَعقوبَ .[٧٢٠٧]

1794. Guidance Being Exclusively from Allah

١٧٩٤ ـ اختِصاصُ الهِدايَةِ بِاللهِ

"You cannot guide whomever you wish, but [it is] Allah [who] guides whomever He wishes, and He knows best those who are guided."[7242]

﴿إنَّكَ لَا تَهْدِي مَنْ أَحْبَبْتَ وَلٰكِنَّ اللهَ يَهْدِي مَنْ يَشاءُ وَهُوَ أَعْلَمُ بِالْمُهْتَدِينَ﴾ .[٧٢٠٨]

6358. **The Prophet (SAWA) said,** 'Allah Almighty said, 'My servants, all of you are astray save he whom I have guided, and all of you are poor except for he whom I have enriched, and all of you are sinners except for he whom I protect from them.'[7243]

٦٣٥٨ . رسولُ اللهِ ﷺ : قالَ اللهُ جلّ جلالُهُ : عِبادِي ، كُلُّكُم ضالٌّ إلّا مَن هَدَيتُهُ ، وكَلُّكُم فَقيرٌ إلّا مَن أغنَيتُهُ ، وكُلُّكُم مُذنِبٌ إلّا مَن عَصَمتُهُ .[٧٢٠٩]

6359. **The Prophet (SAWA) said,** 'I was sent as a caller and a propagator, and I do not have [the power] to guide by myself, and Satan was created to make [people's deeds] decorous [to them], but he does not [have the power to] lead anything astray.'[7244]

٦٣٥٩ . عنه ﷺ : بُعِثتُ داعِياً ومُبَلِّغاً ولَيسَ إلَيَّ مِن الهُدىٰ شَيءٌ ، وخُلِقَ إبليسُ مُزَيِّناً ولَيسَ إلَيهِ مِن الضَّلالَةِ شَيءٌ .[٧٢١٠]

1795. Those Whom Allah Guides

١٧٩٥ ـ مَن يَهديهِمُ اللهُ

"No affliction visits [anyone] except by Allah's leave. Whoever has faith in Allah, He guides his heart, and Allah has knowledge of all things."[7245]

﴿مَا أَصَابَ مِنْ مُصِيبَةٍ إِلَّا بِإِذْنِ اللهِ وَمَنْ يُؤْمِنْ بِاللهِ يَهْدِ قَلْبَهُ وَاللهُ بِكُلِّ شَيْءٍ عَلِيمٌ﴾.[٧٢١١]

"As for those who strive in Us, We shall guide them to Our ways, and Allah is indeed with the virtuous."[7246]

﴿وَالَّذِينَ جَاهَدُوا فِينَا لَنَهْدِيَنَّهُمْ سُبُلَنَا وَإِنَّ اللهَ لَمَعَ الْمُحْسِنِينَ﴾.[٧٢١٢]

"Indeed Allah does not guide the wrongdoing lot."[7247]

﴿إِنَّ اللهَ لَا يَهْدِي الْقَوْمَ الظَّالِمِينَ﴾.[٧٢١٣]

"Indeed Allah does not guide the faithless lot."[7248]

﴿إِنَّ اللهَ لَا يَهْدِي الْقَوْمَ الْكَافِرِينَ﴾.[٧٢١٤]

6360. **Imām al-Bāqir (AS) said** in his letter to Saʿd al-Khair, 'Allah, Blessed and most High, the Clement and all-Knowing, only becomes angry with those who do not accept His satisfaction, and He only prohibits those who do not accept His gifts. Verily, He only causes to go astray those who do not accept from Him His guidance.'[7249]

٦٣٦٠. الإمامُ الباقرُ (ع) ـ في كِتابِهِ إلىٰ سَعدِ الخَيرِ ـ: إنّ اللهَ تباركَ وتعالىٰ الحَليمَ العَليمَ، إنّما غَضَبُهُ علىٰ مَن لَم يَقبَلْ مِنهُ رِضاهُ، وإنّما يَمنَعُ مَن لَم يَقبَلْ مِنهُ عَطاهُ، وإنّما يُضِلُّ مَن لَم يَقبَلْ مِنهُ هُداهُ.[٧٢١٥]

392

THE GIFT

الهَدِيَّة

1796. Encouraging Giving Gifts

١٧٩٦ ـ الحَثُّ عَلَى الهَدِيَّةِ

6361. **The Prophet (SAWA) said,** 'Give gifts to each other and you will love each other; give gifts to each other for it removes grudges.'[7250]

٦٣٦١. رسولُ اللهِ ﷺ: تَهادَوا تَحابُّوا، تَهادُوا فإنَّها تَذهَبُ بالضَّغائنِ.[٧٢١٦]

6362. **The Prophet (SAWA) said,** 'A gift brings about affection, reinforces brotherhood, and removes grudges. Give gifts to each other and you will love each other.'[7251]

٦٣٦٢. عنه ﷺ: الهَدِيَّةُ تُورِثُ المَوَدَّةَ، وتَجدُرُ[٧٢١٧] الأُخُوَّةَ، وتُذهِبُ الضَّغينَةَ، تَهادَوا تَحابُّوا.[٧٢١٨]

6363. **Imām ʿAlī (AS) said,** 'Giving a gift to my Muslim brother that he would benefit from is more beloved to me than giving its like in charity.'[7252]

٦٣٦٣. الإمامُ عليٌّ (ع): لَأَن أُهدِيَ لِأَخي المُسلِمِ هَدِيَّةً تَنفَعُهُ أحَبُّ إلَيَّ مِن أن أتَصَدَّقَ بِمِثلِها.[٧٢١٩]

1797. The Prohibition of Gifts to Administrators

١٧٩٧ ـ حُرمَةُ هَدايا العُمّالِ

6364. **The Prophet (SAWA) said,** 'Gifts to administrators [of the government] are forbidden, all [kinds] of them.'[7253]

٦٣٦٤ . رسولُ اللهِ ﷺ : هَدايا العُمّالِ غُلولٌ.[٧٢٢٠]

6365. Abū Ḥamīd al-Shāhidī said, 'The Prophet (SAWA) employed a man from the tribe of Banī Asad who was called Ibn al-Utbiyya to go and collect some charity and when he came back, he said, 'This is for you, and this is my gift [assuming possession of some of the donation for himself].' So the Prophet (SAWA) ascended the pulpit. He praised Allah and extolled Him, and said, 'What is it with the administrator who we send [to work] and he comes back and says, 'This is for you and this is for me!' He should sit in the house of his mother and father and see if he is given a gift or not?! By He who owns my soul, anything that he takes he will be carrying on his neck on the Day of Resurrection, even if it is a grumbling camel, a bellowing cow, or a moaning sheep.'[7254]

٦٣٦٥ . أبو حميد الشاهدي : استَعمَلَ النَّبيُّ ﷺ رجُلاً مِن بَني أسَدٍ يُقال لَهُ ابنُ الاُتبِيّةِ علىٰ صَدَقَةٍ، فلَمّا قَدِمَ قالَ: هٰذا لَكُم و هٰذا اُهدِيَ لِي، فقامَ النَّبيُّ ﷺ عَلَى المِنبَرِ... فحَمِدَ اللهَ وأثنىٰ علَيهِ ثُمّ قالَ: ما بالُ العامِلِ نَبعَثُهُ، فَيأتي فيقولُ : هٰذا لَكَ و هٰذا لِي ؟! فهَلّا جَلَسَ في بَيتِ أبِيهِ واُمِّهِ فيَنظُرَ أيُهدىٰ لَهُ أم لا ؟ وَالّذي نَفسي بِيَدِهِ لا يَأتي بشَيءٍ إلّا جاءَ بِهِ يَومَ القِيامَةِ يَحمِلُهُ علىٰ رَقَبَتِهِ ، إن كانَ بَعيراً لَهُ رُغاءٌ أو بَقَرَةً لَها خُوارٌ أو شاةً تَيعَرُ.[٧٢٢١]

1798. Prohibition of Accepting Gifts from Polytheists

١٧٩٨ ـ النَّهيُ عَن قَبولِ هَدِيَّةِ المُشرِكِ

6366. **The Prophet (SAWA) said,** 'We do not accept the gift of a polytheist.'[7255]

٦٣٦٦ . رسولُ اللهِ ﷺ : إنّا لا نَقبَلُ هَدِيَةَ مُشرِكٍ.[٧٢٢٢]

6367. **Imām ʿAlī (AS) said,** 'The Prophet (SAWA) prohibited the [acceptance of] gifts from the polytheists, meaning gifts from people who were at war with Muslims.'[7256]

٦٣٦٧ . الإمامُ عليٌّ عليه السلام : إنّ رسولَ اللهِ ﷺ نَهىٰ عَن زَبْدِ المُشرِكينَ ؛ يُريدُ هَدايا أهلِ الحَربِ.[٧٢٢٣]

1799. Enjoinment of Accepting a Gift

١٧٩٩ ـ الحَثُّ عَلىٰ قَبولِ الهَدِيَّةِ

6368. **The Prophet (SAWA) said,** 'If an animal's leg was gifted to me, I would accept it.'[7257]

٦٣٦٨ . رسولُ اللهِ ﷺ : لَو اُهدِيَ إلَيَّ كُراعٌ[٧٢٢٤] لَقَبِلتُهُ.[٧٢٢٥]

6369. **The Prophet (SAWA) said,** 'A person's honouring of his Muslim brother entails accepting his gift, and that he give him from what he has, and that he does not burden himself for him in any way.'[7258]

٦٣٦٩ . عنه ﷺ : مِن تَكرِمَةِ الرّجُلِ لأخيهِ المُسلمِ أن يَقبَلَ تُحفَتَهُ، ويُتحِفَهُ بما عِندَهُ، ولا يَتَكَلّفَ لَهُ شيئاً .[٧٢٢٦]

6370. **The Prophet (SAWA) said** to ʿĀ'isha when a poor lady gave her a gift and she did not accept it in compassion for her, 'Why did you not accept it and recompense her with its equivalent?! Do you not see that you have humiliated her? O ʿĀ'isha, be humble for Allah loves the humble and hates the haughty.'[7259]

٦٣٧٠ . عنه ﷺ ـ لِعائشةَ لَمّا أهدَت إلَيها امرأةٌ مِسكينَةٌ هَدِيَّةً فلَم تَقبَلْها رَحمَةً لَها ـ : ألَا قَبِلتيها مِنها وكافَيتيها مِنها؟! فلا تَرىٰ أنَّكِ حَقَّرتيها ! يا عائشةُ، تَواضَعي فإنَّ اللهَ يُحِبُّ المُتواضِعينَ ويُبغِضُ المُستَكبِرينَ .[٧٢٢٧]

(See also: KINDNESS: section 1597)

(اُنظر) الكرم: باب ١٥٩٧.

1800. Taking Back One's Gift

١٨٠٠ ـ العائِدُ في هِبَتِهِ

6371. **The Prophet (SAWA) said,** 'One who takes back a gift he has given is like one who swallows his own vomit.'[7260]

٦٣٧١ . رسولُ اللهِ ﷺ : العائدُ فِي هِبَتِهِ كالعائدِ في قَيئهِ .[٧٢٢٨]

6372. **Imām al-Ṣādiq (AS) said** regarding a man who goes out with charity to give it to a beggar only to find that he has gone, 'Then he should give it to someone else and not return it back to his wealth.'[7261]

٦٣٧٢ . الإمامُ الصّادقُ عليه السلام ـ في الرّجُلِ يَخرُجُ بِالصَّدَقَةِ لِيُعطِيَها السّائلَ فيَجِدَهُ قد ذَهَبَ ـ : فلْيُعطِها غيرَهُ، ولا يَرُدَّها في مالِهِ .[٧٢٢٩]

393

OLD AGE

الهَرَمُ

1801. Senility

١٨٠١ ـ الهَرَمُ

6373. **The Prophet (SAWA) said,** 'Man is such that ninety nine deaths are decreed for him, and if the deaths were to miss him, he would fall into senility.'[7262]

٦٣٧٣ . رسولُ اللهِ ﷺ : مَثُلَ ابنُ آدَمَ وإلىٰ جَنبِهِ تِسعٌ وتِسعونَ مَنِيَّةً، إن أخطَأتهُ المَنايا وَقَعَ في الهَرَمِ .[٧٢٣٠]

6374. **Imām ʿAlī (AS) said,** 'The outcome of a long life is sickness and senility.'[7263]

٦٣٧٤. الإمامُ عليٌّ ﷺ: ثَمَرَةُ طُولِ الحَياةِ السَّقَمُ والهَرَمُ.٧٢٣١

1802. What Breaks Out in a Human when he Becomes Senile [in Old Age]

١٨٠٢ - مايَشِبُّ فِي الإنسانِ عِندَ هَرَمِهِ

6375. **The Prophet (SAWA) said,** 'Man becomes senile, and two things erupt in him: greed and expectation.'[7264]

٦٣٧٥. رسولُ اللهِ ﷺ: يَهرَمُ ابنُ آدَمَ وتَشِبُّ مِنهُ اثنَتانِ: الحِرصُ والأمَلُ.٧٢٣٢

6376. **The Prophet (SAWA) said,** 'When man becomes senile, two things erupt in him: greed for wealth and greed for age [life].'[7265]

٦٣٧٦. عنه ﷺ: يَهرَمُ ابنُ آدَمَ ويَشِبُّ مِنهُ اثنانِ: الحِرصُ علَى المالِ، والحِرصُ علَى العُمرِ.٧٢٣٣

1803. What Brings About Senility Before its Time

١٨٠٣ - موجِباتُ الهَرَمِ قَبلَ أوانِهِ

6377. **Imām ʿAlī (AS) said,** 'Worry is half of senility.'[7266]

٦٣٧٧. الإمامُ عليٌّ ﷺ: الهَمُّ نِصفُ الهَرَمِ.٧٢٣٤

6378. **Imām al-Ṣādiq (AS) said,** 'There are four things that bring about senility before the time of old age: the eating of dry meat, sitting on humid places, climbing stairs, and copulating old people.'[7267]

٦٣٧٨. الإمامُ الصّادقُ ﷺ: أربَعَةٌ تُهرِمُ قَبلَ أوانِ الهَرَمِ: أكلُ القَديدِ، والقُعودُ علَى النَّداوَةِ، والصُّعودُ فِي الدَّرَجِ، ومُجامَعَةُ العَجوزِ.٧٢٣٥

394

DESTRUCTION

الهَلاكُ

1804. What Brings About Destruction

١٨٠٤ - ما يوجِبُ الهَلاكَ

"We would never destroy the towns except when their people were wrongdoers."[7268]

﴿وَمَا كُنَّا مُهْلِكِي الْقُرَى إِلَّا وَأَهْلُهَا ظَالِمُونَ﴾.٧٢٣٦

(See also: Qur'an: 10:13, 22:45, 8:54, 18:59, 26:139, 44:37, 14:13)

(انظر) يونس ١٣ والحج: ٤٥ والأنفال: ٥٤ والكهف: ٥٩ والشعراء: ١٣٩ والدخان: ٣٧ وإبراهيم: ١٣.

6379. **The Prophet (SAWA) said,** 'As for the destroyers, [they are]: greed obeyed, inclinations [desires] followed, and a man's admiration of himself.'[7269]

٦٣٧٩ . رسولُ اللهِ ﷺ: أمّا المُهلِكاتُ: فشُحٌّ مُطاعٌ، وهَوىً مُتَّبَعٌ، وإعجابُ المَرءِ بنَفسِهِ.[٧٢٣٧]

6380. **The Prophet (SAWA) said,** 'Verily the dinar and the dirham have destroyed those before you, and they will destroy you too.'[7270]

٦٣٨٠ . عنه ﷺ: إنّ الدِّينارَ والدِّرهَمَ أهلَكا مَن كانَ قَبلَكُم، وهُما مُهلِكاكُم.[٧٢٣٨]

6381. **Imām ʿAlī (AS) said,** 'Verily those who perished before you did so because they embarked upon sins, and the priests and clergies did not prohibit them...'[7271]

٦٣٨١ . الإمامُ عليٌّ ﷺ: إنّما هَلَكَ مَن هَلَكَ مِمَّن كانَ قَبلَكُم بِرُكوبِهِمُ المَعاصي، ولَم يَنهَهُم الرَّبّانِيّونَ والأحبارُ...[٧٢٣٩]

6382. **Imām ʿAlī (AS) said,** 'He who sells certainty for doubt, and truth for falsehood, and the Hereafter for the present [life] will perish.'[7272]

٦٣٨٢ . عنه ﷺ: هَلَكَ مَن باعَ اليَقينَ بِالشَّكِّ، والحَقَّ بِالباطِلِ، والآجِلَ بِالعاجِلِ.[٧٢٤٠]

6383. **Imām ʿAlī (AS) said,** 'He who does not know his own value will perish.'[7273]

٦٣٨٣ . عنه ﷺ: هَلَكَ امرُؤٌ لَم يَعرِفْ قَدرَهُ.[٧٢٤١]

6384. **Imām ʿAlī (AS) said,** 'Two kinds of people perish because of me: one who has extreme love [for me] and one who is a debased hater [of me].'[7274]

٦٣٨٤ . عنه ﷺ: هَلَكَ فِيَّ رَجُلانِ: مُحِبٌّ غالٍ، ومُبغِضٌ قالٍ.[٧٢٤٢]

6385. **Imām al-Ṣādiq (AS) said,** 'There are two destructive features: giving verdicts to people with your own opinion, and to yield to something that you do not know.'[7275]

٦٣٨٥ . الإمامُ الصّادقُ ﷺ: خَصلَتَينِ[٧٢٤٣] مُهلِكَتَينِ: تُفتي النّاسَ بِرَأيِكَ، أو تَدينُ بِما لا تَعلَمُ.[٧٢٤٤]

6386. **Imām al-Ṣādiq (AS) said,** 'Allah will destroy six things as a result of six other things: rulers for their oppression, Arabs for their partisanship, chiefs for their haughtiness, merchants for their treachery, villagers for their ignorance, and the jurists for their envy.'[7276]

٦٣٨٦ . عنه ﷺ: يُهلِكُ اللهُ سِتّاً بِسِتٍّ: الأُمَراءَ بِالجَورِ، والعَرَبَ بِالعَصَبِيَّةِ، والدَّهاقينَ بِالكِبرِ، والتُّجّارَ بِالخِيانَةِ، وأهلَ الرَّساتيقِ بِالجَهلِ، والفُقَهاءَ بِالحَسَدِ.[٧٢٤٥]

395

AMBITION

الهِمَّة

1805. The Virtue of High Ambition

١٨٠٥ - فَضلُ عُلُوِّ الهِمَّةِ

6387. **The Prophet (SAWA) said,** 'Allah Almighty loves the highest and the most dignified of things and hates inferior things.'[7277]

٦٣٨٧. رسولُ اللهِ ﷺ: إنّ اللهَ تعالىٰ يُحِبُّ مَعالِيَ الأُمورِ وأشرافَها، ويَكرَهُ سَفسافَها.[٧٢٤٦]

6388. **Imām ʿAlī (AS) said,** 'The worth of a man is according to the extent of his ambition.'[7278]

٦٣٨٨. الإمامُ عليٌّ ﷺ: قَدرُ الرَّجُلِ علىٰ قَدرِ هِمَّتِهِ.[٧٢٤٧]

6389. **Imām ʿAlī (AS) said,** 'He whose ambition is lofty his value is heightened.'[7279]

٦٣٨٩. عنه ﷺ: مَن شَرُفَت هِمَّتُهُ عَظُمَت قيمَتُهُ.[٧٢٤٨]

6390. **Imām Zayn al-ʿĀbidīn (AS),** in a supplication, said, 'I ask You for the most fair witnessing, and the most active of worship ... and the highest ambition.'[7280]

٦٣٩٠. الإمامُ زينُ العابدينَ ﷺ - في الدُّعاءِ -: أسألُكَ مِنَ الشَّهادَةِ أقسَطَها، ومِنَ العِبادَةِ أنشَطَها... ومِنَ الهِمَمِ أعلاها.[٧٢٤٩]

6391. **Imām al-Bāqir (AS) said,** 'There is no dignity like great ambition.'[7281]

٦٣٩١. الإمامُ الباقرُ ﷺ: لا شَرَفَ كَبُعدِ الهِمَّةِ.[٧٢٥٠]

1806. The Benefits of High Ambition

١٨٠٦ - ثَمَراتُ عُلُوِّ الهِمَّةِ

6392. **Imām ʿAlī (AS) said,** 'Tolerance and sobriety are twins, and high ambition produces them.'[7282]

٦٣٩٢. الإمامُ عليٌّ ﷺ: الحِلمُ والأناةُ تَوأمانِ يُنتِجُهُما عُلُوُّ الهِمَّةِ.[٧٢٥١]

6393. **Imām ʿAlī (AS) said,** 'Generosity is the product of high ambition.'[7283]

٦٣٩٣. عنه ﷺ: الكَرَمُ نَتيجَةُ عُلُوِّ الهِمَّةِ.[٧٢٥٢]

6394. **Imām ʿAlī (AS) said,** 'Good action is a sign of high ambition.'[7284]

٦٣٩٤. عنه ﷺ: الفِعلُ الجَميلُ يُنبِئُ عَن عُلُوِّ الهِمَّةِ.[٧٢٥٣]

6395. **Imām ʿAlī (AS) said,** 'Worries are proportionate to the extent of one's ambition.'[7285]

٦٣٩٥. عنه ﷺ: بِقَدرِ الهِمَمِ تَكونُ الهُمومُ.[٧٢٥٤]

6396. **Imām ʿAlī (AS) said,** 'Enthusiasm is proportionate to the extent of one's ambition.'[7286]

٦٣٩٦. عنه ﷺ: عـلىٰ قـدرِ الهِـمَّةِ تكـونُ الحَمِيَّةُ.٧٢٥٥

6397. **Imām ʿAlī (AS) said,** 'The bravery of a man is proportionate to his ambition.[7287]

٦٣٩٧. عنه ﷺ: شَجاعَةُ الرَّجُـلِ عـلىٰ قَـدرِ هِمَّتِهِ.٧٢٥٦

6398. **Imām al-Bāqir (AS) said,** 'Attract the dignity of dismay with far ambition.'[7288]

٦٣٩٨. الإمامُ الباقرُ ﷺ: اِستَجلِبْ عِـزَّ اليأسِ بِبُعدِ الهِمَّةِ.٧٢٥٧

1807. Low Ambition

١٨٠٧ـ قِصَرُ الهِمَّةِ

6399. **Imām ʿAlī (AS) said,** 'He who has low ambition, his virtue ceases.'[7289]

٦٣٩٩. الإمامُ عليٌّ ﷺ: مَن صَغُرَت هِمَّتُهُ بَطَلَت فَضيلَتُهُ.٧٢٥٨

6400. **Imām ʿAlī (AS) said,** 'He whose ambition is short, he will envy a friend in his blessings.'[7290]

٦٤٠٠. عنه ﷺ: مِن صِغَرِ الهِمَّةِ حَسَدُ الصَّديقِ علَى النِّعمَةِ.٧٢٥٩

6401. **Imām ʿAlī (AS) said,** 'A disgraceful person has no ambition.'[7291]

٦٤٠١. عنه ﷺ: لا هِمَّةَ لِمَهينٍ.٧٢٦٠

6402. **Imām al-Ṣādiq (AS) said,** 'There are three things that hinder a person from seeking the lofty: low ambition, few stratagems, and weak opinion.'[7292]

٦٤٠٢. الإمامُ الصّادقُ ﷺ: ثَلاثٌ يَحجُزنَ المرءَ عَن طَلَبِ المَعالي: قِصَرُ الهِمَّةِ، وقِـلَّةُ الحِـيلَةِ، وضَعفُ الرَّأيِ.٧٢٦١

1808. He whose Sole Concern is his Stomach

١٨٠٨ـ مَن كانَت هِمَّتُهُ بَطنَهُ

6403. **The Prophet (SAWA) said,** 'He whose sole concern is his food, his worth is [equivalent] to that which he eats.'[7293]

٦٤٠٣. رسولُ اللهِ ﷺ: مَن كانَت هِمَّتُهُ أكـلَهُ، كانَت قِيمَتُهُ ما أكَلَهُ.٧٢٦٢

6404. **Imām ʿAlī (AS) said,** 'He whose sole concern is what enters his stomach, his worth is [equivalent to] what comes out of it.'[7294]

٦٤٠٤. الإمامُ عليٌّ ﷺ: مَن كانَت هِمَّتُهُ ما يَدخُلُ بَطنَهُ، كانَت قِيمَتُهُ ما يَخرُجُ مِنهُ.٧٢٦٣

6405. **Imām ʿAlī (AS) said,** 'How far away is goodness from he whose sole concern is his stomach and private parts.'[7295]

٦٤٠٥. عنه ﷺ: ما أبعَدَ الخَيرَ مِمَّن هِمَّتُهُ بَطنُهُ وفَرجُهُ!٧٢٦٤

(See also: FOOD: section 64)

(انظر) الأكل: باب ٦٤

396

THE DESIRE

الهَوىٰ

1809. Desire is a Worshipped God

١٨٠٩ ـ الهَوىٰ إلٰهٌ مَعبودٌ

"Have you seen him who has taken his desire to be his god and whom Allah has led astray knowingly, and set a seal upon his hearing and his heart, and drawn a blind on his sight? So who will guide him after Allah? Will you not then take admonition?"[7296]

﴿أَفَرَأَيْتَ مَنِ اتَّخَذَ إِلٰهَهُ هَوَاهُ وأَضَلَّهُ اللهُ عَلَىٰ عِلْمٍ وَخَتَمَ عَلَىٰ سَمْعِهِ وَقَلْبِهِ وَجَعَلَ عَلَىٰ بَصَرِهِ غِشَاوَةً فَمَنْ يَهْدِيهِ مِنْ بَعْدِ اللهِ أَفَلَا تَذَكَّرُونَ﴾.[٧٢٦٥]

6406. **The Prophet (SAWA) said,** 'There is no god worshipped beneath the shadow of the sky other than Allah, considered worse by Allah than a desire pursued.'[7297]

٦٤٠٦. رسولُ اللهِ ﷺ: ما تَحتَ ظِلِّ السَّماءِ مِن إلٰهٍ يُعبَدُ مِن دُونِ اللهِ أعظَمَ عِندَ اللهِ مِن هَوىً مُتَّبَعٍ.[٧٢٦٦]

6407. **Imām ʿAlī (AS) said,** 'The desire is a worshipped god, and the intellect is a praiseworthy friend.'[7298]

٦٤٠٧. الإمامُ عليٌّ عليه السلام: الهَوىٰ إلٰهٌ مَعبودٌ، العَقلُ صَديقٌ مَحمودٌ.[٧٢٦٧]

6408. **Imām ʿAlī (AS) said,** 'An ignorant person is a worshipper of his desires.'[7299]

٦٤٠٨. عنه عليه السلام: الجاهِلُ عَبدُ شَهوَتِهِ.[٧٢٦٨]

1810. Warning Against Following Desire

١٨١٠ ـ التَّحذِيرُ مِن اتِّباعِ الهَوىٰ

6409. **The Prophet (SAWA) said,** 'Desires *(hawā)* have been called thus because they overthrow *(yahwī)* the one who possesses them.'[7300]

٦٤٠٩. رسولُ اللهِ ﷺ: إنّما سُمِّيَ الهَوىٰ لأنّهُ يَهوي بصاحِبِهِ.[٧٢٦٩]

6410. **The Prophet (SAWA) said,** 'Satan said, 'I have destroyed them with sins and they have destroyed me with their seeking for forgiveness from Allah, so when I saw this, I destroyed them with their own desire, so they think that they are guided and they do not seek forgiveness.'[7301]

٦٤١٠. عنه ﷺ: إنّ إبليسَ قالَ: أهلَكتُهُم بالذُّنوبِ فأهلَكوني بالاستِغفارِ، فلَمّا رأيتُ ذلكَ أهلَكتُهُم بالأهواءِ فهُم يَحسَبونَ أنّهُم مُهتَدونَ فلا يَستَغفِرونَ.[٧٢٧٠]

6411. **Imām ʿAlī (AS) said,** 'The onset of calamities is when desires are followed, laws are innovated...'[7302]

٦٤١١. الإمامُ عليٌّ ﷺ: إنّما بَدءُ وُقوعِ الفِتَنِ أهواءٌ تُتَّبَعُ، وأحكامٌ تُبتَدَعُ....٧٢٧١

6412. **Imām ʿAlī (AS),** when asked about the most conquering and strongest of rulers, said, 'The desire.'[7303]

٦٤١٢. عنه ﷺ ـ لمّا سُئلَ عن أغلَبِ السَّلاطينِ وأقواها قالَ ـ: الهَوى.٧٢٧٢

6413. **Imām ʿAlī (AS) said,** 'Heaven is encircled by sufferings and troubles and Hell is encircled with desires.'[7304]

٦٤١٣. عنه ﷺ: إنّ الجَنّةَ حُفَّت بالمَكارِهِ، وإنّ النّارَ حُفَّت (حُجِبَت) بالشَّهَواتِ.٧٢٧٣

6414. **Imām ʿAlī (AS) said,** 'Pleasure deters [from Allah and the hereafter].'[7305]

٦٤١٤. عنه ﷺ: اللَّذّةُ تُلهي.٧٢٧٤

6415. **Imām ʿAlī (AS) said,** 'It is seldom that he who is seduced by pleasures is not destroyed by them.'[7306]

٦٤١٥. عنه ﷺ: قَلَّ مَن غَرِيَ باللَّذّاتِ إلّا كانَ بها هَلاكُهُ.٧٢٧٥

1811. The Effects of Yielding to One's Desires

١٨١١ ـ آثارُ اتّباعِ الهَوى

"Rather the wrongdoers follow their own desires without any knowledge. So who will guide those whom Allah has led astray? They will have no helpers."[7307]

﴿بَلِ اتَّبَعَ الَّذِينَ ظَلَمُوا أَهْوَاءَهُمْ بِغَيْرِ عِلْمٍ فَمَنْ يَهْدِي مَنْ أَضَلَّ اللهُ وَمَالَهُمْ مِنْ نَاصِرِينَ﴾.٧٢٧٦

6416. **The Prophet (SAWA) said,** 'Many a desire of one moment brings about long-lasting grief.'[7308]

٦٤١٦. رسولُ اللهِ ﷺ: رُبَّ شَهوَةِ ساعَةٍ تُورِثُ حُزناً طَويلاً.٧٢٧٧

6417. **Imām ʿAlī (AS) said,** 'I advise you to keep away from desires, for desires instigate blindness, and it is straying both in the Hereafter and in this world.'[7309]

٦٤١٧. الإمامُ عليٌّ ﷺ: أُوصيكُم بمُجانَبَةِ الهَوى؛ فإنّ الهَوى يَدعو إلَى العَمى، وهُوَ الضَّلالُ في الآخِرَةِ والدُّنيا.٧٢٧٨

6418. **Imām ʿAlī (AS) said,** 'The desire is the partner of blindness.'[7310]

٦٤١٨. عنه ﷺ: الهَوى شَريكُ العَمى.٧٢٧٩

6419. **Imām ʿAlī (AS) said,** 'He who follows his desires, it blinds him, deafens him, humiliates him, and leads him astray.'[7311]

٦٤١٩. عنه ﷺ: مَنِ اتَّبَعَ هَواهُ أعماهُ، وأصَمَّهُ، وأذَلَّهُ، وأضَلَّهُ.٧٢٨٠

6420. **Imām ʿAlī (AS) said,** 'The beginning of desire is [heralded] by joy, and its end by ruin.'[7312]

٦٤٢٠. عنه ﷺ: أوَّلُ الشَّهوَةِ طَرَبٌ، وآخِرُها عَطَبٌ.[٧٢٨١]

6421. **Imām ʿAlī (AS) said,** 'Beware of having desires overcome your hearts, for their beginning is an enslavement and their end is ruin.'[7313]

٦٤٢١. عنه ﷺ: إيّاكُم وغَلَبَةَ الشَّهَواتِ علىٰ قُلوبِكُم؛ فإنَّ بِدايَتَها مَلَكَةٌ، ونِهايَتَها هَلَكَةٌ.[٧٢٨٢]

6422. **Imām ʿAlī (AS) said,** 'The associate of the desire has a sick soul and an ill intellect.'[7314]

٦٤٢٢. عنه ﷺ: قَرينُ الشَّهوَةِ مَريضُ النَّفسِ، مَعلولُ العَقلِ.[٧٢٨٣]

6423. **Imām ʿAlī (AS) said,** 'The slave of his own desire is more humiliated than an owned slave.'[7315]

٦٤٢٣. عنه ﷺ: عَبدُ الشَّهوَةِ أذَلُّ مِن عَبدِ الرِّقِّ.[٧٢٨٤]

6424. **Imām ʿAlī (AS) said,** 'How many an imprisoned intellect is under the power of a commanding desire!'[7316]

٦٤٢٤. عنه ﷺ: كَم مِن عَقلٍ أسيرٍ تَحتَ هَوىٰ أميرٍ![٧٢٨٥]

6425. **Imām ʿAlī (AS) said,** 'He who obeys his self in its desires has aided in its destruction.'[7317]

٦٤٢٥. عنه ﷺ: مَن أطاعَ نَفسَهُ في شَهَواتِها فَقَد أعانَها علىٰ هُلْكِها.[٧٢٨٦]

6426. **Imām ʿAlī (AS) said,** 'He who takes pleasure in acts of disobedience to Allah, Allah will strike him with humiliation.'[7318]

٦٤٢٦. عنه ﷺ: مَن تَلَذَّذَ بِمَعاصي اللهِ أورَثَهُ اللهُ ذُلّاً.[٧٢٨٧]

6427. **Imām al-Ṣādiq (AS) said,** 'Be on your guard against your desires as you guard against your enemies, for there is nothing worse as an enemy to men than following their desires and the consequences of their tongues [i.e. speech].'[7319]

٦٤٢٧. الإمامُ الصّادقُ ﷺ: احذَروا أهواءَكُم كما تَحذَرونَ أعداءَكُم، فلَيسَ شيءٌ أعدىٰ لِلرِّجالِ مِن اتِّباعِ أهوائهِم، وحَصائدِ ألسِنَتِهِم.[٧٢٨٨]

1812. Opposing One's Desires

١٨١٢ ـ مُخالَفَةُ الهَوىٰ

"But as for him who is awed to stand before his Lord and forbids the soul from [following] desire, his refuge will indeed be paradise."[7320]

﴿وَأَمَّا مَنْ خَافَ مَقَامَ رَبِّهِ وَنَهَى النَّفْسَ عَنِ الْهَوَىٰ * فَإِنَّ الْجَنَّةَ هِيَ الْمَأْوَىٰ﴾.[٧٢٨٩]

6428. It is narrated in *al-Kāfī*: From what Allah advised Jesus (AS): 'O Jesus, do not wake up disobedient and do not regain consciousness [engaged] in amusement. Wean yourself away from destructive desires, and abandon every passion that distances you from Me.'[7321]

٦٤٢٨. الكافي: فيما وَعَظَ اللهُ تعالىٰ بهِ عيسىٰ ﷺ: يا عيسىٰ، لا تَستَيقِظَنَّ عاصِياً ولا تَستَنبِهَنَّ لاهِياً، وافطِمْ نَفسَكَ عَنِ الشَّهَواتِ المُوبِقاتِ، وكُلُّ شَهوَةٍ تُباعِدُكَ مِنّي فاهجُرْها.[٧٢٩٠]

6429. **Imām ʿAlī (AS) said,** 'The peak of reason is to combat desires.'[7322]

٦٤٢٩. الإمامُ عليٌّ ﷺ: رأسُ العَقلِ مُـجاهَدَةُ الهَوىٰ.[٧٢٩١]

6430. **Imām ʿAlī (AS) said,** 'Prohibiting one's self from desire is the greater struggle (*jihād*).'[7323]

٦٤٣٠. عنه ﷺ: رَدْعُ النَّفسِ عَنِ الهوىٰ الجِهادُ الأكبَرُ.[٧٢٩٢]

6431. **Imām ʿAlī (AS) said,** 'Conquer desire the way you would overcome an opponent, and fight it the way you would fight an enemy.'[7324]

٦٤٣١. عنه ﷺ: غالِبِ الهَوىٰ مُغالَبَةَ الخَصمِ خَصمَهُ، وحارِبْهُ مُحارَبَةَ العَدُوِّ عَدُوَّهُ.[٧٢٩٣]

6432. **Imām ʿAlī (AS) said,** 'Conquer your selves through abandoning habits and you will overcome them, and combat your desires and you will control them.'[7325]

٦٤٣٢. عنه ﷺ: غالِبوا أنفُسَكُم علىٰ تَركِ العاداتِ تَغلِبوها، وجاهِدوا أهواءكُم تَملِكُوها.[٧٢٩٤]

6433. **Imām ʿAlī (AS) said,** 'Take over the desire before it becomes ravenously strong, for if it is empowered it will control you and lead you, and you will not be able to resist it.'[7326]

٦٤٣٣. عنه ﷺ: غالِبِ الشَّهوَةَ قَبلَ قُوَّةِ ضَراوَتِها؛ فإنّها إن قَوِيَت مَلَكَتْكَ واستَقادَتْكَ[٧٢٩٥] ولَم تَقدِرْ علىٰ مُقاوَمَتِها.[٧٢٩٦]

6434. **Imām ʿAlī (AS) said,** 'Maturity lies in opposing desires.'[7327]

٦٤٣٤. عنه ﷺ: الرُّشدُ في خِلافِ الشَّهوَةِ.[٧٢٩٧]

6435. **Imām al-Ṣādiq (AS),** when asked, 'Where does the path to comfort lie? replied, 'In opposing desire.'[7328]

٦٤٣٥. الإمامُ الصّادقُ ﷺ ـ لمّا سُئل ـ: أينَ طَريقُ الرّاحَةِ في خِلافِ الهَوىٰ. قيلَ: فمَتىٰ يَجِدُ عَبدٌ الرّاحَةَ؟ فـقالَ ﷺ: عِـندَ أوَّلِ يَـومٍ يَـصيرُ فـي الجَنَّةِ.[٧٢٩٨]

6436. **Imām al-Kāẓim (AS) said,** 'When two things come your way and you do not know which one is good and correct, then look at which one of them is closer to your desire and then oppose it, for most good is found in opposing your desires.'[7329]

٦٤٣٦. الإمامُ الكاظمُ ﷺ: إذا مَرَّ بكَ[٧٢٩٩] أمرانِ لا تَدري أيُّهُما خَيرٌ وأصوَبُ، فانظُرْ أيُّهُما أقـرَبُ إلىٰ هواكَ فخالِفْهُ؛ فإنَّ كَثيرَ الصَّوابِ في مُخالَفَةِ هَواكَ.[٧٣٠٠]

(See also: JIHĀD (2) 77)

(أُنظر) عنوان ٧٧ «الجهاد (٢)».

1813. Overpowering Desire

١٨١٣ ـ غَلَبَةُ الهَوىٰ

6437. **The Prophet (SAWA) said,** 'Allah Almighty said, 'By My Might and Exaltedness... no sooner does a servant prefer his own desire over My desire than I disperse his affairs, disturb his life with his world, occupy his heart with it, and do not give him

٦٤٣٧. رسولُ اللهِ ﷺ: يقولُ اللهُ عَزَّ وجلَّ: وَعِزَّتي وجَلالي... لا يُؤثِرُ عَبدٌ هَـواهُ عـلىٰ هَـوايَ إلّا شَتَّتُّ علَيهِ أمرَهُ، ولَبَّستُ علَيهِ دُنياهُ، وشَـغَلتُ

thereof other than what I have allotted for him.'[7330]

قَلبَهُ بِها، ولَم أُوْتِهِ مِنها إلّا ما قَدَّرتُ لَهُ.[٧٣٠١]

6438. **The Prophet (SAWA) said,** 'It is forbidden for every heart that is ruled by desires to have piety reside therein.'[7331]

٦٤٣٨. عنه ﷺ: حَرامٌ علىٰ كُلِّ قَلبٍ مُتَوَلِّهٍ بِالشَّهَواتِ أن يَسكُنَهُ الوَرَعُ.[٧٣٠٢]

6439. **The Prophet (SAWA) said,** 'It is forbidden for every heart that is full of desires to journey through the realms of the Heavens.'[7332]

٦٤٣٩. عنه ﷺ: حَرامٌ علىٰ كُلِّ قَلبٍ عزّي[٧٣٠٣] بِالشَّهَواتِ أن يَجُولَ في مَلَكوتِ السَّماواتِ.[٧٣٠٤]

6440. **Imām ʿAlī (AS) said,** 'He whose desire becomes strong, his determination weakens.'[7333]

٦٤٤٠. الإمامُ عليٌّ ؈: مَن قَوِيَ هَواهُ ضَعُفَ عَزمُهُ.[٧٣٠٥]

6441. **Imām ʿAlī (AS) said,** 'It is forbidden for every intellect that is shackled by desires to benefit from wisdom.'[7334]

٦٤٤١. عنه ؈: حَرامٌ علىٰ كُلِّ عَقلٍ مَغلولٍ بِالشَّهوَةِ أن يَنتَفِعَ بِالحِكمَةِ.[٧٣٠٦]

6442. **Imām ʿAlī (AS) said,** 'He who cannot control his desire cannot control his intellect.'[7335]

٦٤٤٢. عنه ؈: مَن لَم يَملِكْ شَهوَتَهُ لَم يَملِكْ عَقلَهُ.[٧٣٠٧]

1814. The Most Courageous of People is he who Overcomes his Desires

١٨١٤ - أشجَعُ النّاسِ مَن غَلَبَ هَواهُ

6443. **Solomon (AS) said,** 'Someone who prevails over his desires is stronger than he who captures a city by himself.'[7336]

٦٤٤٣. سُليمانُ ؈: إنّ الغالِبَ لِهَواهُ أشَدُّ مِنَ الّذي يَفتَحُ المَدينَةَ وَحدَهُ.[٧٣٠٨]

6444. **The Prophet (SAWA) said,** 'The most courageous of people is he who overcomes his desires.'[7337]

٦٤٤٤. رسولُ اللهِ ﷺ: أشجَعُ النّاسِ مَن غَلَبَ هَواهُ.[٧٣٠٩]

6445. **The Prophet (SAWA) said,** 'A strong person is not one who overcomes people, but a strong person is one who overcomes his own self.'[7338]

٦٤٤٥. عنه ﷺ: إنّ الشَّديدَ لَيسَ مَن غَلَبَ النّاسَ، ولٰكِنَّ الشَّديدَ مَن غَلَبَ علىٰ نَفسِهِ.[٧٣١٠]

(See also: COURAGE: section 1014)

(أنظر: الشجاعة: باب ١٠١٤)

1815. That which Weakens Carnal Desires

١٨١٥ ـ مايُضعِفُ الشَّهوَةَ

6446. It is narrated in *al-Kāfī*: 'Allah Almighty revealed unto Prophet Moses (AS), 'Remember that you will be residing in a grave, and that will prevent you from a lot of carnal desires.'[7339]

٦٤٤٦ . الكافي : إنّ موسىٰ عليه السلام ناجاهُ الله تباركَ وتعالىٰ فقال له...: أُذكُرْ أنَّكَ ساكِنُ القَبرِ؛ فَلْيَمنَعكَ ذلكَ مِن الشَّهَواتِ.[٧٣١١]

6447. **Imām ʿAlī (AS) said,** 'The more wisdom is strengthened, carnal desire is weakened.'[7340]

٦٤٤٧ . الإمامُ عليٌّ عليه السلام : كُلَّما قَوِيَتِ الحِكمَةُ ضَعُفَتِ الشَّهوَةُ.[٧٣١٢]

6448. **Imām ʿAlī (AS) said,** 'He whose intellect is complete finds carnal desires insignificant.'[7341]

٦٤٤٨ . عنه عليه السلام: مَن كَمُلَ عَقلُهُ استَهانَ بِالشَّهَواتِ.[٧٣١٣]

6449. **Imām ʿAlī (AS) said,** 'Chastity weakens carnal desire.'[7342]

٦٤٤٩ . عنه عليه السلام: العِفَّةُ تُضعِفُ الشَّهوَةَ.[٧٣١٤]

6450. **Imām ʿAlī (AS) said,** 'He whose own self is dear to him, his carnal desires become insignificant for him.'[7343]

٦٤٥٠ . عنه عليه السلام: مَن كَرُمَت علَيهِ نَفسُهُ هانَت علَيهِ شَهَواتُهُ.[٧٣١٥]

6451. **Imām ʿAlī (AS) said,** 'So have piety in Allah – servants of Allah – with a piety that has a conscience, and a heart occupied with thought....and asceticism that has cleaved his desires.'[7344]

٦٤٥١ . عنه عليه السلام: فاتَّقوا اللهَ ـ عِبادَ اللهِ ـ تَقِيَّةَ ذِي لُبٍّ، شَغَلَ التَّفَكُّرُ قَلبَهُ...، وظَلَفَ الزُّهدُ شَهَواتِهِ[٧٣١٦]. [٧٣١٧]

6452. **Imām ʿAlī (AS) said,** 'He who longs for Heaven will forget desires.'[7345]

٦٤٥٢ . عنه عليه السلام: مَنِ اشتاقَ إلَى الجَنَّةِ سَلا عَنِ الشَّهَواتِ.[٧٣١٨]

1816. He who Overcomes his Desires

١٨١٦ ـ مَن غَلَبَ هَواهُ

6453. **The Prophet (SAWA) said,** 'Allah Almighty said, 'By My Might and Exaltedness...no sooner does a servant prefer My desire over his own desire than I protect him with My angels, and charge the heavens and the earth with his sustenance. I will be for him behind every transaction of every trader, and the world will only come to him forcefully.'[7346]

٦٤٥٣ . رسولُ اللهِ ﷺ: يقولُ اللهُ عَزَّ وجلَّ: وعِزَّتي وجَلالي... لايُؤثِرُ عَبدٌ هَوايَ علىٰ هَواهُ إلّا استَحفَظتُهُ مَلائكَتي، وكَفَّلتُ السَّماواتِ والأرَضِينَ (الأرضَ) رِزقَهُ، وكُنتُ لَهُ مِن وراءِ تِجارَةِ كُلِّ تاجِرٍ، وأتَتهُ الدُّنيا وهِيَ راغِمَةٌ.[٧٣١٩]

6454. **Imām al-Bāqir (AS) said,** 'Allah Almighty has said, 'By My Might and Exaltedness, My

٦٤٥٤ . الإمامُ الباقرُ عليه السلام: قالَ اللهُ عَزَّ وجلَّ: وعِزّتي

Greatness and Loftiness, and by My High Status, no sooner does a servant prefer My desire over his own desire than I will suffice him in his losses, I will guarantee his sustenance upon the Heavens and the earth, and I will be for him behind every transaction of every trader.'[7347]

وجَلالي وعَظَمَتي وبَهائي وعُلُوِّ ارتِفاعي، لا يُؤثِرُ عَبدٌ مُؤمنٌ هَوايَ علىٰ هَواهُ في شيءٍ مِن أمرِ الدُّنيا إلّا جَعَلتُ غِناهُ في نَفسِهِ، وهِمَّتَهُ في آخِرَتِهِ، وضَمَّنتُ السَّماواتِ والأرضَ رِزقَهُ، وكُنتُ لَهُ مِن وَراءِ تِجارَةِ كُلِّ تاجِرٍ.[٧٣٢٠]

6455. **Imām ʿAlī (AS) said,** 'Whoever overcomes his carnal desire his intellect will become manifest.'[7348]

٦٤٥٥. الإمامُ عليٌّ ﷺ: مَن غَلَبَ شَهوَتَهُ ظَهَرَ عَقلُهُ.[٧٣٢١]

6456. **Imām ʿAlī (AS) said,** 'In controlling desire there is immunity from every deficiency.'[7349]

٦٤٥٦. عنه ﷺ: بِمِلكِ الشَّهوَةِ التَّنَزُّهِ عَن كُلِّ عابٍ.[٧٣٢٢]

6457. **Imām ʿAlī (AS) said,** 'Repelling one's desire is the best way to eradicate it, and fulfilling it only strengthens it.'[7350]

٦٤٥٧. عنه ﷺ: رَدُّ الشَّهوَةِ أقضىٰ لَها، وقَضاؤها أشَدُّ لَها.[٧٣٢٣]

397

INHERITANCE

الإرثُ

1817. Inheritance

١٨١٧ ـ الإرثُ

"Allah enjoins you concerning your children: for the male shall be the like of the share of two females, and if there be [two or] more than two females, then for them shall be two-thirds of what he leaves; but if she be alone, then for her shall be a half; and for each of his parents a sixth of what he leaves, if he has children."[7351]

﴿يُوصِيكُمُ اللهُ فِي أَوْلَادِكُمْ لِلذَّكَرِ مِثْلُ حَظِّ الْأُنثَيَيْنِ فَإِنْ كُنَّ نِسَاءً فَوْقَ اثْنَتَيْنِ فَلَهُنَّ ثُلُثَا مَا تَرَكَ وَإِنْ كَانَتْ وَاحِدَةً فَلَهَا النِّصْفُ وَلِأَبَوَيْهِ لِكُلِّ وَاحِدٍ مِنْهُمَا السُّدُسُ مِمَّا تَرَكَ إِنْ كَانَ لَهُ وَلَدٌ﴾.[٧٣٢٤]

(See also: Qur'an: 4:7-12,32,33,127,176, 19:6, 27:16, 89:19)

(أنظر) النساء: ٧ ـ ١٢، ٣٢، ٣٣، ١٢٧، ١٧٦ ومريم: ٦ والنمل: ١٦ والفجر: ١٩.

6458. **Imām al-Ṣādiq (AS),** when he was asked about giving the male the share of two females, said, 'The woman does not have to go for prescribed war *(jihād)*, nor spend money [for household expenses], nor pay blood money, whereas these are compulsory on the man.'[7352]

٦٤٥٨. الإمامُ الصّادقُ ﷺ ـ لَمّا سُئلَ عن عِلَّةِ إعطاءِ الذَّكَرِ مِثلَ حَظِّ الأُنثَيَينِ ـ: إنّ المرأةَ لَيسَ علَيها جِهادٌ ولا نَفَقَةٌ ولا مَعقُلَةٌ[٧٣٢٥]، وإنّما ذلكَ علَى الرِّجالِ.[٧٣٢٦]

6459. **Imām al-Riḍā (AS),** when he was asked about giving the male the share of two females,

٦٤٥٩. الإمامُ الرِّضا ﷺ ـ أيضاً ـ: عِلَّةُ إعطاءِ

said, 'The reason why women are given half of what men are given from the inheritance is because when a woman marries she receives [the *mahr* dowry] and the man gives. Therefore it [i.e. the inheritance] is a greater amount for men. Another reason for giving the male the share of two females is because the female is under the responsibility of the male when she is in need, and he has to support her and provide for her expenses. The female does not have to support the male, nor is it taken from her expenses when he is in need. So because of this, Allah Almighty has saved this for the man, and this is according to Allah's verse: *"Men are the managers of women, because of the advantage Allah has granted some of them over others, and by virtue of their spending out of their wealth.*"'[7353]

النِّساءِ نِصفَ ما يُعطَى الرِّجالُ مِن المِيراثِ لأنَّ المرأةَ إذا تَزَوَّجَت أخَذَت والرّجُلُ يُعطي، فلِذلكَ وُفِّرَ على الرِّجالِ. وعِلَّةٌ اُخرىٰ في إعطاءِ الذَّكَرِ مِثلَي ما يُعطَى الاُنثىٰ، لِأنَّ الاُنثىٰ في عِيالِ الذَّكَرِ إنِ احتاجَت، وعلَيهِ أن يَعُولَها وعلَيهِ نَفَقَتُها، ولَيسَ علَى المَرأةِ أن تَعُولَ الرَّجُلَ، ولا يُؤخَذُ بنَفَقَتِهِ إنِ احتاجَ، فوَفَّرَ اللهُ تعالىٰ علَى الرِّجالِ لِذلكَ، وذلكَ قَولُ اللهِ عزّوجلّ: ﴿الرِّجالُ قَوّامُونَ علَى النِّساءِ بِما فَضَّلَ اللهُ بَعْضَهُمْ علىٰ بَعْضٍ وبِما أنفَقوا مِن أمْوالِهِم﴾ .٧٣٢٧، ٧٣٢٨

1818. Those who are Deprived of Inheritance

١٨١٨ ـ مَوانِعُ الإرثِ

6460. **The Prophet (SAWA) said,** 'There is no inheritance for a murderer [of the deceased].'[7354]

٦٤٦٠. رسولُ اللهِ ﷺ: لا مِيراثَ لِلقاتِلِ. ٧٣٢٩

6461. **The Prophet (SAWA) said,** 'An illegitimate child neither inherits nor is inherited.'[7355]

٦٤٦١. عنه ﷺ: وَلَدُ زِنا لا يَرِثُ ولا يُوَرِّثُ. ٧٣٣٠

6462. **Imām al-Ṣādiq (AS) said,** 'The Muslim can prevent access to the disbeliever [from inheriting him] though he can inherit him, but the disbeliever cannot prevent the believer from access to his inheritance and nor can he inherit from him.'[7356]

٦٤٦٢. الإمامُ الصّادقُ عليه السلام: المُسلِمُ يَحجُبُ الكافِرَ ويَرِثُهُ، والكافِرُ لا يَحجُبُ المُؤمنَ ولا يَرِثُهُ. ٧٣٣١

1819. Inheritance of Prophets

١٨١٩ ـ إرثُ الأنبِياءِ

"Solomon inherited from David, and he said, 'O people! We have been taught the speech of the birds, and we have been given out of everything. Indeed this is a manifest advantage.'"[7357]

﴿وَوَرِثَ سُلَيْمَانُ دَاوُدَ وَقالَ يَا أَيُّهَا النَّاسُ عُلِّمْنَا مَنْطِقَ الطَّيْرِ وَأُوتِينَا مِنْ كُلِّ شَيْءٍ إِنَّ هٰذَا لَهُوَ الْفَضْلُ الْمُبِينُ﴾ . ٧٣٣٢

"Indeed I fear my kinsmen, after me, and my wife is barren. So grant me from Yourself an heir who may

﴿وَإِنِّي خِفْتُ الْمَوالِيَ مِنْ وَرَائِي وَكَانَتِ امْرَأَتِي عَاقِرًا فَهَبْ لِي مِنْ لَدُنْكَ وَلِيًّا * يَرِثُنِي

inherit from me and inherit from the House of Jacob, and make him, my Lord, pleasing [to You]!'[7358]

وَيَرِثُ مِنْ آلِ يَعْقُوبَ وَاجْعَلْهُ رَبِّ رَضِيّاً﴾.[٧٣٣٣]

6463. *al-Ṭabaqāt al-Kubrā*, narrating from Ja'far: 'Fāṭima (AS) came to Abū Bakr asking for her inheritance, and 'Abbās b. 'Abd al-Muṭalib also asked for his inheritance and 'Alī (AS) came with them. Abū Bakr said, 'The Prophet (SAWA) said, 'We do not leave inheritance; whatever we leave is charity', so whoever the Prophet was responsible for in their livelihood, I am responsible for.' 'Alī (AS) said, '*"Solomon inherited from David"*, and Zacharias said, '*"who may inherit from me and inherit from the House of Jacob."* Abū Bakr said, 'That is right, but by Allah you know the same as what I know.' Then 'Alī said, 'This is the Book of Allah talking. So they ['Alī, Fāṭima and 'Abbās] kept quiet and left.'[7359]

٦٤٦٣. الطبقات الكبرىٰ عن جعفر: جاءَت فاطِمَةُ ﵍ إلىٰ أبي بكرٍ تَطلُبُ مِيراثَها، وجاءَ العَبّاسُ بنُ عبدِالمُطَّلبِ يَطلُبُ مِيراثَهُ، وجاءَ مَعَهُما عليٌّ ﵇.
فقالَ أبو بكرٍ: قالَ رسولُ اللهِ ﷺ: «لا نُوَرِّثُ، ما تَرَكناهُ صَدَقَةٌ» وما كانَ النَّبيُّ يَعولُ فَعَلَيَّ، فقالَ عليٌّ ﵇: ﴿وَوَرِثَ سُلَيمانُ داودَ﴾، وقالَ زكريّا: ﴿يَرِثُني ويَرِثُ مِن آلِ يَعقوبَ﴾.
قالَ أبو بكرٍ: هُو هكذا، وأنتَ واللهِ تَعلَمُ مِثلَ ما أعلَمُ.
فقالَ عليٌّ ﵇: هٰذا كِتابُ اللهِ يَنطِقُ. فسَكَتُوا وانصَرَفوا.[٧٣٣٤]

398

PIETY

الوَرَع

1820. The Virtue of Piety

١٨٢٠ـ فَضلُ الوَرَعِ

6464. **The Prophet (SAWA) said,** 'For everything there is a basis, and the basis of faith is piety.'[7360]

٦٤٦٤. رسولُ اللهِ ﷺ: لكلِّ شَيءٍ اُسٌّ، وأُسُّ الإيمانِ الوَرَعُ.[٧٣٣٥]

6465. **The Prophet (SAWA) said,** 'The criterion of religion is piety.'[7361]

٦٤٦٥. عنه ﷺ: مِلاكُ الدِّينِ الوَرَعُ.[٧٣٣٦]

6466. **The Prophet (SAWA) said,** 'The best act in your religion is piety.'[7362]

٦٤٦٦. عنه ﷺ: أفضَلُ دِينِكُمُ الوَرَعُ.[٧٣٣٧]

6467. **Imām 'Alī (AS) said,** 'There is no stronghold better than piety.'[7363]

٦٤٦٧. الإمامُ عليٌّ ﵇: لامَعقِلَ أحسَنُ مِنَ الوَرَعِ.[٧٣٣٨]

6468. **Imām 'Alī (AS) said,** 'Piety is a shield.'[7364]

٦٤٦٨. عنه ﵇: الوَرَعُ جُنَّةٌ.[٧٣٣٩]

6469. **Imām 'Alī (AS) said,** 'He who loves us should do as we do, and seek assistance in piety;

٦٤٦٩. عنه ﵇: مَن أحَبَّنا فلْيَعمَلْ بعَمَلِنا ولْيَستَعِنْ بِالوَرَعِ؛ فإنّهُ أفضَلُ ما يُستعانُ بهِ في

for it is the best assistance in matters of this world and the Hereafter.'[7365]

أمرِ الدُّنيا والآخِرَةِ.[٧٣٤٠]

6470. **Imām al-Bāqir (AS) said,** 'The hardest of worship is piety.'[7366]

٦٤٧٠. الإمامُ الباقرُ عليه السلام: إنّ أشَدَّ العِبادَةِ الوَرَعُ.[٧٣٤١]

6471. **Imām al-Ṣādiq (AS) said,** 'You must have piety; for it is the religion that we adhere to, and with which we devote ourselves to Allah, and we require it from those who accept our guardianship.'[7367]

٦٤٧١. الإمامُ الصّادقُ عليه السلام: علَيكُم بِالوَرَعِ؛ فإنّهُ الدِّينُ الّذي نُلازِمُهُ، ونَدينُ اللهَ بِهِ، ونُريدُهُ مِمَّن يوالِينا.[٧٣٤٢]

6472. **Imām al-Ṣādiq (AS) said,** 'He who lives in a place with a population of one hundred thousand or more and there is in that place someone more pious than him, then he is not [considered] one of us.'[7368]

٦٤٧٢. عنه عليه السلام: لَيسَ مِنّا ـ ولا كَرامَةَ ـ مَن كانَ فِي مِصرٍ فيهِ مِائةُ ألفٍ أو يَزيدونَ، وكانَ في ذلكَ المِصرِ أحَدٌ أورَعَ مِنهُ.[٧٣٤٣]

1821. The Fruit of Piety — ١٨٢١ ـ ثَمَرَةُ الوَرَعِ

6473. **Imām ʿAlī (AS) said,** 'The fruit of piety is the goodness of one's self and one's religion.'[7369]

٦٤٧٣. الإمامُ عليٌّ عليه السلام: ثَمَرَةُ الوَرَعِ صَلاحُ النَّفسِ والدِّينِ.[٧٣٤٤]

6474. **Imām ʿAlī (AS) said,** 'Piety prevents from committing prohibited acts.'[7370]

٦٤٧٤. عنه عليه السلام: الوَرَعُ يحجِزُ عَنِ ارْتِكابِ المَحارِمِ.[٧٣٤٥]

6475. **Imām ʿAlī (AS) said,** 'Abstaining [from sins] is the foundation of piety.'[7371]

٦٤٧٥. عنه عليه السلام: الوَرَعُ أساسُ التَّقوىٰ.[٧٣٤٦]

6476. **Imām ʿAlī (AS) said,** 'Knowledge cannot be developed and purified without piety.'[7372]

٦٤٧٦. عنه عليه السلام: لا يَزكو العِلمُ بغَيرِ وَرَعٍ.[٧٣٤٧]

6477. **Imām al-Ṣādiq (AS) said,** 'Fear Allah and safeguard your faith with piety.'[7373]

٦٤٧٧. الإمامُ الصّادقُ عليه السلام: اِتَّقُوا اللهَ وصُونوا دِينَكُم بِالوَرَعِ.[٧٣٤٨]

1822. The Role of Piety in Worship — ١٨٢٢ ـ دَورُ الوَرَعِ فِي العِبادَةِ

6478. **Imām ʿAlī (AS) said,** 'There is no good in any deed that is devoid of piety.'[7374]

٦٤٧٨. الإمامُ عليٌّ عليه السلام: لا خَيرَ في نُسُكٍ لا وَرَعَ فيهِ.[٧٣٤٩]

6479. **Imām Zayn al-ʿĀbidīn (AS) said,** 'Piety is the structure of worship, and if it is cut, religion

٦٤٧٩. الإمامُ زينُ العابدينَ عليه السلام: الوَرَعُ نِظامُ

will collapse just like when a wire is cut the system follows it!'[7375]

العِبادَةِ، فإذا انقَطَعَ ذَهَبَتِ الدِّيانَةُ؛ كما إذا انقَطَعَ السِّلكُ أتبَعَهُ النِّظامُ.[٧٣٥٠]

6480. **Imām al-Ṣādiq (AS) said,** 'Diligence is of no use without piety.'[7376]

٦٤٨٠. الإمامُ الصّادقُ عليه السلام: لا يَنفَعُ اجتِهادٌ لا وَرَعَ فيهِ.[٧٣٥١]

6481. **Imām al-Ṣādiq (AS),** in his will to ʿAmr b. Saʿīd, said, 'I advise you to be wary of your duty to Allah, to have piety and diligence, and know that diligence that is devoid of piety is of no benefit.'[7377]

٦٤٨١. عنه عليه السلام ـ في وصيَّتِهِ لِعَمرِو بنِ سعيدٍ ـ: اُوصيكَ بتَقوَى اللهِ والوَرَعِ والاجتِهادِ، واعلَم أنّهُ لا يَنفَعُ اجتِهادٌ لا وَرَعَ فيهِ.[٧٣٥٢]

1823. Interpretation of Piety

١٨٢٣ ـ تَفسيرُ الوَرَعِ

6482. **The Prophet (SAWA) said,** 'Piety is the master of action. He who does not have piety to prevent him from an act of disobedience to Allah Almighty when left with it, Allah will not care about any of his other actions. This means that it [piety] is fear of Allah, both in secret and in public, economizing both in poverty and wealth, and fairness both in [times of] contentment and discontentment.'[7378]

٦٤٨٢. رسولُ اللهِ ﷺ: الوَرَعُ سَيِّدُ العَمَلِ، مَن لَم يَكُن لَهُ وَرَعٌ يَرُدُّهُ عَن مَعصيَةِ اللهِ تعالىٰ إذا خَلا بها لَم يَعبَأِ اللهُ بسائرِ عَمَلِهِ، فذلكَ مَخافَةُ اللهِ في السِّرِّ والعَلانِيَةِ، والاقتِصادُ في الفَقرِ والغِنىٰ، والعَدلُ عِندَ الرِّضا والسُّخطِ.[٧٣٥٣]

6483. **Imām ʿAlī (AS) said,** 'The root of piety is keeping away from sins, and restraining oneself from the forbidden.'[7379]

٦٤٨٣. الإمامُ عليٌّ عليه السلام: أصلُ الوَرَعِ تَجَنُّبُ الآثامِ، والتَّنزُّهُ عنِ الحَرامِ.[٧٣٥٤]

6484. **Imām ʿAlī (AS) said,** 'Piety is stopping [in the face of] obscure matters.'[7380]

٦٤٨٤. عنه عليه السلام: الوَرَعُ الوُقوفُ عِندَ الشُّبهَةِ.[٧٣٥٥]

6485. **Imām al-Ṣādiq (AS),** when he was asked about a pious person, said, 'He who restrains himself from what Allah has forbidden.'[7381]

٦٤٨٥. الإمامُ الصّادقُ عليه السلام ـ لَمّا سُئلَ عَن الوَرِعِ مِن النّاسِ ـ: الّذي يَتَوَرَّعُ عَن مَحارِمِ اللهِ عَزَّوجلَّ.[٧٣٥٦]

6486. **Imām al-Ṣādiq (AS) also said,** 'He who restrains himself from what Allah has forbidden, and keeps away from them. And if he does not beware of obscure matters, he will fall into the forbidden without knowing so.'[7382]

٦٤٨٦. عنه عليه السلام ـ أيضاً ـ: الّذي يَتَوَرَّعُ عَن مَحارِمِ اللهِ، ويَجتَنِبُ هؤلاءِ، وإذا لَم يَتَّقِ الشُّبُهاتِ وَقَعَ في الحَرامِ وهُو لا يَعرِفُهُ.[٧٣٥٧]

1824. The Most Pious of People

١٨٢٤ ـ أورَعُ النّاسِ

6487. **Imām al-Bāqir (AS) said,** 'Allah Almighty has said, 'O son of Adam, refrain from what I have forbidden to you and you will be the most pious of people.'[7383]

٦٤٨٧ . الإمامُ الباقرُ عليه السلام : قالَ اللهُ عَزَّ وجلَّ : يا بنَ آدَمَ ، اِجتَنِبْ ما حَرَّمتُ علَيكَ تَكُنْ مِن أورَعِ النّاسِ .[٧٣٥٨]

6488. **The Prophet (SAWA) said,** 'Stop in the face of things that Allah has forbidden and you will be the most pious of people.'[7384]

٦٤٨٨ . رسولُ اللهِ صلى الله عليه وآله : كُفَّ عَن مَحارِمِ اللهِ تَكُن أورَعَ النّاسِ .[٧٣٥٩]

6489. **Imām 'Alī (AS) said,** 'The most pious of people is the most free of wants.'[7385]

٦٤٨٩ . الإمامُ عليٌّ عليه السلام : أورَعُ النّاسِ أنزَهُهُم عَنِ المَطالِبِ .[٧٣٦٠]

6490. **Imām 'Alī (AS) said,** 'The smartest from among you is the most pious of you.'[7386]

٦٤٩٠ . عنه عليه السلام : أكيَسُكُم أورَعُكُم .[٧٣٦١]

399

THE SCALE

المِيزان

1825. Scales of Deeds

١٨٢٥ ـ مَوازينُ الأعمالِ

"The weighing [of deeds] on that Day is a truth. As for those whose deeds weigh heavy in the scales - it is they who are the felicitous. As for those whose deeds weigh light in the scales, - it is they who have ruined their souls, because they used to wrong Our signs."[7387]

﴿وَالْوَزْنُ يَوْمَئِذٍ الْحَقُّ فَمَنْ ثَقُلَتْ مَوَازِينُهُ فَأُولٰئِكَ هُمُ الْمُفْلِحُونَ ۞ وَمَنْ خَفَّتْ مَوَازِينُهُ فَأُولٰئِكَ الَّذِينَ خَسِرُوا أَنْفُسَهُمْ بِمَا كَانُوا بِآيَاتِنَا يَظْلِمُونَ﴾ .[٧٣٦٢]

(See also: Qur'an: 18:105, 23:102, 103, 101:6-11)

(أنظر) الكهف : ١٠٥ والمؤمنون : ١٠٢ ، ١٠٣ والقارعة : ٦ ـ ١١ .

6491. **The Prophet (SAWA) narrated,** 'Allah will say to Adam on the Day of Resurrection: 'Stand at the scale and see what is shown to you from their works. He whose good deeds outweigh his bad deeds even by one atom's worth, he will go to Heaven.'[7388]

٦٤٩١ . رسولُ اللهِ صلى الله عليه وآله ـ في قولِ اللهِ لآدمَ يومَ القِيامَةِ ـ : قُمْ عِندَ المِيزانِ فانظُرْ ما يُرفَعُ إلَيكَ مِن أعمالِهِم ، فمَن رَجَحَ مِنهُم خَيرُهُ علىٰ شَرِّهِ مِثقالَ ذَرَّةٍ فلَهُ الجَنّةُ .[٧٣٦٣]

6492. **Imām al-Bāqir (AS) said,** 'Allah has made the good heavy for the dwellers of this world just like the heaviness of their weight on their scales on the Day of Judgment, and Allah has lightened

٦٤٩٢ . الإمامُ الباقرُ عليه السلام : إنّ اللهَ ثَقَّلَ الخَيرَ علىٰ أهلِ الدُّنيا كثِقْلِهِ في مَوازِينِهِم يَومَ القِيامَةِ ، وإنَّ

the weight of evil on the dwellers of this world just as the lightness of their weight on their scales on the Day of Judgment.'[7389]

اللهَ عَزَّ وجلَّ خَفَّفَ الشَّرَّ علىٰ أهلِ الدُّنيا كـخِفَّتِهِ في مَوازِينِهِم يَومَ القِيامَةِ.[٧٣٦٤]

6493. **Imām al-Ṣādiq (AS),** when an atheist asked him, 'Are deeds not weighed?' replied, 'No. Deeds are not bodies [themselves], but descriptions of what has been done. Only one who is ignorant of things or does not know their weight or lightness would need to weigh, and verily nothing is hidden from Allah.' And he asked, 'So what is the meaning of the scale?' He said, 'Justice.' He said, 'So what does it mean in His Book: *"As for those whose deeds weigh heavy"*?' He (AS) replied, 'He whose [good] deeds outnumber.'[7390]

٦٤٩٣. الاحتجاج: من سؤالِ الزِّنديقِ الذي سألَ أبا عبدِ اللهِ ﵇ عن مسائلَ كثيرةٍ أن قالَ: ... أوَليسَ تُوزَنُ الأعمالُ؟ قالَ ﵇: لا، إنّ الأعمالَ لَيسَت بأجسامٍ، وإنّما هِيَ صِفَةُ ما عَمِلوا، وإنّما يَحتاجُ إلىٰ وَزنِ الشّيءِ مَن جَهِلَ عَدَدَ الأشياءِ ولا يَعرِفُ ثِقلَها وخِفَّتَها، وإنّ اللهَ لا يَخفىٰ علَيهِ شيءٌ.
قالَ: فما معنَى المِيزانِ؟ قالَ ﵇: العَدلُ.
قالَ: فما مَعناهُ في كِتابِهِ: ﴿فَمَنْ ثَقُلَت مَوازِينُهُ﴾؟ قالَ ﵇: فمَن رَجَحَ عَمَلُهُ.[٧٣٦٥]

400

DEVILISH MISGIVINGS

الوَسوَسَةُ

1826. Misgivings in Matters of Belief

١٨٢٦ ـ الوَسوَسَةُ فِي العَقائِدِ

6494. Ibn Mas'ūd narrated, 'We asked the Messenger of Allah (SAWA) about a man who experiences something falling from the sky and being snatched by a bird is more pleasant for him than to talk about it, said, 'That is genuine faith or true faith.'[7391]

٦٤٩٤. ابن مسعودٍ: سألنا رسولَ اللهِ ﷺ عنِ الرّجُلِ يَجِدُ الشّيءَ لَو خَرَّ مِن السّماءِ فتَخطَفُهُ الطَّيرُ كانَ أحَبَّ إلَيهِ مِن أن يَتَكلَّمَ بهِ، قالَ: ذاكَ مَحضُ الإيمانِ، أو صَريحُ الإيمانِ.[٧٣٦٦]

6495. **The Prophet (SAWA) said,** 'Allah overlooks for the people of my community whatever their selves say to them [of misgivings] as long as they neither utter it nor perform it.'[7392]

٦٤٩٥. رسولُ اللهِ ﷺ: تَجاوَزَ اللهُ لأُمَّتي عَمّا حَدَّثَت بِهِ أنفُسَها مالَم تَنطِقْ بِهِ أو تَعمَلْ.[٧٣٦٧]

1827. Caution Against Doubts in Ablution and Prayers

١٨٢٧ ـ التَّحذيرُ مِنَ الوَسوَسَةِ فِي الوُضوءِ وَالصَّلاةِ

6496. **Imām al-Ṣādiq (AS)** – when 'Abdullāh b. Sinān mentioned a man troubled with doubts in his ablution and his prayers, and claimed that he was a sane man,

٦٤٩٦. عبدُ اللهِ بن سنان: ذكرتُ لأبي عبدِ اللهِ ﵇ رجُلاً مُبتَلىً بِالوُضوءِ والصَّلاةِ، وقلتُ: هوَ رجُلٌ عاقِلٌ، فقالَ أبو عبدِ اللهِ ﵇: وأيُّ عَقلٍ لَه وهُو يُطيعُ الشَّيطانَ؟!

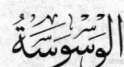

said, 'What kind of mind does he have if he is obeying Satan?!' [He said] So I said to him, 'And how is he obeying Satan?' So he said, 'Ask him this [misgiving] that he has, where does it come from?' And he shall say to you, 'It is an act of Satan.'[7393]

فقلتُ لَهُ: وكيفَ يُطيعُ الشَّيطانَ؟ فقالَ: سَلهُ هٰذا الّذي يَأتِيهِ مِن أيِّ شَيءٍ هُو؟ فإنّهُ يَقولُ لَكَ: مِن عَمَلِ الشَّيطانِ.[٧٣٦٨]

6497. **Imām al-Ṣādiq (AS),** was asked about the extent of doubt that a particular man was having as to how many units of prayer he had performed, such that he neither knew how many he had performed, nor how many he had left. He replied, 'He should repeat it'. So we asked him, 'But this state is so excessive in him that every time he repeats [his prayer] he doubts again.' He said, 'Then he should continue regardless of his doubt.' Then he said, 'Do not accustom the malignant [part] of yourselves to the breaking of the prayer lest you arouse further greed in it, for verily Satan is malignant and gets habituated to whatever he is made accustomed to. So you should ignore that insinuation [and continue], and you should not break your prayers often, and if you do this [i.e. ignore the doubt] often enough, the doubt will not resurface.' Zurāra narrated: Then he (AS) said, 'Verily the malignant wants to be obeyed, so when it is disobeyed, it does not return to you.'[7394]

٦٤٩٧ . زرارةوأبي بصير :قلنالَه[٧٣٦٩]:الرَّجُلُ يشُكّ كثيراً في صلاتِهِ حتّى لا يدري كم صلّي ولا ما بَقِيَ علَيهِ قالَ: يُعيدُ، قُلنا لَهُ: فإنّهُ يَكثُرُ علَيهِ ذلكَ كُلّما عادَ شَكَّ؟ قالَ: يَمضي في شَكِّهِ.
ثُمّ قالَ: لاتُعَوِّدوا الخَبيثَ مِن أنفُسِكُم بِنَقضِ الصَّلاةِ فتُطمِعوهُ؛ فإنَّ الشَّيطانَ خَبيثٌ يَعتادُ لِما عُوِّدَ، فلْيَمضِ أحَدُكُم في الوَهمِ، ولا يُكثِرَنَّ نَقضَ الصَّلاةِ، فإنّهُ إذا فَعَلَ ذلكَ مَرّاتٍ لَم يَعُدْ إلَيهِ الشَّكُّ.
قالَ زُرارَةُ: ثُمّ قالَ: إنّما يُريدُ الخَبيثُ أن يُطاعَ، فإذا عُصِيَ لَم يَعُدْ إلىٰ أحَدِكُم.[٧٣٧٠]

1828. The Treatment of Devilish Misgivings

١٨٢٨ ـ عِلاجُ الوَسواسِ

"And say, 'My Lord! I seek Your protection from the promptings of devils; and I seek Your protection, my Lord, from their presence near me.'"[7395]

﴿وَقُلْ رَبِّ أَعُوذُ بِكَ مِنْ هَمَزاتِ الشَّياطِينِ * وَأَعُوذُ بِكَ رَبِّ أَنْ يَحْضُرُونِ﴾.[٧٣٧١]

"Say, 'I seek the protection of the Lord of humans, Sovereign of humans, God of humans, from the evil of the sneaky tempter who puts temptations into the breasts of humans, from among the jinn and humans.'"[7396]

﴿قُلْ أَعُوذُ بِرَبِّ النَّاسِ * مَلِكِ النَّاسِ * إِلٰهِ النَّاسِ * مِنْ شَرِّ الْوَسْواسِ الْخَنَّاسِ * الَّذِي يُوَسْوِسُ فِي صُدُورِ النَّاسِ * مِنَ الجِنَّةِ وَالنَّاسِ﴾.[٧٣٧٢]

(See also: Qur'an 7:20, 20:120)

(أُنظر) الأعراف: ٢٠ وطه: ١٢٠.

6498. **Imām ʿAlī (AS) said,** 'Fasting for three days of every month – the first and last Thursdays of

٦٤٩٨ . الإمامُ عليٌّ ﷺ: صَومُ ثَلاثَةِ أيّامٍ مِن كُلِّ

the month, and the Wednesday in between the two, and fasting in the month of Shaʿbān removes the misgivings in the breasts and the confusions of the heart.'[7397]

شَهرٍ ـ أربَعاءُ بَينَ خَميسَينِ ـ وصَومُ شَعبانَ يَذهَبُ بوَسواسِ الصَّدرِ، وبَلابِلِ القَلبِ.[٧٣٧٣]

6499. **Imām ʿAlī (AS) said,** 'Remembrance of us, the *Ahl al-Bayt* is a cure from indisposition, ailments and misgivings of doubt.'[7398]

٦٤٩٩. عنه ﷷ : ذِكرُنا أهلَ البَيتِ شِفاءٌ مِن الوَعكِ والأسقامِ ووَسواسِ الرَّيبِ.[٧٣٧٤]

6500. **Imām al-Ṣādiq (AS),** when asked about [devilish] misgivings, and if they happen often, said, 'They are insignificant. Just say: 'There is no God but Allah (*lā ilāha illa Allāh*).'[7399]

٦٥٠٠. الإمامُ الصّادقُ ﷷ ـ وقد سُئلَ عَنِ الوَسوَسَةِ وإن كَثُرَت ـ: لا شيءَ فيها، تقولُ: لاإلهَ إلّا اللهُ.[٧٣٧٥]

401

CONSOLATION

المُواساة

1829. Encouraging Consolation

١٨٢٩ ـ الحَثُّ عَلَى المُواساةِ

6501. **The Prophet (SAWA) said,** 'He who has two shirts should wear one and should give the other to his brother to wear.'[7400]

٦٥٠١. رسولُ اللهِ ﷺ: مَن كانَ لَهُ قَميصانِ فلْيَلبَسْ أحَدَهُما ولْيُلبِسِ الآخَرَ أخاهُ.[٧٣٧٦]

6502. **Imām ʿAlī (AS) said,** 'The best of goodness is giving consolation to one's brothers.'[7401]

٦٥٠٢. الإمامُ عليٌّ ﷷ :أحسَنُ الإحسانِ مُواساةُ الإخوانِ.[٧٣٧٧]

6503. **Imām ʿAlī (AS) said,** 'Do not count as a friend one who does not give assistance [to others] with his wealth.'[7402]

٦٥٠٣. عنه ﷷ : لا تَعُدَّنَّ صَدِيقاً مَن لا يُواسي بمالِهِ.[٧٣٧٨]

6504. **Imām ʿAlī (AS) said,** 'Consolating one's brother for the sake of Allah increases one's sustenance.'[7403]

٦٥٠٤. عنه ﷷ : مُواساةُ الأخِ في اللهِ ﷻ تَزيدُ في الرِّزقِ.[٧٣٧٩]

6505. **Imām al-Ṣādiq (AS) said,** 'Come closer to Allah through supporting your brothers.'[7404]

٦٥٠٥. الإمامُ الصّادقُ ﷷ : تَقَرَّبوا إلَى اللهِ تعالىٰ بِمُواساةِ إخوانِكُم.[٧٣٨٠]

6506. **Imām al-Ṣādiq (AS) said,** 'There are two traits that one should possess, and if not then be

٦٥٠٦. عنه ﷷ : خَصلَتانِ مَن كانَتا فيهِ وإلّا فاعزُبْ ثُمّ اعزُبْ ثُمّ اعزُبْ! قيلَ: وما هُما؟

gone, be gone, be gone!' He was asked, 'And what are they?' He said, 'Performing the prayers at their prescribed times and observing all its laws, and giving consolidation [to others].'[7405]

قالَ: الصَّلاةُ في مَواقيتِها والمحافَظَةُ علَيها، والمُواساةُ.[٧٣٨١]

6507. **Imām al-Kāẓim (AS) said** to Jaʿfar b. Muḥammad al-ʿĀṣimī, 'O ʿĀṣim, how are you at maintaining contact with each other and offering consolidation to each other?' [He said] I said, 'The best that anyone can be.' He said, 'Do any of you come to your brother's shop or his home in times of hardship and you pull out your purse for him to take whatever he needs without disapproving of him?!' He said, 'No.' Imām (AS) said, 'Then you are not at a state of mutual assistance that I love.'[7406]

٦٥٠٧. الإمامُ الكاظمُ عليه السلام ـ لِجَعفرِ بنِ محمّدٍ العاصِميِّ ـ: يا عاصِمُ، كيفَ أنتُم في التَّواصُلِ والتَّواسي؟ [قالَ:] قلتُ: على أفضَلِ ما كانَ علَيهِ أحَدٌ. قالَ: أيَأتي أحَدُكُم إلى دُكّانِ أخيهِ أو مَنزِلِهِ عِندَ الضّائقَةِ فيَستَخرِجُ كِيسَهُ ويأخُذُ ما يَحتاجُ إلَيهِ فلا يُنكِرُ علَيهِ؟! قالَ: لا، قالَ: فَلَستُم على ما اُحِبُّ في التَّواصُلِ.[٧٣٨٢]

402

THE WILL

الوَصيَّة

1830. Encouraging to Make a Will

١٨٣٠ ـ الحَثُّ عَلَى الوَصِيَّةِ

"Prescribed for you, when death approaches any of you and he leaves behind any property, is that he make a bequest for his parents and relatives, in an honourable manner, an obligation on the Godwary."[7407]

﴿كُتِبَ عَلَيْكُمْ إِذَا حَضَرَ أَحَدَكُمُ الْمَوْتُ إِنْ تَرَكَ خَيْراً الْوَصِيَّةُ لِلْوَالِدَيْنِ وَالأَقْرَبِينَ بِالْمَعْرُوفِ حَقّاً عَلَى الْمُتَّقِينَ﴾.[٧٣٨٣]

6508. **The Prophet (SAWA) said,** 'The will is incumbent upon every Muslim.'[7408]

٦٥٠٨. رسولُ اللهِ صلى الله عليه وآله: الوَصِيَّةُ حَقٌّ على كُلِّ مُسلمٍ.[٧٣٨٤]

6509. **The Prophet (SAWA) said,** 'The deprived one is he who has been deprived of [the opportunity to write] a will.'[7409]

٦٥٠٩. عنه صلى الله عليه وآله: المَحرومُ مَن حُرِمَ الوَصيَّةَ.[٧٣٨٥]

6510. **The Prophet (SAWA) said,** 'A Muslim must not sleep a night without his will being beneath his head.'[7410]

٦٥١٠. عنه صلى الله عليه وآله: ما يَنبَغي لامرئٍ مُسلمٍ أن يَبيتَ لَيلَةً إلّا ووَصيَّتُهُ تَحتَ رأسِهِ.[٧٣٨٦]

6511. **Imām al-Bāqir (AS) said,** 'Whoever does not leave a will for those of his family who do not

٦٥١١. الإمامُ الباقرُ عليه السلام: مَن لَم يُوصِ عِندَ مَوتِهِ

automatically inherit him, his deeds end in disobedience [to Allah].'[7411]

لِذَوي قَرابَتِهِ مِمَّن لا يَرِثُهُ فَقَد خَتَمَ عَمَلَهُ بِمَعصِيَةٍ.٧٣٨٧

1831. Forbidding Causing Damages and Losses in One's Will

١٨٣١ ـ النَّهيُ عَنِ الإضرارِ وَالحَيفِ فِي الوَصِيَّةِ

6512. **Imām ʿAlī (AS) said,** 'He who leaves a will and does not wrong or damage is as though he gave it in charity during his lifetime.'[7412]

٦٥١٢. الإمامُ عليٌّ ﷺ: مَن أوصىٰ ولَم يَحِفْ ولَم يُضارَّ كانَ كَمَن تَصَدَّقَ بِهِ في حَياتِهِ.٧٣٨٨

6513. **Imām ʿAlī (AS) said,** 'Causing damages in one's will is among the grave sins.'[7413]

٦٥١٣. عنه ﷺ: الحَيفُ فِي الوَصِيَّةِ مِنَ الكَبائرِ.٧٣٨٩

6514. **Imām al-Ṣādiq (AS) said,** 'He who leaves a will concerning the one third has wronged his heir, and leaving a bequest of a quarter or a fifth [of one's estate] is better than bequesting a third.'[7414]

٦٥١٤. الإمامُ الصّادقُ ﷺ: مَن أوصىٰ بِالثُّلُثِ فَقَد أضَرَّ بِالوَرَثَةِ، والوَصِيَّةُ بِالخُمسِ والرُّبعِ أفضَلُ مِنَ الوَصِيَّةِ بِالثُّلُثِ، ومَن أوصىٰ بِالثُّلُثِ فَلَم يَترُكْ.٧٣٩٠

403

ABLUTION

الوُضوءُ

1832. Ablution

١٨٣٢ ـ الوُضوءُ

"O you who have faith! When you stand up for prayer, wash your faces and your hands up to the elbows, and wipe a part of your heads and your feet, up to the ankles. If you are junub, purify yourselves. But if you are sick, or on a journey, or any of you has come from the toilet, or you have touched women, and you cannot find water, then make tayammum with clean ground and wipe a part of your faces and your hands with it. Allah does not desire to put you to hardship, but He desires to purify you, and to complete His blessing upon you so that you may give thanks." [7415]

﴿يا أيُّهَا الَّذينَ آمَنوا إذا قُمتُم إلَى الصَّلاةِ فَاغسِلوا وُجوهَكُم وأيدِيَكُم إلَى المَرافِقِ وَامسَحوا بِرُؤوسِكُم وأرجُلَكُم إلَى الكَعبَينِ ... ما يُريدُ اللهُ لِيَجعَلَ عَلَيكُم مِن حَرَجٍ ولكِن يُريدُ لِيُطَهِّرَكُم ولِيُتِمَّ نِعمَتَهُ عَلَيكُم لَعَلَّكُم تَشكُرونَ﴾٧٣٩١

6515. **The Prophet (SAWA) said,** 'Ablution is half of faith.'[7416]

٦٥١٥. رسولُ اللهِ ﷺ: الوُضوءُ نِصفُ الإيمانِ.٧٣٩٢

6516. **The Prophet (SAWA) said,** 'He who performs the ablution in the freezing cold weather is given twice the reward, and he who performs the ablution in the extreme heat is given a single share of the reward.'[7417]

٦٥١٦ . عنه ﷺ : مَن أسبَغَ الوُضوءَ في البَردِ الشَّديدِ كانَ لَهُ مِنَ الأجرِ كِفلانِ، ومَن أسبَغَ الوُضوءَ في الحَرِّ الشَّديدِ كانَ لَهُ أجرُ كِفلٍ.[٧٣٩٣]

6517. **The Prophet (SAWA) said,** 'When the Muslim man performs the ablution, mistakes committed by his hearing, his sight, his hands and his feet leave him so that when he sits, he sits forgiven.'[7418]

٦٥١٧ . عنه ﷺ: إذا تَوَضَّأَ الرَّجُلُ المُسلِمُ خَرَجَتْ خَطاياهُ مِن سَمعِهِ وبَصَرِهِ ويَدَيهِ ورِجلَيهِ، فإن قَعَدَ قَعَدَ مَغفوراً لَهُ.[٧٣٩٤]

6518. **The Prophet (SAWA) said,** 'When the servant performs the ablution, his sins shed away from him just as leaves shed from a tree.'[7419]

٦٥١٨ . عنه ﷺ: إذا تَوَضّأَ العَبدُ تَحاطُّ عَنهُ ذُنوبُهُ كما تَحاطُّ وَرَقُ هٰذِهِ الشَّجَرَةِ.[٧٣٩٥]

6519. **Imām ʿAlī (AS) said,** 'He who performs his ablution as best as he can and then walks to the mosque [is considered to be] in a state of prayer as long as he does not nullify it.'[7420]

٦٥١٩ . الإمامُ عليٌّ ؑ: مَن أحسَنَ الطَّهورَ ثُمَّ مَشىٰ إلَى المَسجِدِ، فهُو في صَلاةٍ ما لَم يُحدِثْ.[٧٣٩٦]

6520. **Imām al-Bāqir (AS) said,** 'There is no prayer without ablution.'[7421]

٦٥٢٠ . الإمامُ الباقرُ ؑ: لا صَلاةَ إلّا بِطَهورٍ.[٧٣٩٧]

1833. The Reason for Ablution

١٨٣٣ ـ عِلَّةُ الوُضوءِ

6521. **Imām al-Bāqir (AS) said,** 'Ablution is one of the boundaries of Allah with which He knows who obeys him and who disobeys him.'[7422]

٦٥٢١ . الإمامُ الباقرُ ؑ: إنّما الوُضوءُ حَدٌّ مِن حُدودِ اللهِ؛ لِيَعلَمَ اللهُ مَن يُطيعُهُ ومَن يَعصيهِ.[٧٣٩٨]

6522. **Imām al-Riḍā (AS),** regarding the reason for ablution, said, 'So that the servant is pure when he stands before the Mighty One when engaged in supplication to Him, being obedient to Him through what He has commanded him, purified of filths and impurities, and also because it does away with laziness and repels drowsiness,

٦٥٢٢ . الإمامُ الرِّضا ؑ ـ في عِلَّةِ الوُضوءِ ـ: لأنَّهُ يَكونُ العَبدُ طاهِراً إذا قامَ بَينَ يَدَيِ الجَبّارِ عِندَ مُناجاتِهِ إيّاهُ، مُطيعاً لَهُ فيما أمَرَهُ، نَقِيّاً مِنَ الأدناسِ والنَّجاسَةِ، مَعَ ما فيهِ مِن ذَهابِ الكَسَلِ وطَردِ النُّعاسِ، وتَزكِيَةِ الفُؤادِ

and purifies the heart for standing before the Mighty One.'[7423]

لِلقِيامِ بَينَ يَدَيِ الجَبّارِ.٧٣٩٩

1834. The Effects of Ablution

١٨٣٤ـ آثارُ الوُضوءِ

6523. The Prophet (SAWA) said, 'Allah will resurrect my community on the Day of Resurrection among other communities, having white and illuminated faces from the effects of ablution.'[7424]

٦٥٢٣. رسولُ اللهِ ﷺ: يَحشُرُ اللهُ عَزَّوجلَّ اُمَّتي يَومَ القِيامَةِ بَينَ الاُمَمِ غُرّاً مُحَجَّلينَ مِن آثارِ الوُضوءِ...٧٤٠٠

1835. The Virtue of Frequent and Abundant Ablution

١٨٣٥ـ فَضلُ كَثرَةِ الوُضوءِ

6524. The Prophet (SAWA) said, 'Perform ablution frequently and Allah will increase your life, and if you are able to be in a state of purity throughout the night and day, then do so, for if you die in the state of purity, you will die a martyr.'[7425]

٦٥٢٤. رسولُ اللهِ ﷺ: أكثِرْ مِن الطَّهورِ يَزِدِ اللهُ في عُمرِكَ، وإنِ استَطَعتَ أن تَكونَ بِاللَّيلِ والنَّهارِ على طَهارَةٍ فافعَلْ؛ فإنَّكَ تَكونُ إذا مُتَّ علَى الطَّهارَةِ شَهيداً.٧٤٠١

6525. The Prophet (SAWA) said, 'One who sleeps in a state of purity is as if he is praying [night prayers] and fasting.'[7426]

٦٥٢٥. عنه ﷺ: الطّاهِرُ النّائمُ كالصّائمِ القائمِ.٧٤٠٢

(See also: SLEEPING: section 1779) (اُنظر) النوم: باب ١٧٧٩.

1836. Renewal of Ablution

١٨٣٦ـ تَجديدُ الوُضوءِ

6526. The Prophet (SAWA) said, 'He who performs ablution whilst already in a state of purity is given ten good merits.'[7427]

٦٥٢٦. رسولُ اللهِ ﷺ: مَن تَوَضّأ على طُهرٍ كُتِبَ لَهُ عَشرُ حَسَناتٍ.٧٤٠٣

6527. Imām al-Ṣādiq (AS) said, 'He who renews his ablution without [the need to do so to purify] an impurity, Allah renews his repentance without him [needing to] asking for forgiveness.'[7428]

٦٥٢٧. الإمامُ الصّادقُ ؑ: مَن جَدَّدَ وُضوءَهُ لِغَيرِ حَدَثٍ جَدَّدَ اللهُ تَوبَتَهُ مِن غَيرِ استِغفارٍ.٧٤٠٤

6528. Imām al-Ṣādiq (AS) said, 'Ablution upon ablution is light upon light.'[7429]

٦٥٢٨. عنه ؑ: الوُضوءُ علَى الوُضوءِ نُورٌ على نُورٍ.٧٤٠٥

404

HUMBLENESS التَّواضُعُ

1837. Encouraging Humbleness ١٨٣٧ - الحَثُّ عَلى التَّواضُعِ

6529. **The Prophet (SAWA) said,** 'Why do I not see in you the sweetness of worship?!' They asked, 'What is the sweetness of worship?' He said, 'Humbleness.'[7430]

٦٥٢٩. رسول الله ﷺ: مالي لا أرىٰ عليكُم حَلاوَةَ العِبادَةِ ؟! قالوا: وما حَلاوَةُ العِبادَةِ ؟ قالَ: التَّواضُعُ.٧٤٠٦

6530. **The Prophet (SAWA) said,** 'The best of people is a worshipper who humbles himself when in a high position.'[7431]

٦٥٣٠. عنه ﷺ: إنّ أفضَلَ النّاسِ عَبداً مَن تَواضَعَ عَن رِفعَةٍ.٧٤٠٧

6531. **The Prophet (SAWA) said,** 'Blessed be he who humbles himself before Allah without having any deficiency, and who humiliates himself without poverty.'[7432]

٦٥٣١. عنه ﷺ: طُوبىٰ لِمَن تَواضَعَ للهِ في غَيرِ مَنقَصَةٍ، وأذَلَّ نَفسَهُ في غَيرِ مَسكَنَةٍ.٧٤٠٨

6532. **Imām ʿAlī (AS) said,** 'There is no nobility like humbleness.'[7433]

٦٥٣٢. الإمامُ عليٌّ ﷺ: لا حَسَبَ كالتَّواضُعِ.٧٤٠٩

6533. **Imām ʿAlī (AS) said,** 'The adornment of the noble is humbleness.'[7434]

٦٥٣٣. عنه ﷺ: زينَةُ الشَّريفِ التَّواضُعُ.٧٤١٠

6534. **Imām ʿAlī (AS)**, 'Humbleness is the alms-tax of nobility.'[7435]

٦٥٣٤. عنه ﷺ: التَّواضُعُ زَكاةُ الشَّرَفِ.٧٤١١

6535. **Imām ʿAlī (AS) said,** 'You must be humble, as it is one of the greatest [forms of] worship.'[7436]

٦٥٣٥. عنه ﷺ: عَلَيكَ بِالتَّواضُعِ؛ فإنَّهُ مِن أعظَمِ العِبادَةِ.٧٤١٢

6536. **Imām ʿAlī (AS) said,** describing the pious, 'They are moderate in dressing and humble in manners.'[7437]

٦٥٣٦. عنه ﷺ ـ في صِفَةِ المُتَّقينَ ـ: ومَلبَسُهُمُ الاقتِصادُ، ومَشيُهُمُ التَّواضُعُ.٧٤١٣

6537. **Imām ʿAlī (AS) said,** 'Humbleness spreads virtue.'[7438]

٦٥٣٧. عنه ﷺ: التَّواضُعُ يَنشُرُ الفَضيلَةَ.٧٤١٤

6538. **Imām ʿAlī (AS) said,** 'How good is the humbleness of the wealthy before the poor in seeking what is with Allah, and better than this is the pride of the poor before the wealthy in relying solely on Allah.'[7439]

٦٥٣٨. عنه عليه السلام: ما أحسَنَ تَواضُعَ الأغنياءِ لِلفُقَراءِ طَلَباً لِما عِندَ اللهِ، وأحسَنُ مِنهُ تِيهُ الفُقَراءِ علَى الأغنِياءِ اتِّكالاً علَى اللهِ.[٧٤١٥]

6539. **Imām al-Riḍā (AS) said,** 'Humbleness is to give to people what you yourself like to be given.'[7440]

٦٥٣٩. الإمامُ الرِّضا عليه السلام: التَّواضُعُ أن تُعطِيَ النّاسَ ما تُحِبُّ أن تُعطاهُ.[٧٤١٦]

6540. **Imām al-ʿAskarī (AS) said,** 'Humbleness is a blessing that cannot be envied.'[7441]

٦٥٤٠. الإمامُ العسكريُّ عليه السلام: التَّواضُعُ نِعمَةٌ لا يُحسَدُ علَيها.[٧٤١٧]

1838. Some of the Signs of Humbleness

١٨٣٨ ـ مِن عَلاماتِ التَّواضُعِ

6541. **Imām al-Ṣādiq (AS) said,** 'Humbleness is when a man sits in a place lower than his rank.'[7442]

٦٥٤١. الإمامُ الصّادقُ عليه السلام: إنَّ مِن التَّواضُعِ أن يَجلِسَ الرَّجُلُ دُونَ شَرَفِهِ.[٧٤١٨]

6542. **Imām al-Ṣādiq (AS),** from his fathers (AS) said, 'Humbleness is for a man to be content to sit in any place and not a particular place, to greet those he meets, to leave disputation even if he is right, and to not like to be praised for piety.'[7443]

٦٥٤٢. عنه عن آبائهِ عليهم السلام: إنّ مِن التَّواضُعِ أن يَرضَى الرَّجُلُ بِالمَجلِسِ دُونَ المَجلِسِ، وأن يُسَلِّمَ علىٰ مَن يَلقىٰ، وأن يَترُكَ المِراءَ وإن كانَ مُحِقّاً، ولا يُحِبَّ أن يُحمَدَ علَى التَّقوىٰ.[٧٤١٩]

1839. The Fruit of Humbleness

١٨٣٩ ـ ثَمَرَةُ التَّواضُعِ

6543. **The Prophet (SAWA) said,** 'Humbleness increases the rank of that person, so humble yourselves and Allah will raise you.'[7444]

٦٥٤٣. رسولُ اللهِ ﷺ: إنّ التَّواضُعَ يَزيدُ صاحِبَهُ رِفعَةً، فتَواضَعُوا يَرفَعْكُمُ اللهُ.[٧٤٢٠]

6544. **The Prophet (SAWA) said,** 'He who humbles himself for Allah, Allah will raise him such that he is weak in himself but strong in the eyes of others. And he who is haughty, Allah will degrade him such that he will be small in the eyes of others and big in his own, until he will be more despicable to them than a pig or a dog.'[7445]

٦٥٤٤. عنه ﷺ: مَن تَواضَعَ للهِ رَفَعَهُ اللهُ، فهُو في نَفسِهِ ضَعيفٌ وفي أعيُنِ النّاسِ عَظيمٌ، ومَن تَكبَّرَ وَضَعَهُ اللهُ، فهُو في أعيُنِ النّاسِ صَغيرٌ وفي نَفسِهِ كَبيرٌ؛ حتّىٰ لَهُو أهوَنُ علَيهِم مِن كَلبٍ أو خِنزيرٍ.[٧٤٢١]

6545. **Imām ʿAlī (AS) said,** 'The fruit of humbleness is love, and the result of pride is abuse.'[7446]

٦٥٤٥. الإمامُ عليٌّ عليه السلام: ثَمَرَةُ التَّواضُعِ المَحَبّةُ، ثَمَرَةُ الكِبرِ المَسَبَّةُ.[٧٤٢٢]

6546. **Imām ʿAlī (AS) said,** 'Humbleness clothes you in dignity.'[7447]

٦٥٤٦. عنه عليه السلام: التَّواضُعُ يَكسوكَ المَهابَةَ.[٧٤٢٣]

6547. **Imām ʿAlī (AS) said,** 'With the lowering of one's wing are affairs organised.'[7448]

٦٥٤٧. عنه عليه السلام: بِخَفضِ الجَناحِ تَنتَظِمُ الأُمورُ.[٧٤٢٤]

6548. **Imām ʿAlī (AS) said,** 'Humbleness spreads virtue and haughtiness shows up vice.'[7449]

٦٥٤٨. عنه عليه السلام: التَّواضُعُ يَنشُرُ الفَضيلَةَ، التَّكبُّرُ يُظهِرُ الرَّذيلَةَ.[٧٤٢٥]

6549. **Imām al-Kāẓim (AS) said,** 'A plant grows on level ground and not on the hard terrain, and similarly wisdom flourishes in the heart of the humble, and does not flourish in the heart of the haughty and overbearing, because Allah made humbleness the instrument of the intellect and haughtiness the instrument of ignorance.'[7450]

٦٥٤٩. الإمامُ الكاظمُ عليه السلام: إنّ الزَّرعَ يَنبُتُ في السَّهلِ ولا يَنبُتُ في الصَّفا؛ فكذلكَ الحِكمَةُ تَعمُرُ في قَلبِ المُتَواضِعِ، ولا تَعمُرُ في قَلبِ المُتَكبِّرِ الجَبّارِ؛ لأنّ اللهَ جَعلَ التَّواضُعَ آلَةَ العَقلِ، وجَعَلَ التَّكبُّرَ مِن آلَةِ الجَهلِ.[٧٤٢٦]

6550. **Imām al-Kāẓim (AS) said,** 'Allah does not raise the humble in proportion to their humbleness, rather He raises them according to His own Greatness and Glory.'[7451]

٦٥٥٠. الإمامُ الكاظمُ عليه السلام: إنّ اللهَ لَم يَرفَعِ المُتَواضِعينَ بقَدرِ تَواضُعِهِم، ولٰكنْ رَفَعَهُم بِقَدرِ عَظَمَتِهِ ومَجدِهِ.[٧٤٢٧]

1840. Means to Acquire Humbleness

١٨٤٠ـ ما يُستَعانُ بِهِ عَلَى التَّواضُعِ

6551. **Imām ʿAlī (AS) said,** 'Humbleness cannot be achieved…, unless the heart is healthy.'[7452]

٦٥٥١. الإمامُ عليٌّ عليه السلام: لا يُستَعانُ... علَى التَّواضُعِ إلّا بسَلامَةِ الصَّدرِ.[٧٤٢٨]

6552. **Imām ʿAlī (AS) said,** 'Humbleness is the fruit of knowledge.'[7453]

٦٥٥٢. عنه عليه السلام: التَّواضُعُ ثَمَرَةُ العِلمِ.[٧٤٢٩]

6553. **Imām ʿAlī (AS) said,** 'It is not appropriate for one who knows the Greatness of Allah to consider himself as great, for verily the elevation of those who know His Greatness lies in humbling themselves before Him.'[7454]

٦٥٥٣. عنه عليه السلام: لا يَنبَغي لِمَن عَرَفَ عَظَمَةَ اللهِ أن يَتَعَظَّمَ؛ فإنّ رِفعَةَ الّذينَ يَعلَمونَ ما عَظَمَتُهُ أن يَتَواضَعُوا لَهُ.[٧٤٣٠]

1841. Limits of Humbleness

١٨٤١ـ حَدُّ التَّواضُعِ

6554. **Imām ʿAlī (AS) said,** 'It suffices a man as a sign of humbleness to know his worth.'[7455]

٦٥٥٤. الإمامُ عليٌّ عليه السلام: حَسبُ المَرءِ... مِن تَواضُعِهِ مَعرِفَتُهُ بقَدرِهِ.[٧٤٣١]

6555. **Imām al-Ṣādiq (AS)** when asked about humbleness said, 'Humbleness is that you be content to sit in a meeting where it is below your position, greet whosoever you meet and give up dispute even if you are right.'[7456]

٦٥٥٥. الإمامُ الصّادقُ ﷺ ـ لَـمّا سُئلَ عَنِ التَّواضُعِ ـ: هُو أن تَرضىٰ مِن المَـجلِسِ بِـدُونِ شَرَفِكَ، وأن تُسَلِّمَ علىٰ مَن لَـقِيتَ، وأن تَـترُكَ المِراءَ وإن كُنتَ مُحِقّاً.٧٤٣٢

6556. **Imām al-Riḍā (AS)** when asked about the limits of humbleness said, 'To treat the people in the same manner you like them to treat you.'[7457]

٦٥٥٦. الإمامُ الرِّضا ﷺ ـ لَمّا سُئلَ عَـن حَـدِّ التَّواضُعِ ـ: أن تُعطِيَ النّاسَ مِن نَفسِكَ ما تُحِبُّ أن يُعطوكَ مِثلَهُ.٧٤٣٣

6557. **Imām al-Riḍā (AS)** when asked by Ibn al-Jahm, 'What are the limits of humbleness that makes a servant humble when he observes them?' to which he (AS) replied, 'Humbleness has stages; that one knows the value of his self and places it in its right position with a sincere heart, that he likes to treat people the same way he expects them to treat him, that he responds the wrong with good, that he controls his anger and forgives the people. And Allah likes the good doers.'[7458]

٦٥٥٧. عنه ﷺ ـ لَمّا سألَهُ ابنُ الجَهمِ: ما حَدُّ التَّواضُعِ الّذي إذا فَعَلَهُ العَبدُ كانَ مُتَواضِعاً؟ ـ: التَّواضُعُ دَرَجاتٌ: مِنها أن يَـعرِفَ المَـرءُ قَـدرَ نَفسِهِ فيُنزِلَها مَنزِلَتَها بقَلبٍ سَـليمٍ، لا يُـحِبُّ أن يأتيَ إلى أحَدٍ إلّا مِثلَ مـا يُـؤتىٰ إلَـيهِ؛ إن رأى سَيِّئةً دَرأها بِالحَسنَةِ، كاظِمُ الغَيظِ، عـافٍ عَـنِ النّاسِ، واللهُ يُحِبُّ المُحسِنينَ.٧٤٣٤

405

THE HOMELAND

الوَطَنُ

1842. Patriotism

١٨٤٢ ـ حُبُّ الوَطَنِ

6558. **Imām ʿAlī (AS) said,** 'Countries thrive as a result of patriotism.'[7459]

٦٥٥٨. الإمامُ عليٌّ ﷺ: عَمُرَتِ البُلدانُ بِـحُبِّ الأوطانِ.٧٤٣٥

6559. **Imām ʿAlī (AS) said,** 'The honour of a man lies in his crying over what he has lost from his life, his affection towards his homeland, and his protectiveness of his old brothers.'[7460]

٦٥٥٩. عنه ﷺ: مِن كَرَمِ المَرءِ بُكاؤهُ علىٰ ما مَضىٰ مِن زَمانِهِ، وحَنينُهُ إلىٰ أوطانِهِ، وحِـفظُهُ قَديمَ إخوانِهِ.٧٤٣٦

6560. *Safīnat al-Biḥār*. It is narrated, 'Patriotism is part of faith.'[7461]

٦٥٦٠. سفينة البحار: رُوِيَ: حُبُّ الوَطَنِ مِنَ الإيمانِ.٧٤٣٧

1843. Defending One's Homeland

١٨٤٣ ـ الدِّفاعُ عَنِ الوَطَنِ

6561. **Imām ʿAlī (AS) said,** 'Invade them before they invade you, for by Allah, no sooner are a people invaded in their own homes than they are humiliated. So you were indifferent and treacherous towards each other until invasions were waged upon you, and your homelands were overtaken.'[7462]

٦٥٦١. الإمامُ عليٌّ عليه السلام: اغزُوهُم قَبلَ أن يَغزوكُم، فوَاللهِ ما غُزِيَ قَومٌ قَطُّ في عُقرِ دارِهِم إلّا ذَلّوا، فتواكَلتُم وتَخاذَلتُم حتّىٰ شُنَّت علَيكُمُ الغاراتُ، ومُلِكَت علَيكُمُ الأوطانُ.٧٤٣٨

1844. Separation from One's Homeland

١٨٤٤ ـ الغُربَةُ وَالوَطَنُ

6562. **Imām ʿAlī (AS) said,** 'Wealth in a foreign place is like being in one's homeland, and poverty in one's homeland is like estrangement therein.'[7463]

٦٥٦٢. الإمامُ عليٌّ عليه السلام: الغِنىٰ في الغُربَةِ وَطَنٌ، والفَقرُ في الوَطَنِ غُربَةٌ.٧٤٣٩

6563. **Imām ʿAlī (AS) said,** 'Living in a foreign place is not disgrace, rather poverty in one's homeland is disdain.'[7464]

٦٥٦٣. عنه عليه السلام: لَيسَ في الغُربَةِ عارٌ، إنّما العارُ في الوَطَنِ الافتِقارُ.٧٤٤٠

6564. **Imām ʿAlī (AS) said,** 'Wisdom in a foreign land makes one feel at home while silliness in the homeland is like estrangement therein.'[7465]

٦٥٦٤. عنه عليه السلام: العَقلُ في الغُربَةِ قُربَةٌ، الحُمقُ في الوَطَنِ غُربَةٌ.٧٤٤١

406

THE PROMISE

الوَعد

1845. The Promise of Allah is True

١٨٤٥ ـ وَعدُ اللهِ حَقٌّ

"So be patient! Allah's promise is indeed true. And do not let yourself be upset by those who have no conviction."[7466]

﴿فَاصْبِرْ إِنَّ وَعْدَ اللهِ حَقٌّ وَلَا يَسْتَخِفَّنَّكَ الَّذِينَ لَا يُوقِنُونَ﴾.٧٤٤٢

"Our Lord! You will indeed gather mankind on a day in which there is no doubt. Indeed Allah does not break His promise."[7467]

﴿رَبَّنَا إِنَّكَ جَامِعُ النَّاسِ لِيَوْمٍ لَا رَيْبَ فِيهِ إِنَّ اللهَ لَا يُخْلِفُ الْمِيعَادَ﴾.٧٤٤٣

6565. **The Prophet (SAWA) said,** 'He whom Allah promises a reward for a good deed He will fulfil it, and he whom He has promised punishment for a deed, then it is [ultimately] His choice [whether He punishes or forgives].'[7468]

٦٥٦٥ . رسولُ اللهِ ﷺ : مَن وَعَدَهُ اللهُ علىٰ عَمَلٍ ثَواباً فهُو مُنجِزُهُ لَهُ ، ومَن أوعَدَهُ علىٰ عَمَلٍ عِقاباً فهُو فيهِ بِالخِيارِ .٧٤٤٤

1846. The Promise is a Debt

١٨٤٦ ـ العِدَةُ دَينٌ

6566. **The Prophet (SAWA) said,** 'The promise is a debt. Woe unto he who promises but does not fulfil it. Woe unto he who promises but does not fulfil it. Woe unto he who promises but does not fulfil it.'[7469]

٦٥٦٦ . رسولُ اللهِ ﷺ : العِدَةُ دَينٌ ، وَيلٌ لِمَن وَعَدَ ثُمّ أخلَفَ ، وَيلٌ لِمَن وَعَدَ ثُمّ أخلَفَ ، وَيلٌ لِمَن وَعَدَ ثُمّ أخلَفَ .٧٤٤٥

6567. **The Prophet (SAWA) said,** 'The promise of the believer is a debt and the promise of the believer is like a pledge.'[7470]

٦٥٦٧ . عنه ﷺ : عِدَةُ المُؤمنِ دَينٌ ، وعِدَةُ المُؤمنِ كالأخذِ بِاليَدِ .٧٤٤٦

6568. **Imām ʿAlī (AS) said,** 'The restlessness of a man in his bed during the night whom I have given a promise for the fulfilment of his need the next day is not more than my restlessness in my bed being anxious till the morning to fulfil my promise. I am also fearful lest some obstacles prevent the keeping of my promise, as the breaching of a promise is not of the characteristics of the noble.'[7471]

٦٥٦٨ . الإمامُ عليٌّ ؑ : ما باتَ لِرجُلٍ عِندي مَوعِدٌ قَطُّ فباتَ يَتَمَلمَلُ علىٰ فِراشِهِ لِيَغدُوَ بِالظَّفَرِ بحاجَتِهِ ، أشَدَّ مِن تَمَلمُلي علىٰ فِراشي حِرصاً علَى الخُروجِ إلَيهِ مِن دَينِ عِدَتِهِ ، وخَوفاً مِن عائقٍ يُوجِبُ الخُلفَ ؛ فإنّ خُلفَ الوَعدِ لَيسَ مِن أخلاقِ الكِرامِ .٧٤٤٧

6569. **Imām al-Riḍā (AS) said,** 'We, the *Ahl al-Bayt*, see what we have promised as a debt upon us just as the Prophet (SAWA) used to do.'[7472]

٦٥٦٩ . الإمامُ الرِّضا ؑ : إنّا أهلُ بَيتٍ نَرىٰ ما وَعَدْنا علَينا دَيناً كما صَنَعَ رسولُ اللهِ ﷺ .٧٤٤٨

1847. The Promise is One of Two Types of Bondage

١٨٤٧ ـ الوَعدُ أحَدُ الرِّقَّينِ

6570. **Imām ʿAlī (AS) said,** 'He who is asked is free until he makes a promise.'[7473]

٦٥٧٠ . الإمامُ عليٌّ ؑ : المَسؤولُ حُرٌّ حتّىٰ يَعِدَ .٧٤٤٩

6571. **Imām ʿAlī (AS) said,** 'The promise is one of two bondages; and fulfilment of the promise is one of the two freedoms.'[7474]

٦٥٧١ . عنه ؑ : الوَعدُ أحَدُ الرِّقَّينِ ، إنجازُ الوَعدِ أحَدُ العِتقَينِ .٧٤٥٠

6572. *al-Targhīb wa al-Tarhīb*: "Abdullāh b. Abū al-Ḥumaysā' said, 'I pledged allegiance to the Prophet (SAWA) before he set out [for a place], and I had an appointment with him in a particular place, but I forgot that day and the next, so I came to him on the third day, and the Prophet (SAWA) said, 'Young man, you have brought great difficulty to me, I have been waiting here for three days.'[7475]

٦٥٧٢ . الترغيب والترهيب عن عبدِ اللهِ بنِ أبي لحَمساءِ: بايَعتُ رسولَ اللهِ ﷺ بِبَيعٍ قَبلَ أن يَبعَثَ ، فَبَقِيَت لَهُ بَقيَّةٌ ووَعَدتُهُ أن آتِيَهُ بها في مَكانِهِ، فنَسِيتُ، ثُمّ ذَكَرتُ بَعدَ ثَلاثٍ فَجِئتُ فإذا هُو مَكانَهُ. فقالَ: يافَتىٰ، لَقَد شَقَقتَ علَيَّ، نا هاهُنا مُنذُ ثَلاثٍ أنتَظِرُكَ![٧٤٥١]

6573. **Imām ʿAlī (AS) said,** 'Giving a promise is a sickness and fulfilling it is its remedy.'[7476]

٦٥٧٣ . الإمامُ عليٌّ عليه السلام : الوَعدُ مَرَضٌ وَالبُرءُ نجازُهُ.[٧٤٥٢]

1848. What Should not be Promised

١٨٤٨ ـ ما لا يَنبَغي مِنَ الوَعدِ

6574. **Imām ʿAlī (AS) said,** 'Do not make a promise that you are not confident of fulfilling.'[7477]

٦٥٧٤ . الإمامُ عليٌّ عليه السلام : لا تَعِدَنَّ عِدَةً لا تَثِقُ مِن فسِكَ بإنجازِها.[٧٤٥٣]

6575. **Imām al-Ṣādiq (AS) said,** 'Do not make a promise to your brother that you are incapable of fulfilling.'[7478]

٦٥٧٥ . الإمامُ الصّادقُ عليه السلام : لا تَعِدَنَّ أخاكَ وَعداً يسَ في يَدِكَ وَفاؤُهُ.[٧٤٥٤]

6576. **Imām al-Kāẓim (AS) said,** 'An intelligent person....does not make a promise he cannot fulfil.'[7479]

٦٥٧٦ . الإمامُ الكاظِمُ عليه السلام : إنّ العاقِلَ... لا يَعِدُ ا لا يَقدِرُ عَلَيهِ.[٧٤٥٥]

1849. Reproaching the Breaking of a Promise

١٨٤٩ ـ ذَمُّ خُلفِ الوَعدِ

6577. **Imām al-Ṣādiq (AS) said,** 'The promise of a believer to his brother is a vow for which there is no [prescribed] penance, so he who breaks a promise has first broken his promise to Allah and subjects himself to His discontentment, as Allah says: *"O you who have faith! Why do you say what you do not do?"*'[7480 7481]

٦٥٧٧ . الإمامُ الصّادقُ عليه السلام : عِدَةُ المُؤمِنِ أخاهُ نَذرٌ لا كَفّارَةَ لَهُ ، فمَن أخلَفَ فبِخُلفِ اللهِ بَدأَ ، ولِمَقتِهِ تَعَرَّضَ، وذلكَ قَولُهُ: ﴿يا أيُّها الّذِينَ آمَنُوا لِمَ تَقُولونَ ما لا تَفْعَلُونَ﴾[٧٤٥٦، ٧٤٥٧]

6578. **Imām al-Kāẓim (AS) said,** 'When you make a promise to children then fulfil that promise to them, because they perceive you as the one who provides them with the means of subsistence, and Allah is not angered by anything

٦٥٧٨ . الإمامُ الكاظمُ عليه السلام : إذا وَعَدتُمُ الصِّغارَ فأوفُوا لَهُم ؛ فإنَّهُم يَرَونَ أنّكُم أنتُمُ الّذينَ تَرزُقونَهُم، وإنّ اللهَ لا يَغضَبُ بشَيءٍ كغَضَبِهِ

the way He is angered by [matters pertaining to] the rights of women and children.'[7482] — لِلنِّساءِ والصِّبيانِ.٧٤٥٨

407

EXHORTATION — المَوعِظَة

1850. The Role of Exhortation in the Revival of the Heart — ١٨٥٠ ـ دَورُ المَوعِظَةِ في حَياةِ القَلبِ

6579. **Imām ʿAlī (AS) said** in his will to his son, exhorting him, 'Revive your heart with exhortation.'[7483]

٦٥٧٩. الإمامُ عليٌّ ﷺ ـ في وَصيَّتِهِ لابنِهِ وهُو يَعِظُهُ ـ: أحيِ قَلبَكَ بِالمَوعِظَةِ.٧٤٥٩

6580. **Imām ʿAlī (AS) said,** 'Exhortations are the polishers of the self and the cleansers of the heart.'[7484]

٦٥٨٠. عنه ﷺ: المَواعِظُ صَقالُ النُّفوسِ، وجَلاءُ القُلوبِ.٧٤٦٠

6581. **Imām ʿAlī (AS) said,** 'Through exhortations is inattentiveness cleared.'[7485]

٦٥٨١. عنه ﷺ: بِالمَواعِظِ تَنجَلي الغَفلَةُ.٧٤٦١

(See also: THE HEART: section 1558) — (أنظر) القلب: باب ١٥٥٨.

1851. Types of Exhorters — ١٨٥١ ـ أنواعُ الوُعّاظِ

6582. **The Prophet (SAWA) said,** 'Death suffices as an exhorter.'[7486]

٦٥٨٢. رسولُ اللهِ ﷺ: كَفىٰ بِالمَوتِ واعِظاً.٧٤٦٢

6583. **Imām ʿAlī (AS) said,** 'An intelligent person is he who is exhorted by experience.'[7487]

٦٥٨٣. الإمامُ عليٌّ ﷺ: العاقِلُ مَن وَعَظَتهُ التَّجارِبُ.٧٤٦٣

6584. **Imām ʿAlī (AS) said,** 'The experiences of people of conscience are enough of an exhortation.'[7488]

٦٥٨٤. عنه ﷺ: كَفىٰ عِظَةً لِذَوي الألبابِ ما جَرَّبوا.٧٤٦٤

6585. **Imām ʿAlī (AS) said,** 'When Allah loves a servant, He exhorts him with examples.'[7489]

٦٥٨٥. عنه ﷺ: إذا أحَبَّ اللهُ عَبداً وَعَظَهُ بِالعِبَرِ.٧٤٦٥

6586. **Imām ʿAlī (AS) said,** 'He who understands the exhortations of time will not be at ease with entertaining good opinions about his days.'[7490]

٦٥٨٦. عنه ﷺ: مَن فَهِمَ مَواعِظَ الزَّمانِ لَم يَسكُنْ إلىٰ حُسنِ الظَّنِّ بِالأيّامِ.٧٤٦٦

6587. **Imām ʿAlī (AS) said,** 'That which has exhorted you from your wealth [through loss] is not lost.'[7491]

٦٥٨٧. عنه عليه السلام: لَم يَذهَبْ مِن مالِكَ ما وَعَظَكَ.٧٤٦٧

6588. **Imām ʿAlī (AS) said** in his description of this world, 'The world is the abode of exhortation for he who accepts from it...The world reminds them and so they remember, and it speaks to them so they believe, and it exhorts them so they accept its exhortation.'[7492]

٦٥٨٨. عنه عليه السلام ـ في صِفَةِ الدُّنيا ـ: إنَّ الدُّنيا دارُ مَوعِظَةٍ لِمَنِ اتَّعَظَ بِها... ذَكَّرَتهُمُ الدُّنيا فَتَذَكَّروا، وحَدَّثَتهُم فَصَدَّقوا، ووَعَظَتهُم فاتَّعَظوا.٧٤٦٨

6589. **Imām ʿAlī (AS) said,** 'The sagacious man sees in everything an exhortation.'[7493]

٦٥٨٩. عنه عليه السلام: لِلكَيِّسِ في كُلِّ شَيءٍ اتِّعاظٌ.٧٤٦٩

6590. **Imām ʿAlī (AS) said,** 'The most far-reaching of exhortations is consideration of the fates of dead people.'[7494]

٦٥٩٠. عنه عليه السلام: أبلَغُ العِظاتِ الاعتِبارُ بِمَصارِعِ الأمواتِ.٧٤٧٠

6591. **Imām ʿAlī (AS) said,** 'Allah Almighty has not exhorted anyone like He does through the Qur'an.'[7495]

٦٥٩١. عنه عليه السلام: إنَّ اللهَ سبحانَهُ لَم يَعِظْ أحَداً بِمِثلِ هٰذا القرآنِ.٧٤٧١

6592. **Imām ʿAlī (AS) said,** 'There is no exhorter better than advice.'[7496]

٦٥٩٢. عنه عليه السلام: لا واعِظَ أبلَغُ مِنَ النُّصحِ.٧٤٧٢

6593. **Imām ʿAlī (AS) said,** 'Take lesson from [the lives of] those who passed before you, before those who come after you take lesson from you [i.e. your life].'[7497]

٦٥٩٣. عنه عليه السلام: واتَّعِظوا بِمَن كانَ قَبلَكُم قَبلَ أن يَتَّعِظَ بِكُم مَن بَعدَكُم.٧٤٧٣

6594. **Imām al-Ṣādiq (AS) said,** 'The most truthful saying and the most complete exhortation, and the greatest of stories is the Book of Allah.'[7498]

٦٥٩٤. الإمامُ الصّادقُ عليه السلام: أصدَقُ القَولِ، وأبلَغُ المَوعِظَةِ، وأحسَنُ القَصَصِ: كِتابُ اللهِ.٧٤٧٤

1852. There is Exhortation in Everything

١٨٥٢ـ في كُلِّ شَيءٍ مَوعِظَةٌ

6595. **Imām ʿAlī (AS) said,** 'Verily, there is an exhortation and lesson in everything for those who have wisdom and take lesson.'[7499]

٦٥٩٥. الإمامُ عليٌّ عليه السلام: إنّ في كُلِّ شَيءٍ مَوعِظَةً وعِبرَةً لِذَوي اللُّبِّ والاعتِبارِ.٧٤٧٥

6596. **Imām ʿAlī (AS) said,** 'There is exhortation in everything for the sagacious.'[7500]

٦٥٩٦. عنه ﷺ: لِلكَيِّسِ في كُلِّ شَيءٍ اتِّعاظٌ.٧٤٧٦

6597. **Imām ʿAlī (AS) said,** 'There is exhortation in everything for he who contemplates.'[7501]

٦٥٩٧. عنه ﷺ: مَن كانَت لَهُ فِكرَةٌ فَلَهُ في كُلِّ شَيءٍ عِبرَةٌ.٧٤٧٧

6598. **Imām al-Kāẓim (AS) said** in his letter to Hārūn al-Rashīd, when he asked him for exhortation, 'Every single thing your eye sees contains an exhortation.'[7502]

٦٥٩٨. الإمامُ الكاظمُ ﷺ ـ في كِتابِهِ إلىٰ هارونَ الرَّشيدِ، لَمّا طَلَبَ مِنهُ المَوعِظَةَ ـ: ما مِن شَيءٍ تَراهُ عَينُكَ إلّا وفيهِ مَوعِظَةٌ.٧٤٧٨

(See also: THE MORAL LESSON: section 1206)

1853. Etiquettes of Exhortation

١٨٥٣ـ آدابُ المَوعِظَةِ

"Invite to the way of Your Lord with wisdom and good advice and dispute with them in a manner that is best. Indeed your Lord knows best those who stray from His way, and He knows best those who are guided."[7503]

﴿ادْعُ إِلَىٰ سَبِيلِ رَبِّكَ بِالْحِكْمَةِ وَالْمَوْعِظَةِ الْحَسَنَةِ وَجَادِلْهُمْ بِالَّتِي هِيَ أَحْسَنُ إِنَّ رَبَّكَ هُوَ أَعْلَمُ بِمَنْ ضَلَّ عَنْ سَبِيلِهِ وَهُوَ أَعْلَمُ بِالْمُهْتَدِينَ﴾.٧٤٧٩

6599. **Jābir b. Samura said,** 'The Prophet (SAWA) never prolonged the exhortation on Friday, but rather used simple phrases.'[7504]

٦٥٩٩. جابر بن سَمُرَة: كانَ رسولُ اللهِ ﷺ لا يُطيلُ المَوعِظَةَ يَومَ الجُمُعَةِ، إنَّما هُنَّ كَلِماتٌ يَسيراتٌ.٧٤٨٠

6600. **Imām ʿAlī (AS) said,** 'Your advice to a congregation of people is like chiding.'[7505]

٦٦٠٠. الإمامُ عليٌّ ﷺ: نُصحُكَ بَينَ المَلَأِ تَقريعٌ.٧٤٨١

6601. **Imām al-ʿAskarī (AS) said,** 'He who exhorts his brother in secret has indeed adorned him, and he who exhorts him in public has dishonoured him.'[7506]

٦٦٠١. الإمامُ العسكريُّ ﷺ: مَن وَعَظَ أخاهُ سِرّاً فَقَد زانَهُ، ومَن وَعَظَهُ عَلانِيَةً فَقَد شانَهُ.٧٤٨٢

(See also: PROPAGATION: section 260)

(اُنظر: التبليغ: باب ٢٦٠)

1854. The Personal Exhorter

١٨٥٤ـ الواعِظُ النَّفسيُّ

6602. **Imām ʿAlī (AS) said,** 'He whose inner self is an exhorter to him has been granted a protector by Allah over him.'[7507]

٦٦٠٢. الإمامُ عليٌّ ﷺ: مَن كانَ لَهُ في نَفسِهِ واعِظٌ كانَ عَلَيهِ مِنَ اللهِ حافِظٌ.٧٤٨٣

6603. **Imām Zayn al-ʿĀbidīn (AS) said,** 'O son of Adam, you will continue to be good as long as

٦٦٠٣. الإمامُ زينُ العابدينَ ﷺ ـ كانَ يَقولُ ـ: ابنَ آدَمَ، لا تَزالُ بِخَيرٍ ما كانَ لَكَ واعِظٌ مِن نَفسِكَ،

you have an exhorter within yourself, and as long as taking account of your deeds is your concern, and as long as fear [of Allah] is your basis and caution is your armour.'[7508]

وما كانَتِ المُحاسَبَةُ مِن هَمِّكَ، وما كانَ الخَوفُ لَكَ شِعاراً، والحُـزنُ لَكَ دِثـاراً. ابـنَ آدمَ، إنّكَ مَيِّتٌ وَمبعوثٌ ومَوقوفٌ بَينَ يَدَيِ اللهِ عَـزَّوجلَّ ومَسؤولٌ فأعِدَّ جَواباً.[٧٤٨٤]

6604. **Imām al-Bāqir (AS) said,** 'He for whom Allah has not made an exhorter from his own self, the exhortations of people will not benefit him at all.'[7509]

٦٦٠٤. الإمامُ الباقرُ عليه السلام: مَن لَم يَجعَلِ اللهُ لَهُ مِن نفسِهِ واعِظاً، فإنَّ مَواعِظَ النّاسِ لَن تُغنيَ عَـنهُ شيئاً.[٧٤٨٥]

1855. Those who do not Benefit from Exhortation

١٨٥٥ ـ مَن لا يَنتَفِعُ بِالمَوعِظَةِ

6605. **Imām ʿAlī (AS) said,** 'The ignorant man cannot refrain [from sins], nor does he benefit from exhortations.'[7510]

٦٦٠٥. الإمامُ عليٌّ عليه السلام: الجـاهِلُ لا يَـرتَدِعُ، وبِالمَواعِظِ لا يَنتَفِعُ.[٧٤٨٦]

6606. **Imām ʿAlī (AS) said,** 'He whom Allah does not help against his base self cannot benefit from the exhortation of an adviser.'[7511]

٦٦٠٦. عنه عليه السلام: مَن لَم يُعِنْهُ اللهُ علىٰ نَفسِهِ لَم يَنتَفِعْ بِمَوعِظَةِ واعِظٍ.[٧٤٨٧]

6607. **Imām ʿAlī (AS) said,** 'Between you and [benefitting from] an exhortation is a wall of inadvertency.'[7512]

٦٦٠٧. عنه عليه السلام: بَينَكُم وبَينَ المَوعِظَةِ حِجابٌ مِن الغِرَّةِ.[٧٤٨٨]

1856. The Exhorter who himself is not Exhorted

١٨٥٦ ـ الواعِظُ غَيرُ المُتَّعِظِ

"O you who have faith! Why do you say what you do not do? It is greatly outrageous to Allah that you should say what you do not do."[7513]

﴿يا أَيُّها الَّذِينَ آمَنُوا لِمَ تَقُولُونَ مَا لَا تَفْعَلُونَ ❁ كَبُرَ مَقْتاً عِنْدَ اللهِ أَنْ تَقُولُوا مَا لَا تَفْعَلُونَ﴾.[٧٤٨٩]

6608. **The Prophet (SAWA) said,** 'Allah revealed to Jesus son of Mary, 'Exhort yourself with My wisdom, and once you benefit from it then exhort people, and if not, then be ashamed in front of Me.'[7514]

٦٦٠٨. رسولُ اللهِ صلى الله عليه وآله: أوحَى اللهُ إلىٰ عيسَى بنِ مَريمَ: عِظْ نفسَكَ بحِكمَتي، فإنِ انـتَفَعتَ فَـعِظِ النّاسَ، وإلّا فاستَحيِ مِنّي.[٧٤٩٠]

6609. **Imām ʿAlī (AS) said,** 'Do not be like he who…exhorts extensively but does not take lesson himself, as he is arrogant in his speech and little in

٦٦٠٩. الإمامُ عليٌّ عليه السلام: لا تَكُن مِمَّن... يُبالِغُ في المَوعِظَةِ ولا يَتَّعِظُ، فهُو بِالقَولِ مُدِلٌّ ومِن العَمَلِ

deeds, he challenges for what is to perish, and allows to pass what is eternal, he sees benefits as a loss, and losses as beneficial.'[7515]

مُقِلٌّ، يُنافِسُ فيما يَفنىٰ، ويُسامِحُ فيما يَبقىٰ، يَرَى الغُنمَ مَغرَماً، والغُرمَ مَغنَماً.٧٤٩١

6610. **Imām ʿAlī (AS) said,** 'Many a rebuker is himself not rebuked, and many an exhorter is himself not restrained [from sins].'[7516]

٦٦١٠. عنه ﵇: رُبَّ زاجِرٍ غَيرُ مُزدَجِرٍ، رُبَّ واعِظٍ غَيرُ مُرتَدِعٍ.٧٤٩٢

6611. **Imām ʿAlī (AS) said,** 'O people, seek enlightenment from the torch of the lamp of an exhorter who takes his own advice and from the clear spring that has been filtered of all impurity.'[7517]

٦٦١١. عنه ﵇: أيُّهاالنّاسُ، اِستَصبِحوامِن شُعلَةِ مِصباحِ واعِظٍ مُتَّعِظٍ، وامتاحُوا مِن صَفوِ عَينٍ قَد رُوِّقَت مِنَ الكَدَرِ.٧٤٩٣

6612. **Imām al-Ṣādiq (AS) said,** 'When the knowledgeable man does not act upon his knowledge, his exhortation slips away from the hearts like the rain slips off a flat rock.'[7518]

٦٦١٢. الإمامُ الصّادقُ ﵇: إنّ العالِمَ إذا لم يَعمَلْ بِعلمِهِ زَلَّت مَوعِظَتُهُ عنِ القُلوبِ كَما يَزِلُّ المَطَرُ عنِ الصَّفا.٧٤٩٤

1857. The Silent Propagation

١٨٥٧ ـ الدَّعوَةُ بِغَيرِ اللِّسانِ

6613. **Imām ʿAlī (AS) said,** 'The exhortation which cannot be missed by the hearing, nor matched by any other benefit is that which the tongue of speech remains silent about and the tongue of action expresses.'[7519]

٦٦١٣. الإمامُ عليٌّ ﵇: إنّ الوَعظَ الّذي لا يَمُجُّهُ سَمعٌ، ولا يَعدِلُهُ نَفعٌ، ما سَكَتَ عَنهُ لِسانُ القَولِ ونَطَقَ بِهِ لِسانُ الفِعلِ.٧٤٩٥

408

SUCCESS (*tawfīq*)[7520]

التَّوفيقُ

1858. Success

١٨٥٨ ـ التَّوفيقُ

"He said, "O my people! Have you considered, should I stand on a manifest proof from my Lord, who has provided me a good provision from Himself? I do not wish to oppose you by what I forbid you. I only desire to put things in order, as far as I can, and my success

﴿قَالَ يَا قَوْمِ أَرَأَيْتُمْ إِنْ كُنْتُ عَلَىٰ بَيِّنَةٍ مِنْ رَبِّى وَرَزَقَنِي مِنْهُ رِزْقاً حَسَناً وَمَا أُرِيدُ أَنْ أُخَالِفَكُمْ إِلَىٰ مَا أَنْهَاكُمْ عَنْهُ إِنْ أُرِيدُ إِلَّا الْإِصْلَاحَ مَا

lies only with Allah: in Him I have put my trust, and to Him I turn penitently."[7521]

اسْتَطَعْتُ وَمَا تَوْفِيقِي إِلَّا بِاللهِ عَلَيْهِ تَوَكَّلْتُ وَإِلَيْهِ أُنِيبُ﴾.[٧٤٩٦]

6614. **Imām ʿAlī (AS) said,** 'Success is [divine] care.'[7522]

٦٦١٤. الإمامُ عليٌّ عليه السلام: التَّوفيقُ عِنايَةٌ.[٧٤٩٧]

6615. **Imām ʿAlī (AS) said,** 'Success is [divine] mercy.'[7523]

٦٦١٥. عنه عليه السلام: التَّوفيقُ رَحمَةٌ.[٧٤٩٨]

6616. **Imām ʿAlī (AS) said,** 'Success is from the attractions of the Lord.'[7524]

٦٦١٦. عنه عليه السلام: التَّوفيقُ مِن جَذَباتِ الرَّبِّ.[٧٤٩٩]

6617. **Imām ʿAlī (AS) said,** 'Success is the first blessing.'[7525]

٦٦١٧. عنه عليه السلام: التَّوفيقُ أوَّلُ النِّعمَةِ.[٧٥٠٠]

6618. **Imām ʿAlī (AS) said,** 'Endeavour without divine succour is useless.'[7526]

٦٦١٨. عنه عليه السلام: لا يَنفَعُ اجتِهادٌ بغَيرِ تَوفيقٍ.[٧٥٠١]

6619. **Imām ʿAlī (AS) said,** 'Success is the fountainhead of happiness.'[7527]

٦٦١٩. عنه عليه السلام: التَّوفيقُ رأسُ السَّعادَةِ.[٧٥٠٢]

6620. **Imām ʿAlī (AS) said,** 'There is no leader like success.'[7528]

٦٦٢٠. عنه عليه السلام: لا قائدَ كالتَّوفيقِ.[٧٥٠٣]

6621. **Imām ʿAlī (AS) said,** 'Holding on to experiences is part of success.'[7529]

٦٦٢١. عنه عليه السلام: مِن التَّوفيقِ حِفظُ التَّجرِبَةِ.[٧٥٠٤]

6622. **Imām ʿAlī (AS) said,** 'Stopping in the face of confusion is part of success.'[7530]

٦٦٢٢. عنه عليه السلام: مِن التَّوفيقِ الوُقوفُ عِندَ الحَيرَةِ.[٧٥٠٥]

6623. **Imām al-Bāqir (AS) said,** 'There is no blessing like that of good health, and there is no good health like having the assistance of success.'[7531]

٦٦٢٣. الإمامُ الباقرُ عليه السلام: لا نِعمَةَ كالعافِيَةِ، ولا عافِيَةِ كَمُساعَدَةِ التَّوفيقِ.[٧٥٠٦]

6624. **Imām al-Bāqir (AS),** when asked about the phrase: 'There is no power or strength save in Allah', said, 'It means that we have no power to

٦٦٢٤. عنه عليه السلام ـ لَمّا سُئلَ عن «لا حَولَ ولا قُوَّةَ إلّا باللهِ» ـ: مَعناهُ لا حَولَ لَنا عَن مَعصِيَةِ اللهِ إلّا

keep away from sins except through Allah's help, nor do we have strength to obey Allah, except through Allah's succour.'[7532]

بِعَونِ اللهِ، ولا قُوَّةَ لَنا علىٰ طاعَةِ اللهِ إلّا بِتَوفيقِ اللهِ عَزَّوجلَّ.٧٥٠٧

1859. Success and Failure

١٨٥٩ ـ التَّوفيقُ وَالخِذلانُ

"If Allah helps you, no one can overcome you, but if He forsakes you, who will help you after Him? So in Allah let all the faithful put their trust."[7533]

﴿إِنْ يَنْصُرْكُمُ اللهُ فَلَا غَالِبَ لَكُمْ وَإِنْ يَخْذُلْكُمْ فَمَنْ ذَا الَّذِي يَنْصُرُكُمْ مِنْ بَعْدِهِ وَعَلَى اللهِ فَلْيَتَوَكَّلِ الْمُؤْمِنُونَ﴾.٧٥٠٨

6625. **The Prophet (SAWA) said,** 'Sins bring failure to those who commit them until it lands them in something even worse.'[7534]

٦٦٢٥ . رسولُ اللهِ ﷺ : إنّ المَعاصِيَ يَستَولي بِها الخِذلانُ علىٰ صاحِبِها حتّىٰ تُوقِعَهُ بما هُوَ أعظَمُ مِنها.٧٥٠٩

6626. **Imām ʿAlī (AS) said,** 'Success is an aid for the intellect and failure is an aid for ignorance.'[7535]

٦٦٢٦ . الإمامُ عليٌّ ؑ : التَّوفيقُ مُمِدُّ العَقلِ، الخِذلانُ مُمِدُّ الجَهلِ.٧٥١٠

6627. **Imām ʿAlī (AS) said,** 'O people, those of you who seek advice from Allah will be granted divine succour, and he who takes His advice as a guide is a lead to that which is more stable, for one who takes refuge in Allah is the secure and his enemy is the frightened.'[7536]

٦٦٢٧ . عنه ؑ : أيُّها النّاسُ ؛ إنّهُ مَنِ استَنصَحَ اللهَ وُفِّقَ ، ومَنِ اتَّخَذَ قولَهُ دَليلاً هُدِيَ لِلَّتي هِيَ أقوَمُ ؛ فإنَّ جارَ اللهِ آمِنٌ ، وعَدُوَّهُ خائفٌ.٧٥١١

6628. **Imām al-Ṣādiq (AS),** with regard to Allah's verse in the Qur'an: *"my success lies only with Allah"* and His verse: *"If Allah helps you, no one can overcome you..."*, said, 'When the servant does as Allah has commanded in obedience to Him, his actions are according to Allah's orders, and this servant is called the successful, and when the servant wishes to embark upon a sinful act, then Allah Almighty obstructs between him and that sin so he leaves it, and his abstinence from it is as a result of Allah's divine succour, and when he has his own way in pursuing the sin then Allah will not obstruct him from the sin until he commits it, then He thwarts him and does not support him or give him success.'[7537]

٦٦٢٨ . الإمامُ الصّادقُ ؑ ـ في قَولِهِ تعالىٰ : ﴿وَمَا تَوْفِيقِي إِلَّا بِاللهِ﴾ وقَولِهِ : ﴿إِنْ يَنْصُرْكُمُ اللهُ فَلَا غَالِبَ لَكُمْ وَإِنْ يَخْذُلْكُمْ فَمَنْ ذَا الَّذِي يَنْصُرُكُمْ مِنْ بَعْدِهِ وَعَلَى اللهِ فَلْيَتَوَكَّلِ الْمُؤْمِنُونَ﴾ ـ : إذا فَعَلَ العَبدُ ما أمَرَهُ اللهُ عَزَّوجلَّ بهِ مِن الطّاعَةِ كانَ فِعلُهُ وَفقاً لأمرِ اللهِ عَزَّوجلَّ وسُمِّيَ العَبدُ بهِ مُوَفَّقاً ، وإذا أرادَ العَبدُ أن يَدخُلَ في شيءٍ مِن مَعاصِي اللهِ فَحالَ اللهُ تبارَكَ وتعالىٰ بَينَهُ وبَينَ تِلكَ المَعصِيَةِ فتَرَكَها كانَ تَركُهُ لَها بِتَوفيقِ اللهِ تعالىٰ ذِكرُهُ ، ومَتىٰ خَلّىٰ بَينَهُ وبَينَ تِلكَ المَعصِيَةِ فلَم يَحُلْ بَينَهُ وبَينَها حتّىٰ يَرتَكِبَها فقَد خَذَلَهُ ولَم يَنصُرْهُ ولَم يُوَفِّقْهُ.٧٥١٢

409

LOYALTY

الوَفاءُ

1860. Encouraging of Loyalty

١٨٦٠ ـ الحَثُّ عَلَى الوَفاءِ بِالعَهدِ

"And fulfil the covenants; indeed all covenants are accountable."[7538]

﴿وَأَوْفُوا بِالْعَهْدِ إِنَّ الْعَهْدَ كَانَ مَسْؤُولاً﴾ .[٧٥١٣]

"And those who fulfil their covenants when they pledge themselves."[7539]

﴿وَالْمُوفُونَ بِعَهْدِهِمْ إِذا عَاهَدُوا﴾ .[٧٥١٤]

6629. **The Prophet (SAWA) said,** 'He who believes in Allah and the Day of Judgment must fulfil his promise when he promises.'[7540]

٦٦٢٩ . رسولُ اللهِ ﷺ : مَن كانَ يُؤمِنُ باللهِ واليَومِ الآخِرِ فَلْيَفِ إذا وَعَدَ.[٧٥١٥]

6630. **Imām ʿAlī (AS) said,** 'Loyalty is the fortress of chiefdom.'[7541]

٦٦٣٠ . الإمامُ عليٌّ ؈ :الوَفاءُ حِصنُ السُّؤدَدِ.[٧٥١٦]

6631. **Imām ʿAlī (AS) said,** 'Loyalty is the epitome of the thriving of religion, and the strength of trust.'[7542]

٦٦٣١ . عنه ؈ :الوَفاءُ عُنوانُ وُفورِ الدِّينِ، وقُوَّةِ الأمانَةِ.[٧٥١٧]

6632. **Imām ʿAlī (AS) said,** 'The best trust is fulfilment of promises.'[7543]

٦٦٣٢ . عنه ؈ : أفضَلُ الأمانَةِ الوَفاءُ بِالعَهدِ.[٧٥١٨]

6633. **Imām ʿAlī (AS) said,** 'The best of honesty is fulfilment of promises.'[7544]

٦٦٣٣ . عنه ؈ :أفضَلُ الصِّدقِ الوَفاءُ بِالعُهودِ.[٧٥١٩]

6634. **Imām ʿAlī (AS) said,** 'Do not depend on the friendship of one who does not fulfil his promises.'[7545]

٦٦٣٤ . عنه ؈ : لا تَعتَمِدْ علىٰ مَوَدَّةِ مَن لا يُوفي بعَهدِهِ.[٧٥٢٠]

6635. **Imām Zayn al-ʿĀbidīn (AS),** when he was asked [to summarize] all the laws of religion, said, 'To tell the truth, to judge with fairness and to fulfil a promise.'[7546]

٦٦٣٥ . الإمامُ زينُ العابدينَ ؈ ـ لَمّا سُئلَ عَن جَميعِ شَرايعِ الدِّينِ ـ: قَولُ الحَقِّ، والحُكمُ بِالعَدلِ، والوَفاءُ بِالعَهدِ.[٧٥٢١]

6636. **Imām al-Ṣādiq (AS) said,** 'There are three actions for which no one has an excuse: returning a trust to both the pious and the immoral; fulfilment of a promise to both the pious and the immoral; and goodness to one's parents, whether they be pious or immoral.'[7547]

٦٦٣٦. الإمامُ الصّادقُ ﷺ: ثَلاثَةٌ لا عُذرَ لأحَدٍ فيها: أداءُ الأمانَةِ إلَى البَرِّ والفاجِرِ، والوَفاءُ بالعَهدِ للبَرِّ والفاجِرِ، وبِرُّ الوالِدَينِ بَرَّينِ كانا أو فاجِرَينِ.٧٥٢٢

410

SOLEMNITY

الوَقارُ

1861. Encouraging of Solemnity

١٨٦١ ـ الحَثُّ عَلَى الوَقارِ

"The servants of the All-beneficent are those who walk humbly on the earth and when the ignorant address them, say, peace."[7548]

﴿وَعِبَادُ الرَّحْمَنِ الَّذِينَ يَمْشُونَ عَلَى الْأَرْضِ هَوْناً وَإِذَا خَاطَبَهُمُ الْجَاهِلُونَ قَالُوا سَلَاماً﴾.٧٥٢٣

6637. **The Prophet (SAWA) said,** 'You must adopt tranquillity and solemnity.'[7549]

٦٦٣٧. رسولُ اللهِ ﷺ: عَلَيكُم بِالسَّكينَةِ والوَقارِ.٧٥٢٤

6638. **The Prophet (SAWA) said,** 'Goodness does not lie in good clothes or attire, but goodness lies in tranquillity and solemnity.'[7550]

٦٦٣٨. عنه ﷺ: لَيسَ البِرُّ في حُسنِ اللِّباسِ والزِّيِّ، ولكنَّ البِرَّ في السَّكينَةِ والوَقارِ.٧٥٢٥

6639. **Imām ʿAlī (AS) said,** 'Solemnity is the adornment of the intellect.'[7551]

٦٦٣٩. الإمامُ عليٌّ ﷺ: الوَقارُ حِليَةُ العَقلِ.٧٥٢٦

6640. **Imām ʿAlī (AS) said,** 'Let your prominent feature be solemnity for he who is increasingly clumsy becomes despicable.'[7552]

٦٦٤٠. عنه ﷺ: لِتَكُن شِيمَتُكَ الوَقارَ، فمَن كَثُرَ خُرقُهُ استُرذِلَ.٧٥٢٧

6641. **Imām ʿAlī (AS) said,** 'The beauty of a man is his dignified bearing.'[7553]

٦٦٤١. عنه ﷺ: جَمالُ الرَّجُلِ الوَقارُ.٧٥٢٨

1862. What Brings About Solemnity

١٨٦٢ ـ موجِباتُ الوَقارِ

6642. **Imām ʿAlī (AS) said,** 'The cause of solemnity is clemency.'[7554]

٦٦٤٢. الإمامُ عليٌّ ﷺ: سَبَبُ الوَقارِ الحِلمُ.٧٥٢٩

6643. **Imām ʿAlī (AS) said,** 'With silence solemnity increases.'[7555]

٦٦٤٣. عنه ﷺ : بِالصَّمتِ يَكثُرُ الوَقارُ.[٧٥٣٠]

6644. **Imām ʿAlī (AS) said,** 'He who acts with dignity is dignified.'[7556]

٦٦٤٤. عنه ﷺ : مَن تَوَقَّرَ وُقِّرَ.[٧٥٣١]

6645. **Imām ʿAlī (AS) said,** 'He who is known to have wisdom will be seen with reverence and dignity.'[7557]

٦٦٤٥. عنه ﷺ : مَن عُرِفَ بِالحِكمَةِ لَحظَتهُ العُيونُ بِالوَقارِ وَالهَيبَةِ.[٧٥٣٢]

6646. **Imām ʿAlī (AS) said,** 'Solemnity can only be achieved through adopting a respectful attitude.'[7558]

٦٦٤٦. عنه ﷺ : لا يُستَعانُ... علَى الوَقارِ إلّا بِالمَهابَةِ.[٧٥٣٣]

411

GODWARINESS

التَّقوىٰ

1863. The Virtue of Godwariness

١٨٦٣ ـ فَضلُ التَّقوىٰ

"If the people of the towns had been faithful and Godwary, We would have opened to them blessings from the heaven and the earth. But they denied; so We seized them because of what they used to earn."[7559]

﴿وَلَوْ أَنَّ أَهْلَ الْقُرَىٰ آمَنُوا وَاتَّقَوْا لَفَتَحْنَا عَلَيْهِمْ بَرَكَاتٍ مِنَ السَّمَاءِ وَالأَرْضِ وَلٰكِنْ كَذَّبُوا فَأَخَذْنَاهُم بِمَا كَانُوا يَكْسِبُونَ﴾.[٧٥٣٤]

"This is the Book, there is no doubt in it, a guidance to the Godwary…those who follow their Lord's guidance, and it is they who are the felicitous."[7560]

﴿ذٰلِكَ الْكِتَابُ لَا رَيْبَ فِيهِ هُدىً لِلْمُتَّقِينَ ... أُولٰئِكَ عَلَىٰ هُدىً مِنْ رَبِّهِمْ وَأُولٰئِكَ هُمُ الْمُفْلِحُونَ﴾.[٧٥٣٥]

"To Allah belongs whatever is in the Heavens and whatever is on the earth. We have certainly enjoined those who were given the Book before you, and you, that you should be wary of Allah. But if you are faithless, [you should know that] to Allah indeed belongs whatever is in the Heavens and whatever is on the earth, and Allah is all-sufficient, all-laudable."[7561]

﴿وَلِلّٰهِ مَا فِي السَّمَاوَاتِ وَمَا فِي الْأَرْضِ وَلَقَدْ وَصَّيْنَا الَّذِينَ أُوتُوا الكِتَابَ مِنْ قَبْلِكُمْ وَإِيَّاكُمْ أَنِ اتَّقُوا اللهَ وَإِنْ تَكْفُرُوا فَإِنَّ لِلّٰهِ مَا فِي السَّمَاوَاتِ وَمَا فِي الْأَرْضِ وَكَانَ اللهُ غَنِيّاً حَمِيداً﴾.[٧٥٣٦]

"O Children of Adam! We have certainly sent down to you garments to cover your nakedness, and for adornment. Yet the garment of Godwariness – that is the

﴿يَا بَنِي آدَمَ قَدْ أَنْزَلْنَا عَلَيْكُمْ لِبَاساً يُوَارِي سَوْآتِكُمْ وَرِيشاً وَلِبَاسُ التَّقْوَىٰ ذٰلِكَ خَيْرٌ ذٰلِكَ

best. That is [one] of Allah's signs, so that they may take admonition."[7562]

مِنْ آيَاتِ اللهِ لَعَلَّهُمْ يَذَّكَّرُونَ﴾.[٧٥٣٧]

"O you who have faith! If you are wary of Allah, He shall appoint a criterion for you, and absolve you of your misdeeds, and forgive you, for Allah is dispenser of a great grace."[7563]

﴿يَا أَيُّهَا الَّذِينَ آمَنُوا إِنْ تَتَّقُوا اللهَ يَجْعَلْ لَكُمْ فُرْقَاناً وَيُكَفِّرْ عَنْكُمْ سَيِّئَاتِكُمْ وَيَغْفِرْ لَكُمْ وَاللهُ ذُو الْفَضْلِ الْعَظِيمِ﴾.[٧٥٣٨]

"This is the abode of the Hereafter which We shall grant to those who do not desire to domineer in the earth nor to cause corruption, and the outcome will be in favour of the Godwary."[7564]

﴿تِلْكَ الدَّارُ الآخِرَةُ نَجْعَلُهَا لِلَّذِينَ لَا يُرِيدُونَ عُلُوّاً فِي الأَرْضِ وَلَا فَسَاداً وَالعَاقِبَةُ لِلْمُتَّقِينَ﴾.[٧٥٣٩]

6647. **Imām ʿAlī (AS) said,** 'Godwariness is the leader of moral virtues.'[7565]

٦٦٤٧. الإمامُ عليٌّ عليه السلام: التُّقىٰ رئيسُ الأخلاقِ.[٧٥٤٠]

6648. **Imām ʿAlī (AS) said,** 'Godwariness is the best treasure and the most protective guard. In it is the salvation of every runaway, the goal of every seeker, and the victory of every conqueror.'[7566]

٦٦٤٨. عنه عليه السلام: إنّ التَّقوىٰ أفضَلُ كَنزٍ، وأحرَزُ حِرزٍ، وأعَزُّ عِزٍّ، فيهِ نَجاةُ كُلِّ هارِبٍ، ودَركُ كُلِّ طالِبٍ، وظَفَرُ كُلِّ غالِبٍ.[٧٥٤١]

6649. **Imām ʿAlī (AS) said,** 'Fear Allah with some Godwariness even if it be little, and place a veil [of shame] between yourself and Allah even if it be thin.'[7567]

٦٦٤٩. عنه عليه السلام: اِتَّقِ اللهَ بَعضَ التُّقىٰ وإن قَلَّ، واجعَلْ بَينَكَ وبَينَ اللهِ سِتراً وإن رَقَّ.[٧٥٤٢]

6650. **Imām ʿAlī (AS) said,** 'Godwariness is the ultimate contentment of Allah with His servants and His demand from His creation.'[7568]

٦٦٥٠. عنه عليه السلام: إنّ التَّقوىٰ مُنتَهىٰ رِضَى اللهِ مِن عِبادِهِ وحاجَتِهِ مِن خَلقِهِ.[٧٥٤٣]

6651. **Imām ʿAlī (AS) said,** 'I advise you, O servants of Allah, to be wary of your duty to Allah which is the provision and in it is the refuge; it is ample provision and a successful refuge.'[7569]

٦٦٥١. عنه عليه السلام: أُوصِيكُم عِبادَ اللهِ بتَقوَى اللهِ الّتي هِيَ الزّادُ وبِها المَعاذُ، زادٌ مُبلِغٌ، ومَعاذٌ مُنجِحٌ.[٧٥٤٤]

6652. **Imām ʿAlī (AS) said,** 'I advise you, O servants of Allah, to be wary of your duty to Allah, for it is the rein and the firm foundation. So, hold onto its proofs and cling onto its realities.'[7570]

٦٦٥٢. عنه عليه السلام: أُوصِيكُم عِبادَ اللهِ بتَقوَى اللهِ، فإنَّها الزِّمامُ والقِوامُ، فتَمَسَّكوا بوَثائقِها، واعتَصِموا بحَقائقِها.[٧٥٤٥]

6653. **Imām ʿAlī (AS) said,** 'I advise you to be wary of your duty to Allah, for it is the goal of a

٦٦٥٣. عنه عليه السلام: أُوصِيكُم بتَقوَى اللهِ؛ فإنّها غِبطَةُ

hopeful seeker, the assurance of the runaway refuge, so make Godwariness your inner basis.'[7571]

الطّالِبِ الرّاجي، وثِقَةُ الهارِبِ اللّاجي، واستَشعِروا التَّقوىٰ شِعاراً باطِناً.٧٥٤٦

6654. **Imām ʿAlī (AS) said,** 'I advise you to be wary of your duty to Allah…make your hearts feel it, and rinse out your sins with it… indeed safeguard it and be safeguarded by it.'[7572]

٦٦٥٤. عنه ﵇: أُوصيكُم بتَقوَى اللهِ...وأشعِروها قُلوبَكُم، وارحَضوا بِها ذُنوبَكُم... ألا فَصُونوها وتَصَوَّنوا بِها.٧٥٤٧

6655. **Imām ʿAlī (AS) said,** 'Godwariness of Allah is a guard and a shield for today, and a path to Heaven tomorrow; its trail is clear and the one who traverses it is victorious.'[7573]

٦٦٥٥. عنه ﵇: إنّ التَّقوىٰ في اليَومِ الحِرزُ والجُنَّةُ، وفي غَدٍ الطَّريقُ إلَى الجَنَّةِ، مَسلَكُها واضِحٌ وسالِكُها رابِحٌ.٧٥٤٨

6656. **Imām ʿAlī (AS) said,** 'Godwariness is the key to appropriate behaviour, a store for the Hereafter, freedom from every habit, salvation from every type of ruin, with it a seeker is successful, a runaway is saved, and wishes are acquired.'[7574]

٦٦٥٦. عنه ﵇: إنّ تَقوَى اللهِ مِفتاحُ سَدادٍ، وذَخيرَةُ مَعادٍ، وعِتقٌ مِن كُلِّ مَلَكَةٍ، ونَجاةٌ مِن كُلِّ هَلَكَةٍ، بِها يَنجَحُ الطّالِبُ، ويَنجو الهارِبُ، وتُنالُ الرَّغائبُ.٧٥٤٩

6657. **Imām ʿAlī (AS) said,** 'Whoever plants the trees of Godwariness will reap the fruits of guidance.'[7575]

٦٦٥٧. عنه ﵇: مَن غَرَسَ أشجارَ التُّقىٰ جَنىٰ ثِمارَ الهُدىٰ.٧٥٥٠

6658. **Imām al-Bāqir (AS),** speaking to Saʿd al-Khayr said, 'I advise you to be wary of your duty to Allah, for in it is safety from ruin, and a gain in the Hereafter.'[7576]

٦٦٥٨. الإمامُ الباقرُ ﵇ ـ لِسَعدِ الخَيرِ ـ: أُوصيكَ بِتَقوَى اللهِ؛ فإنّ فيها السَّلامَةَ مِنَ التَّلَفِ، والغَنيمَةَ في المُنقَلَبِ.٧٥٥١

1864. Godwariness is the Key to Nobleness

١٨٦٤ ـ التَّقوىٰ مِفتاحُ الكَرامَةِ

"O mankind! Indeed We created you from a male and a female, and made you nations and tribes that you may identify with one another. Indeed the noblest of you in the sight of Allah is the most Godwary among you. Indeed Allah is all-knowing, all-aware."[7577]

﴿يا أيُّهَا النّاسُ إنّا خَلَقْناكُمْ مِنْ ذَكَرٍ وأُنْثىٰ وجَعَلْناكُمْ شُعُوباً وقَبائلَ لِتَعارَفُوا إنَّ أكْرَمَكُمْ عِنْدَ اللهِ أتْقاكُمْ إنَّ اللهَ عَليمٌ خَبيرٌ﴾.٧٥٥٢

6659. **The Prophet (SAWA) said,** 'Pay more attention to performing deeds with Godwariness than deeds without it, for action with Godwariness is never considered little, and how can an accepted action be little for Allah has said, '*"Allah accepts only from the Godwary."*'[7578 7579]

٦٦٥٩. رسولُ اللهِ ﷺ: كُن بالعَمَلِ بالتَّقوىٰ أشَدَّ اهتِماماً مِنكَ بالعَمَلِ بغَيرِهِ؛ فإنّهُ لا يَقِلُّ عَمَلٌ بالتَّقوىٰ، وكَيفَ يَقِلُّ عَمَلٌ يُتَقَبَّلُ؟! لِقَولِ اللهِ عزّوجلّ: ﴿إنَّما يَتَقَبَّلُ اللهُ مِنَ المُتَّقِينَ﴾.٧٥٥٣ ٧٥٥٤

6660. **The Prophet (SAWA) said,** ‘There is a characteristic that whoever adopts, the world and the Hereafter will obey him, and he will gain Heaven.’ He was asked, ‘What is it O Messenger of Allah (SAWA)?’ He said, ‘Godwariness. Whoever wants to be the most honourable of people should be wary of Allah Almighty.’ He then recited: *“And whoever is wary of Allah, He shall make a way out for him, and provide for him from whence he does not reckon.”*[7580] [7581]

٦٦٦٠. عنه ﷺ: خَصلَةٌ من لَزِمَها أطاعَتهُ الدُّنيا والآخِرَةُ، ورَبِحَ الفوزَ بِالجَنَّةِ. قيلَ: وما هِيَ يا رسولَ اللهِ؟ قالَ: التَّقوىٰ، مَن أرادَ أن يَكونَ أعَزَّ النّاسِ فلْيَتَّقِ اللهَ عَزَّوجلَّ، ثُمَّ تَلا: ﴿وَمَن يَتَّقِ اللهَ يَجْعَلْ لَهُ مَخْرَجاً * وَيَرْزُقْهُ مِن حَيْثُ لا يَحْتَسِبُ﴾ ٧٥٥٥، ٧٥٥٦.

6661. **Imām ʿAlī (AS) said,** ‘There is no dignity more honourable than Godwariness.’[7582]

٦٦٦١. الإمامُ عليٌّ ؑ: لا كَرَمَ أعَزُّ مِنَ التَّقوىٰ. ٧٥٥٧

6662. **Imām ʿAlī (AS) said,** ‘The key to dignity is Godwariness.’[7583]

٦٦٦٢. عنه ؑ: مِفتاحُ الكَرَمِ التَّقوىٰ. ٧٥٥٨

6663. **Imām ʿAlī (AS) said,** ‘He who adopts Godwariness…dignity will pour down on him after having been scarce; mercy will incline towards him after having missed him [previously], blessings will gush onto him after having been barren, and benediction will heavily rain upon him after having merely drizzled.’[7584]

٦٦٦٣. عنه ؑ: مَن أخَذَ بِالتَّقوىٰ… هَطَلَت علَيهِ الكَرامَةُ بَعدَ قُحوطِها، وتَحَدَّبَت علَيهِ الرَّحمَةُ بَعدَ نُفورِها، وتَفَجَّرَت علَيهِ النِّعَمُ بَعدَ نُضوبِها، ووَبَلَتْ علَيهِ البَرَكَةُ بَعدَ إرذاذِها. ٧٥٥٩

6664. **Imām ʿAlī (AS) said,** ‘Godwariness is the remedy for the sickness of your hearts, the sight for the blindness of your hearts, the cure for the sickness of your bodies, the reformation of the corruption of your chests [souls], the purification of the filth of your souls, the enlightenment of the blindness of your eyes, the safety for the fear of your anxiety, and the light to the blackness of your darkness.’[7585]

٦٦٦٤. عنه ؑ: إنَّ تَقوَى اللهِ دَواءُ داءِ قُلوبِكُم، وبَصَرُ عَمىٰ أفئدَتِكُم، وشِفاءُ مَرَضِ أجسادِكُم، وصَلاحُ فَسادِ صُدورِكُم، وطَهورُ دَنَسِ أنفُسِكُم، وجَلاءُ عَشا أبصارِكُم، وأمنُ فَزَعِ جَأشِكُم، وضِياءُ سَوادِ ظُلمَتِكُم. ٧٥٦٠

6665. **Imām ʿAlī (AS) said,** ‘Cling onto Godwariness, for it has a rope with strong links, and a stronghold with an invincible peak.’[7586]

٦٦٦٥. عنه ؑ: فاعتَصِموا بتَقوَى اللهِ؛ فإنَّ لَها حَبلاً وَثيقاً عُروَتُهُ، ومَعقِلاً مَنيعاً ذُروَتُهُ. ٧٥٦١

6666. **Imām Zayn al-ʿĀbidīn (AS) said,** ‘There is no nobility for the Qurayshite, nor the Arab other than through humbleness, and no dignity other than through Godwariness.’[7587]

٦٦٦٦. الإمامُ زينُ العابدينَ ؑ: لا حَسَبَ لِقُرَشيٍّ ولا عَرَبيٍّ إلّا بِتَواضُعٍ، ولا كَرَمَ إلّا بِتَقوىٰ. ٧٥٦٢

6667. **Imām al-Bāqir (AS),** in a letter that he wrote to Saʿd al-Khayr, said, 'Allah guards a servant as a result of his Godwariness when his intellect is distant from him [cannot grasp it], and He illuminates him from blindness and ignorance as a result of his Godwariness. Noah and those with him were saved in the ark and Ṣāliḥ and those with him were saved from the thunderbolt, because of Godwariness. The patient ones are victorious and those groups are saved from destruction through Godwariness.'[7588]

٦٦٦٧ . الإمامُ الباقرُ عليه السلام ـ فيما كَتَبَ إلىٰ سَعدِ الخَيرِ ـ: إنّ اللهَ عَزَّ وجلَّ يَقِي بِالتَّقوىٰ عَنِ العَبدِ ما عَزُبَ عَنهُ عَقلُهُ ، ويُجَلّي بِالتَّقوىٰ عَنهُ عَماهُ وجَهلَهُ ، وبِالتَّقوىٰ نَجا نُوحٌ ومَن مَعهُ فِي السَّفينَةِ ، وصالِحٌ ومَن مَعهُ مِنَ الصّاعِقَةِ ، وبِالتَّقوىٰ فازَ الصّابِرونَ ، ونَجَتْ تِلكَ العُصَبُ مِنَ المَهالِكِ . [٧٥٦٣]

6668. **Imām al-Ṣādiq (AS) said,** 'Whoever clings onto Allah being wary of his duty to Him, Allah will protect him, and whoever Allah comes to protect should not worry even if the sky was to fall onto the earth, or if a calamity was to descend onto the earth and tribulation was to encompass everyone, he will be in the protection of Allah from every tribulation as a result of his Godwariness. Does Allah Almighty not say: *"Indeed the Godwary will be in a secure place."*'[7589 7590]

٦٦٦٨ . الإمامُ الصّادقُ عليه السلام : مَنِ اعتَصَمَ بِاللهِ بِتَقواهُ عَصَمَهُ اللهُ ، ومَن أقبَلَ اللهُ علَيهِ وعَصَمَهُ لَم يُبالِ لَو سَقَطَتِ السَّماءُ علَى الأرضِ ، وإنْ نَزَلَتْ نازِلَةٌ علىٰ أهلِ الأرضِ فشَمِلَهُم بَلِيَّةٌ كانَ في حِرزِ اللهِ بِالتَّقوىٰ مِن كُلِّ بَلِيَّةٍ ، ألَيسَ اللهُ تعالىٰ يَقولُ: ﴿إنَّ المُتَّقِينَ في مَقامٍ أمِينٍ﴾ [٧٥٦٤]؟! [٧٥٦٥]

1865. The Characteristics of the Godwary

١٨٦٥ ـ خَصائِصُ المُتَّقينَ

"Godwariness is not to turn your faces to the east or the west; rather, Godwariness is [personified by] those who have faith in Allah and the Last Day, the angels, the Book, and the prophets, and who give their wealth, for the love of Him, to the needy, the traveller and the beggar, and for [the freeing of] the slaves, and maintain the prayer and give the zakat, and those who fulfil their covenants, when they pledge themselves, and those who are patient in stress and distress, and in the heat of battle. They are the ones who are true [to their covenant], and it is they who are the Godwary. "[7591]

﴿لَيسَ الْبِرَّ أَنْ تُوَلُّوا وُجُوهَكُمْ قِبَلَ الْمَشْرِقِ وَالْمَغْرِبِ وَلٰكِنَّ الْبِرَّ مَنْ آمَنَ بِاللهِ وَالْيَوْمِ الآخِرِ وَالْمَلَائِكَةِ وَالْكِتَابِ وَالنَّبِيِّينَ وَآتَى الْمَالَ عَلىٰ حُبِّهِ ذَوِي الْقُرْبىٰ وَالْيَتَامىٰ وَالْمَسَاكِينَ وَابْنَ السَّبِيلِ وَالسَّائِلِينَ وَفِي الرِّقَابِ وَأَقَامَ الصَّلَاةَ وَآتَى الزَّكَاةَ وَالْمُوفُونَ بِعَهْدِهِمْ إِذَا عَاهَدُوا وَالصَّابِرِينَ فِي الْبَأْسَاءِ وَالضَّرَّاءِ وَحِينَ الْبَأْسِ أُولٰئِكَ الَّذِينَ صَدَقُوا وَأُولٰئِكَ هُمُ الْمُتَّقُونَ﴾ . [٧٥٦٦]

"Indeed the Godwary will be amid gardens and springs, receiving what their Lord has given them, for they had been virtuous aforetime. They used to sleep a little during the night, and at dawns they would plead for forgiveness, and there was a share in their wealth for the beggar and the deprived."[7592]

﴿إِنَّ الْمُتَّقِينَ فِي جَنَّاتٍ وَعُيُونٍ * آخِذِينَ مَا آتَاهُمْ رَبُّهُمْ إِنَّهُمْ كَانُوا قَبْلَ ذٰلِكَ مُحْسِنِينَ * كَانُوا قَلِيلاً مِنَ اللَّيْلِ مَا يَهْجَعُونَ * وَبِالأَسْحَارِ هُمْ يَسْتَغْفِرُونَ * وَفِي أَمْوَالِهِمْ حَقٌّ لِلسَّائِلِ وَالْمَحْرُومِ﴾ . [٧٥٦٧]

(See also: Qur'an 2:2-5, 3:133-136, 39:33, 5:8)

(اُنظر) البقرة: ٢ ـ ٥ و آل عمران: ١٣٣ ـ ١٣٦ والزمر: ٣٣ والمائدة: ٨.

6669. **The Prophet (SAWA) said,** 'The Godwary are those who are wary of Allah for something that does not [necessarily] require wariness, for fear of entering into obscurity.'[7593]

٦٦٦٩ . رسولُ اللهِ ﷺ : إنَّ المُتَّقينَ الّذينَ يَتَّقونَ اللهَ مِن الشّيءِ الّذي لا يُتَّقىٰ مِنهُ خَوفاً مِن الدُّخولِ في الشُّبهَةِ.[٧٥٦٨]

6670. **The Prophet (SAWA),** in his advise to Abū Dharr said, 'O Abū Dharr, a man will not be among the Godwary until he takes account of himself more than a partner would take account of his [business] partner, such that he knows where his food comes from, where his drink comes from, and where his clothes come from – do they come from the lawful or the prohibited?'[7594]

٦٦٧٠ . عنه ﷺ ـ في وصِيَّتِهِ لأبي ذرٍّ ـ : يا أباذرٍّ، لا يكونُ الرّجُلُ مِن المُتَّقينَ حتّىٰ يُحاسِبَ نَفسَهُ أشَدَّ مِن مُحاسَبَةِ الشَّريكِ لِشَريكِهِ، فيَعلَمَ مِن أينَ مَطعَمُهُ، ومِن أينَ مَشرَبُهُ، ومِن أينَ مَلبَسُهُ؟ أمِن حِلٍّ ذلكَ، أم مِن حَرامٍ؟[٧٥٦٩]

6671. *Nahj al-Balāgha*: 'It is related that a companion of the Commander of the Faithful (AS) whose name was Hammām and was a devoted worshipper had said to him, 'O Commander of the Faithful, describe to me the Godwary in such a way as though I was to see them.' So he (AS) praised Allah and extolled Him, and praised the Prophet (SAWA) and then said:

'The Godwary [in this world] are the people of virtue. Their speech is to the point, their dress is moderate and their gait is humble. They keep their eyes closed to what Allah has made unlawful for them, and they put their ears to that knowledge which is beneficial to them. They remain in times of trials as they have been in times of comfort. If there had not been fixed periods [of life] ordained for each, their spirits would not have remained in their bodies even for the twinkling of an eye because of [their] eagerness for the reward and fear of chastisement…

The sign of any one of them is that you will see that he has strength in religion, prudence along with leniency, faith with conviction, eagerness in [seeking] knowledge with forbearance, moderation in wealth, devotion in worship, gracefulness in neediness, endurance in hardship, desire for the lawful, pleasure in guidance and hatred of greed. He performs virtuous deeds but still feels afraid. In the evening he is anxious to offer thanks [to Allah]. In

٦٦٧١ . نهج البلاغة : رُويَ أنّ صاحِباً لأميرِ المؤمنينَ عليه السلام يقالُ لَهُ هَمّامٌ كانَ رجُلاً عابِداً، فقالَ لَهُ : يا أميرَ المؤمِنينَ، صِفْ لِيَ المُتَّقينَ، حتّىٰ كأنّي أنظُرُ إلَيهِم ... فحَمِدَ اللهَ وأثنىٰ علَيهِ وصلّىٰ علَى النَّبيِّ ﷺ ثُمّ قالَ عليه السلام : ... فالمُتَّقونَ فيها هُم أهلُ الفَضائلِ : مَنطِقُهُمُ الصَّوابُ، ومَلبَسُهُمُ الاقتِصادُ، ومَشيُهُمُ التَّواضُعُ، غَضُّوا أبصارَهُم عَمّا حَرَّمَ اللهُ علَيهِم، ووَقَفوا أسماعَهُم علَى العِلمِ النّافِعِ لَهُم، نُزِّلَت أنفُسُهُم مِنهُم في البَلاءِ كالّتي نُزِّلَت في الرَّخاءِ، ولَولا الأجَلُ الّذي كتَبَ اللهُ علَيهِم لَم تَستَقِرَّ أرواحُهُم في أجسادِهِم طَرفَةَ عَينٍ؛ شَوقاً إلَى الثَّوابِ، وخَوفاً مِن العِقابِ...

فمِن عَلامَةِ أحَدِهِم أنَّكَ ترىٰ لَهُ قُوَّةً في دِينٍ، وحَزماً في لِينٍ، وإيماناً في يَقينٍ، وحِرصاً في عِلمٍ، وعِلماً في حِلمٍ، وقَصداً في غِنىً، وخُشوعاً في عِبادَةٍ، وتَجَمُّلاً في فاقَةٍ، وصَبراً في شِدَّةٍ، وطَلَباً في حَلالٍ، ونَشاطاً في هُدىً، وتَحَرُّجاً عَن طَمَعٍ. يَعمَلُ الأعمالَ الصّالِحَةَ وهُو علىٰ وَجَلٍ، يُمسي وَهَمُّهُ الشُّكرُ، ويُصبِحُ وَهَمُّهُ

the morning his anxiety is to remember [Allah]. He passes the night in fear and rises in the morning in joy - fear lest night is passed in forgetfulness, and joy over the favour and mercy received by him.

If his self refuses to endure a thing which it does not like he does not grant its request towards what it likes. The coolness of his eye lies in what is to last forever, while from the things [of this world] that will not last he keeps aloof. He transfuses knowledge with forbearance, and speech with action. You will see his hopes simple, his shortcomings few, his heart fearing, his spirit contented, his meal small and simple, his religion safe, his desires dead and his anger suppressed. Good alone is expected from him. Evil from him is not to be feared.'[7595]

الذِّكرَ، يَبيتُ حَذِراً، ويُصبحُ فَرِحاً؛ حَذِراً لِما حُذِّرَ مِن الغَفلَةِ، وفَرِحاً بما أصابَ مِن الفَضلِ والرَّحمَةِ.

إن اِستَصعَبَت علَيهِ نَفسُهُ فيما تَكرَهُ لَم يُعْطِها سُؤلَها فيما تُحِبُّ. قُرَّةُ عَينِهِ فِيما لا يَزولُ، وزَهادَتُهُ فِيما لا يَبقىٰ، يَمزُجُ الحِلمَ بِالعِلمِ والقَولَ بِالعَمَلِ. تَراهُ قَريباً أمَلُهُ، قَليلاً زَلَلُهُ، خاشِعاً قَلبُهُ، قانِعَةً نَفسُهُ، مَنزوراً أكلُهُ، سَهلاً أمرُهُ، حَريزاً دِينُهُ، مَيِّتَةً شَهوَتُهُ، مَكظوماً غَيظُهُ، الخَيرُ مِنهُ مَأمولٌ، والشَّرُّ مِنهُ مَأمونٌ.[٧٥٧٠]

6672. **Imām al-Bāqir (AS) said,** 'The Commander of the Faithful (AS) would say, 'The Godwary people have signs that they are known by: speaking truthfully, returning trusts, fulfilling promises... spending for good causes, good-naturedness, ample clemency, and the pursuit of knowledge of whatever brings them closer to Allah Almighty'.[7596]

٦٦٧٢. الإمامُ الباقرُ عليه السلام: كانَ أميرُ المؤمنينَ عليه السلام يقولُ: إنّ لِأهلِ التَّقوىٰ عَلاماتٍ يُعرَفونَ بِها: صِدقُ الحَديثِ، وأداءُ الأمانَةِ، والوَفاءُ بِالعَهدِ... وقِلّةُ المُؤاتاةِ لِلنِّساءِ، وبَذلُ المَعروفِ، وحُسنُ الخُلقِ، وسَعَةُ الحِلمِ، واتِّباعُ العِلمِ فيما يُقَرِّبُ إلَى اللهِ عَزَّوجلَّ.[٧٥٧١]

6673. **Imām al-Bāqir (AS) said,** 'The Godwary people have the simplest of expenditures in this world, but are the most helpful to you with their provisions, you only have to mention and they help you, and if you forget [your needs] they remind you. They inform of Allah's commands, guardians over Allah's commands, they have confined their love to loving their Lord. They feel estranged in the world in obedience to their Ruler; they look at Allah and His love with their hearts, and they know that He is the ultimate goal because of the magnitude of His Rank.'[7597]

٦٦٧٣. عنه عليه السلام: إنّ أهلَ التَّقوىٰ أيسَرُ أهلِ الدُّنيا مَؤونَةً، وأكثَرُهُم لكَ مَعونَةً، تَذكُرُ فيُعِينونَكَ، وإن نَسِيتَ ذَكَّروكَ، قَوّالُونَ بأمرِ اللهِ، قَوّامُونَ علىٰ أمرِ اللهِ، قَطَعوا مَحَبَّتَهُم بمَحَبَّةِ رَبِّهِم، ووَحَّشوا الدُّنيا لِطاعَةِ مَليكِهِم، ونَظَروا إلَى اللهِ عَزَّوجلَّ وإلىٰ مَحَبَّتِهِ بِقُلوبِهِم، وعَلِموا أنّ ذلكَ هُو المَنظورُ إلَيهِ، لِعَظيمِ شَأنِهِ.[٧٥٧٢]

(أنظر) الإيمان: باب ١٩٠ ـ ١٩٤.

(See also: FAITH: section 190-194)

1866. What Hinders Godwariness

١٨٦٦ ـ ما يَمنَعُ التَّقوىٰ

6674. **Imām ʿAlī (AS) said,** 'It is forbidden for every heart that is infatuated with the world to have Godwariness reside therein.'[7598]

٦٦٧٤ . الإمامُ عليٌّ ﷷ : حَرامٌ علىٰ كُلِّ قَلبٍ مُتَوَلِّهٍ بِالدُّنيا أن تَسكُنَهُ التَّقوىٰ .[٧٥٧٣]

6675. **Imām ʿAlī (AS) said,** 'By Allah, I cannot see a servant ever having Godwariness that will benefit him unless he guards his tongue.'[7599]

٦٦٧٥ . عنه ﷷ : واللهِ ، ما أرىٰ عَبداً يَتَّقي تَقوىً تَنفَعُهُ حتّىٰ يَخزِنَ لِسانَهُ .[٧٥٧٤]

6676. **Imām ʿAlī (AS) said,** 'One who disputes cannot be wary of Allah.'[7600]

٦٦٧٦ . عنه ﷷ : لا يَستَطيعُ أن يَتَّقِيَ اللهَ مَن خاصَمَ .[٧٥٧٥]

6677. **Imām al-ʿAskarī (AS) said,** 'He who is not wary before people does not have wariness of Allah.'[7601]

٦٦٧٧ . الإمامُ العسكريُّ ﷷ : مَن لَم يَتَّقِ وُجوهَ النّاسِ لَم يَتَّقِ اللهَ .[٧٥٧٦]

1867. The Reality of Godwariness

١٨٦٧ ـ حَقُّ التَّقوىٰ

"O you who have faith! Be wary of Allah with the wariness due to Him and do not die except as muslims."[7602]

﴿يا أَيُّهَا الَّذِينَ آمَنُوا اتَّقُوا اللهَ حَقَّ تُقَاتِهِ وَلَا تَمُوتُنَّ إِلَّا وَأَنْتُمْ مُسْلِمُونَ﴾ .[٧٥٧٧]

6678. **Imām al-Ṣādiq (AS),** when asked about Allah's verse: *"Be wary of Allah with the wariness due to Him"*, said, 'He must be obeyed and not disobeyed, remembered and not forgotten, thanked and not denied.'[7603]

٦٦٧٨ . الإمامُ الصّادقُ ﷷ ـ لَمّا سُئلَ عَن قَولِهِ تعالىٰ : ﴿اتَّقُوا اللهَ حَقَّ تُقاتِهِ﴾ ـ : يُطاعُ فلا يُعصىٰ ، ويُذكَرُ فلا يُنسىٰ ، ويُشكَرُ فلا يُكفَرُ .[٧٥٧٨]

6679. **Abū Baṣīr said,** 'I asked Abū ʿAbdillāh [al-Ṣādiq] (AS) about Allah's verse: *"Be wary of Allah with the wariness due to Him"*, so he said, 'It has been abrogated.' I said, 'With what?' He said, 'Allah's verse: *"Be wary of Allah as far as you can"*'[7604 7605]

٦٦٧٩ . بحار الأنوار عن أبي بَصيرٍ : سَألتُ أبا عبدِ اللهِ ﷷ عَن قَولِ اللهِ : ﴿اتَّقُوا اللهَ حَقَّ تُقاتِهِ﴾[٧٥٧٩] قالَ : مَنسوخَةٌ . قلتُ : وما نَسَختَها ؟ قالَ : قَولُ اللهِ : ﴿اتَّقُوا اللهَ ما اسْتَطَعْتُم﴾[٧٥٨٠] .[٧٥٨١]

1868. Explanation of Godwariness

١٨٦٨ ـ تفسيرُ التَّقوىٰ

6680. **The Prophet (SAWA) said,** 'The completion of Godwariness is that you learn what you

٦٦٨٠ . رسولُ اللهِ ﷺ : تَمامُ التَّقوىٰ أن تَتَعَلَّمَ ما

do not know and you act upon what you do know.'[7606]

جَهِلتَ وتَعمَلَ بِما عَلِمتَ.[٧٥٨٢]

6681. **Imām ʿAlī (AS) said,** 'Godwariness is that a person is wary of everything that tempts him into sin.'[7607]

٦٦٨١. الإمامُ عليٌّ عليه السلام: التَّقوىٰ أن يَتَّقِيَ المَرءُ كُلَّ ما يُؤثِمُهُ.[٧٥٨٣]

6682. **Imām ʿAlī (AS) said,** 'He who controls his desire is Godwary.'[7608]

٦٦٨٢. عنه عليه السلام: مَن مَلَكَ شَهوَتَهُ كانَ تَقِيّاً.[٧٥٨٤]

6683. **Imām al-Ṣādiq (AS),** when asked about the interpretation of Godwariness, said, 'That Allah does not miss you where He has commanded you and does not see you where He has prohibited you.'[7609]

٦٦٨٣. الإمامُ الصّادقُ عليه السلام ـ لَمّا سُئلَ عَن تفسيرِ التَّقوىٰ ـ: أن لا يَفقِدَكَ اللهُ حَيثُ أمَرَكَ، ولا يَراكَ حَيثُ نَهاكَ.[٧٥٨٥]

6684. **Imām al-Ṣādiq (AS) said,** 'The crying of people should not deceive you; indeed Godwariness is in the heart.'[7610]

٦٦٨٤. عنه عليه السلام: لا يَغُرَّنَّكَ بُكاؤهُم، إنّما التَّقوىٰ في القَلبِ.[٧٥٨٦]

(See also: PIETY: section 1825)

(اُنظر) الورع: باب ١٨٢٥.

1869. The Most Godwary of People

١٨٦٩ ـ أتقَى النّاسِ

6685. **The Prophet (SAWA) said,** 'The most Godwary of people is he who speaks the truth, be it for or against himself.'[7611]

٦٦٨٥. رسولُ اللهِ صلى الله عليه وآله: أتقَى النّاسِ مَن قالَ الحَقَّ فيما لَهُ وعلَيهِ.[٧٥٨٧]

6686. **The Prophet (SAWA) said,** 'Perform the duties made incumbent by Allah and you will be the most Godwary of people.'[7612]

٦٦٨٦. عنه صلى الله عليه وآله: اِعمَلْ بفَرائضِ اللهِ تَكُن أتقَى النّاسِ.[٧٥٨٨]

6687. **The Prophet (SAWA) said,** 'Whoever would like to become the most Godwary of people should rely on Allah.'[7613]

٦٦٨٧. عنه صلى الله عليه وآله: مَن أحَبَّ أن يَكونَ أتقَى النّاسِ فلْيَتَوكَّلْ علَى اللهِ.[٧٥٨٩]

(See also: PIETY: section 1826)

(اُنظر) الورع: باب ١٨٢٦.

412

DISSIMULATION (*taqiyya*)

التَّقِيَّة

1870. Legislation of Dissimulation and Instances it Should be Observed

١٨٧٠ ـ تَشرِيعُ التَّقِيَّةِ وَمُورِدُها

"The faithful should not take the faithless for allies instead of the faithful, and whoever does that Allah will have nothing to do with him, except when you are wary of them out of caution. Allah warns you to beware of [disobeying] Him, and toward Allah is the return."[7614]

﴿لَا يَتَّخِذِ الْمُؤْمِنُونَ الْكَافِرِينَ أَوْلِيَاءَ مِنْ دُونِ الْمُؤْمِنِينَ وَمَنْ يَفْعَلْ ذٰلِكَ فَلَيْسَ مِنَ اللهِ فِي شَيْءٍ إِلَّا أَنْ تَتَّقُوا مِنْهُمْ تُقَاةً وَيُحَذِّرُكُمُ اللهُ نَفْسَهُ وَإِلَى اللهِ الْمَصِيرُ﴾.[٧٥٩٠]

"Whoever renounces faith in Allah after [affirming] his faith – barring someone who is compelled while his heart is at rest in faith - but those who open up their breasts to unfaith, upon such shall be Allah's wrath, and there is a great punishment for them."[7615]

﴿مَنْ كَفَرَ بِاللهِ مِنْ بَعْدِ إِيمَانِهِ إِلَّا مَنْ أُكْرِهَ وَقَلْبُهُ مُطْمَئِنٌّ بِالْإِيمَانِ وَلٰكِنْ مَنْ شَرَحَ بِالْكُفْرِ صَدْراً فَعَلَيْهِمْ غَضَبٌ مِنَ اللهِ وَلَهُمْ عَذَابٌ عَظِيمٌ﴾.[٧٥٩١]

6688. **Imām al-Bāqir (AS) said,** 'Dissimulation is in anything that is necessary, and the person [faced with] that situation is more knowledgeable of it when it falls upon him.'[7616]

٦٦٨٨ . الإمامُ الباقرُ عليه السلام : التَّقيَّةُ في كُلِّ ضَرورَةٍ، وصاحِبُها أعلَمُ بِها حِينَ تَنزِلُ بهِ .[٧٥٩٢]

6689. **Imām al-Ṣādiq (AS) said,** 'Dissimulation is Allah's shield between Himself and His creation.'[7617]

٦٦٨٩ . الإمامُ الصّادقُ عليه السلام : التَّقيَّة تُرسُ اللهِ بَينَهُ وبَينَ خَلقِهِ .[٧٥٩٣]

6690. **Imām al-Ṣādiq (AS) said,** 'Be wary for your religion, and protect it through dissimulation, for there is no faith for he who does not have [a place for] dissimulation. You are among people as bees among birds; if the birds knew what the bees harbour within them, they would not leave any of them without eating them.'[7618]

٦٦٩٠ . عنه عليه السلام : اتَّقُوا علىٰ دِينِكُم فاحجِبُوهُ بِالتَّقيَّةِ ؛ فإنّهُ لا إيمانَ لِمَن لا تَقيَّةَ لَهُ ، إنّما أنتُم في النّاسِ كالنَّحلِ في الطَّيرِ ؛ لَو أنَّ الطَّيرَ تَعلَمُ ما في أجوافِ النَّحلِ ما بَقِيَ مِنها شيءٌ إلّا أكَلَتهُ .[٧٥٩٤]

6691. **Imām al-Ṣādiq (AS) said,** 'By Allah, Allah cannot be worshipped with anything more beloved

٦٦٩١ . عنه عليه السلام : واللهِ، ما عُبِدَ اللهُ بشيءٍ أحَبَّ إلَيهِ

to Him than concealment.' I asked, 'What is concealment?' He said, 'Dissimulation.'[7619]

مِن الخَبء، قلتُ: وما الخَبءُ؟ قال: التَّقيَّةُ.٧٥٩٥

6692. **Imām al-Ṣādiq (AS) said,** 'A believer is a struggler because he struggles with the enemies of Allah in a false government through dissimulation, and in a true government with the sword.'[7620]

٦٦٩٢. عنه ﷺ: المُؤمنُ مُجاهِدٌ؛ لأنّهُ يُجاهِدُ أعداءَ اللهِ عزَّوجلَّ في دَولَةِ الباطِلِ بالتَّقيَّةِ، وفي دَولَةِ الحَقِّ بالسَّيفِ.٧٥٩٦

1871. Prohibition of Surpassing the Situations [calling] for Dissimulation

١٨٧١ - النَّهيُ عَن تَجاوُزِ مَواضعِ التَّقيَّةِ

6693. **Imām ʿAlī (AS) said,** 'You will be called to insult me so do so. You will be called to disassociate yourselves from me, so extend your necks [for sacrifice], for I am according to my natural disposition [of Islam and monotheism].'[7621]

٦٦٩٣. الإمامُ عليٌّ ﷺ: سَتُدعَونَ إلى سَبِّي فسُبُّوني، وتُدعَون إلَى البَراءَةِ مِنّي فمُدُّوا الرِّقابَ؛ فإنّي علَى الفِطرَةِ.٧٥٩٧

6694. **Isḥāq ibn ʿAmmār al-Ṣairafī said,** "I visited Abū ʿAbdullah [al-Ṣādiq] (AS) whilst I had not greeted our companions in the mosque of Kūfa out of extreme dissimilation (*taqiyah*) we were observing, so Abū ʿAbdullah said to me: "O Isḥāq, when did you become harsh to your brothers, you go past them and you do not greet them?!" So, I said: "It was because of dissimilation I was observing." He (AS) said: "In dissimilation you do not refrain from greeting, but in dissimilation you try not to reveal yourself."[7622]

٦٦٩٤. إسحاق بن عمّار الصيرفي: دَخَلتُ علىٰ أبي عَبدِاللهِ ﷺ وكُنتُ تَرَكتُ التّسليمَ علىٰ أصحابِنا في مَسجِدِ الكوفَةِ؛ وذلكَ لِتَقيَّةٍ علَينا فيه شَديدَةٍ، فقالَ لي أبو عَبدِاللهِ ﷺ: يا إسحاقُ، متىٰ أحدَثتَ هٰذَا الجَفاءَ لإخوانِكَ تَمُرُّ بِهِم فلا تُسَلِّمُ علَيهِم؟! فقُلتُ لَهُ: ذلكَ لِتَقيَّةٍ كُنتُ فيها. فقالَ: لَيسَ علَيكَ في التَّقيَّةِ تَركُ السَّلامِ، وإنّما علَيكَ في التَّقيَّةِ الإذاعَةُ.٧٥٩٨

6695. **Imām al-Ṣādiq (AS) said,** 'Dissimulation has situations [necessitating it]. Whoever lifts them from their rightful places, they will not uphold him. The explanation of what should be dissimulated is like when there is an evil people whose outer rulings and actions oppose rightful rulings and actions, so everything that a believer does among them in a situation [necessitating]

٦٦٩٥. الإمامُ الصّادقُ ﷺ: لِلتَّقيَّةِ مَواضِعُ، مَن أزالَها عَن مَواضِعِها لَم تَستَقِمْ لَهُ، وتَفسيرُ ما يُتَّقىٰ مِثلُ (أنْ يَكونَ) قَومُ سَوءٍ ظاهِرُ حُكمِهِم وفِعلِهِم علىٰ غَيرِ حُكمِ الحَقِّ وفِعلِهِ، فكُلُّ شيءٍ يَعمَلُ المؤمنُ بَينَهُم لِمَكانِ التَّقيَّةِ مِمّا لا يُؤدّي

dissimulation is permissible, as long as it does not lead to the corruption of his faith.'[7623]

إِلَى الفَسادِ فِي الدِّينِ فَإِنَّهُ جائِزٌ.٧٥٩٩

6696. **Imām al-Ṣādiq (AS) said,** 'Dissimulation was established to withhold blood from being shed, so if dissimulation extends to bloodshed then there is no dissimulation. By Allah, if you are called to aid us you would say: 'We will not, rather we will dissimulate', then dissimulation would be more beloved to you than your fathers and mothers, and if the Awaited Saviour was to appear he would not need to ask you for it, and he would uphold the penalty of Allah among those of you who are hypocrites.'[7624]

٦٦٩٦. عنه عليه السلام: إنّما جُعِلَتِ التَّقِيَّةُ لِيُحقَنَ بِها الدَّمُ، فإذا بَلَغَتِ التَّقِيَّةُ الدَّمَ فلا تَقِيَّةَ. وايمُ اللهِ، لَو دُعِيتُم لِتَنصُرونا لَقُلتُم: لا نَفعَلُ، إنّما نَتَّقي، ولَكانَتِ التَّقِيَّةُ أحَبَّ إلَيكُم مِن آبائكُم واُمَّهاتِكُم، ولَو قد قامَ القائمُ ما احتاجَ إلى مُساءلَتِكُم عَن ذلكَ، ولَأقامَ في كَثيرٍ مِنكُم مِن أهلِ النِّفاقِ حَدَّ اللهِ.٧٦٠٠

(See also: DIVINE LEADERSHIP (IMĀMA): section 105-106)

(اُنظر) الإمامة: باب ١٠٥-١٠٦

413

TRUST (IN ALLAH)

التَّوَكُّلُ

1872. The Virtue of Trust (in Allah)

١٨٧٢ـ فَضلُ التَّوَكُّلِ

"And consult them in the affairs, and once you are resolved, put your trust in Allah. Indeed Allah loves those who trust in Him."[7625]

﴿وَشاوِرْهُمْ فِي الْأَمْرِ فَإِذا عَزَمْتَ فَتَوَكَّلْ عَلَى اللهِ إِنَّ اللهَ يُحِبُّ الْمُتَوَكِّلِينَ﴾.٧٦٠١

"Put your trust in the Living One who does not die, and celebrate His praise. He suffices as one all-aware of the sins of His servants."[7626]

﴿وَتَوَكَّلْ عَلَى الْحَيِّ الَّذِي لا يَمُوتُ وَسَبِّحْ بِحَمْدِهِ وَكَفى بِهِ بِذُنُوبِ عِبادِهِ خَبِيراً﴾.٧٦٠٢

6697. **Imām ʿAlī (AS) said,** 'Faith has four pillars: trust in Allah, handing over matters to Allah, satisfaction with the decree of Allah, and submission to the command of Allah.'[7627]

٦٦٩٧. الإمامُ عليٌّ عليه السلام: الإيمانُ لَهُ أركانٌ أربَعَةٌ: التَّوَكُّلُ عَلَى اللهِ، وتَفويضُ الأمرِ إلَى اللهِ، والرِّضا بِقَضاءِ اللهِ، والتَّسليمُ لأمرِ اللهِ عَزَّوجلَّ.٧٦٠٣

6698. **Imām ʿAlī (AS) said,** 'Trust is the fortress of wisdom.'[7628]

٦٦٩٨. عنه عليه السلام: التَّوَكُّلُ حِصنُ الحِكمَةِ.٧٦٠٤

6699. **Imām ʿAlī (AS) said,** 'Trust in Allah is the salvation from all evil and a protection from every enemy.'[7629]

٦٦٩٩. عنه عليه السلام: التَّوَكُّلُ عَلَى اللهِ نَجاةٌ مِن كُلِّ سُوءٍ، وحِرزٌ مِن كُلِّ عَدُوٍّ.٧٦٠٥

6700. **Imām ʿAlī (AS) said,** 'In trust lies the reality of certainty.'[7630]

٦٧٠٠ . عنه ﵇ : في التَّوكُّلِ حَقيقَةُ الإيقانِ.[٧٦٠٦]

1873. The Explanation of Trust

١٨٧٣ ـ تَفسيرُ التَّوَكُّلِ

"If Allah helps you, no one can overcome you, but if He forsakes you, who will help you after Him? So in Allah let all the faithful put their trust."[7631]

﴿إِنْ يَنْصُرْكُمُ اللهُ فَلَا غَالِبَ لَكُمْ وَإِنْ يَخْذُلْكُمْ فَمَنْ ذَا الَّذِي يَنْصُرُكُمْ مِنْ بَعْدِهِ وَعَلَى اللهِ فَلْيَتَوَكَّلِ الْمُؤْمِنُونَ﴾ .[٧٦٠٧]

"Say, 'Nothing will befall us except what Allah has ordained for us. He is our Master, and in Allah let all the faithful put their trust.'"[7632]

﴿قُلْ لَنْ يُصِيبَنَا إِلَّا مَا كَتَبَ اللهُ لَنَا هُوَ مَوْلَانَا وَعَلَى اللهِ فَلْيَتَوَكَّلِ الْمُؤْمِنُونَ﴾ .[٧٦٠٨]

(See also: Qur'an 35:2, 35:10, 39:38, 42:10, 48:11, 64:13, 72:22, 6:80, 33:17)

(اُنظر) فاطر : ٢، ١٠ والزمر : ٣٨ والشورى : ١٠ والفتح : ١١ والتغابن : ١٣ والجن : ٢٢ والأنعام : ٨٠ والأحزاب : ١٧.

6701. **The Archangel Gabriel (AS)**, when the Prophet (SAWA) asked him about trusting in Allah, said, '[It is] to know that a creature can neither harm nor benefit, nor give nor deny [of itself], and it is to display hopelessness from people, so when a servant is such, then he will not do anything for anyone other than Allah, will neither hope nor fear in anyone other than Allah, and will not seek other than Allah – this is complete trust.'[7633]

٦٧٠١ . جَبرئيلُ ﵇ ـ لَمّا سأَلَهُ النّبيُّ ﷺ عنِ التَّوكُّلِ علَى اللهِ ـ : العِلمُ بأنّ المَخلوقَ لا يَضُرُّ ولا يَنفَعُ ، ولا يُعطي ولا يَمنَعُ ، واستِعمالُ اليَأسِ مِن الخَلقِ ، فإذا كانَ العَبدُ كذلكَ لَم يَعمَلْ لأحَدٍ سِوَى اللهِ ، ولَم يَرْجُ ولَم يَخَفْ سِوَى اللهِ ، ولَم يَطمَعْ في أحَدٍ سِوَى اللهِ ، فهٰذا هُو التَّوكُّلُ.[٧٦٠٩]

6702. **The Prophet (SAWA) said,** 'He who cauterises or resorts to witchcraft has turned away from trust [in Allah].'[7634]

٦٧٠٢ . رسولُ اللهِ ﷺ : مَنِ اكتَوىٰ أو استَرقىٰ ، فَقَد بَرِئَ مِنَ التَّوكُّلِ.[٧٦١٠] [٧٦١١]

6703. **Abū Baṣīr,** narrating from Imām al-Ṣādiq (AS) said, 'Nothing exists without a limit.' I asked, 'May I be sacrificed for you, what is the limit of trust [in Allah]?' He said, 'Certainty.' I said, 'So what is the limit of certainty?' He said, 'That you do not fear anything apart from Allah.'[7635]

٦٧٠٣ . أبو بَصيرٍ عن الإمامِ الصّادقِ ﵇ : لَيسَ شَيءٌ إلّا ولَهُ حَدٌّ . قلتُ : جُعِلتُ فِداكَ ، فما حَدُّ التَّوكُّلِ ؟ قالَ : اليَقينُ . قلتُ : فما حَدُّ اليَقينِ ؟ قالَ : ألّا تَخافَ مَعَ اللهِ شَيئاً .[٧٦١٢]

1874. The Fruit of Trust [in Allah]

١٨٧٤ ـ ثَمَرَةُ التَّوَكُّلِ

"Whoever puts his trust in Allah, He will suffice him. Indeed Allah carries through His command. Certainly Allah has set a measure for everything."[7636]

﴿مَنْ يَتَوَكَّلْ عَلَى اللهِ فَهُوَ حَسْبُهُ إِنَّ اللهَ بَالِغُ أَمْرِهِ قَدْ جَعَلَ اللهُ لِكُلِّ شَيْءٍ قَدْراً﴾ .[٧٦١٣]

6704. **Luqmān (AS) said** to his son, advising him, 'O my son, rely in Allah and then ask people: "Is there anyone who relies in Allah and He does not save him?!" O son, trust in Allah and then ask people: "Who is there among you that has placed his trust in Allah and He has not sufficed him?"'[7637]

٦٧٠٤ . لُقمانُ ﷺ ـ لابنِهِ وهُو يَعِظُهُ ـ : يا بُنَيَّ ، ثِقْ باللهِ عَزَّوجلَّ ثُمّ سَلْ في النّاسِ : هَل مِن أحَدٍ وَثِقَ باللهِ فلَم يُنجِهِ ؟! يا بُنَيَّ ، تَوَكَّلْ علَى اللهِ ثُمّ سَلْ في النّاسِ : مَن ذا الّذي تَوَكَّلَ علَى اللهِ فلَم يَكفِهِ ؟![٧٦١٤]

6705. **The Prophet (SAWA) said,** 'Whoever would like to be the strongest of people should place his trust in Allah, most High.'[7638]

٦٧٠٥ . رسولُ اللهِ ﷺ : مَن أحَبَّ أن يَكونَ أقوَى النّاسِ فلْيَتَوكَّلْ علَى اللهِ تعالىٰ .[٧٦١٥]

6706. **Imām ʿAlī (AS) said,** 'Whoever places his trust in Allah, hardships will become easy for him and all means will be simplified for him.'[7639]

٦٧٠٦ . الإمامُ عليٌّ ﷺ : مَن تَوَكَّلَ علَى اللهِ ذَلَّت لَهُ الصِّعابُ ، وتَسهَّلَت علَيهِ الأسبابُ .[٧٦١٦]

6707. **Imām ʿAlī (AS) said,** 'Whoever relies on Allah, He will show him happiness, and whoever places his trust in Him, He will suffice him in all things.'[7640]

٦٧٠٧ . عنه ﷺ : مَن وَثِقَ باللهِ أراهُ السُّرورَ ، ومَن تَوَكَّلَ علَيهِ كَفاهُ الاُمورَ .[٧٦١٧]

6708. **Imām al-Bāqir (AS) said,** 'Whoever trusts in Allah will never be defeated, and whoever grasps onto Allah will never be put to flight.'[7641]

٦٧٠٨ . الإمامُ الباقرُ ﷺ : مَن تَوَكَّلَ علَى اللهِ لا يُغلَبْ ، ومَنِ اعتَصَمَ باللهِ لا يُهزَمْ .[٧٦١٨]

6709. **Imām al-Ṣādiq (AS) said,** 'Wealth and honour wander around, and when they reach a place where there is trust in Allah they remain there.'[7642]

٦٧٠٩ . الإمامُ الصّادقُ ﷺ : إنّ الغِنىٰ والعِزَّ يَجُولانِ ، فإذا ظَفِرا بمَوضِعِ التَّوكُّلِ أوطَنا .[٧٦١٩]

6710. **Imām al-Ṣādiq (AS) said** to Muʿāwiya b. Wahab, 'Whoever has been given trust has been given sufficiency. He then said, 'Have you not recited from the Book of Allah: *"And whoever puts his trust in Allah, He will suffice him."*'[7643]

٦٧١٠ . عنه ﷺ ـ لمعاوية بن وهب ـ : مَن اُعطي ثلاثاً لم يُمنع ثلاثاً ... : مَن اُعطِيَ التَّوَكُّلَ اُعطِيَ الكِفايَةَ . ثُمّ قالَ : أتَلَوتَ كِتابَ اللهِ عَزَّوجلَّ ﴿ومَن يَتَوكَّلْ علَى اللهِ فَهُوَ حَسْبُهُ﴾ ؟![٧٦٢٠]

6711. **Imām al-Jawād (AS) said,** 'Reliance on Allah is the price for every expensive matter and a ladder to everything high.'[7644]

٦٧١١ . الإمامُ الجوادُ ﷺ : الثِّقَةُ باللهِ تعالىٰ ثَمَنٌ لِكُلِّ غالٍ ، وسُلَّمٌ إلىٰ كُلِّ عالٍ .[٧٦٢١]

(انظر) الغنى : باب ١٤٤٦ .

(See also: WEALTH: section 1446)

1875. The Etiquette of Trust

١٨٧٥ـ أدَبُ التَّوَكُّلِ

6712. **Imām al-Ṣādiq (AS) said,** 'A group from the companions of the Prophet (SAWA), when the verse: *"And whoever is wary of Allah, He shall make a way out for him, and provide for him from whence he does not reckon"* descended, locked their doors and engaged themselves in worship, saying, 'We have been sufficed.' The Prophet (SAWA) found out about this so he sent for them and said, 'What made you do what you are doing?' They said, 'O Messenger of Allah! Our sustenance is being taken care of so we have occupied ourselves in worship.' He said, 'Whoever does this, his call will not be answered [by Allah]. You must seek your livelihood.'[7645]

٦٧١٢. الإمامُ الصّادقُ عليه السلام: إنّ قوماً مِن أصحابِ رسولِ اللهِ صلى الله عليه وآله لَمّا نَزَلَت: ﴿ومَن يَتَّقِ اللهَ يَجْعَلْ لَهُ مَخْرَجاً ويَرْزُقْهُ مِن حَيْثُ لا يَحْتَسِبُ﴾ أغلَقوا الأبوابَ وأقبَلوا على العِبادَةِ وقالوا: قد كُفِينا، فبَلَغَ ذلكَ النَّبيَّ صلى الله عليه وآله فأرسَلَ إلَيهِم فقالَ: ما حَمَلَكُم على ما صَنَعتُم؟ قالوا: يا رسولَ اللهِ! تُكُفِّلَ لَنا بأرزاقِنا فأقبَلنا على العِبادَةِ، فقالَ: إنّهُ مَن فَعَلَ ذلكَ لم يُستَجَبْ لَهُ، علَيكُم بالطَّلَبِ.[٧٦٢٢]

6713. **The Prophet (SAWA) said** to a person who asked him, 'Should I tie it [i.e. my camel] and trust in Allah or leave it loose and trust in Allah?' He said, 'Tie it and then trust.'[7646]

٦٧١٣. رسولُ اللهِ صلى الله عليه وآله ـ لِرجُلٍ قالَ لَهُ: أعقِلُها (يعني دابّته) وأتَوَكَّلُ، أو أُطلِقُها وأتَوَكَّلُ؟ ـ: اِعقِلْها وتَوَكَّلْ.[٧٦٢٣]

6714. **The Prophet (SAWA) said** to a group of people not planting, 'What are you doing?' They said, 'We are placing our trust in Allah.' He said, 'No, rather you are the dependents.'[7647]

٦٧١٤. مستدرك الوسائل: رأى رسولُ اللهِ صلى الله عليه وآله قوماً لا يَزرَعونَ، قالَ: ما أنتُم؟ قالوا: نَحنُ المُتَوَكِّلونَ، قالَ: لا، بَل أنتُمُ المُتَّكِلونَ.[٧٦٢٤]

6715. **Imām 'Alī (AS) said** to his son Muḥammad b. al-Ḥanafiyya when he gave him the standard in the Battle of the Camel, 'Mountains may move from their position but you should not move from yours. Grit your teeth. Lend to Allah your head [i.e. give yourself to Allah]. Plant your feet firmly in the ground. Have your eye on the remotest foe and lower your gaze, and know that victory is from Allah, the Glorified.'[7648]

٦٧١٥. الإمامُ عليٌّ عليه السلام ـ لابنِهِ محمّدِ بنِ الحَنَفيّةِ لَمّا أعطاهُ الرّايَةَ يومَ الجَمَلِ ـ: تَزولُ الجِبالُ ولا تَزُلْ، عَضَّ على ناجِذِكَ، أعِرِ اللهَ جُمجُمَتَكَ، تِدْ في الأرضِ قَدَمَكَ، اِرْمِ بِبَصَرِكَ أقصَى القَومِ، وغُضَّ بَصَرَكَ، واعلَمْ أنَّ النَّصرَ مِن عِندِ اللهِ سبحانَهُ.[٧٦٢٥]

6716. **Imām 'Alī (AS) said** to a group of healthy people sitting down in a corner of the mosque [not working], 'Who are you?' to which they replied, 'We are the ones who place our trust in Allah.' He said, 'No, rather you are the abraded.'[7649]

٦٧١٦. مستدرك الوسائل: إنّه [أميرَ المؤمنين عليه السلام] مَرَّ يَوماً على قَومٍ أصِحّاءَ جالِسينَ في زاوِيَةِ المَسجِدِ فقالَ عليه السلام: مَن أنتُم؟ قالوا: نَحنُ المُتَوَكِّلونَ. قالَ عليه السلام: لا، بَل أنتُمُ المُتَأكِّلَةُ.[٧٦٢٦]

6717. **Imām al-Ṣādiq (AS) said,** 'Do not leave the seeking of lawful sustenance, for it is more helpful to you in your religion, and tie your riding camel, and then trust in Allah.'[7650]

٦٧١٧ . الإمامُ الصّادقُ عليه السلام : لا تَدَعْ طَلَبَ الرِّزقِ مِن حِلِّهِ فإنّهُ أعوَنُ لَك على دِينِكَ، واعقِلْ راحِلَتَكَ وتَوَكَّلْ. ٧٦٢٧

1876. Relying on Other than Allah

١٨٧٦ ـ الاِتّكالُ إلىٰ غَيرِ اللهِ

6718. **The Prophet (SAWA) said,** 'Allah Almighty has said, 'Any creature who resorts to another creature instead of Me, I will shut the doors of Heaven and earth from him, such that if he calls Me, I will not answer him, and if he requests from Me, I will not give him.'[7651]

٦٧١٨ . رسولُ اللهِ صلى الله عليه وآله : يَقولُ اللهُ عَزَّ وجلَّ : ما مِن مَخلوقٍ يَعتَصِمُ بمَخلوقٍ دُوني إلّا قَطَعتُ أبوابَ السَّماواتِ والأرضِ دُونَهُ، فإن دَعاني لَم اُجِبْهُ، وإن سَألَني لَم اُعطِهِ. ٧٦٢٨

6719. **The Prophet (SAWA) said,** 'Do not rely on other than Allah, for Allah will relegate you to him.'[7652]

٦٧١٩ . عنه صلى الله عليه وآله : لا تَتَّكِلْ إلىٰ غَيرِ اللهِ فيَكِلَكَ اللهُ إلَيهِ. ٧٦٢٩

6720. **Imām 'Alī (AS) said,** 'Beware of being completely self-reliant, for that is one of the greatest snares of Satan.'[7653]

٦٧٢٠ . الإمامُ عليٌّ عليه السلام : إيّاكَ والثِّقَةَ بنَفسِكَ ؛ فإنَّ ذلكَ مِن أكبَرِ مَصائدِ الشَّيطانِ. ٧٦٣٠

414

PARENT AND CHILD

الوالِدُ والوَلَدُ

1877. The Virtue of Having Children

١٨٧٧ ـ فَضلُ الوَلدِ

6721. **The Prophet (SAWA) said,** 'For every tree there is a fruit and the fruit of the heart is the child.'[7654]

٦٧٢١ . رسولُ اللهِ صلى الله عليه وآله : إنّ لِكُلِّ شَجَرَةٍ ثَمَرَةً، وثَمَرَةُ القَلبِ الوَلَدُ. ٧٦٣١

6722. **Imām Zayn al-'Ābidīn (AS) said,** 'It is part of the prosperity of a man that he has offspring who can be an aid to him.'[7655]

٦٧٢٢ . الإمامُ زينُ العابدينَ عليه السلام : مِن سَعادَةِ الرَّجُلِ أن يَكونَ لَهُ وُلْدٌ يَستَعينُ بِهِم. ٧٦٣٢

6723. **Imām al-Bāqir (AS) said,** 'It is part of the prosperity of a man that he has a child wherein he can see his own likeness: in his looks, his character, and his virtues.'[7656]

٦٧٢٣ . الإمامُ الباقرُ عليه السلام : مِن سَعادَةِ الرَّجُلِ أن يَكونَ لَهُ الوَلَدُ يَعرِفُ فيهِ شِبهَهُ : خَلقَهُ، وخُلُقَهُ، وشَمائلَهُ. ٧٦٣٣

1878. The Trial of Having a Child

١٨٧٨ ـ فِتنَةُ الوَلَدِ

"Know that your possessions and children are only a test, and that Allah, with Him is a great reward."[7657]

﴿وَاعْلَمُوا أَنَّمَا أَمْوَالُكُمْ وَأَوْلَادُكُمْ فِتْنَةٌ وَأَنَّ اللهَ عِنْدَهُ أَجْرٌ عَظِيمٌ﴾.[٧٦٣٤]

6724. **The Prophet (SAWA) said,** 'Our children are our hearts, the younger ones from among them are our kings and the older ones our enemies. When they are alive they are a trouble for us and when they die they make us grieve.'[7658]

٦٧٢٤. رسولُ اللهِ ﷺ: أولادُنا أكبادُنا، صُغَراؤهُم أُمَراؤنا، وكُبَراؤهُم أعداؤنا، فإن عاشُوا فتَنُونا، وإن ماتُوا أحزَنُونا.[٧٦٣٥]

6725. **The Prophet (SAWA) said,** 'A child is [a source of] cowardice, weakness and sorrow [for the parent].'[7659]

٦٧٢٥. عنه ﷺ: الوَلَدُ مَجبَنَةٌ مَبخَلَةٌ مَحزَنَةٌ.[٧٦٣٦]

6726. **Imām ʿAlī (AS) said,** 'Do not let most of your preoccupation be with your family and children, for if your family and children are lovers of Allah, Allah does not forget His lovers, and if they are the enemies of Allah, then what is your concern and preoccupation with the enemies of Allah?!'[7660]

٦٧٢٦. الإمامُ عليٌّ عليه السلام: لا تَجعَلَنَّ أكثَرَ شُغُلِكَ بأهلِكَ ووَلَدِكَ؛ فإن يَكُن أهلُكَ ووَلَدُكَ أولياءَ اللهِ، فإنَّ اللهَ لا يُضِيعُ أولياءَهُ، وإن يَكُونوا أعداءَ اللهِ فما هَمُّكَ وشُغُلُكَ بأعداءِ اللهِ؟![٧٦٣٧]

1879. Loving Children

١٨٧٩ ـ حُبُّ الوَلَدِ

6727. **The Prophet (SAWA) said,** 'Love children and have mercy on them.'[7661]

٦٧٢٧. رسولُ اللهِ ﷺ: أحِبُّوا الصِّبيانَ وارحَمُوهُم.[٧٦٣٨]

6728. **The Prophet (SAWA)** with regard to a man who stated [proudly], 'I have never kissed a child', said after he had left, 'To me this man is one of the people of Hell.'[7662]

٦٧٢٨. عنه ﷺ ـ في رجُلٍ قالَ: ما قَبَّلتُ صَبِيّاً قَطُّ، فلَمّا ولّى قالَ ـ: هذا رجُلٌ عِندي أنّهُ مِن أهلِ النّارِ.[٧٦٣٩]

6729. **Imām al-Ṣādiq (AS) said,** 'Allah has mercy on a servant because of his strong love for his child.'[7663]

٦٧٢٩. الإمامُ الصّادقُ عليه السلام: إنّ اللهَ عَزَّ وجلَّ لَيَرحَمُ العَبدَ لِشِدَّةِ حُبِّهِ لِوَلَدِهِ.[٧٦٤٠]

1880. Acting Childishly for Children

١٨٨٠ ـ التَّصابي لِلصَّبِيِّ

6730. **The Prophet (SAWA) said,** 'Whoever has a child should act childishly to him.'[7664]

٦٧٣٠. رسولُ اللهِ ﷺ: مَن كانَ عِندَهُ صَبِيٌّ فلْيَتَصابَ لَهُ.[٧٦٤١]

6731. **Jābir said,** 'I visited the Prophet (SAWA) and Ḥasan and Ḥusayn (AS) were on his back and he was kneeling for them, saying, 'What a good camel you have and what good riders you are.'[7665]

٦٧٣١ . بحار الأنوار عن جابِر: دَخَلتُ علَى النَّبيِّ ﷺ والحَسَنُ والحُسَينُ عليهما السلام علىٰ ظَهرِهِ وهُو يَجثو لَهُما ويَقولُ: نِعمَ الجَمَلُ جَمَلُكُما، ونِعمَ العِدلانِ أنتُما.[٧٦٤٢]

1881. The Righteous Child

١٨٨١ ـ الوَلَدُ الصّالِحُ

"And those who say, 'Our Lord! Grant us comfort in our spouses and descendants, and make us Imāms of the Godwary.'"[7666]

﴿وَالَّذِينَ يَقُولُونَ رَبَّنَا هَبْ لَنَا مِنْ أَزْوَاجِنَا وَذُرِّيَّاتِنَا قُرَّةَ أَعْيُنٍ وَاجْعَلْنَا لِلْمُتَّقِينَ إِمَاماً﴾.[٧٦٤٣]

(See also: Qur'an 19:49, 19:50, 21:90)

(أنظر) مريم: ٤٩، ٥٠ والأنبياء: ٩٠.

6732. **The Prophet (SAWA) said,** 'A righteous child is an aromatic plant from the plants of Heaven.'[7667]

٦٧٣٢ . رسولُ اللهِ ﷺ: إنّ الوَلَدَ الصّالِحَ رَيحانَةٌ مِن رَياحِينِ الجَنَّةِ.[٧٦٤٤]

6733. **The Prophet (SAWA) said,** 'A righteous child is an aromatic plant from Allah which He has distributed to His servants.'[7668]

٦٧٣٣ . عنه ﷺ: الوَلَدُ الصّالِحُ رَيحانَةٌ مِن اللهِ، قَسَمَها بَينَ عِبادِهِ.[٧٦٤٥]

6734. **The Prophet (SAWA) said,** 'Part of the prosperity of a man is that he has a righteous child.'[7669]

٦٧٣٤ . عنه ﷺ: مِن سَعادَةِ الرّجُلِ الوَلَدُ الصّالِحُ.[٧٦٤٦]

6735. **Imām 'Alī (AS) said,** 'I never asked my Lord for children with bright faces, nor did I ask Him for a son with a good stature, but I asked my Lord for children who are obedient to Allah and fear Him, so that when I look at the child, seeing him obedient to Allah, it will be a source of comfort for my eyes.'[7670]

٦٧٣٥ . الإمامُ عليٌّ عليه السلام: ماسَألتُ رَبِّي أولاداً نُضْرَ الوَجهِ، ولا سَألتُهُ وَلَداً حسَنَ القامَةِ، ولكنْ سَألتُ رَبِّي أولاداً مُطِيعِينَ للهِ وَجِلِينَ مِنهُ؛ حتّىٰ إذا نَظَرتُ إلَيهِ وهُو مُطيعٌ للهِ قَرَّت عَيني.[٧٦٤٧]

6736. **Imām al-Ṣādiq (AS) said,** 'Allah's inheritance to His pious servant is a righteous child who repents for him.'[7671]

٦٧٣٦ . الإمامُ الصادقُ عليه السلام: مِيراثُ اللهِ مِن عَبدِهِ المؤمنِ وَلَدٌ صالِحٌ يَستَغفِرُ لَهُ.[٧٦٤٨]

1882. Prohibition of Hating Girls

١٨٨٢ ـ النَّهيُ عَن كُرهِ البَناتِ

6737. **The Prophet (SAWA) said,** 'Do not hate girls, for they are the sources of delight and the valuable [ones].'[7672]

٦٧٣٧ . رسولُ اللهِ ﷺ: لا تَكرَهوا البَناتَ؛ فإنَّهُنَّ المُؤنِساتُ الغالِياتُ.[٧٦٤٩]

6738. **The Prophet (SAWA) said,** 'Girls are the compassionate, the ones who have been provided for, the ones who are blessed.'[7673]

٦٧٣٨. عنه ﷺ: البَناتُ هُنَّ المُشفِقاتُ المُجَهَّزاتُ المُباركاتُ. ٧٦٥٠

6739. **The Prophet (SAWA) said,** 'Allah, Blessed and most High, is more affectionate to females than to males, and any man who brings happiness into the heart of a woman he is related to, Allah will make him happy on the Day of Resurrection.'[7674]

٦٧٣٩. عنه ﷺ: إنّ اللهَ تباركَ وتعالىٰ علَى الإناثِ أرأفُ مِنهُ علَى الذُّكورِ، وما مِن رجُلٍ يُدخِلُ فَرحَةً علَى امرأةٍ بَينَهُ وبَينَها حُرمَةٌ، إلّا فَرَّحَهُ اللهُ تعالى يَومَ القِيامَةِ. ٧٦٥١

6740. **Imām al-Ṣādiq (AS) said,** 'Boys are bounties and girls are merits, and Allah asks about bounties but rewards for merits.'[7675]

٦٧٤٠. الإمامُ الصادقُ عليه السلام: البَنونَ نَعيمٌ والبَناتُ حَسَناتٌ، واللهُ يَسألُ عَنِ النَّعيمِ ويُثيبُ علَى الحَسَناتِ. ٧٦٥٢

1883. Enjoinment of being Just between Children

١٨٨٣ ـ الحَثُّ عَلَى العَدلِ بَينَ الأولادِ

6741. **The Prophet (SAWA) said,** 'Maintain justice among your children in gifts, just like you would like them to be just with you in goodness and affection.'[7676]

٦٧٤١. رسولُ اللهِ ﷺ: اِعدِلوا بَينَ أولادِكُم في النُّحْلِ ٧٦٥٣، كما تُحِبّونَ أن يَعدِلوا بَينَكُم في البِرِّ واللُّطفِ. ٧٦٥٤

6742. **Imām ʿAlī (AS) said,** 'The Prophet saw a man with two sons, who kissed one of them but left the other, so the Prophet (SAWA) said, 'Why do you not treat both of them equally?!'[7677]

٦٧٤٢. الإمامُ عليٌّ عليه السلام: أبصَرَ رسولُ اللهِ رجُلاً لَهُ وَلَدانِ فقَبَّلَ أحَدَهُما وتَرَكَ الآخَرَ، فقالَ ﷺ: فَهَلّا واسَيتَ بَينَهُما؟! ٧٦٥٥

1884. Enjoinment of being Good to One's Parents

١٨٨٤ ـ الحَثُّ عَلَى الإحسانِ إلَى الوالِدَينِ

"Your Lord has decreed that you shall not worship anyone except Him, and [He has enjoined] kindness to parents. Should they reach old age at your side – one of them or both -do not say to them, 'Fie'. And do not chide them, but speak to them noble words. Lower the wing of humility to them, out of mercy, and say, 'My Lord! Have mercy on them, just as they reared me when I was [a] small child'."[7678]

﴿وَقَضَىٰ رَبُّكَ أَلَّا تَعْبُدُوا إِلَّا إِيَّاهُ وَبِالْوَالِدَيْنِ إِحْسَاناً إِمَّا يَبْلُغَنَّ عِنْدَكَ الْكِبَرَ أَحَدُهُمَا أَوْ كِلَاهُمَا فَلَا تَقُلْ لَهُمَا أُفٍّ وَلَا تَنْهَرْهُمَا وَقُلْ لَهُمَا قَوْلاً كَرِيماً * وَاخْفِضْ لَهُمَا جَنَاحَ الذُّلِّ مِنَ الرَّحْمَةِ وَقُلْ رَبِّ ارْحَمْهُمَا كَمَا رَبَّيَانِي صَغِيراً﴾. ٧٦٥٦

(Se also: Qur'an 2:83, 19:14, 19:32, 31:14, 46:15)

(أنظر) البقرة: ٨٣ ومريم: ١٤، ٣٢ ولقمان: ١٤ والأحقاف: ١٥.

6743. **The Prophet (SAWA),** when asked about the rights of parents upon their child, said, 'They are your Heaven and your Hell.'[7679]

٦٧٤٣ . رسولُ اللهِ ﷺ ـ لَمّا سُئلَ عَن حقِّ الوالِدَينِ علىٰ وَلَدِهِما ـ: هُما جَنَّتُكَ ونارُكَ.[٧٦٥٧]

6744. *al-Targhīb wa al-Tarhīb*: 'The Prophet (SAWA), when Ibn Masʿūd asked him about the most beloved of acts to Allah Almighty, said, 'Prayer at its prescribed time.' I asked, 'Then what?' He said, 'Being good to one's parents.'[7680]

٦٧٤٤ . الترغيب والترهيب عن رسولِ اللهِ ﷺ ـ وقد سَألَهُ ابنُ مَسعودٍ عَن أحَبِّ الأعمالِ إلَى اللهِ تعالىٰ ـ: الصَّلاةُ علىٰ وَقتِها. قلتُ: ثُمّ أيٌّ؟ قالَ: بِرُّ الوالِدَينِ.[٧٦٥٨]

6745. **The Prophet (SAWA) said,** 'He who is good to his parents, blessings be upon him, Allah will prolong his life.'[7681]

٦٧٤٥ . رسولُ اللهِ ﷺ: مَن بَرَّ والِدَيهِ طُوبىٰ لَهُ، زادَ اللهُ في عُمرِهِ.[٧٦٥٩]

6746. **The Prophet (SAWA) said,** 'Allah's satisfaction lies in the satisfaction of one's parent, and Allah's discontentment lies in the discontentment of one's parent.'[7682]

٦٧٤٦ . عنه ﷺ: رِضا اللهِ في رِضا الوالِدِ، وسَخَطُ اللهِ في سَخَطِ الوالِدِ.[٧٦٦٠]

6747. **Imām al-Ṣādiq (AS) said,** 'Be good to your parents and your children will be good to you.'[7683]

٦٧٤٧ . الإمامُ الصّادقُ عليه السلام: بَرُّوا آباءكُم يَبَرَّكُم أبناؤكُم.[٧٦٦١]

6748. **Imām al-Ṣādiq (AS) said,** 'Being good to one's parents is obligatory, even if they are polytheists, but there is no obedience due to them if it entails disobedience to the Creator.'[7684]

٦٧٤٨ . عنه عليه السلام: بِرُّ الوالِدَينِ واجِبٌ، فإن كانا مُشرِكَينِ فلا تُطِعْهُما ولا غَيرَهُما في المَعصيَةِ؛ فإنّهُ لاطاعَةَ لِمَخلوقٍ في مَعصِيَةِ الخالِقِ.[٧٦٦٢]

6749. **Imām al-Riḍā (AS) said,** 'Allah Almighty… ordered thankfulness to Him and to one's parents, so whoever does not thank their parents does not thank Allah.'[7685]

٦٧٤٩ . الإمامُ الرِّضا عليه السلام: إنّ اللهَ عَزَّ وجلَّ... أمَرَ بالشُّكرِ لَهُ ولِلوالِدَين، فمَن لَم يَشكُرْ والِدَيهِ لَم يَشكُرِ اللهَ.[٧٦٦٣]

1885. Enjoinment of being Good to One's Parents [even] After their Death

١٨٨٥ ـ الحَثُّ عَلىٰ بِرِّ الوالِدَينِ بَعدَ مَوتِهِما

6750. **The Prophet (SAWA),** when asked about being good to one's parents after their death, said, 'Yes, [it entails] praying for them, seeking forgiveness for them, fulfilling their promises after them, maintaining kinship that is not done other than through them, and honouring their friends.'[7686]

٦٧٥٠ . رسولُ اللهِ ﷺ ـ لَمّا سُئلَ عن بِرِّ الوالِدَينِ بَعدَ مَوتِهِما ـ: نَعَم، الصَّلاةُ عَلَيهِما، والاستِغفارُ لَهُما، وإنفاذُ عَهدِهِما مِن بَعدِهِما، وصِلَةُ الرَّحِمِ الّتي لا تُوصَلُ إلّا بِهِما، وإكرامُ صَديقِهِما.[٧٦٦٤]

6751. **Imām al-Bāqir (AS) said,** 'A man could be obedient to his parents during their lifetime, then they die and he does not repay their debts or ask Allah to forgive them, so Allah records him down as being insolent. Or, he could have been insolent to them during their lifetime and not obedient, but after their death he repays their debts and seeks forgiveness from Allah for them, Allah records him down as righteous.'[7687]

٦٧٥١. الإمامُ الباقرُ عليه السلام: إنّ العَبدَ لَيكونُ بـارّاً بِوالِدَيهِ في حياتِهِما، ثُـمّ يَـموتانِ فـلا يَـقضي عَنهُما دُيونَهُما ولا يَستَغفِرُ لَهُما فيَكتُبُهُ اللهُ عاقّاً. وإنّهُ لَيكونُ عاقّاً لَهُما في حياتِهِما غيرَ بارٍّ بِهِما، فإذا ماتا قَضىٰ دَينَهُما واستَغفَرَ لَهُما فـيَكتُبُهُ اللهُ عَزَّوجلَّ بارّاً.[٧٦٦٥]

1886. Heaven is under the Feet of Mothers

١٨٨٦ ـ الجَنَّةُ تَحتَ أقدامِ الأُمَّهاتِ

6752. **The Prophet (SAWA) said,** 'Heaven is under the feet of the mothers.'[7688]

٦٧٥٢. رسولُ اللهِ صلى الله عليه وآله: الجَـنَّةُ تَـحتَ أقـدامِ الأُمَّهاتِ.[٧٦٦٦]

6753. **Imām Zayn al-ʿĀbidīn (AS)** - A man once asked him, 'There is not a single bad deed that I have not committed, but do I still have repentance?' He replied, 'Are any of your parents alive?' He said, 'My father.' He (SAWA) said, 'Then go and be good to him.' The narrator said, 'So when this person left, the Prophet (SAWA) said, 'If only it was his mother!'[7689]

٦٧٥٣. الإمامُ زينُ العابدين عليه السلام: جاءَ رَجلٌ إلىٰ النبيِّ صلى الله عليه وآله فقالَ: يا رسولَ اللهِ ما مِن عَمَلٍ قَبيحٍ إلّا قد عَمِلتُهُ، فهَل لِي مِن تَـوبَةٍ؟ فـقالَ لهُ رسـولُ اللهِ صلى الله عليه وآله: فهَل مِن والِدَيكَ أحَدٌ حَيٌّ؟ قالَ: أبـي، قالَ: فاذهَبْ فَبَرَّهُ. قالَ: فلَمّا ولّىٰ، قالَ رسولُ اللهِ صلى الله عليه وآله: لَو كانَت أُمُّهُ![٧٦٦٧]

6754. **Imām al-Ṣādiq (AS) said,** 'A man came to the Prophet (SAWA) and said, 'O Messenger of Allah, whom shall I be good to?' He said, 'Your mother.' He asked, 'Then who?' He (SAWA) said, 'Your mother.' He asked, 'Then who?' He (SAWA) said, 'Your mother.' He said, 'And then who?' He (SAWA) replied, 'Your father.'[7690]

٦٧٥٤. الإمامُ الصّادقُ عليه السلام: جاءَ رجُلٌ إلَى النَّبيِّ صلى الله عليه وآله فقالَ: يا رسولَ اللهِ، مَن أبَرُّ؟ قالَ: أُمَّكَ، قالَ: ثُمّ مَن؟ قالَ: أُمَّكَ، قالَ: ثُمَّ مَن؟ قالَ: أُمَّكَ، قالَ: ثُمّ مَن؟ قالَ: أباكَ.[٧٦٦٨]

1887. Hurting One's Parents

١٨٨٧ ـ إيذاءُ الوالِدَينِ

6755. **Imām al-Ṣādiq (AS) said,** 'The lowest level of insolence [to one's parents] is saying: 'Fie', and if Allah knew of something more insignificant than that He would have used it.'[7691]

٦٧٥٥. الإمامُ الصّادقُ عليه السلام: أدنَى العُقوقِ: «أُفٍّ»، ولَو عَلِمَ اللهُ عَـزَّوجلَّ شَـيئاً أهـوَنَ مِـنهُ لَـنَهىٰ عَنهُ.[٧٦٦٩]

6756. **Imām al-Ṣādiq (AS),** with regards to Allah's verse in the Qur'an: *"Lower the wing of*

٦٧٥٦. عنه عليه السلام ـ في قولِهِ تعالىٰ: ﴿واخْفِضْ لَهُما

humility to them, out of mercy " said, 'Do not fill your eyes by looking at them other than with compassion and affection, and do not raise your voice over their voices, nor your hand over their hand, and do not walk in front of them.'[7692]

جَناحَ الذُّلِّ مِنَ الرَّحْمَةِ﴾ [٧٦٧٠] ـ: لا تَملَأْ عَينَيكَ مِن النَّظَرِ إلَيهِما إلّا بِرَحمَةٍ ورِقَّةٍ، ولا تَرفَعْ صَوتَكَ فَوقَ أصواتِهِما، ولا يَدَكَ فَوقَ أيديهِما، ولا تَقَدَّمْ قُدّامَهُما. [٧٦٧١]

6757. **Imām al-Ṣādiq (AS),** with regard to Allah's verse in the Qur'an: *"but speak to them noble words"* said, 'If they hit you, then say to them, 'May Allah forgive you.'[7693]

٦٧٥٧. عنه ﷺ ـ في قَولِهِ تعالىٰ: ﴿وقُلْ لَهُما قَوْلاً كَرِيماً﴾ ـ: إن ضَرَباك فَقُلْ لَهُما: غَفَرَ اللهُ لَكُما. [٧٦٧٢]

1888. Insolence to One's Parents

١٨٨٨ ـ عُقوقُ الوالِدَينِ

6758. **The Prophet (SAWA) said,** 'It will be said [by Allah] to the insolent [towards his parents]: Do what you want, for I will not forgive you.'[7694]

٦٧٥٨. رسولُ اللهِ ﷺ: يُقالُ لِلعاقِّ: اِعمَلْ ما شِئتَ فإنّي لا أغفِرُ لَكَ. [٧٦٧٣]

6759. **The Prophet (SAWA) said,** 'Whoever upsets their parents has been insolent to them.'[7695]

٦٧٥٩. عنه ﷺ: مَن أحزَنَ والِدَيهِ فَقَد عَقَّهُما. [٧٦٧٤]

6760. **Imām al-Ṣādiq (AS) said,** 'Insolence to one's parents is a grave sin, because Allah Almighty regards the insolent one as a sinner and a wretched person.'[7696]

٦٧٦٠. الإمامُ الصّادقُ ﷺ: عُقوقُ الوالِدَينِ مِنَ الكَبائرِ؛ لأنَّ اللهَ تعالىٰ جَعَلَ العاقَّ عَصِيّاً شَقِيّاً. [٧٦٧٥]

6761. **Imām al-Ṣādiq (AS) said,** 'Insolence includes a man's looking at his parents with a sharp gaze.'[7697]

٦٧٦١. عنه ﷺ: مِن العُقوقِ أن يَنظُرَ الرَّجُلُ إلىٰ والِدَيهِ فيُحِدَّ النَّظَرَ إلَيهِما. [٧٦٧٦]

6762. **Imām al-Ṣādiq (AS) said,** 'Whoever looks at his parents with hatred, even if they oppress him, Allah will not accept a single prayer from him.'[7698]

٦٧٦٢. عنه ﷺ: مَن نَظَرَ إلىٰ أبَوَيهِ نَظَرَ ماقِتٍ وهُما ظالِمانِ لَهُ، لَم يَقبَلِ اللهُ لَهُ صَلاةً. [٧٦٧٧]

6763. **Imām al-Hādī (AS) said,** 'Insolence brings about lack and leads to humiliation.'[7699]

٦٧٦٣. الإمامُ الهادي ﷺ: العُقوقُ يُعقِبُ القِلَّةَ، ويُؤَدّي إلَى الذِّلَّةِ. [٧٦٧٨]

1889. The Right of the Parent upon the Child

١٨٨٩ ـ حَقُّ الوالِدِ عَلَى الوَلَدِ

6764. **The Prophet (SAWA),** when asked about the right of the parent upon the chid, said, 'He should not call them by their name, nor walk in

٦٧٦٤. رسولُ اللهِ ﷺ ـ لَمّا سُئلَ عَن حَقِّ الوالِدِ علىٰ وَلَدِهِ ـ: لا يُسَمِّيهِ باسمِهِ، ولا يَمشي

front of them, nor sit before they do, nor make himself deserving of abuse from them.'[7700]

بينَ يَدَيهِ، ولا يَجلِسُ قَبلَهُ، ولا يَستَسِبُّ لَهُ.٧٦٧٩

6765. **The Prophet (SAWA)** was once asked by a man, 'My father wants to confiscate my money', to which he replied, 'You and your money belong to your father.'[7701]

٦٧٦٥. عنه ﷺ ـ لرجلٍ قالَ لَهُ: إنّ أبي يُريدُ أن يَستَبيحَ مالي ـ: أنتَ ومالُكَ لأبيكَ.٧٦٨٠

1890. The Right of the Child upon the Parent

١٨٩٠ ـ حَقُّ الوَلَدِ عَلَى الوالِدِ

6766. **The Prophet (SAWA) said,** 'Among the rights of a child upon his parent are three: to give him a good name, to teach him how to write, and to marry him off when he becomes mature.'[7702]

٦٧٦٦. رسولُ اللهِ ﷺ: مِن حَقِّ الوَلَدِ على والِدِهِ ثَلاثَةٌ: يُحَسِّنُ اسمَهُ، ويُعَلِّمُهُ الكِتابَةَ، ويُزَوِّجُهُ إذا بَلَغَ.٧٦٨١

6767. **The Prophet (SAWA) said,** 'The right of the child upon the parent is that he gives him a good name, disciplines him with good manners, and teaches him the Qur'an.'[7703]

٦٧٦٧. عنه ﷺ: حَقُّ الوَلَدِ على والِدِهِ أن يُحَسِّنَ اسمَهُ، ويُحَسِّنَ مَوضِعَهُ، ويُحَسِّنَ أدَبَهُ.٧٦٨٢

6768. **Imām al-Ṣādiq (AS) said,** 'There are three things obligatory upon a father for his child: choose a good mother for him [before he is born], to give him a good name, and to go to lengths in disciplining him.'[7704]

٦٧٦٨. الإمامُ الصّادقُ ﷺ: تَجِبُ لِلوَلَدِ على والِدِهِ ثَلاثُ خِصالٍ: اختِيارُهُ لِوالِدَتِهِ، وتَحسينُ اسمِهِ، والمُبالَغَةُ في تَأديبِهِ.٧٦٨٣

6769. **Imām al-Ṣādiq (AS) said,** 'The parent's goodness towards his child is [tantamount to] his goodness towards his own parents.'[7705]

٦٧٦٩. عنه ﷺ: بِرُّ الرَّجُلِ بِوَلَدِهِ، بِرُّهُ بِوالِدَيهِ.٧٦٨٤

1891. Upbringing of the Child

١٨٩١ ـ تَربِيَةُ الوَلَدِ

6770. **The Prophet (SAWA) said,** 'Honour your children and perfect their manners.'[7706]

٦٧٧٠. رسولُ اللهِ ﷺ: أكرِموا أولادَكُم وأحسِنوا آدابَهُم.٧٦٨٥

6771. **The Prophet (SAWA) said,** 'Discipline your children with three features: the love of your Prophet (SAWA), the love of his Household, and the recitation of the Qur'an.'[7707]

٦٧٧١. عنه ﷺ: أدِّبوا أولادَكُم على ثَلاثِ خِصالٍ: حُبِّ نَبِيِّكُم، وحُبِّ أهلِ بَيتِهِ، وقِراءَةِ القُرآنِ.٧٦٨٦

6772. **The Prophet (SAWA) said,** 'Teach your children swimming and archery.'[7708]

٦٧٧٢ . عنه ﷺ : عَلِّموا أولادَكُم السِّباحَةَ والرِّمايَةَ.[٧٦٨٧]

6773. **The Prophet (SAWA) said,** 'A child is a master for seven years, a servant for seven years, and a minister for seven years. If you are content with assisting him during these twenty one years [and have reached your aim of training him] then be it, or else strike him on his shoulder for you have completed your excuse to Allah in him.'[7709]

٦٧٧٣ . عنه ﷺ : الوَلَدُ سَيِّدٌ سَبعَ سِنينَ، وخادِمٌ سَبعَ سِنينَ، ووَزيرٌ سَبعَ سِنينَ، فإن رضِيتَ مُكانَفَتَهُ لإحدىٰ وعِشرينَ، وإلّا فاضرِبْ علىٰ كَتِفِهِ، قد أعذَرتَ إلَى اللهِ فيهِ.[٧٦٨٨]

6774. **Imām 'Alī (AS) said,** 'Command your children to acquire knowledge.'[7710]

٦٧٧٤ . الإمامُ عليٌّ عليه السلام : مُرُوا أولادَكُم بطَلَبِ العِلمِ.[٧٦٨٩]

6775. **Imām 'Alī (AS) said,** 'Teach your children to pray, and take them to account for it when they reach puberty.'[7711]

٦٧٧٥ . عنه عليه السلام : عَلِّموا صِبيانَكُمُ الصَّلاةَ، وخُذوهُم بها إذا بَلَغوا الحُلُمَ.[٧٦٩٠]

6776. **Imām al-Ṣādiq (AS) said,** 'A child should play for seven years, learn literacy for seven years, and learn the permitted and the prohibited [i.e. jurisprudence] for seven years.'[7712]

٦٧٧٦ . الإمامُ الصّادقُ عليه السلام : الغُلامُ يَلعَبُ سَبعَ سِنينَ، ويَتَعَلَّمُ الكِتابَ سَبعَ سِنينَ، ويَتَعَلَّمُ الحَلالَ والحَرامَ سَبعَ سِنينَ.[٧٦٩١]

(See also: YOUTH: 210; DISCIPLINE: section 50,51)

(أنظر) عنوان ٢١٠ «الشباب»؛ الأدب: باب ٥٠، ٥١.

415

AUTHORITY

الوِلايَة

1892. The Necessity of Obeying those Vested with Authority by Allah

١٨٩٢ ـ وُجوبُ طاعَةِ وُلاةِ الأمرِ مِن قِبَلِ اللهِ

"O you who have faith! Obey Allah and obey the Apostle and those vested with authority among you. And if you dispute concerning anything, refer it to Allah and the Apostle, if you have faith in Allah and the Last Day. That is better and more favourable in outcome."[7713]

﴿يَا أَيُّهَا الَّذِينَ آمَنُوا أَطِيعُوا اللهَ وَأَطِيعُوا الرَّسُولَ وَأُولِي الأَمْرِ مِنْكُمْ فَإِنْ تَنَازَعْتُمْ فِي شَيْءٍ فَرُدُّوهُ إِلَى اللهِ وَالرَّسُولِ إِنْ كُنْتُمْ تُؤْمِنُونَ بِاللهِ وَالْيَوْمِ الآخِرِ ذَلِكَ خَيْرٌ وَأَحْسَنُ تَأْوِيلاً﴾.[٧٦٩٢]

6777. **Jābir b. 'Abdullāh al-Anṣārī said,** 'When Allah revealed the verse: *"Obey Allah and obey the Apostle and*

٦٧٧٧ . كمال الدين عن جابرٍ الجُعفيِّ: سمعتُ

those vested with authority among you..." onto His Prophet Muḥammad (SAWA) I said, 'O Messenger of Allah, we know Allah and His Messenger, but who are those vested with authority that Allah has associated their obedience with your obedience?' He (SAWA) said, 'O Jābir, they are my successors and the leaders of the Muslims after me. The first of them is ʿAlī b. Abī Ṭālib, then Ḥasan, then Ḥusayn, then ʿAlī b. al-Ḥusayn then Muḥammad b, ʿAlī that is known in Torah as al-Bāqir then al-Ṣādiq, Ja'far b. Muḥammad, then Mūsā b. Ja'far, then ʿAlī b. Mūsā then Muḥammad b. ʿAlī, then ʿAlī b. Muḥammad, then Ḥasan b. ʿAlī, then he who carries my name and he whose nickname is as mine –the proof of Allah on His earth and His remainder among His servants, the son of Ḥasan b. ʿAlī....'[7714]

جابرَ بنَ عبدِ اللهِ الأنصاريّ يقول: لَمّا أنـزَلَ اللهُ عَـزّوجلَّ عـلىٰ نَـبيِّهِ مـحمّدٍﷺ: ﴿أطِيعُوا اللهَ وأطِيعُوا الرَّسُولَ وأُولي الأمْرِ مِنْكُم﴾ قلتُ: يـا رسولَ اللهِ، عَرَفْنا اللهَ ورَسولَهُ، فمَن أُولو الأمرِ الّذينَ قَرَنَ اللهُ طاعَتَهُم بطاعَتِكَ؟
فقالَ﵇: هُم خُلَفائي ياجابِرُ، وأئمَّةُ المُسلِمينَ مِن بَعدي، أوَّلُـهُم عـليُّ بـنُ أبـي طـالِبٍ، ثُـمَّ الحَسَنُ، و الحُسَينُ، ثمّ عليّ بن الحسين، ثـمّ محمّد بن عليّ المعروف في التوراة بـالباقر... ثمّ الصّادق جعفر بن محمّد، ثمّ عليّ بن موسى، ثمّ موسى بن جعفر، ثمّ محمّد بن علي، ثمّ عليّ بن محمّد، ثمّ الحسن بن عليّ، ثمّ سميّ وكنيي حجّة الله في أرضه وبقيّته في عباده ابن الحسن بن عليّ....[٧٦٩٣]

1893. What Brings About the Reign of Evil Rulers

١٨٩٣ ـ ما يوجِبُ تَسَلُّطَ وُلاةِ السَّوءِ

"Indeed Allah does not change a people's lot, unless they change what is in their souls. And when Allah wishes to visit ill on a people, there is nothing that can avert it, and they have no protector besides Him."[7715]

﴿إنَّ اللهَ لَا يُغَيِّرُ مَا بِقَوْمٍ حَتَّىٰ يُغَيِّرُوا مَا بِأَنْفُسِهِمْ وَإِذَا أَرادَ اللهُ بِقَوْمٍ سُوءاً فَلَا مَرَدَّ لَهُ وَمَا لَهُمْ مِنْ دُونِهِ مِنْ وَالٍ﴾.[٧٦٩٤]

6778. **The Prophet (SAWA) said,** 'Allah Almighty has said, 'If one of My creation who knows Me disobeys Me, I will cause one of My creation who does not know Me to reign over him.'[7716]

٦٧٧٨. رسولُ اللهِﷺ: قالَ اللهُ عزَّوجلَّ: إذاعَصاني مِن خَلقي مَن يَعرِفُني سَلَّطتُ علَيهِ مِن خَـلقي مَن لا يَعرِفُني.[٧٦٩٥]

6779. **The Prophet (SAWA) said,** 'As you are, so shall you be ruled.'[7717]

٦٧٧٩. عنهﷺ: كَما تَكُونوا يُوَلّىٰ علَيكُم.[٧٦٩٦]

6780. **Imām ʿAlī (AS),** censuring his companions said, 'Verily by He who owns my soul, this group will take control of you, not because they are more rightful than you, but because of their hastening to the wrongfulness of their leader and your slowness at upholding my right.'[7718]

٦٧٨٠. الإمامُ عليٌّ﵇ ـ وهُو يُوَبِّخُ أصحابَهُ ـ: أما والّذي نَفسي بِيَدِهِ لَيَظهَرَنَّ هؤلاءِ القَومُ علَيكُم، لَيس لأنّهُم أولىٰ بِالحَقِّ مِنكُم، ولكنْ لإسراعِهِم إلىٰ باطِلِ صاحِبِهِم (باطِلِهِم)، وإبطائكُم عَن حَقّي.[٧٦٩٧]

(See also: CORRUPTION: section 1480; ENJOINING GOOD AND PROHIBITING WRONG (2): section 1287)

(أنظر) الفساد: باب ١٤٨٠؛ المعروف (٢): باب ١٢٨٧.

1894. Just Rulers — ١٨٩٤ـوُلاةُ العَدلِ

6781. **Imām al-Ṣādiq (AS) said,** 'He who takes control of any of the affairs of people, and is just, opens his door to people, eradicates evil, and examines the affairs of people, it becomes the right of Allah to save him from fear on the Day of Judgment and make him enter Heaven.'[7719]

٦٧٨١. الإمامُ الصّادقُ ﷺ : مَن تَوَلّى أمراً مِن أُمورِ النّاسِ فعَدَلَ وفَتَحَ بابَهُ ورَفَعَ شَرَّهُ ونَظَرَ في أُمورِ النّاسِ، كانَ حَقّاً علَى اللهِ عزّوجلّ أن يُؤمِنَ رَوعَتَهُ يومَ القِيامَةِ ويُدخِلَهُ الجَنَّةَ.٧٦٩٨

1895. Tyrannical Rulers — ١٨٩٥ـوُلاةُ الجَورِ

6782. **The Prophet (SAWA) said,** 'Whoever takes up rule of any of the affairs of the Muslims and deceives them then he is in Hell.'[7720]

٦٧٨٢. رسولُ اللهِ ﷺ: مَن وَلِيَ مِن أمرِ المُسلِمينَ شيئاً فغَشَّهُم فهُو في النّارِ.٧٦٩٩

6783. **Imām 'Alī (AS) said,** 'A ferocious and brutal predator is better than an oppressive and unjust ruler.'[7721]

٦٧٨٣. الإمامُ عليٌّ ﷺ : سَبُعٌ أكُولٌ حَطُومٌ خَيرٌ مِن والٍ ظَلُومٍ غَشُومٍ.٧٧٠٠

6784. **Imām 'Alī (AS) said,** 'The worst of rulers is he whom even the innocent fear.'[7722]

٦٧٨٤. عنه ﷺ :شَرُّ الوُلاةِ مَن يَخافُهُ البَريءُ.٧٧٠١

6785. **Imām 'Alī (AS) said,** 'He whose rule is oppressive, his government will fall apart.'[7723]

٦٧٨٥. عنه ﷺ : مَن جارَت وِلايَتُهُ زالَت دَولَتُهُ.٧٧٠٢

1896. What is Obligatory for the Ruler with Regard to himself — ١٨٩٦ـما يَجِبُ عَلَى الوالي في نَفسِهِ

6786. **Imām 'Alī (AS),** in his letter to Mālik al-Ashtar when he appointed him governor of Egypt, said, 'Surely the virtuous are known by the reputation that Allah circulates for them through the tongues of His creatures. Therefore, the best collection with you should be the collection of good deeds. So control your passions and deprive your heart from doing what is not lawful for you, because depriving the heart means detaining it just half way between what it likes and dislikes.'[7724]

٦٧٨٦. الإمامُ عليٌّ ﷺ ـ مِن كِتابِهِ للأشتَرِ لَمّا وَلّاهُ مِصرَ ـ: إنّما يُستَدَلُّ علَى الصّالحينَ بما يُجري اللهُ لَهُم على ألسُنِ عِبادِهِ، فلْيَكُن أحَبَّ الذَّخائرِ إلَيكَ ذَخيرَةُ العَمَلِ الصّالحِ، فاملِكْ هَواكَ، وشُحَّ بِنَفسِكَ عَمّا لا يَحِلُّ لَكَ؛ فإنَّ الشُّحَّ بالنَّفسِ الإنصافُ مِنها فيما أحَبَّت أو كَرِهَت.٧٧٠٣

6787. **Imām 'Alī (AS),** in his letter to Mālik al-Ashtar when he appointed him governor of Egypt, said, 'Be just to Allah and do justice towards the people, as

٦٧٨٧. عنه ﷺ ـ أيضاً ـ: أنصِفِ اللهَ وأنصِفِ

against yourself, your near ones and those of your subjects for whom you have a liking, because if you do not do so, you will be oppressive.'[7725]

النّاسَ مِن نَفسِكَ، ومِن خاصَّةِ أهلِكَ، ومَن لَكَ فيهِ هَوىً مِن رَعِيَّتِكَ؛ فإنَّكَ إلّا تفعَلْ تَظلِمْ.٧٧٠٤

6788. **Imām ʿAlī (AS),** in his letter to Mālik al-Ashtar when he appointed him governor of Egypt, said, 'Beware of self-admiration, having reliance in what appears good in yourself and love of exaggerated praise because this is one of the most reliable opportunities for Satan to obliterate the good deeds of the virtuous.'[7726]

٦٧٨٨. عنه (ع) ـ أيضاً ـ: وإيّاكَ والإعْجابَ بِنفسِكَ، والثِّقَةَ بما يُعجِبُكَ مِنها، وحُبَّ الإطراءِ؛ فإنَّ ذلكَ مِن أوثَقِ فُرَصِ الشَّيطانِ في نَفسِهِ لِيَمحَقَ ما يَكونُ مِن إحسانِ المُحسِنينَ.٧٧٠٥

1897. The Most Important thing a Ruler Needs in his Rule

١٨٩٧ ـ أهَمُّ ما يَجِبُ عَلَى الوالي في وِلايَتِهِ

6789. **Imām al-Ṣādiq (AS) said:** 'Imām ʿAlī (AS) said to ʿUmar b. al-Khaṭṭāb, 'There are three things which if you observe and act in accordance with, they will suffice you in everything else, and if you abandon them, nothing else will benefit you other than them.' ʿUmar asked, 'What are they Abū al-Ḥasan?' He (AS) said, 'The observance of penalties for the close and the distant, ruling according to the Book of Allah, be it with acceptance or discontentment, and to divide fairly between the black and the red.' ʿUmar said, 'By my life, you have summarised and explained [everything].'[7727]

٦٧٨٩. الإمامُ الصّادقُ (ع): قالَ أميرُ المؤمنينَ (ع) لِعُمَرَ بنِ الخَطّابِ: ثَلاثٌ إن حَفِظتَهُنَّ وعَمِلتَ بِهِنَّ كَفَتكَ ما سِواهُنَّ، وإن تَرَكتَهُنَّ لَم يَنفَعْكَ شيءٌ سِواهُنَّ. قالَ: وما هُنَّ يا أبا الحَسَنِ؟ قالَ: إقامَةُ الحُدودِ علَى القَريبِ والبَعيدِ، والحُكمُ بِكِتابِ اللهِ في الرِّضا والسُّخطِ، والقَسْمُ بالعَدلِ بَينَ الأحمَرِ والأسوَدِ. فقالَ لَهُ عُمَرُ: لَعَمري لَقَد أوجَزتَ وأبلَغتَ.٧٧٠٦

6790. **Imām ʿAlī (AS),** in his letter to Mālik al-Ashtar when he appointed him governor of Egypt, said, 'Habituate your heart to mercy for the subjects and to affection and kindness for them. Do not stand over them like greedy beasts who seeks to devour them, since they are of two kinds, either your brother in religion or one like you in creation. They will commit slips and encounter mistakes. They may act wrongly, wilfully or by neglect. So extend to them your forgiveness and pardon, in the same way as you would like Allah to extend His forgiveness and pardon to you, because you have authority over them, and your

٦٧٩٠. الإمامُ عليٌّ (ع) ـ مِن كِتابِهِ للأشتَرِ لَمّا وَلّاهُ مِصرَ ـ: وأشعِرْ قَلبَكَ الرَّحمَةَ لِلرَّعِيَّةِ، والمَحَبَّةَ لَهُم، واللُّطفَ بِهِم، ولا تَكونَنَّ علَيهِم سَبُعاً ضارِياً تَغتَنِمُ أكلَهُم؛ فإنَّهُم صِنفانِ: إمّا أخٌ لَكَ فِي الدِّينِ، أو نَظيرٌ لَكَ فِي الخَلقِ، يَفرُطُ مِنهُمُ الزَّلَلُ، وتَعرِضُ لَهُمُ العِلَلُ، ويُؤتى على أيديهِم فِي العَمدِ والخَطَأِ، فأعطِهِم مِن عَفوِكَ وصَفحِكَ مِثلَ الّذي تُحِبُّ وتَرضى أن يُعطِيَكَ اللهُ مِن عَفوِهِ

responsible Commander (Imām) has authority over you, while Allah has authority over he who has appointed you.'[7728]

وصَفحِهِ، فإنَّكَ فَوقَهُم، وَوالِي الأمرِ علَيكَ فَوقَكَ، واللهُ فَوقَ مَن وَلّاكَ![٧٧٠٧]

6791. **Imām ʿAlī (AS),** in his letter to Mālik al-Ashtar when he appointed him governor of Egypt, said, 'The way most coveted by you should be that which is the most equitable for the truth, the most universal by way of justice, and the most comprehensive with regard to the agreement among those under you, because the disagreement among the common people sweeps away the arguments of the chiefs while the disagreement among the chiefs can be disregarded when compared to the agreement of the common people. No one among those under you is more burdensome to the ruler in the comfort of life, less helpful in distress, more disliking of equitable treatment, more importunate in asking favours, least thankful when given, least accepting of excuses when refused, and weakest in endurance at the time of discomforts in life than the chiefs. It is the common people of the community who are the pillars of religion, the power of the Muslims and the defence against the enemies. Your leanings should therefore be towards them and your inclination with them.'[7729]

٦٧٩١. الإمامُ عليٌّ عليه السلام ـ مِن كِتابِهِ للأشتَرِ لَمّا وَلّاهُ مِصرَ ـ: ولْيَكُن أحَبَّ الأُمورِ إلَيكَ أوسَطُها فِي الحَقِّ، وأعَمُّها فِي العَدلِ، وأجمَعُها لِرِضا الرَّعِيَّةِ؛ فإنَّ سُخطَ العامَّةِ يُجحِفُ بِرِضا الخاصَّةِ، وإنَّ سُخطَ الخاصَّةِ يُغتَفَرُ مَع رِضا العامَّةِ. ولَيسَ أحَدٌ مِن الرَّعِيَّةِ أثقَلَ علَى الوالِي مَؤونَةً فِي الرَّخاءِ، وأقَلَّ مَعونَةً لَهُ فِي البَلاءِ، وأكرَهَ للإنصافِ، وأسأَلَ بالإلحافِ، وأقَلَّ شُكراً عِندَ الإعطاءِ، وأبطَأَ عُذراً عِندَ المَنعِ، وأضعَفَ صَبراً عِندَ مُلِمّاتِ الدَّهرِ، مِن أهلِ الخاصَّةِ. وإنّما عِمادُ الدِّينِ وجِماعُ المُسلمينَ والعُدَّةُ للأعداءِ: العامَّةُ مِن الأُمَّةِ، فلْيَكُنْ صِغوُكَ لَهُم، ومَيلُكَ مَعهُم.[٧٧٠٨]

6792. **Imām al-Ṣādiq (AS) said,** 'There are three things that are obligatory for a governor, both towards the elite and the general public: rewarding the good-doer with goodness so that he increases in his desire to perform it, forgiving the sins of the wrongful so that he can repent and return from his rebellion, and encompassing all people with goodness and fairness.'[7730]

٦٧٩٢. الإمامُ الصّادقُ عليه السلام: ثَلاثَةٌ تَجِبُ علَى السُّلطانِ لِلخاصَّةِ والعامَّةِ: مُكافأةُ المُحسِنِ بالإحسانِ لِيَزدادُوا رَغبَةً فيهِ، وتَغَمُّدُ ذُنوبِ المُسيءِ لِيَتُوبَ ويَرجِعَ عَن غَيِّهِ (عَتبِهِ)، وتَألُّفُهُم جَميعاً بالإحسانِ والإنصافِ.[٧٧٠٩]

(See also: AMICABLENESS 139)

(أُنظر) عنوان ١٣٩ «المداراة».

1898. What is Obligatory for the Ruler when Employing Workers

١٨٩٨ ـ ما يَجِبُ عَلَى الوالي في استِعمالِ العُمّالِ

6793. **The Prophet (SAWA) said,** 'Whoever employs a worker from a group wherein someone else is more content with Allah than him [the person he chose], then he has betrayed Allah, His Messenger and the believers.'[7731]

٦٧٩٣. رسولُ اللهِ ﷺ : مَنِ استَعمَلَ رجُلاً مِن عِصابَةٍ، وفِيهِم مَن هُو أرضىٰ للهِ مِنهُ، فَقَد خانَ اللهَ ورَسولَهُ والمُؤمنينَ. ٧٧١٠

6794. **The Prophet (SAWA) said,** 'By Allah, we do not appoint for this work someone who has asked for it, nor someone who is avidly eager for it.'[7732]

٦٧٩٤. عنه ﷺ : إنّا واللهِ لانُوَلِّي علىٰ هذا العَمَلِ أحَداً سَألَهُ، ولا أحَداً حَرَصَ علَيهِ. ٧٧١١

6795. **The Prophet (SAWA) said** to 'Abd al-Raḥmān b. Samura, 'O 'Abd al-Raḥmān b. Samura, do not ask for authority, for if you were to be given it by asking for it, then you will be entrusted with it to your own self [and held accountable], and if you are given it without having asked for it, then you will be helped with it.'[7733]

٦٧٩٥. عنه ﷺ ـ لِعَبدِ الرَّحمٰنِ بنِ سَمُرَةَ ـ : يا عبدَ الرَّحمٰنِ بنَ سَمُرَةَ، لاتَسألِ الإمارَةَ؛ فإنَّكَ إذا اُعطِيتَها عَن مَسألَةٍ وُكِلتَ فيها إلىٰ نَفسِكَ، وإن اُعطِيتَها عَن غَيرِ مَسألَةٍ اُعِنتَ علَيها. ٧٧١٢

6796. **Imām 'Alī (AS),** in his letter to Mālik al-Ashtar when he appointed him governor of Egypt, said, 'Thereafter, look into the affairs of your executives. Give them appointment after tests and do not appoint them according to partiality or favouritism, because these two things constitute the sources of injustice and unfairness. Select from among them those who are people of experience and modesty, hailing from virtuous houses, having preceded in [embracing] Islam.'[7734]

٦٧٩٦. الإمامُ عليٌّ عليه السلام ـ فيما كَتَبَ للأشتَرِ لمّا وَلّاهُ مِصرَ ـ : ثُمّ انظُرْ في اُمورِ عُمّالِكَ، فاستَعمِلْهُمُ اختِباراً، ولا تُوَلِّهِم مُحاباةً وأثَرَةً؛ فإنَّهُما جِماعٌ مِن شُعَبِ الجَورِ والخِيانَةِ. وتَوَخَّ مِنهُم أهلَ التَّجرِبَةِ والحَياءِ مِن أهلِ البُيوتاتِ الصّالِحَةِ، والقَدَمِ في الإسلامِ المُتَقَدِّمَةِ. ٧٧١٣

6797. **Imām 'Alī (AS),** in his letter to Mālik al-Ashtar when he appointed him governor of Egypt, said, 'Then you should check their activities and have people report on them, who should be truthful and faithful, because your watching their actions secretly will urge them to preserve trust with and be kind to the people. Be careful of assistants. If any one of them extends his hands towards misappropriation and the reports of your reporters reaching you confirm it, they should be regarded as enough evidence. You should then inflict corporal punishment on him and recover what he has

٦٧٩٧. عنه عليه السلام ـ مِن كِتابِهِ للأشتَرِ لَمّا وَلّاهُ مِصرَ ـ : ثُمّ تَفَقَّدْ أعمالَهُم، وابعَثِ العُيونَ ٧٧١٤ مِن أهلِ الصِّدقِ والوَفاءِ علَيهِم، فإنَّ تَعاهُدَكَ فِي السِّرِّ لاُمورِهِم حَدوَةٌ لَهُم ٧٧١٥ علىٰ استِعمالِ الأمانَةِ، والرِّفقِ بالرَّعِيَّةِ.
وتَحَفَّظْ مِنَ الأعوانِ، فإن أحَدٌ مِنهُم بَسَطَ يَدَهُ

misappropriated. You should put him in a place of disgrace, blacklist him with [the charge of] misappropriation and make him wear the necklace of shame for his offence.'[7735]

إلى خِيانَةٍ اجتَمَعَت بِها علَيهِ عِندَكَ أخبارُ عُيونِكَ، اكتَفَيتَ بذلكَ شاهِداً، فبَسَطتَ علَيهِ العُقوبَةَ في بَدَنِهِ، وأخَذتَهُ بما أصابَ مِن عَمَلِهِ، ثُمّ نَصَبتَهُ بمَقامِ المَذَلَّةِ، ووَسَمتَهُ بالخِيانَةِ، وقَلَّدتَهُ عارَ التُّهَمَةِ.[٧٧١٦]

1899. To not Seclude Oneself [Away from One's Subjects]

١٨٩٩ ـ عَدمُ الإحتِجابِ

6798. **Imām ʿAlī (AS),** in his letter to Mālik al-Ashtar when he appointed him governor of Egypt, said, 'Do not keep yourself secluded from the people for a long time, because the seclusion of those in authority from the subjects is a kind of narrow-sightedness and causes ignorance about their affairs. Seclusion from them also prevents them from the knowledge of those things which they are unaware of and as a result they begin to regard big matters as small and small matters as big, good matters as bad and bad matters as good, while the truth becomes confused with falsehood.'[7736]

٦٧٩٨. الإمامُ عليٌّ عليه السلام ـ من كِتابِهِ للأشتَرِ لَمّا وَلّاهُ مِصرَ ـ: فلا تُطَوِّلَنَّ احتِجابَكَ عَن رَعِيَّتِكَ، فإنَّ احتِجابَ الوُلاةِ عَنِ الرَّعِيَّةِ شُعبَةٌ مِنَ الضِّيقِ، وقِلَّةُ عِلمٍ بالأُمورِ، والاحتِجابُ مِنهُم يَقطَعُ عَنهُم عِلمَ ما احتَجَبوا دُونَهُ، فيَصغُرُ عِندَهُمُ الكَبيرُ، ويَعظُمُ الصَّغيرُ، ويَقبُحُ الحَسَنُ، ويَحسُنُ القَبيحُ، ويُشابُ الحَقُّ بِالباطِلِ....[٧٧١٧]

6799. **Imām al-Ṣādiq (AS) said,** 'Whoever takes up any of the affairs of people and is just, opens his door, uncovers his veils, and fulfils the needs of people, it will become the right of Allah to save him from fear on the Day of Judgment and make him enter Heaven.'[7737]

٦٧٩٩. الإمامُ الصّادقُ عليه السلام: مَن تَولّى أمراً مِن أُمورِ النّاسِ، فعَدَلَ، وفَتَحَ بابَهُ، ورَفَعَ سِترَهُ، ونَظَرَ في أُمورِ النّاسِ، كانَ حَقّاً علَى اللهِ أن يُؤمِنَ رَوعَتَهُ يَومَ القِيامَةِ ويُدخِلَهُ الجَنَّةَ.[٧٧١٨]

1900. The Obligation upon the Ruler to Give Importance to the Abased

١٩٠٠ ـ وُجوبُ اهتِمامِ الوالي بِالمُستَضعَفينَ

6800. **Imām ʿAlī (AS),** in his letter to Mālik al-Ashtar when he appointed him governor of Egypt, said, '[Fear] Allah and keep Allah in view with respect to the lowest class, consisting of those who have few means: the poor, the destitute, the penniless and the disabled; because in this class are both the discontented and those who beg. Take care, for the sake of Allah, of His obligations for which He has made you responsible. Fix for

٦٨٠٠. الإمامُ عليٌّ عليه السلام ـ مِن كِتابِهِ للأشتَرِ لَمّا وَلّاهُ مِصرَ ـ:... ثُمَّ اللهَ اللهَ في الطَّبَقَةِ السُّفلى مِنَ

them a share from the public treasury… Take care of the affairs of those of them who do not approach you because they are of unsightly appearance or those whom people regard as low. Appoint for them some trusted people who are God-fearing and humble. They should inform you of these people's conditions. Then deal with them with a sense of responsibility to Allah on the Day you will meet Him, because of all the subjects, these people are the most deserving of equitable treatment, while for others also you should fulfil their rights so as to render account to Allah.'[7738]

الّذينَ لا حِيلَةَ لَهُم، مِن المَساكينِ والمُحتاجِينَ وأهلِ البُؤسَى والزَّمنى، فإنَّ في هذهِ الطَّبَقَةِ قانِعاً ومُعتَرّاً، واحفَظْ للهِ ما استَحفَظَكَ مِن حَقِّهِ فيهِم واجعَلْ لَهُم قِسْماً مِن بَيتِ مالِكَ... وتَفَقَّدْ أُمورَ مَن لا يَصِلُ إلَيكَ مِنهُم مِمَّن تَقتَحِمُهُ العُيونُ، وتَحقِرُهُ الرِّجالُ، فَفَرِّغْ لأُولئكَ ثِقَتَكَ مِن أهلِ الخَشيَةِ والتَّواضُعِ، فلْيَرفَعْ إلَيكَ أُمورَهُم، ثُمّ اعمَلْ فيهِم بالإعذارِ إلَى اللهِ يَومَ تَلقاهُ؛ فإنَّ هؤلاءِ مِن بَينِ الرَّعِيَّةِ أحوَجُ إلَى الإنصافِ مِن غَيرِهِم، وكلٌّ فأعذِرْ إلَى اللهِ في تَأدِيَةِ حَقِّهِ إلَيهِ.[٧٧١٩]

6801. **Imām ʿAlī (AS),** in his letter to Mālik al-Ashtar when he appointed him governor of Egypt, said, 'And fix a time for the plaintiffs wherein you make yourself free for them, and sit for them in common audience and feel humble therein for the sake of Allah Who created you. [On that occasion] you should keep away your army and your assistants such as the guards and the police so that anyone who would like to speak may speak to you without fear, because I have heard the Messenger of Allah (SAWA) say in more than one place, 'The people among whom the right of the weak is not secured from the strong without fear will never achieve purity.' Tolerate their awkwardness and inability to speak. Keep away narrowness and haughtiness from yourself…'[7739]

٦٨٠١. عنه عليه السلام ـ أيضاً ـ: واجعَلْ لِذَوي الحاجاتِ مِنكَ قِسماً تُفَرِّغُ لَهُم فيهِ شَخصَكَ، وتَجلِسُ لَهُم مَجلِساً عامّاً، فتَتَواضَعُ فيهِ للهِ الّذي خَلَقَكَ، وتُقعِدُ عَنهُم جُندَكَ وأعوانَكَ مِن أحراسِكَ وشُرَطِكَ، حتّى يُكَلِّمَكَ مُتَكَلِّمُهُم غَيرَ مُتَتَعتِعٍ؛ فإنّي سَمِعتُ رسولَ اللهِ ﷺ يَقولُ في غَيرِ مَوطِنٍ: لَن تُقَدَّسَ أُمَّةٌ لا يُؤخَذُ لِلضَّعيفِ فيها حَقُّهُ مِن القَوِيِّ غَيرَ مُتَتَعتِعٍ. ثُمّ احتَمِلِ الخُرقَ مِنهُم والعِيَّ، ونَحِّ عَنهُمُ الضِّيقَ والأنَفَ....[٧٧٢٠]

1901. The Characteristics of the Friends of Allah

١٩٠١ ـ خَصائِصُ أولياءِ الله

"Look! The friends of Allah will indeed have no fear nor will they grieve. Those who have faith, and are Godwary."[7740]

﴿أَلَا إِنَّ أَوْلِيَاءَ اللَّهِ لَا خَوْفٌ عَلَيْهِمْ وَلَا هُمْ يَحْزَنُونَ * الَّذِينَ آمَنُوا وَكَانُوا يَتَّقُونَ﴾.[٧٧٢١]

6802. **Imām ʿAlī (AS) said,** 'The friends of Allah are those who look at the inward aspect of the world while the other people look at its outer aspect; they busy themselves with its remoter benefits while the other people busy themselves in the immediate benefits. They kill those things which they fear would have killed them, and they abandon here in this world what they believe would abandon them. They take the amassing of wealth by others as a small matter and regard it as a loss. They are enemies of those things which others love while they love things which others hate. Through them the Qur'an has been learnt and they have been given knowledge through the Qur'an. With them the Qur'an is staying while they stand by the Qur'an. They do not see any object of hope above what they hope in and no object of fear above what they fear.'[7741]

٦٨٠٢ . الإمامُ عليٌّ ﷺ : إنّ أولياءَ اللهِ هُمُ الذينَ نَـظَروا إلىٰ بـاطِنِ الدُّنـيا إذا نَـظَرَ النّـاسُ إلىٰ ظاهِرِها، واشتَغَلوا بآجِـلِها إذا اشـتَغَلَ النّـاسُ بعاجِلِها، فأماتُوا مِنها مـا خَشَـوا أن يُـميتَهُم، وتَرَكوا مِنها ما عَـلِموا أنّـهُ سَـيَترُكُـهُم، ورَأوا استِكثارَ غَيرِهِم مِنها استِقلالاً، وَدَرَكَـهُم لَـها فَوتاً ، أعداءُ ما سالَمَ النّاسُ، وسِلمُ مـا عـادَى النّاسُ ! بِهِم عُلِمَ الكِتابُ وبِهِ عَلِموا، وبِهِم قـامَ الكِتابُ وبِهِ قاموا، لا يَرَونَ مَـرجُـوّاً فَـوقَ مـا يَرجُونَ، ولا مَخُوفاً فَوقَ ما يَخافونَ.٧٧٢٢

6803. **Imām al-Ṣādiq (AS) said,** 'O Abū Baṣīr, blessed be the followers [*shīʿa*] of our Awaited Saviour [Qāʾim] who wait for his appearance during his occultation, and obey him when he reappears. They are the friends of Allah who indeed have no fear nor will they grieve.'[7742]

٦٨٠٣ . الإمامُ الصّادقُ ﷺ : يا أبا بَصيرٍ ، طُوبىٰ لِشيعَةِ قائِمِنا المُـنتَظِرينَ لِظُهورِهِ فـي غَـيبَتِهِ، والمُطيعينَ لَهُ في ظُهورِهِ، أُولئكَ أولياءُ اللهِ الّذينَ لا خَوفٌ علَيهِم ولاهُم يَحزَنونَ.٧٧٢٣

(See also: FAITH: section 190, GODWARINESS: section 1867)

(انظر) الايمان : باب ١٩٠ ؛ التقوى : باب ١٨٦٧

416

SUSPICION

التُّهَمَة

1902. Warning against Suspicion

١٩٠٢ـ التَّحذيرُ مِنَ التُّهَمَةِ

6804. **Imām al-Ṣādiq (AS) said,** 'When a believer suspects his fellow brother, his faith disappears from his heart like salt disappears in water.'[7743]

٦٨٠٤ . الإمامُ الصّادقُ ﷺ : إذا اتَّهَمَ المؤمنُ أخاهُ انْماثَ الإيمانُ مِن قلبِهِ كما يَنْماثُ المِلحُ فـي الماءِ.٧٧٢٤

6805. **Imām al-Ṣādiq (AS) said,** 'He who suspects the religion of his brother removes the covenant between them.'[7744]

٦٨٠٥. عنه عليه السلام: مَنِ اتَّهمَ أخاهُ في دِينِهِ فلا حُرمَةَ بَينَهُما.[٧٧٢٥]

1903. Prohibition of Placing Oneself in Suspect Circumstances

١٩٠٣ـ النَّهيُ عَن مَواقِفِ التُّهَمَةِ

6806. **The Prophet (SAWA) said,** 'The person most deserving of suspicion is he who sits with suspect people.'[7745]

٦٨٠٦. رسولُ اللهِ ﷺ: أولى النّاسِ بالتُّهمةِ مَن جالَسَ أهلَ التُّهمةِ.[٧٧٢٦]

6807. **Imām ʿAlī (AS) said,** 'Stay away from places of suspicion and suspect gatherings, for an evil friend seduces his companion.'[7746]

٦٨٠٧. الإمامُ عليٌّ عليه السلام: إيّاكَ ومَواطِنَ التُّهْمَةِ والمجلسَ المَظْنونَ بِهِ السّوءُ، فإنَّ قَرينَ السَّوءِ يَغُرُّ جَليسَهُ.[٧٧٢٧]

6808. **Imām ʿAlī (AS) said,** 'A man who places himself in a suspect situation must not blame those who suspect him.'[7747]

٦٨٠٨. عنه عليه السلام: مَن وَقَفَ نَفسَهُ مَوقِفَ التُّهْمةِ فلا يَلُومَنَّ مَن أساءَ بِهِ الظَّنَّ.[٧٧٢٨]

6809. **Imām ʿAlī (AS) said,** 'A man who enters suspect places will be suspected.'[7748]

٦٨٠٩. عنه عليه السلام: مَن دَخلَ مَداخِلَ السُّوءِ اتُّهِمَ.[٧٧٢٩]

(See also: SUSPICION: section 1211)

(أنظر) الظن: باب ١٢١١

417

DESPAIR

اليَأسُ

1904. The Reproaching of Despair

١٩٠٤ـ ذَمُّ اليَأسِ

"If We let man taste a mercy from Us, and then withdraw it from him, he becomes despondent, ungrateful."[7749]

﴿وَلَئِنْ أَذَقْنَا الإنْسَانَ مِنَّا رَحْمَةً ثُمَّ نَزَعْنَاهَا مِنْهُ إِنَّهُ لَيَؤُوسٌ كَفُورٌ﴾[٧٧٣٠]

6810. **Imām ʿAlī (AS) said,** 'The greatest of afflictions is cutting off hope.'[7750]

٦٨١٠. الإمامُ عليٌّ عليه السلام: أعظَمُ البَلاءِ انقِطاعُ الرَّجاءِ.[٧٧٣١]

6811. **Imām ʿAlī (AS) said,** 'Despair destroys who he is hopeless.'[7751]

٦٨١١. عنه عليه السلام: قَتَلَ القُنوطُ صاحِبَهُ.[٧٧٣٢]

1905. The Fruits of Despair in Obtaining What Belongs to Others

١٩٠٥ـ ثَمَراتُ اليَأسِ مِمّا في أيدِي النّاسِ

6812. **Imām ʿAlī (AS) said,** 'The greatest wealth is despair of obtaining what belongs to others.'[7752]

٦٨١٢ . الإمامُ عليٌّ عليه السلام : الغِنَى الأكبَرُ اليَأسُ عَمّا في أيدي النّاسِ.[٧٧٣٣]

6813. **Imām ʿAlī (AS) said,** 'Protecting your own possessions is more beloved to me than asking for what others possess, and the bitterness of despair is better than asking from people.'[7753]

٦٨١٣ . عنه عليه السلام : حِفظُ ما في يَدَيكَ أحَبُّ إلَيَّ مِن طَلَبِ ما في يَدَي غَيرِكَ ، ومَرارَةُ اليَأسِ خَيرٌ مِن الطَّلَبِ إلَى النّاسِ.[٧٧٣٤]

6814. **Imām al-Ṣādiq (AS) said,** 'Despair of what other people possess is dignity for the believer in his religion.'[7754]

٦٨١٤ . الإمامُ الصّادقُ عليه السلام : اليَأسُ مِمّا في أيدي النّاسِ عِزٌّ لِلمُؤمنِ في دِينِهِ.[٧٧٣٥]

(See also: ASKING (2): section 908; HONOUR: section 1292)

(أنظر) السؤال (٢): باب ٩٠٨؛ العزّة: باب ١٢٩٢.

418

THE ORPHAN

اليَتيمُ

1906. Enjoinment of Looking After Orphans

١٩٠٦ـ الحَثُّ عَلىٰ رِعايَةِ الأيتامِ

"And when We took a pledge from the Children of Israel: Worship no one but Allah, do good to parents, relatives, orphans, and the needy."[7755]

﴿وَإِذْ أَخَذْنَا مِيثَاقَ بَنِي إِسْرَائِيلَ لاتَعبُدُونَ إِلَّا اللهَ وَبِالْوَالِدَيْنِ إِحْسَاناً وَذِي الْقُرْبَىٰ وَالْيَتَامَىٰ وَالْمَسَاكِينِ﴾.[٧٧٣٦]

(See also: Qur'an:2:177,220, 89:17-18, 107:2-3)

(أنظر) البقرة: ١٧٧ و٢٢٠ والفجر: ١٧، ١٨ والماعون: ٢، ٣.

6815. **The Prophet (SAWA) said,** 'I and the guardian of an orphan will both be like this in Heaven, if he is wary of his duty to Allah' – raising and joining his index and middle fingers.[7756]

٦٨١٥ . رسولُ اللهِ ﷺ : أنا وكافِلُ اليَتيمِ كَهاتَينِ في الجَنَّةِ إذا اتَّقَى اللهَ عَزَّوجلَّ ـ وأشارَ بِالسَّبّابَةِ والوُسطىٰ ـ.[٧٧٣٧]

6816. **The Prophet (SAWA) said,** 'There is a house in Heaven called the House of Happiness, which none shall enter except those who have made the orphans of the believers happy.'[7757]

٦٨١٦ . عنه ﷺ : إنّ في الجَنَّةِ داراً يُقالُ لَها: دارُ الفَرَحِ ، لايَدخُلُها إلّا مَن فَرَّحَ يَتامَى المُؤمنينَ.[٧٧٣٨]

6817. **The Prophet (SAWA) said** to a person complaining about his hardheartedness, 'Do you want your heart to become soft and acquire your needs? – have mercy on an orphan, stroke his head and feed him from your food, and your heart will become soft and you will achieve your needs.'[7758]

٦٨١٧ . عنه ﷺ ـ لِرجُلٍ يَشكو قسوَةَ قَلبِهِ ـ: أتُحِبُّ أن يَلينَ قَلبُكَ، وتُدرِكَ حاجَتَكَ؟ : اِرحَمِ اليَتيمَ وامسَحْ رأسَهُ، وأطعِمْهُ مِن طَعامِكَ، يَلِنْ قَلبُكَ وتُدرِكْ حاجَتَكَ.[٧٧٣٩]

6818. **Imām ʿAlī (AS),** in his will before his martyrdom said, 'By Allah, by Allah, [pay attention] to orphans. Do not be inconsistent with feeding them, coming one day and abandoning them the next, and do not deprive them of your presence, as I have heard the Prophet (SAWA) say, 'Whoever elevates an orphan until he becomes free from need, Allah will make it incumbent for him to enter Heaven just as He has made Hellfire incumbent for the consumer of the property of the orphan.'[7759]

٦٨١٨ . الإمامُ عليٌّ عليه السلام ـ في وَصِيَّتِهِ قَبلَ شَهادَتِهِ ـ: اللهَ اللهَ في الأيتامِ، فلا تُغِبُّوا[٧٧٤٠] أفواهَهُم، ولا يَضيعوا بحَضرَتِكُم، فقد سَمِعتُ رسولَ اللهِ ﷺ يَقولُ: مَن عالَ يَتيماً حتّىٰ يَستَغنِيَ أوجَبَ اللهُ عَزَّوجلَّ لَهُ بذلكَ الجَنَّةَ كما أوجَبَ لآكِلِ مالِ اليَتيمِ النّارَ.[٧٧٤١]

1907. The Consumption of the Property of the Orphans

١٩٠٧ ـ أكلُ مالِ اليَتيمِ

"Indeed those who consume the property of orphans wrongfully, only ingest fire into their bellies, and soon they will enter the Blaze."[7760]

﴿إنَّ الَّذِينَ يَأْكُلُونَ أَمْوَالَ الْيَتَامَىٰ ظُلْماً إِنَّمَا يَأْكُلُونَ فِي بُطُونِهِمْ نَاراً وَسَيَصْلَوْنَ سَعِيراً﴾.[٧٧٤٢]

(See also: Qur'an 4:2, 4:6, 6:152, 17:34)

(أُنظر) النساء: ٢، ٦ والأنعام: ١٥٢ والاسراء: ٣٤.

6819. **The Prophet (SAWA) said,** 'The most evil of food is the wrongful consumption of the property of the orphans.'[7761]

٦٨١٩ . رسولُ اللهِ ﷺ: شَرُّ المَآكِلِ أكلُ مالِ اليَتيمِ ظُلماً.[٧٧٤٣]

6820. **The Prophet (SAWA) said,** 'On Judgment Day some people will be resurrected from their graves with fire enflaming from their mouths.' The Prophet was asked, 'O Messenger of Allah, who are they?' He said, 'Those who consume the property of orphans…'[7762]

٦٨٢٠ . عنه ﷺ : يُبعَثُ أُناسٌ مِن قُبورِهِم يَومَ القِيامَةِ تأجَّجُ أفواهُهُم ناراً، فقيلَ لَهُ: يا رسولَ اللهِ، مَن هؤلاءِ؟ قالَ: الّذينَ يَأكُلونَ أموالَ اليَتامىٰ....[٧٧٤٤]

6821. **Fāṭima al-Zahrā' (AS),** in one of her sermons said, 'Allah has made it incumbent to

٦٨٢١ . فاطمةُ الزَّهراءُ عليها السلام ـ في خُطبَةٍ لَها ـ:

disassociate oneself from the consumption of the property of orphans in order to protect against oppression.'[7763]

فَرَضَ اللهُ مُجانَبَةَ أكلِ أموالِ اليَتامىٰ إجارَةً مِنَ الظُّلمِ.٧٧٤٥

419

CONVICTION

اليَقين

1908. The Virtue of Conviction

١٩٠٨ـ فَضلُ اليَقينِ

"And among them We appointed imāms who guide [the people] by Our command, when they had conviction in Our signs."[7764]

﴿وَجَعَلْنَا مِنْهُمْ أَئِمَّةً يَهْدُونَ بِأَمْرِنَا لَمَّا صَبَرُوا وَكَانُوا بِآيَاتِنَا يُوقِنُونَ﴾.٧٧٤٦

6822. **The Prophet (SAWA) said,** 'The best of what has been placed in the heart is conviction.'[7765]

٦٨٢٢. رسولُ اللهِ ﷺ: خَيرُ ما اُلقِيَ في القَلبِ اليَقينُ.٧٧٤٧

6823. **Imām ʿAlī (AS) said,** 'O people! Ask Allah for conviction and seek good health from him, for the greatest of blessings is good health and the best thing that can reside in the heart is conviction. A cheated man is he who has been cheated of his religion and an enviable person is he whose conviction is envied.'[7766]

٦٨٢٣. الإمامُ عليٌّ ﷺ: أيُّها النّاسُ، سَلُوا اللهَ اليَقينَ، وارغَبوا إلَيهِ في العافِيَةِ؛ فإنَّ أجَلَّ النِّعمَةِ العافِيَةُ، وخَيرُ مادامَ فِي القَلبِ اليَقينُ، والمَغبونُ مَن غُبِنَ دِينَهُ، والمَغبوطُ مَن غُبِطَ يَقينَهُ.٧٧٤٨

6824. **Imām ʿAlī (AS) said,** 'How great is the prosperity of one whose heart is blessed with the coolness of conviction.'[7767]

٦٨٢٤. عنه ﷺ: ما أعظَمَ سَعادَةَ مَن بُوشِرَ قَلبُهُ بِبَردِ اليَقينِ!٧٧٤٩

6825. **Imām ʿAlī (AS) said,** 'With conviction the ultimate goal can be reached.'[7768]

٦٨٢٥. عنه ﷺ: بِاليَقينِ تُدرَكُ الغايَةُ القُصوىٰ.٧٧٥٠

6826. **Imām ʿAlī (AS) said,** 'The strength of one's conviction is proportionate to the extent of one's faith.'[7769]

٦٨٢٦. عنه ﷺ: علىٰ قَدرِ الدِّينِ تَكونُ قُوَّةُ اليَقينِ.٧٧٥١

6827. **Imām ʿAlī (AS) said,** 'Conviction is the pillar of faith.'[7770]

٦٨٢٧. عنه ﷺ: اليَقينُ عِمادُ الإيمانِ.٧٧٥٢

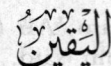

6828. **Imām ʿAlī (AS) said,** 'Sleeping with conviction is better than praying with doubt.'[7771]

٦٨٢٨. عنه ﷺ: نومٌ على يقينٍ خيرٌ مِن صَلاةٍ في شَكٍّ.٧٧٥٣

6829. **Imām al-Bāqir (AS) said,** 'There is nothing least divided among people than conviction.'[7772]

٦٨٢٩. الإمامُ الباقرُ ﷺ: لَم يُقسَمْ بينَ النّاسِ شيءٌ أقَلُّ مِن اليَقينِ.٧٧٥٤

6830. **Imām al-Ṣādiq (AS) said,** 'Faith is better than submission [*islām*] and conviction is better than faith, and there is nothing more honourable than conviction.'[7773]

٦٨٣٠. الإمامُ الصّادقُ ﷺ: إنّ الإيمانَ أفضَلُ مِن الإسلامِ، وإنّ اليَقينَ أفضَلُ مِن الإيمانِ، وما مِن شيءٍ أعَزُّ مِن اليَقينِ.٧٧٥٥

6831. **Imām al-Ṣādiq (AS) said,** 'Continuous but small actions [performed] with conviction are better in the sight of Allah than numerous actions without conviction.'[7774]

٦٨٣١. عنه ﷺ: إنّ العَمَلَ الدّائمَ القَليلَ علَى اليَقينِ أفضَلُ عِندَ اللهِ مِن العَمَلِ الكَثيرِ على غَيرِ يَقينٍ.٧٧٥٦

(See also: DOUBT: section 1058)

(أنظر) الشك: باب ١٠٥٨.

1909. Certain Knowledge

١٩٠٩ ـ عِلمُ اليَقينِ

"No indeed! Were you to know with certain knowledge, you would surely see hell. Again, you will surely see it with the eye of certainty. Then, that day, you will surely be questioned concerning the blessing."[7775]

﴿كَلَّا لَوْ تَعْلَمُونَ عِلْمَ الْيَقِينِ * لَتَرَوُنَّ الْجَحِيمَ * ثُمَّ لَتَرَوُنَّها عَيْنَ الْيَقِينِ * ثُمَّ لَتُسْأَلُنَّ يَوْمَئِذٍ عَنِ النَّعِيمِ﴾.٧٧٥٧

"Thus did We show Abraham the dominions of the heavens and the earth, that he might be of those who possess certitude."[7776]

﴿وَكَذٰلِكَ نُرِي إِبْراهِيمَ مَلَكُوتَ السَّماوَاتِ وَالأَرْضِ وَلِيَكُونَ مِنَ الْمُوقِنِينَ﴾.٧٧٥٨

6832. **The Prophet (SAWA) said,** 'Allah Almighty says, 'There are three things that I have concealed from My servants such that if a person was to see them, they would never do bad: if I was to uncover My veil and they were to see Me such that they had conviction, and if they were to know what I do with My creation when I make them die...'[7777]

٦٨٣٢. رسولُ اللهِ ﷺ: إنّ اللهَ تعالى يَقولُ: ثَلاثُ خِصالٍ غَيَّبتُهُنَّ عَن عِبادِي لَو رآهُنَّ رجُلٌ ما عَمِلَ سُوءاً أبداً: لَو كَشَفتُ غِطائي فَرآني حتّى يَستَيقِنَ، ويَعلَمَ كَيفَ أفعَلُ بخَلقي إذا أمَتُّهُم....٧٧٥٩

1910. Interpretation of Certainty

١٩١٠ ـ تَفسيرُ اليَقينِ

6833. **The Archangel Gabriel (AS),** coming down to the Prophet (SAWA) said, 'O Messenger of Allah, Allah Almighty sent me to you with a gift which He has not given to anyone before you. The Prophet (SAWA) said, 'I asked him, 'And what is it?' He said, 'Patience, and something better than that… until he said, 'I asked, 'So what is the interpretation of conviction?' Gabriel said, 'A person of conviction acts for Allah as if he sees Him, and even though he cannot see Allah, Allah can see him; and it is to know with conviction that whatever afflicts him would not have missed him, and whatever has missed him would not have afflicted him. These are all branches of complete trust [in Allah] and the steps to asceticism.'[7778]

٦٨٣٣ . جَبرئيلُ ﷺ ـ و قد جاء إلَى النَّبيِّ ﷺ ـ: يا رسولَ اللهِ، إنّ اللهَ تبارَكَ وتعالىٰ أرسَلَني إلَيكَ بِهَديَّةٍ لَم يُعطِها أحَداً قَبلَكَ. قالَ رسولُ اللهِ ﷺ: قلتُ: وماهِيَ ؟ قالَ: الصَّبرُ وأحسَنُ مِنهُ ـ إلىٰ أن قالَ ـ قلتُ: فما تَفسيرُ اليَقينِ ؟قالَ: المُوقِنُ يَعمَلُ للهِ كأنّهُ يَراهُ، فإن لَم يَكُن يَرىٰ اللهَ فإنّ اللهَ يَراهُ، وأن يَعلَمَ يَقيناً أنَّ ما أصابَهُ لَم يَكُن لِيُخطِئَهُ، وأنَّ ما أخطأهُ لَم يَكُن لِيُصيبَهُ، وهٰذا كُلُّهُ أغصانُ التَّوكُّلِ ومَدرَجَةُ الزُّهدِ.[٧٧٦٠]

6834. **Imām ʿAlī (AS) said,** 'Islam is submission, submission is conviction, conviction is attestation [to the truth], and attestation is testifying, and testifying is fulfilment [of one's obligations], and fulfilment is action.'[7779]

٦٨٣٤ . الإمامُ عليٌّ ﷺ : الإسلامُ هُو التَّسليمُ، والتَّسليمُ هُو اليَقينُ، واليَقينُ هُو التَّصديقُ، والتَّصديقُ هُو الإقرارُ، والإقرارُ هُو الأداءُ، والأداءُ هُو العَمَلُ.[٧٧٦١]

1911. The Signs of a Person of Conviction

١٩١١ ـ عَلاماتُ المُوقِنِ

6835. **The Prophet (SAWA) said,** 'There are six signs of a person of conviction: he has truly attained conviction in Allah and believed in Him, he is convinced that death is true and he is wary of it, he is convinced that Resurrection is true and he fears shame, he is convinced that Heaven is true and he longs for it, he is convinced that Hell is true and his endeavour is apparent in his wanting to be saved from it, he is convinced that the Account is true and so he takes account of himself.'[7780]

٦٨٣٥ . رسولُ اللهِ ﷺ : أمّا عَلامَةُ المُوقِنِ فَسِتَّةٌ: أيقَنَ باللهِ حَقّاً فآمَنَ بِهِ، وأيقَنَ بأنّ المَوتَ حقٌّ فحَذِرَهُ، وأيقَنَ بأنّ البَعثَ حَقٌّ فخافَ الفَضيحَةَ، وأيقَنَ بأنّ الجَنّةَ حَقٌّ فاشتاقَ إلَيها، وأيقَنَ بأنّ النّارَ حَقٌّ فظَهَرَ سَعيُهُ لِلنَّجاةِ مِنها، وأيقَنَ بأنّ الحِسابَ حَقٌّ فحاسَبَ نَفسَهُ.[٧٧٦٢]

6836. **Imām ʿAlī (AS) said,** 'Conviction can be proved by the shortening of one's expectations, sincerity in one's actions, and abstention from worldliness.'[7781]

٦٨٣٦ . الإمامُ عليٌّ ﷺ : يُستَدَلُّ علَى اليَقينِ بِقِصَرِ الأمَلِ، وإخلاصِ العَمَلِ، والزُّهدِ في الدُّنيا.[٧٧٦٣]

6837. **Imām ʿAlī (AS) said,** 'Whoever has conviction in that he will depart from his loved ones, will dwell in the earth, be faced with the Account, be in no need for what he has left behind but be in need of what he has sent forth, is worthy of having short expectations and lengthy deeds.'[7782]

٦٨٣٧ . عنه ﷺ : مَن أيقَنَ أنّهُ يُفارِقُ الأحبابَ، ويَسكُنُ التُّرابَ، ويُواجِهُ الحِسابَ، ويَستَغني عَمّا خَلَّفَ، ويَفتَقِرُ إلىٰ ما قَدَّمَ، كانَ حَرِيّاً بِقِصَرِ الأمَلِ، وطُولِ العَمَلِ.[٧٧٦٤]

6838. **Imām ʿAlī (AS) said,** 'Whoever has conviction that Allah sees him while he continues to commit sins, then he has considered Him the most insignificant of onlookers.'[7783]

٦٨٣٨ . عنه ﷺ : مَن تَيَقَّنَ أنّ اللهَ سبحانَهُ يَراهُ وهُو يَعمَلُ بِمَعاصيهِ فقَد جَعَلَهُ أهوَنَ النّاظِرينَ.[٧٧٦٥]

(See also: FAITH: section 194; GODWARINESS: section 1867)

(أُنظر) الإيمان: باب ١٩٤؛ التقوى: باب ١٨٦٧.

1912. What Corrupts Conviction

١٩١٢ ـ ما يُفسِدُ اليَقينَ

6839. **Imām ʿAlī (AS) said,** 'Doubt and being overcome by one's desires corrupts conviction.'[7784]

٦٨٣٩ . الإمامُ عليٌّ ﷺ : يُفسِدُ اليَقينَ الشَّكُّ وغَلَبَةُ الهَوىٰ.[٧٧٦٦]

6840. **Imām ʿAlī (AS) said,** 'Disputing about religion corrupts conviction.'[7785]

٦٨٤٠ . عنه ﷺ : الجَدَلُ في الدِّينِ يُفسِدُ اليَقينَ.[٧٧٦٧]

6841. **Imām ʿAlī (AS) said,** 'Associating with worldly people defames religion and weakens conviction.'[7786]

٦٨٤١ . عنه ﷺ : خِلطَةُ أبناءِ الدُّنيا تَشينُ الدِّينَ، وتُضعِفُ اليَقينَ.[٧٧٦٨]

6842. **Imām al-Ṣādiq (AS) said,** 'A greedy person has been deprived of two things, as a result of which he lacks two more things: he is deprived of contentment and so he lacks comfort, and he is deprived of satisfaction and so he lacks conviction.'[7787]

٦٨٤٢ . الإمامُ الصّادقُ ﷺ : حُرِمَ الحَريصُ خَصلَتَينِ ولَزِمَتهُ خَصلَتانِ: حُرِمَ القَناعَةَ فافتَقَدَ الرّاحَةَ، وحُرِمَ الرِّضا فافتَقَدَ اليَقينَ.[٧٧٦٩]

(See also: DOUBT: section 1059)

(أُنظر) الشک: باب ١٠٥٩.

1913. Weakness of Conviction

١٩١٣ ـ ضَعفُ اليَقينِ

6843. **The Prophet (SAWA) said,** 'I do not fear for my community anything other than weakness of conviction.'[7788]

٦٨٤٣ . رسولُ اللهِ ﷺ : ما أخافُ علىٰ اُمَّتي إلّا ضَعفَ اليَقينِ.[٧٧٧٠]

6844. **The Prophet (SAWA) said,** 'Weakness of conviction is that you satisfy people by displeasing

٦٨٤٤ . عنه ﷺ : إنّ مِن ضَعفِ اليَقينِ أن تُرضِيَ

Allah Almighty, and that you praise them for the sustenance that Allah Almighty has given you, and you blame them for what Allah has not given you.'[7789]

النّاسَ بِسَخَطِ اللهِ تعالىٰ، و أن تَحمَدَهُم علىٰ رِزقِ اللهِ تعالىٰ، و أن تَذُمَّهُم علىٰ ما لَم يُؤتِكَ اللهُ.[٧٧٧١]

1914. The Fruits of Conviction

١٩١٤ـ ثَمَراتُ اليَقينِ

6845. **Imām ʿAlī (AS) said,** 'The peak of conviction is sincerity, and the goal of sincerity is salvation.'[7790]

٦٨٤٥. الامامُ عليٌّ عليه السلام: غايَةُ اليَقينِ الإخلاصُ، غايَةُ الإخلاصِ الخَلاصُ.[٧٧٧٢]

6846. **Imām ʿAlī (AS) said,** 'The abstention of a person from all that is perishable is in proportion of his conviction in all that is eternal.'[7791]

٦٨٤٦. عنه عليه السلام: زُهدُ المَرءِ فيما يَفنىٰ علىٰ قَدرِ يَقينِهِ بما يَبقىٰ.[٧٧٧٣]

6847. **Imām ʿAlī (AS) said,** 'Trust [in Allah] is from the strength of conviction.'[7792]

٦٨٤٧. عنه عليه السلام: التَّوكُّلُ مِن قُوَّةِ اليَقينِ.[٧٧٧٤]

6848. **Imām al-Ṣādiq (AS) said,** 'Patience is from conviction.'[7793]

٦٨٤٨. الإمامُ الصّادقُ عليه السلام: الصَّبرُ مِن اليَقينِ.[٧٧٧٥]

6849. **Imām al-Ṣādiq (AS) said,** 'Satisfaction with unpleasant decree is one of the highest levels of conviction.'[7794]

٦٨٤٩. عنه عليه السلام: الرِّضا بِمَكروهِ القَضاءِ مِن أعلىٰ دَرَجاتِ اليَقينِ.[٧٧٧٦]

1915. Increasing Conviction

١٩١٥ـ ازدِيادُ اليَقينِ

6850. **Imām ʿAlī (AS) said,** 'If the veils were to be uncovered for me my conviction would not increase.'[7795]

٦٨٥٠. الإمامُ عليٌّ عليه السلام: لَو كُشِفَ الغِطاءُ ما ازدَدتُ يَقيناً.[٧٧٧٧]

6851. **Imām al-Kāẓim (AS) said,** 'O servants of Allah, make use of His blessings by reforming your selves and your conviction will increase, and you will gain something precious and valuable.'[7796]

٦٨٥١. الإمامُ الكاظمُ عليه السلام: تَعاهَدُوا عِبادَ اللهِ نِعمَهُ بإصلاحِكُم أنفُسَكُم تَزدادُوا يَقيناً، وتَربَحوا نَفِيساً ثَمِيناً.[٧٧٧٨]

6852. **Imām al-Riḍā (AS),** when asked about Allah's saying to Abraham: *"He said, 'Do you not*

٦٨٥٢. الإمامُ الرِّضا عليه السلام ـ لَمّا سُئلَ عَن قَولِ اللهِ

believe?' He said, 'Yes indeed, but in order that my heart may be at rest", and whether there was a doubt in his heart, said, 'No, he had conviction, but he wanted Allah to increase his conviction.'[7797]

لإبراهيمَ: ﴿أوَ لَمْ تُؤْمِنْ قالَ بَلىٰ ولكِنْ لِيَطْمَئنَّ قَلْبي﴾[٧٧٧٩] أكانَ في قَلبِهِ شَكٌّ؟ ـ: لا، كانَ علىٰ يَقينٍ، ولكنَّهُ أرادَ مِن اللهِ الزِّيادَةَ في يَقينِهِ.[٧٧٨٠]

(See also: FAITH: section 178)

(أنظر) الإيمان: باب ١٧٨.

O Allah, bless Muḥammad and the family of Muḥammad. Raise my faith to reach the most perfect faith and make my conviction to be the most excellent of convictions. And accept from me, O Changer of bad deeds to good deeds, O most Merciful of the merciful.

اللّهمّ صلّ على محمّدٍ وآل محمّدٍ، وبلّغ بإيماني أكمل الإيمان، واجعل يقيني أفضل اليقين. وتقبّل منّي يا مبدّل السيّئات بالحسنات يا أرحم الراحمين.

By the grace of Allah, the compiling of this book *Muntakhab Mizān al-Ḥikma* finished on the blessed occasion of the birth anniversary of Fāṭima al-Zahrā' (AS): the twentieth of *Jumādī al-Thānī*, 1429/24th of June 2008. Praise be to Allah, and salutations be to our Master Muḥammad and his Progeny. *Wassalām*.

تمّ الكتاب بحمد الله وتوفيقه، واتّفق الفراغ من منتخب ميزان الحكمة في يوم ولادة سيدة فاطمة الزهراء عليها السلام في العشرين من جمادى الآخرة سنة أربعمائة وتسعة وعشرين بعد الألف من الهجرة، والحمد لله أوّلاً وآخراً، والصلاة علىٰ سيّدنا محمّد وآله، والسلام.

Endnotes

1 *Ghurar al-Ḥikam*, no. 986
2 Ibid. no. 606
3 Ibid. no. 1705
4 Ibid. no. 1148
5 Ibid. no. 2888
6 Ibid. no. 6342
7 Ibid. no. 6361
8 Ibid. no. 4187
9 Qur'an 59:9
10 *Amālī al-Ṭūsī*, p. 185, no. 309
11 *Tanbīh al-Khawāṭir*, v. 1, p. 172
12 *Majma' al-Bayān*, v. 2, p. 792
13 Qur'an 76:8
14 Qur'an 76:22
15 *Tafsīr al-Qummi*, v. 2, p. 398
16 Qur'an 43:32
17 Qur'an 28:26
18 *Wasā'il al-Shī'a*, v. 13, p. 244, no. 3
19 *al-Kāfī*, v. 5, p. 90, no. 3
20 Ibid. p. 273, no. 1
21 *Amālī al-Ṣadūq*, p. 513, no. 707
22 *Biḥār al-Anwār*, v. 103, p. 170, no. 27
23 *Kanz al-'Ummāl*, no. 9126
24 *Kitāb man lā yaḥḍurahi al-Faqīh*, v. 4, p. 10, no. 4968
25 *Nahj al-Balāgha*, Sermon 91
26 *Ghurar al-Ḥikam*, no. 10648
27 Ibid. no. 9905
28 *Nahj al-Balāgha*, Saying 74
29 Qur'an 3:145
30 *Biḥār al-Anwār*, v. 5, p. 142, no. 14
31 *Ghurar al-Ḥikam*, no. 494
32 *Nahj al-Balāgha*, Sermon 190
33 *Ghurar al-Ḥikam*, no. 4778
34 Qur'an 7:34
35 Qur'an 15:4,5
36 Qur'an 6:2
37 *Biḥār al-Anwār*, v. 5, p. 139, no. 3
38 *Ghurar al-Ḥikam*, no. 4239
39 *Biḥār al-Anwār*, v. 5, p. 140, no. 7
40 Qur'an 42:20
41 *Ghurar al-Ḥikam*, no. 694-695
42 Ibid. no. 6080
43 *Nahj al-Balāgha*, Letter 32
44 Qur'an 17:21
45 *Nahj al-Balāgha*, Sermon 114
46 Qur'an 40:39
47 *Ghurar al-Ḥikam*, no. 8298
48 Ibid. no. 4
49 Qur'an 4:77
50 *Ghurar al-Ḥikam*, no. 7502
51 Ibid. no. 5175-5176
52 Ibid. no. 8769
53 *Tanbīh al-Khawāṭir*, v. 2, p. 234
54 *Biḥār al-Anwār*, v. 77, p. 151, no. 104
55 *Ghurar al-Ḥikam*, no. 10829
56 Qur'an 49:10
57 *Amālī al-Mufīd*, p. 187, no. 13
58 *Ghurar al-Ḥikam*, no. 5351
59 *al-Kāfī*, v. 2, p. 166, no. 2 and 7
60 Ibid. no. 3
61 Ibid. no. 4
62 *Kanz al-'Ummāl*, no. 24642
63 *Amālī al-Ṣadūq*, p. 380, no. 483
64 *Biḥār al-Anwār*, v. 74, p. 165, no. 29
65 *al-Ikhtiṣāṣ*, no. 226
66 Ibid. no. 31
67 *Biḥār al-Anwār*, v. 78, p. 291, no. 2
68 *Tuḥaf al-'Uqūl*, p. 322
69 *Biḥār al-Anwār*, v. 74, p. 279, no. 1
70 *Tanbīh al-Khawāṭir*, v. 2, p. 179
71 *Ghurar al-Ḥikam*, no. 6191
72 Ibid. no. 1795
73 Ibid. no. 4225
74 Ibid. no. 8978
75 Ibid. nos. 7776,7777
76 Ibid. no. 8552
77 *al-Maḥāsin*, v. 1, p. 415, no. 953
78 *Biḥār al-Anwār*, v. 74, p. 181, no. 1
79 *Ghurar al-Ḥikam*, no. 5641
80 *Kashf al-Ghamma*, v. 2, p. 331
81 *Biḥār al-Anwār*, v. 74, no. 181
82 *Nahj al-Balāgha*, Letter 31
83 *Biḥār al-Anwār*, v. 77, p. 210, no. 1
84 *al-Maḥāsin*, v. 1, p. 415, no. 950
85 *Nahj al-Balāgha*, Letter 31
86 *Biḥār al-Anwār*, v. 78, p. 121, no. 4
87 *Tuḥaf al-'Uqūl*, p. 54
88 Ibid. no. 323
89 Ibid. no. 324
90 *Ghurar al-Ḥikam*, no. 7503

91 Ibid. no. 10420
92 *al-Irshād*, v. 2, p. 166
93 *al-Khiṣāl*, p. 244, no. 100
94 *Biḥār al-Anwār*, v. 74, p. 282, no. 3
95 *Kanz al-'Ummāl*, no. 24759
96 *Ghurar al-Ḥikam*, no. 2461
97 Ibid. no. 3645
98 *Biḥār al-Anwār*, v. 77, p. 269, no. 1
99 *Ghurar al-Ḥikam*, no. 8166
100 *A'lām al-Dīn*, p. 304
101 *Biḥār al-Anwār*, v. 74, p. 166, no. 29
102 *Ghurar al-Ḥikam*, no. 752
103 Ibid. no. 9079
104 *Tanbīh al-Khawāṭir*, v. 2, p. 123
105 *Ghurar al-Ḥikam*, no. 4978
106 Ibid. no. 4988
107 Ibid. no. 5017
108 Ibid. no. 5021
109 Ibid. no. 5009
110 Ibid. no. 4985
111 *Biḥār al-Anwār*, v. 74, p. 282, no. 4
112 *Nahj al-Balāgha*, Saying 479
113 *Ma'ānī al-Akhbār*, p. 198, no. 4
114 *Kanz al-'Ummāl*, no. 24755
115 *Ghurar al-Ḥikam*, nos. 8921 and 8923
116 *al-Kāfī*, v. 2, p. 672, no. 7
117 *Biḥār al-Anwār*, v. 74, p. 233, no. 29
118 Ibid. p. 166, no. 29
119 Ibid. v. 75, p. 65, no. 2
120 *al-Kāfī*, v. 2, p. 206, no. 4
121 *Biḥār al-Anwār*, v. 74, p. 298, no. 32
122 Ibid. p. 166, no. 29
123 Ibid. p. 322, no. 89
124 Ibid. no. 90
125 *al-Kāfī*, v. 2, p. 198, no. 8
126 *Biḥār al-Anwār*, v. 74, p. 166, no. 30
127 Ibid. p. 171, no. 38
128 Ibid. v. 16, p. 233, no. 35
129 The Arabic word *adab* denotes good manners, etiquette, politeness, and other such propriety characteristic of good breeding and discipline (*ed.*)
130 *Ghurar al-Ḥikam*, no. 998
131 *Mishkāt al-Anwār*, p. 135
132 *Ghurar al-Ḥikam*, no. 967
133 Ibid. no. 5036
134 Ibid. no. 3590
135 Ibid. no. 4853
136 Ibid. no. 6096
137 *Biḥār al-Anwār*, v. 75, p. 68, no. 8
138 Ibid. v. 71, p. 428, no. 78
139 *Tuḥaf al-'Uqūl*, p. 96
140 *Nahj al-Sa'āda*, v. 2, no. 50
141 *Ghurar al-Ḥikam*, no. 10466
142 *Biḥār al-Anwār*, v. 77, p. 131, no. 41
143 *Ghurar al-Ḥikam*, no. 6911
144 Ibid. no. 2004
145 Ibid. no. 8886
146 *Biḥār al-Anwār*, v. 78, p. 111, no. 6
147 *Ghurar al-Ḥikam*, no. 4522
148 *Biḥār al-Anwār*, v. 2, p. 56, no. 33
149 Prophet Jesus (AS) is known in the Arabic tradition as 'Īsā
150 *Tuḥaf al-'Uqūl*, p. 500
151 *Tanbīh al-Khawāṭir*, v. 1, p. 196
152 *Ghurar al-Ḥikam*, no. 4786
153 Ibid. no. 4174
154 Ibid. no. 5520
155 Ibid. no. 8271
156 Ibid. no. 4333
157 *Biḥār al-Anwār*, v. 70, p. 73, no. 27
158 Ibid. v. 94, p. 94, no. 12
159 *Tuḥaf al-'Uqūl*, p. 376
160 *Ghurar al-Ḥikam*, no. 3241
161 Ibid. no. 3298
162 Ibid. no. 5932
163 *Biḥār al-Anwār*, v. 104, p. 95, no. 44
164 *Nahj al-Balāgha*, Letter 31
165 Qur'an 66:6
166 *Da'ā'im al-Islām*, v. 1, p. 82
167 *al-Kāfī*, v. 4, p. 4, no. 10
168 *Kanz al-'Ummāl*, no. 45330
169 *Makārim al-Akhlāq*, v. 1, p. 478, no. 1649
170 *Biḥār al-Anwār*, v. 103, p. 162, no. 6
171 Ibid. v. 79, p. 102, no. 2
172 *Nahj al-Balāgha*, Saying 177
173 *Biḥār al-Anwār*, v. 78, p. 82, no. 81
174 Ibid. v. 71, p. 427, no. 76
175 *Ghurar al-Ḥikam*, no. 2304
176 *Biḥār al-Anwār*, v. 104, p. 99, no. 74
177 Ibid. v. 92, p. 214, no. 13
178 *Ghurar al-Ḥikam*, no. 9001

179 *Biḥār al-Anwār*, v. 81, p. 198, no. 55
180 *Iqbāl al-A'māl*, v. 1, p. 157
181 *Kanz al-'Ummāl*, no. 20954
182 Ibid. no. 20951
183 Ibid. no. 20934
184 *Biḥār al-Anwār*, v. 84, p. 104, no. 2
185 *Da'ā'im al-Islām*, v. 1, p. 147
186 *Tuḥaf al-'Uqūl*, p. 13
187 *Biḥār al-Anwār*, v. 104, p. 122, no. 61
188 Ibid. v. 75, p. 54, no. 19
189 *al-Khiṣāl*, p. 17, no. 60
190 *Tafsīr al-Qummī*, v. 2, p. 146
191 Qur'an 33:58
192 *al-Kāfī*, v. 2, p. 350, no. 1
193 *Biḥār al-Anwār*, v. 67, p. 72, no. 40
194 Ibid. v. 75, p. 150, no. 13
195 Ibid.
196 *al-Kāfī*, v. 5, p. 34, no. 3
197 Ibid. no. 2
198 Qur'an 76:8
199 Qur'an 8:70
200 *Wasā'il al-Shī'a*, v. 11, p. 69, no. 3
201 *Qurb al-Isnād*, p. 143, no. 515
202 *al-Kāfī*, v. 5, p. 35, no. 2
203 *Wasā'il al-Shī'a*, v. 11, p. 69, no. 2
204 *Tanbīh al-Khawāṭir*, v. 1, p. 46
205 *Ghurar al-Ḥikam*, no. 6747
206 *Tanbīh al-Khawāṭir*, v. 2, p. 119
207 Ibid. v. 1, p. 100
208 *Biḥār al-Anwār*, v. 77, p. 182, no. 10
209 *Ghurar al-Ḥikam*, no. 8903
210 *Miṣbāḥ al-Sharī'ah*, p. 239
211 *Ghurar al-Ḥikam*, no. 10572
212 Ibid. no. 4139
213 Ibid. no. 659
214 Ibid. no. 9922
215 *Biḥār al-Anwār*, v. 75, p. 462, no. 17
216 Ibid. v. 77, p. 22, no. 6
217 *Ghurar al-Ḥikam*, no. 9942
218 Ibid. no. 10569
219 *Biḥār al-Anwār*, v. 78, p. 369, no. 4
220 Ibid. v. 62, p. 290
221 Ibid. p. 324
222 *Tanbīh al-Khawāṭir*, v. 1, p. 47
223 *Biḥār al-Anwār*, v. 62, p. 291
224 *Wasā'il al-Shī'a*, v. 16, p. 484, no. 5
225 Ibid. p. 520, no. 3
226 *al-Kāfī*, v. 6, p. 321, no. 1
227 *Wasā'il al-Shī'a*, v. 16, p. 539, no. 1
228 *al-Maḥajjat al-Bayḍā'*, v. 3, p. 6
229 *Wasā'il al-Shī'a*, v. 16, p. 518, no. 1
230 Usually referring to causes of diseases
231 Ibid. v. 16, p. 510, no. 1
232 Ibid. v. 16, p. 513, no. 1
233 *al-Ikhtiṣāṣ*, p. 253
234 Qur'an 8:62,63
235 Qur'an 3:103
236 *Biḥār al-Anwār*, v. 78, p. 11, no. 70
237 *Tuḥaf al-'Uqūl*, p. 373
238 Ibid. no. 45
239 *Biḥār al-Anwār*, v. 75, p. 265, no. 9
240 *al-Tawḥīd*, p. 89, no. 2
241 Ibid. p. 231, no. 5
242 Ibid. p. 89, no. 2
243 *al-Kāfī*, v. 1, p. 115, no. 3
244 *'Uyūn Akhbār al-Riḍā (AS)*, v. 2, p. 93, no. 1
245 *Ansāb al-Ashrāf*, v. 3, p. 135
246 *Kanz al-'Ummāl*, no. 14286
247 Ibid. no. 14366
248 Ibid. no. 31567
249 *Biḥār al-Anwār*, v. 75, p. 358, no. 72
250 Ibid. p. 359, no. 74
251 Qur'an 30:60
252 *Kanz al-'Ummāl*, no. 31618
253 *Tuḥaf al-'Uqūl*, p. 36
254 *al-Manāqib li Ibn Shahr Āshūb*, v. 2, p. 101
255 *Nahj al-Balāgha*, Sermon 33
256 *Biḥār al-Anwār*, v. 40, p. 328, no. 10
257 Ibid. v. 77, p. 173, no. 8
258 *Ghurar al-Ḥikam*, no. 1042
259 *Tanbīh al-Khawāṭir*, v. 1, p. 272
260 *Biḥār al-Anwār*, v. 73, p. 167, no. 31
261 *Ghurar al-Ḥikam*, no. 1010
262 Ibid. no. 639
263 Qur'an 15:3
264 *Ghurar al-Ḥikam*, no. 2572
265 Ibid. no. 1896
266 Ibid. no. 1375
267 Ibid. no. 1828
268 Ibid. no. 4641
269 *Biḥār al-Anwār*, v. 78, p. 35, no. 117
270 Ibid. v. 77, p. 293, no. 2

271 Ibid. v. 71, p. 152, no. 55
272 *Tanbīh al-Khawāṭir*, v. 1, p. 272
273 *Biḥār al-Anwār*, v. 73, p. 95, no. 79
274 *Ghurar al-Ḥikam*, no. 874
275 Ibid. no. 2920-2921
276 Ibid. no. 10844
277 *Biḥār al-Anwār*, v. 77, p. 333, no. 21
278 *A'lām al-Dīn*, p. 305
279 Prophet Moses (AS) is known in the Arabic tradition as Mūsā.
280 *al-Kāfī*, v. 2, p. 329, no. 1
281 *Biḥār al-Anwār*, v. 77, p. 421, no. 40
282 *al-Kāfī*, v. 2, p. 336, no. 3
283 *Biḥār al-Anwār*, v. 77, p. 101, no. 1
284 Ibid. v. 73, p. 167, no. 31
285 *Tuḥaf al-'Uqūl*, p. 286
286 *Ṣaḥīfat al-Imām al-Riḍā (AS)*, p. 276, no. 20
287 *Biḥār al-Anwār*, v. 78, p. 79, no. 61
288 Qur'an 3:110
289 *Kanz al-'Ummāl*, no. 34451
290 Ibid. no. 34452
291 Ibid. no. 34462
292 Ibid. no. 34465
293 *Tanbīh al-Khawāṭīr*, v. 2, p. 123
294 Ibid. v. 2, p. 123
295 Ibid. v. 2, p. 123
296 Qur'an 2:143
297 *Shawāhid al-Tanzīl*, v. 1, p. 119, no. 129
298 *Biḥār al-Anwār*, v. 69, p. 394, no. 77
299 *Tanbīh al-Khawāṭīr*, v. 1, p. 84
300 *Biḥār al-Anwār*, v. 7, p. 130, no. 1
301 Ibid. v. 7, p. 130, no. 3
302 *Al-Malāḥim wa al-Fitan*, p. 307, no. 428
303 *Tanbīh al-Khawāṭir*, v. 1, p. 75
304 *Biḥār al-Anwār*, v. 77, p. 161, no. 178
305 *Amālī al-Ṭūsī*, p. 157, no. 263
306 *al-Khiṣāl*, p. 163, no. 214
307 *Biḥār al-Anwār*, v. 73, p. 158, no. 3
308 Ibid. v. 70, p. 75, no. 3
309 Ibid. v. 72, p. 303, no. 50
310 *Kanz al-'Ummāl*, nos. 28969, 28968, 28970
311 *Tafsīr al-Ṭabarī*, v. 13, part. 25, p. 30
312 *Imāma* in its general sense in Arabic refers to any type of leadership, positive or negative, divinely appointed or otherwise. Within general Islamic terminology, however, it has been coined to refer to leadership within a Muslim community, where an *imām* is the leader of a congregation, of the congregational prayer or of a mosque. In *shī'ī* terminology and creed, in addition to the above, it also refers quite specifically to the divinely appointed leadership of the twelve Imāms (AS) from the lineage of the Prophet (SAWA) for mankind's spiritual and worldly prosperity. In this chapter, where the word *imāma* refers to this last meaning, the word will be left as *'imāma'* in order to differentiate it from other types of leadership referred to in the text. Similarly, Imām will be left as it is wherever it refers to one of the divinely appointed Imāms, and will be specified as 'leader' or otherwise elsewhere. (*ed.*)
313 Qur'an 6:3
314 *Ghurar al-Ḥikam*, no. 1095
315 *al-Kāfī*, v. 2, p. 18, no. 3
316 Qur'an 64:8
317 Ibid. v. 1, p. 196, no. 6
318 Ibid. v. 1, p. 199, no. 1
319 Ibid. v. 1, p. 200, no. 1
320 Ibid.
321 Qur'an 2:124
322 Prophet Abraham (AS) is known in the Arabic tradition as Ibrāhīm.
323 *al-Kāfī*, v. 1, p. 175, no. 2
324 Ibid. v. 1, p. 179, no. 12
325 Ibid. v. 1, p. 178, no. 2
326 Ibid. v. 1, p. 177, no. 2
327 *Biḥār al-Anwār*, v. 23, p. 46, no. 91
328 Ibid. v. 23, p. 23, no. 26
329 *al-Kāfī*, v. 1, p. 179, no. 10
330 *Biḥār al-Anwār*, v. 23, p. 51, no. 101
331 Qur'an 17:71
332 Qur'an 2:166
333 *Biḥār al-Anwār*, v. 8, p. 10, no. 3
334 Ibid. v. 23, p. 76, no. 1
335 *Kanz al-'Ummāl*, no. 464
336 *Biḥār al-Anwār*, v. 23, p. 83, no. 22
337 Qur'an 2:269
338 *al-Kāfī*, v. 1, p. 185, no. 11
339 *Biḥār al-Anwār*, v. 23, p. 88, no. 32
340 *al-Kāfī*, v. 1, p. 187, no. 11

341 Qur'an 32:24
342 Qur'an 10:35
343 *Sharḥ Nahj al-Balāgha li Ibn Abī al-Ḥadīd*, v. 7, p. 36
344 *Ghurar al-Ḥikam*, no. 11010
345 *Nahj al-Balāgha*, Saying 73
346 Ibid. Saying 110
347 *Biḥār al-Anwār*, v. 25, p. 164
348 *Nahj al-Balāgha*, Sermon 131
349 *al-Irshād*, v. 2, p. 39
350 *al-Kāfī*, v. 1, p. 285, no. 4
351 Ibid. v. 1, p. 202, no. 1
352 *Biḥār al-Anwār*, v. 40, p. 336, no. 17
353 *Nahj al-Balāgha*, Sermon 105
354 *Kanz al-'Ummāl*, no. 14313
355 *Nahj al-Balāgha*, Letter 50
356 *Biḥār al-Anwār*, v. 23, p. 30, p. 46
357 Ibid.
358 *al-Kāfī*, v. 1, p. 376, no. 4
359 Ibid. p. 373, no. 6
360 *Amāli al-Ṭūṣi*, p. 417, no. 939
361 Qur'an 28:41
362 *Nahj al-Balāgha*, Sermon 165
363 *al-Kāfī*, v. 1, p. 372, no. 1
364 *Biḥār al-Anwār*, v. 25, p. 112, no. 7
365 Qur'an 33:67
366 *Kanz al-'Ummāl*, no. 14872
367 *al-Khiṣāl*, p. 206, no. 24
368 *Tanbīh al-Khawāṭir*, v. 1, p. 51
369 *al-Durr al-Manthūr*, v. 3, p. 125
370 Such traditions indicate that the Imāms did not have an adequate amount of devoted companions with whose support they could revolt against the tyrant rulers.
371 *Biḥār al-Anwār*, v. 100, p. 49, no. 18
372 *al-Kāfī*, v. 2, p. 243, no. 4.
373 *Kamāl al-Dīn*, p. 461, no. 21
374 *Biḥār al-Anwār*, v. 23, p. 106, no. 7
375 Ibid. p. 105, no. 3
376 *Nahj al-Balāgha*, Sermon 97
377 Ibid. Sermon 100
378 Ibid. Sermon 109
379 Ibid. Sermon 152
380 Ibid. Saying 109
381 *al-Kāfī*, v. 1, p. 204, no. 2
382 *Nahj al-Balāgha*, Sermon 162
383 Ibid. Sermon 131
384 *Amālī al-Mufīd*, p. 155, no. 6
385 *Ṣaḥīḥ Muslim*, v. 3, p. 1452, no. 6
386 *Kanz al-'Ummāl*, no. 14971
387 *al-Kāfī*, v. 1, p. 221, no. 1
388 Qur'an 16:89
389 *al-Kāfī*, v. 1, p. 229, no. 4
390 Ibid. p. 202, no. 1
391 *Kanz al-'Ummāl*, no. 33021
392 Ibid. no. 32900
393 Ibid. no. 33022
394 Ibid. no. 32878
395 Ibid. no. 32909
396 *Tārīkh Dimashq*, Biography of Imām 'Alī (AS), v. 42, p. 303, no. 8835
397 *Amālī al-Ṣadūq*, p. 565, no. 765
398 *Amālī al-Ṭūsī*, p. 602, no. 1244
399 *Kanz al-'Ummāl*, no. 36419
400 *Tārīkh Dimashq*, Biography of Imām 'Alī (AS), v. 42, p. 188, no. 8637
401 Ibid. v. 42, p. 197, no. 8663
402 Ibid. v. 42, p. 207, no. 8683
403 *Sharḥ Nahj al-Balāgha li Ibn Abī al-Ḥadīd*, v. 2, p. 297
404 *al-Kāfī*, v. 1, p. 294, no. 1
405 *Tārīkh Dimashq*, Biography of Imām 'Alī (AS), v. 42, p. 49 no. 9025
406 *Farā'd al-Ṣimṭayn*, v. 1, p. 177 no. 140
407 *Kanz al-'Ummāl*, no. 32890
408 Ibid. no. 32889
409 *Amālī al-Ṣadūq*, p. 642, no. 870
410 *Kanz al-'Ummāl*, no. 32943
411 *Tārīkh Dimashq*, Biography of Imām 'Alī (AS), v. 42, p. 52, no. 8385
412 *Sunan Ibn Māja*, v. 1, p. 44, no. 119
413 *Kanz al-'Ummāl*, no. 32914
414 Ibid. no. 32936
415 *Tārīkh Dimashq*, Biography of Imām 'Alī (AS), v. 42, p. 64
416 Prophet Aaron (AS) is known as Hārūn in the Arabic tradition (*ed.*)
417 *Kanz al-'Ummāl*, no. 32881
418 *Tārīkh Dimashq*, Biography of Imām 'Alī (AS), v. 42, p. 419, no. 9012

419 Prophet Noah (AS) is known as Nūḥ in the Arabic tradition (*ed.*)
420 John the Baptist (AS) is known as Yaḥyā in the Arabic tradition (*ed.*)
421 Prophet Zacharias (AS) is known as Zakariyya in the Arabic tradition (*ed.*)
422 Ibid. v. 42, p. 313, no. 8862
423 *al-Kāfī*, v. 1, p. 294, no. 1
424 Ibid.
425 *Biḥār al-Anwār*, v. 5, p. 69, no. 1
426 *Tārīkh Dimashq,* Biography of Imām ʿAlī (AS), v. 42, p. 304, no. 8838
427 *Biḥār al-Anwār*, v. 36, p. 5, no. 1
428 *Tārīkh Dimashq,* Biography of Imām ʿAlī (AS), v. 42, p. 317, no. 8871
429 Ibid. p. 333, no. 8900
430 Ibid. p. 356, no. 8949
431. Ibid. p. 369, no. 8963
432 *al-Irshād*, v. 1, p. 35
433 *Nahj al-Balāgha*, Sermon 5
434 *Khaṣā'is al-A'imma*, p. 99
435 *Sharḥ Nahj al-Balāgha li Ibn Abī al-Ḥadīd*, v. 4, p. 103
436 *Kanz al-ʿUmmāl*, no. 36541
437 *Nahj al-Balāgha*, Sermon 172
438 *Ghurar al-Ḥikam*, no. 3781
439 *Tanbīh al-Khawāṭir*, v. 2, p. 41
440 *al-Khiṣāl*, p. 580, no. 1
441 *Tārīkh Dimashq,* Biography of Imām ʿAlī (AS), v. 42, p. 489
442 *Ghurar al-Ḥikam*, no. 3761
443 *Nahj al-Saʿāda*, v. 3, p. 79
444 *al-Kāfī*, v. 1, p. 198, no. 3
445 *Nahj al-Balāgha*, Saying 316. Al-Sharīf al-Raḍī said: The meaning to this is: The believers follow me and the debauched and wicked follow wealth the same way the bee follows the queen bee (*yaʿsūb*) which is its leader.
446 *al-Tawḥīd*, p. 164, no. 2
447 *Tārīkh Dimashq,* Biography of Imām ʿAlī (AS), v. 42, p. 475
448 Ibid. p. 31
449 Ibid.
450 *Kanz al-ʿUmmāl*, no. 36477
451 *Nahj al-Balāgha*, Sermon 224
452 *Ghurar al-Ḥikam*, no. 3883
453 *al-Kāfī*, v. 1, p. 207, no. 3
454 *Ghurar al-Ḥikam*, no. 9482
455 The Arabic root *fa-ṭa-ma*, from which the name 'Fāṭima' is derived, means 'to wean' (*ed.*)
456 *Amālī al-Ṭūsī*, p. 300
457 *Amālī al-Ṣadūq*, p. 474, no. 18
458 *Maʿānī al-Akhbār*, p. 64, no. 15
459 *Biḥār al-Anwār*, v. 43, p. 23, no. 17
460 *Amālī al-Ṣadūq*, p. 575, no. 787
461 *Biḥār al-Anwār*, v. 43, p. 22, no. 13
462 *Musnad Aḥmad b. Ḥanbal*, v. 3, p. 80
463 *Amālī al-Ṣadūq*, p. 175, no. 178
464 *Kanz al-ʿUmmāl*, no. 37725
465 *Nahj al-Balāgha*, Sermon 202
466 *al-Kāfī*, v. 1, p. 298, no. 2
467 *Biḥār al-Anwār*, v. 43, p. 306, no. 66
468 *Kanz al-ʿUmmāl*, no. 37640
469 *Amālī al-Ṣadūq*, p. 244, no. 262
470 *al-Manāqib li Ibn Shahr Āshūb*, v. 4, p. 23
471 *Mukhtaṣar Tārīkh Dimashq*, v. 7, p. 26
472 The archangel Gabriel is known as Jibraʿīl in the Islamic tradition (*ed.*)
473 *ʿIlal al-Sharā'iʿ*, p. 137, no. 5
474 *Kifāyat al-Āthār*, no. 194
475 *al-Kāfī*, v. 1, p. 301, no. 2
476 *Amālī al-Ṣadūq*, no. 101
477 *Biḥār al-Anwār*, v. 43, p. 264, no. 16
478 *al-Mustadrak ʿalā al-Ṣaḥiḥayn*, v. 3, p. 177
479 *Sunan al-Tirmidhī*, v. 5, p. 661, no. 3784
480 *al-Manāqib li Ibn Shahr Āshūb*, v. 4, p. 73
481 *ʿUyūn Akhbār al-Riḍā (AS)*, v. 1, p. 59, no. 29
482 The Arabic word '*daʿī*' was used to refer to anyone falsely claiming a certain lineage to secure personal gains of rank or honour. This was the case with both ʿUbaydullāh b. Ziyād and his father Ziyād b. Abīh (*ed.*)
483 *al-Luhūf*, p. 97
484 *al-Irshād*, p. 298
485 *Iḥqāq al-Ḥaqq*, v. 11, p. 431
486 *Amālī al-Ṣadūq*, p. 478, no. 4
487 *al-Manāqib li Ibn Shahr Āshūb*, v. 4, p. 66
488 *al-Luhūf*, p. 170
489 *al-Kāfī*, v. 1, p. 303, no. 1
490 *Biḥār al-Anwār*, v. 46, p. 3, no. 1
491 *al-Manāqib li Ibn Shahr Āshūb*, v. 4, p. 154

492 *Ḥilyat al-Awliyā'*, v. 3, p. 140
493 *al-Kāfī*, v. 3, p. 300, no. 4
494 Qur'an 3:134
495 *I'lām al-Warā*, p. 256
496 *Maṭālib al-Sa'ūl*, p. 77
497 *Ḥilyat al-Awliyā'*, v. 3, p. 138
498 *Kifāyat al-Āthār*, p. 241
499 *Biḥār al-Anwār*, v. 46, p. 225, no. 5
500 *Rabī' al-Abrār*, v. 2, p. 603
501 *Biḥār al-Anwār*, v. 46, p. 227, no, 9
502 *al-Kāfī*, v. 2, p. 499, no. 1
503 Ibid. v. 2, p. 616, no. 11
504 *al-Irshād*, v. 2, p. 167
505 *Biḥār al-Anwār*, v. 47, p. 15, no. 12
506 Ibid.
507 Ibid. v. 47, p. 16, no. 1
508 *al-Kāfī*, v. 4, p. 8, no. 1
509 *Thawāb al-A'māl*, p. 173, no. 2
510 *al-Kāfī*, v. 5, p. 76, no. 13
511 *al-Manāqib li Ibn Shahr Āshūb*, v. 4, no. 317
512 *'Uyūn Akhbār al-Riḍā (AS)*, v. 1, p. 95
513 *Biḥār al-Anwār*, v. 78, p. 329, no. 7
514 *al-Irshād*, v. 2, p. 231
515 *Tārīkh Baghdād*, v. 13, p. 27
516 *Biḥār al-Anwār*, v. 49, p. 17, no. 15
517 *'Uyūn Akhbār al-Riḍā (AS)*, v. 2, p. 139, no. 3
518 *Biḥār al-Anwār*, v. 49, p. 91, no. 5
519 *'Uyūn Akhbār al-Riḍā (AS)*, v. 2, p. 184, no. 7
520 *Kifāyat al-Āthār*, p. 84
521 *Biḥār al-Anwār*, v. 50, p. 35, no. 23
522 *al-Kāfī*, v. 6, p. 360, no. 3
523 *Dalā'il al-Imāma*, p. 211
524 Ibid. p. 212
525 Qur'an 54:24,25
526 *Kashf al-Ghamma*, v. 3, p. 153
527 *Biḥār al-Anwār*, v. 50, p. 118, no. 1
528 Baghā and Waṣīf were two Turkish commanders in the Abbasid army.
529 Ṣāliḥ: A Qur'anic prophet whose equivalent in the biblical tradition is not known (*ed.*)
530 Qur'an 11:65
531 Ibid. v. 50, p. 189, no. 1
532 *Kashf al-Ghamma*, v. 3, p. 179
533 *Biḥār al-Anwār*, v. 50, p. 239, no. 4
534 Ibid. v. 50, p. 308, no. 6
535 *al-Manāqib li Ibn Shahr Āshūb*, v. 4, p. 424
536 Qur'an 17:33
537 *Biḥār al-Anwār*, v. 51, p. 30, no. 8
538 *al-Ghayba li al-Ṭūsī*, p. 471, no. 489
539 *Biḥār al-Anwār*, v. 51, p. 160, no. 7
540 *Kanz al-'Ummāl*, no. 34208
541 Ibid. no. 38666
542 Ibid. no. 38691
543 Ibid. no. 38661
544 Ibid. no. 39675
545 Qur'an 11:86
546 *Nūr al-Thaqalayn*, v. 2, p. 392, no. 194
547 *Biḥār al-Anwār*, v. 52, p. 155, no. 10
548 *Kamāl al-Dīn*, p. 288, no. 7
549 *al-Ghayba li al-Nu'mānī*, p. 169, no. 11
550 *Biḥār al-Anwār*, v. 52, p. 149, no. 73
551 Ibid. v. 52, p. 122, no. 2
552 Ibid. v. 52, p. 122, no. 4
553 Ibid. v. 52, p. 146, no. 69
554 *al-Ghayba li al-Ṭūsī*, p. 459, no. 471
555 *Biḥār al-Anwār*, v. 52, p. 111, no. 20
556 Ibid. v. 52, p. 110, no. 17
557 *al-Ghayba li al-Ṭūsī*, p. 426, no. 411
558 *Biḥār al-Anwār*, v. 52, p. 90, no. 1
559 *Kamāl al-Dīn*, p. 482, no. 11 (narrated by 'Abdullāh b. Faḍl al-Hāshimī)
560 *'Ilal al-Sharā'i'*, p. 147, no. 2
561 *al-Ghayba li al-Nu'mānī*, p. 274, no. 53
562 *Mishkāt al-Anwār*, p. 128, no. 300
563 *Biḥār al-Anwār*, v. 52, p. 92, no. 7
564 Ibid. v. 52, p. 137, no. 42
565 Qur'an 2:155
566 *Kamāl al-Dīn*, p. 649, no. 3
567 *Nūr al-Thaqalayn*, v. 5, p. 461, no. 4
568 *al-Tashrīf bi al-Minan*, p. 129, no. 136. *Kanz al-'Ummāl*, no. 39665
569 *Baṣā'ir al-Darajāt*, p. 44. *Biḥār al-Anwār*, v. 52, p. 318, no. 17
570 *Kashf al-Ghumma*, v. 3, p. 255
571 *al-Kāfī*, v. 8, p. 241, no. 329
572 *al-Ghayba li al-Nu'mānī*, p. 204, no. 6
573 Ibid. p. 317, no. 1
574 *Kanz al-'Ummāl*, no. 38700
575 *Mishkāt al-Anwār*, p. 151, no. 366
576 *al-Kāfī*, v. 8, p. 227, no. 288
577 Qur'an 49:14

578 *Tuḥaf al-ʻUqūl*, p. 297
579 *al-Kāfī*, v. 2, p. 26, no. 3
580 *Biḥār al-Anwār*, v. 69, p. 72, no. 26
581 *Kanz al-ʻUmmāl*, no. 2
582 Ibid. no. 57
583 Ibid. no. 12
584 Ibid. no. 99
585 Ibid. no. 95
586 *Ghurar al-Ḥikam*, no. 873
587 Ibid. no. 1350
588 Ibid. no. 5222
589 *Biḥār al-Anwār*, v. 103, p. 37, no. 79
590 Ibid. v. 70, p. 106, no. 2
591 *Kanz al-ʻUmmāl*, no. 59
592 Ibid. no. 637
593 *Biḥār al-Anwār*, v. 69, p. 19, no. 2
594 *al-Kāfī*, v. 2, p. 38, no. 7
595 *Kanz al-ʻUmmāl*, no. 1333
596 Ibid. no. 205
597 Ibid. no. 223
598 *Biḥār al-Anwār*, v. 69, p. 63, no. 7
599 *Kanz al-ʻUmmāl*, no. 43247
600 Ibid. no. 106
601 *Biḥār al-Anwār*, v. 77, p. 177, no. 10
602 Ibid. v. 71, p. 387, no. 34
603 *Ghurar al-Ḥikam*, no. 4658
604 Ibid. no. 10849
605 *Biḥār al-Anwār*, v. 78, p. 239, no. 78
606 Qur'an, 8:2
607 *Kanz al-ʻUmmāl*, no. 1734
608 *Kanz al-ʻUmmāl*, no. 66
609 Ibid. no. 74
610 Ibid. no. 52
611 *Ghurar al-Ḥikam*, no. 2992
612 *al-Kāfī*, v. 2, p. 45, no. 2
613 Ibid. p. 42, no. 1
614 *Biḥār al-Anwār*, v. 69, p. 175, no. 28
615 Ibid. v. 78, p. 63, no. 154
616 *Ghurar al-Ḥikam*, no. 4838
617 *Kanz al-ʻUmmāl*, no. 43525
618 *Tanbīh al-Khawāṭir*, v. 2, p. 33
619 *Nahj al-Balāgha*, Sermon 189
620 *al-Khiṣāl*, p. 9, no. 29
621 *al-Kāfī*, v. 2, p. 38, no. 6
622 *Kanz al-ʻUmmāl*, no. 72
623 *Biḥār al-Anwār*, v. 72, p. 249, no. 14
624 *al-Kāfī*, v. 2, p. 58, no. 7
625 *Biḥār al-Anwār*, v. 71, p. 85, no. 29
626 *Tanbīh al-Khawāṭir*, v. 2, p. 116
627 *al-Kāfī*, v. 2, p. 128, no. 2
628 *Biḥār al-Anwār*, v. 77, p. 193, no. 11
629 *Tuḥaf al-ʻUqūl*, p. 330
630 *Biḥār al-Anwār*, v. 77, p. 172, no. 8
631 Ibid. p. 173, no. 8
632 *Tuḥaf al-ʻUqūl*, p. 55
633 Ibid. p. 377
634 *Biḥār al-Anwār*, v. 71, p. 158, no. 75
635 *Kanz al-ʻUmmāl*, no. 821
636 *al-Khiṣāl*, p. 27, no. 95
637 *Musnad Ibn Ḥanbal*, v. 6, p. 379, no. 18408
638 *Kanz al-ʻUmmāl*, no. 402
639 Qur'an 8:2-4
640 *Kanz al-ʻUmmāl*, no. 690
641 Ibid. no. 739
642 Ibid. no. 752
643 Ibid. no. 778
644 Ibid. no. 679
645 Ibid. no. 700
646 *Biḥār al-Anwār*, v. 67, p. 71, no. 34 and p. 310, no. 45
647 Ibid. v. 69, p. 410, no. 127
648 *Ghurar al-Ḥikam*, no. 1743
649 Ibid. no. 1901
650 Ibid. no. 1956
651 Ibid. no. 2160
652 *al-Kāfī*, v. 2, p. 231, no. 3
653 Ibid. p. 241, no. 38
654 Ibid. p. 231, no. 4
655 Ibid. p. 235, no. 18
656 *Tuḥaf al-ʻUqūl*, p. 442
657 *al-Kāfī*, v. 2, p. 241, no. 37
658 *Biḥār al-Anwār*, v. 67, p. 303, no. 34
659 *Tārīkh Baghdād*, v. 5, p. 194, and v. 12, p. 111
660 *al-Kāfī*, v. 2, p. 170, no. 5
661 Qur'an 11:40
662 *al-Iḥtijāj*, v. 1, p. 581, no. 137
663 *al-Kāfī*, v. 2, p. 242, no. 1
664 *Biḥār al-Anwār*, v. 67, p. 293, no. 15
665 Ibid. v. 72, p. 336, no. 24
666 *Nahj al-Balāgha*, Letter 69
667 *Ghurar al-Ḥikam*, no. 3278

668 *Kanz al-'Ummāl*, no. 704
669 Ibid. no. 34583
670 Qur'an 23:8
671 *Ghurar al-Ḥikam*, no. 2905-2906
672 *al-Kāfī*, v. 2, p. 162, no. 15
673 *Biḥār al-Anwār*, v. 77, p. 208, no. 1
674 *Amālī al-Ṣadūq*, p. 318, no. 373
675 Ibid. no. 372
676 *Biḥār al-Anwār*, v. 72, p. 198, no. 26. *Ghurar al-Ḥikam*, no. 10767
677 Ibid. v. 75, p. 172, no. 13
678 *Ma'ānī al-Akhbār*, p. 253, no. 1
679 *Biḥār al-Anwār*, v. 75, p. 114, no. 6
680 *Ghurar al-Ḥikam*, no. 4053
681 *Tanbīh al-Khawāṭir*, v. 1, p. 12
682 *Biḥār al-Anwār*, v. 103, p. 179, no. 3
683 *al-Tahdhīb*, v. 7, p. 232, no. 1013
684 *al-Kāfī*, v. 5, p. 301, no. 4
685 *Kanz al-'Ummāl*, no. 10909
686 Ibid. no. 10930
687 *Nahj al-Balāgha*, Saying 155
688 Ibid. Letter 53
689 This refers to the free non-Muslim subjects living in Muslim lands who, in return for paying the capital tax, enjoyed protection and safety therein (*ed.*)
690 *Kanz al-'Ummāl*, no. 10932
691 *Biḥār al-Anwār*, v. 100, p. 46, no. 6
692 *Ghurar al-Ḥikam*, no. 10303
693 *Biḥār al-Anwār*, v. 78, p. 231, no. 25
694 Ibid. v. 70, p. 111, no. 14
695 *al-Durra al-Bāhira*, p. 43
696 *Ghurar al-Ḥikam*, 1772
697 *A'lām al-Dīn*, p. 307
698 *Biḥār al-Anwār*, v. 75, p. 359, no. 74
699 Meaning people who cause one to forget and be distant from Allah Almighty.
700 *Ghurar al-Ḥikam*, no. 8644
701 Qur'an 17:70
702 *Kanz al-'Ummāl*, no. 34621
703 Ibid. no. 34615
704 *Biḥār al-Anwār*, v. 60, p. 299, no. 5
705 Qur'an 51:56
706 Qur'an 11:118,119
707 *Sharḥ Nahj al-Balāgha li Ibn Abī al-Ḥadīd*, v. 3, no. 108
708 *Biḥār al-Anwār*, v. 23, p. 83, no. 22
709 Ibid. v. 10, p. 167, no. 2
710 Ibid v 5 p 314 no 5
711 Qur'an 4:28
712 *Nahj al-Balāgha*, Saying 419
713 *Ghurar al-Ḥikam*, no. 2089
714 The Arabic word *āfa* means 'bane' when translated as accurately as possible into English, denoting something that is a constant source of misery or annoyance for something else, or something that causes the downfall or ruin of something else, though it has been translated differently according to its various contexts in this chapter, where it may denote an affliction in itself, or a misfortune or plague (*ed.*)
715 *Kanz al-'Ummāl*, no. 44091
716 Ibid. no. 44121
717 Ibid. no. 44226
718 *Ghurar al-Ḥikam*, no. 89
719 Ibid. no. 314
720 Ibid. no. 3915
721 Ibid. no. 3916
722 Ibid. no. 3917
723 Ibid. no. 3918
724 Ibid. no. 3919
725 Ibid. no. 3920
726 Ibid. no. 3921
727 Ibid. no. 3923
728 Ibid. no. 3924
729 Ibid. no. 3925
730 Ibid. no. 3922
731 Ibid. no. 3926
732 Ibid. no. 3927
733 Ibid. no. 3928
734 Ibid. no. 3929
735 Ibid. no. 3930
736 Ibid. no. 3931
737 Ibid. no. 3932
738 Ibid. no. 3933
739 Ibid. no. 3934
740 Ibid. no. 3935
741 Ibid. no. 3936
742 Ibid. no. 3937
743 Ibid. no. 3938
744 Ibid. no. 3939

745 Ibid. no. 3940
746 Ibid. no. 3941
747 Ibid. no. 3942
748 Ibid. no. 3943
749 Ibid. no. 3944
750 Ibid. no. 3945
751 Ibid. no. 3946
752 Ibid. no. 3950
753 Ibid. no. 3947
754 Ibid. no. 3948
755 Ibid. no. 3949
756 Ibid. no. 3951
757 Ibid. no. 3952
758 Ibid. no. 3953
759 Ibid. no. 3954
760 Ibid. no. 3955
761 Ibid. no. 3956
762 Ibid. no. 3957
763 Ibid. no. 3958
764 Ibid. no. 3959
765 Ibid. no. 3960
766 Ibid. no. 3961
767 Ibid. no. 3962
768 Ibid. no. 3963
769 Ibid. no. 3964
770 Ibid. no. 3965
771 Ibid. no. 3966
772 Ibid. no. 3969
773 Ibid. no. 3970
774 Ibid. no. 3971
775 Ibid. no. 3972
776 Ibid. no. 5244
777 Ibid. no. 5752
778 Qur'an 4:37
779 Qur'an 47:38
780 *Nahj al-Balāgha*, Saying 378. *Biḥār al-Anwār*, v. 73, p. 307, no. 36
781 *Nahj al-Balāgha*, Saying 3
782 *Biḥār al-Anwār*, v. 77, p. 238, no. 1
783 *Ghurar al-Ḥikam*, no. 1258
784 Ibid. nos. 7921-7922
785 Ibid. no. 1409
786 *Biḥār al-Anwār*, v. 78, p. 357, no. 12
787 Ibid. v. 72, p. 199, no. 27
788 Ibid. v. 73, p. 305, no. 23
789 Ibid. no. 25
790 *Tuḥaf al-'Uqūl*, nos. 371, 372
791 *Biḥār al-Anwār*, v. 73, p. 300, no. 2
792 *Ghurar al-Ḥikam*, no. 464
793 Ibid. no. 7473
794 *Biḥār al-Anwār*, v. 72, p. 199, no. 28
795 Ibid. v. 73, p. 308, no. 37
796 *Amālī al-Ṣadūq*, p. 471, no. 626
797 *Biḥār al-Anwār*, v. 73, p. 307, no. 35
798 *Ma'ānī al-Akhbār*, p. 245, no. 4
799 *Biḥār al-Anwār*, v. 73, p. 306, no. 28
800 Ibid. p. 300, no. 2
801 Ibid. v. 76, p. 4, no. 11
802 *Ghurar al-Ḥikam*, no. 3253
803 Ibid. no. 2038
804 *Wasā'il al-Shī'a*, v. 6, p. 318, no. 1
805 *Biḥār al-Anwār*, v. 77, p. 209, no. 1
806 *Ghurar al-Ḥikam*, no. 1275
807 Introducing into religion something which is not a part of it.
808 *Amālī al-Mufīd*, p. 188, no. 14
809 *Biḥār al-Anwār*, v. 77, p. 104, no. 1
810 *Nahj al-Balāgha*, Sermon 145
811 *Biḥār al-Anwār*, v. 78, p. 92, no. 98
812 *Kanz al-'Ummāl*, nos. 1095, 1126
813 Ibid. no. 1125
814 Ibid. no. 44216
815 *Tuḥaf al-'Uqūl*, p. 375
816 *Kanz al-'Ummāl*, no. 5599
817 *Biḥār al-Anwār*, v. 47, p. 217, no. 4
818 Ibid. v. 72, p. 216, no. 8
819 *Amālī al-Ṭūsī*, p. 385, no. 838
820 *Biḥār al-Anwār*, v. 72, p. 216, no. 8
821 *al-Kāfī*, v. 1, p. 54, no. 2
822 Qur'an 17:26,27
823 *Nahj al-Balāgha*, Saying 33
824 *Ghurar al-Ḥikam*, no. 890
825 Ibid. no. 1043
826 Ibid. no. 9057
827 *Tafsīr al-'Ayyāshī*, v. 2, p. 288, no. 53
828 Ibid. no. 54
829 Qur'an 5:2
830 *Biḥār al-Anwār*, v. 77, p. 166, no. 3
831 *al-Khiṣāl*, p. 110, no. 81
832 *Tuḥaf al-'Uqūl*, p. 8
833 Ibid. no. 295
834 Ibid. no. 21

835 *Kanz al-'Ummāl*, no. 5265
836 Qur'an 23:100
837 *al-Kāfī*, v. 3, p. 242, no. 3
838 Qur'an 3:169
839 *al-Maḥāsin*, v. 1, p. 258, no. 562
840 *Biḥār al-Anwār*, v. 6, p. 270, no. 127
841 Qur'an 19:31
842 *al-Kāfī*, v. 2, p. 165, no. 11
843 Qur'an 7:96
844 *Kanz al-'Ummāl*, no. 9434
845 *Mustadrak al-Wasā'il*, v. 13, p. 9
846 *Biḥār al-Anwār*, v. 79, p. 19, no. 4
847 *Ghurar al-Ḥikam*, no. 4211
848 Ibid. no. 4030
849 *al-Kāfī*, v. 2, p. 103, no. 6
850 Ibid. no. 3
851 Ibid. no. 1
852 *Biḥār al-Anwār*, v. 69, p. 409, no. 120
853 *Ghurar al-Ḥikam*, no. 656
854 Ibid. no. 5546
855 Ibid. no. 3454
856 Ibid. no. 4453
857 *Biḥār al-Anwār*, v. 76, p. 20, no. 3
858 Ibid. v. 78, p. 57, no. 124
859 Qur'an 7:179
860 *Kanz al-'Ummāl*, no. 1220
861 *Ghurar al-Ḥikam*, no. 9972
862 *Nahj al-Balāgha*, Sermon 153
863 Ibid. Saying 281
864 *Ghurar al-Ḥikam*, no. 6536
865 Ibid. no. 3061
866 Qur'an 17:81
867 Qur'an 21:18
868 *Ghurar al-Ḥikam*, no. 549
869 *Nahj al-Balāgha*, Sermon 33
870 *Nahj al-Sa'āda*, v. 3, p. 291
871 *Ghurar al-Ḥikam*, no. 6041
872 *Nahj al-Balāgha*, Sermon 141
873 Qur'an 2:42
874 *Nahj al-Balāgha*, Sermon 50
875 *Ghurar al-Ḥikam*, no. 6969
876 *Biḥār al-Anwār*, v. 5, p. 303, no. 12
877 *Tafsīr al-'Ayyāshī*, v. 2, p. 53, no. 39
878 With the exception of a couple of traditions, the majority of traditions in this chapter deal specifically with Allah's antipathy or hatred towards certain types of people or certain acts (*ed.*)
879 *Tuḥaf al-'Uqūl*, p. 42
880 *Kanz al-'Ummāl*, 28982
881 Ibid. no. 43679
882 *'Uyūn Akhbār al-Riḍā (AS)*, v. 2, p. 28, no. 24
883 *Ghurar al-Ḥikam*, no. 3437
884 *Mustadrak al-Wasā'il*, v. 8, p. 321, no. 9552
885 *Biḥār al-Anwār*, v. 78, p. 176, no. 338
886 *Kanz al-'Ummāl*, no. 21431
887 Ibid. no. 43833
888 *Biḥār al-Anwār*, v. 71, p. 383, no. 17
889 *Kanz al-'Ummāl*, no. 28985
890 Ibid. no. 5184
891 *Ghurar al-Ḥikam*, no. 3128
892 Ibid. no. 3294
893 Ibid. no. 3359
894 *Kanz al-'Ummāl*, no. 44220
895 *Ghurar al-Ḥikam*, no. 3164
896 *Biḥār al-Anwār*, v. 76, p. 180, no. 8
897 *al-Kāfī*, v. 2, p. 323, no. 4
898 *'Uyūn Akhbār al-Riḍā (AS)*, v. 2, p. 36, no. 89
899 *Biḥār al-Anwār*, v. 16, p. 231
900 Ibid. v. 76, p. 180, no. 10
901 *al-Khiṣāl*, p. 89, no. 25
902 *al-Kāfī*, v. 2, p. 290, no. 4
903 *Biḥār al-Anwār*, v. 78, p. 335, no. 16
904 *Ma'ānī al-Akhbār*, p. 367, no. 1
905 *Tuḥaf al-'Uqūl*, p. 316
906 Qur'an 10:23
907 Qur'an 16:90
908 *al-Kāfī*, v. 2, p. 327, no. 1
909 *Nahj al-Balāgha*, Saying 349
910 *Ghurar al-Ḥikam*, no. 382
911 Ibid. no. 795
912 Ibid. no. 2657
913 *al-Kāfī*, v. 2, p. 327, no. 4
914 Ibid. no. 3
915 Qur'an 2:173
916 *Ma'ānī al-Akhbār*, p. 213, no. 1
917 Qur'an 49:9
918 *al-Kāfī*, v. 5, p. 32, no. 2
919 Ibid. v. 5, p. 32, no. 3

920 Ibid. v. 5, p. 32, no. 5
921 *Wasā'il al-Shī'ah*, v. 11, p. 60, no. 5
922 Qur'an 19:58
923 Qur'an 17:109
924 *Biḥār al-Anwār*, v. 93, p. 331, no. 15
925 Ibid. p. 334, no. 25
926 Ibid. v. 84, p. 2, no. 71
927 Ibid. v. 93, p. 336, no. 30
928 *Makārim al-Akhlāq*, v. 2, p. 96, no. 10
929 *Ghurar al-Ḥikam*, no. 2051
930 Ibid. no. 2016
931 *Biḥār al-Anwār*, v. 69, p. 378, no. 31
932 Ibid. v. 7, p. 195, no. 62
933 *'Uddat al-Dā'ī*, p. 161
934 *Biḥār al-Anwār*, v. 93, p. 331, no. 14
935 Ibid. v. 70, p. 52, no. 11
936 Ibid. v. 73, p. 354, no. 60
937 Qur'an 34:15
938 Qur'an 34:18
939 *Nahj al-Balāgha*, Letter 69
940 Ibid. Saying 442
941 *Tuḥaf al-'Uqūl*, p. 321
942 *Ghurar al-Ḥikam*, no. 1881
943 Ibid. no. 2150
944 Ibid. no. 6666
945 *Tuḥaf al-'Uqūl*, . 312
946 Ibid. no. 317
947 *Ghurar al-Ḥikam*, no. 3307
948 Ibid. no. 3304
949 *Kanz al-'Ummāl*, no. 7910
950 Qur'an 9:122
951 *al-Iḥtijāj*, v. 1, p. 157, no. 32
952 *al-Mustadrak 'alā al-Ṣaḥīḥayn*, v. 3, p. 691, no. 6537
953 *al-Mu'jam al-Kabīr*, v. 8, p. 91, no. 7461
954 Ibid. v. 17, p. 285, no. 786
955 *al-Muwaṭṭa'*, v. 1, p. 218, no. 41
956 *Kanz al-'Ummāl*, no. 28779
957 *Amālī al-Ṭūsī*, p. 46, no. 54
958 *al-Firdaws*, v. 1, p. 234, no. 897
959 *Ma'ānī al-Akhbār*, p. 180, no. 1
960 Qur'an 26:145
961 *al-Zuhd li Ibn Ḥanbal*, p. 91
962 Qur'an 33:39
963 *Ḥilyat al-Awliyā'*, v. 1, p. 241
964 *Musnad Ibn Ḥanbal*, v. 4, p. 102, no. 11474
965 *Miṣbāḥ al-Sharī'a*, p. 395
966 *al-Kāfī*, v. 2, p. 104, no. 4
967 *Ṣaḥīḥ al-Bukhārī*, v. 5, p. 2269, no. 5774
968 *Tuḥaf al-'Uqūl*, p. 48
969 *al-Kāfī*, v. 8, p. 334, no. 522
970 Qur'an 7:68
971 *Nahj al-Balāgha*, Sermon 95
972 *Sharḥ Nahj al-Balāgha li Ibn Abī al-Ḥadīd*, v. 20, p. 287, no. 279
973 *al-Kāfī*, v. 2, p. 105, no. 10
974 *Tuḥaf al-'Uqūl*, p. 301
975 Qur'an 21:35
976 *al-Tawḥīd*, p. 354, no. 1
977 Ibid. no. 3
978 Qur'an 3:154
979 Qur'an 47:31
980 Qur'an 67:2
981 *Nahj al-Balāgha*, Sermon 144
982 Ibid. Sermon 192
983 *Biḥār al-Anwār*, v. 5, p. 218, no. 12
984 *Ghurar al-Ḥikam*, no. 10394
985 Qur'an 2:214
986 *Biḥār al-Anwār*, v. 67, p. 222, no. 29
987 *al-Kāfī*, v. 2, p. 252, no. 1
988 Ibid. v. 2, p. 254, no. 12
989 Qur'an 42:30
990 Prophet Job (AS) is known as Ayyūb in the Arabic tradition (*ed.*)
991 *al-Da'awāt*, p. 123, no. 304
992 *Biḥār al-Anwār*, v. 81, p. 174, no. 11
993 Ibid. p. 176, no. 14
994 Ibid. p. 195, no. 52
995 *Jāmi' al-Akhbār*, p. 310, no. 855
996 *al-Kāfī*, v. 2, p. 255, no. 17
997 *Jāmi' al-Akhbār*, p. 313, no. 870
998 *Biḥār al-Anwār*, v. 78, p. 373, no. 34
999 Qur'an 7:130
1000 *Nahj al-Balāgha*, Sermon 143
1001 *Biḥār al-Anwār*, v. 67, p. 211, no. 14
1002 Qur'an 7:182
1003 *Biḥār al-Anwār*, v. 67, p. 229, no. 41
1004 Ibid. p. 232, no. 48
1005 Ibid. p. 178, no. 25
1006 *A'lām al-Dīn*, p. 433

1007 *al-Kāfī*, v. 2, p. 253, no. 6
1008 *Biḥār al-Anwār*, v. 82, p. 148, no. 32
1009 *Jāmi' al-Akhbār*, p. 314, no. 874
1010 *al-Kāfī*, v. 2, p. 253, no. 9
1011 *Biḥār al-Anwār*, v. 67, p. 222, no. 29
1012 Ibid. p. 243, no. 82
1013 Ibid. p. 212, no. 16
1014 *al-Kāfī*, v. 2, p. 257, no. 23
1015 *Biḥār al-Anwār*, v. 72, p. 331, no. 14
1016 Ibid. v. 73, p. 383, no. 8
1017 *Amālī al-Ṭūsī*, p. 146, no. 240
1018 *al-Khiṣāl*, p. 8, no. 27
1019 *Tuḥaf al-'Uqūl*, p. 318
1020 *Biḥār al-Anwār*, v. 78, p. 12, no. 70
1021 *Tuḥaf al-'Uqūl*, p. 357
1022 Qur'an 2:156
1023 *Biḥār al-Anwār*, v. 77, p. 270, no. 1
1024 *Muhj al-Da'awāt*, p. 397
1025 *Biḥār al-Anwār*, v. 71, p. 34, no. 18
1026 Ibid. no. 15
1027 Qur'an 33:58
1028 *Biḥār al-Anwār*, v. 75, p. 194, no. 5
1029 *Ghurar al-Ḥikam*, no. 10455
1030 *Biḥār al-Anwār*, v. 78, p. 31, no. 99
1031 Ibid. p. 160, no. 21
1032 Ibid. v. 75, p. 194, no. 3
1033 Qur'an 3:61
1034 *al-Kāfī*, v. 2, p. 514, no. 4
1035 *Nūr al-Thaqalayn*, v. 1, p. 347, no. 157
1036 Qur'an 48:10
1037 Qur'an 48:18
1038 *Tafsīr al-Qummī*, v. 2, p. 315
1039 *Ṣaḥīḥ Muslim*, v. 3, p. 14 no. 80
1040 Qur'an 60:12
1041 *Tuḥaf al-'Uqūl*, p. 457
1042 Qur'an 16:91
1043 *al-Khiṣāl*, p. 107, no. 70
1044 *Biḥār al-Anwār*, v. 67, p. 186, no. 7
1045 *Kanz al-'Ummāl*, no. 44216
1046 *Biḥār al-Anwār*, v. 67, p. 186, no. 4
1047 *Nahj al-Balāgha*, Letter 1
1048 *al-Irshād*, v. 1, p. 260
1049 Qur'an 4:29
1050 *Wasā'il al-Shī'a*, v. 12, p. 4, no. 6
1051 *al-Kāfī*, v. 5, p. 148, no. 2
1052 Ibid. no. 1
1053 Ibid. p. 149, no. 10
1054 *Biḥār al-Anwār*, v. 103, p. 95, no. 18
1055 *Kanz al-'Ummāl*, no. 9293
1056 *al-Kāfī*, v. 5, p. 150, no. 1
1057 Qur'an 11:84,85
1058 *Biḥār al-Anwār*, v. 78, p. 54, no. 100. *Wasā'il al-Shī'a*, v. 12, p. 284, no. 1
1059 *Wasā'il al-Shī'a*, v. 12, p. 283, no. 4
1060 Ibid. p. 287, no. 4
1061 Qur'an 83:1-3
1062 *Kanz al-'Ummāl*, no. 9442
1063 *al-Kāfī*, v. 5, p. 159, no. 1
1064 *Kanz al-'Ummāl*, no. 9439
1065 Ibid. no. 9453
1066 *Wasā'il al-Shī'a*, v. 12, p. 288, no. 4
1067 *al-Khiṣāl*, p. 245, no. 103
1068 *Rabī' al-Abrār*, v. 4, p. 139
1069 *al-Kāfī*, v. 5, p. 152, no. 10
1070 Ibid. p. 154, no. 22
1071 *Wasā'il al-Shī'a*, v. 12, p. 294, no. 4
1072 *Kanz al-'Ummāl*, no. 9451
1073 Ibid. no. 10043
1074 Ibid. no. 9216
1075 Ibid. no. 9218
1076 *Biḥār al-Anwār*, v. 75, p. 211, no. 6
1077 *al-Kāfī*, v. 5, p. 162, no. 2
1078 *Amālī al-Ṣadūq*, p. 571, no. 775
1079 Qur'an 61:10,11
1080 *Biḥār al-Anwār*, v. 77, p. 106, no. 1
1081 *Tanbīh al-Khawāṭir*, v. 2, p. 120
1082 *Biḥār al-Anwār*, v. 69, p. 409, no. 122
1083 *Ghurar al-Ḥikam*, no. 3076
1084 Ibid. no. 3474
1085 Ibid. no. 8864
1086 Qur'an 24:37
1087 *Biḥār al-Anwār*, v. 103, p. 100, no. 40
1088 *Tuḥaf al-'Uqūl*, p. 223
1089 *Ghurar al-Ḥikam*, no. 8901
1090 Qur'an 42:25
1091 *'Awālī al-La'ālī*, v. 1, p. 237, no. 150
1092 *Kanz al-'Ummāl*, no. 10174
1093 *Ghurar al-Ḥikam*, no. 1355
1094 Qur'an 2:222
1095 *Biḥār al-Anwār*, v. 6, p. 21, no. 15
1096 *al-Durr al-Manthūr*, v. 1, p. 626
1097 *Kanz al-'Ummāl*, no. 10165

1098 *Tuḥaf al-'Uqūl*, p. 20
1099 *Biḥār al-Anwār*, v. 78, p. 72, no. 38
1100 Ibid. v. 94, p. 127, no. 19
1101 Qur'an 42:25
1102 *Biḥār al-Anwār*, v. 69, p. 410, no. 124
1103 Qur'an 4:18
1104 *al-Kāfī*, v. 2, p. 440, no. 2
1105 Ibid. no. 3
1106 *Biḥār al-Anwār*, v. 6, p. 23, no. 25
1107 *Kanz al-'Ummāl*, no. 10301
1108 *Ghurar al-Ḥikam*, no. 1211
1109 Ibid. 9973
1110 Qur'an 9:102
1111 *Ghurar al-Ḥikam*, no. 6334
1112 *Biḥār al-Anwār*, v. 6, p. 36, no. 56
1113 *al-Kāfī*, v. 2, p. 426, no. 2
1114 Qur'an 5:39
1115 Qur'an 20:82
1116 *Biḥār al-Anwār*, v. 78, p. 81, no. 74
1117 *al-Kāfī*, v. 2, p. 331, no. 3
1118 *Biḥār al-Anwār*, v. 77, p. 127, no. 33
1119 Qur'an 65:8
1120 *Kanz al-'Ummāl*, no. 10427
1121 *Biḥār al-Anwār*, v. 6, p. 22, no. 20
1122 Ibid. v. 77, p. 208, no. 1
1123 *Ghurar al-Ḥikam*, no. 9876
1124 *Tuḥaf al-'Uqūl*, p. 456
1125 Ibid. no. 392
1126 *Biḥār al-Anwār*, v. 73, p. 364, no. 96
1127 Ibid. v. 6, p. 28, no. 32
1128 Qur'an 25:70
1129 Prophet David (AS) is known in the Arabic tradition as Dāwūd (*ed.*)
1130 *Biḥār al-Anwār*, v. 6, p. 28, no. 30
1131 *Kanz al-'Ummāl*, no. 7902
1132 *Wasā'il al-Shī'a*, v. 11, p. 267, no. 13
1133 *Ghurar al-Ḥikam*, no. 4688
1134 Ibid. no. 4692
1135 *Nahj al-Balāgha*, Saying 368
1136 *Ghurar al-Ḥikam*, no. 4690
1137 Ibid. no. 3387
1138 Ibid. no. 4695
1139 Ibid. no. 5769
1140 *al-Kāfī*, v. 2, p. 87, no. 2
1141 *Kanz al-'Ummāl*, no. 38657
1142 *al-Malāḥim wa al-Fitan*, p. 314, no. 445
1143 *al-Ghaibah, al-Nu'māni*, p. 329
1144 *al-Tirmidhi*, v. 5, p. 382
1145 *al-Ghayba li al-Nu'mānī*, p. 318, no. 5
1146 *Biḥār al-Anwār*, v. 60, p. 213, no. 22
1147 Since Qā'im (lit. one who will rise) is from the same root as Qum (*ed.*)
1148 Ibid. p. 216, no. 38
1149 Ibid. no. 37
1150 Qur'an 17:5
1151 *Biḥār al-Anwār*, v. 60, p. 216, no. 40
1152 Ibid. v. 5, p. 13, no. 19
1153 Ibid. p. 59, no. 109
1154 Ibid. v. 78, p. 323, no. 23
1155 *al-Tawḥīd*, p. 360, no. 3
1156 *Biḥār al-Anwār*, v. 5, p. 17, no. 27
1157 Ibid. p. 4, no. 3, and p. 56, no. 99, p. 57, no. 104
1158 Ibid. p. 11, no. 17
1159 Qur'an 14:15
1160 Qur'an 11:59
1161 *al-Tawḥīd*, p. 20, no. 9
1162 *Ghurar al-Ḥikam*, no. 10587
1163 *Nahj al-Balāgha*, Sermon 216
1164 *Tanbīh al-Khawāṭir*, v. 1, p. 199
1165 *Ghurar al-Ḥikam*, no. 7697
1166 Ibid. no. 8471
1167 Ibid. no. 2695
1168 *Wasā'il al-Shī'a*, v. 11, p. 304, no. 7
1169 *Nahj al-Balāgha*, Saying 3
1170 *Ghurar al-Ḥikam*, no. 1837
1171 Ibid. no. 2582
1172 Ibid. no. 5773
1173 *Tuḥaf al-'Uqūl*, p. 225
1174 *Da'ā'im al-Islām*, v. 1, p. 342
1175 *Biḥār al-Anwār*, v. 100, p. 49, no. 16
1176 Qur'an 22:3
1177 Qur'an 40:4
1178 *Biḥār al-Anwār*, v. 2, p. 138, no. 52
1179 *al-Khiṣāl*, p. 615, no. 10
1180 Qur'an 16:125
1181 *Sharḥ Nahj al-Balāgha*, v. 20, p. 285, no. 260
1182 *Biḥār al-Anwār*, v. 2, p. 125, no. 2
1183 *Ghurar al-Ḥikam*, no. 1036
1184 *Tuḥaf al-'Uqūl*, p. 70. *Sharḥ Nahj al-Balāgha*, v. 16, p. 66
1185 *Ghurar al-Ḥikam*, no. 7016

1186 Ibid. no. 5426
1187 Ibid. no. 1717
1188 Ibid. no. 673
1189 *Biḥār al-Anwār*, v. 77, p. 420, no. 40
1190 *Ghurar al-Ḥikam*, nos. 8040, 8680
1191 *al-Khiṣāl*, p. 434, no. 20
1192 Qur'an 70:19-21
1193 *Tuḥaf al-'Uqūl*, p. 40
1194 *Biḥār al-Anwār*, v. 82, p. 144, no. 29
1195 *Ghurar al-Ḥikam*, no. 2527
1196 *Nahj al-Balāgha*, Saying 322
1197 *Musakkin al-Fu'ād*, p. 99
1198 *Tuḥaf al-'Uqūl*, p. 414
1199 Qur'an 53:31
1200 *Ghurar al-Ḥikam*, no. 6918
1201 Qur'an 12:22
1202 Qur'an 37:104-105
1203 Qur'an 20:124,127
1204 Qur'an 7:152
1205 Qur'an 7:41
1206 Qur'an 49:12
1207 *Ṣaḥīḥ Muslim*, v. 4, p. 1985, no. 28
1208 *Kanz al-'Ummāl*, nos. 31597, 15035
1209 Ibid. no. 8827
1210 *al-Kāfī*, v. 2, p. 355, no. 5
1211 *al-Tahdhīb*, v. 10, p. 48, no. 177
1212 *Biḥār al-Anwār*, v. 78, p. 253, no. 109
1213 *Sunan Abi Dawūd*, v. 2, p. 453, no. 4888
1214 *Wasā'il al-Shī'a*, v. 11, p. 44, no. 4
1215 *al-Kāfī*, v. 7, p. 431, no. 15
1216 *Biḥār al-Anwār*, v. 75, p. 469, no. 4
1217 *Makārim al-Akhlāq*, v. 1, p. 66, no. 72
1218 Qur'an 58:11
1219 *Biḥār al-Anwār*, v. 84, p. 354, no. 2
1220 Ibid. p. 16, no. 236
1221 *Qurb al-Isnād*, p. 69, no. 222
1222 *Makārim al-Akhlāq*, v. 1, p. 66, no. 71
1223 *Biḥār al-Anwār*, v. 78, p. 304, no. 1
1224 *Ghurar al-Ḥikam*, no. 10283
1225 Qur'an 4:140
1226 *Biḥār al-Anwār*, v. 10, p. 98, no. 1
1227 Ibid. v. 75, p. 468, no. 16
1228 *al-Kāfī*, v. 2, p. 378, no. 10
1229 Ibid. v. 2, p. 377, no. 8
1230 Ibid. p. 374, no. 1
1231 *Biḥār al-Anwār*, v. 77, p. 89, no. 3
1232 Ibid. v. 93, p. 163, no. 42
1233 Ibid v. 74 p. 189 no. 18
1234 Ibid. v. 75, p. 465, no. 6
1235 *Qurb al-Isnād*, p. 36, no. 117
1236 *Biḥār al-Anwār*, v. 75, p. 467, no. 17
1237 *al-Kāfī*, v. 2, p. 504, no. 4
1238 *Biḥār al-Anwār*, v. 1, p. 204, no. 22
1239 *Tuḥaf al-'Uqūl*, p. 44
1240 *Biḥār al-Anwār*, v. 74, p. 188, no. 18
1241 *Tanbīh al-Khawāṭir*, v. 2, p. 120
1242 *Ghurar al-Ḥikam*, no. 4786
1243 Ibid. no. 4787
1244 Ibid. no. 4723
1245 *Biḥār al-Anwār*, v. 78, p. 141, no. 35
1246 *al-Khiṣāl*, p. 569, no. 1
1247 *Tanbīh al-Khawāṭir*, v. 2, p. 32
1248 *Ghurar al-Ḥikam*, no. 5072
1249 *Nahj al-Balāgha*, Sermon 86
1250 *al-Kāfī*, v. 2, p. 375, no. 3
1251 *al-Uṣūl al-Sitta 'Ashar*, p. 57
1252 *Kanz al-'Ummāl*, no. 1028
1253 Ibid. no. 1032
1254 Ibid. no. 20241
1255 Ibid. no. 20242
1256 *Ma'ānī al-Akhbār*, p. 154, no. 2
1257 *Kanz al-'Ummāl*, no. 1644. *Biḥār al-Anwār*, v. 2, p. 266, no. 23
1258 *al-Khiṣāl*, v. 2, p. 383
1259*Biḥār al-Anwār*, v. 89, p. 267, no. 5
1260 Ibid. v. 104, p. 73, no. 24
1261 Ibid. v. 89, p. 283, no. 28
1262 *Thawāb al-A'māl*, p. 220, no. 1
1263 *Biḥār al-Anwār*, v. 81, p. 129, no. 18
1264 Qur'an 7:32
1265 *Kanz al-'Ummāl*, no. 17166
1266 *Makārim al-Akhlāq*, v. 1, p. 85, no. 1
1267 *Qurb al-Isnād*, p. 67, no. 215
1268 *Wasā'il al-Shī'a*, v. 3, p. 340, no. 4
1269 *Kanz al-'Ummāl*, no. 5170
1270 *'Uyūn Akhbār al-Riḍā (AS)*, v. 2, p. 74, no. 344
1271 *Biḥār al-Anwār*, v. 77, p. 59, no. 3
1272 *Ghurar al-Ḥikam*, no. 4848
1273 *Wasā'il al-Shī'a*, v. 1, p. 432, no. 2
1274 Ibid. no. 1
1275 *Tuḥaf al-'Uqūl*, p. 37

1276 *Nahj al-Sa'āda*, v. 1, p. 51
1277 *Biḥār al-Anwār*, v. 77, p. 381, no. 5
1278 Ibid. v. 71, p. 293, no. 63
1279 *A'lām al-Dīn*, p. 313
1280 Qur'an 5:6
1281 *Wasā'il al-Shī'a*, v. 1, p. 501, no. 3
1282 Ibid. p. 495, no. 1
1283 *Nahj al-Balāgha*, Letter 53
1284 Ibid. Letter 53
1285 *Ghurar al-Ḥikam*, no. 8329
1286 Ibid. no. 3932
1287 Qur'an 48:4,7
1288 Qur'an 74:31
1289 Qur'an 9:40
1290 Qur'an 3:133
1291 *Nahj al-Balāgha*, Sermon 28
1292 *Ghurar al-Ḥikam*, no. 1024
1293 Ibid. no. 397
1294 Qur'an 9:111
1295 *Biḥār al-Anwār*, v. 78, p. 13, no. 71
1296 *Ghurar al-Ḥikam*, no. 4698
1297 Ibid. no. 4700
1298 *al-Tawḥīd*, p. 21, no. 13
1299 Qur'an 4:124
1300 Qur'an 19:63
1301 *al-Kāfī*, v. 2, p. 100, no. 6
1302 Ibid. p. 300, no. 2
1303 *Tanbīh al-Khawāṭir*, v. 1, p. 272
1304 *Da'ā'im al-Islām*, v. 1, p. 219
1305 *al-Kāfī*, v. 2, p. 103, no. 2
1306 Qur'an 3:142
1307 *Ghurar al-Ḥikam*, no. 4204
1308 *al-Kāfī*, v. 2, p. 89, no. 7
1309 *Biḥār al-Anwār*, v. 78, p. 356, no. 11
1310 *Ma'ānī al-Akhbār*, p. 411, no. 99
1311 *Amālī al-Ṣadūq*, p. 150, no. 147
1312 Qur'an 5:72
1313 *al-Zuhd li al-Ḥusayn b. Sa'īd*, p. 9, no. 17
1314 *Kanz al-'Ummāl*, no. 43777
1315 *Tanbīh al-Khawāṭir*, v. 2, p. 227
1316 Qur'an 38:50
1317 *Al-Faḍā'īl*, p. 129
1318 *al-Khiṣāl*, p. 408, no. 6
1319 Qur'an 20:75
1320 *al-Khiṣāl*, p. 93, no. 39
1321 *Nahj al-Balāgha*, Sermon 85
1322 *Ghurar al-Ḥikam*, no. 3514
1323 *Biḥār al-Anwār*, v. 8, p. 133, no. 39
1324 Ibid. v. 8, p. 120, no. 11
1325 *al-Mu'jam al-Kabīr*, v. 1, p. 319, no. 950
1326 *Kanz al-'Ummāl*, no. 16636
1327 *Tanbīh al-Khawāṭir*, p. 1, no. 57
1328 *Amālī al-Ṣadūq*, p. 326, no. 383
1329 *Ghurar al-Ḥikam*, no. 5599
1330 Ibid. no. 5591
1331 Ibid. no. 5584
1332 *Kanz al-'Ummāl*, no. 10221
1333 *Biḥār al-Anwār*, v. 74, p. 308, no. 61
1334 *al-Ikhtiṣāṣ*, p. 343
1335 *Nahj al-Balāgha*, Saying 255
1336 *Ma'ānī al-Akhbār*, p. 238, no. 2
1337 *Mishkāt al-Anwār*, p. 469 no. 1675
1338 Ibid. p. 294 no. 898
1339 *Ma'ānī al-Akhbār*, p. 237, no. 1
1340 The Arabic word *jihād* lexically means struggle, fight, or combat, but has adopted a very specific meaning in Islamic terminology. When used in its general sense or as 'the lesser *jihād*', it refers to physical combat or 'holy war' against infidels, disbelievers or hypocrites who wage war against Islam and Muslims. When used in the sense of 'the greater *jihād*'- (*jihād al-nafs*) - coined by the Prophet (SAWA) in his famous tradition (see Ch.78: JIHĀD (2): The Greater Jihād), it refers to one's combat against one's own base self. In this chapter, due to want of an exact English equivalent, the word *jihād* will be left as it is (*ed.*)
1341 Qur'an 66:9
1342 Qur'an 9:24
1343 *Ṣaḥīḥ Muslim*, v. 3, p. 1517, no. 1910
1344 *Awālī al-La'ālī*, v. 1, p. 282, no. 121
1345 *Nahj al-Balāgha*, Sermon 27
1346 *Ghurar al-Ḥikam*, no. 1346
1347 *Wasā'il al-Shī'a*, v. 11, p. 9, no. 15
1348 *Biḥār al-Anwār*, v. 33, p. 447, no. 659
1349 *Sharḥ Nahj al-Balāgha*, v. 3, p. 182
1350 Qur'an 4:95
1351 *Kanz al-'Ummāl*, no. 1068
1352 *Mustadrak al-Wasā'il*, v. 11, p. 13, no. 12293
1353 *Ghurar al-Ḥikam*, no. 1347

1354 *Mustadrak al-Wasā'il,* v. 11, p. 24, no. 12333
1355 *Wasā'il al-Shī'a,* v. 11. p. 14, no. 2
1356 *Kanz al-'Ummāl*, no. 10664
1357 Ibid. no. 10791
1358 *Biḥār al-Anwār*, v. 100, p. 49, no. 23
1359 *Nahj al-Balāgha,* Letter 47
1360 *Amālī al-Ṣadūq*, p. 673, no. 906
1361 *al-Khiṣāl,* p. 232, no. 74
1362 Qur'an 8:60
1363 Qur'an 3:200
1364 *Kanz al-'Ummāl*, no. 10508
1365 Ibid. no. 10611
1366 Ibid. no. 10730
1367 *Sunan al-Tirmidhī*, v. 4, p. 175, no. 1639
1368 *Tuḥaf al-'Uqūl*, p. 243
1369 *al-Khiṣāl,* p. 620, no. 10
1370 *Kanz al-'Ummāl*, no. 11261. *Tanbīh al-Khawāṭir,* v. 1, p. 96
1371 *Ghurar al-Ḥikam*, no. 4755
1372 Ibid. no. 5406
1373 *Tuḥaf al-'Uqūl,* p. 399
1374 *Ma'ānī al-Akhbār*, p. 160, no. 1
1375 *Ghurar al-Ḥikam*, no. 3232
1376 *Tuḥaf al-'Uqūl,* p. 286
1377 *Ghurar al-Ḥikam*, no. 4761
1378 Ibid. no. 2489
1379 *Tanbīh al-Khawāṭir,* v. 2, p. 119
1380 Ibid. v. 2, p. 122
1381 Ibid.
1382 *Ghurar al-Ḥikam*, no. 4760
1383 Ibid. no. 5407
1384 Ibid. no. 4319
1385 *Nahj al-Balāgha*, Sermon 230
1386 *Ghurar al-Ḥikam*, no. 6009
1387 *al-Kāfi,* v. 8 p. 11
1388 *Amālī al-Ṣadūq*, p. 73, no. 41
1389 *al-Maḥāsin,* v. 1, p. 456, no. 1053
1390 Ibid. v. 1, p. 455, no. 1052
1391 *Ghurar al-Ḥikam*, no. 820
1392 Ibid. no. 1464
1393 Ibid. no. 930
1394 Ibid. no. 819
1395 Ibid. no. 1694
1396 *al-Durra al-Bāhira,* no. 44
1397 *Bihār al-Anwār,* v. 1, p. 160, no. 39
1398 *Tuḥaf al-'Uqūl,* p. 29
1399 *Ghurar al-Ḥikam*, no. 1809
1400 Ibid. no. 1125
1401 Ibid. no. 1285
1402 *Nahj al-Balāgha,* Saying 70
1403 *Ghurar al-Ḥikam*, no. 3864
1404 Ibid. no. 449
1405 Ibid. no. 6327
1406 *Tuḥaf al-'Uqūl,* p. 73
1407 *A'lām al-Dīn,* p. 303
1408 *al-Durra al-Bāhira,* no. 41
1409 *Ghurar al-Ḥikam*, no. 3262
1410 Ibid. no. 6371
1411 Ibid. no. 2936
1412 *Maṭālib al-Sa'ūl,* no. 55
1413 *Amālī al-Ṭūsī,* p. 56, no. 78
1414 *Ghurar al-Ḥikam,* no. 7050
1415 Ibid. no. 10187
1416 *Bihār al-Anwār,* v. 70, p. 379, no. 26
1417 *Tanbīh al-Khawāṭir,* v. 2, p. 122
1418 *Nahj al-Balagha,* Saying 384
1419 *Ghurar al-Ḥikam*, no. 5384
1420 *Ma'ānī al-Akhbār*, p. 401, no. 62
1421 *Tuḥaf al-'Uqūl*, p. 317
1422 Ibid. no. 487
1423 *Maṭālib al-Sa'ūl*, no. 57
1424 *Kashf al-Ghamma*, v. 3, p. 137
1425 Qur'an 10:39
1426 *Amālī al-Ṭūsī,* p. 494, no. 1082
1427 *Ghurar al-Ḥikam*, no. 10246
1428 Qur'an 78:21-22
1429 *Ghurar al-Ḥikam*, no. 2620
1430 Ibid. 9995
1431 Qur'an 2:24
1432 Qur'an 2:15
1433 Qur'an 69:30-32
1434 *Biḥār al-Anwār*, v. 8, p. 280, no. 1
1435 Ibid.
1436 Qur'an 88:6-7
1437 Qur'an 69:35-36
1438 *Amālī al-Ṭūsī*, p. 533, no. 1162
1439 *Biḥār al-Anwār*, v. 8, p. 280, no. 1
1440 Qur'an 56:54-55
1441 *Zaqqūm*: bitter fruit from a certain tree in Hell (*ed.*)
1442 *Biḥār al-Anwār*, v. 8, p. 302, no. 58

1443 *'Uyūn Akhbār al-Riḍā (AS)*, v. 2, p. 28, no. 20
1444 *Kanz al-'Ummāl*, no. 39507
1445 Ibid. no. 28977
1446 *al-Durr al-Manthūr*, v. 1, p. 178
1447 *Ghurar al-Ḥikam*, no. 3217
1448 Ibid. no. 3225
1449 *al-Kāfī*, v. 2, p. 310, no. 10
1450 *al-Tawḥīd*, p. 407, no. 6
1451 *Kanz al-'Ummāl*, no. 284
1452 *al-Zuhd li al-Ḥusayn b. Sa'īd*, p. 96, no. 260
1453 Qur'an 17:84
1454 *al-Kāfī*, v. 2, p. 85, no. 5
1455 *Nahj al-Balāgha*, Saying 243
1456 *Ghurar al-Ḥikam*, no. 5378
1457 Ibid. no. 8640
1458 Ibid. no. 9417
1459 Ibid. no. 5136
1460 Ibid. no. 4104
1461 Ibid. no. 5303
1462 *Ma'ānī al-Akhbār*, p. 238, no. 2
1463 *Ghurar al-Ḥikam*, no. 4716
1464 Ibid. no. 4729
1465 *al-Irshād*, v. 1, p. 303
1466 *Ghurar al-Ḥikam*, no. 330
1467 *Kashf al-Ghamma*, v. 2, p. 242
1468 *al-Nawādir al-Rāwandī*, p. 130, no. 183
1469 *Ghurar al-Ḥikam*, no. 3185
1470 *Kashf al-Ghamma*, v. 2, p. 242
1471 *Biḥār al-Anwār*, v. 78, p. 231, no. 27
1472 Qur'an 4:36
1473 *Makārim al-Akhlāq*, v. 1, p. 274, no. 834
1474 *Nahj al-Balāgha*, Letter 47
1475 *al-Kāfī*, v. 2, p. 667, no. 8
1476 *Tuḥaf al-'Uqūl*, p. 409. *al-Kāfī*, v. 2, p. 667, no. 9
1477 *al-Kāfī*, v. 2, p. 667, no. 6
1478 *'Uyūn Akhbār al-Riḍā (AS)*, v. 2, p. 24, no. 2
1479 *Tuḥaf al-'Uqūl*, p. 85
1480 *al-Kāfī*, v. 2, p. 668, no. 14
1481 *Musakkin al-Fu'ād*, no. 105
1482 *al-Khiṣāl*, p. 544, no. 20
1483 *Tuḥaf al-'Uqūl*, p. 97
1484 *Nahj al-Balāgha*, Saying 308
1485 *Ghurar al-Ḥikam*, no. 4684
1486 *Tuḥaf al-'Uqūl*, p. 316
1487 Qur'an 58:22
1488 *Ghurar al-Ḥikam*, no. 10164
1489 Ibid. no. 3124
1490 Ibid. no. 2703
1491 *'Awālī al-La'ālī*, v. 1, p. 290, no. 149
1492 *Ghurar al-Ḥikam*, no. 6314
1493 Ibid. no. 7718
1494 Ibid. no. 7851
1495 Qur'an 9:24
1496 Qur'an 2:165
1497 *Biḥār al-Anwār*, v. 98, p. 226, no. 3
1498 Ibid. v. 70, p. 25, no. 25
1499 *Jāmi' al-Akhbār*, p. 518, no. 1468
1500 *al-Kāfī*, v. 8, p. 129, no. 98
1501 *Irshād al-Qulūb*, no. 199
1502 *al-Kāfī*, v. 2, p. 82, no. 5
1503 Ibid. p. 130, no. 1
1504 Qur'an 2:195
1505 Qur'an 2:222
1506 Qur'an 3:76
1507 Qur'an 2:146
1508 Qur'an 2:159
1509 Qur'an 5:42
1510 Qur'an 61:4
1511 *al-Kāfī*, v. 2, p. 112, no. 8
1512 Ibid. p. 99, no. 30
1513 *al-Maḥāsin*, v. 1, p. 437, no. 1056
1514 Qur'an 2:190
1515 Qur'an 5:64
1516 Qur'an 6:141
1517 Qur'an 16:23
1518 *Tuḥaf al-'Uqūl*, p. 49
1519 *Amālī al-Ṣadūq*, p. 371, no. 467
1520 Qur'an 3:31
1521 *Ghurar al-Ḥikam*, no. 4066
1522 *al-Kāfī*, v. 8, p. 14, no. 1
1523 *Biḥār al-Anwār*, v. 71, p. 156, no. 74. *Kanz al-'Ummāl*, no. 1882
1524 *Kanz al-'Ummāl*, no. 1776
1525 *Amālī al-Ṣadūq*, p. 438, no. 577
1526 *al-Maḥāsin*, v. 1, p. 454, no. 1047
1527 *Tanbīh al-Khawāṭir*, v. 2, p. 122
1528 *al-Kāfī*, v. 8, p. 129, no. 98
1529 *Qaṣaṣ al-Anbiyā'*, p. 205, no. 266
1530 *Kanz al-'Ummāl*, no. 24638
1531 *'Ilal al-Sharā'i'*, p. 140, no. 1

1532 *al-Maḥāsin*, v. 1, p. 411, no. 937
1533 *al-Kāfī*, v. 2, p. 127, no. 16
1534 *Tuḥaf al-'Uqūl*, p. 455
1535 *'Ilal al-Sharā'i'*, p. 140, no. 3
1536 Ibid. p. 139, no. 1
1537 *al-Maḥāsin*, v. 1, p. 232, no. 419. *Mishkāt al-Anwār*, p. 153, no. 373
1538 *al-Da'awāt*, p. 249, no. 699
1539 Qur'an 2:256
1540 *al-Manāqib li Ibn Shahr Āshūb*, v. 4, no. 2
1541 *Wasā'il al-Shī'a*, v. 11, p. 185, no. 4
1542 *Ghurar al-Ḥikam*, no. 6191
1543 Ibid. no. 8977
1544 *Kanz al-'Ummāl*, nos. 24684-24685
1545 Ibid. no. 25553
1546 *Kitāb man lā yaḥḍurahi al-Faqīh,* v. 3, p. 31, no. 3266
1547 *Tahdhīb al-Aḥkām*, v. 10, p. 142, no. 564
1548 *al-Kāfī*, v. 7, p. 263, no. 21
1549 *Wasā'il al-Shī'a*, v. 13, p. 156, no. 1
1550 *al-Kāfī*, v. 7, p. 285, no. 1
1551 *Kitāb man lā yaḥḍurahi al-Faqīh,* v. 4, p. 115
1552 *Tahdhīb al-Aḥkām*, v. 6, p. 314, no. 870
1553 *Da'ā'im al-Islām*, v. 2, p. 539, no.1916
1554 Ibid. v. 2, p. 443, no. 1544
1555 *Kitāb man lā yaḥḍurahi al-Faqīh,* v. 3, p. 31, no. 3265
1556 *Tahdhib al-Aḥkām*, v. 10, p. 174
1557 *Sunan Abi Dawūd*, v. 3, p. 314, no. 3630
1558 Qur'an 33:59
1559 *Nahj al-Balāgha*, Letter 31
1560 *Tanbīh al-Khawāṭir*, v. 2, p. 78
1561 *Ghurar al-Ḥikam*, no. 5820
1562 Qur'an 3:97
1563 Qur'an 22:27
1564 Qur'an 2:196
1565 *Nahj al-Balāgha*, Letter 47
1566 *al-Khiṣāl*, p. 620, no. 10
1567 Ibid. p. 628, no. 10
1568 Ibid. p. 630, no. 10
1569 *Nahj al-Balāgha*, Sermon 1
1570 *Thawāb al-A'māl*, p. 70, no. 3
1571 *Amālī al-Ṭūsī*, p. 296, no. 582
1572 *Amālī al-Ṣadūq*, p. 715, no. 985. *al-Tawḥīd*, p. 253, no. 4
1573 *Biḥār al-Anwār*, v. 99. p. 45, no. 34
1574 *'Uyūn Akhbār al-Riḍā (AS)*, v. 2, p. 119, no. 1
1575 *Tuḥaf al-'Uqūl*, p. 7
1576 *al-Khiṣāl*, p. 117, no. 101
1577 *Amālī al-Ṭūsī*, p. 694, no. 1478
1578 *Thawāb al-A'māl*, p. 70, no. 4
1579 *al-Khiṣāl*, p. 616, no. 10
1580 *'Uyūn Akhbār al-Riḍā (AS)*, v. 2, p. 262, no. 29
1581 Ibid. no. 30
1582 *Biḥār al-Anwār*, v. 77, p. 58, no. 3
1583 *Thawāb al-A'māl*, p. 281, no. 1
1584 Qur'an 5:97
1585 *'Ilal al-Sharā'i'*, p. 452, no. 1
1586 *Biḥār al-Anwār*, v. 27, p. 181, no. 30
1587 Qur'an 2:197
1588 *al-Khiṣāl*, p. 148, no. 180
1589 *Iḥrām:* the state of ritual consecration of the pilgrim in Makkah *(ed.)*
1590 *al-Durr al-Manthūr*, v. 2, p. 63
1591 *Thawāb al-A'māl*, p. 74, no. 16
1592 *al-Khiṣāl*, p. 167, no. 219. *'Ilal al-Sharā'i'*, p. 235, no. 4
1593 *Wasā'il al-Shī'a*, v. 9, p. 3, no. 4
1594 *al-Kāfī*, v. 4, p. 263, no. 45
1595 *Biḥār al-Anwār*, v. 7, p. 302, no. 56
1596 *Kamāl al-Dīn*, p. 346, no. 33
1597 The word *ḥujja* in Arabic literally means: argument, proof, evidence or authority. In the context of these traditions, it refers mainly to the proofs of Allah on this earth in the form of His divine guidance through the prophets, the Imāms, and divine revelation. *(ed.)*
1598 Qur'an 17:15
1599 Qur'an 8:42
1600 *Ghurar al-Ḥikam*, no. 6781
1601 Ibid. no. 8482
1602 *al-Tawḥīd*, p. 459, no. 27
1603 Ibid. p. 410, no. 2
1604 *al-Kāfī*, v. 2, p. 400, no. 8
1605 Qur'an 6:149
1606 *Biḥār al-Anwār*, v. 2, p. 29, no. 10
1607 *al-Kāfī*, v. 1, p. 177, no. 4
1608 Qur'an 4:165
1609 *Ghurar al-Ḥikam*, no. 11004
1610 *Nahj al-Sa'āda*, v. 1, p. 347
1611 *Biḥār al-Anwār*, v. 2, p. 144, no. 5

1612 *Amālī al-Mufīd*, p. 42, no. 10
1613 *Biḥār al-Anwār*, v. 2, p. 152, no. 43
1614 *Amālī al-Ṣadūq*, p. 247, no. 266
1615 *Biḥār al-Anwār*, v. 2, p. 145, no. 9
1616 Ibid. v. 2, p. 150, no. 24
1617 Ibid. p. 156, no. 10
1618 *Kanz al-Fawā'id*, v. 2, p. 31
1619 *Biḥār al-Anwār*, v. 2, p. 160, no. 13
1620 *Ma'ānī al-Akhbār*, p. 2, no. 3
1621 *Amālī al-Ṭūsī*, p. 227, no. 398
1622 *Kanz al-'Ummāl*, no. 29255
1623 *Biḥār al-Anwār*, v. 2, p. 212, no. 114
1624 *Kanz al-'Ummāl*, no. 907
1625 *al-Kāfī*, v. 1, p. 69, no. 4
1626 *Baṣā'ir al-Darajāt*, p. 21, no. 1
1627 *Ma'ānī al-Akhbār*, p. 390, no. 30
1628 *Kanz al-'Ummāl*, no. 29179
1629 *Biḥār al-Anwār*, v. 2, p. 164, no. 24
1630 *Kanz al-'Ummāl*, no. 29284
1631 *al-Kāfī*, v. 1, p. 52, no. 7
1632 Ibid. p. 53, no. 14
1633 Qur'an 5:3
1634 *Biḥār al-Anwār*, v. 2, p. 169, no. 3
1635 *'Uyūn Akhbār al-Riḍā (AS)*, v. 1, p. 290, no. 39
1636 The Arabic word *'ḥadd (pl. ḥudūd)* is a word referring specifically to the punishments prescribed in Islamic law for various crimes. Lexically the word means 'limit, boundary, border', and refers to any such boundary. In Islamic law therefore, the same word applies to both the cause and the effect, where the transgression of Allah's boundaries and overstepping of His limits (*ḥudūd*) necessitates the meting out of due legal punishments (*ḥudūd*) set out in the Islamic penal law. In this chapter therefore, both legal punishment and boundary or limit have been used to translate the same word depending on the individual context. (*ed.*)
1637 *al-Kāfī*, v. 1, p. 59, no. 2
1638 *Kanz al-'Ummāl*, no. 12971
1639 *Kitāb man lā yaḥḍurahi al-Faqīh*, v. 4, p. 74, no. 5146. *Kanz al-'Ummāl*, no. 12972
1640 *Kanz al-'Ummāl*, no. 14599. *al-Kāfī*, v. 7, p. 174, no. 1
1641 *Mustadrak al-Wasā'il*, v. 18, p. 9, no. 21843
1642 *Da'ā'im al-Islām*, v. 2, p. 442, no. 1539
1643 *Kanz al-'Ummāl*, no. 43837
1644 *Kitāb man lā yaḥḍurahi al-Faqīh*, v. 4, p. 74, no. 5146
1645 *Da'ā'im al-Islām*, v. 2, p. 65, no. 181
1646 *Mustadrak al-Wasā'il*, v. 18, p. 24, no. 21901
1647 *al-Kāfī*, v. 7, p. 210, no. 4
1648 Qur'an 2:229
1649 *'Awāli al-La'āli*, v. 2, p. 153, no. 427
1650 *al-Kāfī*, v. 7, p. 260, no. 1. *Tahdhīb al-Aḥkām*, v. 10, p. 148, no. 587
1651 *'Ilal al-Sharā'i'*, p. 545, no. 1
1652 *Kanz al-'Ummāl*, nos. 12964, 12966, 13366, 13367
1653 *Tuḥaf al-'Uqūl*, p. 214
1654 *Tanbīh al-Khawāṭir*, v. 1, p. 116
1655 *Kanz al-'Ummāl*, no. 14002
1656 *Biḥār al-Anwār*, v. 40, p. 277
1657 *al-Ja'fariyāt*, p. 136
1658 *Ghurar al-Ḥikam*, no. 705
1659 Ibid. no. 406
1660 Ibid. no. 2674
1661 *Nahj al-Balāgha*, Sermon 27
1662 *Kanz al-'Ummāl*, nos. 11300, 11396
1663 *Nahj al-Balāgha*, Sermon 55
1664 *Sharḥ Nahj al-Balāgha li Ibn Abī al-Ḥadīd*, v. 3, p. 186
1665 *Tuḥaf al-'Uqūl*, p. 191
1666 *Qurb al-Isnād*, p. 131, no. 456
1667 *Nahj al-Balāgha*, Sermon 124
1668 Ibid. Letter 14
1669 *al-Kāfī*, v. 5, p. 28, no. 2
1670 *'Ilal al-Sharā'i'*, p. 565, no. 1
1671 *Wasā'il al-Shī'a*, v. 11, p. 102, no. 1
1672 Qur'an 8:16
1673 *Nahj al-Balāgha*, Sermon 66. and *Nahj al-Sa'āda*, v. 2, p. 232
1674 *al-Kāfī*, v. 5, p. 34, no. 1
1675 *'Uyūn Akhbār al-Riḍā (AS)*, v. 2, p. 92, no. 1
1676 *Kanz al-'Ummāl*, no. 39878
1677 *Nahj al-Balāgha*, Letter 15
1678 *al-Kāfī*, v. 5, p. 45, no. 8
1679 Qur'an 5:33

1680 *al-Ja'fariyāt*, p. 83
1681 *al-Maḥāsin*, v. 2, p. 107, no. 1289
1682 *Qurb al-Isnad*, p. 158, no. 577
1683 *al-Kāfī*, v. 7, p. 246, no. 6
1684 *Da'ā'im al-Islām*, v. 2, p. 477, no. 1714
1685 *al-Khiṣāl*, p. 284, no. 33
1686 *Nahj al-Sa'āda*, v. 1, p. 198
1687 *Ghurar al-Ḥikam*, no. 10371
1688 Ibid. no. 467
1689 Ibid. no. 3605
1690 Ibid. no. 413
1691 *al-Kāfī*, v. 2, p. 89, no. 6
1692 *Biḥār al-Anwār*, v. 73, p. 167, no. 31
1693 *Ghurar al-Ḥikam*, no. 982
1694 Ibid. no. 1107
1695 Ibid. no. 280
1696 Ibid. no. 1877
1697 Ibid. no. 1370
1698 *Amālī al-Ṣadūq*, p. 478, no. 644
1699 *Ghurar al-Ḥikam*, no. 96
1700 Ibid. no. 1753
1701 Ibid. no. 7723
1702 Ibid. no. 365
1703 *A'lām al-Dīn*, p. 428
1704 *al-Kāfī*, v. 2, p. 316, no. 7
1705 Ibid. p. 138, no. 6
1706 *'Ilal al-Sharā'i'*, p. 559, no. 1
1707 *Kanz al-'Ummāl*, no. 44095
1708 *Ghurar al-Ḥikam*, no. 6195
1709 Ibid. no. 5772
1710 *Kanz al-'Ummāl*, no. 9199
1711 *Jāmi' al-Akhbār*, p. 390, no. 1084
1712 *al-Khiṣāl*, p. 621, no. 10
1713 *Da'ā'im al-Islām*, v. 2, p. 16, no. 14
1714 *Ghurar al-Ḥikam*, no. 4069
1715 Ibid. no. 9382
1716 Ibid. no. 7595
1717 *'Uddat al-Dā'ī*, p. 141
1718 *Tanbīh al-Khawāṭir*, v. 2, p. 120
1719 *Amālī al-Ṭūsī*, p. 680, no. 1447
1720 *al-Kāfī*, v. 2, p. 81, no. 5
1721 *Thawāb al-A'māl*, p. 334, no. 1
1722 *Kanz al-'Ummāl*, no. 43113
1723 *al-Nawādir al-Rāwandī*, p. 152 no 223
1724 Qur'an 5:56
1725 *Ghurar al-Ḥikam*, no. 2828
1726 *al-Tawḥīd*, p. 166, no. 3
1727 Qur'an 58:19
1728 *al-Kāfī*, v. 1, p. 54, no. 1
1729 *Nahj al-Balāgha*, Sermon 194
1730 *Biḥār al-Anwār*, v. 71, p. 339, no. 8
1731 *Ghurar al-Ḥikam*, nos. 7913, 7914
1732 *'Uyūn Akhbār al-Riḍā (AS)*, v. 2, p. 54, no. 204
1733 *Ghurar al-Ḥikam*, no. 3367
1734 *Tuḥaf al-'Uqūl*, p. 356.
1735 Ibid. no. 90
1736 *'Awālī al-La'ālī*, v. 1, p. 292, no. 164
1737 *Ghurar al-Ḥikam*, no. 10682
1738 Ibid. no. 1915
1739 *Tuḥaf al-'Uqūl*, p. 214
1740 *Ghurar al-Ḥikam*, no. 1514
1741 Ibid. no. 1984
1742 Ibid. no. 2026
1743 Ibid. no. 1878
1744 Ibid. no. 2179
1745 *Amālī al-Ṣadūq*, p. 73, no. 41
1746 *A'lām al-Dīn*, p. 333
1747 *Ghurar al-Ḥikam*, no. 2832
1748 *Amālī al-Ṣadūq*, p. 636, no. 853
1749 *Tuḥaf al-'Uqūl*, p. 214
1750 *Ghurar al-Ḥikam*, no. 1039
1751 *al-Da'awāt*, p. 118, no. 276
1752 *A'lām al-Dīn*, p. 294
1753 *Amālī al-Ṭūsī*, p. 533, no. 1162
1754 *Tuḥaf al-'Uqūl*, p. 99
1755 *Biḥār al-Anwār*, v. 73, p. 256, no. 29
1756 *Nahj al-Balāgha*, Saying 127
1757 *Da'ā'im al-Islām*, v. 1, p. 223
1758 Qur'an 10:62
1759 *Tuḥaf al-'Uqūl*, p. 6
1760 *A'lām al-Dīn*, p. 343
1761 *Qurb al-Isnād*, p. 76, no. 244
1762 *Maṭālib al-Sa'ūl*, p. 55
1763 *Biḥār al-Anwār*, v. 77, p. 211, no. 1
1764 *al-Khiṣāl*, p. 612, no. 10
1765 *Amālī al-Ṣadūq*, p. 56, no. 12
1766 *al-Maḥāsin*, v. 2, p. 362, no. 2262
1767 *al-Da'awāt*, p. 120, no. 284
1768 *'Ilal al-Sharā'i'*, p. 93, no. 2
1769 *Biḥār al-Anwār*, v. 74, p. 227, no. 20
1770 *Makārim al-Akhlāq*, v. 2, p. 367, no. 2661

1771 *al-Kāfī*, v. 2, p. 99, no. 30
1772 *al-Tamḥīṣ*, p. 44, no. 55
1773 *al-Kāfī*, v. 2, p. 226, no. 16
1774 *A'lām al-Dīn*, p. 345
1775 *Ghurar al-Ḥikam*, no. 380
1776 Qur'an 59:18
1777 *Biḥār al-Anwār*, v. 70, p. 73, no. 26
1778 *Ghurar al-Ḥikam*, no. 6794
1779 *Tuḥaf al-'Uqūl*, p. 280
1780 *al-Ikhtiṣāṣ*, p. 26
1781 *Ghurar al-Ḥikam*, no. 8927
1782 *Biḥār al-Anwār*, v. 70, p. 73, no. 27
1783 *Ghurar al-Ḥikam*, no. 7887
1784 *'Uyūn Akhbār al-Riḍā (AS)*, v. 2, p. 62, no. 258
1785 *Amālī al-Ṣadūq*, p. 328, no. 388
1786 *Biḥār al-Anwār*, v. 7, p. 261, no. 10
1787 *Amālī al-Ṣadūq*, p. 374, no. 472
1788 *Majma' al-Bayān*, v. 10, p. 812
1789 *al-Khiṣāl*, p. 253, no. 125
1790 *Biḥār al-Anwār*, v. 7, p. 272, no. 39
1791 *A'lām al-Dīn*, p. 344
1792 *Biḥār al-Anwār*, v. 71, p. 383, no. 20
1793 Ibid. v. 74, p. 102, no. 54
1794 *al-Iḥtijāj*, v. 1, p. 572, no. 137
1795 Qur'an 13:21
1796 *Biḥār al-Anwār*, v. 7, p. 266, no. 26
1797 Qur'an 84:7-8
1798 *Ma'ānī al-Akhbār*, p. 262, no. 1
1799 Qur'an 39:10
1800 *Kanz al-'Ummāl*, no. 16635
1801 *Biḥār al-Anwār*, v. 82, p. 138, no. 22
1802 *al-Kāfī*, v. 2, p. 126, no. 8
1803 Ibid. p. 264, no. 19
1804 *Mishkāt al-Anwār*, p. 517, no. 1742
1805 *'Uyūn Akhbār al-Riḍā (AS)*, v. 2, p. 34, no. 66
1806 *Tanbīh al-Khawāṭir*, v. 1, p. 127
1807 *al-Khiṣāl*, p. 80, no. 1
1808 Qur'an 113:5
1809 Known in the Arabic tradition as 'Imrān
1810 *al-Kāfī*, v. 2, p. 307, no. 6
1811 *Ghurar al-Ḥikam*, no. 372
1812 Ibid. no. 332
1813 Ibid.no. 5242
1814 *Sharḥ Nahj al-Balāgha li Ibn Abī al-Ḥadīd*, v. 1, p. 316
1815 *Ghurar al-Ḥikam*, no. 4632
1816 Ibid. no. 1832
1817 *Biḥār al-Anwār*, v. 73, p. 256, no. 29
1818 *Kanz al-Fawā'id*, v. 1, p. 136
1819 *Ghurar al-Ḥikam*, no. 1520
1820 Ibid. no. 1017
1821 *Sharḥ Nahj al-Balāgha li Ibn Abī al-Ḥadīd*, v. 1, p. 316
1822 *al-Kāfī*, v. 2, p. 306, no. 1
1823 Ibid. v. 8, p. 8, no. 1
1824 *al-Khiṣāl*, p. 121, no. 113
1825 Qur'an 19:39
1826 Qur'an 39:56
1827 Qur'an 25:27
1828 *Kanz al-'Ummāl*, no. 14936
1829 *Nahj al-Balāgha*, Saying 429
1830 *Amālī al-Ṭūsī*, p. 663, no. 1386
1831 *Kanz al-'Ummāl*, no. 44084
1832 Qur'an 6:160
1833 *Tuḥaf al-'Uqūl*, p. 281
1834 Qur'an 2:261
1835 *Biḥār al-Anwār*, v. 71, p. 247, no. 7
1836 Qur'an 4:125
1837 *Nūr al-Thaqalayn*, v. 1, p. 553, no. 579
1838 Qur'an 17:7
1839 *Ghurar al-Ḥikam*, nos. 3808, 3809
1840 Qur'an 16:90
1841 *Tuḥaf al-'Uqūl*, p. 37
1842 *Ghurar al-Ḥikam*, no. 6112
1843 Ibid. no. 9912
1844 Ibid. no. 5450
1845 Ibid. no. 8473
1846 Ibid. no. 4339
1847 *Kanz al-Fawā'id*, v. 2, p. 31
1848 *Ghurar al-Ḥikam*, no. 3637
1849 *Kanz al-'Ummāl*, no. 16489
1850 *Biḥār al-Anwār*, v. 3, p. 80
1851 *Kanz al-'Ummāl*, no. 29336
1852 *Biḥār al-Anwār*, v. 62, p. 266, no. 39
1853 *Ghurar al-Ḥikam*, no. 966
1854 Ibid. no. 530
1855 Ibid. no. 422
1856 Ibid. no. 2203
1857 Ibid. no. 5522

1858 Ibid. no. 1962
1859 Ibid. no. 10436
1860 *Biḥār al-Anwār*, v. 78, p. 369, no. 4
1861 *Tuḥaf al-'Uqūl*, p. 488
1862 Ibid. no. 310
1863 *Biḥār al-Anwār*, v. 72, p. 47, no. 57
1864 Ibid. v. 75, p. 147, no. 21
1865 *al-Tamḥīṣ*, p. 50, no. 89
1866 *Biḥār al-Anwār*, v. 72, p. 44, no. 52
1867 *Tanbīh al-Khawāṭir*, v. 1, p. 31
1868 Ibid. v. 2, p. 122
1869 *al-Kāfī*, v. 2, p. 351, no. 5
1870 Qur'an 21:18
1871 *Ghurar al-Ḥikam*, no. 716
1872 *Nahj al-Sa'āda*, v. 3, p. 294
1873 *Tuḥaf al-'Uqūl*, p. 95
1874 *Biḥār al-Anwār*, v. 5, p. 305, no. 24
1875 Qur'an 43:78
1876 *Nahj al-Balāgha*, Saying 376
1877 *Biḥār al-Anwār*, v. 70, p. 184, no. 52
1878 *Amālī al-Ṣadūq*, p. 27, no. 41
1879 *Biḥār al-Anwār*, v. 74, p. 157, no. 2
1880 *Nahj al-Balāgha*, Sermon 125
1881 *Tuḥaf al-'Uqūl*, p. 408
1882 *Kanz al-'Ummāl*, no. 43588
1883 *Tuḥaf al-'Uqūl*, p. 88
1884 *Kanz al-'Ummāl*, no. 43152
1885 *Biḥār al-Anwār*, v. 78, p. 228, no. 105
1886 *Majma' al-Bayān*, v. 1, p. 211
1887 *Nahj al-Balāgha*, Sermon 216
1888 *Ghurar al-Ḥikam*, no. 10328
1889 *Makārim al-Akhlāq*, v. 2, p. 365, no. 2661
1890 *Nahj al-Balāgha*, Sermon 216
1891 *Ghurar al-Ḥikam*, no. 4780
1892 *Nahj al-Balāgha*, Sermon 216
1893 *al-Kāfī*, v. 2, p. 169, no. 1
1894 *Biḥār al-Anwār*, v. 74, p. 287, no. 13
1895 *al-Kāfī*, v. 2, p. 170, no. 4
1896 *al-Khiṣāl*, p. 351, no. 27
1897 *al-Kāfī*, v. 2, p. 174, no. 14
1898 Ibid. p. 169, no. 2
1899 *al-Iḥtijāj*, v. 2, p. 517, no. 340
1900 *Kanz al-'Ummāl*, no. 9738
1901 Ibid. no. 9723
1902 *Ghurar al-Ḥikam*, no. 256
1903 Ibid. no. 607
1904 Ibid. no. 112
1905 *al-Kāfī*, v. 8, p. 19, no. 4
1906 *Ghurar al-Ḥikam*, no. 9349
1907 *Nahj al-Balāgha*, Letter 53
1908 *Da'ā'im al-Islām* v. 2, p. 35, no. 78
1909 *Biḥār al-Anwār*, v. 103, p. 87, no. 3
1910 Ibid. v. 62, p. 292. *Kanz al-'Ummāl*, no. 9716
1911 *Kanz al-'Ummāl*, no. 9717
1912 Ibid. no. 9715
1913 Ibid. no. 9739
1914 *Biḥār al-Anwār*, v. 62, p. 292
1915 *Amālī al-Ṭūsī*, p. 676, no. 1427
1916 *Ghurar al-Ḥikam*, no. 465
1917 Ibid. no. 1842
1918 Qur'an 2:269
1919 *Biḥār al-Anwār*, v. 14, p. 316, no. 17
1920 Ibid. v. 13, p. 432, no. 24
1921 Ibid. v. 77, p. 172, no. 8
1922 *Kanz al-'Ummāl*, no. 44123
1923 *Ghurar al-Ḥikam*, no. 1715
1924 Ibid. no. 1992
1925 *Tuḥaf al-'Uqūl*, p. 97
1926 *Amālī al-Ṭūsī*, p. 625, no. 1290
1927 *Nahj al-Balāgha*, Saying 80
1928 *Ghurar al-Ḥikam*, no. 7499
1929 *Tuḥaf al-'Uqūl*, p. 218
1930 *Ghurar al-Ḥikam*, no. 3052
1931 Ibid. no. 9450
1932 *Biḥār al-Anwār*, v. 1, p. 215, no. 22
1933 Ibid. no. 25
1934 Ibid. v. 13, p. 417, no. 10
1935 *Kanz al-'Ummāl*, no. 5873. *Biḥār al-Anwār*, v. 78, p. 453, no. 23
1936 *Amālī al-Ṣadūq*, p. 576, no. 788
1937 *Kanz al-'Ummāl*, no. 5444
1938 *Ghurar al-Ḥikam*, no. 5258
1939 Ibid. no. 2272
1940 Ibid. no. 10916
1941 *al-Kāfī*, v. 2, p. 128, no. 1
1942 *Tanbīh al-Khawāṭir*, v. 2, p. 119
1943 *Ghurar al-Ḥikam*, no. 10573
1944 *Biḥār al-Anwār*, v. 78, p. 255, no. 129
1945 Ibid. v. 78, p. 312, no. 1
1946 Ibid. p. 370, no. 4
1947 *Ghurar al-Ḥikam*, no. 8706

1948 *Biḥār al-Anwār,* v. 78, p. 247, no. 73
1949 *Qaṣaṣ al-Anbiyā',* p. 160, no. 176
1950 *Biḥār al-Anwār,* v. 78, p. 303, no. 1
1951 Qur'an 2:224
1952 *al-Kāfī,* v. 7, p. 434, no. 1
1953 *Thawāb al-A'māl,* p. 261, no. 2
1954 Ibid. p. 270, no. 3
1955 Ibid. p. 269, no. 1
1956 *Biḥār al-Anwār,* v. 104, p. 209, no. 19
1957 *Nahj al-Balāgha,* Saying 253
1958 Qur'an 5:4
1959 Qur'an 2:168
1960 *Ghurar al-Ḥikam,* no. 6131
1961 *al-Kāfī,* v. 5, p. 161, no. 1
1962 *Kanz al-'Ummāl,* no. 30345, and many more traditions in this regard. See *Kanz al-'Ummāl,* v. 10, p. 637 and v. 1, p. 92
1963 *Biḥār al-Anwār,* v. 43, p. 70, no. 61
1964 *Ghurar al-Ḥikam,* v. 1055
1965 Ibid. no. 1420
1966 Ibid. no. 4718
1967 *al-Kāfī,* v. 2, p. 111, no. 1
1968 *Ghurar al-Ḥikam,* no. 4274
1969 Ibid. no. 6084
1970 *Nahj al-Balāgha,* Saying 460
1971 Ibid. Saying 207
1972 *Biḥār al-Anwār,* v. 77, p. 208, no. 1
1973 *Kanz al-Fawā'id,* v. 1, p. 319
1974 *Jāmi' al-Akhbār,* p. 319, no. 897
1975 *Ghurar al-Ḥikam,* no. 1776
1976 *al-Kāfī,* v. 2, p. 112, no. 6
1977 *Ghurar al-Ḥikam,* no. 1111
1978 *Biḥār al-Anwār,* v. 78, p. 102, no. 2
1979 Ibid. v. 74, p. 178, no. 21
1980 *Amālī al-Ṣadūq,* p. 478, no. 644
1981 *al-Kāfī,* v. 2, p. 112, no. 3
1982 *Ghurar al-Ḥikam,* no. 687
1983 Ibid. no. 2849
1984 *Nahj al-Sa'ada,* v. 3, p. 225
1985 *al-Ikhtiṣāṣ,* p. 221
1986 *Nahj al-Balāgha,* Saying 349
1987 *Ghurar al-Ḥikam,* no. 4520
1988 Ibid. no. 9445
1989 Ibid. no. 10251
1990 *Amālī al-Ṭūsī,* p. 613, no. 1268
1991 *Amālī al-Ṣadūq,* p. 343, no. 409
1992 *Ghurar al-Ḥikam,* no. 3089
1993 Ibid. no. 3283
1994 Ibid. no. 3343
1995 Ibid. no. 1160
1996 *Kitāb man lā yaḥḍurahi al-Faqīh,* v. 1, p. 115, no. 237
1997 *al-Khiṣāl,* p. 155, no. 194
1998 *Biḥār al-Anwār,* v. 76, p. 75, no. 19
1999 *Makārim al-Akhlāq,* v. 1, p. 125, no. 298
2000 *al-Khiṣāl,* p. 420, no. 14
2001 *Ghurar al-Ḥikam,* no. 8610
2002 *al-Kāfī,* v. 2, p. 199, no. 10
2003 *Thawāb al-A'māl,* p. 340, no. 1
2004*Biḥār al-Anwār,* v. 74, p. 315, no. 72
2005 *Amālī al-Ṭūsī,* p. 481, no. 1051
2006 *al-Kāfī,* v. 2, p. 197, no. 6
2007 *Amālī al-Ṭūsī,* p. 97, no. 147
2008 *al-Ṣafā* and *al-Marwā*: hills in Makkah. Running between them seven times is among the obligatory acts performed during the obligatory pilgrimage (*ḥajj*) (*ed.*)
2009 *Tuḥaf al-'Uqūl,* p. 303
2010 *al-Kāfī,* v. 2, p. 193, no. 1
2011 Ibid. no. 4
2012 Ibid. p. 365, no. 4
2013 *Biḥār al-Anwār,* v. 74, p. 287, no. 13
2014 *Thawāb al-A'māl,* p. 297, no. 1
2015 Ibid. p. 286, no. 2
2016 *'Uyūn Akhbār al-Riḍā (AS),* v. 2, p. 179, no. 2
2017 *Biḥār al-Anwār,* v. 78, p. 56, no. 111
2018 *Tuḥaf al-'Uqūl,* p. 278
2019 Ibid. no. 294
2020 *Amālī al-Ṭūsī,* p. 110, no. 168
2021 *Biḥār al-Anwār,* v. 2, p. 259, no. 9
2022 Ibid. v. 2, p. 260, no. 11
2023 *Nahj al-Balāgha,* Sermon 133
2024 Qur'an 21:30
2025 *Tuḥaf al-'Uqūl,* p. 370
2026 Ibid. no. 489
2027 *al-Irshād,* v. 1, p. 296
2028 *Ghurar al-Ḥikam,* no. 540
2029 *Biḥār al-Anwār,* v. 7, p. 276, no. 50
2030 *al-Kāfī,* v. 2, p. 120, no. 12
2031 *Kanz al-'Ummāl,* no. 24957

2032 *al-Ja'fariyyāt,* p. 85. *Mustadrak al-Wasā'il,* v. 8, p. 258, no. 9393
2033 *al-Kāfī,* v. 6, p. 538, no. 4. *al-Khiṣāl,* p. 618 no. 10
2034 *Kanz al-'Ummāl,* no. 43116
2035 Ibid. no. 39968
2036 Ibid. no. 39971
2037 Ibid. no. 24973
2038 Ibid. no. 24982
2039 Ibid. no. 24971
2040 Ibid. no. 39981
2041 *Makārim al-Akhlāq,* v. 1, p. 280, no. 864
2042 *Biḥār al-Anwār,* v. 77, p. 211, no. 1
2043 *Ghurar al-Ḥikam,* no. 340
2044 Ibid. no. 2900
2045 Ibid. no. 1393
2046 Ibid. no. 5527
2047 *Kanz al-'Ummāl,* no. 5757
2048 *al-Kāfī,* v. 2, p. 106, no. 5
2049 *Biḥār al-Anwār,* v. 77, p. 149, no. 75
2050 *Ghurar al-Ḥikam,* no. 6714
2051 Ibid. no. 274
2052 Ibid. no. 8650
2053 *'Uyūn Akhbār al-Riḍā (AS),* v. 2, p. 56, no. 207
2054 *Ghurar al-Ḥikam,* no. 9081
2055 *Biḥār al-Anwār,* v. 78, p. 200, no. 28
2056 *Kanz al-'Ummāl,* no. 5751
2057 *Tuḥaf al-'Uqūl,* p. 394
2058 *Ghurar al-Ḥikam,* no. 6369
2059 *Biḥār al-Anwār,* v. 71, p. 366, no. 13
2060 *Kanz al-'Ummāl,* no. 545
2061 Ibid. no. 589
2062 *Biḥār al-Anwār,* v. 70, p. 392, no. 60
2063 *'Uyūn Akhbār al-Riḍā (AS),* v. 2, p. 4, no. 8
2064 *al-Kāfī,* v. 2, p. 207, no. 1
2065 *Mustadrak al-Wasā'il,* v. 12, p. 429, no. 14524
2066 *al-Kāfī,* v. 2, p. 167, no. 9
2067 *al-Ikhtiṣāṣ,* no. 243
2068 The *Khawārij,* the *Māriqūn* and the *Ḥarūriah* are all the names for one group of people, and they were a group from the Army of Imām 'Alī (AS) who separated from him and revolted against him.
2069 Qur'an 18:103-104
2070 *Kanz al-'Ummāl,* no. 31610
2071 *Sharḥ Nahj al-Balāgha li Ibn Abī al-Ḥadīd,* v. 2, p. 278
2072 Ibid. p. 267
2073 *Nahj al-Balāgha,* Saying 323
2074 Ibid. Sermon 60
2075 Ibid. Sermon 93
2076 *Ibn Abī al-Ḥadīd* said: 'The Imām meant that the Kharijites were misled because of a misconception they had. They were searching for the truth and were relatively religious people defending their faith, although they were wrong in what they believed. As for Mu'āwiah, he was not after the truth, but he was on the wrong path and was not even defending what he wrongly believed. His own lifestyle gives evidence to this fact. Mu'āwiah was not a religious person, and hence it was not permissible for the Muslims were not permitted to defend his rulership. The Kharijites fought against Mu'āwiah, although they were not right, but they were better than him because acted upon forbidding the wrong and considered it obligatory to rise against the oppressor.
2077 Ibid. Sermon 61
2078 *Tanbīh al-Khawāṭir,* v. 2, p. 118
2079 Ibid. p. 119
2080 Qur'an 22:11
2081 *Biḥār al-Anwār,* v. 92, p. 251
2082 Qur'an 18:103-104
2083 *Nahj al-Balāgha,* Saying 430
2084 Qur'an 57:16
2085 *Irshād al-Qulūb,* p. 203
2086 *Ghurar al-Ḥikam,* no. 9945
2087 *Iqbāl al-A'māl,* v. 1, p. 174
2088 *Tuḥaf al-'Uqūl,* p. 20
2089 *Ghurar al-Ḥikam,* no. 8172
2090 Qur'an 38:20
2091 Prophet Lot (AS) is known as Lūṭ in the Arabic tradition *(ed.)*
2092 *al-Durr al-Manthūr,* v. 1, p. 282
2093 *Kanz al-'Ummāl,* no. 17974
2094 *al-Mu'jam al-Kabīr,* v. 8, p. 144, no. 7640, and p. 154, no. 7662
2095 *Sunan Abī Dāwūd,* v. 1, p. 289 no. 1106
2096 Ibid. no. 1107

2097 Qur'an, 29:48
2098 *al-Firdaws,* v. 2, p. 200, no. 2994
2099 Qur'an 46:4
2100 *al-Durr al-Manthūr,* v. 7, p. 434
2101 Ibid.
2102 *Ghurar al-Ḥikam,* no. 706
2103 *Nahj al-Balāgha,* Saying 315
2104 *Ghurar al-Ḥikam,* no. 2465
2105 Qur'an 38:82-83
2106 *Tanbīh al-Khawāṭir,* v. 2, p. 118
2107 *Ghurar al-Ḥikam,* no. 727
2108 Ibid. no. 667
2109 Ibid. no. 859
2110 Ibid. no. 860
2111 *Tanbīh al-Khawāṭir,* v. 2, p. 154
2112 *Tuḥaf al-'Uqūl,* p. 100
2113 *Biḥār al-Anwār,* v. 77, p. 288, no. 1
2114 *al-Kāfī,* v. 2, p. 16, no. 4
2115 Ibid. v. 8, p. 46, no. 8
2116 *Biḥār al-Anwār,* v. 73, p. 175, no. 15
2117 *'Uddat al-Dā'ī,* p. 194
2118 *Tafsīr al-'Ayyāshī,* v. 2, p. 353, no. 94.
2119 *Biḥār al-Anwār,* v. 77, p. 103, no. 1
2120 *Kanz al-'Ummāl,* no. 44399
2121 *Biḥār al-Anwār,* v. 8, p. 359, no. 24
2122 Ibid. v. 72, p. 304, no. 51
2123 *Ghurar al-Ḥikam,* no. 2128
2124 *al-Kāfī,* v. 2, p. 16, no. 4
2125 *Ma'ānī al-Akhbār,* p. 261 no. 1
2126 *Ghurar al-Ḥikam,* no. 5538
2127 Ibid. no. 4642
2128 Ibid. no. 6793
2129 Ibid. no. 3088
2130 *Biḥār al-Anwār,* v. 85, p. 136, no. 16
2131 *'Uyūn Akhbār al-Riḍā (AS),* v. 2, p. 69, no. 321
2132 *Ghurar al-Ḥikam,* no. 8447
2133 *Biḥār al-Anwār,* v. 70, p. 248, no. 21
2134 Qur'an, 10:19
2135 The special origination or innate nature deposited in man by Allah which calls him to his Creator (*ed.*)
2136 *Majma' al-Bayān,* v. 2, p. 543
2137 Qur'an 3:103
2138 *Kanz al-'Ummāl,* no. 929
2139 *Nahj al-Balāgha,* Sermon 127
2140 Ibid. Sermon 25
2141 Ibid. Saying 183
2142 *Ma'ānī al-Akhbār,* p. 157, no. 1
2143 Ibid. p. 154, no. 1
2144 *Nahj al-Balāgha,* Sermon 113
2145 *Biḥār al-Anwār,* v. 78, p. 81, no. 75
2146 *Kanz al-'Ummāl,* no. 15119
2147 Ibid. no. 15188
2148 *Biḥār al-Anwār,* v. 58, p. 104, no. 35
2149 *Kanz al-'Ummāl,* no. 15115
2150 *Biḥār al-Anwār,* v. 1, p. 97, no. 8
2151 Ibid. no. 7
2152 *'Uyūn Akbar al-Riḍā (AS),* v. 1, p. 262, no. 22
2153 *Biḥār al-Anwār,* v. 57, p. 73, no. 49
2154 *al-Tawḥīd,* p. 68, no. 20
2155 Qur'an 21:30
2156 *Nahj al-Balāgha,* Sermon 163
2157 *'Ilal al-Sharā'i',* p. 607, no. 81
2158 *Nahj al-Balāgha,* Sermon 109
2159 *al-Tawḥīd,* p. 277, no. 2
2160 Ibid. p. 298, no. 6
2161 Qur'an 30:30
2162 Qur'an 30:30
2163 *Al-Tawḥīd,* p. 331, no. 9
2164 *Basmala:* This phrase *Bismillāh al-Raḥmānir al-Raḥīm,* meaning 'In the Name of Allah, the all-Beneficent the all-Merciful' (*ed.*)
2165 Ibid. p. 231, no. 5
2166 Qur'an 52:36-37
2167 *al-Tawḥīd,* p. 66, no. 20
2168 Ibid. p. 290, no. 10
2169 *Nahj al-Balāgha,* Sermon 163
2170 *Sharḥ Nahj al-Balāgha li Ibn Abī al-Ḥadīd,* v. 20, p. 255
2171 *Biḥār al-Anwār,* v. 3, p. 28, no. 2
2172 Philosophy here denotes the fallacious philosophy of the atheists, not the commonly known philosophy that is used to provide demonstrations and proofs for the Existence of God (*ed.*)
2173 Ibid. p. 75
2174 Ibid. p. 78
2175 Ibid. p. 55, no. 29
2176 *al-Tawḥīd,* p. 289, no. 8
2177 *Biḥār al-Anwār,* v. 3, p. 67

2178 *Kanz al-'Ummāl,* no. 5225
2179 *al-Khiṣāl,* p. 30, no. 106
2180 *Ghurar al-Ḥikam,* no. 4857
2181 *Biḥār al-Anwār,* v. 77, p. 148, no. 71
2182 Ibid. v. 71, p. 396, no. 77
2183 Ibid. p. 395, no. 73
2184 *'Ilal al-Sharā'i',* p. 560, no. 1
2185 *al-Mu'jam al-Kabīr,* v. 1, p. 260 no. 754
2186 *al-Kāfī,* v. 2, p. 100, no. 5
2187 *'Uyūn Akhbār al-Riḍā (AS),* v. 2, p. 37, no. 98. *Biḥār al-Anwār,* v. 71, p. 383, no. 17
2188 *Biḥār al-Anwār,* v. 71, p. 385, no. 26
2189 *Amālī al-Ṭūsī,* p. 140, no. 227
2190 *Biḥār al-Anwār,* v. 71, p. 392, no. 59
2191 Ibid. p. 394, no. 63
2192 *Ghurar al-Ḥikam,* no. 3404
2193 *Ma'ānī al-Akhbār,* p. 253, no. 1
2194 *Kanz al-'Ummāl,* no. 5180
2195 *Biḥār al-Anwār,* v. 78, p. 53, no. 89
2196 *Ghurar al-Ḥikam,* no. 4712
2197 *Kanz al-'Ummāl,* no. 5217
2198 *Amālī al-Ṣadūq,* p. 290, no. 324
2199 *Ma'ānī al-Akhbār,* p. 191, no. 1
2200 Self-sacrifice: *īthār* - selflessness, the quality of unselfish concern for the welfare of others (*ed.*)
2201 *Ghurar al-Ḥikam,* no. 4953
2202 Ibid. no. 3165
2203 Ibid. no. 2983
2204 *Amālī al-Ṣadūq,* p. 378, no. 308
2205 *al-Kāfī,* v. 2, p. 100, no. 7
2206 *al-Maḥajjat al-Bayḍā',* v. 5, p. 93
2207 *al-Mu'jam al-Kabīr,* v. 1, p. 260, no. 754
2208 *Biḥār al-Anwār,* v. 71, p. 394, no. 63
2209 *Ghurar al-Ḥikam,* no. 5639
2210 Ibid. no. 8595
2211 Ibid. no. 9192
2212 Ibid. no. 8023
2213 *al-Kāfī,* v. 6, p. 309, no. 1
2214 Ibid. v. 2, p. 301, no. 1
2215 *Ghurar al-Ḥikam,* no. 3219
2216 Ibid. no. 3223
2217 *Biḥār al-Anwār,* v. 36, p. 358, no. 228
2218 *Nahj al-Balāgha,* Saying 445
2219 *Amālī al-Ṭūsī,* p. 301, no. 597
2220 *Biḥār al-Anwār,* v. 79, p. 152, no. 64
2221 *Kanz al-'Ummāl,* no. 13181
2222 *Biḥār al-Anwār,* v. 79, p. 148, no. 58
2223 *Nahj al-Balāgha,* Saying 252
2224 *'Uyūn Akhbār al-Riḍā (AS),* v. 2, p. 98, no. 2
2225 *al-Khiṣāl,* p. 632, no. 10
2226 Ibid.
2227 *Biḥār al-Anwār,* v. 79, p. 127, no. 7
2228 Ibid. v. 79, p. 150, no. 64
2229 *Thawāb al-A'māl,* p. 290, no. 5
2230 *Biḥār al-Anwār,* v. 79, p. 150, no. 64
2231 *al-Kāfī,* v. 6, p. 412, no. 2
2232 *Biḥār al-Anwār,* v. 77, p. 133, no. 43
2233 Ibid. v. 77, p. 180, no. 10
2234 Ibid. v. 70, p. 7, no. 5
2235 Ibid. v. 70, p. 393, no. 64
2236 *Ghurar al-Ḥikam,* no. 664
2237 *Amālī al-Ṭūsī,* p. 115, no. 176
2238 al-*Kāfī,* v. 2, p. 71, no. 12
2239 *Kanz al-'Ummāl,* no. 5894
2240 *Biḥār al-Anwār,* v. 70, p. 384, no. 39
2241 *al-Kāfī,* v. 2, p. 67, no. 1
2242 *Biḥār al-Anwār,* v. 75, p. 309, no. 3
2243 Ibid. v. 70, p. 392, no. 61
2244 Ibid. v. 78, p. 244, no. 54
2245 *Ghurar al-Ḥikam,* no. 10234
2246 Ibid. nos. 10161-10162
2247 Ibid. nos. 4027-4028
2248 *Kanz al-'Ummāl,* no. 5885
2249 *Biḥār al-Anwār,* v. 70, p. 379, no. 28
2250 *Ghurar al-Ḥikam,* no. 1987
2251 Ibid. no. 8036
2252 Ibid. no. 4591
2253 *Tanbīh al-Khawāṭir,* v. 2, p. 108
2254 *al-Kāfī,* v. 2. p. 64, no. 3
2255 *Biḥār al-Anwār,* v. 78, p. 366, no. 2
2256 *Kanz al-'Ummāl,* no. 5909
2257 *Biḥār al-Anwār,* v. 77, p. 126, no. 32
2258 *al-Khiṣāl,* p. 526, no. 13
2259 *Nahj al-Balāgha,* Saying 175
2260 *Ghurar al-Ḥikam,* no. 4108
2261 Ibid. no. 8955
2262 Qur'an 17:80
2263 The verse of the Throne in the Holy Qur'an, 2:255-257
2264 *Biḥār al-Anwār,* v. 76, p. 247, no. 37

2265 Ibid. v. 71, p. 174, no. 10
2266 Ibid. v. 103, p. 175, no. 3
2267 Ibid. v. 75, p. 172, no. 14
2268 *Ghurar al-Ḥikam,* no. 969
2269 *al-Ikhtiṣāṣ,* p. 231
2270 *al-Kāfī,* v. 5, p. 98, no. 2
2271 A sect of Muslims who believe in faith alone without action.
2272 *'Ilal al-Sharā'i',* p. 528, no. 7
2273 *Biḥār al-Anwār,* v. 77, p. 89, no. 3
2274 *Tuḥaf al-'Uqūl,* p. 22
2275 *Ghurar al-Ḥikam,* no. 2013
2276 *Biḥār al-Anwār,* v. 75, p. 175, no. 7
2277 Ibid. v. 78, p. 364, no. 4
2278 *Ghurar al-Ḥikam,* no. 6374
2279 Ibid. no. 9310
2280 *Nahj al-Balāgha,* Letter 26
2281 *Biḥār al-Anwār,* v. 77, p. 76, no. 3
2282 *Ghurar al-Ḥikam,* no. 6545
2283 Ibid. no. 6442
2284 Ibid. no. 8177
2285 Ibid. no. 1199
2286 *Tanbīh al-Khawāṭir,* v. 2, p. 122
2287 *Ghurar al-Ḥikam,* no. 4675
2288 Ibid. no. 4735
2289 Ibid. no. 4781
2290 *Biḥār al-Anwār,* v. 73, p. 171, no. 10
2291 *Tuḥaf al-'Uqūl,* p. 278
2292 *al-Ja'fariyyāt,* p. 230
2293 *Biḥār al-Anwār,* v. 74, p. 178, no. 17
2294 *Ghurar al-Ḥikam,* no. 4670
2295 Ibid. no. 9670
2296 Ibid. no. 2142
2297 *Nahj al-Balāgha,* Saying 94
2298 *Tuḥaf al-'Uqūl,* p. 234
2299 *Biḥār al-Anwār,* v. 77, p. 80, no. 3
2300 *Kanz al-'Ummāl,* no. 30765
2301 Ibid. no. 30763
2302 *Ghurar al-Ḥikam,* no. 4115
2303 *Biḥār al-Anwār,* v. 78, p. 292, no. 2
2304 *Kanz al-'Ummāl,* no. 28692
2305 *al-Durr al-Manthūr,* v. 3, p. 270
2306 *Kanz al-'Ummāl,* no. 28691
2307 *Biḥār al-Anwār,* v. 77, p. 165, no. 2
2308 *al-Kāfī,* v. 2, p. 142, no. 4
2309 *al-Khiṣāl,* p. 620, no. 10
2310 *al-Kāfī,* v. 2, p. 142, no. 3
2311 *al-Ikhtiṣāṣ,* p. 342
2312 *Amālī al-Ṣadūq,* p. 576, no. 788
2313 *Ghurar al-Ḥikam,* no. 5032
2314 *Biḥār al-Anwār,* v. 76, p. 292, no. 16
2315 *Nahj al-Balāgha,* Saying 422
2316 *Biḥār al-Anwār,* v. 71, p. 182, no. 37
2317 Ibid. v. 78, p. 41, no. 26
2318 Ibid. v. 77, p. 24, no. 6
2319 *Ghurar al-Ḥikam,* no. 7487
2320 *Amālī al-Ṭūsī,* p. 223, no. 385
2321 *Biḥār al-Anwār,* v. 78, p. 370, no. 4
2322 *Kanz al-'Ummāl,* no. 16052
2323 *Ṣaḥīḥ Muslim,* v. 3, p. 1506, no. 133
2324 *Biḥār al-Anwār,* v. 91, p. 265, no. 19
2325 *Ghurar al-Ḥikam,* no. 9453
2326 Ibid. no. 2346
2327 *Biḥār al-Anwār,* v. 91, p. 224, no. 4
2328 Ibid. p. 256, no. 1
2329 *Tahdhīb al-Aḥkām,* v. 3, p. 310, no. 960
2330 *al-Kāfī,* v. 3, p. 470, no. 1
2331 Ibid. v. 2, p. 117, no. 4
2332 Ibid. no. 5
2333 Ibid. p. 116, no. 1
2334 *Ghurar al-Ḥikam,* no. 4629
2335 Ibid. no. 5610
2336 Ibid. no. 8539
2337 Ibid. no. 8202
2338 *Nahj al-Balāgha,* Sermon 69
2339 Qur'an 25:77
2340 Qur'an 40:60
2341 *Biḥār al-Anwār,* v. 93, p. 300, no. 37
2342 *al-Kāfī,* v. 2, p. 468, no. 1
2343 *Amālī al-Ṭūsī,* p. 89, no. 136
2344 *Tanbīh al-Khawāṭir,* v. 2, p. 237
2345 *Biḥār al-Anwār,* v. 77, p. 204, no. 1
2346 Ibid. v. 93, p. 300, no. 37
2347 *al-Kāfī,* v. 2, p. 467, no. 8
2348 Ibid. p. 468, no. 7
2349 *Makārim al-Akhlāq,* v. 2, p. 12, no. 2008
2350 *al-Kāfī,* v. 2, p. 466, no. 3
2351 Ibid. p. 469, no. 7
2352 Ibid. p. 468, no. 5
2353 *Makārim al- Akhlāq,* v. 2, p. 7, no. 1978
2354 *al-Kāfī,* v. 2, p. 469, no. 5
2355 Ibid. p. 470, no. 8

2356 *Biḥār al-Anwār,* v. 93, p. 288, no. 3
2357 Ibid. p. 301, no. 37
2358 *Makārim al-Akhlāq,* v. 2, p. 10, no. 1992
2359 Qur'an 39:8
2360 Qur'an 27:62
2361 *Makārim al-Akhlāq,* v. 2, p. 10, no. 1991
2362 *Biḥār al-Anwār,* v. 77, p. 87, no. 3
2363 *al-Kāfī,* v. 2, p. 488, no. 1
2364 *Biḥār al-Anwār,* v. 93, p. 303, no. 39
2365 Ibid. p. 295, no. 23
2366 *Makārim al-Akhlāq,* v. 2, p. 97, no. 2275
2367 Qur'an 2:186
2368 *Kanz al-'Ummāl,* no. 3156
2369 *Ghurar al-Ḥikam,* no. 8292
2370 *Biḥār al-Anwār,* v. 78, p. 113, no. 7
2371 Ibid. v. 93, p. 368, no. 4
2372 Qur'an 2:186
2373 *Biḥār al-Anwār,* v. 93, p. 323, no. 37
2374 Qur'an 40:60
2375 *A'lām al-Dīn,* p. 269
2376 *Irshād al-Qulūb,* no. 149
2377 *Makārim al-Akhlāq,* v. 2, p. 20, no. 2045
2378 *Biḥār al-Anwār,* v. 93, p. 321, no. 31
2379 Ibid.
2380 *al-Da'awāt,* p. 30, no. 60
2381 *al-Kāfī,* v. 2, p. 473, no. 1
2382 Ibid. p. 477, no. 5
2383 *Biḥār al-Anwār,* v. 73, p. 329, no. 11
2384 *al-Khiṣāl,* p. 337, no. 40
2385 *Biḥār al-Anwār,* 75, p. 312, no. 20
2386 *Ghurar al-Ḥikam,* no. 3478
2387 *Tanbīh al-Khawāṭir,* v. 1, p. 302
2388 *al-Da'awāt,* p. 52, no. 131
2389 *Biḥār al-Anwār,* v. 93, p. 317, no. 21
2390 *al-Kāfī,* v. 2, p. 491, no. 1
2391 *Makārim al-Akhlāq,* v. 2, p. 19, no. 2040
2392 *al-Da'awāt,* p. 51, no. 127
2393 *Biḥār al-Anwār,* v. 93, p. 318, no. 23
2394 Ibid. p. 314, no. 19
2395 *Makārim al-Akhlāq,* v. 2, p. 8, no. 1981
2396 *Biḥār al-Anwār,* v. 93, p. 314, no. 20
2397 *Amāli al-Ṭusi,* p. 584, no. 1208
2398 *Makārim al-Akhlāq,* v. 2, p. 97, no. 2275
2399 *Biḥār al-Anwār,* v. 77, p. 205, no. 1
2400 *Ṣaḥiḥ ibn Ḥabban,* v. 3, p. 177, no. 896
2401 *Biḥār al-Anwār,* v. 93, p. 313, no. 17
2402 *al-Da'awāt,* p. 18, no. 7
2403 *al-Kāfī,* v. 2, p. 487, no. 2
2404 *Biḥār al-Anwār,* v. 93, p. 305, no. 1
2405 *al-Kāfī,* v. 2, p. 473, no. 1
2406 Prophet Jacob (AS) is known as Ya'qūb in the Arabic tradition (*ed.*)
2407Quran :12 :98
2408 *al-Kāfī,* v. 2, p. 477, no. 6
2409 *Biḥār al-Anwār,* v. 85, p. 321, no. 8
2410 *al-Kāfī,* v. 2, p. 475, no. 6
2411 Ibid. no. 3
2412 *al-Khiṣāl,* p. 635, no. 10
2413 *al-Kāfī,* v. 2, p. 490, no. 8. *Biḥār al-Anwār,* v. 93, p. 374, no. 16
2414 *Biḥār al-Anwār,* v. 71, p. 178, no. 24
2415 Ibid. v. 93, p. 376, no. 16
2416 *Kanz al-'Ummāl,* no. 1874
2417 *Tanbīh al-Khawāṭir,* v. 2, p. 108
2418 *Biḥār al-Anwār,* v. 43, p. 351, no. 25
2419 Ibid. v. 75, p. 110. no. 16
2420 Ibid. v. 74, p. 84, no. 94
2421 Ibid. v. 93, p. 357, no. 14
2422 Ibid. v. 93, p. 313, no. 17
2423 Ibid. p. 378, no. 21
2424 *al-Da'awāt,* p. 33. no. 75
2425 *al-Tamḥīṣ,* p. 33, no. 17
2426 *Kashf al-Maḥajja,* no. 228
2427 *Kanz al-'Ummāl,* no. 3128
2428 *Tuḥaf al-'Uqūl,* p. 280
2429 *al-Kāfī,* v. 2, p. 491, no. 9
2430 *Biḥār al-Anwār,* v. 93, p. 322, no. 36
2431 From the Arabic root da-na-wa: to be low, vile, despicable (*ed.*)
2432 From the Arabic root a-kha-ra: to be last, final; to come after (*ed.*)
2433 *'Ilal al-Sharā'i',* v. 2, no. 1
2434 *'Awālī al-La'ālī,* v. 1, p. 267, no. 66
2435 *Nahj al-Balāgha,* Sermon 156
2436 Ibid. Letter 55
2437 *Biḥār al-Anwār,* v. 73, p. 127, no. 126
2438 *Kanz al-'Ummāl,* no. 6088
2439 *al-Kāfī,* v. 2, p. 317, no. 8
2440 *Biḥār al-Anwār,* v. 73, p. 90, no. 61
2441 *Nahj al-Balāgha,* Sermon 45
2442 *Maṭālib al-Sa'ūl,* no. 52
2443 *Biḥār al-Anwār,* v. 78, p. 193, no. 7

2444 Ibid. v. 77, p. 54, no. 3
2445 Ibid. v. 73, p. 81, no. 43
2446 *Ghurar al-Ḥikam,* no. 9818
2447 *Biḥār al-Anwār,* v. 77, p. 178, no. 10
2448 *Nahj al-Balāgha,* Saying 131
2449 *Ghurar al-Ḥikam,* no. 396
2450 Ibid. no. 921
2451 Ibid. no. 1473
2452 Ibid. no. 401
2453 Ibid. no. 3
2454 *Kanz al-'Ummāl,* no. 6074
2455 *Tanbīh al-Khawāṭir,* v. 2, p. 122
2456 *Kanz al-'Ummāl,* no. 5439
2457 *al-Kāfī,* v. 2, p. 315, no. 1
2458 *Ghurar al-Ḥikam,* no. 4878
2459 Ibid. no. 4872
2460 *al-Kāfī,* v. 2, p. 320, no. 17
2461 Ibid. v. 2, p. 320, no. 16
2462 *Nahj al-Balāgha,* Saying 236
2463 Ibid. Sermon 3
2464 *Biḥār al-Anwār,* v. 40, p. 348, no. 29
2465 *Nahj al-Balāgha,* Letter 45
2466 Qur'an 3:14
2467 Qur'an 31:33
2468 *Amālī al-Ṭūsī,* p. 685, no. 1456
2469 *Biḥār al-Anwār,* v. 73, p. 118, no. 109
2470 *Nahj al-Balāgha,* Sermon 111
2471 Ibid.
2472 *Biḥār al-Anwār,* v. 78, p. 23, no. 88
2473 Ibid. v. 73, p. 108, no. 109
2474 *Nahj al-Balāgha,* Sermon 230
2475 *Amālī al-Ṭūsī,* p. 685, no. 1456
2476 *Ghurar al-Ḥikam,* no. 6413
2477 Ibid. no. 896
2478 Ibid. no. 454
2479 Qur'an 10:7-8
2480 Qur'an 18:82
2481 *Ma'ānī al-Akhbār,* p. 200, no. 1
2482 *Biḥār al-Anwār,* v. 78, p. 20, no. 79
2483 *Ghurar al-Ḥikam,* no. 2386
2484 *Biḥār al-Anwār,* v. 73, p. 88, no. 54
2485 Qur'an, 79:37-39
2486 *Biḥār al-Anwār,* v. 13, p. 422, no. 17
2487 *al-Khiṣāl,* p. 632, no. 10
2488 *Nahj al-Balāgha,* Saying 106
2489 *Kanz al-'Ummāl,* no. 6090
2490 *al-Khiṣāl,* p. 108, no. 74
2491 *Biḥār al-Anwār,* v. 73, p. 81, no. 43
2492 *al-Kāfī,* v. 2, p. 319, no. 15
2493 Qur'an 43:33-35
2494 *al-Tamḥīṣ,* p. 47, no. 73
2495 *Amālī al-Ṭūsī,* p. 531, no. 1162
2496 *Nahj al-Balāgha,* Saying 385
2497 *Biḥār al-Anwār,* v. 44, p. 365
2498 Ibid. v. 73, p. 81, no. 43
2499 *Nahj al-Balāgha,* Saying 103
2500 Ibid. Saying 251
2501 *Ghurar al-Ḥikam,* no. 5995
2502 Ibid. no. 9618
2503 Ibid. no. 4705
2504 *al-Khiṣāl,* p. 64, no. 95
2505 Prophet Solomon (AS) is known as Sulaymān in the Arabic tradition (*ed.*)
2506 *Biḥār al-Anwār,* v. 14, p. 74, no. 16
2507 Qur'an 3:148
2508 *Tārīkh Dimashq,* v. 42 p. 503
2509 *Ghurar al-Ḥikam,* no. 3750-3751
2510 *Biḥār al-Anwār,* v. 78, p. 321, no. 18
2511 Qur'an 18:45
2512 *Biḥār al-Anwār,* v. 73, p. 119, no. 110
2513 *Ghurar al-Ḥikam,* no. 9818
2514 *al-Kāfī,* v. 2, p. 133, no. 16
2515 *Biḥār al-Anwār,* v. 73, p. 126, no. 123
2516 Ibid. v. 78, p. 311, no. 1
2517 *Tuḥaf al-'Uqūl,* p. 396
2518 *Biḥār al-Anwār,* v. 78, p. 311, no. 1
2519 *al-Kāfī,* v. 1, p. 16, no. 12
2520 Qur'an 13:26
2521 *Tanbīh al-Khawāṭir,* v. 1, p. 131
2522 *al-Khiṣāl,* p. 65, no. 95
2523 *Biḥār al-Anwār,* v. 77, p. 164, no. 2
2524 *Ghurar al-Ḥikam,* no. 1802
2525 *Nahj al-Balāgha,* Sermon 203
2526 Ibid. Saying 133
2527 Ibid. Sermon 226
2528 **Translator's Note:** The word *mudāhana* in Arabic has no exact English equivalent, and can be translated with two or three English words depending on the context it is used in. It denotes 'pliability', 'flattery' or 'sycophancy'. In the text it has been translated differently in its different contexts in order to best convey the

meaning of the traditions, though the title has been kept as 'pliability' because of its most general implication.
2529 Qur'an 68:9
2530 Known as Jethro – Prophet Moses's father-in-law - in the biblical tradition (*ed.*)
2531 *Mishkāt al-Anwār,* p. 104, no. 238
2532 *Ghurar al-Ḥikam,* no. 5725
2533 Ibid. no. 9022
2534 *Biḥār al-Anwār,* v. 77, p. 291, no. 2
2535 *Nahj al-Balāgha,* Sermon 24
2536 *Ghurar al-Ḥikam,* no. 5112-5113
2537 Ibid. no. 10965
2538 *Nahj al-Balāgha,* Sermon 216
2539 *Ghurar al-Ḥikam,* no. 9574
2540 Ibid. no. 5831
2541 Ibid. no. 9360
2542 *Biḥār al-Anwār,* v. 62, p. 66, no. 15
2543 *Kanz al-'Ummāl,* no. 28088
2544 *Ghurar al-Ḥikam,* no. 7275
2545 *Biḥār al-Anwār,* v. 81, p. 211, no. 30
2546 *al-Khiṣāl,* p. 620, no. 10
2547 *al-Kāfī,* v. 8, p. 273, no. 409
2548 *Ghurar al-Ḥikam,* no. 903
2549 *Biḥār al-Anwār,* v. 62, p. 140, no. 2
2550 *al-Kāfī,* v. 8, p. 291, no. 442
2551 *Makārim al-Akhlāq,* v. 2, p. 180, no. 2468
2552 *al-Kāfī,* v. 8, p. 291, no. 443
2553 *Biḥār al-Anwār,* v. 101, p. 123, no. 18
2554 *Nahj al-Balāgha,* Letter 31
2555 *Ghurar al-Ḥikam,* no. 9209
2556 *Biḥār al-Anwār,* v. 75, p. 382, no. 47
2557 *Ghurar al-Ḥikam,* no. 8807
2558 Ibid. no. 213
2559 *Biḥār al-Anwār.* v. 77, p. 418, no. 40
2560 *Ghurar al-Ḥikam.* no. 1
2561 Ibid. no. 489
2562 *al-Kāfī,* v. 2, p. 464, no. 6
2563 *Ghurar al-Ḥikam,* no. 3924
2564 Ibid. no. 6554
2565 *al-Kāfī,* v. 2, p. 307, no. 5
2566 Ibid. p. 216, no. 2
2567 *Biḥār al-Anwār,* v. 78, p. 268, no. 183
2568 *al-Kāfī,* v. 2, p. 373, no. 4
2569 *Biḥār al-Anwār,* v. 72, p. 135, no. 19
2570 Ibid. v. 84, p. 252, no. 48
2571 *al-Kāfī,* v. 2, p. 127, no. 16
2572 *Tuḥaf al-'Uqūl,* p. 389
2573 *Kamāl al-Dīn,* p. 371, no. 5
2574 *Kanz al-'Ummāl,* no. 5418
2575 Ibid. no. 900
2576 Ibid. no. 5422
2577 Qur'an 3:85
2578 *al-Kāfī,* v. 2, p. 22, no. 11
2579 *Biḥār al-Anwār,* v. 23, p. 103, no. 11
2580 Ibid. v. 2, p. 105, no. 67
2581 *Ghurar al-Ḥikam,* no. 5861
2582 Ibid. no. 10831
2583 *Kamāl al-Dīn,* p. 352, no. 49
2584 *Ghurar al-Ḥikam,* no. 3912
2585 *Kanz al-'Ummāl,* no. 115
2586 Ibid. no. 28956
2587 *Biḥār al-Anwār,* v. 103, p. 141, no. 4
2588 *Ghurar al-Ḥikam,* no. 7105
2589 *Biḥār al-Anwār,* v. 103, p. 145, no. 21
2590 *al-Kāfī,* v. 5, p. 93, no. 3
2591 Qur'an 2:282
2592 *Biḥār al-Anwār,* v. 104, p. 301, no. 1
2593 Ibid. v. 103, p. 146, no. 3
2594 *al-Muwaṭa,* v. 2, p. 674, no. 84
2595 *Ghurar al-Ḥikam,* no. 3190
2596 Qur'an 63:9
2597 *Biḥār al-Anwār,* v. 77, p. 107, no. 1
2598 *Kanz al-'Ummāl,* no. 3931
2599 *Ghurar al-Ḥikam,* no. 670
2600 Ibid. no. 322
2601 Ibid. no. 5173
2602 Qur'an 33:41-42
2603 *al-Khiṣāl,* p. 525, no. 13
2604 *Biḥār al-Anwār,* v. 93, p. 342, no. 11
2605 *al-Kāfī,* v. 8, p. 7, no. 1
2606 The glorification of Fāṭima al-Zahrā' (AS), otherwise known as *Tasbīḥ al-Zahrā'* is composed of reciting *Allāhu Akbar* (Allah is Greater) 34 times, *Alḥamdulillāh* (Praise be to Allah) 33 times and *Subḥānallāh* (Glory be to Allah) 33 times. Usually it is recommended to recite it after every obligatory prayer (*ed.*)
2607 Ibid. v. 2, p. 500, no. 4
2608 *Kanz al-'Ummāl,* no. 1819
2609 *al-Munājāt al-Sha'bāniyya*: the intimate supplication of the month of Sha'bān recited

by Imām ʿAlī (AS) and the Imāms from his progeny (AS) during the sacred month of Shaʿbān.
2610 *Biḥār al-Anwār,* v. 94, p. 98, no. 13
2611 Ibid. p. 99, no. 13
2612 Qur'an 3:190-191
2613 *Amālī al-Ṭūsī,* p. 8, no. 8
2614 *Biḥār al-Anwār,* v. 80, p. 176, no. 21
2615 *Makārim al-Akhlāq,* v. 2, p. 373, no. 2661
2616 *Biḥār al-Anwār,* v. 81, p. 240, no. 26
2617 Ibid. v. 93, p. 153, no. 11
2618 *Ghurar al-Ḥikam,* no. 8235
2619 Ibid. no. 5159
2620 Qur'an 3:191
2621 *Amālī al-Ṭūsī,* p. 79, no. 116
2622 *Amālī al-Ṣadūq,* p. 550, no. 734
2623 Qur'an 2:152
2624 *Biḥār al-Anwār,* v. 93, p. 158, no. 31
2625 Qur'an 13:28
2626 *Kanz al-ʿUmmāl,* no. 1751
2627 *al-Firdaws,* v. 3, p. 564, no. 5768
2628 *Biḥār al-Anwār,* v. 93, p. 160, no. 39
2629 *Ghurar al-Ḥikam,* no. 8872
2630 Ibid. no. 3083
2631 Ibid. no. 8876
2632 Ibid. no. 5166
2633 Ibid. no. 6103
2634 Ibid. no. 5144
2635 *Nahj al-Balāgha,* Sermon 222
2636 *Iqbāl al-Aʿmāl,* v. 3, p. 337
2637 *Ghurar al-Ḥikam,* no. 541
2638 Ibid. no. 4040-4041
2639 Ibid. no. 5162
2640 Ibid. no. 5165
2641 Ibid. no. 835
2642 Qur'an 8:45
2643 *al-Khiṣāl,* p. 617, no. 10
2644 Ibid. p. 614, no. 10
2645 *Biḥār al-Anwār,* v. 77, p. 171, no. 7
2646 Ibid. v. 75, p. 321, no. 50
2647 *Amālī al-Ṣadūq,* p. 327, no. 384
2648 *Biḥār al-Anwār,* v. 77, p. 86, no. 3
2649 Quran 29:45
2650 *ʿUddat al-Dāʿī,* p. 283
2651 *Biḥār al-Anwār,* v. 93, p. 159, no. 33
2652 Ibid. p. 158, no. 33
2653 Ibid. v. 78, p. 357, no. 11
2654 Ibid. v. 77, p. 22, no. 6
2655 *Ghurar al-Ḥikam,* no. 7851
2656 Qur'an 63:9
2657 Qur'an 5:91
2658 *Ghurar al-Ḥikam,* no. 7520
2659 *Biḥār al-Anwār,* v. 73, p. 157, no. 2
2660 *Tanbīh al-Khawāṭir,* v. 2, p. 170
2661 *Biḥār al-Anwār,* v. 78, p. 129, no. 1
2662 Qur'an 20:124-126
2663 Qur'an 43:36
2664 Qur'an 59:19
2665 *Ghurar al-Ḥikam,* no. 8875
2666 Qur'an 7:205
2667 *Kanz al-ʿUmmāl,* no. 1771
2668 *Biḥār al-Anwār,* v. 5, p. 322, no. 7
2669 *Ghurar al-Ḥikam,* no. 362
2670 *Nahj al-Balāgha,* Saying 396
2671 *Ghurar al-Ḥikam,* no. 5580
2672 *Nahj al-Balāgha,* Sermon 215
2673 lit. 'embarking on a bare backed horse' (*ed.*)
2674 *al-Manāqib li Ibn Shahr Āshūb,* v. 4, p. 68. *Biḥār al-Anwār,* v. 44, p. 192, no. 4
2675 *Tuḥaf al-ʿUqūl,* p. 58
2676 *al-Kāfī,* v. 5, p. 63, no. 3
2677 *Mishkāt al-Anwār,* p. 430, no. 1433
2678 *Kanz al-ʿUmmāl,* no. 10504
2679 *Biḥār al-Anwār,* v. 75, p. 142, no. 2
2680 *Ghurar al-Ḥikam,* no. 2172
2681 *Tuḥaf al-ʿUqūl,* p. 201. *Sharḥ Nahj al-Balāgha,* v. 18, p. 84
2682 *Tuḥaf al-ʿUqūl,* p. 286
2683 *al-Khiṣāl,* p. 120, no. 110
2684 *Kashf al-Ghumma,* p. 21, no. 414. *Biḥār al-Anwār,* v. 78, p. 205, no. 46
2685 Qur'an 6:120
2686 Qur'an 2:81
2687 *Ghurar al-Ḥikam,* no. 1890
2688 *Nahj al-Balāgha,* Sermon 223
2689 *Tuḥaf al-ʿUqūl,* p. 204
2690 *Nahj al-Balāgha,* Saying 290
2691 *Ghurar al-Ḥikam,* no. 1522
2692 *Biḥār al-Anwār,* v. 78, p. 301, no. 1
2693 Ibid. v. 70, p. 286, no. 8
2694 *Ghurar al-Ḥikam,* no. 9811

2695 *Biḥār al-Anwār*, v. 73, p. 356, no. 67
2696 Ibid. p. 364, no. 96
2697 *Ghurar al-Ḥikam*, no. 3131
2698 *al-Kāfī*, v. 2, p. 270, no. 7
2699 Qur'an 4:48
2700 *Biḥār al-Anwār*, v. 77, p. 48, no. 3
2701 *Kanz al-'Ūmmāl*, no. 43770
2702 *Nahj al-Balāgha*, Sermon 153
2703 *al-Khiṣāl*, p. 24, no. 83
2704 *Biḥār al-Anwār*, v. 78, p. 70, no. 25
2705 Ibid. v. 46, p. 247, no. 35
2706 *Amālī al-Ṭūsī*, p. 527, no. 1162
2707 *Biḥār al-Anwār*, v. 73, p. 363, no. 93
2708 Ibid. v. 77, p. 168, no. 6
2709 *Ghurar al-Ḥikam*, no. 3141
2710 *Tuḥaf al-'Uqūl*, p. 286
2711 *Amālī al-Mufīd*, p. 157, no. 8
2712 *Biḥār al-Anwār*, v. 73, p. 353, no. 55
2713 Qur'an 4:31
2714 *Kanz al-'Ummāl*, no. 7798
2715 Ibid. no. 4325
2716 This includes apostasy as well as a mere return to one's previous state of heedlessness and complacency after having believed (*ed.*)
2717 *al-Kāfī*, v. 2, p. 277, no. 3
2718 Qur'an 3:135
2719 *Biḥār al-Anwār*, v. 73, p. 355, no. 62
2720 Ibid. v. 6, p. 32, no. 40
2721 *Ghurar al-Ḥikam*, no. 8823
2722 *Biḥār al-Anwār*, v. 78, p. 159, no. 10
2723 *al-Firdaws*, v. 2, p. 249, no. 3169
2724 *Ilal al-Sharā'i'*, p. 81, no. 1
2725 *Ma'ānī al-Akhbār*, p. 271, no. 2
2726 *Biḥār al-Anwār*, v. 73, p. 329, no. 12
2727 Ibid. p. 327, no. 10
2728 Ibid. p. 339, no. 21
2729 *al-Kāfī*, v. 2, p. 272, no. 16
2730 *Amālī al-Ṭūsī*, p. 701, no. 1498
2731 *Amālī al-Mufīd*, p. 310, no. 2
2732 Ibid. p. 237, no. 1
2733 Ibid. p. 98, no. 8
2734 al-*Ja'fariyāt*, p. 228
2735 *al-Nawādir al-Rāwandī*, p. 97, no. 49
2736 *Biḥār al-Anwār*, v. 67, p. 236, no. 54
2737 *al-Khiṣāl*, p. 236, no. 10
2738 *Biḥār al-Anwār*, v. 81, p. 177, no. 18
2739 Ibid. v. 67, p. 244, no. 83
2740 Ibid. v. 81, p. 186, no. 39
2741 *Da'ā'im al-Islām*, v. 1, p. 218
2742 *Biḥār al-Anwār*, v. 81, p. 186, no. 40
2743 *Tuḥaf al-'Uqūl*, p. 38
2744 *al-Da'awāt*, p. 120, no. 285
2745 *Biḥār al-Anwār*, v. 68, p. 146, no. 94
2746 Qur'an 11:114
2747 *Amālī al-Ṭūsī*, p. 186, no. 312
2748 *al-Kāfī*, v. 2, p. 107, no. 7
2749 *Biḥār al-Anwār*, v. 71, p. 395, no. 74
2750 *Nahj al-Balāgha*, Saying 24
2751 Qur'an 40:7
2752 *Biḥār al-Anwār*, v. 59, p. 196, no. 61
2753 *Amālī al-Ṣadūq*, p. 589, no. 814
2754 *Biḥār al-Anwār*, v. 99, p. 50, no. 46
2755 *Amālī al-Ṣadūq*, p. 131, no. 123
2756 *Amālī al-Mufīd*, p. 283, no. 8
2757 *al-Kāfī*, v. 2, p. 338, no. 1
2758 Ibid. p. 297, no. 3
2759 Ibid. no. 2
2760 Ibid. no. 1
2761 lit. 'an open heart'
2762*Nahj al-Balāgha*, Saying 176
2763 *Tuḥaf al-'Uqūl*, p. 96
2764 *Mustadrak al-Wasā'il*, v. 12, p. 173, no. 13810
2765 Qur'an 10:64
2766 *al-Kāfī*, v. 8, p. 90, no. 60
2767 *Biḥār al-Anwār*, v. 61, p. 177, no. 39
2768 *al-Kāfī*, v. 8, p. 90, no. 59
2769 *Amālī al-Ṣadūq*, p. 209, no. 232
2770 *al-Kāfī*, v. 8, p. 90, no. 61
2771 *Kanz al-'Ummāl*, no. 41392
2772 *al-Kāfī*, v. 8, p. 336, no. 530
2773 Qur'an 8:47
2774 lit. their hearts are wolves' hearts (*ed.*)
2775 *A'lām al-Dīn*, p. 295
2776 *Sijjīn*: proper name given in the Qur'an to a written record of the evildoers' deeds (*ed.*)
2777 *al-Kāfī*, v. 2, p. 295, no. 7
2778 *Munyat al-Murīd*, p. 318
2779 *'Uddat al-Dā'ī*, p. 203
2780 *Tanbīh al-Khawāṭir*, v. 1, p. 187
2781 Ibid. p. 186
2782 *Ghurar al-Ḥikam*, no. 9661

2783 *Nahj al-Balāgha*, Saying 276
2784 *Amālī al-Ṣadūq*, p. 580, no. 798
2785 *al-Kāfī*, v. 2, p. 293, no. 1
2786 *'Uddat al-Dā'ī*, p. 214
2787 *Tuḥaf al-'Uqūl*, p. 151
2788 Qur'an 18:110
2789 *Tafsīr al-Qummī*, v. 2, p. 47
2790 *Mustadrak al-Wasā'il*, v. 1, p. 107, no. 109
2791 *Biḥār al-Anwār*, v. 72, p. 301, no. 44, and *al-Zuhd li al-Ḥusayn ibn Sa'īd*, p. 63, no. 166
2792 *al-Kāfī*, v. 2, p. 295, no. 8
2793 *Kanz al-'Ummāl*, no. 5273
2794 *al-Kāfī*, v. 2, p. 297, no. 18
2795 *'Uddat al-Dā'ī*, p. 221
2796 *Biḥār al-Anwār*, v. 78, p. 81, no. 76
2797 *Ghurar al-Ḥikam*, no. 2567
2798 *Nahj al-Balāgha*, Saying 173
2799 *Ghurar al-Ḥikam*, no. 3152
2800 *Nahj al-Balāgha*, Saying 161
2801 *Ghurar al-Ḥikam*, no. 9471
2802 *Biḥār al-Anwār*, v. 75, p. 105, no. 41
2803 *Nahj al-Balāgha*, Saying 179
2804 *Amālī al-Ṭūsī*, p. 301, no. 595
2805 *Nahj al-Balāgha*, Saying 339
2806 *Kanz al-'Ummāl*, no. 915
2807 Ibid. no. 1640
2808 Ibid. no. 14110
2809 *Waq'at Ṣiffīn*, p. 95
2810 *Amālī al-Ṣadūq*, p. 511, no. 707
2811 *Kanz al-'Ummāl*, no. 31857
2812 *al-Kāfī*, v. 5, p. 147, no. 12
2813 *Tafsīr al-'Ayyāshī*, v. 1, p. 152, no. 503
2814 *Kitāb man lā yaḥḍurahi al-Faqīh*, v. 4, p. 367, no. 5762
2815 *Biḥār al-Anwār*, v. 103, p. 119, no. 24
2816 Ibid. v. 78, p. 201, no. 32
2817 Ibid. v. 103, p. 117, no. 16
2818 *Nahj al-Balāgha*, Saying 447
2819 Qur'an 2:278, 279
2820 *libā'*: colostrum (*ed.*)
2821 *al-Kāfī*, v. 5, p. 147, no. 11
2822 Qur'an 2:218
2823 *Amālī al-Mufīd*, p. 207, no. 38
2824 *Nahj al-Balāgha*, Saying 150
2825 *al-Kāfī*, v. 2, p. 68, no. 5
2826 *Ghurar al-Ḥikam*, no. 2511
2827 *al-raj'a* – the Return, is one of the fundamental beliefs in the return of those of absolutely pure faith or pure evil to the life of this world, for the restoration of justice in this world. This is to take place before the Day of Resurrection (*ed.*)
2828 *Biḥār al-Anwār*, v. 53, p. 102, no. 125
2829 Ibid. p. 62, no. 52
2830 Ibid. p. 46, no. 19
2831 Ibid. p. 39, no. 1
2832 Compassion and mercy have been used interchangeably in this section, as they both come from the same Arabic root ra-ḥa-ma. The main title 'Compassion', however, refers to human compassion and mercy, whereas the title of the following section 'Divine Mercy' refers specifically to Allah's mercy (*ed.*)
2833 Qur'an 48:29
2834 Qur'an 90:17,18
2835 *Kanz al-'Ummāl*, no. 5969
2836 Ibid. no. 5992
2837 *Amālī al-Ṣadūq*, p. 278, no. 308
2838 *Ghurar al-Ḥikam*, no. 6255
2839 *Biḥār al-Anwār*, v. 74, p. 405, no. 2
2840 *Kanz al-'Ummāl*, no. 5983
2841 *Amālī al-Mufīd*, p. 222, no. 1
2842 *Kanz al-'Ummāl*, no. 10464
2843 Ibid. no. 10407
2844 Ibid. no. 10387
2845 *Biḥār al-Anwār*, v. 78, p. 153, no. 17
2846 *Tanbīh al-Khawāṭir*, v. 2, p. 120
2847 *Ghurar al-Ḥikam*, no. 4209
2848 Ibid. no. 4343
2849 *al-Kāfī*, v. 2, p. 152, no. 15
2850 *Biḥār al-Anwār*, v. 74, p. 103, no. 61
2851 Ibid. p. 94, no. 23
2852 Ibid. p. 91, no. 15
2853 *al-Kāfī*, v. 2, p. 150, no. 4
2854 Ibid. p. 152, no. 12
2855 *Amālī al-Ṣadūq*, p. 276, no. 307
2856 *al-Kāfī*, v. 2, p. 347, no. 6
2857 *Biḥār al-Anwār*, v. 74, p. 400, no. 41
2858 Qur'an 47:22,23
2859 *Kanz al-'Ummāl*, no. 6978
2860 *al-Kāfī*, v. 2, p. 348, no. 8
2861 *Biḥār al-Anwār*, v. 74, p. 94, no. 23

2862 *Tuḥaf al-'Uqūl*, p. 57
2863 *al-Kāfī*, v. 2, p. 151, no. 9
2864 Qur'an 51:58
2865 Qur'an 17:30
2866 *Ghurar al-Ḥikam*, no. 10838
2867 *Nahj al-Balāgha*, Sermon 91
2868 Qur'an 11:6
2869 *Biḥār al-Anwār*, v. 77, p. 187, no. 10
2870 *Amālī al-Ṣadūq*, p. 399, no. 515
2871 *Nahj al-Balāgha*, Sermon 185
2872 Ibid. Sermon 91
2873 *al-Irshād*, v. 1, p. 303
2874 *Biḥār al-Anwār*, v. 78, p. 374, no. 22
2875 Ibid. v. 77, p. 68, no. 7
2876 *Amālī al-Mufīd*, p. 207, no. 39
2877 *Amālī al-Ṣadūq*, p. 56, no. 12
2878 *Biḥār al-Anwār*, v. 103, p. 34, no. 63
2879 *al-Kāfī*, v. 2, p. 74, no. 2, and *Kanz al-'Ummāl* nos. 9290,9310,9311,9312,9314,9316
2880 *Nahj al-Balāgha*, Saying 393
2881 *Biḥār al-Anwār*, v. 103, p. 33, no. 63
2882 *Makārim al-Akhlāq*, v. 2, p. 377, no. 2661
2883 *Ghurar al-Ḥikam*, no. 1408
2884 *Nahj al-Balāgha*, Letter 31
2885 *al-Kāfī*, v. 5, p. 84, no. 4
2886 *Biḥār al-Anwār*, v. 77, p. 67, no. 6
2887 *Amālī al-Ṭūsī*, p. 300, no. 593
2888 *Biḥār al-Anwār*, v. 81, p. 195, no. 52
2889 *'Uyūn Akhbār al-Riḍā (AS)*, v. 2, p. 46, no. 171
2890 *Takbīr* or proclaiming *Allāhu akbar*: Allah is the greatest
2891 *Kanz al-'Ummāl*, no. 9325
2892 *Biḥār al-Anwār*, v. 74, p. 362, no. 17
2893 *Kanz al-'Ummāl*, no. 44154
2894 *Biḥār al-Anwār*, v. 77, p. 176, no. 10
2895 Ibid. v. 74, p. 395, no. 22
2896 Ibid. v. 75, p. 172, no. 8
2897 *Nahj al-Balāgha*, Saying 137
2898 *Biḥār al-Anwār*, v. 103, p. 21, no. 18
2899 Ibid. v. 76, p. 60, no. 14
2900 Ibid. v. 96, p. 14, no. 27
2901 Ibid. v. 69, p. 408, no. 117
2902 Ibid. v. 74, p. 81, no. 84
2903 Ibid. v. 71, p. 396, no. 77
2904 *Amālī al-Ṣadūq*, p. 516, no. 707
2905 *al-Kāfī*, v. 2, p. 270, no. 8
2906 *Tuḥaf al-'Uqūl*, p. 372
2907 *Biḥār al-Anwār*, v. 103, p. 9, no. 37
2908 Ibid. p. 13, no. 59
2909 *Kanz al-'Ummāl*, no. 9200
2910 *Jāmi' al-Akhbār*, p. 389, no. 1079
2911 *Ṣirāṭ*: the Bridge extended over Hell, described as being as thin as a hair and as sharp as a sword, leading to Paradise
2912 *Jāmi' al-Akhbār*, p. 390, no. 1085
2913 Ibid. no. 1087
2914 *Biḥār al-Anwār*, v. 103, p. 13, no. 62
2915 Ibid. v. 78, p. 381, no. 1
2916 *al-Kāfī*, v. 2, p. 140, no. 3
2917 *Biḥār al-Anwār*, v. 77, p. 168, no. 4
2918 *Amālī al-Ṣadūq*, p. 576, no. 788
2919 *Biḥār al-Anwār*, v. 104, p. 274, no. 12
2920 *Kanz al-'Ummāl*, no. 15080
2921 *Nahj al-Balāgha*, Letter 79
2922 Ibid. Sermon 131
2923 Qur'an 5:42
2924 *Biḥār al-Anwār*, v. 104, p. 273, no. 5
2925 *al-Kāfī*, v. 7, p. 409, no. 2
2926 Qur'an 2:233
2927 *'Uyūn Akhbār al-Riḍā (AS)*, v. 2, p. 34, no. 69
2928 *al-Kāfī*, v. 6, p. 44, no. 10
2929 Ibid. no. 12
2930 *Biḥār al-Anwār*, v. 103, p. 323, no. 13
2931 Ibid. no. 9
2932 *Nāṣibī* (*f. Nāṣibīyya*): one who declares enmity towards the *Ahl al-Bayt* and their followers
2933 *Wasā'il al-Shī'a*, v. 15, p. 187, no. 1
2934 *Nahj al-Balāgha*, Saying 4
2935 *Biḥār al-Anwār*, v. 78, p. 106, no. 6
2936 Ibid. v. 43, p. 351, no. 25
2937 *al-Kāfī*, v. 2, p. 128, no. 4
2938 *al-Tamḥīṣ*, p. 60, no. 131
2939 *Biḥār al-Anwār*, v. 71, p. 157, no. 75
2940 Ibid. p. 139, no. 28
2941 *Ghurar al-Ḥikam*, no. 3805
2942 *Biḥār al-Anwār*, v. 71, p. 158, no. 75
2943 Ibid. v. 82, p. 142, no. 26
2944 Ibid. v. 69, p. 368, no. 4
2945 *Ghurar al-Ḥikam*, no. 410

2946 Ibid. no. 3397
2947 *Biḥār al-Anwār*, v. 71, p. 159, no. 75
2948 Ibid.
2949 Ibid. v. 78, p. 202, no. 33
2950 Ibid. v. 71, p. 139, no. 26
2951 Qur'an 3:162
2952 *Biḥār al-Anwār*, v. 82, p. 134, no. 17
2953 Ibid. v. 78, p. 81, no. 74
2954 Ibid. v. 70, p. 312, no. 11
2955 *Nahj al-Balāgha*, Sermon 183
2956 *Ghurar al-Ḥikam*, no. 5410
2957 *Biḥār al-Anwār*, v. 78, p. 136, no. 13
2958 Ibid. v. 70, p. 26, no. 29
2959 *Ghurar al-Ḥikam*, no. 6344
2960 *Amālī al-Ṭūsī*, p. 29, no. 31
2961 *Biḥār al-Anwār*, v. 71, p. 208, no. 17
2962 **Translator's Note:** The word *rifq* in Arabic has no exact English equivalent, and can be translated with two or three English words depending on the context it is used in. It denotes 'leniency', 'gentleness' or 'friendliness' when used to depict a trait or virtue, when used to describe one's attitude towards people or when used to describe Allah's leniency towards His creatures, or it can mean 'moderation' when used in an economic or practical context. In the text it has been translated differently in its different contexts in order to best convey the meaning of the traditions, though the title has been kept as 'leniency' because of its most general implication.
2963 *al-Kāfī*, v. 2, p. 119, no. 6
2964 Ibid. p. 120, no. 15
2965 *Sharḥ Nahj al-Balāgha li Ibn Abī al-Ḥadīd*, v. 6, p. 339
2966 *Amālī al-Ṣadūq*, p. 73, no. 41
2967 *Kanz al-'Ummāl*, no. 5370
2968 *Ghurar al-Ḥikam*, no. 294
2969 *al-Kāfī*, v. 2, p. 118, no. 1
2970 Ibid. p. 120, no. 11
2971 Ibid. p. 86, no. 1
2972 *Nahj al-Balāgha*, Letter 69
2973 *al-Kāfī*, v. 2, p. 119, no. 7
2974 *Ghurar al-Ḥikam*, no. 1778
2975 *Biḥār al-Anwār*, v. 78, p. 128, no. 11
2976 Khiḍr: Qur'anic prophet whose equivalent in the biblical tradition in not known (*ed.*)
2977 Ibid. v. 73, p. 386, no. 6
2978 Ibid. v. 78, p. 269, no. 109
2979 *al-Kāfī*, v. 2, p. 120, no. 16
2980 Qur'an 4:1
2981 Qur'an 50:18
2982 *Nahj al-*Balāgha, Sermon 157
2983 *al-Khiṣāl*, p. 525, no. 13. *Ma'ānī al-Akhbār*, p. 334
2984 *Ghurar al-Ḥikam*, no. 2429
2985 Ibid. no. 10947
2986 *Nahj al-*Balāgha, Sermon 76
2987 *Biḥār al-Anwār*, v. 78, p. 6, no. 58
2988 Ibid. v. 14, pp. 289 and 293, no. 14
2989 Ibid. v. 78, p. 277, no. 113
2990 *al-Kāfī*, v. 2, p. 453, no. 2
2991 Qur'an 2:185
2992 Ramaḍān comes from the Arabic root *ra-ma-ḍa*: to scorch, burn up, parch (s.th) (*ed.*)
2993 *Kanz al-'Ummāl*, no. 23688
2994 *Biḥār al-Anwār*, v. 96, p. 344, no. 8
2995 Ibid. p. 346, no. 12
2996 Ibid. p. 348, no. 14
2997 *Amālī al-Ṣadūq*, p. 154, no. 149
2998 Ibid. p. 113, no. 92
2999 *Biḥār al-Anwār*, v. 96, p. 375, no. 63
3000 Ibid. v. 74, p. 74, no. 62
3001 *'Uyūn Akhbār al-Riḍā (AS)*, v. 1, p. 295, no. 53
3002 *Amālī al-Ṣadūq*, p. 107, no. 79
3003 *Biḥār al-Anwār*, v. 96, p. 342, no. 6
3004 Qur'an 17:85
3005 *Biḥār al-Anwār*, v. 61, p. 40, no. 11
3006 Ibid. p. 34, no. 7
3007 *Kanz al-'Ummāl*, 24660
3008 *Ghurar al-Ḥikam*, no. 2057
3009 *Kanz al-'Ummāl*, no. 25560
3010 *Biḥār al-Anwār*, v. 61, p. 40, no. 10
3011 *Jāmi' al-Akhbār*, p. 488, no. 1360
3012 *Biḥār al-Anwār*, v. 61, p. 43, no. 19
3013 *Ghurar al-Ḥikam*, no. 8763
3014 Ibid. no. 1633
3015 *Nahj al-Balāgha*, Saying 371
3016 *Ghurar al-Ḥikam*, no. 1316

3017 *Mishkāt al-Anwār*, p. 74, no. 138
3018 Ibid. p. 324, no. 1026
3019 *Biḥār al-Anwār*, v. 81, p. 195, no. 52
3020 *Ṣaḥīḥ al-Bukhāri*, v. 2, p. 817, no. 2195
3021 *al-Kāfī*, v. 5, p. 260, no. 5
3022 *Qurb al-Isnād*, p. 115, no. 404
3023 *al-Kāfī*, v. 5, p. 261, no. 7
3024 *Biḥār al-Anwār*, v. 103, p. 66, no. 16
3025 Prophet Enoch (AS) is known as Idrīs in the Arabic tradition (*ed.*)
3026 *al-Wasā'il*, v. 12 p. 25, no. 3
3027 Qur'an 9:103
3028 Qur'an 2:110
3029 *Amālī al-Ṭūsī*, p. 693, no. 1474
3030 *Mishkāt al-Anwār*, p. 96, no. 212
3031 *Kitāb man lā yaḥḍurahi al-Faqīh,* v. 2, p. 7, no. 1579
3032 *Biḥār al-Anwār*, v. 96, p. 23, no. 54
3033 Ibid. v. 78, p. 60, no. 138
3034 Ibid. v. 96, p. 23, no. 56
3035 *al-Kāfī*, v. 2, p. 374, no. 2
3036 Ibid. v. 3, p. 498, no. 6
3037 *Biḥār al-Anwār*, v. 73, p. 373, no. 8
3038 Qur'an 3:180
3039 *Biḥār al-Anwār*, v. 96, p. 8, no. 3
3040 Qur'an 23:99-100
3041 *Biḥār al-Anwār*, v. 96, p. 21, no. 50
3042 Ibid. p. 12, no. 15
3043 *Thawāb al-A'māl*, p. 281, no. 7
3044 Qur'an 9:60
3045 *al-Kāfī*, v. 3, p. 501, no. 16
3046 *Zakāt*: in general Islamic terminology and specifically in Islamic jurisprudence and law, this refers to the alms-tax payable on one's wealth or property. Semantically, the word itself means 'purity' and comes from the root *zakā* (to purify, increase, augment, make thrive). Therefore *zakāt* is that which is given out from something in order to purify it and increase its worth, and the traditions in this section indicate that in addition to the *zakāt* payable on wealth, there is also a *zakāt* payable on all other bounties of Allah that He has bestowed on man, in order to purify them, increase their worth and make them thrive. In this section, therefore, the word *zakāt* has been left in the Arabic to differentiate it from the juristic term 'alms-tax' (*ed.*)
3047 *Ghurar al-Ḥikam*, no. 5448
3048 Ibid. no. 5449
3049 Ibid. no. 5453
3050 Ibid. no. 5454
3051 Ibid. no. 5455
3052 *Biḥār al-Anwār*, v. 78, p. 99, no. 1
3053 Ibid. p. 247, no. 77
3054 Ibid. p. 268, no. 182
3055 Termed *zakāt al-fiṭra*. *'Īd al-Fiṭr*: festival marking the end of the month of Ramaḍān (*ed.*)
3056 *Wasā'il al-Shī'a*, v. 6, p. 220, no. 4
3057 *Kitāb man lā yaḥḍurahi al-Faqīh,* v. 2, p. 183, no. 2085
3058 *Biḥār al-Anwār*, v. 78, p. 80, no. 66
3059 *Ghurar al-Ḥikam*, no. 3252
3060 *Tuḥaf al-'Uqūl*, p. 356
3061 *'Uyūn Akhbār al-Riḍā (AS)*, v. 2, p. 54, no. 204
3062 *Ghurar al-Ḥikam*, no. 8028
3063 *Biḥār al-Anwār*, v. 77, p. 213, no. 1
3064 *Ghurar al-Ḥikam*, no. 2093
3065 Ibid. no. 7890
3066 *'Uyūn Akhbār al-Riḍā (AS)*, v. 2, p. 53, no. 204
3067 *Ghurar al-Ḥikam*, no. 9054
3068 *Tuḥaf al-'Uqūl*, p. 85
3069 *'Uyūn Akhbār al-Riḍā (AS)*, v. 2, p. 177, no. 5
3070 Qur'an 17:32
3071 *Biḥār al-Anwār*, v. 76, p. 366, no. 30
3072 *Nahj al-Balāgha*, Saying 305
3073 *Biḥār al-Anwār*, v. 79, p. 26, no. 28
3074 Ibid. p. 24, no. 19
3075 Ibid. p. 22, no. 15
3076 Ibid. p. 23, no. 18
3077 *al-Kāfī*, v. 2, p. 374, no. 2
3078 *al-Tahdhīb*, v. 3, p. 148, no. 318
3079 *Tanbīh al-Khawāṭir*, v. 1, p. 28
3080 Ibid. p. 62
3081 *Kanz al-'Ummāl*, no. 13026
3082 *Biḥār al-Anwār*, v. 70, p. 322
3083 *Ghurar al-Ḥikam*, no. 1713
3084 *al-Kāfī*, v. 2, p. 128, no. 3

3085 *Biḥār al-Anwār*, v. 13, p. 349, no. 37
3086 Ibid. v. 73, p. 49, no. 20
3087 Qur'an 57:23
3088 *Tuḥaf al-'Uqūl*, p. 58
3089 *Biḥār al-Anwār*, v. 77, p. 172, no. 8
3090 Ibid. v. 70, p. 317, no. 23
3091 Ibid. p. 315, no. 20
3092 Ibid. v. 78, p. 37, no. 3
3093 *Nahj al-Balāgha*, Sermon 113
3094 *'Uyūn Akhbār al-Riḍā (AS)*, v. 2, p. 52, no. 199
3095 *Biḥār al-Anwār*, v. 78, p. 349, no. 6
3096 *Ghurar al-Ḥikam*, no. 3209
3097 Ibid. no. 6987
3098 *Biḥār al-Anwār*, v. 73, p. 64, no. 31
3099 Ibid. v. 78, p. 320, no. 9
3100 Ibid. p. 377, no. 3
3101 *Kanz al-'Ummāl*, no. 6060
3102 *Biḥār al-Anwār*, v. 78, p. 63, no. 155
3103 *Ghurar al-Ḥikam*, no. 2275
3104 Ibid. no. 1316
3105 *Tuḥaf al-'Uqūl*, p. 281
3106 *Biḥār al-Anwār*, v. 73, p. 49, no. 20
3107 *Amālī al-Ṣadūq*, p. 72, no. 41
3108 *Biḥār al-Anwār*, v. 78, p. 68, no. 16
3109 *Nahj al-Balāgha*, Saying 28
3110 *Ghurar al-Ḥikam*, nos. 4078-4079
3111 *Biḥār al-Anwār*, v. 78, p. 139, no. 22
3112 Ibid. p. 308, no. 1
3113 Qur'an 24:32
3114 Qur'an 30:21
3115 *Biḥār al-Anwār*, v. 103, p. 220, no. 18
3116 Ibid. p. 222, no. 40
3117 Ibid. p. 220, no. 23
3118 Ibid. p. 221, no. 34
3119 *Kanz al-'Ummāl*, no. 44403
3120 *Biḥār al-Anwār*, v. 103, p. 221, no. 25
3121 Ibid. p. 217, no. 1
3122 Ibid. p. 222, no. 38
3123 Ibid. p. 219, no. 15
3124 Ibid. p. 220, no. 19
3125 *Kanz al-'Ummāl*, no. 44448
3126 *al-Kāfī*, v. 5, p. 331, no. 2
3127 *al-Khiṣāl*, p. 141, no. 162
3128 *Biḥār al-Anwār*, v. 16, p. 223, no. 22
3129 Ibid. v. 103, p. 235, no. 19
3130 *Kanz al-'Ummāl*, no. 44590
3131 *Biḥār al-Anwār*, v. 103, p. 372, no. 3
3132 *Makārim al-Akhlāq*, v. 1, p. 446, no. 1534
3133 *Mahr*: an amount of money or property transferred by a man to his bride when they marry as his gift to her (*ed.*)
3134 *Biḥār al-Anwār*, v. 103, p. 237, no. 25
3135 *Kanz al-'Ummāl*, no. 44707
3136 *Ma'ānī al-Akhbār*, p. 152, no. 1
3137 *Kanz al-'Ummāl*, no. 44559
3138 Ibid. no. 44557
3139 *Biḥār al-Anwār*, v. 103, p. 232, no. 10
3140 Ibid. p. 237, no. 35
3141 *Kanz al-'Ummāl*, no. 44771
3142 *Biḥār al-Anwār*, v. 103, p. 246, no. 24
3143 Ibid. p. 256, no. 1
3144 Ibid. p. 253, no. 58
3145 Ibid. p. 254, no. 60
3146 *al-Kāfī*, v. 5, p. 569, no. 59
3147 *Irshād al-Qulub*, p. 175
3148 *Biḥār al-Anwār*, v. 103, p. 251, no. 49
3149 *al-Kāfī*, v. 5, p. 507, no. 4
3150 *Kanz al-'Ummāl*, no. 44435
3151 *Tanbīh al-Khawāṭir*, v. 2, p. 122
3152 *al-Maḥajjat al-Bayḍā'*, v. 3, p. 70
3153 *Wasā'il al-Shī'a*, v. 14, p. 116, no. 1
3154 *Biḥār al-Anwār*, v. 103, p. 253, no. 55
3155 *Jāmi' al-Akhbār*, p. 447, no. 1259
3156 *Thawāb al-A'māl*, p. 338, no. 1
3157 *Biḥār al-Anwār*, v. 77, p. 229, no. 2
3158 *Thawāb al-A'māl*, p. 339, no. 1
3159 *Biḥār al-Anwār*, v. 103, p. 247, no. 30
3160 *Kanz al-'Ummāl*, no. 44410
3161 Ibid. no. 44451
3162 *al-Kāfī*, v. 5, p. 327, no. 4
3163 *Biḥār al-Anwār*, v. 103, p. 240, no. 52
3164 *Kitāb man lā yaḥḍurahi al-Faqīh*, v. 3, p. 390, no. 4370
3165 *al-Kāfī*, v. 5, p. 326, no. 3
3166 *Biḥār al-Anwār*, v.104, p. 69, no. 2
3167 Ibid. v. 78, p. 136, no. 13
3168 Ibid. v. 103, p. 279, no. 2
3169 *Kanz al-'Ummāl*, no. 44617
3170 Ibid. no. 44536
3171 Ibid. no. 44532
3172 *Biḥār al-Anwār*, v. 77, p. 192, no. 11

3173 *Ghurar al-Ḥikam*, nos. 5392-5393
3174 *Biḥār al-Anwār*, v. 2, p. 144, no. 6
3175 Ibid. v. 74, p. 347, no. 8
3176 *al-Kāfī*, v. 2, p. 186, no. 2
3177 Ibid. p. 188, no. 7
3178 *Biḥār al-Anwār*, v. 74, p. 355, no. 36
3179 Ibid. p. 353, no. 26
3180 Ibid. p. 355, no. 36
3181 Ibid. v. 77, p. 237, no. 1
3182 *Ghurar al-Ḥikam*, no. 4087
3183 *Biḥār al-Anwār*, v. 100, p. 142, no. 18
3184 Ibid. p. 182, no. 4
3185 *'Ilal al-Sharā'i'*, p. 460, no. 5
3186 *Biḥār al-Anwār*, v. 100, p. 141, no. 14
3187 Ibid. v. 102, p. 31, no. 1
3188 Ibid. v. 100, p. 124, no. 34
3189 Ibid. p. 259, no. 7
3190 *Ma'ānī al-Akhbār*, p. 267, no. 1
3191 *Biḥār al-Anwār*, v. 100, p. 257, no. 1
3192 *Amālī al-Ṭūsī*, v. 55, no. 74
3193 *Thawāb al-A'māl*, p. 114, no. 21
3194 *Biḥār al-Anwār*, v. 100, p. 145, no. 34
3195 *al-Kāfī*, v. 4, p. 579, no. 1
3196 *Biḥār al-Anwār*, v. 100, p. 262, no. 14
3197 Ibid. v. 102, p. 1, no. 3
3198 *'Uyūn Akhbār al-Riḍā (AS)*, v. 2, p. 258, no. 16
3199 Ibid. p. 255, no. 2
3200 *al-Kāfī*, v. 5, p. 583, no. 3
3201 *Biḥār al-Anwār*, v. 102, p. 59, no. 1
3202 Ibid. p. 267, no. 5
3203 Ibid. p. 265, no. 3
3204 *Thawāb al-A'māl*, p. 124, no. 1
3205 *Biḥār al-Anwār*, v. 74, p. 354, no. 29
3206 *al-Khiṣāl*, p. 618, no. 10
3207 *Biḥār al-Anwār*, v. 102, p. 296, no. 6
3208 Ibid. v. 78, p. 71, no. 35
3209 Qur'an 7:31
3210 Qur'an 7:32
3211 *Biḥār al-Anwār*, v. 79, p. 307, no. 23
3212 Ibid. p. 298, no. 3
3213 Ibid. v. 71, p. 237, no. 2
3214 *Ghurar al-Ḥikam*, no. 3470
3215 Ibid. no. 9489
3216 Ibid. no. 5503
3217 Ibid. no. 5504
3218 Qur'an 15: 92, 93
3219 *Nahj al-Balāgha*, Sermon 167
3220 *Ṣaḥīḥ Muslim*, v. 3, p. 1459, no. 20
3221 *Ghurar al-Ḥikam*, no. 7254
3222 *Kitāb man lā yaḥḍurahi al-Faqīh*, v. 1, p. 80, no. 177
3223 Qur'an 16:43
3224 *Tuḥaf al-'Uqūl*, p. 41
3225 *Kanz al-'Ummāl*, no. 29260
3226 Ibid. no. 29262
3227 *Nahj al-Balāgha*, Saying 320
3228 Qur'an 5:101
3229 *Kanz al-'Ummāl*, no. 916
3230 *Makārim al-Akhlāq*, v. 2, p. 364, no. 2661
3231 *al-Maḥāsin*, v. 1, p. 328, no. 664
3232 *Nahj al-Balāgha*, Saying 85
3233 *Biḥār al-Anwār*, v. 2, p. 117, no. 15
3234 *al-Kāfī*, v. 1, p. 42, no. 5
3235 Qur'an 2:273
3236 *Kitāb man lā yaḥḍurahi al-Faqīh*, v. 4, p. 375, no. 5762
3237 *Kanz al-'Ummāl*, no. 17142
3238 *Jāmi' al-Akhbār*, p. 379, no. 1061
3239 *Ghurar al-Ḥikam*, no. 7993
3240 *Biḥār al-Anwār*, v. 96, p. 152, no. 16
3241 *Tuḥaf al-'Uqūl*, p. 279
3242 *Wasā'il al-Shī'a*, v. 6, p. 309, no. 15
3243 *Biḥār al-Anwār*, v. 96, p. 156, no. 29
3244 Ibid. p. 158, no. 37
3245 Ibid. p. 155, no. 26
3246 *al-Kāfī*, v. 2, p. 138, no. 2
3247 *Biḥār al-Anwār*, v. 96, p. 158, no. 37
3248 Ibid. v. 96, p. 160, no. 38
3249 *Nahj al-Balāgha*, Saying 346
3250 Ibid. Saying 66
3251 *A'lām al-Dīn*, p. 304
3252 *Tuḥaf al-'Uqūl*, p. 321
3253 Qur'an 93:10
3254 *Biḥār al-Anwār*, v. 96, p. 158, no. 37
3255 *al-Nawādir al-Rāwandī*, p. 86, no. 9
3256 *Tuḥaf al-'Uqūl*, p. 172
3257 *Nahj al-Balāgha*, Saying 67
3258 *Kashf al-Ghamma*, v. 2, p. 244
3259 *Tuḥaf al-'Uqūl*, p. 300

3260 *'Uyūn Akhbār al-Riḍā (AS)*, v. 2, p. 179, no. 2
3261 *'Uddat al-Dā'ī*, p. 91
3262 *Biḥār al-Anwār*, v. 96, p. 159, no. 37
3263 *Kanz al-'Ummāl*, no. 8093
3264 *Biḥār al-Anwār*, v. 75, p. 148, no. 6
3265 Qur'an 6:108
3266*Kanz al-'Ummāl*, no. 2120
3267 *al-Kāfī*, v. 2, p. 360, no. 3
3268 *Amālī al-Mufīd*, p. 118, no. 2
3269 *Tuḥaf al-'Uqūl*, p. 412
3270 *A'lām al-Dīn*, p. 305
3271 *Biḥār al-Anwār*, v.74, p. 46, no. 6
3272 *Musnad Ibn Ḥanbal*, v. 1 p. 309
3273 *'Ilal al-Sharā'i'*, p. 577, no. 1
3274 *Ghurar al-Ḥikam*, no. 10888
3275 *al-Da'awāt*, p. 33, no. 70
3276 *Biḥār al-Anwār*, v. 85, p. 131, no. 6
3277 Ibid. p. 164, no. 12
3278 *al-Khiṣāl*, p. 616, no. 10
3279 *Amālī al-Ṭūsī*, p. 664, no. 1389
3280 *Biḥār al-Anwār*, v. 85, p. 137, no. 17
3281 Qur'an 48:29
3282 *Biḥār al-Anwār*, v. 71, p. 344, no. 4
3283 *'Ilal al-Sharā'i'*, p. 233, no. 1
3284 *Biḥār al-Anwār*, v. 85, p. 153, no. 14
3285 Qur'an 72:18
3286 *Amālī al-Ṣadūq*, p. 440, no. 584
3287 Qur'an 9:18
3288 *Makārim al-Akhlāq*, v. 2, p. 374, no. 2661
3289 *al-Kāfī*, v. 3, p. 368, no. 1
3290 *Biḥār al-Anwār*, v. 76, p. 336, no. 1
3291 Ibid. v. 77, p. 85, no. 3
3292 Ibid. v. 83, p. 379, no. 47
3293 *dhirā'*: cubit – unit of measurement between 0.6 and 0.8 metres (*ed.*)
3294 *al-Khiṣāl*, p. 544, no. 20
3295 *Biḥār al-Anwār*, v. 84, p. 9, no. 83
3296 *Amālī al-Ṣadūq*, p. 509, no. 707
3297 *Kanz al-'Ummāl*, no. 15926
3298 Ibid. no. 16204
3299 *Biḥār al-Anwār*, v. 72, p. 193, no. 9
3300 Ibid. v. 78, p. 7, no. 59
3301 *Ghurar al-Ḥikam*, no. 2145
3302 Ibid. no. 306
3303 Ibid. no. 1600
3304 *Biḥār al-Anwār*, v. 71, p. 355, no. 17
3305 Ibid. p. 350, no. 3
3306 Sāmirī: one of the Israelites accompanying Prophet Moses after he had delivered them from Pharaoh. He led the Israelites to take a golden calf for an idol during Moses's absence (*ed.*)
3307 *al-Kāfī*, v. 4, p. 41, no. 13
3308 *Biḥār al-Anwār*, v. 73, p. 308, no. 37
3309 *Kanz al-'Ummāl*, no. 16212
3310 *Biḥār al-Anwār*, v. 73, p. 307, no. 34
3311 Ibid. v. 71, p. 352, no. 8
3312 Qur'an 17:29
3313 *Biḥār al-Anwār*, v. 77, p. 112, no. 2
3314 *Ghurar al-Ḥikam*, no. 1928
3315 *Biḥār al-Anwār*, v. 71, p. 353, no. 11
3316 Ibid. p. 357, no. 21
3317 Ibid. v. 69, p. 407, no. 115
3318 *Nahj al-Balāgha*, Saying 162
3319 Ibid. Saying 48
3320 *Ghurar al-Ḥikam*, no. 5630
3321 *Nahj al-Balāgha*, Saying 6
3322 *Ghurar al-Ḥikam*, no. 7197
3323 Ibid. no. 2463
3324 Ibid. no. 3284
3325 *Biḥār al-Anwār*, v. 77, p. 269, no. 1
3326 *Tuḥaf al-'Uqūl*, p. 315
3327 *Biḥār al-Anwār*, v. 75, p. 71, no. 15
3328 Qur'an 72:26,27
3329 *Biḥār al-Anwār*, v. 75, p. 68, no. 2
3330 Ibid. p. 71, no. 13
3331 *Ghurar al-Ḥikam*, no. 10265
3332 Ibid. no. 10166
3333 Ibid. no. 2306
3334 *Biḥār al-Anwār*, v. 77, p. 235, no. 3
3335 *Ghurar al-Ḥikam*, no. 8941
3336 *Biḥār al-Anwār*, v. 75, p. 69, no. 4
3337 *Nahj al-Balāgha*, Letter 22
3338 *Biḥār al-Anwār*, v. 78, p. 7, no. 59
3339 *Maṭālib al-Sa'ūl*, no. 50
3340 *Kanz al-'Ummāl*, no. 6008
3341 Ibid. no. 6009
3342 *Nahj al-Balāgha*, Saying 257
3343 *al-Kāfī*, v. 2, p. 189, no. 6
3344 Ibid. p. 188, no. 1
3345 Ibid. p. 199, no. 3

3346 Ibid. p. 190, no. 8
3347 Ibid. p. 200, no. 4
3348 Qur'an 7:31
3349 *Ghurar al-Ḥikam*, no. 10092
3350 *Biḥār al-Anwār*, v. 72, p. 192, no. 9
3351 *al-Saḥīfat al-Sajjādiyya*, Supplication 20
3352 *Tuḥaf al-'Uqūl*, p. 22
3353 *Kanz al-'Ummāl*, no. 7366
3354 *Nahj al-Balāgha*, Sermon 126
3355 *Biḥār al-Anwār*, v. 79, p. 317, no. 1
3356 *al-Durra al-Bāhira*, p. 43,
3357 *al-Kāfī*, v. 4, p. 56, no. 10
3358 *Biḥār al-Anwār*, v. 77, p. 105, no. 2
3359 Ibid. v. 75, p. 303, no. 6
3360 Ibid. v. 79, p. 317, no. 1
3361 Qur'an 5:38
3362 *Nūr al-Thaqalayn*, v. 1, p. 627, no. 183
3363 *Ṣaḥīḥ Muslim*, v. 3, p. 1312, no. 2
3364 *al-Kāfī*, v. 7, p. 226, no. 7
3365 Ibid. no. 6
3366 *Wasā'il al-Shī'a*, v. 18, p. 510, no. 5
3367 *'Ilal al-Sharā'i'*, p. 535, no. 1
3368 *al-Kāfī*, v. 7, p. 231, no. 2
3369 *Tahdhīb al-Aḥkām*, v. 10, p. 122, no. 489
3370 *Amālī al-Ṭūsī*, p. 426, no. 953
3371 *Ghurar al-Ḥikam*, no. 1293
3372 *Tuḥaf al-'Uqūl*, p. 364
3373 *Ghurar al-Ḥikam*, no. 2479
3374 Ibid. no. 4717
3375 Ibid. no. 6489
3376 Ibid. no. 7887
3377 Ibid. nos. 8246-8247
3378 *al-Nawādir al-Rāwandī*, p. 110, no. 93
3379 *Ghurar al-Ḥikam*, no. 5083
3380 Ibid. no. 9296
3381 *Ma'ānī al-Akhbār*, p. 345, no. 1
3382 *Ghurar al-Ḥikam*, no. 6223
3383 *Biḥār al-Anwār*, v. 74, p. 185, no. 2
3384 *Ghurar al-Ḥikam*, no. 3218
3385 *Waq'at Ṣiffīn*, p. 108
3386 *Ghurar al-Ḥikam*, no. 3297
3387 Ibid. no. 3100
3388 *Kanz al-'Ummāl*, no. 17470
3389 *Biḥār al-Anwār*, v. 76, p. 222, no. 7
3390 *al-Maḥāsin*, v. 2, p. 461, no. 2595
3391 *al-Kāfī*, v. 6, p. 326, no. 7
3392 *Kanz al-'Ummāl*, no. 17550
3393 *Makārim al-Akhlāq*, v. 1, p. 536, no. 1866
3394 *Biḥār al-Anwār*, v. 76, p. 283, no. 2
3395 *Nahj al-Balāgha*, Letter 31
3396 *Biḥār al-Anwār*, v. 76, p. 267 no. 8
3397 Ibid. v. 100, p. 103, no. 5
3398 Ibid. v. 76, p. 271, no. 28
3399 *Amālī al-Mufīd*, p. 44, no. 3
3400 *Biḥār al-Anwār*, v. 10, p. 108, no. 1
3401 Ibid. v. 76, p. 222, no. 9
3402 *Kanz al-'Ummāl*, no. 16380
3403 Ibid. no. 16377
3404 *al-Kāfī*, v. 2, p. 201, no. 5
3405 *Biḥār al-Anwār*, v. 96, p. 172, no. 8
3406 Ibid. p. 173, no. 13
3407 Ibid. p. 172, no. 8
3408 Ibid. v. 75, p. 455, no. 24
3409 *Kanz al-'Ummāl*, no. 13139
3410 *Biḥār al-Anwār*, v. 79, p. 131, no. 20
3411 Qur'an 2:18
3412 *Makārim al-Akhlāq*, v. 2, p. 352, no. 266
3413 *Biḥār al-Anwār*, v. 10, p. 114, no. 1
3414 *Ghurar al-Ḥikam*, no. 10948
3415 Ibid. no. 5651
3416 *al-Kāfī*, v. 6, p. 526, no. 7
3417 Ibid. no. 6
3418 *Nahj al-Balāgha*, Sermon 114
3419 *al-Kāfī*, v. 6, p. 531, no. 7
3420 *al-Maḥāsin*, v. 2, p. 446, no. 2531
3421 *Kanz al-'Ummāl*, no. 5440
3422 Ibid. no. 5441
3423 *Sunan Abī Dāwūd*, v. 3, p. 13, no. 2513
3424 Qur'an 4:102
3425 *Biḥār al-Anwār*, v. 100, p. 9, no. 10
3426 *Kanz al-'Ummāl*, no. 10482
3427 *al-Kāfī*, v. 5, p. 7, no. 7
3428 *Kitāb man lā yaḥḍurahu al-Faqīh*, v. 4, p. 356, no. 5762
3429 *Biḥār al-Anwār*, v. 10, p. 368, no. 7
3430 Ibid. v. 75, p. 371, no. 13
3431 Ibid. p. 372, no. 19
3432 *Nahj al-Balāgha*, Saying 263
3433 *Biḥār al-Anwār*, v. 77, p. 215, no. 1
3434 Ibid. v. 76, p. 360, no. 30
3435 *Amālī al-Ṣadūq*, p. 513, no. 707

3436*Thawāb al-A'māl*, p. 294
3437 *Kanz al-'Ummāl*, no. 14589
3438 *Nahj al-Balāgha*, Saying 332
3439 Ibid. Sermon 169
3440 Qur'an 3:19
3441 Qur'an 3:85
3442 *Kitāb man lā yaḥḍurahi al-Faqīh*, v. 4, p. 334, no. 5719
3443 *al-Kāfī*, v. 2, p. 461, no. 2
3444 *Nahj al-Balāgha*, Saying 371
3445 Ibid. Sermon 198
3446 Ibid. Sermon 106
3447 *Kanz al-'Ummāl*, no. 17
3448 Ibid. no. 5225
3449 *Nahj al-Balāgha*, Saying 125
3450 *Ghurar al-Ḥikam*, nos. 6349-6350
3451 *Kanz al-'Ummāl*, no. 745
3452 Ibid. no. 747
3453 Ibid. no. 742
3454 *al-Kāfī*, v. 2, p. 163, no. 1
3455 *Ghurar al-Ḥikam*, no. 4742
3456 Ibid. no. 9220
3457 *Ma'ānī al-Akhbār*, p. 239, no. 1
3458 *al-Maḥāsin*, v. 1, p. 445, no. 1031
3459 *Kanz al-'Ummāl*, no. 37631
3460 *Tuḥaf al-'Uqūl*, p. 196
3461 *Amālī al-Mufīd*, p. 353, no. 4
3462 *al-Kāfī*, v. 1, p. 200, no. 1
3463 Qur'an 10:10
3464 *Kanz al-'Ummāl*, no. 25242
3465 *Amālī al-Ṭūsī*, p. 89, no. 136
3466 *al-Khiṣāl*, p. 181, no. 246
3467 *al-Maḥāsin*, v. 2, p. 143, no. 1371
3468 *Jāmi' al-Akhbār*, p. 231, no. 596
3469 *al-Khiṣāl*, p. 19, no. 67
3470 *Biḥār al-Anwār*, v. 76, p. 12, no. 50
3471 *Kanz al-'Ummāl*, no. 25265
3472 *Biḥār al-Anwār*, v. 76, p. 11, no. 46
3473 Qur'an 24:61
3474 *Biḥār al-Anwār*, v. 76, p. 7, no. 25
3475 Qur'an 4:86
3476 *Kanz al-'Ummāl*, no. 25294
3477 Ibid. no. 25321
3478 *Biḥār al-Anwār*, v. 76, p. 10, no. 38
3479 Ibid. p. 9, no. 35
3480 *al-Kāfī*, v. 5, p. 535, no. 3
3481 Qur'an 4:65
3482 *Biḥār al-Anwār*, v. 82, p. 136, no. 22
3483 Ibid. v. 71, p. 153, no. 63
3484 Ibid. v. 46, p. 301, no. 44
3485 Ibid. v. 2, p. 205, no. 91
3486 *Tanbīh al-Khawāṭir*, v. 2, p. 185, no. 7
3487 *Biḥār al-Anwār*, v. 93, p. 190, no. 25
3488 *Ghurar al-Ḥikam*, no. 4090
3489 *Nahj al-Balāgha*, Sermon 105
3490 Qur'an 67:10
3491 *Nahj al-Balāgha*, Sermon 88
3492 *Ghurar al-Ḥikam*, no. 6234
3493 Ibid. no. 5579
3494 Ibid. no. 9243
3495 Qur'an 17:36
3496 Qur'an 4:140
3497 *Kitāb man lā yaḥḍurahi al-Faqīh*, v. 2, p. 626, no. 3215
3498 *al-Kāfī*, v. 6, p. 19, no. 10
3499 *Makārim al-Akhlāq*, v. 1, p. 474, no. 1626
3500 *Tafsīr al-'Ayyāshī*, v. 1, p. 168, no. 28
3501 *al-Kāfī*, v. 6, p. 18, no. 3
3502 *Biḥār al-Anwār*, v. 104, p. 127, no. 4
3503 Qur'an 27:30
3504 *Kanz al-'Ummāl*, no. 2490
3505 Ibid. no. 2491
3506 *al-Kāfī*, v. 2, p. 672, no. 1
3507 *al-Tawḥīd*, p. 231, no. 5
3508 *Biḥār al-Anwār*, v. 14, p. 113, no. 5
3509 *Kanz al-'Ummāl*, no. 911
3510 *al-Kāfī*, v. 1, p. 70, no. 7
3511 *Kanz al-'Ummāl*, no. 43079
3512 *Nahj al-Balāgha*, Letter 53
3513 *Biḥār al-Anwār*, v. 76, p. 178, no. 3
3514 Ibid. p. 179, no. 5
3515 *Ghurar al-Ḥikam*, p. 666
3516 Ibid. no. 5613
3517 Ibid. no. 3149
3518 *Nahj al-Balāgha*, Sermon 83
3519 *Thawāb al-A'māl*, v. 1, p. 102, no. 2
3520 *Biḥār al-Anwār*, v. 97, p. 88, no. 15
3521 *Kanz al-'Ummāl*, no. 17517
3522 *Biḥār al-Anwār*, v. 72, p. 194, no. 14
3523 *Nahj al-Balāgha*, Saying 224
3524 *Biḥār al-Anwār*, v. 78, p. 82, no. 82

3525 *Ghurar al-Ḥikam*, no. 6559
3526 *Biḥār al-Anwār*, v. 1, p. 94, no. 23
3527 Ibid. v. 78, p. 113, no. 7
3528 *Ghurar al-Ḥikam*, no. 9813
3529 *al-Khiṣāl*, p. 434, no. 20
3530 Ibid. p. 271, no. 10
3531 *Ghurar al-Ḥikam*, no. 17
3532 Ibid. no. 3931
3533 Ibid. no. 4820
3534 Ibid. no. 4818
3535 Ibid. no. 4821
3536 Ibid. no. 5571
3537 Ibid. no. 9714
3538 Ibid. no. 5266
3539 Ibid. no. 772
3540 Ibid. no. 8013
3541 Ibid. no. 5588
3542 Ibid. no. 9333
3543 *Biḥār al-Anwār*, v. 77, p. 75, no. 3
3544 Ibid. v. 73, p. 75, no. 39
3545 *Nahj al-Balāgha*, Saying 285
3546 Ibid. Saying 150
3547 *Biḥār al-Anwār*, v. 98, p. 88, no. 2
3548 Ibid. v. 78, p. 164, no. 1
3549 Ibid. v. 73, p. 365, no. 97
3550 *al-sūq*: market, marketplace – refers to any such public centre for commerce and trade
3551 *Kanz al-'Ummāl*, no. 9330
3552 *Tafsir al-Qūrṭabi*, v. 13, p.16
3553 *Biḥār al-Anwār*, v. 84, p. 11, no. 87
3554 Ibid. v. 103, p. 102, no. 44
3555 *al-Kāfī*, v. 3, p. 22, no. 1
3556 *Biḥār al-Anwār*, v. 77, p. 69, no. 8
3557 Ibid. v. 76, p. 137, no. 48
3558 *Kanz al-'Ummāl*, no. 26200
3559 Ibid. no. 2753
3560 *Biḥār al-Anwār*, v. 76, p. 126, no. 2
3561 Ibid. p. 128, no. 11
3562 This is part of a longer tradition where the Imām cites several other categories of people whom he excludes from the banner of humanity for their various faults, in accordance with the verse of the Qur'an (25:44): *"Do you suppose that most of them listen or apply reason? They are just like cattle; rather they are further astray from the way."* (*ed.*)
3563 Ibid. p. 135, no. 48
3564 *al-Khiṣāl*, p. 481, no. 53
3565 *Biḥār al-Anwār*, v. 76, p. 139, no. 52
3566 Ibid. p. 137, no. 48
3567 *al-Da'awāt*, p. 161, no. 445
3568 *Biḥār al-Anwār*, v. 76, p. 135, no. 47
3569 *Kitāb man lā yaḥḍurahi al-Faqīh*, v. [illegible], p. 480, no. 1390
3570 *al-Ikhtiṣāṣ*, p. 343
3571 *Kanz al-'Ummāl*, no. 43058
3572 *Ghurar al-Ḥikam*, no. 5764
3573 *Tuḥaf al-'Uqūl*, p. 70
3574 *al-Kāfī*, v. 8, p. 93, no. 66
3575 *Biḥār al-Anwār*, v. 1, p. 222, no. 6
3576 *al-Maḥāsin*, v. 1, p. 357, no. 760
3577 *Amālī al-Ṭūsī*, p. 303, no. 604
3578 *Kanz al-'Ummāl*, no. 43057
3579 Ibid. no. 10185
3580 Ibid. no. 43059
3581 Ibid. no. 43060
3582 **Translator's Note:** *fatā*: youth – The Arabic term *fatā* refers to youth but has acquired a meaning related much more to the youth associated with the eternal spring of the life of the spirit than to physical young age. Such a person, possessing *futuwwa* or 'spiritual chivalry', would be adorned with chivalrous characteristics of courage and generosity, and would be regarded with awe, reverence and trust by other Muslims. (See Nasr, Seyyed Hossein, *"Spiritual Chivalry"* in *Islamic Spirituality: Manifestations*, ed. Seyyed Hossein Nasr, 304-315, London: SCM Press, 1991)
3583 *al-Kāfī*, v. 8, p. 395, no. 595
3584 *Nahj al-Balāgha*, Sermon 38
3585 *Tuḥaf al-'Uqūl*, p. 155
3586 *A'lām al-Dīn*, p. 301
3587 *al-Khiṣāl*, p. 16, no. 56
3588 *Tanbīh al-Khawāṭir*, v. 1, p. 52
3589 *al-Kāfī*, v. 1, p. 68, no. 10
3590 *Kanz al-'Ummāl*, no. 9056
3591 Ibid. no. 9051
3592 Ibid. no. 9075

3593 Ibid. no. 9081
3594 *al-Kāfī*, v. 5, p. 264, no. 9
3595 Ibid. no. 8
3596 *Ghurar al-Ḥikam*, no. 572
3597 Ibid. no. 1700
3598 Ibid. no. 7597
3599 *Biḥār al-Anwār*, v. 78, p. 104, no. 2
3600 Ibid. p. 236, no. 66
3601 *Nahj al-Balāgha*, Saying 47
3602 *Ghurar al-Ḥikam*, no. 5763
3603 Ibid. no. 6180
3604 *Maʿānī al-Akhbār*, p. 366, no. 1
3605 *Ghurar al-Ḥikam*, no. 2899
3606 Ibid. no. 3357
3607 Ibid. no. 10591
3608 Ibid. no. 3188
3609 Ibid. no. 3938
3610 *Biḥār al-Anwār*, v. 78, p. 377, no. 3
3611 Qur'an 2:216
3612 Qur'an 17:11
3613 *Nahj al-Balāgha*, Saying 387
3614 Ibid. Sermon 167
3615 *Biḥār al-Anwār*, v. 77, p. 137, no. 2
3616 *Nahj al-Balāgha*, Sermon 114
3617 Ibid. Saying 32
3618 *Biḥār al-Anwār*, v. 72, p. 236, no. 3
3619 Ibid. v. 73, p. 263, no. 4
3620 Ibid. v. 62, p. 293
3621 *Tanbīh al-Khawāṭir*, v. 2, p. 120
3622 *Ghurar al-Ḥikam*, no. 2477
3623 **Translator's Note:** The word *shirk* in Arabic implies a much wider meaning that the English 'polytheism' which has been defined as: worshipping or believing in more than one deity, idolatry. In Islam, its purport, in addition to ascribing partners to Allah, includes any form of association of anything or anyone with Allah's authority, His worship, His Names, His attributes, and His Greatness. This includes, therefore, vices such as self-worth, pride, showing-off, etc... *Shirk* has been translated in the text as polytheism for ease of translation.
3624 Qur'an 31:13
3625 Qur'an 4:116
3626 *Makārim al-Akhlāq*, v. 2, p. 357, no. 2660
3627 *al-Kāfī*, v. 2, p. 415, no. 1
3628 Ibid. p. 397, no. 1
3629 Ibid. no. 2
3630 Qur'an 12:106
3631 *Biḥār al-Anwār*, v. 78, p. 200, no. 28
3632 *Tafsīr al-ʿAyyāshī*, v. 2, p. 200, no. 96
3633 *al-Kāfī*, v. 2, p. 397, no. 4
3634 *Maʿānī al-Akhbār*, p. 379, no. 1
3635 *Biḥār al-Anwār*, v. 58, p. 317, no. 8
3636 *Nahj al-Balāgha*, Sermon 192
3637 Qur'an 23:97,98
3638 Qur'an 16:98
3639 *Nahj al-Balāgha*, Sermon 151
3640 Qur'an 35:6
3641 *Ghurar al-Ḥikam*, no. 2623
3642 *Tuḥaf al-ʿUqūl*, p. 301
3643 Ibid. no. 399
3644 Qur'an 7:27
3645 *al-Khiṣāl*, p. 113, no. 91
3646 Qur'an 36:60
3647 *Nahj al-Balāgha*, Sermon 7
3648 Qur'an 2:268
3649 Qur'an 4:120
3650 Qur'an 6:43
3651 *Bashārat al-Muṣṭafā*, p. 27
3652 *Nahj al-Balāgha*, Sermon 64
3653 *al-Ṣaḥīfat al-Sajjādiyya*, supplication 37, line 144
3654 *al-Kāfī*, v. 2, p. 327, no. 2
3655 Qur'an 16:99
3656 Qur'an 15:42
3657 *Biḥār al-Anwār*, v. 78, p. 9, no. 64
3658 Ibid. p. 164, no. 1
3659 *al-Khiṣāl*, p. 285, no. 37
3660 Qur'an 43:36
3661 *al-Kāfī*, v. 2, p. 314, no. 8
3662 *Nahj al-Balāgha*, Sermon 86
3663 *Tuḥaf al-ʿUqūl*, p. 363
3664 Qur'an 26:224 -227
3665 *Maʿānī al-Akhbār*, p. 385, no. 19
3666 *Majmaʿ al-Bayān*, v. 7, p. 326
3667 *al-Durr al-Manthūr*, v. 6, p. 336
3668 *Amālī al-Ṣadūq*, p. 718, no. 987. *Sunan Abī Dāwūd*, v. 4, p. 303, no. 5011

3669 *'Uyūn Akhbār al-Riḍā (AS)*, v. 1, p. 7, no. 1
3670 Ibid. no. 2
3671 *Da'ā'im al-Islām*, v. 1, p. 370
3672 *al-Ja'fariyāt*, p. 84
3673 *Sharḥ Nahj al-Balāgha li Ibn Abī al-Ḥadīd*, v. 1, p. 262
3674 *al-Kāfī*, v. 5, p. 47, no. 1
3675 *Jāmi' al-Aḥadith li al-Qummī*, p. 89
3676 *Kanz al-'Ummāl*, no. 39030
3677 Ibid. no. 39033
3678 Ibid. no. 6489
3679 Ibid. no. 6496
3680 *Tuḥaf al-'Uqūl*, p. 381
3681 Qur'an 39:44
3682 Qur'an 2:255
3683 Qur'an 19:87
3684 Qur'an 20:109
3685 *Kanz al-'Ummāl*, no. 39057
3686 Ibid. no. 39043
3687 *Amālī al-Ṣadūq*, p. 370, no. 462
3688 *al-Khiṣāl*, p. 29, no. 103
3689 Qur'an 93:5
3690 *Biḥār al-Anwār*, v. 8, p. 57, no. 72
3691 Ibid. p. 36, no. 9
3692 *al-Khiṣāl*, p. 63, no. 93
3693 Ibid. p. 355, no. 36
3694 *al-Maḥāsin*, v. 1, p. 159, no. 323
3695 *'Uyūn Akhbār al-Riḍā (AS)*, v. 1, p. 136, no. 35
3696 *al-Maḥāsin*, v. 1, p. 159, no. 225
3697 Nāṣibī: one who declares enmity towards the *Ahl al-Bayt* and their followers (*ed.*)
3698 Ibid. p. 294, no. 587
3699 *Biḥār al-Anwār*, v. 8, p. 38, no. 16
3700 *al-Khiṣāl*, p. 156, no. 197
3701 *Biḥār al-Anwār*, v. 8, p. 58, no. 75
3702 Ibid. p. 43, no. 39
3703 Ibid. p. 58, no. 75
3704 *Ghurar al-Ḥikam*, no. 5789
3705 *Amālī al-Ṣadūq*, p. 598, no. 826
3706 *Biḥār al-Anwār*, v. 8, p. 58, no. 75
3707 Ibid. p. 43, no. 41
3708 Ibid. v. 8, p. 30
3709 Qur'an 26:100,101
3710 *al-Kāfī*, v. 8, p. 101, no.72
3711 *Nahj al-Balāgha*, Sermon 86
3712 Ibid. Letter 78
3713 *Ghurar al-Ḥikam*, no. 4499
3714 *Kanz al-'Ummāl*, no. 491
3715 *al-Tawḥīd*, p. 357, no. 5
3716 Ibid. p. 358, no. 6
3717 Ibid. p. 356, no. 3
3718 *Ghurar al-Ḥikam*, no. 5516
3719 *Biḥār al-Anwār*, v. 98, p. 218, no. 3
3720 Ibid. v. 2, p. 52, no. 19
3721 *Kanz al-'Ummāl*, no. 16683
3722 *Amālī al-Ṣadūq*, p. 478, no. 644
3723 *al-Khiṣāl*, p. 243, no. 96
3724 *Ghurar al-Ḥikam*, no. 9297
3725 Ibid. no. 9307
3726 Qur'an 2:152
3727 *al-Irshād*, v. 1, p. 300
3728 *Ghurar al-Ḥikam*, no. 3329
3729 *Biḥār al-Anwār*, v. 71, p. 52, no. 77
3730 Qur'an 39:66
3731 *Miṣbāḥ al-Sharī'a*, p. 55
3732 *Tuḥaf al-'Uqūl*, p. 483
3733 *A'lām al-Dīn*, p. 313
3734 Qur'an 14:7
3735 *al-Kāfī*, v. 2, p. 94, no. 2
3736 *Amālī al-Ṭūsī*, p. 580, no. 1197
3737 *Biḥār al-Anwār*, v. 94, p. 146, nc. 21
3738 *Qaṣaṣ al-Anbiyā' li al-Rāwandī*, p. 161, no. 178
3739 *Mishkāt al-Anwār*, p. 75, no. 145
3740 *Nahj al-Balāgha*, Saying 11
3741 *Tuḥaf al-'Uqūl*, p. 285
3742 *al-Kāfī*, v. 2, p. 95, no. 10
3743 Ibid. p. 96, no. 15
3744 Ibid. p. 97, no. 19
3745 *Miṣbāḥ al-Sharī'a*, p. 53
3746 *al-Irshād*, v. 1, p. 304
3747 *al-Kāfī*, v. 2, p. 99, no. 30
3748 *Tuḥaf al-'Uqūl*, p. 233
3749 *al-Khiṣāl*, p. 568, no. 1
3750 *al-Kāfī*, v. 2, p. 99, no. 30
3751 *al-Ikhtiṣāṣ*, p. 241
3752 *'Uyūn Akhbār al-Riḍā (AS)*, v. 2, p. 24, no. 2
3753 *Ghurar al-Ḥikam*, no. 6146
3754 Ibid. no. 9482

3755 *Nahj al-Balāgha*, Sermon 22. *Ghurar al-Ḥikam*, no. 3773
3756 Qur'an 33:33
3757 *al-Kāfī*, v. 1, p. 288, no. 1
3758 *Ghurar al-Ḥikam*, no. 725
3759 *al-Kāfī*, v. 2, p. 392, no. 1
3760 *Biḥār al-Anwār*, v. 2, p. 54, no. 24
3761 *Ghurar al-Ḥikam*, no. 723
3762 Ibid. no. 1242
3763 Ibid. no. 4619
3764 Ibid. no. 4271
3765 *Nahj al-Balāgha*, Saying 126
3766 *Ghurar al-Ḥikam*, no. 9532
3767 *Nahj al-Balāgha*, Saying 31
3768 Qur'an 5:8
3769 *Kanz al-'Ummāl*, no. 17735
3770 *Ghurar al-Ḥikam*, no. 356
3771 Qur'an 65:2
3772 Qur'an 2:282
3773 *Biḥār al-Anwār*, v. 104, p. 311, no. 9
3774 *Tafsīr al-'Ayyāshī*, v. 1, p. 156, no. 524
3775 *al-Tahdhīb*, v. 6, p. 275, no. 752
3776 Qur'an 2:140
3777 Qur'an 2:283
3778 *Kanz al-'Ummāl*, no. 17743
3779 *Thawāb al-A'māl*, p. 333
3780 *Kitāb man lā yaḥḍurahi al-Faqīh*, v. 3, p. 15, no. 3243
3781 *al-Kāfī*, v. 7, p. 395, no. 5
3782 Ibid. p. 396, no. 7
3783 *Wasā'il al-Shī'a*, v. 18, p. 250, no. 3
3784 *al-Kāfī*, v. 7, p. 383, no. 3
3785 Qur'an 3:169
3786 *al-Kāfī*, v. 2, p. 348, no. 4
3787 *Biḥār al-Anwār*, v. 100, p. 8, no. 4
3788 *Ṣaḥīḥ Muslim*, v. 3, p. 1496, no. 103
3789 *Kanz al-'Ummāl*, no. 11110
3790 Ibid. no. 10662
3791 *Ṣaḥīḥ Muslim*, v. 3, p. 1498, no. 108
3792 *al-Irshād*, v. 1, p. 238
3793 *Ṣaḥīḥ Muslim*, v. 3, p. 1517, no. 157
3794 *Kanz al-'Ummāl*, no. 11205
3795 Ibid. no. 11203
3796 *Biḥār al-Anwār*, v. 68, p. 137, no. 76
3797 Ibid. v. 82, p. 173, no. 6
3798 *Kanz al-'Ummāl*, no. 11144
3799 Qur'an 94:4
3800 Qur'an 26:84
3801 *Ṣaḥīḥ Muslim*, v. 4, p. 2034, no. 166
3802 *Biḥār al-Anwār*, v. 70, p. 24, no. 23
3803 Qur'an 28:83
3804 *Sharḥ Nahj al-Balāgha li Ibn Abī al-Ḥadīd*, v. 2, p. 181
3805 *Kanz al-'Ummāl*, no. 6144
3806 *Biḥār al-Anwār*, v. 67, p. 271, no. 3
3807 Ibid. v. 78, p. 252, no. 105
3808 *Mishkāt al-Anwār*, p. 553, no. 1864
3809 *Biḥār al-Anwār*, v. 70, p. 252, no. 5
3810 *al-Kāfī*, v. 6, p. 445, no. 3
3811 Qur'an 42:38
3812 *Nahj al-Balāgha*, Saying 211
3813 Ibid. Saying 54
3814 *Ghurar al-Ḥikam*, no. 3908
3815 *'Ilal al-Sharā'i'*, p. 559, no. 1
3816 *Ghurar al-Ḥikam*, no. 10351
3817 *Makārim al-Akhlāq*, v. 2, p. 98, no. 2280
3818 *Biḥār al-Anwār*, v. 75, p. 105, no. 40
3819 *al-Khiṣāl*, p. 570, no. 1
3820 *al-Maḥāsin*, v. 2, p. 438, no. 2521
3821 *Ghurar al-Ḥikam*, no. 2462
3822 Ibid. no. 2471
3823 Qur'an 30:54
3824 *Biḥār al-Anwār*, v. 77, p. 174, no. 9
3825 *Ghurar al-Ḥikam*, no. 1202
3826 Ibid. no. 7019
3827 Ibid. no. 10099
3828 Ibid. nos. 4169-4170
3829 'Ilal *al-Sharā'i'*, p. 104, no. 2
3830 *Amālī al-Ṭūsī*, p. 699, no. 1492
3831 *al-Kāfī*, v. 2, p. 165, no. 1
3832 *Kanz al-'Ummāl*, no. 6013
3833 *al-Kāfī*, v. 2, p. 165, no. 3
3834 Ibid. no. 2
3835 The word *shī'a* lexically means 'follower', and originally referred to those who followed Imām 'Alī b. Abī Ṭālib and who recognised him as the Prophet (SAWA)'s divinely appointed rightful successor. Today it generally refers to the body of Muslims who recognise the twelve Imāms from Imām 'Alī

(AS) to the rest of the Imāms (AS) from his and Fāṭima, the Prophet's daughter's lineage (*ed.*)
3836 *al-Irshād*, v. 1, p. 43
3837 Ibid. p. 41
3838 *Biḥār al-Anwār*, v. 78, p. 28, no. 95
3839 *Tanbīh al-Khawāṭir*, v. 2, p. 106
3840 *Tuḥaf al-'Uqūl*, p. 295
3841 *al-Kāfī*, v. 2, p. 233, no. 9
3842 *Biḥār al-Anwār*, v. 83, p. 22, no. 40
3843 *al-Kāfī*, v. 8, p. 215, no. 260
3844 *Biḥār al-Anwār*, v. 68, p. 164, no. 13
3845 Ibid. v. 2, p. 80, no. 76
3846 Ibid. v. 69, p. 9, no. 11
3847 *al-Kāfī*, v. 2, p. 173, no. 10
3848 *Baṣā'ir al-Darajāt*, p. 247, no. 10
3849 That they, like glass, cannot keep hidden that which is placed in their trust, like secrets (*ed.*)
3850 *Biḥār al-Anwār*, v. 78, p. 186, no. 24
3851 *al-Khiṣāl*, p. 103, no. 61
3852 *al-Kāfī*, v. 2, p. 75, no. 6
3853 *Biḥār al-Anwār*, v. 2, p. 77, no. 62
3854 *Amālī al-Ṣadūq*, p. 327, no. 17
3855 *'Uyūn Akhbār al-Riḍā (AS)*, v. 2, p. 60, no. 232
3856 Qur'an 56:10,11
3857 *Amālī al-Ṭūsī*, p. 72, no. 104
3858 **Translator's Note:** The Arabic word *sabr* denotes 'patience' as the ability to tolerate and endure, as well as 'perseverance' and 'endurance' in the face of adversity and trial. In the text, translation has not been restricted to just one of these terms, in order to best express the purport of each tradition within its context.
3859 Qur'an 3:146
3860 Qur'an 8:46
3861 *Musakkin al-Fu'ād*, p. 48
3862 Ibid. p. 47
3863 *Ghurar al-Ḥikam*, no. 533
3864 Ibid. no. 1821
3865 *Mishkāt al-Anwār*, p. 59, no. 72
3866 *al-Kāfī*, v. 2, p. 87, no. 1
3867 *Kashf al-Ghamma*, v. 3, p. 139
3868 Qur'an 7:137
3869 Qur'an 32:24
3870 *Ghurar al-Ḥikam*, no. 4276
3871 *Biḥār al-Anwār*, v. 71, p. 95, no. 60
3872 Qur'an 2:249
3873 Qur'an 3:125
3874 *Biḥār al-Anwār*, v. 77, p. 88, no. 2
3875 Ibid. v. 71, p. 96, no. 61
3876 Qur'an 2:155-157
3877 *Nahj al-Balāgha*, Sermon 193
3878 *al-Tamḥīṣ*, p. 59, no. 125
3879 *Ṭibb al-A'imma (AS)*, p. 17
3880 *Kanz al-'Ummāl*, no. 6499
3881 *Ghurar al-Ḥikam*, no. 1874
3882 *Nahj al-Balāgha*, Saying 55
3883 *Sharḥ Nahj al-Balāgha li Ibn Abī al-Ḥadīd*, v. 1, p. 319
3884 Graceful patience (*al-ṣabr al-jamīl*) – mentioned in the Qur'an 12:18, 12:83 (*ed.*)
3885 *al-Kāfī*, v. 2, p. 93, no. 23
3886 Ibid. v2 p 93 no. 25
3887 *Jāmi' al-Akhbār*, p. 316, no. 882
3888 *Nahj al-Balāgha*, Saying 414
3889 *Ghurar al-Ḥikam*, no. 8987
3890 *Nahj al-Balāgha*, Saying 189
3891 *Kanz al-'Ummāl*, no. 6522
3892 *Ghurar al-Ḥikam*, no. 3084
3893 *Nahj al-Balāgha*, Letter 31
3894 *Biḥār al-Anwār*, v. 77, no. 207, no. 1
3895 Qur'an 9:119
3896 *Tārīkh Baghdād*, p. 11, no. 82
3897 *Ghurar al-Ḥikam*, nos. 1552-1553
3898 Ibid. no. 275
3899 Ibid. nos. 1118-1119
3900 Ibid. nos. 1115-1116
3901 Ibid. no. 15
3902 *Nahj al-Balāgha*, Saying 47
3903 Ibid. Saying 458
3904 Ibid. Sermon 86
3905 *al-Kāfī*, v. 2, p. 104, no. 4
3906 *Biḥār al-Anwār*, v. 78, p. 269, no. 109
3907 *al-Kāfī*, v. 2, p. 104, no. 3
3908 Ibid. v. 2, p. 104, no. 2
3909 *Amālī al-Ṭūsī*, p. 223, no. 385
3910 Qur'an 4:87
3911 *Biḥār al-Anwār*, v. 77, p. 378, no. 1
3912 *Ghurar al-Ḥikam*, no. 3302
3913 *Amālī al-Ṭūsī*, p. 518, no. 1135
3914 *Ghurar al-Ḥikam*, no. 674

3915 Ibid. no. 8760
3916 Ibid. no. 2059
3917 *Biḥār al-Anwār*, v. 78, p. 92, no. 100
3918 *Ghurar al-Ḥikam*, no. 6865
3919 *Biḥār al-Anwār*, v. 74, p. 185, no. 2
3920 *Ghurar al-Ḥikam*, no. 3129
3921 Ibid. no. 8775
3922 *Amālī al-Ṭūsī*, p. 646, no. 1339
3923 *Biḥār al-Anwār*, v. 76, p. 267, no. 9
3924 Qur'an 25:27-29
3925 *al-Durra al-Bāhira*, p. 19
3926 *Ghurar al-Ḥikam*, no. 9041
3927 Ibid. no. 2601
3928 Ibid. no. 5829
3929 *Biḥār al-Anwār*, v. 74, p. 199, no. 36
3930 Ibid. p. 198, no. 35
3931 *al-Kāfī*, v. 2, p. 377, no. 7
3932 *Biḥār al-Anwār*, v. 78 p. 352, no. 9
3933 Ibid. v. 74, p. 165, no. 28
3934 *Nahj al-Balāgha*, Saying 218
3935 *Biḥār al-Anwār*, v. 77, p. 207, no. 1
3936 *Ghurar al-Ḥikam*, no. 8582
3937 Ibid. no. 8772
3938 *Biḥār al-Anwār*, v. 78, p. 291, no. 2
3939 *A'lām al-Dīn*, p. 311
3940 *Ghurar al-Ḥikam*, no. 1904
3941 *Biḥār al-Anwār*, v. 74, p. 165, no. 29
3942 Ibid. v. 78, p. 249, no. 90
3943 *Tanbīh al-Khawāṭir*, v. 2, p. 123
3944 *Ghurar al-Ḥikam*, no. 1142
3945 Ibid. no. 10196
3946 *Biḥār al-Anwār*, v. 74, p. 7, no. 1
3947 Qur'an 9:103
3948 *al-Kāfī*, v. 4, p. 3, no. 6
3949 *Kanz al-'Ummāl*, no. 16068
3950 Ibid. no. 16114
3951 *Wasā'il al-Shī'a*, v. 6, p. 258, no. 17
3952 Qur'an 9:104
3953 *Biḥār al-Anwār*, v. 96, p. 134, no. 68
3954 *Kanz al-'Ummāl*, no. 15982
3955 *Biḥār al-Anwār*, v. 96, p. 132, no. 64
3956 *al-Kāfī*, v. 4, p. 2, no. 1
3957 *Kanz al-'Ummāl*, no. 16113
3958 *Nahj al-Balāgha*, Saying 7
3959 *A'lām al-Dīn*, p. 333
3960 *Biḥār al-Anwār*, v. 78, p. 68, no. 13
3961 *Nahj al-Balāgha*, Saying 258
3962 *Biḥār al-Anwār*, v. 78, p. 206, no. 54
3963 Ibid. v. 96, p. 134, no. 68
3964 Ibid. v. 75, p. 50, no. 4
3965 *al-Khiṣāl*, p. 134, no. 145
3966 *al-Kāfī*, v. 2, p. 114, no. 7
3967 *Biḥār al-Anwār*, v. 77, p. 160, no. 168
3968 *al-Kāfī*, v. 2, p. 209, no. 1
3969 *Biḥār al-Anwār*, v. 74, p. 388, no. 1
3970 Ibid. v. 96, p. 178, no. 13
3971 *Kanz al-'Ummāl*. no. 16084
3972 Ibid. no. 16250
3973 *Qaṣaṣ al-Anbiyā'*, p. 188, no. 235
3974 *Kanz al-'Ummāl*, no. 16357
3975 *Thawāb al-A'māl*, p. 171, no. 18
3976 *Kanz al-'Ummāl*, no. 16362
3977 Ibid. no. 16249
3978 *Biḥār al-Anwār*, v. 96, p. 172, no. 8
3979 *Tuḥaf al-'Uqūl*, p. 414
3980 Qur'an 2:271
3981 *Nahj al-Balāgha*, Sermon 110
3982 *Biḥār al-Anwār*, v. 46, p. 89, no. 77
3983 Ibid. v. 78, p. 284, no. 1
3984 *al-Kāfī*, v. 4, p. 8, no. 2
3985 *Biḥār al-Anwār*, v. 96, p. 125, no. 39
3986 Qur'an 17:29
3987 *Kanz al-'Ummāl*, no. 16246
3988 *al-Kāfī*, v. 4, p. 33, no. 2
3989 Qur'an 2:273
3990 *Kanz al-'Ummāl*, no. 16552
3991 *Thawāb al-A'māl*, p. 171, no. 20
3992 *al-Kāfī*, v. 3, p. 500, no. 12
3993 Qur'an 2:264
3994 *Tanbīh al-Khawāṭir*, v. 2, p. 120
3995 *Ghurar al-Ḥikam*, no. 1595
3996 *Nahj al-Balāgha*, Sermon 83
3997 Qur'an 1:6
3998 Qur'an 3:51
3999 Qur'an 3:101
4000 *Biḥār al-Anwār*, v. 24, p. 11, no. 3
4001 *Ma'ānī al-Akhbār*, p. 32, no. 2
4002 *Biḥār al-Anwār*, v. 92, p. 197, no. 3
4003 *Faḍā'il al-Shī'a*, p. 48, no. 3
4004 *Biḥār al-Anwār*, v. 76, p. 4, no. 8
4005 Ibid. v. 8, p. 65, no. 2
4006 Qur'an 89:14

4007 *Thawāb al-A'māl*, p. 321, no. 2
4008 *Amālī al-Ṣadūq*, p. 242, no. 257
4009 *Kanz al-'Ummāl*, no. 30747
4010 *Ghurar al-Ḥikam*, no. 8272
4011 Ibid. no. 8273
4012 Ibid. no. 8937
4013 *Biḥār al-Anwār*, v. 1, p. 183, no. 85
4014 *Kitāb man lā yaḥḍurahi al-Faqīh,* v. 3, p. 493, no. 4748. Playing has a fundamental role in the growth of children. We know that the word 'play' means negligence and wastage of time for the elders but it is contrary in the case of the child which is a prelude to his growth and perfection. Playing in the childhood does not postpone the perfection of the child rather it is the other way round. It is through this way that the potentials and talents of the child grow and progress. Hence, it has been emphasized to allow the children to play. An active child will be a wise and patient man when he grows up.
This tradition describes the role of playing in the perfection and development of man's personality. A child whose instinct is not satisfied through playing will have some childish behaviour in the maturity that is considered as misbehaviour. Among the reasons for this misbehaviour as said above one can mention lack of satisfaction of this instinct in the childhood. This instinct is not satisfied except through playing.
4015 *al-Kāfī*, v. 2, p. 181, no. 11
4016 *Biḥār al-Anwār*, v. 77, p. 158, no. 149
4017 Ibid. p. 165, no. 2
4018 *al-Kāfī*, v. 2, p. 181, no. 13
4019 Ibid. no. 12
4020 Ibid. p. 182, no. 15
4021 *Kanz al-'Ummāl*, no. 475
4022 *al-Kāfī*, v. 5, p. 525, no. 1
4023 Qur'an 8:61
4024 *Ghurar al-Ḥikam*, no. 10138
4025 *Nahj al-Balāgha*, Letter 53
4026 *Nahj al-Sa'āda*, v. 2, p. 742
4027 *Biḥār al-Anwār*, v. 78, p. 287, no. 2
4028 Qur'an 49:10
4029 Qur'an 4:114
4030 *Kanz al-'Ummāl*, no. 5480
4031 *al-Kāfī*, v. 2, p. 209, no. 1
4032 Ibid. p. 3
4033 Ibid. p. 210, no. 5
4034 Ibid. p. 341, no. 16
4035 Qur'an 2:238
4036 Qur'an 4:103
4037 Qur'an 14:40
4038 *Da'ā'im al-Islām*, v. 1, p. 133
4039 *Makārim al-Akhlāq*, v. 2, p. 366, no. 2661
4040 *Ghurar al-Ḥikam*, no. 2214
4041 *Tanbīh al-Khawāṭir*, v. 2, p. 78
4042 *al-Khiṣāl*, p. 620, no. 10
4043 *al-Maḥāsin*, v. 1, p. 116, no. 117
4044 *Kitāb man lā yaḥḍurahi al-Faqīh,* v. 1, p. 210, no. 638
4045 Qur'an 19: 31
4046 *al-Kāfī*, v. 3, p. 264, no. 1
4047 Qur'an 29:45
4048 *Kanz al-'Ummāl*, no. 20083
4049 *Biḥār al-Anwār*, v. 82, p. 198
4050 Ibid. p. 227, no. 54
4051 *al-Khiṣāl*, p. 628, no. 10
4052 *Biḥār al-Anwār*, v. 82, p. 209, no. 19
4053 *al-Kāfī*, v. 3, p. 268, no. 4
4054 *Amālī al-Ṭūsī*, p. 296, no. 582
4055 *Biḥār al-Anwār*, v. 82, p. 236, no. 66
4056 *Makārim al-Akhlāq*, v. 2, p. 366, no. 2661
4057 *al-Khiṣāl*, p. 632, no. 10
4058 Ibid.
4059 Qur'an 23:1-2
4060 *al-Firdaws*, v. 5, p. 195, no. 7935
4061 *Da'ā'im al-Islām*, v. 1, p. 158
4062 *Falāḥ al-Sā'il*, p. 289, no. 182
4063 *al-Khiṣāl*, p. 628, no. 10
4064 *Da'ā'im al-Islām*, v. 1, p. 159
4065 *A'lām al-Dīn*, p. 247
4066 *'Uddat al-Dā'ī*, p. 139
4067 *Biḥār al-Anwār*, v. 80, p. 346, no. 30
4068 *Da'ā'im al-Islām*, v. 1, p. 158
4069 *al-Kāfī*, v. 3, p. 300, no. 4
4070 *Falāḥ al-Sā'il*, p. 290, no. 186
4071 *Biḥār al-Anwār*, v. 84, p. 253, no. 56
4072 Ibid. p. 257, no. 55

4073 *Jāmi' al-Akhbār*, p. 412, no. 1141
4074 *'Ilal al-Sharā'i'*, p. 345, no. 1
4075 *Bashārat al-Muṣṭafā*, p. 28
4076 *al-Manāqib li Ibn Shahr Āshūb*, v. 4, p. 131
4077 *al-Kāfī*, v. 3, p. 266, no. 11
4078 Ibid. v. 2, p. 349, no. 5
4079 *al-Maḥāsin*, v. 1, p. 79, no. 44
4080 Ibid. p. 406, no. 921
4081 *Biḥār al-Anwār*, v. 84, p. 249, no. 41
4082 *Thawāb al-A'māl*, p. 68, no. 1
4083 *Biḥār al-Anwār*, v. 84, p. 260, no. 59
4084 *al-Kāfī*, v. 3, p. 266, no. 12
4085 *Biḥār al-Anwār*, v. 72, p. 198, no. 26
4086 Ibid. v. 84, p. 249, no. 41
4087 *Mishkāt al-Anwār*, p. 96, no. 212
4088 *Amālī al-Ṣadūq*, p. 498, no. 683
4089 Qur'an 4:142
4090 *Biḥār al-Anwār*, v. 77, p. 22, no. 6
4091 Ibid. v. 84, p. 283, no. 5
4092 *Tafsīr al-'Ayyāshī*, v. 1, p. 242, no. 134
4093 Qur'an 107:4,5
4094 Qur'an 23:9-11
4095 *Tanbīh al-Khawāṭir*, v. 2, p. 122
4096 *Biḥār al-Anwār*, v. 83, p. 14, no. 25
4097 *al-Kāfī*, v. 3, p. 274, no. 8
4098 *Thawāb al-A'māl*, p. 58, no. 2
4099 *Biḥār al-Anwār*, v. 83, p. 21, no. 38
4100 Qur'an 74:40-43
4101 *Thawāb al-A'māl*, p. 275, no. 1
4102 *'Ilal al-Sharā'i'*, p. 339, no. 1
4103 *al-Kāfī*, v. 3, p. 269, no. 7
4104 *Mustadrak al-Wasā'il*, v. 3, p. 25, no. 2923
4105 *al-Maḥāsin*, v. 2, p. 126, no. 1348
4106 *Wasā'il al-Shī'a*, v. 3, p. 478, no. 2
4107 *al-Kāfī*, v. 3, p. 371, no. 3
4108 *Amālī al-Ṭūsī*, p. 29, no. 31
4109 *Nahj al-Balāgha*, Letter 52
4110 *al-Kāfī*, v. 3, p. 376, no. 5
4111 Qur'an 17:79
4112 Qur'an 73:6
4113 *Kanz al-'Ummāl*, no. 21425
4114 *Sunan Abī Dāwūd*, v. 2, p. 70, no. 1450
4115 *Amālī al-Ṣadūq*, p. 354, no. 432
4116 *Kanz al-'Ummāl*, no. 21428
4117 *Biḥār al-Anwār*, v. 87, p. 143, no. 17
4118 *al-Harīr*: a celebrated battle between two tribes (*ed.*)
4119 Ibid. v. 41, p. 17, no. 10
4120 *al-Kāfī*, v. 3, p. 488, no. 9
4121 *Ma'ānī al-Akhbār*, p. 342, no. 1
4122 Qur'an 32:16,17
4123 *Biḥār al-Anwār*, v. 8, p. 126, no. 27
4124 *'Ilal al-Sharā'i'*, p. 363, no. 1
4125 *al-Kāfī*, v. 3, p. 450, no. 34
4126 *'Ilal al-Sharā'i'*, p. 362, no. 2
4127 *Kanz al-'Ummāl*, no. 21475
4128 Qur'an 62:9
4129 *Wasā'il al-Shī'a*, v. 5, p. 6, no. 25
4130 *al-Da'awāt*, p. 37, no. 91
4131 *Kitāb man lā yaḥḍurahi al-Faqīh*, v. 1, p. 427, no. 1260
4132 *Imām* as in one of the twelve divinely appointed Imāms (AS) (*ed.*)
4133 *Biḥār al-Anwār*, v. 89, p. 184, no. 21
4134 *Kitāb man lā yaḥḍurahi al-Faqīh*, v. 1, p. 416, no. 1230
4135 Qur'an 33:56
4136 *Kanz al-'Ummāl*, no. 2147
4137 Ibid. no. 2149
4138 Ibid. no. 2243
4139 Ibid. no. 2144
4140 Ibid. no. 2153
4141 *Biḥār al-Anwār*, v. 94, p. 49, no. 9
4142 *Kanz al-'Ummāl*, no. 3993
4143 *Makārim al-Akhlāq*, v. 2, p. 377, no. 2661
4144 *Ghurar al-Ḥikam*, no. 1343
4145 *Nahj al-Balāgha*, Saying 333
4146 *Biḥār al-Anwār*, v. 71, p. 279, no. 19
4147 *Ghurar al-Ḥikam*, no. 2314
4148 Ibid. no. 546
4149 *Biḥār al-Anwār*, v. 78, p. 113, no. 7
4150 *Ma'ānī al-Akhbār*, p. 401, no. 62
4151 *al-Kāfī*, v. 2, p. 113, no. 1
4152 *Nahj al-Balāgha*, Saying 182
4153 Ibid. sermon 193
4154 *A'lām al-Dīn*, p. 297
4155 *Amālī al-Ṣadūq*, p. 479, no. 644
4156 *Ghurar al-Ḥikam*, no. 3081
4157 Ibid. no. 2844
4158 *'Uyūn Akhbār al-Riḍā (AS)*, v. 2, p. 5, no. 10
4159 Qur'an 2:155, 156

4160 *Thawāb al-Aʿmāl*, p. 235, no. 2
4161 *Biḥār al-Anwār*, v. 82, p. 103, no. 50
4162 Ibid.
4163 *Amālī al-Ṭūsī*, p. 388, no. 850
4164 *Sunan al-Nasā'ī*, p. 4, no. 19
4165 *Daʿā'im al-Islām*, v. 1, p. 227
4166 *Kanz al-Fawā'id*, v. 2, p. 163
4167 *Biḥār al-Anwār*, v. 82, p. 84, no. 26
4168 *al-Khiṣāl*, p. 616, no. 10
4169 *Biḥār al-Anwār*, v. 78, p. 268, no. 183
4170 *al-Kāfī*, v. 3, p. 227, no. 1
4171 Ibid. v. 2, p. 359, no. 1
4172 Qur'an 31:19
4173 *Munyat al-Murīd*, p. 213
4174 *Biḥār al-Anwār*, v. 77, p. 82
4175 *Ghurar al-Ḥikam*, no. 4660
4176 Ibid. no. 5073
4177 Qur'an 2:183
4178 *Kanz al-ʿUmmāl*, no. 23610
4179 *Faḍā'il al-Ashhur al-Thalātha*, p. 75, no. 57
4180 *al-Daʿawāt*, p. 76, no. 179
4181 *Thawāb al-Aʿmāl*, p. 75, no. 1
4182 Ibid. p. 77, no. 1
4183 *al-Kāfī*, v. 4, p. 62, no. 1
4184 *Biḥār al-Anwār*, v. 96, p. 368, no. 47
4185 *Amālī al-Ṭūsī*, p. 296, no. 582
4186 *al-Kāfī*, v. 4, p. 63, no. 6
4187 *Kitāb man lā yaḥḍurahi al-Faqīh*, v. 2, p. 76, no. 1783
4188 *al-Kāfī*, v. 4, p. 65, no. 15
4189 Ibid. p. 68, no. 1
4190 *Biḥār al-Anwār*, v. 96, p. 369, no. 50
4191 *Maʿānī al-Akhbār*, p. 409, no. 91
4192 *Amālī al-Ṣadūq*, p. 645, no. 874
4193 Qur'an 6:160
4194 *Daʿā'im al-Islām*, v. 1, p. 283
4195 *al-Kāfī*, v. 4, p. 63, no. 5
4196 *al-Firdaws*, v. 5, p. 242, no. 8075
4197 *Biḥār al-Anwār*, v. 96, p. 294, no. 21
4198 *Daʿā'im al-Islām*, v. 1, p. 268
4199 *al-Kāfī*, v. 4, p. 87, no. 1
4200 *Kitāb man lā yaḥḍurahi al-Faqīh*, v. 4, p. 356, no. 5762
4201 *Biḥār al-Anwār*, v. 96, p. 256, no. 38
4202 *Maʿānī al-Akhbār*, p. 228, no. 1
4203 *Amālī al-Ṭūsī*, p. 522, no. 1156
4204 *al-Kāfī*, v. 2, p. 664, no. 5
4205 Ibid. p. 206, no. 1
4206 *Irshād al-Qulub*, p. 200
4207 *Maʿānī al-Akhbār*, p. 335, no. 1
4208 *Amālī al-Ṣadūq*, p. 289, no. 322. *Nūr al-Thaqalayn*, v. 2, p. 249, no. 261
4209 *Tuḥaf al-ʿUqūl*, p. 96
4210 *al-Kāfī*, v. 2, p. 664, no. 13
4211 Ibid. no. 10
4212 *Biḥār al-Anwār*, v. 76, p. 59, no. 10
4213 *al-Mustaḍʿafīn*: people who are abased, deemed weak, or downtrodden by others. People who are spiritually 'weak' are those who are unable or exempt from carrying out religious obligations due to mental or physical incapacity (*ed.*)
4214 *Kanz al-ʿUmmāl*, no. 5944
4215 Ibid. no. 6019
4216 *al-Durr al-Manthūr*, v. 2, p. 724
4217 Qur'an 28:5
4218 *al Ghaibah al-Ṭūsī*, p. 184, no. 143
4219 Qur'an 4:98,99
4220 *Nahj al-Balāgha*, Sermon 189
4221 *Maʿānī al-Akhbār*, p. 201, no. 4
4222 *al-Kāfī*, v. 8, p. 125, no. 95
4223 Qur'an 2:108
4224 Qur'an 4:136
4225 Qur'an 33:36
4226 Qur'an 45:23
4227 *Nahj al-Balāgha*, Sermon 148
4228 Ibid. Sermon 142
4229 Ibid. Sermon 97
4230 *Ghurar al-Ḥikam*, no. 8501
4231 *Nahj al-Balāgha*, Sermon 164
4232 Ibid. Sermon 17
4233 Ibid. Sermon 194
4234 Ibid. Sermon 176
4235 Ibid. Sermon 198
4236 *Mustadrak al-Wasā'il*, v. 17, p. 88, no. 20819
4237 *al-Jaʿfariyāt*, p. 119
4238 *al-Kāfī*, v. 7, p. 350, no. 3
4239 *Ghurar al-Ḥikam*, no. 10187
4240 *al-Kāfī*, v. 4, p. 33, no. 3
4241 *Kitāb man lā yaḥḍurahi al-Faqīh*, v. 3, p. 97, no. 3405
4242 *al-Kāfī*, v. 5, p. 239, no. 5

4243 *Jāmi' al-Akhbār*, p. 377, no. 1053
4244 *Biḥār al-Anwār*, v. 75, p. 461, no. 14
4245 *al-Maḥāsin*, v. 2, p. 147, no. 1388
4246 *Jāmi' al-Akhbār*, p. 378, no. 1058
4247 *Nahj al-Balāgha*, Sermon 142
4248 *Biḥār al-Anwār*, v. 41, p. 28, no. 1
4249 *Kanz al-'Ummāl*, no. 25881
4250 *al-Da'awāt*, p. 141, no. 358
4251 *al-Maḥāsin*, v. 2, p. 180, no. 1510
4252 *Qurb al-Isnād*, p. 160, no. 583
4253 *Biḥār al-Anwār*, v. 77, p. 84, no. 3
4254 *al-Maḥāsin*, v. 2, p. 186, no. 1533
4255 *Kanz al-'Ummāl*, no. 25876
4256 *al-Maḥāsin*, v. 2, p. 179, no. 1506
4257 *'Uyūn Akhbār al-Riḍā (AS)*, v. 2, p. 42, no. 138
4258 *Tanbīh al-Khawāṭir*, v. 2, p. 116
4259 *al-Maḥāsin*, v. 2, p. 181, no. 1515
4260 *al-Kāfī*, v. 6, p. 283, no. 1
4261 Ibid. no. 2
4262 Ibid. v. 5, p. 368, no. 4
4263 *Biḥār al-Anwār*, v. 75, p. 451, no. 2
4264 *al-Kāfī*, v. 6, p. 283, no. 1
4265 *Kanz al-'Ummāl*, no. 28100-28073
4266 *al-Khiṣāl*, p. 229, no. 67
4267 *Makārim al-Akhlāq*, v. 1, p. 314, no. 1003
4268 Ibid. v. 2, p. 179, no. 2464
4269 *Nahj al-Balāgha*, Saying 27
4270 Qur'an 76:8,9
4271 Qur'an 90:14-16
4272 *Mishkāt al-Anwār*, p. 325
4273 *Ghurar al-Ḥikam*, no. 9634
4274 *al-Maḥāsin*, v. 2, p. 142, no. 1370
4275 Ibid. p. 145, no. 1381
4276 Ibid. p. 279, no. 1901
4277 *Kanz al-'Ummāl*, no. 27871
4278 *al-Kāfī*, v. 6, p. 54, no. 1
4279 Ibid. p. 55, no. 4
4280 Ibid. p. 54, no. 2
4281 Ibid. no. 3
4282 That is, after she has been divorced by the second husband, the two of them may remarry if they think they can maintain a healthy marital relationship.
4283 Qur'an 2:230
4284 Qur'an 2:229
4285 *'Uyūn Akhbār al-Riḍā (AS)*, v. 2, p. 85, no. 27
4286 *'Ilal al-Sharā'i'*, p. 507, no. 1
4287 *Kanz al-'Ummāl*, no. 7576
4288 *Tanbīh al-Khawāṭir*, v. 1, p. 49
4289 *Kanz al-'Ummāl*, no. 8852
4290 *Nahj al-Balāgha*, Saying 180
4291 *Tanbīh al-Khawāṭir*, v. 1, p. 49
4292 *Nahj al-Balāgha*, Saying 226
4293 Ibid. Saying 2
4294 *Ghurar al-Ḥikam*, no. 10593
4295 *Nahj al-Balāgha*, Saying 219
4296 *Ghurar al-Ḥikam*, no. 10578
4297 *al-Kāfī*, v. 2, p. 320, no. 2
4298 *Biḥār al-Anwār*, v. 78, p. 315, no. 1
4299 *al-Durra al-Bāhira*, p. 42
4300 *Biḥār al-Anwār*, v. 78, p. 374, no. 35
4301 **Translator's Note**: Since 'greed' is a word that has intrinsically negative implications, in this sub-section outlining its positive and praiseworthy aspects, we will proceed to refer to it as 'avidity.'
4302 Qur'an 32:16
4303 Qur'an 5:84
4304 *Biḥār al-Anwār*, v. 98, p. 83, no. 2
4305 *Iqbāl al-A'māl*, v. 1, p. 168
4306 Ritual purification (*ṭahūr*): ablution (*wuḍū'*), major ablution (*ghusl*), dry ablution (*tayammum*), as well as cleaning and purifying one's body from all things considered impure in Islam (*ed.*)
4307 *Kanz al-'Ummāl*, no. 25998
4308 Ibid. no. 26010
4309 Ibid. no. 26006
4310 Qur'an 25:48
4311 *Wasā'il al-Shī'a*, v. 1, p. 101, no. 9
4312 Ibid. v. 2, p. 1043, no. 6
4313 *Kitāb man lā yaḥḍurahi al-Faqīh*, v. 1, p. 109, no. 224
4314 *al-Kāfī*, v. 3, p. 330, no. 3
4315 Qur'an 33:33
4316 Qur'an 9:103
4317 *Nahj al-Balāgha*, Saying 252
4318 Ibid. no. 198
4319 *Ghurar al-Ḥikam*, no. 3743
4320 Qur'an 4:59

4477 *Biḥār al-Anwār*, v. 78, p. 160, no. 20
4478 *Ghurar al-Ḥikam*, no. 879
4479 Ibid. no. 5150
4480 Ibid. no. 8056
4481 *Nahj al-Balāgha*, Saying 113
4482 *Ghurar al-Ḥikam*, no. 954
4483 Ibid. no. 62
4484 *Nahj al-Balāgha*, Saying 46
4485 *Ghurar al-Ḥikam*, no. 2642
4486 Ibid. no. 4606
4487 *Tuḥaf al-'Uqūl*, p. 74
4488 *Ghurar al-Ḥikam*, no. 726
4489 *Nahj al-Balāgha*, no. 167
4490 *al-Zuhd li al-Ḥusayn b. Sa'īd*, p. 68, no. 179
4491 *al-Kāfī*, v. 2, p. 313, no. 2
4492 *al-Khiṣāl*, p. 433, no. 17
4493 *Tuḥaf al-'Uqūl*, p. 285
4494 *al-Khiṣāl*, p. 112, no. 86
4495 *Ghurar al-Ḥikam*, no. 9666
4496 *Tuḥaf al-'Uqūl*, p. 285
4497 *Amālī al-Ṣadūq*, p. 56, no. 12
4498 *'Ilal al-Sharā'i'*, p. 122, no. 1
4499 *al-Kāfī*, v. 1, p. 24, no. 20
4500 Qur'an 21:37
4501 Qur'an 17:11
4502 *al-Maḥāsin*, v. 1, p. 340, no. 697
4503 Ibid. no. 698. *Kanz al-'Ummāl*, no. 5674
4504 *Ghurar al-Ḥikam*, no. 432
4505 Ibid. no. 9740
4506 *al-Khiṣāl*, p. 52, no. 100
4507 *al-Kāfī*, v. 2, p. 142, no. 4
4508 *Ghurar al-Ḥikam*, no. 1937
4509 *al-Kāfī*, v. 2, p. 142, no. 3
4510 *Maṭālib al-Sa'ūl*, p. 61
4511 *Ghurar al-Ḥikam*, no. 4789
4512 Ibid. no. 1954
4513 Ibid. no. 1873
4514 Ibid. no. 4215
4515 Ibid. no. 4211
4516 Ibid. no. 774
4517 Ibid. no. 9534
4518 *Nahj al-Balāgha*, Saying 437
4519 *'Ilal al-Sharā'i'*, p. 248, no. 2
4520 *al-Kāfī*, v. 2, p. 146, no. 11
4521 Ibid. p. 147, no. 15
4522 *al-Khiṣāl*, p. 208, no. 28
4523 *Kanz al-Fawā'id*, v. 2, p. 162
4524 Qur'an 5:8
4525 *Tuḥaf al-'Uqūl*, p. 88
4526 *Ghurar al-Ḥikam*, no. 3242
4527 Ibid. no. 3014
4528 Ibid. no. 6368
4529 *al-Kāfī*, v. 2, p. 302, no. 11
4530 *Tuḥaf al-'Uqūl*, p. 42
4531 *Amālī al-Ṭūsī*, p. 512, no. 1119
4532 *Ghurar al-Ḥikam*, no. 5247
4533 *Ḥilyat al-Awliyā'*, v. 3, p. 184, no. 235
4534 *Ghurar al-Ḥikam*, no. 6302
4535 Ibid. 7316
4536 Qur'an 64:14
4537 *Ghurar al-Ḥikam*, no. 4424
4538 *A'lām al-Dīn*, p. 309
4539 *Tanbīh al-Khawāṭir*, v. 1, no. 259
4540 *Ghurar al-Ḥikam*, no. 3269
4541 Ibid. no. 8672
4542 *Nahj al-Balāgha*, Letter 62
4543 *Ghurar al-Ḥikam*, no. 10216
4544 Ibid. no. 8230
4545 Ibid. no. 8043
4546 *Amālī al-Ṣadūq*, p. 766, no. 1031
4547 *Nahj al-Balāgha*, Sayings 172 and 438
4548 *Biḥār al-Anwār*, v. 78, p. 200, no. 28
4549 *Tuḥaf al-'Uqūl*, p. 248
4550 *Mishkāt al-Anwār*, p. 103, no. 235
4551 *Kanz al-'Ummāl*, no. 7032
4552 *Biḥār al-Anwār*, v. 74, p. 165, no. 29
4553 *Ghurar al-Ḥikam*, no. 2988
4554 *Biḥār al-Anwār*, v. 78, p. 141, no. 34
4555 *Ghurar al-Ḥikam*, no. 3190
4556 Ibid. no. 3038
4557 *Nahj al-Balāgha*, Saying 362
4558 *A'lām al-Dīn*, p. 303
4559 *Saḥīfat al-Imām al-Riḍā (AS)*, p. 85, no. 195
4560 *Amālī al-Mufīd*, p. 338, no. 2
4561 *Wasā'il al-Shī'a*, v. 8, p. 606, no. 3
4562 The Arabic *'ma'rifa'* denotes inner knowledge discerned and understood by the heart, often referring to intrinsic knowledge of higher truths, of the soul, and of Allah, which fuels one to perform good deeds and leads one closer to Allah. This is in contrast

to the Arabic *'ilm* which denotes acquired and learned knowledge in any field, which may or may not lead to action or proximity to Allah (*ed.*)
4563 *Jāmi' al-Akhbār*, p. 36, no. 18
4564 *Ghurar al-Ḥikam*, no. 2061
4565 Ibid. no. 538
4566 *Biḥār al-Anwār*, v. 78, p. 128, no. 11
4567 *al-Kāfī*, v. 1, p. 44, no. 2
4568 Qur'an 45:23
4569 *Biḥār al-Anwār*, v. 70, p. 71, no. 20
4570 *Ghurar al-Ḥikam*, no. 9865
4571 Ibid. no. 9965
4572 Ibid. no. 6998
4573 Ibid. nos. 7855-7856
4574 Ibid. nos. 7829-7832
4575 Ibid. no. 3126
4576 Ibid. no. 7946
4577 Ibid.no. 1093
4578 Ibid. no. 10927
4579 Ibid. no. 10937
4580 *Biḥār al-Anwār*, v. 94, p. 128, no. 19
4581 *Tuḥaf al-'Uqūl*, p. 286
4582 *Ghurar al-Ḥikam*, no. 7999
4583 Ibid. no. 9864
4584 *Kanz al-'Ummāl*, no. 36472
4585 *Ghurar al-Ḥikam*, no. 4586
4586 Ibid. no. 8896
4587 *al-Kāfī*, v. 8, p. 247, no. 347
4588 *Amālī al-Ṣadūq*, p. 647, no. 878
4589 *Kanz al-'Ummāl*, no. 5893
4590 *Biḥār al-Anwār*, v. 70, p. 393, no. 64
4591 *Ghurar al-Ḥikam*, no. 10984
4592 *Nahj al-Balāgha*, Sermon 147
4593 *Ghurar al-Ḥikam*, no. 6359
4594 Ibid. no. 3260
4595 *al-Kāfī*, v. 2, p. 62, no. 9
4596 *Tanbīh al-Khawāṭir*, v. 2, p. 185
4597 Ibid. p. 184
4598 *Ghurar al-Ḥikam*, no. 1985
4599 Ibid. no. 855
4600 Ibid. no. 664
4601 Ibid. no. 1791
4602 *Tuḥaf al-'Uqūl*, p. 376
4603 *al-Kāfī*, v. 1, p. 86, no. 1
4604 Ibid. p. 85, no. 1
4605 *Biḥār al-Anwār*, v. 98, p. 225
4606 *Iqbāl al-A'māl*, v. 1, p. 157
4607 *Kanz al-'Ummāl*, no. 5705
4608 *Amālī al-Ṣadūq*, p. 503, no. 690
4609 *al-Maḥāsin*, v. 1, p. 371, no. 808
4610 *Nahj al-Balāgha*, Sermon 160
4611 Ibid. Sermon 109
4612 *Biḥār al-Anwār*, v. 94, p. 150, no. 21
4613 *al-Tawḥīd*, p. 36, no. 2
4614 Ibid. p. 252, no. 3
4615 *Nahj al-Balāgha*, Sermon 152
4616 Ibid. Sermon 94
4617 Ibid. Sermon 185
4618 *al-Kāfī*, v. 1, p. 117, no. 8
4619 Ibid. p. 102, no. 6
4620 *Kashf al-Ghamma*, v. 3, p. 176
4621 *'Uyūn Akhbār al-Riḍā (AS)*, v. 2, p. 35, no. 75
4622 *Ghurar al-Ḥikam*, no. 540
4623 *Nahj al-Balāgha*, Saying 470
4624 *Ma'ānī al-Akhbār*, p. 11, no. 2
4625 *Amālī al-Ṭūsī*, p. 22, no. 28
4626 Qur'an 23:117
4627 *Nahj al-Balāgha*, Letter 31
4628 *al-Tawḥīd*, p. 243, no. 1
4629 Qur'an 21:22
4630 *al-Tawḥīd*, p. 250, no. 2
4631 Ibid. p. 270, no. 6
4632 Qur'an 23:91
4633 *Tafsīr al-Qummī*, v. 2, p. 93
4634 Qur'an 6:103
4635 *al-Tawḥīd*, p. 108, no. 4
4636 *Amālī al-Ṣadūq*, p. 423, no. 560
4637 Ibid. p. 495, no. 673
4638 *al-Kāfī*, v. 1, p. 95, no. 1
4639 *Nahj al-Balāgha*, Sermon 101
4640 Ibid. Letter 31
4641 *Biḥār al-Anwār*, v. 77, p. 331, no. 18
4642 *al-Tawḥīd*, p. 141, no. 5
4643 Qur'an 2:255
4644 *al-Tawḥīd*, p. 137, no. 11
4645 Ibid. p. 142, no. 6
4646 Qur'an 6:59
4647 *Nahj al-Balāgha*, Sermon 178
4648 Ibid. Sermon 198
4649 Ibid. Sermon 108
4650 *al-Kāfī*, v. 1, p. 107, no. 2

4651 *al-Tawḥīd*, p. 137, no. 9
4652 *al-Kāfī*, v. 1, p. 107, no. 1
4653 *al-Tawḥīd*, p. 138, no. 16
4654 Qur'an 4:40
4655 *Nahj al-Balāgha*, Sermon 214
4656 Ibid. Saying 470
4657 *al-Saḥīfat al-Sajjādiyya*, p. 297, Supplication 48
4658 *al-Tawḥīd*, p. 96, no. 1
4659 Qur'an 39:62
4660 *al-Tawḥīd*, p. 295, no. 5
4661 Ibid. p. 98, no. 5
4662 Qur'an 70:40
4663 *al-Tawḥīd*, p. 130, no. 9
4664 Ibid. p. 127, no. 5
4665 Qur'an 4:164
4666 *Nahj al-Balāgha*, Sermon 186
4667 Qur'an 36:82
4668 *al-Tawḥīd*, p. 100, no. 8
4669 Qur'an 57:3
4670 *Nahj al-Balāgha*, Sermon 213
4671 *al-Tawḥīd*, p. 37, no. 2
4672 Qur'an 3:189
4673 *Nahj al-Balāgha*, Sermon 65
4674 Ibid. Saying 404
4675 Qur'an 40:20
4676 *Nahj al-Balāgha*, Sermon 152
4677 *al-Tawḥīd*, p. 144, no. 9
4678 Ibid. p. 65, no. 18
4679 Qur'an 6:103
4680 *al-Kāfī*, v. 1, p. 122, no. 2
4681 Qur'an 11:66
4682 Qur'an 35:10
4683 *Nahj al-Balāgha*, Sermon 65
4684 Ibid. Sermon 109
4685 Ibid. Sermon 65
4686 Ibid. Sermon 192
4687 Qur'an 3:62
4688 *al-Tawḥīd*, p. 397, no. 13
4689 Qur'an 112:2
4690 *al-Tawḥīd*, p. 90, no. 3
4691 Qur'an 57:4
4692 *Nahj al-Balāgha*, Sermon 195
4693 Qur'an 6:3
4694 *al-Tawḥīd*, p. 133, no. 15
4695 Ibid. p. 140, no. 4
4696 Ibid. p. 338, no. 5
4697 *Nahj al-Balāgha*, Sermon 1
4698 The Arabic *ma'rūf* denotes common acts of courtesy, kindly favours towards others, good manners and general acts of goodness to people (*ed.*)
4699 *Ghurar al-Ḥikam*, no. 6585
4700 Ibid. no. 980
4701 *A'lām al-Dīn*, p. 298
4702 *al-Da'awāt*, p. 108, no. 240
4703 *Amālī al-Ṭūsī*, p. 304, no. 610
4704 *Kashf al-Ghamma*, v. 3, p. 137
4705 *Biḥār al-Anwār*, v. 74, p. 401, no. 44
4706 *'Uyūn Akhbār al-Riḍā (AS)*, v. 2, p. 35 no. 76
4707 *Thawāb al-A'māl*, p. 342, no. 1
4708 *al-Kāfī*, v. 4, p. 18, no. 2
4709 *Ghurar al-Ḥikam*, no. 2282
4710 Ibid. nos. 4000-4001
4711 Ibid. no. 9724
4712 *Amālī al-Ṭūsī*, p. 596, no. 1235
4713 *Ghurar al-Ḥikam*, no. 9115
4714 *Tuḥaf al-'Uqūl*, p. 403
4715 *Kanz al-Fawa'id li al-Karājikī*, v. 1, p. 212
4716 *al-Ja'fariyyāt*, p. 233
4717 *Ghurar al-Ḥikam*, no. 4983
4718 *Biḥār al-Anwār*, v. 74, p. 419, no. 47
4719 Ibid. v. 75, p. 15, no. 8
4720 *al-Khiṣāl*, v. 32, p. 111
4721 *Thawāb al-A'māl*, p. 343, no. 1
4722 *al-Kāfī*, v. 5, p. 55, no. 3
4723 *Makārim al-Akhlāq*, v. 1, p. 294, no. 915
4724 Qur'an 3:104
4725 Qur'an 3:110
4726 Qur'an 9:71
4727 *Mustadrak al-Wasā'il*, v. 12, p. 179, no. 13817
4728 *Ma'ānī al-Akhbār*, p. 344, no. 1
4729 *Ghurar al-Ḥikam*, no. 6817
4730 *Nahj al-Balāgha*, Saying 374
4731 *Ghurar al-Ḥikam*, no. 1977
4732 *al-Kāfī*, v. 5, p. 57, no. 6
4733 *Tanbīh al-Khawāṭir*, v. 2, p. 179
4734 *al-Kāfī*, v. 5, p. 56, no. 1
4735 *Wasā'il al-Shī'a*, v. 11, p. 407, no. 12
4736 *Nahj al-Balāgha*, Letter 47
4737 Ibid. Saying 154

4738 *Kashf al-Ghamma*, v. 3, p. 139
4739 *Tuḥaf al-'Uqūl*, p. 456
4740 *Kanz al-'Ummāl*, no. 5523
4741 *Tanbīh al-Khawāṭir*, v. 2, p. 213
4742 *Ghurar al-Ḥikam*, no. 3780
4743 *Nahj al-Balāgha*, Sermon 129
4744 Ibid. Sermon 105
4745 *al-Khiṣāl*, p. 109, no. 79
4746 *al-Targhīb wa al-Tarhīb*, v. 3, p. 223, no. 1
4747 *Kanz al-'Ummāl*, no. 5570
4748 *al-Tahdhīb*, v. 6, p. 181, no. 374
4749 *al-Kāfī*, v. 5, p. 59, no. 10
4750 Ibid. p. 60, no. 1
4751 Qur'an 4:139
4752 *Biḥār al-Anwār*, v. 78, p. 10, no. 67
4753 *Tuḥaf al-'Uqūl*, p. 366
4754 *Nahj al-Balāgha*, Saying 113
4755 *Tuḥaf al-'Uqūl*, p. 283
4756 *Biḥār al-Anwār*, v. 78, p. 228, no. 105
4757 Ibid. p. 453, no. 21
4758 *Qaṣaṣ al-Anbiyā'*, p. 195, p. 244
4759 *Nahj al-Balāgha*, Saying 371
4760 *al-Khiṣāl*, p. 420, no. 14
4761 *al-Kāfī*, v. 2, p. 144, no. 4
4762 *Biḥār al-Anwār*, v. 78, p. 53, no. 90
4763 *al-Kāfī*, v. 2, p. 149, no. 6
4764 Ibid. p. 109, no. 10
4765 *al-Khiṣāl*, p. 169, no. 222
4766 *al-Kāfī*, v. 2, p. 110, no. 5
4767 *Biḥār al-Anwār*, v. 78, p. 374, no. 24
4768 *Tuḥaf al-'Uqūl*, p. 286
4769 *Biḥār al-Anwār*, v. 74, p. 180, p. 28
4770 *al-Kāfī*, v. 8, p. 42, no. 8
4771 *A'lām al-Dīn*, p. 341
4772 *Ghurar al-Ḥikam*, no. 661
4773 Ibid. no. 8644
4774 Ibid. no. 8151
4775 *Biḥār al-Anwār*, v. 47, p. 60, no. 116
4776 Ibid. v. 70, p. 111, no. 14
4777 *Kanz al-'Ummāl*, no. 686
4778 *al-Durr al-Manthūr*, v. 1, p. 161
4779 This refers mainly to a bereaved person who is grieving the loss of a loved one, though it also includes any other type of affliction or misfortune that may befall someone and for which one may express sympathy or condolences (*ed.*)
4780 *Biḥār al-Anwār*, v. 82, p. 94, no. 46
4781 *al-Kāfī*, v. 3, p. 227, no. 3
4782 *Kitāb man lā yaḥḍurahi al-Faqīh*, v. 1, p. 174, no. 505
4783 *Musakkin al-Fu'ād*, p. 108
4784 *Biḥār al-Anwār*, v. 78, p. 353, no. 9
4785 *Nahj al-Balāgha*, Saying 10
4786 *Ma'ānī al-Akhbār*, p. 267, no. 1
4787 *Biḥār al-Anwār*, v. 74, p. 167, no. 34
4788 Qur'an 4:19
4789 *Nahj al-Balāgha*, Letter 31
4790 *Biḥār al-Anwār*, v. 78, p. 236, no. 63
4791 *Amālī al-Ṣadūq*, p. 269, no. 295
4792 *Ghurar al-Ḥikam*, no. 5071
4793 *Biḥār al-Anwār*, v. 78, p. 50, no. 76
4794 Ibid. v. 74, p. 175, no. 6
4795 Ibid. v. 75, p. 151, no. 17
4796 *A'lām al-Dīn*, p. 297
4797 *Tuḥaf al-'Uqūl*, p. 366
4798 Ibid. no. 403
4799 'Āshūrā': The tenth day of Muḥarram, marking the date of Imām Ḥusayn (AS)'s martyrdom at the hands of the Umayyads along with his family and companions in Karbala in 61 A.H (*ed.*)
4800 *Thawāb al-A'māl*, p. 108, no. 1
4801 *Miṣbāḥ al-Mutahajjid*, p. 772
4802 *Thawāb al-A'māl*, p. 110, no. 3
4803 *'Ilal al-Sharā'i'*, p. 227, no. 2
4804 *Wasā'il al-Shī'a*, v. 10, p. 394, no. 8
4805 *Biḥār al-Anwār*, v. 78, p. 11, no. 70
4806 *Nahj al-Balāgha*, Sermon 109
4807 *Amālī al-Ṣadūq*, p. 765, no. 1029
4808 *Kanz al-'Ummāl*, no. 7000
4809 *Nahj al-Balāgha*, Saying 474
4810 *Kanz al-'Ummāl*, no. 1872
4811 Qur'an 48:26
4812 *al-Kāfī*, v. 2, p. 308, no. 2
4813 Ibid. no. 3
4814 *Sunan Abī Dāwūd*, v. 4, p. 332, no. 5121
4815 *Nahj al-Balāgha*, Sermon 192
4816 *al-Kāfī*, v. 2, p. 308, no. 7
4817 *Nahj al-Balāgha*, no. 192
4818 *Ghurar al-Ḥikam*, no. 3738

4819 Qur'an 17:9
4820 *Ma'ānī al-Akhbār*, p. 132, no. 1
4821 Qur'an 3:101
4822 *Ma'ānī al-Akhbār*, p. 132, no. 2
4823 *al-Kāfī*, v. 8, p. 82, no. 39
4824 *Ghurar al-Ḥikam*, no. 8469
4825 Ibid. no. 879
4826 Ibid. no. 3466
4827 Ibid. no. 4316
4828 Ibid. no. 12
4829 *al-Balad al-Amīn*, p. 315
4830 *Biḥār al-Anwār*, v. 78, p. 188, no. 41
4831 The word 'Imām' in this sub-section refers specifically to the Imāms from the Prophet's household, from the progeny of Imām 'Alī (AS) (*ed.*)
4832 *al-Kāfī*, v. 1, p. 204, no. 2
4833 Ibid. p. 269, no. 6
4834 Ibid. p. 200, no. 1
4835 Ibid. p. 203, no. 1
4836 *Āmālī al-Ṣadūq*, p. 347, no. 1
4837 *Biḥār al-Anwār*, v. 16, p. 240
4838 Ibid. v. 76, p. 63, no. 3
4839 *Nahj al-Balāgha*, Saying 37
4840 Qur'an 22:32
4841 Qur'an 22:30
4842 *Kanz al-'Ummāl*, no. 25507
4843 *al-Maḥāsin*, v. 1, p. 364, no. 786
4844 *Tuḥaf al-'Uqūl*, p. 394
4845 Qur'an 24:33
4846 Qur'an 2:273
4847 *Amālī al-Ṭūsī*, p. 39, no. 43
4848 *Nahj al-Balāgha*, Saying 474
4849 *Ghurar al-Ḥikam*, no. 1168
4850 Ibid. no. 529
4851 Ibid. no. 1989
4852 Ibid. no. 5449
4853 *al-Khiṣāl*, p. 55, no. 75
4854 *al-Kāfī*, v. 2, p. 79, no. 5
4855 *Sunan Ibn Māja*, v. 2, p. 817, no. 2444
4856 *al-Kāfī*, v. 2, p. 79, no. 5
4857 *Maṭālib al-Sa'ūl*, p. 50
4858 *Ghurar al-Ḥikam*, no. 1512
4859 *Nahj al-Balāgha*, Saying 47
4860 *Ghurar al-Ḥikam*, no. 7646
4861 *Tuḥaf al-'Uqūl*, p. 17
4862 *Ghurar al-Ḥikam*, no. 2148
4863 Ibid. no. 4637
4864 Ibid. no. 4593
4865 Ibid. no. 8597
4866 Ibid. no. 4238
4867 Qur'an 42:40
4868 Qur'an 3:134
4869 *A'lām al-Dīn*, p. 337
4870 *Kanz al-'Ummāl*, no. 7005
4871 *al-Kāfī*, v. 2, p. 108, no. 5
4872 *A'lām al-Dīn*, p. 315
4873 *Tanbīh al-Khawāṭir*, v. 2, p. 120
4874 *al-Kāfī*, v. 2, p. 108, no. 6
4875 Ibid. p. 107, no. 3
4876 Qur'an 15:85
4877 *Ghurar al-Ḥikam*, no. 9567
4878 *A'lām al-Dīn*, p. 307
4879 *Kanz al-'Ummāl*, no. 7007
4880 *Nahj al-Balāgha*, Saying 11
4881 Ibid. Saying 211
4882 *al-Durra al-Bāhira*, p. 24
4883 *Mustadrak al-Wasā'il*, v. 9, p. 7, no. 10041
4884 *Tuḥaf al-'Uqūl*, p. 87
4885 *Kanz al-Fawa'id li al-Karājikī*, v. 2, p. 182
4886 *Ghurar al-Ḥikam*, p. 4788
4887 Qur'an 4:43
4888 *Sunan Ibn Māja*, v. 2, p. 1265, no. 3850
4889 *Tanbīh al-Khawāṭir*, v. 1, p. 9
4890 *Nahj al-Balāgha*, Letter 27
4891 *Amālī al-Ṣadūq*, p. 138, no. 136
4892 *Nahj al-Balāgha*, Sermon 227
4893 *Biḥār al-Anwār*, v. 78, p. 90, no. 95
4894 *Nahj al-Balāgha*, Sermon 192
4895 *Kashf al-Ghamma*, v. 2, p. 418
4896 *Ghurar al-Ḥikam*, no. 973
4897 *al-Tawḥīd*, v. 74, no. 27
4898 *Ghurar al-Ḥikam*, no. 4207
4899 *Kitāb man lā yaḥdurahi al-Faqīh,* v. 4, p. 406, no. 5878
4900 *Jāmi' al-Akhbār*, p. 153, no. 344
4901 *Tuḥaf al-'Uqūl*, p. 89
4902 *Biḥār al-Anwār*, v. 72, p. 232, no. 2
4903 *Kanz al-'Ummāl*, nos. 4935, 3272
4904 Ibid. nos. 3130-3153
4905 *Sunan Ibn Māja*, v. 2, p. 1265, no. 3849

4906 *al-Da'awāt*, p. 114, no. 262
4907 Ibid. no. 261
4908 Ibid. p. 84, no. 211
4909 *al-Kāfī*, v. 2, p. 462, no. 1
4910 In this chapter the Arabic word *'aql* has been translated as 'intellect' to denote one's mental ability to think, reason and understand (*ed.*)
4911 Qur'an 2:269
4912 Qur'an 67:10
4913 *Rawḍat al-Wā'iẓīn*, p. 9
4914 *Nahj al-Balāgha*, Saying 407
4915 *Ghurar al-Ḥikam*, no. 475
4916 Ibid. no. 1250
4917 Ibid. no. 404
4918 Ibid. no. 1325
4919 Ibid. no. 272
4920 *Nahj al-Balāgha*, Saying 38
4921 *Amālī al-Ṭūsī*, p. 146 no. 240
4922*Tuḥaf al-'Uqūl*, p. 286
4923 *al-Khiṣāl*, p. 589, no. 13
4924 *al-Ikhtiṣāṣ*, p. 244
4925 *al-Kāfī*, v. 1, p. 29, no. 34
4926 *al-Ikhtiṣāṣ*, no. 246
4927 *al-Kāfī*, v. 1, p. 25, no. 24
4928 *Tuḥaf al-'Uqūl*, p. 397
4929 *al-Kāfī*, v. 1, p. 11, no. 4
4930 *Majma' al-Bayān*, v. 10, p. 487
4931 *Tuḥaf al-'Uqūl*, p. 54
4932 *Kashf al-Ghamma*, v. 2, p. 197
4933 *al-Kāfī*, v. 1, p. 26, no. 26
4934 *al-Maḥāsin*, v. 1, p. 308, no. 608
4935 *Ma'ānī al-Akhbār*, p. 1, no. 2
4936 *al-Kāfī*, v. 1, p. 18, no. 12
4937 Ibid. p. 16, no. 12
4938 Ibid.
4939 *Tuḥaf al-'Uqūl*, p. 15
4940 *'Awālī al-La'ālī*, v. 1, p. 248, no. 4
4941 *Ghurar al-Ḥikam*, no. 2141
4942 *Nahj al-Balāgha*, Letter 31
4943 *Maṭālib al-Sa'ūl*, p. 49
4944 *Ma'ānī al-Akhbār*, p. 240, no. 1
4945 Ibid. p. 401, no. 62
4946 *Tuḥaf al-'Uqūl*, p. 28
4947 *Amālī al-Ṣadūq*, p. 73, no. 41
4948 *Nahj al-Balāgha*, Saying 6
4949 Ibid. Saying 235
4950 *al-Ikhtiṣāṣ*, p. 245
4951 *al-Kāfī*, v. 1, p. 11, no. 3
4952 Ibid. v. 2, p. 116, no. 20
4953 *Tuḥaf al-'Uqūl*, p. 390
4954 *al-Kāfī*, v. 1, p. 17, no. 12
4955 *Ghurar al-Ḥikam*, no. 1717
4956 Ibid. no. 4291
4957 *A'lām al-Dīn*, p. 298
4958 *al-Da'awāt*, p. 221, no. 603
4959 *Tuḥaf al-'Uqūl*, p. 364
4960 *al-Ikhtiṣāṣ*, p. 244
4961 *A'lām al-Dīn*, p. 333
4962 *Ghurar al-Ḥikam*, no. 10957
4963 *Nahj al-Balāgha*, Saying 301
4964 *Ghurar al-Ḥikam*, no. 5608
4965 Ibid. no. 5600
4966 Ibid. no. 6221
4967 Ibid. no. 5422
4968 Ibid. no. 7091
4969 *Nahj al-Balāgha*, Saying 71
4970 *Ghurar al-Ḥikam*, no. 8226
4971 Ibid. no. 5180
4972 Ibid. no. 5901
4973 *Kanz al-Fawa'id*, v. 1, p. 200
4974 Ibid. p. 199
4975 *Nahj al-Balāgha*, Saying 450
4976 *Kanz al-Fawa'id*, v. 1, p. 199
4977 *Biḥār al-Anwār*, v. 78, p. 186, no. 16
4978 *Ghurar al-Ḥikam*, no. 4043
4979 Ibid. no. 7985
4980 Ibid. no. 9299
4981 Ibid. no. 7093
4982 Ibid. no. 4589
4983 Ibid. no. 4602
4984 Ibid. no. 4654
4985 Ibid. no. 1254
4986 *Maṭālib al-Sa'ūl*, p. 56
4987 *Nahj al-Balāgha*, Saying 211
4988 Ibid. Saying 252
4989 Ibid. Sermon 86
4990 *al-Durra al-Bāhira*, p. 31
4991 Qur'an 2:125
4992 *Kanz al-'Ummāl*, no. 18091
4993 *Kitāb man lā yaḥḍurahi al-Faqīh*, v. 2, p. 189, no. 2108

4994 *al-Tahdhīb*, v. 4, p. 287, no. 869
4995 *al-Kāfī*, v. 4, p. 176, no. 1
4996 Qur'an 39:9
4997 Qur'an 58:11
4998 *Kanz al-'Ummāl*, no. 28784
4999 *Biḥār al-Anwār*, v. 77, p. 175, no. 9
5000 *Amālī al-Ṭūsī*, p. 488, no. 1069
5001 *Amālī al-Ṣadūq*, p. 73, no. 41
5002 *Kanz al-'Ummāl*, no. 10647
5003 *Tafsīr al-Durr al-Manthūr*, v. 3, no. 423
5004 *Ghurar al-Ḥikam*, nos. 5234,6379
5005 *Tuḥaf al-'Uqūl*, p. 208
5006 *Ghurar al-Ḥikam*, no. 536
5007 Ibid. no. 837
5008 *Kanz al-Fawā'id*, v. 1, p. 319
5009 *'Uyūn Akhbār al-Riḍā (AS)*, v. 2, p. 66, no. 295
5010 *Munyat al-Murīd*, p. 110
5011 *al-Kāfī*, v. 8, p. 19, no. 4
5012 *Nahj al-Balāgha*, Saying 113
5013 Ibid. Saying 205
5014 Ibid. Saying 288
5015 *Ghurar al-Ḥikam*, no. 185
5016 *Amālī al-Ṣadūq*, p. 713, no. 982
5017 *Nahj al-Balāgha*, Saying 147
5018 Ibid.
5019 *Ghurar al-Ḥikam*, nos. 1124,1125
5020 *Amālī al-Ṭūsī*, p. 543, no. 1165
5021 *al-Kāfī*, v. 1, p. 32, no. 2
5022 *Munyat al-Murīd*, p. 105
5023 Ibid. p. 104
5024 *Biḥār al-Anwār*, v. 2, p. 19, no. 49
5025 *Rawḍat al-Wā'iẓīn*, no. 16
5026 Ibid. no. 17
5027 *Kanz al-'Ummāl*, no. 28908
5028 *al-Ikhtiṣāṣ*, p. 245
5029 *al-Da'awāt*, p. 62, no. 153
5030 *Kanz al-'Ummāl*, no. 28858
5031 *al-Nawādir al-Rāwandī*, p. 110, no. 94
5032 *Tanbīh al-Khawāṭir*, v. 1, p. 84
5033 *Kanz al-'Ummāl*, nos. 28697,28698
5034 *al-Kāfī*, v. 1, p. 30, no. 1
5035 *'Awālī al-La'ālī*, v. 1, p. 285, no. 135
5036 Ibid. v. 4, p. 61, no. 9
5037 *Kanz al-'Ummāl*, no. 28726
5038 Ibid.
5039 *al-Targhīb wa al-Tarhīb*, v. 1, p. 97, no. 16
5040 *Kanz al-'Ummāl*, no. 28702
5041 *Munyat al-Murīd*, p. 100
5042 *Kanz al-'Ummāl*, no. 28701
5043 Ibid. no. 28729
5044 Ibid. no. 28745
5045 *Amālī al-Ṣadūq*, p. 116, no. 99
5046 *Kanz al-'Ummāl*, no. 28842
5047 *Amālī al-Mufīd*, p. 29, no. 1
5048 *Majma' al-Bayān*, v. 9, p. 380
5049 *Tanbīh al-Khawāṭir*, v. 2, p. 212
5050 Ibid. v. 1, p. 82
5051 *Munyat al-Murīd*, p. 105
5052 *Amālī al-Ṭūsī*, p. 377, no. 808
5053 *Nahj al-Balāgha*, Saying 478
5054 *Ghurar al-Ḥikam*, no. 6888
5055 *Tuḥaf al-'Uqūl*, p. 297
5056 Ibid. no. 364
5057 *Thawāb al-A'māl*, p. 159, no. 1
5058 *al-Targhīb wa al-Tarhīb*, v. 1, p. 119, no. 5
5059 *Rawḍat al-Wā'iẓīn*, p. 16
5060 *Makārim al-Akhlāq*, v. 2, p. 364, no. 2661
5061 *Kanz al-'Ummāl*, no. 29035
5062 *al-Irshād*, v. 1, p. 230
5063 *Amālī al-Ṭūsī*, p. 167, no. 280
5064 *al-Maḥāsin*, v. 1, p. 359, no. 769
5065 *Kanz al-'Ummāl*, no. 28666
5066 *Ghurar al-Ḥikam*, no. 5048
5067 It can apparently be seen that the traditions in this chapter contradict with that of the previous chapter. This issue has been explained in the book *al-'Ilm wa al-Ḥikmah*. See (*al-'Ilm wa al-Ḥikmah fī al-Kitāb wa al-Sunnah*: section: The Etiquettes of Learning)
5068 *Tuḥaf al-'Uqūl*, p. 387
5069 *Munyat al-Murīd*, p. 193
5070 *'Awālī al-La'ālī*, v. 4, p. 74, no. 54
5071 *Tanbīh al-Khawāṭir*, v. 1, p. 85
5072 Qur'an 31:18
5073 *Munyat al-Murīd*, p. 185
5074 *Tanbīh al-Khawāṭir*, v. 2, p. 212
5075 *Kanz al-'Ummāl*, nos. 29363,29520
5076 Ibid. nos. 29364,28937
5077 *al-Khiṣāl*, p. 567, no. 1
5078 *Kanz al-'Ummāl*, no. 28883
5079 *Ghurar al-Ḥikam*, no. 4044

5080 Ibid. no. 8704
5081 *Kanz al-'Ummāl*, no. 44176
5082 *Tanbīh al-Khawāṭir*, v. 2, p. 112
5083 *Ghurar al-Ḥikam*, no. 6197
5084 Ibid. no. 10758
5085 Ibid. no. 8917
5086 *Kanz al-'Ummāl*, no. 28675
5087 Ibid. no. 28798
5088 *Ghurar al-Ḥikam*, no. 507
5089 *al-Iḥtijāj*, v. 1, p. 13, no. 7
5090 Qur'an 35:28
5091 *Ghurar al-Ḥikam*, no. 4624
5092 Ibid. no. 4600
5093 Ibid. no. 4642
5094 *Biḥār al-Anwār*, v. 2, p. 52, no. 18
5095 *Munyat al-Murīd*, no. 137
5096 *Ghurar al-Ḥikam*, no. 1740
5097 Ibid. no. 1303
5098 *al-Maḥāsin*, v. 1, p. 314, no. 621
5099 *Kanz al-'Ummāl*, no. 28709
5100 *Amālī al-Ṣadūq*, p. 507, no. 705
5101 *Amālī al-Ṭūsī*, p. 126, no. 198
5102 *Kanz al-'Ummāl*, no. 29337
5103 *Makārim al-Akhlāq*, v. 2, p. 364, no. 2661
5104 *Ghurar al-Ḥikam*, no. 3895
5105 *Biḥār al-Anwār*, v. 2, p. 29, no. 9
5106 *Ghurar al-Ḥikam*, nos. 1587,1588
5107 *Munyat al-Murīd*, p. 181
5108 *Nahj al-Balāgha*, Saying 98
5109 *Biḥār al-Anwār*, v. 2, p. 56, no. 33
5110 *Ghurar al-Ḥikam*, no. 6196
5111 *Nahj a-Balāgha*, Saying 366
5112 *Biḥār al-Anwār*, v. 2, p. 34, no. 30
5113 *al-Irshād*, v. 1, p. 230
5114 *Biḥār al-Anwār*, v. 2, p. 58, no. 39
5115 *Tafsīr al-Qummī*, v. 2, p. 146
5116 *Biḥār al-Anwār*, v. 2, p. 37, no. 53
5117 Ibid. v. 2, p. 32, no. 25
5118 *Munyat al-Murīd*, p. 141
5119 *al-Khiṣāl*, p. 113, no. 91
5120 *Munyat al-Murīd*, p. 137
5121 *Tanbīh al-Khawāṭir*, v. 2, p. 21
5122 *Biḥār al-Anwār*, v. 75, p. 381, no. 45
5123 *al-Iḥtijāj*, v. 2, p. 512, no. 337
5124 *al-Kāfī*, v. 1, p. 48, no. 4
5125 *al-Targhīb wa al-Tarhīb*, v. 1, p. 124, no. 1
5126 *Nahj al-Balāgha*, Letter 31
5127 *Amālī al-Ṣadūq*, p. 340, no. 403
5128 It is possible that what is meant by an unambiguous (*muḥkama*) verse here is referring to the principles of belief, an upright obligatory act is good deeds and an established recommended act is good morals. (See: *Sharḥ al-Kāfī*, by al-Māzanderāni, v. 2, p. 23)
5129 *al-Kāfī*, v. 1, p. 32, no. 1
5130 *Biḥār al-Anwār*, v. 1, p. 220, no. 52
5131 *Kanz al-Fawa'id*, v. 2, p. 31
5132 *Amālī al-Ṣadūq*, p. 576, no. 788
5133 *Biḥār al-Anwār*, v. 1, p. 218, no. 42
5134 *Ghurar al-Ḥikam*, no. 4962
5135 *Tuḥaf al-'Uqūl*, p. 286
5136 *al-Maḥāsin*, v. 1, p. 358, no. 765
5137 *Biḥār al-Anwār*, v. 1, p. 225, no. 17
5138 *Kanz al-'Ummāl*, no. 28820
5139 Ibid. nos. 5881,5893
5140 *A'lām al-Dīn*, p. 301
5141 *Amālī al-Ṣadūq*, p. 73, no. 41
5142 *Kanz al-'Ummāl*, no. 44154
5143 *Ghurar al-Ḥikam*, no. 3079
5144 *al-Kāfī*, v. 8, p. 32, no. 5
5145 *Biḥār al-Anwār*, v. 2, p. 92, no. 20
5146 Qur'an 35:11
5147 *Ghurar al-Ḥikam*, no. 3434
5148 *Tanbīh al-Khawāṭir*, v. 2, p. 218
5149 *Makārim al-Akhlāq*, v. 2, p. 364, no. 2661
5150 *A'lām al-Dīn*, p. 336, no. 12
5151 *Ghurar al-Ḥikam*, no. 9840
5152 *Nahj al-Balāgha*, Sermon 188
5153 Qur'an 39:56
5154 *Tanbīh al-Khawāṭir*, v. 2, p. 89
5155 *Ghurar al-Ḥikam*, no. 5214
5156 Ibid. no. 2618
5157 Ibid. no. 3429
5158 Qur'an 35:37
5159 *Kanz al-'Ummāl*, no. 2924
5160 *Nahj al-Balāgha*, Saying 326
5161 Ibid. Sermon 64
5162 *al-Khiṣāl*, p. 545, no. 24
5163 *Amālī al-Mufīd*, p. 60, no. 5
5164 *al-Khiṣāl*, p. 32, no. 112

5165 *'Uyūn Akhbār al-Riḍā (AS)*, v. 2, p. 38, no. 112
5166 *Biḥār al-Anwār*, v. 101, p. 4, no. 12
5167 Ibid. v. 69, p. 408, no. 117
5168 *Amālī al-Ṭūsī*, p. 245, no. 425
5169 *al-Zuhd li al-Ḥusayn b. Sa'īd*, p. 33, no. 87
5170 *Biḥār al-Anwār*, v. 94, p. 225, no. 1
5171 *al-Saḥīfat al-Sajjādiyya*, p. 82, Supplication 20
5172 *Biḥār al-Anwār*, v. 3, p. 83
5173 Qur'an 16:97
5174 *Kanz al-'Ummāl*, no. 42761
5175 *Nahj al-Balāgha*, Sermon 176
5176 Ibid. Saying 23
5177 Ibid. Saying 150
5178 *al-Kāfī*, v. 3, p. 266, no. 11
5179 *Tanbīh al-Khawāṭir*, v. 2, p. 183
5180 *al-Durra al-Bāhira*, p. 41
5181 Qur'an 4:123-124
5182 *Kanz al-'Ummāl*, no. 43676
5183 *Mustadrak al-Wasā'il*, v. 1, p. 130, no. 177
5184 *Nahj al-Balāgha*, Saying 278
5185 *al-Kāfī*, v. 2, p. 82, no. 3
5186 Ibid. no. 1
5187 *Biḥār al-Anwār*, v. 70, p. 191
5188 *Tanbīh al-Khawāṭir*, v. 1, p. 63
5189 *al-Kāfī*, v. 2, p. 191, no. 11
5190 *Biḥār al-Anwār*, v. 78, p. 69, no. 20
5191 *Ghurar al-Ḥikam*, no. 2958
5192 Ibid. no. 3322
5193 *al-Kāfī*, v. 2, p. 158, no. 4
5194 *al-Khiṣāl*, p. 125, no. 121
5195 *Kanz al-'Ummāl*, no. 43824 and 43937
5196 *Biḥār al-Anwār*, v. 77, p. 85
5197 *al-Kāfī*, v. 2, p. 400, no. 7
5198 Ibid. p. 361, no. 8
5199 *Sharḥ Nahj al-Balāgha li Ibn Abī al-Ḥadīd*, v. 18, p. 41
5200 *Nahj al-Balāgha*, Letter 69
5201 *Biḥār al-Anwār*, v. 71, p. 369, no. 19
5202 *Kanz al-'Ummāl*, no. 9128
5203 *Wasā'il al-Shī'a*, v. 2, p. 883, no. 1
5204 Qur'an 9:105
5205 *al-Targhīb wa al-Tarhīb*, v. 3, p. 458, no. 17
5206 *Kitāb man lā yaḥḍurahi al-Faqīh*, v. 1, p. 191, no. 582
5207 *'Uyūn Akhbār al-Riḍā (AS)*, v. 2, p. 44, no. 156
5208 *Biḥār al-Anwār*, v. 23, p. 337, no. 6
5209 *Wasā'il al-Shī'a*, v. 11, p. 392, no. 25
5210 Qur'an 45:29
5211 *Biḥār al-Anwār*, v. 5, p. 327, no. 22
5212 Qur'an 99:7,8
5213 Qur'an 3:30
5214 *Kanz al-'Ummāl*, no. 38963
5215 The Arabic word *'ahd*, here translated as covenant, includes anything by way of a promise, a pledge, a vow, a contract, an oath, a covenant or any such agreement between people (*ed.*)
5216 Qur'an 2:177
5217 *Kanz al-'Ummāl*, no. 10919
5218 Ibid. no. 10924
5219 *Biḥār al-Anwār*, v. 100, p. 46, no. 3
5220 *al-Nawādir al-Rāwandī*, p. 91, no. 27
5221 *Ghurar al-Ḥikam*, no. 3650
5222 *Nahj al-Balāgha*, Letter 53
5223 *Kanz al-'Ummāl*, no. 10937
5224 *Ghurar al-Ḥikam*, no. 9577
5225 *al-Kāfī*, v. 2, p. 162, no. 15
5226 Qur'an 16:92
5227 *Tafsīr al-Qummī*, v. 1, p. 389
5228 *Tafsīr al-'Ayyāshī*, v. 1, p. 289, no. 5
5229 *Biḥār al-Anwār*, v. 7, p. 42, no. 13
5230 *A'lām al-Dīn*, p. 341
5231 *al-Kāfī*, v. 8, p. 73, no. 29
5232 Qur'an 23:115
5233 Qur'an 38:27,28
5234 Qur'an 36:78,79
5235 Qur'an 19:66,67
5236 Qur'an 30:27
5237 Qur'an 30:50
5238 Qur'an 35:9
5239 The Hour refers to the Day of Resurrection (*ed.*)
5240 Qur'an 21:1
5241 *al-Ja'fariyyāt*, p. 212
5242 *Nahj al-Balāgha*, Sermon. 108
5243 Qur'an 33:63
5244 *Qaṣaṣ al-Anbiyā'*, p. 271, no. 346
5245 Qur'an 47:18
5246 Qur'an 39:68

5247 Qur'an 99:1
5248 Qur'an 89:21
5249 Qur'an 52:10
5250 Qur'an 101:5
5251 Qur'an 82:3
5252 Qur'an 81:1,2
5253 Qur'an 82:2
5254 Qur'an 69:16
5255 Qur'an 50:42 and See also 36:51-53
5256 *al-Khiṣāl*, p. 119, no. 108
5257 *Tanbīh al-Khawāṭir*, v. 2, p. 133
5258 Meaning he will be resurrected the way he lived in this world.
5259 *Al-Targhīb wa al-Tarhīb*, v. 4, p. 383, no. 10
5260 *Kanz al-'Ummāl*, no. 38938
5261 *Amālī al-Ṭūsī*, p. 653, no. 1353
5262 *Nahj al-Balāgha*, Sermon 102
5263 Qur'an 19:85
5264 *al-Kāfī*, v. 8, p. 95, no. 69
5265 *Thawāb al-A'māl*, p. 319, no. 1
5266 Ibid. p. 322, no. 8
5267 Ibid. p. 329, no. 1
5268 *al-Kāfī*, v. 2, p. 311, no. 11
5269 Ibid. p. 351, no. 2
5270 Qur'an 17:13,14
5271 *Tafsīr al-Qummī,* v. 2, p. 17
5272 Qur'an 18:49
5273 *Tafsīr al-'Ayyāshī*, v. 2, p. 328, no. 35
5274 Ibid. no. 34
5275 Qur'an 84:7-9
5276 *al-Zuhd li al-Ḥusayn b. Sa'īd*, p. 92, no. 246
5277 Qur'an 84:10-13
5278 *al-Zuhd li al-Ḥusayn b. Sa'īd*, p. 92, no. 246
5279 *Ghurar al-Ḥikam*, no. 702
5280 Ibid. no. 7327
5281 Ibid. no. 6409
5282 Ibid. no. 7634
5283 Ibid. no. 10288
5284 *Nahj al-Balāgha*, Letter 31
5285 A sweet made from water, flour and honey
5286 *Kanz al-'Ummāl*, no. 36549
5287 *Ghurar al-Ḥikam*, no. 6232
5288 *Tanbīh al-Khawāṭir*, v. 2, p. 113
5289 *Ghurar al-Ḥikam*, no. 357
5290 Ibid. no. 2873
5291 Ibid. no. 4300
5292 Ibid. no. 6405
5293 Ibid. no. 5199
5294 Ibid. no. 2969
5295 Ibid. no. 6906
5296 *Nahj al-Balāgha*, Saying 359
5297 Qur'an 5:114
5298 *Nahj al-Balāgha*, Saying 428
5299 *Khaṭīfa*: a food made of flour and milk (*ed.*)
5300 *Milbana*: a food made of bran, milk and honey (*ed.*)
5301 *Biḥār al-Anwār*, v. 40, p. 326, no. 7
5302 *Nayrūz*: The first day of spring, marking the Persian New Year (*ed.*)
5303 *Kitāb man lā yaḥḍurahi al-Faqīh,* v. 3, p. 300, no. 4073
5304 Ibid. no. 4074
5305 *Biḥār al-Anwār*, v. 59, p. 92, no. 1
5306 *Wasā'il al-Shī'a*, v. 7, p. 346, no. 1
5307 One of the Abbasid Caliphs (*ed.*)
5308 *Biḥār al-Anwār*, v. 59, p. 100, no. 2, and v. 48, p. 108, no. 9
5309 After quoting this tradition 'Allāma al-Majlisi says: This tradition is in contradiction with the traditions of al-Mu'allā and indicates that Nayrūz does not possess any religious credit, and the tradition narrated by al-Mu'allā is more authentic in its source and more well known among the scholars of ḥadith. It is possible to interpret this tradition as based on dissimulation (*taqiyya*), as there are some signs in al-Mu'allā's tradition that reveal this fact. (See footnote of *Biḥār al-Anwār,* v. 59, p. 100). [The author says] In our view, both the traditions lack the conditions of credibility, and as we have previously quoted from the Commander of the Faithful (AS) as saying, 'Our Nayrūz is everyday', and also, 'Every day in which Allah is not sinned in is a festive day. Of course, there is no problem with visiting one another on this day which is a good act, as is a custom in Iran.
5310 *Kanz al-'Ummāl*, no. 24094
5311 Ibid. no. 24095
5312 Ibid. no. 18101
5313 *Nahj al-Balāgha*, Sermon 176

5314 *Ghurar al-Ḥikam*, no. 3233
5315 *Tuḥaf al-'Uqūl*, p. 88
5316 *al-Kāfī*, v. 8, p. 243, no. 337
5317 *Mustaṭrafāt al-Sarā'ir*, p. 48, no. 7
5318 *Tuḥaf al-'Uqūl*, p. 501
5319 *Kanz al-'Ummāl*, no. 44141
5320 *al-Khiṣāl*, p. 110, no. 81
5321 *Nahj al-Balāgha*, Saying 349
5322 Ibid. Saying 353
5323 It was a pre-Islamic pagan practice to bury newborn daughters alive as a result of the disgrace they brought to a family, which Islam abolished (*ed.*)
5324 *Kanz al-'Ummāl*, no. 6387
5325 *al-Targhīb wa al-Tarhīb*, v. 3, p. 239, no. 7
5326 *al-Kāfī*, v. 2, p. 207, no. 8
5327 *Tanbīh al-Khawāṭir*, v. 1, p. 117
5328 *Ghurar al-Ḥikam*, no. 8260, 8261
5329 *Nahj al-Balāgha*, Sermon 113
5330 *Tuḥaf al-'Uqūl*, p. 366
5331 Qur'an 104:1
5332 *Thawāb al-A'māl*, p. 288, no. 1
5333 *Ghurar al-Ḥikam*, no. 4489
5334 *Nahj al-Balāgha*, Letter 53
5335 *Ghurar al-Ḥikam*, no. 10294
5336 *Kanz al-Fawā'id li al-Karājikī*, v. 1, p. 279
5337 *al-Kāfī*, v. 2, p. 355, no. 7
5338 *Kanz al-'Ummāl*, no. 28669
5339 *Nahj al-Balāgha*, Saying 6
5340 *Ghurar al-Ḥikam*, no. 6434
5341 *Nahj al-Balāgha*, Saying 223
5342 *Tuḥaf al-'Uqūl*, p. 215
5343 *Nahj al-Balāgha*, Saying 51
5344 *al-Irshād*, v. 1, p. 301
5345 *Kashf al-Ghamma*, v. 3, p. 137
5346 *Qaṣaṣ al-Anbiyā'*, p. 157, no. 171
5347 *Tanbīh al-Khawāṭir*, v. 1, p. 113
5348 *al-Kāfī*, v. 2, p. 356, no. 2
5349 *Tanbīh al-Khawāṭir*, v. 1, p. 57
5350 Ibid. v. 2, p. 155
5351 *al-Kāfī*, v. 2, p. 361, no. 9
5352 Ibid. p. 356, no. 1
5353 Ibid. p. 359, no. 1
5354 *Ghurar al-Ḥikam*, no. 2964
5355 Ibid. no. 2918
5356 Ibid. no. 3295
5357 *'Ilal al-Sharā'i'*, p. 560, no. 1
5358 *Tuḥaf al-'Uqūl*, p. 320
5359 *al-Khiṣāl*, p. 284, no. 34
5360 *Ghurar al-Ḥikam*, no. 5973
5361 Ibid. no. 5651
5362 Ibid. no. 9224
5363 *Nahj al-Balāgha*, no. 282
5364 *Tuḥaf al-'Uqūl*, p. 282
5365 Ibid. no. 319
5366 Qur'an 82:6-8
5367 *Makārim al-Akhlāq*, v. 2, p. 350, no. 2660
5368 *Tuḥaf al-'Uqūl*, p. 150
5369 *Tanbīh al-Khawāṭir*, v. 2, p. 72
5370 *Nahj al-Balāgha*, Saying 116
5371 *Ghurar al-Ḥikam*, no. 2562
5372 Ibid. no. 5650
5373 *Biḥār al-Anwār*, v. 78, p. 83, no. 86
5374 *Ghurar al-Ḥikam*, no. 8744
5375 Qur'an 3:123,124
5376 *Kanz al-'Ummāl*, no. 29942
5377 Ibid. no. 29943
5378 *al-Irshād*, v. 1, p. 73
5379 Qur'an 3:121
5380 *Hubal* and *'Uzza* were two of the idol gods that the pagan Arabs worshipped (*ed.*)
5381 *al-Durr al-Manthūr*, v. 2, p. 345
5382 Qur'an 3:128
5383 *Ṣaḥīḥ Muslim*, v. 3, p. 1417, no. 104
5384 *Kanz al-'Ummāl*, no. 30027
5385 *Biḥār al-Anwār*, v. 20, p. 179, no. 6
5386 *Aḥzāb* : the factions (*ed.*)
5387 *Kanz al-'Ummāl*, no. 30115
5388 Qur'an 90:6
5389 *Tafsīr al-Qummī*, v. 2, p. 422
5390 *al-Kāfī*, v. 8, p. 216, no. 264
5391 *Kanz al-'Ummāl*, no. 30120
5392 Joseph: known as Prophet Yūsuf (AS) in the Arabic tradition (*ed.*)
5393 Qur'an 12:92
5394 *Kanz al-'Ummāl*, no. 30158
5395 *Amālī al-Ṭūsī*, p. 342, no. 701
5396 Qur'an 17:81
5397 *Biḥār al-Anwār*, v. 21, p. 116, no. 11
5398 Ibid. p. 180, no. 16
5399 *Biḥār al-Anwār*, v. 76, p. 365, no. 30

5400 *Kanz al-'Ummāl*, no. 9501
5401 *al-Targhīb wa al-Tarhīb*, v. 2, p. 571, no. 2
5402 *Nahj al-Balāgha*, Letter 26
5403 *Ghurar al-Ḥikam*, no. 8891
5404 *al-Kāfī*, v. 5, p. 160, no. 1
5405 Ibid. no. 6
5406 *'Awālī al-La'ālī,* v.1, p. 364, no. 56
5407 *Kanz al-'Ummāl*, no. 30366
5408 Ibid. no. 30343
5409 *Nahj al-Balāgha*, Saying 240
5410 *Wasā'il al-Shī'a*, v. 17, p. 311, no. 1
5411 Ibid. v.17, p. 309, no. 4
5412 *Biḥār al-Anwār*, v. 73, p. 265, no. 15
5413 *Nahj al-Balāgha*, Saying 255
5414 *al-Kāfī*, v. 2, p. 303, no. 3
5415 Ibid. p. 305, no. 13
5416 *Nathr al-Durar*, v. 1, p. 183
5417 *Tuḥaf al-'Uqūl*, p. 286
5418 *al-Kāfī*, v. 2, p. 305, no. 13
5419 Qur'an 3:134
5420 Qur'an 42:37
5421 *Tanbīh al-Khawāṭir*, v. 1, p. 121
5422 *Biḥār al-Anwār*, v. 73, p. 263, no. 7
5423 *al-Kāfī*, v. 2, p. 110, no. 7
5424 Ibid. p. 109, no. 3
5425 *Tuḥaf al-'Uqūl*, p. 14
5426 *Ghurar al-Ḥikam*, no. 5155
5427 *Wasā'il al-Shī'a*, v. 11, p. 416, no. 3
5428 *al-Maḥajjat al-Bayḍā'*, v. 5, p. 303
5429 *Nahj al-Balāgha*, Saying 31
5430 Qur'an 3:135
5431 Qur'an 4:110
5432 *Mustadrak al-Wasā'il*, v. 12, p. 146, no. 13744
5433 *al-Kāfī*, v. 2, p. 504, no. 1
5434 *al-Kāfī*, v. 2, p. 517, no. 2
5435 *Tanbīh al-Khawāṭir*, v. 1, p. 5
5436 *Nahj al-Balāgha*, Saying 87
5437 *Biḥār al-Anwār*, v. 93, p. 278, no. 7
5438 *Nahj al-Balāgha*, Saying 135
5439 *al-Kāfī*, v. 2, p. 437, no. 1
5440 Qur'an 11:3
5441 Qur'an 11:52
5442 Qur'an 71:10
5443 *Nahj al-Balāgha*, Sermon 143
5444 *Biḥār al-Anwār*, v. 93, p. 277, no. 4
5445 *Ghurar al-Ḥikam*, no. 2228
5446 *Mustadrak al-Wasā'il*, v. 5, p. 320, no. 5987
5447 *Tuḥaf al-'Uqūl*, p. 223
5448 *al-Kāfī*, v. 2, p. 504, no. 3
5449 *Biḥār al-Anwār*, v. 78, p. 356, no. 11
5450 *Ghurar al-Ḥikam*, no. 196
5451 *Nahj al-Balāgha*, Sermon 64
5452 Ibid. Sermon 153
5453 Ibid. Sermon 175
5454 *Biḥār al-Anwār*, v. 77, p. 401, no. 26
5455 Ibid. v. 78, p. 190, no. 1
5456 *Makārim al-Akhlāq*, v. 2, p. 378, no. 2661
5457 *Ghurar al-Ḥikam*, no. 4269
5458 *al-Tawḥīd*, p. 74, no. 27
5459 *al-Kāfī*, v. 3, p. 270, no. 14
5460 *al-Khiṣāl*, p. 121, no. 113
5461 *Biḥār al-Anwār*, v. 78, p. 115, no. 10
5462 *Ghurar al-Ḥikam*, no. 8318
5463 Ibid. no. 8430
5464 Ibid. no. 5146
5465 Ibid. no. 2717
5466 Ibid. no. 2378
5467 *Nahj al-Balāgha*, Saying 222
5468 *Tuḥaf al-'Uqūl*, p. 359
5469 Qur'an 59:10
5470 Qur'an 15:47
5471 *Biḥār al-Anwār*, v. 14, p. 305, no. 17
5472 *Kanz al-'Ummāl*, no. 11044
5473 *Ghurar al-Ḥikam*, no. 547
5474 Ibid. no. 642
5475 Ibid. no. 2932
5476 *Kanz al-'Ummāl*, no. 44272. Ibn Athīr states in *al-Nahāya,* v. 3, p. 381: 'The hearts are reformed through these three things and the hearts of those who acquire these three will be purified from treachery, deception and wrongdoing.
5477 Qur'an 3:161
5478 *al-Durr al-Manthūr*, v. 2, p. 361
5479 *al-Targhīb wa al-Tarhīb*, v. 2, p. 307, no. 4
5480 *Tafsīr al-'Ayyāshī*, v. 1, p. 205, no. 148
5481 *al-ghuluw*: Extremism in religion is a term used specifically to denote people who raise the Imāms or the Prophet (AS) above their statuses designated by Allah, raising them to the level of lordship or divinity. Such

people were severely rebuked and condemned by the Prophet and the Imāms themselves (*ed.*)
5482 Qur'an 4:171
5483 *al-Nawādir al-Rāwandī*, p. 125, no. 143
5484 *Qurb al-Isnād*, p. 64, no. 204
5485 Qur'an 43:57
5486 *Biḥār al-Anwār*, v. 25, p. 284, no. 34
5487 *Nahj al-Balāgha*, Saying 469
5488 *Biḥār al-Anwār*, v. 25, p. 284, no. 32
5489 *al-Khiṣāl*, p. 614, no. 10
5490 *Biḥār al-Anwār*, v. 25, p. 274, no. 20
5491 *Amālī al-Ṭūsī*, p. 650, no. 1349
5492 *Biḥār al-Anwār*, v. 25, p. 294, no. 52
5493 *al-mufawwiḍa*: name given to the adherents of a school of thought that believed in the total empowerment of man as the cause and author of his own deeds, devoid of any involvement therein by God, apart from being the first cause. This was in contrast to the other extreme, *al-jabariyya*, who believed in the absolute predestination of man's deeds by God (*ed.*)
5494 Ibid. p. 273, no. 19
5495 Ibid. p. 274, no. 20
5496 Qur'an 96:6,7
5497 *Kanz al-'Ummāl*, no. 16677
5498 *Nahj al-Balāgha*, Saying 108
5499 *al-Kāfī*, v. 2, p. 262, no. 11
5500 Qur'an 93:8
5501 *al-Ja'fariyyāt*, p. 155
5502 *al-Kāfī*, v. 5, p. 71, no. 4
5503 *Nahj al-Balāgha*, Saying 371
5504 Ibid. Saying 54
5505 *Amālī al-Mufīd*, p. 183, no. 6
5506 *al-Durra al-Bāhira*, p. 41
5507 *al-Kāfī*, v. 2, p. 139, no. 8
5508 *Kanz al-'Ummāl*, no. 7156
5509 *Amālī al-Ṣadūq*, p. 394, no. 1
5510 *Kashf al-Ghamma*, v. 3, p. 137
5511 *Nahj al-Balāgha*, Saying 342
5512 Ibid. Saying 38
5513 *al-Kāfī*, v. 2, p. 139, no. 9
5514 *Tuḥaf al-'Uqūl*, p. 318
5515 *Biḥār al-Anwār*, v. 78, p. 9, no. 65
5516 Ibid. p. 8, no. 64
5517 *Amālī al-Ṭūsī*, p. 580, no. 1198
5518 *Tuḥaf al-'Uqūl*, p. 287
5519 Qur'an 34:37
5520 *Tafsīr al-Qummī*, v. 2, p. 203
5521 *Nahj al-Balāgha*, Saying 328
5522 *Kanz al-'Ummāl*, no. 16840
5523 *Ghurar al-Ḥikam*, no. 10738
5524 The Arabic word *ghinā'* lexically means 'singing' but has been translated in juristic books to denote music in general because of the connotations suggested in the prophetic traditions (*ed.*)
5525 Qur'an 22:30
5526 *Biḥār al-Anwār*, v. 79, p. 250, no. 2
5527 *Kanz al-'Ummāl*, no. 40661
5528 Qur'an 31:6
5529 *Kitāb man lā yaḥḍurahi al-Faqīh*, v. 4, p. 58, no. 5092
5530 *Biḥār al-Anwār*, v. 79, p. 247, no. 26
5531 *lahw*: translated as 'diversionary talk' in the translation of the Qur'an, and often interpreted as music in exegeses of the Qur'an (*ed.*)
5532 Ibid. p. 252, no. 6
5533 Ibid. p. 241, no. 7
5534 *Qaṣaṣ al-Anbiyā'*, p. 308, no. 408
5535 *Nahj al-Balāgha*, Sermon 128
5536 *al-Kāfī*, v. 1, p. 257, no. 4
5537 Ibid. p. 256, no. 1
5538 Qur'an 49:12
5539*Tanbīh al-Khawāṭir*, v. 1, p. 115
5540 *al-Targhīb wa al-Tarhīb*, v. 3, p. 511, no. 24
5541 *Nahj al-Balāgha*, Saying 461
5542 *Tuḥaf al-'Uqūl*, p. 245
5543 *Biḥār al-Anwār*, v. 75, p. 249, no. 16
5544 Ibid. p. 246, no. 8
5545 *al-Kāfī*, v. 2, p. 357, no. 1
5546 *Biḥār al-Anwār*, v. 75, p. 258, no. 53
5547 *Jāmi' al-Akhbār*, p. 412, no. 1144
5548 *Biḥār al-Anwār*, v. 77, p. 89, no. 3
5549 *Kanz al-'Ummāl*, no. 8024
5550 *al-Targhīb wa al-Tarhīb*, v. 3, p. 506, no. 13
5551 *al-Kāfī*, v. 2, p. 358, no. 6
5552 *Biḥār al-Anwār*, v. 75, p. 261, no. 64
5553 *Kanz al-'Ummāl*, no. 8074
5554 *Ghurar al-Ḥikam*, no. 1171
5555 *al-Ikhtiṣāṣ*, p. 225
5556 *al-Khiṣāl*, p. 566, no. 1

5557 *Amālī al-Ṣadūq*, p. 516, no. 707
5558 *Kitāb man lā yaḥḍurahi al-Faqīh,* v. 4, p. 372
5559 *al-Kāfī*, v. 2, p. 357, no. 4
5560 *Kanz al-'Ummāl*, no. 8037
5561 *ghīra*: This word, that has been translated as possessiveness, denotes a possessiveness stemming from a sense of self-honour and self-worth, where a man who has the quality of *ghīra* would be a possessive or jealous husband, seen as a positive trait because of its stemming from self-honour. When *ghīra* is ascribed to Allah, it denotes His being deserving of and demanding exclusive worship, loyalty and adherence. In other texts, *ghīra* has been translated equally as jealousy, zeal, and fervour. In this text therefore, it will be translated according to its connotations in individual traditions (*ed.*)
5562 *Kitāb man lā yaḥḍurahi al-Faqīh,* v. 3, p. 444, no. 4541
5563 *Biḥār al-Anwār*, v. 103, p. 248, no. 33
5564 *Kanz al-'Ummāl*, no. 7072
5565 *Kitāb man lā yaḥḍurahi al-Faqīh,* v. 3, p. 444, no. 4542
5566 *Nahj al-Balāgha*, Saying 47
5567 Ibid. Saying 305
5568 *al-Maḥāsin*, v. 1, p. 204, 355
5569 *al-Kāfī*, v. 5, p. 535, no. 1
5570 *Kanz al-'Ummāl*, no. 7067
5571 *Nahj al-Balāgha*, Letter 31
5572 *Biḥār al-Anwār*, v. 47, p. 214, no. 1
5573 *al-Firdaws*, v. 3, p. 106, no. 4295. *al-Dūr al-Manthūr*, v. 4, p. 326
5574 *al-Kāfī*, v. 5, p. 537, no. 1
5575 Qur'an 29:2-3
5576 Qur'an 9:126
5577 *al-Kāfī*, v. 1, p. 370, no. 4
5578 *Qur'an* 8:28
5579 *Kanz al-'Ummāl*, no. 44129
5580 *al-Targhīb wa al-Tarhīb*, v. 4, p. 184, no. 74
5581 *Biḥār al-Anwār*, v. 73, p. 140, no. 12
5582 *Nahj al-Balāgha*, Saying 322
5583 *al-Targhīb wa al-Tarhīb*, v. 1, p. 54, no. 5
5584 *Kanz al-'Ummāl*, no. 30883
5585 *Nahj al-Balāgha*, Sermon 183
5586 *Kanz al-'Ummāl*, no. 30893
5587 *Ghurar al-Ḥikam*, no. 9163
5588 Ibid. no. 10109
5589 *Nahj al-Balāgha*, Saying 1
5590 The word *'fatwa'* in Arabic specifically denotes a legal verdict or juristic edict (*ed.*)
5591 *Biḥār al-Anwār*, v. 2, p. 123, no. 48
5592 Ibid. v. 2, p. 172, no. 3
5593 Ibid. v. 2, p. 299, no. 25
5594 Ibid. v. 2, p. 260
5595*Nahj al-Balāgha*, letter 67
5596 *Mustadrak al-Wasā'il*. v. 17, p. 315, no. 21452
5597 *Biḥār al-Anwār*, v. 79, p. 111, no. 6
5598 *al-Kāfī*, v. 2, p. 323, no. 3
5599 Ibid. v. 2, p. 325, p. 8
5600 *Ghurar al-Ḥikam*, no. 9478
5601 *al-Kāfī*, v. 2, no. 324, no. 4
5602 *Biḥār al-Anwār*, v. 78, p. 181, no. 67
5603 Ibid. v. 78, p. 185, no. 14
5604 Ibid. v. 79, p. 113, no. 14
5605 *al-Kāfī*, v. 2, p. 327, no. 3
5606 Qur'an 57:20
5607 Qur'an 31:18
5608 *al-Targhīb wa al-Tarhīb*, v. 3, p. 558, no. 1
5609 *al-Kāfī*, v. 2, p. 328, no. 2
5610 *al-Khiṣāl*, p. 69, no. 102
5611 *Nahj al-Balāgha*, Saying 398
5612 *Ghurar al-Ḥikam*, no. 10655
5613 *Nahj al-Balāgha*, Sermon 216
5614 *Mustadrak al-Wasā'il*, v. 12, p. 90, no. 13599
5615 *Nahj al-Balāgha*, Sermon 454
5616 *al-Kāfī*, v. 2, p. 328, no. 1
5617 *Biḥār al-Anwār*, v. 16, p. 341, no. 33
5618 Ibid. v. 72, p. 30
5619 *al-Kāfī*, v. 8, p. 234, no. 311
5620 *Kanz al-'Ummāl*, no. 34126
5621 *Sunan al-Tirmidhī*, v. 5 p. 60
5622 *Majma' al-Bayān*, v. 3 p. 321
5623 *Kanz al-'Ummāl*, no. 34131
5624 *al-Firdaws*, v. 3, p. 360
5625 *Kanz al-'Ummāl*, no. 34128
5626 Ibid. no. 43134
5627 *Biḥār al-Anwār*, v. 77, p. 165, no. 2
5628 *Nahj al-Balāgha*, Saying 21
5629 *Ghurar al-Ḥikam*, no. 2019
5630 Ibid. no. 194
5631 *Nahj al-Balāgha*, Saying 118

5632 *Biḥār al-Anwār*, v. 77, p. 165, no. 2
5633 *Nahj al-Balāgha*, Saying 363
5634 *Biḥār al-Anwār*, v. 78, p. 268, no. 181
5635 *al-Kāfī*, v. 2, p. 82, no. 4
5636 *Nahj al-Balāgha*, Sermon 167
5637 Ibid. Sermon 113
5638 Ibid. Letter 69
5639 Ibid. Saying 113
5640 *Ghurar al-Ḥikam*, no. 3793
5641 *Biḥār al-Anwār*, v. 23, p. 99, no. 3
5642 *al-Kāfī*, v. 2, p. 81, no. 1
5643 Ibid. v. 2, p. 82, no. 5
5644 *Nahj al-Balāgha*, Sermon 209
5645 Ibid. Saying 328
5646 Ibid. Saying 252
5647 Ibid. Saying 382
5648 *Biḥār al-Anwār*, v. 68, p. 388, no. 39
5649 Qur'an 94:7,8
5650 *Tanbīh al-Khawāṭir*, v. 1, p. 60
5651 *Sharḥ Nahj al-Balāgha li B. Abī al-Hadīd*, v. 17, p. 146
5652 *al-Kāfī*, v. 8, p. 152, no. 136
5653 *Ghurar al-Ḥikam*, no. 9251
5654 *Nahj al-Balāgha*, Letter 59
5655 *Ghurar al-Ḥikam*, no. 9684
5656 *Biḥār al-Anwār*, v. 77, p. 419, no. 40
5657 *al-Ṣaḥīfa al-Sajjādiyya*, Supplication 11
5658 Ibid. supplication 20
5659 Ibid. supplication 20
5660 Ibid. supplication 47
5661 *Kitāb man lā yaḥḍurahi al-Faqīh*, v. 3, p. 169, no. 3635
5662 Qur'an 30:41
5663 *Biḥār al-Anwār*, v. 100, p. 74, no. 15
5664 *Amālī al-Mufīd*, p. 235, no. 5
5665 *Biḥār al-Anwār*, v. 77, p. 258, no. 1
5666 Qur'an 5:33
5667 Qur'an 27:34
5668 Qur'an 2:11
5669 Qur'an 26:151,152
5670 *al-Khiṣāl*, p. 37, no. 12
5671 *al-Kāfī*, v. 8, p. 23, no. 4
5672 *Kitāb man lā yaḥḍurahi al-Faqīh*, v. 3, p. 167, no. 3625
5673 *Majma' al-Bayān*, v. 2, p. 621, and *Nūr al-Thaqalayn*, v. 1, p. 253, no. 1007
5674 *Nahj al-Balāgha*, Sermon 178
5675 Qur'an 2:251
5676 *al-Kāfī*, v. 2, p. 451, no. 1
5677 *Ghurar al-Ḥikam*, no. 1925
5678 Ibid. no. 6559
5679 *Nahj al-Balāgha*, Sermon 193
5680 *Ghurar al-Ḥikam*, no. 5139
5681 Ibid. no. 8905
5682 Ibid. no. 7179
5683 *al-Kāfī*, v. 2, p. 107, no. 4
5684 *Kashf al-Ghamma*, v. 3, p. 138
5685 *Ghurar al-Ḥikam*, no. 805
5686 Ibid. no. 4899
5687 Ibid. no. 10625
5688 Ibid. no. 5237
5689 Ibid. no. 6379
5690 *Tanbīh al-Khawāṭir*, v. 1, p. 100
5691 *A'lām al-Dīn*, p. 337, no. 15
5692 *Nahj al-Balāgha*, Sermon 164
5693 Ibid. Sermon 125
5694 *al-Kāfī*, v. 2, p. 307, no. 4
5695 *Kanz al-'Ummāl*, no. 16687
5696 *Jāmi' al-Akhbār*, p. 300 no. 817
5697 *Ghurar al-Ḥikam*, no. 3428
5698 *Jāmi' al-Akhbār*, p. 299, no. 816
5699 *Nahj al-Balāgha*, Saying 319
5700 Ibid. Saying 3
5701 *Jāmi' al-Akhbār*, p. 300, no. 818
5702 *Nahj al-Balāgha*, Saying 319
5703 Ibid. Saying 56
5704 *Uddat al-Dā'ī*, p. 113
5705 *al-Firdaws*, v. 3, p. 157, no. 4423
5706 *Kanz al-'Ummāl*, no. 16669
5707 *al-Kāfī*, v. 2, p. 265, no. 22
5708 Ibid. v. 2, p. 260, no. 2
5709 *Shu'ab al-Imān*, v. 5, p. 388, no. 7040
5710 *Biḥār al-Anwār*, v. 72, p. 56, no. 86
5711 *Ghurar al-Ḥikam*, no. 5904
5712 *al-Kāfī*, v. 2, p. 263, no. 12
5713 *Biḥār al-Anwār*, v. 72, p. 31, no. 26
5714 Qur'an 35:15
5715 Qur'an 9:60
5716 Qur'an 28:24
5717 *Mufradāt Alfāẓ al-Qur'ān*, p. 641
5718 Prophet Enoch (AS) is known as Idrīs in the Arabic tradition (*ed.*)

5719 *Biḥār al-Anwār*, v. 95, p. 462
5720 Ibid. v. 77, p. 150, no. 86
5721 Ibid. v. 72, p. 56, no. 86
5722 *Nahj al-Balāgha*, Saying 54
5723 Ibid. Saying 38
5724 *Biḥār al-Anwār*, v. 77, p. 377, no. 1
5725 *Ghurar al-Ḥikam*, no. 6547
5726 *Nahj al-Balāgha*, Saying 452
5727 *Tuḥaf al-ʿUqūl*, p. 216
5728 Ibid. no. 225
5729 *Biḥār al-Anwār*, v. 78, p. 368, no. 3
5730 *Maʿānī al-Akhbār*, p. 165, no. 1
5731 *al-Kharāʾij wa al-Jarāʾiḥ*, v. 2, p. 739, no. 54
5732 *Kitāb man lā yaḥḍurahi al-Faqīh*, v. 3, p. 166, no. 3614
5733 *al-Kāfī*, v. 2, p. 266, no. 2
5734 *Biḥār al-Anwār*, v. 72, p. 44, no. 52
5735 *al-Khiṣāl*, p. 614, no. 10
5736 *Amālī al-Ṣadūq*, p. 527, no. 714
5737 *Biḥār al-Anwār*, v. 74, p. 103, no. 61
5738 *Ghurar al-Ḥikam*, no. 5156
5739 *Biḥār al-Anwār*, v. 74, p. 81, no. 83
5740 *al-Khiṣāl*, p. 9, no. 32
5741 *Biḥār al-Anwār*, v. 76, p. 316, no. 6
5742 Ibid. v. 75, p. 114, no. 6
5743 *Tuḥaf al-ʿUqūl*, p. 221
5744 *Biḥār al-Anwār*, v. 103, p. 20, no. 4
5745 Ibid. v. 78, p. 184, no. 11
5746 Ibid. v. 76, p. 316, no. 6
5747 Ibid. v. 104, p. 99, no. 77
5748 *al-Kāfī*, v. 2, p. 264, no. 18
5749 Qurʾan 2: 273
5750 *al-Kāfī*, v. 2, p. 260, no. 3
5751 *Nahj al-Balāgha*, Saying 68
5752 *Biḥār al-Anwār*, v. 78, p. 249, no. 87
5753 *al-Kāfī*, v. 2, p. 263, no. 13
5754 *Biḥār al-Anwār*, v. 72, p. 49, no. 58
5755 *Musnad Ibn Ḥanbal*, v. 1, p. 504, no. 2086
5756 *Biḥār al-Anwār*, v. 71, p. 267, no. 17
5757 Ibid. v. 72, p. 52, no. 76
5758 Ibid. v. 72, p. 25, no. 19
5759 Qurʾan 9:122
5760 *Kanz al-ʿUmmāl*, no. 28690
5761 *al-Targhīb wa al-Tarhīb*, v. 1, p. 93, no. 3
5762 *Kanz al-ʿUmmāl*, no. 28768
5763 *Nahj al-Balāgha*, Sermon 110
5764 *Biḥār al-Anwār*, v. 78, p. 321, no. 19
5765 The original meaning of *faqīh* is 'learned man' or 'scholar', but it has acquired a more specific meaning in Islamic terminology, which is a 'jurist' or 'a religious scholar well-versed in Islamic law and jurisprudence (*fiqh*)' (*ed.*)
5766 *Nahj al-Balāgha*, Saying 90
5767 *Tuḥaf al-ʿUqūl*, p. 204
5768 *al-Kāfī*, v. 1, p. 70, no. 8
5769 *Maʿānī al-Akhbār*, v. 2, p. 3
5770 *al-Ikhtiṣāṣ*, p. 232
5771 *Biḥār al-Anwār*, v. 1, p. 177, no. 48
5772 *Kanz al-ʿUmmāl*, no. 28755
5773 *Biḥār al-Anwār*, v. 1, p. 213, no. 10
5774 *al-Kāfī*, v. 1, p. 38, no. 2
5775 Ibid. v. 1, p. 38, no. 1
5776 Qurʾan 2: 219
5777 *al-Kāfī*, v. 2, p. 55, no. 5
5778 *Nahj al-Balāgha*, Letter 31
5779 *Ghurar al-Ḥikam*, no. 8917
5780 *Nahj al-Balāgha*, Saying 113
5781 Ibid. Saying 5
5782 *Biḥār al-Anwār*, v. 78, p. 115, no. 11
5783 *Tanbīh al-Khawāṭir*, v. 1, p. 52
5784 *Biḥār al-Anwār*, v. 71, p. 326, no. 20
5785 *Tanbīh al-Khawāṭir*, v. 1, p. 250
5786 *al-Kāfī*, v. 2, p. 55, no. 3
5787 Qurʾan 39:9
5788 *Biḥār al-Anwār*, v. 71, p. 327, no. 22
5789 *Ghurar al-Ḥikam*, no. 8462
5790 Ibid. no. 6975
5791 Ibid. no. 1278
5792 Ibid. no. 8561
5793 Ibid. no. 8487
5794 *Biḥār al-Anwār*, v. 6, p. 242, no. 64
5795 *Tanbīh al-Khawāṭir*, v. 2, p. 225
5796 *al-Jaʿfariyyāt*, p. 205
5797 *Tanbīh al-Khawāṭir*, v. 1, p. 284
5798 *Ghurar al-Ḥikam*, no. 4800
5799 *al-Kāfī*, v. 3, p. 242, no. 2
5800 *Maʿānī al-Akhbār*, p. 343, no. 1
5801 Qurʾan 14:27
5802 *Biḥār al-Anwār*, v. 6, p. 228, no. 29
5803 *al-Kāfī*, v. 3, p. 241, no. 15
5804 Ibid. v. 3, p. 236, no. 4
5805 *Amālī al-Ṭūsī*, p. 28, no. 31

5806 *Nahj al-Balāgha*, Sermon 20
5807 *Thawāb al-A'māl*, p. 55 no. 1
5808 Qur'an 5:32
5809 *Amālī al-Ṣadūq*, p. 73, no. 41
5810 *Kanz al-'Ummāl*, no. 39887
5811 *al-Targhīb wa al-Tarhīb*, v. 3, p. 293, no. 6
5812 *Kitāb man lā yaḥḍurahi al-Faqīh*, v. 3, p. 565, no. 4934
5813 Qur'an 4:93
5814 *Kanz al-'Ummāl*, no. 39952
5815 Ibid. no. 39895
5816 Qur'an 5:29
5817 *Thawāb al-A'māl*, p. 328, no. 9
5818 *al-Kāfī*, v. 7, p. 276, no. 2
5819 Qur'an 4:29
5820 *al-Kāfī*, v. 3, p. 112, no. 8
5821 *Kitāb man lā yaḥḍurahi al-Faqīh*, v. 4, p. 95, no. 5163
5822 Qur'an 15:87
5823 Qur'an 54:17
5824 *Kanz al-'Ummāl*, no. 4027
5825 *Tafsīr al-'Ayyāshī*, v. 1, p. 6, no. 11
5826 *Kanz al-'Ummāl*, no. 4029
5827 *Biḥār al-Anwār*, v. 92, p. 19, no. 18
5828 Ibid. v. 92, p. 19, no. 18
5829 *Ma'ānī al-Akhbār*, p. 279
5830 Meaning that they should contemplate in its meaning and interpret its exegesis. (See: *al-Nihāya*, v. 1, p. 229)
5831 *Kanz al-'Ummāl*, no. 2454
5832 *Nahj al-Balāgha*, Sermon 147
5833 Ibid. Letter 47
5834 *Tuḥaf al-'Uqūl*, 150
5835 Ibid. Sermon 176
5836 *al-Kāfī*, v. 2, p. 602, no. 13
5837 *Nahj al-Balāgha*, Sermon 156
5838 *Biḥār al-Anwār*, v. 92, p. 15, no. 8
5839 Ibid. v. 92, p. 186, no. 2
5840 *Kanz al-'Ummāl*, no. 2368
5841 Ibid. no. 2382
5842 *Nahj al-Balāgha*, Saying 399
5843 *al-Da'awāt*, p. 220, no. 600
5844 *Kanz al-'Ummāl*, no. 2317
5845 Ibid. no. 2478
5846 Ibid. no. 2849
5847 *Jāmi' al-Akhbār*, p. 115 no. 202
5848 *al-Khiṣāl*, p. 7, no. 21
5849 *al-Kāfī*, v. 2, p. 604, no. 5
5850 *Kanz al-'Ummāl*, no. 2347
5851 *al-Kāfī*, v. 2, p. 603, no. 2
5852 *Thawāb al-A'māl*, p. 283, no. 1
5853 Qur'an 35:29
5854 *Kanz al-'Ummāl*, no. 2257
5855 Ibid. no. 2330
5856 Ibid. no. 2441
5857 *Biḥār al-Anwār*, v. 92, p. 17, no. 18
5858 *Kanz al-'Ummāl*, no. 4032
5859 Ibid. no. 2768
5860 *Biḥār al-Anwār*, v. 92, p. 190, no. 2
5861 Ibid. v. 92, p. 195, no. 10
5862 *Kanz al-'Ummāl*, no. 2777
5863 Qur'an 2:121
5864 Qur'an 38:29
5865 *Tanbīh al-Khawāṭir*, v. 2, p. 236
5866 *Biḥār al-Anwār*, v. 92, p. 213, no. 11
5867 Qur'an 16:98
5868 *Tafsīr al-'Ayyāshī*, v. 2, p. 270, no. 68
5869 Qur'an 73:4
5870 *al-Nawādir al-Rāwandī*, p. 164, no. 247
5871 Qur'an 38:29
5872 *Biḥār al-Anwār*, v. 92, p. 211, no. 4
5873 *al-Kāfī*, v. 2, p. 617, no. 1
5874 Qur'an 57:16
5875 *Biḥār al-Anwār*, v. 92, p. 195, p. 10
5876 *'Uyūn Akhbār al-Riḍā (AS)*, v. 2, p. 182, no. 5
5877 *Biḥār al-Anwār*, v. 92, p. 184, p. 19
5878 *Sharḥ Nahj al-Balāgha li Ibn Abī al-Ḥadīd*, v. 10 p. 23
5879 *Jāmi' al-Akhbār*, p. 130, no. 254
5880 Qur'an 7:204
5881 *Kanz al-'Ummāl*, no. 2472
5882 Ibid. no. 2316
5883 *Biḥār al-Anwār*, v. 92, p. 222, no. 7
5884 Ibid. v. 92, p. 107, no. 1
5885 *Munyat al- Murīd*, p. 369
5886 *Biḥār al-Anwār*, v. 92, p. 110, no. 11
5887 Qur'an 27:10,11
5888 Qur'an 27:88,89
5889 Qur'an 83: 28
5890 *al-Kāfī*, v. 2, p. 352, no. 8
5891 *al-Da'awāt*, p. 292, no. 39

5892 *Iqbāl al-A'māl*, v. 3, p. 299
5893 *Biḥār al-Anwār*, v. 78, p. 380, no. 4
5894 *al-Kāfī*, v. 2, p. 123, no. 11
5895 Ibid. v. 8, p. 69, no. 23
5896 *al-Khiṣāl*, p. 81, no. 5
5897 *Thawāb al-A'māl*, p. 205, no. 1
5898 *Mishkāt al-Anwār*, p. 439, no. 1476
5899 *Ghurar al-Ḥikam*, no. 4477
5900 Ibid. no. 6159
5901 Qur'an 57:11
5902 Kantar (*qinṭār*): a substantial weight of gold varying between 45 and 245 kilos (*ed.*)
5903 *Thawab al-A'māl*, p. 341, no. 1
5904 Ibid. p. 166, no. 1
5905 *Kanz al-'Ummāl*, no. 15398
5906 *Amālī al-Ṣadūq*, p. 516, no. 707
5907 *Nahj al-Balāgha*, Sermon 90
5908 Ibid. Letter 31
5909 *Biḥār al-Anwār*, v. 103, p. 138, no. 2
5910 *Thawāb al-A'māl*, p. 167, no. 4
5911 Qur'an 2: 280
5912 *al-Kāfī*, v. 8, p. 9, no. 1
5913 *Kanz al-'Ummāl*, no. 15424
5914 *Thawāb al-A'māl*, p. 167, no. 5
5915 *Kanz al-'Ummāl*, no. 5434
5916 *Biḥār al-Anwār*, v. 76, p. 269, no. 17
5917 *Tanbīh al-Khawāṭir*, v. 1, p. 167
5918 *Biḥār al-Anwār*, v. 71, p. 342, no. 15
5919 *Ghurar al-Ḥikam*, no. 9165
5920 Ibid 9048
5921 *Amālī al-Ṭūsī*, p. 8, no. 8
5922 *Ghurar al-Ḥikam*, no. 1501
5923 *Tanbīh al-Khawāṭir*, v. 1, p. 167
5924 *Biḥār al-Anwār*, v. 78, p. 10, no. 67
5925 *Ghurar al-Ḥikam*, no. 334, 335
5926 Kitāb man lā yaḥḍurahi al-Faqīh, v. 2, p. 64, no. 1721
5927 Qiṣāṣ: retribution – legal punishment done or given to somebody as a retaliation or requital for a crime he/she has committed, as prescribed by Islamic Law (*ed.*)
5928 Qur'an 2:179
5929 Qur'an 2:194
5930 Qur'an 5:45
5931 *Kanz al-'Ummāl*, no. 39831
5932 *Nahj al-Balāgha*, Saying 252
5933 *Amālī al-Mufīd*, p. 53, no. 15
5934 *Tafsīr al-Imām Ḥasan al-'Askarī (AS)*, p. 595 no. 354
5935 *Kanz al-'Ummāl*, no. 39854
5936 Ibid. no. 39850
5937 *al-Kāfī*, v. 7, p. 358, no. 1
5938 Qur'an 9:51
5939 Qur'an 8:42
5940 Qur'an 55:49
5941 *Kanz al-'Ummāl*, no. 499
5942 Ibid. no. 501
5943 *Nahj al-Balāgha*, Sermon 183
5944 *al-Tawḥīd*, p. 383 no. 32
5945 *Kanz al-'Ummāl*, no. 1567
5946 *Nahj al-Balāgha*, Saying 459
5947 Ibid. Saying 16
5948 *al-Tawḥīd*, p. 364, no. 1
5949 *al-Durra al-Bāhira*, p. 33
5950 *Biḥār al-Anwār*, v. 5, p. 121, no. 64
5951 *A'lām al-Dīn*, p. 311
5952 *al-Kāfī*, v. 6, p. 13, no. 3
5953 Ibid. v. 6, p. 14, no. 4
5954 *'Uyūn Akhbār al-Riḍā (AS)*, v. 1, p. 141, no. 42
5955 *al-Kāfī*, v. 2, p. 62, no. 8
5956 *al-Tamḥiṣ*, p. 59, no. 123
5957 *'Uyūn Akhbār al-Riḍā (AS)*, v. 1, p. 141, no. 42
5958 *Ghurar al-Ḥikam*, no. 3225
5959 *Nahj al-Balāgha*, Saying 228
5960 *Nuzhat al-Nāẓir*, p. 147, no. 21
5961 *Kanz al-'Ummāl*, no. 28082
5962 Ibid. no. 633
5963 Ibid. no. 1560
5964 *Biḥār al-Anwār*, v. 41, p. 2, no. 3
5965 Qur'an 38:26
5966 *al-Kāfī*, v. 7, p. 406, no. 2
5967 *Nahj al-Balāgha*, Letter 53
5968 *al-Kāfī*, v. 7, p. 406, no. 1
5969 Qur'an 4:60
5970 *al-Kāfī*, v. 7, p. 412, no. 5
5971 *Kitāb man lā yaḥḍurahi al-Faqīh*, v. 3, p. 2, no. 3216
5972 *Mustadrak al-Wasā'il*, v. 17, p. 243, no. 21233
5973 *Kanz al-'Ummāl*, no. 14988

5974 *Kitāb man lā yaḥḍurahi al-Faqīh,* v. 3, p. 6, no. 3226
5975 *Kanz al-'Ummāl*, no. 14994
5976 *Biḥār al-Anwār*, v. 104, p. 264, no. 5
5977 *Kanz al-'Ummāl*, no. 15032
5978 *Wasā'il al-Shī'a*, v. 18, p. 155, no. 1
5979 *'Awālī al-La'ālī*, v. 2, p. 343, no. 5
5980 *al-Kāfī*, v. 7, p. 413, no. 1
5981 *Kitāb man lā yaḥḍurahi al-Faqīh,* v. 3, p. 13, no. 3238
5982 *al-Kāfī*, v. 7, p. 413, no. 5
5983 *Da'ā'im al-Islām,* v. 2 p. 537, no. 1907
5984 *Kanz al-'Ummāl*, no. 15040
5985 *al-Kāfī*, v. 7, p. 413, no. 1
5986 Ibid. v. 7, p. 413, no. 4
5987 *Mustadrak al-Wasā'il*, v. 17, p. 350, no. 21549
5988 *Kanz al-'Ummāl*, no. 14993
5989 *al-Kāfī*, v. 7, p. 410, no. 1
5990 Ibid. v. 7, p. 407, no. 1
5991 *Ghurar al-Ḥikam*, no. 3014
5992 *Biḥār al-Anwār*, v. 104, p. 266, no. 20
5993 *Ma'āni al-Akhbār*, p. 279
5994 *Tanbīh al-Khawāṭir*, v. 2, p. 171
5995 *al-Khiṣāl*, p. 311, no. 88
5996 *Biḥār al-Anwār*, v. 14, p. 14, no. 23
5997 *Wasā'il al-Shī'a*, v. 18, p. 582, no. 2
5998 *Kanz al-'Ummāl*, no. 1225
5999 *Amālī al-Ṭūsī*, p. 536, no. 1162
6000 *Nahj al-Balāgha*, Saying 409
6001 Ibid. Saying 147
6002 *Tuḥaf al-'Uqūl*, p. 371
6003 *'Ilal al-Sharā'i'*, p. 109, no. 8
6004 *al-Durra al-Bāhira*, p. 39
6005 Qur'an 26:87-89
6006 *al-Kāfī*, v. 2, p. 16, no. 5
6007 *Majma' al-Bayān*, v. 7, p. 305
6008 *Tuḥaf al-'Uqūl*, p. 504
6009 *Biḥār al-Anwār*, v. 78, p. 8, no. 64
6010 *Tuḥaf al-'Uqūl*, p. 235
6011 *Biḥār al-Anwār*, v. 78, p. 164, no. 1
6012 Ibid. v. 70, p. 59, no. 39
6013 *Iqbāl al-A'māl*, v. 3, p. 299
6014 *al-Kāfī*, v. 8, p. 215, no. 260
6015 *al-Targhīb wa al-Tarhīb*, v. 3, p. 497, no. 3
6016 Qur'an 47:24
6017 *al-Maḥāsin*, v. 1, p. 318, no. 633
6018 *Biḥār al-Anwār*, v. 78, p. 353, no. 9
6019 *al-Dūrrā al-Bāhira*, p. 43
6020 *al-Maḥāsin*, v. 1, p. 457, no. 1058
6021 *Ghurar al-Ḥikam*, no. 6020
6022 Ibid. no. 6777
6023 Qur'an 6:125
6024 Qur'an 94:1
6025 *Majma' al-Bayān*, v. 4, p. 561
6026 Qur'an 83:14
6027 *Sunan Ibn Māja,* v. 2, p. 1418, no. 4244
6028 *Tuḥaf al-'Uqūl*, p. 397
6029 Qur'an 2:74
6030 *al-Kāfī*, v. 2, p. 329, no. 1
6031 *Biḥār al-Anwār*, v. 14, p. 309, no. 17
6032 *Amālī al-Ṭūsī*, v. 3, p. 1
6033 *al-Khiṣāl*, p. 126, no. 122
6034 *'Ilal al-Sharā'i'*, p. 81, no. 1
6035 *Tuḥaf al-'Uqūl*, p. 199
6036 Ibid. no. 214
6037 Ibid. p. 296
6038 Qur'an 2:10
6039 *al-Kāfī*, v. 2, p. 300, no. 1
6040 Ibid. v. 2, p. 275, no. 28
6041 Qur'an 10:57
6042 *Nahj al-Balāgha*, Sermon 198
6043 *Ma'ānī al-Akhbār*, p. 335, no. 1
6044 *Nahj al-Balāgha*, Sermon. 109
6045 Ibid. Saying 349
6046 *Biḥār al-Anwār*, v. 1, p. 204, no. 22
6047 *al-Kāfī*, v. 1, p. 41, no. 6
6048 *Nahj al-Balāgha*, Letter 31
6049 *Biḥār al-Anwār*, v. 77, p. 208, no. 1
6050 *Nahj al-Balāgha*, Letter 31
6051 *Mishkāt al-Anwār*, p. 292, no. 885
6052 *A'lām al-Dīn*, p. 365, no. 33
6053 *Nahj al-Balāgha*, Saying 103
6054 *Tuḥaf al-'Uqūl*, p. 285
6055 *Kanz al-'Ummāl*, no. 42130
6056 *Tanbīh al-Khawāṭir*, v. 2, p. 122
6057 *Nahj al-Balāgha*, Letter 31
6058 *'Uddat al-Dā'ī*, p. 249
6059 Qur'an 5:104
6060 Qur'an 9:31
6061 *al-Maḥāsin*, v. 1, p. 383, no. 847
6062 *Ma'ānī al-Akhbār*, p. 266, no. 1
6063 *al-Iḥtijāj*, v. 2, p. 510, no. 337

6064 Qur'an 5:90,91
6065 These were all pagan pre-Islamic practices of gambling and games of chance (*ed.*)
6066 *al-Kāfī*, v. 5, p. 123, no. 2
6067 *Amālī al-Ṭūsī*, p. 336, no. 681
6068 *al-Khiṣāl*, p. 26, no. 92
6069 *al-Kāfī*, v. 5, p. 122, no. 1
6070 *Tafsīr al-'Ayyāshī*, v. 1, p. 322, no. 116
6071 *'Uddat al-Dā'ī*, p. 166. *Biḥār al-Anwār*, v. 78, p. 453, no. 21
6072 *Kanz al-'Ummāl*, no. 7080
6073 Qur'an 16:97
6074 *Nahj al-Balāgha*, Saying 229
6075 *Biḥār al-Anwār*, v. 77, p. 422, no. 40
6076 Ibid. v. 69, p. 399, no. 91
6077 *Nahj al-Balāgha*, Saying 371
6078 *Biḥār al-Anwār*, v. 78, p. 111, no. 6
6079 *Ghurar al-Ḥikam*, no. 6179
6080 Ibid. no. 7724
6081 *al-Kāfī*, v. 8 p. 244 no. 338
6082 *Biḥār al-Anwār*, v. 77, p. 187, no. 37
6083 *Ghurar al-Ḥikam*, no. 3191
6084 Ibid. no. 7771
6085 Ibid. no. 4244
6086 Ibid. no. 3295
6087 *Biḥār al-Anwār*, v. 78, p. 128, no. 11
6088 *al-Kāfī*, v. 2, p. 138, no. 3
6089 *Biḥār al-Anwār*, v. 78, p. 71, no. 33
6090 *al-Kāfī*, v. 8, p. 243, no. 337
6091 Qur'an 38:73,74
6092 Qur'an 7:13
6093 *Nahj al-Balāgha*, Saying 192
6094 *Biḥār al-Anwār*, v. 78, p. 186, no. 16
6095 Ibid. v. 78, p. 229, no. 5
6096 Ibid. v. 73, p. 215, no. 5
6097 Ibid. v. 77, p. 90, no. 3
6098 Ibid. v. 69, p. 399, no. 91
6099 *al-Kāfī*, v. 2, p. 310, no. 9
6100 Ibid. v. 8, p. 128, no. 98
6101 *Biḥār al-Anwār*, v. 73, p. 231, no. 23
6102 Ibid. v. 73, p. 232, no. 25
6103 Ibid. v. 73, p. 234, no. 33
6104 *Ghurar al-Ḥikam*, no. 9467
6105 *al-Kāfī*, v. 2, p. 312, no. 17
6106 *Tanbīh al-Khawāṭir*, v. 1, p. 201
6107 *Kanz al-'Ummāl*, no. 7793
6108 Ibid. no. 8878
6109 The issue mentioned in these traditions is not a general law indicating lack of arrogance, but it differs because of differences in people, or in times and circumstances. For example, some may dress rough woollen clothes to pretend to be humble while their hearts are full of arrogance.
6110 *Nahj al-Balāgha*, Sermon 192
6111 Ibid. Saying 252
6112 *Biḥār al-Anwār*, v. 78, p. 104, no. 3
6113 *Amālī al-Ṣadūq*, p. 577, no. 778
6114 *Nahj al-Balāgha*, Saying 371
6115 *Ghurar al-Ḥikam*, no. 7464
6116 Ibid. no. 10586
6117 *Biḥār al-Anwār*, v. 77, p. 235, no. 3
6118 *al-Khiṣāl*, p. 434, no. 20
6119 *Tuḥaf al-'Uqūl*, p. 396
6120 Qur'an 16:29
6121 *al-Kāfī*, v. 2, p. 310, no. 10
6122 Qur'an 68:1
6123 *Ghurar al-Ḥikam*, no 991
6124 Ibid. no. 9948
6125 Ibid. no 8126
6126 *Nahj al-Balāgha*, Saying 301
6127 *Ghurar al-Ḥikam*, no. 7260
6128 Ibid. no. 6339
6129 *Kanz al-'Ummāl*, no. 29332
6130 Ibid. no. 28733
6131 *al-Kāfī*, v. 1, p. 52, no. 9
6132 Ibid. v. 1, p. 52, no. 8
6133 *Amālī al-Ṣadūq*, p. 91, no. 64
6134 *Kanz al-'Ummāl*, no. 28951
6135 *al-Durr al-Manthūr*, v. 1, p. 27
6136 *al-Kāfī*, v. 2, p. 672, no. 1
6137*Kanz al-'Ummāl*, no. 29294
6138 *Tuḥaf al-'Uqūl*, p. 358
6139 *al-Kāfī*, v. 2, p. 670, no. 2
6140 *Tuḥaf al-'Uqūl*, p. 223
6141 *al-Kāfī*, v. 2, p. 221, no. 1
6142 Ibid. v. 2, p. 223, no. 7
6143 Ibid. v. 2, p. 226, no. 15
6144 *Biḥār al-Anwār*, v. 75, p. 70, no. 7
6145 *al-Kāfī*, v. 2, p. 370, no. 2
6146 Ibid. v. 2, p. 370, no. 4
6147 Ibid. v. 2, p. 371, no. 10

6148 Qur'an 2:61
6149 *al-Kāfī*, v. 2, p. 371, no. 6
6150 *al-Maḥāsin*, v. 1, p. 403, no. 910
6151 *al-Kāfī*, v. 2, p. 225, no. 12
6152 *Ma'ānī al-Akhbār*, p. 166, no. 1
6153 *Biḥār al-Anwār*, v. 72, p. 263, no. 47
6154 *Sharḥ Nahj al-Balāgha li ibn Abī al-Ḥadīd*, v. 6, p. 357
6155 *Kanz al-'Ummāl*, no. 8212
6156 *Biḥār al-Anwār*, v. 72, p. 262, no. 45
6157 Ibid. v. 72, p. 261, no. 37
6158 *Nahj al-Balāgha*, Sermon 84
6159 Ibid. Saying 458
6160 *Ghurar al-Ḥikam*, no. 339
6161 *Biḥār al-Anwār*, v. 72, p. 259, no. 23
6162 Ibid. v. 78, p. 305, no. 1
6163 Qur'an 16:105
6164 *Nahj al-Balāgha*, Sermon 86
6165 *Biḥār al-Anwār*, v. 72, p. 247, no. 8
6166 Ibid. v. 75, p. 172, no. 11
6167 *Kanz al-'Ummāl*, no. 8217
6168 *Biḥār al-Anwār*, v. 72, p. 236, no. 3
6169 *al-Durra al-Bāhira*, p. 43
6170 *Kanz al-'Ummāl*, no. 8217
6171 Ibid. no. 8215
6172 *Biḥār al-Anwār*, v. 72, p. 249, no. 14
6173 Ibid. v. 72, p. 235, no. 2
6174 *Tanbīh al-Khawāṭir*, v. 2, p. 122
6175 *al-Targhīb wa al-Tarhīb*, v. 3, p. 597, no. 32
6176 Ibid. v. 3, p. 598, no. 34
6177 Qur'an 40:28
6178 Qur'an 9:77
6179 *al-Targhīb wa al-Tarhīb*, v. 3, p. 596, no. 28
6180 Ibid. v. 3, p. 596, no. 29
6181 *Ghurar al-Ḥikam*, no. 4640
6182 Ibid. no. 7123
6183 Ibid. no. 1181
6184 Ibid. no. 7794
6185 Ibid. nos. 8888, 9181
6186 Ibid. no. 11039
6187 *Biḥār al-Anwār*, v. 72, p. 261, no. 36
6188 Ibid. v. 72, p. 192, no. 8
6189 Ibid. v. 72, p. 260, no. 29
6190 Meaning that forgetfulness becomes a way of exposing them, as they may lie about something and forget what it is they had said, and then say something contrary to what they had first said (as is quoted from the footnote of the source reference)
6191 *al-Kāfī*, v. 2, p. 341, no. 15
6192 Qur'an 6:144
6193 Qur'an 39:60
6194 *Nahj al-Balāgha*, Sermon 147
6195 *Qurb al-Isnād*, p. 133, no. 466
6196 *al-Kāfī*, v. 2, p. 340, no. 9
6197 Ibid. v. 2, p. 339, no. 5
6198 *Biḥār al-Anwār*, v. 72, p. 263, no. 48
6199 *al-Kāfī*, v. 2, p. 341, no. 16
6200 Ibid. v. 2, p. 210, no. 5
6201 Meaning someone saying something in such a way that makes it possible for the listener to understand something else.
6202 Qur'an 21:63
6203 *Kanz al-'Ummāl*, no. 8253
6204 *Mustaṭrafāt al-Sarā'ir*, p. 137, no. 1
6205 Qur'an 5:41
6206 *Nahj al-Balāgha*, Letter 10
6207 *Biḥār al-Anwār*, v. 72, p. 264, no. 1
6208 The word *karam* in Arabic has a very wide range of meanings, denoting nobility, high-mindedness, generosity, magnanimity, kindness, graciousness, and all other such qualities associated with someone of high birth or excellent lineage. It has been translated in this chapter with the English term best suited to the individual contexts of the traditions (*ed.*)
6209 *Musnad Ibn Ḥanbal*, v. 3, p. 292, no. 8782
6210 *Kanz al-'Ummāl*, no. 15991
6211 *Biḥār al-Anwār*, v. 77, p. 211, no. 1
6212 Qur'an 25:72
6213 *Ghurar al-Ḥikam*, no. 9130
6214 *Biḥār al-Anwār*, v. 77, p. 209, no. 1
6215 Ibid. v. 78, p. 82, no. 82
6216 *Ghurar al-Ḥikam*, no. 446
6217 Ibid. no. 1528
6218 Ibid. nos. 1298-1299
6219 Ibid. nos. 1566-1567
6220 Ibid. no. 7353
6221 Ibid. no. 5558
6222 *Biḥār al-Anwār*, v. 44, p. 89, no. 2
6223 *al-Durra al-Bāhira*, p. 27

6224 *Tuḥaf al-'Uqūl*, p. 319
6225 *Ghurar al-Ḥikam*, no. 1507
6226 Ibid. no. 7490
6227 Ibid. no. 8958
6228 *Biḥār al-Anwār*, v. 78, p. 113, no. 7
6229 Ibid. v. 46, p. 15, no. 33
6230 Ibid. v. 16, p. 235, no. 35
6231 Ibid. v. 92, p. 184, no. 21
6232 *Kanz al-'Ummāl*, no. 25488
6233 Ibid. no. 25485
6234 Ibid. no. 25490
6235 Ibid. no. 25501
6236 Ibid. no. 25499
6237 *Musnad Ibn Ḥanbal*, v. 5, p. 281, no. 15500
6238 *Sunan Ibn Māja*, v. 2, p. 1211, no. 3671
6239 *Qurb al-Isnād*, p. 92 no. 307
6240 *Biḥār al-Anwār*, v. 77, p. 164, no. 190
6241 *al-Nawādir al-Rāwandī*, p. 101, no. 87
6242 *al-Durra al-Bāhira*, p. 24
6243 *Sunan al-Tirmidhī*, p. 3610
6244 *Kanz al-'Ummāl*, no. 44154
6245 *Nahj al-Balāgha*, Saying 113
6246 *Ghurar al-Ḥikam*, no. 3542
6247 Ibid. no. 6232
6248 *Kanz al-'Ummāl*, no. 9340-9341
6249 Ibid. no. 10516
6250 *Tanbīh al-Khawāṭir*, v. 1, p. 42
6251 *Kanz al- 'Ummal*, no. 9223
6252 *Jāmi' al-Ahādīth*, p. 76
6253 *Kitāb man lā yaḥḍurahi al-Faqīh*, v. 3, p. 163, no. 3596
6254 *al-Tahdhīb*, v. 6, p. 326, no. 895
6255 *Kitāb man lā yaḥḍurahi al-Faqīh*, v. 3, p. 163 no. 3595
6256 *Biḥār al-Anwār*, v. 103, p. 77, no. 1
6257 *Ghurar al-Ḥikam*, no. 3968
6258 *Biḥār al-Anwār*, v. 78, p. 26, no. 92
6259 *Mustadrak al-Wasā'il*, v. 13, p. 45, no. 14695
6260 *Nahj al-Balāgha*, Saying 239
6261 *Ghurar al-Ḥikam*, no. 9284
6262 Ibid. no. 5927
6263 Ibid. no. 4471
6264 *Biḥār al-Anwār*, v. 78, p. 180, no. 64
6265 *al-Kāfī*, v. 5, p. 85, no. 4
6266 Ibid. v. 5, p. 85, no. 1
6267 Ibid. v. 5 p. 85, no. 2
6268 Ibid. v. 2, p. 289, no. 2
6269 Ibid. v. 2, p. 391, no. 1
6270 Ibid. v. 2, p. 387, no. 15
6271 Ibid. v. 2, p. 386, no. 10
6272 *Biḥār al-Anwār*, v. 78, p. 276, no. 112
6273 *Ma'ānī al-Akhbār*, p. 394, no. 47
6274 *al-Kāfī*, v. 2, p. 290, no. 5
6275 Qur'an 4:86
6276 Qur'an 55:60
6277 *Biḥār al-Anwār*, v. 78, p. 311, no. 1
6278 Ibid. v. 75, p. 43, no. 8
6279 *Nahj al-Balāgha*, Saying 216
6280 *Ghurar al-Ḥikam*, no. 2383
6281 *Nahj al-Balāgha*, Saying 62
6282 *al-Durra al-Bāhira*, p. 34
6283 *Biḥār al-Anwār*, v. 78, p. 53, no. 85
6284 *Ghurar al-Ḥikam*, no. 9413
6285 *al-Kāfī*, v. 2, p. 322, no. 2
6286 *Biḥār al-Anwār*, v. 78, p. 278, no. 113
6287 *al-Kāfī*, v. 2, p. 304, no. 10
6288 *Ghurar al-Ḥikam*, no. 10518
6289 Ibid. no. 6766
6290 Ibid. no. 3003
6291 Ibid. no. 7208
6292 *Tuḥaf al-'Uqūl*, p. 88
6293 *Kashf al-Ghummah*, v. 3, p. 136
6294 *Tuḥaf al-'Uqūl*, p. 359
6295 *Nahj al-Balāgha*, Letter 51
6296 Qur'an 38:27
6297 *Nahj al-Balāgha*, Saying 78
6298 Qur'an 2:286
6299 *al-Kāfī*, v. 2, p. 463, no. 2
6300 *al-Tawḥīd*, p. 347, no. 6
6301 *al-Targhīb wa al-Tarhīb*, v. 3, p. 537, no. 45
6302 *Nahj al-Balāgha*, Saying 394
6303 *Biḥār al-Anwār*, v. 71, p. 293, no. 63
6304 *Ghurar al-Ḥikam*, no. 5322
6305 *Tuḥaf al-'Uqūl*, p. 216
6306 *Ghurar al-Ḥikam*, no. 2722
6307 Ibid. no. 2675
6308 Ibid. no. 8496
6309 Ibid. no. 5551
6310 *Biḥār al-Anwār*, v. 2, p. 55, no. 28
6311 *al-Targhīb wa al-Tarhīb*, v. 3, p. 540, no. 51
6312 Ibid. v. 3, p. 537, no. 46
6313 *Amālī al-Ṣadūq*, p. 85, no. 53

6314 *Ghurar al-Ḥikam*, no. 6283
6315 Ibid. no. 2637
6316 *Biḥār al-Anwār*, v. 78, p. 127, no. 10
6317 *Ghurar al-Ḥikam*, no. 2720
6318 *Nahj al-Balāgha*, Saying 123
6319 *Mishkāt al-Anwār*, p. 551, no. 1850
6320 *Kanz al-'Ummāl*, no. 44176
6321 *Amālī al-Ṭūsī*, p. 3, no. 1
6322 *Ghurar al-Ḥikam*, no. 2680
6323 *Nahj al-Balāgha*, Saying 71
6324 Ibid. Saying 381
6325 *Ghurar al-Ḥikam*, no. 4084
6326 *Nahj al-Balāgha*, Saying 349
6327 Ibid. Saying 382
6328 *Ghurar al-Ḥikam*, no. 2182
6329 Ibid. no. 1854
6330 *Sharḥ Nahj al-Balāgha li Ibn Abī al-Ḥadīd*, v. 7, p. 92
6331 *al-Durra al-Bāhira*, p. 41
6332 *Ghurar al-Ḥikam*, no. 1462
6333 *Biḥār al-Anwār*, v. 71, p. 274, no. 1
6334 *al-Kāfī*, v. 8, p. 148, no. 128
6335 *Biḥār al-Anwār*, v. 71, p. 294, no. 64
6336 *Ghurar al-Ḥikam*, no. 5867
6337 Ibid. no. 5865
6338 Ibid. no. 5866
6339 Ibid. no. 283
6340 Ibid. no. 1266
6341 *Sunan al-Nasā'ī*, v. 3, p. 58
6342 *Ghurar al-Ḥikam*, no. 3371
6343 Ibid. no. 3304
6344 Ibid. no. 4929
6345 Qur'an 2:83
6346 Qur'an 17:53
6347 *al-Kāfī*, v. 2, p. 165, no. 10
6348 *Biḥār al-Anwār*, v. 71, p. 312, no. 12
6349 *Amālī al-Ṣadūq*, p. 49, no. 1
6350 Ibid. p. 484, no. 657
6351 *Ghurar al-Ḥikam*, no. 579
6352 Ibid. no. 9442
6353 Ibid. no. 331
6354 *Ma'ānī al-Akhbār*, p. 150, no. 1
6355 *Ghurar al-Ḥikam*, no. 7244
6356 *A'lām al-Dīn*, p. 292
6357 *Ghurar al-Ḥikam*, no. 4536
6358 *Biḥār al-Anwār*, v. 78, p. 172, no. 3
6359 *Tuḥaf al-'Uqūl*, p. 320
6360 *Makārim al-Akhlāq*, v. 2, p. 368, no. 2661
6361 *al-Zuhd li al-Ḥusayn b. Sa'īd*, p. 78, no. 211
6362 *Biḥār al-Anwār*, v. 77, p. 115, no. 8
6363 Ibid. p. 92, no. 250
6364 *Ghurar al-Ḥikam*, no. 1139
6365 Ibid. no. 1797
6366 *Biḥār al-Anwār*, v. 77, p. 378, no. 1
6367 *Ghurar al-Ḥikam*, no. 2839
6368 *al-Targhīb wa al-Tarhīb*, v. 3, p. 88, no. 3
6369 *al-Kāfī*, v. 6, p. 445, no. 2
6370 Ibid. p. 446, no. 4
6371 Ibid. p. 449, no. 1
6372 *Kanz al-'Ummāl*, no. 41172
6373 *Nahj al-Balāgha*, Sermon 193
6374 *Biḥār al-Anwār*, v. 79, p. 304, no. 17
6375 *al-Kāfī*, v. 6, p. 444, no. 15
6376 *Makārim al-Akhlāq*, v. 1, p. 218, no. 642
6377 Ibid. v. 1, p. 220, no. 648
6378 *'Uyūn Akhbār al-Riḍā (AS)*, v. 2, p. 178, no. 1
6379 *al-Kāfī*, v. 6, p. 461, no. 5
6380 *Kanz al-'Ummāl*, no. 41143
6381 *Sunan Abī Dāwūd*, v. 4, p. 54, no. 4076
6382 *al-Kāfī*, v. 6, p. 461, no. 4
6383 *Kanz al-'Ummāl*, no. 41210
6384 Ibid. no. 41203
6385 *al-Kāfī*, v. 6, p. 453, no. 1
6386 *Tuḥaf al-'Uqūl*, p. 14
6387 *Nahj al-Balāgha*, Saying 179
6388 *Ghurar al-Ḥikam*, no. 887
6389 Ibid. no. 7478
6390 Ibid. no. 1718
6391 *Biḥār al-Anwār*, v. 77, p. 208, no. 1
6392 *Nahj al-Balāgha*, Letter 31
6393 *Biḥār al-Anwār*, v. 78, p. 10, no. 68
6394 Ibid. v. 77, p. 212, no. 1
6395 *Ghurar al-Ḥikam*, no. 4975
6396 *Nahj al-Balāgha*, Letter 58
6397 Ibid. Letter 53
6398 *Tuḥaf al-'Uqūl*, p. 37
6399 *Jāmi' al-Akhbār*, p. 247, no. 631
6400 *Ghurar al-Ḥikam*, no. 1282
6401 *Biḥār al-Anwār*, v. 78, p. 56, no. 119
6402 *Nahj al-Balāgha*, Saying 392

6403 *Biḥār al-Anwār*, v. 77, p. 231, no. 2
6404 Ibid. v. 71, p. 286, no. 42
6405 *Saḥīḥ al-Tirmidhī*, v. 4, p. 605, no. 2407
6406 *Tuḥaf al-'Uqūl*, p. 298
6407 *Biḥār al-Anwār*, v. 77, p. 85, no. 3
6408 Ibid. v. 71, p. 286, no. 42
6409 *al-Kāfī*, v. 2, p. 114, no. 7
6410 *Biḥār al-Anwār*, v. 71, p. 283, no. 36
6411 Ibid. v. 71, p. 286, no. 42
6412 *Nahj al-Balāgha*, Saying 60
6413 *Biḥār al-Anwār*, v. 71, p. 277, no. 11
6414 *Nahj al-Balāgha*, Sermon 176
6415 Ibid. Saying 40
6416 *Tuḥaf al-'Uqūl*, p. 298
6417 Qur'an 23:3
6418 Qur'an 26:72
6419 *Amālī al-Ṣadūq*, p. 73, no. 41
6420 *Biḥār al-Anwār*, v. 78, p. 92, no. 101
6421 Ibid. v. 78, p. 7, no. 59
6422 *Tuḥaf al-'Uqūl*, p. 218
6423 *Majma' al-Bayān*, v. 7, p. 157
6424 *al-Maḥajjat al-Bayḍā'*, v. 8, p. 59-61
6425 Ibid. v. 8, p. 62
6426 *Makārim al-Akhlāq*, v. 2, p. 31, no. 2069
6427 *Kanz al-'Ummāl*, no. 42121
6428 *Nahj al-Balāgha*, Letter 62
6429 *Ghurar al-Ḥikam*, no. 8425
6430 Qur'an 57:20
6431 Qur'an 62:11
6432 *Nahj al-Balāgha*, Saying 370
6433 *Ghurar al-Ḥikam*, no. 937
6434 Ibid. no. 5729
6435 *Biḥār al-Anwār*, v. 78, p. 9, no. 66
6436 *Ghurar al-Ḥikam*, no. 2165
6437 Ibid. no. 3333
6438 Ibid. no. 8426
6439 *Nahj al-Balāgha*, Saying 333
6440 *Tanbīh al-Khawāṭir*, v. 1, p. 52
6441 *al-Uṣul al-Sittah 'Ashr*, p. 51
6442 *Kanz al-'Ummāl*, v. 4, p. 344, no. 10812
6443 Ibid. no. 40611
6444 *Tuḥaf al-'Uqūl*, p. 151
6445 *Ghurar al-Ḥikam*, no. 9815
6446 Qur'an 7:80,81
6447 *al-Targhīb wa al-Tarhīb*, v. 3, p. 285, no. 1
6448 *Biḥār al-Anwār*, v. 79, p. 72, no. 24
6449 *Nahj al-Balāgha*, Saying 252
6450 *Biḥār al-Anwār*, v. 79, p. 72, no. 27
6451 *'Ilal al-Sharā'i'*, p. 547, no. 1
6452 *Nahj al-Balāgha*, Sermon 189
6453 Ibid. Sermon 192
6454 Ibid. Saying 434
6455 *Ghurar al-Ḥikam*, no. 6206
6456 Ibid. no. 11026
6457 Ibid. no. 4664
6458 *al-Kāfī*, v. 8, p. 176, no. 196
6459 *al-Khiṣāl*, p. 103, no. 62
6460 *Kanz al-'Ummāl*, no. 8331
6461 *al-Maḥajjat al-Bayḍā'*, v. 5, p. 284
6462 *Tanbīh al-Khawāṭir*, v. 2, p. 122
6463 *Sunan Ibn Māja*, v. 2, p. 1232, no. 3742
6464 *Kanz al-'Ummāl*, no. 8339
6465 *Tuḥaf al-'Uqūl*, p. 208
6466 *Ghurar al-Ḥikam*, no. 3983-3984
6467 *Nahj al-Balāgha*, Sermon 216
6468 Ibid. Saying 100
6469 *al-Kāfī*, v. 2, p. 231, no. 3
6470 Qur'an 3:188
6471 *Makārim al-Akhlāq*, v. 2, p. 353, no. 2660
6472 *Ghurar al-Ḥikam*, no. 9042
6473 *Tanbīh al-Khawāṭir*, v. 2, p. 17
6474 *Nahj al-Balāgha*, Letter 53
6475 *Tuḥaf al-'Uqūl*, p. 284
6476 *A'lām al-Dīn*, p. 313
6477 *Tuḥaf al-'Uqūl*, p. 46
6478 *Amālī al-Ṣadūq*, p. 513, no. 707
6479 Qur'an 53:32
6480 *Ma'ānī al-Akhbār*, p. 243, no. 1
6481 *al-Nawādir al-Rāwandī*, p. 107, no. 86
6482 Qur'an 33:35
6483 *Majma' al-Bayān v 8 p* 560
6484 *al-Durr al-Manthūr*, v. 2, p. 518
6485 *al-Targhīb wa al-Tarhīb*, v. 3, p. 76, no. 6
6486 *Nahj al-Balāgha*, Saying 234
6487 *Irshād al-Qulūb*, v. 1, p. 175
6488 *al-Firdaws*, v. 2, p. 230, no. 3108
6489 *Kanz al-'Ummāl*, v. 16, p. 398, no. 45090
6490 *al-Nawādir al-Rāwandī*, p. 114, no. 109
6491 *Mustaṭrafāt al-Sarā'ir*, p. 143, no. 8
6492 *al-Kāfī*, v. 5, p. 320, no. 1

6493 Islam attaches importance to family life and respects its perimeters. Hence all sexual enjoyments are confined to its perimeters and asks men to pay attention only to their spouses and offer all their loves and affection to them. This is the affection praised and announced by the Holy Prophet. On the other hand Islam warns men not to fall into the trap of Satan and refrain from loving other women, otherwise everyday they will fall in love with a woman and when they could not win their beloved they would destroy their happiness or they will fall into unlawful activities.
6494 Ibid. v. 5, p. 515, no. 5
6495 *al-Khiṣāl*, p. 113, no. 91
6496 *Ghurar al-Ḥikam*, no. 2721
6497 *Kanz al-'Ummāl*, no. 8763
6498 *Tuḥaf al-'Uqūl*, p. 223
6499 Ibid. p. 223
6500 *Ghurar al-Ḥikam*, no. 4201
6501 Ibid. no. 4224
6502 *Tuḥaf al-'Uqūl*, p. 225
6503 Ibid. p. 359
6504 *al-Targhīb wa al-Tarhīb*, v. 4, p. 292, no. 56
6505 Ibid. v. 4, p. 292, no. 55
6506 *al-Kāfī*, v. 3, p. 114, no. 6
6507 Ibid. v. 3, p. 114, no. 7
6508 Ibid. v. 3, p. 115, no. 1
6509 *al-Da'awāt*, p. 167, no. 462
6510 *al-Khiṣāl*, p. 630, no. 10
6511 *Ghurar al-Ḥikam*, no. 8545
6512 Ibid. no. 8612
6513 *al-Da'awāt*, p. 134, no. 334
6514 *Tanbīh al-Khawāṭir*, v. 2, p. 7
6515 *al-Da'awāt*, p. 172, no. 482
6516 *Mishkāt al-Anwār*, p. 487, no. 1626
6517 *al-Targhīb wa al-Tarhīb*, v. 4, p. 317, no. 3
6518 *Kanz al-'Ummāl*, no. 25141
6519 Ibid. no. 25143
6520 *al-Kāfī*, v. 3, p. 120, no. 2
6521 *Kanz al-'Ummāl*, no. 25139
6522 *al-Kāfī*, v. 3, p. 118, no. 6
6523 Ibid. v. 3, p. 118, no. 2
6524 Ibid. v. 3, p. 118, no. 4
6525 Ibid. v. 3, p. 118, no. 3
6526 *Muniyat al-Murīd*, p. 171
6527 *Amālī al-Ṣadūq*, p. 73, no. 41
6528 *al-Kāfī*, v. 2, p. 300, no. 1
6529 *Nahj al-Balāgha*, Saying 362
6530 *Ghurar al-Ḥikam*, no. 5634
6531 *Ma'ānī al-Akhbār*, p. 381, no. 9
6532 *A'lām al-Dīn*, p. 311
6533 *Tuḥaf al-'Uqūl*, p. 486
6534 *Sharḥ Nahj al-Balāgha li Ibn Abī al-Ḥadīd*, v. 6, p. 330
6535 *Tuḥaf al-'Uqūl*, p. 49
6536 Qur'an 56:35,36
6537 *Tanbīh al-Khawāṭir*, v. 1, p. 112
6538 *al-Kāfī*, v. 2, p. 663, no. 4
6539 Ibid. no. 2
6540 Ibid. no. 3
6541 *Makārim al-Akhlāq*, v. 2, p. 321, no. 2656
6542 *Amālī al-Ṣadūq*, p. 344, no. 412
6543 *Nahj al-Balāgha*, Saying 450
6544 *Tuḥaf al-'Uqūl*, p. 86
6545 *Biḥār al-Anwār*, v. 77, p. 235, no. 3
6546 *Tuḥaf al-'Uqūl*, p. 85
6547 *al-Kāfī*, v. 2, p. 665, no. 15
6548 *Amālī al-Ṣadūq*, p. 636, no. 853
6549 *al-Kāfī*, v. 2, p. 664, no. 9
6550 Qur'an 3:26
6551 Qur'an 24:42
6552 *Kanz al-'Ummāl*, no. 45244
6553 *Nahj al-Balāgha*, Sermon 65
6554 *Ghurar al-Ḥikam*, no. 10321
6555 Ibid. no. 2184
6556 *al-Khiṣāl*, p. 223, no. 51
6557 *Ghurar al-Ḥikam*, no. 5005
6558 Ibid. no. 3206
6559 Ibid. no. 3350
6560 Ibid. no. 3261
6561 *Tuḥaf al-'Uqūl*, p. 319
6562 *Ghurar al-Ḥikam*, no. 4940
6563 Ibid. no. 9016-9017
6564 Ibid. no. 4118
6565 Qur'an 35:1
6566 *Tafsīr al-Qummī*, v. 2, p. 206
6567 *Nahj al-Balāgha*, Sermon 91
6568 *al-Ikhtiṣāṣ*, p. 109
6569 *Biḥār al-Anwār*, v. 59, p. 176, no. 7
6570 *Nahj al-Balāgha*, Sermon 109

6571 *Tafsīr al-Qummī*, v. 2, p. 206
6572 Qur'an 6:61
6573 Qur'an 13:11
6574 *Biḥār al-Anwār*, v. 59, p. 179, no. 16
6575 Qur'an 82:10
6576 Qur'an 82:11
6577 *Tafsīr al-Qummī*, v. 2, p. 409
6578 *al-Nawādir al-Rāwandī*, p. 192, no. 349
6579 *al-Kāfī*, v. 3, p. 393, no. 26
6580 Qur'an 67:2
6581 *Kanz al-'Ummāl*, no. 42123
6582 Ibid. no. 42721
6583 *Nahj al-Balāgha*, Sermon 156
6584 *Ghurar al-Ḥikam*, no. 319
6585 *al-Tawḥīd,* p. 401, no. 4
6586 Qur'an 3:185
6587 Qur'an 62:8
6588 Qur'an 7:34
6589 *al-Kāfī*, v. 3, p. 262, no. 44
6590 *Biḥār al-Anwār*, v. 6, p. 137, no. 40
6591 *Nahj al-Balāgha*, Letter 31
6592 Ibid. Letter 27
6593 *Kitāb man lā yaḥḍurahi al-Faqīh,* v. 1, p. 194, no. 596
6594 *Nahj al-Balāgha*, Saying 29
6595 Ibid. Saying 187
6596 *Biḥār al-Anwār*, v. 71, p. 263, no. 2
6597 *Ma'ānī al-Akhbār*, p. 289, no. 4
6598 Ibid. p. 289, no. 6
6599 Ibid. p. 289, no. 5
6600 Qur'an 16:32
6601 *Kanz al-'Ummāl*, no. 42136
6602 Ibid. no. 42110
6603 Qur'an 10:64
6604 *Biḥār al-Anwār*, v. 6, p. 191, no. 36
6605 *Ma'ānī al-Akhbār*, p. 289, no. 7
6606 *Biḥār al-Anwār*, v. 82, p. 167, no. 3
6607 *Kanz al- 'Ummal*, no. 42105
6608 *Nahj al-Balāgha*, Letter 31
6609 *Biḥār al-Anwār*, v. 6, p. 133, no. 32
6610 Ibid. v. 82, p. 168, no. 3
6611 Ibid. v. 78, p. 370, no. 4
6612 Ibid. v. 77, p. 171, no. 7
6613 *Nahj al-Balāgha*, Sermon 64
6614 *Ghurar al-Ḥikam*, no. 3468
6615 Ibid. no. 6253
6616 *Nahj al-Balāgha*, Saying 190
6617 *al-Kāfī*, v. 3, p. 259, no. 30
6618 *Amālī al-Ṣadūq*, p. 172, no. 173
6619 *al-Targhīb wa al-Tarhīb,* v. 4, p. 257, no. 54
6620 *Kanz al-'Ummāl*, no. 42153
6621 *Nahj al-Balāgha*, Letter 69
6622 *Kashf al-Ghamma*, v. 3, p. 42
6623 Qur'an 50:19
6624 *Kanz al-'Ummāl*, no. 42158
6625 *Amālī al-Ṣadūq*, p. 453, no. 1011
6626 *Nahj al-Balāgha*, Saying 221
6627 *al-Khiṣāl*, p. 13, no. 47
6628 *Ma'ānī al-Akhbār*, p. 390, no. 29
6629 *Saḥīfa al-Imām al-Riḍā (AS)*, p. 86, no. 203
6630 *al-Kāfī*, v. 3, p. 127, no. 2
6631 *Tafsīr al-Qummī*, v. 2, p. 265
6632 *al-Kāfī*, v. 3, p. 112, no. 5
6633 *Kanz al-'Ummāl*, no. 42775
6634 *al-Kāfī*, v. 3, p. 261, no. 39
6635 *al-Nawādir al-Rāwandī*, p. 92, no. 29
6636 *Amālī al-Ṣadūq*, p. 383, no. 827
6637 *al-Da'awāt*, p. 259, no. 736
6638 *al-Kāfī*, v. 3, p. 173, no. 3
6639 *'Ilal al-Sharā'i'*, p. 301, no. 1
6640 *al-Kāfī*, v. 3, p. 138, no. 2
6641 *Kanz al-'Ummāl*, no. 42385
6642 Ibid. no. 42386
6643 Ibid. no. 42916
6644 Ibid. no. 42761
6645 *Kitāb man lā yaḥḍurahi al-Faqīh,* v. 1, p. 185, no. 555
6646 Qur'an 18:46
6647 *al-Kāfī*, v. 2, p. 316, no. 6
6648 *al-Targhīb wa al-Tarhīb*, v. 4, p. 182, no. 68
6649 *Nahj al-Balāgha*, Saying 58
6650 *Ghurar al-Ḥikam*, no. 577
6651 Qur'an 89:20
6652 *al-Maḥajjat al-Bayḍā'*, v. 7, p. 328
6653 *Ghurar al-Ḥikam*, no. 1427
6654 Ibid. no. 4876
6655 *Tanbīh al-Khawāṭir*, v. 1, p. 158
6656 *Nahj al-Balāgha*, Saying 56
6657 *al-Kāfī*, v. 1, p. 20, no. 12
6658 Ibid. v. 5, p. 72, no. 5
6659 Qur'an 9:34

6660 *al-Kāfī*, v. 2, p. 135, no. 21
6661 *Kanz al-'Ummāl*, no. 6139
6662 *Ghurar al-Ḥikam*, no. 7109
6663 *al-Durra al-Bāhira*, p. 24
6664 *Amālī al-Ṭūsī*, p. 302, no. 600
6665 *Mustadrak al-Wasā'il*, v. 12, p. 174, no. 13810
6666 *al-Khiṣāl*, p. 282, no. 29
6667 *Amālī al-Ṭūsi*, p. 182, no. 306
6668 *Biḥār al-Anwār*, v. 103, p. 13, no. 63
6669 *Tuḥaf al-'Uqūl*, p. 94
6670 *al-Maḥāsin*, v. 2, p. 445, no. 2528
6671 Meaning he will be caught up with useless and sometimes harmful construction and building.
6672 *Tuḥaf al-'Uqūl*, p. 321
6673 *Kanz al-'Ummāl*, no. 16147
6674 *Biḥār al-Anwār*, v. 71, p. 356, no. 17
6675 *Ghurar al-Ḥikam*, no. 508
6676 Ibid. no. 1838
6677 *Nahj al-Balāgha*, Letter 21
6678 *Biḥār al-Anwār*, v. 78, p. 7, no. 60
6679 Ibid. v. 78, p. 12, no. 70
6680 *Kitāb man lā yaḥḍurahi al-Faqīh*, v. 2, p. 57, no. 1693
6681 *Tanbīh al-Khawāṭir*, v. 2, p. 182
6682 *al-Kāfī*, v. 1, p. 168, no. 1
6683 Qur'an 16:36
6684 *al-Kāfī*, v. 8, p. 386, no. 586
6685 Qur'an 62:2
6686 *Kanz al-'Ummāl*, no. 31969
6687 *al-Ṭabaqāt al-Kūbrā*, v. 1, p. 193
6688 *Nahj al-Balāgha*, Sermon 1
6689 Qur'an 58:25
6690 Qur'an 2:213
6691 *Nahj al-Balāgha*, Sermon 192
6692 *al-Tawḥīd*, p. 45, no. 4
6693 Qur'an 43:51
6694 Prophet Jonah (AS) is known as Yūnus in the Arabic tradition (*ed.*)
6695 Qur'an 37:147
6696 Qur'an 2:124
6697 *al-Kāfī*, v. 1, p. 174, no. 1
6698 *al-Khisal*, p. 524, no. 13
6699 Qur'an 47:35
6700 *Biḥār al-Anwār*, v. 11, p. 33, no. 25
6701 *al-Kāfī*, v. 2, p. 17, no. 2
6702 *Biḥār al-Anwār*, v. 77, p. 140, no. 19
6703 Ibid. v. 16, p. 172, no. 7
6704 *Tanbīh al-Khawāṭir*, v. 1, p. 29
6705 *al-Ṭabaqāt al-Kubrā*, v. 1, p. 376
6706 *Nahj al-Balāgha*, Sermon 192
6707 *'Ilal al-Sharā'i'*, p. 32, no. 1
6708 *al-Kāfī*, v. 4, p. 39, no. 4
6709 *Tuḥaf al-'Uqūl*, p. 442
6710 *al-Kāfī*, v. 6, p. 510, no. 1
6711 Qur'an 4:1
6712 *Nahj al-Balāgha*, Sermon 1
6713 Ibid. Sermon 91
6714 *'Ilal al-Sharā'i'*, p. 4, no. 1
6715 *Biḥār al-Anwār*, v. 11, p. 116, no. 46
6716 *Qurb al-Isnād*, p. 366, no. 1311
6717 Qur'an 19:56,57
6718 In another tradition: He sent down fifty Books, and he is Ukhnūkh, and he is the first person who wrote with a pen. *Biḥār al-Anwār*, v. 11, p. 60, no. 68
6719 *Biḥār al-Anwār*, v. 11, p. 277, no. 5
6720 *Kanz al-'Ummāl*, no. 32269
6721 *Biḥār al-Anwār*, v. 11, p. 284, no. 12
6722 Qur'an 7:59
6723 Qur'an 10:71
6724 *Kanz al-'Ummāl*, no. 32391
6725 *al-Mustadrak 'alā al-Ṣaḥīḥayn*, v. 2, p. 595, no. 4005
6726 Qur'an 11:40
6727 *Biḥār al-Anwār*, v. 11, p. 336, no. 64
6728 *al-Kāfī*, v. 8, p. 283, no. 425
6729 *Kamāl al-Dīn*, p. 214, no. 2
6730 *Tafsīr al-Mizān*, v. 10, p. 270
6731 Prophet Hūd (AS) is not a biblical prophet, and his Christian name is therefore not known (*ed.*)
6732 Qur'an 7:65
6733 *al-Kāfī*, v. 8, p. 115, no. 92
6734 *Kamāl al-Dīn*, p. 136, no. 5
6735 *Aḥqāf* is the plural of *ḥiqf*, meaning sand dunes, and the *aḥqāf* mentioned in the Holy Book is a valley between Oman and the land of Muhrah. It is also said to be between Oman and Haḍramawt. It is a sandy place overseeing the shoreline of the sea. Al-Ḍaḥḥāk has said, 'al-Aḥqāf is a mountain in

Damascus.' [as stated in the footnote of the sourcebook]
6736 *Tafsīr al-Mīzān*, v. 10, p. 307
6737 Prophet Ṣāliḥ is not a biblical prophet, and his Christian name is, therefore, not known (*ed.*)
6738 Qur'an 7:73
6739 Qur'an 26:157
6740 *Nahj al-Balāgha*, Sermon 201
6741 *Biḥār al-Anwār*, v. 11, p. 379, no. 4
6742 *Tafsīr al-Mīzān*, v. 10, p. 317
6743 Qur'an 2:124
6744 *Kanz al-'Ummāl*, no. 32288
6745 *'Ilal al-Sharā'i'*, p. 35, no. 4
6746 *al-Durr al-Manthūr*, v. 1, p. 282
6747 *'Ilal al-Sharā'i'*, p. 34, no. 2
6748 Qur'an 2:124
6749 *al-Kāfī*, v. 1, p. 175, no. 2
6750 This can be understood from Abraham's supplication which is narrated in Ṣūrah Ibrāhīm [as mentioned in the footnote of the source reference]
6751 *Tafsīr al-Mīzān*, v. 7, p. 215
6752 Quran 7:80
6753 *Biḥār al-Anwār*, v. 12, p. 152, no. 5
6754 It is narrated in *Kanz al-'Ummāl*, no. 32361 from Abū Hurayra: 'Allah did not send a prophet after him without being rich among his people. But the correct version is what has been mentioned in the text.
6755 *Biḥār al-Anwār*, v. 12, p. 157, no. 8
6756 Qur'an 29: 26
6757 Qur'an 26: 167
6758 Qur'an 27: 56
6759 Qur'an 11: 80
6760 *Tafsīr al-Mizān*, v. 10, p. 352
6761 Qur'an 2:132,133
6762 *Amālī al-Ṭūsī*, p. 457, no. 1021
6763 *Kanz al-'Ummāl*, no. 32400
6764 Ibid. no. 32404
6765 Qur'an 12:13
6766 *Nūr al-Thaqalayn*, v. 2, p. 415, no. 20
6767 Qur'an 21:83,84
6768 *Kanz al-'Ummāl*, no 32318
6769 Ibid. no. 32316
6770 *al-Da'awāt*, p. 165, no. 456
6771 *'Ilal al-Sharā'i'*, p. 75, no. 3
6772 Ibid. p. 75, no. 4
6773 *Qasas al-Anbiyā'*, p. 139, no. 147
6774 Although Prophet Shu'ayb (AS) is not recognised as a prophet in the Judeo-Christian faiths, he is known in the biblical tradition as Jethro, Moses' father-in-law (*ed.*)
6775 Qur'an 7:85-92
6776 *Qasas al-Anbiyā* ', p. 145, no. 157
6777 *Tafsīr al-Mīzān*, v. 10, p. 377
6778 Qur'an 21:48
6779 Qur'an 4:164
6780 *Amālī al-Ṭūsī*, p. 165, no. 275
6781 *Biḥār al-Anwār*, v. 13, p. 7, no. 5
6782 *al-Ṭabaqāt al-Kubrā*, v. 1, p. 417
6783 *Nahj al-Balāgha*, Sermon 182
6784 Qur'an, 28:24
6785 *Nahj al-Balāgha*, Sermon 160
6786 *Biḥār al-Anwār*, v. 13 p. 47, no. 15
6787 *Tafsīr al-Mizān*, v. 16, p. 40
6788 Qur'an 18:60-82
6789 *Biḥār al-Anwār*, v. 13, p. 284, no. 1
6790 Derived from the Arabic root *kha-ḍa-ra*: green (*ed.*)
6791 *'Ilal al-Sharā'i'*, p. 59, no. 1
6792 *Biḥār al-Anwār*, v. 13, p. 303, no. 25
6793 *Kamāl al-Dīn*, p. 390, no. 4 (These traditions are singular (*āhād*) and are not decisive in narration, so there is no way to authenticate them by the Qur'an, authentic traditions, or the intellect) [as mentioned in the footnote of the source reference]
6794 *Tafsīr al-Mizān*, v. 13, p. 350
6795 Qur'an 19: 54-55
6796 *'Ilal al-Sharā`i'*, p. 77, no. 2
6797 Ibid. p. 78, no. 3
6798 *Tafsīr al-Qummī*, v. 2, p. 51
6799 Qur'an 6:86
6800 *al-Iḥtijāj*, v. 2, p. 407, no. 307
6801 Prophet Dhu'l Kifl (AS) is not one of the biblical prophets and so his Christian name is unknown (*ed.*)
6802 Qur'an 21:85,86
6803 Qur'an 38:48
6804 *Qasas al-Anbiyā'*, p. 213, no. 277
6805 Qur'an 38:17-26

6806 Qur'an 21:105
6807 *Kitāb man lā yaḥḍurahi al-Faqīh,* v. 3, p. 162, no. 3594
6808 *Amālī al-Ṣadūq*, p. 263, no. 280
6809 *Biḥār al-Anwār*, v. 14, p. 40, no. 26
6810 *Kanz al-'Ummāl*, no. 32322
6811 Ibid. no. 32323
6812 *al-Khiṣāl*, p. 248, no. 110
6813 Qur'an 27:16
6814 *Biḥār al-Anwār*, v. 14, p. 95, no. 3
6815 *al-Khiṣāl*, p. 241, no. 91
6816 *Nahj al-Balāgha*, Sermon 183
6817 *al-Da'awāt*, p. 142, no. 363
6818 *Mustaṭrafāt al-Sarā'ir*, p. 41, no. 7
6819 *'Ilal al-Sharā'i'*, p. 73, no. 2
6820 Qur'an 21:89,90
6821 *Kanz al-'Ummāl*, no. 32330
6822 Ibid. no. 32329
6823 Qur'an 19:7,12-15
6824 *Kanz al-'Ummāl*, no. 32425
6825 *al-Kāfī*, v. 2, p. 665, no. 20
6826 *Amālī al-Ṭūsī*, p. 340, no. 692
6827 Qur'an 3:59
6828 Qur'an 4:157-159
6829 *Biḥār al-Anwār*, v. 14, p. 239, no. 17
6830 *al-Khiṣāl*, p. 524, no. 13
6831 *Kanz al-'Ummāl*, no. 32357
6832 Ibid. no. 32358
6833 Ibid. no. 32359
6834 *Nahj al-Balāgha*, Sermon 160
6835 Qur'an 19:31
6836 *Ma'ānī al-Akhbār*, p. 212, no. 1
6837 *Tafsīr al-Mīzān*, v. 3, p. 279
6838 Qur'an 2:259
6839 *al-Kāfī*, v. 8, p. 123, no. 94
6840 *al-Iḥtijāj*, v. 2, p. 230, no. 223
6841 Qur'an 37:139-148
6842 *Kanz al-'Ummāl*, no. 32423
6843 *Biḥār al-Anwār*, v. 14, p. 382, no. 2
6844 *Tafsīr al-Mīzān*, v. 17, p. 165
6845 Qur'an 49:29
6846 Qur'an 10:128
6847 Qur'an 33:45,46
6848 *Ma'ānī al-Akhbār*, p. 52, no. 2
6849 Qur'an 33:40
6850 *al-Ṭabaqāt al-Kubrā*, v. 1, p. 105
6851 *al-Kāfī*, v. 1, p. 269, no. 3
6852 Ibid. v. 2, p. 17, no. 2
6853 *Makārim al-Akhlāq*, v. 1, p. 51, no. 19
6854 *al-Ṭabaqāt al-Kubrā*, v. 1, p. 192
6855 Qur'an 2: 129
6856 *Kanz al-'Ummāl*, no. 31833
6857 *Biḥār al-Anwār*, v. 8, p. 48, no. 51
6858 *Kanz al-'Ummāl*, no. 31883
6859 *al-Kāfī*, v. 2, p. 600, no. 4
6860 *Kanz al-'Ummāl*, no. 31964
6861 *'Uyūn Akhbār al-Riḍā (AS)*, v. 1, p. 262, no. 22
6862 *Amālī al-Ṭūsī*, p. 484, no. 1059
6863 *al-Ṭabaqāt al-Kubrā*, v. 1, p. 410
6864 *Nahj al-Balāgha*, Sermon 105
6865 *Makārim al-Akhlāq*, v. 1, p. 61, no. 55
6866 *al-Kāfī*, v. 1, p. 440, no. 2
6867 *Nahj al-Balāgha*, Saying 108
6868 *al-Tawḥīd*, p. 174, no. 3
6869 Qur'an 34:28
6870 *al-Ṭabaqāt al-Kubrā*, v. 1, p. 191
6871 *Biḥār al-Anwār*, v. 16, p. 316, no. 6
6872 *Nahj al-Balāgha*, Sermon 161
6873 Ibid. Sermon 214
6874 Qur'an 68: 4
6875 *al-Ghārāt*, v. 1, p. 167
6876 *al-Ṭabaqāt al-Kubrā*, v. 1, p. 365
6877 Ibid. v. 1, p. 378
6878 Ibid. v. 1, p. 365
6879 Ibid. v. 1, p. 368
6880 Ibid. v. 1, p. 372
6881 *Kanz al-'Ummāl*, no. 32147
6882 *al-Sīra al-Nabawiyya li Ibn Hishām*, v. 1, p. 210
6883 Ibid. v. 1, p. 199
6884 *al-Kāfī*, v. 8, p. 268, no. 393
6885 *Makārim al-Akhlāq*, v. 1, p. 53, no. 26
6886 *Kanz al-'Ummāl*, no. 35347
6887 *Saḥīḥ Muslim*, v. 4, p. 1802, no. 48
6888 *Makārim al-Akhlāq*, v. 1, p. 55, no. 34
6889 *al-Targhīb wa al-Tarhīb*, v. 3, p. 418, no. 20
6890 *Musnad Aḥmad Ibn Ḥanbal*, v. 10, p. 212, no. 26731
6891 *Makārim al-Akhlāq*, v. 1, p. 50, no. 15
6892 *Amālī al-Ṣadūq*, p. 130, no. 117
6893 *Sunan Ibn Māja*, v. 2, p. 1101, no. 3312

6894 *al-Ṭabaqāt al-Kubrā*, v. 1, p. 370
6895 *al-Kāfī*, v. 8, p. 130, no. 100
6896 *al-Maḥāsin*, v. 2, p. 244, no. 1759
6897 *al-Kāfī*, v. 8, p. 127, no. 97
6898 *Kanz al-'Ummāl*, no. 5818
6899 Ibid. no. 16678
6900 *al-Ṭabaqāt al-Kubrā*, v. 1, p. 378
6901 *al-Targhīb wa al-Tarhīb*, v. 3, p. 419, no. 21
6902 *Makārim al-Akhlāq*, v. 1, p. 64, no. 65
6903 *Qurb al-Isnād*, p. 91, no. 304
6904 *al-Targhīb wa al-Tarhīb*, v. 4, p. 199, no. 120
6905 *Makārim al-Akhlāq*, v. 1, p. 79, no. 124
6906 *al-Kāfī*, v. 8, p. 130, no. 100
6907 *al-Manāqib li Ibn Shahr Āshūb*, v. 1, p. 145, no. 146
6908 *Saḥīḥ Muslim*, v. 4, p. 1814, no. 79
6909 Qur'an 20:1,2
6910 *Tafsīr al-Mīzān*, v. 14, no. 126
6911 *al-Kāfī*, v. 2, p. 95, no. 6
6912 Some of the traditions in this section refer to astronomy and some to astrology, and have been indicated to in their respective cases (*ed.*)
6913 *Nahj al-Balāgha*, Sermon 79
6914 *Biḥār al-Anwār*, v. 58, p. 235, no. 15
6915 *al-Kāfī*, v. 8, p. 195, no. 233
6916 The chapter on astronomy in *al-Makāsib* states: There is no problem in forecasting or guessing on the basis of the position and movement of the stars, that is, some one would forecast the happening of an event in the future on the basis of the position of stars such as closeness, distance, parallelism, and overlapping of two stars... rather apparently there is no problem even if one categorically forecasts the happening of some events if the forecast is based on a definite experience. For instance, there is no problem if someone would say that tonight will definitely rain on the basis of the experience that his dog would come inside the building whenever it rains. It is said that it has happened for an advocator of astronomy. He stayed with a miller in the outskirt of a city when he was travelling. When he entered the house of the miller due to the hot weather he decided to sleep on the roof. The landlord told him to come and sleep inside the room to be safe against the rain. Looking at the stars, he said, there is no sign of rain. The landlord told him; I have a dog who comes inside the building when it feels that it rains. The person did not accept his argument and slept on the roof. However the rain started in the midnight to which surprised him. (*al-Makāsib*, p. 25)
6917 *Biḥār al-Anwār*, v. 58, p. 223, no. 3
6918 It can be understood from these traditions that the science of stars that is prohibited is not astronomy that exists in this present time, but rather it is the study of stars that looks into the effect of stars on the fate of a person and foretelling future events through observing the planets in that they themselves effect human beings.
6919 *Kitāb man lā yaḥḍurahi al-Faqīh,* v. 2, p. 267, no. 2402
6920 Qur'an 3:35
6921 Qur'an 2:270
6922 Qur'an 76:7
6923 *Wasā'il al-Shī'a*, v. 16, p. 190, p. 5
6924 Ibid. v. 16, p. 189, no. 1
6925 Qur'an 7:68
6926 *al-Targhīb wa al-Tarhīb*, v. 2, p. 577, no. 16
6927 *Saḥīḥ Muslim*, v. 1, p. 74, no. 95
6928 *al-Kāfī*, v. 2, p. 208, no. 5
6929 Ibid. no. 4
6930 *Nahj al-Balāgha*, Letter 31
6931 *al-Kāfī*, v. 2, p. 208, no. 2
6932 Ibid. v. 2, p. 208, no. 6
6933 *Tuḥaf al-'Uqūl*, p. 20
6934 *Kashf al-Ghamma*, v. 3, p. 137-138
6935 *Nahj al-Balāgha*, Sermon 86
6936 *al-Durra al-Bāhira*, p. 26
6937 *Biḥār al-Anwār*, v. 78, p. 194, no. 9
6938 *al-Khiṣāl*, p. 46, no. 47
6939 *Ghurar al-Ḥikam*, no. 5944
6940 Ibid. no. 7743
6941 *al-Maḥāsin*, v. 2, p. 440, no. 2526
6942 Qur'an 16: 90
6943 *Nahj al-Balāgha*, Saying 231
6944 *Ghurar al-Ḥikam*, no. 971

6945 Ibid. no. 1130
6946 Ibid. no. 4190
6947 *Nahj al-Balāgha*, Saying 224
6948 *Ghurar al-Ḥikam*, no. 5448
6949 *Biḥār al-Anwār*, v. 78, p. 165, no. 1
6950 *Ghurar al-Ḥikam*, no. 1410
6951 Ibid. no. 3186
6952 *Tuḥaf al-'Uqūl*, p. 305
6953 *al-Khiṣāl*, p. 47, no. 48
6954 *Ghurar al-Ḥikam*, no. 3345
6955 *al-Kāfī*, v. 2, p. 144, no. 4
6956 *Kashf al-Ghamma*, v. 3, p. 137-138
6957 *Nahj al-Balāgha*, Letter 53
6958 *al-Kāfī*, v. 2, p. 148, no. 19
6959 *Ghurar al-Ḥikam*, no. 4674
6960 Ibid. no. 10732-10733
6961 Ibid. no. 368
6962 *Biḥār al-Anwār*, v. 104, p. 41, no. 52
6963 *Nahj al-Balāgha*, Saying 409
6964 *Biḥār al-Anwār*, v. 104, p. 42, no. 52
6965 *Biḥār al-Anwār*, v. 72, p. 199, no. 29
6966 *Ghurar al-Ḥikam*, no. 950
6967 *Tuḥaf al-'Uqūl*, p. 95
6968 *Biḥār al-Anwār*, v. 104, p. 38, no. 33
6969 *al-Kāfī*, v. 5, p. 559, no. 12
6970 *Biḥār al-Anwār*, v. 74, p. 73, no. 59
6971 *Saḥīfa al-Imām al-Riḍā (AS)*, p. 90, no. 19
6972 Qur'an 24:30,31
6973 *Jāmi' al-Akhbār*, p. 408, no. 1129
6974 *Biḥār al-Anwār*, v. 104, p. 41, no. 52
6975 Ibid. v. 76, p. 334, no. 1
6976 *Thawāb al-A'māl*, p. 338, no. 1
6977 *Ghurar al-Ḥikam*, no. 9122
6978 *Kitāb man lā yaḥḍurahi al-Faqīh*, v. 4, p. 18, no. 4969
6979 Qur'an 24:60
6980 *'Uyūn Akhbār al-Riḍā (AS)*, v. 2, p. 97, no. 1
6981 *Kitāb man lā yaḥḍurahi al-Faqīh*, v. 4, p. 19, no. 4971
6982 Ibid. v. 3, p. 474, no. 4658
6983 Ibid. v. 4, p. 18, no. 4970
6984 *Biḥār al-Anwār*, v. 10, p. 115, no. 1
6985 Qur'an 25:63
6986 *Bashārat al-Muṣṭafā*, p. 26
6987 *Biḥār al-Anwār*, v. 2, p. 136, no. 39
6988 Ibid. v. 2, p. 136, no. 41
6989 Ibid. v. 2, p. 135, no. 32
6990 *Sunan al-Tirmidhī*, v. 5, p. 112, no. 2799
6991 *Kanz al-'Ummāl*, no. 26003
6992 *al-Kāfī*, v. 6, p. 439, no. 5
6993 *Sunan Abī Dāwūd*, v. 4, p. 51, no. 4062
6994 *Kanz al-'Ummāl*, no. 26002
6995 Ibid. no. 26000
6996 *al-Kāfī*, v. 6, p. 441, no. 3
6997 Ibid. v. 6, p. 444, no. 14
6998 *Wasā'il al-Shī'a*, v. 3, p. 571, no. 2
6999 *al-Khiṣāl*, p. 54, no. 73
7000 *Biḥār al-Anwār*, v. 78, p. 335, no. 4
7001 *al-Kāfī*, v. 6, p. 439, no. 6
7002 *Kanz al-'Ummāl*, no. 7422
7003 *Wasā'il al-Shī'a*, v. 3, p. 572, no. 3
7004 *Kitāb man lā yaḥḍurahi al-Faqīh*, v. 4, p. 5, no. 4968
7005 *al-Khiṣāl*, p. 620, no. 10
7006 *Wasā'il al-Shī'a*, v. 3, p. 575, no. 2
7007 Qur'an 14:34
7008 *al-Kāfī*, v. 2, p. 316, no. 5
7009 *Nahj al-Balāgha*, Sermon 1
7010 *Bashāra al-Muṣṭafā*, p. 28
7011 *al-Khiṣāl*, p. 35, no. 7
7012 *Biḥār al-Anwār*, v. 81, p. 170, no. 1
7013 Ibid. v. 78, p. 12, no. 70
7014 Ibid. v. 78, p. 115, no. 12
7015 *'Ilal al-Sharā'i'*, p. 464, no. 12
7016 *Nahj al-Balāgha*, Saying 246
7017 *A'lām al-Dīn*, p. 312
7018 Qur'an 7:96
7019 Qur'an 8:53
7020 *Biḥār al-Anwār*, v. 75, p. 353, no. 62
7021 *Nahj al-Balāgha*, Saying 372
7022 Ibid. Saying 330
7023 *Tuḥaf al-'Uqūl*, p. 318
7024 *al-Kāfī*, v. 4, p. 37, no. 1
7025 *Biḥār al-Anwār*, v. 78, p. 327, no. 4
7026 *'Uyūn Akhbār al-Riḍā (AS)*, v. 2, p. 24, no. 52
7027 Qur'an 3:178
7028 *Nahj al-Balāgha*, Saying 25
7029 Ibid. Saying 358
7030 Ibid. Saying 273
7031 *Biḥār al-Anwār*, v. 78, p. 117, no. 7

7032 Qur'an 93:11
7033 *Sunan al-Tirmidhī*, v. 5, p. 124, no. 2819
7034 *Sunan al-Nasā'ī*, v. 8, p. 196
7035 *al-Kāfī*, v. 6, p. 438, no. 1
7036 Ibid. v. 6, p. 438, no. 2
7037 Ibid. v. 6, p. 439, no. 9
7038 *Tuḥaf al-'Uqūl*, p. 36
7039 *Nahj al-Balāgha*, Saying 224
7040 Ibid. Sermon 188
7041 *Ma'ānī al-Akhbār*, p. 408, no. 87
7042 Qur'an 12:53
7043 *Ghurar al-Ḥikam*, no. 2106
7044 *Biḥār al-Anwār*, v. 94, p. 143
7045 Qur'an 75:2
7046 *Makārim al-Akhlāq*, v. 2, p. 353, no. 2660
7047 Qur'an 91:7-10
7048 *Nahj al-Balāgha*, Saying 359
7049 *Ghurar al-Ḥikam*, no. 2489
7050 *Nahj al-Balāgha*, Sermon 198
7051 *Ghurar al-Ḥikam*, no. 2434
7052 Ibid. no. 9103-9104
7053 Ibid. no. 9170
7054 *Amālī al-Ṣadūq*, p. 478, no. 644
7055 *Ghurar al-Ḥikam*, no. 8730
7056 Ibid. no. 8771
7057 Ibid. no. 9130
7058 Qur'an 9:77
7059 *Kanz al-'Ummāl*, no. 1734
7060 *Ghurar al-Ḥikam*, no. 483
7061 Ibid. no. 9559
7062 Ibid. no. 9988
7063 Qur'an 4:142-143
7064 *Biḥār al-Anwār*, v. 72, p. 207, no. 8
7065 *Kanz al-'Ummāl*, no. 854
7066 Ibid. no. 862
7067 *Biḥār al-Anwār*, v. 72, p. 207, no. 8
7068 *al-Kāfī*, v. 2, p. 396, no. 6
7069 *Tuḥaf al-'Uqūl*, p. 212
7070 *Nahj al-Balāgha*, Saying 45
7071 *Amālī al-Ṣadūq*, p. 582, no. 802
7072 *al-Ikhtiṣāṣ*, p. 228
7073 *Ghurar al-Ḥikam*, no. 3214
7074 Ibid. no. 3309
7075 *Nahj al-Balāgha*, Sermon 68
7076 Qur'an 9:68
7077 Qur'an 4:145
7078 *al-Khiṣāl*, p. 38, no. 16
7079 *al-Targhīb wa al-Tarhīb*, v. 3, p. 603, no. 3
7080 *al-Kāfī*, v. 2, p. 492, no. 8
7081 Ibid. v. 2, p. 493, no. 13
7082 Qur'an 2:254
7083 Qur'an 57:7
7084 Qur'an 2:272
7085 *al-Kāfī*, v. 4, p. 3, no. 6
7086 *Amālī al-Ṭūsī*, p. 183, no. 306
7087 *al-Targhīb wa al-Tarhīb*, v. 2, p. 50, no. 8
7088 *Biḥār al-Anwār*, v. 96, p. 117, no. 9
7089 *Ghurar al-Ḥikam*, no. 3834
7090 *Tuḥaf al-'Uqūl*, p. 83
7091 *Ghurar al-Ḥikam*, no. 3827
7092 *Biḥār al-Anwār*, v. 96, p. 133, no. 67
7093 Quran 34:39
7094 *Makārim al-Akhlāq*, v. 2, p. 21, no. 2053
7095 *Biḥār al-Anwār*, v. 96, p. 131, no. 62
7096 *Kanz al-'Ummāl*, no. 16150
7097 *Nahj al-Balāgha*, Saying 138
7098 *Biḥār al-Anwār*, v. 96, p. 130, no. 57
7099 *al-Kāfī*, v. 4, p. 9, no. 1
7100 Qur'an 3:92
7101 *Majma' al-Bayān*, v. 2, p. 792
7102 *al-Kāfī*, v. 4, p. 61, no. 3
7103 *Jāmi' al-Akhbār*, p. 505, no. 1395
7104 *al-Kāfī*, v. 3, p. 504, no. 7
7105 *Tuḥaf al-'Uqūl*, p. 408
7106 *Biḥār al-Anwār*, v. 77, p. 52, no. 3
7107 *Tuḥaf al-'Uqūl*, p. 282
7108 Qur'an 9:53,54
7109 Qur'an 2:267
7110 *Tafsīr al-'Ayyāshī*, v. 1, p. 149, no. 492
7111 *Kitāb man lā yaḥḍurahi al-Faqīh*, v. 2, p. 57, no. 1694
7112 Qur'an 68:10,11
7113 *Kanz al-'Ummāl*, no. 8354
7114 *al-Khiṣāl*, p. 182, no. 249
7115 *Ghurar al-Ḥikam*, no. 2663
7116 Ibid. no. 2939
7117 *Biḥār al-Anwār*, v. 63, p. 21, no. 14
7118 *Kanz al-'Ummāl*, no. 7545
7119 *al-Khiṣāl*, p. 108, no. 73
7120 Qur'an 17:79
7121 *al-Kāfī*, v. 3, p. 454, no. 16
7122 Qur'an 23:9

7123 Qur'an 70:23
7124 *al-Kāfī*, v. 3, p. 269, no. 12
7125 *Bashāra al-Muṣṭafā*, p. 28
7126 *Nahj al-Balāgha*, Saying 279
7127 Ibid. Saying 39
7128 Qur'an 6:122
7129 Qur'an 57:28
7130 *al-Ṣaḥīfa al-Sajjādiyya*, p. 95 supplication 22
7131 *Biḥār al-Anwār*, v. 1, p. 225, no. 17
7132 *Ghurar al-Ḥikam*, no. 3725
7133 *'Ilal al-Sharā'i'*, p. 366, no. 1
7134 *Mustadrak al-Wasā'il*, v. 12, p. 173, no. 13810
7135 *al-Targhīb wa al-Tarhīb*, v. 1, p. 156, no. 22
7136 Ibid. v. 2, p. 281, no. 18
7137 Ibid. v. 2, p. 349, no. 10
7138 *Biḥār al-Anwār*, v. 104, p. 311, no. 9
7139 *al-Kāfī*, v. 2, p. 54, no. 4
7140 Qur'an 57:12
7141 *Kanz al-'Ummāl*, no. 44154
7142 *Ghurar al-Ḥikam*, no. 2097
7143 *Tuḥaf al-'Uqūl*, p. 320
7144 *al-'Uṣūl al-Sitta 'Ashar*, p. 57
7145 *Kanz al-'Ummāl*, no. 24822
7146 *Nahj al-Sa'āda*, v. 2, p. 97
7147 *Biḥār al-Anwār*, v. 78, p. 57, no. 119
7148 *Sharḥ Nahj al-Balāgha li Ibn Abī al-Ḥadīd*, v. 2, p. 200, no. 201
7149 Qur'an 25:44
7150 *al-Khiṣāl*, p. 409, no. 9
7151 *Tuḥaf al-'Uqūl*, p. 413
7152 Qur'an 78:9
7153 Qur'an 39:42
7154 *Kanz al-'Ummāl*, no. 39321
7155 *Biḥār al-Anwār*, v. 62, p. 316
7156 *A'lām al-Dīn*, p. 311
7157 *Qaṣaṣ al-Anbiyā'*, p. 163, no. 185
7158 *al-Ikhtiṣāṣ*, p. 218
7159 *Amālī al-Ṣadūq*, p. 478, no. 644
7160 *Nahj al-Balāgha*, Saying 440, Sermon 241
7161 *al-Kāfī*, v. 5, p. 84, no. 1
7162 *Tafsīr al-'Ayyāshī*, v. 2, p. 115, no. 149
7163 *al-Kāfī*, v. 5, p. 84, no. 2
7164 *al-Durra al-Bāhira*, p. 43
7165 *Biḥār al-Anwār*, v. 81, p. 153, no. 8
7166 *Amālī al-Ṣadūq*, p. 510, no. 707
7167 *Biḥār al-Anwār*, v. 76, p. 183, no. 7
7168 *Thawāb al-A'māl*, p. 35, no. 1
7169 *Biḥār al-Anwār*, v. 76, p. 182, no. 6
7170 *al-Khiṣāl*, p. 229, no. 67
7171 *Biḥār al-Anwār*, v. 76, p. 190, no. 21
7172 *Amālī al-Ṣadūq*, p. 64, no. 27
7173 *Biḥār al-Anwār*, v. 76, p. 196, no. 12
7174 *'Ilal al-Sharā'i'*, p. 589, no. 34
7175 *al-Khiṣāl*, p. 263, no. 140
7176 *Biḥār al-Anwār*, v. 76, p. 218, no. 25
7177 *Kanz al-'Ummāl*, no. 7272
7178 *Amālī al-Ṭūsī*, p. 618, no. 1274
7179 *Ghurar al-Ḥikam*, no. 1040
7180 *al-Kāfī*, v. 2, p. 84, no. 1
7181 *Kitāb man lā yaḥḍurahi al-Faqīh*, v. 4, p. 400, no. 5859
7182 Qur'an 17:84
7183 *al-Kāfī*, v. 2, p. 85, no. 5
7184 *al-Maḥāsin*, v. 1, p. 409, no. 929
7185 *Kanz al-'Ummāl*, no. 7261
7186 *Makārim al-Akhlāq*, v. 2, p. 378, no. 2661
7187 *Ghurar al-Ḥikam*, no. 1624
7188 *Nahj al-Balāgha*, Sermon 12
7189 *Ghurar al-Ḥikam*, no. 6193
7190 *A'lām al-Dīn*, p. 301
7191 *al-Kāfī*, v. 2, p. 84, no. 2
7192 *Amālī al-Ṭūsī*, p. 454, no. 1013
7193 *'Ilal al-Sharā'i'*, p. 524, no. 2
7194 Ibid. no. 1
7195 *Makārim al-Akhlāq*, v. 2, p. 370, no. 2661
7196 *Biḥār al-Anwār*, v. 70, p. 210, no. 32
7197 *Kanz al-'Ummāl*, no. 7238
7198 *Ghurar al-Ḥikam*, no. 4806
7199 Ibid. no. 4766
7200 *al-Maḥāsin*, v. 1, p. 406, no. 922
7201 *al-Kāfī*, v. 2, p. 85, no. 4
7202 *Ghurar al-Ḥikam*, no. 5568
7203 Ibid. no. 6228
7204 Ibid. no. 4021
7205 *Biḥār al-Anwār*, v. 71, p. 247, no. 6
7206 *Kanz al-'Ummāl*, no. 46260
7207 Ibid. no. 46262
7208 This refers to those who are incapacitated, or whom the proof and message of Allah has actually not reached, and thus are not empowered to act (*ed.*)
7209 *Nahj al-Balāgha*, Sermon 189

7210 *al-Kāfī*, v. 8, p. 148, no. 126
7211 Qur'an 74:5
7212 *Kanz al-'Ummāl*, no. 46263
7213 Ibid. no. 46264
7214 Ibid. no. 676
7215 Qur'an 4:97
7216 Qur'an 29:56
7217 *Majma' al-Bayān*, v. 8, p. 455
7218 Ibid. v. 3, p. 153
7219 Returning back to the pre-Islamic age after changing and having accepted Islam.
7220 *Wasā'il al-Shī'a*, v. 11, p. 75, no. 1
7221 *Mustadrak al-Wasā'il*, v. 11, p. 90. no. 1249
7222 *Ma'ānī al-Akhbār*, p. 265
7223 *Wasā'il al-Shī'a*, v. 11, p. 75, no. 2
7224 *Kanz al-'Ummāl*, no. 24789
7225 *Biḥār al-Anwār*, v. 77, p. 89, no. 3
7226 *al-Kāfī*, v. 2, p. 346, no. 7
7227 Ibid. v. 2, p. 344, no. 1
7228 Ibid. v. 2, p. 344, no. 2
7229 *Kanz al-'Ummāl*, no. 24793
7230 *al-Targhīb wa al-Tarhīb*, v. 3, p. 457, no. 7
7231 Ibid. v. 3, p. 457, no. 8
7232 *al-Kāfī*, v. 2, p. 345, no. 5
7233 *Biḥār al-Anwār*, v. 75, p. 188, no. 10
7234 Qur'an 20:50
7235 Qur'an 76:3
7236 *Biḥār al-Anwār*, v. 5, p. 196, no. 4
7237 Qur'an 5:32
7238 *al-Kāfī*, v. 2, p. 210, no. 1
7239 *Biḥār al-Anwār*, v. 14, p. 40, no. 26
7240 *al-Kāfī*, v. 5, p. 28, no. 4
7241 *Wasā'il al-Shī'a*, v. 11, p. 448, no. 5
7242 Qur'an 28:56
7243 *Amālī al-Ṣadūq*, p. 162, no. 161
7244 *Kanz al-'Ummāl*, no. 546
7245 Qur'an 64:11
7246 Qur'an 29:69
7247 Qur'an 28:50
7248 Qur'an 5:67
7249 *al-Kāfī*, v. 8, p. 52, no. 16
7250 Ibid. v. 5, p. 144, no. 14
7251 *Biḥār al-Anwār*, v. 77, p. 166, no. 2
7252 *al-Kāfī*, v. 5, p. 144, no. 12
7253 *Kanz al-'Ummāl*, no. 15068
7254 *Saḥīḥ al-Bukhārī*, v. 6, p. 2624, no. 6753
7255 *Kanz al-'Ummāl*, nos. 14475,14479
7256 *al-Ja'fariyāt,* p. 82
7257 *al-Kāfī*, v. 5, p. 143, no. 8
7258 Ibid. v. 5, p. 143, no. 9
7259 *Kanz al-'Ummāl*, no. 14482
7260 Ibid. no. 46164
7261 *Biḥār al-Anwār*, v. 103, p. 189, no. 5
7262 *Tanbīh al-Khawāṭir*, v. 1, p. 272
7263 *Ghurar al-Ḥikam*, no. 4623
7264 *Tuḥaf al-'Uqūl*, p. 56
7265 *al-Khiṣāl*, p. 73, no. 112
7266 *Nahj al-Balāgha*, Saying 143
7267 *Tuḥaf al-'Uqūl*, p. 317
7268 Qur'an 28: 59
7269 *al-Targhīb wa al-Tarhīb*, v. 1, p. 86, no. 10
7270 *al-Kāfī*, v. 2, p. 316, no. 6
7271 *Nahj al-Sa'āda*, v. 1, p. 477, and *Tārīkh Dimashq*, v. 42, p. 502
7272 *Ghurar al-Ḥikam*, no. 10030
7273 *Nahj al-Balāgha*, Saying 149
7274 Ibid. Saying 117
7275 *Tuḥaf al-'Uqūl*, p. 369
7276 *Biḥār al-Anwār*, v. 78, p. 207, no. 67
7277 *Kanz al-'Ummāl*, no. 43021
7278 *Nahj al-Balāgha*, Saying 47
7279 *Ghurar al-Ḥikam*, no. 8320
7280 *al-Ṣaḥīfa al-Sajjādiyya*, p. 439, no. 199
7281 *Biḥār al-Anwār*, v. 78, p. 165, no. 1
7282 *Nahj al-Balāgha*, Saying 460
7283 *Ghurar al-Ḥikam*, no. 1477
7284 Ibid. no. 1388
7285 Ibid. no. 4277
7286 Ibid. no. 1674
7287 Ibid. no. 5763
7288 *Biḥār al-Anwār*, v. 78, p. 10, no. 164
7289 *Ghurar al-Ḥikam*, no. 8019
7290 Ibid. no. 9256
7291 *Biḥār al-Anwār*, v. 78, p. 10, no. 67
7292 *Tuḥaf al-'Uqūl*, p. 318
7293 *Tanbīh al-Khawāṭir*, v. 1, p. 48
7294 *Ghurar al-Ḥikam*, no. 8830
7295 Ibid. no. 9642
7296 Qur'an 45: 23
7297 *al-Durr al-Manthūr*, v. 6, p. 261
7298 *Ghurar al-Ḥikam*, no. 2217-2218
7299 Ibid. no. 449

7300 *Sunan al-Dārimī*, v. 1, p. 115, no. 401
7301 *al-Targhīb wa al-Tarhīb*, v. 1, p. 87, no. 13
7302 *Nahj al-Balāgha*, Sermon 50
7303 *Biḥār al-Anwār*, v. 70, p. 76, no. 6
7304 *Nahj al-Balāgha*, Sermon 176
7305 *Ghurar al-Ḥikam*, no. 27
7306 Ibid. no. 6813
7307 Qur'an 30: 29
7308 *Biḥār al-Anwār*, v. 77, p. 82, no. 3
7309 *Da'ā'im al-Islām*, v. 2, p. 350
7310 *Nahj al-Balāgha*, Letter 31
7311 *Ghurar al-Ḥikam*, no. 9168
7312 Ibid. no. 3133
7313 Ibid. no. 2746
7314 Ibid. no. 6790
7315 Ibid. no. 6298
7316 *Nahj al-Balāgha*, Saying 211
7317 *Ghurar al-Ḥikam*, no. 8794
7318 Ibid. no. 8823
7319 *al-Kāfī*, v. 2, p. 335, no. 1
7320 Qur'an 80: 40-41
7321 *al-Kāfī*, v. 8, p. 136, no. 103
7322 *Ghurar al-Ḥikam*, no. 5263
7323 Ibid. no. 5393
7324 Ibid. no. 6421
7325 Ibid. no. 6418
7326 Ibid. no. 6444
7327 *Biḥār al-Anwār*, v. 78, p. 53, no. 87
7328 *Tuḥaf al-'Uqūl*, p. 370
7329 Ibid. p. 398
7330 *al-Kāfī*, v. 2, p. 335, no. 2
7331 *Tanbīh al-Khawāṭir*, v. 2, p. 122
7332 Ibid. v. 2, p. 122
7333 *Ghurar al-Ḥikam*, no. 7959
7334 Ibid. no. 4902
7335 Ibid. no. 8995
7336 *Tanbīh al-Khawāṭir*, v. 1, p. 60
7337 *Ma'ānī al-Akhbār*, p. 195, no. 1
7338 *Tanbīh al-Khawāṭir*, v. 2, p. 10
7339 *al-Kāfī*, v. 8, p. 42,46, no. 8
7340 *Ghurar al-Ḥikam*, no. 7205
7341 Ibid. no. 8226
7342 Ibid. no. 2148
7343 *Nahj al-Balāgha*, Saying 449
7344 Ibid. Sermon 83
7345 Ibid. Saying 31
7346 *al-Kāfī*, v. 2, p. 335, no. 2
7347 Ibid. v. 2, p. 137, no. 1
7348 *Ghurar al-Ḥikam*, no. 7953
7349 Ibid. no. 4354
7350 Ibid. no. 5390
7351 Qur'an 4:11
7352 *al-Kāfī*, v. 7, p. 85, no. 3
7353 *'Uyūn Akhbār al-Riḍā (AS)*, v. 2, p. 98, no. 1
7354 *al-Kāfī*, v. 7, p. 141, no. 5
7355 *Kanz al-'Ummāl*, no. 30447
7356 *al-Kāfī*, v. 7, p. 143, no. 5
7357 Qur'an 27:16
7358 Qur'an 19:5,6
7359 *al-Ṭabaqāt al-Kubrā*, v. 2, p. 315
7360 *Kanz al-'Ummāl*, no. 7284
7361 Ibid. no. 7300
7362 *Biḥār al-Anwār*, v. 70, p. 304, no. 18
7363 *Nahj al-Balāgha*, Saying 371
7364 Ibid. Saying 4
7365 *Biḥār al-Anwār*, v. 70, p. 306, no. 30
7366 *al-Kāfī*, v. 2, p. 77, no. 5
7367 *Amālī al-Ṭūsī*, p. 281, no. 544
7368 *al-Kāfī*, v. 2, p. 78, no. 10
7369 *Ghurar al-Ḥikam*, no. 4636
7370 Ibid. no. 1436
7371 Ibid. no. 1107
7372 Ibid. no. 10689
7373 *al-Kāfī*, v. 2, p. 76, no. 2
7374 *al-Maḥāsin*, v. 1, p. 65, no. 9
7375 *Tanbīh al-Khawāṭir*, v. 2, p. 88
7376 *al-Kāfī*, v. 2, p. 77, no. 4
7377 *Biḥār al-Anwār*, v. 70, p. 296, no. 1
7378 *Kanz al-'Ummāl*, no. 7299
7379 *Ghurar al-Ḥikam*, no. 3097
7380 Ibid. no. 2161
7381 *al-Kāfī*, v. 2, p. 77, no. 8
7382 *Biḥār al-Anwār*, v. 70, p. 303, no. 15
7383 *al-Kāfī*, v. 2, p. 77, no. 7
7384 *Biḥār al-Anwār*, v. 69, p. 368, no. 4
7385 *Ghurar al-Ḥikam*, no. 3368
7386 Ibid. no. 2839
7387 Qur'an 7:8,9
7388 *Kanz al-'Ummāl*, no. 39768
7389 *al-Kāfī*, v. 2, p. 143, no. 10
7390 *al-Iḥtijāj*, v. 2, pp. 212-247, no. 223

7391 *Kanz al-'Ummāl*, no. 1709
7392 *Tanbīh al-Khawāṭir*, v. 2, p. 120
7393 *al-Kāfī*, v. 3, p. 358, no. 2
7394 Ibid. v. 1, p. 12, no. 10
7395 Qur'an 23:97,98
7396 Qur'an 114:1-6
7397 *al-Khiṣāl*, p. 612, no. 10
7398 *Biḥār al-Anwār*, v. 81, p. 203, no. 5
7399 *al-Kāfī*, v. 2, p. 424, no. 1
7400 *Makārim al-Akhlāq*, v. 2, p. 380, no. 2661
7401 *Ghurar al-Ḥikam*, no. 3023
7402 Ibid. no. 10276
7403 *Biḥār al-Anwār*, v. 74, p. 395, no. 22
7404 *al-Khiṣāl*, p. 8, no. 26
7405 Ibid. p. 47, no. 50
7406 *Biḥār al-Anwār*, v. 74, p. 231, no. 28
7407 Qur'an 2:180
7408 *Wasā'il al-Shī'a*, v. 13, p. 352, no. 6
7409 *Kanz al-'Ummāl*, no. 46051
7410 *Biḥār al-Anwār*, v. 103, p. 194, no. 3
7411 *Tahdhīb al-Aḥkām*, v. 9, p. 174, no. 708
7412 *al-Kāfī*, v. 7, p. 62, no. 18
7413 *Kitāb man lā yaḥḍurahi al-Faqīh*, v. 4, p. 184, no. 5420
7414 *al-Kāfī*, v. 7, p. 11, no. 5
7415 Qur'an 5:6
7416 *Biḥār al-Anwār*, v. 80, p. 238, no. 12
7417 *Kanz al-'Ummāl*, no. 26059
7418 Ibid. no. 26031
7419 Ibid. no. 26030
7420 *Biḥār al-Anwār*, v. 80, p. 237, no. 11
7421 *Kitāb man lā yaḥḍurahi al-Faqīh*, v. 1, p. 58, no. 129
7422 *'Ilal al-Sharā'i'*, p. 279, no. 1
7423 Ibid. p. 257, no. 9
7424 *Biḥār al-Anwār*, v. 80, p. 237, no. 11
7425 *Amālī al-Mufīd*, p. 60, no. 5
7426 *Kanz al-'Ummāl*, no. 25999
7427 Ibid. no. 26042
7428 *Wasā'il al-Shī'a*, v. 1, p. 264, no. 7
7429 Ibid. v. 1, p. 265, no. 8
7430 *Tanbīh al- Khawāṭir*, v. 1, p. 201
7431 *Biḥār al-Anwār*, v. 77, p. 179, no. 10
7432 *Tanbīh al-Khawāṭir*, v. 2, p. 66
7433 *Nahj al-Balāgha*, Saying 113
7434 *Biḥār al-Anwār*, v. 75, p. 120, no. 11
7435 *Ghurar al-Ḥikam*, no. 939
7436 *Biḥār al-Anwār*, v. 75, p. 119, no. 5
7437 *Nahj al-Balāgha*, Sermon 193
7438 *Ghurar al-Ḥikam*, no. 522
7439*Nahj al-Balāgha*, sermon 406
7440 *al-Kāfī*, v. 2, p. 124, no. 13
7441 *Tuḥaf al-'Uqūl*, p. 489
7442 *al-Kāfī*, v. 2, p. 123, no. 9
7443 *Biḥār al-Anwār*, v. 75, p. 118, no. 3
7444 *al-Kāfī*, v. 2, p. 121, no. 1
7445 *Kanz al-'Ummāl*, no. 5730
7446 *Ghurar al-Ḥikam*, no. 4613-4614
7447 *Biḥār al-Anwār*, v. 77, p. 287, no. 1
7448 *Ghurar al-Ḥikam*, no. 4302
7449 Ibid. nos. 522,523
7450 *Biḥār al-Anwār*, v. 78, p. 312, no. 1
7451 *Tuḥaf al-'Uqūl*, p. 399
7452 *Biḥār al-Anwār*, v. 78, p. 7, no. 59
7453 *Ghurar al-Ḥikam*, no. 301
7454 *Nahj al-Balāgha*, Sermon 147
7455 *Biḥār al-Anwār*, v. 78, p,80 no. 66
7456 Ibid. v. 78, p,277 no. 113
7457 *Uyūn Akhbār al-Riḍā (AS)*, v. 2, p,50 no. 192
7458 *al-Kāfī*, v. 2, p. 124, no. 13
7459 *Biḥār al-Anwār*, v. 78, p45, no. 50
7460 Ibid. v. 74, p. 264, no. 3
7461 *Safīnat al-Biḥār*, v. 8, p. 525
7462 *Nahj al-Balāgha*, Sermon 27
7463 Ibid. Saying 56
7464 *Ghurar al-Ḥikam*, no. 7517
7465 Ibid. nos. 1291,1292
7466 Qur'an 31:60
7467 Qur'an 3:9
7468 *al-Tawḥīd*, p. 406, no. 3
7469 *Kanz al-'Ummāl*, no. 6865
7470 Ibid. no. 6870
7471 *Ghurar al-Ḥikam*, no. 9692
7472 *Biḥār al-Anwār*, v. 75, p. 97, no. 20
7473 *Nahj al-Balāgha*, Saying 336
7474 *Ghurar al-Ḥikam*, no. 1646-1647
7475 *al-Targhīb wa al-Tarhīb*, v. 4, p. 9, no. 12
7476 *Ghurar al-Ḥikam*, no. 1134
7477 Ibid. no. 10297
7478 *Biḥār al-Anwār*, v. 78, p. 250, no. 94
7479 *al-Kāfī*, v. 1, p. 20, no. 12
7480 Qur'an 61:2

7481 *al-Kāfī*, v. 2, p. 363, no. 1
7482 *Biḥār al-Anwār*, v. 104, p. 73, no. 23
7483 *Nahj al-Balāgha*, Letter 31
7484 *Ghurar al-Ḥikam*, no. 1354
7485 Ibid. no. 4191
7486 *Tuḥaf al-'Uqūl*, p. 35
7487 Ibid. p. 85
7488 *Ghurar al-Ḥikam*, no. 7059
7489 Ibid. no. 4032
7490 Ibid. no. 8938
7491 *Nahj al-Balāgha*, Saying 196
7492 Ibid. Saying 131
7493 *Ghurar al-Ḥikam*, no. 7338
7494 Ibid. no. 3123
7495 *Nahj al-Balāgha*, Sermon 176
7496 *Ghurar al-Ḥikam*, no. 10622
7497 *Nahj al-Balāgha*, Sermon 32
7498 *Amālī al-Ṣadūq*, p. 576, no. 778
7499 *Ghurar al-Ḥikam*, no. 3460
7500 Ibid. no. 7338
7501 Ibid. no. 9236
7502 *Biḥār al-Anwār*, v. 71, p. 324, no. 14
7503 Qur'an 16: 125
7504 *Sunan Abī Dāwūd*, v. 1, p. 289, no. 1107
7505 *Ghurar al-Ḥikam*, no. 9968
7506 *Tuḥaf al-'Uqūl*, p. 489
7507 *Biḥār al-Anwār*, v. 78, p. 67, no. 11
7508 *Amālī al-Ṭūsi*, p. 115 no. 176
7509 *Tuḥaf al-'Uqūl*, p. 294
7510 *Ghurar al-Ḥikam*, no. 1729
7511 Ibid. no. 9010
7512 *Nahj al-Balāgha*, Saying 282
7513 Qur'an 61:2,3
7514 *Kanz al-'Ummāl*, no. 43156
7515 *Nahj al-Balāgha*, Saying 150
7516 *Ghurar al-Ḥikam*, no. 5360-5361
7517 *Nahj al-Balāgha*, Sermon 105
7518 *Munyat al-Murīd*, p. 146,181
7519 *Ghurar al-Ḥikam*, no. 3538
7520 The Arabic word *tawfīq* implies a success that comes to man as a result of Allah's divine succour and aid to him, out of His Grace (*ed.*)
7521 Qur'an 11: 88
7522 *Ghurar al-Ḥikam*, no. 73
7523 Ibid. no. 162
7524 Ibid. no. 539
7525 Ibid. no. 545
7526 Ibid. no. 10802
7527 Ibid. no. 858
7528 *Nahj al-Balāgha*, Saying 113
7529 Ibid. Saying 211
7530 *Tuḥaf al-'Uqūl*, p. 83
7531 Ibid. p. 286
7532 *al-Tawḥīd*, p. 242, no. 3
7533 Qur'an 3:160
7534 *Tanbīh al-Khawāṭir*, v. 2, p. 102
7535 *Ghurar al-Ḥikam*, no. 718-719
7536 *Nahj al-Balāgha*, Sermon 147
7537 *al-Tawḥīd*, p. 242, no. 1
7538 Qur'an 17: 34
7539 Qur'an 2: 177
7540 *Biḥār al-Anwār*, v. 77, p. 149, no. 77
7541 *Ghurar al-Ḥikam*, no. 1044
7542 Ibid. no. 1430
7543 Ibid. no. 3018
7544 Ibid. no. 3020
7545 Ibid. no. 10260
7546 *al-Khiṣāl*, p. 113, no. 90
7547 Ibid. p. 123, no. 118
7548 Qur'an 25: 63
7549 *Kanz al-'Ummāl*, no. 6402
7550 Ibid. no. 6401
7551 *Ghurar al-Ḥikam*, no. 270
7552 Ibid. no. 7397
7553 Ibid. no. 4744
7554 Ibid. no. 5534
7555 Ibid. no. 4182
7556 Ibid. no. 7666
7557 *al-Kāfī*, v. 8, p. 23, no. 4
7558 *Biḥār al-Anwār*, v. 78, p. 7, no. 59
7559 Qur'an 7:96
7560 Qur'an 2:2,5
7561 Qur'an 4:31
7562 Qur'an 7:26
7563 Qur'an 8:29
7564 Qur'an 28:83
7565 *Nahj al-Balāgha*, Saying 410
7566 *Biḥār al-Anwār*, v. 77, p. 374, no. 36
7567 *Nahj al-Balāgha*, Saying 242
7568 *Ghurar al-Ḥikam*, no. 3620
7569 *Nahj al-Balāgha*, Sermon 114
7570 Ibid. Sermon 195

7571 *al-Kāfī*, v. 8, p. 17, no. 3
7572 *Nahj al-Balāgha*, Sermon 191
7573 Ibid. Sermon 191
7574 Ibid. Sermon 230
7575 *Biḥār al-Anwār*, v. 78, p. 90, no. 95
7576 *al-Kāfī*, v. 8, p. 52, no. 16
7577 Qur'an 49:13
7578 Qur'an 5:27
7579 *Biḥār al-Anwār*, v. 70, p. 286, no. 8
7580 Qur'an 65:2,3
7581 *Biḥār al-Anwār*, v. 70, p. 285, no. 7
7582 Ibid. v. 70, p. 288, no. 16
7583 Ibid. v. 78, p. 9, no. 65
7584 *Nahj al-Balāgha*, Sermon 198
7585 Ibid. Sermon 198
7586 Ibid. Sermon 190
7587 *Biḥār al-Anwār*, v. 70, p. 288, no. 19
7588 *al-Kāfī*, v. 8, p. 52, no. 16
7589 Qur'an 44:51
7590 *Biḥār al-Anwār*, v. 70, p. 285, no. 8. *'Uddat al-Dā'ī*, p. 288
7591 Qur'an 2:177
7592 Qur'an 51:15-19
7593 *Tanbīh al-Khawāṭir*, v. 2 p. 62
7594 *Kanz al-'Ummāl*, no. 8501
7595 *Nahj al-Balāgha*, Sermon 193
7596 *al-Khiṣāl*, p. 483, no. 56
7597 *al-Kāfī*, v. 2, p. 133, no. 16
7598 *Ghurar al-Ḥikam*, no. 4904
7599 *Nahj al-Balāgha*, Sermon 176
7600 Ibid. Saying 298
7601 *Biḥār al-Anwār*, v. 78, p. 377, no. 3
7602 Qur'an 4: 102
7603 *Biḥār al-Anwār*, v. 70, p. 291, no. 31
7604 Qur'an 64: 16
7605 *Biḥār al-Anwār*, v. 70, p. 287, no. 12
7606 *Tanbīh al-Khawāṭir*, v. 2, p. 120
7607 *Ghurar al-Ḥikam*, no. 2162
7608 Ibid. no. 8284
7609 *Biḥār al-Anwār*, v. 70, p. 285, no. 8
7610 Ibid. v. 70, p. 286, no. 9
7611 *Amālī al-Ṣadūq*, p. 72, no. 41
7612 *Biḥār al-Anwār*, v. 71, p. 196, no. 4
7613 *Ma'ānī al-Akhbār*, p. 196, no. 2
7614 Qur'an 3:28
7615 Qur'an 16:106
7616 *al-Kāfī*, v. 2, p. 219, no. 13
7617 Ibid. v. 2, p. 220, no. 19
7618 Ibid. v. 2, p. 218, no. 5
7619 Ibid. v. 2, p. 219, no. 11
7620 *'Ilal al-Sharā'i'*, p. 467, no. 22
7621 *Amālī al-Ṭūsī*, p. 210, no. 362
7622 *Biḥār al-Anwār*, v. 76, p. 5, no. 18
7623 *al-Kāfī*, v. 2, p. 168, no. 1
7624 *Wasā'il al-Shī'a*, v. 11, p. 483, no. 2
7625 Qur'an 3:159
7626 Qur'an 25:58
7627 *al-Kāfī*, v. 2, p. 47, no. 2
7628 *Ghurar al-Ḥikam*, no. 544
7629 *Biḥār al-Anwār*, v. 78, p. 79, no. 56
7630 *Ghurar al-Ḥikam*, no. 6484
7631 Qur'an 3:160
7632 Qur'an 9:51
7633 *Ma'ānī al-Akhbār*, p. 261, no. 1. See the whole tradition in *Biḥār al-Anwār*, v. 77, p. 20, no. 4
7634 *Sunan Ibn Māja*, v. 2, p. 1154, no. 3489
7635 *al-Kāfī*, v. 2, p. 57, no. 1
7636 Qur'an 65:3
7637 *Biḥār al-Anwār*, v. 71, p. 156, no. 73
7638 *Jāmi' al-Akhbār*, p. 321, no. 904
7639 *Ghurar al-Ḥikam*, no. 9028
7640 *Jāmi' al-Akhbār*, p. 322, no. 905
7641 Ibid. p. 322, no. 907
7642 *al-Kāfī*, v. 2, p. 65, no. 3
7643 Ibid. v. 2, p. 65, no. 6
7644 *Biḥār al-Anwār*, v. 78, no. 364, no. 5
7645 *al-Kāfī*, v. 5, p. 84, no. 5
7646 *Sunan al-Tirmidhī*, v. 4, p. 668, no. 2517
7647 *Mustadrak al-Wasā'il*, v. 11, p. 217, no. 12789
7648 *Nahj al-Balāgha*, Sermon 11
7649 *Mustadrak al-Wasā'il*, v. 11, p. 220, no. 12798
7650 *Amālī al-Ṭūsī*, p. 193, no. 326
7651 *Kanz al-'Ummāl*, no. 8512
7652 *Mustadrak al-Wasā'il*, v. 11, p. 217, no. 12790
7653 *Ghurar al-Ḥikam*, no. 2678
7654 *Kanz al-'Ummāl*, no. 45415
7655 *al-Kāfī*, v. 6, p. 2, no. 2
7656 Ibid. v. 6, p. 4, no. 2
7657 Qur'an 8:28
7658 *Jāmi' al-Akhbār*, p. 283, no. 755
7659 *Biḥār al-Anwār*, v. 104, no. 97, no. 60

7660 *Nahj al-Balāgha*, Saying 352
7661 *al-Kāfī*, v. 6, p. 49, no. 3
7662 Ibid. v. 6, p. 50, no. 7
7663 Ibid. v. 6, p. 50, no. 5
7664 *Kitāb man lā yaḥḍurahi al-Faqīh*, v. 3, p. 483, no. 4707
7665 *Biḥār al-Anwār*, v. 43, p. 285, no. 50
7666 Qur'an 26:74
7667 *al-Kāfī*, v. 6, p. 3, no. 10
7668 Ibid. v. 6, p. 2, no. 1
7669 *Biḥār al-Anwār*, v. 104, p. 98, no. 67
7670 Ibid. v. 104, p. 98, no. 66
7671 *Makārim al-Akhlāq*, v. 1, p. 471, no. 1610
7672 *Kanz al-'Ummāl*, no. 45374
7673 Ibid. no. 45399
7674 *al-Kāfī*, v. 6, p. 6, no. 7
7675 Ibid. v. 6, p. 7, no. 12
7676 *Kanz al-'Ummāl*, no. 45347
7677 *Biḥār al-Anwār*, v. 74, p. 84, no. 94
7678 Qur'an 17:23,24
7679 *al-Targhīb wa al-Tarhīb*, v. 3, p. 316, no. 10
7680 Ibid. v. 3, p. 314, no. 1
7681 Ibid. v. 3, p. 317, no. 17
7682 Ibid. v. 3, p. 322, no. 30
7683 *Biḥār al-Anwār*, v. 74, p. 65, no. 31
7684 *al-Khiṣāl*, p. 608, no. 9
7685 Ibid. p. 156, no. 196
7686 *al-Targhīb wa al-Tarhīb*, v. 3, p. 323, no. 32
7687 *al-Kāfī*, v. 2, p. 163, no. 21
7688 *Kanz al-'Ummāl*, no. 45439
7689 *Biḥār al-Anwār*, v. 74, p. 82, no. 88
7690 *al-Kāfī*, v. 2, p. 159, no. 9
7691 Ibid. v. 2, p. 348, no. 1
7692 Ibid. v. 2, p. 158, no. 1
7693 Ibid. v. 2, p. 158, no. 1
7694 *Biḥār al-Anwār*, v. 74, p. 80, no. 82
7695 *Kanz al-'Ummāl*, no. 45537
7696 *'Ilal al-Sharā'i'*, p. 479, p. 2
7697 *al-Kāfī*, v. 2, p. 349, no. 7
7698 *Biḥār al-Anwār*, v. 74, p. 61, no. 26
7699 Ibid. v. 74, p. 84, no. 95
7700 *al-Kāfī*, v. 2, p. 159, no. 5
7701 *Kanz al-'Ummāl*, no. 45933
7702 *Makārim al-Akhlāq*, v. 1, p. 474, no. 1627
7703 *Kanz al-'Ummāl*, no. 45193
7704 *Biḥār al-Anwār*, v. 78, p. 236, no. 67
7705 *Makārim al-Akhlāq*, v. 1, p. 475, no. 1633
7706 *Kanz al-'Ummāl*, no. 45410
7707 Ibid. no. 45409
7708 *Wasā'il al-Shī'a*, v. 12, p. 247, no. 13
7709 *Kanz al-'Ummāl*, no. 45338
7710 Ibid. no. 45953
7711 *Ghurar al-Ḥikam*, no. 6305
7712 *Wasā'il al-Shī'a*, v. 12, p. 247, no. 12
7713 Qur'an 4:59
7714 *Kamāl al-Dīn*, p. 253, no. 3
7715 Qur'an 13:11
7716 *Kitāb man lā yaḥḍurahi al-Faqīh*, v. 4, p. 404, no. 5871
7717 *Kanz al-'Ummāl*, no. 14972
7718 *Nahj al-Balāgha*, Sermon 97
7719 *Biḥār al-Anwār*, v. 75, p. 340, no. 18
7720 *al-Targhīb wa al-Tarhīb*, v. 3, p. 176, no. 40
7721 *Ghurar al Ḥikam*, no. 5626
7722 Ibid. no. 5687
7723 Ibid. no. 8365
7724 *Nahj al-Balāgha*, Letter 53
7725 Ibid. Letter 53
7726 Ibid. Letter 53
7727 *al-Tahdhīb*, v. 6, p. 227, no. 547
7728 *Nahj al-Balāgha*, Letter 53
7729 Ibid. Letter 53
7730 *Tuḥaf al-'Uqūl*, p. 319
7731 *al-Targhīb wa al-Tarhīb*, v. 3, p. 179, no. 1
7732 *Saḥīḥ Muslim*, v. 3, p. 1456, no. 14
7733 *Sunan Abī Dāwūd*, v. 3, p. 130, no. 2929
7734 *Nahj al-Balāgha*, Letter 53
7735 Ibid. Letter 53
7736 Ibid. Letter 53
7737 *Tanbīh al-Khawāṭir*, v. 2, p. 165
7738 Ibid. Letter 53
7739 *Nahj al-Balāgha*, Letter 53
7740 Qur'an 10:62,63
7741 *Nahj al-Balāgha*, Saying 432
7742 *Kamāl al-Dīn*, p. 357, no. 54
7743 *al-Kāfī*, v. 2, p. 361, no. 1
7744 Ibid. no. 2
7745 *Amālī al-Ṣadūq*, p. 73, no. 41
7746 *Biḥār al-Anwār*, v. 75, p. 90, no. 2
7747 Ibid. no. 4
7748 Ibid. p. 91, no. 8

7749 Qur'an 9:11
7750 *Ghurar al-Ḥikam*, no. 2860
7751 *Ghurar al-Ḥikam*, 6731
7752 *Nahj al-Balāgha*, Saying 342
7753 Ibid. Letter 31
7754 *Wasā'il al-Shī'a*, v. 6, p. 314, no. 5
7755 Qur'an 2:83
7756 *Nūr al-Thaqalayn*, v. 5, p. 597, no. 23
7757 *Kanz al-'Ummāl*, no. 6008
7758 *al-Targhīb wa al-Tarhīb*, v. 3, p. 349, no. 14
7759 *al-Kāfī*, v. 7, p. 51, no. 7
7760 Qur'an 4:10
7761 *Amālī al-Ṣadūq*, p. 577, no. 788
7762 *Tafsīr al-'Ayyāshī*, v. 1, p. 225, no. 47
7763 *Biḥār al-Anwār*, v. 79, p. 268, no. 7
7764 Qur'an 33:24
7765 *Amālī al-Ṣadūq*, p. 576, no. 788
7766 *Biḥār al-Anwār*, v. 70, p. 176, no. 33
7767 *Ghurar al-Ḥikam*, no. 9556
7768 *Nahj al-Balāgha*, Sermon 157
7769 *Ghurar al-Ḥikam*, no. 6184
7770 Ibid. no. 398
7771 Ibid. no. 9958
7772 *al-Kāfī*, v. 2, p. 52, no. 5
7773 Ibid. v. 2, p. 51, no. 1
7774 Ibid. v. 2, p. 57, no. 3
7775 Qur'an 102:5-8
7776 Qur'an 6:75
7777 *Kanz al-'Ummāl*, no. 29858
7778 *Biḥār al-Anwār*, v. 77, p. 20, no. 4
7779 *Nahj al-Balāgha*, Saying 125
7780 *Tuḥaf al-'Uqūl*, p. 20
7781 *Ghurar al-Ḥikam*, no. 10970
7782 *Biḥār al-Anwār*, v. 73, p. 167, no. 31
7783 Ibid. v. 78, p. 92, no. 98
7784 *Ghurar al-Ḥikam*, no. 11011
7785 Ibid. no. 1177
7786 Ibid. no. 5072
7787 *Biḥār al-Anwār*, v. 73, v. 161, p. 6
7788 *Kanz al-'Ummāl*, no. 7332
7789 *Biḥār al-Anwār*, v. 77, p. 185, p. 30
7790 *Ghurar al-Ḥikam*, no. 6347-6348
7791 Ibid. no. 5488
7792 Ibid. no. 699
7793 *Mishkāt al-Anwār*, p. 56, no. 58
7794 *Biḥār al-Anwār*, v. 71, p. 152, no. 60
7795 *Ghurar al-Ḥikam*, no. 7569
7796 *al-Kāfī*, v. 2, p. 268, no. 1
7797 *Biḥār al-Anwār*, v. 79, p. 176, no. 34

Endnotes (Arabic)

١ . غرر الحكم : ٩٨٦ .

٢ . غرر الحكم : ٦٠٦ و ٨٨٢ ، عيون الحكم والمواعظ : ص ٢٣ ح ١٩٧ .

٣ . غرر الحكم : ١٧٠٥ .

٤ . غرر الحكم : ١١٤٨ ، عيون الحكم والمواعظ : ص ٢٩ ح ٤٣٩ .

٥ . غرر الحكم : ٢٨٨٨ ، عيون الحكم والمواعظ : ص ١١١ ح ٢٤٠٥ .

٦ . غرر الحكم : ٦٣٤٢ .

٧ . غرر الحكم : ٦٣٦١ .

٨ . غرر الحكم : ٤١٨٧ .

٩ . الحشر : ٩ .

١٠ . الأمالي للطوسي : ص ١٨٥ ح ٣٠٩ .

١١ . تنبيه الخواطر : ١ / ١٧٢ .

١٢ . مجمع البيان : ٢ / ٧٩٢ .

١٣ . تفسير القمّي : ٢ / ٣٩٨ ، مجمع البيان : ١٠ / ٦١٢ نحوه و كلاهما عن عبدالله بن ميمون القدّاح ، بحار الأنوار : ٣٥ / ٢٤٣ / ٣ .

١٤ . الزخرف : ٣٢ .

١٥ . القصص : ٢٦ .

١٦ . وسائل الشيعة : ١٣ / ٢٤٤ / ٣ .

١٧ . الكافي : ٥ / ٩٠ / ٣ .

١٨ . الكافي : ٥ / ٢٧٣ / ١ .

١٩ . الأمالي للصدوق : ٥١٣ / ٧٠٧ .

٢٠ . بحار الأنوار : ١٠٣ / ١٧٠ / ٢٧ .

٢١ . كنز العمّال : ٩١٢٦ .

٢٢ . كتاب من لا يحضره الفقيه : ٤ / ١٠ / ٤٩٦٨ .

٢٣ . نهج البلاغة : الخطبة ٩١ .

٢٤ . غرر الحكم : ١٠٦٤٨ .

٢٥ . غرر الحكم : ٩٩٠٥ .

٢٦ . نهج البلاغة : الحكمة ٧٤ .

٢٧ . آل عمران : ١٤٥ .

٢٨ . بحار الأنوار : ٥ / ١٤٢ / ١٤ .

٢٩ . غرر الحكم : ٤٩٤ .

٣٠ . نهج البلاغة : الخطبة ١٩٠ .

٣١ . غرر الحكم : ٤٧٧٨ .

٣٢ . الأعراف : ٣٤ .

٣٣ . الحِجر : ٤، ٥ .

٣٤ . الأنعام : ٢ .

٣٥ . الأعراف : ٣٤ .

٣٦ . بحار الأنوار : ٥ / ١٣٩ / ٣ .

وقد جاءت بهذا المعنى روايات اُخرى ، ولكن ينافيها نصُّ خبرِ ابن مُسكان الدّالّ على كون الأجل الأوّل محتوماً والثاني موقوفاً ، وجَمَع العلّامة المجلسيّ ؛ بين الطّائفتَين بوجه . وردَّ العلّامة الطباطبائيّ خبرَ ابن مسكان ، وفسّر الآيةَ طبقاً للرّواية الّتي نقلناها في المتن .

راجع : بحار الأنوار : ٥ / ١٣٩ ـ ١٤٠ ، الميزان في تفسير القرآن : ٧ / ١٥ .

٣٧ . غرر الحكم : ٤٢٣٩ .

٣٨ . بحار الأنوار : ٥ / ١٤٠ / ٧ .

٣٩ . الشورىٰ : ٢٠ .

٤٠ . غرر الحكم : ٦٩٤ و ٦٩٥ .

٤١ . غرر الحكم : ٦٠٨٠ .

٤٢ . نهج البلاغة : الكتاب ٣٢ .

٤٣ . الإسراء : ٢١ .

٤٤ . نهج البلاغة : الخطبة ١١٤ .

٤٥ . غافر : ٣٩ .

٤٦ . غرر الحكم : ٨٢٩٨ .

٤٧ . غرر الحكم : ٤ .

٤٨ . النساء : ٧٧ .

٤٩ . غرر الحكم : ٧٥٠٢ .

٥٠ . غرر الحكم : ٥١٧٥ و ٥١٧٦ .

٥١ . غرر الحكم : ٨٧٦٩ .

٥٢ . تنبيه الخواطر : ٢ / ٢٣٤ .

٥٣ . بحار الأنوار : ٧٧ / ١٥١ / ١٠٤ .

٥٤ . غرر الحكم : ١٠٨٢٩ .

٥٥ . الحجرات : ١٠ .

٥٦ . الأمالي للمفيد : ١٨٧ / ١٣ .

٥٧ . غرر الحكم : ٥٣٥١ .

٥٨ . الكافي : ٢ / ١٦٦ / ٢ و ٧ .

٥٩ . الكافي : ٢ / ١٦٦ / ٣ .

٦٠ . الكافي : ٢ / ١٦٦ / ٤ .

٦١ . كنز العمّال : ٢٤٦٤٢ .

٦٢ . الأمالي للصدوق : ٣٨٠ / ٤٨٣ .

٦٣ . بحار الأنوار : ٧٤ / ١٦٥ / ٢٩ .

٦٤ . الاختصاص : ٢٢٦ .

٦٥ . الاختصاص : ٣١ .

٦٦ . بحار الأنوار : ٧٨ / ٢٩١ / ٢ .

٦٧ . تحف العقول : ٣٢٢ .

٦٨ . بحار الأنوار : ٧٤ / ٢٧٩ / ١ .

٦٩ . تنبيه الخواطر : ٢ / ١٧٩ .

٧٠ . غرر الحكم : ٦١٩١ .

٧١ . غرر الحكم : ١٧٩٥ .

٧٢ . غرر الحكم : ٤٢٢٥ .

٧٣ . غرر الحكم : ٨٩٧٨ .

٧٤ . غرر الحكم : ٧٧٧٦ و ٧٧٧٧ .

٧٥ . غرر الحكم : ٨٥٥٢ .

٧٦ . المحاسن : ١ / ٤١٥ / ٩٥٣ .

٧٧ . بحار الأنوار : ٧٤ / ١٨١ / ١ .

٧٨ . غرر الحكم : ٥٦٤١ .

٧٩ . كشف الغمّة : ٢ / ٣٣١ .

٨٠ . بحار الأنوار : ٧٤ / ١٨١ .

٨١ . نهج البلاغة : الكتاب ٣١ .

٨٢ . بحار الأنوار : ٧٧ / ٢١٠ / ١ .

٨٣ . المحاسن : ١ / ٤١٥ / ٩٥٠ .

٨٤ . نهج البلاغة : الكتاب ٣١ .

٨٥ . بحار الأنوار : ٧٨ / ١٢١ / ٤ .

٨٦ . تحف العقول : ٥٤ .

٨٧ . تحف العقول : ٣٢٣ .

٨٨ . تحف العقول : ٣٢٤ .

٨٩ . غرر الحكم : ٧٥٠٣ .

٩٠ . غرر الحكم : ١٠٤٢٠ .

٩١ . الإرشاد : ٢ / ١٦٦ .

٩٢ . الخصال : ٢٤٤ / ١٠٠ .

٩٣ . بحار الأنوار : ٧٤ / ٢٨٢ / ٣ .

٩٤ . كنز العمّال : ٢٤٧٥٩ .

٩٥ . غرر الحكم : ٢٤٦١ .

٩٦ . غرر الحكم : ٣٦٤٥ .

٩٧ . بحار الأنوار : ٧٧ / ٢٦٩ / ١ .

٩٨ . غرر الحكم : ٨١٦٦ .

٩٩ . أعلام الدين : ٣٠٤ .

١٠٠ . بحار الأنوار : ٧٤ / ١٦٦ / ٢٩ .

١٠١ . غرر الحكم : ٧٥٢ .

١٠٢ . غرر الحكم : ٩٠٧٩ .

١٠٣ . تنبيه الخواطر : ٢ / ١٢٣ .

١٠٤ . غرر الحكم : ٤٩٧٨ .

١٠٥ . غرر الحكم : ٤٩٨٨ .

١٠٦ . غرر الحكم : ٥٠١٧ .

١٠٧ . غرر الحكم : ٥٠٢١ .

١٠٨ . غرر الحكم : ٥٠٠٩ .

١٠٩ . غرر الحكم : ٤٩٨٥ .

١١٠ . بحار الأنوار : ٧٤ / ٢٨٢ / ٤ .

١١١ . نهج البلاغة : الحكمة ٤٧٩ .

١١٢ . معاني الأخبار : ١٩٨ / ٤ .

١١٣ . كنز العمّال : ٢٤٧٥٥ .

١١٤ . غرر الحكم : ٨٩٢١ ، ٨٩٢٣ .

١١٥ . الكافي : ٢ / ٦٧٢ / ٧ .

١١٦ . بحار الأنوار : ٧٤ / ٢٣٣ / ٢٩ .

١١٧ . بحار الأنوار : ٧٤ / ١٦٦ / ٢٩ .

١١٨ . بحار الأنوار : ٧٥ / ٦٥ / ٢ .

١١٩ . الكافي : ٢ / ٢٠٦ / ٤ .

١٢٠ . بحار الأنوار : ٧٤ / ٢٩٨ / ٣٢ .

١٢١ . بحار الأنوار : ٧٤ / ١٦٦ / ٢٩ .

١٢٢ . بحار الأنوار : ٧٤ / ٣٢٢ / ٨٩ .

١٢٣ . بحار الأنوار : ٧٤ / ٣٢٢ / ٩٠ .

١٢٤ . الكافي : ٢ / ١٩٨ / ٨ .

١٢٥ . بحار الأنوار : ٧٤ / ١٦٦ / ٣٠ .

١٢٦ . بحار الأنوار : ٧٤ / ١٧١ / ٣٨ .

١٢٧ . بحار الأنوار : ١٦ / ٢٣٣ / ٣٥ .

١٢٨ . غرر الحكم : ٩٩٨ .

١٢٩ . مشكاة الأنوار : ٢٣٩ / ٦٨٩ .

١٣٠ . غرر الحكم : ٩٦٧ .

١٣١ . غرر الحكم : ٥٠٣٦ .

١٣٢ . غرر الحكم : ٣٥٩٠ .

١٣٣ . غرر الحكم : ٤٨٥٣ .

١٣٤ . غرر الحكم : ٦٠٩٦ .

١٣٥ . بحار الأنوار : ٧٥ / ٦٨ / ٨ .

١٣٦ . بحار الأنوار : ٧١ / ٤٢٨ / ٧٨ .

١٣٧ . تحف العقول : ٩٦ .
١٣٨ . نهج السعادة : ٢ / ٥٠ .
١٣٩ . غرر الحكم : ١٠٤٦٦ .
١٤٠ . بحار الأنوار : ٧٧ / ١٣١ / ٤١ .
١٤١ . غرر الحكم : ٦٩١١ .
١٤٢ . غرر الحكم : ٢٠٠٤ .
١٤٣ . غرر الحكم : ٨٨٨٦ .
١٤٤ . بحار الأنوار : ٧٨ / ١١١ / ٦ .
١٤٥ . غرر الحكم : ٤٥٢٢ .
١٤٦ . بحار الأنوار : ٢ / ٥٦ / ٣٣ .
١٤٧ . تحف العقول : ٥٠٠ .
١٤٨ . تنبيه الخواطر : ١ / ٩٦ .
١٤٩ . غرر الحكم : ٤٧٨٦ .
١٥٠ . غرر الحكم : ٤١٧٤ .
١٥١ . غرر الحكم : ٥٥٢٠ .
١٥٢ . غرر الحكم : ٨٢٧١ .
١٥٣ . غرر الحكم : ٤٣٣٣ .
١٥٤ . بحار الأنوار : ٧٠ / ٧٣ / ٢٧ .
١٥٥ . بحار الأنوار : ٩٤ / ٩٤ / ١٢ .
١٥٦ . تحف العقول : ٣٧٦ .
١٥٧ . غرر الحكم : ٣٢٤١ .
١٥٨ . غرر الحكم : ٣٢٩٨ .
١٥٩ . غرر الحكم : ٥٩٣٢ .
١٦٠ . بحار الأنوار : ١٠٤ / ٩٥ / ٤٤ .
١٦١ . نهج البلاغة : الكتاب ٣١ .
١٦٢ . التحريم : ٦ .
١٦٣ . دعائم الإسلام : ١ / ٨٢ .
١٦٤ . الكافي : ٤ / ٤ / ١٠ .
١٦٥ . كنز العمّال : ٤٥٣٣٠ .
١٦٦ . مكارم الأخلاق : ١ / ٤٧٨ / ١٦٤٩ .
١٦٧ . بحار الأنوار : ١٠٣ / ١٦٢ / ٦ .
١٦٨ . بحار الأنوار : ٧٩ / ١٠٢ / ٢ .
١٦٩ . نهج البلاغة : الحكمة ١٧٧ .
١٧٠ . بحار الأنوار : ٧٨ / ٨٢ / ٨١ .
١٧١ . بحار الأنوار : ٧١ / ٤٢٧ / ٧٦ .
١٧٢ . غرر الحكم : ٢٣٠٤ .
١٧٣ . بحار الأنوار : ١٠٤ / ٩٩ / ٧٤ .
١٧٤ . بحار الأنوار : ٩٢ / ٢١٤ / ١٣ .
١٧٥ . غرر الحكم : ٩٠٠١ .
١٧٦ . بحار الأنوار : ٨١ / ١٩٨ / ٥٥ .
١٧٧ . الإقبال : ١ / ١٥٧ .
١٧٨ . كنز العمّال : ٢٠٩٥٤ .
١٧٩ . كنز العمّال : ٢٠٩٥١ .
١٨٠ . كنز العمّال : ٢٠٩٣٤ .
١٨١ . بحار الأنوار : ٨٤ / ١٠٤ / ٢ .
١٨٢ . دعائم الإسلام : ١ / ١٤٧ .
١٨٣ . تحف العقول : ١٣ .
١٨٤ . بحار الأنوار : ١٠٤ / ١٢٢ / ٦١ .
١٨٥ . بحار الأنوار : ٧٥ / ٥٤ / ١٩ .
١٨٦ . الخصال : ١٧ / ٦٠ .
١٨٧ . تفسير القمّي : ٢ / ١٤٦ .
١٨٨ . الأحزاب : ٥٨ .
١٨٩ . الكافي : ٢ / ٣٥٠ / ١ .
١٩٠ . بحار الأنوار : ٦٧ / ٧٢ / ٤٠ .
١٩١ . بحار الأنوار : ٧٥ / ١٥٠ / ١٣ .
١٩٢ . بحار الأنوار : ٧٥ / ١٥٠ / ١٣ .
١٩٣ . الكافي : ٥ / ٣٤ / ٣ .
١٩٤ . الكافي : ٥ / ٣٤ / ٢ .
١٩٥ . الإنسان : ٨ .
١٩٦ . الأنفال : ٧٠ .
١٩٧ . وسائل الشيعة : ١١ / ٦٩ / ٣ .
١٩٨ . قرب الإسناد : ١٤٣ / ٥١٥ .
١٩٩ . الكافي : ٥ / ٣٥ / ٢ .
٢٠٠ . وسائل الشيعة : ١١ / ٦٩ / ٢ .
٢٠١ . تنبيه الخواطر : ١ / ٤٦ .
٢٠٢ . غرر الحكم : ٦٧٤٧ .
٢٠٣ . تنبيه الخواطر : ٢ / ١١٩ .
٢٠٤ . تنبيه الخواطر : ١ / ١٠٠ .
٢٠٥ . بحار الأنوار : ٧٧ / ١٨٢ / ١٠ .
٢٠٦ . غرر الحكم : ٨٩٠٣ .
٢٠٧ . مصباح الشريعة : ٢٣٩ .
٢٠٨ . غرر الحكم : ١٠٥٧٢ .
٢٠٩ . غرر الحكم : ٤١٣٩ .
٢١٠ . غرر الحكم : ٦٥٩ .

٢١١ . غرر الحكم : ٩٩٢٢ .
٢١٢ . بحار الأنوار : ٧٥ / ٤٦٢ / ١٧ .
٢١٣ . بحار الأنوار : ٧٧ / ٢٢ / ٦ .
٢١٤ . غرر الحكم : ٩٩٤٢ .
٢١٥ . غرر الحكم : ١٠٥٦٩ .
٢١٦ . بحار الأنوار : ٧٨ / ٣٦٩ / ٤ .
٢١٧ . بحار الأنوار : ٦٢ / ٢٩٠ .
٢١٨ . بحار الأنوار : ٦٢ / ٣٢٤ .
٢١٩ . تنبيه الخواطر : ١ / ٤٧ .
٢٢٠ . بحار الأنوار : ٦٢ / ٢٩١ .
٢٢١ . وسائل الشيعة : ١٦ / ٤٨٤ / ٥ ، اُنظر أيضاً : ص ٤٧٩ باب ٥٦ و ص ٤٨٢ باب ٥٧ .
٢٢٢ . وسائل الشيعة : ١٦ / ٥٢٠ / ٣ ، اُنظر أيضاً : ص ٥١٩ باب ٩٥ .
٢٢٣ . الكافي : ٦ / ٣٢١ / ١ .
٢٢٤ . وسائل الشيعة : ١٦ / ٥٣٩ / ١ .
٢٢٥ . المحجّة البيضاء : ٣ / ٦ ، اُنظر وسائل الشيعة : ١٦ / ٤٧٠ باب ٤٩ .
٢٢٦ . وسائل الشيعة : ١٦ / ٥١٨ / ١ .
٢٢٧ . وسائل الشيعة : ١٦ / ٥١٠ / ١ .
٢٢٨ . وسائل الشيعة : ١٦ / ٥١٣ / ١ .
٢٢٩ . الاختصاص : ٢٥٣ .
٢٣٠ . الأنفال : ٦٢ ، ٦٣ .
٢٣١ . آل عمران : ١٠٣ .
٢٣٢ . بحار الأنوار : ٧٨ / ١١ / ٧٠ .
٢٣٣ . تحف العقول : ٣٧٣ .
٢٣٤ . تحف العقول : ٤٥ .
٢٣٥ . بحار الأنوار : ٧٥ / ٢٦٥ / ٩ .
٢٣٦ . التوحيد : ٨٩ / ٢ .
٢٣٧ . التوحيد : ٢٣١ / ٥ .
٢٣٨ . التوحيد : ٨٩ / ٢ .
٢٣٩ . الكافي : ١ / ١١٥ / ٣ .
٢٤٠ . عيون أخبار الرضا : ٢ / ٩٣ / ١ .
٢٤١ . أنساب الأشراف : ٣ / ١٣٥ .
٢٤٢ . كنز العمّال : ١٤٢٨٦ .
٢٤٣ . كنز العمّال : ١٤٣٦٦ .
٢٤٤ . كنز العمّال : ٣١٥٦٧ .
٢٤٥ . بحار الأنوار : ٧٥ / ٣٥٨ / ٧٢ .
٢٤٦ . بحار الأنوار : ٧٥ / ٣٥٩ / ٧٤ .
٢٤٧ . الروم : ٦٠ .
٢٤٨ . كنز العمّال : ٣١٦١٨ .
٢٤٩ . تحف العقول : ٣٦ .
٢٥٠ . المناقب لابن شهرآشوب : ٢ / ١٠١ .
٢٥١ . نهج البلاغة : الخطبة ٣٣ .
٢٥٢ . بحار الأنوار : ٤٠ / ٣٢٨ / ١٠ .
٢٥٣ . بحار الأنوار : ٧٧ / ١٧٣ / ٨ .
٢٥٤ . غرر الحكم : ١٠٤٢ .
٢٥٥ . تنبيه الخواطر : ١ / ٢٧٢ .
٢٥٦ . بحار الأنوار : ٧٣ / ١٦٧ / ٣١ .
٢٥٧ . غرر الحكم : ١٠١٠ .
٢٥٨ . غرر الحكم : ٦٣٩ .
٢٥٩ . الحِجر : ٣ .
٢٦٠ . في المصدر «في أوّل ليلةٍ» والصواب ما أثبتناه .
٢٦١ . غرر الحكم : ٢٥٧٢ .
٢٦٢ . غرر الحكم : ١٨٩٦ .
٢٦٣ . غرر الحكم : ١٣٧٥ .
٢٦٤ . غرر الحكم : ١٨٢٨ .
٢٦٥ . غرر الحكم : ٤٦٤١ .
٢٦٦ . بحار الأنوار : ٧٨ / ٣٥ / ١١٧ .
٢٦٧ . بحار الأنوار : ٧٧ / ٢٩٣ / ٢ .
٢٦٨ . بحار الأنوار : ٧١ / ١٥٢ / ٥٥ .
٢٦٩ . تنبيه الخواطر : ١ / ٢٧٢ .
٢٧٠ . بحار الأنوار : ٧٣ / ٩٥ / ٧٩ ، واُنظر أيضاً : ١٦٤ / ٢٢ و ١٦٦ / ٢٨ .
٢٧١ . غرر الحكم : ٨٧٤ .
٢٧٢ . غرر الحكم : ٢٩٢٠ و ٢٩٢١ .
٢٧٣ . غرر الحكم : ١٠٨٤٤ .
٢٧٤ . بحار الأنوار : ٧٧ / ٣٣٣ / ٢١ .
٢٧٥ . أعلام الدين : ٣٠٥ .
٢٧٦ . الكافي : ٢ / ٣٢٩ / ١ .
٢٧٧ . بحار الأنوار : ٧٧ / ٤٢١ / ٤٠ .
٢٧٨ . الكافي : ٢ / ٣٣٦ / ٣ ، اُنظر تمام الحديث في باب ١٣٦ .
٢٧٩ . بحار الأنوار : ٧٧ / ١٠١ / ١ .
٢٨٠ . بحار الأنوار : ٧٣ / ١٦٧ / ٣١ .
٢٨١ . تحف العقول : ٢٨٦ .

٢٨٢ . صحيفة الإمام الرضا : ٢٧٦ / ٢٠ .

٢٨٣ . بحار الأنوار : ٧٨ / ٧٩ / ٦١ .

٢٨٤ . آل عمران : ١١٠ .

٢٨٥ . كنز العمّال : ٣٤٤٥١ .

٢٨٦ . كنز العمّال : ٣٤٤٥٢ .

٢٨٧ . كنز العمّال : ٣٤٤٦٢ .

٢٨٨ . كنز العمّال : ٣٤٤٦٥ .

٢٨٩ . تنبيه الخواطر : ٢ / ١٢٣ .

٢٩٠ . تنبيه الخواطر : ٢ / ١٢٣ .

٢٩١ . تنبيه الخواطر : ٢ / ١٢٣ .

٢٩٢ . البقرة : ١٤٣ .

٢٩٣ . شواهد التنزيل : ١ / ١١٩ / ١٢٩ .

٢٩٤ . بحار الأنوار : ٦٩ / ٣٩٤ / ٧٧ .

٢٩٥ . تنبيه الخواطر : ١ / ٨٤ وفيه «يزل» بدل «يُزكَ» وهو تصحيف .

٢٩٦ . بحار الأنوار : ٧ / ١٣٠ / ١ .

٢٩٧ . بحار الأنوار : ٧ / ١٣٠ / ٣ .

٢٩٨ . الملاحم والفتن : ٣٠٧ / ٤٢٨ .

٢٩٩ . تنبيه الخواطر : ١ / ٧٥ .

٣٠٠ . بحار الأنوار : ٧٧ / ١٦١ / ١٧٨ .

٣٠١ . الأمالي للطوسي : ١٥٧ / ٢٦٣ .

٣٠٢ . الخصال : ١٦٣ / ٢١٤ .

٣٠٣ . بحار الأنوار : ٧٣ / ١٥٨ / ٣ .

٣٠٤ . بحار الأنوار : ٧٠ / ٧٥ / ٣ .

٣٠٥ . بحار الأنوار : ٧٢ / ٣٠٣ / ٥٠ .

٣٠٦ . كنز العمّال : ٢٨٩٦٩ و ٢٨٩٦٨ و ٢٨٩٧٠ .

٣٠٧ . تفسير الطبري : ١٣ / الجزء ٢٥ / ٣٠ .

٣٠٨ . المائدة : ٣ .

٣٠٩ . غرر الحكم : ١٠٩٥ .

٣١٠ . الكافي : ٢ / ١٨ / ٣ .

٣١١ . التغابن : ٨ .

٣١٢ . الكافي : ١ / ١٩٦ / ٦ .

٣١٣ . الكافي : ١ / ١٩٩ / ١ .

٣١٤ . الكافي : ١ / ٢٠٠ / ١ .

٣١٥ . الكافي : ١ / ٢٠٠ / ١ .

٣١٦ . البقرة : ١٢٤ .

٣١٧ . الكافي : ١ / ١٧٥ / ٢ .

٣١٨ . الكافي : ١ / ١٧٩ / ١٢ .

٣١٩ . الكافي : ١ / ١٧٨ / ٢ .

٣٢٠ . الكافي : ١ / ١٧٧ / ٢ .

٣٢١ . بحار الأنوار : ٢٣ / ٤٦ / ٩١ .

٣٢٢ . بحار الأنوار : ٢٣ / ٢٣ / ٢٦ .

٣٢٣ . الكافي : ١ / ١٧٩ / ١٠ .

٣٢٤ . بحار الأنوار : ٢٣ / ٥١ / ١٠١ .

٣٢٥ . الإسراء : ٧١ .

٣٢٦ . البقرة : ١٦٦ .

٣٢٧ . بحار الأنوار : ٨ / ١٠ / ٣ .

٣٢٨ . بحار الأنوار : ٢٣ / ٧٦ / ١ .

٣٢٩ . كنز العمّال : ٤٦٤ .

٣٣٠ . نَقل ابنُ أبي الحديد أنّ عبدالله بنَ عُمَر امتَنَعَ مِن بَيعةِ عليٍّ ﷺ ، وطَرَقَ على الحجّاج بابَهُ ليلاً لِيُبايعَ لعبدِ الملكِ كي لا يَبيتَ تلكَ اللّيلةَ بلا إمامٍ ، زَعَم لأنّهُ روىٰ عن النّبيِّ ﷺ أنّهُ قالَ : مَن ماتَ ولا إمامَ لَهُ ماتَ مِيتةَ الجاهليّةِ ، وحتّىٰ بَلَغَ مِن احتقارِ الحجّاجِ لهُ واسترذالِهِ حالَهُ أنْ أخرَجَ رِجْلَهُ من الفِراشِ فقالَ : اصْفِقْ بِيَدِكَ عليها ! شرح نهج البلاغة : ١٣ / ٢٤٢ .

٣٣١ . بحار الأنوار : ٢٣ / ٨٣ / ٢٢ .

٣٣٢ . البقرة : ٢٦٩ .

٣٣٣ . الكافي : ١ / ١٨٥ / ١١ .

٣٣٤ . بحار الأنوار : ٢٣ / ٨٨ / ٣٢ .

٣٣٥ . الكافي : ١ / ١٨٧ / ١١ .

٣٣٦ . السجدة : ٢٤ .

٣٣٧ . يونس : ٣٥ .

٣٣٨ . شرح نهج البلاغة : ٧ / ٣٦ .

٣٣٩ . غرر الحكم : ١١٠١٠ .

٣٤٠ . نهج البلاغة : الحكمة ٧٣ .

٣٤١ . نهج البلاغة : الحكمة ١١٠ .

٣٤٢ . بحار الأنوار : ٢٥ / ١٦٤ .

٣٤٣ . نهج البلاغة : الخطبة ١٣١ .

٣٤٤ . الإرشاد : ٢ / ٣٩ .

٣٤٥ . الكافي : ١ / ٢٨٥ / ٤ .

٣٤٦ . الكافي : ١ / ٢٠٢ / ١ .

٣٤٧ . بحار الأنوار : ٤٠ / ٣٣٦ / ١٧ .

٣٤٨ . نهج البلاغة : الخطبة ١٠٥ .

٣٤٩ . كنز العمّال : ١٤٣١٣ .

٣٥٠ . نهج البلاغة : الكتاب ٥٠ .

٣٥١ . بحار الأنوار : ٢٣ / ٣٠ / ٤٦ .

٣٥٢ . بحار الأنوار : ٢٣ / ٣٠ / ٤٦ .

٣٥٣ . الكافي : ١ / ٣٧٦ / ٤ .

٣٥٤ . الكافي : ١ / ٣٧٣ / ٦ .

٣٥٥ . الأمالي للطوسي : ٤١٧ / ٩٣٩ .

٣٥٦ . القصص : ٤١ .

٣٥٧ . نهج البلاغة : الخطبة ١٦٥ .

٣٥٨ . الزمر : ٦٠ .

٣٥٩ . الكافي : ١ / ٣٧٢ / ١ .

٣٦٠ . بحار الأنوار : ٢٥ / ١١٢ / ٧ .

٣٦١ . الأحزاب : ٦٧ .

٣٦٢ . كنز العمّال : ١٤٨٧٢ .

٣٦٣ . الخصال : ٢٠٦ / ٢٤ .

٣٦٤ . تنبيه الخواطر : ١ / ٥١ .

٣٦٥ . الدرّ المنثور : ٣ / ١٢٥ .

٣٦٦ . بحار الأنوار : ١٠٠ / ٤٩ / ١٨ .

٣٦٧ . المراد من هذه الروايات وأمثالها هو أنّ أئمّة أهل البيت عليهم السلام لم يكن لديهم ـ ولو الحدّ الأدنى ـ من القوّات والأعوان الحقيقيّين والصادقين بحيث يتمكّنون عن طريقهم الثورة ضدّ الحكومات الجائرة والظالمة .

٣٦٨ . الكافي : ٢ / ٢٤٣ / ٤ .

٣٦٩ . كمال الدين : ٤٦١ / ٢١ .

٣٧٠ . بحار الأنوار : ٢٣ / ١٠٦ / ٧ ، اُنظر : بحار الأنوار : ٢٣ / ١٠٤ باب ٧ ، كنز العمّال : ٨٧٠ ـ ٨٧٣ ، ٨٩٨ ، ٩٤٢ ـ ٩٤٧ ، ٩٥١ ـ ٩٥٣ ، ٩٥٨ ، ١٦٥٠ ، ١٦٥٧ ، ١٦٦٧ .

٣٧١ . بحار الأنوار : ٢٣ / ١٠٥ / ٣ .

٣٧٢ . نهج البلاغة : الخطبة ٩٧ .

٣٧٣ . نهج البلاغة : الخطبة ١٠٠ .

٣٧٤ . نهج البلاغة : الخطبة ١٠٩ .

٣٧٥ . نهج البلاغة : الخطبة ١٥٢ .

٣٧٦ . نهج البلاغة : الحكمة ١٠٩ .

٣٧٧ . الكافي : ١ / ٢٠٤ / ٢ .

٣٧٨ . نهج البلاغة : الخطبة ١٦٢ .

٣٧٩ . نهج البلاغة : الخطبة ١٣١ .

٣٨٠ . الأمالي للمفيد : ١٥٥ / ٦ .

٣٨١ . صحيح مسلم : ٣ / ١٤٥٢ / ٦ .

٣٨٢ . والأخبار في هذا المعنى كثيرة ، راجع صحيح مسلم : ٣ / ١٤٥١ (كتاب الإمارة) .

٣٨٣ . كنز العمّال : ١٤٩٧١ .

٣٨٤ . الكافي : ١ / ٢٢١ / ١ .

٣٨٥ . إشارة إلى الآية ﴿ونزّلنا عليك الكتاب تبياناً لكلّ شيء﴾ من سورة النحل : ٨٩ .

٣٨٦ . الكافي : ١ / ٢٢٩ / ٤ .

٣٨٧ . الكافي : ١ / ٢٠٢ / ١ .

٣٨٨ . كنز العمّال : ٣٣٠٢١ .

٣٨٩ . كنز العمّال : ٣٢٩٠٠ .

٣٩٠ . كنز العمّال : ٣٣٠٢٢ .

٣٩١ . كنز العمّال : ٣٢٨٧٨ .

٣٩٢ . كنز العمّال : ٣٢٩٠٩ .

٣٩٣ . تاريخ دمشق : ٤٢ / ٣٠٣ / ٨٨٣٥ .

٣٩٤ . يمكن أن يكون تلميحاً للآية ٢٦ من سورة الفتح : ﴿وألزَمَهم كلمةَ التّقوىٰ﴾ ، راجع تفسير نمونه : ٢٢ / ٩٧ .

٣٩٥ . الأمالي للصدوق : ٥٦٥ / ٧٦٥ .

٣٩٦ . الأمالي للطوسي : ٦٠٢ / ١٢٤٤ .

٣٩٧ . كنز العمّال : ٣٦٤١٩ .

٣٩٨ . تاريخ دمشق : ٤٢ / ١٨٨ / ٨٦٣٧ .

٣٩٩ . تاريخ دمشق : ٤٢ / ١٩٧ / ٨٦٦٣ .

٤٠٠ . تاريخ دمشق : ٤٢ / ٢٠٧ / ٨٦٨٣ .

٤٠١ . شرح نهج البلاغة : ٢ / ٢٩٧ .

٤٠٢ . قال ابن أبي الحديد : قد ثبت عنه ـ أي عن النّبيّ صلى الله عليه وآله ـ في الأخبار الصّحيحة أنّه قال : عليٌّ مع الحقّ (شرح نهج البلاغة : ٢ / ٢٩٧) .

٤٠٣ . الكافي : ١ / ٢٩٤ / ١ .

٤٠٤ . تاريخ دمشق : ٤٢ / ٤٤٩ / ٩٠٢٥ .

٤٠٥ . فرائد السمطين : ١ / ١٧٧ / ١٤٠ .

٤٠٦ . كنز العمّال : ٣٢٨٩٠ .

٤٠٧ . كنز العمّال : ٣٢٨٨٩ .

٤٠٨ . الأمالي للصدوق : ٦٤٢ / ٨٧٠ .

٤٠٩ . كنز العمّال : ٣٢٩٤٣ .

٤١٠ . تاريخ دمشق : ٤٢ / ٥٢ / ٨٣٨٥ .

٤١١ . سنن ابن ماجة : ١ / ٤٤ / ١١٩ .

٤١٢ . كنز العمّال : ٣٢٩١٤ .

٤١٣ . كنز العمّال : ٣٢٩٣٦ .

٤١٤ . تاريخ دمشق : ٤٢ / ٦٤ .
٤١٥ . كنزالعمّال : ٣٢٨٨١ .
٤١٦ . تاريخ دمشق : ٤٢ / ٤١٩ / ٩٠١٢ .
٤١٧ . تاريخ دمشق : ٤٢ / ٣١٣ / ٨٨٦٢ .
٤١٨ . الكافي : ١ / ٢٩٤ / ١ .
٤١٩ . الكافي : ١ / ٢٩٤ / ١ .
٤٢٠ . بحار الأنوار : ٥ / ٦٩ / ١ .
٤٢١ . تاريخ دمشق : ٤٢ / ٣٠٤ / ٨٨٣٨ .
٤٢٢ . بحار الأنوار : ٣٦ / ٥ / ١ .
٤٢٣ . تاريخ دمشق : ٤٢ / ٣١٧ / ٨٨٧٢ .
٤٢٤ . تاريخ دمشق : ٤٢ / ٣٣٣ / ٨٩٠٠ .
٤٢٥ . تاريخ دمشق : ٤٢ / ٣٥٦ / ٨٩٤٩ .
٤٢٦ . تاريخ دمشق : ٤٢ / ٣٦٩ / ٨٩٦٣
٤٢٧ . الإرشاد : ١ / ٣٥ .
٤٢٨ . نهج البلاغة : الخطبة ٥ .
٤٢٩ . خصائص الأئمّة عليهم السلام : ٩٩ .
٤٣٠ . شرح نهج البلاغة : ٤ / ١٠٣ .
٤٣١ . كنز العمّال : ٣٦٥٤١ .
٤٣٢ . نهج البلاغة : الخطبة ١٧٢
٤٣٣ . قال ابن أبي الحديد : اعلمْ أنّه قد تواتَرت الأخبارُ عنه عليه السلام بنحوٍ من هذا القول ، نحو :

قوله : ما زِلتُ مظلوماً مُنذُ قَبضَ اللهُ رسولَهُ حتّىٰ يومِ النّاسِ هذا .

وقوله : اللّهمّ أخزِ قُرَيشاً فإنّها مَنَعَتني حقّي ، وغَصَبَتني أمري .

وقوله : فجزىٰ قريشاً عنّي الجَوازي ؛ فإنّهُم ظَلَمُوني حقّي ، واغْتَصَبوني سُلطانَ ابنِ اُمّي .

وقوله ـ وقد سَمِعَ صارخاً يُنادي : أنا مظلومٌ فقالَ ـ : هَلُمَّ فَلْنَصرُخْ معاً ، فإنّي ما زِلتُ مظلوماً .

وقوله : وإنّه لَيعلمُ أنّ مَحَلّي منها مَحَلّ القُطبِ من الرَّحىٰ .

وقوله : أرىٰ تُراثيَ نَهْباً .

وقوله : أصْغَيا بإنائنا ، وحَمَلا النّاسَ علىٰ رقابِنا .

وقوله : إنّ لنا حقّاً إن نُعطَهُ نأخُذْهُ ، وإن نُمْنَعهُ نَركَبْ عجازَ الإبلِ وإنْ طالَ السُّرىٰ .

وقوله : ما زلتُ مُسْتأثَراً عليّ ، مدفوعاً عمّا أستَحِقُّه وأستَوجِبُه . شرح نهج البلاغة : ٣٠٦٩ .

٤٣٤ . غرر الحكم : ٣٧٨١ .
٤٣٥ . تنبيه الخواطر : ٢ / ٤١ .
٤٣٦ . الخصال : ٥٨٠ / ١ .
٤٣٧ . تاريخ دمشق : ٤٢ / ٤٨٩ .
٤٣٨ . غرر الحكم : ٣٧٦١ .
٤٣٩ . نهج السعادة : ٣ / ٧٩ .
٤٤٠ . الكافي : ١ / ١٩٨ / ٣ .
٤٤١ . نهج البلاغة : الحكمة ٣١٦ .
قال الشريف الرضي : ومعنى ذلك أن المؤمنين يتبعونني والفجار يتبعون المال كما تتبع النحل يعسوبها وهو رئيسها .
٤٤٢ . التوحيد : ١٦٤ / ٢ .
٤٤٣ . تاريخ دمشق : ٤٢ / ٤٧٥ .
٤٤٤ . تاريخ دمشق : ٤٢ / ٣١ .
٤٤٥ . تاريخ دمشق : ٤٢ / ٣١ .
٤٤٦ . كنز العمّال : ٣٦٤٧٧ .
٤٤٧ . نهج البلاغة : الخطبة ٢٢٤ .
٤٤٨ . غرر الحكم : ٣٨٨٣ .
٤٤٩ . الكافي : ١ / ٢٠٧ / ٣ .
٤٥٠ . غرر الحكم : ٩٤٨٢ .
٤٥١ . الأمالي للطوسي : ٣٠٠ .
٤٥٢ . الأمالي للصدوق : ٤٧٤ / ١٨ .
٤٥٣ . معاني الأخبار : ٦٤ / ١٥ .
٤٥٤ . بحار الأنوار : ٤٣ / ٢٣ / ١٧ .
٤٥٥ . الأمالي للصدوق : ٥٧٥ / ٧٨٧ .
٤٥٦ . بحار الأنوار : ٤٣ / ٢٢ / ١٣ .
٤٥٧ . مسند ابن حنبل : ٣ / ٨٠ .
٤٥٨ . الأمالي للصدوق : ١٧٥ / ١٧٨ .
٤٥٩ . كنز العمّال : ٣٧٧٢٥ .
٤٦٠ . نهج البلاغة : الخطبة ٢٠٢ .
٤٦١ . الكافي : ١ / ٢٩٨ / ٢ .
٤٦٢ . بحار الأنوار : ٤٣ / ٣٠٦ / ٦٦ .
٤٦٣ . كنز العمّال : ٣٧٦٤٠ .
٤٦٤ . الأمالي للصدوق : ٢٤٤ / ٢٦٢ .
٤٦٥ . المناقب لابن شهرآشوب : ٤ / ٢٣ .
٤٦٦ . مختصر تاريخ دمشق : ٧ / ٢٦ .
٤٦٧ . علل الشرائع : ١٣٧ / ٥ .

٤٦٨ . كفاية الأثر : ١٩٤ .
٤٦٩ . الكافي : ١ / ٣٠١ / ٢ .
٤٧٠ . الأمالي للصدوق : ١٠١ .
٤٧١ . بحار الأنوار : ٤٣ / ٢٦٤ / ١٦ .
٤٧٢ . المستدرك على الصحيحين : ٣ / ١٧٧ .
٤٧٣ . سنن الترمذي : ٥ / ٦٦١ / ٣٧٨٤ .
٤٧٤ . المناقب لابن شهر آشوب : ٤ / ٧٣ .
٤٧٥ . عيون أخبار الرضا : ١ / ٥٩ / ٢٩ .
٤٧٦ . اللهوف : ٩٧ .
٤٧٧ . الإرشاد : ٢ / ٩٨ .
٤٧٨ . إحقاق الحقّ : ١١ / ٤٣١ .
٤٧٩ . الأمالي للصدوق : ٤٧٨ / ٤ .
٤٨٠ . المناقب لابن شهر آشوب : ٤ / ٦٦ .
٤٨١ . اللهوف : ١٧٠ .
٤٨٢ . الكافي : ١ / ٣٠٣ / ١ .
٤٨٣ . بحار الأنوار : ٤٦ / ٣ / ١ .
٤٨٤ . المناقب لابن شهر آشوب : ٤ / ١٥٤ .
٤٨٥ . حلية الأولياء : ٣ / ١٤٠ .
٤٨٦ . الكافي : ٣ / ٣٠٠ / ٤ .
٤٨٧ . آل عمران : ١٣٤ .
٤٨٨ . إعلام الورى : ٢٥٦ .
٤٨٩ . مطالب السؤول : ٧٧ .
٤٩٠ . حلية الأولياء : ٣ / ١٣٨ .
٤٩١ . كفاية الأثر : ٢٤١ .
٤٩٢ . بحار الأنوار : ٤٦ / ٢٢٥ / ٥ .
٤٩٣ . ربيع الأبرار : ٢ / ٦٠٣ .
٤٩٤ . بحار الأنوار : ٤٦ / ٢٢٧ / ٩ .
٤٩٥ . الكافي : ٢ / ٤٩٩ / ١ .
٤٩٦ . الكافي : ٢ / ٦١٦ / ١١ .
٤٩٧ . الإرشاد : ٢ / ١٦٧ .
٤٩٨ . بحار الأنوار : ٤٧ / ١٥ / ١٢ .
٤٩٩ . بحار الأنوار : ٤٧ / ١٥ / ١٢ .
٥٠٠ . بحار الأنوار : ٤٧ / ١٦ / ١ .
٥٠١ . الكافي : ٤ / ٨ / ١ .
٥٠٢ . ثواب الأعمال : ١٧٣ / ٢ .
٥٠٣ . الكافي : ٥ / ٧٦ / ١٣ .
٥٠٤ . المناقب لابن شهر آشوب : ٤ / ٣١٧ .
٥٠٥ . عيون أخبار الرضا : ١ / ٩٥ .
٥٠٦ . بحار الأنوار : ٧٨ / ٣٢٩ / ٧ .
٥٠٧ . الإرشاد : ٢ / ٢٣١ .
٥٠٨ . تاريخ بغداد : ١٣ / ٢٧ .
٥٠٩ . بحار الأنوار : ٤٩ / ١٧ / ١٥ .
٥١٠ . عيون أخبار الرضا : ٢ / ١٣٩ / ٣ .
٥١١ . بحار الأنوار : ٤٩ / ٩١ / ٥ .
٥١٢ . عيون أخبار الرضا : ٢ / ١٨٤ / ٧ .
٥١٣ . كفاية الأثر : ص ٨٤ .
٥١٤ . بحار الأنوار : ٥٠ / ٣٥ / ٢٣ .
٥١٥ . الكافي : ٦ / ٣٦٠ / ٣ .
٥١٦ . دلائل الإمامة : ٢١١ .
٥١٧ . دلائل الإمامة : ٢١٢ .
٥١٨ . القمر : ٢٤ .
٥١٩ . القمر : ٢٥ .
٥٢٠ . كشف الغمّة : ٣ / ١٥٣ .
٥٢١ . بحار الأنوار : ٥٠ / ١١٨ / ١ .
٥٢٢ . هود : ٦٥ .
٥٢٣ . بحار الأنوار : ٥٠ / ١٨٩ / ١ .
٥٢٤ . كشف الغمّة : ٣ / ١٧٩ .
٥٢٥ . بحار الأنوار : ٥٠ / ٢٣٩ / ٤ .
٥٢٦ . بحار الأنوار : ٥٠ / ٣٠٨ / ٦ .
٥٢٧ . المناقب لابن شهر آشوب : ٤ / ٤٢٤ .
٥٢٨ . الإسراء : ٣٣ .
٥٢٩ . بحار الأنوار : ٥١ / ٣٠ / ٨ .
٥٣٠ . الغيبة للطوسي : ٤٧١ / ٤٨٩ .
٥٣١ . بحار الأنوار : ٥١ / ١٦٠ / ٧ .
٥٣٢ . كنز العمّال : ٣٤٢٠٨ .
٥٣٣ . كنز العمّال : ٣٨٦٦٦ .
٥٣٤ . كنز العمّال : ٣٨٦٩١ .
٥٣٥ . كنز العمّال : ٣٨٦٦١ .
٥٣٦ . كنز العمّال : ٣٩٦٧٥ .
٥٣٧ . هود : ٨٦ .
٥٣٨ . نور الثقلين : ٢ / ٣٩٢ / ١٩٤ .
٥٣٩ . بحار الأنوار : ٥٢ / ١٥٥ / ١٠ .
٥٤٠ . كمال الدين : ٢٨٨ / ٧ .
٥٤١ . الغيبة للنعماني : ١٦٩ / ١١ وفي بعض النسخ «فليتّق الله عند

غَيبته» .

٥٤٢ . بحار الأنوار : ٥٢ / ١٤٩ / ٧٣ .

٥٤٣ . بحار الأنوار : ٥٢ / ١٢٢ / ٢ .

٥٤٤ . بحار الأنوار : ٥٢ / ١٢٢ / ٤ .

٥٤٥ . بحار الأنوار : ٥٢ / ١٤٦ / ٦٩ .

٥٤٦ . الغيبة للطوسي : ٤٥٩ / ٤٧١ .

٥٤٧ . بحار الأنوار : ٥٢ / ١١١ / ٢٠ .

٥٤٨ . بحار الأنوار : ٥٢ / ١١٠ / ١٧ .

٥٤٩ . الغيبة للطوسي : ٤٢٦ / ٤١١ .

٥٥٠ . بحار الأنوار : ٥٢ / ٩٠ / ١ ، وقد ذكرت هذه العلّة في روايات كثيرة ، فانظر أيضاً حديث : ٥، ١٠، ١٦ ـ ١٨، ٢٠، ٢٢ و ص ١٤٦ / ٧٠منه .

٥٥١ . كمال الدين : ٤٨٢ / ١١ .

٥٥٢ . علل الشرائع : ١٤٧ / ٢ .

٥٥٣ . الغيبة للنعماني : ٢٧٤ / ٥٣ .

٥٥٤ . مشكاة الأنوار : ١٢٨ / ٣٠٠ .

٥٥٥ . بحار الأنوار : ٥٢ / ٩٢ / ٧ .

٥٥٦ . لعلَّ المُرادُ بالخاطِبِ الطالبُ للخلافَةِ أو الخَـطيبِ الذي يَقومُ بغيرِ الحَقِّ أو بالحاءِ المُهمَلَةِ أي جالِبُ الحَطَبِ .

الغيبة للنعماني : ١٩٥ الهامش الخامس .

٥٥٧ . بحار الأنوار : ٥٢ / ١٣٧ / ٤٢ .

٥٥٨ . البقرة : ١٥٥ .

٥٥٩ . كمال الدين : ٦٤٩ / ٣ .

٥٦٠ . نور الثقلين : ٥ / ٤٦١ / ٤ .

٥٦١ . التشريف بالمنن : ١٢٩ / ١٣٦ ، كنز العمّال : ٣٩٦٦٥ .

٥٦٢ . بصائرالدرجات : ٤٤، بحارالأنوار : ٥٢ / ٣١٨ / ١٧ .

٥٦٣ . كشف الغمة : ٣ / ٢٥٥ .

٥٦٤ . الكافي : ٨ / ٢٤١ / ٣٢٩ .

٥٦٥ . الغيبة للنعماني : ٢٠٤ / ٦ .

٥٦٦ . الغيبة للنعماني : ٣١٧ / ١ .

٥٦٧ . كنز العمّال : ٣٨٧٠٠ .

٥٦٨ . مشكاة الأنوار : ١٥١ / ٣٦٦ .

٥٦٩ . الكافي : ٨ / ٢٢٧ / ٢٨٨ .

٥٧٠ . الحجرات : ١٤ .

٥٧١ . تحف العقول : ٢٩٧ .

٥٧٢ . الكافي : ٢ / ٢٦ / ٣ .

٥٧٣ . بحار الأنوار : ٦٩ / ٧٢ / ٢٦ ، كنز العمّال : ١١ نحوه .

٥٧٤ . كنز العمّال : ٢ .

٥٧٥ . كنز العمّال : ٥٧ .

٥٧٦ . كنز العمّال : ١٢ .

٥٧٧ . كنز العمّال : ٩٩ .

٥٧٨ . كنز العمّال : ٩٥ .

٥٧٩ . غرر الحكم : ٨٧٣ .

٥٨٠ . غرر الحكم : ١٣٥٠ .

٥٨١ . غرر الحكم : ٥٢٢٢ .

٥٨٢ . بحار الأنوار : ١٠٣ / ٣٧ / ٧٩ .

٥٨٣ . بحار الأنوار : ٧٠ / ١٠٦ / ٢ .

٥٨٤ . كنز العمّال : ٥٩ .

٥٨٥ . كنز العمّال : ٦٣٧ .

٥٨٦ . بحار الأنوار : ٦٩ / ١٩ / ٢ .

٥٨٧ . (اُنظر) الكافي : ٢/٣٣ ، باب في أن الايمان مبثوث لجوارح البدن كلها ، وقد اُشير هناك إلى بعض الآيات؛ كالآية ٤٦ من سورة العنكبوت والآية ١٣٩ من سورة النساء والآية ٣٠ و ٣١ من سورة النور .

٥٨٨ . الكافي : ٢ / ٣٨ / ٧ .

٥٨٩ . كنز العمّال : ١٣٣٣ .

٥٩٠ . كنز العمّال : ٢٠٥ .

٥٩١ . كنز العمّال : ٢٢٣ .

٥٩٢ . بحار الأنوار : ٦٩ / ٦٣ / ٧ .

٥٩٣ . كنز العمّال : ٤٣٢٤٧ .

٥٩٤ . كنز العمّال : ١٠٦ .

٥٩٥ . بحار الأنوار : ٧٧ / ١٧٧ / ١٠ .

٥٩٦ . بحار الأنوار : ٧١ / ٣٨٧ / ٣٤ .

٥٩٧ . غرر الحكم : ٤٦٥٨ .

٥٩٨ . غرر الحكم : ١٠٨٤٩ .

٥٩٩ . بحار الأنوار : ٧٨ / ٢٣٩ / ٧٨ .

٦٠٠ . الأنفال : ٢ .

٦٠١ . كنز العمّال : ١٧٣٤ .

٦٠٢ . كنز العمّال : ٦٦ .

٦٠٣ . كنز العمّال : ٧٤ .

٦٠٤ . كنز العمّال : ٥٢ .

٦٠٥ . غرر الحكم : ٢٩٩٢ .

٦٠٦ . الكافي : ٢ / ٤٥ / ٢ .

٦٠٧ . الكافي : ٢ / ٤٢ / ١ ، اُنظر تمام الحديث .

٦٠٨ . بحار الأنوار : ٦٩ / ١٧٥ / ٢٨ .
٦٠٩ . بحار الأنوار : ٧٨ / ٦٣ / ١٥٤ .
٦١٠ . غرر الحكم : ٤٨٣٨ .
٦١١ . كنز العمّال : ٤٣٥٢٥ .
٦١٢ . تنبيه الخواطر : ٢ / ٣٣ .
٦١٣ . نهج البلاغة : الخطبة ١٨٩ .
٦١٤ . الخصال : ٩ / ٢٩ .
٦١٥ . الضمير يرجع إلى المؤمن .
٦١٦ . الكافي : ٢ / ٣٨ / ٦ .
٦١٧ . كنز العمّال : ٧٢ .
٦١٨ . بحار الأنوار : ٧٢ / ٢٤٩ / ١٤ .
٦١٩ . الكافي : ٢ / ٥٨ / ٧ .
٦٢٠ . بحار الأنوار : ٧١ / ٨٥ / ٢٩ .
٦٢١ . تنبيه الخواطر : ٢ / ١١٦ .
٦٢٢ . الكافي : ٢ / ١٢٨ / ٢ .
٦٢٣ . بحار الأنوار : ٧٧ / ١٩٣ / ١١ .
٦٢٤ . تحف العقول : ٣٣٠ ، اُنظر تمام الحديث .
٦٢٥ . بحار الأنوار : ٧٧ / ١٧٢ / ٨ .
٦٢٦ . بحار الأنوار : ٧٧ / ١٧٣ / ٨ .
٦٢٧ . تحف العقول : ٥٥ .
٦٢٨ . تحف العقول : ٣٧٧ .
٦٢٩ . بحار الأنوار : ٧١ / ١٥٨ / ٧٥ .
٦٣٠ . كنز العمّال : ٨٢١ .
٦٣١ . الخصال : ٢٧ / ٩٥ .
٦٣٢ . مسند ابن حنبل : ٦ / ٣٧٩ / ١٨٤٠٨ .
٦٣٣ . كنز العمّال : ٤٠٢ .
٦٣٤ . الأنفال : ٢ـ٤ .
٦٣٥ . كنز العمّال : ٦٩٠ .
٦٣٦ . كنز العمّال : ٧٣٩ .
٦٣٧ . كنز العمّال : ٧٥٢ .
٦٣٨ . كنز العمّال : ٧٧٨ .
٦٣٩ . كنز العمّال : ٦٧٩ .
٦٤٠ . كنز العمّال : ٧٠٠ .
٦٤١ . بحار الأنوار : ٦٧ / ٧١ / ٣٤ و ص ٣١٠ / ٤٥ .
٦٤٢ . بحار الأنوار : ٦٩ / ٤١٠ / ١٢٧ .
٦٤٣ . غرر الحكم : ١٧٤٣ .
٦٤٤ . غرر الحكم : ١٩٠١ .
٦٤٥ . غرر الحكم : ١٩٥٦ .
٦٤٦ . غرر الحكم : ٢١٦٠ .
٦٤٧ . الكافي : ٢ / ٢٣١ / ٣ .
٦٤٨ . الكافي : ٢ / ٢٤١ / ٣٨ .
٦٤٩ . الكافي : ٢ / ٢٣١ / ٤ .
٦٥٠ . الكافي : ٢ / ٢٣٥ / ١٨ .
٦٥١ . تحف العقول : ٤٤٢ .
٦٥٢ . الكافي : ٢ / ٢٤١ / ٣٧ .
٦٥٣ . بحار الأنوار : ٦٧ / ٣٠٣ / ٣٤ .
٦٥٤ . تاريخ بغداد : ٥ / ١٩٤ و ١٢ / ١١١ .
٦٥٥ . الكافي : ٢ / ١٧٠ / ٥ .
٦٥٦ . الاحتجاج : ١ / ٥٨١ / ١٣٧ .
٦٥٧ . الكافي : ٢ / ٢٤٢ / ١ .
٦٥٨ . بحار الأنوار : ٦٧ / ٢٩٣ / ١٥ .
٦٥٩ . بحار الأنوار : ٧٢ / ٣٣٦ / ٢٤ .
٦٦٠ . نهج البلاغة : الكتاب ٦٩ .
٦٦١ . غرر الحكم : ٣٢٧٨ .
٦٦٢ . كنز العمّال : ٧٠٤ .
٦٦٣ . كنز العمّال : ٣٤٥٨٣ .
٦٦٤ . المؤمنون : ٨ .
٦٦٥ . غرر الحكم : ٢٩٠٥ـ٢٩٠٦ .
٦٦٦ . الكافي : ٢ / ١٦٢ / ١٥ .
٦٦٧ . بحار الأنوار : ٧٧ / ٢٠٨ / ١ .
٦٦٨ . الأمالي للصدوق : ٣١٨ / ٣٧٣ .
٦٦٩ . الأمالي للصدوق : ٣١٨ / ٣٧٢ .
٦٧٠ . بحار الأنوار : ٧٢ / ١٩٨ / ٢٦ ، غرر الحكم : ١٠٧٦٧ .
٦٧١ . بحار الأنوار : ٧٥ / ١٧٢ / ١٣ .
٦٧٢ . معاني الأخبار : ٢٥٣ / ١ .
٦٧٣ . بحار الأنوار : ٧٥ / ١١٤ / ٦ .
٦٧٤ . غرر الحكم : ٤٠٥٣ .
٦٧٥ . تنبيه الخواطر : ١ / ١٢ .
٦٧٦ . بحار الأنوار : ١٠٣ / ١٧٩ / ٣ .
٦٧٧ . تهذيب الأحكام : ٧ / ٢٣٢ / ١٠١٣ .
٦٧٨ . الكافي : ٥ / ٣٠١ / ٤ .
٦٧٩ . كنز العمّال : ١٠٩٠٩ .
٦٨٠ . كنز العمّال : ١٠٩٣٠ .
٦٨١ . نهج البلاغة : الحكمة ١٥٥

٦٨٢ . نهج البلاغة : الكتاب ٥٣ .
٦٨٣ . كنز العمّال : ١٠٩٣٢ .
٦٨٤ . بحار الأنوار : ١٠٠ / ٤٦ / ٦ .
٦٨٥ . غرر الحكم : ١٠٣٠٣ .
٦٨٦ . بحار الأنوار : ٧٨ / ٢٣١ / ٢٥ .
٦٨٧ . بحار الأنوار : ٧٠ / ١١١ / ١٤ .
٦٨٨ . الدرّة الباهرة : ٤٣ .
٦٨٩ . غرر الحكم : ١٧٧٢ .
٦٩٠ . أعلام الدين : ٣٠٧ .
٦٩١ . بحار الأنوار : ٧٥ / ٣٥٩ / ٧٤ .
٦٩٢ . غرر الحكم : ٨٦٤٤ .
٦٩٣ . الإسراء : ٧٠ .
٦٩٤ . كنز العمّال : ٣٤٦٢١ .
٦٩٥ . كنز العمّال : ٣٤٦١٥ .
٦٩٦ . بحار الأنوار : ٦٠ / ٢٩٩ / ٥ .
٦٩٧ . الذاريات : ٥٦ .
٦٩٨ . هود : ١١٨ ، ١١٩ .
٦٩٩ . شرح نهج البلاغة : ٣ / ١٠٨ .
٧٠٠ . بحار الأنوار : ٢٣ / ٨٣ / ٢٢ .
٧٠١ . بحار الأنوار : ١٠ / ١٦٧ / ٢ .
٧٠٢ . بحار الأنوار : ٥ / ٣١٤ / ٥ .
٧٠٣ . النساء : ٢٨ .
٧٠٤ . نهج البلاغة : الحكمة ٤١٩ .
٧٠٥ . غرر الحكم : ٢٠٨٩ .
٧٠٦ . كنز العمّال : ٤٤٠٩١ .
٧٠٧ . كنز العمّال : ٤٤١٢١ .
٧٠٨ . كنز العمّال : ٤٤٢٢٦ .
٧٠٩ . غرر الحكم : ٨٩ .
٧١٠ . غرر الحكم : ٣١٤ .
٧١١ . غرر الحكم : ٣٩١٥ .
٧١٢ . غرر الحكم : ٣٩١٦ .
٧١٣ . غرر الحكم : ٣٩١٧ .
٧١٤ . غرر الحكم : ٣٩١٨ .
٧١٥ . غرر الحكم : ٣٩١٩ .
٧١٦ . غرر الحكم : ٣٩٢٠ .
٧١٧ . غرر الحكم : ٣٩٢١ .
٧١٨ . غرر الحكم : ٣٩٢٣ .
٧١٩ . غرر الحكم : ٣٩٢٤ .
٧٢٠ . غرر الحكم : ٣٩٢٥ .
٧٢١ . غرر الحكم : ٣٩٢٢ .
٧٢٢ . غرر الحكم : ٣٩٢٦ .
٧٢٣ . غرر الحكم : ٣٩٢٧ .
٧٢٤ . غرر الحكم : ٣٩٢٨ .
٧٢٥ . غرر الحكم : ٣٩٢٩ .
٧٢٦ . غرر الحكم : ٣٩٣٠ .
٧٢٧ . غرر الحكم : ٣٩٣١ .
٧٢٨ . غرر الحكم : ٣٩٣٢ .
٧٢٩ . غرر الحكم : ٣٩٣٣ .
٧٣٠ . غرر الحكم : ٣٩٣٤ .
٧٣١ . غرر الحكم : ٣٩٣٥ .
٧٣٢ . غرر الحكم : ٣٩٣٦ .
٧٣٣ . غرر الحكم : ٣٩٣٧ .
٧٣٤ . غرر الحكم : ٣٩٣٨ .
٧٣٥ . غرر الحكم : ٣٩٣٩ .
٧٣٦ . غرر الحكم : ٣٩٤٠ .
٧٣٧ . غرر الحكم : ٣٩٤١ .
٧٣٨ . غرر الحكم : ٣٩٤٢ .
٧٣٩ . غرر الحكم : ٣٩٤٣ .
٧٤٠ . غرر الحكم : ٣٩٤٤ .
٧٤١ . غرر الحكم : ٣٩٤٥ .
٧٤٢ . غرر الحكم : ٣٩٤٦ .
٧٤٣ . غرر الحكم : ٣٩٥٠ .
٧٤٤ . غرر الحكم : ٣٩٤٧ .
٧٤٥ . غرر الحكم : ٣٩٤٨ .
٧٤٦ . غرر الحكم : ٣٩٤٩ .
٧٤٧ . غرر الحكم : ٣٩٥١ .
٧٤٨ . غرر الحكم : ٣٩٥٢ .
٧٤٩ . غرر الحكم : ٣٩٥٣ .
٧٥٠ . غرر الحكم : ٣٩٥٤ .
٧٥١ . غرر الحكم : ٣٩٥٥ .
٧٥٢ . غرر الحكم : ٣٩٥٦ .
٧٥٣ . غرر الحكم : ٣٩٥٧ .
٧٥٤ . غرر الحكم : ٣٩٥٨ .
٧٥٥ . غرر الحكم : ٣٩٥٩ .

٧٥٦ . غرر الحكم : ٣٩٦٠ .
٧٥٧ . غرر الحكم : ٣٩٦١ .
٧٥٨ . غرر الحكم : ٣٩٦٢ .
٧٥٩ . غرر الحكم : ٣٩٦٣ .
٧٦٠ . غرر الحكم : ٣٩٦٤ .
٧٦١ . غرر الحكم : ٣٩٦٥ .
٧٦٢ . غرر الحكم : ٣٩٦٦ .
٧٦٣ . غرر الحكم : ٣٩٦٩ .
٧٦٤ . غرر الحكم : ٣٩٧٠ .
٧٦٥ . غرر الحكم : ٣٩٧١ .
٧٦٦ . غرر الحكم : ٣٩٧٢ .
٧٦٧ . غرر الحكم : ٥٢٤٤ .
٧٦٨ . غرر الحكم : ٥٧٥٢ .
٧٦٩ . النساء : ٣٧ .
٧٧٠ . محمّد : ٣٨ .
٧٧١ . نهج البلاغة : الحكمة ٣٧٨، بحار الأنوار : ٣٠٧٧٣ / ٣٦ .
٧٧٢ . نهج البلاغة : الحكمة ٣ .
٧٧٣ . بحار الأنوار : ٧٧ / ٢٣٨ / ١ .
٧٧٤ . غرر الحكم : ١٢٥٨ .
٧٧٥ . غرر الحكم : ٧٩٢١_٧٩٢٢ .
٧٧٦ . غرر الحكم : ١٤٠٩ .
٧٧٧ . بحار الأنوار : ٧٨ / ٣٥٧ / ١٢ .
٧٧٨ . بحار الأنوار : ٧٢ / ١٩٩ / ٢٧ .
٧٧٩ . بحار الأنوار : ٧٣ / ٣٠٥ / ٢٣ .
٧٨٠ . بحار الأنوار : ٧٣ / ٣٠٥ / ٢٥ .
٧٨١ . تحف العقول : ٣٧١، ٣٧٢ .
٧٨٢ . بحار الأنوار : ٧٣ / ٣٠٠ / ٢ .
٧٨٣ . غرر الحكم : ٤٦٤ .
٧٨٤ . غرر الحكم : ٧٤٧٣ .
٧٨٥ . بحار الأنوار : ٧٢ / ١٩٩ / ٢٨ .
٧٨٦ . بحارالأنوار : ٧٣ / ٣٠٨ / ٣٧ .
٧٨٧ . الأمالي للصدوق : ٤٧١ / ٦٢٩ .
٧٨٨ . بحار الأنوار : ٧٣ / ٣٠٧ / ٣٥ .
٧٨٩ . معاني الأخبار : ٢٤٥ / ٤ .
٧٩٠ . بحار الأنوار : ٧٣ / ٣٠٦ / ٢٨ .
٧٩١ . بحار الأنوار : ٧٣ / ٣٠٠ / ٢ .
٧٩٢ . بحار الأنوار : ٧٦ / ٤ / ١١ .

٧٩٣ . غرر الحكم : ٣٢٥٣ .
٧٩٤ . غرر الحكم : ٢٠٣٨ .
٧٩٥ . وسائل الشيعة : ٦ / ٣١٨ / ١ .
٧٩٦ . بحار الأنوار : ٧٧ / ٢٠٩ / ١ .
٧٩٧ . غرر الحكم : ١٢٧٥ .
٧٩٨ . البِدْعَةُ بِالكَسرِ فَالسُّكونِ : الحَدَثُ فِي الدّينِ .
٧٩٩ . الأمالي للمفيد : ١٨٨ / ١٤ .
٨٠٠ . بحار الأنوار : ٧٧ / ١٠٤ / ١ .
٨٠١ . نهج البلاغة : الخطبة ١٤٥ .
٨٠٢ . بحار الأنوار : ٧٨ / ٩٢ / ٩٨ .
٨٠٣ . كنز العمّال : ١٠٩٥، ١١٢٦ .
٨٠٤ . كنز العمّال : ١١٢٥ .
٨٠٥ . كنز العمّال : ٤٤٢١٦ .
٨٠٦ . تحف العقول : ٣٧٥ .
٨٠٧ . كنز العمّال : ٥٥٩٩ .
٨٠٨ . بحار الأنوار : ٤٧ / ٢١٧ / ٤ .
٨٠٩ . بحار الأنوار : ٧٢ / ٢١٦ / ٨ .
٨١٠ . الأمالي للطوسي : ٣٨٥ / ٨٣٨ .
٨١١ . بحار الأنوار : ٧٢ / ٢١٦ / ٨ .
٨١٢ . الكافي : ١ / ٥٤ / ٢ .
٨١٣ . الإسراء : ٢٦، ٢٧ .
٨١٤ . نهج البلاغة : الحكمة ٣٣ .
٨١٥ . غرر الحكم : ٨٩٠ .
٨١٦ . غرر الحكم : ١٠٤٣ .
٨١٧ . غرر الحكم : ٩٠٥٧ .
٨١٨ . تفسير العيّاشي : ٢ / ٢٨٨ / ٥٣ .
٨١٩ . تفسير العيّاشي : ٢ / ٢٨٨ / ٥٤ .
٨٢٠ . المائدة : ٢ .
٨٢١ . بحار الأنوار : ٧٧ / ١٦٦ / ٣ .
٨٢٢ . الخصال : ١١٠ / ٨١ .
٨٢٣ . تحف العقول : ٨ .
٨٢٤ . تحف العقول : ٢٩٥ .
٨٢٥ . تحف العقول : ٢١ .
٨٢٦ . كنز العمّال : ٥٢٦٥ .
٨٢٧ . المؤمنون : ١٠٠ .
٨٢٨ . الكافي : ٣ / ٢٤٢ / ٣ .
٨٢٩ . آل عمران : ١٦٩ .

٨٣٠ . المحاسن : ١ / ٢٨٥ / ٥٦٢ .
٨٣١ . بحار الأنوار : ٦ / ٢٧٠ / ١٢٧ .
٨٣٢ . مريم : ٣١ .
٨٣٣ . الكافي : ٢ / ١٦٥ / ١١ .
٨٣٤ . الأعراف : ٩٦ .
٨٣٥ . كنز العمّال : ٩٤٣٤ .
٨٣٦ . مستدرك الوسائل : ١٣ / ٩ .
٨٣٧ . بحار الأنوار : ٧٩ / ١٩ / ٤ .
٨٣٨ . غرر الحكم : ٤٢١١ .
٨٣٩ . غرر الحكم : ٤٠٣٠ .
٨٤٠ . الكافي : ٢ / ١٠٣ / ٦ .
٨٤١ . الكافي : ٢ / ١٠٣ / ٣ .
٨٤٢ . الكافي : ٢ / ١٠٣ / ١ .
٨٤٣ . بحار الأنوار : ٦٩ / ٤٠٩ / ١٢٠ .
٨٤٤ . غرر الحكم : ٦٥٦ .
٨٤٥ . غرر الحكم : ٥٥٤٦ .
٨٤٦ . غرر الحكم : ٣٤٥٤ .
٨٤٧ . غرر الحكم : ٤٤٥٣ .
٨٤٨ . بحار الأنوار : ٧٦ / ٢٠ / ٣ .
٨٤٩ . بحار الأنوار : ٧٨ / ٥٧ / ١٢٤ .
٨٥٠ . الأعراف : ١٧٩ .
٨٥١ . كنز العمّال : ١٢٢٠ .
٨٥٢ . غرر الحكم : ٩٩٧٢ .
٨٥٣ . نهج البلاغة : الخطبة ١٥٣ .
٨٥٤ . نهج البلاغة : الحكمة ٢٨١ .
٨٥٥ . غرر الحكم : ٦٥٣٦ .
٨٥٦ . غرر الحكم : ٣٠٦١ .
٨٥٧ . الإسراء : ٨١ .
٨٥٨ . الأنبياء : ١٨ .
٨٥٩ . غرر الحكم : ٥٤٩ .
٨٦٠ . نهج البلاغة : الخطبة ٣٣ .
٨٦١ . نهج السعادة : ٣ / ٢٩١ .
٨٦٢ . غرر الحكم : ٦٠٤١ .
٨٦٣ . نهج البلاغة : الخطبة ١٤١ .
٨٦٤ . البقرة : ٤٢ .
٨٦٥ . نهج البلاغة : الخطبة ٥٠ .
٨٦٦ . غرر الحكم : ٦٩٦٩ .
٨٦٧ . بحار الأنوار : ٥ / ٣٠٣ / ١٢ .
٨٦٨ . تفسير العيّاشي : ٢ / ٥٣ / ٣٩ .
٨٦٩ . تحف العقول : ٤٢ .
٨٧٠ . كنز العمّال : ٢٨٩٨٢ .
٨٧١ . كنز العمّال : ٤٣٦٧٩ .
٨٧٢ . عيون أخبار الرضا : ٢ / ٢٨ / ٢٤ .
٨٧٣ . غرر الحكم : ٣٤٣٧ .
٨٧٤ . مستدرك الوسائل : ٨ / ٣٢١ / ٩٥٥٢ .
٨٧٥ . بحار الأنوار : ٧٨ / ١٧٦ / ٣٣٨ .
٨٧٦ . كنز العمّال : ٢١٤٣١ .
٨٧٧ . كنز العمّال : ٤٣٨٣٣ .
٨٧٨ . بحار الأنوار : ٧١ / ٣٨٣ / ١٧ .
٨٧٩ . كنز العمّال : ٢٨٩٨٥ .
٨٨٠ . كنز العمّال : ٥١٨٤ .
٨٨١ . غرر الحكم : ٣١٢٨ .
٨٨٢ . غرر الحكم : ٣٢٩٤ .
٨٨٣ . غرر الحكم : ٣٣٥٩ .
٨٨٤ . كنز العمّال : ٤٤٢٢٠ .
٨٨٥ . غرر الحكم : ٣١٦٤ .
٨٨٦ . بحار الأنوار : ٧٦ / ١٨٠ / ٨ .
٨٨٧ . الكافي : ٢ / ٣٢٣ / ٤ .
٨٨٨ . عيون أخبار الرضا : ٢ / ٣٦ / ٨٩ .
٨٨٩ . بحارالأنوار : ١٦ / ٢٣١ .
٨٩٠ . بحار الأنوار : ٧٦ / ١٨٠ / ١٠ .
٨٩١ . الخصال : ٨٩ / ٢٥ .
٨٩٢ . الكافي : ٢ / ٢٩٠ / ٤ .
٨٩٣ . بحار الأنوار : ٧٨ / ٣٣٥ / ١٦ .
٨٩٤ . معاني الأخبار : ٣٦٧ / ١ .
٨٩٥ . تحف العقول : ٣١٦ .
٨٩٦ . يونس : ٢٣ .
٨٩٧ . النحل : ٩٠ .
٨٩٨ . الكافي : ٢ / ٣٢٧ / ١ .
٨٩٩ . نهج البلاغة : الحكمة ٣٤٩ .
٩٠٠ . غرر الحكم : ٣٨٢ .
٩٠١ . غرر الحكم : ٧٩٥ .
٩٠٢ . غرر الحكم : ٢٦٥٧ .
٩٠٣ . الكافي : ٢ / ٣٢٧ / ٤ .

٩٠٤ . الكافي : ٢ / ٣٢٧ / ٣ .
٩٠٥ . البقرة : ١٧٣ .
٩٠٦ . معاني الأخبار : ٢١٣ / ١ .
٩٠٧ . في الدرّ المنثور عن مجاهد في قوله : ﴿غيرَ باغٍ ولا عادٍ﴾ قال : غير باغ على المسلمين ولا متعدٍّ عليهم . مَن خرج يقطعُ الرّحم أو يقطع السّبيل أو يُفسِدُ في الأرض أو مُفارقاً للجماعة والأئمّة أو خرج في معصيةِ الله فاضْطُرَّ إلى الميتةِ لم تَحِلَّ له . (الدرّ المنثور : ١ / ٤٠٨) .
٩٠٨ . الحجرات : ٩ .
٩٠٩ الكافي : ٥ / ٣٢ / ٢ .
٩١٠ الكافي : ٥ / ٣٢ / ٣ .
٩١١ الكافي : ٥ / ٣٢ / ٥ .
٩١٢ . وسائل الشيعة : ١١ / ٦٠ / ٥ .
٩١٣ . مريم : ٥٨ .
٩١٤ . الإسراء : ١٠٩ .
٩١٥ . بحار الأنوار : ٩٣ / ٣٣١ / ١٥ .
٩١٦ . بحار الأنوار : ٩٣ / ٣٣٤ / ٢٥ .
٩١٧ . بحار الأنوار : ٨٤ / ٢ / ٧١ .
٩١٨ . بحار الأنوار : ٩٣ / ٣٣٦ / ٣٠ .
٩١٩ . مكارم الأخلاق : ٢ / ٩٦ / ١٠ .
٩٢٠ . غرر الحكم : 2051 .
٩٢١ . غرر الحكم : ٢٠١٦ .
٩٢٢ . بحار الأنوار : ٦٩ / ٣٧٨ / ٣١ .
٩٢٣ . بحار الأنوار : ٧ / ١٩٥ / ٦٢ .
٩٢٤ .عدّة الداعي : ١٦١ .
٩٢٥ . بحار الأنوار : ٩٣ / ٣٣١ / ١٤ .
٩٢٦ . بحار الأنوار : ٧٠ / ٥٢ / ١١ .
٩٢٧ . بحار الأنوار : ٧٣ / ٣٥٤ / ٦٠ .
٩٢٨ . سبأ : ١٥ .
٩٢٩ . سبأ : ١٨ .
٩٣٠ . نهج البلاغة : الكتاب ٦٩ .
٩٣١ . نهج البلاغة : الحكمة ٤٤٢ .
٩٣٢ . تحف العقول : ٣٢١ .
٩٣٣ . غرر الحكم : ١٨٨١ .
٩٣٤ . غرر الحكم : ٢١٥٠ .
٩٣٥ . غرر الحكم : ٦٦٦٦ .
٩٣٦ . تحف العقول : ٣١٢ .
٩٣٧ . تحف العقول : ٣١٧ .
٩٣٨ . غرر الحكم : ٣٣٠٧ .
٩٣٩ . غرر الحكم : ٣٣٠٤ .
٩٤٠ . كنزالعمّال : ح ٧٩١٠ .
٩٤١ . التوبة : ١٢٢ .
٩٤٢ . الاحتجاج : ١ / ١٥٧ / ٣٢ .
٩٤٣ . المستدرك على الصحيحين : ٣ / ٦٩١ / ٦٥٣٧ .
٩٤٥_٢ . المعجم الكبير : ٨ / ٩١ / ٧٤٦١، ١٧ / ٢٨٥ / ٧٨٦ .
٩٤٦ . الموطّأ : ١ / ٢١٨ / ٤١ .
٩٤٧ . كنز العمّال : ٢٨٧٧٩ .
٩٤٨ . الأمالي للطوسي : ٤٦ / ٥٤ .
٩٤٩ . الفردوس : ١ / ٢٣٤ / ٨٩٧ .
٩٥٠ . معاني الأخبار : ١٨٠ / ١ .
٩٥١ . الشعراء : ١٤٥ .
٩٥٢ . الزهد لابن حنبل : ٣٩١ .
٩٥٣ . الأحزاب : ٣٩ .
٩٥٤ . حلية الأولياء : ١ / ٢٤١ .
٩٥٥ . مسند ابن حنبل : ٤ / ١٠٢ / ١١٤٧٤ .
٩٥٦ . مصباح الشريعة : ٣٩٥ .
٩٥٧ . الكافي : ٢ / ١٠٤ / ٤ .
٩٥٨ . صحيح البخاري : ٥ / ٢٢٦٩ / ٥٧٧٤ .
٩٥٩ . تحف العقول : ٤٨ .
٩٦٠ . الكافي : ٨ / ٣٣٤ / ٥٢٢ .
٩٦١ . الأعراف : ٦٨ .
٩٦٢ . نهج البلاغة : الخطبة ٩٥ .
٩٦٣ . شرح نهج البلاغة لابن أبي الحديد : ٢٠ / ٢٨٧ / ٢٧٩ .
٩٦٤ . الكافي : ٢ / ١٠٥ / ١٠ .
٩٦٥ . تحف العقول : ٣٠١ .
٩٦٦ . الأنبياء : ٣٥ .
٩٦٧ . التوحيد : ٣٥٤ / ١ .
٩٦٨ . التوحيد : ٣٥٤ / ٣ .
٩٦٩ . آل عمران : ١٥٤ .
٩٧٠ . محمّد : ٣١ .
٩٧١ . الملك : ٢ .
٩٧٢ . نهج البلاغة : الخطبة ١٤٤ .
٩٧٣ . نهج البلاغة : الخطبة ١٩٢ .
٩٧٤ . بحار الأنوار : ٥ / ٢١٨ / ١٢ .

٩٧٥ . غرر الحكم : ١٠٣٩٤ .

٩٧٦ . البقرة : ٢١٤ .

٩٧٧ . بحار الأنوار : ٦٧ / ٢٢٢ / ٢٩ .

٩٧٨ . الكافي : ٢ / ٢٥٢ / ١ .

٩٧٩ . الكافي : ٢ / ٢٥٤ / ١٢ .

٩٨٠ . الشورى : ٣٠ .

٩٨١ . الدعوات : ١٢٣ / ٣٠٤ .

٩٨٢ . بحار الأنوار : ٨١ / ١٧٤ / ١١ .

٩٨٣ . بحار الأنوار : ٨١ / ١٧٦ / ١٤ .

٩٨٤ . بحار الأنوار : ٨١ / ١٩٥ / ٥٢ .

٩٨٥ . جامع الأخبار : ٣١٠ / ٨٥٥ .

٩٨٦ . الكافي : ٢ / ٢٥٥ / ١٧ .

٩٨٧ . جامع الأخبار : ٣١٣ / ٨٧٠ .

٩٨٨ . بحار الأنوار : ٧٨ / ٣٧٤ / ٣٤ .

٩٨٩ . الأعراف : ١٣٠ .

٩٩٠ . نهج البلاغة : الخطبة ١٤٣

٩٩١ . بحار الأنوار : ٦٧ / ٢١١ / ١٤ .

٩٩٢ . الأعراف : ١٨٢ .

٩٩٣ . بحار الأنوار : ٦٧ / ٢٢٩ / ٤١ .

٩٩٤ . بحار الأنوار : ٦٧ / ٢٣٢ / ٤٨ .

٩٩٥ . بحار الأنوار : ٨١ / ١٧٩ / ٢٥ .

٩٩٦ . أعلام الدين : ٤٣٣ .

٩٩٧ . الكافي : ٢ / ٢٥٣ / ٦ .

٩٩٨ . بحار الأنوار : ٨٢ / ١٤٨ / ٣٢ .

٩٩٩ . جامع الأخبار : ٣١٤ / ٨٧٤ .

١٠٠٠ . الكافي : ٢ / ٢٥٣ / ٩ .

١٠٠١ . بحار الأنوار : ٦٧ / ٢٢٢ / ٢٩ .

١٠٠٢ . بحار الأنوار : ٦٧ / ٢٤٣ / ٨٢ .

١٠٠٣ . بحار الأنوار : ٦٧ / ٢١٢ / ١٦ .

١٠٠٤ . الكافي : ٢ / ٢٥٧ / ٢٣ .

١٠٠٥ . بحار الأنوار : ٧٢ / ٣٣١ / ١٤ .

١٠٠٦ . بحار الأنوار : ٧٣ / ٣٨٣ / ٨ .

١٠٠٧ . الأمالي للطوسي : ١٤٦ / ٢٤٠ .

١٠٠٨ . الخصال : ٨ / ٢٧ .

١٠٠٩ . تحف العقول : ٣١٨ .

١٠١٠ . بحار الأنوار : ٧٨ / ١٢ / ٧٠ .

١٠١١ . تحف العقول : ٣٥٧ .

١٠١٢ . البقرة : ١٥٦ .

١٠١٣ . بحار الأنوار : ٧٧ / ٢٧٠ / ١ .

١٠١٤ . مُهج الدعوات : ٣٩٧ .

١٠١٥ . بحار الأنوار : ٧١ / ٣٤ / ١٨ .

١٠١٦ . بحار الأنوار : ٧١ / ٣٤ / ١٥ .

١٠١٧ . الأحزاب : ٥٨ .

١٠١٨ . بحار الأنوار : ٧٥ / ١٩٤ / ٥ .

١٠١٩ . غرر الحكم : ١٠٤٥٥ .

١٠٢٠ . بحار الأنوار : ٧٨ / ٣١ / ٩٩ .

١٠٢١ . بحار الأنوار : ٧٨ / ١٦٠ / ٢١ .

١٠٢٢ . بحار الأنوار : ٧٥ / ١٩٤ / ٣ .

١٠٢٣ . آل عمران : ٦١ .

١٠٢٤ . الكافي : ٢ / ٥١٤ / ٤ .

١٠٢٥ . في نور الثقلين : ١ / ٣٤٧ / ١٥٧ نقلاً عن المصدر : «ففَرِقوا» بدل «فَعرَفوا» .

١٠٢٦ . تفسير القمّي : ١ / ١٠٤ .

١٠٢٧ . الفتح : ١٠ .

١٠٢٨ . تفسير القمّي : ٢ / ٣١٥ .

١٠٢٩ . صحيح مسلم : ٣ / ١٤٨٦ / ٨٠ .

١٠٣٠ . الممتحنة : ١٢ .

١٠٣١ . تحف العقول : ٤٥٧ .

١٠٣٢ . النحل : ٩١ .

١٠٣٣ . الخصال : ١٠٧ / ٧٠ .

١٠٣٤ . بحار الأنوار : ٦٧ / ١٨٦ / ٧ .

١٠٣٥ . كنز العمّال : ٤٤٢١٦ .

١٠٣٦ . بحار الأنوار : ٦٧ / ١٨٦ / ٤ .

١٠٣٧ . نهج البلاغة : الكتاب ١ .

١٠٣٨ . الإرشاد : ١ / ٢٦٠ .

١٠٣٩ . النساء : ٢٩ .

١٠٤٠ . وسائل الشيعة : ١٢ / ٤ / ٦ .

١٠٤١ . الكافي : ٥ / ١٤٨ / ٢ .

١٠٤٢ . الكافي : ٥ / ١٤٨ / ١ .

١٠٤٣ . الكافي : ٥ / ١٤٩ / ١٠ .

١٠٤٤ . بحار الأنوار : ١٠٣ / ٩٥ / ١٨ .

١٠٤٥ . كنز العمّال : ٩٢٩٣ .

١٠٤٦ . الكافي : ٥ / ١٥٠ / ١ .

١٠٤٧ . إشارة إلى الآية ٨٥ من سورة هود .

١٠٤٨ . بحار الأنوار : ٧٨ / ٥٤ / ١٠٠ ، وأُنظر وسائل الشيعة : ١٢ / ٢٨٤ / ١ .
١٠٤٩ . وسائل الشيعة : ١٢ / ٢٨٣ / ٤ .
١٠٥٠ . وسائل الشيعة : ١٢ / ٢٨٧ / ٤ .
١٠٥١ . المطفّفين : ١-٣ .
١٠٥٢ . كنز العمّال : ٩٤٤٢ .
١٠٥٣ . الكافي : ٥ / ١٥٩ / ١ .
١٠٥٤ . كنز العمّال : ٩٤٣٩ .
١٠٥٥ . كنز العمّال : ٩٤٥٣ .
١٠٥٦ . وسائل الشيعة : ١٢ / ٢٨٨ / ٤ .
١٠٥٧ . الخصال : ٢٤٥ / ١٠٣ .
١٠٥٨ . ربيع الأبرار : ٤ / ١٣٩ .
١٠٥٩ . الكافي : ٥ / ١٥٢ / ١٠ .
١٠٦٠ . الكافي : ٥ / ١٥٤ / ٢٢ .
١٠٦١ . وسائل الشيعة : ١٢ / ٢٩٤ / ٤ .
١٠٦٢ . كنز العمّال : ٩٤٥١ .
١٠٦٣ . كنز العمّال : ١٠٠٤٣ .
١٠٦٤ . كنز العمّال : ٩٢١٦ .
١٠٦٥ . كنز العمّال : ٩٢١٨ .
١٠٦٦ . بحار الأنوار : ٧٥ / ٢١١ / ٦ .
١٠٦٧ . الكافي : ٥ / ١٦٢ / ٢ .
١٠٦٨ . الأمالي للصدوق : ٥٧١ / ٧٧٥ .
١٠٦٩ . الصف : ١٠، ١١ .
١٠٧٠ . النحل : ٩٦ .
١٠٧١ . بحار الأنوار : ٧٧ / ١٠٦ / ١ .
١٠٧٢ . تنبيه الخواطر : ٢ / ١٢٠ .
١٠٧٣ . بحار الأنوار : ٦٩ / ٤٠٩ / ١٢٢ .
١٠٧٤ . غرر الحكم : ٣٠٧٦ .
١٠٧٥ . غرر الحكم : ٣٤٧٤ .
١٠٧٦ . غرر الحكم : ٨٨٦٤ .
١٠٧٧ . النور : ٣٧ .
١٠٧٨ . بحار الأنوار : ١٠٣ / ١٠٠ / ٤٠ .
١٠٧٩ . تحف العقول : ٢٢٣ .
١٠٨٠ . غرر الحكم : ٨٩٠١ .
١٠٨١ . الشورىٰ : ٢٥ .
١٠٨٢ . عوالي اللآلي : ١ / ٢٣٧ / ١٥٠ .
١٠٨٣ . كنز العمّال : ١٠١٧٤ .
١٠٨٤ . غرر الحكم : ١٣٥٥ .
١٠٨٥ . البقرة : ٢٢٢ .
١٠٨٦ . بحار الأنوار : ٦ / ٢١ / ١٥ .
١٠٨٧ . الدرّ المنثور : ١ / ٦٢٦ .
١٠٨٨ . كنز العمّال : ١٠١٦٥ .
١٠٨٩ . تحف العقول : ٢٠ .
١٠٩٠ . بحار الأنوار : ٧٨ / ٧٢ / ٣٨ .
١٠٩١ . بحار الأنوار : ٩٤ / ١٢٧ / ١٩ .
١٠٩٢ . الشورى : ٢٥ .
١٠٩٣ . بحار الأنوار : ٦٩ / ٤١٠ / ١٢٤ .
١٠٩٤ . النساء : ١٨ .
١٠٩٥ . الكافي : ٢ / ٤٤٠ / ٢ .
١٠٩٦ . الكافي : ٢ / ٤٤٠ / ٣ .
١٠٩٧ . بحار الأنوار : ٦ / ٢٣ / ٢٥ .
١٠٩٨ . كنز العمّال : ١٠٣٠١ .
١٠٩٩ . غرر الحكم : ١٢١١ .
١١٠٠ . غرر الحكم : ٩٩٧٣ .
١١٠١ . التوبة : ١٠٢ .
١١٠٢ . غرر الحكم : ٦٣٣٤ .
١١٠٣ . بحار الأنوار : ٦ / ٣٦ / ٥٦ .
١١٠٤ . الكافي : ٢ / ٤٢٦ / ٢ .
١١٠٥ . المائدة : ٣٩ .
١١٠٦ . طه : ٨٢ .
١١٠٧ . بحار الأنوار : ٧٨ / ٨١ / ٧٤ .
١١٠٨ . الكافي : ٢ / ٣٣١ / ٣ .
١١٠٩ . بحار الأنوار : ٧٧ / ١٢٧ / ٣٣ .
١١١٠ . التحريم : ٨ .
١١١١ . كنز العمّال : ١٠٤٢٧ .
١١١٢ . بحار الأنوار : ٦ / ٢٢ / ٢٠ .
١١١٣ . بحار الأنوار : ٧٧ / ٢٠٨ / ١ .
١١١٤ . غرر الحكم : ٩٨٧٦ .
١١١٥ . تحف العقول : ٤٥٦ .
١١١٦ . تحف العقول : ٣٩٢ .
١١١٧ . بحار الأنوار : ٧٣ / ٣٦٤ / ٩٦ .
١١١٨ . بحار الأنوار : ٦ / ٢٨ / ٣٢ .
١١١٩ . الفرقان : ٧٠ .
١١٢٠ . بحار الأنوار : ٦ / ٢٨ / ٣٠ .

١١٢١ . كنز العمّال : ٧٩٠٢ .

١١٢٢ . وسائل الشيعة : ١١ / ٢٦٧ / ١٣ .

١١٢٣ . غرر الحكم : ٤٦٨٨ .

١١٢٤ . غرر الحكم : ٤٦٩٢ .

١١٢٥ . نهج البلاغة : الحكمة ٣٦٨ .

١١٢٦ . غرر الحكم : ٤٦٩٠ .

١١٢٧ . غرر الحكم : ٣٣٨٧ .

١١٢٨ . غرر الحكم : ٤٦٩٥ .

١١٢٩ . غرر الحكم : ٥٧٦٩ .

١١٣٠ . الكافي : ٢ / ٨٧ / ٢ .

١١٣١ . كنز العمّال : ٣٨٦٥٧ .

١١٣٢ . الملاحم والفتن : ٣١٤ / ٤٤٥ .

١١٣٣ . الغيبة للنعماني : ص ٣٢٩ .

١١٣٤ . الترمذي : ٥ / ٣٨٢ .

١١٣٥ . الغيبة للنعماني : ٣١٨ / ٥ .

١١٣٦ . بحار الأنوار : ٦٠ / ٢١٣ / ٢٢ .

١١٣٧ . بحار الأنوار : ٦٠ / ٢١٦ / ٣٨ .

١١٣٨ . بحار الأنوار : ٦٠ / ٢١٦ / ٣٧ .

١١٣٩ . الإسراء : ٥ .

١١٤٠ . بحار الأنوار : ٦٠ / ٢١٦ / ٤٠ .

١١٤١ . بحار الأنوار : ٥ / ١٣ / ١٩ .

١١٤٢ . بحار الأنوار : ٥ / ٥٩ / ١٠٩ .

١١٤٣ . بحار الأنوار : ٧٨ / ٣٢٣ / ٢٣ .

١١٤٤ . التوحيد : ٣٦٠ / ٣ .

١١٤٥ . بحار الأنوار : ٥ / ١٧ / ٢٧ .

١١٤٦ . بحار الأنوار : ٥ / ٤ / ٣ وص٥٦ / ٩٩ وص٥٧ / ١٠٤ .

١١٤٧ . بحار الأنوار : ٥ / ١١ / ١٧ .

١١٤٨ . ابراهيم : ١٥ .

١١٤٩ . هود : ٥٩ .

١١٥٠ . التوحيد : ٢٠ / ٩ .

١١٥١ . غرر الحكم : ١٠٥٨٧ .

١١٥٢ . نهج البلاغة : الخطبة ٢١٦ .

١١٥٣ . تنبيه الخواطر : ١ / ١٩٩ .

١١٥٤ . غرر الحكم : ٧٦٩٧ .

١١٥٥ . غرر الحكم : ٨٤٧١ .

١١٥٦ . غرر الحكم : ٢٦٩٥ .

١١٥٧ . وسائل الشيعة : ١١ / ٣٠٤ / ٧ .

١١٥٨ . نهج البلاغة : الحكمة ٣ .

١١٥٩ . غرر الحكم : ١٨٣٧ .

١١٦٠ . غرر الحكم : ٢٥٨٢ .

١١٦١ . غرر الحكم : ٥٧٧٣ .

١١٦٢ . تحف العقول : ٢٢٥ .

١١٦٣ . دعائم الإسلام : ١ / ٣٤٢ .

١١٦٤ . بحار الأنوار : ١٠٠ / ٤٩ / ١٦ .

١١٦٥ . لأجل التعرّف على موضوع الجدال والحوار في تاريخ الفلسفة والأديان يراجع مدخل كتاب «الحواريين الحضارات في الكتاب والسنّة» .

١١٦٦ . الحجّ : ٣ .

١١٦٧ . غافر : ٤ .

١١٦٨ . بحار الأنوار : ٢ / ١٣٨ / ٥٢ .

١١٦٩ . الخصال : ٦١٥ / ١٠ .

١١٧٠ . النحل : ١٢٥ .

١١٧١ . شرح نهج البلاغة : ٢٠ / ٢٨٥ / ٢٦٠ .

١١٧٢ . بحار الأنوار : ٢ / ١٢٥ / ٢ .

١١٧٣ . غرر الحكم : ١٠٣٦ .

١١٧٤ . تحف العقول : ٧٠ ، شرح نهج البلاغة : ١٦ / ٦٦ .

١١٧٥ . غرر الحكم : ٧٠١٦ .

١١٧٦ . غرر الحكم : ٥٤٢٦ .

١١٧٧ . غرر الحكم : ١٧١٧ .

١١٧٨ . غرر الحكم : ٦٧٣ .

١١٧٩ . بحار الأنوار : ٧٧ / ٤٢٠ / ٤٠ .

١١٨٠ . غرر الحكم : ٨٠٤٠ـ٨٦٨٠ .

١١٨١ . الخصال : ٤٣٤ / ٢٠ .

١١٨٢ . المعارج : ١٩ـ٢١ .

١١٨٣ . تحف العقول : ٤٠ .

١١٨٤ . بحار الأنوار : ٨٢ / ١٤٤ / ٢٩ .

١١٨٥ . غرر الحكم : ٢٥٢٧ .

١١٨٦ . نهج البلاغة : الحكمة ٣٢٢ .

١١٨٧ . مسكّن الفؤاد : ٩٩ .

١١٨٨ . تحف العقول : ٤١٤ .

١١٨٩ . النجم : ٣١ .

١١٩٠ . غرر الحكم : ٦٩١٨ .

١١٩١ . يوسف : ٢٢ .

١١٩٢ . الصافّات : ١٠٤، ١٠٥ .

١١٩٣ . طه : ١٢٤، ١٢٧ .

١١٩٤ . الأعراف : ١٥٢ .

١١٩٥ . الأعراف : ٤١ .

١١٩٦ . الحجرات : ١٢ .

١١٩٧ . صحيح مسلم : ٤ / ١٩٨٥ / ٢٨ .

١١٩٨ . كنز العمّال : ٣١٥٩٧، ١٥٠٣٥ .

١١٩٩ . النور : ٢٧ .

١٢٠٠ . كنز العمّال : ٨٨٢٧.

١٢٠١ . الكافي : ٢ / ٣٥٥ / ٥ .

١٢٠٢ . تهذيب الأحكام : ١٠ / ٤٨ / ١٧٧ .

١٢٠٣ . بحار الأنوار : ٧٨ / ٢٥٣ / ١٠٩ .

١٢٠٤ . سنن أبي داود : ٢ / ٤٥٣ / ٤٨٨٨ .

١٢٠٥ . وسائل الشيعة : ١١ / ٤٤ / ٤ .

١٢٠٦ . الكافي : ٧ / ٤٣١ / ١٥ .

١٢٠٧ . بحار الأنوار : ٧٥ / ٤٦٩ / ٤ .

١٢٠٨ . مكارم الأخلاق : ١ / ٦٦ / ٧٢ .

١٢٠٩ . المجادلة : ١١ .

١٢١٠ . بحار الأنوار : ٨٤ / ٣٥٤ / ٢ .

١٢١١ . بحار الأنوار : ١٦ / ٢٣٦ .

١٢١٢ . قرب الإسناد : ٦٩ / ٢٢٢ .

١٢١٣ . مكارم الأخلاق : ١ / ٦٦ / ٧١ .

١٢١٤ . بحار الأنوار : ٧٨ / ٣٠٤ / ١ .

١٢١٥ . غرر الحكم : ١٠٢٨٣ .

١٢١٦ . النساء : ١٤٠ .

١٢١٧ . بحار الأنوار : ١٠ / ٩٨ / ١ .

١٢١٨ . بحارالأنوار ، ٧٥ / ٤٦٨ / ١٦ .

١٢١٩ . الكافي : ٢ / ٣٧٨ / ١٠ .

١٢٢٠ . الكافي : ٢ / ٣٧٧ / ٨ .

١٢٢١ . الكافي : ٢ / ٣٧٤ / ١ .

١٢٢٢ . بحار الأنوار : ٧٧ / ٨٩ / ٣ .

١٢٢٣ . بحار الأنوار : ٩٣ / ١٦٣ / ٤٢ .

١٢٢٤ . كذا في المصدر والصحيح «شاجب» ؛ أي هالك .

١٢٢٥ . بحار الأنوار : ٧٤ / ١٨٩ / ١٨ .

١٢٢٦ . بحار الأنوار : ٧٥ / ٤٦٥ / ٦ .

١٢٢٧ . قرب الإسناد : ٣٦ / ١١٧ .

١٢٢٨ . بحار الأنوار : ٧٥ / ٤٦٧ / ١٧ .

١٢٢٩ . الكافي : ٢ / ٥٠٤ / ٤ .

١٢٣٠ . بحار الأنوار : ١ / ٢٠٤ / ٢٢ .

١٢٣١ . تحف العقول : ٤٤ ، الأمالي للطوسي : ١٥٧ / ٢٦٢ مع تفاوت يسير في اللفظ ، وأُنظر الذكر : باب ١٣٤٣ .

١٢٣٢ . بحار الأنوار : ٧٤ / ١٨٨ / ١٨ .

١٢٣٣ . تنبيه الخواطر : ٢ / ١٢٠ .

١٢٣٤ . غرر الحكم : ٤٧٨٦ .

١٢٣٥ . غرر الحكم : ٤٧٨٧ .

١٢٣٦ . غرر الحكم : ٤٧٢٣ .

١٢٣٧ . بحار الأنوار : ٧٨ / ١٤١ / ٣٥ .

١٢٣٨ . الخصال : ٥٦٩ / ١ .

١٢٣٩ . تنبيه الخواطر : ٢ / ٣٢ .

١٢٤٠ . غرر الحكم : ٥٠٧٢ .

١٢٤١ . نهج البلاغة : الخطبة ٨٦ .

١٢٤٢ . الكافي : ٢ / ٣٧٥ / ٣ .

١٢٤٣ . الأصول الستّة عشر : ٥٧ .

١٢٤٤ . كنز العمّال : ١٠٢٨ .

١٢٤٥ . كنز العمّال : ١٠٣٢ .

١٢٤٦ . كنز العمّال : ٢٠٢٤١ .

١٢٤٧ . كنز العمّال : ٢٠٢٤٢ .

١٢٤٨ . معاني الأخبار : ١٥٤ / ٢ .

١٢٤٩ . كنز العمّال : ١٦٤٤، بحار الأنوار : ٢ / ٢٦٦ / ٢٣ مع تفاوت يسير في اللفظ .

١٢٥٠ . الخصال : ٢ / ٣٨٣ .

١٢٥١ . بحار الأنوار : ٨٩ / ٢٦٧ / ٥ .

١٢٥٢ . بحار الأنوار : ١٠٤ / ٧٣ / ٢٤ .

١٢٥٣ . بحار الأنوار : ٨٩ / ٢٨٣ / ٢٨ .

١٢٥٤ . ثواب الأعمال : ٢٢٠ / ١ .

١٢٥٥ . بحار الأنوار : ٨١ / ١٢٩ / ١٨ .

١٢٥٦ . الأعراف : ٣٢ .

١٢٥٧ . كنز العمّال : ١٧١٦٦ .

١٢٥٨ . مكارم الأخلاق : ١ / ٨٥ / ١ .

١٢٥٩ . قرب الإسناد : ٦٧ / ٢١٥ .

١٢٦٠ . وسائل الشيعة : ٣ / ٣٤٠ / ٤ .

١٢٦١ . كنز العمّال : ٥١٧٠ .

١٢٦٢ . عيون أخبار الرضا ﷺ : ٢ / ٧٤ / ٣٤٤ .

١٢٦٣ . بحار الأنوار : ٧٧ / ٥٩ / ٣ .

١٢٦٤ . غرر الحكم : ٤٨٤٨ .

١٢٦٥ . وسائل الشيعة : ١ / ٤٣٢ / ٢ .

١٢٦٦ . وسائل الشيعة : ١ / ٤٣٢ / ١ .

١٢٦٧ . تحف العقول : ٣٧ .

١٢٦٨ . نهج السعادة : ١ / ٥١ .

١٢٦٩ . بحار الأنوار : ٧٧ / ٣٨١ / ٥ .

١٢٧٠ . بحار الأنوار : ٧١ / ٢٩٣ / ٦٣ .

١٢٧١ . أعلام الدين : ٣١٣ .

١٢٧٢ . المائدة : ٦ .

١٢٧٣ . وسائل الشيعة : ١ / ٥٠١ / ٣ .

١٢٧٤ . وسائل الشيعة : ١ / ٤٩٥ / ١ .

١٢٧٥ . نهج البلاغة : الكتاب ٥٣، اُنظر تمام الكلام .

١٢٧٦ . نهج البلاغة : الكتاب ٥٣، اُنظر تمام الكلام .

١٢٧٧ . غرر الحكم : ٨٣٢٩ .

١٢٧٨ . غرر الحكم : ٣٩٣٢ .

١٢٧٩ . الفتح : ٧ .

١٢٨٠ . المدّثّر : ٣١ .

١٢٨١ . التوبة : ٤٠ .

١٢٨٢ . آل عمران : ١٣٣ .

١٢٨٣ . نهج البلاغة : الخطبة ٢٨ .

١٢٨٤ . غرر الحكم : ١٠٢٤ .

١٢٨٥ . غرر الحكم : ٣٩٧ .

١٢٨٦ . التوبة : ١١١ .

١٢٨٧ . بحار الأنوار : ٧٨ / ١٣ / ٧١ .

١٢٨٨ . غرر الحكم : ٤٦٩٨ .

١٢٨٩ . غرر الحكم : ٤٧٠٠ .

١٢٩٠ . التوحيد : ٢١ / ١٣ .

١٢٩١ . النساء : ١٢٤ .

١٢٩٢ . مريم : ٦٣ .

١٢٩٣ . الكافي : ٢ / ١٠٠ / ٦ .

١٢٩٤ . الكافي : ٢ / ٣٠٠ / ٢ .

١٢٩٥ . تنبيه الخواطر : ١ / ٢٧٢ .

١٢٩٦ . دعائم الإسلام : ١ / ٢١٩ .

١٢٩٧ . الكافي : ٢ / ١٠٣ / ٢ .

١٢٩٨ . آل عمران : ١٤٢ .

١٢٩٩ . غرر الحكم : ٤٢٠٤ .

١٣٠٠ . الكافي : ٢ / ٨٩ / ٧ .
قالَ المجلسيُّ رِضوانُ اللهِ علَيهِ : مَضمونُ الخبرِ متَّفَقٌ علَيهِ بين الخاصّةِ والعامّةِ . (مرآة العقول : ٨ / ١٣٢) .

١٣٠١ . بحار الأنوار : ٧٨ / ٣٥٦ / ١١ .

١٣٠٢ . معاني الأخبار : ٤١١ / ٩٩ .

١٣٠٣ . الأمالي للصدوق : ١٥٠ / ١٤٧ .

١٣٠٤ . المائدة : ٧٢ .

١٣٠٥ . الزهد للحسين بن سعيد : ٩ / ١٧ .

١٣٠٦ . كنز العمّال : ٤٣٧٧٧ .

١٣٠٧ . تنبيه الخواطر : ٢ / ٢٢٧ .

١٣٠٨ . ص : ٥٠ .

١٣٠٩ . الفضائل : ص ١٢٩ .

١٣١٠ . الخصال : ٤٠٨ / ٦ .

١٣١١ . طه : ٧٥ .

١٣١٢ . الخصال : ٩٣ / ٣٩ .

١٣١٣ . نهج البلاغة : الخطبة ٨٥ .

١٣١٤ . غرر الحكم : ٣٥١٤ .

١٣١٥ . بحار الأنوار : ٨ / ١٣٣ / ٣٩ .

١٣١٦ . بحار الأنوار : ٨ / ١٢٠ / ١١ .

١٣١٧ . المعجم الكبير : ١ / ٣١٩ / ٩٥٠ .

١٣١٨ . كنز العمّال : ١٦٦٣٦ .

١٣١٩ . تنبيه الخواطر : ١ / ٥٧ .

١٣٢٠ . الأمالي للصدوق : ٣٢٦ / ٣٨٣ .

١٣٢١ . غرر الحكم : ٥٥٩٩ .

١٣٢٢ . غرر الحكم : ٥٥٩١ .

١٣٢٣ . غرر الحكم : ٥٥٨٤ .

١٣٢٤ . كنز العمّال : ١٠٢٢١ .

١٣٢٥ . بحار الأنوار : ٧٤ / ٣٠٨ / ٦١ .

١٣٢٦ . الاختصاص : ٣٤٣ .

١٣٢٧ . نهج البلاغة : الحكمة ٢٥٥ .

١٣٢٨ . معاني الأخبار : ٢٣٨ / ٢ .

١٣٢٩ . مشكاة الأنوار : ٤٦٩ / ١٥٧١ .

١٣٣٠ . مشكاة الأنوار : ٢٩٤ / ٨٩٨ .

١٣٣١ . معاني الأخبار : ٢٣٧ / ١ .

١٣٣٢ . التحريم : ٩ .

١٣٣٣ . التوبة : ٢٤ .

١٣٣٤ . صحيح مسلم : ٣ / ١٥١٧ / ١٥٨ .

١٣٣٥ . عوالي اللآلي : ١ / ٢٨٢ / ١٢١ .

١٣٣٦ . نهج البلاغة : الخطبة ٢٧ .

١٣٣٧ . غرر الحكم : ١٣٤٦ .

١٣٣٨ . وسائل الشيعة : ١١ / ٩ / ١٥ .

١٣٣٩ . بحار الأنوار : ٣٣ / ٤٤٧ / ٦٥٩ .

١٣٤٠ . شرح نهج البلاغة : ٣ / ١٨٢ .

١٣٤١ . النساء : ٩٥ .

١٣٤٢ . كنز العمّال : ١٠٦٨٠ .

١٣٤٣ . مستدرك الوسائل : ١١ / ١٣ / ١٢٢٩٣ .

١٣٤٤ . غرر الحكم : ١٣٤٧ .

١٣٤٥ . مستدرك الوسائل : ١١ / ٢٤ / ١٢٣٣٣ .

١٣٤٦ . وسائل الشيعة : ١١ / ١٤ / ٢ .

١٣٤٧ . كنز العمّال : ١٠٦٦٤ .

١٣٤٨ . كنز العمّال : ١٠٧٩١ .

١٣٤٩ . بحار الأنوار : ١٠٠ / ٤٩ / ٢٣ .

١٣٥٠ . نهج البلاغة : الكتاب ٤٧ .

١٣٥١ . الأمالي للصدوق : ٦٧٣ / ٩٠٦ .

١٣٥٢ . الخصال : ٢٣٢ / ٧٤ .

١٣٥٣ . الأنفال : ٦٠ .

١٣٥٤ . آل عمران : ٢٠٠ .

١٣٥٥ . كنز العمّال : ١٠٥٠٨ .

١٣٥٦ . كنز العمّال : ١٠٦١١ .

١٣٥٧ . كنز العمّال : ١٠٧٣٠ .

١٣٥٨ . سنن الترمذي : ٤ / ١٧٥ / ١٦٣٩ .

١٣٥٩ . تحف العقول : ٢٤٣ .

١٣٦٠ . الخصال : ٦٢٠ / ١٠ .

١٣٦١ . كنز العمّال : ١١٢٦١؛ تنبيه الخواطر : ١ / ٩٦ .

١٣٦٢ . غرر الحكم : ٤٧٥٥ .

١٣٦٣ . غرر الحكم : ٥٤٠٦ .

١٣٦٤ . تحف العقول : ٣٩٩ .

١٣٦٥ . معاني الأخبار : ١٦٠ / ١ .

١٣٦٦ . غرر الحكم : ٣٢٣٢ .

١٣٦٧ . تحف العقول : ٢٨٦ .

١٣٦٨ . غرر الحكم : ٤٧٦١ .

١٣٦٩ . غرر الحكم : ٢٤٨٩ .

١٣٧٠ . تنبيه الخواطر : ٢ / ١١٩ .

١٣٧١ . تنبيه الخواطر : ٢ / ١٢٢ .

١٣٧٢ . تنبيه الخواطر : ٢ / ١٢٢ .

١٣٧٣ . غرر الحكم : ٤٧٦٠ .

١٣٧٤ . غرر الحكم : ٥٤٠٧ .

١٣٧٥ . غرر الحكم : ٤٣١٩ .

١٣٧٦ . نهج البلاغة : الخطبة ٢٣٠ .

١٣٧٧ . غرر الحكم : ٦٠٠٩ .

١٣٧٨ . الكافي : ٨ / ١١ .

١٣٧٩ . الأمالي للصدوق : ٧٣ / ٤١ .

١٣٨٠ . المحاسن : ١ / ٤٥٦ / ١٠٥٣ .

١٣٨١ . المحاسن : ١ / ٤٥٥ / ١٠٥٢ .

١٣٨٢ . غرر الحكم : ٨٢٠ .

١٣٨٣ . غرر الحكم : ١٤٦٤ .

١٣٨٤ . غرر الحكم : ٩٣٠ .

١٣٨٥ . غرر الحكم : ٨١٩ .

١٣٨٦ . غرر الحكم : ١٦٩٤ .

١٣٨٧ . الدرّة الباهرة : ٤٤ .

١٣٨٨ . بحار الأنوار : ١ / ١٦٠ / ٣٩ .

١٣٨٩ . تحف العقول : ٢٩ .

١٣٩٠ . غرر الحكم : ١٨٠٩ .

١٣٩١ . غرر الحكم : ١١٢٥ .

١٣٩٢ . غرر الحكم : ١٢٨٥ .

١٣٩٣ . نهج البلاغة : الحكمة ٧٠ .

١٣٩٤ . غرر الحكم : ٣٨٦٤ .

١٣٩٥ . غرر الحكم : ٤٤٩ .

١٣٩٦ . غرر الحكم : ٦٣٢٧ .

١٣٩٧ . تحف العقول : ٧٣ .

١٣٩٨ . أعلام الدين : ٣٠٣ .

١٣٩٩ . الدرّة الباهرة : ٤١ .

١٤٠٠ . غرر الحكم : ٣٢٦٢ .

١٤٠١ . غرر الحكم : ٦٣٧١ .

١٤٠٢ . غرر الحكم : ٢٩٣٦ .

١٤٠٣ . مطالب السؤول : ٥٥ .

١٤٠٤ . الأمالي للطوسي : ٥٦ / ٧٨ .

١٤٠٥ . غرر الحكم : ٧٠٥٤ .

١٤٠٦ . غرر الحكم : ١٠١٨٧ .

١٤٠٧ . بحار الأنوار : ٧٠ / ٣٧٩ / ٢٦ .

١٤٠٨ . تنبيه الخواطر : ٢ / ١٢٢ .

١٤٠٩ . نهج البلاغة : الحكمة ٣٨٤ .

١٤١٠ . غرر الحكم : ٥٣٨٤ .

١٤١١ . معاني الأخبار : ٤٠١ / ٦٢ .
١٤١٢ . تحف العقول : ٣١٧ .
١٤١٣ . تحف العقول : ٤٨٧ .
١٤١٤ . مطالب السؤول : ٥٧ .
١٤١٥ . كشف الغمّة : ٣ / ١٣٧ .
١٤١٦ . يونس : ٣٩ .
١٤١٧ . الأمالي للطوسي : ٤٩٤ / ١٠٨٢ .
١٤١٨ . غرر الحكم : ١٠٢٤٦ .
١٤١٩ . النبأ : ٢١، ٢٢ .
١٤٢٠ . غرر الحكم : ٢٦٢٠ .
١٤٢١ . غرر الحكم : ٩٩٩٥ .
١٤٢٢ . البقرة : ٢٤ .
١٤٢٣ . الجنّ : ١٥ .
١٤٢٤ . الحاقّة : ٣٠ـ٣٢ .
١٤٢٥ . بحار الأنوار : ٨ / ٢٨٠ / ١ .
١٤٢٦ . بحار الأنوار : ٨ / ٢٨٠ / ١ .
١٤٢٧ . الغاشية : ٦، ٧ .
١٤٢٨ . الحاقّة : ٣٥، ٣٦ .
١٤٢٩ . الأمالي للطوسي : ٥٣٣ / ١١٦٢ .
١٤٣٠ . بحار الأنوار : ٨ / ٢٨٠ / ١ .
١٤٣١ . الواقعة : ٥٤، ٥٥ .
١٤٣٢ . بحار الأنوار : ٨ / ٣٠٢ / ٥٨ .
١٤٣٣ . عيون أخبار الرّضا عليه السلام : ٢ / ٢٨ / ٢٠ .
١٤٣٤ . كنز العمّال : ٣٩٥٠٧ .
١٤٣٥ . كنز العمّال : ٢٨٩٧٧ .
١٤٣٦ . الدرّ المنثور : ١ / ١٧٨ .
١٤٣٧ . غرر الحكم : ٣٢١٧ .
١٤٣٨ . غرر الحكم : ٣٢٢٥ .
١٤٣٩ . الكافي : ٢ / ٣١٠ / ١٠ ، ثواب الأعمال : ٢٦٥ / ٧ .
١٤٤٠ . التوحيد : ٤٠٧ / ٦ .
١٤٤١ . كنز العمّال : ٢٨٤ .
١٤٤٢ . الزهد للحسين بن سعيد : ٩٦ / ٢٦٠ .
١٤٤٣ . الإسراء : ٨٤ .
١٤٤٤ . الكافي : ٢ / ٨٥ / ٥ .
١٤٤٥ . نهج البلاغة : الحكمة ٢٤٣ .
١٤٤٦ . غرر الحكم : ٥٣٧٨ .
١٤٤٧ . غرر الحكم : ٨٦٤٠ .
١٤٤٨ . غرر الحكم : ٩٤١٧ .
١٤٤٩ . غرر الحكم : ٥١٣٦ .
١٤٥٠ . غرر الحكم : ٤١٠٤ .
١٤٥١ . غرر الحكم : ٥٣٠٣ .
١٤٥٢ . معاني الأخبار : ٢٣٨ / ٢ .
١٤٥٣ . غرر الحكم : ٤٧١٦ .
١٤٥٤ . غرر الحكم : ٤٧٢٩ .
١٤٥٥ . الإرشاد : ١ / ٣٠٣ .
١٤٥٦ . غرر الحكم : ٣٣٠ .
١٤٥٧ . كشف الغمّة : ٢ / ٢٤٢ .
١٤٥٨ . النوادر للراوندي : ١٣٨ / ١٨٣ .
١٤٥٩ . غرر الحكم : ٣١٨٥ .
١٤٦٠ . كشف الغمّة : ٢ / ٢٤٢ .
١٤٦١ . بحار الأنوار : ٧٨ / ٢٣١ / ٢٧ .
١٤٦٢ . النساء : ٣٦ .
١٤٦٣ . مكارم الأخلاق : ١ / ٢٧٤ / ٨٣٤ .
١٤٦٤ . نهج البلاغة : الكتاب ٤٧ .
١٤٦٥ . الكافي : ٢ / ٦٦٧ / ٨ .
١٤٦٦ . تحف العقول : ٤٠٩ ، الكافي : ٢ / ٦٦٧ / ٩ وفيه «صبرك» بدل «الصبر» .
١٤٦٧ . الكافي : ٢ / ٦٦٧ / ٦ .
١٤٦٨ . عيون أخبار الرّضا عليه السلام : ٢ / ٢٤ / ٢ .
١٤٦٩ . تحف العقول : ٨٥ .
١٤٧٠ . الكافي : ٢ / ٦٦٨ / ١٤ .
١٤٧١ . مسكّن الفؤاد : ١٠٥ .
١٤٧٢ . الخصال : ٥٤٤ / ٢٠ .
١٤٧٣ . تحف العقول : ٩٧ .
١٤٧٤ . نهج البلاغة : الحكمة ٣٠٨ .
١٤٧٥ . غرر الحكم : ٤٦٨٤ .
١٤٧٦ . تحف العقول : ٣١٦ .
١٤٧٧ . المجادلة : ٢٢ .
١٤٧٨ . غرر الحكم : ١٠١٦٤ .
١٤٧٩ . غرر الحكم : ٣١٢٤ .
١٤٨٠ . غرر الحكم : ٢٧٠٣ .
١٤٨١ . عوالي اللآلي : ١ / ٢٩٠ / ١٤٩ .
١٤٨٢ . غرر الحكم : ٦٣١٤ .
١٤٨٣ . غرر الحكم : ٧٧١٨ .

١٤٨٤ . غرر الحكم : ٧٨٥١ .

١٤٨٥ . التوبة : ٢٤ .

١٤٨٦ . البقرة : ١٦٥ .

١٤٨٧ . بحار الأنوار : ٩٨ / ٢٢٦ / ٣ .

١٤٨٨ . بحار الأنوار : ٧٠ / ٢٥ / ٢٥ .

١٤٨٩ . جامع الأخبار : ٥١٨ / ١٤٦٨ .

١٤٩٠ . الكافي : ٨ / ١٢٩ / ٩٨ .

١٤٩١ . إرشاد القلوب : ١٩٩ .

١٤٩٢ . الكافي : ٢ / ٨٢ / ٥ .

١٤٩٣ . الكافي : ٢ / ١٣٠ / ١٠ .

١٤٩٤ . البقرة : ١٩٥ .

١٤٩٥ . البقرة : ٢٢٢ .

١٤٩٦ . آل عمران : ٧٦ .

١٤٩٧ . آل عمران : ١٤٦ .

١٤٩٨ . آل عمران : ١٥٩ .

١٤٩٩ . المائدة : ٤٢ .

١٥٠٠ . الصفّ : ٤ .

١٥٠١ . الكافي : ٢ / ١١٢ / ٨ .

١٥٠٢ . الكافي : ٢ / ٩٩ / ٣٠ .

١٥٠٣ . المحاسن : ١ / ٤٥٦ / ١٠٥٦ .

١٥٠٤ . البقرة : ١٩٠ .

١٥٠٥ . المائدة : ٦٤ .

١٥٠٦ . الأنعام : ١٤١ .

١٥٠٧ . النحل : ٢٣ .

١٥٠٨ . تحف العقول : ٤٩ .

١٥٠٩ . الأمالي للصدوق : ٣٧١ / ٤٦٧ .

١٥١٠ . آل عمران : ٣١ .

١٥١١ . غرر الحكم : ٤٠٦٦ .

١٥١٢ . الكافي : ٨ / ١٤ / ١ .

١٥١٣ . بحار الأنوار : ٧١ / ١٥٦ / ٧٤ ، كنز العمّال : ١٨٨٢ نحوه .

١٥١٤ . كنز العمّال : ١٧٧٦ .

١٥١٥ . الأمالي للصدوق : ٤٣٨ / ٥٧٧ .

١٥١٦ . المحاسن : ١ / ٤٥٤ / ١٠٤٧ .

١٥١٧ . تنبيه الخواطر : ٢ / ١٢٢ .

١٥١٨ . الكافي : ٨ / ١٢٩ / ٩٨ .

١٥١٩ . قصص الأنبياء : ٢٠٥ / ٢٦٦ .

١٥٢٠ . كنز العمّال : ٢٤٦٣٨ .

١٥٢١ . علل الشرائع : ١٤٠ / ١ ، عيون أخبار الرضا عليه السلام : ١ / ٢٩١ / ٤١ ، الأمالي للصدوق : ٦١ / ٢١ ، معاني الأخبار : ٣٩٩ / ٥٨ .

١٥٢٢ . المحاسن : ١ / ٤١١ / ٩٣٧ .

١٥٢٣ . الكافي : ٢ / ١٢٧ / ١٦ .

١٥٢٤ . تحف العقول : ٤٥٥ .

١٥٢٥ . علل الشرائع : ١٤٠ / ٣ .

١٥٢٦ . علل الشرائع : ١٣٩ / ١ ، الأمالي للطوسي : ٢٧٨ / ٥٣١ وفيه «بما يغذوكم» بدل «لما يغدوكم» .

١٥٢٧ . المحاسن : ١ / ٢٣٢ / ٤١٩ ، مشكاة الأنوار : ١٥٣ / ٣٧٣ .

١٥٢٨ . الدعوات : ٢٤٩ / ٦٩٩ .

١٥٢٩ . البقرة : ٢٥٦ .

١٥٣٠ . المناقب لابن شهر آشوب : ٤ / ٢ .

١٥٣١ . وسائل الشيعة : ١١ / ١٨٥ / ٤ .

١٥٣٢ . غرر الحكم : ٦١٩١ .

١٥٣٣ . غرر الحكم : ٨٩٧٧ .

١٥٣٤ . كنز العمّال : ٢٤٦٨٤ ـ ٢٤٦٨٥ .

١٥٣٥ . كنز العمّال : ٢٥٥٥٣ .

١٥٣٦ . كتاب من لا يحضره الفقيه : ٣ / ٣١ / ٣٢٦٦ .

١٥٣٧ . تهذيب الأحكام : ١٠ / ١٤٢ / ٥٦٤ .

١٥٣٨ . الكافي : ٧ / ٢٦٣ / ٢١ .

١٥٣٩ . وسائل الشيعة : ١٣ / ١٥٦ / ١ و ح ٢ نحوه .

١٥٤٠ . الكافي : ٧ / ٢٨٥ / ١ .

١٥٤١ . كتاب من لا يحضره الفقيه : ٤ / ١١٥ .

١٥٤٢ . تهذيب الأحكام : ٦ / ٣١٤ / ٨٧٠ .

١٥٤٣ . دعائم الإسلام : ٢ / ٥٣٩ / ١٩١٦ .

١٥٤٤ . دعائم الإسلام : ٢ / ٤٤٣ / ١٥٤٤ .

١٥٤٥ . كتاب من لا يحضره الفقيه : ٣ / ٣١ / ٣٢٦٥ .

١٥٤٦ . تهذيب : ١٠ / ١٧٤ .

١٥٤٧ . سنن ابى داود : ٣ / ٣١٤ / ٣٦٣٠ .

١٥٤٨ . الأحزاب : ٥٩ .

١٥٤٩ . نهج البلاغة : الكتاب ٣١ .

١٥٥٠ . تنبيه الخواطر : ٢ / ٧٨ .

١٥٥١ . غرر الحكم : ٥٨٢٠ .

١٥٥٢ . آل عمران : ٩٧ .

١٥٥٣ . الحجّ : ٢٧ .

١٥٥٤ . البقرة : ١٩٦ .

١٥٥٥ . نهج البلاغة : الكتاب ٤٧ .

١٥٥٦ . الخصال : ٦٢٠ / ١٠ .

١٥٥٧ . الخصال : ٦٢٨ / ١٠ .

١٥٥٨ . الخصال : ٦٣٥ / ١٠ .

١٥٥٩ . نهج البلاغة : الخطبة ١ .

١٥٦٠ . ثواب الأعمال : ٧٠ / ٣ .

١٥٦١ . الأمالي للطوسي : ٢٩٦ / ٥٨٢ .

١٥٦٢ . الأمالي للصدوق : ٧١٥ / ٩٨٥ ، التوحيد : ٢٥٣ / ٤ .

١٥٦٣ . بحار الأنوار : ٩٩ / ٤٥ / ٣٤ .

١٥٦٤ . عيون أخبار الرضا عليه السلام : ٢ / ١١٩ / ١ .

١٥٦٥ . تحف العقول : ٧ .

١٥٦٦ . الخصال : ١١٧ / ١٠١ .

١٥٦٧ . الأمالي للطوسي : ٦٩٤ / ١٤٧٨ .

١٥٦٨ . ثواب الأعمال : ٧٠ / ٤ .

١٥٦٩ . الخصال : ٦١٦ / ١٠ .

١٥٧٠ . عيون أخبار الرضا عليه السلام : ٢ / ٢٦٢ / ٢٩ .

١٥٧١ . عيون أخبار الرضا عليه السلام : ٢ / ٢٦٢ / ٣٠ .

١٥٧٢ . بحار الأنوار : ٧٧ / ٥٨ / ٣ .

١٥٧٣ . ثواب الأعمال : ٢٨١ / ١ .

١٥٧٤ . المائدة : ٩٧ .

١٥٧٥ . علل الشرائع : ٤٥٢ / ١ .

١٥٧٦ . بحار الأنوار : ٢٧ / ١٨١ / ٣٠ .

١٥٧٧ . البقرة : ١٩٧ .

١٥٧٨ . الخصال : ١٤٨ / ١٨٠ .

١٥٧٩ . الدرّ المنثور : ٢ / ٦٣ .

١٥٨٠ . ثواب الأعمال : ٧٤ / ١٦ .

١٥٨١ . الخصال : ١٦٧ / ٢١٩ ، علل الشرائع : ٢٣٥ / ٤ .

١٥٨٢ . في الطبعة المعتمدة «يأمروا» وما أثبتناه من طبعة مؤسسة آل البيت عليهم السلام .

١٥٨٣ . وسائل الشيعة : ٩ / ٣ / ٤ .

١٥٨٤ . الكافي : ٤ / ٢٦٣ / ٤٥ .

١٥٨٥ . بحار الأنوار : ٧ / ٣٠٢ / ٥٦ .

١٥٨٦ . كمال الدين : ٣٤٦ / ٣٣ .

١٥٨٧ . الإسراء : ١٥ .

١٥٨٨ . الأنفال : ٤٢ .

١٥٨٩ . غرر الحكم : ٦٧٨١ .

١٥٩٠ . غرر الحكم : ٨٤٨٢ .

١٥٩١ . التوحيد : ٤٥٩ / ٢٧ .

١٥٩٢ . التوحيد : ٤١٠ / ٢ .

١٥٩٣ . الكافي : ٢ / ٤٠٠ / ٨ .

١٥٩٤ . الأنعام : ١٤٩ .

١٥٩٥ . بحار الأنوار : ٢ / ٢٩ / ١٠ .

١٥٩٦ . الكافي : ١ / ١٧٧ / ٤ .

١٥٩٧ . النساء : ١٦٥ .

١٥٩٨ . غرر الحكم : ١١٠٠٤ .

١٥٩٩ . نهج السعادة : ١ / ٣٤٧ .

١٦٠٠ . بحار الأنوار : ٢ / ١٤٤ / ٥ .

١٦٠١ . الأمالي للمفيد : ٤٢ / ١٠ .

١٦٠٢ . بحار الأنوار : ٢ / ١٥٢ / ٤٣ .

١٦٠٣ . الأمالي للصدوق : ٢٤٧ / ٢٦٦ .

١٦٠٤ . بحار الأنوار : ٢ / ١٤٥ / ٩ .

١٦٠٥ . بحار الأنوار : ٢ / ١٥٠ / ٢٤ .

١٦٠٦ . بحار الأنوار : ٢ / ١٥٦ / ١٠ .

١٦٠٧ . كنز الفوائد : ٢ / ٣١ .

١٦٠٨ . بحار الأنوار : ٢ / ١٦٠ / ١٣ .

١٦٠٩ . معاني الأخبار : ٢ / ٣ .

١٦١٠ . الأمالي للطوسي : ٢٢٧ / ٣٩٨ ، وفي معناه أحاديث كثيرة جدّاً ، فراجع : بحار الأنوار : ٢ / ١٥٨ باب ٢١ و كنزالعمّال : ١٠ / ٢٢١ _ ٢٢٣ وص ٢٣٠ _ ٢٣٧ .

١٦١١ . كنز العمّال : ٢٩٢٥٥ .

١٦١٢ . بحار الأنوار : ٢ / ٢١٢ / ١١٤ .

١٦١٣ . كنز العمّال : ٩٠٧ .

١٦١٤ . الكافي : ١ / ٦٩ / ٤ .

١٦١٥ . بصائر الدرجات : ٢١ / ١ .

١٦١٦ . معاني الأخبار : ٣٩٠ / ٣٠ .

١٦١٧ . كنز العمّال : ٢٩١٧٩ .

١٦١٨ . بحار الأنوار : ٢ / ١٦٤ / ٢٤ .

١٦١٩ . كنز العمّال : ٢٩٢٨٤ .

١٦٢٠ . الكافي : ١ / ٥٢ / ٧ .

١٦٢١ . الكافي : ١ / ٥٣ / ١٤ .

١٦٢٢ . بحار الأنوار : ٢ / ١٦٩ / ٣ .

١٦٢٣ . عيون أخبار الرضا عليه السلام : ١ / ٢٩٠ / ٣٩ .

١٦٢٤ . الكافي : ١ / ٥٩ / ٢ .

١٦٢٥ . كنز العمّال : ١٢٩٧١ .

١٦٢٦ . كتاب من لا يحضره الفقيه : ٤ / ٧٤ / ٥١٤٦ ، كنز العمّال : ١٢٩٧٢ .
١٦٢٧ . كنز العمّال : ١٤٥٩٩؛ الكافي : ٧ / ١٧٤ / ١ مع تفاوت يسير في اللفظ وفيه : «ليلة وأيّامها» .
١٦٢٨ . مستدرك الوسائل : ١٨ / ٩ / ٢١٨٤٣ .
١٦٢٩ . دعائم الإسلام : ٢ / ٤٤٢ / ١٥٣٩ .
١٦٣٠ . كنز العمّال : ٤٣٨٣٧ .
١٦٣١ . كتاب من لا يحضره الفقيه : ٤ / ٧٤ / ٥١٤٦ .
١٦٣٢ . دعائم الإسلام : ٢ / ٦٥ / ١٨١ .
١٦٣٣ . مستدرك الوسائل : ١٨ / ٢٤ / ٢١٩٠١ .
١٦٣٤ . الكافي : ٧ / ٢١٠ / ٤ .
١٦٣٥ . البقرة : ٢٢٩ .
١٦٣٦ . عوالي اللآلي : ٢ / ١٥٣ / ٤٢٧ .
١٦٣٧ . الكافي : ٧ / ٢٦٠ / ١ ، تهذيب الأحكام : ١٠ / ١٤٨ / ٥٨٧ نحوه .
١٦٣٨ . علل الشرائع : ٥٤٥ / ١ .
١٦٣٩ . كنز العمّال : ١٢٩٦٤ ، ١٢٩٦٦ ، ١٣٣٦٦ ، ١٣٣٦٧ مثله معنىً .
١٦٤٠ . تحف العقول : ٢١٤ .
١٦٤١ . تنبيه الخواطر : ١ / ١١٦ .
١٦٤٢ . كنز العمّال : ١٤٠٠٢ .
١٦٤٣ . بحار الأنوار : ٤٠ / ٢٧٧ .
١٦٤٤ . جعفريّات : ١٣٦ .
١٦٤٥ . غرر الحكم : ٧٠٥ .
١٦٤٦ . غرر الحكم : ٤٠٦ .
١٦٤٧ . غرر الحكم : ٢٦٧٤ .
١٦٤٨ . نهج البلاغة : الخطبة ٢٧ .
١٦٤٩ . كنز العمّال : ١١٣٠٠ ، ١١٣٩٦ مع تفاوت يسير في اللفظ .
١٦٥٠ . نهج البلاغة : الخطبة ٥٥ .
١٦٥١ . شرح نهج البلاغة : ٣ / ١٨٦ .
١٦٥٢ . تحف العقول : ١٩١ ، اُنظر تمام الحديث .
١٦٥٣ . قرب الإسناد : ١٣١ / ٤٥٦ .
١٦٥٤ . نهج البلاغة : الخطبة ١٢٤ .
١٦٥٥ . نهج البلاغة : الكتاب ١٤ .
١٦٥٦ . الكافي : ٥ / ٢٨ / ٢ .
١٦٥٧ . علل الشرائع : ٥٦٥ / ١ .
١٦٥٨ . وسائل الشيعة : ١١ / ١٠٢ / ١ .
١٦٥٩ . الأنفال : ١٦ .
١٦٦٠ . في نهج السعادة : «فإنّه عارٌ باقٍ في الأعقابِ والأعناق» .
١٦٦١ . نهج البلاغة : الخطبة ٦٦ ، نهج السعادة : ٢ / ٢٣٢ .
١٦٦٢ . الكافي : ٥ / ٣٤ / ١ .
١٦٦٣ . عيون أخبار الرضا ﷺ : ٢ / ٩٢ / ١ .
١٦٦٤ . كنز العمّال : ٣٩٨٧٨ .
١٦٦٥ . نهج البلاغة : الكتاب ١٥ .
١٦٦٦ . الكافي : ٥ / ٤٥ / ٨ .
١٦٦٧ . المائدة : ٣٣ .
١٦٦٨ . الجعفريّات : ٨٣ .
١٦٦٩ . المحاسن : ٢ / ١٠٧ / ١٢٨٩ .
١٦٧٠ . قرب الأسناد : ص ١٥٨ ح ٥٧٧ .
١٦٧١ . الكافي : ٧ / ٢٤٦ / ٦ ، تهذيب الأحكام : ١٠ / ١٣٤ / ٥٣٠ .
١٦٧٢ . دعائم الإسلام : ٢ / ٤٧٧ / ١٧١٤ ، اُنظر وسائل الشيعة : ١٨ / ٥٣٣ / ٣ .
١٦٧٣ . الخصال : ٢٨٤ / ٣٣ .
١٦٧٤ . نهج السعادة : ١ / ١٩٨ .
١٦٧٥ . غرر الحكم : ١٠٣٧١ .
١٦٧٦ . غرر الحكم : ٤٦٧ .
١٦٧٧ . غرر الحكم : ٣٦٠٥ .
١٦٧٨ . غرر الحكم : ٤١٣ .
١٦٧٩ . الكافي : ٢ / ٨٩ / ٦ .
١٦٨٠ . بحار الأنوار : ٧٣ / ١٦٧ / ٣١ .
١٦٨١ . غرر الحكم : ٩٨٢ .
١٦٨٢ . غرر الحكم : ١١٠٧ .
١٦٨٣ . غرر الحكم : ٢٨٠ .
١٦٨٤ . غرر الحكم : ١٨٧٧ .
١٦٨٥ . غرر الحكم : ١٣٧٠ .
١٦٨٦ . الأمالي للصدوق : ٤٧٨ / ٦٤٤ .
١٦٨٧ . غرر الحكم : ٩٦ .
١٦٨٨ . غرر الحكم : ١٧٥٣ .
١٦٨٩ . غرر الحكم : ٧٧٢٣ .
١٦٩٠ . غرر الحكم : ٣٦٥ .
١٦٩١ . أعلام الدين : ص ٤٢٨ .
١٦٩٢ . الكافي : ٢ / ٣١٦ / ٧ .
١٦٩٣ . الكافي : ٢ / ١٣٨ / ٦ .
١٦٩٤ . علل الشرائع : ٥٥٩ / ١ .
١٦٩٥ . كنز العمّال : ٤٤٠٩٥ .

١٦٩٦ . غرر الحكم : ٦١٩٥ .

١٦٩٧ . غرر الحكم : ٥٧٧٢ .

١٦٩٨ . كنز العمّال : ٩١٩٩ .

١٦٩٩ . جامع الأخبار : ٣٩٠ / ١٠٨٤ .

١٧٠٠ . الخصال : ٦٢١ / ١٠ .

١٧٠١ . دعائم الإسلام : ٢ / ١٦ / ١٤ .

١٧٠٢ . غرر الحكم : ٤٠٦٩ .

١٧٠٣ . غرر الحكم : ٩٣٨٢ .

١٧٠٤ . غرر الحكم : ٧٥٩٥ .

١٧٠٥ . عدّة الداعي : ١٤١ .

١٧٠٦ . تنبيه الخواطر : ٢ / ١٢٠ .

١٧٠٧ . الأمالي للطوسي : ٦٨٠ / ١٤٤٧ .

١٧٠٨ . الفرقان : ٢٣ .

١٧٠٩ . الكافي : ٢ / ٨١ / ٥ .

١٧١٠ . ثواب الأعمال : ٣٣٤ / ١ .

١٧١١ . كنز العمّال : ٤٣١١٣ .

١٧١٢ . النوادر للراوندي : ١٥٢ / ٢٢٣ .

١٧١٣ . المائدة : ٥٦ .

١٧١٤ . غرر الحكم : ٢٨٢٨ .

١٧١٥ . التوحيد : ١٦٦ / ٣ .

١٧١٦ . المجادلة : ١٩ .

١٧١٧ . الكافي : ١ / ٥٤ / ١ .

١٧١٨ . نهج البلاغة : الخطبة ١٩٤

١٧١٩ . بحار الأنوار : ٧١ / ٣٣٩ / ٨ .

١٧٢٠ . غرر الحكم : ٧٩١٣ ، ٧٩١٤ .

١٧٢١ . عيون أخبار الرّضا : ٢ / ٥٤ / ٢٠٤ .

١٧٢٢ . غرر الحكم : ٣٣٦٧ .

١٧٢٣ . تحف العقول : ٣٥٦ . وفي الكافي : ١ / ٢٧ / ٢٩ «الحزم مساءة الظنّ» .

١٧٢٤ . تحف العقول : ٩٠ .

١٧٢٥ . عوالي اللآلي : ١ / ٢٩٢ / ١٦٤ .

١٧٢٦ . غرر الحكم : ١٠٦٨٢ .

١٧٢٧ . غرر الحكم : ١٩١٥ .

١٧٢٨ . تحف العقول : ٢١٤ .

١٧٢٩ . غرر الحكم : ١٥١٤ .

١٧٣٠ . غرر الحكم : ١٩٨٤ .

١٧٣١ . غرر الحكم : ٢٠٢٦ .

١٧٣٢ . غرر الحكم : ١٨٧٨ .

١٧٣٣ . غرر الحكم : ٢١٧٩ .

١٧٣٤ . الأمالي للصدوق : ٧٣ / ٤١ .

١٧٣٥ . أعلام الدين : ٣٣٣ .

١٧٣٦ . غرر الحكم : ٢٨٣٢ .

١٧٣٧ . الأمالي للصدوق : ٦٣٦ / ٨٥٣ .

١٧٣٨ . تحف العقول : ٢١٤ .

١٧٣٩ . غرر الحكم : ١٠٣٩ .

١٧٤٠ . الدعوات : ١١٨ / ٢٧٦ .

١٧٤١ . أعلام الدين : ٢٩٤ .

١٧٤٢ . الأمالي للطوسي : ٥٣٣ / ١١٦٢ .

١٧٤٣ . تحف العقول : ٩٩ .

١٧٤٤ . بحار الأنوار : ٧٣ / ٢٥٦ / ٢٩ .

١٧٤٥ . نهج البلاغة : الحكمة ١٢٧ .

١٧٤٦ . دعائم الإسلام : ١ / ٢٢٣ .

١٧٤٧ . يونس : ٦٢ .

١٧٤٨ . تحف العقول : ٦ .

١٧٤٩ . أعلام الدين : ٣٤٣ .

١٧٥٠ . قرب الإسناد : ٧٦ / ٢٤٤ .

١٧٥١ . مطالب السؤول : ٥٥ .

١٧٥٢ . بحار الأنوار : ٧٧ / ٢١١ / ١ .

١٧٥٣ . الخصال : ٦١٢ / ١٠ .

١٧٥٤ . الأمالي للصدوق : ٥٦ / ١٢ .

١٧٥٥ . المحاسن : ٢ / ٣٦٢ / ٢٢٦٢ .

١٧٥٦ . الدعوات : ١٢٠ / ٢٨٤ .

١٧٥٧ . علل الشرائع : ٩٣ / ٢ .

١٧٥٨ . بحار الأنوار : ٧٤ / ٢٢٧ / ٢٠ .

١٧٥٩ . مكارم الأخلاق : ٢ / ٣٦٧ / ٢٦٦١ .

١٧٦٠ . الكافي : ٢ / ٩٩ / ٣٠ .

١٧٦١ . التمحيص : ٤٤ / ٥٥ .

١٧٦٢ . الكافي : ٢ / ٢٢٦ / ١٦ .

١٧٦٣ . أعلام الدين : ٣٤٥ .

١٧٦٤ . غرر الحكم : ٣٨٠ .

١٧٦٥ . الحشر : ١٨ .

١٧٦٦ . بحار الأنوار : ٧٠ / ٧٣ / ٢٦ .

١٧٦٧ . غرر الحكم : ٦٧٩٤ .

١٧٦٨ . تحف العقول : ٢٨٠ .

١٧٦٩ . الاختصاص : ٢٦ .

١٧٧٠ . غرر الحكم : ٨٩٢٧ .

١٧٧١ . بحار الأنوار : ٧٠ / ٧٣ / ٢٧ .

١٧٧٢ . غرر الحكم : ٧٨٨٧ .

١٧٧٣ . عيون أخبار الرّضا : ٢ / ٦٢ / ٢٥٨ .

١٧٧٤ . الأمالي للصدوق : ٣٢٨ / ٣٨٨ .

١٧٧٥ . بحار الأنوار : ٧ / ٢٦١ / ١٠ .

١٧٧٦ . الأمالي للصدوق : ٣٧٤ / ٤٧٢ .

١٧٧٧ . مجمع البيان : ١٠ / ٨١٢ .

١٧٧٨ . الخصال : ٢٥٣ / ١٢٥ .

١٧٧٩ . بحار الأنوار : ٧ / ٢٧٢ / ٣٩ .

١٧٨٠ . أعلام الدين : ٣٤٤ .

١٧٨١ . بحار الأنوار : ٧١ / ٣٨٣ / ٢٠ .

١٧٨٢ . بحار الأنوار : ٧٤ / ١٠٢ / ٥٤ .

١٧٨٣ . الاحتجاج : ١ / ٥٧٢ / ١٣٧ .

١٧٨٤ . بحار الأنوار : ٧ / ٢٦٦ / ٢٦ .

١٧٨٥ . الانشقاق : ٧، ٨ .

١٧٨٦ . معاني الأخبار : ٢٦٢ / ١ .

١٧٨٧ . الزمر : ١٠ .

١٧٨٨ . كنز العمّال : ١٦٦٣٥ .

١٧٨٩ . بحار الأنوار : ٨٢ / ١٣٨ / ٢٢ .

١٧٩٠ . الكافي : ٢ / ١٢٦ / ٨ .

١٧٩١ . الكافي : ٢ / ٢٦٤ / ١٩ .

١٧٩٢ . مشكاة الأنوار : ٥١٧ / ١٧٤٢ .

١٧٩٣ . عيون أخبار الرّضا : ٢ / ٣٤ / ٦٦ .

١٧٩٤ . تنبيه الخواطر : ١ / ١٢٧ .

١٧٩٥ . الخصال : ٨٠ / ١ .

١٧٩٦ . الفلق : ٥ .

١٧٩٧ . الكافي : ٢ / ٣٠٧ / ٦ .

١٧٩٨ . غرر الحكم : ٣٧٢ .

١٧٩٩ . غرر الحكم : ٣٣٢ .

١٨٠٠ . غرر الحكم : ٥٢٤٢ .

١٨٠١ . شرح نهج البلاغة : ١ / ٣١٦ .

١٨٠٢ . غرر الحكم : ٤٦٣٢ .

١٨٠٣ . غرر الحكم : ١٨٣٢ .

١٨٠٤ . بحار الأنوار : ٧٣ / ٢٥٦ / ٢٩ .

١٨٠٥ . كنز الفوائد : ١ / ١٣٦ .

١٨٠٦ . غرر الحكم : ١٥٢٠ .

١٨٠٧ . غرر الحكم : ١٠١٧ .

١٨٠٨ . شرح نهج البلاغة : ١ / ٣١٦ .

١٨٠٩ . الكافي : ٢ / ٣٠٦ / ١ .

١٨١٠ . الكافي : ٨ / ٨ / ١ .

١٨١١ . الخصال : ١٢١ / ١١٣ .

١٨١٢ . مريم : ٣٩ .

١٨١٣ . الزمر : ٥٦ .

١٨١٤ . الفرقان : ٢٧ .

١٨١٥ . كنز العمّال : ١٤٩٣٦ .

١٨١٦ . نهج البلاغة : الحكمة ٤٢٩ .

١٨١٧ . الأمالي للطوسي : ٦٦٣ / ١٣٨٦ .

١٨١٨ . كنز العمّال : ٤٤٠٨٤ .

١٨١٩ . الأنعام : ١٦٠ .

١٨٢٠ . تحف العقول : ٢٨١ .

١٨٢١ . البقرة : ٢٦١ .

١٨٢٢ . بحار الأنوار : ٧١ / ٢٤٧ / ٧ .

١٨٢٣ . النساء : ١٢٥ .

١٨٢٤ . تفسير نور الثقلين : ١ / ٥٥٣ / ٥٧٩ .

١٨٢٥ . الإسراء : ٧ .

١٨٢٦ . غرر الحكم : ٣٨٠٨ـ٣٨٠٩ .

١٨٢٧ . النحل : ٩٠ .

١٨٢٨ . تحف العقول : ٣٧ .

١٨٢٩ . غرر الحكم : ٦١١٢ .

١٨٣٠ . غرر الحكم : ٩٩١٢ .

١٨٣١ . غرر الحكم : ٥٤٥٠ .

١٨٣٢ . غرر الحكم : ٨٤٧٣ .

١٨٣٣ . غرر الحكم : ٤٣٣٩ .

١٨٣٤ . كنز الفوائد : ٢ / ٣١ .

١٨٣٥ . غرر الحكم : ٣٦٣٧ .

١٨٣٦ . كنز العمّال : ١٦٤٨٩ .

١٨٣٧ . بحار الأنوار : ٣ / ٨٠ .

١٨٣٨ . كنز العمّال : ٢٩٣٣٦ .

١٨٣٩ . بحار الأنوار : ٦٢ / ٢٦٦ / ٣٩ .

١٨٤٠ . غرر الحكم : ٩٦٦ .

١٨٤١ . غرر الحكم : ٥٣٠ .

١٨٤٢ . غرر الحكم : ٤٢٢ .

١٨٤٣ . غرر الحكم : ٢٢٠٣ .

١٨٤٤ . غرر الحكم : ٥٥٢٢ .

١٨٤٥ . غرر الحكم : ١٩٦٢ .

١٨٤٦ . غرر الحكم : ١٠٤٣٦ .

١٨٤٧ . بحار الأنوار : ٧٨ / ٣٦٩ / ٤ .

١٨٤٨ . تحف العقول : ٤٨٨ .

١٨٤٩ . تحف العقول : ٣١٠ .

١٨٥٠ . بحار الأنوار : ٧٢ / ٤٧ / ٥٧ .

١٨٥١ . بحار الأنوار : ٧٥ / ١٤٧ / ٢١ .

١٨٥٢ . التمحيص : ٥٠ / ٨٩ .

١٨٥٣ . بحار الأنوار : ٧٢ / ٤٤ / ٥٢ .

١٨٥٤ . تنبيه الخواطر : ١ / ٣١ .

١٨٥٥ . تنبيه الخواطر : ٢ / ١٢٢ .

١٨٥٦ . الكافي : ٢ / ٣٥١ / ٥ .

١٨٥٧ . الأنبياء : ١٨ .

١٨٥٨ . غرر الحكم : ٧١٦ .

١٨٥٩ . نهج السعادة : ٣ / ٢٩٤ .

١٨٦٠ . تحف العقول : ٩٥ .

١٨٦١ . بحار الأنوار : ٥ / ٣٠٥ / ٢٤ .

١٨٦٢ . الزخرف : ٧٨ .

١٨٦٣ . نهج البلاغة : الحكمة ٣٧٦ .

١٨٦٤ . بحار الأنوار : ٧٠ / ١٨٤ / ٥٢ .

١٨٦٥ . الأمالي للصدوق : ٧٢ / ٤١ .

١٨٦٦ . بحار الأنوار : ٧٤ / ١٥٧ / ٢ .

١٨٦٧ . نهج البلاغة : الخطبة ١٢٥ .

١٨٦٨ . تحف العقول : ٤٠٨ .

١٨٦٩ . كنز العمّال : ٤٣٥٨٨ .

١٨٧٠ . تحف العقول : ٨٨ .

١٨٧١ . كنز العمّال : ٤٣١٥٢ .

١٨٧٢ . بحار الأنوار : ٧٨ / ٢٢٨ / ١٠٥ .

١٨٧٣ . مجمع البيان : ١ / ٢١١ ، روضة الواعظين : ٣٩ .

١٨٧٤ . نهج البلاغة : الخطبة٢١٦ .

١٨٧٥ . غرر الحكم : ١٠٣٢٨ .

١٨٧٦ . مكارم الأخلاق : ٢ / ٣٦٥ / ٢٦٦١ .

١٨٧٧ . نهج البلاغة : الخطبة ٢١٦ .

١٨٧٨ غرر الحكم : ٤٧٨٠ .

١٨٧٩ نهج البلاغة : الخطبة ٢١٦ .

١٨٨٠ . الكافي : ٢ / ١٦٩ / ١ .

١٨٨١ . بحار الأنوار : ٧٤ / ٢٨٧ / ١٣ .

١٨٨٢ . الكافي : ٢ / ١٧٠ / ٤ .

١٨٨٣ . الخصال : ٣٥١ / ٢٧ .

١٨٨٤ . الكافي : ٢ / ١٧٤ / ١٤ .

١٨٨٥ . الكافي : ٢ / ١٦٩ / ٢ .

١٨٨٦ . الاحتجاج : ٢ / ٥١٧ / ٣٤٠ .

١٨٨٧ . كنز العمّال : ٩٧٣٨ .

١٨٨٨ . كنز العمّال : ٩٧٢٣ .

١٨٨٩ . غرر الحكم : ٢٥٦ .

١٨٩٠ . غرر الحكم : ٦٠٧ .

١٨٩١ . غرر الحكم : ١١٢ .

١٨٩٢ . الكافي : ٨ / ١٩ / ٤ .

١٨٩٣ . غرر الحكم : ٩٣٤٩ .

١٨٩٤ . نهج البلاغة : الكتاب ٥٣ .

١٨٩٥ . دعائم الإسلام : ٢ / ٣٥ / ٧٨ .

١٨٩٦ . بحار الأنوار : ١٠٣ / ٨٧ / ٣ .

١٨٩٧ . بحار الأنوار : ٦٢ / ٢٩٢ ؛ كنز العمّال : ٩٧١٦ .

١٨٩٨ . كنز العمّال : ٩٧١٧ .

١٨٩٩ . كنز العمّال : ٩٧١٥ .

١٩٠٠ . كنز العمّال : ٩٧٣٩ .

١٩٠١ . بحار الأنوار : ٦٢ / ٢٩٢ .

١٩٠٢ . الأمالي للطوسي : ٦٧٦ / ١٤٢٧ .

١٩٠٣ . غرر الحكم : ٤٦٥ .

١٩٠٤ . غرر الحكم : ١٨٤٢ .

١٩٠٥ . البقرة : ٢٦٩ .

١٩٠٦ . بحار الأنوار : ١٤ / ٣١٦ / ١٧ .

١٩٠٧ . بحار الأنوار : ١٣ / ٤٣٢ / ٢٤ .

١٩٠٨ . بحار الأنوار : ٧٧ / ١٧٢ / ٨ .

١٩٠٩ . كنز العمّال : ٤٤١٢٣ .

١٩١٠ . غرر الحكم : ١٧١٥ .

١٩١١ . غرر الحكم : ١٩٩٢ .

١٩١٢ . تحف العقول : ٩٧ .

١٩١٣ . الأمالي للطوسي : ٦٢٥ / ١٢٩٠ .

١٩١٤ . نهج البلاغة : الحكمة ٨٠ .

١٩١٥ . غرر الحكم : ٧٤٩٩ .

١٩١٦ . تحف العقول : ٢١٨ .

١٩١٧ . غرر الحكم : ٣٠٥٢ .
١٩١٨ . غرر الحكم : ٩٤٥٠ .
١٩١٩ . بحار الأنوار : ١ / ٢١٥ / ٢٢ .
١٩٢٠ . بحار الأنوار : ١ / ٢١٥ / ٢٥ .
١٩٢١ . بحار الأنوار : ١٣ / ٤١٧ / ١٠ .
١٩٢٢ . كنز العمّال : ٥٨٧٣ ، بحار الأنوار : ٧٨ / ٤٥٣ / ٢٣ .
١٩٢٣ . الأمالي للصدوق : ٥٧٦ / ٧٨٨ .
١٩٢٤ . كنز العمّال : ٥٤٤٤ .
١٩٢٥ . غرر الحكم : ٥٢٥٨ .
١٩٢٦ . غرر الحكم : ٢٢٧٢ .
١٩٢٧ . غرر الحكم : ١٠٩١٦ .
١٩٢٨ . الكافي : ٢ / ١٢٨ / ١ .
١٩٢٩ . تنبيه الخواطر : ٢ / ١١٩ .
١٩٣٠ . غرر الحكم : ١٠٥٧٣ .
١٩٣١ . بحار الأنوار : ٧٨ / ٢٥٥ / ١٢٩ .
١٩٣٢ . بحار الأنوار : ٧٨ / ٣١٢ / ١ .
١٩٣٣ . بحار الأنوار : ٧٨ / ٣٧٠ / ٤ .
١٩٣٤ . غرر الحكم : ٨٧٠٦ .
١٩٣٥ . بحار الأنوار : ٧٨ / ٢٤٧ / ٧٣ .
١٩٣٦ . قصص الأنبياء : ١٦٠ / ١٧٦ .
١٩٣٧ . بحار الأنوار : ٧٨ / ٣٠٣ / ١ .
١٩٣٨ . البقرة : ٢٢٤ .
١٩٣٩ . الكافي : ٧ / ٤٣٤ / ١ .
١٩٤٠ . ثواب الأعمال : ٢٦١ / ٢ .
١٩٤١ . ثواب الأعمال : ٢٧٠ / ٣ .
١٩٤٢ . ثواب الأعمال : ٢٦٩ / ١ .
١٩٤٣ . بحار الأنوار : ١٠٤ / ٢٠٩ / ١٩ .
١٩٤٤ . نهج البلاغة : الحكمة ٢٥٣ .
١٩٤٥ . المائدة : ٤ .
١٩٤٦ . البقرة : ١٦٨ .
١٩٤٧ . غرر الحكم : ٦١٣١ .
١٩٤٨ . في تهذيب الأحكام : ٧ / ١٣ / ٥٨ «مُجالَدَة» وهو الأنسب .
١٩٤٩ . الكافي : ٥ / ١٦١ / ١ .
١٩٥٠ . كنز العمّال : ٣٠٣٤٥ .
١٩٥١ . في معنى الحديث أحاديث كثيرة ، اُنظر كنز العمّال : ١٠ / ٦٣٧ وما بعده ، و ج ١ / ٩٢ .
١٩٥٢ . بحار الأنوار : ٤٣ / ٧٠ / ٦١ .
١٩٥٣ . غرر الحكم : ١٠٥٥ .
١٩٥٤ . غرر الحكم : ١٤٢٠ .
١٩٥٥ . غرر الحكم : ٤٧١٨ .
١٩٥٦ . الكافي : ٢ / ١١١ / ١ .
١٩٥٧ . غرر الحكم : ٤٢٧٤ .
١٩٥٨ . غرر الحكم : ٦٠٨٤ .
١٩٥٩ . نهج البلاغة : الحكمة ٤٦٠ .
١٩٦٠ . نهج البلاغة : الحكمة ٢٠٧ .
١٩٦١ . بحار الأنوار : ٧٧ / ٢٠٨ / ١ .
١٩٦٢ . كنز الفوائد : ١ / ٣١٩ .
١٩٦٣ . جامع الأخبار : ٣١٩ / ٨٩٦ .
١٩٦٤ . غرر الحكم : ١٧٧٦ .
١٩٦٥ . الكافي : ٢ / ١١٢ / ٦ .
١٩٦٦ . غرر الحكم : ١١١١ .
١٩٦٧ . بحار الأنوار : ٧٨ / ١٠٢ / ٢ .
١٩٦٨ . بحار الأنوار : ٧٤ / ١٧٨ / ٢١ .
١٩٦٩ . الأمالي للصدوق : ٤٧٨ / ٦٤٤ .
١٩٧٠ . الكافي : ٢ / ١١٢ / ٣ .
١٩٧١ . غرر الحكم : ٦٨٧ .
١٩٧٢ . غرر الحكم : ٢٨٤٩ .
١٩٧٣ . نهج السعادة : ٣ / ٢٢٥ .
١٩٧٤ . الاختصاص : ٢٢١ .
١٩٧٥ . نهج البلاغة : الحكمة ٣٤٩ .
١٩٧٦ . غرر الحكم : ٤٥٢٠ .
١٩٧٧ . غرر الحكم : ٩٤٤٥ .
١٩٧٨ . غرر الحكم : ١٠٢٥١ .
١٩٧٩ . الأمالي للطوسي : ٦١٣ / ١٢٦٨ .
١٩٨٠ . الأمالي للصدوق : ٣٤٣ / ٤٠٩ .
١٩٨١ . غرر الحكم : ٣٠٨٩ .
١٩٨٢ . غرر الحكم : ٣٢٨٣ .
١٩٨٣ . غرر الحكم : ٣٣٤٣ .
١٩٨٤ . غرر الحكم : ١١٦٠ .
١٩٨٥ . كتاب من لا يحضره الفقيه : ١ / ١١٥ / ٢٣٧ .
١٩٨٦ . الخصال : ١٥٥ / ١٩٤ .
١٩٨٧ . بحار الأنوار : ٧٦ / ٧٥ / ١٩ .
١٩٨٨ . مكارم الأخلاق : ١ / ١٢٥ / ٢٩٨ .
١٩٨٩ . الخصال : ٤٢٠ / ١٤ .

١٩٩٠ . غرر الحكم : ٨٦١٠ .

١٩٩١ . الكافي : ٢ / ١٩٩ / ١٠ .

١٩٩٢ . ثواب الأعمال : ٣٤٠ / ١ .

١٩٩٣ . بحار الأنوار : ٧٤ / ٣١٥ / ٧٢ .

١٩٩٤ . الأمالي للطوسي : ٤٨١ / ١٠٥١ .

١٩٩٥ . الكافي : ٢ / ١٩٧ / ٦ .

١٩٩٦ . الأمالي للطوسي : ٩٧ / ١٤٧ .

١٩٩٧ . تحف العقول : ٣٠٣ .

١٩٩٨ . الكافي : ٢ / ١٩٣ / ١ .

١٩٩٩ . الكافي : ٢ / ١٩٣ / ٤ .

٢٠٠٠ . الكافي : ٢ / ٣٦٥ / ٤ .

٢٠٠١ . بحار الأنوار : ٧٤ / ٢٨٧ / ١٣ .

٢٠٠٢ . ثواب الأعمال : ٢٩٧ / ١ .

٢٠٠٣ . ثواب الأعمال : ٢٨٦ / ٢ .

٢٠٠٤ . عيون أخبار الرّضا : ٢ / ١٧٩ / ٢ .

٢٠٠٥ . بحار الأنوار : ٧٨ / ٥٦ / ١١١ .

٢٠٠٦ . تحف العقول : ٢٧٨ .

٢٠٠٧ . تحف العقول : ٢٩٤ .

٢٠٠٨ . الأمالي للطوسي : ١١٠ / ١٦٨ .

٢٠٠٩ . بحار الأنوار : ٢ / ٢٥٩ / ٩ .

٢٠١٠ . بحار الأنوار : ٢ / ٢٦٠ / ١١ .

٢٠١١ . نهج البلاغة : الخطبة ١٣٣ .

٢٠١٢ . الأنبياء : ٣٠ .

٢٠١٣ . تحف العقول : ٣٧٠ .

٢٠١٤ . تحف العقول : ٤٨٩ .

٢٠١٥ . الإرشاد : ١ / ٢٩٦ .

٢٠١٦ . غرر الحكم : ٥٤٠ .

٢٠١٧ . بحار الأنوار : ٧ / ٢٧٦ / ٥٠ .

٢٠١٨ . الكافي : ٢ / ١٢٠ / ١٢ .

٢٠١٩ . كنز العمّال : ٢٤٩٥٧ .

٢٠٢٠ . في المصدر : «يطيق»، والتصويب من مستدرك الوسائل .

٢٠٢١ . الجعفريّات : ٨٥ ، مستدرك الوسائل : ٨ / ٢٥٨ / ٩٣٩٣ .

٢٠٢٢ . الكافي : ٦ / ٥٣٨ / ٤ ، الخصال : ٦١٨ / ١٠ .

٢٠٢٣ . كنز العمّال : ٤٣١١٦ .

٢٠٢٤ . كنز العمّال : ٣٩٩٦٨ .

٢٠٢٥ . كنز العمّال : ٣٩٩٧١ .

٢٠٢٦ . كنز العمّال : ٢٤٩٧٣ .

٢٠٢٧ . كنز العمّال : ٢٤٩٨٢ .

٢٠٢٨ . كنز العمّال : ٢٤٩٧١ .

٢٠٢٩ . كنز العمّال : ٣٩٩٨١ .

٢٠٣٠ . مكارم الأخلاق : ١ / ٢٨٠ / ٨٦٤ .

٢٠٣١ . بحار الأنوار : ٧٧ / ٢١١ / ١ .

٢٠٣٢ . غرر الحكم : ٣٤٠ .

٢٠٣٣ . غرر الحكم : ٢٩٠٠ .

٢٠٣٤ . غرر الحكم : ١٣٩٣ .

٢٠٣٥ . غرر الحكم : ٥٥٢٧ .

٢٠٣٦ . كنز العمّال : ٥٧٥٧ .

٢٠٣٧ . الكافي : ٢ / ١٠٦ / ٥ .

٢٠٣٨ . بحار الأنوار : ٧٧ / ١٤٩ / ٧٥ .

٢٠٣٩ . غرر الحكم : ٦٧١٤ .

٢٠٤٠ . غرر الحكم : ٢٧٤ .

٢٠٤١ . غرر الحكم : ٨٦٥٠ .

٢٠٤٢ . عيون أخبار الرّضا : ٢ / ٥٦ / ٢٠٧ .

٢٠٤٣ . غرر الحكم : ٩٠٨١ .

٢٠٤٤ . بحار الأنوار : ٧٨ / ٢٠٠ / ٢٨ .

٢٠٤٥ . كنز العمّال : ٥٧٥١ .

٢٠٤٦ . تحف العقول : ٣٩٤ .

٢٠٤٧ . غرر الحكم : ٦٣٦٩ .

٢٠٤٨ . بحار الأنوار : ٧١ / ٣٦٦ / ١٣ .

٢٠٤٩ . كنز العمّال : ٥٤٥ .

٢٠٥٠ . كنز العمّال : ٥٨٩ .

٢٠٥١ . بحار الأنوار : ٧٠ / ٣٩٢ / ٦٠ .

٢٠٥٢ . عيون أخبار الرّضا : ٢ / ٤ / ٨ .

٢٠٥٣ . الكافي : ٢ / ٢٠٧ / ١ .

٢٠٥٤ . مستدرك الوسائل : ١٢ / ٤٢٩ / ١٤٥٢٤ .

٢٠٥٥ . الكافي : ٢ / ١٦٧ / ٩ .

٢٠٥٦ . الاختصاص : ٢٤٣ .

٢٠٥٧ . المارقون ، الخوارج والحرورية ثلاثة إلقاب لمسمّىً واحد ؛ وهم جماعة كانوا في جيش الإمام أمير المؤمنين عليه السلام في صفّين ، ثمّ انفصلوا عنه بعد قضيّة التحكيم وانتفضوا عليه .

٢٠٥٨ . الكهف : ١٠٣ ، ١٠٤ .

٢٠٥٩ . كنز العمّال : ٣١٦١٠ .

٢٠٦٠ . شرح نهج البلاغة : ٢ / ٢٧٨ .

٢٠٦١ . شرح نهج البلاغة : ٢ / ٢٦٧ .

٢٠٦٢ . نهج البلاغة : الحكمة ٣٢٣ .

٢٠٦٣ . نهج البلاغة : الخطبة ٦٠ .

٢٠٦٤ . نهج البلاغة : الخطبة ٩٣ .

٢٠٦٥ . نهج البلاغة : الخطبة ٦١ .

٢٠٦٦ . قال ابنُ أبي الحديد : مُراده أنّ الخوارج ضَلّوا بشُبهةٍ دخَلت عليهم ، كانوا يَطلُبون الحقّ ، ولهم في الجملة تَمسّكٌ بالدِّين ، ومُحاماةٌ عن عقيدةٍ اعتقدوها ، و إنْ أخطَؤوا فيها . وأمّا معاوية فلم يكن يطلب الحقّ ، و إنّما كان ذا باطل ، لا يُحامي عن اعتقادٍ قد بناه على شبهة ، وأحوالُه كانت تدلّ على ذلك ، فإنّه لم يكن من أرباب الدِّين . . . و إذا كان كذلك لم يَجُزْ أن يَنصُر المسلمون سلطانه ، وتحارَبُ الخوارج عليه و إن كانوا أهل ضلال ، لأنّهم أحسن حالاً منه ، فإنّهم كانوا يَنهون عن المنكر ، ويَرَون الخروج على أئمّة الجور واجباً . . . (شرح نهج البلاغة : ٧٨٥) .

٢٠٦٧ . تنبيه الخواطر : ٢ / ١١٨ .

٢٠٦٨ . تنبيه الخواطر : ٢ / ١١٩ .

٢٠٦٩ . الحجّ : ١١ .

٢٠٧٠ . بحار الأنوار : ٩٢ / ٢٥١ .

٢٠٧١ . الكهف : ١٠٣ ، ١٠٤ .

٢٠٧٢ . نهج البلاغة : الحكمة ٤٣٠ .

٢٠٧٣ . الخشوع امام عظمة الله جلّ وعلا .

٢٠٧٤ . الحديد : ١٦ .

٢٠٧٥ . إرشاد القلوب : ٢٠٣ .

٢٠٧٦ . غرر الحكم : ٩٩٤٥ .

٢٠٧٧ . الإقبال : ١ / ١٧٤ .

٢٠٧٨ . تحف العقول : ٢٠ .

٢٠٧٩ . غرر الحكم : ٨١٧٢ .

٢٠٨٠ . ص : ٢٠ .

٢٠٨١ . الدرّ المنثور : ١ / ٢٨٢ .

٢٠٨٢ . كنز العمّال : ١٧٩٧٤ .

٢٠٨٣ . المعجم الكبير : ٨ / ١٤٤ / ٧٦٤٠ و ص ٧٦٦٢١٥٤ .

٢٠٨٤ . سنن أبي داوود : ١ / ٢٨٩ / ١١٠٦ .

٢٠٨٥ . سنن أبي داوود : ١ / ٢٨٩ / ١١٠٧ .

٢٠٨٦ . العنكبوت : ٤٨ .

٢٠٨٧ . الفردوس : ٢ / ٢٠٠ / ٢٩٩٤ .

٢٠٨٨ . الأحقاف : ٤ .

٢٠٨٩ . الدرّ المنثور : ٧ / ٤٣٤ .

٢٠٩٠ . الدرّ المنثور : ٧ / ٤٣٤ .

٢٠٩١ . غرر الحكم : ٧٠٦ .

٢٠٩٢ . نهج البلاغة : الحكمة ٣١٥ .

٢٠٩٣ . غرر الحكم : ٢٤٦٥ .

٢٠٩٤ . ص : ٨٢ ، ٨٣ .

٢٠٩٥ . تنبيه الخواطر : ٢ / ١١٨ .

٢٠٩٦ . غرر الحكم : ٧٢٧ .

٢٠٩٧ . غرر الحكم : ٦٦٧ .

٢٠٩٨ . غرر الحكم : ٨٥٩ .

٢٠٩٩ . غرر الحكم : ٨٦٠ .

٢١٠٠ . تنبيه الخواطر : ٢ / ١٥٤ .

٢١٠١ . تحف العقول : ١٠٠ .

٢١٠٢ . بحار الأنوار : ٧٧ / ٢٨٨ / ١ .

٢١٠٣ . الكافي : ٢ / ١٦ / ٤ .

٢١٠٤ . الكافي : ٨ / ٤٦ / ٨ .

٢١٠٥ . بحار الأنوار : ٧٣ / ١٧٥ / ١٥ .

٢١٠٦ . عدّة الداعي : ١٩٤ .

٢١٠٧ . تفسير العيّاشي : ٢ / ٣٥٣ / ٩٤ .

٢١٠٨ . بحار الأنوار : ٧٧ / ١٠٣ / ١ .

٢١٠٩ . كنز العمّال : ٤٤٣٩٩ .

٢١١٠ . بحار الأنوار : ٨ / ٣٥٩ / ٢٤ .

٢١١١ . بحار الأنوار : ٧٢ / ٣٠٤ / ٥١ .

٢١١٢ . غرر الحكم : ٢١٢٨ .

٢١١٣ . الكافي : ٢ / ١٦ / ٤ .

٢١١٤ . قالَ أبو حامد الغزّاليّ ـ في بيان حقيقة الإخلاص بعد ذكر أقاويل الشّيوخ ـ : الأقاويل في هذا كثيرة ولا فائدة في تكثير النّقل بعد انكشاف الحقيقة ، و إنّما البيان الشافي بيان سيّد الأوّلين والآخرين ﷺ ، إذ سئل عن الإخلاص فقال : هو أن تقول ربّي الله ، ثمّ تستقيم كما امرت . أي لا تعبد هواك ونفسك ، ولا تعبد إلّا ربّك ، وتستقيم في عبادته كما أمرك . وهذه إشارة إلى قطع كلّ ما سوى الله عزّوجلّ عن مجرى النظر ، وهو الإخلاص حقّاً . المحجّة البيضاء : ٨ / ١٣٣ . وأخرج ابن ماجة في السنن تحت رقم ٣٩٧٢ : «أنّ سفيان بن عبدالله الثقفيّ قال : قلت : يا رسول الله ، حدّثني بأمر أعتصم به . قال : قل ربّي الله ، ثمّ استقم» .

٢١١٥ . معاني الأخبار : ٢٦١ / ١ .

٢١١٦ . غرر الحكم : ٥٥٣٨ .
٢١١٧ . غرر الحكم : ٤٦٤٢ .
٢١١٨ . غرر الحكم : ٦٧٩٣ .
٢١١٩ . غرر الحكم : ٣٠٨٨ .
٢١٢٠ . بحار الأنوار : ٨٥ / ١٣٦ / ١٦ .
٢١٢١ . عيون أخبار الرضا : ٢ / ٦٩ / ٣٢١ .
٢١٢٢ . غرر الحكم : ٨٤٤٧ .
٢١٢٣ . بحار الأنوار : ٧٠ / ٢٤٨ / ٢١ .
٢١٢٤ . يونس : ١٩ .
٢١٢٥ . مجمع البيان : ٢ / ٥٤٣ .
٢١٢٦ . آل عمران : ١٠٣ .
٢١٢٧ . كنز العمّال : ٩٢٩ .
٢١٢٨ . نهج البلاغة : الخطبة ١٢٧ .
٢١٢٩ . نهج البلاغة : الخطبة ٢٥ .
٢١٣٠ . نهج البلاغة : الحكمة ١٨٣ .
٢١٣١ . التوبة : ١٢٢ .
٢١٣٢ . معاني الأخبار : ١٥٧ / ١ .
٢١٣٣ . معاني الأخبار : ١٥٤ / ١ .
٢١٣٤ . نهج البلاغة : الخطبة ١١٣ .
٢١٣٥ . بحار الأنوار : ٧٨ / ٨١ / ٧٥ .
٢١٣٦ . كنز العمّال : ١٥١١٩ .
٢١٣٧ . كنز العمّال : ١٥١٨٨ .
٢١٣٨ . بحار الأنوار : ٥٨ / ١٠٤ / ٣٥ .
٢١٣٩ . المراد من الأوّليّة في هذه الروايات هي الأوّليّة النسبيّة ، وبناءً على هذا فلا تعارض بين روايات هذا الباب . وستتطرّق إلى هذا الموضوع بصورة أوضح في موسوعة ميزان الحكمة إن شاء الله تعالى .
٢١٤٠ . كنز العمّال : ١٥١١٥ .
٢١٤١ . بحار الأنوار : ١ / ٩٧ / ٨ .
٢١٤٢ . بحار الأنوار : ١ / ٩٧ / ٧ .
٢١٤٣ . عيون أخبار الرضا : ١ / ٢٦٢ / ٢٢ .
٢١٤٤ . بحار الأنوار : ٥٧ / ٧٣ / ٤٩ .
٢١٤٥ . التوحيد : ٦٧ / ٢٠ .
٢١٤٦ . الأنبياء : ٣٠ .
٢١٤٧ . نهج البلاغة : الخطبة ١٦٣ .
٢١٤٨ . علل الشرائع : ٦٠٧ / ٨١ .
٢١٤٩ . نهج البلاغة : الخطبة ١٠٩ .
٢١٥٠ . التوحيد : ٢٧٧ / ٢ .
٢١٥١ . التوحيد : ٢٩٨ / ٦ .
٢١٥٢ . الروم : ٣٠ .
٢١٥٣ . التوحيد : ٣٣١ / ٩ .
٢١٥٤ . التوحيد : ٢٣١ / ٥ .
٢١٥٥ . الطور : ٣٥، ٣٦ .
٢١٥٦ . التوحيد : ٦٦ / ٢٠ .
٢١٥٧ . التوحيد : ٢٩٠ / ١٠ .
٢١٥٨ . نهج البلاغة : الخطبة ١٦٣ .
٢١٥٩ . شرح نهج البلاغة : ٢٠ / ٢٥٥ .
٢١٦٠ . الإسراء : ٧٢ .
٢١٦١ . بحار الأنوار : ٣ / ٢٨ / ٢ .
٢١٦٢ . بحار الأنوار : ٣ / ٧٥ .
٢١٦٣ . بحار الأنوار : ٣ / ٧٨ .
٢١٦٤ . بحار الأنوار : ٣ / ٥٥ / ٢٩ .
٢١٦٥ . التوحيد : ٢٨٩ / ٨ .
٢١٦٦ . بحار الأنوار : ٣ / ٦٧ .
٢١٦٧ . كنز العمّال : ٥٢٢٥ .
٢١٦٨ . الخصال : ٣٠ / ١٠٦ .
٢١٦٩ . غرر الحكم : ٤٨٥٧ .
٢١٧٠ . بحار الأنوار : ٧٧ / ١٤٨ / ٧١ .
٢١٧١ . بحار الأنوار : ٧١ / ٣٩٦ / ٧٧ .
٢١٧٢ . بحار الأنوار : ٧١ / ٣٩٥ / ٧٣ .
٢١٧٣ . علل الشرائع : ٥٦٠ / ١ .
٢١٧٤ . المعجم الكبير : ١ / ٢٦٠ / ٧٥٤ .
٢١٧٥ . الكافي : ٢ / ١٠٠ / ٥ .
٢١٧٦ عيون أخبار الرضا ٢ / ٣٧ / ٩٨ بحار الأنوار : ٧١ / ٣٨٣ / ١٧ .
٢١٧٧ . بحار الأنوار : ٧١ / ٣٨٥ / ٢٦ .
٢١٧٨ . الأمالي للطوسي : ١٤٠ / ٢٢٧ .
٢١٧٩ . بحار الأنوار : ٧١ / ٣٩٢ / ٥٩ .
٢١٨٠ . بحار الأنوار : ٧١ / ٣٩٤ / ٦٣ .
٢١٨١ . غرر الحكم : ٣٤٠٤ .
٢١٨٢ . معاني الأخبار : ٢٥٣ / ١ .
٢١٨٣ . كنز العمّال : ٥١٨٠ .
٢١٨٤ . بحار الأنوار : ٧٨ / ٥٣ / ٨٩ .
٢١٨٥ . غرر الحكم : ٤٧١٢ .
٢١٨٦ . كنز العمّال : ٥٢١٧ .

٢١٨٧ . الأمالي للصدوق : ٢٩٠ / ٣٢٤ .
٢١٨٨ . معاني الأخبار : ١٩١ / ١ .
٢١٨٩ . غرر الحكم :٤٩٥٣ .
٢١٩٠ . غرر الحكم :٣١٦٥ .
٢١٩١ . غرر الحكم :٢٩٨٣ .
٢١٩٢ . الأمالي للصدوق :٢٧٨ / ٣٠٨ .
٢١٩٣ . الكافي :٢ / ١٠٠ / ٧ .
٢١٩٤ . المحجّة البيضاء : ٥ / ٩٣ .
٢١٩٥ . المعجم الكبير : ١ / ٢٦٠ / ٧٥٤ .
٢١٩٦ . بحار الأنوار : ٧١ / ٣٩٤ / ٦٣ .
٢١٩٧ . غرر الحكم :٥٦٣٩ .
٢١٩٨ . غرر الحكم :٨٥٩٥ .
٢١٩٩ . غرر الحكم :٩١٩٢ .
٢٢٠٠ . غرر الحكم :٨٠٢٣ .
٢٢٠١ . الكافي : ٦ / ٣٠٩ / ١ .
٢٢٠٢ . الكافي :٢ / ٣٢١ / ١ .
٢٢٠٣ . غرر الحكم :٣٢١٩ .
٢٢٠٤ . غرر الحكم :٣٢٢٣ .
٢٢٠٥ . بحار الأنوار :٣٦ / ٣٥٨ / ٢٢٨ .
٢٢٠٦ . نهج البلاغة : الحكمة ٤٤٥ .
٢٢٠٧ . الأمالي للطوسي : ٣٠١ / ٥٩٧ .
٢٢٠٨ . بحار الأنوار :٧٩ / ١٥٢ / ٦٤ .
٢٢٠٩ . كنز العمّال : ١٣١٨١ .
٢٢١٠ . بحار الأنوار : ٧٩ / ١٤٨ / ٥٨ .
٢٢١١ . نهج البلاغة : الحكمة ٢٥٢ .
٢٢١٢ . عيون أخبار الرضا : ٢ / ٩٨ / ٢ .
٢٢١٣ . الخصال : ٦٣٢ / ١٠ .
٢٢١٤ . الخصال : ٦٣٢ / ١٠ .
٢٢١٥ . بحار الأنوار :٧٩ / ١٢٧ / ٧ .
٢٢١٦ . بحار الأنوار :٧٩ / ١٥٠ / ٦٤ .
٢٢١٧ . ثواب الأعمال : ٢٩٠ / ٥ .
٢٢١٨ . بحار الأنوار : ٧٩ / ١٥٠ / ٦٤ .
٢٢١٩ . الكافي :٦ / ٤١٢ / ٢ .
٢٢٢٠ . بحار الأنوار :٧٧ / ١٣٣ / ٤٣ .
٢٢٢١ . بحار الأنوار :٧٧ / ١٨٠ / ١٠ .
٢٢٢٢ . بحار الأنوار : ٧٠ / ٧ / ٥ .
٢٢٢٣ . بحار الأنوار : ٧٠ / ٣٩٣ / ٦٤ .

٢٢٢٤ . غرر الحكم : ٦٦٤ .
٢٢٢٥ . الأمالي للطوسي : ١١٥ / ١٧٦ .
٢٢٢٦ . الكافي : ٢ / ٧١ / ١٢ .
٢٢٢٧ . كنز العمّال : ٥٨٩٤ .
٢٢٢٨ . بحار الأنوار : ٧٠ / ٣٨٤ / ٣٩ .
٢٢٢٩ . الكافي : ٢ / ٦٧ / ١ .
٢٢٣٠ . بحار الأنوار : ٧٥ / ٣٠٩ / ٣ .
٢٢٣١ . بحار الأنوار : ٧٠ / ٣٩٢ / ٦١ .
٢٢٣٢ . بحار الأنوار : ٧٨ / ٢٤٤ / ٥٤ .
٢٢٣٣ . غرر الحكم : ١٠٢٣٤ .
٢٢٣٤ . غرر الحكم : ١٠١٦١_١٠١٦٢ .
٢٢٣٥ . غرر الحكم :٤٠٢٧_٤٠٢٨ .
٢٢٣٦ . كنز العمّال : ٥٨٨٥ .
٢٢٣٧ . بحار الأنوار : ٧٠ / ٣٧٩ / ٢٨ .
٢٢٣٨ . غرر الحكم :١٩٨٧ .
٢٢٣٩ . غرر الحكم :٨٠٣٦ .
٢٢٤٠ . غرر الحكم : ٤٥٩١ .
٢٢٤١ . تنبيه الخواطر : ٢ / ١٠٨ .
٢٢٤٢ . الكافي : ٢ / ٦٨ / ٣ .
٢٢٤٣ . بحار الأنوار :٧٨ / ٣٦٦ / ٢ .
٢٢٤٤ . كنز العمّال : ٥٩٠٩ .
٢٢٤٥ . بحار الأنوار : ٧٧ / ١٢٦ / ٣٢ .
٢٢٤٦ . الخصال :٥٢٦ / ١٣ .
٢٢٤٧ . نهج البلاغة : الحكمة ١٧٥ .
٢٢٤٨ . غرر الحكم :٤١٠٨ .
٢٢٤٩ . غرر الحكم :٨٩٥٥ .
٢٢٥٠ . الإسراء : ٨٠ .
٢٢٥١ . بحار الأنوار :٧٦ / ٢٤٧ / ٣٧ .
٢٢٥٢ . بحار الأنوار : ٧١ / ١٧٤ / ١٠ .
٢٢٥٣ . بحار الأنوار : ١٠٣ / ١٧٥ / ٣ .
٢٢٥٤ . بحار الأنوار : ٧٥ / ١٧٢ / ١٤ .
٢٢٥٥ . غرر الحكم: ٩٦٩ .
٢٢٥٦ . الاختصاص : ٢٣١ .
٢٢٥٧ . الكافي ٥ / ٩٨ / ٢ .
٢٢٥٨ . علل الشرائع : ٥٢٨ / ٧ .
٢٢٥٩ . بحار الأنوار : ٧٧ / ٨٩ / ٣ .
٢٢٦٠ . تحف العقول : ٢٢ .

٢٢٦١ . غرر الحكم : ٢٠١٣ .
٢٢٦٢ . بحار الأنوار : ٧٥ / ١٧٥ / ٧ .
٢٢٦٣ . بحار الأنوار : ٧٨ / ٣٦٤ / ٤ .
٢٢٦٤ . غرر الحكم : ٦٣٧٤ .
٢٢٦٥ . غرر الحكم : ٩٣١٠ .
٢٢٦٦ . نهج البلاغة : الكتاب ٢٦ .
٢٢٦٧ . بحار الأنوار : ٧٧ / ٧٦ / ٣ .
٢٢٦٨ . غرر الحكم : ٦٥٤٥ .
٢٢٦٩ . غرر الحكم : ٦٤٤٢ .
٢٢٧٠ . غرر الحكم : ٨١٧٧ .
٢٢٧١ . غرر الحكم : ١١٩٩ .
٢٢٧٢ . تنبيه الخواطر : ٢ / ١٢٢ .
٢٢٧٣ . غرر الحكم : ٤٦٧٥ .
٢٢٧٤ . غرر الحكم : ٤٧٣٥ .
٢٢٧٥ . غرر الحكم : ٤٧٨١ .
٢٢٧٦ . بحار الأنوار : ٧٣ / ١٧١ / ١٠ .
٢٢٧٧ . تحف العقول : ٢٧٨ .
٢٢٧٨ . الجعفريّات : ٢٣٠ .أنظر وسائل الشيعة : ١٤ / ٢٣ / ٨ .
٢٢٧٩ . بحار الأنوار : ٧٤ / ١٧٨ / ١٧ .
٢٢٨٠ . غرر الحكم : ٤٦٧٠ .
٢٢٨١ . غرر الحكم : ٩٦٧٠ .
٢٢٨٢ . غرر الحكم : ٢١٤٢ .
٢٢٨٣ . نهج البلاغة : الحكمة ٩٤ .
٢٢٨٤ . تحف العقول : ٢٣٤ .
٢٢٨٥ . بحار الأنوار : ٧٧ / ٨٠ / ٣ .
٢٢٨٦ . كنز العمّال : ٣٠٧٦٥ .
٢٢٨٧ . كنز العمّال : ٣٠٧٦٣ .
٢٢٨٨ . غرر الحكم : ٤١١٥ .
٢٢٨٩ . بحار الأنوار : ٧٨ / ٢٩٢ / ٢ .
٢٢٩٠ . كنز العمّال : ٢٨٦٩٢ .
٢٢٩١ . الدرّ المنثور : ٣ / ٢٧٠ .
٢٢٩٢ . كنز العمّال : ٢٨٦٩١ .
٢٢٩٣ . بحار الأنوار : ٧٧ / ١٦٥ / ٢ .
٢٢٩٤ . الكافي : ٢ / ١٤٢ / ٤ .
٢٢٩٥ . الخصال : ٦٢٠ / ١٠ .
٢٢٩٦ . الكافي : ٢ / ١٤٢ / ٣ .
٢٢٩٧ . الاختصاص : ٣٤٢ .
٢٢٩٨ . الأمالي للصدوق : ٥٧٦ / ٧٨٨ .
٢٢٩٩ . غرر الحكم : ٥٠٣٢ .
٢٣٠٠ . بحار الأنوار : ٧٦ / ٢٩٢ / ١٦ .
٢٣٠١ . نهج البلاغة : الحكمة ٤٢٢ .
٢٣٠٢ . بحار الأنوار : ٧١ / ١٨٢ / ٣٧ .
٢٣٠٣ . بحار الأنوار : ٧٨ / ٤١ / ٢٦ .
٢٣٠٤ . بحار الأنوار : ٧٧ / ٢٤ / ٦ .
٢٣٠٥ . غرر الحكم : ٧٤٨٧ .
٢٣٠٦ . الأمالي للطوسي : ٢٢٣ / ٣٨٥ .
٢٣٠٧ . بحار الأنوار : ٧٨ / ٣٧٠ / ٤ .
٢٣٠٨ . كنز العمّال : ١٦٠٥٢ .
٢٣٠٩ . صحيح مسلم : ٣ / ١٥٠٦ / ١٣٣ .
٢٣١٠ . بحار الأنوار : ٩١ / ٢٦٥ / ١٩ .
٢٣١١ . غرر الحكم : ٩٤٥٣ .
٢٣١٢ . غرر الحكم : ٢٣٤٦ .
٢٣١٣ . بحار الأنوار : ٩١ / ٢٢٤ / ٤ .
٢٣١٤ . بحار الأنوار : ٩١ / ٢٥٦ / ١ .
٢٣١٥ . تهذيب الأحكام : ٣ / ٣١٠ / ٩٦٠ .
٢٣١٦ . الكافي : ٣ / ٤٧٠ / ١ .
٢٣١٧ . الكافي : ٢ / ١١٧ / ٤ .
٢٣١٨ . الكافي : ٢ / ١١٧ / ٥ .
٢٣١٩ . الكافي : ٢ / ١١٦ / ١ .
٢٣٢٠ . غرر الحكم : ٤٦٢٩ .
٢٣٢١ . غرر الحكم : ٥٦١٠ .
٢٣٢٢ . غرر الحكم : ٨٥٣٩ .
٢٣٢٣ . غرر الحكم : ٨٢٠٢ .
٢٣٢٤ . نهج البلاغة : الخطبة ٦٩ .
٢٣٢٥ . الفرقان : ٧٧ .
٢٣٢٦ . غافر : ٦٠ .
٢٣٢٧ . بحار الأنوار : ٩٣ / ٣٠٠ / ٣٧ .
٢٣٢٨ . الكافي : ٢ / ٤٦٨ / ١ .
٢٣٢٩ . الأمالي للطوسي : ٨٩ / ١٣٦ .
٢٣٣٠ . تنبيه الخواطر : ٢ / ٢٣٧ .
٢٣٣١ . بحار الأنوار : ٧٧ / ٢٠٤ / ١ .
٢٣٣٢ . بحار الأنوار : ٩٣ / ٣٠٠ / ٣٧ .
٢٣٣٣ . الكافي : ٢ / ٤٦٧ / ٨ .
٢٣٣٤ . الكافي : ٢ / ٤٦٨ / ٤ .

٢٣٣٥ . مكارم الأخلاق : ٢ / ١٢ / ٢٠٠٨ .

٢٣٣٦ . الكافي : ٢ / ٤٦٦ / ٣ .

٢٣٣٧ . الكافي : ٢ / ٤٦٩ / ٧ .

٢٣٣٨ . الكافي : ٢ / ٤٦٨ / ٥ .

٢٣٣٩ . مكارم الأخلاق : ٢ / ٧ / ١٩٧٨ .

٢٣٤٠ . الكافي : ٢ / ٤٦٩ / ٥ .

٢٣٤١ . الكافي : ٢ / ٤٧٠ / ٨ .

٢٣٤٢ . بحار الأنوار : ٩٣ / ٢٨٨ / ٣ .

٢٣٤٣ . بحار الأنوار : ٩٣ / ٣٠١ / ٣٧ .

٢٣٤٤ . مكارم الأخلاق : ٢ / ١٠ / ١٩٩٢ .

٢٣٤٥ . الزمر : ٨ .

٢٣٤٦ . النمل : ٦٢ .

٢٣٤٧ . مكارم الأخلاق : ٢ / ١٠ / ١٩٩١ .

٢٣٤٨ . بحار الأنوار : ٧٧ / ٨٧ / ٣ .

٢٣٤٩ . الكافي : ٢ / ٤٨٨ / ١ .

٢٣٥٠ . بحار الأنوار : ٩٣ / ٣٠٣ / ٣٩ .

٢٣٥١ . بحار الأنوار : ٩٣ / ٢٩٥ / ٢٣ .

٢٣٥٢ . مكارم الأخلاق : ٢ / ٩٧ / ٢٢٧٥ .

٢٣٥٣ . البقرة : ١٨٦ .

٢٣٥٤ . كنز العمّال : ٣١٥٦ .

٢٣٥٥ . غرر الحكم : ٨٢٩٢ .

٢٣٥٦ . بحار الأنوار : ٧٨ / ١١٣ / ٧ .

٢٣٥٧ . بحار الأنوار : ٩٣ / ٣٦٨ / ٤ .

٢٣٥٨ . البقرة : ١٨٦ .

٢٣٥٩ . بحار الأنوار : ٩٣ / ٣٢٣ / ٣٧ .

٢٣٦٠ . غافر : ٦٠ .

٢٣٦١ . أعلام الدين : ٢٦٩ ، اُنظر تمام الحديث .

٢٣٦٢ . إرشاد القلوب : ١٤٩ .

٢٣٦٣ . مابين القوسين أثبتناه من بحار الأنوار : ٩٣ / ٣٥٨ / ١٦ نقلاً عن المصدر .

٢٣٦٤ . مكارم الأخلاق : ٢ / ٢٠ / ٢٠٤٥ .

٢٣٦٥ . بحار الأنوار : ٩٣ / ٣٢١ / ٣١ .

٢٣٦٦ . بحار الأنوار : ٩٣ / ٣٢١ / ٣١ .

٢٣٦٧ . الدعوات : ٣٠ / ٦٠ .

٢٣٦٨ . الكافي : ٢ / ٤٧٤ / ٤ .

٢٣٦٩ . الكافي : ٢ / ٤٧٧ / ٥ .

٢٣٧٠ . ويأتي ما يناسب هذا الباب .

٢٣٧١ . بحار الأنوار : ٧٣ / ٣٢٩ / ١١ .

٢٣٧٢ . الخصال : ٣٣٧ / ٤٠ .

٢٣٧٣ . بحار الأنوار : ٧٥ / ٣١٢ / ٢٠ .

٢٣٧٤ . غرر الحكم : ٣٤٧٨ .

٢٣٧٥ . قال ابن سينا : سبب إجابة الدعاء توافي الأسباب معاً لحكمة إلٰهيّة ، وهو أن يتوافى سبب دعاء رجل فيما يدعو فيه ، وسبب وجود ذلك الشيء معاً عن الباري .

فإن قيل : فهل يصحّ وجود ذلك الشيء من دون الدعاء ، وموافاته لذلك الدعاء ؟ قلنا : لا ، لأنّ علّتهما واحدة ، وهو الباري الذي جعل سبب وجود ذلك الشيء الدعاء ، كما جعل سبب صحّة المريض شرب الدواء ، وما لم يشرب الدواء لم يصحّ ، وكذلك الحال في الدّعاء .

وموافاة ذلك الشيء فلحكمةٍ ما توافيا معاً على حسب ما قدّر وقضى ، فالدّعاء واجب وتوقع الإجابة واجب .... (بحار الأنوار : ٩٣ / ٣٦١ / ٢٣ ، اُنظر تمام الكلام) .

٢٣٧٦ . تنبيه الخواطر : ١ / ٣٠٢ .

٢٣٧٧ . الدعوات : ٥٢ / ١٣١ .

٢٣٧٨ . بحار الأنوار : ٩٣ / ٣١٧ / ٢١ .

٢٣٧٩ . الكافي : ٢ / ٤٩١ / ١ .

٢٣٨٠ . مكارم الأخلاق : ٢ / ١٩ / ٢٠٤٠ .

٢٣٨١ . الدعوات : ٥١ / ١٢٧ .

٢٣٨٢ . بحار الأنوار : ٩٣ / ٣١٨ / ٢٣ .

٢٣٨٣ . بحار الأنوار : ٩٣ / ٣١٤ / ١٩ .

٢٣٨٤ . مكارم الأخلاق : ٢ / ٨ / ١٩٨١ .

٢٣٨٥ . بحار الأنوار : ٩٣ / ٣١٤ / ٢٠ .

٢٣٨٦ . الأمالي للطوسي : ص ٥٨٤ ح ١٢٠٨ .

٢٣٨٧ . مكارم الأخلاق : ٢ / ٩٧ / ٢٢٧٥ .

٢٣٨٨ . لا يتعاظمني : أي لا يعظم عليَّ (النهاية : ٣ : ٢٦٠ «عظم») .

٢٣٨٩ . صحيح ابن حبّان : ٣ / ١٧٧ / ٨٩٦ .

٢٣٩٠ . بحار الأنوار : ٧٧ / ٢٠٥ / ١ .

٢٣٩١ . بحار الأنوار : ٩٣ / ٣١٣ / ١٧ .

٢٣٩٢ . الدعوات : ١٨ / ٧ .

٢٣٩٣ . الكافي : ٢ / ٤٨٧ / ٢ .

٢٣٩٤ . بحار الأنوار : ٩٣ / ٣٠٥ / ١ .

٢٣٩٥ . الكافي : ٢ / ٤٧٣ / ١ .

٢٣٩٦ . يوسف : ٩٨ .

٢٣٩٧ . الكافي : ٢ / ٤٧٧ / ٦ .

٢٣٩٨ . بحار الأنوار : ٨٥ / ٣٢١ / ٨ .

٢٣٩٩ . الكافي : ٢ / ٤٧٥ / ٦ .

٢٤٠٠ . الكافي : ٢ / ٤٧٥ / ٣ .

٢٤٠١ . الخصال : ٦٣٥ / ١٠ .

٢٤٠٢ . الكافي : ٢ / ٤٩٠ / ٨ ، بحار الأنوار : ٩٣ / ٣٧٤ / ١٦ .

٢٤٠٣ . بحار الأنوار : ٧١ / ١٧٨ / ٢٤ .

٢٤٠٤ . بحار الأنوار : ٩٣ / ٣٧٦ / ١٦ .

٢٤٠٥ . كنز العمّال : ١٨٧٤ .

٢٤٠٦ . تنبيه الخواطر : ٢ / ١٠٨ .

٢٤٠٧ . بحار الأنوار : ٤٣ / ٣٥١ / ٢٥ .

٢٤٠٨ . بحار الأنوار : ٧٥ / ١١٠ / ١٦ .

٢٤٠٩ . بحار الأنوار : ٧٤ / ٨٤ / ٩٤ .

٢٤١٠ . بحار الأنوار : ٩٣ / ٣٥٧ / ١٤ .

٢٤١١ . بحار الأنوار : ٩٣ / ٣١٣ / ١٧ .

٢٤١٢ . بحار الأنوار : ٩٣ / ٣٧٨ / ٢١ .

٢٤١٣ . الدعوات : ٣٣ / ٧٥ .

٢٤١٤ . التمحيص : ٣٣ / ١٧ .

٢٤١٥ . كشف المحجّة : ٢٢٨ .

٢٤١٦ . كنز العمّال : ٣١٢٨ .

٢٤١٧ . تحف العقول : ٢٨٠ .

٢٤١٨ . الكافي : ٢ / ٤٩١ / ٩ .

٢٤١٩ . بحار الأنوار : ٩٣ / ٣٢٢ / ٣٦ .

٢٤٢٠ . علل الشرائع : ٢ / ١ .

٢٤٢١ . عوالي اللآلي : ١ / ٢٦٧ / ٦٦ .

٢٤٢٢ . نهج البلاغة : الخطبة ١٥٦ .

٢٤٢٣ . نهج البلاغة : الكتاب ٥٥ .

٢٤٢٤ . بحار الأنوار : ٧٣ / ١٢٧ / ١٢٦ .

٢٤٢٥ . كنز العمّال : ٦٠٨٨ .

٢٤٢٦ . الكافي : ٢ / ٣١٧ / ٨ .

٢٤٢٧ . بحار الأنوار : ٧٣ / ٩٠ / ٦١ .

٢٤٢٨ . نهج البلاغة : الخطبة ٤٥ .

٢٤٢٩ . مطالب السؤول : ٥٢ .

٢٤٣٠ . بحارالأنوار : ٧٨ / ١٩٣ / ٧ .

٢٤٣١ . بحار الأنوار : ٧٧ / ٥٤ / ٣ .

٢٤٣٢ . بحار الأنوار : ٧٣ / ٨١ / ٤٣ .

٢٤٣٣ . غرر الحكم : ٩٨١٨ .

٢٤٣٤ . بحار الأنوار : ٧٧ / ١٧٨ / ١٠ .

٢٤٣٥ . نهج البلاغة : الحكمة ١٣١ .

٢٤٣٦ . غرر الحكم : ٣٩٦ .

٢٤٣٧ . غرر الحكم : ٩٢١ .

٢٤٣٨ . غرر الحكم : ١٤٧٣ .

٢٤٣٩ . غرر الحكم : ٤٠١ .

٢٤٤٠ . غرر الحكم : ٣ .

٢٤٤١ . كنز العمّال : ٦٠٧٤ .

٢٤٤٢ . تنبيه الخواطر : ٢ / ١٢٢ .

٢٤٤٣ . كنز العمّال : ٥٤٣٩ .

٢٤٤٤ . الكافي : ٢ / ٣١٥ / ١ .

٢٤٤٥ . في المصدر : «ويُهِمُّ»، والصحيح ماأثبتناه كما في طبعة النجف وبيروت .

٢٤٤٦ . غرر الحكم : ٤٨٧٨ .

٢٤٤٧ . غرر الحكم : ٤٨٧٢ .

٢٤٤٨ . الكافي : ٢ / ٣٢٠ / ١٧ .

٢٤٤٩ . الكافي : ٢ / ٣٢٠ / ١٦ .

٢٤٥٠ . نهج البلاغة : الحكمة ٢٣٦ .

٢٤٥١ . نهج البلاغة : الخطبة ٣ .

٢٤٥٢ . بحار الأنوار : ٤٠ / ٣٤٨ / ٢٩ .

٢٤٥٣ . نهج البلاغة : الكتاب ٤٥ .

٢٤٥٤ . آل عمران : ١٤ .

٢٤٥٥ . لقمان : ٣٣ .

٢٤٥٦ . الأمالي للطوسي : ٦٨٥ / ١٤٥٦ .

٢٤٥٧ . بحار الأنوار : ٧٣ / ١١٨ / ١٠٩ .

٢٤٥٨ . نهج البلاغة : الخطبة ١١١ .

٢٤٥٩ . نهج البلاغة : الخطبة ١١١ .

٢٤٦٠ . بحار الأنوار : ٧٨ / ٢٣ / ٨٨ .

٢٤٦١ . بحار الأنوار : ٧٣ / ١٠٨ / ١٠٩ .

٢٤٦٢ . نهج البلاغة : الخطبة ٢٣٠ .

٢٤٦٣ . الأمالي للطوسي : ٦٨٥ / ١٤٥٦ .

٢٤٦٤ . غرر الحكم : ٦٤١٣ .

٢٤٦٥ . غرر الحكم : ٨٩٦ .

٢٤٦٦ . غرر الحكم : ٤٥٤ .

٢٤٦٧ . يونس : ٧و ٨ .

٢٤٦٨ . الكهف : ٨٢ .

٢٤٦٩ . معاني الأخبار : ٢٠٠ / ١ .

٢٤٧٠ . بحار الأنوار : ٧٨ / ٢٠ / ٧٩ .

٢٤٧١ . غرر الحكم : ٢٣٨٦ .
٢٤٧٢ . بحار الأنوار : ٧٣ / ٨٨ / ٥٤ .
٢٤٧٣ . النازعات : ٣٧_٣٩ .
٢٤٧٤ . بحار الأنوار : ١٣ / ٤٢٢ / ١٧ .
٢٤٧٥ . الخصال : ٦٣٢ / ١٠ .
٢٤٧٦ . نهج البلاغة : الحكمة ١٠٦ .
٢٤٧٧ . كنز العمّال : ٦٠٩٠ .
٢٤٧٨ . الخصال : ١٠٨ / ٧٤ .
٢٤٧٩ . بحار الأنوار :٧٣ / ٨١ / ٤٣ .
٢٤٨٠ . الكافي : ٢ / ٣١٩ / ١٥ .
٢٤٨١ . الزخرف : ٣٣_٣٥ .
٢٤٨٢ . التمحيص : ٤٧ / ٧٣ .
٢٤٨٣ . الأمالي للطوسي : ٥٣١ / ١١٦٢ .
٢٤٨٤ . نهج البلاغة : الحكمة ٣٨٥ .
٢٤٨٥ . بحار الأنوار : ٤٤ / ٣٦٥ .
٢٤٨٦ . بحار الأنوار : ٧٣ / ٨١ / ٤٣ .
٢٤٨٧ . نهج البلاغة : الحكمة ١٠٣ .
٢٤٨٨ . نهج البلاغة : الحكمة ٢٥١ .
٢٤٨٩ . غرر الحكم : ٥٩٩٥ .
٢٤٩٠ . غرر الحكم : ٩٦١٨ .
٢٤٩١ . غرر الحكم : ٤٧٠٥ .
٢٤٩٢ . الخصال : ٦٤ / ٩٥ .
٢٤٩٣ . بحار الأنوار : ١٤ / ٧٤ / ١٦ .
٢٤٩٤ . آل عمران : ١٤٨ .
٢٤٩٥ . تاريخ دمشق : ٤٢ / ٥٠٣ .
٢٤٩٦ . غرر الحكم : ٣٧٥٠_٣٧٥١ .
٢٤٩٧ . بحار الأنوار : ٧٨ / ٣٢١ / ١٨ .
٢٤٩٨ . الكهف : ٤٥ .
٢٤٩٩ . بحار الأنوار : ٧٣ / ١١٩ / ١١٠ .
٢٥٠٠ . غرر الحكم : ٩٨١٨ .
٢٥٠١ . الكافي : ٢ / ١٣٣ / ١٦ .
٢٥٠٢ . بحارالأنوار : ٧٣ / ١٢٦ / ١٢٣ .
٢٥٠٣ . بحار الأنوار : ٧٨ / ٣١١ / ١ .
٢٥٠٤ . تحف العقول : ٣٩٦ .
٢٥٠٥ . بحارالأنوار : ٧٨ / ٣١١ / ١ .
٢٥٠٦ . الكافي : ١ / ١٦ / ١٢ .
٢٥٠٧ . الرعد : ٢٦ .
٢٥٠٨ . تنبيه الخواطر : ١ / ١٣١ .
٢٥٠٩ . الخصال : ٦٥ / ٩٥ .
٢٥١٠ . بحار الأنوار : ٧٧ / ١٦٤ / ٢ .
٢٥١١ . غرر الحكم : ١٨٠٢ .
٢٥١٢ . نهج البلاغة : الخطبة ٢٠٣ .
٢٥١٣ . نهج البلاغة : الحكمة ١٣٣ .
٢٥١٤ . نهج البلاغة : الخطبة ٢٢٦ .
٢٥١٥ . القلم : ٩ .
٢٥١٦ . مشكاة الأنوار : ١٠٤ / ٢٣٨ .
٢٥١٧ . غرر الحكم : ٥٧٢٥ .
٢٥١٨ . غرر الحكم : ٩٠٢٢ .
٢٥١٩ . بحار الأنوار : ٧٧ / ٢٩١ / ٢ .
٢٥٢٠ . نهج البلاغة : الخطبة ٢٤ .
٢٥٢١ . غرر الحكم : ٥١١٢_٥١١٣ .
٢٥٢٢ . في المصدر : «بالغرور»، والصحيح ما أثبتناه كما في طبعة النجف وبيروت .
٢٥٢٣ . غرر الحكم : ١٠٩٦٥ .
٢٥٢٤ . نهج البلاغة : الخطبة ٢١٦ .
٢٥٢٥ . غرر الحكم : ٩٥٧٤ .
٢٥٢٦ . غرر الحكم : ٥٨٣١ .
٢٥٢٧ . غرر الحكم : ٩٣٦٠ .
٢٥٢٨ . بحار الأنوار : ٦٢ / ٦٦ / ١٥ .
٢٥٢٩ . كنز العمّال : ٢٨٠٨٨ .
٢٥٣٠ . غرر الحكم : ٧٢٧٥ .
٢٥٣١ . بحار الأنوار : ٨١ / ٢١١ / ٣٠ .
٢٥٣٢ . الخصال : ٦٢٠ / ١٠ .
٢٥٣٣ . الكافي : ٨ / ٢٧٣ / ٤٠٩ .
٢٥٣٤ . غرر الحكم : ٩٠٣ .
٢٥٣٥ . بحار الأنوار : ٦٢ / ١٤٠ / ٢ .
٢٥٣٦ . الكافي : ٨ / ٢٩١ / ٤٤٢ .
٢٥٣٧ . مكارم الأخلاق : ٢ / ١٨٠ / ٢٤٦٨ .
٢٥٣٨ . الكافي : ٨ / ٢٩١ / ٤٤٣ .
٢٥٣٩ . بحار الأنوار : ١٠١ / ١٢٣ / ١٨ .
٢٥٤٠ . نهج البلاغة : الكتاب ٣١ .
٢٥٤١ . غرر الحكم : ٩٢٠٩ .
٢٥٤٢ . بحار الأنوار : ٧٥ / ٣٨٢ / ٤٧ .
٢٥٤٣ . غرر الحكم : ٨٨٠٧ .

٢٥٤٤ . غرر الحكم : ٢١٣ .

٢٥٤٥ . بحار الأنوار : ٧٧ / ٤١٨ / ٤٠ .

٢٥٤٦ . غرر الحكم : ١ .

٢٥٤٧ . غرر الحكم : ٤٨٩ .

٢٥٤٨ . الكافي : ٢ / ٤٦٤ / ٦ .

٢٥٤٩ . غرر الحكم : ٣٩٢٤ .

٢٥٥٠ . غرر الحكم : ٦٥٥٤ .

٢٥٥١ . الكافي : ٢ / ٣٠٧ / ٥ .

٢٥٥٢ . الكافي : ٢ / ٢١٦ / ٢ .

٢٥٥٣ . بحار الأنوار : ٧٨ / ٢٦٨ / ١٨٣ .

٢٥٥٤ . الكافي : ٢ / ٣٧٣ / ٤ .

٢٥٥٥ . بحار الأنوار : ٧٢ / ١٣٥ / ١٩ .

٢٥٥٦ . بحار الأنوار : ٨٤ / ٢٥٢ / ٤٧ .

٢٥٥٧ . الكافي : ٢ / ١٢٧ / ١٦ .

٢٥٥٨ . تحف العقول : ٣٨٩ .

٢٥٥٩ . كمال الدين : ٣٧١ / ٥ .

٢٥٦٠ . كنز العمّال : ٥٤١٨ .

٢٥٦١ . كنز العمّال : ٩٠٠ .

٢٥٦٢ . كنز العمّال : ٥٤٢٢ .

٢٥٦٣ . آل عمران : ٨٥ .

٢٥٦٤ . الكافي : ٢ / ٢٢ / ١١ .

٢٥٦٥ . بحار الأنوار : ٢٣ / ١٠٣ / ١١ .

٢٥٦٦ . بحار الأنوار : ٢ / ١٠٥ / ٦٧ .

٢٥٦٧ . غرر الحكم : ٥٨٦١ .

٢٥٦٨ . غرر الحكم : ١٠٨٣١ .

٢٥٦٩ . كمال الدين : ٣٥٢ / ٤٩ .

٢٥٧٠ . غرر الحكم : ٣٩١٢ .

٢٥٧١ . كنز العمّال : ١١٥ .

٢٥٧٢ . كنز العمّال : ٢٨٩٥٦ .

٢٥٧٣ . بحار الأنوار : ١٠٣ / ١٤١ / ٤ .

٢٥٧٤ . غرر الحكم : ٧١٠٥ .

٢٥٧٥ . بحار الأنوار : ١٠٣ / ١٤٥ / ٢١ .

٢٥٧٦ . الكافي : ٥ / ٩٣ / ٣ .

٢٥٧٧ . البقرة : ٢٨٢ .

٢٥٧٨ . بحار الأنوار : ١٠٤ / ٣٠١ / ١ .

٢٥٧٩ . بحار الأنوار : ١٠٣ / ١٤٦ / ٣ .

٢٥٨٠ . الموطّأ : ٢ / ٦٧٤ / ٨٤ .

٢٥٨١ . غرر الحكم : ٣١٩٠ .

٢٥٨٢ . المنافقون : ٩ .

٢٥٨٣ . بحارالأنوار : ٧٧ / ١٠٧ / ١ .

٢٥٨٤ . كنز العمّال : ٣٩٣١ .

٢٥٨٥ . غرر الحكم : ٦٧٠ .

٢٥٨٦ . غرر الحكم : ٣٢٢ .

٢٥٨٧ . غرر الحكم : ٥١٧٣ .

٢٥٨٨ . الأحزاب : ٤١ ، ٤٢ .

٢٥٨٩ . الخصال : ٥٢٥ / ١٣ .

٢٥٩٠ . بحار الأنوار : ٩٣ / ٣٤٢ / ١١ .

٢٥٩١ . الكافي : ٨ / ٧ / ١ .

٢٥٩٢ . الكافي : ٢ / ٥٠٠ / ٤ .

٢٥٩٣ . كنز العمّال : ١٨١٩ .

٢٥٩٤ . بحار الأنوار : ٩٤ / ٩٨ / ١٣ .

٢٥٩٥ . بحار الأنوار : ٩٤ / ٩٩ / ١٣ .

٢٥٩٦ . آل عمران : ١٩٠ ، ١٩١ .

٢٥٩٧ . الأمالي للطوسي : ٨ / ٨ .

٢٥٩٨ . بحار الأنوار : ٨٠ / ١٧٦ / ٢١ .

٢٥٩٩ . مكارم الأخلاق : ٢ / ٣٧٣ / ٢٦٦١ .

٢٦٠٠ . بحار الأنوار : ٨١ / ٢٤٠ / ٢٦ .

٢٦٠١ . بحار الأنوار : ٩٣ / ١٥٣ / ١١ .

٢٦٠٢ . غرر الحكم : ٨٢٣٥ .

٢٦٠٣ . غرر الحكم : ٥١٥٩ .

٢٦٠٤ . آل عمران : ١٩١ .

٢٦٠٥ . الأمالي للطوسي : ٧٩ / ١١٦ .

٢٦٠٦ . الأمالي للصدوق : ٥٥٠ / ٧٣٤ .

٢٦٠٧ . البقرة : ١٥٢ .

٢٦٠٨ . بحار الأنوار : ٩٣ / ١٥٨ / ٣١ .

٢٦٠٩ . الرعد : ٢٨ .

٢٦١٠ . كنز العمّال : ١٧٥١ .

٢٦١١ . الفردوس : ٣ / ٥٦٤ / ٥٧٦٨ .

٢٦١٢ . بحار الأنوار : ٩٣ / ١٦٠ / ٣٩ .

٢٦١٣ . غرر الحكم : ٨٨٧٢ .

٢٦١٤ . غرر الحكم : ٣٠٨٣ .

٢٦١٥ . غرر الحكم : ٨٨٧٦ .

٢٦١٦ . غرر الحكم : ٥١٦٦ .

٢٦١٧ . غرر الحكم : ٦١٠٣ .

٢٦١٨ . غرر الحكم : ٥١٤٤ .

٢٦١٩ . نهج البلاغة : الخطبة ٢٢٢ .

٢٦٢٠ . الإقبال : ٣ / ٣٣٧ .

٢٦٢١ . غرر الحكم : ٥٤١ .

٢٦٢٢ . غرر الحكم : ٤٠٤٠_٤٠٤١ .

٢٦٢٣ . غرر الحكم : ٥١٦٢ .

٢٦٢٤ . غرر الحكم : ٥١٦٥ .

٢٦٢٥ . غرر الحكم : ٨٣٥ .

٢٦٢٦ . الأنفال : ٤٥ .

٢٦٢٧ . الخصال : ٦١٧ / ١٠ .

٢٦٢٨ . الخصال : ٦١٤ / ١٠ .

٢٦٢٩ . بحار الأنوار : ٧٧ / ١٧١ / ٧ .

٢٦٣٠ . بحار الأنوار : ٧٥ / ٣٢١ / ٥٠ .

٢٦٣١ . الأمالي للصدوق : ٣٢٧ / ٣٨٤ .

٢٦٣٢ . بحار الأنوار : ٧٧ / ٨٦ / ٣ .

٢٦٣٣ . العنكبوت : ٤٥ .

٢٦٣٤ . عدّة الداعي : ٢٨٣ .

٢٦٣٥ . بحار الأنوار : ٩٣ / ١٥٩ / ٣٣ .

٢٦٣٦ . بحار الأنوار : ٩٣ / ١٥٨ / ٣٣ .

٢٦٣٧ . بحار الأنوار : ٧٨ / ٣٥٦ / ١١ .

٢٦٣٨ . بحار الأنوار : ٧٧ / ٢٢ / ٦ .

٢٦٣٩ . غرر الحكم : ٧٨٥١ .

٢٦٤٠ . المنافقون : ٩ .

٢٦٤١ . المائدة : ٩١ .

٢٦٤٢ . غرر الحكم : ٧٥٢٠ .

٢٦٤٣ . بحار الأنوار : ٧٣ / ١٥٧ / ٢ .

٢٦٤٤ . تنبيه الخواطر : ٢ / ١٧٠ .

٢٦٤٥ . بحار الأنوار : ٧٨ / ١٢٩ / ١ .

٢٦٤٦ . قال السيد العلامة الطباطبائي : قوله : ﴿فَإِنَّ لَه مَعِيشَةً ضَنْكاً﴾ أي ضيّقة ، وذلك أنّ مَن نسي ربّه وانقطع عن ذكره لم يبق له إلّا أن يتعلّق بالدنيا ويجعلها مطلوبه الوحيد الذي يسعىٰ له، ويهتمّ بإصلاح معيشته والتوسّع فيها والتمتّع منها ، والمعيشة التي أُوتيها لاتسعه سواء كانت قليلة أو كثيرة ؛ لأ نّه كلّما حصل منها واقتناها لم يرض نفسه بها ، وانتزعت إلى تحصيلٍ ما هو أزيد وأوسع من غير أن يقف منها علىٰ حدّ ، فهو دائماً في ضيق صدر وحنق ممّا وجد متعلّق القلب بما وراءه ، مع ما يهجم عليه من الهمّ والغمّ والحزن والقلق والاضطراب والخوف بنزول النوازل وعروض العوارض؛ من موت ومرض وعاهة وحسد حاسد وكيد كائد وخيبة سعيٍ وفراق حبيب .

ولو أ نّه عرف مقام ربّه ذاكراً غير ناس أيقن أنّ له حياة عند ربّه لا يخالطها موت وملكاً لا يعتريه زوال وعزّة لا يشوبها ذلّة وفرحاً وسروراً ورفعة وكرامة لا تقدّر بقدر ولا تنتهي إلى أمد ، وأنّ الدنيا دار مجاز وما حياتها في الآخرة إلّا متاع ، فلو عرف ذلك قنعت نفسه بما قدّر له من الدنيا ووسعه ما اوتيه من المعيشة من غير ضيق وضنك .

الميزان في تفسير القرآن : ١٤ / ٢٢٥ .

قوله : ﴿ومَنْ يَعْشُ عَنْ ذِكْرِ الرَّحمنِ نُقَيِّضْ له شَيْطاناً﴾ أي من تعامىٰ عن ذكر الرحمن ونظر إليه نظر الأعشىٰ جئنا إليه بشيطان ... ﴿فَهُوَ لَهُ قَرِينٌ﴾ أي مصاحب لا يفارقه .

٢٦٤٧ . طه : ١٢٤_١٢٦ .

٢٦٤٨ . الزخرف : ٣٦ .

٢٦٤٩ . الحشر : ١٩ .

٢٦٥٠ . غرر الحكم : ٨٨٧٥ .

٢٦٥١ . الأعراف : ٢٠٥ .

٢٦٥٢ . كنز العمّال : ١٧٧١ .

٢٦٥٣ . بحار الأنوار : ٥ / ٣٢٢ / ٧ .

٢٦٥٤ . غرر الحكم : ٣٦٢ .

٢٦٥٥ . نهج البلاغة : الحكمة ٣٩٦ .

٢٦٥٦ . غرر الحكم : ٥٥٨٠ .

٢٦٥٧ . نهج البلاغة : الخطبة ٢١٥ .

٢٦٥٨ . المناقب لابن شهر آشوب : ٤ / ٦٨ بحار الأنوار : ٤٤ / ١٩٢ / ٤ .

٢٦٥٩ . تحف العقول : ٥٨ .

٢٦٦٠ . الكافي : ٥ / ٦٣ / ٣ .

٢٦٦١ . مشكاة الأنوار : ٤٣٠ / ١٤٣٣ .

٢٦٦٢ . كنز العمّال : ١٠٥٠٤ .

٢٦٦٣ . بحار الأنوار : ٧٥ / ١٤٢ / ٢ .

٢٦٦٤ . غرر الحكم : ٢١٧٢ .

٢٦٦٥ . تحف العقول : ٢٠١، شرح نهج البلاغة : ١٨ / ٨٤ .

٢٦٦٦ . تحف العقول : ٢٨٦ .

٢٦٦٧ . الخصال : ١٢٠ / ١١٠ .

٢٦٦٨ . كشف الغمة : ٢١ / ٤١٤ ، بحار الأنوار : ٧٨ / ٢٠٥ / ٤٦ .

٢٦٦٩ . الأنعام : ١٢٠ .

٢٦٧٠ . البقرة : ٨١ .

٢٦٧١ . غرر الحكم : ١٨٩٠ .
٢٦٧٢ . نهج البلاغة : الخطبة ٢٢٣ .
٢٦٧٣ . تحف العقول : ٢٠٤ .
٢٦٧٤ . نهج البلاغة : الحكمة ٢٩٠ .
٢٦٧٥ . غرر الحكم : ١٥٢٢ .
٢٦٧٦ . بحار الأنوار : ٧٨ / ٣٠١ / ١ .
٢٦٧٧ . بحار الأنوار : ٧٠ / ٢٨٦ / ٨ .
٢٦٧٨ . غرر الحكم : ٩٨١١ .
٢٦٧٩ . بحار الأنوار : ٧٣ / ٣٥٦ / ٦٧ .
٢٦٨٠ . بحار الأنوار : ٧٣ / ٣٦٤ / ٩٦ .
٢٦٨١ . غرر الحكم : ٣١٣١ .
٢٦٨٢ . الكافي : ٢ / ٢٧٠ / ٧ .
٢٦٨٣ . النساء : ٤٨ .
٢٦٨٤ بحار الأنوار : ٧٧ / ٤٨ / ٣ .
٢٦٨٥ . كنزالعمّال : ح ٤٣٧٧٠ .
٢٦٨٦ . نهج البلاغة : الخطبة ١٥٣ .
٢٦٨٧ . الخصال : ٢٤ / ٨٣ .
٢٦٨٨ . بحار الأنوار : ٧٨ / ٧٠ / ٢٥ .
٢٦٨٩ . بحار الأنوار : ٤٦ / ٢٤٧ / ٣٥ .
٢٦٩٠ . الأمالي للطوسي : ٥٢٧ / ١١٦٢ .
٢٦٩١ . بحار الأنوار : ٧٣ / ٣٦٣ / ٩٣ .
٢٦٩٢ . بحارالأنوار : ٧٧ / ١٦٨ / ٦ .
٢٦٩٣ . غرر الحكم : ٣١٤١ .
٢٦٩٤ . تحف العقول : ٢٨٦ .
٢٦٩٥ . الأمالي للمفيد : ١٥٧ / ٨ .
٢٦٩٦ . بحار الأنوار : ٧٣ / ٣٥٣ / ٥٥ .
٢٦٩٧ . النساء : ٣١ .
٢٦٩٨ . كنز العمّال : ٧٧٩٨ .
٢٦٩٩ . كنز العمّال : ٤٣٢٥ .
٢٧٠٠ . الكافي : ٢ / ٢٧٧ / ٣ .
٢٧٠١ . آل عمران : ١٣٥ .
٢٧٠٢ . بحار الأنوار : ٧٣ / ٣٥٥ / ٦٢ .
٢٧٠٣ . بحار الأنوار : ٦ / ٣٢ / ٤٠ .
٢٧٠٤ . غرر الحكم : ٨٨٢٣ .
٢٧٠٥ . بحار الأنوار : ٧٨ / ١٥٩ / ١٠ .
٢٧٠٦ . الفردوس : ٢ / ٢٤٩ / ٣١٦٩ .
٢٧٠٧ . علل الشرائع : ٨١ / ١ .
٢٧٠٨ . معاني الأخبار : ٢٧١ / ٢ .
٢٧٠٩ . بحار الأنوار : ٧٣ / ٣٢٩ / ١٢ .
٢٧١٠ . بحار الأنوار : ٧٣ / ٣٢٧ / ١٠ .
٢٧١١ . بحار الأنوار : ٧٣ / ٣٣٩ / ٢١ .
٢٧١٢ . الكافي : ٢ / ٢٧٢ / ١٦ .
٢٧١٣ . الأمالي للطوسي : ٧٠١ / ١٤٩٨ .
٢٧١٤ . الأمالي للمفيد : ٣١٠ / ٢ .
٢٧١٥ . الأمالي للمفيد : ٢٣٧ / ١ .
٢٧١٦ . الأمالي للمفيد : ٩٨ / ٨ .
٢٧١٧ . الجعفريّات : ٢٢٨ .
٢٧١٨ . النوادر للراوندي : ٩٧ / ٤٩ .
٢٧١٩ . بحار الأنوار : ٦٧ / ٢٣٦ / ٥٤ .
٢٧٢٠ . الخصال : ٦٣٥ / ١٠ .
٢٧٢١ . بحار الأنوار : ٨١ / ١٧٧ / ١٨ .
٢٧٢٢ . بحار الأنوار : ٦٧ / ٢٤٤ / ٨٣ .
٢٧٢٣ . بحار الأنوار : ٨١ / ١٨٦ / ٣٩ .
٢٧٢٤ . دعائم الإسلام : ١ / ٢١٨ .
٢٧٢٥ . بحار الأنوار : ٨١ / ١٨٦ / ٤٠ .
٢٧٢٦ . تحف العقول : ٣٨ .
٢٧٢٧ . الدعوات : ١٢٠ / ٢٨٥ .
٢٧٢٨ . بحار الأنوار : ٦٨ / ١٤٦ / ٩٤ .
٢٧٢٩ . هود : ١١٤ .
٢٧٣٠ . الأمالي للطوسي : ١٨٦ / ٣١٢ .
٢٧٣١ . الكافي : ٢ / ١٠٧ / ٧ .
٢٧٣٢ . بحار الأنوار : ٧١ / ٣٩٥ / ٧٤ .
٢٧٣٣ . نهج البلاغة : الحكمة ٢٤ .
٢٧٣٤ . غافر : ٧ .
٢٧٣٥ . بحار الأنوار : ٥٩ / ١٩٦ / ٦١ .
٢٧٣٦ . الأمالي للصدوق : ٥٨٩ / ٨١٤ .
٢٧٣٧ . بحار الأنوار : ٩٩ / ٥٠ / ٤٦ .
٢٧٣٨ . الأمالي للصدوق : ١٣١ / ١٢٣ .
٢٧٣٩ . الأمالي للمفيد : ٢٨٣ / ٨ .
٢٧٤٠ . الكافي : ٢ / ٣٣٨ / ١ .
٢٧٤١ . الكافي : ٢ / ٢٩٧ / ٣ .
٢٧٤٢ . الكافي : ٢ / ٢٩٧ / ٢ .
٢٧٤٣ . الكافي : ٢ / ٢٩٧ / ١ .
٢٧٤٤ . نهج البلاغة : الحكمة ١٧٦ .

٢٧٤٥ . تحف العقول : ٩٦ .

٢٧٤٦ . مستدرك الوسائل : ١٢ / ١٧٣ / ١٣٨١٠ .

٢٧٤٧ . يونس : ٦٤ .

٢٧٤٨ . الكافي : ٨ / ٩٠ / ٦٠ .

٢٧٤٩ . بحار الأنوار : ٦١ / ١٧٧ / ٣٩ .

٢٧٥٠ . الكافي : ٨ / ٩٠ / ٥٩ .

٢٧٥١ . الأمالي للصدوق : ٢٠٩ / ٢٣٢ .

٢٧٥٢ . الكافي : ٨ / ٩٠ / ٦١ .

٢٧٥٣ . كنز العمّال : ٤١٣٩٢ .

٢٧٥٤ . الكافي : ٨ / ٣٣٦ / ٥٣٠ .

٢٧٥٥ . الأنفال : ٤٧ .

٢٧٥٦ . أعلام الدين : ٢٩٥ .

٢٧٥٧ . الكافي : ٢ / ٢٩٥ / ٧ .

٢٧٥٨ . منية المريد : ٣١٨ .

٢٧٥٩ . عدّة الداعي : ٢٠٣ .

٢٧٦٠ . تنبيه الخواطر : ١ / ١٨٧ .

٢٧٦١ . تنبيه الخواطر : ١ / ١٨٦ .

٢٧٦٢ . غرر الحكم : ٩٦٦١ .

٢٧٦٣ . نهج البلاغة : الحكمة ٢٧٦ وفي شرح نهج البلاغة : ١٩ / ١٦٧ / ٢٨٢ «رثاء» بدل «رياء» .

٢٧٦٤ . الأمالي للصدوق : ٥٨٠ / ٧٩٨ .

٢٧٦٥ . الكافي : ٢ / ٢٩٣ / ١ .

٢٧٦٦ . عدّة الداعي : ٢١٤ .

٢٧٦٧ . تحف العقول : ١٥١ .

٢٧٦٨ . تفسير القمّي : ٢ / ٤٧ .

٢٧٦٩ . مستدرك الوسائل : ١ / ١٠٧ / ١٠٩ .

٢٧٧٠ . ما بين الهلالين أثبتناه من بحار الأنوار : ٧٢ / ٣٠١ / ٤٤ .

٢٧٧١ . الزهد للحسين بن سعيد : ٦٣ / ١٦٦ .

٢٧٧٢ . الكافي : ٢ / ٢٩٥ / ٨ .

٢٧٧٣ . كنز العمّال : ٥٢٧٣ .

٢٧٧٤ . الكافي : ٢ / ٢٩٧ / ١٨ .

٢٧٧٥ . عدّة الداعي : ٢٢١ .

٢٧٧٦ . الفطير : كلّ شيء أعجلته عن إدراكه ، يقال : إيّاك والرأي الفطير (الصحاح : ٢ / ٧٨٢) .

٢٧٧٧ . بحار الأنوار : ٧٨ / ٨١ / ٧٦ .

٢٧٧٨ . غرر الحكم : ٢٥٦٧ .

٢٧٧٩ . نهج البلاغة : الحكمة ١٧٣ .

٢٧٨٠ . غرر الحكم : ٣١٥٢ .

٢٧٨١ . نهج البلاغة : الحكمة ١٦١ .

٢٧٨٢ . غرر الحكم : ٩٤٧١ .

٢٧٨٣ . بحار الأنوار : ٧٥ / ١٠٥ / ٤١ .

٢٧٨٤ . نهج البلاغة : الحكمة ١٧٩ .

٢٧٨٥ . الأمالي للطوسي : ٣٠١ / ٥٩٥ .

٢٧٨٦ . نهج البلاغة : الحكمة ٣٣٩ .

٢٧٨٧ . كنز العمّال : ٩١٥ .

٢٧٨٨ . كنز العمّال : ١٦٤٠ .

٢٧٨٩ . كنز العمّال : ١٤١١٠ .

٢٧٩٠ . وقعة صفّين : ٩٥ .

٢٧٩١ . الأمالي للصدوق : ٥١١ / ٧٠٧ .

٢٧٩٢ . كنز العمّال : ٣١٨٥٧ .

٢٧٩٣ . الكافي : ٥ / ١٤٧ / ١٢ .

٢٧٩٤ . تفسير العيّاشي : ١ / ١٥٢ / ٥٠٣ .

٢٧٩٥ . كتاب من لا يحضره الفقيه : ٤ / ٣٦٧ / ٥٧٦٢ .

٢٧٩٦ . في وسائل الشيعة (١٢ / ٤٢٤ / ٨) : «لِتنفر الناس من الحرام إلى الحلال وإلى التجارات من البيع والشراء ، فيبقى ذلك بينهم في القرض» .

٢٧٩٧ . بحار الأنوار : ١٠٣ / ١١٩ / ٢٤ .

٢٧٩٨ . بحار الأنوار : ٧٨ / ٢٠١ / ٣٢ .

٢٧٩٩ . بحار الأنوار : ١٠٣ / ١١٧ / ١٦ .

٢٨٠٠ . نهج البلاغة : الحكمة ٤٤٧ .

٢٨٠١ . البقرة : ٢٧٨ ، ٢٧٩ .

٢٨٠٢ . الكافي : ٥ / ١٤٧ / ١١ .

٢٨٠٣ . البقرة : ٢١٨ .

٢٨٠٤ . الأمالي للمفيد : ٢٠٧ / ٣٨ .

٢٨٠٥ . نهج البلاغة : الحكمة ١٥٠ .

٢٨٠٦ . الكافي : ٢ / ٦٨ / ٥ .

٢٨٠٧ . غرر الحكم : ٢٥١١ .

٢٨٠٨ . بحار الأنوار : ٥٣ / ١٠٢ / ١٢٥ .

٢٨٠٩ . بحار الأنوار : ٥٣ / ٦٢ / ٥٢ .

٢٨١٠ . بحار الأنوار : ٥٣ / ٤٦ / ١٩ .

٢٨١١ . بحار الأنوار : ٥٣ / ٣٩ / ١ .

٢٨١٢ . الفتح : ٢٩ .

٢٨١٣ . البلد : ١٧ ، ١٨ .

٢٨١٤ . كنز العمّال : ٥٩٦٩ .

٢٨١٥ . كنز العمّال : ٥٩٩٢ .

٢٨١٦ . الأمالي للصدوق : ٢٧٨ / ٣٠٨ .

٢٨١٧ . غرر الحكم : ٦٢٥٥ .

٢٨١٨ . بحار الأنوار : ٧٤ / ٤٠٥ / ٢ .

٢٨١٩ . كنز العمّال : ٥٩٨٣ .

٢٨٢٠ . الأمالي للمفيد : ٢٢٢ / ١ .

٢٨٢١ . كنز العمّال : ١٠٤٦٤ .

٢٨٢٢ . كنز العمّال : ١٠٤٠٧ .

٢٨٢٣ . كنز العمّال : ١٠٣٨٧ .

٢٨٢٤ . بحار الأنوار : ٧٨ / ١٥٣ / ١٧ .

٢٨٢٥ . تنبيه الخواطر : ٢ / ١٢٠ .

٢٨٢٦ . غرر الحكم : ٤٢٠٩ .

٢٨٢٧ . غرر الحكم : ٤٣٤٣ .

٢٨٢٨ . الكافي : ٢ / ١٥٢ / ١٥ .

٢٨٢٩ . بحار الأنوار : ٧٤ / ١٠٣ / ٦١ .

٢٨٣٠ . بحار الأنوار : ٧٤ / ٩٤ / ٢٣ .

٢٨٣١ . بحار الأنوار : ٧٤ / ٩١ / ١٥ .

٢٨٣٢ . الكافي : ٢ / ١٥٠ / ٤ .

٢٨٣٣ . الكافي : ٢ / ١٥٢ / ١٢ .

٢٨٣٤ . نَسَأَ اللهُ أجَلَه وأنسأه : إذا أخَّرَهُ (المصباح المنير : ٦٠٤) .

٢٨٣٥ . الأمالي للصدوق : ٢٧٦ / ٣٠٧ .

٢٨٣٦ . الكافي : ٢ / ٣٤٧ / ٦ .

٢٨٣٧ . بحار الأنوار : ٧٤ / ٤٠٠ / ٤١ .

٢٨٣٨ . محمّد : ٢٢ ، ٢٣ .

٢٨٣٩ . كنز العمّال : ٦٩٧٤ .

٢٨٤٠ . الكافي : ٢ / ٣٤٨ / ٨ .

٢٨٤١ . بحار الأنوار : ٧٤ / ٩٤ / ٢٣ .

٢٨٤٢ . تحف العقول : ٥٧ .

٢٨٤٣ . الكافي : ٢ / ١٥١ / ٩ .

٢٨٤٤ . الذاريات : ٥٨ .

٢٨٤٥ . الإسراء : ٣٠ .

٢٨٤٦ . غرر الحكم : ١٠٨٣٨ .

٢٨٤٧ . نهج البلاغة : الخطبة ٩١ .

٢٨٤٨ . هود : ٦ .

٢٨٤٩ . بحار الأنوار : ٧٧ / ١٨٧ / ١٠ .

٢٨٥٠ . الأمالي للصدوق : ٣٩٩ / ٥١٥ .

٢٨٥١ . نهج البلاغة : الخطبة ١٨٥ .

٢٨٥٢ . نهج البلاغة : الخطبة ٩١ .

٢٨٥٣ . الإرشاد : ١ / ٣٠٣ .

٢٨٥٤ . بحار الأنوار : ٧٨ / ٣٧٤ / ٢٢ .

٢٨٥٥ . بحار الأنوار : ٧٧ / ٦٨ / ٧ .

٢٨٥٦ . الأمالي للمفيد : ٢٠٧ / ٣٩ .

٢٨٥٧ . الأمالي للصدوق : ٥٦ / ١٢ .

٢٨٥٨ . بحار الأنوار : ١٠٣ / ٣٤ / ٦٣ .

٢٨٥٩ . الكافي : ٢ / ٧٤ / ٢ .

٢٨٦٠ . اُنظر : كنز العمّال : ٩٢٩٠ ، ٩٣١٠ ، ٩٣١١ ، ٩٣١٢ ، ٩٣١٤ ، ٩٣١٦ .

٢٨٦١ . نهج البلاغة : الحكمة ٣٩٣ .

٢٨٦٢ . بحار الأنوار : ١٠٣ / ٣٣ / ٦٣ .

٢٨٦٣ . مكارم الأخلاق : ٢ / ٣٧٧ / ٢٦٦١ .

٢٨٦٤ . غرر الحكم : ١٤٠٨ .

٢٨٦٥ . نهج البلاغة : الكتاب ٣١ .

٢٨٦٦ . الكافي : ٥ / ٨٤ / ٤ .

٢٨٦٧ . بحار الأنوار : ٧٧ / ٦٧ / ٦ .

٢٨٦٨ . الأمالي للطوسي : ٣٠٠ / ٥٩٣ .

٢٨٦٩ . بحار الأنوار : ٨١ / ١٩٥ / ٥٢ .

٢٨٧٠ . عيون أخبار الرِّضا : ٢ / ٤٦ / ١٧١ .

٢٨٧١ . كنز العمّال : ٩٣٢٥ .

٢٨٧٢ . بحار الأنوار : ٧٤ / ٣٦٢ / ١٧ .

٢٨٧٣ . كنز العمّال : ٤٤١٥٤ .

٢٨٧٤ . بحار الأنوار : ٧٧ / ١٧٦ / ١٠ .

٢٨٧٥ . بحار الأنوار : ٧٤ / ٣٩٥ / ٢٢ .

٢٨٧٦ . بحار الأنوار : ٧٥ / ١٧٢ / ٨ .

٢٨٧٧ . نهج البلاغة : الحكمة ١٣٧ .

٢٨٧٨ . بحار الأنوار : ١٠٣ / ٢١ / ١٨ .

٢٨٧٩ . بحار الأنوار : ٧٦ / ٦٠ / ١٤ .

٢٨٨٠ . بحار الأنوار : ٩٦ / ١٤ / ٢٧ .

٢٨٨١ . بحار الأنوار : ٦٩ / ٤٠٨ / ١١٧ .

٢٨٨٢ . بحار الأنوار : ٧٤ / ٨١ / ٨٤ .

٢٨٨٣ . بحار الأنوار : ٧١ / ٣٩٦ / ٧٧ .

٢٨٨٤ . الأمالي للصدوق : ٥١٦ / ٧٠٧ .

٢٨٨٥ . الكافي : ٢ / ٢٧٠ / ٨ .

٢٨٨٦ . تحف العقول : ٣٧٢ .

٢٨٨٧ . بحار الأنوار : ١٠٣ / ٩ / ٣٧ .

٢٨٨٨ . بحار الأنوار : ١٠٣ / ١٣ / ٥٩ .

٢٨٨٩ . كنز العمّال : ٩٢٠٠ .

٢٨٩٠ . جامع الأخبار : ٣٨٩ / ١٠٧٩ .

٢٨٩١ . جامع الأخبار : ٣٩٠ / ١٠٨٥ .

٢٨٩٢ . جامع الأخبار : ٣٩٠ / ١٠٨٧ .

٢٨٩٣ . بحار الأنوار : ١٠٣ / ١٣ / ٦٢ .

٢٨٩٤ . بحار الأنوار : ٧٨ / ٣٨١ / ١ .

٢٨٩٥ . الكافي : ٢ / ١٤٠ / ٣ .

٢٨٩٦ . بحار الأنوار : ٧٧ / ١٦٨ / ٤ .

٢٨٩٧ . الأمالي للصدوق : ٥٧٦ / ٧٨٨ .

٢٨٩٨ . بحار الأنوار : ١٠٤ / ٢٧٤ / ١٢ .

٢٨٩٩ . كنز العمّال : ١٥٠٨٠ .

٢٩٠٠ . نهج البلاغة : الكتاب ٧٩ .

٢٩٠١ . نهج البلاغة : الخطبة ١٣١ .

٢٩٠٢ . بحار الأنوار : ١٠٤ / ٢٧٣ / ٥ .

٢٩٠٣ . الكافي : ٧ / ٤٠٩ / ٢ .

٢٩٠٤ . البقرة : ٢٣٣ .

٢٩٠٥ . عيون أخبار الرّضا : ٢ / ٣٤ / ٦٩ .

٢٩٠٦ . الكافي : ٦ / ٤٤ / ١٠ .

٢٩٠٧ . الكافي : ٦ / ٤٤ / ١٢ .

٢٩٠٨ . بحار الأنوار : ١٠٣ / ٣٢٣ / ١٣ .

٢٩٠٩ . بحار الأنوار : ١٠٣ / ٣٢٣ / ٩ .

٢٩١٠ . وسائل الشيعة : ١٥ / ١٨٧ / ١ .

٢٩١١ . نهج البلاغة : الحكمة ٤ .

٢٩١٢ . بحار الأنوار : ٧٨ / ١٠٦ / ٦ .

٢٩١٣ . بحار الأنوار : ٤٣ / ٣٥١ / ٢٥ .

٢٩١٤ . الكافي : ٢ / ١٢٨ / ٤ .

٢٩١٥ . التمحيص : ٦٠ / ١٣١ .

٢٩١٦ . بحار الأنوار : ٧١ / ١٥٧ / ٧٥ .

٢٩١٧ . بحار الأنوار : ٧١ / ١٣٩ / ٢٨ .

٢٩١٨ . غرر الحكم : ٣٠٨٥ .

٢٩١٩ . بحار الأنوار : ٧١ / ١٥٨ / ٧٥ .

٢٩٢٠ . بحار الأنوار : ٨٢ / ١٤٢ / ٢٦ .

٢٩٢١ . بحار الأنوار : ٦٩ / ٣٦٨ / ٤ .

٢٩٢٢ . غرر الحكم : ٤١٠ .

٢٩٢٣ . غرر الحكم : ٣٣٩٧ .

٢٩٢٤ . بحار الأنوار : ٧١ / ١٥٩ / ٧٥ .

٢٩٢٥ . بحار الأنوار : ٧١ / ١٥٩ / ٧٥ .

٢٩٢٦ . بحار الأنوار : ٧٨ / ٢٠٢ / ٣٣ .

٢٩٢٧ . بحار الأنوار : ٧١ / ١٣٩ / ٢٦ .

٢٩٢٨ . آل عمران : ١٦٢ .

٢٩٢٩ . بحار الأنوار : ٨٢ / ١٣٤ / ١٧ .

٢٩٣٠ . بحار الأنوار : ٧٨ / ٨١ / ٧٤ .

٢٩٣١ . بحار الأنوار : ٧٠ / ٣١٢ / ١١ .

٢٩٣٢ . نهج البلاغة : الخطبة١٨٣ .

٢٩٣٣ . غرر الحكم : ٥٤١٠ .

٢٩٣٤ . بحار الأنوار : ٧٨ / ١٣٦ / ١٣ .

٢٩٣٥ . بحار الأنوار : ٧٠ / ٢٦ / ٢٩ .

٢٩٣٦ . غرر الحكم : ٦٣٤٤ .

٢٩٣٧ . الأمالي للطوسي : ٢٩ / ٣١ .

٢٩٣٨ . بحار الأنوار : ٧١ / ٢٠٨ / ١٧ .

٢٩٣٩ . الكافي : ٢ / ١١٩ / ٦ .

٢٩٤٠ . الكافي : ٢ / ١٢٠ / ١٥ .

٢٩٤١ . شرح نهج البلاغة : ٦ / ٣٣٩ .

٢٩٤٢ . الأمالي للصدوق : ٧٣ / ٤١ .

٢٩٤٣ . كنز العمّال : ٥٣٧٠ .

٢٩٤٤ . غرر الحكم : ٢٩٤ .

٢٩٤٥ . الكافي : ٢ / ١١٨ / ١ .

٢٩٤٦ . الكافي : ٢ / ١٢٠ / ١١ .

٢٩٤٧ . الكافي : ٢ / ٨٦ / ١ .

٢٩٤٨ . نهج البلاغة : الكتاب ٦٩ .

٢٩٤٩ . الكافي : ٢ / ١١٩ / ٧ .

٢٩٥٠ . غرر الحكم : ١٧٧٨ .

٢٩٥١ . بحار الأنوار : ٧٨ / ١٢٨ / ١١ .

٢٩٥٢ . بحار الأنوار : ٧٣ / ٣٨٦ / ٦ .

٢٩٥٣ . بحار الأنوار : ٧٨ / ٢٦٩ / ١٠٩ .

٢٩٥٤ . الكافي : ٢ / ١٢٠ / ١٦ .

٢٩٥٥ . النساء : ١ .

٢٩٥٦ . ق : ١٨ .

٢٩٥٧ . نهج البلاغة : الخطبة١٥٧ .

٢٩٥٨ . الخصال : ٥٢٥ / ١٣ ، معاني الأخبار : ٣٣٤ / ١ وفيه «وتفريغ لها» بدل «وتوزيع لها» .

٢٩٥٩ . غرر الحكم : ٢٤٢٩ .

٢٩٦٠ . غرر الحكم : ١٠٩٤٧ .

٢٩٦١ . نهج البلاغة : الخطبة ٧٦ .

٢٩٦٢ . بحار الأنوار : ٧٨ / ٦ / ٥٨ .

٢٩٦٣ . بحار الأنوار : ١٤ / ٢٨٩ و ٢٩٣ / ١٤ .

٢٩٦٤ . بحار الأنوار : ٧٨ / ٢٧٧ / ١١٣ .

٢٩٦٥ . الكافي : ٢ / ٤٥٣ / ٢ .

٢٩٦٦ . البقرة : ١٨٥ .

٢٩٦٧ . كنز العمّال : ٢٣٦٨٨ .

٢٩٦٨ . بحارالأنوار : ٩٦ / ٣٤٤ / ٨ .

٢٩٦٩ . بحار الأنوار : ٩٦ / ٣٤٦ / ١٢ .

٢٩٧٠ . بحار الأنوار : ٩٦ / ٣٤٨ / ١٤ .

٢٩٧١ . الأمالي للصدوق : ١٥٤ / ١٤٩ .

٢٩٧٢ . (أُنظر) الذنب : باب ١٣٦٦ .

٢٩٧٣ . الأمالي للصدوق : ١١٣ / ٩٢ .

٢٩٧٤ . بحار الأنوار : ٩٦ / ٣٧٥ / ٦٣ .

٢٩٧٥ . بحار الأنوار : ٧٤ / ٧٤ / ٦٢ .

٢٩٧٦ . عيون أخبار الرِّضا : ١ / ٢٩٥ / ٥٣ .

٢٩٧٧ . الأمالي للصدوق : ١٠٧ / ٧٩ .

٢٩٧٨ . بحار الأنوار : ٩٦ / ٣٤٢ / ٦ .

٢٩٧٩ . الإسراء : ٨٥ .

٢٩٨٠ . بحار الأنوار : ٦١ / ٤٠ / ١١ .

٢٩٨١ . بحار الأنوار : ٦١ / ٣٤ / ٧ .

٢٩٨٢ . كنز العمّال : ٢٤٦٦٠ .

٢٩٨٣ . غرر الحكم : ٢٠٥٧ .

٢٩٨٤ . كنز العمّال : ٢٥٥٦٠ .

٢٩٨٥ . بحار الأنوار : ٦١ / ٤٠ / ١٠ .

٢٩٨٦ . جامع الأخبار : ٤٨٨ / ١٣٦٠ .

٢٩٨٧ . بحار الأنوار : ٦١ / ٤٣ / ١٩ .

٢٩٨٨ . غرر الحكم : ٨٧٦٣ .

٢٩٨٩ . غرر الحكم : ١٦٣٣ .

٢٩٩٠ . نهج البلاغة : الحكمة ٣٧١ .

٢٩٩١ . غرر الحكم : ١٣١٦ .

٢٩٩٢ . مشكاة الأنوار : ٧٤ / ١٣٨ .

٢٩٩٣ . مشكاة الأنوار : ٣٢٤ / ١٠٢٦ .

٢٩٩٤ . بحار الأنوار : ٨١ / ١٩٥ / ٥٢ .

٢٩٩٥ . صحيح البخاري : ٢ / ٨١٧ / ٢١٩٥ .

٢٩٩٦ . الكافي : ٥ / ٢٦٠ / ٥ .

٢٩٩٧ . قرب الإسناد : ١١٥ / ٤٠٤ .

٢٩٩٨ . الكافي : ٥ / ٢٦١ / ٧ .

٢٩٩٩ . آل عمران : ١٦٠ .

٣٠٠٠ . بحار الأنوار : ١٠٣ / ٦٦ / ١٦ .

٣٠٠١ . وسائل الشيعة : ١٢ / ٢٥ / ٣ .

٣٠٠٢ . التوبة : ١٠٣ .

٣٠٠٣ . البقرة : ١١٠ .

٣٠٠٤ . الأمالي للطوسي : ٦٩٣ / ١٤٧٤ .

٣٠٠٥ . مشكاة الأنوار : ٩٦ / ٢١٢ .

٣٠٠٦ . كتاب من لا يحضره الفقيه : ٢ / ٧ / ١٥٧٩ .

٣٠٠٧ . بحار الأنوار : ٩٦ / ٢٣ / ٥٤ .

٣٠٠٨ . بحار الأنوار : ٧٨ / ٦٠ / ١٣٨ .

٣٠٠٩ . بحار الأنوار : ٩٦ / ٢٣ / ٥٦ .

٣٠١٠ . الكافي : ٢ / ٣٧٤ / ٢ .

٣٠١١ . الكافي : ٣ / ٤٩٨ / ٦ .

٣٠١٢ . بحار الأنوار : ٧٣ / ٣٧٣ / ٨ .

٣٠١٣ . كذا ، ولعلّ الصحيح «زَبيبَتان» (كما في هامش المصدر) .

٣٠١٤ . آل عمران : ١٨٠ .

٣٠١٥ . بحار الأنوار : ٩٦ / ٨ / ٣ .

٣٠١٦ . المؤمنون : ٩٩ـ١٠٠ .

٣٠١٧ . بحار الأنوار : ٩٦ / ٢١ / ٥٠ .

٣٠١٨ . بحار الأنوار : ٩٦ / ١٢ / ١٥ .

٣٠١٩ . ثواب الأعمال : ٢٨١ / ٧ .

٣٠٢٠ . التوبة : ٦٠ .

٣٠٢١ . الكافي : ٣ / ٥٠١ / ١٦ .

٣٠٢٢ . غرر الحكم : ٥٤٤٨ .

٣٠٢٣ . غرر الحكم : ٥٤٤٩ .

٣٠٢٤ . غرر الحكم : ٥٤٥٣ .

٣٠٢٥ . غرر الحكم : ٥٤٥٤ .

٣٠٢٦ . غرر الحكم : ٥٤٥٥ .

٣٠٢٧ . بحار الأنوار : ٧٨ / ٩٩ / ١ .

٣٠٢٨ . بحار الأنوار : ٧٨ / ٢٤٧ / ٧٧ .

٣٠٢٩ . بحار الأنوار : ٧٨ / ٢٦٨ / ١٨٢ .

٣٠٣٠ . وسائل الشيعة : ٦ / ٢٢٠ / ٤ .

٣٠٣١ . كتاب من لا يحضره الفقيه : ٢ / ١٨٣ / ٢٠٨٥ .

٣٠٣٢ . بحار الأنوار : ٧٨ / ٨٠ / ٦٦ .

٣٠٣٣ . غرر الحكم : ٣٢٥٢ .

٣٠٣٤ . تحف العقول : ٣٥٦ .

٣٠٣٥ . عيون أخبار الرّضا : ٢ / ٥٤ / ٢٠٤ .

٣٠٣٦ . غرر الحكم : ٨٠٢٨ .

٣٠٣٧ . بحار الأنوار : ٧٧ / ٢١٣ / ١ .

٣٠٣٨ . غرر الحكم : ٢٠٩٣ .

٣٠٣٩ . غرر الحكم : ٧٨٩٠ .

٣٠٤٠ . عيون أخبار الرّضا : ٢ / ٥٣ / ٢٠٤ .

٣٠٤١ . غرر الحكم : ٩٠٥٤ .

٣٠٤٢ . تحف العقول : ٨٥ .

٣٠٤٣ . عيون أخبار الرّضا : ٢ / ١٧٧ / ٥ .

٣٠٤٤ . الإسراء : ٣٢ .

٣٠٤٥ . بحار الأنوار : ٧٦ / ٣٦٦ / ٣٠ .

٣٠٤٦ . نهج البلاغة : الحكمة ٣٠٥ .

٣٠٤٧ . بحار الأنوار : ٧٩ / ٢٦ / ٢٨ .

٣٠٤٨ . بحار الأنوار : ٧٩ / ٢٤ / ١٩ .

٣٠٤٩ . بحار الأنوار : ٧٩ / ٢٢ / ١٥ .

٣٠٥٠ . بحار الأنوار : ٧٩ / ٢٣ / ١٨ .

٣٠٥١ . الكافي : ٢ / ٣٧٤ / ٢ .

٣٠٥٢ . تهذيب الأحكام : ٣ / ١٤٨ / ٣١٨ .

٣٠٥٣ . تنبيه الخواطر : ١ / ٢٨ .

٣٠٥٤ . تنبيه الخواطر : ١ / ٦٢ .

٣٠٥٥ . كنز العمّال : ١٣٠٢٦ أنظر تمام الحديث .

٣٠٥٦ . بحار الأنوار : ٧٠ / ٣٢٢ .

٣٠٥٧ . غرر الحكم : ١٧١٣ .

٣٠٥٨ . الكافي : ٢ / ١٢٨ / ٣ .

٣٠٥٩ . بحار الأنوار : ١٣ / ٣٤٩ / ٣٧ .

٣٠٦٠ . بحار الأنوار : ٧٣ / ٤٩ / ٢٠ .

٣٠٦١ . الحديد : ٢٣ .

٣٠٦٢ . تحف العقول : ٥٨ .

٣٠٦٣ . بحار الأنوار : ٧٧ / ١٧٢ / ٨ .

٣٠٦٤ . بحار الأنوار : ٧٠ / ٣١٧ / ٢٣ .

٣٠٦٥ . بحار الأنوار : ٧٠ / ٣١٥ / ٢٠ .

٣٠٦٦ . بحار الأنوار : ٧٨ / ٣٧ / ٣ .

٣٠٦٧ . نهج البلاغة : الخطبة ١١٣ .

٣٠٦٨ . عيون أخبار الرّضا : ٢ / ٥٢ / ١٩٩ .

٣٠٦٩ . بحار الأنوار : ٧٨ / ٣٤٩ / ٦ .

٣٠٧٠ . غرر الحكم : ٣٢٠٩ .

٣٠٧١ . غرر الحكم : ٦٩٨٧ .

٣٠٧٢ . بحار الأنوار : ٧٣ / ٦٤ / ٣١ .

٣٠٧٣ . بحار الأنوار : ٧٨ / ٣٢٠ / ٩ .

٣٠٧٤ . بحار الأنوار : ٧٨ / ٣٧٧ / ٣ .

٣٠٧٥ . كنز العمّال : ٦٠٦٠ .

٣٠٧٦ . بحار الأنوار : ٧٨ / ٦٣ / ١٥٥ .

٣٠٧٧ . غرر الحكم : ٢٢٧٥ .

٣٠٧٨ . غرر الحكم : ١٣١٦ .

٣٠٧٩ . تحف العقول : ٢٨١ .

٣٠٨٠ . بحار الأنوار : ٧٣ / ٤٩ / ٢٠ .

٣٠٨١ . الأمالي للصدوق : ٧٢ / ٤١ .

٣٠٨٢ . بحار الأنوار : ٧٨ / ٦٨ / ١٦ .

٣٠٨٣ . نهج البلاغة : الحكمة ٢٨ .

٣٠٨٤ . غرر الحكم : ٤٠٧٨ ـ ٤٠٧٩ .

٣٠٨٥ . بحار الأنوار : ٧٨ / ١٣٩ / ٢٢ .

٣٠٨٦ . بحار الأنوار : ٧٨ / ٣٠٨ / ١ .

٣٠٨٧ . النور : ٣٢ .

٣٠٨٨ . الروم : ٢١ .

٣٠٨٩ . بحار الأنوار : ١٠٣ / ٢٢٠ / ١٨ .

٣٠٩٠ . بحار الأنوار : ١٠٣ / ٢٢٢ / ٤٠ .

٣٠٩١ . بحار الأنوار : ١٠٣ / ٢٢٠ / ٢٣ .

٣٠٩٢ . بحار الأنوار : ١٠٣ / ٢٢١ / ٣٤ .

٣٠٩٣ . كنز العمّال : ٤٤٤٠٣ .

٣٠٩٤ . بحار الأنوار : ١٠٣ / ٢٢١ / ٢٥ .

٣٠٩٥ . بحار الأنوار : ١٠٣ / ٢١٧ / ١ .

٣٠٩٦ . بحار الأنوار : ١٠٣ / ٢٢٢ / ٣٨ .

٣٠٩٧ . بحار الأنوار : ١٠٣ / ٢١٩ / ١٥ .

٣٠٩٨ . بحار الأنوار : ١٠٣ / ٢٢٠ / ١٩ .

٣٠٩٩ . كنز العمّال : ٤٤٤٤٨ .

٣١٠٠ . الكافي : ٥ / ٣٣١ / ٢ .

٣١٠١ . الخصال : ١٤١ / ١٦٢ .

٣١٠٢ . بحار الأنوار : ١٦ / ٢٢٣ / ٢٢ .

٣١٠٣ . بحار الأنوار : ١٠٣ / ٢٣٥ / ١٩ .

٣١٠٤ . كنز العمّال : ٤٤٥٩٠ .

٣١٠٥ . بحار الأنوار : ١٠٣ / ٣٧٢ / ٣ .

٣١٠٦ . مكارم الأخلاق : ١ / ٤٤٦ / ١٥٣٤ .

٣١٠٧ . بحار الأنوار : ١٠٣ / ٢٣٧ / ٢٥ .

٣١٠٨ . كنز العمّال : ٤٤٧٠٧ .

٣١٠٩ . معاني الأخبار : ١٥٢ / ١ .
٣١١٠ . كنز العمّال : ٤٤٥٥٩ .
٣١١١ . كنز العمّال : ٤٤٥٥٧ .
٣١١٢ . بحار الأنوار : ١٠٣ / ٢٣٢ / ١٠ .
٣١١٣ . بحار الأنوار : ١٠٣ / ٢٣٧ / ٣٥ .
٣١١٤ . كنز العمّال : ٤٤٧٧١ .
٣١١٥ . بحار الأنوار : ١٠٣ / ٢٤٦ / ٢٤ .
٣١١٦ . بحارالأنوار : ١٠٣ / ٢٥٦ / ١ .
٣١١٧ . بحار الأنوار : ١٠٣ / ٢٥٣ / ٥٨ .
٣١١٨ . بحار الأنوار : ١٠٣ / ٢٥٤ / ٦٠ .
٣١١٩ . الكافي : ٥ / ٥٦٩ / ٥٩ .
٣١٢٠ . إرشاد القلوب : ١٧٥ .
٣١٢١ . بحار الأنوار : ١٠٣ / ٢٥١ / ٤٩ .
٣١٢٢ . الكافي : ٥ / ٥٠٧ / ٤ .
٣١٢٣ . كنز العمّال : ٤٤٤٣٥ .
٣١٢٤ . تنبيه الخواطر : ٢ / ١٢٢ .
٣١٢٥ . المحجّة البيضاء : ٣ / ٧٠ .
٣١٢٦ . وسائل الشيعة : ١٤ / ١١٦ / ١ .
٣١٢٧ . بحار الأنوار : ١٠٣ / ٢٥٣ / ٥٥ .
٣١٢٨ . جامع الأخبار : ٤٤٧ / ١٢٥٩ .
٣١٢٩ . ثواب الأعمال : ص ٣٣٨ ح ١ .
٣١٣٠ . بحارالأنوار : ٧٧ / ٢٢٩ / ٢ .
٣١٣١ . ثواب الأعمال : ٣٣٩ / ١ .
٣١٣٢ . بحار الأنوار : ١٠٣ / ٢٤٧ / ٣٠ .
٣١٣٣ . كنز العمّال : ٤٤٤١٠ .
٣١٣٤ . كنز العمّال : ٤٤٤٥١ .
٣١٣٥ . الكافي : ٥ / ٣٢٧ / ٤ .
٣١٣٦ . بحار الأنوار : ١٠٣ / ٢٤٠ / ٥٢ .
٣١٣٧ . كتاب من لا يحضره الفقيه : ٣ / ٣٩٠ / ٤٣٧٠ .
٣١٣٨ . الكافي : ٥ / ٣٢٦ / ٣ .
٣١٣٩ . بحار الأنوار : ١٠٤ / ٦٩ / ٢ .
٣١٤٠ . بحار الأنوار : ٧٨ / ١٣٦ / ١٣ .
٣١٤١ . بحار الأنوار : ١٠٣ / ٢٧٩ / ٢ .
٣١٤٢ . كنز العمّال : ٤٤٦١٧ .
٣١٤٣ . كنز العمّال : ٤٤٥٣٦ .
٣١٤٤ . كنز العمّال : ٤٤٥٣٢ .
٣١٤٥ . بحار الأنوار : ٧٧ / ١٩٢ / ١١ .
٣١٤٦ . غرر الحكم : ٥٤٩٢_٥٤٩٣ .
٣١٤٧ . بحار الأنوار : ٢ / ١٤٤ / ٦ .
٣١٤٨ . بحار الأنوار : ٧٤ / ٣٤٧ / ٨ .
٣١٤٩ . الكافي : ٢ / ١٨٦ / ٢ .
٣١٥٠ . الكافي : ٢ / ١٨٨ / ٧ .
٣١٥١ . بحار الأنوار : ٧٤ / ٣٥٥ / ٣٦ .
٣١٥٢ . بحار الأنوار : ٧٤ / ٣٥٣ / ٢٦ .
٣١٥٣ . بحار الأنوار : ٧٤ / ٣٥٥ / ٣٦ .
٣١٥٤ . بحار الأنوار : ٧٧ / ٢٣٧ / ١ .
٣١٥٥ . غرر الحكم : ٤٠٨٧ .
٣١٥٦ . بحار الأنوار : ١٠٠ / ١٤٢ / ١٨ .
٣١٥٧ . بحار الأنوار : ١٠٠ / ١٨٢ / ٤ .
٣١٥٨ . علل الشرائع : ٤٦٠ / ٥ .
٣١٥٩ . بحار الأنوار : ١٠٠ / ١٤١ / ١٤ .
٣١٦٠ . بحار الأنوار : ١٠٢ / ٣١ / ١ .
٣١٦١ . بحار الأنوار : ١٠٠ / ١٢٤ / ٣٤ .
٣١٦٢ . بحار الأنوار : ١٠٠ / ٢٥٩ / ٧ .
٣١٦٣ . معاني الأخبار : ٢٦٧ / ١ .
٣١٦٤ . بحار الأنوار : ١٠٠ / ٢٥٧ / ١ .
٣١٦٥ . الأمالي للطوسي : ٥٥ / ٧٤ .
٣١٦٦ . ثواب‌الأعمال : ١١٤ / ٢١ .
٣١٦٧ . بحار الأنوار : ١٠٠ / ١٤٥ / ٣٤ .
٣١٦٨ . الكافي : ٤ / ٥٧٩ / ١ .
٣١٦٩ . بحار الأنوار : ١٠٠ / ٢٦٢ / ١٤ .
٣١٧٠ . بحار الأنوار : ١٠٢ / ١ / ٣ .
٣١٧١ . عيون أخبار الرّضا : ٢ / ٢٥٨ / ١٦ .
٣١٧٢ . عيون أخبار الرّضا : ٢ / ٢٥٥ / ٢ .
٣١٧٣ . الكافي : ٤ / ٥٨٣ / ٣ .
٣١٧٤ . بحار الأنوار : ١٠٢ / ٥٩ / ١ .
٣١٧٥ . بحار الأنوار : ١٠٢ / ٢٦٧ / ٥ .
٣١٧٦ . بحار الأنوار : ١٠٢ / ٢٦٥ / ٣ .
٣١٧٧ . ثواب الأعمال : ١٢٤ / ١ .
٣١٧٨ . بحار الأنوار : ٧٤ / ٣٥٤ / ٢٩ .
٣١٧٩ . الخصال : ٦١٨ / ١٠ .
٣١٨٠ . بحار الأنوار : ١٠٢ / ٢٩٦ / ٦ .
٣١٨١ . بحار الأنوار : ٧٨ / ٧١ / ٣٥ .
٣١٨٢ . الأعراف : ٣١ .

٣١٨٣ . الأعراف : ٣٢ .
٣١٨٤ . بحار الأنوار : ٧٩ / ٣٠٧ / ٢٣ .
٣١٨٥ . بحار الأنوار : ٧٩ / ٢٩٨ / ٣ .
٣١٨٦ . بحار الأنوار : ٧١ / ٣٣٧ / ٢ .
٣١٨٧ . غرر الحكم : ٣٤٧٠ .
٣١٨٨ . غرر الحكم : ٩٤٨٩ .
٣١٨٩ . غرر الحكم : ٥٥٠٣ .
٣١٩٠ . غرر الحكم : ٥٥٠٤ .
٣١٩١ . الحجر : ٩٢، ٩٣ .
٣١٩٢ . نهج البلاغة : الخطبة ١٦٧ .
٣١٩٣ . صحيح مسلم : ٣ / ١٤٥٩ / ٢٠ .
٣١٩٤ . غرر الحكم : ٧٢٥٤ .
٣١٩٥ . كتاب من لا يحضره الفقيه : ١ / ٨٠ / ١٧٧ .
٣١٩٦ . النحل : ٤٣ .
٣١٩٧ . تحف العقول : ٤١ .
٣١٩٨ . كنز العمّال : ٢٩٢٦٠ .
٣١٩٩ . كنز العمّال : ٢٩٢٦٢ .
٣٢٠٠ . نهج البلاغة : الحكمة ٣٢٠ .
٣٢٠١ . المائدة : ١٠١ .
٣٢٠٢ . كنز العمّال : ٩١٦ .
٣٢٠٣ . مكارم الأخلاق : ٢ / ٣٦٤ / ٢٦٦١ .
٣٢٠٤ . المحاسن : ١ / ٣٢٨ / ٦٦٤ .
٣٢٠٥ . نهج البلاغة : الحكمة ٨٥ .
٣٢٠٦ . بحار الأنوار : ٢ / ١١٧ / ١٥ .
٣٢٠٧ . عنِ القاسمِ بنِ محمّدِ بنِ أبي بكرٍ ـ أحَدِ فُقَهاءِ المَدينةِ المُتَّفَقِ على عِلمِهِ وفِقهِهِ بينَ المسلمينَ ـ أنّه سُئلَ عَن شيءٍ فقالَ : لا اُحسِنُهُ ، فقال السائلُ : إنّي جِئتُ إلَيكَ لا أعرِفُ غَيرَكَ!

فقالَ القاسمُ : لا تَنظُرْ إلى طُولِ لِحيَتي وكَثرَةِ الناسِ حَولي واللهِ ما اُحسِنُهُ ، فقالَ شَيخٌ مِن قُرَيشٍ جالسٌ إلى جَنبِهِ : يا ابنَ أخي الزَمْها ، فقال : فوَاللهِ ما رَأيتُكَ في مجلسٍ أنبَلَ منكَ اليومَ ! فقالَ القاسمُ : واللهِ لأن يُقطَعَ لِساني أحَبُّ إلَيَّ أن أتكَلَّمَ بِما لا عِلمَ لي بِهِ!! بحار الأنوار : ٢ / ١٢٣ / ٥٠ .
٣٢٠٨ . الكافي : ١ / ٤٢ / ٥ .
٣٢٠٩ . البقرة : ٢٧٣ .
٣٢١٠ . كتاب من لا يحضره الفقيه : ٤ / ٣٧٥ / ٥٧٦٢ .
٣٢١١ . كنز العمّال : ١٧١٤٢ .
٣٢١٢ . جامع الأخبار : ٣٧٩ / ١٠٦١ .
٣٢١٣ . غرر الحكم : ٧٩٩٣ .
٣٢١٤ . بحار الأنوار : ٩٦ / ١٥٢ / ١٦ .
٣٢١٥ . تحف العقول : ٢٧٩ .
٣٢١٦ . وسائل الشيعة : ٦ / ٣٠٩ / ١٥ .
٣٢١٧ . بحار الأنوار : ٩٦ / ١٥٦ / ٢٩ .
٣٢١٨ . بحار الأنوار : ٩٦ / ١٥٨ / ٣٧ .
٣٢١٩ . بحار الأنوار : ٩٦ / ١٥٥ / ٢٦ .
٣٢٢٠ . الكافي : ٢ / ١٣٨ / ٢ .
٣٢٢١ . بحار الأنوار : ٩٦ / ١٥٨ / ٣٧ .
٣٢٢٢ . بحار الأنوار : ٩٦ / ١٦٠ / ٣٨ .
٣٢٢٣ . نهج البلاغة : الحكمة ٣٤٦ .
٣٢٢٤ . نهج البلاغة : الحكمة ٦٦ .
٣٢٢٥ . أعلام الدين : ٣٠٤ .
٣٢٢٦ . تحف العقول : ٣٢١ .
٣٢٢٧ . الضحى : ١٠ .
٣٢٢٨ . بحار الأنوار : ٩٦ / ١٥٨ / ٣٧ .
٣٢٢٩ . النوادر للراوندي : ٨٦ / ٩ .
٣٢٣٠ . تحف العقول : ١٧٢ .
٣٢٣١ . نهج البلاغة : الحكمة ٦٧ .
٣٢٣٢ . كشف الغمّة : ٢ / ٢٤٤ .
٣٢٣٣ . تحف العقول : ٣٠٠ .
٣٢٣٤ . عيون أخبار الرِّضا : ٢ / ١٧٩ / ٢ .
٣٢٣٥ . عدّة الداعي : ٩١ .
٣٢٣٦ . بحار الأنوار : ٩٦ / ١٥٩ / ٣٧ .
٣٢٣٧ . كنز العمّال : ٨٠٩٣ .
٣٢٣٨ . بحار الأنوار : ٧٥ / ١٤٨ / ٦ .
٣٢٣٩ . الأنعام : ١٠٨ .
٣٢٤٠ . كنز العمّال : ٢١٢٠ .
٣٢٤١ . الكافي : ٢ / ٣٦٠ / ٣ .
٣٢٤٢ . الأمالي للمفيد : ١١٨ / ٢ .
٣٢٤٣ . تحف العقول : ٤١٢ .
٣٢٤٤ . أعلام الدين : ٣٠٥ .
٣٢٤٥ . بحارالأنوار : ٧٤ / ٤٦ / ٦ .
٣٢٤٦ . مسند احمد بن حنبل : ١ / ٣٠٩ .
٣٢٤٧ . علل الشرائع : ١ / ٥٧٧ .

٣٢٤٨ . غرر الحكم : ١٠٨٨٨ .

٣٢٤٩ . الدعوات : ٣٣ / ٧٠ .

٣٢٥٠ . بحار الأنوار : ٨٥ / ١٣١ / ٦ .

٣٢٥١ . بحار الأنوار : ٨٥ / ١٦٤ / ١٢ .

٣٢٥٢ . الخصال : ٦١٦ / ١٠ .

٣٢٥٣ . الأمالي للطوسي : ٦٦٤ / ١٣٨٩ .

٣٢٥٤ . بحار الأنوار : ٨٥ / ١٣٧ / ١٧ .

٣٢٥٥ . الفتح : ٢٩ .

٣٢٥٦ . بحار الأنوار : ٧١ / ٣٤٤ / ٤ .

٣٢٥٧ . علل الشرائع : ٢٣٣ / ١ .

٣٢٥٨ . بحار الأنوار : ٨٥ / ١٥٣ / ١٤ .

٣٢٥٩ . الجنّ : ١٨ .

٣٢٦٠ . الأمالي للصدوق : ٤٤٠ / ٥٨٤ .

٣٢٦١ . التوبة : ١٨ .

٣٢٦٢ . مكارم الأخلاق : ٢ / ٣٧٤ / ٢٦٦١ .

٣٢٦٣ . الكافي : ٣ / ٣٦٨ / ١ .

٣٢٦٤ . بحار الأنوار : ٧٦ / ٣٣٦ / ١ .

٣٢٦٥ . بحار الأنوار : ٧٧ / ٨٥ / ٣ .

٣٢٦٦ . بحار الأنوار : ٨٣ / ٣٧٩ / ٤٧ .

٣٢٦٧ . الخصال : ٥٤٤ / ٢٠ .

٣٢٦٨ . بحار الأنوار : ٨٤ / ٩ / ٨٣ .

٣٢٦٩ . الأمالي للصدوق : ٥٠٩ / ٧٠٧ .

٣٢٧٠ . كنز العمّال : ١٥٩٢٦ .

٣٢٧١ . كنز العمّال : ١٦٢٠٤ .

٣٢٧٢ . بحار الأنوار : ٧٢ / ١٩٣ / ٩ .

٣٢٧٣ . بحار الأنوار : ٧٨ / ٧ / ٥٩ .

٣٢٧٤ . غرر الحكم : ٢١٤٥ .

٣٢٧٥ . غرر الحكم : ٣٠٦ .

٣٢٧٦ . غرر الحكم : ١٦٠٠ .

٣٢٧٧ . بحار الأنوار : ٧١ / ٣٥٥ / ١٧ .

٣٢٧٨ . بحار الأنوار : ٧١ / ٣٥٠ / ٣ .

٣٢٧٩ . الكافي : ٤ / ٤١ / ١٣ .

٣٢٨٠ . بحار الأنوار : ٧٣ / ٣٠٨ / ٣٧ .

٣٢٨١ . كنز العمّال : ١٦٢١٢ .

٣٢٨٢ . بحار الأنوار : ٧٣ / ٣٠٧ / ٣٤ .

٣٢٨٣ . بحار الأنوار : ٧١ / ٣٥٢ / ٨ .

٣٢٨٤ . الإسراء : ٢٩ .

٣٢٨٥ . بحار الأنوار : ٧٧ / ١١٢ / ٢ .

٣٢٨٦ . غرر الحكم : ١٩٢٨ .

٣٢٨٧ . بحار الأنوار : ٧١ / ٣٥٣ / ١١ .

٣٢٨٨ . بحار الأنوار : ٧١ / ٣٥٧ / ٢١ .

٣٢٨٩ . بحار الأنوار : ٦٩ / ٤٠٧ / ١١٥ .

٣٢٩٠ . نهج البلاغة : الحكمة ١٦٢ .

٣٢٩١ . نهج البلاغة : الحكمة ٤٨ .

٣٢٩٢ . غرر الحكم : ٥٦٣٠ .

٣٢٩٣ . نهج البلاغة : الحكمة ٦ .

٣٢٩٤ . غرر الحكم : ٧١٩٧ .

٣٢٩٥ . غرر الحكم : ٢٤٦٣ .

٣٢٩٦ . غرر الحكم : ٣٢٨٤ .

٣٢٩٧ . بحار الأنوار : ٧٧ / ٢٦٩ / ١ .

٣٢٩٨ . تحف العقول : ٣١٥ .

٣٢٩٩ . بحار الأنوار : ٧٥ / ٧١ / ١٥ .

٣٣٠٠ . الجنّ : ٢٦ و ٢٧ .

٣٣٠١ . بحار الأنوار : ٧٥ / ٦٨ / ٢ .

٣٣٠٢ . بحار الأنوار : ٧٥ / ٧١ / ١٣ .

٣٣٠٣ . غرر الحكم : ١٠٢٦٥ .

٣٣٠٤ . غرر الحكم : ١٠١٦٦ .

٣٣٠٥ . غرر الحكم : ٢٣٠٦ .

٣٣٠٦ . بحار الأنوار : ٧٧ / ٢٣٥ / ٣ .

٣٣٠٧ . غرر الحكم : ٨٩٤١ .

٣٣٠٨ . بحار الأنوار : ٧٥ / ٦٩ / ٤ .

٣٣٠٩ . نهج البلاغة : الكتاب ٢٢ .

٣٣١٠ . بحار الأنوار : ٧٨ / ٧ / ٥٩ .

٣٣١١ . مطالب السؤول : ٥٠ .

٣٣١٢ . كنز العمّال : ٦٠٠٨ .

٣٣١٣ . كنز العمّال : ٦٠٠٩ .

٣٣١٤ . نهج البلاغة : الحكمة ٢٥٧ .

٣٣١٥ . الكافي : ٢ / ١٨٩ / ٦ .

٣٣١٦ . الكافي : ٢ / ١٨٨ / ١ .

٣٣١٧ . الكافي : ٢ / ١٩٩ / ٣ .

٣٣١٨ . الكافي : ٢ / ١٩٠ / ٨ .

٣٣١٩ . الكافي : ٢ / ٢٠٠ / ٤ .

٣٣٢٠ . الأعراف : ٣١ .

٣٣٢١ . غرر الحكم : ١٠٠٩٢ .

٣٣٢٢ . بحار الأنوار :٧٢ / ١٩٢ / ٩ .

٣٣٢٣ . الصحيفة السجّاديّة : الدعاء ٢٠ .

٣٣٢٤ . تحف العقول : ٢٢ .

٣٣٢٥ . كنز العمّال : ٧٣٦٦ .

٣٣٢٦ . نهج البلاغة : الخطبة ١٢٦ .

٣٣٢٧ . بحار الأنوار :٧٩ / ٣١٧ / ١ .

٣٣٢٨ . الدرّة الباهرة : ٤٣ .

٣٣٢٩ . الكافي : ٤ / ٥٦ / ١٠ .

٣٣٣٠ . بحار الأنوار :٧٧ / ١٦٥ / ٢ .

٣٣٣١ . بحار الأنوار : ٧٥ / ٣٠٣ / ٦ .

٣٣٣٢ . بحار الأنوار : ٧٩ / ٣١٧ / ١ .

٣٣٣٣ . المائدة : ٣٨ .

٣٣٣٤ . نور الثقلين : ١ / ٦٢٧ / ١٨٣ .

٣٣٣٥ . صحيح مسلم : ٣ / ١٣١٢ / ٢ .

٣٣٣٦ . الكافي : ٧ / ٢٢٦ / ٧ .

٣٣٣٧ . الكافي : ٧ / ٢٢٦ / ٦ .

٣٣٣٨ . وسائل الشيعة : ١٨ / ٥١٠ / ٥ .

٣٣٣٩ . علل الشرائع : ٥٣٥ / ١ .

٣٣٤٠ . الكافي : ٧ / ٢٣١ / ٢ .

٣٣٤١ . تهذيب الأحكام : ١٠ / ١٢٢ / ٤٨٩ .

٣٣٤٢ . الأمالي للطوسي : ٤٢٦ / ٩٥٣ .

٣٣٤٣ . غرر الحكم : ١٢٩٣ .

٣٣٤٤ . تحف العقول : ٣٦٤ .

٣٣٤٥ . غرر الحكم : ٢٤٧٩ .

٣٣٤٦ . غرر الحكم : ٤٧١٧ .

٣٣٤٧ . غرر الحكم : ٦٤٨٩ .

٣٣٤٨ . غرر الحكم : ٧٨٨٧ .

٣٣٤٩ . غرر الحكم : ٨٢٤٦_٨٢٤٧ .

٣٣٥٠ . النوادر للراوندي : ١١٠ / ٩٣ .

٣٣٥١ . غرر الحكم : ٥٠٨٣ .

٣٣٥٢ . غرر الحكم : ٩٢٩٦ .

٣٣٥٣ . معاني الأخبار : ٣٤٥ / ١ .

٣٣٥٤ . غرر الحكم : ٦٢٢٣ .

٣٣٥٥ . بحار الأنوار : ٧٤ / ١٨٥ / ٢ .

٣٣٥٦ . غرر الحكم : ٣٢١٨ .

٣٣٥٧ . وقعة صفّين : ١٠٨ .

٣٣٥٨ . غرر الحكم : ٣٢٩٧ .

٣٣٥٩ . غرر الحكم : ٣١٠٠ .

٣٣٦٠ . كنز العمّال : ١٧٤٧٠ .

٣٣٦١ . بحار الأنوار : ٧٦ / ٢٢٢ / ٧ .

٣٣٦٢ . المحاسن : ٢ / ٤٦١ / ٢٥٩٥ .

٣٣٦٣ . الكافي : ٦ / ٣٢٦ / ٧ .

٣٣٦٤ . كنز العمّال : ١٧٥٥٠ .

٣٣٦٥ . مكارم الأخلاق : ١ / ٥٣٦ / ١٨٦٦ .

٣٣٦٦ . بحار الأنوار :٧٦ / ٢٨٣ / ٢ .

٣٣٦٧ . نهج البلاغة : الكتاب ٣١ .

٣٣٦٨ . بحار الأنوار :٧٦ / ٢٦٧ / ٨ .

٣٣٦٩ . بحار الأنوار : ١٠٠ / ١٠٣ / ٥ ، وأنظر :٧٦ / ٢٢٦ و ص ٢٢٧ و ٢٣١ و ٢٣٢ و ج ٥٩ / ٢٨ .

٣٣٧٠ . بحار الأنوار :٧٦ / ٢٧١ / ٢٨ .

٣٣٧١ . الأمالي للمفيد : ٤٤ / ٣ .

٣٣٧٢ . بحار الأنوار : ١٠ / ١٠٨ / ١ .

٣٣٧٣ . بحار الأنوار :٧٦ / ٢٢٢ / ٩ .

٣٣٧٤ . كنز العمّال : ١٦٣٨٠ .

٣٣٧٥ . كنز العمّال : ١٦٣٧٧ .

٣٣٧٦ . الكافي : ٢ / ٢٠١ / ٥ .

٣٣٧٧ . بحار الأنوار : ٩٦ / ١٧٢ / ٨ .

٣٣٧٨ . بحار الأنوار : ٩٦ / ١٧٣ / ١٣ .

٣٣٧٩ . بحار الأنوار : ٩٦ / ١٧٢ / ٨ .

٣٣٨٠ . بحار الأنوار : ٧٥ / ٤٥٥ / ٢٤ .

٣٣٨١ . كنز العمّال : ١٣١٣٩ .

٣٣٨٢ . بحار الأنوار : ٧٩ / ١٣١ / ٢٠ .

٣٣٨٣ . البقرة : ١٨ .

٣٣٨٤ . مكارم الأخلاق : ٢ / ٣٥٢ / ٢٦٦ .

٣٣٨٥ . بحار الأنوار : ١٠ / ١١٤ / ١ .

٣٣٨٦ . غرر الحكم : ١٠٩٤٨ .

٣٣٨٧ . غرر الحكم : ٥٦٥١ .

٣٣٨٨ . الكافي : ٦ / ٥٢٦ / ٧ .

٣٣٨٩ . الكافي : ٦ / ٥٢٦ / ٦ .

٣٣٩٠ . نهج البلاغة : الخطبة ١١٤ .

٣٣٩١ . الكافي : ٦ / ٥٣١ / ٧ .

٣٣٩٢ . المحاسن : ٢ / ٤٤٦ / ٢٥٣١ .

٣٣٩٣ . كنز العمّال : ٥٤٤٠ .

٣٣٩٤ . كنز العمّال : ٥٤٤١ .

٣٣٩٥ . سنن أبي داوود : ٣ / ١٣ / 2513 .

٣٣٩٦ . النساء : ١٠٢ .

٣٣٩٧ . بحار الأنوار : ١٠٠ / ٩ / ١٠ .

٣٣٩٨ . كنز العمّال : ١٠٤٨٢ .

٣٣٩٩ . الكافي : ٥ / ٧ / ٧ .

٣٤٠٠ . كتاب من لا يحضره الفقيه : ٤ / ٣٥٦ / ٥٧٦٢ .

٣٤٠١ . بحار الأنوار : ١٠ / ٣٦٨ / ٧ .

٣٤٠٢ . بحار الأنوار : ٧٥ / ٣٧١ / ١٣ .

٣٤٠٣ . بحار الأنوار : ٧٥ / ٣٧٢ / ١٩ .

٣٤٠٤ . نهج البلاغة : الحكمة ٢٦٣ .

٣٤٠٥ . بحار الأنوار :٧٧ / ٢١٥ / ١ .

٣٤٠٦ . بحار الأنوار : ٧٦ / ٣٦٠ / ٣٠ .

٣٤٠٧ . الأمالي للصدوق : ٥١٣ / ٧٠٧ .

٣٤٠٨ . ثواب الأعمال : ٢٩٤ .

٣٤٠٩ . كنز العمّال : ١٤٥٨٩ .

٣٤١٠ . نهج البلاغة : الحكمة ٣٣٢ .

٣٤١١ . نهج البلاغة : الخطبة ١٦٩ .

٣٤١٢ . آل عمران : ١٩ .

٣٤١٣ . آل عمران : ٨٥ .

٣٤١٤ . كتاب من لا يحضره الفقيه : ٤ / ٣٣٤ / ٥٧١٩ .

٣٤١٥ . الكافي : ٢ / ٤٦١ / ٢ .

٣٤١٦ . نهج البلاغة : الحكمة ٣٧١ .

٣٤١٧ . نهج البلاغة : الخطبة ١٩٨ ،اُنظر تمام الخطبة .

٣٤١٨ . نهج البلاغة : الخطبة١٠٦ .

٣٤١٩ . كنز العمّال : ١٧ .

٣٤٢٠ . كنز العمّال : ٥٢٢٥ .

٣٤٢١ . نهج البلاغة : الحكمة ١٢٥ .

٣٤٢٢ . غرر الحكم : (٦٣٤٩ ـ ٦٣٥٠) .

٣٤٢٣ . كنز العمّال : ٧٤٥ .

٣٤٢٤ . كنز العمّال : ٧٤٧ .

٣٤٢٥ . كنز العمّال : ٧٤٢ .

٣٤٢٦ . الكافي : ٢ / ١٦٣ / ١ .

٣٤٢٧ . غرر الحكم : ٤٧٤٢ .

٣٤٢٨ . غرر الحكم : ٩٢٢٠ .

٣٤٢٩ . معاني الأخبار : ٢٣٩ / ١ .

٣٤٣٠ . المحاسن : ١ / ٤٤٥ / ١٠٣١ .

٣٤٣١ . كنز العمّال : ٣٧٦٣١ .

٣٤٣٢ . تحف العقول : ١٩٦ .

٣٤٣٣ . الأمالي للمفيد : ٣٥٣ / ٤ .

٣٤٣٤ . الكافي : ١ / ٢٠٠ / ١ .

٣٤٣٥ . يونس : ١٠ .

٣٤٣٦ . كنز العمّال : ٢٥٢٤٢ .

٣٤٣٧ . الأمالي للطوسي : ٨٩ / ١٣٦ .

٣٤٣٨ . الخصال : ١٨١ / ٢٤٦ .

٣٤٣٩ . المحاسن : ٢ / ١٤٣ / ١٣٧١ .

٣٤٤٠ . جامع الأخبار : ٢٣١ / ٥٩٦ .

٣٤٤١ . الخصال : ١٩ / ٦٧ .

٣٤٤٢ . بحار الأنوار :٧٦ / ١٢ / ٥٠ .

٣٤٤٣ . كنز العمّال : ٢٥٢٦٥ .

٣٤٤٤ . بحار الأنوار :٧٦ / ١١ / ٤٦ .

٣٤٤٥ . النور : ٦١ .

٣٤٤٦ . بحار الأنوار :٧٦ / ٧ / ٢٥ .

٣٤٤٧ . النساء : ٨٦ .

٣٤٤٨ . كنز العمّال : ٢٥٢٩٤ .

٣٤٤٩ . كنز العمّال : ٢٥٣٢١ .

٣٤٥٠ . بحار الأنوار :٧٦ / ١٠ / ٣٨ .

٣٤٥١ . بحار الأنوار :٧٦ / ٩ / ٣٥ .

٣٤٥٢ . الكافي : ٥ / ٥٣٥ / ٣ .

٣٤٥٣ . النساء : ٦٥ .

٣٤٥٤ . بحار الأنوار : ٨٢ / ١٣٦ / ٢٢ .

٣٤٥٥ . بحار الأنوار : ٧١ / ١٥٣ / ٦٣ .

٣٤٥٦ . بحار الأنوار : ٤٦ / ٣٠١ / ٤٤ .

٣٤٥٧ . صدر الحديث في صبيّ له كان مريضاً ثمّ توفّي، وقد كان ﷺ قد أبدى اهتماماً كبيراً واغتمّ غمّاً شديداً في مرضه حتّى تبيّن ذلك أصحابُه منه، لكنّه بعد موته كان منبسط الوجه .

٣٤٥٨ . بحار الأنوار :٢ / ٢٠٥ / ٩١ .

٣٤٥٩ . تنبيه الخواطر : ٢ / ١٨٥ .

٣٤٦٠ . بحار الأنوار :٩٣ / ١٩٠ / ٢٥ .

٣٤٦١ . غرر الحكم : ٤٠٩٠ .

٣٤٦٢ . نهج البلاغة : الخطبة ١٠٥ .

٣٤٦٣ . الملك : ١٠ .

٣٤٦٤ . نهج البلاغة : الخطبة٨٨ .

٣٤٦٥ . غرر الحكم : ٦٢٣٤ .

٣٤٦٦ . غرر الحكم : ٥٥٧٩ .
٣٤٦٧ . غرر الحكم : ٩٢٤٣ .
٣٤٦٨ . الإسراء : ٣٦ .
٣٤٦٩ . كتاب من لا يحضره الفقيه : ٢ / ٦٢٦ / ٣٢١٥ .
٣٤٧٠ . الكافي : ٦ / ١٩ / ١٠ .
٣٤٧١ . مكارم الأخلاق : ١ / ٤٧٤ / ١٦٢٦ .
٣٤٧٢ . آل عمران : ٣١ .
٣٤٧٣ . تفسير العيّاشي : ١ / ١٦٨ / ٢٨ .
٣٤٧٤ . الكافي : ٦ / ١٨ / ٣ .
٣٤٧٥ . بحار الأنوار : ١٠٤ / ١٢٧ / ٤ .
٣٤٧٦ . النمل : ٣٠ .
٣٤٧٧ . كنز العمّال : ٢٤٩٠ .
٣٤٧٨ . مابين المعقوفين سقط من المصدر .
٣٤٧٩ . كنز العمّال : ٢٤٩١ .
٣٤٨٠ . الكافي : ٢ / ٦٧٢ / ١ .
٣٤٨١ . التوحيد : ٢٣١ / ٥ .
٣٤٨٢ . بحار الأنوار : ١٤ / ١١٣ / ٥ .
٣٤٨٣ . كنز العمّال : ٩١١ .
٣٤٨٤ . الكافي : ١ / ٧٠ / ٧ .
٣٤٨٥ . كنز العمّال : ٤٣٠٧٩ .
٣٤٨٦ . نهج البلاغة : الكتاب ٥٣ .
٣٤٨٧ . بحار الأنوار : ٧٦ / ١٧٨ / ٣ .
٣٤٨٨ . بحار الأنوار : ٧٦ / ١٧٩ / ٥ .
٣٤٨٩ . غرر الحكم : ٦٦٦ .
٣٤٩٠ . غرر الحكم : ٥٦١٣ .
٣٤٩١ . غرر الحكم : ٣١٤٩ .
٣٤٩٢ . نهج البلاغة : الخطبة ٨٣ .
٣٤٩٣ . ثواب الأعمال : ١ / ١٠٢ / ٢ .
٣٤٩٤ . بحار الأنوار : ٩٧ / ٨٨ / ١٥ .
٣٤٩٥ . كنز العمّال : ١٧٥١٧ .
٣٤٩٦ . بحار الأنوار : ٧٢ / ١٩٤ / ١٤ .
٣٤٩٧ . نهج البلاغة : الحكمة ٢٢٤ .
٣٤٩٨ . بحار الأنوار : ٧٨ / ٨٢ / ٨٢ .
٣٤٩٩ . غرر الحكم : ٦٥٥٩ .
٣٥٠٠ . بحار الأنوار : ١ / ٩٤ / ٢٣ .
٣٥٠١ . بحار الأنوار : ٧٨ / ١١٣ / ٧ .
٣٥٠٢ . غرر الحكم : ٩٨١٣ .
٣٥٠٣ . الخصال : ٤٣٤ / ٢٠ .
٣٥٠٤ . الخصال : ٢٧١ / ١٠ .
٣٥٠٥ . غرر الحكم : ١٧ .
٣٥٠٦ . غرر الحكم : ٣٩٣١ .
٣٥٠٧ . غرر الحكم : ٤٨٢٠ .
٣٥٠٨ . غرر الحكم : ٤٨١٨ .
٣٥٠٩ . غرر الحكم : ٤٨٢١ .
٣٥١٠ . غرر الحكم : ٥٥٧١ .
٣٥١١ . غرر الحكم : ٩٧١٤ .
٣٥١٢ . غرر الحكم : ٥٢٦٦ .
٣٥١٣ . غرر الحكم : ٧٧٢ .
٣٥١٤ . غرر الحكم : ٨٠١٣ .
٣٥١٥ . غرر الحكم : ٥٥٨٨ .
٣٥١٦ . غرر الحكم : ٩٣٣٣ .
٣٥١٧ . بحار الأنوار : ٧٧ / ٧٥ / ٣ .
٣٥١٨ . بحار الأنوار : ٧٣ / ٧٥ / ٣٩ .
٣٥١٩ . نهج البلاغة : الحكمة ٢٨٥ .
٣٥٢٠ . نهج البلاغة : الحكمة ١٥٠ .
٣٥٢١ . بحار الأنوار : ٩٨ / ٨٨ / ٢ .
٣٥٢٢ . بحار الأنوار : ٧٨ / ١٦٤ / ١ .
٣٥٢٣ . بحار الأنوار : ٧٣ / ٣٦٥ / ٩٧ .
٣٥٢٤ . كنز العمّال : ٩٣٣٠ .
٣٥٢٥ . تفسير القرطبى : ١٣ / ١٦ .
٣٥٢٦ . بحار الأنوار : ٨٤ / ١١ / ٨٧ .
٣٥٢٧ . بحار الأنوار : ١٠٣ / ١٠٢ / ٤٤ .
٣٥٢٨ . الكافي : ٣ / ٢٢ / ١ .
٣٥٢٩ . بحار الأنوار : ٧٧ / ٦٩ / ٨ .
٣٥٣٠ . بحار الأنوار : ٧٦ / ١٣٧ / ٤٨ .
٣٥٣١ . كنز العمّال : ٢٦٢٠٠ .
٣٥٣٢ . كنز العمّال : ٢٧٥٣ .
٣٥٣٣ . بحار الأنوار : ٧٦ / ١٢٦ / ٢ .
٣٥٣٤ . بحار الأنوار : ٧٦ / ١٢٨ / ١١ .
٣٥٣٥ . بحار الأنوار : ٧٦ / ١٣٥ / ٤٨ .
٣٥٣٦ . الخصال : ٤٨١ / ٥٣ .
٣٥٣٧ . بحار الأنوار : ٧٦ / ١٣٩ / ٥٢ .
٣٥٣٨ . بحار الأنوار : ٧٦ / ١٣٧ / ٤٨ .
٣٥٣٩ . الدعوات للراونديّ : ١٦١ / ٤٤٥ .

٣٥٤٠ . بحار الأنوار : ٧٦ / ١٣٥ / ٤٧ .
٣٥٤١ . كتاب من لا يحضره الفقيه : ١ / ٤٨٠ / ١٣٩٠ .
٣٥٤٢ . الاختصاص : ٣٤٣ .
٣٥٤٣ . كنز العمّال : ٤٣٠٥٨ .
٣٥٤٤ . غررالحكم : ٥٧٦٤ .
٣٥٤٥ . تحف العقول : ٧٠ .
٣٥٤٦ . الكافي : ٨ / ٩٣ / ٦٦ .
٣٥٤٧ . بحار الأنوار : ١ / ٢٢٢ / ٦ .
٣٥٤٨ . المحاسن : ١ / ٣٥٧ / ٧٦٠ .
٣٥٤٩ . الأمالي للطوسي : ٣٠٣ / ٦٠٤ .
٣٥٥٠ . كنز العمّال : ٤٣٠٥٧ .
٣٥٥١ . كنز العمّال : ١٠١٨٥ .
٣٥٥٢ . كنز العمّال : ٤٣٠٥٩ .
٣٥٥٣ . كنز العمّال : ٤٣٠٦٠ .
٣٥٥٤ . الكافي : ٨ / ٣٩٥ / ٥٩٥ .
٣٥٥٥ . نهج البلاغة : الخطبة ٣٨ .
٣٥٥٦ . تحف العقول : ١٥٥ .
٣٥٥٧ . أعلام الدين : ٣٠١ .
٣٥٥٨ . الخصال : ١٦ / ٥٦ .
٣٥٥٩ . تنبيه الخواطر : ١ / ٥٢ .
٣٥٦٠ . الكافي : ١ / ٦٨ / ١٠ .
٣٥٦١ . كنز العمّال : ٩٠٥٦ .
٣٥٦٢ . كنز العمّال : ٩٠٥١ .
٣٥٦٣ . كنز العمّال : ٩٠٥٧ .
٣٥٦٤ . كنز العمّال : ٩٠٨١ .
٣٥٦٥ . الكافي : ٥ / ٢٦٤ / ٩ .
٣٥٦٦ . لكافي : ٥ / ٢٦٤ / ٨ .
٣٥٦٧ . غرر الحكم : ٥٧٢ .
٣٥٦٨ . غرر الحكم : ١٧٠٠ .
٣٥٦٩ . غرر الحكم : ٧٥٩٧ .
٣٥٧٠ . بحار الأنوار : ٧٨ / ١٠٤ / ٢ .
٣٥٧١ . بحار الأنوار : ٧٨ / ٢٣٦ / ٦٦ .
٣٥٧٢ . نهج البلاغة : الحكمة ٤٧ .
٣٥٧٣ . غرر الحكم : ٥٧٦٣ .
٣٥٧٤ . غرر الحكم : ٦١٨٠ .
٣٥٧٥ . معاني الأخبار : ٣٦٦ / ١ .
٣٥٧٦ . غرر الحكم : ٢٨٩٩ .
٣٥٧٧ . غرر الحكم : ٣٢٥٧ .
٣٥٧٨ . غرر الحكم : ١٠٥٩١ .
٣٥٧٩ . غرر الحكم : ٣١٨٨ .
٣٥٨٠ . غرر الحكم : ٣٩٣٨ .
٣٥٨١ . بحار الأنوار : ٧٨ / ٣٧٧ / ٣ .
٣٥٨٢ . البقرة : ٢١٦ .
٣٥٨٣ . الإسراء : ١١ .
٣٥٨٤ . نهج البلاغة : الحكمة ٣٨٧ .
٣٥٨٥ . نهج البلاغة : الخطبة ١٦٧ .
٣٥٨٦ . بحار الأنوار : ٧٧ / ١٣٧ / ٢ .
٣٥٨٧ . نهج البلاغة : الخطبة ١١٤ .
٣٥٨٨ . نهج البلاغة : الحكمة ٣٢.
٣٥٨٩ . بحار الأنوار : ٧٢ / ٢٣٦ / ٣ .
٣٥٩٠ . بحار الأنوار : ٧٣ / ٢٦٣ / ٤ .
٣٥٩١ . بحار الأنوار : ٦٢ / ٢٩٣ .
٣٥٩٢ . تنبيه الخواطر : ٢ / ١٢٠ .
٣٥٩٣ . غرر الحكم : ٢٤٧٧ .
٣٥٩٤ . لقمان : ١٣ .
٣٥٩٥ . النساء : ١١٦ .
٣٥٩٦ . مكارم الأخلاق : ٢ / ٣٥٧ / ٢٦٦٠ .
٣٥٩٧ . الكافي : ٢ / ٤١٥ / ١ .
٣٥٩٨ . الكافي : ٢ / ٣٩٧ / ١ .
٣٥٩٩ . الكافي : ٢ / ٣٩٧ / ٢ .
٣٦٠٠ . يوسف : ١٠٦ .
٣٦٠١ . بحار الأنوار : ٧٨ / ٢٠٠ / ٢٨ .
٣٦٠٢ . تفسير العيّاشيّ : ٢ / ٢٠٠ / ٩٦ .
٣٦٠٣ . الكافي : ٢ / ٣٩٧ / ٤ .
٣٦٠٤ . معاني الأخبار : ٣٧٩ / ١ .
٣٦٠٥ . بحار الأنوار : ٥٨ / ٣١٧ / ٨ .
٣٦٠٦ . نهج البلاغة : الخطبة ١٩٢ .
٣٦٠٧ . المؤمنون : ٩٧ ، ٩٨ .
٣٦٠٨ . النحل : ٩٨ .
٣٦٠٩ . نهج البلاغة : الخطبة ١٥١ .
٣٦١٠ . فاطر : ٦ .
٣٦١١ . غرر الحكم : ٢٦٢٣ .
٣٦١٢ . تحف العقول : ٣٠١ .
٣٦١٣ . تحف العقول : ٣٩٩ .

٣٦١٤ . الأعراف : ٢٧ .

٣٦١٥ . الخصال : ١١٣ / ٩١ .

٣٦١٦ . يسٓ : ٦٠ .

٣٦١٧ . نهج البلاغة : الخطبة ٧ .

٣٦١٨ . البقرة : ٢٦٨ .

٣٦١٩ . النساء : ١٢٠ .

٣٦٢٠ . الأنعام : ٤٣ .

٣٦٢١ . بشارة المصطفى : ٢٧ .

٣٦٢٢ . نهج البلاغة : الخطبة ٦٤ .

٣٦٢٣ . الصحيفة السجّاديّة : الدعاء ٣٧ .

٣٦٢٤ . الكافي : ٢ / ٣٢٧ / ٢ .

٣٦٢٥ . النحل : ٩٩ .

٣٦٢٦ . الحِجر : ٤٢ .

٣٦٢٧ . بحار الأنوار : ٧٨ / ٩ / ٦٤ .

٣٦٢٨ . بحار الأنوار : ٧٨ / ١٦٤ / ١ .

٣٦٢٩ . الخصال : ٢٨٥ / ٣٧ .

٣٦٣٠ . الزخرف : ٣٦ .

٣٦٣١ . الكافي : ٢ / ٣١٤ / ٨ .

٣٦٣٢ . نهج البلاغة : الخطبة ٨٦ .

٣٦٣٣ . تحف العقول : ٣٦٣ .

٣٦٣٤ . الشعراء : ٢٢٤ـ٢٢٧ .

٣٦٣٥ . معاني الأخبار : ٣٨٥ / ١٩ .

٣٦٣٦ . مجمع البيان : ٧ / ٣٢٦ .

٣٦٣٧ . الدرّ المنثور : ٦ / ٣٣٦ .

٣٦٣٨ . الأمالي للصدوق : ٧١٨ / ٩٨٧ ، سنن أبي داوود :
٤ / ٣٠٣ / ٥٠١١ نحوه .

٣٦٣٩ . عيون أخبار الرّضا : ١ / ٧ / ١ .

٣٦٤٠ . عيون أخبار الرّضا : ١ / ٧ / ٢ .

٣٦٤١ . دعائم الإسلام : ١ / ٣٧٠ .

٣٦٤٢ . الجعفريّات : ٨٤ .

٣٦٤٣ . شرح نهج البلاغة : ١ / ٢٦٢ .

٣٦٤٤ . الكافي : ٥ / ٤٧ / ١ .

٣٦٤٥ . جامع الأحاديث للقمّي : ٨٩ .

٣٦٤٦ . كنز العمّال : ٣٩٠٣٠ .

٣٦٤٧ . كنز العمّال : ٣٩٠٣٣ .

٣٦٤٨ . كنز العمّال : ٦٤٨٩ .

٣٦٤٩ . كنز العمّال : ٦٤٩٦ .

٣٦٥٠ . تحف العقول : ٣٨١ .

٣٦٥١ . قال العلّامة الطباطبائي في تفسير قوله تعالىٰ : ﴿قُلْ للهِ الشَّفاعَةُ جَميعاً﴾ : توضيح وتأكيد لما مرّ من قوله : ﴿قُلْ أوَلَوْ كانُوا لا يَمْلِكُونَ شَيْئاً﴾ . الزمر : ٤٣ .

واللام في « لله » للملك ، وقوله : ﴿لَهُ مُلْكُ السَّماواتِ والأَرْضِ﴾ . الزمر : ٤٤ .

في مقام التعليل للجملة السابقة ، والمعنى : كلّ شفاعة فإنّها مملوكة لله فإنّه المالك لكلّ شيء ، إلّا أن يأذن لأحد في شيء منها فيملّكه إياها ، وأمّا استقلال بعض عباده كالملائكة بملك الشفاعة مطلقاً ـ كما يقولون ـ فممّا لا يكون ، قال تعالىٰ : ﴿ما مِنْ شَفِيعٍ إلّا مِنْ بَعْدِ إذْنِهِ﴾ .

يونس : ٣ .

وللآية معنى آخر أدقّ إذا انضمّت إلى مثل قوله تعالىٰ : ﴿لَيْسَ لَهُمْ مِنْ دُونِهِ وَلِيٌّ ولا شَفِيعٌ﴾ . الأنعام : ٥١ .

وهو أنّ الشفيع بالحقيقة هو الله سبحانه وغيره من الشفعاء لهم الشفاعة بإذن منه ، فقد تقدّم في بحث الشفاعة في الجزء الأوّل من الكتاب أنّ الشفاعة ينتهي إلى توسّط بعض صفاته تعالىٰ بينه وبين المشفوع له لإصلاح حاله ، كتوسّط الرحمة والمغفرة بينه وبين عبده المذنب لإنجائه من وبال الذنب وتخليصه من العذاب . الميزان في تفسير القرآن : ١٧ / ٢٧٠ .

٣٦٥٢ . الزمر : ٤٤ .

٣٦٥٣ . البقرة : ٢٥٥ .

٣٦٥٤ . مريم : ٨٧ .

٣٦٥٥ . طه : ١٠٩ .

٣٦٥٦ . كنز العمّال : ٣٩٠٥٧ .

٣٦٥٧ . كنز العمّال : ٣٩٠٤٣ .

٣٦٥٨ . الأمالي للصدوق : ٣٧٠ / ٤٦٢ .

٣٦٥٩ . الخصال : ٢٩ / ١٠٣ .

٣٦٦٠ . بحار الأنوار : ٨ / ٥٧ / ٧٢ .

٣٦٦١ . بحار الأنوار : ٨ / ٣٦ / ٩ .

٣٦٦٢ . الخصال : ٦٣ / ٩٣ .

٣٦٦٣ . الخصال : ٣٥٥ / ٣٦ .

٣٦٦٤ . المحاسن : ١ / ١٥٩ / ٢٢٣ .

٣٦٦٥ . عيون أخبار الرّضا : ١ / ١٣٦ / ٣٥ .

٣٦٦٦ . المحاسن : ١ / ١٥٩ / ٢٢٥ .

٣٦٦٧ . المحاسن : ١ / ٢٩٤ / ٥٨٧ ، وانظر بحار الأنوار :

٨ / ٤١ / ٢٧ و ٦٨ / ١٢٦ / ٥٤ .
٣٦٦٨ . بحار الأنوار : ٨ / ٣٨ / ١٦ .
٣٦٦٩ . الخصال : ١٥٦ / ١٩٧ .
٣٦٧٠ . بحار الأنوار : ٨ / ٥٨ / ٧٥ .
٣٦٧١ . بحار الأنوار : ٨ / ٤٣ / ٣٩ .
٣٦٧٢ . بحار الأنوار : ٨ / ٥٨ / ٧٥ .
٣٦٧٣ . غرر الحكم : ٥٧٨٩ .
٣٦٧٤ . الأمالي للصدوق : ٥٩٨ / ٨٢٦ .
٣٦٧٥ . بحار الأنوار : ٨ / ٥٨ / ٧٥ .
٣٦٧٦ . بحار الأنوار : ٨ / ٤٣ / ٤١ .
٣٦٧٧ . بحار الأنوار : ج ٨ ص ٣٠ .
٣٦٧٨ . الشعراء : ١٠٠ و ١٠١ .
٣٦٧٩ . الكافي : ٨ / ١٠١ / ٧٢ .
٣٦٨٠ . نهج البلاغة : الخطبة ٨٦ .
٣٦٨١ . نهج البلاغة : الكتاب ٧٨ .
٣٦٨٢ . غرر الحكم : ٤٤٩٩ .
٣٦٨٣ . كنز العمّال : ٤٩١ .
٣٦٨٤ . التوحيد : ٣٥٧ / ٥ .
٣٦٨٥ . التوحيد : ٣٥٨ / ٦ .
٣٦٨٦ . التوحيد : ٣٥٦ / ٣ .
٣٦٨٧ . غرر الحكم : ٥٥١٦ .
٣٦٨٨ بحار الأنوار : ٩٨ / ٢١٨ / ٣ .
٣٦٨٩ بحار الأنوار : ٢ / ٥٢ / ١٩ .
٣٦٩٠ كنز العمّال : ١٦٦٨٣ .
٣٦٩١ . الأمالي للصدوق : ٤٧٨ / ٦٤٤ .
٣٦٩٢ . الخصال : ٢٤٣ / ٩٦ .
٣٦٩٣ . غرر الحكم : ٩٢٩٧ .
٣٦٩٤ . غرر الحكم : ٩٣٠٧ .
٣٦٩٥ . البقرة : ١٥٢ .
٣٦٩٦ . الإرشاد : ١ / ٣٠٠ .
٣٦٩٧ . غرر الحكم : ٣٣٢٩ .
٣٦٩٨ . بحار الأنوار : ٧١ / ٥٢ / ٧٧ .
٣٦٩٩ . الزمر : ٦٦ .
٣٧٠٠ . مصباح الشريعة : ص ٥٥ .
٣٧٠١ . تحف العقول : ٤٨٣ .
٣٧٠٢ . أعلام الدين : ٣١٣ .
٣٧٠٣ . إبراهيم : ٧ .
٣٧٠٤ . الكافي : ٢ / ٩٤ / ٢ .
٣٧٠٥ . الأمالي للطوسي : ٥٨٠ / ١١٩٧ .
٣٧٠٦ . بحار الأنوار : ٩٤ / ١٤٦ / ٢١ .
٣٧٠٧ . قصص الأنبياء : ١٦١ / ١٧٨ .
٣٧٠٨ . مشكاة الأنوار : ٧٥ / ١٤٦ .
٣٧٠٩ . نهج البلاغة : الحكمة ١١ .
٣٧١٠ . تحف العقول : ٢٨٥ .
٣٧١١ . الكافي : ٢ / ٩٥ / ١٠ .
٣٧١٢ . الكافي : ٢ / ٩٦ / ١٥ .
٣٧١٣ . الكافي : ٢ / ٩٧ / ١٩ .
٣٧١٤ . مصباح الشريعة : ٥٣ .
٣٧١٥ . الإرشاد : ١ / ٣٠٤ .
٣٧١٦ . الكافي : ٢ / ٩٩ / ٣٠ .
٣٧١٧ . تحف العقول : ٢٣٣ .
٣٧١٨ . الخصال : ٥٦٨ / ١ .
٣٧١٩ . الكافي : ٢ / ٩٩ / ٣٠ .
٣٧٢٠ . الاختصاص : ٢٤١ .
٣٧٢١ . عيون أخبار الرِّضا : ٢ / ٢٤ / ٢ .
٣٧٢٢ . غرر الحكم : ٦١٤٦ .
٣٧٢٣ . غرر الحكم : ٩٤٨٢ .
٣٧٢٤ . نهج البلاغة : الخطبة ٢٢ ، غرر الحكم : ٣٧٧٣ .
٣٧٢٥ . الكافي : ١ / ٢٨٨ / ١ .
٣٧٢٦ . غرر الحكم : ٧٢٥ .
٣٧٢٧ . الكافي : ٢ / ٣٩٢ / ١ .
٣٧٢٨ . بحار الأنوار : ٢ / ٥٤ / ٢٤ .
٣٧٢٩ . غرر الحكم : ٧٢٣ .
٣٧٣٠ . غرر الحكم : ١٢٤٢ .
٣٧٣١ . غرر الحكم : ٤٦١٩ .
٣٧٣٢ . غرر الحكم : ٤٢٧١ .
٣٧٣٣ . نهج البلاغة : الحكمة ١٢٦ .
٣٧٣٤ . غرر الحكم : ٩٥٣٢ .
٣٧٣٥ . نهج البلاغة : الحكمة ٣١ .
٣٧٣٦ . المائدة : ٨ .
٣٧٣٧ . كنز العمّال : ١٧٧٣٥ .
٣٧٣٨ . غرر الحكم : ٣٥٦ .
٣٧٣٩ . الطلاق : ٢ .
٣٧٤٠ . البقرة : ٢٨٢ .

٣٧٤١ . بحار الأنوار : ١٠٤ / ٣١١ / ٩ .

٣٧٤٢ . تفسير العيّاشيّ : ١ / ١٥٦ / ٥٢٤ .

٣٧٤٣ . تهذيب الأحكام : ٦ / ٢٧٥ / ٧٥٢ .

٣٧٤٤ . البقرة : ١٤٠ .

٣٧٤٥ . البقرة : ٢٨٣ .

٣٧٤٦ . كنز العمّال : ١٧٧٤٣ .

٣٧٤٧ . ثواب الأعمال : ٣٣٣ .

٣٧٤٨ . كتاب من لا يحضره الفقيه : ٣ / ١٥ / ٣٢٤٣ .

٣٧٤٩ . الكافي : ٧ / ٣٩٥ / ٥ .

٣٧٥٠ . الكافي : ٧ / ٣٩٦ / ٧ .

٣٧٥١ . وسائل الشيعة : ١٨ / ٢٥٠ / ٣ .

٣٧٥٢ . الكافي : ٧ / ٣٨٣ / ٣ .

٣٧٥٣ . آل عمران : ١٦٩ .

٣٧٥٤ . الكافي : ٢ / ٣٤٨ / ٤ .

٣٧٥٥ . بحار الأنوار : ١٠٠ / ٨ / ٤ .

٣٧٥٦ . صحيح مسلم : ٣ / ١٤٩٦ / ١٠٣ .

٣٧٥٧ . كنز العمّال : ١١١١٠ .

٣٧٥٨ . كنز العمّال : ١٠٦٦٢ .

٣٧٥٩ . صحيح مسلم : ٣ / ١٤٩٨ / ١٠٨ .

٣٧٦٠ . الإرشاد : ١ / ٢٣٨ .

٣٧٦١ . صحيح مسلم : ٣ / ١٥١٧ / ١٥٧ .

٣٧٦٢ . كنز العمّال : ١١٢٠٥ .

٣٧٦٣ . كنز العمّال : ١١٢٠٣ .

٣٧٦٤ . بحار الأنوار : ٦٨ / ١٣٧ / ٧٦ .

٣٧٦٥ . بحار الأنوار : ٨٢ / ١٧٣ / ٦ .

٣٧٦٦ . كنز العمّال : ١١١٤٤ .

٣٧٦٧ . الانشراح : ٤ .

٣٧٦٨ . الشعراء : ٨٤ .

٣٧٦٩ . صحيح مسلم : ٤ / ٢٠٣٤ / ١٦٦

٣٧٧٠ . بحار الأنوار : ٧٠ / ٢٤ / ٢٣ .

٣٧٧١ . القصص : ٨٣ .

٣٧٧٢ . شرح نهج البلاغة : ٢ / ١٨١ .

٣٧٧٣ . كنز العمّال : ٦١٤٤ .

٣٧٧٤ . بحار الأنوار : ٦٧ / ٢٧١ / ٣ .

٣٧٧٥ . بحار الأنوار : ٧٨ / ٢٥٢ / ١٠٥ .

٣٧٧٦ . مشكاة الأنوار : ٥٥٣ / ١٨٦٤ .

٣٧٧٧ . بحارالأنوار : ٧٠ / ٢٥٢ / ٥ .

٣٧٧٨ . الكافي : ٦ / ٤٤٥ / ٣ .

٣٧٧٩ . الشورىٰ : ٣٨ .

٣٧٨٠ . نهج البلاغة : الحكمة ٢١١ .

٣٧٨١ . نهج البلاغة : الحكمة ٥٤ .

٣٧٨٢ . غرر الحكم : ٣٩٠٨ .

٣٧٨٣ . علل الشرائع : ٥٥٩ / ١ .

٣٧٨٤ . غرر الحكم : ١٠٣٥١ .

٣٧٨٥ . مكارم الأخلاق : ٢ / ٩٨ / ٢٢٨٠ .

٣٧٨٦ . بحار الأنوار : ٧٥ / ١٠٥ / ٤٠ .

٣٧٨٧ . في الأمالي للصدوق : ٤٥٦ / ٦١٠ « ... له رأياً حسناً » .

٣٧٨٨ . الخصال : ٥٧٠ / ١ .

٣٧٨٩ . المحاسن : ٢ / ٤٣٨ / ٢٥٢١ .

٣٧٩٠ . غرر الحكم : ٢٤٦٢ .

٣٧٩١ . غرر الحكم : ٢٤٧١ .

٣٧٩٢ . الروم : ٥٤ .

٣٧٩٣ . بحار الأنوار : ٧٧ / ١٧٤ / ٩ .

٣٧٩٤ . غرر الحكم : ١٢٠٢ .

٣٧٩٥ . غرر الحكم : ٧٠١٩ .

٣٧٩٦ . غرر الحكم : ١٠٠٩٩ .

٣٧٩٧ . غرر الحكم : ٤١٦٩_٤١٧٠ .

٣٧٩٨ . علل الشرائع : ١٠٤ / ٢ .

٣٧٩٩ . الأمالي للطوسي : ٦٩٩ / ١٤٩٢ .

٣٨٠٠ . الكافي : ٢ / ١٦٥ / ١ .

٣٨٠١ . كنز العمّال : ٦٠١٣ .

٣٨٠٢ . الكافي : ٢ / ١٦٥ / ٣ .

٣٨٠٣ . الكافي : ٢ / ١٦٥ / ٢ .

٣٨٠٤ . الإرشاد : ١ / ٤٣ .

٣٨٠٥ . الإرشاد : ١ / ٤١ .

٣٨٠٦ . بحار الأنوار : ٧٨ / ٢٨ / ٩٥ .

٣٨٠٧ . تنبيه الخواطر : ٢ / ١٠٦ .

٣٨٠٨ . تحف العقول : ٢٩٥ .

٣٨٠٩ . الكافي : ٢ / ٢٣٣ / ٩ .

٣٨١٠ . بحار الأنوار : ٨٣ / ٢٢ / ٤٠ .

٣٨١١ . الكافي : ٨ / ٢١٥ / ٢٦٠ .

٣٨١٢ . بحار الأنوار : ٦٨ / ١٦٤ / ١٣ .

٣٨١٣ . بحار الأنوار : ٢ / ٨٠ / ٧٦ .

٣٨١٤ . بحار الأنوار : ٦٩ / ٩ / ١١ .

٣٨١٥ . الكافي : ٢ / ١٧٣ / ١٠ .

٣٨١٦ . بصائر الدرجات : ٢٤٧ / ١٠ .

٣٨١٧ . يعني : لا يكتم السرّ ويذيع ما في باطنه من الأسرار .

٣٨١٨ . بحار الأنوار : ٧٨ / ١٨٦ / ٢٤ .

٣٨١٩ . الخصال : ١٠٣ / ٦١ .

٣٨٢٠ . الكافي : ٢ / ٧٥ / ٦ .

٣٨٢١ . بحار الأنوار : ٢ / ٧٧ / ٦٢ .

٣٨٢٢ . الأمالي للصدوق : ٣٢٧ / ١٧ .

٣٨٢٣ . عيون أخبار الرّضا : ٢ / ٦٠ / ٢٣٢ .

٣٨٢٤ . الواقعة : ١٠ و ١١ .

٣٨٢٥ . الأمالي للطوسي : ٧٢ / ١٠٤ .

٣٨٢٦ . آل عمران : ١٤٦ .

٣٨٢٧ . الأنفال : ٤٦ .

٣٨٢٨ . مسكّن الفؤاد : ٤٨ .

٣٨٢٩ . مسكّن الفؤاد : ٤٧ .

٣٨٣٠ . غرر الحكم : ٥٣٣ .

٣٨٣١ . غرر الحكم : ١٨٢١ .

٣٨٣٢ . مشكاة الأنوار : ٥٩ / ٧٢ .

٣٨٣٣ . الكافي : ٢ / ٨٧ / ١ .

٣٨٣٤ . كشف الغمّة : ٣ / ١٣٩ .

٣٨٣٥ . الأعراف : ١٣٧ .

٣٨٣٦ . السجدة : ٢٤ .

٣٨٣٧ . غرر الحكم : ٤٢٧٦ .

٣٨٣٨ . بحار الأنوار : ٧١ / ٩٥ / ٦٠ .

٣٨٣٩ . البقرة : ٢٤٩ .

٣٨٤٠ آل عمران : ١٢٥ .

٣٨٤١ بحار الأنوار : ٧٧ / ٨٨ / ٢ .

٣٨٤٢ بحار الأنوار : ٧١ / ٩٦ / ٦١ .

٣٨٤٣ . البقرة : ١٥٥ ـ ١٥٧ .

٣٨٤٤ . نهج البلاغة : الخطبة ١٩٣ .

٣٨٤٥ . التمحيص : ٥٩ / ١٢٥ .

٣٨٤٦ . طبّ الأئمّة لابني بسطام : ١٧ .

٣٨٤٧ . كنز العمّال : ٦٤٩٩ ، ٦٥١٨ .

٣٨٤٨ . غرر الحكم : ١٨٧٤ .

٣٨٤٩ . نهج البلاغة : الحكمة ٥٥ .

٣٨٥٠ . شرح نهج البلاغة : ١ / ٣١٩ .

٣٨٥١ . الكافي : ٢ / ٩٣ / ٢٣ .

٣٨٥٢ . الكافي : ٢ / ٩٣ / ٢٥ .

٣٨٥٣ . جامع الأخبار : ٣١٦ / ٨٨٢ .

٣٨٥٤ . نهج البلاغة : الحكمة ٤١٤ .

٣٨٥٥ . غرر الحكم : ٨٩٨٧ .

٣٨٥٦ . نهج البلاغة : الحكمة ١٨٩ .

٣٨٥٧ . كنز العمّال : ٦٥٢٢ .

٣٨٥٨ . غرر الحكم : ٣٠٨٤ .

٣٨٥٩ . نهج البلاغة : الكتاب ٣١ .

٣٨٦٠ . بحار الأنوار : ٧٧ / ٢٠٧ / ١ .

٣٨٦١ . التوبة : ١١٩ .

٣٨٦٢ . تاريخ بغداد : ١١ / ٨٢ .

٣٨٦٣ . غرر الحكم : ١٥٥٢ ـ ١٥٥٣ .

٣٨٦٤ . غرر الحكم : ٢٧٥ .

٣٨٦٥ . غرر الحكم : ١١١٨ ـ ١١١٩ .

٣٨٦٦ . غرر الحكم : ١١١٥ ـ ١١١٦ .

٣٨٦٧ . غرر الحكم : ١٥ .

٣٨٦٨ . نهج البلاغة : الحكمة ٤٧ .

٣٨٦٩ . نهج البلاغة : الحكمة ٤٥٨ .

٣٨٧٠ . نهج البلاغة : الخطبة ٨٦ .

٣٨٧١ . الكافي : ٢ / ١٠٤ / ٤ .

٣٨٧٢ . بحار الأنوار : ٧٨ / ٢٦٩ / ١٠٩ .

٣٨٧٣ . الكافي : ٢ / ١٠٤ / ٣ .

٣٨٧٤ . الكافي : ٢ / ١٠٤ / ٢ .

٣٨٧٥ . الأمالي للطوسي : ٢٢٣ / ٣٨٥ .

٣٨٧٦ . النساء : ٨٧ .

٣٨٧٧ . بحار الأنوار : ٧٧ / ٣٧٨ / ١ .

٣٨٧٨ . غرر الحكم : ٣٣٠٢ .

٣٨٧٩ . الأمالي للطوسي : ٥١٨ / ١١٣٥ .

٣٨٨٠ . غرر الحكم : ٦٧٤ .

٣٨٨١ . غرر الحكم : ٨٧٦٠ .

٣٨٨٢ . غرر الحكم : ٢٠٥٩ .

٣٨٨٣ . بحار الأنوار : ٧٨ / ٩٢ / ١٠٠ .

٣٨٨٤ . غرر الحكم : ٦٨٦٥ .

٣٨٨٥ . بحار الأنوار : ٧٤ / ١٨٥ / ٢ .

٣٨٨٦ . غرر الحكم : ٣١٢٩ .

٣٨٨٧ . غرر الحكم ٨٧٧٥ .

٣٨٨٨ . الأمالي للطوسي : ٦٤٦ / ١٣٣٩ .

٣٨٨٩ . بحار الأنوار : ٧٦ / ٢٦٧ / ٩ .

٣٨٩٠ . الظاهر أنّ المراد : اصحب من مصاحبته زينة لك وله، ولا تصحب من يتزيّن بك ولا تتزيّن به .

٣٨٩١ . الفرقان : ٢٧_٢٩ .

٣٨٩٢ . الدرّة الباهرة : ١٩ .

٣٨٩٣ . غرر الحكم : ٩٠٤١ .

٣٨٩٤ . غرر الحكم : ٢٦٠١ .

٣٨٩٥ . غرر الحكم : ٥٨٢٩ .

٣٨٩٦ . بحار الأنوار : ٧٤ / ١٩٩ / ٣٦ .

٣٨٩٧ . بحار الأنوار : ٧٤ / ١٩٨ / ٣٥ .

٣٨٩٨ . الكافي : ٢ / ٣٧٧ / ٧ .

٣٨٩٩ . بحار الأنوار : ٧٨ / ٣٥٢ / ٩ .

٣٩٠٠ . بحار الأنوار : ٧٤ / ١٦٥ / ٢٨ .

٣٩٠١ . نهج البلاغة : الحكمة ٢١٨ .

٣٩٠٢ . بحار الأنوار : ٧٧ / ٢٠٧ / ١ .

٣٩٠٣ . غرر الحكم : ٨٥٨٢ .

٣٩٠٤ . غرر الحكم : ٨٧٧٢ .

٣٩٠٥ . بحار الأنوار : ٧٨ / ٢٩١ / ٢ .

٣٩٠٦ . أعلام الدين : ٣١١ .

٣٩٠٧ . غرر الحكم : ١٩٠٤ .

٣٩٠٨ . بحار الأنوار : ٧٤ / ١٦٥ / ٢٩

٣٩٠٩ . بحار الأنوار : ٧٨ / ٢٤٩ / ٩٠ .

٣٩١٠ . تنبيه الخواطر : ٢ / ١٢٣ .

٣٩١١ . غرر الحكم : ١١٤٢ .

٣٩١٢ . غرر الحكم : ١٠١٩٦ .

٣٩١٣ . بحار الأنوار : ٧٤ / ٧ / ١ .

٣٩١٤ . التوبة : ١٠٣ .

٣٩١٥ . الكافي : ٤ / ٣ / ٦ .

٣٩١٦ . كنز العمّال : ١٦٠٦٨ .

٣٩١٧ . كنز العمّال : ١٦١١٤ .

٣٩١٨ . وسائل الشيعة : ٦ / ٢٥٨ / ١٧ .

٣٩١٩ . التوبة : ١٠٤ .

٣٩٢٠ . بحار الأنوار : ٩٦ / ١٣٤ / ٦٨ .

٣٩٢١ . كنز العمّال : ١٥٩٨٢ .

٣٩٢٢ . بحار الأنوار : ٩٦ / ١٣٢ / ٦٤ .

٣٩٢٣ . الكافي : ٤ / ٢ / ١ .

٣٩٢٤ . كنز العمّال : ١٦١١٣ .

٣٩٢٥ . نهج البلاغة : الحكمة ٧ .

٣٩٢٦ . أعلام الدين : ٣٣٣ .

٣٩٢٧ . بحار الأنوار : ٧٨ / ٦٨ / ١٣ .

٣٩٢٨ . نهج البلاغة : الحكمة ٢٥٨ .

٣٩٢٩ . بحار الأنوار : ٧٨ / ٢٠٦ / ٥٤ .

٣٩٣٠ . بحار الأنوار : ٩٦ / ١٣٤ / ٦٨ .

٣٩٣١ . بحار الأنوار : ٧٥ / ٥٠ / ٤ .

٣٩٣٢ . الخصال : ١٣٤ / ١٤٥ .

٣٩٣٣ . الكافي : ٢ / ١١٤ / ٧ .

٣٩٣٤ . بحار الأنوار : ٧٧ / ١٦٠ / ١٦٨ .

٣٩٣٥ . الكافي : ٢ / ٢٠٩ / ١ .

٣٩٣٦ . بحار الأنوار : ٧٤ / ٣٨٨ / ١ .

٣٩٣٧ . بحار الأنوار : ٩٦ / ١٧٨ / ١٣ .

٣٩٣٨ . كنز العمّال : ١٦٠٨٤ .

٣٩٣٩ . كنز العمّال : ١٦٢٥٠ .

٣٩٤٠ . قصص الأنبياء : ١٨٨ / ٢٣٥ .

٣٩٤١ . كنز العمّال : ١٦٣٥٧ .

٣٩٤٢ . ثواب الأعمال : ١٧١ / ١٨ .

٣٩٤٣ . كنز العمّال : ١٦٣٦٢ .

٣٩٤٤ . كنز العمّال : ١٦٢٤٩ .

٣٩٤٥ . بحار الأنوار : ٩٦ / ١٧٢ / ٨ .

٣٩٤٦ . تحف العقول : ٤١٤ .

٣٩٤٧ . البقرة : ٢٧١ .

٣٩٤٨ . نهج البلاغة : الخطبة ١١٠ .

٣٩٤٩ . بحار الأنوار : ٤٦ / ٨٩ / ٧٧ .

٣٩٥٠ . بحار الأنوار : ٧٨ / ٢٨٤ / ١ .

٣٩٥١ . الكافي : ٤ / ٨ / ٢ .

٣٩٥٢ . بحار الأنوار : ٩٦ / ١٢٥ / ٣٩ .

٣٩٥٣ . الإسراء : ٢٩ .

٣٩٥٤ . كنز العمّال : ١٦٢٤٦ .

٣٩٥٥ الكافي : ٤ / ٣٣ / ٢ وانظر وسائل الشيعة : ١١ / ٥٤٣ باب ١٠ .

٣٩٥٦ . البقرة : ٢٧٣ .

٣٩٥٧ . كنز العمّال : ١٦٥٥٢ .

٣٩٥٨ . ثواب الأعمال : ١٧١ / ٢٠ .

٣٩٥٩ . الكافي : ٣ / ٥٠٠ / ١٢ .

٣٩٦٠ . البقرة : ٢٦٣، ٢٦٤ .

٣٩٦١ . تنبيه الخواطر : ٢ / ١٢٠ .

٣٩٦٢ . غرر الحكم : ١٥٩٥ .

٣٩٦٣ . نهج البلاغة : الخطبة ٨٣ .

٣٩٦٤ . الفاتحة : ٦ .

٣٩٦٥ . آل عمران : ٥١ .

٣٩٦٦ . آل عمران : ١٠١ .

٣٩٦٧ . بحار الأنوار : ٢٤ / ١١ / ٣ .

٣٩٦٨ . معاني الأخبار : ٣٢ / ٢ .

٣٩٦٩ . بحار الأنوار : ٩٢ / ١٩٧ / ٣ .

٣٩٧٠ . فضائل الشيعة : ٤٨ / ٣ .

٣٩٧١ . بحار الأنوار : ٧٦ / ٤ / ٨ .

٣٩٧٢ . بحار الأنوار : ٨ / ٦٥ / ٢ .

٣٩٧٣ . ثواب الأعمال : ٣٢١ / ٢ .

٣٩٧٤ . الأمالي للصدوق : ٢٤٢ / ٢٥٧ .

٣٩٧٥ . العُرام : الشدّة والقوّة والشراسة (النهاية : ٣ / ٢٢٣) .

٣٩٧٦ . كنز العمّال : ٣٠٧٤٧ .

٣٩٧٧ . غرر الحكم : ٨٢٧٢ .

٣٩٧٨ . غرر الحكم : ٨٢٧٣ .

٣٩٧٩ . غرر الحكم : ٨٩٣٧ .

٣٩٨٠ . بحار الأنوار : ١ / ١٨٣ / ٨٥ .

٣٩٨١ . إنّ اللّعب له دورٌ أساسي في نموّ الطفل وتطوّره ، ويعتبر اللعب من أهمّ الأُمور في حياته . نحن نعلم أنّ لفظة «اللعب» تساوق اللهو والبطالة والغفلة وغير ذلك بالنسبة إلى الأفراد الكِبار ، وهو يمنع التكامل والعلوّ . وأمّا بالنسبة إلى الأطفال فبالعكس من ذلك فهو يعتبر ممهّداً لنموّه وتكامله .

إنّ اللعب في فترة الطفولة ليس مؤخّراً لتكامل الطفل ، بل هو على العكس من ذلك ؛ فعن طريق اللعب تتفتّح قابليّات الطفل وتنمو استعداداته . ومن هنا جاء التأكيد على السّماح للطفل على أن يلعب وبأنّ الطفل المتحرّك اللعوب يكون عاقلاً وحليماً عند كبره .

يوضّح هذا الحديث الدور الأساسي للّعب في نموّ وتكامل شخصيّة الإنسان . فالطفل الذي لم يُشبع غريزتَه عن طريق اللعب في فترة طفولته تراه في فترة كبره تصدر منه أحياناً أفعالاً تتّسم بالصبيانيّة ، ويعتبر هذا الأمر في عداد الانحرافات التي يصاب بها الأفراد في سنين الشباب وما بعدها . ومن أسباب هذا الانحراف هو ـ وكما أوضحنا ـ عدم إشباع غريزة الطفل في مرحلة طفوليته ، وهذا الإشباع لا يتمّ إلّا عن طريق اللعب .

٣٩٨٢ . كتاب من لا يحضره الفقيه : ٣ / ٤٩٣ / ٤٧٤٨ .

٣٩٨٣ . الكافي : ٢ / ١٨١ / ١١ .

٣٩٨٤ . بحار الأنوار : ٧٧ / ١٥٨ / ١٤٩ .

٣٩٨٥ . بحار الأنوار : ٧٧ / ١٦٥ / ٢ .

٣٩٨٦ . الكافي : ٢ / ١٨١ / ١٣ .

٣٩٨٧ . الكافي : ٢ / ١٨١ / ١٢ .

٣٩٨٨ . الكافي : ٢ / ١٨٢ / ١٥ .

٣٩٨٩ . كنز العمّال : ٤٧٥ .

٣٩٩٠ . الكافي : ٥ / ٥٢٥ / ١ .

٣٩٩١ . الأنفال : ٦١ .

٣٩٩٢ . غرر الحكم : ١٠١٣٨ .

٣٩٩٣ . نهج البلاغة : الكتاب ٥٣ .

٣٩٩٤ . نهج السعادة : ٢ / ٧٤٢ .

٣٩٩٥ . بحار الأنوار : ٧٨ / ٢٨٧ / ٢ .

٣٩٩٦ . الحجرات : ١٠ .

٣٩٩٧ . النساء : ١١٤ .

٣٩٩٨ . كنز العمّال : ٥٤٨٠ .

٣٩٩٩ . الكافي : ٢ / ٢٠٩ / ١ .

٤٠٠٠ . الكافي : ٢ / ٢٠٩ / ٣، وأُنظرح ٤ .

٤٠٠١ . الكافي : ٢ / ٢١٠ / ٥ .

٤٠٠٢ . الكافي : ٢ / ٣٤١ / ١٦ .

٤٠٠٣ . البقرة : ٢٣٨ .

٤٠٠٤ . النساء : ١٠٣ .

٤٠٠٥ . إبراهيم : ٤٠ .

٤٠٠٦ . دعائم الإسلام : ١ / ١٣٣ .

٤٠٠٧ . مكارم الأخلاق : ٢ / ٣٦٦ / ٢٦٦١ .

٤٠٠٨ . غرر الحكم : ٢٢١٤ .

٤٠٠٩ . تنبيه الخواطر : ٢ / ٧٨ .

٤٠١٠ . الخصال : ٦٢٠ / ١٠ .

٤٠١١ . المحاسن : ١ / ١١٦ / ١١٧ .

٤٠١٢ . كتاب من لا يحضره الفقيه : ١ / ٢١٠ / ٦٣٨ .

٤٠١٣ . مريم : ٣١ .

٤٠١٤ . الكافي : ٣ / ٢٦٤ / ١ .

٤٠١٥ . العنكبوت : ٤٥ .

٤٠١٦ . كنز العمّال : ٢٠٠٨٣ .

٤٠١٧ . بحار الأنوار : ٨٢ / ١٩٨ .

٤٠١٨ . بحار الأنوار : ٨٢ / ٢٢٧ / ٥٤ .

٤٠١٩ . الخصال : ٦٢٨ / ١٠ .
٤٠٢٠ . بحار الأنوار : ٨٢ / ٢٠٩ / ١٩ .
٤٠٢١ . الكافي : ٣ / ٢٦٨ / ٤ .
٤٠٢٢ . الأمالي للطوسي : ٢٩٦ / ٥٨٢ .
٤٠٢٣ . بحار الأنوار : ٨٢ / ٢٣٦ / ٦٦ .
٤٠٢٤ . مكارم الأخلاق : ٢ / ٣٦٦ / ٢٦٦١ .
٤٠٢٥ . الخصال : ٦٣٢ / ١٠ .
٤٠٢٦ . الخصال : ٦٣٢ / ١٠ .
٤٠٢٧ . المؤمنون : ١، ٢ .
٤٠٢٨ . الفردوس : ٥ / ١٩٥ / ٧٩٣٥ .
٤٠٢٩ . دعائم الإسلام : ١ / ١٥٨ .
٤٠٣٠ . فلاح السائل : ٢٨٩ / ١٨٢ .
٤٠٣١ . الخصال : ٦٢٨ / ١٠ .
٤٠٣٢ . دعائم الإسلام : ١ / ١٥٩ .
٤٠٣٣ . أعلام الدين : ٢٤٧ .
٤٠٣٤ . عدّة الداعي : ١٣٩ .
٤٠٣٥ . بحار الأنوار : ٨٠ / ٣٤٦ / ٣٠ .
٤٠٣٦ . دعائم الإسلام : ١ / ١٥٨ .
٤٠٣٧ . الكافي : ٣ / ٣٠٠ / ٤ .
٤٠٣٨ . فلاح السائل : ٢٩٠ / ١٨٦ .
٤٠٣٩ . بحار الأنوار : ٨٤ / ٢٥٨ / ٥٦ .
٤٠٤٠ . بحار الأنوار : ٨٤ / ٢٥٧ / ٥٥ .
٤٠٤١ . جامع الأخبار : ٤١٢ / ١١٤١ .
٤٠٤٢ . علل الشرائع : ٣٤٥ / ١ .
٤٠٤٣ . بشارة المصطفى : ٢٨ .
٤٠٤٤ . المناقب لابن شهر آشوب : ٤ / ١٣١ .
٤٠٤٥ . الكافي : ٣ / ٢٦٦ / ١١ .
٤٠٤٦ . الكافي : ٢ / ٣٤٩ / ٥ .
(٤٠٤٧) المحاسن : ١ / ٧٩ / ٤٤ عن ابن القدّاح وص ٤٥٨ / ١٠٥٩ عن عبدالله بن ميمون القدّاح عن الإمام الصادق عن أبيه عليهما السلام، تحف العقول : ٣٠٦ .
٤٠٤٨ . المحاسن : ١ / ٤٠٦ / ٩٢١ .
٤٠٤٩ . بحار الأنوار : ٨٤ / ٢٤٩ / ٤١ .
٤٠٥٠ . ثواب الأعمال : ٦٨ / ١ .
٤٠٥١ . بحار الأنوار : ٨٤ / ٢٦٠ / ٥٩ .
٤٠٥٢ . الكافي : ٣ / ٢٦٦ / ١٢ .
٤٠٥٣ . بحار الأنوار : ٧٢ / ١٩٨ / ٢٦ .
٤٠٥٤ . بحار الأنوار : ٨٤ / ٢٤٩ / ٤١ .
٤٠٥٥ . مشكاة الأنوار : ٩٦ / ٢١٢ .
٤٠٥٦ . الأمالي للصدوق : ٤٩٨ / ٦٨٣ .
٤٠٥٧ . النساء : ١٤٢ .
٤٠٥٨ . بحار الأنوار : ٧٧ / ٢٢ / ٦، أنظر تمام الحديث .
٤٠٥٩ . بحار الأنوار : ٨٤ / ٢٨٣ / ٥ .
٤٠٦٠ . تفسير العيّاشي : ١ / ٢٤٢ / ١٣٤ .
٤٠٦١ . الماعون : ٤، ٥ .
٤٠٦٢ . المؤمنون : ٩ـ١١ .
٤٠٦٣ . تنبيه الخواطر : ٢ / ١٢٢ .
٤٠٦٤ . بحار الأنوار : ٨٣ / ١٤ / ٢٥ .
٤٠٦٥ . الكافي : ٣ / ٢٧٤ / ٨ .
٤٠٦٦ . ثواب الأعمال : ٥٨ / ٢ .
٤٠٦٧ . بحار الأنوار : ٨٣ / ٢١ / ٣٨ .
٤٠٦٨ . المدّثّر : ٤٠ـ٤٣ .
٤٠٦٩ . ثواب الأعمال : ٢٧٥ / ١ .
٤٠٧٠ . علل الشرائع : ٣٣٩ / ١ .
٤٠٧١ . الكافي : ٣ / ٢٦٩ / ٧ .
٤٠٧٢ . كذا في المصدر، والظاهر أنّ الصحيح «يطوف» .
٤٠٧٣ . مستدرك الوسائل : ٣ / ٢٥ / ٢٩٢٣ .
٤٠٧٤ . المحاسن : ٢ / ١٢٦ / ١٣٤٨ .
٤٠٧٥ . وسائل الشيعة : ٣ / ٤٧٨ / ٢ .
٤٠٧٦ . الكافي : ٣ / ٣٧١ / ٣ .
٤٠٧٧ . الأمالي للطوسي : ٢٩ / ٣١ .
٤٠٧٨ . نهج البلاغة : الكتاب ٥٢ .
٤٠٧٩ . الكافي : ٣ / ٣٧٦ / ٥ .
٤٠٨٠ . الإسراء : ٧٩ .
٤٠٨١ . المزمّل : ٦ .
٤٠٨٢ . كنز العمّال : ٢١٤٢٥ .
٤٠٨٣ . سنن أبي داوود : ٢ / ٧٠ / ١٤٥٠ .
٤٠٨٤ . الأمالي للصدوق : ٣٥٤ / ٤٣٢ .
٤٠٨٥ . كنز العمّال : ٢١٤٢٨ .
٤٠٨٦ . بحار الأنوار : ٨٧ / ١٤٣ / ١٧ .
٤٠٨٧ . بحار الأنوار : ٤١ / ١٧ / ١٠ .
٤٠٨٨ . الكافي : ٣ / ٤٨٨ / ٩ .
٤٠٨٩ . معاني الأخبار : ٣٤٢ / ١ .
٤٠٩٠ . السجدة : ١٦ و ١٧ .

٤٠٩١ . بحار الأنوار : ٨ / ١٢٦ / ٢٧ .
٤٠٩٢ . علل الشرائع : ٣٦٣ / ١ .
٤٠٩٣ . الكافي : ٣ / ٤٥٠ / ٣٤ .
٤ ٩٤ . علل الشرائع : ٣٦٢ / ٢ .
٤٠٩٥ . كنز العمّال : ٢١٤٧٥ .
٤٠٩٦ . الجمعة : ٩ .
٤٠٩٧ . وسائل الشيعة : ٥ / ٦ / ٢٥ .
٤٠٩٨ . الدعوات : ٣٧ / ٩١ .
٤٠٦٩ . كتاب من لا يحضره الفقيه : ١ / ٤٢٧ / ١٢٦٠ .
٤١٠٠ . بحار الأنوار : ٨٩ / ١٨٤ / ٢١ .
٤١ ١ . كتاب من لا يحضره الفقيه : ١ / ٤١٦ / ١٢٣٠ .
٤١٠٢ . الأحزاب : ٥٦ .
٤١٠٣ . كنز العمّال : ٢١٤٧ .
٤١٠٤ . كنز العمّال : ٢١٤٩ .
٤١٠٥ . كنز العمّال : ٢٢٤٣ .
٤١٠٦ . كنز العمّال : ٢١٤٤ .
٤١٠٧ . كنز العمّال : ٢١٥٣ .
٤١٠٨ . بحار الأنوار : ٩٤ / ٤٩ / ٩ .
٤١٠٩ . كنز العمّال : ٣٩٩٣ .
٤١١٠ . مكارم الأخلاق : ٢ / ٣٧٧ / ٢٦٦١ .
٤١١١ . غرر الحكم : ١٣٤٣ .
٤١١٢ . نهج البلاغة : الحكمة ٣٣٣ .
٤١١٣ . بحار الأنوار : ٧١ / ٢٧٩ / ١٩ .
٤١١٤ . غرر الحكم : ٢٣١٤ .
٤١١٥ . غرر الحكم : ٥٤٦ .
٤١١٦ . بحار الأنوار : ٧٨ / ١١٣ / ٧ .
٤١١٧ . معاني الأخبار : ٤٠١ / ٦٢ .
٤١١٨ . الكافي : ٢ / ١١٣ / ١ .
٤١١٩ . نهج البلاغة : الحكمة ١٨٢ .
٤١٢٠ . نهج البلاغة : الخطبة ١٩٣ .
٤١٢١ . أعلام الدين : ٢٩٧ .
٤١٢٢ . الأمالي للصدوق : ٤٧٩ / ٦٤٤ .
٤١٢٣ . غرر الحكم : ٣٠٨١ .
٤١٢٤ . غرر الحكم : ٢٨٤٤ .
٤١٢٥ . عيون أخبار الرّضا : ٢ / ٥ / ١٠ .
٤١٢٦ . هو قول : «إنّا لله وإنّا إليه راجعون» .
٤١٢٧ . البقرة : ١٥٥، ١٥٦ .
٤١٢٨ . ثواب الأعمال : ٢٣٥ / ٢ .
٤١٢٩ . بحار الأنوار : ٨٢ / ١٠٣ / ٥٠ .
٤١٣٠ . بحار الأنوار : ٨٢ / ١٠٣ / ٥٠ .
٤١٣١ . الأمالي للطوسي : ٣٨٨ / ٨٥٠ .
٤١٣٢ . سنن النسائي : ٤ / ١٩ .
٤١٣٣ . دعائم الإسلام : ١ / ٢٢٧ .
٤١٣٤ . كنز الفوائد : ٢ / ١٦٣ .
٤١٣٥ . بحار الأنوار : ٨٢ / ٨٤ / ٢٦ .
٤١٣٦ . الخصال : ٦١٦ / ١٠ .
٤١٣٧ . بحار الأنوار : ٧٨ / ٢٦٨ / ١٨٣ .
٤١٣٨ . الكافي : ٣ / ٢٢٧ / ١ .
٤١٣٩ . الكافي : ٢ / ٣٥٩ / ١ .
٤١٤٠ . لقمان : ١٩ .
٤١٤١ . منية المريد : ٢١٣ .
٤١٤٢ . بحار الأنوار : ٧٧ / ٨٢ .
٤١٤٣ . غرر الحكم : ٤٦٦٠ .
٤١٤٤ . غرر الحكم : ٥٠٧٣ .
٤١٤٥ . البقرة : ١٨٣ .
٤١٤٦ . كنز العمّال : ٢٣٦١٠ .
٤١٤٧ . فضائل الأشهر الثلاثة : ٧٥ / ٥٧ .
٤١٤٨ . الدعوات : ٧٦ / ١٧٩ .
٤١٤٩ . ثواب الأعمال : ٧٥ / ١ .
٤١٥٠ . ثواب الأعمال : ٧٧ / ١ .
٤١٥١ . الكافي : ٤ / ٦٢ / ١ .
٤١٥٢ . بحار الأنوار : ٩٦ / ٣٦٨ / ٤٧ .
٤١٥٣ . الأمالي للطوسي : ٢٩٦ / ٥٨٢ .
٤١٥٤ . الكافي : ٤ / ٦٣ / ٦ .
٤١٥٥ . كتاب من لا يحضره الفقيه : ٢ / ٧٦ / ١٧٨٣ .
٤١٥٦ . الكافي : ٤ / ٦٥ / ١٥ .
٤١٥٧ . الكافي : ٤ / ٦٨ / ١، اُنظر تمام الباب .
٤١٥٨ . بحار الأنوار : ٩٦ / ٣٦٩ / ٥٠ .
٤١٥٩ . معاني الأخبار : ٤٠٩ / ٩١ .
٤١٦٠ . الأمالي للصدوق : ٦٤٥ / ٨٧٤ .
٤١٦١ . الأنعام : ١٦٠ .
٤١٦٢ . دعائم الإسلام : ١ / ٢٨٣ .
٤١٦٣ . الكافي : ٤ / ٦٣ / ٥ .
٤١٦٤ . الفردوس : ٥ / ٢٤٢ / ٨٠٧٥ .

٤١٦٥ . بحار الأنوار : ٩٦ / ٢٩٤ / ٢١ .

٤١٦٦ . دعائم الإسلام : ١ / ٢٦٨ .

٤١٦٧ . الكافي : ٤ / ٨٧ / ١ .

٤١٦٨ . كتاب من لا يحضره الفقيه : ٤ / ٣٥٦ / ٥٧٦٢ .

٤١٦٩ . بحار الأنوار : ٩٦ / ٢٥٦ / ٣٨ .

٤١٧٠ . معاني الأخبار : ٢٢٨ / ١ .

٤١٧١ . الأمالي للطوسي : ٥٢٢ / ١١٥٦ .

٤١٧٢ . الكافي : ٢ / ٦٦٤ / ٥ .

٤١٧٣ . الكافي : ٢ / ٢٠٦ / ١ .

٤١٧٤ . إرشاد القلوب : ٢٠٠ .

٤١٧٥ . معاني الأخبار : ٣٣٥ / ١ .

٤١٧٦ الأمالي للصدوق : ٢٨٩ / ٣٢٢ نور الثقلين : ٢ / ٢٤٩ / ٢٦١ .

٤١٧٧ . تحف العقول : ٩٦ .

٤١٧٨ . الكافي : ٢ / ٦٦٤ / ١٣ .

٤١٧٩ . الكافي : ٢ / ٦٦٤ / ١٠ .

٤١٨٠ . بحار الأنوار : ٧٦ / ٥٩ / ١٠ .

٤١٨١ . كنز العمّال : ٥٩٤٤ .

٤١٨٢ . كنز العمّال : ٦٠١٩ .

٤١٨٣ . الدرّ المنثور : ٢ / ٧٢٤ .

٤١٨٤ . القصص : ٥ .

٤١٨٥ . الغيبة للطوسي : ١٨٤ / ١٤٣ .

٤١٨٦ . النساء : ٩٨، ٩٩ .

٤١٨٧ . نهج البلاغة : الخطبة ١٨٩ .

٤١٨٨ . معاني الأخبار : ٢٠١ / ٤ .

٤١٨٩ . الكافي : ٨ / ١٢٥ / ٩٥ .

٤١٩٠ . البقرة : ١٠٨ .

٤١٩١ . النساء : ١٣٦ .

٤١٩٢ . الأحزاب : ٣٦ .

٤١٩٣ . الجاثية : ٢٣ .

٤١٩٤ . نهج البلاغة : الخطبة ١٤٨ .

٤١٩٥ . نهج البلاغة : الخطبة ١٢٠ .

٤١٩٦ . نهج البلاغة : الخطبة ٩٧ .

٤١٩٧ . غرر الحكم : ٨٥٠١ .

٤١٩٨ . نهج البلاغة : الخطبة ١٦٤ .

٤١٩٩ . نهج البلاغة : الخطبة ١٧، اُنظر تمام الكلام .

٤٢٠٠ . نهج البلاغة : الخطبة ١٩٤ .

٤٢٠١ . نهج البلاغة : الخطبة ١٧٦ .

٤٢٠٢ . نهج البلاغة : الخطبة ١٩٨ .

٤٢٠٣ . مستدرك الوسائل : ١٧ / ٨٨ / ٢٠٨١٩ .

٤٢٠٤ . الجعفريّات : ١١٩ .

٤٢٠٥ . الكافي : ٧ / ٣٥٠ / ٣ .

٤٢٠٦ . غرر الحكم : ١٠١٧٨ .

٤٢٠٧ . الكافي : ٤ / ٣٣ / ٣ .

٤٢٠٨ . كتاب من لا يحضره الفقيه : ٣ / ٩٧ / ٣٤٠٥ .

٤٢٠٩ . الكافي : ٥ / ٢٣٩ / ٥ .

٤٢١٠ . جامع الأخبار : ٣٧٧ / ١٠٥٣ .

٤٢١١ . بحار الأنوار : ٧٥ / ٤٦١ / ١٤ .

٤٢١٢ . المحاسن : ٢ / ١٤٧ / ١٣٨٨ .

٤٢١٣ . جامع الأخبار : ٣٧٨ / ١٠٥٨ .

٤٢١٤ . نهج البلاغة : الخطبة ١٤٢ .

٤٢١٥ . بحار الأنوار : ٤١ / ٢٨ / ١ .

٤٢١٦ . كنز العمّال : ٢٥٨٨١ .

٤٢١٧ . الدعوات : ١٤١ / ٣٥٨ .

٤٢١٨ . المحاسن : ٢ / ١٨٠ / ١٥١٠ .

٤٢١٩ . قرب الإسناد : ١٦٠ / ٥٨٣ .

٤٢٢٠ . بحار الأنوار : ٧٧ / ٨٤ / ٣ .

٤٢٢١ . المحاسن : ٢ / ١٨٦ / ١٥٣٣ .

٤٢٢٢ . كنز العمّال : ٢٥٨٧٦ .

٤٢٢٣ . المحاسن : ٢ / ١٧٩ / ١٥٠٦ .

٤٢٢٤ . عيون أخبار الرّضا : ٢ / ٤٢ / ١٣٨ .

٤٢٢٥ . تنبيه الخواطر : ٢ / ١١٦ .

٤٢٢٦ . المحاسن : ٢ / ١٨١ / ١٥١٥ .

٤٢٢٧ . الكافي : ٦ / ٢٨٣ / ١ .

٤٢٢٨ . الكافي : ٦ / ٢٨٣ / ٢ .

٤٢٢٩ . الكافي : ٥ / ٣٦٨ / ٤ .

٤٢٣٠ . بحار الأنوار : ٧٥ / ٤٥١ / ٢ .

٤٢٣١ . الكافي : ٦ / ٢٨٣ / ١ .

٤٢٣٢ . كنز العمّال : ٢٨١٠٠ و ٢٨٠٧٣ .

٤٢٣٣ . الخصال : ٢٢٩ / ٦٧ .

٤٢٣٤ . مكارم الأخلاق : ١ / ٣١٤ / ١٠٠٣ .

٤٢٣٥ . مكارم الأخلاق : ٢ / ١٧٩ / ٢٤٦٤ .

٤٢٣٦ . نهج البلاغة : الحكمة ٢٧ .

٤٢٣٧ . الدهر : ٨، ٩ .

٤٢٣٨ . البلد : ١٤ـ١٦ .

٤٢٣٩ . مشكاة الأنوار : ص ٣٢٥ .

٤٢٤٠ . غرر الحكم : ٩٦٣٤ .

٤٢٤١ . المحاسن : ٢ / ١٤٢ / ١٣٧٠ .

٤٢٤٢ . المحاسن : ٢ / ١٤٥ / ١٣٨١ .

٤٢٤٣ . المحاسن : ٢ / ٢٧٩ / ١٩٠١ .

٤٢٤٤ . كنز العمّال : ٢٧٨٧١ .

٤٢٤٥ . الكافي : ٦ / ٥٤ / ١ .

٤٢٤٦ . الكافي : ٦ / ٥٥ / ٤ .

٤٢٤٧ . الكافي : ٦ / ٥٤ / ٢ .

٤٢٤٨ . الكافي : ٦ / ٥٤ / ٣ .

٤٢٤٩ . البقرة : ٢٣٠ .

٤٢٥٠ . البقرة : ٢٢٩ .

٤٢٥١ . عيون أخبار الرضا : ٢ / ٨٥ / ٢٧ .

٤٢٥٢ . علل الشرائع : ٥٠٧ / ١ .

٤٢٥٣ . كنز العمّال : ٧٥٧٦ .

٤٢٥٤ . تنبيه الخواطر : ١ / ٤٩ .

٤٢٥٥ . كنز العمّال : ٨٨٥٢ .

٤٢٥٦ . نهج البلاغة : الحكمة ١٨٠ .

٤٢٥٧ . تنبيه الخواطر : ١ / ٤٩ .

٤٢٥٨ . نهج البلاغة : الحكمة ٢٢٦ .

٤٢٥٩ . نهج البلاغة : الحكمة ٢ .

٤٢٦٠ . غرر الحكم : ١٠٥٩٣ .

٤٢٦١ . نهج البلاغة : الحكمة ٢١٩ .

٤٢٦٢ . غرر الحكم : ١٠٥٧٨ .

٤٢٦٣ . الكافي : ٢ / ٣٢٠ / ٢ .

٤٢٦٤ . بحار الأنوار : ٧٨ / ٣١٥ / ١ .

٤٢٦٥ . الدرّة الباهرة : ٤٢ .

٤٢٦٦ . بحار الأنوار : ٧٨ / ٣٧٤ / ٣٥ .

٤٢٦٧ . السجدة : ١٦ .

٤٢٦٨ . المائدة : ٨٤ .

٤٢٦٩ . بحار الأنوار : ٩٨ / ٨٣ / ٢ .

٤٢٧٠ . الإقبال : ١ / ١٦٨ .

٤٢٧١ . كنز العمّال : ٢٥٩٩٨ .

٤٢٧٢ . كنز العمّال : ٢٦٠١٠ .

٤٢٧٣ . كنز العمّال : ٢٦٠٠٦ .

٤٢٧٤ . الفرقان : ٤٨ .

٤٢٧٥ . وسائل الشيعة : ١ / ١٠١ / ٩ .

٤٢٧٦ . وسائل الشيعة : ٢ / ١٠٤٣ / ٦ .

٤٢٧٧ . كتاب من لا يحضره الفقيه : ١ / ١٠٩ / ٢٢٤ .

٤٢٧٨ . الكافي : ٣ / ٣٣٠ / ٣ .

٤٢٧٩ . الأحزاب : ٣٣ .

٤٢٨٠ . التوبة : ١٠٣ .

٤٢٨١ . نهج البلاغة : الحكمة ٢٥٢ .

٤٢٨٢ . نهج البلاغة : الخطبة ١٩٨ .

٤٢٨٣ . غرر الحكم : ٣٧٤٣ .

٤٢٨٤ . النساء : ٥٩ .

٤٢٨٥ . وسائل الشيعة : ١١ / ١٨٤ / ٢ .

٤٢٨٦ . غرر الحكم : ٦٠١٢ .

٤٢٨٧ . غرر الحكم : ٣١٩٢ .

٤٢٨٨ . بحار الأنوار : ٧٠ / ٩٥ / ١ .

٤٢٨٩ . بحار الأنوار : ٧٨ / ٣٦٦ / ٢ .

٤٢٩٠ . غرر الحكم : ٢٢٦٣ـ٢٢٦٤ .

٤٢٩١ . غرر الحكم : ٢٣٠٩ .

٤٢٩٢ . عيون أخبار الرضا : ٢ / ٤٣ / ١٤٩ .

٤٢٩٣ . غرر الحكم : ٢٤٧٥ .

٤٢٩٤ . بحار الأنوار : ٧٨ / ٩٠ / ٩٥ .

٤٢٩٥ . بحار الأنوار : ٧٨ / ٣٦٥ / ٤ .

٤٢٩٦ . الأحزاب : ٦٧، ٦٨ .

٤٢٩٧ . عيون أخبار الرضا : ٢ / ٦٩ / ٣١٨ .

٤٢٩٨ . نهج البلاغة : الخطبة ١٩٢ .

٤٢٩٩ . نهج البلاغة : الحكمة ٢٣٩ .

٤٣٠٠ . الكافي : ٦ / ٥١٠ / ٣ .

٤٣٠١ . المصنّف لعبد الرزّاق : ٤ / ٣١٩ / ٧٩٣٣ .

٤٣٠٢ . سنن النسائي : ٨ / ١٨٩ .

٤٣٠٣ . نهج البلاغة : الحكمة ٤٠٠ .

٤٣٠٤ . الكافي : ٦ / ٥١٠ / ٢ .

٤٣٠٥ . الكافي : ٦ / ٥١٢ / ١٨ .

٤٣٠٦ . الكافي : ٦ / ٥١٠ / ٧ .

٤٣٠٧ . الكافي : ٦ / ٥١٠ / ٤ .

٤٣٠٨ . الكافي : ٦ / ٥١٠ / ١ .

٤٣٠٩ . الكافي : ٦ / ٥١٢ / ١٧ .

٤٣١٠ . سنن النسائي : ٨ / ١٥٣ .

٤٣١١ . كنز العمّال : ٢٨٥٦٦ .

٤٣١٢ . كنز العمّال : ٢٨٥٧٠ .

٤٣١٣ . كنز العمّال : ٢٨٥٨٤ .

٤٣١٤ . الترغيب والترهيب : ٤ / ٣٣ / ٤ .

٤٣١٥ . الكافي : ٨ / ١٩٨ / ٢٣٦ .

٤٣١٦ . تفسير نور الثقلين : ٤ / ٣٨٢ / ٣٥ .

٤٣١٧ . مكارم الأخلاق : ٢ / ١٥٣ / ٢٣٧٤ و٢٣٧٥ ، اُنظر كنز العمّال : ٧ / ١٣٦ .

٤٣١٨ . الكافي : ٨ / ١٩٧ / ٢٣٥ .

٤٣١٩ . الكافي : ٦ / ٤٩٠ / ١ .

٤٣٢٠ . الكافي : ٦ / ٤٩٠ / ٦ .

٤٣٢١ . الكافي : ٦ / ٤٩٠ / ٧ .

٤٣٢٢ . من الواضح أنّ الترغيب في إطالة الأظافير للنساء هو في حالة مراعاة نظافتها ، وعدم خروجها عن الحدّ المتعارف عليه .

٤٣٢٣ . الكافي : ٦ / ٤٩١ / ١٥ .

٤٣٢٤ . البقرة : ٢٥٨ .

٤٣٢٥ . الأنعام : ٢١، يوسف : ٢٣ .

٤٣٢٦ . كنز العمّال : ٧٦٣٩ .

٤٣٢٧ . روضة الواعظين : ٥١٢ .

٤٣٢٨ . الكافي : ٢ / ٣٣٢ / ١١ .

٤٣٢٩ . غرر الحكم : ٨٠٤ .

٤٣٣٠ . غرر الحكم : ١٧٣٤ .

٤٣٣١ . نهج البلاغة : الخطبة ٢٢٤ .

٤٣٣٢ . نهج البلاغة : الخطبة ٢٢٤ .

٤٣٣٣ . غرر الحكم : ٢٦٣٨ .

٤٣٣٤ . نهج البلاغة : الكتاب ٥٣، غرر الحكم : ٧٥٢٣ .

٤٣٣٥ . غرر الحكم : ٧٩٤٠ .

٤٣٣٦ . غرر الحكم : ٥٣٩١ .

٤٣٣٧ . غرر الحكم : ٧٨٣٥ .

٤٣٣٨ . الكافي : ٥ / ٣٠٧ / ١١ .

٤٣٣٩ . نهج البلاغة : الخطبة ١٧٦ .

٤٣٤٠ . كنز العمّال : ٧٦٠٥ .

٤٣٤١ . نهج البلاغة : الكتاب ٣١، غرر الحكم : ٦٠٥٤ .

٤٣٤٢ . بحار الأنوار : ٧٥ / ٣٢٠ / ٤٣ .

٤٣٤٣ . غرر الحكم : ٩٢٧٢ .

٤٣٤٤ . الكافي : ٢ / ٣٣١ / ٥ .

٤٣٤٥ . الأنعام : ٤٥ .

٤٣٤٦ . بحار الأنوار : ٧٥ / ٣٢٢ / ٥١ .

٤٣٤٧ . يونس : ٨٩ .

٤٣٤٨ . الخصال : ٥٣٩ / ١١ .

٤٣٤٩ . الفرقان : ٢٧ .

٤٣٥٠ . بحار الأنوار : ٧٥ / ٣٢٢ / ٥٢ .

٤٣٥١ . نهج البلاغة : الحكمة ٣٤١ .

٤٣٥٢ . بحار الأنوار : ٧٥ / ٣١١ / ١٥ .

٤٣٥٣ . هود : ١١٣ .

٤٣٥٤ . بحار الأنوار : ٧٥ / ٣٧٢ / ١٧ .

٤٣٥٥ . الكافي : ٢ / ٣٣٣ / ١٦ .

٤٣٥٦ . الكافي : ٥ / ١٠٦ / ٤، اُنظر تمام الكلام .

٤٣٥٧ . الكافي : ٥ / ١٠٨ / ١٢ .

٤٣٥٨ . النساء : ٨٥ .

٤٣٥٩ . بحار الأنوار : ٧٥ / ٣٥٩ / ٧٥ .

٤٣٦٠ . بحار الأنوار : ١٠٠ / ٩٠ / ٧٥ .

٤٣٦١ . بحار الأنوار : ٧٥ / ٣٤٩ / ٥٦ .

٤٣٦٢ . كنز العمّال : ٧٥٩٧ .

٤٣٦٣ . كنز العمّال : ٧٦٠٢ .

٤٣٦٤ . غرر الحكم : ٢٩٧٩ .

٤٣٦٥ . غرر الحكم : ٦٠٣٨ .

٤٣٦٦ . غرر الحكم : ٦٠٤٠ .

٤٣٦٧ . نهج البلاغة : الحكمة ٣٠٩ .

٤٣٦٨ . بحار الأنوار : ٧٥ / ١٩٧ / ١٥ .

٤٣٦٩ . الأمالي للصدوق : ٣٨٠ / ٤٨٣ .

٤٣٧٠ . غرر الحكم : ٤٨١٦ .

٤٣٧١ . غرر الحكم : ٤٨٢٣ .

٤٣٧٢ . غرر الحكم : ٨٨٤٢ .

٤٣٧٣ . غرر الحكم : ٣٠٢٧ .

٤٣٧٤ . الحجرات : ١٢ .

٤٣٧٥ . بحار الأنوار : ٧٥ / ١٩٥ / ٨ .

٤٣٧٦ . كنز العمّال : ٧٥٨٥ .

٤٣٧٧ . نهج البلاغة : الكتاب ٥٣ .

٤٣٧٨ . غرر الحكم : ١٠٥٣٤ .

٤٣٧٩ . غرر الحكم : ٥٥٧٥ .

٤٣٨٠ . غرر الحكم : ٢٧٠٩ .

٤٣٨١ . غرر الحكم : ١٩٠٣ .

٤٣٨٢ . الأمالي للصدوق : ٣٨٠ / ٤٨٣ .

٤٣٨٣ . كنز الفوائد : ٢ / ١٨٢ .

٤٣٨٤ . بحار الأنوار : ٧٤ / ١٩٧ / ٣١ .

٤٣٨٥ . كنز الفوائد : ٢ / ١٨٢ .

٤٣٨٦ . غرر الحكم : ٩٠٨٤ .

٤٣٨٧ . بحار الأنوار : ٧٧ / ١٥٨ / ١٤٢ .

٤٣٨٨ . نهج البلاغة : الحكمة ١١٤ .

٤٣٨٩ . الكافي : ٥ / ٢٩٨ / ٢ .

٤٣٩٠ . الذاريات : ٥٦ .

٤٣٩١ . الكافي : ٢ / ٨٣ / ٣ .

٤٣٩٢ . تحف العقول : ٣٥ .

٤٣٩٣ . كنز العمّال : ٤٣٦١٤ .

٤٣٩٤ . غرر الحكم : ٤٠٦٦ .

٤٣٩٥ . جامع الأخبار : ٥٠٥ / ١٣٩٧ .

٤٣٩٦ . كنز الفوائد : ١ / ٥٥ .

٤٣٩٧ . كنز العمّال : ٥٢٥٠ .

٤٣٩٨ . تحف العقول : ٢٠٤ .

٤٣٩٩ . تحف العقول : ٢٨٠ .

٤٤٠٠ . تنبيه الخواطر : ١ / ٦٥ .

٤٤٠١ . بحار الأنوار : ١٠٣ / ١٨ / ٨١ .

٤٤٠٢ . تحف العقول : ٤٦ .

٤٤٠٣ . الأمالي للطوسي : ٤٥٤ / ١٠١٥ .

٤٤٠٤ . الدرّة الباهرة : ١٨ .

٤٤٠٥ . غرر الحكم : ١٧٩٢ .

٤٤٠٦ . غرر الحكم : ٣٤٢١ .

٤٤٠٧ . المحاسن : ١ / ٢٤٧ / ٤٦٢ .

٤٤٠٨ . الكافي : ٢ / ٨٤ / ٥ .

٤٤٠٩ . الكافي : ٢ / ٣٩٨ / ٨ .

٤٤١٠ . الكافي : ٦ / ٤٣٤ / ٢٤ .

٤٤١١ . إرشاد القلوب : ٢٠٥ .

٤٤١٢ . الخصال : ٣٠ / ١٤ .

٤٤١٣ . قرب الإسناد : ١٣٥ / ٤٧٥ .

٤٤١٤ . الكافي : ٢ / ٤٦٨ / ٨ .

٤٤١٥ . غرر الحكم : ٢٨٧٣ .

٤٤١٦ . غرر الحكم : ٢٨٧٢ .

٤٤١٧ . تحف العقول : ٣٦٤ .

٤٤١٨ . الكافي : ٢ / ٥٥ / ٣ .

٤٤١٩ . الاختصاص : ٢٨ .

٤٤٢٠ . الخصال : ١٦ / ٥٦ .

٤٤٢١ . تحف العقول : ٤٤٢ .

٤٤٢٢ . تنبيه الخواطر : ٢ / ١٠٩ .

٤٤٢٣ . تحف العقول : ٥٠٧ .

٤٤٢٤ . تحف العقول : ٦ .

٤٤٢٥ . الكافي : ٢ / ٨٦ / ٢ .

٤٤٢٦ . الحشر : ٢ .

٤٤٢٧ . كنز الفوائد : ٢ / ٣١ .

٤٤٢٨ . نهج البلاغة : الحكمة ٣٦٧ .

٤٤٢٩ . غرر الحكم : ٧٨٣٧ .

٤٤٣٠ . بحار الأنوار : ٧٨ / ٩٢ / ١٠١ .

٤٤٣١ . بحار الأنوار : ٧٨ / ٩٢ / ١٠١ .

٤٤٣٢ . نهج البلاغة : الحكمة ٢٠٨ .

٤٤٣٣ . يوسف : ١١١ .

٤٤٣٤ . النور : ٤٤ .

٤٤٣٥ . غرر الحكم : ٦٤٥٣ .

٤٤٣٦ . غرر الحكم : ٧٥٨٩ .

٤٤٣٧ . نهج البلاغة : الخطبة ١٩٢ .

٤٤٣٨ . نهج البلاغة : الخطبة ١٩٢ .

٤٤٣٩ . نهج البلاغة : الحكمة ٢٩٧ .

٤٤٤٠ . بحار الأنوار : ٧٨ / ١٦٠ / ٢٠ .

٤٤٤١ . غرر الحكم : ٨٧٩ .

٤٤٤٢ . غرر الحكم : ٥١٥٠ .

٤٤٤٣ . غرر الحكم : ٨٠٥٦ .

٤٤٤٤ . نهج البلاغة : الحكمة ١١٣ .

٤٤٤٥ . غرر الحكم : ٩٥٤ .

٤٤٤٦ . غرر الحكم : ٦٢ .

٤٤٤٧ . نهج البلاغة : الحكمة ٤٦ .

٤٤٤٨ . غرر الحكم : ٢٦٤٢ .

٤٤٤٩ . غرر الحكم : ٤٦٠٦ .

٤٤٥٠ . تحف العقول : ٧٤ .

٤٤٥١ . غرر الحكم : ٧٢٦ .

٤٤٥٢ . نهج البلاغة : الحكمة ١٦٧ .

٤٤٥٣ . الزهد للحسين بن سعيد : ٦٨ / ١٧٩ .

٤٤٥٤ . الكافي : ٢ / ٣١٣ / ٢ .

٤٤٥٥ . الخصال : ٤٣٣ / ١٧ .

٤٤٥٦ . تحف العقول : ٢٨٥ .

٤٤٥٧ . الخصال : ١١٢ / ٨٦ .

٤٤٥٨ . غرر الحكم : ٩٦٦٦ .
٤٤٥٩ . تحف العقول : ٢٨٥ .
٤٤٦٠ . الأمالي للصدوق : ٥٦ / ١٢ .
٤٤٦١ . علل الشرائع : ١٢٢ / ١ .
٤٤٦٢ . الكافي : ١ / ٢٤ / ٢٠ .
٤٤٦٣ . الأنبياء : ٣٧ .
٤٤٦٤ . الإسراء : ١١ .
٤٤٦٥ . المحاسن : ١ / ٣٤٠ / ٦٩٧ .
٤٤٦٦ . المحاسن : ١ / ٣٤٠ / ٦٩٨؛ كنز العمّال : ٥٦٧٤ .
٤٤٦٧ . غرر الحكم : ٤٣٢ .
٤٤٦٨ . غرر الحكم : ٩٧٤٠ .
٤٤٦٩ . الخصال : ١٠٠ / ٥٢ .
٤٤٧٠ . الكافي : ٢ / ١٤٢ / ٤ .
٤٤٧١ . غرر الحكم : ١٩٣٧ .
٤٤٧٢ . الكافي : ٢ / ١٤٢ / ٣ .
٤٤٧٣ . مطالب السؤول : ٦١ .
٤٤٧٤ . غرر الحكم : ٤٧٨٩ .
٤٤٧٥ . غرر الحكم : ١٩٥٤ .
٤٤٧٦ . غرر الحكم : ١٨٧٣ .
٤٤٧٧ . غرر الحكم : ٤٢١٥ .
٤٤٧٨ . غرر الحكم : ٤٢١١ .
٤٤٧٩ . غررالحكم : ٧٧٤ .
٤٤٨٠ . غررالحكم : ٩٥٤٣ .
٤٤٨١ . نهج البلاغة : الحكمة ٤٣٧ .
٤٤٨٢ . علل الشرائع : ٢٤٨ / ٢ .
٤٤٨٣ . الكافي : ٢ / ١٤٦ / ١١ .
٤٤٨٤ . الكافي : ٢ / ١٤٧ / ١٥ .
٤٤٨٥ . الخصال : ٢٠٨ / ٢٨ .
٤٤٨٦ . كنز الفوائد : ٢ / ١٦٢ .
٤٤٨٧ . المائدة : ٨ .
٤٤٨٨ . تحف العقول : ٨٨ .
٤٤٨٩ . غرر الحكم : ٣٢٤٢ .
٤٤٩٠ . غرر الحكم : ٣٠١٤ .
٤٤٩١ . غرر الحكم : ٦٣٦٨ .
٤٤٩٢ . الكافي : ٢ / ٣٠٢ / ١١ .
٤٤٩٣ . تحف العقول : ٤٢ .
٤٤٩٤ . الأمالي للطوسي : ٥١٢ / ١١١٩ .
٤٤٩٥ . غرر الحكم : ٥٢٤٧ .
٤٤٩٦ . حلية الأولياء : ٣ / ١٨٤ / ٢٣٥ .
٤٤٩٧ . غرر الحكم : ٦٣٠٢ .
٤٤٩٨ . غرر الحكم : ٧٣١٦ .
٤٤٩٩ . التغابن : ١٤ .
٤٥٠٠ . غرر الحكم : ٤٤٢٤ .
٤٥٠١ . أعلام الدين : ٣٠٩ .
٤٥٠٢ . تنبيه الخواطر : ١ / ٢٥٩ .
٤٥٠٣ . غرر الحكم : ٣٢٦٩ .
٤٥٠٤ . غرر الحكم : ٨٦٧٢ .
٤٥٠٥ . نهج البلاغة : الكتاب ٦٢ .
٤٥٠٦ . غرر الحكم : ١٠٢١٦ .
٤٥٠٧ . غرر الحكم : ٨٢٣٠ .
٤٥٠٨ . غرر الحكم : ٨٠٤٣ .
٤٥٠٩ . الأمالي للصدوق : ٧٦٦ / ١٠٣١ .
٤٥١٠ . نهج البلاغة : الحكمة ١٧٢ ، ٤٣٨ .
٤٥١١ . بحار الأنوار : ٧٨ / ٢٠٠ / ٢٨ .
٤٥١٢ . تحف العقول : ٢٤٨ .
٤٥١٣ . مشكاة الأنوار : ١٠٣ / ٢٣٥ .
٤٥١٤ . كنز العمّال : ٧٠٣٢ .
٤٥١٥ . بحار الأنوار : ٧٤ / ١٦٥ / ٢٩ .
٤٥١٦ . غرر الحكم : ٢٩٨٨ .
٤٥١٧ . بحار الأنوار : ٧٨ / ١٤١ / ٣٤ .
٤٥١٨ . غرر الحكم : ٣١٩٠ .
٤٥١٩ . غرر الحكم : ٣٠٣٨ .
٤٥٢٠ . نهج البلاغة : الحكمة ٣٦٢ .
٤٥٢١ . أعلام الدين : ٣٠٣ .
٤٥٢٢ . صحيفة الإمام الرضا ؑ : ٨٥ / ١٩٥ .
٤٥٢٣ . الأمالي للمفيد : ٣٣٨ / ٢ .
٤٥٢٤ . وسائل الشيعة : ٨ / ٦٠٦ / ٣ .
٤٥٢٥ . جامع الأخبار : ٣٦ / ١٨ .
٤٥٢٦ . غرر الحكم : ٢٠٦١ .
٤٥٢٧ . غرر الحكم : ٥٣٨ .
٤٥٢٨ . بحار الأنوار : ٧٨ / ١٢٨ / ١١ .
٤٥٢٩ . الكافي : ١ / ٤٤ / ٢ .
٤٥٣٠ . الجاثية : ٢٣ .
٤٥٣١ . بحار الأنوار : ٧٠ / ٧١ / ٢٠ .

٤٥٣٢ . غرر الحكم : ٩٨٦٥ .

٤٥٣٣ . غرر الحكم : ٩٩٦٥ .

٤٥٣٤ . غرر الحكم : ٦٩٩٨ .

٤٥٣٥ . غرر الحكم : ٧٨٥٥_٧٨٥٦ .

٤٥٣٦ . غرر الحكم : ٧٨٢٩_٧٨٣٢ .

٤٥٣٧ . غرر الحكم : ٣١٢٦ .

٤٥٣٨ . غرر الحكم : ٧٩٤٦ .

٤٥٣٩ . غرر الحكم : ١٠٩٣٠ .

٤٥٤٠ . غرر الحكم : ١٠٩٢٧ .

٤٥٤١ . غرر الحكم : ١٠٩٣٧ .

٤٥٤٢ . بحار الأنوار : ٩٤ / ١٢٨ / ١٩ .

٤٥٤٣ . تحف العقول : ٢٨٦ .

٤٥٤٤ . غرر الحكم : ٧٩٩٩ .

٤٥٤٥ . غرر الحكم : ٩٨٦٤ .

٤٥٤٦ . كنز العمّال : ٣٦٤٧٢ .

٤٥٤٧ . غرر الحكم : ٤٥٨٦ .

٤٥٤٨ . غرر الحكم : ٨٨٩٦ .

٤٥٤٩ . الكافي : ٨ / ٢٤٧ / ٣٤٧ .

٤٥٥٠ . الأمالي للصدوق : ٦٤٧ / ٨٧٨ .

٤٥٥١ . كنز العمّال : ٥٨٩٣ .

٤٥٥٢ . بحار الأنوار : ٧٠ / ٣٩٣ / ٦٤ .

٤٥٥٣ . غرر الحكم : ١٠٩٨٤ .

٤٥٥٤ . نهج البلاغة : الخطبة ١٤٧ .

٤٥٥٥ . غرر الحكم : ٦٣٥٩ .

٤٥٥٦ . غرر الحكم : ٣٢٦٠ .

٤٥٥٧ . الكافي : ٢ / ٦٢ / ٩ .

٤٥٥٨ . تنبيه الخواطر : ٢ / ١٨٥ .

٤٥٥٩ . تنبيه الخواطر : ٢ / ١٨٤ .

٤٥٦٠ . غرر الحكم : ١٩٨٥ .

٤٥٦١ . غرر الحكم : ٨٥٥ .

٤٥٦٢ . غرر الحكم : ٦٦٤ .

٤٥٦٣ . غرر الحكم : ١٧٩١ .

٤٥٦٤ . تحف العقول : ٣٧٦ .

٤٥٦٥ . الكافي : ١ / ٨٦ / ١ .

٤٥٦٦ . الكافي : ١ / ٨٥ / ١ .

٤٥٦٧ . بحار الأنوار : ٩٨ / ٢٢٥ .

٤٥٦٨ . الإقبال : ١ / ١٥٧ .

٤٥٦٩ . كنز العمّال : ٥٧٠٥ .

٤٥٧٠ . الأمالي للصدوق : ٥٠٣ / ٦٩٠ .

٤٥٧١ . المحاسن : ١ / ٣٧١ / ٨٠٨ .

٤٥٧٢ . نهج البلاغة : الخطبة ١٦٠ .

٤٥٧٣ . نهج البلاغة : الخطبة ١٠٩ .

٤٥٧٤ . بحار الأنوار : ٩٤ / ١٥٠ / ٢١ .

٤٥٧٥ . التوحيد : ٣٦ / ٢ .

٤٥٧٦ . التوحيد : ٢٥٢ / ٣ .

٤٥٧٧ . نهج البلاغة : الخطبة ١٥٢ .

٤٥٧٨ . نهج البلاغة : الخطبة ٩٤ .

٤٥٧٩ . نهج البلاغة : الخطبة ١٨٥ .

٤٥٨٠ . الكافي : ١ / ١١٧ / ٨ .

٤٥٨١ . الكافي : ١ / ١٠٢ / ٦ .

٤٥٨٢ . كشف الغمّة : ٣ / ١٧٦ .

٤٥٨٣ . عيون أخبار الرضا : ٢ / ٣٥ / ٧٥ .

٤٥٨٤ . غرر الحكم : ٥٤٠ .

٤٥٨٥ . نهج البلاغة : الحكمة ٤٧٠ .

٤٥٨٦ . معاني الأخبار : ١١ / ٢ .

٤٥٨٧ . الأمالي للطوسي : ٢٢ / ٢٨ .

٤٥٨٨ . المؤمنون : ١١٧ .

٤٥٨٩ . نهج البلاغة : الكتاب ٣١ .

٤٥٩٠ . في الكافي : ١ / ٨١ / ٥ هنا زيادة وهي «والتدبير واحداً» .

٤٥٩١ . التوحيد : ٢٤٣ / ١ .

٤٥٩٢ . التوحيد : ٢٥٠ / ٢ .

٤٥٩٣ . التوحيد : ٢٧٠ / ٦ .

٤٥٩٤ . تفسير القمّي : ٢ / ٩٣ .

٤٥٩٥ . الأنعام : ١٠٣ .

٤٥٩٦ . التوحيد : ١٠٨ / ٤ .

٤٥٩٧ . الأمالي للصدوق : ٤٢٣ / ٥٦٠ .

٤٥٩٨ . الأمالي للصدوق : ٤٩٥ / ٦٧٣ .

٤٥٩٩ . الكافي : ١ / ٩٥ / ١ .

٤٦٠٠ . نهج البلاغة : الخطبة ١٠١ .

٤٦٠١ . نهج البلاغة : الكتاب ٣١ .

٤٦٠٢ . بحار الأنوار : ٧٧ / ٣٣١ / ١٨ .

٤٦٠٣ . التوحيد : ١٤١ / ٥ .

٤٦٠٤ . البقرة : ٢٥٥ .

٤٦٠٥ . التوحيد : ١٣٧ / ١١ .

٤٦٠٦ . التوحيد : ١٤٢ / ٦ .

٤٦٠٧ . الأنعام : ٥٩ .

٤٦٠٨ . نهج البلاغة : الخطبة ١٧٨ .

٤٦٠٩ . نهج البلاغة : الخطبة ١٩٨ .

٤٦١٠ . نهج البلاغة : الخطبة ١٠٨ .

٤٦١١ . الكافي : ١ / ١٠٧ / ٢ .

٤٦١٢ . التوحيد : ١٣٧ / ٩ .

٤٦١٣ . الكافي : ١ / ١٠٧ / ١ .

٤٦١٤ . التوحيد : ١٣٨ / ١٦ .

٤٦١٥ . الآيات في نفي الظلم عنه تعالى تزيد على أربعين آية ، فراجع .

٤٦١٦ . النساء : ٤٠ .

٤٦١٧ . نهج البلاغة : الخطبة ٢١٤ .

٤٦١٨ . نهج البلاغة : الحكمة ٤٧٠ .

٤٦١٩ . الصحيفة السجّادية : ص ٢٠٧ الدعاء ٤٨ .

٤٦٢٠ . التوحيد : ٩٦ / ١ .

٤٦٢١ . الزمر : ٦٢ .

٤٦٢٢ . التوحيد : ٢٩٥ / ٥ .

٤٦٢٣ . التوحيد : ٩٨ / ٥ .

٤٦٢٤ . المعارج : ٤٠ .

٤٦٢٥ . التوحيد : ١٣٠ / ٩ .

٤٦٢٦ . التوحيد : ١٢٧ / ٥ .

٤٦٢٧ . النساء : ١٦٤ .

٤٦٢٨ . نهج البلاغة : الخطبة ١٨٦ .

٤٦٢٩ . يس : ٨٢ .

٤٦٣٠ . التوحيد : ١٠٠ / ٨ .

٤٦٣١ . الحديد : ٣ .

٤٦٣٢ . نهج البلاغة : الخطبة ٢١٣ .

٤٦٣٣ . التوحيد : ٣٧ / ٢ .

٤٦٣٤ . آل عمران : ١٨٩ .

٤٦٣٥ . نهج البلاغة : الخطبة ٦٥ .

٤٦٣٦ . نهج البلاغة : الحكمة ٤٠٤ .

٤٦٣٧ . غافر : ٢٠ .

٤٦٣٨ . نهج البلاغة : الخطبة ١٥٢ .

٤٦٣٩ . التوحيد : ١٤٤ / ٩ .

٤٦٤٠ . التوحيد : ٦٥ / ١٨ .

٤٦٤١ . الأنعام : ١٠٣ .

٤٦٤٢ . الكافي : ١ / ١٢٢ / ٢ .

٤٦٤٣ . هود : ٦٦ .

٤٦٤٤ . فاطر : ١٠ .

٤٦٤٥ . نهج البلاغة : الخطبة ٦٥ .

٤٦٤٦ . نهج البلاغة : الخطبة ١٠٩ .

٤٦٤٧ . نهج البلاغة : الخطبة ٦٥ .

٤٦٤٨ . نهج البلاغة : الخطبة ١٩٢ .

٤٦٤٩ . آل عمران : ٦٢ .

٤٦٥٠ . التوحيد : ٣٩٧ / ١٣ .

٤٦٥١ . الإخلاص : ٢ .

٤٦٥٢ . التوحيد : ٩٠ / ٣ .

٤٦٥٣ . الحديد : ٤ .

٤٦٥٤ . نهج البلاغة : الخطبة ١٩٥ .

٤٦٥٥ . الأنعام : ٣ .

٤٦٥٦ . التوحيد : ١٣٣ / ١٥ .

٤٦٥٧ . التوحيد : ١٤٠ / ٤ .

٤٦٥٨ . التوحيد : ٣٣٨ / ٥ .

٤٦٥٩ . هذه الجملة ليست في غير واحد من النسخ المخطوطة العتيقة ولا في شرحَي ابن ميثم وابن أبي الحديد ، والظاهر أنّها زيادة من النسّاخ . (كما في هامش بحار الأنوار : ٧٧ / ٣٠٠) .

٤٦٦٠ . نهج البلاغة : الخطبة ١ .

٤٦٦١ . غرر الحكم : ٦٥٨٥ .

٤٦٦٢ . غرر الحكم : ٩٨٠ .

٤٦٦٣ . أعلام الدين : ٢٩٨ .

٤٦٦٤ . الدعوات : ١٠٨ / ٢٤٠ .

٤٦٦٥ . الأمالي للطوسي : ٣٠٤ / ٦١٠ .

٤٦٦٦ . كشف الغمّة : ٣ / ١٣٧ .

٤٦٦٧ . بحار الأنوار : ٧٤ / ٤٠١ / ٤٤ .

٤٦٦٨ . عيون أخبار الرضا : ٢ / ٣٥ / ٧٦ .

٤٦٦٩ . ثواب الأعمال : ٣٤٢ / ١ .

٤٦٧٠ . الكافي : ٤ / ١٨ / ٢ .

٤٦٧١ . غرر الحكم : ٢٢٨٢ .

٤٦٧٢ . غرر الحكم : ٤٠٠٠_٤٠٠١ .

٤٦٧٣ . غرر الحكم : ٩٧٢٤ .

٤٦٧٤ . الأمالي للطوسي : ٥٩٦ / ١٢٣٥ ، كنز العمّال : ١٦٢٥٦ .

٤٦٧٥ . غرر الحكم : ٩١١٥ .

٤٦٧٦ . تحف العقول : ٤٠٣ .

٤٦٧٧ . كنز الفوائد : ١ / ٢١٢ .

٤٦٧٨ . الجعفريات : ٢٣٣ .

٤٦٧٩ . غرر الحكم : ٤٩٨٣ .

٤٦٨٠ . بحار الأنوار : ٧٤ / ٤١٩ / ٤٧ .

٤٦٨١ . بحار الأنوار : ٧٥ / ١٥ / ٨ .

٤٦٨٢ . الخصال : ٣٢ / ١١١ .

٤٦٨٣ . ثواب الأعمال : ٣٤٣ / ١ .

٤٦٨٤ . الكافي : ٥ / ٥٥ / ٣ .

٤٦٨٥ . مكارم الأخلاق : ١ / ٢٩٤ / ٩١٥ .

٤٦٨٦ . آل عمران : ١٠٤ .

٤٦٨٧ . آل عمران : ١١٠ .

٤٦٨٨ . التوبة : ٧١ .

٤٦٨٩ . مستدرك الوسائل : ١٢ / ١٧٩ / ١٣٨١٧ .

٤٦٩٠ . معاني الأخبار : ٣٤٤ / ١ .

٤٦٩١ . غرر الحكم : ٦٨١٧ .

٤٦٩٢ . نهج البلاغة : الحكمة ٣٧٤ .

٤٦٩٣ . غرر الحكم : ١٩٧٧ .

٤٦٩٤ . الكافي : ٥ / ٥٧ / ٦ .

٤٦٩٥ . تنبيه الخواطر : ٢ / ١٧٩ .

٤٦٩٦ . الكافي : ٥ / ٥٦ / ١ .

٤٦٩٧ . وسائل الشيعة : ١١ / ٤٠٧ / ١٢ .

٤٦٩٨ . نهج البلاغة : الكتاب ٤٧ .

٤٦٩٩ . نهج البلاغة : الحكمة ١٥٤ .

٤٧٠٠ . كشف الغمّة : ٣ / ١٣٩ .

٤٧٠١ . تحف العقول : ٤٥٦ .

٤٧٠٢ . كنز العمّال : ٥٥٢٣ .

٤٧٠٣ . تنبيه الخواطر : ٢ / ٢١٣ .

٤٧٠٤ . غرر الحكم : ٣٧٨٠ .

٤٧٠٥ . نهج البلاغة : الخطبة ١٢٩ .

٤٧٠٦ . نهج البلاغة : الخطبة ١٠٥ .

٤٧٠٧ . الخصال : ١٠٩ / ٧٩ .

٤٧٠٨ . الترغيب والترهيب : ٣ / ٢٢٣ / ١ .

٤٧٠٩ . كنز العمّال : ٥٥٧٠ .

٤٧١٠ . تهذيب الأحكام : ٦ / ١٨١ / ٣٧٤ .

٤٧١١ . الكافي : ٥ / ٥٩ / ١٠ .

٤٧١٢ . الكافي : ٥ / ٦٠ / ١ .

٤٧١٣ . النساء : ١٣٩ .

٤٧١٤ . بحار الأنوار : ٧٨ / ١٠ / ٦٧ .

٤٧١٥ . تحف العقول : ٣٦٦ .

٤٧١٦ . نهج البلاغة : الحكمة ١١٣ .

٤٧١٧ . تحف العقول : ٢٨٣ .

٤٧١٨ . بحار الأنوار : ٧٨ / ٢٢٨ / ١٠٥ .

٤٧١٩ . بحار الأنوار : ٧٨ / ٤٥٣ / ٢١ .

٤٧٢٠ . قصص الأنبياء : ١٩٥ / ٢٤٤ .

٤٧٢١ . نهج البلاغة : الحكمة ٣٧١ .

٤٧٢٢ . الخصال : ٤٢٠ / ١٤ .

٤٧٢٣ . الكافي : ٢ / ١٤٤ / ٤ .

٤٧٢٤ . بحار الأنوار : ٧٨ / ٥٣ / ٩٠ .

٤٧٢٥ . الكافي : ٢ / ١٤٩ / ٦ .

٤٧٢٦ . الكافي : ٢ / ١٠٩ / ١٠ .

٤٧٢٧ . الخصال : ١٦٩ / ٢٢٢ .

٤٧٢٨ . الكافي : ٢ / ١١٠ / ٥ .

٤٧٢٩ . بحار الأنوار : ٧٨ / ٣٧٤ / ٢٤ .

٤٧٣٠ . تحف العقول : ٢٨٦ .

٤٧٣١ . بحار الأنوار : ٧٤ / ١٨٠ / ٢٨ .

٤٧٣٢ . الكافي : ٨ / ٤٢ / ٨ .

٤٧٣٣ . أعلام الدين : ٣٤١ .

٤٧٣٤ . غرر الحكم : ٦٦١ .

٤٧٣٥ . غرر الحكم : ٨٦٤٤ .

٤٧٣٦ . غرر الحكم : ٨١٥١ .

٤٧٣٧ . بحار الأنوار : ٤٧ / ٦٠ / ١١٦ .

٤٧٣٨ . بحار الأنوار : ٧٠ / ١١١ / ١٤ .

٤٧٣٩ . كنز العمّال : ٦٨٦ .

٤٧٤٠ . الدرّ المنثور : ١ / ١٦١ .

٤٧٤١ . بحار الأنوار : ٨٢ / ٩٤ / ٤٦ .

٤٧٤٢ . الكافي : ٣ / ٢٢٧ / ٣ .

٤٧٤٣ . كتاب من لا يحضره الفقيه : ١ / ١٧٤ / ٥٠٥ .

٤٧٤٤ . مسكّن الفؤاد : ١٠٨ .

٤٧٤٥ . بحار الأنوار : ٧٨ / ٣٥٣ / ٩ .

٤٧٤٦ . نهج البلاغة : الحكمة ١٠ .

٤٧٤٧ . معاني الأخبار : ٢٦٧ / ١ .

٤٧٤٨ . بحار الأنوار : ٧٤ / ١٦٧ / ٣٤ .

٤٧٤٩ . النساء : ١٩ .

٤٧٥٠ . نهج البلاغة : الكتاب ٣١ .
٤٧٥١ . بحار الأنوار : ٧٨ / ٢٣٦ / ٦٣ .
٤٧٥٢ . الأمالي للصدوق : ٢٦٩ / ٢٩٥ .
٤٧٥٣ . غرر الحكم : ٥٠٧١ .
٤٧٥٤ . بحار الأنوار : ٧٨ / ٥٠ / ٧٦ .
٤٧٥٥ . بحار الأنوار : ٧٤ / ١٧٥ / ٦ .
٤٧٥٦ . بحار الأنوار : ٧٥ / ١٥١ / ١٧ .
٤٧٥٧ . أعلام الدين : ٢٩٧ .
٤٧٥٨ . تحف العقول : ٣٦٦ .
٤٧٥٩ . تحف العقول : ٤٠٣ .
٤٧٦٠ . ثواب الأعمال : ١٠٨ / ١ .
٤٧٦١ . مصباح المتهجّد : ٧٧٢ .
٤٧٦٢ . ثواب الأعمال : ١١٠ / ٣ .
٤٧٦٣ . علل الشرائع : ٢٢٧ / ٢ .
٤٧٦٤ . وسائل الشيعة : ١٠ / ٣٩٤ / ٨ .
٤٧٦٥ . بحار الأنوار : ٧٨ / ١١ / ٧٠ .
٤٧٦٦ . نهج البلاغة : الخطبة ١٠٩ .
٤٧٦٧ . الأمالي للصدوق : ٧٦٥ / ١٠٢٩ .
٤٧٦٨ . كنز العمّال : ٧٠٠٠ .
٤٧٦٩ . نهج البلاغة : الحكمة ٤٧٤ .
٤٧٧٠ . كنز العمّال : ١٨٧٢ .
٤٧٧١ . الفتح : ٢٦ .
٤٧٧٢ . الكافي : ٢ / ٣٠٨ / ٢ .
٤٧٧٣ . الكافي : ٢ / ٣٠٨ / ٣ .
٤٧٧٤ . سنن أبي داوود : ٤ / ٣٣٢ / ٥١٢١ .
٤٧٧٥ . نهج البلاغة : الخطبة ١٩٢ .
٤٧٧٦ . الكافي : ٢ / ٣٠٨ / ٧ .
٤٧٧٧ . نهج البلاغة : الخطبة ١٩٢ .
٤٧٧٨ . غرر الحكم : ٣٧٣٨ .
٤٧٧٩ . معاني الأخبار : ١٣٢ / ١ .
٤٧٨٠ . معاني الأخبار : ١٣٢ / ٢ .
٤٧٨١ . الكافي : ٨ / ٨٢ / ٣٩ .
٤٧٨٢ . غرر الحكم : ٨٤٦٩ .
٤٧٨٣ . غرر الحكم : ٨٧٩ .
٤٧٨٤ . غرر الحكم : ٣٤٦٦ .
٤٧٨٥ . غرر الحكم : ٤٣١٦ .
٤٧٨٦ . غرر الحكم : ١٢ .
٤٧٨٧ . البلد الأمين : ٣١٥ .
٤٧٨٨ . بحار الأنوار : ٧٨ / ١٨٨ / ٤١ .
٤٧٨٩ . الكافي : ١ / ٢٠٤ / ٢ .
٤٧٩٠ . الكافي : ١ / ٢٦٩ / ٦ .
٤٧٩١ . الكافي : ١ / ٢٠٠ / ١ .
٤٧٩٢ . الكافي : ١ / ٢٠٣ / ١ .
٤٧٩٣ . أمالي الصدوق : ٣٤٧ / ١ .
٤٧٩٤ . بحار الأنوار : ١٦ / ٢٤٠ .
٤٧٩٥ . بحار الأنوار : ٧٦ / ٦٣ / ٣ .
٤٧٩٦ . نهج البلاغة : الحكمة ٣٧ .
٤٧٩٧ . الحجّ : ٣٢ .
٤٧٩٨ . الحجّ : ٣٠ .
٤٧٩٩ . كنز العمّال : ٢٥٥٠٧ .
٤٨٠٠ . المحاسن : ١ / ٣٦٤ / ٧٨٦ .
٤٨٠١ . تحف العقول : ٣٩٤ .
٤٨٠٢ . النور : ٣٣ .
٤٨٠٣ . البقرة : ٢٧٣ .
٤٨٠٤ . الأمالي للطوسي : ٣٩ / ٤٣ .
٤٨٠٥ . نهج البلاغة : الحكمة ٤٧٤ .
٤٨٠٦ . غرر الحكم : ١١٦٨ .
٤٨٠٧ . غرر الحكم : ٥٢٩ .
٤٨٠٨ . غرر الحكم : ١٩٨٩ .
٤٨٠٩ . غرر الحكم : ٥٤٤٩ .
٤٨١٠ . الخصال : ٥٥ / ٧٥ .
٤٨١١ . الكافي : ٢ / ٧٩ / ٥ .
٤٨١٢ . سنن ابن ماجة : ٢ / ٨١٧ / ٢٤٤٤ .
٤٨١٣ . الكافي : ٢ / ٧٩ / ١ .
٤٨١٤ . مطالب السؤول : ٥٠ .
٤٨١٥ . غرر الحكم : ١٥١٢ .
٤٨١٦ . نهج البلاغة : الحكمة ٤٧ .
٤٨١٧ . غرر الحكم : ٧٦٤٦ .
٤٨١٨ . تحف العقول : ١٧ .
٤٨١٩ . غرر الحكم : ٢١٤٨ .
٤٨٢٠ . غرر الحكم : ٤٦٣٧ .
٤٨٢١ . غرر الحكم : ٤٥٩٣ .
٤٨٢٢ . غرر الحكم : ٨٥٩٧ .
٤٨٢٣ . غرر الحكم : ٤٢٣٨ .

٤٨٢٤ . الشورىٰ : ٤٠ .
٤٨٢٥ . آل عمران : ١٣٤ .
٤٨٢٦ . أعلام الدين : ٣٣٧ .
٤٨٢٧ . كنز العمّال : ٧٠٠٥ .
٤٨٢٨ . الكافي : ٢ / ١٠٨ / ٥ .
٤٨٢٩ . أعلام الدين : ٣١٥ .
٤٨٣٠ . تنبيه الخواطر : ٢ / ١٢٠ .
٤٨٣١ . الكافي : ٢ / ١٠٨ / ٦ .
٤٨٣٢ . الكافي : ٢ / ١٠٧ / ٣ .
٤٨٣٣ . الحجر : ٨٥ .
٤٨٣٤ . غرر الحكم : ٩٥٦٧ .
٤٨٣٥ . أعلام الدين : ٣٠٧ .
٤٨٣٦ . كنز العمّال : ٧٠٠٧ .
٤٨٣٧ . نهج البلاغة : الحكمة ١١ .
٤٨٣٨ . نهج البلاغة : الحكمة ٢١١ .
٤٨٣٩ . الدرّة الباهرة : ٢٤ .
٤٨٤٠ . مستدرك الوسائل : ٩ / ٧ / ١٠٠٤١ .
٤٨٤١ . تحف العقول : ٨٧ .
٤٨٤٢ . كنز الفوائد : ٢ / ١٨٢ .
٤٨٤٣ . غرر الحكم : ٤٧٨٨ .
٤٨٤٤ . النساء : ٤٣ .
٤٨٤٥ . سنن ابن ماجة : ٢ / ١٢٦٥ / ٣٨٥٠ .
٤٨٤٦ . تنبيه الخواطر : ١ / ٩ .
٤٨٤٧ . نهج البلاغة : الكتاب ٢٧ .
٤٨٤٨ . الأمالي للصدوق : ١٣٨ / ١٣٦ .
٤٨٤٩ . نهج البلاغة : الخطبة ٢٢٧ .
٤٨٥٠ . بحار الأنوار : ٧٨ / ٩٠ / ٩٥ .
٤٨٥١ . نهج البلاغة : الخطبة ١٩٢ .
٤٨٥٢ . كشف الغمّة : ٢ / ٤١٨ .
٤٨٥٣ . غرر الحكم : ٩٧٣ .
٤٨٥٤ . التوحيد : ٧٤ / ٢٧ .
٤٨٥٥ . غرر الحكم : ٤٢٠٧ .
٤٨٥٦ . كتاب من لا يحضره الفقيه : ٤ / ٤٠٦ / ٥٨٧٨ .
٤٨٥٧ . جامع الأخبار : ١٥٣ / ٣٤٤ .
٤٨٥٨ . تحف العقول : ٨٩ .
٤٨٥٩ . بحار الأنوار : ٧٢ / ٢٣٢ / ٢ .
٤٨٦٠ . كنز العمّال : ٤٩٣٥ ، ٣٢٧٢ .
٤٨٦١ . كنز العمّال : ٣١٣٠_٣١٥٣ .
٤٨٦٢ . سنن ابن ماجة : ٢ / ١٢٦٥ / ٣٨٤٩ .
٤٨٦٣ . الدعوات : ١١٤ / ٢٦٢ .
٤٨٦٤ . الدعوات : ١١٤ / ٢٦١ .
٤٨٦٥ . الدعوات : ٨٤ / ٢١١ .
٤٨٦٦ . الكافي : ٢ / ٤٦٢ / ١ .
٤٨٦٧ . البقرة : ٢٦٩ .
٤٨٦٨ . الملك : ١٠ .
٤٨٦٩ . روضة الواعظين : ٩ .
٤٨٧٠ . نهج البلاغة : الحكمة ٤٠٧ .
٤٨٧١ . غرر الحكم : ٤٧٥ .
٤٨٧٢ . غرر الحكم : ١٢٥٠ .
٤٨٧٣ . غرر الحكم : ٤٠٤ .
٤٨٧٤ . غرر الحكم : ١٣٢٥ .
٤٨٧٥ . غرر الحكم : ٢٧٢ .
٤٨٧٦ . نهج البلاغة : الحكمة ٣٨ .
٤٨٧٧ . الأمالي للطوسي : ١٤٦ / ٢٤٠ .
٤٨٧٨ . تحف العقول : ٢٨٦ .
٤٨٧٩ . الخصال : ٥٨٩ / ١٣ .
٤٨٨٠ . الاختصاص : ٢٤٤ .
٤٨٨١ . الكافي : ١ / ٢٩ / ٣٤ .
٤٨٨٢ . الاختصاص : ٢٤٦ .
٤٨٨٣ . الكافي : ١ / ٢٥ / ٢٤ .
٤٨٨٤ . تحف العقول : ٣٩٧ .
٤٨٨٥ . الكافي : ١ / ١١ / ٤ .
٤٨٨٦ . مجمع البيان : ١٠ / ٤٨٧ .
٤٨٨٧ . تحف العقول : ٥٤ .
٤٨٨٨ . كذا في المصدر و الظاهر أنّ الصحيح : «حُرِمَ العقلَ» .
٤٨٨٩ . كشف الغمّة : ٢ / ١٩٧ .
٤٨٩٠ . في نقل : أعزّ منك . وفي نقل أ كرم عليّ منك . وفي نقل : ما خلقت خلقاً هو أحبّ إليّ منك . وفي نقل : ما خلقت خلقاً أحسن منك ، ولا أطوع لي منك ، ولا أرفع منك ، ولا أشرف منك ولا أعزّ منك . وفي نقل : فقال جلّ وعزّ : خلقتك خلقاً عظيماً وكرّمتك علىٰ جميع خلقي . وفي نقل : ما خلقت خلقاً أعظم منك ، ولا أطوع منك .
٤٨٩١ . الكافي : ١ / ٢٦ / ٢٦ .
٤٨٩٢ . المحاسن : ١ / ٣٠٨ / ٦٠٨ .

٤٨٩٣ . معاني الأخبار : ١ / ٢ .

٤٨٩٤ . الكافي : ١ / ١٨ / ١٢ .

٤٨٩٥ . الكافي : ١ / ١٦ / ١٢ .

٤٨٩٦ . الكافي : ١ / ١٦ / ١٢ .

٤٨٩٧ . تحف العقول : ١٥ .

٤٨٩٨ . عوالي اللآلي : ١ / ٢٤٨ / ٤ .

٤٨٩٩ . غرر الحكم : ٢١٤١ .

٤٩٠٠ . نهج البلاغة : الكتاب ٣١ .

٤٩٠١ . مطالب السؤول : ٤٩ .

٤٩٠٢ . معاني الأخبار : ٢٤٠ / ١ .

٤٩٠٣ . معاني الأخبار : ٤٠١ / ٦٢ .

٤٩٠٤ . تحف العقول : ٢٨ .

٤٩٠٥ . الأمالي للصدوق : ٧٣ / ٤١ .

٤٩٠٦ . نهج البلاغة : الحكمة ٦ .

٤٩٠٧ . نهج البلاغة : الحكمة ٢٣٥ .

٤٩٠٨ . الإختصاص : ٢٤٥ .

٤٩٠٩ . الكافي : ١ / ١١ / ٣ .

٤٩١٠ . الكافي : ٢ / ١١٦ / ٢٠ .

٤٩١١ . تحف العقول : ٣٩٠ .

٤٩١٢ . الكافي : ١ / ١٧ / ١٢ .

٤٩١٣ . غرر الحكم : ١٧١٧ .

٤٩١٤ . غرر الحكم : ٤٢٩١ .

٤٩١٥ . أعلام الدين : ٢٩٨ .

٤٩١٦ . الدعوات : ٢٢١ / ٦٠٣ .

٤٩١٧ . تحف العقول : ٣٦٤ .

٤٩١٨ . الاختصاص : ٢٤٤ .

٤٩١٩ . أعلام الدين : ٣٣٣ .

٤٩٢٠ . غرر الحكم : ١٠٩٥٧ .

٤٩٢١ . نهج البلاغة : الحكمة ٣٠١ .

٤٩٢٢ . غرر الحكم : ٥٦٠٨ .

٤٩٢٣ . غرر الحكم : ٥٦٠٠ .

٤٩٢٤ . غرر الحكم : ٦٢٢١ .

٤٩٢٥ . غرر الحكم : ٥٤٢٢ .

٤٩٢٦ . غرر الحكم : ٧٠٩١ .

٤٩٢٧ . نهج البلاغة : الحكمة ٧١ .

٤٩٢٨ . غرر الحكم : ٨٢٢٦ .

٤٩٢٩ . غرر الحكم : ٥١٨٠ .

٤٩٣٠ . غرر الحكم : ٥٩٠١ .

٤٩٣١ . كنز الفوائد : ١ / ٢٠٠ .

٤٩٣٢ . كنز الفوائد : ١ / ١٩٩ .

٤٩٣٣ . نهج البلاغة : الحكمة ٤٥٠ .

٤٩٣٤ . كنز الفوائد : ١ / ١٩٩ .

٤٩٣٥ . بحار الأنوار : ٧٨ / ١٨٦ / ١٦ .

٤٩٣٦ . غرر الحكم : ٤٠٤٣ .

٤٩٣٧ . غرر الحكم : ٧٩٨٥ .

٤٩٣٨ . غرر الحكم : ٩٢٩٩ .

٤٩٣٩ . غرر الحكم : ٧٠٩٣ .

٤٩٤٠ . غرر الحكم : ٤٥٨٩ .

٤٩٤١ . غرر الحكم : ٤٦٠٢ .

٤٩٤٢ . غرر الحكم : ٤٦٥٤ .

٤٩٤٣ . غرر الحكم : ١٢٥٤ .

٤٩٤٤ . مطالب السؤول : ٥٦ .

٤٩٤٥ . نهج البلاغة : الحكمة ٢١١ .

٤٩٤٦ . نهج البلاغة : الحكمة ٢٥٢ .

٤٩٤٧ . نهج البلاغة : الخطبة ٨٦ .

٤٩٤٨ . الدرّة الباهرة : ٣١ .

٤٩٤٩ . البقرة : ١٢٥ .

٤٩٥٠ . كنز العمّال : ١٨٠٩١ .

٤٩٥١ . كتاب من لا يحضره الفقيه : ٢ / ١٨٩ / ٢١٠٨ .

٤٩٥٢ . تهذيب الأحكام : ٤ / ٢٨٧ / ٨٦٩ .

٤٩٥٣ . الكافي : ٤ / ١٧٦ / ١ .

٤٩٥٤ . الزمر : ٩ .

٤٩٥٥ . المجادلة : ١١ .

٤٩٥٦ . كنز العمّال : ٢٨٧٨٤ .

٤٩٥٧ . بحار الأنوار : ٧٧ / ١٧٥ / ٩ .

٤٩٥٨ . الأمالي للطوسي : ٤٨٨ / ١٠٦٩ .

٤٩٥٩ . الأمالي للصدوق : ٧٣ / ٤١ .

٤٩٦٠ . كنز العمّال : ١٠٦٤٧ .

٤٩٦١ . الدرّ المنثور : ٣ / ٤٢٣ .

٤٩٦٢ . غرر الحكم : ٥٢٣٤ ـ ٦٣٧٩ .

٤٩٦٣ . فرس حَرُون : لا ينقاد ، وإذا اشتدّ به الجري وقف (الصحاح : ٥ / ٢٠٩٧) .

٤٩٦٤ . تحف العقول : ٢٠٨ .

٤٩٦٥ . غرر الحكم : ٥٣٦ .

٤٩٦٦ . غرر الحكم : ٨٣٧ .

٤٩٦٧ . كنز الفوائد : ١ / ٣١٩ .

٤٩٦٨ . عيون أخبار الرّضا : ٢ / ٦٦ / ٢٩٥ .

٤٩٦٩ . منية المريد : ١١٠ .

٤٩٧٠ . الكافي : ٨ / ١٩ / ٤ .

٤٩٧١ . نهج البلاغة : الحكمة ١١٣ .

٤٩٧٢ . نهج البلاغة : الحكمة ٢٠٥ .

٤٩٧٣ . نهج البلاغة : الحكمة ٢٨٨ .

٤٩٧٤ . غرر الحكم : ١٨٥ .

٤٩٧٥ . الأمالي للصدوق : ٧١٣ / ٩٨٢ .

٤٩٧٦ . الجبّان والجبّانة : الصّحراء ، وتُسمّى بهما المقابر . (النهاية : ١ / ٢٣٦) .

٤٩٧٧ . نهج البلاغة : الحكمة ١٤٧ .

٤٩٧٨ . نهج البلاغة : الحكمة ١٤٧ .

٤٩٧٩ . غرر الحكم : ١١٢٤_١١٢٥ .

٤٩٨٠ . الأمالي للطوسي : ٥٤٣ / ١١٦٥ .

٤٩٨١ . الكافي : ١ / ٣٢ / ٢ .

٤٩٨٢ . منية المريد : ١٠٥ .

٤٩٨٣ . منية المريد : ١٠٤ .

٤٩٨٤ . بحار الأنوار : ٢ / ١٩ / ٤٩ .

٤٩٨٥ . روضة الواعظين : ١٦ .

٤٩٨٦ . روضة الواعظين : ١٧ .

٤٩٨٧ . كنز العمّال : ٢٨٩٠٨ .

٤٩٨٨ . الاختصاص : ٢٤٥ .

٤٩٨٩ . الدعوات : ٦٢ / ١٥٣ .

٤٩٩٠ . كنز العمّال : ٢٨٨٥٨ .

٤٩٩١ . النوادر للراوندي : ١١٠ / ٩٤ .

٤٩٩٢ . تنبيه الخواطر : ١ / ٨٤ .

٤٩٩٣ . كنز العمّال : ٢٨٦٩٧ ، ٢٨٦٩٨ .

٤٩٩٤ . الكافي : ١ / ٣٠ / ١ .

٤٩٩٥ . عوالي اللآلي : ١ / ٢٨٥ / ١٣٥ .

٤٩٩٦ . عوالي اللآلي : ٤ / ٦١ / ٩ .

٤٩٩٧ . كنز العمّال : ٢٨٧٢٦ .

٤٩٩٨ . كنز العمّال : ٢٨٩٣٢ ، ٢٨٩٣٣ نحوه .

٤٩٩٩ . الترغيب والترهيب : ١ / ٩٧ / ١٦ .

٥٠٠٠ . كنز العمّال : ٢٨٧٠٢ .

٥٠٠١ . منية المريد : ١٠٠ .

٥٠٠٢ . كنز العمّال : ٢٨٧٠١ .

٥٠٠٣ . كنز العمّال : ٢٨٧٢٩ .

٥٠٠٤ . كنز العمّال : ٢٨٧٤٥ .

٥٠٠٥ . الأمالي للصدوق : ١١٦ / ٩٩ .

٥٠٠٦ . كنز العمّال : ٢٨٨٤٢ .

٥٠٠٧ . الأمالي للمفيد : ٢٩ / ١ .

٥٠٠٨ . مجمع البيان : ٩ / ٣٨٠ .

٥٠٠٩ . تنبيه الخواطر : ٢ / ٢١٢ .

٥٠١٠ . تنبيه الخواطر : ١ / ٨٢ .

٥٠١١ . منية المريد : ١٠٥ .

٥٠١٢ . الأمالي للطوسي : ٣٧٧ / ٨٠٨ .

٥٠١٣ . نهج البلاغة : الحكمة ٤٧٨ .

٥٠١٤ . غرر الحكم : ٦٨٨٨ .

٥٠١٥ . تحف العقول : ٢٩٧ .

٥٠١٦ . ثواب الأعمال : ١٥٩ / ١ .

٥٠١٧ . تحف العقول : ٣٦٤ .

٥٠١٨ . الترغيب والترهيب : ١ / ١١٩ / ٥ .

٥٠١٩ . روضة الواعظين : ١٦ .

٥٠٢٠ . مكارم الأخلاق : ٢ / ٣٦٤ / ٢٦٦١ .

٥٠٢١ . كنز العمّال : ٢٩٠٣٥ .

٥٠٢٢ . الإرشاد : ١ / ٢٣٠ .

٥٠٢٣ . الأمالي للطوسي : ١٦٧ / ٢٨٠ .

٥٠٢٤ . المحاسن : ١ / ٣٥٩ / ٧٦٩ .

٥٠٢٥ . كنز العمّال : ٢٨٦٦٦ .

٥٠٢٦ . في الطبعة المعتمدة : «تنظره» ، والصحيح ما أثبتناه كما في الطبعات الأُخرى .

٥٠٢٧ . غرر الحكم : ٥٠٤٨ .

٥٠٢٨ . يُلاحَظُ أنّ هناك تعارضاً ظاهرياً بين أحاديث هذا الباب وأحاديث الباب السابق ، وقد بحثنا هذا الأمر في كتاب العلم والحكمة . راجع كتاب : العلم والحكمة في الكتاب والسنة : آداب التَّعَلُّم ، قبولُ الحَقِّ مِمَّن أتى بِهِ .

٥٠٢٩ . تحف العقول : ٣٨٧ .

٥٠٣٠ . منية المريد : ١٩٣ .

٥٠٣١ . عوالي اللآلي : ٤ / ٧٤ / ٥٤ .

٥٠٣٢ . تنبيه الخواطر : ١ / ٨٥ .

٥٠٣٣ . لقمان : ١٨ .

٥٠٣٤ . منية المريد : ١٨٥ .

٥٠٣٥ . تنبيه الخواطر : ٢ / ٢١٢ .

٥٠٣٦ . كذا في المصدر، و لعلّ الصحيح «تُلِحَّ» .

٥٠٣٧ . كنز العمّال : ٢٩٣٦٣ ، ٢٩٥٢٠ نحوه .

٥٠٣٨ . كنز العمّال : ٢٩٣٦٤ و ٢٨٩٣٧ نحوه .

٥٠٣٩ . الخصال : ٥٦٧ / ١ .

٥٠٤٠ . كنز العمّال : ٢٨٨٨٣ .

٥٠٤١ . غرر الحكم : ٤٠٤٤ .

٥٠٤٢ . غرر الحكم : ٨٧٠٤ .

٥٠٤٣ . كنز العمّال : ٤٤١٧٦ .

٥٠٤٤ . تنبيه الخواطر : ٢ / ١١٢ .

٥٠٤٥ . غرر الحكم : ٦١٩٧ .

٥٠٤٦ . غرر الحكم : ١٠٧٥٨ .

٥٠٤٧ . غرر الحكم : ٨٩١٧ .

٥٠٤٨ . كنز العمّال : ٢٨٦٧٥ .

٥٠٤٩ . كنز العمّال : ٢٨٧٩٨ .

٥٠٥٠ . غرر الحكم : ٥٠٧ .

٥٠٥١ . الإحتجاج : ١ / ١٣ / ٧ .

٥٠٥٢ . فاطر : ٢٨ .

٥٠٥٣ . غرر الحكم : ٤٦٢٤ .

٥٠٥٤ . غرر الحكم : ٤٦٠٠ .

٥٠٥٥ . غرر الحكم : ٤٦٤٢ .

٥٠٥٦ . بحارالأنوار : ٢ / ٥٢ / ١٨

٥٠٥٧ . منية المريد : ١٣٧ .

٥٠٥٨ . غرر الحكم : ١٧٤٠ .

٥٠٥٩ . غرر الحكم : ١٣٠٣ .

٥٠٦٠ . المحاسن : ١ / ٣١٤ / ٦٢١ .

٥٠٦١ . كنز العمّال : ٢٨٧٠٩ .

٥٠٦٢ . الأمالي للصدوق : ٥٠٧ / ٧٠٥ .

٥٠٦٣ . الأمالي للطوسي : ١٢٦ / ١٩٨ .

٥٠٦٤ . كنز العمّال : ٢٩٣٣٧ .

٥٠٦٥ . مكارم الأخلاق : ٢ / ٣٦٤ / ٢٦٦١ .

٥٠٦٦ . غرر الحكم : ٣٨٩٥ .

٥٠٦٧ . بحار الأنوار : ٢ / ٢٩ / ٩ .

٥٠٦٨ . غرر الحكم : ١٥٨٧ ، ١٥٨٨ .

٥٠٦٩ . منية المريد : ١٨١ .

٥٠٧٠ . نهج البلاغة : الحكمة ٩٨ .

٥٠٧١ . بحار الأنوار : ٢ / ٥٦ / ٣٣ .

٥٠٧٢ . غرر الحكم : ٦١٩٦ .

٥٠٧٣ . نهج البلاغة : الحكمة ٣٦٦ .

٥٠٧٤ . بحار الأنوار : ٢ / ٣٤ / ٣٠ .

٥٠٧٥ . الإرشاد : ١ / ٢٣٠ .

٥٠٧٦ . بحار الأنوار : ٢ / ٥٨ / ٣٩ .

٥٠٧٧ . تفسير القمّيّ : ٢ / ١٤٦ .

٥٠٧٨ . بحار الأنوار : ٢ / ٣٧ / ٥٣ .

٥٠٧٩ . بحارالأنوار : ٢ / ٣٢ / ٢٥ .

٥٠٨٠ . منية المريد : ١٤١ .

٥٠٨١ . الخصال : ١١٣ / ٩١ .

٥٠٨٢ . منية المريد : ١٣٧ .

٥٠٨٣ . تنبيه الخواطر : ٢ / ٢١ .

٥٠٨٤ . بحار الأنوار : ٧٥ / ٣٨١ / ٤٥ .

٥٠٨٥ . الاحتجاج : ٢ / ٥١٢ / ٣٣٧ .

٥٠٨٦ . الكافي : ١ / ٤٨ / ٤ .

٥٠٨٧ . الترغيب والترهيب : ١ / ١٢٤ / ١ .

٥٠٨٨ . نهج البلاغة : الكتاب ٣١ .

٥٠٨٩ . الأمالي للصدوق : ٣٤٠ / ٤٠٣ .

٥٠٩٠ . يحتمل أن يكون المراد من «آية محكمة» العلم بالأُصول الاعتقاديّة ، والمراد من «فريضة عادلة» العلم بالأعمال الحسنة ، والمراد من «سُنّة قائمة» العلم بمحاسن الأخلاق (راجع شرح أُصول الكافي للمولى محمّد صالح المازندراني : ٢ / ٢٣) .

٥٠٩١ . الكافي : ١ / ٣٢ / ١ .

٥٠٩٢ . بحار الأنوار : ١ / ٢٢٠ / ٥٢ .

٥٠٩٣ . كنز الفوائد : ٢ / ٣١ .

٥٠٩٤ . الأمالي للصدوق : ٥٧٦ / ٧٨٨ .

٥٠٩٥ . بحار الأنوار : ١ / ٢١٨ / ٤٢ .

٥٠٩٦ . غرر الحكم : ٤٩٦٢ .

٥٠٩٧ . تحف العقول : ٢٨٦ .

٥٠٩٨ . المحاسن : ١ / ٣٥٨ / ٧٦٥ .

٥٠٩٩ . بحار الأنوار : ١ / ٢٢٥ / ١٧ .

٥١٠٠ . كنز العمّال : ٢٨٨٢٠ .

٥١٠١ . كنز العمّال : ٥٨٨١ ، ٥٨٩٣ نحوه .

٥١٠٢ . أعلام الدين : ٣٠١ .

٥١٠٣ . الأمالي للصدوق : ٧٣ / ٤١ .

٥١٠٤ . كنز العمّال : ٤٤١٥٤ .

٥١٠٥ . غرر الحكم : ٣٠٧٩ .

٥١٠٦ . الكافي : ٨ / ٣٢ / ٥ .

٥١٠٧ . بحار الأنوار : ٢ / ٩٢ / ٢٠ .

٥١٠٨ . فاطر : ١١ .

٥١٠٩ . غرر الحكم : ٣٤٣٤ .

٥١١٠ . تنبيه الخواطر : ٢ / ٢١٨ .

٥١١١ . مكارم الأخلاق : ٢ / ٣٦٤ / ٢٦٦١ .

٥١١٢ . أعلام الدين : ٣٣٦ / ١٢ .

٥١١٣ . غرر الحكم : ٩٨٤٠ .

٥١١٤ . نهج البلاغة : الخطبة ١٨٨ .

٥١١٥ . الزمر : ٥٦ .

٥١١٦ . تنبيه الخواطر : ٢ / ٨٩ .

٥١١٧ . غرر الحكم : ٥٢١٤ .

٥١١٨ . غرر الحكم : ٢٦١٨ .

٥١١٩ . غرر الحكم : ٣٤٢٩ .

٥١٢٠ . فاطر : ٣٧ .

٥١٢١ . كنز العمّال : ٢٩٢٤ .

٥١٢٢ . نهج البلاغة : الحكمة ٣٢٦ .

٥١٢٣ . نهج البلاغة : الخطبة ٦٤ .

٥١٢٤ . الخصال : ٥٤٥ / ٢٤ .

٥١٢٥ . الأمالي للمفيد : ٦٠ / ٥ .

٥١٢٦ . الخصال : ٣٢ / ١١٢ .

٥١٢٧ . عيون أخبار الرضا : ٢ / ٣٨ / ١١٢ .

٥١٢٨ . بحار الأنوار : ١٠١ / ٤ / ١٢ .

٥١٢٩ . بحار الأنوار : ٦٩ / ٤٠٨ / ١١٧ .

٥١٣٠ . الأمالي للطوسي : ٢٤٥ / ٤٢٥ .

٥١٣١ . الزهد للحسين بن سعيد : ٣٣ / ٨٧ .

٥١٣٢ . بحار الأنوار : ٩٤ / ٢٢٥ / ١ .

٥١٣٣ . الصحيفة السجّاديّة : الدعاء ٢٠ .

٥١٣٤ . المَرَحُ : شِدّة الفرح والنشاط (الصحاح : ١/٤٠٤) .

٥١٣٥ . بحار الأنوار : ٣ / ٨٣ .

٥١٣٦ . النحل : ٩٧ .

٥١٣٧ . كنز العمّال : ٤٢٧٦١ .

٥١٣٨ . نهج البلاغة : الخطبة ١٧٦ .

٥١٣٩ . نهج البلاغة : الحكمة ٢٣ ، ٣٨٩ .

٥١٤٠ . نهج البلاغة : الحكمة ١٥٠ .

٥١٤١ . الكافي : ٣ / ٢٦٦ / ١١ .

٥١٤٢ . تنبيه الخواطر : ٢ / ١٨٣ .

٥١٤٣ . الدرّة الباهرة : ٤١ .

٥١٤٤ . النساء : ١٢٣ و ١٢٤ .

٥١٤٥ . كنز العمّال : ٤٣٦٧٦ .

٥١٤٦ . مستدرك الوسائل : ١ / ١٣٠ / ١٧٧ .

٥١٤٧ . نهج البلاغة : الحكمة ٢٧٨ .

٥١٤٨ . الكافي : ٢ / ٨٢ / ٣ .

٥١٤٩ . الكافي : ٢ / ٨٢ / ١ .

٥١٥٠ . بحار الأنوار : ٧٠ / ١٩١ .

٥١٥١ . تنبيه الخواطر : ١ / ٦٣ .

٥١٥٢ . الكافي : ٢ / ١٩١ / ١١ .

٥١٥٣ . بحار الأنوار : ٧٨ / ٦٩ / ٢٠ .

٥١٥٤ . غرر الحكم : ٢٩٥٨ .

٥١٥٥ . غرر الحكم : ٣٣٢٢ .

٥١٥٦ . الكافي : ٢ / ١٥٨ / ٤ .

٥١٥٧ . الخصال : ١٢٥ / ١٢١ .

٥١٥٨ . كنز العمّال : ٤٣٨٢٤ و ٤٣٩٣٧ .

٥١٥٩ . بحار الأنوار : ٧٧ / ٨٥ .

٥١٦٠ . الكافي : ٢ / ٤٠٠ / ٧ .

٥١٦١ . الكافي : ٢ / ٣٦١ / ٨ .

٥١٦٢ . شرح نهج البلاغة : ١٨ / ٤١ .

٥١٦٣ . نهج البلاغة : الكتاب ٦٩ .

٥١٦٤ . بحار الأنوار : ٧١ / ٣٦٩ / ١٩ .

٥١٦٥ . كنز العمّال : ٩١٢٨ .

٥١٦٦ . وسائل الشيعة : ٢ / ٨٨٣ / ١ .

٥١٦٧ . التوبة : ١٠٥ .

٥١٦٨ . الترغيب والترهيب : ٣ / ٤٥٨ / ١٧ .

٥١٦٩ . كتاب من لا يحضره الفقيه : ١ / ١٩١ / ٥٨٢ .

٥١٧٠ . عيون أخبار الرضا : ٢ / ٤٤ / ١٥٦ .

٥١٧١ . بحار الأنوار : ٢٣ / ٣٣٧ / ٦ .

٥١٧٢ . وسائل الشيعة : ١١ / ٣٩٢ / ٢٥ .

٥١٧٣ . الجاثية : ٢٩ .

٥١٧٤ . بحار الأنوار : ٥ / ٣٢٧ / ٢٢ .

٥١٧٥ . الزلزلة : ٧،٨ .

٥١٧٦ . آل عمران : ٣٠ .

٥١٧٧ . فى المصدر «نورٌ» أو «قائدٌ» .

٥١٧٨ . كنز العمّال : ٣٨٩٦٣ .

٥١٧٩ . البقرة : ١٧٧ .
٥١٨٠ . كنز العمّال : ١٠٩١٩ .
٥١٨١ . كنز العمّال : ١٠٩٢٤ .
٥١٨٢ . بحار الأنوار : ١٠٠ / ٤٦ / ٣ .
٥١٨٣ . النوادر للراوندي : ٩١ / ٢٧ .
٥١٨٤ . غرر الحكم : ٣٦٥٠ .
٥١٨٥ . نهج البلاغة : الكتاب ٥٣ .
٥١٨٦ . كنز العمّال : ١٠٩٣٧ .
٥١٨٧ . غرر الحكم : ٩٥٧٧ .
٥١٨٨ . الكافي : ٢ / ١٦٢ / ١٥ .
٥١٨٩ . النحل : ٩٢ .
٥١٩٠ . تفسير القمّي : ١ / ٣٨٩ .
٥١٩١ . تفسير العيّاشي : ١ / ٢٨٩ / ٥ .
٥١٩٢ . بحار الأنوار : ٧ / ٤٢ / ١٣ .
٥١٩٣ . أعلام الدين : ٣٤١ .
٥١٩٤ . الكافي : ٨ / ٧٣ / ٢٩ .
٥١٩٥ . المؤمنون : ١١٥ .
٥١٩٦ . ص : ٢٧، ٢٨ .
٥١٩٧ . يس : ٧٨، ٧٩ .
٥١٩٨ . مريم : ٦٦، ٦٧ .
٥١٩٩ . الروم : ٢٧ .
٥٢٠٠ . الروم : ٥٠ .
٥٢٠١ . فاطر : ٩ .
٥٢٠٢ . الأنبياء : ١ .
٥٢٠٣ . الجعفريّات : ٢١٢ .
٥٢٠٤ . نهج البلاغة : الخطبة ١٠٨ .
٥٢٠٥ . الأحزاب : ٦٣ .
٥٢٠٦ . قصص الأنبياء : ٢٧١ / ٣٤٦ .
٥٢٠٧ . محمّد : ١٨ .
٥٢٠٨ . الزمر : ٦٨ .
٥٢٠٩ . الزلزلة : ١ .
٥٢١٠ . الفجر : ٢١ .
٥٢١١ . الطور : ١٠ .
٥٢١٢ . القارعة : ٥ .
٥٢١٣ . الانفطار : ٣ .
٥٢١٤ . التكوير : ١، ٢ .
٥٢١٥ . الانفطار : ٢ .
٥٢١٦ . الحاقّة : ١٦ .
٥٢١٧ . ق : ٤٢ .
٥٢١٨ . الخصال : ١١٩ / ١٠٨ .
٥٢١٩ . تنبيه الخواطر : ٢ / ١٣٣ .
٥٢٢٠ . الترغيب والترهيب : ٤ / ٣٨٣ / ١٠ .
٥٢٢١ . كنز العمّال : ٣٨٩٣٨ .
٥٢٢٢ . الأمالي للطوسي : ٦٥٣ / ١٣٥٣ .
٥٢٢٣ . نهج البلاغة : الخطبة ١٠٢ .
٥٢٢٤ . الكافي : ٨ / ٩٥ / ٦٩ .
٥٢٢٥ . ثواب الأعمال : ٣١٩ / ١ .
٥٢٢٦ . ثواب الأعمال : ٣٢٢ / ٨ .
٥٢٢٧ . ثواب الأعمال : ٣٢٩ / ١ .
٥٢٢٨ . الكافي : ٢ / ٣١١ / ١١ .
٥٢٢٩ . الكافي : ٢ / ٣٥١ / ٢ .
٥٢٣٠ . الإسراء : ١٣، ١٤ .
٥٢٣١ . تفسير القمّي : ٢ / ١٧ .
٥٢٣٢ . تفسير العيّاشي : ٢ / ٣٢٨ / ٣٥ .
٥٢٣٣ . تفسير العيّاشي : ٢ / ٣٢٨ / ٣٤ .
٥٢٣٤ . الزهد للحسين بن سعيد : ٩٢ / ٢٤٦ .
٥٢٣٥ . التبكيت : التقريع والتوبيخ ، ويقال : بكته بالحجّة : إذا غلبه (مجمع البحرين : ١ / ١٧٧) .
٥٢٣٦ . الزهد للحسين بن سعيد : ٩٢ / ٢٤٦ .
٥٢٣٧ . غرر الحكم : ٧٠٢ .
٥٢٣٨ . غرر الحكم : ٧٣٢٧ .
٥٢٣٩ . غرر الحكم : ٦٤٠٩ .
٥٢٤٠ . غرر الحكم : ٧٦٣٤ .
٥٢٤١ . غرر الحكم : ١٠٢٨٨ .
٥٢٤٢ . نهج البلاغة : الكتاب ٣١ .
٥٢٤٣ . كنز العمّال : ٣٦٥٤٩ .
٥٢٤٤ . غرر الحكم : ٦٢٣٢ .
٥٢٤٥ . تنبيه الخواطر : ٢ / ١١٣ .
٥٢٤٦ . غرر الحكم : ٣٥٧ .
٥٢٤٧ . غرر الحكم : ٢٨٧٣ .
٥٢٤٨ . غرر الحكم : ٤٣٠٠ .
٥٢٤٩ . غرر الحكم : ٦٤٠٥ .
٥٢٥٠ . غرر الحكم : ٥١٩٩ .
٥٢٥١ . غرر الحكم : ٢٩٦٩ .

٥٢٥٢ . غرر الحكم : ٦٩٠٦ .

٥٢٥٣ . نهج البلاغة : الحكمة ٣٥٩ .

٥٢٥٤ . المائدة : ١١٤ .

٥٢٥٥ . نهج البلاغة : الحكمة ٤٢٨ .

٥٢٥٦ . فاثور : أي خِوانٌ ، والسمراء : الحنطة، والخطيفة : لبن يطبخ بدقيق ويُختطف بالملاعق بسرعة، والملبنة : الملعقة . (النهاية : ٣ / ٤١٢ و ٢ / ٣٩٩ و ص ٤٩ و ج ٤ / ٢٢٩) .

٥٢٥٧ . بحار الأنوار : ٤٠ / ٣٢٦ / ٧ .

٥٢٥٨ . كتاب من لا يحضره الفقيه : ٣ / ٣٠٠ / ٤٠٧٣ .

٥٢٥٩ . كتاب من لا يحضره الفقيه : ٣ / ٣٠٠ / ٤٠٧٤ .

٥٢٦٠ . بحار الأنوار : ٥٩ / ٩٢ / ١ .

٥٢٦١ . وسائل الشيعة : ٧ / ٣٤٦ / ١ .

٥٢٦٢ . بحار الأنوار : ٥٩ / ١٠٠ / ٢ و ٤٨ / ١٠٨ / ٩ .

٥٢٦٣ . قال المجلسيّ بعد نقل الخبر : هذا الخبر مخالف لأخبار المُعلّى ، ويدلّ على عدم اعتبار النيروز شرعاً ، وأخبار المعلّى أقوى سنداً وأشهر بين الأصحاب ، ويمكن حمل هذا على التقيّة ، لاشتمال خبر المعلّى على ما يتّقى فيه . . . .

راجع كلام المحشّي فيما ردّ به على ما قاله المجلسيّ ، بحار الأنوار : ٥٩ / ١٠٠ .

أقول : كِلا الخبرين فاقِد لشرائط الحجّيّة ، وكما مرّ عن أمير المؤمنين ﷺ : نيروزنا كلّ يوم ، وكلّ يوم لا يُعصى الله فيه فهو يوم عيد ، نعم لا بأس بالتزاور كما هو سنّة في إيران .

٥٢٦٤ . كنز العمّال : ٢٤٠٩٤ .

٥٢٦٥ . كنز العمّال : ٢٤٠٩٥ .

٥٢٦٦ . كنز العمّال : ١٨١٠١ .

٥٢٦٧ . نهج البلاغة : الخطبة ١٧٦ .

٥٢٦٨ . غرر الحكم : ٣٢٣٣ .

٥٢٦٩ . تحف العقول : ٨٨ .

٥٢٧٠ . الكافي : ٨ / ٢٤٣ / ٣٣٧ .

٥٢٧١ . مستطرفات السرائر : ٤٨ / ٧ .

٥٢٧٢ . تحف العقول : ٥٠١ .

٥٢٧٣ . كنز العمّال : ٤٤١٤١ .

٥٢٧٤ . الخصال : ١١٠ / ٨١ .

٥٢٧٥ . نهج البلاغة : الحكمة ٣٤٩ .

٥٢٧٦ . نهج البلاغة : الحكمة ٣٥٣ .

٥٢٧٧ . كنز العمّال : ٦٣٨٧ .

٥٢٧٨ . الترغيب والترهيب : ٣ / ٢٣٩ / ٧ .

٥٢٧٩ . الكافي : ٢ / ٢٠٧ / ٨ .

٥٢٨٠ . تنبيه الخواطر : ١ / ١١٧ .

٥٢٨١ . غرر الحكم : ٨٢٦٠ و ٨٢٦١ .

٥٢٨٢ . نهج البلاغة : الخطبة ١١٣ .

٥٢٨٣ . تحف العقول : ٣٦٦ .

٥٢٨٤ . الهُمَزة : الكثير الطعن على غيره بغير حقّ ، العائب له بما ليس بعيب ، وأصل الهَمز الكسر فكأنّ العائب بعيبه إيّاه وطعنه فيه يكسره ويهمزه . . . واللمز العيب أيضاً ، والهمزة واللمزة بمعنى ، وقد قيل : بينهما فرق ؛ فإنّ الهُمزة الذي يَعيبك بظهر الغيب ، واللُّمزة الذي يَعيبك في وجهك . (مجمع البيان : ١٠ / ٨١٧) .

٥٢٨٥ . الهُمَزة : ١ .

٥٢٨٦ . ثواب الأعمال : ٢٨٨ / ١ .

٥٢٨٧ . غرر الحكم : ٤٤٨٩ .

٥٢٨٨ . نهج البلاغة : الكتاب ٥٣ .

٥٢٨٩ . غرر الحكم : ١٠٢٩٤ .

٥٢٩٠ . كنز الفوائد : ١ / ٢٧٩ .

٥٢٩١ . الكافي : ٢ / ٣٥٥ / ٧ .

٥٢٩٢ . كنز العمّال : ٢٨٦٦٩ .

٥٢٩٣ . نهج البلاغة : الحكمة ٦ .

٥٢٩٤ . غرر الحكم : ٦٤٣٤ .

٥٢٩٥ . نهج البلاغة : الحكمة ٢٢٣ .

٥٢٩٦ . تحف العقول : ٢١٥ .

٥٢٩٧ . نهج البلاغة : الحكمة ٥١ .

٥٢٩٨ . الإرشاد : ١ / ٣٠١ .

٥٢٩٩ . كشف الغمّة : ٣ / ١٣٧ .

٥٣٠٠ . قصص الأنبياء : ١٥٧ / ١٧١ .

٥٣٠١ . تنبيه الخواطر : ١ / ١١٣ .

٥٣٠٢ . الكافي : ٢ / ٣٥٦ / ٢ .

٥٣٠٤_٨ . تنبيه الخواطر : ١ / ٥٧ ، ٢ / ١٥٥ .

٥٣٠٥ . الكافي : ٢ / ٣٦١ / ٩ .

٥٣٠٦ . وفي نقل : . . . وكانَ يَتَمَنّى أن يَرجِعَ إلى خَيرٍ . ثواب الأعمال : ٢٨٤ / ١ .

٥٣٠٧ . الكافي : ٢ / ٣٥٦ / ١ .

٥٣٠٨ . الكافي : ٢ / ٣٥٩ / ١ .

٥٣٠٩ . غرر الحكم : ٢٩٦٤ .
٥٣١٠ . غرر الحكم : ٢٩١٨ .
٥٣١١ . غرر الحكم : ٣٢٩٥ .
٥٣١٢ . علل الشرائع : ٥٦٠ / ١ .
٥٣١٣ . تحف العقول : ٣٢٠ .
٥٣١٤ . الخصال : ٢٨٤ / ٣٤ .
٥٣١٥ . غرر الحكم : ٥٩٧٣ .
٥٣١٦ . غرر الحكم : ٥٦٥١ .
٥٣١٧ . غرر الحكم : ٩٢٢٤ .
٥٣١٨ . نهج البلاغة : الحكمة ٢٨٢ .
٥٣١٩ . تحف العقول : ٢٨٢ .
٥٣٢٠ . تحف العقول : ٣١٩ .
٥٣٢١ . الانفطار : ٦ـ٨ .
٥٣٢٢ . مكارم الأخلاق : ٢ / ٣٥٠ / ٢٦٦٠ .
٥٣٢٣ . تحف العقول : ١٥٠ .
٥٣٢٤ . تنبيه الخواطر : ٢ / ٧٢
٥٣٢٥ . نهج البلاغة : الحكمة ١١٦ .
٥٣٢٦ . غرر الحكم : ٢٥٦٢ .
٥٣٢٧ . غرر الحكم : ٥٦٥٠ .
٥٣٢٨ . بحار الأنوار : ٧٨ / ٨٣ / ٨٦ .
٥٣٢٩ . غرر الحكم : ٨٧٤٤ .
٥٣٣٠ . آل عمران : ١٢٣ ، ١٢٤ .
٥٣٣١ . كنز العمّال : ٢٩٩٤٢ .
٥٣٣٢ . كنز العمّال : ٢٩٩٤٣ .
٥٣٣٣ . الإرشاد : ١ / ٧٣ .
٥٣٣٤ . آل عمران : ١٢١ .
٥٣٣٥ . في نقلٍ : إنّ لنا العزّى ولا عُزّى لكم (الدر المنثور : ٣٤٦/٢) .
٥٣٣٦ . في نقل : الله مولانا ولا مولى لكم (الدرّ المنثور : ٢ / ٣٤٦) .
٥٣٣٧ . الدرّ المنثور : ٢ / ٣٤٥ .
٥٣٣٨ . آل عمران : ١٢٨ .
٥٣٣٩ . صحيح مسلم : ٣ / ١٤١٧ / ١٠٤ .
٥٣٤٠ . كنز العمّال : ٣٠٠٢٧ .
٥٣٤١ . بحار الأنوار : ٢٠ / ١٧٩ / ٦ .
٥٣٤٢ . كنز العمّال : ٣٠١١٥ .
٥٣٤٣ . البلد : ٦ .
٥٣٤٤ . تفسير القمّي : ٢ / ٤٢٢ .
٥٣٤٥ . الكافي : ٨ / ٢١٦ / ٢٦٤ .
٥٣٤٦ . كنز العمّال : ٣٠١٢٠ .
٥٣٤٧ . يوسف : ٩٢ .
٥٣٤٨ . كنز العمّال : ٣٠١٥٨ .
٥٣٤٩ . الأمالي للطوسي : ٣٤٢ / ٧٠١ .
٥٣٥٠ . بحار الأنوار : ٢١ / ١١٦ / ١١ .
٥٣٥١ . بحار الأنوار : ٢١ / ١٨٠ / ١٦ .
٥٣٥٢ . بحار الأنوار : ٧٦ / ٣٦٥ / ٣٠ .
٥٣٥٣ . كنز العمّال : ٩٥٠١ .
٥٣٥٤ . الترغيب والترهيب : ٢ / ٥٧١ / ٢ .
٥٣٥٥ . نهج البلاغة : الكتاب ٢٦ .
٥٣٥٦ . غرر الحكم : ٨٨٩١ .
٥٣٥٧ . الكافي : ٥ / ١٦٠ / ١ .
٥٣٥٨ . الكافي : ٥ / ١٦٠ / ٦ .
٥٣٥٩ . عوالي اللآلي : ١ / ٣٦٤ / ٥٦ .
٥٣٦٠ . كنز العمّال : ٣٠٣٦٦ .
٥٣٦١ . كنز العمّال : ٣٠٣٤٣ .
٥٣٦٢ . في شرح نهج البلاغة : ١٩ / ٧٢ «الغصب» بدل «الغصيب» .
٥٣٦٣ . نهج البلاغة : الحكمة ٢٤٠ .
٥٣٦٤ . وسائل الشيعة : ١٧ / ٣١١ / ١ .
٥٣٦٥ . وسائل الشيعة : ١٧ / ٣٠٩ / ٤ .
٥٣٦٦ . بحار الأنوار : ٧٣ / ٢٦٥ / ١٥ .
٥٣٦٧ . نهج البلاغة : الحكمة ٢٥٥ .
٥٣٦٨ . الكافي : ٢ / ٣٠٣ / ٣ .
٥٣٦٩ . الكافي : ٢ / ٣٠٥ / ١٣ .
٥٣٧٠ . نثر الدرر : ١ / ١٨٣ .
٥٣٧١ . تحف العقول : ٢٨٦ .
٥٣٧٢ . الكافي : ٢ / ٣٠٥ / ١٣ .
٥٣٧٣ . آل عمران : ١٣٤ .
٥٣٧٤ . الشورىٰ : ٣٧ .
٥٣٧٥ . تنبيه الخواطر : ١ / ١٢١ .
٥٣٧٦ . بحار الأنوار : ٧٣ / ٢٦٣ / ٧ .
٥٣٧٧ . الكافي : ٢ / ١١٠ / ٧ .
٥٣٧٨ . الكافي : ٢ / ١٠٩ / ٢ .
٥٣٧٩ . تحف العقول : ١٤ .
٥٣٨٠ . غرر الحكم : ٥١٥٥ .
٥٣٨١ . وسائل الشيعة : ١١ / ٤١٦ / ٣ .
٥٣٨٢ . المحجّة البيضاء : ٥ / ٣٠٣ .

٥٣٨٣ . نهج البلاغة : الحكمة ٣١ .

٥٣٨٤ . آل عمران : ١٣٥ .

٥٣٨٥ . النساء : ١١٠ .

٥٣٨٦ . مستدرك الوسائل : ١٢ / ١٤٦ / ١٣٧٤٤ .

٥٣٨٧ . الكافي : ٢ / ٥٠٤ / ١ .

٥٣٨٨ . الكافي : ٢ / ٥١٧ / ٢ .

٥٣٨٩ . تنبيه الخواطر : ١ / ٥ .

٥٣٩٠ . نهج البلاغة : الحكمة ٨٧ .

٥٣٩١ . بحار الأنوار : ٩٣ / ٢٧٨ / ٧ .

٥٣٩٢ . نهج البلاغة : الحكمة ١٣٥ .

٥٣٩٣ . الكافي : ٢ / ٤٣٧ / ١ .

٥٣٩٤ . هود : ٣ .

٥٣٩٥ . هود : ٥٢ .

٥٣٩٦ . نوح : ١٠ .

٥٣٩٧ . نهج البلاغة : الخطبة ١٤٣ .

٥٣٩٨ . بحار الأنوار : ٩٣ / ٢٧٧ / ٤ .

٥٣٩٩ . غرر الحكم : ٢٢٢٨ .

٥٤٠٠ . قال الجزريّ : الغين : الغيم ، وغينت السماء تغان : إذا أطبق عليها الغيم ، وقيل : الغين شجر ملتفّ . أراد ما يغشاه من السهو الذي لا يخلو منه البشر ؛ لأنّ قلبه أبداً كان مشغولاً بالله تعالى، فإن عرض له وقتاً ما عارض بشريّ يشغله من أمور الأمّة والمِلّة ومصالحهما عدّ ذلك ذنباً وتقصيراً ، فيفزع إلى الاستغفار . (النهاية : ٣ / ٤٠٣) .

٥٤٠١ . مستدرك الوسائل : ٥ / ٣٢٠ / ٥٩٨٧ .

٥٤٠٢ . تحف العقول : ٢٢٣ .

٥٤٠٣ . الكافي : ٢ / ٥٠٤ / ٣ .

٥٤٠٤ . بحار الأنوار : ٧٨ / ٣٥٦ / ١١ .

٥٤٠٥ . غرر الحكم : ١٩٦ .

٥٤٠٦ . نهج البلاغة : الخطبة ٦٤ .

٥٤٠٧ . نهج البلاغة : الخطبة ١٥٣ .

٥٤٠٨ . نهج البلاغة : الخطبة ١٧٥ .

٥٤٠٩ . بحار الأنوار : ٧٧ / ٤٠١ / ٢٦ .

٥٤١٠ . بحار الأنوار : ٧٨ / ١٩٠ / ١ .

٥٤١١ . مكارم الأخلاق : ٢ / ٣٧٨ / ٢٦٦١ .

٥٤١٢ . غرر الحكم : ٤٢٦٩ .

٥٤١٣ . التوحيد : ٧٤ / ٢٧ .

٥٤١٤ . الكافي : ٣ / ٢٧٠ / ١٤ .

٥٤١٥ . الخصال : ١٢١ / ١١٣ .

٥٤١٦ . بحار الأنوار : ٧٨ / ١١٥ / ١٠ .

٥٤١٧ . غرر الحكم : ٨٣١٨ .

٥٤١٨ . غرر الحكم : ٨٤٣٠ .

٥٤١٩ . غرر الحكم : ٥١٤٦ .

٥٤٢٠ . غرر الحكم : ٢٧١٧ .

٥٤٢١ . غرر الحكم : ٢٣٧٨ .

٥٤٢٢ . نهج البلاغة : الحكمة ٢٢٢ .

٥٤٢٣ . تحف العقول : ٣٥٩ .

٥٤٢٤ . الحقد والفحشاء .

٥٤٢٥ . الحشر : ١٠ .

٥٤٢٦ . الحِجْر : ٤٧ .

٥٤٢٧ . بحار الأنوار : ١٤ / ٣٠٥ / ١٧ .

٥٤٢٨ . كنز العمّال : ١١٠٤٤ .

٥٤٢٩ . غرر الحكم : ٥٤٧ .

٥٤٣٠ . غرر الحكم : ٦٤٢ .

٥٤٣١ . غرر الحكم : ٢٩٣٢ .

٥٤٣٢ . قال ابن الأثير : «ثلاث لا يغلّ عليهنّ قلب مؤمن» هو من الإغلال :الخيانة في كلّ شيء .ويروى«يَغِلّ» بفتح الياء ، من الغِلّ وهوالحقد والشحناء : أي لايدخله حقد يزيله عن الحقّ . ورُوي «يَغِلُ» بالتخفيف من الوغول : الدخول في الشرّ ، والمعنىٰ : أنّ هذه الخلال الثلاث تُستصلَح بها القلوب ، فمن تمسّك بها طَهُر قلبه من الخيانةوالدَّغَل والشرّ ، و«عليهنّ» في موضع الحال، تقديره لايغلّ كائناً عليهنّ قلب مؤمن . (النهاية : ٣ / ٣٨١) .

٥٤٣٣ . كنز العمّال : ٤٤٢٧٢ .

٥٤٣٤ . محيطة من ورائهم، أى تحوطهم وتكفيهم وتحفظهم (النهاية : ٤ / ١٥٧) . قال العلّامة المجلسي : و يمكن أن يكون على صيغة الموصول أو بالكسر حرف جر . و على التقديرين، يحتمل أن يكون المراد بالدعوة، دعاء النبي إلى الإسلام أو دعاؤه و شفاعته لنجاتهم و سعادتهم أو الأعم منه و من دعاء المؤمنين بعضهم لبعض . بأن يكون اضافة الدعوة الى الفاعل، و على التقدير الأول يحتمل أن يكون المعنى : أن دعوة النبي ليست مختصة بالحاضرين بل تبليغه ـع ـ يشمل الغائبين و من يأتى من بعدهم من المعدومين (بحار الأنوار : ٧٣ / ١١٧) . و على احتمال كون الدعوة بمعنى الدعاء، صار معنى الكلام : فعليكم بجماعة المسلمين

فانّه يشمل دعائهم لأنفسهم و لغيرهم و على تقدير من حرف الجر، يحتمل أن يكون المعنى : فعليكم بجماعة المسلمين ؛لأن دعائهم يشمل كلّهم فيشمل ايّاكم .

5435 . كلّ من خان في شيء خفية فقد غلّ .

5436 . آل عمران : ١٦١ .

5437 . الدرّ المنثور : ٢ / ٣٦١ .

5438 . الترغيب والترهيب : ٢ / ٣٠٧ / ٤ .

5439 . قال ابن الأثير : قد تكرّر ذكر الغلول في الحديث، وهو الخيانة في المَغنَم والسرقة من الغنيمة قبل القِسْمة ، يقال : غلّ في المغنَم يَغُلّ غُلولاً فهو غالٌّ ، وكلّ من خان في شيء خُفيَة فقد غلّ، وسُمّيت غُلولاً لأنّ الأيدي فيها مغلولة : أي ممنوعة مَجعُول فيها غُلٌّ ، وهو الحديدة التي تَجمع يد الأسير إلى عُنقه ، ويقال لها : جامعة أيضاً . (النهاية : ٣ / ٣٨٠) .

5440 . تفسير العيّاشي : ١ / ٢٠٥ / ١٤٨ .

5441 . النساء : ١٧١ .

5442 . النوادر للراوندي : ١٢٥ / ١٤٣ .

5443 . قرب الإسناد : ٦٤ / ٢٠٤ .

5444 . الزخرف : ٥٧ .

5445 . بحار الأنوار : ٢٥ / ٢٨٤ / ٣٤، وأُنظر الغارات : ٢ / ٥٨٩ .

5446 . نهج البلاغة : الحكمة ٤٦٩ .

5447 . بحار الأنوار : ٢٥ / ٢٨٤ / ٣٢ .

5448 . الخصال : ٦١٤ / ١٠ .

5449 . بحارالأنوار : ٢٥ / ٢٧٤ / ٢٠ .

5450 . الأمالي للطوسي : ٦٥٠ / ١٣٤٩ .

5451 . بحار الأنوار : ٢٥ / ٢٩٤ / ٥٢ .

5452 . بحار الأنوار : ٢٥ / ٢٧٣ / ١٩ .

5453 . بحار الأنوار : ٢٥ / ٢٧٤ / ٢٠ .

5454 . العلق : ٦، ٧ .

5455 . كنز العمّال : ١٦٦٧٧ .

5456 . نهج البلاغة : الحكمة ١٠٨ .

5457 . الكافي : ٢ / ٢٦٢ / ١١ .

5458 . الضحىٰ : ٨ .

5459 . الجعفريّات : ١٥٥ .

5460 . الكافي : ٥ / ٧١ / ٤ .

5461 . نهج البلاغة : الحكمة ٣٧١ .

5462 . نهج البلاغة : الحكمة ٥٤ .

5463 . الأمالي للمفيد : ١٨٣ / ٦ .

5464 . الدرّة الباهرة : ٤١ .

5465 . الكافي : ٢ / ١٣٩ / ٨ .

5466 . بِشَوصِ السِّواك : بغُسالته، وقيل : بما يتفتّت منه عند التسوّك . (النهاية : ٢ / ٥٠٩) .

5467 . كنز العمّال : ٧١٥٦ .

5468 . أمالي الصدوق : ٣٩٤ / ١ .

5469 . كشف الغمّة : ٣ / ١٣٧ .

5470 . نهج البلاغة : الحكمة ٣٤٢ .

5471 . نهج البلاغة : الحكمة ٣٨ .

5472 . الكافي : ٢ / ١٣٩ / ٩ .

5473 . تحف العقول : ٣١٨ .

5474 . بحار الأنوار : ٧٨ / ٩ / ٦٥ .

5475 . بحار الأنوار : ٧٨ / ٨ / ٦٤ .

5476 . الأمالي للطوسي : ٥٨٠ / ١١٩٨ .

5477 . تحف العقول : ٢٨٧ .

5478 . سبأ : ٣٧ .

5479 . تفسير القمّي : ٢ / ٢٠٣ .

5480 . نهج البلاغة : الحكمة ٣٢٨ .

5481 . كنز العمّال : ١٦٨٤٠ .

5482 . غرر الحكم : ١٠٧٣٨ .

5483 . الحجّ : ٣٠ .

5484 . بحار الأنوار : ٧٩ / ٢٥٠ / ٢ .

5485 . كنز العمّال : ٤٠٦٦١ .

5486 . كتاب من لا يحضره الفقيه : ٤ / ٥٨ / ٥٠٩٢ .

5487 . بحار الأنوار : ٧٩ / ٢٤٧ / ٢٦ .

5488 . بحارالأنوار : ٧٩ / ٢٥٢ / ٦ .

5489 . بحار الأنوار : ٧٩ / ٢٤١ / ٧ .

5490 . قصص الأنبياء : ٣٠٨ / ٤٠٨ .

5491 . لقمان : ٣٤ .

5492 . نهج البلاغة : الخطبة ١٢٨ .

5493 . الكافي : ١ / ٢٥٧ / ٤ .

5494 . الكافي : ١ / ٢٥٦ / ١ .

5495 . الحجرات : ١٢ .

5496 . تنبيه الخواطر : ١ / ١١٥ .

5497 . الترغيب والترهيب : ٣ / ٥١١ / ٢٤ .

5498 . نهج البلاغة : الحكمة ٤٦١ .

٥٤٩٩ . تحف العقول : ٢٤٥ .

٥٥٠٠ . بحار الأنوار : ٧٥ / ٢٤٩ / ١٦ .

٥٥٠١ . بحار الأنوار : ٧٥ / ٢٤٦ / ٨ .

٥٥٠٢ . الكافي : ٢ / ٣٥٧ / ١ .

٥٥٠٣ . بحار الأنوار : ٧٥ / ٢٥٨ / ٥٣ .

٥٥٠٤ . جامع الأخبار : ٤١٢ / ١١٤٤ .

٥٥٠٥ . بحار الأنوار : ٧٧ / ٨٩ / ٣ .

٥٥٠٦ . كنز العمّال : ٨٠٢٤،

٥٥٠٧ . الترغيب والترهيب : ٣ / ٥٠٦ / ١٣ .

٥٥٠٨ . الكافي : ٢ / ٣٥٨ / ٦ .

٥٥٠٩ . بحار الأنوار : ٧٥ / ٢٦١ / ٦٤ .

٥٥١٠ . كنز العمّال : ٨٠٧٤.

٥٥١١ . غرر الحكم : ١١٧١ .

٥٥١٢ . الاختصاص : ٢٢٥ .

٥٥١٣ . الخصال : ٥٦٦ / ١ .

٥٥١٤ . الأمالي للصدوق : ٥١٦ / ٧٠٧ .

٥٥١٥ . كتاب من لا يحضره الفقيه : ٤ / ٣٧٢ .

٥٥١٦ . الكافي : ٢ / ٣٥٧ / ٤ .

٥٥١٧ . كنز العمّال : ٨٠٣٧ .

٥٥١٨ . كتاب من لا يحضره الفقيه : ٣ / ٤٤٤ / ٤٥٤١ .

٥٥١٩ . بحار الأنوار : ١٠٣ / ٢٤٨ / ٣٣ .

٥٥٢٠ . كنز العمّال : ٧٠٧٢ .

٥٥٢١ . كتاب من لا يحضره الفقيه : ٣ / ٤٤٤ / ٤٥٤٢ .

٥٥٢٢ . نهج البلاغة : الحكمة ٤٧ .

٥٥٢٣ . نهج البلاغة : الحكمة ٣٠٥ .

٥٥٢٤ . المحاسن : ١ / ٢٠٤ / ٣٥٥ .

٥٥٢٥ . الكافي : ٥ / ٥٣٥ / ١ .

٥٥٢٦ . الدر المنثور : ٤ / ٣٢٦ .

٥٥٢٧ . كنز العمّال : ٧٠٦٧ .

٥٥٢٨ . الفردوس : ٣ / ١٠٦ / ٤٢٩٥ .

٥٥٢٩ . في نهج البلاغة : الكتاب ٣١ : «وإيّاك والتغاير في غير موضع غيرة، فإنّ ذلك يدعو الصحيحة إلى السقم، والبريئة إلى الرِّيب» .

٥٥٣٠ . بحار الأنوار : ٧٧ / ٢١٤ / ١ .

٥٥٣١ . الكافي : ٥ / ٥٣٧ / ١ .

٥٥٣٢ . العنكبوت : ٢ و ٣ .

٥٥٣٣ . التوبة : ١٢٦ .

٥٥٣٤ . العنكبوت : ١ و ٢ .

٥٥٣٥ . الكافي : ١ / ٣٧٠ / ٤ .

٥٥٣٦ . الأنفال : ٢٨ .

٥٥٣٧ . كنز العمّال : ٤٤١٢٩ .

٥٥٣٨ . الترغيب والترهيب : ٤ / ١٨٤ / ٧٤ .

٥٥٣٩ . بحار الأنوار : ٧٣ / ١٤٠ / ١٢ .

٥٥٤٠ . نهج البلاغة : الحكمة ٣٢٢ .

٥٥٤١ . الترغيب والترهيب : ١ / ٥٤ / ٥ .

٥٥٤٢ . كنز العمّال : ٣٠٨٨٣ .

٥٥٤٣ . نهج البلاغة : الخطبة ١٨٣ .

٥٥٤٤ . كنز العمّال : ٣٠٨٩٣ .

٥٥٤٥ . غرر الحكم : ٩١٦٣ .

٥٥٤٦ . غرر الحكم : ١٠١٠٩ .

٥٥٤٧ . نهج البلاغة : الحكمة ١ .

٥٥٤٨ . بحار الأنوار : ٢ / ١٢٣ / ٤٨ .

٥٥٤٩ . بحار الأنوار : ٢ / ١٧٢ / ٣ .

٥٥٥٠ . بحار الأنوار : ٢ / ٢٩٩ / ٢٥ .

٥٥٥١ . بحار الأنوار : ٢ / ٢٦٠ .

٥٥٥٢ . نهج البلاغة : الكتاب ٦٧

٥٥٥٣ . في مستدرك الوسائل ١٧ / ٣١٥ / ٢١٤٥٢ : «مسجد» بدل «مجلس» .

٥٥٥٤ . رجال النجاشي : ١ / ٧٣ / ٦ .

٥٥٥٥ . بحار الأنوار : ٧٩ / ١١١ / ٦ .

٥٥٥٦ . الكافي : ٢ / ٣٢٣ / ٣ .

٥٥٥٧ . الكافي : ٢ / ٣٢٥ / ٨ .

٥٥٥٨ . غرر الحكم : ٩٤٧٨ .

٥٥٥٩ . الكافي : ٢ / ٣٢٤ / ٤ .

٥٥٦٠ . بحار الأنوار : ٧٨ / ١٨١ / ٦٧ .

٥٥٦١ . بحار الأنوار : ٧٨ / ١٨٥ / ١٤ .

٥٥٦٢ . بحار الأنوار : ٧٩ / ١١٣ / ١٤ .

٥٥٦٣ . الكافي : ٢ / ٣٢٧ / ٣ .

٥٥٦٤ . الحديد : ٢٠ .

٥٥٦٥ . لقمان : ١٨ .

٥٥٦٦ . الترغيب والترهيب : ٣ / ٥٥٨ / ١ .

٥٥٦٧ . الكافي : ٢ / ٣٢٨ / ٢ .

٥٥٦٨ . الخصال : ٦٩ / ١٠٢ .

٥٥٦٩ . نهج البلاغة : الحكمة ٣٩٨ .

٥٥٧٠ . غرر الحكم : ١٠٦٥٥ .
٥٥٧١ . نهج البلاغة : الخطبة ٢١٦ .
٥٥٧٢ . مستدرك الوسائل : ١٢ / ٩٠ / ١٣٥٩٩ .
٥٥٧٣ . نهج البلاغة : الحكمة ٤٥٤ .
٥٥٧٤ . الكافي : ٢ / ٣٢٨ / ١ .
٥٥٧٥ . بحار الأنوار : ١٦ / ٣٤١ / ٣٣ .
٥٥٧٦ . بحار الأنوار : ٧٢ / ٣٠ .
٥٥٧٧ . الكافي : ٨ / ٢٣٤ / ٣١١ .
٥٥٧٨ . كنز العمّال : ٣٤١٢٦ .
٥٥٧٩ . سنن الترمذي : ٥ / ٦٠ .
٥٥٨٠ . مجمع البيان : ٣ / ٣٢١ .
٥٥٨١ . كنز العمّال : ٣٤١٣١ .
٥٥٨٢ . فردوس : ٣ / ٣٦٠ .
٥٥٨٣ . كنز العمّال : ٣٤١٢٨ .
٥٥٨٤ . كنز العمّال : ٤٣١٣٤ .
٥٥٨٥ . بحار الأنوار : ٧٧ / ١٦٥ / ٢ .
٥٥٨٦ . نهج البلاغة : الحكمة ٢١ .
٥٥٨٧ . غرر الحكم : ٢٠١٩ .
٥٥٨٨ . غرر الحكم : ١٩٤ .
٥٥٨٩ . نهج البلاغة : الحكمة ١١٨ .
٥٥٩٠ . بحار الأنوار : ٧٧ / ١٦٥ / ٢ .
٥٥٩١ . نهج البلاغة : الحكمة ٣٦٣ .
٥٥٩٢ . بحار الأنوار : ٧٨ / ٢٦٨ / ١٨١ .
٥٥٩٣ . الكافي : ٢ / ٨٢ / ٤ .
٥٥٩٤ . نهج البلاغة : الخطبة ١٦٧ .
٥٥٩٥ . نهج البلاغة : الخطبة ١١٣ .
٥٥٩٦ . نهج البلاغة : الكتاب ٦٩ .
٥٥٩٧ . نهج البلاغة : الحكمة ١١٣ .
٥٥٩٨ . غرر الحكم : ٣٧٩٣ .
٥٥٩٩ . بحار الأنوار : ٢٣ / ٩٩ / ٣ .
٥٦٠٠ . الكافي : ٢ / ٨١ / ١ .
٥٦٠١ . الكافي : ٢ / ٨٢ / ٥ .
٥٦٠٢ . نهج البلاغة : الخطبة ٢٠٩ .
٥٦٠٣ . نهج البلاغة : الحكمة ٣٢٨ .
٥٦٠٤ . نهج البلاغة : الحكمة ٢٥٢ .
٥٦٠٥ . نهج البلاغة : الحكمة ٣٨٢ .
٥٦٠٦ . بحار الأنوار : ٦٨ / ٣٨٨ / ٣٩ .
٥٦٠٧ . الشرح : ٧ ، ٨ .
٥٦٠٨ . تنبيه الخواطر : ١ / ٦٠ .
٥٦٠٩ . شرح نهج البلاغة : ١٧ / ١٤٦ .
٥٦١٠ . الكافي : ٨ / ١٥٢ / ١٣٦ .
٥٦١١ . غرر الحكم : ٩٢٥١ .
٥٦١٢ . نهج البلاغة : الكتاب ٥٩ .
٥٦١٣ . غرر الحكم : ٩٦٨٤ .
٥٦١٤ . بحار الأنوار : ٧٧ / ٤١٩ / ٤٠ .
٥٦١٥ . الصحيفة السجّاديّة : الدعاء ١١ .
٥٦١٦ . الصحيفة السجّاديّة : الدعاء ٢٠ .
٥٦١٧ . الصحيفة السجّاديّة : الدعاء ٢٠ .
٥٦١٨ . الصحيفة السجّاديّة : الدعاء ٤٧ .
٥٦١٩ . كتاب من لا يحضره الفقيه : ٣ / ١٦٩ / ٣٦٣٥ .
٥٦٢٠ . الروم : ٤١ .
٥٦٢١ . بحار الأنوار : ١٠٠ / ٧٤ / ١٥ .
٥٦٢٢ . الأمالي للمفيد : ٢٣٥ / ٥ .
٥٦٢٣ . بحار الأنوار : ٧٧ / ٢٥٨ / ١ .
٥٦٢٤ . المائدة : ٣٣ .
٥٦٢٥ . النمل : ٣٤ .
٥٦٢٦ . البقرة : ١١ .
٥٦٢٧ . الشعراء : ١٥١ ، ١٥٢ .
٥٦٢٨ . الخصال : ٣٧ / ١٢ .
٥٦٢٩ . الكافي : ٨ / ٢٣ / ٤ .
٥٦٣٠ . كتاب من لا يحضره الفقيه : ٣ / ١٦٧ / ٣٦٢٥ .
٥٦٣١ . في مجمع البيان : «عبادُ اللهِ»، والتصويب من تفسير نور الثقلين .
٥٦٣٢ مجمع البيان : ٢ / ٦٢١ ،تفسير نور الثقلين : ١ / ٢٥٣ / ١٠٠٧ .
٥٦٣٣ . نهج البلاغة : الخطبة ١٧٨ .
٥٦٣٤ . الكافي : ٢ / ٤٥١ / ١ .
٥٦٣٥ . غرر الحكم : ١٩٢٥ .
٥٦٣٦ . غرر الحكم : ٦٥٥٩ .
٥٦٣٧ . نهج البلاغة : الخطبة ١٩٣ .
٥٦٣٨ . غرر الحكم : ٥١٣٩ .
٥٦٣٩ . غرر الحكم : ٨٩٠٥ .
٥٦٤٠ . غرر الحكم : ٧١٧٩ .
٥٦٤١ . الكافي : ٢ / ١٠٧ / ٤ .
٥٦٤٢ . كشف الغمّة : ٣ / ١٣٨ .

٥٦٤٣. غرر الحكم: ٨٠٥.
٥٦٤٤. غرر الحكم: ٤٨٩٩.
٥٦٤٥. غرر الحكم: ١٠٦٢٥.
٥٦٤٦. غرر الحكم: ٥٢٣٧.
٥٦٤٧. غرر الحكم: ٦٣٧٩.
٥٦٤٨. تنبيه الخواطر: ١ / ١٠٠.
٥٦٤٩. أعلام الدين: ٣٣٧ / ١٥.
٥٦٥٠. نهج البلاغة: الخطبة ١٦٤.
٥٦٥١. نهج البلاغة: الخطبة ١٢٥.
٥٦٥٢. الكافي: ٢ / ٣٠٧ / ٤ عن السكوني عن الإمام الصادق عليه السلام.
٥٦٥٣. كنز العمّال: ١٦٦٨٧.
٥٦٥٤. جامع الأخبار: ٣٠٠ / ٨١٧.
٥٦٥٥. جامع الأخبار: ٢٩٩ / ٨١٦.
٥٦٥٦. غرر الحكم: ح ٣٤٢٨.
٥٦٥٧. نهج البلاغة: الحكمة ١٦٣.
٥٦٥٨. نهج البلاغة: الحكمة ٣.
٥٦٥٩. جامع الأخبار: ٣٠٠ / ٨١٨.
٥٦٦٠. نهج البلاغة: الحكمة ٣١٩.
٥٦٦١. نهج البلاغة: الحكمة ٥٦.
٥٦٦٢. عدّة الداعي: ١١٣.
٥٦٦٣. الفردوس: ٣ / ١٥٧ / ٤٤٢٤.
٥٦٦٤. كنز العمّال: ١٦٦٦٩.
٥٦٦٥. الكافي: ٢ / ٢٦٥ / ٢٢.
٥٦٦٦. الكافي: ٢ / ٢٦٠ / ٢ عن سعدان.
٥٦٦٧. شعب الإيمان: ٥ / ٣٨٨ / ٧٠٤٠.
٥٦٦٨. بحار الأنوار: ٧٢ / ٥٦ / ٨٦.
٥٦٦٩. غرر الحكم: ٥٩٠٤.
٥٦٧٠. الكافي: ٢ / ٢٦٣ / ١٢.
٥٦٧١. بحار الأنوار: ٧٢ / ٣١ / ٢٦.
٥٦٧٢. فاطر: ١٥.
٥٦٧٣. التوبة: ٦٠.
٥٦٧٤. القصص: ٢٤.
٥٦٧٥. مفردات ألفاظ القرآن: ٦٤١.
٥٦٧٦ـ٧. بحار الأنوار: ٩٥ / ٤٦٢ / ٧٧، ١٥٠ / ٨٦، ٥٦٧٢، ٨٦.
٥٦٨٠. نهج البلاغة: الحكمة ٥٤، ٣٨.
٥٦٨١. بحار الأنوار: ٧٧ / ٣٧٧ / ١.
٥٦٨٢. غرر الحكم: ٦٥٤٧.

٥٦٨٣. نهج البلاغة: الحكمة ٤٥٢.
٥٦٨٤ـ٥. تحف العقول: ٢١٦، ٢٢٥.
٥٦٨٦. بحار الأنوار: ٧٨ / ٣٦٨ / ٣.
٥٦٨٧. في بعض النسخ «يروون» (كما في هامش المصدر).
٥٦٨٨. معاني الأخبار: ١ / ١٦٥.
٥٦٨٩. الخرائج والجرائح: ٢ / ٧٣٩ / ٥٤.
٥٦٩٠. كتاب من لا يحضره الفقيه: ٣ / ١٦٦ / ٣٦١٤.
٥٦٩١. الكافي: ٢ / ٢٦٦ / ٢.
٥٦٩٢. بحار الأنوار: ٧٢ / ٤٤ / ٥٢.
٥٦٩٣. الخصال: ٦١٤ / ١٠.
٥٦٩٤. الأمالي للصدوق: ٥٢٧ / ٧١٤.
٥٦٩٥. بحار الأنوار: ٧٤ / ١٠٣ / ٦١.
٥٦٩٦. غرر الحكم: ٥١٥٦.
٥٦٩٧. بحار الأنوار: ٧٤ / ٨١ / ٨٣.
٥٦٩٨. الخصال: ٩ / ٣٢.
٥٦٩٩. بحار الأنوار: ٧٦ / ٣١٦ / ٦.
٥٧٠٠. بحار الأنوار: ٧٥ / ١١٤ / ٦.
٥٧٠١. تحف العقول: ٢٢١.
٥٧٠٢. بحار الأنوار: ١٠٣ / ٢٠ / ٤.
٥٧٠٣. بحار الأنوار: ٧٨ / ١٨٤ / ١١.
٥٧٠٤ و ٥٧٠٥. بحار الأنوار: ١٠٤ / ٩٩ / ٧٧.
٥٧٠٦. الكافي: ٢ / ٢٦٤ / ١٨.
٥٧٠٧. البقرة: ٢٧٣.
٥٧٠٨. الكافي: ٢ / ٢٦٠ / ٣.
٥٧٠٩. نهج البلاغة: الحكمة ٦٨.
٥٧١٠. بحار الأنوار: ٧٨ / ٢٤٩ / ٨٧.
٥٧١١. الكافي: ٢ / ٢٦٣ / ١٣.
٥٧١٢. بحار الأنوار: ٧٢ / ٤٩ / ٥٨.
٥٧١٣. مسند ابن حنبل: ١ / ٥٠٤ / ٢٠٨٦.
٥٧١٤. بحار الأنوار: ٧١ / ٢٦٧ / ١٧.
٥٧١٥. بحار الأنوار: ٧٢ / ٥٢ / ٧٦.
٥٧١٦. بحار الأنوار: ٧٢ / ٢٥ / ١٩.
٥٧١٧. التوبة: ١٢٢.
٥٧١٨. كنز العمّال: ٢٨٦٩٠.
٥٧١٩. الترغيب والترهيب: ١ / ٩٣ / ٣.
٥٧٢٠. كنز العمّال: ٢٨٧٦٨.
٥٧٢١. نهج البلاغة: الخطبة ١١٠.

٥٧٢٢ . بحار الأنوار : ٧٨ / ٣٢١ / ١٩ .

٥٧٢٣ . نهج البلاغة : حكمة ٩٠ .

٥٧٢٤ . تحف العقول : ٢٠٤ .

٥٧٢٥ . الكافي : ١ / ٧٠ / ٨ .

٥٧٢٦ . معاني الأخبار : ٢ / ٣ .

٥٧٢٧ . الاختصاص : ٢٣٢ .

٥٧٢٨ . بحار الأنوار : ١ / ١٧٧ / ٤٨ .

٥٧٢٩ . كنز العمّال : ٢٨٧٥٥ .

٥٧٣٠ . بحار الأنوار : ١ / ٢١٣ / ١٠ .

٥٧٣١ . الكافي : ١ / ٣٨ / ٢ .

٥٧٣٢ . الكافي : ١ / ٣٨ / ١ .

٥٧٣٣ . البقرة : ٢١٩ .

٥٧٣٤ . الكافي : ٢ / ٥٥ / ٥ .

٥٧٣٥ . نهج البلاغة : الكتاب ٣١ .

٥٧٣٦ . غرر الحكم : ٨٩١٧ .

٥٧٣٧ . نهج البلاغة : الحكمة ١١٣ .

٥٧٣٨ . نهج البلاغة : الحكمة ٥ .

٥٧٣٩ . بحار الأنوار : ٧٨ / ١١٥ / ١١ .

٥٧٤٠ . تنبيه الخواطر : ١ / ٥٢ .

٥٧٤١ . بحار الأنوار : ٧١ / ٣٢٦ / ٢٠ .

٥٧٤٢ . تنبيه الخواطر : ١ / ٢٥٠ .

٥٧٤٣ . الكافي : ٢ / ٥٥ / ٣ .

٥٧٤٤ . بحار الأنوار : ٧١ / ٣٢٧ / ٢٢ .

٥٧٤٥ . غرر الحكم : ٨٤٦٢ .

٥٧٤٦ . غرر الحكم : ٦٩٧٥ .

٥٧٤٧ . غرر الحكم : ١٢٧٨ .

٥٧٤٨ . غرر الحكم : ٨٥٦١ .

٥٧٤٩ . غرر الحكم : ح ٨٤٨٧ ، عيون الحكم والمواعظ : ص ٤٤٩ ح ٧٩٧٦ .

٥٧٥٠ . بحار الأنوار : ٦ / ٢٤٢ / ٦٤ .

٥٧٥١ . تنبيه الخواطر : ٢ / ٢٢٥ .

٥٧٥٢ . الجعفريّات : ٢٠٥ .

٥٧٥٣ . تنبيه الخواطر : ١ / ٢٨٤

٥٧٥٤ . غرر الحكم : ٤٨٠٠ .

٥٧٥٥ . الكافي : ٣ / ٢٤٢ / ٢ .

٥٧٥٦ . معاني الأخبار : ٣٤٣ / ١ .

٥٧٥٧ . إبراهيم : ٢٧ .

٥٧٥٨ . بحار الأنوار : ٦ / ٢٢٨ / ٢٩ .

٥٧٥٩ . الكافي : ٣ / ٢٤١ / ١٥ .

٥٧٦٠ . الكافي : ٣ / ٢٣٦ / ٤ .

٥٧٦١ . الأمالي للطوسي : ٢٨ / ٣١ .

٥٧٦٢ . نهج البلاغة : الخطبة ٢٠ .

٥٧٦٣ . قال ابن أبي الحديد : وهذا الكلام يدلُّ علىٰ صحَّة القول بعذاب القبر ، وأصحابنا كلُّهم يذهبون إليه وإن شنَّع عليهم أعداؤهم من الأشعريَّة وغيرهم بجحده . (شرح نهج البلاغة : ١ / ٢٩٨) .

٥٧٦٤ . ثواب الأعمال : ٥٥ / ١ .

٥٧٦٥ . المائدة : ٣٢ .

٥٧٦٦ . الأمالي للصدوق : ٧٣ / ٤١ .

٥٧٦٧ . كنز العمّال : ٣٩٨٨٧ .

٥٧٦٨ . الترغيب والترهيب : ٣ / ٢٩٣ / ٦ .

٥٧٦٩ . كتاب من لا يحضره الفقيه : ٣ / ٥٦٥ / ٤٩٣٤ .

٥٧٧٠ . النساء : ٩٣ .

٥٧٧١ . كنز العمّال : ٣٩٩٥٢ .

٥٧٧٢ . كنز العمّال : ٣٩٨٩٥ ، وراجع وسائل الشيعة : ٨ / ٦١٥ باب ١٦٣ .

٥٧٧٣ . المائدة : ٢٩ .

٥٧٧٤ . ثواب الأعمال : ٣٢٨ / ٩ .

٥٧٧٥ . الكافي : ٧ / ٢٧٦ / ٢ ، راجع وسائل الشيعة : ١٩ / ١٩ باب ٩ .

٥٧٧٦ . النساء : ٢٩ .

٥٧٧٧ . الكافي : ٣ / ١١٢ / ٨ .

٥٧٧٨ . كتاب من لا يحضره الفقيه : ٤ / ٩٥ / ٥١٦٣ .

٥٧٧٩ . الحِجر : ٨٧ .

٥٧٨٠ . القمر : ١٧ .

٥٧٨١ . كنز العمّال : ٤٠٢٧ .

٥٧٨٢ . تفسير العيّاشيّ : ١ / ٦ / ١١ ، اُنظر تمام الحديث .

٥٧٨٣ . كنز العمّال : ٤٠٢٩ .

٥٧٨٤ . بحار الأنوار : ٩٢ / ١٩ / ١٨ .

٥٧٨٥ . بحار الأنوار : ٩٢ / ١٩ / ١٨ .

٥٧٨٦ . معاني الأخبار : ٢٧٩ .

٥٧٨٧ . فليُثَوِّر القرآن : أي لينقّر عنه ويفكّر في معانيه وتفسيره وقراءته . (النهاية : ١ / ٢٢٩) .

٥٧٨٨ . كنز العمّال : ٢٤٥٤ .

٥٧٨٩ . نهج البلاغة : الخطبة ١٤٧

٥٧٩٠ . نهج البلاغة : الكتاب ٤٧ .

٥٧٩١ . تحف العقول : ١٥٠ .

٥٧٩٢ . نهج البلاغة : الخطبة ١٧٦ .

٥٧٩٣ . الكافي : ٢ / ٦٠٢ / ١٣ .

٥٧٩٤ . نهج البلاغة : الخطبة ١٥٦ .

٥٧٩٥ . بحار الأنوار : ٩٢ / ١٥ / ٨ . وعن يعقوب بن السكّيت لنحوي قال : سألت أبا الحسن الثالث ﷺ ما بال القرآن ـ ذ كر نحوه ـ بحار الأنوار : ٩٢ / ١٥ / ٩ .

٥٧٩٦ . بحار الأنوار : ٩٢ / ١٨٦ / ٢ .

٥٧٩٧ . كنزالعمّال : ٢٣٦٨ .

٥٧٩٨ . كنزالعمّال : ٢٣٨٢ .

٥٧٩٩ . نهج البلاغة : الحكمة ٣٩٩ .

٥٩٠٠ . الدعوات : ٢٢٠ / ٦٠٠ .

٥٨٠١ . كنز العمّال : ٢٣١٧ .

٥٨٠٢ . كنز العمّال : ٢٤٧٨ .

٥٨٠٣ . كنز العمّال : ٢٨٤٩ .

٥٨٠٤ . جامع الأخبار : ١١٥ / ٢٠٢ .

٥٨٠٥ . الخصال : ٧ / ٢١ .

٥٨٠٦ . الكافي : ٢ / ٦٠٤ / ٥ .

٥٨٠٧ . كنز العمّال : ٢٣٤٧ .

٥٨٠٨ . الكافي : ٢ / ٦٠٣ / ٢ .

٥٨٠٩ . ثواب الأعمال : ٢٨٣ / ١ .

٥٨١٠ . فاطر : ٢٩ .

٥٨١١ . كنز العمّال : ٢٢٥٧ .

٥٨١٢ . كنزالعمّال : ٢٣٣٠ .

٥٨١٣ . كنز العمّال : ٢٤٤١ .

٥٨١٤ . بحارالأنوار : ٩٢ / ١٧ / ١٨ .

٥٨١٥ . كنز العمّال : ٤٠٣٢ .

٥٨١٦ . كنز العمّال : ٢٧٦٨ .

٥٨١٧ . بحارالأنوار : ٩٢ / ١٩٠ / ٢ .

٥٨١٨ . بحار الأنوار : ٩٢ / ١٩٥ / ١٠ .

٥٨١٩ . كنز العمّال : ٢٧٧٧ .

٥٨٢٠ . ص : ٢٩ .

٥٨٢١ . تنبيه الخواطر : ٢ / ٢٣٦ .

٥٨٢٢ . بحار الأنوار : ٩٢ / ٢١٣ / ١١ .

٥٨٢٣ . النحل : ٩٨ .

٥٨٢٤ . تفسير العيّاشي : ٢ / ٢٧٠ / ٦٨ .

٥٨٢٥ . المزّمّل : ٤ .

٥٨٢٦ . النوادر للراوندي : ١٦٤ / ٢٤٧ .

٥٨٢٧ . ص : ٢٩ .

٥٨٢٨ . بحارالأنوار : ٩٢ / ٢١١ / ٤ .

٥٨٢٩ . الكافي : ٢ / ٦١٧ / ١ .

٥٨٣٠ . الحديد : ١٦ .

٥٨٣١ . بحار الأنوار : ٩٢ / ١٩٥ / ١٠ .

٥٨٣٢ . عيون أخبار الرضا : ٢ / ١٨٢ / ٥ .

٥٨٣٣ . بحار الأنوار : ٩٢ / ١٨٤ / ١٩ .

٥٨٣٤ . شرح نهج البلاغة : ١٠ / ٢٣ .

٥٨٣٥ . جامع الأخبار : ١٣٠ / ٢٥٤ .

٥٨٣٦ . الأعراف : ٢٠٤ .

٥٨٣٧ . كنز العمّال : ٢٤٧٢ .

٥٨٣٨ . كنز العمّال : ٢٣١٦ .

٥٨٣٩ . بحار الأنوار : ٩٢ / ٢٢٢ / ٧ .

٥٨٤٠ . بحارالأنوار : ٩٢ / ١٠٧ / ١ .

٥٨٤١ . منية المريد : ٣٦٩ .

٥٨٤٢ . بحار الأنوار : ٩٢ / ١١٠ / ١١ .

٥٨٤٣ . الواقعة : ١٠ و ١١ .

٥٨٤٤ . الواقعة : ٨٨ و ٨٩ .

٥٨٤٥ . المطفّفين : ٢٨ .

٥٨٤٦ . الكافي : ٢ / ٣٥٢ / ٨ .

٥٨٤٧ . الدعوات : ٢٩٢ / ٣٩ .

٥٨٤٨ . الإقبال : ٣ / ٢٩٩ .

٥٨٤٩ . بحار الأنوار : ٧٨ / ٣٨٠ / ٤ .

٥٨٥٠ . الكافي : ٢ / ١٢٣ / ١١ .

٥٨٥١ . الكافي : ٨ / ٦٩ / ٢٤ .

٥٨٥٢ . الخصال : ٨١ / ٥ .

٥٨٥٣ . ثواب الأعمال : ٢٠٥ / ١ .

٥٨٥٤ . مشكاة الأنوار : ٤٣٩ / ١٤٧٦ .

٥٨٥٥ . غرر الحكم : ٤٤٧٧ .

٥٨٥٦ . غرر الحكم : ٦١٥٩ .

٥٨٥٧ . الحديد : ١١ .

٥٨٥٨ . ثواب الأعمال : ٣٤١ / ١ .

٥٨٥٩ . ثواب الأعمال : ١٦٦ / ١ .

٥٨٦٠ . كنز العمّال : ١٥٣٩٨ .

٥٨٦١ . الأمالي للصدوق : ٥١٦ / ٧٠٧ .

٥٨٦٢ . نهج البلاغة : الخطبة ٩٠ .
٥٨٦٣ . نهج البلاغة : الكتاب ٣١ .
٥٨٦٤ . بحار الأنوار : ١٠٣ / ١٣٨ / ٢ .
٥٨٦٥ . ثواب الأعمال : ١٦٧ / ٤ .
٥٨٦٦ . البقرة : ٢٨٠ .
٥٨٦٧ . الكافي : ٨ / ٩ / ١ .
٥٨٦٨ . كنز العمّال : ١٥٤٢٤ .
٥٨٦٩ . ثواب الأعمال : ١٦٧ / ٥ .
٥٨٧٠ . كنز العمّال : ٥٤٣٤ .
٥٨٧١ . بحار الأنوار : ٧٦ / ٢٦٩ / ١٧ .
٥٨٧٢ . تنبيه الخواطر : ١ / ١٦٧ .
٥٨٧٣ . بحار الأنوار : ٧١ / ٣٤٢ / ١٥ .
٥٨٧٤ . غرر الحكم : ٩١٦٥ .
٥٨٧٥ . غرر الحكم : ٩٠٤٨ .
٥٨٧٦ . الأمالي للطوسي : ٨ / ٨ .
٥٨٧٧ . غرر الحكم : ١٥٠١ .
٥٨٧٨ . تنبيه الخواطر : ١ / ١٦٧ .
٥٨٧٩ . بحار الأنوار : ٧٨ / ١٠ / ٦٧ .
٥٨٨٠ . غرر الحكم : ٣٣٤، ٣٣٥ .
٥٨٨١ . كتاب من لا يحضره الفقيه : ٢ / ٦٤ / ١٧٢١ .
٥٨٨٢ . البقرة : ١٧٩ .
٥٨٨٣ . البقرة : ١٩٤ .
٥٨٨٤ . المائدة : ٤٥ .
٥٨٨٥ . كنز العمّال : ٣٩٨٣١ .
٥٨٨٦ . الأمالي للمفيد : ص ٥٣ ح ١٥ .
٥٨٨٧ . نهج البلاغة : الحكمة ٢٥٢ .
٥٨٨٨ . التفسير المنسوب إلى الإمام العسكري ﷺ : ٥٩٥ / ٣٥٤ .
٥٨٨٩ . كنز العمّال : ٣٩٨٥٤ .
٥٨٩٠ . كنز العمّال : ٣٩٨٥٠ .
٥٨٩١ . الكافي : ٧ / ٣٥٨ / ١ .
٥٨٩٢ . التوبة : ٥١ .
٥٨٩٣ . الأنفال : ٤٢ .
٥٨٩٤ . القمر : ٤٩ .
٥٨٩٥ . كنز العمّال : ٤٩٩ .
٥٨٩٦ . كنز العمّال : ٥٠١ .
٥٨٩٧ . نهج البلاغة : الخطبة ١٨٣ .
٥٨٩٨ . التوحيد : ٣٨٣ / ٣٢ .
٥٨٩٩ . كنز العمّال : ١٥٦٧ .
٥٩٠٠ . نهج البلاغة : الحكمة ٤٥٩ .
٥٩٠١ . نهج البلاغة : الحكمة ١٦ .
٥٩٠٢ . التوحيد : ٣٦٤ / ١ .
٥٩٠٣ . الدّرة الباهرة : ٣٣ .
٥٩٠٤ . بحار الأنوار : ٥ / ١٢١ / ٦٤ .
٥٩٠٥ . أعلام الدين : ٣١١ .
٥٩٠٦ . الكافي : ٦ / ١٣ / ٣ .
٥٩٠٧ . الكافي : ٦ / ١٤ / ٤ .
٥٩٠٨ . عيون أخبار الرّضا : ١ / ١٤١ / ٤٢ .
٥٩٠٩ . الكافي : ٢ / ٦٢ / ٨ .
٥٩١٠ . التمحيص : ٥٩ / ١٢٣ .
٥٩١١ . عيون أخبار الرّضا : ١ / ١٤١ / ٤٢ .
٥٩١٢ . غرر الحكم : ٣٢٢٥ .
٥٩١٣ . نهج البلاغة : الحكمة ٢٢٨ .
٥٩١٤ . نزهة الناظر : ١٤٧ / ٢١ .
٥٩١٥ . كنز العمّال : ٢٨٠٨٢ .
٥٩١٦ . كنز العمّال : ٦٣٣ .
٥٩١٧ . كنز العمّال : ١٥٦٠ .
٥٩١٨ . بحار الأنوار : ٤١ / ٢ / ٣ .
٥٩١٩ . ص : ٢٦ .
٥٩٢٠ . الكافي : ٧ / ٤٠٦ / ٢ .
٥٩٢١ . نهج البلاغة : الكتاب ٥٣ .
٥٩٢٢ . الكافي : ٧ / ٤٠٦ / ١ .
٥٩٢٣ . النساء : ٦٠ .
٥٩٢٤ . الكافي : ٧ / ٤١٢ / ٥ .
٥٩٢٥ . كتاب من لا يحضره الفقيه : ٣ / ٢ / ٣٢١٦ .
٥٩٢٦ . مستدرك الوسائل : ١٧ / ٢٤٣ / ٢١٢٣٣ .
٥٩٢٧ . كنز العمّال : ١٤٩٨٨ .
٥٩٢٨ . موضع في جهنّم .
٥٩٢٩ . كتاب من لا يحضره الفقيه : ٣ / ٦ / ٣٢٢٦ .
٥٩٣٠ . كنز العمّال : ١٤٩٩٤ .
٥٩٣١ . بحار الأنوار : ١٠٤ / ٢٦٤ / ٥ .
٥٩٣٢ . كنز العمّال : ١٥٠٣٢ .
٥٩٣٣ . وسائل الشيعة : ١٨ / ١٥٥ / ١ .
٥٩٣٤ . عوالي اللآلي : ٢ / ٣٤٣ / ٥ .
٥٩٣٥ . الكافي : ٧ / ٤١٣ / ١ .

٥٩٣٦ . كتاب من لا يحضره الفقيه : ٣ / ١٣ / ٣٢٣٨ .
٥٩٣٧ . الكافي : ٧ / ٤١٣ / ٥ .
٥٩٣٨ . دعائم الإسلام : ٢ / ٥٣٧ / ١٩٠٧ .
٥٩٣٩ . كنز العمّال : ١٥٠٤٠ .
٥٩٤٠ . الكافي : ٧ / ٤١٣ / ١ .
٥٩٤١ . الكافي : ٧ / ٤١٣ / ٤ .
٥٩٤٢ . مستدرك الوسائل : ١٧ / ٣٥٠ / ٢١٥٤٩ .
٥٩٤٣ . كنز العمّال : ١٤٩٩٣ .
٥٩٤٤ . الكافي : ٧ / ٤١٠ / ١ .
٥٩٤٥ . الكافي : ٧ / ٤٠٧ / ١ .
٥٩٤٦ . غرر الحكم : ٣٠١٤ .
٥٩٤٧ . بحار الأنوار : ١٠٤ / ٢٦٦ / ٢٠ .
٥٩٤٨ . معاني الأخبار : ٢٧٩ .
٥٩٤٩ . تنبيه الخواطر : ٢ / ١٧١ .
٥٩٥٠ . الخصال : ٣١١ / ٨٨ .
٥٩٥١ . بحار الأنوار : ١٤ / ١٤ / ٢٣ .
٥٩٥٢ . وسائل الشيعة : ١٨ / ٥٨٢ / ٢ .
٥٩٥٣ . كنز العمّال : ١٢٢٥ .
٥٩٥٤ . الأمالي للطوسي : ٥٣٦ / ١١٦٢ .
٥٩٥٥ . نهج البلاغة : الحكمة ٤٠٩ .
٥٩٥٦ . نهج البلاغة : الحكمة ١٤٧ .
٥٩٥٧ . تحف العقول : ٣٧١ .
٥٩٥٨ . علل الشرائع : ١٠٩ / ٨ .
٥٩٥٩ . الدّرة الباهرة : ٣٩ .
٥٩٦٠ . الشعراء : ٨٧-٨٩ .
٥٩٦١ . الكافي : ٢ / ١٦ / ٥ .
٥٩٦٢ . مجمع البيان : ٧ / ٣٠٥ .
٥٩٦٣ . تحف العقول : ٥٠٤ .
٥٩٦٤ . بحار الأنوار : ٧٨ / ٨ / ٦٤ .
٥٩٦٥ . تحف العقول : ٢٣٥ .
٥٩٦٦ . بحارالأنوار : ٧٨ / ١٦٤ / ١ .
٥٩٦٧ . بحار الأنوار : ٧٠ / ٥٩ / ٣٩ .
٥٩٦٨ . الإقبال : ٣ / ٢٩٩ .
٥٩٦٩ . الكافي : ٨ / ٢١٥ / ٢٦٠ .
٥٩٧٠ . الترغيب والترهيب : ٣ / ٤٩٧ / ٣ .
٥٩٧١ . محمّد : ٢٤ .
٥٩٧٢ . المحاسن : ١ / ٣١٨ / ٦٣٣ .
٥٩٧٣ . بحار الأنوار : ٧٨ / ٣٥٣ / ٩ .
٥٩٧٤ . الدّرة الباهرة : ٤٣ .
٥٩٧٥ . المحاسن : ١ / ٤٥٧ / ١٠٥٨ .
٥٩٧٦ . غرر الحكم : ٦٠٢٠ .
٥٩٧٧ . غرر الحكم : ٦٧٧٧ .
٥٩٧٨ . الأنعام : ١٢٥ .
٥٩٧٩ . الشرح : ١ .
٥٩٨٠ . مجمع البيان : ٤ / ٥٦١ .
٥٩٨١ . المطففين : ١٤ .
٥٩٨٢ . سنن ابن ماجة : ٢ / ١٤١٨ / ٤٢٤٤ .
٥٩٨٣ . تحف العقول : ٣٩٧ .
٥٩٨٤ . البقرة : ٧٤ .
٥٩٨٥ . الكافي : ٢ / ٣٢٩ / ١ .
٥٩٨٦ . بحار الأنوار : ١٤ / ٣٠٩ / ١٧ .
٥٩٨٧ . الأمالي للطوسي : ٣ / ١ .
٥٩٨٨ . الخصال : ١٢٦ / ١٢٢ .
٥٩٨٩ . علل الشرائع : ٨١ / ١ .
٥٩٩٠ . تحف العقول : ١٩٩ .
٥٩٩١ . تحف العقول : ٢١٤ .
٥٩٩٢ . تحف العقول : ٢٩٦ .
٥٩٩٣ . البقرة : ١٠ .
٥٩٩٤ . الكافي : ٢ / ٣٠٠ / ١ .
٥٩٩٥ . الكافي : ٢ / ٢٧٥ / ٢٨ .
٥٩٩٦ . يونس : ٥٧ .
٥٩٩٧ . نهج البلاغة : الخطبة ١٩٨ .
٥٩٩٨ . معاني الأخبار : ٣٣٥ / ١ .
٥٩٩٩ . نهج البلاغة : الخطبة ١٠٩ .
٦٠٠٠ . نهج البلاغة : الحكمة ٣٤٩ .
٦٠٠١ . بحار الأنوار : ١ / ٢٠٤ / ٢٢ .
٦٠٠٢ . الكافي : ١ / ٤١ / ٦ .
٦٠٠٣ . نهج البلاغة : الكتاب ٣١ .
٦٠٠٤ . بحار الأنوار : ٧٧ / ٢٠٨ / ١ .
٦٠٠٥ . نهج البلاغة : الكتاب ٣١ .
٦٠٠٦ . مشكاة الأنوار : ٢٩٢ / ٨٨٥ .
٦٠٠٧ . أعلام الدين : ٣٦٥ / ٣٣ .
٦٠٠٨ . نهج البلاغة: الحكمة١٠٣ .
٦٠٠٩ . تحف العقول : ٢٨٥ .

٦٠١٠ . كنز العمّال : ٤٢١٣٠ .

٦٠١١ . تنبيه الخواطر : ٢ / ١٢٢ .

٦٠١٢ . نهج البلاغة : الكتاب ٣١ .

٦٠١٣ .عدّة الداعي : ٢٤٩ .

٦٠١٤ . المائدة : ١٠٤ .

٦٠١٥ . المحاسن : ١ / ٣٨٣ / ٨٤٧ .

٦٠١٦ . معاني الأخبار : ٢٦٦ / ١ .

٦٠١٧ . الاحتجاج : ٢ / ٥١٠ / ٣٣٧ .

٦٠١٨ . المائدة : ٩٠ و ٩١ .

٦٠١٩ . الكافي : ٥ / ١٢٣ / ٢ .

٦٠٢٠ . الأمالي للطوسي : ٣٣٦ / ٦٨١ .

٦٠٢١ . الخصال : ٢٦ / ٩٢ .

٦٠٢٢ . البقرة : ١٨٨ .

٦٠٢٣ . الكافي : ٥ / ١٢٢ / ١ .

٦٠٢٤ . تفسير العيّاشيّ : ١ / ٣٢٢ / ١١٦ .

٦٠٢٥ .عدّة الداعي : ١٦٦ .

٦٠٢٦ . كنز العمّال : ٧٠٨٠ .

٦٠٢٧ . نهج البلاغة : الحكمة ٢٢٩ .

٦٠٢٨ . بحار الأنوار : ٧٧ / ٤٢٢ / ٤٠ .

٦٠٢٩ . بحار الأنوار : ٦٩ / ٣٩٩ / ٩١ .

٦٠٣٠ . نهج البلاغة : الحكمة ٣٧١ .

٦٠٣١ . بحار الأنوار : ٧٨ / ١١١ / ٦ .

٦٠٣٢ . غرر الحكم : ٦١٧٩ .

٦٠٣٣ . غرر الحكم : ٧٧٢٤ .

٦٠٣٤ . الكافي : ٨ / ٢٤٤ / ٣٣٨ .

٦٠٣٥ . بحار الأنوار : ٧٧ / ١٨٧ / ٣٧ .

٦٠٣٦ . غرر الحكم : ٣١٩١ .

٦٠٣٧ . غرر الحكم : ٧٧٧١ .

٦٠٣٨ . غرر الحكم : ٤٢٤٤ .

٦٠٣٩ . غرر الحكم : ٣٢٩٥ .

٦٠٤٠ . بحار الأنوار : ٧٨ / ١٢٨ / ١١ .

٦٠٤١ . الكافي : ٢ / ١٣٨ / ٣ .

٦٠٤٢ . بحار الأنوار : ٧٨ / ٧١ / ٣٣ .

٦٠٤٣ . الكافي : ٨ / ٢٤٣ / ٣٣٧ .

٦٠٤٤ . ص : ٧٣ ، ٧٤ .

٦٠٤٥ . الأعراف : ١٣ .

٦٠٤٦ . نهج البلاغة : الخطبة ١٩٢ .

٦٠٤٧ . بحار الأنوار : ٧٨ / ١٨٦ / ١٦ .

٦٠٤٨ . بحار الأنوار : ٧٨ / ٢٢٩ / ٥ .

٦٠٤٩ . بحار الأنوار : ٧٣ / ٢١٥ / ٥ .

٦٠٥٠ . بحار الأنوار : ٧٧ / ٧٤ ، ٩٠ / ٣ .

٦٠٥١ . بحار الأنوار : ٦٩ / ٣٩٩ / ٩١ .

٦٠٥٢ . الكافي : ٢ / ٣١٠ / ٩ .

٦٠٥٣ . الكافي : ٨ / ١٢٨ / ٩٨ .

٦٠٥٤ . بحار الأنوار : ٧٣ / ٢٣١ / ٢٣ .

٦٠٥٥ . بحار الأنوار : ٧٣ / ٢٣٢ / ٢٥ .

٦٠٥٦ . بحار الأنوار : ٧٣ / ٢٣٤ / ٣٣ .

٦٠٥٧ . غرر الحكم : ٩٤٦٧ .

٦٠٥٨ . الكافي : ٢ / ٣١٢ / ١٧ .

٦٠٥٩ . في بعض النسخ : مَهنأة (كما في هامش المصدر) .

٦٠٦٠ . تنبيه الخواطر : ١ / ٢٠١ .

٦٠٦١ . كنز العمّال : ٧٧٩٣ .

٦٠٦٢ . كنز العمّال : ٨٨٧٨ .

٦٠٦٣ . الأُمور المذكورة في الأحاديث ليست قانوناً كلّيّاً تكشف عن عدم وجود الكبر ، بل تختلف باختلاف الأشخاص والأعصار والموارد، فقد قيل : «إنّ من النّاس ناساً يلبسون الصوف إرادة التواضع وقلوبهم مملوءة عُجباً وكِبراً» فليُتأمّل .

٦٠٦٤ . نهج البلاغة : الخطبة ١٩٢ .

٦٠٦٥ . نهج البلاغة : الحكمة ٢٥٢ .

٦٠٦٦ . بحار الأنوار : ٧٨ / ١٠٤ / ٣ .

٦٠٦٧ . الأمالي للصدوق : ٥٧٧ / ٧٨٨ .

٦٠٦٨ . نهج البلاغة : الحكمة ٣٧١ .

٦٠٦٩ . غرر الحكم : ٧٤٦٤ .

٦٠٧٠ . غرر الحكم : ١٠٥٨٦ .

٦٠٧١ . بحار الأنوار : ٧٧ / ٢٣٥ / ٣ .

٦٠٧٢ . الخصال : ٤٣٤ / ٢٠ .

٦٠٧٣ . تحف العقول : ٣٩٦ .

٦٠٧٤ . النحل : ٢٩ .

٦٠٧٥ . الكافي : ٢ / ٣١٠ / ١٠ .

٦٠٧٦ . القلم : ١ .

٦٠٧٧ . غرر الحكم : ٩٩١ .

٦٠٧٨ . غرر الحكم : ٩٩٤٨ .

٦٠٧٩ . غرر الحكم : ٨١٢٦ .

٦٠٨٠ . نهج البلاغة : الحكمة ٣٠١ .

٦٠٨١ . غرر الحكم : ٧٢٦٠ .

٦٠٨٢ . غرر الحكم : ٦٣٣٩ .

٦٠٨٣ . كنز العمّال : ٢٩٣٣٢ .

٦٠٨٤ . كنز العمّال : ٢٨٧٣٣ .

٦٠٨٥ . الكافي : ١ / ٥٢ / ٩ .

٦٠٨٦ . الكافي : ١ / ٥٢ / ٨ .

٦٠٨٧ . الأمالي للصدوق : ٩١ / ٦٤ .

٦٠٨٨ . كنز العمّال : ٢٨٩٥١ .

٦٠٨٩ . الدرّ المنثور : ١ / ٢٧ .

٦٠٩٠ . الكافي : ٢ / ٦٧٢ / ١ .

٦٠٩١ . كنز العمّال : ٢٩٢٩٤ .

٦٠٩٢ . تحف العقول : ٣٥٨ .

٦٠٩٣ . الكافي : ٢ / ٦٧٠ / ٢ .

٦٠٩٤ . تحف العقول : ٢٢٣ .

٦٠٩٥ . النَّزَق : الخِفّة و الطَّيش . (لسان العرب : ١٠ / ٣٥٢) .

٦٠٩٦ . الكافي : ٢ / ٢٢١ / ١ .

٦٠٩٧ . الكافي : ٢ / ٢٢٣ / ٧ .

٦٠٩٨ . الكافي : ٢ / ٢٢٦ / ١٥ .

٦٠٩٩ . بحار الأنوار : ٧٥ / ٧٠ / ٧ .

٦١٠٠ . الكافي : ٢ / ٣٧٠ / ٢ .

٦١٠١ . الكافي : ٢ / ٣٧٠ / ٤ .

٦١٠٢ . الكافي : ٢ / ٣٧١ / ١٠ .

٦١٠٣ . الكافي : ٢ / ٣٧١ / ٦ .

٦١٠٤ . المحاسن : ١ / ٤٠٣ / ٩١٠ .

٦١٠٥ . حلية الأولياء : ١ / ٧٦ ، وأنظر الكافي : ٢ / ٢٢٥ / ١٢ .

٦١٠٦ . معاني الأخبار : ١٦٦ / ١ .

٦١٠٧ . بحار الأنوار : ٧٢ / ٢٦٣ / ٤٧ .

٦١٠٨ . شرح نهج البلاغة : ٦ / ٣٥٧ .

٦١٠٩ . كنز العمّال : ٨٢١٢ .

٦١١٠ . بحار الأنوار : ٧٢ / ٢٦٢ / ٤٥ .

٦١١١ . بحار الأنوار : ٧٢ / ٢٦١ / ٣٧ .

٦١١٢ . نهج البلاغة : الخطبة : ٨٤ .

٦١١٣ . نهج البلاغة : الحكمة ٤٥٨ .

٦١١٤ . غرر الحكم : ٣٣٩ .

٦١١٥ . بحار الأنوار : ٧٢ / ٢٥٩ / ٢٣ .

٦١١٦ . بحار الأنوار : ٧٨ / ٣٠٥ / ١ .

٦١١٧ . النحل : ١٠٥ .

٦١١٨ . نهج البلاغة : الخطبة ٨٦ .

٦١١٩ . بحار الأنوار : ٧٢ / ٢٤٧ / ٨ .

٦١٢٠ . بحار الأنوار : ٧٥ / / ١٧٢ / ١١ .

٦١٢١ . كنز العمّال : ٨٢١٧ .

٦١٢٢ . بحار الأنوار : ٧٢ / ٢٣٦ / ٣ .

٦١٢٣ . الدرّة الباهرة : ٤٣ .

٦١٢٤ . كنز العمّال : ٨٢١٧ .

٦١٢٥ . كنز العمّال : ٨٢١٥ .

٦١٢٦ . بحار الأنوار : ٧٢ / ٢٤٩ / ١٤ .

٦١٢٧ . بحار الأنوار : ٧٢ / ٢٣٥ / ٢ .

٦١٢٨ . تنبيه الخواطر : ٢ / ١٢٢ .

٦١٢٩ . الترغيب والترهيب : ٣ / ٥٩٧ / ٣٢ .

٦١٣٠ . الترغيب والترهيب : ٣ / ٥٩٨ / ٣٤ .

٦١٣١ . غافر : ٢٨ .

٦١٣٢ . التوبة : ٧٧ .

٦١٣٣ . الترغيب والترهيب : ٣ / ٥٩٦ / ٢٨ .

٦١٣٤ . الترغيب والترهيب : ٣ / ٥٩٦ / ٢٩ .

٦١٣٥ . غرر الحكم : ٤٦٤٠ .

٦١٣٦ . غرر الحكم : ٧١٢٣ .

٦١٣٧ . غرر الحكم : ١١٨١ .

٦١٣٨ . غرر الحكم : ٧٧٩٤ .

٦١٣٩ . غرر الحكم : ٨٨٨٨ و ٩١٨١ .

٦١٤٠ . غرر الحكم : ١١٠٣٩ .

٦١٤١ . بحار الأنوار : ٧٢ / ٢٦١ / ٣٦ .

٦١٤٢ . بحار الأنوار : ٧٢ / ١٩٢ / ٨ .

٦١٤٣ . بحار الأنوار : ٧٢ / ٢٦٠ / ٢٩ .

٦١٤٤ . يعني أنّ النسيان يصير سبباً لفضيحتهم ، وذلك لأنّهم ربّما قالوا شيئاً فنسوا أنّهم قالوه فيقولون خلاف ما قالوه أوّلاً فيفتضحون (كما في هامش المصدر) .

٦١٤٥ . الكافي : ٢ / ٣٤١ / ١٥ .

٦١٤٦ . الأنعام : ١٤٤ .

٦١٤٧ . الزمر : ٦٠ .

٦١٤٨ . نهج البلاغة : الخطبة ١٤٧ .

٦١٤٩ . قرب الإسناد : ١٣٣ / ٤٦٦ .

٦١٥٠ . الكافي : ٢ / ٣٤٠ / ٩ .

٦١٥١ . الكافي : ٢ / ٣٣٩ / ٥ .

٦١٥٢ . بحار الأنوار : ٧٢ / ٢٦٣ / ٤٨ .

٦١٥٣ . الكافي : ٢ / ٣٤١ / ١٦ .

٦١٥٤ . الكافي : ٢ / ٢١٠ / ٥ .

٦١٥٥ . الأنبياء : ٦٣ .

٦١٥٦ . كنز العمّال : ٨٢٥٣ .

٦١٥٧ . مستطرفات السرائر : ١٣٧ / ١ .

٦١٥٨ . قال الشيخ الأنصاريّ في «المكاسب» بعد ذكر الحديث : فإنّ سلب الكذب مبنيّ على أنّ المشار إليه بقوله «هاهنا» موضعٌ خالٍ مِن الدّار ، إذ لا وجه له سوىٰ ذلك . (المكاسب : ٥١) .

٦١٥٩ . المائدة : ٤١ .

٦١٦٠ . نهج البلاغة : الكتاب ١٠ .

٦١٦١ . بحار الأنوار : ٧٢ / ٢٦٤ / ١ .

٦١٦٢ . مسند ابن حنبل : ٣ / ٢٩٢ / ٨٧٨٢ .

٦١٦٣ . كنز العمّال : ١٥٩٩١ .

٦١٦٤ . بحار الأنوار : ٧٧ / ٢١١ / ١ .

٦١٦٥ . الفرقان : ٧٢ .

٦١٦٦ . غرر الحكم : ٩١٣٠ .

٦١٦٧ . بحار الأنوار : ٧٧ / ٢٠٩ / ١ .

٦١٦٨ . بحار الأنوار : ٧٨ / ٨٢ / ٨٢ .

٦١٦٩ . غرر الحكم : ٤٤٦ .

٦١٧٠ . غرر الحكم : ١٥٢٨ .

٦١٧١ . غرر الحكم : ١٢٩٨ و ١٢٩٩ .

٦١٧٢ . غرر الحكم : ١٥٦٦ و ١٥٦٧ .

٦١٧٣ . غرر الحكم : ٧٣٥٣ .

٦١٧٤ . غرر الحكم : ٥٥٥٨ .

٦١٧٥ . بحار الأنوار : ٤٤ / ٨٩ / ٢ .

٦١٧٦ . الدّرة الباهرة : ٢٧ .

٦١٧٧ . تحف العقول : ٣١٩ .

٦١٧٨ . غرر الحكم : ١٥٠٧ .

٦١٧٩ . غرر الحكم : ٧٤٩٠ .

٦١٨٠ . غرر الحكم : ٨٩٥٨ .

٦١٨١ . بحار الأنوار : ٧٨ / ١١٣ / ٧ .

٦١٨٢ . بحار الأنوار : ٤٦ / ١٥ / ٣٣ .

٦١٨٣ . بحار الأنوار : ١٦ / ٢٣٥ / ٣٥ .

٦١٨٤ . بحار الأنوار : ٩٢ / ١٨٤ / ٢١ .

٦١٨٥ . كنز العمّال : ٢٥٤٨٨ .

٦١٨٦ . كنز العمّال : ٢٥٤٨٥ .

٦١٨٧ . كنز العمّال : ٢٥٤٩٠ .

٦١٨٨ . كنز العمّال : ٢٥٥٠١ .

٦١٨٩ . كنز العمّال : ٢٥٤٩٩ .

٦١٩٠ . مسند ابن حنبل : ٥ / ٢٨١ / ١٥٥٠٠ .

٦١٩١ . سنن ابن ماجة : ٢ / ١٢١١ / ٣٦٧١ .

٦١٩٢ . قرب الاسناد : ٩٢ / ٣٠٧ .

٦١٩٣ . بحار الأنوار : ٧٧ / ١٦٤ / ١٩٠ .

٦١٩٤ . النوادر للراوندي : ١٠٧ / ٨٧ .

٦١٩٥ . الدّرة الباهرة : ٢٤ .

٦١٩٦ . سنن الترمذي : ٥ / ٥٨٥ / ٣٦١٠ .

٦١٩٧ . كنز العمّال : ٤٤١٥٤ .

٦١٩٨ . نهج البلاغة : الحكمة ١١٣ .

٦١٩٩ . غرر الحكم : ٣٥٤٢ .

٦٢٠٠ . غرر الحكم : ٦٢٣٢ .

٦٢٠١ . كنز العمّال : ٩٣٤٠ و ٩٣٤١ .

٦٢٠٢ . كنز العمّال : ١٠٥١٦ .

٦٢٠٣ . تنبيه الخواطر : ١ / ٤٢ .

٦٢٠٤ . كنز العمّال : ٩٢٢٣ .

٦٢٠٥ . جامع الأحاديث للقمّي : ٧٦ .

٦٢٠٦ . كتاب من لا يحضره الفقيه : ٣ / ١٦٣ / ٣٥٩٦ .

٦٢٠٧ . تهذيب الأحكام : ٦ / ٣٢٦ / ٨٩٥ .

٦٢٠٨ . كتاب من لا يحضره الفقيه : ٣ / ١٦٣ / ٣٥٩٥ .

٦٢٠٩ . بحار الأنوار : ١٠٣ / ٧٧ / ١ .

٦٢١٠ . غرر الحكم : ٣٩٦٨ .

٦٢١١ . بحار الأنوار : ٧٨ / ٢٦ / ٩٢ .

٦٢١٢ . مستدرك الوسائل : ١٣ / ٤٥ / ١٤٦٩٥ .

٦٢١٣ . نهج البلاغة : الحكمة ٢٣٩ .

٦٢١٤ . غرر الحكم : ٩٢٨٤ .

٦٢١٥ . غرر الحكم : ٥٩٢٧ .

٦٢١٦ . غرر الحكم : ٤٤٧١ .

٦٢١٧ . بحار الأنوار : ٧٨ / ١٨٠ / ٦٤ .

٦٢١٨ . الكافي : ٥ / ٨٥ / ٤ .

٦٢١٩ . الكافي : ٥ / ٨٥ / ١ .

٦٢٢٠ . الكافي : ٥ / ٨٥ / ٢ .

٦٢٢١ . الكافي : ٢ / ٢٨٩ / ٢ .

٦٢٢٢ . الكافي : ٢ / ٣٩١ / ١ .

٦٢٢٣ . الكافي : ٢ / ٣٨٧ / ١٥ .
٦٢٢٤ . الكافي : ٢ / ٣٨٦ / ١٠ .
٦٢٢٥ . بحار الأنوار : ٧٨ / ٢٧٦ / ١١٢ .
٦٢٢٦ . معاني الأخبار : ٣٩٤ / ٤٧ .
٦٢٢٧ . الكافي : ٢ / ٢٩٠ / ٥ .
٦٢٢٨ . النساء : ٨٦ .
٦٢٢٩ . الرحمٰن : ٦٠ .
٦٢٣٠ . بحار الأنوار : ٧٨ / ٣١١ / ١ .
٦٢٣١ . بحار الأنوار : ٧٥ / ٤٣ / ٨ .
٦٢٣٢ . نهج البلاغة : الخطبة ٢١٦ .
٦٢٣٣ . غرر الحكم : ٢٣٨٣ .
٦٢٣٤ . نهج البلاغة : الحكمة ٦٢ .
٦٢٣٥ . الدّرة الباهرة : ٣٤ .
٦٢٣٦ . بحار الأنوار : ٧٨ / ٥٣ / ٨٥ .
٦٢٣٧ . غرر الحكم : ٩٤١٣ .
٦٢٣٨ . الكافي : ٢ / ٣٢٢ / ٢ .
٦٢٣٩ . بحار الأنوار : ٧٨ / ٢٧٨ / ١١٣ .
٦٢٤٠ . الكافي : ٢ / ٣٠٤ / ١٠ .
٦٢٤١ . غرر الحكم : ١٠٥١٨ .
٦٢٤٢ . غرر الحكم : ٦٧٦٦ .
٦٢٤٣ . غرر الحكم : ٣٠٠٣ .
٦٢٤٤ . غرر الحكم : ٧٢٠٨ .
٦٢٤٥ . تحف العقول : ٨٨ .
٦٢٤٦ . كشف الغمّة : ٣ / ١٣٦ .
٦٢٤٧ . تحف العقول : ٣٥٩ .
٦٢٤٨ . نهج البلاغة : الكتاب ٥١ .
٦٢٤٩ . ص : ٢٧ .
٦٢٥٠ . نهج البلاغة : الحكمة ٧٨ .
٦٢٥١ . البقرة : ٢٨٦ .
٦٢٥٢ . الكافي : ٢ / ٤٦٣ / ٢ .
٦٢٥٣ . التوحيد : ٣٤٧ / ٦ .
٦٢٥٤ . الترغيب والترهيب : ٣ / ٥٣٧ / ٤٥ .
٦٢٥٥ . نهج البلاغة : الحكمة ٣٩٤ .
٦٢٥٦ . بحار الأنوار : ٧١ / ٢٩٣ / ٦٣ .
٦٢٥٧ . غرر الحكم : ٥٣٢٢ .
٦٢٥٨ . تحف العقول : ٢١٦ .
٦٢٥٩ . غرر الحكم : ٢٧٢٢ .
٦٢٦٠ . غرر الحكم : ٢٦٧٥ .
٦٢٦١ . غرر الحكم : ٨٤٩٦ .
٦٢٦٢ . غرر الحكم : ٥٥٥١ .
٦٢٦٣ . بحار الأنوار : ٢ / ٥٥ / ٢٨ .
٦٢٦٤ . الترغيب والترهيب : ٣ / ٥٤٠ / ٥١ .
٦٢٦٥ . الترغيب والترهيب : ٣ / ٥٣٧ / ٤٦ .
٦٢٦٦ . الأمالي للصدوق : ٨٥ / ٥٣ .
٦٢٦٧ . غرر الحكم : ٦٢٨٣ .
٦٢٦٨ . غرر الحكم : ٢٦٣٧ .
٦٢٦٩ . بحار الأنوار : ٧٨ / ١٢٧ / ١٠ .
٦٢٧٠ . غرر الحكم : ٢٧٢٠ .
٦٢٧١ . نهج البلاغة : الحكمة ١٢٣ .
٦٢٧٢ . مشكاة الأنوار : ٥٥١ / ١٨٥٠ .
٦٢٧٣ . كنز العمّال : ٤٤١٧٦ .
٦٢٧٤ . الأمالي للطوسي : ٣ / ١ .
٦٢٧٥ . غرر الحكم : ٢٦٨٠ .
٦٢٧٦ . نهج البلاغة: الحكمة ٧١ .
٦٢٧٧ . نهج البلاغة : الحكمة ٣٨١ .
٦٢٧٨ . غرر الحكم : ٤٠٨٤ .
٦٢٧٩ . نهج البلاغة : الحكمة ٣٤٩ .
٦٢٨٠ . نهج البلاغة : الحكمة ٣٨٢ .
٦٢٨١ . غرر الحكم: ٢١٨٢ .
٦٢٨٢ . غرر الحكم: ١٨٥٤ .
٦٢٨٣ . شرح نهج البلاغة : ٧ / ٩٢ .
٦٢٨٤ . الدّرة الباهرة : ٤١ .
٦٢٨٥ . غرر الحكم : ١٤٦٢ .
٦٢٨٦ . بحار الأنوار : ٧١ / ٢٧٤ / ١ .
٦٢٨٧ . الكافي : ٨ / ١٤٨ / ١٢٨ .
٦٢٨٨ . بحار الأنوار : ٧١ / ٢٩٤ / ٦٤ .
٦٢٨٩ . غرر الحكم : ٥٨٦٧ .
٦٢٩٠ . غرر الحكم : ٥٨٦٥ .
٦٢٩١ . غرر الحكم : ٥٨٦٦ .
٦٢٩٢ . غرر الحكم : ٢٨٣ .
٦٢٩٣ . غرر الحكم : ١٢٦٦ .
٦٢٩٤ . سنن النسائي : ٣ / ٥٨ .
٦٢٩٥ . غرر الحكم : ٣٣٧١ .
٦٢٩٦ . غرر الحكم : ٣٣٠٤ .

٦٢٩٧ . غرر الحكم : ٤٩٦٩ .
٦٢٩٨ . البقرة : ٨٣ .
٦٢٩٩ . الإسراء : ٥٣ .
٦٣٠٠ . البقرة : ٨٣ .
٦٣٠١ . الكافي : ٢ / ١٦٥ / ١٠ .
٦٣٠٢ . بحار الأنوار : ٧١ / ٣١٢ / ١٢ .
٦٣٠٣ . الأمالي للصدوق : ٤٩ / ١ .
٦٣٠٤ . الأمالي للصدوق : ٤٨٤ / ٦٥٧ .
٦٣٠٥ . غرر الحكم : ٥٧٩ .
٦٣٠٦ . غرر الحكم : ٩٤٤٢ .
٦٣٠٧ . غرر الحكم: ٣٣١ .
٦٣٠٨ . معاني الأخبار : ١٥٠ / ١ .
٦٣٠٩ . غرر الحكم : ٧٢٤٤ .
٦٣١٠ . أعلام الدين : ٢٩٢ .
٦٣١١ . غرر الحكم : ٤٥٣٦ .
٦٣١٢ . بحار الأنوار : ٧٨ / ١٧٢ / ٣ .
٦٣١٣ . تحف العقول : ٣٢٠ .
٦٣١٤ . مكارم الأخلاق : ٢ / ٣٦٨ / ٢٦٦١ .
٦٣١٥ . الزهد للحسين بن سعيد : ٧٨ / ٢١١ .
٦٣١٦ . بحار الأنوار : ٧٧ / ١١٥ / ٨ .
٦٣١٧ . بحار الأنوار : ٩٢ / ٢٥٠ .
٦٣١٨ . غرر الحكم : ١١٣٩ .
٦٣١٩ . غرر الحكم : ١٧٩٧ .
٦٣٢٠ . بحار الأنوار : ٧٧ / ٣٧٨ / ١ .
٦٣٢١ . غرر الحكم : ٢٨٣٩ .
٦٣٢٢ . الترغيب والترهيب : ٣ / ٨٨ / ٣ .
٦٣٢٣ . الكافي : ٦ / ٤٤٥ / ٢ .
٦٣٢٤ . الكافي : ٦ / ٤٤٦ / ٤ .
٦٣٢٥ . الكافي : ٦ / ٤٤٩ / ١ .
٦٣٢٦ . كنز العمّال : ٤١١٧٢ .
٦٣٢٧ . نهج البلاغة : الخطبة ١٩٣ .
٦٣٢٨ . بحار الأنوار : ٧٩ / ٣٠٤ / ١٧ .
٦٣٢٩ . الكافي : ٦ / ٤٤٤ / ١٥ .
٦٣٣٠ . مكارم الأخلاق : ١ / ٢١٨ / ٦٤٢ .
٦٣٣١ . مكارم الأخلاق : ١ / ٢٢٠ / ٦٤٨ .
٦٣٣٢ . المِسحُ : الكساء من الشعر (لسان العرب : ٢ / ٥٩٦) .
٦٣٣٣ . عيون أخبار الرِّضا : ٢ / ١٧٨ / ١ .
٦٣٣٤ . الكافي : ٦ / ٤٦١ / ٥ ؛ كنز العمّال : ٤١١٣٢ .
٦٣٣٥ . كنز العمّال : ٤١١٤٣ .
٦٣٣٦ . سنن أبي داوود : ٤ / ٥٤ / ٤٠٧٦ .
٦٣٣٧ . الكافي: ٦ / ٤٦١ / ٤ .
٦٣٣٨ . كنز العمّال : ٤١٢١٠ .
٦٣٣٩ . كنز العمّال : ٤١٢٠٣ .
٦٣٤٠ . الكافي : ٦ / ٤٥٣ / ١ .
٦٣٤١ . تحف العقول : ١٤ .
٦٣٤٢ . نهج البلاغة : الحكمة ١٧٩ .
٦٣٤٣ . غرر الحكم : ٨٨٧ .
٦٣٤٤ . غرر الحكم : ٧٤٧٨ .
٦٣٤٥ . غرر الحكم : ١٧١٨ .
٦٣٤٦ . بحار الأنوار : ٧٧ / ٢٠٨ / ١ .
٦٣٤٧ . نهج البلاغة : الكتاب ٣١ .
٦٣٤٨ . بحار الأنوار : ٧٨ / ١٠ / ٦٨ .
٦٣٤٩ . بحار الأنوار : ٧٧ / ٢١٢ / ١ .
٦٣٥٠ . غرر الحكم : ٤٩٧٥ .
٦٣٥١ . نهج البلاغة : الكتاب ٥٨ .
٦٣٥٢ . نهج البلاغة : الكتاب ٥٣ .
٦٣٥٣ . تحف العقول : ٣٧ .
٦٣٥٤ . جامع الأخبار : ٢٤٧ / ٦٣١ .
٦٣٥٥ . غرر الحكم : ١٢٨٢ .
٦٣٥٦ . بحار الأنوار : ٧٨ / ٥٦ / ١١٩ .
٦٣٥٧ . نهج البلاغة : الحكمة ٣٩٢ .
٦٣٥٨ . بحار الأنوار : ٧٧ / ٢٣١ / ٢ .
٦٣٥٩ . بحار الأنوار : ٧١ / ٢٨٦ / ٤٢ .
٦٣٦٠ . سنن الترمذي : ٤ / ٦٠٥ / ٢٤٠٧ .
٦٣٦١ . تحف العقول : ٢٩٨ .
٦٣٦٢ . بحار الأنوار : ٧٧ / ٨٥ / ٣ .
٦٣٦٣ . بحار الأنوار : ٧١ / ٢٨٦ / ٤٢ .
٦٣٦٤ . الكافي : ٢ / ١١٤ / ٧ .
٦٣٦٥ . بحار الأنوار : ٧١ / ٢٨٣ / ٣٦ .
٦٣٦٦ . بحار الأنوار : ٧١ / ٢٨٦ / ٤٢ .
٦٣٦٧ . نهج البلاغة: الحكمة ٦٠ .
٦٣٦٨ . بحار الأنوار : ٧١ / ٢٧٧ / ١١ .
٦٣٦٩ . نهج البلاغة : الخطبة ١٧٦ .
٦٣٧٠ . نهج البلاغة : الحكمة ٤٠ .

٦٣٧١ . تحف العقول : ٢٩٨ .

٦٣٧٢ . المؤمنون : ٣ .

٦٣٧٣ . الفرقان : ٧٢ .

٦٣٧٤ . الأمالي للصدوق : ٧٣ / ٤١ .

٦٣٧٥ . بحار الأنوار : ٧٨ / ٩٢ / ١٠١ .

٦٣٧٦ . بحار الأنوار : ٧٨ / ٧ / ٥٩ .

٦٣٧٧ . تحف العقول : ٢١٨ .

٦٣٧٨ . مجمع البيان : ٧ / ١٥٧ .

٦٣٧٩ . المحجّة البيضاء : ٨ / ٥٩ و ٦١ .

٦٣٨٠ . المحجّةالبيضاء: ٨ / ٦٢ .

٦٣٨١ . مكارم الأخلاق : ٢ / ٣١ / ٢٠٦٩ .

٦٣٨٢ . كنز العمّال : ٤٢١٢١ .

٦٣٨٣ . نهج البلاغة: الكتاب ٦٢ .

٦٣٨٤ . غرر الحكم : ٨٤٢٥ .

٦٣٨٥ . الحديد : ٢٠ .

٦٣٨٦ . الجمعة : ١١ .

٦٣٨٧ . نهج البلاغة : الحكمة ٣٧٠ .

٦٣٨٨ . غرر الحكم : ٩٣٧ .

٦٣٨٩ . غرر الحكم : ٥٧٢٩ .

٦٣٩٠ . بحار الأنوار: ٧٨ / ٩ / ٦٦ .

٦٣٩١ . غرر الحكم : ٢١٦٥ .

٦٣٩٢ . غرر الحكم : ٣٣٣٣ .

٦٣٩٣ . غرر الحكم : ٨٤٢٦ .

٦٣٩٤ . نهج البلاغة : الحكمة ٣٣٣ .

٦٣٩٥ . تنبيه الخواطر : ١ / ٥٢ .

٦٣٩٦ . الأُصول الستّة عشر : ٥١ .

٦٣٩٧ . كنز العمّال : ١٠٨١٢ .

٦٣٩٨ . كنز العمّال : ٤٠٦١١ .

٦٣٩٩ . تحف العقول : ١٥١ .

٦٤٠٠ . غرر الحكم : ٩٨١٥ .

٦٤٠١ . الأعراف : ٨٠، ٨١ .

٦٤٠٢ . الترغيب والترهيب : ٣ / ٢٨٥ / ١ .

٦٤٠٣ . بحار الأنوار : ٧٩ / ٧٢ / ٢٤ .

٦٤٠٤ . نهج البلاغة : الحكمة ٢٥٢ .

٦٤٠٥ . بحار الأنوار : ٧٩ / ٧٢ / ٢٧ .

٦٤٠٦ . علل الشرائع : ٥٤٧ / ١ .

٦٤٠٧ . نهج البلاغة : الخطبة ١٨٩ .

٦٤٠٨ . نهج البلاغة : الخطبة ١٩٢ .

٦٤٠٩ . نهج البلاغة : الحكمة ٤٣٤ .

٦٤١٠ . قال الرضيّ : ومن النّاس من يروي هذا للرسول ﷺ ، وممّا يقوّي أنّه من كلام أمير المؤمنين ﵇ ما حكاه ثعلبٌ عن ابن الأعرابيّ ، قال المأمون : لولا أنّ عليّاً قال : «اُخبر تـقله» لقلت : اقله تخبر .

٦٤١١ . غرر الحكم : ٦٢٠٦ .

٦٤١٢ . غرر الحكم : ١١٠٢٦ .

٦٤١٣ . غرر الحكم : ٤٦٦٤ .

٦٤١٤ . الكافي : ٨ / ١٧٦ / ١٩٦ .

٦٤١٥ . الخصال : ١٠٣ / ٦٢ .

٦٤١٦ . كنز العمّال : ٨٣٣١ .

٦٤١٧ . المحجّة البيضاء : ٥ / ٢٨٤ .

٦٤١٨ . تنبيه الخواطر : ٢ / ١٢٢ .

٦٤١٩ . سنن ابن ماجة : ٢ / ١٢٣٢ / ٣٧٤٢ .

٦٤٢٠ . كنز العمّال : ٨٣٣٩ .

٦٤٢١ . تحف العقول : ٢٠٨ .

٦٤٢٢ . غرر الحكم : ٣٩٨٣ و ٣٩٨٤ .

٦٤٢٣ . نهج البلاغة : الخطبة ٢١٦ .

٦٤٢٤ . نهج البلاغة : الحكمة ١٠٠ .

٦٤٢٥ . الكافي : ٢ / ٢٣١ / ٣ .

٦٤٢٦ . مكارم الأخلاق : ٢ / ٣٥٣ / ٢٦٦٠ .

٦٤٢٧ . غررالحكم : ٩٠٤٢ .

٦٤٢٨ . تنبيه الخواطر : ٢ / ١٧ .

٦٤٢٩ . نهج البلاغة : الكتاب : ٥٣ .

٦٤٣٠ . تحف العقول : ٢٨٤ .

٦٤٣١ . أعلام الدين : ٣١٣ .

٦٤٣٢ . تحف العقول : ٤٦ .

٦٤٣٣ . الأمالي للصدوق : ٥١٣ / ٧٠٧ .

٦٤٣٤ . النجم : ٣٢ .

٦٤٣٥ . معاني الأخبار : ٢٤٣ / ١ .

٦٤٣٦ . النوادر للراوندي : ١٠٧ / ٨٦ .

٦٤٣٧ . الأحزاب : ٣٥ .

٦٤٣٨ . مجمع البيان : ٨ / ٥٦٠ .

٦٤٣٩ . هكذا في المصدر ، والظاهر «وربّينا لكم أ ولادكم» .

٦٤٤٠ . الدرّ المنثور : ٢ / ٥١٨ .

٦٤٤١ . الترغيب والترهيب : ٣ / ٧٦ / ٦ .

٦٤٤٢ . نهج البلاغة : الحكمة ٢٣٤ .

٦٤٤٣ . إرشاد القلوب : ١ / ١٧٥ .

٦٤٤٤ . فردوس : ٢ / ٢٣٠ / ٣١٠٨ .

٦٤٤٥ . كنز العمال : ١٦ / ٣٩٨ / ٤٥٠٩٠ .

٦٤٤٦ . النوادر للراوندي : ١١٤ / ١٠٩ .

٦٤٤٧ . مستطرفات السرائر : ١٤٣ / ٨ .

٦٤٤٨ . الكافي : ٥ / ٣٢٠ / ١ .

٦٤٤٩ . أعطى الإسلام الأهميّة البالغة للحياة العائليّة ، واهتمّ اهتماماً كبيراً بحفظ حدودها واحترامها . ولذلك فقد قيّد كلّ اللذات والأفعال الجنسيّة بما يتناسب مع هذا الأمر الأساسي ؛ وذلك بهدف صرف الرجال عن الاهتمام بغير زوجاتهم ، وحثّهم على اعطاء الحظّ الوافر من الحبّ والشوق وإبراز العلاقة لهنّ ، وهذا هو الحبّ الممدوح والذي أكّد عليه الرسول الأكرمﷺ . ومن جهة أخرى فالإسلام يريد من الرجال ألّا يقعوا في فخّ الشيطان وحبائله وأن يقطعوا رغباتهم عن أن تنال غير زوجاتهم ؛ وإلّا سيقعون كلّ يوم بحبّ امرأة ، وبما أنّهم لا يستطيعون نيل مرادهم فستكون حياتهم عرضةً للخيبة والضياع ، أو أنّهم يتورّطون في الحرام ويكون مصيرهم الهلاك والخسران .

٦٤٥٠ . الكافي : ٥ / ٥١٥ / ٥ .

٦٤٥١ . الخصال : ١١٣ / ٩١ .

٦٤٥٢ . غرر الحكم : ٢٧٢١ .

٦٤٥٣ . كنز العمّال : ٨٧٦٣ .

٦٤٥٤ . تحف العقول : ٢٢٣ .

٦٤٥٥ . تحف العقول : ٢٢٣ .

٦٤٥٦ . غرر الحكم : ٤٢٠١ .

٦٤٥٧ . غرر الحكم : ٤٢٢٤ .

٦٤٥٨ . تحف العقول : ٢٢٥ .

٦٤٥٩ . تحف العقول : ٣٥٩ .

٦٤٦٠ . الترغيب والترهيب : ٤ / ٢٩٢ / ٥٦ .

٦٤٦١ . الترغيب والترهيب : ٤ / ٢٩٢ / ٥٥ .

٦٤٦٢ . الكافي : ٣ / ١١٤ / ٦ .

٦٤٦٣ . الكافي : ٣ / ١١٤ / ٧ .

٦٤٦٤ . الكافي : ٣ / ١١٥ / ١ .

٦٤٦٥ . الدعوات : ١٦٧ / ٤٦٢ .

٦٤٦٦ . الخصال : ٦٣٠ / ١٠ .

٦٤٦٧ . غرر الحكم : ٨٥٤٥ .

٦٤٦٨ . غرر الحكم : ٨٦١٢ .

٦٤٦٩ . الدعوات : ١٣٤ / ٣٣٤ .

٦٤٧٠ . تنبيه الخواطر : ٢ / ٧ .

٦٤٧١ . الدعوات: ١٧٢ / ٤٨٢ .

٦٤٧٢ . مشكاة الأنوار : ٤٨٧ / ١٦٢٦ .

٦٤٧٣ . الترغيب والترهيب : ٤ / ٣١٧ / ٣ .

٦٤٧٤ . كنز العمّال : ٢٥١٤١ .

٦٤٧٥ . كنز العمّال : ٢٥١٤٣ .

٦٤٧٦ . الكافي : ٣ / ١٢٠ / ٢ .

٦٤٧٧ . كنز العمّال : ٢٥١٣٩ .

٦٤٧٨ . الكافي : ٣ / ١١٨ / ٦ .

٦٤٧٩ . الكافي : ٣ / ١١٨ / ٢ .

٦٤٨٠ . الكافي : ٣ / ١١٨ / ٤ .

٦٤٨١ . الكافي : ٣ / ١١٨ / ٣ .

٦٤٨٢ . منية المريد : ١٧١ .

٦٤٨٣ . الأمالي للصدوق : ٧٣ / ٤١ .

٦٤٨٤ . الكافي : ٢ / ٣٠٠ / ١ .

٦٤٨٥ . نهج البلاغة : الحكمة ٣٦٢ .

٦٤٨٦ . غرر الحكم : ٥٦٣٤ .

٦٤٨٧ . معاني الأخبار : ٣٨١ / ٩ .

٦٤٨٨ . أعلام الدين : ٣١١ .

٦٤٨٩ . تحف العقول : ٤٨٦ .

٦٤٩٠ . شرح نهج البلاغة : ٦ / ٣٣٠ .

٦٤٩١ . تحف العقول : ٤٩ .

٦٤٩٢ . الواقعة : ٣٥ و ٣٦ .

٦٤٩٣ . تنبيه الخواطر : ١ / ١١٢ .

٦٤٩٤ . الكافي : ٢ / ٦٦٣ / ٤ ، الرَّفَثُ : الفحش من القول (مجمع البحرين : ٢ / ٧١٦) ، وفي بعض النسخ «يحبّ المداعبة» . (كما في هامشه) .

٦٤٩٥ . الكافي : ٢ / ٦٦٣ / ٢ .

٦٤٩٦ . المداعبة : المُمازحة (لسان العرب : ١ / ٣٧٥) . أي فلا تفعلوا ما تفعلون من قلّة المداعبة ، بل كونوا على حدّ الوسط (كما في هامش المصدر) ، وفي مكارم الأخلاق: ١ / ٥٨ / ٤٧ «هلّا تفعلوا» وهو الأصوب .

٦٤٩٧ . الكافي : ٢ / ٦٦٣ / ٣ .

٦٤٩٨ . مكارم الأخلاق : ٢ / ٣٢١ / ٢٦٥٦ .

٦٤٩٩ . الأمالي للصدوق : ٣٤٤ / ٤١٢ .

٦٥٠٠ . نهج البلاغة : الحكمة ٤٥٠ .

٦٥٠١ . تحف العقول : ٨٦ .

٦٥٠٢ . بحار الأنوار : ٧٧ / ٢٣٥ / ٣ .

٦٥٠٣ . هزل في كلامه هزلاً : مزح (المصباح المنير : ٦٣٨) .

٦٥٠٤ . تحف العقول : ٨٥ .

٦٥٠٥ . الكافي : ٢ / ٦٦٥ / ١٥ .

٦٥٠٦ . الأمالي للصدوق : ٦٣٦ / ٨٥٣ .

٦٥٠٧ . الكافي : ٢ / ٦٦٤ / ٩ .

٦٥٠٨ . آل عمران : ٢٦ .

٦٥٠٩ . النور : ٤٢ .

٦٥١٠ . كنز العمّال : ٤٥٢٤٤ .

٦٥١١ . نهج البلاغة : الخطبة ٦٥ .

٦٥١٢ . غرر الحكم : ١٠٣٢١ .

٦٥١٣ . غرر الحكم : ٢١٨٤ .

٦٥١٤ . الخصال : ٢٢٣ / ٥١ .

٦٥١٥ . غرر الحكم : ٥٠٠٥ .

٦٥١٦ . غرر الحكم : ٣٢٠٦ .

٦٥١٧ . غرر الحكم : ٣٣٥٠ .

٦٥١٨ . غرر الحكم : ٣٢٦١ .

٦٥١٩ . تحف العقول : ٣١٩ .

٦٥٢٠ . غرر الحكم : ٤٩٤٠ .

٦٥٢١ . غرر الحكم : ٩٠١٦ و ٩٠١٧ .

٦٥٢٢ . غرر الحكم : ٤١١٨ .

٦٥٢٣ . فاطر : ١ .

٦٥٢٤ . تفسير القمّي : ٢ / ٢٠٦ .

٦٥٢٥ . نهج البلاغة : الخطبة ٩١ .

٦٥٢٦ . الاختصاص : ١٠٩ .

٦٥٢٧ . بحار الأنوار : ٥٩ / ١٧٦ / ٧ .

٦٥٢٨ . نهج البلاغة : الخطبة ١٠٩ .

٦٥٢٩ . تفسير القمّي : ٢ / ٢٠٦ .

٦٥٣٠ . الأنعام : ٦١ .

٦٥٣١ . الرعد : ١١ .

٦٥٣٢ . بحار الأنوار : ٥٩ / ١٧٩ / ١٦ .

٦٥٣٣ . انفطار : ١٠ .

٦٥٣٤ . انفطار : ١١ .

٦٥٣٥ . تفسير القمّي : ٢ / ٤٠٩ .

٦٥٣٦ . البراجم : هي العقد التي في ظهور الأصابع يجتمع فيها
الوسخ ،الواحدة «بُرجُمة» بالضمّ (النهاية : ١ / ١١٣) .

٦٥٣٧ . النوادر للراوندي : ١٩٢ / ٣٤٩ .

٦٥٣٨ . الكافي : ٣ / ٣٩٣ / ٢٦ .

٦٥٣٩ . الملك : ٢ .

٦٥٤٠ . كنز العمّال : ٤٢١٢٣ .

٦٥٤١ . كنز العمّال : ٤٢٧٢١ .

٦٥٤٢ . نهج البلاغة: الخطبة ١٥٦ .

٦٥٤٣ . غرر الحكم : ٣١٩ .

٦٥٤٤ . في نسخة «ويربّيهم» وفي نسخ أُخرى «ويوصّيهم» . (كما في هامش المصدر) .

٦٥٤٥ . التوحيد : ٤٠١ / ٤ .

٦٥٤٦ . آل عمران : ١٨٥ .

٦٥٤٧ . الجمعة : ٨ .

٦٥٤٨ . الأعراف : ٣٤ .

٦٥٤٩ . الكافي : ٣ / ٢٦٢ / ٤٤ .

٦٥٥٠ . بحار الأنوار : ٦ / ١٣٧ / ٤٠ .

٦٥٥١ . نهج البلاغة : الكتاب ٣١ .

٦٥٥٢ . نهج البلاغة : الكتاب ٢٧ .

٦٥٥٣ . كتاب من لا يحضره الفقيه : ١ / ١٩٤ / ٥٩٦ .

٦٥٥٤ . نهج البلاغة : الحكمة ٢٩ .

٦٥٥٥ . نهج البلاغة : الحكمة ١٨٧ .

٦٥٥٦ . بحار الأنوار : ٧١ / ٢٦٣ / ٢ .

٦٥٥٧ . معاني الأخبار : ٢٨٩ / ٤ .

٦٥٥٨ . معاني الأخبار : ٢٨٩ / ٦ .

٦٥٥٩ . معاني الأخبار : ٢٨٩ / ٥ .

٦٥٦٠ . النحل : ٣٢ .

٦٥٦١ . كنز العمّال : ٤٢١٣٦ .

٦٥٦٢ . كنز العمّال : ٤٢١١٠ .

٦٥٦٣ . يونس : ٦٤ .

٦٥٦٤ . بحار الأنوار : ٦ / ١٩١ / ٣٦ .

٦٥٦٥ . معاني الأخبار : ٢٨٩ / ٧ .

٦٥٦٦ . بحار الأنوار : ٨٢ / ١٦٧ / ٣ .

٦٥٦٧ . كنز العمّال : ٤٢١٠٥ .

٦٥٦٨ . في بحار الأنوار : (٧٧ / ٢٠٥) «واجعله أمامك حيث (تراه حتّى) يأتيك وقد أخذت منه حذرك» .

٦٥٦٩ . نهج البلاغة : الكتاب ٣١ .

٦٥٧٠ . بحار الأنوار : ٦ / ١٣٣ / ٣٢ .

٦٥٧١ . بحار الأنوار: ٨٢ / ١٦٨ / ٣ .

٦٥٧٢ . بحار الأنوار: ٧٨ / ٣٧٠ / ٤ .

٦٥٧٣ . بحار الأنوار: ٧٧ / ١٧١ / ٧ .

٦٥٧٤ . نهج البلاغة: الخطبة ٦٤ .

٦٥٧٥ . غرر الحكم: ٣٤٦٨ .

٦٥٧٦ . غرر الحكم: ٦٢٥٣ .

٦٥٧٧ . نهج البلاغة: الخطبة ١٩٠ .

٦٥٧٨ . الكافي: ٣ / ٢٥٩ / ٣٠ .

٦٥٧٩ . الأمالي للصدوق: ١٧٢ / ١٧٣ .

٦٥٨٠ . الترغيب والترهيب: ٤ / ٢٥٧ / ٥٤ .

٦٥٨١ . كنز العمّال: ٤٢١٥٣ .

٦٥٨٢ . نهج البلاغة: الكتاب ٦٩ .

٦٥٨٣ . كشف الغمّة: ٣ / ٤٢ .

٦٥٨٤ . ق: ١٩ .

٦٥٨٥ . كنز العمّال: ٤٢١٥٨ .

٦٥٨٦ . الأمالي للطوسي: ٤٥٣ / ١٠١١ .

٦٥٨٧ . نهج البلاغة: الخطبة ٢٢١ .

٦٥٨٨ . الخصال: ١٣ / ٤٧ .

٦٥٨٩ . معاني الأخبار: ٣٩٠ / ٢٩ .

٦٥٩٠ . صحيفة الإمام الرّضا: ٨٦ / ٢٠٣ .

٦٥٩١ . الكافي: ٣ / ١٢٧ / ٢ .

٦٥٩٢ . تفسير القمّي: ٢ / ٢٦٥ .

٦٥٩٣ . الكافي: ٣ / ١١٢ / ٥ .

٦٥٩٤ . كنز العمّال: ٤٢٧٧٥ .

٦٥٩٥ . الكافي: ٣ / ٢٦١ / ٣٩ .

٦٥٩٦ . النوادر للراوندي: ٩٢ / ٢٩ .

٦٥٩٧ . الأمالي للطوسي: ٣٨٣ / ٨٢٧ .

٦٥٩٨ . الدعوات: ٢٥٩ / ٧٣٦ .

٦٥٩٩ . الكافي: ٣ / ١٧٣ / ٣ .

٦٦٠٠ . علل الشرائع: ٣٠١ / ١ .

٦٦٠١ . الكافي: ٣ / ١٣٨ / ٢ .

٦٦٠٢ . كنز العمّال: ٤٢٣٨٥ .

٦٦٠٣ . كنز العمّال: ٤٢٣٨٦ .

٦٦٠٤ . كنز العمّال: ٤٢٩١٦ .

٦٦٠٥ . كنز العمّال: ٤٢٧٦١ .

٦٦٠٦ . كتاب من لا يحضره الفقيه: ١ / ١٨٥ / ٥٥٥ .

٦٦٠٧ . الكهف: ٤٦ .

٦٦٠٨ . الكافي: ٢ / ٣١٦ / ٦ .

٦٦٠٩ . الترغيب والترهيب: ٤ / ١٨٢ / ٦٨ .

٦٦١٠ . نهج البلاغة: الحكمة ٥٨ .

٦٦١١ . غرر الحكم: ٥٧٧ .

٦٦١٢ . الفجر: ٢٠ .

٦٦١٣ . المحجّة البيضاء: ٧ / ٣٢٨ .

٦٦١٤ . غرر الحكم: ١٤٢٧ .

٦٦١٥ . غرر الحكم: ٤٨٧٦ .

٦٦١٦ . تنبيه الخواطر: ١ / ١٥٨ .

٦٦١٧ . نهج البلاغة: الحكمة ٥٦ .

٦٦١٨ . الكافي: ١ / ٢٠ / ١٢ .

٦٦١٩ . الكافي: ٥ / ٧٢ / ٥ .

٦٦٢٠ . التوبة: ٣٤ .

٦٦٢١ . الكافي: ٢ / ١٣٥ / ٢١ .

٦٦٢٢ . كنز العمّال: ٦١٣٩ .

٦٦٢٣ . غرر الحكم: ٧١٠٩ .

٦٦٢٤ . الدرّة الباهرة: ٢٤ .

٦٦٢٥ . ولنعم ما قيل في تفسير الزّهد أنّه «ليس الزُّهدُ أن لا تَملِكَ شيئاً ، بل الزُّهدُ أن لا يَملِكَكَ شيءٌ» .

٦٦٢٦ . الأمالي للطوسي: ٣٠٢ / ٦٠٠ .

٦٦٢٧ . مستدرك الوسائل: ١٢ / ١٧٤ / ١٣٨١٠ .

٦٦٢٨ . الخصال: ٢٨٢ / ٢٩ .

٦٦٢٩ . الأمالي للطوسي: ١٨٢ / ٣٠٦ .

٦٦٣٠ . بحار الأنوار: ١٠٣ / ١٣ / ٦٣ .

٦٦٣١ . تحف العقول: ٩٤ .

٦٦٣٢ . المحاسن: ٢ / ٤٤٥ / ٢٥٢٨ .

٦٦٣٣ . تحف العقول: ٣٢١ .

٦٦٣٤ . كنز العمّال: ١٦١٤٧ .

٦٦٣٥ . بحار الأنوار: ٧١ / ٣٥٦ / ١٧ .

٦٦٣٦ . غرر الحكم: ٥٠٨ .

٦٦٣٧ . غرر الحكم: ١٨٣٨ .

٦٦٣٨ . نهج البلاغة: الكتاب ٢١ .

٦٦٣٩ . بحار الأنوار: ٧٨ / ٧ / ٦٠ .

٦٦٤٠ . بحار الأنوار: ٧٨ / ١٢ / ٧٠ .

٦٦٤١ . كتاب من لا يحضره الفقيه: ٢ / ٥٧ / ١٦٩٣ .

٦٦٤٢ . تنبيه الخواطر: ٢ / ١٨٢ .

٦٦٤٣ . الكافي: ١ / ١٦٨ / ١ .

٦٦٤٤ . النحل : ٣٦ .

٦٦٤٥ . الكافي : ٨ / ٣٨٦ / ٥٨٦ .

٦٦٤٦ . الجمعة : ٢ .

٦٦٤٧ . كنز العمّال : ٣١٩٦٩ .

٦٦٤٨ . الطبقات الكبرىٰ : ١ / ١٩٣ .

٦٦٤٩ . نهج البلاغة : الخطبة ١ .

٦٦٥٠ . الحديد : ٢٥ .

٦٦٥١ . البقرة : ٢١٣ .

٦٦٥٢ . نهج البلاغة : الخطبة ١٩٢ ، اُنظر تمام الكلام .

٦٦٥٣ . التوحيد : ٤٥ / ٤ .

٦٦٥٤ . الشورىٰ : ٥١ .

٦٦٥٥ . الصافّات : ١٤٧ .

٦٦٥٦ . البقرة : ١٢٤ .

٦٦٥٧ . الكافي : ١ / ١٧٤ / ١ .

٦٦٥٨ . الخصال : ٥٢٤ / ١٣ .

٦٦٥٩ . الأحقاف : ٣٥ .

٦٦٦٠ . بحار الأنوار : ١١ / ٣٣ / ٢٥ .

٦٦٦١ . الكافي : ٢ / ١٧ / ٢ ، اُنظر تمام الحديث .

٦٦٦٢ . بحار الأنوار : ٧٧ / ١٤٠ / ١٩ .

٦٦٦٣ . بحار الأنوار : ١٦ / ١٧٢ / ٧ .

٦٦٦٤ . تنبيه الخواطر : ١ / ٢٩ .

٦٦٦٥ . الطبقات الكبرىٰ : ١ / ٣٧٦ .

٦٦٦٦ . نهج البلاغة : الخطبة ١٩٢ .

٦٦٦٧ . علل الشرائع : ٣٢ / ٢ .

٦٦٦٨ . الكافي : ٤ / ٣٩ / ٤ .

٦٦٦٩ . تحف العقول : ٤٤٢ .

٦٦٧٠ . الكافي : ٦ / ٥١٠ / ١ .

٦٦٧١ . النساء : ١ .

٦٦٧٢ . نهج البلاغة : الخطبة ١ .

٦٦٧٣ . أي خلقته .

٦٦٧٤ . نهج البلاغة : الخطبة ٩١ .

٦٦٧٥ . علل الشرائع : ١٤ / ١ .

٦٦٧٦ . بحار الأنوار : ١١ / ١١٦ / ٤٦ .

٦٦٧٧ . قرب الإسناد : ٣٦٦ / ١٣١١ .

٦٦٧٨ . مريم : ٥٦ و ٥٧ .

٦٦٧٩ . وفي خبر : ... أنزل على إدريس خمسين صحيفة ، وهو اُخنوخ ، وهو أوّل من خطّ بالقلم . (بحار الأنوار : ١١ / ٦٠ / ٦٨) .

٦٦٨٠ . بحار الأنوار : ١١ / ٢٧٧ / ٥ .

٦٦٨١ . كنز العمّال : ٣٢٢٦٩ .

٦٦٨٢ . بحار الأنوار : ١١ / ٢٨٤ / ١٢ .

٦٦٨٣ . الأعراف : ٥٩ .

٦٦٨٤ . يونس : ٧١ .

٦٦٨٥ . كنز العمّال : ٣٢٣٩١ .

٦٦٨٦ . المستدرك على الصحيحين : ٢ / ٥٩٥ / ٤٠٠٥ .

٦٦٨٧ . هود : ٤٠ .

٦٦٨٨ . بحار الأنوار : ١١ / ٣٣٦ / ٦٤ .

٦٦٨٩ . الكافي : ٨ / ٢٨٣ / ٤٢٥ .

٦٦٩٠ . كمال الدين : ٢١٤ / ٢ .

٦٦٩١ . تفسير الميزان : ١٠ / ٢٧٠ .

٦٦٩٢ . الأعراف : ٦٥ .

٦٦٩٣ . الكافي : ٨ / ١١٥ / ٩٢ .

٦٦٩٤ . كمال الدين : ١٣٦ / ٥ .

٦٦٩٥ . الأحقاف : جمع حِقْف : من الرمل، والعرب تسمّي الرمل المعوّج حقافاً ... ، والأحقاف المذكور في الكتاب العزيز وادٍ بين عُمان وأرض مهرة ، قال ابن إسحاق : رمال فيما بين عُمان إلىٰ حضرموت ، وقال قتادة الأحقاف : رمال مشرفة علَى البحر بالشحر من أرض اليمن . وقال الضحّاك : الأحقاف جبل بالشام . (معجم البلدان : ١ / ١١٥) .

٦٦٩٦ . تفسير الميزان : ١٠ / ٣٠٧ .

٦٦٩٧ . الأعراف : ٧٣ .

٦٦٩٨ . الشعراء : ١٥٧ .

٦٦٩٩ . نهج البلاغة : الخطبة : ٢٠١ .

٦٧٠٠ . بحار الأنوار : ١١ / ٣٧٩ / ٤ .

٦٧٠١ . تفسير الميزان : ١٠ / ٣١٧ .

٦٧٠٢ . البقرة : ١٢٤ .

٦٧٠٣ . كنز العمّال : ٣٢٢٨٨ .

٦٧٠٤ . علل الشرائع : ٣٥ / ٤ .

٦٧٠٥ . الدرّ المنثور : ١ / ٢٨٢ .

٦٧٠٦ . علل الشرائع : ٣٤ / ٢ .

٦٧٠٧ . الكافي : ١ / ١٧٥ / ٢ .

٦٧٠٨ . وقد تقدّم استفادة ذلك من دعائه المنقول في سورة إبراهيم . (كما في هامش المصدر) .

٦٧٠٩ . تفسير الميزان : ٧ / ٢١٥ .

٦٧١٠ . الأعراف : ٨٠ .

٦٧١١ . بحار الأنوار : ١٢ / ١٥٢ / ٥ .

٦٧١٢ . بحار الأنوار : ١٢ / ١٥٧ / ٨ .

٦٧١٣ . العنكبوت : ٢٦ .

٦٧١٤ . الشعراء : ١٦٧ .

٦٧١٥ . النمل : ٥٦ .

٦٧١٦ . هود : ٨٠ .

٦٧١٧ . تفسير الميزان : ١٠ / ٣٥٢ .

٦٧١٨ . البقرة : ١٣٢ ، ١٣٣ .

٦٧١٩ . الأمالي للطوسي : ٤٥٧ / ١٠٢١ .

٦٧٢٠ . كنز العمّال : ٣٢٤٠٠ .

٦٧٢١ . كنز العمّال : ٣٢٤٠٤ .

٦٧٢٢ . يوسف : ١٣ .

٦٧٢٣ . نور الثقلين : ٢ / ٤١٥ / ٢٠ .

٦٧٢٤ . الأنبياء : ٨٣ ، ٨٤ .

٦٧٢٥ . ما بين المعقوفين سقط من المصدر و أضفناه من الفردوس : ٣ / ١٧٤ / ٤٤٦٨ .

٦٧٢٦ . كنز العمّال : ٣٢٣١٨ .

٦٧٢٧ . كنز العمّال : ٣٢٣١٦ .

٦٧٢٨ . الدعوات : ١٦٥ / ٤٥٦ .

٦٧٢٩ . علل الشرائع : ٧٥ / ٣ .

٦٧٣٠ . علل الشرائع : ٧٥ / ٤ .

٦٧٣١ . قصص الأنبياء : ١٣٩ / ١٤٧ .

٦٧٣٢ . الأعراف : ٨٥_٩٢ .

٦٧٣٣ . قصص الأنبياء : ١٤٥ / ١٥٧ .

٦٧٣٤ . تفسير الميزان : ١٠ / ٣٧٧ .

٦٧٣٥ . الأنبياء : ٤٨ .

٦٧٣٦ . النساء : ١٦٤ .

٦٧٣٧ . الأمالي للطوسي : ١٦٥ / ٢٧٥ .

٦٧٣٨ . بحار الأنوار : ١٣ / ٧ / ٥ .

٦٧٣٩ . الطبقات الكبرى : ١ / ٤١٧ .

٦٧٤٠ . نهج البلاغة : الخطبة ١٨٢ .

٦٧٤١ . القصص : ٢٤ .

٦٧٤٢ . نهج البلاغة : الخطبة ١٦٠ .

٦٧٤٣ . بحار الأنوار : ١٣ / ٤٧ / ١٥ .

٦٧٤٤ . تفسير الميزان : ١٦ / ٤٠ .

٦٧٤٥ . الكهف : ٦٠_٨٢ .

٦٧٤٦ . بحار الأنوار : ١٣ / ٢٨٤ / ١ .

٦٧٤٧ . علل الشرائع : ٥٩ / ١ .

٦٧٤٨ . بحار الأنوار : ١٣ / ٣٠٣ / ٢٥ .

٦٧٤٩ . كمال الدين : ٣٩٠ / ٤ .

٦٧٥٠ . تفسير الميزان : ١٣ / ٣٥٠ .

٦٧٥١ . مريم : ٥٤ ، ٥٥ .

٦٧٥٢ . الفروة : جلدة الرأس . (القاموس المحيط : ٤ / ٣٧٣) .

٦٧٥٣ . علل الشرائع : ٧٧ / ٢ .

٦٧٥٤ . علل الشرائع : ٧٨ / ٣ .

٦٧٥٥ . تفسير القمّي : ٢ / ٥١ .

٦٧٥٦ . قال العلّامة الطباطبائيّ رضوان الله عليه بعد نقل الحديث : وعده ﷺ - وهو أن يثبت في مكانه في انتظار صاحبه - كان مطلقاً لم يقيّده بساعة أو يوم ونحوه ، فألزمه مقامُ الصِّدق أن يفي به بإطلاقه ، ويصبّر نفسه في المكان الذي وعد صاحبه أن يقيم فيه حتّىٰ يرجع إليه .

وصفة الوفاء - كسائر الصفات النفسانيّة من الحبّ والإرادة والعزم والإيمان والثقة والتسليم - ذات مراتب مختلفة باختلاف العلم واليقين ، فكما أنّ من الإيمان ما يجتمع مع أيّ خطيئة وإثم وهو أنزل مراتبه ولا يزال ينمو ويصفو حتّىٰ يخلص من كلّ شرك خفيّ فلا يتعلّق القلب بشيء غير الله ولو بالتفات إلىٰ من دونه - وهو أعلىٰ مراتبه - كذلك الوفاء بالوعد ذو مراتب ؛ فمن مراتبه في المقال مثلاً : إقامة ساعة أو ساعتين حتّىٰ تعرض حاجة اُخرىٰ توجب الانصراف إليها ، وهو الذي يصدق عليه الوفاء عرفاً . وأعلىٰ منه مرتبة : الإقامة بالمكان حتّى ييأس من رجوع الصديق إليه عادة بمجيء اللّيل ونحوه ، فيقيّد به إطلاق الوعد . وأعلىٰ منه مرتبة : الأخذ بإطلاق القول والإقامة حتّىٰ يرجع وإن طال الزمان . فالنفوس القويّة التي تراقب قولها وفعلها لا تلقي من القول إلّا ما في وسعها أن تصدّقه بالفعل ، ثمّ إذا لفظت لم يصرفها عن إتمام الكلمة وإنفاذ العزيمة أيّ صارف .

وفي الرواية : أنّ النبيّ ﷺ وعد بعض أصحابه بمكّة أن ينتظره عند الكعبة حتّىٰ يرجع إليه ، فمضى الرجل لشأنه ونسي الأمر ، فبقي ﷺ ثلاثة أيّام هناك ينتظره ، فاطّلع بعض الناس عليه فأخبر الرجل بذلك فجاء واعتذر إليه ، وهذا مقام الصدّيقين لا يقولون إلّا ما يفعلون . الميزان في تفسير القرآن : ١٤ / ٦٥ .

٦٧٥٧ . الأنعام : ٨٦ .

٦٧٥٨ . الاحتجاج : ٢ / ٤٠٧ / ٣٠٧ .

٦٧٥٩ . الأنبياء : ٨٥، ٨٦ .

٦٧٦٠ . ص : ٤٨ .

٦٧٦١ . قصص الأنبياء : ٢١٣ / ٢٧٧ .

٦٧٦٢ . ص : ١٧ـ٢٦ .

٦٧٦٣ . الأنبياء : ١٠٥ .

٦٧٦٤ . كتاب من لا يحضره الفقيه : ٣ / ١٦٢ / ٣٥٩٤ .

٦٧٦٥ . الأمالي للصدوق : ٢٦٣ / ٢٨٠ .

٦٧٦٦ . بحار الأنوار : ١٤ / ٤٠ / ٢٦ .

٦٧٦٧ . كنز العمّال : ٣٢٣٢٢ .

٦٧٦٨ . كنز العمّال : ٣٢٣٢٣ .

٦٧٦٩ . الخصال : ٢٤٨ / ١١٠ .

٦٧٧٠ . النمل : ١٦ .

٦٧٧١ . بحار الأنوار : ١٤ / ٩٥ / ٣ .

٦٧٧٢ . الخصال : ٢٤١ / ٩١ .

٦٧٧٣ . نهج البلاغة : الخطبة ١٨٢ .

٦٧٧٤ . الدعوات : ١٤٢ / ٣٦٣ .

٦٧٧٥ . مستطرفات السرائر : ٤١ / ٧ .

٦٧٧٦ . علل الشرائع : ٧٣ / ٢ .

٦٧٧٧ . الأنبياء : ٨٩ و ٩٠ .

٦٧٧٨ . كنز العمّال : ٣٢٣٣٠ .

٦٧٧٩ . كنز العمّال : ٣٢٣٢٩ .

٦٧٨٠ . مريم : ٧ و ١٢ـ١٥ .

٦٧٨١ . كنز العمّال : ٣٢٤٢٥ .

٦٧٨٢ . الأمالي للطوسي : ٣٤٠ / ٦٩٢ .

٦٧٨٣ . الكافي : ٢ / ٦٦٥ / ٢٠ .

٦٧٨٤ . آل عمران : ٥٩ .

٦٧٨٥ . النساء : ١٥٧ـ١٥٩ .

٦٧٨٦ . في المصدر : أبيت وليس معي شيء ، وأصبحت وليس لي شيء . (كما في هامش بحار الأنوار) .

٦٧٨٧ . بحار الأنوار : ١٤ / ٢٣٩ / ١٧ .

٦٧٨٨ . الخصال : ٥٢٤ / ١٣ .

٦٧٨٩ . كنز العمّال : ٣٢٣٥٧ .

٦٧٩٠ . كنز العمّال : ٣٢٣٥٨ .

٦٧٩١ . المبطَّن : الضامر البطن (النهاية : ١ / ١٣٧) .

٦٧٩٢ . كنز العمّال : ٣٢٣٥٩ .

٦٧٩٣ . نهج البلاغة : الخطبة ١٦٠ .

٦٧٩٤ . مريم : ٣١ .

٦٧٩٥ . معاني الأخبار : ٢١٢ / ١ .

٦٧٩٦ . فكان هذا الكلام منه ﷺ كبراعة الاستهلال بالنسبة إلى ما سينهض علّى البغي والظلم ، وإحياء شريعة موسى ﷺ وتقويمه ، وتجديد ما اندرس من معارفه ، وبيان ما اختلفوا فيه من آياته .

٦٧٩٧ . تفسير الميزان : ٣ / ٢٧٩ .

٦٧٩٨ . البقرة : ٢٥٩ .

٦٧٩٩ . الكافي : ٨ / ١٢٣ / ٩٤ .

٦٨٠٠ . البقرة : ٢٥٩ .

٦٨٠١ . الاحتجاج : ٢ / ٢٣٠ / ٢٢٣ .

٦٨٠٢ . الصافّات : ١٣٩ـ١٤٨ .

٦٨٠٣ . كنز العمّال : ٣٢٤٢٢ .

٦٨٠٤ . بحار الأنوار : ١٤ / ٣٨٢ / ٢ .

٦٨٠٥ . تفسير الميزان : ١٧ / ١٦٥ .

٦٨٠٦ . الفتح : ٢٩ .

٦٨٠٧ . التوبة : ١٢٨ .

٦٨٠٨ . الأحزاب : ٤٥ و ٤٦ .

٦٨٠٩ . معاني الأخبار : ٥٢ / ٢ .

٦٨١٠ . الأحزاب : ٤٠ .

٦٨١١ . الطبقات الكبرىٰ : ١ / ١٠٥ .

٦٨١٢ . الكافي : ١ / ٢٦٩ / ٣ .

٦٨١٣ . الكافي : ٢ / ١٧ / ٢ .

٦٨١٤ . مكارم الأخلاق : ١ / ٥١ / ١٩ .

٦٨١٥ . الطبقات الكبرىٰ : ١ / ١٩٢ .

٦٨١٦ . البقرة : ١٢٩ .

٦٨١٧ . كنز العمّال : ٣١٨٣٣ .

٦٨١٨ . بحار الأنوار : ٨ / ٤٨ / ٥١ .

٦٨١٩ . كنز العمّال : ٣١٨٨٣ .

٦٨٢٠ . الكافي : ٢ / ٦٠٠ / ٤ .

٦٨٢١ . كنز العمّال : ٣١٩٦٤ .

٦٨٢٢ . عيون أخبار الرّضا : ١ / ٢٦٢ / ٢٢ .

٦٨٢٣ . الأمالي للطوسيّ : ٤٨٤ / ١٠٥٩ .

٦٨٢٤ . الطبقات الكبرىٰ : ١ / ٤١٠ .

٦٨٢٥ . نهج البلاغة : الخطبة ١٠٥ .

٦٨٢٦ . مكارم الأخلاق : ١ / ٦١ / ٥٥ .

٦٨٢٧ . الكافي : ١ / ٤٤٠ / ٢ .
٦٨٢٨ . نهج البلاغة : الخطبة ١٠٨ .
٦٨٢٩ . التوحيد : ١٧٤ / ٣ .
٦٨٣٠ . سبأ : ٢٨ .
٦٨٣١ . الطبقات الكبرى : ١ / ١٩١ .
٦٨٣٢ . بحار الأنوار : ١٦ / ٣١٦ / ٦ .
٦٨٣٣ . نهج البلاغة : الخطبة ١٦١ .
٦٨٣٤ . نهج البلاغة : الخطبة ٢١٤ .
٦٨٣٥ . القلم : ٤ .
٦٨٣٦ . الغارات : ١ / ١٦٧ .
٦٨٣٧ . الطبقات الكبرىٰ : ١ / ٣٦٥ .
٦٨٣٨ . الطبقات الكبرىٰ : ١ / ٣٧٨ .
٦٨٣٩ . الطبقات الكبرىٰ : ١ / ٣٦٥ .
٦٨٤٠ . الطبقات الكبرىٰ : ١ / ٣٦٨ .
٦٨٤١ . الطبقات الكبرىٰ : ١ / ٣٧٢ .
٦٨٤٢ . كنز العمّال : ٣٢١٤٧ .
٦٨٤٣ . السيرة النبويّة لابن هشام : ١ / ٢١٠ .
٦٨٤٤ . السيرة النبويّة لابن هشام : ١ / ١٩٩ .
٦٨٤٥ . الكافي : ٨ / ٢٦٨ / ٣٩٣ .
٦٨٤٦ . مكارم الأخلاق : ١ / ٥٣ / ٢٦ .
٦٨٤٧ . كنز العمّال : ٣٥٣٤٧ .
٦٨٤٨ . صحيح مسلم : ٤ / ١٨٠٢ / ٤٨ .
٦٨٤٩ . مكارم الأخلاق : ١ / ٥٥ / ٣٤ .
٦٨٥٠ . الترغيب والترهيب : ٣ / ٤١٨ / ٢٠ .
٦٨٥١ . مسند ابن حنبل : ١٠ / ٢١٢ / ٢٦٧٣١ .
٦٨٥٢ . مكارم الأخلاق : ١ / ٥٠ / ١٥ .
٦٨٥٣ . الأمالي للصدوق : ١٣٠ / ١١٧ .
٦٨٥٤ . سنن ابن ماجة : ٢ / ١١٠١ / ٣٣١٢ .
٦٨٥٥ . الطبقات الكبرىٰ : ١ / ٣٧٠ .
٦٨٥٦ . الكافي : ٨ / ١٣٠ / ١٠٠ .
٦٨٥٧ . المحاسن : ٢ / ٢٤٤ / ١٧٥٩ .
٦٨٥٨ . الكافي : ٨ / ١٢٧ / ٩٧ .
٦٨٥٩ . كنز العمّال : ٥٨١٨ .
٦٨٦٠ . كنز العمّال : ١٦٦٧٨ .
٦٨٦١ . الطبقات الكبرىٰ : ١ / ٣٧٨ .
٦٨٦٢ . الترغيب والترهيب : ٣ / ٤١٩ / ٢١ .
٦٨٦٣ . مكارم الأخلاق : ١ / ٦٤ / ٦٥ .
٦٨٦٤ . قرب الإسناد : ٩١ / ٣٠٤ .
٦٨٦٥ . الترغيب والترهيب : ٤ / ١٩٩ / ١٢٠ .
٦٨٦٦ . مكارم الأخلاق : ١ / ٧٩ / ١٢٤ .
٦٨٦٧ . الكافي : ٨ / ١٣٠ / ١٠٠ .
٦٨٦٨ . المناقب لابن شهراشوب : ١ / ١٤٥ و ١٤٦ .
٦٨٦٩ . صحيح مسلم : ٤ / ١٨١٤ / ٧٩ .
٦٨٧٠ . طه : ١ و ٢ .
٦٨٧١ . المزَّمِّل : ١ و ٢ .
٦٨٧٢ . المزَّمِّل : ٢٠ .
٦٨٧٣ . الميزان في تفسير القرآن : ١٤ / ١٢٦ .
٦٨٧٤ . الكافي : ٢ / ٩٥ / ٦ .
٦٨٧٥ . نهج البلاغة : الخطبة ٧٩ .
٦٨٧٦ . بحار الأنوار : ٥٨ / ٢٣٥ / ١٥ .
٦٨٧٧ . الكافي : ٨ / ١٩٥ / ٢٣٣ .

أقول : قال الشيخ الأنصاريّ في كتاب «المكاسب» في مبحث التّنجيم : يجوز الإخبار بحدوث الأحكام عند الاتّصالات والحركات المذكورة ؛ بأن يحكم بوجود كذا في المستقبل عند الوضع المعيّن من القرب والبعد والمقابلة والاقتران بين الكوكبَين إذا كان علىٰ وجه الظنّ . . . بل الظاهر حينئذٍ جواز الإخبار علىٰ وجه القطع إذا استند إلىٰ تجربة قطعيّة ؛ إذ لا حرج علىٰ من حكم قطعاً بالمطر في هذه الليلة نظراً إلىٰ ما جرّبه من نزول كلبه عن السطح إلىٰ داخل البيت مثلاً ، كماحكي أنّه اتّفق ذلك لمروّج هذا العلم بل محييه نصير الملّة والدين حيث نزل في بعض أسفاره علىٰ طحّان له طاحونة خارج البلد ، فلمّا دخل منزله صعد السطح لحرارة الهواء فقال له صاحب المنزل : انزل ونَم في البيت تحفّظاً من المطر ، فنظر المحقق إلَى الأوضاع الفلكيّة فلم يرَ شيئاً فيما هو مظنّة للتأثير في المطر ، قال صاحب المنزل : إنّ لي كلباً ينزل في كلّ ليلة يحسّ المطر فيها إلَى البيت ، فلم يقبل منه المحقّق ذلك وبات فوق السطح فجاءه المطر في الليل وتعجّب المحقق . (المكاسب : ٢٥) .

٦٨٧٨ . بحار الأنوار : ٥٨ / ٢٢٣ / ٣ .

تعليق :

يتبيّن بالتأمّل في نصوص هذه الأحاديث أنّ المقصود من علم النجوم المحرّم تعلّمه ليس العلم بمفهومه المعاصر ، بل المقصود هو تعلّم النجوم الأحكامي الّذي يبحث عن تأثير النجوم في مصير الإنسان والتنبؤ بحوادث المستقبل عن

طريق المطالعة في سير الكواكب على أنّها هي المؤثّرات ، كما أن النّظر في الطالع أيضاً بهذا الهدف مذموم .

٦٨٧٩ . كتاب من لايحضره الفقيه : ٢ / ٢٦٧ / ٢٤٠٢ .

٦٨٨٠ . آل عمران : ٣٥ .

٦٨٨١ . البقرة : ٢٧٠ .

٦٨٨٢ . الإنسان : ٧ .

٦٨٨٣ . وسائل الشيعة : ١٦ / ١٩٠ / ٥ .

٦٨٨٤ . وسائل الشيعة : ١٦ / ١٨٩ / ١ .

٦٨٨٥ . الأعراف : ٦٢ .

٦٨٨٦ . الترغيب والترهيب : ٢ / ٥٧٧ / ١٦ .

٦٨٨٧ . صحيح مسلم : ١ / ٧٤ / ٩٥ .

٦٨٨٨ . الكافي : ٢ / ٢٠٨ / ٥ .

٦٨٨٩ . الكافي : ٢ / ٢٠٨ / ٤ .

٦٨٩٠ . نهج البلاغة : الكتاب ٣١ .

٦٨٩١ . الكافي : ٢ / ٢٠٨ / ٢ .

٦٨٩٢ . الكافي : ٢ / ٢٠٨ / ٦ .

٦٨٩٣ . تحف العقول : ٢٠ .

٦٨٩٤ . كشف الغمّة : ٣ / ١٣٧، ١٣٨ .

٦٨٩٥ . نهج البلاغة : الخطبة ٨٦ .

٦٨٩٦ . الدرّة الباهرة : ٢٦ .

٦٨٩٧ . بحار الأنوار : ٧٨ / ١٩٤ / ٩ .

٦٨٩٨ . الخصال : ٤٦ / ٤٧ .

٦٨٩٩ . غرر الحكم : ٥٩٤٤ .

٦٩٠٠ . غرر الحكم : ٧٧٤٣ .

٦٩٠١ . المحاسن : ٢ / ٤٤٠ / ٢٥٢٦ .

٦٩٠٢ . النحل : ٩٠ .

٦٩٠٣ . نهج البلاغة : الحكمة ٢٣١ .

٦٩٠٤ . غرر الحكم : ٩٧١ .

٦٩٠٥ . غرر الحكم: ١١٣٠ ، وفي الطبعة المعتمدة «يألف» والصحيح ما أثبتناه كما في طبعة طهران .

٦٩٠٦ . غرر الحكم : ٤١٩٠ .

٦٩٠٧ . نهج البلاغة : الحكمة ٢٢٤ .

٦٩٠٨ . غرر الحكم : ٥٤٤٨ .

٦٩٠٩ . بحار الأنوار : ٧٨ / ١٦٥ / ١ .

٦٩١٠ . غرر الحكم : ١٤١٠ .

٦٩١١ . غرر الحكم : ٣١٨٦ .

٦٩١٢ . تحف العقول : ٣٠٥ .

٦٩١٣ . الخصال : ٤٧ / ٤٨ .

٦٩١٤ . غرر الحكم : ٣٣٤٥ .

٦٩١٥ . الكافي : ٢ / ١٤٤ / ٤ .

٦٩١٦ . كشف الغمّة : ٣ / ١٣٧، ١٣٨ .

٦٩١٧ . نهج البلاغة : الكتاب ٥٣ .

٦٩١٨ . الكافي : ٢ / ١٤٨ / ١٩ .

٦٩١٩ . غرر الحكم : ٤٦٧٤ .

٦٩٢٠ . غرر الحكم : ١٠٧٣٢ و ١٠٧٣٣ .

٦٩٢١ . غرر الحكم : ٣٦٨ .

٦٩٢٢ . بحار الأنوار : ١٠٤ / ٤١ / ٥٢ .

٦٩٢٣ . أي ما يتناوله البصر يُحفظ في القلب كأنّه يُكتب فيه . (كما في هامش نهج البلاغة ضبط الدكتور صبحي الصالح) .

٦٩٢٤ . نهج البلاغة: الحكمة ٤٠٩ .

٦٩٢٥ . بحار الأنوار : ١٠٤ / ٤٢ / ٥٢ .

٦٩٢٦ . بحار الأنوار : ٧٢ / ١٩٩ / ٢٩ .

٦٩٢٧ . غرر الحكم: ٩٥٠ .

٦٩٢٨ . تحف العقول : ٩٥ .

٦٩٢٩ . بحار الأنوار : ١٠٤ / ٣٨ / ٣٣ .

٦٩٣٠ . الكافي : ٥ / ٥٥٩ / ١٢ .

٦٩٣١ . بحار الأنوار : ٧٤ / ٧٣ / ٥٩ .

٦٩٣٢ . صحيفة الإمام الرّضا : ٩٠ / ١٩ .

٦٩٣٣ . النور : ٣٠ و ٣١ .

٦٩٣٤ . جامع الأخبار : ٤٠٨ / ١١٢٩ .

٦٩٣٥ . بحار الأنوار : ١٠٤ / ٤١ / ٥٢ .

٦٩٣٦ . بحار الأنوار : ٧٦ / ٣٣٤ / ١ .

٦٩٣٧ . ثواب الأعمال : ٣٣٨ / ١ .

٦٩٣٨ . غرر الحكم : ٩١٢٢ .

٦٩٣٩ . كتاب من لايحضره الفقيه : ٤ / ١٨ / ٤٩٦٩ .

٦٩٤٠ . النور : ٦٠ .

٦٩٤١ . عيون أخبار الرّضا : ٢ / ٩٧ / ١ .

٦٩٤٢ . كتاب من لايحضره الفقيه : ٤ / ١٩ / ٤٩٧١ .

٦٩٤٣ . كتاب من لايحضره الفقيه : ٣ / ٤٧٤ / ٤٦٥٨ .

٦٩٤٤ . كتاب من لايحضره الفقيه : ٤ / ١٨ / ٤٩٧٠ .

٦٩٤٥ . بحار الأنوار : ١٠ / ١١٥ / ١ .

٦٩٤٦ . الفرقان : ٦٣ .

٦٩٤٧ . بشارة المصطفى : ٢٦ .

٦٩٤٨ . بحار الأنوار : ٢ / ١٣٦ / ٣٩ .

٦٩٤٩ . بحار الأنوار : ٢ / ١٣٦ / ٤١ .
٦٩٥٠ . بحار الأنوار : ٢ / ١٣٥ / ٣٢ .
٦٩٥١ . سنن الترمذي : ٥ / ١١٢ / ٢٧٩٩ .
٦٩٥٢ . كنز العمّال : ٢٦٠٠٣ .
٦٩٥٣ . الكافي : ٦ / ٤٣٩ / ٥ .
٦٩٥٤ . سنن أبي داوود : ٤ / ٥١ / ٤٠٦٢ .
٦٩٥٥ . كنز العمّال : ٢٦٠٠٢ .
٦٩٥٦ . كنز العمّال : ٢٦٠٠٠ .
٦٩٥٧ . الكافي : ٦ / ٤٤١ / ٣ .
٦٩٥٨ . الكافي : ٦ / ٤٤٤ / ١٤ .
٦٩٥٩ . وسائل الشيعة : ٣ / ٥٧١ / ٢ .
٦٩٦٠ . الخصال : ٥٤ / ٧٣ .
٦٩٦١ . بحار الأنوار : ٧٨ / ٣٣٥ / ٤ .
٦٩٦٢ . الكافي : ٦ / ٤٣٩ / ٦ .
٦٩٦٣ . كنز العمّال : ٧٤٢٢ .
٦٩٦٤ . وسائل الشيعة : ٣ / ٥٧٢ / ٣ .
٦٩٦٥ . كتاب من لا يحضره الفقيه : ٤ / ٥ / ٤٩٦٨ .
٦٩٦٦ . الخصال : ٦٢٠ / ١٠ .
٦٩٦٧ . وسائل الشيعة : ٣ / ٥٧٥ / ٢ .
٦٩٦٨ . إبراهيم : ٣٤ .
٦٩٦٩ . الكافي : ٢ / ٣١٦ / ٥ .
٦٩٧٠ . نهج البلاغة : الخطبة ١ .
٦٩٧١ . بشارة المصطفى : ٢٨ .
٦٩٧٢ . الخصال : ٣٥ / ٧ .
٦٩٧٣ . بحار الأنوار : ٨١ / ١٧٠ / ١ .
٦٩٧٤ . بحار الأنوار : ٧٨ / ١٢ / ٧٠ .
٦٩٧٥ . بحار الأنوار : ٧٨ / ١١٥ / ١٢ .
٦٩٧٦ . علل الشرائع : ٤٦٤ / ١٢ .
٦٩٧٧ . نهج البلاغة : الحكمة ٢٤٦ .
٦٩٧٨ . أعلام الدين : ٣١٢ .
٦٩٧٩ . الأعراف : ٩٦ .
٦٩٨٠ . الأنفال : ٥٣ .
٦٩٨١ . بحار الأنوار : ٧٥ / ٣٥٣ / ٦٢ .
٦٩٨٢ . نهج البلاغة : الحكمة ٣٧٢ .
٦٩٨٣ . نهج البلاغة : الحكمة ٣٣٠ .
٦٩٨٤ . تحف العقول : ٣١٨ .
٦٩٨٥ . الكافي : ٤ / ٣٧ / ١ .
٦٩٨٦ . بحار الأنوار : ٧٨ / ٣٢٧ / ٤ .
٦٩٨٧ . عيون أخبار الرّضا : ٢ / ٢٤ / ٥٢ .
٦٩٨٨ . آل عمران : ١٧٨ .
٦٩٨٩ . نهج البلاغة : الحكمة ٢٥ .
٦٩٩٠ . نهج البلاغة : الحكمة ٣٥٨ .
٦٩٩١ . نهج البلاغة : الحكمة ٢٧٣ .
٦٩٩٢ . بحار الأنوار : ٧٨ / ١١٧ / ٧ .
٦٩٩٣ . الضحىٰ : ١١ .
٦٩٩٤ . سنن الترمذي : ٥ / ١٢٤ / ٢٨١٩ .
٦٩٩٥ . سنن نسائي : ٨ / ١٩٦ .
٦٩٩٦ . الكافي : ٦ / ٤٣٨ / ١ .
٦٩٩٧ . الكافي : ٦ / ٤٣٨ / ٢ .
٦٩٩٨ . الكافي : ٦ / ٤٣٩ / ٩ .
٦٩٩٩ . تحف العقول : ٣٦ .
٧٠٠٠ . نهج البلاغة : الحكمة ٢٢٤ .
٧٠٠١ . نهج البلاغة : الخطبة ١٨٨ .
٧٠٠٢ . معاني الأخبار : ٤٠٨ / ٨٧ .
٧٠٠٣ . يوسف : ٥٣ .
٧٠٠٤ . غرر الحكم : ٢١٠٦ .
٧٠٠٥ . بحار الأنوار : ٩٤ / ١٤٣ .
٧٠٠٦ . القيامة : ٢ .
٧٠٠٧ . مكارم الأخلاق : ٢ / ٣٥٣ / ٢٦٦٠ .
٧٠٠٨ . الشمس : ٧ـ١٠ .
٧٠٠٩ . نهج البلاغة : الحكمة ٣٥٩ .
٧٠١٠ . غرر الحكم : ٢٤٨٩ .
٧٠١١ . نهج البلاغة : الخطبة ١٩٨ .
٧٠١٢ . غرر الحكم : ٢٤٣٤ .
٧٠١٣ . غرر الحكم : ٩١٠٣ و ٩١٠٤ .
٧٠١٤ . غرر الحكم : ٩١٧٠ .
٧٠١٥ . الأمالي للصدوق : ٤٧٨ / ٦٤٤ .
٧٠١٦ . غرر الحكم : ٨٧٣٠ .
٧٠١٧ . غرر الحكم : ٨٧٧١ .
٧٠١٨ . غرر الحكم : ٩١٣٠ .
٧٠١٩ . التوبة : ٧٧ .
٧٠٢٠ . كنز العمّال : ١٧٣٤ .
٧٠٢١ . غرر الحكم : ٤٨٣ .
٧٠٢٢ . غرر الحكم : ٩٥٥٩ .

٧٠٢٣ . غرر الحكم : ٩٩٨٨ .
٧٠٢٤ . النساء : ١٤٢ و ١٤٣ .
٧٠٢٥ . في المصدر : أساء . (كما في هامش بحار الأنوار) .
٧٠٢٦ . بحار الأنوار : ٧٢ / ٢٠٧ / ٨ .
٧٠٢٧ . كنز العمّال : ٨٥٤ .
٧٠٢٨ . كنز العمّال : ٨٦٢ .
٧٠٢٩ . بحار الأنوار : ٧٢ / ٢٠٧ / ٨ .
٧٠٣٠ . الكافي : ٢ / ٣٩٦ / ٦ .
٧٠٣١ . تحف العقول : ٢١٢ .
٧٠٣٢ . نهج البلاغة: الحكمة ٤٥ .
٧٠٣٣ . الأمالي للصدوق : ٥٨٢ / ٨٠٢ .
٧٠٣٤ . الاختصاص : ٢٢٨ .
٧٠٣٥ . غرر الحكم : ٣٢١٤ .
٧٠٣٦ . غرر الحكم : ٣٣٠٩ .
٧٠٣٧ . نهج البلاغة : الخطبة ٦٨ .
٧٠٣٨ . التوبة : ٦٨ .
٧٠٣٩ . النساء : ١٤٥ .
٧٠٤٠ . الخصال : ٣٨ / ١٦ .
٧٠٤١ . الترغيب والترهيب : ٣ / ٦٠٣ / ٣ .
٧٠٤٢ . الكافي : ٢ / ٤٩٢ / ٨ .
٧٠٤٣ . الكافي : ٢ / ٤٩٣ / ١٣ .
٧٠٤٤ . البقرة : ٢٥٤ .
٧٠٤٥ . الحديد : ٧ .
٧٠٤٦ . البقرة : ٢٧٢ .
٧٠٤٧ . الكافي : ٤ / ٣ / ٦ ، ثواب الأعمال : ١٦٩ / ٩ .
٧٠٤٨ . الأمالي للطوسيّ : ١٨٣ / ٣٠٦ .
٧٠٤٩ . الترغيب والترهيب : ٢ / ٥٠ / ٨ .
٧٠٥٠ . بحار الأنوار : ٩٦ / ١١٧ / ٩ .
٧٠٥١ . غرر الحكم : ٣٨٣٤ .
٧٠٥٢ . تحف العقول : ٨٣ .
٧٠٥٣ . غرر الحكم : ٣٨٢٧ .
٧٠٥٤ . بحار الأنوار : ٩٦ / ١٣٣ / ٦٧ .
٧٠٥٥ . سبأ : ٣٩ .
٧٠٥٦ . مكارم الأخلاق : ٢ / ٢١ / ٢٠٥٣ .
٧٠٥٧ . بحار الأنوار : ٩٦ / ١٣١ / ٦٢ .
٧٠٥٨ . كنز العمّال : ١٦١٥٠ .
٧٠٥٩ . نهج البلاغة : الحكمة ١٣٨ .
٧٠٦٠ . بحار الأنوار : ٩٦ / ١٣٠ / ٥٧ .
٧٠٦١ . الكافي : ٤ / ٩ / ١ .
٧٠٦٢ . آل عمران : ٩٢ .
٧٠٦٣ . مجمع البيان : ٢ / ٧٩٢ .
٧٠٦٤ . الكافي : ٤ / ٦١ / ٣ .
٧٠٦٥ . جامع الأخبار : ٥٠٥ / ١٣٩٥ .
٧٠٦٦ . الكافي : ٣ / ٥٠٤ / ٧ .
٧٠٦٧ . تحف العقول : ٤٠٨ .
٧٠٦٨ . بحار الأنوار : ٧٧ / ٥٢ / ٣ .
٧٠٦٩ . تحف العقول : ٢٨٢ .
٧٠٧٠ . التوبة : ٥٣ و ٥٤ .
٧٠٧١ . البقرة : ٢٦٧ .
٧٠٧٢ . تفسير العيّاشيّ : ١ / ١٤٩ / ٤٩٢ .
٧٠٧٣ . كتاب من لا يحضره الفقيه : ٢ / ٥٧ / ١٦٩٤ .
٧٠٧٤ . القلم : ١٠ و ١١ .
٧٠٧٥ . كنز العمّال : ٨٣٥٤ .
٧٠٧٦ . الخصال : ١٨٢ / ٢٤٩ .
٧٠٧٧ . غرر الحكم : ٢٦٦٣ .
٧٠٧٨ . غرر الحكم : ٢٩٣٩ .
٧٠٧٩ . بحار الأنوار : ٦٣ / ٢١ / ١٤ .
٧٠٨٠ . كنز العمّال : ٧٥٤٥ .
٧٠٨١ . الخصال : ١٠٨ / ٧٣ .
٧٠٨٢ . الإسراء : ٧٩ .
٧٠٨٣ . الكافي : ٣ / ٤٥٤ / ١٦ .
٧٠٨٤ . المؤمنون : ٩ .
٧٠٨٥ . المعارج : ٢٣ .
٧٠٨٦ . الكافي : ٣ / ٢٦٩ / ١٢ .
٧٠٨٧ . بشارة المصطفى : ٢٨ .
٧٠٨٨ . نهج البلاغة : الحكمة ٢٧٩ .
٧٠٨٩ . نهج البلاغة : الحكمة ٣٩ .
٧٠٩٠ . الأنعام : ١٢٢ .
٧٠٩١ . الحديد : ٢٨ .
٧٠٩٢ . الصحيفة السجّاديّة : الدعاء ٢٢ .
٧٠٩٣ . بحار الأنوار : ١ / ٢٢٥ / ١٧ .
٧٠٩٤ . غرر الحكم : ٣٧٢٥ .
٧٠٩٥ . علل الشرائع : ٣٦٦ / ١ .
٧٠٩٦ . مستدرك الوسائل : ١٢ / ١٧٣ / ١٣٨١٠ .

٧٠٩٧ . الترغيب والترهيب : ١ / ١٥٦ / ٢٢ .

٧٠٩٨ . الترغيب والترهيب : ٢ / ٢٨١ / ١٨ .

٧٠٩٩ . الترغيب والترهيب : ٢ / ٣٤٩ / ١٠ .

٧١٠٠ . بحار الأنوار : ١٠٤ / ٣١١ / ٩ .

٧١٠١ . الكافي : ٢ / ٥٤ / ٤ .

٧١٠٢ . الحديد : ١٢ .

٧١٠٣ . كنز العمّال : ٤٤١٥٤ .

٧١٠٤ . غرر الحكم : ٢٠٩٧ .

٧١٠٥ . تحف العقول : ٣٢٠ .

٧١٠٦ . الأُصول الستّة عشر : ٥٧ .

٧١٠٧ . كنز العمّال : ٢٤٨٢٢ .

٧١٠٨ . نهج السعادة : ٢ / ٩٧ .

٧١٠٩ . بحار الأنوار : ٧٨ / ٥٧ / ١١٩ .

٧١١٠ . شرح نهج البلاغة : ٢ / ٢٠٠ .

٧١١١ . الخَلَنْج شجرٌ، فارسي معرّب، تتّخذ من خشبه الأواني . (لسان العرب : ٢ / ٢٦١) .

٧١١٢ . الفرقان : ٤٤ .

٧١١٣ . الخصال : ٤٠٩ / ٩ .

٧١١٤ . النجد : الطريق الواضح المرتفع (القاموس المحيط : ١ / ٣٤٠)، وقوله عليه السلام : «إنّما هما نجدان» فالظاهر إشارة إلىٰ قوله في سورة البلد : ١٠﴿وهدَيناه النجدَين﴾ . (كما في هامش المصدر) .

٧١١٥ . تحف العقول : ٤١٣ .

٧١١٦ . السُّبات بالضمّ : أي النوم الثقيل ، وأصله الراحة، ومعناه : جعلنا نومكم راحةً لأبدانكم (مجمع البحرين : ٢ / ٨٠٢) .

٧١١٧ . النبأ : ٩ .

٧١١٨ . الزمر : ٤٢ .

٧١١٩ . كنز العمّال : ٣٩٣٢١ .

٧١٢٠ . بحار الأنوار : ٦٢ / ٣١٦ .

٧١٢١ . أعلام الدين : ٣١١ .

٧١٢٢ . قصص الأنبياء : ١٦٣ / ١٨٥ .

٧١٢٣ . الاختصاص : ٢١٨ .

٧١٢٤ . الأمالي للصدوق : ٤٧٨ / ٦٤٤ .

٧١٢٥ . نهج البلاغة : الحكمة ٤٤٠ و الخطبة ٢٤١ .

٧١٢٦ . الكافي : ٥ / ٨٤ / ١ .

٧١٢٧ . تفسير العيّاشيّ : ٢ / ١١٥ / ١٤٩ .

٧١٢٨ . الكافي : ٥ / ٨٤ / ٢ .

٧١٢٩ . الدرّة الباهرة : ٤٣ .

٧١٣٠ . بحار الأنوار : ٨١ / ١٥٣ / ٨ .

٧١٣١ . الأمالي للصدوق : ٥١٠ / ٧٠٧ .

٧١٣٢ . بحار الأنوار : ٧٦ / ١٨٣ / ٧ .

٧١٣٣ . ثواب الأعمال : ٣٥ / ١ .

٧١٣٤ . بحار الأنوار : ٧٦ / ١٨٢ / ٦ .

٧١٣٥ . الخصال : ٢٢٩ / ٦٧ .

٧١٣٦ . بحار الأنوار : ٧٦ / ١٩٠ / ٢١ .

٧١٣٧ . الأمالي للصدوق : ٦٤ / ٢٧ .

٧١٣٨ . بحار الأنوار : ٧٦ / ١٩٦ / ١٢ .

٧١٣٩ . علل الشرائع : ٥٨٩ / ٣٤ .

٧١٤٠ . الخصال : ٢٦٣ / ١٤٠ .

٧١٤١ . بحار الأنوار : ٧٦ / ٢١٨ / ٢٥ .

٧١٤٢ . كنز العمّال : ٧٢٧٢ .

٧١٤٣ . الأمالي للطوسيّ : ٦١٨ / ١٢٧٤ .

٧١٤٤ . غرر الحكم : ١٠٤٠ .

٧١٤٥ . الكافي : ٢ / ٨٤ / ١ .

٧١٤٦ . كتاب من لا يحضره الفقيه : ٤ / ٤٠٠ / ٥٨٥٩ .

٧١٤٧ . الإسراء : ٨٤ .

٧١٤٨ . الكافي: ٢ / ٨٥ / ٥، إشارة إلىٰ رسوخ الملَكات بحيث يبطل في النفس استعداد ما يقابلها .(الميزان في تفسير القرآن:١٣ / ٢١٢) .

٧١٤٩ . المحاسن : ١ / ٤٠٩ / ٩٢٩ .

٧١٥٠ . كنز العمّال : ٧٢٦١ .

٧١٥١ . مكارم الأخلاق : ٢ / ٣٧٨ / ٢٦٦١ .

٧١٥٢ . غرر الحكم : ١٦٢٤ .

٧١٥٣ . يرعف بهم الزمان : يجود علىٰ غير انتظار كما يجود الأنف بالرعاف . (كما في هامش نهج البلاغة ضبط الدكتور صبحي الصالح) . والرُعاف : خروج الدم من الأنف (المصباح المنير : ٢٣٠) .

٧١٥٤ . نهج البلاغة : الخطبة ١٢ .

٧١٥٥ . غرر الحكم : ٦١٩٣ .

٧١٥٦ . أعلام الدين : ٣٠١ .

٧١٥٧ . الكافي : ٢ / ٨٤ / ٢ .

٧١٥٨ . الأمالي للطوسيّ : ٤٥٤ / ١٠١٣ .

٧١٥٩ . علل الشرائع : ٥٢٤ / ٢ .

٧١٦٠ . علل الشرائع : ٥٢٤ / ١ .

٧١٦١ . مكارم الأخلاق : ٢ / ٣٧٠ / ٢٦٦١ .

٧١٦٢ . بحار الأنوار : ٧٠ / ٢١٠ / ٣٢ .

٧١٦٣ . كنز العمّال : ٧٢٣٨ .

٧١٦٤ . غرر الحكم : ٤٨٠٦ .

٧١٦٥ . غرر الحكم : ٤٧٦٦ .

٧١٦٦ . المحاسن : ١ / ٤٠٦ / ٩٢٢ .

٧١٦٧ . الكافي : ٢ / ٨٥ / ٤ .

٧١٦٨ . غرر الحكم : ٥٥٦٨ .

٧١٦٩ . غرر الحكم : ٦٢٢٨ .

٧١٧٠ . غرر الحكم : ٤٠٢١ .

٧١٧١ . بحار الأنوار : ٧١ / ٢٤٧ / ٦، ثواب الأعمال : ٢٨٨ / ١ .

٧١٧٢ . كنز العمّال : ٤٦٢٦٠ .

٧١٧٣ . كنز العمّال : ٤٦٢٦٢ .

٧١٧٤ . نهج البلاغة : الخطبة ١٨٩ .

٧١٧٥ . الكافي : ٨ / ١٤٨ / ١٢٦ .

٧١٧٦ . المدّثّر : ٥ .

٧١٧٧ . كنز العمّال : ٤٦٢٦٣ .

٧١٧٨ . كنز العمّال : ٤٦٢٦٤ .

٧١٧٩ . كنز العمّال : ٦٧٦ .

٧١٨٠ . النساء : ٩٧ .

٧١٨١ . العنكبوت : ٥٦ .

٧١٨٢ . مجمع البيان : ٨ / ٤٥٥ .

٧١٨٣ . مجمع البيان : ٣ / ١٥٣ .

٧١٨٤ . وسائل الشيعة : ١١ / ٧٥ / ١ .

٧١٨٥ . مستدرك الوسائل : ١١ / ٩٠ / ١٢٤٩ .

٧١٨٦ . معاني الأخبار : ٢٦٥ / ١ .

٧١٨٧ . وسائل الشيعة : ١١ / ٧٥ / ٢ .

٧١٨٨ . كنز العمّال : ٢٤٧٨٩ .

٧١٨٩ . بحار الأنوار : ٧٧ / ٨٩ / ٣ .

٧١٩٠ . اصطَكّتْ رُكبتاه : اضطَربتا، والتخلّع : التفكّك، الوَصل : المِفصل، أو مجتمع العظام (المعجم الوسيط : ١ / ٥١٩ و ٢٥٠ و ج ٢ / ١٠٣٧) .

٧١٩١ . الكافي : ٢ / ٣٤٦ / ٧ .

٧١٩٢ . «يتغامس» في أكثر النسخ بالغين المعجمة، والظاهر أنّه بالمهملة كما في بعضها، وفي القاموس تعامس : تغافل . وتعامسَ عليّ : تعامىٰ عليَّ، وبالمعجمة : غمسه في الماء، والغميس : الليل المظلم . (أُنظر القاموس المحيط : ٢ / ٢٣٣ وص ٢٣٥) .

7193 . الكافي : ٢ / ٣٤٤ / ١ .

7194 . الكافي : ٢ / ٣٤٤ / ٢ .

7195 . كنز العمّال : ٢٤٧٩٣ .

7196 . الترغيب والترهيب : ٣ / ٤٥٧ / ٧ .

7197 . الترغيب والترهيب : ٣ / ٤٥٧ / ٨ .

7198 . الكافي : ٢ / ٣٤٥ / ٥ .

7199 . بحار الأنوار : ٧٥ / ١٨٨ / ١٠ .

7200 . طه : ٥٠ .

7201 . الإنسان : ٣ .

7202 . بحار الأنوار : ٥ / ١٩٦ / ٤ .

7203 . المائدة : ٣٢ .

7204 . الكافي : ٢ / ٢١٠ / ١ .

7205 . بحار الأنوار : ١٤ / ٤٠ / ٢٦ .

7206 . الكافي : ٥ / ٢٨ / ٤ .

7207 . وسائل الشيعة : ١١ / ٤٤٨ / ٥ .

7208 . القصص : ٥٦ .

7209 . الأمالي للصدوق : ١٦٢ / ١٦١ .

7210 . كنز العمّال : ٥٤٦ .

7211 . التغابن : ١١ .

7212 . العنكبوت : ٦٩ .

7213 . القصص : ٥٠ .

7214 . المائدة : ٦٧ .

7215 . الكافي : ٨ / ٥٢ / ١٦ .

7216 . الكافي : ٥ / ١٤٤ / ١٤ .

7217 . جَدَرَه يَجْدُرُه : حَوَّطه، والضغينة : الحقد (لسان العرب : ٤ / ١٢١ و ١٣ / ٢٥٥) .

7218 . بحار الأنوار : ٧٧ / ١٦٦ / ٢ .

7219 . الكافي : ٥ / ١٤٤ / ١٢ .

7220 . كنز العمّال : ١٥٠٦٧ .

7221 . صحيح البخاري : ٦ / ٢٦٢٤ / ٦٧٥٣ .

7222 . كنز العمّال : ١٤٤٧٥، ١٤٤٧٩ .

7223 . الجعفريّات : ٨٢ .

7224 . الكُراع : هو مادون الرُّكبة من الساق (النهاية : ٤/١٦٥) .

7225 . الكافي : ٥ / ١٤٣ / ٩ .

7226 . الكافي : ٥ / ١٤٣ / ٨ .

7227 . كنز العمّال : ١٤٤٨٢ .

٧٢٢٨ . كنز العمّال : ٤٦١٦٤ .

٧٢٢٩ . بحار الأنوار : ١٠٣ / ١٨٩ / ٥ .

٧٢٣٠ . تنبيه الخواطر : ١ / ٢٧٢ .

٧٢٣١ . غرر الحكم : ٤٦٢٣ .

٧٢٣٢ . تحف العقول : ٥٦ .

٧٢٣٣ . الخصال : ٧٣ / ١١٢ .

٧٢٣٤ . نهج البلاغة : الحكمة ١٤٣ .

٧٢٣٥ . تحف العقول : ٣١٧ .

٧٢٣٦ . القصص : ٥٩ .

٧٢٣٧ . الترغيب والترهيب : ١ / ٨٦ / ١٠ .

٧٢٣٨ . الكافي : ٢ / ٣١٦ / ٦ .

٧٢٣٩ . تاريخ دمشق : ٤٢ / ٥٠٢ .

٧٢٤٠ . غرر الحكم : ١٠٠٣٠ .

٧٢٤١ . نهج البلاغة : الحكمة ١٤٩ .

٧٢٤٢ . نهج البلاغة : الحكمة ١١٧ .

٧٢٤٣ . مفعول به لفعل محذوف تقديره «احذر» .

٧٢٤٤ . تحف العقول : ٣٦٩ .

٧٢٤٥ . بحار الأنوار : ٧٨ / ٢٠٧ / ٦٧ .

٧٢٤٦ . كنز العمّال : ٤٣٠٢١ .

٧٢٤٧ . نهج البلاغة : الحكمة ٤٧ .

٧٢٤٨ . غرر الحكم : ٨٣٢٠ .

٧٢٤٩ . الصحيفة السجّاديّة الجامعة : الدعاء ١٩٩ .

٧٢٥٠ . بحار الأنوار : ٧٨ / ١٦٥ / ١ .

٧٢٥١ . نهج البلاغة : الحكمة ٤٦٠ .

٧٢٥٢ . غرر الحكم : ١٤٧٧ .

٧٢٥٣ . غرر الحكم : ١٣٨٨ .

٧٢٥٤ . غرر الحكم : ٤٢٧٧ .

٧٢٥٥ . غرر الحكم : ١٦٧٤ .

٧٢٥٦ . غرر الحكم : ٥٧٦٣ .

٧٢٥٧ . بحار الأنوار: ٧٨ / ١٦٤ / ١ .

٧٢٥٨ . غرر الحكم : ٨٠١٩ .

٧٢٥٩ . غرر الحكم : ٩٢٥٦ .

٧٢٦٠ . بحار الأنوار : ٧٨ / ١٠ / ٦٧ .

٧٢٦١ . تحف العقول : ٣١٨ .

٧٢٦٢ . تنبيه الخواطر : ١ / ٤٨ .

٧٢٦٣ . غرر الحكم : ٨٨٣٠ .

٧٢٦٤ . غرر الحكم : ٩٦٤٢ .

٧٢٦٥ . الجاثية : ٢٣ .

٧٢٦٦ . الدرّ المنثور : ٦ / ٢٦١ .

٧٢٦٧ . غرر الحكم : ٢٢١٧، ٢٢١٨ .

٧٢٦٨ . غرر الحكم : ٤٤٩ .

٧٢٦٩ . سنن الدارمي : ١ / ١١٥ / ٤٠١ .

٧٢٧٠ . الترغيب والترهيب : ١ / ٨٧ / ١٣ .

٧٢٧١ . نهج البلاغة : الخطبة ٥٠ .

٧٢٧٢ . بحار الأنوار : ٧٠ / ٧٦ / ٦ .

٧٢٧٣ . نهج البلاغة : الخطبة ١٧٦ .

٧٢٧٤ . غرر الحكم : ٢٧ .

٧٢٧٥ . غرر الحكم : ٦٨١٣ .

٧٢٧٦ . الروم : ٢٩ .

٧٢٧٧ . بحار الأنوار : ٧٧ / ٨٢ / ٣ .

٧٢٧٨ . دعائم الإسلام : ٢ / ٣٥٠ .

٧٢٧٩ . نهج البلاغة : الكتاب ٣١ .

٧٢٨٠ . غرر الحكم : ٩١٦٨ .

٧٢٨١ . غرر الحكم : ٣١٣٣ .

٧٢٨٢ . غرر الحكم : ٢٧٤٦ .

٧٢٨٣ . غرر الحكم : ٦٧٩٠ .

٧٢٨٤ . غرر الحكم : ٦٢٩٨ .

٧٢٨٥ . نهج البلاغة : الحكمة ٢١١ .

٧٢٨٦ . غرر الحكم : ٨٧٩٤ .

٧٢٨٧ . غرر الحكم : ٨٨٢٣ .

٧٢٨٨ . الكافي : ٢ / ٣٣٥ / ١ .

٧٢٨٩ . النازعات : ٤٠، ٤١ .

٧٢٩٠ . الكافي : ٨ / ١٣٦ / ١٠٣ .

٧٢٩١ . غرر الحكم : ٥٢٦٣ .

٧٢٩٢ . غرر الحكم : ٥٣٩٣ .

٧٢٩٣ . غرر الحكم : ٦٤٢١ .

٧٢٩٤ . غرر الحكم : ٦٤١٨ .

٧٢٩٥ . في الطبعة المعتمدة «واستفادتك»، والصحيح ما أثبتناه كما في طبعة النجف وطهران وبيروت .

٧٢٩٦ . غرر الحكم : ٦٤٤٤ .

٧٢٩٧ . بحار الأنوار : ٧٨ / ٥٣ / ٨٧ .

٧٢٩٨ . تحف العقول : ٣٧٠ .

٧٢٩٩ . في بعض النسخ «وإذا خرّبك أمران» وخرّبه أمر : أي نزل به وأهمّه . (كما في هامش المصدر) .

٧٣٠٠ . تحف العقول : ٣٩٨ .

٧٣٠١ . الكافي : ٢ / ٣٣٥ / ٢ .

٧٣٠٢ . تنبيه الخواطر : ٢ / ١٢٢ .

٧٣٠٣ . كذا في المصدر، ولعلّ الصواب «غَرِيَ» من غَرِيَ بالشيء: أُولِعَ به .

٧٣٠٤ . تنبيه الخواطر : ٢ / ١٢٢ .

٧٣٠٥ . غرر الحكم : ٧٩٥٩ .

٧٣٠٦ . غرر الحكم : ٤٩٠٢ .

٧٣٠٧ . غرر الحكم : ٨٩٩٥ .

٧٣٠٨ . تنبيه الخواطر : ١ / ٦٠ .

٧٣٠٩ . معاني الأخبار : ١٩٥ / ١ .

٧٣١٠ . تنبيه الخواطر : ٢ / ١٠ .

٧٣١١ . الكافي : ٨ / ٤٢ و ص ٤٦ / ٨ .

٧٣١٢ . غرر الحكم : ٧٢٠٥ .

٧٣١٣ . غرر الحكم : ٨٢٢٦ .

٧٣١٤ . غرر الحكم : ٢١٤٨ .

٧٣١٥ . نهج البلاغة : الحكمة ٤٤٩ .

٧٣١٦ . ظَلَفَ الزُهدُ شَهَوَاتِه : أي كَفَّها ومَنَعَها . (النهاية : ٣ / ١٥٩) .

٧٣١٧ . نهج البلاغة : الخطبة ٨٣ .

٧٣١٨ . نهج البلاغة : الحكمة ٣١ .

٧٣١٩ . الكافي : ٢ / ٣٣٥ / ٢ .

٧٣٢٠ . الكافي : ٢ / ١٣٧ / ٢ .

٧٣٢١ . غرر الحكم : ٧٩٥٣ .

٧٣٢٢ . غرر الحكم : ٤٣٥٤ .

٧٣٢٣ . غرر الحكم : ٥٣٩٠ .

٧٣٢٤ . النساء : ١١ .

٧٣٢٥ . العاقلة : الدِّية (النهاية : ٣ / ٢٨٧) . أي لا تصير عاقلة في دية الخطأ . (كما في هامش المصدر) .

٧٣٢٦ . الكافي : ٧ / ٨٥ / ٣ .

٧٣٢٧ . النساء : ٣٤ .

٧٣٢٨ . عيون أخبار الرضا : ٢ / ٩٨ / ١ .

٧٣٢٩ . الكافي : ٧ / ١٤١ / ٥ .

٧٣٣٠ . كنز العمّال : ٣٠٤٤٧ .

٧٣٣١ . الكافي : ٧ / ١٤٣ / ٥ .

٧٣٣٢ . النمل : ١٦ .

٧٣٣٣ . مريم : ٥، ٦ .

٧٣٣٤ . الطبقات الكبرى : ٢ / ٣١٥ .

٧٣٣٥ . كنز العمّال : ٧٢٨٤ .

٧٣٣٦ . كنز العمّال : ٧٣٠٠ .

٧٣٣٧ . بحار الأنوار : ٧٠ / ٣٠٤ / ١٨ .

٧٣٣٨ . نهج البلاغة : الحكمة ٣٧١ .

٧٣٣٩ . نهج البلاغة : الحكمة ٤ .

٧٣٤٠ . بحار الأنوار : ٧٠ / ٣٠٦ / ٣٠ .

٧٣٤١ . الكافي : ٢ / ٧٧ / ٥ .

٧٣٤٢ . الأمالي للطوسي : ٢٨١ / ٥٤٤ .

٧٣٤٣ . الكافي : ٢ / ٧٨ / ١٠ .

٧٣٤٤ . غرر الحكم : ٤٦٣٦ .

٧٣٤٥ . غرر الحكم : ١٤٣٦ .

٧٣٤٦ . غرر الحكم : ١١٠٧ .

٧٣٤٧ . غرر الحكم : ١٠٦٨٩ .

٧٣٤٨ . الكافي : ٢ / ٧٦ / ٢ .

٧٣٤٩ . المحاسن : ١ / ٦٥ / ٩ .

٧٣٥٠ . تنبيه الخواطر : ٢ / ٨٨ .

٧٣٥١ . الكافي : ٢ / ٧٧ / ٤ .

٧٣٥٢ . بحار الأنوار : ٧٠ / ٢٩٦ / ١ .

٧٣٥٣ . كنز العمّال : ٧٢٩٩ .

٧٣٥٤ . غرر الحكم : ٣٠٩٧ .

٧٣٥٥ . غرر الحكم : ٢١٦١ .

٧٣٥٦ . الكافي : ٢ / ٧٧ / ٨ .

٧٣٥٧ . بحار الأنوار : ٧٠ / ٣٠٣ / ١٥ .

٧٣٥٨ . الكافي : ٢ / ٧٧ / ٧ .

٧٣٥٩ . بحار الأنوار : ٦٩ / ٣٦٨ / ٤ .

٧٣٦٠ . غرر الحكم : ٣٣٦٨ .

٧٣٦١ . غرر الحكم : ٢٨٣٩ .

٧٣٦٢ . الأعراف : ٨، ٩ .

٧٣٦٣ . كنز العمّال : ٣٩٧٦٨ .

٧٣٦٤ . الكافي : ٢ / ١٤٣ / ١٠ .

٧٣٦٥ . الاحتجاج : ٢ / ٢١٢ و ٢٤٧ / ٢٢٣ .

قال العلّامة الطباطبائيّ : وفي الرواية تأييد ما قدّمناه في تفسير الوزن ، ومن ألطف ما فيها قوله عليه السلام : «وإنّما هي صفة ما عملوا» يشير عليه السلام إلى أن ليس المراد بالأعمال في هذه الأبواب هو الحركات الطبيعيّة الصادرة عن الإنسان لاشتراكها بين الطاعة والمعصية ، بل الصفات الطارئة عليها التي تعتبر لها بالنظر إلى السّنن والقوانين الإجتماعيّة أو

الدينيّة مثل الحركات الخاصّة التي تسمّىٰ وقاعاً بالنظر إلىٰ طبيعة نفسها ثمّ تسمّىٰ نكاحاً إذا وافقت السنّة الاجتماعيّة أو الإذن الشرعيّ، وتسمّى زناً إذا لم توافق ذلك، وطبيعة الحركات الصادرة واحدة. وقد استدلّ ﷺ لما ذكره من طريقين: أحدهما: أنّ الأعمال صفات لا وزن لها، والثاني: أنّ الله سبحانه لايحتاج إلىٰ توزين الأشياء لعدم اتّصافه بالجهل تعالىٰ شأنه. (الميزان في تفسير القرآن: ٨ / ١٦).

٧٣٦٦ . كنز العمّال: ١٧٠٩ . والترديد من الرّاوي .

٧٣٦٧ . تنبيه الخواطر: ٢ / ١٢٠ .

٧٣٦٨ . الكافي: ١ / ١٢ / ١٠ .

٧٣٦٩ . هكذا جاء الحديث في المصدر مضمراً .

٧٣٧٠ . الكافي: ٣ / ٣٥٨ / ٢ .

٧٣٧١ . المؤمنون: ٩٧ و ٩٨ .

٧٣٧٢ . الناس: ١ـ٦ .

٧٣٧٣ . الخصال: ٦١٢ / ١٠ .

٧٣٧٤ . بحار الأنوار: ٨١ / ٢٠٣ / ٥ .

٧٣٧٥ . الكافي: ٢ / ٤٢٤ / ١ .

٧٣٧٦ . مكارم الأخلاق: ٢ / ٣٨٠ / ٢٦٦١ .

٧٣٧٧ . غرر الحكم: ٣٠٢٣ .

٧٣٧٨ . غرر الحكم: ١٠٢٧٦ .

٧٣٧٩ . بحار الأنوار: ٧٤ / ٣٩٥ / ٢٢ .

٧٣٨٠ . الخصال: ٨ / ٢٦ .

٧٣٨١ . الخصال: ٤٧ / ٥٠ .

٧٣٨٢ . بحار الأنوار: ٧٤ / ٢٣١ / ٢٨ .

٧٣٨٣ . البقرة: ١٨٠ .

٧٣٨٤ . وسائل الشيعة: ١٣ / ٣٥٢ / ٦ .

٧٣٨٥ . كنز العمّال: ٤٦٠٥١ .

٧٣٨٦ . بحار الأنوار: ١٠٣ / ١٩٤ / ٣ .

٧٣٨٧ . تهذيب الأحكام: ٩ / ١٧٤ / ٧٠٨ .

٧٣٨٨ . الكافي: ٧ / ٦٢ / ١٨ .

٧٣٨٩ . كتاب من لايحضره الفقيه: ٤ / ١٨٤ / ٥٤٢٠ .

٧٣٩٠ . الكافي: ٧ / ١١ / ٥ .

٧٣٩١ . المائدة: ٦ .

٧٣٩٢ . بحار الأنوار: ٨٠ / ٢٣٨ / ١٢ .

٧٣٩٣ . كنز العمّال: ٢٦٠٥٩ .

٧٣٩٤ . كنز العمّال: ٢٦٠٣١ .

٧٣٩٥ . كنز العمّال: ٢٦٠٣٠ .

٧٣٩٦ . بحار الأنوار: ٨٠ / ٢٣٧ / ١١ .

٧٣٩٧ . كتاب من لايحضره الفقيه: ١ / ٥٨ / ١٢٩ .

٧٣٩٨ . علل الشرائع: ٢٧٩ / ١ .

٧٣٩٩ . علل الشرائع: ٢٥٧ / ٩ .

٧٤٠٠ . بحار الأنوار: ٨٠ / ٢٣٧ / ١١ .

٧٤٠١ . الأمالي للمفيد: ٦٠ / ٥ .

٧٤٠٢ . كنز العمّال: ٢٥٩٩٩ .

٧٤٠٣ . كنز العمّال: ٢٦٠٤٢ .

٧٤٠٤ . وسائل الشيعة: ١ / ٢٦٤ / ٧ .

٧٤٠٥ . وسائل الشيعة: ١ / ٢٦٥ / ٨، عوالي اللآلي: ١ / ٢٣ / ٢ .

٧٤٠٦ . تنبيه الخواطر: ١ / ٢٠١ .

٧٤٠٧ . بحار الأنوار: ٧٧ / ١٧٩ / ١٠ .

٧٤٠٨ . تنبيه الخواطر: ٢ / ٦٦ .

٧٤٠٩ . نهج البلاغة: الحكمة ١١٣ .

٧٤١٠ . بحار الأنوار: ٧٥ / ١٢٠ / ١١ .

٧٤١١ . غرر الحكم: ٩٣٩ .

٧٤١٢ . بحار الأنوار: ٧٥ / ١١٩ / ٥ .

٧٤١٣ . نهج البلاغة: الخطبة ١٩٣ .

٧٤١٤ . غرر الحكم: ٥٢٢ .

٧٤١٥ . نهج البلاغة: الحكمة ٤٠٦ .

٧٤١٦ . الكافي: ٢ / ١٢٤ / ١٣ .

٧٤١٧ . تحف العقول: ٤٨٩ .

٧٤١٨ . الكافي: ٢ / ١٢٣ / ٩ .

٧٤١٩ . بحار الأنوار: ٧٥ / ١١٨ / ٣ .

٧٤٢٠ . الكافي: ٢ / ١٢١ / ١ .

٧٤٢١ . كنز العمّال: ٥٧٣٠ .

٧٤٢٢ . غرر الحكم: ٤٦١٣، ٤٦١٤ .

٧٤٢٣ . بحار الأنوار: ٧٧ / ٢٨٧ / ١ .

٧٤٢٤ . غرر الحكم: ٤٣٠٢ .

٧٤٢٥ . غرر الحكم: ٥٢٢، ٥٢٣ .

٧٤٢٦ . بحار الأنوار: ٧٨ / ٣١٢ / ١ .

٧٤٢٧ . تحف العقول: ٣٩٩ .

٧٤٢٨ . بحار الأنوار: ٧٨ / ٧ / ٥٩ .

٧٤٢٩ . غرر الحكم: ٣٠١ .

٧٤٣٠ . نهج البلاغة: الخطبة ١٤٧ .

٧٤٣١ . بحار الأنوار: ٧٨ / ٨٠ / ٦٦ .

٧٤٣٢ . بحار الأنوار: ٧٨ / ٢٧٧ / ١١٣ .

٧٤٣٣ . عيون أخبار الرّضا عليه السلام : ٢ / ٥٠ / ١٩٢ .
٧٤٣٤ . الكافي : ٢ / ١٢٤ / ١٣ .
٧٤٣٥ . بحار الأنوار : ٧٨ / ٤٥ / ٥٠ .
٧٤٣٦ . بحار الأنوار : ٧٤ / ٢٦٤ / ٣ .
٧٤٣٧ . سفينة البحار : ٨ / ٥٢٥ .
٧٤٣٨ . نهج البلاغة : الخطبة ٢٧ .
٧٤٣٩ . نهج البلاغة : الحكمة ٥٦ .
٧٤٤٠ . غرر الحكم : ٧٥١٧ .
٧٤٤١ . غرر الحكم : ١٢٩١ و ١٢٩٢ .
٧٤٤٢ . الروم : ٦٠ .
٧٤٤٣ . آل عمران : ٩ .
٧٤٤٤ . التوحيد : ٤٠٦ / ٣ .
٧٤٤٥ . كنز العمّال : ٦٨٦٥ .
٧٤٤٦ . كنز العمّال : ٦٨٧٠ .
٧٤٤٧ . غرر الحكم : ٩٦٩٢ .
٧٤٤٨ . بحار الأنوار : ٧٥ / ٩٧ / ٢٠ .
٧٤٤٩ . نهج البلاغة : الحكمة ٣٣٦ .
٧٤٥٠ . غرر الحكم : ١٦٤٦ و ١٦٤٧ .
٧٤٥١ . الترغيب والترهيب : ٤ / ٩ / ١٢ .
٧٤٥٢ . غرر الحكم : ح ١١٣٤ .
٧٤٥٣ . غرر الحكم : ١٠٢٩٧ .
٧٤٥٤ . بحار الأنوار : ٧٨ / ٢٥٠ / ٩٤ .
٧٤٥٥ . الكافي : ١ / ٢٠ / ١٢ .
٧٤٥٦ . الصفّ : ٢ .
٧٤٥٧ . الكافي : ٢ / ٣٦٣ / ١ .
٧٤٥٨ . بحار الأنوار : ١٠٤ / ٧٣ / ٢٣ .
٧٤٥٩ . نهج البلاغة : الكتاب ٣١ .
٧٤٦٠ . غرر الحكم : ١٣٥٤ .
٧٤٦١ . غرر الحكم : ٤١٩١ .
٧٤٦٢ . تحف العقول : ٣٥ .
٧٤٦٣ . تحف العقول : ٨٥ .
٧٤٦٤ . غرر الحكم : ٧٠٥٩ .
٧٤٦٥ . غرر الحكم : ٤٠٣٢ .
٧٤٦٦ . غرر الحكم : ٨٩٣٨ .
٧٤٦٧ . نهج البلاغة : الحكمة ١٩٦ .
٧٤٦٨ . نهج البلاغة : الحكمة ١٣١ .
٧٤٦٩ . غرر الحكم : ٧٣٣٨ .
٧٤٧٠ . غرر الحكم : ٣١٢٣ .
٧٤٧١ . نهج البلاغة : الخطبة ١٧٦ .
٧٤٧٢ . غرر الحكم : ١٠٦٢٢ .
٧٤٧٣ . نهج البلاغة : الخطبة ٣٢ .
٧٤٧٤ . الأمالي للصدوق : ٥٧٦ / ٧٨٨ .
٧٤٧٥ . غرر الحكم : ٣٤٦٠ .
٧٤٧٦ . غرر الحكم : ٧٣٣٨ .
٧٤٧٧ . غرر الحكم : ٩٢٣٦ .
٧٤٧٨ . بحار الأنوار : ٧١ / ٣٢٤ / ١٤ .
٧٤٧٩ . النحل : ١٢٥ .
٧٤٨٠ . سنن أبي داوود : ١ / ٢٨٩ / ١١٠٧ .
٧٤٨١ . غرر الحكم : ٩٩٦٨ .
٧٤٨٢ . تحف العقول : ٤٨٩ .
٧٤٨٣ . بحار الأنوار : ٧٨ / ٦٧ / ١١ .
٧٤٨٤ . الأمالي للطوسي: ١١٥ / ١٧٦ .
٧٤٨٥ . تحف العقول : ٢٩٤ .
٧٤٨٦ . غرر الحكم : ١٧٢٩ .
٧٤٨٧ . غرر الحكم : ٩٠١٠ .
٧٤٨٨ . نهج البلاغة : الحكمة ٢٨٢ .
٧٤٨٩ . الصفّ : ٢، ٣ .
٧٤٩٠ . كنز العمّال : ٤٣١٥٦ .
٧٤٩١ . نهج البلاغة : الحكمة ١٥٠ .
٧٤٩٢ . غرر الحكم : ٥٣٦٠ ـ ٥٣٦١ .
٧٤٩٣ . نهج البلاغة : الخطبة ١٠٥ .
٧٤٩٤ . منية المريد : ١٤٦ و ١٨١ .
٧٤٩٥ . غرر الحكم : ٣٥٣٨ .
٧٤٩٦ . هود : ٨٨ .
٧٤٩٧ . غرر الحكم : ٧٣ .
٧٤٩٨ . غرر الحكم : ١٦٢ .
٧٤٩٩ . غرر الحكم : ٥٣٩ .
٧٥٠٠ . غرر الحكم : ٥٤٥ .
٧٥٠١ . غرر الحكم : ١٠٨٠٢ .
٧٥٠٢ . غرر الحكم : ٨٥٨ .
٧٥٠٣ . نهج البلاغة : الحكمة ١١٣ .
٧٥٠٤ . نهج البلاغة : الحكمة ٢١١ .
٧٥٠٥ . تحف العقول : ٨٣ .
٧٥٠٦ . تحف العقول : ٢٨٦ .

٧٥٠٧ . التوحيد : ٢٤٢ / ٣ .
٧٥٠٨ . آل عمران : ١٦٠ .
٧٥٠٩ . تنبيه الخواطر : ٢ / ١٠٢ .
٧٥١٠ . غرر الحكم : ٧١٨ و ٧١٩ .
٧٥١١ . نهج البلاغة : الخطبة ١٤٧ .
٧٥١٢ . التوحيد : ٢٤٢ / ١ .
٧٥١٣ . الإسراء : ٣٤ .
٧٥١٤ . البقرة : ١٧٧ .
٧٥١٥ . بحار الأنوار : ٧٧ / ١٤٩ / ٧٧ .
٧٥١٦ . غرر الحكم : ١٠٤٤ .
٧٥١٧ . غرر الحكم : ١٤٣٠ .
٧٥١٨ . غرر الحكم: ٣٠١٨ .
٧٥١٩ . غرر الحكم: ٣٠٢٠ .
٧٥٢٠ . غرر الحكم : ١٠٢٦٠ .
٧٥٢١ . الخصال : ١١٣ / ٩٠ .
٧٥٢٢ . الخصال : ١٢٣ / ١١٨ .
٧٥٢٣ . الفرقان : ٦٣ .
٧٥٢٤ . كنز العمّال : ٦٤٠٢ .
٧٥٢٥ . كنز العمّال : ٦٤٠١ .
٧٥٢٦ . غرر الحكم : ٢٧٠ .
٧٥٢٧ . غرر الحكم : ٧٣٩٧ .
٧٥٢٨ . غرر الحكم : ٤٧٤٤ .
٧٥٢٩ . غرر الحكم : ٥٥٣٤ .
٧٥٣٠ . غرر الحكم : ٤١٨٢ .
٧٥٣١ . غرر الحكم : ٧٦٦٦ .
٧٥٣٢ . الكافي : ٨ / ٢٣ / ٤ .
٧٥٣٣ . بحار الأنوار : ٧٨ / ٧ / ٥٩ .
٧٥٣٤ . الأعراف : ٩٦ .
٧٥٣٥ . البقرة : ٢ و ٥ .
٧٥٣٦ . النساء : ١٣١ .
٧٥٣٧ . الأعراف : ٢٦ .
٧٥٣٨ . الأنفال : ٢٩ .
٧٥٣٩ . القصص : ٨٣ .
٧٥٤٠ . نهج البلاغة : الحكمة ٤١٠ .
٧٥٤١ . بحار الأنوار : ٧٧ / ٣٧٤ / ٣٦ .
٧٥٤٢ . نهج البلاغة : الحكمة ٢٤٢ .
٧٥٤٣ . غرر الحكم : ٣٦٢٠ .
٧٥٤٤ . نهج البلاغة : الخطبة ١١٤ .
٧٥٤٥ . نهج البلاغة : الخطبة ١٩٥ .
٧٥٤٦ . الكافي : ٨ / ١٧ / ٣ .
٧٥٤٧ . نهج البلاغة : الخطبة ١٩١ .
٧٥٤٨ . نهج البلاغة : الخطبة ١٩١ .
٧٥٤٩ . نهج البلاغة : الخطبة ٢٣٠ .
٧٥٥٠ . بحار الأنوار : ٧٨ / ٩٠ / ٩٥ .
٧٥٥١ . الكافي : ٨ / ٥٢ / ١٦ .
٧٥٥٢ . الحجرات : ١٣ .
٧٥٥٣ . المائدة : ٢٧ .
٧٥٥٤ . بحار الأنوار : ٧٠ / ٢٨٦ / ٨ .
٧٥٥٥ . الطلاق : ٢ و ٣ .
٧٥٥٦ . بحار الأنوار : ٧٠ / ٢٨٥ / ٧ .
٧٥٥٧ . بحار الأنوار : ٧٠ / ٢٨٨ / ١٦ .
٧٥٥٨ . بحار الأنوار : ٧٨ / ٩ / ٦٥ .
٧٥٥٩ . نهج البلاغة : الخطبة ١٩٨ .
٧٥٦٠ . نهج البلاغة : الخطبة ١٩٨ .
٧٥٦١ . نهج البلاغة : الخطبة ١٩٠ .
٧٥٦٢ . بحار الأنوار : ٧٠ / ٢٨٨ / ١٩ .
٧٥٦٣ . الكافي : ٨ / ٥٢ / ١٦ .
٧٥٦٤ . الدخان : ٥١ .
٧٥٦٥ . بحار الأنوار: ٧٠ / ٢٨٥ / ٨ .
٧٥٦٦ . البقرة : ١٧٧ .
٧٥٦٧ . الذاريات : ١٥ـ١٩ .
٧٥٦٨ . تنبيه الخواطر : ٢ / ٦٢ .
٧٥٦٩ . كنز العمّال : ٨٥٠١ .
٧٥٧٠ . نهج البلاغة : الخطبة ١٩٣ .
٧٥٧١ . الخصال : ٤٨٣ / ٥٦ .
٧٥٧٢ . الكافي : ٢ / ١٣٣ / ١٦ .
٧٥٧٣ . غرر الحكم : ٤٩٠٤ .
٧٥٧٤ . نهج البلاغة : الخطبة ١٧٦ .
٧٥٧٥ . نهج البلاغة : الحكمة ٢٩٨ .
٧٥٧٦ . بحار الأنوار : ٧٨ / ٣٧٧ / ٣ .
٧٥٧٧ . آل عمران : ١٠٢ .
٧٥٧٨ . بحار الأنوار : ٧٠ / ٢٩١ / ٣١ .
٧٥٧٩ . آل عمران : ١٠٢ .
٧٥٨٠ . التغابن : ١٦ .

٧٥٨١ . بحار الأنوار : ٧٠ / ٢٨٧ / ١٢.
٧٥٨٢ . تنبيه الخواطر : ٢ / ١٢٠ .
٧٥٨٣ . غرر الحكم : ٢١٦٢.
٧٥٨٤ . غرر الحكم : ٨٢٨٤ .
٧٥٨٥ . بحار الأنوار : ٧٠ / ٢٨٥ / ٨.
٧٥٨٦ . بحار الأنوار : ٧٠ / ٢٨٦ / ٩ .
٧٥٨٧ . الأمالي للصدوق : ٧٢ / ٤١ .
٧٥٨٨ . بحار الأنوار : ٧١ / ١٩٦ / ٤ .
٧٥٨٩ . معاني الأخبار : ١٩٦ / ٢ .
٧٥٩٠ . آل عمران : ٢٨ .
٧٥٩١ . النحل : ١٠٦.
٧٥٩٢ . الكافي : ٢ / ٢١٩ / ١٣ .
٧٥٩٣ . الكافي : ٢ / ٢٢٠ / ١٩ .
٧٥٩٤ . الكافي : ٢ / ٢١٨ / ٥.
٧٥٩٥ . الكافي : ٢ / ٢١٩ / ١١.
٧٥٩٦ . علل الشرائع : ٤٦٧ / ٢٢.
٧٥٩٧ . أمالي الطوسي : ٢١٠ / ٣٦٢ .
٧٥٩٨ . بحار الأنوار : ٧٦ / ٥ / ١٨ .
٧٥٩٩ . الكافي : ٢ / ١٦٨ / ١.
٧٦٠٠ . وسائل الشيعة : ١١ / ٤٨٣ / ٢.
٧٦٠١ . آل عمران : ١٥٩ .
٧٦٠٢ . الفرقان : ٥٨ .
٧٦٠٣ . الكافي : ٢ / ٤٧ / ٢.
٧٦٠٤ . غرر الحكم : ٥٤٤ .
٧٦٠٥ . بحار الأنوار : ٧٨ / ٧٩ / ٥٦.
٧٦٠٦ . غرر الحكم : ٦٤٨٤ .
٧٦٠٧ . آل عمران : ١٦٠
٧٦٠٨ . التوبة : ٥١ .
٧٦٠٩ . معاني الأخبار : ٢٦١ / ١، أُنظر تمام الحديث في بحار الأنوار : ٧٧ / ٢٠ / ٤ .
٧٦١٠ . سنن ابن ماجة : ٢ / ١١٥٤ / ٣٤٨٩ .
٧٦١١ . في الماضي القديم كان الناس ـ وخصوصاً العرب ـ يعالجون مرضاهم بالكيّ اذا يئسوا من الدواء، وكانوا يربطون الرُّقى التى يبتدعوها من انفسهم على أعناق وأيدي الأفراد لئلا يصيبهم داء، وهذا الحديث يرى أن الاتكال و الاعتماد على كلا الأمرين المذكورين بالكلية منافٍ للتوكل .

٧٦١٢ . الكافي : ٢ / ٥٧ / ١ .
٧٦١٣ . الطلاق : ٣ .
٧٦١٤ . بحار الأنوار : ٧١ / ١٥٦ / ٧٣ .
٧٦١٥ . جامع الأخبار : ٣٢١ / ٩٠٤ .
٧٦١٦ . غرر الحكم : ٩٠٢٨.
٧٦١٧ . جامع الأخبار : ٣٢٢ / ٩٠٥.
٧٦١٨ . جامع الأخبار : ٣٢٢ / ٩٠٧ .
٧٦١٩ . الكافي : ٢ / ٦٥ / ٣.
٧٦٢٠ . الكافي : ٢ / ٦٥ / ٦ .
٧٦٢١ . بحار الأنوار : ٧٨ / ٣٦٤ / ٥ .
٧٦٢٢ . الكافي : ٥ / ٨٤ / ٥ .
٧٦٢٣ . سنن الترمذي : ٤ / ٦٦٨ / ٢٥١٧ .
٧٦٢٤ . مستدرك الوسائل : ١١ / ٢١٧ / ١٢٧٨٩ .
٧٦٢٥ . نهج البلاغة : الخطبة ١١ .
٧٦٢٦ . مستدرك الوسائل : ١١ / ٢٢٠ / ١٢٧٩٨ .
٧٦٢٧ . الأمالي للطوسيّ : ١٩٣ / ٣٢٦.
٧٦٢٨ . كنز العمّال : ٨٥١٢.
٧٦٢٩ . مستدرك الوسائل : ١١ / ٢١٧ / ١٢٧٩٠ .
٧٦٣٠ . غرر الحكم : ٢٦٧٨ .
٧٦٣١ . كنز العمّال : ٤٥٤١٥ .
٧٦٣٢ . الكافي : ٦ / ٢ / ٢ .
٧٦٣٣ . الكافي : ٦ / ٤ / ٢ .
٧٦٣٤ . الأنفال : ٢٨ .
٧٦٣٥ . جامع الأخبار : ٢٨٣ / ٧٥٥ .
٧٦٣٦ . بحار الأنوار:١٠٤ / ٩٧ / ٦٠.
٧٦٣٧ . نهج البلاغة : الحكمة ٣٥٢.
٧٦٣٨ . الكافي : ٦ / ٤٩ / ٣.
٧٦٣٩ . الكافي : ٦ / ٥٠ / ٧ .
٧٦٤٠ . الكافي : ٦ / ٥٠ / ٥ .
٧٦٤١ . كتاب من لايحضره الفقيه : ٣ / ٤٨٣ / ٤٧٠٧ .
٧٦٤٢ . بحار الأنوار : ٤٣ / ٢٨٥ / ٥٠ .
٧٦٤٣ . الفرقان : ٧٤ .
٧٦٤٤ . الكافي : ٦ / ٣ / ١٠ .
٧٦٤٥ . الكافي : ٦ / ٢ / ١.
٧٦٤٦ . بحار الأنوار : ١٠٤ / ٩٨ / ٦٧.
٧٦٤٧ . بحار الأنوار : ١٠٤ / ٩٨ / ٦٦ .
٧٦٤٨ . مكارم الأخلاق : ١ / ٤٧١ / ١٦١٠ .

٧٦٤٩ . كنز العمّال : ٤٥٣٧٤ .

٧٦٥٠ . كنز العمّال : ٤٥٣٩٩ .

٧٦٥١ . الكافي : ٦ / ٦ / ٧ .

٧٦٥٢ . الكافي : ٦ / ٧ / ١٢ .

٧٦٥٣ . النُّحل : العطيّة والهبة ابتداءً من غير عِوَض ولا استحقاق . (النهاية : ٥ / ٢٩) .

٧٦٥٤ . كنز العمّال : ٤٥٣٤٧ .

٧٦٥٥ . بحار الأنوار : ٧٤ / ٨٤ / ٩٤ .

٧٦٥٦ . الإسراء : ٢٣ و ٢٤ .

٧٦٥٧ . الترغيب والترهيب : ٣ / ٣١٦ / ١٠ .

٧٦٥٨ . الترغيب والترهيب : ٣ / ٣١٤ / ١ .

٧٦٥٩ . الترغيب والترهيب : ٣ / ٣١٧ / ١٧ .

٧٦٦٠ . الترغيب والترهيب : ٣ / ٣٢٢ / ٣٠ .

٧٦٦١ . بحار الأنوار : ٧٤ / ٦٥ / ٣١ .

٧٦٦٢ . الخصال : ٦٠٨ / ٩ .

٧٦٦٣ . الخصال : ١٥٦ / ١٩٦ .

٧٦٦٤ . الترغيب والترهيب : ٣ / ٣٢٣ / ٣٢ .

٧٦٦٥ . الكافي : ٢ / ١٦٣ / ٢١ .

٧٦٦٦ . كنز العمّال : ٤٥٤٣٩ .

٧٦٦٧ . بحار الأنوار : ٧٤ / ٨٢ / ٨٨ .

٧٦٦٨ . الكافي : ٢ / ١٥٩ / ٩ .

٧٦٦٩ . الكافي : ٢ / ٣٤٨ / ١ .

٧٦٧٠ . الإسراء : ٢٤ .

٧٦٧١ . الكافي : ٢ / ١٥٨ / ١ .

٧٦٧٢ . الكافي : ٢ / ١٥٨ / ١ .

٧٦٧٣ . بحار الأنوار : ٧٤ / ٨٠ / ٨٢ .

٧٦٧٤ . كنز العمّال : ٤٥٥٣٧ .

٧٦٧٥ . علل الشرائع : ٤٧٩ / ٢ .

٧٦٧٦ . الكافي : ٢ / ٣٤٩ / ٧ .

٧٦٧٧ . بحار الأنوار : ٧٤ / ٦١ / ٢٦ .

٧٦٧٨ . بحار الأنوار : ٧٤ / ٨٤ / ٩٥ .

٧٦٧٩ . الكافي : ٢ / ١٥٩ / ٥ .

٧٦٨٠ . كنز العمّال : ٤٥٩٣٣ .

٧٦٨١ . مكارم الأخلاق : ١ / ٤٧٤ / ١٦٢٧ .

٧٦٨٢ . كنز العمّال : ٤٥١٩٣ .

٧٦٨٣ . بحار الأنوار : ٧٨ / ٢٣٦ / ٦٧ .

٧٦٨٤ . مكارم الأخلاق : ١ / ٤٧٥ / ١٦٣٣ .

٧٦٨٥ . كنز العمّال : ٤٥٤١٠ .

٧٦٨٦ . كنز العمّال : ٤٥٤٠٩ .

٧٦٨٧ . وسائل الشيعة : ١٢ / ٢٤٧ / ١٣ .

٧٦٨٨ . كنز العمّال : ٤٥٣٣٨ .

٧٦٨٩ . كنز العمّال : ٤٥٩٥٣ .

٧٦٩٠ . غرر الحكم : ٦٣٠٥ .

٧٦٩١ . وسائل الشيعة : ١٢ / ٢٤٧ / ١٢ .

٧٦٩٢ . النساء : ٥٩ .

٧٦٩٣ . كمال الدين : ٢٥٣ / ٣ .

٧٦٩٤ . الرعد : ١١ .

٧٦٩٥ . كتاب من لا يحضره الفقيه : ٤ / ٤٠٤ / ٥٨٧١ .

٧٦٩٦ . كنز العمّال : ١٤٩٧٢ .

٧٦٩٧ . نهج البلاغة : الخطبة ٩٧ .

٧٦٩٨ . بحار الأنوار : ٧٥ / ٣٤٠ / ١٨ .

٧٦٩٩ . الترغيب والترهيب : ٣ / ١٧٦ / ٤٠ .

٧٧٠٠ . غرر الحكم : ٥٦٢٦ .

٧٧٠١ . غرر الحكم : ٥٦٨٧ .

٧٧٠٢ . غرر الحكم : ٨٣٦٥ .

٧٧٠٣ . نهج البلاغة : الكتاب ٥٣ .

٧٧٠٤ . نهج البلاغة : الكتاب ٥٣ .

٧٧٠٥ . نهج البلاغة : الكتاب ٥٣ .

٧٧٠٦ . تهذيب الأحكام : ٦ / ٢٢٧ / ٥٤٧ .

٧٧٠٧ . نهج البلاغة : الكتاب ٥٣ .

٧٧٠٨ . نهج البلاغة: الكتاب٥٣ .

٧٧٠٩ . تحف العقول : ٣١٩ .

٧٧١٠ . الترغيب والترهيب: ٣ / ١٧٩ / ١ .

٧٧١١ . صحيح مسلم : ٣ / ١٤٥٦ / ١٤ .

٧٧١٢ . سنن أبي داوود : ٣ / ١٣٠ / ٢٩٢٩ .

٧٧١٣ . نهج البلاغة : الكتاب ٥٣ .

٧٧١٤ . العَين : الذي يُبعَث ليتجسّس الخبر (لسان العرب: ١٣ / ٣٠١) .

٧٧١٥ . تحدوني : تبعثني وتسوقني، وهو من حَدْو الإبل فإنّه من أكبر الأشياء على سوقها (النهاية : ١ / ٣٥٥) .

٧٧١٦ . نهج البلاغة : الكتاب ٥٣ .

٧٧١٧ . نهج البلاغة : الكتاب ٥٣ .

٧٧١٨ . تنبيه الخواطر : ٢ / ١٦٥ .

٧٧١٩ . نهج البلاغة : الكتاب ٥٣ .

٧٧٢٠ . نهج البلاغة : الكتاب ٥٣ .

٧٧٢١ . يونس : ٦٢، ٦٣ .

٧٧٢٢ . نهج البلاغة : الحكمة ٤٣٢ .

٧٧٢٣ . كمال الدين : ٣٥٧ / ٥٤ .

٧٧٢٤ . الكافي : ٢ / ٣٦١ / ١ .

٧٧٢٥ . الكافي : ٢ / ٣٦١ / ٢ .

٧٧٢٦ . الأمالي للصدوق : ٧٣ / ٤١ .

٧٧٢٧ . بحار الأنوار : ٧٥ / ٩٠ / ٢ .

٧٧٢٨ . بحار الأنوار : ٧٥ / ٩٠ / ٤ .

٧٧٢٩ . بحار الأنوار : ٧٥ / ٩١ / ٨ .

٧٧٣٠ . هود : ٩ـ ١١ .

٧٧٣١ . غرر الحكم : ٢٨٦٠ .

٧٧٣٢ . غرر الحكم : ٦٧٣١ .

٧٧٣٣ . نهج البلاغة : الحكمة ٣٤٢ .

٧٧٣٤ . نهج البلاغة : الكتاب ٣١ .

٧٧٣٥ . وسائل الشيعة : ٦ / ٣١٤ / ٥ .

٧٧٣٦ . البقرة : ٨٣ .

٧٧٣٧ . تفسير نور الثقلين : ٥ / ٥٩٧ / ٢٣ .

٧٧٣٨ . كنز العمّال : ٦٠٠٨ .

٧٧٣٩ . الترغيب والترهيب : ٣ / ٣٤٩ / ١٤ .

٧٧٤٠ . أغبَّ القومَ : جاءهم يوماً وترك يوماً (القاموس المحيط : ١ / ١٠٩) أي : صِلُوا أفواههم بالإطعام ولا تقطعوه عنها . (كما في هامش نهج البلاغة ضبط الدكتور صبحي الصالح) .

٧٧٤١ . الكافي : ٧ / ٥١ / ٧ .

٧٧٤٢ . النساء : ١٠ .

٧٧٤٣ . الأمالي للصدوق : ٥٧٧ / ٧٨٨ .

٧٧٤٤ . تفسير العيّاشيّ : ١ / ٢٢٥ / ٤٧ .

٧٧٤٥ . بحار الأنوار : ٧٩ / ٢٦٨ / ٧ .

٧٧٤٦ . السجدة : ٢٤ .

٧٧٤٧ . الأمالي للصدوق : ٥٧٦ / ٧٨٨ .

٧٧٤٨ . بحار الأنوار : ٧٠ / ١٧٦ / ٣٣ .

٧٧٤٩ . غرر الحكم : ٩٥٥٦ .

٧٧٥٠ . نهج البلاغة : الخطبة ١٥٧ .

٧٧٥١ . غرر الحكم : ٦١٨٤ .

٧٧٥٢ . غرر الحكم : ٣٩٨ .

٧٧٥٣ . غرر الحكم : ٩٩٥٨ .

٧٧٥٤ . الكافي : ٢ / ٥٢ / ٥ .

٧٧٥٥ . الكافي : ٢ / ٥١ / ١ .

٧٧٥٦ . الكافي : ٢ / ٥٧ / ٣ .

٧٧٥٧ . التكاثر : ٥ـ ٨ .

٧٧٥٨ . الأنعام : ٧٥ .

٧٧٥٩ . كنز العمّال : ٢٩٨٥٨ .

٧٧٦٠ . بحار الأنوار : ٧٧ / ٢٠ / ٤ .

٧٧٦١ . نهج البلاغة : الحكمة ١٢٥ .

٧٧٦٢ . تحف العقول : ٢٠ .

٧٧٦٣ . غرر الحكم : ١٠٩٧٠ .

٧٧٦٤ . بحار الأنوار : ٧٣ / ١٦٧ / ٣١ .

٧٧٦٥ . بحار الأنوار : ٧٨ / ٩٢ / ٩٨ .

٧٧٦٦ . غرر الحكم : ١١٠١١ .

٧٧٦٧ . غرر الحكم : ١١٧٧ .

٧٧٦٨ . غرر الحكم : ٥٠٧٢ .

٧٧٦٩ . بحار الأنوار : ٧٣ / ١٦١ / ٦ .

٧٧٧٠ . كنز العمّال : ٧٣٣٢ .

٧٧٧١ . بحار الأنوار : ٧٧ / ١٨٥ / ٣٠ .

٧٧٧٢ . غرر الحكم : ٦٣٤٧ و ٦٣٤٨ .

٧٧٧٣ . غرر الحكم : ٥٤٨٨ .

٧٧٧٤ . غرر الحكم : ٦٩٩ .

٧٧٧٥ . مشكاة الأنوار : ٥٦ / ٥٨ .

٧٧٧٦ . بحار الأنوار : ٧١ / ١٥٢ / ٦٠ .

٧٧٧٧ . غرر الحكم : ٧٥٦٩ .

٧٧٧٨ . الكافي : ٢ / ٢٦٨ / ١ .

٧٧٧٩ . البقرة : ٢٦٠ .

٧٧٨٠ . بحار الأنوار : ٧٠ / ١٧٦ / ٣٤ .

Bibliography

Al-Iḥtijāj ʿalā ahl al-Lijāj, Aḥmad ibn ʿAli al-Ṭabrasi [620AH], researched by: Ibrāhim al-Bahāduri and Muḥammad Hādibeh, Tehran: Dār al-Uswah, 1413 AH. First Edition

Iḥqāq al-Ḥaqq wa Iẓhāq al-Bāṭel, Nurullah ibn al-Seyyed Sharīf al-Shushtari (al-Qāḍi al-Tustari) [1019AH], with commentary by: al-Seyyed Shahāb al-Dīn al-Marʿashi, Qum: Maktabah Āyatullah al-Marʿashi, 1411 AH. First Edition

Al-Ikhtiṣāṣ, attributed to Muḥammad ibn Muḥammad ibn al-Nuʿmān al-ʿAkbari al-Baghdādi (al-Shaikh al-Mufīd) [413AH], researched by: ʿAli Akbar al-Ghaffāri, Qum: Muʾassasah al-Nashr al-Islāmi, 1414 AH. Forth Edition

Al-Irshād fi Maʿrifah Ḥujjaj Allah ʿalā al-ʿIbād, Muḥammad ibn Muḥammad ibn al-Nuʿmān al-ʿAkbari al-Baghdādi (al-Shaikh al-Mufīd) [413AH], researched by: Muʾassasah Āl al-Bayt (AS), Qum, Muʾassasah Āl al-Bayt (AS), 1413 AH. First Edition

Irshād al-Qulūb, al-Ḥasan ibn Muḥammad al-Daylami [711 AH], Beyrūt: Muʾassasah al-Aʿlami, 1398 AH. Forth Edition

Al-Uṣūl al-Sittah ʿAshar, by a group of narrators, Qum: Dār al-Shabestari, 1405 AH. Second Edition

Aʿlām al-Dīn fi Ṣifāt al-Muʾminīn, al-Ḥasan ibn Muḥammad al-Daylami [711AH], researched by: Muʾassasah Āl al-Bayt (AS), Qum, Muʾassasah Āl al-Bayt (AS)

Iʿlām al-Warā bi Aʿlām al-Hudā, al-Faḍl ibn al-Ḥasan al-Ṭabrasi [548AH], Muʾassasah Āl al-Bayt (AS), Qum, Muʾassasah Āl al-Bayt (AS). First Edition

Al-Iqbāl bi al-Aʿmāl al-Ḥasanah fi ma yuʿmal marrah fi al-Sanah, ʿAli ibn Mūsā al-Ḥilli (al-Seyyed Ibn Ṭāwūs) [664AH], researched by: Jawād al-Qayyūmi, Qum: Maktab al-Iʿlām al-Islāmi, 1414 AH. First Edition

Al-Amāli, Muḥammad ibn al-Ḥasan al-Ṭūsi [460AH], researched by: Muʾassasah al-Biʿthah, Qum: Dār al-Thaqāfah, 1414 AH. First Edition

Al-Amāli, Muḥammad ibn ʿAli Ibn Bābwayh al-Qummi (al-Shaikh al-Ṣadūq) [d. 381 AH], researched by: Muʾassasah al-Biʿthah, Qum: Dār al-Thaqāfah, 1414 AH. First Edition

Al-Amāli, Muḥammad ibn Muḥammad ibn al-Nuʿmān al-ʿAkbari al-Baghdādi (al-Shaikh al-Mufīd) [413AH], researched by: Ḥusain Ustād Wali and ʿAli Akbar al-Ghaffāri, Qum: Muʾassasah al-Nashr al-Islāmi, 1404 AH. Second Edition

Ansāb al-Ashrāf, Aḥmad ibn Yaḥyā al-Bilādhari [279AH], researched by: Suhail Zakkār and Riyāḍ Zarkali, Beyrūt: Dār al-Fikr, 1417 AH. First Edition

Biḥār al-Anwār al-Jāmiʿah li Durar Akhbār al-Aʾimmah al-Aṭhār (AS), Muḥammad Bāqir ibn Muḥammad Taqi al-Majlisi (al-ʿAllāmah al-Majlisi) [1111 AH], Beyrūt: Muʾassasah al-Wafā, 1403 AH. Second Edition

Bishārah al-Muṣṭafā li Shiʿah al-Murtaḍā, Muḥammad ibn Muḥammad al-Ṭabari [525 AH], Najaf: al-Maṭbaʿah al-Ḥaidariyah, 1383 AH, Second Edition

Baṣāʾīr al-Darajāt, Muḥammad ibn al-Ḥasan al-Ṣaffār al-Qummi (Ibn Farrukh) [290AH], Qum: Maktabah Āyatullah al-Marʿashi, 1404 AH. First Edition

Al-Balad al-Amīn wa al-Dirʿ al-Ḥaṣīn, Ibrāhim ibn Zain al-Dīn al-Kafʿami [905 AH]

Tārikh Dimashq, ʿAli ibn al-Ḥasan ibn Hibatullah (Ibn ʿAsākir al-Dimashqi) [571 AH], researched by: ʿAli Shīri, Beyrūt: Dār al-Fikr, 1415 AH. First Edition

Tuḥaf al-ʿUqūl ʿan Āl al-Rasūl (ṣ.a.w.), al-Ḥasan ibn ʿAli al-Ḥarrāni (Ibn Shuʿbah) [381 AH], researched by: ʿAli Akbar al-Ghaffāri, Qum: Muʾassasah al-Nashr al-Islāmi, 1404 AH. Second Edition

Al-Targhīb wa al-Tarhīb min al-Ḥadīth al-Sharīf, Zaki al-Dīn ʿAbd al-ʿAḍīm ibn ʿAbd al-Qawwi al-Mundhiri [656AH], compiled and commented upon by: Muṣṭafā Muḥammad ʿAmārah, Beyrūt: Dār al-Fikr, 1408 AH

Tafsīr al-Ṭabari = Jāmiʿ al-Bayān ʿan Taʾwīl Āy al-Qurʾān

Tafsīr al-ʿAyyāshi, Muḥammad ibn Masʿūd al-Silmi al-Samarqandi (al-ʿAyyāshi) [320 AH], researched by: Hāshim al-Rasūli al-Maḥalāti, Tehran: al-Maktabah al-ʿIlmiyah, 1380 AH. First Edition

Tafsīr al-Qurṭubi = al-Jāmiʿ li Aḥkām al-Qurʾān

Tafsīr al-Qummi, ʿAli ibn Ibrāhim al-Qummi [307 AH], researched by: al-Seyyed al-Ṭayyeb al-Mūsawi al-Jazaʾiri, Maṭbaʿah al-Najaf al-Ashraf

Tafsīr Nūr al-Thaqalayn = Nūr al-Thaqalayn

Al-Tafsīr al-Mansūb ilā al-Imām al-'Askari (AS), researched by: Madrasa al-Imām al-Mahdi (AS), Qum: Madrasa al-Imām al-Mahdi (AS), 1409 AH. First Edition

Tafsīr al-Mizān = al-Mizān fi Tafsīr al-Qur'ān

Al-Tamḥīṣ, Muḥammad ibn Humām al-Iskāfi [336 AH], researched by: Madrasa al-Imām al-Mahdi (AS), Qum: Madrasa al-Imām al-Mahdi (AS)

Tanbīh al-Khawāṭir wa Nuzhaht al-Nawāẓir (Majmū'ah Warrām), Warrām ibn abū Firās al-Ḥamdān [605 AH], Beyrūt: Dār al-Ta'āruf wa Dār Ṣa'b

Tahdhīb al-Aḥkām fi sharḥal-Muqni'ah, Muḥammad ibn al-Ḥasan al-Ṭūsi (al-Shaikh al- Ṭūsi) [460 AH], Beyrūt: Dār al-Ta'āruf, 1401 AH. First Edition

Al-Tawḥid, Muḥammad ibn 'Ali Ibn Babwayh al-Qummi (al-Shaikh al-Ṣadūq) [381 AH], researched by: Hāshim al-Ḥusaini al-Ṭehrāni, Qum: Mu'assasah al-Nashr al-Islāmi, 1398 AH. First Edition

Thawāb al-A'māl wa 'Iqāb al-A'māl, Muḥammad ibn 'Ali Ibn Babwayh al-Qummi (al-Shaikh al-Ṣadūq) [381 AH], researched by: 'Ali Akbar al-Ghaffāri, Tehran: Maktabah al- Ṣadūq

Jāmi' al-Aḥādith, Ja'far ibn Aḥmad al-Qummi (Ibn al-Rāzi) [4th century AH], researched by: al-Seyyed Muḥammad al-Ḥusaini al-Nisābūri, Mashhad: Mu'assasah al-Ṭab' wa al-Nashr al-tābi'ah li al-Ḥaḍrah al-Raḍawiyah al-Muqadasah, 1413 AH. First Edition

Jāmi' al-Akhbār aw Ma'ārij al-Yaqīn fi Uṣūl al-Dīn, Muḥammad ibn Muḥammad al-Shu'airi al-Sabziwāri [7th century AH] researched by: Mu'assasah Āl al-Bayt (AS), Qum: Mu'assasah Āl al-Bayt (AS), 1414 AH. First Edition

Jāmi' al-Bayān 'an Ta'wīl Āy al-Qur'ān (Tafsīr al-Ṭabari), Muḥammad ibn Jarīr al-Ṭabari [d. 310 AH], Beyrūt: Dār al-Fikr, 1480 AH. First Edition

Al-Jāmi' li Aḥkām al-Qur'ān (Tafsīr al-Qurṭabi), Muḥammad ibn Aḥmad al-Anṣāri al- Qurṭubi [d. 671 AH], researched by: Muḥammad 'Abd al-Raḥmān al-Mar'ashl., Beyrūt: Dār Iḥyā' al-Turāth al-'Arabi, 1405 AH. Second Edition

Al-Ja'fariyāt (al-Ash'athiyāt), Muḥammad ibn Muḥammad ibn al-Ash'ath al-Kūfi [4th century AH], Tehran: Maktabah Naynawā

Al-Kharā'ij wa al-Jarā'iḥ, Sa'īd ibn 'Abdullah al-Rāwandi (Quṭb al-Dīn al-Rāwandi) [d. 573 AH], researched by: Mu'assasah al-Imām al-Mahdi (AS), Qum: Mu'assasah al-Imām al-Mahdi (AS), 1409 AH. First Edition

Khaṣā'iṣ al-A'immah (AS) (Khaṣā'iṣ Amir al-Mu'minīn(AS)), Muḥammad ibn al-Ḥusain al-Musawi (al-Sharīf al-Raḍi) [d. 406 AH], researched by: Muḥammad Hādi al-Amini, Mashhad: Majma' al-Buḥūth al-Islāmiyah al-tābi'ah li al-Ḥaḍrah al-Raḍawiyah al-Muqadasah, 1406 AH

Al-Khiṣāl, Muḥammad ibn 'Ali Ibn Babwayh al-Qummi (al-Shaikh al-Ṣadūq) [381 AH], Qum: Mu'assasah al-Nashr al-Islāmi, 1414 AH. Forth Edition

Ḥilyah al-Awliyā wa Ṭabaqāt al-Aṣfiyā', Aḥmad ibn 'Abdullah al-Iṣbahāni (Abū Na'īm) [d. 430 AH], Beyrūt: Dār al-Kitāb al-'Arabi, 1387 AH. Second Edition

Al-Durr al-Manthūr fi al-Tafsīr al-Ma'thūr, 'Abd al-Raḥmān ibn Abū Bakr al-Suyūṭī [d. 911 AH], Beyrūt: Dār al-Fikr, 1414 AH. First Edition

Al-Durrah al-Bāhirah min al-Aṣdāf al-Ṭāhirah, Muḥammad ibn Makki al-'Āmili (al-Shahīd al-Awwal), Mashhad: Mu'assasah al-ṭab' wa al-Nashr al-tābi'ah li al-Ḥaḍrah al-Raḍawiyah al-Muqadasah, 1365 Solar

Al-Da'awāt, Sa'īd ibn 'Abdullah al-Rāwandi (Quṭb al-Dīn al-Rāwandi) [d. 573 AH], researched by: Mu'assasah al-Imām al-Mahdi (AS), Qum: Mu'assasah al-Imām al-Mahdi (AS), 1407 AH. First Edition

Da'ā'im al-Islām wa Dikr al-Ḥalāl wa al-Ḥarām wa al-Qaḍāyā wa al-Aḥkām, al-Nu'mān ibn Muḥammad al-Tamimi al-Maghribi [d. 363 AH], researched by: Āṣif ibn 'Ali Aṣghar Fayḍi, Egypt: Dār al-Ma'ārif, 1389 AH. Third Edition

Dalā'il al-Imāmah, Muḥammad ibn Jarīr al-Ṭabari [d. 310 AH], researched by: Mu'assasah al-Bi'thah, Qum: Mu'assasah al-Bi'thah, 1413 AH. First Edition

Rabī' al-Abrār wa Nuṣūṣ al-Akhbār, Maḥmūd ibn 'Umar al-Zamakhshari [d. 538 AH], researched by: Salīm al-Na'īmi, Qum: Manshūrāt al-Sharīf al-Raḍi, 1410 AH. First Edition

Rawḍah al-Wā'iẓīn, Muḥammad ibn al-Ḥasan al-Fattāl al-Nisābūri [d. 508 AH], researched by: Ḥusain al-A'lami, Beyrūt: Mu'assasah al-A'lami, 1406 AH. First Edition

Al-Zuhd, Ḥusain ibn Sa'īd al-Kūfi al-Ahwāzi [3d century AH], Qum: al-Maṭba'ah al-'Ālamiyah

Safīnah al-Biḥār wa Madina al-Ḥikam wa al-Āthār, al-Shaikh ʿAbbās al-Qummi ibn Muḥammad Riḍā [d. 1359 AH], Mashhad: Majmaʿ al-Buḥūth al-Islāmiyah

Sunan Ibn Mājah, Muḥammad ibn Yazīd al-Qazwini (Ibn Mājah) [d. 275 AH], researched by: Muḥammad Fu'ād ʿAbd al-Bāqi, Beyrūt: Dār Iḥyā' al-Turāth, 1395 AH. First Edition

Sunan al-Tirmidhi (al-Jāmi ʿal-Ṣaḥiḥ), Muḥammad ibn ʿIsā al-Tirmidhi [d. 297 AH], researched by: Aḥmad Muḥammad Shākir, Beyrūt: Dār Iḥyā' al-Turāth

Sunan al-Nisā'i bi sharḥ al-Ḥāfiẓ Jalāl al-Dīn al-Suyūṭi wa ḥāshiyah al-Imām al-Sindi, Aḥmad ibn Shuʿayb al-Nisā'i [d. 303 AH], Beyrūt: Dār al-Jīl, 1407 AH. First Edition

Sharḥ Nahj al-Balāghah, ʿAbd al-Ḥamīd ibn Muḥammad al-Muʿtazili (Ibn Abi al-Ḥadid) [d. 656 AH], researched by: Muḥammad Abū al-Faḍl Ibrāhim, Beyrūt: Dār Iḥyā' al-Turāth, 1387 AH. Second Edition

Sharḥ Nahj al-Balāghah, Maytham ibn ʿAli al-Baḥrāni [d. 689 AH], Beyrūt: Dār al-Āthār li al-Nashr, 1402 AH

Shuʿb al-Imān, Aḥmad ibn al-Ḥusain al-Bayhaqi [d. 458 AH], researched by: Muḥammad ibn al-Saʿīd Basyūni Zaghlūl, Beyrūt: Dār al-Kutub al-ʿIlmiyah, 1410 AH. First Edition

Shawāhid al-Tanzīl li Qawāʿid al-Tafḍīl, ʿUbaydullah ibn ʿAbdullah al-Nisābūri (al-Ḥākim al-Ḥasakāni) [5th century AH], researched by: Muḥammad Bāqir al-Maḥmūdi, Tehran: Mu'assasah al-Ṭabʿ wa al-Nashr al-Tabiʿah li Wizārah al-Thaqāfa wa al-Irshād al-Islāmi, 1411 AH. First Edition

Ṣaḥiḥ al-Bukhāri, Muḥammad ibn Ismāʿī al-Bukhāri [d. 256 AH], researched by: Muṣṭafā Dayb al-Baghā, Beyrūt: Dār Ibn Kathīr, 1410 AH. Forth Edition

Ṣaḥiḥ Muslim, Muslim ibn al-Ḥajjāj al-Qushayri al-Nisābūri [d. 261 AH], researched by: Muḥammad Fu'ād ʿAbd al-Bāqi, Cairo: Dār al-Ḥadīth, 1412 AH. First Edition

Ṣaḥifah al-Imām al-Riḍā (AS), attribute to al-Imām al-Riḍā (AS), researched by: Muʿassasah al-Imām al-Mahdi (AS), Qum: Muʿassasah al-Imām al-Mahdi (AS), 1408 AH. First Edition

Al-Ṣaḥifah al-Sajādiyah, attribute to al-Imām ʿAli ibn al-Ḥusain (AS), edited by: ʿAli Anṣāriyān, Dimashq: al-Mustashāriyah al-Thaqāfiyah li al-Jumhūriyah al-Islāmiyah al-Irāniyah, 1405 AH

Al-Ṭabaqāt al-Kubrā, Muḥammad ibn Saʿd (Kātib al-Wāqidi) [d. 230 AH], Beyrūt: Dār Ṣādir

ʿUddaht al-Dāʿi wa Najāḥ al-Sāʿi, Aḥmad ibn Muḥammad al-Ḥilli al-Asadi [d. 841 AH], researched by: Aḥmad al-Muwaḥidi, Tehran: Maktabah Wejdāni

ʿIlal al-Sharāʾiʿ, Muḥammad ibn ʿAli ibn Bābwayh al-Qummi (al-Shaikh al-Ṣadūq) [d. 381 Ah], Beyrūt: Dār Iḥyāʾ al-Turāth, 1408 AH. First Edition

ʿAwāli al-Laʾāli al-ʿAziziyah fi al-Aḥādīth al-Diniyah, Muḥammad ibn ʿAli al-Aḥsāʾi (Ibn Abi Jumhūr) [d. 940 AH], researched by: Mujtabā al-ʿIrāqi, Qum: Maṭbaʿah Seyyed al-Shuhadāʾ (AS), 1403 AH. First Edition

ʿUyūn Akhbār al-Riḍā (AS), Muḥammad ibn ʿAli ibn Bābwayh al-Qummi (al-Shaikh al-Ṣadūq) [d. 381 Ah], researched by: al-Seyyed Mahdi al-Ḥusaini al-Lājawardi, Tehran: Manshūrāt Jahān

Al-Ghārāt, Ibrāhim ibn Muḥammad (Ibn Hilāl al-Thaqafi) [d. 283 AH], researched by: Mīr Jalāl al-Dīn al-Muḥadith al-Urmawi, Tehran: Anjuman Āthār Melli, 1395 AH. First Edition

Ghurar al-Ḥikam wa Durar al-Kalim, ʿAbd al-Wāḥid al-Āmadi al-Tamimi [d. 550 AH], researched by: Mīr Jalāl al-Dīn al-Muḥadith al-Urmawi, Tehran: Tehran University, 1360 Solar. Third Edition

Al-Ghaybah, Muḥammad ibn Ibrāhim al-Kātib al-Nuʿmāni [d. 350 AH], researched by: ʿAli Akbar al-Ghaffāri, Tehran: al-Ṣadūq library

Al-Ghaybah, Muḥammad ibn al-Ḥasan al-Ṭūsi [d. 460 AH], researched by: ʿIbādullah al-Ṭahrāni and ʿAli Aḥmad Nāṣih, Qum: Muʾassasah al-Maʿārif al-Islāmiyah, 1411 AH. First Editiion

Farāʾid al-Simṭain fi Faḍāʾil al-Murtaḍā wa al-Batūl wa al-Sibṭain wa al-Aʾimmah min Dhuriyatihim, Ibrāhim ibn Muḥammad al-Juwayni [d. 730AH], researched by: Bāqir al-Maḥmūdi, Beyrūt: Muʾassasah al-Maḥmūdi, 1398 AH. First Edition

Al-Firdaws bi Maʾthūr al-Khiṭāb, Shirwayh ibn Shahrdār al-Daylami al-Hamedāni [d. 509 AH], researched by: Muḥammad al-Saʾīd Basyūni Zaghlūl, Beyrūt: Dār al-Kutub al-ʿIlmiyah, 1406 AH. First Edition

Al-Faḍā'il, Shādhān ibn Jabra'īl al-Qummi [d. 660 AH], Najaf: al-Maṭba'h al-Ḥaydariyah, 1338 AH

Faḍā'il al-Ashhur al-Thalāthah, Muḥammad ibn 'Ali ibn Bābwayh al-Qummi (al-Shaikh al-Ṣadūq) [d. 381 Ah], researched by: Ghulāmriḍā 'Irfāniyān, Qum: al-Dāwari library, 1396 AH. First Edition

Faḍā'il al-Shi'a, Muḥammad ibn 'Ali ibn Bābwayh al-Qummi (al-Shaikh al-Ṣadūq) [d. 381 Ah], researched by: Mu'assasah al-Imām al-Mahdi (AS), Qum: Mu'assasah al-Imām al-Mahdi (AS), 1410 AH. First Edition

Falāḥ al-Sā'il, 'Ali ibn Mūsā al-Ḥilli (al-Seyyed Ibn Ṭāwūs) [d.664 AH], researched by: Ghulāmḥusain Majidi, Qum: Maktab al-I'lām al-Islāmi, 1419 AH. First Edition

Qurb al-Isnād, 'Abdullah ibn Ja'far al-Ḥimyari, al-Qummi [d. after 304 AH], researched by: Mu'assasah Āl al-Bayt (AS), Qum: Mu'assasah Āl al-Bayt (AS), 1413 AH. First Edition

Qiṣaṣ al-Anbiyā', Sa'īd ibn 'Abdullah (Quṭb al-Dīn al-Rāwandi) [d. 573 AH], researched by: Ghulāmriḍā 'Irfāniyān, Mashhad: Majma' al-Buḥūth al-Islāmiya al-Tābi' li al-Āstāneh al-Raḍawiyah, 1409 AH. First Edition

Al-Kāfi, Muḥammad ibn Ya'qūb al-Kulayni al-Rāzi [d. 329 AH], researched by: 'Ali Akbar al-Ghaffāri, Beyrūt: Dār Ṣa'b wa Dār al-Ta'āruf, 1401 AH. First Edition

Kitāb man lā Yaḥḍurhu al-Faqih, Muḥammad ibn 'Ali ibn Bābwayh al-Qummi (al-Shaikh al-Ṣadūq) [d. 381 Ah], researched by: 'Ali Akbar al-Ghaffāri, Qum: Mu'assasah al-Nashr al-Islāmi, Second Edition

Kashf al-Ghummah fi Ma'rifah al-A'immah, 'Ali ibn 'Isā al-Irbali [d. 687 AH], edited by: al-Seyyed Hāshim al-Rasūli al-Maḥlāti, Beyrūt: Dār al-Kitāb, 1401 AH. First Edition

Kashf al-Maḥajjah li Thamarah al-Muhjah, 'Ali ibn Mūsā al-Ḥilli (al-Seyyed Ibn Ṭāwūs) [d. 664 AH], researched by: Muḥammad al-Ḥassūn, Qum: Maktab al-I'lām al-Islāmi, 1412 AH. First Edition

Kifāyah al-Athar fi al-Naṣṣ 'Alā al-A'immah al-Ithnā 'Ashar, 'Ali ibn Muḥammad al-Khazzāz al-Qummi [4th century AH], researched by: al-Seyyed 'Abd al-Laṭīf al-Ḥusaini al-Kūh Kamari, Qum: Bidār, 1401 AH

Kamāl al-Dīn wa Itmām al-Niʿmah, Muḥammad ibn ʿAli ibn Bābwayh al-Qummi (al-Shaikh al-Ṣadūq) [d. 381 AH], researched by: ʿAli Akbar al-Ghaffāri, Qum: Muʾassasah al-Nashr al-Islāmi, 1405 AH. First Edition

Kanz al-ʿUmmāl fi Sunan al-Aqwāl wa al-Afʿāl, ʿAli al-Mutaqi ibn Ḥisām al-Dīn al-Hindi [d. 975 AH], edited by: Ṣafwah al-Saqqā, Beyrūt: Maktabah al-Turāth al-Islāmi, 1397 AH. First Edition

Kanz al-Fawāʾid, Muḥammad ibn ʿAli al-Karājaki al-Ṭarāblasi [d. 449 AH], researched by: ʿAbdullah Niʿmah, Qum: Dār al-Dhakhāʾir, 1410 AH. First Edition

Al-Maḥāsin, Aḥmad ibn Muḥammad al-Barqi [d. 280 AH], researched by: al-Seyyed Mahdi al-Rajāʾi, Qum: al-Majmaʿ al-ʿĀlami li Ahl al-Bayt (AS), 1413 AH. First Edition

Majmaʿ al-Bayān fi Tafsīr al-Qurʾān, al-Faḍl ibn al-Ḥasan al-Ṭabrasi (Amīn al-Islām) [d. 548 AH], researched by: al-Seyyed Hāshim al-Rasūli al-Maḥallāti and al-Seyyed Faḍlullah al-Yazdi al-Ṭabāṭabāʾi, Beyrūt: Dār al-Maʿrifah, 1408 AH. Second Edition

Al-Maḥajjah al-Bayḍāʾ fi Tahdhīb al-Aḥyāʾ, Muḥammad Muḥsin ibn Shāh Murtaḍā al-Fayḍ al-Kāshāni [d. 1091 AH], with footnotes by: ʿAli Akbar al-Ghaffāri, Qum: Jamāʿah al-Mudarisīn fi al-Ḥawzah al-ʿIlmiyah, 1383 AH

Mukhtaṣar Tārikh Dimashq, Muḥammad ibn Mukram al-Miṣri al-Anṣāri (Ibn Manẓūr) [d. 711 AH], researched by: Rātib Ḥammūsh, Dimashq: Dār al-Fikr

Al-Mustadrak ʿalā al-Ṣaḥiḥain, Muḥammad ibnʿAbdullah al-Ḥākim al-Nisābūri [d. 405 AH], researched by: Muṣṭafā ʿAbd al-Qādir ʿAṭā, Beyrūt: Dār al-Kutub al-ʿIlmiya, 1411 AH. First Edition

Mustadrak al-Wasāʾil wa Mustanbaṭ al-Masāʾil, Ḥusain al-Nūri al-Ṭabrasi [d. 1320 AH], Qum: Muʾassasah Āl al-Bayt (AS), 1407 AH. First Edition

Musakkin al-Fuʾād, Zayn al-Dīn ibn ʿAli al-Jibʿi al-ʿĀmili (al-Shahīd al-Thāni) [d. 965 AH], researched by: Muʾassasah Āl al-Bayt (AS): li Iḥyāʾ al-Turāth, Qum: Muʾassasah Āl al-Bayt (AS), 1412 AH. Second Editions

Al-Musnad, Aḥmad ibn Muḥammad al-Shaybāni (Ibn Ḥanbal) [d. 241 AH], researched by: ʿAbdullah Muḥammad al-Darwīsh, Beyrūt: Dār al-Fikr, 1414 AH. Second Edition

Mishkāt al-Anwār fī Ghurar al-Akhbār, ʿAli ibn al-Ḥasan al-Ṭabrasi [d. 7th century AH], researched by: Mahdi Hūshmand, Qum: Dār al-Ḥadīth, 1418 AH. First Edition

Miṣbāḥ al-Shariʿah wa Miftāḥ al-Ḥaqiqah, attribute to Imām al-Ṣādiq (AS), commentary by: ʿAbd al-Razzāq Gilāni, Tehran: Nashr Ṣadūq, 1407 AH. Third Edition

Miṣbāḥ al-Mutahajjid, Muḥammad ibn al-Ḥasan al-Ṭūsi (al-Shaikh al-Ṭūsi) [d. 460 AH], researched by: ʿAli Aṣghar Murwārīd, Beyrūt: Muʾassasah Fiqh al-Shiʿh, 1411 AH. First Edition

Al-Muṣaniff, ʿAbd al-Razzāq ibn Hammām al-Ṣanʿāni [d. 211 AH], researched by: Ḥabib al-Raḥmān al-Aʿẓami, Beyrūt: Manshūrāt al-Majlis al-ʿIlmi

Maṭālib al-Suʾūl fī Manāqib Āl al-Rasūl, Muḥammad ibn Ṭalḥah al-Shāfiʿi [d. 654 AH], Qum: manuscript in Āyahtullah al-Marʿashi's library

Maʿāni al-Akhbār, Muḥammad ibn ʿAli ibn Bābwayh al-Qummi (al-Shaikh al-Ṣadūq) [d. 381 Ah], researched by: ʿAli Akbar al-Ghaffāri, Qum: Muʾassasah al-Nashr al-Islāmi, 1361 Sailor. First Edition

Al-Muʿjam al-Kabīr, Sulaymān ibn Aḥmad al-Lakhmi al-Ṭabarāni [d. 360 AH], researched by: Ḥamdi ʿAb al-Majīd al-Salafi, Beyrūt: Dār Iḥyāʾ al-Turāth al-ʿArab_, 1404 AH. Second Edition

Mufradāt Alfāẓ al-Qurʾān, Ḥusain ibn Muḥammad al-Rāghib al-Iṣfahāni [d. 425 AH], researched by: Ṣafwān ʿAdnān Dāwūdi, Beyrūt: Dār al-Qalam, 1412 AH. First Edition

Makārim al-Akhlāq, al-Faḍl ibn al-Ḥasan al-Ṭabrasi [d. 548 AH], researched by:ʿAlāʾ Āl Jaʿfar, Qum: Muʾassasah al-Nashr al-Islāmi, 1414 AH. First Edition

Al-Malāḥim wa al-Fitan (al-Tashrīf bi al-Minan fi Taʿrīf bi al-Fitan), ʿAli ibn Mūsā al-Ḥilli (al-Seyyed Ibn Ṭāwūs) [d.664 AH], researched and published by: Muʾassasah Ṣāḥib al-Amr, 1416 AH. First Edition

Al-Malhūf ʿalā Qatla al-Ṭufūf, ʿAli ibn Mūsā al-Ḥilli (al-Seyyed Ibn Ṭāwūs) [d.664 AH], researched by: Fāres Tabriziyān, Tehran: Dār al-Uswah, 1414 AH. First Edition

Manāqib Āl Abū Ṭālib (al-Manāqib li Ibn Shahr Āshūb), Muḥammad ibn ʿAli al-Māzandarāni (Ibn Shahr Āshūb) [d. 588 AH], Qum: al-Maṭbaʿh al-ʿIlmiya

Munyat al-Murīd, Zayn al-Dīn ʿAli al-ʿĀmili (al-Shahīd al-Thāni) [d. 965 AH], Qum: Maktab al-Iʿlām al-Islāmi, 1415 AH

Muhajt al-Daʿawāt wa Manhaj al-ʿIbādāt, ʿAli ibn Mūsā al-Ḥilli (al-Seyyed Ibn Ṭāwūs) [d.664 AH], researched by: Ḥusain al-Aʿlami, Beyrūt: Muʾassasah al-Aʿlami, 1414 AH. First Edition

Al-Muwaṭṭa', Mālik ibn Anas [d. 158 AH], researched by: Muḥammad Fuʾād ʿAbd al-Bāqi, Beyrūt: Dār Iḥyāʾ al-Turāth al-ʿArabi, 1406 AH. First Edition

Al-Mizān fi Tafsīr al-Qurʾān, al-Seyyed Muḥammad Ḥusain al-Ṭabāṭabāʾi [d. 1402 AH], Qum: Ismāʿiliyān, 1394 AH. Third Edition

Nuzhat al-Nāẓir wa Tanbīh al-Khawāṭit, al-Ḥusain ibn Muḥammad al-Ḥalwāni [d. 5th century AH], researched by: Muʾassasah al-Imām al-Mahdi (AS), Qum: Muʾassasah al-Imām al-Mahdi (AS), 1408 AH. First Edition

Al-Nawādir, Faḍlullah ibn ʿAli al-Ḥasani al-Rāwandi [d. 571 AH], researched by: Saʿīd Riḍā ʿAli ʿAskari, Qum: Dār al-Ḥdīth, 1377 Sailor. First Edition

Nūr al-Thaqalayn, ʿAbd ʿAli ibn Jumʿh al-ʿArūsi al-Ḥuwayzi [d. 1112 AH], researched by: al-Seyyed Hāshim al-Rasūli al-Maḥallāti, Qum: Muʾssasah Ismāʿiliyān, 1412 AH. Forth Edition

Nahj al-Balāghah, Muḥammad ibn al-Ḥusain al-Mūsawi (al-Sharīf al-Raḍi) [d. 406 AH], edited by: Muḥammad ʿAbduh, Beyrūt: Muʾssasah al-Aʿlami

Nahj al-Saʿādah fi Mustadrak Nahj al-Balāghah, Muḥammad Bāqir al-Maḥmūdi (d. 1104 AH), Beyrūt: Muʾssasah al-Aʿlami

Wasāʾil al-Shiʿa, Muḥammad ibn al-Ḥasan al-Ḥurr al-ʿĀmili [d. 1104 AH], researched by: Muʾssasah Āl al-Bayt (AS), Qum: Muʾassasah Āl al-Bayt (AS), 1409 AH. First Edition

Waqʿat Ṣiffin, Naṣr ibn Muzāḥim al-Munqari [d. 212 AH], researched by: ʿAbd al-Salām Muḥammad Hārūn, Qum: Āyatullah al-Marʿashi's library, 1382 AH. Second Edition

Index

adornment, 21, 77, 204, 207, 292, 499, 500, 521, 537, 551, 582, 602, 697, 884, 904, 969, 1012, 1151, 1166, 1167

advice, 13, 15, 16, 154, 187, 223, 225, 233, 265, 368, 441, 463, 467, 487, 489, 503, 533, 554, 612, 639, 650, 701, 706, 761, 763, 821, 836, 841, 928, 929, 951, 965, 1077, 1078, 1084, 1088, 1093, 1124, 1159, 1160, 1162, 1164

Ahl al-Bayt, 78, 100, 153, 212, 243, 259, 284, 285, 418, 538, 546, 568, 573, 578, 599, 606, 791, 890, 1085, 1146, 1156

allegiance (*bay'a*), 65, 85, 131, 166, 167, 168, 196, 865, 1124, 1157

amusement, 305, 839, 927, 962, 981, 982, 1028, 1093, 1134

angels, 57, 69, 109, 119, 120, 177, 180, 181, 184, 221, 222, 287, 324, 334, 339, 374, 417, 429, 433, 443, 447, 463, 464, 513, 540, 542, 555, 558, 577, 593, 605, 634, 641, 644, 645, 649, 651, 657, 660, 711, 751, 777, 782, 802, 808, 826, 828, 831, 874, 905, 910, 912, 917, 920, 935, 944, 947, 964, 967, 974, 992, 994, 1000-02, 1005, 1009, 1010, 1020, 1035, 1047, 1053, 1057, 1071, 1085, 1111, 1119, 1137, 1171

creation of angels, 1000

guardian angels, 1001

anger, 17, 24, 78, 88, 221, 252, 262, 278, 295, 308, 312, 353, 397, 414, 422, 562, 572, 606, 611, 737, 746, 753, 767, 812, 834, 835, 874, 875, 893, 951, 958, 990, 998, 1010, 1037, 1051, 1082, 1154, 1173

anxiety, 192, 607

Arabia, 745

Arch-Prophets (*Ulū al-ʿAzm*), 1020

argument, 92, 231, 243, 254, 255, 260, 437, 715, 750, 995, 999

arrogance, 122, 126, 200, 289, 531, 539, 779, 863, 868, 935, 936, 937, 938, 939, 1026

asking, 83, 138, 144, 178, 180, 272, 404, 504, 506, 507, 620, 720, 762, 788, 802, 837, 874, 989, 1124, 1140, 1150, 1194, 1195, 1200

astrology, 1074, 1075

astronomy, 790, 1074

backbiting, 302, 506, 852-5

barzakh, 135

bathing, 204, 206

battle, 98, 146, 192, 267, 573, 826-31, 914, 1116, 1181

Badr, 55, 62, 98, 573, 592, 826, 830, 841

of the Camel, 146, 573, 1116, 1181

Siffīn, 146, 192, 914

believers, 1, 9, 34, 47, 62, 64, 67, 75, 97, 98, 109, 110, 114, 135, 146, 159, 195, 230, 242, 326, 346, 358, 371, 431, 451, 471, 519, 577, 578, 626, 636, 682, 810, 819, 856, 858, 862, 923, 930, 959, 971, 1005, 1006, 1010, 1027, 1032, 1036, 1046, 1053, 1122, 1195, 1200

bounties, 22, 52, 159, 289, 300, 325, 343, 361, 399, 418, 420, 426, 452, 475, 583, 677, 679, 707, 757, 797, 878, 923, 1028, 1085, 1087-89, 1090, 1091, 1092, 1185

charity, 2, 6, 24, 27, 52, 77, 114, 134, 170, 204, 210, 248, 304, 452, 460, 471, 472, 492, 528, 530, 551, 560, 614, 615-21, 626, 627, 643, 648, 662, 670, 728, 778, 882, 906, 909, 910, 977, 988, 993, 1012, 1017, 1075, 1099, 1100-03, 1107, 1125-27, 1140, 1148

cheerfulness, 137, 138, 210, 446

children, 2, 23, 24, 74, 76, 90, 167, 183, 232, 235-37, 265, 294, 301, 381, 388, 394, 395, 408, 416, 428, 456, 457, 467, 478, 488, 501, 519, 544, 545, 569, 656, 700, 848, 859, 873, 891, 922, 923, 933, 946, 953, 954, 958, 962, 989, 1003, 1009, 1012, 1026, 1033, 1036, 1041, 1054, 1063, 1070, 1076, 1109, 1113, 1138, 1157, 1183, 1184, 1185, 1186, 1189, 1190

cleanliness, 1022, 1085, 1086, 1112

clothing, 972, 973

turban, 973

companions

Jābir b. ʿAbdullāh, 79, 1086, 1190

Ubayy ibn Kaʿb, 75

'Abdullāh b. Mas'ūd, 86

condolences, 78, 739

congregation, 202, 203, 338, 513, 638, 639, 1003, 1160

conjecture, 682, 712, 805, 817, 962

contentment, 104, 106, 124, 176, 280, 348, 360, 362, 380, 514, 723, 752, 753, 822, 823, 846, 847, 933, 934, 1022, 1029, 1096, 1142, 1168, 1205

conviction, 36, 50, 105, 106, 112, 189, 280, 281, 324, 335, 536, 558, 586, 604, 607, 686, 758, 766, 804, 847, 1013, 1155, 1172, 1202-07

courtesy, 440, 521, 550, 663, 726-30, 951

cowardice, 15, 185, 189, 272, 561, 595, 684, 989, 1183

crying, 147, 148, 192, 460, 482, 555, 742, 743

death, 5, 37, 40, 44, 49, 69, 71, 73, 75-7, 84, 93, 121, 125, 126, 145, 154, 156, 157, 160, 167, 177, 179, 198, 209, 218, 223, 229, 267, 272, 279, 281, 298, 302, 319, 320, 324, 361, 400, 401, 410, 418, 428, 431, 441, 446, 447, 451, 465, 469, 474, 478, 479, 482, 495, 496, 540, 549, 552, 573, 576, 597, 615, 619, 638, 649, 658, 664, 679, 717, 747, 775, 776, 777, 795, 796, 798, 805, 806, 808, 822, 837, 864, 876, 877, 881, 887, 891, 912, 926, 927, 930, 941, 956, 969, 970, 971, 979, 993, 1001-12, 1036, 1051, 1053, 1055, 1059, 1060, 1094, 1110, 1111, 1147, 1158, 1186, 1187, 1204

  lifespan, 80, 134, 446, 619, 720, 754, 792-5, 1007

debate, 190, 1031, 1084, 1085

debating, 190, 588, 714, 1048, 1084

deeds

  bad, 286, 434, 1008, 1118, 1143, 1207

  book of, 287, 334, 853

  evil, 159, 421, 428, 429, 513, 677, 802, 870, 1096

  good, 23, 53, 120, 147, 161, 174, 180, 187, 207, 286, 292, 317, 414, 416, 421, 429, 430, 433, 434, 435, 467, 513, 525, 538, 540, 552, 553, 555, 616, 652, 677, 681, 691, 694, 727, 730, 747, 793, 800, 802, 811, 832, 837, 841, 853, 870, 914, 951, 968, 1001, 1005, 1007-09, 1143, 1192, 1193, 1207

delusions, 388, 825

desertion, 1121

destiny, 120, 185, 186, 281, 607, 911-4

disputation, 45, 209, 703, 767, 995, 996, 1085, 1152

dissimulation (*taqīyyah*), 742, 1176-78

divine displeasure, 141-4, 594, 649, 666, 831

divorce, 491, 665, 666

Egypt, 207, 303, 547, 625, 639, 804, 819, 915, 980, 1039, 1041, 1042, 1192-97

enemies, 33, 76, 98, 99, 138, 236, 268, 294, 318, 337, 367, 389, 393, 399, 493, 558, 568, 596, 600, 633, 700, 707, 732, 891, 918, 965, 984, 1000, 1010, 1116, 1134, 1177, 1183, 1194, 1198

enmity, 94, 100, 212, 360, 416, 568, 618, 699, 700, 810, 909, 932, 1104

extremism, 843, 958

fairness, 1, 11, 91, 94, 182, 183, 326, 614, 741, 918, 991, 1079, 1080, 1102, 1142, 1165, 1194

faith, 1, 18, 23, 42, 46, 88, 90, 95, 100-18, 122, 127, 161, 168, 173, 179, 180, 197, 202, 206, 212, 218, 230, 234, 236, 237, 242, 249, 270, 272, 283, 287, 290, 291, 316, 323, 327, 329, 332, 340, 341, 346, 350, 367, 372, 382, 396, 404, 407, 408, 409, 412, 413, 416, 431, 440, 443, 452, 453, 462, 480, 483, 485, 487, 493, 494, 500, 529, 534, 535, 555, 564, 565, 569, 570-2, 575, 586, 587, 588, 594, 596, 604, 608, 618, 620, 630, 643, 644, 646, 647, 649, 651, 656, 657, 660, 669, 671, 683, 684, 698, 700, 704, 713, 716, 719, 731, 734, 740, 745, 763, 771, 784, 804-6, 842, 848, 852, 856, 865, 868, 877, 880, 881, 890, 893, 900, 909, 926, 932, 938, 944-6, 958, 960, 977, 982, 983, 990, 995, 1003, 1013, 1019, 1027, 1030, 1083, 1092, 1099, 1102, 1103, 1106, 1116, 1119, 1125, 1140, 1141, 1144, 1148, 1155, 1157, 1161, 1168, 1171, 1172, 1174, 1176, 1178, 1190, 1197, 1198, 1202, 1203, 1207

falsehood, 67, 79, 111, 118, 139, 140, 165, 203, 277, 297, 298, 299, 328, 337, 570, 656, 717, 780, 830, 871, 894, 948, 1129, 1196

fame, 594, 595

family, 28, 32, 57, 61, 77, 84, 114, 158, 166, 184, 212, 215, 243, 269, 301, 310, 347, 349, 366, 376, 388, 406, 410, 444, 453-5, 490-2, 527, 528, 566, 578, 628, 645, 648, 649, 662, 741, 742, 795, 797, 827, 847, 857, 889, 937, 969,

1007, 1012, 1026, 1030, 1035, 1037, 1039, 1042, 1047, 1052, 1066, 1072, 1080, 1147, 1183, 1207

Fāṭima, 2, 68-70, 73, 77, 94, 166, 380, 409, 446, 496, 498, 630, 632, 651, 653, 698, 750, 795, 1010, 1076, 1140, 1201, 1207

fasting, 46, 81, 103, 219, 222, 242, 284, 295, 316, 404, 475, 489, 609, 627, 633, 651-54, 688, 689, 708, 770, 776, 844, 852, 869, 884, 890, 897, 948, 1146, 1150

fate, 123, 168, 281, 329, 369, 913, 914, 1017, 1075

fault-finding, 195

fear of Allah, 84, 147, 148, 209, 219, 225, 275, 307, 352, 353, 356, 631, 632, 686, 709, 779, 927, 930, 1050, 1142

feeding others, 664

forgiveness, 84, 110, 157, 159, 167, 176, 177, 178, 179, 180, 200, 208, 248, 249, 284, 361, 420, 424, 425, 427, 430, 452, 460, 465, 466, 467, 471, 513, 569, 570, 624, 645, 651, 652, 665, 777, 778, 801, 835-8, 846, 855, 856, 926, 930, 985, 987, 988, 994, 1012, 1132, 1150, 1171, 1186, 1187, 1193

fraud, 581, 831

Friday, 203, 204, 246, 643, 674, 719, 989, 1160

friendship, 10-12, 16, 18, 61, 189, 216, 236, 242, 244, 280, 296, 297, 314, 360, 389, 461, 493, 497, 498, 525, 548, 558, 568, 569, 610, 611, 613, 638, 673, 681, 701, 707, 810, 877, 1010, 1099, 1104, 1109, 1165, 1186, 1197, 1198

gallantry, 271, 486, 561, 699, 991, 992, 1014

gambling, 416, 932, 933

generosity, 1, 67, 122, 123, 125, 137, 211, 235, 293, 514, 515, 550, 614, 652, 697, 741, 752, 769, 828, 951, 952, 953, 999, 1071

good opinion, 625, 638, 672, 683, 685, 979, 1158

governance, 35, 36, 64, 273, 398, 399, 438, 767, 916, 1126, 1177, 1192

greed, 2, 15, 45, 85, 107, 124, 128, 129, 133, 143, 189, 360, 387, 419, 449, 450, 581, 667, 668, 684, 736, 737, 748, 765, 879, 880, 915, 923, 1006, 1015, 1056, 1096, 1097, 1128, 1129, 1145, 1172

grief, 39, 70, 111, 193, 272, 281, 282, 353, 389, 391, 429, 496, 647, 650, 726, 739, 743, 808, 905, 1011, 1086, 1133

guidance, 50, 57, 61, 67, 75, 112, 178, 465, 521, 595, 600, 622, 658, 778, 788, 859, 907, 928, 943, 1026, 1033, 1042, 1074, 1123, 1125, 1167, 1169, 1172

habit, 31, 124, 303, 689, 812-14, 844, 951, 964, 1169

happiness, 111, 114, 137, 280-82, 482, 496, 519, 520, 542, 562, 652, 740, 741, 743, 799, 824, 989, 997, 1052, 1053, 1090, 1134, 1163, 1173, 1180, 1185

hard-heartedness, 30, 425, 926, 927, 981

haste, 696

heart (*qalb*), 30, 31, 34, 39, 58, 95, 101, 105, 107, 125, 138, 140, 148, 149, 155, 162, 174, 175, 177, 178, 194, 200, 237, 249, 256, 266, 279, 292, 305, 307, 308, 374, 375, 387, 405, 412, 413, 415, 417, 425, 483, 502, 544, 555, 557, 581, 585, 587, 593, 607, 649, 652, 654, 667, 673, 683, 693, 698, 699, 704, 716, 718, 727, 738, 749, 750, 763, 764, 773, 784, 790, 791, 805, 812, 833, 841, 845, 849, 880, 885, 888, 895, 896, 898, 900, 922-30, 935, 964, 966, 975, 977, 979, 995, 1006, 1014, 1022, 1081, 1083, 1095, 1096, 1106, 1107, 1117, 1146, 1150, 1153, 1158, 1162, 1175, 1182, 1185, 1192, 1202

hell, 54, 57, 60, 67, 71, 113, 130, 131, 135, 138, 139, 167, 194, 210, 215, 227, 228, 230, 231, 243, 267, 304, 315, 349, 368, 390, 459, 406, 467, 489, 497, 533, 579, 601, 622, 637, 694, 785, 810, 824, 834, 852, 890, 892, 894, 901, 917, 921, 939, 948, 967, 987, 1015, 1062, 1074, 1098, 1115, 1119, 1133, 1183, 1186, 1192, 1203, 1204

the bridge, 497

hereafter, 116, 583, 846, 935, 1133

honour, 47, 51, 89, 128, 160, 196, 216, 232, 293, 325, 399, 418, 455, 487, 538, 609, 614, 634, 641, 660, 680, 723, 735, 736, 737, 754, 773, 825, 877, 909, 936, 938, 952-54, 977, 997, 1014, 1154, 1180

hospitality, 1046

hypocrisy, 144, 188, 200, 202, 215, 305, 357, 412, 636, 658, 699, 781, 850, 863, 895, 923, 944, 947, 981, 995, 1095, 1096, 1099

hypocrites, 64, 215, 277, 384, 635, 658, 673, 850, 1095-98, 1178

idleness, 143, 869, 870

Imam

ʿAlī ibn Abī Tālib, 67, 129, 171, 190, 201, 213, 216, 244, 264

ʿAlī ibn al-Ḥusayn, 71, 72

ʿAlī ibn Musa al-Riḍā, 24, 31, 35, 46, 47, 51, 59, 96, 112, 119, 128, 144, 163, 168, 177, 187, 196, 210, 234, 249, 253, 260, 267, 311, 351, 356, 369, 403, 415, 421, 424, 426, 429, 430, 431, 432, 473, 477, 478, 482, 486, 497, 515, 517, 520, 523, 527, 538, 549, 555, 586, 594, 612, 646, 662, 666, 674, 689, 711, 713, 714, 716, 720-3, 725, 739, 743, 748, 754, 762, 801, 830, 837, 838, 844, 858, 864, 872, 882, 886, 892, 900, 925, 973, 983, 1006, 1015, 1022, 1024, 1045, 1048, 1083, 1086, 1090, 1110, 1120, 1138, 1149, 1152, 1154, 1156, 1186, 1206

Ḥasan al-ʿAskarī, 91, 931

Ḥusayn ibn ʿAlī, 14, 120, 219, 232, 233, 237, 265, 271, 376, 392, 401, 418, 442, 446, 447, 461, 463, 494, 496, 498, 507, 549, 580, 702, 704, 710, 724, 726, 732, 755, 766, 801, 852, 953, 965

Jaʿfar al-Ṣādiq, *passim*

Muḥammad ibn al-Ḥasan

Qā'im, 73, 91, 94, 95, 96, 97, 98, 99, 100, 183, 921

Muḥammad ibn ʿAlī al-Bāqir, 10, 12, 13, 15, 35, 41, 46-8, 51, 53-5, 71, 77-80, 93, 94, 97, 99-101, 113, 115, 117, 134, 141, 143, 148, 157, 158, 160, 161, 164, 177, 178, 182, 183, 186, 193, 197, 204, 206, 210, 213, 221, 222, 230, 234, 239, 243, 245, 249, 250, 252, 254, 256, 258, 260, 262, 263, 267-9, 272, 274, 282, 285, 287, 290, 298, 301, 306, 317, 319, 337, 340, 342, 343, 350, 371, 374, 377, 379, 384, 395, 397, 403, 411, 414, 417, 419, 421-3, 425-7, 431-6, 439, 446, 453, 456, 462, 466, 471, 473, 479, 480, 482, 489, 493, 505, 507, 511, 524, 529, 530, 531, 538, 539, 541, 542, 545, 546, 553, 556-9, 564, 566, 571, 572, 576-9, 584, 597, 599, 600-2, 606, 609, 619, 624, 629, 630, 632, 634, 636, 638, 643, 645, 652, 655, 656, 659, 663, 665, 668, 670, 676, 679, 680, 693, 694, 696, 699, 706, 708, 717, 718, 722, 724, 732, 736, 737, 740, 742, 748, 752, 754, 759-63, 768, 773, 774, 775, 778, 790, 791, 792, 794, 795, 798, 800, 804, 810, 818, 822, 828, 834, 839, 847, 851, 861, 862, 882, 883, 886, 887, 891-3, 904, 912, 924, 927, 930, 932, 935, 942, 945, 957, 958, 967, 969, 970, 977, 986, 992, 994, 997, 1001, 1002, 1023, 1025, 1027, 1031, 1034, 1050, 1059, 1070, 1072-80, 1086, 1103, 1110, 1116, 1119, 1122, 1125, 1130, 1131, 1137, 1141, 1143, 1147, 1149, 1161, 1163, 1169, 1171, 1173, 1176, 1180, 1182, 1187, 1203

Musa ibn Jaʿfar al-Kāzim, 25, 83, 85-7, 153, 466, 1076, 1193

infallibility, 747

infatuation, 123, 126, 647, 743

inner knowledge, 101, 106, 306, 341, 373, 583, 621, 704-9, 713, 763, 844

innovation, 130, 132, 202, 203, 422, 774

insight, 39, 50, 138, 139, 265, 361, 362, 690-2, 785, 839, 971

insulting, 509, 984

intention, 24, 222, 231, 333, 336, 344, 360, 375, 382, 439, 452, 474, 490, 571, 730, 748, 1045, 1114-18

jihād, 156, 173, 182, 209, 210, 215-23, 237, 248, 299, 333, 419, 441, 454, 490, 654, 799, 989, 1073, 1135, 1138

joking, 528, 997

Judgement Day, 10, 31, 49, 71, 77, 135, 142, 148, 164, 170, 172, 173, 188, 808, 874, 882, 892, 895, 906, 913, 917, 921, 937, 941, 1050, 1064, 1070, 1077, 1082, 1098, 1099, 1107, 1108, 1110, 1115, 1122, 1143, 1165, 1192, 1196

judgment, 425, 456, 541, 916-21

witnesses, 13, 43, 154, 439, 588-90, 698, 733, 869, 920, 1019, 1036

justice, 51, 65, 67, 90, 91, 94, 98, 99, 125, 136, 146, 169, 182, 183, 229, 291, 293, 300, 308, 349, 399, 551, 588, 680, 697-99, 709, 719, 732, 741, 746, 757, 868, 874, 889, 915, 918, 919, 922, 999, 1000, 1018, 1025, 1028, 1029, 1049, 1078, 1079, 1090, 1108, 1185, 1192, 1194

knowledge, 20, 22, 32, 49, 50, 57, 59, 62, 64, 65, 79, 81, 104, 106, 121, 122, 125, 132, 143, 165, 190, 191, 193, 200, 216, 224, 225, 226, 227, 229, 256, 306, 311, 314, 323, 331-33, 335, 345, 361, 362, 365, 375, 395, 396, 424, 440, 458, 468, 469, 475, 476, 483, 502, 503, 508, 525, 531, 544, 546, 548, 549, 581, 596, 606,

618, 629, 630, 634, 666, 668, 672, 694, 704-8, 710, 713, 717, 718, 721, 723, 725, 745, 750, 761, 763, 766, 771-96, 806, 807, 820, 824, 849, 850, 856, 860, 861, 865, 875, 886, 887, 888, 894, 916, 917, 922, 924, 929, 940, 941, 948, 967, 1027, 1045, 1055, 1063, 1065, 1075, 1089, 1102, 1109, 1121, 1125, 1133, 1153, 1162, 1172, 1173, 1190, 1196, 1198, 1203
of religion, 361, 362
laughter, 86, 654, 655
liability, 117, 574, 1067
liberality, 101, 105, 111, 122, 126, 133, 134, 171, 186, 348, 349, 403, 407, 515, 703
lifestyle, 822, 823
light, 31, 46, 61, 69, 112, 113, 150, 153, 200, 265, 282, 292, 298, 304, 339, 354, 368, 401, 409, 412, 434, 494, 515, 520, 528, 544, 558, 587-89, 598, 604, 628, 634, 641, 644, 666, 704, 705, 707, 710, 716, 717, 730, 761, 764, 773, 790, 795, 802, 847, 860, 895, 896, 901, 903, 924, 926, 929, 953, 979, 987, 997, 998, 1000, 1013, 1040, 1065, 1106-08, 1143, 1150, 1170
lower self, 694, 700
Luqmān (the Sage), 116, 200, 290, 296, 305, 306, 312, 390, 396, 528, 565, 638, 701, 736, 805, 836, 839, 929, 1180
lying, 97, 107, 109, 122, 125, 173, 289, 309, 357, 410, 411, 442, 564, 608, 609, 627, 628, 774, 944-51, 1067
madness, 88, 214, 215, 328, 833
Makkah, 87, 142, 171, 196, 248, 249, 251, 253, 357, 639, 815, 830, 973, 1033, 1066
malice, 144, 627
Mary (Maryam), 38, 465, 629, 720, 807, 814, 842, 843, 1055, 1056, 1058, 1161
medicine, 14, 32, 399, 400, 401, 420, 659, 663, 664, 695, 790, 914, 966, 1112
Medina, 275, 639
memorization, 108, 896, 897, 941
memorizing, 899, 958
men, 27, 28, 36, 51, 59, 62, 75, 76, 83, 85, 91, 94, 100, 164, 171, 173, 183, 185, 198, 265, 267, 269, 275, 300, 308, 327, 332, 336, 338, 404, 450, 478, 502, 558, 598, 603, 656, 667, 674, 676, 688, 731, 767, 808, 809, 865, 896, 916, 921, 982, 983, 988, 989, 990, 1009, 1016, 1023, 1041, 1042, 1043, 1067, 1068, 1076, 1082, 1083, 1092, 1098, 1107, 1116, 1121, 1134, 1139
migration, 1066, 1114, 1118, 1119, 1120
miracle, 694, 1042, 1044
miserliness, 109, 124, 126, 128, 130, 189, 272, 684, 1015
mistrust, 127, 129
mosque, 12, 36, 84, 184, 275, 493, 512-14, 638, 770, 789, 839, 861, 971, 1057, 1064, 1096, 1149, 1177, 1181
nails, 676, 851
narrators
Abū Dharr, 503, 504, 512, 513, 552, 645, 650, 661, 749, 839, 853, 881, 888, 928, 936, 1020, 1115, 1117, 1121, 1172
Abū Hurayra, 2, 648
al-Sayyid Ibn al-Ṭāwūs, 76
Ḥudhayfa b. al-Yamān, 76
Muḥammad b. Muslim, 4, 81, 98, 259, 529, 653, 1073
Shuʿayb b. ʿAbd al-Raḥmān al-Khuzāʿī, 76
ʿAmmār al-Sābāṭī, 4
ʿĀʾisha, 2, 1101, 1127
negligence, 291, 325, 414, 469, 553, 625, 679, 793, 838, 839, 840, 1065
nobility, 122, 123, 232, 646, 950, 951, 1151, 1170
obedience, 30, 43, 49, 50, 54, 55, 66, 74, 75, 88, 89, 106, 119, 120, 121, 123, 124, 133, 160, 168, 174, 214, 222, 240, 243, 249, 287, 291, 301, 306, 307, 336, 396, 403, 434, 445, 450, 458, 460, 461, 475, 500, 525, 535, 548, 558, 567, 570, 606, 614, 628, 671, 672, 693, 694, 706, 736, 737, 746, 793, 795, 813, 839, 844, 853, 870, 881, 1018, 1019, 1097, 1102, 1117, 1164, 1173, 1186, 1191
obscene language, 509, 862
old age, 279, 295, 400, 443, 597, 598, 952, 1128, 1185
omen, 674, 675, 684, 963
opinion, 131, 191, 192, 224, 272, 313, 437, 438, 439, 550, 595, 596, 597, 612, 684, 687, 757, 861, 902, 974, 991, 1129, 1131
opportunity, 126, 148, 226, 278, 363, 373, 637, 642, 764, 836, 866, 906, 1147

oppression, 58, 91, 144, 183, 282, 322, 354, 358, 374, 407, 680, 881, 999, 1022, 1029, 1129, 1202

orphans, 2, 29, 67, 76, 77, 233, 245, 424, 519, 664, 842, 930, 953, 1003, 1044, 1047, 1200, 1201, 1202

paradise, 157, 393, 569, 1003, 1005, 1134

pardon, 84, 182, 195, 325, 584, 612, 669, 694, 736, 753, 754, 755, 756, 757, 828, 1067, 1193

partisanship, 745, 746, 1129

patience, 31, 70, 78, 101, 102, 104, 105, 106, 112, 114, 159, 192, 193, 210, 215, 239, 270, 348, 360, 361, 396, 443, 582, 604, 606, 607, 758, 759, 767, 859, 884, 903, 970, 1044, 1045, 1046, 1092

peacemaking, 991

perfume, 479, 673, 674, 816, 953, 995

Persians, 815, 816, 851, 865

possessiveness, 741, 856, 857, 858

prayer, 26, 43, 46, 56, 69, 86, 110, 112, 136, 152, 174, 206, 217, 239, 240, 246, 284, 349, 366, 377, 404, 411, 416, 429, 435, 436, 472, 475, 485, 486, 490, 496, 499, 512, 513, 514, 521, 528, 529, 538, 541, 548, 554, 556, 577, 594, 595, 600, 609, 628, 629, 630, 631, 632, 633, 634, 635, 636, 637, 638, 639, 640, 641, 642, 643, 644, 654, 655, 669, 686, 758, 769, 770, 780, 797, 799, 829, 844, 850, 852, 864, 868, 869, 889, 890, 891, 897, 932, 938, 984, 1037, 1047, 1053, 1057, 1058, 1061, 1063, 1076, 1084, 1095, 1103, 1107, 1145, 1148, 1149, 1171, 1188

- prostration, 78, 83, 84, 147, 510, 511, 630, 635, 670, 1042, 1064
- supererogatory, 241, 867, 902, 1105, 1106

predestination, 120, 185, 186, 911

pride, 75, 122, 123, 125, 133, 402, 521, 613, 630, 727, 736, 757, 768, 863, 864, 954, 986, 989, 1063, 1064, 1072, 1152

propagation (*da'wa*), 1018

Prophet

- Aaron (Hārūn), 64, 66, 73, 680, 1040, 1041, 1042, 1058
- Abraham, 47, 64, 193, 330, 464, 597, 598, 645, 769, 856, 1020, 1021, 1030, 1031, 1032, 1033, 1034, 1036, 1040, 1047, 1063, 1120, 1203, 1206
- Adam, 64, 77, 119, 120, 121, 156, 175, 187, 260, 269, 272, 283, 297, 353, 380, 409, 411, 414, 484, 499, 521, 553, 569, 571, 686, 745, 778, 805, 864, 954, 961, 994, 1003, 1009, 1016, 1020, 1022, 1023, 1024, 1025, 1055, 1063, 1090, 1108, 1143, 1160, 1167
- David (Dāwūd), 180, 195, 241, 371, 380, 393, 499, 542, 736, 787, 903, 915, 922, 926, 933, 955, 979, 993, 1048, 1049, 1050, 1051, 1052, 1123, 1139, 1140
- Elisha (al-Yasaʿ), 1048, 1049
- Enoch, 472, 879, 1024
- Hūd, 1026, 1027, 1028, 1029, 1030, 1038, 1039
- Irmiyā' (ʿUzair), 1059
- Ishmael b. Ḥazqīl, 1047
- Jacob, 378, 1033, 1036, 1037, 1124, 1140
- Jesus (ʿĪsā), 21, 22, 38, 55, 87, 93, 165, 180, 200, 279, 304, 313, 374, 376, 395, 396, 465, 479, 581, 604, 629, 687, 689, 695, 720, 777, 780, 788, 807, 814, 817, 818, 840, 842, 843, 923, 927, 1013, 1021, 1040, 1048, 1055, 1056, 1058, 1081, 1134, 1161
- Job (Ayyūb), 491, 1037
- John the Baptist (Yaḥyā), 84, 87, 1054
- Jonah (Yūnus), 997, 1020, 1048, 1060, 1061, 1109
- Joseph, 193, 270, 830, 1036, 1037
- Lot (Lūṭ), 251, 330, 982, 1020, 1031, 1032, 1034, 1035, 1039, 1048
- Moses (Mūsā), 40, 59, 64, 73, 143, 162, 240, 289, 333, 371, 410, 414, 446, 460, 463, 480, 515, 571, 584, 622, 680, 695, 721, 737, 752, 762, 777, 783, 821, 835, 878, 904, 925, 927, 937, 965, 1014, 1021, 1038, 1040, 1041, 1042, 1043, 1044, 1045, 1046, 1047, 1055, 1110, 1137
- Muḥammad, 57, 73, 203, 255, 258, 376, 404, 430, 577, 695, 851, 865, 1010, 1017, 1038, 1063, 1064, 1065, 1066, 1191
- Ṣāliḥ, 89, 91, 153, 184, 333, 723, 1028, 1029, 1030, 1038, 1039, 1171
- Noah, 57, 64, 66, 113, 337, 396, 1021, 1024, 1025, 1026, 1027, 1028, 1039, 1171
- Shuʿayb, 76, 397, 1038, 1039, 1042

Solomon, 80, 393, 545, 857, 884, 1048, 1050, 1051, 1052, 1053, 1136, 1139, 1140
Zacharias, 64, 392, 1053, 1054, 1055, 1057, 1140
prophethood, 47, 1017, 1022
prosperity, 10, 25, 47, 58, 111, 116, 192, 270, 278, 448, 475, 492, 525, 526, 531, 579, 580, 793, 942, 1019, 1182, 1184, 1202
purity, 176, 452, 500, 794, 1047, 1054, 1085, 1086, 1111, 1150, 1197
Qum, 184, 185, 498
religious invitation (*daʿwa*)
eloquence, 121, 150, 151, 695, 970
good advice, 190, 1160
honesty, 102, 106, 154, 429, 561, 1165
kindness, 1, 14, 52, 115, 186, 207, 235, 242, 293, 453, 506, 545, 585, 687, 699, 727, 953, 954, 960, 1079, 1185, 1193
repentance, 175, 176, 177, 178, 179, 199, 422, 425, 441, 552, 553, 578, 615, 893, 1061, 1093, 1118, 1150, 1187
reputation, 111, 407, 561, 668, 703, 704, 996, 1192
reward, 26, 43, 141, 147, 152, 153, 156, 160, 161, 166, 174, 181, 182, 185, 189, 192, 193, 216, 217, 220, 221, 252, 278, 283, 287, 288, 301, 314, 316, 326, 329, 333, 346, 364, 365, 382, 383, 394, 417, 430, 434, 446, 459, 462, 491, 495, 497, 541, 547, 564, 585, 592, 593, 600, 605, 606, 619, 620, 621, 622, 624, 627, 639, 642, 643, 647, 652, 654, 664, 681, 688, 719, 727, 728, 730, 739, 742, 744, 751, 753, 762, 769, 778, 796, 797, 822, 848, 859, 884, 885, 897, 899, 901, 905, 906, 910, 914, 918, 941, 953, 962, 965, 987, 988, 989, 992, 994, 1005, 1012, 1022, 1090, 1099, 1114, 1122, 1124, 1149, 1156, 1172, 1183
Satan, 26, 33, 132, 170, 202, 221, 276, 277, 310, 327, 337, 413, 416, 423, 433, 439, 485, 494, 508, 509, 510, 534, 553, 564, 567, 568, 569, 570, 571, 572, 588, 611, 631, 646, 655, 676, 688, 691, 694, 696, 720, 745, 774, 784, 795, 833, 838, 845, 886, 887, 899, 932, 935, 950, 963, 969, 980, 990, 991, 1009, 1013, 1054, 1083, 1112, 1113, 1121, 1124, 1132, 1145, 1182, 1193
satans, 132
scholars, 22, 43, 123, 126, 200, 224, 245, 257, 289, 362, 525, 577, 772, 773, 775, 779, 782, 783, 784, 788, 872, 886, 901, 929, 931, 940, 1129
secrets, 97, 112, 115, 156, 334, 360, 516, 517, 500, 718, 781, 791, 911, 942, 984
self-admiration, 122, 125, 144, 481, 692, 693, 694, 1193
self-restraint, 30, 400, 688, 692, 706, 752, 753, 847, 875, 934
self-sacrifice, 1, 348
shaking hands, 1021
sickness, 162, 302, 469, 664, 895, 928, 992, 993, 1006, 1094, 1118, 1128, 1157, 1170
sight, 39, 67, 138, 148, 149, 219, 266, 305, 327, 390, 395, 479, 544, 548, 555, 581, 589, 637, 649, 716, 718, 722, 727, 773, 864, 1022, 1035, 1060, 1081, 1082, 1097, 1107, 1152, 1203
silence, 72, 95, 111, 190, 232, 315, 333, 509, 528, 646, 647, 652, 688, 758, 766, 835, 886, 907, 967, 968, 1067, 1106, 1167
singing, 195, 649, 978
slander, 27, 164, 167, 351, 561, 1104
sleep, 24, 31, 41, 143, 206, 216, 234, 344, 364, 432, 466, 469, 531, 548, 549, 635, 636, 640, 641, 643, 652, 701, 711, 724, 761, 774, 836, 860, 875, 987, 1005, 1020, 1021, 1055, 1056, 1070, 1072, 1097, 1110, 1111, 1112, 1113, 1147, 1171
smiling, 86, 137, 528, 654
society, 1026, 1029
sodomy, 982, 1034
solitude, 209, 601, 641, 705, 738, 770, 797
soul, 5, 10, 20, 22, 23, 40, 50, 73, 110, 111, 123, 137, 173, 177, 189, 201, 208, 222, 243, 280, 283, 284, 293, 296, 320, 324, 325, 327, 329, 349, 355, 393, 418, 420, 422, 424, 428, 450, 462, 464, 525, 572, 592, 610, 630, 664, 668, 677, 713, 750, 751, 763, 772, 774, 790, 802, 806, 810, 812, 813, 825, 846, 858, 867, 891, 896, 962, 988, 1000, 1003, 1009, 1010, 1022, 1046, 1049, 1053, 1073, 1092, 1093, 1094, 1113, 1123, 1126, 1134, 1191
sovereignty, 124, 998, 999
speech, 75, 87, 89, 92, 112, 122, 126, 151, 153, 154, 200, 206, 223, 232, 239, 240, 254, 281,

307, 330, 331, 333, 361, 413, 538, 539, 573, 603, 608, 609, 640, 695, 721, 749, 767, 780, 782, 797, 849, 874, 886, 894, 895, 918, 927, 942, 943, 944, 949, 963, 964, 965, 966, 967, 968, 969, 972, 1041, 1050, 1058, 1066, 1084, 1098, 1100, 1134, 1139, 1161, 1162, 1172, 1173

spying, 226

squandering, 126, 132, 133, 407, 516, 522, 551

stubbornness, 974, 975

supplication, 90, 176, 329, 330, 368, 369, 370, 373, 374, 375, 376, 378, 379, 381, 382, 409, 410, 413, 451, 466, 552, 571, 580, 583, 628, 645, 652, 655, 680, 719, 736, 747, 756, 789, 795, 836, 870, 871, 903, 924, 979, 1093, 1106, 1130, 1149

sustenance, 2, 9, 109, 154, 160, 172, 249, 250, 271, 273, 323, 343, 346, 349, 381, 406, 446, 448, 449, 450, 451, 452, 453, 467, 470, 478, 485, 486, 549, 566, 571, 584, 616, 642, 655, 660, 665, 676, 686, 692, 732, 734, 777, 794, 795, 823, 831, 837, 847, 868, 912, 947, 969, 1052, 1056, 1057, 1072, 1078, 1086, 1092, 1096, 1117, 1118, 1137, 1138, 1146, 1181, 1182, 1206

talebearing, 1104

tongue, 101, 140, 151, 155, 178, 206, 305, 608, 721, 875, 963, 976, 977, 1097, 1162, 1192

theft, 136, 261, 523, 524

throne, 148, 173, 603, 632, 910, 987, 1001

travel, 462, 527, 528, 611, 675, 942, 1011, 1017

trial, 158, 162, 384, 391, 691, 775, 858, 859, 870, 999, 1061, 1090

truthfulness, 17, 114, 116, 365, 608, 944, 972, 986, 991, 1104

tyrants, 184, 188, 985, 1026, 1070

vain talk (*lahw*), 512, 950, 978

veneration, 750

vitality, 757, 758, 759, 846, 867

vow, 1076, 1157

war, 28, 53, 185, 189, 217, 218, 226, 265, 267, 268, 289, 309, 367, 369, 441, 455, 490, 524, 842, 872, 974, 1031, 1126, 1138

wastefulness, 30, 122, 521, 522

wealth, 14, 31, 37, 51, 52, 64, 67, 78, 90, 99, 100, 112, 114, 119, 126, 128, 129, 157, 158, 161, 168, 200, 201, 217, 229, 232, 233, 237, 250, 269, 273, 274, 285, 291, 299, 302, 318, 319, 329, 361, 381, 393, 402, 407, 419, 428, 432, 446, 447, 450, 452, 453, 455, 472, 473, 475, 487, 499, 504, 505, 516, 521, 522, 528, 531, 532, 569, 582, 597, 600, 605, 613, 619, 620, 648, 660, 677, 680, 686, 691, 698, 703, 737, 741, 761, 763, 767, 773, 785, 788, 796, 797, 820, 828, 842, 845, 846, 847, 848, 859, 868, 878, 879, 880, 881, 882, 883, 893, 923, 932, 933, 969, 970, 983, 984, 990, 993, 1009, 1012, 1013, 1014, 1015, 1016, 1017, 1026, 1051, 1056, 1068, 1091, 1099, 1100, 1101, 1102, 1127, 1128, 1139, 1142, 1146, 1159, 1171, 1172, 1198, 1200

women, 3, 27, 69, 164, 165, 167, 192, 247, 266, 268, 327, 388, 487, 488, 490, 541, 564, 569, 572, 625, 648, 656, 666, 667, 674, 676, 731, 740, 751, 795, 808, 827, 859, 962, 981, 982, 988, 989, 990, 991, 1009, 1023, 1035, 1041, 1082, 1083, 1098, 1107, 1109, 1116, 1139, 1148, 1158

world (*dunyā*), 3, 7, 8, 42, 43, 44, 45, 47, 49, 58, 66, 69, 77, 85, 104, 153, 183, 194, 209, 210, 228, 231, 241, 271, 272, 286, 291, 326, 328, 329, 361, 383, 384, 385, 386, 387, 388, 389, 390, 391, 392, 393, 394, 396, 415, 473, 474, 480, 483, 484, 535, 539, 584, 591, 598, 603, 650, 679, 680, 690, 714, 720, 726, 743, 762, 824, 849, 859, 860, 870, 879, 882, 898, 907, 913, 929, 941, 979, 982, 983, 994, 1003, 1006, 1007, 1009, 1034, 1042, 1047, 1057, 1060, 1072, 1094, 1097, 1098, 1114, 1115, 1117, 1137, 1170, 1173, 1174, 1198

worship, 1, 4, 11, 65, 84, 91, 100, 120, 122, 123, 132, 148, 194, 204, 215, 219, 221, 222, 261, 282, 293, 305, 328, 332, 335, 346, 361, 368, 380, 422, 435, 462, 466, 480, 490, 510, 512, 548, 550, 556, 567, 569, 582, 619, 621, 633, 646, 651, 652, 684, 685, 686, 687, 688, 689, 690, 699, 711, 713, 716, 738, 757, 762, 774, 775, 784, 813, 815, 824, 836, 844, 867, 870, 874, 885, 887, 888, 900, 904, 927, 928, 987, 992, 1001, 1024, 1025, 1027, 1028, 1031, 1036, 1038, 1053, 1057, 1059, 1077, 1082, 1105, 1117, 1119, 1130,1141, 1151, 1172, 1181, 1185

writing, 295, 557, 644, 912, 922, 940, 941, 992

wrongdoing, 37, 817

youth, 23, 43, 74, 214, 285, 485, 515, 531, 556, 557, 558, 597, 843, 1058

ʿUzra, 1059

Achevé d'imprimer en décembre 2008
dans les ateliers de Normandie Roto Impression s.a.s.
61250 Lonrai (Orne)
N° d'impression : 08-4289
Dépôt légal : décembre 2008

Imprimé en France